Street by Street

LONDON

Extended Coverage of the Capital

2nd edition July 2003

Original edition printed May 2001

Published by AA Publishing (a trading name of Automobile Association Developments Limited, whose registered office is Millstream, Maidenhead Road, Windsor, Berkshire SL4 5GD. Registered number 1878835).

Mapping produced by the Cartography Department of The Automobile Association. (A1708)

A CIP Catalogue record for this book is available from the British Library.

Printed by G. Canale & C. S.P.A., Torino, Italy

Ref: MX039z

Key to map pages ii-iii

Key to map symbols iv–1

Enlarged map pages 2-19

Main map pages 20-181

Index – towns & villages 182

Index – streets 183-257

Index – featured places 258-275

Acknowledgements 276

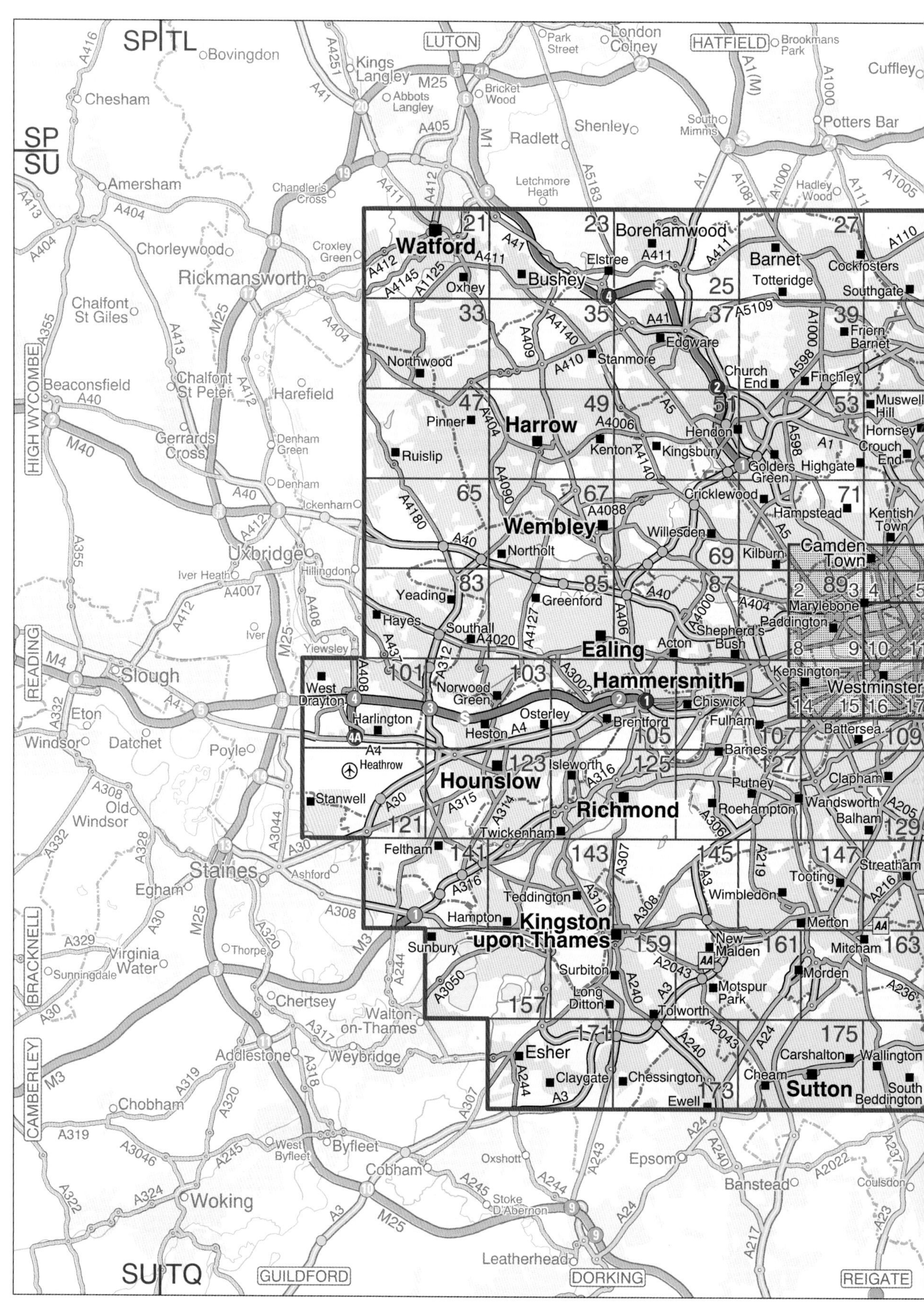

Scale of enlarged map pages **1:10,000** 6.3 inches to 1 mile

0 1/4 miles 1/2 3/4

0 1/4 1/2 kilometres 3/4 1 1 1/4

National Grid references are shown on the map frame of each page.
Red figures denote the 100 km square and blue figures the 1 km square.
Example, page 3 : Regent's Park 528 183

The reference can also be written using the National Grid two-letter prefix shown on this page, where 4 and 3 are replaced by TQ to give TQ2883.

4.2 inches to 1 mile **Scale of main map pages** **1:15,000**

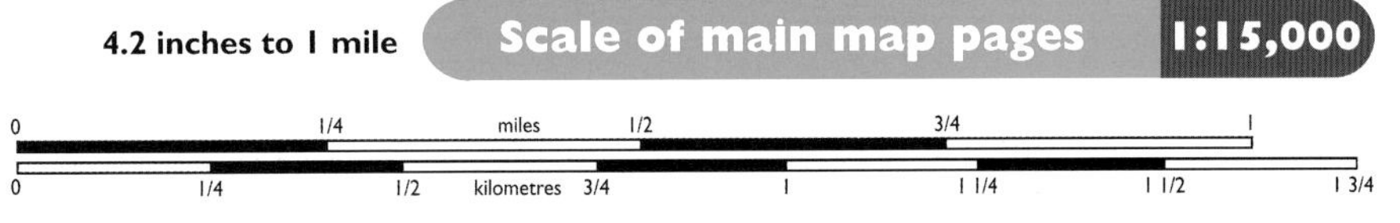

Symbol	Description	Symbol	Description
Junction 9	Motorway & junction		Underground station
Services	Motorway service area		Light railway & station
	Primary road single/dual carriageway		Preserved private railway
Services	Primary road service area	LC	Level crossing
	A road single/dual carriageway		Tramway
	B road single/dual carriageway		Ferry route
	Other road single/dual carriageway		Airport runway
	Minor/private road, access may be restricted		County, administrative boundary
	One-way street		Congestion Charging Zone *
	Pedestrian area		Mounds
	Track or footpath	93	Page continuation 1:15,000
	Road under construction	7	Page continuation to enlarged scale 1:10,000
	Road tunnel		River/canal, lake, pier
AA	AA Service Centre		Aqueduct, lock, weir
P	Parking	465 Winter Hill	Peak (with height in metres)
P+	Park & Ride		Beach
	Bus/coach station		Woodland
	Railway & main railway station		Park
	Railway & minor railway station		Cemetery

* The AA central London congestion charging map is also available

	Built-up area
	Featured building
	City wall
A&E	Hospital with 24-hour A&E department
PO	Post Office
	Public library
	Tourist Information Centre
	Petrol station, 24 hour Major suppliers only
	Church/chapel
	Public toilets
	Toilet with disabled facilities
PH	Public house AA recommended
	Restaurant AA inspected
	Theatre or performing arts centre
	Cinema
	Golf course
	Camping AA inspected
	Caravan site AA inspected
	Camping & caravan site AA inspected
	Theme park

	Abbey, cathedral or priory
	Castle
	Historic house or building
Wakehurst Place NT	National Trust property
	Museum or art gallery
	Roman antiquity
	Ancient site, battlefield or monument
	Industrial interest
	Garden
	Arboretum
	Farm or animal centre
	Zoological or wildlife collection
	Bird collection
	Nature reserve
	Aquarium
	Visitor or heritage centre
	Country park
	Cave
	Windmill
	Distillery, brewery or vineyard

2
71
88
8
A
B
C
D
E
F
1
2
3
4
5
6
7
8
9
525
26
IVERSON ROAD
B520
KILBURN HIGH ROAD
West Hampstead Station
Blackburn Rd
West Hampstead Station
Works
Netherwood St
Sherriff Road
Linstead St
Lowfield Rd
Kylemore Rd
Gladys Road
Hilltop Road
West Hampstead Clinic
Broadhurst Gardens
Broadhurst Cl
Compayne Gardens
Fairhazel Gardens
Canfield Pl
Edgware Coll
Finchley Road Stn
Optimax Laser Eye Clinic
Sumpter Close
Holy Trinity CE Primary School
FINCHLEY ROAD
College
Naseby Cl
Surgery
Broadhurst School
Canfield Gardens
Greencroft Gardens
Goldhurst Terrace
Marston Close
Fairfax Place
Fairfax Road
Fairfax Pl
Belsize Road
Harben Rd
Brondesbury Station
Surgery
Palmerston Road
Hemstal Road
Cleve Road
Dynham Road
Cotleigh Road
WEST END LANE
Priory Road
Woodchurch Road
Kingsgate Infant School
Tricycle Theatre
Junior School
Kingsgate Road
Surgery
Avenue
Messina Avenue
Grangeway
Drakes Ctyd
Dunster Gdns
Streatley Road
Buckley Road
Tricycle
Callcott Road
Burton Road
Gascony Avenue
Grange Place
Eresby Place
Smyrna Road
Queensgate Place
Kings Gardens
St Eugene de Mazenod RC Primary School
Mazenod Avenue
Acol Road
Wavel Ms
St Mary's Ms
Aberdare Gardens
Coleridge Gardens
Goldhurst Terrace
HILGROVE ROAD
South Hampstead Station
Alexandra Road
Langtry Walk
Alexandra Place
Christ Church Brondesbury CE Primary School
NW6
A4003
Tennyson Road
Douglas Road
Kingsley Road
Kenilworth Road
Aldershot Road
B4
St Julian's Rd
The Ter
Kingsgate Pl
QUEX ROAD
B510
Primary School
Abbot's Place
ABBEY ROAD
B509
ROAD
Jack Taylor School
Rowley Way
College of North West London
Quex Mews
Mutrix Road
Bransdale Close
Priory Road
Priory Terrace
BELSIZE
Ainsworth Way
Boundary Road
Loudoun Road
Priory Road
Glengall Road
Victoria Ms
Victoria Road
Birchington Road
West End Lane
B507
Esmond Road
Charteris Road Sports Centre
Kilburn Square
Kilburn Vale
Kilburn Place
Springfield Road
Hazelmere Road
Algernon Road
Charteris Road
Works
Langtry Road
Mortimer Crs
Abbey Medical Centre
Rutland Ms
Clifton Hill
Donaldson Rd
KILBURN
ROAD
Kilburn High Road Station
Mortimer Place
Springfield Wk
Belgrave Gdns
Bolton Road
St John's Wood
Marlborough
Lynton Road
Honiton Road
Kilburn Bridge
Mallard Cl
A5
Springfield La
Greville Ms
Kilburn Priory
Greville Road
Carlton Hill
Hazelmere Road
Villas
Coventry Cl
Manor Ms
BRONDESBURY
Brondesbury
Cambridge Avenue
Oxford Road
Hotel
Blenheim Road
Marlborough Pl
Alpha Pl
Kilburn Park Station
Tollgate Gardens
Primary School
Boundary Road
Hillside Cl
Carlton Hill
Blenheim Ter
Marlborough Day Hospital
New London Synagogue
B451
Gorefield Pl
St Marys RC Primary School
KILBURN PARK ROAD
The Lane
Langford Pl
Canterbury Ter
Canterbury Rd
Chichester Road
Surgery
School
Naima Jewish Preparatory School
Andover Place
Randolph Gdns
MAIDA VALE
Albert Road
Denmark Road
Denmark Rd
Princess Road
Cambridge Gdns
Rudolph Rd
Marlborough Place
Abbey Gardens
Aubrey Place
Abercorn Place School
B507
Neville Rd
Peel Precinct
Surgery
Granville Road
Granville Road
Cambridge Rd
B414
Vale
St Georges RC School
Hamilton Terrace
Violet Hill
Alma Square
St Lukes CE Primary School
CARLTON VALE
B413
Kilburn Park Junior School
Carlton Vale
Carlton
Lanark Road
North West London Medical Centre
Abercorn Cl
Nugent Ter
Abercorn Place
Hill Road
Hamilton Gdns
Ashmore Rd
Marban Rd
Malvern Pl
Carlton Vale Infant School
Nelson Cl
Stafford Rd
Paddington Recreation Ground
Maida Vale
Randolph Avenue
Fernhead Road
Bradiston Road
Dennolme Rd
Saltram Crescent
Macroom Rd
Malvern Road
Surgery
Cambridge Rd
Paddington Recreation Ground Athletics Track
Pavilion
The Lanark Medical Centre
Wellesley Ct
Elgin Ms Nth
Surgery
Maida Vale Station
Elgin Ms Sth
Vale Close
Hampton Close
Croxley Road
College
Malvern Ms
Park Business Cen
Grantully Road
Ashworth Road
Morshead Road
Avenue
Stafford Cl
Stuart Rd
Fordingley Road
Shirland Road
Riverton Cl
Portnall Road
Saltram Crs
Essendine Primary School
Essendine Rd
Maida Vale Medical Cen
Biddulph Road
Spanish & Portuguese Synagogue
Sutherland Av
Primary School
Cropthorne Ct
Hall Road
Hamilton Terrace
Surgery
Shirland Mews
Wymering Road
City of Westminster College
Lauderdale Road
Lapford Cl
Lydford Road
Elmfield Way
Widley Road
Elgin
Lanark Road
Ada Court
Maida Vale Hospital
Warlock Road
Portgate Cl
Abinger Ms
CHIPPENHAM ROAD
Lanhill Rd
SHIRLAND
Delaware
Castellain Road
Paddington Bowling & Sports Club
Warrington Crescent
Randolph Crs
Randolph Av
A5
Coryton Path
Drayford Cl
Barnsdale Rd
Walterton Road
Burlington Close
Grittleton Rd
Secondary School
Thorngate Road
BBC Studios
Sutherland Avenue
Avenue
Elgin Avenue
B413 CLIFTON RD
Kennet Rd
Errington Rd
A404
Queen Elizabeth II School
Westbourne Green
Oakington Road
Edbrooke Road
Warwick Place
Pindock Ms
Formosa St
CLIFTON GARDENS
Lanark Place
Robert Cl
Clarendon Gardens
Randolph Ms
Fermoy Road
B414
Chantry Cl
Fleming Cl
Goldney Road
Maryland Rd
Surrendale Pl
Elnathan Ms
Primary School
FORMOSA ST
WARWICK AV
Randolph Road
Works
Prim Sch
Elgin Estate
Chippenham Ms
Downfield Cl
Clearwell Dr
Barnwood Cl
Bristol Mews
Warwick Avenue Station
Sutherland Avenue
Aldsworth Cl
Blomfield Road
Avenue
1 grid square represents 250 metres
A404 HARROW
School
Police
W9

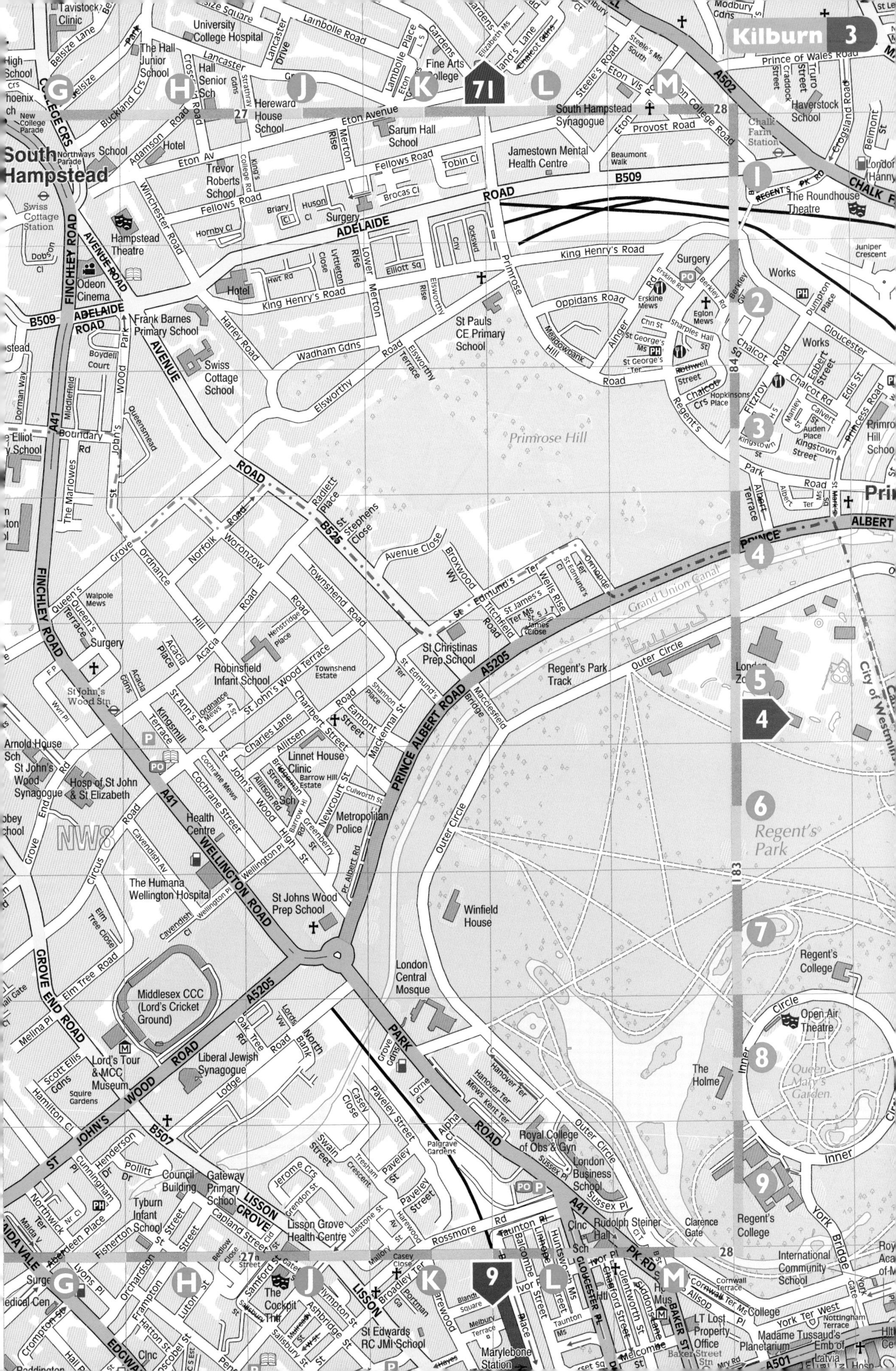
South Hampstead
Swiss Cottage Station
University College Hospital
The Hall Junior School
Hall Senior Sch
Hereward House School
Fine Arts College
71
South Hampstead Synagogue
Sarum Hall School
Jamestown Mental Health Centre
Chalk Farm Station
Haverstock School
Prince of Wales Road
The Roundhouse Theatre
Trevor Roberts School
Hampstead Theatre
Odeon Cinema
Frank Barnes Primary School
Swiss Cottage School
St Pauls CE Primary School
Primrose Hill
Adelaide Road
King Henry's Road
Finchley Road
Avenue Road
Eton Avenue
Fellows Road
Elsworthy Road
Regent's Park Road
Gloucester Avenue
Chalcot Road
Prince Albert Road
Grand Union Canal
London Zoo
City of Westminster
Regent's Park
St Christinas Prep School
Robinsfield Infant School
Linnet House Clinic
Metropolitan Police
St John's Wood Stn
St John's Wood Synagogue
Hosp of St John & St Elizabeth
Arnold House Sch
NW8
The Humana Wellington Hospital
Health Centre
Wellington Road
St Johns Wood Prep School
Winfield House
London Central Mosque
Middlesex CCC (Lord's Cricket Ground)
Lord's Tour & MCC Museum
Liberal Jewish Synagogue
St John's Wood Road
Grove End Road
Regent's College
Open Air Theatre
Queen Mary's Garden
The Holme
Royal College of Obs & Gyn
London Business School
Park Road
Lisson Grove
Gateway Primary School
Council Building
Tyburn Infant School
Lisson Grove Health Centre
Rudolph Steiner Hall
Clarence Gate
International Community School
The Cockpit Thtr
St Edwards RC JMI School
Marylebone Station
LT Lost Property Office
Madame Tussaud's
Planetarium
Baker Street Stn
Edgware Road
9
4
27
28
83
84

4
72
10
3
A
B
C
D
E
F
1
2
3
4
5
6
7
8
9
528
29
84
83
Modbury Gdns
Queen's
Prince of Wales Road
St Leonards Square
Newbury Mews
Steele's Ms South
Steele's Road
Eton Vls
Eton College Road
South Hampstead Synagogue
Provost Road
Beaumont Walk
B509
Haverstock School
Chalk Farm Station
Crogsland Road
Belmont St
Powlett Place
Ferdinand Place
FERDINAND ST
Chalcot School
Lewis St
Castlehaven Rd
Collard Pl
London Zendo (Hannya Temple)
Holy Trinity Haverstock Hill CE Prim Sch
Works
Clarence Way
Hartland Rd
Hawley Rd
HAWLEY RD
CASTLEHAVEN RD
Ly Rd
Water Lane
Kelly St
Church Avenue
Healey St
Grafton Crs
Hadley St
Surgery
Castle Road
Castle Place
Farrier St
KENTISH TOWN ROAD
A400
Lawford Road
Kentish Town Health Centre
St Andrews Greek School
Bartholomew Road
Rochester Road
Rochester Terrace
Rochester Place
Reed's Pl
Wilmot Pl
Whitcher Pl
Rochester Ms
Rochester Sq
Camden School for Girls
Camden Mews Day Hospital
Spiritualist Temple
ROYAL COLLEGE STREET
ST PANCRAS WAY
A503
Jeffrey's Sq
Prowse Pl
Ivor St
Camden Road Station
Rousden St
Wrotham Rd
Bonny St
Randolph St
Bruges Place
BAYNES ST
Lyme Terrace
Lyme Street
A5202
Barker Dr
REGENT'S PK RD
BRIDGE AP
The Roundhouse Theatre
CHALK FARM RD
King Henry's Road
Surgery
PO
Erskine Rd
Erskine Mews
Berkley Rd
Berkley Gv
Juniper Crescent
Camden Market
CAMDEN TOWN
Camden Lock Pl
Gilbeys Yard
Works
PH
Dumpton Place
Gloucester Av
Chalcot Sq
Chalcot Road
Egbert Street
Chalcot Rd
Edis St
Fitzroy Rd
Manley St
Calvert St
Auden Place
Kingstown Street
Princess Road
Primrose Hill School
St Mark's Crs
Cecil Sharpe House
Oppidans Road
Ainger Rd
Chn St
Sharples Hall St
St George's Ms
St George's Ter
Rothwell Street
Chalcot Crs
Hopkinsons Place
Regent's Park Road
Albert Terrace
Park
Road
Albert Ter
St Mark's Sq
Primrose Hill
PRINCE ALBERT ROAD
A5205
Regal Lane
Grand Union Canal
Ormonde Ter
St Edmund's Ter
Outer Circle
Regent's Park
London Zoo
City of Westminster
Camden
Gloucester Gate
Gloucester Ga
Gloucester Ga Ms
North Bridge House Senior School
Pk Village W
Park Village East
Regent's Park Barracks
NW1
Bridge
Cumberland Terrace
Cm T Ms
A4201
ALBANY STREET
Cumberland Gate
Regent's College
Open Air Theatre
Inner Circle
Queen Mary's Garden
Chester Road
Holme
London Business School
Sussex Pl
Rudolph Steiner Hall
Clarence Gate
York Bridge
York Gate
International University
Royal Academy of Music
Jamestown Road
Arlington Road
Early Ms
Inverness St
Oval Road
Gloucester Crs
Regent's Pk Ter
The Cavendish School
Odeon
Camden Town Station
CAMDEN HIGH ST
PKWY
London Capital College
Mornington Sports & Fitness Cen
Friends of the Hebrew University
The Jewish Museum
DELANCEY ST
A503
Delancey Passage
Mary Ter
Albert Street
Arlington Road
Mornington Terrace
Mornington St
Miller St
Carlow St
Underhill St
Hawley Infant School
Hawley Crs
Stucley Pl
Buck St
Greenland Rd
Carol St
Greenland Pl
Works
St Michael's CE Prim Sch
St Martin's Cl
BAYHAM ST
CAMDEN ROAD
Georgiana St
Primary School
Pratt St
PRATT ST
Pratt Ms
King's Ter
Bayham Street
Plender Street
Bayham Pl
College Place
Mandela Street
Surgery
Royal Veterinary College
Richard Cobden Primary School
College
Camden Thtr
CROWNDALE ROAD
Oakley Sq
OAKLEY SQ
Crowndale Hlth Cen
EVERSHOLT ST
Mornington Crescent Stn
Nelsons Yard
Mornington Crs
Mornington Place
Clarkson Row
Harrington Sq
Ampthill Square Medical Centre
Ampthill Estate
Ampthill Square
Cranleigh St
Barnby Street
EVERSHOLT
Regent's Park
Christ Church School
Granby Ter
Augustus Street
Harrington St
Silverdale
HAMPSTEAD ROAD
Redhill Street
Redhill St
Stanhope Parade
Stanhope Street
Mackworth St
Harrington Street
Varndell St
Cumberland Medical Cen
Market
Nash St
Robert St
Compton Close
Everton Buildings
Clarence Gdns
Netley Primary School
Netley St
Prince Regent Mews
William Road
National Temperance Hospital
Lower School
Hotel
Starcross St
Cobourg St
Euston Street
Drummond St
Camden Peoples Thtr
University of Westminster
Euston Centre
Euston Tower
Longford St
Hotel
Osnaburgh St
Diana Place
Works
Police Station
Colosseum Terrace
Munster Sq
Cambridge Ga Ms
Cambridge Ga
Chester Terrace
Chester Cl North
Chester Pl
Chester Ga
Chester Cl South
Outer Circle
Royal College of Physicians
St Andrew's Pl
Park Sq East
Park Square
Regent's Park Stn
Peto Pl
EUSTON ROAD
Euston Sq Station
A501
Warren Street Stn
Whitfield Pl
Beaumont Pl
Grafton Way
University Coll Hosp
TOTTENHAM
University Street
UCL Hospitals
Obs Hosp
A&E
Great Portland Street Stn
Royal National Orthopaedic Hosp
Emb of Croatia
Emb of Mozambique
Medical Cen
London Foot Hosp
Union of Liberal
Coll
W1T
MARYLEBONE ROAD
Central London Co Court
Consulate
The London Clinic
Brunswick Place
Ulster Pl
Sherlock Holmes Mus
Allsop Pl
Cornwall Terrace
Cornwall Ter Ms
College
York Ter West
Nottingham Terrace
Madame Tussaud's
London Planetarium
Emb of Latvia
LT Lost Property
Baker Street Stn
Melcombe St
Glentworth St
Chagford St
Ivor Pl
Dorset Sq
GLOUCESTER PL
PK RD
A41
Hlth Cen
Regent's Park
Harley St
Marylebone High St
1 grid square represents 250 metres

Camden Town
5
72
6
11
Islington Tennis Centre
Robert Blair Primary School
Knowledge Point School
HM Prison
Caledonian Road & Barnsbury Station
Barnsbury
Barnsbury School for Girls
ISLINGTON
Cedar Way Industrial Estate
St Pancras Hospital
Central School Speech & Drama
Depot
YORK WAY
CALEDONIAN ROAD
A5203
A5200
A5202
A501
A4200
B514
B504
COPENHAGEN ST B514
Cally Pool
St Andrews Primary School
True Buddha School
Blessed Sacrament RC Primary School
Copenhagen Primary School
The London Canal Museum
Killick Street Medical Centre
Vittoria Primary School
Samuel Rhodes School
Pentonville
Elizabeth Garrett Anderson School
Somers Town
Edith Neville Primary School
St Mary & St Pancras CE Primary School
Maria Fidelis Convent Upper School
St Aloysius RC Infant School
King's Cross Station
St Pancras Station
British Library
St Pancras International Youth Hostel
Camden Town Hall & St Pancras Library
Euston Station
PENTONVILLE ROAD
EUSTON ROAD
GRAY'S INN RD
KING'S CROSS RD
PENTON RISE
Kingsway College
Royal National Throat Nose & Ear Hosp
Magistrates Court
FINSBURY
St Pancras
Elizabeth Garrett Anderson Hosp
University College
British Medical Association
The Foundling Museum
The Treehouse School
Coram's Fields Playground
The Charles Dickens Mus
National Hosp for Sick Children (Great Ormond St)
Mount Pleasant (Postal Office)
Family Records Centre
Finsbury Health Centre
Clerkenwell
The Alchemy Gal
Eastman Dental Hosp
Brunswick Housing & Shopping Cen
British Cartoon Centre
Bloomsbury Theatre
Wellcome Institute
Friends House
National Hosp for Neurology
Russell Square Station
WC1H
WC1N
WC1X
FARRINGDON
ROSEBERY AVENUE
UPR WOBURN PL
WOBURN PLACE
BERNARD ST

6
Prison
A
B
73
C
D
E
F
HIGHBURY CORNER
Canonbury JMI School
Primary School
Canonbury
Barnsbury School for Girls
Caledonian Road & Barnsbury Sta
Ellington Street
Arundel Square
Highbury Station Rd
Barnsbury Park
Islington Park St
LIVERPOOL RD
UPPER STREET
CANONBURY ROAD
ESSEX ROAD
ISLINGTON
Islington Town Hall
William Tyndale Primary School
Essex Road Station
River Place Health Cen
CALEDONIAN ROAD
Bridgeman
Thornhill Square
Almeida Theatre
Maples Bus Centre
Kings Head Theatre
Charles Lamb Primary School
Rosemary Primary School
Islington Business Centre
Richmond Avenue
Samuel Rhodes School
St Andrews Primary School
Theberton Street
Screen on the Green Cinema
Islington Green Medical Cen
ISLINGTON GREEN
Islington Green School
True Buddha School
Copenhagen St
Vittoria Primary School
The Business Design Centre
Barford Street
Carnegie Street
Colebrooke Works
Primary School
Museum of London (Archaeological Research Centre)
N1 Shopping Centre
Pentonville
5
Police Stn
Consulate of Eritrea
Angel Station
Elizabeth Anderson School
Chapel Market
White Lion St
Crafts Council
Noel Road
Vincent Terrace
Hanover Primary School
Faircharm Trading Estate
PENTONVILLE ROAD
A501
CITY ROAD
Cosmopolitan Coll
Brewery Industrial Estate
SHEPHERDESS WALK
Kingsway College
Pop Up Theatre
City Uni
City University
London Open College
Lilian Baylis Thtr
Sadler's Wells Theatre
PENTON RISE
KING'S CROSS RD
Magistrates Court
FINSBURY
Primary School
Moreland Primary School
GOSWELL ROAD
The City University
City & Islington College
Family Records Centre
Town Hall
ROSEBERY AVENUE
Ironmonger Row Baths
Finsbury Leisure Centre
Eastman Dental Hosp
Mount Pleasant Postal Sorting Office
FARRINGDON
CALTHORPE STREET
SKINNER ST
PERCIVAL ST
City Business Coll
Clerkenwell
Finsbury Health Cen
Records Office
Rosemary Secondary Sch
Kingsway Coll
House of Detention
The Alchemy Gal
St Luke's
12
The Charles Dickens Mus
Central School of Ballet
Clerkenwell Heritage Cen
Mus of the Order
St Bartholomews Medical Sch
Charterhouse Buildings
Golden Lane Estate
CLERKENWELL ROAD
1 grid square represents 250 metres

Finsbury 7
Kingsland
Dalston
De Beauvoir Town
Haggerston
Hoxton
SHOREDITCH
EC2A
74
92
13
G
H
J
K
L
M
33
34
1
2
3
4
5
6
7
8
9
ESSEX ROAD
Ockendon Road
Englefield Road
Oakley Road
Northchurch Road
SOUTHGATE ROAD
B102
Southgate Road Medical Centre
Culford Road
Ufton Road
De Beauvoir Road
Mortimer Road
Hertford Road
Kingsland Health Cen
KINGSLAND ROAD
A10
Stamford Road
Holy Trinity Primary School
Primary School
Tottenham Road
Buckingham Road
Ardleigh Road
Wall St
Richmond Road
Forest Rd
Forest Gv
Holly Street
Queensbridge Sports Centre
QUEENSBRIDGE ROAD
B108
Lenthall Road
Gayhurst Road
Mapledene Road
Lavender Grove
Middleton Road
Queensbridge Infant School
Albion Drive
Albion Sq
Shrubland Road
Livermere Rd
Haggerston Road
Metropolitan Business Cen
Downham Road
Balmes Road
Benyon Road
Canal Walk
Branch Place
De Beauvoir Crs
Orsman Road
Mill Row
Phillipp Street
Hyde Road
Whitmore Road
Penn Street
Gopsall St
Whitmore Primary School
Britannia Leisure Centre
Shoreditch Park
NORTH ROAD
B144
BARING ST
Poole Street
Mintern Street
Ivy St
Burbage School
Hemsworth St
Hoxton Street
Nuttall St
St Leonards Hospital
Hoxton Hall Community Thtr
Purcell Street
Buckland St
Cherbury Street
NEW N ROAD
B101
Crondall Street
Myrtle Walk
St John the Baptist CE Primary Sch
Hackney Community College
Falkirk St
Pitfield Street
Haberdasher Street
Bevenden Street
City Coll of Higher Education
Chart St
EAST ROAD
A1200
Moorfields Eye Hospital
Old Street Station
OLD STREET
A5201
CITY ROAD
A501
Bunhill Row
Wesley's Chapel, House & Museum
Honourable Artillery Company HQ
Worship Street
Great Eastern Street
Curtain Road
Charlotte Rd
Rivington St
Brick Lane Music Hall
SHOREDITCH HIGH ST
CALVERT AVENUE
Virginia Primary Sch
Arnold Circus
Boundary St
Club Row
B122
Redchurch St
Bethnal Green Technology College
Columbia Primary School
COLUMBIA ROAD
A1208
HACKNEY ROAD
Geffrye Mus
Trans Atlantic College
Haggerston School
Haggerston Swimming Pool
Haggerston Park
Whiston Road
Laburnum Primary Sch
Regent's Row
Dove Row
Sebright Primary School
Hackney City Farm
B108 WARNER PLACE
Gosset Street
Tower Hamlets College
BETHNAL GREEN
Cheshire Street
Sclater Street
B135
St Matthias CE Primary School
Shoreditch Station
Spitalfields Community Farm
Thomas Buxton Primary School
Pedley Street
Buxton St
Quaker Street
Hewett St
Scrutton Street
Shoreditch County Court
Moorfields Primary School
Provost Street
Britannia Walk
Crusoe House Sch
Fairbank Estate
Cranston Estate
Geffrye Estate
Wilks Pl Comprehensive School
Shenfield Street
Cremer Bus Cen
Columbia Road Market
Midway Mission Hosp
Virginia Road
Ravenscroft Street
Gascoigne Pl
Hare Wk
Dunloe Street
Weymouth Terrace
Council Building

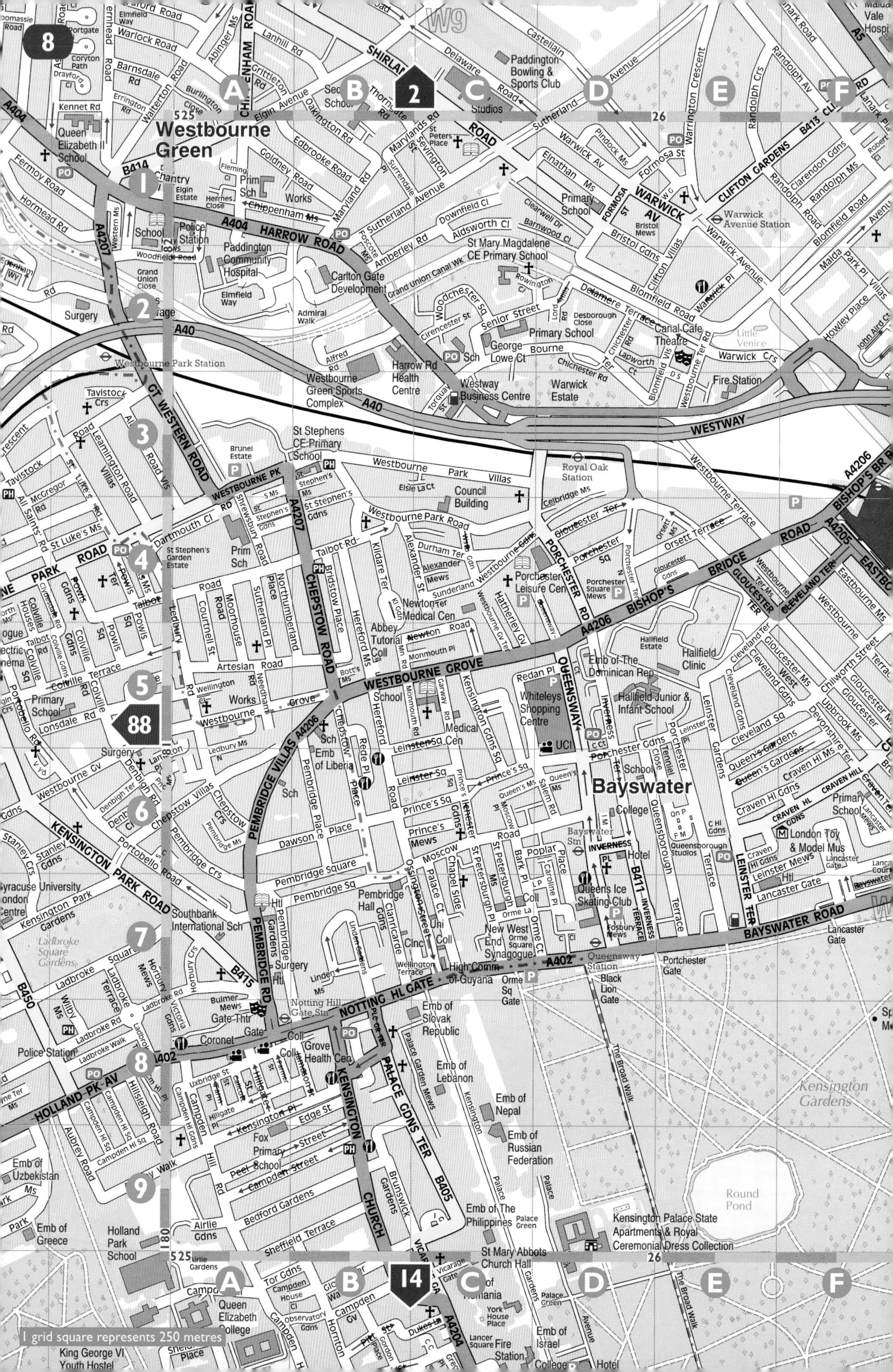

8
2
W9
Westbourne Green
Bayswater
Kensington Gardens
Round Pond
Ladbroke Square Gardens
Little Venice
A B C D E F
A B C D E F
1
2
3
4
5
6
7
8
9
525
26
525
26
180
181
88
14
Paddington Bowling & Sports Club
Studios
Queen Elizabeth II School
Police Station
School
Paddington Community Hospital
Carlton Gate Development
Primary School
St Mary Magdalene CE Primary School
Warwick Avenue Station
Canal Cafe Theatre
Primary School
George Lowe Ct
Harrow Rd Health Centre
Westbourne Green Sports Complex
Westway Business Centre
Warwick Estate
Fire Station
Westbourne Park Station
Surgery
Brunel Estate
St Stephens CE Primary School
Royal Oak Station
Council Building
St Stephen's Garden Estate
Prim Sch
Porchester Leisure Cen
Newton Medical Cen
Abbey Tutorial Coll
Hallfield Estate
Hallfield Clinic
Emb of The Dominican Rep
Hallfield Junior & Infant School
Whiteleys Shopping Centre
UCI
Medical Cen
Emb of Liberia
Primary School
Surgery
College
Bayswater Stn
Hotel
Queen's Ice Skating Club
Queensborough Studios
London Toy & Model Mus
Primary School
Syracuse University London Centre
Southbank International Sch
Pembridge Hall
New West End Synagogue
Uni Coll
Clnc
High Comm of Guyana
Queensway Station
Black Lion Gate
Porchester Gate
Lancaster Gate
Notting Hill Gate Stn
Gate Thtr
Coronet
Police Station
Grove Health Cen
Emb of Slovak Republic
Emb of Lebanon
Emb of Nepal
Emb of Russian Federation
Emb of The Philippines
Kensington Palace State Apartments & Royal Ceremonial Dress Collection
St Mary Abbots Church Hall
Fox Primary School
Emb of Uzbekistan
Emb of Greece
Holland Park School
Queen Elizabeth College
King George VI Youth Hostel
Emb of Romania
York House Place
Fire Station
Emb of Israel
HARROW ROAD
A404
A40
WESTWAY
A4207
GT WESTERN ROAD
WESTBOURNE GROVE
A4206
BISHOP'S BRIDGE ROAD
QUEENSWAY
PORCHESTER RD
CHEPSTOW ROAD
PEMBRIDGE VILLAS
PEMBRIDGE RD
KENSINGTON PARK ROAD
NOTTING HL GATE
A402
BAYSWATER ROAD
HOLLAND PK AV
KENSINGTON CHURCH
PALACE GDNS TER
B405
LEINSTER TER
INVERNESS TERRACE
B411
CLIFTON GARDENS
WARWICK AV
FORMOSA ST
Elgin Avenue
Sutherland Avenue
Shirland
Delaware Road
Castellain
Warrington Crescent
Randolph Av
Maida Vale
Blomfield Road
Westbourne Terrace
Gloucester Ter
Ledbury Road
Portobello Road
Westbourne Park Road
Westbourne Park Villas
Talbot Road
Colville Terrace
Pembridge Square
Moscow Road
Palace Gardens Terrace
Kensington Palace Gardens
The Broad Walk
Campden Hill
Holland Park Av
Ladbroke Grove
1 grid square represents 250 metres

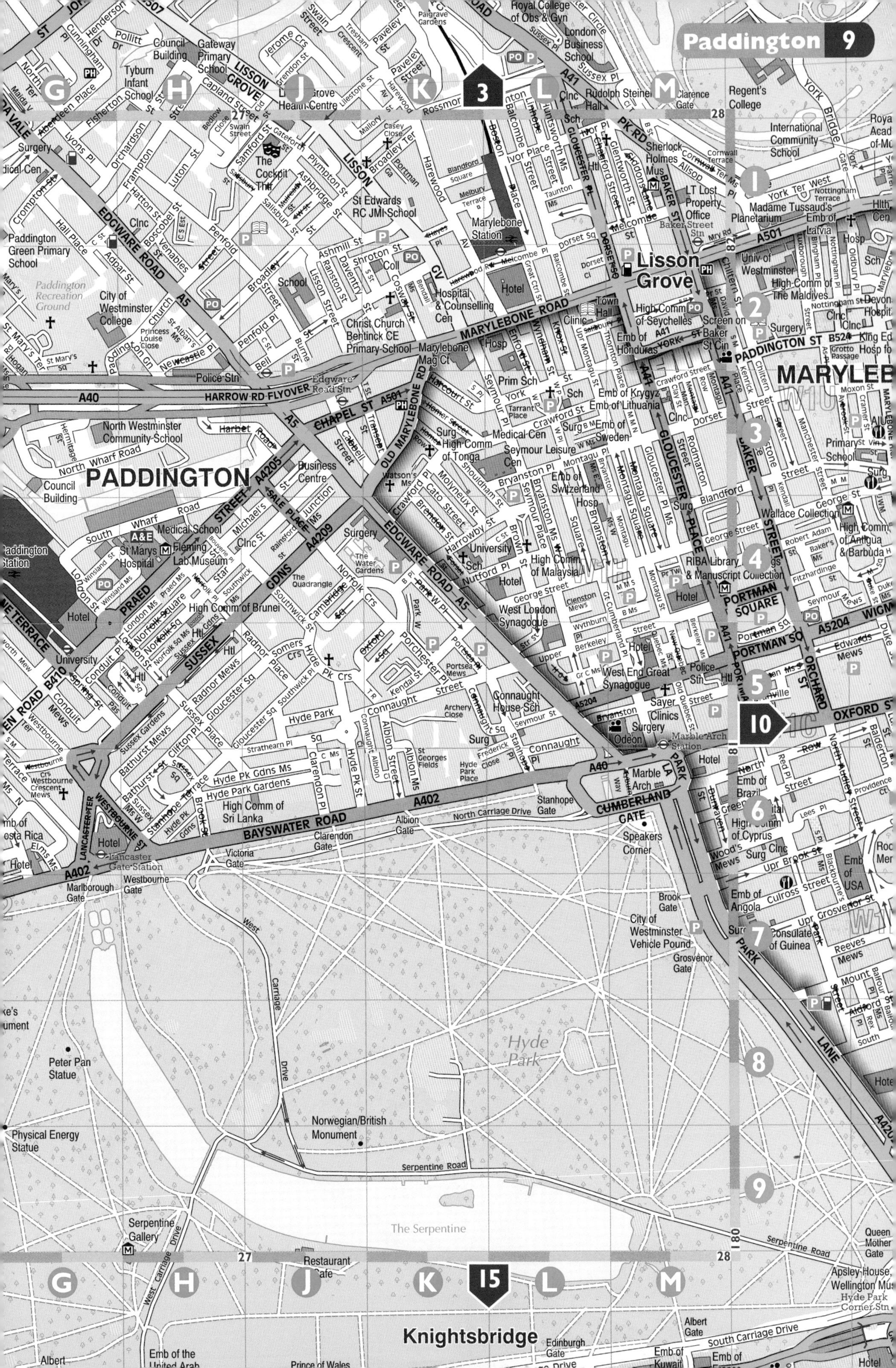
PADDINGTON
MARYLEBONE
Lisson Grove
Knightsbridge
Hyde Park
The Serpentine
Serpentine Road
Serpentine Gallery
West Carriage Drive
North Carriage Drive
South Carriage Drive
Peter Pan Statue
Physical Energy Statue
Norwegian/British Monument
Restaurant Cafe
Speakers Corner
Marble Arch
Marble Arch Station
Cumberland Gate
Brook Gate
Grosvenor Gate
Stanhope Gate
Albion Gate
Clarendon Gate
Victoria Gate
Marlborough Gate
Westbourne Gate
Lancaster Gate Station
Queen Mother Gate
Apsley House, Wellington Mus
Hyde Park Corner Stn
Albert Gate
Edinburgh Gate
City of Westminster Vehicle Pound
BAYSWATER ROAD
EDGWARE ROAD
MARYLEBONE ROAD
HARROW RD FLYOVER
PRAED STREET
SUSSEX GDNS
OLD MARYLEBONE RD
CHAPEL ST
LISSON GROVE
GLOUCESTER PLACE
BAKER STREET
PORTMAN SQUARE
OXFORD ST
PARK LANE
ORCHARD ST
Paddington Station
St Marys Hospital
Fleming Lab Museum
Marylebone Station
Baker Street Stn
Edgware Road Stn
Regent's College
Madame Tussaud's
Planetarium
Wallace Collection
RIBA Library & Manuscript Collection
West London Synagogue
West End Great Synagogue
Odeon
The Cockpit Thtr
Paddington Green Primary School
City of Westminster College
North Westminster Community School
Royal College of Obs & Gyn
London Business School
Sherlock Holmes Mus
Seymour Leisure Cen
Emb of USA
Hotel
28
27
G
H
J
K
L
M
3
10
15
1
2
3
4
5
6
7
8
9

10
4
16
9
A
B
C
D
E
F
1
2
3
4
5
6
7
8
9
528
29
Inner
York Bridge
Regent's College
Clarence Gate
Rudolph Steiner Hall
International Community School
Royal Academy of Music
Royal College of Physicians
Park Square
Colosseum Terrace
Longford St
University of Westminster
Euston Centre
Euston Tower
EUSTON
ROAD
Euston Sq Station
A&E
GRAFTON WY
Warren Street Stn
Works
A501
Sherlock Holmes Mus
BAKER ST
Baker Street Stn
Madame Tussaud's
Planetarium
MARYLEBONE ROAD
Regent's Park Stn
Central London Co Court
Great Portland Street Stn
Royal National Orthopaedic Hosp
Emb of Croatia
Emb of Mozambique
London Foot Hosp
Union of Liberal & Prog Synagogues
UCL Hospital
TOTTENHAM
Lisson Grove
Property Office
Melcombe St
Dorset Sq
DORSET SQ
GLOUCESTER PL
Univ of Westminster
High Comm of The Maldives
Emb of Latvia
Consulate of Chile
Medical Express Clnc
PORTLAND PL
Hallam
British Telecom Twr
RIBA
College
University
Town Hall
High Comm of Seychelles
Screen on Baker St
Emb of Honduras
YORK ST
PADDINGTON ST
B524
King Edward VII Hosp for Officers
Devonshire Hospital
Emb of Poland
High Comm of Kenya
Emb of China
Sch Cen Synagogue
New Cavendish St
Nurses Home
Sch of Physiotherapy
MARYLEBONE
Emb of Krygyz
Emb of Lithuania
Emb of Sweden
Montagu Sq
Bryanston Sq
Medical Cen
The Heart Hosp
Surgeries
GT PORTLAND STREET
Duchess St
Primary School
Middlesex Hosp
Wallace Collection
George St
High Comm of Antigua & Barbuda
Wigmore Hall
Lister Ho Clinic
Harley Medical
Queens Coll
Allergey Clnc
British Dental Ass
High Comm of Namibia
A4201 LANGHAM PL
MORTIMER ST
Emb of Bosnia
London Fo Temple
Emb of Turkmenistan
Consulate of Colombia
Library Drawings & Manuscript Collection
PORTMAN SQUARE
WIGMORE STREET
A5204
Emb of Slovenia
High Comm of Belize
CAVENDISH PL
Royal Society of Medicine
Eastcastle St
OXFORD STREET
High Comm of Sierra Leone
Radcliffe College
West End Great Synagogue
Sayer Clinic
Surgery
Odeon
PORTMAN ST
ORCHARD ST
Edwards Mews
St Christopher's Place
Oxford Circus Station
High Comm of Botswana
(0700-1900 Mon-Sat Buses and taxis only)
Hotel
Palladium Thtr
Gt Marlborough St
Marshall St Leis Cen
Marble Arch
CUMBERLAND GATE
PARK LA
A40
Emb of Brazil
Hospital
High Comm of Cyprus
OXFORD ST
Bond Street Stn
Medical Cen
Shop Cen
NEW BOND STREET
The Ford College
Bus College
Handel's House
High Comm of Cyprus
REGENT STREET
A4201
CONDUIT ST
Police Stn
Speakers Corner
Emb of Argentina
Emb of Italy
High Comm of Malawi
High Comm of Angola
Roosevelt Memorial
Grosvenor Square
Emb of USA
Emb of Angola
Emb of Indonesia
Brook Gate
City of Westminster Vehicle Pound
Grosvenor Gate
Consulate of Guinea
Reeves Mews
Royal Institution's Faraday Museum
Royal Academy of Arts
High Comm of Malta
Mayfair
Berkeley Sq
Primary School
PARK LANE
PICCADILLY
Burlington Arcade
Princes Arcade
Masons Yard
Emb of Myanmar
Emb of Saudi Arabia
Emb of Qatar
High Comm of Bahamas
Curzon
Crewe Ho
Emb of Egypt
A4202
Emb of Mexico
Consulate of Panama
Emb of Japan
Emb of Qatar
A4
Green Park Station
ST JAMES'S ST
King Street
Spencer House
Emb of Sudan
St James's Palace
Clarence Ho
Lancaster House
Stable Yard Rd
Serpentine Road
Queen Mother Gate
Apsley House
Wellington Mus
Hyde Park Corner Stn
HYDE PK CORNER
Green Park
Wellington Arch
Constitution Hill
The Mall
Emb of Kuwait
1 grid square represents 250 metres

Marylebone 11
5
17
12
G
H
J
K
L
M
1
2
3
4
5
6
7
8
9
30
31
Bloomsbury
Holborn
St Giles
Soho
China Town
Strand
St James
Clerkenwell
WC1H
WC1N
WC1E
WC1B
WC1R
WC1V
WC1A
WC2H
WC2B
WC2A
WC2E
WC2R
WC2N
W1D
EC1
EC4
Wellcome Institute
University College
British Medical Association
Woolf Mews
Health Centre
The Foundling Museum
The Treehouse School
Dental Hosp
Brunswick Medical Centre
Brunswick Housing & Shopping Cen
British Cartoon Centre
Bloomsbury Theatre
Birkbeck Coll
University of London
University College London
Dep of Clinical Haematology
Percival David Fndtn
College
Grant Mus
Russell Square Station
The Charles Dickens Mus
National Hosp for Sick Children (Great Ormond St)
National Hosp for Neurology & Neurosurgery
Royal London Homeopathic Hosp
Vanbrugh Thtr
RADA
London Sch of Hygiene & Tropical Medicine
Uni of London
Royal College of Anaesthetists
Goodge St Station
Cavendish Coll
New York Uni in London
British Museum
Coll of Art & Design
Police Station
Conway Hall
Cochrane Thtr
Inns of Court School of Law
Gray's Inn
Chancery Lane Stn
London Silver Vaults
Staple Inn Blds
Patent Off
Public Record Office
Lincoln's Inn
Sir John Soane's Mus
Royal College of Surgeons
Old Curiosity Shop
Museums
Royal Courts of Justice
London School of Economics
YMCA
High Comm of Barbados
Dominion Thtr
Oxford Hse Coll
Tottenham Court Road Stn
Centre Point
Eye Clinc
Shaftesbury
Embassy of Cuba
LSE
Oasis Sports Cen
Martan Coll
Primary School
Holborn Station
Holborn Town Hall
Stationery Office
New London Thtr
Kings Coll
New Connaught Rooms
The Peacock Thtr
Hse of St Barnabus
Phoenix Thtr
Medical Cen
Donmar Warehouse
London Int Film Sch
Royal Ballet Sch
Royal Opera House
Thtr Mus
Fortune Thtr
Thtr Royal
Aldwych
Bush Ho (BBC)
Australia House
India House
Kings College London
Roman Bath
Courtauld Institute
Somerset House
Gilbert Collection
Temple Stn
Thames Police Station
HQS Wellington (Master Mariners)
Covent Garden Station
Africa Cen
The Mkt
Jubilee Mkt
LT Mus
St Peter's Hosp
Duchess
Lyceum
Savoy Thtr
Royal Society of Arts
Coliseum
Police Stn
High Comm of Zimbabwe
Charing Cross Stn
Embankment Station
Victoria Embankment Gardens
Cleopatra's Needle
Savoy Pier
Embankment Pier
Festival Pier
Waterloo Bridge
Queen Elizabeth Hall
Hungerford Bridge
Hayward Gallery
Royal Festival Hall
BFI London IMAX Cinema
National Film Theatre
The London Television Centre (LWT)
London City College
Shell Centre
Jubilee Gardens
International Rail Terminal
Waterloo Station
County Hall
Dali Universal Exhibition
Queens
Gielgud
Apollo
Lyric
Piccadilly
Trocadero
London Pav
Piccadilly Circus Stn
Eros
Prince of Wales
Odeon
Visitor Cen
High Comm of Singapore
Her Majesty's
Royal
High Comm of New Zealand
High Comm of Papua New Guinea
Canada House
High Com of Uganda
National Gallery
National Portrait Gal
Garrick
Trafalgar Square
Nelson's Column
High Comm of South Africa
Players Thtr
High Comm of Nigeria
Government Offices
The Playhouse
DEFRA
Admiralty Arch
Whitehall Thtr
Old Admiralty
Mall Galleries
ICA
Duke of York Column
Carlton House
The Royal College of Pathology
Horse Guards Parade
Old War Office
Banqueting House
Ministry of Defence
Privy Council Office
Old Treas
Foreign & Commonwealth Office
Cenotaph
Department of Hlth
Norman Shaw Building (MP's Offices)
Hispaniola
York Water Gate
Proud Gal
Capital Radio
Alby
Wyn
Leicester Square Stn
Curzon
Prince Edward Thtr
St Martins
Photo Gal
Arts Thtr
New Amb
Camb
Cncl Bldg
Warner
Empire
UCI
Odeon
Cmdy
Uni of Notre Dame
St Albans CE Primary School
London Weather Centre
University
Mt Pleasant
Rosebery Avenue
Clerkenwell Road
Hatton Garden
The Alchemy Gal
Holborn
High Holborn
Fleet St
Strand
Kingsway
Southampton Row
Theobald's Road
Gray's Inn Road
Russell Sq
Montague Place
Bedford Wy
Tavistock
Woburn Place
New Oxford St
Shaftesbury Av
Charing Cross Rd
Long Acre
Aldwych
Victoria Embankment
Waterloo Rd
Stamford Street
Whitehall
Pall Mall
The Mall
Haymarket
Regent St
Northumberland Av
Lancaster Pl
Chancery La
Middle Temple Hall
Inner Temple
High Comm of Nigeria
Oxo Tower Wharf
Gabriel's Wharf
Thames Path
Entrance to Strand Underpass (northbound only)

12
6
11
18
A
B
C
D
E
F
1
2
3
4
5
6
7
8
9
Clerkenwell
Holborn
St Luke's
CITY OF LONDON
River Thames
City of London
Southwark
Mount Pleasant (Postal Sorting Office)
Clerkenwell Road
Theobald's Road
High Holborn
Holborn Circus
Holborn Viad
Newgate St
Fleet St
Strand
Victoria Emb
Embankment
Upper Thames
Southwark Street
Stamford St
Union Street
Farringdon Road
Farringdon Street
New Bridge Street
Blackfriars Road
Blackfriars Bridge
Waterloo Bridge
Southwark Bridge Road
Aldersgate St
Rosebery Avenue
Chancery La
Hatton Garden
Beech St (Below)
Queen Victoria St
Farringdon Station
Chancery Lane Stn
Barbican Station
St Paul's Station
City Thameslink Station
Blackfriars Stn
Temple Stn
Waterloo Station
Waterloo East Stn
Southwark Station
Mansion House Station
St Paul's Cathedral
St Bartholomews Hospital
Central London Mkts
Central Criminal Court
Royal Courts of Justice
London School of Economics
Kings College London
Somerset House
The Barbican
Barbican Cinema
Mus of London
Tate Modern
Shakespeare's Globe Theatre
Oxo Tower Wharf
Royal National Theatre
National Film Theatre
Royal Festival Hall
Hayward Gallery
BFI London IMAX Cinema
Sir John Soane's Mus
Lincoln's Inn
Gray's Inn
The Charles Dickens Mus
Dr Johnson's House
Millennium Bridge
Blackfriars Millennium Pier
HQS Wellington (Master Mariners)
HMS President
Savoy Pier
Festival Pier
Bankside Gallery
Financial Times
Bank of England Ext
College of Arms
Inner Temple
Middle Temple Hall
WC1R
WC2R
WC1V
WC2A
EC1R
EC1M
EC1N
EC1A
EC1Y
EC4A
EC4M
EC4Y
EC4V
EC4N
EC2Y
EC2V
1 grid square represents 250 metres

SPITALFIELDS
Whitechapel
City of London
Southwark
EC2A
EC2M
EC2N
EC2R
EC3A
EC3V
EC3M
EC3R
EC3N
Liverpool Street Station
Spitalfields Market Hall
Exchange Square
Broadgate
Ice Arena
Finsbury Circus
Bank of England (& Mus)
Royal Exchange
Stock Exchange
Lloyd's
Leadenhall Market
Fenchurch Street Stn
Tower Gateway Stn
Tower Hill Stn
Tower of London
Tower Bridge
The Monument
Cannon Street Stn
London Bridge
London Bridge Station
London Bridge City Pier
Tower Millennium Pier
RNLI Lifeboat Station
HMS Belfast
Southwark Cath
Borough Market
Greater London Authority Headquarters (City Hall)
Winston Churchill's Britain at War Exp
London Dungeon
Tower Bridge Experience
St Katharine Docks
St Katharine Pier
Butler's Wharf Pier
Honourable Artillery Company HQ
Wesley's Chapel, House & Museum
Shoreditch Station
Aldgate East Stn
Aldgate Stn
Aldgate Bus Station
Whitechapel Art Gal
Toynbee Hall & Curtain Thtr
CITY ROAD
BISHOPSGATE
COMMERCIAL STREET
COMMERCIAL ROAD
WHITECHAPEL ROAD
WHITECHAPEL HIGH ST
SHOREDITCH HIGH STREET
GRACECHURCH ST
KG WILLIAM ST
BOROUGH HIGH ST
TOOLEY STREET
TOWER BR RD
LONDON WALL
HOUNDSDITCH
MINORIES
MANSELL ST
EAST SMITHFIELD
LWR THAMES ST
CHISWELL ST
MOORGATE
7
19
92

A
B
C
D
E
F
1
2
3
4
5
6
7
8
9
8
107
108
525
526
79
78
80
KENSINGTON
Earl's Court
South Kensington
West Brompton
W8
SW5
SW10
Holland Park
Round Pond
The Broad Walk
Kensington Palace State Apartments & Royal Ceremonial Dress Collection
Emb of the Russian Federation
Emb of The Philippines
Palace Green
St Mary Abbots Church Hall
Emb of Romania
Emb of Israel
College
Hotel
Fire Station
Emb of Greece
Holland Park School
Queen Elizabeth College
King George VI Youth Hostel
Holland House
Holland Park Theatre
Cricket Ground
Commonwealth Institute
Leighton House Museum & Art Gallery
Odeon Cinema
Kensington & Chelsea Town Hall
Linley Sambourne Ho
Emb of Jordan
Holland St Clinic
Primary School
Emb of Georgia
Kensington Mkt
High Street Kensington Stn
Heythrop College
Scarsdale Place Medical Cen
Emb of Armenia
The Kensington Clinic
High Comm of The Gambia
Emb of Belarus
Emb of Mongolia
High Comm of St Vincent & the Grenadines
Emb of South Vietnam
Richmond Coll
Lady Edens School
Emb of Paraguay
Emb of Bahrain
Emb of Morocco
Superstore
David Lloyd Leisure Centre
Cromwell Hospital
Hotel
Emb of the Netherlands
High Comm of Zambia
Emb of Estonia
High Comm of Fiji
Consulate of Guinea Bissau
Emb of Iraq
High Comm of Mauritius
Emb of Gabon
Huron Coll
Gloucester Rd Stn
Police Stn
Primary School
Surgeries
International Medical Cen
Eden Medical Centre
Avon Trading Estate
The Clinic
West Kensington Station
Gibbs Green Special School
Earl's Court Station
Earl's Court Exhibition Centre
On Sai Clnc
Courtfield Medical Cen
High Comm of Dominica
College
YMCA
Bousfield Primary School
Brompton Medical Centre
West Brompton Station
Imperial College of Science
Fulham Clinic
Normand Park Primary School
Redcliffe Sch
Emb of Guatemala
Primary School
Chelsea & Westminster Hosp
A&E
Brompton Cemetery
Farm Lane Trading Est
Turtle Key Arts Centre
Surgery
KENSINGTON ROAD
HYDE PARK GATE
KENSINGTON HIGH ST
CROMWELL ROAD A4
EARL'S COURT RD
WARWICK ROAD
OLD BROMPTON ROAD
GLOUCESTER ROAD
REDCLIFFE GARDENS
FINBOROUGH ROAD
LILLIE ROAD
NORTH END ROAD
FULHAM ROAD
CHURCH ST
PEMBROKE ROAD
A315
A4204
A3220
A3218
B316
B405
1 grid square represents 250 metres

Knightsbridge
Brompton
Belgravia
CHELSEA
KENSINGTON ROAD
KNIGHTSBRIDGE
A4 BROMPTON ROAD
CROMWELL ROAD
FULHAM ROAD
KING'S ROAD
SLOANE STREET
PONT STREET
BEAUCHAMP PL
THURLOE PLACE
SYDNEY STREET
OAKLEY STREET
ROYAL HOSPITAL ROAD
CHELSEA BRIDGE
PIMLICO RD
EMBANKMENT
BEAUFORT STREET
The Serpentine
Serpentine Road
South Carriage Drive
Harrods Store
Victoria & Albert Museum
Natural History Museum
Science Museum
Royal Albert Hall
Albert Memorial
Imperial College
Brompton Oratory
Royal Marsden Hosp
Royal Brompton & National Heart Hospitals
Chelsea Physic Garden
National Army Museum
Royal Hospital Chelsea
Carlyle's House (NT)
Cadogan Pier
Albert Bridge
Kensington & Chelsea
Wandsworth

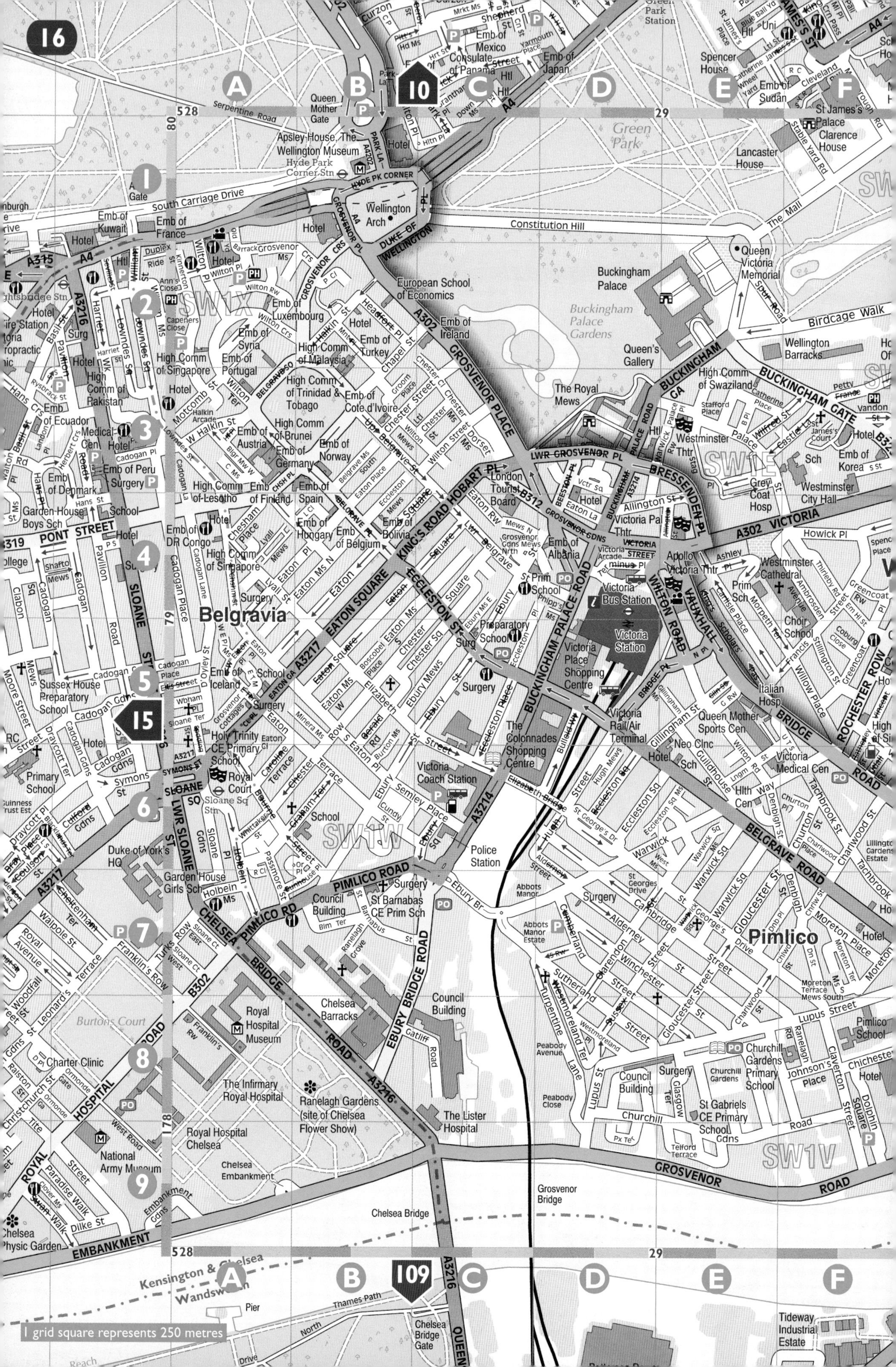
16
A
B
C
D
E
F
10
Curzon
Shepherd St
Emb of Mexico
Consulate of Panama
Emb of Japan
Green Park Station
Spencer House
Emb of Sudan
St James's Palace
Clarence House
Lancaster House
Cleveland
Serpentine Road
Queen Mother Gate
Apsley House, The Wellington Museum
Hyde Park Corner Stn
PARK LA
A4202
HYDE PK CORNER
Green Park
Wellington Arch
Constitution Hill
The Mall
South Carriage Drive
Emb of Kuwait
Emb of France
Hotel
Barrack
Grosvenor Ms
GROSVENOR CRS
GROSVENOR PL
DUKE OF WELLINGTON
Queen Victoria Memorial
Buckingham Palace
Buckingham Palace Gardens
Birdcage Walk
Wellington Barracks
European School of Economics
Emb of Ireland
Queen's Gallery
The Royal Mews
Knightsbridge Stn
A315
A4
A3216
Harriet St
Lowndes St
Lowndes Sq
Wilton Pl
Wilton Crs
Emb of Luxembourg
Emb of Syria
Emb of Portugal
High Comm of Singapore
High Comm of Malaysia
Emb of Turkey
Headfort Pl
Halkin St
Chapel St
High Comm of Trinidad & Tobago
Emb of Cote d'Ivoire
High Comm of Brunei
Emb of Norway
Emb of Austria
Emb of Germany
Emb of Finland
Emb of Spain
Emb of Hungary
Emb of Belgium
Emb of Bolivia
High Comm of Lesotho
Emb of DR Congo
High Comm of Singapore
Chester Street
Wilton Street
GROSVENOR PLACE
A302
Motcomb St
W Halkin St
High Comm of Pakistan
Emb of Ecuador
Emb of Peru
Emb of Denmark
Medical Cen
Surgery
School
Garden House Boys Sch
PONT STREET
B319
Cadogan Sq
Cadogan Place
Cadogan Lane
Pavilion Road
SLOANE ST
Chesham Place
Eaton Pl
Eaton Sq
Belgravia
EATON SQUARE
KING'S ROAD
HOBART PL
ECCLESTON ST
Eccleston Sq
LWR GROSVENOR PL
BRESSENDEN PL
BUCKINGHAM GATE
BUCKINGHAM PALACE ROAD
High Comm of Swaziland
Westminster Thtr
Grey Coat Hosp
Emb of Korea
Westminster City Hall
SW1E
London Tourist Board
Emb of Albania
Victoria Palace Thtr
VICTORIA STREET
A302 VICTORIA
Apollo Victoria Thtr
Westminster Cathedral
Victoria Bus Station
Victoria Station
Victoria Place Shopping Centre
WILTON ROAD
VAUXHALL BRIDGE ROAD
ROCHESTER ROW
Francis St
Willow Place
Italian Hosp
Queen Mother Sports Cen
Victoria Rail/Air Terminal
Victoria Medical Cen
Preparatory School
Prim School
Emb of Iceland
Sussex House Preparatory School
Holy Trinity CE Primary School
Royal Court
Sloane Sq Stn
SLOANE SQ
15
Cadogan Gdns
Draycott Pl
Primary School
A3217
LWR SLOANE ST
Duke of York's HQ
Garden House Girls Sch
Chester Terrace
Ebury Street
Victoria Coach Station
The Colonnades Shopping Centre
Elizabeth Bridge
SW1W
Police Station
PIMLICO ROAD
PIMLICO RD
Council Building
St Barnabas CE Prim Sch
Ebury Br
Warwick Sq
Warwick Way
BELGRAVE ROAD
Pimlico
Cambridge St
Alderney Street
Abbots Manor Estate
Churchill Gardens Primary School
St Gabriels CE Primary School
Council Building
Lupus Street
Pimlico School
SW1V
Chelsea Barracks
EBURY BRIDGE ROAD
CHELSEA BRIDGE ROAD
A3216
Royal Hospital Museum
The Infirmary Royal Hospital
Ranelagh Gardens (site of Chelsea Flower Show)
Royal Hospital Chelsea
Chelsea Embankment
The Lister Hospital
Burtons Court
Charter Clinic
ROYAL HOSPITAL ROAD
National Army Museum
Franklin's Row
Chelsea Physic Garden
EMBANKMENT
GROSVENOR ROAD
Grosvenor Bridge
Chelsea Bridge
Kensington & Chelsea
Wandsworth
Pier
Thames Path
Chelsea Bridge Gate
QUEENSTOWN ROAD
109
Tideway Industrial Estate
528
29
1 grid square represents 250 metres

Westminster 17
St James
WC2N
11
G
H
J
K
L
M
College of Pathology
Carlton House Ter
Duke of York Column
Old Admiralty
Horse Guards Parade
Horse Guards Road
Whitehall Ct
Old War Office
Hotel
Horse Guards Avenue
Royal Festival Hall
Gallery
Schiller College
Privy Council
Banqueting House
Privy Council Office
Old Treasury
Downing St
Ministry of Defence
Whitehall
Victoria Emb
A3212
A3211
Jubilee Gardens
British Airways London Eye
Shell Centre
York Road
A3200
International Rail Terminal
Waterloo Station
Waterloo Rd
Exton St
Mepham St
Alaska St
Sandell St
Wootton Street
Roupell Street
Young Vic Theatre
Old Vic Theatre
Richmond Ter
Department of Hlth
Cenotaph
Foreign & Commonwealth Office
Norman Shaw Building (MP's Offices)
King Charles St
Derby Ga
Parliament St
Canon Rw
St Stephens Parade
Portcullis House
Westminster Pier
Westminster Station
Dali Universal Exhibition
Saatchi Gallery
London Aquarium
County Hall
Forum Magnum Square
Belvedere Road
Chicheley Street
Leake Street
Spur Road
Coral St
Marsh
Launcelot St
Grindal St
Johanna Primary School
Frazier St
Baylis Road
Waterloo Health Centre
St James's Park
Cabinet War Rooms
Treasury
Great George Street
Birdcage Walk
Bridge Street
A302
A23
Westminster Bridge Road
The Nightingale School
Big Ben
Westminster Bridge
Florence Nightingale Museum
Old Queen Street
Q E Conf Centre
Storey's Gate
Middlesex Guildhall
Parliament Sq
Central Hall
Tothill St
Broadway
St James's Park Stn
Department of Trade & Industry
Caxton Hall
New Scotland Yard
Dacre St
Westminster Abbey
Little Cloisters
Deans Yard
Choir School
Little Deans Yard
Jewel Tower
Westminster School
Church House
College St
Abingdon Street
Houses of Parliament
Victoria Tower Gardens
City of Westminster
Lambeth
Thames Path
A&E
St Thomas's Hospital
United Medical & Dental Schools
Lambeth Palace Road
Upper Marsh
Royal Street
Carlisle Lane
Lambeth North Station
Lambeth
Police Stn
Westminster
Centaur St
Virgil St
Cosser Street
Hercules Rd
Archbishop's Park
Imperial War Museum
Old Pye St
Great Peter St
Surgery
Tufton Street
Civil Service Recreation Cen
St John's Concert Hall
Fire Station
Greycoat Hosp Sch
Westminster
Royal Horticultural Society New Hall
Medway St
Magistrates Court
Transport House
Horseferry Road
B323
A3203
Lambeth Palace
Museum of Garden History
Lambeth Road
Sidford Place
Kennington Road
Hotel
Old Paradise St
Norfolk Row
Pratt Walk
Juxon St
Lambeth Walk
Walnut Tree Walk
Walnut Tree Walk Primary School
18
Walcot Sq
Coroners Court
Marsham Street
Thames House
Dean Ryle St
Page Street
Lambeth Bridge
Millbank
Fire Brigade HQ
Lambeth High Street
Whitgift Street
Newport Street
Lollard Street
SW1P
SE11
John Islip St
Thorney St
Millbank Tower
Clore Gallery
Millbank Estate
Erasmus St
Herrick St
B326
Tate Britain
Millbank Millennium Pier
Works
Salamanca Place
Salamanca Street
Black Prince Rd
Lilac Pl
Gibson Road
Lillian Baylis School
Beaufoy Walk
Marylee Way
Vincent St
Regency St
Chapter St
Greycoat Hosp
Millbank Primary School
Fairley House Sch
Causton St
Cureton St
Atterbury St
The London Institute
A3036 Albert Embankment
Randall Road
Citadel Place
Jonathan Street
School Road
St Thomas' Childrens Day Hosp
Imperial College Sch of Medicine
A202
Vauxhall Br Rd
Pimlico Station
Rampayne St
Bessborough St
Primary School
Lindsay Sq
Ponsonby Pl
Tinworth Street
Graphite Square
Vauxhall Walk
Glasshouse Walk
Laud Street
Tyers Ter
Wickham St
Primary School
Newburn Street
Orsett St
Sancroft Street
Courtenay Street
Cardigan Street
Stables Way
Vauxhall Bridge
Grosvenor Road
Goding Street
London Balloon
Vauxhall
Vauxhall Station
Five Bridges Special School
Dolland St
Surgery
Kennington Lane
Windmill Row
A3212
St George's Square
Aylesford Street
St George's Sq Mews
Pimlico Gardens
River Thames
St George Wharf
Wandsworth Road
Bondway
Lambeth Rd
A3204
St Annes RC Primary School
Durham St
Harleyford Rd
Westminster Business Square
Oval Business Centre
Farnham Royal
Vauxhall St
Works
Kennington Grove
St Marks CE Prim School
Montford Place
Pegasus Pl
Henry Fawcett Primary School
Clayton St
Bowling Gn St
Surrey County Cricket Club (The Oval)
Nine Elms Lane
Parry St
A3205
Langley Lane
Bonnington Square
Lawn Lane
Lilian Baylis School
Ebbisham Drive
Bedser Close
Kennington Oval
Barrington Centre
New Covent Garden Market
30
31
Covent Garden Flower Market
Miles St
Young England RFC
109
Kennington
Archbishop Tenison's School
Oval Ho-Thtr
Ashmole St
Ashmole Primary School
Oval Station
Southbank Business Cen
Fentiman

18
12
17
110
A
B
C
D
E
F
1
2
3
4
5
6
7
8
9
531
32
LAMBETH
Newington
SE11
SE1
Walw
The Borou
Jubilee Gardens
Archbishop's Park
Lambeth Palace
BFI London IMAX Cinema
Schiller International School
Shell Centre
County Hall
International Rail Terminal
Waterloo Station
Waterloo East Stn
Young Vic Theatre
THE CUT
Old Vic Theatre
WATERLOO RD
WATERLOO ROAD
YORK ROAD
A3200
BLACKFRIARS ROAD
A201
UNION STREET
B300
BOROUGH ROAD
SOUTHWARK BRIDGE ROAD
MARSHALSEA RD
Crown Court at the Borough
Fire Brigade Mus
Friars Primary Foundation School
Johanna Primary School
Waterloo Health Centre
The Nightingale School
Florence Nightingale Museum
A&E
BAYLIS ROAD
WESTMINSTER BR RD
A3202
Lambeth North Station
Metropolitan Hospital
St George's Cathedral RC Primary School
St George's Cathedral
Churchill Clinic
Girls School
South Bank University
ST GEORGE'S CIRCUS
LONDON RD
Eden College
NEWINGTON CSWY
Inner London Sessions Ho (Crown Court)
Newington Gardens
HARPER RD
Council Building
Imperial War Museum
Geraldine Mary Harmsworth Park
IWM Annexe
ST GEORGE'S RD
Elephant and Castle Stn
Newington Court Business Cen
London Coll of Printing
Metropolitan Tabernacle
Elephant & Castle Shopping Centre
Elephant and Castle Stn
Castle Industrial Est
Elephant & Castle Leisure Cen
NEW KENT RD
A201
LAMBETH ROAD
A3203
KENNINGTON ROAD
A23
Walnut Tree Walk Primary School
The Michael Tippett School
Archbishop Sumners CE Primary School
London College of Further Education
NEWINGTON BUTTS
A3204
KENNINGTON LANE
Hinley Clinic
WALWORTH ROAD
Walworth Town Hall
Newington Industrial Est
John Smith House
The Cuming Mus
Crampton Primary School
Police Station
Surgery
Robert Browning Primary Sch
St Thomas Childrens Day Hosp
Lambeth County Court
Art School
Art College
KENNINGTON PARK ROAD
Kennington Station
Keyworth Primary School
St Pauls CE Primary School
Five Bridges Special School
Oval Business Centre
Westminster Business Square
St Marks CE Prim School
Surrey County Cricket Club (The Oval)
Henry Fawcett Primary School
HARLEYFORD RD
KENNINGTON OVAL
Archbishop Tenison's School
Oval Ho Thtr
Oval Station
Aspen House School
John Ruskin Primary School
A215
A3
PARK ROAD
1 grid square represents 250 metres

Old Operating Theatre Museum
St Thomas Hosp Operation Theatre
Winston Churchill's Britain at War Exp
Guys Hospital
London Bridge Station
Greater London Authority Headquarters (City Hall)
Tower Bridge Experience
Butler's Wharf Pier
Butlers Wharf
Tower Stairs
Wapping Head
TOOLEY STREET
ST THOMAS ST
A200
Magdalen St
Holyrood St
Vine Lane
Abbots La
Shand St
Cayenne Court
Barnham St
London City Mission
Tower Bridge Rd
Horselydown
Shad Thames
Copper Row
Brewery Square
Gainsford St
Lafone St
Curlew St
Maguire St
Design Mus
Butler's Wharf Business Centre
Police Stn
Magistrates Court
Queen Elizabeth St
Millennium Square
St Saviour's Dock
Mill Street
Jacob St
Providence Square
Chambers Street
Wolseley Street
Secondary School
Dockhead
Parkers Row
John Felton Rd
BERMONDSEY
JAMAICA ROAD
Scott Lidgett
Dickens Estate
St James CE J&I School
Old Jamaica Rd
Bus Est
Marine St
Thurland Rd
Frean St
Voyager Bus Est
Spa Road
Dockley Rd
Dockley Road Industrial Est
Lucey Rd
Amina Way
Goodwin Cl
Woolstaplers Wy
Yalding Rd
Rouel Rd
Lynsey Street
Eveline Lowe Estate
Alma Junior & Infant School
Alexis Str
Macks Road
SOUTHWARK PK RD
Longley St
Works
Spa School
Thorburn Square
Strathnairn St
Simms Rd
Esmeralda Rd
Lynton Rd
Paterson Pk
Monnow Rd
Welsford St
Abercorn Wy
ROLLS ROAD
Avocet Close
Avondale Estate
Avondale Sq
Avondale Pavement
School
Marlborough Gv
Six Bridges Trading Estate
B204
Malt St
Cantium Retail Park
North Peckham Civic Centre
Council Building
Olmar St
Works
Haymerle School
Haymerle Rd
Latona Rd
Bianca Rd
Unwin Close
Maismore St
Frensham Street
Bridale Close
Pennack Rd
Glengall Rd
Cator Street
Davey St
Alder Close
Ebley Cl
Gloucester Primary
Longhope
Bibury Cl
St George's Way
Winchcombe Business Centre
Brockworth Cl
Dragon Road
Birdlip Cl
St Georges
Trinity
Neate St
Church Road
Works
Depot St
ALBANY ROAD
Canal Street
Keesey Street
Neate Street
SUMMER RD
WILLOW
B214
Westmoreland Road
Bradenham Cl
Queen's Rw
Horsley
Phelp Street
Sondes St
Michael Faraday Primary School
Hopwood Rd
Beaconsfield Road
Aylesbury Estate
Thurlow St
Inville Road
Roland Wy
Lytham St
Merrow St
Saltwood Grove
Worth Grove
Liverpool Grove
Portland St
Burton Grove
Villa St
Brettell St
Aylesbury Rd
St Peters CE Primary School
Faraday Gardens
Wooler St
Date St
Trafalgar
Walworth Lower School
Sandford Rw
Merrow Wk
The New Aylesbury Medical Centre
Surgery
Townley St
Blackwood St
East Street
Dawes St
Dean's Buildings
Orb St
Nursery Row
English Martyrs RC Primary School
Stead St
Wadding St
Sedan Way
Alsace Rd
Thurlow Wk
Alvey Street
Surrey Square Park
Surrey Square Primary School
Surrey Grove
Aldbridge Street
Kinglake Street
Bagshot Street
Smyrk's Road
Mina Road
Walworth Upper School
Upnor Wy
Burgess Park Lake
Calmington Rd
Loncroft Road
Cobourg Road
Cobourg Primary School
Waite St
New Peckham Mosque
TRAFALGAR AV
B215
Glengall Ter
Nile Ter
Oakley Place
Surgery
Fire Station
Brodie St
Cooper's Road
Mawbey Place
Rowcross Street
Humphrey St
Shorncliffe Rd
Superstore
Madron St
Marcia Road
Surgery
Freemantle St
Exon St
East Street
Minnow Walk
Surgery
Beckway St
Tisdall Pl
Elsted St
Huntsman St
Tatum St
Flint Street
Kennedy Walk
Catesby St
Crail Rw
Hillery Cl
Barlow St
Darwin Street
Mason St
Townsend St
Comus Pl
Congreve Street
Massinger St
Stanford Pl
Hendre Rd
OLD KENT ROAD
A2
Townsend Primary School
Salisbury Cl
Hemp Walk
Chatham Street
Henshaw Street
John Maurice Cl
Searles Road
Balfour St
Rodney Road
Mandela Way
Bricklayer Arms Industrial Estate
DUNTON ROAD
B203
MANDELA WY
Milton Cl
Lynton Estate
Lynton Road
Bushwood Drive
Rich Industrial Estate
Oxley Close
Chaucer Dr
Cadet Dr
Alma Grove
Balaclava Road
Fort Road
Longfield Estate
Setchell Estate
Setchell Road
Alscot Wy
Council Building
Aylwin Girls School
Henley Dr
Alscot Rd Ind Est
Cadbury Wy
Keyse Road
Canon Murnane Rd
Boutcher CE Primary School
Hazel Way
Curtis Way
Setchell Way
Willow Walk
Bacon Gv
A2206
GRANGE ROAD
Rich Industrial Estate
Crimscott Street
Rich Industrial Est
Pages Walk
Page's Walk
Guinness Sq
Leroy Street
Aberdour St
TOWER BRIDGE RD
NEW KENT RD
St Saviour and St Olaves Sch
Bartholomew St
Rephidim St
Prioress St
Potier St
Chrysolyta Prim School
Law St
Bushbaby Close
Swan Md
Webb St
Tower Bridge Primary School
Southwark Coll
Wood's Pl
Grange Walk Mews
Grange Walk
Fendall St
The Grange
Grange Yd
Works
Bermondsey Town Hall
Neckinger Estate
Spa Road
Vauban Estate
Vauban St
Dunlop Pl
Alscot Rd
ABBEY STREET
Maltby Street
Bridewain St
Neckinger
Enid St
Old Jamaica Rd
Gedling Pl
B202
Millstream Rd
St Saviour's Estate
Riley Road
Purbrook Street
Stevens Street
Tanner Street
Pope St
Druid Street
Phoenix Wharf Road
Sweeney Crs
Arnold Estate
Caledonian Market
Newham's Row
Works
BERMONDSEY ST
Decima St
Cluny Estate
Cluny Pl
Works
Alice St
Rothsay St
Wild's Rents
Elim St
Graduate Pl
A2198
LONG LANE
Weston Street
Tabard Garden Estate
Staple Street
Manciple Street
Tabard Garden
Tabard Street
Pardoner St
GREAT DOVER STREET
A2
Spurgeon St
Chettle Close
Burbage Close
Deverell St
Theobald St
Geoffrey Chaucer School
Alderney Mews
Becket St
Pilgrimage Street
Globe St
Sterry St
Hankey Pl
Kipling St
Kipling Estate
Dunsterville Way
Council Building
Leathermarket Street
Leathermarket Court
Leathermarket Gardens
Tyers Gate
Fashion & Textile Design Museum
Tanner St
Hatchers Mews
Morocco St
Lamb Wk
A220
Black Swan Yd
Whites Grounds Estate
Brunswick Ct
Roper La
A100
TOWER BRIDGE RD
School
St John's Estate
DRUID ST
JAMAICA RD
Three Oak La
Coxson Wy
CRUCIFIX LANE
Primary School
Kirby Gv
City Banking College
Weston St
Melior St
Snowsfields
Guy St
Hamlet Way
Porlock St
Beormund School
Plantain Pl
Baden Place
Crosby Row
Tabard Garden Estate
Chapel Court
Newcomen St
Mermaid Ct
Tennis St
Bloomfield Clinic Guys
Greenwood Thtr
Providence Square
York Clinic
Talbot Yard
White Hart Yard
Bgh H St
A3
ST
Southwark Coroners Court
Tabard St
ROAD
Elephant ...
Decima St
33
34
79
80
178
111
13

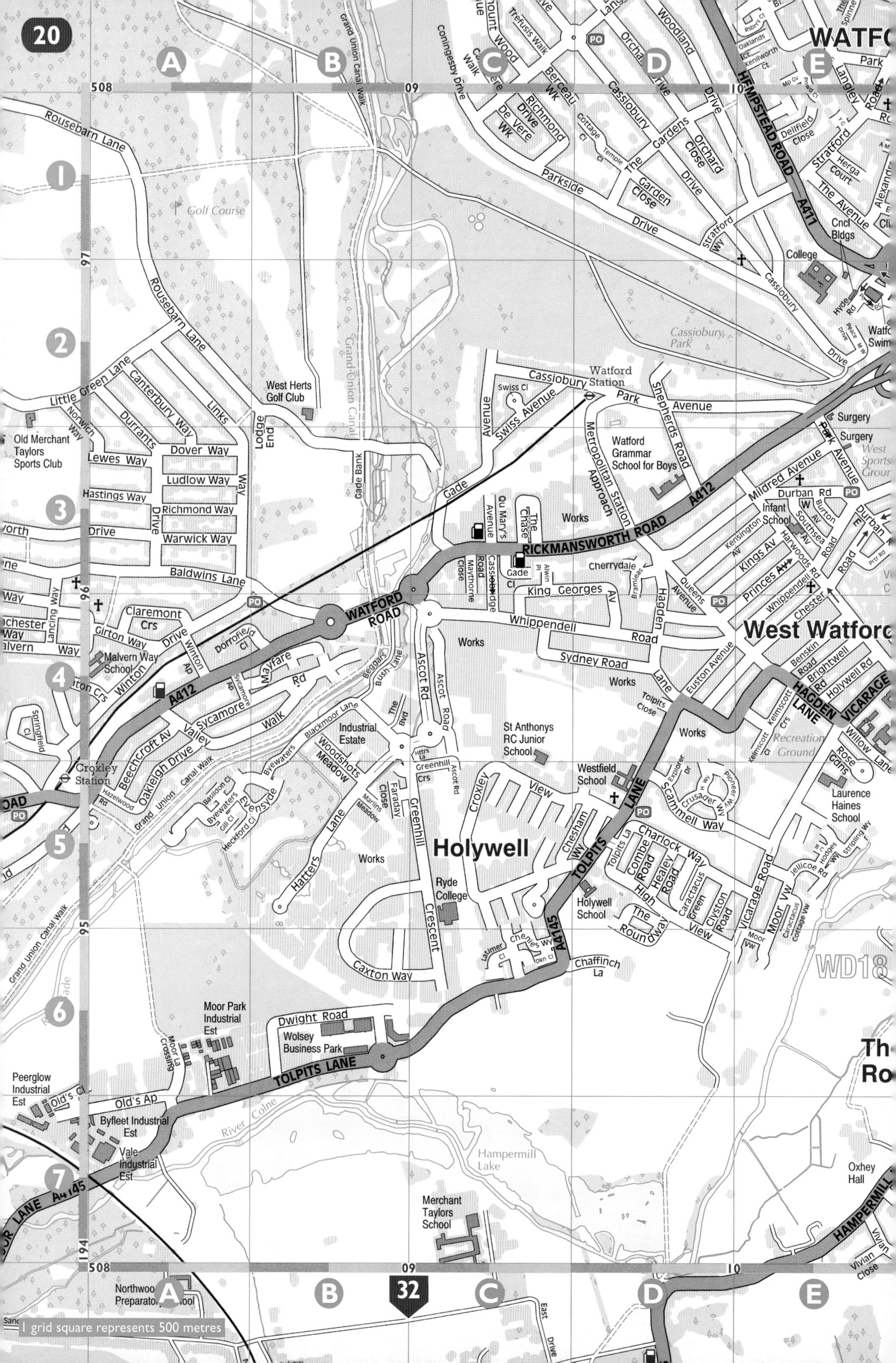

20
WATFORD
508
09
10
97
96
95
194
Rousebarn Lane
Golf Course
Grand Union Canal Walk
Grand Union Canal
Coningesby Drive
Trefusis Walk
Berceau Wk
Richmond Drive
De Vere Wk
Cottage Cl
Temple Cl
Cassiobury Drive
The Gardens
Orchard Close
Orchard Drive
Woodland Drive
Garden Close
Parkside Drive
Stratford Wy
HEMPSTEAD ROAD
A411
Oaklands
Kenilworth Ct
Park
Langley
Dellfield Close
Stratford Court
Herga Court
The Avenue
Cncl Bldgs
College
Hyde Rd
Peace Drive
Cassiobury Park
Little Green Lane
Canterbury Way
Durrants
Links Way
West Herts Golf Club
Lodge End
Norwich Way
Old Merchant Taylors Sports Club
Lewes Way
Dover Way
Ludlow Way
Hastings Way
Richmond Way
Warwick Way
Drive
Baldwins Lane
Cade Bank
Cassiobury
Swiss Cl
Swiss Avenue
Avenue
Watford Station
Park Avenue
Shepherds Road
Metropolitan Station Approach
Watford Grammar School for Boys
Surgery
Mildred Avenue
Park Avenue
West Watford
Durban Rd
Infant School
Burton Av
Southsea Av
Kensington Av
Kings Av
Harwoods Rd
Princes Av
Whippendell Rd
Chester
Works
A412
RICKMANSWORTH ROAD
Gade
Qu Mary's Avenue
The Chase
Maythorne Close
Cassiobridge Road
Gade Cl
Alwin Pl
Cherrydale
Bramleas
King Georges Av
Queens Avenue
Hagden Lane
Lancing Way
Claremont Crs
Girton Way
Malvern Way
Malvern Way School
Winton Drive
Winton Ap
Dorrofield Cl
WATFORD ROAD
Mayfare
Sycamore Ap
Rd
Whippendell Road
Sydney Road
Euston Avenue
Benskin Road
Brightwell Rd
Holywell Rd
HAGDEN LANE
VICARAGE
Kelmscott Crs
Kelmscott Cl
Recreation Ground
Willow Lane
Rose Gdns
Laurence Haines School
Springfield Cl
Winton Crs
Beechcroft Av
Valley
Sycamore Walk
Oakleigh Drive
Croxley Station
Hazelwood Rd
Grand Union Canal Walk
Blackmoor Lane
Beggars Bush Lane
Ascot Rd
Ascot Road
The Bvd
Industrial Estate
Woodshots Meadow
Bywaters
Basildon Cl
Evensyde
Gill Cl
Heckford Cl
Greenhill Crs
Faraday Close
Marlins Meadow
Greenhill Crescent
Hatters Lane
Works
St Anthonys RC Junior School
Croxley View
Westfield School
Scammell Way
Explorer Dr
Crusader Wy
Pioneer Wy
TOLPITS LANE
Holywell
Ryde College
Chesham Wy
Holywell School
Tolpits La
Charlock Way
Combe Road
Healey Road
High View
The Roundway
Caractacus Green
Clyston Road
Vicarage Road
Moor Vw
Jellicoe Rd
Hodges Wy
Stripling Wy
Caractacus Cottage Vw
Caxton Way
Latimer Cl
Chenies Wy
Dkn Cl
A4145
Chaffinch La
WD18
Moor Park Industrial Est
Dwight Road
Wolsey Business Park
Moor La Crossing
TOLPITS LANE
Peerglow Industrial Est
Old's Cl
Old's Ap
Byfleet Industrial Est
Vale Industrial Est
River Colne
Hampermill Lake
A4145
Merchant Taylors School
Oxhey Hall
HAMPERMILL
Vivian Close
Northwood Preparatory School
32
East Drive
1 grid square represents 500 metres

WD24
Watford Junction Station
Colonial Business Park
Colonial Wy
Ind Est
Industrial Park
A4008
Highwood Primary School
Hartspring Sports Centre
HARTSPRING
B462
Station Rd
Reeds Cres
Hallam Cl
Exeter Cl
Orphanage Rd
Monica Cl
Raphael Dr
Radlett Road
Rhodes Way
Link Rd
Park Av
Park Avenue
Scottswood Rd
Mead Way
Mill Way
Maple Cl
Surgery
Bushey Mill Lane
The Purcell School
Police Station
Mag Court
Woodford Road
St John's Rd
Clarendon Rd
Estcourt Road
Sotheron Rd
Queen's Road
Sutton Rd
Prince St
Cross St
Duke St
Works
Recreation Ground
Brocklesbury Cl
Ver-Colne Valley Walk
River Colne
STEPHENSON WAY
Golf Cl
Park Cl
West Herts College
Golf Course
Queens School
ALDENHAM ROAD
ST ALBANS ROAD
A412
BEECHEN GROVE
A411
Town Hall
Business Cen
Pal Theatre
Indoor Market
BEECHEN GV
Gladstone Road
Grosvenor Rd
Primary School
Ebury Rd
Woolmerdine Ct
Greatham Rd
William St
Ashdon Road
Bendysh Rd
Arthur St
Walton Road
Greatham Road Industrial Estate
Bushey Hall Golf Club
Bushey Hall Dr
Finch
UPTON RD
CASSIO ROAD
Telephone Exchange
Marlborough Rd
Francis Rd
Market Street
St Mary's Rd
Harlequin Shopping Cen
High St
EXCHANGE RD
VICARAGE RD
MERTON RD
Surgery
King St
Watford High Street Stn
Mosque
Lady's Cl
Water Lane
Hotel
A411 WATERFIELDS WAY
Bushey Hall Road
New Rd
Superstore
Lambert Ct
Bushey Grove Road
St Leonards Cl
Napier Dr
Grove Hall Rd
Ashlyn Cl
Fishers Close
Heathfield Road
Woodlands Road
Belmont Road
The Avenue
International University
University Cl
WIGGENHALL ROAD
Watford Grammar School for Girls
Museum
Lwr High St
Watford Fld Rd
Neal St
Junior School
Muriel Av
Theatre
Gazelda Industrial Est
Superstore
Colne Valley Retail Park
LWR HIGH ST
Malden Flds
Three Valleys Wy
Beechcroft Road
Silverdale Rd
Hillside Road
Highfield Rd
Grange Road
Vale Rd
Bushey Hall Swimming Pool
22
Clifton Rd
St James Rd
Liverpool Rd
Occupation Rd
Watford FC & Saracens RFC (Vicarage Road Stadium)
Watford General Hospital
Fisher Industrial Est
Watford Arches Retail Park
Colne Bridge Retail Park
The Larches
Bushey Manor Junior School
Falconer School
Cardiff Rd
Cardiff Road Industrial Est
Oxhey Park
DALTON WAY A411
Ye Corner
Oxhey Infant School
CHALK HILL A411
LONDON ROAD
Haydon Rd
Bushey Health Centre
Bushey Hall School
Bushey Mus & Art Gallery
Rudolph Road
ALDENHAM RD
Edward Rd
Cross Road
Works
Capel Rd
Villiers Rd
Field Rd
Lwr Paddock Rd
Paddock Cl
Sacred Heart Junior Middle & Infant School
The Clover Fld
Hayden Dell
Kemp Place
Riverside Road
Crossmead
Coine Avenue
The Coppice
DEACONS HILL
Blackwell Dr
ROAD
A4125
Oxhey
Bushey Station
PINNER ROAD
Cedar Road
Kingsfield Road
Grover Road
Upr Paddock Road
Firbank Dr
Haydon Hill
Long Cft
Silk Mill Road
Russell Wy
Brookside Road
Ransom Cl
Woodwave
Oxhey Rd
Heathfield Cl
Bromet School
Heath Rd
Oxhey Avenue
Bucks Av
Wilcot Cl
Talbot Av
EASTBURY
Thorpe Crs
Sonia Cl
Lane
Blenheim Cl
Sheridan Rd
Watford Heath
Merry Hill
kery
A4125
BROOKDENE AVENUE
B4542
The Pastures
Meadowbank
Nancy Downs
Green
Watford Heath
Sherwoods Road
Elm Avenue
Lowson Grove
OXHEY PINNER RD
A4008
The Oaks
The Pathway
Anthony Cl
Raglan Gardens
Broadfields Lane
Oaklands
Francis Cl
Avenue
Hillcroft
Beaulieu Close
Green La
Highlands
Oxhey Park Golf Centre
Upr Hitch
PRESTWICK
Crescent
Oxhey Warren
33
The Margehoe
The Hill
Wood
The Courtway
Avenue
OXHEY
South Oxhey Playing Fields
F
G
H
J
K
1
2
3
4
5
6
7
11
12
13
94
95
96
97

22
21
34
Patchetts Green
BUSHEY
Merry Hill
Bushey Heath
Hartspring Sports Centre
Hartspring Industrial Park
Cp House Business Centre
Superstore
The Purcell School
Queens School
International University
Bushey Hall Swimming Pool
Bushey Hall School
Bushey Museum & Art Gallery
Bournehall Junior & Infant School
Little Reddings Primary School
Meadow Wood School
Bushey Meads School
Bushey Golf & Country Club
Golf Course
St Hildas School
St Margarets School
Ashfield Junior School
Police Station
Council Building
Bushey & District Synagogue
Primary School
Immanuel College
Hartsbourne JMI School
Cemetery
NORTH WESTERN AVENUE
A41
M1
A411
A4140
B462
HIGH STREET
SPARROWS HERNE
ELSTREE RD
HIGH ROAD
ALDENHAM ROAD
HARTSPRING LA
Little Bushey Lane
Hilfield Lane
Finch Lane
Merry Hill Road
1 grid square represents 500 metres

Aldenham School
Aldenham Road
North Medburn Farm
Slades Farm
Butterfly Lane
Elstree Golf Club
Haberdashers' Aske's Boys' School
Elstree Aerodrome
Aldenham Road
A5183
Tykes Water Lake
Hogg Lane
Dagger Lane
Haberdashers' Aske's Girls' School
Home Farm
Aldenham Road
Hilfield Park Reservoir
Aldenham Country Park
ELSTREE HILL N
Elstree
Surgery
St Nicholas Cl
School
Hertsmere Progressive Synagogue
(TYLERS WAY)
Dagger Lane
Aldenham Reservoir
Lands' End
WATFORD ROAD
HIGH ST
Schubert Rd
Rodgers Cl
Delius Cl
Beethoven Rd
ELSTREE ROAD
A411
Lismarrine Industrial Park
M1
A411 ELSTREE ROAD
N WESTERN AV (WATFORD BY-PASS)
A41
Sullivan Way
Elgar Close
Coates Rd
ELSTREE HILL SOUTH
Summer Gv
May Gdns
Fortune La
A411
Caldecote Hill
A409
Paynesfield Rd
Centennial Avenue
ELSTREE HL S
HEATHBOURNE ROAD
Brockley Hill Farm
Junction 4
M1
Royal National Orthopaedic Hospital
Works
Nutt Gv
A41
A5 BROCKLEY
ALLUM
Golf Cou
Cemet
Hertfordsh
24
35

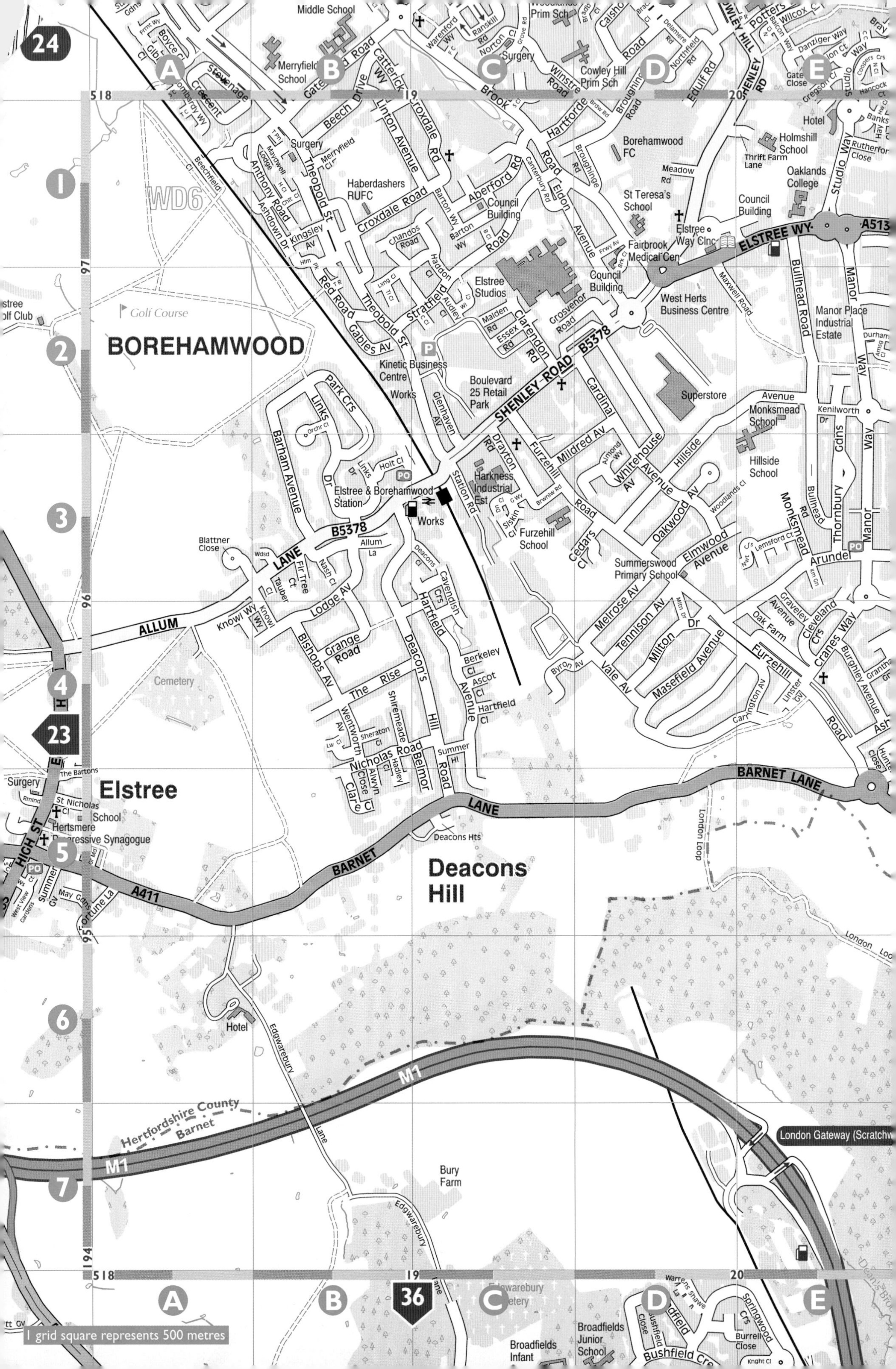

24
23
36
A
B
C
D
E
1
2
3
4
5
6
7
518
19
20
97
96
95
194
BOREHAMWOOD
Elstree
Deacons Hill
WD6
Middle School
Merryfield School
Gateshead Road
Catterick Wy
Stevenage Crescent
Boyce Cl
Lombardy Wy
Beech Drive
Linton Avenue
Croxdale Rd
Croxdale Road
Surgery
Merryfield Cl
Theobold St
Anthony Road
Ashdown Dr
Kingsley Av
Haberdashers RUFC
Aberford Rd
Council Building
Barton Wy
Barton Road
Chandos Road
Haddon Cl
Elstree Studios
Stratfield Rd
Audley Cl
Red Road
Gables Av
Golf Course
Beechfield Cl
Malden Rd
Essex Rd
Clarendon Rd
Grosvenor Road
Kinetic Business Centre
Works
Boulevard 25 Retail Park
SHENLEY ROAD
B5378
Glenhaven Av
Park Crs
Links Dr
Orchard Cl
Barham Avenue
Holt Cl
PO
P
Elstree & Borehamwood Station
Station Rd
Drayton Rd
Harkness Industrial Est
Furzehill Road
Furzehill School
Cardinal Av
Mildred Av
Whitehouse Avenue
Almond Wy
Blattner Close
LANE
Allum La
ALLUM
Fir Tree Ct
Nash Cl
Tauber Cl
Knowl Wy
Lodge Av
Deacons Cl
Cavendish Crs
Hartfield Avenue
Grange Road
Bishops Av
The Rise
Deacon's Hill Road
Berkeley Cl
Ascot Cl
Hartfield Cl
Wentworth Av
Sheraton Cl
Shiremeade
Nicholas Road
Belmor
Hadley Cl
Alwyn Close
Clare Cl
Summer Hl
Cemetery
Brook Road
Winstre Road
Cowley Hill Prim Sch
Hartforde Road
Broughinge Road
Eldon Avenue
Canterbury Rd
Northfield Rd
Eduif Rd
SHENLEY RD
Potters
Wilcox Cl
Danziger Way
Gate Close
Gregson Cl
Studio Way
Hotel
Holmshill School
Thrift Farm Lane
Oaklands College
Rutherford Close
Banks
Hancock
Borehamwood FC
Meadow Rd
St Teresa's School
Elstree Way Clnc
Fairbrook Medical Cen
Council Building
ELSTREE WY
A5135
West Herts Business Centre
Maxwell Road
Bullhead Road
Manor Way
Manor Place Industrial Estate
Durham
Superstore
Avenue
Monksmead School
Kenilworth Dr
Hillside Av
Hillside School
Oakwood Av
Woodlands Cl
Monksmead Rd
Thornbury Gdns
Manor Way
Cedars Cl
Elmwood Avenue
Summerswood Primary School
Lemsford Ct
Arundel
Melrose Av
Tennison Av
Milton Dr
Masefield Avenue
Byron Av
Vale Av
Graveley Avenue
Oak Farm
Cleveland Crs
Cranes Way
Burghley Avenue
Furzehill Road
Carrington Av
Linster Gv
BARNET LANE
London Loop
Surgery
The Bartons
St Nicholas Cl
School
Hertsmere Progressive Synagogue
HIGH ST
Summer Gv
May Gdns
West View Gardens
Fortune La
A411
BARNET LANE
Deacons Hts
Hotel
Edgwarebury Lane
M1
Hertfordshire County
Barnet
London Gateway (Scratchwood)
Bury Farm
Edgwarebury
Edgwarebury Cemetery
Broadfields Junior School
Broadfields Infant
Bushfield Close
Bushfield Cre
Springwood Crs
Burrell Close
Knight Cl
Warren Shawe La
1 grid square represents 500 metres

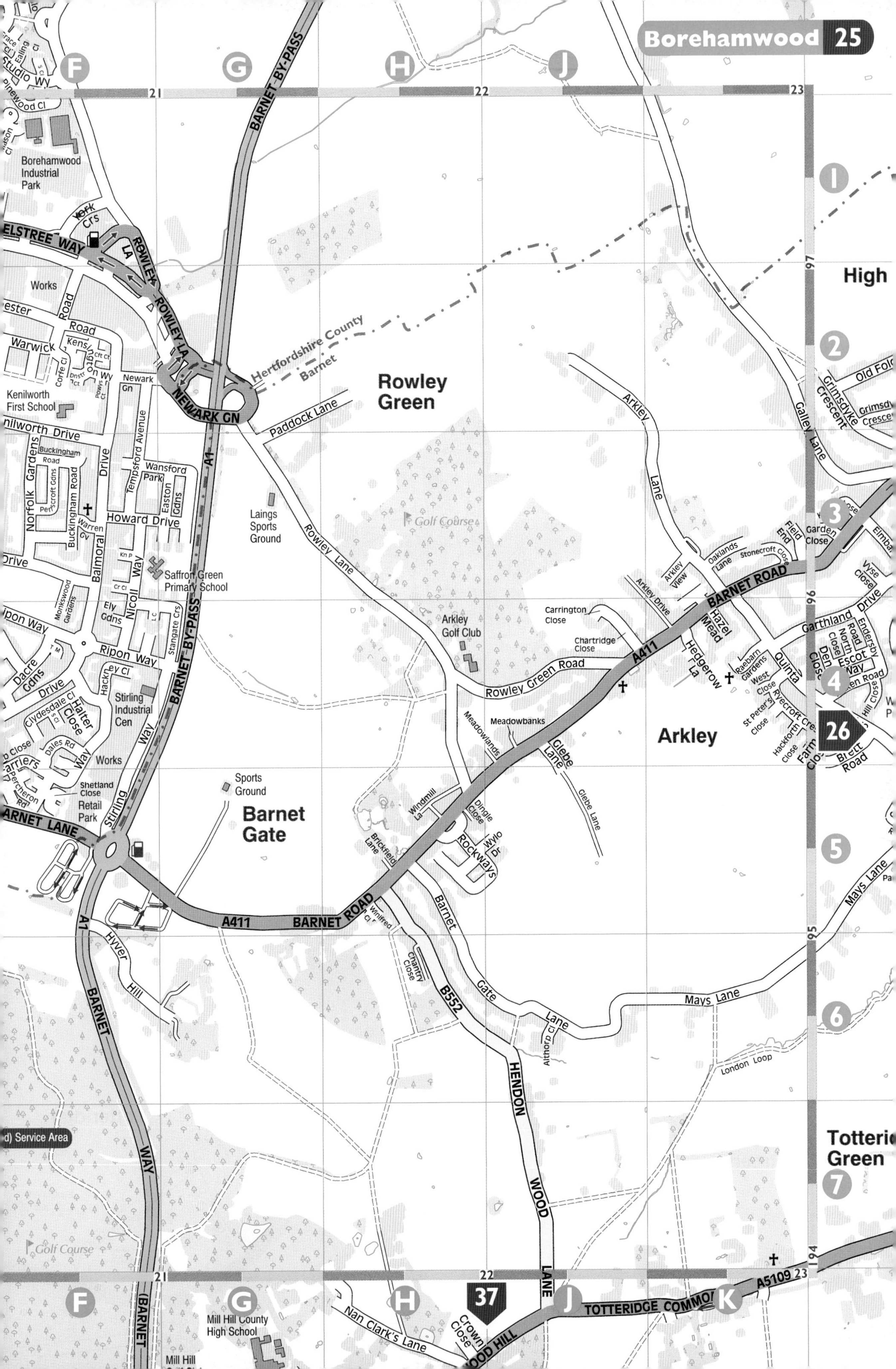
F
G
H
J
K
21
22
23
97
96
95
94
BARNET BY-PASS
Borehamwood Industrial Park
ELSTREE WAY
Works
Warwick
Kenilworth First School
Hertfordshire County
Barnet
Rowley Green
Paddock Lane
NEWARK GN
Laings Sports Ground
Golf Course
Rowley Lane
Arkley Golf Club
Rowley Green Road
Saffron Green Primary School
Howard Drive
Balmoral Drive
Ripon Way
Stirling Industrial Cen
Sports Ground
Barnet Gate
Shetland Close
Retail Park
BARNET LANE
A411
BARNET ROAD
A1
Arkley
Arkley Lane
Galley Lane
Mays Lane
London Loop
HENDON WOOD LANE
B552
Barnet Gate Lane
Glebe Lane
Meadowbanks
Carrington Close
Chartridge Close
Hedgerow La
Quinta
Garthland Drive
High
Totteridge Green
TOTTERIDGE COMMON
A5109
Nan Clark's Lane
Crown Close
Mill Hill County High School
Mill Hill
Golf Course
Service Area
BARNET WAY
Hyver Hill
Chantry Close
Brickfield Lane
Windmill La
Dingle Close
Rockways
26
37

Monken Hadley
High Barnet
Hadley
Chipping Barnet
BARNET
Underhill
Ducks Island
Totteridge Green
Totteridge
EN5
N20
ST ALBANS ROAD
HADLEY GREEN
A1000
WOOD STREET
A411
HIGH ST
BARNET HILL
GT NORTH
BARNET ROAD
TOTTERIDGE COMMON
A5109
TOTTERIDGE VILLAGE
Christ Church CE Primary School
Queen Elizabeths Boys School
Foulds School
Barnet Hospital Chest Clinic
Barnet General Hospital
Whitings Hill Primary School
Underhill J&I School
Barnet Hill JMI School
The Spires Shopping Centre
Barnet Museum
Barnet College
The Bull Theatre
Police Station
Queen Elizabeth Centre
Queen Elizabeths Girls School
High Barnet Station
Barnet Health Centre
Barnet FC (Underhill)
Ravenscroft School
Grasvenor Avenue Infant School
St Andrews CE JMI School
South Herts Golf Club
Monken Hadley CE Primary School
St Marthas Convent Senior School
Old Fold Manor Golf Club
Barnet Trading Estate
King George's Field
Old Court House Rec Gnd
Playing Field
Golf Course
London Loop
Cemetery
Works
Surgery
1 grid square represents 500 metres

25
38

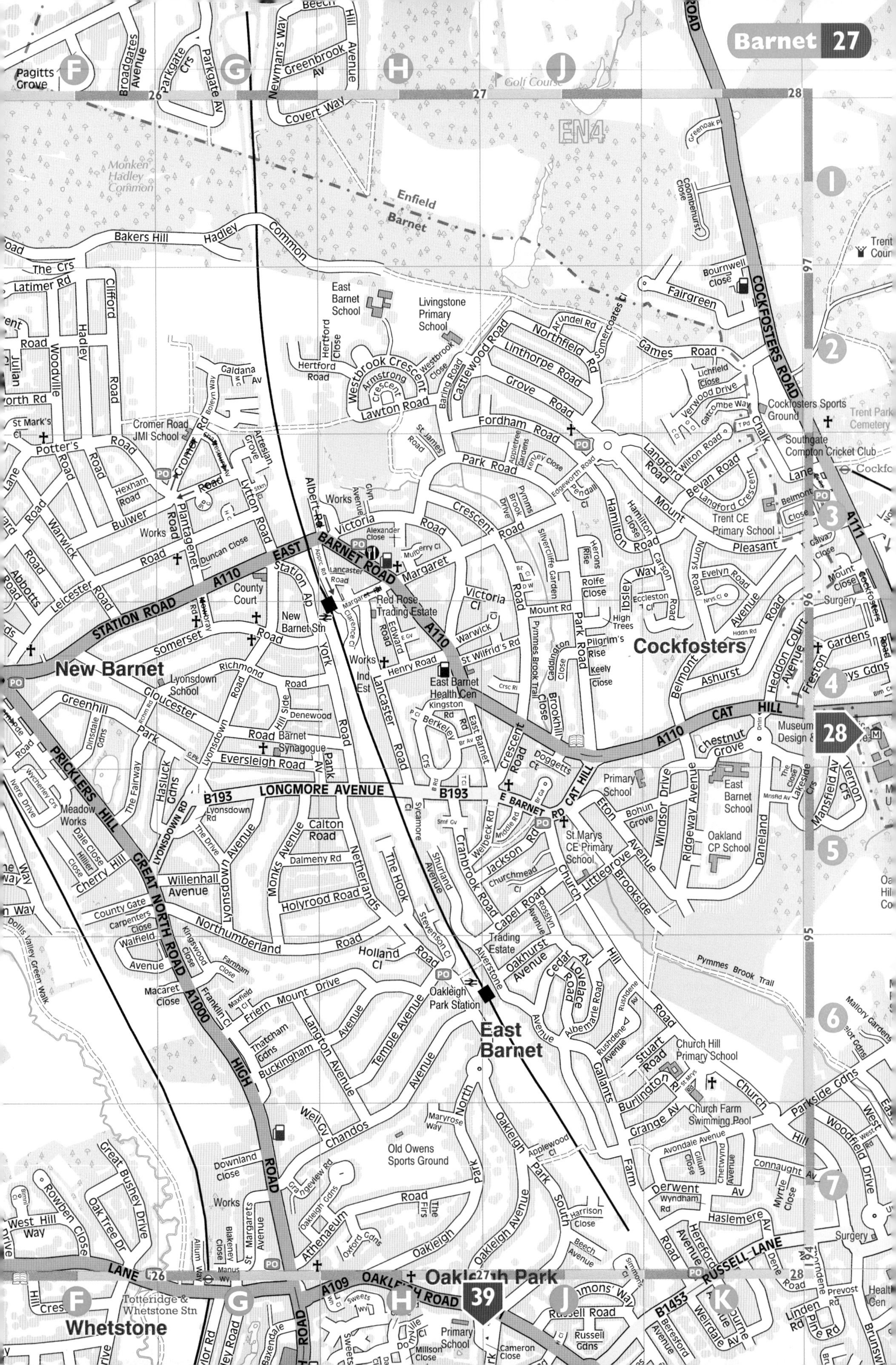Barnet 27
F
G
H
J
I
K
26
27
28
97
96
95
94
2
3
4
5
6
7
28
39
EN4
Golf Course
Monken Hadley Common
Enfield
Barnet
Pagitts Grove
Broadgates Avenue
Parkgate Crs
Parkgate Av
Newman's Way
Greenbrook Av
Beech Hill Avenue
Covert Way
Bakers Hill
Hadley Common
The Crs
Latimer Rd
Clifford Road
Hadley Road
Woodville Road
Julian
North Rd
St Mark's Cl
Potter's Road
East Barnet School
Livingstone Primary School
Hertford Close
Hertford Road
Westbrook Crescent
Armstrong Crescent
Westbrook Close
Lawton Road
Baring Road
Castlewood Road
Caldana Av
Bolelyn Way
Cromer Road JMI School
Cromer Rd
Artesian Grove
Lytton Road
Hexham Road
Bulwer Road
Warwick Road
Leicester Road
Abbotts Road
Plantagenet Road
Works
Duncan Close
Station Road
A110
East Barnet Road
County Court
New Barnet Stn
Station Ap
Albert Rd
Victoria Road
Alexander Close
Lancaster Road
Margaret Road
Mulberry Cl
Red Rose Trading Estate
Clarence Ct
Edward Road
New Barnet
Somerset Road
Richmond Road
Lyonsdown School
Gloucester Road
Greenhill Park
Dinsdale Gdns
The Fairway
Hasluck Gdns
Lyonsdown Road
Hill Side
Denewood Road
York Road
Barnet Synagogue
Eversleigh Road
Park Road
Ind Est
Lancaster Road
Henry Road
East Barnet Health Cen
Kingston Rd
Berkeley Crs
East Barnet Road
Longmore Avenue
B193
Prickler's Hill
Great North Road
Meadow Works
Dale Close
Hillier Close
Cherry Hill
Lyonsdown Rd
The Drive
Lyonsdown Avenue
Willenhall Avenue
County Gate
Carpenters Close
Walfield Avenue
Kingswood Close
Monks Avenue
Calton Road
Dalmeny Rd
Holyrood Road
Netherlands
The Hook
Northumberland Road
Holland Cl
Stevenson Cl
Shurland Avenue
Sycamore Cl
Cranbrook Road
Macaret Close
Farnham Close
Franklin Cl
Maxfield Cl
Friern Mount Drive
Thatcham Gdns
Buckingham Road
Langton Avenue
Temple Avenue
Oakleigh Park Station
East Barnet
A1000
High Road
Well Cv
Chandos Avenue
Maryrose Way
Old Owens Sports Ground
Downland Close
Works
Oakleigh Gdns
Athenaeum Road
The Firs
Oxford Gdns
Oakleigh Road
Oakleigh Avenue
Oakleigh Park South
Applewood Cl
Harrison Close
Beech Avenue
North
Park
Great Bushey Drive
Oak Tree Dr
Rowben Close
West Hill Way
Blakeney Close
St Margarets Avenue
Allum Way
Manus Wy
Lane
Totteridge & Whetstone Stn
Whetstone
Oakleigh Park
Oakleigh Road
A109
Sweets Wy
Domville Cl
Millson Close
Primary School
Cameron Close
Russell Road
Russell Gdns
Simmons Way
Russell Lane
B1453
Weirdale Av
Beresford Avenue
Northfield Rd
Arundel Rd
Somercoates Cl
Linthorpe Road
Grove Road
Fordham Road
St James Road
Park Road
Appletree Gardens
Kenley Close
Edgeworth Road
Pendall Cl
Crescent Road
Pymms Brook Drive
Victoria Cl
Warwick Cl
St Wilfrid's Rd
Silvercliffe Gardens
Herons Rise
Rolfe Close
Mount Rd
Pymmes Brook Trail
Caddington Close
Brookhill Close
Park Road
Pilgrim's Rise
Keely Close
High Trees
Cockfosters
Hamilton Road
Hamilton Close
Ibsley Way
Eccleston Cl
Carson Road
Mount Road
Langford Road
Games Road
Lichfield Close
Verwood Drive
Catcombe Way
Wilton Road
Bevan Road
Langford Crescent
Chalk Lane
Trent CE Primary School
Pleasant
Norrys Road
Evelyn Road
Avenue Road
Belmont Close
Ashurst
Heddon Court Avenue
Bournwell Close
Fairgreen
Coombehurst Close
Greenoak Pl
Cockfosters Road
Cockfosters Sports Ground
Southgate Compton Cricket Club
Trent Park Cemetery
Trent Cour
A111
Galva Close
Mount Close
Surgery
Freston Gardens
Norrys Gdns
Museum Design
Cat Hill
Chestnut Grove
Doggetts Ct
Cat Hill
E Barnet Rd
St Marys CE Primary School
Primary School
Bohun Grove
Eton Avenue
Windsor Drive
Ridgeway Avenue
East Barnet School
Oakland CP School
Daneland
The Close
Lakeside Crs
Mansfield Av
Vernon Crs
Welbeck Rd
Middle Rd
Jackson Rd
Churchmead Cl
Church Hill Road
Littlegrove
Brookside
Capel Road
Rosslyn Avenue
Trading Estate
Alverstone Avenue
Oakhurst Avenue
Cedar Av
Lovelace Road
Albemarle Road
Rushdene Avenue
Rushdene Av
Pymmes Brook Trail
Stuart Road
Church Hill Primary School
Burlington Ri
St Mrys
Church Farm Swimming Pool
Grange Av
Gallants Farm Road
Avondale Avenue
Gillum Close
Chetwynd Avenue
Connaught Av
Myrtle Close
Derwent Av
Wyndham Rd
Haslemere Av
Hereford Avenue
Church Hill Road
Parkside Gdns
Woodfield Drive
West Rd
Mallory Gardens
Surgery
Dene Road
Prevost Rd
Linden Rd
Pine Rd
Health Cen
Brunswick

28
A
B
C
D
E
528
29
30
97
96
95
194
1
2
3
4
5
6
7
University of Middlesex
Trent Country Park
Snakes Lane
Golf Course
ENFIELD ROAD
ENFIELD RD
A110
Cockfosters Sports Ground
Trent Park Cemetery
Southgate Compton Cricket Club
Cockfosters Station
COCKFOSTERS ROAD
A111
Norfolk Close
West Close
East Close
Trent Park Golf Club
Westpole Avenue
Gloucester Gardens
Kent Drive
Southgate School
Sussex Way
BRAMLEY ROAD
Oakwood Station
Oakwood Medical Cen
Chicken Shed Theatre
Museum of Domestic Design & Architecture
Middlesex University
East Barnet School
Oak Hill College
CHASE SIDE
Reservoir Road
De Bohun Primary School
Addison Av
The Fairway
Cowper Gardens
Green Road
Hood Avenue
Trent Gardens
De Bohun Av
Merrivale
Sheringham Avenue
Oakwood
Saxon Wy
Dalrymple Cl
Primary School
Chase Road
Linden Way
Orchard Av
Nursery Rd
Synagogue
Ivy Road
West Grove Primary School
Salcombe School
Oakwood Av
Oakwood Park Rd
Fountains Crs
Winchmore Hill
Wynchgate
Queen Elizabeth's Drive
South Lodge Drive
Lonsdale Drive
Lowther Drive
Merryhills Drive
Prince George Av
Brantwood Gardens
Sir Thomas Lipton Memorial Hospital
OSIDGE LANE
B1453
Monkfrith Primary School
Brookside
Fernley Road
Knoll Drive
Osidge JMI School
Crown Lane Clinic
Police Station
Southgate Stn
Southgate Leisure Cen
Burleigh Gardens
Ashmole Centre
Ashmole School
Southgate College
HIGH STREET
THE BOURNE
Grovelands Priory Hospital
Bourneside Sports Club
N14
Brunswick Park JMI School
Osidge
40
27
Pymmes Brook Trail
Surgery
1 grid square represents 500 metres

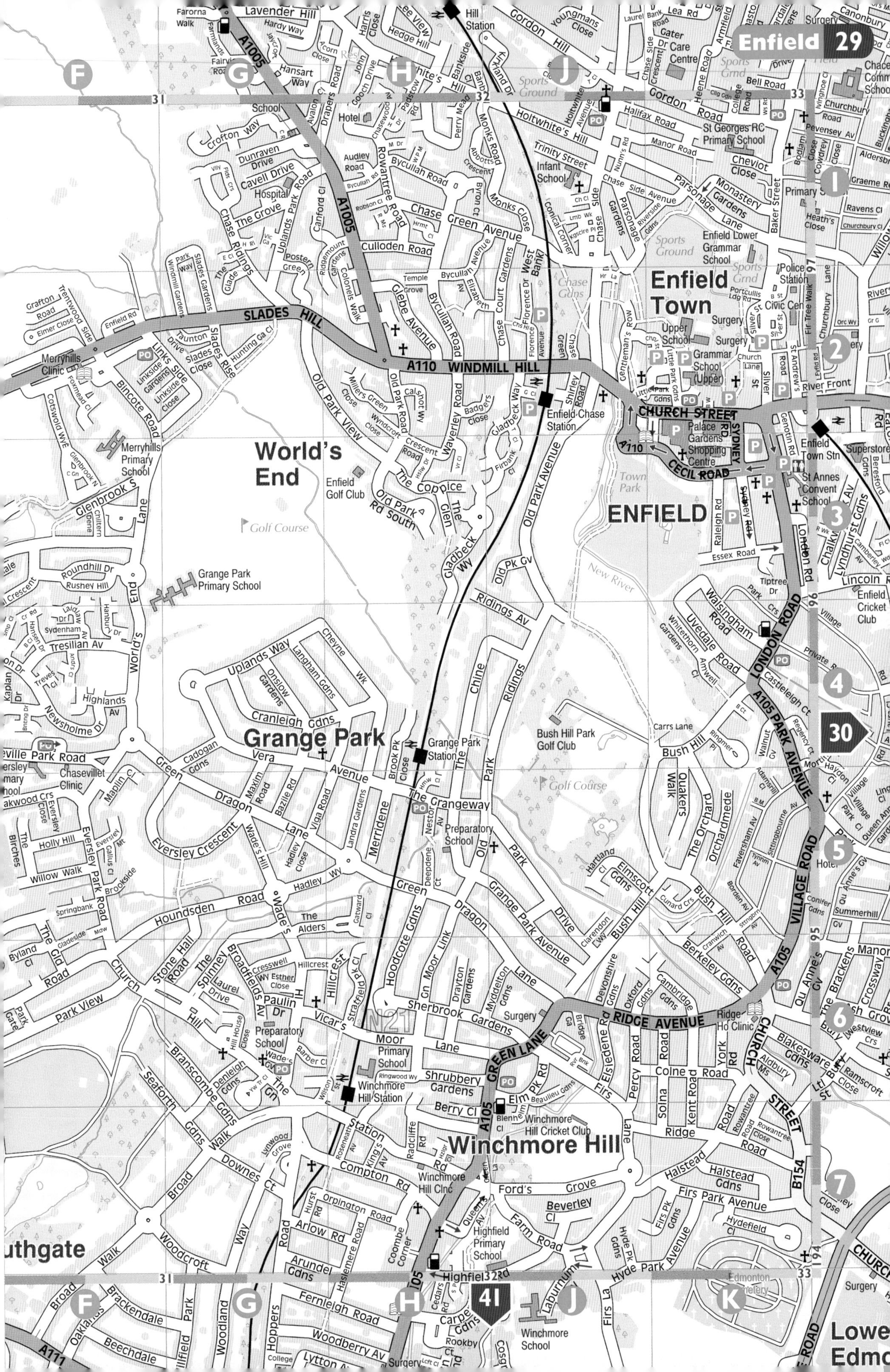

Enfield Town
ENFIELD
World's End
Grange Park
Winchmore Hill
Enfield Golf Club
Golf Course
Bush Hill Park Golf Club
Town Park
New River
Enfield Chase Station
Enfield Town Stn
Grange Park Station
Winchmore Hill Station
Hill Station
Gordon Hill
Lavender Hill
Hardy Way
Hansart Way
Crofton Way
Dunraven Drive
Cavell Drive
Hospital
The Grove
Chase Ridings
Uplands Park Road
Canford Cl
Culloden Road
Chase Green Avenue
Bycullah Road
Rowantree Road
Glebe Avenue
Bycullah Avenue
Chase Court Gardens
Florence Dr
Holtwhite's Hill
Halifax Road
Manor Road
Gordon Road
Trinity Street
Infant School
Chase Side
Parsonage Lane
Monastery Gardens
Baker Street
Cheviot Close
St Georges RC Primary School
Enfield Lower Grammar School
Police Station
Upper School
Grammar School (Upper)
Civic Cen
Surgery
Churchbury Lane
Fir Tree Walk
River Front
Sports Ground
Chase Gdns
SLADES HILL
A110 WINDMILL HILL
A1005
CHURCH STREET
CECIL ROAD
SYDNEY RD
Palace Gardens Shopping Centre
St Annes Convent School
Enfield Cricket Club
Merryhills Clinic
Merryhills Primary School
Bincote Road
Slades Gardens
Windmill Gardens
Links Side
Old Park View
Old Park Road
Waverley Road
Badgers Close
Gladbeck Way
The Coppice
The Glen
Old Park Rd South
Old Park Avenue
Old Pk Gv
Ridings Av
Chine
Ridings
Glenbrook S
Chiltern Dene
Roundhill Dr
Rushey Hill
Grange Park Primary School
Sydenham Av
Tresilian Av
Highlands Av
Newsholme Dr
World's End Lane
Chaseville Park Road
Chaseville Clinic
Uplands Way
Onslow Gardens
Langham Gdns
Cheyne Wk
Cranleigh Gdns
Cadogan Gdns
Vera Avenue
Maxim Road
Bazile Rd
Viga Road
Landra Gardens
Merridene
Brook Pk Close
The Grangeway
Nestor Av
Preparatory School
Green Dragon Lane
Eversley Crescent
Wade's Hill
Hadley Close
Hadley Wy
Eversley Park Road
Holly Hill
Willow Walk
Brookside
Houndsden Road
Springbank
The Alders
Oatward Cl
Deepdene Ct
Hoodcote Gdns
Gn Moor Link
Drayton Gardens
Myddelton Gdns
Grange Park Avenue
Park Drive
Hartland Cl
Elmscott Gdns
Bush Hill
Clarendon Wy
Cunard Crs
Bush Hill Road
Berkeley Gdns
Walsingham Road
Uvedale Road
Whitethorn Gardens
Amwell
Carrs Lane
Quakers Walk
The Orchard
Orchardmede
Faversham Av
Sittingbourne Av
LONDON ROAD
A105 PARK AVENUE
A105
VILLAGE ROAD
Essex Road
Tiptree Dr
London Rd
Private Rd
Castleleigh Ct
Lincoln Rd
Chalkwell Pk Av
Lyndhurst Gdns
Superstore
Hotel
Summerhill
Qu Anne's Gv
Manor
The Brackens
Crossway
Conifer Gdns
Church Hill
Stone Hall Road
The Spinney
Broadfields Av
Laurel Drive
Cresswell Wy
Hillcrest
Strafield Pk Cl
Paulin Dr
Vicar's Moor Lane
Moor Primary School
Preparatory School
N21
Sherbrook Gardens
Surgery
Shrubbery Gardens
Ringwood Wy
Berry Cl
GREEN LANE
RIDGE AVENUE
Ridge Ho Clinic
Eversley Park Road
Devonshire Gdns
Oxford Gdns
Cambridge Gdns
Elsiedene Rd
Percy Road
Solna Road
Kent Road
Colne Road
York Rd
Ridge Road
Firs Lane
Elm Pk Rd
Winchmore Hill Cricket Club
Rowantree Road
Blakesware Gdns
Aldbury Ms
CHURCH STREET
B154
Ramscroft Close
Halstead Road
Halstead Gdns
Firs Park Avenue
Firs Pk Gdns
Hydefield Cl
Hyde Park Avenue
Hyde Pk Gdns
Ford's Grove
Beverley Cl
Farm Road
Highfield Primary School
Laburnum
Winchmore Hill Clnc
Compton Rd
Station Rd
King's Av
Radcliffe Rd
Roseneath Av
Orpington Road
Arlow Rd
Arundel Gdns
Haslemere Road
Coombe Corner
Fernleigh Road
Woodberry Av
Lytton Av
College
Surgery
Hoppers Road
Woodland Way
Broad Walk
Woodcroft
Downes Ct
Lynwood Grove
Seaforth Gdns
Branscombe Gdns
Denleigh Gdns
The Glenbrook
Old Road
The Old Road
Park View
Park Gate
Byland Cl
Gladeside
Southgate
Brackendale
Beechdale
Oaklands
Fernfield Park
A111
Winchmore School
Carpenter Gdns
Rookby Ct
Cedars Rd
Edmonton Cemetery
Lower Edmonton
Surgery
Golf Course
31
32
33
F
G
H
I
J
K
2
3
4
5
6
7
30
41

30
29
42
A
B
C
D
E
1
2
3
4
5
6
7
533
34
35
96
95
Forty Hill
Enfield
EN1
Enfield Playing Fields
Ponders End
Bush Hill Park
Edmonton
N9
Adath Yisroel Cemetery
Community School
Carterhatch Lane
Carterhatch Primary School
House School
Queen Elizabeth Stadium
Sports Centre & Swimming Pool
Donkey Lane
Tenniswood Road
Carisbrook Close
Willow Road
Churchbury Road
Baker St
Primary School
Police Station
Civic Cen
Fir Tree Walk
Riversfield Rd
Peartree Road
Apple Grove
River Front
Surgery
Enfield Town Stn
Superstore
St Annes Convent School
London Road
Lincoln Road
Enfield Cricket Club
Village Road
Private Road
Wellington Road
Martindale Ind Estate
George Spicer Primary School
Southbury Road
A110
Kingsmead School
UGC
Bush Hill Park
Recreation Ground
Main Av
Bush Hill Park Primary School
Bush Hill Park Stn
Great Cambridge Road
A10
Crown Road
Baird Road
Dearsley Road
Works
Northgate Business Centre
Southbury Station
De Mandeville Gate
Haslemere Business Centre
Martinbridge Industrial Estate
Great Cambridge Industrial Est
Progress Way
Bishop Stopford School
Suffolks Primary School
Broadfield Sq
Enfield College
Enfield Business Centre
Cemetery
Waverley School
Asquith Sch
Queensway Business Cen
Queensway
Nags Head
University
Hertford Road High St
A1010
Lincoln Rd
Northfield Road
Southfield Road
Elmcroft Avenue
Galliard Rd
Oaklands Av
Galliard Primary School
Bedford Road
Hadleigh Rd
Lanford Obesity Clnc
Houndsfield Primary School
Hertford Road
Nightingale Road
Salisbury School
St Joseph's Road
Forest Road
Lowden Rd
Woodlands Road
Eldon JMI School
Eldon Road
Chester Rd
Bounces Road
Enfield FC
Claverings Industrial Est
Infant School
Hotel
Park Avenue
Village Road
A105
Church Street
B154
Raglan Junior School
Countisbury Avenue
Edmonton Upper School
Bush Hill Park Medical Cen
Lawn Cl
Bury St
Harrow Dr
Churchfield Primary School
Winchester Road
Chichester Road
Junction Rd
Croyland
Church Street
Cedars Ct
Fire Station
Redford Lodge Psychiatric Hosp
Durham Rd
Catward
Edmonton Cemetery
Clinic
1 grid square represents 500 metres

Highway
Brimsdown
EN3
King George's Reservoir
William Girling Reservoir
Ponders End Industrial Estate
Brimsdown Station
Ponders End Station
Lee Valley Campsite
Lee Valley Leisure Golf Club
Lee Valley Leisure Centre Camping & Caravan
Chingford School
MOLLISON AVENUE
LEA VALLEY ROAD
SEWARDSTONE ROAD
MERIDIAN WAY
KINGS HEAD HILL
MANSFIELD HILL
WALTHAM WAY
43

32
20
46
A
B
C
D
E
1
2
3
4
5
6
7
508
09
10
94
93
92
91
Merchant Taylors School
Oxhey Hall
Northwood Preparatory School
Sandy Lodge Road
Sandy Lodge Lane
Askew Road
East Drive
The Dell
North Approach
Main Av
Wolsey Road
Sandy Lodge Golf Club
Moor Park Station
Golf Course
Pembroke Road
Main Avenue
Russell Rd
South Approach
Temple Gdns
Astons Road
Thornhill Rd
Russell Road
Bedford Road
Ormonde Rd
Moor Park
Close
Anson Walk
Old Gannon Cl
Oxford Cl
Russell Cl
Nevill Cl
Heathside Rd
Heathside Cl
Batchworth Lane
Farm Rd
Ebury Cl
Treetops Cl
Grove Farm Park
Hertfordshire County
Hillingdon
St Martins School
Kewferry Road
Kewferry Drive
Langton Gv
Mezen Cl
Grove Road
Moor Park Road
Thirlmere Gdns
RICKMANSWORTH ROAD A404
Gateway Cl
Holy Trinity School
Harrison Cl
High Elms Cl
Hill Road
Sherborne Pl
Wildwood
Halland Way
Sandy Lodge Way
Woodridge Wy
School
Dene Rd
Woodlea Gv
College Wy
Firs Wk
Foxdell
London Bible College
HA6
Trinity Cl
Northwood Pinner Liberal Synagogue
Cygnet Cl
Eaton Gate
The Avenue
Mallard Wy
Chlw Cl
Langland Ct
GREEN LANE B469
Myrtleside Close
The Gln
Wilford Cl
Anthus Mews
Surgery
Police Station
Northwood United Synagogue
College
Equestrian Centre
Denville Hall
Buttsmead
Northgate Way
Manor House Drive
A4180 DUCK'S HILL ROAD
Treal Drive
Maxwell Road
Falcon Cl
Hwksw Close
Dormans Cl
Leaf Cl
Lingfield Cl
Murray Road
Greenheys Cl
Northbrook Dr
Elgin Dr
Northwood Golf Club
Hurst Place
Fringewood Cl
The Covert
Copse Wood Way
Silverwood Cl
Links Way
NORTHWOOD
Golf Course
Hills Lane
Highfield Crs
Highfield Road
Highfield Cl
Oak Glade
Nicholas Way
Rogers Ruff
Lowswood Cl
Copse Close
Broad Walk
Links Way
Haste Hill Golf Club
Northwood Hills
1 grid square represents 500 metres
Westbury Road
The Roughs
Bishops Avenue
Eastbury Farm JMI School
Ross Wy
Wildacres
Bourne End Road
The Fairway
Crofters Road
Crofters Rd
Woodfield Av
Farm Way
Heron Wk
Eastbury
Batchworth Lane
Valency Cl
Orion Way
Phoenix Cl
Canopus Wy
Avior Dr
Capella Rd
Altair Way
Aquarius Wy
Vega Crs
Apollo Av
Ardross Av
Shelley Close
Davenham Avenue
Grosvenor Road
Parkside Road
Holbein Gate
Eastgrade
Wellesley Av
The Lee
Sirus Rd
Atria Rd
St Mary's Avenue
Eastbury Avenue
Ltl Stream Cl
Rofant Road
Eastbury Road
Kiln Way
Pine Cl
Morgan Cl
Frithwood Avenue
Kirby Cl
Kings Cl
Cullera Cl
Canterbury Cl
Martins
The Mountview
Bayhurst Drive
Chartwell Rd
Carew Rd
Primary School
St Helens School
Ashb Sq
Little St Helens School
Maycock Gv
Wild Oaks Cl
Foxfield Cl
WATFORD ROAD
Brookdene Drive
Elgood Av
Woodside Rd
Gatehill Rd
Ravenswood Pk
Willow End
Woodgate Crs
Wieland Rd
Elgood Av
Gate End
Shelton Rd
Madison Bowl
Northwood Stn
Crvn Ct
Hawes Close
Bennett Cl
Chester Road
School
Forge Lane
Hallowell Road
Roy Road
Barker Cl
Reginald Road
GREEN LANE
CHURCH RD
Northwood Way
Townsend Way
Emmanuel Road
Hillside Primary School
Hillside Road
Hillside Rise
Hillside Crescent
Addison Way
Addison Cl
Northwood Way
Hilliard Road
A4125 HIGH STREET
PO
Works
Acre Way
Neal Cl
Northwood and Pinner Community Hosp
Stanley Ro
New Farm Lane
The Drive
Athena Pl
Lynwood Dr
Lees Av
Chestnut Av
The Knoll
Jasmin Cl
Works
A404 PINNER ROAD
Robina Cl
Waller Dr
Windsor
Oakdale Av
Briarwood Drive
Ferndown
Northwood FC
Northwood Cemetery
SANDY LANE A4125
Hayling Rd
Ashburnham Dr
Dumfries Cl
Handsworth Cl
Nairn Gn
Fairhaven Crs
Brampton Rd
Oxhey Close
THE WOODS
Sandy Lodge
HAMPERMILL
Vivian Close
Hospital

Carpenders Park
South Oxhey
Hatch End
Pinnerwood Park
Pinner Green
Oxhey Warren
South Oxhey Playing Fields
Oxhey Park Golf Centre
Carpenders Park Station
Carpenders Park Cemetery
Oxhey Woods
Hertfordshire County
Harrow
Hillingdon
Pinnerwood House
Pinner Hill Golf Club
Golf Course
Grimsdyke First & Middle School
Hatch End Station
Public Swimming Pool
Colnbrook School
Warren Dell School
St Josephs RC School
Little Furze School
Oxhey Wood Primary Sch
The St Meryl Junior Middle & Infant School
Council Building
Police Stn
Primary School
Pinner Wood Primary School
Northwood School
Northwood Sports Centre
Oxheylane Farm
Grims Dyke Golf Club
Pinner Park
Pinner Park Farm
River Pinn
Prestwick Road
Oxhey Lane
Little Oxhey Lane
Oxhey Drive
Hayling Road
Gosforth Lane
Fairfield Avenue
Penrose Avenue
Greenfield Avenue
Carpenders Avenue
St George's Drive
Compton Place
Harrow Way
Romilly Drive
Woodhall Lane
Lytham Avenue
Uxbridge Road (Pinner)
The Broadway
St Thomas' Drive
Grimsdyke Road
Colburn Avenue
Sylvia Avenue
Albury Drive
Evelyn Drive
Woodhall Avenue
Royston Park
Royston Grove
Potter Street
Potter Street Hill
Hillside Road
Park View Road
Lyndhurst Avenue
Athol Gardens
Norman Crescent
Blythwood Road
Buckland Ri
Marsworth Avenue
Old Hall Dr
Nugent's Park
Wellington Road
Devonshire Rd
Woodridings Avenue
Anselm Road
Jubilee Cl
Greenway
Crossway
Moss Lane
Ltl Moss Lane
A4008
A404
A410
B4542
21
47
34
F
G
H
J
K
1
2
3
4
5
6
7
11
12
13
91
92
93
94

34
Merry Hill
22
33
48
A
B
C
D
E
1
2
3
4
5
6
7
513
14
15
94
93
92
91
Carpenders Park
Rose Lawn
Warren Road
Downalong
Robinson Cr
Allard Crs
Prowse Avenue
Finucane Rise
Treacy Close
Cleed Av
Giant Tree Hl
Florida Close
Hartsbourne Road
Hive Rd
Westwood School
Rutherford Way
Windmill
Lime Tree Walk
Elder Ct
Alpine Wk
MAGPIE HALL RD
A4140
Broadfield Ct
Greenacres
Hartsbourne JMI School
Hartsbourne Av
Hartsbourne Close
Lake Dr
Laurino Pl
Hartsbourne Golf & Country Club
Tanglewood Cl
Peterborough & St Margarets High School
COMMON ROAD
A409
Golf Course
Hertfordshire County
Harrow
Harrow Weald Common
The Kiln
Ass House La
Old Redding
Hotel
Clamp Hill
Brookshill Drive
Brookshill Av
Grims Dyke Golf Club
Oxheylane Farm
OXHEY LANE
A4008
B4542
White Craig Cl
Park Road
Saddlers Close
Highbanks Rd
Royston Park
Royston Grove
Royston Gv
Oakleigh Road
Witney Cl
Clonard Way
Thornton Grove
Ashcroft
Oakmeade
Hazelcroft Drive
Rowlands Avenue
Sequoia Pk
Pinewood Cl
Pinewood Av
Oxhey La
Cedar
Walpole Cl
Hillview Close
Avenue
Hatch End Station
Milne Fld
Furham Field
Sherington Av
The Lawns
Surgery
UXBRIDGE RD (HATCH END)
A410
UXBRIDGE ROAD (HARROW WEALD)
UXBRIDGE RD (HARROW WEALD)
Superstore
Hatch End Swimming Pool
Harrow Arts Centre
Boniface Wk
Boniface Gdns
Ufford Rd
Ufford Av
Courtenay Av
Tillotson Road
Winston Ct
Hatch End High School
Shaftesbury School
School
Headstone La
Chantry Rd
Chantry Pl
Headstone Lane
Headstone Lane Station
Long Elmes
Augustine Road
Old Millhillians Sports Ground
Pinner Park
Pinner Park Farm
River
Woodridings Avenue
Park View
Gable Cl
Anseim Road
Dove Pk
Westfield Park
Roger Bannister Sports Ground
Bannister Stadium
Birch Pk
Ross Close
Hutton Wk
Chicheley Road
Mepham Crs
Langton Rd
Whittlesea School
Whittlesea Road
Cedars First School
Cedars Middle School
Stafford Rd
Hutton Lane
Boxtree Rd
Greer Rd
Bellfield Av
Timbers Clinic
Harrow Weald Pk
Lakeland Cl
West Drive
West Dr Gdns
BROOKSHILL
Weald College
Harrow Weald Cemetery
All Saints Ms
Park Dr
Belsize Road
Silver Cl
Boxtree Road
Kynaston Wd
Kynaston Close
High Rd
A409 HIGH ROAD
Fontwell Cl
Monro Gdns
Kelvin Crs
Elms
College Cl
College Hill Road
Lorraine Pk
Superstore
Harrow Weald
Hithermell Drive
Marlcas Av
Colmer Place
Blackwell Cl
Elm Ter
Weighton Road
College Avenue
College Rd
Park Crescent
Long Elmes
Mead Cl
Stanhope Av
Stox Md
Derby Av
Clewer Crs
Windsor Road
Hampden Road
Carmelite Road
Sefton Av
Medical Centre
Enderley Rd
Farmst Road
The Meadow Way
HIGH ROAD A409
Whitefriars Dr
Nicola Cl
Brinsley Road
Toorack Road
Bengarth Dr
Salvatorian College
School
Parkfield Avenue
Broadfields
Bancroft Rd
Courtenay Avenue
Barmor Cl
Fernleigh Ct
1 grid square represents 500 metres

Junction 4
Stanmore 35
23
36
49
F
G
H
I
J
K
Royal Natl Orthopaedic Hospital
Stanmore Common
Works
Wood Lane
Warren Lane
COMMON
A5 BROCKLEY HILL
Barnet
Harrow
A41 EDGWARE WAY
Nutt Gv
Harrow RFC
Priory Drive
Priory Cl
Springfield Close
Park La
Hilltop Wy
A4140
STANMORE HILL
Fallowfield
Aylmer Cl
Aylwards Rise
Heriots Cl
Pine Cl
Hall Farm Cl
Dennis Lane
Spring Lake
Old Forge Cl
Adelaide Cl
St Johns CE Middle School
First School
Hill Close
Eaton Close
Rec Gnd
Stangate Gdns
Halsbury Cl
Knights Road
Valencia Road
Kerry Av
Glanleam Road
Stanmore Synagogue
London Rd
LONDON ROAD
Berry Hill
Grantham Close
Newlands Close
Hamlyn Close
Rees Dr
Snaresbrook Dr
Tintagel Drive
Brockley Cl
Court Dr
Stanmore Station
Westbere Dr
Morecambe Gdns
Pangbourne Dr
Doverco Gard
Heronslea Dr
Grove
Aylward First & Middle Schools
Dalkeith
North London Collegiate School
Canons Dr
Embry Close
Embry Way
Surgery
Green Lane
Ben Hale Cl
Woodside Cl
Oldfield Close
Old Lodge Way
Winscombe Wy
Holland Wk
Bowls Close
Linden Cl
Pynnacles Cl
Tennis Club
Ray Gdns
Dennis Gdns
A410
The Broadway
THE BROADWAY
CHURCH ROAD
Hall
Tel Ex
A4140
London Rd
Copley Rd
Merrion Avenue
Bentley Wood Girls School
Flecker Close
Bridges Rd
Masefield Avenue
Sitwell Gv
Chenduit Way
Algar Cl
White Orchards
Bentley Way
Dearne Close
Binyon Crs
Brockhurst Cl
UXBRIDGE ROAD (STANMORE)
HA7
STANMORE
Rectory Lane
Rectory Cl
Tudor Well Close
Lady Aylesford Avenue
Elm Park
Glebe Rd
Haig Rd
Marsh La
Marsh Lane
Dene Gdns
Beech Tree Close
Craigwell Dr
Sandymount Avenue
Charlbury Av
Craigwell Close
Elizabeth Gdns
Malcolm Ct
Nelson Road
Beatty Road
Du Cros Drive
Peters Cl
Howberry Rd
Cheyneys
Douglas Cl
Elliott Rd
Jellicoe Gdns
Boyle Av
Cherry Tree Wy
Old Church La
Stanmore College
Bernays Cl
Silverston Way
Talman Gv
Wychwood Avenue
Wychwood Close
Wychwood Av
Woodlands Dr
Chartley Avenue
Cairn Wy
Holme Wy
Heather Wy
Ashdale Gv
Conway Close
Dowding Pl
Embry Drive
Robb Rd
Trenchard Cl
Temple Md Close
Capuchin Cl
Kenneth Gardens
The Chase
Leavesden Rd
Water Gdns
September Wy
The Ridgeway
MARSH
Barn Crs
Lansdowne Road
Howberry Road
Howberry Cl
Winston
Richmond Gdns
Kenton Lane
Ash Cl
Gordon Av
Maytree La
Weymouth Wk
Links Vw Cl
Gordon
Rosedale Cl
Georgian Close
Sunningdale Cl
Greenacres Drive
Gleneagles
Stanmore Golf Club
Wolverton Rd
Courten Ms
Old Church Lane
Cranmer Cl
Gn Verges
Gas Works
Cloyster Wd
Longcrofte Rd
Cornbury Road
Howberry Road
Avenue
Donnefield Avenue
Surgery
Canons Park Station
WHIT
Drummond Dr
Woodward Gdns
Daventer Dr
Dromey Gdns
Golf Cl
Abercorn Road
Sports Ground
Stanmore Marsh
LANE
Watersfield Wy
B461
Golf Course
Alton Av
Weald First & Middle School
Laurel Cl
Hood Drive
Weald Rise
Chestnut Dr
The Drive
The Hwy
Woodcroft Av
Acorn Close
Belmont Lane
Stanburn Middle Sch
Wemborough Road
Bush Gv
Bromefield
Brick La
HONEYPOT
Honeypot Lane Centre
Honister Gdns
Honister Close
Honister Pl
Gyles Park
St Andrews Dr
The Avenue
Three Mdw Ms
Mountside
Vernon Drive
St Edmunds Drive
Hermitage Way
Beverley Gardens
Felbridge Av
Curzon Av
College Hill Rd
Adderley Rd
Connaught Rd
Dryden Rd
Kenton Road
Floriston Close
Floriston Gdns
Drive
Bellamy Dr
Coledale Drive
Braithwaite Gdns
Lyon Meade
Bush Grove
Pickett Cft
Crowshott Av
Surgery
Ladycroft Walk
Ammersham Gardens
Pearse Grove
Honeypot Lane
Parr Rd
Honeypot Business Cen
Wigton Gdns
Dalston Gardens
Aldridge Av
Church Lane Way
Weston
Ventnor Av
York Avenue
Wetheral Dr
Kynance Gdns
Burnell Gardens
Lamorna Gdns
Thistlecroft
Fisher Road
Hibbert Road
Lime Close
Surgery
Belmont
Belmont First & Middle School
School
Dobbin
Clifton
Kenton Avenue
Grange Avenue
Derwent Crs
Culver
High School
Carisbrooke Close
Broadcroft Avenue
Collins Av
Fairways
A41

36
A
B
24
C
D
E
518
19
20
94
93
92
91
1
2
3
4
5
6
7
35
50
Edgwarebury Cemetery
Broadfields Junior School
Broadfields Infant School
Meadfield
Bushfield Close
Springwood Crs
Burrell Close
Bushfield Crescent
Hartland Close
Hartland Drive
Hamonde Cl
Pentland Av
Luther Close
Luther
Morley Crescent
Kenilworth Road
Tayside Dr
Rosh Pinah School
Aldridge Avenue
Bellamy Close
Franklyn Gardens
Harrowes Meade
Avenue
Glengall Rd
Bullescroft Road
Parsons Gv
Parsons Cres
Edgwarebury Lane
Edgwarebury Park
Beulah Close
Cranmer Rd
Marlborough Av
Wyre Grove
Warwick Av
Harcourt Avenue
Fairmead Crescent
Crossgate
Wolmer Gdns
Broadfields
Windsor Av
Lynford Gardens
Rosens Wk
Parkside Dr
Blackwell Gdns
Mowbray Rd
Holland House School
Surgery
Broadhurst Av
Edgware United Synagogue
Parnell Cl
EDGWARE WAY (WATFORD BY-PASS)
Edgware Way
A41
EDGWARE WAY (WATFORD BY-PASS)
HILL
Grantham Close
Newlands Close
Hamlyn Close
Pipers Gn Lane
Brockley Avenue
SPUR ROAD A410
The Edgware School
Sterling Avenue
Glendale Avenue
Ranelagh Cl
Ranelagh Drive
Ashcombe Gdns
Hazel Gdns
Hillcrest Avenue
The Grove
Priory Field Drive
Highview Avenue
Highview Gardens
Ash Close
Berry Hill
Rees Dr
London Rd
LONDON ROAD
London Road
Surgery
Lacey Dr
Green Lane
Hillside Gardens
Shelley Cl
Fairview Wy
Edgware
Upcroft Av
Stoneyfields Lane
Snaresbrook Dr
Court Dr
The Spinney
Stone Grove
Tintagel Drive
Brockley Cl
Edgware Reform Synagogue
King's Dr
Drive
Pangbourne Dr
Jesmond Wy
Morecambe Gdns
Westbere Dr
Pangbourne Dr
Heronslea Dr
Dovercourt Gardens
Grove
Orchard Dr
Surgery
Oakleigh Gdns
Purcells Av
Campbell Cft
The Drive
The Rise
Heather Walk
A5100
HALE LA
Cloister Gdns
Aylward First & Middle Schools
Stonegrove Gdns
Hillersdon Av
Park Grove
Savoy Cl
HA8
Surgery
Gardens
Farm Road
Alders
Grange Hill
STONE GROVE
A5
Stone Grove Park
Princes Cl
Queen's Cl
Heronsgate
Edgwarebury Gd
Penshurst Gardens
St Margarets Road
Orchard Crs
Keith
The Lake
North London Collegiate School
Rose Gdn Cl
Dukes Av
Lake View
Stone Grove
Mill Rdg
Hillside Drive
Carltone Close
Manor Pk Gdns
Hall
Rectory La
STATION ROAD A5100
Masorti Synagogue
Brook Av
Lovatt Cl
Brook Av
Stanway Gdns
Deans Way
Oakwood Dr
Meadow Gdns
West Way
DEAN'S LANE
Rudyard Grove
Deansbrook Primary School
Church Cl
Canons Dr
Canons Close
Powell Close
Handel Close
Drive
The Basin
Yeshurun Synagogue
Manor Pk Crs
Belle Vue Cinema
Broadwalk Shopping Cen
Edgware Station
Bus Station & Depot
Hale
Chestnut Av
Whitchurch Gardens
Cavendish Dr
Dorset Drive
Gresham Rd
Churchill Rd
Montgomery Rd
War Meml
Sharp Sports Cen
The Forum
Edgware Clnc
Telephone Exchange
Junior School
Parkfield Close
Banstock Rd
Dryfield Walk
Walter Walk
Crispin Rd
Langham Rd
A5109
Woodstead Gv
Howberry Road
Cloyster Wd
Longcrofte Road
Cornbury Road
Howberry Avenue
Donnefield Avenue
Canons Park
Canons Park Station
St Lawrence Close
Stratton Close
Mead Rd
Police Stn
Boys' Club
Forumside
Infant School
Garratt Rd
Heming Road
Fairfield Av
Fairfield Crs
Wenlock Rd
Edrick Rd
Deans Cl
Langham Gdns
Surgery
Waterfield Cl
Whitchurch La
WHITCHURCH LANE
B461
HONEYPOT
Winton Gdns
Overbrook Wk
Edgware FC & Wealdstone FC
EDGWARE RD
HIGH ST
Elmer Gdns
Works
A5109 DEANSBROOK RD
Blood Transfusion Centre
Littlefield Rd
The Menorah Foundation School
Colchester Rd
Whitchurch Av
Chandos Crs
Road
Methuen Close
Methuen Road
Summit Cl
Albany Crs
TA Centre
Edgware Community Hospital
Pavilion Way
Littlefield
Boston Rd
Orange Hill Road
Briar Wk
Norwich Wk
Torbridge Close
Buckingham
Chandos Recreation Ground
A5 BURNT OAK BROADWAY
Buckingham Gdns
Bransgrove Rd
Merlin Crs
Avenue
Oak Lodge Medical Centre
North Rd
East Rd
The Cft
Blessbury Rd
Honeypot Lane Centre
Little Stanmore
Bacon Lane
Northolme Gdns
Little Stanmore First & Middle School
Parr Rd
Garland Road
Honeypot Business Cen
Camrose Av
Appledore Close
Tavistock Rd
Bideford Close
William Ellis Sports Ground
Broomgrove
Orchard
Axholme Av
The Chase
Vancouver Road
Broadway Clnc
South Road
East Road
Burnt Oak Flds
Burnt Oak Station
Watling Medical Centre
Back Lane
Market Lane
Silkstream
Barnfield Primary School
Wigton Gdns
Dalston Gardens
Aldridge Avenue
Works
Peareswood Gardens
Annesmere Gardens
Ladycroft Walk
Honeypot La
St David's Dr
St Bride's Av
Prescelly Place
Nolton Place
Haverford Wy
Tenby Road
Roch Av
Raeburn Road
Hogarth Road
Constable Gardens
Westleigh Gdns
Greencourt Av
Cardens
Grove
Axeholm Av
Oakleigh Avenue
Camrose Avenue
Shaldon Rd
Bridgewater Gdns
Dale
School
Avenue
Whistler Gdns
Cotman Gdns
School
Landseer Close
Leighton Close
Mollison
The Highlands
Gordon Gdns
Stag La
Redhill Dr
Millfield Road
A41
1 grid square represents 500 metres

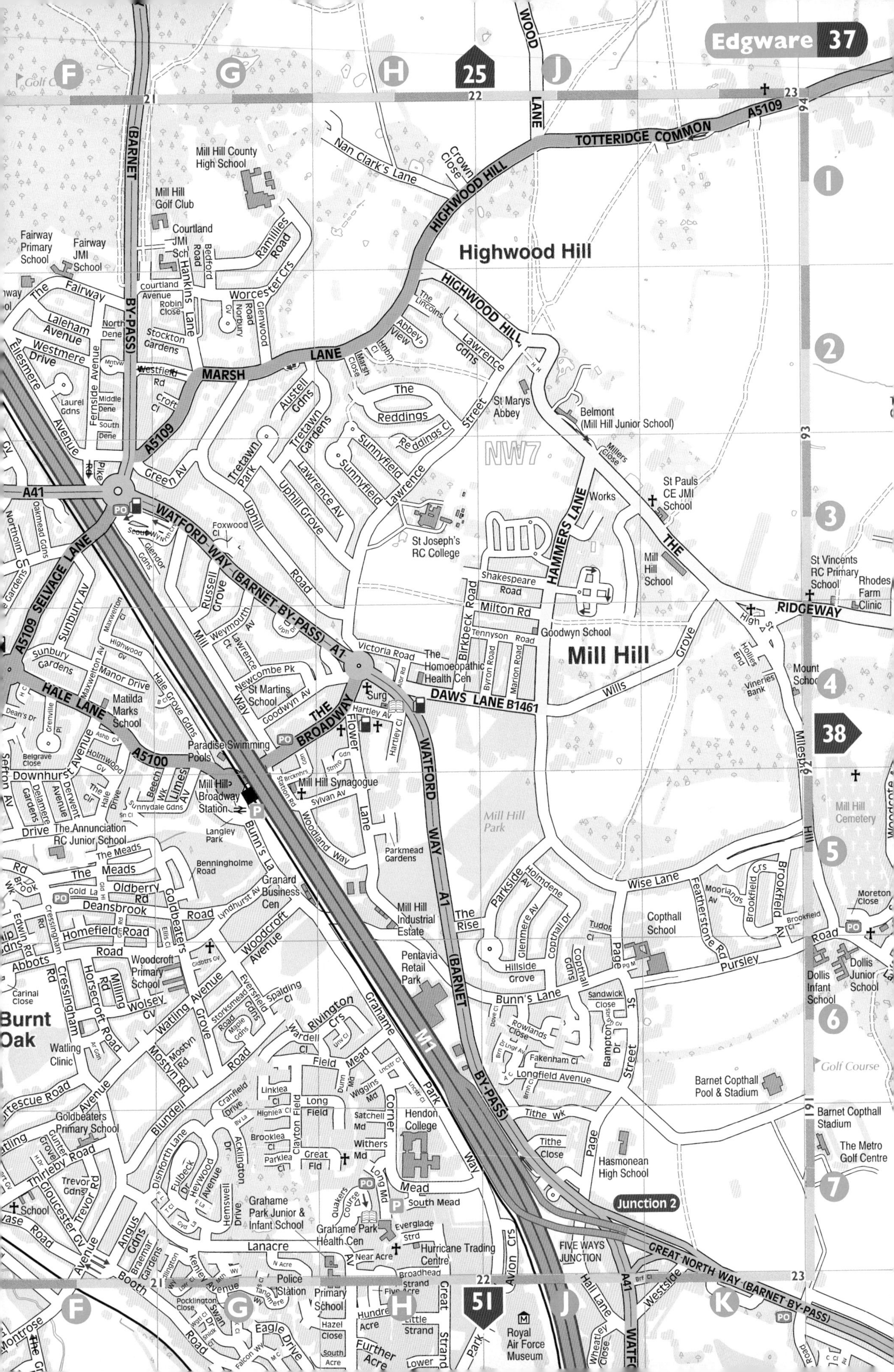
Highwood Hill
Mill Hill
Burnt Oak
NW7
25
38
51
Totteridge Common
A5109
Highwood Hill
Wood Lane
Nan Clark's Lane
Crown Close
Marsh Lane
Barnet By-Pass
Watford Way (Barnet By-Pass) A1
Mill Hill County High School
Mill Hill Golf Club
Courtland JMI Sch
Fairway Primary School
Fairway JMI School
The Fairway
Laleham Avenue
Westmere Drive
Ellesmere Avenue
Fernside Avenue
Laurel Gdns
North Dene
Middle Dene
South Dene
Westfield Rd
Croft Cl
Pike Rd
Courtland Avenue
Robin Close
Hankins Lane
Bedford Road
Stockton Gardens
Worcester Crs
Ramillies Road
Norbury Gv
Glenwood Road
Green Av
A41
Selvage Lane
A5109
Sunbury Av
Sunbury Gardens
Hale Lane
A5100
Manor Drive
Maxwelton Av
Highwood Gv
Matilda Marks School
Hale Grove Gdns
Paradise Swimming Pools
Mill Hill Broadway Station
Langley Park
Bunn's La
The Broadway
Flower Lane
Mill Hill Synagogue
Sylvan Av
Woodland Way
Station Rd
Hartley Av
Hartley Cl
Daws Lane B1461
The Homoeopathic Health Cen
Victoria Road
St Martins School
Goodwyn Av
Newcombe Pk
Lawrence Way
Weymouth Av
Russell Grove
Mill Way
Uphill Road
Uphill Grove
Tretawn Park
Tretawn Gardens
Austell Gdns
Lawrence Av
Sunnyfield
The Reddings
Reddings Cl
Lawrence Street
Lawrence Gdns
The Lincoins
Abbey View
Marsh Close
St Marys Abbey
Belmont (Mill Hill Junior School)
Millers Close
St Joseph's RC College
Hammers Lane
Works
St Pauls CE JMI School
The Ridgeway
Mill Hill School
St Vincents RC Primary School
Rhodes Farm Clinic
High St
Hollies End
Vineries Bank
Mount School
Shakespeare Road
Milton Rd
Tennyson Road
Birkbeck Road
Byron Road
Marion Road
Goodwyn School
Wills Grove
Milespit Hill
Mill Hill Cemetery
Mill Hill Park
Wise Lane
Parkside Av
Holmdene Av
Glenmere Av
Copthall Dr
Copthall Gdns
Tudor Cl
Copthall School
Featherstone Rd
Moorlands Av
Brookfield Crs
Brookfield Av
Pursley Road
Dollis Infant School
Dollis Junior School
Moreton Close
The Rise
Hillside Grove
Bunn's Lane
Sandwick Close
Page Street
Rowlands Close
Fakenham Cl
Bampton Dr
Longfield Avenue
Barnet Copthall Pool & Stadium
Golf Course
Barnet Copthall Stadium
The Metro Golf Centre
Tithe Wk
Tithe Close
Hasmonean High School
Junction 2
Five Ways Junction
Great North Way (Barnet By-Pass)
Hall Lane
Westside
M1
Mill Hill Industrial Estate
Pentavia Retail Park
Parkmead Gardens
Grahame Park Way
Granard Business Cen
Benningholme Road
Lyndhurst Av
Woodcroft Avenue
Woodcroft Primary School
Goldbeaters Grove
The Annunciation RC Junior School
The Meads
Oldberry Rd
Deansbrook Road
Gold La
Homefield Road
Cressingham Rd
Abbots Road
Horsecroft Road
Milling Rd
Wolsey Gv
Watling Avenue
Mostyn Rd
Storksmead Road
Eversfield Gdns
Spalding Cl
Maple Gdns
Watling Clinic
Carinal Close
Rivington Crs
Wardell Cl
Field Mead
Linklea Cl
Long Field
Satchell Md
Withers Md
Clayton Field
Great Fld
Hendon College
Goldbeaters Primary School
Fortescue Road
Blundell Road
Cranfield Drive
Acklington Dr
Dishforth Lane
Fulbeck Dr
Heywood Avenue
Hemswell Drive
Grahame Park Junior & Infant School
Grahame Park Health Cen
Quakers Course
South Mead
Everglade Strd
Hurricane Trading Centre
Near Acre
Broadhead Strand
Lanacre Av
Police Station
Primary School
Hundred Acre
Five Acre
Little Strand
Great Strand
Further Acre
Lower Strand
Hazel Close
South Acre
Eagle Drive
Swan Dr
Booth Road
Kenley Avenue
Pocklington Close
Angus Gdns
Braemar Gardens
Thirleby Road
Trevor Rd
Trevor Gdns
Gloucester Gv
Avion Crs
Royal Air Force Museum
Montrose Avenue
Dean's Dr
Grenville Pl
Belgrave Close
Downhurst Avenue
Delamere Gardens
Derwent Avenue
The Hale
Holmwood Gv
Beech Wk
Limes Av
Sunnydale Gdns
Oakmead Gdns
Northolm Gn
Foxwood Cl
Glendor Gdns
Junction 2
PO
P

38
26
37
52
A
B
C
D
E
1
2
3
4
5
6
7
523
24
25
94
93
92
91
A5109
TOTTERIDGE
TOTTERIDGE VILLAGE
A5109 TOTTERIDGE
Chestnut
Pine
Grove
Harmsworth Way
South Herts Golf Club
N20
The Close
St Andrews CE JMI School
Willow
End
Close
Elmstead Cl
Greenway
Totteridge Cricket Club
Coppice Walk
Laurel
Woodridge Primary School
Southover
Chiddingfold
Arlington
Framfield Cl
Northiam
Shortgate
Michleham Down
Woodside Park
Woodside Park Golf Club
Twine Green
The Mill Hill Cricket Club
Golf Course
Burtonhole Lane
Burtonhole Cl
Hillview Road
Eleanor Crescent
St Vincents RC Primary School
Rhodes Farm Clinic
RIDGEWAY
High St
Hollies End
Mount School
Milespit Hill
B552
Partingdale Lane
Reading Way
Reading Wy
Sevright Drive
Charles
Henry Darlot Dr
PO
Holmes Av
Ross Av
Roberts Road
Lidbury Rd
Kenny Rd
Price Cl
Kelly Rd
Drew Av
Warren Way
Twinn Rd
Approach La
Lullington
Pycombe Corner
Chanctonbury
Rodmell Slope
Cissbury Ring North
Garth
Offham Slope
Wolstonbury
Ring South
Singleton Scarp
Argyle
Saddlescombe Wy
Poynings Wy
Steynings Wy
Walmington Fold
Folkington Corner
Cissbury
Linkside
Chesterfield Road
Nethercourt Av
Fursby Avenue
West Avenue
Brent Way
Hamilton Wy
Penstemon Cl
Finchley Wy
The Dr
Surgery
Howcroft Crescent
Woodcote Avenue
Rushden Gdns
Mill Hill Cemetery
Bittacy Park Av
Bittacy Rise
Engel Park
Salcombe Gdns
Bittacy Cl
Curry Rise
BITTACY HILL B552
Road
Bray Wy
Walden
Westlinton Close
Frith Lane
Finchley Golf Club
Brookfield Crs
Brookfield Av
Dorlands
Moreton Close
Surgery
Road
Pursley
Dollis Infant School
Dollis Junior School
Sanders Lane
Grants Cl
Hendon Golf Club
Sanders La
Bittacy Rd
Mill Hill East Station
Bittacy Business Centre
Oakdene Pk
Lansdowne Road
Gordon Road
Grosvenor Rd
Eversleigh Road
Elm Park Road
Nether Street
Nether Cl
Sellers Hall Close
Cornwall
Devonshire Crs
Devonshire Road
Ashley Lane
Osborn Gdns
Aberdare Gardens
Oakhampton Rd
Lee Rd
Vineyard Avenue
New Road
Abercorn Road
Mallow Md
Frith Court
B1462 DOLLIS RD
Links Vw
B1462
Copthall & Stadium
Barnet Copthall Stadium
The Metro Golf Centre
Hendon Crematorium
Hendon Cemetery
Thornfield Av
Christ's College Playing Fields
St Marys CE Primary School
Dollis Av
Crescent Rd
NETHER ST
Surgery
Falkland Av
The Grove
Popes Dr
Shopping Precinct
Finchley Central Synagogue
Telephone Exchange
Finchley Central Stn
Holders Hill
ROAD
Claremont Pk
Lyndhurst Gardens
Grass Park
Tennis & Squash Club
Dollis
Clifton Av
Church Crs
Park
Victoria Hall
County Court
Victoria Av
Rectory Close
Works
Lichfield
Station
N3
REGENT'S PK ROAD
Arcadia Avenue
Hendon Avenue
Grenville Close
Rathgar Close
School
Chur
WAY (BARNET-BY-PASS)
Ashley
Woodtree Cl
Linksway
Linksway
HOLDERS
Cyprus Gardens
St Mary's Av
Freston Pk
Works
HENDON LANE
GRAVEL
Spencer Cl
Cyprus Av
Manor Av
Playing Fields
1 grid square represents 500 metres

F
G
H
27
J
Oakleigh Park
Whetstone
Totteridge & Whetstone Stn
A109 OAKLEIGH ROAD NORTH
RUSSELL LANE
B1453
Russell Road
Simmons' Way
Cameron Close
Loring Road
Pollard Road
Queensway Infant School
Primary School
Police Stn
Superstore
A1000 HIGH ROAD
B550
Golf Course
North Middlesex Golf Club
FRIERN BARNET
Friary Park
Friary Road
Torrington Park
Friern Park
Woodside Park Rd
Lodge Lane
Percy Road
Nether Street
North Finchley
Woodhouse Road
A1003
Woodhouse Sixth Form College
Christchurch CE School
Summerside JMI School
The Compton School
Sports Centre
Colney Hatch
COLNEY HATCH LANE
Ballards Lane
Finchley Reform Synagogue
Finchley Progressive Synagogue
Woodside Park Synagogue
Finchley Memorial Hospital
Victoria Park
Sports Club
Wingate & Finchley FC
Swimming Pool
Warner Village
TA Centre
A406
NORTH CIRCULAR ROAD
Islington Crematorium
St Pancras and Islington Cemetery
Greenfields Special School
Coppetts Wood Hospital
Coppetts Wood Primary School
Coppetts Rd
Tudor Primary School
Manorside Primary School
Coldfall Wood
Finchley Park High School
The North London Hospice
Woodside Park School
Northside Primary School
Grammar School
Barnet Coll
Park Health Cen
Torrington Clnc
Archgate Business Cen
Finchley Industrial Cen
St Johns CE Primary School
Friern Barnet School
Oakleigh Sch
Health Cen
N12
West Finchley Stn
Dollis Valley Green Walk
I
2
3
4
5
6
7
40
K
53
26
28

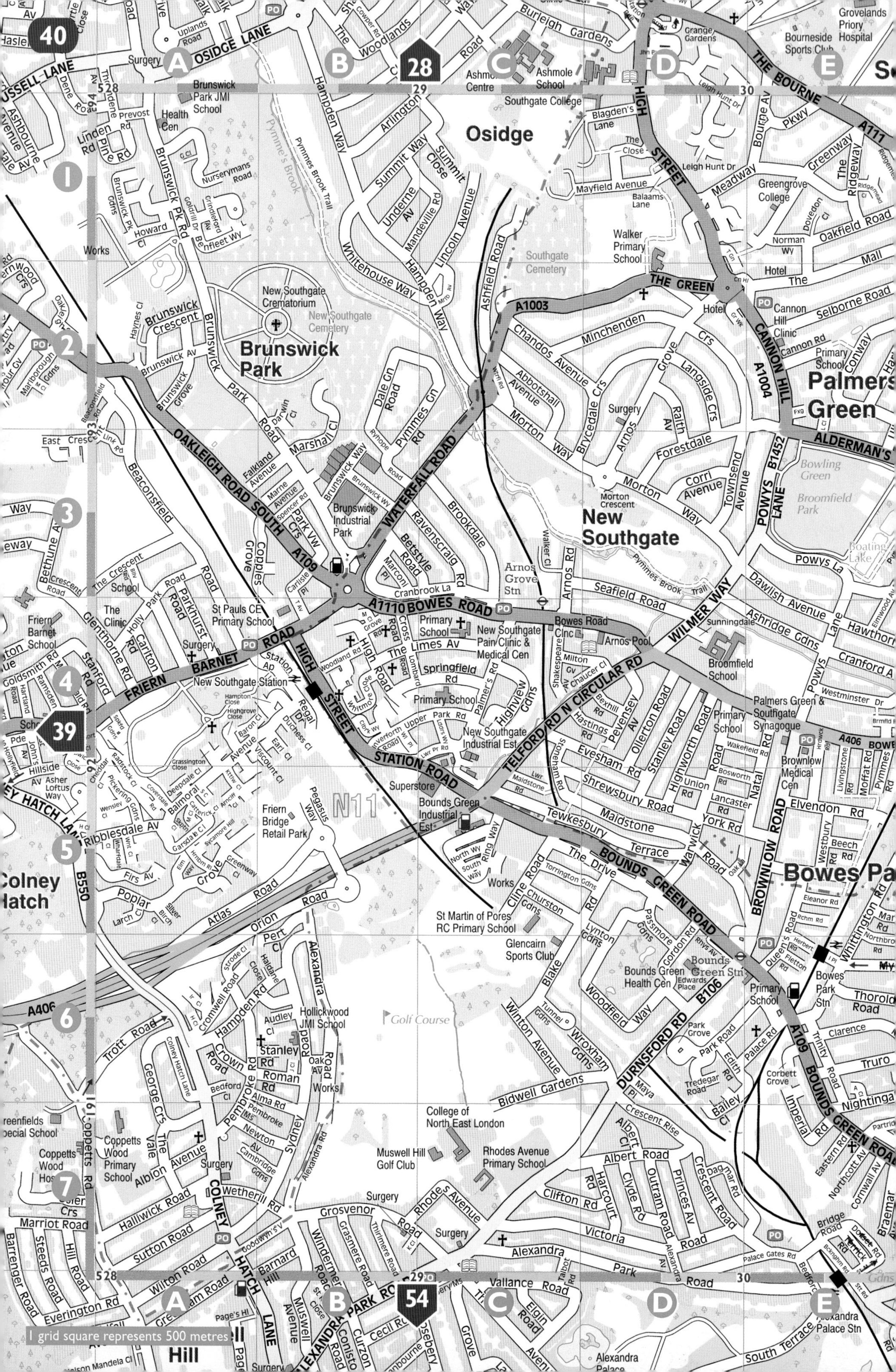

40
28
39
54
A
B
C
D
E
1
2
3
4
5
6
7
528
29
30
94
93
92
91
Osidge Lane
Uplands Road
Surgery
Russell Lane
Dene Road
Thirlmere Road (?)
Prevost Rd
Health Cen
Brunswick Park JMI School
Linden Rd
Pine Rd
Ashbourne Avenue
Brunswick Pk Rd
Brunswick Pk Gdns
Howard Cl
Nurserymans Road
Crindleford
Benfleet Wy
Works
The Woodlands
Hampden Way
Pymmes Brook Trail
Pymme's Brook
Arlington
Summit Way
Summit Close
Underne Av
Mandeville Rd
Lincoln Avenue
Whitehouse Way
Road
Burleigh Gardens
Ashmole Centre
Ashmole School
Southgate College
Osidge
Blagden's Lane
The Close
Mayfield Avenue
Balaams Lane
Walker Primary School
Southgate Cemetery
Ashfield Road
High Street
Grange Gardens
Grovelands Priory Hospital
Bourneside Sports Club
The Bourne
Leigh Hunt Dr
Bourne Av
Pkwy
A111
Greenway
The Ridgeway
Meadway
Greengrove College
Oakfield Road
Norman Wy
Hotel
The Mall
The Green
A1003
Cannon Hill
Cannon Hill Clinic
Cannon Rd
Selborne Road
Primary School
Conway
A1004
Palmers Green
Alderman's Hill
New Southgate Crematorium
New Southgate Cemetery
Brunswick Park
Brunswick Crescent
Brunswick Av
Brunswick Grove
Brunswick Park Road
Haynes Cl
Darwin Cl
Marshall Cl
Falkland Avenue
Marne Avenue
Spencer Rd
Park Vw Crs
Brunswick Way
Brunswick Industrial Park
Dale Gn Road
Pymmes Gn Rd
Rynope Road
Waterfall Road
Ravenscraig Rd
Brookdale
Betstyle Road
Marconi Pl
Oakleigh Road South
A109
Chandos Avenue
Minchenden Crs
Abbotshall Avenue
Morton Way
Brycedale Crs
Arnos Grove
Raith Av
Langside Crs
Forestdale
Surgery
Corri Avenue
Townsend Avenue
Morton Crescent
Powys Lane
B1452
Bowling Green
Broomfield Park
Boating Lake
New Southgate
Pymmes Brook Trail
Powys La
Dawlish Avenue
Ashridge Gdns
Hawthorn
Cranford Av
Westminster Dr
Elmwood Av
Arnos Grove Stn
Walker Cl
Arnos Rd
Seafield Road
Wilmer Way
Sunningdale
Broomfield School
Bowes Road
Bowes Road Clnc
Arnos Pool
A1110 Bowes Road
Cranbrook La
Carlisle Pl
Primary School
New Southgate Pain Clinic & Medical Cen
The Limes Av
Springfield Rd
Palmer's Rd
Highview Gdns
Primary School
Milton Gv
Chaucer Cl
Shakespeare Av
Telford Rd N Circular Rd
Bexhill Rd
Hastings Rd
Pevensey Av
Ollerton Road
Stanley Road
Highworth Road
Palmers Green & Southgate Synagogue
A406
Bowes Rd
East Crescent
Beaconsfield Road
Link Rd
Way
Bethune Av
Crescent Road
The Crescent
School
The Clinic
Holly Park Road
Parkhurst Road
St Pauls CE Primary School
Friern Barnet School
Glenthorne Rd
Goldsmith Rd
Hartland Road
Ramsden Road
Stanford Rd
Carlton Rd
Surgery
Friern Barnet Road
Station Ap
New Southgate Station
High Street
Woodland Rd
High Road
Cross Road
Lombard Av
Regal Dr
Duchess Cl
Earl Cl
Viscount Cl
Hampton Close
Highgrove Close
Baron Cl
Avenue
Grassington Close
Deepdale Cl
Balmoral Av
Coverdale Rd
Pickering Gdns
Radstock Cl
Cheddar Cl
Wensley Cl
Ribblesdale Av
Wharfdale Cl
Firs Av
Grove Rd
Greenway Cl
Poplar Rd
Larch Cl
Silver Birch
Sycamore Hill
Hillside
Asher Loftus Way
Colney Hatch Lane
Colney Hatch
B550
Upper Park Rd
Inverforth Road
Station Road
Stoneham Rd
Maidstone Rd
Evesham Rd
Shrewsbury Road
Union Rd
Bosworth Rd
Lancaster Rd
York Rd
Natal Rd
Brownlow Road
Brownlow Medical Cen
Wakefield Rd
Livingstone Rd
Moffat Rd
Pymmes Rd
Elvendon Rd
New Southgate Industrial Est
Superstore
Bounds Green Industrial Est
N11
Friern Bridge Retail Park
Pegasus Way
Ring Way
North Wy
South Wy
Works
Tewkesbury Terrace
Maidstone Road
The Drive
Bounds Green Road
Warwick Road
Torrington Gdns
Churston Gdns
Cline Road
Atlas Road
Orion Road
Pert Cl
Alexandra Road
Strode Cl
Haldane Close
Cromwell Road
Hampden Rd
St Martin of Pores RC Primary School
Glencairn Sports Club
Lynton Gdns
Blake Rd
Passmore Gdns
Gordon Rd
Rhys Av
Bounds Green Health Cen
Edwards Place
Bounds Green Stn
Woodfield Way
Durnsford Rd
B106
Primary School
Bowes Park
Westbury Rd
Beech Rd
Eleanor Rd
Queen's Road
Herbert Rd
Fletton Rd
Whittington Rd
Northbrook Rd
Bowes Park Stn
Thorold Road
Clarence Rd
Truro Rd
Nightingale Rd
Trinity Road
Imperial Rd
Corbett Grove
A109 Bounds Green Road
Eastern Rd
Northcott Av
Cornwall Av
Braemar
Golf Course
Hollickwood JMI School
Audley Cl
Stanley Rd
Roman Rd
Alma Rd
Pembroke Rd
Pembroke Ms
Newton Av
Cambridge Gdns
Oak Av
Works
Sydney Road
Trott Road
George Crs
Coppetts Wood Primary School
Greenfields Special School
Coppetts Wood Hospital
Coppetts Rd
The Vale
Albion Avenue
Surgery
Wetherill Rd
Halliwick Road
Sutton Road
Marriot Road
Barrenger Road
Steeds Road
Hill Road
Everington Rd
Wilton Road
Gresham Road
Barnard Hill
Colney Hatch Lane
Muswell Avenue
Page's Hl
Hill
Alexandra Park Road
Coniston Road
Curzon Road
Cecil Rd
Rosebery
Winton Avenue
Tunnel Gdns
Wroxham Gdns
Bidwell Gardens
Maya Pl
Crescent Rise
Albert Road
Harcourt Rd
Clyde Rd
Outram Road
Princes Av
Dagmar Rd
Crescent Road
Clifton Rd
Victoria Road
Alexandra Park Road
Palace Gates Rd
Bedford Rd
Bridge Road
Park Grove
Park Road
Tredegar Road
Edith Rd
Palace Rd
Bailey Cl
College of North East London
Muswell Hill Golf Club
Rhodes Avenue Primary School
Rhodes Avenue
Grosvenor Road
Grasmere Road
Windermere
Thirlmere Road
Surgery
Alexandra
Vallance Road
Elgin Road
Alexandra Palace Stn
South Terrace
Alexandra Palace
1 grid square represents 500 metres

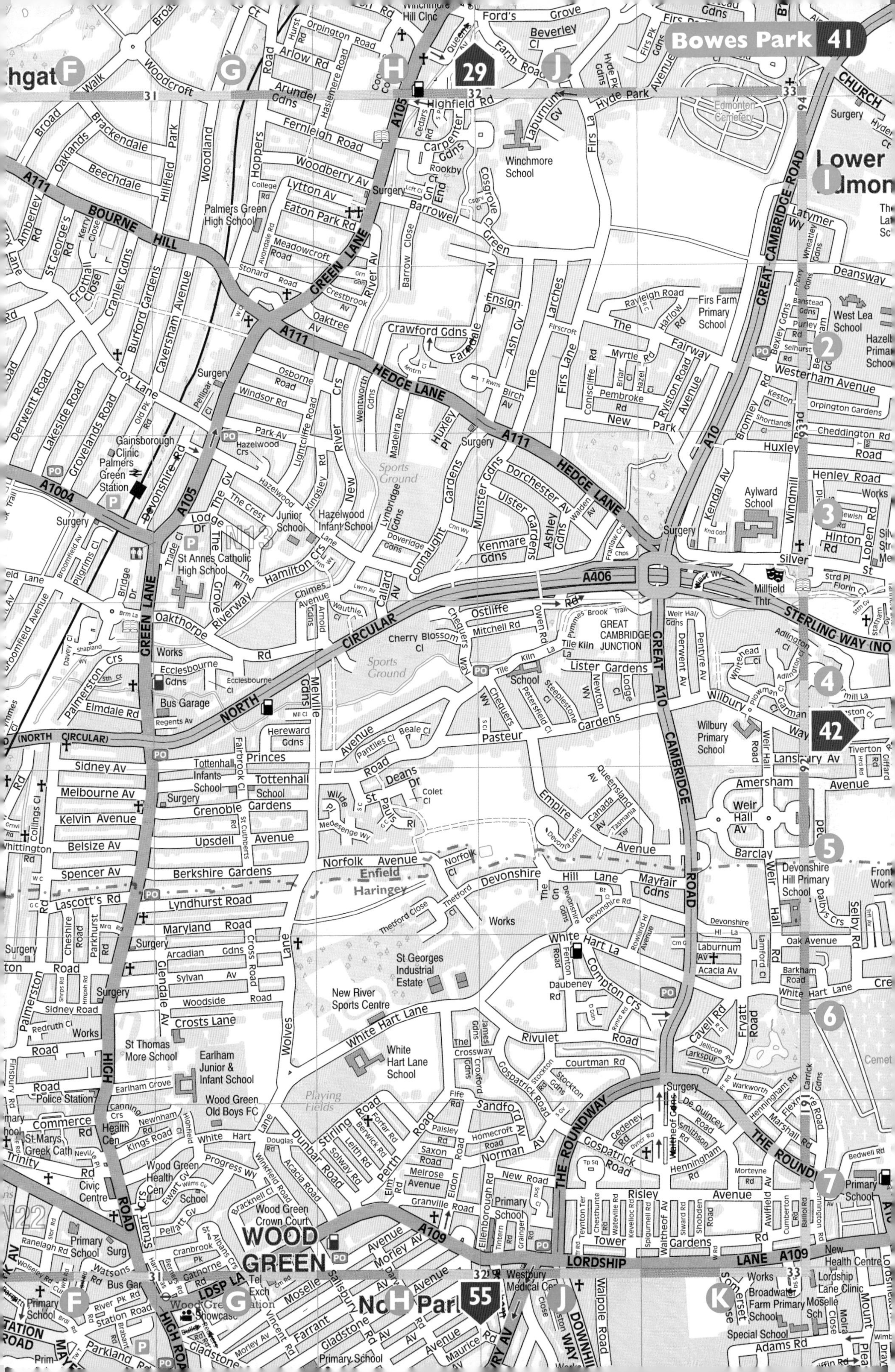
29
55
42
F
G
H
J
I
K
2
3
4
5
6
7
31
32
33
Winchmore Hill Clnc
Ford's Grove
Beverley Cl
Farm Road
Hurst
Orpington Road
Arlow Rd
Arundel Gdns
Highfield Rd
Fernleigh Road
Woodberry Av
Lytton Av
Eaton Park Rd
Barrowell Green
Winchmore School
Hyde Park Avenue
Firs La
Laburnum Gv
Edmonton Cemetery
Lower Edmonton
Surgery
Church
Great Cambridge Road
Latymer Wy
Deansway
West Lea School
Westerham Avenue
Orpington Gardens
Cheddington Rd
Huxley Road
Henley Road
Works
Aylward School
Windmill
Hinton Rd
Silver St
Millfield Thtr
Sterling Way (North Circular)
Firs Farm Primary School
Rayleigh Road
The Fairway
Myrtle Rd
Pembroke Rd
New Park Avenue
Rylston Road
Hedge Lane
A111
A10
A406
A105
A1004
A109
Bourne Hill
Green Lane
Fox Lane
Broad Walk
Woodcroft
Brackendale
Oaklands
Beechdale
Hillfield Park
Woodland
Hoppers Road
Palmers Green High School
Caversham Avenue
Burford Gardens
Cranley Gdns
Derwent Road
Lakeside Road
Grovelands Road
Gainsborough Clinic
Palmers Green Station
Devonshire Rd
Osborne Road
Windsor Rd
Park Av
Hazelwood Crs
Hazelwood Junior School
Hazelwood Infant School
Lightcliffe Road
Kingsley Rd
New River Crs
Wentworth Gdns
Madeira Rd
Crawford Gdns
Farndale
Sports Ground
Lynbridge Gdns
Doveridge Gdns
Connaught Gardens
Huxley Pl
Munster Gdns
Dorchester Av
Ulster Gardens
Kenmare Gdns
Ashley Gdns
Walden Av
Ensign Dr
Ash Gv
The Larches
Firs Lane
Birch Av
St Annes Catholic High School
N13
Hamilton Crs
Riverway
Oakthorpe Road
Chimes Avenue
Arnold Gdns
Callard Av
Ostliffe Rd
Mitchell Rd
Owen Rd
Pymmes Brook Trail
Great Cambridge Junction
Cherry Blossom Cl
Chequers Way
Tile Kiln La
Lister Gardens
Newton Wy
Lodge Cl
Derwent Av
Pentyre Av
Weir Hall Gdns
Wilbury Way
Wilbury Primary School
Lansbury Av
Amersham Avenue
Weir Hall Av
Barclay
Devonshire Hill Primary School
Selby Rd
Oak Avenue
Works
Ecclesbourne Gdns
Bus Garage
Regents Av
Elmdale Rd
Palmerston Crs
North Circular
Melville Gdns
Hereward Gdns
Princes Avenue
Pasteur Gardens
Queensland Av
Empire Avenue
Canada Av
Tasmania Ter
Devonia Gdns
Deans Dr
Colet Cl
St Pauls Ri
Medesenge Wy
Sidney Av
Melbourne Av
Kelvin Avenue
Belsize Av
Spencer Av
Tottenhall Infants School
Tottenhall School
Grenoble Gardens
Upsdell Avenue
Berkshire Gardens
Norfolk Avenue
Norfolk Cl
Enfield
Haringey
Devonshire Hill Lane
Mayfair Gdns
Thetford Close
Lascott's Rd
Lyndhurst Road
Maryland Road
Arcadian Gdns
Sylvan Av
Woodside Road
Crosts Lane
Cross Road
Glendale Av
Cheshire Road
Parkhurst Rd
St Georges Industrial Estate
New River Sports Centre
White Hart Lane
White Hart Lane School
White Hart La
Compton Crs
Daubeney Rd
Fenton Road
Rivulet Road
Courtman Rd
Gospatrick Road
Stockton Gdns
The Crossway
Laburnum Av
Acacia Av
Barkham Road
Fryatt Road
Cavell Rd
Larkspur Cl
The Roundway
Surgery
De Quincey Road
Henningham Rd
Risley Avenue
Tower Gardens
Lordship Lane
Sandford Av
Norman Av
New Road
Primary School
Palmerston Road
Sidney Road
Police Station
Commerce Rd
Health Cen
St Marys Greek Cath
Trinity Rd
Civic Centre
High Road
St Thomas More School
Earlham Junior & Infant School
Earlham Grove
Wood Green Old Boys FC
Playing Fields
Kings Road
Progress Wy
Wood Green Health Cen
Stirling Road
Dunbar Road
Acacia Road
Perth Road
Eldon Road
Melrose Avenue
Saxon Road
Granville Road
Wood Green Crown Court
Wood Green
Morley Av
Westbury Medical Cen
Walpole Road
Noel Park
Moselle Av
Gladstone Av
Lordship Lane Clinic
Broadwater Farm Primary School
Moselle Sch
Somerset Close
Special School
Adams Rd
New Health Centre
Station Road
Parkland Rd
Bedwell Rd
Primary School

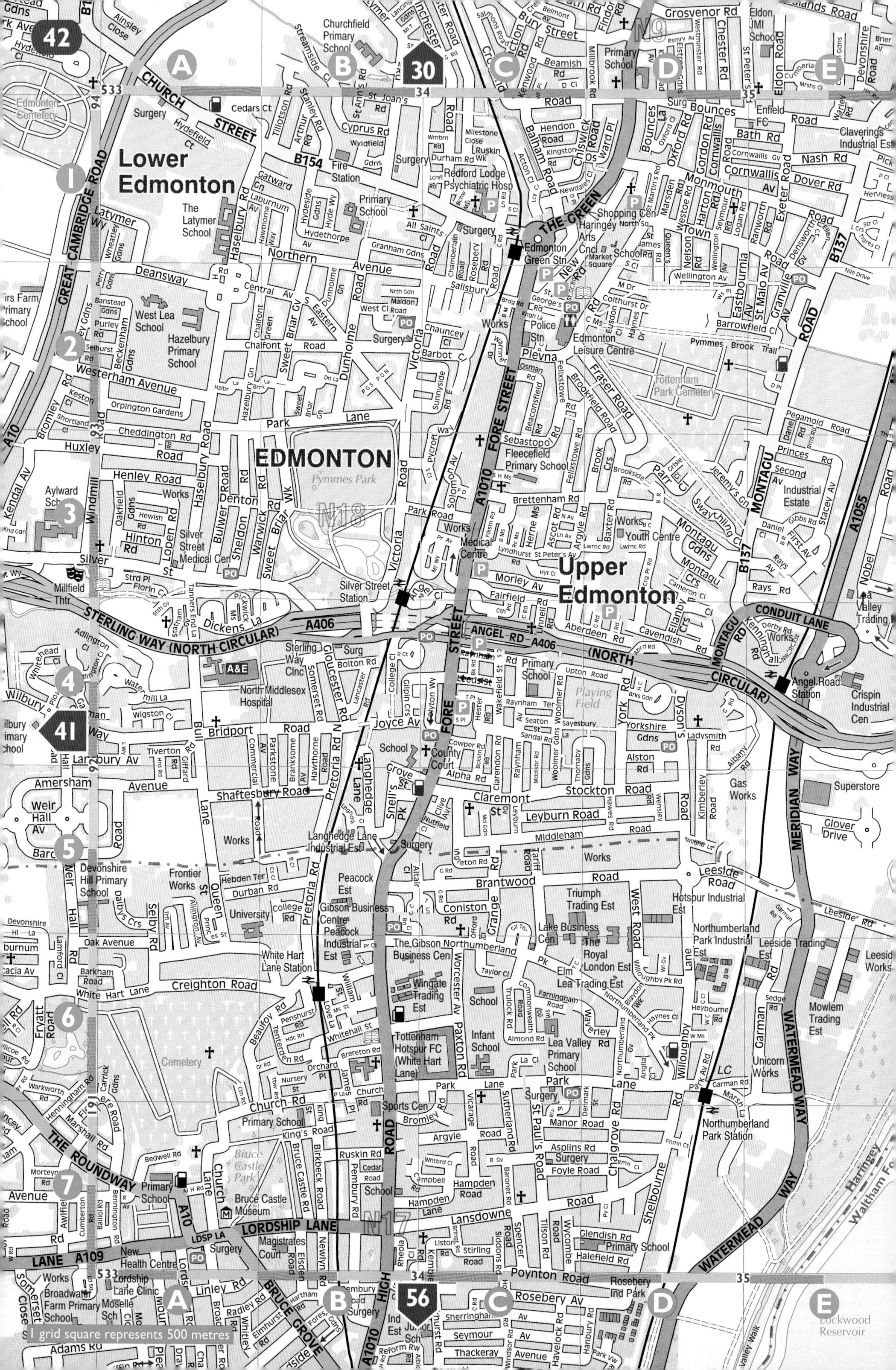

42
30
A
B
C
D
E
Lower Edmonton
EDMONTON
Upper Edmonton
Pymmes Park
N18
N9
N17
CHURCH STREET
Cedars Ct
Hydefield Ct
Surgery
Edmonton Cemetery
Ainsley Close
Churchfield Primary School
Streamside Cl
St Joan's Rd
Cyprus Rd
Tillotson Rd
Stanley Rd
Arthur Rd
B154
Fire Station
Wyldfield Gdns
Milestone Close
Ruskin Wk
Durham Rd
Redford Lodge Psychiatric Hosp
Grosvenor Rd
Chester Rd
Eldon JMI School
Eldon Road
Devonshire Road
Bury Street
Beamish Rd
Millbrook Rd
Primary School
Hendon Road
Kingston
Balham Road
Acton Cl
THE GREEN
Haringey Arts Cncl
Shopping Cen
Market Square
Edmonton Green Stn
Bounces Rd
Bounces La
Oxford Rd
Gordon Rd
Cornwallis Rd
Cornwallis Av
Bath Rd
Enfield FC
Claverings Industrial Est
Nash Rd
Dover Rd
Monmouth Rd
Town Rd
Exeter Road
B137
GREAT CAMBRIDGE ROAD
A10
Latymer Wy
The Latymer School
Haselbury Rd
Laburnum Av
Gatward Cl
Hyde Wy
Hydethorpe Av
Primary School
All Saints Cl
Granham Gdns
Northern Avenue
Surgery
Deansway
Central Av
West Lea School
Hazelbury Primary School
Firs Farm Primary School
Chalfont Road
Sweet Briar Gv
Dunholme Road
Victoria Road
Chauncey Cl
Barbot Cl
Salisbury Rd
Police Stn
Plevna
Edmonton Leisure Centre
Westerham Avenue
Orpington Gardens
Keston
Shortland
Bromley Rd
Cheddington Rd
Huxley Road
Park Lane
Henley Road
Haselbury Road
Works
Aylward School
Windmill Road
Oakfield Gdns
Hewish Rd
Hinton Rd
Lopen Rd
Bulwer Rd
Denton
Sheldon Rd
Warwick Rd
Sweet Briar Wk
Silver Street Medical Cen
Silver St
Millfield Thtr
Strd Pl
Florin Cl
Dickens La
Silver Street Station
STERLING WAY (NORTH CIRCULAR)
A406
FORE STREET
A1010
Fleecefield Primary School
Sebastopol Rd
Brettenham Rd
Felixstowe Rd
Fraser Road
Brookfield Road
Beaconsfield Rd
Osman Rd
Tottenham Park Cemetery
Pymmes Brook Trail
Barrowfield Cl
Pegamoid Road
Princes Rd
Second Av
Industrial Estate
MONTAGU ROAD
A1055
Montagu Gdns
Montagu Crs
Youth Centre
Baxter Rd
Argyle Rd
Ascot Rd
Medical Centre
Morley Av
Fairfield Rd
Aberdeen Rd
Cavendish Rd
Rays Rd
Nobel Road
Lea Valley Trading
CONDUIT LANE
Angel Road Station
Crispin Industrial Cen
ANGEL RD A406 (NORTH CIRCULAR)
Primary School
Upton Road
Playing Field
York Rd
Dyson's Rd
Ladysmith Rd
Yorkshire Gdns
Alston Rd
Gas Works
Superstore
MERIDIAN WAY
Glover Drive
A&E
North Middlesex Hospital
Sterling Way Clnc
Bolton Rd
Gloucester Rd
Somerset Rd
Bridport Road
Joyce Av
Parkstone Av
Commercial Rd
Branksome Av
Hawthorne Rd
Pretoria Rd N
Langhedge Lane
Snell's Pk
County Court
Grove St
Alpha Rd
Clarendon Rd
Raynham Av
Woolmer Rd
Claremont St
Leyburn Road
Stockton Road
Middleham Road
Kimberley Road
Watermill La
Wigston Cl
Tiverton Rd
Clifford Rd
Larbury Av
Amersham Avenue
Weir Hall Av
Shaftesbury Road
Works
Langhedge Lane Industrial Est
Surgery
Devonshire Hill Primary School
Frontier Works
Hebden Ter
Durban Rd
University
College Cl
Queen St
Selby Rd
Weir Hall Rd
Oak Avenue
Barkham Road
Lamford Cl
White Hart Lane
Creighton Road
White Hart Lane Station
Peacock Est
Gibson Business Centre
Peacock Industrial Est
The Gibson Business Cen
Wingate Trading Est
Tottenham Hotspur FC (White Hart Lane)
Worcester Av
Paxton Rd
Northumberland Pk
Brantwood Road
Coniston Rd
Grange Rd
Triumph Trading Est
Lake Business Cen
The Royal London Est
Lea Trading Est
West Road
Leeside Road
Hotspur Industrial Est
Northumberland Park Industrial Est
Leeside Trading Est
Mowlem Trading Est
Unicorn Works
WATERMEAD WAY
Taylor Cl
Commonwealth Road
Trulock Rd
School
Infant School
Almond Rd
Lea Valley Primary School
Waverley Rd
Willoughby La
Park Lane
Surgery
Northumberland Park Station
Garman Rd
Cemetery
Fryatt Road
Beaufoy Rd
Penshurst Rd
Tenterden Rd
Whitehall St
Orchard Pl
Nursery St
Church Rd
Primary School
King's Road
Bruce Castle Rd
Birkbeck Road
Ruskin Rd
Pembury Rd
Sports Cen
Bromley Rd
Argyle Rd
Vicarage Road
Sutherland Rd
St Paul's Road
Manor Road
Asplins Rd
Foyle Road
Chalgrove Rd
Shelbourne Rd
Hampden Road
Hampden Lane
Campbell
School
Bruce Castle Park
Bruce Castle Museum
Church Lane
THE ROUNDWAY
Henningham Rd
Marshall Rd
Warkworth Rd
Bedwell Rd
Primary School
LORDSHIP LANE
LANE A109
Magistrates Court
New Health Centre
Lordship Lane Clinic
Surgery
Lansdowne Road
Spencer Rd
Tilson Rd
Wycombe Rd
Glendish Rd
Primary School
Halefield Rd
Stirling Road
Poynton Road
Rosebery Ind Park
Rosebery Av
Linley Rd
Radley Rd
BRUCE GROVE
HIGH ROAD
A1010
Broadwater Farm Primary School
Moselle Sch
Somerset Close
Adams Rd
Sherringham Av
Seymour Av
Thackeray Avenue
Windsor Rd
Havelock Rd
Hanbury Rd
Park Vw
Lockwood Reservoir
Haringey
Waltham Fo
Valley Walk
56
41
1
2
3
4
5
6
7
533
34
35
1 grid square represents 500 metres

Golf Course
Pickett's Lock La
Pymmes Brook Trail
Lea Valley Wk
Ardra Rd
Works
River Lea or Lee
Lee Park Way
Advent Way
Lwr Hall La
Chingford Industrial Cen
Service Centre
A406
COOKS FERRY ROUNDABOUT
Ravenside Retail Park
Hawley Rd
Stonehill Business Park
Stonehill Business Cen
Harbet Rd
Haslingwood Trading Est
Lea Valley Trading Estate
Shadbolt Avenue
Lee Valley Watersports Cen
Banbury Reservoir
Folly La
WALTHAMSTOW AVENUE (NORTH CIRCULAR)
Enfield
Lea Valley Walk
A1037 WALTHAM WAY
A1009 HALL LANE
Russell Road
Heriot Av
Leadale Avenue
Brindwood Road
Rectory Close
Priory Avenue
Priory Close
Mayhew Close
Cherrydown Close
Cherrydown Avenue
Middleton Close
Middleton Avenue
Marmion Cl
Marmion Avenue
Hurst Av
Hurst Cl
Churchill Terrace
Eatons Md
Lansdowne Rd
Lawrence Hl
Lambourne Gdns
Denner Road
St Catherines Road
Silverthorn Gardens
Mulberry Cl
Peel Cl
Walmer Cl
Wellington Avenue
Chingford Avenue
OLD CHURCH ROAD A112
B169
Nevin
Surgery
Cemetery
Moreland Wy
Heathfield
Gunners Gv
Heathcote Gv
Hale Cl
Alpha Road
Salisbury Rd
Mount Av
Templeton Avenue
Medical Centre
Brook Cr
Brook Crs
Brook Gdns
Windsor Rd
Primary School
Chivers Rd
St John's Rd
Suffield Rd
Morris Court
Flaxen Road
Grove
Harold Road
Tiptree Cl
NEW ROAD
Drive
Normanshire
Chase Lane Primary School
Chingford Health Centre
Hall Gdns
Chase Gdns
Tufton Road
Albert Av
Orchard Cl
Frankland Road
Norbury Rd
Norton Cl
Soper Cl
Hampton Road
Burnham Road
Sinclair Road
Westward Road
York Road
Warwick Rd
Titley Cl
Larkswood Road
Larkswood Playing Fields
Ainslie Wood Gdns
Bourne Gdns
Lynton Rd
Underwood Road
Palace Vw Rd
Kingsley Gdns
Genever Cl
Finch Gdns
Ainslie Wood Road
Broad Oak Cl
Rolls Pk
Ainslie Wood Primary School
Royston Avenue
Rolls Park Av
Edward Av
Bateman Rd
Ashley Rd
Frances Rd
Leonard Rd
May Rd
George Rd
Cranston Gdns
Coningsby Gdns
Woodside Gdns
CHINGFORD MOUNT ROAD
CHINGFORD ROAD A112
Maple Avenue
Hazel Way
Lilac Sq
Silver Birch Av
Rowan
Cabinet Way
Burnside Av
Primary School
Superstore
Adam Rd
Ching Way
Keatley Grn
Iris Wy
Trinity Wy
Justin Rd
Avenue Industrial Est
Higham Station Avenue
United Synagogue
Tudor Rd
Marlborough Road
Nelson Road
Rowden Road
Loxham Rd
Ascham Dr
Rushcroft Road
Rush Croft School
Walthamstow Greyhound Stadium
Empress Av
Grove Pk Av
CROOKED BILLET ROUNDABOUT
Wadham Av
Higham Park
Bellamy Rd
Long Leys
Selwyn Av
Selwyn Primary School
Cavendish
Lena Kennedy Cl
Aldriche Wy
NORTH CIRCULAR
B179
Banbury Road
Swift Cl
Cormorant Cl
Cogan Av
Valognes Av
Amber Av
School
Cooper Av
Lawrence Av
Waterhall Cl
Travers Cl
Gurney Close
Sinnott Rd
McEntee Av
William Morris School
Kimberley Industrial Est
Kimberley Road
Durban Rd
Stow Crs
Cheney Rw
Asch End
Billet Works
McEntee Sch
Britannia Sports Ground
Waltham Pk
Cecil Rd
Knebworth Avenue
Mansel Gv
Lewis Av
Douglas Av
Douglas Ter
Monoux Gv
Penrhyn Avenue
Penrhyn Crs
Brettenham Road
Chapel End Infant School
Roberts Road
Beresford Road
Kitchener Road
Junior School
Wadham Lodge Sports Centre
Brookscroft
Galeborough Road
FULBOURNE ROAD
Bridge End
BILLET ROAD
Lee Close
Sutton Road
Fair View Cl
Millfield Av
Whittingham Community Primary School
Higham Hill Road
Carlton Road
Hecham Cl
Folly La
Lyne Crs
Guildsway
Primary School
Wigton Rd
Countess Rd
Ardleigh Rd
Keith Rd
Williams Av
Thorpe Crs
Warwick Road
Manor Road
Mount Pleasant Rd
Rodney Pl
Windsor Rd
Priors Croft
Heron Cl
Pennant Ter
Elphinstone
Fleeming Rd
Worcester Road
Gloucester Road
Mayfield Rd
Clarence Rd
Lancaster Rd
Lockwood Wy
Waltham Forest College
Surgery
Aveling Pk Rd
Marten Road
Evesham Av
Cazenove Rd
Chapel End Infant School
Sturge Av
Warburton Ter
Sir George Monoux College
Northbank Rd
Woodend Rd
Thorpe Rd
St John's Rd
Victoria Rd
Works
Higham Hill
F
G
H
J
K
31
44
57
36
37
38
92
93
94
91
2
3
4
5
6
7

44
43
58
A
B
C
D
E
1
2
3
4
5
6
7
538
39
40
94
93
92
91
Chingford
Friday Hill
Chingford Hatch
Hale End
Highams Park
Woodford
South
THE RIDGEWAY
KING'S ROAD
WHITEHALL ROAD
A110
B169
B146
B160
A1009
A104
A406
A503
A11
B168
LARKSHALL ROAD
FRIDAY HILL
NEW ROAD
HATCH LA
CHINGFORD LANE
HIGH RD WOODFORD GREEN
WOODFORD NEW ROAD
WINCHESTER ROAD
FULBOURNE ROAD
NORTH CIRCULAR
SOUTHEND ROAD (NORTH CIRCULAR)
SOUTHEND RD (NORTH CIRCULAR)
BROADMEAD ROAD
HIGH RD WOODFORD GN
GEORGE LANE
SHRUBBERIES
Larkshall Business Centre
Heathcote School
Whitehall Primary School
Junior School
Infant School
Surgery
Friday Hill Primary School
Larkswood Playing Fields
Jubilee Sports Ground
Woodford Golf Club
Woodford Green Primary School
High School
Primary School
Trinity Catholic Lower High School
Avon House School
Bancrofts School
Woodford Green Prep School
Woodford County High School
St Aubyns School
Handsworth Hlth Clinic
Highams Park School
Highams Park Station
Special School
Selwyn Primary School
Rush Croft School
Walthamstow Greyhound Stadium
Chapel End Infant School
Wadham Lodge Sports Centre
Whitefield School & Leisure Centre
South Woodford Health Centre
Churchfields J&I School
College
The Synagogue
Ainslie Primary School
Works
Hotel
Centenary Walk
Centenary Wk
Odeon
Superstore
1 grid square represents 500 metres

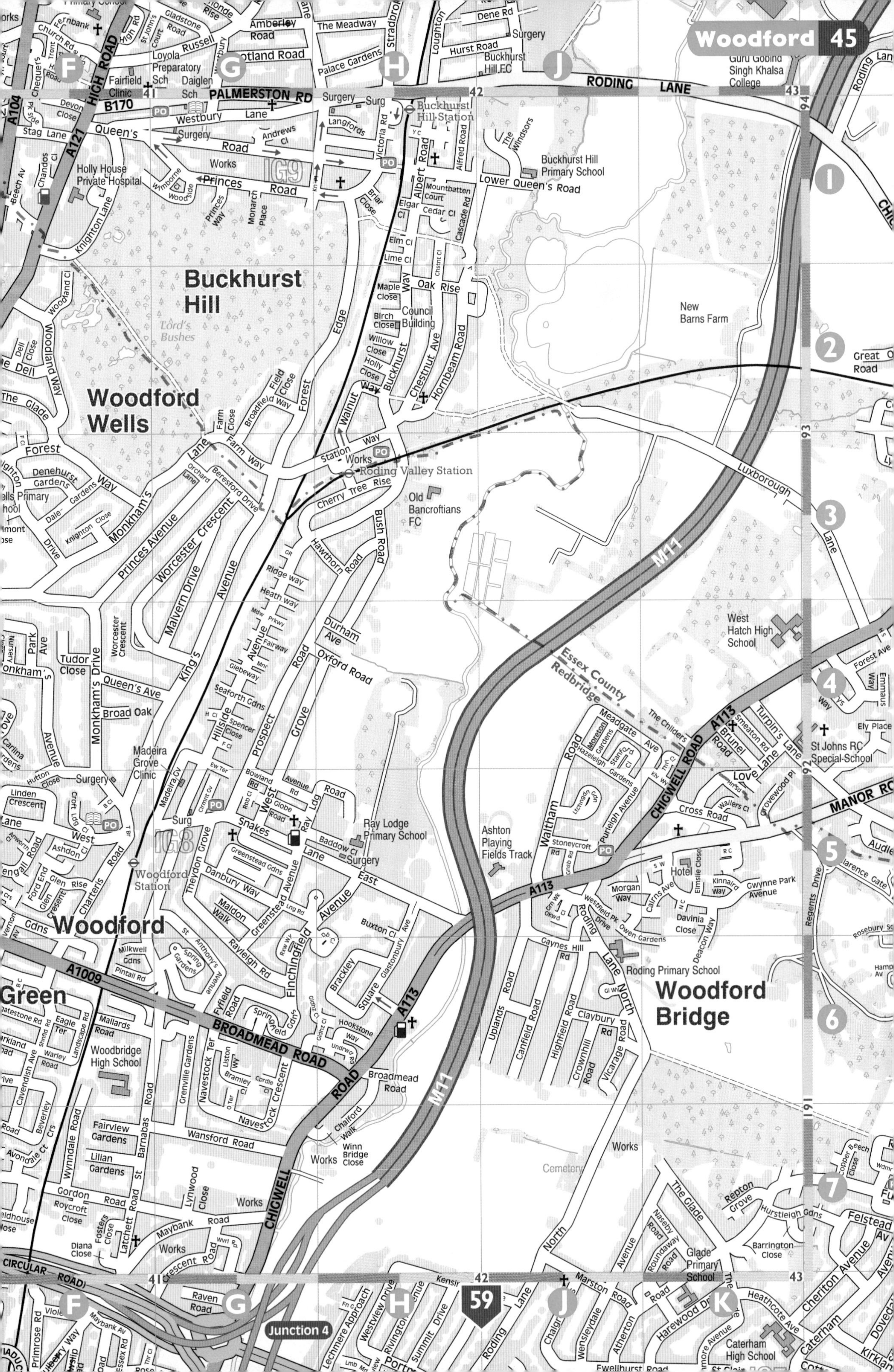
Buckhurst Hill
Woodford Wells
Woodford
Woodford Bridge
Green
Lord's Bushes
New Barns Farm
RODING LANE
PALMERSTON RD
B170
A104
A121
HIGH ROAD
Queen's Road
Westbury Lane
Stag Lane
Princes Road
Lower Queen's Road
Buckhurst Hill Station
Roding Valley Station
Woodford Station
Buckhurst Hill Primary School
Holly House Private Hospital
Loyola Preparatory Sch
Fairfield Clinic
Daiglen Sch
Guru Gobind Singh Khalsa College
Buckhurst Hill FC
Old Bancroftians FC
Council Building
West Hatch High School
St Johns RC Special School
Ray Lodge Primary School
Ashton Playing Fields Track
Roding Primary School
Glade Primary School
Woodbridge High School
Caterham High School
Madeira Grove Clinic
Hotel
Cemetery
Works
Surgery
Luxborough Lane
Great Cullen Road
CHIGWELL ROAD
A113
MANOR ROAD
BROADMEAD ROAD
A1009
CIRCULAR ROAD
M11
Junction 4
Essex County
Redbridge
IG8
IG9
Monkham's Lane
Princes Avenue
Worcester Crescent
Malvern Drive
King's Avenue
Forest Edge
Buckhurst Way
Chestnut Ave
Hornbeam Road
Hawthorn Road
Bush Road
Prospect Road
Grove Road
Snakes Lane
Oxford Road
Durham Ave
Ridge Way
Heath Way
Theydon Grove
Danbury Way
Greenstead Avenue
Finchingfield Avenue
Rayleigh Rd
Navestock Crescent
Grenville Gardens
Wansford Road
Maybank Road
Uplands Road
Canfield Road
Highfield Road
Crownhill Road
Vicarage Road
Roding Lane North
Waltham Road
Puteaux Avenue
Cross Road
Love Lane
Turpin's Lane
Brunel Road
Regents Drive
Cheriton Avenue
Heathcote Ave
Harewood Dr
The Glade
Repton Grove
Hurstleigh Gdns
Felstead Av
Gaynes Hill Rd
Claybury Rd
Monkham's Drive
Woodland Way
Knighton Lane
Queen's Ave
Broad Oak
Tudor Close
Linden Crescent
Charteris Road
Wynndale Road
Gordon Road
Latchett Road
Fairview Gardens
Lilian Gardens
Barnabas Road
Lynwood Close
Raven Road
Primrose Rd
Lechmere Approach
Westview Drive
Summit Drive
Roding Lane
Wensleydale
Atherton
Marston Road
Kirkland
Dovedale
Caterham
42
43
41
91
92
93
94
59
F
G
H
J
K
1
2
3
4
5
6
7

46
32
64
A
B
C
D
E
1
2
3
4
5
6
7
508
09
10
90
89
88
187
Northwood Hills
Ruislip Common
RUISLIP
West Ruislip
Haste Hill Golf Club
Golf Course
Northwood Cemetery
Northwood FC
Northwood & Pinner Community Hosp
PINNER ROAD
A404
JOEL STREET
Northwood Hills Stn
Copse Wood
Poor's Field
Ruislip Lido
Park Wood
Mad Bess Wood
St Vincents Hospital
Haydon Sch
Kings College Sports Ground
Breakspear Crematorium
Hillingdon Borough FC
Hillingdon Trail
A4180
BURY STREET
HIGH STREET
EASTCOTE ROAD
B466
ICKENHAM ROAD
Reservoir Road
Dell Farm Road
Withy Lane
Nicholas Way
Rogers Ruff
Copse Close
The Broad Walk
Oak Glade
Broadwood Avenue
Park Avenue
Kings College Road
Evelyn Avenue
Pinn Way
Ladygate Lane
Mead Way
Sharps Lane
Manor Road
Kg Edward's Road
Kingsend
Pembroke Road
Brickwall Lane
Manor Way
Windmill Hill
The Ridgeway
Warrender Way
Westholme Gdns
Park Way
Wood Lane
Willow Grove
Shenley Avenue
Fore Street
Wiltshire Lane
Salisbury Road
Coniston Gdns
Wentworth Dr
Grangewood School
Coteford Infant School
Whiteheath Infant School
Whiteheath Junior School
Bishop Winnington-Ingram CE Primary School
St Martins Medical Centre
Bishop Ramsey CE School
Warrender School
Police Station
King Edwards Road Clinic
Wood Lane Medical Centre
Ruislip Station
Ruislip Manor Station
West Ruislip Station
Ruislip Manor FC
The Synagogue
HA4
Pond Green
Airbase Unity
The Greenway
Golf Course
Ravenscourt Close
Glovers Grove
1 grid square represents 500 metres

Pinner Green
Pinner
Eastcote Village
Eastcote
North Harrow
Rayners Lane
33
48
65

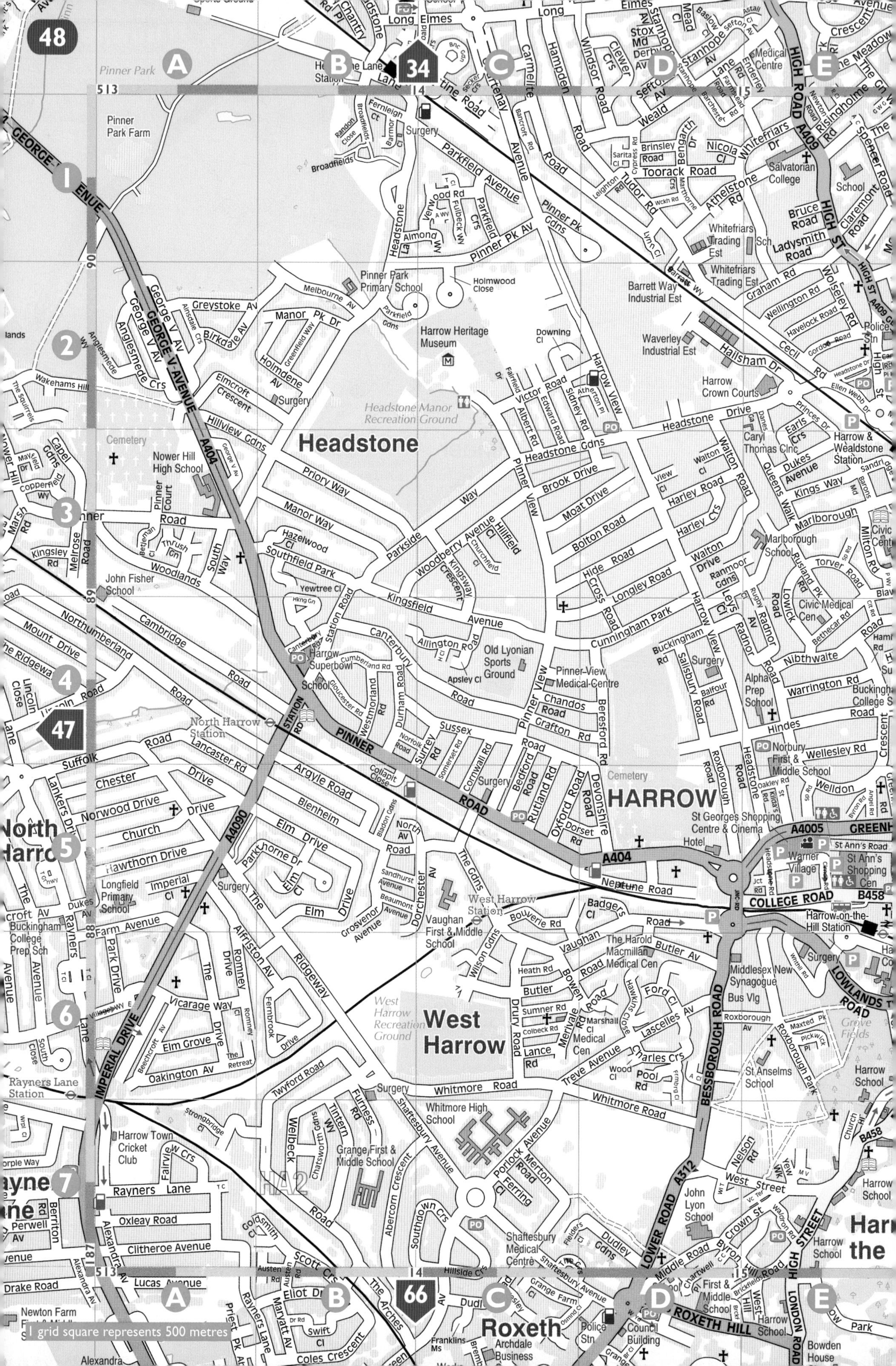

34
47
66
A
B
C
D
E
1
2
3
4
5
6
7
513
14
15
90
89
88
187
Pinner Park
Pinner Park Farm
Headstone Lane Station
Long Elmes
Headstone
Harrow Heritage Museum
Headstone Manor Recreation Ground
Pinner Park Primary School
Holmwood Close
Nower Hill High School
Cemetery
John Fisher School
North Harrow Station
Harrow Superbowl
Old Lyonian Sports Ground
Pinner View Medical Centre
HARROW
St Georges Shopping Centre & Cinema
Harrow & Wealdstone Station
Harrow Crown Courts
Salvatorian College
Whitefriars Trading Est
Barrett Way Industrial Est
Waverley Industrial Est
Marlborough School
Civic Medical Cen
Alpha Prep School
Norbury First & Middle School
Harrow-on-the-Hill Station
St Ann's Shopping Cen
Warner Village
Middlesex New Synagogue
Bus Vlg
West Harrow Station
Vaughan First & Middle School
The Harold Macmillan Medical Cen
West Harrow Recreation Ground
West Harrow
Whitmore High School
Grange First & Middle School
Harrow Town Cricket Club
Rayners Lane Station
Longfield Primary School
Buckingham College Prep Sch
St Anselms School
Harrow School
John Lyon School
Shaftesbury Medical Centre
Roxeth
Police Stn
Council Building
Archdale Business
Grove Fields
HA2
GEORGE V AVENUE
A404
A4090
PINNER ROAD
IMPERIAL DRIVE
HIGH ROAD A409
HIGH ST
A4005
COLLEGE ROAD
B458
LOWLANDS ROAD
BESSBOROUGH ROAD
LOWER ROAD A312
ROXETH HILL
HIGH STREET
LONDON ROAD
North Harrow
Rayners Lane
1 grid square represents 500 metres

35
50
67
F
G
H
J
I
K
16
17
18
2
3
4
5
6
7
Belmont
Wealdstone
Greenhill
Kenton
North Wembley
Preston
HA3
HA1
College Hill Rd
Connaught Rd
Dryden Rd
Kenton
Addersley Rd
Church Lane
Beverley Gardens
Hermitage Way
Felbridge Av
Bellamy
Ventnor Av
York Avenue
Kynance Gdns
Crowshott Av
Pickett Cft
Lyon
Grove
Lamorna Grove
Ladycroft Walk
Amherst Gardens
Honeypot La
Aldridge
Fisher Road
Bishop Ken
Hibbert Road
Lime Close
Grasmere Gardens
Dobbin Cl
Surgery
School
Belmont First & Middle School
Byron Road
Warham Road
Locket Road
Lorne Rd
Sancroft Road
Radcliffe Road
Borrowdale Av
Elgin Avenue
Tenby Avenue
Kenton Lane
Clifton Av
Grange Avenue
Rocklands Dr
Jersey Avenue
Crowshott Av
Derwent Crs
Culver Grove
Burnell Gardens
Thistlecroft Gdns
High School
Carisbrooke Close
Broadcroft Avenue
Portland Crescent
Langland Crs
Fairways
Collins Av
A4140
Honeypot Medical Centre
Talbot Road
Ivanhoe Drive
Hilliary Gdns
Morley Crs East
Morley Crs West
Charmian Av
Clydesdale Av
Portland Crs W
Streatfield Rd
Medical Centre
Priestmead First & Middle Schools
Queens Avenue
Ennerdale Av
Uppingham Av
Formby Avenue
Dudley Avenue
Streatfield Road
Archery Cl
Avondale Road
Ronart St
Belmont Road
Canning Road
Stuart Rd
Cemetery
Pembroke Av
Irvine Av
Hartford Avenue
Radstock Av
Beaufort Avenue
Kingshill Dr
Alveston Av
Oakfield Av
Larkfield Av
Moorhouse Road
Kenmore Park School
Cody Cl
Warneford Road
Wagorn Road
Hinkler Road
Brancker Road
Kenmore Road
Glebe Avenue
Peel Road
Palmerston Rd
Oxford Rd
Driving School & Road Safety Centre
Christchurch Av
Christchurch Gdns
Kenmore Avenue
Rowland Avenue
Shooters Avenue
Paulhan Road
Hamel Cl
Liddell Cl
Glebe First & Middle School
D'Arcy Gardens
Glenalvon Rd
Cheltenham Pl
Loretto Gdns
Masons Av
Herga Road
Forward Dr
The Hollies
Coxe Pl
Burnham Cl
Christchurch Avenue
Bradenham Rd
Wykeham Road
Boxmoor Rd
Brampton Grove
Alicia Gardens
Elmsleigh Avenue
Hunters Grove
Kenton Pk Crs
Kenton Cricket Club
Westfield Lane
Westfield Gdns
Westfield Dr
Charlton Road
The Bridge
Railway App
Station Road
Mag Cts
Rosslyn Crs
Harrow Central Mosque
Frognal Av
Cullington Close
Daintry Close
Elmgrove First & Middle School
Prestwood Av
Prestwood Close
Penn Cl
Alicia Avenue
Kenton Pk Rd
Kenton Pk Cl
Kenton Pk Av
D'Arcy Dr
Lodge Av
Morland Road
Phoenix Industrial Est
Hawthorn Centre
Kenmore Av
Kenton Recreation Ground
Hughenden Av
Addiscombe Close
St Leonards Av
St Marys Vw
Kenton Gdns
Tenby Rd
Brookside Cl
Gooseacre La
KENTON
Surgery
Hillview
Oakdale Av
Safari Cinema & Bingo
Woodlands Rd
Crystal Wy
Glenwood Cl
Elmgrove Crs
Francis Road
Moelyn Ms
Becmead Avenue
Hillbury Avenue
Willowcourt Av
Woodgrange Av
Retreat Cl
Tottenhoe Cl
Lidding Rd
Cranleigh Gdns
Greenway
TA Centre
Troy Ind Est
Catherine Pl
Duffield Cl
Richards Cl
Hill Crs
Carlton Avenue
Mayfield Av
A4006
Sedgecombe Av
Kenton
St Gregorys High School
Kenton Synagogue
Brookfield Crs
Greenhill Coll
Grange Rd
Crofts Road
Bonnersfield Road
Elmwood Avenue
Hotel
Briar Road
Northwick Cir
Norcombe Gdns
Winchfield Cl
Woodcock Hill
Donnington Road
Falcon
Regal
Bonnersfield Lane
Magistrates Court
Manor Road
Woodway Crs
Medical Centre
Upton Gdns
Nash Wy
Draycott Close
Wellacre Road
Dovedale Avenue
Illmington Rd
Sheepcote Road
Station Road
Hotel
Hall
St John's Road
Lyon Rd
Gerard Road
Surgery
Hawthorne Av
Superstore
Kenton Station
Mentmore Close
Lapstone Gdns
Greystone Gdns
Ebrington Road
Shaftesbury Av
Palace
Regent Cl
Westward Wy
Hotel
Gayton Road
Flambard Road
Rufford Cl
Rushout Av
Churchill Avenue
Asquith Court School
Draycott Avenue
Ashridge Close
Woodhill Crs
Bouverie Gdns
Harrow High School
Kenton Road
Northwick Avenue
A409
The Ridgeway
Sheridan Gdns
Mount Stewart Primary School
Carlisle Gdns
College
Gayton Road
Ashburnham Av
Aston Av
Mount Stewart Avenue
Grenfell Gdns
Trevelyan Crs
A404
Northwick Park Station
Golf Course
University of Westminster (Harrow Campus)
Northwick Park
Bulmer Gdns
Abercorn Gdns
Caverley Gdns
Manning Gdns
Woodcock Hill
Northwick Park Hospital & Clinical Research Centre
Lulworth Av
Conway Gdns
Woodcock Dell Avenue
Silverholme Cl
Viewfield Cl
Woodcock Ct
Tenterden Sports Gro
Playing Fields
A&E
Ntgale Av
Derwent Gdns
Coniston Gdns
Rydal Gdns
Ambleside Gdns
Arnside Gdns
Grasmere Avenue
Rifle Range La
Football La
Windermere Avenue
Thirlmere Gardens
Preston Waye
Preston Park Primary School
Preston Road Station
North Wembley
Brent
Harrow
A404
Ennerdale Gdns
Montpelier Rise
College Road
Woodford Pl
Glendale Gdns
Longfield Av
Norval Road
The Link
South Kenton Station
Preston
East Lane
Fernleigh Ct
Watford Road
Audrey Gdns
Byron Court Primary School
Nathans Road
Carlton Av
Second Av
First Av
Warren
Logan Road
Walton Gdns
Pellatt Road
Abbotts Drive
Fairway
Pebworth Road
Carlton Avenue
The Crs
West
Eskdale Close
East Lane

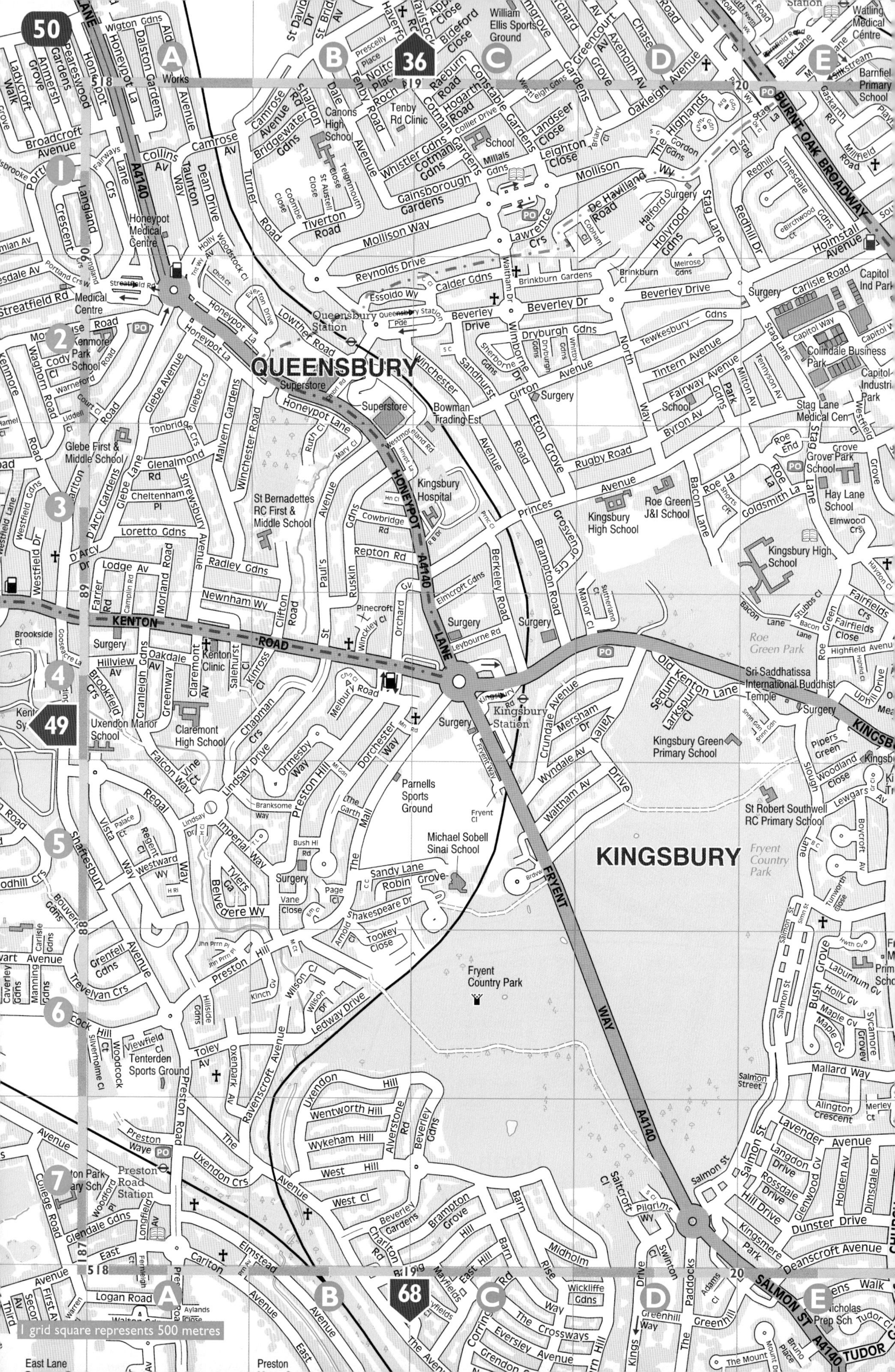

50
36
49
68
A
B
C
D
E
1
2
3
4
5
6
7
518
519
520
187
188
189
190
QUEENSBURY
KINGSBURY
William Ellis Sports Ground
Watling Medical Centre
Barnfield Primary School
BURNT OAK BROADWAY
Works
Canons High School
Tenby Rd Clinic
School
Millais Gdns
Surgery
Honeypot Medical Centre
Medical Centre
Kenmore Park School
Glebe First & Middle School
Queensbury Station
Superstore
Bowman Trading Est
Kingsbury Hospital
St Bernadettes RC First & Middle School
Pinecroft
Kenton Clinic
Claremont High School
Uxendon Manor School
Parnells Sports Ground
Michael Sobell Sinai School
Kingsbury Station
Fryent Country Park
Roe Green Park
Sri Saddhatissa International Buddhist Temple
Kingsbury Green Primary School
St Robert Southwell RC Primary School
Kingsbury High School
Roe Green J&I School
Hay Lane School
Grove Park School
Stag Lane Medical Cen
Colindale Business Park
Capitol Ind Park
Capitol Industrial Park
Tenterden Sports Ground
Preston Road Station
Prep Sch
KENTON ROAD
HONEYPOT LANE
FRYENT WAY
A4140
SALMON ST
Honeypot La
Camrose Av
Collins Av
Taunton Way
Dean Drive
Turner Road
Mollison Way
Reynolds Drive
Tiverton Road
Gainsborough Gardens
Whistler Gdns
Cotman Gdns
Constable Gardens
Landseer Close
Leighton Close
Lawrence Crs
De Havilland Road
Holyrood Gdns
Stag Lane
Redhill Dr
Holmstall Avenue
Carlisle Road
Beverley Drive
Beverley Dr
Brinkburn Gardens
Calder Gdns
Wimborne Dr
Dryburgh Gdns
Tewkesbury Gdns
Tintern Avenue
Fairway Avenue
Byron Av
Rugby Road
Princes Avenue
Eton Grove
Girton Avenue
Sandhurst Avenue
Winchester Road
Malvern Gardens
Shrewsbury Avenue
Glebe Avenue
Glenalmond Rd
Cheltenham Pl
Loretto Gdns
Radley Gdns
Newnham Wy
Clifton Road
Lodge Av
Morland Road
Farrer Rd
Westfield Dr
Streatfield Rd
Broadcroft Avenue
Langland Crescent
Waghorn Road
Kenton Road
Hillview Av
Oakdale Av
Cranleigh Gdns
Greenway
Claremont Av
Brookfield Crs
Falcon Way
Vine Ct
Lindsay Drive
Chapman Crs
Ormesby Way
Preston Hill
Dorchester Way
Melbury Road
Crundale Avenue
Mersham Dr
Valley Drive
Wyndale Av
Waltham Av
Old Kenton Lane
Sedum Cl
Larkspur Cl
Berkeley Road
Brampton Road
Grosvenor Crs
Manor Cl
Elmcroft Gdns
Leybourne Rd
Repton Rd
Cowbridge Rd
Ruskin Gdns
St Paul's Avenue
Orchard Gv
Sandy Lane
Robin Grove
Shakespeare Dr
Tookey Close
Bush Hl Rd
The Mall
The Garth
Regal Way
Vista Way
Westward Wy
Imperial Way
Belvedere Wy
Tylers Ga
Shaftesbury Av
Preston Hill
Grenfell Gdns
Trevelyan Crs
Woodcock Hill
Viewfield Cl
Toley Av
Oxenpark Av
Ravenscroft Avenue
Preston Road
Ledway Drive
Wilson Dr
Kinch Gv
Uxendon Hill
Wentworth Hill
Wykeham Hill
West Hill
West Cl
Alverstone Rd
Beverley Gdns
Brampton Grove
Barn Hill
Barn Rise
Midholm
East Hill
Uxendon Crs
Preston Waye
Glendale Gdns
Longfield Av
Woodford Pl
College Road
Elmstead Avenue
Carlton Avenue
East Lane
Logan Road
Mallard Way
Alington Crescent
Lavender Avenue
Langdon Drive
Rossdale Drive
Hill Drive
Glenwood Gv
Holden Av
Dimsdale Dr
Dunster Drive
Deanscroft Avenue
Kingsmere Park
Salmon St
Pilgrims Wy
Saltcroft Cl
The Paddocks
Greenhill Way
Kings Drive
Wicklife Gdns
The Crossways
Eversley Avenue
Laburnum Gv
Holly Gv
Maple Gv
Sycamore Grove
Bush Grove
Tunworth Close
Boycroft Av
Slough Lane
Pipers Green
Woodland Close
Lewgars Av
Fairfields Crs
Fairfields Close
Highfield Avenue
Uphill Drive
Bacon Lane
Goldsmith La
Roe Green
Roe La
Roe End
Grove Park
Elmwood Crs
Oakleigh Avenue
Chase Road
Axeholm Av
Greencourt Av
Mollison Way
Tenby Road
Dale Avenue
Camrose Avenue
Bridgewater Gdns
Shaldon Rd
Honeypot Lane
Dalston Gardens
Annesmere Gardens
Pearswood Gardens
Ladycroft Walk
Wigton Gdns
Back Lane
Gaskarth Rd
Millfield Road
Station
1 grid square represents 500 metres

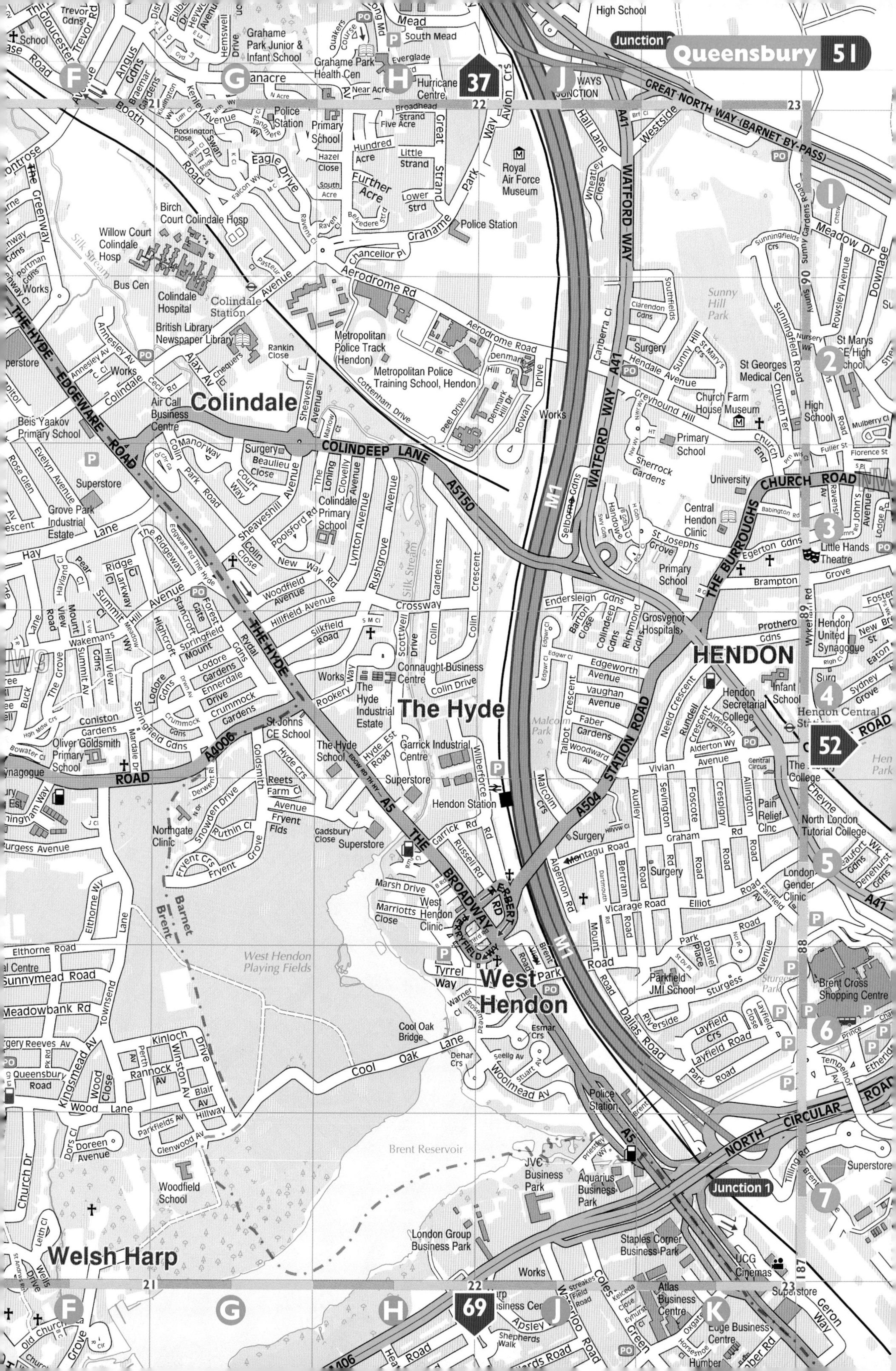

Queensbury 51
37
52
69
F
G
H
J
I
K
21
22
23
1
2
3
4
5
6
7
87
88
89
90
Junction 2
Junction 1
High School
Trevor Gdns
Trevor Rd
Gloucester
School
Angus Gdns
Braemar Gardens
Hemswell Drive
Grahame Park Junior & Infant School
Grahame Park Health Cen
Quakers Course
South Mead
Everglade
Hurricane Centre
Ganacre
Near Acre
Booth Road
Kenley Avenue
Police Station
Primary School
Five Acre
Broadhead Strand
Great Strand
Hundred Acre
Little Strand
Hazel Close
Further Acre
South Acre
Lower Strd
Belvedere Strd
Grahame Park Way
Avion Crs
Royal Air Force Museum
Police Station
Pocklington Close
Swan Dr
Eagle Drive
Falcon Wy
Ravens Cl
Raven Cl
Chancellor Pl
Great North Way (Barnet By-Pass)
Ways Junction
Hall Lane
Westside
Wheatley Close
Watford Way
A41
M1
Meadow Dr
Sunningfields Crs
Sunny Gardens Road
Downage
Rowsley Avenue
Sunny Hill Park
St Marys CE High School
St Georges Medical Cen
Sunningfield Road
Church Ter
Church Farm House Museum
Greyhound Hill
Hendale Avenue
Sunny Hill Crs
St Mary's Crs
Clarendon Gdns
Southfields
Surgery
Canberra Cl
Montrose
The Greenway
Birch Court Colindale Hosp
Willow Court Colindale Hosp
Silk Stream
Portman Gdns
Works
Bus Cen
Pasteur Cl
Colindale Hospital
Colindale Station
Colindale Avenue
British Library Newspaper Library
Aerodrome Rd
Aerodrome Road
Metropolitan Police Track (Hendon)
Metropolitan Police Training School, Hendon
Cottenham Drive
Denmark Hill Dr
Peel Drive
Rowan Drive
Rankin Close
Annesley Av
Superstore
Ajax Av
Chequers Cl
Cecil Rd
Colindale
Air Call Business Centre
Beis Yaakov Primary School
Edgware Road
Sheaveshill Avenue
Colindeep Lane
A5150
Manor Way
Colin Park Road
Court Way
Beaulieu Close
Surgery
The Loning
Marlow Ct
Clovelly Avenue
Colindale Primary School
Lynton Avenue
Rushgrove Avenue
Poolsford Rd
Rose Glen
Evelyn Avenue
Superstore
Grove Park Industrial Estate
Hay Lane
The Ridgeway
Ridge Cl
Larkway Cl
Pear Cl
Summit Cl
Hayland Cl
Mount View Road
Wakemans Hill Avenue
Summit Av
Hill View Gdns
The Grove
Colin Close
New Way Rd
Woodfield Avenue
Hillfield Avenue
Crossway
Highcroft
Stancroft
Forest Gate
Springfield Mount
Rydal Gdns
Lodore Gardens
Ennerdale Drive
Crummock Gardens
Silkfield Road
Scottwell Drive
Colin Gardens
Colin Crescent
Colin Drive
Connaught Business Centre
Rookery Way
Works
The Hyde Industrial Estate
The Hyde
Coniston Gardens
Springfield Gdns
Oliver Goldsmith Primary School
Mardale Dr
St Johns CE School
Hyde Crs
Goldsmith
Reets Farm Cl
Fryent Avenue
Fryent Flds
The Hyde School
Hyde Est Road
Garrick Industrial Centre
Superstore
Wilberforce Rd
Hendon Station
A4006 Road
Synagogue
Derwent Ri
Snowden Drive
Ruthin Cl
Northgate Clinic
Fryent Crs
Fryent Grove
Gadsbury Close
Superstore
A5
The Broadway
Garrick Rd
Russell Rd
Marsh Drive
West Hendon Clinic
Marriotts Close
Perryfield Way
Egbert Rd
Surgery
Burgess Avenue
Eithorne Wy
Elthorne Road
Sunnymead Road
Meadowbank Rd
Townsend Lane
Barnet Brent
West Hendon Playing Fields
Tyrrel Way
West Hendon
Warner Cl
Rosemead
Cool Oak Bridge
Cool Oak Lane
Dehar Crs
Kinloch Drive
Winston Av
Perth Av
Rannock Av
Blair Av
Hillway
Reeves Av
Queensbury Road
Kingsmead Av
Wood Close
Wood Lane
Parkfields Av
Doreen Avenue
Glenwood Av
Church Dr
Woodfield School
Welsh Harp
Leith Cl
Wells Drive
Old Church
Brent Reservoir
Esmar Crs
Seelig Av
Stuart Av
Woolmead Av
Police Station
JVC Business Park
Aquarius Business Park
London Group Business Park
Works
Staples Corner Business Park
UCG Cinemas
Atlas Business Centre
Edge Business Centre
Superstore
Geron Way
Coles Green
Waterloo Road
Apsley
Shepherds Walk
Business Cen
A406
Selborne Gdns
Handowe Cl
St Josephs Grove
Primary School
Central Hendon Clinic
University
Sherrock Gardens
Primary School
Church Road
The Burroughs
Church End
Babington Rd
Ravenshurst Av
St John's Avenue
Lodge Rd
Little Hands Theatre
Egerton Gdns
Brampton Grove
Fuller St
Florence St
Mulberry Cl
High School
Endersleigh Gdns
Barton Close
Colindeep Gdns
Richmond Gdns
Grosvenor Hospitals
Prothero Gdns
Wykeham Rd
Hendon United Synagogue
New Brent St
Foster
Eaton
HENDON
Infant School
Sydney Grove
Hendon Central Station
Road
Hendon Secretarial College
Edgeworth Avenue
Vaughan Avenue
Faber Gardens
Woodward Av
Talbot Crescent
Malcolm Park
Malcolm Crs
Station Road
A504
Neeld Crescent
Rundell Crescent
Alderton Crs
Alderton Wy
Vivian Avenue
Audley
Sevington
Foscote
Crespigny
Allington
Central Circus
The Albany College
Cheyne
Pain Relief Clnc
North London Tutorial College
Graham Rd
Montagu Road
Algernon Rd
Dartmouth Rd
Bertram Road
Surgery
Road
Beaufort Gdns
Denehurst Gdns
London Gender Clinic
Fairfield
Vicarage Road
Elliot Road
Park Road
Mount Road
Park Place
Daniel Place
Avenue
Brent Park
Parkfield JMI School
Sturgess Avenue
Sturgess Park
Riverside
Layfield Crs
Layfield Road
Layfield Close
Dallas Road
Park Road
Brent Cross Shopping Centre
Prince
Tempelhof Av
North Circular Road
Tilling Rd
Brent Ter
Superstore

A
B
C
D
E
38
Holders Hill
Hendon
Claremont Pk
Lyndhurst Gardens
Grass Park
Tennis & Squash Club
Dollis
Church Crs
Clifton Av
Victoria Hall
Victoria Av
County Court
Rectory Close
Exchange
Synagogue
Finchley Central Stn
N3
Station
Lichfield
Arcadia Avenue
Surgery
Glenhill Cl
School
Spencer Cl
Playing Fields
523
24
25
WAY (BARNET-BY-PASS)
PO
Ashley Close
Woodtree Cl
Manor Av
Hall
Linksway
Village Rd
Cyprus Gardens
St Mary's Av
Freston Pk
Works
Ratngar Close
Cyprus Av
HENDON LANE
GRAVEL HL
REGENT'S PK ROAD
Bibsworth Rd
A504 EAST END ROAD
1
Sunny Gardens Rd
Meadow Dr
Downage
Ashley La
Manor Hall Dr
Garrick Pk
B552 HOLDERS
Hasmonean High School
Holders Hl Gdns
Holders Hl Dr
Dollis Valley Gn Wk
Windsor Road
Kensit Memorial Coll
Wickliffe Av
Cyprus Road
North Crs
Salisbury Av
Stanhope Avenue
Cavendish Avenue
Templars Crs
Holmwood Gdns
Avenue
Sunningfields Crs
Sunningfield Road
Sunny Hill Park
90
Sunny Gardens
Rowsley Avenue
Sherwood Rd
Sherwood Road
Surg
Garrick Dr
Ashley Lane
A1
Holders Hl Crs
Brook
Broughton Av
Rawlins Cl
Arden
Road
Mountfield Rd
Cavendish Av
Surg
Fitzalan
Road
Nursery Wk
St Marys CE High School
Surgery
PARSON STREET B552
Westchester Dr
GREAT NORTH WAY
Waverley Gv
Cedars Close
Dollis
Allandale
Avenue
Regents Pk Rd
Holly Park Gdns
Orchard Avenue
Windermere
Amberden Avenue
Kingsgate Avenue
Clandon Gdns
2
St G Medical Cen
Church Ter
Church Farm Hse Museum
High School
Gardens
Road
Mulberry Cl
Hanbury Close
Lingfield Cl
Westhorpe Gdns
Preparatory School
Tenterden Gardens
Tenterden Gv
Mills Gv
Brinsdale Rd
Tenterden Drive
HENDON LANE
(BARNET
Crooked Usage
Highview Gdns
Drive
Parklands Drive
Chalgrove Gdns
Chalgrove Primary School
Chessington Av
Fairholme Gdns
Haslemere Gdns
Gardens
Kinloss Gdns
Finchley Synagogue
Holly Park
Beechwood Avenue
Tillingbourne Gdns
Edge Hill Av
NORTH CIRC
Church End
Fuller St
Florence St
Garrick Way
A504
FINCHLEY LANE
BY-PASS)
Hillcrest Gardens
Fairholme Close
CHARTER WY
ROAD
A1
A406
University
CHURCH ROAD
NW4
Babington Rd
THE BURROUGHS
Ravenshurst Av
John's Av
Lodge Rd
BRENT STREET
Aprey Gdns
First Av
Second Av
Alexandra Road
Albert Rd
Jews College London
Avenue
Kings Close
Boyne Av
Southbourne Av
Greenbank Crs
NORTH
CIRCULAR
Dollis Valley Green Walk
Beaufort Drive
Connaught Drive
Gloucester Drive
3
Egerton Gdns
Little Hands Theatre
Victoria
Road
Bell Lane JMI School
Bell Lane
Surgery
Hurstwood Road
Monkville Avenue
Eastside Rd
Alberon Gardens
Creswick Walk
Addison
Way
Coleridge Walk
Erskine
FALLODE
Brampton
Grove
Foster St
Bell
Lane
Wk
Green
Courtleigh Gdns
Decoy Av
Hogarth Hill
Wordsworth Walk
89
Wykeham Rd
Prothero Gdns
Hendon United Synagogue
New Brent St
North St
Cowley Pl
The Crest
Hendon School
Green Walk
Independent Jewish Sch
Holmbrook Drive
Bridge
Hillcrest Av
Ashbourne Avenue
Childs Way
Garden Suburb Primary School
Woodside
Denman Dr
HENDON
Eaton Rd
Surg
Sydney Grove
Heriot Road
West Av
Holmfield Av
Holmdale Gardens
Hendon Reform Synagogue
Green Lane
Century Cl
Woods Cl
Harmony Close
Avenue
Lane
Cranbourne Gardens
Hallswelle Road
Hayes Crs
Bridge Wy
FINCHLEY ROAD
Asmuns Place
Asmuns Hill
Willifield Way
Denman Drive
Hill
4
Hendon Secretarial College
Hendon Central Station
The Albany College
B551
BRENT STREET
Brent Green
Synagogue
Danescroft Gdns
NORTH-CIRCULAR-ROAD
Park Way
Cranbourne
The Orch
Temple Fortune Hill
Chatham Close
51
QUEEN'S ROAD
Hendon Park
Elm Pk Gdns
Elms Avenue
Elm Cl
Primary School
Park View Gardens
Woodlands
Woodlands
Princes
Park
Oakfields Road
Grosvenor Gdns
Eastville Av
Hampstead Way
North Sq
Crespigny Road
Allington Road
Pain Relief Clnc
The Albany College
Cheyne
North London Tutorial College
Shirehall Lane
Shirehall Cl
Shirehall Gdns
Shirehall Park
Mayfield Gdns
Haslemere Avenue
Wentworth Tutorial College
Leeside Crs
Temple Gdns
Shaare Zedek Medical Cen
Temple Fortune Lane
St George's Close
St George's Road
Golders Green
NW11
5
Road
London Gender Clinic
Beaufort Gdns
Denehurst Gdns
Renters Av
Shirehall Pk
Sinclair Grove
Golders Manor Drive
Heather Gdns
PO
Highfield Gardens
Alba Gardens
Russell Gardens
Brookside Rd
Garrick Avenue
Ambrose Avenue
Portsdown Avenue
Wentworth
Templars Avenue
Alyth Gdns
Reform Synagogue
Jewish Cemetery
Fairfield Av
Road
A41
Haley Road
A406
Heathfield Gdns
Western Av
Avenue
GOLDERS
Sneath Av
Gloucester Gdns
St Andrew's Road
St John's Road
School
Forres Gdns
Hoop Lane
Wild Hatch
88
Sturgess Avenue
Spalding Road
BRENT CROSS FLYOVER
Brent Cross Station
Highfield Av
St Mary's Road
Grammar School
Limes Av
The Drive
The Grove
Surgery
Ravenscroft Medical Centre
Ravenscroft Av
Rd
Elmcroft Av
Golders Green Crematorium
Surgery
Corringham
Brent Cross Shopping Centre
Drive
Charles
Prince
Etheridge Rd
Woodville Road
GREEN
Menorah Prim Sch
Beechcroft Av
Hoop Lane
Middleton Rd
Rotherwick Road
School
6
field Road
Tempelhof Av
Tilling Rd
Mapledown School
Hendon Youth Sports Centre
Superstores
Hamilton Road
Elmcroft Crs
Montpelier Ri
Sandringham Road
Sinai Synagogue
Woodstock Avenue
Golders Gdns
Gainsborough Gdns
Powis Gdns
The Riding
ROAD
Broadwalk La
Golders Crs
Golders Way
Golders Gn
A598
Golders Green Station
Works
ROAD
Hotel
Claremont Rd
Whitefield Avenue
Whitefield School
Prayle Grove
Wallcote Av
Pearl Cl
Amber Gv
Jade Cl
Marble Dr
Golders Green Beth Hamedrash Synagogue
Surgery
Woodstock Road
Accommodation Rd
A502
University
School
NORTH CIRCULAR
Superstore
Claremont Way
Primary School
Wessex Way
Wessex Gdns
Ridge Hill
Gresham Gardens
Armitage Road
Surgery
Basing Hill
The Ridgeway
Vale Rise
Hodford Road
Rodborough Road
St Albans La
West Heath Dr
West Heath
Junction 7
Tilling Rd
Brent Terrace
Claremont Way Industrial Estate
Prayle Grove
A41
Recreation Ground
Grampian Gardens
Cotswold Gate
HENDON
Wayside
The Vale
Surgery
Helenslea Av
Dunstan Road
UCG Cinemas
187
Clitterhouse Crs
Clitterhouse Rd
Claremont Road
Superstore
Geron Way
Brent Terrace
Hendon FC
Purbeck Drive
Cotswold
70
Pennine Dr
Malvern Gdns
WAY
Child's Hill
Granville Road Estate
Wycombe Gdns
Finchley Rd
Carlton Rd
Bus
Edge Business Cent
1 grid square represents 500 metres
Clitterhouse Primary School
Cleveland
Surgery
Gardens
LEY ROAD

39
54
71
East Finchley
N2
Fortis Green
Hampstead Garden Suburb
Highgate
N6
North End
Sandy Heath
Hampstead Heath
Coldfall Wood
HIGH ROAD
NORTH CIRCULAR
EAST END ROAD
A504
FORTIS GREEN
GREAT NORTH ROAD
A1
LYTTELTON ROAD
AYLMER ROAD
CHERRY TREE HILL
ARCHWAY ROAD
NORTH HILL
B519
HAMPSTEAD LANE
SPANIARDS ROAD
A502
Haringey
Barnet
Camden
Manorside Primary School
Tudor Primary School
Martin Infant School
Fortismere School
Bishop Douglas RC School
Christs College School
Christs College
St Marylebone Crematorium
East Finchley Cemetery
Finchley Cricket Club
Brookland Primary School
Oak Lodge School
Finchley Youth Theatre
Primary School
Police Station
Clinic
Tetherdown Primary School
East Finchley Station
Kerem House School
The Kerem School
Hampstead Garden Suburb Synagogue
Golders Hill Health Centre
Annemount School
Golf Course
Highgate Golf Club
Hampstead Golf Club
Coll of Fuel Technology
Highgate Private Hospital
Highgate Pre-Preparatory School
Highgate School
Highgate Junior School
Athlone House Hospital
Kenwood House
Spaniards Inn
Golders Green Health Centre
King Alfred School
Manor House Hospital
Middlesex University
The Gatehouse Theatre
Secondary School
Highgate Synagogue
Creighton Avenue
Chandos Road
Church Vale
Twyford Avenue
Durham Road
Leicester Rd
Huntingdon Road
Bedford Road
Hertford Road
Brim Hill
Winnington Road
Bishops Avenue
Kingsley Way
Wildwood Road
Ingram Avenue
Hampstead Way
Stormont Road
Sheldon Avenue
Denewood Road
Broadlands Road
Bishopswood Road
Compton Avenue
Courtenay Avenue
Southern Road
Lauradale Road
Everington Rd
Coldfall Avenue
Colney Hatch Lane
Long Lane
Summerlee Avenue
Linden Lea
Neville Drive
Meadway
Northway
Middleway
Thornton Way
Litchfield Way
Norrice Lea
Church Mount
Spaniards Close
Kenwood Close
Merton Lane
Highgate West Hill
Fitzroy Park

54
40
53
72
A
B
C
D
E
1
2
3
4
5
6
7
528
29
30
90
89
88
187
Muswell Hill
Fortis Green
Cranley Gardens
Crouch End
Highgate
Upper Holloway
Dartmouth
HORNS
N10
N6
N19
Alexandra Palace Ice Rink
Alexandra Palace (Historic House)
Alexandra Park
Alexandra Palace Stn
Highgate Wood
Queen's Wood
Highgate Cemetery
Highgate Station
Archway Stn
Hornsey Central Hospital
Highgate Wood School
Swimming Centre
Muswell Hill Primary School
Muswell Hill Synagogue
Muswell Hill Bowling Club
Odeon Cinema
St Lukes Woodside Hospital
Tetherdown Primary School
St James CE Primary School
Coll of Fuel Technology
Haringey Magistrates Court
Highgate Private Hospital
Highgate Synagogue
Southwood Hospital
Highgate School
Highgate Junior School
The Gatehouse Theatre
Channing Sch
Emb of Ghana
St Aloysius College
The London Irish Youth Theatre
Whittington Hospital
A&E
Archway Leisure Centre
Hillgate Hill-Murugan Temple
Milton Natural Health Centre
The Beehive School
Coleridge Primary School
Crouch Hill Recreation Cen
Hornsey Rise Health Cen
St Johns Way Medical Cen
Campsbourne Junior School
Campsbourne Inf Sch
St Marys CE Junior School
Crouch End Health Centre
Town Hall
Park Road Clinic
Fortismere School
Secondary School
Norfolk House School
Police Station
Ante Natal Clinic
Alexandra Park Road
Queens Av
Fortis Gn Rd
A504 Muswell Hill
Priory Road
A1201 Park Road
Muswell Hill Road
Archway Road
North Hill
Highgate High Street
Highgate Hill
Hornsey Lane
A103 Tottenham Lane
The Broadway
Crouch End Hill
Hornsey Rise
Colney Hatch Lane
Alexandra Park
South Terrace
Haringey
Islington
1 grid square represents 500 metres

Wood Green
Noel Park
West Green
Hornsey Vale
Harringay
Stroud Green
Finsbury Park
Downhills Park
Turnpike Lane Station
Wood Green Station
Hornsey Station
Harringay Station
Harringay Green Lanes Stn
Manor House Station
Crouch Hill Station
Finsbury Park Station
Finsbury Park Track
St Ann's General Hospital
Lordship Lane A109
Westbury Avenue
High Road A105
Green Lane A105
West Green Road A504
St Ann's Road B152
Seven Sisters Road
Stroud Green Road A1201
Turnpike Lane
Wightman Road B138
Hornsey Park Road
Belmont Road B155
Downhills Way
Endymion Road B150
Tollington Park
Woodstock Road
Amhurst Park
N4
N15
N22
41
56
73

56
42
55
74
A
B
C
D
E
1
2
3
4
5
6
7
533
34
35
N17
N15
N16
TOTTENHAM
Tottenham Hale
South Tottenham
Stamford Hill
Upper Clapton
STOKE
LORDSHIP LANE
LANE A109
BRUCE GROVE
HIGH RD
A1010
A10
HIGH ROAD
WATERMEAD WAY
FERRY LANE
A503
FOREST ROAD
WEST GREEN ROAD
A504
PHILIP LANE
B153
SEVEN SISTERS ROAD
B152
AMHURST PARK
A107
CLAPTON COMMON
STAMFORD HILL
MANOR ROAD
B105
BROAD LANE
A503 FOUNTAYNE RD
MONUMENT WAY
HALE ROAD
THE HALE
Bruce Castle Museum
Magistrates Court
New Health Centre
Lordship Lane Clinic
Broadwater Farm Primary School
Moselle Sch
Special School
Bruce Grove Stn
Fire Station
Police Station
Retail Park
Down Lane Recreation Ground
Milmead Industrial Cen
Lockwood Ind Park
Tottenham Hale Station
Lockwood Reservoir
Lea Valley Walk
Tottenham Hale Retail Park
Fountayne Business Centre
High Cross Centre
Ferry Lane Primary School
Tottenham Grn Leisure Cen
Town Hall
College of North East London
Haringey Hlth Care
Bus Cen
Seven Sisters Station
Superstore
South Tottenham Stn
South Tottenham District Synagogue
Gladesmore Community School
Warwick Reservoir
Copper Mills Works
Coppermill Lane
Stamford Hill Stn
Torah Sch
Beis Rochel D'satmar Girls School
Jewish School
United Synagogue
Boys School
Beth Hamedrash Skver Synagogue
Sir Thomas Abney Primary School
Holmleigh Primary School
St Thomas CE Primary School
Oldhill Medical Centre
Jubilee JMI School
Yetev Lev Day School for Boys
Springfield Park
Nature Reserve
Healy Medical Cen
Fountayne Road Health Cen
Stoke Newington Station
George Downing Estate
Council Building
Abney Park Cemetery
Ziam Trading Estate
1 grid square represents 500 metres

Higham Hill
WALTHAMSTOW
Blackhorse Road Station
Walthamstow Central Station
Walthamstow Queens Road Stn
St James St Stn
Leyton Midland Road Station
Forest Road
A503
A112
A1006
A104
B179
Hoe Street
Chingford Road
Blackhorse Road
Blackhorse La
Markhouse Road
Lea Bridge Road
High Road Leyton
Church Road
Billet Road
Carlton Road
Manor Road
Mount Pleasant Rd
Gloucester Road
Winns Avenue
Higham Hill Road
St Andrews Rd
Sutherland Road
Blenheim Rd
Selborne Road
Cranbrook Ms
Warner Road
Palmerston Road
Hatherley Road
Hatherley Road
Erskine Road
High Street
Coppermill Lane
Leucha Road
Markhouse Av
Boundary Road
Farmilo Road
Capworth Street
Vicarage Rd
Melville Road
Greenleaf Rd
Church Hill
Prospect Hill
Grove Road
Pembroke Road
Hale End
Brettenham Road
Whittingham Community Primary School
Waltham Forest College
Uplands Business Park
Forest Trading Estate
Highams Lodge Business Cen
Willowfield Adult Education Centre
Willowfield School
William Morris Gallery
Waltham Forest Theatre
Forest Road Medical Cen
Police Station
Aveling Park School
Chapel End Infant School
Sir George Monoux College
Waltham Forest Pool & Track
Waltham Forest Magistrates Court
Waltham Forest College
Ashgrove College
Council Building
Holy Family College
Holy Family Technology College
St Marys CE Primary Sch
School for Girls
The Hiltongrove Business Centre
Cinema
Vestry House Mus
Coppermill Primary School
Alpha Business Cen
St James's Health Cen
Cemetery
Coroners Court
Kelmscott Leisure Centre
Kelmscott School
Barn Croft Primary School
Low Hall Sports Ground
Forest Business Park
Leyton Industrial Village
Roxwell Trading Park
Cromwell Industrial Estate
Burwell Industrial Est
Dorma Tdg Park
Lea Park Trading Est
Leyton FC
St Saviours CE Primary School
Church Mead Junior School
St Josephs Catholic Inf School
Orient Ind Park
Fairways Business Park
Lea Valley Ice Centre
Leyton Leisure Centre
Superstore
Leyton Youth Sports Ground
George Mitchell School
E17
E10
F
G
H
I
J
K
1
2
3
4
5
6
7
36
37
38
43
58
75

58
44
57
76
A
B
C
D
E
1
2
3
4
5
6
7
Upper Walthamstow
South Woodford
Leytonstone
E18
E11
Whipps Cross Hospital
Snaresbrook Crown Court
Wood Street Station
Leyton Midland Road Station
Leytonstone Stn
Leytonstone High Road Stn
Snaresbrook Station
FOREST ROAD
WOODFORD NEW ROAD
WHIPPS CROSS ROAD
LEA BRIDGE ROAD
HOLLYBUSH HILL
WOODFORD ROAD
NEW WANSTEAD
BLAKE HALL ROAD
BUSH ROAD A114
Snaresbrook Road
Forest School
Hyland House School
Walthamstow Business Cen
Leyton VI Form College
Barclay Junior & Infant School
Leytonstone School
Gwyn Jones Primary School
Leyton Leisure Centre
Leyton Youth Sports Ground
Norlington Sch
Police Cadet School
Police Station
1 grid square represents 500 metres

45
60
77
F
G
H
J
I
K
2
3
4
5
6
7
41
42
43
Junction 4
Clayhall
IG5
IG4
Redbridge
Gants Hill
WANSTEAD
Aldersbrook
NORTH CIRCULAR ROAD
A406
SOUTHEND ROAD A1400
A1400 WOODFORD
EASTERN AVENUE A12
CHIGWELL ROAD
A113
GEORGE LANE
B168
BEEHIVE LANE
B192
CRANBROOK ROAD
A123
CIRCULAR ROAD
Gordon Road
Roycroft Close
Fosters Close
Latchett Road
Lynwood Close
Works
Maybank Road
Crescent Road
Raven Road
Violet Rd
Primrose Rd
Maybank Av
Mulberry Way
Cowslip Road
Essex Rd
Rose Av
Infant School
Oakdale Rd
Junior School
Woodville Road
Ashford Rd
Granville Road
Old Mill Court
Victoria Rd
Albert Rd
Pulteney Road
Pelham Road
Orford Rd
Onslow Gardens
Cadogan Gardens
Southview Drive
Southwood Av
Sherwood Av
Monmouth Avenue
Admirals Close
Hurstwood Av
Charnwood Drive
Lancaster Avenue
Broxbourne Avenue
Alexandra Rd
Cranbourne Avenue
Ashbourne Avenue
Nightingale Primary School
Victory Road
Wanstead Hospital
Colvin Gdns
Rodney Road
Elmcroft Av
Florence Court
Foxglove
Merino Cl
Lorne Gdns
Deynecourt Gardens
Eaton Rise
Buckingham Rd
Limes Av
Rutland Rd
Warwick Rd
Eastway
Leicester Road
Hereford Road
Gloucester Road
Nightingale Lane
Cowley Rd
Grosvenor Rd
Stanstead Rd
Park Grove
Nutter Lane
Eaton Manor RFC
Preston Drive
Reydon Av
The Avenue
Kendon Cl
Elm Hall Gdns
Gardner Cl
High St
Wanstead Station
Mansfield Road
Chester Rd
Oak Hall Rd
Elm Cl
Redbridge Lane
Wigram Road
Drummond Rd
Corbett Rd
River Close
West
Wanstead Leisure Centre
Wanstead High School
Langley Drive
Langley Crs
Warren Road
Colebrooke Drive
Overton Drive
St Mary's Av
Draycot Road
The Gn
Wanstead Golf Club
The Warren Dr
Raynes Avenue
Wanstead Cricket Club
Golf Course
Lincoln Island
Wanstead Park
Woodlands Avenue
St Gabriel's Cl
Brading
Primary Sch
Secondary Sch
Northumberland Av
Park Rd
Harpenden Road
Herongate Road
Margaret's
Surgery
Wanstead Park Avenue
Clavering Road
Arran Drive
Westmorland
Lechmere Approach
Westview Drive
Rivington Avenue
Summit Drive
Kensington Drive
Roding Lane
Portman Dr
Northview Dr
Woodford Trading Est
Embroidery World Business Centre
Unity Trading Estate
Anderson Road
Hatton School
Animal Cemetery
PDSA Hospital
BUPA Roding Hospital
Woodford Bridge Rd
Roding Lane South
Carswell Close
Whitney Av
Lakeside Av
Leigh Avenue
Merrivale Avenue
Peaketon Avenue
Falmouth
Torquay Gardens
Mighell Avenue
Fowey Avenue
Tryfan Close
Vista Drive
Rosemary Drive
Fernhall Drive
Fairmead Gdns
Edwina Gdns
Cobbetts Av
The Ms
Avondale Crs
Hotel
Redbridge
Redbridge Station
Margaret Way
Works
Beal High School
Lodge Hill
Babbacombe Gdns
Widecombe Gardens
Coniston Gdns
Derwent Gdns
Braintree Avenue
Bergholt Av
Keswick
Primary School
Ambleside Gdns
Brantwood Gardens
Grasmere Gardens
College Gdns
Grangeway Gardens
Ridgeway Gardens
Highcliffe Gardens
East
Danehurst Gdns
Inglehurst Gardens
Somersby Gdns
Windermere Gardens
Ellesmere Gdns
Hedgeley
Beehive Preparatory School
Gosford Primary School
Radnor Crs
Sussex Cl
Wycombe Road
Avery Gdns
Ethelbert Gdns
Gants Hill Station
Studley Drive
Evanston Gardens
Surgery
Castle Drive
Castle View Gardens
Devonport Gdns
Hill Vw Crs
Preston Gdns
Lane
The Drive
Stonehall Avenue
Carlisle Gdns
Wakefield Gdns
Ripon Gdns
Royston Gdns
Wanstead
Worcester Gdns
Hereford Gdns
Gloucester Gardens
Canterbury
Wells Gdns
Lincoln Gardens
Chelmsford Gdns
Truro Gdns
Chichester Gdns
Rochester Gdns
Exeter Gdns
Infant Sch
Prim Sch
Highlands Gardens
St George's Road
St Andrew's Road
Vaughan Gardens
Wilson Rd
Cowley Road
Clarendon Gardens
Ranelagh Gardens
Redcliffe Gardens
Cavendish Gdns
Stanhope Gardens
Sackville Gdns
Seymour Gdns
Seymour Gardens
Medical Centre
Kensington Gardens
Endsleigh Gdns
De Vere Gardens
Arlington Gdns
Wanstead Pk Road
Ilford Golf Club
Belgrave
Courtland Avenue
Mayfair Avenue
Empress Avenue
Clarence Avenue
St Helen's Road
Cranbrook Rise
St Edmund's Road
Mornington Av
Ilford Synagogue
Marston Road
Chalgrove Crs
Wensleydale Avenue
Atherton Road
Naseby Road
Roundaway Road
Glade Primary School
The Glade
Harewood Drive
Couchmore Avenue
Heathcote Ave
Barrington Close
Cheriton Avenue
Caterham High School
Caterham Avenue
Cottesmore Av
St Clair Close
Ewellhurst Road
Peel Place
Clayhall Avenue
Coburg Gdns
Vienna Cl
Clayhall Clnc
Stradbroke Grove
Peel Drive
Brinkworth Road
Marlborough Drive
Marlands Road
Surgery
Gayfere Road
Chadacre Avenue
Mellows Road
Heatherley Drive
Stoneleigh Road
Parkhill Primary School
Rushden Gardens
Dymchurch Cl
Tiverton Av
Wernet Road
Abbotsford Gardens
Herent Drive
Lord Avenue
Lord Gdns
Orlet Gdns
Monkswood Gdns
Eariswood Gdns
Clayhall Park
Parkview Gardens
Longwood Gardens
Wychwood Gdns
Highwood Gardens
Beechwood Gardens
Hedgewood Gdns
Collinwood Gardens
Glenwood Gardens
Kirkland
Dover

60
59
78
A
B
C
D
E
1
2
3
4
5
6
7
543
44
45
Fullwell Cross
Barkingside
Clayhall
Gants Hill
Newbury Park
Cranbrook
Aldborough Hatch
Valentines Park
Clayhall Park
IG5
IG8
IG2
IG1
A123
A12
A118
A1400
B192
Redbridge Sports Centre
Fairlop Station
King Solomon High School
Fullwell Cross Health Cen
Pool & Rec Cen
Ilford County High School
Mossford Green Primary School
Gilbert Colvin Primary School
Caterham High Sch
Parkhill Primary School
Barkingside Cemetery
Ilford Jewish Primary School
Superstore
Fullwood Primary School
Barkingside FC
Barkingside Station
Gearies Junior School
Infant School
Lower School
Primary Sch
Gants Hill Medical Cen
Gants Hill Station
Odeon Cinema
Valentine High School
Ilford Synagogue
Newbury Park Health Centre
Newbury Park Primary School
Newbury Park Station
South-West Essex Reform Synagogue
William Torbitt Junior & Infant School
Seven Kings High School
St Aidans RC Primary School
Downshall Primary School
Canon Palmer RC High School
Seven Kings
Seven Kings Health Cen
Christchurch Primary Sch
Cranbrook College
College High School
New Rush Hall School
Ilford County Court
Ilford Swimming Pool
Buckingham Road Cemetery
Ilford Retail Park
Seymour Gdns Medical Centre
Starch House Lane
Works
Surgery
Fullwell Avenue
Basildon Avenue
Cheriton Avenue
Dovedale Avenue
Strafford Avenue
Kirkland Avenue
Cottesmore Av
Clayhall Avenue
Tiptree Crescent
Rushden Gardens
Beaminster Gardens
Mossford Green
Mossford Lane
Waterloo Rd
Fairlop Road
Fremantle Rd
Horace Rd
High Street
Cranbrook Road
Craven Gardens
Heybridge Drive
Tanners Lane
Station Rd
Princes Rd
Crown Rd
Duke Road
Longwood Gardens
Woodville Gdns
Glenthorne Gdns
Beattyville Gardens
Queenborough Gardens
Northwood Gdns
Kenwood Gardens
Highwood Gardens
Collinwood Gardens
Glenwood Gardens
Woodford Avenue
Beehive Lane
Ethelbert Gdns
Gantshill Crescent
Roll Gardens
Shere Road
Gaysham Avenue
Sunnymede Dr
Hamilton Avenue
Bute Road
Hatley Avenue
Hastings Avenue
Campbell Avenue
Aldwych Av
Poplar Wy
Donington Av
Emmott Av
Ardwell Av
Springfield Drive
Icknield Dr
Glenham Dr
Martley Drive
Parham Dr
Otley Drive
Headley Drive
Ashurst Drive
Brockham Dr
Denham Drive
Bentley Drive
Cantley Gdns
Yoxley Drive
Horns Road
Perryman's Farm Rd
Perkins Road
Birkbeck Road
Abbey Road
Netley Road
Kg George Av
Eastern Avenue
Perth Road
Albemarle Gardens
Middleton Gardens
Milton Crescent
Quebec Road
Westernville Gardens
Cranley Rd
Ley Street
Lynn Road
Wards Road
Raymond Road
Charter Avenue
Glebelands Avenue
Lancing Road
Stainforth Road
Buxton Road
Brook Road
Suffolk Road
Aldborough Road
Devonshire Road
St Johns Road
Ladysmith Avenue
Kimberley Avenue
Glencoe Av
Colenso Road
Norfolk Road
Elgin Road
Cameron Road
Benton Road
Bradford Road
Vicarage Lane
Dunedin Rd
Balfour Road
Thorold Road
Colombo Road
Brisbane Road
Auckland Road
Toronto Road
Christchurch Road
Melbourne Road
Ingleby Road
Coventry Road
Wellesley Road
Granville Road
Park Avenue
Aden Road
Montreal Road
Bethell Avenue
Tillotson Rd
Cowley Road
Vaughan Gardens
Ranelagh Gardens
Redcliffe Gardens
Cavendish Gdns
De Vere Gardens
Kensington Gardens
The Drive
Cranbrook Rise
1 grid square represents 500 metres

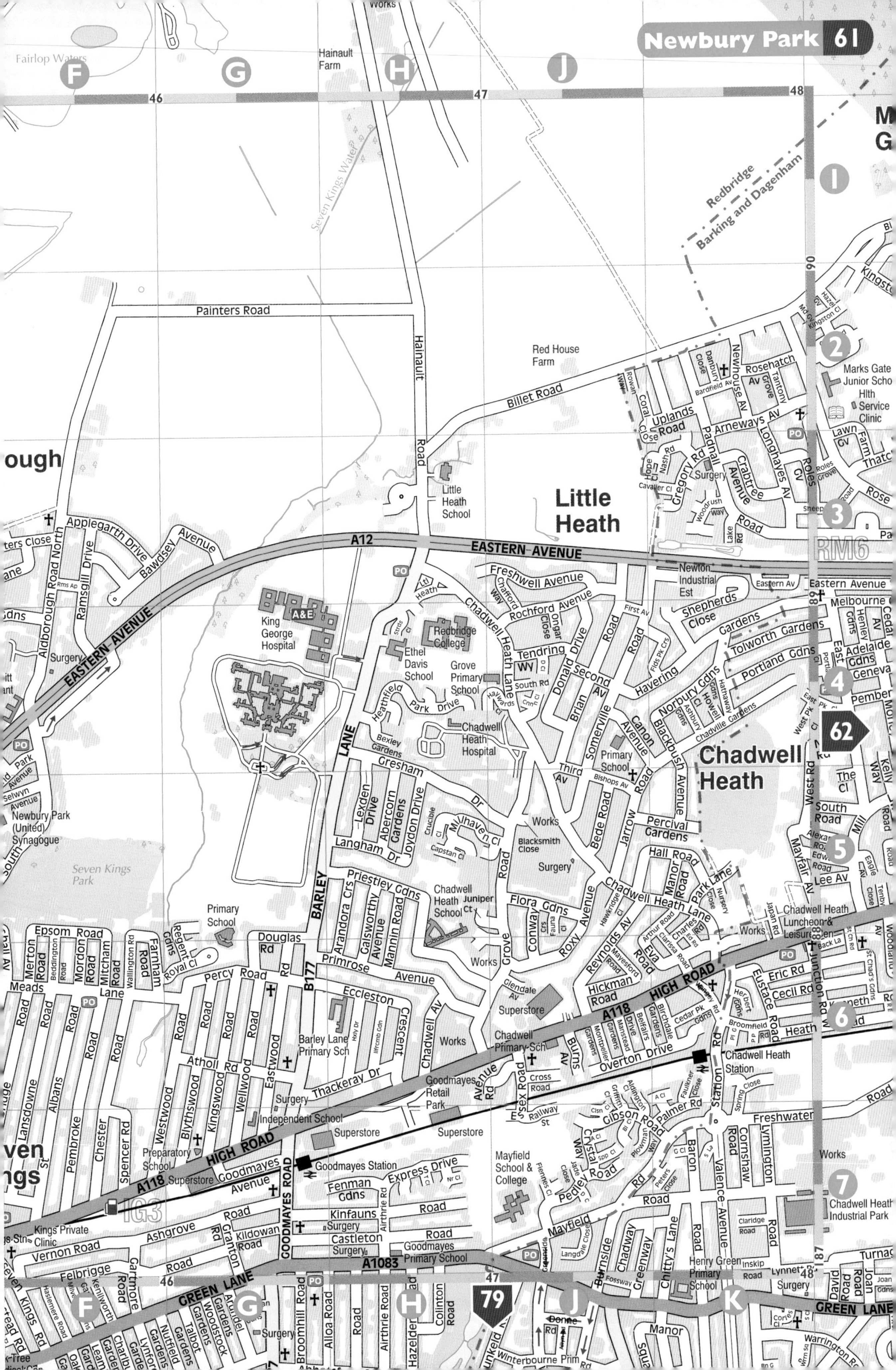
Fairlop Waters
Hainault Farm
Works
F
G
H
J
46
47
48
Seven Kings Water
Redbridge
Barking and Dagenham
I
Painters Road
Hainault Road
Red House Farm
Billet Road
Little Heath School
Little Heath
A12
EASTERN AVENUE
Applegarth Drive
Bawdsey Avenue
Aldborough Road North
Ramsgill Drive
Surgery
King George Hospital
A&E
Redbridge College
Ethel Davis School
Grove Primary School
Chadwell Heath Hospital
Chadwell Heath Lane
Freshwell Avenue
Rochford Avenue
Tendring Wy
Donald Drive
Second Av
Third Av
First Av
Somerville Road
Canon Avenue
Blackbush Avenue
Primary School
Newton Industrial Est
Shepherds Close
Tolworth Gardens
Portland Gdns
Norbury Gdns
Chadwell Heath
Gresham Dr
Lexden Drive
Abercorn Gardens
Joydon Drive
Millhaven Cl
Langham Dr
BARLEY LANE
B177
Priestley Gdns
Arandora Crs
Galsworthy Avenue
Mannin Road
Chadwell Heath School
Juniper Ct
Blacksmith Close
Works
Flora Gdns
Conway Crs
Roxy Avenue
Reynolds Av
Hickman Road
Bede Road
Jarrow Road
Percival Gardens
Hall Road
Manor Road
Park Lane
Chadwell Heath Lane
Seven Kings Park
Newbury Park (United) Synagogue
Primary School
Epsom Road
Douglas Rd
Percy Road
Primrose Avenue
Eccleston Crescent
Barley Lane Primary Sch
Chadwell Av
Thackeray Dr
Goodmayes Retail Park
Superstore
Chadwell Primary Sch
A118
HIGH ROAD
Overton Drive
Chadwell Heath Station
Cross Road
Railway St
Gibson Road
Palmer Rd
Freshwater Road
Lymington Road
Cornshaw Road
Baron Road
Valence Avenue
Mayfield School & College
Goodmayes Station
GOODMAYES ROAD
Goodmayes Avenue
Express Drive
Fenman Gdns
Kinfauns Road
Castleton Road
Goodmayes Primary School
Independent School
Preparatory School
Kings Private Clinic
Vernon Road
Ashgrove Road
Felbrigge Road
Lansdowne
Albans
Pembroke
Chester
Spencer Rd
Westwood Road
Blythswood
Kingswood
Wellwood
Eastwood
Atholl Rd
A1083
GREEN LANE
Mayfield
Chittys Lane
Chadway
Greenway
Burnside
Henry Green Primary School
Chadwell Heath Industrial Park
Works
Chadwell Heath Luncheon & Leisure Cen
Eric Rd
Cecil Rd
Eustace Road
Heath
Junction Rd
Mill Road
Mayfair Av
South Road
West Rd
Lee Av
Marks Gate Junior Scho
Hlth Service Clinic
Rosehatch Av
Arneways Av
Uplands Road
Padnall Road
Crabtree Avenue
Longhayes Av
Roles Gv
Gregory Rd
Lake Rd
Melbourne
Eastern Avenue
Adelaide Gdns
Geneva
RM6
IG3
62
79
2
3
4
5
6
7
K
Broomhill Road
Alloa Road
Airthrie Road
Colinton Road
Winterbourne Prim
Manor
Warrington Rd

62
A
B
C
D
E
548
49
50
Marks Gate
Collier Row
Works
Collier Row FC
Northgate Ind Park
School
Elizabeth Close
Lynton
Rodney Way
White
Clovelly Gardens
Hood Wa
Goring Cl
Hillfoot Avenue
Hornchurch Road
Horndon Green
Mowbrays Close
Mowbrays
Orchard Rd
Peartree Gardens
Victory
Anson Close
Elm Road
Ashdown Walk
Kenway
COLLIER ROW LANE
Crownfield Primary School
Hart
Lane
Vanguard Close
Barham Close
Mawney Rd
Redriff Road
Walmer Close
Dunster Cl
Dove Cl
Maidstone Av
Surgery
B174
Percy Rd
Linley Crs
Abbotts Cl
Birch Road
Birch Close
Forest Road
Silver Way
Epping Close
Essex Road
Works
Essex Close
Marlborough Road
Blandford Close
Winston Close
Pitcairn Close
Cross Road
Kings Oak
Mawney Road
Susan Cl
Beaufort Cl
Surgery
Blenheim Cl
Hubbinet Ind Est
King George Cl
EASTERN AVENUE
Edinburgh's Dr
Poplar Street
Cedar St
Maple
Beech St
Willow
Barking and Dagenham
Havering
Billet Road
Kingston Hill Avenue
Beansland Gv
Kingston Cl
Gibbfield Close
Rosehatch Av
Tantony Grove
Marks Gate Junior School
Hlth Service Clinic
Cemetery
Lawn Farm Gv
Thatches Grove
Bagleys Spring
Rams Gv
Rose Lane
Padnall Rd
Hatch Grove
Longhayes Av
Roles Gv
Crabtree Avenue
Sheepcotes Road
Lake Rd
Newhouse Av
WHALEBONE LANE NORTH
A1112
RM6
Warren Farm
EASTERN AVENUE WEST A12
Eastern Av
Eastern Avenue West
Melbourne Gdns
Henley Gdns
Cedar Av
Yew Tree Gdns
Tolworth Gardens
Portland Gdns
Adelaide Gdns
Geneva Gardens
Pemberton Gdns
East Pk Cl
North Rd
Morley Road
Kelly Way
Lansbury Avenue
The Cl
South Road
Mill Lane
Willow Road
Ashton Gardens
Warren Comprehensive School
Warren Sports Centre
Warren Junior School
Hainault Gore
Millbrook Gdns
Gordon Road
Albany Road
Hainault Road
Kings Avenue
Sylvan Av
Lime Cl
Pretoria
Oak St
RM7
Mildmay Rd
Palm Road
Barkwood Close
Vine
Works
Jubilee Avenue
Jubilee Close
Recreation Av
Spring Gdns
Marina Gdns
Lowland Gdns
Richards Avenue
A118 LONDON ROAD
Primary School
Crowlands Avenue
Burlington Avenue
Lonsdale Av
Aston Av
Derby Av
Lessington Av
Cromer Rd
Norfolk Road
Kensington Rd
Sheringham
Kimberley Av
Ainsley Av
Jutsums Lane
Jutsums Av
Bridport Av
Eddy Close
Weald Way
Bear Cl
Stanford Close
Fernden Way
Southern Way
Bracken Ms
St Edwards CE Comprehensive School
Viking Business Centre
Danes Road
Maldon Rd
Bernard Rd
Beechfield Gardens
Crow Lane
Romford Cemetery
Works
Vignoles Rd
Braithwaite Av
HIGH ROAD
Salcombe Drive
Coombewood Drive
Saville Road
Grantham Gdns
Furze Infant School
Chadwell Heath Luncheon & Leisure Cen
West Rd
Alexandra Road
Edward Road
Lee Av
Mayfair Av
Eagle Close
Cromer Road
Tenby Road
Woodlands Av
Farrance Road
Bennett Rd
Wadeville Av
Morden Road
Merten Road
Burlington Gdns
Kenneth Road
Junction Rd W
Eric Rd
Cecil Rd
Eustace Road
Back La
Works
Heath Road
Chadwell Heath Station
Mirravale Trading Estate
Coppen Road
Selinas Lane
Road
Spring Close
Freshwater
Lymington
Cornshaw
Works
WHALEBONE LANE SOUTH
Rosslyn Av
Warley Avenue
Laneside Avenue
Alan Gdns
Goldsmith Avenue
Seabrook Gardens
Stanley Avenue
Torrington Road
Mount Road
Gray Av
Brendon Road
Albert Rd
James Av
Temple Avenue
Grosvenor Road
Superstore
Eldenwall Industrial Estate
Purland Cl
Rosemary Gdns
Chadwell Heath Industrial Park
Claridge Road
Inskip Road
Lamberhurst Rd
Winifred Road
Gerald Rd
Ross Avenue
Tenterden Road
Robert Clack School
All Saints Catholic School
Wood Lane Sports Centre
Meadow Road
Bell House Road
A124 RUSH
Barton Av
Wisdons Cl
Gosfield Road
WOOD LANE A124
Legon Av
Turnage Road
Lynnett Rd
Surgery
Fordyke Rd
Grafton Gdns
GREEN LANE A1083
Terling Road
Dagenham Civic Centre
Laburnum Health Centre
Bentry Road
Stockdale Rd
Bradwell Av
Stour Rd
Central
1 grid square represents 500 metres
61
80

Gidea Park
ROMFORD
Heath Park
Rush Green
RM1
RM2
Golf Course
Gidea Park Sports Ground
Eastern Avenue
A12
A118
Main Road
A125 North Street
St Edwards Way
Waterloo Road
Mercury Gdns
A1251
Thurloe Gdns
Oldchurch Rd
Rom Valley Wy
Roneo Cnr
A124 Hornchurch Road
Green Road
Upr Rainham Rd
Heath Park Road
Balgores Lane
Carlton Road
Brentwood Road
Victoria Road
South Street
Marshalls Park School
Romford Golf Club
Gidea Park Primary School
Romford County Court
Havering Magistrates Court
The Dolphin Leisure Centre
Liberty Centre
Romford Shop Hall
Odeon
Romford Station
Gidea Park Station
Ster Century Cinema
Oldchurch Hospital
A&E
Romford Ice Rink
Superstore
Frances Bardsley School for Girls
Squirrels Heath Junior School
Royal Liberty School
St Marys Hare Park School
Havering College of Further & Higher Education
Edwin Lambert School
Raphael School
The Manor Primary School
St Peters Catholic Primary School
St Edwards CE Primary School
North Havering College of Adult Education
Diane Matthews Clinic
The Mawney School
Rush Green Primary School
St Marys RC JM&I School
Wykeham Primary School
Hornchurch Sports Centre
Brooke Trading Est
Medical Centre
Surgery
Works
Hotel
College
81

West Ruislip
Ruislip Golf Club
West Ruislip Station
Airbase Unity Elementary School
West Ruislip Elementary School
Ickenham Clinic
Compass Theatre
Ickenham Station
The Douay Martyrs RC School
Glebe Primary School
Ickenham Manor
UB10
Ruislip Station
Pond Green
Ruislip RFC
Sacred Heart RC Junior & Infant School
Ruislip Manor FC
Ruislip Manor
Queensmead Sports Cen
The Synagogue
HA4
Works
Ruislip Gardens
Ruislip Gardens Primary School
Ruislip Gardens Station
Northolt Aerodrome
North Hillingdon
Ryefield Primary School
Gutteridge Wood
Hillingdon Trail
Dog Rose Ramble
Sports Ground Pavilion
Swakeleys School
Wood Lane Medical Centre
Road Clnc
ICKENHAM ROAD
HIGH ROAD
LONG LANE
B466
A4180
WEST END ROAD
A40
WESTERN AVENUE
A437
Brickwall Lane
Pembroke Road
Willow Grove
Shenley Avenue
Cornwall Road
Torrington Road
Sidmouth Drive
Austin's Lane
Glebe Avenue
Tavistock Road
Sussex Road
Granville Road
Richmond Avenue
Merton Avenue
Lynhurst Crescent
Berkeley Road
Oakleigh Road
Midhurst Gardens
Leybourne Road
Sutton Court Road
Cowdray Road
Charville Lane
508
09
10
87
86
85
84
A
B
C
D
E
1
2
3
4
5
6
7
46
82
1 grid square represents 500 metres

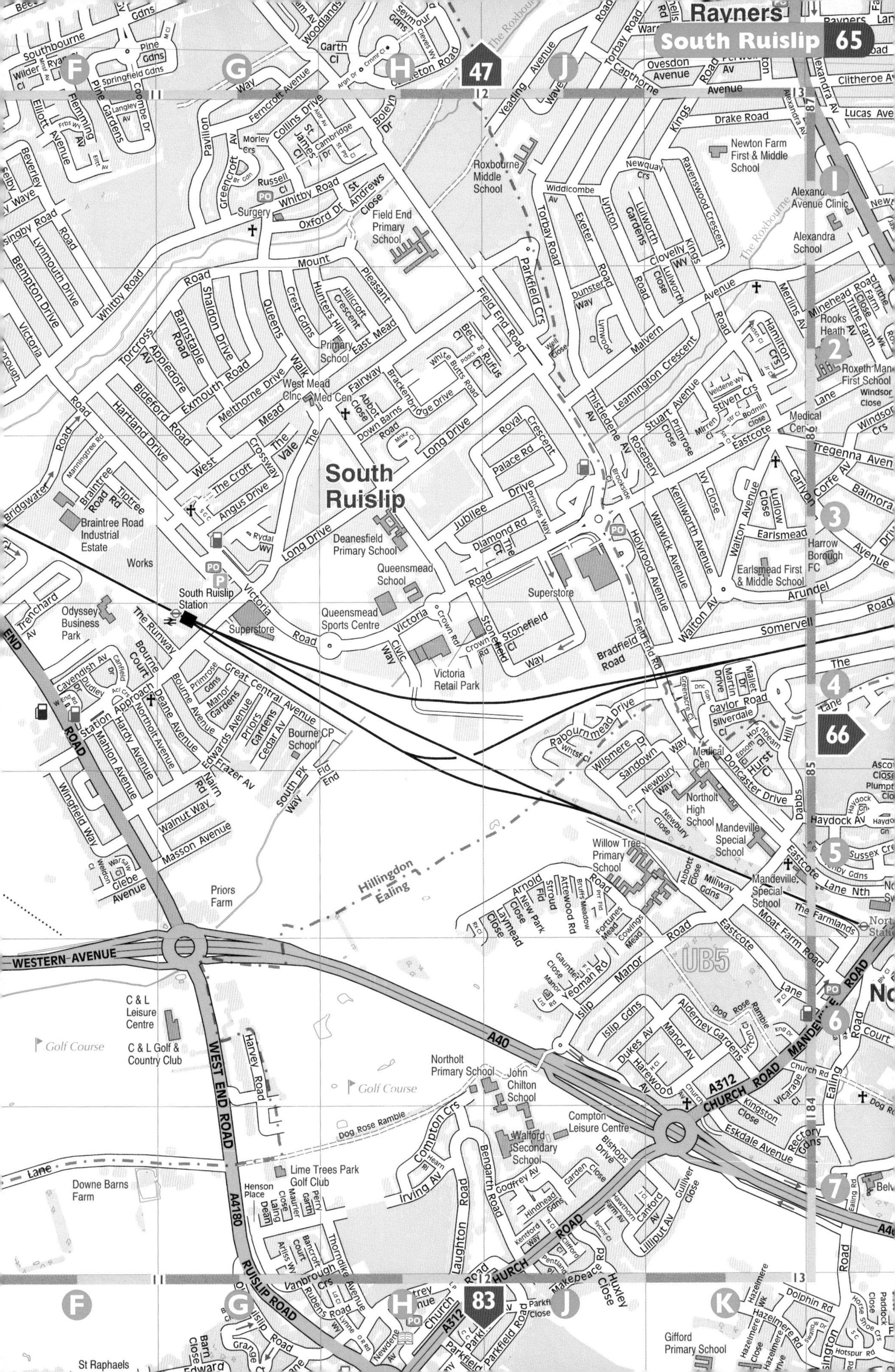

South Ruislip 65
Rayners
47
66
83
F
G
H
J
K
I
2
3
4
5
6
7
11
12
13
87
86
85
84
South Ruislip
Southbourne Gdns
Pine Gdns
Springfield Gdns
Pine Gardens
Coombe Dr
Langley Av
Flemming Av
Elliott Avenue
Beverley Road
Lynmouth Drive
Bempton Drive
Victoria Road
Whitby Road
Woodlands
Garth Cl
Seymour Gdns
Cleves Wy
Castleton Road
Ferncroft Avenue
Pavilion Way
Morley Crs
Collins Drive
St James Cl
Cambridge Dr
Boleyn Dr
Greencroft Av
Russell Cl
Whitby Road
St Andrews Close
Oxford Dr
Surgery
Field End Primary School
Mount Pleasant
Queens Walk
Crest Gdns
Hunters Hill
Hillcroft Crescent
Primary School
East Mead
Road
Shaldon Drive
Barnstaple Road
Torcross Av
Appledore
Exmouth Road
Bideford Road
Hartland Drive
Melthorne Drive
West Mead
West Mead Clnc
Med Cen
Mead
The Vale
The Croft
Crossway
Angus Drive
Fairway
Abbot Close
Down Barns Road
Brackenbridge Drive
White Butts Road
Bec Cl
Rufus Cl
Long Drive
Field End Road
Roxbourne Middle School
Yeading Avenue
Wave
Torbay Road
Capthorne Avenue
Ovesdon Avenue
Drake Road
Kings
Newton Farm First & Middle School
Widdicombe Av
Exeter Road
Lynton Road
Lulworth Gardens
Newquay Crs
Ravenswood Crescent
Clovelly Wy
Lulworth Close
Dunster Way
Lynwood Cl
Parkfield Crs
Malvern Avenue
Leamington Crescent
Thistledene Av
Rosebery Av
Stuart Avenue
Primrose Close
Stiven Crs
Veldene Wy
Eastcote
Hamilton Crs
Merlins Av
Minehead Road
Tithe Farm Close
Rooks Heath
Roxeth Manor First School
Alexandra Avenue Clinic
Alexandra School
Clitheroe Av
Lucas Avenue
Medical Cen
Tregenna Avenue
Windsor Crs
Corfe Av
Carlyon
Balmoral
Ludlow Close
Walton Avenue
Earlsmead
Harrow Borough FC
Earlsmead First & Middle School
Arundel
Road
Royal Crescent
Palace Rd
Jubilee Drive
Princes Way
Diamond Rd
The Ct
Kenilworth Avenue
Warwick Avenue
Holyrood Avenue
Ivy Close
Walton Av
Somervell Road
Superstore
Stonefield Way
Stonefield Cl
Bradfield Road
Field End Rd
Bridgwater Road
Braintree Road
Tiptree Rd
Braintree Road Industrial Estate
Works
South Ruislip Station
Victoria Road
Deanesfield Primary School
Queensmead School
Queensmead Sports Centre
Crown Rd
Civic Way
Victoria Retail Park
Trenchard Av
Odyssey Business Park
The Runway
Bourne Court
Cavendish Av
Dudley Dr
Station Approach
Great Central Avenue
Primrose Gdns
Manor Gardens
Bourne Avenue
Deane Avenue
Northolt Avenue
Hardy Avenue
Mahlon Avenue
Edwards Avenue
Priors Gardens
Cedar Av
Bourne CP School
South Pk Way
Fld End
Frazer Av
Nairn Rd
Walnut Way
Masson Avenue
Wingfield Way
Glebe Avenue
Priors Farm
END ROAD
Rabournmead Drive
Wilsmere Dr
Sandown Way
Newbury Way
Newbury Close
Gaylor Road
Silverdale Cl
Hornbeam
Doncaster Drive
Hurst Cl
Martin Dr
Mallet Dr
Medical Cen
Northolt High School
Mandeville Special School
Dabbs Hill
The Lane
Haydock Av
Sussex Crs
Eastcote Lane Nth
The Farmlands
Moat Farm Road
Willow Tree Primary School
Arnold Rd
Stroud Fld
Attewood Rd
Abbott Close
Millway Gdns
New Park Close
Laymead Close
Fortunes Mead
Cowings Mead
Eastcote Lane
Mandeville Road
Gauntlett Close
Yeoman Rd
Manor Road
Islip Manor
Islip Gdns
UB5
Dog Rose Ramble
Alderney Gardens
Dukes Av
Manor Av
Harewood Av
Hillingdon
Ealing
WESTERN AVENUE
A40
A312
CHURCH ROAD
Church Rd
Vicarage Cl
Kingston Close
Eskdale Avenue
Rectory Gdns
Ealing Road
Court
C & L Leisure Centre
C & L Golf & Country Club
Golf Course
Harvey Road
WEST END ROAD
Northolt Primary School
John Chilton School
Compton Leisure Centre
Walford Secondary School
Compton Crs
Bengarth Road
Bishops Drive
Godfrey Av
Garden Close
Hindhead Gdns
Irving Av
Laughton Road
Lime Trees Park Golf Club
Downe Barns Farm
Lane
A4180
RUISLIP ROAD
Henson Place
Dean
Laing Close
Maurier Close
Perry Garth
Bancroft Court
Thorndike Avenue
Vanbrough Crs
Rubens Road
Kentford Way
Clifford
Hawthorn Farm Av
Canford Av
Gulliver Close
Lilliput Av
Makepeace Rd
Huxley Close
Parkfield Road
Hazelmere
Dolphin Rd
Gifford Primary School
Barn Close
Grange
Islip Road
Edward
St Raphaels
Newdene Av
Lynne Wy

66
48
65
84
A
B
C
D
E
1
2
3
4
5
6
7
513
514
515
86
85
84
HA2
Rayners Lane
Oxley Road
Clitheroe Avenue
Alexandra Av
Lucas Avenue
Drake Road
Newton Farm First & Middle School
Alexandra Avenue Clinic
Alexandra School
The Roxbourne
Austen Rd
Eliot Drive
Swift Cl
Coles Crescent
Maryatt Av
Priest Pk Av
Abbots Dr
Newton Close
Roxbourne Medical Centre
Eastleigh Avenue
Sandringham Crs
Scott Crs
The Arches
Abercorn Cres
Hillside Crs
Dudley Road
Shaftesbury Medical Centre
Shaftesbury Avenue
Grange Farm Cl
Roxeth
Archdale Business Cen
Franklins Ms
Works
Stanley Road
Sherwood Road
Police Stn
Council Building
A4005 ROXETH HILL
John Lyon School
West Street
Crown St
Middle Road
Byron Hill Road
First & Middle School
West Street
Harrow School
HIGH STREET
LONDON ROAD
Harrow Park
Bowden House Clinic
Julian Hill
Georgian Way
Mount Pk Avenue
College
Cowen Avenue
Wendela Ct
Gooden Court
Fircroft Gdns
A4005
Inglety Dr
Park
The Purcell School
Orley Farm School
South Hill Avenue
Harrow Fields Gardens
Runnelfield
South Hill Av
Orley Farm Road
Harrow Cricket Club
South Vale
Tyrell Cl
Hartington Cl
Cavendish Avenue
Sudbury Hill Station
GREENFORD ROAD
A312
South Harrow Station
Brooke Av
Ashneal Gdns
Sackville Cl
Arden Cl
South Hill Av
Minehead Road
Rooks Heath School
Tithe Farm Close
Roxeth Manor First School
Windsor Close
Windsor Crs
Medical Centre
Eastcote Lane
Eastcote Lane Cem
South Harrow
Beechwood Av
Park Mead
Northolt Road Clnc
Whitby Road
Parkfield Road
Eastcote Road
Scarsdale Rd
Kingsley Road
Middle School
Roxeth Gv
Torrington Drive
Brendon Gdns
Paddocks Close
ALEXANDRA AVENUE
Tregenna Avenue
Balmoral Drive
Carlyon Avenue
Corfe Av
Walton Avenue
Earlsmead
Harrow Borough FC
Earlsmead First & Middle School
Arundel
Somervell Road
Wood End Av
Westwood Av
Northolt Park Station
Acock Grove
Halsbury Road
Clauson Avenue
Russell Road
Killowen Avenue
Gdns
Ealing Northern Sports Centre
Bannister Close
Mary Peters Dr
Bedser Drive
Lilian Board Wy
Harrow
Ealing
East End Road
A4090 PETT'S HILL
The Heights
Reading Road
Wood End Way
WHITTON AV WEST
A4090
Merton Av
Keble Cl
Primary School
Wood End J&I Schools
Dimmock Drive
Greenford Green Clinic
Surgery
Newmarket Avenue
Bangor Cl
Infant School
Kempton Avenue
Ascot Close
Plumpton Close
Haydock Av
Sussex Crescent
Lewes Close
Tenby Gdns
Southwell Close
Thirsk Cl
Wetherby Cl
Redcar Close
Mildred Av
Wood End Lane
Newnham Gdns
Barnabas Medical Cen
Currey Gdns
Wadham Gardens
Malden Avenue
Rugby Av
Ennismore Avenue
Sherwood
Burwell Av
Horsenden Primary School
Berkeley Av
Oldfield Lane North
Clare Road
Hadden Way
Rothesay Av
Worcester Road
The Fairway
Carr Road
Girton Close
Lancaster Road
Blenheim Road
Gonville Crs
Castle Road
Ribblesdale Av
Briar Crs
A312 MANDEVILLE ROAD
Mandeville Special School
Eastcote Lane Nth
Northolt Swimarama
The Farmlands
Northolt Station
Moat Farm Road
Dabbs
Doncaster Drive
Northolt
Belvue Road
Sandringham Rd
Summit Rd
Court Farm Rd
Fort Rd
Belvue Business Cen
Cherry Gdns
Auriol Drive
Grand Union Canal
Church Rd
Vicarage
Kingston Close
Eskdale Avenue
Rectory Gdns
Dog Rose Ramble
Rowdell
Belvue School
Ealing Rd
Taunton Road
Derby Road
Greenford Industrial Estate
Halifax Road
Bridport Road
Bristol Road
Field Way
Kelvin Ind Est
Superstore
A40 WESTERN AVENUE
Fairway Dr
Chartwell Cl
Stanley Avenue
Lincoln Close
Jeymer Drive
Birkbeck Avenue
Station Approach
Allington Close
Hill Rise
Belle Vue
Hillbeck Wy
Greenford Station
Rockware Business Cen
Works
Uneeda Drive
Bennetts Avenue
Rockware Av
Lyon Way
Oldfield La North
Ingram Way
Oldfield Farm Gdns
Courthope Rd
Community Rd
Downing Drive
Greenford Road Medical Centre
Middleton Avenue
Oldfield Primary School
Hotel
Darlington Drive
WESTERN AVENUE
Hazelmere Wk
Dolphin Rd
Meadow Close
Union Road
Hotspur Rd
Evesham Close
Chesterton Close
Melrose Av
Bledlow Rise
1 grid square represents 500 metres

Wembley 67
Wembley
Preston
49
85
68
F
G
H
J
K
I
2
3
4
5
6
7
16
17
18
84
85
86
87
Sudbury
WEMBLEY
HA0
Perivale
Alperton
WATFORD ROAD
A404
A4127
SUDBURY COURT DRIVE A4127
HARROW ROAD
A4005
EAST LANE
A4088
WHITTON AVENUE EAST
BRIDGEWATER ROAD
EALING ROAD
A4089
South Kenton Station
North Wembley Station
Sudbury & Harrow Road Station
Sudbury Town Station
Alperton Station
Perivale Station
Byron Court Primary School
Wembley High School
Playing Fields
East Lane Business Park
Council Building
Works
Sudbury Court Sports Club
Vale Farm Sports Centre
Wembley FC
Sudbury Primary School
Perrin Road Clnc
St Georges RC First & Middle School
Thomas a'Beckett Close
Barham Park
Barham Primary School
Police Station
Fire Station
Health Centre
Wembley Hospital
Ambulance Station
Lancelot Medical Cen
Buxlow Preparatory School
King Edward VII Park
Horsenden Hill Golf Club
Sudbury Golf Club
Golf Course
Alperton Cem
Alperton High School
Abercorn Trading Estate
Grand Union Canal
Phoenix Trading Est
Perivale Industrial Park
Perivale Ind Park
Eden Close Superstore
Capital Business Centre
Athlon Industrial Estate
The One Stanley Medical Centre
Surgery
Community Centre
Market
Mosque
Abbotts Drive
Carlton Avenue
Paxford Road
Blockley Road
Holt Road
Norval Road
Pebworth Road
Amery Road
Mulgrave Road
Littleton Road
Littleton Crescent
The Green
Heritage View
Grantchester Close
Sudbury Court Road
Sudbury Hill
Priory Gdns
St Andrews Av
Foxlees
Church Gdns
Homefield Road
Medway Gdns
Rosebank Avenue
Fernbank Av
Maybank Avenue
Greenbank Av
Eastcote Avenue
District Road
Central Road
Saunderton Road
Roundtree Road
Northwood Gdns
Bourne View
Drew Gdns
Robin Hood Way
Rosewood Av
Bracewell Av
Woodland Rise
Oakwood Crs
Ashness Gdns
Orchard Gate
Horsenden Lane North
Horsenden Lane South
Jubilee Road
Bilton Road
George V Way
Jordan Road
Lynmouth Road
Launceston Road
Torrington Road
Empire Road
Walmgate Road
Aintree Road
Fraser Rd
Federal Rd
Fairfield Dr
Perimeade Road
Wadsworth Road
Colwyn Av
Woodhouse Av
Eton Avenue
Rugby Avenue
Beaumont Avenue
Charterhouse Avenue
Sylvester Road
Pettsgrove Av
Crawford Avenue
Copland Av
Talbot Road
Napier Road
Ranelagh Road
Chaplin Road
Farm Avenue
Danethorpe Rd
Bassingham Road
Norton Road
Thurlby Road
Scarle Road
Eagle Road
Bowrons Ave
Braemar Av
Swinderby Road
Lancelot Road
Harrowdene Road
Sudbury Avenue
Peel Road
Byron Road
Strathcona Road
Oldborough Road
Llanover Road
Meadow Way
Carlton Av
Eskdale Close
Logan Road
Walton Gdns
Chamberlayne Av
Keswick Gdns
St John's Road
Clarendon Gdns
Burnside Crescent
Clifford Rd
Brindley Cl
Glacier Way

68
50
67
86
A
B
C
D
E
1
2
3
4
5
6
7
518
519
520
187
186
185
184
Wembley Park
Tokyngton
Alperton
HA9
Preston Park Primary Sch
Preston Road Station
Glendale Gdns
Carlton
Elmstead Avenue
Logan Road
Walton Gdns
Pellatt Road
East Lane Business Park
Works
Council Building
Preston Road
Preston Manor School
Preston Medical Centre
Buxlow Preparatory School
Wembley Synagogue
Wembley Manor Primary School
Forty Avenue
Forty Lane
A4088
A4089
A479
A404
A406
A4140
A4005
B4557
Salmon St
Tudor
Barn Hill
Sports Ground
British Transport Police Stn
Wembley Park Station
Bridge Road
Coll of North West London
Brook Avenue
Wembley Park Drive
Empire Way
Park Lane
Wembley Hill Road
High Road
Harrow Road
Ealing Road
Stadium Retail Park
TV Studios
Fulton Road
Wembley Stadium Industrial Estate
Olympic Retail Park
Olympic Ind Est
Metro Trading Cen
Wembley Park Business Cen
MSP Business Cen
Chalkhill Primary School
Stadium Business Cen
Engineers Way
Lakeside Way
Wembley Arena
Conference Centre
Exhibition Halls
Wembley Stadium (under development)
Olympic Trading Est
Market Area
Cannon Trading Est
Towers Business Park
Hallmark Trading Estate
Great Central Way
South Way
Adams Bridge Bus Cen
Stadium Industrial Est
Wembley Stadium Station
Wembley Central Station
Central Square Shopping Centre
Copland Community School & Technology Centre
St Josephs Junior School
St Josephs RC School
Elsley Primary School
Playing Fields
King Edward VII Park
Park Lane Primary School
Princes Court
Oakington Manor School
Tokyngton Community Centre
St Raphaels Way Medical Cen
Hazeldene Medical Cen
Stonebridge Park Station
Bridge Park Business & Leisure Centre
Brentfield
Our Lady of Lourdes RC Primary School
North Circular Road
Alperton Community School
Lyon Park Junior & Infant School
The One Stanley Medical Centre
Alperton High School
Abbey Industrial Est
Northfields Industrial Est
Townsend Industrial Estate
Mill Trading Estate
Grand Union Industrial Estate
Grand Union Canal
Grand Union Canal Walk
Capital Business Centre
Athlon Industrial Estate
River Brent
Mosque
1 grid square represents 500 metres

Wembley Park 69
Junction 1
51
70
87
F
G
H
J
I
K
2
3
4
5
6
7
21
22
23
85
86
87
Welsh Harp
Woodfield School
London Grove Business
Business Park
Staples Corner Business Park
UCG Cinemas
Superstore
Works
Harp Business Centre
Atlas Business Centre
Edge Business Centre
Humber Trading Estate
Dollis Hill
Neasden
Dudden Hill
WILLESDEN
Church End
Willesden Green
Harlesden
NW10
NORTH CIRCULAR ROAD
A406
A4088
A407
A404
A5
B4557
B453
B4492
NEASDEN LANE
DUDDEN HILL LA
HIGH ROAD
CHURCH ROAD
CRAVEN PK RD
MANOR PK ROAD
KINGS ROAD
HILLSIDE
ACTON LANE
GREAT CENTRAL WAY
DRURY WAY
Drury Way Industrial Estate
Neasden Station
Dollis Hill Station
Harlesden Station
Brent Trading Estate
Central Business Cen
Superstore
Braincroft Primary School
John Kelly Boys & Girls Technology College
The Grange Mus
Gladstone Medical Centre
Brent Arts Council
The Stables Gallery & Art Centre
Gladstone Park
Synagogue & Torah Temimah Primary School
Wykeham Primary School
Falcon Park Industrial Est
Brent Child & Family Clnc
Coll of North West London
Trading Cen
Cygnus Business Cen
Brent Magistrates Court Ho
Chapman Park Industrial Est
Community Centre
Bus Depot
Willesden Medical Cen
Police Stn
Islamic College
Belle Vue
Helena Road Clinic
Burnley Road Clnc
Brentfield Medical Centre
Mitchell Brook Primary School
Hindu Temple
Swaminarayan School
Brentfield Primary School
Church End Medical Centre
Cobbold Est
Trojan Business Cen
Spiritualist University
Cemetery
Roundwood Park Medical Centre
Fire Stn
Willesden Community Hospital
Roundwood Park
Newfield Primary School
Donnington Primary School
Belvedere Day Hospital
Willesden High School
Swimming Pool
Willesden Sports Stadium
Cardinal Hinsley High School
Convent Primary School
Greenhill Park Medical Cen
Craven Park Medical Cen
Stonebridge Shopping Centre
Health Cen
College
Police Stn
Surgery
Willesden Co Court
Pippin Close
Junior School

70
52
69
88
A
B
C
D
E
1
2
3
4
5
6
7
523
24
25
86
85
84
87
NW2
NW6
Child's Hill
Cricklewood
Brondesbury
Brondesbury Park
Willesden Green
Kilburn
Kensal Rise
Queens Park
Claremont Way Industrial Estate
Recreation Ground
UCG Cinemas
Superstore
Edge Business Centre
Hendon FC
Clitterhouse Primary School
Granville Road Industrial Estate
Cricklewood Trading Estate
Childs Hill Primary School
All Saints CE Primary School
Welbeck Clinic
Greenfield Medical Centre
Cricklewood Station
Broadway Retail Park
Britannia Business Centre
The Mosque & Islamic Centre of Brent
Anson Primary School
Cricklewood Synagogue
Hampstead School
Cemetery
Shomrei Hadath Synagogue
Mill Lane Medical Cen
Fire Station
Solent Road Health Cen
Mulberry House Sch
Walm Lane Clinic
Willesden Green Station
Kilburn Station
West Hampstead Station
Brondesbury Station
North West London Jewish J&I School
Tricycle Cinema
Kingsgate Primary School
London Welsh School
Council Building
Synagogue
Islamic College
Belle Vue
Emb of Senegal
Cricket Ground
South Hampstead Cricket Club
Avenue Primary School
Brondesbury College for Boys
Malorees Junior & Infant School
Queens Park Community School GM
Brondesbury Park Station
Islamia Girls School
Bus Park
Coll of North West London
Charteris Road Sports Centre
Kilburn Square
St Marys RC Primary School
Kilburn Park Stn
Queens Park Station
Willesden Sports Stadium
Swimming Pool
Special School
Kensal Rise Station
Police Stn
EDGWARE ROAD CRICKLEWOOD BROADWAY
CRICKLEWOOD BROADWAY
SHOOT-UP HILL
CRICKLEWOOD LANE
HENDON WAY
FINCHLEY ROAD
WALM LANE
CHICHELE ROAD
WILLESDEN LANE
IVERSON ROAD
KILBURN HIGH
BRONDESBURY ROAD
FORTUNE GN RD
QUEX RD
A5
A407
A41
A4003
B520
B451
B150
Barnet
Camden
Brent
1 grid square represents 500 metres

North End
Sandy Heath
West Heath
Golders Hill Park
Golders Green Health Centre
Manor House Hospital
King Alfred School
Spaniards Inn
SPANIARDS ROAD
NORTH END WAY
A502
B519
53
Hampstead Heath
Highgate Ponds
Millfield Lane
Highgate West Hill
Hampstead Pond
Whitestone Pond
Vale of Health
HEATH STREET
West Heath Road
Telegraph Hill
Templewood Av
Redington Road
Branch Hill
Fenton House
New End Thtr
Christchurch Hill
Well Walk
HAMPSTEAD
Parliament Hill
Parliament Hill Fields Athletics Track
La Sainte Union Convent School
Gospel Oak Primary School
Hampstead Heath Stn
Keats House Museum
Keats Gv
Police Station
University
NW3
ROSSLYN HILL
Royal Free Hospital
A&E
POND ST
FLEET RD
AGINCOURT RD
MANSFIELD ROAD
CONSTANTINE RD
Nassington Rd
Hampstead Hill School
Downshire Hill
Pilgrim's La
Willoughby Rd
Flask Wk
Frognal
Frognal Lane
Church Rw
University College School
Devonshire House Sch
St Margarets School
FINCHLEY ROAD
A41
Finchley Road & Frognal Station
Hampstead Cricket Club
Arkwright
Arts Centre
Warner Village 02 Centre Cinema
Finchley Road Station
West Hampstead Station
Broadhurst Gardens
FITZJOHN'S AVENUE
HEATH ST B511
St Anthony's School
St Marys School
Maresfield Gdns
Freud Mus
The Portman Clinic
Tavistock Clinic
Lyndhurst Road
Wedderburn Rd
St Christophers School
Belsize Park Stn
Screen on the Hill
Belsize Av
Belsize Pk
Belsize Square Synagogue
Belsize Sq
Lambolle Rd
Coll Hosp
Lancaster Grove
A502 HAVERSTOCK HILL
Maitland Park
The Village School
Rhyl Primary School
Haverstock Sch
Council Building
St Dominics RC Primary School
72
Chalk Farm Station
South Hampstead
South Hampstead Synagogue
Swiss Cottage Stn
Odeon
Hampstead Theatre
Trevor Roberts School
Sarum Hall School
ADELAIDE ROAD
B509
HILGROVE ROAD
South Hampstead Station
BELSIZE ROAD
Jack Taylor School
George Eliot Junior & Infant School
Swiss Cottage School
AVENUE ROAD
Elsworthy Rd
St Pauls CE Primary School
Primrose Hill
PRINCE ALBERT ROAD
Grand Union Canal
London Zoo
Regent's Park Track
Outer Circle
Camden
Westminster
Abbey Medical Centre
Kilburn High Road Station
ABBEY ROAD
Boundary Road
Springfield Road
Greville
St John's Wood
St John's Wood Stn
89
Naima Jewish Preparatory School
Synagogue
St Christina's RC Prep Sch
Queen's Grove
Acacia
B525
Townshend Rd
FINCHLEY ROAD
B507

72
54
71
90
4
5
A
B
C
D
E
1
2
3
4
5
6
7
528
29
30
87
86
85
84
Upper Holloway
Dartmouth Park
Tufnell Park
Gospel Oak
Kentish Town
CAMDEN TOWN
Barnsb
NW5
N19
N7
Highgate Cemetery
Whittington Hospital
Archway Stn
Archway Leisure Centre
St Aloysius College
Upper Holloway Stn
HOLLOWAY ROAD
JUNCTION ROAD
A400
FORTESS ROAD
KENTISH TOWN ROAD
CAMDEN ROAD
BRECKNOCK ROAD
YORK WAY
HIGHGATE RD
MANSFIELD ROAD
PARKHURST RD
HILLMARTON RD
PRINCE ALBERT ROAD
DELANCEY ST
CAMDEN HIGH ST
ROYAL COLLEGE ST
PANCRAS WAY
CAMDEN ST
A5200
A503
A4201
A5202
B518
B517
B512
Tufnell Park Station
Kentish Town Station
Kentish Town West Stn
Gospel Oak Station
Chalk Farm Station
Camden Town Stn
Camden Road Stn
Mornington Crescent Stn
Parliament Hill
Parliament Hill Fields Athletics Track
Highgate Ponds
HM Prison
City & Islington College
Holloway School
Kentish Town Industrial Est
The Roundhouse Theatre
Camden Market
Jewish Museum
London Zoo
London Canal Museum
St Pancras Hospital
Grand Union Canal
Cedar Way Industrial Est
Camden School for Girls
Islington Tennis Centre
Robert Blair Primary School
National Youth Thtr of GB
Ecole De Mime Thtr De Lange
1 grid square represents 500 metres

Finsbury Park
Lower Holloway
Highbury
Canonbury
ISLINGTON
Hoxton
Kingsla
De Bea
Town
N5
N1
Clissold Park
Highbury Fields
Hackney
STROUD GREEN ROAD
SEVEN SISTERS ROAD
BLACKSTOCK ROAD
BROWNSWOOD ROAD
LORDSHIP PARK
GREEN LANE
HORNSEY ROAD
HOLLOWAY ROAD
TOLLINGTON ROAD
CALEDONIAN ROAD
HIGHBURY PARK
A1201 HIGHBURY GROVE
ST PAUL'S RD
BALLS POND ROAD
NEWINGTON GN RD
ALBION ROAD
A1200 CANONBURY ROAD
ESSEX ROAD
UPPER STREET
LIVERPOOL ROAD
ISLINGTON GN
NEW NORTH ROAD
BARING STREET
SOUTHGATE ROAD
EAGLE WHF ROAD
Finsbury Park Station
Arsenal Station
Drayton Park Station
Holloway Road Stn
Canonbury Stn
Highbury & Islington Stn
Essex Road Station
Caledonian Road & Barnsbury Stn
Angel Stn
Arsenal FC (Highbury)
Highbury Fields School
HM Prison
Islington Town Hall
Almeida Thtr
Kings Head Thtr
Little Angel Thtr
Tower Theatre
The Anna Scher Thtr
Theatre De Complicite
N1 Shopping Centre
Sobell Leisure Centre
Clissold Leisure Cen
Highbury Pool
Cally Pool
Watersports Centre
Britannia Leisure Centre
HIGHBURY CORNER
55
74
91
6
F G H J K
1 2 3 4 5 6 7
31 32 33

74
56
73
92
7
A
B
C
D
E
1
2
3
4
5
6
7
533
34
35
STOKE NEWINGTON
Shacklewell
Hackney Downs
HACKNEY
Kingsland
Dalston
De Beauvoir Town
South Hackney
London Fields
N16
E5
E8
Abney Park Cemetery
STOKE NEWINGTON HIGH ST
STOKE NEWINGTON ROAD
KINGSLAND HIGH ST
KINGSLAND ROAD
UPPER CLAPTON ROAD
LOWER CLAPTON ROAD
NORTHWOLD ROAD
RECTORY ROAD
ALBION ROAD
BALLS POND ROAD
DALSTON LANE
GRAHAM ROAD
AMHURST RD
PEMBURY RD
CRICKETFIELD RD
MARE STREET
MORNING LANE
URSWICK RD
VICTORIA PARK
WELL ST
SOUTHGATE RD
QUEENSBRIDGE ROAD
MANOR ROAD
Stoke Newington Station
Rectory Road Station
Hackney Downs Stn
Hackney Ctrl Stn
London Fields Stn
Kingsland Shopping Cen
Hackney Empire Variety Thr
Town Hall
1 grid square represents 500 metres

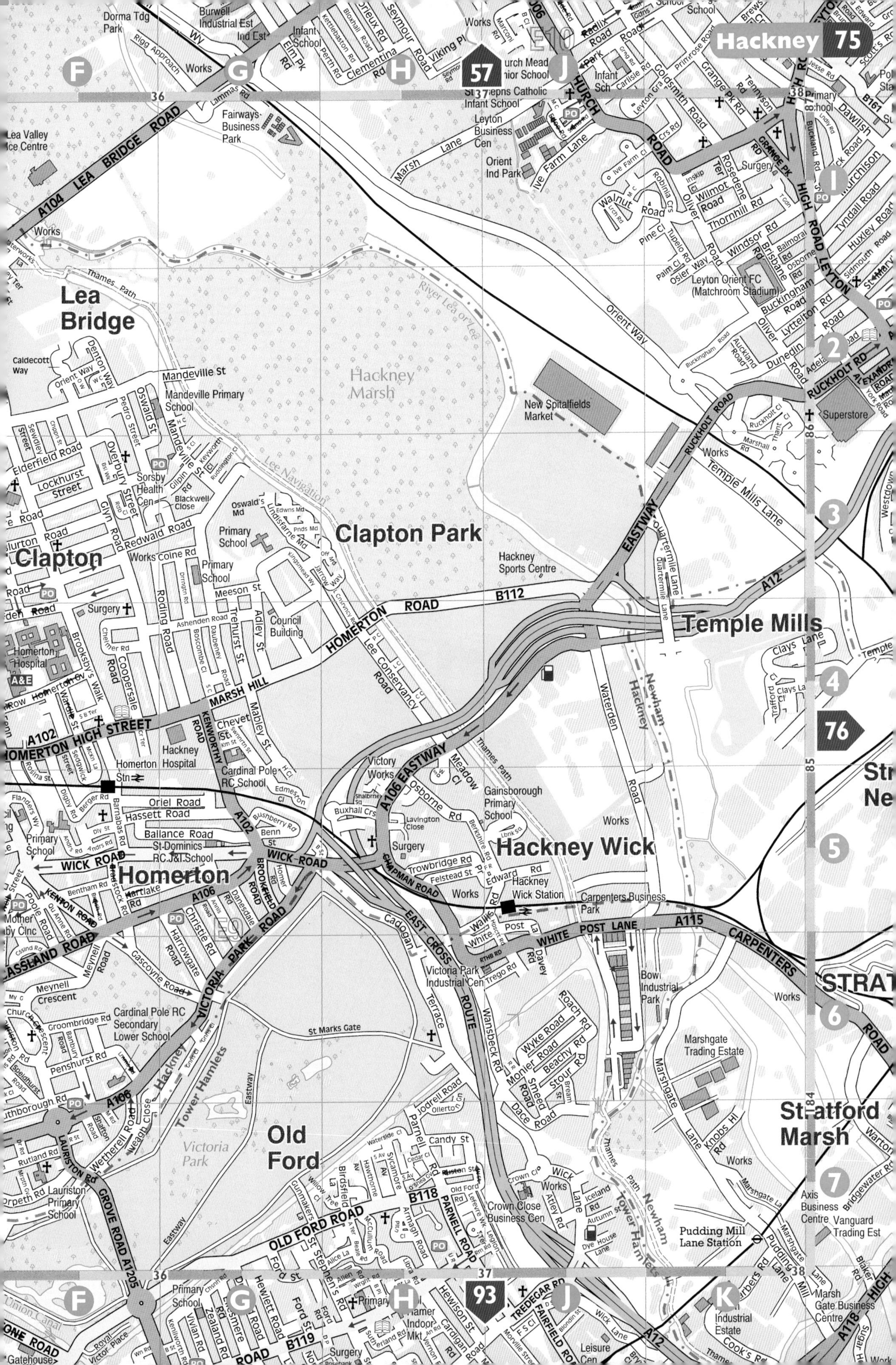
57
76
93
F
G
H
J
K
I
2
3
4
5
6
7
36
37
38
Lea Bridge
Clapton
Clapton Park
Hackney Marsh
Temple Mills
Hackney Wick
Homerton
Old Ford
Stratford Marsh
Victoria Park
E10
E9
A104 LEA BRIDGE ROAD
Lea Valley Ice Centre
Dorma Tdg Park
Burwell Industrial Est
Rigg Approach
Works
Fairways Business Park
Lammas Rd
Infant School
Elm Pk Rd
Perth Rd
Clementina Rd
Seymour Road
Viking Pl
Leyton Business Cen
Marsh Lane
Orient Ind Park
Ive Farm Lane
Church Mead Junior School
St Stephens Catholic Infant School
Church Road
Radlix Road
Goldsmith Road
Grange Pk Rd
Tennyson Rd
Primary School
Dawlish
Buckland Rd
Murchison
Tyndall Road
Huxley Road
Sidmouth Road
HIGH ROAD LEYTON
Walnut Road
Pine Cl
Robinia Crs
Oliver Road
Wilmot
Rosedene Ter
Thornhill Rd
Windsor Rd
Brisbane Rd
Balmoral Rd
Osborne Rd
Surgery
Leyton Orient FC (Matchroom Stadium)
Orient Way
Buckingham Road
Lyttelton Rd
Dunedin Road
Auckland Road
Adelaide Road
RUCKHOLT RD
RUCKHOLT ROAD
ALEXANDRA ROAD
Superstore
Ruckholt Cl
Marshall Rd
Temple Mills Lane
Westdown
River Lea or Lee
Lee Navigation
Thames Path
New Spitalfields Market
EASTWAY
Quartermile Lane
Hackney Sports Centre
A12
B112
HOMERTON ROAD
Clays Lane
Trafford Cl
Temple
Caldecott Way
Denton Way
Orient Way
Mandeville St
Mandeville Primary School
Oswald St
Pedro Street
Overbury Street
Elderfield Road
Lockhurst Street
Sorsby Health Cen
Gilpin Rd
Blackwell Close
Redwald Road
Glyn Road
Oswald's Md
Lindisfarne Md
Primary School
Kingsmead Way
Jarrow Way
Works
Colne Rd
Roding Road
Meeson St
Ashenden Road
Trehurst St
Adley St
Council Building
Lee Conservancy Road
Surgery
Homerton Hospital
A&E
Brooksby's Walk
Chelmer Rd
Coopersale Road
Homerton Gv
Marsh Hill
A102
HOMERTON HIGH STREET
Sedgwick Street
Hackney Hospital
Homerton Stn
KENWORTHY ROAD
Chevet St
Mabley St
Cardinal Pole RC School
Edmeston Cl
Oriel Road
Hassett Road
Ballance Road
St Dominics RC J&I School
Bushberry Rd
Benn St
WICK ROAD
Primary School
Berger Rd
Barnabas Rd
Digby Rd
Kenton Road
Bentham Rd
Hartlake Rd
A106
Brookfield Road
Homer Rd
Mother & Baby Clnc
Cassland Road
Meynell Road
Meynell Crescent
Christie Rd
Harrowgate Road
Danesdale Road
Gascoyne Road
VICTORIA PARK ROAD
Cardinal Pole RC Secondary Lower School
Groombridge Rd
Penshurst Rd
Church Crescent
Hackney
Tower Hamlets
Wetherell Road
Lauriston Rd
Lauriston Primary School
GROVE ROAD A1205
Rutland Rd
Victoria Park
St Marks Gate
Eastway
Victory Works
A106 EASTWAY
Meadow Cl
Osborne Rd
Gainsborough Primary School
Lavington Close
Surgery
Buxhall Crs
Trowbridge Rd
Felstead St
CHAPMAN ROAD
EAST CROSS ROUTE
Cadogan Terrace
Edward Rd
Hackney Wick Station
Works
Waterden Road
Newham
Carpenters Business Park
White Post Lane
WHITE POST LANE
A115
CARPENTERS ROAD
Victoria Park Industrial Cen
Trego Rd
Davey Rd
Wansbeck Rd
Roach Rd
Wyke Road
Monier Road
Beachy Rd
Stour Rd
Smeed Road
Dace Road
Bow Industrial Park
Marshgate Trading Estate
Marshgate Lane
Knobs Hl Rd
Works
STRATFORD
Works
Axis Business Centre
Vanguard Trading Est
Bridgewater Rd
Pudding Mill Lane Station
Pudding Mill Lane
Marsh Gate Business Centre
Baker Rd
A118 HIGH
Sugar
Jodrell Road
Candy St
Parnell Road
PARNELL ROAD
Sycamore Av
Hawthorne Av
Birdsfield La
Gunmakers La
Old Ford Rd
B118
OLD FORD ROAD
Armagh Road
McCullum Road
Crown Close Business Cen
Wick Lane
Iceland Rd
Autumn St
Dye House Lane
Atley Rd
Leyton
Primary School
Ford St
St Stephen's Rd
Hewlett Road
Zealand Rd
Vivian Rd
Ellesmere Road
B119
Roman Road
Tredegar Rd
Fairfield Rd
Hewison St
Cardigan Rd
Roman Indoor Mkt
Surgery
Industrial Estate
Leisure Cen
Cook's Rd
Union Canal
Royal Victor Place
Gatehouse
Wick Lane
A12

76
58
75
94
A
B
C
D
E
1
2
3
4
5
6
7
538
39
40
87
86
85
84
Leytonstone
LEYTON
Forest Gate
Stratford New Town
STRATFORD
Stratford Marsh
HIGH ROAD LEYTON
HIGH ROAD LEYTONSTONE
LEYTONSTONE RD
LEYTON ROAD
MAJOR RD
CHOBHAM ROAD A112
ANGEL LANE
A106 GROVE GREEN ROAD
GROVE GREEN RD
A106 WARREN ROAD
RUCKHOLT RD
HARROW ROAD
ROMFORD ROAD
WATER LANE
THE GROVE
BROADWAY
HIGH ST
EASTERN ROAD
VICARAGE LA
WEST HAM LANE
NEW PLAISTOW RD
PLAISTOW ROAD
PORTWAY B165
PORTWAY
STOPFORD ROAD
DAMES ROAD
CARPENTERS ROAD
MANOR ROAD
Temple Mills Lane
Clays Lane
Leyton Stn
Leytonstone High Road Stn
Maryland Stn
Stratford Station
Forest Gate Station
Plaistow Station
Superstore
Orient FC
Cemetery
Langthorne Hospital
Langthorne Health Centre
Cathall Leisure Cen
Drapers Sports Ground
Atherton Leisure Centre
Stratford Shopping Cen
Royal Thtr
County Court
West Ham Park
Police Stn
Police Station
Acacia Business Cen
Maryland Industrial Est
Axis Business Centre
Vanguard Trading Est
Marsh Gate Business Centre
Ramgarhia Sikh Gurdwara Temple
Portway Primary School
Davies Lane Infant School
Stratford School
St Bonaventure School
Rokeby School
Sarah Bonnell Sch
Works
1 grid square represents 500 metres

Aldersbrook
Leyton 77
59
F
G
H
J
42
43
Woodlands Avenue
Northumberland Av
Primary Sch
Secondary Sch
Park Road
Harpenden Road
Dover Road
Herongate Road
St Margaret's Road
Empress Avenue
Wanstead Park Avenue
Clavering Road
Arran Drive
Westmorland Close
Sunderland Way
Merlin Road
Brading Crs
Heatherwood Close
Surgery
ALDERSBROOK ROAD
City of London Cemetery
City of London Crematorium
Golf Course
Ilford Golf Club
Wanstead Flats
Centenary Walk
FOREST DRIVE
A117
A116
A406
NORTH CIRCULAR ROAD
Courtland Avenue
Mayfair Avenue
Empress Avenue
Wanstead Pk Rd
Westbrook Road
Belgrave Road
Selborne Road
York Ms
Maytime School
Aldersbrook Lane
Daines Close
Grantham Road
Capel Road
Tylney Road
Cranmer Road
Latimer Road
Lorne Road
Godwin Road
Ridley Road
Godwin Junior Sch
Chestnut Avenue
Forest View Road
Manor Park Crematorium
Manor Park Cemetery
Manor Park Station
The Chase
Whitta Road
Gladding Road
RABBITS RD
Washington Av
ROMFORD RD
Gloucester Rd
Worcester Rd
Eighth Avenue
Seventh Avenue
Sixth Avenue
Fifth Avenue
Fourth Avenue
Third Avenue
Second Avenue
First Avenue
B165
LTL ILFORD LANE
Sheringham Avenue
Dersingham Avenue
Junior School
Wolferton Rd
Jack Cornwell St
Lawrence Avenue
Parkhurst Road
Walton Road
Carlyle Road
Ravandos Sikh Temple
Mosque
Manor Park
Kubrick Business Estate
Wanstead Park Stn
Woodgrange Infant School
Sebert Road
Works
Balmoral Road
Durham Road
Carlton Road
Albany Road
Manor Pk
STATION RD
Clarence Road
Primary School
Avenue Primary School
Snowshill Road
Herbert Road
Meanley Road
Nine Acres Close
Harcourt Avenue
Trevelyan Av
Dersingham Infant School
Church Road
Gainsborough Road
Landseer Avenue
Hampton Road
Osborne Road
Claremont Road
Windsor Road
Richmond Road
Claremont Clinic
ROMFORD ROAD
A118
Woodgrange Park Stn
Salisbury Road
Bluebell Avenue
Woodgrange Park Cemetery
Tenbury Cl
Queensberry Pl
HIGH ST NORTH
Church Rd
London Sri Murugan Temple
Morris Av
CHURCH RD
Little Ilford School
Rectory Rd
Chesterford Rd
Barrington Rd
Hathaway Crs
78
Police Station
Post Office
Sandringham Road
Primary School
Rosedale Road
Birchdale Road
Nigel Road
Quakers Pl
Monega Primary School
Sherrard Road
Halley Road
Monega Road
Strone Road
Berkeley Road
Stanley Road
Coleridge Avenue
Ruskin Avenue
Goldsmith Avenue
Rosebery Avenue
Warwick Road
Sheridan Road
BROWNING ROAD
Ruskin Av
Dashmesh Darbar Sikh Temple
Kensington Avenue
Kensington Primary School
Shakespeare Crescent
Stevenage Road
NTGB Sports
Leigh Road
5
Katherine Road Medical Centre
Henderson Rd
Health Cen
Shrewsbury Road
Plashet Jewish Cemetery
Colston Rd
Clifton Rd
Vale Road
Glenparke Road
Whyteville Road
Medical Centre
Studley Road
Kitchener Road
Grosvenor Road
RC Sch
6th Form Centre
St George's Road
UPTON LA
B167
GREEN STREET
South Esk Road
Marlborough Road
Rothsay Road
Lansdown Road
Woodstock Road
Cromwell Road
Prestbury Road
B109
Bristol Road
Stafford Road
Derby Road
Rutland Road
Chester Road
Prim School
Surgery
Primary School
Plashet
Shrewsbury Road Health Centre
Plashet Park
Woodhouse Grove
Shelley Avenue
Byron Avenue
Wordsworth Avenue
Tennyson Avenue
Gladstone Avenue
EAST AVENUE
Sibley Grove
Keppel Road
Bridge Road
Shoebury Road
Springfield Road
Northfield Road
Ashford Road
Burges Road
6
Elmhurst Road
Elmhurst Primary School
Upton Park Road
Upton
Shaftesbury Road
Independent School
East Ham Memorial Hospl
B165
Plashet School
Works
East Ham Stn
Lathom Junior School
Lathom Road
Clements Road
Caulfield Road
Caledon Road
Altmore Avenue
Altmore Infant School
Wall End Road
Holland Road
St Antony's Rd
Stukeley Road
Plashet Road Medical Centre
St Stephens Road
Wortley Road
GROVE
Milton Avenue
Heigham Road
Covelee Rd
KATHERINE ROAD
PLASHET ROAD
PLASHET
Elizabeth Road
Lawrence Road
Benedict Road
RON LEIGHTON WAY
High Street North
Skeffington Road
Kempton Road
Latimer Avenue
Streatfield Avenue
Norfolk Road
Bedford Road
Calverton Road
St Olave's Road
7
B165
Lucas Avenue
Thorngrove Road
Ferndale Road
Claude Road
Dacre Road
Churston Avenue
Gwendoline Avenue
Harold Road
Upton Cross Primary School
Upton Park Station
Park Road
King's Rd
Redclyffe Road
William Morley Close
Primary School
Grangewood Street
Victoria Avenue
Eversleigh Road
Spencer Road
Outram Road
Malvern Road
Stamford Road
Oakfield Road
Holme Road
Wakefield Street
Campbell Road
Hartley Avenue
Altrincham Avenue
Winter Av
Primary School
The Shop Hall
Thorpe Rd
Lloyd Rd
Works
Surgery
A124
BARKING ROAD
Ranelagh Road
Napier Road
Primary Sch
East Ham Leisure Cen
Wellington Road
Melbourne Road
Talbot
Nelson St
College
K
Market Street
St Michaels RC Primary
Works
Rochester Av
Queens Road West
Queen's Ter
Waghorn Road
Orwell Road
Selsdon Road
Kirton Rd
Walton Rd
Upton Park
West Ham United FC (Upton Park)
Priory Rd
Tudor Road
Boleyn Rd
Rochford Cl
Parr Rd
Arragon Road
Abbots Road
Friar's Road
St Bernard's Road
ROAD
95
Kimberley Avenue
Lady smith Avenue
Gillett Avenue
Ernald Avenue
Henry Road
Lister Community Sch
Southern Rd Primary School
St Mary's Road
Eastern Road
Credon Road
Western Road
Bushey Road
Newham Medical Centre
Castle St
Cinema
Dickens Rd
Thackeray Rd
Macaulay Rd
Plaistow Hosp
Glasgow Road
Southern Road

60
ILFORD
Little Ilford
Loxford
Wallend
BARKING
NORTH CIRCULAR ROAD
HIGH ROAD
GREEN LANE
A1083
A118
A406
A123
A124
A12
ILFORD LANE
WINSTON WAY
ILFORD HL
CHAPEL RD
FANSHAWE AVENUE
NORTHERN RELIEF ROAD
LONGBRIDGE ROAD
HIGHBRIDGE ROAD
ABBEY RD
LONDON ROAD
ST PAULS RD
LTL ILFORD LANE
CHURCH RD
B165
IG1
Ilford Station
Barking Station
Seven Kings
Cranbrook College
Ilford County High School
Ilford Retail Park
The Exchange
The Business Centre
Kenneth More Theatre
Ilford Medical Cen
Ilford Swimming Pool
Buckingham Road Cemetery
Cricklefield Stadium
South Park
South Park Terrace
St Peter & Pauls RC Primary School
Gordon Infant School
Woodlands Infant & Junior School
Loxford School of Science and Technology
Hyleford School
Barking Abbey Comprehensive School
Barking Park
Jamia Mosque
Northbury Primary School
NTGB Sports Ground
Singh Sabha Temple
The Vicarage Field Shopping Cen
Magistrates Court
Abbey Sports Centre
Barking Abbey Industrial Est
Fresh Wharf Est
Eastbury Comprehensive School
Ripple Junior & Infant School
The Orchard Health Cen
Dersingham Infant School
Maytime School
River Roding
543
44
45
81
86
85
84
A
B
C
D
E
1
2
3
4
5
6
7
77
96
1 grid square represents 500 metres

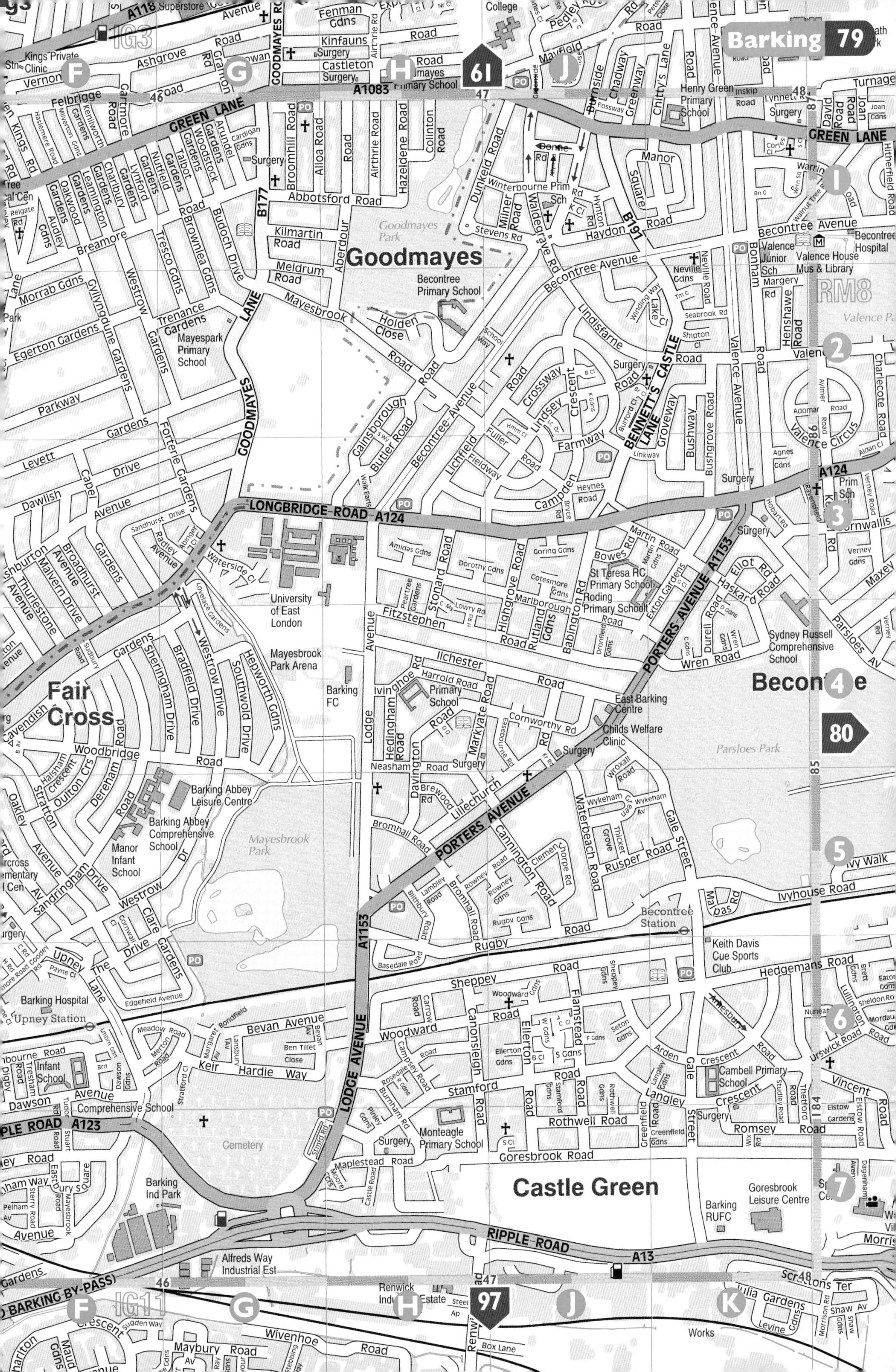

Barking 79
61
Goodmayes
Goodmayes Park
Becontree Primary School
Mayesbrook Park Arena
University of East London
Barking FC
Fair Cross
Barking Abbey Leisure Centre
Barking Abbey Comprehensive School
Manor Infant School
Mayesbrook Park
Parsloes Park
Becontree
Becontree Station
Castle Green
Barking RUFC
Goresbrook Leisure Centre
Barking Ind Park
Alfreds Way Industrial Est
Cemetery
Barking Hospital
Upney Station
Sydney Russell Comprehensive School
Valence House Mus & Library
Becontree Hospital
Valence Park
GREEN LANE
LONGBRIDGE ROAD A124
PORTERS AVENUE A1153
LODGE AVENUE A1153
GOODMAYES LANE
BENNETT'S CASTLE LANE
RIPPLE ROAD A13
RIPPLE ROAD A123
BARKING BY-PASS
Becontree Avenue
Valence Avenue
Mayesbrook Road
Goresbrook Road
Rugby Road
Ivyhouse Road
Hedgemans Road
Sheppey Road
Woodward Road
Bevan Avenue
Keir Hardie Way
Stamford Road
Rothwell Road
Gale Street
Monteagle Primary School
Cambell Primary School
St Teresa RC Primary School
Roding Primary School
East Barking Centre
Childs Welfare Clinic
Mayespark Primary School
Henry Green Primary School
Keith Davis Cue Sports Club
RM8
IG3
IG11
F G H J I K
80
97

80
62
79
98
A
B
C
D
E
1
2
3
4
5
6
7
548
49
50
Chadwell Heath Industrial Park
Wood Lane Sports Centre
All Saints Catholic School
Robert Clack School
Turnage Road
Lynnett Surgery
Inskip Road
Winifred Road
Gerald Rd
Ross Avenue
Tenterden Rd
Fordyke Rd
Grafton Gdns
Joan Gdns
David Road
Lamberhurst Rd
Brendon Road
Albert Avenue
Purland Cl
Rosemary Gdns
SOUTH
A1112
Gosfield Road
WOOD LANE
Terling Road
Barton Av
Wisdons Cl
GREEN LANE
A1083
Laburnum Health Centre
Dagenham Civic Centre
Central Park
Warrington Road
Walnut Tree Rd
Bentry Road
Bentry Cl
Hitherfield Road
Stockdale Rd
Green La
Morris Road
Dagenham Swimming Pool
Althorne Way
Bradwell Av
Stour Rd
RAINHAM ROAD NORTH A1112
Trefgarne Road
William Bellamy Junior & Infant School
Calverley Crs
Becontree Avenue
Valence Junior Sch
Valence House Mus & Library
Becontree Day Hospital
Grafton Primary School
Surgery
Homestead Road
Boulton Rd
Stanhope Road
Nicholas Road
Rowlands Road
Danette Gdns
Stansgate Road
Listowel Road
Bull Lane
Bonham Road
Margery Rd
RM8
Valence Park
Grafton Road
Brittain Road
Coote Rd
Ogilethorpe Road
Kershaw Road
Uvedale Road
Listowel Road
Lawrence Crescent
Hamden Crescent
Bell Farm Avenue
Woodshire Rd
Highland Av
Wheel Farm Dr
Park Drive
Ely Gdns
Birch Gdns
Valence Avenue
Valence Wood Road
Charlecote Road
Windsor Road
Wellington Road
Weylond Road
Five Elms Primary School
LANE
Marston
Rusholme Avenue
Woodshire Rd
Hardie Rd
Fels Farm
Dagenham Chest Clnc
Thompson Road
Dunbar Avenue
Naseby Road
Wythenshawe Rd
Bosworth Road
Frizlands
Crescent Road
Central Pk Avenue
Macdonald Av
Adomar Road
Aylmer Road
Valence Circus
WOOD
Aidan Cl
Halbutt St
Boyne Road
Heathway Med Cen
Trinity School
Avenue
Glencoe Road
Greenwood Av
Dagenham Road
Eastbrook Av
Agnes Gdns
A124
Weston Road
Boxoll Rd
Five Elms Road
Elms Gdns
Joyners Cl
Connor Road
Bainbridge Road
Robinson Road
Sedgemoor Drive
Webbscroft Rd
Health Centre
Prim Sch
Keppel Rd
Ravensfield
Verney Road
Beverley Rd
Maxey Gdns
St Georges Rd
School
Northfield Road
HEATHWAY
Oxlow Lane
Kingsley Cl
Surgery
Eastbrook Comprehensive School
Cornwallis Road
Carey Road
Verney Gdns
Sidney Russell School
Osborne Square
Powell Gardens
Eastfield Rd
Hunters Square
Croppath Road
Midas Business Cen
Midas Industrial Est
Hunters Hall Road
Wantz Road
Heathway Industrial Estate
Sterling Ind Est
RAINHAM RD SOUTH
Eliot Rd
Haskard Road
Maxey
St Georges Road
Westfield Road
Sterry Road
Primary School
Cranmer Gardens
Foxlands Crs
Gay Gardens
Winstead Gdns
Sydney Russell Comprehensive School
Parsloes Av
Raydons Road
Raydons Gdns
Pasture Road
Cherry Gdns
Spinney Gdns
Springpond Road
Street
Wayside Gdns
Sterry Crs
Alibon Road
Dagenham & Redbridge FC
Bury Rd
Victoria Rd
Becontree
Fanshawe Crescent
Monmouth Road
Harris Road
Barnmead Rd
Barnmead Gdns
Kingsmill Rd
Singleton
Lake Gdns
Berry Cl
Standfield Road
Witham Road
Rockwell Road
Hunters Hall Primary School
Surrey Road
Kent Road
Norfolk Road
Suffolk Rd
Essex Rd
Durham Rd
Reede Rd
Foxlands Road
Cambeys Road
Parsloes
Terrace Walk
Parsloes Avenue
Kingsmill Gdns
Pettit's Road
Pettit's Place
Rogers Gdns
Dunbar Gdns
Pondfield Road
Holgate Road
Reede Road
Reede Way
Dagenham East Station
Meadow Road
Aylofe Road
Parsloes Primary School
Spurling Road
Council Building
Sterry Gdns
Shafter Rd
Dewey Road
Dewey Rd
Ivy Walk
Ivyhouse Road
Hunsdon Cl
Dagenham Heathway Stn
Blackborne Road
Payet Cl
Radleys Md
Coopers Cl
Lewis Way
Exeter Road
Honey Cl
Plumtree Cl
Sandown Av
Aldborough Rd
Crown St
Ibscott Cl
A1112
Tilney Road
Medical Centre
Manning Road
Crane Close
Hrsfld Rd
Church Elm Lane
Inglebry Rd
Buttfield Close
Salisbury Road
Church St
Crown St
Cadiz Road
Smith Davis Sports
Hedgemans Road
Hedgemans Way
Surgery
Walfrey Gdns
Brett Gdns
Eaton Gdns
Langhorne Road
Rectory Road
Vicarage Road
Hollidge Way
St Giles Avenue
Church La
Sivliter Way
Church La
B178
Sheldon Road
Finnymore Road
Lullington Road
Mordaunt Gdns
Godwin Primary School
Dagenham Avenue
Ford Road
Moss Road
William Ford CE Junior School
Brook Avenue
Acre Rd
Beech Gdns
Farm Cl
Nuneaton Road
Urswick Road
Bluebird La
Village Infant School
Welling
The Leys Primary School
Campbell Primary School
Studley Road
Vincent Road
Primary School
Comyns Road
Morgan Close
Armstead Wk
Broad
Dagenham Priory Comprehensive School
Crescent
Elstow Road
Elstow Gardens
Downing Road
Rowdowns Road
Arnold Road
A1240
Morland Road
Chantress Cl
Clemence
Romsey Road
Treswell Road
Coombes Road
D'Arcy Gdns
Digby Gdns
Lwr Broad St
School Road
BALLARDS ROAD
Ridgewell Cl
Gores Leisure Centre
Sports Centre
Dagenham Avenue
Goresbrook Road
Starmans Close
Blossom Cl
Nurbrowne Road
Baddow Close
Marsh Green Road
Street
Orchard Road
Ballards Cl
Oval Road North
Warner Village Cinema
Wallers Cl
St Peters RC Primary School
Burdetts Road
Surgery
North Close
South Close
Whitebarn Lane
Review Road
B178
Crosby Road
Beam Avenue
Third Avenue
Second Avenue
Centre Road
Oval Rd North
Morrison Rd
A1306
Merrielands Retail Pk
Dagenham Superbowl
Scrattons Ter
RIPPLE ROAD
Julia Gardens
Shaw Av
Polesworth Rd
Marsh Green School
NEW ROAD
Beam Avenue
Oval Rd South
Third Av
Beam Primary School
Link Road
Works
1 grid square represents 500 metres

63
99
Elm Park
Dagenham
South Hornchurch
RM10
RM
Eastbrookend Country Park
Eastbrook End Cemetery
Harrow Lodge Park
Hornchurch Sports Centre
Barking College
Rush Green Primary School
Wykeham Primary School
The Albany School
Benhurst JMI School
Ayloff Primary School
Elm Park Station
Kings Estate
Dunningford Primary School
Rosewood Medical Centre
R J Mitchell Primary School
John Perry Primary School
Brittons School
Whybridge Infant School
Whybridge Junior School
Health & Welfare Clinic
Bretons
Albyns Farm
Works
Barking & Dagenham
Havering
Beam River
UPPER RAINHAM ROAD
RAINHAM ROAD
A125
A1112
DAGENHAM RD
The Chase
Dagenham Road
Warren Drive
Eyhurst Avenue
Woodcote Avenue
Northwood Avenue
Elm Park Avenue
St Nicholas Av
The Broadway
Maylands Av
Coronation Dr
Ambleside Av
Rosewood Av
Windermere Avenue
Andrews Avenue
Carnforth Gardens
Coniston Wy
Mungo Park Road
South End Road
Maybank Avenue
Abbs Cross Lane
Chestnut Avenue
Hartland Road
Broadstone Road
Gordon Avenue
Crescent Avenue
Milton Av
Valentines Way
Eastbrook Drive
Foxglove Road
Gorseway
Ford Lane
Fyfield Road
Stanley Road
Blacksmith's Lane
Grove Park Road
Avelon Road
Gainsborough Road
Hayes Dr
Airfield Way
Tangmere Crs
Elms Farm Road
Rosebank Avenue
Fernbank
Laburnum
Lancaster
Calbourne Av
Arbour Way
Simpson Road
Beamway
Castle Av
Thorogood Way
Lowen Road
Frederick Road
Maytree Cl
Nelson Road
Victory Rd
Newtons Primary
51
52
53
84
85
86
87

82
64
101
A
B
C
D
E
1
2
3
4
5
6
7
508
09
10
83
82
81
80
Sutton Court Road
Sports Ground Pavilion
Swakeleys School
Abbotsfield School
Highfield School
Works
Charville Lane
Charville Primary School
Hedgewood School
Gainsborough Road
Lawrence Rd
Hayman Crs
Raeburn Rd
Bury Avenue
Goshawk Gardens
Weymouth
Dorset Avenue
Adelphi Crs
Kingshill Avenue
Grosvenor Road
Lansbury Drive
Brook House FC
Raynton Dr
Dog Rose Ramble
Hillingdon Trail
Yeading Brook
Harrow View
Hill Road
Nelson Rd
Marlborough Road
Pole Hill Road
Mellow Lane East
Mellow Lane School
Hewens Road
Heath Rd
Star Road
Uxbridge Road
Hayes End
Hayes End Road
Hayes End Dr
Mead House Lane
Wilmar Close
Blacklands Drive
Frogmore Gardens
Balmoral Dr
Park Lane
Mansfield Dr
Frogmore Avenue
Fairholme Crs
Hayes Park Junior & Infant School
Surgery
Grange Park Primary School
Grange Park Clinic
Hurstfield Crs
Westacott
Derwent Drive
Woodrow Avenue
Whittington Avenue
Gledwood Dr
Balmoral Road
Gledwood Av
Gledwood Gdns
Shelley Close
Keats Close
Chaucer Av
Spencer Av
Warley Avenue
Belmore Av
Coleridge Way
Marvell Av
Hillingdon
Heath
Sibley Ct
Haig Road
New Road
Fountain Cl
West Drayton Rd
Green Lane
DRAYTON ROAD
HAYES
Morgan's La
Angel La
Newport Road
Pronto Trading Estate
Wood End Green
Uxbridge Co Court
Grange Rd
The Beck Theatre
Queens Road
Albion Road
The Hayes Manor School
Hayes Stadium Sports Centre
Hayes Cricket Club
Wood End
Church Walk
Church Road
Dr Tripletts School
Hemmen Lane
B465 WEST
Kingsway
Surgery
Saxony Pde
Hanover
Stuart Crs
Normandy Drive
Tudor Road
Bishop's Road
York Avenue
Cromwell Road
Victoria Cranmer Road
HARLINGTON ROAD
Harlington Road
Dawley Av
Cherry Grove
Corwell Lane
Judge Heath Lane
Junior Sch
Mcmillan Clinic
Princes Park Avenue
Beechwood Av
Freemans Lane
Sycamore Avenue
Manton Close
Willenhall Dr
Botwell Common Road
Botwell Lane
Hayes FC
Hayes Social and Sports Club
Compton Road
A437
DAWLEY ROAD
Golf Course
Stockley Park Golf Club
UB11
Stockley Park Business Centre
Furzeground Way
The Square
Bollingbroke Way
Roundwood Av
Longwalk Road
Grand Union Canal Wk
Rostrever Gardens
Hayes Pool
Sikh Temple
Rec Gnd
Golden Crs
Moray Avenue
Forris Avenue
Lannock Road
Central Avenue
Uxbridge College
Orchard Road
Silverdale Industrial Estate
Birchway
Minet Drive
Hunters Grove
Caxton Trading Est
Crown Trading Cen
Printinghouse Lane
Primary School
Aberglen Industrial Est
Betam Rd
Clayton
Pump
Provident
UXBRIDGE
1 grid square represents 500 metres

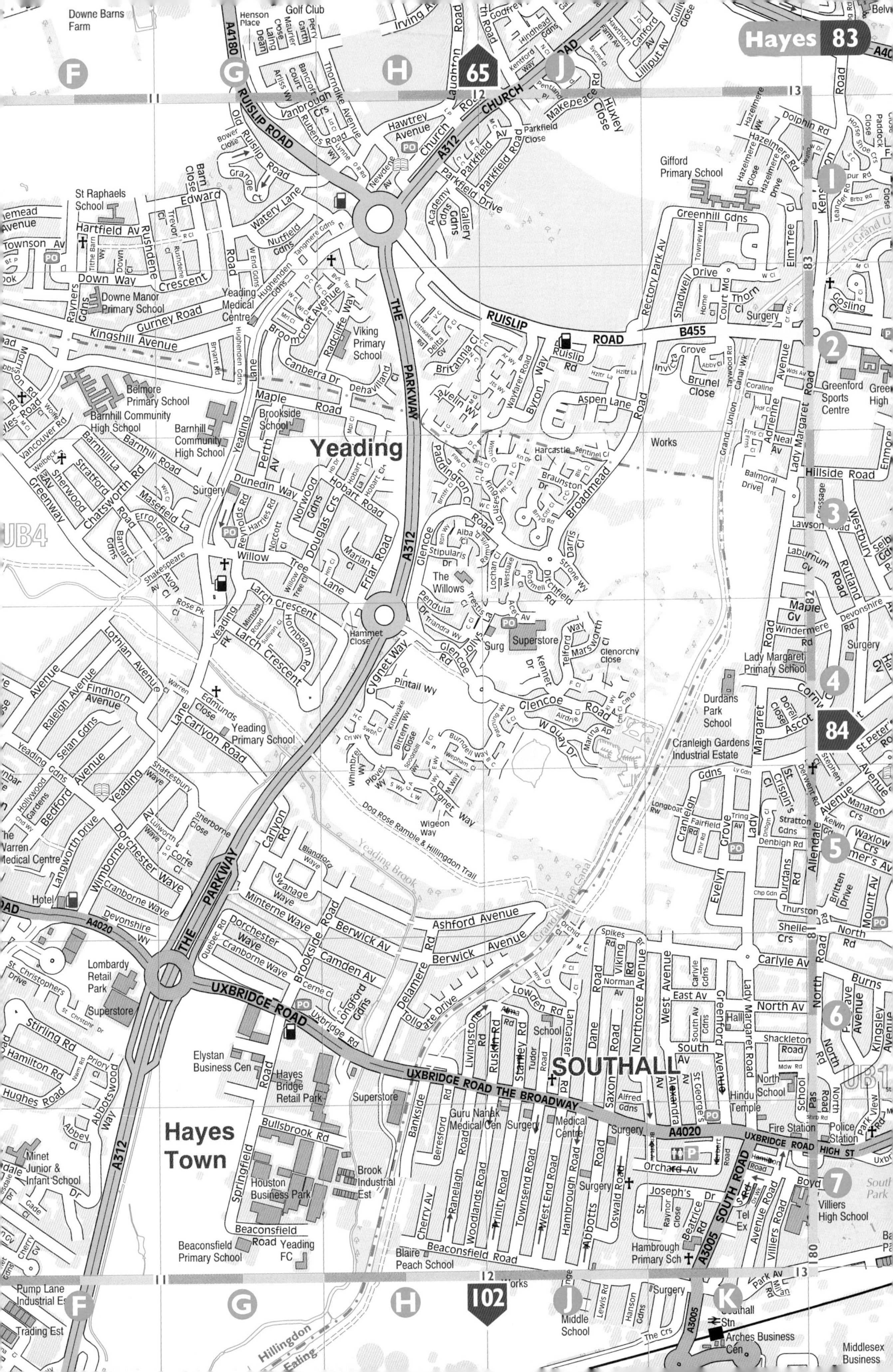
Yeading
SOUTHALL
Hayes Town
UB4
UB1
Downe Barns Farm
Golf Club
St Raphaels School
Downe Manor Primary School
Belmore Primary School
Barnhill Community High School
Yeading Medical Centre
Viking Primary School
Brookside School
Gifford Primary School
Greenford Sports Centre
Lady Margaret Primary School
Durdans Park School
Cranleigh Gardens Industrial Estate
Yeading Primary School
Lombardy Retail Park
Superstore
Elystan Business Cen
Hayes Bridge Retail Park
Houston Business Park
Brook Industrial Est
Beaconsfield Primary School
Yeading FC
Blaire Peach School
Minet Junior & Infant School
Guru Nanak Medical Cen
Hambrough Primary Sch
Villiers High School
Southall Stn
Arches Business Cen
Pump Lane Industrial Est
Trading Est
Middle School
Fire Station
Police Station
Hindu Temple
The Willows
Works
RUISLIP ROAD
A4180
CHURCH ROAD
A312
THE PARKWAY
B455
UXBRIDGE ROAD
A4020
UXBRIDGE ROAD THE BROADWAY
SOUTH ROAD
A3005
HIGH ST
Grand Union Canal
Yeading Brook
Dog Rose Ramble & Hillingdon Trail
Kingshill Avenue
Broadmead Road
Lady Margaret Road
Greenford Avenue
North Road
Allendale Avenue
Springfield Road
Beaconsfield Road
Ashford Avenue
Berwick Avenue
Glencoe Road
Cygnet Way
Larch Crescent
Yeading Lane
Rectory Park Av
Greenhill Gdns
Hillside Road
65
84
102
11
12
13
80
81
82
83

66
83
103
A
B
C
D
E
1
2
3
4
5
6
7
513
14
15
83
82
81
80
WESTERN AVENUE
Belvue School
Kelvin Ind Est
Bristol Road
Field Way
Jeymer
Stanley
Oldfields Primary School
Greenford Road Medical Centre
Courthope Rd
Middleton Avenue
Darygton Drive
Runnymede Gdns
Cayton Rd
Conway
Bennetts Avenue
Rockware
Lyon Way
Downing Drive
Hotel
Dolphin Rd
Hazelmere Rd
Farrier Road
Union Road
Kensington
Grand Union Canal
Elm Tree Cl
Evesham Close
Chesterton Close
Melrose Av
Melrose Cl
Chinnor Crs
Bleddow Rise
Ferrymead Avenue
Ferrymead Gdns
Goring Way
Ormsby Gdns
Barnham Road
Farndale Crs
Girls School
Greenford Gardens
Millet Road
Marnham Crs
Penn Cl
Gosling Cl
Crossmead Avenue
Primary School
Rosedene Avenue
Greenway Gardens
Beechwood Avenue
Eastmead Avenue
Ravenor Park Road
Greenford Synagogue
South
Betham CE Primary School
Costons La
Costons Av
Cowgate Rd
Wessex
Leaver Gardens
Anthony
Hicks
David Av
Avenue
South Greenford Station
Kelvin Ind Est
UB6
Perivale Park Athletics Track
Perivale Park Golf Club
Golf Course
Surgery
Thorn Cl
Court Md
Greenford Sports Centre
Greenford High School
Allenby Rd
RUISLIP ROAD
Stickleton Cl
Pembroke Rd
Oldfield Lane
Croyde Av
Surgery
A4127
Oakfield Gdns
Costons Lane
Wedmore Road
Betham Road
Shelley Av
Locarno Rd
GREENFORD
Clifton Rd
Coraline Cl
Neal Av
Adrienne Av
Lady Margaret Road
Enmore Rd
Towers Rd
Verulam Rd
Avon Road
Ruislip Close
Braund Avenue
Warren Dr
Lyric Dr
Carrick Road
School
B455
RUISLIP ROAD
Brentside High School
Riverside
Balmoral Drive
Hillside Road
Cressage Close
Lawson Road
Westbury
Rose Gdns
Selby Gdns
Rosecroft Rd
Bycroft Road
Upper Town Rd
Mornington Road
Portland House Medical Centre
Ellesmere Rd
Otter Rd
GREENFORD ROAD
Our Lady of the Visitation RC Combined Primary School
Brentside Primary School
Brants Wk
Cuckoo
Laburnum Gv
Rutland Road
Sunnycroft Road
Allenby Road
Fermoy Rd
Portland Crs
Lane Road
Bingley Rd
The Cardinal Wiseman ARC School Technology and Art College
Brookbank Av
Elmbank Way
Cuckoo Dene
Gifford Gardens
Beechmount Av
Beresford Av
Kennedy Road
Elfwine Rd
Laurie Rd
Hillyard Road
Greenford Avenue
Brent First
Bordars
Maple Gv
Windermere Rd
Devonshire Rd
Cedar Gv
Ash Gv
Purcell Rd
Mansell
Portland Crs
Windmill
Stanhope
Lady Margaret Primary School
Surgery
Hart Gv
Gdns
Cornwall
Somerset Road
Dale Road
Keats Way
Hurley Road
Greenford Park Cemetery
River Brent
Brent River Pk Wk
Bridge Avenue
Benham Rd
St Peter's Road
Jubilee Gdns
Canterbury Close
Barbican Rd
Bassett Wy
Queen's Av
The Gv
St Stephen's
Avenue
St Ursula Rd
Allenby Road
King's Avenue
Mayfield Primary School
High Lane
Mayfield Gardens
Greenford Avenue Medical Centre
Hanway Rd
Highland Av
Hobbayne Rd
Studland Road
Westview
Crispin's
Lady
Grove
Stratton Gdns
Manaton Crs
Kelvin Gdns
Allendale
Allenby Infant School
Lovell Rd
Walls Road
Swan Rd
Darwin Dr
Howard Rd
Kings Avenue Medical Centre
Waxlow Crs
Dormer's Av
Dormers Wells School
Dormers Wells Leisure Centre
Edison Dr
Fleming Road
Durdans Rd
Britten Drive
Mount Av
Telford Rd
Marconi Way
Longridge Lane
Dormers Ri
Redcroft Rd
A4127
High Lane
Golf Course
Grove Avenue
Greenford Avenue
Elmwood Gardens
Thurston Rd
Sherry Crs
North Rd
Medical Centre
Dormer's Wells La
Faraday Rd
Haldane Rd
Carlyle Av
Masefield Av
Farm Cl
Baird Avenue
Brindley Way
Brent Valley Golf Club
Surgery
Cuckoo Lane
Church Road
Oakley Close
Burns Avenue
North Road
Palgrave Avenue
Kingsley Avenue
Oakwood Av
Kenton Av
Milford Road
Longford Avenue
KS Medical Centre
Dormer's Wells
Dormers Wells Primary School
West Middlesex Golf Club
GREENFORD ROAD
Manor Ct Road
Golden Manor
Manor House School
Lady Margaret Road
Shackleton Road
North School
Hindu Temple
UB1
School
Pas Road
North Road
Park View Rd
Melrose Dr
Atherton Pl
Dormer's Lane
Golf Course
Alwyne Rd
Hanwell Stn
Primary School
Hanwell
York Av
Fire Station
Police Station
UXBRIDGE ROAD HIGH ST
Uxbridge Rd
Green Drive
UXBRIDGE ROAD
A4020
Works
Brentvale Av
Blackmore Av
Conolly Rd
Lawn Gdns
Myrtle Gdns
Laurel Gdns
Station Rd
Half Acre Rd
SOUTH ROAD
Boyd Av
Southall Park
Villiers High School
Argyll Av
Knowsley Avenue
Morland Gdns
Windmill Business Centre
WINDMILL LANE
Ellis Cl
Alderson Place
Alexander Cl
West Park Road
A&E
A3002
Tel Ex
Villiers Road
Avenue Rd
Barrett Ind Park
Park
Park Av
Walker Cl
Westminster Rd
BOSTON RD
Great Western Industrial Park
Dean Way
Navigator Drive
Chaucer Clinic
Ealing Hospital
St Marks Primary School
Southall Stn
Armstrong Way
Middlesex Business
Three Bridges Business
1 grid square represents 500 metres

Perivale
Alperton
67
86
104
F
G
H
J
K
I
2
3
4
5
6
7
16
17
18
81
82
83
Perivale Industrial Park
Works
Phoenix Trading Est
Sunley Gdns
Woodhouse Cl
Woodhouse Av
Selborne School
Thames Avenue
Medway Drive
Hodder Drive
Barmouth Avenue
Colwyn Av
Perivale Station
Horsenden Lane South
Perivale Ind Park
Sarsfield Road
Primary School
Perivale New Business Cen
Perimeade Road
Athlon Rd
Glacier Way
Capital Business Centre
Superstore
Eden Close
Athlon Industrial Estate
Alperton Sports Ground
Ealing Road
Wadsworth Business Cen
Wadsworth Road
Fleetway Business Park
Sheraton Business Cen
Silicon Business Cen
Tavistock Av
Ealing Central Sports Ground
Welland Gdns
B456
A40
Bideford Av
Crescent
Coniston Avenue
St John Fisher School
Alperton Lane
Nagi Business Centre
Lily Gdns
May Gardens
Pleasant Way
Primrose Way
Manor Farm Rd
W Links
Marsh Road
Stockdove Way
Perivale Lane
Hotel
Ealing Golf Club
Golf Course
River Brent
Brent River Pk Wk
Argyle Road
Gurnell Leisure Centre
B455
East
Gurnell Gv
Avalon Close
Crossway
Downside Crescent
Royle Crs
Lynwood Road
Brunswick Road
Mulgrave Road
Clarendon Rd
Kingsfield Rd
Fowler's Walk
Brentham Way
Neville Rd
Ludlow Road
Denison Rd
Holyoake Walk
Meadvale Road
Selby Road
Barnfield Road
Lindfield Road
Harrow Vw
Curzon Road
Perivale Gdns
Bellevue Rd
Brentcot Cl
Woodbury Pk Rd
Primary School
Pitshanger Lane
Princes Gdns
Queen's Walk
Mount Pleasant
Woodfield Rd
Woodfield Crs
St Gregorys RC Primary School
Ainsdale Rd
Birkdale Road
Scotch Common
Kent Gardens
Castlebar Road
Glencairn Dr
Castlebar Mews
Buckingham Cl
Queen's Gdns
Lanark Close
Mount Avenue
Helena Rd
Montpelier Primary School
Montpelier Road
Montpelier Av
Eaton Rise
St Benedicts School
The Firs
Park Hill
Kings Road
Queen's Rd
Corfton Road
West Croft
Hathaway Primary School
Castlebar Special School
Vallis Way
Fosse Way
Bruton Way
Hathaway Gdns
Claremont Road
Castle Bar Park Station
Harp Road
Greatdown Rd
Copley Close
Templeman Road
Alcott Close
Kent Avenue
Templewood
The Md
The Dene
Victoria Rd
Castlebar Hill
Park
The Knoll
Ealing Abbey Scriptorium
Ealing Abbey
Marchwood Crs
Eaton Rise
Elmcroft Close
Hillcroft
Mount Pk Road
Kings Av
Aston House School
Cleveland Road
Cavendish Avenue
Kingsley Av
Highview Road
Rosemount Rd
Rosebery Gdns
Charles Rd
Hollingbourne Gdns
North Avenue
Sherborne Gdns
High School
Edgehill Rd
St Stephen's Rd
Surg
Colebrooke Av
Egerton Gardens
Bradley Gdns
Avenue House School
Mortimer Road
Amherst Avenue
White Ledges
Charbury Gv
Blakesley Av
Castlebar Road
Durston House School
Haven Green Clnc
Cavendish Special School
Springhallow School
Lynton Av
Ealing Liberal Synagogue
Courtfield Gdns
Argyle Road
Ealing College Upper School
Waldeck Rd
Arlington Road
Albany Road
Sports Ground
Harvington School
Longfield Rd
Haven Gn
Mountfield Rd
Madeley Road
Ealing Broadway Stn
Sports Cen
Homefarm Road
Framfield Road
Dryden Av
Browning Av
Drayton Green Station
Drayton Manor High School
Drayton Br Road
Cowper Road
Shakespeare Road
Milton Road
Allingham Cl
Tennyson Road
Sutherland Rd
Primary School
Drayton Gdns
Drayton Green Road
Manor Av
West Ealing Station
Langham Gardens
Carlton Road
Saint Leonard's Road
W5
W13
W7
Gordon Road
EALING
Arcadia Shopping Centre
Town Hall
Middle School
Ealing Civic Centre
Craven Avenue
Craven Road
Bowling Club
New Broadway
The Broadway
The Mall
Ealing Broadway Centre
Windsor Road
Hastings Road
Fire Station
Police Station
College
UGC
Clifton Lodge Sch
The Questors Theatre
Bond St
High Street
Works
West Ealing Business Centre
Alexandria Road
Felix Road
St Johns Primary School
Mag Ct
Cemetery
West Ealing
Uxbridge Road
Broadway
A4020
Gosai Snooker Club
St Johns Ambulance Station
Gordon House Hlth Cen
Mattock Lane
Pitshanger Manor Mus
Ealing Tertiary College
Telephone Exchange
University
Walpole Park
Ealing Film Studios
Ealing Green
Ealing & Acton Synagogue
Grange Road
Park Pl
The Park
Disraeli Road
Sunnyside Road
Cairn Av
Lammas Pk Gdns
City of Westminster Cemetery
Barchester Cl
Michael Gaynor Cl
Grosvenor Road
Oaklands Primary School
Seward Road
St Kilda Road
Adelaide Road
Thames Valley University
Beaconsfield Rd
Ranelagh Road
Church Place
Church La
Richmond Road
Ascott Avenue
Elm Grove
Melbourne Road
Leighton Road
Hessel Road
Northfield Rd
Glenfield Road
Kingsdown Av
Camborne Av
Carew Rd
Walpole Road
Somerset Rd
Culmington Road
Rathgar Av
Waldemar Av
Churchfield Road
Loveday Rd
Lavington Rd
Regina Road
Sydney Rd
Westfield Road
Seaford Rd
Leeland Terrace
Singapore Road
Shirley Gdns
Broughton Road
Denmark Rd
Arden Rd
Dane Rd
Broomfield Rd
Hartington Road
Chapel Rd
Kitchener Rd
Bedford Rd
Witham Rd
Netheravon Road
Holly Pk Rd
Church Road
Balfour Av
Eccleston Road
Tewkesbury Rd
Endsleigh Rd
Florence Rd
Harriers Cl
Grove Road
Sch
University
Balmain Close
Webster Gdns
Kenilworth Road
Grange Park
Oxford Rd
Westfield Rd
Oak Rd
Spring Br Rd
Hlth Cen
Montague Av
Nightingale Road
Azalea
Oaklands Rd
Croft Gdns
Hillcroft Crs
Woodville Rd
Westbury Road
Ealing Cricket
Sandall

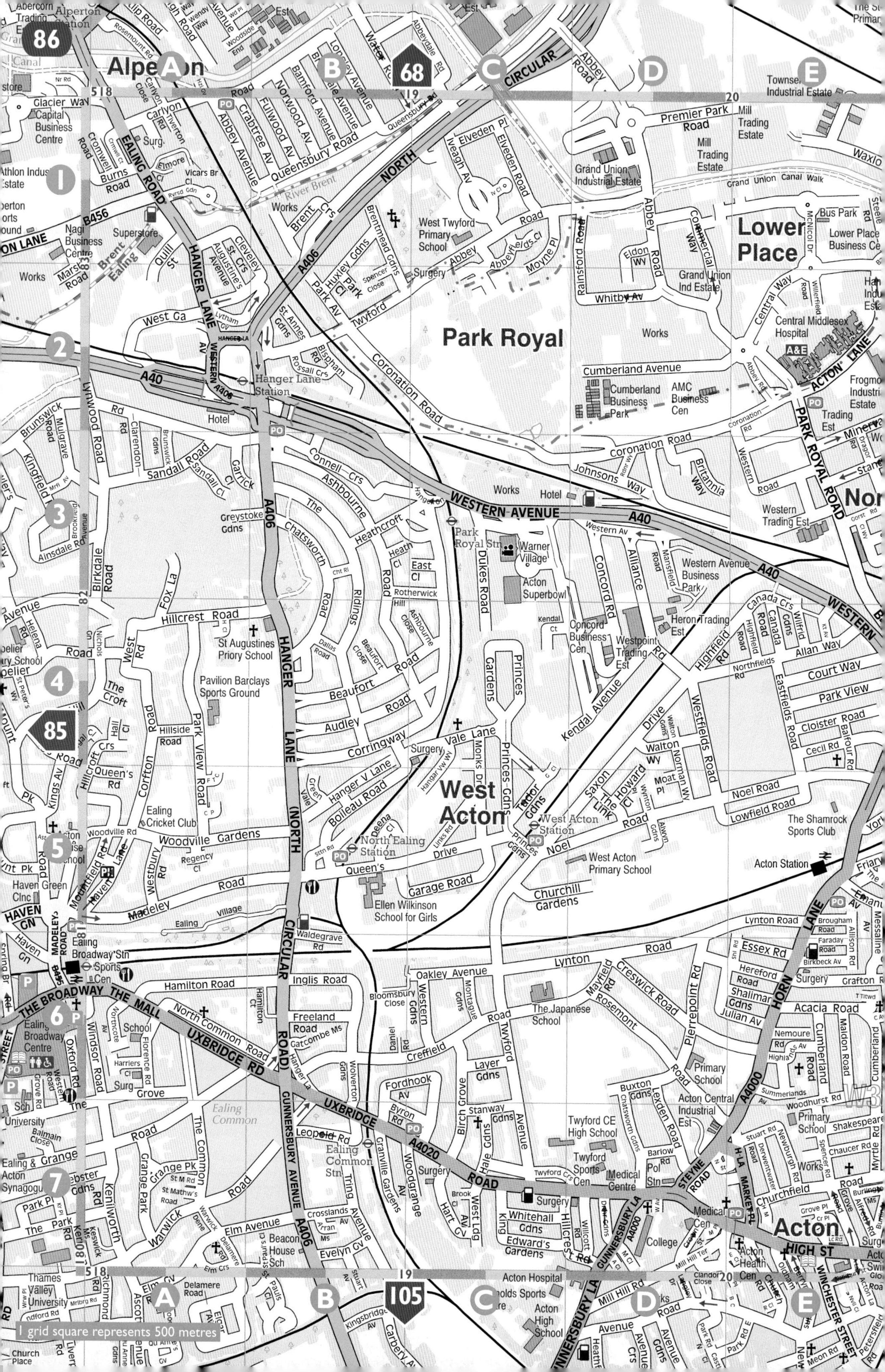

86
68
85
105
Alperton
Alperton Station
Park Royal
West Acton
Acton
Lower Place
Hanger Lane Station
Park Royal Stn
West Acton Station
North Ealing Station
Acton Station
Ealing Broadway Stn
Ealing Common Stn
NORTH CIRCULAR
NORTH CIRCULAR ROAD
HANGER LANE
EALING ROAD
WESTERN AVENUE
A40
A406
A4020
A4000
UXBRIDGE RD
UXBRIDGE ROAD
GUNNERSBURY AVENUE
GUNNERSBURY LA
HORN LANE
HIGH ST
STEYNE ROAD
PARK ROYAL ROAD
ACTON LANE
THE BROADWAY
THE MALL
HAVEN GN
WINCHESTER STREET
Coronation Road
Cumberland Avenue
Abbey Road
Premier Park Road
Queensbury Road
Twyford Abbey Road
Noel Road
Lynton Road
Twyford Avenue
Creswick Road
Pierrepoint Rd
Westfields Road
Queen's Drive
Hillcrest Road
Vale Lane
Woodville Gardens
Madeley Road
Hamilton Road
North Common Road
Elm Avenue
Acacia Road
Churchfield
Central Middlesex Hospital
A&E
St Augustines Priory School
Pavilion Barclays Sports Ground
Ealing Cricket Club
Ellen Wilkinson School for Girls
West Acton Primary School
The Japanese School
Twyford CE High School
Acton Central Industrial Est
Acton Hospital
Acton High School
West Twyford Primary School
Warner Village
Acton Superbowl
The Shamrock Sports Club
Ealing Common
Ealing Broadway Centre
Cumberland Business Park
Grand Union Industrial Estate
Mill Trading Estate
Western Trading Est
Heron Trading Est
Westpoint Trading Est
Concord Business Cen
Western Avenue Business Park
Park Royal
Lower Place Business Cen
Nagi Business Centre
Capital Business Centre
Hotel
Works
Superstore
Grand Union Canal Walk
River Brent
1 grid square represents 500 metres

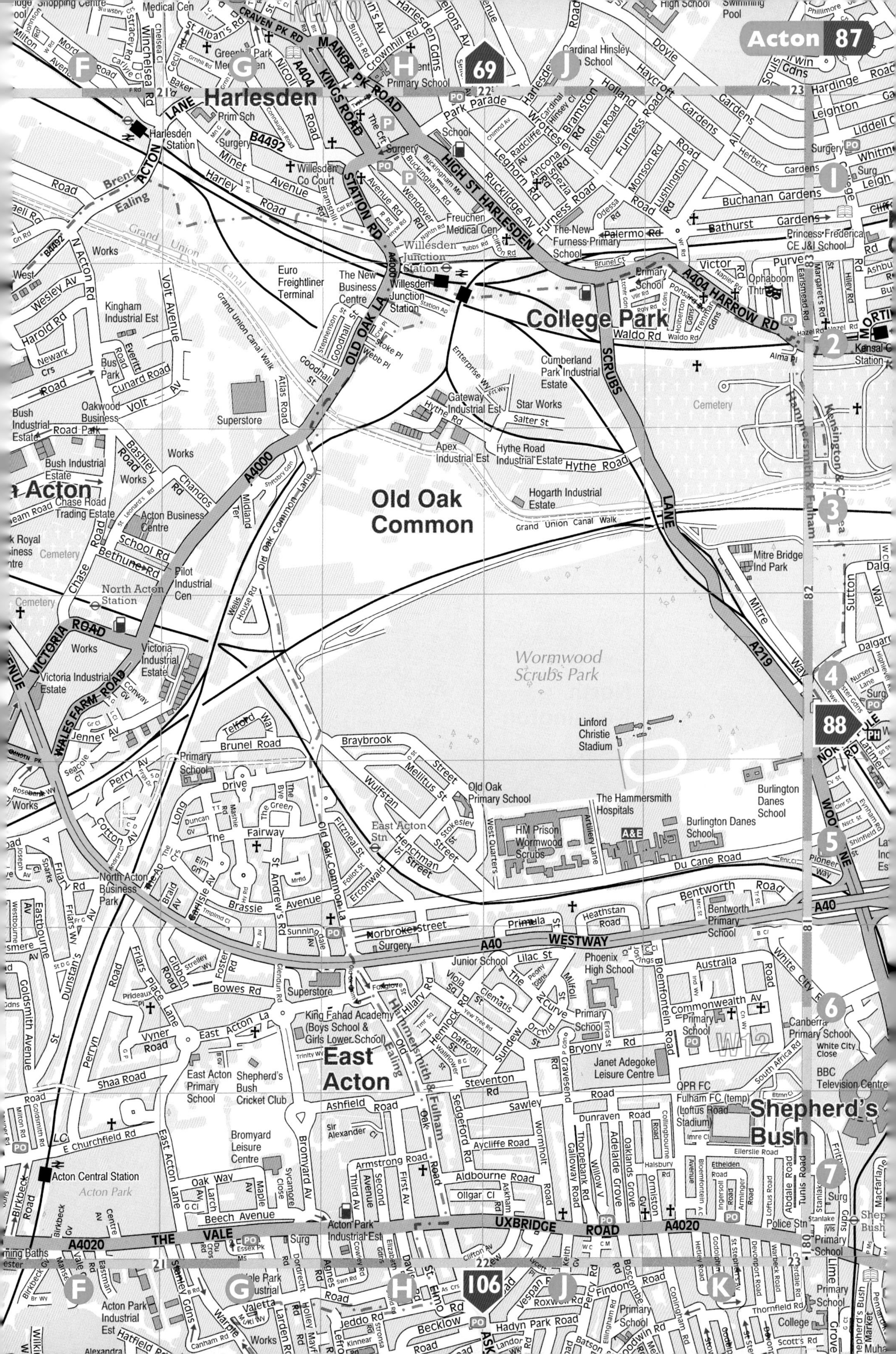

Harlesden
College Park
Old Oak Common
Wormwood Scrubs Park
East Acton
Shepherd's Bush
Acton
Acton Park
Cemetery
Harlesden Station
Willesden Junction Station
North Acton Station
East Acton Stn
Acton Central Station
Kensal Green Station
Euro Freightliner Terminal
Superstore
Linford Christie Stadium
The Hammersmith Hospitals
HM Prison Wormwood Scrubs
Burlington Danes School
Old Oak Primary School
Phoenix High School
Janet Adegoke Leisure Centre
QPR FC Fulham FC (temp) (Loftus Road Stadium)
BBC Television Centre
King Fahad Academy (Boys School & Girls Lower School)
Shepherd's Bush Cricket Club
Bromyard Leisure Centre
East Acton Primary School
Acton Park Industrial Est
Kingham Industrial Est
Bush Industrial Estate
Oakwood Business Park
Acton Business Centre
Chase Road Trading Estate
Pilot Industrial Cen
Victoria Industrial Estate
North Acton Business Park
Gateway Industrial Est
Apex Industrial Est
Hythe Road Industrial Estate
Hogarth Industrial Estate
Star Works
Cumberland Park Industrial Estate
Mitre Bridge Ind Park
Grand Union Canal
Grand Union Canal Walk
A404 HARROW RD
HIGH ST HARLESDEN
OLD OAK LA
SCRUBS LANE
A40 WESTWAY
UXBRIDGE ROAD
A4020 THE VALE
VICTORIA ROAD
WALES FARM ROAD
Du Cane Road
Hythe Road
Bentworth Road
Old Oak Common Lane
East Acton Lane
Hammersmith & Fulham
Ealing
Brent
NW10
W12
69
88
106
F G H J
I 2 3 4 5 6 7
21 22 23

88
70
87
107
A
B
C
D
E
1
2
3
4
5
6
7
Kensal Rise
Kensal Green
Queens Park
Kilburn
West Kilburn
Kensal Town
North Kensington
Westbourne Green
Notting Hill
Shepherd's Bush
W10
W11
W12
HARVIST ROAD
KILBURN LANE
HARROW ROAD
MORTIMER RD
BANISTER ROAD
CHAMBERLAYNE RD
BRONDESBURY ROAD
CARLTON VALE
LADBROKE GROVE
WESTWAY
ST QUINTIN AVENUE
ST MARK'S RD
WOOD LANE
WEST CROSS ROUTE A3220 (A40)
HOLLAND PK AVENUE
UXBRIDGE ROAD
WESTBOURNE PK RD
CHEPSTOW ROAD
PEMBROKE VILLAS
GT WESTERN RD
ELGIN AV
Grand Union Canal Walk
Kensal Rise Station
Kensal Green Station
Queens Park Station
Kilburn Park Stn
Westbourne Park Station
Ladbroke Grove Stn
Latimer Road Station
White City Station
Shepherd's Bush Station
Holland Park Stn
Notting Hill Gate Stn
Mitre Bridge Ind Park
St Charles Hospital
Princess Louise Hosp
BBC Television Centre
Portobello Market
LTR Depot
Holland Park
1 grid square represents 500 metres

Primrose Hill
St John's Wood
St John's Wood Stn
NW8
Maida Vale
Maida Vale Stn
Lisson Grove
Marylebone Station
Regent's Park
London Zoo
Outer Circle
Prince Albert Road
Regent's Canal
London Central Mosque
Winfield House
Boating Lake
Open Air Theatre
Queen Mary's Garden
London Business School
Middlesex CCC (Lord's Cricket Ground)
Lord's Tour & MCC Mus
The Humana Wellington Hosp
Liberal Jewish Synagogue
Spanish & Portuguese Synagogue
Warwick Avenue Stn
Little Venice
Puppet Thtr Barge
PADDINGTON
Paddington Station
St Marys Hosp
Edgware Road Stn
Marylebone Road
Baker Street
Madame Tussauds
Planetarium
Academy of Music
Harrow Road
Harrow Rd Flyover
A40
Westway
Royal Oak Stn
Bishop's Br Rd
Bayswater
Bayswater Stn
Queensway
Queensway Station
Bayswater Road
Lancaster Gate
Lancaster Gate Station
Marble Arch
Marble Arch Stn
Speakers Corner
Hyde Park
Kensington Gardens
W2
Round Pond
The Serpentine
Serpentine Road
Speke's Monument
Peter Pan Statue
Physical Energy Statue
Norwegian/British Monument
Kensington Palace
Emb of Russian Federation
Knightsbridge
Albert Memorial
Alexandra Gate
Prince of Wales Gate
Edinburgh Gate
Albert Gate
Apsley House Wellington Mus
Hyde Park Corner
Park Lane
Edgware Road
Sussex Gdns
Praed Street
Eastbourne Ter
Craven Rd
Gloucester Pl
Portman St
Oxford St
Grosvenor Gate
Brook Gate
Cumberland Gate
Victoria Gate
Marlborough Gate
Black Lion Gate
Clarence Gate
City of Westminster Vehicle Pound
71
90
108
F G H J K
1 2 3 4 5 6 7 8 9
26 27 28
180 181 182 183

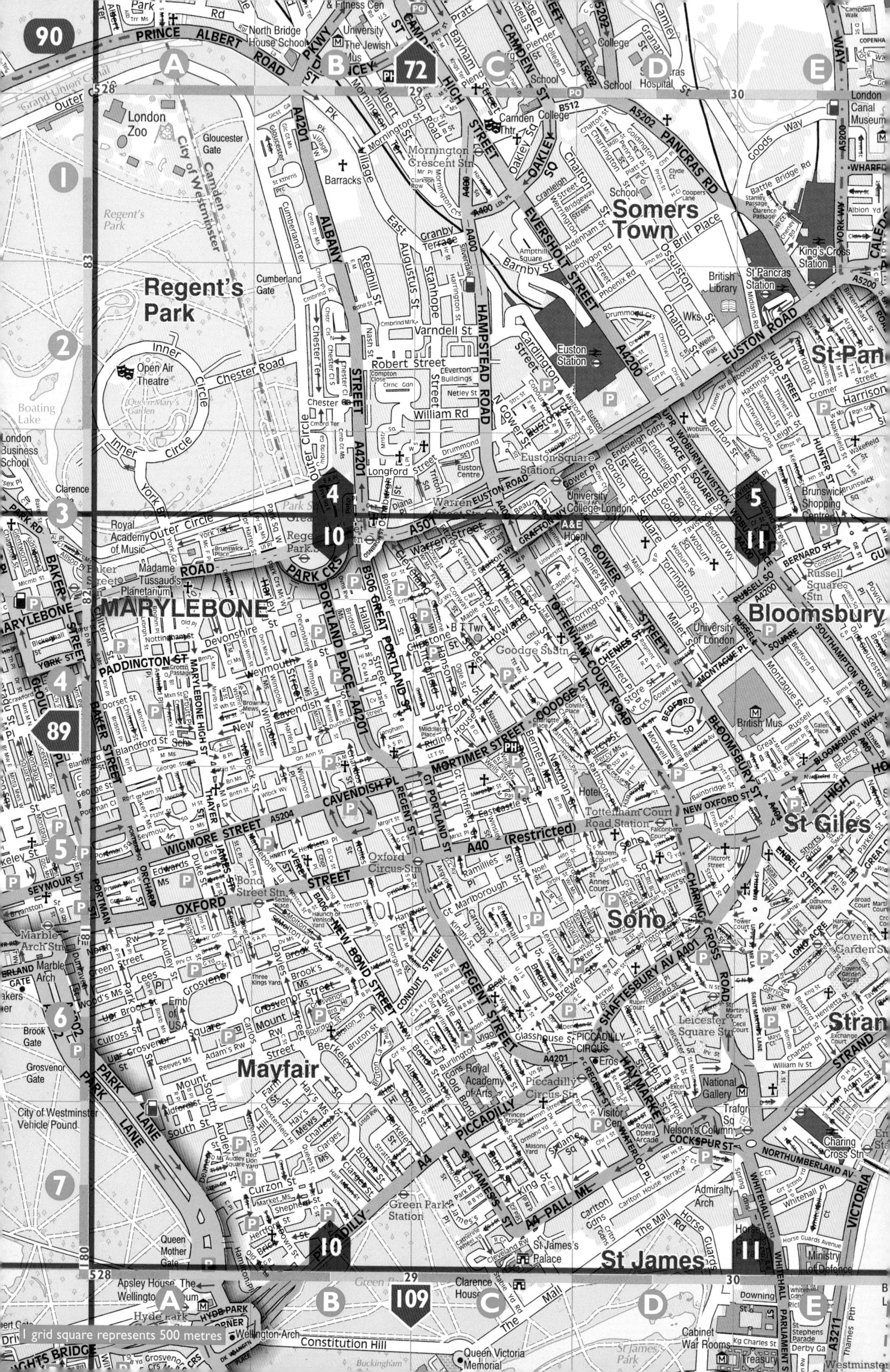

90
72
89
109
4
10
5
11
A
B
C
D
E
1
2
3
4
5
6
7
528
29
30
83
82
81
80
Regent's Park
London Zoo
Open Air Theatre
Queen Mary's Garden
Boating Lake
London Business School
Royal Academy of Music
Madame Tussaud's
Planetarium
MARYLEBONE
Somers Town
Bloomsbury
St Giles
Soho
Mayfair
St James
Strand
Camden Thtr
Mornington Crescent Stn
Euston Station
Euston Square Station
St Pancras Station
King's Cross Station
British Library
University College London
University of London
British Mus
Goodge St Stn
Tottenham Court Road Station
Oxford Circus Stn
Bond Street Stn
Marble Arch Stn
Marble Arch
Green Park Station
Piccadilly Circus Stn
PICCADILLY CIRCUS
Royal Academy of Arts
National Gallery
Leicester Square Stn
Charing Cross Stn
Nelson's Column
Admiralty Arch
Horse Guards
Ministry of Defence
St James's Palace
Clarence House
Apsley House, The Wellington Mus
Hyde Park Corner
Wellington Arch
Queen Victoria Memorial
Queen Mother Gate
Grosvenor Gate
Brook Gate
City of Westminster Vehicle Pound
Cabinet War Rooms
Downing St
London Canal Museum
Barracks
PRINCE ALBERT ROAD
CAMDEN HIGH STREET
HAMPSTEAD ROAD
EVERSHOLT STREET
PANCRAS RD
EUSTON ROAD
ALBANY STREET
PORTLAND PLACE
GREAT PORTLAND ST
TOTTENHAM COURT ROAD
GOWER STREET
BAKER STREET
MARYLEBONE HIGH ST
WIGMORE STREET
OXFORD STREET
REGENT STREET
NEW BOND STREET
PICCADILLY
PARK LANE
SHAFTESBURY AV
CHARING CROSS ROAD
HAYMARKET
PALL MALL
The Mall
WHITEHALL
STRAND
NORTHUMBERLAND AV
VICTORIA
BLOOMSBURY WAY
NEW OXFORD ST
SOUTHAMPTON ROW
Constitution Hill
1 grid square represents 500 metres

City 91
73
92
110
6
12
Pentonville
FINSBURY
Clerkenwell
Hoxton
St Luke's
Holborn
CITY
PENTONVILLE ROAD
CITY ROAD
OLD STREET
CLERKENWELL ROAD
FARRINGDON ROAD
GOSWELL ROAD
ROSEBERY AVENUE
GRAY'S INN ROAD
KING'S CROSS ROAD
THEOBALD'S ROAD
HOLBORN
HOLBORN VIADUCT
NEWGATE ST
LONDON WALL
FLEET ST
ALDWYCH
KINGSWAY
CHANCERY LANE
FETTER LANE
NEW FETTER LA
HATTON GARDEN
LEVER STREET
PERCIVAL STREET
SKINNER ST
CHISWELL ST
FINSBURY PAVEMENT
MOORGATE
BUNHILL ROW
BATH STREET
EAGLE WHF ROAD
SHEPHERDESS WALK
NEW NORTH ROAD
VESTRY STREET
GT EASTERN STREET
VICTORIA EMBANKMENT
UPPER THAMES STREET
QU VICTORIA ST
CANNON ST
CHEAPSIDE
BLACKFRIARS ROAD
SOUTHWARK BRIDGE ROAD
SOUTHWARK STREET
STAMFORD STREET
UNION STREET
KG WILLIAM ST
TOOLEY STREET
LOWER THAMES ST
Angel Stn
Farringdon Stn
Barbican Stn
Moorgate Stn
Old Street Station
Chancery Lane Stn
Holborn Stn
St Paul's Station
City Thameslink Stn
Blackfriars Station
Mansion House Stn
Cannon Street Station
Monument Stn
Bank Stn
London Bridge Stn
Temple Station
Waterloo East Stn
Waterloo Station
Borough Stn
St Paul's Cathedral
Bank of England (& Mus)
The Barbican
City Road Basin
PO Sorting Office
London Weather Centre
Crafts Council
Blackfriars Bridge
Millennium Bridge
Southwark Bridge
London Bridge
Waterloo Bridge
Hungerford Bridge
Tate Modern
Shakespeare's Globe Theatre
Bankside Gallery
Royal Festival Hall
Queen Elizabeth Hall
National Film Theatre
Royal National Theatre
The London Television Centre (LWT)
Oxo Tower Wharf
HMS President
HQS Wellington (Master Mariners)
Somerset House
Courtauld Institute
Kings College London
Gilbert Collection
Cleopatra's Needle
Golden Hinde Educational Museum
Vinopolis City of Wine
Clink St
London Dungeon
Hays Galleria
Guys Hospital
The Monument
Mus of Tea & Coffee
Shell Centre
London Eye
County Hall
Saatchi Gallery
International Rail Terminal
Temple
Smithfield
Central London Markets
Lloyds
Broadgate Ice Arena
Thames Path

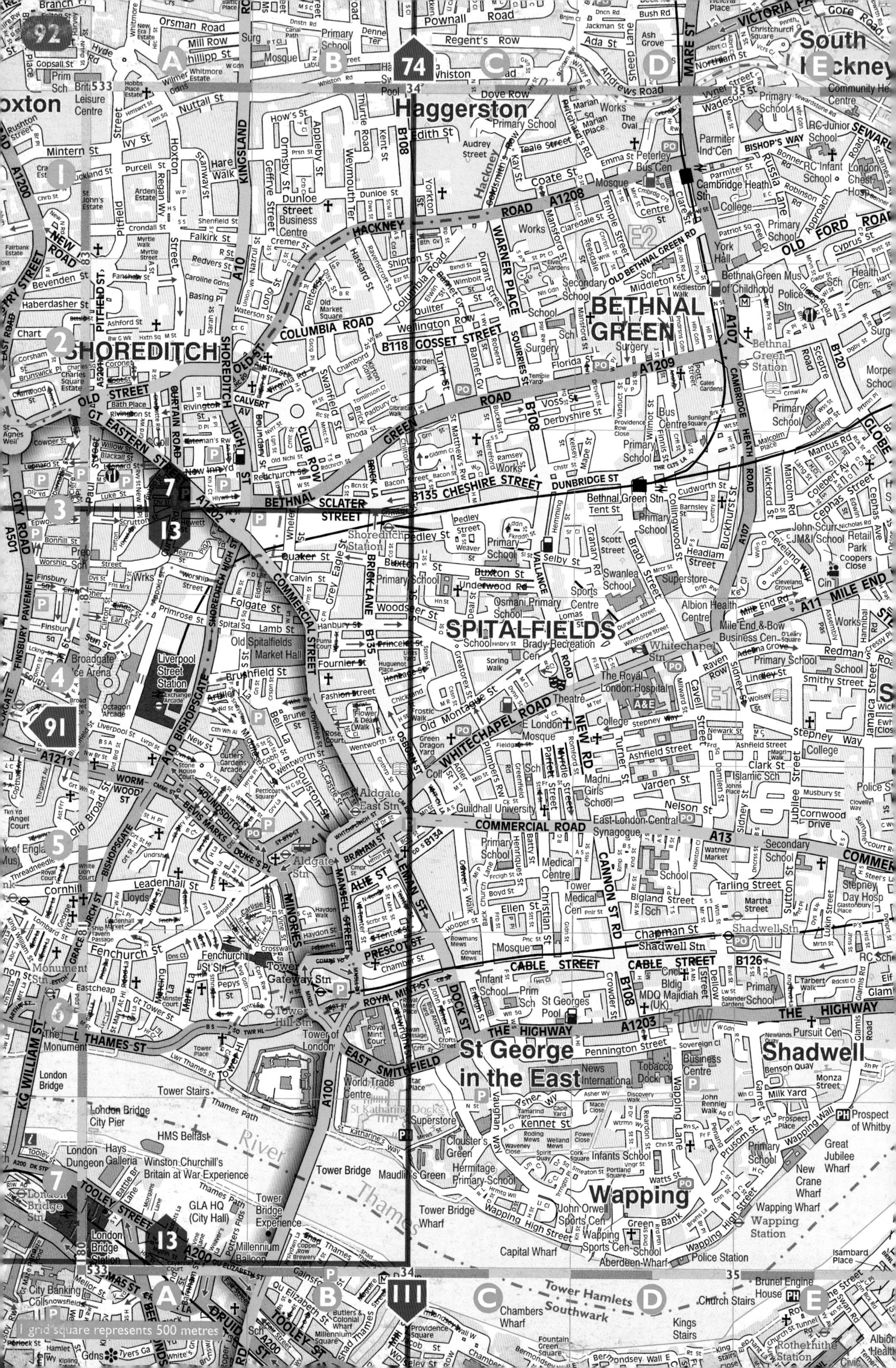
92
74
91
13
7
111
A
B
C
D
E
1
2
3
4
5
6
7
South Hackney
Haggerston
Hoxton
SHOREDITCH
BETHNAL GREEN
SPITALFIELDS
St George in the East
Shadwell
Wapping
River Thames
Tower Hamlets
Southwark
Orsman Road
Mill Row
Regent's Row
Pownall Road
Dove Row
Andrews Road
VICTORIA PARK
Gore Road
MARE ST
Nuttall St
Mintern St
Kingsland
Hackney Road
A1208
Columbia Road
Gosset Street
B118
Warner Place
Old Bethnal Green Rd
Old Ford Road
Bishop's Way
Cambridge Heath Road
A107
Roman Road
A1209
Bethnal Green Road
Old Street
Great Eastern Street
Curtain Road
Shoreditch High St
City Road
A501
Finsbury Pavement
Bethnal Green Stn
Cheshire Street
B135
Dunbridge St
Sclater Street
Commercial Street
Brick Lane
Shoreditch Station
Liverpool Street Station
A10 Bishopsgate
A1202
Folgate St
Old Spitalfields Market Hall
Brushfield St
Fournier St
Fashion Street
Whitechapel Road
Whitechapel Stn
The Royal London Hospital
New Rd
Vallance Road
Mile End Rd
A11 Mile End
Stepney Way
Commercial Road
A13
Cannon St Rd
Cable Street
B126
Aldgate East Stn
Aldgate Stn
Houndsditch
Bevis Marks
Leadenhall St
Lloyds
Fenchurch St
Fenchurch St Stn
Minories
Mansell Street
Leman St
Alie St
Prescot St
Royal Mint St
Dock St
Tower Gateway Stn
Tower Hill Stn
Tower of London
East Smithfield
The Highway
A1203
Lwr Thames St
Thames St
Monument Stn
The Monument
KG William St
London Bridge
Tower Stairs
London Bridge City Pier
HMS Belfast
Hays Galleria
Winston Churchill's Britain at War Experience
Tower Bridge
Tower Bridge Experience
GLA HQ (City Hall)
Tooley Street
A200
London Bridge Station
London Dungeon
St Katharine Docks
Maudlin's Green
Pennington Street
News International
Tobacco Dock
Wapping High Street
Wapping Lane
Wapping Station
Wapping Wall
Prospect of Whitby
Shadwell Stn
Capital Wharf
Aberdeen Wharf
Police Station
Church Stairs
Chambers Wharf
Kings Stairs
Brunel Engine House
Rotherhithe Station
Jamaica Street
Globe Road
Sidney St
Jubilee Street
E1
E2
E1W
Gt Tower St
Eastcheap
Cornhill
Threadneedle St
Old Broad St
Gracechurch St
Broadgate Ice Arena
1 grid square represents 500 metres

Globe Town
BOW
Bromley
Mile End
Bow Common
Limehouse
Ratcliff
POPLAR
Canary Wharf
EPNEY
GROVE ROAD A1205
OLD FORD ROAD
ROMAN ROAD
BOW ROAD
A11
A12
BURDETT ROAD
ST PAUL'S WAY
BEN JONSON ROAD
COMMERCIAL ROAD
A13
EAST INDIA DOCK ROAD
LIMEHOUSE LINK
W INDIA DOCK RD
WESTFERRY RD
WESTFERRY CIRC
SALTER ROAD
Rotherhithe Street
Narrow Street
DEVONS ROAD
NORTHERN
BLACKWALL
COTTON STREET
A1261
Pudding Mill Lane Station
Mile End Stn
Bow Road Stn
Bow Church Stn
Devons Rd Stn
Limehouse Stn
Westferry Stn
Poplar Station
West India Quay Station
Canary Wharf Station
Heron Quays Station
Bromley by Bow Station
Stepney Green Station
Queen Mary & Westfield College
Mile End Hospital
St Clements Hospital
St Andrews Hospital
Mile End Stadium
Cemetery
Tower Hamlets
Southwark
Lower Pool
Shadwell Dock Stairs
Surrey Docks
Museum in Docklands
Canada Square
Billingsgate Fish Market
Half Moon Theatre
Limehouse Town Hall
Ian Mikardo High School
75
94
112
F
G
H
J
K
1
2
3
4
5
6
7
36
37
38
80
81
82
83

94
76
93
113
A
B
C
D
E
1
2
3
4
5
6
7
538
39
40
Mill Meads
Plaistow
South Bromley
Blackwall
River Thames
Dome
Channelsea Business Centre
Three Mills Heritage Centre
Invicta Industrial Estate
Hedges & Butler Estate
Marsh Gate Business Centre
Axis Business Centre
Vanguard Trading Est
Bromley by Bow Station
Ian Mikardo High School
St Andrews Hospital
Gas Works
Barratt Industrial Park
Datapoint Business Cen
Pylon Trading Estate
Blackwall Trading Estate
Culloden Primary School
West Ham Station
Canning Town Station
East India Station
Blackwall Station
Poplar Station
All Saints Stn
Plaistow Station
Royal Victoria Station
North Greenwich Station
East London RUFC
East London Crematorium
East London Cemetery
Memorial Recreation Ground
Ranelagh Primary School
Grange Infant School
St Helens RC Primary School
Comprehensive School
Community School
Community College
St Luke's Health Cen
Royal Victoria Docks Watersports Centre
Mace Gateway
Greenshields Industrial Est
Minerva Works
Billingsgate Fish Market
Poplar Business Park
Financial Times
Tunnel Avenue Trading Est
Pumping Station
Portway Primary School
MANOR ROAD
STEPHENSON STREET
BARKING ROAD
NEWHAM WAY A13
SILVERTOWN WAY
LOWER LEA CROSSING
EAST INDIA DOCK ROAD
ABBOTT ROAD
NORTHERN APPROACH
BLACKWALL TUNNEL
COTTON STREET
ASPEN WAY
PRESTON'S ROAD
HIGH STREET
NEW PLAISTOW RD
PLAISTOW ROAD
Tower Hamlets
Greenwich
Newham
1 grid square represents 500 metres

Upton Park
Upton Park Station
Upton Cross Primary School
West Ham United FC (Upton Park)
77
Queen's Road West
Barking Road
A124
Lister Community School
Southern Rd Primary School
Plaistow Hosp
Nightingale Clinic
Newham Medical Centre
Cinema
Central Pk Road
B167
East Ham
Central Park
East Ham Leisure Cen
College
High Street
A117
Rancliffe Rd B167
Greengate St
E13
University of East London
Greengate Medical Cen
Tunmarsh Lane
Humberstone Road
Newham General Hospital
A&E
Lonsdale Avenue
East Ham Jewish Cemetery
Synagogue
Brampton Primary School
Roman Road Primary School
Brampton Manor School
Kingford Community School
Prince Regent Lane
A112
Newham Sixth Form College
Tollgate Primary School
Terence McMillan Stadium
Newham Leisure Centre
Newham Way
A13
East Ham Industrial Est
Beckton Ski Centre
E6
Woolwich Manor Way
Canning Town Recreation Ground
Rosetta Primary School
Beckton Special School
Scott Wilkie Primary School
West Becton Health Cen
King George V Park
Beckton Globe
Beckton
East Beckton District Centre
Superstore
Health Centre
Beckton District Park
New Beckton Park
Winsor Primary School
Royal Docks Medical Cen
96
Custom House
Custom House for ExCeL Station
Prince Regent Station
Royal Albert Station
Beckton Park Station
Royal Albert Way
A1020
Victoria Dock Rd
Strait Road
ExCeL Exhibition Centre
Western Gateway
Royal Victoria Dock
E16
Royal Albert Dock
Connaught Br
London City Airport
Hartmann Road
Drew Primary School
St Marks Industrial Estate
North Woolwich Road
Albert Rd
Silvertown & City Airport Stn
Thameside Ind Est
Thames Road
Primary School
Factory Road
Standard Industrial Estate
114
Silvertown
Works
F
G
H
J
K
1
2
3
4
5
6
7
41
42
43

96
78
95
115
A
B
C
D
E
1
2
3
4
5
6
7
Wallend
Creekm
NORTH CIRCULAR ROAD
A406
A124
A13
NEWHAM WAY
ALFRED'S WAY
EAST HAM-AN
A1020
ROYAL DOCKS ROAD
WOOLWICH MNR WAY
A117
WOOLWICH MANOR WAY
ROYAL ALBERT WAY
ROYAL ALBERT RD
ALBERT ROAD
SOUTH STREET
E6
ST PAULS RD
Sussex Road
Langdon School
St Michaels RC Primary School
Abbey Park Industrial Est
The Orchard Health Cen
New England Industrial Est
Abbey Wharf Industrial Estate
Showcase Newham Cinema
River Road Business Park
Katella Trading Est
Cromwell Business Cen
Lyon Business Pa
Jenkins Lane
Eric Clarke Lane
Beckton Triangle Retail Park
Superstore
Gateway Retail Park
East Ham Nature Reserve
Beckton Ski Centre
Eastbury Road
Alpine Way
Alpine Bus Cen
GX Superbowl
The London Ind Estate
London Ind Park
Roding Road
Beckton Station
East Beckton District Centre
Cygnet Clinic Beckton
Gallions Primary School
Winsor Primary School
Royal Docks Medical Cen
New Beckton Park
Gallions Reach Station
Armada Way
Cyprus Station
University of East London Campus
University Way
Gallions Road
Royal Albert Dock
King George V Dock
Storey Primary School
North Woolwich Station
Gallions Reach
Newham
Greenwich
Margaret or Tripcock Ness
Barking Creek
Works
1 grid square represents 500 metres

Castle Green
Barking Ind Park
Goresbrook
Sports Centre
79
A13
Altmore Way Industrial Est
BARKING BY-PASS
IG11
Renwick Industrial Estate
Steel Ap
Renwick Road
Box Lane
Scrattons Ter
Julia Gardens
Shaw Av
Levine Gdns
Morrison Rd
Works
Crescent
Sugden Way
Wivenhoe Road
Maybury Road
Roxwell Road
Crouch Av
Abridge Way
Charlton
Maud Gdns
Roycraft Avenue
Avenue
Bastable Avenue
Thames View Clinic
Thames View Junior & Infant School
Stanley Avenue
Curzon Crs
Glenmore Wy
Endeavour Wy
Alderman Av
Havering Way
Stern Close
Keel Close
Choats Road
Blessing Way
Wanderer Drive
Sovereign Road
Gt Galley Close
Skillion Business Park
Riverside Industrial Est
Twine Cl
Estuary Cl
Thames Road
Radford Way
Crossness Road
Gallions Cl
Bankside Park Industrial Est
Marine Dr
Anchor Cl
Galleons Drive
Mallards Rd
Marine Drive
Atlantis Cl
Buzzard Creek Industrial Est
Creek Road
Creekmouth Industrial Park
Long Reach Road
Works
Trafalgar Business Centre
Anglian Industrial Estate
Balmoral Trading Estate
River Road
Buzzard Creek Industrial Estate
Atcost Road
Works
Barking and Dagenham
Newham
River Thames
Barking and Dagenham
Bexley
98
Cross Ness
Barking Reach
Barking and Dagenham
Greenwich
Bexley
Greenwich
St Andrews Cl
Fairway Drive
Riverside Golf Club
Voyagers Cl
Thamesbank Place
Copperfield Rd
Watersmeet Way
Castilion Primary School
Nickelby Cl
Crossway
Manordene Road
Summerton Way
Cherbury Close
Longworth Cl
Golf Course
Greenhaven Drive
Greenhaven Dr
Thamesmead Leisure Centre
Primary School
Superstore
Thamesmere Dr
Thamesmead Shopping Centre
Superstore
CENTRAL WAY
Bishop John Robinson CE Primary
Kingfisher Close
Walsham Cl
Wroxham Rd
Courtland Gv
Fleming Way
Goldcrest Close
Crossway
Kinder Cl
Glendale Way
Crowden Way
Howden Cl
Haldane Road
Wallace Cl
Titmuss Avenue
Police Station
CARLYLE ROAD
Saunders Way
Attlee Rd
Blyth Rd
Hawksmoor Primary School
Booth Close
Applegarth Rd
Arnott Cl
Byron Cl
Owen Cl
Poplar Pl
Jubilee Primary School
Green Chain Walk
EASTERN WAY
Belvedere Road
Thamesmead
Waldstock Rd
Hutchins Road
Dean Rd
A2041
Woolwich Polytechnic School
SE28
Hampstead Cl
Bentham Road
Epstein Rd
Austen Close
Primary School
Disraeli Cl
Newmarsh Rd
Grasshaven Way
Silver Birch Cl
Birchdene Dr
Pitfield Crs
Roman Sq
Sorrel Cl
Courtauld Cl
Sunset Road
Lakeside Av
Chervil Mews
Celandine Dr
Southwood Rd
Cole Cl
Shaw Close
St Margaret Clitherow RC Primary
Sewell Road
HARROW MNR WAY
Harrow Mnr Wy
Marathon Wy
Sunset Road
EASTERN WAY
J16
116
Works
Binsley Wk
Tavy Clinic
Hartslock Drive
Seacourt Road
Southlake
Green Chain Wk
St Edmunds Cl
Saint Brides Close
St Katherines
St Helens
46
47
48
83
82
81
80
F
G
H
J
K
2
3
4
5
6
7

98
80
97
117
A
B
C
D
E
1
2
3
4
5
6
7
548
49
50
83
82
81
80
Goresbrook
Sports Centre
Warner Village Cinema
Starmans Close
Burdetts Road
St Peters RC Primary School
Surgery
Marsh Green Road
South Close
North Close
Whitebarn Lane
Review Road
B178
Crosby Road
Oval Road North
Beam Avenue
Oval Rd North
Centre Road
Second Avenue
First Avenue
Third Av
Oval Rd South
Oval Rd S
Beam Primary School
Ripple Road
Rd
Scrattons Ter
Julia Gardens
Levine Gdns
Morrison Rd
Shaw Av
Merrielands Retail Park
Merrielands Crs
Polesworth Rd
Chequers Lane
Marsh Green School
Dagenham Superbowl
A1306
New Road
Link Road
E Entrance
Sierra Drive
Sierra Dr
Works
RM9
Dagenham Dock Station
LC
A13
Avenue
Kent Avenue
Ford Industrial Park
Thames Avenue
Breach Lane
Power Station
Choats Road
Hindmans Way
Lake Road
Lake Rd
Courier
Thames Av
Fiesta Drive
Industrial Estate
Hindmans Way
Thunderer Road
Hornchurch Marshes
River Thames
Halfway Reach
St Andrews
Fairway Drive
Riverside Golf Club
Summerton Way
Cherbury Close
Longworth Cl
Golf Course
Courtland Gv
Fleming Way
Chadwick
Bayliss Av
Wallace Cl
Eastern Way
A2016
Road
Norman Road
Norman Rd
Capital Industrial Est
Crabtree Manorway North
Fisher's Way
Erith Marshes
Thamesmead
East
Manorway
Anderson Way
Jenningtree Way
Mulberry
1 grid square represents 500 metres

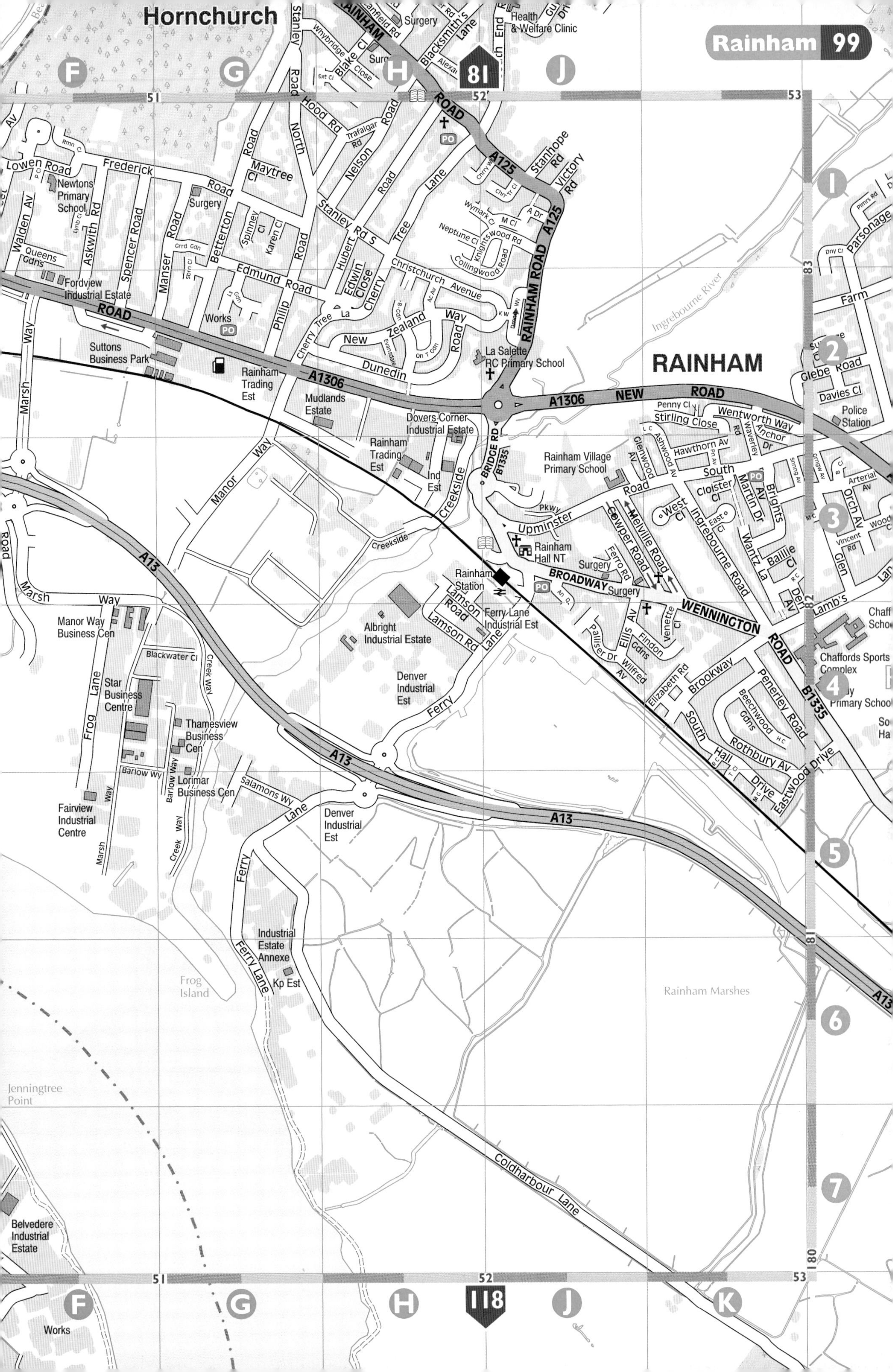
Hornchurch
RAINHAM
Rainham Marshes
Frog Island
Jenningtree Point
Ingrebourne River
RAINHAM ROAD
A125
A1306
NEW ROAD
A13
B1335
BRIDGE RD
BROADWAY
WENNINGTON ROAD
Upminster Road
Frederick Road
Edmund Road
Lowen Road
Walden Av
Askwith Rd
Spencer Road
Manser Road
Betterton Road
Maytree Cl
Philip Road
North Road
Stanley Road
Hood Rd
Nelson Road
Trafalgar Rd
Stanley Rd S
Hubert Rd
Edwin Close
Cherry Tree Lane
Christchurch Avenue
New Zealand Way
Dunedin Rd
Stanhope Rd
Victory Rd
Neptune Cl
Knightswood Rd
Collingwood Road
Blacksmith's Lane
Whybridge Cl
Blake Cl
Queens Gdns
Newtons Primary School
Fordview Industrial Estate
Suttons Business Park
Rainham Trading Est
Mudlands Estate
Dovers Corner Industrial Estate
Ind Est
Creekside
Manor Way
Marsh Way
Marsh Road
Manor Way Business Cen
Blackwater Cl
Creek Way
Frog Lane
Star Business Centre
Thamesview Business Cen
Barlow Way
Lorimar Business Cen
Salamons Wy
Fairview Industrial Centre
Ferry Lane
Denver Industrial Est
Albright Industrial Estate
Lamson Road
Ferry Lane Industrial Est
Rainham Station
Rainham Hall NT
Industrial Estate Annexe
Kp Est
Coldharbour Lane
Belvedere Industrial Estate
Works
La Salette RC Primary School
Rainham Village Primary School
Surgery
Health & Welfare Clinic
Penny Cl
Stirling Close
Wentworth Way
Anchor Dr
Hawthorn Av
Glenwood Av
Ashwood Av
Waverley Rd
West Cl
Cloister Cl
East Cl
Martin Dr
Brights Av
Wantz La
Ingrebourne Road
Cowper Road
Melville Road
Ferro Rd
Baillie Cl
Dern Av
Ellis Av
Findon Gdns
Venette Cl
Palliser Dr
Wilfred Av
Elizabeth Rd
Brookway
South Hall Drive
Penerley Road
Beechwood Gdns
Rothbury Av
Eastwood Drive
Lamb's La
Glebe Road
Davies Cl
Police Station
Parsonage
Farm
Arterial Av
Orch Av
Vincent Rd
Glen
Chafford Sports Complex
Primary School
F G H J K
1 2 3 4 5 6 7
51 52 53
83 82 81 180
81
118

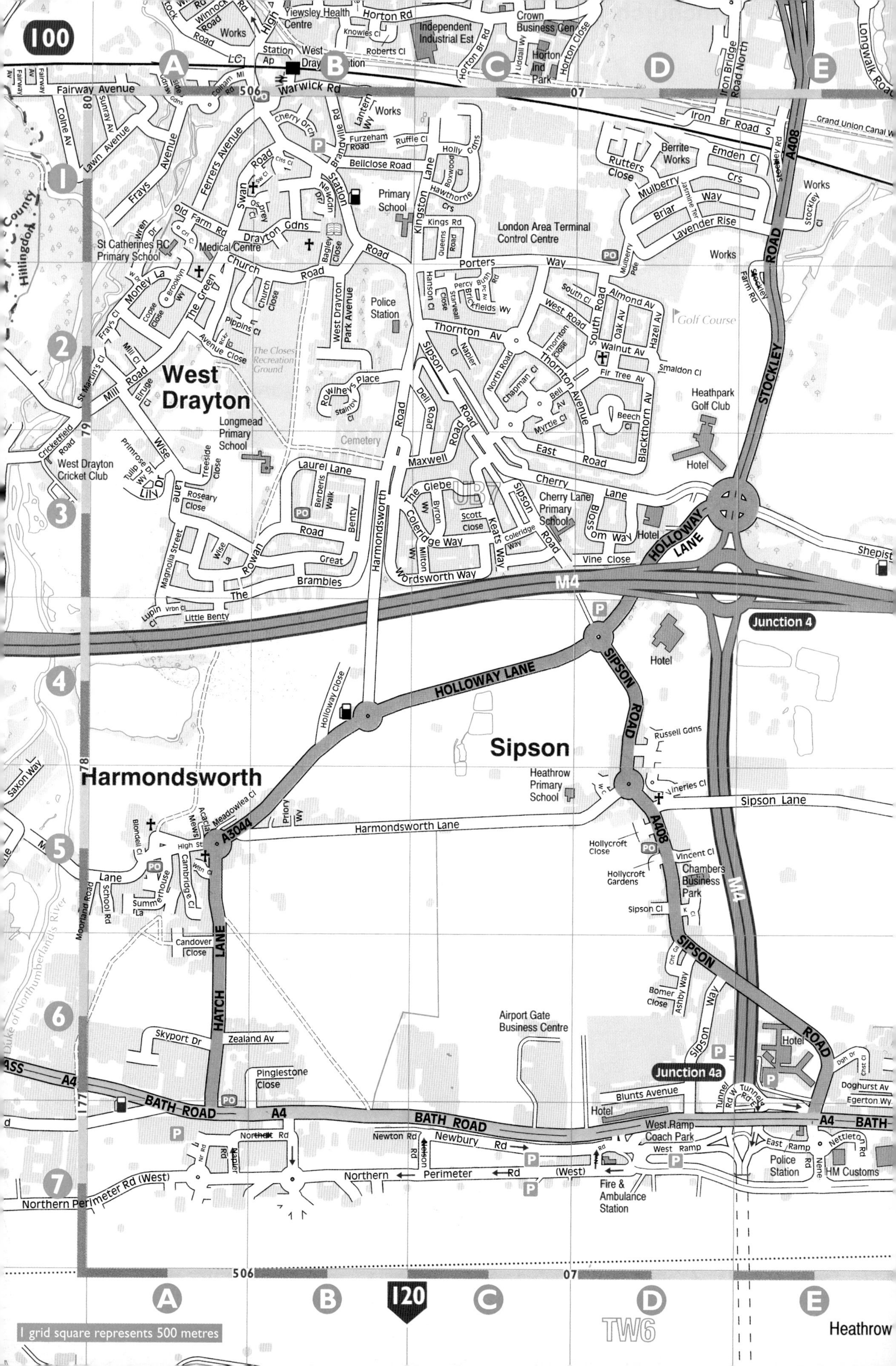
100
West Drayton
Harmondsworth
Sipson
Yiewsley Health Centre
Horton Rd
Independent Industrial Est
Crown Business Cen
Horton Ind Park
Horton Close
Iron Bridge Road North
Longwalk Road
Station Ap
West Drayton
Fairway Avenue
Warwick Rd
Grand Union Canal Walk
Iron Br Road S
Colne Av
Lawn Avenue
Frays Avenue
Ferrers Avenue
Swan Road
Cherry Orch
Brandville Road
Furzeham Road
Ruffle Cl
Bellclose Road
Holly Gdns
Boxwood Cl
Hawthorne Crs
Kingston Lane
Station Road
Primary School
London Area Terminal Control Centre
Berrite Works
Emden Cl
Rutters Close
Mulberry Crs
Briar Way
Lavender Rise
Works
Stockley Cl
County Hillingdon
Old Farm Rd
Drayton Gdns
St Catherines RC Primary School
Medical Centre
Church Road
Money La
The Green
Church Close
Bagley Close
West Drayton Park Avenue
Police Station
Porters Way
Kings Rd
Hanson Cl
Brickfields Wy
Thornton Av
South Road
Almond Av
Oak Av
Hazel Av
Golf Course
Walnut Av
Fir Tree Av
Smaldon Cl
Heathpark Golf Club
Hotel
Pippins Cl
Avenue Close
The Closes Recreation Ground
Frays Cl
Mill Cl
Mill Road
Elruge Cl
St Martin's Cl
Rowlheys Place
Stainby Cl
Sipson Road
Dell Road
Napier Cl
North Road
Chapman Cl
Bell Av
Myrtle Cl
Thornton Avenue
Beech Cl
Blackthorn Av
East Road
Longmead Primary School
Cemetery
Cricketfield Road
West Drayton Cricket Club
Primrose Dr
Tulip Wy
Lily Dr
Wise Lane
Treeside Close
Laurel Lane
Berberis Walk
Maxwell Road
The Glebe
Byron Wy
Cherry Lane
Cherry Lane Primary School
Blossom Way
Holloway Lane
UB7
Roseary Close
Benty
Scott Close
Keats Way
Coleridge Way
Vine Close
Magnolia Street
Wise La
Rowan Road
Great Brambles
The Brambles
Harmondsworth Road
Milton Wy
Wordsworth Way
Shepiston
M4
Lupin Cl
Little Benty
Junction 4
Holloway Close
HOLLOWAY LANE
SIPSON ROAD
Russell Gdns
Heathrow Primary School
Vineries Cl
Sipson Lane
Saxon Way
Meadowlea Cl
Acacia Mews
A3044
Priory Wy
Harmondsworth Lane
A408
Hollycroft Close
Hollycroft Gardens
Vincent Cl
Chambers Business Park
Sipson Cl
Blondell Cl
High St
Cambridge Cl
Lane
School Rd
Summerhouse La
Moorland Road
Duke of Northumberland's River
Candover Close
HATCH LANE
Bomer Close
Ashby Way
Sipson Way
Airport Gate Business Centre
Skyport Dr
Zealand Av
Junction 4a
ROAD
Doghurst Av
Egerton Wy
Pinglestone Close
Blunts Avenue
A4
BATH ROAD
West Ramp Coach Park
Tunnel Rd W
Tunnel Rd E
Northolt Rd
Newton Rd
Newbury Rd
Nelson Rd
East Ramp
Nettleton Rd
Police Station
HM Customs
Nene Rd
Northern Perimeter Rd (West)
Fire & Ambulance Station
Heathrow
TW6
A
B
C
D
E
1
2
3
4
5
6
7
506
07
120
1 grid square represents 500 metres

Stockley Park Business Centre
Roundwood Av
Furze Ground Way
The Square
Stroke Way
A437
Rostrever Gardens
82
Lannock Road
Hayes Pool
Central Avenue
Rec Gnd
Silverdale Industrial
Birchway
Temple
Caxton Trading Est
Warnford Industrial Est
Swallowfield Wy
Speedway Industrial Est
Rigby Lane
Works
Aberglen Industrial Est
Betam Rd
Kestrel Way
Adler Ind Est
Crown Trading Cen
Clayton Road
Printinghouse Lane
Primary School
Anselms Road
Nield Road
Botwell La
Crown Close
Mount Rd
Pump Lane
Fairdale Gdns
Silverdale
Hunters Grove
East Walk
Pump Lane Industrial Est
Trading Est
Provident Ind Est
Chailey Industrial Est
Superstore
Silverdale Industrial Est
Regent Business Cen
Peter James Business Cen
Halls Business Cen
Fairview Industrial Est
Frogmore Industrial Est
Blyth Rd
Station Rd
Cranford Park Primary School
Works
Johnsons Industrial Estate
Trinity Trading Est
A437 DAWLEY ROAD
UB3
Hayes & Harlington Station
Denbigh Dr
Stormount Dr
Snowdon Crs
Conway Drive
Clevedon Gdns
Burnham Gdns
Marlow Gdns
Windsor Gdns
Guinness Cl
Bourne Avenue
Keith Road
N HYDE RD
Grand Union Canal Wk
Gardens
North Hyde
Glamis Crs
Waltham Avenue
Colbrook Av
Millington Rd
Millington Road
Albert Rd
Station Road
Viveash Cl
Squirrels Trading Est
Nestle's Avenue
Bulls Bridge
Superstore
Bullsbridge Industrial Estate
Skipton Drive
Carnarvon Drive
Seaton Road
Mildred Avenue
Wentworth Crs
Elers Clinic
Ross Cl
Elers Road
Dawley Road
Woodhouse Cl
Redmead Rd
STATION ROAD
Northfield Pk
Fairey Av
A437
Hyde Way
Dallas Ter
Harold Av
Gordon Crs
Monmouth Road
Crowland Avenue
A312 NORTH HYDE RD
Pinkwell Lane
Pinkwell Avenue
Harlington Community School
Pinkwell Primary School
Copthorne Ms
Bushey Rd
Station Rd
Gardens
Crane Gdns
Granville Road
Wyre Gv
Blair Cl
Laburnum Rd
Coronation Rd
Watersplash Lane
A312
Oakington Avenue
Repton Avenue
Clement Gdns
Bedwell Gdns
Woolacombe Wy
Lundy Dr
Croyde Avenue
Cranford Drive
Phelps Way
Cranford Park Junior School
Carlton Av
Bedwell
Cleave Avenue
Savoy Av
St Dunstans Cl
Carfax Rd
Hillborne Cl
Road
Hillingdon Trail
Hotel
Fuller Wy
Moston Cl
Wilkins Close
Roseville
M4
Junction 3
St Pauls Cl
St Peters Wy
HARLINGTON
Heathrow Medical Centre
STREET
HIGH
Gravel Works
102
Church
The Hartlands
Imperial College Athletic Ground
William Byrd School
Victoria Lane
Hudson Road
Bletchmore Cl
Brickfield La
Kiln Cl
Pmbry Ct
Richards Cl
Hillingdon
Hounslow
Cranford Park
Cranford Community College
Sipson Lane
Shortlands
Cranford Lane
Manse Close
Harlington
Manor La
Gilbin Ct
Works
THE
Fleld Cl
The Crescent
West End Lane
Cranford Lane
Quinton Close
The Cedars Primary School
Raywood Close
Tasker Cl
Croft Cl
New Road
Pennine Wy
Pennine Wy
Little Elms
Acorn Gv
Saunton Av
Pendell Av
Langley Crs
Cranford
Browngraves Road
Brendon Cl
Cheviot
Hall La
HIGH ST HARLINGTON
Marlborough Rd
Oxford Av
Eton Road
Sheepcote Cl
Hawthorn Dr
Bolton's La
Mondial Way
Hotel
Heath Close
David Cl
Caroline Pl
Nobel Dr
Winchester Road
Malvern Road
Windsor Park Rd
Craneswater
Park Lane
Cole Gdns
The Avenue
Firs Dr
Royston Cl
Hotel
Triumph Cl
Hotel
Hotel
ROAD
BATH ROAD
A4
Norwood Crs
World Business Cen Heathrow
Newall Road
Hatton Rd North
Northrop Road
Cranford Lane
Dudset Lane
Wave Av
Sandown Cl
Berkeley Avenue
BAA Heathrow Visitor Centre
Northern Perimeter Rd
Northern Perimeter Road
Surgery
Wave Avenue
Meadowbank Gdns
Clevedon Gardens
Burnham West Gdns
08
09
10
F
G
H
J
K
I
2
3
4
5
6
7
121
Esher Crs
Business Park
Byron Avenue
Chaucer Avenue
Airport
Cranfor

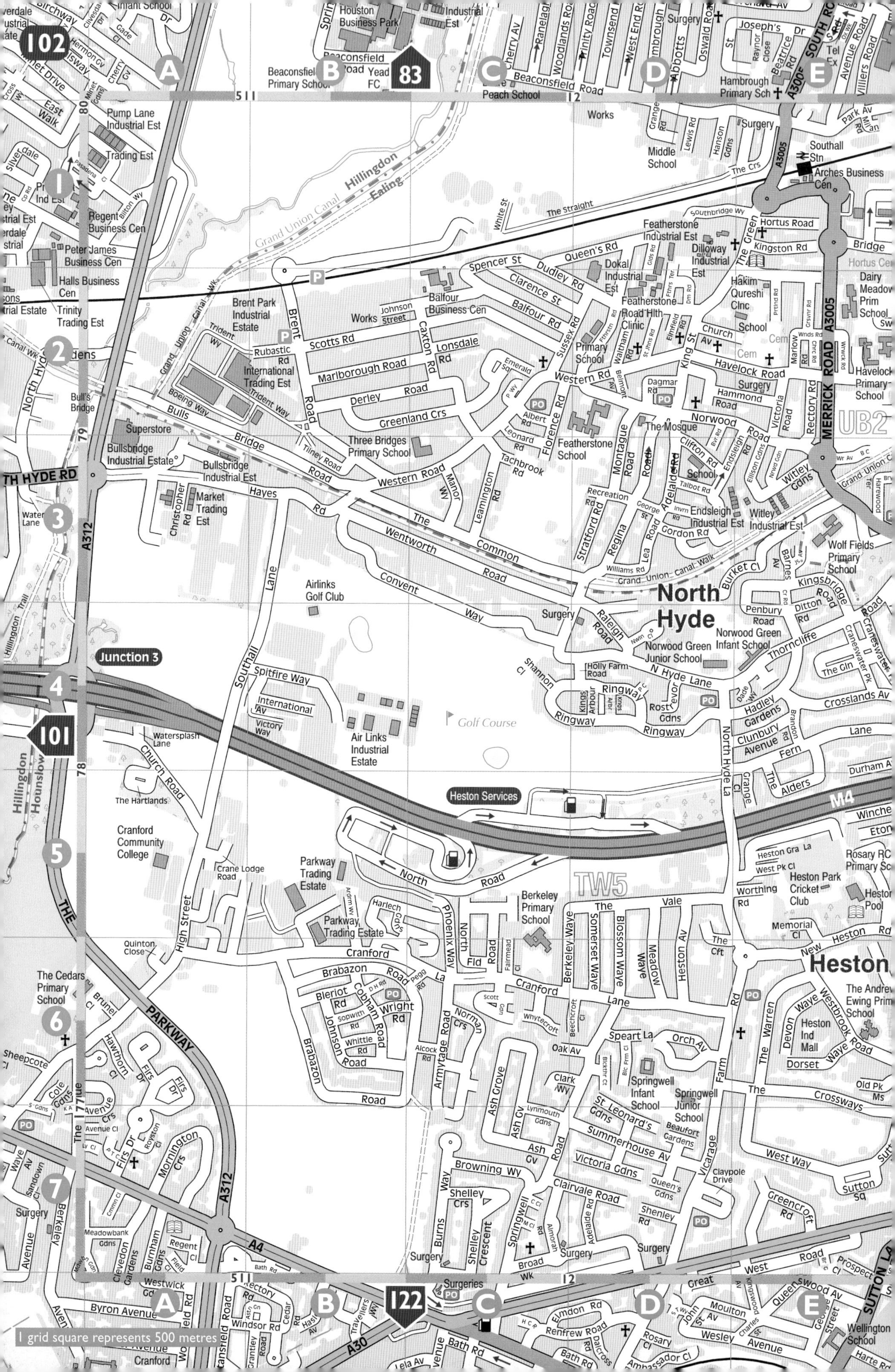

102
83
101
122
A
B
C
D
E
1
2
3
4
5
6
7
511
12
80
79
78
77
Birchway
Infant School
Hermon Gv
Cherry Gv
Minet Gdns
Minet Drive
East Walk
Silverdale
Pump Lane Industrial Est
Trading Est
Pasadena Cl
Bilton Wy
Ind Est
Regent Business Cen
Peter James Business Cen
Halls Business Cen
Trinity Trading Est
Houston Business Park
Industrial Est
Beaconsfield Road
Beaconsfield Primary School
Yeading FC
Peach School
Beaconsfield Road
Woodlands Road
Ranelagh Rd
Trinity Road
Townsend Rd
West End Rd
Abbotts
Oswald Road
Surgery
Joseph's Dr
Raynor Close
Beatrice Rd
Hambrough Primary Sch
SOUTH RD
A3005
Avenue Road
Villiers Road
Tel Ex
Park Av
Milan
Works
Grange Rd
Lewis Rd
Hanson Gdns
Middle School
The Crs
Southall Stn
Arches Business Cen
Hillingdon
Ealing
Grand Union Canal
White St
The Straight
Southbridge Wy
Hortus Road
Kingston Rd
Bridge
Featherstone Industrial Est
Dilloway Industrial Est
The Green
Queen's Rd
Dudley Rd
Spencer St
Clarence St
Dokal Industrial Est
Featherstone Road Hlth Clinic
Hakim Qureshi Clnc
School
Balfour Rd
Balfour Business Cen
Johnson Street
Works
Brent Park Industrial Estate
Brent Road
Scotts Rd
Caxton Rd
Lonsdale Rd
Rubastic Rd
Trident Wy
International Trading Est
Trident Way
Marlborough Road
Derley Road
Greenland Crs
Emerald Sq
Sussex Rd
Primary School
Western Rd
Church Av
Havelock Road
Cem
Marlow Av
Merrick Road
A3005
Havelock Primary School
Dairy Meadow Prim School
Dagmar Rd
Hammond Road
Surgery
Victoria Road
Rectory Rd
UB2
Albert Rd
Leonard Rd
Florence Rd
Featherstone School
The Mosque
Norwood Road
Clifton Rd
Endsleigh Rd
Ellison Gdns
Witley Gdns
Grand Union Canal
Bull's Bridge
Boeing Way
Bulls Bridge Road
Superstore
Bullsbridge Industrial Estate
Bullsbridge Industrial Est
Tilney Road
Three Bridges Primary School
Western Road
Manor Wy
Leamington Rd
Tachbrook Rd
Montague Road
Lea Road
Adelaide Rd
School
Talbot Rd
Endsleigh Industrial Est
Witley Industrial Est
NORTH HYDE RD
A312
North Hyde Gdns
Water Lane
Christopher Rd
Market Trading Est
Hayes Rd
The Common
Wentworth Road
Recreation Rd
Stratford Rd
Regina Rd
George St
Gordon Rd
Williams Rd
Grand Union Canal Walk
Wolf Fields Primary School
Burket Cl
Barnes Av
Kingsbridge Road
Southall Lane
Airlinks Golf Club
Convent Way
Surgery
Raleigh Road
North Hyde
Nwin Cl
Norwood Green Junior School
Norwood Green Infant School
Penbury Road
Ditton Rd
Thorncliffe
Craneswater Pk
The Gln
Hillingdon Trail
Junction 3
Shannon Cl
Holly Farm Road
N Hyde Lane
Ringway
Kings Arbour
Rost Gdns
Trevor
Dade Wy
Hadley Gardens
Crosslands Av
Clunbury Avenue
Brandon Rd
Lane
Fern
Durham Av
Spitfire Way
International Av
Victory Way
Air Links Industrial Estate
Golf Course
Watersplash Lane
Church Road
The Hartlands
Hillingdon
Hounslow
North Hyde La
Grange Cl
The Alders
Heston Services
M4
Cranford Community College
Crane Lodge Road
High Street
Parkway Trading Estate
North Road
Heston Gra La
West Pk Cl
Rosary RC Primary Sc
Heston Park Cricket Club
Worthing Rd
Heston Pool
TW5
Berkeley Primary School
Harlech Gdns
Phoenix Way
North Fld Road
Fairmead Cl
Berkeley Wave
The Somerset Wave
Blossom Wave
Meadow Wave
Vale
Heston Av
The Cft
Memorial Cl
New Heston Rd
Heston
Quinton Close
Cranford
Brabazon Road
Pegg Rd
Cranford Lane
The Cedars Primary School
Brunel Cl
Bleriot Rd
Cobham Road
Wright Rd
Sopwith Rd
Whittle Rd
Johnson Road
Brabazon Road
Armytage Road
Alcock Rd
Norman Crs
Scott Gdn
Whytecroft
Beechcroft Cl
Speart La
Orch Av
Oak Av
Clark Wy
Springwell Infant School
Springwell Junior School
Farm Rd
The Warren
Devon Waye
Westbrook Road
Heston Ind Mall
Dorset Waye
The Andrew Ewing Prim School
Old Pk Ms
The Crossways
THE PARKWAY
Sheepcote
Hawthorn Dr
Firs Dr
Cole Gdns
Avenue Crs
Avenue Cl
Royston Cl
Firs Dr
Mornington Crs
Ash Grove
Ash Gv
Lynmouth Gdns
Ash Gv
Ash Road
St Leonard's Gdns
Summerhouse Av
Beaufort Gardens
Victoria Gdns
Queen's Gdns
Vicarage
Claypole Drive
West Way
Sutton Sq
Greencroft Rd
Browning Wy
Shelley Crs
Shelley Crescent
Burns Way
Springwell Rd
Clairvale Road
Almorah Rd
Adelaide Rd
Shenley Rd
Wayside Av
Sandown Cl
Surgery
Berkeley Avenue
The Avenue
Meadowbank Gdns
Clevedon Gardens
Burnham Gdns
Regent Cl
Field
A312
A4
Bath Rd
Surgery
Surgery
Surgery
Broad Wk
Surgeries
Great West Road
Prospect
SUTTON LA
Westwick Gdns
Byron Avenue
Rectory Rd
Windsor Rd
Cedar Rd
Travellers Wy
A30
Renfrew Road
Dalcross Rd
Bath Rd
Rosary Cl
Ambassador Cl
Moulton Av
Wesley Avenue
Queenswood Av
Charles St
George Street
Wellington School
Harte Rd
Cranford
1 grid square represents 500 metres

Heston 103
84
104
123
Southall Park
Villiers High School
Knowsley Avenue
Argyll Av
Park
Avenue
Morland Gdns
Windmill Business Centre
Windmill Lane
A4020
Works
Brentvale Av
Blackmore Av
Iron Br Cl
Alexander Cl
Ellis Road
Jessamine Road
A3002
A&E
Ealing Hospital
Chaucer Clinic
Navigator Drive
Chevy Rd
Great Western Industrial Park
Dean Way
Armstrong Way
Three Bridges Business Centre
Middlesex Business Cen
Grand Union Canal Walk
Glade Lane
The Bridge Business Cen
Quaker La
Hillary Rd
Wylie Rd
Gregory Rd
Waterside
Hunt Rd
Havelock Road
Cookham Cl
Baxter Cl
Cayley Rd
Post
McNair Rd
Trubshaw Rd
Works
Poplar Av
Tentelow Lane
A4127
Wolsey Cl
Osterley RFC
Three Bridges Primary School
Melbury Avenue
Shaftesbury Avenue
Stour Av
Minterne Av
Sherborne Av
Dorset Av
Norwood Green
Wimborne Av
Cranborne Avenue
Manston Av
St Marys Av
Norwood Gn Rd
Norwood Road
St Marys Av
The Lawn
Boundary Cl
Green Wk
Osterley Lane
Windmill Lane
The Aviary
Ealing
Hounslow
River Brent
St Marks Primary School
Green Lane
Bishop's Rd
St Mark's Road
St Dunstan's Road
Rosebank Road
St Margaret's Road
Osterley Vw Rd
Studley Grange Rd
Humes Avenue
Billetts Hart
Belvedere
Trumpers Way
Lambourn Cl
Works
Montague Rd
The Waterside Trading Cen
Grand Union Canal Wk
Boston Business Park
River Brent Business Park
Golf Course
Wyke Green Golf Club
Syon Lane
B454
Osterley Lane
Osterley Park House
Osterley Park
Osterley
Jersey Road
Ashley Dr
Wood Lane
Grasshoppers RFC
Crowntree Close
Stags Wy
Braybourne Dr
Lingwood Gardens
Ridgeway Road North
Hotel
Great W Rd
Great West Road
Brunel University (Osterley Campus) Track
Brunel University
Borough Rd
Osterley Crs
Highfield Rd
College Road
Musgrave Rd
Crown Court
Ferraro Cl
Biscoe Cl
Wheatlands
Old Cote Drive
Heston Junior School
Heston Community Sports Hall
Heston Infant School
Heston Community School
Church Road
Eldon Av
Hogarth Gdns
Sonia Gardens
Sutton Hall Rd
Sark Cl
Guernsey Cl
Heston Road
Herm Close
Jersey Road
Bassett Gdns
Thistleworth Cl
Bassett Gardens
Thornbury Road
St Mary's Crs
Osterley Av
Osterley Station
Alderney Avenue
Pevensey Cl
Penwerris Av
Stucley Rd
Lulworth Av
Surgery
Lime Tree Rd
Jersey Rd
Thornbury Av
Campion House College
Church Rd
Isleworth & Syon School for Boys
Ridgeway
Osterley Rd
Deborah Cl
Spring Grove
Kilberry Close
Oakley Cl
Aplin Way
More House School
The Harvard Rd
Grove Rd
Naseby Cl
Ashton House Sch
Sutton Road
Camborne Wy
Channel Cl
Upr Sutton La
Hotel
Great W Rd
North Dene
Berwyn Av
Lampton Av
Lampton School
Harris Cl
Sutton Dene
Neville Cl
Lampton Road
Brookwood Rd
Brackendale Cl
Spring Gv Crs
Surgery
Lampton
Gresham Road
Palmerston Rd
Taylor Cl
Spring Grove
Farnell Hse Medical Centre
Addison Av
Spencer Rd
Burlington Rd
Eversley Crs
Vincent Rd
Witham Rd
Road B363
West Thames College
Grove Rd
Avenue
Works
Surgery
Kingsley Av
Taunton Av
Worton Gdns
Drive
Primary School
Thornbury Rd
Clifton Rd
London Road
Metro Industrial Centre
Crawford Cl
Sidmouth
Isleworth Sta
Loring Rd
Newton
Castle
B363
Civic Centre
Avonwick Rd
Ellesworth Av
Denbigh Rd
Sunnycroft Rd
Alexandra
Primary
Hounslow
F
G
H
J
K
I
2
3
4
5
6
7
14
15

104
85
103
124
A
B
C
D
E
1
2
3
4
5
6
7
UXBRIDGE ROAD
BOSTON ROAD
A3002
BOSTON MANOR ROAD
NORTHFIELD AVENUE
B452
B4491 LITTLE EALING LANE
SOUTH EALING RD
B455
EALING ROAD
WINDMILL ROAD
WINDMILL LANE
SYON LANE
B454
SYON LA
SPUR ROAD
A310
LONDON ROAD
A315
A4
M4
HALF ACRE
POPE'S
Great W Rd
St Johns Ambulance Station
Ealing Film Studios
University
Acton Synagogue
Walpole Park
City of Westminster Cemetery
Oaklands Primary School
Elthorne Park High School
Elthorne Sports Centre
Boston Business Park
River Brent Business Park
River Brent
Fielding Primary School
Northfields Station
Boston Manor Station
South Ealing Stn
Grange Primary School
Thames Valley University
Primary School
Ealing Park Health Cen
Laurel Clinic
King Fahad Academy (Girls Upper School)
Gunnersbury Catholic School
Reynard Mills Trading Estate
Our Lady of St Johns
Burden Close
Golf Course
Wyke Green Golf Club
Centaurs RFC
Centaurs Business Cen
Centaurs Business Centre
Grasshoppers RFC
Superstore
Hotel
Great West Trading Estate
Brentford End
Rock Works
Brentford Business Cen
Brentford Stn
BRENTFORD
TW8
Brook Lane Bus Cen
Health Cen
Brentford School for Girls
St Paul's CE Primary School
Brentford County Court
Police Station
Pump Alley
Brentford Medical Cen
Catherine Wheel Rd
Brentwaters Business Park
Butterfly House
Syon House
River Thames
Thames Path
Syon Lane Station
The Green School for Girls
Marlborough Primary School
Syon Park School
Brunel University (Osterley Campus) Track
Brunel University
Crown Court
West Thames College
TW7
Metro Industrial Centre
Isleworth Station
Smallberry Green Primary School
Isleworth Town Primary School
A&E
Middlesex University
Hounslow
Richmond upon Thames
1 grid square represents 500 metres

Brentford 105
86
106
125
F
G
H
J
K
19
20
I
2
3
4
5
6
7
Acton
HIGH ST
Acton Swimming Baths
Acton Health Cen
Medical Cen
Churchfield Road
Acton Hospital
Reynolds Sports Centre
Acton High School
GUNNERSBURY LA
Mill Hill Rd
Works
Avenue Road
Beacon House Sch
Elm Avenue
Crosslands Av
Evelyn Gv
Whitehall Gdns
Edward Gardens
Surgery
Kingsbridge Av
Carbery Av
Tudor Wy
Gunnersbury Gdns
Gunnersbury Crs
Lillian Av
A4000 GUNNERSBURY AVENUE
Acton Town Station
Heathfield Rd
Enfield Rd
Berrymede Junior Sch
Infant Sch
Osborne Rd
Bollo Br Rd
Roslin Rd
Rowley Ind Park
Stirling Rd
Stanley Road
South Acton Stn
Bollo La
WINCHESTER STREET
ACTON LANE
Petersfield
Bollo Br
All Saints
Ramsay Rd
Fletcher Rd
Beaumont Road
Bridgman Rd
Kent Road
Church Path
Antrobus
Rothschild Rd
Cunnington St
Weston Rd
Ivy Crs
Bell Industrial Est
Chiswick Park Station
Ealing Hounslow
BEACONSFIELD RD
Kingscote Rd
B491
Acton Lane Medical Cen
Graham Rd
Somerset Road
Berrymede
Baronsmede
Old Actonians Sports Club
B4491
LANE
Elm Gv
Delamere Road
Elgar Av
Ascott Avenue
Richmond
Elderberry Road
Willow Rd
Rowan Rd
Avenue
Aspen Cl
Beech Gdns
Ash Grove
Almond
Berry Wy
Grove
The Ridgeway
Park Drive
Princes Avenue
A406
Gunnersbury Park Museum
Gunnersbury Park
Lionel Road
Sterling Place
Claypond Hospital
Carville Crs
Crowther Av
North Road
Lionel Road Primary School
Junction 2
Junction 1
International School of London
Cemetery
Manor Gdns
GUNNERSBURY AVE
Park Pl
Works
Power Rd
Power Road
Thorney Hedge Rd
Silver Crs
Chiswick Business Park
Chiswick Road
Superstore
Essex Rd
Essex Pl
A315 CHISWICK HIGH RD
CHISWICK HIGH ROAD
Works
Marlborough Rd
Arlington Gdns
Sutton La
A3000
HEATHFIELD TER
Gunnersbury Station
WELLESLEY RD
Grange Road
Surgery
Walpole Gdns
W4
Capital Int Way
Brentford Fountain Leisure Centre
Works
Lionel Rd South
Kew Bridge Station
WELLESLEY RD
Stile Hall Gardens
Oxford Rd South
Regent St
Chiswick Village
Harvard Rd
Grosvenor Rd
Sutton Lane
Heathfield Gdns
Barrowgate Road
A4
GREAT WEST RD
Wolseley Gdns
Elmwood Road
Court
Green Dragon Lane
Burford Rd
Green Dragon School
Kew Bridge Steam Museum
Works
KEW BR RD
The Musical Museum
A315
North Road
Netley Rd
Pottery
The Church School
Watermans Arts, Cinema & Theatre Centre
The Brentford Clinic
Thames Pth
Spring Gv
Waldeck Road
Strand-On-The-Green
Kew Bridge
Infant School
Thames
Magnolia Rd
Herbert Gdns
Ernest Gdns
Loraine Rd
Whitehall Pk Rd
St Mary's Gv
Gordon Rd
Burnaby Gdns
Falconberg
Hazeldene Rd
Compton Crs
Primary School
Thomas'
Sutton
Staveley
Chatsworth
Chesterfield
Eastbourne Rd
Garth Road
Park
KEW ROAD
A205
Ferry La
Bush Rd
Bushwood Road
Priory Road
Kew Gn
Kew Green
Kew Palace
Broad
Queen Charlotte's Cottage
Maze Rd
Forest Rd
Gloucester Rd
Princess of Wales Conservatory
Queens CE Primary School
Surgery
Royal Botanic Gardens Kew School
Kew
Palm House
Kew Gardens (Royal Botanic Gardens)
Thames Path
Kew Coll
Leyborne Park
MORTLAKE ROAD
Public Record Office Museum
Defoe Avenue
Ruskin Av
River Thames
Grove Park Rd
Grove Park Ter
Grove Pk Gdns
Hartington Road
Grove Pk Rd
Kinnaird Av
Devonshire Gdns
Bolton Road
Spencer Road
Lawford Rd
Crofton Av
Chrysanthemum Clnc
Burlington
Chiswick Station
Wilmington Av
Surg
Coniston Cl
Chiswick Village
Cavendish Road
University of Westminster
A316
Ibis La
Thames Path
Bessant Dr
Kew Retail Park
Kew Meadow Pth
Marlborough Trading Estate
Melliss Ave
Whitcombe Ms
Broomfield Rd
Broomfield House Sch
Surgery
Lichfield Rd
Princes Rd
Lindley Pl
Layton Pl
Station Pde
Kew Gardens Stn
Burlington Av
Beechwood Avenue
West Pk Rd
High Pk Rd
Brick Farm Cl
W Hall Rd
A205
Unicorn School
Branstone Rd
Elizabeth Cottages
Clarence Rd
Victoria Cottages
Hatherley Rd
ROAD
Nylands Av
Pensford Avenue
Evolution House
Temperate House
Lawn Crs
The Avenue
Enderdale
Eversfield Rd
Alexandra Rd
Atwood
Pavilion
North Sheen
Mortlake Crematorium
Townmead Rd
Chiswick Bridge
SW14
18

106
87
105
126
A
B
C
D
E
1
2
3
4
5
6
7
Acton Central Station
Acton Park
THE VALE
UXBRIDGE ROAD
A4020
Acton Swimming Baths
Vale Park Industrial
Acton Park Industrial Est
Alexandra Road
Southfield First & Middle Sch
Cobbold Primary School
Primary School
Bedford Park
ACTON LANE
B491 SOUTHFIELD ROAD
B491 THE AVENUE
BATH ROAD
B409 SOUTH PDE
Acton Green
Tabard Thtr
Turnham Green Stn
STAMFORD BROOK RD
GOLDHAWK RD
A402
Queen Charlottes & Chelsea Hosp
Ravenscourt Square
John Betts Primary School
W6
Stamford Clinic
Stamford Brook Stn
Ravenscourt Park Stn
PADDENSWICK RD
Goldhawk Industrial Estate
Brackenbury Health Cen
Flora Gardens Primary School
GLENTHORNE RD
The Craven Clinic
KING STREET
A315
CHISWICK
CHISWICK HIGH ROAD
A316 CHISWICK LANE
Airedale Physiotherapy Clnc
UGC Cinema
Town Hall
GREAT W ROAD
HEATHFIELD TER
A3000
Superstore
Swan Bus Cen
Pol Stn
GREAT WEST RD ELLESMERE RD GT W RD HOGARTH LA
GREAT WEST ROAD CHISWICK A4
Hogarth's House
Hogarth Business Park
BURLINGTON LANE
Chiswick House
Thames Path
Hounslow
Richmond upon Thames
Hammersmith & Fulham
St Pauls Preparatory School
Swedish School
Hammersmith Bridge
B350
FERRY ROAD
CASTELNAU
A306
SW13
Harrodian School
LONSDALE
Lowther Prim Sch
Barnes Sports Club
London Wetland Centre
BARNES
Queen Elizabeth Walk
St Osmunds RC Primary School
CHURCH ROAD
Police Station
Barnes Bridge
Barnes Bridge Station
Barn Elms
Chiswick Station
Chrysanthemum Clnc
Chiswick Community School
Cavendish Primary School
New Chiswick Pool
GREAT CHERTSEY ROAD
A316
Fuller Smith & Turner Sports Club
United Services Sports Ground
Grove Park
SW14
Duke's Meadows
University of West...
Old Barnes
1 grid square represents 500 metres

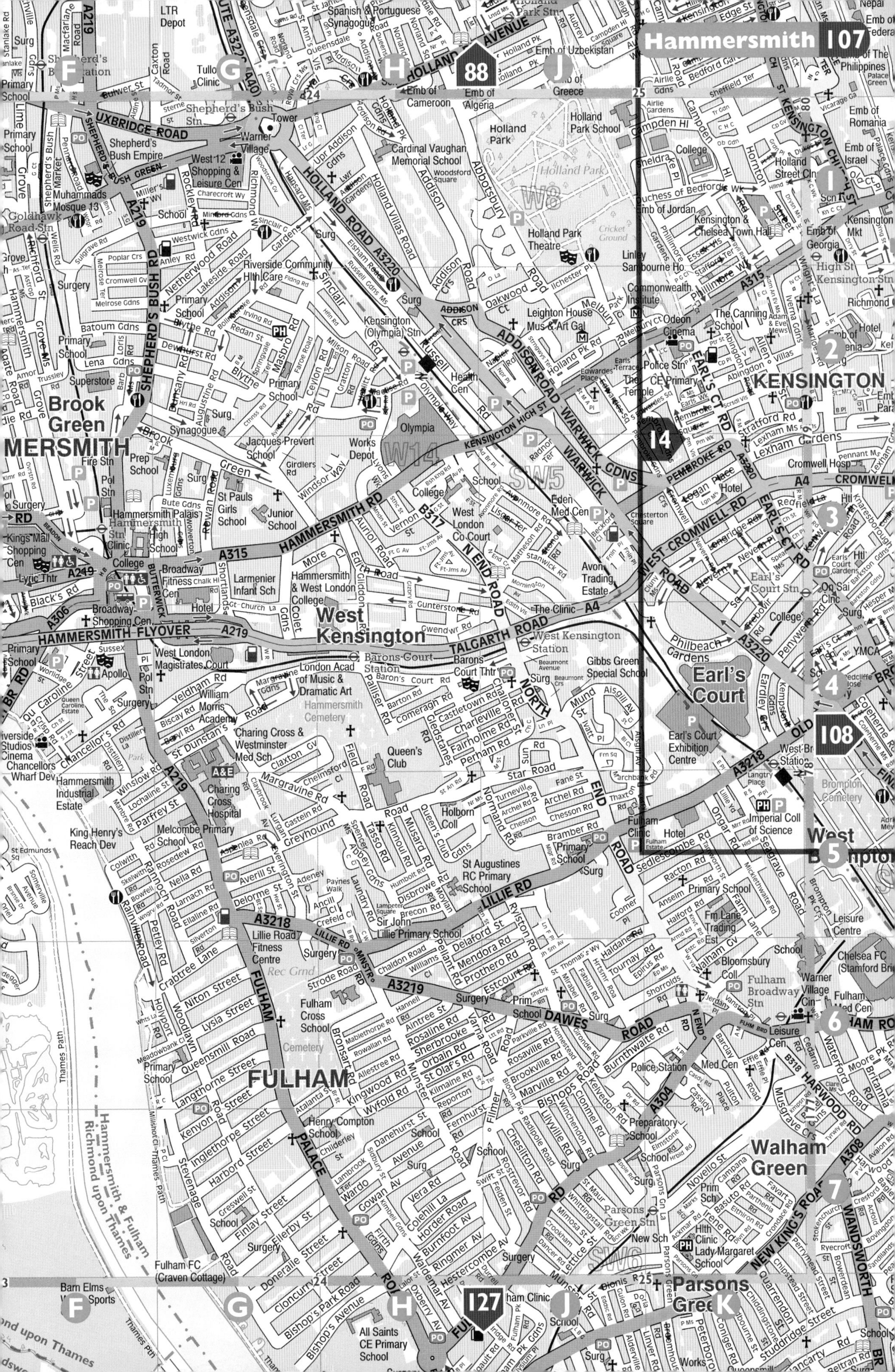
Hammersmith 107
88
108
127
14
F
G
H
J
I
K
2
3
4
5
6
7
24
25
LTR Depot
Spanish & Portuguese Synagogue
Shepherd's Bush Stn
Tullo Clinic
Emb of Uzbekistan
Emb of Greece
Emb of Cameroon
Emb of Algeria
Holland Park
Holland Park School
Holland Park Theatre
Cricket Ground
W8
Cardinal Vaughan Memorial School
Woodsford Square
UXBRIDGE ROAD
HOLLAND ROAD A3220
HOLLAND PARK AVENUE
SHEPHERD'S BUSH RD
SHEPHERD'S BUSH GREEN
Shepherd's Bush Empire
Shepherd's Bush Market
Muhammads Mosque 13
Goldhawk Road Stn
Warner Village
Tower
West 12 Shopping & Leisure Cen
Riverside Community Hlth Care
Kensington (Olympia) Stn
Olympia
Olympia Way
W14
SW5
Works Depot
Jacques Prevert School
Leighton House Mus & Art Gal
Commonwealth Institute
Linley Sambourne Ho
Kensington & Chelsea Town Hall
Emb of Jordan
Emb of Georgia
High St Kensington Stn
Emb of Romania
Emb of Israel
Emb of the Philippines
Kensington Mkt
KENSINGTON
KENSINGTON HIGH ST
ADDISON ROAD
WARWICK GDNS
EARL'S CT RD
PEMBROKE RD
WEST CROMWELL RD
CROMWELL
Cromwell Hosp
Earl's Court Stn
Earl's Court
Earl's Court Exhibition Centre
West Brompton Station
Brompton Cemetery
Imperial Coll of Science
Brook Green
HAMMERSMITH
Hammersmith Stn
Hammersmith Palais
Kings Mall Shopping Cen
Lyric Thtr
Broadway Shopping Cen
HAMMERSMITH FLYOVER
HAMMERSMITH RD
A315
A4
A219
A306
TALGARTH ROAD
West Kensington
West Kensington Station
Barons Court Station
Barons Court Thtr
London Acad of Music & Dramatic Art
Hammersmith Cemetery
Queen's Club
Charing Cross Hospital
Charing Cross & Westminster Med Sch
West London Magistrates Court
Hammersmith & West London College
Riverside Studios Cinema
Chancellors Wharf Dev
Hammersmith Industrial Estate
King Henry's Reach Dev
Gibbs Green Special School
Avon Trading Estate
N END ROAD
NORTH END ROAD
LILLIE RD
A3218
A3219
DAWES ROAD
FULHAM PALACE ROAD
FULHAM
Fulham Cross School
Cemetery
Henry Compton School
Fulham FC (Craven Cottage)
Thames Path
Hammersmith & Fulham
Richmond upon Thames
Barn Elms Sports
Fulham Broadway Stn
Chelsea FC (Stamford Bridge)
Walham Green
Parsons Green Stn
Parsons Green
NEW KING'S ROAD
WANDSWORTH BRIDGE RD
SW6
A304
A308
Lady Margaret School
All Saints CE Primary School
HARWOOD RD
Fulham Clinic
Police Station

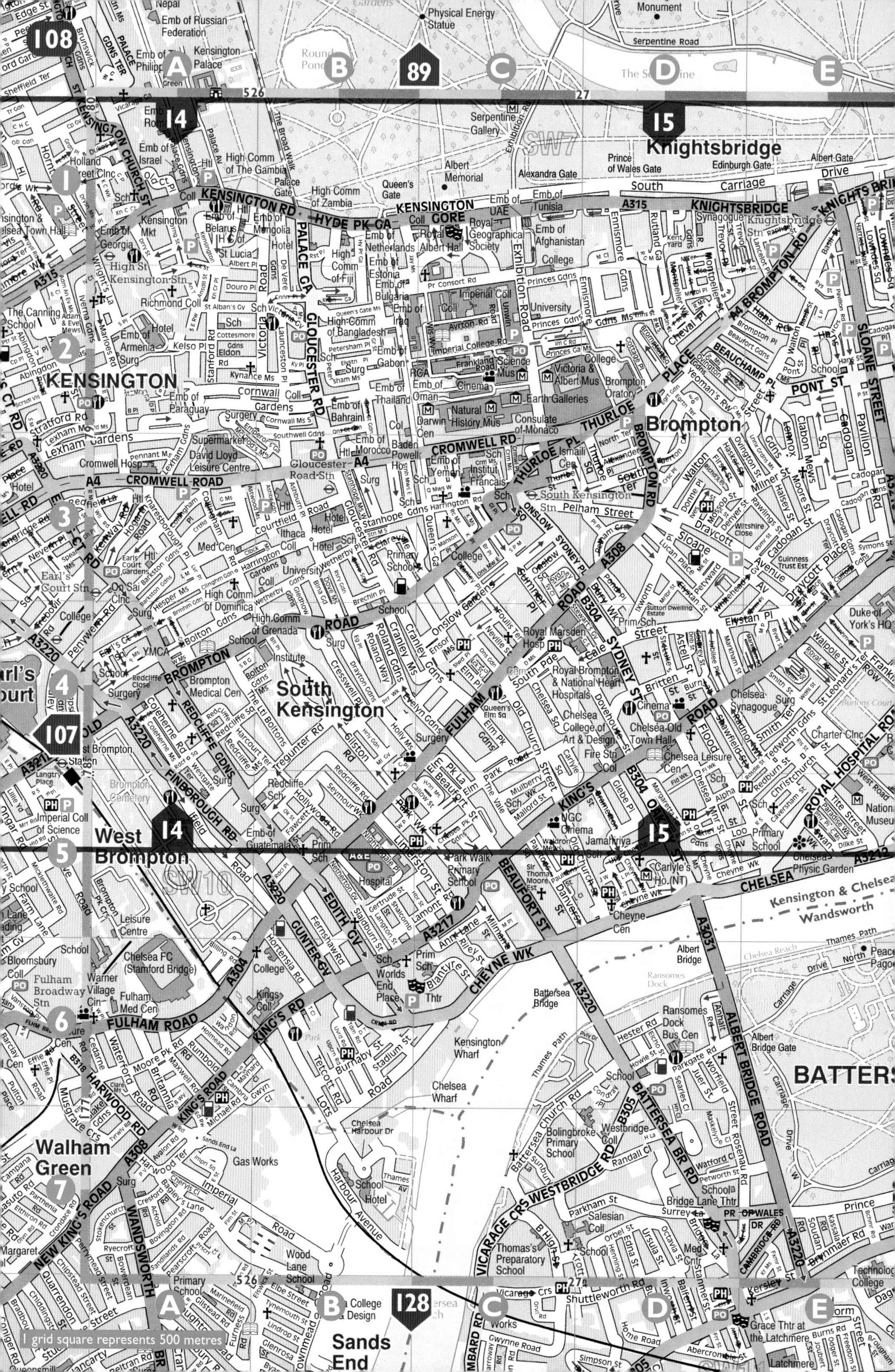
108
89
14
15
107
14
15
128
A
B
C
D
E
1
2
3
4
5
6
7
Kensington Palace
Emb of Russian Federation
Physical Energy Statue
Monument
Serpentine Road
The Serpentine
Round Pond
The Broad Walk
Serpentine Gallery
SW7
Knightsbridge
Prince of Wales Gate
Albert Gate
Edinburgh Gate
Alexandra Gate
Queen's Gate
Albert Memorial
South Carriage Drive
KENSINGTON RD
HYDE PK GA
KENSINGTON GORE
KNIGHTSBRIDGE
A315
Royal Albert Hall
Royal Geographical Society
Imperial Coll
Science Mus
Victoria & Albert Mus
Natural History Mus
Earth Galleries
Brompton Oratory
High St Kensington Stn
Kensington Mkt
KENSINGTON
Kensington & Chelsea Town Hall
GLOUCESTER RD
Gloucester Road Stn
CROMWELL RD
CROMWELL ROAD
A4
Earl's Court Stn
Brompton
South Kensington Stn
A4 BROMPTON RD
SLOANE STREET
PONT ST
Cadogan Sq
Sloane Sq
South Kensington
BROMPTON ROAD
FULHAM ROAD
Royal Marsden Hosp
Royal Brompton & National Heart Hospitals
Chelsea Old Town Hall
KING'S RD
ROYAL HOSPITAL RD
Chelsea Physic Garden
Carlyle's Ho (NT)
CHEYNE WK
CHELSEA EMB
Kensington & Chelsea
Wandsworth
Albert Bridge
Battersea Bridge
Brompton Cemetery
West Brompton
SW10
Chelsea FC (Stamford Bridge)
Fulham Broadway Stn
Walham Green
Worlds End Place
Chelsea Harbour
Gas Works
Imperial Road
Wandsworth Bridge Rd
NEW KING'S ROAD
BATTERSEA BR RD
ALBERT BRIDGE ROAD
BATTERSEA
Westbridge Rd
Sands End
Grace Thtr at the Latchmere
1 grid square represents 500 metres

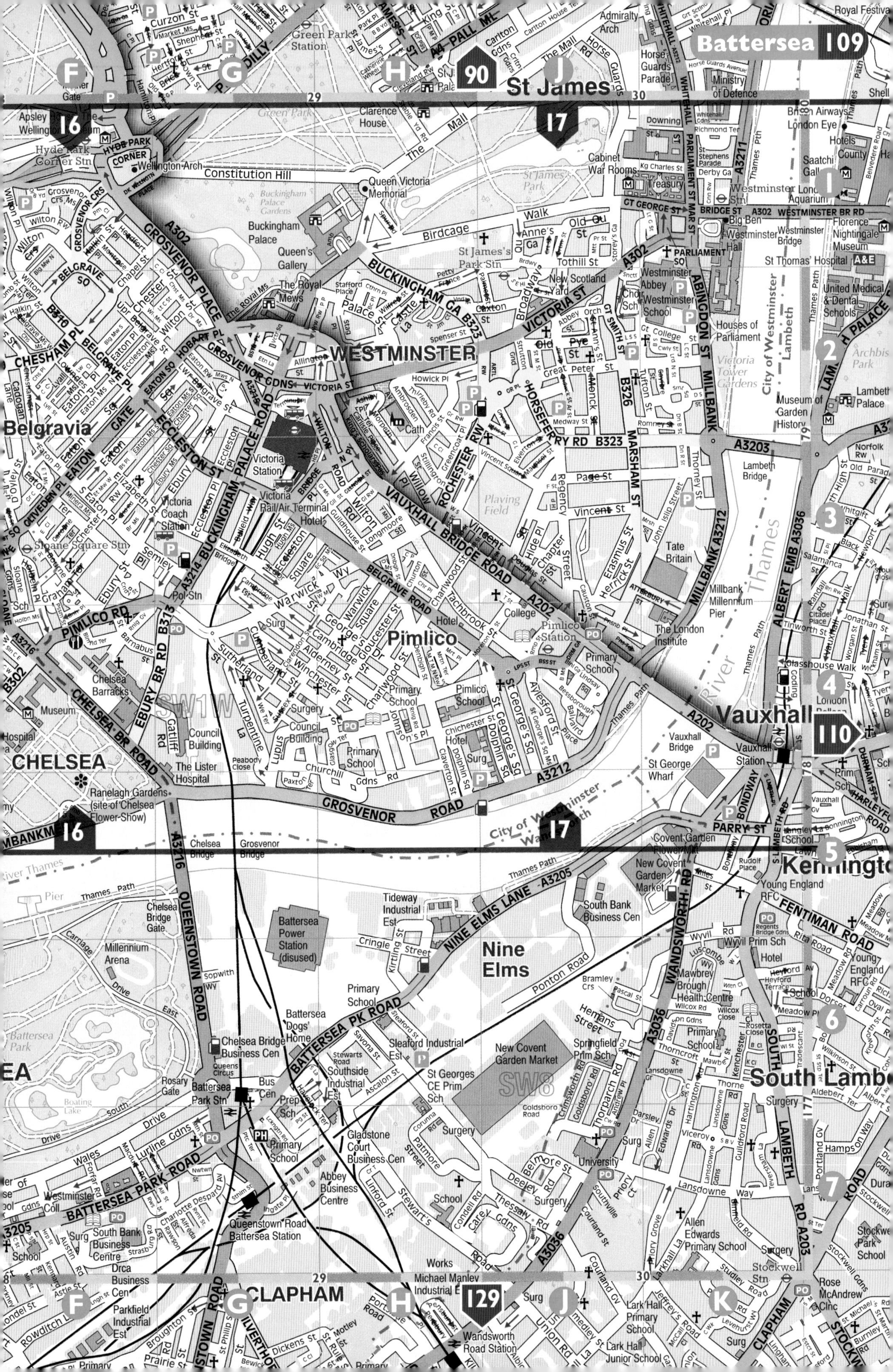

St James
Green Park Station
Green Park
Clarence House
Constitution Hill
Wellington Arch
Hyde Park Corner Stn
Buckingham Palace
Buckingham Palace Gardens
Queen's Gallery
The Royal Mews
Queen Victoria Memorial
St James's Park
St James's Park Stn
Birdcage Walk
The Mall
Horse Guards Parade
Admiralty Arch
Ministry of Defence
Cabinet War Rooms
Treasury
Westminster Stn
Big Ben
Westminster Hall
Westminster Abbey
Westminster School
Houses of Parliament
Victoria Tower Gardens
Westminster Bridge
London Eye
London Aquarium
County Hall
Florence Nightingale Museum
St Thomas' Hospital
A&E
United Medical & Dental Schools
Archbishop's Park
Lambeth Palace
Museum of Garden History
Lambeth Bridge
WESTMINSTER
New Scotland Yard
VICTORIA ST
BUCKINGHAM GA B323
GROSVENOR PLACE
GROSVENOR GDNS
BUCKINGHAM PALACE ROAD
Victoria Station
Victoria Coach Station
Victoria Rail/Air Terminal
VAUXHALL BRIDGE ROAD
HORSEFERRY RD B323
MARSHAM ST
MILLBANK
Millbank Millennium Pier
Tate Britain
The London Institute
Belgravia
BELGRAVE SQ
EATON SQ
ECCLESTON ST
CHESHAM PL
EATON GATE
Sloane Square Stn
PIMLICO RD
Chelsea Barracks
Pimlico
Pimlico Station
BELGRAVE ROAD
Playing Field
CHELSEA
Ranelagh Gardens (site of Chelsea Flower Show)
The Lister Hospital
CHELSEA BR ROAD
EBURY BR RD B313
GROSVENOR ROAD
Chelsea Bridge
Grosvenor Bridge
River Thames
Thames Path
City of Westminster
Lambeth
Wandsworth
Vauxhall
Vauxhall Bridge
Vauxhall Station
St George Wharf
ALBERT EMB A3036
Kennington
Young England RFC
FENTIMAN ROAD
New Covent Garden Market
NINE ELMS LANE A3205
Nine Elms
Battersea Power Station (disused)
Tideway Industrial Est
Ponton Road
QUEENSTOWN ROAD
Millennium Arena
Battersea Park
Boating Lake
Battersea 'Dogs' Home
BATTERSEA PK ROAD
Battersea Park Stn
Queenstown Road Battersea Station
Chelsea Bridge Business Cen
South Bank Business Centre
WANDSWORTH RD A3036
South Lambeth
SOUTH LAMBETH RD A203
Stockwell Stn
CLAPHAM
Wandsworth Road Station
Michael Manley Industrial Est
SW1W
SW8
16
17
90
110
129

110
91
18
109
130
A
B
C
D
E
1
2
3
4
5
6
7
Royal Festival Hall
Hungerford Bridge
Shell Centre
Waterloo East Stn
Waterloo Station
International Rail Terminal
STAMFORD
SOUTHWARK STREET
UNION STREET
Mus of Tea & Coffee
Guys Hospital
London Bridge Stn
Ministry of Defence
British Airways London Eye
County Hall
Saatchi Gallery
London Aquarium
Westminster Stn
Big Ben
Westminster Hall
Westminster Bridge
WESTMINSTER BR RD
Florence Nightingale Museum
St Thomas' Hospital
A&E
United Medical & Dental Schools
Houses of Parliament
Victoria Tower Gardens
Archbishop's Park
Lambeth Palace
Museum of Garden History
Lambeth Bridge
LAMBETH PALACE RD
ALBERT EMB
YORK RD
THE CUT
WATERLOO ROAD
BAYLIS RD
BLACKFRIARS RD
BOROUGH RD
Lambeth Nth Stn
ST GEORGES CIRCUS
LAMBETH
LAMBETH ROAD
Imperial War Museum
Newington
ST GEORGE'S RD
LONDON RD
Elephant and Castle Stn
Elephant & Castle Station
Elephant & Castle Shopping Cen
The Borough
Borough Stn
BOROUGH HIGH ST
MARSHALSEA RD
GREAT DOVER STREET
LONG LANE
NEWINGTON CSWY
HARPER RD
NEW KENT ROAD
WALWORTH RD
KENNINGTON ROAD
KENNINGTON LA
KENNINGTON PARK ROAD
NEWINGTON BUTTS
Kennington Stn
SE11
SE17
Vauxhall
Vauxhall Station
Millbank Millennium Pier
Thames
River
London Balloon
HARLEYFORD ROAD
KENNINGTON OV
Surrey CCC (The Oval)
Oval Stn
Kennington
Young England RFC
FENTIMAN ROAD
Walworth
ALBANY ROAD
CAMBERWELL ROAD A215
CAMBERWELL NEW ROAD
CAMBERWELL CHURCH ST
DENMARK HILL
SOUTHAMPTON WAY
Royal National Thtr
South Lambeth
SOUTH LAMBETH RD A203
Stockwell Stn
The Type Museum
Temple of Bacchus
Camberwell Trading Est
Flaxman Sports Cen
MEDLAR ST
1 grid square represents 500 metres

Bermondsey 111
Wapping
92
19
112
131
BERMONDSEY
CAMBERWELL
Peckham
SE16
SE15
F
G
H
J
I
K
2
3
4
5
6
7
34
35
Britain at War Experience
Tower Bridge Experience
GLA HQ (City Hall)
Millennium Balloon
Thames Path
Tower Bridge Wharf
Capital Wharf
Aberdeen Wharf
Police Station
John Orwell Cen
Wapping High St
Tower Hamlets
Southwark
Thames
Design Museum
Butlers & Colonial Wharf
Millennium Square
Chambers Wharf
Fountain Green Square
Church Stairs
Kings Stairs
Brunel Engine House
Rotherhithe Station
Rotherhithe Street
Albion Street Health Cen
Civic Cen
Infant School
City Bus Cen
Canada Water Station
Canada Water Retail Park
UCI Cinema
Surrey Quays
Shopping Centre
Dock Offices
Police Station
Seven Islands Leisure Cen
Primary School
LOWER ROAD
A200
JAMAICA ROAD
JAMAICA RD
BRUNEL RD
ROTH TNL
TOOLEY ST
DRUID ST
TOWER BRIDGE RD
BERMONDSEY STREET
A2205
A100
B202 ABBEY STREET
A2206 GRANGE ROAD
Tyers Ga
Leathermarket
Tanner St
White's Grounds
Morocco St
Graduate Place
Cluny Estate
Decima St
Rothsay St
Alice St
Grigg's Place
Webb St
Bushbaby Close
Pages Walk
Swan Md
Leroy Street
Page's Walk
Willow Walk
Rich Industrial Estate
Curtis St
Bacon Grove
Spa Road
Grange Walk
Grange Yd
The Grange
Neckinger
Alscot Rd
Vaudan St
Dunlop Pl
Dockley Road Industrial Est
Voyager Business Est
Discovery Business Park
Toussaint Walk
Collett Rd
Webster Road
Clement's Road
Southwark College
Drummond Road
Lockwood Square
Southwark Park Road
Slippers Pl
Marden Square
Southwark Park Primary School
Southwark Park
Southwark Park Sports Centre
Abbeyfield Estate
Park Med Cen
Prim Sch
Hawkstone Road
Old Rd
Rotherhithe New Rd
Bermondsey Trading Est
St Helena Road
Oldfield Grove
Crane Md
Corbett's La
Eugenia Rd
Jarrow Rd
Reculver Rd
Silwood Street
Sketchley Gdns
Millwall FC (The New Den)
Stockholm Road
Surrey Canal
Rollins St
Bridge House
Canterbury Ind Est
John Williams Cl
Hunsdon Rd
Edric Rd
Farrow La
Pump La
Avonley Road
New Cross Rd A2
B2227
Kender St
Kender Primary School
Besson Street
Queen's Road
Mona Rd
Waller Rd
Erlanger Rd
Sherwin Rd
Arbuthnot Rd
Bousfield Rd
Dennett's Rd
Bermondsey Wall E
Bermondsey Wall W
Cathay St
Paradise St
Fulford St
West La
Cherry Gdn St
Marigold St
Wilson Gv
Emba St
Prim Sch
Chambers St
George Row
Providence Square
Jacob St
Wolseley St
Dockhead
Primary School
Scott Lidgett Crs
Old Jamaica Rd
Bermondsey Stn
John Dixon Clnc
Keetons Rd
Perryn Rd
Frean St
Thurland Rd
Southwark Park Rd
A2206
Raymouth Road
Almond Road
Trading Est
Primary School
Admiral Hyson Industrial Est
Rennie Estate
Camilla Road
Beatrice Road
Rosebery St
Anchor Street
Galleywall Road
Aylwin Girls Sch
Alexis St
Lucey Road
Lucey Way
Rouel Rd
Linsey St
Macks Rd
Prim Sch
Valding Rd
Amina Way
Eveline Lowe Estate
Henley Dr
Cadbury Wy
Mandela Way
Setchell Way
Dunton Road
B203
Fort Rd
Balaclava Rd
Alma Grove
Reverdy Road
Longley St
Strathnairn St
Simms Rd
Thorburn Square
Monnow Road
Welsford St
St James's Road
Mason Cl
Stevenson Crs
Rossetti Rd
Stubbs Dr
Sheppard Dr
Rolls Road B204
Catlin St
A2208
Abercorn Wy
Oxley Close
Cadet Dr
Bushwood Dr
Lynton Rd
Chaucer Dr
Mandela Wy
Humphrey St
Superstore
Surgery
Rowcross St
Old Kent Road
A2
Marcia Road
Madron St
Congreve St
Hendre Rd
Minnow Walk
Freemantle St
Surrey Sq
Aldbridge
Surrey Square School
Kinglake Street
Bagshot St
Smyrk's Rd
Upnor Wy
Mina Road
Walworth Upper School
Albany Road
B214
Calmington Road
Loncroft Road
Lake
Cobourg Primary School
Cobourg Road
New Peckham Mosque
Waite St
B215
Trafalgar Av
Fire Stn
Cooper's Rd
Avondale Square
Primary School
Six Bridges Trading Est
St James's Road
Marlborough Gv
Sherwood Gdns
Ryder Drive
Verney Road
Masters Dr
Credon Rd
Cranswick Rd
Ablett St
Enterprise Industrial Est
Zampa Rd
South Bermondsey Station
Bolina Road
Sandgate Trading Est
Sandgate Street
Kent Park Industrial Est
Rich Industrial Est
Ruby St
Devonshire Gv
Primary School
Ilderton Road
Record St
Penarth St
Hatcham Rd
Ormside St
Manor Gv
Pilgrims Way Junior & Infant School
Patterdale Rd
Works
Old Kent Road A2
Livesey Museum for Children
Primary School
Wales Close
Asylum Road
Cardine Ms
Naylor Road
Albert Way
Clifton Crs
Culmore Road
Clifton Way
Studholme St
Leo St
Drovers Pl
Montague
Loder St
Pomeroy Street
Coll's Road
Astbury Rd
Dayton Gv
York Gv
Station Passage
Queen's Road Peckham Stn
Bath Cl
Queen's Road
Lausanne Road
St Mary's Rd
St Thomas the Apostle College
Belfort Road
Dundas Rd
Ansdell Road
Gautrey Rd
Hollydale Rd
Lugard Rd
Caulfield Rd
Hathorne Cl
Kirkwood Road
Cossall Wk
Wood's Road
Prim Sch
Tuke Sch
A202
Peckham High St
Pulse Healthy Living Centre
The Aylesham Centre
Bellenden Rd Retail Park
Hanover Pk
Rye Lane
Cncl Bldng
Highshore School
Oliver Ms
Mkt
Premier
Agora Shop Cen
South London Temple
Peckham Rye Stn
Bellenden Road Business Cen
Holly Gv
Bournemouth Rd
Blackpool Rd
Clayton Rd
Consort Rd
Surgery
Pol Stn
Meeting House La
Marmont Rd
Goldsmith Rd
Primary School
Surgery
Peckham Pk Road
B216
Peckham Hill Street
B215 Peckham
Bullar Cl
Furley Road
Leontine Cl
Friary Rd
Ledbury St
Commercial Way
Holbeck Rw
Fenham Rd
Kincaid Rd
Geldart Rd
Bewick Mews
Bird in Bush Rd
Lympstone Gardens
St Francis RC Primary School
Haymerle Sch
Horizon Ind Est
Haymerle Rd
Latona Road
Unwin Rd
Colegrove Road
Glengall Road
Bianca Rd
Works
Willowbrook Rd
Neate Street
Burgess Park
Ossory Road
Malt St
Olmar St
Quantum Retail Park
Council Building
Livesey Pl
Canal Gv
Green Hundred Rd
Ethnard Rd
St George's Way
Winchcombe Business Cen
Primary School
Coll Cen
Daniel Gardens
Hordle Prom East
Nutt St
Garnies Cl
Rosemary Rd
Jowett St
Surgery
Sumner Road
Council Building
Damilola Taylor Cen
Cator St
Diamond St
Commercial Wy
Blake's Rd
Peckham Gv
Coleman Rd
Southwark Coll
Bonsor St
Stanswood Gdns
Sedgmoor Pl
Wells Place
Dalwood St
South London Gallery
Prim Sch
Camberwell College of Arts
Surgery
School
Peckham Road
Camberwell College of Arts
Shenley Road
Crofton Rd
Vestry Road
Maude Road
Surgery
Talfourd Pl
Talfourd Road
Denman Road
Lyndhurst Way
Grummant Rd
Warwick Park School
Bushey Hl Rd
Linnell Rd
Oswyth Rd
Gairloch Rd
Cross Rd
Grace's Road
Lyndhurst Grove
McNeil Road
St Giles Rd
Havil St
Gables Cl
Ada Rd
Rainbow St
Newent Cl
Tilson Cl
Pentridge St
Cronin St
E Surrey Gv
Kelly Av
Gatonby St
Sumner Av
Lisford St
Pioneer St
Jocelyn St
Neville Cl
Bonar Rd
Surgery

112
93
111
132
A
B
C
D
E
1
2
3
4
5
6
7
Rotherhithe
Canary Wharf
Millwall
DEPTFORD
New Cross Gate
New Cross
St Johns
SE8
SE14
River Thames
Limehouse Reach
Tower Hamlets
Southwark
Lewisham
SALTER ROAD
REDRIFF RD
LOWER ROAD
A200
PLOUGH WAY
B206
GROVE ST
EVELYN STREET
CREEK ROAD
DEPTFORD CHURCH STREET
WESTFERRY ROAD
A1206
NEW CROSS RD
A2
LEWISHAM WAY
BROOKMILL RD
BLACKHEATH RD
GREENWICH HIGH ROAD
B207 TRUNDLEY'S ROAD
SANFORD STREET
EDWARD ST
PAGNELL ST
AMERSHAM RD
FLORENCE ROAD
POMEROY STREET
KENDER ST
LAUSANNE ROAD
BESSON STREET
NORMAN RD
Surrey Quays Station
Canada Water Station
Surrey Quays Shopping Centre
Greenland Dock
Surrey Docks Watersports Centre
Deptford Park
Deptford Park Primary School
Deptford Stn
Deptford Bridge Station
New Cross Station
New Cross Gate Stn
St Johns Stn
South Quay Station
Heron Quays Station
Crossharbour & London Arena Stn
Daily Telegraph
London Arena
Millwall Docks
Goldsmiths College
University of London
Haberdashers Askes Hatcham College
Laban Cen
Millwall FC
1 grid square represents 500 metres

Greenwich 113
94
114
133
F
G
H
J
K
I
2
3
4
5
6
7
39
40
80
79
78
77
Blackwall Basin
Lovegrove Wk
Medical Cen
A1206
A102
Dome
Newham
Greenwich
Bell
Works
Minerva Works
Greenshields Industrial Est
Greenshields Industrial Estate
Knights Rd
Bradfield Rd
Works
Wood Wharf Business Park
S W India Dock Entrance
Glen Ter
Lawn House Cl
Pumping Station
Delta Wharf
Tunnel Avenue Trading Est
North Greenwich Station
Bugsby's Reach
Blackwall Reach
Chipka St
Folly Wall
Capstan Square
River Barge Close
Stewart Street
Island Clinic
Plevna St
Galbraith St
Marshfield St
New Union Cl
Adult Education Cen
Strattondale St
Amsterdam Rd
Rotterdam Dr
Rembrandt Cl
Cubitt Town Primary School
Friars Md
Superstore
Schooner Cl
Millennium Dr
Millennium Whf
Millennium Wharf Development
Pier
Greenwich
Tower Hamlets
Tunnel Avenue
Ordnance Crs
Edmund Halley
West
East
Millennium Way
Parkside
Annandale Primary School
River Wy
John Harrison Wy
Thames Path
Gas Works
Dreadnought St
Boord St
Thames Pth
Morden Whf Road
Peterboat Cl
Cubitt Town
Mudchute City Farm
Millwall Park
Pier St
Ch Wy
Sextant Av
Mariners Ms
Plymouth Whf
Storers Quay
Primary School
Caledonian Wharf Road
Empire Whf Rd
Seyssel St
Kingfield St
Billson St
Parsonage St
Glengarnock Av
Saunders Ness Rd
Pol Stn
ROAD
ISLE OF DOGS
Community Centre (Island History Trust)
Island Gardens Station
Stebondale Street
MANCHESTER
Grosvenor Whf Rd
Newcastle Drawdock
George Green Mixed School
Ferry St
Greenwich Foot Tunnel
Lawrence Trading Est
Maritime Mus
Mauritius Road
Azof Street
BLACKWALL LANE
A2203
Tunnel Av
BUGSBY'S WAY
UCI-Filmworks Cinema
W Parkside
Peartree Wy
Horn Link Wy
Brocklebank Industrial Estate
Willoughby Way
Lombard Wall
BUGSBY'S WAY
Maritime Industrial Estate
Superstore
Angerstein Business Park
Horn Lane
A102
Peninsular Pk Rd
Fearon St
Felltram Way
Ind Est
Ramac Way
WOOLWICH ROAD
Victoria Way
East Greenwich Christ Church CE Prim Sch
Armitage Rd
Armitage Road
Lenthorp Rd
Glenforth St
Fingal St
Glenister Rd
Chilver St
Dandridge Cl
Cadet Pl
Derwent St
Bellot St
Flavell Ms
Commerell St
Prim School
Lovell's Wharf
Banning St
Enderby St
Pelton Rd
Caradoc St
Hadrian St
Christchurch Wy
Whitworth St
Lassell St
Hoskins St
Trinity Hospital
Greenwich Hospital
A&E
Vanbrugh Hill
Calvert Rd
Annandale Rd
Chevening Rd
Halstow Rd
Kemsing Rd
Combedale Rd
Police Stn
Farmdale Rd
Fairthorn Rd
Gurdon Road
A206
GREENWICH
TRAFALGAR ROAD
Tyler St
Colomb St
Primary School
Primary School
Ormiston Rd
Westcombe Park Stat
Station Crs
University
Old Royal Naval College
Meridian Prim Sch
Tuskar St
Woodlands Pk Rd
Annandale Rd
Humber Road
Bernard Ashley Dr
Eastcombe Avenue
Angerstein Works
Sandtoft Road
Eversley Road
Greenwich Pier
Cutty Sark Clipper Ship
Gypsy Moth
Thames St
Trinity College of Music
Cutty Sark Station
Library
Thames Path
Eastney St
Park Row
Arches Leisure Cen
School
Maze Hill Station
Restell Close
Dinsdale Rd
Coleraine Rd
Ruthin Road
Westcombe Hill
CREEK ROAD
ROMNEY ROAD
Feathers Pl
Park Vista
The Queens House
National Maritime Museum
Maze Hill
Ulundi Rd
Foyle Road
Coleraine Road
Webb Rd
Beaconsfield Road
Mycenae Road
Kirkside Rd
Glenluge Rd
Siebert Rd
Invicta Primary School
Invicta Rd
Hopedale Road
Sherington Road
Roan St
Council Building
Royal Observatory Greenwich
SE10
Greenwich Park
Hardy Rd
Ingleside Gv
John Roan Lower School
Westcombe Park Rd
Blackheath High Senior School
Broad Bri
CHARLTON RD
B210
Furzefield Rd
Hassendean Rd
Banchory Rd
Randall Pl
A206
Burney St
Nevada St
Greenwich Theatre & Art Gallery
Greenwich Cinema
Fan Mus
Welfare Clinic
Police Stn
Flamsteed House Museum
Highmore Rd
Vanbrugh Flds
John Roan School
Wycherley Cl
Vanbrugh Pk Rd W
Combe Av
Vanbrugh Pk
VANBRUGH PK B210
B211
OLD DOVER
Dornberg Cl
Greenwich Coll
ROYAL HL
Croom's Hill
King George St
School
Conduit House
The Avenue
Great Cross Av
Blackheath Av
Vanbrugh Park
Mary Lawrencson Pl
Heathway
STRATHEDEN ROAD
St John's Park
Circus St
Brand St
Prior St
Greenwich Natural Health Cen
Luton Pl
Georgette Pl
St Ursulas Convent School
Old Royal Observatory Greenwich
St John's Pk
Gregor Ms
Langton Way
A2211
Royal Hl
HYDE VALE
Hill
B210
Angerstein Lane
Vanbrugh Ter
School
Langton Way
Blissett St
Winforton St
Dutton St
Maidenstone Hl
Point Hill
Westgrove Lane
Hotel
B209
General Wolfe Rd
Bower Avenue
Blackheath Avenue
Rangers House (The Wernher Collection)
CHARLTON WAY
Pr Charles Rd
SHOOTERS HILL ROAD
A2
B212
KIDBROOKE PARK RD
Rosse Mews
Annesley Rd
Point Cl
West Gv
Cade Rd
Christs College
Shooters Hill Road
BLACKHEATH HILL A2
SHOOTERS HILL RD A2
St German's Place
Greenwich
Lewisham
Kidbrooke Gardens
Liskeard Gdns
Westbrook Road
Dartmouth Hl
Long Pond Road
PR OF WALES RD B212
Blackheath Business Est
Dartmouth Gv
Wat Tyler Road
Hare And Billet Road
Whitfield Rd
Goffers Rd
Talbot Place
Duke Humphrey Rd
Manor Brook Medical Centre
Morden Lane
Sparta Street
Blackheath
South Row
St German's Pl
SE3
Surgery
LEWISHAM
Blackheath Ri
Mounts Pond Rd
All Saints Primary Sch
Duke Humphrey Road
The Paragon
Morden College Homes
Morden Rd
Mounts Pond Road
Aberdeen Ter
The Orchard
Orchard Dr
Eliot Pl
All Saints
Montpelier Row
Hotel
Blackheath High School
Fulthorp Rd
Rycullf Sq
The Plantation
St Austell Rd

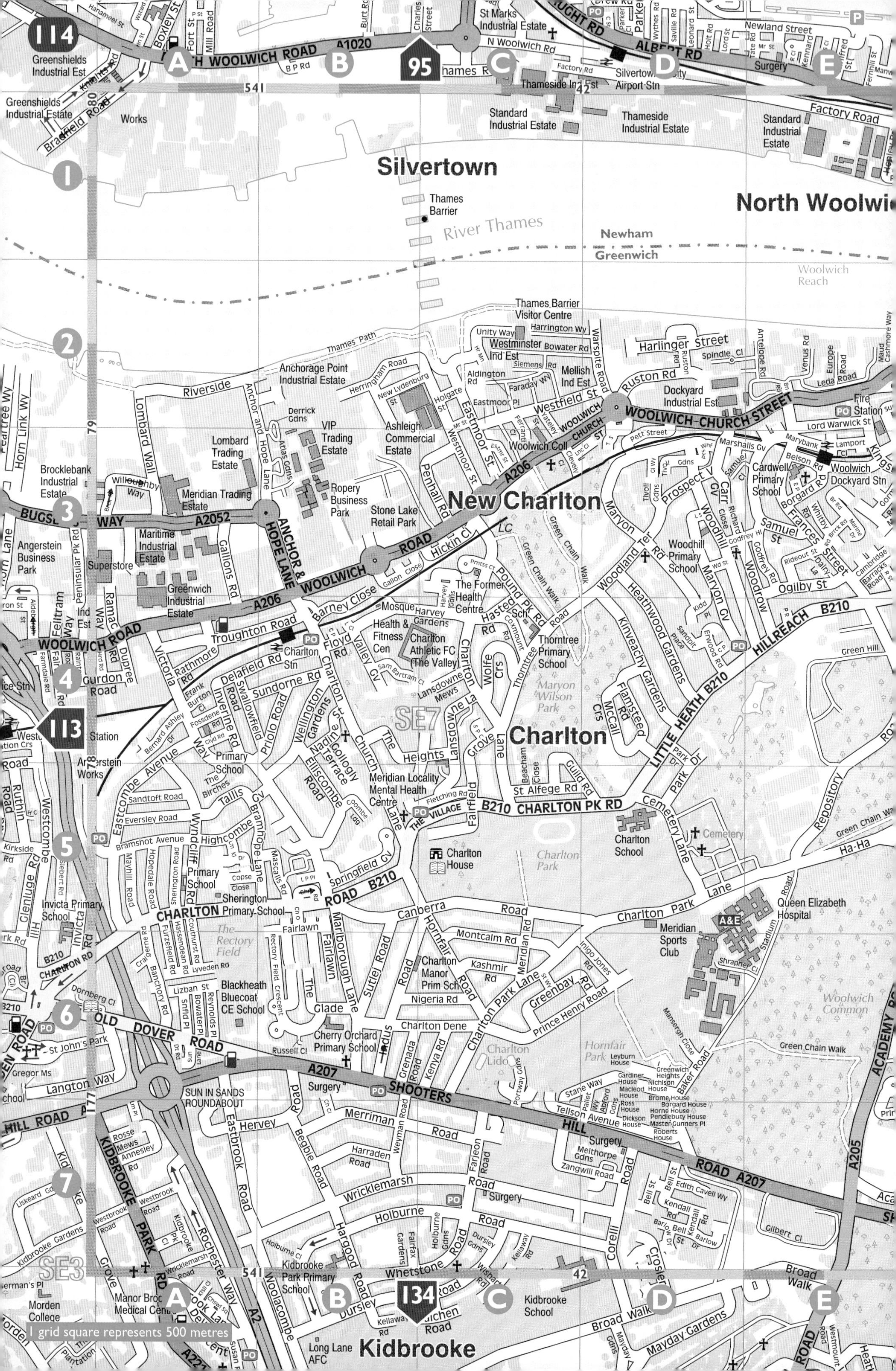

114
95
113
134
A
B
C
D
E
1
2
3
4
5
6
7
541
42
80
79
78
177
Greenshields Industrial Est
Greenshields Industrial Estate
Bradfield Road
Works
Hanameel St
Boxley St
Fort St
Mill Road
Burt Rd
Charles Street
NORTH WOOLWICH ROAD
A1020
B P Rd
St Marks Industrial Estate
N Woolwich Rd
ALBERT RD
Newland Street
Surgery
Factory Rd
Silvertown City Airport Stn
Thameside Ind Est
Standard Industrial Estate
Thameside Industrial Estate
Factory Road
Silvertown
Thames Barrier
River Thames
North Woolwi
Newham
Greenwich
Woolwich Reach
Thames Barrier Visitor Centre
Harrington Wy
Unity Way
Westminster Ind Est
Bowater Rd
Thames Path
Harlinger Street
Spindle Cl
Antelope Rd
Venus Rd
Europe Road
Leda Road
Fire Station
Anchorage Point Industrial Estate
Riverside
Herringham Road
New Lydenburg St
Aldington Rd
Faraday Wy
Mellish Ind Est
Warspite Road
Ruston Rd
Dockyard Industrial Est
WOOLWICH CHURCH STREET
Lord Warwick St
Lombard Wall
Anchor and Hope Lane
Derrick Gdns
VIP Trading Estate
Ashleigh Commercial Estate
Holgate St
Eastmoor Pl
Eastmoor St
Westfield St
Woolwich Coll
Pett Street
Marshalls Gv
Marybank
Lamport Cl
Woolwich Dockyard Stn
Belson Rd
Cardwell Primary School
Lombard Trading Estate
Brocklebank Industrial Estate
Willoughby Way
Meridian Trading Estate
Ropery Business Park
Stone Lake Retail Park
Penhall Rd
Westmoor St
A206
New Charlton
Maryon Rd
Prospect V
Woodhill Gv
Borgard Rd
Frances Street
Samuel St
BUGSBYS WAY
A2052
ANCHOR & HOPE LANE
Maritime Industrial Estate
Angerstein Business Park
Superstore
Gallions Rd
Greenwich Industrial Estate
Peninsular Pk Rd
Horn Link Way
Hickin Cl
Gallon Close
WOOLWICH ROAD
LC
Green Chain Walk
Woodland Ter
Woodhill Primary School
Ogilby St
Feltram Way
Ind Est
Barney Close
Mosque
Harvey Gardens
The Former Health Centre
Pound Pk Rd
Heathwood Gardens
Kinveachy Gardens
HILLREACH B210
Green Hill
Troughton Road
Charlton Stn
Floyd Rd
Health & Fitness Cen
Charlton Athletic FC (The Valley)
Hasted Rd
Thorntree Primary School
Maryon Wilson Park
Flamsteed Rd
McCall Crs
Gurdon Road
Rathmore Rd
Delafield Rd
Sundorne Rd
Victoria Way
Lansdowne Mews
Wolfe Crs
SE7
Charlton
LITTLE HEATH B210
Station
Westcombe
Angerstein Works
Eastcombe Avenue
Primary School
The Birches
Wellington Gardens
Nadine St
Elliscombe Road
Church Lane
The Heights
Meridian Locality Mental Health Centre
Grove
Lane
Beacham Close
Guild Rd
St Alfege Rd
Park Dr
Repository Rd
Sandtoft Road
Eversley Road
Tallis Gv
Highcombe
Bramshot Avenue
Wyndcliff Rd
Primary School
Sherington Primary School
Springfield Gv
THE VILLAGE
B210 CHARLTON PK RD
Fairfield
Charlton House
Charlton Park
Charlton School
Cemetery
Cemetery Lane
Green Chain Wa
Ha-Ha
Invicta Primary School
Invicta Rd
CHARLTON
ROAD B210
Canberra Road
Charlton Park Lane
Queen Elizabeth Hospital
A&E
Meridian Sports Club
The Rectory Field
Fairlawn
Marlborough Lane
Sutlej Road
Hornfair Road
Montcalm Rd
Meridian Rd
Charlton Manor Prim Sch
Kashmir Rd
Greenbay Rd
Inigo Jones Rd
Prince Henry Road
Stadium Rd
Shrapnel Cl
Woolwich Common
Blackheath Bluecoat CE School
The Glade
Nigeria Rd
Charlton Dene
Charlton Lido
Hornfair Park
Mansergh Close
Green Chain Walk
OLD DOVER ROAD
Cherry Orchard Primary School
Russell Cl
Kenya Rd
Baker Road
ACADEMY
St John's Park
Gregor Ms
Langton Way
SUN IN SANDS ROUNDABOUT
A207
SHOOTERS HILL ROAD A207
Surgery
Merriman Road
Tellson Avenue
Stane Way
Melthorpe Gdns
Zangwill Road
HILL ROAD
KIDBROOKE PARK RD
Eastbrook Road
Hervey
Begbie Road
Harraden Road
Weyman Road
Farjeon Rd
Wricklemarsh Road
Surgery
Edith Cavell Wy
Kendall Rd
Bell St
Barlow Dr
Gilbert Cl
A205
Holburne Road
Hargood Road
Kidbrooke Park Primary School
Whetstone Rd
Corelli Road
Crosier
Broad Walk
Rochester Way
Westbrook Road
Kidbrooke Gardens
SE3
A2
Woolacombe Road
Manor Brook Medical Centre
Morden College
Kidbrooke School
Mayday Gardens
Long Lane AFC
Kidbrooke
1 grid square represents 500 metres

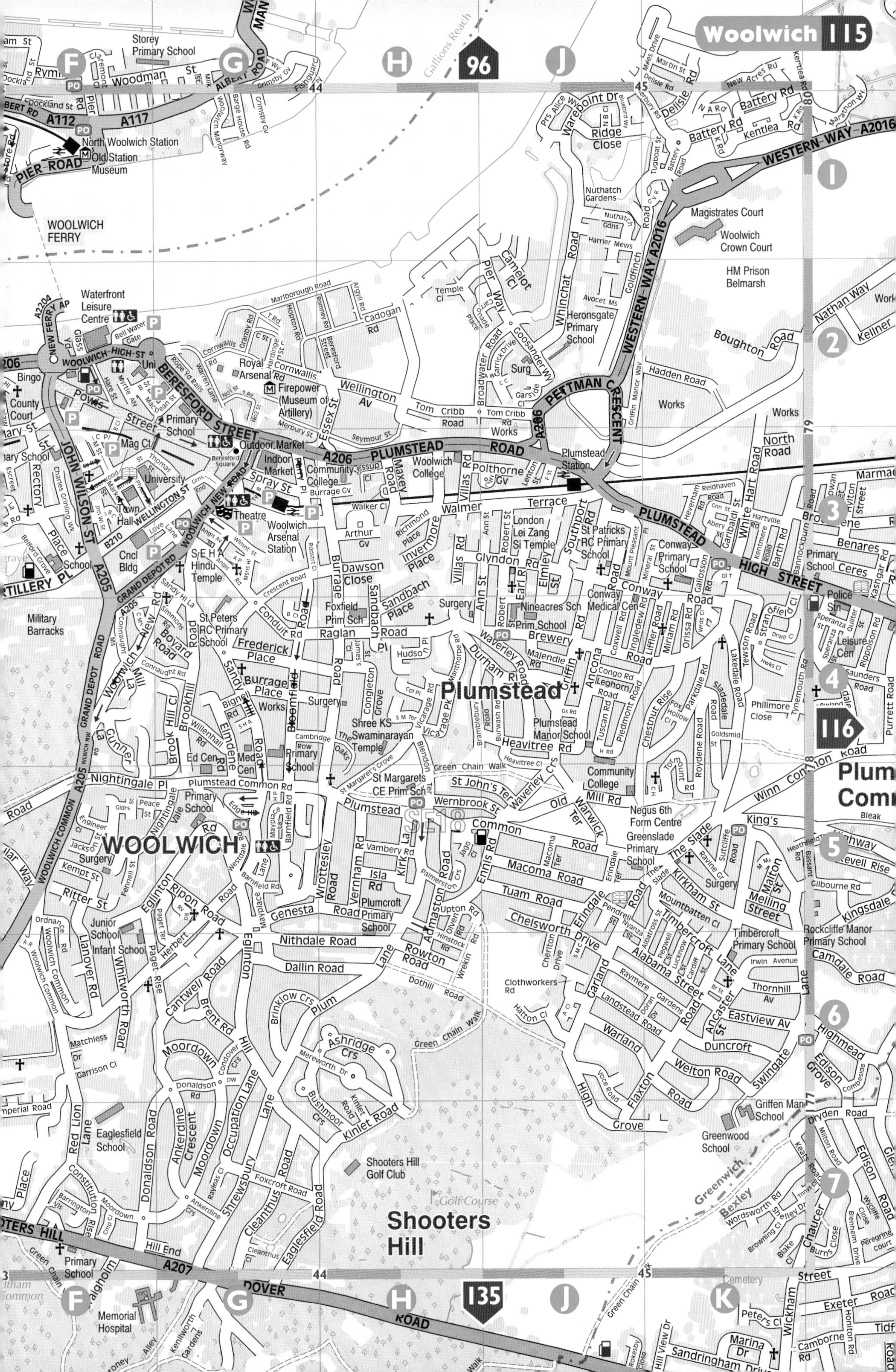

Woolwich 115
96
116
135
North Woolwich Station
Old Station Museum
Pier Road
Albert Road
Woodman St
Storey Primary School
Woolwich Ferry
Waterfront Leisure Centre
Woolwich High St
Beresford Street
Royal Arsenal
Firepower (Museum of Artillery)
Wellington Av
Cadogan Rd
Tom Cribb Road
Plumstead Road
A206
Outdoor Market
Indoor Market
Community College
Woolwich College
Woolwich Arsenal Station
Theatre
University
Town Hall
Wellington St
John Wilson St
A205
Grand Depot Road
Woolwich New Road
Military Barracks
County Court
S/E H A Hindu Temple
St Peters RC Primary School
Burrage Road
Sandbach Place
Raglan Road
Foxfield Prim Sch
Plumstead
Plumstead Station
Pettman Crescent
Western Way A2016
Magistrates Court
Woolwich Crown Court
HM Prison Belmarsh
Heronsgate Primary School
Whinchat Road
Goldfinch Road
Nuthatch Gardens
Boughton Road
Hadden Road
Works
North Road
Plumstead High Street
White Hart Road
Conway Primary School
St Patricks RC Primary School
London Lei Zang Si Temple
Walmer Terrace
Glyndon Rd
Nineacres Sch Prim School
Conway Medical Cen
Brewery Road
Plumstead Manor School
Heavitree Rd
Community College
Negus 6th Form Centre
Greenslade Primary School
Police Stn
Leisure Cen
Winn Common Road
Plumstead Common Road
Plumstead Common
SE18
St Margarets CE Prim Sch
Shree KS Swaminarayan Temple
Cambridge Row Primary School
Bloomfield Road
WOOLWICH
Nightingale Pl
Primary School
Ripon Road
Eglinton Hill
Genesta Road
Nithdale Road
Dallin Road
Plumcroft Primary School
Vernham Rd
Wrottesley Road
Admaston Road
Ennis Rd
Macoma Road
Tuam Road
Chelsworth Drive
Erindale
Timbercroft Lane
Timbercroft Primary School
Rockcliffe Manor Primary School
Alabama Street
Garland Rd
Wariand
Duncroft
Welton Road
Swingate Lane
Eastview Av
Thornhill Av
Griffen Manor School
Greenwood School
Greenwich
Bexley
Junior School
Infant School
Whitworth Road
Cantwell Road
Brent Rd
Moordown
Occupation Lane
Shrewsbury Lane
Donaldson Road
Ankerdine Crescent
Eaglesfield School
Eaglesfield Road
Cleanthus Road
Foxcroft Road
Kinlet Road
Ashridge Crs
Bushmoor Crs
Plum Lane
Dothill Road
Green Chain Walk
Shooters Hill Golf Club
Golf Course
Shooters Hill
A207
Dover Road
Shooters Hill
Red Lion Lane
Constitution Rise
Primary School
Memorial Hospital
Kenilworth Gardens
Cemetery
Wickham Street
Exeter Road
Marina Dr
Sandringham Drive
Hill View Dr
Edison Road
Dryden Road
Chaucer
Wordsworth Rd
Highmead
Edison Grove
Camdale Road
Kingsdale
Plum Comm

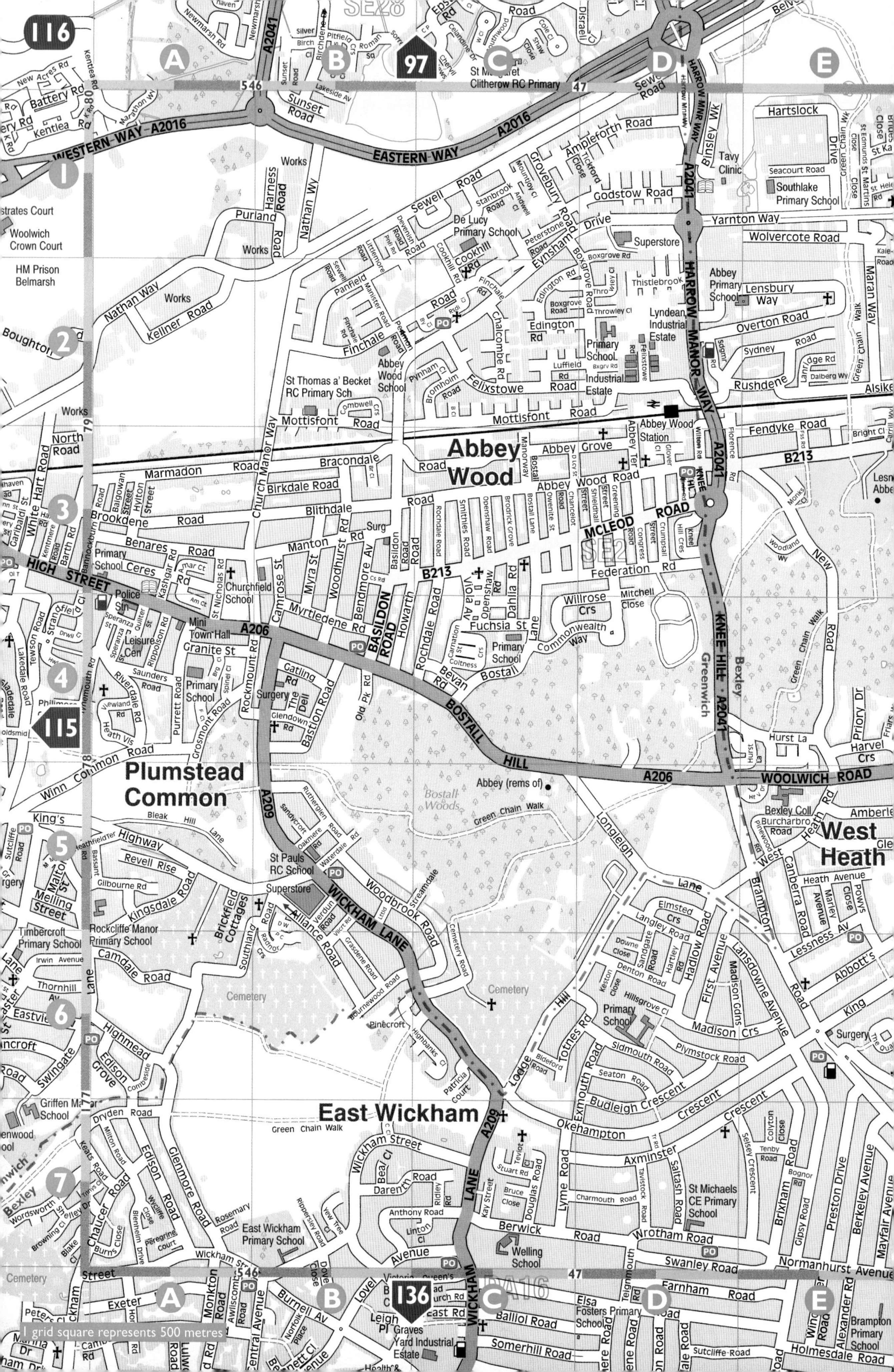
116
97
115
136
A
B
C
D
E
1
2
3
4
5
6
7
WESTERN WAY A2016
EASTERN WAY A2016
HARROW MANOR WAY A2041
KNEE HILL A2041
HIGH STREET A206
BOSTALL HILL A206
WOOLWICH ROAD
WICKHAM LANE A209
Abbey Wood
Plumstead Common
East Wickham
West Heath
Bostall Woods
Greenwich
Bexley
Woolwich Crown Court
HM Prison Belmarsh
Abbey Wood Station
De Lucy Primary School
St Thomas a' Becket RC Primary Sch
Abbey Wood School
Abbey Primary School
Southlake Primary School
Tavy Clinic
Lyndean Industrial Estate
Churchfield School
Mini Town Hall
Leisure Cen
Police Stn
Rockcliffe Manor Primary School
Timbercroft Primary School
St Pauls RC School
Superstore
East Wickham Primary School
St Michaels CE Primary School
Welling School
Fosters Primary School
Bexley Coll
Brampton Primary School
Graves Yard Industrial Estate
St Margaret Clitherow RC Primary
Abbey (rems of)
Cemetery
Green Chain Walk
Works
1 grid square represents 500 metres

Abbey Wood 117
98
F
G
H
J
49
50
80
79
78
77
A2016
EASTERN WAY
PICARDY MANORWAY
Norman Rd
Erith Marshes
Thamesmead Community College
East Thamesmead Business Park
DA18
Hailey Road Business Park
Hailey Rd
Hailey Road
Waldrist Way
Norman Road
North Road
Caldy Road
Yarnton Way
John Fisher Primary School
Pkwy
Glimpsing Green
Northwood Pl
Leatherbottle Gn
Aspen Green
Parkway Primary School
Northwood Primary School
Centurian Way
Works
Sutherland Road
Waterfield Close
Maida Rd
Station Rd
Belvedere Station
Superstore
B253
Elbourne Trading Estate
Crabtree Manorway South
Keats Rd
Cables Cl
Viking Way
Belvedere Link Business Park
BRONZE AGE WAY
Anderson Way
St Thomas Rd
Crabtree Manorway
Jenningtree Way
Mulberry Way
Works
Industrial Estate
Capital
GILBERT ROAD
B213
PICARDY ST
Dylan Rd
LOWER ROAD
Halifield Dr
Holcote Close
Tunstock Wy
Laymarsh Close
Beckett Cl
St Augustines Primary School
Paroma Road
Monarch Rd
Ambrook Rd
Sikh Temple
Mitchell Cl
Elstree Gardens
Kingswood Av
Hadley Road
St Augustine's Rd
Ripley Rd
Coleman Rd
Edwards Rd
Sheridan Road
Gertrude Rd
Lyndon Rd
B250
Lower Pk Rd
Belvedere Primary School
Woodside Sch
Methuen Rd
Poplar Mt
Beltwood Rd
Bullbanks Rd
Mayfield Road
Ashburnham Road
Gordon Rd
Stanmore Road
Glendale Rd
Upper Abbey Road
Halt Robin Rd
Halt Robin Road
Parkside Road
Green Chain Walk
Abbey Crs
Brigstock Rd
Regent Sq
Capital Industrial Estate
DA17
Lesnes Abbey Woods
Hattersfield Cl
Heron Hill
Draper Cl
Clive Rd
Ruskin Road
Cowper Rd
Milton Rd
Kentish Road
Orchard Rd
PICARDY ROAD
Fremantle Rd
Mossdown Close
Calvert Close
Heathdene Drive
Elmbourne Dr
Fox House Rd
Trinity Sch Belvedere
Tower Rd
Bexley College
Bramble Croft
Pembroke Road
Sandcliff Road
Raglan Rd
Wellington Rd
Napier Rd
Lessness Pk
Nelson Rd
Smarden Cl
Berkhampstead Rd
Essenden Rd
Eardley Road
Upper Pk Rd
Belvedere
A206
Upr Holly Hill Rd
Holmhurst Rd
Church Rd
Crusoe Rd
Alford Rd
Vickers Rd
Valley Rd
Walden Cl
Court Av
Abbey Mt
The View
Treetops Cl
ERITH ROAD
Surgery
WOOLWICH ROAD
Tyeshurst Cl
Croft Cl
Harold Avenue
Albert Rd
Victoria St
Surgery
Bedwell Rd
Cheshunt Rd
Hoddesdon Rd
Standard Rd
Roberts Rd
Salmon Road
Chapman Road
Lessness Heath Primary School
Rutland Gate
Holly Hill Road
Athol Rd
FRASER ROAD
Hawthorn Pl
Europa Trading Estate
118
Med Cen
The Abbey Clinic
Alfred Rd
Fairmont Cl
Stapley Rd
Albany Rd
Barnfield Rd
Nuxley Rd
Grosvenor Road
Wadeville Cl
Lumley Cl
Brook St
Riverdale Road
Lessness Heath
Cemetery
Milford Cl
Westergate Road
Osborne Road
Upper Gv Rd
Dryhill Rd
Stream Way
Walsingham Walk
Silver Spring Cl
Kempton Cl
Bedonwell Clinic
Orchard Av
Orchard Avenue
Bedonwell Road
Bedonwell Primary School
Redleaf Cl
Matfield Rd
Trosley Road
Cray Road
Swaylands Rd
Belliring Close
Manorway
Carlton Rd
Carlton Road
Thorne Close
Thwaite Cl
Vicarage Close
Lochmere Cl
Collindale Av
Cavendish Av
Oakdene Av
Primary School
Park Crs
Ling Rd
Erith & District Hosp
Northumberland Heath Medical Cen
Clovelly Road
Walk Way
Edwin Cl
Iris Crs
Brabourne Crs
Parsonage Manorway
Shinglewell Rd
Luddesdon Road
Eastry Road
Plaxtol Road
Swanton Road
The Drive
Brook Street
Brantwood Av
Hengist Rd
Horsa Rd
Emes Rd
Buxton Rd
Elm Gv
Avenue Road
Lwd
Pembury Road
Lenham Road
Knowle Av
Whitfield Road
Stapleton Road
Lydd Rd
Avenue
Harolds Rd
Barry Av
Ashbourne Av
Chessington Avenue
Hythe Avenue
The Pantiles
Hurlingham Rd
Ightham Road
Nurstead Road
Sussex Rd
Cookson Gv
Dickens Cl
Byron Drive
Primary School
Northumberland Park
Mill Road
Stonecroft Rd
BEXLEY ROAD
Hurst Road
Erith School
Erith School Community Sports Centre
Northumberland Heath
Ramsden Rd
Bostall Park Av
Malvern Av
Cumberland Drive
Winchelsea Avenue
Heath Road
Belmont Primary School
Belmont Road
Austen Rd
Wilde Rd
Bronte Cl
York Ter
Becton Pl
Brook St
Colyers La
Heath Way
Long Lane
Little Heath
Surgery
Romney Gdns
Norfolk Gdns
Hollingbourne Avenue
Cranbrook Road
Cartmel Rd
Arnside Rd
Langdale Crescent
Birchington Cl
Dalmeny Road
Rydal Drive
A220
Alberta Road
Doris Av
Courteen Dr
Barnehurst Close
Primary Sch
Fairford Avenue
Kipling Road
Kingsgate Cl
Shakespeare Road
Ferndale Cl
Orchard Close
Bowford Avenue
Franklin Road
Coote Rd
Harris Road
Cannon Road
Bristow Road
Dunwich Road
Long Lane
Sheldon Road
Cloudesley Road
Penshurst Rd
Bedonwell Road
The Ennerdale Rd
Green
Keswick Rd
Eskdale Rd
Eversham Road
Silecroft Road
Swanbridge Rd
Francis Avenue
Coniston Road
Coniston Close
Thirlmere Rd
Barnehurst Avenue
Appledore Avenue
Beechcroft Avenue
Castleton Avenue
Pickford Lane Medical Centre
Heathside Av
Jenton Avenue
Albury Av
Hamilton Road
Stanhope Road
Harding Road
Hudson
Ambleside Rd
137
Bursted Wood Primary School
Bursted Wood
DA7
Grasmere Rd
Windermere Rd
Merewood Road
K
Surgery
Dorcis Avenue
Herbert Road
St Thomas More RC Primary School
Grace Av
Long Lane
Hyde Rd
Lavernock Rd
Somersham Rd
Surgery
1
2
3
4
5
6
7

118
99
117
138
A
B
C
D
E
551
52
80
79
78
77
1
2
3
4
5
6
7
Belvedere Industrial Estate
Works
Mulberry Way
Jenningtree Way
Belvedere Link Business Park
Cables Cl
Viking Way
Church Manorway
B213
Ashburnham Road
Gordon Rd
Stanmore Road
Dale Rd
Battle Rd
Valley Rd
Bramble Croft
Park Gdns
Tower Rd
Bexley College
Pembroke Road
Sandcliff Road
Vickers Rd
St John's Rd
Lower Rd
Corinthian Manorway
Galleon Close
Jessett Cl
West Street
St Fidelis Rd
Chandlers Dr
A2016
Nrd Rd
Mildred Rd
Maxim Rd
Winifred Road
Maximfeldt Rd
Chichester Whf
Church Rd
Crusoe Rd
Friday Rd
Alford Rd
Athol Rd
FRASER ROAD
Europa Trading Estate
Hamlet International Industrial Estate
Erith Station
A206
Ron Gn Ct
Cricketers Cl
Ind Park
Riverside Swimming Centre
Erith
Erith High St
Erith Theatre Guild
Library & Mus
Saltford Cl
Walnut Tree Rd
Erith Reach
Coldharbour
Erith Rands
Havering
Bexley
Coldharbour Lane
A220
B252
Pier Road
ERITH HIGH ST
Colebrk St Business Centre
Superstore
James Watt Way
Wheatley Ter Road
Crescent Road
Appold St
Elrick Cl
Health Centre
Christ Church Av
Arran Close
Debrabant Close
Park Crescent
Victoria Road
Glebe Way
QUEENS ROAD
Lesney Park Primary School
Lesney Park Road
Meyer Rd
Randall Cl
Ward Cl
Park Crs
Erith & District Hosp
Surgery
Ling Rd
Mortimer Road
Northumberland Heath Medical Cen
Grovebury Close
Clydon Close
Avenue Road
Erith Stadium
Erith Sports Centre
DA8
Manor Road
Compton Pl
Britannia Cl
Alexandra Rd
Springhead Road
Lydia Rd
Aperfield Road
Cornwallis Close
Frobisher Rd
Turpin Lane
Works
Manford Industrial Estate
Ray Lamb Way
Reddy Road
Raleigh Close
Bilton Road
Mayn
Betsham Road
Festival Close
Canada Road
Durlun Way
Snipe Cl
Sandpiper Dr
Longreach Rd
Jenningtree Rd
Beacon Rd
Widgeon Rd
Shepey Cl
Slade Green Primary School
Alderney Road
Hilden Dr
Brompton Dr
Hollywood Wy
Rodeo Cl
Fern Cl
Hazel Dr
Leycroft Gdns
Slade Green FC
Moat Lane
Slade Green
Church Trading Estate
Richmer Rd
Slade Green Road
Elm Road
Larkswood Cl
Hazel Road
Kempton Cl
Vicarage Close
BEXLEY ROAD
Emes Rd
Hind Crs
Buxton Road
Elm Gv
Broadoak Rd
Beechfield Rd
Conistone Close
Thanet Road
Larner Rd
Badlow Cl
SOUTH ROAD
Guild Rd
Ind Est
Boundary St
Arthur St
Nursery
The Page Crs
Avenue Road
Lwd
Erith School
Erith School Community Sports Centre
Ramsden Rd
Frinsted Road
Valence Rd
Stelling Rd
Detling Rd
Stuart Mantle Way
Hemsted Rd
Twigg Cl
Brasted Rd
Waterhead Close
Chipstead Rd
Northumberland Heath
Birling Road
Halstead Rd
Colyers Lane Medical Centre
Colyers Primary School
Colyers La
West Holme
East Holme
Colyers Cl
Heath Way
Colyers Lane
Health Centre
North End Trading Est
Pearewood Road
Northend Primary School
Cloudesley Rd
Newbery Road
Burns Cl
Scott Crs
Craydene Rd
Slade Gdns
Power Ind Estate
Plantation Rd
Bridge Road
North End
Forest Road
Clark Cl
Cedar Rd
Willow Road
Slade Green Station
Barnehurst Close
Primary Sch
Northumberland Way
Pear Tree Cl
Normandy Primary School
Swallow Cl
Normandy Way
Brendon Close
Doyle Close
Drummond Cl
Selkirk Drive
Myrtle Close
NORTHEND ROAD
Mendip Road
Pennine Way
Chiltern Crs
Hurstwood Avenue
Fairford Avenue
Barnehurst Avenue
Appledore Avenue
Beechcroft Avenue
Castleton Avenue
Downbank Avenue
Erith Road
Coniston Close
Cheviot Cl
Cotswold Close
Venners Cl
Eversley Avenue
Ranworth Cl
Barnett Cl
Lincoln Cl
Lincoln Rd
Sun Ct
Dale View
Whitehall Lane
Lane
Oak Rd
Howbury
Ely Cl
Lincoln Road
Works
A206
A20
1 grid square represents 500 metres

Wennington Marshes
Havering
Thurrock
Aveley Marshes
Purfleet Ind Park
Juliette Way
Kerry Avenue
LONDON ROAD
LONDON RD
A1306
A13
Fanns Farm
LC
Milehams Industrial Estate
Water Lane
Surgery
Marlow Av
Fanns Rise
Council Building
Marine Court
Centurion Way
Crusader Close
TANK HILL
ROAD
Thamley
Rapier Cl
Chieftan Drive
Saladin Dr
Comet Cl
Mulberry Drive
PO
Tank Lane
Purfleet Primary School
Beacon Hill Industrial Estate
A1090
Hotel
The Limes
Church Lane
Harrisons Wharf
Works
Purfleet Station
Purfleet
River Thames
Crayford Ness
Landau Way
Darent Industrial Park
Dayton Drive
Maypole Crescent
Burnett Road
Ness Road
Works
Wallhouse Road
Long Reach
Dartford Marshes
Darent Valley Path
Joyce Green Lane
Crayford Marshes
Marsh Street
Kent
139
F
G
H
J
K
54
55
80
79
78
77
1
2
3
4
5
6
7

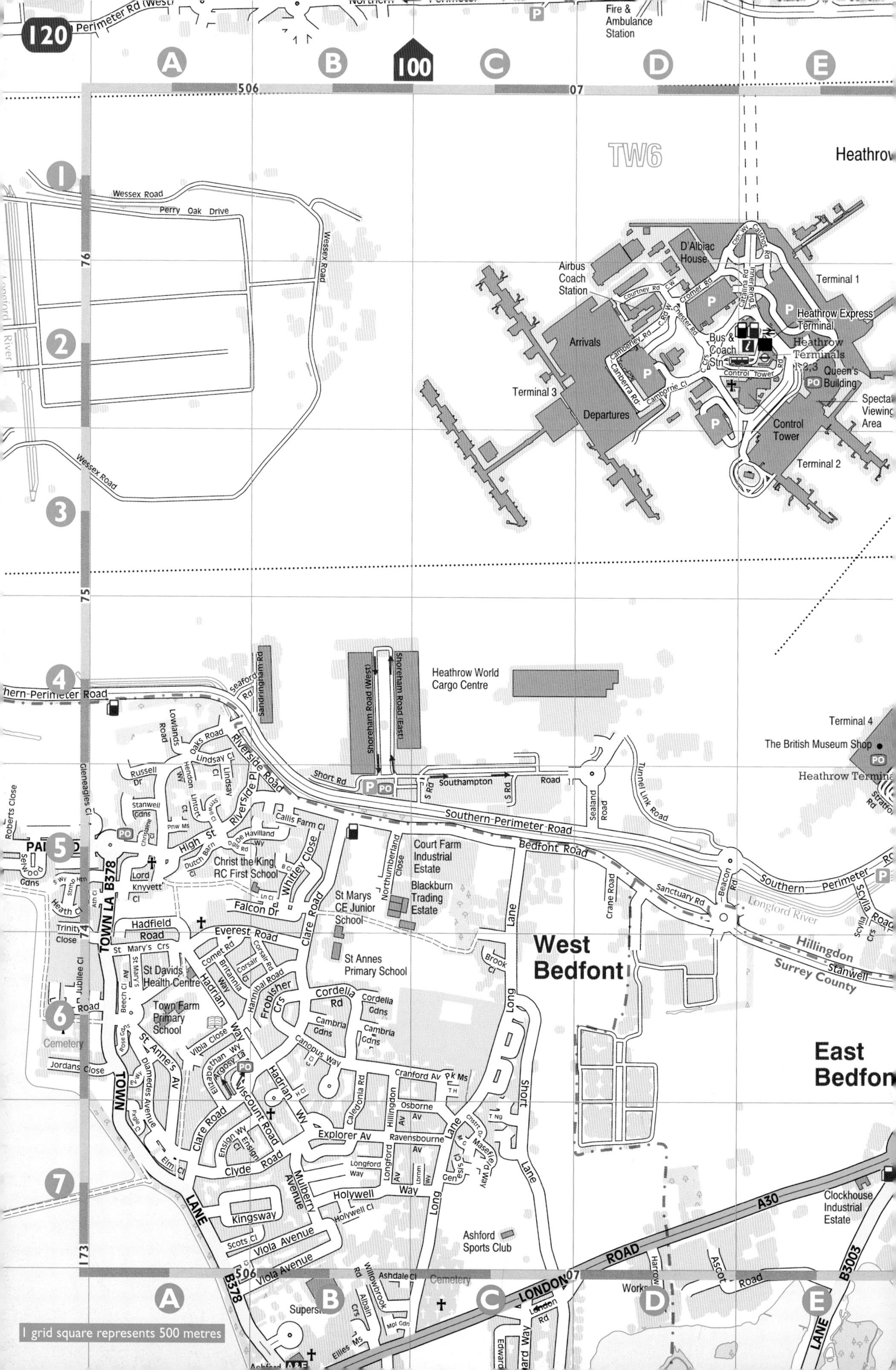

120
100
A
B
C
D
E
Perimeter Rd (West)
Fire & Ambulance Station
TW6
Heathrow
Wessex Road
Perry Oak Drive
Longford River
Airbus Coach Station
D'Albiac House
Courtney Rd
Cromer Rd
Chester Rd
Camberley Rd
Canberra Rd
Camborne Cl
Arrivals
Departures
Terminal 3
Terminal 1
Terminal 2
Heathrow Express Terminal
Bus & Coach Stn
Heathrow Terminals 1,2,3
Control Tower
Queen's Building
Spectator Viewing Area
Inner Ring E
Heathrow World Cargo Centre
Sandringham Rd
Seaford Rd
Shoreham Road (West)
Shoreham Road (East)
Short Rd
Southampton Road
Terminal 4
The British Museum Shop
Heathrow Terminal 4
Stratford Rd
Tunnel Link Road
Sealand Road
Southern Perimeter Road
Bedfont Road
Sanctuary Rd
Beacon Rd
Crane Road
Scylla Road
Hillingdon
Stanwell
Surrey County
Lowlands Road
Oaks Road
Lindsay Cl
Riverside Road
Riverside Pl
Russell Dr
Stanwell Gdns
Hendon Way
Lintort Ct
High St
De Havilland Way
Dutch Barn Cl
Callis Farm Cl
Whitley Close
Christ the King RC First School
Lord Knyvett Cl
Gleneagles Cl
Roberts Close
Town La B378
Heath Cl
Trinity Close
Jubilee Cl
Hadfield Road
Falcon Dr
Clare Road
Northumberland Close
Court Farm Industrial Estate
Blackburn Trading Estate
St Marys CE Junior School
St Annes Primary School
Everest Road
Comet Rd
Britannia Way
Corsair Cl
Hannibal Road
Frobisher Crs
Cordelia Rd
Cordelia Gdns
Cambria Gdns
St Mary's Crs
St Davids Health Centre
Hadrian Way
Town Farm Primary School
Vibia Close
Elizabethan Wy
Argosy La
Canopus Way
Cranford Av
Osborne Av
Hillingdon Av
Caledonia Rd
Explorer Av
Ravensbourne Av
Longford Way
Long Lane
Short Lane
Brook Cl
Masefield Way
West Bedfont
East Bedfont
St Anne's Av
Diamedes Avenue
Cemetery
Jordans Close
Town Lane
Clyde Road
Ensign Way
Viscount Road
Mulberry Avenue
Holywell Way
Holywell Cl
Kingsway
Scots Cl
Viola Avenue
Ashford Sports Club
Clockhouse Industrial Estate
A30
London Road
Harrow Rd
Ascot Road
B3003
Lane
Ashdale Cl
Willowbrook
Albain Crs
Ellies Ms
Edward Way
B378
506
07
76
75
74
173
1
2
3
4
5
6
7
1 grid square represents 500 metres

Northern Perimeter Rd
F
G
H
J
101
09
10
Eastern Perimeter Rd
Eastern Business Park
Esher Crs
Eastchurch Rd
Exeter Wy
Vanguard Wy
Exeter Road
Eastchurch Road
Eastern Perimeter Road
River Crane
Cranford Infant School
Cranford Junior School
Byron Avenue
Chaucer Avenue
Electra Av
Eagle Rd
Elmdon Rd
Cranford La
Girling Way
Sun Life Trading Estate
Viscount Way
Works
Lithgow's Rd
Hatton
Hatton Cross Stn
GT SOUTH-WEST RD
GREAT SOUTH-WEST ROAD
A30
Faggs Rd
Dockwell Close
Green Man Lane
St Theresa's Road
St Anthony's Wy
Fagg's Road
Hatton Gn
CAUSEWAY
A312
Heron Wy
Hatton Road
Myrtle Av
Wellington Rd
Haslemere Industrial Estate
Armadale Rd
Space Waye
Pier Road
FAGG'S ROAD
Cem
122
Cain's Lane
Orchard Av
Edward Rd
Perimeter Road
Southern Perimeter Rd
Swindon Rd
The Marjory Kinnon School
Surgery
Bedfont J&I School
Hazelmere Cl
Marriott Cl
The Gardens
Shrewsbury Road
Swansea Road
Hillingdon
Hounslow
Clive Road
Minimax Close
Engineer Dr
Pentelow Gdns
Kingston Av
Peninsular Cl
Target Cl
Northumberland Crs
Richmond Av
Longford Avenue
Elmcroft Cl
A315
STAINES ROAD
Staines Rd
Ruskin Av
Burns Avenue
Shaftesbury Avenue
Shakespeare Avenue
Buckingham Av
Gladstone Av
HARLINGTON ROAD
Bedfont Cl
Montrose Rd
Horsham Rd
North Rd
North Cl
New Road
Page Road
Dorchester Dr
Bethany Waye
East Road
West Road
Hatton Road
Benedict Dr
Cassiobury Avenue
Letchworth Av
Longford Community School
Tachbrook Rd
Feltham & Hounslow Boro FC
TW14
Stanwell Rd
Longleat Wy
Pates Mnr Dr
Burlington Cl
Gould Rd
Warfield Rd
Colonial Rd
Imperial Road
BEDFONT LANE
Bedfont Health Clinic
Fruen Road
Feltham Athletics Arena
Nursery Close
Fern Grove
GREAT SOUTH-WEST ROAD
West View
Spinney Drive
St Mary's Drive
Natalie Cl
Grovestile Waye
Beech Road
Monarch Cl
Southville Road
Walker Cl
Westmacott Dr
Stone Crs
Shore Cl
Hawkes Rd
B3377
BEDFONT LA
Locomotive Dr
Station Est Rd
NEW ROAD
Feltham Station
Hatchett Rd
Bedfont Green Close
Fawns Manor Rd
Elm Road
Sherborne Rd
Cedar Rd
Peacock Avenue
Dudley Road
Kilross Rd
Grove Village Medical Cen
Southville Close
Southville Crs
Oak Way
Beattie Cl
Chandlers Close
Southville Junior School
Westminster Cl
Southern Av
Proctors Cl
Sandycombe Rd
Fairholme J&I School
Padbury Cl
Bowden Close
Loxwood Cl
Elsworth Close
Sandy Dr
Ash Gv
Watermead
Derwent Cl
Trevithick Cl
Jubilee Wy
Eldridge Cl
Railway Terrace
Cardinal Road Infant School
A244
Victoria Rd
Waterloo Cl
Highfield Road
Plum Cl
Hanover Av
Cemetery
Bedfont Road
Padstow Walk
140
Guildford Rd
Superstore
School
Industrial Estate
Edward Pauling School
Bedfont Lakes
K
Surgery
I
2
3
4
5
6
7

122
102
121
141
A
B
C
D
E
1
2
3
4
5
6
7
Hounslow West
North Feltham
TW4
A4
A30
A312
A315
A3063
A244
A314
B3377
Bath Rd
Great South-West Road
South-West
Causeway
Fagg's
Staines Road
Wellington Road North
Harlington Road West
Harlington Road East
Hounslow Road
Hanworth Road
New Road
Bedfont La
Uxbridge Road
Great West Road
Beavers Lane
Green Lane
Green La
Hounslow West Station
Feltham Station
Heathrow International Trading Est
Wallbrook Business Cen
Sun Life Trading Estate
Reservoir
North Feltham Trading Est
River Gardens Business Cen
Haslemere Industrial Estate
Dockwell's Industrial Est
Maple Grove Business Cen
Tamian Industrial Est
Freehold Industrial Cen
Superstore
Works
Cranford Infant School
Cranford Junior School
Community Primary School
Hounslow Heath Infant School
Junior School
Hounslow Cricket Club
Wellington School
Hounslow Heath Golf Club
Golf Course
Hounslow Heath
Heathland School
The Sparrow Farm Infant School
Sparrow Farm Junior School
Feltham & Hounslow Boro FC
Feltham Athletics Arena
Mill Farm Business Park
South West Middlesex Crematorium
Hounslow Cem
Cardinal Road Infant School
Junior School
Cineworld Cinema
Lawrence Business Cen
Feltham Community College
Surgery
Surgeries
Crane
Hounslow Cem
1 grid square represents 500 metres

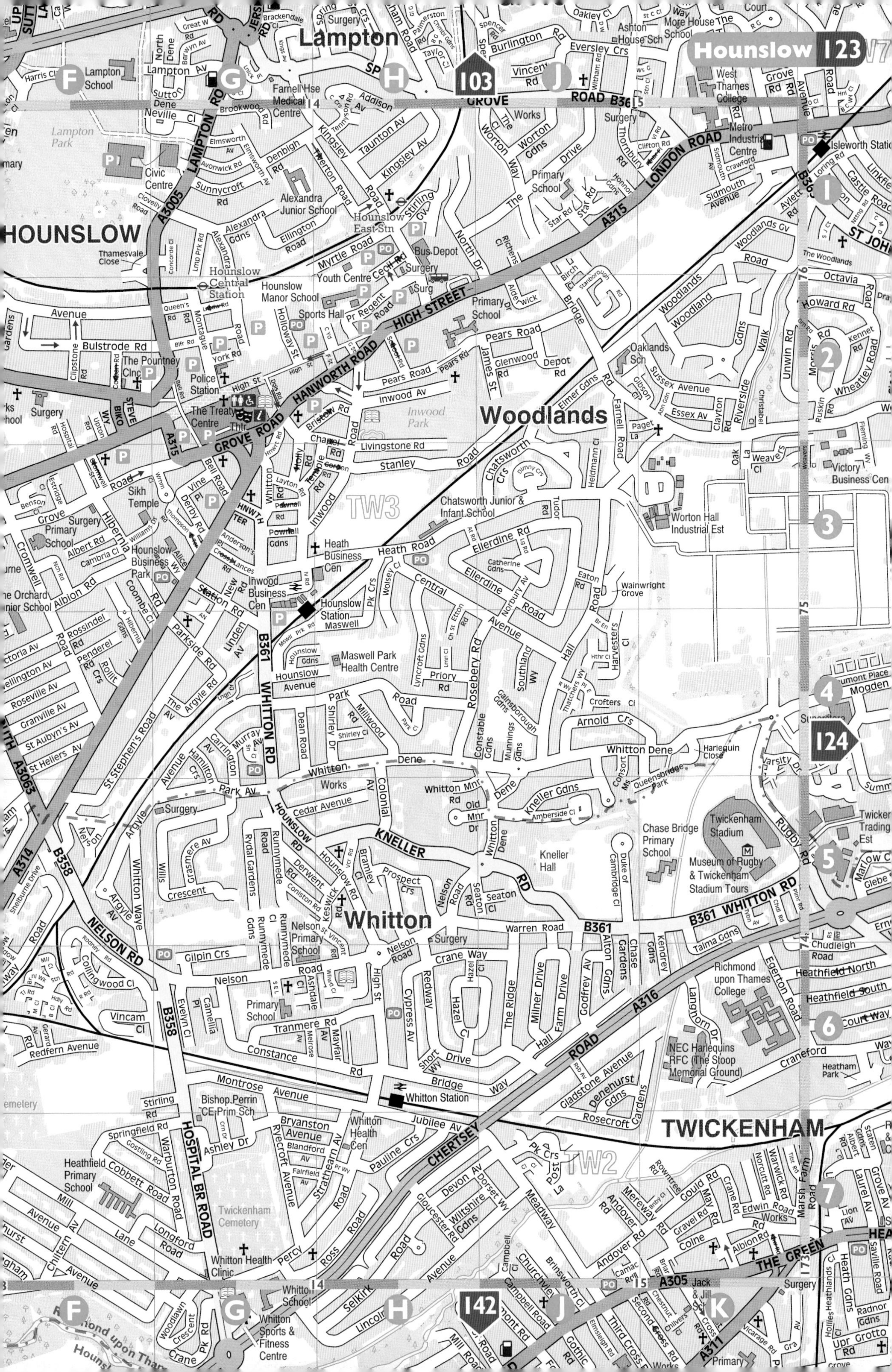

Hounslow 123
103
124
142
Lampton
HOUNSLOW
Woodlands
Whitton
TWICKENHAM
TW3
TW2
F
G
H
J
I
K
2
3
4
5
6
7
14
15
75
74
173
Lampton School
Lampton Park
Civic Centre
Hounslow Central Station
Hounslow Manor School
Hounslow East Stn
Bus Depot
Youth Centre
Sports Hall
Police Station
The Treaty Centre
The Pountney Clnc
Sikh Temple
Hounslow Business Park
Inwood Business Cen
Heath Business Cen
Hounslow Station
Maswell Park Health Centre
Inwood Park
Chatsworth Junior & Infant School
Oaklands Sch
Worton Hall Industrial Est
Victory Business Cen
Isleworth Station
West Thames College
Metro Industrial Centre
Alexandra Junior School
Farnell Hse Medical Centre
Kneller Hall
Chase Bridge Primary School
Twickenham Stadium
Museum of Rugby & Twickenham Stadium Tours
Twickenham Trading Est
Richmond upon Thames College
NEC Harlequins RFC (The Stoop Memorial Ground)
Heatham Park
Whitton Station
Whitton Health Cen
Bishop Perrin CE Prim Sch
Heathfield Primary School
Twickenham Cemetery
Whitton Health Clinic
Whitton School
Whitton Sports & Fitness Centre
Nelson Primary School
LAMPTON RD
A3005
GROVE ROAD B3615
LONDON ROAD
A315
HIGH STREET
HANWORTH ROAD
GROVE ROAD
B361
WHITTON RD
HOUNSLOW RD
KNELLER RD
WHITTON DENE
B361 WHITTON RD
NELSON RD
B358
HOSPITAL BR ROAD
A316
CHERTSEY ROAD
A305
THE GREEN
A311
A314
A3063
Richmond upon Thames

124
104
123
143
A
B
C
D
E
1
2
3
4
5
6
7
TW7
TW1
516
17
76
75
74
173
ISLEWORTH
St Margarets
Cole Park
West Thames College
Metro Industrial Centre
Isleworth Station
Syon Park School
Syon House
Syon Park
Smallberry Green Primary School
Isleworth Cem
Isleworth Town Primary School
Middlesex University Hospital
A&E
Snowy Fielder Waye
Hounslow
Richmond upon Thames
Thames Path
River Thames
Old Deer Park
Golf Course
Royal Mid-Surrey Golf Club
Pools in the Park
Community College
Richmond Magistrates Court
Richmond
Richmond Theatre
Richmond Green
Green Med Cen
Old Palace Yard
Odeon
Film House
Museum
Richmond Bridge
Twickenham Bridge
Brewery Mews Bus Centre
Convent School
Prim Sch
School
Surgery
Works
Victory Business Cen
Isleworth Recreation Centre
Waterside Business Cen
Railshead Road
University
Primary School
Lion Whf
Herons Place
Ivybridge Retail Park
Superstore
Twickenham Stadium
Twickenham Trading Est
Junior School
Twickenham Park Health Cen
St Margarets Business Centre
St Margaret's Stn
Infant School
Cambridge Park Bowling & Sports Club
Marble Hill House
Marble Hill Park
Orleans Park School
Orleans House Gallery
Richmond upon Thames College
Heatham Park
Twickenham Stn
Health Centre
Oak Lane Medical Cen
Civic Centre
Council Building
Richmond Adult & Community College
Mary Wallace Theatre
Eel Pie Island
Ham House (NT)
Deutsche Schule
The Russell School
Strathmore School
TWICKENHAM ROAD
SOUTH STEET
RICHMOND ROAD
ST JOHN'S ROAD
ST MARGARET'S RD
THE AVENUE
CHERTSEY RD A316
LONDON ROAD
TWICKENHAM RD
ST MARGARET'S RD
CROWN RD
RICHMOND ROAD
BRIDGE ST
HEATH ROAD A305
THE GREEN
YORK ST
KING ST
WHITTON RD
A310
A315
A3004
A305
A316
B363
Mill Plat
North St
Church St
Clock Tower Rd
Worton Road
Brantwood Av
Cleveland Rd
Chestnut Gv
Napier Road
Woodstock Av
Northcote Av
Worple Rd
Crane Avenue
Haliburton Road
Kilmorey Road
Ranelagh Drive
St Peter's Road
St George's Rd
Heathcote Rd
Cassilis Rd
Ravensbourne Rd
Rosslyn Rd
Sandycoombe Rd
Cambridge Park
Beaufort Rd
Meadowside
Riverside
River Lane
Ham Street
Meadlands Drive
Lebanon Park
Orleans Road
Montpelier Row
Station Rd
Grosvenor Rd
Queens Rd
Lion Rd
Marsh Farm Road
Egerton Road
Heathfield North
Heathfield South
Court Way
Craneford Way
Chudleigh Road
Mogden Lane
Beaumont Place
Summerwood Road
Rugby Rd
Gordon Av
Allsa Av
Netherton Rd
Orchard Rd
Octavia Road
Howard Rd
Wheatley Road
Unwin Rd
Riverside
Woodlands Gv
Linkfield
Castle Road
Smallberry Av
Mandeville Rd
Hartham Rd
Deepwell Cl
Teesdale Gdns
Busch Close
1 grid square represents 500 metres

North Sheen
Mortlake
Richmond
Richmond Hill
Petersham
Kew Gardens Stn
North Sheen Station
Richmond Stn
Mortlake Stn
Mortlake Crematorium
Hammersmith New Cemetery
East Sheen Common
East Sheen Cemetery
Chiswick Bridge
Evolution House
Temperate House
Pavilion Restaurant
London Welsh FC
Royal Hospital
Marlborough Trading Estate
University of Westminster
Holy Trinity CE Primary School
Sheen Mount Primary School
Tower House School
Kings House School
Queens Medical Cen
St Elizabeths RC Primary School
The Vineyard Primary School
Richmond College
Star & Garter Home
Sheen Lane Health Centre
Superstores
Bog Lodge
Pembroke Lodge
Pen Ponds
Sawyer's Hill
LOWER RICHMOND ROAD
UPPER RICHMOND ROAD WEST
SHEEN ROAD
LWR MORTLAKE ROAD
CLIFFORD AVENUE
MORTLAKE ROAD
MANOR ROAD
SANDYCOMBE ROAD
KEW ROAD
KINGS ROAD
QUEEN'S ROAD
RICHMOND HILL
STAR AND GARTER HILL
PETERSHAM ROAD
SHEEN LANE
A316
A307
A305
A205
A3003
B353
B322
B321
B351
TW9
TW10
SW14
105
126
144

126
106
145
145
BARNES
Grove Park
Mortlake
Roehampton
East Sheen
SW14
SW15
Duke's Meadows
River Thames
Thames Path
Chiswick Bridge
Barnes Bridge
Barnes Bridge Station
Barnes Station
Mortlake Stn
United Services Sports Ground
Police Station
MORTLAKE HIGH STREET
THE TER
BARNES HIGH ST
CHURCH RD
STATION ROAD
ROCKS LANE
MILL HILL ROAD
QUEEN'S RIDE
UPPER RICHMOND
RICHMOND RD
SHEEN LANE
ROEHAMPTON LANE
KINGSTON
A3003
A316
A306
A205
B349
B306
B351
Westmoreland Rd
Gerard Road
Melville Rd
Queen Elizabeth Walk
Barn Elms Athletics Track
Old Barnes Cemetery
Putney Lower Common Cemetery
Barnes Common
St Osmunds RC Primary School
Westfields Primary School
Mortlake Cem
Barnes Hospital
Sheen Lane Health Centre
Tower House School
East Sheen Primary School
Sheen Sch
Sheen Sports Centre
Paddock School
Rosslyn Park RFC
Southlands College
Roehampton Golf Club
The Priory
The Roehampton Priory Hospital
Priory Lane
Bank Lane
Roedean Crescent
Roehampton Gate
Clarence Lane
Ibstock Place School
Golf Course
Roehampton Institute
Grove House
Froebel College
Queen Mary's University Hospital
Douglas Bader Foundation
South Thames College / Wandsworth Adult College
Sacred Heart RC Primary School
Richmond Park Golf Club
Richmond Park
The Royal Ballet School
Beverley Brook
Richmond upon Thames
Wandsworth
Roehampton Recreation Centre
Westmoor Community Clnc
Roehampton Church School
Royal Hospital & Home
Granard Primary School
Chartfield Sch
Alton Primary School
Putney Vale Crematorium
Putney Vale Cemetery
Vicarage Road
Palewell Common Dr
Stonehill Road
Clare Lawn Avenue
Danebury Av
Harbridge Av
Laverstoke Gdns
Fontley Way
Dover House Road
Parkstead Road
Crestway
Westmead
Medfield St
Roehampton High St
A
B
C
D
E
1
2
3
4
5
6
7
521
22
173
74
76
1 grid square represents 500 metres

Putney
Putney Heath
West Hill
Parsons Green
Wandsworth
Southfields
SW6
SW18
River Thames
Thames Path
Fulham FC (Craven Cottage)
Barn Elms Water Sports Centre
Bowls Club
Imperial College
All Saints CE Primary School
Fulham Palace
Bishops Park
Museum of Fulham Palace
Preparatory School
Putney Bridge Station
Putney Bridge
Hurlingham House
Hurlingham Business Park
Hurlingham Private School
Hurlingham & Chelsea School
Sullivan Primary School
Queensmill School
Peterborough Primary School
Fulham Clinic
Lady Margaret School
ABC Cinema
Shopping Centre
Putney Station
Putney Leisure Centre
Putneymead Medical Centre
Lion House School
Arts Theatre
Hawkins Clnc
Health Cen
Prim Sch
Wandsworth Park
Wandsworth County Court
East Putney Station
Bective Ho Clinic
Northfields Prospect Business Cen
Osier Ind Est
Wandsworth Stn
Ferrier Industrial Est
St Josephs Primary School
The Roche School
Ram Brewery
Police Station
Fire Station
ADT Technology College
South Thames College
Merlin School
Putney High School
Elliott Foundation School
The Wandsworth Arndale Centre
Arndale Health Centre
The Southfields Clnc
Wandle Recreation Centre
Wandsworth Trading Estate
King George's Park
Roehampton Institute
Royal Hospital for Neuro-Disability
Prospect House Sch
Ronald Rose Primary Sch
Tudor Lodge Health Cen
Southmead Primary School
Theatre of the Dispossessed
Linden Lodge School
Southfields Station
Sheringdale Primary School
Grammar School
Merton Road Industrial Estate
Riverside Business Centre
Community School
Wimbledon
LWR RICHMOND ROAD
UPPER RICHMOND RD
PUTNEY BRIDGE ROAD
PUTNEY HILL
WEST HILL
TIBBET'S RIDE
WIMBLEDON PARK SIDE
MERTON ROAD
FULHAM ROAD
NEW KINGS ROAD
ARMOURY WY
A3
A205
A217
A218
A219
A308
B306
107
128
146
F
G
H
J
K
1
2
3
4
5
6
7

128
108
127
147
A
B
C
D
E
1
2
3
4
5
6
7
Sands End
WANDSWORTH
Earlsfield
Southfields
SW11
SW18
Wandsworth Common
Wandsworth Bridge
Wandsworth Town Stn
Clapham Junction Station
Wandsworth Common Station
Earlsfield Station
Chelsea College of Art & Design
Battersea Reach
Atlas Transport Est
Trading Estate
Lombard Bus Cen
Heliport Ind Est
Westland Heliport
Library & Community Centre
Consulate of Burkina Faso
Townmead Business Cen
Superstore
Works
Carnwath Road Industrial Est
Hurlingham Business Park
Hurlingham & Chelsea School
Peterborough Primary School
Queensmill School
Ram Brewery & Visitor Centre
The Wandsworth Arndale Centre
Arndale Health Centre
Wandle Recreation Centre
Sergeant Industrial Est
Wandsworth Trading Estate
King George's Park
Merton Road Industrial Estate
Riverside Business Centre
Community School
Haslemere Industrial Est
Brocklebank Health Cen
Council Building
Wandsworth Cemetery
HM Prison
Lombard Business Park
Emanuel School
Bolingbroke Hosp
St Mary's Cemetery
Northcote Lodge School
Highfield School
Beatrix Potter Primary School
St Walter & St John Sports Ground
Upper Tooting Independent High School
Finton House Sch
Nightingale School
Latchmere Leisure Cen
Grace Thtr at the Latchmere
Technology College
Middle School Primary School
Infant School
Fire Station
Police Station & Magistrates Court
Falcon Business Cen
Superstore
High View Primary School
St John's Hospital Day Cen
Battersea Sports Cen
Charterhouse Works
The Roche School
Osier Ind Est
Ferrier Industrial Est
Town Hall
Cncl Building
JMI School
Medical Cen
On the Road Tours
Bridge Lane Thtr
Salesian Coll
Thomas's Preparatory School
WANDSWORTH BRIDGE ROAD
NEW KING'S ROAD
YORK ROAD A3205
FALCON RD A3207
LATCHMERE ROAD A3220
ST JOHN'S HL
BATTERSEA RISE
NORTH SIDE WANDSWORTH COMMON
SWANDON WY
ARMOURY WY
WANDSWORTH HIGH ST
HUGUENOT PL
TRINITY ROAD
WINDMILL RD
SPENCER PARK
EARLSFIELD ROAD
GARRATT LANE
MERTON ROAD
BOLINGBROKE GROVE
ST JAMES'S DRIVE
BURNTWOOD LA
BELLEVUE RD
ELSPETH RD
LAVENDER
A3
A214
A217
A218
A3205
A3207
A3220
A3036
B229
B234
B237
B526
27
526
1 grid square represents 500 metres

CLAPHAM
Stockwell
Clapham Park
Streatham Hill
Balham
Clapham Common
SW4
SW12
CLAPHAM COMMON NORTH SIDE
LONG ROAD
CLAPHAM HIGH STREET
CLAPHAM ROAD
STOCKWELL ROAD
WANDSWORTH ROAD
QUEENSTOWN ROAD
CEDARS ROAD
NORTH ST
CLAPHAM COMMON SOUTH SIDE
THE AVENUE
CAVENDISH ROAD
A205 POYNDERS ROAD
BALHAM HILL
BALHAM HIGH RD
NIGHTINGALE LANE
KINGS AVENUE
BEDFORD ROAD
BRIXTON HILL
STREATHAM HILL
STREATHAM PL
ACRE LA
BATTERSEA PARK
Wandsworth Road Station
Clapham High Street Stn
Clapham North Stn
Clapham Common Stn
Clapham South Station
Balham Station
Queenstown Road Battersea Station
109
130
148

130
110
129
149
A
B
C
D
E
1
2
3
4
5
6
7
Stockwell
BRIXTON
Herne Hill
Knight's Hill
Tulse Hill
West Dulwich
SW9
SW2
SE24
SE5
Brockwell Park
Belair Park
STOCKWELL ROAD
BRIXTON ROAD
BRIXTON HILL
COLDHARBOUR LANE
ACRE LANE
EFFRA RD
ATLANTIC ROAD
RAILTON ROAD
DULWICH ROAD
MILKWOOD ROAD
HERNE HILL
DENMARK HILL
HALF MOON LANE
VILLAGE WAY
NORWOOD ROAD
TULSE HILL
A205 CHRISTCHURCH ROAD
THURLOW PARK ROAD
CAMBERWELL CHURCH ST
CHAMPION PK
Brixton Stn
Loughborough Junction Stn
Herne Hill Station
North Dulwich Station
Tulse Hill Station
West Dulwich Station
Denmark Hill Stn
King's College Hospital
The Maudsley Hosp
HM Prison
Brockwell Lido
Lloyds Register Cricket Club
Herne Hill Stadium (Cycle Centre)
1 grid square represents 500 metres

Brixton 131
132
150
Peckham
Nunhead
East Dulwich
Dulwich Village
Honor Oak
SE22
PECKHAM ROAD
PECKHAM HIGH ST
RYE LANE A2215
PECKHAM RYE
EAST DULWICH RD
A2214
NUNHEAD LANE
EVELINA ROAD
DOG KENNEL HILL
A2216
LORDSHIP LANE
EAST DULWICH GROVE
GROVE VALE
FOREST HILL ROAD
PECKHAM RYE B238
BARRY ROAD
LORDSHIP LANE A205
LONDON ROAD
HONOR OAK PARK
DULWICH COMMON
WALDRAM PK RD
SUSANNE ROAD
GELLATLY RD
B2142 DRAKE
Peckham Rye Park
Peckham Rye Stn
Nunhead Stn
East Dulwich Stn
Forest Hill Station
Dulwich Park
Southwark Sports Ground
Marlborough Cricket Club
Dulwich College
Dulwich Hospital
The Horniman Museum & Gardens
Goose Green Trading Est
Dulwich Leisure Centre
Premier Cinema
Cemetery
Camberwell New Cemetery
Old Cemetery
Golf Course
Aquarius Golf Club
Waverley School
Waverley Lower Secondary School
Alleyns Sch
Dulwich Hamlet FC
Superstore
F
G
H
J
K
I
2
3
4
5
6
7
34
35

132
112
131
151
A
B
C
D
E
1
2
3
4
5
6
7
New Cross Gate
New Cross
St Johns
Nunhead
Ladywell
Brockley
Honor Oak
Honor Oak Park
Forest Hill
SE4
SE23
Haberdashers Askes Hatcham College
University of London
Goldsmiths Coll
Lewisham College
Edmund Waller Primary School
Telegraph Hill School
Brockley Cross Business Cen
Brockley Stn
Crofton Park Station
Honor Oak Park Station
Ladywell Stn
Catford Bridge Station
Catford Station
Forest Hill Station
St Johns Stn
Nunhead Stn
Goldsmiths College
Meadowgate Sch
Ivydale Primary School
Bredinghurst School
Honor Oak Health Centre
Honor Oak Crematorium
Camberwell New Cemetery
Aquarius Golf Club
Ladywell Cemetery
Hilly Fields Medical Centre
Prendergast School
Police Stn
Crofton Leisure Centre
Crofton School
Stillness Primary School
St Dunstans College
Jenner Health Cen
Malham Road Industrial Est
Rathfern Primary School
Holbeach Primary School
Phoenix Leisure Centre
ABC Cinema
Rushey Green Prim Sch
Catford Cricket & Sports Club
Priory House School
Catford Trading Estate
Kilmorie Primary School
University Hospital
Lambeth Southwark & Lewisham Health Authority
Ladywell Arena
Register Office
Watergate School
Thurston Industrial Est
B2142 DRAKEFELL ROAD
LOAMPIT HILL
LEWISHAM WAY
MALPAS ROAD
BROCKLEY ROAD
ADELAIDE AV
LADYWELL ROAD
STANSTEAD ROAD
CATFORD ROAD
CATFORD HILL
HONOR OAK PARK
STONDON PK
BROCKLEY RI
RUSHEY GN
LEWISHAM HIGH ST
THURSTON RD
WALDRAM PK RD
SUNDERLAND RD
Ravensbourne River
1 grid square represents 500 metres

BLACKHEATH HILL A2
SHOOTERS HILL RD A2
113
PR OF WALES RD B212
Blackheath
SE3
LEWISHAM RD A2211
Hare And Billet Road
Mounts Pond Road
All Saints CE Primary Sch
Tranquil Vale
Montpelier Rw
Royal Pde
Blackheath High School GDST
Prep School
Camden Ho Clinic
Primary School
Blackheath Stn
Blackheath Park
Morden College Homes
Manor Brook Medical Centre
Lewisham Centre
Clock Tower
Our Lady of Lourdes RC Primary School
St Josephs Academy RC School
Christ the King 6th Form College
LEE TERRACE
BELMONT HILL B220
Blackheath Hosp
LEE ROAD B212
Brooklands Primary School
Wingfield Primary School
Huntsman Sports Club
The Blackheath Clinic
LEWISHAM
HIGH ROAD
LEE
Goldsmiths Coll
Northbrook CE School
A2212 BURNT ASH ROAD
A20
ELTHAM ROAD
Riverston School
134
Old Colfeian Sports Club
Ladywell Leisure Centre
Lewisham Park
SE13
Ennersdale Primary School
St Winifreds RC Infant School
Lee Manor Primary School
Complementary Health Cen
Hither Green Stn
Hither Green
Lee
Lee Station
Chiltonian Industrial Est
WESTHORNE AVENUE
St Winifreds Junior School
Mountsfield Park
BROWNHILL ROAD A205
ST MILDREDS ROAD A205
Baring Primary School
SE12
Sandhurst Primary School
Holy Cross RC Primary School
CATFORD
152
Hither Green Cemetery
Torridon Primary School
BARING ROAD
F
G
H
J
K
I
2
3
4
5
6
7
38
39
40
74
75
76
173

134
114
133
153
A
B
C
D
E
1
2
3
4
5
6
7
SE3
SE12
Kidbrooke
ELTHAM
Mottingham
Wricklemarsh Road
Holburne Road
Whetstone Road
Dursley Road
Balchen Road
Kidbrooke Park Primary School
Kidbrooke School
Broad Walk
Mayday Gardens
Long Lane AFC
Manor Brook Medical Centre
Morden College Homes
Rochester Way
Woolacombe Road
Kidbrooke Park Road
Brook Lane
Delme Crescent
Sports Ground
Thomas Tallis School
Superstore
Kidbrooke Station
Wingfield Primary School
Moorhead Way
Pinto Way
Huntsman Sports Club
Surgery
Elford Cl
Primary School
Ryan Close
Tudway Road
Meadowside Leisure Centre
Lyme Farm Road
Riverston School
Sutcliffe Park
Sutcliffe Park Athletics Track
Eltham Road
Sidcup Road
Westhorne Avenue
Colfes Prep School
Civil Service Sports Ground
Old Brockleians Sports Ground
Leathersellers Sports Ground
Horn Park Primary School
Simnel Road
Sibthorpe Road
Paston Crescent
Mottingham Lane
Hadlow College
Eltham College Junior School
Eric Liddell Sports Centre
Infant School
Nelson Mandela Rd
Birdbrook Road
Tilbrook Rd
Ridgebrook Road
Langbrook Road
Bournbrook Road
Appleton Road
Ross Way
St Thomas More RC Primary School
Winchcomb Gardens
Kingsholm Gardens
Rancliffe Gdns
Odeon
Kidbrooke Lane
University of Greenwich Sports Ground
The Pleasance
Cemetery
Arbroath Road
Dunblane Road
Allenswood Rd
Well Hall Road
Westmount Road
Heatherbank
Granby Road
Arsenal Road
Congreve Road
Gordon Primary School
Craigton Rd
Eltham Station
Rochester Way
Eltham Bus Station
Eltham Hill
Eltham Health Clinic
Eltham Pools
Bingo Hall
Police Station
Council Building
The Bob Hope Theatre
Eltham High St
Eltham Green School
Eltham Hill Technology College
Queenscroft Road
Moatbridge School
King's Orchard
Court Yard
Eltham Palace (remains)
Royal Blackheath Golf Club
Kingsground
Middle Park Avenue
Middle Park Primary School
Gregory Crs
Greenwich
Bromley
Green Chain Walk
Park Avenue
Shrubsall Cl
Mottingham Station
Sidcup Road
Luxfield Road
West Park
Court Road
Tarnwood Pk
Woodmere
Woodyates Rd
Burnt Ash Hill
Baring Road
Lewisham
Senlac Road
Jevington Way
Coopers School
1 grid square represents 500 metres

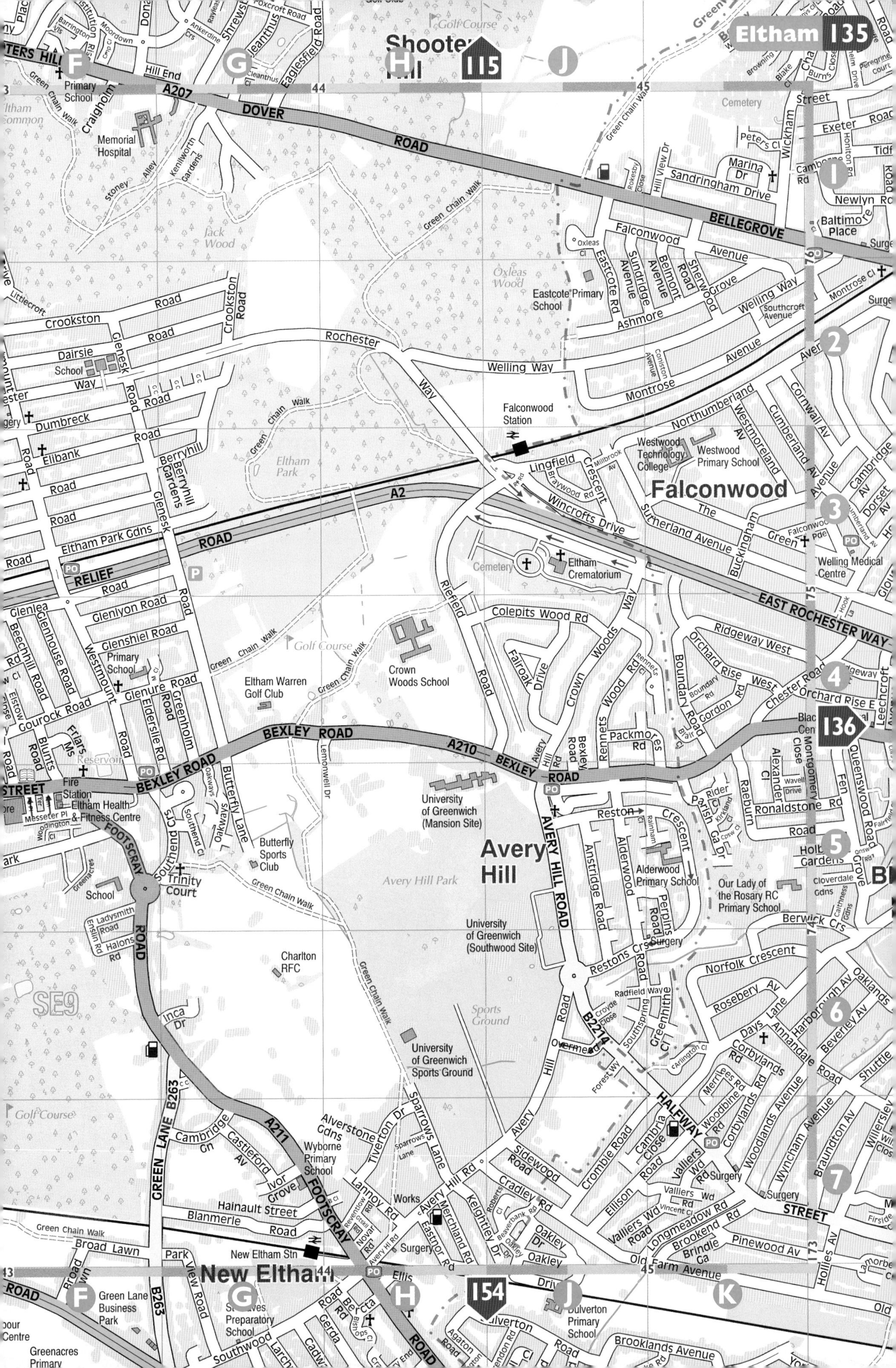
Shooters Hill
115
Golf Course
F
G
H
J
Primary School
A207
DOVER ROAD
Memorial Hospital
Stoney Alley
Kenilworth Gardens
Green Chain Walk
Jack Wood
Oxleas Wood
Cemetery
Wickham Street
Exeter Road
Marina Dr
Sandringham Drive
BELLEGROVE
Falconwood Avenue
Eastcote Rd
Sundridge Avenue
Belmont Road
Sherwood Grove
Eastcote Primary School
Ashmore
Welling Way
Montrose Cl
Southcroft Avenue
Crookston Road
Dairsie Road
Glenesk Road
School
Rochester Way
Welling Way
Coniston Avenue
Montrose Avenue
Dumbreck Road
Elibank Road
Falconwood Station
Northumberland Av
Westmoreland Av
Cumberland Av
Cornwall Av
Cambridge Av
Dorset Av
Eltham Park
Lingfield Crescent
Westwood Technology College
Westwood Primary School
Falconwood
Berryhill Gardens
A2
ROAD
Wincrofts Drive
Sutherland Avenue
The Green
Buckingham
Welling Medical Centre
Eltham Park Gdns
RELIEF ROAD
Cemetery
Eltham Crematorium
EAST ROCHESTER WAY
Glenlea
Glenlyon Road
Glenshiel Road
Riefield Road
Colepits Wood Rd
Fairoak Drive
Crown Woods Way
Ridgeway West
Orchard Rise West
Boundary Road
Primary School
Golf Course
Crown Woods School
Eltham Warren Golf Club
Beechhill Road
Glenhouse Road
Westmount Road
Gourock Road
Glenure Road
Eldersie Rd
Greenholm Road
Rennets Wood Rd
Packmores Rd
Chester Road
Orchard Rise E
136
BEXLEY ROAD
A210
Lemonwell Dr
BEXLEY ROAD
Avery Hill Rd
Bexley Road
Blunts Road
Friars Ms
Reservoir
Butterfly Lane
STREET
Fire Station
Eltham Health & Fitness Centre
Southend Crs
Oakways
University of Greenwich (Mansion Site)
Reston
Crescent
Alexander Cl
Montgomery Close
Ronaldstone Rd
Raeburn
Parish Ga Dr
FOOTSCRAY
Butterfly Sports Club
Avery Hill
AVERY HILL ROAD
Anstridge Road
Alderwood
Alderwood Primary School
Holbeck Gardens
Our Lady of the Rosary RC Primary School
Trinity Court
Avery Hill Park
Green Chain Walk
School
Ladysmith Road
Halons Rd
ROAD
Charlton RFC
University of Greenwich (Southwood Site)
Perpins Road
Surgery
Restons Crs
Berwick Crs
Norfolk Crescent
Rosebery Av
SE9
Inca Dr
Sports Ground
Radfield Way
Southspring
Greenhithe Cl
Days Lane
Annandale Road
Harborough Av
Beverley Av
B2214
University of Greenwich Sports Ground
Corbylands Rd
Shuttle
Golf Course
GREEN LANE B263
A211
Cambridge Gn
Castleford Av
Alverstone Gdns
Tiverton Dr
Sparrows Lane
Wyborne Primary School
Avery Hill Rd
Sidewood Road
Crombie Road
Cambria Close
HALFWAY
Woodbine Rd
Woodlands Avenue
Wyncham Avenue
Braundton Av
Ivor Grove
FOOTSCRAY
Lannoy Rd
Works
Merchland Rd
Keightley Dr
Cradley Rd
Ellison Road
Valliers Wd Rd
Surgery
STREET
Hainault Street
Blanmerle Road
Green Chain Walk
Broad Lawn
Park View Road
New Eltham Stn
Novar Rd
Surgery
Eastnor Rd
Oakley Dr
Valliers Wd Road
Longmeadow Rd
Brookend Rd
Brindle Ga
Pinewood Av
Hollies Av
New Eltham
Old Farm Avenue
154
Ellis
Broad Lawn
F
Green Lane Business Park
B263
G
St Olaves Preparatory School
H
J
Dulverton Primary School
K
ROAD
Southwood
Gerda Rd
Larch
Dulverton Rd
Brooklands Avenue
Greenacres Primary

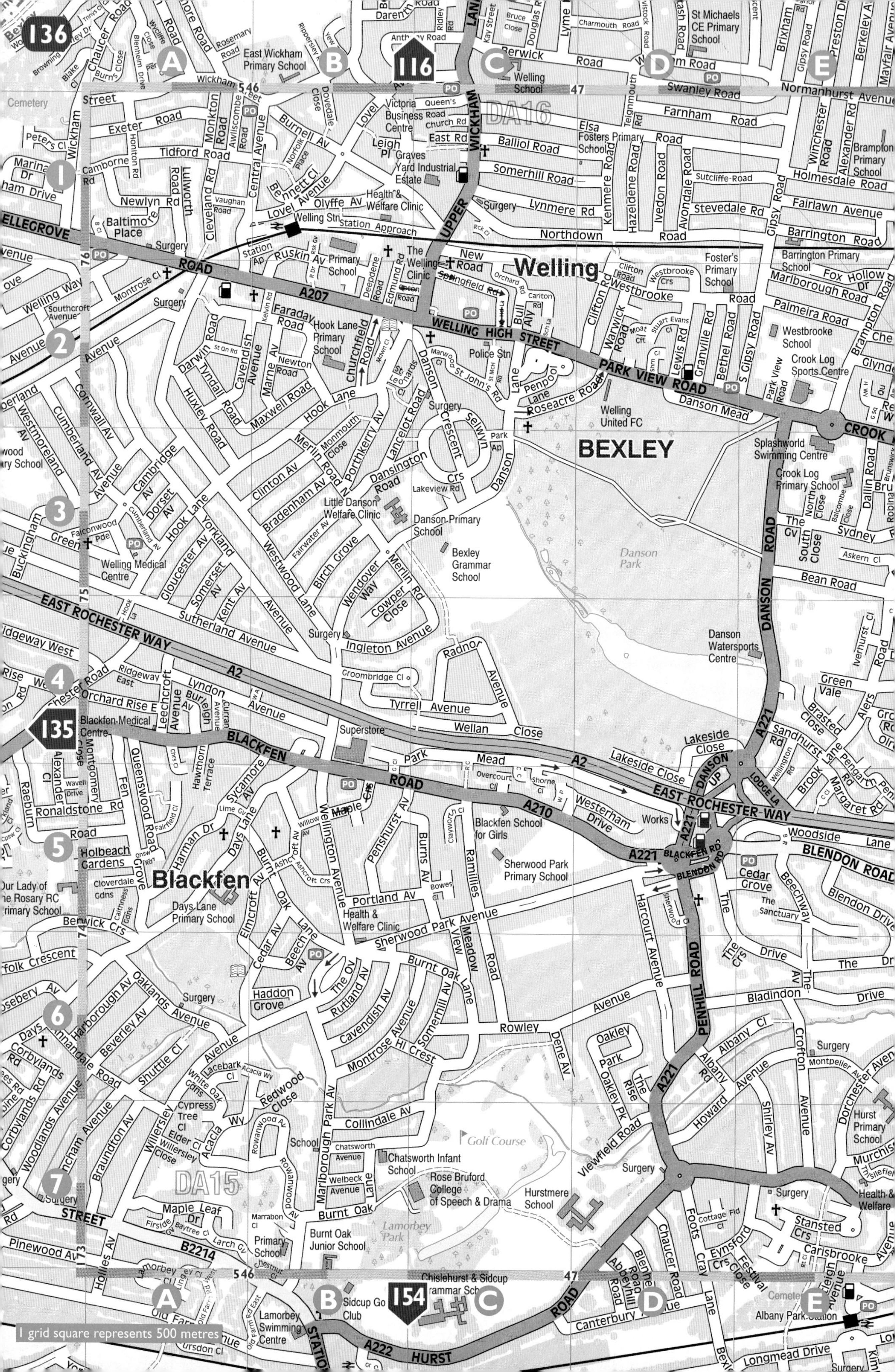
136
116
135
154
A
B
C
D
E
1
2
3
4
5
6
7
546
47
76
75
74
173
DA16
DA15
Welling
BEXLEY
Blackfen
Cemetery
Wickham Street
Exeter Road
Tidford Road
Newlyn Rd
Baltimore Place
Marina Dr
Camborne Rd
Monkton Road
Awliscombe Road
Central Avenue
Cleveland Rd
Vaughan Road
Lullworth Road
Honiton Rd
Peters Cl
Wickham
Welling Stn
Station Approach
Station Ap
Ruskin Av
Primary School
Burnell Av
Norfolk Place
Bennett Cl
Olyffe Av
Lovel Avenue
Dovedale Close
Victoria Business Centre
Queen's Road
Church Rd
East Rd
Leigh Pl
Graves Yard Industrial Estate
Health & Welfare Clinic
UPPER WICKHAM LANE
Anthony Road
Darenth Road
Ripon Road
Kay Street
Bruce Close
Douglas Rd
Berwick Road
Welling School
Charmouth Road
Lyme
St Michaels CE Primary School
Wickham Road
Swanley Road
Normanhurst Avenue
Farnham Road
Elsa Road
Fosters Primary School
Balliol Road
Somerhill Road
Lynmere Rd
Surgery
Northdown Road
Kenmere Road
Hazeldene Road
Iveдon Road
Avondale Road
Sutcliffe Road
Stevedale Rd
Holmesdale Road
Fairlawn Avenue
Barrington Road
Barrington Primary School
Fox Hollow Dr
Marlborough Road
Palmeira Road
Brampton Road
Brampton Primary School
Winchester Road
Alexander Rd
Gipsy Road
Brixham
Preston Dr
Berkeley Av
Mayfair Avenue
ELLEGROVE ROAD
A207
WELLING HIGH STREET
PARK VIEW ROAD
New Road
Springfield Rd
Orchard Rd
Carlton Rd
The Welling Clinic
Edmund Rd
Deepdene Road
Clifton Rd
Westbrooke Road
Westbrooke Crs
Foster's Primary School
Stuart Evans Cl
Lewis Rd
Granville Rd
Bethel Road
S Gipsy Road
Westbrooke School
Crook Log Sports Centre
Welling Way
Southcroft Avenue
Montrose Cl
Faraday Road
Kelvin Rd
Darwin Road
Tyndall Road
Cavendish Avenue
Marne Av
Newton Road
Maxwell Road
Hook Lane Primary School
Churchfield Road
Hook Lane
Danson Crescent
Marwood Cl
St John's Rd
Police Stn
Penpool Lane
Roseacre Road
Welling United FC
Danson Mead
Park View Road
CROOK LOG
Splashworld Swimming Centre
Crook Log Primary School
North Close
Balcombe Close
Dallin Road
The Gv
South Close
Sydney Road
Askern Cl
Bean Road
Westmoreland Av
Cumberland Av
Cornwall Av
Cambridge Av
Dorset Av
Huxley Road
Merlin Road N
Monmouth Close
Porthkerry Av
Lancelot Road
Selwyn Crs
Lakeview Rd
Park Ap
Danson Road
Clinton Av
Bradenham Av
Dansington Road
Little Danson Welfare Clinic
Danson Primary School
Bexley Grammar School
Danson Park
Falconwood Pde
Green
Buckingham
Welling Medical Centre
Hook Lane
Yorkland Av
Gloucester Av
Somerset Av
Kent Av
Westwood Avenue
Westwood Lane
Birch Grove
Fairwater Av
Wendover Way
Merlin Rd
Cowper Close
Ingleton Avenue
Radnor Avenue
Danson Watersports Centre
DANSON ROAD
EAST ROCHESTER WAY
Sutherland Avenue
Hook La
Ridgeway West
Ridgeway East
Chester Road
Orchard Rise E
Leechcroft Avenue
Lyndon Avenue
Burleigh Av
Curran Avenue
A2
Groombridge Cl
Tyrrell Avenue
Wellan Close
Blackfen Medical Centre
BLACKFEN ROAD
Superstore
Park Mead
Lakeside Close
DANSON UP
A221
Montgomery Close
Alexander Cl
Wavell Drive
Queenswood Road
Hawthorn Terrace
Sycamore Av
Overcourt Cl
Shorne Cl
Westerham Drive
Works
A210
Raeburn
Ronaldstone Rd
Road
Lime Gv
Harman Dr
Days Lane
Burnt Oak Lane
Ashcroft Av
Willow Av
Maple Crs
Wellington Avenue
Penshurst Av
Burns Av
Clayworth Cl
Ramillies Road
Blackfen School for Girls
Sherwood Park Primary School
BLACKFEN RD
BLENDON RD
Woodside Lane
BLENDON ROAD
Cedar Grove
Beechway
The Sanctuary
Blendon Drive
Holbeach Gardens
Our Lady of the Rosary RC Primary School
Cloverdale Gdns
Caithness Gdns
Grove
Days Lane Primary School
Berwick Crs
Elmcroft Av
Portland Av
Bowes Cl
Health & Welfare Clinic
Sherwood Park Avenue
Meadow View
Harcourt Avenue
PENHILL ROAD
The Crs
Drive
The Av
Bladindon Drive
Norfolk Crescent
Rosebery Av
Harborough Av
Oaklands Avenue
Beverley Av
Cedar Av
Beech Av
The Ov
Rutland Av
Haddon Grove
Cavendish Av
Burnt Oak Lane
Somerhill Av
Rowley Avenue
Dene Av
Oakley Park
Oakley Pk
The Rise
Albany Cl
Albany Rd
Crofton Avenue
Montpelier Av
Dorchester Avenue
Hurst Primary School
Days Lane
Annandale Road
Corbylands Rd
Shuttle Cl
Lacebark Cl
Acacia Wy
White Oak Gdns
Cypress Tree Cl
Elder Cl
Redwood Close
Montrose Avenue
Hill Crest
Collindale Av
Marlborough Park Av
Rowanwood Av
School
Chatsworth Avenue
Chatsworth Infant School
Golf Course
Viewfield Road
Howard Avenue
Shirley Av
Murchison
Woodlands Avenue
Wincham Avenue
Braundton Av
Willersley Close
Acacia Wy
Welbeck Avenue
Rose Bruford College of Speech & Drama
Hurstmere School
Surgery
Health & Welfare
Stansted Crs
Carisbrooke Avenue
STREET
Maple Leaf Dr
Firside Gv
Baytree Cl
Larch Gv
B2214
Pinewood Av
Hollies Av
Marrabon Cl
Primary School
Burnt Oak Junior School
Lamorbey Park
Burnt Oak Lane
Foots Cray Lane
Cottage Fld Cl
Eynsford Crs
Festival Close
Chaucer Road
Blenheim Road
Abbeyhill Road
Lamorbey Cl
Chestnut Cl
Sidcup Golf Club
Chislehurst & Sidcup Grammar School
Lamorbey Swimming Centre
Old Farm Road
Old Farm Rd East
Ursdon Cl
STATION
A222
HURST ROAD
Canterbury Avenue
Longmead Drive
Albany Park Station
Cemetery
1 grid square represents 500 metres

Bexley 137
117
138
F
G
H
J
K
I
2
3
4
5
6
7
49
50
76
75
74
73
DA7
DA6
DA5
Bexleyheath
Old Bexley
Coldblow
Bursted Wood
Russell Park
Bexley Woods
Hall Place
River Cray
A207 BROADWAY
A221
ALBION ROAD
ALBION RD A207
BROADWAY
WATLING STREET
A207 LONDON
A2 EAST ROCHESTER WAY
A220
ERITH ROAD
GRAVEL HILL
BOURNE RD
A223
BOURNE
BRIDGEN ROAD B2210
PARKHILL RD B2210
BEXLEY HIGH ST
A222
HURST ROAD
NORTH CRAY ROAD
A2018 VICARAGE ROAD
DARTFORD ROAD A2018
MAYPLACE RD W
ARNSBERG WAY
Bexleyheath Station
Barnehurst Station
Bexley Station
Bursted Wood Primary School
St Thomas More RC Primary School
Upland Primary School
Bexleyheath School
Pelham Primary School
Gravel Hill Primary School
St Catherines RC Girls School
St Columbas RC Boys School
Upton Road School
Upton Primary School
Townley Grammar School for Girls
Bexley Erith Technical High School
Old Bexley CE Primary School
The Medical Centre
Pickford Lane Medical Centre
London Transport Bus Depot
Police Station
Shopping Centre
Broadway Sh Ctr
Cineworld
Civic Offices
Bexleyheath Centre
Super Bowl
Superstore
Bexleyheath Golf Club
Golf Course
Cemetery
Playing Field
Recn Gnd
Old Bexley Business Park
Bexley RFC
Bexley Cricket Club
Hotel
Fire Stn
Amb Stn
Clock Tower
Hospital
Barnehurst Pay & Play
Shakespeare Road
Orchard Close
Bowford Avenue
Pickford Lane
Heathside Av
Albury Avenue
Dorcis Avenue
Herbert Road
Oldfield Road
Percy Rd
Station Road
Woodlands Road
Sheridan Road
Stratton Close
Rowan Road
Ethronvi Road
Standard Road
Paddock Rd
Windsor Rd
Hansol Road
Sibley Cl
Fairway
Iris Av
Sheldon Road
Fairfield Road
Belvedere Road
Nursery Avenue
Garden Avenue
Palmar Crs
Woolwich Road
Haslemere Road
Long Lane
Grace Av
Hyde Rd
Ambleside Rd
Francis Avenue
St Audrey Avenue
Wenvoe Avenue
Lavernock Rd
Rydal Drive
Silecroft Road
Bowness Rd
Silverdale Road
Brantwood Road
Lyndhurst Road
Barnehurst Road
Northumberland Av
Coniston Rd
Grasmere Road
Windermere Road
Merewood Road
Northall Road
Beverley Road
Eastleigh Rd
Westfield Rd
Hillingdon Road
Mayplace Rd East
Mayplace Road
Stephen Road
Inglewood Road
Oakwood Drive
Martens Avenue
Leysdown Avenue
Halcot Avenue
Grazeley Close
Chieveley Road
Springfield Road
Pinnacle Hill
Pelham Road
Latham Road
Broomfield Road
Broom Md
Rochester Drive
Horsham Rd
Midhurst Hill
Highland Rd
Martin Dene
Bellevue Road
Freta Road
Oaklands Road
Townley Road
Upton Road
Meadow Close
Basing Drive
Arcadian Av
Arbuthnot Lane
Meadowview Rd
Riverdale Road
Willow Close
Finsbury Way
Love Lane
Hartford Road
Albert Road
The Ridge
Cross La
Parkhurst Rd
Thanet Rd
Bradbourne Road
Lesley Cl
Parkwood Road
Chilham Close
Salisbury Road
Manor Rd
Manor Way
Glenhurst Avenue
Camden Road
Maiden Erlegh Av
Ravenswood
Hurst Springs
Valentine Av
Heath Road
Wansunt Road
Ashdown Cl
Ridgecroft Cl
Hill Crs
Cold Blow Crs
Betterton Dr
Davenport Road

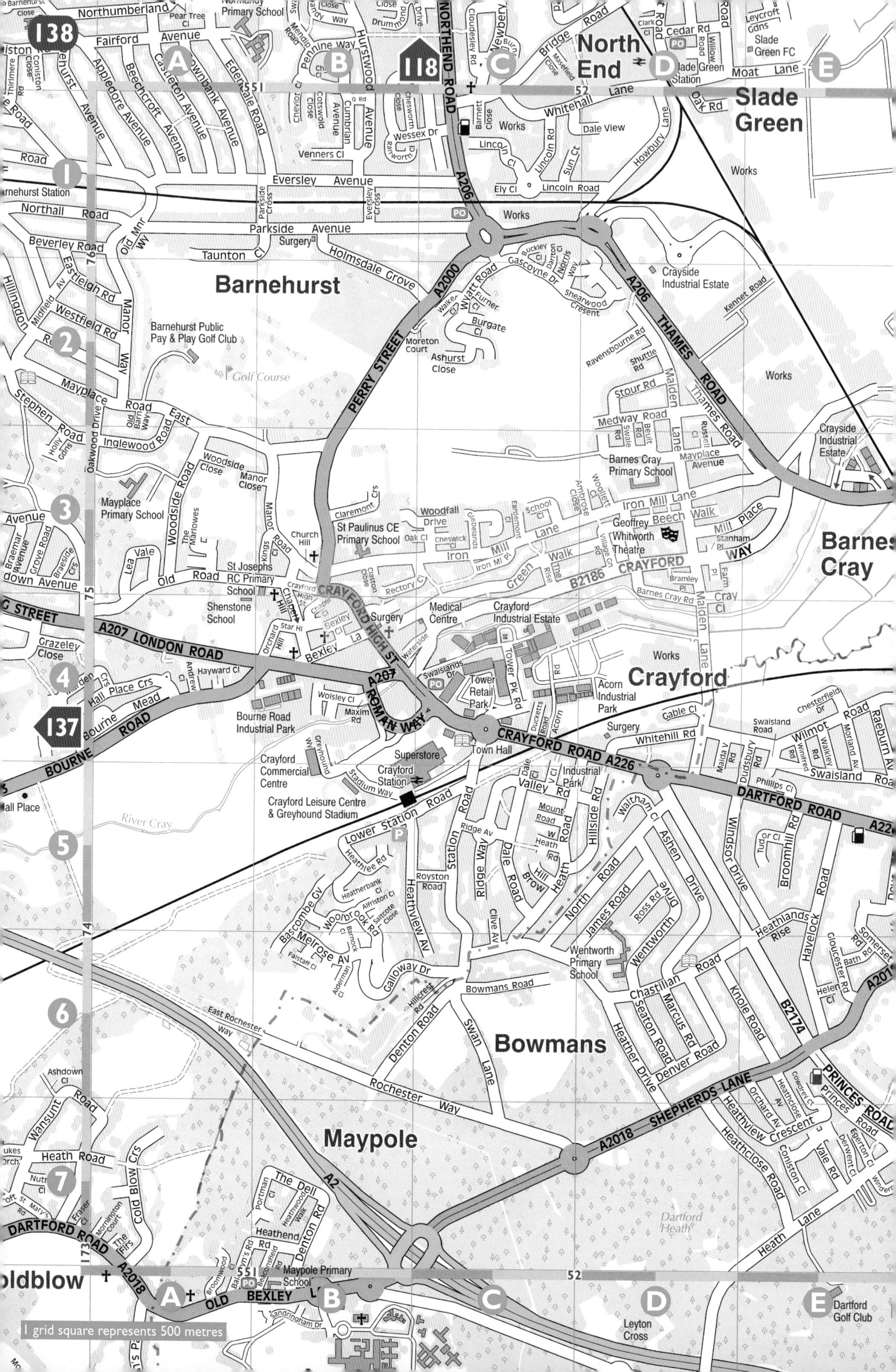

138
118
137
North End
Slade Green
Barnehurst
Crayford
Barnes Cray
Bowmans
Maypole
Oldblow
A B C D E
1 2 3 4 5 6 7
NORTHEND ROAD
PERRY STREET
THAMES ROAD
A207 LONDON ROAD
CRAYFORD HIGH ST
CRAYFORD ROAD A226
DARTFORD ROAD
BOURNE ROAD
A2018 SHEPHERDS LANE
PRINCES ROAD
CRAYFORD WAY
Barnehurst Public Pay & Play Golf Club
Mayplace Primary School
St Paulinus CE Primary School
St Josephs RC Primary School
Shenstone School
Barnes Cray Primary School
Geoffrey Whitworth Theatre
Crayford Industrial Estate
Crayside Industrial Estate
Bourne Road Industrial Park
Crayford Commercial Centre
Crayford Leisure Centre & Greyhound Stadium
Crayford Station
Town Hall
Superstore
Wentworth Primary School
Maypole Primary School
Slade Green Station
Slade Green FC
Barnehurst Station
Dartford Heath
Dartford Golf Club
Leyton Cross
1 grid square represents 500 metres

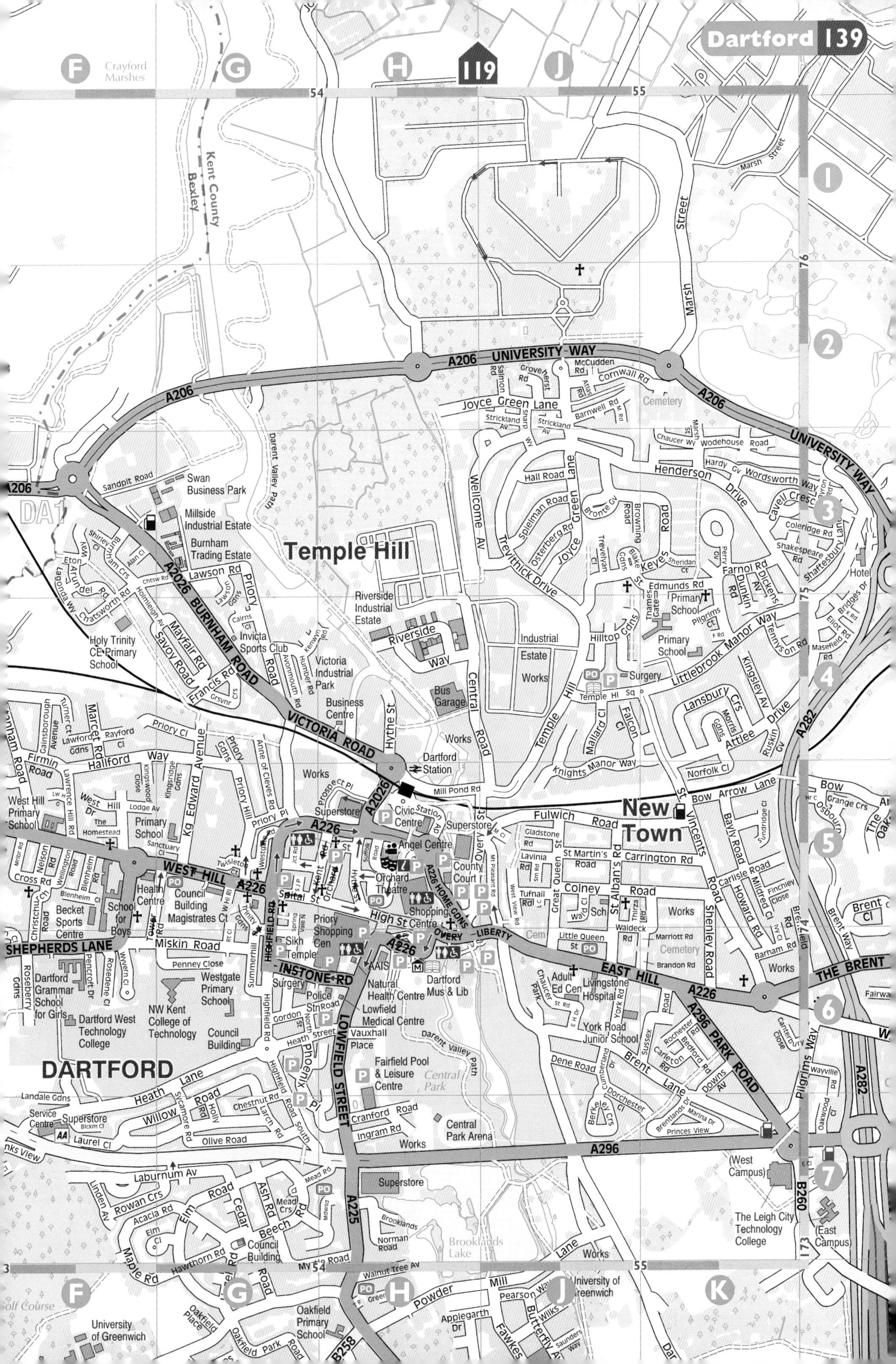

119
Crayford Marshes
Kent County
Bexley
A206 UNIVERSITY WAY
Temple Hill
New Town
DARTFORD
DA1
Swan Business Park
Millside Industrial Estate
Burnham Trading Estate
A2026 BURNHAM ROAD
VICTORIA ROAD
Riverside Industrial Estate
Riverside Way
Victoria Industrial Park
Business Centre
Industrial Estate Works
Bus Garage
Central Road
Dartford Station
Mill Pond Rd
Wellcome Av
Joyce Green Lane
Marsh Street
Cemetery
Henderson Drive
Littlebrook Manor Way
Knights Manor Way
Temple Hill
Holy Trinity CE Primary School
Invicta Sports Club
West Hill Primary School
WEST HILL A226
SHEPHERDS LANE
Dartford Grammar School for Girls
Dartford West Technology College
NW Kent College of Technology
Westgate Primary School
Council Building
Magistrates Ct
School for Boys
Becket Sports Centre
HIGHFIELD RD
INSTONE RD
Priory Shopping Cen
Orchard Theatre
Angel Centre
County Court
Civic Centre
Superstore
A226 HOME GDNS
OVERY LIBERTY
EAST HILL A226
Dartford Mus & Lib
Natural Health Centre
Lowfield Medical Centre
LOWFIELD STREET
Fairfield Pool & Leisure Centre
Central Park
Central Park Arena
Darent Valley Path
Fulwich Road
Carrington Rd
St Vincents Road
Shenley Road
A296 PARK ROAD
A296
THE BRENT
Livingstone Hospital
York Road Junior School
Adult Ed Cen
Brent Lane
Heath Lane
Princes View
Pilgrims Way
A282
B260
(West Campus)
The Leigh City Technology College
(East Campus)
A225
Brooklands Lake
Powder Mill Lane
University of Greenwich
Oakfield Primary School
B258
54
55
F G H J K
1 2 3 4 5 6 7

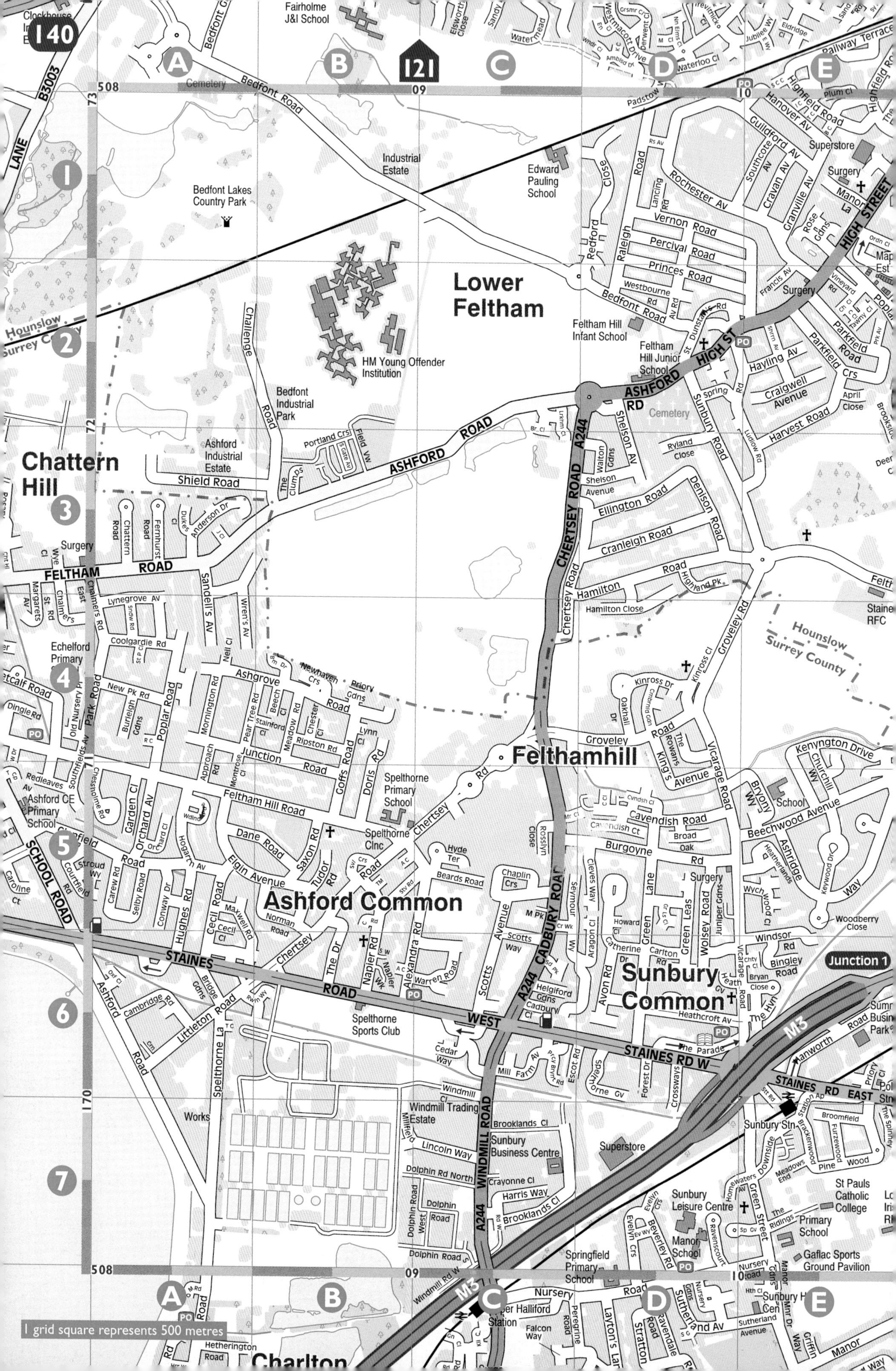

140
121
A
B
C
D
E
1
2
3
4
5
6
7
508
09
10
73
72
170
Fairholme J&I School
Bedfont Road
Cemetery
Industrial Estate
Bedfont Lakes Country Park
Edward Pauling School
Lower Feltham
HM Young Offender Institution
Bedfont Industrial Park
Challenge Road
Ashford Industrial Estate
Shield Road
Chattern Hill
Hounslow
Surrey County
Feltham Hill Infant School
Feltham Hill Junior School
ASHFORD HIGH ST
ASHFORD RD
ASHFORD ROAD
CHERTSEY ROAD
A244
Rochester Av
Vernon Road
Percival Road
Princes Road
Westbourne Rd
Bedfont Road
Superstore
Surgery
HIGH STREET
Hanover Av
Highfield Road
Guildford Av
Cravan Av
Granville Av
Parkfield Road
Hayling Av
Craigwell Avenue
Harvest Road
Sunbury Road
Spring Rd
Shelson Av
Shelson Avenue
Ellington Road
Denison Road
Cranleigh Road
Hamilton Road
Hamilton Close
Groveley Rd
Staines RFC
FELTHAM ROAD
Echelford Primary
Park Road
Sandell's Av
Wren's Av
Coolgardie Rd
Lynegrove Av
Ashgrove Road
New Pk Rd
Poplar Road
Mornington Rd
Junction Road
Goffs Road
Doris Rd
Feltham Hill Road
Dane Road
Elgin Avenue
Saxon Rd
Spelthorne Primary School
Spelthorne Clnc
Felthamhill
Groveley Road
Kinross Dr
King's Avenue
Vicarage Road
Kenyngton Drive
Beechwood Avenue
Cavendish Road
Burgoyne Rd
School
Ashford CE Primary School
SCHOOL ROAD
Ashford Common
Orchard Av
Hogarth Av
Hughes Rd
Cecil Road
Maxwell Rd
Norman Road
Chertsey Rd
The Dr
Napier Rd
Alexandra Rd
Warren Road
Beards Road
Chaplin Crs
Scotts Avenue
Scotts Way
CADBURY ROAD
Sunbury Common
Green Lane
Green Leas
Wolsey Road
Woodberry Close
Junction 1
STAINES ROAD
WEST
STAINES RD W
STAINES RD EAST
The Parade
Heathcroft Av
M3
Spelthorne Sports Club
Littleton Road
Ashford Road
Spelthorne La
Works
Windmill Trading Estate
WINDMILL ROAD
Brooklands Cl
Sunbury Business Centre
Lincoln Way
Dolphin Rd North
Dolphin Road
Harris Way
Brooklands Cl
Superstore
Sunbury Stn
Sunbury Leisure Centre
Manor School
Springfield Primary School
St Pauls Catholic College
Primary School
Gaflac Sports Ground Pavilion
Green Street
Nursery Road
Sunbury Hth Cen
Upper Halliford Station
Sutherland Av
Stratton Road
Ravendale Road
Charlton
Hetherington Road
1 grid square represents 500 metres

Feltham 141
122
142
156
F
G
H
J
I
K
2
3
4
5
6
7
11
12
13
FELTHAM
Hanworth
TW13
TW16
Hanworth Park
HANWORTH ROAD
UXBRIDGE ROAD
HOUNSLOW ROAD
A314
HAMPTON ROAD WEST
TWICKENHAM ROAD
GREAT CHERTSEY ROAD
TWICKENHAM RD
HAMPTON RD E
A312
A316
COUNTRY WAY
A308
STAINES ROAD
EAST
UPPER SUNBURY
B3377
A244
Surgery
Crematorium
Cardinal Road Infant School
Junior School
Cineworld Cinema
St Lawrence Business Cen
Feltham Superbowl
Feltham Community College
Feltham Airparcs Leisure Centre
Mount Medical Cen
Crane Junior School
Crane Infant School
Hampton Fm Industrial Est
Hanworth Trading Est
Apex Retail Park
Medical Centre
Superstore
Felthambrook Industrial Estate
Five Ways Business Cen
Works
Oriel Primary School
Little Eden & Eden High School
Hounslow College Independent School
Lindon Bennett School
Forge Lane Primary School
Richmond House School
Primary School
Kempton Park East Reservoir (disused)
Reservoir
Richmond upon Thames
Surrey County
Kempton Park Station
Kempton Park Racecourse
Lazards Sports Club
Kingsway Business Park
Oldfield House Special School
Infant School
The Hampton Medical Centre
Athelstan House School
Jnr Sch
Hampton Cem
Hampton Community College
Chennestone Community School
Victoria Rd
Browell's Lane
Forest Road
Elmwood
Sandalwood Rd
Pinewood Rd
Plane Tree Crs
Poplar Wy
Roebuck Cl
Beagle
Felthambrook Way
Felthambrook Wy
Road
Fernside Av
Clifton
Camrose Av
Castle Way
Seymour Gdns
Elizabeth Way
Moat Side
Queens Wy
Queens Av
Shakespeare Wy
Sunbury Wy
Raleigh Wy
Boundaries Road
De Brome Rd
Slattery Rd
Elthorne Court
Wigley Road
Westbury Rd
Marlborough Rd
Amesbury Road
Eastbourne Rd
Woodlawn Dr
Little Pk Dr
Meadow Rd
Oaks Av
Bexhill Cl
Pevensey Rd
Saxon Av
Sunningdale Av
Canterbury Rd
Braid Cl
Norman Av
Towfield Rd
Barnlea
Saxon
Water Mill Way
Fountains Av
Winchester Road
York Wy
Lincoln Rd
Exeter Rd
Churchfields Av
Butts Crs
Broadlands
Mt Rd
Winslow Way
Cottington Rd
Cresswell Rd
Devonshire Rd
Swift Rd
Swift
Park Rd
Crispen Rd
Cross Rd
St George's Rd
Grove Crs
Hampton La
Millbourne Rd
St John's Road
Riverdale Rd
Stourton Av
Fairlawn Cl
Wordsworth Rd
Browning Cl
Byron Cl
Rectory Grove
Bishops Grove
Buckingham Road
Hanworth Road
Dukes Cl
The Alders
Swan Cl
Swan
Oxford Wy
Bear Road
St Albans Av
Conway Rd
New Road
Green Lane
Forge La
Armstrong Rd
Robin Cl
Lebanon Av
Street
Main
Fir Rd
Birch Rd
South Road
Church Road
Nallhead Road
Dickenson Rd
Osborne Cl
Oak Avenue
Fulmer Cl
Briar Cl
Fearnley Crs
Morland Cl
Maple Cl
Stewart Cl
Page Cl
Houghton Cl
Sonning Gdns
South Rd
Coombe Rd
Coombe Crs
Old
Courtlands Av
Broad Lane
Westbrook Av
Cleveland Av
Falcon Rd
Hatherop Road
Cambridge Rd
Orchard Road
Percy
Holly
Bush
Lane
Chestnut Avenue
Ripley Road
Lawrence Rd
Cleves Way
Priory
Priory Gdns
Priory Cl
Broome Road
Hill Field Road
Bloxham Crs
Heather Close
Linden Road
Chandler Cl
Oldfield
Hammond Close
Lacey Drive
Mason Cl
Templar Place
Marlingdene Close
Farm
Partridge Rd
Gresham Rd
Cotswold Rd
The Avenue
Rumsey Cl
Park Road
Grove
Hamilton Pl
Kempton Court
Kempton Avenue
Belgrave Road
Belgrave Crs
Elmbrook Cl
Batavia Road
Claremont Avenue
Allen Close
Allen Road
Manor Lane
Elm Drive
Sunbury Ct Rd
Oakington Dr
Oakington Drive
Bramwell Close
French
Woodlands Drive
Kempton Road
Avenue
Hanworth Road
Ellerman
Sheringham Av
Cheyne Av
Chiltern Av
Glasbrook Av
Gatfield Gv
Evans Gv
Beach Gv
Camden Av
Alfred Rd
Danesbury Road
Ashfield Av
Florence Rd
Cardinal Rd
Kings Rd
Hampton Rd

142
123
141
157
A
B
C
D
E
1
2
3
4
5
6
7
513
14
15
Twickenham Cemetery
Whitton Health Clinic
Whitton School
Whitton Sports & Fitness Centre
Richmond upon Thames
Hounslow
River Crane
HOSPITAL BR RD
GREAT CHERTSEY ROAD A316
TWICKENHAM ROAD
A305
STAINES ROAD
SIXTH CROSS ROAD
B358
Medical Centre
Twickenham Golf Club
Golf Course
HAMPTON RD E
A312
UXBRIDGE ROAD
Superstore
Burton's Road
Hampton Hill
A313
PARK ROAD
Pigeon Lane
Hampton Community College
Hampton School
The Lady Eleanor Holles School
Hanworth Road
Jack & Jill School
Clarendon School
Carlisle Infant School
Longford Industrial Estate
Broad Lane
Templar Place
Hampton Cem
TW12
Denmead School
The Hampton Medical Centre
Athelstan House Sch
Hampton Station
Oldfield Road
SUNBURY ROAD
THAMES STREET
HIGH STREET
CHURCH STREET
A311
Hampton
Hampton FC
King's Paddock
Hampton Open Air Pool
Bushy Park
Bartons Cottage
Works
TEDDINGTON
St Clare Business Park
National Physical Laboratory
Teddington Memorial Hospital
Teddington Clinic
HAMPTON ROAD
STANLEY ROAD
WELLINGTON ROAD
FULWELL ROAD
B360
Fulwell Golf Club
Fulwell Station
SOUTH ROAD
Strawberry Hi
Stanley Junior School
Teddington Cemetery
Stanley Infant School
St James RC Primary School
The Mall School
Waldegrave Girls School
Trafalgar Primary School
Jack & Jill School
Primary School
Strawberry Hill Golf Club
Surgery
Richmond upon Thames
Surrey County
HAMPTON
1 grid square represents 500 metres

124
144
158
F
G
H
J
K
1
2
3
4
5
6
7
16
17
18
Deutsche Schule
Mary Wallace Theatre
Works
Eel Pie Island
Ham House (NT)
Strathmore School
School
Heath Road
A305
Surgery
Heath Gdns
Radnor Road
Tennyson Avenue
Poulett Gdns
Radnor Gdns
Cross Deep Gdns
Upr Grotto Rd
Grotto Road
St Catherines School
Grove
Orford Gardens
Radnor Road
Hotel
Holmes Road
Bonser Road
River Vw Gdns
Cross Deep A310
School
Thames Path
Ham Street
The Orangery
Meadlands Drive
Clifford Road
Buckingham Rd
Sandpits Road
Dickens Lane
Sudbrook Lane
Golf Course
Riverside Drive
Murray Rd
Russell Gdns
Stretton Rd
Neville Rd
Perryfield Wy
Link Wy
Stuart Road
Woodville Road
Sandy Lane
Arlington Rd
Ashley Gdns
Lauderdale Drive
Petersham Road
A307
Back La
Grey Court School
Ham Health Clinic
Bank
Willow
Breamwater Gdns
Ashburnham Road
St Richards with St Andrews CE Primary School
Martingales Cl
Bishop Cl
Sudbrook Gardens
Ham
Ham Common
Evelyn Rd
Lovell Rd
Back La
Cleves Rd
Mowbray Rd
Sheridan Rd
Mead Rd
Surgery
Croft Wy
Riverside Drive
Fellbrook
Mariner Gdns
Meadlands Prim Sch
Surg Rd
New Road
Mornington Wk
Upr Ham Road
B352
Ham
The Cassel Hospital
Langham House Close
Kingfisher Dr
Broughton Av
Lock Rd
Lawrence Rd
Craig Rd
Hardwicke Rd
Langham Gdns
Randle Rd
Dukes
Ham & Petersham Cricket Club
Church Road
Dysart School
Maguire Dr
Beaufort Rd
Lammas Rd
Burnell Av
Dysart Avenue
Avenue
Parkleys
Barnfield
Barnfield Av
Beech
Teddington Lock
Thames Path
River Thames
Weald La
Camel Gv
St Georges Industrial Est
Tudor Drive
Wittering Cl
Chivenor
Lancaster Gdns
The Hawker Centre
Fernhill
Wolsey
Kingston upon Thames
Richmond upon Thames
Richmond Road
Tiffin Girls School
Ferry Rd
Broom Road
Marston Road
Rivermead Cl
Broom Water W
Broom Water
River Reach
Bucklands Rd
Sycamore Way
Trowlock Av
Melbourne Rd
Trowlock Island
Lower Ham Road
Albany Park Canoe & Sailing Cen
Albany Pk Road
Teddington School
Trowlock Wy
The Vine Clinic
Surgery
Durlston
St Albans
Mallard Pl
Michelham Gdns
Strawberry V
Works
St Marys University College
Waldegrave Road
A309
Waldegrave Gdns
Downside
Strawberry Hill
Surgery
Clive Road
A310
Waldegrave Park
Newland House School
Fieldend
Arlington Rd
Teddington Park Road
Teddington Park
Claremont Rd
Cambridge
The Gv
Gv Gdns
Ter
Grove
Twickenham Rd
Manor Road
Manor Rd
Twickenham Rd
St Alban's Gdns
The Waldegrave Clinic
Elmfield Av
Teddington Pool & Fitness Centre
Vicarage Rd
Wade's La
Watt's La
Road
High Street
A313
Ferry Rd
Works
Teddington Business Park
Broad St
Field La
Spr Rd
Cedar Rd
Bridgeman Rd
Station Rd
Gomer Pl
Udney Park Road
Kingston Lane
Langham Road
A310
Kingston Rd
St Winifred's Road
Atbara Road
King Edward's Grove
Keepers Ms
Munster Road
Pond Wy
Holmesdale Road
Langwood Cha
Broom Road
TW11
Middle La
North La
North Pl
Park Lane
Surgery
Teddington Station
Bolton Gdns
Cromwell Road
Kingston Close
Kingsmead Cl
Addison Rd
Borland Rd
Down Rd
Collis Primary School
Sacred Heart RC Primary School
St Mark's Road
Bushy Park Road
Fairfax Road
Surgery
Albert Rd
Clarence Road
Victoria Rd
Avenue Gdns
Avenue Rd
Park Road
B358
Queen's Road
Maddison Cl
Admiralty Rd
The Link
Glazebrook Rd
Harrowdene Gardens
Shaef Way
Sandy Lane
Park Road
Chestnut Avenue
Admiralty Road
Walk
Wick Road
Lindum Rd
Fairways
Thameside
Broom Cl
Broom Pk
Broom Park
Hampton Wick Infant School
Normansfield Av
Raeburn Cl
Glamorgan Rd
Monmouth Av
Elton Close
St John the Baptist CE Junior Sch
Thames Path
Bank Lane
Berkeley Rd
Chestnut Road
Eastbury Road
Richmond Road
Woffington Close
Works
Upr Teddington Rd
Sandy Lane
Cedars Rd
Vicarage Road
Surgery
Seymour Road
Lower Teddington Road
Hampton Wick Stn
Samuel Gray Gdns
Henry Macaulay Avenue
May Bate Avenue
B357
Skerne Rd
Kingsgate Business Centre
Kingsgate Rd
Kingston Stn
Wood Street
Down Hall Rd
Park Road
Bennet Cl
Jubilee Cl
High Street
Hotel
Church Grove
St John's Rd
Becketts Pl
Hampton Wick
Bushy Park
Old Br St
A308
Bentalls Shopping Cen
Fife Rd
The Rotunda
Clarence Street
Eden Walk Shopping Cen
Riverside Walk
Diana Fountain

1 grid square represents 500 metres

Richmond Park 145
126
146
160
F
G
H
J
K
I
2
3
4
5
6
7
21
22
23
73
72
71
70
Putney Vale
Putney Vale Crematorium
Putney Vale Cemetery
Superstore
ROEHAMPTON VALE
A3
Norstead Pl
Friars Av
Stag Lane
Frensham Dr
Stroud Crescent
Hall School Wimbledon
London Scottish Golf Club
Wandsworth
Merton
Golf Course
Windmill Road
Wimbledon Common
KINGSTON VALE
A308
Robinwood Place
Woodview Cl
Cedar Cl
Derwent Avenue
Robin Hood Lane
Robin Hood Way
Grasmere Avenue
Ullswater Crs
Vale Crs
ROBIN HOOD WAY (KINGSTON BY PASS)
Robin Hood Road
Windermere Rd
Kingston University
Robin Hood Primary School
Bowness Crescent
Rydal Gdns
Keswick Avenue
Coombe Park
Kingston Vale
Merton
Kingston upon Thames
Robin Hood Rd
Windmill Rd
Sunset Road
Wimbledon Common Golf Club
North Vw
West Pl
Camp Vw
Camp Road
Caesar's Camp
Warren Farm
Eversley Park
Royal Wimbledon Golf Club
Crooked Billet
Warren House
Wool Rd
Dunstall Road
McKay Rd
Sycamore Rd
High Coombe Pl
Warren Cutting
Warren Rd
Coombe Hill Golf Club
Golf Club Drive
Coombe
Edgecombe Cl
Coombe End
Kingston University
Ballard Close
Greenwood Pk
Henley Dr
Coombe Hill Road
Beverley La
Coombe Hill Gld
Moor Pk Gdns
Devey Cl
Warbank La
New Victoria Hospital
Hawkins Clnc
A238
COOMBE LANE W
Fitzgeorge Av
Coombe Houses Chase
B283
Oakcombe Close
Wonford Close
Coombe Bank
The Chesters
The Moat
Warren Rise
Neville Av
Fairway
Burghley Av
Coombe Hill J&I School
Woodlands
Matlock Way
Cromford Way
Buxton Dr
Badgers Walk
Soames Walk
Coombe Girls School
Bakewell Way
Darley Dr
Langley Grove
TRAPS LANE
Malden
Ely Close
Perth Close
BEVERLEY WAY
Beverley Way
COOMBE LANE
Wimbledon RFC
Ellerton Road
Barham Road
Almer Road
Drax Av
Rowans School
Wolsey Close
Grange Pk Pl
Thurstan Rd
Rokeby Pl
Ernle Road
B281
Surgery
Copse Hill
Wolfson Medical Centre
Atkinson Morley Hospital
Prospect Pl
Cottenham Dr
High Cedar Dr
COPSE HL
COTTENHAM PK RD
Preston Road
Hood Road
Holland Avenue
Copse Hill Av
Burdett Av
Melville Av
Lindisfarne Rd
Copse Hill
Heights Cl
Cottenham Park Road
St Matthews CE Primary School
Cottenham Park
Melbury Gardens
Oakwood Road
Laurel Road
Pannuir Road
Cambridge Close
Cambridge Road
DURHAM ROAD
SW20
Westcoombe Avenue
Coombe Gardens
Richmond Road
Parkfields Av
Spencer Road
Health Centre
Surgery
Amity Grove
Primary School
Kenwyn Road
Rosevine Rd
Lambton Road
Tolverne Road
Raynes Park Station
Camberley Avenue
Somerset Av

146
127
145
161
A
B
C
D
E
1
2
3
4
5
6
7
523
24
25
73
72
71
170
1 grid square represents 500 metres
WIMBLEDON
SW19
WIMBLEDON PARK
PARKSIDE
A219
B281
CANNIZARO RD
W SIDE COMMON
WOODHAYES RD
HIGH ST
WIMBLEDON HL ROAD
THE BROADWAY
HARTFIELD RD
HARTFIELD ROAD
B285
B235
ALEXANDRA RD
WORPLE ROAD
KINGSTON ROAD
DURNSFORD ROAD
MERTON ROAD
LEOPOLD RD
COTTENHAM PK RD
COPSE HL
Augustus Road
Theatre of the Disp
Linden Lodge School
Surgery
Brookwood Rd
Albemarle Primary School
Southdean Gardens
Wimbledon Park
Wimbledon Park Athletics Track
Boating Lake
Wimbledon Park Golf Club
Wimbledon Park Station
Golf Course
London Scottish Golf Club
Windmill Road
Apostolic Nuncio
Parkside Hospital
The All England Lawn Tennis & Croquet Club
Church Road
Home Park Road
Arthur Road
Queensmere Road
Synagogue
Somerset Rd
Calonne Road
Buddhapadipa Temple
Parkside Gardens
Margin Drive
Marryat Road
Burghley Road
Parkhouse Middle School
High School
Primary School
Preparatory School
The Causeway
Camp Road
Wimbledon Common Golf
Royal Wimbledon Golf Club
Helston Court Business Centre
Hotel
Crooked Billet
Chester Rd
Beech Close
King's College School
Wimbledon Common Pre-Preparatory School
The Norwegian School
Dunstall Road
Ernle Road
Copse Hill
The Grange
Murray Road
Lauriston Road
Clifton Road
Ridgway
Telephone Exchange
Spencer Hill
Denmark Road
Thornton Road
Wimbledon College High School
Edge Hill
Ursuline High School
Hazelhurst School
Blossom House School
Primary School
Wimbledon High School
Wimbledon Station
Centre Court Shopping Centre
Police Station
Wimbledon Theatre
Odeon Cinema
Railway Engineering Works
Squash and Badminton Club
Sorting Office
Dundonald First School
Wimbledon School of Art
Wimbledon Chase Middle School
Wimbledon Chase Stn
Wimbledon House School
Merton Park Primary School
Willington Sch
Wimbledon Magistrates Court
Holy Trinity First School
Dudley Road
Prince's Road
Gladstone Road
Sheridan
Nelson Hospital
Health Centre
Works
Rutlish School
Manor Gdns
Watery Lane
Erridge Road
Melrose Road

Wimbledon 147
128
162
148
Summerstown
Upper Tooting
South Wimbledon
Tooting Graveney
TOOTING
Collier's Wood
ERTON
SW17
Earlsfield Station
Earlsfield Primary School
Beatrix Potter Primary School
Haslemere Industrial Est
Rufus Business Centre
Wimbledon Stadium Business Cen
Wimbledon Stadium
Lambeth Crematorium
Lambeth Cemetery
Streatham Cemetery
Central London Golf Club
Burntwood School
Nightingale School
Springfield Hospital
Ernest Bevin School
St Walter & St John Sports Ground
Upper Tooting Independent High School
Finton House Sch
Churchill Coll
Phoenix Coll
Police Station
Battersea Tutorial Colle
Tooting Bec Stn
Balham Preparatory School
Hillbrook Primary School
Tooting Leisure Centre
St Georges Hospital
A&E
Tooting Broadway Stn
Superstore
Trident Business Cen
Health Trust
Tooting Station
Haydons Road Station
Priory CE Middle School
Garfield Primary School
Shree Ghanapathy Temple
Wimbledon Recreation Centre
Albany Clinic
South Wimbledon Station
Collier's Wood Stn
Singlegate First School
Priory Retail Park
Tandem Centre
College Fields Business Cen
Chelsea Fields Industrial Est
Riverside Business Park
Abbey Mills
Merton Ind Park
Roan Industrial Estate
Blenheim Business Centre
Liberty Middle School
Bond Road School
Menin Works
Lombard Business Park
Saxon Business
Wimbledon (Gap Road) Cemetery
GARRATT LANE
BURNTWOOD LANE
PLOUGH LANE
DURNSFORD ROAD
HAYDON'S RD
MERTON HIGH STREET A238
MERTON ROAD
MERANTUN WAY
CHRISTCHURCH RD
TOOTING HIGH STREET A24
HIGH ST COLLIER'S WOOD
UPPER TOOTING ROAD
TRINITY RD A214
MITCHAM RD
SUMMERSTOWN
A217
A218
A24
B229
B235
F
G
H
J
K
I
2
3
4
5
6
7
26
27
28

148
129
147
163
A
B
C
D
E
1
2
3
4
5
6
7
528
29
30
Streatham Hill
Streatham Park
Furzedown
Streatham Vale
SW16
Balham Station
Balham Station Rd
Sistova Rd
Rossiter Rd
Fernlea
Oakmead Rd
Chrysalis Thtr
Trinity St Marys Primary School
Ravenstone Primary School
Balham Leisure Centre
Balham Health Cen
Elmfield Road
Byrne Road
Bedford
Cornford Gv
Emmanuel
Telferscot Primary School
Thornton Av
Sternhold Av
Kirkstall Road
Megabowl
Streatham Hill Station
Upper Tooting Park
Police Station
Trinity Rd A214
Battersea Tutorial College
Tooting Bec Stn
Ritherdon Road
Huron Road
Streathbourne Road
Drakefield Road
Louisville Road
Manville Road
Veronica Road
Terrapin Road
Hillbury Road
Culverden Road
Hill
B242
Dr Johnson Avenue
Wandsworth Lambeth
Mortimer Close
Waldorf School of S W London
Streatham & Clapham High School
Tooting Bec Common
Lido
Mortimer School
Drewstead Road
Hoadly Road
Woodfield Av
De Montfort Road
Bowls Club
ABC
Streatham High Rd
Norfolk House Road
Kingscourt Road
Mount Ephraim Lane
Garrad's Road
Woodbourne Av
South London Liberal Synagogue
Becmead Av
Odeon
Gracefield Gdns
Pendennis
Pinfold Road
Refuge Temple
Police Stn
Tooting Bec Road
Tooting Bec Gdns
A214
Tooting Road
Hillbrook Primary School
Balham Preparatory School
Lessingham
Franciscan Primary School
Moring Road
Mantilla Road
Lucien Road
Church Lane
Tooting Bec Athletics Track
West Drive
North Dr
Ullathorne Road
Abbotsleigh Road
Aldrington Road
Fir Tree Cl
Furzedown Road
Birchwood Rd
Natural Therapy Clnc
Brookview Rd
Thrale
Colwyn Cl
Heybridge Av
Fayland Av
Surgery
Riggindale Road
Rydal Road
Ambleside Av
Bethel Temple
St Leonards CE Primary School
Babington Road
Fairmile Av
Gleneagle
Conyer's Road
Eardley Road
Streatham Swimming Pool
Streatham Ice Rink
Streatham Stn
Hambro Rd
Ellora Rd
Lewin Mead Community Mental Health Cen
Lewin Road
Barrow Road
Pathfield Road
Greyhound La
War Memorial
Streatham High Road
Superstore
Tooting
Mitcham Rd
Wandsworth Community Health Trust
Trident Business Cen
Crowborough
Graveney School
Furzedown Primary School
Welham
Ramsdale Rd
Chillerton Road
Idlecombe Rd
Salterford Rd
Southcroft Road
Seely Road
Links Primary School
Links Road
Penwortham Primary School
Penwortham Road
Pendle Road
Ribblesdale Road
Pretoria Road
Mitcham Lane
A216
Dahomey Rd
Fernthorpe Rd
Eardley Primary School
Besley Street
Streatham Common Station
Streatham Vale Sports Club
Ellison Road
Tankerville Rd
Kempshott Road
Primary School
Tooting Station
A217
Ashbourne Road
Edenvale Child Health Clinic
Streatham Road
Ridge Rd
Caithness Road
Park Avenue
Melrose Avenue
Garden Avenue
Elmhurst Av
Hill Road
Woodland Way
St Barnabas Road
St James' Road
Framfield Road
Middle School
Mitcham Industrial Est
Tooting & Mitcham United FC
First School
Service Centre
Streatham Vale
B272
Sherwood Av
Woodmansterne Road
Woodmansterne Primary School
Greyhound Ter
Marian Road
Hassocks Road
Stanford Middle School
Norbury Manor Primary School
Bishops Park Road
Shree Swaminarayan Temple
Streatham Vale Park
Caplan Estate
Meopham Road
Windermere Rd
Works
Eastfield High School
Loneson First Sch
South London Crematorium
Longthornton Road
Lymington Close
Turle Rd
Semley Rd
Tylecroft
Streatham Park
London Road
1 grid square represents 500 metres

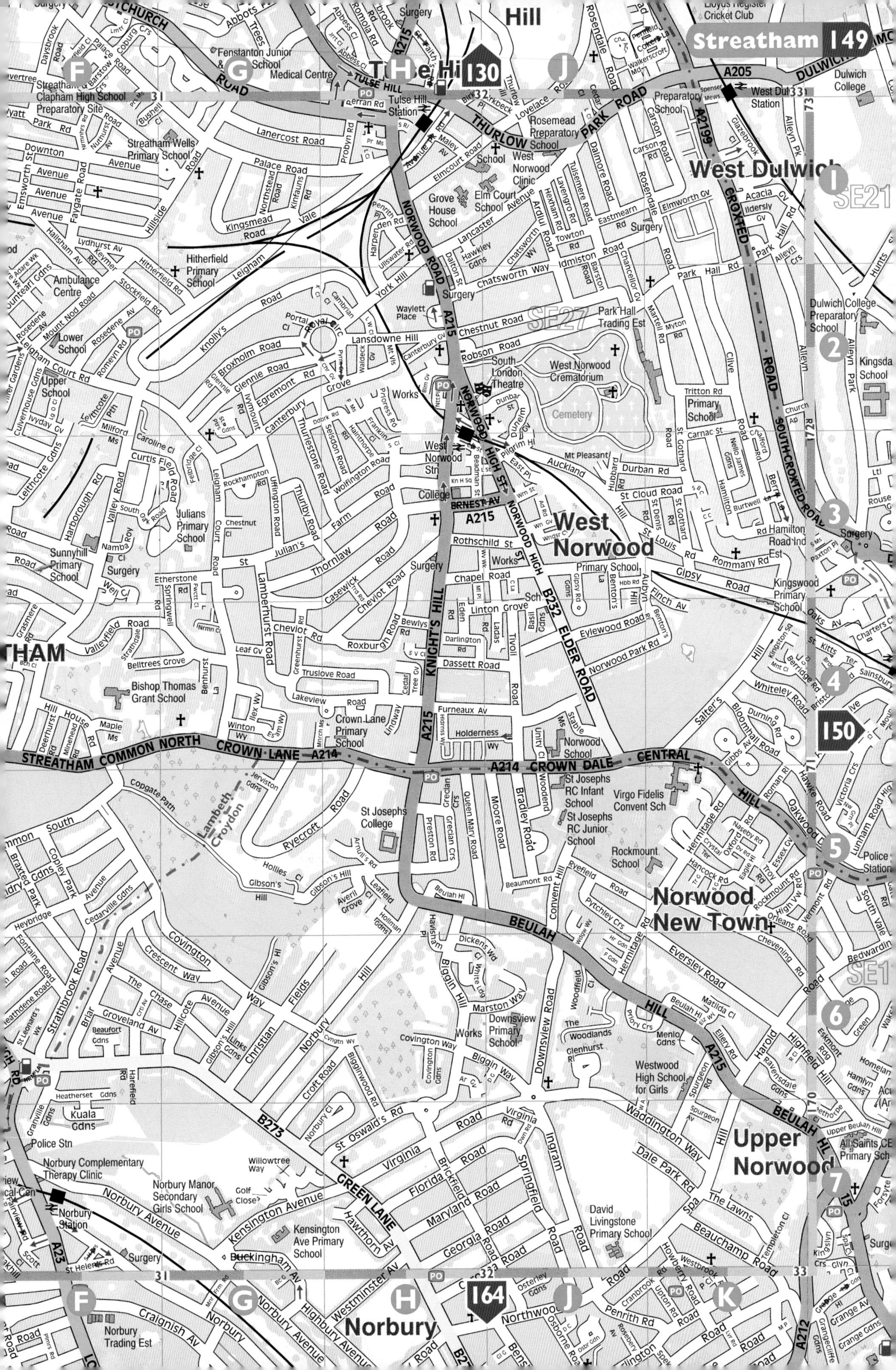

Streatham 149
130
150
164
Tulse Hill
Tulse Hill Station
Thurlow Park Road
West Dulwich
West Dulwich Station
Croxted Road
South Croxted Road
Dulwich College
Dulwich College Preparatory School
SE21
SE27
SE19
West Norwood
West Norwood Station
West Norwood Cemetery
West Norwood Crematorium
South London Theatre
Norwood Road
Norwood High St
Knight's Hill
Elder Road
Gipsy Road
Crown Lane
Crown Dale
Central Hill
Beulah Hill
Streatham Common North
Norwood New Town
Upper Norwood
Norbury
Norbury Station
Green Lane
Norbury Avenue
Kensington Avenue
Leigham Court Road
Knolly's Road
Lansdowne Hill
Chatsworth Way
Park Hall Road
Park Hall Trading Est
Hamilton Road Ind Est
Rosemead Preparatory School
Elm Court School
Grove House School
Hitherfield Primary School
Streatham Wells Primary School
Fenstanton Junior School
Julians Primary School
Sunnyhill Primary School
Bishop Thomas Grant School
Crown Lane Primary School
Kingswood Primary School
Norwood School
St Josephs College
St Josephs RC Infant School
St Josephs RC Junior School
Virgo Fidelis Convent Sch
Rockmount School
Downsview Primary School
Westwood High School for Girls
David Livingstone Primary School
Kensington Ave Primary School
Norbury Manor Secondary Girls School
Norbury Complementary Therapy Clinic
Norbury Trading Est
Police Stn
Police Station
Ambulance Centre
A215
A214
A205
A2199
B232
B273
A23
A212
F
G
H
J
K
1
2
3
4
5
6
7
31
32
33

150
131
149
165
A
B
C
D
E
1
2
3
4
5
6
7
533
34
35
DULWICH COMMON
A205
West Dulwich Station
Dulwich College
Golf Course
Dulwich College Track
Hambledon Pl
LORDSHIP LANE A205
The Horniman Museum & Gardens
Lapse Wd Wk
LONDON ROAD
Forest Hill Station
West Dulwich
SE21
CROXTED ROAD
Acacia Gv
Park Hall Rd
Alleyn Pk
Alleyn Crs
Grange Lane
Dulwich & Sydenham Hill Golf Club
Dulwich
Hunts Slip Road
Tollgate Dr
Ferrings
Constable Walk
College Road
Dulwich College Preparatory School
Kingsdale School
Alleyn Park
Sydenham Hill Station
Langbourne Primary School
Bowen Drive
Woodhall Dr
Woodhall Avenue
Stonehills Ct
Peckarmans Wood
Peckarmans Wd
Crescent Wood Road
Sydenham Hill
Droitwich Cl
Crouchmans Cl
Gt Brownings
Woodsyre
Mountacre Cl
Rock Hill
Dome Hl Pk
Chestnut Place
Bluebell Cl
Vigilant Cl
The Gradient
High Level Dr
Hillcrest Cl
Wells Pk Road
Sydenham Rd
Eliot Bank
Primary School
Kirkdale
Thorpewood Av
Mount Gdns
Mount Ash Rd
Panmure Road
Charlecote Gv
Kelvin Grove
Sydenham Girls School
Cheseman St
Holy Trinity CE Prim Sch
Round Hill
Forest Hills Pools
Derby Hill
DARTMOUTH ROAD
Police Station
Willow Business Park
Sydenham Park Road
Sydenham Park
St Bartholomews CE Primary School
Surgery
Upper Sydenham
Taylor's Lane
Infant School
Longton Grove
Longton Av
KIRKDALE A2216
Collingtree Rd
Kinver Rd
Peak Hill
Jews Walk
Beaulieu Av
Sydenham Junior High School
Sydenham High School
WESTWOOD HILL
A212
Sydenham Station
SE26
Lawrie Park Av
Hall Drive
Lawrie Park Gardens
Border Rd
Border Crs
Chulsa Road
Lawrie Pk Crs
Cobden Ms
CRYSTAL PALACE PARK ROAD
Springfield Rd
Venner Road
Byne Road
Wiverton Road
Homecroft Rd
Tredown
Crystal Palace
Crystal Palace Athletics Stadium
A234
Penge East Station
Station Road
Crampton Rd
Kingswood Rd
Lucas Rd
HIGH ST
Malcolm Rd
Primary School
PENGE
Parkside Cl
Laurel Gv
Oakfield Road Industrial Est
James Dixon Primary School
Anerley Station
Penge West Station
Anerley Pk
Rosebank
Trenholme Rd
Ivychurch Cl
Hawthorn Grove
Jasmine Grove
Padua Road
Melvin Road
Stodart Rd
Howard Rd
Franklin Industrial Est
Maple Road
Genoa Rd
ANERLEY ROAD
A214
ELMERS END ROAD
Oak Grove
Chesham Crs
Surgery
Works
DULWICH WOOD PARK
Paxton Pl
Kingswood Primary School
Oaks Av
Rusholme Gv
Dulwich Wd Av
Farquhar Road
Fountain Dr
Tylney Av
Lymer Av
A2199
COLLEGE RD
CRYSTAL PALACE PDE
A212
Gipsy Hill Station
Sainsbury Rd
Colby Rd
Alexandra Drive
Bristow Road
St Kitts Ter
Beckondale
Mountbatten Cl
Woodland Hill
Woodland Rd
Cawnpore St
Primary School
Gipsy Hill
Victoria Crs
Hawke Road
Oakwood Drive
Roman Ri
Lunham Road
Highland Rd
Camden Hl Rd
Jasper Rd
Crystal Palace Museum
Police Station
WESTOW HILL
Westow St
Shopping Centre
SE19
Bedwardine Dr
Coxwell Road
Gatestone Rd
South Vale
Vermont Rd
Rockmount Rd
High Vw Rd
Chevening Rd
Orleans Road
College Green
Highfield Hill
Eskmont Rdg
Harold Rd
Ravensdale Gdns
BEULAH HL
Upper Norwood
Upper Beulah Hill
All Saints CE Primary School
Tree View Close
Acumen (Anglo School)
Turkey Oak Cl
Stambourne Way
Sylvan Hl
Sylvan Road
Harris City Technology College
Mowbray Rd
Maberley Rd
Auckland Ri
Auckland Gdns
Acorn Gdns
Kitley Gdns
Cantley Gdns
CHURCH ROAD
A212
Fox Hill
Fox Hl Gdns
Tudor Rd
Belvedere Rd
Chipstead Cl
Waldegrave Road
Hamlet Road
Maberley Crs
Palace Grove
Patterson Rd
Milestone Rd
Cintra Park
Pleydell Av
A214 ANERLEY HILL
Crystal Palace Station
Orchard Grove
Lullington Rd
Versailles Rd
Madeline Rd
Anerley School
Anerley Primary School
Seymour Vls
Seymour Ter
Cranleigh Cl
Betts Way
A215
Templeton Cl
Lawns
Infant Sch
Auckland
Anerley
SE20
CROYDON
Selby Road
Worbeck Road
Samos
Ash Gv
Pelham
Raven
1 grid square represents 500 metres

Penge 151
132
152
166
F
G
H
J
I
K
2
3
4
5
6
7
Forest Hill
Lower Sydenham
Bell Green
Bellingham
New Beckenham
STANSTEAD ROAD
WALDRAM PK RD
PERRY VALE
PERRY RISE
PERRY HILL
A212
B227
SYDENHAM ROAD
BELL GN
SOUTHEND LA
STANTON WY
A2218
SOUTHEND LANE
BROMLEY ROAD A21
BROMLEY ROAD
BECKENHAM HILL ROAD
SOUTHEND ROAD A2015
A2015
SOUTHEND RD
HIGH ST
BROMLEY ROAD
B230
MANOR ROAD
A222
BECKENHAM ROAD
A234
PARISH LANE
A213
GREEN LANE
RECTORY ROAD
Vancouver Road
Catford Cyphers Cricket Club
Kilmorie Primary School
Christ Church CE Primary School
The Vale Medical Centre
Our Lady & St Philip Neri RC Primary School
Forest Hill School
London Living Theatre
Brent Knoll School
Greenvale School
Superstore
The Bridge Leisure Centre
Lower Sydenham Stn
Lower Sydenham Industrial Est
Abbey Trading Estate
Kangley Business Cen
Gardener Industrial Est
Orchard Business Cen
Laker Industrial Est
Metro Business Cen
Beckenham Business Cen
Broomsleigh Business Park
Alexandra Junior School
Athelney Primary School
Bellingham Stn
Bellingham Trading Est
Catford Trading Estate
Bromley Road Retail Park
Catford & Bromley Synagogue
Catford Synagogue
Council Building
Elfrida Primary School
Police Station
South Lewisham Health Centre
Catford Wanderers Sports Club
London Ladies & Girls FC
Primary School
Beckenham Hill Stn
Sedgehill School
Cornhill Sports Club
Natwest Sports Club
Cuaco Sports Ground
Hong Kong & Shanghai Sports Club
New Beckenham Station
Cator Park School for Girls
Beckenham Place Park Golf Course
Beckenham Place Park
Golf Course
Green Chain Walk
Worsley Bridge Junior School
Beckenham Cricket Club
Alexandra Infant School
Royston Primary School
Kent House Station
Beckenham Junction Station
Woodbrook Sch
Beckenham Leisure Centre
Clock House Station
Christian Meeting Hall
Telephone Exchange
Infant School
Police Stn
Theatre Ctr
Fire Station
Odeon Cinema
Worsley Bridge Road
Copers Cope Road
The Avenue
Albemarle Road
Foxgrove
Brackley Road
Bridge Road
Kings Hall Road
Kent House Road
Lennard Road
Cator Road
Trewsbury Road
Sydenham Road
Winchfield Road
Randlesdown Rd
Moremead Road
Brookehowse Road
Overbrae
Braeside
Westgate Road
Court Downs

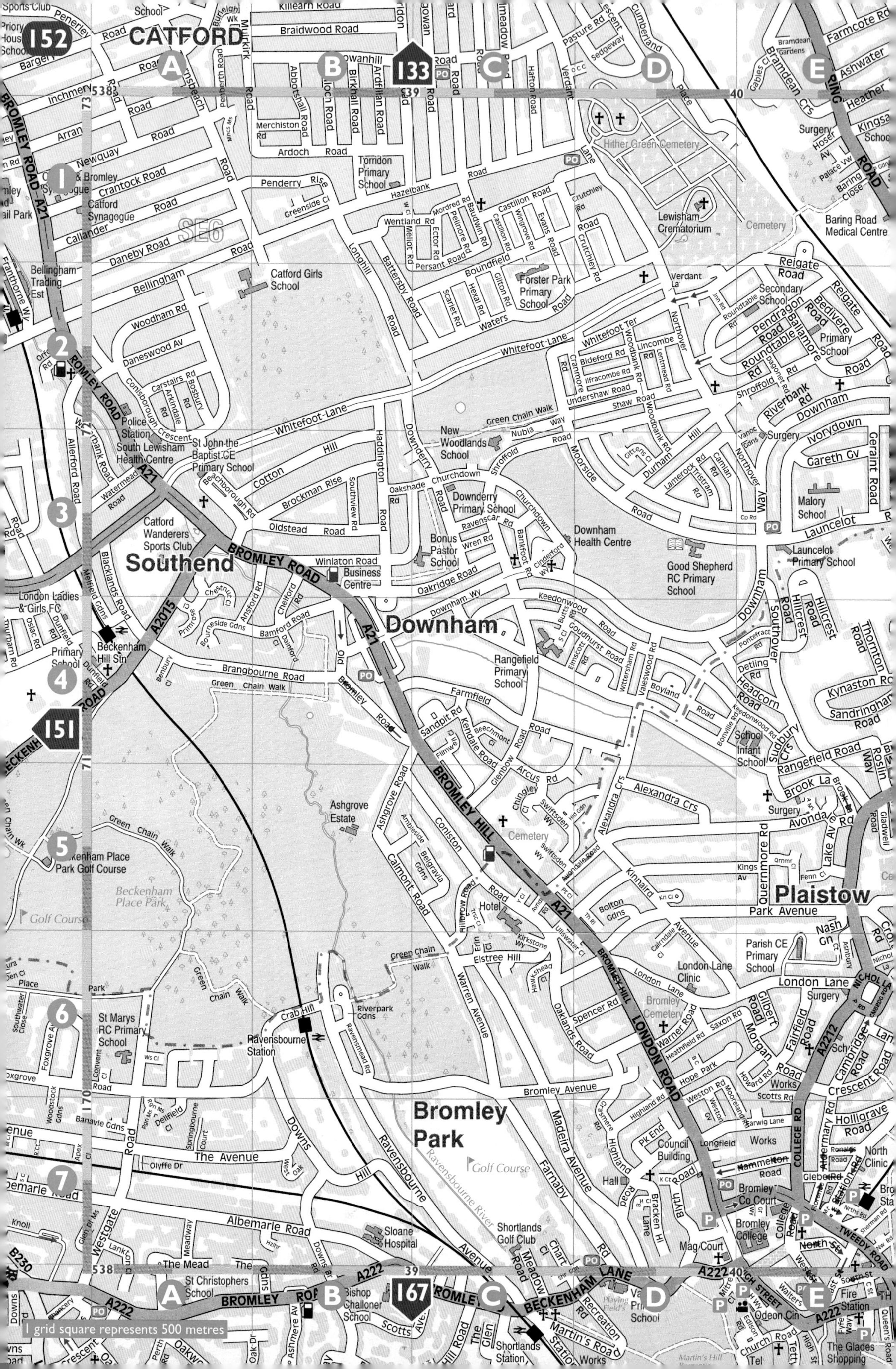
152
CATFORD
133
151
167
A
B
C
D
E
1
2
3
4
5
6
7
538
39
40
73
71
170
Braidwood Road
Killearn Road
Abbotshall Road
Birkhall Road
Ardfillan Road
Merchiston Rd
Ardoch Road
Torridon Primary School
Hazelbank
Penderry Rise
Greenside Cl
Inchmery Road
Arran Road
Newquay Road
Crantock Road
Callander Road
Catford Synagogue
Catford & Bromley Synagogue
Daneby Road
SE6
Bellingham Road
Bellingham Trading Est
Catford Girls School
Woodham Rd
Daneswood Av
Carstairs Rd
Arkindale Rd
Bosbury Rd
Conisborough Crescent
Police Station
South Lewisham Health Centre
St John the Baptist CE Primary School
Whitefoot Lane
Cotton Hill
Brockman Rise
Southview Rd
Haddington Road
Oldstead Road
Beachborough Rd
Watermead Road
Allerford Road
Catford Wanderers Sports Club
Southend
BROMLEY ROAD
A21
A2015
Winlaton Road
Business Centre
Blacklands Road
Melfield Gdns
London Ladies & Girls FC
Beckenham Hill Stn
Primary School
Brangbourne Road
Green Chain Walk
Ansford Rd
Chelford Rd
Bamford Road
Bourneside Gdns
Chestnut Cl
Primrose Cl
Benbury Cl
Old Bromley Road
PO
Downham
Oakridge Road
Downham Wy
Bonus Pastor School
Wren Rd
Ravenscar Rd
Downderry Primary School
Downderry Road
Churchdown
Oakshade Rd
New Woodlands School
Green Chain Walk
Nubia Way
Shroffold Road
Moorside Road
Downham Health Centre
Bankfoot Rd
Cinderford Wy
Keedonwood Road
Coudhurst Road
Rangefield Primary School
Good Shepherd RC Primary School
Whitefoot Ter
Bideford Rd
Ilfracombe Rd
Undershaw Road
Shaw Road
Woodbank Rd
Lincombe Rd
Lentmead Rd
Durham Hill
Northover
Lamerock Rd
Tristram Rd
Camlan Rd
Northover Way
Forster Park Primary School
Boundfield Road
Waters Road
Scarlet Rd
Hexal Rd
Glitton Rd
Battersby Road
Longhill Road
Wentland Rd
Mordred Rd
Pellinore Rd
Ector Rd
Persant Road
Castillon Road
Wingrove Rd
Evans Road
Crutchley Rd
Baudwin Rd
Hither Green Cemetery
Lewisham Crematorium
Cemetery
Verdant Lane
Verdant La
Cumberland Place
Pasture Rd
Sedgeway
Hafton Road
Reigate Road
Secondary School
Pendragon Road
Roundtable Road
Ballamore Road
Bedivere Road
Primary School
Dagonet Rd
Riverbank Rd
Downham Road
Ivorydown
Gareth Gv
Geraint Road
Malory School
Launcelot Road
Launcelot Primary School
Surgery
Baring Road Medical Centre
Bramdean Crs
Bramdean Gardens
Farmcote Rd
Ashwater
Heather
Kingsa
Hoser Av
Palace Vw
Baring Close
RING ROAD
Southover
Hillcrest Road
Thornton Road
Kynaston Road
Sandringham Road
Headcorn Road
Boyland Road
Valeswood Rd
Wittersham Rd
Detling Rd
Pontefract Rd
Bonville Rd
Sudbury Crs
Infant School
Rangefield Road
Roslin Way
Brook La
Avondale Rd
Alexandra Crs
Kinnaird Avenue
Quernmore Rd
Kings Av
Lake Av
Plaistow
Park Avenue
Nash Gn
Parish CE Primary School
London Lane Clinic
London Lane
Bromley Cemetery
Warner Road
Saxon Rd
Gilbert Road
Morgan Road
Fairfield Road
Cambridge Road
Crescent Road
Hollingrave Road
COLLEGE RD
A2212
Heathfield Rd
Hope Park
Weston Rd
Highland Rd
Highland Road
Council Building
Longfield
Works
Hammelton Road
Bromley Co Court
Bromley College
Mag Court
North Clinic
Gleneldre
Farwig Lane
Scotts Rd
TWEEDY ROAD
North St
Fire Station
Odeon Cin
The Glades Shopping
HIGH STREET
Farmfield
Sandpit Rd
Kendale Road
Beechmont Cl
Glenbow Road
Arcus Rd
Chingley Cl
Swiftsden Wy
Cemetery
BROMLEY HILL
Ashgrove Road
Ambleside
Belgravia Gdns
Calmont Road
Coniston Road
Hotel
Hillbrow Road
Elstree Hill
Erin Cl
Kirkstone Wy
Ullswater Cl
Bolton Gdns
Hawkshead Cl
Oaklands Road
Spencer Rd
LONDON ROAD
Ashgrove Estate
Beckenham Place Park Golf Course
Beckenham Place Park
Golf Course
Green Chain Walk
Crab Hill
Riverpark Gdns
Ravensbourne Station
Ravensmead Rd
Warren Avenue
Bromley Avenue
Bromley Park
Golf Course
Ravensbourne River
Madeira Avenue
Farnaby Road
Hall
Bracken Hl
Blyth Road
Pk End
St Marys RC Primary School
Convent Cl
Foxgrove Road
Foxgrove Av
Southwater Close
Place
Park
Woodstock Gdns
Banavie Gdns
Delfield Cl
Springbourne Court
The Avenue
Olyffe Dr
Albemarle Road
Downs Hill
Ravensbourne Avenue
Westgate Road
Meadway
Sloane Hospital
Shortlands Golf Club
Meadow Road
Chart Cl
The Mead
St Christophers School
BROMLEY ROAD
A222
B230
Bishop Challoner School
Scotts Av
BECKENHAM LANE
Recreation Rd
Playing Fields
Vale Primary School
Shortlands Station
Martin's Road
Church Road
1 grid square represents 500 metres

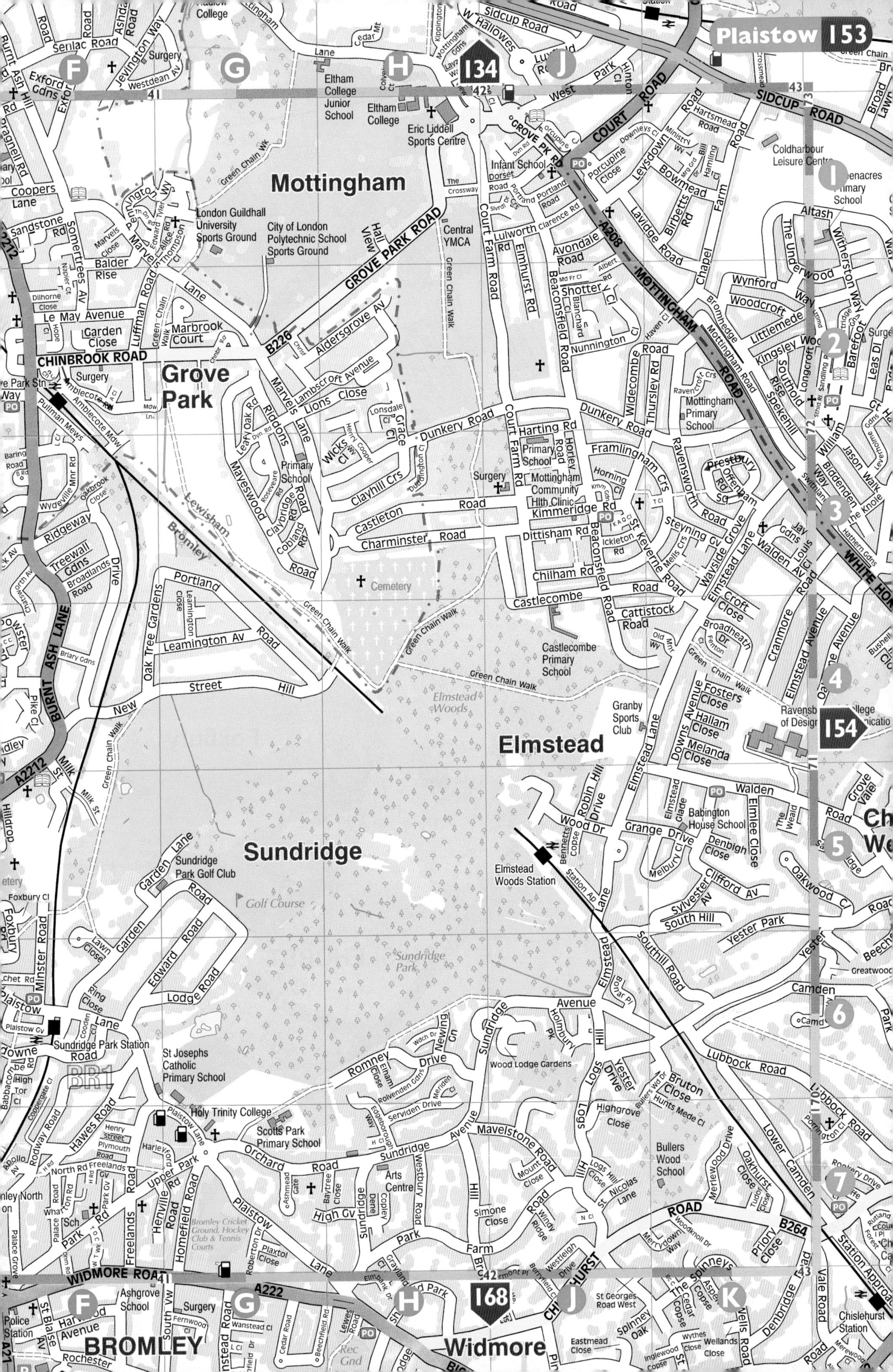
Plaistow 153
134
154
168
Mottingham
Grove Park
Elmstead
Sundridge
Widmore
BROMLEY
BR1
Eltham College Junior School
Eltham College
Eric Liddell Sports Centre
London Guildhall University Sports Ground
City of London Polytechnic School Sports Ground
Central YMCA
Infant School
Coldharbour Leisure Centre
Mottingham Primary School
Primary School
Mottingham Community Hlth Clinic
Surgery
Cemetery
Castlecombe Primary School
Granby Sports Club
Elmstead Woods
Elmstead Woods Station
Babington House School
Sundridge Park Golf Club
Golf Course
Sundridge Park
Sundridge Park Station
St Josephs Catholic Primary School
Holy Trinity College
Scotts Park Primary School
Arts Centre
Wood Lodge Gardens
Bullers Wood School
Bromley Cricket Ground, Hockey Club & Tennis Courts
Ashgrove School
Chislehurst Station
Grove Park Stn
Green Chain Walk
Lewisham
Bromley
GROVE PARK ROAD
CHINBROOK ROAD
MOTTINGHAM ROAD
COURT ROAD
SIDCUP ROAD
WIDMORE ROAD
BURNT ASH LANE
A208
A2212
A222
B226
B264
Dunkery Road
Court Farm Road
Beaconsfield Road
Castleton Road
Charminster Road
Elmstead Lane
Elmstead Avenue
Marvels Lane
Portland Road
Leamington Av
New Street Hill
Garden Road
Edward Road
Lodge Road
Plaistow Lane
Sundridge Avenue
Orchard Road
Mavelstone Road
Southill Road
Lubbock Road
Lower Camden
Chislehurst Road
Station Approach
Walden Road
Grange Drive
Wood Dr
Robin Hill Drive
Yester Park
Camden Park
Bickley Park Road

154
135
153
169
A
B
C
D
E
1
2
3
4
5
6
7
New Eltham
Longlands
Foxbury
Chislehurst West
CHISLEHURST
SIDCUP ROAD
A20 SIDCUP ROAD
SIDCUP-BY-PASS ROAD
WHITE HORSE HILL
A208 RED HILL
CHISLEHURST HIGH ST
CENTRE COMMON ROAD
BROMLEY ROAD
BROMLEY LANE
ROYAL PARADE
PRINCE IMPERIAL RD
A222
A211
B263
B264
GREEN LANE
OLD HILL
SUMMER HILL
WATT'S LANE
MANOR PARK ROAD
Hainault Street
Blanmerle Road
New Eltham Stn
Green Lane Business Park
Coldharbour Leisure Centre
Greenacres Primary School
Coldharbour Sports Ground
St Olaves Preparatory School
Dulverton Primary School
Montbelle Primary School
Ruxley Manor School
Edgebury Primary School
Kemnal Manor
Kemnal Road
Belmont Lane
Cemetery
Old Elthamians Sports Club
Beaverwood School for Girls
St Barts Hospital Sports Ground
Farrington & Stratford House School
Farrington Place
Ravensbourne College Design & Communication
The Willows Clinic
Junior School
Chislehurst Natural Health Centre
Mead Road Infant School
Chislehurst Common
Golf Course
Chislehurst Golf Club
Chislehurst Caves
Chislehurst
Coopers School
School
Greenwich
Bromley
BR7
1 grid square represents 500 metres

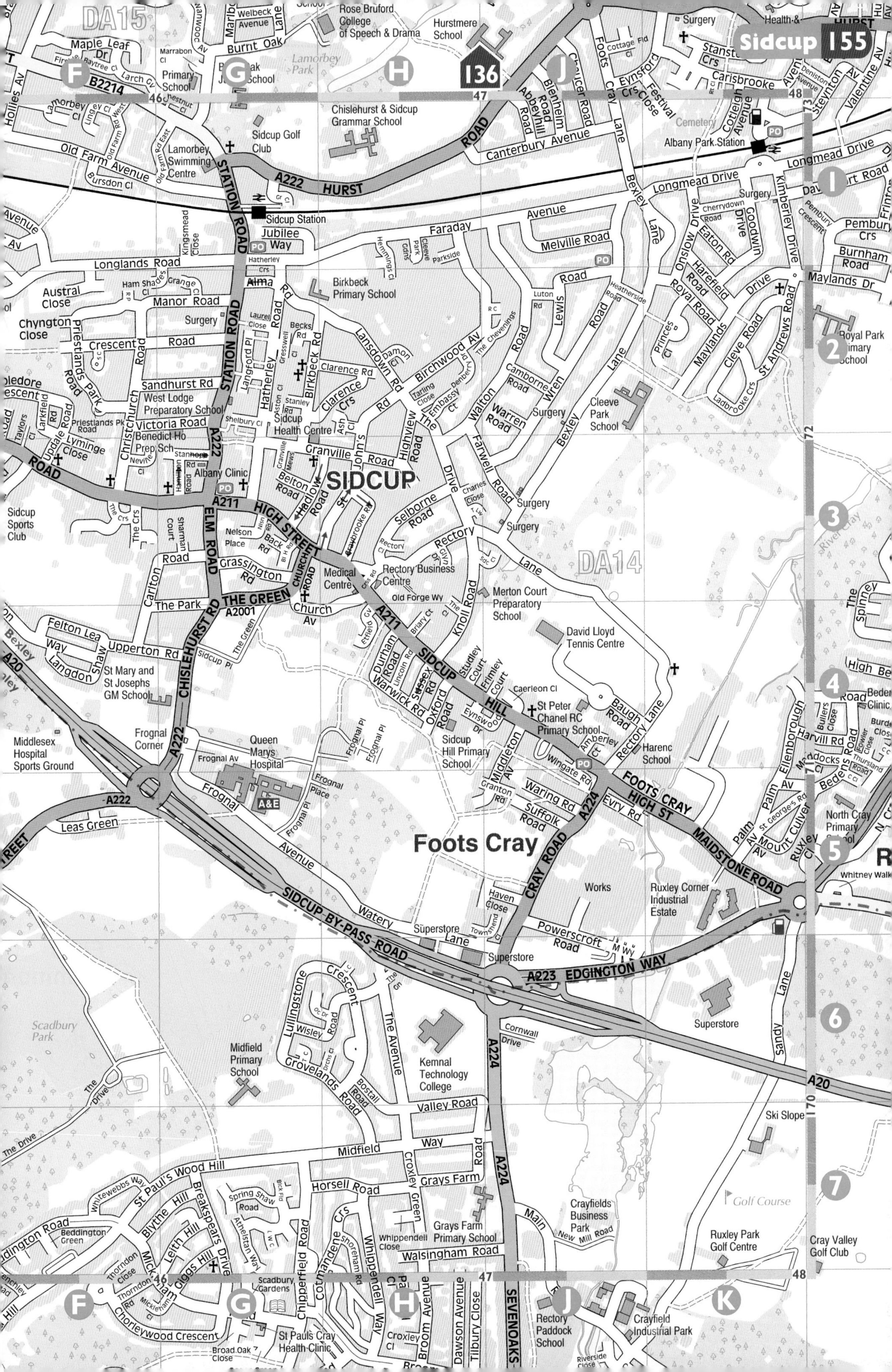
DA15
136
Rose Bruford College of Speech & Drama
Hurstmere School
Lamorbey Park
Maple Leaf Dr
Burnt Oak
Primary School
Chislehurst & Sidcup Grammar School
Sidcup Golf Club
Lamorbey Swimming Centre
Old Farm Avenue
Bursdon Cl
Canterbury Avenue
Albany Park Station
Cemetery
Longmead Drive
Station Road
A222 Hurst Road
Sidcup Station
Jubilee Way
Faraday Avenue
Melville Road
Longlands Road
Austral Close
Manor Road
Chyngton Close
Crescent Road
Birkbeck Primary School
Sandhurst Rd
West Lodge Preparatory School
Victoria Road
Benedict Ho Prep Sch
Albany Clinic
Sidcup Health Centre
Granville Road
SIDCUP
High Street
Elm Road
Grassington Rd
The Green
Church Road
Medical Centre
Rectory Business Centre
Rectory Lane
Selborne Road
Merton Court Preparatory School
David Lloyd Tennis Centre
DA14
Cleeve Park School
Royal Park Primary School
Sidcup Sports Club
The Park
Felton Lea
Upperton Rd
Langdon Shaw
St Mary and St Josephs GM School
Chislehurst Rd
A20
Middlesex Hospital Sports Ground
Frognal Corner
Queen Marys Hospital
A&E
Frognal Avenue
Sidcup Hill
St Peter Chanel RC Primary School
Sidcup Hill Primary School
Harenc School
Foots Cray High St
Maidstone Road
Foots Cray
Cray Road
Works
Ruxley Corner Industrial Estate
North Cray Primary School
Whitney Walk
Leas Green
Watery Lane
Sidcup By-Pass Road
Superstore
Powerscroft Road
A223 Edgington Way
Scadbury Park
Midfield Primary School
Kemnal Technology College
Valley Road
Midfield Way
Grays Farm Road
Grays Farm Primary School
Cornwall Drive
Ski Slope
Golf Course
Crayfields Business Park
Ruxley Park Golf Centre
Cray Valley Golf Club
St Paul's Wood Hill
Horsell Road
Walsingham Road
Sevenoaks Road
Chipperfield Road
Broom Avenue
Dawson Avenue
Tilbury Close
Rectory Paddock School
Crayfield Industrial Park
Scadbury Gardens
St Pauls Cray Health Clinic
Chorleywood Crescent
Broad Oak Close
F
G
H
J
K
1
2
3
4
5
6
7
46
47
48

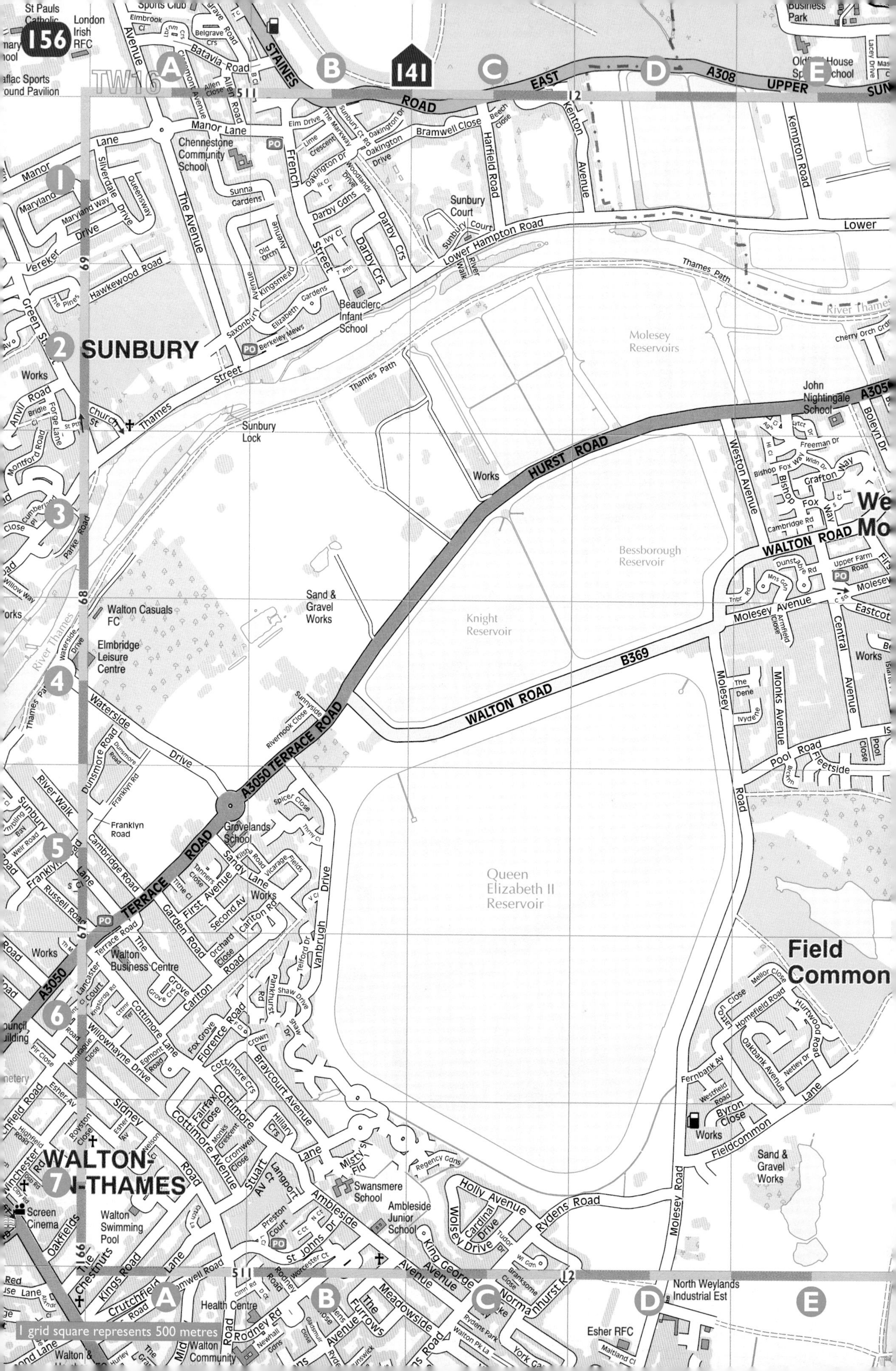

156
141
SUNBURY
WALTON-ON-THAMES
Field Common
A308 UPPER SUNBURY ROAD
EAST
A3050 TERRACE ROAD
HURST ROAD
WALTON ROAD
B369
Thames Street
River Thames
Thames Path
Sunbury Lock
Molesey Reservoirs
Bessborough Reservoir
Knight Reservoir
Queen Elizabeth II Reservoir
Sand & Gravel Works
Works
Chennestone Community School
Beauclerc Infant School
John Nightingale School
Grovelands School
Swansmere School
Ambleside Junior School
Walton Casuals FC
Elmbridge Leisure Centre
Walton Business Centre
Walton Swimming Pool
Screen Cinema
Health Centre
North Weylands Industrial Est
Esher RFC
London Irish RFC
Lower Hampton Road
Molesey Road
Molesey Avenue
Cottimore Lane
Rydens Road
Fieldcommon Lane
1 grid square represents 500 metres

West Molesey 157
142
158
170
Hampton Station
Oldfield Road
Hammond Close
Station Road
Hampton FC
HIGH STREET
CHURCH STREET
A311
Park Close
King's Paddock
Hogarth Way
THAMES STREET
Thames Cl
Sunbury Road
Richmond upon Thames
Surrey County
Thames Path
Works
HAMPTON COURT ROAD
A308
Hurst Park
Sadlers Ride
Buckingham Gdns
Buckingham Avenue
Victoria Avenue
Beldham Gardens
Tufton Gdns
Bedster Gdns
Carlyle Cl
Winchilsea Crs
Rivermead
East Molesey Cricket Club
Tagg's Island
Ash Island
Graburn Way
Hurst Park School
Hurstfield Rd
Garrick Gdns
HURST ROAD
Wilton Gardens
Windsor Avenue
New Road
Park Way
The Fairway
Dunstall Way
Kings Chase
HURST A3050 ROAD
Thames Path
Molesey Lock
Hotel
Hampton Court Palace
Balmoral Crescent
Dundas Gdns
Mole Abbey Gdns
Abbey Road
Merton Way
Adecroft Way
Lane
Palace Road
Parsons Md
Church Road
St Lawrence Junior School
Palace Road
RIVERBANK
Feltham Av
Vine Medical Centre
KT8
Wolsey Road
Cemetery
Rosemary Avenue
Council Building
St Peter's Rd
WALTON ROAD
B369
Molesham Way
Walk
Second Cl
Third Close
Hurst Road
Dennis Road
Vine Road
Pemberton Road
Park Road
Kent Road
Church Rd
Manor Road
Arnison Road
Grove Road
Challoners Close
School Road
St John's Road
BRIDGE RD
CREEK RD
HAMPTON COURT WAY
Hampton Court Station
Cannon Way
High Street
Yeend Close
Groveland's
Palmers Gv
Faraday Road
Chalford Cl
Odard Road
Grange Close
Grange Road
Spreighton Road
Surgery
Avern Road
Avern Gdns
Spring Gardens
Langton Road
Seymour Road
Clinton Avenue
Spencer Road
Hansler Grove
Bridge Gardens
Cedar Road
Molember Road
Helen Close
Brende Gdns
Glebelands
Priory La
Street
Chandlers Field Primary School
Beauchamp Road
Green Lane
Nightingale Rd
Primary School
St Mary's Road
The Orchard School
Mathan Road
Summer Road
Grist Memorial Sports Club
East Molesey
Bell Road
Aldersgrove
Riverside Avenue
Summer Gdns
Summer Avenue
Leaf Close
Works
Down
High Street
Molesey Hospital
Waverley Close
Approach Road
St Barnabas' Gdns
Farm Road
Ray Road
Molesey Road
Park Road
The Wilderness
Glenlyn Medical Cen
Molesey Park Close
The Teddington Theatre Club
Old Tiffinians Sports Ground
Fleetside
Ember Farm Way
Ember Farm Avenue
ESHER ROAD
B3379
Broadfields
Southfields
A309
Ennismore Gardens
Thistledene
Sterry Drive
Elsworthy
Speer Road
Orchard Lane
River Ember
Island Barn Reservoir
Imber Court Trading Estate
Metropolitan Police FC
B364
EMBERCOURT ROAD
Ember Gdns
St Pauls RC Primary School
College Drive
Thames Ditton Station
Basingfield Road
Esher College
EMBER LANE
Elm Tree Av
Woodside Avenue
Hampton Ct Way
Weston Av
Weston Green
Longmead Rd
Ember Lane
Works
Grove Way
Ember Sports Club
Imber Grove
Sandon Cl
Chestnut Avenue
Lime Tree Av
Imber Park Road
The Drive
Grove End Lane
The Broadway
Weston Green School
Onslow Way
Newlands Avenue
Weston Green
River Mole
Grove Way
Parkwood Avenue
Oaklands Avenue
Orchard Gate
Carleton Cl
Cranbrook Drive
Cranleigh Road
Woodlands
EMBER LANE STATION ROAD
Weston Green Road
Alma Road
HAMPTON COURT WAY
Weston Park
River Mole Business Park
Farm Road
Sandown Industrial Park
Works
Blair Avenue
Arran Way
The Woodend
Road
Douglas Road
Mill Road
Works
Esher Station
Macaulay Avenue
Woodfield Road
Hotel
PORTSMOUTH
Green

158
143
157
171
Hampton Wick
Bushy Park
Diana Fountain
Chestnut Avenue
HAMPTON COURT ROAD
A308
Hampton Court Palace
Hampton Court Station
HAMPTON COURT WAY
Stud House
Hampton Court Park
Golf Course
Home Park Golf Club
River Thames
Thames Path
Thames Ditton Island
Richmond upon Thames
Kingston upon Thames
Surrey County
Seething Wells
PORTSMOUTH ROAD
A307
Thames Ditton
Giggshill
Weston Green
Long Ditton
SURBITON
Thames Ditton Station
Thames Ditton Infant School
Thames Ditton Junior School
St Pauls RC Primary School
Council Building
EMBERCOURT ROAD
B364
STATION ROAD
WATTS ROAD
GIGGS HILL RD
Kingston Liberal Synagogue
St Marys CE Junior School
Infant School
Cemetery
Surbiton Business Centre
BRIGHTON ROAD
A243
VICTORIA ROAD
UPPER
HIGH STREET
TAVR Centre
Synagogue
Guildhall
Works
Hotel
Surgery
1 grid square represents 500 metres

Norbiton
KINGSTON UPON THAMES
Berrylands
Tolworth
Old Malden
KT1
KT5
KT6
Norbiton Station
Berrylands Station
Surbiton Station
Kingston Stn
Kingston Hospital
Kingston Crematorium
Kingsmeadow Athletics Centre
Kingstonian FC
Fairfield Industrial Estate
Cemetery
Surbiton Cemetery
Kingston University
Hogsmill River
Thames Down Link
Tiffin School
Grammar School
St Josephs RC Primary School
Sports Centre
Eden Walk Shopping Centre
Odeon
ABC
The Rotunda
Telephone Exchange
Council Building
University Primary School
The Mount Infant School
Superstore
Health Clinic
Roselands Clinic
Leigh Close Industrial Esta
Beech Grove Junior School
LSE Sports Club
Christ Church CE Primary School
The Hollyfield School
Assembly Rooms
High School
Hillcroft College
Surbiton Hosp
Oak Hill Health Cen
Fire Station
St Matthews CE Primary School
Dysart Special School
Grand Avenue Primary School
Our Lady Immaculate RC Primary School
Tolworth CP School
Tolworth Tower
Knollmead Primary School
Coombe Hill J&I School
CAMBRIDGE ROAD
A2043 KINGSTON RD
OLD LONDON RD
A238
CROMWELL RD
PENRHYN ROAD
A240
SURBITON HILL ROAD
EWELL ROAD
EWELL ROAD A240
CLAREMONT RD
B3363
B3370
ST MARK'S HILL
BRIGHTON ROAD A243
UPPER BRIGHTON ROAD
KINGSDOWNE ROAD
DITTON ROAD
KINGSTON BY-PASS
A3
WARREN DRIVE NORTH
BROADWAY
144
160
172

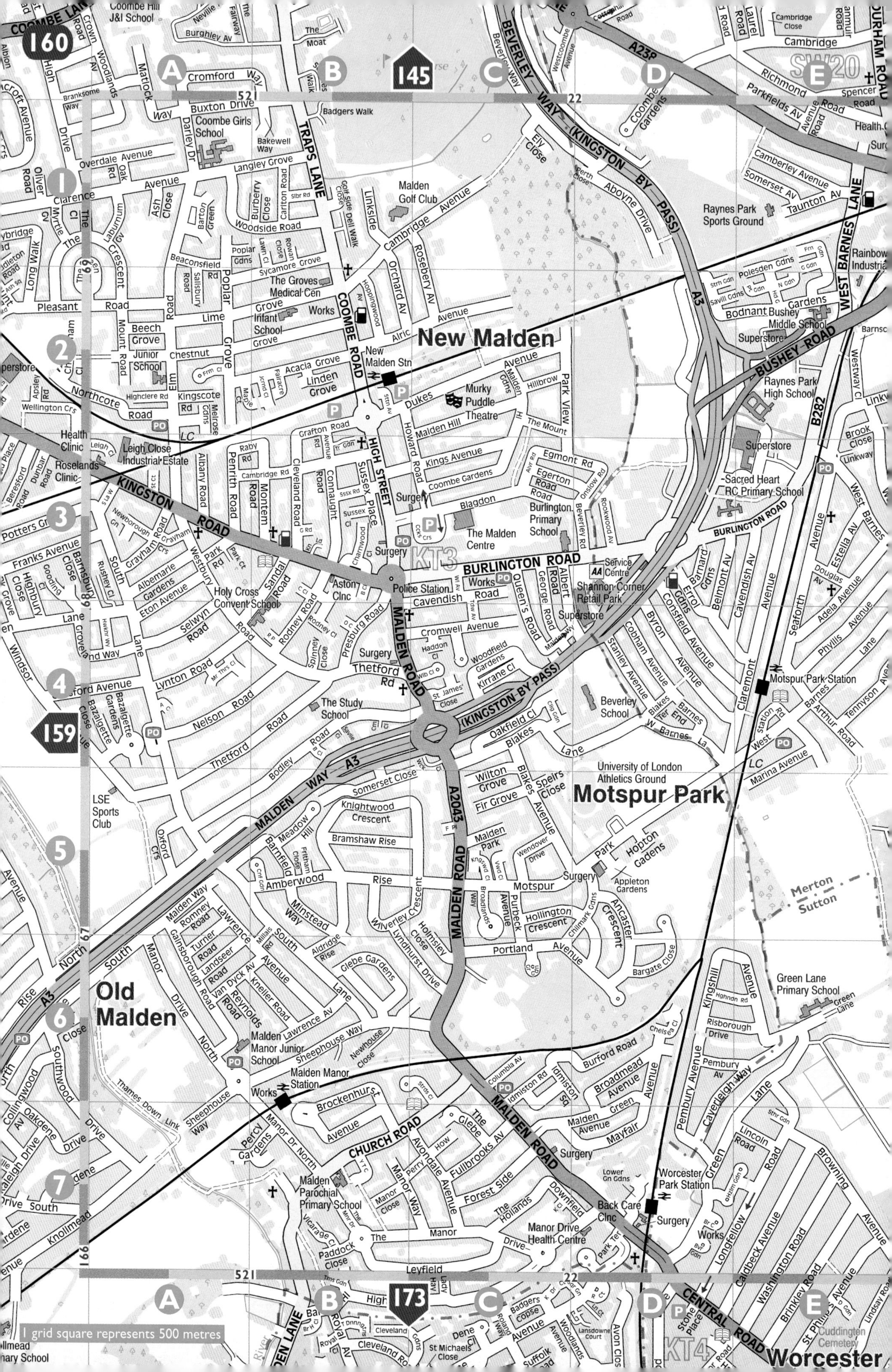
160
145
159
173
A
B
C
D
E
1
2
3
4
5
6
7
521
22
SW20
KT3
KT4
New Malden
Motspur Park
Old Malden
Worcester
Coombe Hill J&I School
Coombe Girls School
Malden Golf Club
Raynes Park Sports Ground
The Groves Medical Cen
Grove Infant School
Beech Grove Junior School
New Malden Stn
Murky Puddle Theatre
Health Clinic
Roselands Clinic
Leigh Close Industrial Estate
Bushey Middle School
Superstore
Raynes Park High School
Sacred Heart RC Primary School
The Malden Centre
Burlington Primary School
Service Centre
Shannon Corner Retail Park
Police Station
Aston Clnc
Holy Cross Convent School
The Study School
Beverley School
University of London Athletics Ground
LSE Sports Club
Motspur Park Station
Green Lane Primary School
Malden Manor Junior School
Malden Manor Station
Malden Parochial Primary School
Manor Drive Health Centre
Back Care Clnc
Worcester Park Station
Cuddington Cemetery
Merton
Sutton
KINGSTON BY PASS
MALDEN WAY
MALDEN ROAD
KINGSTON ROAD
BURLINGTON ROAD
BUSHEY ROAD
WEST BARNES LANE
HIGH STREET
COOMBE ROAD
TRAPS LANE
CHURCH ROAD
CENTRAL ROAD
BEVERLEY WAY
DURHAM ROAD
COOMBE LANE
A3
A238
A2043
B282
1 grid square represents 500 metres

MERTON
146
162
174
Raynes Park
Merton Park
Bushey Mead
Cannon Hill
Morden
West Barnes
Morden Park
SM4
KINGSTON ROAD A238
BUSHEY ROAD A298
GRAND DRIVE
WORPLE ROAD
MARTIN WAY
B286
B279
CROWN LANE
LONDON ROAD A24
A239 CENTRAL
GREEN LANE
EPSOM ROAD
STONECOT HILL
SUTTON COMMON ROAD
TUDOR DRIVE
OLD LODGE ROAD
REIGATE AVENUE
Wimbledon Chase Middle School
Wimbledon Chase Stn
Nelson Hospital
Merton Park Primary School
Rutlish School
South Merton Station
Poplar First School
Morden Station
Morden South Station
St Helier Station
Merton Adult College
Hillcross Primary School
Merton College
Morden Park Pool
Morden First School
Raynes Park Vale FC
St Catherines RC Middle School
St John Fisher RC Primary School
North East Surrey Crematorium
Morden Cemetery
The Garth Road Industrial Cen
Beverley Trading Est
Dorchester Primary Sch
St Anthony's Hospital
Brookfield Primary School
Glenthorne High School
St Raphaels Hospice
Kimpton Industrial Estate
THE BEVERLY
Churchill College
Raynes Park Station
F
G
H
J
I
K
1
2
3
4
5
6
7
24
25

162
MERTON
147
161
175
A
B
C
D
E
1
2
3
4
5
6
7
526
27
Melbourne
Nelson Trading Estate
Merton Ind Park
Abbey Mills
Liberty Avenue
Windsor Av
Jubilee Way
Chelsea Fields Industrial Est
Works
Business Cen
Lavender Park
Biggin Avenue
Avenue
Poplar Av
Reynolds Close
Silbury Av
Mortlake Drive
Lavender
Lavender Grove
Oakmead
Mortimer Road
Evelyn Road
Blenheim Business Centre
Dorset Road
Poplar Road
Hazelbury Close
Willmore End
Nursery Road
Saxon Business Centre
Brangwyn Crs
Primary School
Western Road
Moan Industrial Estate
Playing Fields
Surgery
Heyford Rd
Lavender Grove
Lewis Road
Liberty Middle School
Dorset Rd
Menin Works
Bond Road School
Bond First School
London Road
Downe Road
St Mark Prim Sch
Sadler Cl
Holborn Wy
A236
A24
Lombard Road
Lombard Business Park
Deer Park
Homefield Gdns
Sheldrick Cl
Church Road
Mount Rd
Haslemere Av
Roslyn Close
Primary School
Foxton Grove
Bourne Dr
Rock Cl
Batsworth Road
Goodwin Cl
Belgrave Road
Bank Av
Glebe Av
Abbeyfield Cl
Rodney Rd
Boundary Bus Park
Dalton Avenue
Ashtree Avenue
Hawthorne Av
Lowry Crs
Borough Road
Portland Road
Seaton Rd
Miles Road
Frimley Gdns
Edmund Road
Raleigh Gdns
Upper Gn W
Charnwood Avenue
Charminster Avenue
Sandbourne Avenue
Daybrook Road
Morden Road
Circle Gdns
Poplar Road South
Kenley Road
Windermere Avenue
Grasmere Av
Morden Road Clnc
Morden Hall Medical Centre
Morden Station
Crown La
Crown Lane
Aberconway Road
Police Stn
Morden Hall Road
Morden Hall Park
New Close
Bridge Road
Queen's Road
Oxted Close
Illingworth Cl
Benedict Rd
Belgrave Wk
Hallowfield Wy
Church Pth
Vicarage Gdns
Melrose Special School
Nursery Rd
Works
Love La
Church Rd
Harwood Av
Russell Rd
Glebe Path
Surgery
Lower Gn W
Fire Stn
Vestry Hall
Cricket Green
Birches Close
Chart Close
Primary Sch
The Ca Leisure
Elmwood Rd
Whitford Gdns
Albert Road
Langdale Avenue
Kingsleigh Place
A217
Stanley Road
Camrose Close
Cedars Road
Links Avenue
York Close
Morden Court
Bordesley Road
Abbotsbury Road
Hazelwood Avenue
Beeleigh Road
Bayham Road
Bardney Rd
Central Medical Centre
Buckfast Road
Birchwood Close
Morden
Morden South Station
School
Abbotsbury First School
Bodmin Grove
Burnham Road
Blanchland Road
Surgery
Phoenix College
Willows Avenue
Farm Road
Jarrow Cl
Central Road
Rosedene Avenue
Chalgrove Av
London Road
A24
A239
Morden Road
Rutter Gdns
Ravensbury Grove
Hengelo Gdns
Ravensbury La
Morden Gdns
Runes Cl
Heatherdene Cl
Crescent Gv
Octavia Cl
Taplow Ct
Works
Mitcham Cricket Club
Baron Gv
Linden Pl
Mitcham Park
Pol Stn
Branscome Av
Denham Crs
The Close
Cranmer School
Cranmer Road
Madeira
Tramway Path
Brookfields Av
Riverside Drive
Wandle Way
Forval Close
Osier Way
Bunting Close
Capital Business Cen
Connaught Business Centre
Abbey Industrial Est
The Willow Cent
Grace Business
Eagle Trading Estate
Wates Way
Ellis Road
Works
River Wandle
Surgery
Bruton Rd
Bristol Rd
Connaught Gdns
Arras Av
Rose Av
Ravensbury Av
Victory Avenue
Leonard Avenue
Florence Av
Johns Lane
Williams Lane
Langdon Road
Wandle Road
The Drive
Freeman Rd
Edward Av
Milner Road
Morton Road
Pollard Road
Seddon Road
Gavina Cl
Hillfield Avenue
Garth Primary School
Watermeads High School
Lessness Rd
Llanthony Road
Leominster Road
Merevale Crescent
Muchelney Road
Lilleshall Road
Montacute Road
Combermere Rd
Canterbury Road
Crowland Wk
Faversham Rd
St Helier Avenue
Middleton Road
Evesham Green
Egleston Rd
Easby Crs
Furness Road
Surgery
St Helier Station
Yenston Cl
Goldcliff Cl
Flaxley Road
Torrington Way
Love Lane
Green Lane
Pilgrim Close
Dorchester Road
Haines Wk
Malmesbury Middle School
Newminster Rd
Malmesbury Rd
Primary School
Netley Rd
Bishopsford Road
Surgery
Rewley Road
Roche Walk
Green Wrythe Primary School
Tosney Walk
Pershore Grove
Pipewell Road
Quarr Road
Revesby Road
Peterborough Road
Shrewsbury Road
Selby Green
Selby Road
Stoneleigh Road
Sherborne Crs
Shaftesbury Road
Middleton Road
Sawtry Close
Maynooth Gdns
Watermead La
Mill Gr Business
Wandle Trading Est
Rivers Tradin
Hartland Road
Garendon Road
Halesowen Road
Hexham Rd
Iona Close
Keynsham Road
Kirksted Road
Hunston Road
Glastonbury Road
Claymore Cl
Shearing Dr
Newstead Walk
Stavordale Road
Kelso Rd
Robertsbridge Road
Lindores Road
Tweeddale Junior School
Sutton Arena
Winchcombe Road
Infant School
Paisley Road
Titchfield Road
Thornton Road
St Paul's Cl
Blake Cl
St Alban's Grove
Welbeck Rd
Lark Way
Tull St
Bisham Cl
Batley Cl
Shap Crs
Newent Cl
Bramblewood Close
Oakfield Gardens
Buckhurst Avenue
Elm Cl
Limes Avenue
St Helier
Rosehill Avenue
B278
B2230
Twyford Rd
Tweeddale Road
Tewkesbury Road
Tintern Road
Whitland Road
Waltham Road
Tavistock Road
Welbeck Road
Woburn Road
Green Wrythe Lane
Wrythe
St Helier Hospital
A&E
Glenthorne Close
Glenthorne High School
Rosehill
Reigate Avenue A217
Anderson Cl
Surgery
Hurstcourt Road
Rose Hill
Hill
Rose Hill Park West
Gloucester Gdns
Rosehill Gardens
Kendal Gdns
Grennell
Greenshaw High School
Wendling Road
Whitby Road
Westminster
Welbeck Road
Wrythe
Carshalton High School for Boys
Groveside
Bakers Gdns
Muschamp
Winchcombe
Culvers Avenue
Culvers Retreat
Millside
Ash Close
Beech Close
Fairlands Av
Aultone Way
1 grid square represents 500 metres

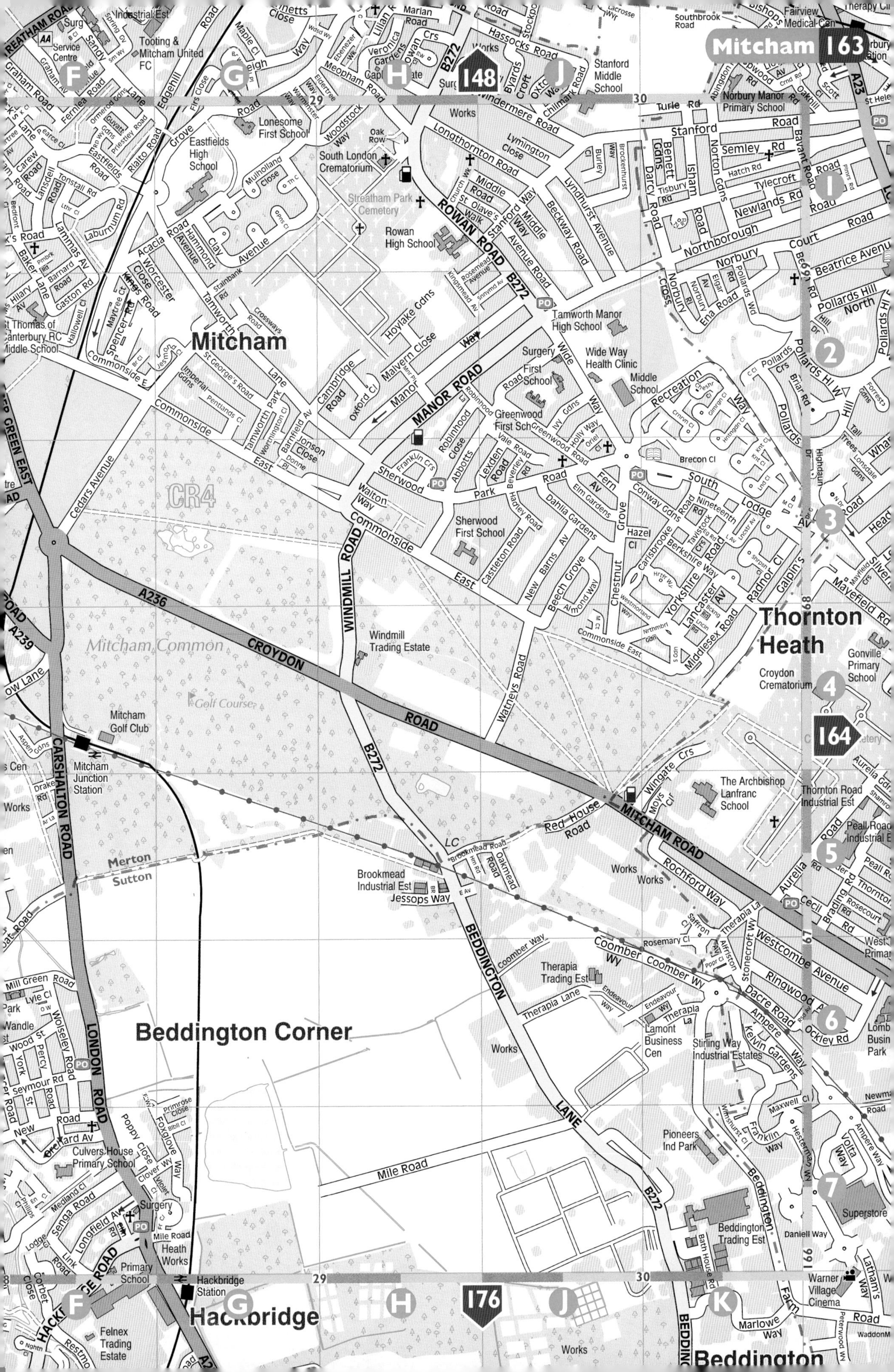

Mitcham
163
148
164
176
F
G
H
J
K
I
2
3
4
5
6
7
29
30
Mitcham
Thornton Heath
Beddington Corner
Hackbridge
Beddington
Mitcham Common
CR4
Golf Course
Mitcham Golf Club
Mitcham Junction Station
Hackbridge Station
Merton
Sutton
A236
CROYDON ROAD
MITCHAM ROAD
A239
CARSHALTON ROAD
LONDON ROAD
WINDMILL ROAD
B272
BEDDINGTON LANE
ROWAN ROAD
MANOR ROAD
Commonside East
Commonside
Cedars Avenue
Watneys Road
Red House Road
Mile Road
Rochford Way
Westcombe Avenue
Ringwood Av
Dacre Road
Coomber Way
Therapia Lane
Stanford Way
Longthornton Road
Windermere Road
Lyndhurst Avenue
Beckway Road
Northborough Road
Norbury Cross
Pollards Hill
Recreation Way
Tamworth Lane
Eastfields Road
Edgehill Road
Streatham Park Cemetery
South London Crematorium
Rowan High School
Tamworth Manor High School
Wide Way Health Clinic
Lonesome First School
Eastfields High School
Sherwood First School
Greenwood First Sch
Windmill Trading Estate
Brookmead Industrial Est
Jessops Way
Therapia Trading Est
Lamont Business Cen
Stirling Way Industrial Estates
Pioneers Ind Park
Beddington Trading Est
Warner Village Cinema
Superstore
The Archbishop Lanfranc School
Croydon Crematorium
Gonville Primary School
Thornton Road Industrial Est
Norbury Manor Primary School
Stanford Middle School
Tooting & Mitcham United FC
St Thomas of Canterbury RC Middle School
Culvers House Primary School
Felnex Trading Estate
Works
Surgery
Fairview Medical Cen
Southbrook Road

164
149
163
177
A
B
C
D
E
1
2
3
4
5
6
7
531
32
196
67
68
69
Norbury
Thornton Heath
Broad Green
Selhurst
Wandle Park
Beddington
CR7
Norbury Station
Thornton Heath Station
West Croydon Stn
East Croydon Station
Norbury Manor Secondary Girls School
Norbury Manor Primary School
David Livingstone Primary School
Norbury Trading Est
Norbury Health Centre
St James The Great RC Primary School
Sports Ground
Infant School
Parchmore Medical Centre
Thornton Heath Pools & Fitness Cen
Thornton Heath Health Centre
Primary School
St Lukes School
Junior Girls School
Gonville Primary School
Croydon Crematorium
Croydon Cemetery
The Archbishop Lanfranc School
Thornton Road Industrial Est
Peall Road Industrial Est
West Thornton Primary School
Lombard Business Park
Brigstock Medical Centre
Streatham & Croydon RFC
Croydon Mosque & Islamic Cen
Mayday University Hospital
North Croydon Medical Cen
A&E
London Road Medical Centre
Eversley Medical Cen
Manor School
Ecclesbourne Primary School
Queen's Rd Cemetery
Council Building
Hampton Rd Ind Park
St James Medical Cen
St Marys High School
Croydon Hlth Authority
St Marys RC Junior School
St Marys RC Infant School
Beddington Trading Est
Superstore
Warner Village Cinema
Mosque
Safari
Works
Surgery
LONDON ROAD
A23
A235
A236
A212
A222
B266
B273
BRIGSTOCK ROAD
THORNTON ROAD
MITCHAM ROAD
PURLEY WAY
A213 SUMNER ROAD
PARCHMORE ROAD
GRANGE ROAD
WHITEHORSE ROAD
WINDMILL ROAD
NORTHCOTE ROAD
WELLESLEY ROAD
ST JAMES'S RD
HIGH ST
GREEN LANE
1 grid square represents 500 metres

Selhurst 165
150
166
178
Anerley
SE20
SE25
Woodside
Addiscombe
Monks Orchard
Anerley Primary School
Aucklands Gdns
Auckland Rd
Sylvan Road
Kitley Gdns
Cantley Gdns
Acorn Gdns
Surgery
Infant Sch
Grange Av
Grange Gdns
Spurgeons Coll
Cypress Road
Cypress Junior School
High Vw Cl
Howden Road
Wharncliffe Gdns
Falkland Park Av
South Norwood Hill Medical Centre
SOUTH NORWOOD HILL
Woodvale Avenue
Court Road
Lancaster Road
Sundial Avenue
Norhyrst Av
Southern Av
Warminster Road
Coleman Cl
Avenue Rd
Pittville Gardens
Selby Road
Derwent Rd
Tovil Cl
Wadhurst Cl
Weighton Rd
Thornsett Pl
Thornsett Road
Wheathill Rd
Cambridge Road
Stembridge Road
Tremaine Road
Samos Road
Worbeck Road
Bourdon Rd
CROYDON ROAD
A213
A214
ANERLEY ROAD
ELMERS END ROAD
Oak Grove Rd
Ash Gv
Chesham Crs
Pelham Road
Ravenscroft
Birkbeck
Blandford
Allen Road
Birkbeck Station
Arrol Road
Beck
Witham Rd
Felmingham
Piquet Rd
Sheringham
Ashleigh
Marlow
Warwick Road
Stewart Fleming Primary School
Beckenham Crematorium
Cemetery
Bromley
Croydon
Elmers End Station
South Norwood Country Park
Superstore
Croydon Road Industrial Est
Tannery Cl
Puffin Cl
Kingfisher Way
Longheath Gardens
Mardell Rd
Chaffinch Av
Bywood Av
Brookside
Gladeside
Fairhaven Avenue
Gwynne Av
Woodmere Gdns
Honeysuckle Gdns
Laburnum Gdns
Primrose La
Marigold Wy
Teasel Cl
Shirley Oaks Road
Nugent Rd
Dixon Road
Whitworth Road
WHITEHORSE LANE
Canham Road
St Mary's Rd
Michael Rd
Parry Road
Egerton Rd
Holmewood
Huntly Rd
Claret Gdns
Sangley Rd
Oliver Av
Oliver Gv
South Norwood Medical Cen
Crystal Palace FC
Wimbledon FC
(Selhurst Park)
Clifton
Holmesdale
Bungalow Rd
Upper Gv
Burgoyne Rd
Police Stn
Lawrence Rd
Priory Special School
Priory Gdns
Cargreen Road
Station Rd
HIGH STREET A213
Chalfont Rd
High School
Cumberlow Av
PENGE ROAD
MANOR RD
King's Rd
Camille Cl
Regina Rd
Sunny Bank
Bevill Cl
Lincoln Rd
Cromer Rd
Hambrook Rd
Chartham Rd
Malden Av
Waverley Rd
Brooklyn Rd
Love La
Sunnycroft Rd
Twr Industrial Est
Eldon Pk
Archer Rd
Lonsdale Rd
Albert Road
Westgate Rd
Belgrave Rd
Norwood Junction Stn
Clifford Rd
Doyle Rd
Farley Pl
Crowther Rd
Balfour Road
Stanger Rd
School
Works
Addison Rd
Cresswell Rd
Pembury Rd
Harrington
Apsley Road
Belfast Rd
Notson Rd
Aylett
Watcombe Rd
Sandown Road
Oakley Road
Ferndale Road
Dundee Rd
Belmont Rd
PORTLAND ROAD
Prince Road
Dinsdale Gardens
Alverston Gdns
Wynton Gdns
Tennison Road
South Norwood Primary School
Carmichael Road
Holland Road
Alfred Rd
Enmore Av
Elborough
Merton Road
Pools & Fitness Centre
Health Cen
Portland Medical Cen
Denmark Rd
Enmore Road
Ryelands Primary School
Croydon Sports Arena
Croydon FC
Macclesfield Rd
SELHURST
St Chads RC Primary School
Heavers Farm Primary School
Selhurst Station
Works
Follys End Christian High School
Towpath Way
Canal Walk
Davidson Road
Birchanger Road
Howard Road
Cobden Road
Woodside Av
Woodside Pk
Woodside Gn
Christie Dr
Rendle Cl
Pickering Gdns
Gunnell Cl
Backley Gdns
Becket Cl
Primary School
Anthony Rd
Dickenson's La
Coe Av
Grasmere Road
Cumberland Rd
Southcote Rd
Tudor Rd
St Luke's Cl
Estcourt Road
Shoreham Cl
Rusthall Cl
Tollgate Primary School
Stockbury Rd
Longhurst Rd
Ashburton Primary School
Ritchie Rd
LONG LANE
A222
Keats Wy
Delamare Crs
Swinburne Crs
Coleridge
Green Way
WOODSIDE GREEN
A215
SPRING LANE
Cleaverholme Cl
Woodside Road
Stroud Rd
Salisbury Rd
Elmers Rd
B243
Tenterden Rd
Willow Wd Crs
Selhurst New Rd
Rees Gdns
Beckford Rd
Adams Wy
Davies Cl
Goodhew Rd
Malcolm Rd
Sonning Rd
Westbourne Rd
Northway Rd
Lindfield Rd
Meadvale Rd
Hermitage La
Ashurch Rd
Alderton Road
Junior School
Brampton Rd
Dominion Rd
Laurier Rd
Davidson J&I School
Jesmond Rd
Bredon Rd
Kemerton Rd
Edward Road
Rymer Road
Dartnell Road
Exeter Road
Fullerton Rd
MORLAND ROAD
Tait Rd
Davidson Rd
Alexandra Road
Vincent Rd
Stretton Rd
Leicester Rd
Morland Avenue
Gordon Crs
Surgery
Chaucer Green
Council Building
Ashburton High School
Stroud Green
Pagehurst Rd
Wydenhurst Rd
Blackhorse La
Teevan Road
Woodside Ct Rd
Coniston Rd
Camborne Rd
Addiscombe Av
Dalmally Rd
Capri Rd
Highbarrow Rd
Everton Rd
Sundridge Rd
Brockenhurst Rd
Kingscote Rd
Sherwood Road
Elmgrove Rd
Fernhurst Rd
Parkview Road
SHIRLEY ROAD
Shirley Park Road
Glenthorne Avenue
Blackthorne Avenue
Poppy Lane
Peabody Close
Shirley Clinic
Primrose Lane
Barnfield Av
Valley Walk
LOWER ADDISCOMBE ROAD
ORCHARD ROAD
Leslie Park Rd
Primary School
Warren Rd
Hastings Rd
Grant Road
Nicholson Rd
Inglis Rd
Fisher Cl
Academy Gdns
Claremont Road
Ashling Rd
Baring Road
Bingham Rd
Sefton Road
Compton Road
Craven Rd
Ashburton Avenue
Selwood Road
Craigen Av
Lebanon Road
Addiscombe Court Rd
Tunstall Rd
Canning Road
Clyde Road
Havelock Rd
Outram Road
Ashburton Road
Mulberry La
Northampton Road
Harriet Gdns
Annandale Rd
Ashurst Walk
Birch Tree Way
Shirley Park Golf Club
Trinity
SHIRLEY ROAD
Cedar Road
A232
Addiscombe Road
F
G
H
J
I
K
1
2
3
4
5
6
7
34
35
67

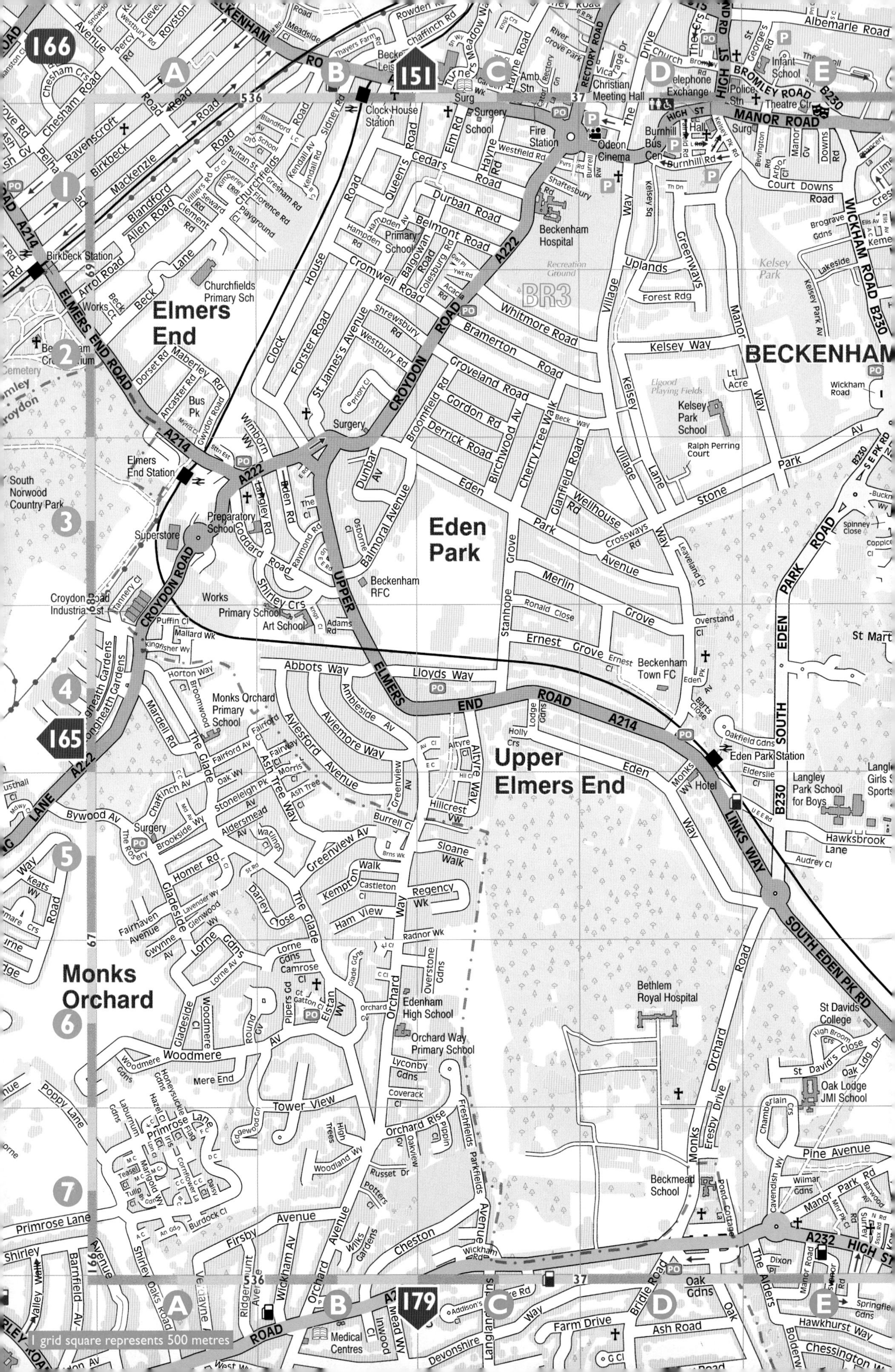

166
151
165
179
A
B
C
D
E
1
2
3
4
5
6
7
Elmers End
Eden Park
Upper Elmers End
Monks Orchard
BECKENHAM
BR3
Clock House Station
Birkbeck Station
Elmers End Station
Eden Park Station
Beckenham Hospital
Bethlem Royal Hospital
Churchfields Primary Sch
Kelsey Park School
Langley Park School for Boys
Oak Lodge JMI School
Edenham High School
Orchard Way Primary School
Monks Orchard Primary School
Beckmead School
St Davids College
Beckenham RFC
Beckenham Town FC
South Norwood Country Park
Croydon Road Industrial Est
Odeon Cinema
Christian Meeting Hall
Fire Station
Telephone Exchange
Elgood Playing Fields
Ralph Perring Court
Recreation Ground
Kelsey Park
Medical Centres
ELMERS END ROAD
CROYDON ROAD
UPPER ELMERS END ROAD
SOUTH EDEN PK RD
SOUTH EDEN PARK ROAD
WICKHAM ROAD B230
BROMLEY ROAD
MANOR ROAD
HIGH ST
A214
A222
A232
B230
Eden Way
Stone Park Av
Village Way
Kelsey Way
Manor Way
Whitmore Road
Bramerton Road
Groveland Road
Cromwell Road
Durban Road
Belmont Road
Cedars Road
Abbots Way
Lloyds Way
Aylesford Avenue
Aviemore Way
Ernest Grove
Merlin Grove
Stanhope Grove
Links Way
Orchard Way
Monks Orchard Road
Woodmere Av
Primrose Lane
Tower View
1 grid square represents 500 metres

Beckenham 167
152
168
180
F
G
H
J
K
I
2
3
4
5
6
7
39
40
66
67
68
Shortlands
Park Langley
West Wickham
Hayes
Albemarle Road
Sloane Hospital
Shortlands Golf Club
Bromley Co Coll
Bromley College
Bromley North
Mag Court
The Mead
St Christophers School
A222
BROMLEY ROAD
BROMLEY RD
BECKENHAM LANE
HIGH STREET
TWEEDY ROAD
Bishop Challoner School
Scotts Avenue
Valley Primary School
Playing Fields
Recreation Rd
Martin's Road
Odeon Cin
Fire Station
Police Station
Walters Yard
Westmoreland Rd
Church Road
Tel Exchange
Tetty Way
The Glades Shopping Centre
Queens Gardens
The Pavilion Leisure Cen
Churchill Theatre
Indoor Market
Church House Gardens
Martin's Hill Recreation Ground
Queens Mead
Bowling Green
Works
Shortlands Station
Station Road
Queen's Md Rd
Pumping Station
Valley Rd
Park Hill Road
The Glen
Beckenham Grove
Bromley Grove
Oakwood Avenue
Clare House Primary School
Holmdene Cl
Oakhill Rd
Perth Rd
Ashmere Av
White Oak Dr
Courtenay Dr
Oakway
Lane
Stanley Avenue
Springpark Dr
Kenwood Drive
Ferguson Cl
Quinton Cl
Tulse Cl
Thorne's Cl
Tudor Cl
Scott's Lane
Oates Cl
Shortlands Gv
Shortlands Rd
Waldron Gardens
Foxes Dl
Church Road
Green Cl
May's Hill Rd
Iden Cl
Hill
Hillside Rd
Dykes Wy
Bromley Crs
Bromley Gdns
Glassmill La
Gwydyr Rd
Mill Vale
Forstal Close
Ethelbert Close
Ethelbert Road
Ringer's Road
Ravensbourne Road
Ridley Road
High Street
Elmfield Park
Elmfield Road
Surgery
Bromley South Station
Superstore
Langdon
Kentish Way
A21
Rafford Way
Stockwell Cl
Civic Centre
St Blaise Av
Harwood Avenue
MASONS HL
B228
Bromley Hospital
A&E
Cromwell Avenue
Tiger Lane
Pinewood Rd
Sandford Road
Streamside Close
The Ravensbourne School
HAYES LANE
Castle Cl
Kingswood
St Mary's Avenue
Winchester Pk
Winchester Rd
Primary School
Newbury Rd
Aylesbury Rd
Simpson's Rd
Queen Anne Avenue
WESTMORELAND ROAD
Den Road
Den Cl
Celtic Av
Valan Leas
Cumberland Road
Avenue
Chiltern Gdn
Caygill Cl
HAYES
Hayes Way
Fyfield Cl
Druids Way
Kingswood Avenue
South Hill Road
Highfield Junior School
Highfield Drive
Highfield Infant School
Durham Avenue
Lancaster Cl
Elwill Way
Whitecroft Cl
Wickham Way
Malmains Way
Malmains Cl
Styles Way
Whitecroft
Hengist Wy
Romanhurst Gdns
Romanhurst Av
Tootswood Road
Br Cl
Stamford Dr
Rutland Gate
D'Arcy Pl
Whitehaven Cl
New Farm Avenue
Oakham Drive
Langham Dr
Tall Elms Cl
Stone Road
Cameron Road
Beadon Road
HAYES ROAD B2212
Rise
B251
Top Park
Surgery
Broad Oaks Wy
Knowlton Gn
Hayesford Park Dr
Letchworth Drive
Brambie Cl
Wagtail Wk
Limewood Cl
Brabourne Rise
Woodmere Way
Overhill Way
Bushey Way
Wickham Way
Dunstan's Lane
Chase
Wood
Road
Westmoreland Rd
Pickhurst La
Woodlea Dr
Pickhurst Park
Penshurst Gn
Hayesford Pk Dr
Cheriton Av
Matfield Close
Barnhill Avenue
Fair Acres
Cornford Cl
Mead Way
Link Field
Heath Rise
Hazelmere Way
Cranbrook Cl
Wolfe Close
Montcalm Close
Fairway
Barnfield
Barnfield Wd
Langley Park Golf Club
Hawksbrook La
Hayes Way
The Crescent
Surgery
West Wy
Goodhart Way
The Avenue
Pickhurst Lane
Pickhurst Junior School
Pickhurst Infant School
Eastry Av
Shoreham Wy
Kingsdown Way
Marden Avenue
Oakmead Avenue
Northbourne
Gardens
Sedgewood Cl
Malling Way
Boughton Av
Pembury Cl
Chilham Way
Farleigh Av
Vale
Southway
Eastway
Dartmouth Road
C G Rd
Kechill
Golf Course
Road
Lodge
Long Meadow Cl
The Avenue
The Drive
Wickham Chase
Langley Way
Pickhurst Rise
Pickhurst Gn
Pickhurst Md
Mounthurst Road
Pittsmead Avenue
Southbourne
The Green
Trevor Cl
Chatham Av
Constance Crescent
Bourne Way
Chatham Avenue
Sackville Avenue
Cecil Way
Stuart Av
Cherry Walk
Hambro Av
Everard Avenue
Alexander Close
Husseywell Crs
Stanhope Av
Georgian Close
HAYES STREET
Hayes Wood Avenue
Glebe House Drive
Burwood Avenue
B265
Hayes School
West Wickham Station
Rays Rd
Red
HAYES
Crest Rd
Hilldown Rd
Courtlands Av
B251
Hayes Hill Rd
Brian Gdns
Dene Cl
Hurstdene Av
Hurst Close
Hayes Station
Station Ap
PICKHURST LANE
Surgery
Forge Close
Forge Clinic
The Knoll
Hayes Garden
Saville Rw
Close
BECKENHAM ROAD
West Wickham Swimming Baths
A214
STATION ROAD
Ravenswood Crs
Ravenswood Av
Surgery
Hawes Lane
Links Road
The Mead
Croft Av
Oak Gv
Ash Gv
Hawes Down Primary School
Glebe School
Old Wilsonians Sports Club
Hayes Md Rd
Pondfield Road
Hayes Hill
Keswick Road
Prickley Wd
Hp Gdn
Glebe Wy
Wickham Crs
Rose Walk
GLEBE
Linden Leas
Rose Wk
Lane
Hawes Down Clnc
Phoenix Cl
Hawes Lane
Mount Ct
Windermere Rd
Rydal Dr
Holland Cl
Holland Way
Hillside Lane
Station Hill
Warren Road
Ridge Way
Grove Close

168
153
167
181
A
B
C
D
E
1
2
3
4
5
6
7
541
42
BROMLEY
Widmore
Bickley
Bromley Common
Hayes
Bromley North Station
Bromley South Station
Bickley Station
WIDMORE ROAD
A222
A21
KENTISH WAY
MASONS HILL
BROMLEY COMMON
HASTINGS ROAD
HAYES ROAD B2212
HAYES STREET
HAYES LANE
B265
B228
BICKLEY ROAD
BICKLEY PARK ROAD
CHISLEHURST
PAGE HEATH LANE
HOMESDALE ROAD
Police Station
Fire Station
Ashgrove School
Surgery
Civic Centre & Bromley Palace
Widmore Centre
St Georges CE Primary School
Playing Field
Works
Rec Gnd
The Pavilion Leisure Cen.
Indoor Market
Bromley Hospital
A&E
Superstore
Tennis Club
Waldo Industrial Est
Chartwell Business Centre
Bickley Park Prep School
Bickley Park Cricket Club
The Ravensbourne School
Raglan Primary School
Old Bromlians Cricket Club
Bromley FC
Norman Park
Norman Park Athletics Track
Bromley College of Further & Higher Education
Bromley Common
Oakley House
Bromley Golf Club
Golf Course
Cemetery
Hayes Primary School
Forge Close Clinic
Newton Terrace
Rookery Lane
George Lane
Church Lane
Lower Gravel Road
Jackson Road
Southborough Lane
Oldfield Road
Hawthorne Road
St Georges Road
Turpington Lane
Magpie Hall Lane
BR2
1 grid square represents 500 metres

154
F
G
H
J
I
K
1
2
3
4
5
6
7
44
45
Chislehurst Station
Station Approach
SUMMER HILL
BROMLEY ROAD
OLD HILL
A222
Cricket Ground Road
Onslow Crescent
Norlands Crescent
Ravenshill
Sheridan Crescent
Penn Gardens
Lindenfield
Longmead
Roundwood
Gosshill Road
Faro Close
Coates Hill Road
Hever Gardens
Wellsmoor Gardens
Barfield Road
Otford Close
Golf Road
Thornet Wood Road
Northumberland Gardens
Lane
Bromley High School
Jubilee Country Park
Hawkwood Farm
Tongs Farm
Botany Bay Lane
Hawkwood Lane
Coopers School
Bishops Walk
Consort Drive
Queens Gate Gardens
Park
Cookham Dene Close
Manor Place
Manor Park
Riverwood Lane
Walsingham Park
ST PAUL'S CRAY ROAD
ORPINGTON ROAD
A208
CHISLEHURST ROAD
Beddington
Beddington Green
Brenchley Road
St Paul's Wood Hill
Bridgewater Close
The Drive
Leesons Hill
Kenley Close
Clarendon
Berens Way
Marlings Park Av
Marlings Close
Kevington Drive
Scotsdale Close
Sefton Close
Sefton Road
Ascot
Sherborne
Poverest
Pets Wood
Petts Wood
Little Thrift
Great Thrift
Hazelmere Road
Silverdale Road
Manor Way
Towncourt Crescent
Woodland Way
Crossway
Birchwood Road
Wood Ride
Kingsway
Petts Wood Road
Greencourt Road
Princes Avenue
Ladywood Avenue
The Chenies
Willett Way
Station Sq
West Way
Petts Wood Station
Maple Close
Acacia Close
Hawthorn Close
Ash Cl
Fairway
Tudor Way
Priory Avenue
St Georges Rd
St John's Road
Willett Close
Oaklands Close
Greenwood Close
St Francis Close
Berger Cl
The Close
The Covert
Grosvenor Road
Sutherland Avenue
Elysian Av
Covet Wood Close
Kedleston
Scads Hill Close
Grampian Cl
Clovelly Way
Denver Cl
Plesham Rd
Fordwich Cl
Wye Cl
Cowden
Bicknor Road
Melbourne Close
Irvine Way
Westholme
Broom Hill
Mayfield Avenue
Eastcote
Broxbourne
Bancroft Gardens
Hall
Surgery
Hillview Crescent
Elm Grove
Hill View Road
Oakhill Rd
Orpington Station
Station Ap
Crofton Lane
Lynwood Grove
Dale Wood Road
Pondwood Rise
Claywood Cl
Cedars Rd
Red Cedars Rd
Homesdale Road
Buckingham Close
Fairfield Road
Beaumont Road
Eastbury Road
Fieldway
Towncourt Lane
Bushey Av
Jersey Dr
Ryecroft Rd
Kenilworth Road
Transmere Road
Ad Cl
Shepperton Road
Kydbrook Cl
Eynsford Cl
Queensway
West Ap
Lakeswood Road
Franks Wood Avenue
Crest View Drive
Merton Gdns
Crest View Drive
Maybury Close
St James RC Primary School
London Loop
Tent Peg La
Southborough Lane
Southborough Primary School
Funtwell Drive
Oxhawth Crescent
Langley Gardens
Chesham Avenue
Woodhurst Av
Nightingale Road
Drive
Crescent
Diameter Rd
Rolleston Avenue
Rolleston Close
Fairoak Close
Ember Close
Felton Close
Prescott Avenue
Hollingworth Road
Faringdon Av
Faringdon Avenue
Laburnum Way
Lovelace Avenue
Thorn Cl
Hazel Walk
Ash Row
Birch Row
Hornbeam Way
Larch Way
Whitebeam Avenue
Almond Way
Almond Close
Southborough
Derwent Drive
Greenfield Gardens
Beckford Drive
Broadcroft Road
Heath Side
Branston Crs
Kennedy Close
Honeybourne Way
Birkdale Cl
Woodcote Drive
Place Farm Av
Sparrow Drive
Abbots Close
Monks Way
St Thomas' Drive
Romany Rise
Crofton Lane
Tandridge Drive
Ferndown Av
Gleneagles Close
Allington Road
Andover Road
Cathcart Drive
York Rise
Kelvin Parade
Oregon Square
Yeovil Cl
Bramley Close
Lansdowne Avenue
Wyndham Close
Drayton Avenue
St Anthony's Court
Rose Dale
Lime Grove
Wistaria Close
Cedar Avenue
Jasmine Close
Fairbank Av
Birch Mead
Wood Way
Hazel Grove
Cumping Road
Ormond Av
Clarendon Road
Crofton
A232
Allington Road
Orchard Green
Oakwood

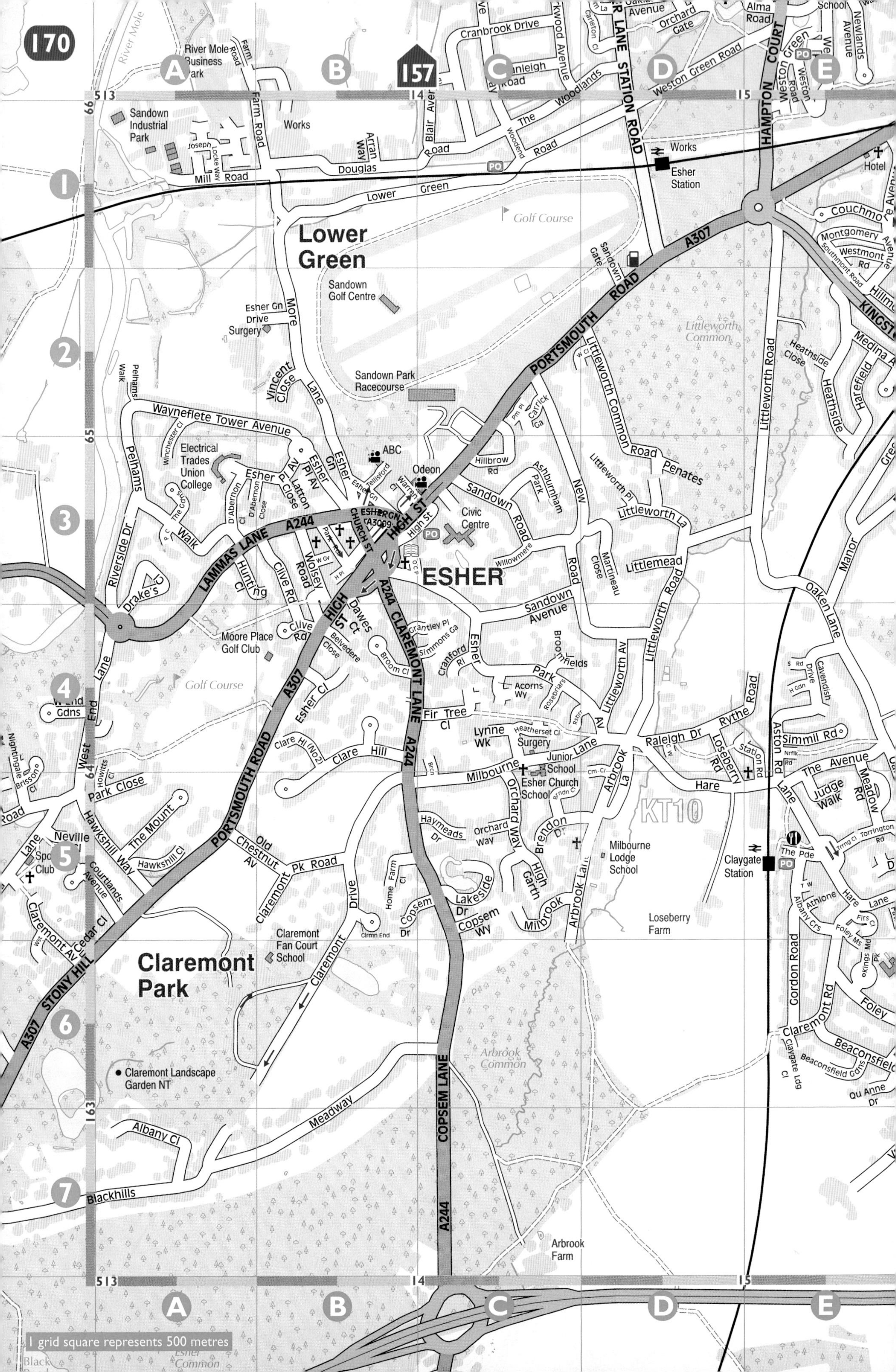

170
157
A
B
C
D
E
1
2
3
4
5
6
7
513
14
15
66
65
64
163
River Mole
River Mole Business Park
Farm Road
Sandown Industrial Park
Works
Arran Way
Blair Avenue
Cranbrook Drive
Kirkwood Avenue
Orchard Gate
Alma Road
Weston Green Road
Weston Green
Newlands Avenue
The Woodlands
Woodend
Road
Douglas
Mill Road
Lower Green
Lower Green
Golf Course
Station Road
Hampton Court
Esher Station
Hotel
Couchmore Avenue
Montgomery Avenue
Westmont Rd
Southmont Road
Kingston
Sandown Gate
A307
Portsmouth Road
Sandown Golf Centre
Littleworth Common
Littleworth Road
Heathside Close
Heathside
Harefield
Medina Av
Esher Gn Drive
Surgery
More Lane
Vincent Close
Sandown Park Racecourse
Pelhams Walk
Wayneflete Tower Avenue
Winchester Cl
Electrical Trades Union College
Pelhams
Esher Pl Av
Latton Close
Esher Gn
ABC
Odeon
Warren Cl
Hillbrow Rd
Ashburnham Park
Sandown Road
Littleworth Common Road
Penates
Littleworth Pl
Littleworth La
New Road
Civic Centre
High St
Church St
Esher Pl Av
D'Abernon Cl
D'Abernon Close
Walk
Riverside Dr
Drake's Cl
Lammas Lane
A244
Hunting Cl
Clive Rd
Wolsey Road
Park Rd
Willowmere
ESHER
Martineau Close
Littlemead
Littleworth Road
Sandown Avenue
Manor
Oaken Lane
Moore Place Golf Club
Clive Rd
Dawes Ct
High St
Belvedere Close
Broom Cl
Grantley Pl
Simmons Ga
Cranford Rl
Esher Park Av
Broomfields
Acorns Wy
Rosebriars
Littleworth Av
Golf Course
Esher Cl
Claremont Lane
West End Lane
W End Gdns
Fir Tree Cl
Lynne Wk
Heatherset Cl
Surgery
Raleigh Dr
Rythe Road
Station Rd
Aston Rd
Cavendish
Simmil Rd
Nightingale
Brisson Cl
Clare Hill (No2)
Clare Hill
Milbourne Lane
Junior School
Esher Church School
Orchard Way
Loseberry Rd
Hare Lane
The Avenue
Meadow Rd
Judge Walk
Howitts Cl
Park Close
The Mount
Hawkshill Way
Hawkshill Cl
Neville Cl
Sports Club
Courtlands Avenue
Old Chestnut Av
Claremont Pk Road
Haymeads Dr
Home Farm Cl
Brendon Dr
Arbrook La
KT10
Milbourne Lodge School
Claygate Station
The Pde
Torrington Rd
Athlone
High Garth
Lakeside Dr
Copsem Dr
Copsem Wy
Milbrook
Arbrook Lane
Loseberry Farm
Albany Crs
Hare Lane
Firs Cl
Foley Ms
Claremont Av
Cedar Cl
Stony Hill
Claremont Drive
Claremont Fan Court School
Claremont Park
Gordon Road
Claremont Rd
Foley
Beaconsfield
Beaconsfield Gdns
Claygate Ldg Cl
Qu Anne Dr
Arbrook Common
Claremont Landscape Garden NT
Albany Cl
Meadway
Copsem Lane
Blackhills
Arbrook Farm
1 grid square represents 500 metres
Esher Common

Esher 171
Weston Green
Long Ditton 158
PORTSMOUTH ROAD
Lynwood Road
Woodfield Road
Bourne Cl
Wessex Cl
Lynwood
North Gdns
Dene Gardens
Greenwood Road
Sugden Road
Mayfield Close
Orchard Avenue
Bankside Drive
Rectory Lane
Infant School
Ditton Hl Rd
Church Road
Ditton Grange Drive
Ditton Gra Cl
Oaks Way
Saffron Way
Mandeville Drive
Devonshire Drive
Ditton Hill
Shrewsbury House School
Rickards Close
Shrewsbury Close
Herne Road
HOOK ROAD
Cemetery
Woodstock Lane North
Church Meadow
Summerfield Lane
Wentworth Close
Love Lane
Brook Road
Gladstone Road
Haycroft Road
Claygate Lane
Hinchley Wood School
Cumberland Drive
Chesterfield Drive
Severn Drive
Hill Rise
Cotswold Close
Manor Road
Hinchley Wood
Hinchley Way
KINGSTON BY-PASS
A309
HOOK UNDERPASS (KINGSTON BY-PASS)
Manor Drive
Hinchley Wood Stn
Station Ap
Avondale Av
Southwood Gdns
Claygate La
Hinchley Dr
Hillcrest Gdns
Hinchley Close
South
Kelvin Gv
Surgery
Coniston Way
Priory
A243
St Pauls CE Prim Sch
Grange
The Waffrons
Surbiton Golf Club
Woodstock Lane South
Oaklands Close
Somerset Avenue
Vallis Way
Selwood Road
Clayton Road
Cecil Cl
Rosemary Gdns
Elm Rd
Hook
Golf Course
Telegraph Lane
Surrey County
Kingston upon Thames
A3
Beverley Close
Devon Wy
Newlands Wy
Cricketers Cl
Hereford Way
HOOK ROAD
Meadow Way
Moorfield
Rhodrons Avenue
Lovelace Primary School
Ripon Gdns
Tiverton Way
Holsworthy Wy
Woodgate Av
Hartfield Rd
Stormont Way
Mansfield Road
Court Crs
Field Cl
172
Chessington North
Bridge
Applegarth
Crediton Wy
Old Claygate Lane
Langbourne Wy
Woodbourne Drive
The Roundway
Oaken Dr
Surgery
Cedar Walk
Red Lane
Trystings Close
Merrilyn Cl
Hermitage Cl
Rosehill
Lower Wd Rd
Bridle Rd
Melbury Cl
Coppard Gdns
Benham Cl
Arnold Dr
Cheshire Gdns
Sussex Gardens
Hillier Pl
Merritt Gdns
Works
St Catherines Cl
Ellingham Rd
Bolton Close
Bolton Road
Parbury Rise
Carlton Close
Chessington
Claygate
St Leonard's Rd
High St
Elm Gdns
Blakeden Drive
Church Rd
Dalmore Avenue
Common Road
Glenavon Close
Glenavon Cl
Klinside
Oakhill
Close
Forge Dr
Stevens' Lane
Berkeley Gardens
Mount View Rd
Hill View Road
Cornwall Road
The Cswy
Fee Farm Rd
Ruxley Rdg
Ruxley Crs
Common Lane
Ashlyns Way
LEATHERHEAD ROAD
Chessington Hall Gdns
School
Prim Sch
Lofthouse Place
Woodgall Close
Burton Close
Chessington South Stn
York Way
Bransby
Crayke Hl
Garrison
Fisher
Rythe Close
Orchid Cl
Grapsome Cl
Nigel
Charles Babbage Cl
Winey Cl
Chessington Community College & Sports Cen
Huntin
Chessington Golf Club
Barwell
KT9
Road
Wdl Cl
Coverts Road
Foxwarren
Chessington Cricket Club
Barwell Business Park
Almshouse Lane
Green
Golf Course
Holroyd Road
Glebelands
Chalky Lane
Chessington World of Adventures
Park Farm

172
159
171
KT6
KT9
KT19
A
B
C
D
E
1
2
3
4
5
6
7
518
19
20
65
64
163
HOOK ROAD
A243
HOOK-UNDERPASS (KINGSTON-BY-PASS)
KINGSTON BY-PASS
Hook Rise South
Hook Rise North
EWELL RD
WARREN DRIVE NORTH
A240
BROADWAY
KINGSTON ROAD
Tolworth Tower
Tolworth Station
Charrington Bowl
Primary School
Warren Drive South
Barnsbury La
Hazel Bank
Meadway
Alpine Avenue
Knollmead Primary School
Tolworth CP Sch
School Lane
Dennan Road
Douglas Road
Ellerton Road
Cotterill Road
Malvern Rd
Mayfair Cl
Ravenscar Road
Tolworth Park Road
Tankerton Road
Bond Road
Thornhill Road
Thornhill Av
Hamilton Avenue
Kingsmead Av
Princes Avenue
Oakleigh Avenue
Lion Road
Draycot Road
Largewood Avenue
Ravenswood Avenue
Ladywood Road
Cranborne Avenue
Selbourne Av
Red Lion Business Park
Tolworth Girls School & Centre for Continuing Education
Tolworth Recreation Cen
Kingston Business Cen
Fullers Av
Fullers Wy N
Fullers Wy S
Kent Way
Verona Drive
Vale Road
Tolworth Road
Works
Shrewsbury Close
Shrewsbury House School
Rickards Close
Brook Road
Gladstone Road
Haycroft Road
Southborough Sch
Elmcroft Dr
Willcocks Cl
Coniston Way
Priory Road
Hunters Road
Grange Rd
Lynton Close
Cumberland Dr
Ranyard Cl
Ashcroft Rd
Oakcroft Road
Oakcroft Vls
Cedarcroft Road
Fircroft Road
Hook Rise South Industrial Park
Corinthian Casuals FC
Jubilee Way
Old Kingston Road
Davis Rd
Davis Road
Cox Lane
Cox La
Works
Lion Pk Av
Foxglove Lane
Mount Rd
Mount Road
Mt Road
Roebuck Road
Drake Road
Wolsey Way
Angus Cl
Hurst Cl
Lockwood Wy
Chantry Road
Buckland Infant School
Buckland Road
Moor Lane Junior School
Moor Lane
Chessington Hl Pk
St Pauls CE Prim Sch
Orchard Road
Gosbury Hill Health Cen
Gosbury Hill
Durbin Road
The Causeway
Rosemary Gdns
Orchard Gdns
Elm Rd
Cecil Cl
Hook
Romney Cl
Tudor Cl
Meadow Way
Moorfield Road
Sherborne Rd
Rhodrons Avenue
Sanger Avenue
Station Road
Holmwood Road
Albury Rd
Frimley Rd
Hartfield Rd
Chessington North Stn
Sopwith Av
North Pde
Bridge Road
Compton Crs
Marston Av
Wilson Rd
Church Rise
Church Lane
Bolton Close
Bolton Road
Parbury Rise
Court Crs
Ellingham Rd
Salmons Road
Carlton Close
Chessington
Chessington Hall Gdns
School
Prim Sch
Chessington South Stn
Chessington Community College & Sports
Chessington Golf Club
Golf Course
Barwell Business Park
St Marys CE Primary School
Bransby Road
York Way
Crayke Hl
Garrison La
Reynolds Av
Vivien Cl
Selby Cl
Hunting Ga Dr
Green Lane
Stokesby Rd
St Mary's Cl
Leas Cl
Gilders Road
Green View
Billockby Close
Hemsby Road
Filby Road
Thrigby Road
May Cl
Gilders Road
Thames Down Link
Woodland Walk
Chessington Road
Ashby Av
Maltby Road
Rollesby Road
Headley Close
Hartford Rd
Collier Cl
Carnforth Cl
Derek Av
Derek Cl
Stanton Close
Gatley Avenue
Amis Avenue
Iris Rd
Pemberley Cha
Ruxley Cl
Jasmine Road
Lavender Rd
B284 RUXLEY LANE
B284
CHESSINGTON ROAD
Larch Crs
Nightingale Dr
Poplar Crs
Godwin Cl
Surgery
Cox La
Magnolia Wy
Larkspur Way
Hogsmill Way
Holman Road
Millais Way
Rowden Road
Watersedge
Longford Court
Wey Court
Mole Ct
Ash Court
Colne Court
Wandle Court
Riverview
Curtis Rd
Fendall Road
Brumfield Road
Scott Cl
Ruxley Lane
Epsom & Ewell High School
Scotts Farm Road
Poplar Farm Close
Chessington Close
Vernon Close
Gadesden Road
Danetree School
Danetree Cl
Chessington Rd
Horton Park Golf & Country Club
HOOK ROAD
Cemetery
St Ebba's Hospital
Horton Lane
Oakwood Av
Sandy Md
Hendon Gv
Monro Pl
Harewood Wy
Nelson Wk
Lady Forsdyke Wy
Horton Country Park
Kingston upon Thames
Surrey County
Mckenzie Way
Grove Cl
Horton Park Farm
Long
Park Farm
Lane
Gainsborough Road
1 grid square represents 500 metres

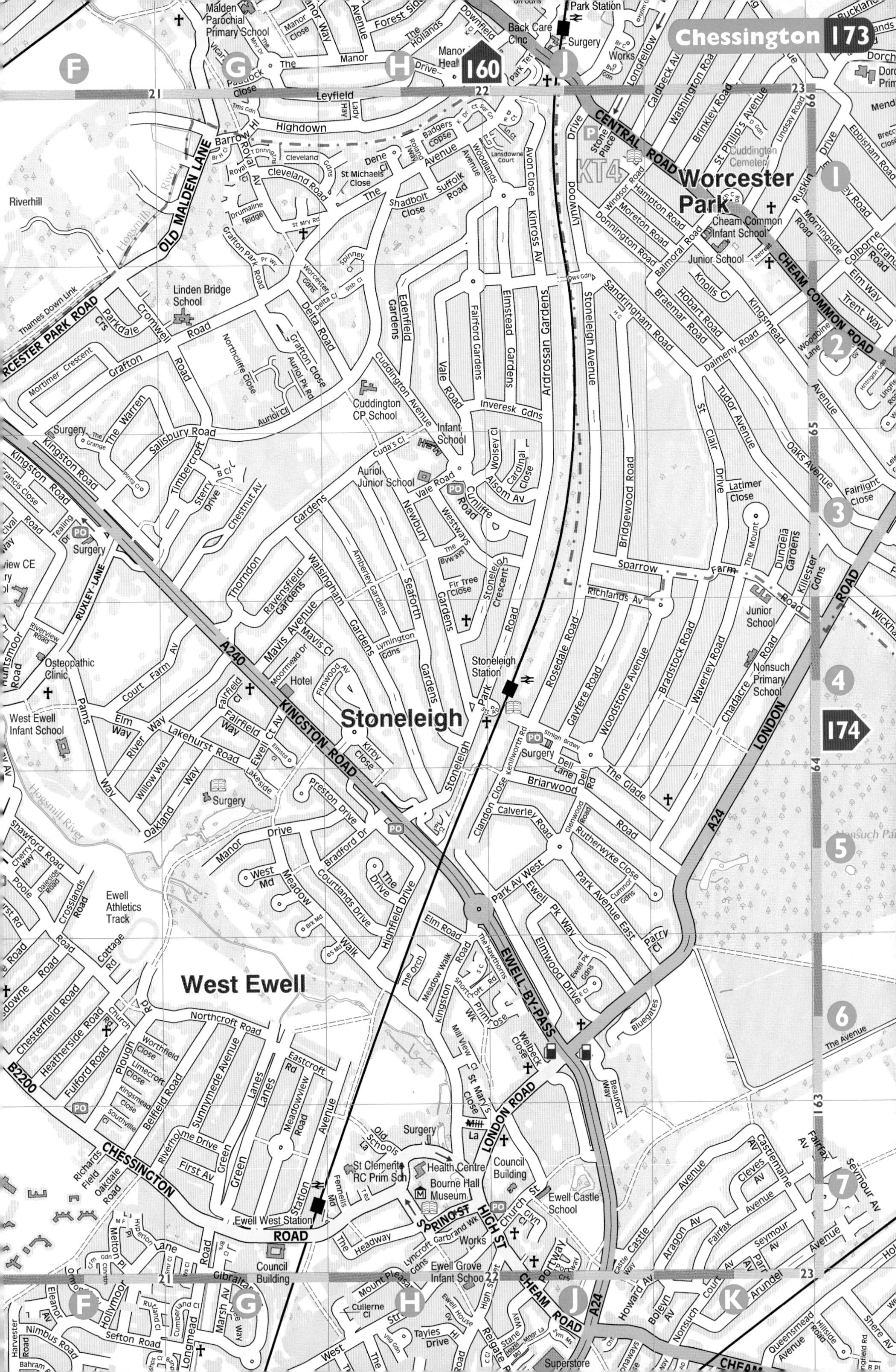

Chessington 173
160
174
Worcester Park
Stoneleigh
West Ewell
KT4
Central Road
Cheam Common Road
Old Malden Lane
Worcester Park Road
Kingston Road
A240
Ewell-By-Pass
London Road
A24
Chessington Road
B2200
Cheam Road
High St
Spring St
Manor Drive
Highdown
Leyfield
Cleveland Road
The Avenue
Woodlands Avenue
Cuddington Avenue
Delta Road
Grafton Road
Cromwell Road
Salisbury Road
Timbercroft
Sterry Drive
Chestnut Av
Thorndon Gardens
Ravensfield Gardens
Walsingham Gardens
Mavis Avenue
Seaforth Gardens
Newbury Gardens
Vale Road
Edenfield Gardens
Fairford Gardens
Elmstead Gardens
Ardrossan Gardens
Kinross Av
Avon Close
Stoneleigh Avenue
Stoneleigh Crescent
Stoneleigh Park Road
Sandringham Road
Bridgewood Road
St Clair Drive
Tudor Avenue
Oaks Avenue
Sparrow Farm Road
Richlands Av
Rosedale Road
Gayfere Road
Woodstone Avenue
Bradstock Road
Waverley Road
Chadacre Road
The Glade
Briarwood Road
Calverley Road
Rutherwyke Close
Park Avenue East
Park Av West
Elmwood Drive
Preston Drive
Highfield Drive
Courtlands Drive
Bradford Dr
Meadow Walk
West Md
Northcroft Road
Sunnymede Avenue
Meadowview Road
Eastcroft Rd
Riverholme Drive
First Av
Beaufort Way
Castlemaine Av
Fairfax Av
Seymour Av
Cleves Av
Aragon Av
Boleyn Av
Howard Av
Nonsuch Court Av
Arundel
Queensmead Avenue
Sefton Road
Hollymoor
Longmead
Marsh Av
Gibraltar
Pams Way
Ruxley Lane
Court Farm Av
Lakehurst Road
Willow Way
Oakland Way
River Way
Elm Way
Fairfield Way
Ewell Ct Av
Cottage Rd
Crosslands Road
Chesterfield Road
Heatherside Road
Fulford Road
Beresford Road
Plough Lane
Church Rd
Malden Parochial Primary School
Linden Bridge School
Cuddington CP School
Infant School
Auriol Junior School
Cheam Common Infant School
Junior School
Nonsuch Primary School
Cuddington Cemetery
Stoneleigh Station
Park Station
Ewell West Station
Ewell Athletics Track
Hogsmill River
Riverhill
Thames Down Link
West Ewell Infant School
Osteopathic Clinic
Hotel
Surgery
Back Care Clinc
Health Centre
Bourne Hall Museum
Council Building
St Clements RC Prim Sch
Ewell Castle School
Ewell Grove Infant School
Works
Superstore
Nonsuch Park
The Avenue
F
G
H
J
I
K
1
2
3
4
5
6
7
21
22
23
63
64
65
66

174
161
173
A
B
C
D
E
1
2
3
4
5
6
7
523
24
25
66
65
64
163
North Cheam
Cheam
SUTTON
SM3
SM2
LONDON ROAD
CHEAM COMMON ROAD
MALDEN ROAD
A2043
ST DUNSTAN'S HILL
A217
OLDFIELDS ROAD
CHEAM ROAD
HIGH STREET
THE BROADWAY
STATION WAY
EWELL ROAD
SANDY LANE
BELMONT RISE
BURDON
B283
A232
Ridge Road
Charminster Road
Trafalgar Ave
Merrilands Road
Manchester Road
Manchester Primary Sch
Mendip Close
Cotswold Way
Brecon Close
Clarkes Avenue
Langley Av
Burnham Drive
St Raphaels Hospice
Primary School
Tonfield Primary School
Sutton Cemetery
Four Seasons Crs
Minden Road
Kimpton Industrial Estate
Sandiford Rd
Wealdstone Road
Kimpton Road
Willow Walk
Whittaker Road
Cuddington Cemetery
St Philip's Avenue
Lindsay Rd
Ruskin Drive
Ebbisham Road
Beverley Road
Morningside Road
Colborne Way
Grandison Road
Bedford Road
Hill Crs
Glyn Road
Lloyd Road
Courtenay Road
Lavender Avenue
Elm Way
Trent Way
Farm Way
Cheam Common Infant School
Woodbine Lane
Kingsmead Av
Oaks Avenue
Tudor Avenue
Latimer Close
The Mount
Dundela Gardens
Killester Gdns
Junior School
Nonsuch Primary School
Chadacre Road
Fairlight Close
Leicester Close
Lingfield Road
Wellington Avenue
Hemingford Rd
The Spinney
Wordsworth Drive
Kenley Walk
Palmer Avenue
Wickham Avenue
Newbolt Avenue
Ashmere Close
Nonsuch Park
Fir Walk
The Avenue
Sutton
Surrey County
Superstore
Sennouse Road
Hilbert Road
Wrayfield Road
Hayes Crs
D'Arcy Rd
Church Hill Road
Surgery
Malden Road Baths
Cheam Leisure Cen
Priory Crs
Priory Av
Priory Road
Staines Avenue
Egham Crs
Marlow Drive
Camberley Close
Sunbury Road
The Meads
Henley Avenue
Esher Av
Frogmore Close
Caversham Av
Warner Avenue
Hamilton Avenue
Watson Avenue
Gander Green Lane
Chertsey Drive
Molesey Drive
Brocks Drive
St Margaret's Avenue
Kingston Avenue
Kew Crs
Walton Avenue
Cheam Park Farm Junior School
Windsor Avenue
Works
Buxton Crescent
Carlton Crescent
Abbots Road
Chartwell Place
Hanover Rd
Chelsea Gdns
Matlock Crescent
Matlock Gdns
Chatsworth Road
Cheam High Sch
Cheam Fields Prim Sch
Stoughton Av
Netley Close
Tilehurst Road
Kingsdown Road
Fromondes Road
Lumley Road
Tudor Close
Cookes Lane
Mickleham Gdns
Cheam Pk Way
Parkside Surg
Park La
Love La
Park Road
Stafford Close
Alberta Av
Alma Crescent
Sunningdale Road
Westfield Road
Silverdale Cl
St Albans Road
Elmbrook Rd
Jeffs Road
Hilldale Road
Frederick Road
Denbigh Close
Shearwater Rd
Cheam Works
Grebe Ct
Petersham Cl
Antrobus Close
Carlisle Road
Fairholme Road
Revell Road
Quarry Road
Quarry Rise
Park Rd
Gander Gn Lane
Cricket Ground
Recreation Ground
Sutton United FC
West Sutton Station
Sutton West Centre
Norman Road
St James Av
St James' Road
Sydney Road
Beulah Rd
Beauchamp Road
Orchard Road
Wings Cl
Robin Hood Lane
School
Western Road
Tate Road
Cheam Road
Hotel
Derby Road
Rosebery Road
Cecil Road
Bridgefield Road
Landseer Road
Beggar's Roost Lane
Grove Av
Tormead Close
Grove Road
Surgery
Summerville Gdns
Salisbury Avenue
Tabor Gdns
Scotsdale Cl
Cheam Station
St Dunstans CE Primary School
Kings Rd
Forge La
Jubilee Rd
Queens Acre
Anne Boleyn's Walk
Nonsuch High School for Girls
Upr Mulgrave Rd
Mulgrave Road
Hillside Rd
Arundel Road
Beresford Road
Cornwall Road
Burdon Pk
Manor Road
Old Barn Close
Peaches Close
Cheam Sports Club
Holmwood Close
Glebe Road
Villiers Gv
Wonersh Wy
Merrow Road
Ranmore Road
Bramley Road
Abinger Avenue
Ewhurst Close
Buckland Road
Albury Avenue
Holmwood Road
West Drive
The Glade
Devon Road
Meadowside Road
The Wray Rd
Harefield Avenue
Rugby Lane
Hays Walk
Cheyham Gardens
Northey Avenue
South Drive
Shirley Av
Dorset Road
The Avenue Primary School
Balmoral Way
Heather Gdns
Village Rw
Overton Road
Worcester Road
Frampton Cl
Chalcot Cl
Grange Road
Wyndham Cl
Sackville Rd
York Road
Holland Avenue
Courtenay Av
Henderson Hosp
Moore Wy
Sutton Bowling Club
Fir Rd
Morley Road
Acacia Drive
Taunton Cl
Barrington Rd
Sherborne Road
Alcorn Cl
Glenthorne High Sch
Clensham Lane
Leafield Rd
Burford Road
Dibdin Road
Oldfields Trading Est
Stayton Road
Northspur Road
Anton Crs
Westbourne Primary School
Alexandra Av
Milton Road
Chaucer Gdns
Collingwood Road
Bus Depot
Busney Road
Fairlawn Road
Lymescote Gdns
Castleton Av
Cleves Av
Seymour Av
Fairfax Av
Pair Av
Arundel Av
Avenue Road
1 grid square represents 500 metres

Rosehill
Benhilton
The Wrythe
Carshalton
Carshalton Beeches
Belmont
Carshalton on the Hill
Sutton
St Helier Hospital
Greenshaw High School
Carshalton High School for Boys
Muschamp Primary School
Carshalton College of FE
Carshalton High School for Girls
Carshalton AFC
War Mem Sports Ground
Benhill Recreation Ground
Palmerston Business Cen
Grammar School
St Nicholas Centre
Times Square Shopping Centre
Sutton Station
Carshalton Station
Carshalton Beeches Station
St Marys Infant School
St Marys RC Infant School
St Philomenas RC High School
Carshalton War Memorial Hospital
Westcroft Leisure Centre
Council Building
Lewis Clinic
Stanley Park Primary School
Devonshire Primary School
Stowford College
Overton Grange School
Barrow Hedges Primary School
Queen Marys Hospital for Children
Sutton General Hospital
Seaton House School
Royal Marsden
Sutton High School for Girls
Police Stn
Health Cen
Superbowl
Sports Club
Gas Works
Works
Cemetery
The Warren
CARSHALTON ROAD
A232
B2230
B278
B277
HIGH STREET
ANGEL HILL
ROSE HILL
REIGATE
WRYTHE LANE
NIGHTINGALE ROAD
HACKBRIDGE
NORTH STREET
WEST STREET
POUND ST
PARK HILL
THE BEECHES AV
BRIGHTON ROAD
HIGH ST
THROWLEY WAY
ST NICHOLAS WAY
GROVE RD
WOODMANSTERNE
SM1
SM5
162
176
F
G
H
J
K
I
26
27
28
2
3
4
5
6
7
63
64
65

176
163
175
A
B
C
D
E
1
2
3
4
5
6
7
528
29
30
Hackbridge
Hackbridge Station
Primary School
Surgery
Heath Works
Mile Road
HACKBRIDGE ROAD
NIGHTINGALE ROAD
Felnex Trading Estate
Edes Business Park
Restmor Way
Wandle Road
Elmwood Close
Birchwood Avenue
LONDON ROAD
A237
Beddington Park
Carew Manor School
Church Paddock Ct
Church Road
Church Lane
Works
Beddington Park Primary School
Crispin Crs
Mallinson Road
Harrington Close
BEDDINGTON LANE
B272
Beddington Lane Ind Est
Bath House Rd
Marlowe Way
Beddingt
Richmond
HILLIER'S LA B272
Bridle Pth
Tritton Av
The Link Day Primary School
Beddington Medical Cen
CROYDON ROAD
Sherwood Park School
Beddington Infants School
Dell Close
Bloxworth Close
Paston Close
Bampfylde Close
Wallington Grammar School
The Holt Junior School
Infant School
Stannet Way
Northway
Southway
Rectory Lane
Demesne Road
Ferrers Av
Raleigh Av
Rookwood Av
Qu Elizabeth's Wk
Royston Av
Iberian Av
Sandhills
Queenswood Avenue
Collyer Av
Oakley Av
Bristow Road
Claydon Dr
Carshalton College of FE
Council Building
Denmark Road
Westcroft Leisure Centre
The Grove
Westcroft Road
Scawen Close
Sycamore Close
West St Lane
Council Building
Lewis Clinic
HIGH STREET
A232
ACRE LANE
MANOR RD
Derek Av
Quinton Close
Chestnut Mnr
The Mnr Way
Harcourt Road
Harcourt Av
Danbury Ms
Lavender Road
Lavender Close
Park Lane
Rotherfield Road
Alcester Road
Arran Close
Bute Road
Montagu Gardens
Crichton Avenue
Bandon Hill Cemetery
Bandonhill
Plough La Cl
PLOUGH LANE
Maldon Road
Morton Gardens
Park Road
Surgery
Parkgate Road
Talbot Road
Cemetery
RUSKIN ROAD B271
Woodstock Road
Carshalton Park
Taylor Road
St George's Road
Clifton Road
Osmond Gdns
Bute Gdns
The Bridle Way
Springfield Rd
Collingwood Prep Sch
Belmont Road
Bute Gdns W
Tharp Road
Beddington Gv
Sandy La N
Upper Road
Works
Primary School
Central Av
Gomshall Av
Reigate Way
Garden Clo
Melbourne Road
Mellows Road
Bandon Ri
Surgery
SM6
Wallington
PARK LANE B271
Ashcombe Road
Grosvenor Road
Wallington Station
Ross Pde
Ross Road
Clarendon Road
St Michael's Rd
Clyde Road
Carew Road
Police Station
STAFFORD ROAD
South Beddington
Bandon Hill Prim Sch
Wilsons
Mollison Drive
Carshalton War Memorial Hospital
Salisbury Road
Cedar Cl
Park Av
Avenue
Grosvenor
Beddington Gdns
Magistrates Court
Shotfield
Superstore
Chandos Bus Cen
Woodcote Ms
Elgin Rd
Charlotte Road
Francis Road
Milton Road
Works
Lavender Vale
Link Lane
SANDY LANE S
The Mead
Redford
BOUNDARY ROAD
Northwood Rd
Anglesey Gdns
Anglesey Ct Road
Beddington Gdns
Stanley Park High School
STANLEY PARK RD B271
Holmwood Gardens
Shotfield Health Clinic
WOODCOTE ROAD
Blenheim Gardens
Stanley Gdns
Hinton Road
Cowper Gdns
Wordsworth Road
Waterer Rise
Foresters Primary School
Hermes Way
Carter Cl
Shaw Way
Cobham Cl
Olley Cl
McIntosh Cl
Douglas Cl
St Elphege's RC Primary School
Roe Way
Stanley Park
Woodfield Av
Stanley Park Primary School
Dalmeny Road
Hawthorne Av
Hawthorn Road
Turpin Way
Willow Rd
Cranley Gdns
Grosvenor Gardens
Onslow Gardens
Cosdach Av
Foresters Close
B272
FORESTERS DRIVE
Avenue
Defiant Wy
Avro Wy
De Havilland Rd
Park
Fir Tree
Oaks Way
Stanhope Rd
Windborough Road
Heathdene Road
Park Hill
South Oaklands Way
Tudor Cl
Brown Close
Mollison Drive Health Cen
Mollison
Kingsford Av
Brambledown Road
Hillside Gdns
The Newlands
Lindbergh Rd
Brabazon Av
Moore Cl
Bristol Cl
Amy Johnson Primary School
Carshalton on the Hill
Pine Ridge
Mount Park Road
Boundary Road
Woodcote Avenue
Glen Rd
Hall Road
Elystan Cl
Avenue Rd
Marchmont Road
Sandy Lane
Ingleby Way
Carleton Avenue
Lawford Cl
Mariette Wy
Sunkist Wy
Apeldoorn Drive
Clarice Wy
Stanley Square
Cranfield Rd East
Mount Close
Mount Way
Briar Lane
Briar Bank
Bramble Banks
Dower Av
Shirley Rd
Oakwood
High School
Mallard Way
Buckingham Way
Allington Grove
Hamilton Way
Stratton Avenue
Ambrey Way
Sprucedale Gdns
Great Woodcote Park
Kenny Dr
Ftn Dr
Lawson Wk
Woodcote Green
The Drive
Ridge Park
Lordsbury Field
Purley Sports Club
Ridge
John Fisher Sch
Church Hill Road
Peaks Hill
St Marys Hospital School
1 grid square represents 500 metres
Track

164
178
F
G
H
J
I
K
2
3
4
5
6
7
31
32
33
63
64
65
66
Wandle Park
Waddon
CROYDON
South Croydon
Roundshaw
Superstore
Works
Warner Village Cinema
Latham's Way
Peterwood Wy
Progress Way
Progress Business Park
Commerce Way
PURLEY WAY
A23
Enterprise Cl
Factory Lane
Drury Crs
Trafalgar Wy
Turners Wy
Trojan Wy
Jennett Rd
Mill Lane Trading Est
Mill La
Limes Av
Lodge Av
Godson Road
Alton Rd
Rigby Cl
Courtney Rd
Benson Rd
Waddon Cl
Vicarage Rd
Siddons Rd
Kemble Rd
Waddon New Rd
Waddon Park Av
Waddon Ct Rd
Waddon Station
Sayer Clinic
Court Dr
The Ridgeway
Aldwick Road
Lavington Rd
ROAD
The Link Secondary School
A232
Willoughby Av
Cherry Hl Gdns
Lynwood Gdns
EPSOM RD
STAFFORD RD
Stafford Rd
Epsom Road
Duppas Rd
Glen Gdns
DUPPAS HILL ROAD A232
THE CROYDON FLYOVER A232
Euston Road
Miller Road
Martin Crs
Sumner Rd
South Rd
Bute Rd
Grafton Rd
Leighton St
Parson's Mead
Nelson Close
Rodney Close
Works
A236
ROMAN WAY
A236 OLD TOWN
Derby Rd
Pitlake
Pilton Estate
Clarendon Rd
Theobald Rd
Westfield
Cornwall Rd
Cuthbert Rd
Ruskin Road
Drayton Rd
Tamworth Road
Keeley Rd
North End
Whitgift Shopping Centre
West Croydon Stn
Station Rd
Poplar Wk
WELLESLEY ROAD
A212
Drummond Shopping Centre
Whitgift Almshouses
George St
Church St
Old Palace School
Old Palace Rd
Church Road
Howley Rd
Cranmer Rd
Fawcett Rd
Salem Pl
Rectory Gv
Sylverdale Rd
Wks
Waddon Rd
Eland Rd
Borough Hill
Harrison's Ri
Warrington Rd
Parish Church CE Prim Sch
Abbey Rd
Duppas Hill Ter
Fire Station
Katharine St
Clocktower
Mint Wk
Town Hall
Taberner House
Fell Rd
Park St
PARK LA
Croydon Coll
Fairfield Halls
Coll Ct
Mag Courts
The Law Courts
BARCLAY RD
FAIRFIELD RD
Surgery
Friends' Rd
Police Stn
Beech House Rd
Woodstock Rd
Chatsworth Road
Occupational Health Centre
Mulgrave Rd
Eden Rd
Wrencote
Edridge Road
Mason's Av
Queen St
West St
LWR COOMBE ST
COOMBE ROAD
A212
SOUTHBRIDGE ROAD
Tanfield Rd
Parker Rd
South End
Spices Yd
Aberdeen Rd
Ledbury Rd
ST PETER'S ROAD
Temple Road
Galloway Pth
Dean Rd
Hurst Rd
Elmhurst School
South Croydon Station
B243
CROHAM RD
Sydenham Rd
Bedford Pk
Dingwall Rd
Lansdowne Rd
Wellesley Gv
Warehouse Thtr
East Croydon Station
A222
ADDISCOMBE GV
Cedar Road
Colson Rd
Oval Road
Park Hill Rd
Stanhope Road
Chichester Rd
Water Tower Hill
Steep Hill
PARK HILL ROAD
SOUTH PARK B243
Birdhurst Av
Birdhurst Rd
Birdhurst Rise
Hotel
Ashley La
Lane
Bramley Hill
Bramley Cl
Nottingham Rd
Howard Primary School
Barham Rd
Whitstable Pl
Waldronhyrst
Cooper Road
Coombe Rd
Hillside Rd
Price Rd
Heighton Gdns
Raglan Ct
Violet Lane
DENNING AVENUE B275
Cosedge Crs
Layton Crs
WARHAM ROAD B275
Croydon Indoor Bowling Club
Whitgift Av
Nottingham Rd
Duppas Junior School
Goodwin Road
Violet Gdns
Crowley Crs
Thorneloe Gdns
Barrow Road
Coldharbour Rd
Coldharbour Wy
Stapleton Gdns
Hillier Gdns
Waddon Clinic
Waddon Infant School
Charles Cobb Gdns
Foss Av
Bates Crs
Williams Ter
Burgos Cl
Houlder Crs
Waddon Way
Haling Park Rd
Heath Cl
Goodwin Gdns
Whitgift School
Health Centre
Drovers Rd
Upland Rd
Junction Rd
SELSDON ROAD
St Peter's Street
Sussex Road
Birchend Cl
Haling Rd
Helder St
Jarvis Rd
Newark Rd
Mansfield Rd
Crunden Road
Napier Rd
Bynes Rd
Purley Oaks Primary School
Selsdon Rd Ind Estate
Two Bridges Business Park
Chelsham Rd
Carlton Rd
Carlton Av
Normanton Road
Whitmead Close
St Peter's Primary School
Rockhampton Cl
Moreton Road
Croham Rd
Ward Cl
Elm Cl
Surgery
B275
Essenden Road
Brambledown Rd
Heathhurst Road
Beechwood
Mayfield Rd
Sanderstead Station
Chase
High Vw Av
East Av
Headley Av
Merebank La
Capel Av
Kings Way
Princes Way
Queensway
Stafford Cross Business Park
Silver Wing Industrial Estate
Lysander Rd
Imperial Way
Hannibal Way
Connaught Business Cen
Hotel
Pegasus Rd
PURLEY WAY A23
Croydon Airport Industrial Estate
Merlin Cl
Dove Cl
Vickers Cl
Dakota Cl
Morton Cl
Jean Batten Cl
Page Rd
Cubitt St
Stone St
Park Road
St Ann's Way
St Giles School
Nicola Cl
St Augustine's Avenue
Vauxhall Gdns
Avondale Rd
South Croydon Medical Cen
Tirlemont Rd
Regina Coeli RC Primary School
Columbine Av
Kendra Hall Rd
Haling Manor High School
Alder Wy
Joshua Cl
Knighton Cl
Hamond Cl
Chancellor Gdns
Blackford Cl
Pampisford Road
Cumnor House Sch
Lynscott Way
Barnards Pl
Mount Park Avenue
Coningsby Rd
Culmington Rd
Blenheim Crs
Blenheim Park Road
Haling Gv
Churchill Road
Darmaine Cl
BRIGHTON ROAD
A235
Purley Rd
Wyche Gv
Surgery
Works
SANDERSTEAD ROAD
Broomhall Rd
Glossop Rd
Parrs Cl
Florence Rd
Kendall Av
Junior School
Edgar Rd
Brantwood Rd
Kingsdown Av
Allenby Av
Grange Road
Braemar Av
Purley Oaks Stn
Biddulph Rd
Croydon
Sutton
B272
Sovereign
Wellington Dr
Hilldeane Rd
Overhill Rd
Road
Highfield Road
Margaret Roper RC Primary School
Ensign Cl
Atalanta Cl
Edgehill
Wyvern Rd
The Close
Montpelier Road
Norman Avenue
Kendall Avenue South
Derrick Av
Purley
Montana
Mary's Rd
East Hill

178
165
177
A
B
C
D
E
1
2
3
4
5
6
7
533
34
35
Addiscombe
CROYDON
Shirley
Upper Shirley
LOWER ADDISCOMBE
CHERRY ORCHARD ROAD
Leslie Park Rd
Lebanon Road
Addiscombe Court Rd
Tunstall Rd
Canning Road
Clyde Road
Elgin Road
Havelock Rd
Outram Road
Ashburton Road
Northampton Road
Carlyle Road
Harriet Gdns
Annandale Rd
Sefton Road
Compton Road
Ashburton Avenue
Selwood Road
Birch Tree Wy
Fryston Av
Ashurst Walk
Cragien Av
Peabody Close
Shirley Clinic
Primrose Lane
SHIRLEY ROAD
Shirley Park Golf Club
Trinity School
Barnfield Av
Valley Walk
Eldon
Works
Primary School
Surgery
Cedar Road
Colson Rd
East Croydon Station
Addiscombe Road
ADDISCOMBE ROAD
A232
A222
St Clair's Rd
Park Hill Rd
Garrick Cres
Granville Cl
Leafy Wy
Park Hill Ri
Tpk Link
CHEPSTOW ROAD
Woodbury Cl
Radcliffe Road
Paul Gardens
Savile Gdns
Harding Cl
Harland Av
Sandilands
Fitzjames Avenue
Upfield
Grimwade Avenue
Mapledale Avenue
Golf Course
The Law Courts
Mag Ct
Coll Ct
FAIRFIELD RD
Park Hill Junior Sch
The Av
Cotelands
Chepstow Rd
Chichester Rd
Park Hill Rd
Dartcourt Gdns
Acres Gdns
Lyndhurst Cl
Engadine Cl
Archbishop Tenisons CE School
Addiscombe Cricket Club
Ranmore Av
Deepdene Av
Selborne Road
Waldegrave Rd
Chatsworth Road
Occupational Health Centre
Stanhope Road
Chichester Rd
Merlin Cl
Minster Dr
Langton Wy
Reynolds Wy
Rushmead Cl
PARK HILL ROAD
A2039
Water Tower Hill
Steep Hill
Brownlow Road
COOMBE ROAD
A212
Vanguard Way
Lloyd Pk Av
Larcombe Close
Coombe Av
Rutland Gdns
Hotel
Birdhurst Av
Birdhurst Gdns
SOUTH PARK HILL ROAD
B243
Birdhurst Road
Campion Cl
Witherby Cl
South Croydon Sports Club
Campden Road
Croham Park Avenue
Castlemaine Avenue
Binfield Rd
Ballater Road
Melville Avenue
Blossom Cl
Pilgrim's Way
COOMBE ROAD
Oaks Road
Hotel
London Loop
Elmhurst School
South Croydon Station
Birdhurst Rise
Beech Copse
Spencer Road
Croham Road
Wells Cl
Hollycroft Cl
Ward Cl
Regents Cl
Croham Hurst School
Bench Fld
Conduit Lane
Vanguard Way
COOMBE LANE
Sunken Rd
St Peter's Street
Birchend Cl
Sussex Road
Whitmead Close
Normanton Road
Harewood Road
St Peters Primary School
Manor Way
Winchelsey Ri
Manor Gdns
Croham Hurst Golf Club
Ballards Farm Road
Croham Valley Road
Royal Russell School
Hollingsworth Road
Ballards Way
Riesco Dr
Heathfield
Rayleigh Ri
Hurst Wy
Surgery
Bankside
Croham Manor Road
Golf Course
Ruffetts Close
Crest Rd
The Ruffetts
Chapel Vw
Chestnut Gv
The Gallop
Croham Va Rd
Two Bridges Business Park
Selsdon Rd Ind Estate
Carlton Av
Carlton Rd
Hurst Vw Rd
High Beech
Croham Mt
B275
Lytchgate Cl
Croham Hurst
Essenden Road
Sandhurst Way
UPPER SELSDON ROAD
Farley Road
Brambledown Rd
Heathhurst Road
Sandhurst Close
Trinity Cl
Elmfield Way
Ewhurst Avenue
Wisborough Rd
Littleheath Road
Vanguard Way
Brent Rd
Foxearth Sp
Selsdon Primary School
Glossop Rd
Sanderstead Station
Beechwood
West Hill
Barnfield Road
Kirkly Cl
Ellenbridge Way
Arkwright Road
Moir Cl
SELSDON ROAD
Farley Rd
Queenhill Rd
Rylandes Rd
Foxearth Road
The Rise
A2022
Cowley Cl
Ridgeway Primary School
St Mary's Rd
Montana Cl
Purley
Southcote Road
Day's Acre
Morley Road
Courtlands Cl
Langley Oaks Av
Crozier Dr
Surgery
Byron Road
Dulverton Road
Sundale
1 grid square represents 500 metres

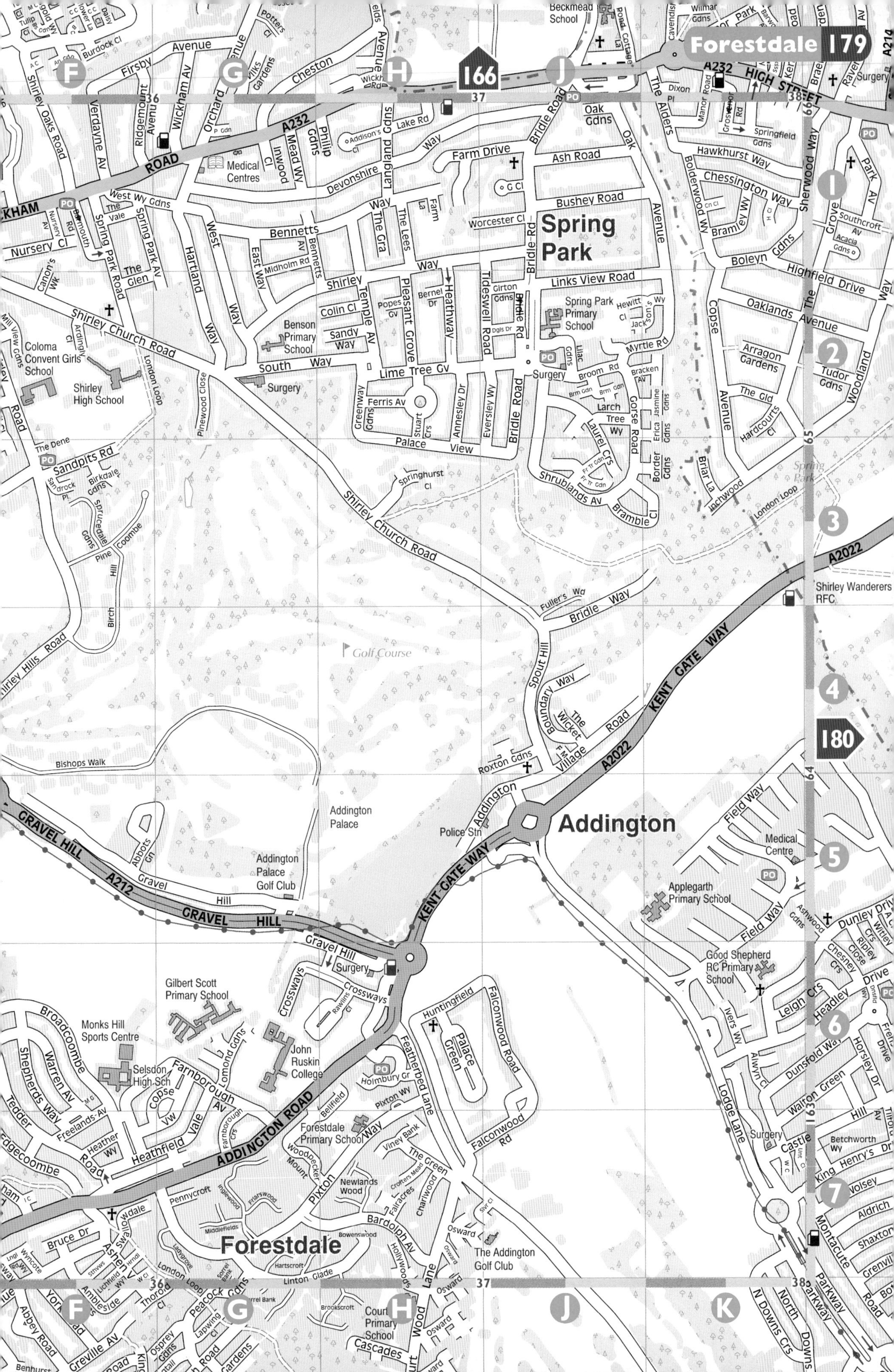
166
180
F
G
H
J
I
K
36
37
38
2
3
4
5
6
7
65
64
63
Spring Park
Addington
Forestdale
A232
ROAD
HIGH STREET
A214
A2022
KENT GATE WAY
A212
GRAVEL HILL
ADDINGTON ROAD
Beckmead School
Firsby
Avenue
Burdock Cl
Cheston
Avenue
Verdayne Av
Shirley Oaks Road
Ridgemount Avenue
Wickham Av
Orchard
Wilks Gardens
Potters
Medical Centres
Inwood Cl
Mead Wy
Philip Gdns
Langland Gdns
Lake Rd
Addison's Cl
Devonshire
Way
Farm Drive
Bridle Road
Oak Gdns
Ash Road
Oak
Avenue
The Alders
Dixon
Manor Road
Springfield Gdns
Hawkhurst Way
Chessington Way
Bolderwood Way
Bramley Wy
Sherwood Way
Park Av
Southcroft Av
Acacia Gdns
Grove
Bushey Road
Worcester Cl
G Cl
Farm La
The Lees
The Gra
Bennetts
Bennetts Av
Midholm Rd
East Way
Hartland
Way
West
Way
West Wy Gdns
The Vale
Spring Park Av
Spring Park Road
Barmouth Rd
Nursery Av
Nursery Cl
Canon's Wk
The Glen
Shirley
Colin Cl
Temple Av
Popes Gv
Pleasant Grove
Bernel Dr
Heathway
Tideswell Road
Girton Gdns
Bridle Rd
Dgls Dr
Links View Road
Spring Park Primary School
Hewitt Cl
Jackson's Wy
Myrtle Rd
Bracken Av
Boleyn Gdns
Highfield Drive
Oaklands Avenue
The
Copse
Avenue
Arragon Gardens
Tudor Gdns
Woodland
Way
The Gld
Hardcourts Cl
Benson Primary School
Sandy Way
South Way
Lime Tree Gv
Surgery
Lilac Gdns
Broom Rd
Brm Gdn
Larch Tree Wy
Gorse Road
Erica Gdns
Jasmine Gdns
Border Gdns
Laurel Crs
Shrublands Av
Bramble Cl
Briar La
Inchwood
London Loop
Spring Park
Ferris Av
Greenway Gdns
Stuart Crs
Annesley Dr
Eversley Wy
Bridle Road
Palace View
Springhurst Cl
Shirley Church Road
Coloma Convent Girls School
Shirley High School
Ardingly Cl
London Loop
Pinewood Close
Mill View Gdns
Road
The Dene
Sandpits Rd
Sandrock Pl
Birkdale Gdns
Sprucedale Gdns
Pine Coombe
Birch Hill
Shirley Hills Road
Golf Course
Fuller's Wd
Bridle Way
Spout Hill
Boundary Way
The Wicket
Village Road
Roxton Gdns
Shirley Wanderers RFC
Bishops Walk
Addington Palace
Addington Palace Golf Club
Abbots Gn
Gravel Hill
Addington
Police Stn
Field Way
Medical Centre
Applegarth Primary School
Ashwood Gdns
Dunley Drive
Witley Cres
Ripley Close
Chesney Crs
Headley Drive
Dunsfold Wy
Good Shepherd RC Primary School
Leigh Crs
Ivers Wy
Alwyn Cl
Dunsfold Way
Horsley Dr
Walton Green
Hill
Lodge Lane
Surgery
Castle
Betchworth Wy
King Henry's Dr
Volsey
Aldrich
Shaxton
Grenville
Montacute Road
Parkway
North Downs
N Downs Crs
Gravel Hill
Crossways
Rawlins Cl
Gilbert Scott Primary School
Monks Hill Sports Centre
Selsdon High Sch
John Ruskin College
Broadcoombe
Warren Av
Shepherds Way
Tedder
Edgecoombe
Freelands Av
Heather Wy
Farnborough Av
Copse Vw
Lomond Gdns
Heathfield Vale
Farnborough Crs
Road
Huntingfield
Palace Green
Falconwood Road
Falconwood Rd
Featherbed Lane
Holmbury Gr
Pixton Wy
Bellfield
Forestdale Primary School
Woodpecker Mount
Pixton Way
Viney Bank
The Green
Newlands Wood
Crofters Mead
Fairacres
Chartwood
Bardolph Av
Oswald
Hollywoods
The Addington Golf Club
Pennycroft
Middlefields
Bowenswood
Swallowdale
Bruce Dr
Ashen V
Ambleside
Lichfield Wy
London Loop
Linton Glade
Hartscroft
Peacock Gdns
Thorold Cl
Court Primary School
Cascades
Brookscroft
Wood Lane
Lapwing
Osprey Gdns
Abbey Road
York Road
Greville Av
Benhurst

180
167
179
A
B
C
D
E
1
2
3
4
5
6
7
538
39
40
66
65
64
63
BR4
Works
HIGH STREET
232
A214
STATION ROAD
Wickham Swimming Baths
Links Road
The Mead
Down School
Old Wilsonians Sports Club
Hayes
Hayes Station
PICKHURST LANE
Surgery
Croft Av
Glebe Wy
GLEBE WAY
A232
Keswick Road
Windermere Road
Ridgeway
Warren Road
Hawes Down Clnc
Hawes Lane
Holland Way
Westland Dr
Abbotsbury Rd
Coney Hill School
Metropolitan Police Hayes Sports Club
Hayes Grove Priory Hospital
Prestons Road
Wickham Court Rd
Rose Walk
Silver Lane
Sherwood Way
Park Av
Highfield Drive
Oaklands Avenue
Boleyn Gdns
Wickham Theatre
Corkscrew Hill
Stambourne Wy
Wood Lodge Lane
Courtfield Rise
Addington Road
Coney Hill Rd
Lennard Av
Dukes Wy
Croydon Rd
Addington Rd
South Walk
Church Drive
Farm Close
Kingsway
Old Beckenhamian RFC
London Loop
Harvest Bank Road
Robins Grove
Hartfield Crescent
Lawrence Road
Gates
Coney Hall
Layhams Road
Sylvan Way
Chestnut Avenue
Birch Tree Avenue
Lime Tree Walk
Cherry Tree Wk
Queensway
Monarch Cl
Hawthorn Dr
Spring Park
ADDINGTON ROAD
A2022
St John Rigby Catholic College
Shirley Wanderers RFC
Rouse Farm
Bromley
Croydon
North Pole Lane
Nash Lane
Field Way
Medical
Dunley Drive
Headley Drive
Frimley Close
Netley Close
Brockham Crs
Mickleham Wy
Alford Gn
Claygate Crs
Pirbright Crs
Merrow Wy
Burford Wy
Surgery
New Addington
Goldcrest Wy
Kestrel Way
Frensham Drive
Horsley Dr
Dunsfold Way
Walton Green
Castle Hill Av
Tilford Av
Betchworth Wy
King Henry's Drive
Wolsey Crescent
Aldrich Crescent
Shaxton Crescent
Grenville Road
Rothwell Road
Montacute Road
Lodge Lane
Queen Elizabeth's Drive
Gascoigne Road
Godric Crs
Stowell Av
Rowdown Crs
Vulcan Business Cen
Vulcan Way
Addington Business Centre
Layhams Farm
N Downs
Parkway
1 grid square represents 500 metres

168
Keston Mark
Keston
Nash
BR2
CROYDON ROAD
BASTON ROAD
OAKLEY ROAD
HASTINGS ROAD
WESTERHAM ROAD
HEATHFIELD ROAD
A233
A232
A21
B265
Hayes School
Baston School
Park House RFC
Ravens Wood School
Keston CE Primary School
Heathfield College
Baston Manor
Hayes Common
Keston Court
Holwood
Holwood Farm
Lower Hook Farm
Bromley Hospitals
Hassock Wood
Poulters Wood
Swires Shaw
Barnet Wood Road
Five Elms Road
Commonside
Lakes Road
Fishponds Road
Jackass Lane
Church Road
Downe Road
New Road Hill
Farthing Street
Shire Lane
Blackness Lane
Rectory Road
Leafy Grove
Fox Hill
Heritage Hill
Jackson Road
Beverley Road
Barnet Drive
Kemble Drive
Lakeside Drive
Rowan Walk
Holwood Park Av
Pine Glade
Beech Dell
Forest Drive
Forest Ridge
Keston Park Close
Cedar Crescent
Longdon Wood
Mark Close
Beechwood Drive
Brockdene Dr
The Dale
Rushley Close
Rolinsden Way
Quiet Nook
Phoenix Dr
The Drift
Oakfield Lane
Windmill Drive
Keston Gdns
Keston Av
Greys Park Cl
Regents Drive
Redgate Drive
Burwood Avenue
Baston Manor Road
West Common Road
Cross Road
Doves Cl
Gravel Road
Weald Close
Knowle Road
Copthorne Avenue
Cherry Orchard Road
Daerwood Cl
Holwydale Drive
Ebury Close
Oakley Drive
Cedar Close
Crofton Road
Pallant Way
The Birch
Primary School
F G H J K
41 42 43
1 2 3 4 5 6 7
66 65 64 163

Abbey Wood 116 C3
Acton 86 E7
Acton Green 106 A3
Addington 179 J5
Addiscombe 165 G7
Aldborough Hatch 60 E3
Aldersbrook 59 G7
Alperton 68 A7
Anerley 165 H1
Arkley 25 K4
Ashford Common 140 B5
Avery Hill 135 H5
Balham 128 E6
Bandonhill 176 D4
Barking 78 D6
Barkingside 60 B2
Barnehurst 138 A2
Barnes 106 E7
Barnes Cray 138 E3
Barnet 26 D5
Barnet Gate 25 G5
Barnsbury 5 L1
Barwell 171 J6
Battersea 108 E6
Bayswater 8 D6
Beckenham 166 E2
Beckton 95 K5
Becontree 79 K4
Beddington 176 E1
Beddington Corner 163 F6
Bedford Park 106 C2
Belgravia 16 A5
Bell Green 151 H2
Bellingham 151 J3
Belmont 49 G1
Belmont 174 E7
Belvedere 117 J4
Benhilton 175 F2
Berrylands 159 G5
Bethnal Green 92 D2
Bexley 136 D3
Bexleyheath 137 G3
Bickley 168 D1
Blackfen 136 A5
Blackheath 133 J1
Blackheath Park 133 K3
Blackwall 94 B6
Bloomsbury 11 H2
Borehamwood 24 A2
The Borough 18 F2
Bow 93 J1
Bow Common 93 J4
Bowes Park 40 E5
Bowmans 138 C6
Brentford 104 E5
Brentford End 104 C5
Brimsdown 31 G1
Brixton 130 B3
Broad Green 164 C6
Brockley 132 C4
Bromley 93 K2
Bromley 168 A1
Bromley Common 168 C5
Bromley Park 152 C7
Brompton 15 J4
Brondesbury 70 C5
Brondesbury Park 70 B7
Brook Green 107 F2
Brunswick Park 40 A2
Buckhurst Hill 45 G2
Burnt Oak 37 F6
Bushey 22 C6
Bushey Heath 22 E6
Bushey Mead 161 G2
Bush Hill Park 30 A5
Caldecote Hill 23 F6
Camberwell 111 G7
Camden Town 4 B2
Canary Wharf 93 K7
Cannon Hill 161 G3
Canonbury 6 F1
Canonbury 73 J5
Canons Park 36 A6
Carpenders Park 33 K1
Carshalton 175 J3
Carshalton Beeches 175 J7
Carshalton on the Hill 175 K6
Castle Green 79 J7
Catford 133 F7
Chadwell Heath 61 K4
Charlton 114 C4
Cheam 174 D4
Chelsea 15 H8
Chessington 172 A5
Child's Hill 70 C1
China Town 11 G6
Chingford 44 A1
Chingford Hatch 44 C3
Chipping Barnet 26 C4
Chislehurst 154 C6
Chislehurst West 154 A5
Chiswick 106 C3
Church End 52 E1
Church End 69 H6
City of London 12 D6
Clapham 129 G1
Clapham Park 129 J5
Clapton Park 75 H3
Claremont Park 170 A6
Claygate 171 F5
Clayhall 59 K1
Clerkenwell 6 A9
Cockfosters 27 J4
Coldharbour 118 D3
Cole Park 124 B5
Colindale 51 G2
College Park 87 J2
Collier's Wood 147 H6
Colney Hatch 39 K5
Coney Hall 180 C3
Coombe 145 G6
Copse Hill 145 J6
Cottenham Park 145 K7
Cranbrook 60 A6
Cranford 101 K6
Cranley Gardens 54 A3
Crayford 138 D4
Creekmouth 96 E4
Cricklewood 70 B3
Crooked Billet 145 K5
Crouch End 54 C5
Croydon 177 K2
Crystal Palace 150 C4
Cubitt Town 113 F3
Custom House 95 J6
Dagenham 81 F6
Dartford 139 F6
Dartmouth Park 72 A1
Deacons Hill 24 C5
De Beauvoir Town 7 J3
Deptford 112 C5
Dollis Hill 69 K2
Dormer's Wells 84 B6
Downham 152 B4
Ducks Island 26 B6
Dudden Hill 69 J4
Dulwich 150 B1
Dulwich Village 131 F6
Ealing 85 J6
Earl's Court 14 A6
Earlsfield 128 B7
East Acton 87 H6
East Barnet 27 H6
East Bedfont 120 E6
Eastbury 32 D3
Eastcote 47 F6
Eastcote Village 47 F4
East Dulwich 131 H4
East Finchley 53 H2
East Ham 95 J1
East Molesey 157 H4
East Sheen 126 A4
East Wickham 116 B7
Eden Park 166 C3
Edgware 36 D3
Edmonton 42 A3
Elmers End 166 A2
Elm Park 81 K4
Elmstead 153 J4
Elstree 24 A5
Eltham 134 D5
Enfield 29 J3
Enfield Highway 30 E1
Enfield Town 29 K2
Erith 118 C4
Esher 170 C3
Fair Cross 79 F4
Falconwood 135 K3
Feltham 141 F1
Felthamhill 140 C4
Field Common 156 E6
Finchley 38 E7
Finsbury 6 A7
Finsbury Park 73 F1
Foots Cray 155 H5
Forestdale 179 G7
Forest Gate 76 E4
Forest Hill 132 A7
Fortis Green 53 K3
Foxbury 154 D4
Friday Hill 44 B2
Friern Barnet 39 J3
Fulham 107 G6
Furzedown 148 B3
Gants Hill 59 K5
Gidea Park 63 H1
Giggshill 158 B6
Globe Town 93 F2
Golders Green 52 C5
Goodmayes 79 H1
Gospel Oak 72 A4
Grange Park 29 G4
Greenford 84 D3
Greenhill 49 F4
Greenwich 113 G4
Grove Park 106 A7
Grove Park 153 G2
Hackbridge 176 B1
Hackney 74 E5
Hackney Wick 75 J5
Hadley 26 E2
Haggerston 7 M5
Hale End 44 B5
Ham 143 K2
Hammersmith 106 E3
Hampstead 71 H3
Hampstead Garden Suburb 53 F4
Hampton 142 B7
Hampton Hill 142 C3
Hampton Wick 143 H7
Hanwell 84 E7
Hanworth 141 H2
Harlesden 87 G1
Harlington 101 F5
Harringay 55 G4
Harrow 48 D5
Harrow on the Hill 48 E7
Harrow Weald 34 E6
Hatch End 33 J6
Hatton 121 H3
Hayes 82 A4
Hayes 168 A6
Hayes End 82 B3
Hayes Town 83 G7
Headstone 48 B3
Heath Park 63 K5
Hendon 51 K4
Herne Hill 130 D5
Heston 102 E6
Higham Hill 57 G1
Highams Park 43 K6
High Barnet 26 A2
Highbury 73 H3
Highgate 53 K6
Highwood Hill 37 H1
Hinchley Wood 171 F2
Hither Green 133 H5
Holborn 11 L3
Holders Hill 38 B7
Holywell 20 C5
Homerton 75 F5
Honor Oak 132 A5
Honor Oak Park 132 B5
Hook 172 A4
Hornsey 54 E3
Hornsey Vale 55 F4
Hounslow 123 F1
Hounslow West 122 C2
Hoxton 7 J6
Hurst Park 157 H1
The Hyde 51 H4
Ilford 78 B2
Isle of Dogs 113 F3
Isleworth 124 C2
Islington 6 A3
Kennington 109 K5
Kensal Green 88 A1
Kensal Rise 88 B1
Kensal Town 88 C3
Kensington 14 C4
Kentish Town 72 C5
Kenton 49 J4
Keston 181 H3
Keston Mark 181 H2
Kew 105 G6
Kidbrooke 134 B1
Kilburn 70 C7
Kingsbury 50 D5
Kingsland 7 J1
Kingston upon Thames 159 G2
Kingston Vale 145 F4
Knightsbridge 15 K1
Knight's Hill 130 D7
Ladywell 132 D3
Lambeth 18 A3
Lampton 103 G7
Lea Bridge 75 F2
Lee 133 J5
Lessness Heath 117 J5
Lewisham 133 F3
Leyton 76 B2
Leytonstone 58 D7
Limehouse 93 H5
Lisson Grove 9 M2
Little Heath 61 J3
Little Ilford 78 A4
Little Stanmore 36 B7
Long Ditton 158 C7
Longlands 154 C2
Lower Clapton 74 E3
Lower Edmonton 42 A1
Lower Feltham 140 C2
Lower Green 170 B1
Lower Holloway 73 F4
Lower Place 86 E1
Lower Sydenham 151 F3
Loxford 78 C4
Maida Vale 2 C7
Maitland Park 71 K5
Manor Park 77 J3
Marks Gate 62 A1
Marylebone 10 A3
Mayfair 10 C7
Maypole 138 B7
Merry Hill 22 B7
Merton 146 E7
Merton Park 161 J1
Mile End 93 G3
Mill Hill 37 J4
Mill Meads 94 B1
Millwall 112 D2
Mitcham 163 G2
Monken Hadley 26 C1
Monks Orchard 165 K6
Moor Park 32 A3
Morden 161 K3
Morden Park 161 H5
Mortlake 125 K1
Motspur Park 160 D5
Mottingham 153 G1
Muswell Hill 54 A1
Nash 181 F5
Neasden 69 F3
New Addington 180 B6
New Barnet 27 F4
New Beckenham 151 G5
Newbury Park 60 D5
New Charlton 114 C3
New Cross 132 B1
New Cross Gate 112 B7
New Eltham 154 B1
Newington 18 B4
New Malden 160 C2
New Southgate 40 C3
New Town 139 J5
Nine Elms 109 J6
Noel Park 55 H1
Norbiton 159 G1
Norbury 164 C1
North Acton 86 E3
North Cheam 174 B2
North End 53 G7
North End 118 C7
North Feltham 122 A4
North Finchley 39 G5
North Harrow 47 K5
North Hyde 102 D3
North Kensington 88 B4
Northolt 66 A6
North Sheen 125 J1
Northumberland Heath 117 K6
North Wembley 49 H7
Northwood 32 A7
Northwood Hills 46 B1
North Woolwich 114 D1
Norwood Green 103 F3
Norwood New Town 149 K5
Notting Hill 88 C6
Nunhead 131 K3
Oakleigh Park 39 H1
Oakwood 28 D5
Old Bexley 137 H6
Old Ford 75 G7
Old Malden 160 A6
Old Oak Common 87 H3
Osidge 40 C1
Osterley 103 H6
Oxhey 21 H5
Paddington 9 G3
Palmers Green 40 E2
Park Langley 167 F5
Park Royal 86 C2
Parsons Green 127 K1
Peckham 131 J1
Penge 150 E6
Pentonville 5 M5
Perivale 67 J7
Petersham 125 F7
Petts Wood 169 J3
Pimlico 16 E7
Pinner 47 H3
Pinner Green 47 G1
Pinnerwood Park 33 G6
Plaistow 94 D2
Plaistow 152 E5
Plashet 77 H5
Plumstead 115 H4
Plumstead Common 116 A5
Ponders End 30 E4
Poplar 93 J6
Preston 49 K7
Primrose Hill 4 B4
Purfleet 119 K5
Putney 127 G4
Putney Heath 127 F6
Putney Vale 145 J2
Queensbury 50 A2
Queens Park 88 C1
Rainham 99 K2
Ratcliff 93 G6
Rayners Lane 47 K7
Raynes Park 161 F2
Redbridge 59 G4
Regent's Park 4 D6
Richmond 125 F4
Richmond Hill 125 F5
Roehampton 126 C4
Romford 63 F4
The Rookery 20 E6
Rosehill 162 A7
Rotherhithe 112 A2
Roundshaw 177 F5
Rowley Green 25 H2
Roxeth 66 C1
Ruislip 46 C5
Ruislip Common 46 B3
Ruislip Gardens 64 C2
Ruislip Manor 64 E1
Rush Green 63 G6
St George in the East 92 C6
St Giles 11 H4
St Helier 162 B7
St James 11 G9
St Johns 132 D1
St John's Wood 2 F4
St Luke's 6 F9
St Margarets 124 D5
St Pancras 5 K8
Sands End 128 B1
Sandy Heath 71 G1
Seething Wells 158 C5
Selhurst 164 E4
Seven Kings 60 E7
Shacklewell 74 C3
Shadwell 92 E6
Shepherd's Bush 87 K7
Shirley 178 E1
Shooters Hill 115 H7
Shoreditch 7 H8
Shortlands 167 H2
Sidcup 155 H3
Silvertown 114 B1
Sipson 100 C4
Slade Green 138 D1
Soho 11 G5
Somers Town 5 G6
Southall 83 J6
South Beddington 176 D5
Southborough 168 E5
South Bromley 94 B5
South Croydon 177 J5
Southend 152 A3
Southfields 127 K7
Southgate 28 E7
South Hackney 74 E7
South Hampstead 3 G1
South Harrow 66 B2
South Hornchurch 81 F7
South Kensington 14 E6
South Lambeth 109 K6
South Norwood 164 E2
South Oxhey 33 F2
South Ruislip 65 H3
South Tottenham 56 A4
South Wimbledon 147 G4
South Woodford 58 E1
Spitalfields 13 L2
Spring Grove 103 J7
Spring Park 179 J1
Stamford Hill 56 B6
Stanmore 35 H4
Stepney 92 E4
Stockwell 129 K2
Stoke Newington 74 B1
Stoneleigh 173 H4
Strand 11 K6
Stratford 76 A6
Stratford Marsh 75 K7
Stratford New Town 76 A5
Strawberry Hill 142 D2
Streatham 148 E4
Streatham Hill 129 K7
Streatham Park 148 B3
Streatham Vale 148 B6
Stroud Green 55 G5
Sudbury 67 F4
Summerstown 147 H1
Sunbury Common 140 D6
Sundridge 153 G5
Surbiton 158 E7
Sutton 174 E4
Teddington 142 D5
Temple Hill 139 G3
Temple Mills 75 K4
Thames Ditton 158 B6
Thamesmead 97 F7
Thornton Heath 163 K4
Tokyngton 68 D5
Tolworth 159 H7
Tooting 147 K4
Tooting Graveney 147 H4
Tottenham 56 A1
Tottenham Hale 56 B2
Totteridge 26 E7
Totteridge Green 26 A7
Tufnell Park 72 C3
Tulse Hill 130 C7
Twickenham 123 K7
Underhill 26 E5
Upper Clapton 56 C7
Upper Edmonton 42 C3
Upper Elmers End 166 C4
Upper Holloway 72 C1
Upper Norwood 149 K7
Upper Shirley 178 E3
Upper Sydenham 150 C3
Upper Tooting 147 J2
Upper Walthamstow 58 A3
Upton 77 F6
Upton Park 77 G7
Vale of Health 71 H2
Vauxhall 17 L8
Waddon 177 F1
Walham Green 107 K7
Wallend 78 A7
Wallington 176 B4
Walthamstow 57 J2
Walworth 18 F8
Wandle Park 177 G1
Wandsworth 127 K3
Wanstead 59 F6
Wapping 92 D7
Watford Heath 21 J6
Wealdstone 49 G2
Welling 136 C2
Welsh Harp 51 F7
Wembley 67 J4
Wembley Park 68 C2
West Acton 86 C5
West Barnes 161 F4
West Bedfont 120 C6
West Brompton 14 C9
West Drayton 100 A2
West Dulwich 149 K1
West Ealing 85 G7
West Ewell 173 G6
West Green 55 J2
West Hampstead 70 E4
West Harrow 48 C6
West Heath 71 F1
West Heath 116 E5
West Hendon 51 J6
West Hill 127 H6
West Kensington 107 G4
West Kilburn 88 C2
Westminster 16 F4
West Molesey 156 E3
West Norwood 149 J3
Weston Green 157 K7
West Ruislip 46 A7
West Watford 20 E4
West Wickham 167 G7
Whetstone 39 F1
Whitechapel 13 M6
Whitton 123 H5
Widmore 168 C1
Willesden 69 J5
Willesden Green 69 K6
Wimbledon 146 C4
Winchmore Hill 29 H7
Wood End 82 C5
Wood End Green 82 C4
Woodford 45 F5
Woodford Bridge 45 K6
Woodford Green 44 E6
Woodford Wells 45 F2
Wood Green 41 G7
Woodlands 123 J2
Woodside 165 H5
Woodside Park 38 E3
Woolwich 115 F5
Worcester Park 173 K1
World's End 29 G3
The Wrythe 175 J1
Yeading 83 G3

USING THE STREET INDEX

Street names are listed alphabetically. Each street name is followed by its postal town or area locality, the Postcode District, the page number, and the reference to the square in which the name is found.

Standard index entries are shown as follows:

Aaron Hill Rd *EHAM* E6 ....**96** A4

Street names and selected addresses not shown on the map due to scale restrictions are shown in the index with an asterisk:

Abbeville Ms *CLAP* * SW4......................**129** J4

GENERAL ABBREVIATIONS

ACC	ACCESS
ALY	ALLEY
AP	APPROACH
AR	ARCADE
ASS	ASSOCIATION
AV	AVENUE
BCH	BEACH
BLDS	BUILDINGS
BND	BEND
BNK	BANK
BR	BRIDGE
BRK	BROOK
BTM	BOTTOM
BUS	BUSINESS
BVD	BOULEVARD
BY	BYPASS
CATH	CATHEDRAL
CEM	CEMETERY
CEN	CENTRE
CFT	CROFT
CH	CHURCH
CHA	CHASE
CHYD	CHURCHYARD
CIR	CIRCLE
CIRC	CIRCUS
CL	CLOSE
CLFS	CLIFFS
CMP	CAMP
CNR	CORNER
CO	COUNTY
COLL	COLLEGE
COM	COMMON
COMM	COMMISSION
CON	CONVENT
COT	COTTAGE
COTS	COTTAGES
CP	CAPE
CPS	COPSE
CR	CREEK
CREM	CREMATORIUM
CRS	CRESCENT
CSWY	CAUSEWAY
CT	COURT
CTRL	CENTRAL
CTS	COURTS
CTYD	COURTYARD
CUTT	CUTTINGS
CV	COVE
CYN	CANYON
DEPT	DEPARTMENT
DL	DALE
DM	DAM
DR	DRIVE
DRO	DROVE
DRY	DRIVEWAY
DWGS	DWELLINGS
E	EAST
EMB	EMBANKMENT
EMBY	EMBASSY
ESP	ESPLANADE
EST	ESTATE
EX	EXCHANGE
EXPY	EXPRESSWAY
EXT	EXTENSION
F/O	FLYOVER
FC	FOOTBALL CLUB
FK	FORK
FLD	FIELD
FLDS	FIELDS
FLS	FALLS
FLS	FLATS
FM	FARM
FT	FORT
FWY	FREEWAY
FY	FERRY
GA	GATE
GAL	GALLERY
GDN	GARDEN
GDNS	GARDENS
GLD	GLADE
GLN	GLEN
GN	GREEN
GND	GROUND
GRA	GRANGE
GRG	GARAGE
GT	GREAT
GTWY	GATEWAY
GV	GROVE
HGR	HIGHER
HL	HILL
HLS	HILLS
HO	HOUSE
HOL	HOLLOW
HOSP	HOSPITAL
HRB	HARBOUR
HTH	HEATH
HTS	HEIGHTS
HVN	HAVEN
HWY	HIGHWAY
IMP	IMPERIAL
IN	INLET
IND EST	INDUSTRIAL ESTATE
INF	INFIRMARY
INFO	INFORMATION
INT	INTERCHANGE
IS	ISLAND
JCT	JUNCTION
JTY	JETTY
KG	KING
KNL	KNOLL
L	LAKE
LA	LANE
LDG	LODGE
LGT	LIGHT
LK	LOCK
LKS	LAKES
LNDG	LANDING
LTL	LITTLE
LWR	LOWER
MAG	MAGISTRATE
MAN	MANSIONS
MD	MEAD
MDW	MEADOWS
MEM	MEMORIAL
MKT	MARKET
MKTS	MARKETS
ML	MALL
ML	MILL
MNR	MANOR
MS	MEWS
MSN	MISSION
MT	MOUNT
MTN	MOUNTAIN
MTS	MOUNTAINS
MUS	MUSEUM
MWY	MOTORWAY
N	NORTH
NE	NORTH EAST
NW	NORTH WEST
O/P	OVERPASS
OFF	OFFICE
ORCH	ORCHARD
OV	OVAL
PAL	PALACE
PAS	PASSAGE
PAV	PAVILION
PDE	PARADE
PH	PUBLIC HOUSE
PK	PARK
PKWY	PARKWAY
PL	PLACE
PLN	PLAIN
PLNS	PLAINS
PLZ	PLAZA
POL	POLICE STATION
PR	PRINCE
PREC	PRECINCT
PREP	PREPARATORY
PRIM	PRIMARY
PROM	PROMENADE
PRS	PRINCESS
PRT	PORT
PT	POINT
PTH	PATH
PZ	PIAZZA
QD	QUADRANT
QU	QUEEN
QY	QUAY
R	RIVER
RBT	ROUNDABOUT
RD	ROAD
RDG	RIDGE
REP	REPUBLIC
RES	RESERVOIR
RFC	RUGBY FOOTBALL CLUB
RI	RISE
RP	RAMP
RW	ROW
S	SOUTH
SCH	SCHOOL
SE	SOUTH EAST
SER	SERVICE AREA
SH	SHORE
SHOP	SHOPPING
SKWY	SKYWAY
SMT	SUMMIT
SOC	SOCIETY
SP	SPUR
SPR	SPRING
SQ	SQUARE
ST	STREET
STN	STATION
STR	STREAM
STRD	STRAND
SW	SOUTH WEST
TDG	TRADING
TER	TERRACE
THWY	THROUGHWAY
TNL	TUNNEL
TOLL	TOLLWAY
TPK	TURNPIKE
TR	TRACK
TRL	TRAIL
TWR	TOWER
U/P	UNDERPASS
UNI	UNIVERSITY
UPR	UPPER
V	VALE
VA	VALLEY
VIAD	VIADUCT
VIL	VILLA
VIS	VISTA
VLG	VILLAGE
VLS	VILLAS
VW	VIEW
W	WEST
WD	WOOD
WHF	WHARF
WK	WALK
WKS	WALKS
WLS	WELLS
WY	WAY
YD	YARD
YHA	YOUTH HOSTEL

POSTCODE TOWNS AND AREA ABBREVIATIONS

ABYW	Abbey Wood
ACT	Acton
ALP/SUD	Alperton/Sudbury
ARCH	Archway
ASHF	Ashford (Surrey)
BAL	Balham
BANK	Bank
BAR	Barnet
BARB	Barbican
BARK	Barking
BARK/HLT	Barkingside/Hainault
BARN	Barnes
BAY/PAD	Bayswater/Paddington
BCTR	Becontree
BECK	Beckenham
BELMT	Belmont
BELV	Belvedere
BERM/RHTH	Bermondsey/Rotherhithe
BETH	Bethnal Green
BFN/LL	Blackfen/Longlands
BGVA	Belgravia
BKHH	Buckhurst Hill
BKHTH/KID	Blackheath/Kidbrooke
BLKFR	Blackfriars
BMLY	Bromley
BMSBY	Bloomsbury
BORE	Borehamwood
BOW	Bow
BROCKY	Brockley
BRXN/ST	Brixton north/Stockwell
BRXS/STRHM	Brixton south/ Streatham Hill
BRYLDS	Berrylands
BTFD	Brentford
BTSEA	Battersea
BUSH	Bushey
BXLY	Bexley
BXLYHN	Bexleyheath north
BXLYHS	Bexleyheath south
CAMTN	Camden Town
CAN/RD	Canning Town/Royal Docks
CANST	Cannon Street station
CAR	Carshalton
CAT	Catford
CAVSQ/HST	Cavendish Square/ Harley Street
CDALE/KGS	Colindale/Kingsbury
CEND/HSY/T	Crouch End/Hornsey/ Turnpike Lane
CHARL	Charlton
CHCR	Charing Cross
CHDH	Chadwell Heath
CHEAM	Cheam
CHEL	Chelsea
CHIG	Chigwell
CHING	Chingford
CHSGTN	Chessington
CHST	Chislehurst
CHSWK	Chiswick
CITYW	City of London west
CLAP	Clapham
CLAY	Clayhall
CLKNW	Clerkenwell
CLPT	Clapton
CMBW	Camberwell
CONDST	Conduit Street
COVGDN	Covent Garden
CRICK	Cricklewood
CROY/NA	Croydon/New Addington
CRW	Collier Row
DAGE	Dagenham east
DAGW	Dagenham west
DART	Dartford
DEN/HRF	Denham/Harefield
DEPT	Deptford
DUL	Dulwich
E/WMO/HCT	East & West Molesey/ Hampton Court
EA	Ealing
EBAR	East Barnet
EBED/NFELT	East Bedfont/ North Feltham
ECT	Earl's Court
ED	Edmonton
EDGW	Edgware
EDUL	East Dulwich
EFNCH	East Finchley
EHAM	East Ham
ELTH/MOT	Eltham/Mottingham
EMB	Embankment
EMPK	Emerson Park
EN	Enfield
ENC/FH	Enfield Chase/Forty Hill
ERITH	Erith
ERITHM	Erith Marshes
ESH/CLAY	Esher/Claygate
EW	Ewell
FARR	Farringdon
FBAR/BDGN	Friern Barnet/ Bounds Green
FELT	Feltham
FENCHST	Fenchurch Street
FITZ	Fitzrovia
FLST/FETLN	Fleet Street/Fetter Lane
FNCH	Finchley
FSBYE	Finsbury east
FSBYPK	Finsbury Park
FSBYW	Finsbury west
FSTGT	Forest Gate
FSTH	Forest Hill
FUL/PGN	Fulham/Parsons Green
GDMY/SEVK	Goodmayes/Seven Kings
GFD/PVL	Greenford/Perivale
GINN	Gray's Inn
GLDGN	Golders Green
GNTH/NBYPK	Gants Hill/Newbury Park
GNWCH	Greenwich
GPK	Gidea Park
GSTN	Garston
GTPST	Great Portland Street
GWRST	Gower Street
HACK	Hackney
HAMP	Hampstead
HAYES	Hayes
HBRY	Highbury
HCH	Hornchurch
HCIRC	Holborn Circus
HDN	Hendon
HDTCH	Houndsditch
HEST	Heston
HGDN/ICK	Hillingdon/Ickenham
HGT	Highgate
HHOL	High Holborn
HMSMTH	Hammersmith
HNHL	Herne Hill
HNWL	Hanwell
HOL/ALD	Holborn/Aldwych
HOLWY	Holloway
HOM	Homerton
HOR/WEW	Horton/West Ewell
HPTN	Hampton
HRW	Harrow
HSLW	Hounslow
HSLWW	Hounslow west
HTHAIR	Heathrow Airport
HYS/HAR	Hayes/Harlington
IL	Ilford
IS	Islington
ISLW	Isleworth
KENS	Kensington
KIL/WHAMP	Kilburn/West Hampstead
KTBR	Knightsbridge
KTN/HRWW/WS	Kenton/Harrow Weald/ Wealdstone
KTTN	Kentish Town
KUT	Kingston upon Thames
KUTN/CMB	Kingston upon Thames north/Coombe
LBTH	Lambeth
LEE/GVPK	Lee/Grove Park
LEW	Lewisham
LEY	Leyton
LINN	Lincoln's Inn
LOTH	Lothbury
LSQ/SEVD	Leicester Square/Seven Dials
LVPST	Liverpool Street
MANHO	Mansion House
MBLAR	Marble Arch
MHST	Marylebone High Street
MLHL	Mill Hill
MNPK	Manor Park
MON	Monument
MORT/ESHN	Mortlake/East Sheen
MRDN	Morden
MTCM	Mitcham
MUSWH	Muswell Hill
MV/WKIL	Maida Vale/West Kilburn
MYFR/PICC	Mayfair/Piccadilly
MYFR/PKLN	Mayfair/Park Lane
NFNCH/WDSPK	North Finchley/Woodside Park
NKENS	North Kensington
NOXST/BSQ	New Oxford Street/ Bloomsbury Square
NRWD	Norwood
NTGHL	Notting Hill
NTHLT	Northolt
NTHWD	Northwood
NWCR	New Cross
NWDGN	Norwood Green
NWMAL	New Malden
OBST	Old Broad Street
ORP	Orpington
OXHEY	Oxhey
OXSTW	Oxford Street west
PECK	Peckham
PEND	Ponders End
PGE/AN	Penge/Anerley
PIM	Pimlico
PIN	Pinner
PLMGR	Palmers Green
PLSTW	Plaistow
POP/IOD	Poplar/Isle of Dogs
PUR	Purfleet
PUR/KEN	Purley/Kenley
PUT/ROE	Putney/Roehampton
RAIN	Rainham (Gt Lon)
RCH/KEW	Richmond/Kew
RCHPK/HAM	Richmond Park/Ham
RDART	Rural Dartford
REDBR	Redbridge
REGST	Regent Street
RKW/CH/CXG	Rickmansworth/ Chorleywood/Croxley Green
ROM	Romford
ROMW/RG	Romford west/Rush Green
RSLP	Ruislip
RSQ	Russell Square
RYLN/HDSTN	Rayners Lane/Headstone
RYNPK	Raynes Park
SAND/SEL	Sanderstead/Selsdon
SCUP	Sidcup
SDTCH	Shoreditch
SEVS/STOTM	Seven Sisters/South Tottenham
SHB	Shepherd's Bush
SHPTN	Shepperton
SKENS	South Kensington
SNWD	South Norwood
SOCK/AV	South Ockendon/Aveley
SOHO/CST	Soho/Carnaby Street
SOHO/SHAV	Soho/Shaftesbury Avenue
SRTFD	Stratford
STAN	Stanmore
STBT	St Bart's
STHGT/OAK	Southgate/Oakwood
STHL	Southall
STHWK	Southwark
STJS	St James's
STJSPK	St James's Park
STJWD	St John's Wood
STKPK	Stockley Park
STLK	St Luke's
STMC/STPC	St Mary Cray/St Paul's Cray
STNW/STAM	Stoke Newington/ Stamford Hill
STP	St Paul's
STPAN	St Pancras
STRHM/NOR	Streatham/Norbury
STWL/WRAY	Stanwell/Wraysbury
SUN	Sunbury
SURB	Surbiton
SUT	Sutton
SWFD	South Woodford
SYD	Sydenham
TEDD	Teddington
THDIT	Thames Ditton
THHTH	Thornton Heath
THMD	Thamesmead
TOOT	Tooting
TOTM	Tottenham
TPL/STR	Temple/Strand
TRDG/WHET	Totteridge/Whetstone
TWK	Twickenham
TWRH	Tower Hill
UED	Upper Edmonton
UX/CGN	Uxbridge/Colham Green
VX/NE	Vauxhall/Nine Elms
WALTH	Walthamstow
WALW	Walworth
WAN	Wanstead
WAND/EARL	Wandsworth/Earlsfield
WAP	Wapping
WAT	Watford
WATN	Watford north
WATW	Watford west
WBLY	Wembley
WBPTN	West Brompton
WCHMH	Winchmore Hill
WCHPL	Whitechapel
WDGN	Wood Green
WDR/YW	West Drayton/Yiewsley
WEA	West Ealing
WELL	Welling
WEST	Westminster
WESTW	Westminster west
WFD	Woodford
WHALL	Whitehall
WHTN	Whitton
WIM/MER	Wimbledon/Merton
WKENS	West Kensington
WLGTN	Wallington
WLSDN	Willesden
WNWD	West Norwood
WOOL/PLUM	Woolwich/Plumstead
WOT/HER	Walton-on-Thames/Hersham
WPK	Worcester Park
WWKM	West Wickham
YEAD	Yeading

I

1 Av WOOL/PLUM SE18 ...115 G2

A

Aaron Hill Rd EHAM E6 ...96 A4
Abbess Cl BRXS/STRHM SW2 ...130 C7
Abbeville Ms CLAP * SW4 ...129 J4
Abbeville Rd CEND/HSY/T N8 ...54 D3
CLAP SW4 ...129 H5
Abbey Av ALP/SUD HA0 ...86 A1
Abbey Cl HYS/HAR UB3 ...83 F7
NTHLT UB5 ...83 K2
PIN HA5 ...47 F2
ROM RM1 ...63 H5
Abbey Crs BELV DA17 ...117 H3
Abbeydale Rd ALP/SUD HA0 ...68 B7
Abbey Dr TOOT SW17 ...148 A4
Abbeyfield Cl MTCM CR4 ...162 D1
Abbeyfield Est
BERM/RHTH SE16 ...111 K3
Abbeyfield Rd
BERM/RHTH SE16 ...111 K3
Abbeyfields Cl WLSDN NW10 ...86 C2
Abbey Gdns BERM/RHTH SE16 ...111 H3
HMSMTH W6 ...107 H5
STJWD NW8 ...2 E6
Abbey Gv ABYW SE2 ...116 C3
Abbeyhill Rd BFN/LL DA15 ...136 D7
Abbey La BECK BR3 ...151 J6
SRTFD E15 ...94 B1
Abbey Ms WALTH E17 ...57 J4
Abbey Mt BELV DA17 ...117 G4
Abbey Orchard St WEST SW1P ...17 H3
Abbey Pk BECK BR3 ...151 J6
Abbey Pl DART * DA1 ...139 G4
Abbey Rd BARK IG11 ...78 B7
BELV DA17 ...116 E3
BXLYHS DA6 ...137 F3
CROY/NA CR0 ...177 H2
EN EN1 ...30 A4
GNTH/NBYPK IG2 ...60 D4
KIL/WHAMP NW6 ...2 C3
SRTFD E15 ...94 B1
WIM/MER SW19 ...147 G6
WLSDN NW10 ...68 D7
Abbey St PLSTW E13 ...94 E3
STHWK SE1 ...19 L3
Abbey Ter ABYW SE2 ...116 D2
Abbey Vw MLHL NW7 ...37 H2
Abbey Wk E/WMO/HCT KT8 ...157 G2
Abbey Wood Rd ABYW SE2 ...116 C3
Abbot Cl RSLP HA4 ...65 H2
Abbotsbury Cl SRTFD E15 ...94 A1
WKENS * W14 ...107 J1
Abbotsbury Gdns PIN HA5 ...47 G5
Abbotsbury Ms PECK SE15 ...131 K2
Abbotsbury Rd MRDN SM4 ...162 A3
WKENS W14 ...107 H1
WWKM BR4 ...180 D1
Abbots Cl STMC/STPC BR5 ...169 H7
Abbots Dr RYLN/HDSTN HA2 ...66 A1
Abbotsford Av
SEVS/STOTM N15 ...55 J3
Abbotsford Gdns WFD IG8 ...44 E6
Abbotsford Rd GDMY/SEVK IG3 ...79 G1
Abbots Gdns EFNCH N2 ...53 H3
Abbots Gn CROY/NA CR0 ...179 F5
Abbotshade Rd
BERM/RHTH * SE16 ...93 F7
Abbotshall Av STHGT/OAK N14 ...40 C2
Abbotshall Rd CAT SE6 ...133 G7
Abbots La STHWK SE1 ...13 K9
Abbotsleigh Cl BELMT SM2 ...175 F6
Abbotsleigh Rd
STRHM/NOR SW16 ...148 C3
Abbots Mnr PIM SW1V ...16 C7
Abbots Manor Est PIM SW1V ...16 C7
Abbotsmede Cl TWK TW1 ...143 F1
Abbots Pk BRXS/STRHM SW2 ...130 B7
Abbot's Pl KIL/WHAMP NW6 ...2 C3
Abbots Rd CHEAM SM3 ...174 C3
EDGW HA8 ...37 F6
EHAM E6 ...77 H7
Abbots Ter CEND/HSY/T N8 ...54 E5
Abbotstone Rd PUT/ROE SW15 ...127 F2
Abbot St HACK E8 ...74 B5
Abbots Wk KENS * W8 ...14 C4
Abbots Wy BECK BR3 ...166 B4
Abbotswell Rd BROCKY SE4 ...132 C4
Abbotswood Cl BELV DA17 ...117 F2
Abbotswood Gdns CLAY IG5 ...59 K2
Abbotswood Rd EDUL SE22 ...131 F3
STRHM/NOR SW16 ...148 D2
Abbotswood Wy HYS/HAR UB3 ...83 F7
Abbott Av RYNPK SW20 ...161 G1
Abbott Cl HPTN TW12 ...141 J5
NTHLT UB5 ...65 K5
Abbott Rd POP/IOD E14 ...94 A4
Abbotts Cl IS * N1 ...6 E1
ROMW/RG RM7 ...62 D2
THMD SE28 ...97 J6
Abbotts Crs CHING E4 ...44 B3
ENC/FH EN2 ...29 H1
Abbotts Dr ALP/SUD HA0 ...67 H1
Abbotts Md
RCHPK/HAM * TW10 ...143 J3
Abbotts Park Rd LEY E10 ...58 A6
Abbotts Rd BAR EN5 ...27 F3
MTCM CR4 ...163 H3
STHL UB1 ...83 J7
Abbott's Wk BXLYHN DA7 ...116 E6
Abchurch La MANHO EC4N ...13 H6
Abdale Rd SHB W12 ...87 K7
Aberavon Rd BOW E3 ...93 G2
Abercairn Rd
STRHM/NOR SW16 ...148 C6
Aberconway Rd MRDN SM4 ...162 A2
Abercorn Cl MLHL NW7 ...38 C6
STJWD NW8 ...2 E6
Abercorn Crs RYLN/HDSTN HA2 ...48 B7
Abercorn Gdns CHDH RM6 ...61 H5
KTN/HRWW/W HA3 ...49 K6
Abercorn Gv RSLP HA4 ...46 B3
Abercorn Pl STJWD NW8 ...2 E7
Abercorn Rd MLHL NW7 ...38 C6
STAN HA7 ...35 J6
Abercorn Wy STHWK SE1 ...111 H4
Abercrombie St BTSEA SW11 ...128 D1
Aberdare Cl WWKM BR4 ...180 A1
Aberdare Gdns KIL/WHAMP NW6 ...2 D2
MLHL NW7 ...38 B6
Aberdare Rd PEND EN3 ...30 E3
Aberdeen Cottages STAN * HA7 ...35 J6
Aberdeen La HBRY N5 ...73 H4
Aberdeen Pde UED * N18 ...42 D4
Aberdeen Pk HBRY N5 ...73 H4
Aberdeen Pl STJWD NW8 ...9 G1
Aberdeen Rd CROY/NA CR0 ...177 J3
HBRY N5 ...73 J3
KTN/HRWW/W HA3 ...49 F2
UED N18 ...42 D4
WLSDN NW10 ...69 H4
Aberdeen Ter BKHTH/KID SE3 ...133 G1
Aberdour Rd BCTR RM8 ...79 H2
Aberdour St STHWK SE1 ...19 J5
Aberfeldy St POP/IOD E14 ...94 A5
Aberford Gdns
WOOL/PLUM SE18 ...114 D7
Aberford Rd BORE WD6 ...24 C1
Aberfoyle Rd
STRHM/NOR SW16 ...148 D5
Abergeldie Rd LEE/GVPK SE12 ...134 A5
Abernethy Rd LEW SE13 ...133 H3
Abersham Rd HACK E8 ...74 B4
Abery St WOOL/PLUM SE18 ...115 K3
Abingdon Cl STHWK * SE1 ...19 M6
WIM/MER SW19 ...147 G5
Abingdon Rd FNCH N3 ...53 G1
KENS W8 ...14 B4
STRHM/NOR SW16 ...148 E7
Abingdon St WEST SW1P ...17 J2
Abingdon Vls KENS W8 ...14 B4
Abinger Av BELMT SM2 ...174 A7
Abinger Cl BMLY BR1 ...168 D2
CROY/NA CR0 ...180 A5
GDMY/SEVK IG3 ...79 G3
WLGTN SM6 ...176 E4
Abinger Gdns ISLW TW7 ...123 K2
Abinger Gv DEPT SE8 ...112 C5
Abinger Ms MV/WKIL W9 ...2 A9
Abinger Rd CHSWK W4 ...106 C2
Ablett St BERM/RHTH SE16 ...111 K4
Abney Park Ter
STNW/STAM * N16 ...74 B1
Aboyne Dr RYNPK SW20 ...160 D1
Aboyne Rd TOOT SW17 ...147 H2
WLSDN NW10 ...69 G2
Abridge Wy BARK IG11 ...97 H1
Abyssinia Cl BTSEA SW11 ...128 D3
Abyssinia Rd BTSEA * SW11 ...128 D3
Acacia Av BTFD TW8 ...104 C6
HCH RM12 ...81 H1
RSLP HA4 ...46 E7
TOTM N17 ...41 K6
WBLY HA9 ...68 A4
YEAD UB4 ...82 D5
Acacia Cl DEPT SE8 ...112 B3
KTN/HRWW/W HA3 ...34 E5
STMC/STPC BR5 ...169 J4
Acacia Dr CHEAM SM3 ...161 J7
Acacia Gdns STJWD NW8 ...3 H5
WWKM BR4 ...180 A1
Acacia Gv DUL SE21 ...149 K1
NWMAL KT3 ...160 B2
Acacia Ms WDR/YW UB7 ...100 A5
Acacia Pl STJWD NW8 ...3 H5
Acacia Rd ACT W3 ...86 E6
BECK BR3 ...166 C2
DART DA1 ...139 F7
HPTN TW12 ...142 A5
MTCM CR4 ...163 F1
STJWD NW8 ...3 H5
STRHM/NOR SW16 ...148 E7
WALTH E17 ...57 G5
WAN E11 ...76 C1
WDGN N22 ...41 G7
The Acacias EBAR * EN4 ...27 H4
Acacia Wy BFN/LL DA15 ...136 A7
Academy Gdns CROY/NA CR0 ...165 G7
NTHLT UB5 ...83 H1
Academy Pl WOOL/PLUM SE18 ...114 E7
Academy Rd
WOOL/PLUM SE18 ...114 E6
Acanthus Dr STHWK SE1 ...111 H4
Acanthus Rd BTSEA SW11 ...129 F2
Accommodation Rd
GLDGN NW11 ...52 D6
Ace Pde CHSGTN * KT9 ...172 A2
Acer Av YEAD UB4 ...83 J3
Acfold Rd FUL/PGN SW6 ...108 A7
Achilles Cl STHWK SE1 ...111 H4
Achilles Rd KIL/WHAMP NW6 ...70 E4
Achilles St NWCR SE14 ...112 B6
Acklam Rd NKENS W10 ...88 D4
Acklington Dr CDALE/KGS NW9 ...37 G7
Ackmar Rd FUL/PGN SW6 ...107 K7
Ackroyd Dr BOW E3 ...93 H4
Ackroyd Rd FSTH SE23 ...132 A6
Acland Cl WOOL/PLUM SE18 ...115 J6
Acland Crs CMBW SE5 ...130 E3
Acland Rd WLSDN NW2 ...69 K5
Acock Gv NTHLT UB5 ...66 B3
Acol Crs RSLP HA4 ...65 F4
Acol Rd KIL/WHAMP NW6 ...2 B2
Acorn Cl CHING E4 ...43 K4
CHST BR7 ...154 C4
HPTN TW12 ...142 B5
STAN HA7 ...35 H6
Acorn Gdns ACT W3 ...87 F4
NRWD SE19 ...150 B7
Acorn Gv HYS/HAR UB3 ...101 J6
RSLP HA4 ...64 D3
Acorn Pde PECK * SE15 ...111 J6
Acorn Rd DART DA1 ...138 C4
Acorns Wy ESH/CLAY KT10 ...170 C4
Acorn Wy FSTH SE23 ...151 F2
Acre Dr EDUL SE22 ...131 H3
Acre La BRXS/STRHM SW2 ...130 A3
CAR SM5 ...176 A3
Acre Rd DAGE RM10 ...80 D6
KUTN/CMB KT2 ...144 A7
WIM/MER SW19 ...147 H5
Acre Wy NTHWD HA6 ...32 D7
Acris St WAND/EARL SW18 ...128 B4
Acton Cl ED N9 ...42 C1
Acton Hill Ms ACT * W3 ...86 D7
Acton La ACT W3 ...86 E7
WLSDN NW10 ...86 E2
Acton Ms HACK E8 ...7 L3
Acton St FSBYW WC1X ...5 L8
Acuba Rd WAND/EARL SW18 ...147 F1
Acworth Pl DART * DA1 ...139 F5
Ada Ct STJWD NW8 ...2 F8
Ada Gdns POP/IOD E14 ...94 B5
SRTFD E15 ...76 D7
Adair Cl SNWD SE25 ...165 J2
Adair Rd NKENS W10 ...88 C3
Adam & Eve Ms KENS W8 ...14 B3
Adam Rd CHING E4 ...43 H5
Adams Cl BRYLDS KT5 ...159 G5
CDALE/KGS NW9 ...68 D1
FNCH N3 ...38 E6
Adams Ms WDGN * N22 ...41 F6
Adamson Rd CAN/RD E16 ...94 E5
HAMP NW3 ...3 H1
Adams Pl HOLWY N7 ...73 F4
Adamsrill Rd SYD SE26 ...151 F3
Adams Rd BECK BR3 ...166 B4
TOTM N17 ...55 K1
Adam's Rw MYFR/PKLN W1K ...10 B7
Adams Sq BXLYHS DA6 ...137 F2
Adam St TPL/STR WC2R ...11 K7
Adams Wk KUT KT1 ...159 F1
Adams Wy SNWD SE25 ...165 G5
Adam Wk FUL/PGN * SW6 ...107 F6
Ada Pl BETH E2 ...74 C7
Adare Wk STRHM/NOR SW16 ...148 E1
Ada Rd ALP/SUD * HA0 ...67 J2
CMBW SE5 ...111 F6
Ada St HACK E8 ...74 D7
Adderley Gdns ELTH/MOT SE9 ...154 A3
Adderley Gv BTSEA SW11 ...129 F4
Adderley Rd KTN/HRWW/W HA3 ...35 F7
Adderley St POP/IOD E14 ...94 A5
Addington Dr
NFNCH/WDSP N12 ...39 H5
Addington Gv SYD SE26 ...151 G3
Addington Rd BOW E3 ...93 J2
CAN/RD E16 ...94 C3
CROY/NA CR0 ...164 B7
FSBYPK N4 ...55 G6
WWKM BR4 ...180 A3
Addington Sq CMBW SE5 ...110 D6
Addington Village Rd
CROY/NA CR0 ...179 H5
Addiscombe Av CROY/NA CR0 ...165 H6
Addiscombe Cl
KTN/HRWW/W HA3 ...49 J4
Addiscombe Court Rd
CROY/NA CR0 ...165 F7
Addiscombe Gv CROY/NA CR0 ...177 K1
Addiscombe Rd CROY/NA CR0 ...178 A1
WATW WD18 ...21 F3
Addison Av HSLW TW3 ...103 H7
NTGHL W11 ...88 C7
STHGT/OAK N14 ...28 B5
Addison Bridge Pl WKENS W14 ...107 H3
Addison Cl NTHWD HA6 ...32 E7
STMC/STPC BR5 ...169 H5
Addison Crs WKENS W14 ...107 H2
Addison Dr LEE/GVPK SE12 ...134 A4
Addison Gdns BRYLDS KT5 ...159 G3
WKENS W14 ...107 G2
Addison Gv CHSWK W4 ...106 B2
Addison Pl NTGHL W11 ...88 C7
Addison Rd HAYES BR2 ...168 C4
NTGHL W11 ...107 H1
SNWD SE25 ...165 H3
TEDD TW11 ...143 H5
WALTH E17 ...57 K4
WAN E11 ...58 E5
Addison's Cl CROY/NA CR0 ...179 H1
Addison Ter CHSWK * W4 ...105 K3
Addison Wy GLDGN NW11 ...52 D3
NTHWD HA6 ...32 E7
YEAD UB4 ...82 E5
Addle Hl BLKFR EC4V ...12 D6
Addle St CITYW * EC2V ...12 F4
Adecroft Wy E/WMO/HCT KT8 ...157 H2
Adela Av NWMAL KT3 ...160 E4
Adelaide Av BROCKY SE4 ...132 D3
Adelaide Cl STAN HA7 ...35 G3
Adelaide Ct HNWL W7 ...104 A1
Adelaide Gdns CHDH RM6 ...62 A4
Adelaide Gv SHB W12 ...87 J7
Adelaide Rd CHST BR7 ...154 B4
HAMP NW3 ...3 G2
HEST TW5 ...102 D7
IL IG1 ...78 B1
LEY E10 ...76 A2
NWDGN UB2 ...102 D3
RCH/KEW TW9 ...125 G3
SURB KT6 ...159 F4
TEDD TW11 ...143 F5
WAND/EARL SW18 ...127 K4
WEA W13 ...104 B1
Adelaide St CHCR * WC2N ...11 J7
Adelaide Ter BTFD * TW8 ...104 E4
Adela St NKENS W10 ...88 C3
Adelina Gv WCHPL E1 ...92 E4
Adelina Ms BAL SW12 ...129 J7
Adeline Pl RSQ WC1B ...11 H3
Adeliza Cl BARK IG11 ...78 C6
Adelphi Crs HCH RM12 ...81 J1
YEAD UB4 ...82 C2
Adelphi Ter CHCR WC2N ...11 K7
Adelphi Wy YEAD UB4 ...82 D2
Adeney Cl HMSMTH W6 ...107 G5
Aden Gv STNW/STAM N16 ...73 K3
Adenmore Rd CAT SE6 ...132 D6
Aden Rd IL IG1 ...60 B6
PEND EN3 ...31 G3
Adhara Rd NTHWD HA6 ...32 D4
Adie Rd HMSMTH W6 ...107 F2
Adine Rd PLSTW E13 ...94 E3
Adler St WCHPL E1 ...92 C4
Adley St HOM E9 ...75 G4
Adlington Cl UED N18 ...41 K4
Admaston Rd
WOOL/PLUM SE18 ...115 H6
Admiral Ms NKENS W10 ...88 B3
Admiral Pl BERM/RHTH SE16 ...93 G7
Admirals Cl SWFD E18 ...59 F3
Admiral Seymour Rd
ELTH/MOT SE9 ...134 E3
Admiral's Ga GNWCH SE10 ...112 E7
Admiral Sq WBPTN * SW10 ...108 B7
Admiral St DEPT SE8 ...112 D7
Admiral's Wk HAMP NW3 ...71 G2
Admirals Wy POP/IOD E14 ...112 E1
Admiralty Rd TEDD TW11 ...143 F6
Admiral Wk MV/WKIL W9 ...8 B2
Adnams Wk RAIN RM13 ...81 J4
Adolf St CAT SE6 ...151 J3
Adolphus Rd FSBYPK N4 ...73 H1
Adolphus St DEPT SE8 ...112 C6
Adomar Rd BCTR RM8 ...79 K2
Adpar St BAY/PAD W2 ...9 G2
Adrian Ms WBPTN SW10 ...14 D9
Adrienne Av STHL UB1 ...83 K3
Advance Rd WNWD SE27 ...149 J3
Advent Wy UED N18 ...43 F4
Adys Lawn CRICK * NW2 ...69 K5
Adys Rd PECK SE15 ...131 G2
Aerodrome Rd CDALE/KGS NW9 ...51 H2
Aerodrome Wy HEST TW5 ...102 B5
Affleck St IS * N1 ...5 M6
Afghan Rd BTSEA SW11 ...128 D1
Aftab Ter WCHPL * E1 ...92 D3
Agamemnon Rd
KIL/WHAMP NW6 ...70 D4
Agar Cl SURB KT6 ...172 B1
Agar Gv CAMTN NW1 ...5 H1
Agar Pl CAMTN NW1 ...4 F2
Agar St CHCR WC2N ...11 J7
Agate Cl CAN/RD E16 ...95 H5
Agate Rd HMSMTH W6 ...107 F2
Agatha Cl WAP E1W ...92 D7
Agaton Rd ELTH/MOT SE9 ...154 C1
Agave Rd CRICK NW2 ...70 A3
Agdon St FSBYE EC1V ...6 C9
Agincourt Rd HAMP NW3 ...71 K3
Agnes Av IL IG1 ...78 A3
Agnes Cl EHAM E6 ...96 A6
Agnesfield Cl NFNCH/WDSP N12 ...39 J5
Agnes Gdns BCTR RM8 ...79 K3
Agnes Riley Gdns CLAP * SW4 ...129 H6
Agnes Rd ACT W3 ...106 C1
Agnes St POP/IOD E14 ...93 H5
Agnew Rd FSTH SE23 ...132 B6
Agricola Pl EN EN1 ...30 B4
Aidan Cl DAGW RM9 ...80 A3
Ailsa Av TWK TW1 ...124 B4
Ailsa Rd TWK TW1 ...124 C4
Ailsa St POP/IOD E14 ...94 A4
Ainger Rd HAMP NW3 ...3 M2
Ainsdale Cl ORP BR6 ...169 J7
Ainsdale Crs PIN HA5 ...48 A2
Ainsdale Dr STHWK SE1 ...111 H4
Ainsdale Rd EA W5 ...85 K3
OXHEY WD19 ...33 G2
Ainsley Av ROMW/RG RM7 ...62 E5
Ainsley Cl ED N9 ...30 A7
Ainsley St BETH E2 ...92 D2
Ainslie Wood Crs CHING E4 ...43 K4
Ainslie Wood Gdns CHING E4 ...43 K3
Ainslie Wood Rd CHING E4 ...43 J4
Ainsty St BERM/RHTH * SE16 ...111 K1
Ainsworth Cl CMBW * SE5 ...131 F1
CRICK NW2 ...69 J2
Ainsworth Rd CROY/NA CR0 ...164 C7
HOM E9 ...74 E6
Ainsworth Wy STJWD NW8 ...2 E3
Aintree Av EHAM E6 ...77 J7
Aintree Crs BARK/HLT IG6 ...60 C1
Aintree Rd GFD/PVL UB6 ...85 H1
Aintree St FUL/PGN SW6 ...107 H6
Airdrie Cl IS N1 ...5 L2
YEAD UB4 ...83 J4
Airedale Av CHSWK W4 ...106 C4
Airedale Av South
CHSWK * W4 ...106 C4
Airedale Rd BAL SW12 ...128 E6
EA W5 ...104 D2
Airfield Wy HCH RM12 ...81 K5
Airlie Gdns IL IG1 ...60 B7
KENS W8 ...8 A9
Air St REGST W1B ...10 F7
Airthrie Rd GDMY/SEVK IG3 ...61 H7
Aisgill Av WKENS W14 ...107 J4
Aisher Rd THMD SE28 ...97 J6
Aislibie Rd LEW SE13 ...133 H3
Aiten Pl HMSMTH W6 ...106 D3
Aitken Cl HACK E8 ...74 C7
MTCM CR4 ...162 E6
Aitken Rd BAR EN5 ...26 A4
CAT SE6 ...151 K1
Aitman Dr CHSWK * W4 ...105 H4
Ajax Av CDALE/KGS NW9 ...51 G2
Ajax Rd KIL/WHAMP NW6 ...70 D3
Akabusi Cl SNWD SE25 ...165 H5
Akehurst St PUT/ROE SW15 ...126 D5
Akenside Rd HAMP NW3 ...71 H4
Akerman Rd CMBW SE5 ...110 C7
SURB KT6 ...158 D5
Alabama St WOOL/PLUM SE18 ...115 J6
Alacross Rd EA W5 ...104 D1
Alan Cl DART DA1 ...139 F3
Alandale Dr PIN HA5 ...33 F7
Alan Dr BAR EN5 ...26 C5
Alan Gdns ROMW/RG RM7 ...62 C6
Alan Hocken Wy SRTFD E15 ...94 C1
Alan Rd WIM/MER SW19 ...146 C4
Alanthus Cl LEE/GVPK SE12 ...133 J5
Alaska St STHWK SE1 ...12 A9
Alba Cl YEAD UB4 ...83 H3
Albacore Crs LEW SE13 ...132 E5
Alba Gdns GLDGN NW11 ...52 C5
The Albany KUTN/CMB KT2 ...143 K5
Albany Cl BUSH WD23 ...22 D5
BXLY DA5 ...136 D6
ESH/CLAY KT10 ...170 A7
MORT/ESHN SW14 ...125 J3
SEVS/STOTM N15 ...55 H3
Albany Cottages HNWL * W7 ...84 E7
Albany Ctyd MYFR/PICC * W1J ...10 F7
Albany Crs EDGW HA8 ...36 C6
ESH/CLAY KT10 ...170 E5
Albany Ms BMLY BR1 ...152 E5
IS N1 ...6 B1
KUTN/CMB * KT2 ...143 K5
SUT SM1 ...175 F4
WALW SE17 ...110 D5
Albany Pde BTFD * TW8 ...105 F5
Albany Park Rd
KUTN/CMB KT2 ...143 K5
Albany Pl BTFD TW8 ...104 E5
HOLWY N7 ...73 G3
Albany Rd BELV DA17 ...117 G5
BTFD TW8 ...104 E5
BXLY DA5 ...136 D6
CHDH RM6 ...62 B5
CHST BR7 ...154 B4
CMBW SE5 ...19 H9
FSBYPK N4 ...55 F5
HCH RM12 ...63 J7
MNPK E12 ...77 H3
NWMAL KT3 ...160 A3
RCHPK/HAM * TW10 ...125 G4
UED N18 ...42 D4
WALTH E17 ...57 G5
WEA W13 ...85 H6
WIM/MER SW19 ...147 F4
Albany Rw EFNCH * N2 ...53 J3
Albany St CAMTN NW1 ...4 D7
Albany Ter
RCHPK/HAM * TW10 ...125 G4
Alba Pl NTGHL W11 ...88 D5
Albatross St WOOL/PLUM SE18 ...115 K6
Albemarle Ap GNTH/NBYPK IG2 ...60 B5
Albemarle Av WHTN TW2 ...122 E7
Albemarle Gdns
GNTH/NBYPK IG2 ...60 B5
NWMAL KT3 ...160 A3
Albemarle Pk BECK * BR3 ...151 K7
STAN * HA7 ...35 J4
Albemarle Rd BECK BR3 ...151 K7
EBAR EN4 ...27 J6
Albemarle St CONDST W1S ...10 E7
Albemarle Wy FARR EC1M ...12 C1
Alberon Gdns GLDGN NW11 ...52 D3
Alberta Av SUT SM1 ...174 C3
Alberta Est WALW SE17 ...18 D7
Alberta Rd BXLYHN DA7 ...117 K7
EN EN1 ...30 B5
Alberta St WALW SE17 ...18 D7
Albert Av CHING E4 ...43 J3
VX/NE SW8 ...110 A6
Albert Br BTSEA SW11 ...108 D6
Albert Bridge Ga BTSEA SW11 ...108 E6
Albert Bridge Rd BTSEA SW11 ...108 D6
Albert Carr Gdns
STRHM/NOR SW16 ...148 E4
Albert Cl HOM E9 ...74 D7
WDGN N22 ...40 D7
Albert Cottages WCHPL * E1 ...92 C4
Albert Crs CHING E4 ...43 J3
Albert Dr WIM/MER SW19 ...146 C1
Albert Emb LBTH SE11 ...17 K7
Albert Gdns WCHPL E1 ...93 F5
Albert Ga KTBR SW1X ...15 M1
Albert Gv WIM/MER SW19 ...146 B7
Albert Ms BROCKY * SE4 ...132 C3
FSBYPK * N4 ...55 F7
KENS W8 ...14 E3
POP/IOD * E14 ...93 G6
Albert Pl FNCH N3 ...38 E7
KENS W8 ...14 D2
Albert Rd BCTR RM8 ...62 B7
BELMT SM2 ...175 H4
BELV DA17 ...117 G4
BKHH IG9 ...45 H1
BXLY DA5 ...137 H5
CAN/RD E16 ...95 J7
EA W5 ...85 H3
EBAR EN4 ...27 G3
ELTH/MOT SE9 ...153 J2
FSBYPK N4 ...55 F7
HAYES BR2 ...168 C4
HDN NW4 ...52 B3
HPTN TW12 ...142 C4
HSLW TW3 ...123 F3
HYS/HAR UB3 ...101 H2
IL IG1 ...78 C2
KIL/WHAMP NW6 ...88 D1
KUT KT1 ...159 G1
LEY E10 ...76 A1
MLHL NW7 ...37 H4
MTCM CR4 ...162 E2
NWDGN UB2 ...102 C2
NWMAL KT3 ...160 C3
PGE/AN SE20 ...151 F6
RCHPK/HAM TW10 ...125 F4
ROM RM1 ...63 H5
RYLN/HDSTN HA2 ...48 C2
SEVS/STOTM N15 ...56 A5
SNWD SE25 ...165 J3
SWFD E18 ...59 F2
TEDD TW11 ...143 F5
TWK TW1 ...124 A7
WALTH E17 ...57 J4
WDGN N22 ...40 D7
Albert Rd North WAT * WD17 ...21 F2
Albert Rd South WATW * WD18 ...21 F2
Albert Sq SRTFD E15 ...76 C4
VX/NE SW8 ...110 A6
Albert St CAMTN NW1 ...4 D4
NFNCH/WDSP N12 ...39 G4
Albert Ter CAMTN NW1 ...4 A3
EA * W5 ...85 H3
WLSDN * NW10 ...69 F7
Albert Terrace Ms CAMTN NW1 ...4 A3
Albert Wy PECK SE15 ...111 J6
Albion Av MUSWH N10 ...40 A7
VX/NE SW8 ...129 J1
Albion Cl BAY/PAD W2 ...9 K6
ROMW/RG RM7 ...63 F5
Albion Dr HACK E8 ...7 M2
Albion Est BERM/RHTH * SE16 ...111 K1
Albion Gdns HMSMTH W6 ...106 E3
Albion Ga BAY/PAD W2 ...9 K6
Albion Gv STNW/STAM N16 ...74 A3
Albion Ms BAY/PAD W2 ...9 K5
IS * N1 ...6 A3
Albion Pl FARR EC1M ...12 C2
HMSMTH W6 ...106 E3
SNWD * SE25 ...165 H2
Albion Rd BELMT SM2 ...175 H5
BXLYHS DA6 ...137 G3
HSLW TW3 ...123 F3
HYS/HAR UB3 ...82 C5
KUTN/CMB KT2 ...144 E7
STNW/STAM N16 ...73 K4
TOTM N17 ...56 B1
WALTH E17 ...58 A2
WHTN TW2 ...123 K7
Albion Sq HACK E8 ...7 L2
Albion St BAY/PAD W2 ...9 K5
BERM/RHTH SE16 ...111 K1
CROY/NA CR0 ...164 C7
Albion Ter CHING * E4 ...31 K3
HACK E8 ...7 L2
Albion Villas Rd FSTH SE23 ...150 E2
Albion Wy LEW SE13 ...133 F3
STBT EC1A ...12 E3
WBLY HA9 ...68 C2
Albion Yd IS N1 ...5 K6
Albrighton Rd EDUL SE22 ...131 F2
Albury Av BELMT SM2 ...174 A7
BXLYHN DA7 ...137 F1
ISLW TW7 ...104 A6
Albury Cl HOR/WEW KT19 ...172 D7
HPTN TW12 ...142 A5
Albury Dr PIN HA5 ...33 G7
Albury Ms MNPK E12 ...59 G7
Albury Rd CHSGTN KT9 ...172 A4
Albury St DEPT SE8 ...112 D5
Albyfield BMLY BR1 ...168 E2
Albyn Rd DEPT SE8 ...112 D7
Alcester Crs CLPT E5 ...74 D1
Alcester Rd WLGTN SM6 ...176 B3
Alcock Cl WLGTN SM6 ...176 D6
Alcock Rd HEST TW5 ...102 C6
Alconbury Rd CLPT E5 ...74 C1
Alcorn Cl CHEAM SM3 ...174 E1
Alcott Cl HNWL W7 ...85 F4
Aldborough Rd DAGE RM10 ...80 E5
Aldborough Rd North
GNTH/NBYPK IG2 ...61 F4
Aldborough Rd South
GDMY/SEVK IG3 ...60 E7
Aldbourne Rd ACT W3 ...87 H7
Aldbridge St WALW SE17 ...19 K7
Aldburgh Ms MHST W1U ...10 B4
Aldbury Av WBLY HA9 ...68 D6
Aldbury Ms ED N9 ...29 K6
Aldebert Ter VX/NE SW8 ...110 A6
Aldeburgh Pl WFD IG8 ...44 E3
Aldeburgh St GNWCH SE10 ...113 K4
Alden Av SRTFD E15 ...94 D2
Aldenham Rd GSTN WD25 ...23 F1
OXHEY WD19 ...21 H5
Aldenham St CAMTN NW1 ...4 F6
Alden Md PIN * HA5 ...34 A6

Aldensley Rd HMSMTH W6 106 E2
Alderbrook Rd BAL SW12 129 G5
Alderbury Rd BARN SW13 106 D5
Alder Cl PECK SE15 111 G5
Alder Gv CRICK NW2 69 J1
Alderholt Wy PECK * SE15 111 F6
Alderman Av BARK IG11 97 G2
Aldermanbury CITYW * EC2V 12 F4
Aldermanbury Sq CITYW EC2V 12 F3
Alderman Cl DART DA1 138 B6
Alderman Judge Ml KUT * KT1 159 F1
Alderman's Hl PLMGR N13 40 E3
Aldermary Rd BMLY BR1 152 E7
Aldermoor Rd CAT SE6 151 H2
Alderney Av HEST TW5 103 G6
Alderney Gdns NTHLT UB5 65 K6
Alderney Ms STHWK SE1 19 G3
Alderney Rd ERITH DA8 118 D6
WCHPL E1 93 F3
Alderney St PIM SW1V 16 C6
Alder Rd MORT/ESHN SW14 126 A2
SCUP DA14 154 E2
Alders Av WFD IG8 44 C5
Aldersbrook Av EN EN1 30 A1
Aldersbrook Dr KUTN/CMB KT2 144 B5
Aldersbrook La MNPK E12 77 K2
Aldersbrook Rd MNPK E12 77 G1
Alders Cl EA W5 104 E2
EDGW HA8 36 E4
WAN E11 77 F1
Aldersey Gdns BARK IG11 78 D5
The Alders FELT TW13 141 J4
NWDGN UB2 102 E5
STRHM/NOR * SW16 148 C3
WCHMH N21 29 G5
WWKM BR4 166 E7
Aldersford Cl BROCKY SE4 132 A3
Aldersgate St STBT EC1A 12 E4
Aldersgrove E/WMO/HCT KT8 157 J4
Aldersgrove Av ELTH/MOT SE9 153 G2
Aldershot Rd KIL/WHAMP NW6 70 D7
Aldershot Ter
WOOL/PLUM * SE18 115 F6
Aldersmead Av CROY/NA CR0 166 A5
Aldersmead Rd BECK BR3 151 G6
Alderson Pl NWDGN UB2 84 C7
Alderson St NKENS W10 88 C3
Alders Rd EDGW HA8 36 E4
Alderton Cl WLSDN NW10 69 F1
Alderton Crs HDN NW4 51 K4
Alderton Rd CROY/NA CR0 165 G6
HNHL SE24 130 D2
Alderton Wy HDN NW4 51 K4
Alderville Rd FUL/PGN SW6 127 J1
Alderwick Dr HSLW TW3 123 J2
Alderwood Rd ELTH/MOT SE9 135 J5
Aldford St MYFR/PKLN W1K 10 A8
Aldgate FENCHST EC3M 13 K5
Aldgate Barrs WCHPL * E1 13 M4
Aldgate High St TWRH EC3N 13 L5
Aldine St SHB W12 107 F1
Aldingham Gdns HCH RM12 81 J4
Aldington Cl CHDH RM6 61 J6
Aldington Rd
WOOL/PLUM SE18 114 C2
Aldis Ms TOOT SW17 147 J4
Aldis St TOOT SW17 147 J4
Aldred Rd KIL/WHAMP NW6 70 E4
Aldren Rd TOOT SW17 147 G2
Aldrich Crs CROY/NA CR0 180 A7
Aldriche Wy CHING E4 44 A5
Aldrich Gdns CHEAM SM3 174 D2
Aldrich Ter WAND/EARL SW18 147 G1
Aldridge Av EDGW HA8 36 D2
RSLP HA4 65 G1
STAN HA7 36 A7
Aldridge Ri NWMAL KT3 160 B6
Aldridge Road Vls NTGHL W11 88 D4
Aldridge Wk STHGT/OAK N14 28 E6
Aldrington Rd
STRHM/NOR SW16 148 C4
Aldsworth Cl MV/WKIL W9 8 C1
Aldwick Cl CHST BR7 154 D2
Aldwick Rd CROY/NA CR0 177 F2
Aldworth Gv LEW SE13 133 F5
Aldworth Rd SRTFD E15 76 C6
Aldwych TPL/STR WC2R 11 L6
Aldwych Av BARK/HLT IG6 60 C3
Aldwych Cl HCH RM12 81 J1
Alers Rd BXLYHS DA6 136 E4
Alesia Cl WDGN N22 40 E6
Alestan Beck Rd CAN/RD E16 95 H5
Alexander Av WLSDN NW10 69 K6
Alexander Cl BFN/LL DA15 135 K4
EBAR EN4 27 H3
HAYES BR2 167 K7
NWDGN UB2 84 C7
WHTN TW2 142 E1
Alexander Evans Ms
FSTH SE23 151 F1
Alexander Ms BAY/PAD W2 8 C4
Alexander Pl SKENS SW7 15 J5
Alexander Rd ARCH N19 72 E2
BXLYHN DA7 136 E1
CHST BR7 154 B5
Alexander Sq CHEL SW3 15 J5
Alexander St BAY/PAD W2 8 B4
Alexander Ter ABYW * SE2 116 C4
Alexandra Av BTSEA * SW11 109 F7
RYLN/HDSTN HA2 47 K7
STHL UB1 83 K6
SUT SM1 174 E2
WDGN N22 40 D7
Alexandra Cl ASHF TW15 140 B6
RYLN/HDSTN HA2 66 A2
Alexandra Cottages
NWCR * SE14 112 C7
Alexandra Ct ASHF TW15 140 B5
Alexandra Crs BMLY BR1 152 D5
Alexandra Dr BRYLDS KT5 159 H6
NRWD SE19 150 A4
Alexandra Gdns CAR SM5 176 A7
HSLW TW3 123 G1
MUSWH N10 54 B3
Alexandra Ga SKENS SW7 15 G1
Alexandra Gv FSBYPK N4 55 H7
NFNCH/WDSP N12 39 F4
Alexandra Ms EFNCH N2 53 K2
WAT WD17 20 E1
Alexandra Palace Wy
CEND/HSY/T N8 54 C3
Alexandra Pde
RYLN/HDSTN * HA2 66 B3
Alexandra Park Rd MUSWH N10 54 B1
Alexandra Pl CROY/NA CR0 165 F7
SNWD SE25 164 E4
STJWD NW8 2 F3
Alexandra Rd ASHF TW15 140 B6
BTFD * TW8 104 E5
CEND/HSY/T N8 55 G2
CHDH RM6 61 K5
CHSWK W4 106 A1
CROY/NA CR0 165 F7
ED * N9 30 D6
EHAM E6 96 A2
ERITH DA8 118 C5
HDN NW4 52 B3
HSLW TW3 123 G1
KUTN/CMB KT2 144 C6
LEY E10 76 A2
MORT/ESHN SW14 126 A2
MUSWH N10 40 B7
PEND EN3 31 F3
RAIN RM13 81 H7
RCH/KEW TW9 125 G1
ROM RM1 63 H5
SEVS/STOTM N15 55 K4
STJWD NW8 2 F3
SWFD E18 59 F2
SYD SE26 151 F5
THDIT KT7 158 A4
TWK TW1 124 D5
WALTH E17 57 H5
WAT WD17 20 E1
WIM/MER SW19 146 E4
WIM/MER SW19 147 J6
Alexandra Sq MRDN SM4 161 K4
Alexandra St CAN/RD E16 94 E4
NWCR SE14 112 B6
Alexandria Rd WEA W13 85 G6
Alexis St BERM/RHTH SE16 111 H3
Alfearn Rd CLPT E5 74 E3
Alford Gn CROY/NA CR0 180 B5
Alford Pl IS * N1 6 F6
Alford Rd ERITH DA8 117 K4
Alfoxton Av SEVS/STOTM N15 55 H3
Alfreda St BTSEA SW11 109 G7
Alfred Cl CHSWK W4 106 A3
Alfred Gdns STHL UB1 83 J6
Alfred Ms FITZ W1T 11 G2
Alfred Pl FITZ W1T 11 G2
Alfred Rd ACT W3 86 E7
BAY/PAD W2 8 B2
BELV DA17 117 G4
BKHH IG9 45 H1
FELT TW13 122 B7
KUT KT1 159 F2
SNWD SE25 165 H4
SRTFD E15 76 D4
SUT SM1 175 G4
Alfred's Gdns BARK IG11 96 E1
Alfred St BOW E3 93 H2
Alfred's Wy
(East Ham & Barking By-Pass)
BARK IG11 96 E1
Alfred Vls WALTH * E17 58 A3
Alfreton Cl WIM/MER SW19 146 B2
Alfriston BRYLDS KT5 159 G5
Alfriston Av CROY/NA CR0 163 K6
RYLN/HDSTN HA2 48 A5
Alfriston Cl BRYLDS KT5 159 G5
DART DA1 138 B5
Alfriston Rd CLAP SW4 128 E4
Algar Cl STAN HA7 35 F4
Algar Rd ISLW TW7 124 B2
Algarve Rd WAND/EARL SW18 128 A7
Algernon Rd HDN NW4 51 J5
KIL/WHAMP NW6 2 A4
LEW SE13 132 E3
Algiers Rd LEW SE13 132 D3
Alguin Ct STAN * HA7 35 J5
Alibon Gdns DAGE RM10 80 C4
Alibon Rd DAGE RM10 80 C4
Alice La BOW E3 75 H7
Alice Ms TEDD TW11 143 F4
Alice St STHWK SE1 19 J4
Alice Thompson Cl
LEE/GVPK SE12 153 G1
Alice Walker Cl HNHL * SE24 130 C3
Alice Wy HSLW TW3 123 G3
Alicia Av KTN/HRWW/W HA3 49 H3
Alicia Cl KTN/HRWW/W HA3 49 J3
Alicia Gdns KTN/HRWW/W HA3 49 H3
Alie St WCHPL E1 13 M5
Alington Crs CDALE/KGS NW9 50 E7
Alington Gv WLGTN SM6 176 D7
Alison Cl CROY/NA CR0 166 A7
EHAM E6 96 A5
Aliwal Ms BTSEA * SW11 128 D3
Aliwal Rd BTSEA SW11 128 D3
Alkerden Rd CHSWK W4 106 B4
Alkham Rd STNW/STAM N16 74 B1
Allan Barclay Cl
STNW/STAM N16 56 B5
Allan Cl NWMAL KT3 160 A4
Allandale Av FNCH N3 52 C2
Allandale Rd EMPK RM11 63 H6
Allan Wy ACT W3 86 E4
Allard Crs BUSH WD23 34 C1
Allardyce St BRXN/ST SW9 130 A3
Allbrook Cl TEDD TW11 142 E4
Allcot Cl EBED/NFELT TW14 121 J7
Allcroft Rd KTTN NW5 72 A4
Allder Wy SAND/SEL CR2 177 H6
Allenby Av SAND/SEL CR2 177 J7
Allenby Cl GFD/PVL UB6 84 A2
Allenby Rd FSTH SE23 151 G2
STHL UB1 84 A5
Allen Cl MTCM CR4 148 B7
SUN TW16 141 F7
Allendale Av STHL UB1 84 A5
Allendale Cl CMBW SE5 130 E1
SYD SE26 151 F4
Allendale Rd GFD/PVL UB6 67 H5
Allen Edwards Dr VX/NE SW8 109 K7
Allen Rd BECK BR3 166 A1
BOW E3 93 H1
CROY/NA CR0 164 A6
STNW/STAM N16 74 A3
SUN TW16 141 F7
Allensbury Pl CAMTN NW1 5 H2
Allens Rd PEND EN3 30 E4
Allen St KENS W8 14 B3
Allenswood Rd ELTH/MOT SE9 134 D2
Allerford Rd CAT SE6 151 K3
Allerton Rd STNW/STAM N16 73 J1
Allestree Rd FUL/PGN SW6 107 H6
Alleyn Crs DUL SE21 149 K1
Alleyndale Rd BCTR RM8 79 J1
Alleyn Pk DUL SE21 149 K1
NWDGN UB2 102 E4
Alleyn Rd DUL SE21 149 K2
Allfarthing La
WAND/EARL SW18 128 B5
Allgood Cl MRDN SM4 161 G5
Allgood St BETH E2 7 M6
Allhallows La CANST EC4R 13 G7
Allhallows Rd EHAM E6 95 J5
All Hallows Rd TOTM N17 42 A7
Alliance Cl ALP/SUD HA0 67 K3
Alliance Rd ACT W3 86 D3
PLSTW E13 95 G3
WOOL/PLUM SE18 116 B5
Allied Wy ACT * W3 106 B1
Allingham Cl HNWL W7 85 F6
Allington Av TOTM N17 42 A5
Allington Cl GFD/PVL UB6 66 C6
WIM/MER SW19 146 B4
Allington Rd HDN NW4 51 K4
NKENS W10 88 C2
ORP BR6 169 K7
RYLN/HDSTN HA2 48 C4
Allington St WESTW SW1E 16 E4
Allison Cl GNWCH SE10 113 F7
Allison Gv DUL SE21 131 F7
Allison Rd ACT W3 86 E5
CEND/HSY/T N8 55 G4
Allitsen Rd STJWD NW8 3 J6
Allitson Rd STJWD NW8 3 J6
Allnutt Wy CLAP SW4 129 J4
Alloa Rd DEPT SE8 112 A4
GDMY/SEVK IG3 79 H1
Allonby Gdns WBLY HA9 49 J7
Alloway Rd BOW E3 93 G2
Allport Ms WCHPL * E1 92 E4
All Saints' Cl ED N9 42 B1
All Saints Dr BKHTH/KID SE3 133 J1
All Saints Ms
KTN/HRWW/W HA3 34 E5
All Saints Pas
WAND/EARL * SW18 127 K4
All Saints' Rd ACT W3 105 K1
NTGHL W11 88 D4
SUT SM1 175 F2
WIM/MER SW19 147 G6
All Saints St IS N1 5 L5
Allsop Pl CAMTN NW1 9 M1
All Souls' Av WLSDN NW10 87 K1
All Souls' Pl REGST W1B 10 D3
Allum La BORE WD6 24 A4
Allum Wy TRDG/WHET N20 27 G7
Allwood Cl SYD SE26 151 F3
Alma Av CHING E4 44 A6
Almack Rd CLPT E5 74 E3
Alma Cl MUSWH * N10 40 B7
Alma Ct RYLN/HDSTN * HA2 66 D1
Alma Crs SUT SM1 174 C4
Alma Gv STHWK SE1 19 M6
Alma Pl NRWD SE19 150 B6
THHTH CR7 164 B4
WLSDN NW10 87 K2
Alma Rd CAR SM5 175 J4
ESH/CLAY KT10 157 K7
MUSWH N10 40 A6
PEND EN3 31 G4
SCUP DA14 155 G2
STHL UB1 83 J6
WAND/EARL SW18 128 B4
Alma Rw KTN/HRWW/W * HA3 34 D7
Alma Sq STJWD NW8 2 F7
Alma St KTTN NW5 72 B5
SRTFD E15 76 B5
Alma Ter BOW E3 75 H7
KENS W8 14 B4
WAND/EARL SW18 128 C6
Almeida St IS N1 6 C3
Almeric Rd BTSEA SW11 128 E3
Almer Rd RYNPK SW20 145 J6
Almington St FSBYPK * N4 54 E7
Almond Av CAR SM5 175 K1
EA W5 105 F2
WDR/YW UB7 100 D2
Almond Cl HAYES BR2 169 F6
HYS/HAR UB3 82 C6
RSLP HA4 64 D2
Almond Gv BTFD TW8 104 C6
Almond Rd BERM/RHTH SE16 111 J3
TOTM N17 42 C6
Almonds Av BKHH IG9 44 E1
Almond Wy BORE WD6 24 D3
HAYES BR2 169 F6
MTCM CR4 163 J4
RYLN/HDSTN HA2 48 C1
Almorah Rd HEST TW5 102 C7
IS N1 7 G2
Almshouse La CHSGTN KT9 171 J7
Alnwick Gv MRDN SM4 162 A3
Alnwick Rd CAN/RD E16 95 G5
LEE/GVPK SE12 134 A6
Alperton La ALP/SUD HA0 85 K2
Alperton St NKENS W10 88 C3
Alphabet Gdns CAR SM5 162 C5
Alpha Cl CAMTN NW1 3 K9
Alpha Est HYS/HAR * UB3 101 H1
Alpha Gv POP/IOD E14 112 D1
Alpha Pl CHEL SW3 15 K9
KIL/WHAMP NW6 2 B5
MRDN * SM4 161 G6
Alpha Rd BRYLDS KT5 159 G5
CHING E4 43 J2
CROY/NA CR0 165 F7
HPTN TW12 142 D4
NWCR SE14 112 C7
PEND EN3 31 G3
UED N18 42 C5
Alpha St PECK SE15 131 H1
Alphea Cl WIM/MER SW19 147 J6
Alpine Av BRYLDS KT5 172 E1
Alpine Cl CROY/NA CR0 178 A2
Alpine Copse BMLY BR1 169 F1
Alpine Gv HOM * E9 74 E6
Alpine Rd BERM/RHTH SE16 111 K3
Alpine Vw SUT SM1 175 J4
Alpine Wk BUSH WD23 34 E1
Alpine Wy EHAM E6 96 A4
Alric Av NWMAL KT3 160 B2
WLSDN NW10 69 F6
Alroy Rd FSBYPK N4 55 G6
Alsace Rd WALW SE17 19 J7
Alscot Rd BERM/RHTH SE16 19 M4
Alscot Wy STHWK SE1 19 L5
Alsike Rd BELV DA17 116 E3
Alsom Av HOR/WEW KT19 173 H3
Alston Cl THDIT KT7 158 C6
Alston Rd BAR EN5 26 C2
TOOT SW17 147 H3
UED N18 42 D4
Altair Cl UED N18 42 B5
Altair Wy NTHWD HA6 32 D4
Altash Wy ELTH/MOT SE9 153 K1
Altenburg Av WEA W13 104 C2
Altenburg Gdns BTSEA SW11 128 E3
Alt Gv WIM/MER SW19 146 D6
Altham Ct RYLN/HDSTN * HA2 34 B7
Altham Rd PIN HA5 33 J6
Althea St FUL/PGN SW6 128 A1
Althorne Gdns SWFD E18 58 D3
Althorne Wy DAGE RM10 80 C1
Althorp Cl TRDG/WHET N20 25 J6
Althorpe Rd HRW * HA1 48 C4
Althorp Rd TOOT SW17 128 E7
Altmore Av EHAM E6 77 K6
Alton Av STAN HA7 35 F6
Alton Cl BXLY DA5 137 F7
ISLW TW7 124 A1
Alton Gdns BECK BR3 151 J6
WHTN TW2 123 J5
Alton Rd CROY/NA CR0 177 G3
PUT/ROE SW15 126 D7
RCH/KEW TW9 125 F3
TOTM N17 55 K2
Alton St POP/IOD E14 93 K4
Altyre Cl BECK BR3 166 C4
Altyre Rd CROY/NA CR0 177 K1
Altyre Wy BECK BR3 166 C4
Alvanley Gdns HAMP NW3 71 F4
Alva Wy OXHEY WD19 33 H1
Alverstone Av EBAR EN4 27 H6
WAND/EARL SW18 146 E1
Alverstone Gdns
ELTH/MOT SE9 135 G7
Alverstone Rd CRICK NW2 70 A6
MNPK E12 78 A3
NWMAL KT3 160 C3
WBLY HA9 50 B7
Alverston Gdns SNWD SE25 165 F4
Alverton St DEPT SE8 112 C4
Alveston Av KTN/HRWW/W HA3 49 H2
Alvey St WALW SE17 19 J7
Alvia Gdns SUT SM1 175 G3
Alvington Crs HACK E8 74 B4
Alway Av HOR/WEW KT19 172 E4
Alwin Pl WATW WD18 20 C3
Alwold Crs LEE/GVPK SE12 134 B5
Alwyn Av CHSWK W4 106 A4
Alwyn Cl BORE WD6 24 B5
CROY/NA CR0 179 K6
Alwyne La IS N1 6 D1
Alwyne Pl IS N1 6 E1
Alwyne Rd HNWL W7 84 E6
IS N1 6 E1
WIM/MER SW19 146 D5
Alwyne Sq IS N1 73 J5
Alwyne Vls IS N1 6 D1
Alwyn Gdns ACT W3 86 D5
Alyn Bank CEND/HSY/T * N8 54 D5
Alyth Gdns GLDGN NW11 52 D5
Amalgamated Dr BTFD TW8 104 B5
Amanda Ms ROMW/RG RM7 62 E4
Amar Ct WOOL/PLUM SE18 116 A3
Amardeep Ct
WOOL/PLUM SE18 116 A4
Amazon St WCHPL E1 92 D5
Ambassador Cl HSLW TW3 122 D1
Ambassador Gdns EHAM E6 95 K4
Ambassador Sq POP/IOD E14 112 E3
Amber Av WALTH E17 43 G7
Amberden Av FNCH N3 52 E2
Ambergate St WALW SE17 18 C7
Amber Gv CRICK NW2 52 B7
Amberley Cl PIN HA5 47 K2
Amberley Ct SCUP DA14 155 J4
Amberley Gdns
HOR/WEW KT19 173 H3
Amberley Gv CROY/NA CR0 165 G6
SYD SE26 150 D3
Amberley Rd ABYW SE2 116 E5
EN EN1 30 B6
LEY E10 57 J6
MV/WKIL W9 8 B2
PLMGR N13 41 F1
Amberley Wy HSLWW TW4 122 B4
MRDN SM4 161 J6
ROMW/RG RM7 62 D3
Amberside Cl ISLW TW7 123 J5
Amber St SRTFD * E15 76 B5
Amberwood Cl WLGTN SM6 176 E4
Amberwood Ri NWMAL KT3 160 B5
Amblecote Cl LEE/GVPK SE12 153 F2
Amblecote Meadow
LEE/GVPK SE12 153 F2
Amblecote Rd LEE/GVPK SE12 153 F2
Ambler Rd FSBYPK N4 73 H2
Ambleside BMLY BR1 152 B5
Ambleside Av BECK BR3 166 B4
HCH RM12 81 K4
STRHM/NOR SW16 148 D3
WOT/HER KT12 156 B7
Ambleside Cl LEY E10 57 K6
Ambleside Crs PEND EN3 31 F2
Ambleside Dr
EBED/NFELT TW14 121 J7
Ambleside Gdns BELMT SM2 175 G5
REDBR IG4 59 J3
WBLY HA9 49 K7
Ambleside Rd BXLYHN DA7 137 H1
WLSDN NW10 69 H6
Ambrey Wy WLGTN SM6 176 D7
Ambrook Rd BELV DA17 117 H2
Ambrosden Av WEST SW1P 16 F4
Ambrose Av GLDGN NW11 52 D5
Ambrose Cl DART DA1 138 C3
Ambrose St BERM/RHTH SE16 111 J3
Amelia Cl ACT W3 86 D7
Amelia St WALW SE17 18 D7
Amen Cnr STP EC4M 12 D5
Amen Ct STP EC4M 12 D5
America Sq TWRH * EC3N 13 L6
America St STHWK SE1 12 E9
Ameriand Rd
WAND/EARL SW18 127 J5
Amersham Av UED N18 41 K5
Amersham Gv NWCR SE14 112 C6
Amersham Rd CROY/NA CR0 164 D5
NWCR SE14 112 C7
Amersham V NWCR SE14 112 C6
Amery Gdns WLSDN NW10 69 K7
Amery Rd HRW HA1 67 G1
Amesbury Av
BRXS/STRHM SW2 148 E1
Amesbury Cl WPK KT4 161 F7
Amesbury Dr CHING E4 31 K5
Amesbury Rd BMLY BR1 168 C2
DAGW RM9 79 K6
FELT TW13 141 H1
Ames Cottages POP/IOD * E14 93 G4
Amethyst Rd WAN E11 76 B3
Amherst Av WEA W13 85 J5
Amherst Gdns WEA * W13 85 J5
Amherst Rd WEA W13 85 J5
Amhurst Gdns ISLW TW7 104 A7
Amhurst Pde STNW/STAM * N16 56 B6
Amhurst Pk STNW/STAM N16 56 A6
Amhurst Rd STNW/STAM N16 74 B2
STNW/STAM N16 74 B3
Amhurst Ter HACK E8 74 C3
Amidas Gdns BCTR RM8 79 H3
Amiel St WCHPL E1 92 E3
Amies St BTSEA SW11 128 E2
Amina Wy BERM/RHTH SE16 111 H2
Amis Av HOR/WEW KT19 172 C5
Amity Gv RYNPK SW20 146 A7
Amity Rd SRTFD E15 76 D6
Ammanford Gn
CDALE/KGS * NW9 51 G5
Amner Rd BTSEA SW11 129 F5
Amor Rd HMSMTH W6 107 F2
Amott Rd PECK SE15 131 H2
Ampere Wy CROY/NA CR0 163 K6
Ampleforth Rd ABYW SE2 116 C1
Ampthill Est CAMTN NW1 4 E6
Ampthill Sq CAMTN NW1 4 F6
Ampton St FSBYW WC1X 5 L8
Amroth Cl FSTH SE23 131 J7
Amroth Gn CDALE/KGS * NW9 51 G5
Amsterdam Rd POP/IOD E14 113 F2
Amwell Cl WCHMH N21 29 K4
Amwell St CLKNW EC1R 6 A7
Amyand Cottages TWK TW1 124 C5
Amyand Park Gdns TWK TW1 124 C6
Amyand Park Rd TWK TW1 124 B6
Amy Cl WLGTN SM6 176 E6
Amyruth Rd BROCKY SE4 132 D4
Amy Warne Cl EHAM E6 95 J4
Ancaster Crs NWMAL KT3 160 D5
Ancaster Rd BECK BR3 166 A2
Ancaster St WOOL/PLUM SE18 115 K6
Anchorage Cl WIM/MER SW19 146 E4
Anchor Cl BARK IG11 97 H2
Anchor Dr RAIN RM13 99 K2
Anchor & Hope La CHARL SE7 114 A2
Anchor St BERM/RHTH SE16 111 J3
Anchor Ter WCHPL * E1 92 E3
Anchor Yd FSBYE * EC1V 6 F9
Ancill Cl HMSMTH W6 107 G5
Ancona Rd WLSDN NW10 87 J1
WOOL/PLUM SE18 115 J4
Andace Park Gdns BMLY * BR1 153 G7
Andalus Rd BRXN/ST SW9 129 K2
Ander Cl ALP/SUD HA0 67 K3
Anderson Cl ACT W3 87 F5
CHEAM SM3 161 K7
WCHMH N21 29 F4
Anderson Dr ASHF TW15 140 A3
Anderson Rd HOM E9 75 F5
WFD IG8 59 H2
Anderson's Pl HSLW TW3 123 G3
Anderson Sq IS N1 6 C4
Anderson St CHEL SW3 15 L7
Anderson Wy BELV DA17 117 J1
Andover Av CAN/RD E16 95 H5
Andover Cl EBED/NFELT TW14 121 J7
GFD/PVL UB6 84 B3
Andover Pl KIL/WHAMP NW6 2 C6
Andover Rd HOLWY N7 73 F1
ORP BR6 169 K7
WHTN TW2 123 J7
Andover Ter HMSMTH * W6 106 E3
Andre St HACK E8 74 C4
Andrew Borde St
LSQ/SEVD * WC2H 11 H4
Andrew Cl DART DA1 138 A4
Andrewes Gdns EHAM E6 95 J5
Andrew Pl VX/NE SW8 109 J7
Andrews Cl BKHH IG9 45 G1
HRW HA1 48 D6
WPK KT4 174 B1
Andrews Rd HACK E8 74 D7
Andrew St POP/IOD E14 94 A5
Andrews Wk WALW SE17 110 C5
Andwell Cl ABYW SE2 116 C1
Anerley Gv NRWD SE19 150 B6
Anerley Hl NRWD SE19 150 B5
Anerley Pk PGE/AN SE20 150 D6
Anerley Park Rd PGE/AN SE20 150 D6
Anerley Rd NRWD SE19 150 C6
Anerley Station Rd
PGE/AN SE20 150 D7
Anerley V NRWD SE19 150 B6
Anfield Cl BAL SW12 129 H6
Angel Cl UED N18 42 B4
Angel Corner Pde UED * N18 42 C4
Angel Ct LOTH EC2R 13 H4
Angelfield HSLW TW3 123 G4
Angel Hl SUT SM1 175 F2
Angel Hill Dr SUT SM1 175 F2
Angelica Dr EHAM E6 96 A4
Angelica Gdns CROY/NA CR0 166 A7
Angel La HYS/HAR UB3 82 B4
SRTFD E15 76 B5
Angell Park Gdns
BRXN/ST SW9 130 B2
Angell Rd BRXN/ST SW9 130 C2
Angell Town Est
BRXN/ST * SW9 130 B1
Angel Ms WCHPL E1 92 D6
Angel Pas CANST EC4R 13 G7
Angel Rd HRW HA1 48 E5
THDIT KT7 158 B7
Angel Rd (North Circular)
UED N18 42 C4
Angel Sq FSBYE * EC1V 6 C6
Angel St STBT EC1A 12 E4
Angel Wk HMSMTH W6 107 F3
Angel Wy ROM RM1 63 G4
Angerstein La BKHTH/KID SE3 113 J6
Anglers La KTTN NW5 72 B5
Anglers Reach SURB * KT6 158 E4
Anglesea Av WOOL/PLUM SE18 115 G3
Anglesea Rd KUT KT1 158 E3
WOOL/PLUM SE18 115 G3
Anglesey Court Rd CAR SM5 176 A5
Anglesey Dr RAIN RM13 99 J3
Anglesey Gdns CAR SM5 176 A5
Anglesey Rd OXHEY WD19 33 G4
PEND EN3 30 D3
Anglesmede Crs PIN HA5 48 A2
Anglesmede Wy PIN HA5 47 K2
Angles Rd STRHM/NOR SW16 148 E3
Anglia Cl TOTM N17 42 D6
Anglian Cl WATN WD24 21 G1
Anglian Rd WAN E11 76 B2
Anglo Rd BOW E3 93 H1
Angus Cl CHSGTN KT9 172 C4
Angus Dr RSLP HA4 65 G3
Angus Gdns CDALE/KGS NW9 37 F7
Angus Rd PLSTW E13 95 G2
Angus St NWCR SE14 112 B6
Anhalt Rd BTSEA SW11 108 D6
Ankerdine Crs
WOOL/PLUM SE18 115 G7
Anlaby Rd TEDD TW11 142 E4
Anley Rd HMSMTH W6 107 G1
Anmersh Gv STAN HA7 35 K7
Annabel Cl POP/IOD E14 93 K5
Anna Cl HACK E8 7 M3
Annandale Gv HGDN/ICK UB10 64 A2
Annandale Rd BFN/LL DA15 135 K6
CHSWK W4 106 B3
CROY/NA CR0 178 C1

GNWCH SE10 113 J5
Anna Neagle Cl FSTGT E7 76 E3
Anne Boleyn's Wk BELMT SM2 174 B6
KUTN/CMB KT2 144 A4
Anne Case Ms NWMAL * KT3 160 A2
Anne Compton Ms
LEE/GVPK SE12 133 J6
Anne of Cleves Rd DART DA1 139 G4
Annesley Av CDALE/KGS NW9 51 F2
Annesley Cl WLSDN NW10 69 G2
Annesley Dr CROY/NA CR0 179 H2
Annesley Rd BKHTH/KID SE3 114 A7
Anne St PLSTW E13 94 E3
Annette Cl KTN/HRWW/W HA3 48 E1
Annette Rd HOLWY N7 73 F3
Annexe Market WCHPL * E1 13 L2
Annie Besant Cl BOW * E3 75 H7
Anning St SDTCH EC2A 7 K9
Annington Rd EFNCH N2 53 K2
Annis Rd HOM E9 75 G5
Ann La WBPTN SW10 108 C6
Ann Moss Wy
BERM/RHTH SE16 111 K2
Ann's Cl KTBR SW1X 15 M2
Ann St WOOL/PLUM SE18 115 J4
Annsworthy Av THHTH CR7 164 E2
Ansar Gdns WALTH E17 57 G4
Ansdell Rd PECK SE15 131 K1
Ansdell St KENS W8 14 D3
Ansdell Ter KENS W8 14 D3
Ansell Gv CAR SM5 162 E7
Ansell Rd TOOT SW17 147 J2
Anselm Cl CROY/NA CR0 178 B2
Anselm Rd FUL/PGN SW6 107 K5
PIN HA5 33 K6
Ansford Rd BMLY BR1 152 A4
Ansleigh Pl NTGHL W11 88 B6
Anson Cl ROMW/RG RM7 62 D1
Anson Rd CRICK NW2 69 K4
HOLWY N7 72 C3
Anson Wk NTHWD HA6 32 A3
Anstead Dr RAIN RM13 99 J1
Anstey Rd PECK SE15 131 H2
Anstice Cl CHSWK W4 106 B6
Anstridge Rd ELTH/MOT SE9 135 J5
Antelope Rd WOOL/PLUM SE18 114 E2
Anthony Cl OXHEY WD19 21 H7
Anthony Rd BORE WD6 24 A1
GFD/PVL UB6 84 E1
SNWD SE25 165 H5
WELL DA16 116 B7
Anthony's Cl WAP E1W 92 C7
Anthony St WCHPL E1 92 D5
Anthus Ms NTHWD HA6 32 B6
Antill Rd BOW E3 93 G2
SEVS/STOTM N15 56 C3
Antill Ter WCHPL E1 93 F5
Antlers Hl CHING E4 31 K4
Anton Crs SUT SM1 174 E2
Antoneys Cl PIN HA5 47 H1
Anton St HACK E8 74 C4
Antrim Rd HAMP NW3 71 K5
Antrobus Cl SUT SM1 174 D4
Antrobus Rd CHSWK W4 105 K3
Anvil Cl STRHM/NOR SW16 148 C6
Anworth Cl WFD IG8 45 F5
Apeldoorn Dr WLGTN SM6 176 E7
Aperfield Rd ERITH DA8 118 C5
Apex Cl BECK BR3 151 K7
Apex Pde MLHL * NW7 37 F3
Aplin Wy ISLW TW7 103 K7
Apollo Av BMLY BR1 153 F7
NTHWD HA6 32 E4
Apollo Cl EMPK RM11 81 K1
Apollo Pl WAN E11 76 C2
WBPTN * SW10 108 C6
Apollo Wy WOOL/PLUM SE18 115 J2
Apothecary St BLKFR * EC4V 12 C5
Appach Rd BRXS/STRHM SW2 130 B4
Apple Blossom Ct VX/NE * SW8 109 J6
Appleby Cl CHING E4 44 A5
SEVS/STOTM N15 55 K4
WHTN TW2 142 D1
Appleby Gdns
EBED/NFELT * TW14 121 J7
Appleby Rd CAN/RD E16 94 E5
HACK E8 74 C6
Appleby St BETH E2 7 L5
Appledore Av BXLYHN DA7 117 K7
RSLP HA4 65 F2
Appledore Cl EDGW HA8 36 C7
HAYES BR2 167 J4
TOOT SW17 147 K1
Appledore Crs BFN/LL DA15 154 E2
Appleford Rd NKENS W10 88 C3
Apple Garth BTFD TW8 104 E3
Applegarth ESH/CLAY KT10 171 F4
Applegarth Dr GNTH/NBYPK IG2 61 F3
Applegarth Rd THMD SE28 97 H7
WKENS * W14 107 G2
Apple Gv CHSGTN KT9 172 A3
EN EN1 30 A2
Apple Ldg ALP/SUD * HA0 67 J2
Apple Market KUT KT1 158 E1
Apple Rd WAN E11 76 C2
Appleton Gdns NWMAL KT3 160 D5
Appleton Rd ELTH/MOT SE9 134 D2
Appletree Cl PGE/AN SE20 150 D7
Appletree Gdns EBAR EN4 27 J3
Apple Tree Yd STJS SW1Y 10 F8
Applewood Cl CRICK NW2 69 K2
TRDG/WHET N20 27 J7
Appold St ERITH DA8 118 C5
SDTCH EC2A 13 J2
Apprentice Wy CLPT E5 74 D3
The Approach ACT W3 87 F5
EN EN1 30 D1
HDN NW4 52 B4
Approach La MLHL NW7 38 C4
Approach Rd ASHF TW15 140 A5
BETH E2 92 E1
E/WMO/HCT KT8 157 F4
EBAR EN4 27 G3
RYNPK SW20 161 F1
Aprey Gdns HDN NW4 52 A3
April Cl FELT TW13 140 E2
HNWL W7 84 E6
April Gln FSTH SE23 151 F2
April St STNW/STAM N16 74 B3
Apsley Cl HRW HA1 48 C4
Apsley Rd NWMAL KT3 159 K2
SNWD SE25 165 J3
Apsley Wy CRICK NW2 69 J1
MYFR/PICC * W1J 10 C9
Aquarius TWK * TW1 124 C7
Aquarius Wy NTHWD HA6 32 E4
Aquila St STJWD NW8 3 H5
Aquinas St STHWK SE1 12 B9
Arabella Dr PUT/ROE SW15 126 B3
Arabin Rd BROCKY SE4 132 B3
Aragon Av EW KT17 173 K7
THDIT KT7 158 A4
Aragon Cl HAYES BR2 168 E7
SUN TW16 140 D6
Aragon Dr RSLP HA4 47 H7
Aragon Rd KUTN/CMB KT2 144 A4
MRDN SM4 161 G6
Arandora Crs CHDH RM6 61 H6
Arbery Rd BOW E3 93 G2
Arbor Cl BECK BR3 166 E1
Arborfield Cl
BRXS/STRHM SW2 130 A7
Arbor Rd CHING E4 44 B2
Arbour Rd PEND EN3 31 F3
Arbour Sq WCHPL E1 92 E5
Arbour Wy HCH RM12 81 K4
Arbroath Gn OXHEY WD19 32 E2
Arbroath Rd ELTH/MOT SE9 134 D2
Arbrook La ESH/CLAY KT10 170 D5
Arbuthnot La BXLY DA5 137 F5
Arbuthnot Rd NWCR SE14 132 A1
Arbutus St HACK E8 7 L3
The Arcade ELTH/MOT * SE9 135 F5
LVPST * EC2M 13 J3
WALTH * E17 57 J3
Arcade Chambers
ELTH/MOT * SE9 135 F5
Arcade Pde CHSGTN * KT9 172 A3
Arcade Pl ROM RM1 63 G4
Arcadia Av FNCH N3 38 E7
Arcadia Cl CAR SM5 176 A3
Arcadian Av BXLY DA5 137 F5
Arcadian Cl BXLY DA5 137 F5
Arcadian Gdns WDGN N22 41 G6
Arcadian Rd BXLY DA5 137 F6
Arcadia St POP/IOD E14 93 J5
Archangel St
BERM/RHTH SE16 112 A1
Archbishop's Pl
BRXS/STRHM SW2 130 A5
Archdale Ct SHB W12 87 K7
Archdale Pl NWMAL KT3 159 J2
Archdale Rd EDUL SE22 131 G4
Archel Rd WKENS W14 107 J5
Archer Cl KUTN/CMB KT2 144 A6
Archer Rd SNWD SE25 165 J3
Archers Dr PEND EN3 30 E1
Archer Sq DEPT SE8 112 B5
Archer St SOHO/SHAV W1D 11 G6
Archery Cl BAY/PAD W2 9 K5
KTN/HRWW/W HA3 49 F2
Archery Rd ELTH/MOT SE9 134 E4
The Arches CHCR * WC2N 11 K8
RYLN/HDSTN HA2 66 B1
Archibald Ms MYFR/PICC W1J 10 B7
Archibald Rd HOLWY N7 72 D3
Arch St STHWK SE1 18 E4
Archway Cl ARCH * N19 72 C1
CROY/NA * CR0 176 E2
NKENS W10 88 B4
WIM/MER SW19 147 F3
Archway Rd HGT N6 53 K4
Archway St BARN SW13 126 B2
Arcola St HACK E8 74 B4
Arctic St KTTN NW5 72 B4
Arcus Rd BMLY BR1 152 C5
Ardbeg Rd HNHL SE24 130 E5
Arden Cl BUSH WD23 23 F6
HRW HA1 66 D2
THMD SE28 97 K5
Arden Court Gdns EFNCH N2 53 H5
Arden Crs DAGW RM9 79 K6
POP/IOD E14 112 D3
Arden Est IS N1 7 J6
Arden Mhor PIN HA5 47 F3
Arden Rd FNCH N3 52 D2
WEA W13 85 J6
Ardent Cl SNWD SE25 165 F2
Ardfern Av STRHM/NOR SW16 164 B2
Ardfillan Rd CAT SE6 133 G7
Ardgowan Rd CAT SE6 133 H7
Ardilaun Rd HBRY N5 73 J3
Ardingly Cl CROY/NA CR0 179 F2
Ardleigh Gdns CHEAM SM3 161 K7
Ardleigh Rd IS N1 74 A5
WALTH E17 43 H7
Ardleigh Ter WALTH E17 43 H7
Ardley Cl FSTH SE23 151 G2
WLSDN NW10 69 G2
Ardlui Rd WNWD SE27 149 J1
Ardmay Gdns SURB * KT6 159 F4
Ardmere Rd LEW SE13 133 G5
Ardoch Rd CAT SE6 152 B1
Ardra Rd ED N9 43 F2
Ardrossan Gdns WPK KT4 173 J2
Ardross Av NTHWD HA6 32 C4
Ardshiel Cl PUT/ROE SW15 127 G2
Ardwell Av BARK/HLT IG6 60 C4
Ardwell Rd BRXS/STRHM SW2 148 E1
Ardwick Rd CRICK NW2 70 E3
The Arena STKPK * UB11 82 A7
Arena Est FSBYPK * N4 55 H5
Argall Av LEY E10 57 G6
Argall Wy LEY E10 57 F7
Argenta Wy WLSDN NW10 68 D6
Argent Ct SURB * KT6 172 C1
Argon Ms FUL/PGN SW6 107 K6
Argon Rd UED N18 43 F4
Argosy La STWL/WRAY TW19 120 A6
Argus Wy NTHLT UB5 83 J2
Argyle Av HSLW TW3 123 F5
Argyle Cl WEA W13 85 F3
Argyle Cnr WEA * W13 85 H6
Argyle Ct WATW * WD18 20 D3
Argyle Pl HMSMTH W6 106 E3
Argyle Rd BAR EN5 26 A3
CAN/RD E16 95 F5
GFD/PVL UB6 85 F2
HSLW TW3 123 G4
IL IG1 78 A1
NFNCH/WDSP N12 38 E4
RYLN/HDSTN HA2 48 B5
SRTFD E15 76 C3
TOTM N17 42 C7
UED N18 42 C3
WCHPL E1 93 F3
Argyle Sq STPAN WC1H 5 K7
Argyle St STPAN WC1H 5 K8
Argyle Wk STPAN * WC1H 5 J8
Argyle Wy STHWK SE1 111 H4
Argyll Av STHL UB1 84 B7
Argyll Cl BRXN/ST SW9 130 A2
Argyll Gdns EDGW HA8 50 D1
Argyll Rd KENS W8 14 A2
WOOL/PLUM SE18 115 H2
Argyll St REGST W1B 10 E5
Arica Rd BROCKY SE4 132 B3
Ariel Rd KIL/WHAMP NW6 70 E5
Ariel Wy HSLWW TW4 122 A2
SHB W12 88 A7
Aristotle Rd CLAP SW4 129 J2
Arkell Gv NRWD SE19 149 H6
Arkindale Rd CAT SE6 152 A2
Arkley Crs WALTH * E17 57 H4
Arkley Dr BAR EN5 25 J3
Arkley La BAR EN5 25 J2
Arkley Rd WALTH E17 57 H4
Arkley Vw BAR EN5 25 K3
Arklow Rd NWCR SE14 112 C5
Arkwright Rd HAMP NW3 71 G4
Arlesford Rd BRXN/ST SW9 129 K2
Arlingford Rd
BRXS/STRHM * SW2 130 B4
Arlington NFNCH/WDSP N12 38 E2
Arlington Av IS N1 6 F4
Arlington Cl BFN/LL DA15 135 K6
LEW * SE13 133 G4
SUT SM1 174 E1
TWK * TW1 124 D5
Arlington Ct HYS/HAR UB3 101 G4
Arlington Dr CAR SM5 175 K1
RSLP HA4 46 B5
Arlington Gdns CHSWK W4 105 K4
IL IG1 59 K6
Arlington Pde
BRXS/STRHM * SW2 130 A3
Arlington Rd CAMTN NW1 4 D4
RCHPK/HAM TW10 143 K1
STHGT/OAK N14 40 B1
SURB KT6 158 E5
TWK TW1 124 D5
TWK TW1 143 F3
WEA W13 85 H5
WFD IG8 44 E7
Arlington Sq IS N1 6 F4
Arlington St MYFR/PICC W1J 10 E8
Arlington Wy CLKNW EC1R 6 B7
Arliss Wy NTHLT UB5 65 G7
Arlow Rd WCHMH N21 29 G7
Armadale Cl TOTM N17 56 D3
Armadale Rd
EBED/NFELT TW14 121 K4
FUL/PGN SW6 107 K6
Armada St DEPT SE8 112 D5
Armada Wy EHAM E6 96 C5
Armagh Rd BOW E3 75 H7
Armfield Cl E/WMO/HCT KT8 156 E4
Armfield Crs MTCM CR4 162 E1
Arminger Rd SHB W12 87 K7
Armitage Rd GLDGN NW11 52 C7
GNWCH SE10 113 J4
Armour Cl HOLWY N7 73 F5
Armoury Rd DEPT SE8 132 E1
Armoury Wy
WAND/EARL SW18 127 K4
Armstead Wk DAGE RM10 80 C6
Armstrong Av WFD IG8 44 C5
Armstrong Cl BCTR RM8 61 K6
BMLY BR1 168 D2
BORE WD6 24 E2
EHAM E6 95 K5
RSLP HA4 46 E5
Armstrong Crs EBAR EN4 27 H2
Armstrong Rd ACT W3 87 H7
FELT TW13 141 J4
Armstrong Wy NWDGN UB2 103 H1
Armytage Rd HEST TW5 102 C6
Arnal Crs WAND/EARL SW18 127 H6
Arncliffe Cl FBAR/BDGN N11 40 A5
Arne St LSQ/SEVD WC2H 11 K5
Arnett Sq CHING E4 43 H5
Arne Wk BKHTH/KID SE3 133 J3
Arneways Av CHDH RM6 61 K3
Arneway St WEST SW1P 17 H4
Arney's La MTCM CR4 163 F5
Arngask Rd CAT SE6 133 G6
Arnheim Pl POP/IOD E14 112 D2
Arnison Rd E/WMO/HCT KT8 157 J3
Arnold Cl KTN/HRWW/W HA3 50 B6
Arnold Crs ISLW TW7 123 J4
Arnold Dr CHSGTN KT9 171 K5
Arnold Est STHWK SE1 19 M2
Arnold Gdns PLMGR N13 41 H4
Arnold Rd BOW E3 93 J2
DAGW RM9 80 B6
NTHLT UB5 65 J5
TOOT SW17 147 K6
TOTM N17 56 B2
Arnold Ter STAN * HA7 35 F4
Arnos Gv STHGT/OAK N14 40 D3
Arnos Rd FBAR/BDGN N11 40 C4
Arnott Cl CHSWK W4 106 A3
THMD SE28 97 J7
Arnould Av CMBW SE5 130 E3
Arnsberg Wy BXLYHN DA7 137 H3
Arnside Gdns WBLY HA9 49 K7
Arnside Rd BXLYHN DA7 117 H7
Arnside St WALW SE17 18 F9
Arnulf St CAT SE6 151 K3
Arnull's Rd STRHM/NOR SW16 149 H5
Arodene Rd BRXS/STRHM SW2 130 A5
Arosa Rd TWK TW1 124 E5
Arragon Gdns
STRHM/NOR SW16 148 E6
WWKM BR4 179 K2
Arragon Rd EHAM E6 77 H7
TWK TW1 124 B6
WAND/EARL SW18 127 K7
Arran Cl ERITH DA8 118 A5
WLGTN SM6 176 C3
Arran Dr MNPK E12 59 H7
STAN HA7 35 J3
Arran Gn OXHEY * WD19 33 H3
Arran Ms EA W5 86 B7
Arranmore Ct BUSH * WD23 21 J3
Arran Rd CAT SE6 151 K1
Arran Wk IS N1 6 E1
Arran Wy ESH/CLAY KT10 170 B1
Arras Av MRDN SM4 162 B4
Arrol Rd BECK BR3 165 K2
Arrow Rd BOW E3 93 K2
Arsenal Rd ELTH/MOT SE9 134 E1
Arterberry Rd RYNPK SW20 146 A6
Artesian Cl ROM RM1 63 H5
WLSDN NW10 69 F6
Artesian Gv BAR EN5 27 G3
Artesian Houses NTGHL * W11 8 A5
Artesian Rd NTGHL W11 8 A5
Arthingworth St SRTFD E15 76 C7
Arthurdon Rd LEW SE13 132 D4
Arthur Gv WOOL/PLUM SE18 115 H3
Arthur Rd CHDH RM6 61 J6
ED N9 42 B1
EHAM E6 95 K1
HOLWY N7 73 F3
KUTN/CMB KT2 144 C6
NWMAL KT3 160 E4
WIM/MER SW19 146 E3
Arthur St BUSH WD23 21 H2
CANST EC4R 13 H7
ERITH DA8 118 C6
Artichoke Hl WAP E1W 92 D6
Artichoke Pl CMBW * SE5 110 E7
Artillery Cl GNTH/NBYPK IG2 60 C5
Artillery La LVPST EC2M 13 K3
SHB W12 87 J5
Artillery Pas WCHPL * E1 13 K3
Artillery Pl WOOL/PLUM SE18 114 E4
Artizan St WCHPL E1 13 K4
Arundel Av MRDN SM4 161 J3
Arundel Cl BTSEA SW11 128 D4
BXLY DA5 137 G5
CROY/NA * CR0 177 H2
HPTN TW12 142 B4
SRTFD E15 76 C3
Arundel Dr BORE WD6 24 E3
RYLN/HDSTN HA2 65 K3
WFD IG8 44 E6
Arundel Gdns EDGW HA8 37 F6
GDMY/SEVK IG3 79 G1
NTGHL W11 88 D6
WCHMH N21 29 G7
Arundel Gv STNW/STAM N16 74 A4
Arundel Pl IS N1 73 G5
Arundel Rd BELMT SM2 174 D6
CROY/NA CR0 164 E5
DART DA1 139 F3
EBAR EN4 27 J2
HSLWW TW4 122 B2
KUT KT1 159 K1
Arundel Sq HOLWY N7 73 G5
Arundel St TPL/STR WC2R 11 M6
Arundel Ter BARN SW13 106 E5
Arvon Rd HBRY N5 73 G4
Asbaston Ter IL IG1 78 C4
Ascalon St VX/NE SW8 109 H6
Ascham Dr CHING E4 43 K6
Ascham End WALTH E17 43 G7
Ascham St KTTN NW5 72 C4
Aschurch Rd CROY/NA CR0 165 G6
Ascot Cl BORE WD6 24 C4
NTHLT UB5 66 A4
Ascot Gdns STHL UB1 83 K4
Ascot Ms WLGTN SM6 176 C7
Ascot Pde CLAP * SW4 129 K3
Ascot Rd ASHF TW15 120 D7
EHAM E6 95 K2
SEVS/STOTM N15 55 K4
TOOT SW17 148 A5
UED N18 42 C3
WATW WD18 20 C5
Ascott Av EA W5 105 F1
Ascott Ct PIN * HA5 46 E3
Ashanti Ms HACK * E8 74 D5
Ashborurne Sq NTHWD HA6 32 C5
Ashbourne Av BXLYHN DA7 117 F6
GLDGN NW11 52 D4
RYLN/HDSTN * HA2 66 D1
SWFD E18 59 F3
TRDG/WHET N20 39 K1
Ashbourne Cl EA W5 86 B4
NFNCH/WDSP N12 39 F3
Ashbourne Gv CHSWK W4 106 B4
EDUL SE22 131 G4
MLHL NW7 37 F4
Ashbourne Pde EA * W5 86 B3
GLDGN * NW11 52 D3
Ashbourne Rd EA W5 86 B3
MTCM CR4 148 A5
Ashbourne Ter
WIM/MER SW19 146 E6
Ashbourne Wy GLDGN NW11 52 D4
Ashbridge Rd WAN E11 58 C6
Ashbridge St STJWD NW8 9 J1
Ashbrook EDGW * HA8 36 B5
Ashbrook Rd ARCH N19 54 D7
DAGE RM10 80 D2
Ashburn Gdns SKENS SW7 14 E5
Ashburnham Av HRW HA1 49 F6
Ashburnham Cl EFNCH N2 53 H2
OXHEY * WD19 32 E2
Ashburnham Dr OXHEY WD19 32 E2
Ashburnham Gdns HRW HA1 49 F5
Ashburnham Gv GNWCH SE10 112 E6
Ashburnham Pk
ESH/CLAY KT10 170 C3
Ashburnham Pl GNWCH SE10 112 E6
Ashburnham Retreat
GNWCH SE10 112 E6
Ashburnham Rd BELV DA17 117 K3
RCHPK/HAM TW10 143 H2
WBPTN * SW10 108 B6
WLSDN NW10 88 A2
Ashburn Pl SKENS SW7 14 E6
Ashburton Av CROY/NA CR0 165 J7
GDMY/SEVK IG3 79 F3
Ashburton Cl CROY/NA CR0 165 H7
Ashburton Gdns CROY/NA CR0 178 C1
Ashburton Gv HOLWY N7 73 G3
Ashburton Rd CAN/RD E16 94 E5
CROY/NA CR0 178 C1
RSLP HA4 64 E1
Ashbury Ct BMLY BR1 152 E6
Ashbury Gdns CHDH RM6 61 K4
Ashbury Pl WIM/MER SW19 147 G5
Ashbury Rd BTSEA SW11 128 E2
Ashby Av CHSGTN KT9 172 C5
Ashby Gv IS N1 6 F1
Ashby Ms BROCKY SE4 132 C2
Ashby Rd BROCKY SE4 132 C1
SEVS/STOTM N15 56 C4
Ashby St FSBYE EC1V 6 D8
Ashby Wk CROY/NA CR0 164 D5
Ashby Wy WDR/YW UB7 100 D6
Ashchurch Gv SHB W12 106 D1
Ashchurch Park Vls SHB W12 106 D2
Ashchurch Ter SHB W12 106 C2
Ash Cl CAR SM5 175 K1
EDGW HA8 36 E3
NWMAL KT3 160 A1
PGE/AN SE20 165 K1
SCUP DA14 155 H2
STAN HA7 35 G5
STMC/STPC BR5 169 J4
Ashcombe Av SURB KT6 158 E6
Ashcombe Gdns EDGW HA8 36 C3
Ashcombe Pk CRICK NW2 69 G2
Ashcombe Rd CAR SM5 176 A5
WIM/MER SW19 146 E4
Ashcombe Sq NWMAL KT3 159 K2
Ashcombe St FUL/PGN * SW6 128 A1
Ash Ct HOR/WEW KT19 172 E3
Ashcroft PIN HA5 34 A5
Ashcroft Av BFN/LL DA15 136 B5
Ashcroft Crs BFN/LL DA15 136 B5
Ashcroft Rd BOW E3 93 G2
CHSGTN KT9 172 B2
Ashdale Cl WHTN TW2 123 G6
Ashdale Gv STAN HA7 35 F5
Ashdale Rd LEE/GVPK SE12 134 A7
Ashdene PIN HA5 47 G2
Ashdene Cl ASHF * TW15 140 A6
Ashdon Cl WFD IG8 45 F5
Ashdon Rd BUSH WD23 21 H2
Ashdown WEA * W13 85 H4
Ashdown Cl BECK BR3 166 E1
BXLY DA5 137 K6
Ashdown Crs KTTN * NW5 72 A4
Ashdown Dr BORE WD6 24 B1
Ashdown Pl THDIT KT7 158 B5
Ashdown Rd KUT KT1 159 F1
PEND EN3 30 E2
WLSDN NW10 69 G7
Ashdown Wy TOOT SW17 148 A1
Ashenden Rd CLPT E5 75 G4
Ashen Dr DART DA1 138 D5
Ashen Gv WIM/MER SW19 146 E2
Ashen V SAND/SEL CR2 179 F7
Asher Loftus Wy
FBAR/BDGN N11 39 K5
Asher Wy WAP E1W 92 C7
Ashfield Av BUSH WD23 22 B5
FELT TW13 122 A7
Ashfield Cl BECK BR3 151 J6
RCHPK/HAM TW10 125 F7
Ashfield Ct EA * W5 86 A6
Ashfield La CHST BR7 154 C5
Ashfield Rd ACT W3 87 H7
FSBYPK N4 55 J5
STHGT/OAK N14 40 C2
Ashfield St WCHPL E1 92 E4
Ashfield Yd WCHPL * E1 92 E4
Ashford Av CEND/HSY/T N8 54 E3
YEAD UB4 83 H5
Ashford Cl WALTH E17 57 H5
Ashford Crs PEND EN3 30 E1
Ashford Gn OXHEY WD19 33 H4
Ashford Rd CRICK NW2 70 B3
EHAM E6 77 K5
FELT TW13 140 B3
SHPTN TW17 140 A6
SWFD E18 59 F1
Ashford St IS N1 7 J7
Ash Gv ALP/SUD HA0 67 G3
CRICK NW2 70 B3
EA W5 105 F1
EBED/NFELT TW14 121 H7
EN EN1 30 A6
HACK E8 74 D7
HEST TW5 102 C7
HYS/HAR UB3 82 B6
PGE/AN SE20 165 K1
PLMGR N13 41 J2
STHL UB1 84 A4
WWKM BR4 180 A1
Ashgrove Rd ASHF TW15 140 A4
BMLY BR1 152 B5
GDMY/SEVK IG3 61 F7
Ash Hill Cl BUSH WD23 22 B7
Ash Hill Dr PIN HA5 47 G2
Ashingdon Cl CHING E4 44 A3
Ashington Rd FUL/PGN * SW6 127 J1
Ashlake Rd STRHM/NOR SW16 148 E3
Ashland Pl MHST W1U 10 A2
Ashlar Pl WOOL/PLUM SE18 115 G3
Ashleigh Gdns SUT SM1 175 F1
Ashleigh Rd MORT/ESHN SW14 126 B2
PGE/AN SE20 165 J2
Ashley Av BARK/HLT IG6 60 B1
MRDN SM4 161 K4
Ashley Cl HDN NW4 52 A1
PIN HA5 47 F1
Ashley Crs BTSEA SW11 129 F2
WDGN N22 55 G1
Ashley Dr BORE WD6 24 E4
ISLW TW7 103 K5
WHTN TW2 123 G7
Ashley Gdns PLMGR N13 41 J3
RCHPK/HAM TW10 143 K2
WBLY HA9 68 A1
Ashley La CROY/NA CR0 177 H3
HDN NW4 52 A1
MLHL NW7 38 A6
Ashley Pl WEST SW1P 16 E4
Ashley Rd ARCH N19 54 E7
CHING E4 43 J4
FSTGT E7 77 G6
HPTN TW12 142 A7
PEND EN3 30 E1
RCH/KEW TW9 125 F2
THDIT KT7 158 A5
THHTH CR7 164 A3
TOTM N17 56 C2
WIM/MER SW19 147 F5
Ashling Rd CROY/NA CR0 165 H7
Ashlin Rd SRTFD E15 76 B3
Ashlone Rd PUT/ROE SW15 127 F2
Ashlyn Cl BUSH WD23 21 J3
Ashlyns Wy CHSGTN KT9 171 K5
Ashmead STHGT/OAK N14 28 C4
Ashmead Ga BMLY BR1 153 G7
Ashmead Ms DEPT * SE8 112 D7
Ashmead Rd DEPT SE8 132 D1
EBED/NFELT TW14 121 K7
Ashmere Av BECK BR3 167 G1
Ashmere Cl CHEAM SM3 174 B4
Ashmere Gv CLAP SW4 129 K3
Ash Ms KTTN * NW5 72 C4
Ashmill St STJWD NW8 9 J2
Ashmole St VX/NE SW8 110 A5
Ashmore Cl PECK SE15 111 H6
Ashmore Gv WELL DA16 135 J2
Ashmore Rd MV/WKIL W9 88 D2
Ashmount Rd HGT N6 54 C6
SEVS/STOTM N15 56 B4
Ashmount Ter EA * W5 104 E3
Ashmour Gdns ROM RM1 63 F1
Ashneal Gdns HRW HA1 66 D2
Ashness Gdns GFD/PVL UB6 67 H5
Ashness Rd BTSEA SW11 128 E4
Ashridge Cl KTN/HRWW/W HA3 49 J5
Ashridge Crs
WOOL/PLUM SE18 115 H6
Ashridge Dr OXHEY WD19 33 G4
Ashridge Gdns PIN HA5 47 J3
PLMGR N13 40 E4
Ashridge Wy MRDN SM4 161 J3
SUN TW16 140 E5
Ash Rd CROY/NA CR0 179 J1
DART DA1 139 G7
MRDN SM4 161 H7
SRTFD E15 76 C4
Ash Rw HAYES BR2 169 F5
Ashtead Rd CLPT E5 56 C6
Ashton Cl SUT SM1 174 E3
Ashton Gdns CHDH RM6 62 A5
HSLWW TW4 122 E3
Ashton Rd SRTFD E15 76 B4
Ashton St POP/IOD E14 94 A6

Ashtree Av MTCM CR4 162 C1
Ash Tree Cl CROY/NA CR0 166 B5
SURB KT6 159 F7
Ash Tree Dell CDALE/KGS NW9 50 E4
Ash Tree Wy CROY/NA CR0 166 B4
Ashurst Cl DART DA1 138 C2
NTHWD HA6 32 C6
PGE/AN SE20 150 D7
Ashurst Dr GNTH/NBYPK IG2 60 B5
Ashurst Gdns
BRXS/STRHM * SW2 130 B7
Ashurst Rd EBAR EN4 27 K4
NFNCH/WDSP N12 39 J4
Ashurst Wk CROY/NA CR0 178 D1
Ashvale Rd TOOT SW17 147 K4
Ashville Rd WAN E11 76 B1
Ash Wk ALP/SUD HA0 67 J3
Ashwater Rd LEE/GVPK SE12 133 K7
Ashwin St HACK E8 74 B5
Ashwood Av RAIN RM13 99 K2
Ashwood Gdns CROY/NA CR0 179 K5
HYS/HAR UB3 101 J3
Ashwood Rd CHING E4 44 B2
Ashworth Cl CMBW SE5 130 E1
Ashworth Rd MV/WKIL W9 2 D7
Askern Cl BXLYHS DA6 136 E3
Aske St IS N1 7 J7
Askew Crs SHB W12 106 C1
Askew Rd NTHWD HA6 32 B1
SHB W12 106 C1
Askew Vls PLMGR * N13 41 H2
Askham Rd SHB W12 87 J7
Askill Dr PUT/ROE SW15 127 H4
Askwith Rd RAIN RM13 99 F1
Asland Rd SRTFD E15 76 B7
Aslett St WAND/EARL SW18 128 A6
Asmara Rd CRICK NW2 70 C4
Asmuns Hl GLDGN NW11 52 E4
Asmuns Pl GLDGN NW11 52 D4
Asolando Dr WALW SE17 18 F7
Aspen Cl EA W5 105 G1
Aspen Copse BMLY BR1 168 E1
Aspen Dr ALP/SUD HA0 67 G2
Aspen Gdns MTCM CR4 163 F4
Aspen Gn ERITHM DA18 117 G2
Aspen La NTHLT UB5 83 J2
Aspenlea Rd HMSMTH W6 107 G5
Aspen Wy FELT TW13 141 F2
POP/IOD E14 93 L6
Aspern Gv HAMP NW3 71 J4
Aspinall Rd BROCKY SE4 132 A2
Aspinden Rd BERM/RHTH SE16 111 J3
Aspley Rd WAND/EARL SW18 128 A4
Asplins Rd TOTM N17 42 C7
Asplins Vls TOTM * N17 42 C7
Asquith Cl BCTR RM8 61 J7
Assam St WCHPL E1 92 C5
Assata Ms IS N1 73 H5
Assembly Pas WCHPL E1 92 E4
Assembly Wk CAR SM5 162 D6
Ass House La
KTN/HRWW/W HA3 34 B3
Astall Cl KTN/HRWW/W HA3 34 D7
Astbury Rd PECK SE15 111 K7
Astell St CHEL SW3 15 K7
Asteys Rw IS N1 6 C1
Astle St BTSEA SW11 129 F1
Astley Av CRICK NW2 70 A4
Aston Av KTN/HRWW/W HA3 49 J6
Aston Cl BUSH WD23 22 C5
SCUP DA14 155 G2
WATN WD24 21 G1
Aston Gn HEST TW5 122 B1
Aston Rd EA W5 85 K5
ESH/CLAY KT10 170 E4
RYNPK SW20 161 F1
Astons Rd NTHWD HA6 32 A2
Aston St WCHPL E1 93 G5
Aston Ter BAL * SW12 129 G5
Astonville St
WAND/EARL SW18 127 K7
Astor Av ROMW/RG RM7 62 D5
Astor Cl KUTN/CMB KT2 144 D5
Astoria Pde
STRHM/NOR * SW16 148 E2
Astoria Wk BRXN/ST SW9 130 B2
Astra Cl HCH RM12 81 K5
Astrop Ms HMSMTH W6 107 F2
Astrop Ter HMSMTH W6 107 F2
Astwood Ms SKENS SW7 14 D5
Asylum Rd PECK SE15 111 J6
Atalanta St FUL/PGN SW6 107 G7
Atbara Rd TEDD TW11 143 H5
Atcham Rd HSLW TW3 123 H3
Atcost Rd BARK IG11 97 G4
Atheldene Rd
WAND/EARL SW18 128 A7
Athelney St CAT SE6 151 J2
Athelstane Gv BOW E3 93 H1
Athelstane Ms FSBYPK N4 55 G7
Athelstan Gdns
KIL/WHAMP * NW6 70 C6
Athelstan Rd KUT KT1 159 G3
Athelstan Wy STMC/STPC BR5 155 G7
Athelstone Rd
KTN/HRWW/W HA3 48 D1
Athena Cl KUT KT1 159 G2
RYLN/HDSTN HA2 66 D1
Athenaeum Pl MUSWH N10 54 B2
Athenaeum Rd
TRDG/WHET N20 27 G7
Athena Pl NTHWD HA6 32 D7
Athenlay Rd PECK SE15 132 A4
Athens Gdns MV/WKIL * W9 8 A1
Atherden Rd CLPT E5 74 E3
Atherfold Rd BRXN/ST SW9 129 K2
Atherley Wy HSLWW TW4 122 E6
Atherstone Ms SKENS SW7 14 F5
Atherton Cl STWL/WRAY TW19 120 A5
Atherton Dr WIM/MER SW19 146 B3
Atherton Hts ALP/SUD HA0 67 J5
Atherton Ms FSTGT E7 76 E5
Atherton Pl RYLN/HDSTN HA2 48 C2
STHL UB1 84 A6
Atherton Rd BARN SW13 106 D6
CLAY IG5 59 J1
FSTGT E7 76 D4
Atherton St BTSEA SW11 128 D1
Athlone ESH/CLAY KT10 170 E5
Athlone Cl CLPT E5 74 D4
Athlone Ct WALTH E17 58 B2
Athlone Rd BRXS/STRHM SW2 130 A6
Athlone St KTTN NW5 72 A5
Athlon Rd ALP/SUD HA0 85 K1
Athol Cl PIN HA5 33 F7
Athole Gdns EN EN1 30 A4
Athol Gdns PIN HA5 33 F7
Atholl Rd GDMY/SEVK IG3 61 G6
Athol Rd ERITH DA8 117 K4
Athol Sq POP/IOD E14 94 A5
Atkins Dr WWKM BR4 180 B2
Atkinson Rd CAN/RD E16 95 G4
Atkins Rd BAL SW12 129 H6
LEY E10 57 K5
Atlanta Bvd ROM RM1 63 G5
Atlantic Rd BRXN/ST SW9 130 B3
Atlantis Cl BARK IG11 97 H2
Atlas Gdns CHARL SE7 114 B3
Atlas Ms HACK E8 74 B5
Atlas Rd DART DA1 139 J2
FBAR/BDGN N11 40 A5
PLSTW E13 94 E1
WBLY HA9 68 E3
WLSDN NW10 87 G2
Atley Rd BOW E3 75 J7
Atlip Rd ALP/SUD HA0 68 A7
Atney Rd PUT/ROE SW15 127 H3
Atria Rd NTHWD HA6 32 E3
Attenborough Cl OXHEY WD19 33 J2
Atterbury Rd FSBYPK N4 55 G5
Atterbury St WEST SW1P 17 H6
Attewood Av CRICK NW2 69 G2
Attewood Rd NTHLT UB5 65 J5
Attfield Cl TRDG/WHET N20 39 H1
Attlee Cl CROY/NA CR0 164 D5
NTHLT * UB5 83 F2
Attlee Dr DART DA1 139 K4
Attlee Rd THMD SE28 97 H6
YEAD UB4 82 E2
Attlee Ter WALTH E17 57 K3
Attneave St FSBYW WC1X 6 A9
Atwell Rd PECK * SE15 131 H1
Atwood Av RCH/KEW TW9 125 H1
Atwood Rd HMSMTH W6 106 E3
Aubert Pk HBRY N5 73 G3
Aubert Rd HBRY N5 73 H3
Aubrey Pl STJWD NW8 2 E6
Aubrey Rd CEND/HSY/T * N8 54 E4
KENS W8 88 D7
WALTH E17 57 J2
Aubrey Wk KENS W8 88 D7
Auburn Cl NWCR SE14 112 B6
Aubyn Hl WNWD SE27 149 J3
Aubyn Sq PUT/ROE SW15 126 D3
Auckland Av RAIN RM13 99 H2
Auckland Cl NRWD SE19 150 B7
Auckland Hl WNWD SE27 149 J3
Auckland Ri NRWD SE19 150 A7
Auckland Rd BTSEA SW11 128 D3
IL IG1 60 B7
KUT KT1 159 G3
LEY E10 75 K2
NRWD SE19 150 B7
Aucklands Gdns NRWD SE19 150 A7
Auckland St LBTH SE11 17 L8
Aucuba Vls WELL * DA16 136 C2
Audax CDALE/KGS * NW9 51 H1
Auden Pl CAMTN NW1 4 A3
CHEAM * SM3 174 A3
Audley Cl BORE WD6 24 C2
MUSWH N10 40 B6
Audley Ct PIN HA5 47 G1
SWFD E18 58 D3
Audley Dr CAN/RD E16 95 F7
Audley Gdns GDMY/SEVK IG3 79 F1
Audley Pl BELMT SM2 175 F6
Audley Rd EA W5 86 B4
ENC/FH EN2 29 H1
HDN NW4 51 J5
RCHPK/HAM TW10 125 G4
Audley Sq MYFR/PKLN * W1K 10 B8
Audrey Cl BECK BR3 166 E5
Audrey Gdns ALP/SUD HA0 67 H1
Audrey Rd IL IG1 78 B2
Audrey St BETH E2 92 C1
Audric Cl KUTN/CMB KT2 144 C7
Augurs La PLSTW E13 95 F2
Augusta Cl E/WMO/HCT KT8 156 E2
Augusta Rd WHTN TW2 142 C1
Augustine Rd
KTN/HRWW/W HA3 34 B7
WKENS W14 107 G2
Augustus Cl BTFD TW8 104 E6
SHB W12 106 E1
Augustus Rd WIM/MER SW19 127 H7
Augustus St CAMTN NW1 4 D6
Aultone Wy CAR SM5 175 K2
SUT SM1 175 F1
Aulton Pl LBTH SE11 18 B8
Aurelia Gdns THHTH CR7 164 A4
Aurelia Rd CROY/NA CR0 163 K5
Auriel Av DAGE RM10 81 F5
Auriga Ms IS N1 73 K4
Auriol Cl HOR/WEW KT19 173 G2
Auriol Dr GFD/PVL UB6 66 D6
Auriol Park Rd WPK KT4 173 G2
Auriol Rd WKENS W14 107 H3
Austell Gdns MLHL NW7 37 G2
Austen Cl THMD SE28 97 H7
Austen Rd ERITH DA8 117 J6
RYLN/HDSTN HA2 66 B1
Austin Av HAYES BR2 168 D5
Austin Cl CAT SE6 132 B6
Austin Friars OBST EC2N 13 H4
Austin Friars Sq OBST * EC2N 13 H4
Austin Rd BTSEA SW11 109 F7
HYS/HAR UB3 101 J1
Austin's La HGDN/ICK UB10 64 A2
Austin St BETH E2 7 L8
Austral Cl BFN/LL DA15 155 F2
Australia Rd SHB W12 87 K6
Austral St LBTH SE11 18 C5
Austyn Gdns BRYLDS * KT5 159 J7
Autumn Cl EN EN1 30 D1
WIM/MER SW19 147 G5
Autumn Dr BELMT SM2 175 F7
Autumn St BOW E3 75 J7
Avalon Cl ENC/FH EN2 29 G1
RYNPK SW20 161 H1
WEA W13 85 G4
Avalon Rd FUL/PGN SW6 108 A7
WEA W13 85 G3
Avarn Rd TOOT SW17 147 K5
Avebury Pk SURB * KT6 158 E5
Avebury Rd WAN E11 58 B7
WIM/MER SW19 146 D7
Avebury St IS N1 7 G4
Aveley Cl ERITH DA8 118 C5
Aveline St LBTH SE11 17 M7
Aveling Park Rd WALTH E17 57 J1
Avelon Rd RAIN RM13 81 J7
Avenell Rd HBRY N5 73 H2
Avening Rd WAND/EARL SW18 127 K6
Avening Ter WAND/EARL SW18 127 K5
Avenons Rd PLSTW E13 94 E4
The Avenue BAR EN5 26 C2
BECK BR3 151 K7
BELMT SM2 174 D7
BMLY BR1 168 C2
BRYLDS KT5 159 G5
BUSH WD23 21 K3
BXLY DA5 136 E6
CAR SM5 176 A6
CEND/HSY/T N8 55 G2
CHING E4 44 B5
CHSWK W4 106 B2
CLAP SW4 129 F4
CROY/NA CR0 178 A2
ESH/CLAY KT10 170 E5
EW KT17 174 A6
FBAR/BDGN N11 40 B4
GNWCH SE10 113 G6
HEST TW5 101 K7
HPTN TW12 141 K5
HSLW TW3 123 G4
KIL/WHAMP NW6 70 B7
KTN/HRWW/W HA3 35 F7
MUSWH N10 54 C1
NTHWD HA6 32 A5
PIN HA5 33 K5
PIN HA5 47 K5
RCH/KEW TW9 125 G1
ROM RM1 63 F3
STMC/STPC BR5 155 H6
SUN TW16 141 F7
TOTM N17 56 A1
TWK TW1 124 C5
WAN E11 59 F5
WAT WD17 20 E1
WBLY HA9 50 A7
WEA W13 85 H6
WPK KT4 173 H1
WWKM BR4 167 G6
Avenue Cl HEST TW5 102 A7
STHGT/OAK N14 28 C5
STJWD NW8 3 K4
WDR/YW UB7 100 A2
Avenue Crs ACT W3 105 J1
HEST TW5 101 K7
Avenue Elmers SURB KT6 159 F4
Avenue Gdns ACT W3 105 J1
HEST * TW5 101 K6
MORT/ESHN SW14 126 B2
TEDD TW11 143 F6
Avenue Ms MUSWH N10 54 B2
Avenue Pde SUN * TW16 156 A2
WCHMH * N21 29 K6
Avenue Park Rd WNWD SE27 149 H1
Avenue Ri BUSH WD23 22 A4
Avenue Rd ACT W3 105 J1
BTFD TW8 104 D4
BXLYHS DA6 137 F2
ERITH DA8 117 K6
FELT TW13 140 D2
FSTGT E7 77 F4
GDMY/SEVK IG3 61 H6
HGT N6 54 C6
HPTN TW12 142 B7
ISLW TW7 103 K7
KIL/WHAMP NW6 3 G1
KUT KT1 159 F2
NFNCH/WDSP N12 39 G3
NWMAL KT3 160 B2
PGE/AN SE20 150 E7
PIN HA5 47 J2
RYNPK SW20 160 E1
SEVS/STOTM N15 55 K4
SNWD SE25 165 H1
STHGT/OAK N14 28 C6
STHL UB1 83 K7
STRHM/NOR SW16 163 J1
TEDD TW11 143 G6
WFD IG8 45 G5
WLGTN SM6 176 C6
WLSDN NW10 87 H1
Avenue South BRYLDS KT5 159 G6
Avenue Ter NWMAL KT3 159 K2
OXHEY WD19 21 J5
Averil Gv STRHM/NOR SW16 149 H5
Averill St HMSMTH W6 107 G5
Avern Gdns E/WMO/HCT KT8 157 G3
Avern Rd E/WMO/HCT KT8 157 G3
Avery Farm Rw BGVA * SW1W 16 C6
Avery Gdns GNTH/NBYPK IG2 59 K4
Avery Hill Rd ELTH/MOT SE9 135 H7
Avery Rw MYFR/PKLN W1K 10 C6
Aviary Cl CAN/RD E16 94 D4
Aviemore Cl BECK BR3 166 C4
Aviemore Wy BECK BR3 166 B4
Avignon Rd BROCKY SE4 132 A2
Avington Gv PGE/AN SE20 150 E6
Avington Wy PECK * SE15 111 G6
Avion Crs CDALE/KGS NW9 51 J1
Avior Dr NTHWD HA6 32 D3
Avis Sq WCHPL E1 93 F5
Avoca Rd TOOT SW17 148 A3
Avocet Ms THMD SE28 115 J2
Avon Cl SUT SM1 175 G3
WPK KT4 173 J1
YEAD UB4 83 G3
Avon Ct PIN * HA5 34 A6
Avondale Av CRICK NW2 69 G2
EBAR EN4 27 K7
ESH/CLAY KT10 171 G2
NFNCH/WDSP N12 39 F4
WPK KT4 160 C7
Avondale Ct WFD IG8 45 F7
Avondale Crs PEND EN3 31 G2
REDBR IG4 59 H4
Avondale Dr HYS/HAR UB3 82 E7
Avondale Gdns HSLWW TW4 122 E4
Avondale Park Gdns
NTGHL * W11 88 C6
Avondale Park Rd NTGHL W11 88 C6
Avondale Pavement
STHWK * SE1 111 H4
Avondale Ri PECK SE15 131 G2
Avondale Rd BMLY BR1 152 C5
CAN/RD E16 94 C4
ELTH/MOT SE9 153 J1
FNCH N3 39 G7
KTN/HRWW/W HA3 49 F2
MORT/ESHN SW14 126 A2
PLMGR N13 41 G1
SAND/SEL CR2 177 J5
SEVS/STOTM N15 55 H4
WALTH E17 57 J6
WELL DA16 136 D1
WIM/MER SW19 147 F4
Avondale Sq STHWK SE1 111 H4
Avonley Rd NWCR SE14 111 K6
Avonmore Gdns WKENS * W14 107 J3
Avonmore Pl WKENS W14 107 H3
Avonmore Rd WKENS W14 107 J3
Avonmouth Rd DART DA1 139 G4
Avonmouth St STHWK SE1 18 E3
Avon Rd BROCKY SE4 132 D2
GFD/PVL UB6 84 A3
SUN TW16 140 D6
WALTH E17 58 B2
Avon Wy SWFD E18 58 E2
Avonwick Rd HSLW TW3 123 G1
Avril Wy CHING E4 44 A4
Avro Wy WLGTN SM6 176 E6
Awberry Ct WATW * WD18 20 B5
Awlfield Av TOTM N17 41 K7
Awliscombe Rd WELL DA16 136 A1
Axeholm Av EDGW HA8 36 D7
Axe St BARK IG11 78 C7
Axholme Av EDGW HA8 36 C7
Axminster Crs WELL DA16 116 D7
Axminster Rd HOLWY N7 72 E2
Aybrook St MHST W1U 10 A3
Aycliff Ct KUT * KT1 159 H1
Aycliffe Cl BMLY BR1 168 E3
Aycliffe Rd SHB W12 87 H7
Aylands Cl WBLY HA9 68 A1
Aylesbury Cl FSTGT E7 76 D5
Aylesbury Est WALW SE17 19 H8
Aylesbury Rd HAYES BR2 167 K2
WALW SE17 19 H8
Aylesbury St CLKNW EC1R 12 C1
WLSDN NW10 69 F2
Aylesford Av BECK BR3 166 B4
Aylesford St PIM SW1V 17 G8
Aylesham Cl MLHL NW7 37 J6
Aylesham Rd ORP BR6 169 K6
Ayles Rd YEAD UB4 83 F2
Aylestone Av KIL/WHAMP NW6 70 B6
Aylett Rd ISLW TW7 123 K1
SNWD SE25 165 J3
Ayley Cft EN EN1 30 C4
Ayliffe Cl KUT KT1 159 H1
Aylmer Cl STAN HA7 35 G3
Aylmer Dr STAN HA7 35 G3
Aylmer Pde EFNCH * N2 53 K4
Aylmer Rd BCTR RM8 80 A2
EFNCH N2 53 J4
SHB W12 106 B1
WAN E11 58 D6
Ayloffe Rd DAGW RM9 80 B5
Aylsham Dr HGDN/ICK UB10 64 A1
Aylton Est BERM/RHTH * SE16 111 K1
Aylward Rd FSTH SE23 151 F1
RYNPK SW20 161 J1
Aylwards Ri STAN HA7 35 G3
Aylward St WCHPL E1 93 F5
Aynhoe Rd WKENS W14 107 G3
Aynho St WATW WD18 21 F4
Ayres Cl PLSTW E13 94 E2
Ayres Crs WLSDN NW10 69 F6
Ayres St STHWK SE1 18 F1
Ayrsome Rd STNW/STAM N16 74 A2
Ayrton Rd SKENS SW7 15 G3
Aysgarth Rd DUL SE21 130 E5
Aytoun Pl BRXN/ST SW9 130 A1
Aytoun Rd BRXN/ST SW9 130 A1
Azalea Cl HNWL W7 85 F7
IL IG1 78 B4
Azalea Ct WFD * IG8 44 C6
Azalea Wk PIN HA5 47 F5
Azania Ms KTTN NW5 72 B4
Azenby Rd PECK SE15 131 G1
Azof St GNWCH SE10 113 H3

B

Baalbec Rd HBRY N5 73 H4
Babbacombe Cl CHSGTN KT9 171 K4
Babbacombe Gdns REDBR IG4 59 J3
Babbacombe Rd BMLY BR1 153 F7
Baber Bridge Pde
EBED/NFELT * TW14 122 B5
Baber Dr EBED/NFELT TW14 122 B5
Babington Ri WBLY HA9 68 C5
Babington Rd BCTR RM8 79 J4
HCH RM12 63 K7
HDN NW4 51 K3
STRHM/NOR SW16 148 D4
Babmaes St STJS SW1Y 11 G7
Bache's St IS N1 7 H8
Back Church La WCHPL E1 92 C5
Back Hl CLKNW EC1R 12 B1
Back La BTFD TW8 104 E6
BXLY DA5 137 H6
CEND/HSY/T N8 54 E4
CHDH RM6 62 A6
EDGW HA8 36 E7
HAMP NW3 71 G3
RCHPK/HAM TW10 143 J2
Backley Gdns SNWD SE25 165 H5
Back Rd SCUP DA14 155 G3
TEDD TW11 142 E6
Bacon Gv STHWK SE1 19 L5
Bacon La CDALE/KGS NW9 50 D3
EDGW HA8 36 C7
Bacon's La HGT N6 54 A7
Bacon St BETH E2 7 M9
Bacton St BETH E2 92 E2
Baddow Cl DAGE RM10 80 C7
WFD IG8 45 H5
Baden Pl STHWK SE1 19 G1
Baden Powell Cl DAGW RM9 80 A7
SURB KT6 172 B1
Baden Rd CEND/HSY/T N8 54 D3
IL IG1 78 B4
Bader Wy HCH RM12 81 J5
Badger Cl FELT TW13 141 F2
HSLWW TW4 122 B2
Badgers Cl BORE * WD6 24 B1
ENC/FH EN2 29 H2
HRW HA1 48 D5
HYS/HAR UB3 82 C7
Badgers Copse WPK KT4 173 H1
Badgers Ct WPK * KT4 173 H1
Badgers Cft ELTH/MOT SE9 154 A2
TRDG/WHET N20 26 C6
Badgers Wk NWMAL KT3 160 B1
Badlis Rd WALTH E17 57 J1
Badlow Cl ERITH DA8 118 B6
Badminton Cl BORE WD6 24 C1
HRW * HA1 48 E3
NTHLT UB5 66 A5
Badminton Ms CAN/RD E16 94 E7
Badminton Rd BAL SW12 129 F5
Badsworth Rd CMBW SE5 110 D6
Bagley Cl WDR/YW UB7 100 B1
Bagley's La FUL/PGN SW6 108 A7
Bagleys Spring CHDH RM6 62 A3
Bagshot Ct
WOOL/PLUM * SE18 115 F7
Bagshot Rd EN EN1 30 B6
Bagshot St WALW SE17 19 K8
Baildon St DEPT SE8 112 C6
Bailey Cl WDGN N22 40 D7
Bailey Cottages POP/IOD * E14 93 G4
Bailey Crs CHSGTN KT9 171 K6
Bailey Pl SYD SE26 150 E5
Baillie Cl RAIN RM13 99 K3
Bainbridge Cl KUTN/CMB KT2 144 A4
Bainbridge Rd DAGW RM9 80 B3
Bainbridge St
NOXST/BSQ WC1A 11 H4
Baines Cl SAND/SEL CR2 177 K4
Baird Av STHL UB1 84 B6
Baird Cl BUSH WD23 22 B5
CDALE/KGS NW9 50 E5
LEY E10 57 J7
Baird Gdns NRWD SE19 150 A3
Baird Memorial Cottages
STHGT/OAK * N14 40 D1
Baird Rd EN EN1 30 D2
Baird St STLK EC1Y 6 F9
Baizdon Rd BKHTH/KID SE3 133 H1
Baker La MTCM CR4 163 F1
Baker Rd WLSDN NW10 69 G7
WOOL/PLUM SE18 114 D6
Bakers Av WALTH E17 57 K5
Bakers End RYNPK SW20 161 H1
Bakers Gdns CAR SM5 175 J1
Bakers Hl BAR EN5 27 F1
CLPT E5 56 D7
Baker's Ms MHST W1U 10 A4
Bakers Rents BETH E2 7 L8
Baker's Rw CLKNW EC1R 12 A1
SRTFD E15 94 C1
Baker St CAMTN NW1 9 M1
EN EN1 29 K1
MHST W1U 10 A3
Baker's Yd CLKNW EC1R 12 A1
Bakery Cl BRXN/ST * SW9 110 A6
Bakewell Wy NWMAL KT3 160 B1
Balaams La STHGT/OAK N14 40 D1
Balaam St PLSTW E13 94 E2
Balaclava Rd STHWK SE1 19 M6
SURB KT6 158 D6
Bala Gn CDALE/KGS * NW9 51 G5
Balcaskie Rd ELTH/MOT SE9 134 E4
Balchen Rd BKHTH/KID SE3 134 C1
Balchier Rd EDUL SE22 131 J5
Balcombe Cl BXLYHS DA6 136 E3
Balcombe St CAMTN NW1 3 L9
Balcorne St HOM E9 74 E6
Balder Ri LEE/GVPK SE12 153 F1
Balderton St MYFR/PKLN W1K 10 B5
Baldock St BOW E3 93 K1
Baldry Gdns STRHM/NOR SW16 148 E5
Baldwin Crs CMBW SE5 110 D7
Baldwin Gdns HSLW TW3 103 H7
Baldwin's Gdns FSBYW WC1X 12 A2
Baldwin St FSBYE EC1V 7 G8
Baldwin Ter IS N1 6 E5
Baldwyn Gdns ACT W3 86 E6
Bale Rd WCHPL E1 93 G4
Bales Ter ED * N9 42 B2
Balfern Gv CHSWK W4 106 B4
Balfern St BTSEA SW11 128 D1
Balfe St IS N1 5 K6
Balfour Av HNWL W7 85 F7
Balfour Gv TRDG/WHET N20 39 K2
Balfour Ms ED N9 42 C2
MYFR/PKLN W1K 10 B8
Balfour Pl MYFR/PKLN W1K 10 B7
Balfour Rd ACT W3 86 E4
CAR SM5 175 K6
HAYES BR2 168 C4
HBRY N5 73 J3
HRW HA1 48 D4
HSLW TW3 123 G2
IL IG1 78 B1
NWDGN UB2 102 C3
SNWD SE25 165 H3
WEA W13 104 C1
WIM/MER SW19 147 F6
Balfour St STHWK SE1 19 G5
Balgores Crs GPK RM2 63 K2
Balgores La GPK RM2 63 K3
Balgores Sq GPK RM2 63 K3
Balgowan Cl NWMAL KT3 160 B3
Balgowan Rd BECK BR3 166 B2
Balgowan St
WOOL/PLUM SE18 116 A3
Balham Gv BAL SW12 129 F6
Balham High Rd BAL SW12 129 G7
Balham Hl BAL SW12 129 G6
Balham New Rd BAL SW12 129 G6
Balham Park Rd TOOT SW17 128 E7
Balham Rd ED N9 42 C1
Balham Station Rd BAL SW12 129 F7
Balkan Wk WAP * E1W 92 D6
Ballamore Rd BMLY BR1 152 E2
Ballance Rd HOM E9 75 F5
Ballantine St
WAND/EARL SW18 128 B3
Ballard Cl KUTN/CMB KT2 145 F6
Ballards Cl DAGE RM10 80 D7
Ballards Farm Rd
SAND/SEL CR2 178 C5
Ballards La FNCH N3 39 F6
Ballards Ri SAND/SEL CR2 178 C5
Ballards Rd CRICK NW2 69 J1
DAGE RM10 80 D7
Ballards Wy SAND/SEL CR2 178 C5
Ballast Quay GNWCH SE10 113 G4
Ballater Cl OXHEY WD19 33 G3
Ballater Rd CLAP SW4 129 K3
SAND/SEL CR2 178 B4
Ballina St FSTH SE23 132 A6
Ballingdon Rd BTSEA SW11 129 F5
Balliol Av CHING E4 44 B3
Balliol Rd NKENS W10 88 A5
TOTM N17 42 A7
WELL DA16 136 C1
Balloch Rd CAT SE6 133 G7
Ballogie Av WLSDN NW10 69 G3
Ballow Cl CMBW * SE5 110 E6
Ball's Pond Pl IS * N1 73 K5
Balls Pond Rd IS N1 73 K5
Balmain Cl EA W5 85 K7
Balmer Rd BOW E3 93 H1
Balmes Rd IS N1 7 H3
Balmoral Av BECK BR3 166 B3
FBAR/BDGN N11 40 A5
Balmoral Cl PUT/ROE * SW15 127 G5
Balmoral Crs E/WMO/HCT KT8 157 F2
Balmoral Dr BORE WD6 25 F3
STHL UB1 83 K3
YEAD UB4 82 C3
Balmoral Gdns BXLY DA5 137 G6
HNWL W7 104 B2
Balmoral Gv HOLWY N7 73 F5
Balmoral Ms SHB W12 106 C2
Balmoral Rd CRICK NW2 69 K5
FSTGT E7 77 G3
GPK RM2 63 K3
KUT KT1 159 G3
LEY E10 75 K1

RYLN/HDSTN HA2 66 A3
WPK KT4 173 K2
Balmore Crs EBAR EN4 28 A4
Balmore St ARCH N19 72 B1
Balmuir Gdns PUT/ROE SW15 127 F3
Balnacraig Av WLSDN NW10 69 G3
Baltic Cl WIM/MER SW19 147 H6
Baltic Pl IS N1 7 K3
Baltic St East STLK EC1Y 12 E1
Baltic St West FARR EC1M 12 E1
Baltimore Pl WELL DA16 136 A1
Balvaird Pl PIM SW1V 17 H8
Balvernie Gv
WAND/EARL SW18 127 J6
Bamborough Gdns SHB W12 107 F1
Bamford Av ALP/SUD HA0 68 B7
Bamford Rd BMLY BR1 152 B4
Bampfylde Cl WLGTN SM6 176 C2
Bampton Dr MLHL NW7 37 J6
Bampton Rd FSTH SE23 151 F2
Banavie Gdns BECK BR3 151 K7
Banbury Ct BELMT * SM2 174 E6
COVGDN * WC2E 11 J6
Banbury Rd HOM E9 75 F6
WALTH E17 43 G6
Banbury St BTSEA * SW11 128 D1
WATW WD18 20 E4
Banchory Rd BKHTH/KID SE3 114 A6
Bancroft Av EFNCH N2 53 J4
Bancroft Cha HCH RM12 81 H1
Bancroft Ct NTHLT UB5 65 G7
Bancroft Gdns
KTN/HRWW/W HA3 34 C7
Bancroft Rd KTN/HRWW/W HA3 48 C1
WCHPL E1 92 E3
Bandon Ri WLGTN SM6 176 D5
Banfield Rd PECK SE15 131 J2
Bangalore St PUT/ROE SW15 127 F2
Bangor Cl NTHLT UB5 66 B4
Banim St HMSMTH W6 106 E2
Banister Rd NKENS W10 88 B2
The Bank HGT N6 54 B7
Bank Av MTCM CR4 162 C1
Bank Buildings CHING * E4 44 B5
Bank End STHWK SE1 12 F8
Bankfoot Rd BMLY BR1 152 C3
Bankhurst Rd CAT SE6 132 C6
Bank La KUTN/CMB KT2 144 A6
PUT/ROE SW15 126 B4
Banksia Rd UED N18 42 E4
Bankside SAND/SEL CR2 178 B5
STHL UB1 83 H7
STHWK SE1 12 E7
Bankside Av NTHLT UB5 82 E1
Bankside Cl CAR SM5 175 J4
ISLW TW7 124 A3
Bankside Dr THDIT KT7 171 H1
Bankside Rd IL IG1 78 C4
Banks La BXLYHS DA6 137 G3
Banks Rd BORE WD6 24 E1
Bankton Rd BRXS/STRHM SW2 130 B3
Bankwell Rd LEW SE13 133 H3
Bank Willow
RCHPK/HAM TW10 143 H2
Banner St STLK EC1Y 12 F1
Banning St GNWCH SE10 113 H4
Bannister Cl BRXS/STRHM SW2 130 B7
GFD/PVL UB6 66 D4
Bannockburn Rd
WOOL/PLUM SE18 115 K3
Bannow Cl HOR/WEW KT19 173 G3
Banstead Gdns ED N9 41 K2
Banstead Rd BELMT SM2 175 H6
Banstead St PECK SE15 131 K2
Banstead Wy WLGTN SM6 176 E4
Banstock Rd EDGW HA8 36 E5
Banting Dr WCHMH N21 29 F4
Banton Cl EN EN1 30 D1
Bantry St CMBW SE5 110 E6
Banwell Rd BXLY DA5 136 E5
Banyard Rd BERM/RHTH SE16 111 J2
Baptist Gdns HAMP NW3 72 A5
Barandon Wk NTGHL * W11 88 B6
Barbara Hucklesbury Cl
WDGN N22 55 H1
Barbauld Rd STNW/STAM N16 74 A2
Barber Cl WCHMH N21 29 G6
Barbers Rd SRTFD E15 93 K1
Barbican BARB EC2Y 12 F2
Barbican Rd GFD/PVL UB6 84 B5
Barb Ms HMSMTH W6 107 F2
Barbon Cl BMSBY WC1N 11 K2
Barbot Cl ED N9 42 B2
Barchard St WAND/EARL SW18 128 A4
Barchester Cl HNWL W7 85 F7
Barchester Rd
KTN/HRWW/W HA3 34 D7
Barchester St POP/IOD E14 93 K4
Barclay Cl FUL/PGN * SW6 107 K6
WATW WD18 20 E5
Barclay Ov WFD IG8 44 E3
Barclay Rd CROY/NA CR0 177 K2
FUL/PGN SW6 107 K6
PLSTW E13 95 G3
UED N18 41 K5
WALTH E17 58 A4
WAN E11 58 D7
Barcombe Av
BRXS/STRHM SW2 148 E1
Barden St WOOL/PLUM SE18 115 K6
Bardfield Av CHDH RM6 61 K2
Bardney Rd MRDN SM4 162 A3
Bardolph Av CROY/NA CR0 179 H7
Bardolph Rd HOLWY N7 72 E3
RCH/KEW TW9 125 G3
Bard Rd NKENS W10 88 B6
Bardsey Pl WCHPL E1 92 E4
Bardsey Wk IS * N1 73 J5
Bardsley Cl CROY/NA CR0 178 B2
Bardsley La GNWCH SE10 113 F5
Barfett St NKENS W10 88 D3
Barfield Av TRDG/WHET N20 39 K1
Barfield Rd BMLY BR1 169 F2
WAN * E11 58 D7
Barford Cl HDN NW4 51 J1
Barford St IS N1 6 B4
Barforth Rd PECK SE15 131 J2
Barfreston Wy PGE/AN SE20 150 D7
Bargate Cl NWMAL KT3 160 D6
WOOL/PLUM SE18 116 A4
Barge House Rd CAN/RD E16 115 G1
Barge House St STHWK SE1 12 B8
Bargery Rd CAT SE6 132 E7
Barge Wk KUT KT1 158 E1
Bargrove Cl PGE/AN SE20 150 C6
Bargrove Crs CAT SE6 151 H1
Barham Av BORE WD6 24 B2
Barham Cl ALP/SUD HA0 67 H5
CHST BR7 154 B4
HAYES BR2 168 D7
ROMW/RG RM7 62 D1
Barham Ct ALP/SUD HA0 67 J5
Barham Rd CHST BR7 154 B4
CROY/NA CR0 177 J3
DART DA1 139 K6
RYNPK SW20 145 J6
Baring Cl LEE/GVPK SE12 152 E1
Baring Rd BMLY BR1 153 F3
CROY/NA CR0 165 H7
EBAR EN4 27 H2
LEE/GVPK SE12 133 K7
LEE/GVPK SE12 153 F3
Baring St IS N1 7 G4
Barker Cl KUT KT1 159 J3
NTHWD HA6 32 D6
Barker Dr CAMTN NW1 4 F2
Barkham Rd TOTM N17 41 K6
Barking Rd POP/IOD E14 94 C5
Bark Pl BAY/PAD W2 8 C6
Barkston Gdns ECT SW5 14 C7
Barkwood Cl ROMW/RG RM7 62 E4
Barkworth Rd
BERM/RHTH SE16 111 J4
Barlborough St NWCR SE14 112 A6
Barlby Gdns NKENS W10 88 B3
Barlby Rd NKENS W10 88 A4
Barley Cl BUSH WD23 22 B4
Barley La GDMY/SEVK IG3 61 G5
Barley Mow Pas CHSWK W4 106 A4
Barlow Cl WLGTN SM6 176 E5
Barlow Dr WOOL/PLUM SE18 114 D7
Barlow Pl MYFR/PICC W1J 10 D7
Barlow Rd ACT W3 86 D7
CRICK NW2 70 D5
HPTN TW12 142 A6
Barlow St WALW SE17 19 H5
Barlow Wy DAGW RM9 99 F5
Barmeston Rd CAT SE6 151 K1
Barmor Cl RYLN/HDSTN HA2 48 B1
Barmouth Av GFD/PVL UB6 85 F1
Barmouth Rd CROY/NA CR0 179 F1
WAND/EARL SW18 128 B5
Barnabas Rd HOM E9 75 F5
Barnaby Cl RYLN/HDSTN HA2 66 C1
Barnaby Pl SKENS SW7 15 G6
Barnard Cl CHST BR7 154 D7
SUN TW16 141 F6
WLGTN SM6 176 D6
Barnard Gdns NWMAL KT3 160 D3
YEAD UB4 83 F3
Barnard Hl MUSWH N10 54 B1
Barnard Ms BTSEA SW11 128 D3
Barnardo Dr BARK/HLT IG6 60 C3
Barnardo Gdns WCHPL * E1 93 F5
Barnardo St WCHPL E1 93 F5
Barnard Rd BTSEA SW11 128 D3
EN EN1 30 D1
MTCM CR4 163 F2
Barnards Pl SAND/SEL CR2 177 H7
Barnby St CAMTN NW1 4 F6
SRTFD E15 76 C7
Barn Cl KTTN * NW5 72 D4
NTHLT UB5 83 G1
Barn Crs STAN HA7 35 J5
Barneby Cl WHTN TW2 123 K7
Barnehurst Av BXLYHN DA7 117 K7
Barnehurst Cl ERITH DA8 117 K7
Barnehurst Rd BXLYHN DA7 137 K1
Barnes Av BARN SW13 106 D6
NWDGN UB2 102 E3
Barnes Br CHSWK W4 126 B1
Barnes Cl MNPK E12 77 H3
Barnes Cray Rd DART DA1 138 D3
Barnes End NWMAL KT3 160 D4
Barnes High St BARN SW13 126 C1
Barnes Rd IL IG1 78 C4
UED N18 42 E3
Barnes St POP/IOD E14 93 G5
Barnes Ter DEPT SE8 112 C4
Barnet By-pass BORE WD6 25 G4
Barnet Dr HAYES BR2 181 J1
Barnet Gate La BAR EN5 25 H5
Barnet Gv BETH E2 92 C2
Barnet Hl BAR EN5 26 D3
Barnet La BORE WD6 24 B5
TRDG/WHET N20 26 D7
Barnet Rd MLHL NW7 25 G5
Barnett Cl ERITH DA8 138 C1
Barnetts Ct RYLN/HDSTN * HA2 66 B2
Barnett St WCHPL E1 92 D5
Barnet Wy (Barnet By-Pass)
MLHL NW7 25 F6
Barnet Wood Rd HAYES * BR2 181 F2
Barney Cl CHARL SE7 114 B4
Barn Fld HAMP * NW3 71 K4
Barnfield NWMAL KT3 160 B5
Barnfield Av CROY/NA CR0 165 K7
KUTN/CMB KT2 143 K3
MTCM CR4 163 G3
Barnfield Gdns KUTN/CMB KT2 144 A4
WOOL/PLUM * SE18 115 G5
Barnfield Rd BELV DA17 117 G5
EA W5 85 J3
EDGW HA8 36 E7
SAND/SEL CR2 178 A7
WOOL/PLUM SE18 115 G5
Barnfield Wood Cl BECK BR3 167 G5
Barnfield Wood Rd BECK BR3 167 G5
Barnham Rd GFD/PVL UB6 84 C2
Barnham St STHWK SE1 19 K1
Barnhill PIN HA5 47 G4
Barn Hl WBLY HA9 68 D1
Barnhill Av HAYES BR2 167 K4
Barnhill La YEAD UB4 83 F2
Barnhill Rd WBLY HA9 68 E2
YEAD UB4 83 F3
Barnhurst Pth OXHEY WD19 33 G4
Barningham Wy
CDALE/KGS NW9 50 E5
Barnlea Cl FELT TW13 141 J1
Barnmead Gdns DAGW RM9 80 B4
Barnmead Rd BECK BR3 151 F7
DAGW RM9 80 B4
Barnock Cl DART DA1 138 B5
Barn Ri WBLY HA9 50 C7
Barnsbury Cl NWMAL KT3 159 K3
Barnsbury Crs BRYLDS KT5 159 K7
Barnsbury Est IS N1 5 M4
Barnsbury Gv HOLWY N7 5 M1
Barnsbury La BRYLDS KT5 172 D1
Barnsbury Pk IS N1 6 A1
Barnsbury Rd IS N1 6 A5
Barnsbury Sq IS N1 6 A2
Barnsbury St IS N1 6 B2
Barnsbury Ter IS N1 5 M2
Barnscroft RYNPK SW20 160 E2
Barnsdale Av POP/IOD E14 112 E3
Barnsdale Rd MV/WKIL W9 88 D3
Barnsley St WCHPL E1 92 D3
Barnstaple La LEW SE13 133 F3
Barnstaple Rd RSLP HA4 65 G2
Barnston Wk IS * N1 6 E3
Barn St STNW/STAM N16 74 A1
Barn Wy WBLY HA9 50 C7
Barnwell Rd DART DA1 139 J2
HNHL SE24 130 B4
Barnwood Cl MV/WKIL W9 8 C1
RSLP HA4 64 B1
Baron Cl FBAR/BDGN N11 40 A4
Baroness Rd BETH E2 7 M7
Baronet Gv TOTM N17 42 C7
Baronet Rd TOTM N17 42 C7
Baron Gdns BARK/HLT IG6 60 C2
Baron Gv MTCM CR4 162 D3
Baron Rd BCTR RM8 61 K7
The Barons TWK TW1 124 C5
Barons Cl IS * N1 6 A5
Baron's Court Rd WKENS W14 107 H4
Baronsfield Rd TWK * TW1 124 C5
Barons Ga EBAR EN4 27 J5
Barons Keep WKENS * W14 107 H4
Barons Md HRW HA1 48 E3
Baronsmead Rd BARN SW13 106 D7
Baronsmede EA W5 105 G1
Baronsmere Ct BAR * EN5 26 C3
Baronsmere Rd EFNCH N2 53 J3
Baron's Pl STHWK SE1 18 B2
Baron St IS N1 6 B6
Baron's Wk CROY/NA CR0 166 B5
Barque Ms DEPT SE8 112 D5
Barrack Rd HSLWW TW4 122 C3
Barra Hall Rd HYS/HAR UB3 82 C6
Barratt Av WDGN N22 55 F1
Barratt Wy KTN/HRWW/W HA3 48 D2
Barrenger Rd MUSWH N10 39 K7
Barrett Rd WALTH E17 58 A3
Barrett's Green Rd
WLSDN NW10 86 E1
Barrett's Gv STNW/STAM N16 74 A4
Barrett St MBLAR W1H 10 B5
Barrhill Rd BRXS/STRHM SW2 148 E1
Barriedale NWCR SE14 112 B7
Barrier Point Rd CAN/RD E16 95 G7
Barringer Sq TOOT SW17 148 A3
Barrington Cl CLAY IG5 45 K7
KTTN NW5 72 A4
Barrington Rd BRXN/ST SW9 130 C2
BXLYHN DA7 136 E1
CEND/HSY/T N8 54 D4
CHEAM SM3 161 K7
MNPK E12 78 A5
Barrington Vls
WOOL/PLUM SE18 115 F7
Barrington Wk NRWD * SE19 150 A5
Barrow Av CAR SM5 175 K6
Barrow Cl WCHMH N21 41 H2
Barrowdene Cl PIN HA5 47 J1
Barrowell Gn WCHMH N21 41 H1
Barrowfield Cl ED N9 42 D2
Barrowgate Rd CHSWK W4 105 K4
Barrow Hedges Cl CAR SM5 175 J6
Barrow Hedges Wy CAR SM5 175 J6
Barrow Hl WPK KT4 173 G1
Barrow Hill Cl WPK KT4 173 G1
Barrow Hill Est STJWD NW8 3 J6
Barrow Hill Rd STJWD NW8 3 J6
Barrow Point Av PIN HA5 47 J1
Barrow Point La PIN HA5 47 J1
Barrow Rd CROY/NA CR0 177 G4
STRHM/NOR SW16 148 D5
Barrs Rd WLSDN NW10 69 F6
Barry Av BXLYHN DA7 117 F6
SEVS/STOTM N15 56 B5
Barry Pde EDUL * SE22 131 H3
Barry Rd EDUL SE22 131 H5
EHAM E6 95 J5
WLSDN NW10 68 E6
Barset Rd PECK SE15 131 K2
Barsons Cl PGE/AN SE20 150 E6
Barston Rd WNWD SE27 149 J1
Barstow Crs BRXS/STRHM SW2 130 A7
Barter St NOXST/BSQ WC1A 11 K3
Bartholomew Cl STBT EC1A 12 E3
WAND/EARL SW18 128 B3
Bartholomew La LOTH EC2R 13 H5
Bartholomew Rd KTTN NW5 72 C5
Bartholomew Sq FSBYE EC1V 6 F9
Bartholomew St STHWK SE1 19 H4
Bartholomew Vls KTTN NW5 72 C5
Barth Rd WOOL/PLUM SE18 115 K3
Bartle Av EHAM E6 95 J1
Bartle Rd NTGHL W11 88 B5
Bartlett Cl POP/IOD E14 93 J5
Bartlett Ct FLST/FETLN * EC4A 12 B4
Bartlett St SAND/SEL CR2 177 K4
Barton Av DAGE RM10 62 E7
Barton Cl BXLYHS DA6 137 F4
HDN NW4 51 J4
PECK SE15 131 J2
Barton Gn NWMAL KT3 160 A1
Barton Mdw BARK/HLT IG6 60 B3
Barton Rd HCH RM12 63 J7
WKENS W14 107 H4
The Bartons BORE WD6 23 K5
Barton St WEST SW1P 17 J4
Barton Wy BORE WD6 24 C1
Bartram Rd BROCKY SE4 132 B4
Bartrip St HOM E9 75 G5
Barts Cl BECK BR3 166 D4
Barward Cl WOOL/PLUM SE18 115 F3
Barwell Ct CHSGTN * KT9 171 J6
Barwick Rd FSTGT E7 77 F3
Barwood Av WWKM BR4 166 E7
Bascombe Gv DART DA1 138 B6
Basden Gv FELT TW13 142 A1
Basedale Rd DAGW RM9 79 H6
Baseing Cl EHAM E6 96 A6
Basevi Wy DEPT SE8 112 D5
Bashley Rd WLSDN NW10 87 F3
Basil Av EHAM E6 95 J2
Basildene Rd HSLWW TW4 122 C2
Basildon Cl BELMT SM2 175 F7
WATW WD18 20 A5
Basildon Rd ABYW SE2 116 B4
Basil Gdns CROY/NA CR0 166 A7
WNWD SE27 149 J4
Basilon Rd BXLYHN DA7 137 F1
Basil St CHEL SW3 15 L3
Basin Ap POP/IOD E14 93 G5
Basingdon Wy CMBW SE5 130 E3
Basing Dr BXLY DA5 137 G5
Basingfield Rd THDIT KT7 158 A6
Basinghall Av CITYW EC2V 13 G4
Basinghall Gdns BELMT SM2 175 F7
Basinghall St CITYW EC2V 13 G4
Basing Hl GLDGN NW11 52 D7
WBLY HA9 68 B1
Basing Pl BETH E2 7 K7
Basing St NTGHL W11 88 D5
Basing Wy FNCH N3 52 E2
THDIT KT7 158 A6
Basire St IS N1 6 F3
Baskerville Gdns WLSDN NW10 69 G3
Baskerville Rd
WAND/EARL SW18 128 D6
Basket Gdns ELTH/MOT SE9 134 D4
Baslow Cl KTN/HRWW/W HA3 34 D7
Baslow Wk CLPT E5 75 F3
Basnett Rd BTSEA * SW11 129 F2
Bassano St EDUL SE22 131 G4
Bassant Rd WOOL/PLUM SE18 116 A5
Bassein Park Rd SHB W12 106 C1
Bassett Cl BELMT SM2 175 F7
Bassett Gdns ISLW TW7 103 H6
Bassett Rd NKENS W10 88 B5
Bassett St KTTN NW5 72 A5
Bassett Wy GFD/PVL UB6 84 B5
Bassingham Rd ALP/SUD HA0 67 K5
WAND/EARL SW18 128 B6
Basswood Cl PECK SE15 131 J2
Bastable Av BARK IG11 97 G1
Bastion Rd ABYW SE2 116 B4
Baston Manor Rd WWKM BR4 181 F2
Baston Rd HAYES BR2 181 F1
Bastwick St FSBYE EC1V 6 D9
Basuto Rd FUL/PGN SW6 107 K7
Batavia Cl SUN TW16 141 G7
Batavia Rd NWCR SE14 112 B6
SUN TW16 141 F7
Batchelor St IS N1 6 A5
Batchworth La NTHWD HA6 32 A4
Bateman Cl BARK IG11 78 C5
Bateman Rd CHING E4 43 J5
Batemans Cnr CHSWK * W4 106 A3
Bateman's Rw SDTCH EC2A 7 K9
Bateman St SOHO/SHAV W1D 11 G5
Bates Crs CROY/NA CR0 177 G5
STRHM/NOR SW16 148 C6
Bate St POP/IOD E14 93 H6
Bath Cl PECK SE15 111 J6
Bathgate Rd WIM/MER SW19 146 B2
Bath Gv BETH E2 92 C1
Bath House Rd CROY/NA CR0 163 K7
Bath Pas KUT KT1 158 E1
Bath Pl IS N1 7 J8
Bath Rd CHSWK W4 106 B3
DART DA1 138 E6
ED N9 42 D1
FSTGT E7 77 H5
HEST TW5 102 B7
HSLWW TW4 122 C1
WDR/YW UB7 100 A7
Baths Ap FUL/PGN * SW6 107 J6
Bath St FSBYE EC1V 6 F8
Bath Ter STHWK SE1 18 E4
Bathurst Av WIM/MER SW19 147 F7
Bathurst Gdns WLSDN NW10 87 K1
Bathurst Ms BAY/PAD W2 9 H6
Bathurst Rd IL IG1 60 B7
Bathurst St BAY/PAD W2 9 H6
Bathway WOOL/PLUM SE18 115 F3
Batley Cl MTCM CR4 162 E6
Batley Pl STNW/STAM N16 74 B2
Batley Rd STNW/STAM N16 74 B2
Batman Cl SHB W12 87 K7
Batoum Gdns HMSMTH W6 107 F2
Batson St SHB W12 106 D1
Batsworth Rd MTCM CR4 162 C2
Batten Cottages POP/IOD * E14 93 G4
Batten St BTSEA SW11 128 D2
Battersby Rd CAT SE6 152 B1
Battersea Br BTSEA SW11 108 C6
Battersea Bridge Rd
BTSEA SW11 108 D6
Battersea Church Rd
BTSEA SW11 108 C7
Battersea High St BTSEA SW11 108 C7
Battersea Park Rd
BTSEA SW11 109 F7
Battersea Ri BTSEA SW11 128 D4
Battersea Sq BTSEA * SW11 108 D6
Battery Rd THMD SE28 115 K1
Battishill St IS N1 6 C2
Battle Bridge La STHWK SE1 13 J9
Battle Bridge Rd CAMTN NW1 5 J6
Battle Cl WIM/MER SW19 147 G5
Battledean Rd HBRY N5 73 H4
Battle Rd ERITH DA8 117 K3
Batty St WCHPL E1 92 C5
Baudwin Rd CAT SE6 152 C1
Baugh Rd SCUP DA14 155 J4
The Baulk WAND/EARL SW18 127 K6
Bavant Rd STRHM/NOR SW16 163 K1
Bavaria Rd ARCH N19 72 E1
Bavent Rd CMBW SE5 130 D1
Bawdale Rd EDUL SE22 131 G4
Bawdsey Av CHTH/NBYPK IG2 61 F3
Bawtree Rd NWCR SE14 112 B6
Bawtry Rd TRDG/WHET N20 39 K2
Baxendale TRDG/WHET N20 39 G1
Baxendale St BETH E2 92 C2
Baxter Cl NWDGN UB2 103 G2
Baxter Rd CAN/RD E16 95 G5
IL IG1 78 B4
IS N1 73 K5
UED N18 42 D3
Bay Ct EA * W5 105 F2
Baycroft Cl PIN * HA5 47 G2
Bayfield Rd ELTH/MOT SE9 134 C3
Bayford Ms HACK * E8 74 D6
Bayford Rd WLSDN NW10 88 B2
Bayford St HACK E8 74 D6
Bayham Pl CAMTN NW1 4 E4
Bayham Rd CHSWK W4 106 A2
MRDN SM4 162 A3
WEA W13 85 H6
Bayham St CAMTN NW1 4 E4
Bayhurst Dr NTHWD HA6 32 D5
Bayleaf Cl HPTN TW12 142 D4
Bayley St FITZ W1T 11 G3
Baylis Rd STHWK SE1 18 A3
Bayliss Av THMD SE28 97 K6
Bayliss Cl STHGT/OAK N14 28 E4
Bayly Rd DART DA1 139 K5
Bayne Cl EHAM E6 95 K5
Baynes Ms HAMP NW3 71 H5
Baynes St CAMTN NW1 4 F2
Baynham Cl BXLY DA5 137 G5
Bayonne Rd FUL/PGN SW6 107 H5
Bays Cl SYD SE26 150 E4
Bayston Rd STNW/STAM N16 74 B2
Bayswater Rd BAY/PAD W2 8 D7
Baythorne St BOW E3 93 H4
Baytree Cl BFN/LL DA15 136 A7
BMLY BR1 153 H7
Baytree Rd BRXS/STRHM SW2 130 A3
Bazalgette Cl NWMAL KT3 159 K4
Bazalgette Gdns NWMAL KT3 160 A4
Bazely St POP/IOD E14 94 A6
Bazile Rd WCHMH N21 29 G5
Beacham Cl CHARL SE7 114 C5
Beachborough Rd BMLY BR1 152 A3
Beachcroft Rd WAN E11 76 C2
Beach Gv FELT TW13 142 A2
Beachy Rd BOW E3 75 J6
Beacon Hl HOLWY N7 72 E4
Beacon Pl CROY/NA CR0 176 E2
Beacon Rd ERITH DA8 118 E6
HTHAIR TW6 120 D5
LEW SE13 133 G5
Beaconsfield Cl
BKHTH/KID SE3 113 K5
CHSWK W4 105 K4
Beaconsfield Cottages
TRDG/WHET * N20 38 E2
Beaconsfield Gdns
ESH/CLAY KT10 170 E6
Beaconsfield Rd
BKHTH/KID SE3 113 K5
BMLY BR1 168 C2
BRYLDS KT5 159 G6
CAN/RD E16 94 D3
CHSWK W4 106 A2
CROY/NA CR0 164 E5
EA W5 104 D1
ED N9 42 C2
ELTH/MOT SE9 153 J2
ESH/CLAY KT10 170 E6
HYS/HAR UB3 83 G7
LEY * E10 76 A2
NWMAL KT3 160 A1
SEVS/STOTM N15 56 A3
TRDG/WHET N20 39 K2
TWK TW1 124 C6
WALTH E17 57 H5
WALW SE17 19 H9
WLSDN NW10 69 H5
Beaconsfield Terrace Rd
WKENS W14 107 H2
Beaconsfield Wk
FUL/PGN SW6 107 J7
Beacontree Av WALTH E17 44 B7
Beacontree Rd WAN E11 58 D6
Beadlow Cl MRDN SM4 162 C5
Beadman Pl WNWD * SE27 149 H3
Beadman St WNWD SE27 149 H3
Beadnell Rd FSTH SE23 132 A7
Beadon Rd HAYES BR2 167 K3
HMSMTH W6 107 F3
Beaford Gv RYNPK SW20 161 H2
Beagle Cl FELT TW13 141 F3
Beak St REGST W1B 10 E6
Beal Cl WELL DA16 116 B7
Beale Cl PLMGR N13 41 H4
Beale Pl BOW E3 93 H1
Beale Rd BOW E3 75 H7
Beal Rd IL IG1 78 A1
Beam Av DAGE RM10 80 D7
Beaminster Gdns BARK/HLT IG6 60 B2
Beamish Dr BUSH WD23 22 C7
Beamish Rd ED N9 30 C7
Beamway DAGE RM10 81 F6
Beanacre Cl HOM * E9 75 H5
Bean Rd BXLYHS DA6 136 E3
Beanshaw ELTH/MOT SE9 154 A3
Beansland Gv CHDH RM6 62 A1
Bear Cl ROMW/RG RM7 62 D5
Beardell St NRWD SE19 150 B5
Beardow Gv STHGT/OAK * N14 28 C5
Beard Rd RCHPK/HAM TW10 144 B4
Beardsfield PLSTW E13 76 E7
Beard's Hl HPTN TW12 142 A7
Beard's Hill Cl HPTN TW12 142 A7
Beardsley Wy ACT W3 106 A1
Beards Rd ASHF TW15 140 C5
Bearfield Rd KUTN/CMB KT2 144 A6
Bear Gdns STHWK SE1 12 E8
Bear La STHWK SE1 12 D8
Bear Rd FELT TW13 141 H3
Bearstead Ri BROCKY SE4 132 C4
Bearstead Ter BECK * BR3 151 J7
Bear St LSQ/SEVD WC2H 11 H6
Beasant House WATN * WD24 21 H1
Beatrice Av STRHM/NOR SW16 164 A2
WBLY HA9 68 A4
Beatrice Cl PIN HA5 46 E3
PLSTW E13 94 E3
Beatrice Pl KENS W8 14 C4
Beatrice Rd ED N9 30 E6
FSBYPK N4 55 G6
RCHPK/HAM TW10 125 G4
STHL UB1 83 K7
STHWK SE1 111 H3
WALTH E17 57 J4
Beattie Cl EBED/NFELT TW14 121 J7
Beattock Ri MUSWH N10 54 B3
Beatty Rd STAN HA7 35 J5
STNW/STAM N16 74 A3
Beatty St CAMTN * NW1 4 E5
Beattyville Gdns CLAY IG5 60 A2
Beauchamp Pl CHEL SW3 15 K3
Beauchamp Rd BTSEA SW11 128 D3
E/WMO/HCT KT8 157 G4
FSTGT E7 77 F6
SUT SM1 174 E4
THHTH CR7 149 K7
TWK TW1 124 B6
Beauchamp St HCIRC EC1N 12 A3
Beauchamp Ter
PUT/ROE SW15 126 E2
Beauclerc Rd HMSMTH W6 106 E2
Beauclerk Cl FELT TW13 122 A7
Beaufort EHAM E6 96 A4
Beaufort Av KTN/HRWW/W HA3 49 G3
Beaufort Cl CHING E4 43 K5
EA W5 86 B4
PUT/ROE SW15 127 F7
ROMW/RG RM7 62 E3
Beaufort Dr GLDGN NW11 52 E3
Beaufort Gdns CHEL SW3 15 K3
HDN NW4 52 A5
HEST TW5 102 D7
IL IG1 60 A7
STRHM/NOR SW16 149 F6
Beaufort Rd EA W5 86 B4
KUT KT1 159 F3
RCHPK/HAM TW10 143 J3
RSLP * HA4 64 B1
TWK TW1 124 D6
Beaufort St CHEL SW3 15 G9
Beaufort Wy EW KT17 173 J6
Beaufoy Rd TOTM N17 42 A6
Beaufoy Wk LBTH SE11 17 M6
Beaulieu Av CAN/RD E16 95 F7
SYD SE26 150 D3
Beaulieu Cl CDALE/KGS NW9 51 G3
CMBW SE5 130 E2
HSLWW TW4 122 E4
MTCM CR4 148 A7

OXHEY WD19 21 G7
TWK TW1 124 E5
Beaulieu Dr PIN HA5 47 H5
Beaulieu Gdns WCHMH N21 29 J6
Beaulieu Pl CHSWK W4 105 K2
Beaumaris Gn
CDALE/KGS * NW9 51 G5
Beaumont Av ALP/SUD HA0 67 J4
RCH/KEW TW9 125 G2
RYLN/HDSTN HA2 48 B5
WKENS W14 107 J4
Beaumont Cl KUTN/CMB * KT2 144 C6
Beaumont Ct ALP/SUD HA0 67 J4
Beaumont Crs RAIN RM13 81 J5
WKENS W14 107 J4
Beaumont Dr ASHF TW15 140 B4
Beaumont Gdns HAMP NW3 70 E2
Beaumont Gv WCHPL E1 93 F3
Beaumont Ms MHST * W1U 10 B2
PIN * HA5 47 J2
Beaumont Pl FITZ W1T 4 F9
ISLW TW7 124 A4
Beaumont Ri ARCH N19 54 D7
Beaumont Rd CHSWK W4 105 K2
LEY E10 57 K6
NRWD SE19 149 J5
PLSTW E13 95 F2
STMC/STPC BR5 169 J5
WAND/EARL SW18 127 H6
Beaumont Sq WCHPL E1 93 F4
Beaumont St MHST W1U 10 B2
Beaumont Ter LEW * SE13 133 H6
Beaumont Wk HAMP NW3 3 M1
Beauvais Ter NTHLT UB5 83 H2
Beauval Rd EDUL SE22 131 G5
Beaverbank Rd ELTH/MOT SE9 135 J7
Beaver Cl HPTN TW12 142 B7
PGE/AN * SE20 150 C6
Beavers Crs HSLWW TW4 122 C3
Beavers La HSLWW TW4 122 B2
Beaverwood Rd CHST BR7 154 E4
Beavor La HMSMTH W6 106 D3
Bebbington Rd
WOOL/PLUM * SE18 115 K3
Beccles St POP/IOD E14 93 H5
Bec Cl RSLP HA4 65 H2
Beck Cl LEW SE13 112 E7
Beck Ct BECK BR3 166 A2
Beckenham Gdns ED N9 42 A2
Beckenham Gv HAYES BR2 167 G1
Beckenham Hill Rd BECK BR3 151 K5
Beckenham La HAYES BR2 167 H1
Beckenham Place Pk
BECK BR3 151 K6
Beckenham Rd BECK BR3 151 F7
WWKM BR4 166 E6
Becket Av EHAM E6 96 A2
Becket Cl SNWD SE25 165 H5
WIM/MER * SW19 147 F7
Becket Fold HRW * HA1 49 F4
Becket Rd UED N18 42 E3
Becket St STHWK SE1 19 G3
Beckett Cl BELV DA17 117 F2
STRHM/NOR SW16 148 D1
WLSDN NW10 69 F5
Becketts Cl EBED/NFELT TW14 122 A5
Becketts Pl KUT KT1 143 K7
Beckett Wk BECK BR3 151 G5
Beckford Cl WKENS W14 107 J3
Beckford Dr STMC/STPC BR5 169 J6
Beckford Pl WALW * SE17 18 F8
Beckford Rd CROY/NA CR0 165 G5
Beck La BECK BR3 166 A2
Becklow Rd SHB W12 106 D1
Beck River Pk BECK BR3 151 H7
Beck Rd HACK E8 74 D7
Becks Rd SCUP DA14 155 G2
Beckton Rd CAN/RD E16 94 D4
Beck Wy BECK BR3 166 C2
Beckway Rd
STRHM/NOR SW16 163 J1
Beckway St WALW SE17 19 H6
Beckwith Rd HNHL SE24 130 E5
Beclands Rd TOOT SW17 148 A5
Becmead Av
KTN/HRWW/W HA3 49 H4
STRHM/NOR SW16 148 D3
Becondale Rd NRWD SE19 150 A4
Becontree Av BCTR RM8 79 H3
Bective Rd FSTGT E7 76 E3
PUT/ROE SW15 127 J3
Becton Pl ERITH DA8 117 J6
Bedale St STHWK * SE1 13 G9
Beddington Farm Rd
CROY/NA CR0 163 K7
Beddington Gdns CAR SM5 176 A5
Beddington Gn
STMC/STPC BR5 155 F7
Beddington Gv WLGTN SM6 176 D4
Beddington La CROY/NA CR0 176 E1
MTCM CR4 163 H5
Beddington Rd GDMY/SEVK IG3 61 F6
STMC/STPC BR5 154 E7
Beddington Ter
CROY/NA * CR0 164 A6
Bede Cl PIN HA5 33 H7
Bede Rd CHDH RM6 61 J5
Bedfont Cl EBED/NFELT TW14 121 F5
MTCM CR4 163 F1
Bedfont Green Cl
EBED/NFELT TW14 121 F7
Bedfont La EBED/NFELT TW14 121 H6
Bedfont Rd EBED/NFELT TW14 121 F7
STWL/WRAY TW19 120 C5
Bedford Av BAR EN5 26 D4
RSQ WC1B 11 H3
YEAD UB4 83 F5
Bedfordbury CHCR WC2N 11 J6
Bedford Cl CHSWK W4 106 B5
MUSWH N10 40 A6
Bedford Cnr CHSWK * W4 106 B3
Bedford Ct CHCR WC2N 11 J7
Bedford Gdns KENS W8 8 A9
Bedford Hl BAL SW12 148 B1
Bedford Pk CROY/NA CR0 164 D7
Bedford Pl CROY/NA CR0 164 E7
RSQ WC1B 11 J2
Bedford Rd BFN/LL DA15 154 E2
CEND/HSY/T N8 54 D5
CHSWK W4 106 A2
CLAP SW4 129 K3
DART DA1 139 K6
ED N9 30 D6
EFNCH N2 53 J2
EHAM E6 78 A7
HRW HA1 48 C5
IL IG1 78 B2
MLHL NW7 37 G1
NTHWD HA6 32 A3
RSLP HA4 64 D3
SEVS/STOTM N15 55 K3
SWFD E18 58 E1
WALTH E17 57 J1
WDGN N22 40 E7
WEA W13 85 H6
WHTN TW2 142 D2
WPK KT4 174 A1
Bedford Rw FSBYW WC1X 11 M2
Bedford Sq RSQ WC1B 11 H3
Bedford St COVGDN WC2E 11 J6
Bedford Vls KUT * KT1 159 G1
Bedford Wy STPAN WC1H 11 H1
Bedgebury Gdns
WIM/MER SW19 146 C1
Bedgebury Rd ELTH/MOT SE9 134 C3
Bedivere Rd BMLY BR1 152 E2
Bedlow Cl STJWD NW8 9 H1
Bedlow Wy CROY/NA CR0 177 F3
Bedonwell Rd BELV DA17 117 F5
Bedser Cl LBTH SE11 17 M9
THHTH CR7 164 D2
Bedser Dr GFD/PVL UB6 66 D4
Bedster Gdns E/WMO/HCT KT8 157 G1
Bedwardine Rd NRWD SE19 150 A6
Bedwell Gdns HYS/HAR UB3 101 H4
Bedwell Rd BELV DA17 117 H4
TOTM N17 42 A7
Beeby Rd CAN/RD E16 95 F4
Beech Av ACT W3 87 G7
BFN/LL DA15 136 B6
BKHH IG9 45 F1
BTFD TW8 104 C6
RSLP HA4 47 F7
TRDG/WHET N20 27 J7
Beech Cl ASHF TW15 140 B4
CAR SM5 175 K1
DEPT SE8 112 C5
ED N9 30 C5
HCH RM12 81 K2
PUT/ROE SW15 126 D6
RYNPK SW20 146 A5
STWL/WRAY TW19 120 A6
SUN TW16 156 C1
WDR/YW UB7 100 D2
Beech Copse BMLY BR1 168 E1
SAND/SEL CR2 178 A4
Beech Ct ELTH/MOT * SE9 134 D5
Beechcroft CHST BR7 154 A6
Beechcroft Av BXLYHN DA7 118 A7
GLDGN NW11 52 D6
NWMAL KT3 144 E7
RKW/CH/CXG WD3 20 A5
RYLN/HDSTN HA2 48 A6
STHL UB1 83 K7
Beechcroft Cl HEST TW5 102 D6
STRHM/NOR SW16 149 F4
Beechcroft Gdns WBLY HA9 68 B2
Beechcroft Rd BUSH WD23 21 J4
CHSGTN KT9 172 B3
MORT/ESHN * SW14 125 K2
SWFD E18 59 F1
TOOT SW17 147 J2
Beechdale WCHMH N21 41 F1
Beechdale Rd
BRXS/STRHM SW2 130 A5
Beech Dell HAYES BR2 181 K3
Beech Dr BORE WD6 24 B1
EFNCH N2 53 K2
Beechen Cliff Wy ISLW TW7 124 A1
Beechengrove PIN HA5 47 K2
Beechen Gv WAT WD17 21 F2
Beechen Pl FSTH SE23 150 E1
The Beeches HNWL * W7 104 A1
WATW * WD18 21 F2
The Beeches Av CAR SM5 175 J6
Beeches Cl PGE/AN SE20 150 E7
Beeches Rd CHEAM SM3 161 H7
TOOT SW17 147 J2
Beeches Wk CAR SM5 175 H7
Beechfield Cl BORE WD6 24 A1
Beechfield Gdns
ROMW/RG RM7 62 E6
Beechfield Rd BMLY BR1 168 B1
CAT SE6 132 C7
ERITH DA8 118 B6
FSBYPK N4 55 J5
Beech Gdns DAGE RM10 80 D6
EA W5 105 F1
Beech Gv MTCM CR4 163 J4
NWMAL KT3 160 A2
Beech Hall Crs CHING E4 44 B6
Beech Hall Rd CHING E4 44 B6
Beechhill Rd ELTH/MOT SE9 135 F4
Beech House Rd CROY/NA CR0 177 K2
Beech Lawns
NFNCH/WDSP * N12 39 H4
Beechmont Cl BMLY BR1 152 C4
Beechmore Gdns CHEAM SM3 174 B1
Beechmore Rd BTSEA SW11 108 E7
Beechmount Av HNWL W7 84 D4
Beecholme Av MTCM CR4 148 B7
Beecholme Est CLPT * E5 74 E2
Beech Rd DART DA1 139 G7
EBED/NFELT TW14 121 H6
FBAR/BDGN N11 40 E5
STRHM/NOR SW16 163 K1
Beechrow KUTN/CMB KT2 144 A3
Beech St ROMW/RG RM7 62 E3
Beech St (Below) BARB EC2Y 12 E2
Beech Tree Cl IS N1 6 A1
STAN HA7 35 J4
Beech Tree Pl SUT SM1 175 F4
Beechvale Cl NFNCH/WDSP N12 39 J4
Beech Wk DART DA1 138 D3
MLHL NW7 37 F5
Beechway BXLY DA5 136 E5
Beech Wy FELT TW13 142 A2
WLSDN NW10 69 F6
Beechwood Av FNCH N3 52 D2
GFD/PVL UB6 84 B2
HYS/HAR UB3 82 B6
RCH/KEW TW9 105 H7
RSLP HA4 64 D1
RYLN/HDSTN HA2 66 B1
SUN TW16 140 E5
THHTH CR7 164 C3
Beechwood Cl EFNCH * N2 53 K3
MLHL NW7 37 G4
SURB KT6 158 D6
Beechwood Crs BXLYHN DA7 136 E2
Beechwood Dr HAYES BR2 181 H3
WFD IG8 44 D4
Beechwood Gdns CLAY IG5 59 K4
RAIN RM13 99 K4
RYLN/HDSTN HA2 66 B2
Beechwood Gv ACT W3 87 G6
Beechwood Ms ED N9 42 C1
Beechwood Pk SWFD E18 58 E2
Beechwood Ri CHST BR7 154 B3
Beechwood Rd CEND/HSY/T N8 54 D3
HACK E8 74 B5
SAND/SEL CR2 178 A7
Beechworth Cl HAMP NW3 71 F1
Beecroft La BROCKY SE4 132 B4
Beecroft Ms BROCKY SE4 132 B4
Beecroft Rd BROCKY SE4 132 B4
Beehive Cl BORE WD6 23 K5
HACK E8 7 L1
Beehive La REDBR IG4 59 K4
Beehive Pl BRXN/ST SW9 130 B2
Beeleigh Rd MRDN SM4 162 A3
Beeston Cl HACK E8 74 C4
OXHEY WD19 33 H3
Beeston Pl BGVA SW1W 16 D4
Beeston Rd EBAR EN4 27 H5
Beeston Wy EBED/NFELT TW14 122 B5
Beethoven Rd BORE WD6 23 J6
Beethoven St NKENS W10 88 C2
Beeton Cl PIN HA5 34 A6
Begbie Rd BKHTH/KID SE3 114 B7
Beggars Bush La WATW WD18 20 B4
Beggar's Roost La SUT SM1 174 E5
Begonia Cl EHAM E6 95 J4
Begonia Pl HPTN TW12 142 A5
Beira St BAL SW12 129 G6
Bekesbourne St POP/IOD * E14 93 G5
Belcroft Cl BMLY BR1 152 D6
Beldham Gdns
E/WMO/HCT KT8 157 G2
Belfairs OXHEY WD19 33 H4
Belfairs Dr CHDH RM6 61 J6
Belfast Rd SNWD SE25 165 J3
STNW/STAM N16 74 B1
Belfield Rd HOR/WEW KT19 173 F7
Belford Gv WOOL/PLUM SE18 115 F3
Belfort Rd PECK SE15 131 K1
Belfry Cl BERM/RHTH * SE16 111 J4
Belgrade Rd HPTN TW12 142 B7
STNW/STAM N16 74 A3
Belgrave Cl ACT W3 105 K1
MLHL NW7 37 F4
STHGT/OAK N14 28 C4
Belgrave Crs SUN TW16 141 F7
Belgrave Gdns STHGT/OAK N14 28 D4
STJWD NW8 2 D4
Belgrave Ms South KTBR SW1X 16 B3
Belgrave Ms West KTBR SW1X 16 A3
Belgrave Pl KTBR SW1X 16 B4
Belgrave Rd BARN SW13 106 C6
HSLWW TW4 122 E2
IL IG1 78 A1
LEY E10 58 A7
MTCM CR4 162 C2
PIM SW1V 16 E6
PLSTW E13 95 G3
SNWD SE25 165 G3
SUN TW16 141 F7
WALTH E17 57 J5
WAN E11 58 E7
Belgrave Sq KTBR SW1X 16 A3
Belgrave St WCHPL E1 93 F5
Belgrave Wk MTCM CR4 162 C2
Belgravia Cl BAR EN5 26 D2
Belgravia Gdns BMLY BR1 152 C5
Belgravia Ms KUT KT1 158 E3
Belgrove St CAMTN NW1 5 J7
Belinda Rd BRXN/ST SW9 130 C2
Belitha Vls IS N1 5 M1
Bellamy Cl EDGW HA8 36 E2
POP/IOD E14 112 D1
WKENS W14 107 J4
Bellamy Dr STAN HA7 35 H7
Bellamy Rd CHING E4 43 K5
ENC/FH * EN2 29 K1
Bellamy St BAL SW12 129 G6
Bel La FELT TW13 141 J2
Bellasis Av BRXS/STRHM SW2 129 K7
Bell Av WDR/YW UB7 100 C2
Bell Cl PIN HA5 47 G2
Bellclose Rd WDR/YW UB7 100 B1
Bell Dr WAND/EARL SW18 127 H6
Bellefields Rd BRXN/ST SW9 130 A2
Bellegrove Cl WELL DA16 136 A1
Bellegrove Rd WELL DA16 135 K1
Bellenden Rd PECK SE15 131 G1
Belle Staines Pleasaunce
CHING E4 43 J1
Belleville Rd BTSEA SW11 128 E4
Belle Vue GFD/PVL UB6 66 D7
Belle Vue La BUSH WD23 22 D7
Bellevue Pk THHTH CR7 164 D2
Bellevue Pl WCHPL * E1 92 E3
Belle Vue Rd WALTH E17 58 B1
Bellevue Rd BARN SW13 126 D1
BXLYHS DA6 137 G4
FBAR/BDGN N11 40 A3
KUT KT1 159 F2
TOOT SW17 128 E6
WEA W13 85 H3
Bellew St TOOT SW17 147 G2
Bell Farm Av DAGE RM10 80 E2
Bellfield CROY/NA CR0 179 H7
Bellfield Av KTN/HRWW/W HA3 34 D5
Bell Gdns LEY * E10 57 J7
Bellgate Ms KTTN NW5 72 B3
Bell Gn CAT SE6 151 G3
Bell Green La SYD SE26 151 H4
Bell House Rd ROMW/RG RM7 62 E7
Bellina Ms KTTN NW5 72 B3
Bellingham Gn CAT SE6 151 J2
Bellingham Rd CAT SE6 152 A2
Bell La CAN/RD E16 94 E7
HDN NW4 52 B3
TWK TW1 124 B7
WBLY * HA9 67 K1
WCHPL E1 13 L3
Bell Meadow NRWD SE19 150 A3
Bello Cl BRXS/STRHM SW2 130 C7
Bellot St GNWCH SE10 113 H4
Bell Pde HSLW * TW3 123 G3
WWKM * BR4 180 A1
Bellring Cl BELV DA17 117 H5
Bell Rd E/WMO/HCT KT8 157 J4
HSLW TW3 123 G3
Bells Hl BAR EN5 26 B4
Bell St BAY/PAD W2 9 J2
WOOL/PLUM SE18 114 D7
Belltrees Gv STRHM/NOR SW16 149 F4
Bell Water Ga
WOOL/PLUM SE18 115 F2
Bell Wharf La CANST EC4R 12 F7
Bellwood Rd PECK SE15 132 A3
Bell Yd LINN WC2A 12 A5
Belmont Av ALP/SUD HA0 68 B7
EBAR EN4 27 K4
ED N9 30 C7
NWDGN UB2 102 D2
NWMAL KT3 160 D4
PLMGR N13 40 E4
TOTM N17 55 J2
WELL DA16 135 K1
Belmont Cir
KTN/HRWW/W * HA3 35 H7
Belmont Cl CHING E4 44 B4
CLAP SW4 129 H2
EBAR EN4 27 K3
TRDG/WHET N20 27 F7
WFD IG8 45 F3
Belmont Gv CHSWK W4 106 A3
LEW SE13 133 G2
Belmont Hl LEW SE13 133 G2
Belmont La CHST BR7 154 C3
STAN HA7 35 J6
Belmont Pde CHST * BR7 154 B4
GLDGN * NW11 52 D4
Belmont Pk LEW SE13 133 G3
Belmont Park Cl LEW SE13 133 H3
Belmont Park Rd LEY E10 57 K5
Belmont Ri BELMT SM2 174 D6
Belmont Rd BECK BR3 166 B1
BUSH WD23 21 J4
CHST BR7 154 B4
CLAP SW4 129 H2
ERITH DA8 117 H6
IL IG1 78 C2
KTN/HRWW/W HA3 49 F2
SEVS/STOTM N15 55 J3
SNWD SE25 165 J4
WHTN TW2 142 D1
WLGTN SM6 176 C4
Belmont St CAMTN NW1 4 B1
Belmont Ter CHSWK W4 106 A3
Belmor BORE WD6 24 C4
Belmore Av YEAD UB4 82 E5
Belmore La HOLWY * N7 72 D4
Belmore St VX/NE SW8 109 J7
Beloe Cl BARN SW13 126 D3
Belsham St HOM E9 74 E5
Belsize Av HAMP NW3 71 J4
PLMGR N13 41 F5
WEA W13 104 C2
Belsize Ct Garages HAMP NW3 71 H4
Belsize Crs HAMP NW3 71 H4
Belsize Gdns SUT SM1 175 F3
Belsize Gv HAMP NW3 71 J5
Belsize La HAMP NW3 71 H5
Belsize Ms HAMP * NW3 71 H5
Belsize Pk HAMP NW3 71 H5
Belsize Park Gdns HAMP NW3 71 H5
Belsize Park Ms HAMP NW3 71 H5
Belsize Pl HAMP NW3 71 H4
Belsize Rd KIL/WHAMP NW6 2 C3
KIL/WHAMP NW6 2 F2
KTN/HRWW/W HA3 34 D6
Belsize Sq HAMP NW3 71 H5
Belsize Ter HAMP NW3 71 H5
Belson Rd WOOL/PLUM SE18 114 E3
Beltane Dr WIM/MER SW19 146 B2
Belthorn Crs BAL SW12 129 H6
Belton Rd FSTGT E7 77 F6
SCUP DA14 155 G3
TOTM N17 56 A2
WAN E11 76 C3
WLSDN NW10 69 J5
Belton Wy BOW E3 93 J4
Beltran Rd FUL/PGN SW6 128 A1
Beltwood Rd BELV DA17 117 K3
The Belvedere WBPTN * SW10 108 B7
Belvedere Av CLAY IG5 60 B1
WIM/MER SW19 146 C4
Belvedere Buildings STHWK SE1 18 D2
Belvedere Cl ESH/CLAY KT10 170 B4
TEDD TW11 142 E4
Belvedere Ct BELV DA17 117 G2
Belvedere Dr WIM/MER SW19 146 C4
Belvedere Gdns
E/WMO/HCT KT8 156 E4
Belvedere Gv WIM/MER SW19 146 C4
Belvedere Ms PECK SE15 131 K2
Belvedere Rd BXLYHN DA7 137 G2
HNWL W7 103 K2
LEY E10 57 G7
NRWD SE19 150 B6
STHWK SE1 17 L1
THMD SE28 97 K7
Belvedere Sq WIM/MER SW19 146 C4
Belvedere Strd CDALE/KGS NW9 51 H1
Belvedere Wy
KTN/HRWW/W HA3 50 A5
Belvoir Rd EDUL SE22 131 H6
Belvue Cl NTHLT UB5 66 A6
Belvue Rd NTHLT UB5 66 A6
Bembridge Cl KIL/WHAMP NW6 70 C6
Bembridge Gdns RSLP HA4 64 B1
Bemerton Est IS N1 5 L2
Bemerton St IS N1 5 L3
Bemish Rd PUT/ROE SW15 127 G2
Bempton Dr RSLP HA4 65 F1
Bemsted Rd WALTH E17 57 H2
Benares Rd WOOL/PLUM SE18 116 A3
Benbow Rd HMSMTH W6 106 E2
Benbow St DEPT SE8 112 D5
Benbury Cl BMLY BR1 152 A4
The Bench RCHPK/HAM * TW10 143 J2
Bench Fld SAND/SEL CR2 178 B5
Bencroft Rd
STRHM/NOR SW16 148 C6
Bencurtis Pk WWKM BR4 180 B2
Bendall Ms CAMTN NW1 9 K2
Bendemeer Rd PUT/ROE SW15 127 G2
Bendish Rd EHAM E6 77 J6
Bendmore Av ABYW SE2 116 B4
Bendon Va WAND/EARL SW18 128 A6
Bendysh Rd BUSH WD23 21 J2
Benedict Dr EBED/NFELT TW14 121 G6
Benedict Rd BRXN/ST SW9 130 A2
MTCM CR4 162 C2
Benedict Wy EFNCH * N2 53 G2
Benedict Whf MTCM CR4 162 D2
Benenden Gn HAYES BR2 167 K4
Benett Gdns
STRHM/NOR SW16 163 K1
Benfleet Cl SUT SM1 175 G2
Benfleet Wy FBAR/BDGN N11 40 A1
Bengal Rd IL IG1 78 A4
Bengarth Dr KTN/HRWW/W HA3 48 D1
Bengarth Rd NTHLT UB5 65 H7
Bengeworth Rd HRW HA1 67 G1
Ben Hale Cl STAN HA7 35 G4
Benham Cl BTSEA SW11 128 C2
CHSGTN KT9 171 J5
Benham Gdns HSLW TW3 122 E4
Benham Rd HNWL W7 84 E4
Benhill Av SUT SM1 175 G3
Benhill Rd CMBW SE5 110 E6
SUT SM1 175 H2
Benhill Wood Rd SUT SM1 175 G3
Benhilton Gdns SUT SM1 175 F2
Benhurst Av HCH RM12 81 K3
Benhurst La STRHM/NOR SW16 149 G4
Benin St LEW SE13 133 G6
Benjafield Cl UED N18 42 D3
Benjamin Cl EMPK RM11 63 J5
HACK E8 74 C7
Benjamin St FARR EC1M 12 C2
Ben Jonson Rd WCHPL E1 93 G4
Benledi St POP/IOD E14 94 B5
Bennelong Cl SHB W12 87 K6
Bennerley Rd BTSEA SW11 128 E4
Bennet Cl KUT KT1 143 J7
Bennet's Hl BLKFR EC4V 12 D6
Bennett Cl NTHWD HA6 32 D6
WELL DA16 136 B1
Bennett Gv LEW SE13 112 E7
Bennett Pk BKHTH/KID SE3 133 J2
Bennett Rd CHDH RM6 62 A5
PLSTW E13 95 G3
Bennetts Av CROY/NA CR0 179 G1
GFD/PVL UB6 66 E7
Bennett's Castle La BCTR RM8 79 J3
Bennetts Cl MTCM CR4 148 B7
TOTM N17 42 B5
Bennetts Copse CHST BR7 153 J5
Bennett St CHSWK W4 106 B5
WHALL SW1A 10 E8
Bennetts Wy CROY/NA CR0 179 G1
Benningholme Rd EDGW HA8 37 G5
Bennington Rd TOTM N17 42 A7
WFD * IG8 44 C6
Benn St HOM E9 75 G5
Bensbury Cl PUT/ROE SW15 126 E6
Bensham Cl THHTH CR7 164 D3
Bensham Gv THHTH CR7 164 D1
Bensham La THHTH CR7 164 C3
Bensham Manor Rd
THHTH CR7 164 D3
Benskin Rd WATW WD18 20 E4
Ben Smith Wy
BERM/RHTH SE16 111 H2
Benson Av PLSTW E13 95 G1
Benson Cl HSLW TW3 123 F3
Benson Quay WAP E1W 92 E6
Benson Rd CROY/NA CR0 177 G2
FSTH SE23 131 K7
Benthal Rd STNW/STAM N16 74 B1
Bentham Rd HOM E9 75 F5
THMD SE28 97 H7
Ben Tillet Cl BARK IG11 79 G6
CAN/RD * E16 95 K7
Bentinck Ms MHST W1U 10 B4
Bentinck St MHST W1U 10 B4
Bentley Dr GNTH/NBYPK IG2 60 C5
Bentley Ms EN EN1 29 K5
Bentley Rd IS N1 74 A5
Bentley Wy STAN HA7 35 G4
WFD IG8 44 E2
Benton Rd IL IG1 60 D7
OXHEY WD19 33 H4
Benton's La WNWD SE27 149 J3
Benton's Ri WNWD SE27 149 K4
Bentry Cl BCTR RM8 80 A1
Bentry Rd BCTR RM8 80 A1
Bentworth Rd SHB W12 87 K5
Benwell Ct SUN * TW16 140 E7
Benwell Rd HOLWY N7 73 G3
Benwick Cl BERM/RHTH SE16 111 J3
Benworth St BOW E3 93 H2
Benyon Rd IS N1 7 H3
Berberis Wk WDR/YW UB7 100 B3
Berber Rd BTSEA * SW11 128 E4
Bercta Rd ELTH/MOT SE9 154 C1
Berenger Wk WBPTN * SW10 108 C6
Berens Rd WLSDN NW10 88 B2
Beresford Av ALP/SUD HA0 68 C7
BRYLDS KT5 159 J7
HNWL W7 84 D4
TRDG/WHET N20 39 K1
TWK TW1 124 D5
Beresford Dr BMLY BR1 168 C2
WFD IG8 45 G3
Beresford Gdns CHDH RM6 62 A4
EN EN1 30 A3
HSLWW TW4 122 E4
Beresford Rd BELMT SM2 174 D6
CEND/HSY/T N8 55 G4
EFNCH N2 53 J2
HBRY N5 73 K4
HRW HA1 48 D4
KUTN/CMB KT2 144 B7
NWMAL KT3 159 K3
STHL UB1 83 H7
WALTH E17 43 K7
Beresford St
WOOL/PLUM SE18 115 H2
Beresford Ter HBRY N5 73 J4
Berestede Rd HMSMTH W6 106 C4
Bere St WAP E1W 93 F6
Berger Cl STMC/STPC BR5 169 J5
Berger Rd HOM E9 75 F5
Berghem Ms WKENS W14 107 G2
Bergholt Av REDBR IG4 59 J4
Bergholt Crs STNW/STAM N16 56 A6
Bergholt Ms CAMTN NW1 4 F2
Bering Wk CAN/RD E16 95 H5
Berisford Ms
WAND/EARL SW18 128 B5
Berkeley Av BXLYHN DA7 116 E7
CLAY IG5 60 A1
GFD/PVL UB6 66 E5
HEST TW5 101 K7
Berkeley Cl BORE WD6 24 C4
KUTN/CMB KT2 144 A6
ORP BR6 169 K6
RSLP HA4 64 E2
Berkeley Ct RKW/CH/CXG * WD3 20 B4
WLGTN SM6 176 C2
Berkeley Crs DART DA1 139 J7
EBAR EN4 27 H4
Berkeley Dr E/WMO/HCT KT8 156 E2
Berkeley Gdns ESH/CLAY KT10 171 G6
WCHMH N21 29 K6
Berkeley Ms MBLAR W1H 9 M4
SUN TW16 156 B2
Berkeley Pl WIM/MER SW19 146 B5
Berkeley Rd BARN SW13 106 D7
CDALE/KGS NW9 50 C3
CEND/HSY/T N8 54 D4
HGDN/ICK UB10 64 A6
MNPK E12 77 J4
SEVS/STOTM N15 55 K5
The Berkeleys SNWD * SE25 165 H3
Berkeley Sq MYFR/PICC W1J 10 D7
Berkeley St MYFR/PICC W1J 10 D7
Berkeley Waye HEST TW5 102 D6
Berkhampstead Rd BELV DA17 117 H4
Berkhamsted Av WBLY HA9 68 B5
Berkley Cl WHTN * TW2 142 E2
Berkley Gv CAMTN NW1 4 A2
Berkley Rd CAMTN NW1 3 M2
Berkshire Gdns PLMGR N13 41 G5

UED N18 42 D4
Berkshire Rd HOM E9 75 H5
Berkshire Wy MTCM CR4 163 K3
Bermans Wy WLSDN NW10 69 G3
Bermondsey St STHWK SE1 13 J9
Bermondsey Wall East
BERM/RHTH SE16 111 H1
Bermondsey Wall West
BERM/RHTH SE16 111 H1
Bernal Cl THMD SE28 97 K6
Bernard Ashley Dr CHARL SE7 114 A4
Bernard Av WEA W13 104 C2
Bernard Cassidy St
CAN/RD * E16 94 D4
Bernard Gdns WIM/MER SW19 146 D4
Bernard Rd ROMW/RG RM7 62 E6
SEVS/STOTM N15 56 B4
WLGTN SM6 176 B4
Bernard St BMSBY WC1N 11 J1
Bernays Cl STAN HA7 35 J5
Bernay's Gv BRXN/ST SW9 130 A3
Bernel Dr CROY/NA CR0 179 H2
Berne Rd THHTH CR7 164 C4
Berners Dr WEA W13 85 G6
Berners Ms FITZ W1T 10 F3
Berners Pl FITZ W1T 10 F4
Berners Rd IS N1 6 C4
WDGN N22 41 G7
Berners St FITZ W1T 10 F3
Berner Ter WCHPL * E1 92 C5
Berney Rd CROY/NA CR0 164 E6
Bernhart Cl EDGW HA8 36 E6
Bernwell Rd CHING E4 44 C2
Berridge Gn EDGW HA8 36 C6
Berridge Ms KIL/WHAMP NW6 70 E4
Berridge Rd NRWD SE19 149 K4
Berriman Rd HOLWY N7 73 F2
Berriton Rd RYLN/HDSTN HA2 47 K7
Berrybank Cl CHING E4 44 A1
Berry Cl DAGE RM10 80 C4
WCHMH N21 29 H7
WLSDN NW10 69 G6
Berry Cottages POP/IOD * E14 93 G5
Berrydale Rd YEAD UB4 83 J3
Berryfield Cl BMLY BR1 153 J7
Berry Field Cl WALTH E17 57 K3
Berryfield Rd WALW SE17 18 D7
Berryhill ELTH/MOT SE9 135 G3
Berry Hl STAN HA7 35 K3
Berryhill Gdns ELTH/MOT SE9 135 G3
Berrylands BRYLDS KT5 159 H4
RYNPK SW20 161 F2
Berrylands Rd BRYLDS KT5 159 G5
Berry La DUL SE21 149 K3
Berryman Cl BCTR RM8 79 J2
Berryman's La SYD SE26 151 F3
Berrymead Gdns ACT W3 86 E7
Berrymede Rd CHSWK W4 106 A2
Berry Pl FSBYE EC1V 6 D8
Berry St FSBYE EC1V 12 D1
Berry Wy EA W5 105 F2
Bertal Rd TOOT SW17 147 H3
Berthons Gdns WALTH * E17 58 B4
Berthon St DEPT SE8 112 D6
Bertie Rd SYD SE26 151 F5
WLSDN NW10 69 J5
Bertram Rd EN EN1 30 C3
HDN NW4 51 J5
KUTN/CMB KT2 144 C6
Bertram St KTTN NW5 72 B2
Bertrand St LEW SE13 132 E2
Bertrand Wy THMD SE28 97 H6
Bert Rd THHTH CR7 164 D4
Bert Wy EN EN1 30 B3
Berwick Av YEAD UB4 83 H6
Berwick Cl STAN HA7 35 F5
Berwick Crs BFN/LL DA15 135 K5
Berwick Rd CAN/RD E16 95 F5
WDGN N22 41 H7
WELL DA16 116 C7
Berwick St SOHO/CST W1F 10 F5
Berwyn Av HSLW TW3 103 G7
Berwyn Rd HNHL SE24 130 C7
RCHPK/HAM TW10 125 J3
Beryl Av EHAM E6 95 J4
Beryl Rd HMSMTH W6 107 G4
Berystede KUTN/CMB KT2 144 D6
Besant Cl CRICK * NW2 70 C2
Besant Rd CRICK NW2 70 C3
Besant Wy WLSDN NW10 68 E4
Besley St STRHM/NOR SW16 148 C5
Bessant Dr RCH/KEW TW9 105 J7
Bessborough Pl PIM SW1V 17 G8
Bessborough Rd HRW HA1 48 D7
PUT/ROE SW15 126 D7
Bessborough St PIM SW1V 17 G7
Bessemer Rd CMBW SE5 130 D1
Bessie Lansbury Cl EHAM E6 96 A5
Bessingby Rd RSLP HA4 64 E1
Besson St NWCR SE14 112 A7
Bessy St BETH * E2 92 E2
Bestwood St DEPT SE8 112 A3
Beswick Ms KIL/WHAMP NW6 71 F4
Betam Rd HYS/HAR UB3 101 G1
Betchworth Cl SUT SM1 175 H4
Betchworth Rd GDMY/SEVK IG3 78 E1
Betchworth Wy CROY/NA CR0 180 A7
Betham Rd GFD/PVL UB6 84 D2
Bethany Waye
EBED/NFELT TW14 121 H6
Bethecar Rd HRW HA1 48 E4
Bethell Av CAN/RD E16 94 D3
IL IG1 60 A6
Bethel Rd WELL DA16 136 D2
Bethersden Cl BECK BR3 151 H6
Bethnal Green Rd BETH E2 7 M9
Bethune Av FBAR/BDGN N11 39 K3
Bethune Rd STNW/STAM N16 55 K6
WLSDN NW10 87 F3
Bethwin Rd CMBW SE5 110 C6
Betjeman Cl RYLN/HDSTN HA2 48 A3
Betony Cl CROY/NA CR0 166 A7
Betoyne Av CHING E4 44 C3
Betsham Rd ERITH DA8 118 C6
Betstyle Rd FBAR/BDGN N11 40 B3
Betterton Rd RAIN RM13 99 G1
Betterton St LSQ/SEVD WC2H 11 J5
Bettons Pk SRTFD E15 76 C7
Bettridge Rd FUL/PGN SW6 127 J1
Betts Cl BECK BR3 166 B1
Betts Rd CAN/RD E16 95 F5
Betts St WCHPL * E1 92 D6
Betts Wy PGE/AN SE20 165 J1
THDIT KT7 158 C7
Beulah Av THHTH * CR7 164 D1
Beulah Cl EDGW HA8 36 D2
Beulah Crs THHTH CR7 164 D1
Beulah Gv CROY/NA CR0 164 D5
Beulah Hl NRWD SE19 149 H5
Beulah Rd SUT SM1 174 E3
THHTH CR7 164 D2
WALTH E17 57 K4
WIM/MER SW19 146 D6
Beult Rd DART DA1 138 D2
Bevan Av BARK IG11 79 G6
Bevan Ct CROY/NA CR0 177 G4
Bevan House WATN WD24 21 H1
Bevan Rd ABYW SE2 116 C4
EBAR EN4 27 K3
Bevan St IS N1 6 F4
Bev Callender Cl VX/NE SW8 129 G2
Bevenden St IS N1 7 H7
Beveridge Rd WLSDN NW10 69 G6
Beverley Av BFN/LL DA15 136 A6
HSLWW TW4 122 E3
RYNPK SW20 145 H7
Beverley Cl BARN SW13 126 D1
BTSEA SW11 128 C3
CHSGTN KT9 171 J3
WCHMH N21 29 J7
Beverley Ct BROCKY SE4 132 C2
Beverley Crs WFD IG8 45 F7
Beverley Dr EDGW HA8 50 D2
Beverley Gdns BARN SW13 126 C2
GLDGN NW11 52 C6
STAN HA7 35 G7
WBLY HA9 50 C7
WPK KT4 160 D7
Beverley La KUTN/CMB KT2 145 G6
Beverley Rd BARN SW13 126 C2
BXLYHN DA7 137 K1
CHING E4 44 B5
CHSWK W4 106 C4
DAGW RM9 80 A3
EHAM E6 95 H2
HAYES BR2 181 J1
KUT KT1 143 J7
MTCM CR4 163 J3
NWDGN UB2 102 D3
NWMAL KT3 160 D3
PGE/AN SE20 165 J1
RSLP HA4 65 F1
SUN TW16 140 D7
WPK KT4 174 A1
Beverley Wy NWMAL KT3 145 H7
Beverley Wy
(Kingston By-Pass)
NWMAL KT3 145 H7
The Beverly MRDN SM4 161 G5
Beversbrook Rd ARCH N19 72 D2
Beverstone Rd
BRXS/STRHM SW2 130 A4
THHTH CR7 164 B3
Beverston Ms MBLAR W1H 9 L3
Bevill Cl SNWD SE25 165 H2
Bevin Cl BERM/RHTH SE16 93 G7
Bevington Rd BECK BR3 166 E1
NKENS * W10 88 C4
Bevington St
BERM/RHTH SE16 111 H1
Bevin Rd YEAD UB4 82 E2
Bevin Sq TOOT SW17 147 K2
Bevin Wy IS N1 6 A6
Bevis Marks HDTCH EC3A 13 K4
Bewcastle Gdns ENC/FH EN2 28 E3
Bewdley St IS N1 6 A1
Bewick Ms PECK SE15 111 J6
Bewick St VX/NE SW8 129 G1
Bewley St WCHPL E1 92 D6
WIM/MER SW19 147 G5
Bewlys Rd WNWD SE27 149 H4
Bexhill Cl FELT TW13 141 J1
Bexhill Rd BROCKY SE4 132 C5
FBAR/BDGN N11 40 D4
MORT/ESHN SW14 125 K2
Bexley Cl DART DA1 138 B4
Bexley Gdns CHDH RM6 61 H4
ED N9 41 K2
Bexley High St BXLY DA5 137 H6
Bexley La DART DA1 138 B4
SCUP DA14 155 J1
Bexley Rd ELTH/MOT SE9 135 F5
ERITH DA8 117 K6
Beynon Rd CAR SM5 175 K4
Bianca Rd PECK SE15 111 G5
Bibsworth Rd FNCH N3 52 D1
Bibury Cl PECK SE15 111 F5
Bicester Rd RCH/KEW TW9 125 H2
Bickenhall St MHST W1U 9 M2
Bickersteth Rd TOOT SW17 147 K5
Bickerton Rd ARCH N19 72 B1
Bickley Crs BMLY BR1 168 D3
Bickley Park Rd BMLY BR1 168 E2
Bickley Rd BMLY BR1 168 C1
LEY E10 57 K6
Bickley St TOOT SW17 147 J4
Bicknell Rd CMBW SE5 130 D2
Bicknor Rd ORP BR6 169 K6
Bidborough Cl HAYES BR2 167 J4
Bidborough St STPAN WC1H 5 J8
Biddenden Wy ELTH/MOT SE9 154 A3
Bidder St CAN/RD E16 94 C4
Biddestone Rd HOLWY N7 73 F3
Biddulph Rd MV/WKIL W9 2 D8
SAND/SEL CR2 177 J7
Bideford Av GFD/PVL UB6 85 H2
Bideford Cl EDGW HA8 36 C7
FELT TW13 141 K2
Bideford Gdns EN EN1 30 A6
Bideford Rd BMLY BR1 152 D2
RSLP HA4 65 F2
WELL DA16 116 C6
Bidwell Gdns FBAR/BDGN N11 40 C7
Bidwell St PECK * SE15 111 J7
Biggerstaff Rd SRTFD E15 76 A7
Biggerstaff St FSBYPK N4 73 G1
Biggin Av MTCM CR4 147 K7
Biggin Hl NRWD SE19 149 H6
Biggin Wy NRWD SE19 149 H6
Bigginwood Rd
STRHM/NOR SW16 149 H6
Bigg's Rw PUT/ROE SW15 127 G2
Bigland St WCHPL E1 92 D5
Bignell Rd WOOL/PLUM SE18 115 G4
Bignold Rd FSTGT E7 76 E3
Bigwood Rd GLDGN NW11 53 F5
Billet Rd CHDH RM6 61 J2
WALTH E17 43 F7
Billetts Hart Cl HNWL W7 103 K1
Bill Hamling Cl ELTH/MOT SE9 135 K1
Billingford Cl BROCKY SE4 132 A3
Billing Pl WBPTN * SW10 108 A6
Billing Rd WBPTN SW10 108 A6
Billings Cl DAGW RM9 79 J6
Billing St WBPTN * SW10 108 A6
Billington Rd NWCR SE14 112 A6
Billiter Sq FENCHST * EC3M 13 K5
Billiter St FENCHST EC3M 13 K5
Billockby Cl CHSGTN KT9 172 B5
Billson St POP/IOD E14 113 F3
Bilton Rd ERITH DA8 118 D6
GFD/PVL UB6 67 H7
Bilton Wy HYS/HAR UB3 102 A1
Bina Gdns ECT SW5 14 E6
Bincote Rd ENC/FH EN2 29 F2
Binden Rd SHB W12 106 C2
Binfield Rd SAND/SEL CR2 178 B4
VX/NE SW8 109 K7
Bingfield St IS N1 5 K3
Bingham Ct IS * N1 6 D1
Bingham Pl MHST W1U 10 A1
Bingham Rd CROY/NA CR0 165 H7
Bingham St IS N1 73 K5
Bingley Rd CAN/RD E16 95 G5
GFD/PVL UB6 84 C3
SUN TW16 140 E6
Binney St MYFR/PKLN W1K 10 B6
Binns Rd CHSWK W4 106 B4
Binsey Wk ABYW SE2 116 D1
Binstead Cl YEAD UB4 83 J4
Binyon Crs STAN HA7 35 F4
Birbetts Rd ELTH/MOT SE9 153 K1
Birchanger Rd SNWD SE25 165 H4
Birch Av PLMGR N13 41 J2
Birch Cl BKHH IG9 45 H2
BTFD TW8 104 C6
CAN/RD E16 94 C4
HSLW TW3 123 J2
ROMW/RG RM7 62 D2
TEDD TW11 143 G4
Birchdale Gdns CHDH RM6 61 K6
Birchdale Rd FSTGT E7 77 G4
Birchdene Dr THMD SE28 97 G7
Birchen Cl CDALE/KGS NW9 69 F1
Birchend Cl SAND/SEL CR2 177 K5
Birchen Gv CDALE/KGS NW9 69 F1
Birchen La BANK EC3V 13 H5
The Birches BUSH WD23 22 C4
CHARL SE7 114 A5
CMBW * SE5 131 F2
HSLWW * TW4 122 E6
STHGT/OAK N14 29 F5
Birches Cl MTCM CR4 162 E2
PIN HA5 47 J4
Birchfield St POP/IOD E14 93 J6
Birch Gdns DAGE RM10 80 E2
Birch Gv ACT W3 86 C7
LEE/GVPK SE12 133 J6
WAN E11 76 C2
WELL DA16 136 B3
Birch Hl CROY/NA CR0 179 F4
Birchington Cl BXLYHN DA7 117 J7
Birchington Rd BRYLDS KT5 159 G6
CEND/HSY/T N8 54 D5
KIL/WHAMP NW6 2 B3
Birchlands Av BAL SW12 128 E6
Birchmead Av PIN HA5 47 G3
Birchmore Wk HBRY N5 73 J2
Birch Pk KTN/HRWW/W HA3 34 C6
Birch Rd FELT TW13 141 H4
ROMW/RG RM7 62 D2
Birch Rw HAYES BR2 169 F6
Birch Tree Av WWKM BR4 180 D4
Birch Tree Wy CROY/NA CR0 178 D1
Birch Wk MTCM CR4 163 B1
Birchway HYS/HAR UB3 82 E7
Birchwood Av BECK BR3 166 C3
MUSWH N10 54 A2
SCUP DA14 155 H2
WLGTN SM6 176 A2
Birchwood Cl MRDN SM4 162 A3
Birchwood Ct EDGW HA8 50 E1
Birchwood Dr HAMP NW3 71 F2
Birchwood Gv HPTN TW12 142 A5
Birchwood Rd STMC/STPC BR5 169 J3
TOOT SW17 148 B4
Birdbrook Cl DAGE RM10 80 E6
Birdbrook Rd BKHTH/KID SE3 134 B2
Birdcage Wk STJSPK SW1H 16 F2
Birdham Cl BMLY BR1 168 D4
Birdhurst Av SAND/SEL CR2 177 K3
Birdhurst Gdns SAND/SEL CR2 177 K3
Birdhurst Ri SAND/SEL CR2 178 A4
Birdhurst Rd SAND/SEL CR2 178 A4
WAND/EARL SW18 128 B3
WIM/MER SW19 147 J5
Bird In Bush Rd PECK SE15 111 H6
Bird-in-hand La BMLY BR1 168 C1
Bird-in-hand Pas FSTH * SE23 150 E1
Birdlip Cl PECK SE15 111 F5
Birdsfield La HOM E9 75 H7
Bird St MHST W1U 10 B5
Bird Wk WHTN TW2 122 E7
Birdwood Cl TEDD TW11 142 E3
Birkbeck Av ACT W3 86 E6
GFD/PVL UB6 66 C7
Birkbeck Gv ACT W3 87 F7
Birkbeck Hl DUL SE21 149 H1
Birkbeck Ms ACT * W3 87 F6
HACK E8 74 B4
Birkbeck Pl DUL SE21 130 C7
Birkbeck Rd ACT W3 87 F7
BECK BR3 166 A1
CEND/HSY/T N8 54 E3
EA W5 104 D3
GNTH/NBYPK IG2 60 D4
HACK E8 74 B4
MLHL NW7 37 H4
NFNCH/WDSP N12 39 G4
ROMW/RG RM7 63 F7
SCUP DA14 155 G2
TOTM N17 42 B7
WIM/MER SW19 147 F4
Birkbeck St BETH E2 92 D2
Birkbeck Wy GFD/PVL UB6 66 D7
Birkdale Av PIN HA5 48 A2
Birkdale Cl
BERM/RHTH * SE16 111 J4
ORP BR6 169 J6
Birkdale Gdns CROY/NA CR0 179 F3
OXHEY WD19 33 H2
Birkdale Rd ABYW SE2 116 B3
EA W5 86 A3
Birkenhead Av
KUTN/CMB KT2 159 G1
Birkenhead St IS N1 5 K7
Birkhall Rd CAT SE6 133 G7
Birkwood Cl BAL SW12 129 J6
Birley Rd TRDG/WHET N20 39 G1
Birley St BTSEA SW11 129 F1
Birling Rd ERITH DA8 118 A6
Birnam Rd HOLWY N7 73 F1
Birse Crs WLSDN NW10 69 G3
Birstal Gn OXHEY WD19 33 H3
Birstall Rd SEVS/STOTM N15 56 A4
Biscay Rd HMSMTH W6 107 G4
Biscoe Cl HEST TW5 103 F5
Biscoe Wy LEW * SE13 133 G3
Bisenden Rd CROY/NA CR0 178 A1
Bisham Cl MTCM CR4 162 E6
Bisham Gdns HGT N6 54 A7
Bishop Cl RCHPK/HAM TW10 143 K2
Bishop Fox Wy
E/WMO/HCT KT8 156 E3
Bishop Ken Rd
KTN/HRWW/W HA3 49 F1
Bishop King's Rd WKENS W14 107 H3
Bishop Rd STHGT/OAK N14 28 B6
The Bishops Av EFNCH N2 53 H5
Bishops Av BMLY BR1 168 B2
BORE WD6 24 B4
CHDH RM6 61 J5
FUL/PGN SW6 127 G1
NTHWD HA6 32 C3
PLSTW E13 77 F7
Bishop's Bridge Rd BAY/PAD W2 8 D4
Bishops Cl BAR EN5 26 B5
CHSWK W4 105 K4
ELTH/MOT SE9 154 C1
EN EN1 30 D1
SUT SM1 174 E2
WALTH E17 57 K3
Bishop's Ct STP EC4M 12 C4
Bishops Dr EBED/NFELT TW14 121 G5
NTHLT UB5 65 J7
Bishopsford Rd MRDN SM4 162 B6
Bishopsgate LVPST EC2M 13 K3
Bishopsgate Ar LVPST EC2M 13 J3
Bishops Gn BMLY * BR1 153 G7
Bishops Gv EFNCH N2 53 H5
HPTN TW12 141 K3
Bishop's Hall KUT KT1 158 E1
Bishops Md CMBW * SE5 110 D6
Bishop's Park Rd
FUL/PGN SW6 127 G1
STRHM/NOR SW16 148 E7
Bishop's Pl SUT SM1 175 G4
Bishop's Rd CROY/NA CR0 164 C6
FUL/PGN SW6 107 J7
HGT N6 54 A5
HNWL W7 103 K1
HYS/HAR UB3 82 A5
Bishop's Ter LBTH SE11 18 B5
Bishopsthorpe Rd SYD SE26 150 E3
Bishop St IS N1 6 E3
Bishops Wk CHST BR7 154 C7
CROY/NA CR0 179 F4
Bishop's Wy BETH E2 92 E1
Bishopswood Rd HGT N6 53 K6
Bishop Wy WLSDN NW10 69 G6
Bisley Cl WPK KT4 161 F7
Bispham Rd WLSDN NW10 86 B2
Bisson Rd SRTFD E15 94 A1
Bistern Av WALTH E17 58 B2
Bittacy Cl MLHL NW7 38 B5
Bittacy Hl MLHL NW7 38 B5
Bittacy Park Av MLHL NW7 38 B5
Bittacy Ri MLHL NW7 38 B5
Bittacy Rd MLHL NW7 38 B5
Bittern Cl YEAD UB4 83 H4
Bittern Pl WDGN * N22 55 F1
Bittern St STHWK SE1 18 E2
The Bittoms KUT KT1 158 E2
Bittoms Ct KUT * KT1 158 E2
Bixley Cl NWDGN UB2 102 E3
Blackall St SDTCH EC2A 7 J9
Blackberry Farm Cl HEST TW5 102 D6
Blackberry Fld
STMC/STPC BR5 155 G7
Blackbird Hl CDALE/KGS NW9 68 E1
Blackbird Yd BETH E2 7 M7
Blackborne Rd DAGE RM10 80 C5
Black Boy La SEVS/STOTM N15 55 J4
Blackbrook La HAYES BR2 169 F4
Blackburne's Ms
MYFR/PKLN W1K 10 A6
Blackburn Rd KIL/WHAMP NW6 71 F5
Blackbush Av CHDH RM6 61 K4
Blackbush Cl BELMT SM2 175 F6
Blackdown Cl EFNCH N2 53 G1
Blackdown Ter
WOOL/PLUM * SE18 114 E7
Blackenham Rd TOOT SW17 147 K3
Blackett St PUT/ROE SW15 127 G2
Blackfen Pde BFN/LL * DA15 136 B5
Blackfen Rd BFN/LL DA15 136 A4
Blackford Cl SAND/SEL CR2 177 H7
Blackford Rd OXHEY WD19 33 H4
Blackfriars Br STHWK SE1 12 C7
Black Friars La BLKFR EC4V 12 C5
Blackfriars Pas BLKFR EC4V 12 C6
Blackfriars Rd STHWK SE1 12 C8
Blackfriars U/P BLKFR EC4V 12 D6
Blackheath Av GNWCH SE10 113 H6
Blackheath Gv BKHTH/KID SE3 133 J1
Blackheath Hl GNWCH SE10 113 F7
Blackheath Pk BKHTH/KID SE3 133 K2
Blackheath Ri LEW SE13 133 F1
Blackheath Rd GNWCH SE10 112 E7
Blackheath V BKHTH/KID SE3 133 H1
Black Horse Ct STHWK * SE1 19 H4
Blackhorse La CROY/NA CR0 165 H6
WALTH E17 57 F2
Black Horse Pde PIN * HA5 47 F4
Blackhorse Rd DEPT SE8 112 B5
Black Horse Rd SCUP DA14 155 G3
Blackhorse Rd WALTH E17 57 F2
Blacklands Dr YEAD UB4 82 A3
Blacklands Rd CAT SE6 152 A3
Blacklands Ter CHEL SW3 15 L6
Black Lion Ga KENS W8 8 D7
Black Lion La HMSMTH W6 106 D3
Blackmans Cl DART DA1 139 F7
Blackmans Yd BETH * E2 7 M9
Blackmoor La WATW WD18 20 B4
Blackmore Av STHL UB1 84 D7
Blackmore's Gv TEDD TW11 143 G5
Blackness Cottages
HAYES * BR2 181 H7
Blackness La HAYES BR2 181 H7
Blackpool Gdns YEAD UB4 82 C3
Blackpool Rd PECK SE15 131 J1
Black Prince Rd LBTH SE11 17 L6
Black Rod Cl HYS/HAR UB3 101 J2
Blackshaw Rd TOOT SW17 147 H4
Blacksmith Cl CHDH RM6 61 J5
Blacksmith's La RAIN RM13 81 H7
Black's Rd HMSMTH W6 107 F4
Blackstock Rd FSBYPK N4 73 H1
Blackstone Est HACK E8 74 C6
Blackstone Rd CRICK NW2 70 A4
Black Swan Yd STHWK SE1 19 J1
Blackthorn Av WDR/YW UB7 100 D3
Blackthorn Ct HEST TW5 102 D6
Blackthorne Av CROY/NA CR0 165 K7
Blackthorne Dr CHING E4 44 B3
Blackthorn Gv BXLYHN DA7 137 F2
Blackthorn St BOW E3 93 J3
Blacktree Ms BRXN/ST * SW9 130 B2
Blackwall La GNWCH SE10 113 H4
Blackwall Tunnel Northern Ap
BOW E3 93 K2
Blackwall Wy POP/IOD E14 94 A6
Blackwater Cl RAIN RM13 99 F4
Blackwater St EDUL SE22 131 G4
Blackwell Cl CLPT E5 75 G3
KTN/HRWW/W HA3 34 D6
Blackwell Dr OXHEY WD19 21 G5
Blackwell Gdns EDGW HA8 36 C3
Blackwood St WALW SE17 19 G7
Bladindon Dr BXLY DA5 136 E6
Bladon Gdns RYLN/HDSTN HA2 48 B5
Blagden's La STHGT/OAK N14 40 D1
Blagdon Rd LEW SE13 132 E5
NWMAL KT3 160 C3
Blagdon Wk TEDD TW11 143 J5
Blagrove Rd NKENS W10 88 C4
Blair Av CDALE/KGS NW9 51 G6
ESH/CLAY KT10 170 C1
Blair Cl BFN/LL DA15 135 K4
HYS/HAR UB3 101 K3
IS N1 73 J5
Blairderry Rd BRXS/STRHM SW2 148 E1
Blairhead Dr OXHEY WD19 33 F2
Blair St POP/IOD E14 94 A5
Blake Av BARK IG11 78 E7
Blake Cl CAR SM5 162 D7
NKENS W10 88 A4
RAIN RM13 81 H7
WELL DA16 115 K7
Blakeden Dr ESH/CLAY KT10 171 F6
Blake Gdns DART DA1 139 J3
FUL/PGN SW6 107 K7
Blakehall Rd CAR SM5 175 K5
Blake Hall Rd WAN E11 58 E7
Blakemore Rd
STRHM/NOR SW16 148 E2
THHTH CR7 164 A4
Blakemore Wy BELV DA17 117 F2
Blakeney Av BECK BR3 151 H7
Blakeney Cl CAMTN NW1 5 G5
CAMTN NW1 5 G2
HACK E8 74 C4
TRDG/WHET N20 27 G7
Blakeney Rd BECK BR3 151 H7
Blaker Ct CHARL * SE7 114 B6
Blake Rd CAN/RD E16 94 D3
CROY/NA CR0 178 A1
FBAR/BDGN N11 40 C6
MTCM CR4 162 D2
Blaker Rd SRTFD E15 76 A7
Blakes Av NWMAL KT3 160 C4
Blake's Gn WWKM BR4 167 F6
Blakes La NWMAL KT3 160 C4
Blakesley Av EA W5 85 J5
Blake's Rd PECK SE15 111 F6
Blakes Ter NWMAL KT3 160 D4
Blakesware Gdns ED N9 29 K6
Blakewood Cl FELT TW13 141 G3
Blanchard Cl ELTH/MOT SE9 153 J2
Blanchard Wy HACK * E8 74 C5
Blanch Cl PECK SE15 111 K6
Blanchedowne CMBW SE5 130 E3
Blanche St CAN/RD E16 94 D3
Blanchland Rd MRDN SM4 162 A4
Blandfield Rd BAL SW12 129 F5
Blandford Av BECK BR3 166 B1
WHTN TW2 123 G7
Blandford Cl CROY/NA CR0 176 E2
EFNCH N2 53 G4
ROMW/RG RM7 62 D3
Blandford Rd BECK BR3 166 A1
CHSWK W4 106 B2
EA W5 104 E1
NWDGN UB2 103 F3
TEDD TW11 142 D4
Blandford Sq CAMTN NW1 9 K1
Blandford St MHST W1U 9 M4
Blandford Waye YEAD UB4 83 G5
Bland St ELTH/MOT SE9 134 C3
Blaney Crs EHAM E6 96 B2
Blanmerle Rd ELTH/MOT SE9 135 G7
Blann Cl ELTH/MOT SE9 134 C5
Blantyre St WBPTN SW10 108 C6
Blantyre Wk WBPTN * SW10 108 C6
Blashford St LEW SE13 133 G6
Blattner Cl BORE WD6 24 A3
Blawith Rd HRW HA1 48 E3
Blaydon Cl RSLP HA4 46 C6
TOTM * N17 42 D6
Blaydon Wk TOTM N17 42 D6
Bleak Hill La WOOL/PLUM SE18 116 A5
Blean Gv PGE/AN SE20 150 E6
Bleasdale Av GFD/PVL UB6 85 G1
Blechynden St NKENS * W10 88 B6
Bledlow Cl THMD SE28 97 J6
Bledlow Ri GFD/PVL UB6 84 C1
Bleeding Heart Yd
HCIRC * EC1N 12 B3
Blegborough Rd
STRHM/NOR SW16 148 C5
Blendon Dr BXLY DA5 136 E5
Blendon Rd BXLY DA5 136 E5
Blendon Ter WOOL/PLUM SE18 115 H4
Blendworth Wy PECK SE15 111 F6
Blenheim CDALE/KGS * NW9 51 H1
Blenheim Av GNTH/NBYPK IG2 60 A5
Blenheim Cl DART DA1 139 F5
GFD/PVL * UB6 84 D1
OXHEY WD19 21 G6
ROMW/RG RM7 62 E3
RYNPK SW20 161 F2
WCHMH N21 29 J7
WLGTN SM6 176 C6
Blenheim Ct BFN/LL DA15 154 D2
WFD IG8 45 F6
Blenheim Crs NTGHL W11 88 C6
RSLP HA4 64 B1
SAND/SEL CR2 177 J6
Blenheim Dr WELL DA16 116 A7
Blenheim Gdns
BRXS/STRHM SW2 130 A5
CRICK NW2 70 A4
KUTN/CMB KT2 144 D6
WBLY HA9 68 A2
WLGTN SM6 176 C5
Blenheim Gv PECK SE15 131 G1
Blenheim Park Rd
SAND/SEL CR2 177 J7
Blenheim Pas STJWD * NW8 2 E5
Blenheim Ri SEVS/STOTM * N15 56 B3
Blenheim Rd BAR EN5 26 B2
BFN/LL DA15 136 D7
CHSWK W4 106 B2
DART DA1 139 F5
EHAM E6 95 H2
HAYES BR2 168 D3
NTHLT UB5 66 B5
PGE/AN SE20 150 E6
RYLN/HDSTN HA2 48 B5

RYNPK SW20 161 F2
STJWD NW8 2 F5
SUT SM1 174 E2
WALTH E17 57 F2
WAN E11 76 C3
Blenheim St MYFR/PKLN W1K 10 C5
Blenheim Ter STJWD NW8 2 E5
Blenheim Wy ISLW TW7 104 B7
Blenkarne Rd BTSEA SW11 128 E5
Bleriot Rd HEST TW5 102 B6
Blessbury Rd EDGW HA8 36 E7
Blessington Rd LEW SE13 133 G3
Blessing Wy BARK IG11 97 J1
Bletchingly Cl THHTH CR7 164 C3
Bletchley St IS N1 6 F6
Bletchmore Cl HYS/HAR UB3 101 G4
Bletsoe Wk IS N1 6 F5
Blincoe Cl WIM/MER SW19 146 B1
Blissett St GNWCH SE10 113 F7
Bliss Ms NKENS W10 88 C2
Blisworth Cl YEAD UB4 83 J3
Blithbury Rd DAGW RM9 79 H5
Blithdale Rd ABYW SE2 116 B3
Blithfield St KENS W8 14 C4
Blockley Rd ALP/SUD HA0 67 H1
Bloemfontein Av SHB W12 87 K7
Bloemfontein Rd SHB W12 87 K6
Blomfield Rd BAY/PAD W2 8 D2
Blomfield St LVPST EC2M 13 H3
Blomfield Vls BAY/PAD W2 8 D3
Blomville Rd BCTR RM8 80 A1
Blondell Cl WDR/YW UB7 100 A5
Blondel St BTSEA SW11 129 F1
Blondin Av EA W5 104 D3
Blondin St BOW E3 93 J1
Bloomfield Crs
GNTH/NBYPK IG2 60 B5
Bloomfield Pl MYFR/PKLN W1K 10 D6
Bloomfield Rd HAYES BR2 168 C4
HGT N6 54 A5
KUT KT1 159 F3
WOOL/PLUM SE18 115 G4
Bloomfield Ter BGVA SW1W 16 B7
Bloom Gv WNWD SE27 149 H2
Bloomhall Rd NRWD SE19 149 K4
Bloom Park Rd FUL/PGN SW6 107 J6
Bloomsbury Cl EA W5 86 B6
Bloomsbury Pl
NOXST/BSQ WC1A 11 K3
Bloomsbury Sq
NOXST/BSQ WC1A 11 K3
Bloomsbury St RSQ WC1B 11 H3
Bloomsbury Wy
NOXST/BSQ WC1A 11 J3
Blore Cl VX/NE SW8 109 J7
Blossom Cl DAGW RM9 80 B7
EA W5 105 F1
SAND/SEL CR2 178 B4
Blossom St WCHPL E1 13 K2
Blossom Wy WDR/YW UB7 100 D3
Blossom Waye HEST TW5 102 D5
Blount St POP/IOD E14 93 G5
Bloxam Gdns ELTH/MOT SE9 134 D4
Bloxhall Rd LEY E10 57 H7
Bloxham Crs HPTN TW12 141 K7
Bloxworth Cl WLGTN SM6 176 C2
Blucher Rd CMBW SE5 110 D6
Blue Anchor La
BERM/RHTH SE16 111 H3
Blue Anchor Yd WCHPL E1 92 C6
Blue Ball Yd WHALL SW1A 10 E9
Bluebell Av FSTGT E7 77 H4
Bluebell Cl HOM E9 74 E7
ROMW/RG RM7 81 G1
SYD SE26 150 B3
WLGTN SM6 163 G7
Bluebell Wy IL IG1 78 B5
Blueberry Cl WFD IG8 44 E5
Bluebird La DAGE RM10 80 C6
Bluebird Wy THMD SE28 115 J1
Blue Br CAMTN NW1 4 C6
Bluefield Cl HPTN TW12 142 A4
Bluegates EW KT17 173 J6
Bluehouse Rd CHING E4 44 C2
Blue Riband Est
CROY/NA * CR0 177 H1
Blundell Rd EDGW HA8 37 F7
Blundell St HOLWY N7 5 K1
Blunden Cl BCTR RM8 61 J7
Blunt Rd CROY/NA CR0 177 K4
Blunts Av WDR/YW UB7 100 D6
Blunts Rd ELTH/MOT SE9 135 F4
Blurton Rd CLPT E5 75 F3
Blyth Cl TWK TW1 124 A5
Blythe Cl CAT SE6 132 C6
Blythe Hl CAT SE6 132 C6
STMC/STPC BR5 155 F7
Blythe Hill La CAT SE6 132 C6
Blythe Hill Pl FSTH * SE23 132 B6
Blythe Ms WKENS * W14 107 G2
Blythe Rd WKENS W14 107 G2
Blythe V CAT SE6 132 C7
Blyth Rd BMLY BR1 152 D7
HYS/HAR UB3 101 H1
THMD SE28 97 J6
WALTH E17 57 H6
Blyth's Whf POP/IOD * E14 93 G6
Blythswood Rd GDMY/SEVK IG3 61 G7
Blythwood Rd FSBYPK N4 54 E6
PIN HA5 33 H7
Boadicea St IS N1 5 L4
Boardman Av CHING E4 31 K4
Boardman Cl BAR EN5 26 C4
Boardwalk Pl POP/IOD E14 94 A7
Boathouse Wk PECK SE15 111 G6
Boat Lifter Wy
BERM/RHTH SE16 112 B3
Bob Anker Cl PLSTW E13 94 E2
Bobbin Cl CLAP SW4 129 H2
Bob Marley Wy BRXN/ST SW9 130 B3
Bockhampton Rd
KUTN/CMB KT2 144 B6
Bocking St HACK E8 74 D7
Boddicott Cl WIM/MER SW19 146 C1
Bodiam Cl EN EN1 29 K1
Bodiam Rd STRHM/NOR SW16 148 D7
Bodley Cl NWMAL KT3 160 B4
Bodley Rd NWMAL KT3 160 B5
Bodmin Cl RYLN/HDSTN HA2 65 K2
Bodmin Gv MRDN SM4 162 A3
Bodmin St WAND/EARL SW18 127 K7
Bodnant Gdns RYNPK SW20 160 D2
Bodney Rd CLPT E5 74 D4
Boeing Wy NWDGN UB2 102 A2
Bognor Gdns OXHEY * WD19 33 G4
Bognor Rd WELL DA16 116 E7
Bohemia Pl HACK E8 74 E5
Bohn Rd WCHPL E1 93 G4
Bohun Gv EBAR EN4 27 J5
Boileau Rd BARN SW13 106 D6
EA W5 86 B5
Bolden St DEPT SE8 132 E1
Boldero Pl STJWD * NW8 9 J1
Bolderwood Wy WWKM BR4 179 K1
Boldmere Rd PIN HA5 47 G6
Boleyn Ct WALTH E17 57 J3
Boleyn Dr E/WMO/HCT KT8 156 E2
RSLP HA4 65 H1
Boleyn Gdns DAGE RM10 80 E6
WWKM BR4 179 K1
Boleyn Rd EHAM E6 95 H1
FSTGT E7 76 E6
STNW/STAM N16 74 A4
Boleyn Wy BAR EN5 27 G2
Bolina Rd BERM/RHTH SE16 111 K4
Bolingbroke Gv BTSEA SW11 128 D4
Bolingbroke Rd WKENS W14 107 G2
Bolingbroke Wk BTSEA * SW11 108 C6
Bolingbroke Wy HYS/HAR UB3 82 B7
Bollo Bridge Rd ACT W3 105 J2
Bollo La ACT W3 105 J2
Bolney Ga SKENS SW7 15 J2
Bolney St VX/NE SW8 110 A6
Bolsover St GTPST W1W 10 D1
Bolstead Rd MTCM CR4 148 B7
Bolster Gv WDGN * N22 40 D7
Bolt Ct FLST/FETLN * EC4A 12 B5
Bolton Cl CHSGTN KT9 171 K5
Bolton Crs CMBW SE5 110 B5
Bolton Gdns BMLY BR1 152 D5
ECT SW5 14 D7
TEDD TW11 143 G5
WLSDN NW10 88 B1
Bolton Gardens Ms
WBPTN SW10 14 D7
Bolton Rd CHSGTN KT9 171 K5
CHSWK W4 105 K6
FSTGT E7 76 D5
HRW HA1 48 C3
KIL/WHAMP NW6 2 D4
UED N18 42 B4
WLSDN NW10 69 G7
The Boltons ALP/SUD HA0 67 F3
WBPTN SW10 14 E7
WFD * IG8 44 E3
Bolton's La WDR/YW UB7 101 F6
Bolton St MYFR/PICC W1J 10 D8
Bombay St BERM/RHTH SE16 111 J3
Bomer Cl WDR/YW UB7 100 D6
Bomore Rd NTGHL W11 88 B6
Bonaparte Ms PIM SW1V 17 G7
Bonar Pl CHST BR7 153 J6
Bonar Rd PECK SE15 111 H6
Bonchester Cl CHST BR7 154 A6
Bonchurch Cl BELMT SM2 175 F6
Bonchurch Rd NKENS W10 88 C4
WEA W13 85 H7
Bondfield Av YEAD UB4 82 E2
Bond Gdns WLGTN SM6 176 C3
Bond Rd MTCM CR4 162 E1
SURB KT6 172 B1
Bond St EA W5 85 K6
SRTFD E15 76 C4
Bondway VX/NE SW8 17 K9
Boneta Rd WOOL/PLUM SE18 114 E2
Bonfield Rd LEW SE13 133 F3
Bonham Gdns BCTR RM8 79 K1
Bonham Rd BCTR RM8 79 K1
BRXS/STRHM SW2 130 A4
Bonheur Rd CHSWK W4 106 A1
Bonhill St SDTCH EC2A 13 H1
Boniface Gdns
KTN/HRWW/W HA3 34 B6
Boniface Wk
KTN/HRWW/W HA3 34 B6
Bonita Ms BROCKY SE4 132 A2
Bonner Hill Rd KUT KT1 159 G2
Bonner Rd BETH E2 92 E1
Bonnersfield Cl HRW HA1 49 G5
Bonnersfield La HRW HA1 49 G5
Bonner St BETH * E2 92 E1
Bonneville Gdns CLAP SW4 129 H5
Bonnington Sq VX/NE SW8 17 L9
Bonny St CAMTN NW1 4 E2
Bonser Rd TWK TW1 143 F1
Bonsor St CMBW SE5 111 F6
Bonville Gdns HDN NW4 51 J3
Bonville Rd BMLY BR1 152 D4
Booker Rd UED N18 42 C4
Boones Rd LEW SE13 133 H3
Boone St LEW SE13 133 H3
Boord St GNWCH SE10 113 H2
Boothby Rd ARCH N19 72 D1
Booth Cl THMD SE28 97 H6
Booth La BLKFR EC4V 12 E6
Booth Rd CDALE/KGS NW9 37 F7
CROY/NA * CR0 177 H1
Boot Pde EDGW * HA8 36 C5
Boot St IS N1 7 J8
Bordars Rd HNWL W7 84 E4
Bordars Wk HNWL W7 84 E4
Borden Av WCHMH N21 29 K5
Border Crs SYD SE26 150 D4
Border Gdns CROY/NA CR0 179 K3
Border Ga MTCM CR4 147 J7
Border Rd SYD SE26 150 D4
Bordesley Rd MRDN SM4 162 A3
Bordon Wk PUT/ROE SW15 126 D6
Boreas Wk IS N1 6 D6
Boreham Av CAN/RD E16 94 E5
Boreham Rd WDGN N22 41 J7
Borgard House
WOOL/PLUM SE18 114 D7
Borgard Rd WOOL/PLUM SE18 114 E3
Borland Rd PECK SE15 131 K3
TEDD TW11 143 H5
Borneo St PUT/ROE SW15 127 F2
Borough High St STHWK SE1 18 F2
Borough Hl CROY/NA CR0 177 H2
Borough Rd ISLW TW7 103 K7
KUTN/CMB KT2 144 C7
MTCM CR4 162 D1
STHWK SE1 18 C3
Borough Sq STHWK SE1 18 E2
Borrett Cl WALW SE17 18 E8
Borrodaile Rd
WAND/EARL SW18 128 A5
Borrowdale Av
KTN/HRWW/W HA3 49 G1
Borrowdale Cl REDBR IG4 59 J3
Borthwick Ms WAN * E11 76 C3
Borthwick Rd CDALE/KGS NW9 51 H5
SRTFD E15 76 C3
Borthwick St DEPT SE8 112 D4
Borwick Av WALTH E17 57 H2
Bosbury Rd CAT SE6 152 A2
Boscastle Rd KTTN NW5 72 B2
Boscobel Pl BGVA SW1W 16 B5
Boscobel St BAY/PAD W2 9 H2
Boscombe Av LEY E10 58 B6
Boscombe Cl CLPT E5 75 G4
Boscombe Rd SHB W12 106 D1
TOOT SW17 148 A5
WIM/MER SW19 146 E7
WPK KT4 161 F7
Boss St STHWK * SE1 19 L1
Bostall Heath ABYW * SE2 116 D4
Bostall Hl ABYW SE2 116 C4
Bostall La ABYW SE2 116 C4
Bostall Manorway ABYW SE2 116 C3
Bostall Park Av BXLYHN DA7 117 F6
Bostall Rd STMC/STPC BR5 155 H6
Boston Gdns BTFD TW8 104 B3
CHSWK W4 106 B5
Boston Gv RSLP HA4 46 A5
Boston Manor Rd BTFD TW8 104 B3
Boston Pde HNWL * W7 104 B3
Boston Park Rd BTFD TW8 104 D4
Boston Pl CAMTN NW1 9 L1
Boston Rd CROY/NA CR0 164 A5
EDGW HA8 36 E6
EHAM E6 95 J2
HNWL W7 84 E7
Bostonthorpe Rd HNWL * W7 103 K1
Boston V HNWL W7 104 B3
Boswell Ct BMSBY WC1N 11 K2
Boswell Rd THHTH CR7 164 D3
Boswell St BMSBY WC1N 11 K2
Bosworth Cl WALTH E17 43 H7
Bosworth Rd BAR EN5 26 E2
DAGE RM10 80 C3
FBAR/BDGN N11 40 D5
NKENS W10 88 C3
Botany Bay La CHST BR7 169 H1
Botany Cl EBAR EN4 27 J3
Botany Ter PUR * RM19 119 K4
Boteley Cl CHING E4 44 B1
Botham Cl EDGW HA8 36 E6
Botha Rd PLSTW E13 95 F4
Bothwell Cl CAN/RD E16 94 E4
Bothwell St HMSMTH W6 107 G5
Botolph Aly MON EC3R 13 J7
Botolph La MON EC3R 13 J7
Botsford Rd RYNPK SW20 161 H1
Bott's Ms BAY/PAD W2 8 B5
Botwell Common Rd
HYS/HAR UB3 82 B6
Botwell Crs HYS/HAR UB3 82 C5
Botwell La HYS/HAR UB3 82 C6
Boucher Cl TEDD TW11 143 F4
Boughton Av HAYES BR2 167 J6
Boughton Rd THMD SE28 115 K2
Boulcott St WCHPL E1 93 F5
The Boulevard WATW WD18 20 B4
Boulevard WATW * WD18 20 B4
Boulogne Rd CROY/NA CR0 164 D5
Boulter Gdns RAIN RM13 81 J5
Boulton Rd BCTR RM8 80 A1
Boultwood Rd EHAM E6 95 K5
Bounces La ED N9 42 D1
Bounces Rd ED N9 42 D1
Boundaries Rd BAL SW12 147 K1
FELT TW13 122 B7
Boundary Av WALTH E17 57 H6
Boundary Cl GDMY/SEVK IG3 78 E3
KUT KT1 159 H2
NWDGN UB2 103 F4
Boundary La PLSTW E13 95 H3
WALW SE17 110 D5
Boundary Ms STJWD * NW8 2 F3
Boundary Rd BARK IG11 78 D7
BARK IG11 96 C1
BFN/LL DA15 135 K4
ED N9 30 E5
PIN HA5 47 H5
PLSTW E13 95 G1
ROM RM1 63 J5
STJWD NW8 2 E4
WALTH E17 57 H6
WDGN N22 55 H2
WIM/MER SW19 147 H5
WLGTN SM6 176 A7
Boundary Rw STHWK SE1 18 C1
Boundary St BETH E2 7 L8
ERITH DA8 118 C6
Boundary Wy CROY/NA CR0 179 J4
Boundfield Rd CAT SE6 152 C2
Bounds Green Rd
FBAR/BDGN N11 40 D5
Bourchier St SOHO/CST W1F 11 G6
Bourdon Pl MYFR/PKLN W1K 10 D6
Bourdon Rd PGE/AN SE20 165 K1
Bourdon St MYFR/PKLN W1K 10 C7
Bourke Cl CLAP SW4 129 K5
WLSDN NW10 69 G5
Bourlet Cl FITZ W1T 10 E3
The Bourne STHGT/OAK N14 28 E7
Bourn Av EBAR EN4 27 H4
SEVS/STOTM N15 55 K3
Bournbrook Rd
BKHTH/KID SE3 134 C2
Bourne Av HYS/HAR UB3 101 F2
RSLP HA4 65 G4
STHGT/OAK N14 40 E1
Bourne Cl ESH/CLAY KT10 171 F1
Bourne Ct RSLP HA4 65 F4
Bourne Dr MTCM CR4 162 C1
Bourne End Rd NTHWD HA6 32 C3
Bourne Est HCIRC * EC1N 12 A2
Bourne Gdns CHING E4 43 K3
Bournehall BUSH * WD23 22 A5
Bournehall Av BUSH WD23 22 A4
Bournehall La BUSH WD23 22 A5
Bournehall Rd BUSH WD23 22 A5
Bourne Hl PLMGR N13 41 F1
Bourne Hill Cl PLMGR * N13 41 F1
Bourne Md BXLY DA5 137 K4
Bournemead Av NTHLT UB5 82 E1
Bournemead Cl NTHLT UB5 82 E1
Bournemouth Cl PECK SE15 131 H1
Bournemouth Rd PECK SE15 131 H1
WIM/MER SW19 146 E7
Bourne Pde BXLY * DA5 137 J6
Bourne Rd BUSH WD23 22 A4
BXLY DA5 137 J6
CEND/HSY/T N8 54 E5
FSTGT E7 76 D2
HAYES BR2 168 C3
Bourneside Crs STHGT/OAK N14 28 D7
Bourneside Gdns CAT SE6 152 A4
Bourne St BGVA SW1W 16 A6
CROY/NA CR0 177 H1
Bourne Ter BAY/PAD W2 8 C2
Bourne V HAYES BR2 167 K7
Bournevale Rd
STRHM/NOR SW16 148 E3
Bourne Vw GFD/PVL UB6 67 F5
Bourne Wy HAYES BR2 180 E1
HOR/WEW KT19 172 E3
SUT SM1 174 D4
Bournewood Rd
WOOL/PLUM SE18 116 B6
Bournville Rd CAT SE6 132 D6
Bournwell Cl EBAR EN4 27 K2
Bourton Cl HYS/HAR UB3 82 E7
Bousfield Rd NWCR SE14 132 A1
Boutflower Rd BTSEA SW11 128 D3
Boutique Hall LEW * SE13 133 F3
Bouverie Gdns
KTN/HRWW/W HA3 49 K5
Bouverie Ms STNW/STAM N16 74 A1
Bouverie Pl BAY/PAD W2 9 H4
Bouverie Rd HRW HA1 48 C5
STNW/STAM N16 74 A1
Bouverie St EMB EC4Y 12 B5
Boveney Rd FSTH SE23 132 A6
Bovill Rd FSTH SE23 132 A6
Bovingdon Av WBLY HA9 68 C5
Bovingdon La CDALE/KGS NW9 37 G7
Bovingdon Rd FUL/PGN SW6 108 A7
Bow Arrow La DART DA1 139 K5
Bowater Cl BRXS/STRHM SW2 129 K5
CDALE/KGS NW9 51 F4
Bowater Pl BKHTH/KID SE3 114 A6
Bowater Rd WOOL/PLUM SE18 114 C2
Bow Bridge Est BOW E3 93 K2
Bow Churchyard STP * EC4M 12 F5
Bow Common La BOW E3 93 H3
Bowden Cl EBED/NFELT TW14 121 H7
Bowden St LBTH SE11 18 B7
Bowditch DEPT SE8 112 C4
Bowdon Rd LEY E10 57 J6
Bowen Dr DUL SE21 150 A2
Bowen Rd HRW HA1 48 C6
Bowen St POP/IOD E14 93 K5
Bowens Wd CROY/NA * CR0 179 H7
Bowenswood CROY/NA CR0 179 H7
Bower Av GNWCH SE10 113 H7
Bower Cl NTHLT UB5 83 G1
Bowerdean St FUL/PGN SW6 108 A7
Bowerman Av NWCR SE14 112 B5
Bower St WCHPL * E1 93 F5
Bowes Cl BFN/LL DA15 136 C5
Bowes Rd ACT W3 87 G6
BCTR RM8 79 J3
FBAR/BDGN N11 40 B4
Bowes Rd (North Circular)
PLMGR N13 40 E4
Bowfell Rd HMSMTH W6 107 F5
Bowford Av BXLYHN DA7 117 F7
Bowhill Cl BRXN/ST SW9 110 B6
Bowie Cl CLAP SW4 129 J6
Bowland Rd CLAP SW4 129 J3
WFD IG8 45 G5
Bowland Yd KTBR * SW1X 15 M2
Bow La FNCH N3 39 G6
STP EC4M 12 F5
Bowley Cl NRWD * SE19 150 B5
Bowley La NRWD SE19 150 B4
Bowley St POP/IOD E14 93 H6
Bowling Green Cl
PUT/ROE SW15 126 E6
Bowling Green Ct WBLY HA9 68 B1
Bowling Green La CLKNW EC1R 12 B1
Bowling Green Pl STHWK * SE1 19 G1
Bowling Green Rw
WOOL/PLUM * SE18 114 E3
Bowling Green St LBTH SE11 18 A9
Bowling Green Wk IS N1 7 J7
Bow Locks BOW * E3 94 A3
Bowls Cl STAN HA7 35 H4
Bowman Av CAN/RD E16 94 D5
Bowman Ms WAND/EARL SW18 127 J7
Bowmans Cl WEA W13 85 H7
Bowmans Lea FSTH SE23 131 K6
Bowman's Meadow
WLGTN SM6 176 B2
Bowman's Ms HOLWY N7 72 E2
WCHPL E1 92 C6
Bowman's Pl HOLWY N7 72 E2
Bowmans Rd DART DA1 138 C6
Bowmead ELTH/MOT SE9 153 K1
Bowmore Wk CAMTN NW1 5 H2
Bowness Cl HACK * E8 74 B5
Bowness Crs PUT/ROE SW15 145 G4
Bowness Dr HSLWW TW4 122 D3
Bowness Rd BXLYHN DA7 137 J1
CAT SE6 132 E6
Bowness Wy HCH RM12 81 J4
Bowood Rd CLAP SW4 129 F3
PEND EN3 31 F1
Bowring Gn OXHEY WD19 33 G4
Bow Rd BOW E3 93 J2
Bowrons Av ALP/SUD HA0 67 K6
Bowsley Ct FELT TW13 140 E1
Bow St COVGDN WC2E 11 K5
SRTFD E15 76 C4
Bowyer Cl EHAM E6 95 K4
Bowyer Pl CMBW SE5 110 D6
Bowyer St CMBW SE5 110 D6
Boxall Rd DUL SE21 131 F5
Boxelder Cl EDGW * HA8 36 E4
Boxgrove Rd ABYW SE2 116 C1
Box La BARK IG11 97 H1
Boxley Rd MRDN SM4 162 B3
Boxley St CAN/RD E16 95 F7
Boxmoor Rd
KTN/HRWW/W HA3 49 H3
Boxoll Rd DAGW RM9 80 B3
Boxtree La KTN/HRWW/W HA3 34 C7
Boxtree Rd KTN/HRWW/W HA3 34 D6
Boxwood Cl WDR/YW UB7 100 C1
Boxworth Gv IS N1 5 M3
Boyard Rd WOOL/PLUM SE18 115 G4
Boyce Wy PLSTW E13 94 E3
Boycroft Av CDALE/KGS NW9 50 E5
Boyd Av STHL UB1 83 K7
Boyd Cl KUTN/CMB KT2 144 C6
Boydell Ct STJWD NW8 3 G2
Boyd Rd WIM/MER SW19 147 H5
Boyd St WCHPL E1 92 C5
Boyfield St STHWK SE1 18 D2
Boyland Rd BMLY BR1 152 D4
Boyle Av STAN HA7 35 G5
Boyle Farm Rd THDIT KT7 158 B5
Boyne Av HDN NW4 52 B3
Boyne Rd DAGE RM10 80 C2
LEW SE13 133 G2
Boyne Terrace Ms NTGHL * W11 88 D7
Boyson Rd WALW SE17 18 F9
Boyton Cl CEND/HSY/T N8 54 E2
WCHPL E1 93 F3
Boyton Rd CEND/HSY/T N8 54 E2
Brabant Rd WDGN N22 55 F1
Brabazon Av WLGTN SM6 176 E7
Brabazon Rd HEST TW5 102 B6
NTHLT UB5 84 A1
Brabazon St POP/IOD E14 93 K5
Brabourne Cl NRWD SE19 150 A4
Brabourne Crs BXLYHN DA7 117 G5
Brabourne Ri BECK BR3 167 G4
Brabourn Gv PECK SE15 131 K1
Bracewell Av GFD/PVL UB6 67 F4
Bracewell Rd NKENS W10 88 A4
Bracewood Gdns
CROY/NA CR0 178 B2
Bracey St FSBYPK * N4 72 E1
The Bracken CHING E4 44 A1
Bracken Av BAL SW12 129 F5
CROY/NA CR0 179 J2
Brackenbridge Dr RSLP HA4 65 H2
Brackenbury Gdns
HMSMTH W6 106 E2
Brackenbury Rd EFNCH N2 53 G2
HMSMTH W6 106 E2
Bracken Cl EHAM E6 95 K4
SUN * TW16 140 D5
WHTN TW2 123 F6
Brackendale WCHMH N21 41 F1
Brackendale Cl HEST TW5 103 G7
Bracken End ISLW TW7 123 J4
Bracken Gdns BARN SW13 126 D1
Brackenhill RSLP * HA4 65 J3
Bracken Hill Cl BMLY BR1 152 D7
Bracken Hill La BMLY BR1 152 D7
Bracken Ms ROMW/RG RM7 62 C5
The Brackens EN EN1 30 A6
Brackenwood SUN TW16 140 E7
Brackley Cl WLGTN SM6 176 E6
Brackley Rd BECK BR3 151 H6
CHSWK W4 106 B3
Brackley Sq WFD IG8 45 H6
Brackley St BARB EC2Y 12 F2
Brackley Ter CHSWK W4 106 B4
Bracklyn St IS N1 7 G5
Bracknell Cl WDGN N22 41 G7
Bracknell Gdns HAMP NW3 71 F4
Bracknell Wy HAMP NW3 71 F3
Bracondale ESH/CLAY KT10 170 C4
Bracondale Rd ABYW SE2 116 B3
Bradbourne Rd BXLY DA5 137 H6
Bradbourne St FUL/PGN SW6 127 K1
Bradbury Cl NWDGN UB2 102 E3
Bradbury St STNW/STAM N16 74 A4
Braddock Cl ISLW TW7 124 A2
Braddon Ct BAR * EN5 26 C2
Braddon Rd RCH/KEW TW9 125 G2
Braddyll St GNWCH SE10 113 H4
Bradenham Av WELL DA16 136 B3
Bradenham Cl WALW SE17 19 G9
Bradenham Rd
KTN/HRWW/W HA3 49 H3
YEAD UB4 82 C2
Braden St MV/WKIL * W9 8 C1
Bradfield Dr BARK IG11 79 G4
Bradfield Rd CAN/RD E16 113 K1
RSLP HA4 65 J4
Bradford Cl HAYES BR2 168 E7
SYD SE26 150 D3
UED N18 42 B5
Bradford Dr HOR/WEW KT19 173 H5
Bradford Rd ACT W3 106 B1
IL IG1 60 D7
Bradgate Rd CAT SE6 132 D5
Brading Crs WAN E11 77 F1
Brading Rd BRXS/STRHM SW2 130 A6
CROY/NA CR0 164 A5
Brading Ter SHB W12 106 D2
Bradiston Rd MV/WKIL W9 88 D2
Bradley Gdns WEA W13 85 H5
Bradley Rd NRWD SE19 149 J5
WDGN N22 55 F1
Bradley's Cl IS N1 6 A5
Bradley Stone Rd EHAM E6 95 K5
Bradman Rw EDGW * HA8 36 E6
Bradmead VX/NE * SW8 109 G7
Bradmore Park Rd
HMSMTH W6 106 E2
Bradshaw Cl WIM/MER SW19 146 E5
Bradshaw Cottages
POP/IOD * E14 93 G5
Bradshaws Cl SNWD SE25 165 H2
Bradstock Rd EW KT17 173 K4
HOM E9 75 F5
Brad St STHWK SE1 12 B9
Bradwell Av DAGE RM10 80 C1
Bradwell Cl HCH RM12 81 K5
SWFD E18 58 D3
Bradwell Ms UED N18 42 C3
Bradymead EHAM E6 96 A5
Brady St WCHPL E1 92 D3
Braemar Av ALP/SUD HA0 67 K6
BXLYHN DA7 137 K3
THHTH CR7 164 C2
WAND/EARL SW18 146 E1
WDGN N22 40 E7
WLSDN NW10 69 F2
Braemar Gdns BFN/LL DA15 154 D2
CDALE/KGS NW9 37 F7
WWKM BR4 167 F7
Braemar Rd BTFD TW8 104 E5
PLSTW E13 94 E3
SEVS/STOTM N15 56 A4
WPK KT4 173 K2
Braeside BECK BR3 151 J4
Braeside Av WIM/MER SW19 146 C7
Braeside Cl PIN HA5 34 A6
Braeside Crs BXLYHN DA7 137 K3
Braeside Rd STRHM/NOR SW16 148 C6
Braes St IS N1 6 D2
Braesyde Cl BELV DA17 117 G3
Brafferton Rd CROY/NA CR0 177 J3
Braganza St WALW SE17 18 C8
Bragg Rd TEDD TW11 142 E6
Braham St WCHPL E1 13 M5
Braid Av ACT W3 87 G5
Braid Cl FELT TW13 141 K1
Braidwood Rd CAT SE6 133 G7
Brailsford Cl WIM/MER SW19 147 J6
Brailsford Rd
BRXS/STRHM SW2 130 B5
Brainton Av EBED/NFELT TW14 122 A6
Braintree Av REDBR IG4 59 J4
Braintree Rd DAGE RM10 80 C2
RSLP HA4 65 F3
Braintree St BETH * E2 92 E2
Brair Bank CAR SM5 176 A7
Braithwaite Av ROMW/RG RM7 62 C6
Braithwaite Gdns STAN HA7 35 J7
Braithwaite Rd PEND EN3 31 H2
Bramall Cl SRTFD E15 76 D4
Bramber Rd NFNCH/WDSP N12 39 J4
WKENS W14 107 J5
Bramble Acres Cl BELMT SM2 174 E6
Bramble Banks CAR SM5 176 A7
Bramblebury Rd
WOOL/PLUM SE18 115 J4
Bramble Cl BECK BR3 167 F4
CROY/NA CR0 179 J3
SEVS/STOTM N15 56 C3

STAN HA7 35 K6
Bramble Cft ERITH DA8 117 K3
Brambledown Cl HAYES BR2 167 H5
Brambledown Rd CAR SM5 176 A6
SAND/SEL CR2 178 A6
Bramble Gdns SHB W12 87 H6
Bramble La HPTN TW12 141 K5
The Brambles SUT * SM1 175 H1
WDR/YW UB7 100 A4
WIM/MER * SW19 146 D4
Brambles Cl BTFD TW8 104 C6
Bramblewood Cl CAR SM5 162 D7
Brambling Cl BUSH WD23 21 J3
The Bramblings CHING E4 44 B3
Bramcote Av MTCM CR4 162 E3
Bramcote Gv
BERM/RHTH SE16 111 K4
Bramcote Rd PUT/ROE SW15 126 E3
Bramdean Crs LEE/GVPK SE12 133 K7
Bramdean Gdns
LEE/GVPK SE12 133 K7
Bramerton Rd BECK BR3 166 C2
Bramerton St CHEL SW3 15 J9
Bramfield Rd BTSEA SW11 128 D5
Bramford Rd WAND/EARL SW18 128 B3
Bramham Ct NTHWD * HA6 32 C4
Bramham Gdns CHSGTN * KT9 171 K4
ECT SW5 14 C7
Bramhope La CHARL SE7 114 A5
Bramlands Cl BTSEA SW11 128 D2
Bramleas WATW WD18 20 D4
Bramley Cl HYS/HAR UB3 82 E6
ORP BR6 169 G7
RSLP HA4 46 D2
SAND/SEL CR2 177 H4
STHGT/OAK N14 28 B4
WALTH E17 57 G1
WFD IG8 45 G6
WHTN TW2 123 H5
Bramley Crs GNTH/NBYPK IG2 60 A5
VX/NE SW8 109 J6
Bramley Gdns OXHEY WD19 33 G5
Bramley Hl SAND/SEL CR2 177 J3
Bramley Hyrst SAND/SEL * CR2 177 J4
Bramley Ldg ALP/SUD HA0 67 K3
Bramley Pl DART DA1 138 D3
Bramley Rd BELMT SM2 174 B7
EA W5 104 D2
NTGHL W11 88 B6
STHGT/OAK N14 28 B4
SUT SM1 175 H4
Bramley Wy HSLWW TW4 122 E4
WWKM BR4 179 K1
Brampton Cl CLPT E5 74 D1
Brampton Gv HDN NW4 51 K3
KTN/HRWW/W HA3 49 G3
WBLY HA9 50 C7
Brampton La HDN NW4 52 A3
Brampton Park Rd WDGN N22 55 G2
Brampton Rd BXLYHN DA7 136 E2
CDALE/KGS NW9 50 C3
CROY/NA CR0 165 G6
EHAM E6 95 H3
FSBYPK N4 55 J4
OXHEY WD19 32 E2
Bramshaw Gdns OXHEY WD19 33 J4
Bramshaw Ri NWMAL KT3 160 B5
Bramshaw Rd HOM E9 75 F5
Bramshill Gdns ARCH N19 72 B2
Bramshill Rd WLSDN NW10 87 G1
Bramshot Av CHARL SE7 114 A5
Bramston Rd WLSDN NW10 87 J1
Bramwell Cl SUN TW16 156 C1
Bramwell Ms IS N1 5 M3
Brancaster Dr MLHL NW7 37 J6
Brancaster Rd GNTH/NBYPK IG2 60 E5
STRHM/NOR SW16 148 E2
Brancepeth Gdns BKHH IG9 44 E1
Branch Hl HAMP NW3 71 G2
Branch Pl IS N1 7 H3
Branch Rd POP/IOD E14 93 G6
Branch St CMBW SE5 111 F6
Brancker Rd KTN/HRWW/W HA3 49 K2
Brand Cl FSBYPK N4 55 H7
Brandlehow Rd
PUT/ROE SW15 127 J3
Brandon Est WALW SE17 18 E9
Brandon Ms BARB * EC2Y 13 G2
Brandon Rd DART DA1 139 K6
HOLWY N7 5 J1
NWDGN UB2 102 E4
SUT SM1 175 F3
WALTH * E17 58 A3
Brandon St WALW SE17 18 F6
Brandram Ms LEW * SE13 133 H3
Brandram Rd LEW SE13 133 H2
Brandreth Ct HRW * HA1 49 F5
Brandreth Rd EHAM E6 95 K5
TOOT SW17 148 B1
The Brandries WLGTN SM6 176 D2
Brand St GNWCH SE10 113 F6
Brandville Gdns BARK/HLT IG6 60 B3
Brandville Rd WDR/YW UB7 100 B1
Brandy Wy BELMT SM2 174 E6
Brangbourne Rd BMLY BR1 152 A4
Brangton Rd LBTH SE11 17 M8
Brangwyn Crs
WIM/MER SW19 147 H7
Branksea St FUL/PGN SW6 107 H6
Branksome Av UED N18 42 B5
Branksome Rd
BRXS/STRHM SW2 129 K4
WIM/MER SW19 146 E7
Branksome Wy
KTN/HRWW/W HA3 50 B5
NWMAL KT3 159 K1
Bransby Rd CHSGTN KT9 172 A6
Branscombe Gdns WCHMH N21 29 G6
Branscombe St LEW SE13 132 E2
Bransdale Cl KIL/WHAMP NW6 2 B3
Bransgrove Rd EDGW HA8 36 B7
Branston Crs STMC/STPC BR5 169 J7
Branstone Rd RCH/KEW TW9 105 G7
Brants Wk HNWL W7 84 E3
Brantwood Av ERITH DA8 117 K6
ISLW TW7 124 B3
Brantwood Cl WALTH * E17 57 K2
Brantwood Gdns ENC/FH EN2 28 E3
REDBR IG4 59 J4
Brantwood Rd BXLYHN DA7 137 J1
HNHL SE24 130 D4
SAND/SEL CR2 177 J7
TOTM N17 42 C5
Brasenose Dr BARN SW13 107 F5
Brasher Cl GFD/PVL UB6 66 D4
Brassey Cl EBED/NFELT * TW14 121 K7
Brassey Rd KIL/WHAMP NW6 70 D5
Brassey Sq BTSEA SW11 129 F2
Brassie Av ACT W3 87 G5
Brasted Cl BXLYHS DA6 136 E4
SYD SE26 150 E3
Brasted Rd ERITH DA8 118 B6
Brathway Rd
WAND/EARL SW18 127 K6
Bratley St WCHPL E1 92 C3
Braund Av GFD/PVL UB6 84 B3
Braundton Av BFN/LL DA15 136 A7
Braunston Dr YEAD UB4 83 J3
Bravington Pl MV/WKIL W9 88 D3
Bravington Rd MV/WKIL W9 88 D2
Braxfield Rd BROCKY SE4 132 B3
Braxted Pk STRHM/NOR SW16 149 F5
Brayard's Rd PECK SE15 131 J1
Braybourne Dr ISLW TW7 104 A6
Braybrooke Gdns NRWD SE19 150 A6
Braybrook St SHB W12 87 H4
Brayburne Av VX/NE SW8 129 H1
Braycourt Av WOT/HER KT12 156 B6
Bray Crs BERM/RHTH SE16 112 A1
Braydon Rd STNW/STAM N16 56 B7
Bray Dr CAN/RD E16 94 D6
Brayfield Ter IS N1 6 A2
Brayford Sq WCHPL * E1 92 E5
Bray Pl CHEL SW3 15 L7
Bray Rd MLHL NW7 38 B5
Brayton Gdns ENC/FH EN2 28 D3
Braywood Rd ELTH/MOT SE9 135 J3
Breach La DAGW RM9 98 C2
Bread St BLKFR EC4V 12 F6
Breakspears Dr
STMC/STPC BR5 155 G7
Breakspears Ms BROCKY SE4 132 D1
Breakspears Rd BROCKY SE4 132 C2
Bream Cl TOTM N17 56 D3
Bream Gdns EHAM E6 96 A2
Breamore Cl PUT/ROE SW15 126 D7
Breamore Rd GDMY/SEVK IG3 79 F1
Bream's Buildings LINN WC2A 12 A4
Bream St BOW E3 75 J6
Breamwater Gdns
RCHPK/HAM TW10 143 H2
Brearley Cl EDGW HA8 36 E6
Breasley Cl PUT/ROE SW15 126 E3
Breasy Pl HDN * NW4 51 K3
Brechin Pl SKENS SW7 14 F7
Brecknock Rd ARCH N19 72 C3
Brecknock Road Est ARCH * N19 72 D4
Brecon Cl MTCM CR4 163 K3
WPK KT4 174 A1
Brecon Gn CDALE/KGS * NW9 51 G5
Brecon Ms KTTN NW5 72 D5
Brecon Rd HMSMTH W6 107 H5
PEND EN3 30 E3
Brede Cl EHAM E6 96 A2
Bredgar Rd ARCH N19 72 C1
Bredhurst Cl PGE/AN SE20 150 E5
Bredon Rd CROY/NA CR0 165 G6
Breer St FUL/PGN SW6 128 A2
Breezer's Hl WAP * E1W 92 C6
Brember Rd RYLN/HDSTN HA2 66 C1
Bremer Ms WALTH E17 57 K3
Bremner Rd SKENS SW7 14 F3
Brenchley Cl CHST BR7 154 A7
HAYES BR2 167 J4
Brenchley Gdns FSTH SE23 131 K5
Brenchley Rd STMC/STPC BR5 154 E7
Brenda Rd TOOT SW17 147 K1
Brende Gdns E/WMO/HCT KT8 157 G3
Brendon SCUP * DA14 155 G3
Brendon Av WLSDN NW10 69 G3
Brendon Cl ERITH DA8 118 B7
ESH/CLAY KT10 170 C5
HYS/HAR UB3 101 F6
Brendon Dr ESH/CLAY KT10 170 C5
Brendon Gdns
RYLN/HDSTN HA2 66 B3
Brendon Gv EFNCH N2 53 G1
Brendon Rd BCTR RM8 62 B7
CHST BR7 154 D1
Brendon St MBLAR W1H 9 K4
Brendon Vls WCHMH * N21 29 J7
Brendon Wy EN EN1 30 A6
Brenley Cl MTCM CR4 163 F2
Brenley Gdns ELTH/MOT SE9 134 C3
Brent Cl BXLY DA5 137 F7
Brentcot Cl WEA W13 85 H3
Brent Crs WLSDN NW10 86 B1
Brent Cross F/O HDN NW4 52 A5
Brentfield WLSDN NW10 68 D6
Brentfield Cl WLSDN NW10 69 F5
Brentfield Gdns CRICK * NW2 52 B6
Brentfield Rd DART DA1 139 K5
WLSDN NW10 69 F5
Brentford Cl YEAD UB4 83 H3
Brent Gn HDN NW4 52 A4
Brentham Wy EA W5 85 K3
Brenthouse Rd HACK E8 74 D6
Brenthurst Rd WLSDN NW10 69 H5
Brentlands Dr DART DA1 139 K7
Brent La DART DA1 139 J6
Brent Lea BTFD TW8 104 D6
Brentmead Cl HNWL W7 84 E6
Brentmead Gdns WLSDN NW10 86 B1
Brenton St POP/IOD E14 93 G5
Brent Park Rd CDALE/KGS NW9 51 J7
Brent Pl BAR EN5 26 E4
Brent River Park Wk WEA W13 85 H2
Brent Rd BTFD TW8 104 D5
CAN/RD E16 94 E5
NWDGN UB2 102 B2
SAND/SEL CR2 178 D7
WOOL/PLUM SE18 115 G6
Brentside BTFD TW8 104 D5
Brentside Cl WEA W13 85 F3
Brent St HDN NW4 52 A3
Brent Ter CRICK NW2 52 A7
Brentvale Av ALP/SUD HA0 68 B7
STHL UB1 84 D7
Brent View Rd CDALE/KGS NW9 51 J5
Brent Wy BTFD TW8 104 E6
FNCH N3 38 E5
WBLY HA9 68 D5
Brentwick Gdns BTFD TW8 105 F3
Brentwood Cl ELTH/MOT SE9 135 H7
Brentwood Rd ROM RM1 63 H5
Brereton Rd TOTM N17 42 B6
Bressenden Pl WESTW SW1E 16 D3
Bressey Gv SWFD E18 58 D1
Brett Cl NTHLT UB5 83 H2
STNW/STAM N16 74 A1
Brett Crs WLSDN NW10 69 F6
Brettell St WALW SE17 19 H8
Brettenham Av WALTH E17 43 J7
Brettenham Rd UED N18 42 C3
WALTH E17 57 J1
Brett Gdns DAGW RM9 80 A6
Brett Pas HACK E8 74 D4
Brett Rd BAR EN5 26 A4
HACK E8 74 D4
Brett Vls ACT * W3 87 F4
Brewer St REGST W1B 10 F6
Brewery Cl ALP/SUD HA0 67 G4
Brewery Rd HAYES BR2 168 D7
WOOL/PLUM SE18 115 J4
Brewery Sq STHWK SE1 13 L9
Brewhouse La WAP E1W 92 D7
Brewhouse Rd
WOOL/PLUM SE18 114 E3
Brewhouse St PUT/ROE SW15 127 H3
Brewhouse Wk
BERM/RHTH SE16 93 G7
Brewhouse Yd FSBYE EC1V 6 C9
Brewood Rd BCTR RM8 79 H5
Brewster Gdns NKENS W10 88 A4
Brewster Rd LEY E10 57 K7
Brian Cl HCH RM12 81 K3
Brian Rd CHDH RM6 61 J4
Briants Cl PIN HA5 33 J7
Briant St NWCR SE14 112 A7
Briar Av STRHM/NOR SW16 149 F6
Briarbank Rd WEA W13 85 G5
Briar Cl BKHH IG9 45 H1
EFNCH N2 53 G1
HPTN TW12 141 K4
ISLW TW7 124 A4
PLMGR N13 41 J2
Briar Crs NTHLT UB5 66 B5
Briardale Gdns CRICK NW2 70 E2
Briarfield Av EFNCH N2 53 F2
Briar Gdns HAYES BR2 167 J7
Briar La CAR SM5 176 A7
CROY/NA CR0 179 K3
Briar Rd CRICK NW2 70 A3
KTN/HRWW/W HA3 49 J4
STRHM/NOR SW16 163 K2
WHTN TW2 123 K7
Briar Wk EDGW HA8 36 E6
NKENS * W10 88 C3
PUT/ROE SW15 126 E3
Briar Wy WDR/YW UB7 100 D1
Briarwood Cl CDALE/KGS * NW9 50 E5
FELT TW13 140 C2
Briarwood Ct WPK * KT4 160 D7
Briarwood Dr NTHWD HA6 46 E1
Briarwood Rd CLAP SW4 129 J4
EW KT17 173 J5
Briary Cl EDGW HA8 50 D1
HAMP NW3 3 J1
Briary Ct SCUP DA14 155 H4
Briary Gdns BMLY BR1 153 F4
Briary La ED N9 42 A2
Brickbarn Cl WBPTN * SW10 108 B6
Brick Ct EMB * EC4Y 12 A5
Brickett Cl RSLP HA4 46 A4
Brick Farm Cl RCH/KEW TW9 105 J7
Brickfield Cl BTFD TW8 104 D6
Brickfield Cottages
WOOL/PLUM SE18 116 A6
Brickfield La BAR EN5 25 H5
HYS/HAR UB3 101 G5
Brickfield Rd BOW E3 93 K3
THHTH CR7 149 H7
WIM/MER SW19 147 F3
Brickfields RYLN/HDSTN HA2 66 D1
Brickfields Wy WDR/YW UB7 100 C2
Brickfield Vls SUT * SM1 175 J2
Brick Kiln Cl BUSH WD23 21 J5
Brick La EN EN1 30 D1
STAN HA7 35 K6
WCHPL E1 13 M1
Brick St MYFR/PICC W1J 10 C9
Brickwall La RSLP HA4 46 C7
Brickwood Cl SYD SE26 150 D2
Brickwood Rd CROY/NA CR0 178 A1
Brideale Cl PECK * SE15 111 G5
Bride Ct BLKFR * EC4V 12 C5
Bride La EMB EC4Y 12 C5
Bridel Ms FSBYE EC1V 6 C6
Bride St HOLWY N7 73 F5
Bridewain St STHWK SE1 19 L3
Bridewell Pl BLKFR EC4V 12 C5
WAP E1W 92 D7
Bridford Ms REGST W1B 10 D2
The Bridge EA * W5 86 B7
KTN/HRWW/W HA3 49 F2
Bridge Ap CAMTN NW1 4 A1
Bridge Av HMSMTH W6 107 F4
HNWL W7 84 D4
Bridge Cl EN EN1 30 D1
NKENS W10 88 B5
ROM RM1 63 G5
Bridge Dr PLMGR N13 41 F3
Bridge End WALTH E17 44 A7
Bridgefield Rd SUT SM1 174 E5
Bridge Gdns ASHF TW15 140 A6
E/WMO/HCT KT8 157 J3
Bridge Ga WCHMH N21 29 J6
Bridge House Quay
POP/IOD E14 94 A7
Bridgeland Rd CAN/RD E16 94 E6
Bridge La BTSEA SW11 108 D7
GLDGN NW11 52 C4
Bridgeman Rd IS N1 5 M2
TEDD TW11 143 G5
Bridgeman St STJWD NW8 3 J6
Bridge Mdw NWCR SE14 112 A5
Bridgen Rd BXLY DA5 137 F6
Bridge Pde
STRHM/NOR * SW16 148 E4
WCHMH * N21 29 J6
Bridge Pl CROY/NA CR0 164 E7
PIM SW1V 16 D5
WAT WD17 21 H4
Bridgeport Pl WAP * E1W 92 C7
Bridge Rd BECK BR3 151 H6
BXLYHN DA7 137 F2
CHSGTN KT9 172 A4
E/WMO/HCT KT8 157 K3
ED N9 42 C2
EHAM E6 77 K6
ERITH DA8 118 D7
HSLW TW3 123 J2
NWDGN UB2 102 E1
RAIN RM13 99 J3
SRTFD E15 76 B7
SUT SM1 175 F5
TWK TW1 124 C5
WALTH E17 57 H6
WBLY HA9 68 C2
WDGN N22 40 E7
WLGTN SM6 176 B4
WLSDN NW10 69 G5
Bridge Rw CROY/NA * CR0 164 E7
Bridges Ct BTSEA SW11 128 C2
Bridges La CROY/NA CR0 176 E3
Bridges Rd STAN HA7 35 F4
Bridge St CHSWK W4 106 A3
PIN HA5 47 H2
TWK TW1 124 E5
WEST SW1P 17 J2
Bridge Ter LEW * SE13 133 G3
SRTFD E15 76 B6
Bridgetown Cl NRWD SE19 150 A4
Bridgeview HMSMTH W6 107 F4
Bridge Vls WIM/MER * SW19 146 E4
Bridgewater Cl CHST BR7 169 K2
Bridgewater Gdns EDGW HA8 50 B1
Bridgewater Rd ALP/SUD HA0 67 H5
SRTFD E15 76 A7
Bridgewater Sq BARB * EC2Y 12 E2
Bridgewater St BARB EC2Y 12 E2
Bridgewater Wy BUSH WD23 22 B5
Bridgeway ALP/SUD HA0 68 A6
BARK IG11 79 F6
Bridge Wy GLDGN NW11 52 D4
WHTN TW2 123 H6
Bridgeway St CAMTN NW1 4 F6
Bridgewood Cl PGE/AN SE20 150 D6
Bridgewood Rd
STRHM/NOR SW16 148 D6
WPK KT4 173 J3
Bridgford St WAND/EARL SW18 147 G2
Bridgman Rd CHSWK W4 105 K2
Bridgwater Rd RSLP HA4 65 F3
Bridle Cl HOR/WEW KT19 172 E3
KUT KT1 158 E3
Bridle La SOHO/CST W1F 10 F6
TWK TW1 124 C5
The Bridle Pth WFD IG8 44 C6
Bridle Pth CROY/NA CR0 176 E2
WAT WD17 21 F1
Bridlepath Wy
EBED/NFELT TW14 121 H6
Bridle Rd CROY/NA CR0 179 J3
ESH/CLAY KT10 171 H5
PIN HA5 47 G5
The Bridle Wy WLGTN SM6 176 C3
Bridle Wy CROY/NA CR0 179 J4
Bridlington Rd ED N9 30 D6
OXHEY WD19 33 H2
Bridport Av ROMW/RG RM7 62 D5
Bridport Pl IS N1 7 H5
Bridport Rd NTHLT UB5 66 B7
THHTH CR7 164 B2
UED N18 42 A4
Bridstow Pl BAY/PAD W2 8 B4
Brief St CMBW SE5 110 C7
Brierley Av ED N9 30 E7
Brierley Cl SNWD SE25 165 H3
Brierley Rd BAL SW12 148 C1
WAN E11 76 B3
Brierly Gdns BETH * E2 92 E1
Brigade Cl RYLN/HDSTN HA2 66 D1
Brigade St BKHTH/KID * SE3 133 J1
Briggeford Cl CLPT E5 74 C1
Briggs Cl MTCM CR4 148 B7
Bright Cl BELV DA17 116 E3
Brightfield Rd LEW SE13 133 H4
Brightling Rd BROCKY SE4 132 C5
Brightlingsea Pl POP/IOD E14 93 H6
Brightman Rd
WAND/EARL SW18 128 C7
Brighton Av WALTH E17 57 H4
Brighton Dr NTHLT * UB5 66 A5
Brighton Rd BELMT SM2 175 G6
EFNCH N2 53 G1
EHAM E6 96 A2
SAND/SEL CR2 177 J7
STNW/STAM N16 74 A3
SURB KT6 158 D5
Brighton Ter BRXN/ST SW9 130 A3
Brights Av RAIN RM13 99 K3
Brightside Rd LEW SE13 133 G5
Bright St POP/IOD E14 93 K5
Brightwell Cl CROY/NA CR0 164 B7
Brightwell Crs TOOT SW17 147 K4
Brightwell Rd WATW WD18 20 E4
Brig Ms DEPT SE8 112 D5
Brigstock Rd BELV DA17 117 J3
THHTH CR7 164 C4
Brill Pl CAMTN NW1 5 H6
Brim Hl EFNCH N2 53 G3
Brimpsfield Cl ABYW SE2 116 C2
Brindle Ga BFN/LL DA15 135 K7
Brindley Cl BXLYHN DA7 137 H2
GFD/PVL UB6 67 J7
Brindley St NWCR SE14 112 C7
Brindley Wy BMLY BR1 152 E4
STHL UB1 84 B6
Brindwood Rd CHING E4 43 J2
Brinkburn Cl ABYW SE2 116 B3
EDGW HA8 50 D2
Brinkburn Gdns EDGW HA8 50 C2
Brinkley Rd WPK KT4 173 K1
Brinklow Crs
WOOL/PLUM SE18 115 G6
Brinkworth Rd CLAY IG5 59 J2
Brinkworth Wy HOM * E9 75 H5
Brinsdale Rd HDN NW4 52 B2
Brinsley Rd KTN/HRWW/W HA3 48 D1
Brinsley St WCHPL * E1 92 D5
Brinsworth Cl WHTN TW2 123 J7
Brinton Wk STHWK SE1 12 C9
Brion Pl POP/IOD E14 94 A4
Brisbane Av WIM/MER SW19 147 F7
Brisbane Rd IL IG1 60 C6
LEY E10 75 K1
Brisbane St CMBW SE5 110 E6
Briscoe Cl WAN E11 76 D1
Briscoe Rd WIM/MER SW19 147 H5
Briset Rd ELTH/MOT SE9 134 C2
Briset St FARR EC1M 12 C2
Briset Wy HOLWY N7 73 F1
Bristol Cl STWL/WRAY TW19 120 B5
WLGTN SM6 176 E7
Bristol Gdns MV/WKIL W9 8 D1
Bristol Ms MV/WKIL W9 8 D1
Bristol Park Rd WALTH * E17 57 G3
Bristol Rd FSTGT E7 77 G5
GFD/PVL UB6 66 B7
MRDN SM4 162 B4
Briston Gv CEND/HSY/T N8 54 E5
Bristow Rd BXLYHN DA7 117 F7
CROY/NA CR0 176 E3
HSLW TW3 123 G2
NRWD SE19 150 A4
Britannia Cl CLAP SW4 129 J3
ERITH DA8 118 C5
NTHLT UB5 83 H2
Britannia Ga CAN/RD E16 94 E7
Britannia Rd BRYLDS KT5 159 G6
FUL/PGN SW6 108 A6
IL IG1 78 B2
NFNCH/WDSP N12 39 G2
POP/IOD E14 112 D3
Britannia Rw IS N1 6 D3
Britannia St FSBYW WC1X 5 L7
Britannia Wk IS N1 7 G7
Britannia Wy FUL/PGN SW6 108 A6
STWL/WRAY TW19 120 A6
WLSDN NW10 86 D3
British Est BOW E3 93 H2
British Gv CHSWK W4 106 C4
British Grove Pas CHSWK * W4 106 C4
British Legion Rd CHING E4 44 D1
British St BOW E3 93 H2
Brittain Rd BCTR RM8 80 A2
Britten Cl BORE WD6 23 K5
GLDGN NW11 53 F7
Britten Dr STHL UB1 84 A5
Britten St CHEL SW3 15 J8
Britton Cl CAT SE6 133 G6
Britton St FARR EC1M 12 C1
Brixham Crs RSLP HA4 46 E7
Brixham Gdns GDMY/SEVK IG3 78 E4
Brixham Rd WELL DA16 116 E7
Brixham St CAN/RD E16 95 K7
Brixton Hl BRXS/STRHM SW2 130 A5
Brixton Hill Pl
BRXS/STRHM SW2 129 K6
Brixton Ov BRXN/ST SW9 130 B3
Brixton Rd BRXN/ST SW9 130 B1
LBTH SE11 110 B5
Brixton Station Rd
BRXN/ST SW9 130 B2
Brixton Water La
BRXS/STRHM SW2 130 B4
Broadbent St
MYFR/PKLN * W1K 10 C6
Broad Bridge Cl
BKHTH/KID SE3 113 K6
Broad Common Est
STNW/STAM * N16 56 C7
Broadcoombe SAND/SEL CR2 179 F6
Broad Ct COVGDN * WC2E 11 K5
Broadcroft Av STAN HA7 49 K1
Broadcroft Rd STMC/STPC BR5 169 J6
Broadeaves Cl SAND/SEL CR2 178 A4
Broadfield Cl CRICK NW2 70 A2
ROM RM1 63 H4
Broadfield Ct BUSH WD23 34 E1
Broadfield La CAMTN NW1 5 J2
Broadfield Pde EDGW * HA8 36 D2
Broadfield Rd CAT SE6 133 H7
Broadfields E/WMO/HCT KT8 157 J5
PIN HA5 48 B1
Broadfields Av EDGW HA8 36 D3
WCHMH N21 29 G6
Broadfields Hts EDGW HA8 36 D3
Broadfields La OXHEY WD19 21 F7
Broadfield Sq EN EN1 30 D2
Broadfields Wy WLSDN NW10 69 H4
Broadfield Wy BKHH IG9 45 G2
Broadgates Rd
WAND/EARL SW18 128 C7
Broad Green Av CROY/NA CR0 164 C6
Broadhead Strd
CDALE/KGS NW9 51 H1
Broadheath Dr CHST BR7 153 K4
Broadhinton Rd CLAP SW4 129 G2
Broadhurst Av EDGW HA8 36 D3
GDMY/SEVK IG3 79 F3
Broadhurst Cl KIL/WHAMP NW6 71 G5
Broadhurst Gdns
KIL/WHAMP NW6 71 F5
RSLP HA4 65 G1
Broadlands FELT TW13 141 K2
Broadlands Av PEND EN3 30 D2
STRHM/NOR SW16 148 E1
Broadlands Cl HGT N6 54 A6
PEND EN3 30 D2
STRHM/NOR SW16 148 E1
Broadlands Rd BMLY BR1 153 F3
HGT N6 53 K6
Broadlands Wy NWMAL KT3 160 C5
Broad La HPTN TW12 141 K6
SEVS/STOTM N15 56 B4
Broad Lawn ELTH/MOT SE9 135 F7
Broadlawns Ct
KTN/HRWW/W HA3 35 F7
Broadley St STJWD NW8 9 J2
Broadley Ter STJWD NW8 9 K1
Broadmead CAT SE6 151 J2
Broadmead Av WPK KT4 160 D6
Broadmead Cl HPTN TW12 142 A5
PIN * HA5 33 J6
Broadmead Rd WFD IG8 44 E5
YEAD UB4 83 J3
Broad Oak SUN TW16 140 D5
WFD IG8 45 F4
Broad Oak Cl CHING E4 43 J4
Broadoak Rd ERITH DA8 118 A6
Broad Oaks SURB KT6 159 J7
Broad Oaks Wy HAYES BR2 167 J4
Broadstone Pl MHST W1U 10 A3
Broadstone Rd HCH RM12 81 J1
Broad St DAGE RM10 80 C6
TEDD TW11 143 F5
Broad Street Av LVPST EC2M 13 J3
Broad Street Pl LVPST EC2M 13 H3
Broadview CDALE/KGS NW9 50 C5
Broadview Rd
STRHM/NOR SW16 148 D6
The Broad Wk KENS W8 8 D8
NTHWD HA6 46 A1
Broad Wk BKHTH/KID SE3 134 B1
HEST TW5 102 C7
RCH/KEW TW9 105 G6
WCHMH N21 29 G7
Broadwalk RYLN/HDSTN * HA2 48 B4
SWFD E18 58 D2
Broadwalk La GLDGN NW11 52 D6
Broadwall STHWK SE1 12 B8
Broadwater Rd TOOT SW17 147 J3
TOTM N17 56 A1
WOOL/PLUM SE18 115 J2
The Broadway ACT * W3 105 H1
BCTR RM8 80 B1
CDALE/KGS NW9 51 H5
CEND/HSY/T N8 54 E5
CHEAM SM3 174 C5
EA W5 85 K6
FBAR/BDGN * N11 39 K4
HCH RM12 81 K3
KTN/HRWW/W HA3 48 E1
MLHL NW7 37 G4
PIN HA5 33 K6
PLSTW E13 94 E1
RYLN/HDSTN * HA2 66 D1
STAN HA7 35 J4
THDIT KT7 157 K7
WAT WD17 21 G2
WFD IG8 45 F5
WIM/MER SW19 146 D5
Broadway BARK IG11 78 C7
BXLYHS DA6 137 F3
GPK RM2 63 J2
HNWL W7 84 E7
RAIN RM13 99 J3
SRTFD E15 76 B6

STJSPK SW1H 17 G3
SURB KT6 159 J7
SUT SM1 175 G3
Broadway Av
CROY/NA CR0 164 E4
TWK TW1 124 C5
Broadway Cl WFD IG8 45 F5
Broadway Ct
WIM/MER * SW19 146 E5
Broadway Gdns MTCM CR4 162 D3
Broadway Market HACK E8 74 D7
Broadway Market Ms
HACK * E8 74 C7
Broadway Ms STNW/STAM N16 56 B6
Broadway Pde CHING * E4 44 A5
HYS/HAR * UB3 101 J1
RYLN/HDSTN * HA2 48 B4
WDR/YW * UB7 100 B1
Broadwell Pde
KIL/WHAMP * NW6 71 G5
Broadwick St SOHO/CST W1F 10 F5
Broadwood Av RSLP HA4 46 D5
Broadwood Ter WKENS * W14 107 J3
Broad Yd FARR EC1M 12 C1
Brocas Cl HAMP NW3 3 K1
Brockdene Dr HAYES BR2 181 H3
Brockdish Av BARK IG11 79 F4
Brockenhurst
E/WMO/HCT KT8 156 E4
Brockenhurst Av WPK KT4 160 B7
Brockenhurst Gdns IL IG1 78 C4
MLHL NW7 37 G5
Brockenhurst Rd
CROY/NA CR0 165 J6
Brockenhurst Wy
STRHM/NOR SW16 163 J1
Brockham Cl WIM/MER SW19 146 D4
Brockham Crs CROY/NA CR0 180 B6
Brockham Dr
BRXS/STRHM SW2 130 A6
GNTH/NBYPK IG2 60 C5
Brockham St STHWK SE1 18 F3
Brockhurst Cl STAN HA7 35 F5
Brockill Crs BROCKY SE4 132 B3
Brocklebank Rd CHARL SE7 114 A3
WAND/EARL SW18 128 B6
Brocklehurst St NWCR SE14 112 A6
Brocklesbury Cl WATN WD24 21 G2
Brocklesby Rd SNWD SE25 165 J3
Brockley Av EDGW HA8 36 A2
Brockley Cl STAN HA7 36 A3
Brockley Cross BROCKY SE4 132 B2
Brockley Gv BROCKY SE4 132 C4
Brockley Hall Rd BROCKY SE4 132 B5
Brockley Hl STAN HA7 35 J1
Brockley Ms BROCKY SE4 132 B4
Brockley Pk FSTH SE23 132 B6
Brockley Ri FSTH SE23 132 B6
Brockley Rd BROCKY SE4 132 B5
Brockleyside STAN * HA7 36 A3
Brockley Vw FSTH SE23 132 B6
Brockley Wy FSTH SE23 132 A4
Brockman Ri BMLY BR1 152 B3
Brock Pl BOW E3 93 K3
Brock Rd PLSTW E13 95 F4
Brocks Dr CHEAM SM3 174 C2
Brockshot Cl BTFD TW8 104 E5
Brock St PECK * SE15 131 K2
Brockton Cl ROM RM1 63 H3
Brockway Cl WAN E11 76 C1
Brockwell Park Gdns
HNHL SE24 130 C6
Brockworth Cl PECK SE15 111 F5
Brodewater Rd BORE WD6 24 D1
Brodia Rd STNW/STAM N16 74 A2
Brodie St STHWK SE1 19 M7
Brodlove La WAP E1W 93 F6
Brodrick Gv ABYW SE2 116 C3
Brodrick Rd TOOT SW17 147 J1
Brograve Gdns BECK BR3 166 E1
Brokesley St BOW E3 93 H3
Broke Wk HACK * E8 74 C7
Bromar Rd CMBW SE5 131 F2
Bromborough Gn OXHEY WD19 33 G4
Bromefield STAN HA7 35 J7
Bromehead St WCHPL E1 92 E5
Brome House
WOOL/PLUM SE18 114 D6
Bromell's Rd CLAP SW4 129 H3
Brome Rd ELTH/MOT SE9 134 E2
Bromfelde Rd CLAP SW4 129 J2
Bromfield St IS N1 6 B5
Bromhall Rd DAGW RM9 79 H5
Bromhedge ELTH/MOT SE9 153 K2
Bromholm Rd ABYW SE2 116 C2
Bromley Av BMLY BR1 152 C6
Bromley Common HAYES BR2 168 D6
Bromley Crs HAYES BR2 167 J2
RSLP HA4 64 D3
Bromley Gdns HAYES BR2 167 J1
Bromley Gv HAYES BR2 167 G1
Bromley Hall Rd POP/IOD E14 94 A4
Bromley High St BOW E3 93 K2
Bromley Hl BMLY BR1 152 C5
Bromley La CHST BR7 154 C6
Bromley Rd BECK BR3 151 K7
CAT SE6 151 K2
CHST BR7 154 B7
HAYES BR2 167 H1
LEY E10 57 K5
TOTM N17 42 B7
UED N18 41 K3
WALTH E17 57 J2
Bromley St WCHPL E1 93 F4
Brompton Ar KTBR * SW1X 15 L2
Brompton Cl HSLWW TW4 122 E4
Brompton Dr ERITH DA8 118 E6
Brompton Gv EFNCH N2 53 J3
Brompton Park Crs
FUL/PGN SW6 108 A5
Brompton Pl CHEL SW3 15 K3
Brompton Rd CHEL SW3 15 J5
Brompton Sq CHEL SW3 15 J3
Brompton Ter
WOOL/PLUM * SE18 115 F7
Bromwich Av HGT N6 72 A1
Bromyard Av ACT W3 87 G7
Brondesbury Ms
KIL/WHAMP * NW6 2 A2
Brondesbury Pk CRICK NW2 70 A6
Brondesbury Rd
KIL/WHAMP NW6 88 D1
Brondesbury Vls
KIL/WHAMP NW6 88 D1
Bronhill Ter TOTM * N17 42 C7
Bronsart Rd FUL/PGN SW6 107 H6
Bronson Rd RYNPK SW20 161 G1
Bronte Cl ERITH DA8 117 J6
FSTGT * E7 76 E3
GNTH/NBYPK IG2 60 A4
Bronte Gv DART DA1 139 J3
Bronti Cl WALW SE17 18 F7
Bronze Age Wy BELV DA17 117 K2
Bronze St DEPT SE8 112 D6
Brook Av DAGE RM10 80 D6
EDGW HA8 36 D5
WBLY HA9 68 C2
Brookbank Av HNWL W7 84 D4
Brookbank Rd LEW SE13 132 E2
Brook Cl ACT W3 86 C7
BORE WD6 24 D2
HOR/WEW KT19 173 G7
RSLP HA4 46 C6
RYNPK SW20 160 E2
STWL/WRAY TW19 120 C6
TOOT SW17 148 A1
Brook Ct BECK * BR3 151 H7
Brook Crs CHING E4 43 J3
ED N9 42 D3
Brookdale FBAR/BDGN N11 40 C3
Brookdale Rd BXLY DA5 137 F5
CAT SE6 132 E6
WALTH E17 57 J2
Brookdene Av OXHEY WD19 21 F6
Brookdene Dr NTHWD HA6 32 D6
Brookdene Rd
WOOL/PLUM SE18 115 K3
Brook Dr RSLP HA4 46 C5
RYLN/HDSTN HA2 48 C3
STHWK SE1 18 B4
Brooke Av RYLN/HDSTN HA2 66 C2
Brooke Cl BUSH WD23 22 C6
Brookehowse Rd CAT SE6 151 K2
Brookend Rd BFN/LL DA15 135 K7
Brooke Rd CLPT E5 74 C2
WALTH E17 58 A3
Brooke's Market HCIRC * EC1N 12 A2
Brooke St HCIRC EC1N 12 A3
Brooke Wy BUSH WD23 22 C6
Brookfield Av EA W5 85 K3
MLHL NW7 37 K5
SUT SM1 175 J2
WALTH E17 58 A3
Brookfield Cl MLHL NW7 37 K5
Brookfield Crs
KTN/HRWW/W HA3 50 A4
MLHL NW7 37 K5
Brookfield Gdns
ESH/CLAY KT10 171 F5
Brookfield Pk KTTN NW5 72 B2
Brookfield Pth CHING E4 44 B5
Brookfield Rd CHSWK W4 106 A1
ED N9 42 C2
HOM E9 75 G5
Brookfields PEND EN3 31 F3
Brookfields Av MTCM CR4 162 D4
Brook Gdns BARN SW13 126 C2
CHING E4 43 K3
KUTN/CMB KT2 144 E7
Brook Ga BAY/PAD W2 9 M7
Brook Gn HMSMTH W6 107 F2
Brookhill Cl EBAR EN4 27 J4
Brook Hill Cl WOOL/PLUM SE18 115 G4
Brookhill Rd WOOL/PLUM SE18 115 G4
Brookhouse Gdns CHING E4 44 C3
Brooking Cl BCTR RM8 79 J2
Brooking Rd FSTGT E7 76 E4
Brookland Cl GLDGN NW11 52 E3
Brookland Garth GLDGN NW11 53 F3
Brookland Hl GLDGN NW11 52 E3
Brookland Ri GLDGN NW11 52 E3
The Brooklands ISLW * TW7 103 J7
Brooklands DART DA1 139 H7
Brooklands Ap ROM RM1 63 F3
Brooklands Av BFN/LL DA15 154 D1
WAND/EARL SW18 147 F1
Brooklands Cl ROMW/RG RM7 63 F3
SUN TW16 140 C7
Brooklands Ct
KIL/WHAMP * NW6 70 D6
WCHMH N21 29 K4
Brooklands Dr GFD/PVL UB6 67 J7
Brooklands La ROMW/RG RM7 63 F3
Brooklands Pk BKHTH/KID SE3 133 K2
Brooklands Rd ROMW/RG RM7 63 F3
THDIT KT7 158 A7
Brook La BKHTH/KID SE3 134 A1
BMLY BR1 152 E5
BXLY DA5 136 E5
Brook La North BTFD TW8 104 E4
Brooklea Cl CDALE/KGS NW9 37 G7
Brooklyn Av SNWD SE25 165 J3
Brooklyn Cl CAR SM5 175 J1
Brooklyn Gv SNWD SE25 165 J3
Brooklyn Rd HAYES BR2 168 C4
SNWD SE25 165 J3
Brooklyn Wy WDR/YW UB7 100 A2
Brook Md HOR/WEW KT19 173 G5
Brookmead MTCM CR4 163 H5
Brookmead Av HAYES BR2 168 E4
Brook Meadow
NFNCH/WDSP N12 39 F3
Brook Meadow Cl WFD IG8 44 C5
Brookmead Rd CROY/NA CR0 163 H5
Brook Ms North BAY/PAD W2 8 F6
Brookmill Cl OXHEY * WD19 21 F6
Brookmill Rd DEPT SE8 112 D7
Brook Park Cl WCHMH N21 29 H5
Brook Pl BAR EN5 26 E4
Brook Rd BKHH IG9 44 E1
CEND/HSY/T N8 54 E3
CRICK NW2 69 J1
GNTH/NBYPK IG2 60 E5
GPK RM2 63 H1
SURB KT6 172 A1
THHTH CR7 164 D3
TWK TW1 124 B5
WDGN * N22 55 F1
Brook Rd South BTFD TW8 105 F5
Brooks Av EHAM E6 95 K3
Brooksbank St HOM * E9 75 F5
Brooksby Ms IS N1 6 A1
Brooksby St IS N1 6 A2
Brooksby's Wk HOM E9 75 F4
Brookscroft CROY/NA * CR0 179 H7
Brookscroft Rd WALTH E17 43 K7
Brookshill KTN/HRWW/W HA3 34 E5
Brookshill Av
KTN/HRWW/W HA3 34 D4
Brookshill Dr
KTN/HRWW/W HA3 34 D4
Brookside CAR SM5 176 A4
EBAR EN4 27 J5
WCHMH N21 29 F5
Brookside Cl BAR EN5 26 B5
FELT TW13 140 E2
KTN/HRWW/W HA3 49 K4
RSLP HA4 65 J3
Brookside Crs WPK KT4 160 D7
Brookside Rd ED N9 42 D3
GLDGN NW11 52 C5
OXHEY WD19 21 F6
YEAD UB4 83 G6
Brookside South EBAR EN4 28 A6
Brookside Wy CROY/NA CR0 166 A5
Brooks La CHSWK W4 105 H5
Brook's Ms MYFR/PKLN W1K 10 C6
Brooks Rd CHSWK W4 105 H4
PLSTW E13 76 E7
Brook St BAY/PAD W2 9 H6
BELV DA17 117 J4
KUT KT1 159 F1
MYFR/PKLN W1K 10 C6
Brooksville Av
KIL/WHAMP NW6 70 C7
Brookview Rd
STRHM/NOR SW16 148 C4
Brookville Rd FUL/PGN SW6 107 J6
Brook Wk EDGW HA8 37 F5
EFNCH * N2 39 H7
Brook Water La HDN * NW4 52 B4
Brookway BKHTH/KID SE3 133 K2
RAIN RM13 99 K4
Brookwood Av BARN SW13 126 C2
Brookwood Cl HAYES BR2 167 J3
Brookwood Rd HSLW TW3 123 G1
WAND/EARL SW18 127 J7
Broom Cl ESH/CLAY KT10 170 B4
HAYES BR2 168 D5
TEDD TW11 143 K6
Broomcroft Av NTHLT UB5 83 G2
Broome Rd HPTN TW12 141 K7
Broome Wy CMBW SE5 110 E6
Broomfield SUN TW16 140 E7
WALTH E17 57 H6
Broomfield Av PLMGR N13 41 F3
Broomfield Cottages
WEA * W13 85 H7
Broomfield La PLMGR N13 40 E3
Broomfield Pl WEA W13 85 H7
Broomfield Rd BECK BR3 166 B3
BRYLDS KT5 159 G7
BXLYHS DA6 137 H4
CHDH RM6 61 K6
PLMGR N13 40 E4
RCH/KEW TW9 105 G7
TEDD TW11 143 J5
WEA W13 85 H7
Broomfields ESH/CLAY KT10 170 C4
Broomfield St POP/IOD E14 93 J4
Broom Gdns CROY/NA CR0 179 J2
Broomgrove Gdns EDGW HA8 36 C7
Broomgrove Rd BRXN/ST SW9 130 A1
Broomhall Rd SAND/SEL CR2 177 K7
Broomhill Ri BXLYHS DA6 137 H4
Broomhill Rd DART DA1 138 E5
GDMY/SEVK IG3 79 G1
WAND/EARL SW18 127 K4
WFD IG8 44 E5
Broomhouse La FUL/PGN SW6 127 K1
Broomhouse Rd FUL/PGN SW6 127 K1
Broomloan La SUT SM1 174 E1
Broom Lock TEDD * TW11 143 J4
Broom Md BXLYHS DA6 137 H5
Broom Pk KUT KT1 143 K6
Broom Rd CROY/NA CR0 179 J2
TEDD TW11 143 H4
Broomsleigh St
KIL/WHAMP * NW6 70 E4
Broom Water TEDD TW11 143 J5
Broom Water West
TEDD TW11 143 J4
Broomwood Cl CROY/NA CR0 166 A4
Broomwood Rd BTSEA SW11 128 E5
Broseley Gv SYD SE26 151 G4
Broster Gdns SNWD SE25 165 G2
Brougham Rd ACT W3 86 E5
HACK E8 74 C7
Brougham St BTSEA SW11 128 E1
Brough Cl KUTN/CMB * KT2 143 K4
VX/NE SW8 109 K6
Broughinge Rd BORE WD6 24 D1
Broughton Av FNCH N3 52 C2
RCHPK/HAM TW10 143 J3
Broughton Dr BRXN/ST SW9 130 B3
Broughton Gdns HGT N6 54 C5
Broughton Rd FUL/PGN SW6 128 A1
THHTH CR7 164 B5
WEA W13 85 H6
Broughton Road Ap
FUL/PGN * SW6 128 A1
Broughton St VX/NE SW8 129 F1
Brouncker Rd ACT W3 105 K1
Browell's La FELT TW13 141 G1
Brown Cl WLGTN SM6 176 D6
Brownfield St POP/IOD E14 94 A5
Browngraves Rd WDR/YW UB7 101 F6
Brown Hart Gdns
MYFR/PKLN W1K 10 B6
Brownhill Rd CAT SE6 133 F6
Browning Av HNWL W7 85 F5
SUT SM1 175 J3
WPK KT4 160 E7
Browning Cl HPTN TW12 141 K3
MV/WKIL * W9 8 F1
WALTH E17 58 A3
WELL DA16 115 K7
Browning Ms CAVSQ/HST * W1G 10 B3
Browning Rd DART DA1 139 J3
MNPK E12 77 K5
WAN E11 58 D6
Browning St WALW SE17 18 F7
Browning Wy HEST TW5 102 C7
Brownlea Gdns GDMY/SEVK IG3 79 G1
Brownlow Ms FSBYW WC1X 5 M9
Brownlow Rd BORE WD6 24 C3
CROY/NA CR0 178 A3
FBAR/BDGN N11 40 E5
FNCH N3 39 F6
FSTGT E7 76 E3
HACK E8 7 M3
WEA * W13 85 G7
WLSDN NW10 69 G6
Brownlow St GINN WC1R 11 M3
Brownspring Dr
ELTH/MOT SE9 154 B3
Brown's Rd BRYLDS KT5 159 G6
WALTH E17 57 J2
Brown St MBLAR W1H 9 L4
Brownswell Rd EFNCH N2 53 H1
Brownswood Rd FSBYPK N4 73 J1
Broxash Rd BTSEA SW11 129 F5
Broxbourne Av WAN E11 59 F3
Broxbourne House BOW E3 93 K3
Broxbourne Rd FSTGT E7 76 E2
Broxholm Rd WNWD SE27 149 G2
Broxted Rd CAT SE6 151 H1
Broxwood Wy STJWD NW8 3 K4
Bruce Castle Rd TOTM N17 42 B7
Bruce Cl NKENS W10 88 B4
WELL DA16 116 C7
Bruce Dr SAND/SEL CR2 179 F7
Bruce Gdns TRDG/WHET N20 39 K2
Bruce Gv TOTM N17 56 B1
Bruce Rd BAR * EN5 26 C2
BOW E3 93 K2
KTN/HRWW/W HA3 48 E1
MTCM CR4 148 A6
SNWD SE25 164 E3
WLSDN NW10 69 F6
Bruckner St NKENS W10 88 C2
Brudenell Rd TOOT SW17 147 K2
Bruffs Meadow NTHLT UB5 65 J5
Bruges Pl CAMTN NW1 4 F2
Brumfield Rd HOR/WEW KT19 172 E4
Brunel Cl HEST TW5 102 A6
NRWD SE19 150 B5
NTHLT UB5 83 K2
ROM RM1 63 G3
Brunel Ct WLSDN NW10 87 J2
Brunel Est BAY/PAD W2 8 A3
Brunel Rd ACT W3 87 G4
BERM/RHTH SE16 92 E7
WALTH E17 57 G5
WFD IG8 45 K4
Brunel St CAN/RD E16 94 D5
Brunel Wk WHTN TW2 123 F6
Brune St WCHPL E1 13 L3
Brunner Cl GLDGN NW11 53 F4
Brunner Rd EA W5 85 K3
WALTH E17 57 H4
Bruno Pl CDALE/KGS NW9 68 E1
Brunswick Av FBAR/BDGN N11 40 A2
Brunswick Cl BXLYHS DA6 136 E3
PIN HA5 47 J5
THDIT KT7 158 A7
WHTN TW2 142 D2
Brunswick Ct STHWK SE1 19 K2
Brunswick Crs FBAR/BDGN N11 40 A2
Brunswick Gdns EA W5 86 A2
KENS W8 8 B9
Brunswick Gv FBAR/BDGN N11 40 A2
Brunswick Ms MBLAR W1H 9 M4
STRHM/NOR SW16 148 D5
Brunswick Pk CMBW SE5 110 E7
Brunswick Park Gdns
FBAR/BDGN N11 40 A1
Brunswick Park Rd
FBAR/BDGN N11 40 A1
Brunswick Pl CAMTN NW1 10 B1
IS N1 7 H8
NRWD SE19 150 C6
Brunswick Quay
BERM/RHTH SE16 112 A2
Brunswick Rd BXLYHS DA6 136 E3
EA W5 85 K3
KUTN/CMB KT2 144 C7
LEY E10 58 A7
SEVS/STOTM N15 56 A4
SUT SM1 175 F3
Brunswick Sq BMSBY WC1N 5 K9
Brunswick St WALTH E17 58 A4
Brunswick Vls CMBW SE5 111 F7
Brunswick Wy FBAR/BDGN N11 40 B3
Brunton Pl POP/IOD E14 93 G5
Brushfield St WCHPL E1 13 K2
Brussels Rd BTSEA SW11 128 C3
Bruton Cl CHST BR7 153 K6
Bruton La MYFR/PICC W1J 10 D7
Bruton Pl MYFR/PKLN W1K 10 D7
Bruton Rd MRDN SM4 162 B3
Bruton St MYFR/PICC W1J 10 D7
Bruton Wy WEA W13 85 G4
Bryan Av WLSDN NW10 69 K6
Bryan Cl SUN TW16 140 E6
Bryan Rd BERM/RHTH SE16 112 C1
Bryanston Av WHTN TW2 123 G7
Bryanston Cl NWDGN UB2 102 E3
Bryanstone Rd CEND/HSY/T N8 54 D4
Bryanston Ms East MBLAR W1H 9 L3
Bryanston Ms West MBLAR W1H 9 L3
Bryanston Pl MBLAR W1H 9 L3
Bryanston Sq MBLAR W1H 9 L4
Bryanston St MBLAR W1H 9 L5
Bryant Cl BAR EN5 26 D4
Bryant Rd NTHLT UB5 83 G2
Bryant St SRTFD E15 76 B6
Bryantwood Rd HOLWY N7 73 G4
Brycedale Crs STHGT/OAK N14 40 D3
Bryce Rd BCTR RM8 79 J3
Bryden Cl SYD SE26 151 G4
Brydges Pl CHCR WC2N 11 J7
Brydges Rd SRTFD E15 76 B4
Brydon Wk IS N1 5 K3
Bryett Rd HOLWY N7 72 E2
Brymay Cl BOW E3 93 J1
Brynmaer Rd BTSEA SW11 108 E7
Bryn-y-Mawr Rd EN EN1 30 B3
Bryony Rd SHB W12 87 J6
Bryony Wy SUN TW16 140 E5
Buchanan Cl WCHMH N21 29 F4
Buchanan Ct BORE * WD6 24 E1
Buchanan Gdns WLSDN NW10 87 K1
Buchan Rd PECK SE15 131 K2
Bucharest Rd
WAND/EARL SW18 128 B6
Buckden Cl LEE/GVPK SE12 133 J5
Buckfast Rd MRDN SM4 162 A3
Buckfast St BETH E2 92 C2
Buckhold Rd
WAND/EARL SW18 127 K5
Buckhurst Av CAR SM5 162 D7
Buckhurst St WCHPL E1 92 D3
Buckhurst Wy BKHH IG9 45 H2
Buckingham Av
E/WMO/HCT KT8 157 G1
EBED/NFELT TW14 122 A5
GFD/PVL UB6 67 G7
THHTH CR7 149 G7
TRDG/WHET N20 27 G6
WELL DA16 135 K3
Buckingham Cl EA W5 85 J4
EN EN1 30 A1
HPTN TW12 141 K4
STMC/STPC BR5 169 K6
Buckingham Ct BELMT * SM2 174 E7
Buckingham Dr CHST BR7 154 B4
Buckingham Gdns
E/WMO/HCT KT8 157 G1
STAN HA7 36 A6
THHTH CR7 164 B1
Buckingham Ga WESTW SW1E 16 E3
Buckingham La FSTH SE23 132 B6
Buckingham Ms WESTW * SW1E 16 E3
WLSDN NW10 87 H1
Buckingham Palace Rd
BGVA SW1W 16 C6
Buckingham Pde STAN * HA7 35 J4
Buckingham Pl WESTW SW1E 16 E3
Buckingham Rd BORE WD6 25 F3
EDGW HA8 36 B6
FELT TW13 141 K3
HRW HA1 48 D4
IL IG1 78 D1
IS N1 74 A5
KUT KT1 159 G3
LEY E10 75 K2
MTCM CR4 163 K4
RCHPK/HAM TW10 143 K1
SRTFD E15 76 D4
SWFD E18 44 D7
WAN E11 59 F3
WDGN N22 40 E7
WLSDN NW10 87 H1
Buckingham St CHCR WC2N 11 K7
Buckingham Wy WLGTN SM6 176 C7
Buckland Crs HAMP NW3 3 G1
Buckland Ri PIN HA5 33 G7
Buckland Rd CHSGTN KT9 172 B4
LEY E10 76 A1
Bucklands OXHEY * WD19 33 H2
Bucklands Rd TEDD TW11 143 J5
Buckland St IS N1 7 H6
Bucklands Whf KUT * KT1 158 E1
Buckland Wk MRDN SM4 162 B3
Buckland Wy WPK KT4 161 F7
Buck La CDALE/KGS NW9 51 F4
Buckleigh Av RYNPK SW20 161 J2
Buckleigh Rd
STRHM/NOR SW16 148 D5
Buckleigh Wy NRWD SE19 150 B7
Bucklersbury MANHO * EC4N 13 G5
Bucklers' Wy CAR SM5 175 K2
Buckle St WCHPL E1 13 M4
Buckley Cl DART DA1 138 C1
Buckley Rd KIL/WHAMP NW6 70 D6
Buckmaster Rd BTSEA SW11 128 D3
Bucknall St NOXST/BSQ WC1A 11 J4
Bucknall Wy BECK BR3 166 E3
Buckner Rd BRXS/STRHM SW2 130 A3
Buckrell Rd CHING E4 44 B1
Bucks Av OXHEY WD19 21 J6
Buckstone Cl FSTH SE23 131 K5
Buckstone Rd UED N18 42 C5
Buck St CAMTN NW1 4 D3
Buckters Rents
BERM/RHTH SE16 93 G7
Buckthorne Rd BROCKY SE4 132 B5
Budd Cl NFNCH/WDSP N12 39 F3
Buddings Cir WBLY HA9 68 E2
Bude Cl WALTH E17 57 H4
Budge La MTCM CR4 162 E6
Budge Rw MANHO EC4N 13 G6
Budleigh Crs WELL DA16 116 D7
Budoch Dr GDMY/SEVK IG3 79 G1
Buer Rd FUL/PGN SW6 127 H1
Bugsby's Wy GNWCH SE10 113 K3
Bulganak Rd THHTH CR7 164 D3
Bulinca St WEST * SW1P 17 J6
Bullace Rw CMBW SE5 110 E7
Bull Aly WELL DA16 136 C2
Bullar Cl PECK SE15 111 H6
Bullard Rd TEDD * TW11 143 F5
Bullards Pl BETH E2 93 F2
Bullbanks Rd BELV DA17 117 K3
Bulleid Wy PIM SW1V 16 D6
Bullen St BTSEA SW11 128 D1
Buller Rd BARK IG11 78 E6
THHTH CR7 164 E2
TOTM N17 56 C1
WDGN N22 55 G1
WLSDN NW10 88 B2
Bullers Wood Dr CHST BR7 153 J7
Bullescroft Rd EDGW HA8 36 C2
Bullhead Rd BORE WD6 24 E1
Bullivant St POP/IOD E14 94 A6
Bull La CHST BR7 154 D6
DAGE RM10 80 D2
UED N18 42 A4
Bull Rd SRTFD E15 94 D1
Bullrush Cl CROY/NA CR0 165 F5
Bulls Aly MORT/ESHN * SW14 126 A2
Bull's Br HYS/HAR UB3 101 K2
Bulls Bridge Rd NWDGN UB2 102 A2
Bullsbrook Rd HYS/HAR UB3 83 G7
Bull Yd PECK SE15 111 H7
Bulmer Gdns
KTN/HRWW/W HA3 49 K6
Bulmer Ms NTGHL W11 8 A8
Bulstrode Av HSLW TW3 122 E2
Bulstrode Gdns HSLW TW3 123 F2
Bulstrode Pl MHST W1U 10 B3
Bulstrode Rd HSLW TW3 123 F2
Bulstrode St MHST W1U 10 B4
Bulwer Court Rd WAN E11 58 B7
Bulwer Gdns BAR EN5 27 G3
Bulwer Rd BAR EN5 27 F3
UED N18 42 A3
WAN E11 58 B7
Bulwer St SHB W12 88 A7
Bunces La WFD IG8 44 D6
The Bungalows
RYLN/HDSTN * HA2 65 K2
STRHM/NOR SW16 148 B6
Bungalow Rd SNWD SE25 165 F3
Bunhill Rw STLK EC1Y 7 G9
Bunhouse Pl BGVA SW1W 16 A7
Bunning Wy HOLWY N7 5 K1
Bunn's La MLHL NW7 37 G5
Bunsen St BOW E3 93 G1
Bunting Cl ED N9 31 F7
MTCM CR4 162 E4
Bunton St WOOL/PLUM SE18 115 F2
Bunyan Rd WALTH E17 57 G2
Burbage Cl HYS/HAR UB3 82 B5
STHWK SE1 19 G4
Burbage Rd HNHL SE24 130 E5
Burberry Cl NWMAL KT3 160 B1
Burbridge Wy TOTM N17 56 C1
Burcham St POP/IOD E14 93 K5
Burcharbro Rd ABYW SE2 116 E5
Burchell Ct BUSH WD23 22 C6
Burchell Rd LEY E10 57 K7
PECK SE15 111 J7
Burcote Rd WAND/EARL SW18 128 C7
Burden Cl BTFD TW8 104 D4
Burdenshott Av
RCHPK/HAM TW10 125 J3
Burden Wy WAN E11 77 F1
Burder Cl IS N1 74 A5
Burder Rd IS N1 74 A5
Burdett Av RYNPK SW20 145 J7
Burdett Cl HNWL * W7 85 F7
Burdett Rd BOW E3 93 H3
CROY/NA CR0 164 E5
RCH/KEW TW9 125 G1
Burdetts Rd DAGW RM9 80 B7
Burdock Cl CROY/NA CR0 166 A7
Burdock Rd TOTM N17 56 C2
Burdon La BELMT SM2 174 D7

Burdon Pk BELMT SM2 174 D7
Burfield Cl TOOT SW17 147 G3
Burford Cl BARK/HLT IG6 60 C3
BCTR RM8 79 J2
Burford Gdns PLMGR N13 41 F2
Burford Rd BMLY BR1 168 D3
BTFD TW8 85 F5
CAT SE6 151 H1
EHAM E6 95 J2
SRTFD E15 76 B6
SUT SM1 174 E1
WPK KT4 160 D6
Burford Wk FUL/PGN * SW6 108 A6
Burford Wy CROY/NA CR0 180 A6
Burgate Cl DART DA1 138 C2
Burges Gv BARN SW13 106 E6
Burges Rd EHAM E6 78 A6
Burgess Av CDALE/KGS NW9 51 F5
Burgess Cl FELT TW13 141 J3
Burgess Hl CRICK NW2 70 E3
Burgess Rd SRTFD E15 76 C3
SUT SM1 175 F3
Burgess St POP/IOD E14 93 J4
Burge St STHWK SE1 19 H4
Burghill Rd SYD SE26 151 F3
Burghley Av BORE WD6 24 E4
NWMAL KT3 145 F7
Burghley Hall Cl
WIM/MER * SW19 127 H7
Burghley Pl MTCM CR4 162 E3
Burghley Rd CEND/HSY/T N8 55 G2
KTTN NW5 72 B3
WAN * E11 58 C7
WIM/MER SW19 146 C3
Burgh St IS N1 6 D5
Burgon St BLKFR EC4V 12 D5
Burgon Street Hl BLKFR EC4V 12 D5
Burgos Cl CROY/NA CR0 177 G5
Burgos Gv GNWCH SE10 112 E7
Burgoyne Rd BRXN/ST SW9 130 A2
FSBYPK N4 55 H5
SNWD SE25 165 G3
SUN TW16 140 D5
Burham Cl PGE/AN SE20 150 E6
Burhill Gv PIN HA5 47 J1
Burke Cl PUT/ROE SW15 126 B3
Burke St CAN/RD E16 94 D5
Burket Cl NWDGN UB2 102 D3
Burland Rd BTSEA SW11 128 E4
Burleigh Av BFN/LL DA15 136 A4
WLGTN SM6 176 A2
Burleigh Ct BUSH * WD23 21 J3
Burleigh Gdns ASHF TW15 140 A4
STHGT/OAK N14 28 C7
Burleigh Pde STHGT/OAK * N14 28 D7
Burleigh Pl PUT/ROE SW15 127 G4
Burleigh Rd CHEAM SM3 161 H7
EN EN1 30 A3
Burleigh St COVGDN WC2E 11 K6
Burleigh Wk CAT SE6 133 F7
Burleigh Wy ENC/FH EN2 29 K2
Burley Cl CHING E4 43 J4
STRHM/NOR SW16 163 J1
Burley Rd CAN/RD E16 95 G5
Burlington Ar CONDST W1S 10 E7
Burlington Av RCH/KEW TW9 105 H7
ROMW/RG RM7 62 D5
Burlington Cl
EBED/NFELT TW14 121 G6
EHAM E6 95 J5
MV/WKIL W9 2 A9
Burlington Gdns ACT W3 86 E7
CHDH RM6 62 A6
CHSWK W4 105 K4
CONDST W1S 10 E7
Burlington La CHSWK W4 105 K6
Burlington Ms ACT W3 86 E7
Burlington Pde CRICK * NW2 70 B3
Burlington Pl FUL/PGN SW6 127 H1
PIN HA5 47 F2
WFD IG8 44 E2
Burlington Ri EBAR EN4 27 J7
Burlington Rd CHSWK * W4 105 K4
FUL/PGN SW6 127 H1
ISLW TW7 103 J7
MUSWH N10 54 A2
NWMAL KT3 160 C3
THHTH CR7 164 D1
TOTM N17 42 C7
Burma Rd STNW/STAM N16 73 K3
Burma Ter NRWD * SE19 150 A4
Burmester Rd TOOT SW17 147 G2
Burnaby Crs CHSWK W4 105 J5
Burnaby Gdns CHSWK W4 105 J5
Burnaby St WBPTN SW10 108 B6
Burnbrae Cl FNCH N3 39 F5
Burnbury Rd BAL SW12 129 H7
Burn Cl GSTN * WD25 22 D3
Burncroft Av PEND EN3 30 E2
Burndell Wy YEAD UB4 83 H4
Burnell Av RCHPK/HAM TW10 143 J4
WELL DA16 136 B1
Burnell Gdns STAN HA7 49 K1
Burnell Rd SUT SM1 175 F3
Burnell Wk STHWK * SE1 19 M7
Burnels Av EHAM E6 96 A2
Burness Cl HOLWY N7 73 F5
Burne St CAMTN NW1 9 J2
Burnett Rd ERITH DA8 119 G5
Burney Av BRYLDS KT5 159 G4
Burney St GNWCH SE10 113 F6
Burnfoot Av FUL/PGN SW6 107 H7
Burnham Av HGDN/ICK UB10 64 A3
Burnham Cl KTN/HRWW/W HA3 49 G3
MLHL NW7 37 J6
STHWK SE1 19 M6
Burnham Crs DART DA1 139 F3
WAN E11 59 G3
Burnham Dr WPK KT4 174 B1
Burnham Gdns CROY/NA CR0 165 G6
HEST TW5 102 A7
HYS/HAR UB3 101 G2
Burnham Rd CHING E4 43 H4
DAGW RM9 79 H6
DART DA1 139 G4
MRDN SM4 162 A4
ROMW/RG RM7 62 E2
Burnham St BETH E2 92 E2
KUTN/CMB KT2 144 C7
Burnham Ter DART * DA1 139 G4
Burnham Wy SYD SE26 151 H4
WEA W13 104 C3
Burnhill Rd BECK BR3 166 D1
Burnley Cl OXHEY WD19 33 G4
Burnley Rd BRXN/ST SW9 130 A1
WLSDN NW10 69 H4
Burnsall St CHEL SW3 15 K7
Burns Av BFN/LL DA15 136 C5
CHDH RM6 61 J6
EBED/NFELT TW14 121 K5
STHL UB1 84 A6
Burns Cl ERITH DA8 118 C7
WALTH E17 58 A3
WELL DA16 116 A7
WIM/MER SW19 147 H5
YEAD UB4 82 E4
Burnside Av CHING E4 43 H5
Burnside Cl BAR EN5 26 E2
BERM/RHTH SE16 93 F7
TWK TW1 124 B5
Burnside Crs ALP/SUD HA0 67 K7
Burnside Rd BCTR RM8 79 J1
Burns Rd ALP/SUD HA0 86 A1
BTSEA SW11 128 E1
WEA * W13 104 C1
WLSDN NW10 69 H7
Burns Wy HEST TW5 102 C7
Burnt Ash Hl LEE/GVPK SE12 133 J5
Burnt Ash La BMLY BR1 153 F4
Burnt Ash Rd LEE/GVPK SE12 133 J4
Burnthwaite Rd FUL/PGN SW6 107 J6
Burnt Oak Broadway
EDGW HA8 36 D6
Burnt Oak Flds EDGW HA8 36 E7
Burnt Oak La BFN/LL DA15 136 B5
Burntwood Cl
WAND/EARL * SW18 128 C7
Burntwood Grange Rd
WAND/EARL SW18 128 C7
Burntwood La TOOT SW17 147 G2
Burntwood Vw NRWD * SE19 150 B4
Buross St WCHPL E1 92 D5
Burpham Cl YEAD UB4 83 H4
Burrage Gv WOOL/PLUM SE18 115 G3
Burrage Pl WOOL/PLUM SE18 115 G4
Burrage Rd WOOL/PLUM SE18 115 H3
Burrard Rd CAN/RD E16 94 E5
KIL/WHAMP NW6 70 E4
Burr Cl BXLYHN DA7 137 G2
WAP * E1W 92 C7
Burrell Cl CROY/NA CR0 166 B5
EDGW HA8 36 D1
Burrell Rw BECK BR3 166 D1
Burrell St STHWK SE1 12 C8
Burritt Rd KUT KT1 159 H1
The Burroughs HDN NW4 51 K3
Burroughs Cottages
POP/IOD * E14 93 G4
Burroughs Gdns HDN NW4 51 K3
Burrow Rd EDUL SE22 131 F3
Burrows Ms STHWK SE1 18 C1
Burrows Rd WLSDN NW10 88 A2
Burr Rd WAND/EARL SW18 127 K7
Bursar St STHWK * SE1 13 J9
Bursdon Cl BFN/LL DA15 155 F1
Bursland Rd PEND EN3 31 F3
Burslem St WCHPL E1 92 D5
Burstock Rd PUT/ROE SW15 127 H3
Burston Rd PUT/ROE SW15 127 G4
Burstow Rd RYNPK SW20 146 C7
Burtenshaw Rd THDIT KT7 158 B6
Burtley Cl FSBYPK N4 55 J7
Burton Av WATW WD18 20 E3
Burton Bank IS * N1 7 G2
Burton Cl CHSGTN KT9 171 K6
THHTH CR7 164 E2
Burton Gdns HEST TW5 102 E7
Burton Gv WALW SE17 19 G8
Burtonhole Cl MLHL NW7 38 B3
Burtonhole La MLHL NW7 38 B4
Burton La BRXN/ST * SW9 130 B1
Burton Ms BGVA SW1W 16 B6
Burton Pl STPAN WC1H 5 H9
Burton Rd BRXN/ST SW9 130 C1
KIL/WHAMP NW6 70 D6
KUTN/CMB KT2 144 A6
SWFD E18 59 F2
Burtons Ct SRTFD E15 76 B6
Burton's Rd HPTN TW12 142 B3
Burton St STPAN WC1H 5 H9
Burt Rd CAN/RD E16 95 G7
Burtwell La WNWD SE27 149 K3
Burwash Rd WOOL/PLUM SE18 115 J4
Burwell Av GFD/PVL UB6 66 E5
Burwell Cl WCHPL * E1 92 D5
Burwell Rd LEY E10 57 G7
Burwood Av HAYES BR2 181 F1
PIN HA5 47 G4
Burwood Cl SURB KT6 159 H7
Burwood Gdns RAIN RM13 99 H2
Burwood Pl BAY/PAD W2 9 K4
Bury Av RSLP HA4 46 A5
YEAD UB4 82 C1
Bury Cl BERM/RHTH SE16 93 F7
Bury Ct HDTCH EC3A 13 K4
Bury Gv MRDN SM4 162 A4
Bury Pl NOXST/BSQ WC1A 11 J3
Bury Rd DAGE RM10 80 E4
WDGN N22 55 G1
Bury St ED N9 30 B6
HDTCH EC3A 13 K5
RSLP HA4 46 B5
STJS SW1Y 10 E8
Bury St West ED N9 30 A6
Bury Wk CHEL SW3 15 J6
Busby Pl KTTN NW5 72 D5
Busch Cl ISLW TW7 104 C7
Bushbaby Cl STHWK SE1 19 J4
Bushberry Rd HOM E9 75 G5
Bush Cl GNTH/NBYPK IG2 60 D4
Bush Cottages
WAND/EARL SW18 127 K4
Bushell Cl BRXS/STRHM SW2 149 F1
Bushell Gn BUSH WD23 34 D1
Bushell Wy CHST BR7 154 A4
Bush Elms Rd EMPK RM11 63 J6
Bushey Av STMC/STPC BR5 169 J6
SWFD E18 58 D2
Bushey Cl CHING E4 44 A2
Bushey Grove Rd BUSH WD23 21 H3
Bushey Hall Dr BUSH WD23 21 J3
Bushey Hall Pk BUSH * WD23 21 J3
Bushey Hall Rd BUSH WD23 21 H3
Bushey Hill Rd CMBW SE5 111 G7
Bushey La SUT SM1 174 E2
Bushey Lees BFN/LL * DA15 136 A5
Bushey Mill La BUSH WD23 21 K1
Bushey Rd CROY/NA CR0 179 J1
HYS/HAR UB3 101 H3
PLSTW E13 95 G1
RYNPK SW20 161 F1
SEVS/STOTM N15 56 A5
SUT SM1 174 E3
Bushey Wy BECK BR3 167 G5
Bushfield Cl EDGW HA8 36 D1
Bushfield Crs EDGW HA8 36 D1
Bush Gv CDALE/KGS NW9 50 E6
STAN HA7 35 K7
Bushgrove Rd BCTR RM8 79 K3
Bush Hl WCHMH N21 29 J6
Bush Hill Pde EN * EN1 29 K6
Bush Hill Rd KTN/HRWW/W HA3 50 B5
WCHMH N21 29 K5
Bush La CANST EC4R 13 G6
Bushmead Cl
SEVS/STOTM * N15 56 B3
Bushmoor Crs
WOOL/PLUM SE18 115 G6
Bushnell Rd TOOT SW17 148 B1
Bush Rd BERM/RHTH SE16 112 A3
BKHH IG9 45 H3
HACK E8 74 D7
RCH/KEW TW9 105 G5
WAN E11 58 D6
Bushway BCTR RM8 79 K3
Bushwood WAN E11 58 D7
Bushwood Dr STHWK SE1 19 M6
Bushwood Rd RCH/KEW TW9 105 H5
Bushy Park Gdns HPTN * TW12 142 D4
Bushy Park Rd TEDD TW11 143 H6
Bushy Rd TEDD TW11 142 E5
Butcher Rw POP/IOD E14 93 F6
Butchers Rd CAN/RD E16 94 E5
Bute Av RCHPK/HAM TW10 144 A1
Bute Gdns HMSMTH W6 107 G3
RCHPK/HAM * TW10 125 F7
WLGTN SM6 176 C4
Bute Gdns West WLGTN SM6 176 C4
Bute Rd BARK/HLT IG6 60 B4
CROY/NA CR0 164 B7
WLGTN SM6 176 C3
Bute St SKENS SW7 15 G5
Bute Wk IS * N1 73 K5
Butler Av HRW HA1 48 D6
Butler Rd BCTR RM8 79 H3
HRW HA1 48 C6
WLSDN NW10 69 H6
Butlers & Colonial Whf
STHWK SE1 19 M1
Butler St BETH * E2 92 E2
Buttercup Sq
STWL/WRAY * TW19 120 A7
Butterfield Cl
BERM/RHTH * SE16 111 H1
TOTM N17 41 J5
TWK TW1 124 A5
Butterfields WALTH E17 58 A4
Butterfield Sq EHAM E6 95 K5
Butterfly La BORE WD6 23 H2
ELTH/MOT SE9 135 G5
Butterfly Wk CMBW * SE5 110 E7
Butter Hl WLGTN SM6 176 A2
Butteridges Cl DAGW RM9 80 B7
Buttermere Cl
EBED/NFELT TW14 121 J7
MRDN SM4 161 G5
STHWK SE1 19 L5
WAN E11 76 B3
Buttermere Dr PUT/ROE SW15 127 H4
Buttermere Wk HACK * E8 74 B5
Butterwick HMSMTH W6 107 F3
Butterworth Gdns WFD IG8 44 E5
Buttesland St IS N1 7 H7
Buttfield Cl DAGE RM10 80 D5
Buttmarsh Cl
WOOL/PLUM SE18 115 G4
The Butts BTFD TW8 104 E5
Buttsbury Rd IL IG1 78 C4
Butts Crs FELT TW13 142 A2
Buttsmead NTHWD HA6 32 A6
Butts Piece NTHLT UB5 83 F1
Butts Rd BMLY BR1 152 C4
Buxhall Crs HOM E9 75 H5
Buxted Rd EDUL SE22 131 F3
HACK E8 7 L1
NFNCH/WDSP N12 39 J4
Buxton Cl WFD IG8 45 H5
Buxton Crs CHEAM SM3 174 C3
Buxton Dr NWMAL KT3 160 A1
WAN E11 58 C3
Buxton Gdns ACT W3 86 D6
Buxton Pth OXHEY * WD19 33 G2
Buxton Rd ARCH N19 54 D7
CRICK NW2 69 K5
EHAM E6 95 J2
ERITH DA8 118 A6
GNTH/NBYPK IG2 60 E5
MORT/ESHN SW14 126 B2
SRTFD E15 76 C4
THHTH CR7 164 C4
WALTH E17 57 G3
Buxton St WCHPL E1 13 M1
Byam St FUL/PGN SW6 128 B1
Byards Cft STRHM/NOR SW16 148 D7
Bychurch End TEDD * TW11 143 F4
Bycroft Rd STHL UB1 84 A4
Bycroft St PGE/AN SE20 151 F6
Bycullah Av ENC/FH EN2 29 H2
Bycullah Rd ENC/FH EN2 29 H2
The Bye ACT W3 87 G5
Byefield Cl BERM/RHTH SE16 112 B1
Byelands Cl BERM/RHTH SE16 93 F7
Byewaters WATW WD18 20 B5
The Bye Wy KTN/HRWW/W HA3 34 E7
The Byeway
MORT/ESHN SW14 125 K2
Bye Ways WHTN TW2 142 B2
The Byeways BRYLDS KT5 159 H4
Byfeld Gdns BARN SW13 106 D7
Byfield Cl BERM/RHTH SE16 112 B1
Byfield Rd ISLW TW7 124 B2
Byford Cl SRTFD E15 76 C6
Bygrove Rd WIM/MER SW19 147 H5
Bygrove St POP/IOD E14 93 K5
Byland Cl ABYW SE2 116 C2
WCHMH N21 29 F6
Byne Rd CAR SM5 175 J1
SYD SE26 150 E5
Bynes Rd SAND/SEL CR2 177 K6
Byng Pl GWRST WC1E 11 H1
Byng Rd BAR EN5 26 B2
Byng St POP/IOD E14 112 D1
Bynon Av BXLYHN DA7 137 F2
Byre Rd STHGT/OAK N14 28 A5
Byrne Rd BAL SW12 129 G7
Byron Av BORE WD6 24 C4
CDALE/KGS NW9 50 D3
HSLWW TW4 122 A1
MNPK E12 77 J5
NWMAL KT3 160 D4
SUT SM1 175 H3
SWFD E18 58 D2
Byron Av East SUT SM1 175 H3
Byron Cl HACK E8 74 C7
HPTN TW12 141 K3
PGE/AN * SE20 165 J2
SYD * SE26 151 G3
THMD SE28 97 J7
WOT/HER KT12 156 D7
Byron Ct ENC/FH EN2 29 H1
Byron Dr EFNCH N2 53 H5
ERITH DA8 117 J6
Byron Gdns SUT SM1 175 H3
Byron Hill Rd RYLN/HDSTN HA2 48 D7
Byron Ms HAMP NW3 71 J4
Byron Rd ALP/SUD HA0 67 J1
CRICK NW2 69 K1
EA W5 86 B7
HRW HA1 48 E5
KTN/HRWW/W HA3 49 F2
LEY E10 57 K7
MLHL NW7 37 J4
WALTH E17 57 J2
Byron St POP/IOD E14 94 A5
Byron Ter ED * N9 30 E6
Byron Wy NTHLT UB5 83 H2
WDR/YW UB7 100 C3
YEAD UB4 82 C3
By the Wd OXHEY WD19 33 H1
Bythorn St BRXN/ST SW9 130 A2
Byton Rd TOOT SW17 147 K5
Byward Av EBED/NFELT TW14 122 B5
Byward St MON EC3R 13 K7
Bywater Pl BERM/RHTH SE16 93 G7
Bywater St CHEL SW3 15 L7
The Byway BELMT SM2 175 H7
The Byways HOR/WEW KT19 173 H3
Bywell Pl GTPST * W1W 10 E3
Bywood Av CROY/NA CR0 165 K5

C

Cabbell St CAMTN NW1 9 J3
Cabinet Wy CHING E4 43 H5
Cable Pl GNWCH SE10 113 F7
Cables Cl BELV DA17 117 K2
Cable St TWRH EC3N 13 M6
WCHPL E1 92 D6
Cabot Sq POP/IOD E14 93 J7
Cabot Wy EHAM E6 77 H7
Cabul Rd BTSEA SW11 128 D1
Cactus Cl CMBW * SE5 131 F1
Cadbury Cl ISLW TW7 104 B7
SUN TW16 140 C6
Cadbury Rd SUN TW16 140 C6
Cadbury Wy BERM/RHTH SE16 19 M4
Caddington Cl EBAR EN4 27 J4
Caddington Rd CRICK NW2 70 C2
Caddis Cl STAN * HA7 35 F6
Cadell Cl BETH E2 7 M6
Cade Rd GNWCH SE10 113 G7
Cader Rd WAND/EARL SW18 128 B5
Cadet Dr STHWK SE1 19 M7
Cadet Pl GNWCH SE10 113 H4
Cadiz Rd DAGE RM10 80 E6
Cadiz St WALW SE17 18 F8
Cadman Cl BRXN/ST SW9 110 C6
Cadmer Cl NWMAL KT3 160 B3
Cadogan Cl HOM * E9 75 H6
RYLN/HDSTN HA2 66 B3
TEDD TW11 142 E4
Cadogan Ct BELMT SM2 175 F5
Cadogan Gdns CHEL SW3 15 M6
FNCH * N3 39 F7
SWFD E18 59 F2
WCHMH N21 29 G4
Cadogan Ga KTBR SW1X 15 M5
Cadogan La KTBR SW1X 16 A4
Cadogan Pl KTBR SW1X 15 M5
Cadogan Rd SURB KT6 158 E4
WOOL/PLUM SE18 115 H2
Cadogan Sq KTBR SW1X 15 M4
Cadogan St CHEL SW3 15 L6
Cadogan Ter HOM E9 75 H5
Cadoxton Av SEVS/STOTM N15 56 B5
Cadwallon Rd ELTH/MOT SE9 154 B1
Caedmon Rd HOLWY N7 73 F3
Caerleon Cl ESH/CLAY KT10 171 H6
SCUP DA14 155 J4
Caernarvon Cl MTCM CR4 163 K2
Caesars Wk MTCM CR4 162 E4
Cahill St STLK * EC1Y 12 F1
Cahir St POP/IOD E14 112 E3
Cain's La EBED/NFELT TW14 121 G4
Caird St NKENS W10 88 C2
Cairn Av EA W5 85 K7
Cairndale Cl BMLY BR1 152 D6
Cairnfield Av CRICK NW2 69 G2
Cairns Av WFD IG8 45 K5
Cairns Cl DART DA1 139 G4
Cairns Rd BTSEA SW11 128 D4
Cairn Wy STAN HA7 35 F5
Cairo New Rd CROY/NA CR0 177 H1
Cairo Rd WALTH * E17 57 J3
Caistor Park Rd SRTFD E15 76 D7
Caistor Rd BAL SW12 129 G6
Caithness Gdns BFN/LL DA15 136 A5
Caithness Rd MTCM CR4 148 B6
WKENS W14 107 G2
Calabria Rd HBRY N5 73 H5
Calais St CMBW SE5 110 C7
Calbourne Av HCH RM12 81 K4
Calbourne Rd BAL SW12 128 E6
Caldbeck Av WPK KT4 173 K1
Caldecote Gdns BUSH WD23 22 E5
Caldecote La BUSH WD23 23 F6
Caldecot Rd CMBW SE5 130 D1
Caldecott Wy CLPT E5 75 F2
Calder Av GFD/PVL UB6 85 F1
Calder Gdns EDGW HA8 50 C2
Calderon Rd WAN E11 76 A3
Calder Rd MRDN SM4 162 B4
Caldervale Rd CLAP SW4 129 J4
Calderwood St
WOOL/PLUM SE18 115 F3
Caldicote Gn CDALE/KGS * NW9 51 G5
Caldwell Rd OXHEY WD19 33 H3
Caldwell St BRXN/ST SW9 110 A6
Caldy Rd BELV DA17 117 J2
Caldy Wk IS * N1 73 J5
Caledonian Cl GDMY/SEVK * IG3 61 H7
Caledonian Rd HOLWY N7 73 F4
IS N1 5 L2
Caledonian Wharf Rd
POP/IOD E14 113 G3
Caledonia Rd
STWL/WRAY TW19 120 B7
Caledonia St IS N1 5 K6
Caledon Rd EHAM E6 77 K7
WLGTN SM6 176 A3
Cale St CHEL SW3 15 J7
Calidore Cl BRXS/STRHM * SW2 130 A5
California La BUSH WD23 22 D7
California Rd NWMAL KT3 159 K3
Callaby Ter IS * N1 73 K5
Callaghan Cottages WCHPL * E1 92 E4
Callander Rd CAT SE6 151 K1
The Callanders BUSH * WD23 22 E7
Callard Av PLMGR N13 41 H4
Callcott Rd KIL/WHAMP NW6 70 D6
Callcott St KENS W8 8 A8
Callendar Rd SKENS SW7 15 G3
Callingham Cl POP/IOD E14 93 H4
Callis Farm Cl
STWL/WRAY TW19 120 B5
Callis Rd WALTH E17 57 H5
Callow St CHEL SW3 15 G9
Calmington Rd CMBW SE5 19 K8
Calmont Rd BMLY BR1 152 B5
Calonne Rd WIM/MER SW19 146 B3
Calshot Rd HTHAIR TW6 120 E1
Calshot St IS N1 5 L5
Calshot Wy ENC/FH EN2 29 H2
HTHAIR TW6 120 D1
Calthorpe Gdns EDGW HA8 36 B4
SUT SM1 175 G2
Calthorpe St FSBYW WC1X 5 M9
Calton Av DUL SE21 131 F5
Calton Rd BAR EN5 27 G5
Calverley Cl BECK BR3 151 K5
Calverley Crs DAGE RM10 80 C1
Calverley Gv ARCH N19 54 D7
Calverley Rd EW KT17 173 J5
Calvert Av BETH E2 7 K8
Calvert Cl BELV DA17 117 H3
Calverton Rd EHAM E6 78 A7
Calvert Rd BAR EN5 26 B1
GNWCH SE10 113 J4
Calvert St CAMTN NW1 4 A3
Calvin St WCHPL E1 13 L1
Calydon Rd CHARL SE7 114 A4
Calypso Wy BERM/RHTH SE16 112 C2
Camac Rd WHTN TW2 123 J7
Camarthen Gn
CDALE/KGS * NW9 51 G5
Cambalt Rd PUT/ROE SW15 127 G4
Camberley Av EN EN1 30 A3
RYNPK SW20 160 E1
Camberley Cl CHEAM SM3 174 B2
Camberley Rd HTHAIR TW6 120 D2
Cambert Wy BKHTH/KID SE3 134 A3
Camberwell Church St
CMBW SE5 110 E7
Camberwell Glebe CMBW SE5 110 E7
Camberwell Gn CMBW SE5 110 E7
Camberwell Gv CMBW SE5 110 E7
Camberwell New Rd
CMBW SE5 110 C6
Camberwell Rd CMBW SE5 110 D5
Camberwell Station Rd
CMBW SE5 110 D7
Cambeys Rd DAGE RM10 80 E4
Camborne Av WEA W13 104 C1
Camborne Cl HTHAIR TW6 120 D2
Camborne Crs HTHAIR TW6 120 D2
Camborne Rd BELMT SM2 174 E6
CROY/NA CR0 165 H6
MRDN SM4 161 G5
SCUP DA14 155 J2
WAND/EARL SW18 127 K6
WELL DA16 135 K1
Camborne Wy HEST TW5 103 F7
Cambourne Av ED N9 31 F6
Cambourne Ms NTGHL W11 88 C5
Cambray Rd BAL SW12 129 H7
Cambria Cl BFN/LL DA15 135 J7
HSLW TW3 123 F3
Cambria Ct EBED/NFELT TW14 122 A6
Cambria Gdns
STWL/WRAY TW19 120 B6
Cambrian Av GNTH/NBYPK IG2 60 E4
Cambrian Cl WNWD SE27 149 H2
Cambrian Gn CDALE/KGS * NW9 51 G4
Cambrian Rd LEY E10 57 J6
RCHPK/HAM TW10 125 G5
Cambria Rd CMBW SE5 130 D2
Cambria St FUL/PGN SW6 108 A6
Cambridge Av GFD/PVL UB6 67 F4
KIL/WHAMP NW6 2 B5
NWMAL KT3 160 C1
WELL DA16 136 A3
Cambridge Barracks Rd
WOOL/PLUM SE18 114 E3
Cambridge Cl HSLWW TW4 122 D3
RYNPK SW20 145 K7
WALTH E17 57 H5
WDGN * N22 41 G7
WDR/YW UB7 100 A5
WLSDN NW10 68 E2
Cambridge Crs BETH E2 92 D1
TEDD * TW11 143 G4
Cambridge Dr LEE/GVPK SE12 133 K4
RSLP HA4 65 G1
Cambridge Gdns EN EN1 30 C1
KIL/WHAMP NW6 2 B5
KUT KT1 159 H1
NKENS W10 88 B5
TOTM N17 41 K6
WCHMH N21 29 K6
Cambridge Ga CAMTN NW1 4 C8
Cambridge Gate Ms
CAMTN NW1 4 D8
Cambridge Gn ELTH/MOT SE9 135 G7
Cambridge Gv HMSMTH W6 106 E3
PGE/AN * SE20 150 D7
Cambridge Grove Rd KUT KT1 159 H1
Cambridge Heath Rd BETH E2 92 D2
Cambridge Pde EN * EN1 30 C1
Cambridge Pk TWK TW1 124 E6
WAN E11 58 E5
Cambridge Park Rd WAN E11 58 E6
Cambridge Pas HOM E9 74 E6
Cambridge Pl KENS * W8 14 D2
Cambridge Rd ASHF TW15 140 A6
BARK IG11 78 C6
BMLY BR1 152 E6
BTSEA SW11 108 E7
CAR SM5 175 J5
E/WMO/HCT KT8 156 E3
GDMY/SEVK IG3 60 E7
HNWL W7 104 A1
HPTN TW12 141 K6
HSLWW TW4 122 D3
KIL/WHAMP NW6 2 B7
KUT KT1 159 H1
MTCM CR4 163 H2
NWMAL KT3 160 A3
PGE/AN SE20 165 H2
RCH/KEW TW9 105 H6
RYLN/HDSTN HA2 48 A4
RYNPK SW20 145 K7
SCUP DA14 154 E3
STHL * UB1 83 K7
TEDD TW11 143 G3
TWK TW1 124 E5
WAN E11 58 E5
WATW * WD18 21 G3
WOT/HER KT12 156 A5

Cambridge Rd North
CHSWK W4 105 J4
Cambridge Rd South
CHSWK W4 105 J4
Cambridge Rw
WOOL/PLUM SE18 115 G4
Cambridge Sq BAY/PAD W2 9 J4
Cambridge St PIM SW1V 16 D7
Cambridge Ter CAMTN NW1 4 C8
ED * N9 30 B6
Cambridge Terrace Ms
CAMTN * NW1 4 D8
Cambridge Yd HNWL * W7 104 A1
Cambus Cl YEAD UB4 83 J4
Cambus Rd CAN/RD E16 94 E4
Camdale Rd WOOL/PLUM SE18 116 A6
Camden Av FELT TW13 141 G1
YEAD UB4 83 G6
Camden Cl CHST BR7 154 C7
Camden Gdns CAMTN NW1 4 D2
SUT SM1 175 F4
THHTH CR7 164 C2
Camden Gv CHST BR7 154 B5
Camden High St CAMTN NW1 4 D2
Camden Hill Rd NRWD SE19 150 A5
Camdenhurst St POP/IOD E14 93 G5
Camden Lock Pl CAMTN NW1 4 C2
Camden Ms CAMTN NW1 5 G1
HOLWY N7 72 D5
Camden Park Rd CAMTN NW1 72 C5
CHST BR7 153 K6
Camden Pas IS N1 6 C5
Camden Rd BXLY DA5 137 G7
CAMTN NW1 4 E2
CAR SM5 175 K3
HOLWY N7 72 E3
SUT SM1 175 F4
WALTH E17 57 H5
WAN E11 59 F5
Camden Rd Permanent Wy
CAMTN * NW1 5 G4
Camden Rw BKHTH/KID SE3 133 H1
PIN * HA5 47 G2
Camden Sq CAMTN NW1 5 G1
Camden St CAMTN NW1 4 D2
Camden Ter CAMTN NW1 72 D5
Camden Wk IS N1 6 C4
Camden Wy CHST BR7 153 K6
THHTH CR7 164 C2
Camelford Wk NTGHL * W11 88 C5
Camel Gv KUTN/CMB KT2 143 K4
Camellia Pl WHTN TW2 123 G6
Camellia St VX/NE SW8 109 K6
Camelot Cl WIM/MER SW19 146 D3
WOOL/PLUM SE18 115 J1
Camel Rd CAN/RD E16 95 H7
Camera Pl WBPTN SW10 108 C5
Cameron Cl TRDG/WHET N20 39 J1
UED N18 42 D3
Cameron Rd CAT * SE6 151 H1
CROY/NA CR0 164 C5
GDMY/SEVK IG3 60 E7
HAYES BR2 167 K4
Cameron Ter LEE/GVPK * SE12 153 F2
Camerton Cl HACK E8 74 B5
Camilla Cl SUN * TW16 140 C5
Camilla Rd BERM/RHTH SE16 111 J3
Camille Cl SNWD SE25 165 H2
Camlan Rd BMLY BR1 152 D3
Camlet St BETH E2 7 L9
Camlet Wy EBAR EN4 26 E1
Camley St CAMTN NW1 5 G3
Camm Gdns KUT * KT1 159 G1
THDIT KT7 157 K6
Camomile Av MTCM CR4 147 K7
Camomile St HDTCH EC3A 13 K4
Camomile Rd ROMW/RG RM7 81 F1
Campana Rd FUL/PGN SW6 107 K7
Campbell Av BARK/HLT IG6 60 C3
Campbell Cl RSLP HA4 46 E5
STRHM/NOR * SW16 148 D4
WHTN TW2 123 J7
WOOL/PLUM SE18 115 F7
Campbell Cottages
MTCM * CR4 163 F1
Campbell Cft EDGW HA8 36 C4
Campbell Gordon Wy
CRICK NW2 69 K3
Campbell Rd BOW E3 93 J2
CROY/NA CR0 164 C6
EHAM E6 77 J7
HNWL W7 84 E6
SRTFD E15 76 C3
TOTM N17 42 B7
WALTH E17 57 H3
WHTN TW2 142 D1
Campbell Wk IS * N1 5 K3
Campdale Rd ARCH N19 72 D2
Campden Crs ALP/SUD HA0 67 H2
BCTR RM8 79 J3
Campden Gv KENS W8 14 B1
Campden Hl KENS W8 14 A1
Campden Hill Gdns KENS W8 8 A8
Campden Hill Pl KENS * W8 88 D7
Campden Hill Rd KENS W8 8 A8
Campden Hill Sq KENS W8 88 D7
Campden House Cl KENS W8 14 A1
Campden House Ter KENS * W8 8 B9
Campden Rd SAND/SEL CR2 178 A4
Campden St KENS W8 8 A9
Campden Ter CHSWK * W4 106 B4
Campen Cl WIM/MER SW19 146 C1
Camperdown St WCHPL E1 13 M5
Campfield Rd ELTH/MOT SE9 134 C6
Campion Cl EHAM E6 95 K6
KTN/HRWW/W HA3 50 B5
ROMW/RG RM7 81 F1
SAND/SEL CR2 178 A3
Campion Ct ALP/SUD * HA0 86 A1
Campion Gdns WFD IG8 44 E4
Campion Pl THMD SE28 97 H7
Campion Rd ISLW TW7 104 A7
PUT/ROE SW15 127 F3
Campion Wy EDGW HA8 36 E3
Camplin Rd KTN/HRWW/W HA3 50 A4
Camplin St NWCR SE14 112 A6
Camp Rd WIM/MER SW19 145 K4
The Campsbourne
CEND/HSY/T N8 54 E3
Campsbourne Pde
CEND/HSY/T * N8 54 E3
Campsbourne Rd
CEND/HSY/T N8 54 E2
Campsey Rd DAGW RM9 79 H6
Campshill Pl LEW SE13 133 F4
Campshill Rd LEW SE13 133 F4
Campus Rd WALTH E17 57 H5
Camp Vw WIM/MER SW19 145 K4
Cam Rd SRTFD E15 76 B7
Camrose Av EDGW HA8 36 B7
ERITH DA8 117 J5
FELT TW13 141 F3
STAN HA7 50 A1
Camrose Cl CROY/NA CR0 166 B6
MRDN SM4 161 K3
Camrose St ABYW SE2 116 B4
Canada Av UED N18 41 J5
Canada Crs ACT W3 86 E4
Canada Park Pde EDGW * HA8 36 D7
Canada Rd ACT W3 86 E4
ERITH DA8 118 E6
Canada St BERM/RHTH SE16 112 A1
Canada Wy SHB W12 87 K6
Canadian Av CAT SE6 132 E7
Canal Ap DEPT SE8 112 B5
Canal Cl NKENS W10 88 B3
WCHPL E1 93 G3
Canal Gv PECK SE15 111 H5
Canal Pth HACK E8 7 L4
Canal Rd WCHPL E1 93 G3
Canal St CMBW SE5 110 E5
Canal Wk CROY/NA CR0 165 F5
IS N1 7 H3
WLSDN * NW10 68 E6
Canal Wy NKENS W10 88 B3
Canal Whf GFD/PVL * UB6 67 G7
Canal Yd NWDGN * UB2 102 A3
Canberra Cl DAGE RM10 81 F6
HDN NW4 51 J2
Canberra Crs DAGE RM10 81 F6
Canberra Dr NTHLT UB5 83 G2
Canberra Rd HTHAIR TW6 120 D2
ABYW SE2 116 E5
CHARL SE7 114 B5
EHAM E6 77 K7
Canbury Av KUTN/CMB KT2 144 B7
Canbury Ms SYD SE26 150 C2
Canbury Park Rd
KUTN/CMB KT2 144 A7
Cancell Rd BRXN/ST SW9 110 B7
Candahar Rd BTSEA SW11 128 D1
Candler Ms TWK TW1 124 B6
Candler St SEVS/STOTM * N15 55 K5
Candover Cl WDR/YW UB7 100 A6
Candover Rd EMPK RM11 63 K6
Candover St GTPST * W1W 10 E3
Candy St BOW E3 75 H7
Caney Ms CRICK NW2 70 B1
Canfield Dr RSLP HA4 65 F4
Canfield Gdns KIL/WHAMP NW6 2 D1
Canfield Pl KIL/WHAMP NW6 71 G5
Canfield Rd RAIN RM13 81 H7
WFD IG8 45 J6
Canford Av NTHLT UB5 65 J7
Canford Cl ENC/FH EN2 29 G1
Canford Gdns NWMAL KT3 160 B5
Canford Pl TEDD TW11 143 J5
Canford Rd CLAP SW4 129 F3
Canham Rd CHSWK W4 106 B1
SNWD SE25 165 F2
Canmore Gdns
STRHM/NOR SW16 148 C6
Cann Hall Rd WAN E11 76 D3
Canning Crs WDGN N22 41 F7
Canning Cross CMBW SE5 131 F1
Canning Pl KENS W8 14 E3
Canning Rd CROY/NA CR0 178 B1
HBRY N5 73 H2
KTN/HRWW/W HA3 48 E2
SRTFD E15 94 C1
WALTH E17 57 G3
Cannington Rd DAGW RM9 79 J5
Cannizaro Rd
WIM/MER SW19 146 A5
Cannonbury Av PIN HA5 47 H5
Cannon Cl HPTN TW12 142 B5
RYNPK SW20 161 F2
Cannon Dr POP/IOD E14 93 J6
Cannon Hl KIL/WHAMP NW6 71 F4
STHGT/OAK N14 40 E2
Cannon Hill La MRDN SM4 161 G4
Cannon La HAMP NW3 71 H2
PIN HA5 47 J4
Cannon Pl CHARL SE7 114 D4
HAMP NW3 71 G2
Cannon Rd BXLYHN DA7 117 F7
STHGT/OAK N14 40 E2
WATW WD18 21 G4
Cannon St STP EC4M 12 E5
Cannon Street Rd WCHPL E1 92 D5
Cannon Wy E/WMO/HCT KT8 157 F3
Canon Av CHDH RM6 61 J4
Canon Beck Rd
BERM/RHTH SE16 111 K1
Canonbie Rd FSTH SE23 131 K6
Canonbury Crs IS N1 6 F1
Canonbury Gv IS N1 6 E1
Canonbury La IS N1 6 C1
Canonbury Pk North IS N1 73 J5
Canonbury Pk South IS N1 73 J5
Canonbury Rd IS N1 6 D1
Canonbury Sq IS N1 6 D1
Canonbury St IS N1 6 E1
Canonbury Vls IS N1 6 D2
Canon Mohan Cl EBAR EN4 28 A5
Canon Murnane Rd STHWK SE1 19 L4
Canon Rd BMLY BR1 168 B2
Canon Rw WHALL SW1A 17 J2
Canons Cl EDGW HA8 36 B5
EFNCH N2 53 H6
Canons Cottages EDGW * HA8 36 B5
Canons Ct EDGW * HA8 36 B5
Canons Dr EDGW HA8 36 B5
Canonsleigh Rd DAGW RM9 79 H6
Canon St IS N1 6 E4
Canon's Wk CROY/NA CR0 179 F2
Canopus Wy NTHWD HA6 32 E3
STWL/WRAY TW19 120 B6
Canrobert St BETH E2 92 D1
Cantelowes Rd CAMTN NW1 72 D5
Canterbury Av BFN/LL DA15 155 J1
IL IG1 59 J6
Canterbury Cl BECK BR3 151 K7
CMBW * SE5 130 D1
DART DA1 139 K6
EHAM E6 95 K5
GFD/PVL UB6 84 B4
NTHWD HA6 32 D5
Canterbury Crs BRXN/ST SW9 130 B2
Canterbury Gv WNWD SE27 149 H2
Canterbury Pl WALW SE17 18 D6
Canterbury Rd BORE WD6 24 C1
CROY/NA CR0 164 A6
FELT TW13 141 J1
KIL/WHAMP NW6 2 A6
LEY E10 58 A6
MRDN SM4 162 B5
RYLN/HDSTN HA2 48 B4
WAT * WD17 21 F1
Canterbury Ter KIL/WHAMP NW6 2 A5
Canterbury Wy
RKW/CH/CXG WD3 20 A2
Cantley Gdns GNTH/NBYPK IG2 60 C5
NRWD SE19 150 B7
Cantley Rd HNWL W7 104 B2
Canton St POP/IOD E14 93 J5
Cantrell Rd BOW E3 93 J3
Cantwell Rd WOOL/PLUM SE18 115 G6
Canvey St STHWK SE1 12 E8
Cape Cl BARK IG11 78 B6
Capel Av WLGTN SM6 177 F4
Capel Cl HAYES BR2 168 D7
TRDG/WHET N20 39 G2
Capel Gdns GDMY/SEVK IG3 79 F3
PIN HA5 47 K3
Capella Rd NTHWD HA6 32 D4
Capel Rd EBAR EN4 27 J5
FSTGT E7 77 F3
OXHEY WD19 21 H5
Capeners Cl KTBR SW1X 15 M2
Capern Rd WAND/EARL SW18 128 B7
Cape Rd TOTM N17 56 C2
Cape Yd WAP E1W 92 C7
Capital Interchange Wy
CHSWK W4 105 H4
Capitol Wy CDALE/KGS NW9 50 E2
Capland St STJWD NW8 3 H9
Caple Pde WLSDN * NW10 87 H1
Caple Rd WLSDN NW10 87 H1
Caprea Cl YEAD UB4 83 H4
Capri Rd CROY/NA CR0 165 G7
Capstan Cl CHDH RM6 61 H5
Capstan Ride ENC/FH EN2 29 G1
Capstan Rd DEPT SE8 112 C3
Capstan Sq POP/IOD E14 113 F1
Capstan Wy BERM/RHTH SE16 93 G7
Capstone Rd BMLY BR1 152 E3
Capthorne Av RYLN/HDSTN HA2 47 J7
Capuchin Cl STAN HA7 35 H5
Capulet Ms CAN/RD E16 94 E7
Capworth St LEY E10 57 J7
Caractacus Cottage Vw
WATW WD18 20 E6
Caractacus Gn WATW WD18 20 D5
Caradoc Evans Cl
FBAR/BDGN * N11 40 B4
Caradoc St GNWCH SE10 113 H4
Caradon Ct WAN * E11 58 C7
Caradon Wy SEVS/STOTM * N15 55 K3
Caravel Ms DEPT * SE8 112 D5
Caraway Cl PLSTW E13 95 F4
Caraway Pl WLGTN * SM6 176 B2
Carberry Rd NRWD SE19 150 A5
Carbery Av ACT W3 105 G1
Carbis Rd POP/IOD E14 93 H5
Carburton St GTPST W1W 10 D2
Cardale St POP/IOD E14 113 F2
Carden Rd PECK SE15 131 J2
Cardiff Rd HNWL W7 104 B2
PEND EN3 30 D3
WATW WD18 21 F5
Cardiff St WOOL/PLUM SE18 115 K6
Cardigan Gdns GDMY/SEVK IG3 79 G1
Cardigan Pl BKHTH/KID * SE3 133 G1
Cardigan Rd BARN SW13 126 D1
BOW E3 93 H1
RCHPK/HAM TW10 125 F5
WIM/MER SW19 147 G5
Cardigan St LBTH SE11 18 A7
Cardigan Wk IS * N1 6 F1
Cardinal Av BORE WD6 24 D2
KUTN/CMB KT2 144 A4
MRDN SM4 161 H5
Cardinal Bourne St
STHWK * SE1 19 H4
Cardinal Cl CHST BR7 154 D7
EDGW HA8 37 F6
MRDN SM4 161 H5
WPK KT4 173 J3
Cardinal Crs NWMAL KT3 159 K1
Cardinal Dr WOT/HER KT12 156 C7
Cardinal Hinsey Cl
WLSDN NW10 87 J1
Cardinal Pl PUT/ROE SW15 127 G3
Cardinal Rd FELT TW13 122 A7
RSLP HA4 47 H7
Cardinal's Wk HPTN TW12 142 C6
SUN TW16 140 C5
Cardinals Wy ARCH N19 54 D7
Cardinal Wy
KTN/HRWW/W * HA3 48 E2
Cardine Ms PECK SE15 111 J6
Cardington Sq HSLWW TW4 122 C3
Cardington St CAMTN NW1 4 F7
Cardozo Rd HOLWY N7 72 E4
Cardrew Av NFNCH/WDSP N12 39 H4
Cardross St HMSMTH W6 106 E2
Cardwell Rd HOLWY * N7 72 E3
Cardwell Ter HOLWY * N7 72 E3
Carew Cl HOLWY N7 73 F1
Carew Rd ASHF TW15 140 A5
MTCM CR4 163 F1
NTHWD HA6 32 C5
THHTH CR7 164 C2
TOTM N17 56 C1
WEA W13 104 D1
WLGTN SM6 176 C5
Carew St CMBW SE5 130 D1
Carew Wy OXHEY WD19 33 K2
Carey Gdns VX/NE SW8 109 H7
Carey La CITYW EC2V 12 E4
Carey Pl WEST SW1P 17 G6
Carey Rd DAGW RM9 80 A3
Carey St LINN WC2A 11 M5
Carey Wy WBLY HA9 68 D3
The Carfax SYD * SE26 150 E2
Carfax Pl CLAP SW4 129 J3
Carfax Rd HCH RM12 81 H3
HYS/HAR UB3 101 K4
Carfree Cl IS N1 6 B1
Cargill Rd WAND/EARL SW18 128 B7
Cargreen Rd SNWD SE25 165 G3
Carholme Rd FSTH SE23 132 C7
Carisbrooke Av BXLY DA5 136 E7
Carisbrooke Cl STAN HA7 49 K1
Carisbrooke Ct NTHLT * UB5 65 K7
Carisbrooke Gdns PECK * SE15 111 G6
Carisbrooke Rd HAYES * BR2 168 B3
MTCM CR4 163 K3
WALTH * E17 57 G3
Carleton Av WLGTN SM6 176 D7
Carleton Cl ESH/CLAY KT10 157 J7
Carleton Gdns ARCH * N19 72 C4
Carleton Rd DART DA1 139 K6
HOLWY N7 72 D4
Carleton Vls KTTN * NW5 72 C4
Carlie Cl BOW E3 93 H1
Carlina Gdns WFD IG8 45 F4
Carlingford Rd HAMP NW3 71 H3
MRDN SM4 161 G5
SEVS/STOTM N15 55 H2
Carlisle Av ACT W3 87 G5
TWRH EC3N 13 K5
Carlisle Cl KUTN/CMB KT2 144 C7
Carlisle Gdns IL IG1 59 J5
KTN/HRWW/W HA3 49 K6
Carlisle La STHWK SE1 17 M3
Carlisle Pl FBAR/BDGN N11 40 B3
WEST SW1P 16 E4
Carlisle Rd CDALE/KGS NW9 50 E2
DART DA1 139 K5
FSBYPK N4 55 G7
HPTN TW12 142 B6
KIL/WHAMP NW6 70 C7
LEY E10 57 J7
ROM RM1 63 H4
SUT SM1 174 D5
Carlisle St SOHO/CST W1F 11 G5
Carlisle Wk HACK E8 74 B5
Carlisle Wy TOOT SW17 148 A4
Carlos Pl MYFR/PKLN W1K 10 B7
Carlow St CAMTN NW1 4 E5
Carlton Av EBED/NFELT TW14 122 B5
HYS/HAR UB3 101 H3
KTN/HRWW/W HA3 49 H4
SAND/SEL CR2 177 K6
STHGT/OAK N14 28 D4
Carlton Av East WBLY HA9 67 K1
Carlton Av West ALP/SUD HA0 67 H1
Carlton Cl BORE WD6 25 F3
CHSGTN KT9 171 K5
EDGW HA8 36 C4
HAMP NW3 70 E1
Carlton Crs CHEAM SM3 174 C3
Carlton Dene EW * KT17 173 K4
Carlton Dr BARK/HLT IG6 60 D2
PUT/ROE SW15 127 G4
Carlton Gdns EA W5 85 J5
STJS SW1Y 11 G9
Carlton Gn SCUP * DA14 155 F3
Carlton Gv PECK SE15 111 J7
Carlton Hl STJWD NW8 2 E5
Carlton House Ter STJS SW1Y 11 G9
Carlton Ms KIL/WHAMP * NW6 70 E4
Carlton Pde WBLY * HA9 50 A7
Carlton Park Av RYNPK SW20 161 F1
Carlton Rd CHSWK W4 106 A1
EA W5 85 J6
ERITH DA8 117 K5
FBAR/BDGN N11 40 A4
FSBYPK N4 55 G6
GPK RM2 63 J4
MNPK E12 77 H3
MORT/ESHN SW14 125 K2
NWMAL KT3 160 B1
SAND/SEL CR2 177 K6
SCUP DA14 155 F4
SUN TW16 140 D6
WALTH E17 43 G7
WAN E11 58 D7
WELL DA16 136 C2
WOT/HER KT12 156 A6
Carlton Sq WCHPL * E1 93 F3
Carlton St STJS SW1Y 11 G7
Carlton Ter SYD SE26 150 E2
UED * N18 41 K3
WAN * E11 59 F4
Carlton Tower Pl KTBR SW1X 15 M3
Carlton V KIL/WHAMP NW6 2 A7
Carlwell St TOOT SW17 147 J4
Carlyle Av BMLY BR1 168 C2
STHL UB1 83 K6
Carlyle Cl E/WMO/HCT KT8 157 G1
EFNCH N2 53 G5
WLSDN NW10 69 F7
Carlyle Ct WBPTN * SW10 108 B7
Carlyle Gdns STHL UB1 83 K6
Carlyle Rd CROY/NA CR0 178 C1
EA W5 104 D3
MNPK E12 77 J3
THMD SE28 97 H6
Carlyle Sq CHEL SW3 15 H8
Carlyon Av RYLN/HDSTN HA2 65 K3
Carlyon Cl ALP/SUD HA0 68 A7
Carlyon Rd ALP/SUD HA0 86 A1
YEAD UB4 83 G5
Carlys Cl BECK BR3 166 A1
Carmalt Gdns PUT/ROE SW15 127 F3
Carmel Ct KENS W8 14 C1
Carmelite Rd
KTN/HRWW/W HA3 34 C7
Carmelite St EMB EC4Y 12 B6
Carmen St POP/IOD E14 93 K5
Carmichael Cl BTSEA * SW11 128 C2
RSLP HA4 64 E3
Carmichael Rd SNWD SE25 165 H4
Carminia Rd BAL SW12 148 B1
Carnaby St REGST W1B 10 E6
Carnac St WNWD SE27 149 K3
Carnanton Rd WALTH E17 44 B7
Carnarvon Av EN EN1 30 B1
Carnarvon Dr HYS/HAR UB3 101 F2
Carnarvon Rd BAR EN5 26 C2
LEY E10 58 A5
SRTFD E15 76 D5
SWFD E18 44 D7
Carnation Cl ROMW/RG RM7 81 G1
Carnation St ABYW SE2 116 C4
Carnbrook Rd BKHTH/KID SE3 134 C2
Carnecke Gdns ELTH/MOT SE9 134 D4
Carnegie Cl SURB KT6 172 B1
Carnegie Pl WIM/MER SW19 146 B2
Carnegie St IS N1 5 L4
Carnforth Cl HOR/WEW KT19 172 D5
Carnforth Gdns HCH RM12 81 J4
Carnforth Rd
STRHM/NOR SW16 148 D6
Carnoustie Dr IS N1 5 L2
Carnoustie Cl THMD SE28 97 K5
Carnwath Rd FUL/PGN SW6 127 K2
Carolina Cl SRTFD E15 76 C4
Carolina Rd THHTH CR7 164 C1
Caroline Cl BAY/PAD W2 8 D7
CROY/NA CR0 178 A3
STRHM/NOR SW16 149 F3
WDR/YW UB7 100 A1
Caroline Ct STAN * HA7 35 G5
Caroline Gdns BETH E2 7 K7
PECK * SE15 111 J6
Caroline Pl BAY/PAD W2 8 D6
HYS/HAR UB3 101 H6
OXHEY WD19 21 J5
VX/NE SW8 129 F1
Caroline Place Ms BAY/PAD * W2 8 D7
Caroline Rd WIM/MER SW19 146 D6
Caroline St WCHPL E1 93 F5
Caroline Ter BGVA SW1W 16 A6
Caroline Wk HMSMTH W6 107 H5
Carol St CAMTN NW1 4 E3
Carpenders Av OXHEY WD19 33 J2
Carpenter Gdns WCHMH N21 41 H1
Carpenters Cl TRDG/WHET N20 27 F5
Carpenters Ms HOLWY * N7 72 E4
Carpenter's Pl CLAP SW4 129 J3
Carpenters Rd SRTFD E15 75 K6
Carpenter St MYFR/PKLN W1K 10 C7
Carrara Ms HACK E8 74 C4
Carr Gv WOOL/PLUM SE18 114 D3
Carriage Dr East BTSEA SW11 109 F5
Carriage Dr North BTSEA SW11 108 E6
Carriage Dr South BTSEA SW11 108 E7
Carriage Dr West BTSEA SW11 108 E6
Carriage Ms IL IG1 78 C1
Carrick Cl ISLW TW7 124 B2
Carrick Gdns TOTM N17 42 A6
Carrick Ga ESH/CLAY KT10 170 C2
Carrick Ms DEPT SE8 112 D5
Carrill Wy BELV DA17 116 E3
Carrington Av BORE WD6 24 D4
HSLW TW3 123 G4
Carrington Cl BAR EN5 25 J4
CROY/NA CR0 166 B6
Carrington Gdns FSTGT E7 76 E3
Carrington Pl ESH/CLAY * KT10 170 B3
Carrington Rd DART DA1 139 J5
RCHPK/HAM TW10 125 H3
Carrington Sq
KTN/HRWW/W HA3 34 C6
Carrington St MYFR/PICC W1J 10 C9
Carrol Cl KTTN NW5 72 B3
Carroll Cl SRTFD E15 76 D4
Carronade Pl
WOOL/PLUM SE18 115 H2
Carron Cl POP/IOD E14 93 K5
Carroun Rd VX/NE SW8 110 A6
Carroway La GFD/PVL UB6 84 D2
Carrow Rd DAGW RM9 79 H6
Carr Rd NTHLT UB5 66 B6
WALTH E17 57 H1
Carrs La WCHMH N21 29 K4
Carr St POP/IOD E14 93 G5
Carshalton Gv SUT SM1 175 H3
Carshalton Park Rd CAR SM5 175 K5
Carshalton Pl CAR SM5 176 A3
Carshalton Rd MTCM CR4 163 F4
SUT SM1 175 G4
Carslake Rd PUT/ROE SW15 127 F5
Carson Rd CAN/RD E16 94 E4
DUL SE21 149 K1
EBAR EN4 27 K3
Carstairs Rd CAT SE6 152 A2
Carston Cl LEE/GVPK SE12 133 J4
Carswell Cl REDBR IG4 59 H3
Carswell Rd CAT SE6 133 F6
Carter Cl WLGTN SM6 176 D6
Carteret St STJSPK SW1H 17 G2
Carteret Wy DEPT SE8 112 B3
Carterhatch La EN EN1 30 C1
Carterhatch Rd PEND EN3 31 G1
Carter La BLKFR EC4V 12 D5
Carter Pl WALW SE17 18 F8
Carter Rd PLSTW E13 77 F7
WIM/MER SW19 147 H5
Carters Cl KTTN * NW5 72 D5
WPK KT4 174 B1
Carters Hill Cl ELTH/MOT SE9 134 B7
Carter St WALW SE17 18 E9
Carter's Yd
WAND/EARL * SW18 127 K4
Carthew Rd HMSMTH W6 106 E2
Carthew Vls HMSMTH W6 106 E2
Carthusian St FARR EC1M 12 E2
Carting La TPL/STR WC2R 11 K7
Cartmel Cl TOTM N17 42 D6
Cartmel Ct NTHLT UB5 65 J5
Cartmel Gdns MRDN SM4 162 B4
Cartmel Rd BXLYHN DA7 117 H7
Cartwright Gdns STPAN WC1H 5 J9
Cartwright St TWRH EC3N 13 M6
Cartwright Wy BARN SW13 106 E6
Carver Rd HNHL SE24 130 D5
Carville Crs BTFD TW8 105 F4
Cary Rd WAN E11 76 C3
Carysfort Rd CEND/HSY/T N8 54 D4
STNW/STAM N16 73 K2
Cascade Av MUSWH N10 54 C3
Cascade Rd BKHH IG9 45 H1
Casella Rd NWCR SE14 112 A6
Casewick Rd WNWD SE27 149 H4
Casey Cl STJWD NW8 3 J8
Casimir Rd CLPT E5 74 D2
Casino Av HNHL SE24 130 D4
Caspian St CMBW SE5 110 E6
Caspian Wk CAN/RD E16 95 H5
Cassandra Cl NTHLT UB5 66 D3
Casselden Rd WLSDN NW10 69 F6
Cassidy Rd FUL/PGN SW6 107 K6
Cassilda Rd ABYW SE2 116 B3
Cassilis Rd TWK TW1 124 C5
Cassiobridge Rd WATW WD18 20 C3
Cassiobridge Ter
RKW/CH/CXG * WD3 20 B4
Cassiobury Av
EBED/NFELT TW14 121 J6
Cassiobury Dr WAT WD17 20 E2
Cassiobury Park Av
WATW WD18 20 C2
Cassiobury Rd WALTH E17 57 F4
Cassio Rd WATW WD18 21 F3
Cassio Whf WATW * WD18 20 B4
Cassland Rd HOM E9 75 F6
THHTH CR7 164 E3
Casslee Rd CAT SE6 132 C6
Casson St WCHPL E1 92 C4
Castellain Rd MV/WKIL W9 2 C9
Castellan Av GPK RM2 63 K2
Castellane Cl STAN HA7 35 F6
Castello Av PUT/ROE SW15 127 F4
Castelnau BARN SW13 106 E6
Casterbridge Rd
BKHTH/KID SE3 133 K2
Casterton St HACK E8 74 D5
Castile Rd WOOL/PLUM SE18 115 F3
Castillon Rd CAT SE6 152 C1
Castlands Rd CAT SE6 151 H1
Castle Av CHING E4 44 B5
EW KT17 173 J7
RAIN RM13 81 G6
Castlebar Hl WEA W13 85 H4
Castlebar Ms EA W5 85 H4
Castlebar Pk EA W5 85 H4
Castlebar Rd WEA W13 85 J5
Castle Baynard St BLKFR EC4V 12 D6
Castlebrook Cl LBTH SE11 18 C5
Castle Cl ACT W3 105 J1
BUSH WD23 22 B5
HAYES BR2 167 G2
WIM/MER SW19 146 B2
Castlecombe Dr
WIM/MER SW19 127 G6

Castlecombe Rd
ELTH/MOT SE9 153 J4
Castle Ct BANK * EC3V 13 H5
SYD SE26 151 G3
Castledine Rd PGE/AN SE20 150 D6
Castle Dr REDBR IG4 59 J5
Castleford Av ELTH/MOT SE9 135 G7
Castleford Cl UED N18 42 B5
Castlegate RCH/KEW TW9 125 G2
Castlehaven Rd CAMTN NW1 4 C2
Castle Hill Av CROY/NA CR0 179 K7
Castle Hill Pde WEA * W13 85 H6
Castle La WESTW SW1E 16 E3
Castleleigh Ct ENC/FH EN2 29 K4
Castlemaine Av EW KT17 173 K7
SAND/SEL CR2 178 B4
Castle Md CMBW * SE5 110 D6
Castle Ms CAMTN NW1 72 B5
NFNCH/WDSP N12 39 G4
Castle Pde EW * KT17 173 J6
Castle Pl CAMTN NW1 72 B5
Castlereagh St MBLAR W1H 9 L4
Castle Rd CAMTN NW1 72 B5
DAGW RM9 79 H7
ISLW TW7 124 A1
NFNCH/WDSP N12 39 G4
NTHLT UB5 66 B5
NWDGN * UB2 102 E2
Castle Rw CHSWK * W4 106 A4
Castle St EHAM E6 95 G1
KUT * KT1 159 F1
Castleton Av BXLYHN DA7 118 A7
WBLY HA9 68 A3
Castleton Cl CROY/NA CR0 166 B5
Castleton Gdns WBLY HA9 68 A2
Castleton Rd ELTH/MOT SE9 153 H3
GDMY/SEVK IG3 61 H7
MTCM CR4 163 J3
RSLP HA4 47 H7
WALTH E17 58 B1
Castletown Rd WKENS W14 107 H4
Castleview Cl FSBYPK N4 55 J7
Castle View Gdns IL IG1 59 J5
Castle Vls CRICK * NW2 69 J5
Castle Wk SUN * TW16 156 B2
Castle Wy FELT TW13 141 G3
WIM/MER SW19 146 B2
Castlewood Dr ELTH/MOT SE9 134 E1
Castlewood Rd EBAR EN4 27 H2
SEVS/STOTM N15 56 C5
Castle Yd HGT N6 54 A6
RCHPK/HAM TW10 124 E4
STHWK * SE1 12 D8
Castor La POP/IOD E14 93 K6
Catalina Rd HTHAIR TW6 120 E2
Caterham Av CLAY IG5 60 A1
Caterham Rd LEW SE13 133 F2
Catesby St WALW SE17 19 H6
Catford Broadway CAT SE6 132 E6
Catford Hl CAT SE6 151 H1
Catford Island CAT * SE6 132 E6
Catford Rd CAT SE6 132 D7
Cathall Rd WAN E11 76 B1
Cathay St BERM/RHTH SE16 111 J1
Cathcart Hl KTTN NW5 72 C2
Cathcart Rd WBPTN SW10 14 E9
Cathcart St KTTN NW5 72 B5
Cathedral St STHWK SE1 13 G8
Catherall Rd HBRY N5 73 J2
Catherine Ct STHGT/OAK N14 28 C4
Catherine Dr RCH/KEW TW9 125 F3
SUN TW16 140 D6
Catherine Gdns HSLW TW3 123 J3
Catherine Griffiths Ct
CLKNW * EC1R 6 B9
Catherine Gv GNWCH SE10 112 E7
Catherine Pl HRW HA1 49 F4
WESTW SW1E 16 E3
Catherine Rd GPK RM2 63 K4
SURB KT6 158 E4
Catherines Cl WDR/YW * UB7 100 A1
Catherine St HOL/ALD * WC2B 11 L6
Catherine Vls RYNPK * SW20 145 K6
Catherine Wheel Aly
LVPST EC2M 13 K3
Catherine Wheel Rd BTFD TW8 104 E6
Catherine Wheel Yd
WHALL SW1A 10 E9
Cat Hl EBAR EN4 27 J5
Cathles Rd BAL SW12 129 G5
Cathnor Rd SHB W12 106 E1
Catling Cl FSTH SE23 150 E2
Catlin's La PIN HA5 47 F2
Catlin St BERM/RHTH SE16 111 H4
Cator La BECK BR3 166 C1
Cato Rd CLAP SW4 129 J2
Cator Rd CAR SM5 175 K4
SYD SE26 151 F5
Cator St PECK SE15 111 G5
Cato St MBLAR W1H 9 K3
Catsey La BUSH WD23 22 C6
Catsey Wd BUSH WD23 22 C6
Catterick Cl FBAR/BDGN N11 40 A5
Cattistock Rd ELTH/MOT SE9 153 J4
Cattley Cl BAR EN5 26 C3
Catton St RSQ WC1B 11 L3
Caudwell Ter
WAND/EARL * SW18 128 C5
Caulfield Rd EHAM E6 77 K6
PECK SE15 131 J1
The Causeway BELMT SM2 175 G7
CAR SM5 176 A2
CHSGTN KT9 172 A3
EFNCH N2 53 H3
ESH/CLAY KT10 171 F6
TEDD TW11 143 F5
WAND/EARL SW18 128 A4
WIM/MER SW19 146 A4
Causeway EBED/NFELT TW14 122 A3
Causeyware Rd ED N9 30 D6
Causton Cottages
POP/IOD * E14 93 G4
Causton Rd HGT * N6 54 B6
Causton Sq DAGE RM10 80 C6
Causton St WEST SW1P 17 H6
Cautley Av CLAP SW4 129 H4
Cavalier Cl CHDH RM6 61 J3
Cavalier Gdns HYS/HAR UB3 82 B5
Cavalry Crs HSLWW TW4 122 C3
Cavalry Gdns PUT/ROE SW15 127 H4
Cavan Pl PIN * HA5 33 K7
Cavaye Pl WBPTN SW10 14 F8
Cavell Crs DART DA1 139 K3
Cavell Dr ENC/FH EN2 29 G1
Cavell Rd TOTM N17 41 K6
Cavell St WCHPL E1 92 D4
Cavendish Av BFN/LL DA15 136 B6
ERITH DA8 117 K5
FNCH N3 52 E2
HCH RM12 81 K5
HRW HA1 66 D3
NWMAL KT3 160 E4
RSLP HA4 65 F4
STJWD NW8 3 H6
WEA W13 85 G4
WELL DA16 136 A2
WFD IG8 45 F6
Cavendish Cl KIL/WHAMP NW6 70 D5
STJWD NW8 3 H7
SUN TW16 140 D5
UED * N18 42 D4
YEAD UB4 82 C4
Cavendish Ct
RKW/CH/CXG * WD3 20 B4
SUN TW16 140 D5
Cavendish Crs BORE WD6 24 C3
HCH RM12 81 K5
Cavendish Dr EDGW HA8 36 B5
ESH/CLAY KT10 170 E4
WAN E11 58 B7
Cavendish Gdns BARK IG11 79 F4
CHDH RM6 62 A4
CLAP * SW4 129 H5
IL IG1 60 A7
Cavendish Ms North
REGST W1B 10 D2
Cavendish Ms South
GTPST * W1W 10 D3
Cavendish Pde CLAP * SW4 129 H3
HSLWW * TW4 122 D1
Cavendish Pl KIL/WHAMP NW6 70 B6
MHST W1U 10 C4
Cavendish Rd BAL SW12 129 G5
BAR EN5 26 A2
BELMT SM2 175 G6
CHING E4 43 K6
CHSWK W4 105 K7
CROY/NA CR0 164 C7
FSBYPK N4 55 H5
KIL/WHAMP NW6 70 C6
NWMAL KT3 160 C4
SUN TW16 140 D5
UED N18 42 D4
WIM/MER SW19 147 J6
Cavendish Sq CAVSQ/HST W1G 10 D4
Cavendish St IS N1 7 G6
Cavendish Ter BOW * E3 93 H2
FELT * TW13 140 E1
Cavendish Wy WWKM BR4 166 E7
Cavenham Gdns IL IG1 78 D2
Caverleigh Wy WPK KT4 160 D7
Caverley Gdns
KTN/HRWW/W HA3 49 K6
Cave Rd PLSTW E13 95 F1
RCHPK/HAM TW10 143 J3
Caversham Av CHEAM SM3 174 C1
PLMGR N13 41 G2
Caversham Rd KTTN * NW5 72 C5
KUT KT1 159 G1
SEVS/STOTM N15 55 J3
Caversham St CHEL SW3 15 L9
Caverswall St SHB W12 88 A5
Cawdor Crs HNWL W7 104 B3
Cawnpore St NRWD SE19 150 A4
Caxton Gv BOW E3 93 J2
Caxton Ms BTFD * TW8 104 E6
Caxton Rd NWDGN UB2 102 C2
SHB W12 88 B7
WDGN N22 55 F1
WIM/MER SW19 147 G4
The Caxtons CMBW * SE5 110 C6
Caxton St STJSPK SW1H 16 F3
Caxton St North CAN/RD E16 94 D5
Caxton Wy ROM RM1 63 G3
WATW WD18 20 B6
Cayenne Ct STHWK SE1 19 K1
Caygill Cl HAYES BR2 167 J3
Cayley Rd NWDGN UB2 103 G2
Cayton Rd GFD/PVL UB6 84 E1
Cayton St FSBYE EC1V 7 G8
Cazenove Rd STNW/STAM N16 74 B1
WALTH E17 43 J7
Cecil Av BARK IG11 78 D6
EN EN1 30 B3
WBLY HA9 68 B4
Cecil Cl ASHF TW15 140 A5
CHSGTN KT9 171 K3
EA * W5 85 K4
Cecil Ct BAR EN5 26 B2
LSQ/SEVD WC2H 11 H7
Cecile Pk CEND/HSY/T N8 54 E5
Cecilia Cl EFNCH N2 53 G2
Cecilia Rd HACK E8 74 B4
Cecil Pk PIN HA5 47 J3
Cecil Pl MTCM CR4 162 E4
Cecil Rd ACT W3 86 E4
ASHF TW15 140 A6
CDALE/KGS NW9 51 F2
CHDH RM6 61 K6
CROY/NA CR0 163 K5
ENC/FH EN2 29 K3
HSLW TW3 123 H2
IL IG1 78 B3
KTN/HRWW/W HA3 48 E2
MUSWH N10 54 B1
PLSTW E13 76 E7
STHGT/OAK N14 28 B7
SUT SM1 174 D5
WALTH E17 43 J7
WAN E11 76 C1
WIM/MER SW19 147 F6
WLSDN NW10 69 G7
Cecil Wy HAYES BR2 167 K7
Cedar Av BFN/LL DA15 136 B6
CHDH RM6 62 A4
EBAR EN4 27 J6
HYS/HAR UB3 82 E5
PEND EN3 30 E1
RSLP HA4 65 G4
WHTN TW2 123 G5
Cedar Cl BKHH IG9 45 H1
BOW E3 75 H7
CAR SM5 175 K5
DUL SE21 130 D7
HAYES BR2 181 J2
KUTN/CMB KT2 145 F3
ROMW/RG RM7 62 E3
Cedar Copse BMLY BR1 168 E1
Cedar Ct CHARL * SE7 114 B5
ELTH/MOT * SE9 134 D5
WIM/MER SW19 146 B2
Cedar Crs HAYES BR2 181 J2
Cedarcroft Rd CHSGTN KT9 172 B3
Cedar Dr EFNCH N2 53 J3
PIN HA5 34 A5
Cedar Gdns BELMT SM2 175 G5
Cedar Gv BXLY DA5 136 E5
EA W5 104 E2
STHL UB1 84 A4
Cedar Hts RCHPK/HAM TW10 125 F7
Cedarhurst BMLY * BR1 152 C6
Cedarhurst Dr ELTH/MOT SE9 134 B4
Cedar Lawn Av BAR EN5 26 C4
Cedar Mt ELTH/MOT SE9 134 C7
Cedarne Rd FUL/PGN SW6 107 K6
Cedar Park Gdns CHDH RM6 61 K6
Cedar Pl CHARL SE7 114 B4
Cedar Ri STHGT/OAK N14 28 A6
Cedar Rd BELMT SM2 175 G5
BMLY BR1 168 B1
CRICK NW2 70 A3
CROY/NA CR0 178 A1
DART DA1 139 G7
E/WMO/HCT KT8 157 K3
EBED/NFELT TW14 121 G7
ERITH DA8 118 D7
HEST TW5 122 B1
OXHEY WD19 21 G5
ROMW/RG RM7 62 E3
TEDD TW11 143 G4
TOTM N17 42 B7
Cedars Av MTCM CR4 163 F3
WALTH E17 57 J4
Cedars Cl BORE WD6 24 C3
HDN NW4 52 B2
LEW SE13 133 G2
Cedars Cottages
PUT/ROE * SW15 126 D5
Cedars Ct ED N9 42 A1
Cedars Ms CLAP * SW4 129 G3
Cedars Rd BARN SW13 126 C1
BECK BR3 166 B1
CLAP SW4 129 G2
CROY/NA CR0 176 E2
E/WMO/HCT KT8 143 J7
ED N9 42 C1
MRDN SM4 161 K3
SRTFD E15 76 C5
WCHMH N21 41 H1
The Cedars HOM * E9 75 F6
SRTFD * E15 76 D7
TEDD TW11 143 F5
Cedar Ter RCH/KEW TW9 125 F3
Cedar Tree Gv WNWD SE27 149 H4
Cedarville Gdns
STRHM/NOR SW16 149 F5
Cedar Wk ESH/CLAY KT10 171 F5
Cedar Wy CAMTN NW1 5 G2
SUN TW16 140 C6
Cedric Av ROM RM1 63 G2
Cedric Rd ELTH/MOT SE9 154 C2
Celadon Cl PEND EN3 31 G2
Celandine Cl POP/IOD * E14 93 J4
Celandine Dr HACK E8 7 M1
THMD SE28 97 H7
Celandine Wy SRTFD E15 94 C2
Celbridge Ms BAY/PAD W2 8 D4
Celestial Gdns LEW SE13 133 G3
Celia Rd ARCH N19 72 C3
Celtic Av HAYES BR2 167 H2
Celtic St POP/IOD E14 93 K4
Cemetery La CHARL SE7 114 D5
Cemetery Rd ABYW SE2 116 C5
FSTGT E7 76 D4
TOTM N17 42 A6
Cenacle Cl HAMP NW3 70 E2
Centaur Ct BTFD * TW8 105 F4
Centaur St STHWK SE1 17 M3
Centenary Rd PEND EN3 31 H3
Centenary Wk WAN E11 58 E7
WFD IG8 44 C5
Centennial Av BORE WD6 23 J6
Centennial Pk BORE * WD6 23 J6
Central Av E/WMO/HCT KT8 156 E4
ED N9 42 A2
EFNCH N2 53 H1
EN EN1 30 D1
HSLW TW3 123 H3
HYS/HAR UB3 82 D7
PIN HA5 47 K5
WAN E11 76 B1
WELL DA16 136 B1
WLGTN SM6 176 E4
Central Buildings EA * W5 85 K6
Central Circ HDN NW4 51 K4
Central Hall Buildings
ARCH * N19 72 C1
Central Hl NRWD SE19 149 J4
Central Pde ACT * W3 105 H1
E/WMO/HCT * KT8 156 E3
GFD/PVL * UB6 85 G2
HRW HA1 49 F4
PEND * EN3 30 E1
PGE/AN * SE20 151 F6
SCUP * DA14 155 G2
STRHM/NOR * SW16 148 E4
SURB * KT6 159 F5
WALTH * E17 57 J3
Central Park Av DAGE RM10 80 E2
Central Park Est HSLWW * TW4 122 C3
Central Park Rd EHAM E6 95 H1
Central Pl SNWD * SE25 165 H3
Central Rd ALP/SUD HA0 67 H4
DART DA1 139 H4
MRDN SM4 161 K4
WPK KT4 173 J1
Central Sq E/WMO/HCT KT8 156 E3
GLDGN NW11 52 E5
Central St FSBYE EC1V 6 E8
Central Ter BECK * BR3 166 A2
Central Wy CAR SM5 175 J6
EBED/NFELT TW14 122 A4
NTHWD HA6 32 C6
THMD SE28 97 H6
WLSDN NW10 86 E2
The Centre FELT TW13 140 E1
Centre Av ACT W3 87 F7
EFNCH N2 53 J1
Centre Common Rd CHST BR7 154 C6
Centre Rd DAGE RM10 98 D1
WAN E11 76 E1
Centre St BETH E2 92 D1
Centre Wy ED N9 42 E1
Centric Cl CAMTN * NW1 4 C3
Centurian Wy ERITHM DA18 117 G2
Centurion Cl HOLWY N7 5 L1
Centurion Ct WLGTN * SM6 176 B1
Centurion La BOW E3 93 H1
Centurion Wy PUR RM19 119 J3
Century Cl HDN NW4 52 B4
Century Ct WATW * WD18 20 A6
Century Ms CLPT * E5 74 E3
Century Pk WAT * WD17 21 G4
Century Rd WALTH E17 57 G2
Cephas Av WCHPL E1 92 E3
Cephas St WCHPL E1 92 E3
Ceres Rd WOOL/PLUM SE18 116 A3
Cerise Rd PECK SE15 111 H7
Cerne Cl YEAD UB4 83 G6
Cerne Rd MRDN SM4 162 B5
Cervantes Ct BAY/PAD W2 8 D5
NTHWD HA6 32 D6
Ceylon Rd WKENS W14 107 G2
Chadacre Av CLAY IG5 59 K2
Chadacre Rd EW KT17 173 K4
Chadbourn St POP/IOD E14 93 K4
Chadd Dr BMLY BR1 168 D2
Chadville Gdns CHDH RM6 61 K4
Chadway BCTR RM8 79 J1
Chadwell Av CHDH RM6 61 H6
Chadwell Heath La CHDH RM6 61 H3
Chadwell St CLKNW EC1R 6 B7
Chadwick Av CHING E4 44 B3
WCHMH * N21 29 F4
WIM/MER SW19 146 E5
Chadwick Cl TEDD TW11 143 G5
Chadwick Pl SURB KT6 158 D5
Chadwick Rd CMBW SE5 131 G1
IL IG1 78 B2
WAN E11 58 C6
WLSDN NW10 69 H7
Chadwick St WEST SW1P 17 G4
Chadwick Wy THMD SE28 97 K6
Chadwin Rd PLSTW E13 95 F4
Chadworth Wy ESH/CLAY KT10 170 D4
Chaffinch Av CROY/NA CR0 166 A5
Chaffinch Cl CROY/NA CR0 166 A4
ED N9 31 F7
SURB KT6 172 C2
Chaffinch La WATW WD18 20 D6
Chaffinch Rd BECK BR3 151 G7
Chafford Wy CHDH RM6 61 J3
Chagford St CAMTN NW1 9 L1
Chailey Av EN EN1 30 B1
Chailey Cl HEST TW5 102 C7
Chailey St CLPT E5 74 E2
Chalbury Wk IS N1 5 M5
Chalcombe Rd ABYW SE2 116 C2
Chalcot Cl BELMT SM2 174 E6
Chalcot Crs CAMTN NW1 3 M3
Chalcot Gdns HAMP NW3 71 K5
Chalcot Ms STRHM/NOR SW16 148 E2
Chalcot Rd CAMTN NW1 4 A3
Chalcot Sq CAMTN NW1 4 A2
Chalcott Gdns SURB * KT6 158 D7
Chalcroft Rd LEW SE13 133 H4
Chaldon Rd FUL/PGN SW6 107 H6
Chale Rd BRXS/STRHM SW2 129 K5
Chalet Est MLHL * NW7 37 J3
Chalfont Av WBLY HA9 68 D5
Chalfont Gn ED N9 42 A2
Chalfont Rd ED N9 42 A2
HYS/HAR UB3 101 K1
SNWD SE25 165 G2
Chalfont Wk PIN * HA5 47 G1
Chalfont Wy WEA W13 104 C2
Chalford Cl E/WMO/HCT KT8 157 F3
Chalforde Gdns GPK RM2 63 K3
Chalford Rd DUL SE21 149 K3
Chalford Wk WFD IG8 45 H7
Chalgrove Av MRDN SM4 161 K4
Chalgrove Crs CLAY IG5 59 J1
Chalgrove Gdns FNCH N3 52 C2
Chalgrove Rd BELMT SM2 175 H6
HOM E9 74 E5
TOTM N17 42 D7
Chalice Cl WLGTN SM6 176 D5
Chalkenden Cl PGE/AN SE20 150 D6
Chalk Farm Pde HAMP * NW3 4 A1
Chalk Farm Rd CAMTN NW1 4 A1
Chalk Hl OXHEY WD19 21 J5
Chalk Hill Rd HMSMTH W6 107 G3
Chalkhill Rd WBLY HA9 68 E2
Chalklands WBLY HA9 68 E2
Chalk La EBAR EN4 27 K2
Chalkley Cl MTCM CR4 162 E1
Chalk Pit Rd SUT SM1 175 G4
Chalk Rd PLSTW E13 95 F4
Chalkstone Cl WELL DA16 116 B7
Chalkwell Park Av EN EN1 30 A3
Chalky La CHSGTN KT9 171 K7
Challenge Cl WLSDN NW10 69 G7
Challenge Rd FELT TW13 140 A2
Challice Wy BRXS/STRHM SW2 130 A7
Challin St PGE/AN SE20 150 E7
Challis Rd BTFD TW8 104 E4
Challoner Cl EFNCH N2 53 H1
Challoner Crs WKENS W14 107 J4
Challoners Cl E/WMO/HCT KT8 157 J3
Challoner St WKENS W14 107 J4
Chalmers Wk WALW * SE17 110 C5
Chalmers Wy
EBED/NFELT TW14 122 A4
Chalsey Rd BROCKY SE4 132 C3
Chalton Dr EFNCH N2 53 G5
Chalton St CAMTN NW1 5 G5
Chamberlain Cl
WOOL/PLUM SE18 115 J2
Chamberlain Cottages
CMBW * SE5 110 E7
Chamberlain Crs WWKM BR4 166 E7
Chamberlain Gdns HSLW TW3 103 H7
Chamberlain La PIN HA5 46 E3
Chamberlain Pl WALTH * E17 57 G2
Chamberlain Rd ED N9 42 C2
EFNCH N2 53 G1
WEA W13 104 B1
Chamberlain St HAMP NW3 3 M2
Chamberlain Wy PIN HA5 47 F2
SURB KT6 159 F6
Chamberlayne Av WBLY HA9 68 A2
Chamberlayne Rd WLSDN NW10 70 A7
Chamberlens Garages
HMSMTH * W6 106 E3
Chambers Gdns EFNCH N2 39 H7
Chambers La WLSDN NW10 69 K6
Chambers Rd HOLWY N7 72 E3
Chambers St BERM/RHTH SE16 111 H1
Chamber St WCHPL E1 13 M6
Chambon Pl HMSMTH W6 106 D3
Chambord St BETH E2 7 M8
Champion Crs SYD SE26 151 G3
Champion Gv CMBW SE5 130 E2
Champion Hl CMBW SE5 130 E3
Champion Pk CMBW SE5 130 E2
Champion Rd SYD SE26 151 G3
Champness Cl WNWD SE27 149 K3
Champness Rd BARK IG11 79 F6
Champneys OXHEY * WD19 33 J1
Champneys Cl BELMT SM2 174 D6
Chancellor Gdns
SAND/SEL CR2 177 H7
Chancellor Gv DUL SE21 149 J1
Chancellor Pl CDALE/KGS NW9 51 H1
Chancellor's Rd HMSMTH W6 107 F4
Chancellors St HMSMTH W6 107 F4
Chancellors Whf
HMSMTH * W6 107 F4
Chancelot Rd ABYW SE2 116 C3
Chancel St STHWK SE1 12 C8
Chancery La BECK BR3 166 E1
LINN WC2A 11 M3
Chance St BETH E2 7 L9
Chanctonbury Cl
ELTH/MOT SE9 154 B2
Chanctonbury Gdns
BELMT SM2 175 F6
Chanctonbury Wy
NFNCH/WDSP N12 38 E3
Chandler Av CAN/RD E16 94 E4
Chandler Cl HPTN TW12 141 K7
Chandlers Cl
EBED/NFELT TW14 121 J6
Chandlers Ct LEE/GVPK * SE12 153 F1
Chandlers Dr ERITH DA8 118 A3
Chandlers Ms POP/IOD E14 112 D1
Chandler St WAP E1W 92 D7
Chandlers Wy ROM RM1 63 G4
Chandler Wy PECK SE15 111 G6
Chandos Av EA W5 104 D3
STHGT/OAK N14 40 C2
TRDG/WHET N20 27 H7
WALTH * E17 57 J1
Chandos Cl BKHH IG9 45 F1
Chandos Crs EDGW HA8 36 B6
Chandos Pl CHCR WC2N 11 J7
Chandos Rd BORE WD6 24 B1
CRICK NW2 70 A4
EFNCH N2 53 H1
HRW HA1 48 C4
PIN HA5 47 G6
SRTFD E15 76 B4
TOTM N17 56 A1
WLSDN NW10 87 G3
Chandos St CAVSQ/HST W1G 10 D3
Chandos Wy GLDGN NW11 53 F7
Channel Cl HEST TW5 103 F7
Channel Islands Est IS N1 73 J5
Channelsea Rd SRTFD E15 76 B7
Chantress Cl DAGE RM10 80 E7
Chantrey Rd BRXN/ST SW9 130 A2
Chantry Cl KTN/HRWW/W HA3 50 B4
MLHL NW7 25 H6
MV/WKIL * W9 88 D3
SUN TW16 140 E6
Chantry La HAYES BR2 168 C4
Chantry Pl RYLN/HDSTN HA2 34 B7
Chantry Rd CHSGTN KT9 172 B4
KTN/HRWW/W HA3 34 B7
Chantry Sq KENS W8 14 C4
Chantry St IS N1 6 D4
Chantry Wy MTCM CR4 162 C2
Chant Sq SRTFD * E15 76 B6
Chant St SRTFD E15 76 B6
Chapel Cl DART DA1 138 B4
Chapel Ct EFNCH N2 53 J2
STHWK SE1 19 G1
Chapel Farm Rd
ELTH/MOT SE9 153 K2
Chapel Hl DART DA1 138 B3
EFNCH N2 53 J1
Chapel House St POP/IOD E14 112 E4
Chapel La PIN HA5 47 H2
Chapel Market IS N1 6 A5
Chapel Pl CAVSQ/HST W1G 10 C5
IS N1 6 B5
TOTM N17 42 B6
Chapel Rd BXLYHN DA7 137 H3
HSLW TW3 123 G2
IL IG1 78 A2
TWK TW1 124 C6
WEA W13 85 H7
WNWD SE27 149 H3
Chapel Side BAY/PAD W2 8 C6
Chapel St BAY/PAD W2 9 J3
ENC/FH EN2 29 J2
KTBR SW1X 16 B3
Chapel Vw SAND/SEL CR2 178 E6
Chaplemount Rd WFD * IG8 45 K5
Chaplin Cl ALP/SUD * HA0 67 K5
STHWK SE1 18 B1
Chaplin Crs SUN TW16 140 C5
Chaplin Rd ALP/SUD HA0 67 J5
CRICK NW2 69 J5
SRTFD E15 94 C1
TOTM * N17 56 B2
Chapman Cl WDR/YW UB7 100 C2
Chapman Crs
KTN/HRWW/W HA3 50 A4
Chapman Rd BELV DA17 117 H4
CROY/NA CR0 164 B7
HOM E9 75 H5
Chapmans Gn WDGN * N22 41 G7
Chapman Sq WIM/MER SW19 146 B1
Chapman St WCHPL E1 92 D6
Chapmans Yd WAT WD17 21 G3
Chapman Ter WDGN * N22 41 H7
Chapter Rd CRICK NW2 69 J4
WALW SE17 18 D8
Chapter St WEST SW1P 17 G6
Chapter Wy HPTN TW12 142 A3
Chara Pl CHSWK W4 106 A5
Charcroft Gdns PEND EN3 31 F3
Chardin Rd CHSWK * W4 106 B3
Chardmore Rd STNW/STAM N16 56 C7
Chardwell Cl EHAM E6 95 J5
Charecroft Wy WKENS W14 107 G1
Charford Rd CAN/RD E16 94 E4
Chargeable La PLSTW E13 94 E3
Chargeable St CAN/RD E16 94 D3
Charing Cross CHCR * WC2N 11 J8
Charing Cross Rd
LSQ/SEVD WC2H 11 H6
Charlbert St STJWD NW8 3 J5
Charlbury Av STAN HA7 35 K4
Charlbury Gdns GDMY/SEVK IG3 79 F1
Charlbury Gv EA W5 85 J5
Charldane Rd ELTH/MOT SE9 154 B2
Charlecote Gv SYD SE26 150 D2
Charlecote Rd BCTR RM8 80 A2
Charlemont Rd EHAM E6 95 K2
Charles Babbage Cl
CHSGTN KT9 171 J6
Charles Barry Cl CLAP * SW4 129 H2
Charles Cl SCUP DA14 155 H3
Charles Cobb Gdns
CROY/NA CR0 177 G4
Charles Coveney Rd
PECK * SE15 111 G7
Charles Crs HRW HA1 48 D6
Charles Dickens Ter
PGE/AN * SE20 150 E6
Charlesfield ELTH/MOT SE9 153 G2
Charles Flemwell Ms
CAN/RD * E16 94 E7
Charles Grinling Wk
WOOL/PLUM SE18 115 F3
Charles Haller St
BRXS/STRHM SW2 130 B6
Charles II Pl CHEL SW3 15 K8

Charles II St STJS SW1Y 11 G8
Charles La STJWD NW8 3 J6
Charles Pl CAMTN * NW1 4 F8
Charles Rd CHDH RM6 61 K6
DAGE RM10 81 F5
FSTGT E7 77 G6
WEA W13 85 G5
WIM/MER SW19 146 E7
Charles Sevright Dr MLHL NW7 38 B4
Charles Sq IS N1 7 H8
Charles Square Est IS N1 7 H8
Charles St BARN SW13 126 B2
CAN/RD E16 95 G7
CROY/NA CR0 177 J2
EN EN1 30 B4
HSLW TW3 122 E1
MYFR/PICC W1J 10 C8
Charleston Cl FELT TW13 140 E2
Charleston St WALW SE17 18 F6
Charleville Circ SYD SE26 150 C4
Charleville Rd WKENS W14 107 H4
Charlieville Rd ERITH DA8 117 K6
Charlmont Rd TOOT SW17 147 J5
Charlock Wy WATW WD18 20 D5
Charlotte Cl BXLYHS DA6 137 F4
Charlotte Despard Av
BTSEA SW11 109 G7
Charlotte Ms ESH/CLAY * KT10 170 B3
FITZ W1T 10 F2
NKENS W10 88 B5
Charlotte Pde FSTH * SE23 151 G1
Charlotte Park Av BMLY BR1 168 D2
Charlotte Pl FITZ W1T 10 F3
Charlotte Rd BARN SW13 106 C7
IS N1 7 J8
WLGTN SM6 176 C5
Charlotte Rw CLAP SW4 129 H2
Charlotte St FITZ W1T 10 F2
Charlotte Ter IS N1 5 M4
Charlow Cl FUL/PGN SW6 128 B1
Charlton Church La CHARL SE7 114 B4
Charlton Crs BARK IG11 97 F1
Charlton Dene CHARL SE7 114 B6
Charlton King's Rd HOLWY N7 72 D4
Charlton La CHARL SE7 114 C4
Charlton Park La CHARL SE7 114 C6
Charlton Park Rd CHARL SE7 114 C5
Charlton Pl IS N1 6 C5
Charlton Rd BKHTH/KID SE3 113 K6
ED N9 31 F7
KTN/HRWW/W HA3 49 K3
WBLY HA9 50 B7
WLSDN NW10 69 G7
Charlton Wy BKHTH/KID SE3 113 H7
Charlwood CROY/NA CR0 179 H7
Charlwood Cl
KTN/HRWW/W HA3 34 E5
Charlwood Pl PIM SW1V 16 F6
Charlwood Rd PUT/ROE SW15 127 G3
Charlwood St PIM SW1V 16 E8
Charlwood Ter PUT/ROE SW15 127 G3
Charmian Av STAN HA7 49 K2
Charminster Av
WIM/MER SW19 161 K1
Charminster Rd ELTH/MOT SE9 153 H3
WPK KT4 161 G7
Charmouth Rd WELL DA16 116 D7
Charnock Rd CLPT E5 74 D2
Charnwood Av
WIM/MER SW19 161 K1
Charnwood Cl NWMAL KT3 160 B3
Charnwood Dr SWFD E18 59 F2
Charnwood Gdns
POP/IOD E14 112 D3
Charnwood Pl TRDG/WHET N20 39 G2
Charnwood Rd SNWD SE25 164 E4
Charnwood St CLPT * E5 74 C1
Charrington Rd CROY/NA CR0 177 H1
Charrington St CAMTN NW1 5 G5
Charsley Rd CAT SE6 151 K1
Chart Cl CROY/NA CR0 165 K5
HAYES BR2 152 C7
MTCM CR4 162 E3
Charter Av GNTH/NBYPK IG2 60 D7
Charter Crs HSLWW TW4 122 D3
Charter Dr BXLY DA5 137 F6
The Charterhouse FARR * EC1M 12 D1
Charterhouse Av ALP/SUD HA0 67 J4
Charterhouse Bldgs FARR EC1M 12 E1
Charterhouse Ms FARR EC1M 12 D2
Charterhouse Rd HACK E8 74 C4
Charterhouse St HCIRC EC1N 12 B3
Charteris Rd FSBYPK N4 55 F7
KIL/WHAMP NW6 70 D7
WFD IG8 45 F5
Charter Pl WAT * WD17 21 F3
The Charter Rd WFD IG8 44 C5
Charter Rd KUT KT1 159 J2
Charters Cl NRWD SE19 150 A4
Charter Sq KUT KT1 159 J1
Charter Wy GLDGN NW11 52 D3
STHGT/OAK N14 28 C5
Chartfield Av PUT/ROE SW15 126 E4
Chartfield Sq PUT/ROE * SW15 127 G4
Chartham Gv WNWD SE27 149 G2
Chartham Rd SNWD SE25 165 J2
Chart Hills Cl THMD SE28 98 A5
Chartley Av CRICK NW2 69 G2
STAN HA7 35 F5
Chartley Pde WLSDN * NW10 69 G2
Charton Cl BELV DA17 117 G5
Chartridge OXHEY * WD19 33 H1
Chartridge Cl BAR EN5 25 J4
BUSH WD23 22 C5
Chart St IS N1 7 H7
Chartwell Cl CHST BR7 154 D1
CROY/NA CR0 164 E7
GFD/PVL UB6 66 B7
Chartwell Pl CHEAM SM3 174 C3
RYLN/HDSTN HA2 66 D1
Chartwell Rd NTHWD HA6 32 D5
Chartwell Wy PGE/AN SE20 150 D7
Charville La HGDN/ICK UB10 82 A2
Charwood STRHM/NOR * SW16 149 G3
The Chase BMLY BR1 168 A2
BXLYHN DA7 137 J2
CLAP SW4 129 G2
DAGE RM10 81 F2
EDGW HA8 36 D7
MNPK E12 77 H3
PIN HA5 47 G5
PIN HA5 47 K3
ROM RM1 63 G2
STAN HA7 35 G5
STRHM/NOR SW16 149 F6
SUN TW16 141 F7
WATW WD18 20 C3
WLGTN SM6 176 E4
Chase Ct RYNPK SW20 161 H1
Chase Court Gdns ENC/FH EN2 29 J2
Chasefield Rd TOOT SW17 147 K3
Chase Gdns CHING E4 43 J3
WHTN TW2 123 J5
Chase Gn ENC/FH EN2 29 J2
Chase Green Av ENC/FH EN2 29 H1
Chase Hl ENC/FH EN2 29 J2
Chase La BARK/HLT IG6 60 D4
Chaseley Ct CHSWK W4 105 J4
Chaseley St POP/IOD * E14 93 G5
Chasemore Cl MTCM CR4 162 E6
Chasemore Gdns
CROY/NA CR0 177 G4
Chase Ridings ENC/FH EN2 29 G1
Chase Rd ACT W3 87 F3
STHGT/OAK N14 28 C4
Chase Side EBAR EN4 28 A4
ENC/FH EN2 29 J1
Chase Side Av ENC/FH EN2 29 J1
Chaseside Av RYNPK SW20 146 C7
Chaseville Pde WCHMH * N21 29 F4
Chaseville Park Rd WCHMH N21 28 E4
Chase Wy STHGT/OAK N14 28 B7
Chasewood Av ENC/FH EN2 29 H1
Chasewood Pk HRW * HA1 66 E2
Chastilian Rd DART DA1 138 D6
Chatfield Rd BTSEA SW11 128 B2
CROY/NA CR0 164 C7
Chatham Av HAYES BR2 167 K6
Chatham Cl CHEAM SM3 161 J6
GLDGN NW11 52 E4
Chatham Pl HOM E9 74 E5
Chatham Rd BTSEA SW11 128 E5
KUTN/CMB KT2 159 H1
SWFD E18 58 D1
WALTH E17 57 G2
Chatham St WALW SE17 19 G5
WOOL/PLUM SE18 115 G2
Chatsfield Pl EA W5 86 A5
Chatsworth Av BFN/LL DA15 136 B7
BMLY BR1 153 F4
HDN NW4 52 A1
RYNPK SW20 146 C7
WBLY HA9 68 B4
Chatsworth Cl BORE WD6 24 C2
CHSWK * W4 105 K5
HDN NW4 52 A1
WWKM BR4 180 D1
Chatsworth Crs HSLW TW3 123 J3
Chatsworth Dr EN EN1 30 C6
Chatsworth Est CLPT * E5 75 F3
Chatsworth Gdns ACT W3 86 D6
NWMAL * KT3 160 C4
RYLN/HDSTN HA2 48 B7
Chatsworth Pl MTCM CR4 162 E2
TWK TW1 143 G3
Chatsworth Ri EA W5 86 B3
Chatsworth Rd CHEAM SM3 174 B3
CHSWK W4 105 K5
CLPT E5 74 E2
CRICK NW2 70 B5
CROY/NA CR0 177 K3
DART DA1 139 F4
EA W5 86 B3
SRTFD E15 76 D4
YEAD UB4 83 F3
Chatsworth Wy WNWD SE27 149 H2
Chattern Rd ASHF TW15 140 A3
Chatterton Ms FSBYPK * N4 73 H2
Chatterton Rd FSBYPK N4 73 H2
HAYES BR2 168 C4
Chatto Rd BTSEA SW11 128 E4
Chaucer Av HSLWW TW4 122 A1
RCH/KEW TW9 125 H2
YEAD UB4 82 E4
Chaucer Cl FBAR/BDGN N11 40 C4
Chaucer Dr STHWK SE1 19 M6
Chaucer Gdns SUT SM1 174 E3
Chaucer Gn CROY/NA CR0 165 J6
Chaucer Pk DART DA1 139 J6
Chaucer Rd ACT W3 86 E7
BFN/LL DA15 136 D7
FSTGT E7 76 E5
HNHL SE24 130 B4
SUT SM1 174 E3
WALTH E17 44 A7
WAN E11 58 E5
WELL DA16 116 A7
Chaucer Wy DART DA1 139 K3
Chauncey Cl ED N9 42 C2
Chaundrye Cl ELTH/MOT SE9 134 E5
Chauntler Rd CAN/RD E16 95 F5
Cheam Common Rd WPK KT4 173 K1
Cheam Man CHEAM * SM3 174 C5
Cheam Park Wy CHEAM SM3 174 B5
Cheam Rd BELMT SM2 174 B7
Cheam St PECK * SE15 131 J2
Cheapside CITYW EC2V 12 F5
EFNCH * N2 53 K2
PLMGR N13 41 J3
WDGN * N22 55 G2
Cheddar Cl FBAR/BDGN N11 39 K5
Cheddar Waye YEAD UB4 83 F5
Cheddington Rd UED N18 42 A3
Cheeseman Cl HPTN TW12 141 J5
Cheesemans Ter WKENS * W14 107 J4
Chelford Rd BMLY BR1 152 B4
Chelmer Crs BARK IG11 97 H1
Chelmer Rd HOM E9 75 F4
Chelmsford Cl BELMT SM2 174 E7
EHAM E6 95 K5
HMSMTH W6 107 G5
Chelmsford Gdns IL IG1 59 J6
Chelmsford Rd
STHGT/OAK N14 28 C6
SWFD E18 44 D7
WALTH E17 57 J5
WAN E11 58 B7
Chelmsford Sq WLSDN NW10 70 A7
Chelsea Br CHEL SW3 16 B9
Chelsea Bridge Ga BTSEA SW11 109 F5
Chelsea Bridge Rd BGVA SW1W 16 A7
Chelsea Cl HPTN TW12 142 C5
WLSDN NW10 69 F7
WPK KT4 160 D6
Chelsea Crs CRICK * NW2 70 D5
WBPTN * SW10 108 B7
Chelsea Emb CHEL SW3 16 A9
Chelsea Gdns CHEAM SM3 174 C3
Chelsea Harbour Dr
WBPTN SW10 108 B7
Chelsea Manor Gdns CHEL SW3 15 J9
Chelsea Manor St CHEL SW3 15 J7
Chelsea Park Gdns CHEL SW3 15 G9
Chelsea Sq CHEL SW3 15 H8
Chelsea Village WBPTN * SW10 108 A6
Chelsfield Av ED N9 31 F6
Chelsfield Gdns SYD SE26 150 E2
Chelsham Rd CLAP SW4 129 J2
SAND/SEL CR2 177 K6
Chelston Rd RSLP HA4 64 E1
Chelsworth Dr
WOOL/PLUM SE18 115 J5
Cheltenham Av TWK TW1 124 B6
Cheltenham Cl NTHLT UB5 66 B5
NWMAL KT3 159 K2
Cheltenham Gdns EHAM E6 95 J1
Cheltenham Pl ACT W3 105 K1
KTN/HRWW/W HA3 50 A3
Cheltenham Rd LEY E10 58 A5
PECK SE15 131 K3
Cheltenham Ter CHEL SW3 15 M7
Chelverton Rd PUT/ROE SW15 127 G3
Chelwood Cl CHING E4 31 K5
Chelwood Gdns RCH/KEW TW9 125 H1
Chenappa Cl PLSTW E13 94 E2
Chenduit Wy STAN HA7 35 F4
Cheney Rd CAMTN NW1 5 J6
Cheney Rw WALTH E17 43 H7
Cheneys Rd WAN E11 76 C2
Cheney St PIN HA5 47 G3
The Chenies ORP BR6 169 K5
Chenies Ms GWRST WC1E 11 G1
Chenies Pl CAMTN NW1 5 H5
Chenies St FITZ W1T 11 G2
Chenies Wy WATW WD18 20 C6
Cheniston Gdns KENS W8 14 B3
Chepstow Cl PUT/ROE SW15 127 H4
Chepstow Cnr BAY/PAD * W2 8 B5
Chepstow Crs GDMY/SEVK IG3 60 E5
NTGHL W11 8 A6
Chepstow Gdns STHL UB1 83 K5
Chepstow Pl BAY/PAD W2 8 B5
Chepstow Ri CROY/NA CR0 178 A2
Chepstow Rd BAY/PAD W2 8 B4
CROY/NA CR0 178 A2
HNWL W7 104 B2
Chepstow Vls NTGHL W11 88 D6
Chepstow Wy PECK SE15 111 G7
The Chequers PIN * HA5 47 H2
Chequers Cl CDALE/KGS NW9 51 G2
Chequers La DAGW RM9 98 B3
Chequers Pde PLMGR * N13 41 J4
Chequer St STLK EC1Y 12 F1
Chequers Wy PLMGR N13 41 H4
Cherbury Cl THMD SE28 97 K5
Cherbury St IS N1 7 H6
Cherimoya Gdns
E/WMO/HCT KT8 157 G2
Cherington Rd HNWL * W7 85 F7
Cheriton Av CLAY IG5 60 A1
HAYES BR2 167 J4
Cheriton Cl EA W5 85 J4
EBAR EN4 27 K2
Cheriton Ct WOT/HER KT12 156 B7
Cheriton Dr WOOL/PLUM SE18 115 J6
Cheriton Sq TOOT SW17 148 A1
Cherry Av STHL UB1 83 H7
Cherry Blossom Cl PLMGR N13 41 H4
Cherry Cl BRXS/STRHM * SW2 130 B6
CAR SM5 175 K1
EA W5 104 E2
MRDN SM4 161 H3
RSLP HA4 64 D2
Cherry Ct PIN HA5 47 H1
Cherry Crs BTFD TW8 104 C6
Cherry Croft Gdns PIN * HA5 33 K6
Cherrydale WATW WD18 20 D3
Cherrydown Av CHING E4 43 H2
Cherrydown Cl CHING E4 43 H2
Cherrydown Rd SCUP DA14 155 K1
Cherrydown Wk
ROMW/RG RM7 62 D1
Cherry Gdns DAGW RM9 80 B4
NTHLT UB5 66 B6
Cherry Garden St
BERM/RHTH SE16 111 J1
Cherry Garth BTFD TW8 104 E4
Cherry Gv HYS/HAR UB3 83 F7
UX/CGN UB8 82 A4
Cherry Hl BAR EN5 27 F5
KTN/HRWW/W HA3 34 E5
Cherry Hill Gdns CROY/NA CR0 177 F3
Cherry Hills OXHEY WD19 33 J4
Cherrylands Cl
CDALE/KGS * NW9 68 E1
Cherry La WDR/YW UB7 100 C3
Cherry Orch CHARL SE7 114 B5
WDR/YW UB7 100 B1
Cherry Orchard Gdns
CROY/NA CR0 164 E7
E/WMO/HCT KT8 156 E2
Cherry Orchard Rd
CROY/NA CR0 164 E7
E/WMO/HCT KT8 157 F2
HAYES BR2 181 J1
Cherry St ROMW/RG RM7 63 F4
Cherry Tree Cl ALP/SUD HA0 67 G3
RAIN RM13 99 J1
Cherry Tree Ct CHARL * SE7 114 B5
Cherry Tree Dr
STRHM/NOR * SW16 148 E2
Cherry Tree Hl EFNCH N2 53 J4
Cherry Tree La RAIN RM13 99 H2
Cherry Tree Ri BKHH IG9 45 H3
Cherry Tree Rd EFNCH N2 53 K3
SRTFD E15 76 C4
Cherry Tree Wk BECK BR3 166 C3
STLK EC1Y 12 F1
WWKM BR4 180 D3
Cherry Tree Wy STAN HA7 35 H5
Cherry Wk HAYES BR2 167 K7
RAIN RM13 99 H1
Cherry Wy HOR/WEW KT19 173 F5
Cherrywood Cl BOW E3 93 G2
KUTN/CMB KT2 144 C6
Cherrywood Dr
PUT/ROE SW15 127 G4
Cherrywood La MRDN SM4 161 H3
Chertsey Dr CHEAM SM3 174 C1
Chertsey Rd ASHF TW15 140 B6
FELT TW13 140 D3
IL IG1 78 D3
TWK TW1 124 B5
WAN E11 76 B1
WHTN TW2 123 H7
Chertsey St TOOT SW17 148 A4
Chervil Cl FELT TW13 140 D2
Chervil Ms THMD SE28 97 H7
Cherwell Ct HOR/WEW KT19 172 E3
Cherwell Wy RSLP HA4 46 A5
Cheryls Cl FUL/PGN SW6 108 A7
Cheseman St SYD SE26 150 D2
Chesfield Rd KUTN/CMB KT2 144 A6
Chesham Av HAYES BR2 169 G5
Chesham Cl KTBR * SW1X 16 A4
ROMW/RG RM7 63 F3
Chesham Crs PGE/AN SE20 150 E7
Chesham Ms KTBR SW1X 16 A3
Chesham Pl KTBR SW1X 16 A4
Chesham Rd KUTN/CMB KT2 144 C7
PGE/AN SE20 165 K1
Chesham St KTBR SW1X 16 A4
WLSDN NW10 69 F2
Chesham Ter WEA W13 104 C1
Chesham Wy WATW WD18 20 C5
Cheshire Cl MTCM CR4 163 K2
WALTH E17 43 K7
Cheshire Gdns CHSGTN KT9 171 K5
Cheshire Rd WDGN N22 41 F6
Cheshire St BETH E2 92 C3
Chesholm Rd STNW/STAM N16 74 A2
Cheshunt Rd BELV DA17 117 H4
FSTGT E7 77 F5
Chesilton Rd FUL/PGN SW6 107 J7
Chesil Wy YEAD UB4 82 D2
Chesley Gdns EHAM E6 95 H1
Chesney Crs CROY/NA CR0 180 A6
Chesney St BTSEA SW11 109 F7
Chesnut Av North WALTH E17 58 B3
Chesnut Gv TOTM N17 56 C2
Chesnut Rd TOTM N17 56 C2
Chesnut Rw FNCH * N3 38 E6
Chessholme Rd ASHF TW15 140 A5
Chessington Av BXLYHN DA7 117 F6
FNCH N3 52 C2
Chessington Cl
HOR/WEW KT19 172 E5
Chessington Ct PIN HA5 47 K3
Chessington Hall Gdns
CHSGTN KT9 171 K6
Chessington Hill Pk
CHSGTN KT9 172 C5
Chessington Pde
CHSGTN * KT9 171 K4
Chessington Rd CHSGTN KT9 172 C5
Chessington Wy WWKM BR4 179 K1
Chesson Rd WKENS W14 107 J5
Chesswood Wy PIN HA5 47 H1
Chester Av RCHPK/HAM TW10 125 G5
WHTN TW2 122 E7
Chester Cl ASHF TW15 140 B4
BARN * SW13 126 E2
KTBR SW1X 16 B2
SUT SM1 174 E1
Chester Cl North CAMTN NW1 4 D7
Chester Cl South CAMTN NW1 4 D8
Chester Crs HACK E8 74 B4
Chester Dr RYLN/HDSTN HA2 48 A5
Chesterfield Dr DART DA1 138 E4
ESH/CLAY KT10 171 G1
Chesterfield Gdns FSBYPK N4 55 H4
GNWCH * SE10 113 G6
MYFR/PICC * W1J 10 C8
Chesterfield Gv EDUL SE22 131 G4
Chesterfield Hl MYFR/PICC W1J 10 C7
Chesterfield Rd BAR EN5 26 B4
CHSWK W4 105 K5
FNCH N3 38 E5
HOR/WEW KT19 173 F6
LEY E10 58 A6
Chesterfield St MYFR/PICC W1J 10 C8
Chesterfield Wy
HYS/HAR * UB3 101 K1
PECK SE15 111 K6
Chesterford Gdns HAMP NW3 71 F3
Chesterford Rd MNPK E12 77 K4
Chester Gdns ED N9 30 D5
MRDN SM4 162 B4
WEA * W13 85 H5
Chester Ga CAMTN NW1 4 C8
Chester Ms KTBR SW1X 16 C3
Chester Pl CAMTN NW1 4 C7
NTHWD * HA6 32 C6
Chester Rd ARCH N19 72 B1
BFN/LL DA15 135 K4
BORE WD6 24 E2
CAMTN NW1 4 B8
CAN/RD E16 94 C3
ED N9 30 D7
FSTGT E7 77 H6
GDMY/SEVK IG3 61 F7
HSLWW TW4 122 A2
HTHAIR TW6 120 D2
NTHWD HA6 32 D6
TOTM N17 55 K2
WALTH E17 57 F4
WAN E11 59 F5
WATW WD18 20 E4
WIM/MER SW19 146 A5
Chester Rw BGVA SW1W 16 A6
Chester Sq BGVA SW1W 16 B5
Chester Square Ms
BGVA * SW1W 16 C4
The Chesters NWMAL KT3 145 G7
Chester St BETH * E2 74 C7
BETH E2 92 C3
KTBR SW1X 16 B3
Chester Ter CAMTN NW1 4 C7
Chesterton Cl GFD/PVL UB6 84 B1
WAND/EARL SW18 127 K4
Chesterton Ct EA * W5 85 K5
Chesterton Dr
STWL/WRAY TW19 120 C7
Chesterton Rd NKENS W10 88 B4
PLSTW E13 94 E2
Chesterton Sq WKENS W14 107 J3
Chesterton Ter KUT KT1 159 H1
PLSTW E13 94 E2
Chester Wy LBTH SE11 18 B6
Chesthunte Rd TOTM N17 41 J7
Chestnut Aly FUL/PGN * SW6 107 J5
Chestnut Av ALP/SUD HA0 67 H4
BKHH IG9 45 H2
BTFD TW8 104 E4
CEND/HSY/T N8 54 E4
E/WMO/HCT KT8 158 A2
EDGW HA8 36 A5
ESH/CLAY KT10 157 J6
FSTGT E7 77 F3
HCH RM12 81 H1
HOR/WEW KT19 173 G3
HPTN TW12 142 A6
MORT/ESHN * SW14 126 A2
NTHWD HA6 46 D1
TEDD TW11 143 F6
WWKM BR4 180 C4
Chestnut Av South WALTH E17 58 A3
Chestnut Cl BFN/LL DA15 155 G1
BKHH IG9 45 H2
CAR SM5 162 E7
CAT SE6 152 A3
HYS/HAR UB3 82 C6
NWCR SE14 112 C7
STHGT/OAK N14 28 C4
STRHM/NOR SW16 149 G3
SUN TW16 140 D5
WDR/YW UB7 100 E6
Chestnut Cottages
TRDG/WHET * N20 26 C7
Chestnut Dr BXLYHN DA7 136 E2
KTN/HRWW/W HA3 35 F6
PIN HA5 47 H5
WAN E11 58 E5
Chestnut Gln HCH RM12 81 H1
Chestnut Gv ALP/SUD HA0 67 H4
BAL SW12 129 F6
EA W5 104 E2
EBAR EN4 27 K4
ISLW TW7 124 B3
MTCM CR4 163 J4
NWMAL KT3 160 A2
SAND/SEL CR2 178 D6
Chestnut La TRDG/WHET N20 26 C7
Chestnut Mnr WLGTN SM6 176 B3
Chestnut Pl SYD SE26 150 B3
Chestnut Ri BUSH WD23 22 B6
WOOL/PLUM SE18 115 K4
Chestnut Rd DART DA1 139 G7
KUTN/CMB KT2 144 A6
RYNPK SW20 161 G1
WHTN TW2 142 E1
WNWD SE27 149 H2
The Chestnuts BECK * BR3 166 A2
PIN * HA5 33 K6
Chestnut Ter SUT * SM1 175 F3
Chestnut Wy FELT TW13 141 F2
Cheston Av CROY/NA CR0 166 B7
Cheswick Cl DART DA1 138 C3
Chesworth Cl ERITH DA8 118 B7
Chettle Cl STHWK SE1 19 G3
Chetwode Rd TOOT SW17 147 K2
Chetwynd Av EBAR EN4 27 K7
Chetwynd Rd KTTN NW5 72 B3
Chetwynd Vls KTTN * NW5 72 B3
Chevalier Cl STAN HA7 35 K2
Cheval Pl SKENS SW7 15 K3
Cheval St POP/IOD E14 112 D2
Cheveney Wk HAYES BR2 167 K2
The Chevenings SCUP DA14 155 H2
Chevening Rd GNWCH SE10 113 J4
KIL/WHAMP NW6 88 B1
NRWD SE19 149 K6
Cheverton Rd ARCH N19 54 D7
Chevet St HOM E9 75 G4
Chevington CRICK * NW2 70 D5
Cheviot Cl BELMT SM2 175 H7
BUSH WD23 22 C5
BXLYHN DA7 138 B1
ENC/FH EN2 29 K1
HYS/HAR UB3 101 G6
Cheviot Gdns GLDGN NW11 70 B1
Cheviot Rd EMPK RM11 63 J6
WNWD SE27 149 H4
Cheviot Wy GNTH/NBYPK IG2 60 E4
Chevron Cl CAN/RD E16 94 E5
Chevy Rd NWDGN UB2 103 H1
Chewton Rd WALTH E17 57 G3
Cheyne Av SWFD E18 58 D2
WHTN TW2 122 E7
Cheyne Cl HAYES BR2 181 J2
Cheyne Ct BUSH * WD23 21 J3
Cheyne Gdns CHEL SW3 15 K9
Cheyne Hl BRYLDS KT5 159 G3
Cheyne Pth WEA W13 85 F4
Cheyne Pl CHEL SW3 15 L9
Cheyne Rd ASHF TW15 140 B5
Cheyne Rw CHEL SW3 108 D5
Cheyne Wk CROY/NA CR0 178 C1
HDN NW4 52 A5
WBPTN SW10 108 C6
WCHMH N21 29 G4
Cheyneys Av EDGW HA8 35 K5
Chichele Gdns CROY/NA CR0 178 A3
Chichele Rd CRICK NW2 70 B4
Chicheley Rd
KTN/HRWW/W HA3 34 C6
Chicheley St STHWK SE1 17 M1
Chichester Av RSLP HA4 64 B1
Chichester Cl BKHTH/KID SE3 114 B6
EHAM E6 95 J5
HPTN TW12 141 K5
Chichester Ct EW * KT17 173 H7
STAN HA7 50 A2
Chichester Gdns IL IG1 59 J6
Chichester Rd BAY/PAD W2 8 D2
CROY/NA CR0 178 A2
ED N9 30 B7
KIL/WHAMP NW6 2 A6
WAN E11 76 C2
Chichester St PIM SW1V 16 F8
Chichester Wy
EBED/NFELT TW14 122 B6
POP/IOD E14 113 G3
Chichester Whf ERITH DA8 118 B4
Chicksand St WCHPL E1 13 M3
Chiddingfold NFNCH/WDSP N12 38 E2
Chiddingstone Av BXLYHN DA7 117 G5
Chiddingstone St
FUL/PGN SW6 127 K1
Chieftan Dr PUR RM19 119 K3
Chieveley Pde BXLYHN * DA7 137 J2
Chieveley Rd BXLYHN DA7 137 J3
Chignell Pl WEA W13 85 G7
Chigwell Hl WAP E1W 92 D6
Chigwell Rd SWFD E18 59 F2
WFD IG8 45 J5
Chilcott Cl ALP/SUD HA0 67 J3
Childebert Rd TOOT SW17 148 B1
Childeric Rd NWCR SE14 112 B6
Childerley St FUL/PGN SW6 107 H7
The Childers WFD IG8 45 K4
Childers St DEPT SE8 112 B5
Childs Ct HYS/HAR UB3 82 E6
Childs La NRWD * SE19 150 A5
Child's Pl ECT SW5 14 B6
Child's St ECT SW5 14 B5
Child's Wk ECT * SW5 14 B5
Childs Wy GLDGN NW11 52 D4
Chilham Cl BXLY DA5 137 G6
GFD/PVL UB6 85 G1
Chilham Rd ELTH/MOT SE9 153 J3
Chilham Wy HAYES BR2 167 K6
Chillerton Rd TOOT SW17 148 A4
Chillingworth Gdns TWK * TW1 143 F1
Chillingworth Rd HOLWY N7 73 G4
Chilmark Gdns NWMAL KT3 160 C5
Chilmark Rd
STRHM/NOR SW16 163 J1
Chiltern Av BUSH WD23 22 C5
WHTN TW2 123 F7
Chiltern Cl BORE WD6 24 B1
BUSH WD23 22 B5
BXLYHN DA7 118 B7
CROY/NA CR0 178 A2
WPK KT4 174 A1
Chiltern Dene ENC/FH EN2 29 F3
Chiltern Dr BRYLDS KT5 159 J5
Chiltern Gdns CRICK NW2 70 B2
HAYES BR2 167 J3
Chiltern Rd BOW E3 93 J3

GNTH/NBYPK IG2 60 E3
PIN HA5 47 G4
The Chilterns BELMT * SM2 175 F7
Chiltern St MHST W1U 10 A2
Chiltern Wy WFD IG8 44 E2
Chilthorne Cl CAT SE6 132 C6
Chilton Av EA W5 104 E3
Chilton Gv DEPT SE8 112 A3
Chilton Rd EDGW HA8 36 C5
RCH/KEW TW9 125 H2
Chilton St BETH E2 7 M9
Chilvers Cl WHTN TW2 142 E1
Chilver St GNWCH SE10 113 J4
Chilwell Gdns OXHEY WD19 33 G3
Chilworth Gdns SUT SM1 175 G2
Chilworth Ms BAY/PAD W2 8 F5
Chilworth St BAY/PAD W2 8 F5
Chimes Av PLMGR N13 41 G3
Chinbrook Crs LEE/GVPK SE12 153 F2
Chinbrook Rd ELTH/MOT SE9 153 G2
Chinchilla Dr HSLWW TW4 122 B1
The Chine ALP/SUD HA0 67 H4
MUSWH N10 54 C3
WCHMH N21 29 H5
Chingdale Rd CHING E4 44 C2
Chingford Av CHING E4 43 K2
Chingford La WFD IG8 44 C3
Chingford Mount Rd CHING E4 43 J4
Chingford Rd CHING E4 43 J6
WALTH E17 57 K1
Chingley Cl BMLY BR1 152 C5
Ching Wy CHING E4 43 H5
Chinnor Crs GFD/PVL UB6 84 C1
Chipka St POP/IOD E14 113 F1
Chipley St NWCR SE14 112 B5
Chippendale St CLPT E5 75 F2
Chippenham Cl RSLP * HA4 46 D3
Chippenham Ms MV/WKIL W9 8 A1
Chippenham Rd MV/WKIL W9 2 A9
Chipping Cl BAR EN5 26 C2
Chipstead Av THHTH CR7 164 C3
Chipstead Cl BELMT SM2 175 F7
NRWD SE19 150 B6
Chipstead Gdns CRICK NW2 69 K1
Chipstead Rd ERITH DA8 118 B6
Chipstead St FUL/PGN SW6 107 K7
Chirk Cl YEAD UB4 83 J3
Chisenhale Rd BOW E3 93 G1
Chisholm Rd CROY/NA CR0 178 A1
RCHPK/HAM TW10 125 G5
Chislehurst Av FNCH N3 39 G6
Chislehurst High St CHST BR7 154 B5
Chislehurst Rd BMLY BR1 168 D1
RCHPK/HAM TW10 125 F5
SCUP DA14 155 G4
STMC/STPC BR5 169 K3
Chislet Cl BECK BR3 151 J6
Chisley Rd SEVS/STOTM N15 56 A5
Chiswell Sq BKHTH/KID SE3 134 A1
Chiswell St STLK EC1Y 13 G2
Chiswick Br MORT/ESHN SW14 125 K1
Chiswick Cl CROY/NA CR0 177 F2
Chiswick Common Rd
CHSWK W4 106 A3
Chiswick High Rd CHSWK W4 105 J4
Chiswick House Grounds
CHSWK * W4 106 A5
Chiswick La CHSWK W4 106 B4
Chiswick La South CHSWK W4 106 C5
Chiswick Ml CHSWK W4 106 C5
Chiswick Pk CHSWK * W4 105 K2
Chiswick Pier CHSWK * W4 106 C6
Chiswick Quay CHSWK W4 105 K7
Chiswick Rd CHSWK W4 105 K3
ED N9 42 C1
Chiswick Sq CHSWK W4 106 B5
Chiswick Staithe CHSWK W4 105 J7
Chiswick Village CHSWK W4 105 H5
Chitterfield Ga WDR/YW UB7 100 D6
Chitty's La BCTR RM8 79 K1
Chitty St FITZ W1T 10 F2
Chivalry Rd BTSEA SW11 128 D4
Chivenor Gv KUTN/CMB KT2 143 K4
Chivers Rd CHING E4 43 K2
Choats Rd BARK IG11 97 J1
Chobham Gdns
WIM/MER SW19 146 B1
Chobham Rd SRTFD E15 76 C4
Cholmeley Cl HGT * N6 54 B6
Cholmeley Crs HGT N6 54 B6
Cholmeley Pk HGT N6 54 B7
Cholmley Gdns
KIL/WHAMP NW6 70 E4
Cholmley Rd THDIT KT7 158 C5
Cholmley Ter THDIT * KT7 158 C6
Cholmley Vls THDIT * KT7 158 C6
Cholmondeley Av WLSDN NW10 87 J1
Chopwell Cl SRTFD * E15 76 B6
Choumert Gv PECK SE15 131 H1
Choumert Rd PECK SE15 131 G2
Chow Sq HACK * E8 74 B4
Chrislaine Cl STWL/WRAY TW19 120 A5
Chrisp St POP/IOD E14 93 K5
Christabel Cl ISLW TW7 123 K2
Christ Church Av ERITH DA8 118 A5
Christchurch Av ALP/SUD HA0 68 A5
KIL/WHAMP NW6 70 B7
KTN/HRWW/W HA3 49 G3
NFNCH/WDSP N12 39 G5
RAIN RM13 99 H1
TEDD TW11 143 G4
Christchurch Cl ENC/FH EN2 29 J1
NFNCH/WDSP * N12 39 H6
WIM/MER SW19 147 H6
Christchurch Gdns
KTN/HRWW/W HA3 49 G3
Christchurch Hl HAMP NW3 71 H2
Christ Church La BAR EN5 26 C1
Christchurch Ldg EBAR * EN4 27 K3
Christchurch Pk BELMT SM2 175 G6
Christchurch Pas HAMP NW3 71 H2
Christ Church Rd BECK * BR3 166 D1
BRYLDS KT5 159 G6
CEND/HSY/T N8 54 E5
Christchurch Rd BFN/LL DA15 155 F3
BRXS/STRHM SW2 130 A7
DART DA1 139 F6
IL IG1 60 B7
MORT/ESHN SW14 125 J4
WIM/MER SW19 147 H7
Christchurch Sq HOM E9 74 E7
Christchurch St CHEL SW3 15 L9
Christchurch Ter CHEL * SW3 15 L9
Christchurch Wy GNWCH SE10 113 H4
Christian Flds
STRHM/NOR SW16 149 G6
Christian St WCHPL E1 92 C5
Christie Dr SNWD SE25 165 H4
Christie Rd HOM E9 75 G5
Christina Sq FSBYPK N4 55 H7
Christina St SDTCH EC2A 7 J9
Christopher Av HNWL W7 104 B2
Christopher Cl BFN/LL DA15 136 A4
Christopher Gdns DAGW RM9 79 K4
Christopher Pl CAMTN * NW1 5 H7
Christopher Rd NWDGN UB2 102 A3
Christophers Ms NTGHL * W11 88 C7
Christopher St SDTCH EC2A 13 H1
Chryssell Rd BRXN/ST SW9 110 B6
Chubworthy St NWCR SE14 112 B5
Chudleigh Crs GDMY/SEVK IG3 78 E3
Chudleigh Gdns SUT SM1 175 G2
Chudleigh Rd BROCKY SE4 132 C4
KIL/WHAMP NW6 70 A6
WHTN TW2 123 K5
Chudleigh St WCHPL E1 93 F5
Chudleigh Wy RSLP HA4 46 E7
Chulsa Rd SYD SE26 150 D4
Chumleigh St CMBW SE5 19 J9
Chumleigh Wk BRYLDS KT5 159 G3
Church Ap DUL SE21 149 K2
Church Av BECK BR3 151 J7
CAMTN NW1 72 B5
CHING E4 44 B5
EFNCH N2 53 H1
MORT/ESHN SW14 126 A3
NTHLT UB5 65 K6
NWDGN UB2 102 D2
PIN HA5 47 J5
RSLP HA4 46 B7
SCUP DA14 155 G4
Churchbury Cl EN EN1 30 A1
Churchbury La EN EN1 30 A2
Churchbury Rd ELTH/MOT SE9 134 C6
EN EN1 30 A1
Church Cl EDGW HA8 36 E4
HSLW TW3 122 E1
NTHWD HA6 32 D6
TRDG/WHET N20 39 J2
WDR/YW UB7 100 B2
YEAD UB4 82 B4
Church Crs FNCH N3 38 D7
HOM E9 75 F6
MUSWH N10 54 B3
TRDG/WHET N20 39 J2
Churchcroft Cl BAL * SW12 129 F6
Churchdown BMLY BR1 152 C3
Church Dr CDALE/KGS NW9 51 F7
RYLN/HDSTN HA2 48 A5
WWKM BR4 180 C2
Church Elm La DAGE RM10 80 C5
Church End HDN NW4 51 K2
WALTH * E17 57 K3
Church Farm EBAR * EN4 27 K6
Church Farm La CHEAM SM3 174 C5
Churchfield Av
NFNCH/WDSP N12 39 G5
Churchfield Cl HYS/HAR UB3 82 D6
RYLN/HDSTN HA2 48 C3
Churchfield Rd ACT W3 86 E7
HNWL W7 103 K1
WEA W13 85 H7
WELL DA16 136 B2
Churchfields E/WMO/HCT KT8 157 F2
GNWCH SE10 113 F5
SWFD E18 44 E7
Churchfields Av FELT TW13 141 K2
Churchfields Rd BECK BR3 166 A1
Churchfield Wy
NFNCH/WDSP N12 39 G5
Church Gdns ALP/SUD HA0 67 G3
EA W5 104 E1
Church Garth ARCH * N19 72 D1
Church Ga FUL/PGN SW6 127 H2
Church Gn BRXN/ST * SW9 130 B1
HYS/HAR UB3 82 D5
Church Gv KUT KT1 143 J7
LEW SE13 132 E3
Church Hl CAR SM5 175 K4
DART DA1 138 B3
HRW HA1 48 E7
WALTH E17 57 J3
WCHMH N21 29 F6
WIM/MER SW19 146 D4
WOOL/PLUM SE18 114 E2
Church Hill Rd CHEAM SM3 174 B3
EBAR EN4 27 J5
SURB KT6 159 F4
WALTH E17 57 K3
Church Hollow PUR RM19 119 K4
Church Hyde
WOOL/PLUM SE18 115 K5
Churchill Av KTN/HRWW/W HA3 49 H5
Churchill Cl EBED/NFELT TW14 121 J7
Churchill Gdns ACT W3 86 C5
PIM SW1V 16 E8
Churchill Gardens Rd PIM SW1V 16 D8
Churchill Pl POP/IOD E14 93 K7
Churchill Rd CAN/RD E16 95 G5
CRICK NW2 69 K5
EDGW HA8 36 B5
KTTN NW5 72 B3
SAND/SEL CR2 177 J7
Churchill Ter CHING E4 43 J3
Churchill Wk HOM E9 74 E4
Churchill Wy BMLY BR1 167 K1
SUN TW16 140 E4
Church La CDALE/KGS NW9 50 E7
CEND/HSY/T N8 55 F3
CHSGTN KT9 172 B5
CHST BR7 154 C7
DAGE RM10 80 D5
ED * N9 42 C1
EFNCH N2 53 H2
ENC/FH EN2 29 K2
HAYES BR2 168 D7
KTN/HRWW/W HA3 35 F7
PIN HA5 47 J2
PUR RM19 119 K4
ROM RM1 63 G3
TEDD TW11 143 F4
THDIT KT7 158 A5
TOOT SW17 148 A4
TOTM N17 42 A7
TWK TW1 124 B7
WALTH E17 57 K3
WAN E11 58 C7
WEA W13 104 D1
WIM/MER SW19 161 K1
WLGTN SM6 176 D2
Churchley Rd SYD SE26 150 D3
Church Manor Wy ABYW SE2 116 B3
Church Manorway ERITH DA8 118 D3
Church Md CMBW * SE5 110 D6
Churchmead Cl EBAR EN4 27 J5
Church Meadow SURB KT6 171 J1
Churchmead Rd WLSDN NW10 69 J5
Churchmore Rd
STRHM/NOR SW16 148 C7
Church Mt EFNCH N2 53 H4
Church Paddock Ct
WLGTN SM6 176 D2
Church Pas BAR * EN5 26 D2
Church Pth CHSWK W4 105 K2
CROY/NA CR0 177 J1
MTCM CR4 162 D2
NFNCH/WDSP * N12 39 G4
WAN E11 58 E4
WIM/MER SW19 161 J1
Church Pl EA W5 104 E1
MTCM CR4 162 D2
Church Ri CHSGTN KT9 172 B5
FSTH SE23 132 A7
Church Rd ACT W3 105 K1
BARK IG11 78 C5
BARN SW13 126 D1
BXLYHN DA7 137 G1
CHEAM SM3 174 C5
CROY/NA CR0 177 J2
E/WMO/HCT KT8 157 J2
EFNCH N2 39 H7
ERITH DA8 117 K4
ESH/CLAY KT10 171 F5
FELT TW13 141 G4
GNTH/NBYPK IG2 60 E5
HAYES BR2 167 H2
HAYES BR2 167 K1
HAYES BR2 181 H6
HDN NW4 51 K3
HEST TW5 102 A4
HEST TW5 103 F6
HNWL W7 84 E6
HOR/WEW KT19 173 F6
HYS/HAR UB3 82 D7
IS N1 73 J5
ISLW TW7 103 J7
KUT KT1 159 G1
LEY E10 57 J7
MNPK E12 77 K4
MTCM CR4 162 C1
NRWD SE19 150 A6
NTHLT UB5 65 K6
NTHLT UB5 83 H1
NTHWD HA6 32 D6
NWDGN UB2 102 E2
PEND EN3 30 E5
RCHPK/HAM TW10 125 F4
RCHPK/HAM TW10 144 A3
SCUP DA14 155 G3
STAN HA7 35 H4
SURB KT6 158 D7
TEDD TW11 142 E3
TOTM N17 42 A7
WALTH E17 57 G1
WDR/YW UB7 100 A1
WELL DA16 136 C1
WIM/MER SW19 146 C3
WLGTN SM6 176 C2
WLSDN NW10 69 G6
WPK KT4 160 B7
Church Rd South EFNCH N2 53 H1
Church Rw CHST BR7 154 C7
FUL/PGN * SW6 108 A6
HAMP NW3 71 G3
WAND/EARL * SW18 127 K4
Church Row Ms CHST BR7 154 C6
Church St BAY/PAD W2 9 H2
CHSWK W4 106 B5
CROY/NA CR0 177 H2
DAGE RM10 80 D6
ED N9 29 J7
ENC/FH EN2 29 J2
ESH/CLAY KT10 170 B3
EW KT17 173 J7
HPTN TW12 142 C7
HSLW TW3 123 H4
ISLW TW7 124 C2
KUT KT1 158 E1
SRTFD E15 76 C7
TWK TW1 124 B7
WATW * WD18 21 G3
Church Street Est STJWD NW8 9 H1
Church St North SRTFD E15 76 C7
Church Ter FUL/PGN * SW6 128 A1
HDN NW4 51 K2
LEW SE13 133 H2
RCHPK/HAM TW10 124 E4
Church V EFNCH N2 53 K2
FSTH SE23 150 E1
Churchview Rd WHTN TW2 123 J7
Church Wk BTFD TW8 104 D5
BUSH WD23 22 A5
CDALE/KGS NW9 69 F1
CRICK NW2 70 D2
HYS/HAR UB3 82 C5
RYNPK SW20 161 F2
STNW/STAM N16 73 K4
STNW/STAM N16 73 K2
STRHM/NOR SW16 163 H1
THDIT KT7 158 A5
Churchway CAMTN NW1 5 H8
Church Wy TRDG/WHET N20 39 J2
Churchyard Rw LBTH SE11 18 D5
Churston Av PLSTW E13 77 F7
Churston Cl
BRXS/STRHM * SW2 130 C7
Churston Dr MRDN SM4 161 G4
Churston Gdns FBAR/BDGN N11 40 C5
Churton Pl CHSWK * W4 105 J5
PIM SW1V 16 F6
Churton St PIM SW1V 16 F6
Chyngton Cl BFN/LL DA15 155 F2
Cibber Rd FSTH SE23 151 F1
Cicada Rd WAND/EARL SW18 128 B5
Cicely Rd PECK SE15 111 H7
Cinderford Wy BMLY BR1 152 C3
Cinema Pde EDGW * HA8 36 C5
Cinnamon Cl CROY/NA * CR0 163 K6
Cinnamon St WAP E1W 92 D7
Cintra Pk NRWD SE19 150 B6
The Circle CRICK NW2 69 G2
MLHL NW7 37 F5
Circle Gdns WIM/MER SW19 161 K2
Circle Rd EFNCH N2 53 H1
The Circuits PIN HA5 47 G3
Circular Rd TOTM N17 56 B2
Circular Wy
WOOL/PLUM SE18 114 E5
Circus Ms MBLAR * W1H 9 L2
Circus Pl LVPST * EC2M 13 H3
Circus Rd STJWD NW8 3 G7
Circus St GNWCH SE10 113 F6
Cirencester St BAY/PAD W2 8 C2
Cissbury Ring North
NFNCH/WDSP N12 38 D4
Cissbury Ring South
NFNCH/WDSP N12 38 D4
Cissbury Rd SEVS/STOTM N15 55 K4
Citadel Pl LBTH SE11 17 L7
Citizen Rd HOLWY N7 73 G2
Citron Ter PECK * SE15 131 J2
City Barracks SHB * W12 88 A7
City Gdn EDGW HA8 36 C5
City Garden Rw IS N1 6 D6
City Rd FSBYE EC1V 6 C6
STLK EC1Y 13 H1
Civic Wy BARK/HLT IG6 60 C3
RSLP HA4 65 H4
Clabon Ms KTBR SW1X 15 L4
Clack St BERM/RHTH SE16 111 K1
Clacton Rd TOTM * N17 56 B1
WALTH E17 57 G5
Claire Ct NFNCH/WDSP N12 39 G2
Claire Gdns STAN HA7 35 J4
Claire Pl POP/IOD E14 112 D2
Clairvale Rd HEST TW5 102 C7
Clairview Rd TOOT SW17 148 B4
Clairville Gdns HNWL W7 84 E7
Clamp Hl KTN/HRWW/W HA3 34 D3
Clancarty Rd FUL/PGN SW6 127 K1
Clandon Cl ACT W3 105 J1
EW KT17 173 H5
Clandon Gdns FNCH N3 52 E2
Clandon Rd GDMY/SEVK IG3 78 E1
Clandon St DEPT SE8 132 D1
Clandon Ter RYNPK * SW20 161 G1
Clanricarde Gdns BAY/PAD W2 8 B7
Clapgate Rd BUSH WD23 22 B5
Clapham Common North Side
CLAP SW4 129 G3
Clapham Common South Side
CLAP SW4 129 G5
Clapham Common West Side
CLAP SW4 128 E3
Clapham Court Ter
BRXS/STRHM * SW2 129 K4
Clapham Crs CLAP SW4 129 J3
Clapham High St CLAP SW4 129 J3
Clapham Manor St CLAP SW4 129 H2
Clapham Park Est CLAP * SW4 129 J6
Clapham Park Rd CLAP SW4 129 H3
Clapham Park Ter
BRXS/STRHM * SW2 129 K4
Clapham Rd BRXN/ST SW9 129 K1
Clapham Rd South IS N1 73 K5
Claps Gate La EHAM E6 96 B3
Clapton Common
STNW/STAM N16 56 C6
Clapton Sq CLPT E5 74 E4
Clapton Ter STNW/STAM N16 56 C6
Clapton Wy CLPT E5 74 C3
Clara Pl WOOL/PLUM SE18 115 F3
Clare Cl BORE WD6 24 B5
EFNCH N2 53 G2
Clare Cnr ELTH/MOT SE9 135 G6
Clare Ct NTHWD HA6 32 C4
Claredale St BETH E2 92 C1
Clare Gdns BARK IG11 79 F5
FSTGT E7 76 E3
NTGHL * W11 88 C5
Clare Hl ESH/CLAY KT10 170 B4
Clare Hl (No 2) ESH/CLAY KT10 170 B4
Clare La IS N1 6 F2
Clare Lawn Av
MORT/ESHN SW14 126 A4
Clare Ms FUL/PGN SW6 108 A6
Claremont Av
KTN/HRWW/W HA3 50 A4
NWMAL KT3 160 E4
SUN TW16 141 F7
Claremont Cl
BRXS/STRHM SW2 130 A7
CAN/RD E16 96 A7
IS N1 6 B6
Claremont Crs DART DA1 138 B3
RKW/CH/CXG WD3 20 A4
Claremont Dr ESH/CLAY KT10 170 B6
Claremont End ESH/CLAY KT10 170 B5
Claremont Gdns
GDMY/SEVK IG3 78 E1
SURB KT6 159 F3
Claremont Gv CHSWK W4 106 B6
WFD IG8 45 G5
Claremont House WATW * WD18 20 B5
Claremont La ESH/CLAY KT10 170 B4
Claremont Pk FNCH N3 38 C7
Claremont Park Rd
ESH/CLAY KT10 170 B5
Claremont Rd BMLY BR1 168 D3
CRICK NW2 52 A6
CROY/NA CR0 165 H7
ESH/CLAY KT10 170 E6
FSTGT E7 77 F4
HGT N6 54 B6
KIL/WHAMP NW6 88 C1
KTN/HRWW/W HA3 48 E1
ROM RM1 63 J5
SURB KT6 159 F4
TEDD TW11 143 F4
TWK TW1 124 C6
WALTH E17 57 G1
WAN E11 76 B2
WEA W13 85 G4
Claremont Sq IS N1 6 A6
Claremont St GNWCH SE10 112 E5
UED N18 42 C5
Claremont Ter THDIT * KT7 158 C6
Claremont Vls CMBW * SE5 110 E6
KUT * KT1 159 G1
Claremont Wy CRICK NW2 52 A7
Clarence Av CLAP SW4 129 J6
HAYES BR2 168 D3
IL IG1 59 K5
NWMAL KT3 159 K1
Clarence Cl BUSH WD23 23 F6
EBAR EN4 27 H4
Clarence Ct MLHL * NW7 37 H4
Clarence Crs CLAP SW4 129 J5
SCUP DA14 155 H2
Clarence Gdns CAMTN NW1 4 D8
Clarence Ga CAMTN NW1 3 M9
Clarence La PUT/ROE SW15 126 C5
Clarence Ms CLPT E5 74 D4
Clarence Pas CAMTN * NW1 5 J6
Clarence Pl CLPT E5 74 D4
Clarence Rd BMLY BR1 168 D2
BXLYHS DA6 137 F3
CAN/RD E16 94 C3
CHSWK W4 105 H4
CLPT E5 74 D3
CROY/NA CR0 164 E6
DEPT SE8 112 E5
ELTH/MOT SE9 153 J1
FSTGT E7 77 G3
KIL/WHAMP NW6 70 D6
PEND EN3 30 E4
RCH/KEW TW9 105 G7
SCUP DA14 155 H2
SEVS/STOTM N15 55 J4
SUT SM1 175 F3
TEDD TW11 143 F5
WALTH E17 57 F1
WDGN N22 40 E6
WIM/MER SW19 147 F5
WLGTN SM6 176 B4
Clarence St KUT KT1 158 E1
NWDGN UB2 102 C2
RCH/KEW TW9 125 F3
Clarence Ter CAMTN NW1 3 M9
HSLW TW3 123 G3
Clarence Vls KUT * KT1 159 G1
Clarence Wk CLAP SW4 129 K1
Clarence Wy CAMTN NW1 4 C1
Clarendon Cl BAY/PAD * W2 9 J6
HOM E9 74 E6
Clarendon Crs WHTN TW2 142 D2
Clarendon Cross NTGHL W11 88 C6
Clarendon Dr PUT/ROE SW15 127 F3
Clarendon Gdns HDN NW4 51 J2
IL IG1 59 K7
MV/WKIL W9 8 F1
WBLY HA9 67 K2
Clarendon Ga BAY/PAD W2 9 J6
Clarendon Gv MTCM CR4 162 E2
Clarendon Ms BAY/PAD W2 9 J6
BORE * WD6 24 C2
Clarendon Pl BAY/PAD W2 9 J6
Clarendon Ri LEW SE13 133 F2
Clarendon Rd BORE WD6 24 C2
CEND/HSY/T N8 55 F2
CROY/NA CR0 177 H1
EA W5 86 A2
HRW HA1 48 E5
HYS/HAR UB3 101 J1
NTGHL W11 88 C6
SEVS/STOTM N15 55 H3
SWFD E18 58 E2
UED N18 42 C5
WALTH E17 57 K5
WAN E11 58 B7
WAT WD17 21 F2
WIM/MER SW19 147 J6
WLGTN SM6 176 C4
Clarendon St PIM SW1V 16 D7
Clarendon Ter MV/WKIL W9 2 F9
Clarendon Wy WCHMH N21 29 J6
Clarens St CAT SE6 151 H1
Clare Pde GFD/PVL * UB6 66 D5
Clare Rd GFD/PVL UB6 66 D5
HSLWW TW4 122 E2
NWCR SE14 132 C1
STWL/WRAY TW19 120 A7
WAN E11 58 B5
WLSDN NW10 69 J6
Clare St BETH E2 92 D1
Claret Gdns SNWD SE25 165 F3
Clareville Gv SKENS SW7 14 F6
Clareville St SKENS SW7 14 F6
Clare Wy BXLYHN DA7 117 F7
Clarges Ms MYFR/PICC W1J 10 C8
Clarges St MYFR/PICC W1J 10 D8
Claribel Rd BRXN/ST SW9 130 C1
Clarice Wy WLGTN SM6 176 E7
Claridge Rd BCTR RM8 61 K7
Clarissa Rd CHDH RM6 61 K5
Clarissa St HACK E8 7 L3
Clark Cl ERITH DA8 118 D7
Clarke Ms ED N9 42 D2
Clarkes Av WPK KT4 161 G7
Clarkes Ms CAVSQ/HST W1G 10 B2
Clarks Md BUSH WD23 22 C6
Clarkson Rd CAN/RD E16 94 D5
Clarkson Rw CAMTN NW1 4 D6
Clarkson St BETH * E2 92 D2
Clark's Rd IL IG1 78 D1
Clark St WCHPL E1 92 E5
Clark Wy HEST TW5 102 C6
Classon Cl WDR/YW UB7 100 B1
Claston Cl DART DA1 138 B3
Claude Rd LEY E10 58 A7
PECK SE15 131 J1
PLSTW E13 77 F7
Claude St POP/IOD E14 112 D3
Claudia Pl WIM/MER SW19 127 H7
Claughton Rd PLSTW E13 95 G1
Clauson Av NTHLT UB5 66 B4
Clavell St GNWCH SE10 113 F5
Claverdale Rd
BRXS/STRHM SW2 130 A6
Clavering Av BARN SW13 106 E5
Clavering Cl TWK TW1 143 G3
Clavering Rd MNPK E12 59 H7
Claverley Gv FNCH N3 38 F7
Claverley Vls FNCH N3 39 F6
Claverton St PIM SW1V 16 F8
Clave St WAP E1W 92 E7
Claxton Gv HMSMTH W6 107 G4
Clay Av MTCM CR4 163 G1
Claybank Gv LEW SE13 132 E2
Claybridge Rd LEE/GVPK SE12 153 G3
Claybrook Cl EFNCH N2 53 H2
Claybrook Rd HMSMTH W6 107 G5
Claybury BUSH WD23 22 B6
Claybury Rd WFD IG8 45 J6
Claydon Dr CROY/NA CR0 176 E3
Claydown Ms
WOOL/PLUM SE18 115 F4
Clayfarm Rd ELTH/MOT SE9 154 C1
Claygate Cl HCH RM12 81 J3
Claygate Crs CROY/NA CR0 180 A5
Claygate La ESH/CLAY KT10 171 G1
THDIT KT7 158 B7
Claygate Lodge Cl
ESH/CLAY KT10 170 E6
Claygate Rd WEA W13 104 C2
Clayhall Av CLAY IG5 59 K1
Clayhill Crs ELTH/MOT SE9 153 H3
Claylands Pl BRXN/ST SW9 110 B6
Claylands Rd VX/NE SW8 110 A5
Clay La BUSH WD23 22 E6
Claymore Cl MRDN SM4 161 K6
Claypole Dr HEST TW5 102 D7
Claypole Rd SRTFD * E15 94 A1
Clayponds Av BTFD TW8 105 F3
Clayponds Gdns EA W5 104 E3
Clayponds La BTFD TW8 105 F4
Clays La SRTFD E15 75 K4
Clays Lane Cl SRTFD E15 75 K4
Clay St MHST W1U 9 M3
Clayton Av ALP/SUD HA0 68 A6
Clayton Cl EHAM E6 95 K5
Clayton Crs BTFD TW8 104 E4
Clayton Dr DEPT SE8 112 B4
Clayton Fld CDALE/KGS NW9 37 G7
Clayton Ms GNWCH SE10 113 G7
Clayton Rd CHSGTN KT9 171 J3
HYS/HAR UB3 101 H1
ISLW TW7 123 K2
PECK SE15 111 H7
ROMW/RG RM7 62 E7

Clayton St LBTH SE11 18 A9
Clayton Ter YEAD * UB4 83 H4
Claytonville Ter BELV * DA17 117 K1
Clay Wood Cl ORP BR6 169 K6
Clayworth Cl BFN/LL DA15 136 C5
Cleanthus Cl WOOL/PLUM SE18 115 G7
Cleanthus Rd
WOOL/PLUM SE18 115 G7
Clearbrook Wy WCHPL E1 92 E5
Clearwater Pl SURB KT6 158 D5
Clearwater Ter NTGHL W11 107 G1
Clearwell Dr MV/WKIL W9 8 C1
Cleave Av HYS/HAR UB3 101 H3
Cleaveland Rd SURB KT6 158 E4
Cleaverholme Cl SNWD SE25 165 J5
Cleaver Sq LBTH SE11 18 B8
Cleeve Hl FSTH SE23 131 J7
Cleeve Park Gdns SCUP DA14 155 H1
Clegg St PLSTW E13 94 E1
WAP E1W 92 D7
Clematis Cottages SHB * W12 87 J6
Clematis Gdns WFD IG8 44 E4
Clematis St SHB W12 87 H6
Clem Attlee Ct FUL/PGN * SW6 107 J5
Clem Attlee Pde
FUL/PGN * SW6 107 J5
Clemence Rd DAGE RM10 80 E7
Clemence St POP/IOD E14 93 H4
Clement Av CLAP SW4 129 J3
Clement Cl CHSWK W4 106 A3
KIL/WHAMP NW6 70 A6
Clement Gdns HYS/HAR UB3 101 H3
Clementhorpe Rd DAGW RM9 79 J5
Clementina Rd LEY E10 57 H7
Clementine Cl WEA W13 104 C1
Clement Rd BECK BR3 166 A1
WIM/MER SW19 146 C4
Clements Av CAN/RD E16 94 E6
Clements Inn LINN WC2A 11 M5
Clements La IL IG1 78 B2
MANHO EC4N 13 H6
Clements Pl BTFD TW8 104 E4
Clement's Rd
BERM/RHTH SE16 111 H2
EHAM E6 77 K6
IL IG1 78 B2
Clendon Wy WOOL/PLUM SE18 115 J3
Clennam St STHWK * SE1 18 F1
Clensham La SUT SM1 174 E1
Clenston Ms MBLAR W1H 9 L4
Clephane Rd IS N1 73 J5
Clere Pl SDTCH EC2A 7 H9
Clere St SDTCH EC2A 7 H9
Clerkenwell Cl CLKNW EC1R 6 B9
Clerkenwell Gn CLKNW EC1R 12 C1
Clerkenwell Rd CLKNW EC1R 12 A1
Clermont Rd HOM E9 74 E7
Clevedon Gdns HEST TW5 122 A1
HYS/HAR UB3 101 G2
Clevedon Rd KUT KT1 159 H1
PGE/AN SE20 151 F7
TWK TW1 124 E5
Cleveland Av CHSWK W4 106 C3
HPTN TW12 141 K6
Cleveland Crs BORE WD6 24 E4
Cleveland Gdns BARN SW13 126 C1
BAY/PAD W2 8 E5
CRICK NW2 70 B1
FSBYPK N4 55 J6
WPK KT4 173 G1
Cleveland Gv WCHPL E1 92 E3
Cleveland Ms FITZ W1T 10 E2
Cleveland Park Av WALTH E17 57 J3
Cleveland Park Crs WALTH E17 57 J3
Cleveland Pl STJS SW1Y 10 F8
Cleveland Ri MRDN SM4 161 G6
Cleveland Rd BARN SW13 126 C1
CHSWK W4 105 K2
ED * N9 30 D6
IL IG1 78 B2
IS N1 7 H2
ISLW TW7 124 B3
NWMAL KT3 160 B3
SWFD E18 58 E2
WEA W13 85 G4
WELL DA16 136 A1
WPK KT4 173 G1
Cleveland Rw WHALL SW1A 10 F9
Cleveland Sq BAY/PAD W2 8 E5
Cleveland St CAMTN NW1 10 D1
Cleveland Ter BAY/PAD W2 8 E5
Cleveland Wy WCHPL E1 92 E3
Cleveley Crs EA W5 86 A1
Cleveleys Rd CLPT E5 74 D2
Clevely Cl CHARL SE7 114 C3
Cleverly Est SHB * W12 87 J7
Cleve Rd KIL/WHAMP NW6 2 B1
SCUP DA14 155 K2
Cleves Av EW KT17 173 K7
Cleves Rd EHAM E6 77 H7
RCHPK/HAM TW10 143 J2
Cleves Wy HPTN TW12 141 K6
RSLP HA4 47 H7
SUN TW16 140 D5
Clewer Crs KTN/HRWW/W HA3 34 D7
Clifden Rd BTFD TW8 104 E5
CLPT E5 74 E4
TWK TW1 124 A7
Cliffe Rd SAND/SEL CR2 177 K4
Clifford Av CHST BR7 153 K5
RCH/KEW TW9 125 J2
WLGTN SM6 176 C3
Clifford Cl NTHLT UB5 65 J7
PLSTW * E13 95 F2
Clifford Dr BRXN/ST SW9 130 C3
Clifford Gdns HYS/HAR UB3 101 G3
WLSDN NW10 88 A1
Clifford Rd ALP/SUD HA0 67 K7
BAR EN5 27 F2
CAN/RD E16 94 D3
ED N9 30 E5
HSLWW TW4 122 C2
RCHPK/HAM TW10 143 K1
SNWD SE25 165 H3
WALTH E17 58 A1
Clifford St CONDST W1S 10 E7
Clifford Wy WLSDN NW10 69 H3
Cliff Rd HOLWY N7 72 D5
Cliff Ter DEPT SE8 132 D1
Cliffview Rd LEW SE13 132 D2
Cliff Vls HOLWY N7 72 D5
Cliff Wk CAN/RD E16 94 D4
Clifton Av FELT TW13 141 G2
FNCH N3 38 D7
KTN/HRWW/W HA3 49 H1
SHB W12 106 C1
WALTH E17 57 F3
WBLY HA9 68 B5
Clifton Ct BECK * BR3 151 K7
Clifton Crs PECK SE15 111 J6
Clifton Gdns CHSWK W4 106 A3
ENC/FH EN2 28 E3
GLDGN NW11 52 D6
MV/WKIL W9 8 E1
SEVS/STOTM N15 56 B5
Clifton Gv HACK E8 74 C5
Clifton Hl KIL/WHAMP NW6 2 D5
Clifton Ms SNWD SE25 165 F3
Clifton Pde FELT * TW13 141 G3
Clifton Park Av RYNPK SW20 161 F1
Clifton Pl BAY/PAD W2 9 H6
BERM/RHTH SE16 111 K1
KUTN/CMB * KT2 144 C7
Clifton Ri NWCR SE14 112 B6
Clifton Rd CAN/RD E16 94 C4
CEND/HSY/T N8 54 D5
EMPK RM11 63 J5
FNCH N3 39 G7
FSTGT E7 77 H5
GFD/PVL UB6 84 C3
GNTH/NBYPK IG2 60 D5
HTHAIR * TW6 120 E3
ISLW TW7 123 K1
KTN/HRWW/W HA3 50 B4
KUTN/CMB KT2 144 C7
MV/WKIL W9 2 F9
NWDGN UB2 102 D3
SCUP DA14 154 E3
SNWD SE25 165 F3
TEDD TW11 142 E3
WATW WD18 21 F4
WDGN N22 40 C7
WELL DA16 136 D2
WIM/MER SW19 146 B5
WLGTN SM6 176 B4
WLSDN NW10 87 J1
Clifton St SDTCH EC2A 13 J2
Clifton Ter FSBYPK N4 73 G1
Clifton Vls MV/WKIL W9 8 D2
Clifton Wy ALP/SUD HA0 68 A7
PECK SE15 111 K6
Cline Rd FBAR/BDGN N11 40 C5
Clink St STHWK SE1 13 G8
Clinton Av E/WMO/HCT KT8 157 H3
WELL DA16 136 B3
Clinton Rd BOW E3 93 G2
FSTGT E7 76 E3
SEVS/STOTM N15 55 K3
Clinton Ter DEPT * SE8 112 D5
SUT * SM1 175 G3
Clipper Cl BERM/RHTH SE16 112 A1
Clipper Wy LEW SE13 133 F3
Clippesby Cl CHSGTN * KT9 172 B5
Clipstone Ms GTPST W1W 10 E1
Clipstone Rd HSLW TW3 123 F2
Clipstone St GTPST W1W 10 D2
Clissold Crs STNW/STAM N16 73 K3
Clissold Rd STNW/STAM N16 73 K2
Clitheroe Av RYLN/HDSTN HA2 48 A7
Clitheroe Gdns OXHEY WD19 33 H2
Clitheroe Rd BRXN/ST SW9 129 K1
Clitherow Av HNWL W7 104 B2
Clitherow Rd BTFD TW8 104 C4
Clitterhouse Crs CRICK NW2 52 A7
Clitterhouse Rd CRICK NW2 52 A7
Clive Av DART DA1 138 C5
UED N18 42 C5
Clive Ct WLSDN * NW10 69 H6
Cliveden Cl NFNCH/WDSP N12 39 G3
Cliveden Pl BGVA SW1W 16 A5
Cliveden Rd WIM/MER SW19 146 D7
Clivedon Ct WEA W13 85 H4
Clivedon Rd CHING E4 44 C4
Clive Rd BELV DA17 117 H3
DUL SE21 149 K2
EBED/NFELT TW14 121 K5
EN EN1 30 C3
ESH/CLAY KT10 170 B3
GPK RM2 63 K4
TWK TW1 143 F3
WIM/MER SW19 147 J5
Clivesdale Dr HYS/HAR UB3 82 E7
Clive Wy EN EN1 30 C3
Cloak La BLKFR EC4V 12 F6
Clockhouse Av BARK IG11 78 C7
Clockhouse Cl WIM/MER SW19 146 A2
Clock House Pde PLMGR * N13 41 G4
Clockhouse Pl PUT/ROE SW15 127 H4
Clock House Rd BECK BR3 166 B2
Clock Pde EN * EN1 29 K4
Clock Tower Ms IS N1 6 F4
THMD SE28 97 H6
Clock Tower Pl HOLWY * N7 72 E5
Clock Tower Rd ISLW TW7 124 A2
Cloister Cl RAIN RM13 99 K3
TEDD TW11 143 H4
Cloister Gdns EDGW HA8 36 E4
SNWD SE25 165 J5
Cloister Rd ACT W3 86 E4
CRICK NW2 70 D2
Cloisters Av HAYES BR2 168 E4
Clonard Wy PIN HA5 34 A5
Clonbrock Rd STNW/STAM N16 74 A3
Cloncurry St FUL/PGN SW6 127 G1
Clonmel Cl RYLN/HDSTN HA2 48 D7
Clonmell Rd TOTM N17 55 K2
Clonmel Rd FUL/PGN SW6 107 J6
HPTN TW12 142 D3
Clonmore St WAND/EARL SW18 127 J7
Clorane Gdns HAMP NW3 70 E2
The Close ALP/SUD HA0 68 A5
BECK BR3 166 B3
BUSH * WD23 22 A5
BXLY DA5 137 H5
CAR SM5 175 J7
CHDH RM6 62 A5
CHEAM SM3 161 J6
CHING E4 44 A6
EBAR EN4 27 K5
GNTH/NBYPK IG2 60 E5
ISLW TW7 123 J1
MTCM CR4 162 E3
NWMAL KT3 159 K1
PIN HA5 47 G6
PIN HA5 47 K6
RCH/KEW TW9 125 J2
SCUP DA14 155 H4
SNWD * SE25 165 H5
STHGT/OAK N14 40 D1
STMC/STPC BR5 169 K5
SURB KT6 159 F6
TRDG/WHET N20 38 D1
WBLY HA9 68 E2
Closemead Cl NTHWD HA6 32 A5
Cloth Ct STBT EC1A 12 D3
Cloth Fair STBT EC1A 12 D3
Clothier St HDTCH * EC3A 13 K4
Cloth St STBT * EC1A 12 E2
Clothworkers Rd
WOOL/PLUM SE18 115 J6
Cloudesdale Rd TOOT SW17 148 B1
Cloudesley Pl IS N1 6 B4
Cloudesley Rd BXLYHN DA7 117 G7
ERITH DA8 118 C7
IS N1 6 A4
Cloudesley Sq IS N1 6 B3
Cloudesley St IS N1 6 B4
Clouston Cl WLGTN SM6 176 E4
Clova Rd FSTGT E7 76 E5
Clove Crs POP/IOD E14 94 A6
Clovelly Av CDALE/KGS NW9 51 H3
HGDN/ICK UB10 64 A3
Clovelly Cl HGDN/ICK UB10 64 A3
PIN HA5 47 F2
Clovelly Gdns EN EN1 30 A6
Clovelly Rd BXLYHN DA7 117 F5
CEND/HSY/T N8 54 D3
CHSWK * W4 106 A1
HSLW TW3 123 F1
WEA W13 104 D1
Clovelly Wy RYLN/HDSTN HA2 65 K2
WCHPL E1 92 E5
Clover Cl WAN * E11 76 B1
Cloverdale Gdns BFN/LL DA15 136 A5
The Clover Fld BUSH WD23 21 K5
Clover Ms CHEL SW3 15 L9
Clover Wy WLGTN SM6 163 F7
Clove St PLSTW E13 94 E3
Clowders Rd CAT SE6 151 H2
Clowser Cl SUT SM1 175 G4
Cloysters Gn WAP * E1W 92 C7
Cloyster Wd EDGW HA8 35 K6
Club Gardens Rd HAYES BR2 167 K6
Club Rw BETH E2 7 L9
The Clumps FELT TW13 140 B3
Clunbury Av NWDGN UB2 102 E4
Cluny Est STHWK SE1 19 J3
Cluny Ms ECT SW5 14 A6
Cluny Pl STHWK SE1 19 J3
Clutton St POP/IOD E14 93 K4
Clydach Rd EN EN1 30 B3
Clyde Circ SEVS/STOTM N15 56 A3
Clyde Ct CAMTN NW1 5 H5
Clyde Flats FUL/PGN * SW6 107 J6
Clyde Pl LEY E10 57 K6
Clyde Rd CROY/NA CR0 178 B1
SEVS/STOTM N15 56 A3
STWL/WRAY TW19 120 A7
SUT SM1 174 E4
WDGN N22 40 D7
WLGTN SM6 176 C4
Clydesdale PEND EN3 31 F3
Clydesdale Av
KTN/HRWW/W HA3 49 K2
Clydesdale Cl BORE WD6 25 F4
ISLW TW7 124 A2
Clydesdale Gdns
RCHPK/HAM TW10 125 J3
Clydesdale Pth BORE * WD6 25 F4
Clydesdale Rd EMPK RM11 63 H6
NTGHL W11 88 D5
Clyde St DEPT SE8 112 C5
Clyde Ter FSTH SE23 150 E1
Clyde V FSTH SE23 150 E1
Clydon Cl ERITH DA8 118 B5
Clyfford Rd RSLP HA4 64 D3
Clymping Dene
EBED/NFELT TW14 122 A6
Clyston Rd WATW WD18 20 D5
Clyston St VX/NE SW8 129 H1
Coach & Horses Yd
CONDST W1S 10 D6
Coach House La HBRY * N5 73 H3
WIM/MER SW19 146 B3
Coach House Ms FSTH SE23 131 K5
NWCR * SE14 112 A7
Coach House Yd
WAND/EARL * SW18 128 A3
Coalecroft Rd PUT/ROE SW15 127 F3
Coates Av WAND/EARL SW18 128 D5
Coates Hill Rd BMLY BR1 169 F1
Coates Rd BORE WD6 23 K6
Coate St BETH E2 92 C1
Cobbett Rd ELTH/MOT SE9 134 D2
WHTN TW2 123 F7
Cobbetts Av REDBR IG4 59 H4
Cobbett St VX/NE SW8 110 A6
Cobble La IS N1 6 B1
Cobble Ms FSBYPK N4 73 J2
Cobbler's Wk TEDD TW11 142 E6
Cobblestone Pl CROY/NA CR0 164 D7
Cobbold Ms SHB * W12 106 C1
Cobbold Rd SHB W12 106 C1
WAN E11 76 D2
WLSDN NW10 69 H5
Cobb's Rd HSLWW TW4 122 E3
Cobb St WCHPL E1 13 L4
Cob Cl BORE WD6 24 E4
Cobden Ms SYD SE26 150 D4
Cobden Rd SNWD SE25 165 H4
WAN E11 76 C2
Cobham Av NWMAL KT3 160 D4
Cobham Cl BFN/LL DA15 136 C5
BTSEA * SW11 128 D5
EDGW HA8 50 D1
EN EN1 30 C2
HAYES BR2 168 D6
WLGTN SM6 176 E5
Cobham Ms CAMTN NW1 5 G1
Cobham Pl BXLYHS DA6 136 E4
Cobham Rd GDMY/SEVK IG3 78 E1
HEST TW5 102 B6
KUT KT1 159 H1
WALTH E17 44 A7
WDGN N22 55 H2
Cobland Rd LEE/GVPK SE12 153 G3
Coborn Rd BOW E3 93 H2
Coborn St BOW E3 93 H2
Cobourg Rd CMBW SE5 19 L8
Cobourg St CAMTN NW1 4 F8
Coburg Cl WEST SW1P 16 F5
Coburg Crs BRXS/STRHM SW2 130 A7
Coburg Dwellings WCHPL * E1 92 E6
Coburg Gdns CLAY IG5 59 H1
Coburg Rd WDGN N22 55 F1
Cochrane Ms STJWD NW8 3 H6
Cochrane Rd WIM/MER SW19 146 C6
Cochrane St STJWD NW8 3 H6
Cockcrow Hl SURB * KT6 158 E7
Cockerell Rd WALTH E17 57 G6
Cockfosters Pde EBAR * EN4 28 A3
Cockfosters Rd EBAR EN4 28 A3
Cock La STBT EC1A 12 C3
Cocks Crs NWMAL KT3 160 C3
Cockspur Ct STJS SW1Y 11 H8
Cockspur St STJS * SW1Y 11 H8
Code St WCHPL E1 13 M1
Codling Cl WAP E1W 92 C7
Codling Wy ALP/SUD HA0 67 K3
Codrington Hl FSTH SE23 132 B6
Codrington Ms NTGHL W11 88 C5
Cody Cl KTN/HRWW/W HA3 49 K2
WLGTN SM6 176 D6
Cody Rd CAN/RD E16 94 B3
Coe Av SNWD SE25 165 H5
Cofers Cir WBLY HA9 68 D2
Coffey St DEPT SE8 112 D6
Cogan Av WALTH E17 43 G7
Coin St STHWK SE1 12 A8
Coity Rd KTTN NW5 72 A5
Cokers La DUL SE21 130 D7
Coke St WCHPL E1 92 C5
Colbeck Ms ECT SW5 14 D6
Colbeck Rd HRW HA1 48 C6
Colberg Pl STNW/STAM * N16 56 B6
Colborne Wy WPK KT4 174 A2
Colbrook Av HYS/HAR UB3 101 G2
Colbrook Cl HYS/HAR UB3 101 G2
Colburn Av PIN HA5 33 K5
Colburn Wy SUT SM1 175 H2
Colby Rd NRWD SE19 150 A4
Colchester Dr PIN HA5 47 H4
Colchester Rd EDGW HA8 36 E6
NTHWD HA6 46 E1
WALTH E17 57 J5
Colchester St WCHPL E1 13 M4
Coldbath Sq CLKNW * EC1R 6 A9
Coldbath St LEW SE13 112 E7
Cold Blow Crs BXLY DA5 138 A7
Coldblow La NWCR SE14 112 A6
Coldershaw Rd HNWL W7 104 B1
Coldfall Av MUSWH N10 53 K1
Coldharbour POP/IOD E14 94 A7
Coldharbour Crest
ELTH/MOT * SE9 154 A2
Coldharbour La BRXN/ST SW9 130 B3
BUSH WD23 22 B5
HYS/HAR UB3 101 J1
RAIN RM13 99 J7
Coldharbour Pl CMBW SE5 130 D1
Coldharbour Rd CROY/NA CR0 177 G4
Coldharbour Wy CROY/NA CR0 177 G4
Coldstream Gdns
PUT/ROE SW15 127 J5
Colebeck Ms IS N1 73 H5
Colebert Av WCHPL E1 92 E3
Colebrooke Av WEA W13 85 H5
Colebrooke Dr WAN E11 59 F6
Colebrooke Pl IS N1 6 D4
Colebrooke Rw IS N1 6 C6
Colebrook Ri HAYES BR2 167 H1
Colebrook Rd
STRHM/NOR SW16 148 E7
Colebrook St ERITH DA8 118 C5
Colebrook Wy FBAR/BDGN N11 40 B4
Coleby Pth CMBW * SE5 110 E6
Cole Cl THMD SE28 97 H7
Coledale Dr STAN HA7 35 J7
Coleford Rd WAND/EARL SW18 128 B4
Cole Gdns HEST TW5 101 K6
Colegrave Rd SRTFD E15 76 B4
Colegrove Rd PECK SE15 111 G5
Coleherne Ms WBPTN SW10 14 C8
Coleherne Rd WBPTN SW10 14 C8
Colehill Gdns FUL/PGN * SW6 107 H7
Colehill La FUL/PGN SW6 107 H7
Coleman Cl SNWD SE25 165 H1
Coleman Flds IS N1 6 F3
Coleman Rd BELV DA17 117 H2
CMBW SE5 111 F6
Colemans Heath
ELTH/MOT SE9 154 A2
Coleman St LOTH EC2R 13 G4
Colenso Rd CLPT E5 74 E3
GNTH/NBYPK IG2 60 E7
Cole Park Gdns TWK TW1 124 B5
Cole Park Rd TWK TW1 124 B6
Colepits Wood Rd
ELTH/MOT SE9 135 J4
Coleraine Rd BKHTH/KID SE3 113 K5
CEND/HSY/T N8 55 G2
Coleridge Av MNPK E12 77 J5
SUT SM1 175 J3
Coleridge Cl VX/NE SW8 129 G1
Coleridge Gdns KIL/WHAMP NW6 2 E2
Coleridge Rd CEND/HSY/T N8 54 D5
CROY/NA CR0 165 K6
DART DA1 139 K3
FSBYPK N4 73 G1
NFNCH/WDSP N12 39 G4
WALTH E17 57 H3
Coleridge Sq WEA * W13 85 G5
Coleridge Wk GLDGN NW11 52 E3
Coleridge Wy WDR/YW UB7 100 C3
YEAD UB4 82 E5
Cole Rd TWK TW1 124 B5
Colesburg Rd BECK BR3 166 C2
Coles Crs RYLN/HDSTN HA2 66 B1
Coles Gn BUSH WD23 22 C7
Coles Green Rd CRICK NW2 51 J7
Coleshill Rd TEDD TW11 142 E5
Colestown St BTSEA SW11 128 D1
Cole St STHWK SE1 18 F2
Colet Cl PLMGR N13 41 H5
Colet Gdns WKENS W14 107 G4
Coley St FSBYW WC1X 11 M1
Colfe & Hatcliffe Glebe
LEW * SE13 132 E4
Colfe Rd FSTH SE23 132 B7
Colham Mill Rd WDR/YW UB7 100 A1
Colina Ms SEVS/STOTM N15 55 H3
Colina Rd CEND/HSY/T N8 55 H4
Colin Cl CDALE/KGS NW9 51 G3
CROY/NA CR0 179 H2
WWKM BR4 180 D2
Colin Crs CDALE/KGS NW9 51 H4
Colindale Av CDALE/KGS NW9 51 F2
Colindeep Gdns HDN NW4 51 J4
Colindeep La CDALE/KGS NW9 51 H3
Colin Dr CDALE/KGS NW9 51 H4
Colinette Rd PUT/ROE SW15 127 F3
Colin Gdns CDALE/KGS NW9 51 H4
Colin Park Rd CDALE/KGS NW9 51 G2
Colin Rd WLSDN NW10 69 J5
Colinton Rd GDMY/SEVK IG3 79 H1
Coliston Rd WAND/EARL SW18 127 K6
Collamore Av
WAND/EARL SW18 128 D7
Collapit Cl RYLN/HDSTN HA2 48 B5
Collard Pl CAMTN NW1 4 C1
College Ap GNWCH SE10 113 F5
College Av KTN/HRWW/W HA3 34 E7
College Cl KTN/HRWW/W HA3 34 E6
UED N18 42 B4
WHTN TW2 123 J7
College Ct EA * W5 86 A6
College Crs KIL/WHAMP NW6 71 G5
College Cross IS N1 6 B1
College Dr RSLP HA4 46 E6
THDIT KT7 157 K6
College East WCHPL * E1 13 M3
College Gdns CHING E4 31 K6
NWMAL KT3 160 C4
REDBR IG4 59 J4
TOOT SW17 147 J1
UED * N18 42 B4
College Gn NRWD SE19 150 A6
College Gv CAMTN NW1 5 G4
College Hl CANST * EC4R 12 F6
College Hill Rd
KTN/HRWW/W HA3 34 E6
College Ms IS N1 6 B2
WEST SW1P 17 J3
College Pde KIL/WHAMP * NW6 70 C7
College Park Cl LEW SE13 133 G3
College Pl CAMTN NW1 4 F3
WALTH E17 58 C3
WBPTN * SW10 108 B6
College Rd BMLY BR1 152 E7
CROY/NA CR0 177 K1
DUL SE21 131 F6
ENC/FH EN2 29 K1
HRW HA1 48 E5
ISLW TW7 104 A7
KTN/HRWW/W HA3 34 E7
NRWD SE19 150 B4
TOTM N17 42 B5
WALTH E17 58 A4
WBLY HA9 49 K7
WCHMH N21 41 G1
WEA W13 85 H5
WIM/MER SW19 147 H5
WLSDN NW10 88 A1
College St CANST * EC4R 12 F6
College Ter FNCH N3 38 D7
College Vw ELTH/MOT SE9 134 C7
College Wy HYS/HAR UB3 82 E6
NTHWD HA6 32 B5
College Yd KIL/WHAMP * NW6 70 C7
KTTN * NW5 72 B4
Collent St HOM E9 74 E5
Colless Rd SEVS/STOTM N15 56 B4
Collett Rd BERM/RHTH SE16 111 H2
Collier Cl EHAM E6 96 B6
HOR/WEW KT19 172 C5
Collier Dr EDGW HA8 50 C1
Collier St IS N1 5 L6
Colliers Water La THHTH CR7 164 B4
Colliers Wd HAYES BR2 181 H4
Collindale Av BFN/LL DA15 136 B7
CDALE/KGS NW9 51 G2
ERITH DA8 117 J5
Collingbourne Rd SHB W12 87 K7
Collingham Gdns ECT SW5 14 D6
Collingham Pl ECT SW5 14 C6
Collingham Rd ECT SW5 14 D5
Collings Cl WDGN N22 41 F5
Collington St GNWCH * SE10 113 G4
Collingtree Rd SYD SE26 150 E3
Collingwood Av BRYLDS KT5 159 K7
MUSWH N10 54 A2
Collingwood Cl HSLW TW3 123 F6
Colling Wood Cl PGE/AN SE20 150 D7
Collingwood Rd MTCM CR4 162 D1
RAIN RM13 99 H1
SEVS/STOTM N15 56 A3
SUT SM1 174 E3
Collingwood St WCHPL E1 92 D3
Collins Av STAN HA7 50 A1
Collins Dr RSLP HA4 65 G1
Collinson St STHWK SE1 18 E2
Collinson Wk STHWK SE1 18 E2
Collins Rd HBRY N5 73 J3
Collins St BKHTH/KID SE3 133 H1
Collinwood Av PEND EN3 30 E2
Collinwood Gdns
GNTH/NBYPK IG2 59 K4
Coll's Rd PECK SE15 111 K7
Collyer Av CROY/NA CR0 176 E3
Collyer Pl PECK SE15 111 H7
Collyer Rd CROY/NA CR0 176 E3
Colman Pde EN * EN1 30 A2
Colman Rd CAN/RD E16 95 G4
Colmar Cl WCHPL E1 93 F3
Colmer Pl KTN/HRWW/W HA3 34 D6
Colmer Rd STRHM/NOR SW16 148 E6
Colmore Ms PECK SE15 111 J7
Colmore Rd PEND EN3 30 E3
Colnbrook St STHWK SE1 18 C4
Colne Av OXHEY WD19 21 F5
Colne Ct HOR/WEW KT19 172 E3
Colne Ldg BUSH * WD23 21 H3
Colne Rd CLPT E5 75 F3
WCHMH N21 29 K6
WHTN TW2 123 K7
Colne St PLSTW E13 94 E2
Colney Hatch La
FBAR/BDGN N11 39 K5
Colney Rd DART DA1 139 J5
Cologne Rd BTSEA SW11 128 C3
Colombo Rd IL IG1 60 C7
Colombo St STHWK SE1 12 C9
Colomb St GNWCH SE10 113 H4
Colonels Wk ENC/FH EN2 29 H1
Colonial Av HSLW TW3 123 H5
Colonial Dr CHSWK W4 105 K3
Colonial Rd EBED/NFELT TW14 121 H6
The Colonnade DEPT * SE8 112 C3
Colonnade BMSBY WC1N 11 J1
Colosseum Ter CAMTN NW1 4 D9
Colson Rd CROY/NA CR0 177 K1
Colson Wy STRHM/NOR SW16 148 C3
Colsterworth Rd
SEVS/STOTM N15 56 B3
Colston Av CAR SM5 175 J3
Colston Rd FSTGT E7 77 H5
MORT/ESHN SW14 125 K3
Colthurst Crs FSBYPK N4 73 H1
Colthurst Dr ED N9 42 D2
Coltness Crs ABYW SE2 116 C4
Colton Gdns TOTM N17 55 J2
Colton Rd HRW HA1 48 E4
Columbas Dr HAMP * NW3 53 H7
Columbia Av EDGW HA8 36 D7
RSLP HA4 47 F7
WPK KT4 160 C6
Columbia Rd BETH E2 7 M7
PLSTW * E13 94 D3
Columbia Whf PEND * EN3 31 G4
Columbine Av EHAM E6 95 J4
SAND/SEL CR2 177 H6
Columbine Wy LEW * SE13 133 F1
Columbus Gdns NTHWD HA6 32 E7
Colvestone Crs HACK E8 74 B4
Colview Ct ELTH/MOT SE9 134 C7
Colville Est IS N1 7 H4
Colville Gdns NTGHL W11 88 D5
Colville Houses NTGHL * W11 88 D5
Colville Ms NTGHL W11 88 D5
Colville Pl FITZ W1T 10 F3

Colville Rd ACT W3 105 J2
ED N9 30 D7
NTGHL W11 88 D5
WALTH E17 57 G1
WAN E11 76 A2
Colville Sq NTGHL * W11 88 D5
Colville Square Ms NTGHL * W11 88 D5
Colville Ter NTGHL W11 88 D5
Colvin Cl SYD SE26 150 E4
Colvin Gdns CHING E4 44 A2
SWFD E18 59 F3
Colvin Rd EHAM E6 77 J6
THHTH CR7 164 B4
Colwall Gdns WFD IG8 44 E4
Colwell Rd EDUL SE22 131 G4
Colwick Cl HGT N6 54 D6
Colwith Rd HMSMTH W6 107 F5
Colwood Gdns
WIM/MER SW19 147 H6
Colworth Gv WALW SE17 18 F6
Colworth Rd CROY/NA CR0 165 H7
WAN E11 58 C5
Colwyn Av GFD/PVL UB6 85 F1
Colwyn Cl STRHM/NOR SW16 148 C4
Colwyn Crs HSLW TW3 103 H7
Colwyn Gn CDALE/KGS * NW9 51 G5
Colwyn Rd CRICK NW2 69 K2
Colyer Cl ELTH/MOT SE9 154 B1
Colyers Cl ERITH DA8 118 A7
Colyers La ERITH DA8 117 K7
Colyton Cl ALP/SUD HA0 67 J5
WELL DA16 116 E7
Colyton Rd EDUL SE22 131 J4
Colyton Wy UED N18 42 C4
Combe Av BKHTH/KID SE3 113 J6
Combedale Rd GNWCH SE10 113 K4
Combemartin Rd
WAND/EARL SW18 127 H6
Comber Cl CRICK NW2 69 J2
Comber Gv CMBW SE5 110 D6
Combermere Rd BRXN/ST SW9 130 A2
MRDN SM4 162 A5
Combe Rd WATW WD18 20 D5
Comberton Rd CLPT E5 74 D1
Combeside WOOL/PLUM SE18 116 A6
Combes Rd DAGW RM9 80 B6
Combwell Crs ABYW SE2 116 B2
Comely Bank Rd WALTH E17 58 A4
Comeragh Ms WKENS * W14 107 H4
Comeragh Rd WKENS W14 107 H4
Comerford Rd BROCKY SE4 132 B3
Comet Cl MNPK E12 77 H3
PUR RM19 119 K3
Comet Pl DEPT SE8 112 D6
Comet Rd STWL/WRAY TW19 120 A6
Comet St DEPT SE8 112 D6
Commerce Rd BTFD TW8 104 D5
WDGN N22 41 F7
Commerce Wy CROY/NA CR0 177 F2
Commercial Rd UED N18 42 A4
WCHPL E1 13 M4
Commercial St WCHPL E1 13 L1
Commercial Wy PECK SE15 111 G7
WLSDN NW10 86 D1
Commerell Pl GNWCH SE10 113 J4
Commerell St GNWCH SE10 113 H4
Commodore Pde
STRHM/NOR * SW16 149 F6
Commodore St WCHPL E1 93 F4
The Common EA W5 86 A7
NWDGN UB2 102 C3
STAN HA7 35 F1
Commondale PUT/ROE SW15 127 F1
Common La ESH/CLAY KT10 171 G6
Common Rd BARN SW13 126 D2
ESH/CLAY KT10 171 G5
STAN HA7 34 D2
Commonside HAYES BR2 181 G3
Commonside East MTCM CR4 163 F2
Commonwealth Av
HYS/HAR UB3 82 B5
SHB W12 87 K6
Commonwealth Rd TOTM N17 42 C6
Commonwealth Wy ABYW SE2 116 C4
Community Cl HEST TW5 102 A7
Community Rd GFD/PVL UB6 66 C7
SRTFD E15 76 B4
Como Rd FSTH SE23 151 G1
Como St ROMW/RG RM7 63 F4
Compass Hl RCHPK/HAM TW10 124 E5
Compayne Gdns
KIL/WHAMP NW6 2 C1
Compton Av ALP/SUD HA0 67 H3
EHAM E6 95 H1
GPK RM2 63 K2
HGT N6 53 J6
IS N1 73 H5
Compton Cl CAMTN NW1 4 D8
CRICK NW2 70 B2
EDGW HA8 36 E6
ESH/CLAY KT10 170 D5
WEA W13 85 G5
Compton Crs CHSGTN KT9 172 A5
CHSWK W4 105 K5
NTHLT UB5 65 H7
TOTM N17 41 J6
Compton Pas FSBYE EC1V 6 D9
Compton Pl ERITH DA8 118 C5
OXHEY WD19 33 J3
STPAN WC1H 5 J9
Compton Ri PIN HA5 47 J4
Compton Rd CROY/NA CR0 165 J7
HYS/HAR UB3 82 C6
IS N1 73 H5
WCHMH N21 29 H7
WIM/MER SW19 146 D5
WLSDN NW10 88 B2
Compton St FSBYE EC1V 6 C9
Compton Ter IS N1 73 H5
WCHMH * N21 29 G7
Comus Pl WALW SE17 19 J6
The Comyns BUSH WD23 22 C7
Comyn Rd BTSEA SW11 128 D3
Comyns Cl CAN/RD E16 94 D4
Comyns Rd DAGW RM9 80 C6
Conant Ms WCHPL E1 92 C6
Concanon Rd
BRXS/STRHM SW2 130 A3
Concert Hall Ap STHWK SE1 11 M9
Concord Cl NTHLT UB5 83 H2
Concorde Cl HSLW TW3 123 G1
Concorde Dr EHAM E6 95 K4
Concord Rd ACT W3 86 D3
PEND EN3 30 E4
Condell Rd VX/NE SW8 109 H7
Conder St POP/IOD E14 93 G5
Condover Crs
WOOL/PLUM SE18 115 G6
Condray Pl BTSEA SW11 108 D6
Conduit Ct COVGDN * WC2E 11 J6
Conduit La SAND/SEL CR2 178 C4
UED N18 42 E4
Conduit Ms BAY/PAD W2 9 G5
Conduit Pas BAY/PAD W2 9 G5
Conduit Pl BAY/PAD W2 9 G5
Conduit Rd WOOL/PLUM SE18 115 G4
Conduit St CONDST W1S 10 D6
Conduit Wy WLSDN NW10 68 E6
Conewood St HBRY N5 73 H2
Coney Acre DUL SE21 130 D7
Coney Burrows CHING E4 44 C1
Coney Hall Pde WWKM * BR4 180 C2
Coney Hill Rd WWKM BR4 180 C1
Coney Wy VX/NE SW8 110 A5
Conference Cl CHING E4 44 A1
Conference Rd ABYW SE2 116 D3
Congleton Gv
WOOL/PLUM SE18 115 H4
Congo Rd WOOL/PLUM SE18 115 J4
Congress Rd ABYW SE2 116 D3
Congreve Rd ELTH/MOT SE9 134 E2
Congreve St WALW SE17 19 J6
Conical Cnr ENC/FH EN2 29 J1
Conifer Gdns EN EN1 29 K5
STRHM/NOR SW16 149 F2
SUT SM1 175 F1
Conifers Cl TEDD TW11 143 H6
Conifer Wy ALP/SUD HA0 67 J2
HYS/HAR UB3 82 E6
Coniger Rd FUL/PGN SW6 127 K1
Coningham Ms SHB W12 87 J7
Coningham Rd SHB W12 106 E1
Coningsby Cottages EA W5 104 E1
Coningsby Gdns CHING E4 43 K5
Coningsby Rd EA W5 104 D1
FSBYPK N4 55 H6
SAND/SEL CR2 177 J7
Conington Rd LEW SE13 132 E1
Conisbee Ct STHGT/OAK N14 28 C4
Conisborough Crs CAT SE6 152 A2
Coniscliffe Cl CHST BR7 154 A7
Coniscliffe Rd PLMGR N13 41 J2
Coniston Av BARK IG11 78 E6
GFD/PVL UB6 85 H2
WELL DA16 135 K2
Coniston Cl BARN SW13 106 C6
BXLYHN DA7 117 K7
CHSWK W4 105 K7
DART DA1 138 E7
ERITH DA8 118 B6
MRDN SM4 161 G5
Coniston Ct BAY/PAD * W2 9 K5
Conistone Wy HOLWY N7 5 K1
Coniston Gdns BELMT * SM2 175 H5
CDALE/KGS NW9 51 F4
ED N9 30 E7
PIN HA5 46 E3
REDBR IG4 59 J3
WBLY HA9 49 J7
Coniston Rd BMLY BR1 152 C5
BXLYHN DA7 117 K7
CROY/NA CR0 165 H6
MUSWH N10 54 B1
TOTM N17 42 C5
WHTN TW2 123 G5
Coniston Wy CHSGTN KT9 172 A2
HCH RM12 81 J4
Conlan St NKENS W10 88 C3
Conley Rd WLSDN NW10 69 G5
Conley St GNWCH * SE10 113 H4
Connaught Av EBAR EN4 27 K7
EN EN1 30 A1
HSLWW TW4 122 D4
MORT/ESHN SW14 125 K2
Connaught Br CAN/RD E16 95 H7
Connaught Cl BAY/PAD W2 9 J5
EN EN1 30 A1
LEY * E10 75 G1
SUT SM1 175 H1
UX/CGN * UB8 82 A4
Connaught Dr GLDGN NW11 52 E3
Connaught Gdns MRDN SM4 162 B4
MUSWH N10 54 B4
PLMGR N13 41 H3
Connaught La IL IG1 78 C1
Connaught Ms FUL/PGN * SW6 107 H7
HAMP * NW3 71 J4
WOOL/PLUM SE18 115 F4
Connaught Pl BAY/PAD W2 9 L6
Connaught Rd BAR EN5 26 B5
CAN/RD E16 95 H6
FSBYPK N4 55 G6
HPTN TW12 142 D4
IL IG1 78 D1
KTN/HRWW/W HA3 35 F7
NWMAL KT3 160 B3
RCHPK/HAM * TW10 125 G4
SUT SM1 175 H1
WALTH * E17 57 J4
WAN E11 58 B7
WEA W13 85 H6
WLSDN * NW10 69 G7
WOOL/PLUM SE18 115 F4
Connaught Sq BAY/PAD W2 9 K5
Connaught St BAY/PAD W2 9 K5
Connaught Wy PLMGR N13 41 H3
Connell Crs EA W5 86 B3
Connemara Cl BORE * WD6 24 E5
Connington Crs CHING E4 44 B2
Connor Rd DAGW RM9 80 B3
Connor St HOM * E9 75 F7
Conolly Rd HNWL W7 84 E7
Conrad Dr WPK KT4 161 F7
Consfield Av NWMAL KT3 160 D3
Consort Cl FBAR/BDGN N11 39 K4
Consort Ms ISLW TW7 123 J5
Consort Rd PECK SE15 131 J1
Cons St STHWK * SE1 18 B1
Constable Av CAN/RD E16 95 F7
Constable Cl GLDGN NW11 53 F5
YEAD UB4 82 A1
Constable Crs SEVS/STOTM N15 56 C4
Constable Gdns EDGW HA8 36 C7
ISLW TW7 123 J4
Constable Ms BCTR RM8 79 H4
Constable Wk DUL SE21 150 A2
Constance Crs HAYES BR2 167 J7
Constance Rd CROY/NA CR0 164 C6
EN EN1 30 A5
SUT SM1 175 G3
WHTN TW2 123 G6
Constance St CAN/RD E16 95 J7
Constantine Rd HAMP NW3 71 J4
Constitution Hl WHALL SW1A 16 C1
Constitution Ri
WOOL/PLUM SE18 115 F7
Content St WALW SE17 18 F6
Control Tower Rd HTHAIR TW6 120 D2
Convent Cl BECK BR3 152 A6
Convent Gdns EA W5 104 D3
NTGHL W11 88 D5
Convent Hl NRWD SE19 149 J5
Convent Wy NWDGN UB2 102 B3
Conway Cl RAIN RM13 81 J6
STAN HA7 35 G5
Conway Crs CHDH RM6 61 J6
GFD/PVL UB6 84 E1
Conway Dr ASHF TW15 140 A5
BELMT SM2 175 F5
HYS/HAR UB3 101 F2
Conway Gdns MTCM CR4 163 J3
WBLY HA9 49 J6
Conway Gv ACT W3 87 F4
Conway Ms FITZ W1T 10 E2
Conway Rd CRICK NW2 70 A1
FELT TW13 141 H4
HSLWW TW4 122 E6
RYNPK SW20 146 A7
SEVS/STOTM N15 55 J4
STHGT/OAK N14 40 E2
WOOL/PLUM SE18 115 J3
Conway St FITZ W1T 10 E1
Conybeare HAMP NW3 3 K1
Conyer's Rd STRHM/NOR SW16 148 D4
Conyer St BOW * E3 93 G1
Cooden Cl BMLY BR1 153 F6
Cookes Cl WAN E11 76 D1
Cookes La CHEAM SM3 174 C5
Cookham Cl NWDGN UB2 103 G2
Cookham Dene Cl CHST BR7 154 D7
Cookhill Rd ABYW SE2 116 C1
Cooks Ferry Rbt UED N18 43 G4
Cooks Md BUSH WD23 22 B5
Cookson Gv ERITH DA8 117 J6
Cook's Rd SRTFD E15 93 K1
WALW SE17 18 C9
Coolfin Rd CAN/RD E16 94 E5
Coolgardie Av CHING E4 44 B4
Coolgardie Rd ASHF TW15 140 A4
Coolhurst Rd CEND/HSY/T N8 54 D5
Cool Oak Br CDALE/KGS NW9 51 H6
Cool Oak La CDALE/KGS NW9 51 H6
Coomassie Rd MV/WKIL W9 88 D3
Coombe Av CROY/NA CR0 178 A3
Coombe Bank NWMAL KT3 145 G7
Coombe Cl EDGW HA8 50 B1
HSLW TW3 123 F3
Coombe Cnr WCHMH N21 29 H7
Coombe Crs HPTN TW12 141 J6
Coombe Dr RSLP HA4 47 F7
Coombe End KUTN/CMB KT2 145 F6
Coombefield Cl NWMAL KT3 160 B4
Coombe Gdns NWMAL KT3 160 C3
RYNPK SW20 160 D1
Coombe Hill Gld
KUTN/CMB KT2 145 G6
Coombe Hill Rd
KUTN/CMB KT2 145 G6
Coombe House Cha
NWMAL KT3 145 F7
Coombehurst Cl EBAR EN4 27 K1
Coombe La CROY/NA CR0 178 D4
RYNPK SW20 145 H7
Coombe La West
KUTN/CMB KT2 144 E7
Coombe Lea BMLY BR1 168 D2
Coombe Ldg CHARL SE7 114 B5
Coombe Neville
KUTN/CMB KT2 144 E6
Coombe Pk KUTN/CMB KT2 144 E4
Coombe Ridings
KUTN/CMB KT2 144 E4
Coombe Ri KUTN/CMB KT2 144 E7
Coombe Rd BUSH WD23 22 C6
CHSWK W4 106 B4
HPTN TW12 141 K5
KUTN/CMB KT2 144 C7
NWMAL KT3 160 B2
SAND/SEL CR2 178 A3
SYD SE26 150 D3
WDGN N22 55 G1
WEA W13 104 C2
WLSDN NW10 69 F2
Coomber Wy CROY/NA CR0 163 K6
Coombes Rd DAGW RM9 80 B7
Coombe Vls
WAND/EARL * SW18 127 K6
Coombewood Dr CHDH RM6 62 B5
Coombe Wood Rd
KUTN/CMB KT2 144 E4
Coombs St IS N1 6 D6
Coomer Ms FUL/PGN * SW6 107 J5
Coomer Pl FUL/PGN SW6 107 J5
Cooperage Cl TOTM N17 42 B5
Cooper Av WALTH E17 43 F7
Cooper Cl STHWK SE1 18 B2
Cooper Crs CAR SM5 175 K2
Cooperdale Cl WFD IG8 45 G6
Cooper Rd CRICK NW2 69 J4
CROY/NA CR0 177 G4
HDN NW4 52 B5
Coopersale Rd HOM E9 75 F4
Coopers Cl DAGE RM10 80 D5
WCHPL E1 92 E3
Coopers La CAMTN NW1 5 H6
LEE/GVPK SE12 153 F1
LEY E10 57 K7
Cooper's Rd STHWK SE1 19 M8
Cooper's Rw TWRH EC3N 13 L6
Cooper St CAN/RD E16 94 D4
Cooper's Yd NRWD SE19 150 A5
Coote Rd BCTR RM8 80 B2
BXLYHN DA7 117 G7
Copeland Rd PECK SE15 131 H1
WALTH E17 57 K4
Copeman Cl SYD SE26 150 E4
Copenhagen Pl POP/IOD E14 93 H5
Copenhagen St IS N1 5 K4
Cope Pl KENS W8 14 A4
Copers Cope Rd BECK BR3 151 H6
Cope St BERM/RHTH SE16 112 A3
Copford Wk IS * N1 6 E3
Copgate Pth
STRHM/NOR SW16 149 F5
Copland Av ALP/SUD HA0 67 K4
Copland Cl ALP/SUD HA0 67 J4
Copland Ms ALP/SUD HA0 68 A5
Copland Rd ALP/SUD HA0 68 A5
Copleston Rd PECK SE15 131 G2
Copley Cl HNWL W7 85 F4
WALW SE17 110 C5
Copley Dene BMLY BR1 153 H7
Copley Pk STRHM/NOR SW16 149 F5
Copley Rd STAN HA7 35 J4
Coppard Gdns CHSGTN KT9 171 J5
Coppelia Rd BKHTH/KID SE3 133 J3
Coppen Rd BCTR RM8 62 B6
Copperas St DEPT SE8 112 E5
Copper Cl NRWD SE19 150 B6
Copperdale Rd HYS/HAR UB3 101 K1
Copperfield Dr
SEVS/STOTM N15 56 B3
Copperfield Rd BOW E3 93 G3
THMD SE28 97 J5
Copperfields SUN * TW16 140 D5
Copperfield St STHWK SE1 18 D1
Copperfield Wy CHST BR7 154 C5
PIN HA5 47 K3
Coppergate Cl BMLY BR1 153 F7
Coppermead Cl CRICK NW2 70 A2
Copper Mill Dr ISLW TW7 124 A1
Copper Mill La TOOT SW17 147 G3
Coppermill La WALTH E17 56 E5
Coppetts Cl NFNCH/WDSP N12 39 K6
Coppetts Rd MUSWH N10 39 K7
The Coppice BAR * EN5 27 F5
ENC/FH EN2 29 H3
OXHEY WD19 21 G5
Coppice Cl BECK BR3 166 E3
KTN/HRWW/W HA3 35 F5
RSLP * HA4 46 A5
RYNPK SW20 161 F2
Coppice Dr PUT/ROE SW15 126 D5
Coppice Wk TRDG/WHET N20 38 E2
Coppice Wy SWFD E18 58 D3
Coppies Gv FBAR/BDGN N11 40 B3
Copping Cl CROY/NA CR0 178 A3
The Coppins KTN/HRWW/W HA3 34 E5
Coppock Cl BTSEA SW11 128 D1
Coppsfield E/WMO/HCT KT8 157 F2
The Copse EFNCH * N2 53 K2
Copse Av WWKM BR4 179 K2
Copse Cl CHARL SE7 114 A5
NTHWD HA6 32 A7
WDR/YW UB7 100 A2
Copse Gld SURB KT6 158 E7
Copse Hl BELMT SM2 175 F6
RYNPK SW20 145 J7
Copsem Dr ESH/CLAY KT10 170 B5
Copsem La ESH/CLAY KT10 170 C7
Copsem Wy ESH/CLAY KT10 170 C5
Copse Vw SAND/SEL CR2 179 F6
Copsewood Cl BFN/LL DA15 135 K5
Copse Wood Wy NTHWD HA6 32 A7
Coptefield Dr BELV DA17 116 E2
Copthall Av LOTH EC2R 13 H4
Copthall Dr MLHL NW7 37 J6
Copthall Gdns MLHL NW7 37 J6
TWK * TW1 124 B7
Copthorne Av BAL SW12 129 J6
HAYES BR2 181 K1
Copthorne Ms HYS/HAR UB3 101 H3
Coptic St NOXST/BSQ WC1A 11 J3
Copton Cl BOW E3 93 J4
Copwood Cl NFNCH/WDSP N12 39 H3
Coral Cl CHDH RM6 61 J2
Coraline Cl STHL UB1 83 K2
Coral St STHWK SE1 18 B2
Coram St STPAN WC1H 11 J1
Coran Cl ED N9 31 F6
Corban Rd HSLW TW3 123 F2
Corbet Cl WLGTN SM6 163 F7
Corbet Pl WCHPL E1 13 L2
Corbett Gv FBAR/BDGN N11 40 E6
Corbett Rd WALTH E17 58 B1
WAN E11 59 G5
Corbett's La BERM/RHTH SE16 111 K3
Corbicum WAN E11 58 C6
Corbin's La RYLN/HDSTN HA2 66 B2
Corbridge Crs BETH E2 92 D1
Corbridge Ms ROM RM1 63 H4
Corby Crs ENC/FH EN2 28 E3
Corbylands Rd BFN/LL DA15 135 K7
Corbyn St FSBYPK N4 54 E7
Corby Rd WLSDN NW10 86 E1
Cordelia Cl HNHL SE24 130 C3
Cordelia Gdns
STWL/WRAY TW19 120 B6
Cordelia Rd STWL/WRAY TW19 120 B6
Cordelia St POP/IOD E14 93 K5
Cordingley Rd RSLP HA4 46 B7
Cording St POP/IOD E14 93 K4
Cordova Rd BOW E3 93 G2
Cordwell Rd LEW SE13 133 G4
Corelli Rd BKHTH/KID SE3 114 D7
Corfe Av RYLN/HDSTN HA2 66 A3
Corfe Cl BORE WD6 25 F2
YEAD UB4 83 G5
Corfield Rd WCHMH N21 29 F4
Corfield St BETH E2 92 D3
Corfton Rd EA W5 86 A5
Coriander Av POP/IOD E14 94 B5
Cories Cl BCTR RM8 79 K1
Corinium Cl WBLY HA9 68 B3
Corinne Rd HOLWY N7 72 C3
Corinthian Manorway
ERITH DA8 118 A3
Corinthian Rd ERITH DA8 118 A3
Corkran Rd SURB KT6 158 E6
Cork St Ms CONDST W1S 10 E7
Corkscrew Hl WWKM BR4 180 A1
Cork Sq WAP E1W 92 C7
Cork St CONDST W1S 10 E7
Cork Tree Wy CHING E4 43 G4
Corlett St STJWD NW8 9 J2
Cormont Rd CMBW SE5 110 C7
Cormorant Cl WALTH E17 43 F7
Cormorant Rd FSTGT E7 76 D4
Cornbury Rd EDGW HA8 35 K6
Cornelia St HOLWY N7 73 F5
The Corner EA * W5 86 A7
Corner Fielde
BRXS/STRHM * SW2 130 A7
Corner Gn BKHTH/KID SE3 133 K1
Corner Md CDALE/KGS NW9 37 H6
Cornerside ASHF TW15 140 A6
Corney Reach Wy CHSWK W4 106 B6
Corney Rd CHSWK W4 106 B5
Cornfield Rd BUSH WD23 22 B3
Cornflower La CROY/NA CR0 166 A7
Cornflower Ter EDUL SE22 131 J5
Cornford Cl HAYES BR2 167 K4
Cornford Gv BAL SW12 148 B1
Cornhill BANK EC3V 13 H5
Cornish Gv PGE/AN SE20 150 D7
Cornmill La LEW SE13 132 E2
Cornmow Dr WLSDN NW10 69 H4
Cornshaw Rd BCTR RM8 61 K7
Cornthwaite Rd CLPT E5 74 E2
Cornwall Av BETH E2 92 E2
ESH/CLAY KT10 171 F6
FNCH N3 38 E6
STHL UB1 83 K4
WDGN N22 40 E7
WELL DA16 135 K2
Cornwall Cl BARK IG11 79 F5
Cornwall Crs NTGHL W11 88 C6
Cornwall Dr STMC/STPC BR5 155 J6
Cornwall Gdns SKENS SW7 14 E4
SNWD * SE25 165 G3
WLSDN NW10 69 K5
Cornwall Gv CHSWK W4 106 B4
Cornwallis Av BFN/LL DA15 154 D1
ED N9 42 D1
Cornwallis Cl ERITH DA8 118 C5
Cornwallis Gv ED N9 42 D1
Cornwallis Rd ARCH N19 72 E1
DAGW RM9 80 A3
ED N9 42 D1
WALTH E17 57 F3
WOOL/PLUM SE18 115 G2
Cornwallis Sq ARCH N19 72 E1
Cornwallis Wk ELTH/MOT SE9 134 E2
Cornwall Ms South SKENS SW7 14 E4
Cornwall Ms West SKENS * SW7 14 D4
Cornwall Rd BELMT SM2 174 D6
CROY/NA CR0 177 H1
DART DA1 139 J2
FSBYPK N4 55 G6
HRW HA1 48 C5
PIN HA5 33 K6
RSLP HA4 64 D1
SEVS/STOTM N15 55 K4
STHWK SE1 12 A8
TWK TW1 124 B6
UED N18 42 C4
Cornwall St WCHPL * E1 92 D6
Cornwall Ter CAMTN NW1 9 M1
Cornwall Terrace Ms
CAMTN NW1 9 M1
Corn Wy WAN E11 76 B2
Cornwood Cl EFNCH N2 53 H4
Cornwood Dr WCHPL E1 92 E5
Cornworthy Rd BCTR RM8 79 J4
Corona Rd LEE/GVPK SE12 133 K6
Coronation Cl BARK/HLT IG6 60 C3
BXLY DA5 136 E5
Coronation Dr HCH RM12 81 K4
Coronation Rd HYS/HAR UB3 101 J3
PLSTW E13 95 G2
WLSDN NW10 86 B2
Coronation Vls WLSDN * NW10 86 D3
Coronet Pde ALP/SUD * HA0 68 A5
Coronet St IS N1 7 J8
Corporation Av HSLWW TW4 122 D3
Corporation Rw CLKNW EC1R 6 B9
Corporation St HOLWY N7 72 E4
SRTFD E15 94 C1
Corrance Rd CLAP SW4 129 K3
Corri Av STHGT/OAK N14 40 D3
Corrib Dr SUT SM1 175 J4
Corrigan Cl HDN NW4 52 A2
Corringham Rd GLDGN NW11 52 E6
WBLY HA9 68 C1
Corringway EA W5 86 B4
GLDGN NW11 53 F6
Corris Gn CDALE/KGS * NW9 51 G5
Corsair Cl STWL/WRAY TW19 120 A6
Corsair Rd STWL/WRAY TW19 120 B6
Corscombe Cl KUTN/CMB KT2 144 E4
Corsehill St STRHM/NOR SW16 148 C5
Corsham St IS N1 7 H8
Corsica St HBRY N5 73 H5
Cortayne Rd FUL/PGN * SW6 127 J1
Cortina Dr DAGW RM9 98 E2
Cortis Rd PUT/ROE SW15 126 E5
Cortis Ter PUT/ROE SW15 126 E4
Corunna Rd VX/NE SW8 109 H7
Corunna Ter VX/NE SW8 109 H7
Corwell Gdns UX/CGN UB8 82 A5
Corwell La UX/CGN UB8 82 A5
Coryton Pth MV/WKIL W9 88 D3
Cosbycote Av HNHL SE24 130 D4
Cosdach Av WLGTN SM6 176 D6
Cosedge Crs CROY/NA CR0 177 G4
Cosgrove Cl WCHMH N21 41 H1
YEAD UB4 83 H3
Cosmo Pl RSQ WC1B 11 K2
Cosmur Cl SHB W12 106 C2
Cossall Wk PECK SE15 111 J7
Cosser St STHWK SE1 18 A3
Costa St PECK SE15 131 H1
Costons Av GFD/PVL UB6 84 D2
Costons La GFD/PVL UB6 84 D2
Cosway St CAMTN NW1 9 K2
Cotall St POP/IOD E14 93 J5
Coteford Cl PIN HA5 46 E4
Coteford St TOOT SW17 147 K3
Cotelands CROY/NA CR0 178 A2
Cotesbach Rd CLPT E5 74 E2
Cotesmore Gdns BCTR RM8 79 J3
Cotford Rd THHTH CR7 164 D3
Cotham St WALW SE17 18 F6
Cotherstone HOR/WEW KT19 173 F7
Cotherstone Rd
BRXS/STRHM SW2 130 A7
Cotleigh Av BXLY DA5 155 K1
Cotleigh Rd KIL/WHAMP NW6 2 A1
ROMW/RG RM7 63 F5
Cotman Cl EFNCH N2 53 G5
Cotman Gdns EDGW HA8 50 C1
Cotmans Cl HYS/HAR UB3 82 E7
Coton Rd WELL DA16 136 B2
Cotsford Av NWMAL KT3 159 K4
Cotswold Av BUSH WD23 22 C5
Cotswold Cl BXLYHN DA7 118 B7
ESH/CLAY KT10 171 F1
KUTN/CMB KT2 144 E5
Cotswold Gdns CRICK NW2 70 B1
EHAM E6 95 H2
GNTH/NBYPK IG2 60 D6
Cotswold Ga CRICK NW2 52 C7
Cotswold Gn ENC/FH EN2 29 F3
Cotswold Rd HPTN TW12 142 A5
Cotswold St WNWD SE27 149 H3
Cotswold Wy ENC/FH EN2 29 F2
WPK KT4 174 A1
Cottage Av HAYES BR2 168 D7
Cottage Cl RSLP HA4 46 B7
WAT WD17 20 D1
Cottage Field Cl SCUP DA14 136 D7
Cottage Gn CMBW SE5 110 E6
Cottage Gv BRXN/ST SW9 129 K2
SURB KT6 158 E5
Cottage Pl SKENS SW7 15 J3
Cottage Rd HOR/WEW KT19 173 F6
The Cottages EDGW * HA8 36 D6
Cottage St POP/IOD E14 93 K6
Cottenham Dr CDALE/KGS NW9 51 H2
RYNPK SW20 145 K6
Cottenham Park Rd
RYNPK SW20 145 J7
Cottenham Pl RYNPK SW20 145 K6
Cottenham Rd WALTH E17 57 H3
Cotterill Rd SURB KT6 172 B1
Cottesbrook St NWCR SE14 112 B6
Cottesloe Ms STHWK SE1 18 B3
Cottesmore Av CLAY IG5 59 K1
Cottesmore Gdns KENS W8 14 D3

Cottimore Av WOT/HER KT12 156 A7
Cottimore Crs WOT/HER KT12 156 A6
Cottimore La WOT/HER KT12 156 A6
Cottimore Ter WOT/HER KT12 156 A6
Cottingham Cha RSLP HA4 64 E2
Cottingham Rd PGE/AN SE20 151 F6
VX/NE SW8 110 A6
Cottington Rd FELT TW13 141 H3
Cottington St LBTH SE11 18 B7
Cotton Av ACT W3 87 F5
Cotton Cl DAGW RM9 79 J6
Cotton Gardens Est LBTH SE11 18 C6
Cottongrass Cl CROY/NA CR0 166 A7
Cotton Hl BMLY BR1 152 B3
Cotton Rw BTSEA SW11 128 B2
Cottons Ap ROMW/RG RM7 63 F4
Cottons Centre STHWK * SE1 13 J8
Cotton's Gdns BETH E2 7 K7
Cotton St POP/IOD E14 94 A6
Couchmore Av CLAY IG5 59 K1
ESH/CLAY KT10 170 E1
Coulgate St BROCKY SE4 132 B2
Coulson Cl BCTR RM8 61 J7
Coulson St CHEL SW3 15 L7
Coulter Cl YEAD UB4 83 J3
Coulter Rd HMSMTH W6 106 E2
Councillor St CMBW SE5 110 D6
Counter St STHWK SE1 13 J8
Countess Rd KTTN NW5 72 C4
Countisbury Av EN EN1 30 B6
Country Wy FELT TW13 141 G4
County Ga CHST BR7 154 C2
TRDG/WHET N20 27 F5
County Gv CMBW SE5 110 D7
County Pde BTFD * TW8 104 E6
County Rd EHAM E6 96 B4
THHTH CR7 164 C1
County St STHWK SE1 18 F4
Coupland Pl WOOL/PLUM SE18 115 H4
Courcy Rd CEND/HSY/T N8 55 G2
Courier Rd DAGW RM9 98 E3
Courland Gv VX/NE SW8 109 J7
Courland St VX/NE SW8 109 J7
The Course ELTH/MOT SE9 154 A2
The Court MUSWH * N10 54 C3
RSLP HA4 65 J3
Courtauld Rd ARCH N19 54 D7
Courtaulds Cl THMD SE28 97 G7
Court Av BELV DA17 117 G4
Court Cl FELT TW13 142 B2
HAMP * NW3 3 G2
KTN/HRWW/W HA3 49 K2
Court Close Av FELT TW13 142 B2
Court Crs CHSGTN KT9 171 K5
Court Downs Rd BECK BR3 166 E1
Court Dr CROY/NA CR0 177 F3
STAN HA7 36 A3
SUT SM1 175 J3
Courtenay Av BELMT SM2 174 E7
HGT N6 53 J6
KTN/HRWW/W HA3 34 C6
Courtenay Dr BECK BR3 167 G1
Courtenay Ms WALTH E17 57 G4
Courtenay Rd PGE/AN SE20 151 F6
WALTH E17 57 F4
WAN * E11 76 D2
WBLY * HA9 67 K2
WPK KT4 174 A2
Courtenay Sq LBTH SE11 18 A8
Courtenay St LBTH SE11 17 M7
Courten Ms STAN HA7 35 J6
Court Farm Av HOR/WEW KT19 173 F4
Court Farm Rd ELTH/MOT SE9 153 H1
NTHLT UB5 66 A6
Courtfield Av HRW * HA1 49 F4
Courtfield Crs HRW HA1 49 F4
Courtfield Gdns ECT SW5 14 D6
RSLP HA4 64 D1
WEA W13 85 G5
Courtfield Ms SKENS * SW7 14 E6
Courtfield Ri WWKM BR4 180 B2
Courtfield Rd SKENS SW7 14 E6
Court Gdns HOLWY N7 73 G5
Courthill Rd LEW SE13 133 F4
Courthope Rd GFD/PVL UB6 84 D1
HAMP NW3 71 K3
WIM/MER SW19 146 C4
Courthope Vls
WIM/MER SW19 146 C6
Court House Rd FNCH N3 39 F5
Courtland Av CHING E4 44 D1
IL IG1 77 K1
MLHL NW7 37 F2
STRHM/NOR SW16 149 F6
Courtland Gv THMD SE28 97 K6
Courtland Rd EHAM E6 77 J7
Courtlands RCHPK/HAM TW10 125 H4
Courtlands Av HAYES BR2 167 H7
HPTN TW12 141 K5
LEE/GVPK SE12 134 A4
RCH/KEW TW9 125 J1
Courtlands Cl RSLP HA4 46 D6
Courtlands Dr HOR/WEW KT19 173 G5
Courtlands Rd BRYLDS KT5 159 H6
Court La DUL SE21 131 G6
Court Lane Gdns DUL SE21 131 F6
Courtleet Dr BXLYHN DA7 117 J7
Courtleigh Gdns GLDGN NW11 52 C3
Courtman Rd TOTM N17 41 J6
Court Md NTHLT UB5 83 K2
Courtmead Cl HNHL SE24 130 D5
Courtnell St BAY/PAD W2 8 A4
Courtney Cl NRWD * SE19 150 A5
Courtney Crs CAR SM5 175 K6
Courtney Rd CROY/NA CR0 177 G2
HOLWY N7 73 G4
HTHAIR TW6 120 D2
WIM/MER SW19 147 J6
Courtney Wy HTHAIR TW6 120 D2
Courtrai Rd BROCKY SE4 132 B5
Court Rd ELTH/MOT SE9 134 E7
NWDGN UB2 102 E3
SNWD SE25 165 G1
The Courts STRHM/NOR SW16 148 E6
Courtside CEND/HSY/T N8 54 D5
SYD * SE26 150 E2
Court St BMLY BR1 167 K1
WCHPL E1 92 D4
Court Vw HGT * N6 72 B1
The Courtway OXHEY WD19 33 J1
Court Wy ACT W3 86 E4
BARK/HLT IG6 60 C2
CDALE/KGS NW9 51 G3
WHTN TW2 124 A6
The Courtyard IS N1 5 M1
Court Yd ELTH/MOT SE9 134 E5
The Courtyards WATW * WD18 20 B6
Cousin La CANST EC4R 13 G7
Couthurst Rd BKHTH/KID SE3 114 A5
Coutts Av CHSGTN KT9 172 A4
Coutts Crs KTTN * NW5 72 A2
Coval Gdns MORT/ESHN SW14 125 J3
Coval La MORT/ESHN SW14 125 J3
Coval Rd MORT/ESHN SW14 125 K3
Covelees Wall EHAM E6 96 A5
Covent Gdn COVGDN WC2E 11 K6
Covent Garden Piazza
COVGDN WC2E 11 K6
Coventry Cl EHAM E6 95 K5
KIL/WHAMP NW6 2 B5
Coventry Cross Est BOW E3 94 A3
Coventry Rd IL IG1 60 B7
SNWD SE25 165 H3
WCHPL E1 92 D3
Coventry St MYFR/PICC W1J 11 G7
Coverack Cl CROY/NA CR0 166 B6
STHGT/OAK N14 28 C5
Coverdale Gdns CROY/NA CR0 178 B2
Coverdale Rd FBAR/BDGN N11 40 A5
KIL/WHAMP NW6 70 C6
SHB W12 87 K7
The Coverdales BARK IG11 96 D1
Coverley Cl WCHPL * E1 92 C4
The Covert NRWD * SE19 150 B6
NTHWD HA6 32 A7
ORP BR6 169 K5
Coverton Rd TOOT SW17 147 J3
Coverts Rd ESH/CLAY KT10 171 F6
Covert Wy EBAR EN4 27 G1
Covey Cl WIM/MER SW19 162 A1
Covington Gdns
STRHM/NOR SW16 149 H6
Covington Wy
STRHM/NOR SW16 149 G6
Cowbridge La BARK IG11 78 B6
Cowbridge Rd
KTN/HRWW/W HA3 50 B3
Cowcross St FARR EC1M 12 C2
Cowdenbeath Pth IS N1 5 L3
Cowden St CAT SE6 151 J3
Cowdray Rd HGDN/ICK UB10 64 A7
Cowdray Wy HCH RM12 81 J3
Cowdrey Cl EN EN1 30 A1
Cowdrey Ct DART DA1 138 E6
Cowdrey Rd WIM/MER SW19 147 F5
Cowen Av RYLN/HDSTN HA2 66 D1
Cowgate Rd GFD/PVL UB6 84 D2
Cowick Rd TOOT SW17 147 K3
Cowings Md NTHLT UB5 65 J6
Cowland Av PEND EN3 30 E3
Cow La BUSH * WD23 22 A5
Cow Leaze EHAM E6 96 A5
Cowleaze Rd KUTN/CMB KT2 144 A7
Cowley Cl SAND/SEL CR2 178 E7
Cowley La WAN * E11 76 C2
Cowley Pl HDN NW4 52 A4
Cowley Rd ACT W3 87 H7
BRXN/ST SW9 110 B7
IL IG1 59 K6
MORT/ESHN SW14 126 B2
WAN E11 59 F4
Cowley St WEST SW1P 17 J4
Cowling Cl NTGHL W11 88 C6
Cowper Av EHAM E6 77 J6
SUT SM1 175 H3
Cowper Cl HAYES BR2 168 C3
WELL DA16 136 B4
Cowper Gdns STHGT/OAK N14 28 C5
WLGTN SM6 176 C5
Cowper Rd ACT W3 87 G7
BELV DA17 117 G3
HAYES BR2 168 C3
HNWL W7 85 F6
RAIN RM13 99 J3
RCHPK/HAM TW10 144 B4
STHGT/OAK N14 28 B7
STNW/STAM N16 74 A3
UED N18 42 C4
WIM/MER SW19 147 G5
Cowper St STLK EC1Y 7 H9
Cowper Ter NKENS * W10 88 B4
Cowslip Rd SWFD E18 59 F2
Cowthorpe Rd VX/NE SW8 109 J7
Coxe Pl KTN/HRWW/W HA3 49 G3
Cox La CHSGTN KT9 172 B3
HOR/WEW KT19 172 E4
Coxmount Rd CHARL SE7 114 C4
Coxson Wy STHWK SE1 19 L2
Coxwell Rd NRWD SE19 150 A6
WOOL/PLUM SE18 115 J4
Crab Hl BECK BR3 152 B6
Crabtree Av ALP/SUD HA0 86 A1
CHDH RM6 61 K3
Crabtree Cl BETH E2 7 L6
BUSH WD23 22 B4
Crabtree La FUL/PGN SW6 107 G6
Crabtree Manorway North
BELV DA17 117 K1
Crabtree Manorway South
BELV DA17 117 K2
Craddock Rd EN EN1 30 B2
Craddock St CAMTN * NW1 72 A5
Cradley Rd ELTH/MOT SE9 135 J7
Cragie Lea MUSWH * N10 54 B1
Craigdale Rd ROM RM1 63 H5
Craigen Av CROY/NA CR0 165 J7
Craigerne Rd BKHTH/KID SE3 114 A6
Craig Gdns SWFD E18 58 D1
Craigholm WOOL/PLUM SE18 135 F1
Craigmuir Pk ALP/SUD HA0 68 B7
Craignair Rd BRXS/STRHM SW2 130 A6
Craignish Av
STRHM/NOR SW16 164 A1
Craig Park Rd UED N18 42 D3
Craig Rd RCHPK/HAM TW10 143 J3
Craig's Ct WHALL SW1A 11 J8
Craigton Rd ELTH/MOT SE9 134 E3
Craigweil Cl STAN HA7 35 K4
Craigweil Dr STAN HA7 35 K4
Craigwell Av FELT TW13 140 E2
Crail Rw WALW SE17 19 H6
Crakers Md WATW * WD18 21 F2
Cramer St MHST W1U 10 B3
Crammond Cl HMSMTH W6 107 H5
Crampton Rd PGE/AN SE20 150 E5
Crampton St WALW SE17 18 E7
Cranberry Cl NTHLT UB5 83 H1
Cranberry La CAN/RD E16 94 C3
Cranborne Av NWDGN UB2 103 F3
SURB KT6 172 C2
Cranborne Rd BARK IG11 78 D7
Cranborne Waye YEAD UB4 83 F5
Cranbourne Av WAN E11 59 F3
Cranbourne Cl
STRHM/NOR SW16 163 K2
Cranbourne Dr PIN HA5 47 H4
Cranbourne Gdns BARK/HLT IG6 60 C2
GLDGN NW11 52 D4
Cranbourne Rd MNPK E12 77 J4
MUSWH N10 54 B1
NTHWD HA6 46 D2
SRTFD E15 76 A3
Cranbourn St LSQ/SEVD WC2H 11 H6
Cranbrook Cl HAYES BR2 167 K5
Cranbrook Dr ESH/CLAY KT10 157 H7
GPK RM2 63 K3
WHTN TW2 123 G7
Cranbrook La FBAR/BDGN N11 40 B3
Cranbrook Ms WALTH E17 57 H4
Cranbrook Pk WDGN N22 41 G7
Cranbrook Ri IL IG1 59 K5
Cranbrook Rd BXLYHN DA7 117 G7
CHSWK W4 106 B4
DEPT SE8 112 D7
EBAR EN4 27 H5
HSLWW TW4 122 E3
IL IG1 60 A6
THHTH CR7 164 D1
WIM/MER SW19 146 C6
Cranbrook St BETH E2 93 F1
Cranbury Rd FUL/PGN SW6 128 A1
Crane Av ACT W3 86 E6
ISLW TW7 124 B4
Cranebank Ms TWK * TW1 124 C4
Cranebrook WHTN TW2 142 C1
Crane Cl DAGE RM10 80 C5
Crane Ct FLST/FETLN EC4A 12 B5
MORT/ESHN * SW14 125 K3
Craneford Cl WHTN TW2 124 A6
Craneford Wy WHTN TW2 123 K6
Crane Gdns HYS/HAR UB3 101 J3
Crane Gv HOLWY N7 73 G5
Crane Lodge Rd HEST TW5 102 A5
Crane Md BERM/RHTH SE16 112 A3
Crane Park Rd WHTN TW2 142 B1
Crane Rd STWL/WRAY TW19 120 D5
WHTN TW2 123 K7
Cranesbill Cl CDALE/KGS NW9 51 F2
Cranes Dr BRYLDS KT5 159 F3
Cranes Pk SURB KT6 159 F3
Cranes Park Av SURB KT6 159 F3
Cranes Park Crs BRYLDS KT5 159 G3
Crane St PECK SE15 111 G7
Craneswater HYS/HAR UB3 101 J6
Craneswater Pk NWDGN UB2 102 E4
Cranes Wy BORE WD6 24 E4
Crane Wy WHTN TW2 123 H6
Cranfield Dr CDALE/KGS NW9 37 G6
Cranfield Rd BROCKY SE4 132 C2
Cranfield Rd East CAR SM5 176 A7
Cranfield Rd West CAR * SM5 175 K7
Cranford Av PLMGR N13 40 E4
STWL/WRAY TW19 120 B6
Cranford Cl RYNPK * SW20 145 K7
STWL/WRAY TW19 120 B6
Cranford Cottages WAP * E1W 93 F6
Cranford Dr HYS/HAR UB3 101 J3
Cranford La HEST TW5 102 C6
HTHAIR TW6 101 J7
HYS/HAR UB3 101 G5
Cranford Park Rd
HYS/HAR UB3 101 J3
Cranford Ri ESH/CLAY KT10 170 C4
Cranford Rd DART DA1 139 H7
Cranford St WAP E1W 93 F6
Cranford Wy CEND/HSY/T N8 55 F4
Cranham Rd EMPK RM11 63 K5
Cranhurst Rd CRICK NW2 70 A4
Cranleigh Cl BXLY * DA5 137 J5
PGE/AN SE20 165 J1
Cranleigh Gdns BARK IG11 78 D6
KTN/HRWW/W HA3 50 A4
KUTN/CMB KT2 144 B5
SNWD SE25 165 F2
STHL UB1 83 K5
SUT SM1 175 F1
WCHMH N21 29 G4
Cranleigh Ms BTSEA SW11 128 D1
Cranleigh Rd ESH/CLAY KT10 157 H7
FELT TW13 140 D3
SEVS/STOTM N15 55 J4
WIM/MER SW19 161 K2
Cranleigh St CAMTN NW1 4 F6
Cranley Dr GNTH/NBYPK IG2 60 C6
RSLP HA4 64 D1
Cranley Gdns MUSWH N10 54 B3
PLMGR N13 41 F2
SKENS SW7 14 F7
WLGTN SM6 176 C6
Cranley Ms SKENS SW7 14 F7
Cranley Pl SKENS SW7 15 G6
Cranley Rd GNTH/NBYPK IG2 60 C5
PLSTW E13 95 F4
Cranley Ter HDN * NW4 52 B1
Cranmer Av WEA W13 104 C2
Cranmer Cl MRDN SM4 161 G5
RSLP HA4 47 G7
STAN HA7 35 J6
Cranmer Ct HPTN TW12 142 B4
Cranmer Farm Cl MTCM CR4 162 E3
Cranmer Gdns DAGE RM10 80 E3
Cranmer Rd BRXN/ST SW9 110 B6
CROY/NA CR0 177 H2
EDGW HA8 36 D2
FSTGT E7 77 F3
HPTN TW12 142 B4
HYS/HAR UB3 82 B5
KUTN/CMB KT2 144 A4
MTCM CR4 162 E3
Cranmer Ter TOOT SW17 147 H4
Cranmore Rd BMLY BR1 152 C2
CHST BR7 153 K4
Cranmore Wy MUSWH N10 54 C3
Cranston Cl HGDN/ICK UB10 64 B1
HSLW TW3 122 D1
Cranston Est IS N1 7 H5
Cranston Gdns CHING E4 43 K5
Cranston Rd FSTH SE23 132 B7
Cranswick Rd
BERM/RHTH SE16 111 J4
Crantock Rd CAT SE6 152 A1
Cranwell Cl BOW E3 93 K3
Cranwich Av WCHMH N21 29 K6
Cranwich Rd STNW/STAM N16 56 A6
Cranwood St FSBYE EC1V 7 H8
Cranworth Gdns
BRXN/ST SW9 110 B7
Craster Rd BRXS/STRHM SW2 130 A6
Crathie Rd LEE/GVPK SE12 134 A5
Cravan Av FELT TW13 140 E1
Craven Av WEA W13 85 J6
Craven Cl STNW/STAM * N16 56 C6
YEAD UB4 82 E5
Craven Gdns BARK IG11 96 E1
BARK/HLT IG6 60 D1
WIM/MER SW19 147 F4
Craven Hl BAY/PAD W2 8 F6
Craven Hill Gdns BAY/PAD W2 8 E6
Craven Hill Ms BAY/PAD W2 8 F6
Craven Ms BTSEA SW11 129 F2
Craven Pk WLSDN NW10 69 F7
Craven Park Ms WLSDN NW10 69 G6
Craven Park Rd
STNW/STAM N16 56 B5
WLSDN NW10 69 G7
Craven Rd BAY/PAD W2 8 F6
CROY/NA CR0 165 J7
KUTN/CMB KT2 144 B7
WEA W13 85 J6
WLSDN NW10 69 F7
Craven St CHCR WC2N 11 J8
Craven Ter BAY/PAD W2 8 F6
Craven Wk STNW/STAM N16 56 C6
Crawford Av ALP/SUD HA0 67 K4
Crawford Cl ISLW TW7 123 K1
Crawford Gdns NTHLT UB5 83 K2
PLMGR N13 41 H2
Crawford Pas CLKNW EC1R 12 A1
Crawford Pl BAY/PAD W2 9 K4
Crawford Rd CMBW SE5 130 D1
Crawford St MBLAR W1H 9 M3
Crawley Rd ED N9 30 B6
LEY E10 57 K7
WDGN N22 55 J1
Crawthew Gv EDUL SE22 131 G3
Craybrooke Rd SCUP DA14 155 H3
Craybury End ELTH/MOT SE9 154 C1
Cray Cl DART DA1 138 D4
Craydene Rd ERITH DA8 118 C7
Crayford High St DART DA1 138 B4
Crayford Rd DART DA1 138 C4
HOLWY N7 72 E3
Crayford Wy DART DA1 138 D3
Crayke Hl CHSGTN KT9 172 A6
Crayleigh Ter SCUP * DA14 155 J5
Crayonne Cl SUN TW16 140 C7
Cray Rd BELV DA17 117 H5
SCUP DA14 155 J5
Crealock Gv WFD IG8 44 D4
Crealock St WAND/EARL SW18 128 A5
Creasey Cl EMPK RM11 81 K1
Crebor St EDUL SE22 131 H5
Credenhall Dr HAYES BR2 168 E7
Credenhill St
STRHM/NOR SW16 148 C5
Crediton Hl KIL/WHAMP NW6 71 F4
Crediton Rd WLSDN NW10 70 B7
Crediton Wy ESH/CLAY KT10 171 G4
Credon Rd BERM/RHTH SE16 111 J4
PLSTW E13 95 G1
Creechurch La HDTCH EC3A 13 K5
Creechurch Pl HDTCH * EC3A 13 K5
Creed La BLKFR EC4V 12 D5
Creek Cottages
E/WMO/HCT * KT8 157 K3
Creek Rd BARK IG11 97 F2
DEPT SE8 112 D5
E/WMO/HCT KT8 157 K3
Creekside DEPT SE8 112 D6
RAIN RM13 99 H3
Creek Wy RAIN RM13 99 G4
Creeland Gv CAT SE6 132 C7
Crefeld Cl FUL/PGN SW6 107 G5
Creffield Rd EA W5 86 C6
Creighton Av EFNCH N2 53 K1
EHAM E6 95 H1
Creighton Cl SHB W12 87 K6
Creighton Rd EA W5 104 E2
KIL/WHAMP NW6 88 B1
TOTM N17 42 A6
Creigton Av EFNCH N2 53 J2
Cremer St BETH E2 7 L6
Cremorne Est WBPTN * SW10 108 C5
Cremorne Gdns
HOR/WEW KT19 173 F7
Cremorne Rd WBPTN SW10 108 B6
The Crescent ACT W3 87 G5
ALP/SUD HA0 67 H1
BAR EN5 27 F2
BARN SW13 126 C1
BECK BR3 151 J7
BXLY DA5 136 D6
CRICK NW2 69 K2
E/WMO/HCT KT8 156 E3
FBAR/BDGN N11 39 K3
GNTH/NBYPK IG2 60 A5
HYS/HAR UB3 101 F6
NWDGN UB2 102 D1
NWMAL KT3 159 K1
RYLN/HDSTN HA2 48 C7
SCUP DA14 155 F3
SNWD SE25 164 E5
SURB KT6 159 F4
SUT SM1 175 H4
WALTH E17 57 G4
WATW WD18 21 G3
WIM/MER SW19 146 E2
WWKM BR4 167 H5
Crescent TWRH EC3N 13 L6
Crescent Ar GNWCH SE10 113 F5
Crescent Av HCH RM12 81 H1
Crescent Dr STMC/STPC BR5 169 H5
Crescent Gdns RSLP HA4 47 F6
WIM/MER SW19 146 E2
Crescent Gv CLAP SW4 129 H3
MTCM CR4 162 D3
Crescent La CLAP SW4 129 J4
Crescent Pl CHEL SW3 15 J5
Crescent Ri EBAR EN4 27 J4
FNCH * N3 38 D7
WDGN N22 40 D7
Crescent Rd BECK BR3 166 E1
BFN/LL DA15 155 F2
BMLY BR1 152 E6
CEND/HSY/T N8 54 D5
DAGE RM10 80 D3
EBAR EN4 27 H3
ED N9 30 C7
ENC/FH EN2 29 H3
ERITH DA8 118 C5
FBAR/BDGN N11 39 K3
FNCH N3 38 D7
KUTN/CMB KT2 144 C6
LEY E10 75 K1
PLSTW E13 76 E7
RYNPK SW20 146 B7
SEVS/STOTM * N15 55 H2
SWFD E18 59 G1
WDGN N22 40 D7
WOOL/PLUM SE18 115 G4
Crescent Rw STLK EC1Y 12 E1
Crescent St IS N1 5 M1
Crescent Wy BROCKY SE4 132 D2
STRHM/NOR SW16 149 F6
Crescentway NFNCH/WDSP N12 39 J5
Crescent Wood Rd SYD SE26 150 C2
Cresford Rd FUL/PGN SW6 108 A7
Crespigny Rd HDN NW4 51 K5
Cressage Cl STHL UB1 84 A3
Cresset Rd HOM E9 74 E5
Cresset St CLAP SW4 129 J2
Cressfield Cl KTTN NW5 72 A4
Cressida Rd ARCH N19 54 C7
Cressingham Gv SUT SM1 175 G3
Cressingham Rd EDGW HA8 37 F6
LEW SE13 133 F2
Cressington Cl STNW/STAM N16 74 A4
Cresswell Gdns ECT * SW5 14 E7
Cresswell Pk BKHTH/KID SE3 133 J2
Cresswell Pl ECT SW5 14 E7
Cresswell Rd FELT TW13 141 J2
SNWD SE25 165 H3
TWK TW1 124 E5
Cresswell Wy WCHMH N21 29 G6
Cressy Ct HMSMTH W6 106 E2
Cressy Houses WCHPL * E1 92 E4
Cressy Pl WCHPL E1 92 E4
Cressy Rd HAMP NW3 71 K3
Cressys Cnr HSLW * TW3 123 G2
Crestbrook Av PLMGR N13 41 H2
Crestbrook Pl PLMGR * N13 41 G2
The Crest BRYLDS KT5 159 H4
HDN NW4 52 A4
HOLWY * N7 72 D4
PLMGR N13 41 G3
Crestfield St CAMTN NW1 5 K7
Crest Gdns RSLP HA4 65 G2
Creston Wy WPK KT4 161 G7
Crest Rd CRICK NW2 69 J1
HAYES BR2 167 J6
SAND/SEL CR2 178 D6
Crest Vw PIN HA5 47 H3
Crest View Dr STMC/STPC BR5 169 G4
Crestway PUT/ROE SW15 126 D5
Crestwood Wy HSLWW TW4 122 E4
Creswick Rd ACT W3 86 D6
Creswick Wk GLDGN NW11 52 D3
Crewdson Rd BRXN/ST SW9 110 A6
Crewe Pl WLSDN NW10 87 H2
Crews St POP/IOD * E14 112 D3
Crewys Rd CRICK NW2 70 D1
PECK SE15 131 J1
Crichton Av WLGTN SM6 176 D4
Crichton Rd CAR SM5 175 K6
Crichton St VX/NE * SW8 129 H1
Cricketers Arms Rd
ENC/FH * EN2 29 J1
Cricketers Cl CHSGTN KT9 171 K4
ERITH DA8 118 B4
STHGT/OAK N14 28 C6
Cricketers Wk SYD SE26 150 E4
Cricketfield Rd CLPT E5 74 D3
Cricket Gn MTCM CR4 162 E2
Cricket Ground Rd CHST BR7 154 B7
Cricket La BECK BR3 151 G5
Cricket Rw EFNCH * N2 53 H2
Cricklade Av BRXS/STRHM SW2 148 E1
Cricklewood Broadway
CRICK NW2 70 A2
Cricklewood La CRICK NW2 70 C3
Cridland St SRTFD E15 76 D7
Crieff Rd WAND/EARL SW18 128 B5
Criffel Av BRXS/STRHM SW2 148 D1
Crimscott St STHWK SE1 19 K4
Crimsworth Rd VX/NE SW8 109 J7
Crinan St IS N1 5 K5
Cringle St VX/NE SW8 109 H6
Cripplegate St BARB * EC2Y 12 E2
Crispen Rd FELT TW13 141 J3
Crispian Cl WLSDN NW10 69 G3
Crispin Crs CROY/NA CR0 176 D2
Crispin Rd EDGW HA8 36 E5
Crispin St WCHPL E1 13 L3
Crisp Rd HMSMTH W6 107 F4
Cristowe Rd FUL/PGN * SW6 127 J1
Criterion Ms ARCH N19 72 D1
Cricketers Ms
WAND/EARL SW18 128 A4
Crockerton Rd TOOT SW17 147 K1
Crockham Wy ELTH/MOT SE9 154 A3
Crocus Cl CROY/NA CR0 166 A7
Crocus Fld BAR EN5 26 D5
The Croft ALP/SUD HA0 67 J4
BAR EN5 26 C3
CHING E4 44 C1
EA W5 86 A4
EDGW HA8 36 D7
HEST TW5 102 D6
RSLP HA4 65 G3
WLSDN NW10 87 H1
Croft Av WWKM BR4 167 F7
Croft Cl BELV DA17 117 G4
CHST BR7 153 K4
HYS/HAR UB3 101 F6
MLHL NW7 37 G2
Croft Ct BORE WD6 25 F2
RSLP * HA4 46 D7
SUT * SM1 175 H1
Croftdown Rd KTTN NW5 72 A2
Crofters Cl ISLW TW7 123 J4
Crofters Ct DEPT SE8 112 B3
Crofters Md CROY/NA CR0 179 H7
Crofters Rd NTHWD HA6 32 C3
Crofters Wy CAMTN NW1 5 G3
Croft Gdns HNWL W7 104 B1
RSLP HA4 46 C7
Croft Lodge Cl WFD IG8 45 F5
Croft Ms NFNCH/WDSP N12 39 G2
Crofton Av BXLY DA5 136 E6
CHSWK W4 105 K6
Crofton Gate Wy BROCKY SE4 132 B4
Crofton Gv CHING E4 44 B3
Crofton La STMC/STPC BR5 169 J7
Crofton Park Rd BROCKY SE4 132 C5
Crofton Rd CMBW SE5 111 F7
PLSTW E13 95 F3
Crofton Ter RCH/KEW TW9 125 G3
Crofton Wy BAR * EN5 27 F5
ENC/FH EN2 29 G1
Croft Rd BMLY BR1 152 E5
STRHM/NOR SW16 149 G6
SUT SM1 175 H4
WIM/MER SW19 147 G6
Crofts Rd HRW HA1 49 G5
Crofts St WCHPL E1 92 C6
Croft St DEPT SE8 112 B3
WCHPL E1 92 C6
Croft Wy BFN/LL DA15 154 E2
RCHPK/HAM TW10 143 H2
Crogsland Rd CAMTN NW1 4 A1
Croham Cl SAND/SEL CR2 178 A5
Croham Manor Rd
SAND/SEL CR2 178 A6
Croham Mt SAND/SEL CR2 178 A6
Croham Park Av
SAND/SEL CR2 178 B4
Croham Rd SAND/SEL CR2 177 K4
Croham Valley Rd
SAND/SEL CR2 178 C5

Croindene Rd
STRHM/NOR SW16 .....148 E7
Cromartie Rd ARCH N19 .....54 D6
Cromarty Rd EDGW * HA8 .....36 D1
Cromarty Vls BAY/PAD * W2 .....8 E6
Crombie Cl REDBR IG4 .....59 K4
Crombie Ms BTSEA * SW11 .....128 D1
Crombie Rd BFN/LL DA15 .....135 J7
Cromer Cl UX/CGN UB8 .....82 A5
Cromer Hyde MRDN * SM4 .....162 A4
Cromer Rd BAR EN5 .....27 G3
CHDH RM6 .....62 A5
HTHAIR TW6 .....120 D2
LEY E10 .....58 B6
ROMW/RG RM7 .....62 E5
SNWD SE25 .....165 J2
TOOT SW17 .....148 A5
TOTM N17 .....56 C1
Cromer Rd West HTHAIR TW6 .....120 D2
Cromer St STPAN WC1H 5 K8
Cromer Ter HACK E8 .....74 C4
Cromer Villas Rd
WAND/EARL SW18 .....127 J5
Cromford Rd PUT/ROE SW15 .....127 J4
Cromford Wy NWMAL KT3 .....145 F7
Cromlix Cl CHST BR7 .....169 G1
Crompton St BAY/PAD W2 .....9 G1
Cromwell Av HAYES BR2 .....168 A2
HGT N6 .....54 B7
HMSMTH W6 .....106 E4
NWMAL KT3 .....160 C4
Cromwell Cl CHSWK * W4 .....105 J4
EFNCH N2 .....53 H3
WOT/HER KT12 .....156 A7
Cromwell Ct ALP/SUD HA0 .....86 A1
Cromwell Crs ECT SW5 .....14 A5
Cromwell Gv HMSMTH W6 .....107 F2
Cromwell Ms SKENS * SW7 .....15 G5
Cromwell Pde ALP/SUD * HA0 .....86 A1
Cromwell Pl ACT W3 .....86 E7
HGT * N6 .....54 B7
MORT/ESHN SW14 .....125 K2
SKENS SW7 .....15 H5
Cromwell Rd ALP/SUD HA0 .....85 K1
BECK BR3 .....166 B1
BRXN/ST SW9 .....110 C7
CROY/NA CR0 .....164 E6
FELT TW13 .....122 A7
FNCH N3 .....53 G1
FSTGT E7 .....77 G6
HSLW TW3 .....123 F3
HYS/HAR UB3 .....82 B5
KUTN/CMB KT2 .....144 A7
MUSWH N10 .....40 A6
SKENS SW7 .....15 G5
TEDD TW11 .....143 G5
WALTH E17 .....58 A4
WIM/MER SW19 .....146 E4
WPK KT4 .....173 F2
Cromwell St HSLW TW3 .....123 F3
Cromwell Ter HSLW * TW3 .....123 F3
Crondace Rd FUL/PGN SW6 .....107 K7
Crondall St IS N1 .....7 H6
Cronin St PECK SE15 .....111 G6
Crooked Billet Rbt CHING E4 .....43 K6
Crooked Usage FNCH N3 .....52 C2
Crooke Rd DEPT SE8 .....112 B4
Crookham Rd FUL/PGN SW6 .....107 J7
Crook Log BXLYHN DA7 .....136 E2
Crookston Rd ELTH/MOT SE9 .....135 G2
Croombs Rd CAN/RD E16 .....95 G4
Croom's Hl GNWCH SE10 .....113 G6
Croom's Hill Gv GNWCH SE10 .....113 F6
Cropley St IS N1 .....7 G5
Croppath Rd DAGE RM10 .....80 C3
Cropthorne Ct STJWD NW8 .....2 F8
Crosby Cl FELT TW13 .....141 J3
Crosby Rd DAGE RM10 .....98 D1
FSTGT E7 .....76 E5
Crosby Rw STHWK SE1 .....19 G2
Crosby Wk HACK E8 .....74 B5
Crosier Cl WOOL/PLUM SE18 .....114 D7
Crosier Rd HGDN/ICK UB10 .....64 A3
Crosier Wy RSLP HA4 .....64 C2
Crossbrook Rd BKHTH/KID SE3 .....134 D1
Cross Deep TWK TW1 .....143 F2
Cross Deep Gdns TWK TW1 .....143 F1
Crossfield Est DEPT SE8 .....112 D6
Crossfield Rd HAMP NW3 .....71 H5
TOTM N17 .....55 J2
Crossfield St DEPT SE8 .....112 D6
Crossford St BRXN/ST SW9 .....130 A1
Crossgate EDGW HA8 .....36 C2
GFD/PVL UB6 .....67 H5
Cross Keys Cl MHST W1U 10 B3
Cross Lances Rd HSLW TW3 .....123 G3
Crossland Rd THHTH CR7 .....164 C5
Crosslands Av EA W5 .....86 B7
NWDGN UB2 .....102 E4
Crosslands Pde NWDGN * UB2 .....103 F4
Crosslands Rd HOR/WEW KT19 .....173 F5
Cross La BXLY DA5 .....137 G6
CEND/HSY/T N8 .....55 F2
Crosslet St WALW SE17 .....19 H5
Crosslet V GNWCH SE10 .....112 E7
Crossley St HOLWY N7 .....73 G5
Crossmead ELTH/MOT SE9 .....134 E7
OXHEY WD19 .....21 F5
Crossmead Av GFD/PVL UB6 .....84 A2
Crossness Rd BARK IG11 .....97 F2
Cross Rd BUSH WD23 .....21 J5
CHDH RM6 .....61 J6
CMBW SE5 .....131 F1
CROY/NA CR0 .....164 E7
DART DA1 .....139 F5
EN EN1 .....30 B3
FBAR/BDGN N11 .....40 B4
FELT TW13 .....141 J3
HAYES BR2 .....181 J1
HRW HA1 .....48 D3
KTN/HRWW/W HA3 .....49 G1
KUTN/CMB KT2 .....144 B6
ROMW/RG RM7 .....62 C2
RYLN/HDSTN HA2 .....66 A2
SCUP DA14 .....155 H3
SUT SM1 .....175 H4
WDGN N22 .....41 G5
WFD IG8 .....45 K5
WIM/MER SW19 .....146 E6
Cross St BARN SW13 .....126 B1
ERITH DA8 .....118 B5
HPTN TW12 .....142 C4
IS N1 .....6 D3
UED N18 .....42 C4
WAT WD17 .....21 G2
Crossthwaite Av HNHL SE24 .....130 E3
Crosswall TWRH EC3N 13 L6
The Cross Wy
KTN/HRWW/W HA3 .....48 E1
The Crossway ELTH/MOT SE9 .....153 H1

WDGN N22 .....41 H6
Cross Wy HYS/HAR UB3 .....101 K1
Crossway BCTR RM8 .....79 J2
CDALE/KGS NW9 .....51 H3
EN EN1 .....30 A6
NFNCH/WDSP N12 .....39 H5
NWMAL KT3 .....161 F3
PIN HA5 .....47 F1
RSLP HA4 .....65 G3
STMC/STPC BR5 .....169 J3
STNW/STAM N16 .....74 A4
THMD SE28 .....97 J6
WEA W13 .....85 F3
Crossway Pde WDGN * N22 .....41 H6
The Crossways BRYLDS * KT5 .....159 J7
HEST TW5 .....102 E6
WBLY HA9 .....68 C1
Crossways BELMT SM2 .....175 H7
GPK RM2 .....63 K2
SAND/SEL CR2 .....179 H6
SUN TW16 .....140 D7
Crossways Rd BECK BR3 .....166 D3
MTCM CR4 .....163 G2
Crossways Ter CLPT * E5 .....74 E3
Croston St HACK E8 .....74 C7
Crosts La WDGN N22 .....41 G6
Crothall Cl PLMGR N13 .....41 F2
Crouch Av BARK IG11 .....97 H1
Crouch Cl BECK BR3 .....151 J5
Crouch Cft ELTH/MOT SE9 .....154 A2
Crouch End Hl ARCH N19 .....54 D6
Crouch Hall Rd CEND/HSY/T N8 .....54 D5
Crouch Hl ARCH N19 .....54 E6
Crouchmans Cl SYD SE26 .....150 B2
Crouch Rd WLSDN NW10 .....69 F6
Crowborough Pth OXHEY WD19 .....33 H3
Crowborough Rd TOOT SW17 .....148 A4
Crowden Wy THMD SE28 .....97 J6
Crowder St WCHPL E1 .....92 D6
Crowfoot Cl HOM E9 .....75 H4
Crowhurst Cl BRXN/ST SW9 .....130 B1
Crowland Av HYS/HAR UB3 .....101 H3
Crowland Gdns STHGT/OAK N14 .....28 E6
Crowland Rd SEVS/STOTM N15 .....56 B4
THHTH * CR7 .....164 E3
Crowlands Av ROMW/RG RM7 .....62 D5
Crowland Ter IS N1 .....7 G1
Crowland Wk MRDN SM4 .....162 A5
Crow La ROMW/RG RM7 .....62 B6
Crowley Crs CROY/NA CR0 .....177 G4
Crowline Wk IS * N1 .....73 J5
Crown Ar KUT * KT1 .....158 E1
Crownbourne Ct SUT * SM1 .....175 F3
Crown Cl BOW E3 .....75 J7
HYS/HAR UB3 .....101 J1
KIL/WHAMP NW6 .....71 F5
MLHL NW7 .....37 H1
WOT/HER KT12 .....156 B6
Crown Ct HOL/ALD WC2B 11 K5
Crown Dl NRWD SE19 .....149 J5
Crowndale Rd CAMTN NW1 .....4 F5
Crownfield Av GNTH/NBYPK IG2 .....60 E4
Crownfield Rd SRTFD E15 .....76 B4
Crown Hl CROY/NA * CR0 .....177 J1
Crownhill Rd WFD IG8 .....45 J6
WLSDN NW10 .....69 H7
Crown La CHST BR7 .....154 C7
HAYES BR2 .....168 C4
STHGT/OAK N14 .....28 C7
STRHM/NOR SW16 .....149 G4
WIM/MER SW19 .....161 K2
Crown Lane Gdns
WNWD * SE27 .....149 G4
Crown Lane Sp HAYES BR2 .....168 C5
Crown Office Rw EMB EC4Y 12 A6
Crown Pde MRDN * SM4 .....162 A3
STHGT/OAK * N14 .....28 C7
Crown Pas STJS SW1Y 10 F9
Crown Pl KTTN NW5 .....72 B5
SDTCH EC2A 13 J1
Crown Rd BARK/HLT IG6 .....60 D3
EN EN1 .....30 C2
MUSWH N10 .....40 A6
NWMAL KT3 .....144 E7
RSLP HA4 .....65 H4
SUT SM1 .....174 E3
TWK TW1 .....124 C5
WIM/MER SW19 .....161 K3
Crownstone Rd
BRXS/STRHM SW2 .....130 B4
Crown St ACT W3 .....86 D7
CMBW SE5 .....110 D6
DAGE RM10 .....80 E5
RYLN/HDSTN HA2 .....48 D7
Crown Ter CRICK * NW2 .....70 B3
RCH/KEW TW9 .....125 G3
STHGT/OAK * N14 .....28 D7
Crowntree Cl ISLW TW7 .....104 A5
Crown Vls ACT * W3 .....105 K1
Crown Wk WBLY HA9 .....68 B2
Crown Woods Wy
ELTH/MOT SE9 .....135 J4
Crown Yd HSLW TW3 .....123 H2
Crowshott Av STAN HA7 .....35 J7
Crows Rd BARK IG11 .....78 B5
SRTFD E15 .....94 B2
Crowther Av BTFD TW8 .....105 F4
Crowther Rd SNWD SE25 .....165 H3
Crowthorne Cl
WAND/EARL SW18 .....127 J6
Crowthorne Rd NKENS W10 .....88 B5
Croxdale Rd BORE WD6 .....24 B1
Croxden Cl EDGW HA8 .....50 C2
Croxden Wk MRDN SM4 .....162 B5
Croxford Gdns WDGN N22 .....41 H6
Croxford Wy ROMW/RG RM7 .....63 F7
Croxley Gn STMC/STPC BR5 .....155 H7
Croxley Rd MV/WKIL W9 .....88 D2
Croxley Vw WATW WD18 .....20 C5
Croxted Cl DUL SE21 .....130 D6
Croxted Rd DUL SE21 .....149 K1
Croyde Av GFD/PVL UB6 .....84 C2
HYS/HAR UB3 .....101 H3
Croyde Cl ELTH/MOT SE9 .....135 J6
The Croydon F/O
CROY/NA CR0 .....177 H3
Croydon Gv CROY/NA CR0 .....164 C7
Croydon Rd BECK BR3 .....166 B2
CROY/NA CR0 .....166 A4
MTCM CR4 .....163 G4
PGE/AN SE20 .....165 J1
PLSTW E13 .....94 D3
WLGTN SM6 .....176 B3
WWKM BR4 .....180 C2
Croyland Rd ED N9 .....30 C7
Croylands Dr SURB KT6 .....159 F6
Crozier Ter HOM E9 .....75 F4
Crucible Cl CHDH RM6 .....61 H5
Crucifix La STHWK SE1 .....19 J1
Cruden St IS N1 .....6 D4

Cruickshank St FSBYW WC1X 6 A7
Cruikshank Rd SRTFD E15 .....76 C3
Crummock Gdns
CDALE/KGS NW9 .....51 G4
Crumpsall St ABYW SE2 .....116 D3
Crundale Av CDALE/KGS NW9 .....50 C4
Crunden Rd SAND/SEL CR2 .....177 K6
Crusader Cl PUR RM19 .....119 K3
Crusader Gdns CROY/NA CR0 .....178 A2
Crusader Wy WATW WD18 .....20 D5
Crusoe Ms STNW/STAM N16 .....73 K1
Crusoe Rd ERITH DA8 .....118 A4
MTCM CR4 .....147 K6
Crutched Friars TWRH EC3N 13 K6
Crutchfield La WOT/HER KT12 .....156 A7
Crutchley Rd CAT SE6 .....152 C1
Crystal Palace NRWD * SE19 .....150 C6
Crystal Palace Pde NRWD SE19 .....150 B5
Crystal Palace Park Rd
SYD SE26 .....150 C4
Crystal Palace Rd EDUL SE22 .....131 G5
Crystal Ter NRWD SE19 .....149 K5
Crystal Wy BCTR RM8 .....61 J7
HRW HA1 .....49 F4
Cuba Dr PEND EN3 .....30 E1
Cuba St POP/IOD E14 .....112 D1
Cubitt Sq NWDGN * UB2 .....84 C7
Cubitt St CROY/NA CR0 .....177 F4
FSBYW WC1X 5 M8
Cubitt Ter CLAP SW4 .....129 H2
Cuckoo Av HNWL W7 .....84 E3
Cuckoo Dene HNWL W7 .....84 D4
Cuckoo Hall La ED N9 .....30 E6
Cuckoo Hl PIN HA5 .....47 G2
Cuckoo Hill Dr PIN HA5 .....47 G2
Cuckoo Hill Rd PIN HA5 .....47 H3
Cuckoo La HNWL W7 .....84 E6
Cuda's Cl HOR/WEW KT19 .....173 H3
Cuddington Av WPK KT4 .....173 H2
Cudham St CAT SE6 .....132 E6
Cudworth St WCHPL E1 .....92 D3
Cuff Crs ELTH/MOT SE9 .....134 C6
Culford Gdns CHEL SW3 .....15 M6
Culford Gv IS N1 .....74 A5
Culford Ms IS N1 .....73 K5
Culford Rd IS N1 .....7 J1
Culgaith Gdns ENC/FH EN2 .....28 E3
Cullen Wy WLSDN NW10 .....86 E3
Cullera Cl NTHWD HA6 .....32 D5
Culling Rd BERM/RHTH SE16 .....111 K2
Cullington Cl
KTN/HRWW/W HA3 .....49 G3
Cullingworth Rd WLSDN NW10 .....69 J4
Culloden Cl STHWK SE1 .....111 H4
Culloden Rd ENC/FH EN2 .....29 H1
Culloden St POP/IOD E14 .....94 A5
Cullum St FENCHST EC3M 13 J6
Culmington Pde WEA * W13 .....85 J6
Culmington Rd SAND/SEL CR2 .....177 J6
WEA W13 .....85 J7
Culmore Rd PECK SE15 .....111 J6
Culmstock Rd BTSEA SW11 .....129 F4
Culross Cl SEVS/STOTM N15 .....55 J3
Culross St MYFR/PKLN W1K 10 A7
Culsac Rd SURB KT6 .....172 A1
Culverden Rd BAL SW12 .....148 C2
OXHEY WD19 .....33 F2
Culver Gv STAN HA7 .....49 J1
Culverhouse Gdns
STRHM/NOR SW16 .....149 F3
Culverlands Cl STAN HA7 .....35 H3
Culverley Rd CAT SE6 .....132 E7
Culvers Av CAR SM5 .....175 K1
Culvers Retreat CAR SM5 .....162 E7
Culverstone Cl HAYES BR2 .....167 J5
Culvers Wy CAR SM5 .....175 K1
Culvert Pl BTSEA SW11 .....129 F1
Culvert Rd BTSEA SW11 .....128 E1
SEVS/STOTM N15 .....56 A4
Culworth St STJWD NW8 .....3 J6
Cumberland Av WELL DA16 .....135 K2
WLSDN NW10 .....86 D2
Cumberland Cl HACK E8 .....74 B5
RYNPK SW20 .....146 B6
TWK TW1 .....124 C5
Cumberland Dr BXLYHN DA7 .....117 F6
CHSGTN KT9 .....172 A2
DART DA1 .....139 J6
ESH/CLAY KT10 .....171 G1
Cumberland Gdns FSBYW WC1X 5 M7
HDN * NW4 .....52 B1
Cumberland Ga CAMTN NW1 .....4 C7
MBLAR W1H 9 L6
Cumberland Market CAMTN NW1 .....4 D7
Cumberland Pk ACT W3 .....86 E6
Cumberland Pl CAMTN NW1 .....4 C7
CAT SE6 .....133 J7
Cumberland Rd ACT W3 .....86 E6
BARN SW13 .....106 C7
ED N9 .....30 E7
HAYES BR2 .....167 H3
HNWL W7 .....104 A1
HRW HA1 .....48 B4
KTN/HRWW/W HA3 .....50 B5
MNPK E12 .....77 H3
PLSTW E13 .....95 F4
RCH/KEW TW9 .....105 H7
SNWD SE25 .....165 J5
WALTH E17 .....57 G1
WDGN N22 .....55 F1
Cumberland St PIM SW1V 16 D7
Cumberland Ter CAMTN NW1 .....4 C6
PGE/AN * SE20 .....150 D6
Cumberland Terrace Ms
CAMTN NW1 .....4 C6
Cumberlow Av SNWD SE25 .....165 H2
Cumbernauld Gdns SUN TW16 .....140 D4
Cumberton Rd TOTM N17 .....41 K7
Cumbrae Gdns SURB KT6 .....171 K1
Cumbrian Av BXLYHN DA7 .....138 B1
Cumbrian Gdns CRICK NW2 .....70 B1
Cumming St IS N1 .....5 M6
Cumnor Cl BRXN/ST * SW9 .....130 A1
Cumnor Gdns EW KT17 .....173 J5
Cumnor Rd BELMT SM2 .....175 G5
Cunard Crs WCHMH N21 .....29 K5
Cunard Rd WLSDN NW10 .....87 F2
Cundy Rd CAN/RD E16 .....95 G5
Cundy St BGVA SW1W 16 B6
Cunliffe Rd HOR/WEW KT19 .....173 H3
Cunliffe St STRHM/NOR SW16 .....148 C5
Cunningham Cl CHDH RM6 .....61 J4
WWKM BR4 .....179 K1
Cunningham Pk HRW HA1 .....48 D4
Cunningham Pl STJWD NW8 .....3 G9
Cunningham Rd
SEVS/STOTM * N15 .....56 C3
Cunnington St CHSWK W4 .....105 K2
Cupar Rd BTSEA SW11 .....109 F7
Cupola Cl BMLY BR1 .....153 F4

Cureton St WEST SW1P 17 H7
Curlew Cl THMD SE28 .....97 K6
Curlew St STHWK SE1 .....19 L1
Curlew Wy YEAD UB4 .....83 H4
Curnick's La WNWD SE27 .....149 J3
Curran Av BFN/LL DA15 .....136 A4
WLGTN SM6 .....176 A2
Currey Rd GFD/PVL UB6 .....66 C5
Curricle St ACT W3 .....87 G7
Currie Hill Cl WIM/MER SW19 .....146 D3
Curry Ri MLHL NW7 .....38 B5
Cursitor St FLST/FETLN EC4A 12 A4
Curtain Pl SDTCH EC2A 7 K9
Curtain Rd SDTCH EC2A 13 J1
Curthwaite Gdns ENC/FH EN2 .....28 D3
Curtis Dr ACT W3 .....87 F5
Curtis Field Rd
STRHM/NOR SW16 .....149 F3
Curtis La ALP/SUD HA0 .....68 A5
Curtis Rd HOR/WEW KT19 .....172 E3
HSLWW TW4 .....122 E6
Curtis St STHWK SE1 .....19 L5
Curtis Wy STHWK SE1 .....19 L5
The Curve SHB W12 .....87 J6
Curwen Av FSTGT E7 .....77 F3
Curwen Rd SHB W12 .....106 D1
Curzon Av PEND EN3 .....31 F4
STAN HA7 .....35 G7
Curzon Crs BARK IG11 .....97 F2
WLSDN NW10 .....69 G6
Curzon Pl MYFR/PKLN W1K 10 B9
PIN HA5 .....47 G4
Curzon Rd EA W5 .....85 H3
MUSWH N10 .....54 B1
THHTH CR7 .....164 B5
Curzon St MYFR/PKLN W1K 10 B9
Cusack Cl TWK * TW1 .....143 F3
Custom House Reach
BERM/RHTH * SE16 .....112 C2
The Cut STHWK SE1 .....18 B1
Cutcombe Rd CMBW SE5 .....130 D1
Cuthberga Cl BARK IG11 .....78 C6
Cuthbert Gdns SNWD SE25 .....165 F2
Cuthbert Rd CROY/NA CR0 .....177 H1
UED N18 .....42 C4
WALTH E17 .....58 A2
Cuthbert St BAY/PAD W2 .....9 G1
Cutlers Gardens Ar LVPST EC2M 13 K4
Cutler St HDTCH EC3A 13 K4
Cuxton Cl BXLYHS DA6 .....137 F4
Cyclamen Cl HPTN TW12 .....142 A5
Cyclamen Wy HOR/WEW KT19 .....172 E4
Cygnet Av EBED/NFELT TW14 .....122 C6
Cygnet Cl NTHWD HA6 .....32 A6
WLSDN NW10 .....69 F4
The Cygnets FELT TW13 .....141 J3
Cygnet St WCHPL E1 .....7 M9
Cygnet Wy YEAD UB4 .....83 H5
Cymbeline Ct HRW * HA1 .....49 F5
Cynthia St IS N1 .....5 M6
Cypress Av WHTN TW2 .....123 H6
Cypress Gdns BROCKY SE4 .....132 B4
Cypress Rd KTN/HRWW/W HA3 .....48 D1
SNWD SE25 .....165 F1
Cypress Tree Cl BFN/LL DA15 .....136 A7
Cyprus Av FNCH N3 .....52 C1
Cyprus Cl FSBYPK N4 .....55 G5
Cyprus Gdns FNCH N3 .....52 C1
Cyprus Pl BETH E2 .....92 E1
EHAM E6 .....96 A6
Cyprus Rd ED N9 .....42 B1
FNCH N3 .....52 D1
Cyprus St BETH E2 .....92 E1
Cyrena Rd EDUL SE22 .....131 G5
Cyril Rd BXLYHN DA7 .....137 F1
Cyrus St FSBYE EC1V 6 D9
Czar St DEPT SE8 .....112 D5

D

Dabbling Cl ERITH * DA8 .....118 E6
Dabbs Hill La NTHLT UB5 .....65 K5
D'Abernon Cl ESH/CLAY KT10 .....170 A3
Dabin Crs GNWCH SE10 .....113 F7
Dacca St DEPT SE8 .....112 C5
Dace Rd BOW E3 .....75 J7
Dacre Av CLAY IG5 .....60 A1
Dacre Cl GFD/PVL UB6 .....84 B1
Dacre Gdns BORE WD6 .....25 F4
LEW * SE13 .....133 H3
Dacre Pk LEW SE13 .....133 H2
Dacre Pl LEW SE13 .....133 H2
Dacre Rd CROY/NA CR0 .....163 K6
PLSTW E13 .....77 F7
WAN E11 .....58 D7
Dacres Est FSTH * SE23 .....151 F2
Dacres Rd FSTH SE23 .....151 F2
Dacre St STJSPK SW1H 17 G3
Dade Wy NWDGN UB2 .....102 E4
Daerwood Cl HAYES BR2 .....168 E7
Daffodil Cl CROY/NA CR0 .....166 A7
HPTN TW12 .....142 A5
Daffodil Gdns IL IG1 .....78 B4
Daffodil St SHB W12 .....87 H6
Dafforne Rd TOOT SW17 .....147 K2
Dagenham Av DAGW RM9 .....80 A7
Dagenham Rd DAGE RM10 .....80 E3
LEY E10 .....57 H7
RAIN RM13 .....81 F6
ROMW/RG RM7 .....63 F6
Dagger La BORE WD6 .....23 G5
Dagmar Av WBLY HA9 .....68 B3
Dagmar Gdns WLSDN NW10 .....88 B1
Dagmar Pas IS N1 .....6 C3
Dagmar Rd CMBW SE5 .....111 F7
DAGE RM10 .....80 E6
FSBYPK N4 .....55 G6
KUTN/CMB KT2 .....144 B7
NWDGN UB2 .....102 D2
SEVS/STOTM N15 .....55 K3
SNWD SE25 .....165 F3
WDGN N22 .....40 D7
Dagmar Ter IS N1 .....6 D3
Dagnall Pk SNWD SE25 .....165 F4
Dagnall Rd SNWD SE25 .....165 F4
Dagnall St BTSEA SW11 .....128 E1
Dagnan Rd BAL SW12 .....129 G6
Dagonet Rd BMLY BR1 .....152 E2
Dahlia Gdns IL IG1 .....78 B5
MTCM CR4 .....163 J3
Dahlia Rd ABYW SE2 .....116 C4
Dahomey Rd
STRHM/NOR SW16 .....148 C5
Daimler Wy WLGTN SM6 .....176 E6
Daines Cl MNPK E12 .....77 K2
Dainford Cl BMLY BR1 .....152 B4
Daintry Cl KTN/HRWW/W HA3 .....49 G3
Dairsie Rd ELTH/MOT SE9 .....135 F2

Dairy Cl BMLY * BR1 .....153 F6
THHTH CR7 .....164 D1
Dairy La WOOL/PLUM SE18 .....114 E3
Dairyman Cl CRICK * NW2 .....70 B3
Daisy Cl CROY/NA CR0 .....166 A7
Daisy La FUL/PGN SW6 .....127 K2
Daisy Rd SWFD E18 .....59 F1
Dakota Cl CROY/NA CR0 .....177 F6
Dakota Gdns EHAM E6 .....95 J3
Dalberg Rd BRXS/STRHM SW2 .....130 B4
Dalberg Wy ABYW SE2 .....116 E2
Dalby Rd WAND/EARL SW18 .....128 B3
Dalbys Crs TOTM N17 .....42 A5
Dalby St KTTN NW5 .....72 B5
Dalcross Rd HEST TW5 .....122 D1
The Dale HAYES BR2 .....181 H3
Dale Av EDGW HA8 .....36 B7
HSLWW TW4 .....122 D2
Dalebury Rd TOOT SW17 .....147 K1
Dale Cl BAR EN5 .....27 F5
BKHTH/KID SE3 .....133 K2
DART DA1 .....138 C5
PIN HA5 .....33 F7
Dale Dr YEAD UB4 .....82 D3
Dale Gdns WFD IG8 .....45 F3
Dale Green Rd FBAR/BDGN N11 .....40 B2
Dale Gv NFNCH/WDSP N12 .....39 G4
Daleham Gdns HAMP NW3 .....71 H4
Daleham Ms HAMP * NW3 .....71 H5
Dale Park Av CAR SM5 .....175 K1
Dale Park Rd NRWD SE19 .....149 J7
Dale Rd DART DA1 .....138 C5
GFD/PVL UB6 .....84 B4
KTTN NW5 .....72 A4
SUN * TW16 .....140 D6
SUT SM1 .....174 D3
WALW SE17 .....110 C5
Dale Rw NTGHL W11 .....88 C5
Daleside Rd HOR/WEW KT19 .....173 F5
STRHM/NOR SW16 .....148 B4
Dales Pth BORE * WD6 .....25 F4
Dales Rd BORE WD6 .....25 F4
Dale St CHSWK W4 .....106 B4
Dale Vw BAR * EN5 .....26 D2
ERITH DA8 .....138 D1
Dale View Av CHING E4 .....44 A1
Dale View Crs CHING E4 .....44 A2
Dale View Gdns CHING E4 .....44 B2
Daleview Rd SEVS/STOTM N15 .....56 A5
Dalewood Gdns WPK KT4 .....173 K1
Dale Wood Rd ORP BR6 .....169 K6
Daley St HOM E9 .....75 F5
Daley Thompson Wy
VX/NE SW8 .....129 G1
Dalgarno Gdns NKENS W10 .....88 A4
Dalgarno Wy NKENS W10 .....88 A3
Dalkeith Gv STAN HA7 .....35 K4
Dalkeith Rd DUL SE21 .....130 D7
IL IG1 .....78 C2
Dallas Rd CHEAM SM3 .....174 C5
EA W5 .....86 B4
HDN NW4 .....51 J6
SYD SE26 .....150 D3
Dallas Ter HYS/HAR UB3 .....101 J2
Dallega Cl HYS/HAR UB3 .....82 B6
Dallinger Rd LEE/GVPK SE12 .....133 J5
Dalling Rd HMSMTH W6 .....106 E3
Dallington Sq FSBYE EC1V 6 D9
Dallington St FSBYE EC1V 6 D9
Dallin Rd BXLYHS DA6 .....136 E3
WOOL/PLUM SE18 .....115 G6
Dalmain Rd FSTH SE23 .....132 A7
Dalmally Rd CROY/NA CR0 .....165 G6
Dalmeny Av HOLWY N7 .....72 D3
STRHM/NOR SW16 .....164 B1
Dalmeny Cl ALP/SUD HA0 .....67 J5
Dalmeny Crs HSLW TW3 .....123 J3
Dalmeny Rd BAR EN5 .....27 G5
CAR SM5 .....176 A6
ERITH DA8 .....117 J7
HOLWY N7 .....72 D3
WPK KT4 .....173 K2
Dalmeyer Rd WLSDN NW10 .....69 H5
Dalmore Av ESH/CLAY KT10 .....171 F5
Dalmore Rd DUL SE21 .....149 J1
Dalrymple Cl STHGT/OAK N14 .....28 D6
Dalrymple Rd BROCKY SE4 .....132 B3
Dalston Gdns STAN HA7 .....36 A7
Dalston La HACK E8 .....74 B5
Dalton Av MTCM CR4 .....162 D1
Dalton Cl YEAD UB4 .....82 B3
Dalton St WNWD SE27 .....149 H1
Dalton Wy WAT WD17 .....21 H4
Dalwood St CMBW SE5 .....111 F7
Dalyell Rd BRXN/ST SW9 .....130 A2
Damask Crs CAN/RD E16 .....94 C3
Damer Ter WBPTN SW10 .....108 B6
Dames Rd FSTGT E7 .....76 E3
Dame St IS N1 .....6 E5
Damien St WCHPL E1 .....92 D4
Damon Cl SCUP DA14 .....155 H2
Damsel Ct BERM/RHTH * SE16 .....111 H1
Damson Dr HYS/HAR UB3 .....82 E6
Damsonwood Rd NWDGN UB2 .....103 F2
Danbrook Rd
STRHM/NOR SW16 .....148 E7
Danbury Cl CHDH RM6 .....61 K2
Danbury Ms CAR SM5 .....176 B3
Danbury Rd RAIN RM13 .....81 H7
Danbury St IS N1 .....6 D5
Danbury Wy WFD IG8 .....45 G5
Danby St PECK SE15 .....131 G2
Dancer Rd FUL/PGN SW6 .....107 J7
RCH/KEW TW9 .....125 H2
Dandelion Cl ROMW/RG RM7 .....81 G1
Dando Crs BKHTH/KID SE3 .....134 A2
Dandridge Cl GNWCH SE10 .....113 J4
Danebury Av PUT/ROE SW15 .....126 C6
Daneby Rd CAT SE6 .....152 A2
Dane Cl BXLY DA5 .....137 H6
Danecourt Gdns CROY/NA CR0 .....178 B2
Danecroft Rd HNHL SE24 .....130 D4
Danehurst Gdns REDBR IG4 .....59 J4
Danehurst St FUL/PGN SW6 .....107 H7
Daneland EBAR EN4 .....27 K4
Danemead Gv NTHLT UB5 .....66 B4
Danemere St PUT/ROE SW15 .....127 F2
Dane Pl BOW E3 .....93 G1
Dane Rd ASHF TW15 .....140 A5
IL IG1 .....78 C4
STHL UB1 .....83 J6
UED N18 .....42 E3
WEA W13 .....85 J6
WIM/MER SW19 .....147 G7
Danesbury Rd FELT TW13 .....122 A7
Danescombe LEE/GVPK SE12 .....133 K7
Danescourt Crs SUT SM1 .....175 G1
Danescroft Av HDN * NW4 .....52 B4
Danescroft Gdns GLDGN NW11 .....52 B4
Danesdale Rd HOM E9 .....75 G5

Danes Ga HRW HA1 48 E2
Danes Rd ROMW/RG RM7 62 E6
Dane St GINN WC1R 11 L3
Daneswood Av CAT SE6 152 A2
Danethorpe Rd ALP/SUD HA0 67 K5
Danetree Cl HOR/WEW KT19 172 E6
Danetree Rd HOR/WEW KT19 172 E6
Danette Gdns DAGE RM10 80 B1
Daneville Rd CMBW SE5 110 E7
Dangan Rd WAN E11 58 E5
Daniel Bolt Cl POP/IOD E14 93 K4
Daniel Cl HSLWW TW4 122 E6
UED N18 42 E3
WIM/MER SW19 147 J5
Daniel Gdns PECK SE15 111 G6
Daniell Wy CROY/NA CR0 163 K7
Daniel Pl HDN NW4 51 K5
Daniel Rd EA W5 86 B6
Daniel's Rd PECK SE15 131 K2
Dan Leno Wk FUL/PGN * SW6 108 A6
Dansey Pl SOHO/SHAV W1D 11 G6
Dansington Rd WELL DA16 136 B3
Danson Crs WELL DA16 136 C2
Danson La WELL DA16 136 C3
Danson Md WELL DA16 136 D2
Danson Rd BXLYHS DA6 136 E4
Danson U/P BFN/LL DA15 136 D5
Dante Rd LBTH SE11 18 C5
Danube St CHEL SW3 15 K7
Danvers Rd CEND/HSY/T N8 54 D3
Danvers St CHEL SW3 108 C5
Daphne Gdns CHING E4 44 A2
Daphne St WAND/EARL SW18 128 B5
Daplyn St WCHPL E1 92 C4
D'arblay St SOHO/CST W1F 10 F5
Darby Crs SUN TW16 156 B1
Darby Gdns SUN TW16 156 B1
Darcy Av WLGTN SM6 176 C3
Darcy Cl TRDG/WHET N20 39 H1
D'arcy Dr KTN/HRWW/W HA3 49 K3
D'arcy Gdns DAGW RM9 80 B7
KTN/HRWW/W HA3 50 A3
D'arcy Pl HAYES BR2 167 K3
D'arcy Rd CHEAM SM3 174 B3
ISLW TW7 104 B7
STRHM/NOR SW16 163 K1
Darell Rd RCH/KEW TW9 125 H2
Darenth Rd STNW/STAM N16 56 B6
WELL DA16 116 B7
Darent Valley Pth DART DA1 119 G7
Darfield Rd BROCKY SE4 132 C4
Darfield Wy NKENS W10 88 B6
Darfur St PUT/ROE SW15 127 G2
Dargate Cl NRWD SE19 150 B6
Darien Rd BTSEA SW11 128 C2
Darlands Dr BAR EN5 26 B4
Darlan Rd FUL/PGN SW6 107 J6
Darlaston Rd WIM/MER SW19 146 B6
Darley Cl CROY/NA CR0 166 A5
Darley Dr NWMAL KT3 160 A1
Darley Gdns MRDN SM4 162 A5
Darley Rd BTSEA SW11 128 E5
ED N9 30 B7
Darling Rd BROCKY SE4 132 D2
Darling Rw WCHPL E1 92 D3
Darlington Rd WNWD SE27 149 H4
Darlton Cl DART DA1 138 C2
Darmaine Cl SAND/SEL CR2 177 J6
Darndale Cl WALTH E17 57 H1
Darnley Rd HACK E8 74 D5
WFD IG8 44 E7
Darnley Ter NTGHL W11 88 B7
Darrell Rd EDUL SE22 131 H4
Darren Cl FSBYPK N4 55 F6
Darris Cl NTHLT UB5 83 J3
Darsley Dr VX/NE SW8 109 J7
Dartford Av ED N9 30 E5
Dartford Rd BXLY DA5 137 K7
DART DA1 138 D5
Dartford St WALW SE17 18 F9
Dartmoor Wk POP/IOD * E14 112 D3
Dartmouth Cl NTGHL W11 88 D5
Dartmouth Gv GNWCH SE10 113 F7
Dartmouth Hl GNWCH SE10 113 F7
Dartmouth Park Av KTTN NW5 72 B2
Dartmouth Park Hl ARCH N19 54 B7
KTTN NW5 72 B2
Dartmouth Park Rd KTTN NW5 72 B2
Dartmouth Pl CHSWK W4 106 B5
FSTH SE23 150 E1
Dartmouth Rd CRICK NW2 70 B5
HAYES BR2 167 K6
HDN NW4 51 J5
RSLP HA4 64 E2
SYD SE26 150 D2
Dartmouth Rw GNWCH SE10 133 F1
Dartmouth St STJSPK SW1H 17 G2
Dartmouth Ter GNWCH SE10 113 G7
Dartnell Rd CROY/NA CR0 165 G6
Dartrey Wk WBPTN * SW10 108 B6
Dart St MV/WKIL W9 88 D2
Darville Rd STNW/STAM N16 74 B2
Darwell Cl EHAM E6 96 A1
Darwin Cl FBAR/BDGN N11 40 B2
Darwin Dr STHL UB1 84 B5
Darwin Gdns OXHEY WD19 33 G4
Darwin Rd EA W5 104 D4
WDGN N22 41 H7
WELL DA16 136 A2
Darwin St WALW SE17 19 H5
Darygton Dr GFD/PVL UB6 84 D1
Dashwood Cl BXLYHS DA6 137 H4
Dashwood Rd CEND/HSY/T N8 55 F5
Dassett Rd WNWD SE27 149 H4
Datchelor Pl CMBW * SE5 110 E7
Datchet Rd CAT SE6 151 H2
Date St WALW SE17 19 G8
Daubeney Gdns TOTM N17 41 J6
Daubeney Rd CLPT E5 75 G4
TOTM N17 41 J6
Dault Rd WAND/EARL SW18 128 B5
Davenant Rd ARCH N19 72 D1
Davenant St WCHPL E1 92 C4
Davenham Av NTHWD HA6 32 D3
Davenport Cl TEDD * TW11 143 G5
Davenport Rd LEW SE13 132 E5
SCUP DA14 155 K1
Daventer Dr STAN HA7 35 F6
Daventry Av WALTH E17 57 J5
Daventry St CAMTN NW1 9 J2
Davern Cl GNWCH SE10 113 J3
Davey Cl HOLWY N7 73 F5
PLMGR N13 41 F4
Davey Rd HOM E9 75 J6
Davey St PECK SE15 111 G5
David Av GFD/PVL UB6 84 E2
David Cl HYS/HAR UB3 101 G6
Davidge St STHWK SE1 18 C2
David Ms MHST W1U 9 M2
David Rd BCTR RM8 80 A1
Davidson Gdns VX/NE SW8 109 K6
Davidson Rd CROY/NA CR0 165 F7
Davidson Wy ROMW/RG RM7 63 G5
David's Rd FSTH SE23 131 K7
David St SRTFD E15 76 B5
David Twigg Cl KUTN/CMB KT2 144 A7
Davies Cl SNWD SE25 165 G5
Davies La WAN E11 76 C1
Davies Ms MYFR/PKLN W1K 10 C6
Davies St MYFR/PKLN W1K 10 C6
Davies Wk ISLW TW7 103 J7
Davington Gdns BCTR RM8 79 H4
Davington Rd BCTR RM8 79 H5
Davinia Cl WFD IG8 45 K5
Davis Rd ACT W3 87 H7
CHSGTN KT9 172 C3
Davis St PLSTW E13 95 F1
Davisville Rd SHB W12 106 D1
Dawes Av ISLW TW7 124 B4
Dawes Ct ESH/CLAY KT10 170 B3
Dawes Rd FUL/PGN SW6 107 J6
Dawes St WALW SE17 19 H7
Dawley Pde HYS/HAR UB3 82 A6
Dawley Rd HYS/HAR UB3 82 B6
Dawlish Av GFD/PVL UB6 85 G1
PLMGR N13 40 E3
WAND/EARL SW18 147 F1
Dawlish Dr GDMY/SEVK IG3 79 F3
PIN HA5 47 J4
RSLP HA4 64 E1
Dawlish Rd CRICK NW2 70 B5
LEY E10 76 A1
TOTM N17 56 C2
Dawnay Gdns
WAND/EARL SW18 147 H1
Dawnay Rd WAND/EARL SW18 147 G1
Dawn Cl HSLWW TW4 122 D2
Dawn Crs SRTFD E15 76 B7
Dawpool Rd CRICK NW2 69 H1
Daws La MLHL NW7 37 H4
Dawson Av BARK IG11 79 F6
Dawson Cl HYS/HAR UB3 82 B4
WOOL/PLUM SE18 115 H3
Dawson Dr RAIN RM13 81 K6
Dawson Gdns BARK IG11 79 F6
Dawson Pl BAY/PAD W2 8 A6
Dawson Rd CRICK NW2 70 A4
KUT KT1 159 G2
Dawson St BETH E2 7 M6
Dawson Ter ED * N9 30 E6
Daybrook Rd WIM/MER SW19 162 A1
Daylesford Av PUT/ROE SW15 126 D3
Daymer Gdns PIN HA5 47 G3
Daysbrook Rd
BRXS/STRHM SW2 130 A7
Days La BFN/LL DA15 135 K6
Dayton Dr ERITH DA8 119 G5
Dayton Gv PECK SE15 111 K7
Deacon Cl PUR/KEN CR8 176 E7
The Deacon Est CHING * E4 43 H5
Deacon Ms IS N1 7 H2
Deacon Rd CRICK NW2 69 J5
KUTN/CMB KT2 144 B7
Deacons Cl BORE WD6 24 C3
PIN HA5 47 F1
Deacons Hts BORE WD6 24 C5
Deacons Hl OXHEY WD19 21 G5
Deacon's Hill Rd BORE WD6 24 B4
Deacons Ri EFNCH N2 53 H5
Deacons Ter IS * N1 73 J5
Deacons Wk HPTN TW12 142 A3
Deacon Wy WALW SE17 18 E5
WFD IG8 45 K6
Deakin Cl WATW WD18 20 C6
Deal Porters Wy
BERM/RHTH SE16 111 K2
Deal Rd TOOT SW17 148 A5
Deal St WCHPL E1 92 C4
Dealtry Rd PUT/ROE SW15 127 F3
Deal Wk BRXN/ST SW9 110 B6
Dean Bradley St WEST SW1P 17 J4
Dean Ct ALP/SUD HA0 67 H2
Deancross St WCHPL E1 92 E5
Dean Dr STAN HA7 50 A1
Deane Av RSLP HA4 65 F4
Deane Ct NTHWD * HA6 32 C7
Deane Croft Rd PIN HA5 47 G5
Deanery Cl EFNCH N2 53 J3
Deanery Ms MYFR/PKLN * W1K 10 B8
Deanery Rd SRTFD E15 76 C5
Deanery St MYFR/PKLN W1K 10 B8
Deane Wy RSLP HA4 47 F5
Dean Farrar St STJSPK SW1H 17 H3
Deanfield Gdns
CROY/NA * CR0 177 K3
Dean Gdns WALTH E17 58 B3
Deanhill Ct
MORT/ESHN * SW14 125 J3
Deanhill Rd MORT/ESHN SW14 125 J3
Dean Rd CRICK NW2 70 A5
CROY/NA CR0 177 K3
HPTN TW12 142 A4
HSLW TW3 123 G4
THMD SE28 97 G6
Dean Ryle St WEST SW1P 17 J5
Deansbrook Cl EDGW HA8 36 E6
Deansbrook Rd EDGW HA8 36 D6
Dean's Buildings WALW SE17 19 H6
Deans Cl CHSWK W4 105 J5
CROY/NA CR0 178 B2
EDGW HA8 36 E5
Dean's Ct BLKFR EC4V 12 D5
Deanscroft Av CDALE/KGS NW9 68 E1
Dean's Dr MLHL NW7 37 F4
PLMGR N13 41 H5
Deans Gate Cl FSTH SE23 151 F2
Dean's La EDGW HA8 36 E5
Dean's Ms CAVSQ/HST * W1G 10 D4
Dean's Rd HNWL W7 104 A1
SUT SM1 175 F2
Dean Stanley St WEST * SW1P 17 J4
Dean St FSTGT E7 76 E4
SOHO/CST W1F 11 G4
Deans Wy EDGW HA8 36 E4
Deansway ED N9 42 A2
EFNCH N2 53 H3
Deans Yd WEST SW1P 17 H3
Dean Trench St WEST * SW1P 17 J4
Dean Wy NWDGN UB2 103 G1
Dearne Cl STAN HA7 35 G4
De'arn Gdns MTCM CR4 162 D2
Dearsley Rd EN EN1 30 C2
Deason St SRTFD * E15 76 A7
De Barowe Ms HBRY * N5 73 H3
Debden Cl KUTN/CMB KT2 143 K4
WFD IG8 45 H6
De Beauvoir Crs IS N1 7 J3
De Beauvoir Est IS N1 7 J3
De Beauvoir Rd IS N1 7 J2
De Beauvoir Sq IS N1 7 K2
Debnams Rd BERM/RHTH SE16 111 K3
De Bohun Av STHGT/OAK N14 28 B5
Deborah Cl ISLW TW7 103 K7
Debrabant Cl ERITH DA8 118 A5
De Broome Rd FELT TW13 122 B7
Deburgh Rd WIM/MER SW19 147 G6
Decima St STHWK SE1 19 J3
Decimus Cl SNWD * SE25 164 E3
Deck Cl BERM/RHTH SE16 93 F7
Decoy Av GLDGN NW11 52 C4
De Crespigny Pk CMBW SE5 130 E1
Deeley Rd VX/NE SW8 109 J7
Deena Cl EA W5 86 B5
Deepdale WIM/MER SW19 146 B3
Deepdale Av HAYES BR2 167 J3
Deepdale Cl FBAR/BDGN N11 40 A5
Deepdene Av CROY/NA CR0 178 B2
Deepdene Cl WAN E11 58 E3
Deepdene Ct WCHMH N21 29 H5
Deepdene Gdns
BRXS/STRHM SW2 130 A6
Deepdene Rd HNHL SE24 130 D3
WELL DA16 136 B2
Deepwell Cl ISLW TW7 104 B7
Deepwood La GFD/PVL UB6 84 D2
Deerbrook Rd
BRXS/STRHM SW2 130 C7
Deerdale Rd HNHL SE24 130 D3
Deere Av RAIN RM13 81 J5
Deerhurst Cl FELT TW13 140 E3
Deerhurst Crs HPTN TW12 142 C4
Deerhurst Rd KIL/WHAMP NW6 70 B6
STRHM/NOR SW16 149 F4
Deerings Dr PIN HA5 46 E4
Deerleap Gv CHING E4 31 K4
Dee Rd RCH/KEW TW9 125 G3
Deer Park Cl KUTN/CMB KT2 144 D6
Deer Park Gdns MTCM * CR4 162 C3
Deer Park Rd WIM/MER SW19 162 A1
Deer Park Wy WWKM BR4 180 D1
Deeside Rd TOOT SW17 147 H2
Dee St POP/IOD E14 94 A5
Defiant Wy WLGTN SM6 176 E6
Defoe Av RCH/KEW TW9 105 H6
Defoe Cl WIM/MER SW19 147 J5
Defoe Rd BERM/RHTH SE16 112 C1
STNW/STAM N16 74 A1
De Frene Rd SYD SE26 151 F3
Degema Rd CHST BR7 154 B4
Dehar Crs CDALE/KGS NW9 51 H6
Dehavilland Cl NTHLT UB5 83 H2
De Havilland Rd EDGW HA8 50 D1
HEST TW5 102 B6
WLGTN SM6 176 E6
De Havilland Wy
STWL/WRAY TW19 120 A5
Dekker Rd DUL SE21 131 F5
Delacourt Rd BKHTH/KID SE3 114 A6
Delafield Rd CHARL SE7 114 A4
Delaford Rd BERM/RHTH SE16 111 J4
Delaford St FUL/PGN SW6 107 H6
Delamare Crs CROY/NA CR0 165 K5
Delamere Gdns MLHL NW7 37 F5
Delamere Rd EA W5 86 A7
RYNPK SW20 146 B7
YEAD UB4 83 H6
Delamere St BAY/PAD W2 8 E3
Delamere Ter BAY/PAD W2 8 D2
Delancey Pas CAMTN NW1 4 D4
Delancey St CAMTN NW1 4 D4
De Laune St WALW SE17 18 C8
Delaware Rd MV/WKIL W9 2 C9
Delawyk Crs HNHL SE24 130 E5
Delcombe Av WPK KT4 161 F7
Delhi Rd EN EN1 30 B6
Delhi St IS N1 5 K4
Delia St WAND/EARL SW18 128 A6
Delisle Rd THMD SE28 96 E7
Delius Cl BORE WD6 23 J5
The Dell ABYW SE2 116 B4
ALP/SUD HA0 67 H4
BECK * BR3 151 J6
BTFD TW8 104 D5
BXLY DA5 138 B7
EBED/NFELT TW14 122 A6
NRWD SE19 150 B7
NTHWD HA6 32 C1
PIN HA5 47 H1
WFD IG8 45 F2
Dellbow Rd EBED/NFELT TW14 122 A4
Dell Cl SRTFD E15 76 B7
WFD IG8 45 F2
WLGTN SM6 176 C3
Dell Farm Rd RSLP HA4 46 B4
Dellfield Cl BECK BR3 152 A7
WAT WD17 20 E1
Dell La EW KT17 173 J4
Dellors Cl BAR EN5 26 B4
Dellow Cl GNTH/NBYPK IG2 60 D6
Dellow St WCHPL E1 92 D6
Dell Rd EW KT17 173 J5
WDR/YW UB7 100 C2
Dells Cl CHING E4 31 K6
Dell's Ms PIM * SW1V 16 F6
Dell Wk NWMAL KT3 160 B1
Dell Wy WEA W13 85 J5
Dellwood Gdns CLAY IG5 60 A2
Delme Crs BKHTH/KID SE3 134 A1
Delmey Cl CROY/NA CR0 178 B2
Deloraine St DEPT SE8 112 D7
Delorme St HMSMTH W6 107 G5
Delta Cl WPK KT4 173 G2
Delta Est BETH * E2 92 C2
Delta Gain OXHEY WD19 33 H1
Delta Gv NTHLT UB5 83 H2
Delta Rd WPK KT4 173 G2
Delta St BETH * E2 92 C2
De Luci Rd ERITH DA8 117 K4
De Lucy St ABYW SE2 116 C3
Delvers Md DAGE RM10 80 E3
Delverton Rd WALW SE17 18 D7
Delvino Rd FUL/PGN SW6 107 K7
De Mandeville Ga EN EN1 30 C3
Demesne Rd WLGTN SM6 176 D3
Demeta Cl WBLY HA9 68 E2
De Montfort Pde
STRHM/NOR * SW16 148 E2
De Montfort Rd
STRHM/NOR SW16 148 D1
De Morgan Rd FUL/PGN SW6 128 A2
Dempster Rd
WAND/EARL SW18 128 B4
Denberry Dr SCUP DA14 155 H2
Denbigh Cl CHST BR7 153 K5
NTGHL W11 88 D6
STHL UB1 83 K5
SUT SM1 174 D4
WLSDN NW10 69 G6
Denbigh Dr WDR/YW UB7 101 F1
Denbigh Gdns
RCHPK/HAM TW10 125 G4
Denbigh Pl PIM SW1V 16 E7
Denbigh Rd EHAM E6 95 H2
HSLW TW3 123 G1
NTGHL W11 88 D6
STHL UB1 83 K5
WEA W13 85 H6
Denbigh St PIM SW1V 16 E6
Denbigh Ter NTGHL W11 88 D6
Denbridge Rd BMLY BR1 168 E1
Den Cl BECK BR3 167 G3
Dendy St BAL SW12 129 F7
The Dene CROY/NA CR0 179 F3
E/WMO/HCT KT8 156 E4
WBLY HA9 68 A3
WEA W13 85 H4
Dene Av BFN/LL DA15 136 C6
HSLW TW3 122 E2
Dene Cl BROCKY SE4 132 B2
HAYES BR2 167 J7
WPK KT4 173 H1
Dene Gdns STAN HA7 35 J4
THDIT KT7 171 G1
Denehurst Gdns ACT W3 86 D7
HDN NW4 52 A5
RCHPK/HAM TW10 125 H3
WFD IG8 45 F3
WHTN TW2 123 J6
Dene Rd DART DA1 139 J6
NTHWD HA6 32 A5
TRDG/WHET N20 27 K7
Denewood BAR EN5 27 G4
Denewood Rd HGT N6 53 K5
Dengie Wk IS N1 6 E3
Dengil Crs KTTN NW5 72 A4
Denham Crs MTCM CR4 162 E3
Denham Dr GNTH/NBYPK IG2 60 C5
Denham Rd EBED/NFELT TW14 122 B6
TRDG/WHET N20 39 K2
Denham Wy BARK IG11 78 E7
Denholme Rd MV/WKIL W9 88 D2
Denholme Wk RAIN RM13 81 H5
Denison Cl EFNCH N2 53 G2
Denison Rd EA W5 85 J3
FELT TW13 140 D3
WIM/MER SW19 147 H5
Deniston Av BXLY DA5 136 E7
Denleigh Gdns THDIT * KT7 157 K5
WCHMH N21 29 G6
Denman Dr ESH/CLAY KT10 171 G4
GLDGN NW11 52 E4
Denman Dr North GLDGN NW11 52 E4
Denman Dr South GLDGN NW11 52 E4
Denman Rd PECK SE15 111 G7
Denman St REGST W1B 10 F7
Denmark Av WIM/MER SW19 146 C6
Denmark Ct MRDN SM4 161 K4
Denmark Gdns CAR SM5 175 K2
Denmark Gv IS N1 6 A5
Denmark Hl CMBW SE5 110 E7
HNHL SE24 130 E3
Denmark Hill Dr
CDALE/KGS NW9 51 J2
Denmark Rd BMLY BR1 153 F7
CAR SM5 175 K2
CEND/HSY/T N8 55 F3
CMBW SE5 110 D7
KIL/WHAMP NW6 88 D1
KUT KT1 159 F2
SNWD SE25 165 H4
WEA W13 85 H6
WHTN TW2 142 D2
WIM/MER SW19 146 B5
Denmark St LSQ/SEVD WC2H 11 H5
PLSTW E13 95 F4
TOTM N17 42 D7
WAN E11 76 C2
WAT WD17 21 F1
Denmark Ter EFNCH * N2 53 K2
Denmead Rd CROY/NA CR0 164 C7
Dennan Rd SURB KT6 159 G7
Denner Rd CHING E4 43 J1
Denne Ter HACK E8 7 M4
Dennett Rd CROY/NA CR0 164 B6
Dennett's Gv NWCR SE14 132 A1
Dennett's Rd NWCR SE14 111 K7
Denning Av CROY/NA CR0 177 G4
Denning Cl HPTN TW12 141 K5
STJWD NW8 2 F7
Denning Rd HAMP NW3 71 H3
Dennington Park Rd
KIL/WHAMP NW6 70 E5
The Denningtons WPK KT4 173 G1
Dennis Av WBLY HA9 68 B4
Dennis Gdns STAN HA7 35 J4
Dennis La STAN HA7 35 H3
Dennis Pde STHGT/OAK * N14 28 D7
Dennis Park Crs RYNPK SW20 146 C7
Dennis Reeve Cl MTCM CR4 147 K7
Dennis Rd E/WMO/HCT KT8 157 H3
Dennis Wy CLAP SW4 129 J2
Denny Crs LBTH SE11 18 B7
Denny Rd ED N9 30 D7
Denny St LBTH SE11 18 B7
Den Rd HAYES BR2 167 G2
Densham Rd SRTFD E15 76 C7
Densole Cl BECK * BR3 151 G7
Densworth Gv ED N9 42 E1
Denton Cl BAR EN5 26 A4
Denton Rd CEND/HSY/T N8 55 F4
DART DA1 138 B6
TWK TW1 124 E5
UED N18 42 A3
WELL DA16 116 D6
Denton St WAND/EARL SW18 128 A5
Denton Wy CLPT E5 75 F2
Dents Rd BTSEA SW11 128 E5
Denver Cl ORP BR6 169 K5
Denver Rd DART DA1 138 D6
STNW/STAM N16 56 A6
Denyer St CHEL SW3 15 K5
Denzil Rd WLSDN NW10 69 H4
Deodar Rd PUT/ROE SW15 127 H3
Deodora Cl TRDG/WHET N20 39 J2
Depot Ap CRICK NW2 70 B3
Depot Rd HSLW TW3 123 J2
Depot St CMBW SE5 110 E5
Deptford Br GNWCH SE10 112 D7
Deptford Broadway DEPT SE8 112 D7
Deptford Church St DEPT SE8 112 D6
Deptford Gn DEPT SE8 112 D5
Deptford High St DEPT SE8 112 D5
Deptford Market DEPT * SE8 112 D6
Deptford Whf DEPT SE8 112 C3
De Quincey Rd TOTM N17 41 K7
Derby Av KTN/HRWW/W HA3 34 D7
NFNCH/WDSP N12 39 G4
ROMW/RG RM7 62 D5
Derby Ga WHALL SW1A 17 J1
Derby Hl FSTH SE23 150 E1
Derby Hill Crs FSTH SE23 150 E1
Derby Rd BRYLDS KT5 159 H7
CROY/NA CR0 177 H1
FSTGT E7 77 H6
GFD/PVL UB6 66 B7
HOM E9 75 F7
HSLW TW3 123 G3
MORT/ESHN SW14 125 J3
PEND EN3 30 D4
SUT SM1 174 D5
SWFD E18 44 D7
UED N18 42 E4
WAT WD17 21 G3
WIM/MER SW19 146 E6
Derbyshire St BETH E2 92 D2
Derby St MYFR/PICC W1J 10 B9
Dereham Pl SDTCH EC2A 7 K9
Dereham Rd BARK IG11 79 F5
Derek Av HOR/WEW KT19 172 C5
WBLY HA9 68 D6
WLGTN SM6 176 B2
Derek Cl HOR/WEW KT19 172 D4
Derek Walcott Cl HNHL * SE24 130 C4
Deri Av RAIN RM13 99 K3
Dericote St HACK E8 74 C7
Deri Dene Cl
STWL/WRAY * TW19 120 B5
Derifall Cl EHAM E6 95 K4
Dering Pl CROY/NA CR0 177 J3
Dering Rd CROY/NA CR0 177 J3
Dering St CONDST W1S 10 C5
Derinton Rd TOOT SW17 148 A3
Derley Rd NWDGN UB2 102 B2
Dermody Gdns LEW * SE13 133 G4
Dermody Rd LEW SE13 133 G4
Deronda Rd BRXS/STRHM SW2 130 C7
Deroy Cl CAR SM5 175 K5
Derrick Gdns CHARL SE7 114 B2
Derrick Rd BECK BR3 166 C2
Derry Rd CROY/NA CR0 176 E2
Derry St KENS W8 14 C2
Dersingham Av MNPK E12 77 K3
Dersingham Rd CRICK NW2 70 C2
Derwent Av CDALE/KGS NW9 51 G4
EBAR EN4 27 K7
MLHL NW7 37 F5
PIN HA5 33 J5
PUT/ROE SW15 145 G3
UED N18 41 K4
Derwent Cl DART DA1 138 E7
EBED/NFELT TW14 121 J7
ESH/CLAY KT10 170 E5
Derwent Crs BXLYHN DA7 137 H1
NFNCH/WDSP N12 39 G2
STAN HA7 49 J1
Derwent Dr STMC/STPC BR5 169 J6
YEAD UB4 82 C4
Derwent Gdns REDBR IG4 59 J3
WBLY HA9 49 J6
Derwent Gv EDUL SE22 131 G3
Derwent Ri CDALE/KGS NW9 51 G5
Derwent Rd EA W5 104 D2
MRDN SM4 161 G5
PGE/AN SE20 165 H1
PLMGR N13 41 F3
STHL UB1 83 K5
WHTN TW2 123 G5
Derwent St GNWCH SE10 113 H4
Derwentwater Rd ACT W3 86 E7
Derwent Wy HCH RM12 81 K4
Derwent Yd EA * W5 104 D2
De Salis Rd HGDN/ICK UB10 82 A3
Desborough Cl BAY/PAD W2 8 D2
Desenfans Rd DUL SE21 131 F5
Desford Rd CAN/RD E16 94 C3
Desmond St NWCR SE14 112 B5
Despard Rd ARCH N19 54 C7
Detling Rd BMLY BR1 152 E4
ERITH DA8 118 A6
Detmold Rd CLPT E5 74 D1
Devalls Cl EHAM E6 96 A6
Devana End CAR SM5 175 K2
Devas Rd RYNPK SW20 146 A7
Devas St BOW E3 93 K3
Devema Cl CHST BR7 154 A7
Devenay Rd SRTFD E15 76 D6
Devenish Rd ABYW SE2 116 B1
De Vere Gdns IL IG1 77 K1
KENS W8 14 E2
Deverell St STHWK SE1 19 G4
De Vere Ms KENS W8 14 E3
Devereux Ct TPL/STR WC2R 12 A5
Devereux La BARN SW13 106 E6
Devereux Rd BTSEA SW11 128 E5
De Vere Wk WAT WD17 20 C1
Devey Cl KUTN/CMB KT2 145 H6
Devizes St IS * N1 7 H4
Devon Av WHTN TW2 123 H7
Devon Cl BKHH IG9 45 F1
GFD/PVL UB6 67 J7
TOTM N17 56 B2
Devoncroft Gdns TWK TW1 124 B6
Devon Gdns FSBYPK N4 55 H5
Devonhurst Pl CHSWK * W4 106 A4
Devonia Gdns UED N18 41 J5
Devonia Rd IS N1 6 D5
Devon Man
KTN/HRWW/W * HA3 49 J4
Devonport Gdns IL IG1 59 K5
Devonport Ms SHB * W12 87 K7
Devonport Rd SHB W12 87 K7
Devonport St WCHPL E1 92 E5
Devon Ri EFNCH N2 53 H3
Devon Rd BARK IG11 78 E7
BELMT SM2 174 C7
Devons Est BOW E3 93 K2
Devonshire Av BELMT SM2 175 G6
DART DA1 138 E5
Devonshire Cl CAVSQ/HST W1G 10 C2
SRTFD E15 76 C3
Devonshire Ct FELT * TW13 141 F1
Devonshire Crs MLHL NW7 38 B6
Devonshire Dr GNWCH SE10 112 E7
SURB KT6 158 E7
Devonshire Gdns CHSWK W4 105 K6
TOTM N17 41 J5
WCHMH N21 29 J6
Devonshire Gv PECK SE15 111 J5
Devonshire Hill La TOTM N17 41 K5
Devonshire Ms South
CAVSQ/HST W1G 10 C2
Devonshire Ms West
CAVSQ/HST W1G 10 B1
Devonshire Pl
CAVSQ/HST W1G 10 B1
CRICK NW2 70 E2
KENS * W8 14 C4
Devonshire Place Ms
MHST W1U 10 B1

Devonshire Rd BELMT SM2 175 G6
BXLYHS DA6 137 F3
CAN/RD E16 95 F5
CAR SM5 176 A3
CHSWK W4 106 B4
CROY/NA CR0 164 E6
EA W5 104 D2
ED N9 30 E7
ELTH/MOT SE9 153 J1
FELT TW13 141 J2
FSTH SE23 132 A6
GNTH/NBYPK IG2 60 D6
HRW HA1 48 D5
MLHL NW7 38 B6
PIN HA5 33 K7
PIN HA5 47 G5
PLMGR N13 41 F3
STHL UB1 84 A4
TOTM N17 41 J5
WALTH E17 57 J5
WIM/MER SW19 147 J6
Devonshire Rw LVPST EC2M 13 K3
Devonshire Sq HAYES BR2 168 A3
LVPST EC2M 13 K4
Devonshire St CAVSQ/HST W1G 10 B2
CHSWK W4 106 B4
Devonshire Ter BAY/PAD W2 8 F5
EDUL * SE22 131 H3
Devonshire Wy CROY/NA CR0 179 H1
YEAD UB4 83 F5
Devons Rd BOW E3 93 J4
Devon St PECK SE15 111 J5
Devon Wy CHSGTN KT9 171 J3
HOR/WEW KT19 172 D4
Devon Waye HEST TW5 102 E6
De Walden St CAVSQ/HST W1G 10 B3
Dewar St PECK SE15 131 H2
Dewberry Gdns EHAM E6 95 J4
Dewberry St POP/IOD E14 94 A5
Dewey Rd DAGE RM10 80 E5
IS N1 6 A5
Dewey St TOOT SW17 147 K4
Dewhurst Rd WKENS W14 107 G2
Dewsbury Cl PIN HA5 47 J5
Dewsbury Gdns WPK KT4 173 J2
Dewsbury Rd WLSDN NW10 69 J4
Dexter Rd BAR EN5 26 B5
Deyncourt Rd TOTM N17 41 J7
Deynecourt Gdns WAN E11 59 G3
D'eynsford Rd CMBW SE5 110 E7
Diadem Ct SOHO/SHAV * W1D 11 G4
Diamedes Av
STWL/WRAY TW19 120 A6
Diameter Rd STMC/STPC BR5 169 G6
Diamond Cl BCTR RM8 61 J7
Diamond Rd RSLP HA4 65 H3
Diamond St PECK SE15 111 F6
WLSDN NW10 68 E6
Diana Cl DEPT SE8 112 C5
SWFD E18 45 F7
Diana Gdns SURB KT6 172 B1
Diana Pl CAMTN NW1 4 D9
Diana Rd WALTH E17 57 H2
Dianne Wy EBAR EN4 27 J3
Dianthus Cl ABYW * SE2 116 C4
Diban Av HCH RM12 81 K3
Dibden St IS N1 6 E3
Dibdin Cl SUT SM1 174 E2
Dibdin Rd SUT SM1 174 E2
Dicey Av CRICK NW2 70 A4
Dickens Av DART DA1 139 K3
FNCH N3 39 G7
Dickens Cl ERITH DA8 117 J6
HYS/HAR UB3 101 H3
RCHPK/HAM TW10 144 A1
Dickens Dr CHST BR7 154 C5
Dickens Est
BERM/RHTH * SE16 111 H2
Dickens La UED N18 42 A4
Dickens Ms FARR EC1M 12 C1
Dickenson Cl ED N9 30 C7
Dickenson Rd CEND/HSY/T N8 54 E6
FELT TW13 141 G4
Dickenson's La SNWD SE25 165 H5
Dickenson's Pl SNWD SE25 165 H5
Dickens Rd EHAM E6 95 H1
Dickens Sq STHWK SE1 18 F3
Dickens St VX/NE SW8 129 G1
Dickens Wy ROM RM1 63 G3
Dickens Wood Cl NRWD SE19 149 H6
Dickerage Hl NWMAL KT3 159 K1
Dickerage La NWMAL KT3 159 K2
Dickerage Rd KUT KT1 144 E7
NWMAL KT3 159 K1
Dickson Fold PIN HA5 47 H3
Dickson House
WOOL/PLUM SE18 114 D7
Dickson Rd ELTH/MOT SE9 134 D2
Dick Turpin Wy
EBED/NFELT TW14 121 J3
Didsbury Cl EHAM E6 77 K7
Digby Crs FSBYPK N4 73 J1
Digby Gdns DAGE RM10 80 C7
Digby Pl CROY/NA CR0 178 B2
Digby Rd BARK IG11 79 F6
HOM E9 75 F5
Digby St BETH E2 92 E2
Diggon St WCHPL E1 93 F4
Dighton Rd WAND/EARL SW18 128 B4
Dignum St IS * N1 6 A5
Digswell St HOLWY * N7 73 G5
Dilhorne Cl LEE/GVPK SE12 153 F2
Dilke St CHEL SW3 15 M9
Dillwyn Cl SYD SE26 151 G3
Dilston Cl NTHLT UB5 83 G2
Dilton Gdns PUT/ROE SW15 126 D7
Dimes Pl HMSMTH W6 106 E3
Dimmock Dr GFD/PVL UB6 66 D4
Dimond Cl FSTGT E7 76 E3
Dimsdale Dr CDALE/KGS NW9 50 E7
EN EN1 30 C6
Dimson Crs BOW E3 93 J3
Dingle Cl BAR EN5 25 H5
Dingle Gdns POP/IOD * E14 93 J6
Dingley La STRHM/NOR SW16 148 D1
Dingley Pl FSBYE EC1V 6 F8
Dingley Rd FSBYE EC1V 6 E8
Dingwall Av CROY/NA CR0 177 J1
Dingwall Gdns GLDGN NW11 52 E5
Dingwall Rd CAR SM5 175 K7
CROY/NA CR0 177 K1
WAND/EARL SW18 128 B6
Dinmont St BETH E2 92 D1
Dinsdale Gdns BAR EN5 27 F4
SNWD SE25 165 F3
Dinsdale Rd BKHTH/KID SE3 113 J5
Dinsmore Rd BAL SW12 129 G6
Dinton Rd KUTN/CMB KT2 144 B6
WIM/MER SW19 147 H5
Diploma Av EFNCH N2 53 J3
Dirleton Rd SRTFD E15 76 D7
Disbrowe Rd HMSMTH W6 107 H5
Discovery Wk WAP E1W 92 D6
Dishforth La CDALE/KGS NW9 37 G7
Disney Pl STHWK SE1 18 F1
Disney St STHWK SE1 18 F1
Disraeli Cl THMD SE28 97 H7
Disraeli Rd EA W5 85 K7
FSTGT E7 76 E5
PUT/ROE SW15 127 H3
WLSDN NW10 86 E1
Diss St BETH E2 7 L7
Distaff La BLKFR EC4V 12 E6
Distillery La HMSMTH W6 107 F4
Distillery Rd HMSMTH W6 107 F4
Distin St LBTH SE11 18 A6
District Rd ALP/SUD HA0 67 H4
Ditchburn St POP/IOD E14 94 A6
Ditchfield Rd YEAD UB4 83 J3
Dittisham Rd ELTH/MOT SE9 153 J3
Ditton Cl THDIT KT7 158 B6
Dittoncroft Cl SAND/SEL CR2 178 A3
Ditton Grange Cl SURB KT6 158 E7
Ditton Grange Dr SURB KT6 158 E7
Ditton Hl SURB KT6 158 D7
Ditton Hill Rd SURB KT6 158 D7
Ditton Lawn THDIT KT7 158 B7
Ditton Pl PGE/AN * SE20 150 D7
Ditton Reach THDIT KT7 158 C5
Ditton Rd BXLYHS DA6 136 E4
NWDGN UB2 102 E4
SURB KT6 159 F7
Dixey Cottages EFNCH * N2 53 J4
Dixon Cl EHAM E6 95 K5
Dixon Pl WWKM BR4 166 E7
Dixon Rd NWCR SE14 112 B7
SNWD SE25 165 F2
Dobbin Cl KTN/HRWW/W HA3 49 G1
Dobell Rd ELTH/MOT SE9 134 E4
Dobree Av WLSDN NW10 69 K6
Dobson Cl KIL/WHAMP NW6 3 G2
Dockers Tanner Rd
POP/IOD E14 112 D3
Dockhead STHWK SE1 19 M2
Dock Hill Av BERM/RHTH SE16 112 A1
Dockland St CAN/RD E16 96 A7
Dockley Rd BERM/RHTH SE16 111 H2
Dock Rd BTFD * TW8 104 E6
CAN/RD E16 94 D6
Dockside Rd CAN/RD E16 95 H6
Dock St WCHPL E1 92 C6
Dockwell Cl EBED/NFELT TW14 121 K3
Doctors Cl SYD SE26 150 E4
Dodbrooke Rd WNWD SE27 149 G2
Doddington Gv WALW SE17 18 C9
Doddington Pl WALW SE17 18 C9
Dodsley Pl ED N9 42 E2
Dodson St STHWK SE1 18 B2
Dod St POP/IOD E14 93 H5
Doebury Wk
WOOL/PLUM SE18 116 B5
Doel Cl WIM/MER SW19 147 G6
Doggett Rd CAT SE6 132 D6
Doggetts Ct EBAR EN4 27 J4
Doghurst Av WDR/YW UB7 100 E6
Doghurst Dr WDR/YW UB7 100 E6
Dog Kennel Hl EDUL SE22 131 F2
Dog La WLSDN NW10 69 G3
Dog Rose Ramble NTHLT UB5 64 E7
Dog Rose Ramble &
Hillingdon Trail
YEAD UB4 64 D7
Doherty Rd PLSTW E13 94 E3
Dolben Ct DEPT * SE8 112 C3
Dolben St STHWK * SE1 12 D9
Dolby Rd FUL/PGN SW6 127 J1
Dolland St LBTH SE11 17 M8
Dollary Pde KUT * KT1 159 J2
Dollis Av FNCH N3 38 D7
Dollis Crs RSLP HA4 47 G7
Dollis Hill Av CRICK NW2 69 K2
Dollis Hill Est CRICK * NW2 69 J2
Dollis Hill La CRICK NW2 69 H3
Dollis Pk FNCH N3 38 D7
Dollis Rd FNCH N3 38 C7
Dollis Valley Green Wk
GLDGN NW11 52 C3
TRDG/WHET N20 27 F5
Dollis Valley Wy BAR EN5 26 D4
Dolman Cl FNCH N3 53 G1
Dolman Rd CHSWK W4 106 A3
Dolman St BRXN/ST SW9 130 A3
Dolphin Ap ROM RM1 63 H3
Dolphin Cl SURB KT6 158 E5
THMD SE28 97 J5
Dolphin Est SUN * TW16 140 C7
Dolphin La POP/IOD E14 93 K6
Dolphin Rd NTHLT UB5 83 K1
SUN TW16 140 C7
Dolphin Rd North SUN TW16 140 B7
Dolphin Rd South SUN TW16 140 B7
Dolphin Rd West SUN TW16 140 C7
Dolphin Sq CHSWK * W4 106 B6
PIM SW1V 16 F8
Dolphin St KUT KT1 159 F1
Dombey St BMSBY WC1N 11 L2
Dome Buildings
RCHPK/HAM * TW10 124 E4
Dome Hill Pk SYD SE26 150 B3
Domett Cl CMBW SE5 130 E3
Domingo St FSBYE EC1V 6 E9
Dominica Cl PLSTW E13 95 H2
Dominion Pde HRW * HA1 49 F4
Dominion Rd CROY/NA CR0 165 G6
NWDGN UB2 102 D2
Dominion St LVPST EC2M 13 H2
Dominion Wy RAIN RM13 99 J2
Domonic Dr ELTH/MOT SE9 154 B2
Domville Cl TRDG/WHET N20 39 H1
Donald Dr CHDH RM6 61 J4
Donald Rd CROY/NA CR0 164 A5
PLSTW E13 77 F7
Donaldson Rd KIL/WHAMP NW6 70 D7
WOOL/PLUM SE18 115 F7
Donald Woods Gdns
BRYLDS KT5 172 D1
Doncaster Dr NTHLT UB5 65 K4
Doncaster Gdns FSBYPK * N4 55 J5
NTHLT UB5 65 K4
Doncaster Gn OXHEY WD19 33 G4
Doncaster Rd ED N9 30 D6
Donegal St IS N1 5 M6
Doneraile St FUL/PGN SW6 127 G1
Dongola Rd PLSTW E13 95 F2
TOTM N17 56 A2
WCHPL E1 93 G4
Dongola Rd West PLSTW E13 95 F2
Donington Av BARK/HLT IG6 60 C4
Donkey Aly EDUL SE22 131 H6
Donkey La EN EN1 30 C1
Donnefield Av EDGW HA8 36 A5
Donne Pl CHEL SW3 15 K5
MTCM CR4 163 G3
Donne Rd BCTR RM8 79 J1
Donnington Rd
KTN/HRWW/W HA3 49 K5
WLSDN NW10 69 K7
WPK KT4 173 J1
Donnybrook Rd
STRHM/NOR SW16 148 C6
Donoghue Cottages
POP/IOD * E14 93 G4
Donovan Av MUSWH N10 54 B1
Don Phelan Cl CMBW SE5 110 E7
Doone Cl TEDD TW11 143 G5
Doon St STHWK SE1 12 A9
Doral Wy CAR SM5 175 K4
Dorando Cl SHB * W12 87 K6
Doran Gv WOOL/PLUM SE18 115 K6
Dora Rd WIM/MER SW19 146 E4
Dora St POP/IOD E14 93 H5
Dorchester Av BXLY DA5 136 E7
PLMGR N13 41 J3
RYLN/HDSTN HA2 48 C5
Dorchester Cl DART DA1 139 J6
NTHLT UB5 66 B4
STMC/STPC BR5 155 H6
Dorchester Ct CRICK NW2 70 B2
HNHL SE24 130 D4
RKW/CH/CXG * WD3 20 A4
STHGT/OAK N14 28 B6
Dorchester Dr
EBED/NFELT TW14 121 H5
HNHL SE24 130 D4
Dorchester Gdns CHING E4 43 J3
GLDGN * NW11 52 E3
Dorchester Gv CHSWK W4 106 B5
Dorchester Ms TWK TW1 124 D5
Dorchester Pde
STRHM/NOR * SW16 148 E1
Dorchester Rd MRDN SM4 162 A6
NTHLT UB5 66 B4
WPK KT4 161 F7
Dorchester Ter HDN * NW4 52 B1
Dorchester Wy
KTN/HRWW/W HA3 50 B5
Dorchester Waye YEAD UB4 83 G5
Dorcis Av BXLYHN DA7 137 F1
Dordrecht Rd ACT W3 87 G7
Dore Av MNPK E12 78 A4
Doreen Av CDALE/KGS NW9 51 F7
Dore Gdns MRDN SM4 162 A6
Dorell Cl STHL UB1 83 K4
Dorian Rd HCH RM12 63 J7
Doria Rd FUL/PGN SW6 127 J1
Doric Wy CAMTN NW1 5 G7
Dorien Rd RYNPK SW20 161 G1
Doris Av BXLYHN DA7 117 K7
Doris Rd ASHF TW15 140 B5
FSTGT E7 76 E6
Dorking Cl DEPT SE8 112 C5
WPK KT4 174 B1
Dorlcote Rd WAND/EARL SW18 128 C6
Dorman Pl ED N9 42 C1
Dormans Cl NTHWD HA6 32 B6
Dorman Wy STJWD NW8 3 G3
Dormay St WAND/EARL SW18 128 A4
Dormer Cl BAR EN5 26 B4
SRTFD E15 76 D5
Dormer's Av STHL UB1 84 A5
Dormers Ri STHL UB1 84 B5
Dormer's Wells La STHL UB1 84 A5
Dormywood RSLP HA4 46 D4
Dornberg Cl BKHTH/KID SE3 113 K6
Dornberg Rd BKHTH/KID * SE3 114 A6
Dorncliffe Rd FUL/PGN SW6 127 H1
Dorney Wy HSLWW TW4 122 D4
Dornfell St KIL/WHAMP NW6 70 D4
Dornton Rd BAL SW12 148 B1
SAND/SEL CR2 178 A4
Dorothy Av ALP/SUD HA0 68 A6
Dorothy Evans Cl BXLYHN DA7 137 J3
Dorothy Gdns BCTR RM8 79 H3
Dorothy Rd BTSEA SW11 128 E2
Dorrington St HCIRC EC1N 12 A2
Dorrit St STHWK * SE1 18 F1
Dorrit Wy CHST BR7 154 C5
Dorrofield Cl RKW/CH/CXG WD3 20 A4
Dors Cl CDALE/KGS NW9 51 F7
Dorset Av NWDGN UB2 103 F3
ROM RM1 63 F2
WELL DA16 136 A3
YEAD UB4 82 C2
Dorset Buildings EMB * EC4Y 12 C5
Dorset Cl CAMTN NW1 9 L2
YEAD * UB4 82 C2
Dorset Dr EDGW HA8 36 B5
Dorset Gdns
STRHM/NOR SW16 164 A3
Dorset Ms FNCH N3 38 E7
KTBR SW1X 16 C3
Dorset Pl SRTFD E15 76 B5
Dorset Ri EMB EC4Y 12 C5
Dorset Rd BECK BR3 166 A2
EA W5 104 D2
ELTH/MOT SE9 153 J1
HRW HA1 48 C6
MTCM CR4 162 D1
SEVS/STOTM N15 55 K3
VX/NE SW8 110 A6
WDGN N22 40 E7
WIM/MER SW19 146 E7
Dorset Sq CAMTN NW1 9 L2
Dorset St MHST W1U 9 M3
Dorset Wy WHTN TW2 123 H7
Dorset Waye HEST TW5 102 E6
Dorton Cl PECK * SE15 111 F6
Dorville Crs HMSMTH W6 106 E2
Dorville Rd LEE/GVPK SE12 133 K4
Dothill Rd WOOL/PLUM SE18 115 H6
Douai Gv HPTN TW12 142 C7
Doughty Ms BMSBY WC1N 11 L1
Doughty St BMSBY WC1N 5 L9
Douglas Av ALP/SUD HA0 68 A6
NWMAL KT3 160 E3
WALTH E17 43 J7
Douglas Cl STAN HA7 35 G4
WLGTN SM6 176 E5
Douglas Crs YEAD UB4 83 G3
Douglas Dr CROY/NA CR0 179 J2
Douglas Est IS * N1 73 J5
Douglas Ms CRICK NW2 70 C2
Douglas Pl POP/IOD * E14 113 F4
Douglas Rd CAN/RD E16 94 E4
ESH/CLAY KT10 170 B1
GDMY/SEVK IG3 61 G6
HSLW TW3 123 G2
IS N1 6 E1
KIL/WHAMP NW6 70 D7
KUT KT1 159 J1
ROM RM1 63 H5
STWL/WRAY TW19 120 A5
SURB KT6 172 B1
WDGN N22 41 G7
WELL DA16 116 C7
Douglas Rd North IS N1 73 J5
Douglas Rd South IS * N1 73 J5
Douglas St WEST SW1P 17 G6
Douglas Ter WALTH E17 43 H7
Douglas Vls KUT * KT1 159 G1
Douglas Wy NWCR SE14 112 C6
Doulton Ms KIL/WHAMP NW6 71 F5
Dounesforth Gdns
WAND/EARL SW18 128 A7
Douro Pl KENS W8 14 D3
Douro St BOW E3 93 J1
Douthwaite Sq WAP E1W 92 C7
Dove Ap EHAM E6 95 J4
Dove Cl CROY/NA CR0 177 F6
MLHL NW7 37 J6
NTHLT UB5 83 H3
Dovecot Cl PIN HA5 47 G4
Dove Ct LOTH * EC2R 13 G5
Dovedale Av CLAY IG5 60 A1
KTN/HRWW/W HA3 49 J5
Dovedale Cl WELL DA16 116 B7
Dovedale Ri MTCM CR4 147 K6
Dovedale Rd EDUL SE22 131 J4
Dovedon Cl STHGT/OAK N14 40 E1
Dove House Gdns CHING E4 43 J1
Dovehouse Md BARK IG11 96 D1
Dovehouse St CHEL SW3 15 J8
Dove Ms ECT SW5 14 E6
Dove Pk PIN HA5 33 K6
Dover Cl CRICK NW2 70 B1
ROMW/RG RM7 62 E1
Dovercourt Av THHTH CR7 164 B3
Dovercourt Est IS N1 73 K5
Dovercourt Gdns STAN HA7 36 A4
Dovercourt La SUT SM1 175 G2
Dovercourt Rd EDUL SE22 131 F5
Doverfield Rd
BRXS/STRHM SW2 129 K5
Dover Gdns CAR SM5 175 K2
Dover House Rd
PUT/ROE SW15 126 D3
Doveridge Gdns PLMGR N13 41 H3
Dove Rd IS N1 73 K5
Dove Rw BETH E2 92 C1
Dover Park Dr PUT/ROE SW15 126 E5
Dover Patrol BKHTH/KID SE3 134 A1
Dover Rd ED N9 42 E1
MNPK E12 77 G1
NRWD SE19 149 K5
WOOL/PLUM SE18 135 G1
Dover St MYFR/PICC W1J 10 D7
Dover Ter RCH/KEW * TW9 125 H1
Dover Wy RKW/CH/CXG WD3 20 A3
Doves Cl HAYES BR2 181 J1
Doves Yd IS N1 6 A4
Doveton Rd SAND/SEL CR2 177 K4
Doveton St WCHPL E1 92 E3
Dowanhill Rd CAT SE6 133 G7
Dowdeswell Cl PUT/ROE SW15 126 B3
Dowding Cl HCH RM12 81 K6
Dowding Pl STAN HA7 35 G5
Dowdney Cl KTTN NW5 72 C4
Dower Av WLGTN SM6 176 B7
Dowgate Hl CANST EC4R 13 G6
Dowland St NKENS W10 88 C2
Dowlas St CMBW SE5 111 F6
Dowman Cl WIM/MER SW19 147 F7
Downage HDN NW4 52 A2
Downalong BUSH WD23 22 D7
Downbank Av BXLYHN DA7 118 A7
Down Barns Rd RSLP HA4 65 H3
Down Cl NTHLT UB5 83 F2
Downderry Rd BMLY BR1 152 B2
Downe Cl WELL DA16 116 D6
Downend WOOL/PLUM SE18 115 G6
Downe Rd HAYES BR2 181 J7
MTCM CR4 162 E1
Downer's Cottages CLAP SW4 129 H3
Downes Cl TWK TW1 124 C5
Downes Ct WCHMH N21 29 G7
Downfield WPK KT4 160 C7
Downfield Cl MV/WKIL W9 8 C1
Down Hall Rd KUTN/CMB KT2 143 K7
Downham Rd IS N1 7 G2
Downham Wy BMLY BR1 152 C4
Downhills Av TOTM N17 55 K2
Downhills Park Rd TOTM N17 55 J2
Downhills Wy TOTM N17 55 J1
Downhurst Av MLHL NW7 37 F5
Downing Cl RYLN/HDSTN HA2 48 C2
Downing Dr GFD/PVL UB6 66 E7
Downing Rd DAGW RM9 80 B7
Downings EHAM E6 96 A5
Downing St WHALL SW1A 17 J1
Downland Cl TRDG/WHET N20 27 G7
Downleys Cl ELTH/MOT SE9 153 J1
Downman Rd ELTH/MOT SE9 134 D2
Down Pl HMSMTH W6 106 E3
Down Rd TEDD TW11 143 H5
The Downs RYNPK SW20 146 B6
Downs Av CHST BR7 153 K4
DART DA1 139 K6
PIN HA5 47 K5
Downs Bridge Rd BECK BR3 152 B7
Downs Court Pde CLPT * E5 74 D4
Downsell Rd WAN E11 76 B3
Downsfield Rd WALTH E17 57 G5
Downshall Av GDMY/SEVK IG3 60 E5
Downs Hl BECK BR3 152 B7
Downshire Hl HAMP NW3 71 H3
Downside BECK * BR3 151 J7
SUN TW16 140 E7
TWK TW1 143 F2
Downside Cl WIM/MER SW19 147 G5
Downside Crs HAMP NW3 71 J4
WEA W13 85 G3
Downside Rd BELMT SM2 175 H5
Downs La CLPT E5 74 D3
Downs Park Rd HACK E8 74 C4
Downs Rd BECK BR3 166 E1
CLPT E5 74 D3
EN EN1 30 A3
THHTH CR7 149 J7
Down St E/WMO/HCT KT8 157 F4
MYFR/PICC W1J 10 C9
Down Street Ms
MYFR/PICC W1J 16 C1
Downs Vw ISLW TW7 104 A7
Downsview Gdns NRWD SE19 149 J6
Downsview Rd NRWD SE19 149 J6
The Downsway BELMT SM2 175 G7
Downton Av
BRXS/STRHM SW2 149 F1
Downtown Rd
BERM/RHTH SE16 112 B1
Downway NFNCH/WDSP N12 39 J6
Down Wy NTHLT UB5 83 F2
Dowrey St IS * N1 6 A3
Dowsett Rd TOTM N17 56 C1
Dowson Cl CMBW * SE5 130 E3
Doyce St STHWK * SE1 18 E1
Doyle Cl ERITH DA8 118 B7
Doyle Gdns WLSDN NW10 69 K7
Doyle Rd SNWD SE25 165 H3
D'oyley St KTBR SW1X 16 A5
Doynton St ARCH * N19 72 B1
Draco Ga PUT/ROE * SW15 127 F2
Draco St WALW SE17 18 E9
Dragonfly Cl PLSTW E13 95 F2
Dragon Rd PECK * SE15 111 F5
Dragoon Rd DEPT SE8 112 C4
Dragor Rd WLSDN NW10 86 E3
Drake Cl BERM/RHTH SE16 112 A1
Drake Crs THMD SE28 97 J5
Drakefell Rd NWCR SE14 132 A1
Drakefield Rd TOOT SW17 148 A2
Drake Ms HCH RM12 81 J6
Drake Rd BROCKY SE4 132 D2
CHSGTN KT9 172 C4
CROY/NA CR0 164 A6
MTCM CR4 163 F5
RYLN/HDSTN HA2 65 K1
Drake's Cl ESH/CLAY KT10 170 A4
Drakes Ctyd KIL/WHAMP NW6 70 D6
Drake St BMSBY WC1N 11 L3
Drakewood Rd
STRHM/NOR SW16 148 D6
Draper Cl BELV DA17 117 G3
Draper Est WALW SE17 18 D5
Draper Pl IS N1 6 D3
Drapers Rd ENC/FH EN2 29 H1
SRTFD E15 76 A3
TOTM N17 56 B2
Drappers Wy
BERM/RHTH SE16 111 H3
Draven Cl HAYES BR2 167 J6
Drawell Cl WOOL/PLUM SE18 115 K4
Drax Av RYNPK SW20 145 J6
Draxmont WIM/MER SW19 146 C5
Draycot Rd SURB KT6 159 H7
WAN E11 59 F5
Draycott Av CHEL SW3 15 K6
KTN/HRWW/W HA3 49 H5
Draycott Cl CRICK NW2 70 B2
KTN/HRWW/W HA3 49 H5
Draycott Pl CHEL SW3 15 L6
Draycott Ter CHEL SW3 15 L5
Dray Ct ALP/SUD * HA0 67 J5
Drayford Cl MV/WKIL * W9 88 D3
Draymans Wy ISLW TW7 124 A2
Drayson Ms KENS W8 14 B2
Drayton Av ORP BR6 169 G7
WEA W13 85 G6
Drayton Bridge Rd HNWL W7 85 F6
Drayton Cl HSLWW TW4 122 E4
IL IG1 60 D7
Drayton Ct WDR/YW * UB7 100 C3
Drayton Ct Chambers
WEA * W13 85 H6
Drayton Gdns WBPTN SW10 14 F7
WCHMH N21 29 H6
WDR/YW UB7 100 A1
WEA W13 85 G6
Drayton Gn WEA W13 85 G6
Drayton Green Rd WEA W13 85 H6
Drayton Gv WEA W13 85 G6
Drayton Pk HOLWY N7 73 G4
Drayton Park Ms HOLWY * N7 73 G4
Drayton Rd BORE WD6 24 C3
CROY/NA CR0 177 H1
TOTM N17 56 A1
WAN E11 58 B7
WEA W13 85 G5
WLSDN NW10 69 H7
Dreadnought St GNWCH SE10 113 H2
Drenon Sq HYS/HAR UB3 82 D6
Dresden Cl HAMP NW3 71 F5
Dresden Rd ARCH N19 54 C7
Dressington Av BROCKY SE4 132 D5
Drew Av MLHL NW7 38 C5
Drewery Ct BKHTH/KID * SE3 133 H2
Drew Gdns GFD/PVL UB6 67 F5
Drew Rd CAN/RD E16 95 J7
Drews Cottages BAL * SW12 148 D1
Drewstead Rd
STRHM/NOR SW16 148 D1
Driffield Rd BOW E3 93 G1
The Drift HAYES BR2 181 H2
The Driftway MTCM CR4 148 A7
Drinkwater Rd
RYLN/HDSTN HA2 66 B1
The Drive ACT W3 86 E5
ASHF TW15 140 B6
BAR EN5 26 C2
BAR EN5 27 G5
BARK IG11 79 F6
BECK BR3 166 D1
BXLY DA5 136 D5
CHST BR7 155 F7
EBED/NFELT TW14 122 A6
EDGW HA8 36 C4
ERITH DA8 117 J6
ESH/CLAY KT10 157 H7
FBAR/BDGN N11 40 C5
FNCH N3 38 E6
GLDGN NW11 52 C6
HGT N6 53 K4
HOLWY N7 73 F5
HOR/WEW KT19 173 H5
HSLW TW3 123 J1
IL IG1 59 J5
KUTN/CMB KT2 144 E6
MRDN SM4 162 B4
NTHWD HA6 32 C7
RYLN/HDSTN HA2 48 A6
RYNPK SW20 146 A6
SCUP DA14 155 H2
SURB * KT6 159 F6
SWFD E18 58 E2
THHTH CR7 164 E3
WALTH E17 57 K2
WBLY HA9 68 E1
WWKM BR4 167 G6
Drive Ct EDGW * HA8 36 C4
Dr Johnson Av TOOT SW17 148 B2
Droitwich Cl SYD SE26 150 C2
Dromey Gdns
KTN/HRWW/W HA3 35 F6
Dromore Rd PUT/ROE SW15 127 H5
Dronfield Gdns BCTR RM8 79 J4
Droop St NKENS W10 88 C3
Drovers Pl PECK SE15 111 J6
Drovers Rd SAND/SEL CR2 177 K4
Druce Rd DUL SE21 131 F5
Druid St STHWK SE1 19 L2

Druids Wy HAYES BR2 167 G3
Drumaline Rdg WPK KT4 173 G1
Drummond Av ROMW/RG RM7 63 F3
Drummond Cl ERITH DA8 118 B7
Drummond Crs CAMTN NW1 5 G7
Drummond Dr
KTN/HRWW/W HA3 35 F6
Drummond Ga PIM SW1V 17 H7
Drummond Rd
BERM/RHTH SE16 111 J2
CROY/NA CR0 177 J1
ROMW/RG RM7 62 E3
WAN E11 59 F5
Drummonds Pl RCH/KEW TW9 125 F3
Drummond St CAMTN NW1 4 E9
Drum St WCHPL E1 13 M4
Drury Crs CROY/NA CR0 177 G1
Drury La HOL/ALD WC2B 11 K5
Drury Rd HRW HA1 48 C6
Drury Wy WLSDN NW10 69 F4
Dryad St PUT/ROE SW15 127 G2
Dryburgh Gdns
CDALE/KGS NW9 50 C2
Dryburgh Rd PUT/ROE SW15 126 E2
Dryden Av HNWL W7 85 F5
Dryden Rd EN EN1 30 A5
KTN/HRWW/W HA3 35 F7
WIM/MER SW19 147 G5
WOOL/PLUM SE18 116 A7
Dryden St COVGDN WC2E 11 K5
Dryfield Cl WLSDN NW10 68 E5
Dryfield Rd EDGW HA8 36 E5
Dryhill Rd BELV DA17 117 G5
Drylands Rd CEND/HSY/T N8 54 E5
Drysdale Av CHING E4 31 K5
Drysdale Cl NTHWD HA6 32 C6
Drysdale Dwellings HACK * E8 74 B4
Drysdale Pl BETH E2 7 K7
Drysdale St IS N1 7 K8
Dublin Av HACK E8 74 C7
Du Burstow Ter HNWL W7 103 K1
Ducal St BETH E2 7 M8
Du Cane Cl SHB * W12 88 A5
Du Cane Rd SHB W12 87 K5
Duchess Cl FBAR/BDGN N11 40 B4
SUT SM1 175 G3
Duchess Gv BKHH * IG9 45 F1
Duchess Ms CAVSQ/HST W1G 10 D3
Duchess of Bedford's Wk
KENS W8 107 J1
Duchess St REGST W1B 10 D3
Duchy St STHWK SE1 12 B8
Ducie St BRXN/ST SW9 129 K3
Duckett Rd FSBYPK N4 55 H5
Ducketts Rd DART DA1 138 C4
Duckett St WCHPL E1 93 F4
Ducking Stool Ct ROM RM1 63 G3
Duck La SOHO/CST W1F 11 G5
Duck Lees La PEND EN3 31 G3
Du Cros Dr STAN HA7 35 K5
Du Cros Rd ACT W3 87 G7
Dudden Hill La WLSDN NW10 69 H3
Dudden Hill Pde WLSDN * NW10 69 H3
Duddington Cl ELTH/MOT SE9 153 H3
Dudley Av KTN/HRWW/W HA3 49 J2
Dudley Dr MRDN SM4 161 H7
RSLP HA4 65 F4
Dudley Gdns RYLN/HDSTN HA2 48 D7
WEA W13 104 C1
Dudley Rd EBED/NFELT TW14 121 G7
FNCH N3 53 F1
IL IG1 78 B3
KIL/WHAMP NW6 88 C1
KUT KT1 159 G2
NWDGN UB2 102 C1
RCH/KEW TW9 125 G1
RYLN/HDSTN HA2 66 C1
WALTH E17 57 J1
WIM/MER SW19 146 E5
Dudley St BAY/PAD * W2 9 G3
Dudlington Rd CLPT E5 74 E1
Dudmaston Ms CHEL SW3 15 H7
Dudsbury Rd DART DA1 138 E5
Dudset La HEST TW5 101 K7
Dufferin Av STLK EC1Y 13 G1
Dufferin St STLK EC1Y 12 F1
Duffield Cl HRW HA1 49 F4
Duffield Dr SEVS/STOTM N15 56 B3
Duff St POP/IOD E14 93 K5
Dufour's Pl SOHO/CST W1F 10 F5
Duke Humphrey Rd
BKHTH/KID SE3 113 H7
Duke of Cambridge Cl
WHTN TW2 123 J5
Duke of Edinburgh Rd
SUT SM1 175 H2
Duke of Wellington Pl
WHALL SW1A 16 B2
Duke of York St STJS SW1Y 10 F8
Duke Rd BARK/HLT IG6 60 D3
CHSWK W4 106 A4
Duke's Av CHSWK W4 106 A4
EDGW HA8 36 B5
FNCH N3 39 F7
HRW HA1 48 E3
HSLWW TW4 122 D3
MUSWH N10 54 C2
NTHLT UB5 65 J6
NWMAL KT3 160 B2
PIN HA5 47 K5
RCHPK/HAM TW10 143 J3
Dukes Cl ASHF TW15 140 A3
HPTN TW12 141 K4
Dukes Ga CHSWK * W4 105 K3
Dukes La KENS W8 14 C1
Duke's Ms MHST W1U 10 B4
MUSWH N10 54 B2
Dukes Orch BXLY DA5 137 K7
Duke's Pl HDTCH EC3A 13 L5
Dukes Rd ACT W3 86 C3
CAMTN NW1 5 H8
EHAM E6 78 A7
Dukesthorpe Rd SYD SE26 151 F3
Duke St MBLAR W1H 10 B4
RCH/KEW TW9 124 E3
SUT SM1 175 H3
WAT WD17 21 G2
Duke Street Hl STHWK SE1 13 H8
Duke Street St James's
MYFR/PICC W1J 10 F8
Dukes Wy WWKM BR4 180 C2
Duke's Yd MYFR/PKLN W1K 10 B6
Dulas St FSBYPK N4 55 F7
Dulford St NTGHL W11 88 C6
Dulka Rd BTSEA SW11 128 E4
Dulverton Rd ELTH/MOT SE9 154 C1
RSLP HA4 64 E1
Dulwich Common DUL SE21 130 E7
The Dulwich Oaks DUL * SE21 150 B2
Dulwich Rd HNHL SE24 130 B4
Dulwich Village DUL SE21 130 E5
Dulwich Wood Av NRWD SE19 150 A4
Dulwich Wood Pk NRWD SE19 150 A3
Dumbarton Rd
BRXS/STRHM SW2 129 K5
Dumbleton Cl KUT KT1 144 D7
Dumbreck Rd ELTH/MOT SE9 135 F3
Dumfries Cl OXHEY WD19 32 E2
Dumont Rd STNW/STAM N16 74 A2
Dumpton Pl CAMTN NW1 4 A2
Dunbar Av BECK BR3 166 B3
DAGE RM10 80 C2
STRHM/NOR SW16 164 B1
Dunbar Cl YEAD UB4 82 E4
Dunbar Gdns DAGE RM10 80 C4
Dunbar Rd FSTGT E7 76 E5
NWMAL KT3 159 K3
WDGN N22 41 G7
Dunbar St WNWD SE27 149 J2
Dunblane Rd ELTH/MOT SE9 134 D2
Dunboyne Rd HAMP NW3 71 K4
Dunbridge St BETH E2 92 C3
Duncan Cl BAR EN5 27 G3
Duncan Gv ACT W3 87 G5
Duncannon St CHCR WC2N 11 J7
Duncan Rd HACK E8 74 D7
RCH/KEW TW9 125 F3
Duncan St IS N1 6 C5
Duncan Ter IS N1 6 C6
Duncan Wy BUSH WD23 21 K1
Dunch St WCHPL * E1 92 D5
Duncombe Hl FSTH SE23 132 B6
Duncombe Rd ARCH N19 54 D7
Duncrievie Rd LEW SE13 133 G5
Duncroft WOOL/PLUM SE18 115 K6
Dundalk Rd BROCKY SE4 132 B2
Dundas Gdns E/WMO/HCT KT8 157 G2
Dundas Rd PECK SE15 131 K1
Dundee Rd PLSTW E13 95 F1
SNWD SE25 165 J4
Dundee St WAP E1W 92 D7
Dundee Wy PEND EN3 31 G2
Dundela Gdns WPK KT4 173 K3
Dundonald Cl EHAM E6 95 J5
Dundonald Rd WIM/MER SW19 146 D6
WLSDN NW10 70 B7
Dunedin Rd IL IG1 60 C7
LEY E10 75 K2
RAIN RM13 99 H2
Dunedin Wy YEAD UB4 83 G3
Dunelm Gv WNWD SE27 149 J3
Dunelm St WCHPL E1 93 F5
Dunfield Rd CAT SE6 151 K4
Dunford Rd HOLWY N7 73 F3
Dungarvan Av PUT/ROE SW15 126 D3
Dunheved Cl THHTH CR7 164 B5
Dunheved Rd North
THHTH CR7 164 B5
Dunheved Rd South
THHTH CR7 164 B5
Dunheved Rd West
THHTH CR7 164 B5
Dunholme Gn ED N9 42 B2
Dunholme La ED N9 42 B2
Dunholme Rd ED N9 42 B2
Dunkeld Rd BCTR RM8 79 H1
SNWD SE25 164 E3
Dunkery Rd ELTH/MOT SE9 153 H3
Dunkin Rd DART DA1 139 K3
Dunkirk St WNWD * SE27 149 J3
Dunlace Rd CLPT E5 74 E4
Dunleary Cl HSLWW TW4 122 E6
Dunley Dr CROY/NA CR0 180 A5
Dunloe Av TOTM N17 55 K2
Dunloe St BETH E2 7 M6
Dunlop Pl BERM/RHTH SE16 19 M4
Dunmore Rd KIL/WHAMP NW6 70 C7
RYNPK SW20 146 A7
Dunmow Cl CHDH RM6 61 J4
FELT * TW13 141 J3
Dunmow Dr RAIN RM13 81 H7
Dunmow Rd SRTFD E15 76 B3
Dunmow Wk IS * N1 6 E3
Dunningford Cl HCH RM12 81 H4
Dunn Md CDALE/KGS NW9 37 H6
Dunnock Cl BORE WD6 24 C3
ED N9 31 F7
Dunnock Rd EHAM E6 95 J5
Dunn St HACK E8 74 B4
Dunollie Pl KTTN NW5 72 C4
Dunollie Rd KTTN NW5 72 C4
Dunoon Gdns FSTH * SE23 132 A6
Dunoon Rd FSTH SE23 131 K6
Dunraven Dr ENC/FH EN2 29 G1
Dunraven Rd SHB W12 87 J7
Dunraven St MYFR/PKLN W1K 9 M6
Dunsany Rd WKENS W14 107 G2
Dunsbury Cl BELMT SM2 175 F7
Dunsfold Wy CROY/NA CR0 179 K6
Dunsmore OXHEY * WD19 33 H1
Dunsmore Cl BUSH WD23 22 D5
YEAD UB4 83 H3
Dunsmore Rd WOT/HER KT12 156 A4
Dunsmore Wy BUSH WD23 22 C5
Dunsmure Rd STNW/STAM N16 56 A7
Dunspring La CLAY IG5 60 B1
Dunstable Ms CAVSQ/HST W1G 10 B2
Dunstable Rd E/WMO/HCT KT8 156 E3
RCH/KEW TW9 125 F3
Dunstall Rd RYNPK SW20 145 K5
Dunstall Wy E/WMO/HCT KT8 157 G2
Dunstall Welling Est
WELL * DA16 136 C1
Dunstan Cl EFNCH * N2 53 G2
Dunstan Gld STMC/STPC * BR5 169 J5
Dunstan Houses WCHPL * E1 92 E4
Dunstan Rd GLDGN NW11 52 D7
Dunstan's Gv EDUL SE22 131 J5
Dunstan's Rd EDUL SE22 131 H6
Dunster Av MRDN SM4 161 G7
Dunster Cl BAR EN5 26 B3
ROMW/RG RM7 62 E1
Dunster Ct BORE WD6 25 F2
FENCHST EC3M 13 J6
Dunster Dr CDALE/KGS NW9 50 E7
Dunster Gdns KIL/WHAMP NW6 70 D6
Dunsterville Wy STHWK SE1 19 H2
Dunster Wy RYLN/HDSTN HA2 65 J2
Dunston Rd BTSEA SW11 129 F2
HACK E8 7 L4
Dunston St HACK E8 7 K3
Dunton Cl SURB KT6 159 F7
Dunton Rd LEY E10 57 K6
ROM RM1 63 G3
STHWK SE1 19 L6
Duntshill Rd WAND/EARL SW18 128 A7
Dunvegan Cl E/WMO/HCT KT8 157 G3
Dunvegan Rd ELTH/MOT SE9 134 E3
Dunwich Rd BXLYHN DA7 117 G7
Dunworth Ms NTGHL * W11 88 D5
Duplex Ride KTBR SW1X 15 M2
Dupont Rd RYNPK SW20 161 G1
Dupont St POP/IOD E14 93 G5
Duppas Av CROY/NA CR0 177 H3
Duppas Hill Rd CROY/NA CR0 177 G3
Duppas Hill Ter CROY/NA CR0 177 H2
Duppas Rd CROY/NA CR0 177 G2
Dupree Rd CHARL SE7 114 A4
Dura Den Cl BECK BR3 151 K6
Durand Gdns BRXN/ST SW9 110 A7
Durand Wy WLSDN NW10 68 E6
Durants Park Av PEND EN3 31 F3
Durants Rd PEND EN3 30 E3
Durant St BETH E2 92 C1
Durban Gdns DAGE RM10 80 E6
Durban Rd BECK BR3 166 C1
GNTH/NBYPK IG2 60 E7
SRTFD E15 94 C2
TOTM N17 42 A5
WALTH E17 43 H7
WNWD SE27 149 J3
Durban Rd East WATW WD18 20 E3
Durban Rd West WATW WD18 20 E3
Durbin Rd CHSGTN KT9 172 A3
Durdans Rd STHL UB1 83 K5
Durell Gdns DAGW RM9 79 K4
Durell Rd DAGW RM9 79 K4
Durford Crs PUT/ROE SW15 126 D7
Durham Av HAYES BR2 167 J3
HEST TW5 102 E5
WFD IG8 45 H4
Durham Hl BMLY BR1 152 D3
Durham House St CHCR * WC2N 11 K7
Durham Pl CHEL SW3 15 L8
Durham Ri WOOL/PLUM SE18 115 H4
Durham Rd BORE WD6 24 E2
CAN/RD E16 94 C3
DAGE RM10 80 E4
EA W5 104 E2
EBED/NFELT TW14 122 B6
ED N9 42 C1
EFNCH N2 53 J2
HAYES BR2 167 K3
HOLWY N7 73 F1
HRW HA1 48 B4
MNPK E12 77 H3
RYNPK SW20 145 K7
SCUP DA14 155 H4
Durham Rw WCHPL E1 93 F4
Durham St LBTH SE11 17 L8
Durham Ter BAY/PAD W2 8 C4
PGE/AN * SE20 150 D6
Durham Yd BETH * E2 92 D2
Duriun Wy ERITH DA8 118 E6
Durley Av PIN HA5 47 J5
Durley Rd STNW/STAM N16 56 A6
Durlston Rd CLPT E5 74 C1
KUTN/CMB KT2 144 A5
Durnford St SEVS/STOTM N15 56 A4
Durning Rd NRWD SE19 149 K4
Durnsford Av
WAND/EARL SW18 146 E1
Durnsford Rd FBAR/BDGN N11 40 D6
WAND/EARL SW18 146 E1
Durrants Dr RKW/CH/CXG WD3 20 A2
Durrell Rd FUL/PGN SW6 107 H7
Durrington Av RYNPK SW20 146 A6
Durrington Park Rd
RYNPK SW20 146 A7
Durrington Rd CLPT E5 75 G3
Dursley Cl BKHTH/KID SE3 134 B1
Dursley Gdns BKHTH/KID SE3 114 C7
Dursley Rd BKHTH/KID SE3 134 B1
Durward St WCHPL E1 92 D4
Durweston Ms MHST * W1U 9 M2
Dutch Barn Cl
STWL/WRAY TW19 120 A5
Dutch Gdns KUTN/CMB KT2 144 D5
Dutch Yd WAND/EARL SW18 127 K4
Duthie St POP/IOD E14 94 A6
Dutton St GNWCH SE10 113 F7
Duxford Cl HCH RM12 81 K5
Dwight Rd WATW WD18 20 B6
Dye House La BOW E3 75 J7
Dyer's Buildings
FLST/FETLN EC4A 12 A3
Dyers Hall Rd WAN E11 58 C7
Dyer's La PUT/ROE SW15 126 E2
Dykes Wy HAYES BR2 167 J2
Dylan Cl BORE * WD6 23 K6
Dylan Rd BELV DA17 117 H2
Dylways CMBW SE5 130 E3
Dymchurch Cl CLAY IG5 60 A1
Dymock St FUL/PGN SW6 128 A2
Dymoke Rd ROM RM1 63 H6
Dyneley Rd LEE/GVPK SE12 153 G3
Dyne Rd KIL/WHAMP NW6 70 D6
Dynevor Rd RCHPK/HAM TW10 125 F4
STNW/STAM N16 74 A2
Dynham Rd KIL/WHAMP NW6 2 A1
Dyott St RSQ WC1B 11 H3
Dysart Av KUTN/CMB KT2 143 J4
Dysart St SDTCH EC2A 13 H1
Dyson Ct ALP/SUD HA0 67 G3
Dyson Rd FSTGT E7 76 D5
WAN E11 58 C5
Dyson's Rd UED N18 42 D4

E

Eade Rd FSBYPK N4 55 J6
Eagans Cl EFNCH * N2 53 H2
Eagle Av CHDH RM6 62 A5
Eagle Cl HCH RM12 81 K5
PEND EN3 30 E3
WLGTN SM6 176 E5
Eagle Ct FARR EC1M 12 C2
Eagle Dr CDALE/KGS NW9 51 G1
Eagle Hl NRWD SE19 149 K5
Eagle La WAN E11 58 E3
Eagle Ms IS N1 74 A5
Eagle Pl WBPTN SW10 14 F7
Eagle Rd ALP/SUD HA0 67 K6
HTHAIR TW6 121 J2
Eaglesfield Rd
WOOL/PLUM SE18 115 G7
Eagle St GINN WC1R 11 L3
Eagle Ter WFD IG8 45 F6
Eagle Wharf Rd IS N1 6 F5
Ealdham Sq ELTH/MOT SE9 134 B3
Ealing Gn EA W5 85 K7
Ealing Park Gdns EA W5 104 D3
Ealing Rd ALP/SUD HA0 86 A1
BOW E3 93 K2
EA W5 104 E3
NTHLT UB5 66 A7
Ealing Village EA W5 86 A5
Eamont St STJWD NW8 3 J5
Eardemont Cl DART DA1 138 C3
Eardley Crs ECT SW5 14 B7
Eardley Rd BELV DA17 117 H4
STRHM/NOR SW16 148 C5
Earl Cl FBAR/BDGN N11 40 B4
Earldom Rd PUT/ROE SW15 127 F3
Earle Gdns KUTN/CMB KT2 144 A6
Earlham Gv FSTGT E7 76 D4
WDGN N22 41 F6
Earlham St LSQ/SEVD WC2H 11 H5
Earl Ri WOOL/PLUM SE18 115 J4
Earl Rd MORT/ESHN SW14 125 K3
Earl's Court Gdns ECT SW5 14 C6
Earl's Court Rd KENS W8 14 A4
Earl's Court Sq ECT SW5 14 C7
Earls Crs HRW HA1 48 E3
Earlsferry Wy IS N1 5 K2
Earlsfield Rd
WAND/EARL SW18 128 B7
Earlshall Rd ELTH/MOT SE9 134 E3
Earlsmead RYLN/HDSTN HA2 65 K3
Earlsmead Rd SEVS/STOTM N15 56 B4
WLSDN NW10 87 K2
Earls Ter KENS * W8 14 A4
Earlsthorpe Ms BAL SW12 129 F5
Earlsthorpe Rd SYD SE26 151 F3
Earlstoke Est FSBYE EC1V 6 C7
Earlstoke St FSBYE EC1V 6 C7
Earlston Gv HOM E9 74 D7
Earl St SDTCH EC2A 13 J2
WAT WD17 21 G2
Earls Wk BCTR RM8 79 H3
KENS W8 14 A4
Earlswood Av THHTH CR7 164 B4
Earlswood Gdns CLAY IG5 60 A2
Earlswood St GNWCH SE10 113 H4
Early Ms CAMTN NW1 4 D3
Earnshaw St NOXST/BSQ WC1A 11 H4
Earsby St WKENS W14 107 H3
Easby Crs MRDN SM4 162 A5
Easebourne Rd BCTR RM8 79 J4
Easedale Dr HCH RM12 81 K4
East Acton Ar ACT * W3 87 H5
East Acton La ACT W3 87 G6
East Arbour St WCHPL E1 93 F5
East Av CROY/NA CR0 177 F4
HYS/HAR UB3 101 J1
MNPK E12 77 J6
STHL UB1 83 K6
WALTH E17 57 K3
East Bank STNW/STAM N16 56 A6
Eastbank Rd HPTN TW12 142 C4
East Barnet Rd BAR EN5 27 G3
Eastbourne Av ACT W3 87 F5
Eastbourne Gdns
MORT/ESHN SW14 125 K2
Eastbourne Ms BAY/PAD W2 8 F4
Eastbourne Rd BTFD TW8 104 E4
CHSWK W4 105 K5
EHAM E6 96 A2
FELT TW13 141 H1
SEVS/STOTM N15 56 A5
SRTFD E15 76 C7
TOOT SW17 148 A5
Eastbourne Ter BAY/PAD W2 8 F4
Eastbournia Av ED N9 42 D2
Eastbrook Av DAGE RM10 80 E3
ED N9 30 E6
Eastbrook Dr DAGE RM10 81 G2
Eastbrook Rd BKHTH/KID SE3 114 A7
Eastbury Av BARK IG11 78 E7
NTHWD HA6 32 C4
Eastbury Ct OXHEY * WD19 21 G6
Eastbury Gv CHSWK W4 106 B4
Eastbury Rd EHAM E6 96 A3
KUTN/CMB KT2 144 A6
NTHWD HA6 32 C5
OXHEY WD19 21 G6
ROMW/RG RM7 63 F5
STMC/STPC BR5 169 J5
Eastbury Sq BARK IG11 79 F7
Eastbury Ter WCHPL E1 93 F3
Eastcastle St GTPST W1W 10 E4
Eastcheap FENCHST EC3M 13 H6
East Churchfield Rd ACT W3 87 F7
Eastchurch Rd HTHAIR TW6 121 H2
East Cl EA W5 86 C3
EBAR EN4 28 A3
GFD/PVL UB6 84 C1
RAIN RM13 99 K3
Eastcombe Av CHARL SE7 114 A5
Eastcote Av E/WMO/HCT KT8 156 E4
GFD/PVL UB6 67 G4
RYLN/HDSTN HA2 66 B1
Eastcote La NTHLT UB5 65 K5
RYLN/HDSTN HA2 65 K3
Eastcote La North NTHLT UB5 65 K5
Eastcote Rd PIN HA5 47 H4
RSLP HA4 46 C6
RYLN/HDSTN HA2 66 C2
WELL DA16 135 J1
Eastcote St BRXN/ST SW9 129 K1
Eastcote Vw PIN HA5 47 G3
East Ct ALP/SUD HA0 67 J1
East Crs EN EN1 30 A4
TRDG/WHET N20 39 K3
Eastcroft Rd HOR/WEW KT19 173 G6
East Cross Route HOM E9 75 H5
Eastdown Pk LEW SE13 133 G3
East Dr CAR SM5 175 J7
NTHWD HA6 32 C1
East Duck Lees La PEND EN3 31 G3
East Dulwich Gv EDUL SE22 131 F4
East Dulwich Rd EDUL SE22 131 H3
East End Rd FNCH N3 52 E1
East End Wy PIN HA5 47 J2
East Entrance DAGE RM10 98 D1
Eastern Av GNTH/NBYPK IG2 61 F4
PIN HA5 47 H6
REDBR IG4 59 H5
Eastern Av East ROM RM1 63 F2
Eastern Av West CHDH RM6 62 A3
ROMW/RG RM7 62 E3
Eastern Perimeter Rd
HTHAIR TW6 121 H1
Eastern Rd BROCKY SE4 132 D3
EFNCH N2 53 K2
PLSTW E13 95 F1
ROM RM1 63 H4
WALTH E17 58 A4
WDGN N22 40 E7
Easternville Gdns
GNTH/NBYPK IG2 60 C5
Eastern Wy THMD SE28 116 B1
East Ferry Rd POP/IOD E14 112 E3
Eastfield Gdns DAGE RM10 80 C3
Eastfield Rd CEND/HSY/T N8 54 E2
DAGE RM10 80 C3
WALTH E17 57 J3
Eastfields PIN HA5 47 G4
Eastfields Rd ACT W3 86 E4
MTCM CR4 163 F1
Eastfield St POP/IOD E14 93 G4
East Gdns WIM/MER SW19 147 J5
Eastgate Cl THMD SE28 97 K5
Eastglade NTHWD HA6 32 C4
PIN HA5 47 K2
Eastham Cl BAR EN5 26 D4
East Ham Manor Wy EHAM E6 96 A5
East Harding St
FLST/FETLN EC4A 12 B4
East Heath Rd HAMP NW3 71 H2
East Hl DART DA1 139 J6
WAND/EARL SW18 128 B4
WBLY HA9 68 C1
East Hill Dr DART DA1 139 J6
Eastholm GLDGN NW11 53 F3
East Holme ERITH DA8 118 A7
Eastholme HYS/HAR UB3 82 E7
East India Dock Rd
POP/IOD E14 93 J5
Eastlake Rd CMBW SE5 130 C1
Eastlands Crs EDUL SE22 131 G5
East La ALP/SUD HA0 67 J2
BERM/RHTH SE16 111 H1
KUT KT1 158 E2
Eastlea Ms CAN/RD E16 94 C3
Eastleigh Av RYLN/HDSTN HA2 66 B1
Eastleigh Cl BELMT SM2 175 F6
CRICK NW2 69 G2
Eastleigh Rd BXLYHN DA7 137 K1
WALTH E17 57 H1
Eastleigh Wy
EBED/NFELT TW14 121 K7
Eastman Rd ACT W3 106 A1
East Md RSLP HA4 65 H2
Eastmead Av GFD/PVL UB6 84 B2
Eastmead Cl BMLY BR1 168 D1
Eastmearn Rd DUL SE21 149 J1
Eastmont Rd ESH/CLAY KT10 171 F1
Eastmoor Pl WOOL/PLUM SE18 114 C2
Eastmoor St CHARL SE7 114 C3
East Mount St WCHPL * E1 92 D4
Eastney Rd CROY/NA CR0 164 C7
Eastney St GNWCH SE10 113 G4
Eastnor Rd ELTH/MOT SE9 135 H7
Easton Gdns BORE WD6 25 G3
Easton St FSBYW WC1X 6 A9
East Park Cl CHDH RM6 61 K4
East Parkside GNWCH SE10 113 H1
East Pl WNWD SE27 149 J3
East Pole Cottages EBAR * EN4 28 D3
East Poultry Av FARR EC1M 12 C3
East Rp HTHAIR TW6 100 E7
East Rd CHDH RM6 62 A4
EBAR EN4 28 A7
EBED/NFELT TW14 121 G6
EDGW HA8 36 E7
EFNCH N2 39 J7
IS N1 7 G8
KUTN/CMB KT2 144 A7
ROMW/RG RM7 63 F6
SRTFD E15 76 E7
WDR/YW UB7 100 C3
WELL DA16 136 C1
WIM/MER SW19 147 G5
East Rochester Wy
BFN/LL DA15 135 K4
DART DA1 138 A6
East Rw NKENS W10 88 C3
WAN E11 58 E5
Eastry Av HAYES BR2 167 J5
Eastry Rd ERITH DA8 117 H6
East Sheen Av
MORT/ESHN SW14 126 A4
East Side SHB * W12 107 F1
Eastside Rd GLDGN NW11 52 D3
East Smithfield WAP E1W 13 M7
East St BARK IG11 78 C6
BMLY BR1 167 K1
BTFD TW8 104 D6
BXLYHN DA7 137 H3
WALW SE17 18 F7
East Surrey Gv PECK SE15 111 G6
East Tenter St WCHPL E1 13 M5
East Ter BFN/LL * DA15 135 K7
East Towers PIN HA5 47 H5
East V ACT * W3 87 H7
East Vw BAR EN5 26 D2
CHING E4 44 A4
Eastview Av WOOL/PLUM SE18 115 K6
Eastville Av GLDGN NW11 52 D4
East Wk EBAR EN4 28 A7
HYS/HAR UB3 101 K1
East Wy CROY/NA CR0 179 G1
HYS/HAR UB3 82 E7
RSLP HA4 46 E7
Eastway HAYES BR2 167 K6
HOM E9 75 G7
MRDN SM4 161 G4
WAN E11 59 F4
WLGTN SM6 176 C3
Eastwell Cl BECK BR3 151 G7
Eastwood Cl SWFD E18 58 E1
TOTM * N17 42 D6
Eastwood Dr RAIN RM13 99 K5
Eastwood Rd GDMY/SEVK IG3 61 G6
MUSWH N10 54 A1
SWFD E18 58 E1
Eastwood St
STRHM/NOR SW16 148 C5
Eatington Rd LEY E10 58 B4
Eaton Cl BGVA SW1W 16 A5
STAN HA7 35 H3
Eaton Dr BRXN/ST SW9 130 C3
KUTN/CMB KT2 144 C6
Eaton Gdns DAGW RM9 80 A6
Eaton Ga BGVA SW1W 16 A5
NTHWD HA6 32 A5
Eaton La BGVA SW1W 16 D4
Eaton Ms North KTBR SW1X 16 B4
Eaton Ms South BGVA SW1W 16 B5
Eaton Ms West BGVA SW1W 16 B5
Eaton Park Rd PLMGR N13 41 G1
Eaton Pl KTBR SW1X 16 A5
Eaton Ri EA W5 85 J4
WAN E11 59 G4
Eaton Rd BELMT SM2 175 H5
EN EN1 30 A2
HDN NW4 52 A4
ISLW TW7 123 J3
SCUP DA14 155 K1
Eaton Rw BGVA SW1W 16 C3
Eatons Md CHING E4 43 J1
Eaton Sq BGVA SW1W 16 B5
Eaton Ter BOW * E3 93 G2
KTBR SW1X 16 A5
Eaton Terrace Ms KTBR SW1X 16 A5
Eatonville Rd TOOT SW17 147 K1
Eatonville Vls TOOT SW17 147 K1

Ebbisham Dr VX/NE SW8 17 L9
Ebbisham Rd WPK KT4 174 A1
Ebbsfleet Rd CRICK NW2 70 C4
Ebdon Wy BKHTH/KID SE3 134 A2
Ebenezer St IS N1 7 G7
Ebenezer Wk MTCM CR4 148 C7
Ebley Cl PECK SE15 111 G5
Ebner St WAND/EARL SW18 128 A4
Ebor St BETH E2 7 L9
Ebrington Rd
KTN/HRWW/W HA3 49 J5
Ebsworth St FSTH SE23 132 A6
Eburne Rd HOLWY N7 72 E2
Ebury Bridge Rd BGVA SW1W 16 B8
Ebury Cl HAYES BR2 181 J2
NTHWD HA6 32 A4
Ebury Ms BGVA SW1W 16 B5
Ebury Ms East BGVA SW1W 16 C5
Ebury Rd WAT WD17 21 H2
Ebury Sq BGVA SW1W 16 C6
Ebury St BGVA SW1W 16 B6
Ecclesbourne Cl PLMGR N13 41 G4
Ecclesbourne Gdns PLMGR N13 41 G4
Ecclesbourne Rd IS N1 6 F2
THHTH CR7 164 D4
Eccles Rd BTSEA SW11 128 E3
Eccleston Cl EBAR EN4 27 J4
ORP * BR6 169 J7
Eccleston Crs CHDH RM6 61 H6
Ecclestone Ct WBLY HA9 68 A4
Ecclestone Ms WBLY HA9 68 A4
Ecclestone Pl WBLY HA9 68 B4
Eccleston Ms KTBR SW1X 16 B4
Eccleston Pl BGVA SW1W 16 C6
Eccleston Rd HNWL W7 85 E6
Eccleston Sq PIM SW1V 16 D6
Eccleston Square Ms PIM SW1V 16 D6
Eccleston St BGVA SW1W 16 B4
Echo Hts CHING * E4 31 K7
Eckford St IS N1 6 A5
Eckstein Rd BTSEA SW11 128 D3
Eclipse Rd PLSTW E13 95 F4
Ector Rd CAT SE6 152 C1
Edans Ct SHB W12 106 C1
Edbrooke Rd MV/WKIL W9 8 A1
Eddiscombe Rd FUL/PGN SW6 127 J1
Eddy Cl ROMW/RG RM7 62 D5
Eddystone Rd BROCKY SE4 132 B4
Ede Cl HSLW TW3 122 E2
Edenbridge Cl
BERM/RHTH * SE16 111 J4
Edenbridge Rd EN EN1 30 A5
HOM * E9 75 F6
Eden Cl ALP/SUD HA0 67 K7
HAMP NW3 70 E1
KENS W8 14 B3
Edencourt Rd
STRHM/NOR SW16 148 B5
Edendale Rd BXLYHN DA7 118 A7
Edenfield Gdns WPK KT4 173 H2
Eden Gv HOLWY N7 73 F4
Edenham Wy MV/WKIL W9 88 D3
Edenhurst Av FUL/PGN SW6 127 J2
Eden Pde BECK * BR3 166 B3
Eden Park Av BECK BR3 166 C3
Eden Rd BECK BR3 166 B3
CROY/NA CR0 177 K3
WALTH E17 57 K4
WNWD SE27 149 H4
Edensor Rd CHSWK W4 106 B6
Eden St KUT KT1 158 E1
Edenvale Rd MTCM CR4 148 A6
Edenvale St FUL/PGN SW6 128 A1
Eden Wk KUT * KT1 159 F1
Eden Wy BECK BR3 166 D4
Ederline Av STRHM/NOR SW16 164 A2
Edgar Kail Wy CMBW SE5 131 F2
Edgarley Ter FUL/PGN * SW6 107 H7
Edgar Rd BOW E3 93 J2
HSLWW TW4 122 E6
Edgeborough Wy BMLY BR1 153 H7
Edgebury CHST BR7 154 B3
Edgecombe Cl KUTN/CMB KT2 145 F6
Edgecoombe SAND/SEL CR2 179 F7
Edgecote Cl ACT W3 86 E7
Edgefield Av BARK IG11 79 F6
Edge Hl WIM/MER SW19 146 B6
WOOL/PLUM SE18 115 G5
Edge Hill Av GLDGN NW11 52 E3
Edgehill Ct WOT/HER * KT12 156 B7
Edgehill Gdns DAGE RM10 80 C3
Edgehill Rd CHST BR7 154 C2
MTCM CR4 163 G1
WEA W13 85 J5
Edgeley La CLAP SW4 129 J2
Edgeley Rd CLAP SW4 129 J2
Edgel St WAND/EARL SW18 128 A3
Edgepoint Cl WNWD * SE27 149 H4
Edge St KENS W8 8 B8
Edgewood Gn CROY/NA CR0 166 A7
Edgeworth Av HDN NW4 51 J4
Edgeworth Cl HDN NW4 51 J4
Edgeworth Rd EBAR EN4 27 J3
ELTH/MOT SE9 134 B3
Edgington Rd
STRHM/NOR SW16 148 D5
Edgington Wy SCUP DA14 155 J6
Edgwarebury Gdns EDGW HA8 36 C4
Edgwarebury La BORE WD6 24 B6
Edgware Rd BAY/PAD W2 9 G1
CDALE/KGS NW9 51 F2
CRICK NW2 70 A2
Edgware Rd
Burnt Oak Broadway
EDGW HA8 36 D6
Edgware Rd High St EDGW HA8 36 C5
Edgware Rd The Hyde
CDALE/KGS NW9 51 G3
Edgware Wy (Watford By-Pass)
EDGW HA8 36 A1
Edinburgh Cl BETH E2 92 E1
PIN HA5 47 J6
Edinburgh Ct KUT * KT1 159 F2
Edinburgh Ga BAY/PAD W2 15 L1
Edinburgh Rd HNWL W7 104 A1
PLSTW E13 95 F1
SUT SM1 175 G1
UED * N18 42 C4
WALTH E17 57 J4
Edinburgh's Dr ROMW/RG RM7 62 E3
Edington Rd ABYW SE2 116 C2
PEND EN3 30 E1
Edison Av HCH RM12 63 H7
Edison Cl HCH RM12 63 H7
Edison Dr STHL UB1 84 B5
WBLY HA9 68 A1
Edison Gv WOOL/PLUM SE18 116 A6
Edison Rd CEND/HSY/T N8 54 D5
HAYES BR2 167 K1
PEND EN3 31 H1
WELL DA16 116 A7
Edis St CAMTN NW1 4 A3
Edith Cavell Wy
WOOL/PLUM SE18 114 D7
Edith Gdns BRYLDS KT5 159 J6
Edith Gv WBPTN SW10 108 B5
Editha St BRXN/ST SW9 129 K2
Edith Rd CHDH RM6 61 K6
EHAM E6 77 H6
FBAR/BDGN N11 40 D6
SNWD SE25 164 E4
SRTFD E15 76 B4
WIM/MER SW19 147 F5
WKENS W14 107 H3
Edith Rw FUL/PGN SW6 108 A7
Edith St BETH E2 7 M5
Edith Ter WBPTN * SW10 108 B6
Edith Vls WKENS W14 107 J3
Edison Cl WALTH E17 57 J4
Edmeston Cl HOM E9 75 G5
Edmund Gv FELT TW13 141 K1
Edmund Halley Wy
GNWCH SE10 113 H1
Edmund Hurst Dr EHAM E6 96 B4
Edmund Rd MTCM CR4 162 D2
RAIN RM13 99 G2
WELL DA16 136 B2
Edmunds Cl YEAD UB4 83 G4
Edmund St CMBW SE5 110 E6
Edmunds Wk EFNCH N2 53 J3
Edna Rd RYNPK SW20 161 G1
Edna St BTSEA SW11 108 D7
Edrick Rd EDGW HA8 36 E5
Edrick Wk EDGW HA8 36 E5
Edric Rd NWCR SE14 112 A6
Edridge Cl BUSH WD23 22 C4
Edridge Rd CROY/NA CR0 177 J2
Edulf Rd BORE WD6 24 D1
Edward Av CHING E4 43 K4
MRDN SM4 162 C4
Edward Cl ED N9 30 B6
HPTN TW12 142 C4
Edward Ct CAN/RD E16 94 E4
Edwardes Pl WKENS W14 107 J2
Edwardes Sq KENS W8 14 A4
Edward Gv EBAR EN4 27 H4
Edward Mann Cl East
WCHPL * E1 93 F5
Edward Mann Cl West
WCHPL * E1 93 F5
Edward Ms CAMTN * NW1 4 D7
Edward Pl DEPT SE8 112 C5
Edward Rd BMLY BR1 153 F6
CHDH RM6 62 A5
CHST BR7 154 B4
CROY/NA CR0 165 F6
EBAR EN4 27 H4
EBED/NFELT TW14 121 G4
HPTN TW12 142 C4
NTHLT UB5 83 G1
PGE/AN SE20 151 F6
RYLN/HDSTN HA2 48 C2
WALTH E17 57 F3
Edwards Av RSLP HA4 65 G4
Edwards Cl WPK KT4 174 B1
Edward's La STNW/STAM N16 73 K1
Edwards Ms IS N1 6 B1
MBLAR W1H 10 A5
Edwards Pl FBAR/BDGN N11 40 D6
Edward Sq IS N1 5 L4
Edwards Rd BELV DA17 117 H3
Edward St CAN/RD E16 94 E3
NWCR SE14 112 B6
Edward Temme Av SRTFD E15 76 D6
Edward Tyler Rd
LEE/GVPK SE12 153 F1
Edwina Gdns REDBR IG4 59 J4
Edwin Av EHAM E6 96 A1
Edwin Cl BXLYHN DA7 117 G5
RAIN RM13 99 H2
Edwin Rd EDGW HA8 37 F5
WHTN TW2 123 K7
Edwin's Md HOM E9 75 G3
Edwin St CAN/RD E16 94 E4
WCHPL E1 92 E3
Edwin Ware Ct PIN * HA5 47 G1
Edwyn Cl BAR EN5 26 A4
Effie Pl FUL/PGN SW6 107 K6
Effie Rd FUL/PGN SW6 107 K6
Effingham Cl BELMT SM2 175 F6
Effingham Rd CEND/HSY/T N8 55 G4
CROY/NA CR0 164 A6
LEW SE13 133 H4
SURB KT6 158 C6
Effort St TOOT SW17 147 J4
Effra Pde BRXS/STRHM SW2 130 B4
Effra Rd BRXS/STRHM SW2 130 A3
WIM/MER SW19 147 F5
Egan Wy HYS/HAR UB3 82 C6
Egbert St CAMTN NW1 4 A3
Egerton Cl DART DA1 138 E7
PIN HA5 46 E3
Egerton Crs CHEL SW3 15 K5
Egerton Dr GNWCH SE10 112 E7
Egerton Gdns CHEL SW3 15 J5
GDMY/SEVK IG3 79 F2
HDN NW4 51 K3
WEA W13 85 H5
WLSDN * NW10 70 A7
Egerton Gardens Ms CHEL SW3 15 K4
Egerton Pl CHEL * SW3 15 K4
Egerton Rd ALP/SUD HA0 68 B6
NWMAL KT3 160 C3
SNWD SE25 165 F2
STNW/STAM * N16 56 B6
WHTN TW2 123 K6
Egerton Ter CHEL SW3 15 K4
Egerton Wy WDR/YW UB7 100 E6
Egham Cl CHEAM SM3 174 C1
Egham Crs CHEAM SM3 174 B2
Egham Rd PLSTW E13 95 F4
Eglantine Rd
WAND/EARL SW18 128 B4
Egleston Rd MRDN SM4 162 A5
Eglinton Hl WOOL/PLUM SE18 115 G5
Eglinton Rd WOOL/PLUM SE18 115 F5
Egliston Ms PUT/ROE SW15 127 F2
Egliston Rd PUT/ROE SW15 127 F2
Eglon Ms CAMTN NW1 3 M2
Egmont Av SURB KT6 159 H7
Egmont Rd BELMT SM2 175 G6
NWMAL KT3 160 C3
SURB KT6 159 G7
WOT/HER KT12 156 A6
Egmont St NWCR SE14 112 A6
Egremont Rd WNWD SE27 149 G2
Egret Wy YEAD UB4 83 H5
Eider Cl FSTGT E7 76 D4
Eighteenth Rd MTCM CR4 163 K3
Eighth Av HYS/HAR UB3 82 E7
MNPK E12 77 K3
Eileen Rd SNWD SE25 164 E4
Eindhoven Cl MTCM CR4 163 F7
Eisenhower Dr EHAM E6 95 J4
Elaine Gv KTTN NW5 72 A4
Elam Cl CMBW SE5 130 C1
Elam St CMBW SE5 130 C1
Eland Rd BTSEA SW11 128 E2
CROY/NA CR0 177 H2
Elba Pl WALW * SE17 18 F5
Elberon Av CROY/NA CR0 163 H5
Elbe St FUL/PGN SW6 128 B1
Elborough Rd SNWD SE25 165 H4
Elborough St
WAND/EARL SW18 127 K7
Elbury Dr CAN/RD E16 94 E5
Elcho St BTSEA SW11 108 D6
Elcot Av PECK SE15 111 J6
Elder Av CEND/HSY/T N8 54 E4
Elderberry Rd EA W5 105 F1
Elder Cl BFN/LL DA15 136 A7
Elder Ct BUSH WD23 34 E1
Elderfield Rd CLPT E5 75 F3
Elderfield Wk WAN E11 59 F4
Elderflower Wy SRTFD E15 76 C6
Elder Oak Cl PGE/AN SE20 150 D7
Elder Rd WNWD SE27 149 J4
Elderslie Cl BECK BR3 166 D5
Elderslie Rd ELTH/MOT SE9 135 F4
Elder St WCHPL E1 13 L2
Elderton Rd SYD SE26 151 G3
Eldertree Wy MTCM CR4 148 B7
Elder Wk IS N1 6 D3
Eldon Av BORE WD6 24 C1
CROY/NA CR0 178 E1
HEST TW5 103 F6
Eldon Gv HAMP NW3 71 H4
Eldon Pde WDGN * N22 41 H7
Eldon Pk SNWD SE25 165 J3
Eldon Rd ED N9 30 E7
KENS W8 14 D4
WALTH E17 57 H3
WDGN N22 41 H7
Eldon St LVPST EC2M 13 H3
Eldon Wy WLSDN NW10 86 D1
Eldridge Cl EBED/NFELT TW14 121 K7
Eleanora Ter SUT * SM1 175 G4
Eleanor Cl TOTM N17 56 B2
Eleanor Crs MLHL NW7 38 B3
Eleanor Gdns BAR EN5 26 B4
Eleanor Gv BARN SW13 126 B2
Eleanor Rd FBAR/BDGN N11 40 E5
HACK E8 74 D6
SRTFD E15 76 D5
Eleanor St BOW E3 93 J2
Electra Av HTHAIR TW6 121 J2
Electric Av BRXN/ST SW9 130 B3
Electric La BRXN/ST * SW9 130 B3
Electric Pde SURB KT6 158 E5
Elephant & Castle STHWK SE1 18 D5
Elephant La BERM/RHTH SE16 111 K1
Elephant Rd WALW SE17 18 E5
Elers Rd HYS/HAR UB3 101 F3
WEA W13 104 D1
Eley Rd UED N18 43 F4
Elfindale Rd HNHL SE24 130 D4
Elfin Gv TEDD TW11 143 F4
Elford Cl BKHTH/KID SE3 134 B3
Elfort Rd HBRY N5 73 G3
Elfrida Crs CAT SE6 151 J3
Elfrida Rd WATW WD18 21 G4
Elf Rw WAP E1W 92 E6
Elfwine Rd HNWL W7 84 E4
Elgar Av BRYLDS KT5 159 J7
EA W5 105 F1
STRHM/NOR SW16 163 K2
WLSDN NW10 69 F5
Elgar Cl BKHH IG9 45 H1
BORE WD6 23 J6
DEPT SE8 112 D6
PLSTW E13 95 G1
Elgar St BERM/RHTH SE16 112 B1
Elgin Av ASHF TW15 140 A5
KTN/HRWW/W HA3 49 H1
MV/WKIL W9 2 D8
SHB W12 106 D1
Elgin Crs HTHAIR TW6 121 H1
NTGHL W11 88 C6
Elgin Dr NTHWD HA6 32 C6
Elgin Est MV/WKIL W9 8 A1
Elgin Ms NTGHL W11 88 C5
Elgin Ms North MV/WKIL W9 2 D7
Elgin Ms South MV/WKIL W9 2 D8
Elgin Rd CROY/NA CR0 178 B1
GDMY/SEVK IG3 60 E7
SUT SM1 175 G2
WDGN N22 54 C1
WLGTN SM6 176 C5
Elgood Av NTHWD HA6 32 E6
Elgood Cl NTGHL W11 88 C6
Elham Cl BMLY BR1 153 H6
Elia Ms IS N1 6 C6
Elias Pl LBTH SE11 110 B5
Elia St IS N1 6 C6
Elibank Rd ELTH/MOT SE9 135 F3
Elim St STHWK SE1 19 H3
Elim Wy PLSTW E13 94 D2
Eliot Bank FSTH SE23 150 D1
Eliot Dr RYLN/HDSTN HA2 66 B1
Eliot Gdns PUT/ROE SW15 126 D3
Eliot Hl LEW SE13 133 F1
Eliot Pk LEW SE13 133 F2
Eliot Pl BKHTH/KID SE3 133 H1
Eliot Rd DAGW RM9 79 K3
Eliot V BKHTH/KID SE3 133 G1
Elizabethan Wy
STWL/WRAY TW19 120 A6
Elizabeth Av ENC/FH EN2 29 H2
IL IG1 78 D1
IS N1 6 F2
Elizabeth Barnes Ct
FUL/PGN * SW6 128 A1
Elizabeth Br BGVA SW1W 16 C6
Elizabeth Cl BAR EN5 26 B2
MV/WKIL * W9 8 F1
SUT SM1 174 D3
Elizabeth Clyde Cl
SEVS/STOTM N15 56 A3
Elizabeth Cottages
RCH/KEW TW9 105 G7
Elizabeth Gdns ACT W3 87 H7
STAN HA7 35 J5
SUN TW16 156 B2
Elizabeth Ms HAMP NW3 71 J5
Elizabeth Pl SEVS/STOTM N15 55 K3
Elizabeth Ride ED N9 30 D6
Elizabeth Rd EHAM E6 77 H7
RAIN RM13 99 K4
SEVS/STOTM N15 56 A4
Elizabeth Sq BERM/RHTH SE16 93 G6
Elizabeth St BGVA SW1W 16 B5
Elizabeth Wy FELT TW13 141 G3
NRWD SE19 149 K6
Elkington Rd PLSTW E13 95 F3
The Elkins ROM RM1 63 G1
Elkstone Rd NKENS W10 88 D4
Ellaline Rd HMSMTH W6 107 G5
Ella Ms HAMP NW3 71 K3
Ellanby Crs UED N18 42 D4
Elland Rd PECK SE15 131 K3
Ella Rd CEND/HSY/T N8 54 E6
Ellement Cl PIN HA5 47 H4
Ellenborough Pl
PUT/ROE SW15 126 D3
Ellenborough Rd SCUP DA14 155 K5
WDGN N22 41 J7
Ellenbridge Wy SAND/SEL CR2 178 A7
Ellen Cl BMLY BR1 168 C2
Ellen Ct ED N9 42 E1
Ellen St WCHPL E1 92 C5
Ellen Webb Dr
KTN/HRWW/W HA3 48 E2
Elleray Rd TEDD TW11 143 F5
Ellerby St FUL/PGN SW6 107 G7
Ellerdale Rd HAMP NW3 71 G4
Ellerdale St LEW SE13 132 E3
Ellerdine Rd HSLW TW3 123 H3
Ellerker Gdns
RCHPK/HAM TW10 125 F5
Ellerman Av WHTN TW2 122 E7
Ellerslie Rd SHB W12 87 K7
Ellerton Gdns DAGW RM9 79 J6
Ellerton Rd BARN * SW13 106 D7
DAGW RM9 79 J6
RYNPK SW20 145 J6
SURB KT6 172 B1
WAND/EARL SW18 128 C7
Ellery Rd NRWD SE19 149 K6
Ellery St PECK SE15 131 J1
Ellesborough Cl OXHEY WD19 33 G4
Ellesmere Av BECK BR3 166 E1
MLHL NW7 37 F2
Ellesmere Cl RSLP HA4 46 A6
WAN E11 58 D4
Ellesmere Gdns REDBR IG4 59 J4
Ellesmere Gv BAR EN5 26 D4
Ellesmere Rd BOW E3 93 G1
GFD/PVL UB6 84 C3
TWK TW1 124 D5
WLSDN NW10 69 J4
Ellesmere St POP/IOD E14 93 K5
Ellingfort Rd HACK E8 74 D6
Ellingham Rd CHSGTN KT9 171 K5
SHB W12 106 D1
WAN E11 76 B3
Ellington Rd FELT TW13 140 D3
HSLW TW3 123 G1
MUSWH N10 54 B3
Ellington St HOLWY N7 73 G5
Elliot Cl SRTFD E15 76 C6
WBLY HA9 68 B2
Elliot Rd HDN NW4 51 K5
Elliott Av RSLP HA4 65 F1
Elliott Rd BRXN/ST SW9 110 C6
CHSWK W4 106 B3
HAYES BR2 168 C3
STAN HA7 35 G5
THHTH CR7 164 C3
Elliott's Pl IS N1 6 D4
Elliott Sq HAMP NW3 3 K2
Elliott's Rw LBTH SE11 18 D5
Ellis Av RAIN RM13 99 J4
Ellis Cl CRICK NW2 70 A5
EDGW HA8 37 G5
ELTH/MOT SE9 154 C1
Elliscombe Mt CHARL * SE7 114 B5
Elliscombe Rd CHARL SE7 114 B4
Ellisfield Dr PUT/ROE SW15 126 C6
Ellison Gdns NWDGN UB2 102 E3
Ellison Rd BARN SW13 126 C1
BFN/LL DA15 135 J7
STRHM/NOR SW16 148 D6
Ellis Rd MTCM CR4 162 E5
NWDGN UB2 84 C7
Ellis St KTBR SW1X 15 M5
Ellora Rd STRHM/NOR SW16 148 D4
Ellsworth St BETH * E2 92 D2
Elmar Rd SEVS/STOTM N15 55 K3
Elm Av EA W5 86 A7
OXHEY WD19 21 J6
RSLP HA4 46 E7
Elmbank WCHMH N21 28 E6
Elmbank Av BAR EN5 26 A3
Elmbank Dr BMLY BR1 168 C1
Elm Bank Gdns BARN SW13 126 B1
Elmbank Wy HNWL W7 84 D4
Elmbourne Dr BELV DA17 117 J3
Elmbourne Rd TOOT SW17 148 B2
Elmbridge Av BRYLDS KT5 159 K5
Elmbridge Cl RSLP HA4 46 E5
Elmbridge Dr RSLP HA4 46 E5
Elmbridge Wk HACK * E8 74 C6
Elmbrook Cl SUN TW16 141 H7
Elmbrook Gdns ELTH/MOT SE9 134 D3
Elmbrook Rd SUT SM1 174 D3
Elm Cl BKHH IG9 45 H1
BRYLDS KT5 159 K6
CAR SM5 162 E7
DART DA1 139 F7
HDN NW4 52 B4
HYS/HAR UB3 82 E5
RYLN/HDSTN HA2 48 B5
RYNPK SW20 161 F3
SAND/SEL CR2 177 K5
STWL/WRAY TW19 120 A7
WAN E11 59 F5
WHTN TW2 142 B1
Elm Cottages MTCM * CR4 162 E1
Elm Ct WAT * WD17 21 F2
Elmcourt Rd WNWD SE27 149 H1
Elm Crs EA W5 105 F1
KUTN/CMB KT2 144 A7
Elmcroft CEND/HSY/T N8 55 F4
Elmcroft Av BFN/LL DA15 136 A6
ED N9 30 D5
GLDGN NW11 52 D6
WAN E11 59 F4
Elmcroft Cl CHSGTN * KT9 172 A2
EA W5 85 K5
EBED/NFELT TW14 121 J5
Elmcroft Crs GLDGN NW11 52 B6
RYLN/HDSTN HA2 48 A2
Elmcroft Dr CHSGTN KT9 172 A2
Elmcroft Gdns CDALE/KGS NW9 50 C4
Elmcroft St CLPT E5 74 E3
Elmdale Rd PLMGR N13 41 F4
Elmdene BRYLDS KT5 159 K7
Elmdene Cl BECK BR3 166 C4
Elmdene Rd WOOL/PLUM SE18 115 G4
Elmdon Rd HEST TW5 122 C1
HTHAIR TW6 121 J2
Elm Dr RYLN/HDSTN HA2 48 B5
SUN TW16 156 B1
Elmer Cl ENC/FH EN2 29 F2
RAIN RM13 81 J6
Elmer Gdns EDGW HA8 36 D6
ISLW TW7 123 J2
RAIN RM13 81 J6
Elmer Rd CAT SE6 133 F6
Elmer's Dr TEDD TW11 143 H5
Elmers End Rd BECK BR3 165 K2
Elmerside Rd BECK BR3 166 B3
Elmers Rd CROY/NA CR0 165 H6
Elmfield Av CEND/HSY/T N8 54 E4
MTCM CR4 148 A7
TEDD TW11 143 F4
Elmfield Cl HRW HA1 66 E1
Elmfield Pk BMLY BR1 167 K2
Elmfield Rd BAL SW12 148 B1
BMLY BR1 167 K2
CHING E4 44 A1
EFNCH N2 53 H2
NWDGN UB2 102 D2
WALTH E17 57 F5
Elmfield Wy MV/WKIL W9 8 A2
SAND/SEL CR2 178 B7
Elm Friars Wk CAMTN NW1 5 H2
Elm Gdns EFNCH N2 53 G2
ESH/CLAY KT10 171 F5
MTCM CR4 163 J3
Elmgate Av FELT TW13 141 F2
Elmgate Gdns EDGW HA8 36 E4
Elm Gn ACT W3 87 G5
Elmgreen Cl SRTFD E15 76 C7
Elm Gv CEND/HSY/T N8 54 E5
CRICK NW2 70 B3
ERITH DA8 118 A6
KUTN/CMB KT2 144 A7
PECK SE15 131 H1
RYLN/HDSTN HA2 48 A6
SUT SM1 175 F3
WIM/MER SW19 146 C6
Elmgrove Crs HRW HA1 49 F4
Elmgrove Gdns HRW HA1 49 G4
Elm Grove Pde WLGTN SM6 176 A2
Elm Grove Rd BARN SW13 106 D7
EA W5 105 F1
Elmgrove Rd CROY/NA CR0 165 J6
HRW HA1 49 F4
Elm Hall Gdns WAN E11 59 F5
Elm Hatch PIN HA5 33 K6
Elmhurst BELV DA17 117 F5
Elmhurst Av EFNCH * N2 53 H2
MTCM CR4 148 A6
Elmhurst Cl BUSH WD23 21 J3
Elmhurst Crs EFNCH N2 53 H2
Elmhurst Dr SWFD E18 58 E1
Elmhurst Rd ELTH/MOT SE9 153 J1
FSTGT E7 77 F6
TOTM N17 56 A1
Elmhurst St CLAP SW4 129 J2
Elmington Cl BXLY DA5 137 J6
Elmington Est CMBW SE5 110 D6
Elmington Rd CMBW SE5 110 E7
Elmira St LEW SE13 132 E2
Elm La CAT SE6 151 H1
Elmlee Cl CHST BR7 153 K5
Elmley St WOOL/PLUM SE18 115 J3
Elmore Cl ALP/SUD HA0 86 A1
Elmore Rd WAN E11 76 A2
Elmore St IS N1 7 G1
Elm Pde SCUP * DA14 155 G3
Elm Pk BRXS/STRHM SW2 130 A5
STAN HA7 35 H4
Elm Park Av HCH RM12 81 K3
SEVS/STOTM N15 56 B4
Elm Park Gdns CHEL SW3 15 G8
HDN NW4 52 B4
Elm Park La CHEL SW3 15 G8
Elm Park Rd CHEL SW3 15 G9
FNCH N3 38 D6
LEY E10 57 G7
PIN HA5 47 G1
SNWD SE25 165 G2
WCHMH N21 29 J6
Elm Pl SKENS SW7 15 G7
Elm Rd BAR EN5 26 D3
BECK BR3 166 C1
CHSGTN KT9 172 A3
DART DA1 139 G7
EBED/NFELT TW14 121 G7
ERITH DA8 118 D7
ESH/CLAY KT10 171 F5
EW KT17 173 H5
FSTGT E7 76 D5
KUTN/CMB KT2 144 B7
MORT/ESHN SW14 125 K2
NWMAL KT3 160 A2
ROMW/RG RM7 62 D1
SCUP DA14 155 G3
THHTH CR7 164 D3
WALTH E17 58 A4
WAN E11 76 B1
WBLY HA9 68 A4
WDGN N22 41 H7
WLGTN SM6 163 F7
Elm Rd West MRDN SM4 161 J6
Elm Rw HAMP NW3 71 G2
The Elms BARN SW13 126 C2
ESH/CLAY * KT10 171 F6
NFNCH/WDSP * N12 39 J4
TOOT * SW17 148 A2
WLGTN * SM6 176 C3
Elms Av HDN NW4 52 A4
MUSWH N10 54 B2
Elmscott Gdns WCHMH N21 29 J5
Elmscott Rd BMLY BR1 152 C4
Elms Ct ALP/SUD HA0 67 F3
Elms Crs CLAP SW4 129 H5
Elmsdale Rd WALTH E17 57 H3
Elms Gdns ALP/SUD HA0 67 G3
DAGW RM9 80 B3
Elmshaw Rd PUT/ROE SW15 126 D4
Elmshurst Crs EFNCH N2 53 H3
Elmside Rd WBLY HA9 68 C2
Elms La ALP/SUD HA0 67 G3
Elmsleigh Av
KTN/HRWW/W HA3 49 H3
Elmsleigh Rd WHTN TW2 142 D1
Elmslie Cl WFD IG8 45 K5
Elms Ms BAY/PAD W2 9 G6
Elms Park Av ALP/SUD HA0 67 G3
Elms Rd CLAP SW4 129 H4
KTN/HRWW/W HA3 34 E6
Elmstead Av CHST BR7 153 K4
WBLY HA9 50 A7
Elmstead Cl HOR/WEW KT19 173 G4
TRDG/WHET N20 38 E1
Elmstead Gdns WPK KT4 173 J2
Elmstead Gld CHST BR7 153 K5

Elmstead La CHST BR7 153 J6
Elmstead Rd ERITH DA8 118 B7
GDMY/SEVK IG3 78 E1
Elmsted Crs WELL DA16 116 D5
Elmstone Rd FUL/PGN SW6 107 K7
Elm St FSBYW WC1X 11 M1
Elmsworth Av HSLW TW3 123 G1
Elm Ter CRICK NW2 70 E2
ELTH/MOT SE9 135 F5
KTN/HRWW/W HA3 34 D6
Elmton Wy STNW/STAM N16 74 C2
Elm Tree Av ESH/CLAY KT10 157 J6
Elm Tree Cl NTHLT UB5 83 K2
STJWD NW8 3 G7
Elm Tree Ct CHARL * SE7 114 B5
Elm Tree Rd STJWD NW8 3 G8
Elmtree Rd TEDD TW11 142 E4
Elm Vls HNWL * W7 84 E6
Elm Wk GPK RM2 63 J2
HAMP NW3 70 E1
ORP BR6 181 K2
RYNPK SW20 161 F3
Elm Wy FBAR/BDGN N11 40 A5
HOR/WEW KT19 173 F4
WLSDN NW10 69 G3
WPK KT4 174 A2
Elmwood Av BORE WD6 24 D3
FELT TW13 141 F2
KTN/HRWW/W HA3 49 G4
PLMGR N13 40 E4
Elmwood Cl EW KT17 173 J6
WLGTN SM6 176 B1
Elmwood Crs CDALE/KGS NW9 50 E3
Elmwood Dr BXLY DA5 137 F6
EW KT17 173 J6
Elmwood Gdns HNWL W7 84 E5
Elmwood Rd CHSWK W4 105 K5
CROY/NA CR0 164 C6
HNHL SE24 130 E4
MTCM CR4 162 E2
Elmworth Gv DUL SE21 149 K1
Elnathan Ms MV/WKIL W9 8 D1
Elphinstone Rd WALTH E17 57 H1
Elphinstone St HBRY N5 73 H3
Elrick Cl ERITH DA8 118 B5
Elrington Rd HACK E8 74 C5
WFD IG8 44 E4
Elruge Cl WDR/YW UB7 100 A2
Elsa Cottages POP/IOD * E14 93 G4
Elsa Rd WELL DA16 136 D1
Elsa St WCHPL * E1 93 G4
Elsdale St HOM E9 74 E5
Elsden Ms BETH * E2 92 E1
Elsden Rd TOTM N17 42 B7
Elsenham Rd MNPK E12 78 A4
Elsenham St WAND/EARL SW18 127 J7
Elsham Rd WAN E11 76 C2
WKENS W14 107 H1
Elsham Ter WKENS * W14 107 H1
Elsiedene Rd WCHMH N21 29 J6
Elsie Lane Ct BAY/PAD W2 8 B3
Elsiemaud Rd BROCKY SE4 132 C4
Elsie Rd EDUL SE22 131 G3
Elsinore Av
STWL/WRAY * TW19 120 B6
Elsinore Gdns CRICK * NW2 70 C2
Elsinore Rd FSTH SE23 132 B7
Elsinore Wy RCH/KEW TW9 125 J2
Elsley Rd BTSEA SW11 128 E2
Elspeth Rd ALP/SUD HA0 68 A4
BTSEA SW11 128 E3
Elsrick Av MRDN SM4 161 K4
Elstan Wy CROY/NA CR0 166 B6
Elsted St WALW SE17 19 H6
Elstow Cl ELTH/MOT SE9 134 E4
RSLP HA4 47 H6
Elstow Gdns DAGW RM9 80 A7
Elstow Rd DAGW RM9 80 A6
Elstree Gdns BELV DA17 117 F3
ED N9 30 D7
IL IG1 78 C4
Elstree Ga BORE * WD6 25 F1
Elstree Hl BMLY BR1 152 C6
Elstree Hl North BORE WD6 23 K4
Elstree Hl South BORE WD6 23 K6
Elstree Pk MLHL * NW7 25 F5
Elstree Rd BUSH WD23 22 D7
Elstree Wy BORE WD6 24 E1
Elswick Rd LEW SE13 132 E2
Elswick St FUL/PGN SW6 128 B1
Elsworth Cl EBED/NFELT TW14 121 H7
Elsworthy THDIT KT7 157 K5
Elsworthy Ri HAMP NW3 3 K2
Elsworthy Rd HAMP NW3 3 J3
Elsworthy Ter HAMP NW3 3 K2
Elsynge Rd WAND/EARL SW18 128 C4
Eltham Gn ELTH/MOT SE9 134 B4
Eltham Green Rd
ELTH/MOT SE9 134 B4
Eltham High St ELTH/MOT SE9 134 E5
Eltham Hl ELTH/MOT SE9 134 C4
Eltham Palace Rd
ELTH/MOT SE9 134 C5
Eltham Park Gdns
ELTH/MOT SE9 135 F3
Eltham Rd ELTH/MOT SE9 134 B4
Elthiron Rd FUL/PGN SW6 107 K7
Elthorne Av HNWL W7 104 A1
Elthorne Ct FELT TW13 122 B7
Elthorne Park Rd HNWL W7 104 A2
Elthorne Rd ARCH N19 72 D1
CDALE/KGS NW9 51 F6
Elthorne Wy CDALE/KGS NW9 51 F5
Elthruda Rd LEW SE13 133 G5
Eltisley Rd IL IG1 78 B3
Elton Av BAR EN5 26 D4
GFD/PVL UB6 67 F5
Elton Cl E/WMO/HCT KT8 143 J6
Elton Pk WAT WD17 20 E1
Elton Pl STNW/STAM N16 74 A4
Elton Rd KUTN/CMB KT2 144 B7
Eltringham St
WAND/EARL SW18 128 B3
Elvaston Ms SKENS SW7 14 E4
Elvaston Pl SKENS SW7 14 E4
Elveden Pl WLSDN NW10 86 C1
Elveden Rd WLSDN NW10 86 C1
Elvendon Rd FBAR/BDGN N11 40 E5
Elver Gdns BETH E2 92 C2
Elverson Ms DEPT * SE8 112 C6
Elverson Rd DEPT SE8 132 E1
Elverton St WEST SW1P 17 G5
Elvington Gn HAYES BR2 167 J4
Elvington La CDALE/KGS NW9 37 G7
Elvino Rd SYD SE26 151 F4
Elvis Rd CRICK NW2 70 A5
Elwill Wy BECK BR3 167 G3
Elwin St BETH E2 92 C2
Elwood St HBRY N5 73 H2
Elwyn Gdns LEE/GVPK SE12 133 K6
Ely Cl ERITH DA8 138 C1
NWMAL KT3 160 C1
Ely Cottages VX/NE * SW8 110 A6
Ely Gdns BORE WD6 25 F4
DAGE RM10 80 E2
Elyne Rd FSBYPK N4 55 G5
Ely Pl HCIRC EC1N 12 B3
Ely Rd CROY/NA CR0 164 E4
HSLWW TW4 122 B2
HTHAIR TW6 121 J1
LEY E10 58 A5
Elysian Av STMC/STPC BR5 169 K5
Elysium Pl FUL/PGN SW6 127 J1
Elysium St FUL/PGN SW6 127 J1
Elystan Cl WLGTN SM6 176 C7
Elystan Pl CHEL SW3 15 K7
Elystan St CHEL SW3 15 J6
Elystan Wk IS N1 6 A4
Emanuel Av ACT W3 86 E5
The Embankment TWK TW1 124 B7
Embankment PUT/ROE SW15 127 G2
Embankment Gdns CHEL SW3 15 M9
Embankment Pl CHCR WC2N 11 K8
Embassy Ct SCUP DA14 155 H2
WLGTN * SM6 176 B5
Emba St BERM/RHTH SE16 111 H1
Ember Cl STMC/STPC BR5 169 H6
Embercourt Rd THDIT KT7 157 K5
Ember Farm Av
E/WMO/HCT KT8 157 J5
Ember Farm Wy
E/WMO/HCT KT8 157 J4
Ember Gdns ESH/CLAY KT10 157 K6
Ember La ESH/CLAY KT10 157 J7
Embleton Rd LEW SE13 132 E3
OXHEY WD19 32 E2
Embry Cl STAN HA7 35 G3
Embry Dr STAN HA7 35 G5
Embry Wy STAN HA7 35 G4
Emden Cl WDR/YW UB7 100 D1
Emden St FUL/PGN SW6 108 A7
Emerald Cl CAN/RD E16 95 J5
Emerald Gdns BCTR RM8 62 C7
Emerald Sq NWDGN UB2 102 C2
Emerald St BMSBY WC1N 11 L2
Emerson Gdns
KTN/HRWW/W HA3 50 B5
Emerson St STHWK SE1 12 E8
Emerton Cl BXLYHS DA6 137 F3
Emery Hill St WEST SW1P 16 F4
Emery St STHWK SE1 18 B3
Emes Rd ERITH DA8 117 K6
Emilia Cl PEND EN3 30 D4
Emily Pl HOLWY N7 73 G3
Emily St CAN/RD E16 94 D5
Emlyn Rd SHB W12 106 B1
Emmanuel Rd BAL SW12 129 H7
NTHWD HA6 32 D6
Emma Rd PLSTW E13 94 D2
Emma St BETH E2 92 D1
Emma Ter RYNPK * SW20 146 A6
Emmott Av BARK/HLT IG6 60 C4
Emmott Cl EFNCH N2 53 G5
WCHPL E1 93 G3
Emperor's Ga SKENS SW7 14 E5
Empire Av UED N18 41 J5
Empire Pde UED * N18 41 K5
WBLY * HA9 68 C2
Empire Rd GFD/PVL UB6 67 J7
Empire Wy WBLY HA9 68 B3
Empire Wharf Rd
POP/IOD E14 113 G3
Empress Av CHING E4 43 K6
IL IG1 77 K1
MNPK E12 77 G1
WFD IG8 44 D6
Empress Dr CHST BR7 154 B5
Empress Pde CHING * E4 43 J6
Empress Pl ECT SW5 14 A8
Empress St WALW SE17 18 F9
Empson St BOW E3 93 K3
Emsworth Cl ED N9 30 E7
Emsworth Rd BARK/HLT IG6 60 B1
Emsworth St
BRXS/STRHM SW2 149 F1
Emu Rd VX/NE SW8 129 G1
Ena Rd STRHM/NOR SW16 163 K2
Enbrook St NKENS W10 88 C2
Enclave Ct FSBYE EC1V 6 D9
Endale Cl CAR SM5 175 K1
Endeavour Wy BARK IG11 97 G1
CROY/NA CR0 163 K6
WIM/MER SW19 147 F3
Endell St LSQ/SEVD WC2H 11 J4
Enderby St GNWCH SE10 113 H4
Enderley Rd KTN/HRWW/W HA3 34 D7
Endersby Rd BAR EN5 26 A4
Endersleigh Gdns HDN NW4 51 J3
Endlebury Rd CHING E4 44 A1
Endlesham Rd BAL SW12 129 F6
Endsleigh Gdns IL IG1 59 K7
STPAN WC1H 5 G9
SURB KT6 158 D5
Endsleigh Pl STPAN WC1H 5 H9
Endsleigh Rd HNWL W7 85 G7
NWDGN UB2 102 D3
Endsleigh St STPAN WC1H 5 H9
Endway BRYLDS KT5 159 H6
Endwell Rd BROCKY SE4 132 B2
Endymion Rd
BRXS/STRHM SW2 130 A6
FSBYPK N4 55 H6
Energen Cl WLSDN NW10 69 G5
Enfield Rd ACT W3 105 J1
BTFD TW8 104 E4
EBAR EN4 28 D3
HTHAIR TW6 121 H1
IS N1 7 K2
Enford St MBLAR W1H 9 L2
Engadine Cl CROY/NA CR0 178 B2
Engadine St WAND/EARL SW18 127 J7
Engate St LEW SE13 133 F3
Engel Pk MLHL NW7 38 A5
Engineer Cl WOOL/PLUM SE18 115 F5
Engineers Wy WBLY HA9 68 C3
England's La HAMP NW3 71 K5
England Wy NWMAL KT3 159 J3
Englefield Cl CROY/NA CR0 164 D5
ENC/FH EN2 29 G1
Englefield Rd IS N1 7 H1
Engleheart Dr
EBED/NFELT TW14 121 J5
Engleheart Rd CAT SE6 132 E6
Englewood Rd BAL SW12 129 G5
English St BOW E3 93 H3
Enid St STHWK SE1 19 M3
Enmore Av SNWD SE25 165 H4
Enmore Gdns
MORT/ESHN SW14 126 A4
Enmore Rd PUT/ROE SW15 127 F3
SNWD SE25 165 H4
STHL UB1 84 A3
Ennerdale Av HCH RM12 81 J4
STAN HA7 49 J2
Ennerdale Cl
EBED/NFELT TW14 121 J7
SUT SM1 174 D3
Ennerdale Dr CDALE/KGS NW9 51 G4
Ennerdale Gdns WBLY HA9 49 J7
Ennerdale Rd BXLYHN DA7 117 H7
RCH/KEW TW9 125 G1
Ennersdale Rd LEW SE13 133 G4
Ennismore Av CHSWK W4 106 C3
GFD/PVL UB6 66 E5
Ennismore Gdns SKENS SW7 15 H3
THDIT KT7 157 K5
Ennismore Gardens Ms
SKENS SW7 15 H3
Ennismore Ms SKENS SW7 15 J2
Ennismore St SKENS SW7 15 J3
Ennis Rd FSBYPK N4 55 G7
WOOL/PLUM SE18 115 J5
Ensign Cl STWL/WRAY TW19 120 A7
Ensign Dr PLMGR N13 41 J2
Ensign St WCHPL E1 92 C6
Ensign Wy STWL/WRAY TW19 120 A7
Enslin Rd ELTH/MOT SE9 135 F5
Ensor Ms SKENS SW7 15 G7
Enstone Rd PEND EN3 31 G2
Enterprise Cl CROY/NA CR0 164 B7
Enterprise Rw
SEVS/STOTM N15 56 B4
Enterprise Wy TEDD TW11 143 F4
WAND/EARL SW18 127 K3
WLSDN NW10 87 H2
Enterprize Wy DEPT * SE8 112 C3
Epcot Ms NKENS * W10 88 B2
Epirus Ms FUL/PGN SW6 107 K6
Epirus Rd FUL/PGN SW6 107 J6
Epping Cl POP/IOD E14 112 D3
ROMW/RG RM7 62 D2
Epping Pl HOLWY N7 73 G5
Epping Wy CHING E4 31 K5
Epple Rd FUL/PGN SW6 107 J7
Epsom Cl BXLYHN DA7 137 J2
NTHLT UB5 65 K4
Epsom Rd CROY/NA CR0 177 G3
GDMY/SEVK IG3 61 F5
LEY E10 58 A5
MRDN SM4 161 J5
Epsom Sq HTHAIR * TW6 121 J1
Epstein Rd THMD SE28 97 H7
Epworth Rd ISLW TW7 104 C6
Epworth St SDTCH EC2A 13 H1
Equity Sq BETH E2 7 M8
Erasmus St WEST SW1P 17 H6
Erconwald St ACT W3 87 H5
Eresby Dr BECK BR3 166 D7
Eresby Pl KIL/WHAMP NW6 2 A2
Erica Gdns CROY/NA CR0 179 K3
Erica St SHB W12 87 J6
Eric Clarke La BARK IG11 96 B3
Ericcson Cl WAND/EARL SW18 127 K4
Eric Est BOW E3 93 H3
Eric Rd CHDH RM6 61 K6
FSTGT E7 76 E3
WLSDN NW10 69 H5
Eric St BOW E3 93 H3
Eridge Rd CHSWK W4 106 A2
Erin Cl BMLY BR1 152 C6
Erindale WOOL/PLUM SE18 115 J5
Erindale Ter WOOL/PLUM SE18 115 J5
Erin Ms WDGN * N22 41 H7
Erith Ct PUR RM19 119 K3
Erith High St ERITH DA8 118 B4
Erith Rd BELV DA17 117 J4
BXLYHN DA7 137 J2
Erlanger Rd NWCR SE14 112 A7
Erlesmere Gdns HNWL W7 104 B2
Erlich Cottages WCHPL * E1 92 E4
Ermine Cl HSLWW TW4 122 B1
Ermine Rd LEW SE13 132 E3
SEVS/STOTM N15 56 B5
Ermine Side EN EN1 30 C4
Ermington Rd ELTH/MOT SE9 154 C1
Ernald Av EHAM E6 95 J1
Erncroft Wy TWK TW1 124 A5
Ernest Av WNWD SE27 149 H3
Ernest Cl BECK BR3 166 D4
Ernest Gdns CHSWK W4 105 J5
Ernest Gv BECK BR3 166 C4
Ernest Rd KUT KT1 159 J1
Ernest St WCHPL E1 93 F3
Ernle Rd RYNPK SW20 145 K6
Ernshaw Pl PUT/ROE SW15 127 H4
Erpingham Rd PUT/ROE SW15 127 F2
Erridge Rd WIM/MER SW19 161 K1
Errington Rd MV/WKIL W9 88 D3
Errol Gdns NWMAL KT3 160 D3
YEAD UB4 83 F3
Erroll Rd ROM RM1 63 H3
Errol St STLK EC1Y 12 F1
Erskine Cl SUT SM1 175 J2
Erskine Crs TOTM N17 56 D3
Erskine Hl GLDGN NW11 52 E3
Erskine Ms HAMP NW3 3 M2
Erskine Rd HAMP NW3 3 M2
SUT SM1 175 H3
WALTH E17 57 H3
Erwood Rd CHARL SE7 114 D4
Esam Wy STRHM/NOR SW16 149 G4
Escot Rd SUN TW16 140 C6
Escot Wy BAR EN5 26 A4
Escreet Gv WOOL/PLUM SE18 115 F3
Esher Av CHEAM SM3 174 B2
ROMW/RG RM7 62 E5
WOT/HER KT12 156 A7
Esher Cl BXLY DA5 137 F7
ESH/CLAY KT10 170 B4
Esher Crs HTHAIR TW6 121 J1
Esher Gn ESH/CLAY KT10 170 B3
Esher Green Dr ESH/CLAY KT10 170 A2
Esher Ms MTCM CR4 163 F2
Esher Park Av ESH/CLAY KT10 170 C4
Esher Place Av ESH/CLAY KT10 170 B3
Esher Rd E/WMO/HCT KT8 157 J5
GDMY/SEVK IG3 78 E2
Eskdale Av NTHLT UB5 65 K7
Eskdale Cl WBLY HA9 67 K1
Eskdale Rd BXLYHN DA7 137 H1
Eskmont Rdg NRWD SE19 150 A6
Esk Rd PLSTW E13 95 F3
Esmar Crs CDALE/KGS NW9 51 J6
Esmeralda Rd STHWK SE1 111 H3
Esmond Cl RAIN * RM13 81 K6
Esmond Gdns CHSWK * W4 106 A3
Esmond Rd CHSWK W4 106 A2
KIL/WHAMP NW6 70 D7
Esmond St PUT/ROE SW15 127 H3
Esparto St WAND/EARL SW18 128 A6
Essenden Rd BELV DA17 117 H4
SAND/SEL CR2 178 A6
Essendine Rd MV/WKIL W9 2 B9
Essex Av ISLW TW7 123 K2
Essex Cl MRDN SM4 161 G6
ROMW/RG RM7 62 D3
RSLP HA4 47 H7
WALTH E17 57 G3
Essex Ct BARN SW13 126 C1
TPL/STR * WC2R 12 A5
Essex Gdns FSBYPK N4 55 H5
Essex Gv NRWD SE19 149 K5
Essex Pk FNCH N3 39 F5
Essex Park Ms ACT W3 87 G7
Essex Pl CHSWK W4 105 K3
Essex Place Sq CHSWK * W4 106 A3
Essex Rd ACT W3 86 E6
BARK IG11 78 D6
BORE WD6 24 C2
CHDH RM6 61 J7
CHSWK W4 106 A3
DAGE RM10 80 E4
DART * DA1 139 G5
ENC/FH EN2 29 K3
IS N1 6 D3
LEY E10 58 A5
ROMW/RG RM7 62 D3
SWFD E18 59 F1
WALTH E17 57 G5
WAT WD17 20 E1
WLSDN NW10 69 G6
Essex Rd South LEY E10 58 B6
Essex St FSTGT E7 76 E4
TPL/STR WC2R 12 A5
WOOL/PLUM SE18 115 H3
Essex Vls KENS W8 14 A2
Essex Whf CLPT * E5 75 F1
Essian St WCHPL E1 93 G4
Essoldo Wy EDGW HA8 50 B2
Estate Wy LEY E10 57 H7
Estcourt Rd FUL/PGN SW6 107 J6
SNWD SE25 165 J5
WAT WD17 21 G2
Estella Av NWMAL KT3 160 E3
Estelle Rd HAMP NW3 71 K3
Esterbrooke St WEST SW1P 17 G6
Este Rd BTSEA SW11 128 D2
Esther Cl WCHMH N21 29 G6
Esther Rd WAN E11 58 C6
Estoria Cl BRXS/STRHM SW2 130 B6
Estreham Rd
STRHM/NOR SW16 148 D5
Estridge Cl HSLW TW3 123 F3
Estuary Cl BARK IG11 97 H2
Eswyn Rd TOOT SW17 147 K3
Etchingham Park Rd FNCH N3 39 F6
Etchingham Rd SRTFD E15 76 A3
Etfield Gv SCUP DA14 155 H4
Ethelbert Cl HAYES BR2 167 K1
Ethelbert Gdns
GNTH/NBYPK IG2 59 K4
Ethelbert Rd BMLY BR1 167 K2
ERITH DA8 117 K6
RYNPK SW20 146 B7
Ethelbert St BAL SW12 129 G7
Ethelburga St BTSEA * SW11 108 D7
Ethelden Av MUSWH N10 54 C3
Ethelden Rd SHB W12 87 K7
Ethelred Est LBTH SE11 18 A6
Ethel Rd CAN/RD E16 95 F6
Ethel St WALW * SE17 18 F6
Etheridge Rd CRICK NW2 52 A6
Etherley Rd SEVS/STOTM N15 55 J4
Etherow St EDUL SE22 131 H5
Etherstone Rd
STRHM/NOR SW16 149 F3
Ethnard Rd PECK SE15 111 J5
Ethronvi Rd BXLYHN DA7 137 F2
Etloe Rd LEY E10 75 J1
Eton Av ALP/SUD HA0 67 J3
EBAR EN4 27 J5
HAMP NW3 3 H1
HEST TW5 102 E5
NFNCH/WDSP N12 39 G6
NWMAL KT3 160 A4
Eton Cl WAND/EARL SW18 128 A6
Eton College Rd HAMP NW3 71 K5
Eton Garages HAMP NW3 71 J5
Eton Gv CDALE/KGS NW9 50 C2
LEW SE13 133 H2
Eton Pl HAMP * NW3 4 A1
Eton Ri HAMP * NW3 71 K5
Eton Rd HAMP NW3 3 M1
HYS/HAR UB3 101 J6
IL IG1 78 C3
Eton St RCHPK/HAM TW10 124 E4
Eton Vls HAMP NW3 71 K5
Eton Wy DART DA1 139 F3
Etta St DEPT SE8 112 B5
Etton Rd HSLW TW3 123 H4
Ettrick St POP/IOD E14 94 A5
Etwell Pl BRYLDS KT5 159 G5
Eugenia Rd BERM/RHTH SE16 111 K4
Eureka Rd KUT KT1 159 H1
Europa Pl FSBYE EC1V 6 E8
Europe Rd WOOL/PLUM SE18 114 E2
Eusdon Cl ED N9 42 B2
Eustace Pl WOOL/PLUM SE18 114 E3
Eustace Rd CHDH RM6 61 K6
EHAM E6 95 J2
FUL/PGN SW6 107 K6
Euston Av WATW WD18 20 D4
Euston Rd CAMTN NW1 5 J7
CROY/NA CR0 164 B7
Euston Sq CAMTN NW1 5 G8
Euston St CAMTN NW1 4 F9
Evandale Rd BRXN/ST SW9 130 B1
Evangelist Rd KTTN NW5 72 B3
Evans Cl HACK E8 74 B5
Evansdale RAIN RM13 99 H2
Evans Gv FELT TW13 142 A1
Evans Rd CAT SE6 152 C1
Evanston Av CHING E4 44 A6
Evanston Gdns REDBR IG4 59 J5
Eva Rd CHDH RM6 61 J6
Evelina Rd PECK SE15 131 K2
PGE/AN SE20 150 E6
Eveline Lowe Est
BERM/RHTH SE16 111 H2
Eveline Rd MTCM CR4 147 K7
Evelyn Av CDALE/KGS NW9 51 F3
RSLP HA4 46 D6
Evelyn Cl WHTN TW2 123 G6
Evelyn Crs SUN TW16 140 D7
Evelyn Denington Rd EHAM E6 95 J3
Evelyn Dr PIN HA5 33 H6
Evelyn Est DEPT SE8 112 B5
Evelyn Gdns RCH/KEW TW9 125 F3
WBPTN SW10 14 F8
Evelyn Gv EA W5 86 B7
STHL UB1 83 K5
Evelyn Rd CAN/RD E16 94 E7
CHSWK W4 106 A2
EBAR EN4 27 K3
RCH/KEW TW9 125 F2
RCHPK/HAM TW10 143 J2
WALTH E17 58 A3
WIM/MER SW19 147 F4
Evelyn St DEPT SE8 112 B4
Evelyn Ter RCH/KEW TW9 125 F2
Evelyn Wk IS N1 7 G6
Evelyn Wy SUN TW16 140 D7
WLGTN SM6 176 D3
Evensyde WATW WD18 20 A5
Evenwood Cl PUT/ROE * SW15 127 H4
Everard Av HAYES BR2 167 K7
Everard Wy WBLY HA9 68 A2
Everatt Cl WAND/EARL * SW18 127 J5
Everdon Rd BARN SW13 106 D5
Everest Pl POP/IOD E14 94 A4
Everest Rd ELTH/MOT SE9 134 D4
STWL/WRAY TW19 120 A6
Everett Cl BUSH WD23 22 E7
PIN HA5 46 D2
The Everglades HSLW * TW3 123 H2
Everglade Strd
CDALE/KGS NW9 37 H7
Evergreen Cl PGE/AN SE20 150 E6
Evergreen Ct
STWL/WRAY * TW19 120 A6
Evergreen Sq HACK E8 7 L1
Evergreen Wy HYS/HAR UB3 82 D6
STWL/WRAY TW19 120 A6
Everilda St IS N1 5 M4
Evering Rd CLPT E5 74 C2
Everington Rd MUSWH N10 53 K1
Everington St HMSMTH W6 107 G5
Everitt Rd WLSDN NW10 87 F2
Everleigh St FSBYPK N4 55 F7
Eve Rd ISLW TW7 124 B3
SRTFD E15 94 C1
TOTM N17 56 A2
WAN E11 76 C3
Eversfield Gdns EDGW HA8 37 G6
Eversfield Rd RCH/KEW TW9 125 G1
Evershot St CAMTN NW1 4 F6
Evershot Rd FSBYPK N4 55 F7
Eversleigh Rd BAR EN5 27 G4
BTSEA SW11 128 E2
EHAM E6 77 H7
FNCH N3 38 D6
Eversley Av BXLYHN DA7 138 B1
WBLY HA9 68 C1
Eversley Cl WCHMH N21 29 F5
Eversley Crs ISLW TW7 103 J7
RSLP HA4 64 C1
WCHMH N21 29 F5
Eversley Cross BXLYHN DA7 138 B1
Eversley Mt WCHMH N21 29 F5
Eversley Pk WIM/MER SW19 145 K4
Eversley Park Rd WCHMH N21 29 F5
Eversley Rd BRYLDS KT5 159 G3
CHARL SE7 114 A5
NRWD SE19 149 K6
Eversley Wy CROY/NA CR0 179 J2
Everthorpe Rd PECK SE15 131 G2
Everton Buildings CAMTN NW1 4 E8
Everton Dr STAN HA7 50 B2
Everton Rd CROY/NA CR0 165 H7
Evesham Av WALTH E17 57 J1
Evesham Cl BELMT SM2 174 E6
GFD/PVL UB6 84 B1
Evesham Gn MRDN SM4 162 A5
Evesham Rd FBAR/BDGN N11 40 C4
MRDN SM4 162 A5
SRTFD E15 76 D6
Evesham St NTGHL W11 88 B6
Evesham Ter SURB * KT6 158 E5
Evesham Wk BRXN/ST SW9 130 B1
CMBW SE5 130 E1
Evesham Wy BTSEA SW11 129 F2
CLAY IG5 60 A2
Evry Rd SCUP DA14 155 J5
Ewald Rd FUL/PGN SW6 127 J1
Ewanrigg Ter WFD IG8 45 G4
Ewart Gv WDGN N22 41 G7
Ewart Pl BOW * E3 93 H1
Ewart Rd FSTH SE23 132 A6
Ewe Cl HOLWY N7 72 E5
Ewell By-Pass EW KT17 173 J6
Ewell Court Av
HOR/WEW KT19 173 G4
Ewellhurst Rd CLAY IG5 59 J1
Ewell Park Gdns EW KT17 173 J6
Ewell Park Wy EW KT17 173 J5
Ewell Rd CHEAM SM3 174 B5
SURB KT6 159 G5
THDIT KT7 158 C6
Ewelme Rd FSTH SE23 131 K7
Ewen Crs BRXS/STRHM SW2 130 B6
Ewer St STHWK SE1 12 E9
Ewhurst Av SAND/SEL CR2 178 B7
Ewhurst Cl BELMT SM2 174 A7
WCHPL E1 92 E4
Ewhurst Rd BROCKY SE4 132 D5
Exbury Rd CAT SE6 151 J1
Excel Ct LSQ/SEVD WC2H 11 H7
Excelsior Cl KUT KT1 159 H1
Exchange Ar LVPST EC2M 13 J3
Exchange Ct COVGDN * WC2E 11 K7
Exchange Rd WATW WD18 21 F3
Exchange Sq SDTCH * EC2A 13 K2
Exchange St ROM RM1 63 G5
Exeter Cl EHAM E6 95 K5
WATN WD24 21 G1
Exeter Gdns IL IG1 59 K7
Exeter Ms FUL/PGN * SW6 107 K6
Exeter Pde CRICK * NW2 70 C5
Exeter Rd CAN/RD E16 94 E4
CRICK NW2 70 C4
CROY/NA CR0 165 F6
DAGE RM10 80 D5
ED N9 42 E1
FELT TW13 141 K2
HTHAIR TW6 121 H2
PEND EN3 31 F2
RYLN/HDSTN HA2 65 J1
STHGT/OAK N14 28 B7
WALTH E17 57 J4
WELL DA16 136 A1
Exeter St COVGDN WC2E 11 K6
Exeter Wy HTHAIR TW6 121 H1
NWCR SE14 112 C6
Exford Gdns LEE/GVPK SE12 134 A7
Exford Rd LEE/GVPK SE12 153 F1
Exhibition Rd SKENS SW7 15 H2
Exit Rd EFNCH N2 53 H1
Exmoor St NKENS W10 88 B3
Exmouth Market CLKNW EC1R 6 A9
Exmouth Ms CAMTN * NW1 4 F8

Exmouth Pl HACK E8 74 D7
Exmouth Rd RSLP HA4 65 G2
WALTH E17 57 H4
WELL DA16 116 D7
YEAD UB4 82 C2
Exmouth St WCHPL E1 92 E5
Exning Rd CAN/RD E16 94 D3
Exon St WALW SE17 19 J6
Explorer Av STWL/WRAY TW19 120 B7
Explorer Dr WATW WD18 20 D5
Express Dr GDMY/SEVK IG3 61 H7
Exton Crs WLSDN NW10 68 E6
Exton Gdns BCTR RM8 79 K4
Exton St STHWK SE1 12 A9
Eyhurst Av HCH RM12 81 J2
Eyhurst Cl CRICK NW2 69 J1
Eylewood Rd WNWD SE27 149 J4
Eynella Rd DUL SE21 131 G6
Eynham Rd SHB W12 88 A5
Eynsford Cl STMC/STPC BR5 169 H6
Eynsford Crs SCUP DA14 136 D7
Eynsford Rd GDMY/SEVK IG3 78 E1
Eynsham Dr ABYW SE2 116 C2
Eynswood Dr SCUP DA14 155 H4
Eyot Gdns HMSMTH W6 106 C4
Eyre Cl GPK RM2 63 K3
Eyre Street Hl CLKNW EC1R 12 A1
Eythorne Rd BRXN/ST SW9 110 B7
Ezra St BETH E2 7 M7

F

Faber Gdns HDN NW4 51 J4
Fabian Rd FUL/PGN SW6 107 J6
Fabian St EHAM E6 95 K3
The Facade FSTH * SE23 150 E1
Factory La CROY/NA CR0 177 G1
TOTM N17 56 B1
Factory Pl POP/IOD E14 113 F4
Factory Rd CAN/RD E16 95 H7
Factory Yd HNWL W7 84 E7
Faggs Rd EBED/NFELT TW14 121 J3
Fairacre ISLW * TW7 103 J7
NWMAL KT3 160 B2
Fairacres CROY/NA CR0 179 H7
Fair Acres HAYES BR2 167 K4
Fairacres RSLP HA4 46 D6
Fairbank Est IS N1 7 G6
Fairbanks Rd TOTM N17 56 C2
Fairbourne Rd TOTM N17 56 A2
Fairbridge Rd ARCH N19 72 D1
Fairbrook Cl PLMGR N13 41 G4
Fairby Rd LEE/GVPK SE12 134 A4
Fairchild Cl BTSEA SW11 128 C1
Fairchild Pl SDTCH * EC2A 13 K1
Fairchild St SDTCH EC2A 13 K1
Fair Cl BUSH WD23 22 B6
Fairclough St WCHPL E1 92 C5
Faircross Av BARK IG11 78 C5
Fairdale Gdns HYS/HAR UB3 101 K1
PUT/ROE SW15 126 E3
Fairey CDALE/KGS * NW9 51 H1
Fairey Av HYS/HAR UB3 101 J2
Fairfax Av EW KT17 173 K7
Fairfax Cl WOT/HER KT12 156 A7
Fairfax Gdns BKHTH/KID SE3 114 B7
Fairfax Ms CEND/HSY/T * N8 55 H3
PUT/ROE SW15 127 F3
Fairfax Pl KIL/WHAMP NW6 2 F2
Fairfax Rd CEND/HSY/T N8 55 G3
CHSWK W4 106 B2
KIL/WHAMP NW6 2 F2
TEDD TW11 143 G6
Fairfax Wy MUSWH * N10 40 A6
Fairfield Av EDGW HA8 36 D5
HDN NW4 51 K5
OXHEY WD19 33 G2
RSLP HA4 46 A6
WHTN TW2 123 G7
Fairfield Cl BFN/LL DA15 136 A5
HCH RM12 63 J7
HOR/WEW KT19 173 G4
NFNCH/WDSP N12 39 G3
PEND EN3 31 G3
WIM/MER SW19 147 J6
Fairfield Cnr KUT * KT1 159 G1
Fairfield Ct RSLP HA4 46 B7
Fairfield Crs EDGW HA8 36 D5
Fairfield Dr GFD/PVL UB6 67 J7
RYLN/HDSTN HA2 48 C2
WAND/EARL SW18 128 A4
Fairfield East KUT KT1 159 F1
Fairfield Gdns CEND/HSY/T N8 54 E4
Fairfield Gv CHARL SE7 114 C5
Fairfield North KUT KT1 159 F1
Fairfield Pth CROY/NA CR0 177 K2
Fairfield Pl KUT KT1 159 F2
Fairfield Rd BECK BR3 166 D1
BMLY BR1 152 E6
BOW E3 93 J1
BXLYHN DA7 137 G1
CEND/HSY/T N8 54 E4
CROY/NA CR0 177 K2
IL IG1 78 B5
KUT KT1 159 F1
STHL UB1 83 K5
STMC/STPC BR5 169 J6
UED N18 42 C3
WALTH E17 57 G1
WFD IG8 44 E5
Fairfields CAT SE6 132 E6
Fairfields Cl CDALE/KGS NW9 50 E4
Fairfields Crs CDALE/KGS NW9 50 E3
Fairfield South KUT KT1 159 F2
Fairfield St WAND/EARL SW18 128 A4
Fairfield Wy BAR EN5 26 E4
HOR/WEW KT19 173 G4
Fairfield West KUT KT1 159 F1
Fairfoot Rd BOW * E3 93 J3
Fairford Av BXLYHN DA7 117 K7
CROY/NA CR0 166 A4
Fairford Cl CROY/NA CR0 166 A4
Fairford Ct BELMT * SM2 175 F6
Fairford Gdns WPK KT4 173 H2
Fairgreen EBAR EN4 27 K2
Fairgreen Ct EBAR * EN4 27 K2
Fairgreen Rd THHTH CR7 164 C4
Fairhaven Av CROY/NA CR0 166 A5
Fairhaven Crs OXHEY WD19 32 E2
Fairhazel Gdns KIL/WHAMP NW6 2 E1
Fairholme EBED/NFELT TW14 121 G6
Fairholme Av GPK RM2 63 J4
Fairholme Cl FNCH N3 52 C3
Fairholme Ct PIN * HA5 34 A5
Fairholme Crs YEAD UB4 82 D3
Fairholme Gdns FNCH N3 52 C2
Fairholme Rd CROY/NA CR0 164 B6
HRW HA1 48 E4
IL IG1 59 K6
SUT SM1 174 D5
WKENS W14 107 H4
Fairholt Rd STNW/STAM N16 55 K7
Fairholt St SKENS SW7 15 K3
Fairland Rd SRTFD E15 76 D5
Fairlands Av BKHH IG9 44 E1
SUT SM1 174 E1
THHTH CR7 164 A3
Fairlawn CHARL SE7 114 B6
Fairlawn Av BXLYHN DA7 136 E1
CHSWK W4 105 K3
EFNCH N2 53 J3
Fairlawn Cl ESH/CLAY KT10 171 F5
FELT TW13 141 K3
KUTN/CMB KT2 144 E5
STHGT/OAK N14 28 D5
Fairlawn Ct CHARL * SE7 114 B6
Fairlawn Dr WFD IG8 44 E6
Fairlawn Gdns STHL * UB1 83 K6
Fairlawn Gv CHSWK W4 105 K3
Fairlawn Pk SYD SE26 151 G4
Fairlawn Rd WIM/MER SW19 146 D6
Fairlawns TWK TW1 124 D5
Fairlea Pl EA W5 85 J4
Fairlie Gdns FSTH SE23 131 K6
Fairlight Av CHING E4 44 B1
WFD IG8 44 E5
WLSDN NW10 87 G1
Fairlight Cl CHING E4 44 B1
WPK KT4 174 A3
Fairlight Rd TOOT SW17 147 H3
Fairlop Cl HCH RM12 81 K5
Fairlop Rd BARK/HLT IG6 60 C1
WAN E11 58 B6
Fairmead BMLY BR1 168 E3
SURB KT6 159 J7
Fairmead Cl BMLY BR1 168 E3
HEST TW5 102 C6
NWMAL KT3 160 A2
Fairmead Crs EDGW HA8 36 E3
Fairmead Gdns REDBR IG4 59 H4
Fairmead Rd CROY/NA CR0 164 B6
HOLWY N7 72 E2
Fairmile Av STRHM/NOR SW16 148 D4
Fairmont Cl BELV DA17 117 G4
Fairmount Rd
BRXS/STRHM SW2 130 A5
Fairoak Cl STMC/STPC BR5 169 G6
Fairoak Dr ELTH/MOT SE9 135 J4
Fairoak Gdns ROM RM1 63 G1
Fair Oak Pl BARK/HLT IG6 60 C1
Fairseat Cl BUSH WD23 34 E1
Fairstead Wk IS * N1 6 E3
Fair St HSLW TW3 123 H2
STHWK SE1 19 K1
Fairthorn Rd CHARL SE7 113 K4
Fairview ERITH DA8 118 C6
Fairview Av ALP/SUD HA0 67 K5
Fairview Cl SYD * SE26 151 G3
Fair View Cl WALTH E17 43 G7
Fairview Ct HDN * NW4 52 B1
Fairview Crs RYLN/HDSTN HA2 48 A7
Fairview Gdns WFD IG8 45 F7
Fairview Pl BRXS/STRHM SW2 130 A6
Fairview Rd SEVS/STOTM N15 56 B5
STRHM/NOR SW16 149 F7
SUT SM1 175 H4
Fairview Vls CHING * E4 43 J6
Fairview Wy EDGW HA8 36 C3
Fairwater Av WELL DA16 136 B3
The Fairway ACT W3 87 G5
ALP/SUD HA0 67 H1
BAR EN5 27 F5
BMLY BR1 168 E4
E/WMO/HCT KT8 157 G2
HNWL * W7 84 E6
MLHL NW7 37 F2
NTHLT UB5 66 C5
NTHWD HA6 32 C3
NWMAL KT3 145 F7
PLMGR N13 41 J2
RSLP HA4 65 G3
STHGT/OAK N14 28 B5
Fairway BXLYHS DA6 137 F4
RYNPK SW20 161 F2
STMC/STPC BR5 169 J5
WFD IG8 45 G4
Fairway Av BORE WD6 24 D1
CDALE/KGS NW9 50 D2
Fairway Cl CROY/NA CR0 166 B4
GLDGN NW11 53 G6
HOR/WEW KT19 172 E3
Fairway Ct MLHL * NW7 37 F2
Fairway Dr GFD/PVL UB6 66 B6
THMD SE28 97 K5
Fairway Gdns BECK BR3 167 G5
IL IG1 78 D4
Fairways ISLW * TW7 103 K7
STAN HA7 50 A1
TEDD TW11 143 K6
WALTH * E17 58 A3
Fairweather Cl
SEVS/STOTM N15 56 A3
Fairweather Rd
STNW/STAM N16 56 C5
Fairwyn Rd SYD SE26 151 G2
Faithfield BUSH * WD23 21 J5
Fakenham Cl MLHL NW7 37 J6
NTHLT UB5 66 A5
Fakruddin St WCHPL E1 92 C3
Falaize Av IL IG1 78 B3
Falcon Av BMLY BR1 168 D2
Falconberg Ct
SOHO/SHAV * W1D 11 G4
Falcon Cl CHSWK W4 105 J5
DART DA1 139 J4
NTHWD HA6 32 C6
STHWK SE1 12 D8
Falcon Ct IS N1 6 D6
Falcon Crs PEND EN3 31 F4
Falcon Dr STWL/WRAY TW19 120 A5
Falconer Rd BUSH WD23 22 A5
Falcon Gv BTSEA SW11 128 D2
Falcon La BTSEA SW11 128 D2
Falcon Rd BTSEA SW11 128 D2
HPTN TW12 141 K6
PEND EN3 31 F4
Falcon St PLSTW E13 94 E3
Falcon Ter BTSEA * SW11 128 D2
Falcon Wy CDALE/KGS NW9 51 G1
KTN/HRWW/W HA3 50 A4
WAN E11 58 E3
Falconwood Av WELL DA16 135 J1
Falconwood Pde WELL DA16 135 K3
Falconwood Rd
CROY/NA CR0 179 H7
Falcourt Cl SUT SM1 175 F4
Falkirk Gdns OXHEY WD19 33 H4
Falkirk St IS N1 7 K6
Falkland Av FBAR/BDGN N11 40 A3
FNCH N3 38 E6
Falkland Park Av SNWD SE25 165 F2
Falkland Pl KTTN NW5 72 C4
Falkland Rd BAR EN5 26 C1
CEND/HSY/T N8 55 G3
KTTN NW5 72 C4
Falloden Wy GLDGN NW11 52 E3
Fallow Ct STHWK * SE1 111 H4
Fallow Court Av
NFNCH/WDSP N12 39 G6
Fallowfield STAN HA7 35 G2
Fallowfield Ct STAN HA7 35 G2
Fallowfields Dr
NFNCH/WDSP N12 39 J5
Fallows Cl EFNCH N2 53 G1
Fallsbrook Rd
STRHM/NOR SW16 148 B5
Falman Cl ED N9 30 C7
Falmer Rd EN EN1 30 A3
SEVS/STOTM N15 55 J4
WALTH E17 57 K2
Falmouth Av CHING E4 44 B4
Falmouth Cl LEE/GVPK SE12 133 J4
Falmouth Gdns REDBR IG4 59 H3
Falmouth Rd STHWK SE1 18 F4
Falmouth St SRTFD E15 76 B4
Falstaff Cl DART DA1 138 B6
Fambridge Cl SYD SE26 151 H3
Fambridge Rd BCTR RM8 62 C7
Fane St WKENS W14 107 J5
Fanns Ri PUR RM19 119 K3
Fann St FARR EC1M 12 E1
Fanshawe Av BARK IG11 78 C5
Fanshawe Crs DAGW RM9 80 A4
Fanshawe Rd
RCHPK/HAM TW10 143 J3
Fanshaw St IS N1 7 J7
Fanthorpe St PUT/ROE SW15 127 F2
Faraday Av SCUP DA14 155 H1
Faraday Cl HOLWY N7 73 F5
WATW WD18 20 B5
Faraday Rd ACT W3 86 E6
E/WMO/HCT KT8 157 F3
NKENS W10 88 C4
SRTFD E15 76 D5
STHL UB1 84 B6
WELL DA16 136 B2
WIM/MER SW19 147 F5
Faraday Wy WOOL/PLUM SE18 114 C2
Fareham Rd
EBED/NFELT TW14 122 B6
Fareham St SOHO/CST * W1F 11 G4
Farewell Pl MTCM CR4 147 H7
Faringdon Av HAYES BR2 169 F6
Faringford Rd SRTFD E15 76 C6
Farjeon Rd BKHTH/KID SE3 114 C7
Farleigh Av HAYES BR2 167 J6
Farleigh Pl STNW/STAM N16 74 B3
Farleigh Rd STNW/STAM N16 74 B3
Farley Dr GDMY/SEVK IG3 60 E7
Farley Pl SNWD SE25 165 H3
Farley Rd CAT SE6 133 F6
SAND/SEL CR2 178 D6
Farlington Pl PUT/ROE SW15 126 E6
Farlow Rd PUT/ROE SW15 127 G2
Farlton Rd WAND/EARL SW18 128 A6
The Farm WIM/MER * SW19 127 G6
Farman Ter
KTN/HRWW/W * HA3 49 K3
Farm Av ALP/SUD HA0 67 J5
CRICK NW2 70 C2
RYLN/HDSTN HA2 48 A6
STRHM/NOR SW16 148 E3
Farmborough Cl HRW HA1 48 D6
Farm Cl BAR EN5 25 K4
BELMT SM2 175 H6
BKHH IG9 45 G2
DAGE RM10 80 E6
FUL/PGN * SW6 107 K6
STHL UB1 84 B6
WWKM BR4 180 D2
Farmcote Rd LEE/GVPK SE12 133 K7
Farm Cottages
E/WMO/HCT * KT8 158 B3
Farmdale Rd CAR SM5 175 J6
GNWCH SE10 113 K4
Farm Dr CROY/NA CR0 179 H1
Farmer Rd LEY E10 57 K7
Farmers Rd CMBW SE5 110 C6
Farmer St KENS W8 8 A8
Farmfield Rd BMLY BR1 152 C4
Farmhouse Rd
STRHM/NOR SW16 148 C6
Farmilo Rd WALTH E17 57 J6
Farmington Av SUT SM1 175 H2
The Farmlands NTHLT UB5 65 K5
Farmlands PIN HA5 46 E3
Farmland Wk CHST BR7 154 B4
Farm La CROY/NA CR0 179 H1
FUL/PGN SW6 107 K5
STHGT/OAK N14 28 A5
Farmleigh STHGT/OAK N14 28 C6
Farm Pl DART DA1 138 D3
KENS W8 8 A8
Farm Rd BELMT SM2 175 H6
EDGW HA8 36 E4
ESH/CLAY KT10 157 F7
HSLWW TW4 122 D7
MRDN SM4 162 A4
NTHWD HA6 32 A4
WCHMH N21 29 J7
WLSDN NW10 69 F7
Farmstead Rd CAT SE6 151 K3
KTN/HRWW/W HA3 34 D7
Farm St MYFR/PICC W1J 10 C7
Farm V BXLY DA5 137 J5
Farmway BCTR RM8 79 J3
Farm Wy BKHH IG9 45 G3
BUSH WD23 22 B3
HCH RM12 81 K3
NTHWD HA6 32 C3
WPK KT4 174 A2
Farnaby Rd BMLY BR1 152 C7
ELTH/MOT SE9 134 B3
Farnan Av WALTH E17 57 J1
Farnan Rd STRHM/NOR SW16 148 E4
Farnborough Av
SAND/SEL CR2 179 G6
WALTH * E17 57 G2
Farnborough Cl WBLY HA9 68 D1
Farnborough Common
ORP BR6 181 K2
Farnborough Crs HAYES BR2 167 J7
SAND/SEL CR2 179 G7
Farnborough Wy PECK SE15 111 F6
Farncombe St
BERM/RHTH SE16 111 H1
Farndale Av PLMGR N13 41 H2
Farndale Crs GFD/PVL UB6 84 C2
Farnell Ms ECT SW5 14 C7
Farnell Rd ISLW TW7 123 J2
Farnham Cl TRDG/WHET N20 27 G6
Farnham Gdns RYNPK SW20 160 E1
Farnham Pl STHWK SE1 12 D9
Farnham Rd GDMY/SEVK IG3 61 F5
WELL DA16 136 D1
Farnham Royal LBTH SE11 17 M8
Farningham Rd TOTM N17 42 C6
Farnley Rd THHTH CR7 164 E3
Farnol Rd DART DA1 139 K4
Faro Cl BMLY BR1 169 F1
Faroe Rd WKENS W14 107 G2
Farquhar Rd NRWD SE19 150 B4
WIM/MER SW19 146 E2
Farquharson Rd CROY/NA CR0 164 D6
Farraline Rd WATW WD18 21 F3
Farrance Rd CHDH RM6 62 A5
Farrance St POP/IOD E14 93 J5
Farrant Av WDGN N22 55 G1
Farr Av BARK IG11 97 G1
Farren Rd FSTH SE23 151 G1
Farrer Ms CEND/HSY/T N8 54 C3
Farrer Rd CEND/HSY/T N8 54 C3
KTN/HRWW/W HA3 50 A4
Farrier Cl BMLY BR1 168 C2
Farrier Rd NTHLT UB5 84 A1
Farrier St CAMTN NW1 4 D1
Farriers Wy BORE WD6 25 F5
Farrier Wk WBPTN SW10 14 E9
Farringdon La CLKNW EC1R 12 B1
Farringdon Rd FSBYW WC1X 6 A9
HCIRC EC1N 12 C3
Farringdon St STBT EC1A 12 C4
Farrington Pl CHST BR7 154 D6
Farrins Rents BERM/RHTH SE16 93 G7
Farrow La NWCR SE14 111 K6
Farrow Pl BERM/RHTH SE16 112 B2
Farthing Aly STHWK * SE1 111 H1
Farthing Flds WAP E1W 92 D7
The Farthings KUTN/CMB KT2 144 C7
Farthings Cl CHING E4 44 C2
PIN HA5 47 F5
Farthing St ORP BR6 181 K6
Farwell Rd SCUP DA14 155 H3
Farwig La BMLY BR1 152 E7
Fashion St WCHPL E1 13 L3
Fashoda Rd HAYES BR2 168 C3
Fassett Rd HACK E8 74 C5
KUT KT1 159 F3
Fassett Sq HACK E8 74 C5
Fauconberg Rd CHSWK W4 105 K5
Faulkner Cl BCTR RM8 61 K6
Faulkner St NWCR SE14 111 K7
Fauna Cl CHDH RM6 61 J5
Faunce St WALW SE17 18 C8
Favart Rd FUL/PGN SW6 107 K7
Faversham Av EN EN1 29 K5
Faversham Rd BECK BR3 166 C1
CAT SE6 132 C6
MRDN SM4 162 A5
Fawcett Cl BTSEA SW11 128 C1
STRHM/NOR SW16 149 G3
Fawcett Est CLPT * E5 56 C7
Fawcett Rd CROY/NA CR0 177 H2
WLSDN NW10 69 H6
Fawcett St WBPTN SW10 14 E9
Fawcus Cl ESH/CLAY KT10 170 E5
Fawe Park Rd PUT/ROE SW15 127 J3
Fawe St POP/IOD E14 93 K4
Fawley Rd KIL/WHAMP NW6 71 F4
Fawnbrake Av HNHL SE24 130 C4
Fawn Rd PLSTW E13 95 G1
Fawns Manor Rd
EBED/NFELT TW14 121 G7
Fawood Av WLSDN NW10 69 F6
Faygate Crs BXLYHS DA6 137 H4
Faygate Rd BRXS/STRHM SW2 149 F1
Fayland Av STRHM/NOR SW16 148 C4
Fearnley Crs HPTN TW12 141 J4
Fearnley St WATW WD18 21 F3
Fearon St GNWCH SE10 113 K4
Featherbed La CROY/NA CR0 179 H6
Feathers Pl GNWCH SE10 113 G5
Featherstone Av FSTH SE23 150 D1
Featherstone Gdns BORE WD6 25 F3
Featherstone Rd MLHL NW7 37 K5
NWDGN UB2 102 D2
Featherstone St STLK EC1Y 7 G9
Featherstone Ter NWDGN UB2 102 D2
Featley Rd BRXN/ST SW9 130 C2
Federal Rd GFD/PVL UB6 85 J1
Federation Rd ABYW SE2 116 D3
Fee Farm Rd ESH/CLAY KT10 171 F6
Felbridge Av STAN HA7 35 G7
Felbridge Cl BELMT SM2 175 F7
STRHM/NOR SW16 149 G3
Felbrigge Rd GDMY/SEVK IG3 79 F1
Felday Rd LEW SE13 132 E5
Felden Cl PIN HA5 33 J6
Felden St FUL/PGN SW6 107 J7
Feldman Cl STNW/STAM N16 56 C7
Felgate Ms HMSMTH W6 106 E3
Felhampton Rd ELTH/MOT SE9 154 B2
Felix Av CEND/HSY/T N8 54 E5
Felix Rd HNWL W7 85 G6
Felixstowe Rd ABYW SE2 116 D2
ED N9 42 C3
TOTM N17 56 B2
WLSDN * NW10 87 K2
Felix St BETH * E2 92 D1
Fellbrigg Rd EDUL SE22 131 G4
Fellbrigg St WCHPL E1 92 D3
Fellbrook RCHPK/HAM TW10 143 H2
Fellmongers Yd CROY/NA CR0 177 J2
Fellowes Cl YEAD UB4 83 H3
Fellowes Rd CAR SM5 175 J2
Fellows Rd HAMP NW3 3 H1
Fell Pth BORE * WD6 25 F4
Fell Rd CROY/NA CR0 177 J2
Felltram Wy CHARL SE7 113 K4
Felmersham Cl CLAP SW4 129 K3
Felmingham Rd PGE/AN SE20 165 K1
Felsberg Rd BRXS/STRHM SW2 129 K5
Fels Cl DAGE RM10 80 D2
Fels Farm Av DAGE RM10 80 E2
Felsham Rd PUT/ROE SW15 127 G2
Felspar Cl WOOL/PLUM SE18 116 A4
Felstead Rd HOM E9 75 J5
WAN E11 58 E6
Felstead St HOM E9 75 H5
Felsted Rd CAN/RD E16 95 H5
Feltham Av E/WMO/HCT KT8 157 K3
Felthambrook Wy FELT TW13 141 F3
Feltham Hill Rd ASHF TW15 140 A5
Felthamhill Rd FELT TW13 140 E3
Feltham Rd MTCM CR4 162 E1
Felton Cl STMC/STPC BR5 169 G5
Felton Lea SCUP DA14 155 F4
Felton Rd BARK IG11 96 E1
WEA W13 104 D1
Felton St IS N1 7 H4
Fenchurch Av FENCHST EC3M 13 J5
Fenchurch Buildings
FENCHST EC3M 13 K5
Fenchurch Pl FENCHST * EC3M 13 K6
Fenchurch St FENCHST EC3M 13 J6
Fendall Rd HOR/WEW KT19 172 E4
Fendall St STHWK SE1 19 K4
Fendt Cl CAN/RD E16 94 D5
Fendyke Rd ABYW SE2 116 E3
Fenelon Pl WKENS W14 107 J3
Fen Gv BFN/LL DA15 136 A5
Fenham Rd PECK SE15 111 H6
Fenman Ct TOTM N17 42 D7
Fenman Gdns GDMY/SEVK IG3 61 H7
Fenn Cl BMLY BR1 152 E5
Fennel Cl CAN/RD E16 94 C3
CROY/NA CR0 166 A7
Fennells Md HOR/WEW KT19 173 H7
Fennell St WOOL/PLUM SE18 115 F5
Fenner Cl BERM/RHTH SE16 111 J3
Fenner Sq BTSEA * SW11 128 C2
Fenning St STHWK SE1 19 J1
Fenn St HOM E9 75 F4
Fenstanton Av
NFNCH/WDSP N12 39 H4
Fen St CAN/RD E16 94 D6
Fentiman Rd VX/NE SW8 109 K5
Fenton Cl BRXN/ST * SW9 130 A1
CHST BR7 153 K4
HACK E8 74 B5
Fenton Rd TOTM N17 41 J6
Fenton's Av PLSTW E13 95 F2
Fenwick Gv PECK SE15 131 H2
Fenwick Pl BRXN/ST SW9 129 K2
SAND/SEL CR2 177 H6
Fenwick Rd PECK SE15 131 H2
Ferdinand Pl CAMTN NW1 4 B1
Ferdinand St CAMTN NW1 4 B1
Ferguson Av BRYLDS KT5 159 G4
Ferguson Cl BECK BR3 167 F2
Ferguson Dr ACT W3 87 F5
Ferguson's Cl POP/IOD E14 112 D3
Fergus Rd HBRY N5 73 H4
Ferme Park Rd CEND/HSY/T N8 54 E4
Fermor Rd FSTH SE23 132 B7
Fermoy Rd GFD/PVL UB6 84 B3
MV/WKIL W9 88 D3
Fern Av MTCM CR4 163 J3
Fernbank Av ALP/SUD HA0 67 F3
WOT/HER KT12 156 D6
Fernbank Ms CLAP SW4 129 G5
Fernbrook Dr RYLN/HDSTN HA2 48 B6
Fernbrook Rd LEW SE13 133 H5
Ferncliff Rd HACK E8 74 C4
Fern Cl ERITH DA8 118 E7
IS * N1 7 J5
Ferncroft Av HAMP NW3 70 E2
NFNCH/WDSP N12 39 J5
RSLP HA4 65 G1
Ferndale BMLY BR1 168 B1
Ferndale Av HSLWW TW4 122 D2
WALTH E17 58 B4
Ferndale Cl BXLYHN DA7 117 F7
Ferndale Rd CLAP SW4 129 K3
CRW RM5 62 E1
FSTGT E7 77 F6
SEVS/STOTM N15 56 B5
SNWD SE25 165 J4
WAN E11 76 D1
Ferndale St EHAM E6 96 B6
Ferndale Ter HRW HA1 49 F3
Ferndene Rd HNHL SE24 130 D3
Fernden Wy ROMW/RG RM7 62 D5
Ferndown NTHWD HA6 46 E1
Ferndown Av ORP BR6 169 J7
Ferndown Cl BELMT SM2 175 H5
PIN HA5 33 J6
Ferndown Rd ELTH/MOT SE9 134 C6
OXHEY WD19 33 G2
Ferney Meade Wy ISLW TW7 124 B1
Ferney Rd EBAR EN4 28 A6
Fern Gv EBED/NFELT TW14 122 A6
Fernhall Dr REDBR IG4 59 H4
Fernham Rd THHTH CR7 164 D3
Fernhead Rd MV/WKIL W9 88 D2
Fernhill Ct WALTH E17 58 B1
Fernhill Gdns KUTN/CMB KT2 143 K4
Fernhill St CAN/RD E16 95 K7
Fernholme Rd PECK SE15 132 A4
Fernhurst Gdns EDGW HA8 36 C5
Fernhurst Rd ASHF TW15 140 A3
CROY/NA CR0 165 H6
FUL/PGN SW6 107 H7
Fern La NWDGN UB2 102 E4
Fernlea Rd BAL SW12 129 G7
MTCM CR4 163 F1
Fernleigh Cl CROY/NA CR0 177 G3
MV/WKIL W9 88 D2
Fernleigh Ct RYLN/HDSTN HA2 48 B1
WBLY HA9 50 A7
Fernleigh Rd WCHMH N21 41 G1
Fernley Cl PIN HA5 46 E3
Fernsbury St FSBYW WC1X 6 A8
Fernshaw Cl WBPTN * SW10 108 B5
Fernshaw Rd WBPTN SW10 108 B5
Fernside Av FELT TW13 141 F3
MLHL NW7 37 F2
Fernside Rd BAL SW12 128 E7
Ferns Rd SRTFD E15 76 C5
Fern St BOW E3 93 J3
Fernthorpe Rd
STRHM/NOR SW16 148 C5
Ferntower Rd HBRY N5 73 K4
Fern Wk STHWK SE1 111 H4
Fernways IL IG1 78 B2
Fernwood Av ALP/SUD HA0 67 J5
STRHM/NOR SW16 148 D3
Fernwood Cl BMLY BR1 168 B1
Fernwood Crs TRDG/WHET N20 39 K2
Ferranti Cl WOOL/PLUM SE18 114 C2
Ferraro Cl HEST TW5 103 F5
Ferrers Av WDR/YW UB7 100 A1
WLGTN SM6 176 D3
Ferrers Rd STRHM/NOR SW16 148 D4
Ferrestone Rd CEND/HSY/T N8 55 F3
Ferrey Ms BRXN/ST SW9 130 B1
Ferriby Cl IS N1 6 A1
Ferrier St WAND/EARL SW18 128 A3
Ferring Cl RYLN/HDSTN HA2 48 C7
Ferrings DUL SE21 150 A1
Ferris Av CROY/NA CR0 179 H2
Ferris Rd EDUL SE22 131 H3
Ferron Rd CLPT * E5 74 D2
Ferro Rd RAIN RM13 99 J3
Ferryhills Cl OXHEY WD19 33 G2
Ferry La BARN SW13 106 C5
BTFD TW8 105 F5
RAIN RM13 99 G5

TOTM N17 56 D3
Ferrymead Av GFD/PVL UB6 84 A1
Ferrymead Dr GFD/PVL UB6 84 A2
Ferrymead Gdns GFD/PVL UB6 84 C1
Ferrymoor RCHPK/HAM TW10 143 H2
Ferry Rd BARN SW13 106 D6
E/WMO/HCT KT8 157 F2
TEDD TW11 143 H4
THDIT KT7 158 C5
TWK TW1 124 C7
Ferry Sq BTFD TW8 105 F5
Ferry St POP/IOD E14 113 F4
Festing Rd PUT/ROE SW15 127 G2
Festival Cl BXLY DA5 136 E7
ERITH DA8 118 C6
Fetter La FLST/FETLN EC4A 12 B5
Ffinch St DEPT SE8 112 D6
Fidler Pl BUSH WD23 22 B5
Field Cl BKHH IG9 45 G2
BMLY BR1 168 B1
CHING E4 43 K5
CHSGTN KT9 171 J4
E/WMO/HCT KT8 157 G4
HSLWW TW4 102 A7
HYS/HAR UB3 101 F6
RSLP HA4 46 A7
Fieldcommon La
WOT/HER KT12 156 D7
Field Cottages EFNCH * N2 53 K2
FUL/PGN * SW6 127 J1
Field Ct GINN WC1R 11 M3
Field End BAR EN5 25 K3
RSLP HA4 65 G5
Fieldend TEDD TW11 143 F3
Field End Cl OXHEY WD19 21 J6
Field End Rd PIN HA5 47 F4
RSLP HA4 65 H2
Fieldend Rd STRHM/NOR SW16 148 C7
Fielders Cl EN EN1 30 A3
RYLN/HDSTN HA2 48 C7
Fieldfare Rd THMD SE28 97 J6
Fieldgate St WCHPL E1 92 C4
Fieldhouse Cl SWFD E18 45 F7
Fieldhouse Rd BAL SW12 129 H7
Fielding Av WHTN TW2 142 C2
Fielding Rd CHSWK W4 106 B2
WKENS W14 107 G2
The Fieldings FSTH SE23 131 K7
Fielding St WALW SE17 18 E9
Fielding Ter EA * W5 86 B6
Field La BTFD TW8 104 D6
TEDD TW11 143 G4
Field Md CDALE/KGS NW9 37 G6
Field Pl NWMAL KT3 160 C5
Field Rd EBED/NFELT TW14 122 A5
FSTGT E7 76 E3
HMSMTH W6 107 H5
OXHEY WD19 21 J5
TOTM N17 55 K2
Fieldsend Rd CHEAM SM3 174 C4
Fields Est HACK * E8 74 C6
Fieldside Cottages
TRDG/WHET * N20 26 D6
Fields Park Crs CHDH RM6 61 K4
Field St FSBYW WC1X 5 L7
Field Vw FELT TW13 140 B3
Fieldview WAND/EARL SW18 128 C7
Fieldview Cottages
STHGT/OAK * N14 40 D1
Field Wy CROY/NA CR0 179 K6
GFD/PVL UB6 66 B7
RSLP HA4 46 A7
WLSDN NW10 68 E6
Fieldway BCTR RM8 79 H3
STMC/STPC BR5 169 J5
Fieldway Crs HBRY N5 73 G4
Fiennes Cl BCTR RM8 61 J7
Fiesta Dr DAGW RM9 98 E3
Fife Rd CAN/RD E16 94 E4
KUT KT1 159 F1
MORT/ESHN SW14 125 K4
WDGN N22 41 H6
Fife Ter IS N1 5 M5
Fifield Pth FSTH SE23 151 F2
Fifth Av MNPK E12 77 K3
NKENS W10 88 C3
Fifth Cross Rd WHTN TW2 142 D1
Fifth Wy WBLY HA9 68 D3
Figge's Rd MTCM CR4 148 A6
Filby Rd CHSGTN KT9 172 B5
Filey Av STNW/STAM N16 56 C7
Filey Cl BELMT SM2 175 G6
Filey Waye RSLP HA4 64 E1
Fillebrook Av EN EN1 30 A1
Fillebrook Rd WAN E11 58 B7
Filmer Chambers
FUL/PGN * SW6 107 J7
Filmer Rd FUL/PGN SW6 107 J7
Finborough Rd TOOT SW17 147 K6
WBPTN SW10 14 D9
Finchale Rd ABYW SE2 116 C2
Fincham Cl HGDN/ICK UB10 64 A2
Finch Av WNWD SE27 149 K3
Finch Cl BAR EN5 26 E4
Finch Dr EBED/NFELT TW14 122 C6
Finch Gdns CHING E4 43 J4
Finchingfield Av WFD IG8 45 G6
Finch La BANK EC3V 13 H5
BUSH WD23 22 A4
Finchley Cl DART DA1 139 K5
Finchley La HDN NW4 52 B3
Finchley Pk NFNCH/WDSP N12 39 G3
Finchley Pl STJWD NW8 3 G5
Finchley Rd GLDGN NW11 52 D4
HAMP NW3 70 E3
STJWD NW8 3 G4
Finchley Vls
NFNCH/WDSP * N12 39 H3
Finchley Wy FNCH N3 38 E5
Finch Ms PECK * SE15 111 G7
Finden Rd FSTGT E7 77 F4
Findhorn Av YEAD UB4 83 F4
Findhorn St POP/IOD E14 94 A5
Findon Cl RYLN/HDSTN * HA2 66 B2
WAND/EARL SW18 127 K5
Findon Gdns RAIN RM13 99 J4
Findon Rd ED N9 30 D7
SHB W12 106 D1
Fingal St GNWCH SE10 113 J4
Finland Rd BROCKY SE4 132 B2
Finland St BERM/RHTH SE16 112 B2
Finlays Cl CHSGTN KT9 172 C4
Finlay St FUL/PGN SW6 127 G1
Finnis St BETH E2 92 D2
Finnymore Rd DAGW RM9 80 A6
Finsbury Av LVPST * EC2M 13 H3
Finsbury Cir LVPST EC2M 13 H3
Finsbury Cottages WDGN N22 40 E6
Finsbury Est CLKNW EC1R 6 B8
Finsbury Market SDTCH * EC2A 13 J2
Finsbury Park Av FSBYPK N4 55 J5
Finsbury Park Rd FSBYPK N4 73 H1
Finsbury Pavement
SDTCH EC2A 13 H2
Finsbury Rd WDGN N22 41 F7
Finsbury Sq SDTCH EC2A 13 H2
Finsbury St STLK EC1Y 13 G2
Finsbury Wy BXLY DA5 137 G5
Finsen Rd HNHL SE24 130 D3
Finstock Rd NKENS W10 88 B5
Finucane Gdns RAIN RM13 81 J5
Finucane Ri BUSH WD23 34 C1
Finway Ct WATW * WD18 20 D4
Fiona Ct ENC/FH * EN2 29 H2
Firbank Cl CAN/RD E16 95 H4
ENC/FH EN2 29 J3
Firbank Dr OXHEY WD19 21 J6
Firbank Rd PECK SE15 131 J1
Fircroft Gdns HRW HA1 66 E2
Fircroft Rd CHSGTN KT9 172 B3
TOOT SW17 147 K2
Firdene BRYLDS KT5 159 K7
Fir Dene ORP BR6 181 K2
Fire Bell Aly SURB KT6 159 F5
Firebell Ms SURB KT6 159 F5
Firecrest Dr HAMP NW3 71 F2
Firefly Gdns EHAM E6 95 J3
Fir Gv NWMAL KT3 160 C5
Firhill Rd CAT SE6 151 J2
Firmin Rd DART DA1 139 F4
Fir Rd CHEAM SM3 161 J7
FELT TW13 141 H4
The Firs BXLY DA5 138 A7
EA W5 85 K4
EBED/NFELT * TW14 121 H5
EDGW * HA8 37 F3
TRDG/WHET N20 27 H7
Firs Av FBAR/BDGN N11 40 A5
MORT/ESHN SW14 125 K3
MUSWH N10 54 A2
Firsby Av CROY/NA CR0 166 A7
Firsby Rd STNW/STAM N16 56 B7
Firs Cl ESH/CLAY KT10 170 E5
FSTH SE23 132 A6
MTCM CR4 163 G1
Firscroft PLMGR N13 41 J2
Firs Dr HEST TW5 102 A6
Firside Gv BFN/LL DA15 136 A7
Firs La PLMGR N13 41 J2
Firs Park Av WCHMH N21 29 K7
Firs Park Gdns WCHMH N21 29 K7
First Av ACT W3 87 H7
BXLYHN DA7 116 D6
CHDH RM6 61 J4
DAGE RM10 98 D1
E/WMO/HCT KT8 156 E3
EN EN1 30 B4
HDN NW4 52 A3
HOR/WEW KT19 173 G7
HYS/HAR UB3 82 D7
MNPK E12 77 J3
MORT/ESHN SW14 126 B1
MV/WKIL W9 88 D3
PLSTW E13 94 E2
UED N18 42 E3
WALTH E17 57 K4
WBLY HA9 67 K1
WOT/HER KT12 156 A5
First Cl E/WMO/HCT KT8 157 H3
First Cross Rd WHTN TW2 142 E1
First Dr WLSDN NW10 68 E6
First St CHEL SW3 15 K5
Firstway RYNPK SW20 161 F1
First Wy WBLY HA9 68 D3
Firs Wk NTHWD HA6 32 B5
WFD IG8 44 E4
Firswood Av HOR/WEW KT19 173 G4
Firth Gdns FUL/PGN SW6 107 H7
Firtree Av MTCM CR4 163 F1
Fir Tree Av WDR/YW UB7 100 D2
Fir Tree Cl EA W5 86 A5
ESH/CLAY KT10 170 C4
HOR/WEW KT19 173 H3
ROM RM1 63 F2
STRHM/NOR SW16 148 C4
Fir Tree Ct BORE WD6 24 B3
Fir Tree Gdns CROY/NA CR0 179 J3
Fir Tree Gv CAR SM5 175 K6
Fir Tree Rd HSLWW TW4 122 D3
Fir Trees Cl BERM/RHTH SE16 93 G7
Fir Tree Wk EN EN1 30 A2
Fir Wk EW KT17 174 B5
Fisher Cl CROY/NA CR0 165 G7
GFD/PVL UB6 84 A2
Fisherdene ESH/CLAY KT10 171 G6
Fisherman Cl
RCHPK/HAM TW10 143 J3
Fishermans Dr
BERM/RHTH SE16 112 A1
Fisher Rd KTN/HRWW/W HA3 49 F1
Fishers Cl BUSH WD23 21 J3
Fishers Ct NWCR SE14 112 A7
Fisher's La CHSWK W4 106 A3
Fisher St CAN/RD E16 94 E4
RSQ WC1B 11 L3
Fisher's Wy BELV DA17 98 E7
Fisherton St STJWD NW8 9 G1
Fishguard Wy CAN/RD E16 96 B7
Fishponds Rd HAYES BR2 181 H4
TOOT SW17 147 J3
Fish Street Hl MON EC3R 13 H7
Fisons Rd CAN/RD E16 94 E7
Fitzalan Rd ESH/CLAY KT10 170 E6
FNCH N3 52 C2
Fitzalan St LBTH SE11 17 M5
Fitzgeorge Av NWMAL KT3 145 F7
Fitz-George Av WKENS W14 107 H3
Fitzgerald Av
MORT/ESHN SW14 126 B2
Fitzgerald Rd
MORT/ESHN SW14 126 A2
THDIT KT7 158 B5
WAN E11 58 E4
Fitzhardinge St MBLAR W1H 10 A4
Fitzhugh Gv WAND/EARL SW18 128 C5
Fitzjames Av CROY/NA CR0 178 C1
Fitz-James Av WKENS W14 107 H3
Fitzjohn Av BAR EN5 26 C4
Fitzjohn's Av HAMP NW3 71 H4
Fitzmaurice Pl MYFR/PICC W1J 10 D8
Fitzneal St ACT W3 87 H5
Fitzroy Cl HGT N6 53 K7
Fitzroy Crs CHSWK * W4 106 A6
Fitzroy Gdns NRWD SE19 150 A6
Fitzroy Ms GTPST W1W 10 E1
Fitzroy Pk HGT N6 53 K7
Fitzroy Rd CAMTN NW1 4 A3
Fitzroy Sq FITZ W1T 10 E1
Fitzroy St CAMTN NW1 10 E1
Fitzstephen Rd BCTR RM8 79 H4
Fitzwarren Gdns ARCH N19 54 C7
Fitzwilliam Av RCH/KEW TW9 125 G1
Fitzwilliam Ms CAN/RD E16 94 E7
Fitzwilliam Rd CLAP SW4 129 H2
Fitz Wygram Cl HPTN TW12 142 C4
Five Acre CDALE/KGS NW9 51 H1
Fiveacre Cl THHTH CR7 164 B5
Five Elms Rd DAGW RM9 80 B2
HAYES BR2 181 G2
Five Fields Cl OXHEY WD19 33 K1
Five Ways Jct HDN NW4 37 J7
Fiveways Rd BRXN/ST SW9 130 B1
Fladbury Rd SEVS/STOTM N15 55 K5
Fladgate Rd WAN E11 58 C5
Flag Cl CROY/NA CR0 166 A7
Flag Wk PIN HA5 46 E5
Flambard Rd HRW HA1 49 G5
Flamborough Rd RSLP HA4 64 E2
Flamborough St POP/IOD E14 93 G5
Flamingo Wk HCH RM12 81 J6
Flamstead Gdns DAGW RM9 79 J6
Flamstead Rd DAGW RM9 79 J6
Flamsted Av WBLY HA9 68 C5
Flamsteed Rd CHARL SE7 114 D4
Flanchford Rd SHB W12 106 C2
Flanders Crs TOOT SW17 147 K6
Flanders Rd CHSWK W4 106 B3
EHAM E6 95 K1
Flanders Wy HOM E9 75 F5
Flank St WCHPL E1 92 C6
Flask Wk HAMP NW3 71 G3
Flavell Ms GNWCH SE10 113 H4
Flaxen Cl CHING E4 43 K2
Flaxen Rd CHING E4 43 K2
Flaxley Rd MRDN SM4 162 A5
Flaxman Rd CMBW SE5 130 C1
Flaxman Ter STPAN WC1H 5 H8
Flaxton Rd WOOL/PLUM SE18 115 J7
Flecker Cl STAN HA7 35 F4
Fleece Dr ED N9 42 C3
Fleece Rd SURB KT6 158 D7
Fleece Wk HOLWY * N7 72 E5
Fleeming Cl WALTH E17 57 H1
Fleeming Rd WALTH E17 57 H1
Fleet Cl E/WMO/HCT KT8 156 E4
RSLP HA4 46 A5
Fleet Pl STP EC4M 12 C4
Fleet Rd HAMP NW3 71 J4
Fleetside E/WMO/HCT KT8 156 E5
Fleet Sq FSBYW WC1X 5 L8
Fleet St EMB EC4Y 12 B5
Fleet Street Hl BETH * E2 92 C3
Fleet Ter CAT * SE6 133 F6
Fleetwood Cl CAN/RD E16 95 H4
CHSGTN KT9 171 K6
CROY/NA CR0 178 B2
Fleetwood Rd NWMAL KT3 159 J2
WLSDN NW10 69 J4
Fleetwood Sq NWMAL KT3 159 J2
Fleetwood St STNW/STAM N16 74 A1
Fleetwood Wy OXHEY WD19 33 G3
Fleming Cl MV/WKIL W9 8 A1
Fleming Ct CROY/NA CR0 177 G4
Fleming Md WIM/MER SW19 147 J6
Fleming Rd STHL UB1 84 B5
WALW SE17 18 D9
Fleming Wk CDALE/KGS * NW9 51 G1
Fleming Wy ISLW TW7 124 A2
THMD SE28 97 K6
Flemming Av RSLP HA4 47 F7
Flempton Rd WALTH E17 57 G7
Fletcher Cl EHAM E6 96 B6
Fletcher La LEY E10 58 A6
Fletcher Rd CHSWK W4 105 K2
Fletchers Cl HAYES BR2 168 A3
Fletcher St WCHPL E1 92 C6
Fletching Rd CHARL SE7 114 C5
CLPT E5 74 E2
Fletton Rd FBAR/BDGN N11 40 E6
Fleur De Lis St WCHPL E1 13 L1
Flexmere Rd TOTM N17 41 K7
Flight Ap CDALE/KGS * NW9 37 H7
Flimwell Cl BMLY BR1 152 C4
Flint Down Cl
STMC/STPC * BR5 155 G7
Flintmill Crs BKHTH/KID SE3 134 D1
Flinton St WALW SE17 19 K7
Flint St WALW SE17 19 H6
Flitcroft St LSQ/SEVD WC2H 11 H5
Flock Mill Pl WAND/EARL SW18 128 A7
Flockton St BERM/RHTH SE16 111 H1
Flodden Rd CMBW SE5 110 D7
Flood La TWK * TW1 124 B7
Flood St CHEL SW3 15 K8
Flood Wk CHEL SW3 15 K9
Flora Cl POP/IOD E14 93 K5
Flora Gdns CHDH RM6 61 J5
Floral Pl IS N1 73 K4
Floral St COVGDN WC2E 11 K6
Flora St BELV DA17 117 G4
Florence Av ENC/FH EN2 29 J2
MRDN SM4 162 B4
Florence Cl WOT/HER KT12 156 A6
Florence Ct WAN E11 59 F3
Florence Dr ENC/FH EN2 29 J2
Florence Gdns CHSWK W4 105 K5
Florence Rd ABYW SE2 116 D2
BECK BR3 166 A1
BMLY BR1 152 E7
CHSWK W4 106 A2
EA W5 86 A6
EHAM E6 77 G7
FELT TW13 122 A7
FSBYPK N4 55 F6
KUTN/CMB KT2 144 B6
NWCR SE14 112 C7
NWDGN UB2 102 C3
PLSTW E13 94 E1
SAND/SEL CR2 177 K7
WIM/MER SW19 147 F5
WOT/HER KT12 156 A6
Florence St CAN/RD E16 94 D3
HDN NW4 52 A3
IS N1 6 C2
Florence Ter NWCR SE14 112 C7
Florence Vls HGT * N6 54 B6
Florence Wy BAL SW12 128 E7
Florfield Rd HACK E8 74 D5
Florian Av SUT SM1 175 H3
Florian Rd PUT/ROE SW15 127 H3
Florida Cl BUSH WD23 34 D1
Florida Rd THHTH CR7 149 H7
Florida St BETH E2 92 C2
Florin Ct UED N18 42 A3
Floriston Av HGDN/ICK UB10 64 A6
Floriston Cl STAN HA7 35 H7
Floriston Gdns STAN HA7 35 H7
Floss St PUT/ROE SW15 127 F1
Flower & Dean Wk WCHPL E1 13 M3
Flower La MLHL NW7 37 H4
Flowers Cl CRICK NW2 69 J2
Flowers Ms ARCH N19 72 C1
Floyd Rd CHARL SE7 114 B4
Fludyer St LEW SE13 133 H3
Foley Ms ESH/CLAY KT10 170 E5
Foley Rd ESH/CLAY KT10 170 E6
Foley St GTPST W1W 10 E3
Folgate St WCHPL E1 13 K2
Foliot St ACT W3 87 H5
Folkestone Rd EHAM E6 96 A1
UED N18 42 C3
WALTH E17 57 K3
Folkingham La CDALE/KGS NW9 37 F7
Folkington Cnr
NFNCH/WDSP N12 38 D4
Follett St POP/IOD E14 94 A5
Folly La WALTH E17 43 G7
Folly Wall POP/IOD E14 113 F1
Fontaine Rd
STRHM/NOR SW16 149 F5
Fontarabia Rd BTSEA SW11 129 F3
Fontayne Av RAIN RM13 81 G6
ROM RM1 63 G1
Fontenoy Rd BAL SW12 148 B1
Fonteyne Gdns WFD IG8 59 H1
Fonthill Ms FSBYPK N4 73 F1
Fonthill Rd FSBYPK N4 73 F1
Font Hills EFNCH N2 53 G1
Fontley Wy PUT/ROE SW15 126 D6
Fontwell Cl KTN/HRWW/W HA3 34 E6
NTHLT UB5 66 A5
Fontwell Dr HAYES BR2 169 F4
Football La HRW HA1 49 F7
The Footpath PUT/ROE * SW15 126 D4
Foots Cray High St SCUP DA14 155 J5
Foots Cray La BXLY DA5 136 D7
Footscray Rd ELTH/MOT SE9 135 F5
Forbes Cl CRICK NW2 69 J2
EMPK RM11 63 K7
Forbes St WCHPL E1 92 C5
Forbes Wy RSLP HA4 65 F1
Forburg Rd STNW/STAM N16 56 C7
Ford Cl BUSH WD23 22 C3
HRW HA1 48 D6
RAIN RM13 81 H6
THHTH CR7 164 C5
Forde Av BMLY BR1 168 B2
Fordel Rd CAT SE6 133 G7
Ford End WFD IG8 45 F5
Fordham Rd EBAR EN4 27 H2
Fordham St WCHPL E1 92 C5
Fordhook Av EA W5 86 B6
Fordingley Rd MV/WKIL W9 88 D2
Fordington Rd HGT N6 53 K3
Ford La RAIN RM13 81 H6
Fordmill Rd CAT SE6 151 J1
Ford Rd BOW E3 93 G1
DAGE RM10 80 C6
Ford's Gv WCHMH N21 29 J7
Fords Park Rd CAN/RD E16 94 E5
Ford Sq WCHPL E1 92 D4
Ford St BOW E3 75 G7
CAN/RD E16 94 D5
Fordwych Rd CRICK NW2 70 C4
Fordyce Rd LEW SE13 133 F5
Fordyke Rd BCTR RM8 80 A1
Foreland Ct HDN NW4 38 C7
Foreland St WOOL/PLUM SE18 115 J3
Foreshore DEPT SE8 112 C3
Forest Ap WFD IG8 44 E6
Forest Cl CHST BR7 154 A7
WAN E11 58 D4
WFD IG8 45 F3
Forest Ct WAN E11 58 C3
Forestdale STHGT/OAK N14 40 D3
Forest Dr HAYES BR2 181 J3
MNPK E12 77 H2
SUN TW16 140 D6
WFD IG8 44 B6
Forest Dr East WAN E11 58 B6
Forest Dr West WAN E11 58 A6
Forest Edge BKHH IG9 45 G2
Forester Rd PECK SE15 131 J3
Foresters Cl WLGTN SM6 176 D6
Foresters Crs BXLYHN DA7 137 J3
Foresters Dr WALTH E17 58 B3
WLGTN SM6 176 D6
Forest Gdns TOTM N17 56 B1
Forest Ga CDALE/KGS NW9 51 G3
Forest Gld CHING E4 44 C4
WAN E11 58 C5
Forest Gv HACK E8 7 L1
Forest Hill Rd EDUL SE22 131 J5
Forestholme Cl FSTH * SE23 150 E1
Forest La FSTGT E7 76 E4
Forest Mount Rd WFD IG8 44 B6
Fore St BARB EC2Y 13 G3
ED N9 42 C3
PIN HA5 46 D3
The Forest WALTH E17 58 C3
Forest Rdg BECK BR3 166 D2
HAYES BR2 181 J3
Forest Ri WALTH E17 58 B2
Forest Rd CHEAM SM3 161 K7
ED N9 30 D7
ERITH DA8 118 D7
FELT TW13 141 G2
FSTGT E7 76 E3
HACK E8 74 B5
RCH/KEW TW9 105 H6
ROMW/RG RM7 62 D2
WALTH E17 56 E3
WALTH E17 58 B1
WAN E11 58 B6
WFD IG8 44 E2
Forest Side FSTGT E7 77 F3
WPK KT4 160 C7
Forest St FSTGT E7 76 E4
Forest Vw WAN E11 58 D4
Forest View Av WAN E11 58 D6
Forest View Rd MNPK E12 77 J3
WALTH E17 44 A7
Forest Wy BFN/LL DA15 135 J6
WFD IG8 45 F3
Forfar Rd BTSEA SW11 109 F7
WDGN N22 41 H7
Forge Cl HAYES BR2 167 K7
Forge Cottages EA * W5 85 K7
Forge Dr ESH/CLAY KT10 171 G6
Forge La BELMT SM2 174 C6
FELT TW13 141 J4
NTHWD HA6 32 C6
Forge Ms CROY/NA CR0 179 J4
Forge Pl CAMTN NW1 72 A5
Forman Pl STNW/STAM N16 74 B3
Formby Av KTN/HRWW/W HA3 49 J2
Formosa St MV/WKIL W9 8 D1
Formunt Cl CAN/RD E16 94 D4
Forres Gdns GLDGN NW11 52 E5
Forrester Pth SYD SE26 150 E3
Forrest Gdns
STRHM/NOR SW16 164 A2
Forris Av HYS/HAR UB3 82 D7
Forset St MBLAR W1H 9 K4
Forstal Cl HAYES BR2 167 K2
Forster Cl CHING E4 44 B6
Forster Rd BECK BR3 166 B2
BRXS/STRHM SW2 129 K6
TOTM N17 56 B2
WALTH E17 57 G5
Forsters Cl CHDH RM6 62 B5
Forston St IS N1 6 F5
Forsyte Crs NRWD SE19 150 A7
Forsyth Gdns WALW SE17 18 D9
Forsythia Cl IL IG1 78 B4
Forsyth Pl EN EN1 30 A4
Forterie Gdns GDMY/SEVK IG3 79 G2
Fortescue Av WHTN TW2 142 C2
Fortescue Rd EDGW HA8 37 F7
WIM/MER SW19 147 H6
Fortess Gv KTTN NW5 72 C4
Fortess Rd KTTN NW5 72 C3
Fortess Wk KTTN NW5 72 B4
Forthbridge Rd BTSEA SW11 129 F3
Fortis Cl CAN/RD E16 95 G5
Fortis Gn EFNCH N2 53 K2
Fortis Green Av EFNCH N2 54 A2
Fortis Green Rd MUSWH N10 54 A2
Fortismere Av MUSWH N10 54 A2
Fortnam Rd ARCH N19 72 D1
Fortnums Acre STAN HA7 35 F5
Fort Rd NTHLT UB5 66 A6
STHWK SE1 19 M6
Fortrose Gdns
BRXS/STRHM SW2 129 K7
Fort St CAN/RD E16 95 F7
WCHPL * E1 13 K3
Fortuna Cl HOLWY * N7 73 F5
Fortunegate Rd WLSDN NW10 69 G7
Fortune Green Rd
KIL/WHAMP NW6 70 E4
Fortune La BORE WD6 23 K5
Fortunes Md NTHLT UB5 65 J5
Fortune St STLK EC1Y 12 F1
Fortune Wy WLSDN NW10 87 J2
Forty Acre La CAN/RD E16 94 E4
Forty Av WBLY HA9 68 B2
Forty Cl WBLY HA9 68 B2
Forty La WBLY HA9 68 E1
The Forum E/WMO/HCT KT8 157 G3
Forum Magnum Sq STHWK SE1 17 L1
Forumside EDGW HA8 36 C5
Forum Wy EDGW HA8 36 C5
Forval Cl MTCM CR4 162 E4
Forward Dr KTN/HRWW/W HA3 49 F3
Fosbury Ms BAY/PAD W2 8 D7
Foscote Ms MV/WKIL W9 8 B1
Foscote Rd HDN NW4 51 K5
Foskett Rd FUL/PGN SW6 127 J1
Foss Av CROY/NA CR0 177 G4
Fossdene Rd CHARL SE7 114 A4
Fossdyke Cl YEAD UB4 83 J4
Fosse Wy WEA W13 85 G4
Fossil Rd LEW SE13 132 D2
Fossington Rd BELV DA17 116 E3
Foss Rd TOOT SW17 147 H3
Fossway BCTR RM8 79 J1
Foster La CITYW EC2V 12 E4
Foster Rd ACT W3 87 G6
CHSWK W4 106 A4
PLSTW E13 94 E3
Fosters Cl CHST BR7 153 K4
SWFD E18 45 F7
Foster St HDN NW4 52 A3
Foster Wk HDN NW4 52 A3
Fothergill Cl PLSTW E13 76 E7
Fothergill Dr WCHMH N21 28 E4
Fotheringham Rd EN EN1 30 B3
Foubert's Pl SOHO/CST W1F 10 E5
Foulden Rd STNW/STAM N16 74 B3
Foulden Ter STNW/STAM N16 74 B3
Foulis Ter SKENS SW7 15 G6
Foulser Rd TOOT SW17 147 K2
Foulsham Rd THHTH CR7 164 D2
Founders Gdns NRWD SE19 149 J6
Foundry Cl BERM/RHTH SE16 93 G7
Foundry Ms CAMTN NW1 4 F9
Foundry Pl
WAND/EARL * SW18 128 A6
Fountain Cl UX/CGN UB8 82 A4
Fountain Dr CAR SM5 175 K7
NRWD SE19 150 B3
Fountain Green Sq
BERM/RHTH SE16 111 H1
Fountain Ms HAMP * NW3 71 K5
Fountain Pl BRXN/ST SW9 110 B7
Fountain Rd THHTH CR7 164 D1
TOOT SW17 147 H4
Fountains Av FELT TW13 141 K2
Fountains Cl FELT TW13 141 K1
Fountains Crs STHGT/OAK N14 28 E6
Fountayne Rd SEVS/STOTM N15 56 C3
STNW/STAM N16 74 C1
Fount St VX/NE SW8 109 J6
Fourland Wk EDGW HA8 36 E5
Fournier St WCHPL E1 13 M2
Four Seasons Cl BOW E3 93 J1
Four Seasons Crs CHEAM SM3 174 D1
Fourth Av HYS/HAR UB3 82 D7
MNPK E12 77 K3
NKENS W10 88 C3
ROMW/RG RM7 62 E7
Fourth Cross Rd WHTN TW2 142 D1
Fourth Wy WBLY HA9 68 E3
The Four Tubs BUSH WD23 22 D6
The Four Wents CHING E4 44 B1
Fowey Av REDBR IG4 59 H4
Fowey Cl WAP E1W 92 D7
Fowler Cl BTSEA SW11 128 C2
Fowler Rd FSTGT E7 76 E3
IS N1 6 D3
Fowler's Wk EA W5 85 K3
Fownes St BTSEA SW11 128 D2
Fox And Knot St FARR * EC1M 12 D2
Foxberry Rd BROCKY SE4 132 B3
Foxborough Gdns BROCKY SE4 132 D5
Foxbourne Rd TOOT SW17 148 A1
Foxbury Av CHST BR7 154 D5
Foxbury Cl BMLY BR1 153 F5
Foxbury Rd BMLY BR1 153 F5
Fox Cl BORE WD6 23 K5
BUSH WD23 22 B4
CAN/RD E16 94 E4
WCHPL E1 92 E3
Foxcroft Rd WOOL/PLUM SE18 115 G7
Foxdell NTHWD HA6 32 B5
Foxearth Sp SAND/SEL CR2 178 E7
Foxes Dl BKHTH/KID SE3 133 K2
HAYES BR2 167 G2
Foxfield Cl NTHWD HA6 32 D5

Foxglove Cl STHL UB1 83 J6
STWL/WRAY TW19 120 A7
Foxglove Dr WAN E11 59 G3
Foxglove La CHSGTN KT9 172 C3
Foxglove Rd ROMW/RG RM7 81 G1
Foxglove St ACT W3 87 H6
Foxglove Wy MTCM CR4 163 F6
Foxgrove STHGT/OAK N14 40 E2
Fox Gv WOT/HER KT12 156 A6
Foxgrove Av BECK BR3 151 K6
Foxgrove Pth OXHEY WD19 33 H4
Foxgrove Rd BECK BR3 151 K6
Foxham Rd ARCH N19 72 D2
Fox Hl NRWD SE19 150 B6
Fox Hill Gdns NRWD SE19 150 B6
Foxhole Rd ELTH/MOT SE9 134 D4
Fox Hollow Cl
WOOL/PLUM SE18 115 K4
Fox Hollow Dr BXLYHN DA7 136 E2
Foxholt Gdns WLSDN NW10 68 E6
Foxhome Cl CHST BR7 154 A5
Fox House Rd BELV DA17 117 J3
Foxlands Crs DAGE RM10 80 E4
Foxlands Rd DAGE RM10 80 E4
Fox La EA W5 86 A4
HAYES BR2 181 F4
PLMGR N13 41 F1
Foxlees ALP/SUD HA0 67 G3
Foxley Cl HACK E8 74 C4
Foxley Rd CMBW SE5 110 B6
THHTH CR7 164 C3
Foxleys OXHEY WD19 33 J2
Foxley Sq BRXN/ST * SW9 110 C6
Foxmead Cl ENC/FH EN2 29 F2
Foxmore St BTSEA SW11 108 E7
Fox Rd CAN/RD E16 94 D4
Foxton Gv MTCM CR4 162 C1
Foxwarren ESH/CLAY KT10 171 F7
Foxwell St BROCKY SE4 132 B2
Foxwood Cl FELT TW13 141 F2
MLHL NW7 37 G3
Foxwood Green Cl EN EN1 30 A5
Foxwood Rd BKHTH/KID SE3 133 J3
Foyle Rd BKHTH/KID SE3 113 J5
TOTM N17 42 C7
Framfield Cl NFNCH/WDSP N12 38 E3
Framfield Rd HBRY N5 73 H4
HNWL W7 85 F5
MTCM CR4 148 A6
Framlingham Crs
ELTH/MOT SE9 153 J3
Frampton Cl BELMT SM2 174 E6
Frampton Park Rd HOM E9 74 E5
Frampton Rd HSLWW TW4 122 D4
Frampton St STJWD NW8 9 H1
Francemary Rd LEW SE13 132 D4
Frances Rd CHING E4 43 J5
Frances St WOOL/PLUM SE18 114 E3
Franche Court Rd TOOT SW17 147 G2
Francis Av BXLYHN DA7 137 H1
FELT TW13 140 E2
IL IG1 78 D1
Francis Barber Cl
STRHM/NOR * SW16 149 F3
Franciscan Rd TOOT SW17 148 A3
Francis Chichester Wy
BTSEA * SW11 109 F7
Francis Cl HOR/WEW KT19 173 F3
Francis Gv WIM/MER SW19 146 D5
Francis Ms LEE/GVPK * SE12 133 J5
Francis Rd CROY/NA CR0 164 C6
DART DA1 139 G4
EFNCH * N2 53 K3
GFD/PVL UB6 85 J1
HRW HA1 49 G4
HSLWW TW4 122 C1
LEY E10 76 A1
PIN HA5 47 G4
WATW WD18 21 F3
WLGTN SM6 176 C5
Francis St SRTFD E15 76 C4
WEST SW1P 16 F5
Francis Ter ARCH N19 72 C2
Francis Wk IS N1 5 L3
Francklyn Gdns EDGW HA8 36 C2
Francombe Gdns ROM RM1 63 J5
Franconia Rd CLAP SW4 129 H4
Frank Burton Cl CHARL SE7 114 A4
Frank Dixon Cl DUL SE21 131 F6
Frank Dixon Wy DUL SE21 131 F7
Frankfurt Rd HNHL SE24 130 D4
Frankham St DEPT SE8 112 D6
Frankland Cl
BERM/RHTH SE16 111 J2
WFD IG8 45 G4
Frankland Rd CHING E4 43 J4
SKENS SW7 15 G4
Franklin Cl KUT KT1 159 H2
LEW SE13 112 E7
TRDG/WHET N20 27 G6
WNWD SE27 149 H2
Franklin Crs MTCM CR4 163 H3
Franklin Rd BXLYHN DA7 117 F7
PGE/AN SE20 150 E6
WAT WD17 21 F1
Franklins Ms RYLN/HDSTN HA2 66 C1
Franklin Sq WKENS W14 107 J4
Franklin's Rw CHEL SW3 15 M7
Franklin St BOW E3 93 K2
SEVS/STOTM N15 56 A5
Franklin Wy CROY/NA CR0 163 K7
Franklyn Rd WLSDN NW10 69 H6
WOT/HER KT12 156 A5
Franks Av NWMAL KT3 159 K3
Franks Wood Av
STMC/STPC BR5 169 G4
Franlaw Crs PLMGR N13 41 J3
Franmil Rd EMPK RM11 63 H6
Fransfield Gv SYD SE26 150 D2
Franshams BUSH * WD23 34 E1
Frant Cl PGE/AN SE20 150 E6
Franthorne Wy CAT SE6 151 K1
Frant Rd THHTH CR7 164 C4
Fraser Cl BXLY DA5 137 K7
Fraser Rd ED N9 42 D2
ERITH DA8 117 K4
GFD/PVL UB6 67 J7
WALTH E17 57 K4
Fraser St CHSWK W4 106 B4
Frating Crs WFD IG8 44 E5
Frays Av WDR/YW UB7 100 A1
Frays Cl WDR/YW UB7 100 A2
Frazer Av RSLP HA4 65 G4
Frazer Cl ROMW/RG RM7 63 H6
Frazier St STHWK SE1 18 A2
Frean St BERM/RHTH SE16 111 H2
Freda Corbett Cl PECK SE15 111 H6
Frederica St HOLWY N7 5 L1
Frederick Cl BAY/PAD W2 9 K6
SUT SM1 174 D3
Frederick Crs BRXN/ST SW9 110 C6
PEND EN3 30 E1
Frederick Gdns CROY/NA CR0 164 C5
SUT SM1 174 D4
Frederick Pl
WOOL/PLUM SE18 115 G4
Frederick Rd RAIN RM13 99 F1
SUT SM1 174 D4
WALW * SE17 18 D8
Frederick's Pl LOTH * EC2R 13 G5
NFNCH/WDSP N12 39 G3
Frederick Sq BERM/RHTH SE16 93 G6
Frederick's Rw FSBYE EC1V 6 C7
Frederick St FSBYW WC1X 5 L8
Frederick Ter HACK E8 7 L2
Frederic Ms KTBR * SW1X 16 A2
Frederic St WALTH E17 57 G4
Fredora Av YEAD UB4 82 D3
Freeborne Gdns RAIN RM13 81 J5
Freedom Cl WALTH E17 57 F3
Freedom St BTSEA SW11 128 E1
Freegrove Rd HOLWY N7 72 E4
Freeland Pk HDN NW4 52 C1
Freeland Rd EA W5 86 B6
Freelands Av SAND/SEL CR2 179 F7
Freelands Gv BMLY BR1 153 F7
Freelands Rd BMLY BR1 153 F7
Freeland Wy ERITH DA8 118 D7
Freeling St IS * N1 5 L2
Freeman Cl NTHLT UB5 65 J6
Freeman Dr E/WMO/HCT KT8 156 E3
Freeman Rd MRDN SM4 162 C4
Freemans La HYS/HAR UB3 82 C6
Freemantle Av PEND EN3 31 F4
Freemantle St WALW SE17 19 J7
Freemasons Rd CAN/RD E16 95 F5
CROY/NA CR0 165 F7
Freethorpe Cl NRWD SE19 150 A7
Freightmaster Est
RAIN * RM13 118 D3
Freke Rd BTSEA SW11 129 F2
Fremantle Rd BARK/HLT IG6 60 B1
BELV DA17 117 H3
Fremont St HOM E9 74 E7
French Pl SDTCH EC2A 7 K8
French St SUN TW16 156 B1
Frendsbury Rd BROCKY SE4 132 B3
Frensham Cl STHL UB1 83 K3
Frensham Dr CROY/NA CR0 180 A6
PUT/ROE SW15 145 J2
Frensham Rd BFN/LL DA15 154 D1
Frensham St PECK SE15 111 H5
Frere St BTSEA SW11 128 D1
Freshfield Av HACK E8 7 L1
Freshfield Cl LEW SE13 133 G3
Freshfield Dr STHGT/OAK N14 28 B6
Freshfields CROY/NA CR0 166 C6
Freshford St TOOT SW17 147 G2
Freshwater Cl TOOT SW17 148 A5
Freshwater Rd BCTR RM8 61 K7
TOOT SW17 148 A5
Freshwell Av CHDH RM6 61 J3
Fresh Wharf Rd BARK IG11 78 B7
Freshwood Cl BECK BR3 151 K7
Freshwood Wy WLGTN SM6 176 C7
Freston Gdns EBAR EN4 28 A4
Freston Pk FNCH N3 52 D1
Freston Rd NKENS W10 88 B6
Freta Rd BXLYHS DA6 137 G4
Frewin Rd WAND/EARL SW18 128 C7
Friar Ms WNWD SE27 149 H2
Friar Rd YEAD UB4 83 H3
Friars Av PUT/ROE SW15 145 H2
TRDG/WHET N20 39 J2
Friars Cl CHING E4 44 A2
NTHLT UB5 83 G2
STHWK * SE1 12 D8
Friars Gdns ACT W3 87 F5
Friars Gate Cl WFD IG8 44 E3
Friars La RCH/KEW TW9 124 E4
Friars Md POP/IOD E14 113 F2
Friars Ms ELTH/MOT SE9 135 F4
Friars Place La ACT W3 87 F6
Friar's Rd EHAM E6 77 H7
Friars Stile Rd
RCHPK/HAM TW10 125 F5
Friars Wk ABYW SE2 116 E4
STHGT/OAK N14 28 B7
Friars Wy ACT W3 87 F5
Friars Wd CROY/NA * CR0 179 G7
Friarswood CROY/NA CR0 179 G7
Friary Cl NFNCH/WDSP N12 39 J4
Friary Est PECK * SE15 111 H6
Friary La WFD IG8 44 E3
Friary Pk TRDG/WHET * N20 39 J3
Friary Park Ct ACT * W3 86 E5
Friary Rd ACT W3 86 E5
NFNCH/WDSP N12 39 H3
PECK SE15 111 H6
Friary Wy NFNCH/WDSP N12 39 J3
Friday Hl CHING E4 44 C2
Friday Hl East CHING E4 44 C2
Friday Hl West CHING E4 44 C1
Friday Rd ERITH DA8 118 A4
MTCM CR4 147 K6
Friday St BLKFR EC4V 12 E6
Frideswide Pl KTTN NW5 72 C4
Friendly Pl GNWCH SE10 112 E7
Friendly St DEPT SE8 112 D7
Friendly Street Ms DEPT SE8 132 D1
Friends' Rd CROY/NA CR0 177 K2
Friend St FSBYE EC1V 6 C7
Friern Barnet La
TRDG/WHET N20 39 H2
Friern Barnet Rd
FBAR/BDGN N11 40 A4
Friern Mount Dr
TRDG/WHET N20 27 G6
Friern Pk NFNCH/WDSP N12 39 H4
Friern Rd EDUL SE22 131 H5
Friern Watch Av
NFNCH/WDSP N12 39 H3
Frigate Ms DEPT SE8 112 D5
Frimley Av WLGTN SM6 176 E4
Frimley Cl CROY/NA CR0 180 A6
WIM/MER SW19 146 C1
Frimley Ct SCUP DA14 155 J4
Frimley Crs CROY/NA CR0 180 A6
Frimley Gdns MTCM CR4 162 D2
Frimley Rd CHSGTN KT9 171 K4
GDMY/SEVK IG3 78 E2
Frimley Wy WCHPL * E1 93 F3
Frinsted Rd ERITH DA8 118 A6
Frinton Cl OXHEY WD19 33 F1
Frinton Dr WFD IG8 44 B6
Frinton Ms IL IG1 60 A5
Frinton Rd EHAM E6 95 H2
SEVS/STOTM N15 56 A5
TOOT SW17 148 A5
Friston St FUL/PGN SW6 128 A1
Friswell Pl BXLYHN DA7 137 H3
Fritham Cl NWMAL KT3 160 B5
Frith Ct MLHL NW7 38 C6
Frith La MLHL NW7 38 C5
Frith Manor Farm Cotts
NFNCH/WDSP * N12 38 C4
Frith Rd CROY/NA CR0 177 J1
WAN E11 76 A3
Frith St SOHO/SHAV W1D 11 G5
Frithville Gdns SHB W12 88 A7
Frithwood Av NTHWD HA6 32 D5
Frizlands La DAGE RM10 80 D2
Frobisher Cl BUSH WD23 22 A5
PIN HA5 47 H6
Frobisher Crs BARB * EC2Y 12 F2
STWL/WRAY TW19 120 B6
Frobisher Gdns LEY * E10 57 K5
Frobisher Rd CEND/HSY/T N8 55 G3
EHAM E6 95 K5
ERITH DA8 118 D6
Frog La DAGW RM9 99 F4
Frogley Rd EDUL SE22 131 G3
Frogmore WAND/EARL SW18 127 K4
Frogmore Av YEAD UB4 82 C3
Frogmore Cl CHEAM SM3 174 B2
Frogmore Est HBRY * N5 73 J3
Frogmore Gdns CHEAM SM3 174 C3
YEAD UB4 82 C3
Frognal HAMP NW3 71 G3
Frognal Av HRW HA1 49 F3
SCUP DA14 155 G5
Frognal Cl HAMP NW3 71 G4
Frognal Gdns HAMP NW3 71 G3
Frognal La HAMP NW3 71 F4
Frognal Man HAMP * NW3 71 G3
Frognal Pde HAMP NW3 71 G5
Frognal Pl SCUP DA14 155 G5
Frognal Ri HAMP NW3 71 G2
Frognal Wy HAMP NW3 71 G3
Froissart Rd ELTH/MOT SE9 134 D4
Frome Rd SEVS/STOTM N15 55 H2
Frome St IS N1 6 E5
Fromondes Rd CHEAM SM3 174 C4
Fromows Cnr CHSWK * W4 105 K4
Frostic Wk WCHPL E1 13 M3
Froude St VX/NE SW8 129 G1
Fruen Rd EBED/NFELT TW14 121 J6
Fryatt Rd TOTM N17 41 K6
Fryent Cl KTN/HRWW/W HA3 50 C5
Fryent Crs CDALE/KGS NW9 51 G5
Fryent Flds CDALE/KGS NW9 51 G5
Fryent Gv CDALE/KGS NW9 51 G5
Fryent Wy CDALE/KGS NW9 50 C5
Frying Pan Aly WCHPL E1 13 K3
Fry Rd EHAM E6 77 H6
WLSDN NW10 69 H7
Fryston Av CROY/NA CR0 178 C1
Fuchsia St ABYW SE2 116 C4
Fulbeck Dr CDALE/KGS NW9 37 G7
Fulbeck Wy RYLN/HDSTN HA2 48 C1
Fulbourne Rd WALTH E17 44 A7
Fulbourne St WCHPL E1 92 D4
Fulbrook Rd ARCH N19 72 C3
Fulford Gv OXHEY WD19 33 F1
Fulford Rd HOR/WEW KT19 173 F6
Fulford St BERM/RHTH SE16 111 J1
Fulham Broadway
FUL/PGN SW6 107 K6
Fulham Cl HGDN/ICK UB10 82 A3
Fulham High St FUL/PGN SW6 127 H2
Fulham Palace Rd
FUL/PGN SW6 107 G6
Fulham Park Gdns
FUL/PGN SW6 127 J1
Fulham Park Rd
FUL/PGN SW6 127 J1
Fulham Rd FUL/PGN SW6 127 H1
WBPTN SW10 14 F9
Fullbrooks Av WPK KT4 160 C7
Fuller Cl BETH * E2 92 C3
Fuller Rd BCTR RM8 79 J2
Fullers Av SURB KT6 172 B1
WFD IG8 44 D6
Fuller's Rd SWFD E18 44 D7
Fuller St HDN NW4 52 A3
Fullers Wy North SURB KT6 172 B2
Fullers Wy South CHSGTN KT9 172 A3
Fuller's Wd CROY/NA CR0 179 J4
Fullerton Rd CAR SM5 175 J7
CROY/NA CR0 165 G6
WAND/EARL SW18 128 B4
Fuller Wy HYS/HAR UB3 101 J4
Fullwood's Ms IS * N1 7 H7
Fulmar Ct BRYLDS KT5 159 G5
Fulmar Rd HCH RM12 81 J6
Fulmead St FUL/PGN SW6 108 A7
Fulmer Cl HPTN TW12 141 J4
Fulmer Rd CAN/RD E16 95 H4
Fulmer Wy WEA W13 104 C2
Fulready Rd LEY E10 58 B4
Fulstone Cl HSLWW TW4 122 E3
Fulthorp Rd BKHTH/KID SE3 133 K1
Fulton Ms BAY/PAD W2 8 E6
Fulton Rd WBLY HA9 68 C2
Fulwell Park Av WHTN TW2 142 C1
Fulwell Rd HPTN TW12 142 D3
Fulwich Rd DART DA1 139 J5
Fulwood Av ALP/SUD HA0 86 B1
Fulwood Gdns TWK TW1 124 A5
Fulwood Pl GINN WC1R 11 M3
Fulwood Wk WIM/MER SW19 127 H7
Furber St HMSMTH W6 106 E2
Furham Fld PIN HA5 34 A6
Furley Rd PECK SE15 111 H6
Furlong Cl WLGTN SM6 163 G7
Furlong Rd HOLWY N7 73 G5
Furmage St
WAND/EARL SW18 128 A6
Furneaux Av WNWD SE27 149 H4
Furner Cl DART DA1 138 C2
Furness Rd FUL/PGN SW6 128 A1
MRDN SM4 162 A5
RYLN/HDSTN HA2 48 B6
WLSDN NW10 87 J1
Furness Wy HCH RM12 81 J4
Furnival St FLST/FETLN EC4A 12 A4
Furrow La HOM E9 74 E4
Fursby Av FNCH N3 38 E5
Further Acre CDALE/KGS NW9 51 H1
Furtherfield Cl CROY/NA CR0 164 B5
Further Green Rd CAT SE6 133 H6
Furze Cl OXHEY WD19 33 G4
Furzedown Dr TOOT SW17 148 B4
Furzedown Rd TOOT SW17 148 B4
Furze Farm Cl CHDH RM6 62 A1
Furzefield Cl CHST BR7 154 B5
Furzefield Rd BKHTH/KID SE3 114 A5
Furzeground Wy STKPK UB11 82 A7
Furzeham Rd WDR/YW UB7 100 B1
Furzehill Pde BORE * WD6 24 C3
Furzehill Rd BORE WD6 24 E4
Furze Rd THHTH CR7 164 D2
Furze St BOW * E3 93 J4
Furzewood SUN TW16 140 E7
Fye Foot La BLKFR * EC4V 12 E6
Fyfe Wy BMLY BR1 167 K1
Fyfield Cl BECK BR3 167 G3
Fyfield Rd BRXN/ST SW9 130 B2
EN EN1 30 A2
RAIN RM13 81 H7
WALTH E17 58 B2
WFD IG8 45 G6
Fynes St WEST SW1P 17 G5

G

Gable Cl DART DA1 138 D4
PIN HA5 34 A6
Gable Ct SYD SE26 150 D3
The Gables NRWD * SE19 150 A7
WBLY HA9 68 B2
Gables Av BORE WD6 24 B2
Gables Cl CMBW SE5 111 F7
LEE/GVPK SE12 133 K7
Gabriel Cl FELT TW13 141 J3
Gabrielle Cl WBLY HA9 68 B2
Gabriel St FSTH SE23 132 A6
Gabriel's Whf STHWK SE1 12 A8
Gad Cl PLSTW E13 95 F2
Gaddesden Av WBLY HA9 68 B5
Gade Av WATW WD18 20 C3
Gade Bank RKW/CH/CXG WD3 20 B3
Gade Cl HYS/HAR UB3 83 F7
WATW WD18 20 C3
Gadesden Rd HOR/WEW KT19 172 E5
Gadsbury Cl CDALE/KGS NW9 51 H5
Gadwall Cl CAN/RD E16 95 F5
Gage Rd CAN/RD E16 94 C4
Gainford St IS N1 6 A3
Gainsboro Gdns GFD/PVL UB6 66 E4
Gainsborough Av DART DA1 139 F4
MNPK E12 78 A4
Gainsborough Cl BECK BR3 151 J6
ESH/CLAY * KT10 157 J7
Gainsborough Ct SHB W12 107 F1
Gainsborough Gdns EDGW HA8 50 B1
GLDGN NW11 52 D6
HAMP NW3 71 H2
HSLW TW3 123 J4
Gainsborough Rd BCTR RM8 79 H3
CHSWK W4 106 C3
NFNCH/WDSP N12 39 F4
NWMAL KT3 160 A5
RAIN RM13 81 J7
RCH/KEW TW9 125 G1
SRTFD E15 94 C2
WAN E11 58 C6
WFD IG8 45 J5
YEAD UB4 82 A1
Gainsborough Sq BXLYHN DA7 136 E2
Gainsborough Ter
BELMT * SM2 174 D6
Gainsford Rd WALTH E17 57 H3
Gainsford St STHWK SE1 13 L9
Gairloch Rd CMBW SE5 131 F1
Gaisford St KTTN NW5 72 C5
Gaitskell Rd ELTH/MOT SE9 135 H7
Galahad Rd BMLY BR1 152 E2
Galata Rd BARN SW13 106 D6
Galatea Sq PECK SE15 131 J2
Galbraith St POP/IOD E14 113 F2
Galdana Av BAR EN5 27 G2
Galeborough Av WFD IG8 44 B6
Gale Cl HPTN TW12 141 J5
MTCM CR4 162 C2
Galena Rd HMSMTH W6 106 E3
Galen Pl NOXST/BSQ WC1A 11 J3
Galesbury Rd
WAND/EARL SW18 128 B5
Gales Gdns BETH E2 92 D2
Gale St BOW E3 93 J4
DAGW RM9 79 K5
Gales Wy WFD IG8 45 J6
Galgate Cl WIM/MER SW19 127 G7
Gallants Farm Rd EBAR EN4 27 J6
Galleon Cl BERM/RHTH SE16 111 K1
ERITH DA8 118 A3
Galleons Dr BARK IG11 97 G2
The Galleries IS * N1 6 C5
Gallery Gdns NTHLT UB5 83 H1
Gallery Rd DUL SE21 130 E7
Galleywall Rd
BERM/RHTH SE16 111 J3
Galliard Crs ED N9 30 C6
Galliard Rd ED N9 30 C6
Gallia Rd HBRY N5 73 H4
Gallions Cl BARK IG11 97 G2
Gallions Rd CAN/RD E16 96 B6
CHARL SE7 114 A3
Gallions View Rd THMD SE28 115 K1
Gallon Cl CHARL SE7 114 B3
The Gallop BELMT SM2 175 H7
SAND/SEL CR2 178 D6
Gallosson Rd
WOOL/PLUM SE18 115 K3
Galloway Dr DART DA1 138 B6
Galloway Pth CROY/NA CR0 177 K3
Galloway Rd SHB W12 87 J7
Gallus Cl WCHMH N21 29 F5
Gallus Sq BKHTH/KID SE3 134 A2
Galpin's Rd THHTH CR7 163 K3
Galsworthy Av CHDH RM6 61 H6
Galsworthy Cl THMD SE28 97 H7
Galsworthy Crs
BKHTH/KID * SE3 114 B7
Galsworthy Rd CRICK NW2 70 C3
KUTN/CMB KT2 144 D7
Galton St NKENS W10 88 C3
Galva Cl EBAR EN4 28 A3
Galveston Rd PUT/ROE SW15 127 J4
Galway Cl BERM/RHTH * SE16 111 J4
Galway St FSBYE EC1V 6 F8
Gambetta St VX/NE SW8 129 G1
Gambia St STHWK SE1 12 D9
Gambole Rd TOOT SW17 147 J3
Games Rd EBAR EN4 27 J2
Gamlen Rd PUT/ROE SW15 127 G3
Gamuel Cl WALTH E17 57 J5
Gander Green Crs HPTN TW12 142 A7
Gander Green La CHEAM SM3 174 C1
SUT SM1 174 E5
Gandhi Cl WALTH E17 57 J5
Gandhi Ct WATN WD24 21 H1
Ganton St SOHO/CST * W1F 10 F5
Ganton Wk OXHEY * WD19 33 J3
Gantshill Crs GNTH/NBYPK IG2 60 A4
Gap Rd WIM/MER SW19 146 E4
Garage Rd ACT W3 86 C5
Garbrand Wk EW KT17 173 H7
Garbutt Pl MHST * W1U 10 B2
Garden Av BXLYHN DA7 137 G2
MTCM CR4 148 B6
Garden Cl ASHF TW15 140 A5
BAR EN5 26 A3
CHING E4 43 J4
HPTN TW12 141 K4
LEE/GVPK SE12 153 F2
NTHLT UB5 65 J7
PUT/ROE SW15 126 E6
RSLP HA4 64 C1
WAT WD17 20 D1
WLGTN SM6 176 E4
Garden Ct TPL/STR * WC2R 12 A6
Gardeners Rd CROY/NA CR0 164 C7
Garden Flats HMSMTH * W6 107 G5
Gardenia Rd EN EN1 30 A5
Gardenia Wy WFD IG8 44 E5
Garden La BMLY BR1 153 F5
BRXS/STRHM SW2 130 A7
Garden Lodge Ct EFNCH * N2 53 H2
Garden Pl HACK E8 7 M3
Garden Rd BMLY BR1 153 F6
PGE/AN SE20 150 E7
RCH/KEW TW9 125 H2
STJWD NW8 2 F7
WOT/HER KT12 156 A5
Garden Rw STHWK SE1 18 C4
The Gardens BECK BR3 167 F1
CEND/HSY/T * N8 54 E3
EBED/NFELT TW14 121 G5
EDUL SE22 131 H3
ESH/CLAY KT10 170 A3
HRW HA1 48 C5
PIN * HA5 47 K5
STNW/STAM * N16 56 B6
WAT WD17 20 D1
Garden St WCHPL E1 93 F4
Garden Studios BAY/PAD * W2 8 E3
Garden Ter PIM SW1V 17 G7
Garden Vls ESH/CLAY * KT10 171 F6
Garden Wk BECK BR3 151 H7
SDTCH EC2A 7 J9
Garden Wy WLSDN NW10 68 E5
Gardiner Av CRICK * NW2 70 A4
Gardiner Cl BCTR RM8 79 K3
PEND EN3 31 F5
Gardiner House
WOOL/PLUM SE18 114 D6
Gardner Cl WAN E11 59 F5
Gardner Pl EBED/NFELT TW14 122 A5
Gardner Rd PLSTW E13 95 F3
Gardners Cl FBAR/BDGN N11 40 A1
Gardners La BLKFR EC4V 12 E6
Gardnor Rd HAMP NW3 71 H3
Gard St FSBYE EC1V 6 D7
Garendon Gdns MRDN SM4 162 A6
Garendon Rd MRDN SM4 162 A6
Gareth Cl WPK KT4 174 B1
Gareth Gv BMLY BR1 152 E3
Garfield Rd BTSEA SW11 129 F2
PEND EN3 30 E3
PLSTW E13 94 D3
TWK TW1 124 B7
WIM/MER SW19 147 G5
Garford St POP/IOD E14 93 J6
Garibaldi St WOOL/PLUM SE18 115 K3
Garland Rd STAN HA7 36 A7
WOOL/PLUM SE18 115 J6
Garlick Hl BLKFR EC4V 12 F6
Garlies Rd FSTH SE23 151 G2
Garlinge Rd CRICK NW2 70 D5
Garman Cl UED N18 41 K4
Garman Rd TOTM N17 42 E6
Garnault Ms CLKNW EC1R 6 B8
Garnault Pl CLKNW EC1R 6 B8
Garner Cl BCTR RM8 61 K7
Garner Rd WALTH E17 44 A7
Garner St BETH E2 92 C1
Garnet Rd THHTH CR7 164 D3
WLSDN NW10 69 G5
Garnet St WAP E1W 92 E6
Garnett Cl ELTH/MOT SE9 134 E2
Garnett Rd HAMP NW3 71 K4
Garnham St STNW/STAM N16 74 B1
Garnies Cl PECK SE15 111 G6
Garrad's Rd STRHM/NOR SW16 148 D2
Garrard Cl BXLYHN DA7 137 H2
CHST BR7 154 B4
Garrard Wk WLSDN * NW10 69 G5
Garratt Cl CROY/NA CR0 176 E3
Garratt La WAND/EARL SW18 128 A6
Garratt Rd EDGW HA8 36 C6
Garratts Rd BUSH WD23 22 C6
Garratt Ter TOOT SW17 147 J3
Garrett Cl ACT W3 87 F4
Garrett St STLK EC1Y 12 E1
Garrick Av GLDGN NW11 52 C5
Garrick Cl BTSEA SW11 128 B3
EA W5 86 A3
RCH/KEW TW9 124 D4
Garrick Crs CROY/NA CR0 178 A1
Garrick Dr HDN NW4 52 A1
WOOL/PLUM SE18 115 J2
Garrick Gdns E/WMO/HCT KT8 157 F2
Garrick Pk HDN NW4 52 B1
Garrick Rd CDALE/KGS NW9 51 H5
GFD/PVL UB6 84 B3
RCH/KEW TW9 125 H1
Garrick St COVGDN WC2E 11 J6
Garrick Wy HDN NW4 52 B3
Garrick Yd CHCR WC2N 11 J6
Garrison Cl HSLWW TW4 122 E4
WOOL/PLUM SE18 115 F6
Garrison La CHSGTN KT9 172 A6
Garsdale Cl FBAR/BDGN N11 40 A5
Garsdale Ter WKENS * W14 107 J4
Garside Cl HPTN TW12 142 B6
WOOL/PLUM SE18 115 J2
Garsington Ms BROCKY SE4 132 C2
The Garth HPTN TW12 142 B5
KTN/HRWW/W HA3 50 B5
NFNCH/WDSP * N12 39 F4
Garth Cl KUTN/CMB KT2 144 B4
MRDN SM4 161 G6
RSLP HA4 47 H7
Garthland Dr BAR EN5 25 K4
Garth Ms EA * W5 86 A3
Garthorne Rd FSTH SE23 132 A6
Garth Rd CHSWK W4 106 A4
CRICK NW2 70 D1
KUTN/CMB KT2 144 B4
MRDN SM4 161 G7
Garthside KUTN/CMB KT2 144 A4
Garthway NFNCH/WDSP N12 39 J5
Gartlet Rd WAT WD17 21 G2
Gartmoor Gdns
WIM/MER SW19 127 J7
Gartmore Rd GDMY/SEVK IG3 61 F7

Garton Pl WAND/EARL SW18 128 B5
Gartons Cl PEND EN3 30 E4
Gartons Wy BTSEA SW11 128 B2
Garvary Rd CAN/RD E16 95 F5
Garway Rd BAY/PAD W2 8 C5
Gascoigne Gdns WFD IG8 44 C6
Gascoigne Pl BETH E2 7 L7
Gascoigne Rd BARK IG11 78 C7
Gascony Av KIL/WHAMP NW6 2 A2
Gascoyne Dr DART DA1 138 C2
Gascoyne Rd HOM E9 75 F6
Gaselee St POP/IOD E14 94 A6
Gasholder Pl LBTH SE11 17 M8
Gaskarth Rd BAL SW12 129 G5
EDGW HA8 36 E7
Gaskell Rd HGT N6 53 K5
Gaskell St CLAP SW4 129 K1
Gaskin St IS N1 6 C3
Gaspar Cl ECT * SW5 14 D5
Gaspar Ms ECT SW5 14 D5
Gassiot Rd TOOT SW17 147 K3
Gassiot Wy SUT SM1 175 H2
Gastein Rd HMSMTH W6 107 G5
Gaston Bell Cl RCH/KEW TW9 125 G2
Gaston Rd MTCM CR4 163 F2
Gataker St BERM/RHTH SE16 111 J2
Gatcombe Ms EA W5 86 B6
Gatcombe Rd ARCH N19 72 D2
Gatcombe Wy EBAR EN4 27 K2
Gate Cottages EDGW * HA8 36 C1
Gate End NTHWD HA6 32 E6
Gateforth St STJWD NW8 9 J1
Gatehill Rd NTHWD HA6 32 E6
Gatehouse Cl KUTN/CMB KT2 144 E6
Gatehouse Sq STHWK SE1 12 F8
Gateley Rd BRXN/ST SW9 130 A2
Gate Ms SKENS SW7 15 K2
Gates Green Rd WWKM BR4 180 E3
Gateshead Rd BORE WD6 24 B1
Gateside Rd TOOT SW17 147 K2
Gatestone Rd NRWD SE19 150 A5
Gate St HHOL WC1V 11 L4
Gateway WALW SE17 18 F9
Gateway Ar IS * N1 6 C5
Gateway Cl NTHWD HA6 32 A5
Gateway Ms HACK * E8 74 B4
The Gateways RCH/KEW * TW9 124 E3
Gatfield Gv FELT TW13 142 A1
Gathorne Rd WDGN N22 55 G1
Gathorne St BETH E2 93 F1
Gatley Av HOR/WEW KT19 172 D4
Gatliff Rd BGVA SW1W 16 B8
Gatling Rd ABYW SE2 116 B4
Gatonby St PECK SE15 111 G7
Gatton Cl BELMT * SM2 175 F7
Gatton Rd TOOT SW17 147 J3
Gatward Cl WCHMH N21 29 H5
Gatward Gn ED N9 42 A1
Gatwick Rd WAND/EARL SW18 127 J6
Gauden Cl CLAP SW4 129 J2
Gauden Rd CLAP SW4 129 J2
Gaumont Ap WATW WD18 21 F2
Gaumont Ter SHB * W12 107 F1
Gauntlet Cl NTHLT UB5 65 J6
Gauntlett Ct ALP/SUD HA0 67 G4
Gauntlett Rd SUT SM1 175 H4
Gaunt St STHWK SE1 18 D3
Gautrey Rd PECK SE15 131 K1
Gavel St WALW * SE17 19 H5
Gaverick St POP/IOD E14 112 D3
Gavestone Crs LEE/GVPK SE12 134 A7
Gavestone Rd LEE/GVPK SE12 134 A6
Gavina Cl MRDN SM4 162 D4
Gawber St BETH E2 92 E2
Gawsworth Cl SRTFD E15 76 D4
Gawthorne Av MLHL NW7 38 C4
Gay Cl CRICK NW2 69 K4
Gaydon La CDALE/KGS NW9 37 G7
Gayfere Rd CLAY IG5 59 K2
EW KT17 173 J4
Gayfere St WEST SW1P 17 J4
Gayford Rd SHB W12 106 C1
Gay Gdns DAGE RM10 80 E3
Gayhurst Rd HACK E8 74 C6
Gaylor Rd NTHLT UB5 65 K4
Gaynesford Rd CAR SM5 175 K6
FSTH SE23 151 F1
Gaynes Hill Rd WFD IG8 45 J6
Gay Rd SRTFD E15 94 B1
Gaysham Av GNTH/NBYPK IG2 60 A4
Gayton Crs HAMP NW3 71 H3
Gayton Rd HAMP NW3 71 H3
HRW HA1 49 G5
Gayville Rd BTSEA SW11 128 E5
Gaywood Cl BRXS/STRHM SW2 130 A7
Gaywood Rd WALTH E17 57 J2
Gaywood St STHWK SE1 18 D4
Gaza St WALW SE17 18 C8
Gearlesville Gdns BARK/HLT IG6 60 B3
Geary Rd WLSDN NW10 69 J4
Geary St HOLWY N7 73 F4
Geddes Pl BXLYHN DA7 137 H3
Geddes Rd BUSH * WD23 22 C3
Gedeney Rd TOTM N17 41 J7
Gedling Pl STHWK SE1 19 L3
Geere Rd SRTFD E15 76 D7
Gees Ct MHST W1U 10 B5
Gee St FSBYE EC1V 6 E9
Geffrye Est IS N1 7 K6
Geffrye St BETH E2 7 L5
Geldart Rd PECK SE15 111 J6
Geldeston Rd CLPT E5 74 C1
Gellatly Rd PECK SE15 131 K1
General Wolfe Rd GNWCH SE10 113 G7
Genesis Cl STWL/WRAY TW19 120 C7
Genesta Rd WOOL/PLUM SE18 115 G5
Geneva Dr BRXN/ST SW9 130 B3
Geneva Gdns CHDH RM6 62 A4
Geneva Rd KUT KT1 159 F3
THHTH CR7 164 D4
Genever Cl CHING E4 43 J4
Genista Rd UED N18 42 D4
Genoa Av PUT/ROE SW15 127 F4
Genoa Rd PGE/AN SE20 150 E7
Genotin Rd EN EN1 29 K2
Gentleman's Rw ENC/FH EN2 29 J2
Geoffrey Cl CMBW SE5 130 D1
Geoffrey Gdns EHAM E6 95 J1
Geoffrey Rd BROCKY SE4 132 C2
George Beard Rd DEPT SE8 112 C3
George Crs MUSWH N10 40 A6
George Downing Est
STNW/STAM N16 74 B1
George Gange Wy
KTN/HRWW/W HA3 48 E2
George Groves Rd PGE/AN SE20 150 C7
George La HAYES BR2 168 A7
LEW SE13 133 F5
SWFD E18 58 E1
George Mathers Rd LBTH * SE11 18 C5
George Ms CAMTN NW1 4 E8
George Rd CHING E4 43 J5
KUTN/CMB KT2 144 E6
NWMAL KT3 160 C3
George Rw BERM/RHTH SE16 111 H1
Georges Md BORE WD6 24 A5
Georges Rd HOLWY N7 73 F5
George St BARK IG11 78 C6
CAN/RD E16 94 D5
CROY/NA CR0 177 K1
HNWL W7 84 E7
HSLW TW3 122 E1
MBLAR W1H 9 M4
NWDGN UB2 102 D3
RCHPK/HAM TW10 124 E4
ROM RM1 63 H5
WATW WD18 21 G3
Georgetown Cl NRWD SE19 149 K4
Georgette Pl GNWCH SE10 113 F6
George V Av PIN HA5 47 K1
Georgeville Gdns BARK/HLT IG6 60 B3
George V Wy GFD/PVL UB6 67 H6
George Wyver Cl
WAND/EARL SW18 127 H6
George Yd BANK EC3V 13 H5
MYFR/PKLN W1K 10 B6
Georgiana St CAMTN NW1 4 E3
Georgian Cl HAYES BR2 168 A7
STAN HA7 35 G6
Georgian Ct WBLY HA9 68 C5
Georgian Wy HRW HA1 66 D1
Georgia Rd NWMAL KT3 159 K3
THHTH CR7 149 H7
Georgina Gdns BETH * E2 7 M7
Geraint Rd BMLY BR1 152 E2
Geraldine Rd CHSWK W4 105 H5
WAND/EARL SW18 128 B4
Geraldine St LBTH SE11 18 C4
Gerald Rd BCTR RM8 80 B1
BGVA SW1W 16 B5
CAN/RD E16 94 D3
Gerard Av HSLWW TW4 123 F6
Gerard Gdns RAIN RM13 99 G1
Gerard Rd BARN SW13 106 C7
HRW HA1 49 G5
Gerards Cl BERM/RHTH SE16 111 K5
Gerda Rd ELTH/MOT SE9 154 B1
Germander Wy SRTFD E15 94 C2
Gernon Rd BOW E3 93 G1
Geron Wy CRICK NW2 70 A1
Gerrard Gdns PIN HA5 46 E4
Gerrard Pl SOHO/SHAV * W1D 11 H6
Gerrard Rd IS N1 6 C5
Gerrards Cl STHGT/OAK N14 28 C4
Gerrard St SOHO/SHAV W1D 11 G6
Gerridge St STHWK SE1 18 B2
Gertrude Rd BELV DA17 117 H3
Gertrude St WBPTN SW10 108 B5
Gervase Cl WBLY HA9 68 E2
Gervase Rd EDGW HA8 36 E7
Gervase St PECK SE15 111 J6
Ghent St CAT SE6 151 J1
Ghent Wy HACK E8 74 B5
Giant Arches Rd HNHL SE24 130 D6
Giant Tree Hl BUSH WD23 34 D1
Gibbfield Cl CHDH RM6 62 A2
Gibbins Rd SRTFD E15 76 A6
Gibbon Rd ACT W3 87 G6
KUTN/CMB KT2 144 A7
PECK SE15 131 K1
Gibbons Rd WLSDN NW10 69 F5
Gibbon Wk PUT/ROE * SW15 126 D3
Gibbs Av NRWD SE19 149 K5
Gibbs Cl NRWD * SE19 149 K4
Gibbs Couch OXHEY WD19 33 H2
Gibbs Gn EDGW HA8 36 E3
WKENS * W14 107 J4
Gibbs Rd UED N18 42 E3
Gibbs Sq NRWD * SE19 149 K4
Gibraltar Wk BETH E2 7 M8
Gibson Cl CHSGTN * KT9 171 J4
ISLW TW7 123 J2
WCHPL E1 92 E3
Gibson Gdns STNW/STAM * N16 74 B1
Gibson Rd BCTR RM8 61 J7
LBTH SE11 17 M6
SUT SM1 175 F4
Gibson's Hl STRHM/NOR SW16 149 G6
Gibson Sq IS N1 6 B3
Gibson St GNWCH SE10 113 H4
Gidea Av GPK RM2 63 J2
Gidea Cl GPK RM2 63 J2
Gideon Cl BELV DA17 117 J3
Gideon Ms EA * W5 104 E1
Gideon Rd BTSEA SW11 129 F2
Giesbach Rd ARCH N19 72 D1
Giffard Rd UED N18 42 A4
Giffin St DEPT SE8 112 D6
Gifford Gdns HNWL W7 84 D4
Gifford St IS N1 5 K2
Gift La SRTFD E15 76 C7
Giggs Hill Gdns THDIT KT7 158 B7
Giggs Hill Rd THDIT KT7 158 B6
Gilbert Cl WIM/MER * SW19 147 F7
WOOL/PLUM SE18 114 E7
Gilbert Gv EDGW HA8 36 E7
Gilbert Pl NOXST/BSQ WC1A 11 J3
Gilbert Rd BELV DA17 117 H2
BMLY BR1 152 E6
LBTH SE11 18 B5
PIN HA5 47 H3
ROM RM1 63 H3
WIM/MER SW19 147 G6
Gilbert St HSLW TW3 123 H2
MYFR/PKLN W1K 10 B5
SRTFD E15 76 C3
Gilbey Rd TOOT SW17 147 J3
Gilbeys Yd CAMTN NW1 4 B2
Gilbourne Rd
WOOL/PLUM SE18 116 A5
Gilda Av PEND EN3 31 G4
Gilda Crs STNW/STAM N16 56 C7
Gildea Cl PIN HA5 34 A6
Gildea St REGST W1B 10 D3
Gildersome St WOOL/PLUM SE18 115 F5
Gilders Rd CHSGTN KT9 172 B6
Giles Coppice NRWD SE19 150 B3
Gilkes Crs DUL SE21 131 F5
Gilkes Pl DUL SE21 131 F5
Gillam Wy RAIN RM13 81 J5
Gillan Gn BUSH WD23 34 C1
Gillards Ms WALTH E17 57 J3
Gillards Wy WALTH E17 57 J3
Gill Av CAN/RD E16 94 E5
Gill Cl WATW WD18 20 A5
Gillender St BOW E3 94 A3
Gillespie Rd HBRY N5 73 G2
Gillett Av EHAM E6 95 J1
Gillett Pl HACK E8 74 B4
Gillett Rd THHTH CR7 164 E3
Gillett St STNW/STAM N16 74 A4
Gillham Ter TOTM N17 42 C5
Gillian Park Rd CHEAM SM3 161 J7
Gillian St LEW SE13 132 E4
Gillian Ter BRYLDS * KT5 159 G5
Gillingham Ms PIM SW1V 16 D5
Gillingham Rd CRICK NW2 70 C2
Gillingham Rw PIM SW1V 16 E5
Gillingham St PIM SW1V 16 D6
Gillison Wk BERM/RHTH * SE16 111 H2
Gillman Dr SRTFD E15 76 C7
Gill St POP/IOD E14 93 H5
Gillum Cl EBAR EN4 27 K7
Gilmore Rd LEW SE13 133 G3
Gilpin Av MORT/ESHN SW14 126 A3
Gilpin Cl BAY/PAD W2 8 F3
MTCM CR4 162 D1
Gilpin Crs HSLW TW3 123 G6
UED N18 42 B4
Gilpin Rd CLPT E5 75 G3
Gilpin Wy HYS/HAR UB3 101 G6
Gilroy Cl RAIN RM13 81 H5
Gilsland Rd THHTH CR7 164 E3
Gilstead Rd FUL/PGN SW6 128 A1
Gilston Rd WBPTN SW10 14 F8
Gilton Rd CAT SE6 152 C2
Giltspur St STBT EC1A 12 D4
Gilwell Cl CHING E4 31 K3
Gippeswyck Cl PIN HA5 33 H7
Gipsy Hl NRWD SE19 150 A4
Gipsy La BARN SW13 126 D2
Gipsy Rd WELL DA16 136 E1
WNWD SE27 149 K3
Gipsy Road Gdns WNWD SE27 149 J3
Giralda Cl CAN/RD E16 95 H4
Giraud St POP/IOD E14 93 K5
Girdlers Rd WKENS W14 107 G3
Girdwood Rd
WAND/EARL SW18 127 H6
Girling Wy EBED/NFELT TW14 121 K2
Gironde Rd FUL/PGN SW6 107 J6
Girtin Rd BUSH WD23 22 B4
Girton Av CDALE/KGS NW9 50 C2
Girton Cl NTHLT UB5 66 C5
Girton Gdns CROY/NA CR0 179 J2
Girton Rd NTHLT UB5 66 C5
SYD SE26 151 F4
Girton Wy RKW/CH/CXG WD3 20 A4
Gisbourne Cl WLGTN SM6 176 D2
Gisburn Rd CEND/HSY/T N8 55 F3
Gissing Wk IS N1 6 B2
Gittens Cl BMLY BR1 152 D3
Glacier Wy ALP/SUD HA0 85 K1
Gladbeck Wy WCHMH N21 29 H3
Gladding Rd MNPK E12 77 H3
The Glade BELMT SM2 174 C7
BMLY BR1 168 C1
CHARL SE7 114 B6
CLAY IG5 45 K7
CROY/NA CR0 166 A4
ENC/FH EN2 29 G2
EW KT17 173 J5
HACK * E8 74 B5
NFNCH/WDSP * N12 39 H3
SHB * W12 106 E1
WCHMH N21 29 F5
WFD IG8 45 F2
WWKM BR4 179 K2
Glade Cl SURB * KT6 171 K1
Glade Gdns CROY/NA CR0 166 B6
Glade La NWDGN UB2 103 G1
Gladeside CROY/NA CR0 166 A6
WCHMH N21 29 F6
Gladesmore Rd
SEVS/STOTM N15 56 B5
Gladiator St FSTH SE23 132 B5
Glading Ter STNW/STAM N16 74 B2
Gladioli Cl HPTN TW12 142 A5
Gladsdale Dr PIN HA5 46 E3
Gladsmuir Rd ARCH N19 54 C7
BAR EN5 26 C1
Gladstone Av
EBED/NFELT TW14 121 K5
MNPK E12 77 J6
WDGN N22 55 H1
WHTN TW2 123 J6
Gladstone Gdns HSLW TW3 103 H7
Gladstone Ms KIL/WHAMP NW6 70 D5
PGE/AN SE20 150 E6
WDGN N22 55 G1
Gladstone Pde CRICK * NW2 70 A2
Gladstone Park Gdns
CRICK NW2 69 K2
Gladstone Pl BAR * EN5 26 B3
E/WMO/HCT * KT8 157 K4
Gladstone Rd CHSWK * W4 106 A2
CROY/NA CR0 164 E6
DART DA1 139 J5
KUT KT1 159 H2
NWDGN UB2 102 D1
SURB KT6 171 K1
WAT WD17 21 G2
WIM/MER SW19 146 E6
Gladstone St STHWK SE1 18 C3
Gladstone Ter VX/NE * SW8 109 G7
WNWD * SE27 149 J3
Gladstone Wy
KTN/HRWW/W HA3 48 E2
Gladwell Rd BMLY BR1 152 E5
CEND/HSY/T N8 55 F5
Gladwyn Rd PUT/ROE SW15 127 G2
Gladys Rd KIL/WHAMP NW6 2 B1
Glaisher St DEPT SE8 112 E5
Glamis Crs HYS/HAR UB3 101 F2
Glamis Pl WAP E1W 92 E6
Glamis Rd WAP E1W 92 E6
Glamis Wy NTHLT UB5 66 C5
Glamorgan Cl MTCM CR4 163 K2
Glamorgan Rd KUT KT1 143 J6
Glanfield Rd BECK BR3 166 C3
Glanleam Rd STAN HA7 35 K3
Glanville Rd BRXS/STRHM SW2 129 K4
HAYES BR2 168 A2
Glasbrook Av WHTN TW2 122 E7
Glasbrook Rd ELTH/MOT SE9 134 C6
Glaserton Rd STNW/STAM N16 56 A6
Glasford St TOOT SW17 147 K5
Glasgow Rd PLSTW E13 95 F1
UED N18 42 D4
Glasgow Ter PIM SW1V 16 E8
Glasse Cl WEA W13 85 G6
Glasshill St STHWK SE1 18 D1
Glasshouse Flds WAP E1W 93 F6
Glasshouse St REGST W1B 10 F7
Glasshouse Wk LBTH SE11 17 K7
Glasshouse Yd STBT EC1A 12 E1
Glasslyn Rd CEND/HSY/T N8 54 D4
Glassmill La HAYES BR2 167 J1
Glass St BETH * E2 92 D3
Glass Yd WOOL/PLUM SE18 115 F2
Glastonbury Av WFD IG8 45 H6
Glastonbury Pl WCHPL E1 92 E5
Glastonbury Rd ED N9 30 C7
MRDN SM4 161 K6
Glastonbury St
KIL/WHAMP NW6 70 D4
Glaston Ct EA * W5 85 K7
Glaucus St BOW E3 93 K4
Glazbury Rd WKENS W14 107 H3
Glazebrook Cl DUL SE21 149 K1
Glazebrook Rd TEDD TW11 143 F6
The Glebe BKHTH/KID SE3 133 H2
CHST BR7 154 C7
STRHM/NOR * SW16 148 D3
WDR/YW UB7 100 B3
WPK KT4 160 C7
Glebe Av ENC/FH EN2 29 H2
HGDN/ICK UB10 64 A3
KTN/HRWW/W HA3 50 A2
MTCM CR4 162 D1
RSLP HA4 65 F5
WFD IG8 44 E5
Glebe Cl CHSWK * W4 106 B4
HGDN/ICK UB10 64 A3
Glebe Ct BKHTH/KID * SE3 133 H2
EA * W5 85 K7
STAN HA7 35 J4
Glebe Crs HDN NW4 52 A3
KTN/HRWW/W HA3 50 A2
Glebe Gdns NWMAL KT3 160 B6
Glebe House Dr HAYES BR2 168 A7
Glebelands DART DA1 138 C3
E/WMO/HCT KT8 157 G4
ESH/CLAY KT10 171 F7
Glebelands Av GNTH/NBYPK IG2 60 D6
SWFD E18 58 E1
Glebelands Cl CMBW * SE5 131 F2
Glebelands Rd
EBED/NFELT TW14 121 K6
Glebe La BAR EN5 25 J5
KTN/HRWW/W HA3 50 A3
Glebe Pth MTCM CR4 162 E2
Glebe Pl CHEL SW3 15 J9
Glebe Rd BARN SW13 126 D1
BELMT SM2 174 C7
BMLY BR1 152 E7
CAR SM5 175 K5
CEND/HSY/T N8 55 F3
DAGE RM10 80 D6
FNCH N3 39 G7
HACK E8 7 L1
RAIN RM13 99 K2
STAN HA7 35 J4
WLSDN NW10 69 J5
Glebe Side TWK TW1 124 A5
Glebe Sq MTCM * CR4 162 E2
Glebe St CHSWK W4 106 A4
Glebe Ter BOW E3 93 K2
Glebe Wy ERITH DA8 118 B5
FELT TW13 142 A2
WWKM BR4 180 B1
Glebeway WFD IG8 45 G4
Gledhow Gdns ECT SW5 14 E6
Gledstanes Rd WKENS W14 107 H4
Gledwood Av YEAD UB4 82 E4
Gledwood Crs YEAD UB4 82 D4
Gledwood Dr YEAD UB4 82 D4
Gledwood Gdns YEAD UB4 82 E4
Gleed Av BUSH WD23 34 D1
Glegg Pl PUT/ROE * SW15 127 G3
The Glen BELMT * SM2 175 G5
CROY/NA CR0 179 F2
ENC/FH EN2 29 H3
HAYES BR2 167 H1
NTHWD HA6 32 B6
NWDGN UB2 102 E4
ORP BR6 181 K2
PIN HA5 47 F4
PIN HA5 47 J6
WBLY HA9 67 K3
Glenaffric Av POP/IOD E14 113 F3
Glen Albyn Rd WIM/MER SW19 146 B1
Glenalla Rd RSLP HA4 46 D6
Glenalmond Rd
KTN/HRWW/W HA3 50 A3
Glenalvon Wy
WOOL/PLUM SE18 114 D3
Glena Mt SUT SM1 175 G3
Glenarm Rd CLPT E5 74 E3
Glenavon Cl ESH/CLAY KT10 171 G5
Glenavon Rd SRTFD E15 76 C6
Glenbarr Cl ELTH/MOT SE9 135 G2
Glenbow Rd BMLY BR1 152 C5
Glenbrook North ENC/FH EN2 29 F3
Glenbrook Rd KIL/WHAMP NW6 70 E4
Glenbrook South ENC/FH EN2 29 F3
Glenbuck Rd SURB KT6 158 E5
Glenburnie Rd TOOT SW17 147 K2
Glencairn Dr EA W5 85 H3
Glencairne Cl CAN/RD E16 95 H4
Glencairn Rd
STRHM/NOR SW16 148 E6
Glencoe Av GNTH/NBYPK IG2 60 E6
Glencoe Rd BUSH WD23 22 A5
DAGE RM10 80 C3
YEAD UB4 83 H4
Glencorse Gn OXHEY * WD19 33 H3
Glen Crs WFD IG8 45 F5
Glendale Av CHDH RM6 61 J6
EDGW HA8 36 B3
WDGN N22 41 G6
Glendale Cl ELTH/MOT SE9 135 F2
Glendale Gdns WBLY HA9 49 K7
Glen Dale Ms BECK BR3 151 K7
Glendale Rd ERITH DA8 117 K3
Glendale Wy THMD SE28 97 J7
Glendall St BRXN/ST SW9 130 A3
Glendarvon St PUT/ROE SW15 127 G2
Glendevon Cl EDGW HA8 36 D2
Glendish Rd TOTM N17 42 C7
Glendor Gdns MLHL NW7 37 F3
Glendower Gdns
MORT/ESHN SW14 126 A2
Glendower Rd
MORT/ESHN SW14 126 A2
Glendown Rd ABYW SE2 116 B4
Glendun Rd ACT W3 87 G6
Gleneagle Ms
STRHM/NOR SW16 148 D4
Gleneagle Rd
STRHM/NOR SW16 148 D4
Gleneagles STAN HA7 35 H5
Gleneagles Cl
BERM/RHTH * SE16 111 J4
ORP BR6 169 J7
OXHEY * WD19 33 H4
Gleneldon Ms
STRHM/NOR SW16 148 E3
Gleneldon Rd
STRHM/NOR SW16 148 E3
Glenelg Rd BRXS/STRHM SW2 129 K4
Glenesk Rd ELTH/MOT SE9 135 F3
Glenfarg Rd CAT SE6 133 G7
Glenfield Crs RSLP HA4 46 B6
Glenfield Rd BAL SW12 129 H7
WEA W13 104 C1
Glenfinlas Wy CMBW SE5 110 C6
Glenforth St GNWCH SE10 113 J3
Glengall Br POP/IOD E14 112 E2
Glengall Gv POP/IOD E14 112 E2
Glengall Rd BXLYHN DA7 137 F2
EDGW HA8 36 D2
KIL/WHAMP NW6 70 D7
PECK SE15 19 M9
WFD IG8 44 E5
Glengall Ter PECK SE15 19 M9
Glen Gdns CROY/NA CR0 177 G2
Glengarnock Av POP/IOD E14 113 F3
Glengarry Rd EDUL SE22 131 F3
Glenham Dr GNTH/NBYPK IG2 60 B4
Glenhaven Av BORE WD6 24 C2
Glenhead Cl ELTH/MOT SE9 135 G2
Glenhill Cl FNCH N3 52 E1
Glenhouse Rd ELTH/MOT SE9 135 F4
Glenhurst Av BXLY DA5 137 G7
KTTN NW5 72 A3
RSLP HA4 46 A6
Glenhurst Ri NRWD SE19 149 J6
Glenhurst Rd BTFD TW8 104 D5
NFNCH/WDSP N12 39 H3
Glenilla Rd HAMP NW3 71 J5
Glenister Park Rd
STRHM/NOR SW16 148 D6
Glenister Rd GNWCH SE10 113 J4
Glenlea Rd ELTH/MOT SE9 135 F4
Glenloch Rd HAMP NW3 71 J5
PEND EN3 30 E1
Glenluge Rd BKHTH/KID SE3 113 K5
Glenlyon Rd ELTH/MOT SE9 135 F4
Glenmere Av MLHL NW7 37 J6
Glenmore Lawns WEA * W13 85 G5
Glenmore Pde ALP/SUD * HA0 68 A7
Glenmore Rd HAMP NW3 71 J5
WELL DA16 116 A7
Glenmore Wy BARK IG11 97 G2
Glennie Rd WNWD SE27 149 G2
Glenny Rd BARK IG11 78 C5
Glenorchy Cl YEAD UB4 83 J4
Glenparke Rd FSTGT E7 77 F5
Glen Ri WFD IG8 45 F5
Glen Rd CHSGTN KT9 172 A2
PLSTW E13 95 G3
WALTH E17 57 H4
WLGTN SM6 176 B7
Glenrosa St FUL/PGN SW6 128 B1
Glenroy St SHB W12 88 A5
Glensdale Rd BROCKY SE4 132 C2
Glenshiel Rd ELTH/MOT SE9 135 F4
Glentanner Wy TOOT SW17 147 H2
Glen Ter POP/IOD E14 113 F1
Glentham Cottages
BARN * SW13 106 D5
Glentham Gdns BARN SW13 106 E4
Glentham Rd BARN SW13 106 D5
Glenthorne Av CROY/NA CR0 165 K7
Glenthorne Cl CHEAM SM3 161 K7
Glenthorne Gdns BARK/HLT IG6 60 A2
CHEAM SM3 161 K7
Glenthorne Rd FBAR/BDGN N11 39 K4
HMSMTH W6 106 E3
KUT KT1 159 G3
WALTH E17 57 G4
Glenthorpe Rd MRDN SM4 161 G4
Glenton Rd LEW SE13 133 H3
Glentworth St CAMTN NW1 9 M1
Glenure Rd ELTH/MOT SE9 135 F4
Glenview ABYW SE2 116 E5
Glen View Rd BMLY BR1 168 C1
Glenville Gv DEPT SE8 112 C6
Glenville Rd KUTN/CMB KT2 144 C7
Glenwood Av CDALE/KGS NW9 51 G7
RAIN RM13 99 J3
Glenwood Cl HRW HA1 49 F4
Glenwood Dr GPK RM2 63 J4
Glenwood Gdns
GNTH/NBYPK IG2 60 A4
Glenwood Gv CDALE/KGS NW9 50 E7
Glenwood Rd CAT SE6 132 C7
EW KT17 173 J5
HSLW TW3 123 J2
MLHL NW7 37 G2
SEVS/STOTM N15 55 H4
Glenwood Rw NRWD * SE19 150 B7
Glenwood Wy CROY/NA CR0 166 A5
Glenworth Av POP/IOD E14 113 G3
Gliddon Rd WKENS W14 107 H3
Glimpsing Gn ERITHM DA18 117 F2
Globe Pond Rd
BERM/RHTH SE16 93 G7
Globe Rd BETH E2 92 E2
EMPK RM11 63 J5
SRTFD E15 76 D4
WFD IG8 45 G5
Globe St STHWK SE1 19 G2
Globe Ter BETH E2 92 E2
Glossop Rd SAND/SEL CR2 177 K7
Gloster Rd NWMAL KT3 160 B3
Gloucester Av BFN/LL DA15 154 E1
CAMTN NW1 4 A2
WELL DA16 136 A4
Gloucester Circ GNWCH SE10 113 F6
Gloucester Cl THDIT * KT7 158 B7
WLSDN NW10 69 F6
Gloucester Ct MON EC3R 13 K7
MTCM * CR4 163 K4
RCH/KEW * TW9 105 H6
Gloucester Crs CAMTN NW1 4 C3
Gloucester Dr FSBYPK N4 73 H1
GLDGN NW11 52 E3
Gloucester Gdns BAY/PAD W2 8 D4
EBAR EN4 28 A3
GLDGN NW11 52 D6
IL IG1 59 J6
SUT SM1 175 F1
Gloucester Ga CAMTN NW1 4 C5
Gloucester Gate Ms CAMTN NW1 4 C5
Gloucester Gv EDGW HA8 37 F7
Gloucester Ms BAY/PAD W2 8 F5
Gloucester Ms West BAY/PAD W2 8 E5
Gloucester Pde BFN/LL * DA15 136 B4
HYS/HAR * UB3 101 F2
Gloucester Pl CAMTN NW1 9 L1
MHST W1U 9 M3
Gloucester Place Ms MBLAR W1H 9 M3
Gloucester Rd ACT W3 105 K1
BAR EN5 27 F4
BELV DA17 117 G4
CROY/NA CR0 164 E6
DART DA1 138 E5
EA W5 104 D1

FELT TW13 122 B7
HPTN TW12 142 B6
HSLWW TW4 122 D3
KUT KT1 159 H1
LEY E10 57 J6
MNPK E12 77 K6
RCH/KEW TW9 105 H6
ROM RM1 63 G5
RYLN/HDSTN HA2 48 B4
SKENS SW7 14 E3
TEDD TW11 142 E4
TOTM N17 55 K2
UED N18 42 B4
WALTH E17 57 F1
WAN E11 59 F4
WHTN TW2 123 H7
Gloucester Sq BAY/PAD W2 9 H6
BETH E2 74 C7
Gloucester St PIM SW1V 16 E8
Gloucester Ter BAY/PAD W2 8 E4
STHGT/OAK * N14 28 D7
Gloucester Wk KENS W8 14 B1
Gloucester Wy CLKNW EC1R 6 B8
Glover Cl ABYW SE2 116 D3
Glover Dr UED N18 42 E5
Glover Rd PIN HA5 47 H5
Glycena Rd BTSEA SW11 128 E2
Glyn Av EBAR EN4 27 H3
Glyn Cl EW KT17 173 J7
SNWD SE25 165 F1
Glynde Ms CHEL SW3 15 K4
Glynde Rd BXLYHN DA7 136 E2
Glynde St BROCKY SE4 132 C5
Glyndon Rd WOOL/PLUM SE18 115 H3
Glyn Dr SCUP DA14 155 H3
Glynfield Rd WLSDN NW10 69 G6
Glynne Rd WDGN N22 55 G1
Glyn Rd CLPT E5 75 F3
PEND EN3 30 E3
WPK KT4 174 B1
Glyn St LBTH SE11 17 L8
Goat Rd MTCM CR4 163 F6
Goat Whf BTFD TW8 105 F5
Godalming Av WLGTN SM6 176 E4
Godalming Rd POP/IOD E14 93 K4
Godbold Rd SRTFD E15 94 C3
Goddard Pl ARCH N19 72 C2
Goddard Rd BECK BR3 166 A3
Goddards Wy IL IG1 60 D7
Godfrey Av NTHLT UB5 65 J7
WHTN TW2 123 J6
Godfrey Hl WOOL/PLUM SE18 114 D3
Godfrey Rd WOOL/PLUM SE18 114 E3
Godfrey St CHEL SW3 15 K7
SRTFD E15 94 A1
Godfrey Wy HSLWW TW4 122 D6
Goding St LBTH SE11 17 K8
Godley Rd WAND/EARL SW18 128 C7
Godliman St BLKFR * EC4V 12 D5
Godman Rd PECK * SE15 131 J1
Godolphin Cl PLMGR N13 41 H5
Godolphin Pl ACT W3 87 F6
Godolphin Rd SHB W12 87 K7
Godric Crs CROY/NA CR0 180 B7
Godson Rd CROY/NA CR0 177 G2
Godstone Rd SUT SM1 175 G3
TWK TW1 124 B5
Godstow Rd ABYW SE2 116 D1
Godwin Cl HOR/WEW KT19 172 E5
IS N1 6 F5
Godwin Rd FSTGT E7 77 F3
HAYES BR2 168 B2
Goffers Rd BKHTH/KID SE3 113 H7
Goffs Rd ASHF TW15 140 B5
Goidel Cl WLGTN SM6 176 D3
Golborne Gdns NKENS * W10 88 C3
Golborne Ms NKENS W10 88 C4
Golborne Rd NKENS W10 88 C4
Golda Cl BAR EN5 26 B5
Goldbeaters Gv EDGW HA8 37 G6
Goldcliff Cl MRDN SM4 161 K6
Goldcrest Cl CAN/RD E16 95 H4
THMD SE28 97 J6
Goldcrest Ms EA * W5 85 K4
Goldcrest Wy BUSH WD23 22 C7
CROY/NA CR0 180 B7
Golden Crs HYS/HAR UB3 82 C7
Golden Cross Ms NTGHL * W11 88 D5
Golden Hind Pl DEPT * SE8 112 C3
Golden La STLK EC1Y 6 E9
Golden Lane Est STLK EC1Y 12 E1
Golden Mnr HNWL W7 84 E6
Golden Pde WALTH * E17 58 A2
Golden Plover Cl CAN/RD E16 94 E5
Golden Sq SOHO/CST W1F 10 F6
Golden Yd HAMP * NW3 71 G3
Golders Cl EDGW HA8 36 D4
Golders Gdns GLDGN NW11 52 C6
Golders Green Crs GLDGN NW11 52 D6
Golders Green Rd GLDGN NW11 52 C5
Golders Hl HAMP * NW3 71 F1
Golderslea GLDGN * NW11 52 E7
Golders Manor Dr GLDGN NW11 52 B5
Golders Park Cl GLDGN NW11 52 E7
Golders Ri HDN NW4 52 B4
Golders Wy GLDGN NW11 52 D6
Goldfinch Rd THMD SE28 115 J2
Goldfinch Wy BORE WD6 24 C3
Goldhawk Ms SHB W12 106 E1
Goldhawk Rd HMSMTH W6 106 C3
Goldhaze Cl WFD IG8 45 H6
Gold Hl EDGW HA8 37 F5
Goldhurst Ter KIL/WHAMP NW6 2 D2
Golding St WCHPL E1 92 C5
Goldington Crs CAMTN NW1 5 G5
Goldington St CAMTN NW1 5 G5
Gold La EDGW HA8 37 F5
Goldman Cl BETH E2 92 C3
Goldney Rd MV/WKIL W9 8 A1
Goldrill Dr FBAR/BDGN N11 40 A1
Goldsboro Rd VX/NE SW8 109 J7
Goldsborough Crs CHING E4 43 K1
Goldsdown Cl PEND EN3 31 G1
Goldsdown Rd PEND EN3 31 F1
Goldsmid St WOOL/PLUM SE18 115 K4
Goldsmith Av ACT W3 87 F6
CDALE/KGS NW9 51 G4
MNPK E12 77 J5
ROMW/RG RM7 62 B6
Goldsmith Cl RYLN/HDSTN HA2 48 A7
Goldsmith La CDALE/KGS NW9 50 E3
Goldsmith Pl KIL/WHAMP * NW6 2 C4
Goldsmith Rd ACT W3 87 F7
FBAR/BDGN N11 39 K4
LEY E10 57 K7
PECK SE15 111 H7
WALTH E17 57 F1
Goldsmiths Cl ACT * W3 87 F7
Goldsmith's Rw BETH E2 74 C7
Goldsmith St CITYW EC2V 12 F4
Goldsworthy Gdns
BERM/RHTH SE16 111 K3
Goldwell Rd THHTH CR7 164 A3
Goldwing Cl CAN/RD E16 94 E5
Golf Cl BUSH WD23 21 H2
STAN HA7 35 J6
STRHM/NOR SW16 149 G7
Golf Club Dr KUTN/CMB KT2 145 F6
Golfe Rd IL IG1 78 D2
Golf Rd BMLY BR1 169 F2
EA * W5 86 B5
Golf Side WHTN TW2 142 D2
Golf Side Cl NWMAL KT3 160 B1
Golfside Cl TRDG/WHET N20 39 J2
Gollogly Ter CHARL SE7 114 B4
Gomer Gdns TEDD TW11 143 G5
Gomer Pl TEDD TW11 143 G5
Gomm Rd BERM/RHTH SE16 111 K2
Gomshall Av WLGTN SM6 176 E4
Gondar Gdns KIL/WHAMP NW6 70 D4
Gonson St DEPT SE8 112 E5
Gonston Cl WIM/MER SW19 146 C1
Gonville Crs NTHLT UB5 66 B5
Gonville Rd THHTH CR7 164 A4
Gonville St FUL/PGN SW6 127 H2
Goodall Rd WAN E11 76 A2
Gooden Ct HRW HA1 66 E2
Goodenough Rd
WIM/MER SW19 146 D6
Goodey Rd BARK IG11 79 F6
Goodge Pl FITZ W1T 10 F3
Goodge St FITZ W1T 10 F3
Goodhall St WLSDN NW10 87 H2
Goodhart Wy WWKM BR4 167 H5
Goodhew Rd SNWD SE25 165 H5
Gooding Cl NWMAL KT3 159 K3
Goodinge Cl HOLWY N7 72 E4
Goodinge Rd HOLWY N7 72 E5
Goodison Cl BUSH WD23 22 C4
Goodman Ct ALP/SUD * HA0 67 K3
Goodman Crs
BRXS/STRHM SW2 148 E1
Goodman Rd LEY E10 58 A6
Goodmans Ct ALP/SUD HA0 67 K3
Goodman's Stile WCHPL E1 92 C5
Goodman's Yd TWRH EC3N 13 L6
Goodmayes Av GDMY/SEVK IG3 61 G7
Goodmayes La GDMY/SEVK IG3 79 G3
Goodmayes Rd GDMY/SEVK IG3 61 G7
Goodrich Rd EDUL SE22 131 G5
Goodson Rd WLSDN NW10 69 G6
Goods Wy CAMTN NW1 5 J5
Goodway Gdns POP/IOD E14 94 B5
Goodwin Cl BERM/RHTH SE16 19 M4
MTCM CR4 162 C2
Goodwin Dr SCUP DA14 155 K1
Goodwin Gdns CROY/NA CR0 177 H5
Goodwin Rd CROY/NA CR0 177 H4
ED N9 30 E7
SHB W12 106 D1
Goodwins Ct CHCR WC2N 11 J6
Goodwin St FSBYPK N4 73 G1
Goodwood Cl MRDN SM4 161 K3
Goodwood Dr NTHLT UB5 66 A5
Goodwood Pde BECK * BR3 166 B3
Goodwood Rd NWCR SE14 112 B6
Goodwyn Av MLHL NW7 37 G4
Goodwyn's V MUSWH N10 40 A7
Goodyers Gdns HDN NW4 52 B4
Goosander Wy
WOOL/PLUM SE18 115 J2
Gooseacre La
KTN/HRWW/W HA3 49 K4
Gooseley La EHAM E6 96 A2
Goossens Cl SUT SM1 175 G4
Gophir La CANST * EC4R 13 G6
Gopsall St IS N1 7 H4
Gordon Av CHING E4 44 C5
HCH RM12 81 H1
MORT/ESHN SW14 126 B3
STAN HA7 35 F5
TWK TW1 124 B4
Gordonbrock Rd BROCKY SE4 132 D4
Gordon Cl WALTH E17 57 J5
Gordon Crs CROY/NA CR0 165 F7
HYS/HAR UB3 101 K3
Gordondale Rd
WIM/MER SW19 146 E1
Gordon Gdns EDGW HA8 50 D1
Gordon Gv CMBW SE5 130 C1
Gordon House Rd KTTN NW5 72 A3
Gordon Pl KENS W8 14 B1
Gordon Rd BARK IG11 78 E7
BECK BR3 166 C2
BELV DA17 117 K3
BFN/LL DA15 135 K4
BRYLDS KT5 159 G6
CAR SM5 175 K5
CHDH RM6 62 B5
CHSWK W4 105 J5
DART DA1 139 G6
EA W5 85 J6
ED N9 42 D1
ESH/CLAY KT10 170 E6
FBAR/BDGN N11 40 D6
FNCH N3 38 D6
HSLW TW3 123 H3
IL IG1 78 D2
KTN/HRWW/W HA3 48 E2
KUTN/CMB KT2 144 B7
NWDGN UB2 102 D3
PECK SE15 131 J1
RCH/KEW TW9 125 G1
SRTFD E15 76 A3
SWFD E18 45 F7
WAN E11 58 E5
Gordon Sq STPAN WC1H 5 H9
Gordon St PLSTW E13 94 E2
STPAN WC1H 5 G9
Gordon Wy BAR EN5 26 D3
BMLY BR1 152 E7
Gorefield Pl KIL/WHAMP NW6 2 A5
Gore Rd HOM E9 74 E7
RYNPK SW20 161 F1
Goresbrook Rd DAGW RM9 79 J7
Gore St SKENS SW7 14 F3
Gorham Pl NTGHL W11 88 C6
Goring Gdns BCTR RM8 79 J3
Goring Rd DAGE RM10 81 F5
FBAR/BDGN * N11 40 E5
Goring St HDTCH EC3A 13 K4
Goring Wy GFD/PVL UB6 84 C1
Gorleston Rd SEVS/STOTM N15 55 K4
Gorleston St WKENS W14 107 H3
Gorman Rd WOOL/PLUM SE18 114 E3
Gorringe Park Av MTCM CR4 147 K6
Gorse Ri TOOT SW17 148 A4
Gorse Rd CROY/NA CR0 179 J2
Gorseway ROMW/RG RM7 81 G1
Gorst Rd BTSEA SW11 128 E5
WLSDN NW10 86 E3
Gorsuch Pl BETH E2 7 L7
Gorsuch St BETH E2 7 L7
Gosberton Rd BAL SW12 128 E7
Gosbury Hl CHSGTN KT9 172 A3
Gosfield Rd BCTR RM8 62 C7
Gosfield St GTPST W1W 10 E2
Gosford Gdns REDBR IG4 59 K4
Gosforth La OXHEY WD19 32 E2
Gosforth Pth OXHEY WD19 32 E2
Goshawk Gdns YEAD UB4 82 C2
Goslett Yd SOHO/SHAV W1D 11 H4
Gosling Cl GFD/PVL UB6 84 A2
Gosling Wy BRXN/ST SW9 110 B7
Gospatrick Rd TOTM N17 41 J7
Gosport Rd WALTH E17 57 H4
Gosport Wy PECK SE15 111 G6
Gossage Rd WOOL/PLUM SE18 115 J4
Gosset St BETH E2 92 C2
Gosshill Rd CHST BR7 169 F1
Gossington Cl CHST BR7 154 B3
Gosterwood St DEPT SE8 112 B5
Gostling Rd WHTN TW2 123 F7
Goston Gdns THHTH CR7 164 B2
Goswell Pl FSBYE EC1V 6 D8
Goswell Rd FSBYE EC1V 6 D7
Gothic Ct HYS/HAR UB3 101 G5
Gothic Rd WHTN TW2 142 D1
Gottfried Ms KTTN NW5 72 C3
Goudhurst Rd BMLY BR1 152 C4
Gough Rd EN EN1 30 D1
FSTGT E7 76 D3
Gough Sq FLST/FETLN EC4A 12 B4
Gough St FSBYW WC1X 5 M9
Goulding Gdns THHTH CR7 164 D1
Gould Rd EBED/NFELT TW14 121 H6
WHTN TW2 123 K7
Gould Ter HACK E8 74 D4
Goulston St WCHPL E1 13 L4
Goulton Rd CLPT E5 74 D4
Gourley Pl SEVS/STOTM N15 56 A4
Gourley St SEVS/STOTM N15 56 A4
Gourock Rd ELTH/MOT SE9 135 F4
Govan St BETH E2 74 C7
Govier Cl SRTFD E15 76 C6
Gowan Av FUL/PGN SW6 107 H7
Gowan Rd WLSDN NW10 69 K6
Gower Cl CLAP SW4 129 H5
Gower Ms GWRST WC1E 11 H3
Gower Pl STPAN WC1H 4 F9
Gower Rd FSTGT E7 76 E5
ISLW TW7 104 A5
Gower St GWRST WC1E 4 F9
Gower's Wk WCHPL E1 92 C5
Gowland Pl BECK BR3 166 C1
Gowlett Rd PECK SE15 131 H2
Gowrie Rd BTSEA SW11 129 F2
Graburn Wy E/WMO/HCT KT8 157 J2
Grace Av BXLYHN DA7 137 G1
Gracechurch St BANK EC3V 13 H6
Grace Cl EDGW HA8 36 E6
ELTH/MOT SE9 153 H2
Gracedale Rd
STRHM/NOR SW16 148 B4
Gracefield Gdns
STRHM/NOR SW16 148 E2
Grace Jones Cl HACK * E8 74 B5
Grace Pl BOW E3 93 K2
Grace Rd CROY/NA CR0 164 D5
Grace's Ms CMBW SE5 130 E1
STJWD * NW8 2 F6
Grace's Rd CMBW SE5 131 F1
Grace St BOW E3 93 K2
The Gradient SYD SE26 150 C3
Graduate Pl STHWK SE1 19 J3
Graeme Rd EN EN1 30 A1
Graemesdyke Av
MORT/ESHN SW14 125 J2
Grafton Cl HSLWW TW4 122 D7
WEA W13 85 G5
WPK KT4 173 G2
Grafton Crs CAMTN NW1 72 B5
Grafton Gdns BCTR RM8 80 A1
FSBYPK N4 55 J5
Grafton Ms FITZ W1T 10 E1
Grafton Park Rd WPK KT4 173 G1
Grafton Pl CAMTN NW1 5 G8
Grafton Rd ACT W3 86 E6
BCTR RM8 80 A1
CROY/NA CR0 164 B7
ENC/FH EN2 29 F2
HRW HA1 48 C4
KTTN NW5 72 A4
NWMAL KT3 160 B3
WPK KT4 173 F2
Grafton Sq CLAP SW4 129 H3
Grafton St MYFR/PICC W1J 10 D7
Grafton Ter KTTN NW5 71 K4
Grafton Wy E/WMO/HCT KT8 156 E3
GTPST W1W 10 E2
Grafton Yd KTTN NW5 72 B5
Graham Av MTCM CR4 148 A7
WEA W13 104 C1
Graham Cl CROY/NA CR0 179 J1
Grahame Park Wy MLHL NW7 37 H6
Graham Gdns SURB KT6 159 F7
Graham Rd BXLYHN DA7 137 G3
CHSWK W4 106 A2
HACK E8 74 C5
HDN NW4 51 K5
HPTN TW12 142 A3
KTN/HRWW/W HA3 48 E2
MTCM CR4 148 A7
PLSTW E13 94 E3
SEVS/STOTM N15 55 H2
WIM/MER SW19 146 D6
Graham St IS N1 6 D6
Graham Ter BFN/LL * DA15 136 C5
BGVA SW1W 16 B6
Grainger Cl NTHLT UB5 66 C4
Grainger Rd ISLW TW7 124 A1
WDGN N22 41 J7
Gramer Cl WAN E11 76 B1
Grampian Cl BELMT SM2 175 G6
HYS/HAR UB3 101 G6
Grampian Gdns CRICK NW2 52 C7
Granada St TOOT SW17 147 K4
Granard Av PUT/ROE SW15 126 E4
Granard Rd BAL SW12 128 E6
Granary Cl ED N9 30 E6
Granary Rd WCHPL E1 92 D3
Granary Sq IS * N1 73 G5
Granary St CAMTN NW1 5 G4
Granby Rd ELTH/MOT SE9 134 E1
WOOL/PLUM SE18 115 G2
Granby St BETH E2 7 M9
Granby Ter CAMTN NW1 4 E6
Grand Av BRYLDS KT5 159 J5
FARR EC1M 12 D2
MUSWH N10 54 A3
WBLY HA9 68 C4
Grand Av East WBLY HA9 68 D4
Grand Depot Rd
WOOL/PLUM SE18 115 F4
Grand Dr NWDGN UB2 103 H1
RYNPK SW20 161 F2
Granden Rd
STRHM/NOR * SW16 163 K1
Grandison Rd CLAP SW4 128 E4
WPK KT4 174 A1
Grand Junction Whf IS * N1 6 E6
Grand Pde FSBYPK * N4 55 H5
MORT/ESHN * SW14 125 K3
SURB * KT6 159 H7
WBLY * HA9 68 D1
Grand Union Canal Wk
BAY/PAD W2 8 B2
NWDGN UB2 102 A2
STHL UB1 83 K3
STKPK UB11 100 E1
WLSDN NW10 86 D1
Grand Union Cl MV/WKIL W9 88 D4
Grand Union Crs HACK * E8 74 C7
Grand Union Wk CAMTN * NW1 4 D2
Grand Wk WCHPL * E1 93 G3
Granfield St BTSEA * SW11 108 C7
The Grange ALP/SUD HA0 68 C6
CROY/NA CR0 179 H1
HOR/WEW KT19 173 F3
NWMAL * KT3 160 D4
STHWK SE1 19 L3
WIM/MER SW19 146 B5
WKENS * W14 107 J3
Grange Av EBAR EN4 27 J7
KTN/HRWW/W HA3 49 H1
NFNCH/WDSP N12 39 G4
SNWD SE25 165 F1
TRDG/WHET N20 26 C6
WFD IG8 44 E5
WHTN TW2 142 E1
Grangecliffe Gdns SNWD SE25 165 F1
Grange Cl BFN/LL DA15 155 G2
E/WMO/HCT KT8 157 G3
HYS/HAR UB3 82 C4
NWDGN UB2 102 E4
WFD IG8 44 E6
Grange Ct ALP/SUD * HA0 67 J4
BELMT * SM2 175 F6
HRW * HA1 67 F2
NTHLT UB5 83 G1
PIN * HA5 47 J2
WLGTN * SM6 176 B2
Grangecourt Rd
STNW/STAM N16 56 A7
Grange Crs THMD SE28 97 J5
Grangedale Cl NTHWD HA6 32 C7
Grange Dr CHST BR7 153 J5
Grange Farm Cl
RYLN/HDSTN HA2 66 C1
Grange Gdns HAMP NW3 71 F2
PIN HA5 47 K3
SNWD SE25 165 F1
STHGT/OAK N14 28 D7
Grange Gv IS N1 73 J5
Grange Hl EDGW HA8 36 E4
SNWD SE25 165 F1
Grangehill Pl ELTH/MOT SE9 134 E2
Grangehill Rd ELTH/MOT SE9 134 E3
Grange Houses HBRY * N5 73 J3
Grange La DUL SE21 150 B1
Grange Ms FELT * TW13 140 B2
Grangemill Rd CAT SE6 151 J2
Grangemill Wy CAT SE6 151 J1
Grange Pk EA W5 86 A7
Grange Park Av WCHMH N21 29 H5
Grange Park Pl RYNPK SW20 145 K6
Grange Park Rd LEY E10 57 K7
THHTH CR7 164 E2
Grange Pl KIL/WHAMP NW6 2 A2
Grange Rd BARN SW13 106 D7
BELMT SM2 174 E6
BORE WD6 24 B4
BUSH WD23 21 J4
CHSGTN KT9 172 A3
CHSWK W4 105 J4
E/WMO/HCT KT8 157 G3
EA W5 85 K7
EDGW HA8 37 F5
HGT N6 54 A5
HRW HA1 49 G5
HYS/HAR UB3 82 C5
IL IG1 78 C3
KUT KT1 159 F2
LEY E10 57 J7
PLSTW E13 94 E2
RYLN/HDSTN HA2 66 D1
SNWD SE25 164 E2
STHL UB1 102 D1
STHWK SE1 19 K4
TOTM N17 42 C5
WALTH E17 57 G4
WLSDN NW10 69 K5
Granger Wy ROM RM1 63 J5
Grange St IS N1 7 H4
Grange V BELMT SM2 175 F6
Grangeview Rd
TRDG/WHET N20 27 G7
Grange Wk STHWK SE1 19 K3
Grange Walk Ms STHWK SE1 19 K4
Grange Wy ERITH DA8 118 E6
Grangeway KIL/WHAMP NW6 2 A2
NFNCH/WDSP N12 39 F3
WFD IG8 45 G3
Grangeway Gdns REDBR IG4 59 J4
The Grangeway WCHMH N21 29 H5
Grangewood BXLY DA5 137 G7
Grangewood Cl PIN HA5 46 E4
Grangewood La BECK BR3 151 H5
Grangewood St EHAM E6 77 H7
Grange Yd STHWK SE1 19 L4
Granham Gdns ED N9 42 B1
Granite St WOOL/PLUM SE18 116 A4
Granleigh Rd WAN E11 76 C1
Gransden Av HACK E8 74 D6
Gransden Rd SHB W12 106 C1
Grantbridge St IS N1 6 D5
Grantchester KUT * KT1 159 H1
Grantchester Cl HRW HA1 67 F2
Grant Cl STHGT/OAK N14 28 C6
Grantham Cl EDGW HA8 36 A2
Grantham Gdns CHDH RM6 62 B5
Grantham Gn BORE WD6 24 E4
Grantham Pl MYFR/PICC W1J 10 C9
Grantham Rd BRXN/ST SW9 129 K2
CHSWK W4 106 B6
MNPK E12 78 A3
Grantley Pl ESH/CLAY KT10 170 B4
Grantley Rd HSLWW TW4 122 B1
Grantley St WCHPL E1 93 F2
Grantock Rd WALTH E17 44 B7
Granton Rd GDMY/SEVK IG3 61 G7
SCUP DA14 155 H5
STRHM/NOR SW16 148 C7
Grant Rd BTSEA SW11 128 D2
CROY/NA CR0 165 G7
KTN/HRWW/W HA3 48 E2
Grants Cl MLHL NW7 38 A6
Grant St IS N1 6 A5
PLSTW E13 94 E2
Grant Ter STNW/STAM * N16 56 C6
Grantully Rd MV/WKIL W9 2 C8
Grant Wy ISLW TW7 104 B5
Granville Ar BRXN/ST * SW9 130 B3
Granville Av ED N9 42 E2
FELT TW13 140 E1
HSLW TW3 123 F4
Granville Cl CROY/NA CR0 178 A1
Granville Gdns EA W5 86 B7
STRHM/NOR SW16 149 F7
Granville Gv LEW SE13 133 F2
Granville Ms SCUP DA14 155 G3
Granville Pk LEW SE13 133 F2
Granville Pl FUL/PGN * SW6 108 A6
MBLAR W1H 10 A5
NFNCH/WDSP * N12 39 G6
PIN HA5 47 H2
Granville Rd BAR EN5 26 A3
CRICK NW2 70 D1
FSBYPK N4 55 F5
HYS/HAR UB3 101 J3
IL IG1 60 B7
KIL/WHAMP NW6 2 A6
NFNCH/WDSP N12 39 G6
PLMGR N13 41 F5
SCUP DA14 155 G3
SWFD E18 59 F1
WALTH E17 57 K5
WAND/EARL SW18 127 K6
WATW * WD18 21 G3
WDGN N22 41 H7
WELL DA16 136 D2
WIM/MER SW19 146 E6
Granville Sq PECK * SE15 111 F6
Granville St FSBYW WC1X 5 M8
Grape St LSQ/SEVD WC2H 11 J4
Graphite Sq LBTH SE11 17 L7
Grapsome Cl CHSGTN KT9 171 J6
Grasdene Rd
WOOL/PLUM SE18 116 B6
Grasmere Av ACT W3 86 E6
HSLW TW3 123 G5
PUT/ROE SW15 145 F3
RSLP HA4 46 A6
WBLY HA9 49 K6
WIM/MER SW19 161 K2
Grasmere Cl EBED/NFELT TW14 121 J7
Grasmere Ct WDGN N22 41 F5
Grasmere Gdns
KTN/HRWW/W HA3 49 G1
REDBR IG4 59 J4
Grasmere Rd BMLY BR1 152 D7
BXLYHN DA7 117 K7
MUSWH N10 40 B7
PLSTW E13 94 E1
SNWD SE25 165 J5
STRHM/NOR SW16 149 F4
TOTM N17 42 C5
Grasshaven Wy THMD SE28 97 F7
Grassington Cl FBAR/BDGN N11 40 A4
Grassington Rd SCUP DA14 155 G3
Grassmount FSTH SE23 150 D1
Grass Pk FNCH N3 38 D7
Grassway WLGTN SM6 176 C3
Grasvenor Av BAR EN5 26 E5
Grately Wy PECK * SE15 111 F6
Gratton Rd WKENS W14 107 H2
Graveley Av BORE WD6 24 E3
Gravel Hl BXLYHS DA6 137 J4
CROY/NA CR0 179 F5
FNCH N3 52 D1
Gravel Hill Cl BXLY DA5 137 J5
Gravel La WCHPL E1 13 L4
Gravel Rd HAYES BR2 181 J1
WHTN TW2 123 K7
Gravelwood Cl CHST BR7 154 C2
Gravenel Gdns TOOT * SW17 147 J4
Graveney Gv PGE/AN SE20 150 E6
Graveney Rd TOOT SW17 147 J3
Gravesend Rd SHB W12 87 J6
Gray Av BCTR RM8 62 B7
Gray Gdns HCH RM12 81 J5
Grayham Crs NWMAL KT3 160 A3
Grayham Rd NWMAL KT3 160 A3
Grayland Cl BMLY BR1 153 H7
Grayling Cl CAN/RD E16 94 C3
Grayling Ct EA * W5 85 K7
Grayling Rd STNW/STAM N16 73 K1
Grayling Sq BETH * E2 92 C2
Grays Cottages
STMC/STPC * BR5 155 J7
Grayscroft Rd
STRHM/NOR SW16 148 D6
Grays Farm Rd
STMC/STPC BR5 155 H7
Grayshott Rd BTSEA SW11 129 F2
Gray's Inn Rd FSBYW WC1X 5 K7
Gray's Inn Sq GINN WC1R 12 A2
Gray St STHWK SE1 18 C1
Grayswood Gdns RYNPK SW20 160 E1
Gray's Yd MHST * W1U 10 B5
Graywood Ct NFNCH/WDSP N12 39 G6
Grazebrook Rd
STNW/STAM N16 73 K1
Grazeley Cl BXLYHS DA6 137 K4
Great Benty WDR/YW UB7 100 B3
Great Brownings SYD SE26 150 B3
Great Bushey Dr
TRDG/WHET N20 27 F7
Great Cambridge Jct
PLMGR N13 41 J4
Great Cambridge Rd UED N18 41 K4
Great Castle St REGST W1B 10 E4
Great Central Av RSLP HA4 65 G4
Great Central St CAMTN NW1 9 L2
Great Central Wy WBLY HA9 68 E4
Great Chapel St SOHO/CST W1F 11 G4
Great Chertsey Rd CHSWK W4 106 A7
FELT TW13 141 K2
Great Church La HMSMTH W6 107 G4
Great College St WEST SW1P 17 J3
Great Cross Av GNWCH SE10 113 H6
Great Cullings ROMW/RG RM7 81 G1
Great Cumberland Ms
MBLAR W1H 9 L5
Great Cumberland Pl
MBLAR W1H 9 L4
Great Dover St STHWK SE1 19 G3
Greatdown Rd HNWL W7 85 F4
Great Eastern Rd SRTFD E15 76 B6
Great Eastern St SDTCH EC2A 7 J9

Great Eastern Whf
BTSEA * SW11 108 D6
Great Elms Rd HAYES BR2 168 B3
Great Fld CDALE/KGS NW9 37 G7
Greatfield Av EHAM E6 95 K3
Greatfield Cl LEW SE13 132 D3
Greatfields Rd BARK IG11 78 D7
Great Galley Cl BARK IG11 97 H2
Great Gardens Rd EMPK RM11 63 K5
Great Gatton Cl CROY/NA CR0 166 B6
Great George St STJSPK SW1H 17 H2
Great Gv BUSH WD23 22 B3
Great Guildford St STHWK SE1 12 E9
Greatham Rd BUSH WD23 21 H2
Great Harry Dr ELTH/MOT SE9 154 A2
Great James St BMSBY WC1N 11 L2
Great Marlborough St
SOHO/CST W1F 10 E5
Great Maze Pond STHWK SE1 13 H9
Great New St
FLST/FETLN * EC4A 12 B4
Great North Rd BAR EN5 27 F5
EFNCH N2 53 J3
Great North Wy (Barnet By-Pass)
HDN NW4 37 K7
Greatorex St WCHPL E1 92 C4
Great Ormond St BMSBY WC1N 11 K2
Great Percy St FSBYW WC1X 5 M7
Great Peter St WEST SW1P 17 G4
Great Portland St GTPST W1W 10 E4
Great Pulteney St
SOHO/CST W1F 10 F6
Great Queen St DART DA1 139 J5
HOL/ALD WC2B 11 L4
Great Russell St RSQ WC1B 11 J3
Great St Helen's HDTCH EC3A 13 J5
Great St Thomas Apostle
BLKFR EC4V 12 F6
Great Scotland Yd WHALL SW1A 11 J9
Great Smith St WEST SW1P 17 H3
Great South-west Rd
EBED/NFELT TW14 121 F6
Great Spilmans EDUL SE22 131 F4
Great Strd CDALE/KGS NW9 51 H1
Great Suffolk St STHWK SE1 12 D9
Great Sutton St FSBYE EC1V 12 D1
Great Swan Aly LOTH EC2R 13 G4
Great Thrift STMC/STPC BR5 169 H3
Great Titchfield St GTPST W1W 10 D1
Great Tower St MON EC3R 13 J6
Great Trinity La BLKFR EC4V 12 F6
Great Turnstile HHOL * WC1V 11 M3
Great Western Rd BAY/PAD W2 88 D4
Great West Rd CHSWK W4 105 K5
HEST TW5 122 D1
HMSMTH W6 106 E4
ISLW TW7 103 K6
Great West Rd Chiswick
CHSWK W4 106 C5
Great West Rd Ellesmere Rd
CHSWK W4 105 K5
Great West Rd Hogarth La
CHSWK W4 106 A5
Great Winchester St OBST EC2N 13 H4
Great Windmill St
SOHO/SHAV W1D 11 G7
Greatwood CHST BR7 154 A6
Greaves Cl BARK IG11 78 D6
Greaves Cottages
POP/IOD * E14 93 G4
Greaves Pl TOOT SW17 147 J3
Grebe Av YEAD UB4 83 H5
Grebe Cl BARK IG11 97 G3
FSTGT E7 76 D4
WALTH E17 43 G6
Grebe Ct SUT SM1 174 D4
Grebe Ter KUT * KT1 159 F2
Grecian Crs NRWD SE19 149 H5
Greek St SOHO/SHAV W1D 11 H5
The Green ACT W3 87 G5
BXLYHN DA7 117 H7
CAR * SM5 176 A3
CROY/NA CR0 179 H7
ED N9 42 C1
FELT TW13 141 F1
HAYES BR2 167 K6
HEST TW5 103 F5
HGDN/ICK UB10 64 A1
HRW HA1 67 G1
MRDN SM4 161 H3
NWDGN UB2 102 E1
NWMAL KT3 159 K2
RCH/KEW TW9 124 E4
SCUP DA14 155 G4
SRTFD E15 76 D5
STHGT/OAK N14 40 D2
STMC/STPC BR5 155 H6
SUT SM1 175 F2
TOTM N17 41 J5
WAN E11 59 F5
WCHMH N21 29 G6
WDR/YW UB7 100 A2
WELL DA16 135 K3
WHTN TW2 123 K7
Greenacre Cl NTHLT UB5 65 K4
Greenacre Pl WLGTN SM6 176 B1
Green Acres CROY/NA CR0 178 B2
SCUP * DA14 155 F3
Greenacres BUSH WD23 34 D1
ELTH/MOT SE9 135 F5
Greenacres Dr STAN HA7 35 H6
Greenacre Sq
BERM/RHTH * SE16 112 A1
Greenacre Wk STHGT/OAK N14 40 D2
Green Arbour Ct STP * EC4M 12 C4
Green Av MLHL NW7 37 F3
WEA W13 104 C2
Greenaway Av UED * N18 43 F4
Greenaway Gdns HAMP NW3 71 F3
Green Bank NFNCH/WDSP N12 39 F3
WAP E1W 92 D7
Greenbank Av ALP/SUD HA0 67 G4
Greenbank Cl CHING E4 44 A1
Greenbank Crs FNCH N3 52 C3
Greenbay Rd CHARL SE7 114 C6
Greenberry St STJWD NW8 3 J6
Green Chain Wk BECK BR3 152 A6
CHARL SE7 114 C3
ELTH/MOT SE9 135 G4
SYD SE26 151 F5
THMD SE28 97 K7
Green Cl CAR SM5 175 K1
CDALE/KGS NW9 50 E5
EFNCH N2 53 G6
FELT TW13 141 J4
HAYES BR2 167 H2
Greencoat Pl WEST SW1P 16 F5
Greencoat Rw WEST SW1P 16 F4
Green Court Av CROY/NA CR0 178 D1
Greencourt Av EDGW HA8 36 C7
Green Court Gdns
CROY/NA CR0 178 D1
Greencourt Rd
STMC/STPC BR5 169 K4
Greencroft EDGW HA8 36 E4
Greencroft Av RSLP HA4 65 G1
Greencroft Gdns EN EN1 30 A2
KIL/WHAMP NW6 2 E1
Greencroft Rd HEST TW5 102 E7
Green Dl EDUL SE22 131 F4
Green Dragon La BTFD TW8 105 F4
WCHMH N21 29 F4
Green Dragon Yd WCHPL E1 92 C4
Green Dr STHL UB1 84 A7
Green End CHSGTN KT9 171 K3
WCHMH N21 41 H1
Greenend Rd CHSWK W4 106 B1
Greenfell Man DEPT * SE8 112 C4
Greenfield Av BRYLDS KT5 159 J6
OXHEY WD19 33 J1
Greenfield Dr BMLY BR1 168 B1
EFNCH N2 53 K3
Greenfield Gdns CRICK NW2 70 C1
DAGW RM9 79 J7
STMC/STPC BR5 169 H6
Greenfield Rd DAGW RM9 79 J7
SEVS/STOTM N15 56 A4
WCHPL E1 92 C4
Greenfields STHL UB1 84 A6
Greenfield Wy
RYLN/HDSTN HA2 48 B2
Greenford Av HNWL W7 84 E3
STHL UB1 83 K6
Greenford Gdns GFD/PVL UB6 84 B2
Greenford Rd GFD/PVL UB6 66 E4
STHL UB1 84 C6
SUT SM1 175 F3
Greengate GFD/PVL UB6 67 H5
Greengate St PLSTW E13 95 F1
Greenhalgh Wk EFNCH N2 53 G3
Greenham Cl STHWK SE1 18 A2
Greenham Crs CHING E4 43 H5
Greenham Rd MUSWH N10 54 A1
Greenhaven Dr THMD SE28 97 H5
Greenheys Cl NTHWD HA6 32 C7
Greenheys Dr SWFD E18 58 D2
Greenhill HAMP NW3 71 H3
SUT SM1 175 G1
WBLY HA9 68 D1
Green Hl WOOL/PLUM SE18 114 E4
Greenhill Ct BAR * EN5 27 F4
Greenhill Crs WATW WD18 20 C5
Greenhill Gdns NTHLT UB5 83 K1
Greenhill Gv MNPK E12 77 J3
Greenhill Pde BAR * EN5 27 F4
Greenhill Pk BAR EN5 27 G4
WLSDN NW10 69 G7
Greenhill Rd HRW HA1 48 E5
WLSDN NW10 69 G7
Greenhill's Rents FARR * EC1M 12 C2
Greenhills Ter IS N1 73 K5
Greenhill Ter NTHLT * UB5 83 K1
Greenhill Wy HRW HA1 48 E5
WBLY HA9 68 D1
Greenhithe Cl ELTH/MOT SE9 135 K6
Greenholm Rd ELTH/MOT SE9 135 G4
Green Hundred Rd PECK SE15 111 H5
Greenhurst Rd WNWD SE27 149 G4
Greening St ABYW SE2 116 D3
Greenland Crs NWDGN UB2 102 B2
Greenland Ms DEPT SE8 112 A4
Greenland Pl CAMTN NW1 4 D3
Greenland Quay
BERM/RHTH SE16 112 A3
Greenland Rd BAR EN5 26 A5
CAMTN NW1 4 E3
Greenlands HOR/WEW KT19 172 D4
Greenland St CAMTN NW1 4 D3
Green La BCTR RM8 80 B1
CHSGTN KT9 172 A7
E/WMO/HCT KT8 157 G4
EDGW HA8 36 B3
ELTH/MOT SE9 135 F7
ELTH/MOT SE9 154 A1
FELT TW13 141 J4
HDN NW4 52 B4
HNWL W7 103 K1
HSLWW TW4 122 B3
IL IG1 78 D1
MRDN SM4 162 A6
NTHWD HA6 32 B6
NWMAL KT3 159 K4
OXHEY WD19 21 G7
PGE/AN SE20 151 F6
STAN HA7 35 H3
SUN TW16 140 D6
THHTH CR7 149 H7
UX/CGN UB8 82 A4
WPK KT4 160 D7
Green Lane Cottages
STAN * HA7 35 H3
Green Lane Gdns THHTH CR7 164 D1
Green Lanes CEND/HSY/T N8 55 H2
FSBYPK N4 55 H5
HOR/WEW KT19 173 G7
PLMGR N13 41 F4
WCHMH N21 29 H7
Greenlaw Ct EA * W5 85 K5
Greenlaw Gdns NWMAL KT3 160 C6
Green Lawns
NFNCH/WDSP * N12 39 F5
RSLP * HA4 47 G7
Greenlaw St WOOL/PLUM SE18 115 F2
Green Leaf Av WLGTN SM6 176 D3
Greenleaf Cl
BRXS/STRHM * SW2 130 B6
Greenleafe Dr BARK/HLT IG6 60 B2
Greenleaf Rd EHAM E6 77 G7
WALTH E17 57 H2
Greenlea Pk WIM/MER * SW19 147 J7
Green Leas SUN TW16 140 D6
Green Leas Cl SUN TW16 140 D6
Green Man La
EBED/NFELT TW14 121 K3
WEA W13 85 G6
Greenman St IS N1 6 E2
Greenmead Cl SNWD SE25 165 H4
Green Moor Link WCHMH N21 29 H6
Greenmoor Rd PEND EN3 30 E1
Greenoak Pl EBAR EN4 27 K1
Green Oaks NWDGN * UB2 102 C3
Greenoak Wy WIM/MER SW19 146 B3
Greenock Rd ACT W3 105 J2
STRHM/NOR SW16 148 D7
Green Pde HSLW * TW3 123 G5
Green Pond Cl WALTH E17 57 G2
Green Pond Rd WALTH E17 57 G2
Green Rd STHGT/OAK N14 28 B5
TRDG/WHET N20 39 G2
Greens Ct NTGHL * W11 88 D7
SOHO/CST W1F 11 G6
Greens End WOOL/PLUM SE18 115 G3
Greenshank Cl WALTH E17 43 G6
Greenside BCTR RM8 79 J1
BXLY DA5 137 F7
Greenside Cl CAT SE6 152 B1
TRDG/WHET N20 39 H1
Greenside Rd CROY/NA CR0 164 B6
SHB W12 106 D2
Greenslade Rd BARK IG11 78 D6
Greenstead Av WFD IG8 45 G5
Greenstead Gdns
PUT/ROE SW15 126 D4
WFD IG8 45 G5
Greenstone Ms WAN E11 58 E5
Green St FSTGT E7 77 F4
MYFR/PKLN W1K 9 M6
PEND EN3 31 F2
SUN TW16 140 E7
Green Street Green Rd
DART DA1 139 K7
Greenstreet Hl NWCR * SE14 132 A2
Greensward BUSH WD23 22 B5
Green Ter CLKNW EC1R 6 B8
Green V BXLYHS DA6 136 E4
EA W5 86 B5
Greenvale Rd ELTH/MOT SE9 134 E3
Green Verges STAN HA7 35 K6
Green Vw CHSGTN KT9 172 B6
Greenview Av BECK BR3 166 B5
Greenview Cl ACT W3 87 G7
Green Wk DART DA1 138 C3
HDN NW4 52 B4
NWDGN UB2 103 F4
RSLP HA4 46 D7
STHWK SE1 19 J4
WFD IG8 45 J5
The Green Wy
KTN/HRWW/W HA3 34 E7
The Greenway CDALE/KGS NW9 51 F1
HSLWW * TW4 122 E3
PIN HA5 47 K5
Green Wy ELTH/MOT SE9 134 C4
HAYES BR2 168 D5
Greenway BCTR RM8 79 J1
CHST BR7 154 A4
KTN/HRWW/W HA3 50 A4
PIN HA5 47 F1
RYNPK SW20 161 F3
STHGT/OAK N14 40 E1
TRDG/WHET N20 38 E1
WLGTN SM6 176 C3
YEAD UB4 83 F3
Greenway Av WALTH E17 58 B3
Greenway Cl CDALE/KGS NW9 51 F1
FBAR/BDGN N11 40 A5
FSBYPK N4 73 J1
TRDG/WHET N20 38 E1
Greenway Ct IL IG1 60 A7
Greenway Gdns
CDALE/KGS NW9 50 E1
CROY/NA CR0 179 H2
GFD/PVL UB6 84 A2
Green Way Gdns
KTN/HRWW/W HA3 48 E1
The Greenways TWK * TW1 124 B5
Greenways BECK BR3 166 D1
ESH/CLAY KT10 170 E3
NFNCH/WDSP * N12 39 G5
Greenwell St GTPST W1W 10 D1
Greenwich Church St
GNWCH * SE10 113 F5
Greenwich Crs EHAM E6 95 J4
Greenwich Foot Tnl
GNWCH SE10 113 F4
Greenwich Hts
WOOL/PLUM SE18 114 D6
Greenwich High Rd
GNWCH SE10 112 E6
Greenwich Park St
GNWCH * SE10 113 G5
Greenwich Quay DEPT SE8 112 E5
Greenwich South St
GNWCH SE10 112 E7
Greenwich Vw POP/IOD E14 112 E2
Greenwood Av DAGE RM10 80 D3
Greenwood Cl BFN/LL DA15 155 G1
MRDN SM4 161 H3
STMC/STPC BR5 169 K5
THDIT KT7 158 B7
Greenwood Dr CHING E4 44 A4
Greenwood Gdns PLMGR N13 41 H2
Greenwood La HPTN TW12 142 B4
Greenwood Pk KUTN/CMB KT2 145 G6
Greenwood Pl KTTN NW5 72 B4
Greenwood Rd CROY/NA CR0 164 C6
HACK E8 74 C5
ISLW TW7 123 K2
MTCM CR4 163 J2
PLSTW E13 94 D1
THDIT KT7 158 B7
Greenwood Ter WLSDN * NW10 69 F7
Green Wrythe Crs CAR SM5 162 D7
Green Wrythe La MRDN SM4 162 C5
Green Yd FSBYW WC1X 5 M9
Greer Rd KTN/HRWW/W HA3 34 C7
Greet St STHWK SE1 12 B9
Greg Cl LEY E10 58 A5
Gregor Ms BKHTH/KID SE3 113 K6
Gregory Crs ELTH/MOT SE9 134 C6
Gregory Pl KENS W8 14 C1
Gregory Rd CHDH RM6 61 K3
NWDGN UB2 103 F2
Gregson Cl BORE WD6 24 E1
Greig Cl CEND/HSY/T N8 54 E4
Greig Ter WALW SE17 18 D9
Grenaby Av CROY/NA CR0 164 E6
Grenaby Rd CROY/NA CR0 164 E6
Grenada Rd CHARL SE7 114 B6
Grenade St POP/IOD E14 93 H6
Grenadier St CAN/RD E16 96 A7
Grena Gdns RCH/KEW TW9 125 G3
Grenard Cl PECK * SE15 111 H6
Grena Rd RCH/KEW TW9 125 G3
Grendon Gdns WBLY HA9 68 C1
Grendon St STJWD NW8 3 J9
Grenfell Av HCH RM12 63 H7
Grenfell Ct MLHL * NW7 37 K5
Grenfell Gdns
KTN/HRWW/W HA3 50 A6
Grenfell Rd NTGHL W11 88 B6
TOOT SW17 147 K5
Grenfell Wk NTGHL W11 88 B6
Grennell Cl SUT SM1 175 H1
Grennell Rd SUT SM1 175 G1
Grenoble Gdns PLMGR N13 41 G5
Grenville Cl BRYLDS KT5 159 K7
FNCH N3 38 D7
Grenville Gdns WFD IG8 45 G6
Grenville Ms HPTN TW12 142 B4
Grenville Pl MLHL NW7 37 F4
SKENS SW7 14 E5
Grenville Rd ARCH N19 54 E7
Grenville St BMSBY WC1N 11 K1
Gresham Av TRDG/WHET N20 39 K3
Gresham Cl BXLY DA5 137 F5
ENC/FH EN2 29 J2
Gresham Dr CHDH RM6 61 H4
Gresham Gdns CRICK NW2 52 C7
Gresham Rd BECK BR3 166 B1
BRXN/ST SW9 130 B2
CAN/RD E16 95 F5
EDGW HA8 36 B5
EHAM E6 95 K1
HEST TW5 103 H7
HPTN TW12 142 A5
SNWD * SE25 165 H3
WLSDN NW10 69 F4
Gresham St CITYW EC2V 12 E4
Gresham Wy WIM/MER SW19 146 E2
Gresley Cl SEVS/STOTM * N15 55 K3
WALTH E17 57 G5
Gresley Rd ARCH N19 54 C7
Gressenhall Rd
WAND/EARL SW18 127 J5
Gresse St FITZ W1T 11 G3
Gresswell Cl SCUP DA14 155 G2
Greswell St FUL/PGN SW6 107 G7
Gretton Rd TOTM N17 42 A6
Greville Cl TWK TW1 124 C6
Greville Ms KIL/WHAMP NW6 2 C4
Greville Rd KIL/WHAMP NW6 2 C4
RCHPK/HAM TW10 125 G5
WALTH E17 58 A3
Greville St HCIRC EC1N 12 B3
Grey Cl EFNCH N2 53 G5
Greycoat Pl WEST SW1P 17 G4
Greycoat St WEST SW1P 17 G4
Greycot Rd BECK BR3 151 J4
Grey Eagle St WCHPL E1 13 M2
Greyfell Cl STAN HA7 35 H4
Greyhound Hl HDN NW4 51 J2
Greyhound La
STRHM/NOR SW16 148 E5
Greyhound Rd HMSMTH W6 107 G5
SUT SM1 175 G4
TOTM N17 56 A2
WLSDN * NW10 87 K2
Greyhound Ter
STRHM/NOR SW16 148 C7
Greyhound Wy DART DA1 138 B4
Greyladies Gdns
GNWCH * SE10 133 F1
Greys Park Cl HAYES BR2 181 G4
Greystead Rd FSTH SE23 131 K6
Greystoke Av PIN HA5 48 A2
Greystoke Cottages EA * W5 86 A3
Greystoke Gdns EA W5 86 A3
ENC/FH EN2 28 D3
Greystone Gdns BARK/HLT IG6 60 C1
KTN/HRWW/W HA3 49 J5
Greyswood Av UED * N18 43 F4
Greyswood St
STRHM/NOR SW16 148 B5
Grierson Rd FSTH SE23 132 B5
Griffin Centre
EBED/NFELT * TW14 122 A5
Griffin Cl WLSDN NW10 69 K4
Griffin Manor Wy THMD SE28 115 J2
Griffin Rd TOTM N17 56 A1
WOOL/PLUM SE18 115 J4
Griffith Cl CHDH RM6 61 J6
Griffiths Rd WIM/MER SW19 146 E6
Griggs Ap IL IG1 78 C1
Grigg's Pl STHWK SE1 19 K4
Griggs Rd LEY E10 58 A5
Grimsby Gv CAN/RD E16 96 B7
Grimsby St WCHPL E1 13 M1
Grimsdyke Crs BAR EN5 26 A2
Grimsdyke Rd PIN HA5 33 J6
Grimsel Pth CMBW SE5 110 C6
Grimshaw Cl HGT * N6 54 A6
Grimshaw Wy ROM RM1 63 G4
Grimston Rd FUL/PGN SW6 127 J1
Grimwade Av CROY/NA CR0 178 C2
Grimwood Rd TWK TW1 124 A6
Grindall Cl CROY/NA CR0 177 H3
Grindal St STHWK SE1 18 A2
Grindleford Av FBAR/BDGN N11 40 A1
Grindley Gdns CROY/NA * CR0 165 G5
Grinling Pl DEPT SE8 112 D5
Grinstead Rd DEPT SE8 112 B4
Grisle Cl ED N9 42 D3
Grittleton Av WBLY HA9 68 D5
Grittleton Rd MV/WKIL W9 2 A9
Grocers' Hall Ct LOTH * EC2R 13 G5
Groombridge Cl WELL DA16 136 B4
Groombridge Rd HOM E9 75 F6
Groom Cl HAYES BR2 168 A3
Groom Crs WAND/EARL SW18 128 C6
Groomfield Cl TOOT SW17 148 A3
Groom Pl KTBR SW1X 16 B3
Grooms Dr RSLP HA4 46 E4
Grosmont Rd
WOOL/PLUM SE18 116 A4
Grosse Wy PUT/ROE SW15 126 E5
Grosvenor Av CAR SM5 175 K5
HBRY N5 73 J4
MORT/ESHN SW14 126 B2
RYLN/HDSTN HA2 48 B6
YEAD UB4 82 D1
Grosvenor Br PIM SW1V 16 D9
Grosvenor Cottages KTBR SW1X 16 A5
Grosvenor Ct
RKW/CH/CXG * WD3 20 B4
Grosvenor Crs CDALE/KGS NW9 50 C3
DART DA1 139 G4
KTBR SW1X 16 B2
Grosvenor Crescent Ms
KTBR SW1X 16 A2
Grosvenor Gdns BGVA SW1W 16 D4
CRICK NW2 70 A5
GLDGN NW11 52 D5
KUTN/CMB KT2 143 K5
MORT/ESHN SW14 126 B2
MUSWH N10 54 C2
STHGT/OAK N14 28 D4
WFD IG8 44 E5
WLGTN SM6 176 C6
Grosvenor Gardens Ms East
BGVA * SW1W 16 D3
Grosvenor Gardens Ms North
BGVA SW1W 16 C4
Grosvenor Ga BAY/PAD W2 9 M7
Grosvenor Hl MYFR/PKLN W1K 10 C6
WIM/MER SW19 146 C5
Grosvenor Pde EA * W5 86 C7
Grosvenor Pk CMBW SE5 110 D6
Grosvenor Park Rd WALTH E17 57 J4
Grosvenor Pl KTBR SW1X 16 B1
Grosvenor Ri East WALTH E17 57 K4
Grosvenor Rd BCTR RM8 62 B7
BELV DA17 117 G5
BORE WD6 24 C2
BTFD TW8 104 E5
BXLYHS DA6 136 E4
CHSWK W4 105 K4
ED N9 30 D7
FNCH N3 38 D6
FSTGT E7 77 F5
HNWL W7 85 G7
HSLW TW3 122 E2
IL IG1 78 C2
LEY E10 58 A7
MUSWH N10 40 B7
NTHWD HA6 32 D4
NWDGN UB2 102 E2
PIM SW1V 16 D9
PIM SW1V 17 H8
RCHPK/HAM TW10 125 F4
ROMW/RG RM7 63 F6
SNWD SE25 165 H3
STMC/STPC BR5 169 K5
TWK TW1 124 B6
WAN E11 59 F4
WAT WD17 21 G3
WLGTN SM6 176 B5
WWKM BR4 179 K1
Grosvenor Sq MYFR/PKLN W1K 10 B6
Grosvenor St MYFR/PKLN W1K 10 B6
Grosvenor Ter CMBW SE5 110 D6
Grosvenor V RSLP HA4 64 D1
Grosvenor Wy CLPT E5 74 E1
Grosvernor Wharf Rd
POP/IOD E14 113 G3
Grote's Buildings
BKHTH/KID SE3 133 H1
Grote's Pl BKHTH/KID SE3 133 H1
Groton Rd WAND/EARL SW18 147 F1
Grotto Ct STHWK * SE1 18 E1
Grotto Pas MHST W1U 10 A2
Grotto Rd TWK TW1 143 F1
The Grove BXLYHS DA6 136 E3
CDALE/KGS NW9 51 F4
CEND/HSY/T N8 54 D4
EA W5 85 K7
EDGW HA8 36 D3
ENC/FH EN2 29 G1
FNCH N3 38 E6
FSBYPK N4 55 F6
GFD/PVL UB6 84 C5
GLDGN NW11 52 C6
HGT N6 54 A7
ISLW TW7 103 K7
PLMGR N13 41 G3
SRTFD E15 76 C6
TEDD TW11 143 G3
WOT/HER KT12 156 A6
WWKM BR4 180 A2
Grove Av HNWL W7 84 E5
MUSWH N10 54 C1
PIN HA5 47 J3
SUT SM1 174 E5
TWK TW1 124 A7
Grove Bank OXHEY * WD19 21 H7
Grovebury Cl ERITH DA8 118 A5
Grovebury Ct STHGT/OAK N14 28 C6
Grovebury Rd THMD SE28 116 C1
Grove Cl FSTH SE23 132 A7
HAYES BR2 180 E1
KUT KT1 159 F3
STHGT/OAK * N14 28 B6
Grove Cottages CHSWK * W4 106 B5
Grove Ct E/WMO/HCT KT8 157 J4
EA * W5 86 A7
Grove Crs CDALE/KGS NW9 50 E3
FELT TW13 141 J3
KUT KT1 159 F2
SWFD E18 58 D1
WOT/HER KT12 156 A6
Grove Crescent Rd SRTFD E15 76 B5
Grovedale Rd ARCH N19 72 D1
Grove Dwellings WCHPL * E1 92 E4
Grove End KTTN NW5 72 B3
SWFD E18 58 D1
Grove End La ESH/CLAY KT10 157 J7
Grove End Rd STJWD NW8 3 G7
Grove Farm Pk NTHWD HA6 32 B4
Grove Footpath SURB KT6 159 F3
Grove Gdns HDN * NW4 51 J4
STJWD NW8 3 K8
TEDD TW11 143 G3
Grove Green Rd LEY E10 76 A2
Grove Hall Rd BUSH WD23 21 J3
Groveherst Rd DART DA1 139 J2
Grove Hl HRW HA1 48 E6
SWFD E18 58 D1
Grove Hill Rd CMBW SE5 131 F2
HRW HA1 49 F6
Grove House Rd
CEND/HSY/T N8 54 E3
Groveland Av
STRHM/NOR SW16 149 F6
Groveland Ct STP EC4M 12 F5
Groveland Rd BECK BR3 166 C2
Grovelands E/WMO/HCT KT8 157 F3
Grovelands Cl CMBW SE5 131 F1
RYLN/HDSTN HA2 66 B2
Grovelands Rd PLMGR N13 41 F3
SEVS/STOTM N15 56 C5
STMC/STPC BR5 155 G6
Groveland Wy NWMAL KT3 159 K4
Grove La CMBW SE5 110 E7
KUT KT1 159 F3
Groveley Rd SUN TW16 140 D4
Grove Market Pl
ELTH/MOT * SE9 134 E5
Grove Ms HMSMTH W6 107 F2
Grove Pk CDALE/KGS NW9 50 E3
CMBW SE5 131 F1
WAN E11 59 F4
Grove Park Av CHING E4 43 K6
Grove Park Br CHSWK W4 105 K6
Grove Park Gdns CHSWK W4 105 J6
Grove Park Rd CHSWK W4 105 K6
ELTH/MOT SE9 153 J1
RAIN RM13 81 J7
SEVS/STOTM N15 56 A3
Grove Park Ter CHSWK W4 105 J6
Grove Pl ACT W3 86 E7
BAL SW12 129 G5
HAMP NW3 71 H2
Grove Rd ACT W3 86 E7
BARN SW13 126 C1
BELV DA17 117 G5
BOW E3 93 G1
BTFD TW8 104 D4
BXLYHN DA7 137 K3
CHDH RM6 61 J6
CHING E4 44 A2

CRICK NW2 70 A5
E/WMO/HCT KT8 157 J3
EA W5 85 K6
EBAR EN4 27 J2
EDGW HA8 36 C5
FBAR/BDGN N11 40 B4
HOM E9 75 F7
HSLW TW3 123 G3
ISLW TW7 103 K7
MTCM CR4 163 G1
NFNCH/WDSP N12 39 H4
NTHWD HA6 32 B4
PIN HA5 47 K4
RCHPK/HAM TW10 125 G5
SEVS/STOTM N15 56 A4
SURB KT6 158 E4
SUT SM1 174 E5
SWFD E18 58 D1
THHTH CR7 164 B3
WALTH E17 57 K4
WAN E11 58 D6
WHTN TW2 142 D2
WIM/MER SW19 147 G6
Grover Rd *OXHEY* WD19 21 H5
Groveside Cl *ACT* W3 86 C5
CAR SM5 175 J1
Groveside Rd *CHING* E4 44 C2
Grovestile Waye
EBED/NFELT TW14 121 G6
Grove St *BERM/RHTH* SE16 112 C3
UED N18 42 B5
Grove Ter *KTTN* NW5 72 A2
STHL * UB1 84 A6
TEDD TW11 143 G3
Grove V *CHST* BR7 154 A5
EDUL SE22 131 F3
Groveway *BCTR* RM8 79 K3
BRXN/ST SW9 110 A7
Grove Wy *ESH/CLAY* KT10 157 H7
WBLY HA9 68 E4
Grovewood Pl *WFD* IG8 45 K5
Grummant Rd *PECK* SE15 111 G7
Grundy St *POP/IOD* E14 93 K5
Gruneisen Rd *FNCH* N3 39 F6
Guardian Cl *EMPK* RM11 81 K1
Gubyon Av *HNHL* SE24 130 D4
Guernsey Cl *HEST* TW5 103 F7
Guernsey Gv *HNHL* SE24 130 D6
Guernsey Rd *IS* N1 73 J5
LEY E10 58 B7
Guibal Rd *LEE/GVPK* SE12 134 A7
Guildersfield Rd
STRHM/NOR SW16 148 E6
Guildford Av *FELT* TW13 140 E1
Guildford Gv *GNWCH* SE10 112 E7
Guildford Rd *CROY/NA* CR0 164 E5
EHAM E6 95 J5
GDMY/SEVK IG3 78 E1
VX/NE SW8 109 K7
WALTH E17 44 A7
Guildford Wy *WLGTN* SM6 176 E4
Guildhall Buildings
CITYW EC2V 12 F4
Guildhall Yd *CITYW* EC2V 12 F4
Guildhouse St *PIM* SW1V 16 E6
Guildown Av *NFNCH/WDSP* N12 39 F3
Guild Rd *CHARL* SE7 114 C4
ERITH DA8 118 C6
Guildsway *WALTH* E17 43 H7
Guilford Av *BRYLDS* KT5 159 G4
Guilford Pl *BMSBY* WC1N 11 L1
Guilford St *BMSBY* WC1N 11 L1
Guillemot Pl *WDGN* * N22 55 F1
Guilsborough Cl *WLSDN* NW10 69 G6
Guinness Cl *HOM* E9 75 G6
HYS/HAR UB3 101 G2
Guinness Ct *CROY/NA* * CR0 178 B1
Guinness Sq *STHWK* SE1 19 J4
Guinness Trust Est *CHEL* SW3 15 L6
SRTFD * E15 76 D7
STNW/STAM * N16 56 B7
Guion Rd *FUL/PGN* SW6 127 J1
Gulland Cl *BUSH* WD23 22 C4
Gulland Wk *IS* * N1 73 J5
Gull Cl *WLGTN* SM6 176 E6
Gulliver Cl *NTHLT* UB5 65 K7
Gulliver Rd *BFN/LL* DA15 154 D1
Gulliver St *BERM/RHTH* SE16 112 C2
Gumleigh Rd *EA* W5 104 D3
Gumley Gdns *ISLW* TW7 124 B2
Gundulph Rd *HAYES* BR2 168 B2
Gunmakers La *HOM* E9 75 G7
Gunnell Cl *SNWD* SE25 165 G5
SYD * SE26 150 C3
Gunner La *WOOL/PLUM* SE18 115 F4
Gunnersbury Av *ACT* W3 105 H3
Gunnersbury Av
(North Circular Rd)
EA W5 86 B6
Gunnersbury Cl *CHSWK* * W4 105 J4
Gunnersbury Crs *ACT* W3 105 H1
Gunnersbury Dr *EA* W5 105 G1
Gunnersbury Gdns *ACT* W3 105 H1
Gunnersbury La *ACT* W3 105 H1
Gunners Gv *CHING* E4 44 A2
Gunners Rd *WAND/EARL* SW18 147 H1
Gunning St *WOOL/PLUM* SE18 115 K3
Gunstor Rd *STNW/STAM* * N16 74 A3
Gun St *WCHPL* E1 13 L3
Gunter Gv *EDGW* HA8 37 F7
WBPTN SW10 108 B5
Gunterstone Rd *WKENS* W14 107 H4
Gunthorpe St *WCHPL* E1 13 M3
Gunton Rd *CLPT* E5 74 D2
TOOT SW17 148 A5
Gunwhale Cl *BERM/RHTH* SE16 93 F7
Gurdon Rd *CHARL* SE7 113 K4
Gurnell Gv *WEA* W13 85 F3
Gurney Cl *BARK* IG11 78 B5
SRTFD E15 76 C4
WALTH E17 43 F7
Gurney Crs *CROY/NA* CR0 164 A7
Gurney Dr *EFNCH* N2 53 G4
Gurney Rd *CAR* SM5 176 A3
FUL/PGN SW6 128 B2
NTHLT UB5 83 F2
SRTFD E15 76 C4
Guthrie St *CHEL* SW3 15 J7
Gutter La *CITYW* EC2V 12 E4
Guyatt Gdns *MTCM* CR4 163 F1
Guy Barnett Gv
BKHTH/KID SE3 133 K2
Guy Rd *CROY/NA* CR0 176 E2
Guyscliff Rd *LEW* SE13 133 F4
Guysfield Cl *RAIN* RM13 81 J7
Guysfield Dr *RAIN* RM13 81 J7
Guy St *STHWK* SE1 19 H1
Gwalior Rd *PUT/ROE* SW15 127 G3
Gwendolen Av *PUT/ROE* SW15 127 G4
Gwendoline Av *PLSTW* E13 77 F7
Gwendwr Rd *WKENS* W14 107 H4
Gweneth Cottages *EDGW* * HA8 36 C5
Gwillim Cl *BFN/LL* DA15 136 B5
Gwydor Rd *BECK* BR3 166 A3
Gwydyr Rd *HAYES* BR2 167 J2
Gwyn Cl *FUL/PGN* SW6 108 B6
Gwynne Av *CROY/NA* CR0 166 A6
Gwynne Park Av *WFD* IG8 45 K5
Gwynne Rd *BTSEA* SW11 128 C1
Gwynne Whf *CHSWK* W4 106 C5
Gylcote Cl *CMBW* SE5 130 E3
Gyles Pk *STAN* HA7 35 J7
Gyllyngdune Gdns
GDMY/SEVK IG3 79 F2

H

Haarlem Rd *WKENS* W14 107 G2
Haberdasher Pl *IS* N1 7 H7
Haberdasher St *IS* N1 7 H7
Haccombe Rd *WIM/MER* SW19 147 G5
Hackbridge Park
Gdns *CAR* SM5 175 K1
Hackbridge Rd *CAR* SM5 176 A1
Hackford Rd *BRXN/ST* SW9 110 A7
Hackford Wk *BRXN/ST* SW9 110 A7
Hackforth Cl *BAR* EN5 25 K4
Hackington Crs *BECK* BR3 151 J5
Hackney Cl *BORE* WD6 25 F4
Hackney Gv *HACK* E8 74 D5
Hackney Rd *BETH* E2 7 L7
Haddenham Ct *OXHEY* * WD19 33 H2
Hadden Rd *THMD* SE28 115 K2
Hadden Wy *GFD/PVL* UB6 66 D5
Haddington Rd *BMLY* BR1 152 B2
Haddon Cl *BORE* WD6 24 C1
EN EN1 30 C5
NWMAL KT3 160 C4
Haddon Gv *BFN/LL* DA15 136 B6
Haddon Rd *SUT* SM1 175 F3
Haddo St *GNWCH* SE10 112 E5
Hadfield Cl *STHL* UB1 83 K2
Hadfield Rd *STWL/WRAY* TW19 120 A5
Hadleigh Cl *RYNPK* SW20 161 J1
WCHPL E1 92 E3
Hadleigh Dr *BELMT* SM2 174 E7
Hadleigh Rd *ED* N9 30 D6
Hadleigh St *BETH* E2 92 E3
Hadley Cl *BORE* WD6 24 B4
WCHMH N21 29 G5
Hadley Common *BAR* EN5 27 G1
Hadley Gdns *CHSWK* W4 106 A4
NWDGN UB2 102 E4
Hadley Gn *BAR* EN5 26 D2
Hadley Green Rd *BAR* EN5 26 D1
Hadley Gn West *BAR* EN5 26 C1
Hadley Gv *BAR* EN5 26 C1
Hadley Pde *BAR* * EN5 26 C2
Hadley Rdg *BAR* EN5 26 D2
Hadley Rd *BAR* EN5 27 F2
BELV DA17 117 G3
MTCM CR4 163 J3
Hadley St *KTTN* NW5 72 B5
Hadley Wy *WCHMH* N21 29 G5
Hadley Wood Rd *BAR* EN5 26 E1
Hadlow Rd *SCUP* DA14 155 G3
WELL DA16 116 D6
Hadrian Cl *STWL/WRAY* TW19 120 B6
Hadrian Est *BETH* * E2 92 C1
Hadrian's Ride *EN* EN1 30 B4
Hadrian St *GNWCH* SE10 113 H4
Hadrian Wy *STWL/WRAY* TW19 120 B6
Hadyn Park Rd *SHB* W12 106 D1
Hafer Rd *BTSEA* SW11 128 E3
Hafton Rd *CAT* SE6 133 H7
Hagden La *WATW* WD18 20 D3
Haggard Rd *TWK* TW1 124 C6
Hagger Ct *WALTH* * E17 58 B2
Haggerston Rd *HACK* E8 7 L2
Hague St *BETH* E2 92 C2
Ha-ha Rd *WOOL/PLUM* SE18 114 E5
Haig Rd *STAN* HA7 35 J4
Haig Rd East *PLSTW* E13 95 G2
Haig Rd West *PLSTW* E13 95 G2
Haigville Gdns *BARK/HLT* IG6 60 B3
Hailes Cl *WIM/MER* SW19 147 G5
Haileybury Av *EN* EN1 30 B5
Hailey Rd *ERITHM* DA18 117 H1
Hailsham Av *BRXS/STRHM* SW2 149 F1
Hailsham Cl *SURB* KT6 158 E6
Hailsham Dr *HRW* HA1 48 D2
Hailsham Rd *TOOT* SW17 148 A5
Hailsham Ter *PLMGR* * N13 41 K4
Haimo Rd *ELTH/MOT* SE9 134 C4
Hainault Buildings *LEY* * E10 58 A7
Hainault Gore *CHDH* RM6 62 A4
Hainault Rd *CHDH* RM6 62 B5
ROM RM1 63 F2
WAN E11 58 A7
Hainault St *ELTH/MOT* SE9 135 G7
IL IG1 78 B1
Haines Wk *MRDN* SM4 162 A6
Hainford Cl *BROCKY* SE4 132 A3
Haining Cl *CHSWK* W4 105 H4
Hainthorpe Rd *WNWD* SE27 149 H2
Hainton Cl *WCHPL* E1 92 D5
Halbutt St *DAGW* RM9 80 B3
Halcomb St *IS* N1 7 J4
Halcot Av *BXLYHS* DA6 137 J4
Halcrow St *WCHPL* * E1 92 D4
Haldane Cl *MUSWH* N10 40 B6
Haldane Pl *WAND/EARL* SW18 128 A7
Haldane Rd *EHAM* E6 95 H2
FUL/PGN SW6 107 J6
STHL UB1 84 C6
THMD SE28 97 K6
Haldan Rd *CHING* E4 44 A5
Haldon Rd *WAND/EARL* SW18 127 J5
The Hale *CHING* E4 44 B6
TOTM N17 56 C2
Hale Cl *CHING* E4 44 A2
EDGW HA8 36 E4
Hale Dr *EDGW* HA8 36 E5
Hale End Cl *RSLP* HA4 46 E5
Hale End Rd *WALTH* E17 44 B7
Halefield Rd *TOTM* N17 42 C7
Hale Gdns *ACT* W3 86 C7
TOTM N17 56 C2
Hale Grove Gdns *MLHL* NW7 37 F4
Hale La *EDGW* HA8 36 E4
Hale Rd *EHAM* E6 95 J3
TOTM N17 56 C2
Halesowen Rd *MRDN* SM4 162 A6
Hales St *DEPT* SE8 112 D6
Hale St *POP/IOD* E14 93 K6
Halesworth Rd *LEW* SE13 132 E2
Haley Rd *HDN* NW4 52 A5
Half Acre *BTFD* TW8 104 E5
Half Acre Ms *BTFD* TW8 104 E6
Half Acre Rd *HNWL* W7 84 E7
Half Moon Crs *IS* N1 5 M5
Half Moon La *HNHL* SE24 130 E5
Half Moon Pas *WCHPL* E1 13 M5
Half Moon St *MYFR/PICC* W1J 10 D8
Halford Cl *EDGW* HA8 50 D1
Halford Rd *FUL/PGN* SW6 107 K5
RCHPK/HAM TW10 125 F4
WALTH E17 58 B4
Halfway Ct *PUR* RM19 119 K3
Halfway St *BFN/LL* DA15 135 K7
Haliburton Rd *TWK* TW1 124 B4
Haliday Wk *IS* N1 73 K5
Halifax Cl *TEDD* TW11 142 E5
Halifax Rd *ENC/FH* EN2 29 J1
GFD/PVL UB6 66 B7
Halifax St *SYD* SE26 150 D2
Halifield Dr *BELV* DA17 117 F2
Haling Gv *SAND/SEL* CR2 177 J6
Haling Park Gdns
SAND/SEL CR2 177 H5
Haling Park Rd *SAND/SEL* CR2 177 H5
Haling Rd *SAND/SEL* CR2 177 K5
Halkin Ar *KTBR* SW1X 16 A3
Halkin Ms *KTBR* * SW1X 16 A3
Halkin Pl *KTBR* SW1X 16 A3
Halkin St *KTBR* SW1X 16 B2
The Hall *BKHTH/KID* SE3 133 K2
Hallam Cl *CHST* BR7 153 K4
WATN WD24 21 G1
Hallam Gdns *PIN* HA5 33 J6
Hallam Ms *REGST* W1B 10 D2
Hallam Rd *SEVS/STOTM* N15 55 H3
Hallam St *GTPST* W1W 10 D2
Halland Wy *NTHWD* HA6 32 B5
Hall Cl *EA* W5 86 A4
Hall Ct *TEDD* TW11 143 F4
Hall Dr *SYD* SE26 150 E4
Halley Rd *FSTGT* E7 77 G5
Halley St *POP/IOD* E14 93 G4
Hall Farm Cl *STAN* HA7 35 H3
Hall Farm Dr *WHTN* TW2 123 J6
Hallfield Est *BAY/PAD* W2 8 D5
Hallford Wy *DART* DA1 139 F5
Hall Gdns *CHING* E4 43 H3
Hall Ga *STJWD* NW8 2 F8
Halliday Sq *NWDGN* UB2 84 D7
Halliford St *IS* N1 6 F1
Halliwell Rd *BRXS/STRHM* SW2 130 A5
Halliwick Court Pde
FBAR/BDGN * N11 39 K4
Halliwick Rd *MUSWH* N10 40 A7
Hall La *CHING* E4 43 H4
HDN NW4 51 J1
HYS/HAR UB3 101 G6
Hallmead Rd *SUT* SM1 175 F2
Hall Oak Wk *KIL/WHAMP* NW6 70 D5
Hallowell Av *CROY/NA* CR0 176 E3
Hallowell Cl *MTCM* CR4 163 F2
Hallowell Rd *NTHWD* HA6 32 C6
Hallowes Crs *OXHEY* WD19 32 E2
Hallowfield Wy *MTCM* CR4 162 C2
Hall Pl *BAY/PAD* W2 9 G1
Hall Place Crs *BXLY* DA5 137 K4
Hall Rd *CHDH* RM6 61 J5
DART DA1 139 J3
EHAM E6 77 K7
GPK RM2 63 K2
ISLW TW7 123 J4
STJWD NW8 2 F8
WAN E11 76 B3
WLGTN SM6 176 B7
Hall St *FSBYE* EC1V 6 D7
NFNCH/WDSP N12 39 G4
Hallsville Rd *CAN/RD* E16 94 D5
Hallswelle Pde *GLDGN* * NW11 52 D4
Hallswelle Rd *GLDGN* NW11 52 D4
Hall Vw *ELTH/MOT* SE9 153 H1
Hallywell Crs *EHAM* E6 95 K4
Halons Rd *ELTH/MOT* SE9 135 F6
Halpin Pl *WALW* SE17 19 H6
Halsbrook Rd *BKHTH/KID* SE3 134 B2
Halsbury Cl *STAN* HA7 35 H4
Halsbury Rd *SHB* W12 87 K7
Halsbury Rd East *NTHLT* UB5 66 C3
Halsbury Rd West *NTHLT* UB5 66 B4
Halsend *HYS/HAR* * UB3 83 F7
Halsey Rd *WATW* WD18 21 F2
Halsey St *CHEL* SW3 15 L5
Halsham Crs *BARK* IG11 79 F5
Halsmere Rd *CMBW* SE5 110 C7
Halstead Cl *CROY/NA* CR0 177 J2
Halstead Gdns *WCHMH* N21 29 K7
Halstead Rd *EN* EN1 30 A3
ERITH DA8 118 B7
WAN E11 59 F4
WCHMH N21 29 K7
Halstow Rd *GNWCH* SE10 113 K4
WLSDN NW10 88 B2
Halsway *HYS/HAR* UB3 82 E7
Halter Cl *BORE* WD6 25 F4
Halton Cl *FBAR/BDGN* N11 39 K5
Halton Cross St *IS* * N1 6 D3
Halton Pl *IS* * N1 6 E3
Halton Rd *IS* N1 6 D2
Halt Pde *CDALE/KGS* * NW9 51 F3
Halt Robin Rd *BELV* DA17 117 H3
The Ham *BTFD* TW8 104 D6
Hambalt Rd *CLAP* SW4 129 H4
Hamble Cl *RSLP* HA4 64 C1
Hambledon Ct *EA* * W5 86 A6
Hambledon Gdns *SNWD* SE25 165 G2
Hambledon Pl *DUL* SE21 131 G7
Hambledon Rd
WAND/EARL SW18 127 J6
Hambledown Rd
ELTH/MOT * SE9 135 J6
Hamble St *FUL/PGN* SW6 128 A2
Hambleton Cl *WPK* KT4 174 A1
Hambro Av *HAYES* BR2 167 K7
Hambrook Rd *SNWD* SE25 165 J2
Hambro Rd *STRHM/NOR* SW16 148 D5
Hambrough Rd *STHL* UB1 83 J7
Ham Common
RCHPK/HAM TW10 143 K2
Hamden Crs *DAGE* RM10 80 D2
Hamel Cl *KTN/HRWW/W* HA3 49 K3
Hameway *EHAM* E6 96 A3
Ham Farm Rd
RCHPK/HAM TW10 143 K3
Hamfrith Rd *SRTFD* E15 76 D5
Ham Gate Av
RCHPK/HAM TW10 144 B3
Hamilton Av *BARK/HLT* IG6 60 B3
CHEAM SM3 174 C1
ED N9 30 C6
ROM RM1 63 F1
SURB KT6 172 C1
Hamilton Cl *BERM/RHTH* SE16 112 B1
EBAR EN4 27 J3
FELT TW13 140 D4
STJWD NW8 3 G8
TOTM N17 56 B2
Hamilton Ct *EA* W5 86 B6
Hamilton Crs *HSLW* TW3 123 G4
PLMGR N13 41 G3
RYLN/HDSTN HA2 65 K2
Hamilton Gdns *STJWD* NW8 2 F7
Hamilton Pde *FELT* * TW13 140 E3
Hamilton Pk *HBRY* N5 73 H3
Hamilton Pk West *HBRY* N5 73 H3
Hamilton Pl *MYFR/PKLN* W1K 10 B9
SUN TW16 141 F6
Hamilton Rd *BFN/LL* DA15 155 G3
BTFD TW8 104 E5
BXLYHN DA7 137 F1
CHSWK W4 106 B2
EA W5 86 A6
EBAR EN4 27 J3
ED N9 30 C6
EFNCH N2 53 G2
FELT TW13 140 C4
GLDGN NW11 52 B6
GPK RM2 63 K4
HRW HA1 48 E4
HYS/HAR UB3 83 F6
IL IG1 78 B3
OXHEY WD19 33 F2
SRTFD E15 94 C2
STHL UB1 83 K7
THHTH CR7 164 E2
WALTH E17 57 G1
WHTN * TW2 123 K7
WIM/MER SW19 147 F6
WLSDN NW10 69 J4
WNWD SE27 149 K3
Hamilton Road Ms
WIM/MER SW19 147 F6
Hamilton Sq
NFNCH/WDSP * N12 39 G5
Hamilton St *DEPT* SE8 112 D5
WATW WD18 21 G4
Hamilton Ter *STJWD* NW8 2 E6
Hamilton Wy *FNCH* N3 38 E5
PLMGR N13 41 H3
WLGTN SM6 176 D7
Hamlea Cl *BKHTH/KID* SE3 133 K4
The Hamlet *CMBW* SE5 130 E2
Hamlet Cl *LEW* SE13 133 H3
Hamlet Gdns *HMSMTH* W6 106 D3
Hamlet Rd *NRWD* SE19 150 B6
Hamlet Sq *CRICK* NW2 70 C2
Hamlets Wy *BOW* E3 93 H3
Hamlet Wy *STHWK* SE1 19 H2
Hamlin Crs *PIN* HA5 47 G4
Hamlyn Cl *EDGW* HA8 36 A2
Hamlyn Gdns *NRWD* SE19 150 A6
Hammelton Rd *BMLY* BR1 152 E7
Hammers La *MLHL* NW7 37 J3
Hammersmith Br *HMSMTH* W6 106 E4
Hammersmith Bridge Rd
BARN SW13 106 E5
Hammersmith Broadway
HMSMTH W6 107 F3
Hammersmith Emb
BARN * SW13 107 F4
Hammersmith F/O
HMSMTH W6 107 F4
Hammersmith Gv
HMSMTH W6 107 F2
Hammersmith Rd
HMSMTH W6 107 F3
Hammersmith Ter
HMSMTH * W6 106 D4
Hammet Cl *YEAD* UB4 83 H4
Hammett St *TWRH* EC3N 13 L6
Hammond Av *MTCM* CR4 163 G1
Hammond Cl *GFD/PVL* UB6 66 D4
HPTN TW12 142 A7
Hammond Rd *EN* EN1 30 D2
NWDGN UB2 102 D2
Hammonds Cl *BCTR* RM8 79 J2
Hammond St *KTTN* NW5 72 C5
Hamond Cl *SAND/SEL* CR2 177 H7
Hamonde Cl *EDGW* HA8 36 D1
Hamond Sq *IS* N1 7 J5
Ham Park Rd *FSTGT* E7 76 E6
Hampden Av *BECK* BR3 166 B1
Hampden Cl *CAMTN* NW1 5 H6
Hampden Gurney St *MBLAR* W1H 9 L5
Hampden La *TOTM* N17 42 B7
Hampden Rd *ARCH* N19 72 D1
BECK BR3 166 B1
CEND/HSY/T N8 55 G3
KTN/HRWW/W HA3 34 C7
KUT KT1 159 H2
MUSWH N10 40 A6
TOTM N17 42 C7
Hampden Wy *STHGT/OAK* N14 28 B7
Hampermill La *OXHEY* WD19 20 E7
Hampshire Cl *UED* N18 42 D4
Hampshire Hog La
HMSMTH * W6 106 E3
Hampshire Rd *WDGN* N22 41 F6
Hampshire St *KTTN* * NW5 72 D5
Hampson Wy *VX/NE* SW8 110 A7
Hampstead Cl *THMD* SE28 97 H7
Hampstead Gdns *GLDGN* NW11 52 E5
Hampstead Ga *HAMP* NW3 71 G4
Hampstead Gn *HAMP* NW3 71 J4
Hampstead Gv *HAMP* NW3 71 G3
Hampstead Hill Gdns
HAMP NW3 71 J3
Hampstead La *HGT* N6 53 K6
Hampstead Rd *CAMTN* NW1 4 E6
Hampstead Sq *HAMP* NW3 71 G2
Hampstead Wy *GLDGN* NW11 52 E4
Hampton Cl *FBAR/BDGN* N11 40 A4
KIL/WHAMP NW6 2 A8
RYNPK * SW20 146 A6
Hampton Ct *IS* N1 73 H5
Hampton Court Av
E/WMO/HCT KT8 157 J5
Hampton Court Crs
E/WMO/HCT * KT8 157 J2
Hampton Court Est
THDIT * KT7 157 K4
Hampton Court Rd
HPTN TW12 157 J1
Hampton Court Wy
E/WMO/HCT KT8 157 K3
Hampton La *FELT* TW13 141 J3
Hampton Ri *KTN/HRWW/W* HA3 50 A5
Hampton Rd *CHING* E4 43 H4
CROY/NA CR0 164 D5
FSTGT E7 77 F4
HPTN TW12 142 D4
IL IG1 78 C3
WAN E11 58 B7
WPK KT4 173 J1
Hampton Rd East *FELT* TW13 141 K3
Hampton Rd West *FELT* TW13 141 J1
Hampton St *WALW* SE17 18 D6
Ham Ridings
RCHPK/HAM TW10 144 B4
Ham Shades Cl *BFN/LL* DA15 155 F2
Ham St *RCHPK/HAM* TW10 143 J1
Ham Vw *CROY/NA* CR0 166 B5
Ham Yd *SOHO/SHAV* * W1D 11 G6
Hanameel St *CAN/RD* E16 94 E7
Hanbury Cl *HDN* NW4 52 A2
Hanbury Ct *HRW* * HA1 49 F5
Hanbury Dr *WCHMH* N21 29 F3
Hanbury Rd *ACT* W3 105 J1
TOTM N17 56 D1
Hanbury St *WCHPL* E1 92 C4
Hancock Rd *BOW* E3 94 A2
NRWD SE19 149 K5
Handa Wk *IS* N1 73 J5
Hand Ct *HHOL* WC1V 11 M3
Handcroft Rd *CROY/NA* CR0 164 C7
Handel Cl *EDGW* HA8 36 B5
Handel Pde *EDGW* * HA8 36 C5
Handel Pl *WLSDN* NW10 69 F5
Handel St *BMSBY* WC1N 5 K9
Handel Wy *EDGW* HA8 36 C6
Handen Rd *LEW* SE13 133 H4
Handforth Rd *BRXN/ST* SW9 110 B6
IL IG1 78 B2
Handley Gv *CRICK* NW2 70 B2
Handley Page Rd *WLGTN* SM6 177 F6
Handley Rd *HOM* E9 74 E6
Handowe Cl *HDN* NW4 51 J3
Handside Cl *WPK* KT4 161 G7
Handsworth Av *CHING* E4 44 B5
Handsworth Cl *OXHEY* WD19 32 E2
Handsworth Rd *TOTM* N17 55 K2
Handtrough Wy *BARK* IG11 96 B1
Hanford Cl *WAND/EARL* SW18 127 K7
Hangar Ruding *OXHEY* WD19 33 K2
Hangar View Wy *ACT* W3 86 C5
Hanger Gn *EA* W5 86 C3
Hanger La *EA* W5 86 A1
Hanger La (North Circular Rd)
EA W5 86 A2
Hanger Vale La *EA* W5 86 B5
Hankey Pl *STHWK* SE1 19 H2
Hankins La *MLHL* NW7 37 G1
Hanley Gdns *ARCH* N19 55 F7
Hanley Pl *BECK* BR3 151 J6
Hanley Rd *FSBYPK* N4 54 E7
Hannah Cl *BECK* BR3 166 E2
WLSDN * NW10 68 E3
Hannah Mary Wy *STHWK* * SE1 111 H3
Hannan Cl *WLSDN* NW10 68 E3
Hannay La *ARCH* N19 54 D6
Hannell Rd *FUL/PGN* SW6 107 H6
Hannen Rd *WNWD* * SE27 149 H2
Hannibal Rd *STWL/WRAY* TW19 120 B6
WCHPL E1 92 E4
Hannibal Wy *CROY/NA* CR0 177 F4
Hannington Rd *CLAP* SW4 129 G2
Hanover Av *CAN/RD* E16 94 E7
FELT TW13 121 K7
Hanover Cir *HYS/HAR* UB3 82 A5
Hanover Cl *CHEAM* SM3 174 C3
RCH/KEW TW9 105 H6
Hanover Dr *CHST* BR7 154 C3
Hanover Gdns *LBTH* SE11 110 B5
Hanover Pk *PECK* SE15 111 H7
Hanover Pl *COVGDN* WC2E 11 K5
Hanover Rd *SEVS/STOTM* N15 56 B3
WIM/MER SW19 147 G6
WLSDN NW10 70 A6
Hanover Sq *CONDST* W1S 10 D5
Hanover Steps *BAY/PAD* * W2 9 K5
Hanover St *CONDST* W1S 10 D5
CROY/NA CR0 177 H2
Hanover Ter *CAMTN* NW1 3 K8
Hanover Terrace Ms *CAMTN* NW1 3 K8
Hanover Wy *BXLYHN* DA7 136 E2
Hanover Yd *IS* * N1 6 D5
Hansard Ms *NTGHL* W11 107 G1
Hans Crs *CHEL* SW3 15 L3
Hanselin Cl *STAN* HA7 35 F4
Hansen Dr *WCHMH* N21 29 F4
Hanshaw Dr *EDGW* HA8 37 F7
Hansler Gv *E/WMO/HCT* KT8 157 J4
Hansler Rd *EDUL* SE22 131 G4
Hansol Rd *BXLYHS* DA6 137 F4
Hansom Ter *BMLY* * BR1 153 F7
Hanson Cl *BAL* SW12 129 G6
BECK * BR3 151 K5
MORT/ESHN SW14 125 K2
WDR/YW UB7 100 C2
Hanson Gdns *STHL* UB1 102 D1
Hanson St *GTPST* W1W 10 E2
Hans Pl *KTBR* SW1X 15 L3
Hans Rd *CHEL* SW3 15 L3
Hans St *KTBR* SW1X 15 M4
Hanway Pl *FITZ* W1T 11 G4
Hanway Rd *HNWL* W7 84 D5
Hanway St *FITZ* W1T 11 G4
Hanworth Rd *FELT* TW13 122 A7
HPTN TW12 141 K3
HSLW TW3 123 G3
HSLWW TW4 122 E6
SUN TW16 140 E6
Hanworth Ter *HSLW* TW3 123 G3
Hapgood Cl *GFD/PVL* UB6 66 D4
Harben Pde *HAMP* * NW3 3 G1
Harben Rd *KIL/WHAMP* NW6 2 F1
Harberson Rd *BAL* SW12 129 G7
SRTFD E15 76 D7
Harberton Rd *ARCH* N19 54 C7
Harbet Rd *BAY/PAD* W2 9 H3
UED N18 43 F4
Harbex Cl *BXLY* DA5 137 J6
Harbinger Rd *POP/IOD* E14 112 E3
Harbledown Rd *FUL/PGN* SW6 107 K7
Harbord Cl *CMBW* SE5 130 E1
Harbord St *FUL/PGN* SW6 107 G7
Harborne Cl *OXHEY* WD19 33 G4
Harborough Av *BFN/LL* DA15 135 K6
Harborough Rd
STRHM/NOR SW16 149 F3
Harbour Av *WBPTN* SW10 108 B7
Harbour Rd *CMBW* SE5 130 D2
Harbour Yd *WBPTN* * SW10 108 B7
Harbridge Av *PUT/ROE* SW15 126 C6
Harbury Rd *CAR* SM5 175 J7
Harbut Rd *BTSEA* SW11 128 C3
Harcastle Cl *NTHLT* UB5 83 J3
Harcombe Rd *STNW/STAM* N16 74 A2
Harcourt Av *BFN/LL* DA15 136 D5
EDGW HA8 36 E2
MNPK E12 77 K3
WLGTN SM6 176 B3
Harcourt Buildings *EMB* * EC4Y 12 A6

Harcourt Cl ISLW TW7 124 B2
Harcourt Fld WLGTN SM6 176 B3
Harcourt Ms ROM RM1 63 H4
Harcourt Rd BROCKY SE4 132 C3
BUSH WD23 22 C4
BXLYHS DA6 137 F3
SRTFD E15 94 D1
THHTH CR7 164 A5
WDGN N22 40 D7
WIM/MER SW19 146 E6
WLGTN SM6 176 B3
Harcourt St CAMTN NW1 9 K3
Harcourt Ter WBPTN SW10 14 D8
Hardcastle Cl SNWD SE25 165 H5
Hardcourts Cl WWKM BR4 179 K3
Hardel Wk BRXS/STRHM SW2 130 B6
Hardens Manorway
WOOL/PLUM SE18 114 C2
Harders Rd PECK SE15 131 J1
Hardess St HNHL SE24 130 D2
Hardie Cl WLSDN NW10 69 F4
Hardie Rd DAGE RM10 80 E2
Harding Cl CROY/NA CR0 178 B2
KUTN/CMB KT2 144 B7
WALW SE17 18 E9
Hardinge Rd UED N18 42 A4
WLSDN NW10 70 A7
Hardinge St WCHPL E1 92 E5
WOOL/PLUM SE18 115 G2
Harding Rd BXLYHN DA7 137 G1
Hardings La PGE/AN SE20 151 F5
Hardman Rd CHARL SE7 114 A4
KUTN/CMB KT2 159 F1
Hardwick Cl STAN HA7 35 J4
Hardwicke Av HEST * TW5 103 F7
Hardwicke Ms FSBYW * WC1X 5 M8
Hardwicke Rd CHSWK W4 105 K3
PLMGR N13 40 E4
RCHPK/HAM TW10 143 J3
Hardwicke St BARK IG11 78 C7
Hardwick Gn WEA W13 85 H4
Hardwick St CLKNW EC1R 6 B8
Hardwick's Wy
WAND/EARL SW18 127 K4
Hardwidge St STHWK SE1 19 J1
Hardy Av CAN/RD E16 94 E7
RSLP HA4 65 F4
Hardy Cl BAR EN5 26 C4
BERM/RHTH SE16 112 A1
PIN HA5 47 H6
Hardy Cottages GNWCH * SE10 113 G5
Hardy Gv DART DA1 139 K3
Hardy Pas WDGN N22 41 F7
Hardy Rd BKHTH/KID SE3 113 J5
CHING E4 43 H5
WIM/MER SW19 147 F6
Hare & Billet Rd
BKHTH/KID SE3 113 G7
Harebell Dr EHAM E6 96 A4
Hare Ct EMB * EC4Y 12 A5
Harecourt Rd IS N1 73 J5
Haredale Rd HNHL SE24 130 D3
Haredon Cl FSTH SE23 131 K6
Harefield ESH/CLAY KT10 170 E2
Harefield Av BELMT SM2 174 C7
Harefield Ms BROCKY SE4 132 C2
Harefield Rd BROCKY SE4 132 C2
CEND/HSY/T N8 54 D4
SCUP DA14 155 K1
STRHM/NOR SW16 149 F6
Hare Hall La GPK RM2 63 K3
Hare La ESH/CLAY KT10 170 E5
Hare Marsh BETH E2 92 C3
Hare Rw BETH E2 92 D1
Haresfield Rd DAGE RM10 80 C5
Hare St WOOL/PLUM SE18 115 F2
Hare Wk IS N1 7 K6
Harewood Av NTHLT UB5 65 J6
STJWD NW8 3 K9
Harewood Cl NTHLT UB5 65 K6
Harewood Dr CLAY IG5 59 K1
Harewood Pl CONDST W1S 10 D5
Harewood Rd ISLW TW7 104 A6
OXHEY WD19 33 F1
SAND/SEL CR2 178 A5
WIM/MER SW19 147 J5
Harewood Rw CAMTN NW1 9 K2
Harewood Ter NWDGN UB2 102 E3
Harfield Gdns CMBW * SE5 131 F2
Harfield Rd SUN TW16 156 C1
Harford Cl CHING E4 31 K6
Harford Rd CHING E4 31 K6
Harford St WCHPL E1 93 G3
Harford Wk EFNCH N2 53 H3
Harglaze Ter CDALE/KGS * NW9 51 G2
Hargood Cl KTN/HRWW/W HA3 50 A5
Hargood Rd BKHTH/KID SE3 114 B7
Hargrave Pk ARCH N19 72 C1
Hargrave Rd ARCH N19 72 C1
Hargwyne St BRXN/ST SW9 130 A2
Haringey Pk CEND/HSY/T N8 54 E5
Haringey Rd CEND/HSY/T N8 54 E3
Harington Ter UED * N18 41 K3
Harkett Cl KTN/HRWW/W HA3 49 F1
Harland Av BFN/LL DA15 154 D2
CROY/NA CR0 178 B2
Harland Cl WIM/MER SW19 162 A2
Harland Rd LEE/GVPK SE12 133 K7
Harlech Gdns HEST TW5 102 B5
RSLP HA4 47 H6
Harlech Rd STHGT/OAK N14 40 D2
The Harlequin WAT * WD17 21 G3
Harlequin Av BTFD TW8 104 B5
Harlequin Cl ISLW TW7 123 K4
YEAD UB4 83 H4
Harlequin Ct WEA * W13 85 J6
Harlequin Rd TEDD * TW11 143 H6
Harlescott Rd PECK SE15 132 A3
Harlesden Gdns WLSDN NW10 69 H7
Harlesden Rd WLSDN NW10 69 J7
Harley Cl ALP/SUD * HA0 67 K5
Harley Crs HRW HA1 48 D3
Harleyford BMLY BR1 153 F7
Harleyford Rd LBTH SE11 17 L9
Harley Gdns WBPTN SW10 14 F8
Harley Gv BOW E3 93 H2
Harley Pl CAVSQ/HST W1G 10 C3
Harley Rd HAMP NW3 3 H2
HRW HA1 48 D3
WLSDN NW10 87 G1
Harley St CAVSQ/HST W1G 10 C2
Harley Vls WLSDN * NW10 87 G1
Harlinger St WOOL/PLUM SE18 114 D2
Harlington Cl HYS/HAR UB3 101 F6
Harlington Rd BXLYHN DA7 137 F2
Harlington Rd East
EBED/NFELT TW14 122 A6
Harlington Rd West
EBED/NFELT TW14 122 A5
Harlow Rd PLMGR N13 41 K2
RAIN RM13 81 H7
Harlyn Dr PIN HA5 47 F2
Harman Av WFD IG8 44 D6
Harman Cl CHING E4 44 B3
CRICK NW2 70 C2
STHWK * SE1 111 H4
Harman Dr BFN/LL DA15 136 A5
CRICK NW2 70 C2
Harman Rd EN EN1 30 B4
Harmondsworth La
WDR/YW UB7 100 B5
Harmondsworth Rd
WDR/YW UB7 100 B2
Harmony Cl GLDGN NW11 52 C4
WLGTN SM6 176 E7
Harmony Wy HAYES BR2 167 K1
HDN NW4 52 A3
Harmood Gv CAMTN * NW1 4 C1
Harmood St CAMTN NW1 72 B5
Harmsworth Ms STHWK SE1 18 B4
Harmsworth St WALW SE17 18 C8
Harmsworth Wy
TRDG/WHET N20 26 D7
Harness Rd THMD SE28 116 B1
Harold Av BELV DA17 117 G4
HYS/HAR UB3 101 J2
Harold Rd CEND/HSY/T N8 55 F4
CHING E4 44 A2
NRWD SE19 149 K6
PLSTW E13 77 F7
SEVS/STOTM N15 56 B4
SUT SM1 175 H3
WAN E11 58 C7
WFD IG8 44 E7
WLSDN NW10 87 F2
Haroldstone Rd WALTH E17 57 F4
Harp Cross La MON EC3R 13 J7
Harpenden Rd MNPK E12 77 G1
WNWD SE27 149 H1
Harper Cl STHGT/OAK N14 28 C4
Harper Rd EHAM E6 95 K5
STHWK SE1 18 F3
Harpers Yd ISLW * TW7 124 A1
Harp Island Cl WLSDN NW10 69 F1
Harpley Sq WCHPL E1 92 E3
Harpour Rd BARK IG11 78 C5
Harp Rd HNWL W7 85 F3
Harpsden St BTSEA SW11 109 F7
Harpur St BMSBY WC1N 11 L2
Harraden Rd BKHTH/KID SE3 114 B7
Harrier Cl HCH RM12 81 K5
Harrier Ms THMD SE28 115 J1
Harriers Cl EA W5 86 A6
Harrier Wy EHAM E6 95 K4
Harries Rd YEAD UB4 83 G3
Harriet Cl BRXS/STRHM SW2 130 B6
HACK E8 74 C7
Harriet Gdns CROY/NA CR0 178 C1
Harriet St KTBR SW1X 15 M2
Harriet Wk KTBR SW1X 15 M2
Harriet Wy BUSH WD23 22 D6
Harringay Gdns
CEND/HSY/T N8 55 H3
Harringay Rd CEND/HSY/T N8 55 H4
Harrington Cl CROY/NA CR0 176 E1
WLSDN NW10 69 F2
Harrington Ct MV/WKIL * W9 88 D2
Harrington Gdns SKENS SW7 14 E6
Harrington Hl CLPT E5 56 D7
Harrington Rd SKENS SW7 15 G5
SNWD SE25 165 H3
WAN E11 58 C7
Harrington Sq CAMTN NW1 4 E5
Harrington St CAMTN NW1 4 E7
Harrington Wy
WOOL/PLUM SE18 114 C2
Harriott Cl GNWCH SE10 113 J3
Harris Cl HEST TW5 103 F7
Harrison Cl NTHWD HA6 32 A5
TRDG/WHET N20 27 J7
Harrison Rd DAGE RM10 80 D5
Harrison's Ri CROY/NA CR0 177 H2
Harrison St STPAN WC1H 5 K8
Harrisons Whf PUR RM19 119 K4
Harris Rd BXLYHN DA7 117 F7
DAGW RM9 80 B4
Harris St CMBW SE5 110 E6
WALTH E17 57 H6
Harris Wy SUN TW16 140 C7
Harrods Gn EDGW * HA8 36 C4
Harrogate Rd OXHEY WD19 33 G2
Harrold Rd BCTR RM8 79 H4
Harrow Av EN EN1 30 B5
Harroway Rd BTSEA SW11 128 C1
Harrowby St MBLAR W1H 9 K4
Harrow Cl CHSGTN KT9 171 K6
Harrowdene Cl ALP/SUD HA0 67 K3
Harrowdene Gdns TEDD TW11 143 G6
Harrowdene Rd ALP/SUD HA0 67 K3
Harrow Dr ED N9 30 B7
Harrowes Meade EDGW HA8 36 C2
Harrow Fields Gdns HRW HA1 66 E2
Harrowgate Rd HOM E9 75 G6
Harrow Gn WAN E11 76 C2
Harrow La POP/IOD E14 94 A6
Harrow Manor Wy ABYW SE2 116 D2
THMD SE28 97 J7
Harrow Pk HRW HA1 66 E1
Harrow Pl WCHPL E1 13 K4
Harrow Rd ALP/SUD HA0 67 G3
ALP/SUD HA0 67 J4
ASHF TW15 120 D7
BARK IG11 78 E7
CAR SM5 175 J5
EHAM * E6 77 J7
IL IG1 78 C3
WAN E11 76 D2
WBLY HA9 68 B4
WLSDN NW10 87 K2
Harrow Rd F/O BAY/PAD W2 9 H3
Harrow St CAMTN * NW1 9 K2
Harrow Vw HGDN/ICK UB10 82 A2
HYS/HAR UB3 82 E6
RYLN/HDSTN HA2 48 D2
Harrow View Rd EA W5 85 H3
Harrow Wy OXHEY WD19 33 J2
Harrow Weald Pk
KTN/HRWW/W HA3 34 D5
Hartcliff Ct HNWL * W7 104 A1
Harte Rd HSLW TW3 122 E1
Hartfield Av BORE WD6 24 C3
NTHLT UB5 83 F1
Hartfield Cl BORE WD6 24 C4
Hartfield Crs WIM/MER SW19 146 D6
WWKM BR4 180 E2
Hartfield Gv PGE/AN SE20 150 D7
Hartfield Rd CHSGTN KT9 171 K4
WIM/MER SW19 146 D6
WWKM BR4 180 E3
Hartfield Ter BOW E3 93 J1
Hartford Av KTN/HRWW/W HA3 49 G2
Hartforde Rd BORE WD6 24 C1
Hartford Rd BXLY DA5 137 H5
HOR/WEW KT19 172 C5
Hart Gv ACT W3 86 C7
STHL UB1 84 A4
Hartham Cl HOLWY N7 72 E4
ISLW TW7 104 B7
Hartham Rd HOLWY N7 72 E4
ISLW TW7 104 A7
TOTM N17 56 B1
Harting Rd ELTH/MOT SE9 153 J3
Hartington Cl HRW HA1 66 E3
Hartington Rd CAN/RD E16 95 F5
CHSWK W4 105 J6
NWDGN * UB2 102 D2
TWK TW1 124 C6
VX/NE SW8 109 K7
WALTH E17 57 G5
WEA W13 85 H6
Hartismere Rd FUL/PGN SW6 107 J6
Hartlake Rd HOM E9 75 F5
Hartland Cl EDGW HA8 36 C1
WCHMH N21 29 J5
Hartland Dr EDGW HA8 36 C1
RSLP HA4 65 F2
Hartland Rd CAMTN NW1 4 C1
FBAR/BDGN N11 39 K4
HCH RM12 81 J1
HPTN TW12 142 B3
ISLW TW7 124 B2
KIL/WHAMP NW6 88 D1
MRDN SM4 161 K6
SRTFD E15 76 D6
Hartland Rd Arches
CAMTN * NW1 4 B1
The Hartlands HEST TW5 102 A5
Hartlands Cl BXLY DA5 137 G5
Hartland Wy CROY/NA CR0 179 G1
MRDN SM4 161 J6
Hartley Av EHAM E6 77 J7
MLHL NW7 37 H4
Hartley Cl BMLY BR1 168 E1
MLHL NW7 37 H4
Hartley Rd CROY/NA CR0 164 D6
WAN E11 58 D7
WELL DA16 116 D6
Hartley St BETH E2 92 E2
Hartmann Rd CAN/RD E16 95 H7
Hartnoll St HOLWY N7 73 F4
Harton Cl BMLY BR1 153 H7
Harton Rd ED N9 42 D1
Harton St DEPT SE8 112 D7
Hartsbourne Av BUSH WD23 34 C1
Hartsbourne Cl BUSH WD23 34 D1
Hartsbourne Rd BUSH WD23 34 D1
Harts Cl BUSH WD23 22 A1
Hartscroft CROY/NA CR0 179 G7
Harts Gv WFD IG8 44 E4
Hartshorn Gdns EHAM E6 96 A3
Harts La BARK IG11 78 B6
NWCR SE14 112 B6
Hartslock Dr ABYW SE2 116 E1
Hartsmead Rd ELTH/MOT SE9 153 K1
Hartspring La GSTN WD25 22 A1
Hart Sq MRDN * SM4 162 A4
Hart St MON EC3R 13 K6
Hartsway PEND EN3 30 D3
Hartswood Gdns SHB * W12 106 C2
Hartswood Gn BUSH WD23 34 D1
Hartswood Rd SHB W12 106 C1
Hartsworth Cl PLSTW E13 94 D1
Hartville Rd WOOL/PLUM SE18 115 K3
Hartwell Dr CHING E4 44 A5
Hartwell St HACK E8 74 B5
Harvard Hl CHSWK W4 105 J4
Harvard Rd CHSWK W4 105 J4
ISLW TW7 103 K7
LEW SE13 133 F4
Harvel Crs ABYW SE2 116 E4
Harvest Bank Rd WWKM BR4 180 E2
Harvesters Cl ISLW TW7 123 J4
Harvest La THDIT KT7 158 B5
Harvest Rd BUSH WD23 22 B3
FELT TW13 140 E3
Harvey Dr HPTN TW12 142 B7
Harvey Gdns CHARL SE7 114 C4
Harvey Rd CEND/HSY/T N8 55 F4
CMBW SE5 110 E7
HSLWW TW4 122 E6
IL IG1 78 B4
NTHLT UB5 65 G6
WAN E11 58 C7
Harvey's La ROMW/RG RM7 81 F1
Harvey St IS N1 7 H4
Harvill Rd SCUP DA14 155 K4
Harvington Wk HACK * E8 74 C6
Harvist Rd KIL/WHAMP NW6 88 C1
Harwell Cl RSLP HA4 46 B7
Harwood Av BMLY BR1 168 A1
MTCM CR4 162 D2
Harwood Cl ALP/SUD HA0 67 K3
NFNCH/WDSP N12 39 J5
Harwood Ms FUL/PGN * SW6 108 A6
Harwood Rd FUL/PGN SW6 107 K6
Harwoods Rd WATW WD18 20 E3
Harwood Ter FUL/PGN SW6 108 A7
Hascombe Ter CMBW * SE5 130 E1
Haselbury Rd ED N9 42 A2
Haseley End FSTH * SE23 131 K6
Haselrigge Rd CLAP SW4 129 J3
Haseltine Rd SYD SE26 151 H3
Haselwood Dr ENC/FH EN2 29 H3
Haskard Rd DAGW RM9 79 K3
Hasker St CHEL SW3 15 K5
Haslam Av CHEAM SM3 161 H7
Haslam Cl HGDN/ICK UB10 64 A1
IS N1 6 B1
Haslam St PECK SE15 111 G7
Haslemere Av EBAR EN4 27 K7
HDN NW4 52 B5
HEST TW5 122 B1
HNWL W7 104 B2
MTCM CR4 162 C1
WAND/EARL SW18 147 F1
Haslemere Cl HPTN TW12 141 K4
WLGTN SM6 176 E4
Haslemere Gdns FNCH N3 52 D2
Haslemere Heathrow Est
HSLWW * TW4 122 A1
Haslemere Rd BXLYHN DA7 137 G1
CEND/HSY/T N8 54 E6
GDMY/SEVK IG3 79 F1
THHTH CR7 164 C4
WCHMH N21 41 H1
Hasler Cl THMD SE28 97 H6
Hasluck Gdns BAR EN5 27 G5
Hassard St BETH E2 7 M6
Hassendean Rd
BKHTH/KID SE3 114 A5
Hassett Rd HOM E9 75 F5
Hassocks Cl SYD SE26 150 D2
Hassocks Rd
STRHM/NOR SW16 148 D7
Hassock Wd HAYES BR2 181 H3
Hassop Rd CRICK NW2 70 B3
Hasted Rd CHARL SE7 114 C4
Hastings Av BARK/HLT IG6 60 C3
Hastings Cl ALP/SUD HA0 67 J3
BAR EN5 27 G3
PECK * SE15 111 H6
Hastings Dr SURB KT6 158 D5
Hastings Rd CROY/NA CR0 165 G7
FBAR/BDGN N11 40 C4
GPK RM2 63 K4
HAYES BR2 168 D7
TOTM * N17 55 K2
WEA W13 85 H6
Hastings St STPAN WC1H 5 J8
Hastings Ter SEVS/STOTM * N15 55 J4
Hastings Wy BUSH WD23 21 J3
Hastoe Cl YEAD UB4 83 J3
Hatcham Park Ms NWCR SE14 112 A7
Hatcham Park Rd NWCR SE14 112 A7
Hatcham Rd PECK SE15 111 K5
Hatchard Rd ARCH N19 72 D1
Hatchcroft HDN NW4 51 K2
Hatchers Ms STHWK SE1 19 K2
Hatchett Rd EBED/NFELT TW14 121 F7
Hatch Gv CHDH RM6 62 A3
Hatch La CHING E4 44 B3
WDR/YW UB7 100 A6
Hatch Pl RCHPK/HAM TW10 144 B4
Hatch Rd STRHM/NOR SW16 163 K1
Hatchwoods WFD IG8 44 D3
Hatcliffe Cl BKHTH/KID SE3 133 J2
Hatcliffe St GNWCH SE10 113 J4
Hatfield Cl BARK/HLT IG6 60 B2
BELMT SM2 174 E7
MTCM * CR4 162 C3
Hatfield Ct BKHTH/KID * SE3 113 K6
Hatfield Rd CHSWK W4 106 A1
HNWL W7 85 G7
SRTFD E15 76 C4
Hatfields STHWK SE1 12 B8
Hathaway Cl HAYES BR2 168 E7
RSLP HA4 64 D3
STAN HA7 35 G4
Hathaway Crs MNPK E12 77 K5
Hathaway Gdns CHDH RM6 61 K4
WEA W13 85 F4
Hathaway Rd CROY/NA CR0 164 C6
Hatherleigh Cl CHSGTN KT9 171 K4
MRDN SM4 161 K3
Hatherleigh Rd RSLP HA4 64 E1
Hatherley Crs SCUP DA14 155 G1
Hatherley Gdns CEND/HSY/T N8 54 E5
EHAM E6 95 H2
Hatherley Gv BAY/PAD W2 8 C4
Hatherley Rd RCH/KEW TW9 105 G7
SCUP DA14 155 G2
WALTH E17 57 H3
Hatherley St WEST SW1P 16 F6
Hathern Gdns ELTH/MOT SE9 154 A3
Hatherop Rd HPTN TW12 141 K6
Hathorne Cl PECK SE15 131 J1
Hathorne Ter ARCH * N19 54 D7
Hathway St PECK SE15 131 K1
Hatley Av BARK/HLT IG6 60 C3
Hatley Cl FBAR/BDGN N11 39 K4
Hatley Rd HOLWY N7 73 F1
Hat & Mitre Ct FARR EC1M 12 D1
Hatteraick St
BERM/RHTH SE16 111 K1
Hattersfield Cl BELV DA17 117 G3
Hatters La WATW WD18 20 B5
Hatton Cl WOOL/PLUM SE18 115 J6
Hatton Cross Est
HTHAIR * TW6 121 J3
Hatton Gdn CLKNW EC1R 12 B1
Hatton Gdns MTCM CR4 162 E4
Hatton Gn EBED/NFELT TW14 121 K3
Hatton Gv WDR/YW * UB7 100 A1
Hatton Pl HCIRC EC1N 12 B1
Hatton Rd CROY/NA CR0 164 B7
EBED/NFELT TW14 121 F6
HTHAIR TW6 121 J3
Hatton Rd North HTHAIR TW6 101 G7
Hatton Rw STJWD * NW8 9 H1
Hatton St STJWD NW8 9 H1
Hatton Wall HCIRC EC1N 12 A2
Haunch of Venison Yd
MYFR/PKLN W1K 10 C5
Havana Cl ROM RM1 63 G4
Havana Rd WIM/MER SW19 146 E1
Havannah St POP/IOD E14 112 D1
Havant Rd WALTH E17 58 A2
Havelock Cl SHB * W12 87 K6
Havelock Pl HRW HA1 48 E5
Havelock Rd BELV * DA17 117 G3
CROY/NA CR0 178 B1
DART DA1 138 E6
HAYES BR2 168 B3
KTN/HRWW/W HA3 48 E2
NWDGN UB2 102 D2
TOTM N17 56 C1
WIM/MER SW19 147 G4
Havelock St IL IG1 78 B1
IS N1 5 K3
Havelock Ter VX/NE SW8 109 G6
Havelock Wk FSTH SE23 131 K7
The Haven RCH/KEW TW9 125 H2
SUN TW16 140 E6
Haven Cl ELTH/MOT SE9 153 K2
SCUP DA14 155 J5
WIM/MER SW19 146 B2
YEAD UB4 82 C4
Haven Ct BRYLDS * KT5 159 G5
Haven Gn EA W5 85 K6
Havenhurst Ri ENC/FH EN2 29 G1
Haven La EA W5 86 A5
Haven St CAMTN * NW1 4 C2
Havenwood WBLY HA9 68 D2
Haverfield Est BTFD TW8 105 F5
Haverfield Gdns
RCH/KEW TW9 105 H6
Haverfield Rd BOW E3 93 F2
Haverford Wy EDGW HA8 36 B7
Havergal Vls CEND/HSY/T * N8 55 H3
Haverhill Rd BAL SW12 129 H7
Havering Dr ROM RM1 63 G3
Havering Gdns CHDH RM6 61 J4
Havering Rd ROM RM1 63 F2
Havering St WCHPL E1 93 F5
Havering Wy BARK IG11 97 H2
Haversham Cl TWK TW1 124 E6
Haverstock Hl HAMP NW3 71 J5
Haverstock Pl IS N1 6 B6
Haverstock Rd KTTN NW5 72 A4
Haverstock St IS N1 6 D6
Havil St CMBW SE5 111 F7
Havisham Pl NRWD SE19 149 H5
Hawarden Gv HNHL SE24 130 D6
Hawarden Hl CRICK NW2 69 J2
Hawarden Rd WALTH E17 57 F3
Hawbridge Rd WAN E11 58 B7
Hawes Cl NTHWD HA6 32 D6
Hawes La WWKM BR4 167 F7
Hawes Rd BMLY BR1 153 F7
UED N18 42 D5
Hawes St IS N1 6 D2
Hawgood St BOW E3 93 J4
Hawkdene CHING E4 31 K5
Hawke Park Rd WDGN N22 55 H2
Hawke Pl BERM/RHTH * SE16 112 A1
Hawke Rd NRWD SE19 149 K5
Hawkesbury Rd
PUT/ROE SW15 126 E4
Hawkesfield Rd FSTH SE23 151 G1
Hawkesley Cl TWK TW1 143 G3
Hawkes Rd EBED/NFELT TW14 121 K6
MTCM CR4 147 J7
Hawkesworth Cl NTHWD HA6 32 C6
Hawkewood Rd SUN TW16 156 A2
Hawkhurst Rd
STRHM/NOR SW16 148 D7
Hawkhurst Wy NWMAL KT3 160 A4
WWKM BR4 179 K1
Hawkins Cl BORE WD6 24 E1
EDGW HA8 37 F4
HRW HA1 48 D6
Hawkins Rd TEDD TW11 143 H5
Hawkins Wy CAT SE6 151 J4
Hawkley Gdns WNWD SE27 149 H1
Hawkridge Cl CHDH RM6 61 J5
Hawksbrook La BECK BR3 166 E5
Hawkshead Cl BMLY BR1 152 C6
Hawkshead Rd CHSWK W4 106 B2
WLSDN * NW10 69 H6
Hawkshill Cl ESH/CLAY KT10 170 A5
Hawkshill Pl ESH/CLAY * KT10 170 A5
Hawkslade Rd PECK SE15 132 A4
Hawksley Rd STNW/STAM N16 73 K2
Hawks Ms GNWCH * SE10 113 F6
Hawksmoor Cl EHAM E6 95 J5
WOOL/PLUM SE18 115 K4
Hawksmoor Ms WCHPL E1 92 D6
Hawksmoor St HMSMTH W6 107 G5
Hawksmouth CHING E4 31 K6
Hawks Rd KUT KT1 159 G1
Hawkstone Rd
BERM/RHTH SE16 111 K3
Hawkwell Wk IS * N1 6 F3
Hawkwood Crs CHING E4 31 K5
Hawkwood La CHST BR7 154 C7
Hawkwood Mt CLPT E5 56 D7
Hawlands Dr PIN HA5 47 J6
Hawley Cl HPTN TW12 141 K5
Hawley Crs CAMTN NW1 4 D2
Hawley Rd CAMTN NW1 4 D1
UED N18 43 F4
Hawley St CAMTN NW1 4 C2
Hawstead Rd LEW SE13 132 E5
Hawthorn Av PLMGR N13 40 E4
RAIN RM13 99 K3
THHTH CR7 149 H7
Hawthorn Cl HEST TW5 102 A6
HPTN TW12 142 A4
STMC/STPC BR5 169 J5
Hawthornden Cl
NFNCH/WDSP N12 39 J5
Hawthorndene Cl HAYES * BR2 180 D1
Hawthorndene Rd HAYES BR2 180 E1
Hawthorn Dr RYLN/HDSTN HA2 48 A5
WWKM BR4 180 C3
Hawthorne Av CAR SM5 176 A6
HOM E9 75 H7
HRW HA1 49 G5
MTCM CR4 162 C1
RSLP HA4 47 F5
Hawthorne Cl BMLY BR1 168 E2
IS N1 74 A5
Hawthorne Ct
STWL/WRAY * TW19 120 A6
Hawthorne Crs WDR/YW UB7 100 C1
Hawthorne Gv CDALE/KGS NW9 50 E6
Hawthorne Rd BMLY BR1 168 E2
UED N18 42 B5
WALTH E17 57 J2
Hawthorne Wy ED N9 42 B1
Hawthorn Farm Av NTHLT UB5 65 J7
Hawthorn Gdns EA W5 104 E2
Hawthorn Gv PGE/AN SE20 150 D7
Hawthorn Hatch BTFD TW8 104 C6
Hawthorn Ms HDN NW4 38 C7
Hawthorn Pl ERITH DA8 117 K4
HYS/HAR * UB3 82 D6
Hawthorn Rd BKHH IG9 45 G3
BTFD TW8 104 C6
BXLYHS * DA6 137 G3
CEND/HSY/T N8 54 D2
SUT SM1 175 H4
WLGTN SM6 176 B6
WLSDN NW10 69 J6
The Hawthorns EW KT17 173 H5
Hawthorns WFD IG8 44 E2
Hawthorn Ter BFN/LL DA15 136 A5
Hawthorn Wk NKENS W10 88 C3
Hawtrey Av NTHLT UB5 83 H1
Hawtrey Dr RSLP HA4 46 E6
Hawtrey Rd HAMP NW3 3 J2
Haxted Rd BMLY BR1 153 F7
Hayburn Wy HCH RM12 63 H7
Hay Cl BORE WD6 24 E1
SRTFD E15 76 C6
Haycroft Gdns WLSDN NW10 69 J7
Haycroft Rd BRXS/STRHM SW2 129 K4
SURB KT6 171 K1
Hay Currie St POP/IOD E14 93 K5
Hayday Rd CAN/RD E16 94 E4
Hayden Dell BUSH WD23 21 K5
Hayden's Pl NTGHL W11 88 D5
Hayden Wy CRW RM5 62 E1
Haydock Av NTHLT UB5 66 A5
Haydock Gn NTHLT UB5 66 A5
Haydon Cl CDALE/KGS NW9 50 E3
EN EN1 30 A5
Haydon Dell Farm BUSH * WD23 21 K6
Haydon Dr PIN HA5 46 E3
Haydon Park Rd
WIM/MER SW19 146 E4
Haydon Rd BCTR RM8 79 J1
OXHEY WD19 21 J5
Haydon's Rd WIM/MER SW19 147 F4
Haydon St TWRH EC3N 13 L6
Haydon Wk WCHPL E1 13 L5
Haydon Wy BTSEA SW11 128 B3
Hayes Cha WWKM BR4 167 G5
Hayes Cl HAYES BR2 180 E1
Hayes Crs CHEAM SM3 174 B3

GLDGN NW11 52 D4
Hayes Dr RAIN RM13 81 K6
Hayes End Dr YEAD UB4 82 B4
Hayes End Rd YEAD UB4 82 B3
Hayesford Park Dr HAYES BR2 167 J4
Hayes Gdn HAYES BR2 180 E1
Hayes Hl HAYES BR2 167 H7
Hayes Hill Rd HAYES BR2 167 J7
Hayes La BECK BR3 167 G2
HAYES BR2 167 K5
Hayes Mead Rd HAYES BR2 167 H7
Hayes Pl CAMTN NW1 9 K1
Hayes Rd HAYES BR2 167 K3
NWDGN UB2 102 B3
Hayes St HAYES BR2 168 A7
Hayes Wy BECK BR3 167 F3
Hayes Wood Av HAYES BR2 168 A7
Hayfield Cl BUSH WD23 22 B3
Hayfield Pas WCHPL E1 92 E3
Haygarth Pl WIM/MER SW19 146 B4
Haygreen Cl KUTN/CMB KT2 144 D5
Hay Hl MYFR/PICC W1J 10 D7
Hayland Cl CDALE/KGS NW9 51 F3
Hay La CDALE/KGS NW9 51 F3
Hayles St LBTH SE11 18 C5
Haylett Gdns KUT * KT1 158 E3
Hayling Av FELT TW13 140 E2
Hayling Cl STNW/STAM N16 74 A4
Hayling Rd OXHEY WD19 32 D2
Hayman Crs YEAD UB4 82 B1
Haymarket STJS SW1Y 11 G7
Haymeads Dr ESH/CLAY KT10 170 C5
Haymer Gdns WPK KT4 173 J2
Haymerle Rd STHWK SE1 111 H5
Haymill Cl GFD/PVL UB6 85 F2
Hayne Rd BECK BR3 151 H7
Haynes Cl BKHTH/KID SE3 133 H2
FBAR/BDGN N11 40 A2
TOTM N17 42 D6
Haynes Dr ED N9 42 D2
Haynes La NRWD SE19 150 A5
Haynes Rd ALP/SUD HA0 68 A6
Hayne St STBT EC1A 12 D2
Haynt Wk RYNPK SW20 161 H2
Hays La STHWK SE1 13 J8
Haysleigh Gdns PGE/AN SE20 165 H1
Hay's Ms MYFR/PICC W1J 10 C8
Haysoms Cl ROM RM1 63 G3
Haystall Cl YEAD UB4 82 C1
Hay St BETH E2 74 C7
Hayter Rd BRXS/STRHM SW2 129 K4
Hayton Cl HACK E8 74 B5
Hayward Cl DART DA1 138 A4
WIM/MER SW19 147 F6
Hayward Gdns PUT/ROE SW15 127 F5
Hayward Rd THDIT KT7 158 A7
TRDG/WHET N20 39 G1
Haywards Cl CHDH RM6 61 J4
Hayward's Pl CLKNW * EC1R 12 C1
Haywood Cl PIN HA5 47 H1
Haywood Rd HAYES BR2 168 C3
Hazel Av WDR/YW UB7 100 D2
Hazel Bank BRYLDS KT5 159 K7
Hazelbank Rd CAT SE6 152 B1
Hazelbourne Rd BAL SW12 129 G5
Hazelbury Cl WIM/MER SW19 161 K1
Hazelbury Gn ED N9 42 A2
Hazelbury La ED N9 42 A2
Hazel Cl BTFD * TW8 104 C6
CDALE/KGS NW9 51 H1
CROY/NA CR0 166 A6
HCH RM12 81 K4
MTCM CR4 163 J3
PLMGR N13 41 K2
WHTN TW2 123 H6
Hazelcroft PIN HA5 34 A5
Hazeldean Rd WLSDN NW10 69 F6
Hazeldene Dr PIN HA5 47 G2
Hazeldene Gdns
HGDN/ICK UB10 64 A7
Hazeldene Rd BCTR RM8 79 H1
WELL DA16 136 D1
Hazeldon Rd BROCKY SE4 132 B4
Hazel Dr ERITH DA8 118 D7
Hazeleigh Gdns WFD IG8 45 J4
Hazel Gdns EDGW HA8 36 D3
Hazelgreen Cl WCHMH N21 29 H7
Hazel Gv ALP/SUD HA0 68 A7
CHDH RM6 62 A2
EN * EN1 30 C5
SYD SE26 151 F3
Hazelhurst BECK BR3 152 B7
Hazelhurst Rd TOOT SW17 147 G3
Hazellville Rd ARCH N19 54 D6
Hazel Md BAR EN5 25 K4
Hazelmere Cl
EBED/NFELT TW14 121 G5
NTHLT UB5 83 K1
Hazelmere Dr NTHLT UB5 83 K1
Hazelmere Gdns EMPK RM11 63 K4
Hazelmere Rd
KIL/WHAMP NW6 70 D7
NTHLT UB5 83 K1
STMC/STPC BR5 169 H3
Hazelmere Wk NTHLT UB5 83 K1
Hazelmere Wy HAYES BR2 167 K5
Hazel Rd ERITH DA8 118 D7
SRTFD * E15 76 C4
WLSDN NW10 88 A2
Hazel Rw NFNCH/WDSP * N12 39 H4
Hazeltree La NTHLT UB5 83 J2
Hazel Wk HAYES BR2 169 F5
Hazel Wy CHING E4 43 H5
STHWK SE1 19 L5
Hazelwood Av MRDN SM4 162 A3
Hazelwood Cl CLPT E5 75 G2
EA W5 105 F1
RYLN/HDSTN HA2 48 B3
Hazelwood Ct SURB KT6 159 F5
Hazelwood Crs PLMGR N13 41 G3
Hazelwood Dr PIN HA5 47 F1
Hazelwood La PLMGR N13 41 G3
Hazelwood Rd EN EN1 30 B5
RKW/CH/CXG WD3 20 A6
WALTH E17 57 G4
Hazlebury Rd FUL/PGN SW6 128 A1
Hazledean Rd CROY/NA CR0 177 K1
Hazledene Rd CHSWK W4 105 K5
Hazlemere Gdns WPK KT4 160 D7
Hazlewell Rd PUT/ROE SW15 127 F4
Hazlewood Crs NKENS W10 88 C3
Hazlitt Cl FELT TW13 141 J3
Hazlitt Ms WKENS * W14 107 H2
Hazlitt Rd WKENS W14 107 H2
Heacham Av HGDN/ICK UB10 64 A2
Headcorn Rd BMLY BR1 152 D4
THHTH CR7 164 A3
TOTM N17 42 B6
Headfort Pl KTBR SW1X 16 B2
Headington Rd
WAND/EARL SW18 128 B7
Headlam Rd CLAP SW4 129 J6
Headlam St WCHPL E1 92 D3
Headley Ap IL IG1 60 A4
Headley Av WLGTN SM6 177 F4
Headley Cl CHSGTN KT9 172 C5
Headley Dr CROY/NA CR0 180 A6
GNTH/NBYPK IG2 60 B5
Headstone Dr HRW HA1 48 D3
Headstone Gdns
RYLN/HDSTN HA2 48 C3
Headstone La
KTN/HRWW/W HA3 34 B7
RYLN/HDSTN HA2 48 B1
Headstone Pde HRW * HA1 48 D3
Headstone Rd HRW HA1 48 E5
Head St WCHPL E1 93 F5
The Headway EW KT17 173 H7
Headway Cl RCHPK/HAM TW10 143 J3
Heald St NWCR SE14 112 C7
Healey Rd WATW WD18 20 D5
Healey St CAMTN * NW1 72 B5
Hearne Rd CHSWK W4 105 H4
Hearn Ri NTHLT UB5 65 H7
Hearn Rd ROM RM1 63 H5
Hearn's Buildings WALW SE17 19 H6
Hearn St SDTCH EC2A 13 K1
Hearnville Rd BAL SW12 129 F7
The Heath HNWL * W7 103 K1
Heatham Pk WHTN TW2 124 A6
Heath Av BXLYHN DA7 116 E5
Heathbourne Rd STAN HA7 34 E1
Heath Brow HAMP NW3 71 G2
Heath Cl EA W5 86 B3
GLDGN NW11 53 F6
GPK RM2 63 J2
HYS/HAR UB3 101 G6
SAND/SEL CR2 177 H5
Heathclose Av DART DA1 138 E6
Heathclose Rd DART DA1 138 D7
Heathcote Av CLAY IG5 45 K7
Heathcote Gv CHING E4 44 A2
Heathcote Rd TWK TW1 124 C5
Heathcote St BMSBY WC1N 5 L9
Heathcroft EA W5 86 B3
Heathcroft Av SUN TW16 140 D6
Heathcroft Gdns WALTH E17 44 B7
Heathdale Av HSLWW TW4 122 D2
Heathdene Dr BELV DA17 117 J3
Heathdene Rd
STRHM/NOR SW16 149 F6
WLGTN SM6 176 B6
Heath Dr BELMT SM2 175 G7
HAMP NW3 71 F3
RYNPK SW20 161 F3
Heathedge SYD * SE26 150 D1
Heathend Rd BXLY DA5 138 B7
Heather Av ROM RM1 63 F1
Heatherbank CHST BR7 169 F1
ELTH/MOT SE9 134 E1
Heatherbank Cl DART DA1 138 B5
Heather Cl EHAM E6 96 A5
HPTN TW12 141 K7
ISLW TW7 123 J4
LEW SE13 133 G6
VX/NE SW8 129 G2
Heatherdale Cl KUTN/CMB KT2 144 C5
Heatherdene Cl FNCH N3 39 G6
MTCM CR4 162 C3
Heather Dr DART DA1 138 D6
ENC/FH EN2 29 H1
ROM RM1 63 F1
Heatherfold Wy PIN HA5 46 D2
Heather Gdns BELMT SM2 174 E5
GLDGN NW11 52 C5
ROM RM1 63 F1
Heather Gln ROM RM1 63 F1
Heatherlands SUN TW16 140 E5
Heatherley Dr CLAY IG5 59 K2
Heather Park Dr ALP/SUD HA0 68 C6
Heather Park Pde
ALP/SUD * HA0 68 B6
Heather Pl ESH/CLAY KT10 170 B3
Heather Ri BUSH WD23 21 K1
Heather Rd CHING E4 43 H5
CRICK NW2 69 H1
LEE/GVPK SE12 152 E1
The Heathers
STWL/WRAY TW19 120 C6
Heatherset Cl ESH/CLAY KT10 170 C4
Heatherset Gdns
STRHM/NOR SW16 149 F6
Heatherside Rd
HOR/WEW KT19 173 F6
SCUP DA14 155 J2
Heather Wk EDGW HA8 36 D4
NKENS W10 88 C3
Heather Wy SAND/SEL CR2 179 F7
STAN HA7 35 F5
Heatherwood Cl MNPK E12 77 F1
Heatherwood Dr YEAD UB4 82 B1
Heathfield CHING E4 44 A2
CHST BR7 154 C5
HRW * HA1 49 F6
Heathfield Av
WAND/EARL SW18 128 C6
Heathfield Cl CAN/RD E16 95 H4
HAYES BR2 181 G4
OXHEY WD19 21 G6
Heathfield Dr MTCM CR4 147 J7
Heathfield Gdns CHSWK W4 105 K4
CROY/NA * CR0 177 J3
GLDGN NW11 52 B5
WAND/EARL SW18 128 C5
Heathfield La CHST BR7 154 C5
Heathfield North WHTN TW2 123 K6
Heathfield Pk CRICK NW2 70 A5
Heathfield Park Dr CHDH RM6 61 H4
Heathfield Ri RSLP HA4 46 A6
Heathfield Rd ACT W3 105 J1
BMLY BR1 152 D6
BUSH WD23 21 J3
BXLYHS DA6 137 G3
CROY/NA CR0 177 K4
HAYES BR2 181 G4
WAND/EARL SW18 128 B5
Heathfield South WHTN TW2 124 A6
Heathfield Sq
WAND/EARL SW18 128 C6
Heathfield Ter CHSWK W4 105 K4
WOOL/PLUM SE18 115 K5
Heathfield V SAND/SEL CR2 179 F7
Heath Gdns DART * DA1 139 F7
TWK TW1 124 A7
Heathgate GLDGN NW11 53 F5
Heathgate Pl HAMP NW3 71 K4
Heath Gv PGE/AN SE20 150 E6
SUN TW16 140 D6
Heathhurst Rd SAND/SEL CR2 178 A7
Heathland Rd STNW/STAM N16 56 A7
Heathlands Cl TWK TW1 143 F1
Heathlands Ct HSLWW TW4 122 D4
Heathlands Ri DART DA1 138 E6
Heathlands Wy HSLWW TW4 122 D4
Heath La BKHTH/KID SE3 133 G1
DART DA1 138 E7
Heathlee Rd BKHTH/KID SE3 133 J3
DART DA1 138 B5
Heathley End CHST BR7 154 C5
Heath Ldg BUSH * WD23 22 D7
Heathman's Rd
FUL/PGN * SW6 107 J7
Heath Md WIM/MER SW19 146 B2
Heath Park Dr BMLY BR1 168 D2
Heath Park Rd GPK RM2 63 J4
Heath Ri HAYES BR2 167 K5
PUT/ROE SW15 127 G5
Heath Rd BXLY DA5 137 K7
CHDH RM6 61 K6
DART DA1 138 C5
HGDN/ICK UB10 82 A3
HRW HA1 48 C6
HSLW TW3 123 H3
OXHEY WD19 21 H6
THHTH CR7 164 D2
TWK TW1 124 A7
VX/NE SW8 129 G1
Heath's Cl EN EN1 29 K1
Heathside ESH/CLAY KT10 170 E2
HAMP NW3 71 H3
HSLWW TW4 122 E6
Heath Side STMC/STPC BR5 169 H7
Heathside Av BXLYHN DA7 137 F1
Heathside Cl ESH/CLAY KT10 170 E2
GNTH/NBYPK IG2 60 D4
NTHWD HA6 32 B4
Heathside Rd NTHWD HA6 32 B3
Heathstan Rd SHB W12 87 J5
Heath St DART DA1 139 G6
HAMP NW3 71 G3
Heath Vw EFNCH N2 53 G3
Heathview Av DART DA1 138 B5
Heath View Cl EFNCH N2 53 G3
Heathview Crs DART DA1 138 D6
Heath View Dr ABYW SE2 116 E5
Heathview Gdns
PUT/ROE SW15 127 F6
Heathview Rd THHTH CR7 164 B3
Heath Vls WAND/EARL * SW18 128 B7
WOOL/PLUM SE18 116 A4
Heathville Rd ARCH N19 54 E6
Heathwall St BTSEA SW11 128 E2
Heath Wy ERITH DA8 117 K7
Heathway BKHTH/KID SE3 113 K6
CROY/NA CR0 179 H2
DAGW RM9 80 B3
NWDGN * UB2 102 C3
WFD IG8 45 G3
Heathwood Gdns CHARL SE7 114 D3
Heathwood Wk BXLY DA5 138 B7
Heaton Cl CHING E4 44 A2
Heaton Rd MTCM CR4 148 A6
PECK SE15 131 J2
Heaver Rd BTSEA * SW11 128 C2
Heavitree Cl WOOL/PLUM SE18 115 J4
Heavitree Rd
WOOL/PLUM SE18 115 J4
Hebden Ter TOTM N17 42 A5
Hebdon Rd TOOT SW17 147 J2
Heber Rd CRICK NW2 70 B4
EDUL SE22 131 G5
Hebron Rd HMSMTH W6 106 E2
Hecham Cl WALTH E17 57 G1
Heckfield Pl FUL/PGN SW6 107 K6
Heckford Cl WATW WD18 20 A5
Heckford St WAP E1W 93 F6
Hector St WOOL/PLUM * SE18 115 K3
Heddington Gv HOLWY N7 73 F4
Heddon Cl ISLW TW7 124 B3
Heddon Court Av EBAR EN4 27 K4
Heddon Court Pde EBAR * EN4 28 A4
Heddon Rd EBAR EN4 27 K4
Heddon St CONDST W1S 10 E7
Hedge La PLMGR N13 41 H2
Hedgeley REDBR IG4 59 K3
Hedgemans Rd DAGW RM9 79 K6
Hedgemans Wy DAGW RM9 80 A5
Hedgerley Gdns GFD/PVL UB6 84 C1
Hedgerow La BAR EN5 25 K4
Hedger's Gv HOM * E9 75 G5
Hedger St LBTH SE11 18 C5
Hedgewood Gdns CLAY IG5 60 A3
Hedgley St LEE/GVPK SE12 133 J4
Hedingham Cl IS N1 6 E2
Hedingham Rd BCTR RM8 79 H4
Hedley Rd WHTN TW2 123 F6
Hedley Rw HBRY N5 73 K4
Heenan Cl BARK IG11 78 C5
Heene Rd ENC/FH EN2 29 K1
Heidegger Crs BARN SW13 106 E6
Heigham Rd EHAM E6 77 H6
Heighton Gdns CROY/NA CR0 177 H4
The Heights BECK * BR3 152 A6
CHARL SE7 114 B4
NTHLT UB5 66 A4
Heights Cl RYNPK SW20 145 K6
Heiron St WALW SE17 110 C5
Helby Rd CLAP SW4 129 J5
Helder Gv LEE/GVPK SE12 133 J6
Helder St SAND/SEL CR2 177 K5
Heldmann Cl ISLW TW7 123 J3
Helena Pl HOM E9 74 D7
Helena Rd EA W5 85 K4
PLSTW E13 94 D1
WALTH E17 57 J4
WLSDN NW10 69 K4
Helena Sq BERM/RHTH SE16 93 G6
Helen Av EBED/NFELT TW14 122 A6
Helen Cl DART DA1 138 E6
E/WMO/HCT KT8 157 G3
EFNCH N2 53 G2
Helenslea Av GLDGN NW11 52 E7
Helen's Pl BETH E2 92 E2
Helen St WOOL/PLUM * SE18 115 G3
Helford Cl RSLP HA4 64 C1
Helgiford Gdns SUN TW16 140 C6
Helix Gdns BRXS/STRHM SW2 130 A5
Helix Rd BRXS/STRHM SW2 130 A5
Hellings St WAP E1W 92 C7
Helme Cl WIM/MER SW19 146 D4
Helmet Rw FSBYE EC1V 6 F9
Helmore Rd BARK IG11 78 E6
Helmsdale Cl YEAD * UB4 83 J3
Helmsdale Rd
STRHM/NOR SW16 148 C7
Helmsley Pl HACK E8 74 D6
Helmsley St HACK E8 74 D7
Helperby Rd WLSDN NW10 69 G6
Helsinki Sq BERM/RHTH SE16 112 C2
Helston Cl PIN HA5 33 K6
Helvetia St CAT SE6 151 H1
Hemans St VX/NE SW8 109 J6
Hemery Rd GFD/PVL UB6 66 D4
Hemingford Rd
CHEAM SM3 174 A3
IS N1 5 M3
Heming Rd EDGW HA8 36 D5
Hemington Av FBAR/BDGN N11 39 K4
Hemlock Rd SHB W12 87 H6
Hemmen La HYS/HAR UB3 82 D6
Hemming Cl HPTN TW12 142 A7
Hemmings Cl SCUP DA14 155 H1
Hemming St WCHPL E1 92 C3
Hemmingway Cl KTTN NW5 72 A3
Hempstead Cl BKHH IG9 44 E1
Hempstead Rd WALTH E17 58 B2
WAT WD17 20 E1
Hemp Wk WALW SE17 19 H5
Hemsby Rd CHSGTN KT9 172 B5
Hemstal Rd KIL/WHAMP NW6 2 A1
Hemsted Rd ERITH DA8 118 B7
Hemswell Dr CDALE/KGS NW9 37 G7
Hemsworth St IS N1 7 J5
Henbury Wy OXHEY WD19 33 H2
Henchman St SHB W12 87 H5
Hendale Av HDN NW4 51 J2
Henderson Cl EMPK RM11 81 K1
WLSDN NW10 68 E5
Henderson Dr DART DA1 139 K3
STJWD NW8 3 G9
Henderson Rd CROY/NA CR0 164 E5
ED N9 30 D7
FSTGT E7 77 G5
WAND/EARL SW18 128 D6
YEAD UB4 82 E2
Hendham Rd TOOT SW17 147 J1
Hendon Av FNCH N3 38 C7
Hendon Gv HOR/WEW KT19 172 C7
Hendon Hall Ct HDN * NW4 52 B2
Hendon La FNCH N3 52 C2
Hendon Park Rw
GLDGN * NW11 52 D5
Hendon Rd ED N9 42 C1
Hendon Ter ASHF * TW15 140 B5
Hendon Wy CRICK NW2 52 C7
STWL/WRAY TW19 120 A4
Hendon Wood La MLHL NW7 25 J6
Hendren Cl GFD/PVL UB6 66 D4
Hendre Rd STHWK SE1 19 K6
Hendrick Av BAL SW12 128 E5
Heneage La HDTCH EC3A 13 K5
Heneage St WCHPL E1 13 M3
Henfield Cl ARCH N19 54 C7
BXLY DA5 137 H5
Henfield Rd WIM/MER SW19 146 D7
Hengelo Gdns MTCM CR4 162 C3
Hengist Rd ERITH DA8 117 K6
LEE/GVPK SE12 134 A6
Hengist Wy HAYES BR2 167 G3
Hengrave Rd FSTH SE23 132 A6
Hengrove Ct BXLY DA5 137 F7
Henley Av CHEAM SM3 174 C2
Henley Cl BERM/RHTH * SE16 111 K1
GFD/PVL * UB6 84 C1
ISLW TW7 104 A7
Henley Dr BERM/RHTH SE16 19 M5
KUTN/CMB KT2 145 H6
Henley Gdns CHDH RM6 62 A4
PIN HA5 47 F2
Henley Rd CAN/RD E16 114 E1
IL IG1 78 C3
UED N18 42 A3
WLSDN NW10 70 A7
Henley St BTSEA SW11 129 F1
Henley Wy FELT TW13 141 H4
Hennel Cl FSTH SE23 150 E2
Hennessy Rd ED N9 42 E1
Henniker Gdns EHAM E6 95 H2
Henniker Ms CHEL SW3 15 G9
Henniker Rd SRTFD E15 76 B4
Henningham Rd TOTM N17 41 K7
Henning St BTSEA SW11 108 D7
Henrietta Cl DEPT SE8 112 D5
Henrietta Ms BMSBY WC1N 5 K9
Henrietta Pl CAVSQ/HST W1G 10 C4
Henrietta St COVGDN WC2E 11 K6
SRTFD E15 76 A4
Henriques St WCHPL E1 92 C5
Henry Addlington Cl EHAM E6 96 B4
Henry Cooper Wy
ELTH/MOT SE9 153 H2
Henry Darlot Dr MLHL NW7 38 C4
Henry Dickens Ct NTGHL W11 88 B6
Henry Doulton Dr TOOT SW17 148 A3
Henry Jackson Rd
PUT/ROE SW15 127 G2
Henry Macaulay Av
KUTN/CMB KT2 143 K7
Henry Peters Dr TEDD TW11 142 E4
Henry Rd EBAR EN4 27 H4
EHAM E6 95 J1
FSBYPK N4 55 J7
Henry's Av WFD IG8 44 D4
Henryson Rd BROCKY SE4 132 D4
Henry St BMLY BR1 153 F7
Hensford Gdns SYD SE26 150 D3
Henshall St IS N1 73 K5
Henshawe Rd BCTR RM8 79 K2
Henshaw St WALW SE17 19 G5
Henslowe Rd EDUL SE22 131 H4
Henson Av CRICK NW2 70 A4
Henson Pl NTHLT UB5 65 G7
Henstridge Pl STJWD NW8 3 J5
Henty Cl BTSEA SW11 108 D6
Henty Wk PUT/ROE SW15 126 E4
Henville Rd BMLY BR1 153 F7
Henwick Rd ELTH/MOT SE9 134 C2
Henwood Side WFD IG8 45 K5
Hepburn Gdns HAYES BR2 167 J7
Hepple Cl ISLW TW7 124 C1
Hepscott Rd HOM E9 75 J5
Hepworth Gdns BARK IG11 79 G4
Hepworth Rd
STRHM/NOR SW16 148 E6
Herald Gdns WLGTN SM6 176 B2
Heralds Pl LBTH SE11 18 C5
Herald St BETH E2 92 D3
Herbal Hl CLKNW EC1R 12 B1
Herbert Crs KTBR SW1X 15 M3
Herbert Gdns CHDH RM6 61 K6
CHSWK W4 105 J5
WLSDN NW10 88 A1
Herbert Pl WOOL/PLUM SE18 115 G5
Herbert Rd BXLYHN DA7 137 F1
CDALE/KGS NW9 51 J5
FBAR/BDGN N11 40 E6
GDMY/SEVK IG3 78 E1
HAYES BR2 168 C4
KUT KT1 159 G2
MNPK E12 77 J3
SEVS/STOTM N15 56 B4
STHL UB1 83 K7
WALTH E17 57 H6
WIM/MER SW19 146 D6
WOOL/PLUM SE18 115 G6
Herbert St KTTN NW5 72 A5
PLSTW E13 94 E1
Herbrand St BMSBY WC1N 5 J9
Hercules Pl HOLWY N7 72 E2
Hercules Rd STHWK SE1 17 M4
Hercules St HOLWY N7 72 E2
Hereford Av EBAR EN4 27 K7
Hereford Gdns IL IG1 59 J6
PIN HA5 47 J4
WHTN * TW2 123 H7
Hereford Ms BAY/PAD W2 8 B4
Hereford Pl NWCR * SE14 112 C6
Hereford Retreat PECK SE15 111 H6
Hereford Rd ACT W3 86 E6
BAY/PAD W2 8 B5
EA W5 104 D2
FELT TW13 122 B7
WAN E11 59 F4
Hereford Sq SKENS SW7 14 F6
Hereford St BETH E2 92 C3
Hereford Wy CHSGTN KT9 171 J4
Herent Dr CLAY IG5 59 K2
Hereward Gdns PLMGR N13 41 G4
Hereward Rd TOOT SW17 147 J3
Herga Ct WAT WD17 20 E1
Herga Rd KTN/HRWW/W HA3 49 F3
Heriot Av CHING E4 43 J1
Heriot Rd HDN NW4 52 A4
Heriots Cl STAN HA7 35 G3
Heritage Hl HAYES BR2 181 G4
Heritage Pl
WAND/EARL * SW18 128 C5
Heritage Vw HRW HA1 67 F2
Herkomer Cl BUSH WD23 22 B5
Herkomer Rd BUSH WD23 22 A4
Herlwyn Av RSLP HA4 64 C2
Herlwyn Gdns TOOT SW17 147 K3
Herm Cl ISLW TW7 103 H6
Hermes Cl MV/WKIL W9 8 A1
Hermes St IS N1 6 A6
Hermes Wy WLGTN SM6 176 D6
Hermiston Av CEND/HSY/T N8 54 E4
The Hermitage BARN * SW13 106 C7
FELT * TW13 140 D2
FSTH SE23 131 K7
KUT * KT1 158 E3
LEW * SE13 133 F1
RCHPK/HAM TW10 125 F4
Hermitage Cl ENC/FH EN2 29 H1
ESH/CLAY KT10 171 G5
RCHPK/HAM * TW10 124 E4
SWFD E18 58 D3
Hermitage Cottages
STAN * HA7 34 E4
Hermitage Gdns HAMP NW3 70 E2
NRWD SE19 149 J6
Hermitage La CRICK NW2 70 E2
CROY/NA CR0 165 G6
STRHM/NOR SW16 149 F6
Hermitage Rd FSBYPK N4 55 J6
NRWD SE19 149 J6
Hermitage Rw HACK * E8 74 C4
Hermitage St BAY/PAD W2 9 G3
Hermitage Wk SWFD E18 58 D3
Hermitage Wall WAP E1W 92 C7
Hermitage Wy STAN HA7 35 G7
Hermit Rd CAN/RD E16 94 D4
Hermit St FSBYE EC1V 6 C7
Hermon Gv HYS/HAR UB3 82 E7
Hermon Hl WAN E11 58 E3
Herndon Rd WAND/EARL SW18 128 B4
Herne Cl WLSDN NW10 69 F4
Herne Ct BUSH * WD23 22 C7
Herne Hl HNHL SE24 130 D4
Herne Hill Rd HNHL SE24 130 D2
Herne Ms UED N18 42 C3
Herne Pl HNHL SE24 130 C5
Herne Rd BUSH WD23 22 B5
SURB KT6 171 K1
Heron Cl WALTH E17 57 H1
WLSDN NW10 69 G5
Heron Ct HAYES BR2 168 B3
KUT * KT1 159 F2
Heron Crs SCUP DA14 154 E3
Herondale SAND/SEL CR2 179 F7
Herondale Av
WAND/EARL SW18 128 C7
Heron Dr FSBYPK N4 73 J1
Heron Flight Av HCH RM12 81 J6
Herongate Rd MNPK E12 77 G1
Heron Hl BELV DA17 117 G3
Heron Ms IL IG1 78 B1
Heron Quays POP/IOD E14 93 J7
Heron Rd CROY/NA * CR0 165 F7
HNHL SE24 130 D3
TWK TW1 124 B3
Heronsforde WEA W13 85 J5
Heronsgate EDGW HA8 36 C4
Herons Lea HGT * N6 53 K5
Heronslea Dr STAN HA7 36 A6
Herons Pl ISLW TW7 124 C2
Herons Ri EBAR EN4 27 J3
Heron Wk NTHWD HA6 32 C3
Heron Wy EBED/NFELT TW14 121 K3
Herrick Rd HBRY N5 73 J2
Herrick St WEST SW1P 17 H6
Herries St NKENS W10 88 C1
Herringham Rd CHARL SE7 114 B2
Herrongate Cl EN EN1 30 A1
Hersant Cl WLSDN NW10 69 J7
Herschell Rd FSTH SE23 132 A6
Hersham Cl PUT/ROE SW15 126 D6
Hershell Ct
MORT/ESHN * SW14 125 J3
Hertford Av MORT/ESHN SW14 126 A4
Hertford Cl EBAR EN4 27 H2
Hertford Ct STAN * HA7 35 K6
Hertford End Ct NTHWD * HA6 32 C4
Hertford Rd BARK IG11 78 B6
EBAR EN4 27 G2
ED N9 30 D7
EFNCH N2 53 J2
GNTH/NBYPK IG2 60 E5
IS N1 7 K1
PEND EN3 30 E1
Hertford Road High St
PEND * EN3 30 E3
Hertford St MYFR/PICC W1J 10 C8
Hertford Wy MTCM CR4 163 K3
Hertslet Rd HOLWY N7 73 F2
Hertsmere Rd POP/IOD E14 93 J6
Hertswood Ct BAR * EN5 26 C3
Hervey Cl FNCH N3 38 E7
Hervey Park Rd WALTH E17 57 G3

Hesa Rd HYS/HAR UB3 82 E5
Hesewall Cl VX/NE SW8 129 H1
Hesketh Pl NTGHL W11 88 C6
Hesketh Rd FSTGT E7 76 E2
Heslop Rd BAL SW12 128 E7
Hesper Ms ECT SW5 14 C7
Hesperus Crs POP/IOD E14 112 E3
Hessel Rd WEA W13 104 B1
Hessel St WCHPL E1 92 D5
Hesselyn Dr RAIN RM13 81 K6
Hestercombe Av
FUL/PGN SW6 127 H1
Hesterman Wy CROY/NA CR0 163 K7
Hester Rd BTSEA SW11 108 D6
UED N18 42 C4
Hester Ter RCH/KEW TW9 125 H2
Heston Av HEST TW5 102 D6
Heston Grange La HEST TW5 102 E5
Heston Rd HEST TW5 103 F6
Heston St DEPT SE8 112 C7
Heswell Gn OXHEY * WD19 32 E2
Hetherington Rd CLAP SW4 129 K3
Hetley Rd SHB W12 87 K7
Heton Gdns HDN NW4 51 J3
Hevelius Cl GNWCH SE10 113 J4
Hever Cft ELTH/MOT SE9 154 A3
Hever Gdns BMLY BR1 169 F1
Heverham Rd
WOOL/PLUM SE18 115 K3
Heversham Rd BXLYHN DA7 137 H1
Hewens Rd HGDN/ICK UB10 82 A2
Hewer St NKENS W10 88 B4
Hewett Cl STAN HA7 35 H3
Hewett St SDTCH EC2A 13 K1
Hewish Rd UED N18 42 A3
Hewison St BOW E3 93 H1
Hewitt Av WDGN N22 55 H1
Hewitt Cl CROY/NA CR0 179 J2
Hewitt Rd CEND/HSY/T N8 55 G4
Hewlett Rd BOW E3 93 G1
The Hexagon HGT N6 53 K7
Hexal Rd CAT SE6 152 C2
Hexham Gdns ISLW TW7 104 B6
Hexham Rd BAR EN5 27 F3
MRDN SM4 162 A7
WNWD SE27 149 J1
Heybourne Rd TOTM N17 42 D6
Heybridge Av
STRHM/NOR SW16 149 F5
Heybridge Dr BARK/HLT IG6 60 D2
Heybridge Wy WALTH E17 57 G6
Heyford Av RYNPK SW20 161 J2
VX/NE SW8 109 K6
Heyford Rd MTCM CR4 162 D1
Heyford Ter VX/NE SW8 109 K6
Heygate Est WALW SE17 18 F5
Heygate St WALW SE17 18 E6
Heynes Rd BCTR RM8 79 J3
Heysham Dr OXHEY WD19 33 G4
Heysham La HAMP NW3 71 G2
Heysham Rd SEVS/STOTM N15 55 K5
Heythorp St WAND/EARL SW18 127 J7
Heywood Av CDALE/KGS NW9 37 G7
Heyworth Rd CLPT E5 74 D3
SRTFD E15 76 D4
Hibbert Rd KTN/HRWW/W HA3 49 F1
WALTH E17 57 H6
Hibbert St BTSEA SW11 128 B2
Hibernia Gdns HSLW TW3 123 F4
Hibernia Rd HSLW TW3 123 F3
Hichisson Rd PECK SE15 131 K4
Hickin Cl CHARL SE7 114 C3
Hickin St POP/IOD E14 113 F2
Hickling Rd IL IG1 78 B4
Hickman Av CHING E4 44 A5
Hickman Cl CAN/RD E16 95 H4
Hickman Rd CHDH RM6 61 J6
Hicks Av GFD/PVL UB6 84 D2
Hicks Cl BTSEA SW11 128 D2
Hicks St DEPT SE8 112 B4
Hidcote Gdns RYNPK SW20 160 E2
Hide Pl WEST SW1P 17 G6
Hide Rd HRW HA1 48 D3
Higham Hill Rd WALTH E17 43 G7
Higham Pl WALTH E17 57 G2
Higham Rd TOTM N17 55 K2
WFD IG8 44 E5
Higham Station Av CHING E4 43 K5
The Highams WALTH * E17 44 A7
Higham St WALTH E17 57 G2
Highbank Pl
WAND/EARL * SW18 128 A6
Highbanks Cl WELL DA16 116 B6
Highbanks Rd PIN HA5 34 B5
Highbank Wy CEND/HSY/T N8 55 G5
Highbarrow Rd CROY/NA CR0 165 G7
High Beech SAND/SEL CR2 178 A6
Highbridge Rd BARK IG11 78 A6
Highbrook Rd BKHTH/KID SE3 134 C2
High Broom Crs WWKM BR4 166 E6
Highbury Av THHTH CR7 164 B1
Highbury Cl NWMAL KT3 159 K3
WWKM BR4 179 K1
Highbury Cnr IS N1 73 H5
Highbury Crs HBRY N5 73 H4
Highbury Est HBRY N5 73 J4
Highbury Gdns GDMY/SEVK IG3 78 E1
Highbury Gra HBRY N5 73 H3
Highbury Gv HBRY N5 73 H4
Highbury Hl HBRY N5 73 H3
Highbury New Pk HBRY N5 73 H5
Highbury Pk HBRY N5 73 H3
Highbury Pl HBRY N5 73 H5
Highbury Qd HBRY N5 73 J2
Highbury Rd WIM/MER SW19 146 C4
Highbury Station Pde IS * N1 73 H5
Highbury Station Rd IS * N1 73 G5
Highbury Ter HBRY N5 73 H4
Highbury Terrace Ms HBRY N5 73 H4
High Cedar Dr RYNPK SW20 145 K6
Highclere Rd NWMAL KT3 160 A2
Highclere St SYD SE26 151 G3
Highcliffe Dr PUT/ROE SW15 126 C5
Highcliffe Gdns REDBR IG4 59 J4
Highcombe CHARL SE7 114 A5
Highcombe Cl ELTH/MOT SE9 134 C7
High Coombe Pl
KUTN/CMB KT2 145 F6
Highcroft CDALE/KGS NW9 51 G4
Highcroft Av ALP/SUD HA0 68 B6
Highcroft Gdns GLDGN NW11 52 D5
Highcroft Rd ARCH N19 54 E6
High Cross Rd TOTM N17 56 C2
Highdaun Dr
STRHM/NOR SW16 164 A3
Highdown WPK KT4 173 G1
Highdown Rd PUT/ROE SW15 126 E5
High Dr NWMAL KT3 144 E7
High Elms WFD IG8 44 E4
High Elms Cl NTHWD HA6 32 A5
Highfield OXHEY WD19 33 K2
Highfield Av CDALE/KGS NW9 50 E4
ERITH DA8 117 J5
GFD/PVL UB6 66 E4
GLDGN NW11 52 B6
PIN HA5 47 K4
WBLY HA9 68 A2
Highfield Cl CDALE/KGS NW9 50 E4
LEW SE13 133 G5
NTHWD HA6 32 C7
SURB KT6 158 D7
WDGN N22 41 G7
Highfield Ct STHGT/OAK N14 28 C5
Highfield Crs NTHWD HA6 32 C7
Highfield Dr HAYES BR2 167 H3
HOR/WEW KT19 173 H6
WWKM BR4 179 K2
Highfield Gdns GLDGN NW11 52 C5
Highfield Hl NRWD SE19 149 K6
Highfield Rd ACT W3 86 E4
BMLY BR1 168 E3
BRYLDS KT5 159 K6
BUSH WD23 21 J4
BXLYHS DA6 137 G4
DART DA1 139 G6
FELT TW13 121 K7
GLDGN * NW11 52 C5
ISLW TW7 104 A7
NTHWD HA6 32 C7
SUT SM1 175 J4
WCHMH N21 41 H1
WFD IG8 45 J6
Highfield Rd South DART DA1 139 G6
Highfields Gv HGT N6 54 A7
High Foleys ESH/CLAY KT10 171 H6
High Garth ESH/CLAY KT10 170 C5
Highgate Av HGT N6 54 B6
Highgate Cl HGT N6 54 A6
Highgate Edge EFNCH * N2 53 J4
Highgate High St HGT N6 54 A7
Highgate Hl ARCH N19 54 B7
Highgate Rd KTTN NW5 72 A2
Highgate Spinney
CEND/HSY/T * N8 54 D5
Highgate West Hl HGT N6 72 A1
High Gv BMLY BR1 153 G7
WOOL/PLUM SE18 115 J6
Highgrove Cl CHST BR7 153 J7
FBAR/BDGN N11 40 A4
Highgrove Ms CAR SM5 175 J2
Highgrove Rd BCTR RM8 79 J4
Highgrove Wy RSLP HA4 46 E5
High Hill Ferry CLPT E5 56 D7
High Holborn HHOL WC1V 11 K4
Highland Av DAGE RM10 80 E2
HNWL W7 84 E5
Highland Cottages
WLGTN * SM6 176 B3
Highland Cft BECK BR3 151 K4
Highland Dr BUSH WD23 22 B6
Highland Pk FELT TW13 140 D3
Highland Rd BMLY BR1 152 D7
BXLYHS DA6 137 H4
NRWD SE19 150 A5
NTHWD HA6 46 E1
The Highlands BAR * EN5 27 F3
EDGW HA8 50 D1
Highlands OXHEY WD19 21 G7
Highlands Av ACT W3 86 E6
WCHMH N21 29 F4
Highlands Cl HSLW TW3 103 G7
Highlands Gdns IL IG1 59 K7
Highlands Rd BAR EN5 26 E3
Highland Ter LEW * SE13 132 E2
High La HNWL W7 84 D5
Highlea Cl CDALE/KGS NW9 37 G7
High Level Dr SYD SE26 150 C3
Highlever Rd NKENS W10 88 A4
High Limes NRWD * SE19 150 A5
High Md HRW HA1 48 E4
Highmead WOOL/PLUM SE18 116 A6
High Md WWKM BR4 180 B1
Highmead Crs ALP/SUD HA0 68 B6
High Meadow Cl PIN HA5 47 F3
High Meadow Crs
CDALE/KGS NW9 51 F4
High Meads Rd CAN/RD E16 95 H5
Highmore Rd BKHTH/KID SE3 113 H6
High Mt HDN * NW4 51 J5
The High Pde
STRHM/NOR * SW16 148 E2
High Park Rd RCH/KEW TW9 105 H7
High Pth WIM/MER SW19 147 F7
High Point ELTH/MOT SE9 154 B2
High Rdg MUSWH * N10 40 B7
High Rd BKHH IG9 45 F1
BUSH WD23 22 D7
CHDH RM6 62 B5
FBAR/BDGN N11 40 B4
FNCH N3 39 G7
GDMY/SEVK IG3 61 G7
IL IG1 78 B2
KTN/HRWW/W HA3 34 E7
LEY E10 57 K5
NFNCH/WDSP N12 39 G2
NFNCH/WDSP N12 39 G5
SEVS/STOTM N15 56 B4
TRDG/WHET N20 27 G6
WBLY HA9 68 A4
WDGN N22 41 F6
WLSDN NW10 69 G5
High Rd Eastcote PIN HA5 47 F4
High Rd Great North Rd
EFNCH N2 53 H1
High Rd Ickenham
HGDN/ICK UB10 64 A1
High Rd Leyton LEY E10 75 K1
High Rd Leytonstone WAN E11 76 C2
High Rd Woodford Gn WFD IG8 44 E3
WFD IG8 44 D7
Highshore Rd PECK SE15 131 H1
Highstead Crs ERITH DA8 118 B7
Highstone Av WAN E11 58 E5
High St ACT W3 86 E7
BAR EN5 26 D3
BARK/HLT IG6 60 C2
BECK BR3 166 D1
BELMT SM2 175 F5
BMLY BR1 167 K2
BORE WD6 23 K5
BTFD TW8 104 E5
BUSH WD23 22 A5
CAR SM5 175 K4
CEND/HSY/T N8 54 E3
CHEAM SM3 174 C5
CROY/NA CR0 177 J2
DART DA1 139 H5
E/WMO/HCT KT8 157 F3
EA W5 85 K6
ESH/CLAY KT10 170 B4
ESH/CLAY KT10 171 F5
EW KT17 173 H7
FBAR/BDGN N11 40 B4
FELT TW13 140 D2
HEST TW5 102 A6
HPTN TW12 142 B7
HRW HA1 66 E1
HSLW TW3 123 H2
HYS/HAR UB3 101 G5
KTN/HRWW/W HA3 48 E2
KUT KT1 143 J7
KUT KT1 158 E2
MLHL NW7 37 K4
NTHWD HA6 32 D7
NWMAL KT3 160 B3
PGE/AN SE20 150 E6
PIN HA5 47 J2
PLSTW E13 94 E1
ROM RM1 63 G4
RSLP HA4 46 C7
SCUP DA14 155 G3
SNWD SE25 165 G3
SRTFD E15 94 A1
STHGT/OAK N14 28 D7
STWL/WRAY TW19 120 A5
SUT SM1 175 F3
TEDD TW11 143 G4
THDIT KT7 158 B6
THHTH CR7 164 D3
WALTH E17 57 H3
WAN E11 59 F5
WAT WD17 21 F2
WBLY HA9 68 B3
WDR/YW UB7 100 A5
WHTN TW2 123 H6
WIM/MER SW19 146 B4
WWKM BR4 166 E7
High St Collier's Wd
WIM/MER SW19 147 H6
High St Harlesden
WLSDN NW10 87 H1
High St Harlington
HYS/HAR UB3 101 G5
High Street Ms
WIM/MER SW19 146 C4
High St North MNPK E12 77 J5
High St South EHAM E6 95 K1
High Timber St BLKFR EC4V 12 E6
High Tor Cl BMLY BR1 153 F6
High Trees BRXS/STRHM SW2 130 B7
CROY/NA CR0 166 B7
EBAR EN4 27 J4
High Vw PIN HA5 47 G3
WATW WD18 20 D5
Highview Av EDGW HA8 36 E3
High View Av WLGTN SM6 177 F4
High View Cl NRWD SE19 165 G1
Highview Gdns EDGW HA8 36 E4
FBAR/BDGN N11 40 C4
FNCH N3 52 C2
High View Rd NRWD SE19 149 K5
SWFD E18 58 D1
Highview Rd SCUP DA14 155 H3
WEA W13 85 G5
Highview Ter DART * DA1 139 G4
The Highway BELMT SM2 175 G7
STAN HA7 35 F7
WAP E1W 92 C6
Highwood Av
NFNCH/WDSP N12 39 G3
Highwood Gdns CLAY IG5 59 K4
Highwood Gv MLHL NW7 37 F4
Highwood Hl MLHL NW7 37 H2
Highwood Rd ARCH N19 72 E2
High Worple RYLN/HDSTN HA2 47 J6
Highworth Rd FBAR/BDGN N11 40 D5
Highworth St CAMTN * NW1 9 K2
Hilary Av MTCM CR4 163 F2
Hilary Cl BXLYHN DA7 117 J7
FUL/PGN * SW6 108 A6
Hilary Rd ACT W3 87 H6
Hilberry Ct BUSH * WD23 22 B6
Hilbert Rd CHEAM SM3 174 B3
Hilborough Cl WIM/MER SW19 147 G6
Hilborough Rd HACK * E8 7 M2
Hilda Rd CAN/RD E16 94 C3
EHAM E6 77 H6
Hilda Ter BRXN/ST * SW9 130 B1
Hildenborough Gdns
BMLY BR1 152 C5
Hilden Dr ERITH DA8 118 E6
Hildenlea Pl HAYES BR2 167 H1
Hildreth St BAL SW12 129 G7
Hildyard Rd FUL/PGN SW6 14 B9
Hiley Rd WLSDN NW10 88 A2
Hilgrove Rd KIL/WHAMP NW6 2 F2
Hiliary Gdns STAN HA7 49 J1
Hillary Crs WOT/HER KT12 156 B7
Hillary Dr ISLW TW7 124 A3
Hillary Ri BAR EN5 26 E3
Hillary Rd NWDGN UB2 103 F2
Hillbeck Cl PECK SE15 111 K6
Hillbeck Wy GFD/PVL UB6 66 D7
Hillborne Cl HYS/HAR UB3 101 K4
Hillborough Cl
WIM/MER * SW19 147 G6
Hillbrook Rd TOOT SW17 147 K2
Hill Brow BMLY BR1 153 H7
DART DA1 138 C5
Hillbrow NWMAL KT3 160 C2
Hillbrow Rd BMLY BR1 152 C6
ESH/CLAY KT10 170 C3
Hill Bunker's BELV DA17 117 H3
Hillbury Av KTN/HRWW/W HA3 49 H4
Hillbury Rd TOOT SW17 148 B2
Hill Cl BAR EN5 26 A4
CHST BR7 154 B4
CRICK NW2 69 K2
GLDGN NW11 52 E5
HRW HA1 66 E2
STAN HA7 35 H3
Hillcote Av STRHM/NOR SW16 149 G6
Hillcourt Av NFNCH/WDSP N12 39 F5
Hillcourt Rd EDUL SE22 131 J5
Hill Crs BRYLDS KT5 159 G4
BXLY DA5 137 K7
HRW HA1 49 G4
TRDG/WHET N20 39 F1
WPK KT4 174 A1
Hill Crest BFN/LL DA15 136 B6
SURB * KT6 159 F6
Hillcrest CMBW * SE5 130 E3
HGT N6 54 A6
WCHMH N21 29 H6
Hillcrest Av EDGW HA8 36 D3
GLDGN NW11 52 C4
PIN HA5 47 H3
Hillcrest Cl BECK BR3 166 C5
SYD SE26 150 C3
Hill Crest Gdns CRICK NW2 69 J2
Hillcrest Gdns ESH/CLAY KT10 171 F3
FNCH N3 52 C3
Hillcrest Rd ACT W3 86 C7
BMLY BR1 152 E3
DART DA1 138 B6
EA W5 86 A4
EMPK RM11 63 J6
WALTH E17 58 B1
Hillcrest Vw BECK BR3 166 C5
Hillcroft Av PIN HA5 47 K5
Hillcroft Crs EA W5 85 K5
OXHEY WD19 21 F7
RSLP HA4 65 H2
WBLY HA9 68 B3
Hillcroft Rd EHAM E6 96 B4
Hillcroome Rd BELMT SM2 175 H5
Hillcross Av MRDN SM4 161 H5
Hilldale Rd SUT SM1 174 D3
Hilldown Rd HAYES BR2 167 H7
STRHM/NOR SW16 148 E6
Hill Dr CDALE/KGS NW9 50 E7
STRHM/NOR SW16 164 A2
Hilldrop Crs HOLWY N7 72 D4
Hilldrop Est HOLWY N7 72 D4
Hilldrop La HOLWY N7 72 D4
Hilldrop Rd BMLY BR1 153 F5
HOLWY N7 72 D4
Hill End WOOL/PLUM SE18 115 F7
Hillersdon Av BARN SW13 126 D1
EDGW HA8 36 B4
Hillery Cl WALW SE17 19 H6
Hill Farm Rd NKENS W10 88 A4
Hillfield Av ALP/SUD HA0 68 A6
CDALE/KGS NW9 51 G4
CEND/HSY/T N8 55 F3
MRDN SM4 162 D5
Hillfield Cl RYLN/HDSTN HA2 48 C3
Hillfield La South BUSH WD23 22 E5
Hillfield Pde MRDN * SM4 162 C5
Hillfield Pk MUSWH N10 54 B2
WCHMH N21 41 G1
Hillfield Park Ms MUSWH N10 54 B3
Hill Field Rd HPTN TW12 141 K6
Hillfield Rd KIL/WHAMP NW6 70 D4
Hill Gardens Craven
BAY/PAD * W2 8 E6
Hillgate Pl BAL SW12 129 G5
KENS W8 8 A8
Hillgate St KENS W8 8 A8
Hill Gv FELT TW13 141 K1
ROM RM1 63 G2
Hill House Av STAN HA7 35 F6
Hill House Cl WCHMH N21 29 G6
Hill House Dr HPTN TW12 142 A7
Hill House Rd
STRHM/NOR SW16 149 F4
Hilliard Rd NTHWD HA6 32 D7
Hilliard's Ct WAP E1W 92 E7
Hillier Cl BAR EN5 27 F5
Hillier Gdns CROY/NA CR0 177 G4
Hillier Pl CHSGTN KT9 171 K5
Hillier Rd BTSEA SW11 128 E5
Hillier's La CROY/NA CR0 176 E2
Hillingdon Av
STWL/WRAY TW19 120 B7
Hillingdon Rd BXLYHN DA7 137 K2
Hillingdon St WALW SE17 110 C5
Hillingdon Trail HYS/HAR UB3 101 K4
Hill La RSLP HA4 46 A7
Hillman St HACK E8 74 D5
Hillmarton Rd HOLWY N7 72 E4
Hillmarton Ter HOLWY * N7 72 E4
Hillmead Dr BRXN/ST SW9 130 C3
Hillmont Rd ESH/CLAY KT10 170 E2
Hillmore Gv SYD SE26 151 F4
Hillreach WOOL/PLUM SE18 114 E4
Hill Ri ED N9 30 D5
ESH/CLAY KT10 171 H1
GFD/PVL UB6 66 C7
GLDGN NW11 53 F3
RCHPK/HAM TW10 124 E4
RSLP HA4 46 A7
Hillrise Rd ARCH N19 54 E6
Hill Rd ALP/SUD HA0 67 H2
CAR SM5 175 J5
HRW HA1 49 G4
MTCM CR4 148 B7
MUSWH N10 39 K7
NTHWD HA6 32 B5
PIN HA5 47 J5
STJWD NW8 2 F6
SUT SM1 175 F4
Hillsboro Rd EDUL SE22 131 F4
Hillsborough Gn OXHEY * WD19 32 E2
Hillsgrove Cl WELL DA16 116 D6
Hill Side BAR EN5 27 G4
Hillside BAR * EN5 25 J4
CDALE/KGS NW9 51 F3
ESH/CLAY * KT10 170 B4
WIM/MER SW19 146 B5
WLSDN NW10 69 F7
Hillside Av BORE WD6 24 E2
FBAR/BDGN N11 39 K5
WBLY HA9 68 B3
WFD IG8 45 G4
Hillside Cl KIL/WHAMP NW6 2 D5
MRDN SM4 161 H3
WFD IG8 45 G4
Hillside Crs NTHWD HA6 32 E7
OXHEY WD19 21 H5
RYLN/HDSTN HA2 66 C1
Hillside Dr EDGW HA8 36 C5
Hillside Gdns BAR EN5 26 C3
BRXS/STRHM * SW2 149 G1
EDGW HA8 36 B3
FBAR/BDGN * N11 40 C5
HGT N6 54 A5
KTN/HRWW/W HA3 50 A6
NTHWD HA6 32 E6
WLGTN SM6 176 C6
Hillside Gv MLHL NW7 37 J6
STHGT/OAK N14 28 D6
Hillside La HAYES BR2 180 E1
Hillside Ri NTHWD HA6 32 E6
Hillside Rd BELMT SM2 174 D6
BRXS/STRHM SW2 149 F1
BUSH WD23 21 J4
CROY/NA CR0 177 H4
DART DA1 138 D5
EA W5 86 A4
HAYES BR2 167 J2
NTHWD HA6 32 E6
STHL UB1 84 A3
STNW/STAM N16 56 A6
Hills La NTHWD HA6 32 C7
Hillsleigh Rd KENS W8 88 D7
Hills Ms EA * W5 86 A6
Hills Pl SOHO/CST W1F 10 E5
Hillstowe St CLPT E5 74 E1
Hill St MYFR/PICC W1J 10 C8
RCHPK/HAM TW10 124 E4
Hill Top GLDGN NW11 53 F3
MRDN SM4 161 J6
Hilltop WALTH * E17 57 K2
Hilltop Cottages SYD * SE26 150 D3
Hilltop Gdns DART DA1 139 J4
Hilltop Rd KIL/WHAMP NW6 2 B1
Hill Top Vw WFD * IG8 45 K5
Hilltop Wy STAN HA7 35 G2
Hillview RYNPK SW20 145 K6
Hillview Av KTN/HRWW/W HA3 50 A4
Hillview Cl PIN HA5 33 K5
Hill View Crs IL IG1 59 K5
Hillview Crs ORP BR6 169 K7
Hill View Dr WELL DA16 135 K1
Hill View Gdns CDALE/KGS NW9 51 F4
Hillview Gdns HDN NW4 52 B3
PIN HA5 48 A2
Hill View Rd ESH/CLAY KT10 171 G6
TWK TW1 124 B5
Hillview Rd CHST BR7 154 A4
MLHL NW7 38 B3
PIN HA5 33 K6
SUT SM1 175 G2
Hillway CDALE/KGS NW9 51 G7
HGT N6 72 A1
Hillworth BECK * BR3 166 E1
Hillworth Rd
BRXS/STRHM SW2 130 B6
Hillyard Rd HNWL W7 84 E4
Hillyard St BRXN/ST SW9 110 B7
Hillyfield WALTH E17 57 G1
Hillyfield Cl HOM E9 75 G4
Hilly Flds BROCKY * SE4 132 D3
Hilly Fields Crs BROCKY SE4 132 D3
Hilsea St CLPT E5 74 E3
Hilton Av NFNCH/WDSP N12 39 H4
Himalayan Wy WATW WD18 20 D5
Himley Rd TOOT SW17 147 J4
Hinchley Cl ESH/CLAY KT10 171 F2
Hinchley Dr ESH/CLAY KT10 171 F2
Hinchley Wy ESH/CLAY KT10 171 G2
Hinckley Rd EDUL SE22 131 H3
Hind Ct FLST/FETLN * EC4A 12 B5
Hind Crs ERITH DA8 117 K6
Hinde Ms MHST * W1U 10 B4
Hindes Rd HRW HA1 48 E4
Hinde St MHST W1U 10 B4
Hind Gv POP/IOD E14 93 J5
Hindhead Gdns NTHLT UB5 65 J7
Hindhead Gn OXHEY WD19 33 G4
Hindhead Wy WLGTN SM6 176 E4
Hindmans Rd EDUL SE22 131 H4
Hindmans Wy DAGW RM9 98 B3
Hindmarsh Cl WCHPL E1 92 C6
Hindrey Rd CLPT E5 74 D4
Hindsley's Pl FSTH SE23 150 E1
Hinkler Rd KTN/HRWW/W HA3 49 K2
Hinstock Rd WOOL/PLUM SE18 115 H6
Hinton Av HSLWW TW4 122 C3
Hinton Cl ELTH/MOT SE9 134 D7
Hinton Rd BRXN/ST SW9 130 C2
UED N18 42 A3
WLGTN SM6 176 C5
Hippodrome Pl NTGHL W11 88 C6
Hitcham Rd WALTH E17 57 H6
Hitherbroom Rd HYS/HAR UB3 82 E7
Hither Farm Rd
BKHTH/KID SE3 134 B2
Hitherfield Rd BCTR RM8 80 A1
STRHM/NOR SW16 149 F1
Hither Green La LEW SE13 133 F4
Hitherwell Dr
KTN/HRWW/W HA3 34 D7
Hitherwood Dr DUL SE21 150 B3
Hive Rd BUSH WD23 34 D1
Hoadly Rd STRHM/NOR SW16 148 D2
Hobart Cl TRDG/WHET N20 39 J1
YEAD UB4 83 H3
Hobart Dr YEAD UB4 83 H3
Hobart Gdns THHTH CR7 164 E2
Hobart La YEAD UB4 83 H3
Hobart Pl BGVA SW1W 16 C4
RCHPK/HAM TW10 125 G6
Hobart Rd BARK/HLT IG6 60 C1
DAGW RM9 79 K3
WPK KT4 173 K2
YEAD UB4 83 H3
Hobbayne Rd HNWL W7 84 D5
Hobbes Wk PUT/ROE SW15 126 E4
Hobbs Gn EFNCH N2 53 G2
Hobbs Pl IS N1 7 J4
Hobbs Place Est IS N1 7 J5
Hobbs Rd WNWD SE27 149 J3
Hobday St POP/IOD E14 93 K5
Hoblands End CHST BR7 154 E5
Hobsons Pl WCHPL * E1 92 C4
Hobury St WBPTN SW10 108 B5
Hocker St BETH * E2 7 L8
Hockley Av EHAM E6 95 J1
Hockley Dr GPK RM2 63 K1
Hockley Ms BARK IG11 96 E1
Hocroft Av CRICK NW2 70 D2
Hocroft Rd CRICK NW2 70 D3
Hocroft Wk CRICK NW2 70 D2
Hodder Dr GFD/PVL UB6 85 F1
Hoddesdon Rd BELV DA17 117 H4
Hodford Rd GLDGN NW11 52 D7
Hodges Wy WATW WD18 20 E5
Hodgkins Cl THMD SE28 97 K6
Hodister Cl CMBW SE5 110 D6
Hodson Cl RYLN/HDSTN HA2 65 K2
The Hoe OXHEY WD19 33 H1
Hoe St WALTH E17 57 J4
Hoffman Sq IS * N1 7 H7
Hofland Rd WKENS W14 107 H2
Hogan Ms BAY/PAD W2 9 G2
Hogarth Av ASHF TW15 140 A5
Hogarth Cl CAN/RD E16 95 H4
EA W5 86 A4
Hogarth Crs CROY/NA CR0 164 D6
WIM/MER SW19 147 H7
Hogarth Gdns HEST TW5 103 F6
Hogarth Hl GLDGN NW11 52 D3
Hogarth Pl ECT * SW5 14 C6
Hogarth Rd BCTR RM8 79 H4
ECT SW5 14 C6
EDGW HA8 50 C1
Hogarth Ter CHSWK * W4 106 B5
Hogarth Wy HPTN TW12 142 C7
Hogg La BORE WD6 23 G3
Hogshead Pas WAP * E1W 92 D6
Hogsmill Wy HOR/WEW KT19 172 E4
Holbeach Gdns BFN/LL DA15 135 K5
Holbeach Rd CAT SE6 132 D6
Holbeck Rw PECK SE15 111 H6
Holbein Ga NTHWD HA6 32 C4
Holbein Ms BGVA SW1W 16 A7
Holbein Pl BGVA SW1W 16 A6
Holberton Gdns WLSDN NW10 87 K2

Holborn HCIRC EC1N 12 A3
Holborn Circ HCIRC EC1N 12 B3
Holborn Pl HHOL WC1V 11 L3
Holborn Rd PLSTW E13 95 F4
Holborn Viad STBT EC1A 12 C4
Holborn Wy MTCM CR4 162 E1
Holbrooke Ct HOLWY N7 72 E2
Holbrook La CHST BR7 154 D6
Holbrook Rd SRTFD E15 94 D1
Holbrook Wy HAYES BR2 168 E5
Holburne Cl BKHTH/KID SE3 114 B7
Holburne Gdns BKHTH/KID SE3 114 C7
Holburne Rd BKHTH/KID SE3 114 B7
Holcombe Hl MLHL NW7 37 J2
Holcombe Rd TOTM N17 56 B2
Holcombe St HMSMTH W6 106 E4
Holcote Cl BELV DA17 117 F2
Holcroft Rd HOM E9 74 E6
Holden Av CDALE/KGS NW9 50 E7
NFNCH/WDSP N12 39 F4
Holdenby Rd BROCKY SE4 132 B4
Holden Cl BCTR RM8 79 H2
Holdenhurst Av FNCH N3 39 F6
Holden Rd NFNCH/WDSP N12 39 F3
Holden St BTSEA SW11 129 F1
Holdernesse Rd ISLW TW7 104 B7
TOOT SW17 147 K2
Holderness Wy WNWD SE27 149 H4
Holders Hill Av HDN NW4 52 B1
Holders Hill Crs HDN NW4 52 B2
Holders Hill Dr HDN NW4 52 B1
Holders Hill Gdns HDN NW4 52 B1
Holders Hill Pde HDN * NW4 38 C7
Holders Hill Rd HDN NW4 52 B1
Holford Ms FSBYW * WC1X 5 L7
Holford Rd HAMP NW3 71 G2
Holford St FSBYW WC1X 6 A7
Holford Yd IS * N1 6 A6
Holgate Av BTSEA SW11 128 C2
Holgate Rd DAGE RM10 80 C4
Holgate St CHARL SE7 114 C2
Holland Av BELMT SM2 174 E6
RYNPK SW20 145 H7
Holland Cl BAR EN5 27 H6
HAYES BR2 180 D1
ROMW/RG RM7 62 E4
STAN HA7 35 H4
Holland Dr FSTH SE23 151 G2
Holland Gdns WKENS W14 107 H2
Holland Gv BRXN/ST SW9 110 B6
Holland Pk KENS W8 107 J1
NTGHL W11 88 D7
Holland Park Av
GDMY/SEVK IG3 60 E5
NTGHL W11 88 C7
Holland Park Gdns NTGHL W11 88 D7
Holland Park Ms NTGHL W11 88 D7
Holland Park Rd WKENS W14 107 J2
Holland Park Ter NTGHL * W11 88 C7
Holland Pas IS N1 6 E3
Holland Pl KENS * W8 14 C1
Holland Rd ALP/SUD HA0 67 K5
EHAM E6 77 K7
SNWD SE25 165 H4
SRTFD E15 94 C2
WKENS W14 107 G1
WLSDN NW10 69 J7
The Hollands WPK KT4 160 C7
Holland St KENS W8 14 B2
STHWK SE1 12 D8
Holland Villas Rd WKENS W14 107 H1
Holland Wk STAN HA7 35 G4
Holland Wy HAYES BR2 180 D1
Hollar Rd STNW/STAM N16 74 B2
Hollen St SOHO/CST W1F 10 F5
Holles Cl HPTN TW12 142 A5
Holles St CAVSQ/HST W1G 10 D4
Holley Rd ACT W3 106 B1
Hollickwood Av
NFNCH/WDSP N12 39 K5
Holliday Sq BTSEA SW11 128 C2
Hollidge Wy DAGE RM10 80 D6
The Hollies BAR * EN5 25 J4
KTN/HRWW/W HA3 49 G3
Hollies Av BFN/LL DA15 155 F1
Hollies Cl STRHM/NOR SW16 149 G5
TWK TW1 143 F1
Hollies End MLHL NW7 37 K4
Hollies Rd EA W5 104 D3
Hollies Wy BAL * SW12 129 F6
Holligrave Rd BMLY BR1 152 E7
Hollingbourne Av BXLYHN DA7 117 G7
Hollingbourne Gdns WEA W13 85 H4
Hollingbourne Rd HNHL SE24 130 D4
Hollingsworth Rd
SAND/SEL CR2 178 D5
Hollington Crs NWMAL KT3 160 C5
Hollington Rd EHAM E6 95 K2
TOTM N17 56 C1
Hollingworth Cl
E/WMO/HCT KT8 156 E3
Hollingworth Rd
STMC/STPC BR5 169 G6
Hollman Gdns
STRHM/NOR SW16 149 H5
The Hollow WFD IG8 44 D3
Holloway Cl WDR/YW UB7 100 B4
Holloway La WDR/YW UB7 100 A5
Holloway Rd ARCH N19 72 D1
EHAM E6 95 K2
WAN E11 76 B2
Holloway St HSLW TW3 123 G2
Holly Av STAN HA7 50 A1
WOT/HER KT12 156 C7
Holly Bank MUSWH * N10 54 C3
Hollybank Cl HPTN TW12 142 A4
Hollybrake Cl CHST BR7 154 D6
Hollybush Cl OXHEY WD19 21 G6
WAN E11 58 E4
Hollybush Gdns BETH E2 92 D2
Hollybush Hl WAN E11 58 D6
Holly Bush La HPTN TW12 141 K6
Hollybush Pl BETH E2 92 D2
Hollybush Rd KUTN/CMB KT2 144 A4
Hollybush St PLSTW E13 95 F2
Hollybush Ter NRWD * SE19 150 A5
Holly Bush Vale HAMP * NW3 71 G3
Holly Cl BECK BR3 167 F3
BKHH IG9 45 H2
FELT TW13 141 J4
WLSDN NW10 69 G6
Holly Crs BECK BR3 166 C4
WFD IG8 44 B6
Hollycroft Av HAMP NW3 70 E2
WBLY HA9 68 A1
Hollycroft Cl SAND/SEL CR2 178 A4
WDR/YW UB7 100 D5
Hollycroft Gdns WDR/YW UB7 100 D5
Hollydale Cl NTHLT UB5 66 B4
Hollydale Dr HAYES BR2 181 K2
Hollydale Rd PECK SE15 131 K1
Hollydown Wy WAN E11 76 B2
Holly Dr CHING E4 31 K6
Holly Farm Rd NWDGN UB2 102 D4
Hollyfield Av FBAR/BDGN N11 39 K4
Hollyfield Rd BRYLDS KT5 159 G6
Holly Gdns BXLYHN DA7 137 K3
WDR/YW UB7 100 C1
Hollygrove BUSH WD23 22 D6
Holly Gv CDALE/KGS NW9 50 E6
PECK SE15 131 G1
PIN HA5 33 J7
Hollygrove Cl HSLW TW3 122 E3
Holly Hedge Ter LEW SE13 133 F4
Holly Hl HAMP NW3 71 G3
WCHMH N21 29 F5
Holly Hill Rd BELV DA17 117 J4
Holly Lodge Gdns HGT N6 72 A1
Hollymead CAR SM5 175 K2
Holly Ms WBPTN SW10 14 F8
Holly Mt HAMP * NW3 71 G3
Hollymount Cl GNWCH SE10 113 F7
Holly Pk FNCH N3 52 D2
FSBYPK N4 54 E6
Holly Park Gdns FNCH N3 52 E2
Holly Park Rd FBAR/BDGN N11 40 A4
HNWL W7 85 F7
Holly Rd CHSWK * W4 106 A3
DART DA1 139 G7
HPTN TW12 142 C5
HSLW TW3 123 G3
TWK TW1 124 B7
Hollytree Cl WIM/MER SW19 127 G7
Hollytree Pde SCUP * DA14 155 J4
Hollyview Cl HDN NW4 51 J5
Holly Vls HMSMTH * W6 106 E2
Holly Wk HAMP NW3 71 G3
Holly Wy MTCM CR4 163 J3
Hollywood Gdns YEAD UB4 83 F5
Hollywood Ms WBPTN SW10 14 E9
Hollywood Rd CHING E4 43 G4
WBPTN SW10 14 E9
Hollywoods CROY/NA CR0 179 H7
Hollywood Wy ERITH DA8 118 E7
WFD IG8 44 B6
Holman Ct EW * KT17 173 J7
Holman Rd BTSEA SW11 128 C1
HOR/WEW KT19 172 E4
Holmbridge Gdns PEND EN3 31 F3
Holmbrook Dr HDN NW4 52 B4
Holmbury Cl BUSH WD23 34 E1
Holmbury Ct WIM/MER SW19 147 J6
Holmbury Gdns HYS/HAR UB3 82 D7
Holmbury Gv CROY/NA CR0 179 H6
Holmbury Mnr SCUP * DA14 155 G3
Holmbury Pk CHST BR7 153 J6
Holmbury Vw CLPT E5 56 D7
Holmbush Rd PUT/ROE SW15 127 H5
Holmcote Gdns HBRY N5 73 J4
Holmcroft Wy HAYES BR2 168 E4
Holmdale Cl BORE WD6 24 B1
Holmdale Gdns HDN NW4 52 B4
Holmdale Rd CHST BR7 154 C4
KIL/WHAMP NW6 70 E4
Holmdale Ter SEVS/STOTM N15 56 A5
Holmdene Av HNHL SE24 130 D4
MLHL NW7 37 J5
RYLN/HDSTN HA2 48 B2
Holmdene Cl BECK BR3 167 F1
Holmdene Ct BMLY BR1 168 D2
Holmead Rd FUL/PGN SW6 108 A6
Holmebury Cl BUSH * WD23 34 E1
Holme Lacey Rd
LEE/GVPK SE12 133 J5
Holme Pk BORE WD6 24 B1
Holme Rd EHAM E6 77 J7
Holmes Av MLHL NW7 38 C4
WALTH E17 57 H2
Holmesdale Av
MORT/ESHN SW14 125 J2
Holmesdale Cl SNWD SE25 165 G2
Holmesdale Rd BXLYHN DA7 136 E1
CROY/NA CR0 164 E4
HGT N6 54 B6
RCH/KEW TW9 105 G7
TEDD TW11 143 J6
Holmesley Rd BROCKY SE4 132 B5
Holmes Rd KTTN NW5 72 B4
TWK TW1 143 F1
WIM/MER SW19 147 G6
Holmes Ter STHWK SE1 18 A1
Holme Wy STAN HA7 35 F5
Holmewood Gdns
BRXS/STRHM SW2 130 A6
Holmewood Rd
BRXS/STRHM SW2 129 K6
SNWD SE25 165 F2
Holmfield Av HDN NW4 52 B4
Holmhurst Rd BELV DA17 117 J4
Holmleigh Av DART DA1 139 F3
Holmleigh Rd STNW/STAM N16 56 A7
Holm Oak Cl PUT/ROE SW15 127 J5
Holm Oak Pk WATW * WD18 20 E4
Holmsdale Gv BXLYHN DA7 138 B1
Holmshaw Cl SYD SE26 151 G3
Holmside Ri OXHEY WD19 33 F2
Holmside Rd BAL SW12 129 F5
Holmsley Cl NWMAL KT3 160 C5
Holmstall Av EDGW HA8 50 E1
Holmstall Pde EDGW * HA8 50 E1
Holmwood Cl BELMT SM2 174 B7
NTHLT UB5 66 B5
RYLN/HDSTN HA2 48 C2
Holmwood Gdns FNCH N3 52 E1
WLGTN SM6 176 B5
Holmwood Gv MLHL NW7 37 F4
Holmwood Rd BELMT SM2 174 A7
CHSGTN KT9 172 A4
GDMY/SEVK IG3 78 E1
Holne Cha EFNCH N2 53 G5
MRDN SM4 161 K5
Holness Rd SRTFD E15 76 D5
Holroyd Rd ESH/CLAY KT10 171 G7
PUT/ROE SW15 127 F3
Holstock Rd IL IG1 78 C1
Holsworth Cl RYLN/HDSTN HA2 48 C4
Holsworthy Sq FSBYW WC1X 11 M1
Holsworthy Wy CHSGTN KT9 171 J4
The Holt MRDN * SM4 161 K3
WLGTN SM6 176 C3
Holt Cl BORE WD6 24 B3
MUSWH N10 54 A3
THMD SE28 97 H6
Holton St WCHPL E1 93 F3
Holt Rd ALP/SUD HA0 67 H2
CAN/RD E16 95 J7
Holtwhite Av ENC/FH EN2 29 J1
Holtwhite's Hl ENC/FH EN2 29 J1
Holwell Pl PIN HA5 47 J3
Holwood Park Av ORP BR6 181 K3
Holwood Pl CLAP SW4 129 J3
Holybourne Av PUT/ROE SW15 126 D6
Holyhead Cl BOW E3 93 J2
Holyoake Ct BERM/RHTH SE16 112 B1
Holyoake Wk EA W5 85 J3
EFNCH N2 53 G2
Holyoak Rd LBTH SE11 18 C5
Holyport Rd FUL/PGN SW6 107 F6
Holyrood Av RYLN/HDSTN HA2 65 J3
Holyrood Gdns EDGW HA8 50 D1
Holyrood Rd BAR EN5 27 G5
Holyrood St STHWK SE1 13 J9
Holywell Cl BERM/RHTH * SE16 111 J4
BKHTH/KID SE3 113 K5
STWL/WRAY TW19 120 B7
Holywell La SDTCH EC2A 7 K9
Holywell Rd WATW WD18 20 E4
Holywell Rw SDTCH EC2A 13 J1
Holywell Wy STWL/WRAY TW19 120 B7
Home Cl CAR SM5 175 K1
NTHLT UB5 83 K2
Home Ct FELT * TW13 121 K7
SURB * KT6 158 E4
Homecroft Rd SYD SE26 150 E4
WDGN N22 41 H7
Home Farm Cl ESH/CLAY KT10 170 B5
THDIT KT7 158 A6
Homefarm Rd HNWL W7 84 E5
The Homefield MRDN * SM4 161 K3
Homefield Av GNTH/NBYPK IG2 60 E4
Homefield Cl WLSDN NW10 68 E5
YEAD UB4 83 H3
Homefield Gdns EFNCH N2 53 H2
WIM/MER SW19 162 B1
Homefield Ms BECK * BR3 151 J7
Homefield Pk SUT SM1 175 F5
Homefield Rd ALP/SUD HA0 67 G3
BMLY BR1 153 G7
BUSH WD23 22 A4
CHSWK W4 106 C3
EDGW HA8 37 F5
WIM/MER SW19 146 C5
WOT/HER KT12 156 E6
Homefield St IS * N1 7 J6
Home Gdns DAGE RM10 80 E2
DART DA1 139 H5
Homeland Dr BELMT SM2 175 F7
Homelands Dr NRWD SE19 150 A6
Homeleigh Rd PECK SE15 132 A4
Home Md STAN HA7 35 J7
Homemead Rd CROY/NA CR0 163 H5
HAYES BR2 168 E4
Home Park Ct KUT * KT1 158 E3
Home Park Rd
WIM/MER SW19 146 D3
Home Park Wk SURB KT6 158 E3
Homer Cl BXLYHN DA7 117 K7
Homer Dr POP/IOD E14 112 D3
Home Rd BTSEA SW11 128 D1
Homer Rd CROY/NA CR0 166 A5
HOM E9 75 G5
Homer Rw CAMTN NW1 9 K3
Homersham Rd KUT KT1 159 H1
Homer St CAMTN NW1 9 K3
Homerton Gv HOM E9 75 F4
Homerton High St HOM E9 75 F4
Homerton Rd HOM E9 75 H4
Homerton Rw HOM E9 74 E4
Homerton Ter HOM E9 74 E5
Homesdale Cl WAN E11 58 E4
Homesdale Rd HAYES BR2 168 B3
ORP BR6 169 K6
Homesfield GLDGN NW11 52 E4
Homestall Rd EDUL SE22 131 K4
The Homestead DART DA1 139 F5
Homestead Gdns
ESH/CLAY KT10 170 E4
Homestead Paddock
STHGT/OAK N14 28 B4
Homestead Pk CRICK NW2 69 H2
Homestead Rd BCTR RM8 80 B1
FUL/PGN SW6 107 J6
Homewaters Av SUN TW16 140 D7
Homewillow Cl WCHMH N21 29 H5
Homewood Cl HPTN TW12 141 K5
Homewood Crs CHST BR7 154 E5
Homewood Gdns SNWD * SE25 165 F4
Honduras St FSBYE EC1V 6 E9
Honeybourne Rd
KIL/WHAMP NW6 71 F4
Honeybourne Wy
STMC/STPC BR5 169 H7
Honeybrook Rd BAL SW12 129 H6
Honey Cl DAGE RM10 80 E5
Honeyman Cl CRICK NW2 70 B6
Honeypot Cl KTN/HRWW/W HA3 50 B3
Honeypot La STAN HA7 35 K7
STAN HA7 50 A2
Honeysett Rd TOTM N17 56 B1
Honeysuckle Cl STHL UB1 83 J6
Honeysuckle Gdns
CROY/NA CR0 166 A6
Honeywell Rd BTSEA SW11 128 D5
Honeywood Rd ISLW * TW7 124 B3
WLSDN NW10 87 H1
Honeywood Wk CAR SM5 175 K3
Honister Cl STAN HA7 35 H7
Honister Gdns STAN HA7 35 H6
Honister Pl STAN HA7 35 H7
Honiton Gdns PECK * SE15 131 K1
Honiton Rd KIL/WHAMP NW6 88 D1
ROMW/RG RM7 63 F5
WELL DA16 136 A1
Honley Rd CAT SE6 132 E6
Honnor Gdns ISLW TW7 123 J1
Honor Oak Pk FSTH SE23 131 K6
Honor Oak Ri FSTH SE23 131 K5
Honor Oak Rd FSTH SE23 131 K7
Hood Av MORT/ESHN SW14 125 K4
STHGT/OAK N14 28 B5
Hood Cl CROY/NA CR0 164 C7
Hoodcote Gdns WCHMH N21 29 H6
Hood Rd RAIN RM13 81 G7
RYNPK SW20 145 H6
The Hook BAR EN5 27 H5
Hooker's Rd WALTH E17 57 F2
Hook Farm Rd HAYES BR2 168 C4
Hooking Gn RYLN/HDSTN HA2 48 B4
Hook La WELL DA16 136 A4
Hook Ri North SURB KT6 172 C2
Hook Ri South CHSGTN KT9 172 B2
Hook Rd CHSGTN KT9 171 K4
HOR/WEW KT19 172 E6
SURB KT6 172 A1
Hooks Hall Dr DAGE RM10 80 E2
Hookstone Wy WFD IG8 45 H6
Hook U/P (Kingston By-Pass)
SURB KT6 171 K2
Hook Wk EDGW HA8 36 E5
Hooper Rd CAN/RD E16 94 E5
Hooper's Ms ACT W3 86 E7
Hooper St WCHPL E1 92 C6
Hoop La GLDGN NW11 52 D6
Hop Ct ALP/SUD * HA0 67 J5
Hope Cl BTFD TW8 105 F4
CHDH RM6 61 K3
IS N1 73 J5
LEE/GVPK SE12 153 F2
SUT SM1 175 G4
Hopedale Rd CHARL SE7 114 A5
Hopefield Av KIL/WHAMP NW6 88 C1
Hope Pk BMLY BR1 152 D6
Hopes Cl HEST TW5 103 F5
Hope St BTSEA SW11 128 C2
Hopetown St WCHPL * E1 13 M3
Hopewell St CMBW SE5 110 E6
Hopewell Yd CMBW SE5 110 E6
Hop Gdns CHCR WC2N 11 J7
Hopgood St SHB W12 88 A7
Hopkins Cl MUSWH N10 40 A6
Hopkinsons Pl CAMTN NW1 3 M3
Hopkins St SOHO/CST W1F 10 F5
Hoppers Rd WCHMH N21 41 G1
Hoppett Rd CHING E4 44 C2
Hopping La IS * N1 73 H5
Hoppingwood Av NWMAL KT3 160 B2
Hoppner Rd YEAD UB4 82 B1
Hopton Gdns NWMAL KT3 160 D5
Hopton Pde
STRHM/NOR * SW16 148 E4
Hopton Rd STRHM/NOR SW16 148 E4
WOOL/PLUM SE18 115 G2
Hoptons Gdns STHWK * SE1 12 D8
Hopton St STHWK SE1 12 D8
Hopwood Cl TOOT SW17 147 G2
Hopwood Rd WALW SE17 19 H9
Hopwood Wk HACK * E8 74 C6
Horace Av ROMW/RG RM7 63 F7
Horace Rd BARK/HLT IG6 60 C2
FSTGT E7 77 F3
KUT KT1 159 G2
Horatio Pl POP/IOD E14 113 F1
Horatio St BETH E2 7 M6
Horatius Wy CROY/NA CR0 177 F5
Horbury Crs NTGHL W11 8 A7
Horbury Ms NTGHL W11 88 D6
Horder Rd FUL/PGN SW6 107 H7
Hordle Prom East PECK SE15 111 G6
Hordle Prom North
PECK * SE15 111 G6
Hordle Prom West PECK SE15 111 F6
Horley Cl BXLYHS DA6 137 H4
Horley Rd ELTH/MOT SE9 153 J3
Hormead Rd MV/WKIL W9 88 D3
Hornbeam Cl IL IG1 78 D4
LBTH SE11 18 A5
MLHL NW7 37 H2
NTHLT UB5 65 K4
Hornbeam Crs BTFD TW8 104 C6
Hornbeam Gv CHING E4 44 C2
Hornbeam Rd BKHH IG9 45 H2
YEAD UB4 83 G4
Hornbeams Ri FBAR/BDGN N11 40 A5
Hornbeam Wy HAYES BR2 169 F5
Hornbuckle Cl RYLN/HDSTN HA2 66 D1
Hornby Cl HAMP NW3 3 H1
Horncastle Cl LEE/GVPK SE12 133 K6
Horncastle Rd LEE/GVPK SE12 133 K6
Hornchurch Cl KUTN/CMB KT2 143 K4
Hornchurch Rd EMPK RM11 63 K7
Horndean Cl PUT/ROE SW15 126 D7
Horne House
WOOL/PLUM SE18 114 D7
Horner La MTCM CR4 162 C1
The Hornets WATW WD18 21 F3
Horne Wy PUT/ROE SW15 127 F1
Hornfair Rd CHARL SE7 114 C5
Hornford Wy ROMW/RG RM7 63 G6
Horniman Dr FSTH SE23 131 J7
Horniman Gdns FSTH * SE23 131 J7
Horning Cl ELTH/MOT SE9 153 J3
Horn La ACT W3 86 E7
GNWCH SE10 113 K3
WFD IG8 44 E5
Horn Link Wy GNWCH SE10 113 K3
Horn Park Cl LEE/GVPK SE12 134 A4
Horn Park La LEE/GVPK SE12 134 A4
Horns End Pl PIN HA5 47 G3
Hornsey Chambers CLPT * E5 74 D1
Hornsey La ARCH N19 54 C6
Hornsey Lane Est ARCH * N19 54 D6
Hornsey Lane Gdns HGT N6 54 C6
Hornsey Park Rd
CEND/HSY/T N8 55 F2
Hornsey Ri ARCH N19 54 D6
Hornsey Rise Gdns ARCH N19 54 D6
Hornsey Rd ARCH N19 54 E7
HOLWY N7 73 F2
Hornsey St HOLWY N7 73 F4
Hornshay St PECK SE15 111 K5
Horns Rd BARK/HLT IG6 60 C4
Hornton Pl KENS W8 14 B2
Hornton St KENS W8 14 B1
Horsa Rd ERITH DA8 117 K6
LEE/GVPK SE12 134 B6
Horsebridges Cl DAGW RM9 80 A7
Horsecroft Rd EDGW HA8 37 F6
Horse Fair KUT KT1 158 E1
Horseferry Pl GNWCH SE10 113 F5
Horseferry Rd POP/IOD E14 93 G6
WEST SW1P 17 G4
Horse Guards Av WHALL SW1A 11 J9
Horse Guards Rd WHALL SW1A 11 H9
Horse Leaze EHAM E6 96 B5
Horsell Rd HBRY N5 73 G4
STMC/STPC BR5 155 G7
Horselydown La STHWK SE1 19 L1
Horsenden Av GFD/PVL UB6 66 E4
Horsenden Crs GFD/PVL UB6 67 F4
Horsenden La North
GFD/PVL UB6 66 E5
Horsenden La South
GFD/PVL UB6 67 G7
Horseshoe Cl CRICK NW2 69 K1
POP/IOD E14 113 F4
Horse Shoe Crs NTHLT UB5 84 A1
Horseshoe La ENC/FH EN2 29 J2
TRDG/WHET N20 26 B7
Horse Yd IS N1 6 D3
Horsfeld Gdns ELTH/MOT SE9 134 D4
Horsfeld Rd ELTH/MOT SE9 134 C4
Horsford Rd BRXS/STRHM SW2 130 A4
Horsham Av NFNCH/WDSP N12 39 J4
Horsham Rd BXLYHS DA6 137 G5
EBED/NFELT TW14 121 F5
Horsley Dr CROY/NA CR0 180 A6
KUTN/CMB KT2 143 K4
Horsley Rd BMLY BR1 153 F7
CHING E4 44 A1
Horsley St WALW SE17 19 G9
Horsmans Pl DART * DA1 139 H6
Horsman St CMBW SE5 110 D5
Horsmonden Cl ORP BR6 169 K6
Horsmonden Rd BROCKY SE4 132 C4
Hortensia Rd WBPTN SW10 108 B5
Horticultural Pl CHSWK W4 106 A4
Horton Av CRICK NW2 70 C3
Horton Rd HACK E8 74 D5
Horton St LEW SE13 132 E2
Horton Wy CROY/NA CR0 166 A4
Hortus Rd NWDGN UB2 102 E1
Hosack Rd BAL SW12 147 K1
Hoser Av LEE/GVPK SE12 152 E1
Hosier La STBT EC1A 12 C3
Hoskin's Cl CAN/RD E16 95 G5
HYS/HAR UB3 101 J4
Hoskins St GNWCH SE10 113 G4
Hospital Bridge Rd WHTN TW2 123 G7
Hospital Rd HSLW TW3 123 F2
Hospital Wy LEW SE13 133 G5
Hotham Cl E/WMO/HCT KT8 157 F2
Hotham Rd PUT/ROE SW15 127 F2
WIM/MER SW19 147 G6
Hotham St SRTFD E15 76 C7
Hothfield Pl BERM/RHTH SE16 111 K2
Hotspur Rd NTHLT UB5 84 A1
Hotspur St LBTH SE11 18 A7
Houblon Rd RCHPK/HAM TW10 125 F4
Houghton Cl HACK * E8 74 B5
HPTN TW12 141 J5
Houghton Rd SEVS/STOTM N15 56 B3
Houghton St HOL/ALD * WC2B 11 M5
Houlder Crs CROY/NA CR0 177 H5
Houndsden Rd WCHMH N21 29 F5
Houndsditch HDTCH EC3A 13 K4
Houndsfield Rd ED N9 30 D6
Hounslow Av HSLW TW3 123 G4
Hounslow Gdns HSLW TW3 123 G4
Hounslow Rd
EBED/NFELT TW14 122 A6
FELT TW13 141 H2
HSLW TW3 123 G5
Houseman Wy CMBW SE5 110 E6
Houston Rd FSTH SE23 151 G1
SURB KT6 158 C5
Hove Av WALTH E17 57 H4
Hoveden Rd CRICK NW2 70 B4
Hove Gdns SUT SM1 162 A7
Hoveton Rd THMD SE28 97 J5
Howard Av BXLY DA5 136 D7
Howard Cl ACT W3 86 D5
BUSH WD23 22 E6
CRICK * NW2 70 C3
FBAR/BDGN N11 40 A1
HPTN TW12 142 C6
SUN TW16 140 D5
Howard Dr BORE WD6 25 F3
Howard Rd BARK IG11 78 D7
BMLY BR1 152 E6
BRYLDS KT5 159 G5
CRICK NW2 70 B3
DART DA1 139 K5
EHAM E6 95 K1
IL IG1 78 B3
ISLW TW7 124 A2
NWMAL KT3 160 B2
PGE/AN SE20 150 E7
SEVS/STOTM N15 56 A5
SNWD SE25 165 H4
STHL UB1 84 B5
STNW/STAM N16 73 K3
WALTH E17 57 J2
WAN E11 76 C2
Howards Cl PIN * HA5 47 F1
Howards Crest Cl BECK BR3 167 F1
Howard's La PUT/ROE SW15 127 F3
Howard's Rd PLSTW E13 94 E2
Howard St THDIT KT7 158 C6
Howard Wk EFNCH N2 53 G3
Howard Wy BAR EN5 26 B4
Howarth Rd ABYW SE2 116 B4
Howberry Cl EDGW HA8 35 K5
Howberry Rd EDGW HA8 35 K6
THHTH CR7 149 K7
Howbury La ERITH DA8 138 D1
Howbury Rd PECK SE15 131 K2
Howcroft Crs FNCH N3 38 E6
Howcroft La GFD/PVL UB6 84 D2
Howden Cl THMD SE28 97 J6
Howden Rd SNWD SE25 165 G1
Howden St PECK SE15 131 H2
Howell Cl CHDH RM6 61 K4
Howell Wk WALW SE17 18 D6
Howfield Pl TOTM * N17 56 B2
Howgate Rd
MORT/ESHN SW14 126 A2
Howick Pl WEST SW1P 16 F4
Howie St BTSEA SW11 108 D6
Howitt Cl HAMP NW3 71 J5
Howitt Rd HAMP NW3 71 J5
Howitts Cl ESH/CLAY KT10 170 A5
Howland Ct PIN * HA5 34 A5
Howland Ms East FITZ W1T 10 F2
Howland St FITZ W1T 10 F2
Howland Wy
BERM/RHTH SE16 112 B1
Howletts La RSLP HA4 46 A5
Howletts Rd HNHL SE24 130 D5
Howley Pl BAY/PAD W2 8 F2
Howley Rd CROY/NA CR0 177 H2
Howsman Rd BARN SW13 106 D5
Howson Rd BROCKY SE4 132 B3
Howson Ter
RCHPK/HAM * TW10 125 F5
How's St BETH E2 7 L5
Howton Pl BUSH WD23 22 D7
Hoxton Market IS N1 7 J8
Hoxton Sq IS N1 7 J8
Hoxton St IS N1 7 J4
Hoylake Gdns MTCM CR4 163 H2
OXHEY WD19 33 H3
RSLP HA4 47 F7
Hoylake Rd ACT W3 87 G5
Hoyland Cl PECK * SE15 111 J6
Hoyle Rd TOOT SW17 147 J4
Hoy St CAN/RD E16 94 D5
Hubbard Dr CHSGTN KT9 171 J5
Hubbard Rd WNWD SE27 149 J3
Hubbard St SRTFD E15 76 C7
Hubert Cl WIM/MER * SW19 147 G7
Hubert Gv BRXN/ST SW9 129 K2
Hubert Rd EHAM E6 95 H2
RAIN RM13 99 H2
Huddart St BOW E3 93 H4
Huddleston Cl BETH * E2 92 E1
Huddlestone Rd CRICK NW2 69 K5
FSTGT E7 76 D3
Huddleston Rd ARCH N19 72 C2
Hudson Cl SHB * W12 87 K6
Hudson Pl WOOL/PLUM SE18 115 H4

Hudson Rd BXLYHN DA7 137 G1
HYS/HAR UB3 101 G5
Huggin Hl BLKFR EC4V 12 F6
Huggins Pl BRXS/STRHM SW2 130 A7
Hughan Rd SRTFD E15 76 B4
Hugh Dalton Av
FUL/PGN * SW6 107 J5
Hughenden Av
KTN/HRWW/W HA3 49 H4
Hughenden Gdns NTHLT UB5 83 G2
Hughenden Rd WPK KT4 160 D6
Hughes Rd ASHF TW15 140 A6
HYS/HAR UB3 83 F6
Hughes Ter CAN/RD * E16 94 D4
Hughes Wk CROY/NA CR0 164 D6
Hugh Gaitskell Cl
FUL/PGN * SW6 107 J5
Hugh Ms PIM SW1V 16 D6
Hugh Pl WEST SW1P 17 G5
Hugh St PIM SW1V 16 D6
Hugo Gdns RAIN RM13 81 H5
Hugon Rd FUL/PGN SW6 128 A2
Hugo Rd ARCH N19 72 C3
Huguenot Pl
WAND/EARL SW18 128 B4
WCHPL E1 13 M2
Hullbridge Ms IS N1 7 G3
Hull Cl BERM/RHTH * SE16 93 F7
Hull St FSBYE EC1V 6 E8
Hulme Pl STHWK SE1 18 F2
Hulse Av BARK IG11 78 D5
Humber Dr NKENS W10 88 B3
Humber Rd BKHTH/KID SE3 113 K5
CRICK NW2 69 K1
DART DA1 139 G4
Humberstone Rd PLSTW E13 95 G2
Humbolt Rd HMSMTH W6 107 H5
Humes Av HNWL W7 104 A2
Hume Wy RSLP HA4 46 E5
Humphrey Cl CLAY * IG5 45 K7
Humphrey St STHWK SE1 19 L7
Humphries Cl DAGW RM9 80 B3
Hundred Acre CDALE/KGS NW9 51 H1
Hungerford Br STHWK SE1 11 L8
Hungerford Rd HOLWY N7 72 D5
Hungerford St WCHPL * E1 92 D5
Hunsdon Cl DAGW RM9 80 A5
Hunsdon Rd NWCR SE14 112 A6
Hunslett St BETH * E2 92 E1
Hunston Rd MRDN SM4 162 A7
Hunt Cl BKHTH/KID * SE3 133 K1
Hunter Cl BAL SW12 129 F7
BORE WD6 24 E4
STHWK SE1 19 H4
Hunter Ct CMBW * SE5 130 E3
Huntercrombe Gdns
OXHEY WD19 33 G4
Hunter Rd RYNPK SW20 146 A7
THHTH CR7 164 E2
Hunters Ct RCH/KEW TW9 124 E4
Hunters Gv HYS/HAR UB3 82 E7
KTN/HRWW/W HA3 49 J3
Hunters Hall Rd DAGE RM10 80 C3
Hunters Hl RSLP HA4 65 G2
Hunters Meadow NRWD SE19 150 A3
Hunters Rd CHSGTN KT9 172 A2
IL IG1 78 B4
Hunters Sq DAGE RM10 80 C3
Hunter St BMSBY WC1N 5 K9
Hunters Wy CROY/NA CR0 178 A3
Hunting Cl ESH/CLAY KT10 170 A3
Huntingdon Cl MTCM CR4 163 K3
Huntingdon Gdns CHSWK * W4 105 K6
WPK KT4 174 A2
Huntingdon Rd ED N9 30 E7
EFNCH N2 53 J2
Huntingdon St CAN/RD E16 94 D5
IS N1 5 M1
Huntingfield CROY/NA CR0 179 H6
Huntingfield Rd
PUT/ROE SW15 126 D3
Hunting Gate Cl ENC/FH EN2 29 G2
Hunting Gate Dr CHSGTN KT9 172 A6
Hunting Gate Ms WHTN * TW2 123 K7
Huntings Rd DAGE RM10 80 C5
Huntland Cl RAIN RM13 99 K4
Huntley St GWRST WC1E 10 F1
Huntley Wy RYNPK * SW20 160 D1
Huntly Dr FNCH N3 38 E5
Huntly Rd SNWD SE25 165 F3
Hunton St WCHPL E1 92 C4
Hunt Rd NWDGN UB2 103 F2
Hunt's La SRTFD E15 94 A1
Huntsman Cl FELT TW13 141 F3
Huntsman St WALW SE17 19 J6
Hunts Md PEND EN3 31 F2
Hunts Mede Cl CHST BR7 153 K6
Huntsmoor Rd
HOR/WEW KT19 173 F4
Huntspill St TOOT SW17 147 G2
Hunts Slip Rd DUL SE21 150 A2
Huntsworth Ms CAMTN NW1 3 L9
Hurdwick Pl CAMTN * NW1 4 E5
Hurley Rd GFD/PVL UB6 84 B4
Hurlingham Gdns
FUL/PGN SW6 127 J2
Hurlingham Pk
FUL/PGN * SW6 127 J2
Hurlingham Rd BXLYHN DA7 117 G6
FUL/PGN SW6 127 J1
Hurlingham Sq
FUL/PGN * SW6 127 K2
Hurlock St HBRY N5 73 H2
Hurlstone Rd SNWD SE25 164 E4
Hurn Court Rd HEST TW5 122 C1
Huron Rd TOOT SW17 148 A1
Hurren Cl BKHTH/KID SE3 133 H2
Hurricane Rd WLGTN SM6 177 F6
Hurry Cl SRTFD E15 76 C6
Hurst Av CHING E4 43 J2
HGT N6 54 C5
Hurstbourne Gdns BARK IG11 78 D5
Hurstbourne Rd FSTH SE23 132 B7
Hurst Cl CHING E4 43 J2
CHSGTN KT9 172 C4
GLDGN NW11 53 F5
HAYES BR2 167 J7
NTHLT UB5 65 K5
Hurstcourt Rd SUT SM1 162 A7
Hurstdene Av HAYES BR2 167 J7
Hurstdene Gdns
SEVS/STOTM N15 56 A6
Hurstfield HAYES BR2 167 K4
Hurstfield Crs YEAD UB4 82 C4
Hurstfield Rd E/WMO/HCT KT8 157 F2
Hurst La ABYW SE2 116 E4
E/WMO/HCT KT8 157 H3
Hurstleigh Gdns CLAY IG5 45 K7
Hurst Pl DART * DA1 139 F5
Hurst Ri BAR EN5 26 E2
Hurst Rd BFN/LL DA15 155 H1
CROY/NA CR0 177 K4
E/WMO/HCT KT8 157 H2
ERITH DA8 117 K6
WALTH E17 57 K2
WCHMH N21 29 G7
WOT/HER KT12 156 C3
Hurst Springs BXLY DA5 137 F7
Hurst St HNHL SE24 130 C5
Hurst View Rd SAND/SEL CR2 178 A6
Hurst Wy SAND/SEL CR2 178 A5
Hurstway Wk NKENS * W10 88 B6
Hurstwood Av BXLY DA5 137 F7
ERITH DA8 118 B7
SWFD E18 59 F3
Hurstwood Dr BMLY BR1 168 E2
Hurstwood Rd GLDGN NW11 52 C3
Hurtwood Rd WOT/HER KT12 156 E6
Huson Cl HAMP NW3 3 J2
Hussain Cl HRW HA1 67 F3
Hussars Cl HSLWW TW4 122 D2
Husseywell Crs HAYES BR2 167 K7
Hutching's St POP/IOD E14 112 D1
Hutchings Wk GLDGN NW11 53 F3
Hutchins Cl SRTFD E15 76 A6
Hutchinson Ter WBLY HA9 67 K2
Hutchins Rd THMD SE28 97 G6
Hutton Cl GFD/PVL UB6 66 D4
WFD IG8 45 F5
Hutton Gv NFNCH/WDSP N12 39 F4
Hutton La KTN/HRWW/W HA3 34 C6
Hutton Rw EDGW HA8 36 E6
Hutton St EMB EC4Y 12 B5
Hutton Wk KTN/HRWW/W HA3 34 C6
Huxbear St BROCKY SE4 132 C4
Huxley UED * N18 41 K4
Huxley Cl NTHLT UB5 83 J1
Huxley Dr CHDH RM6 61 H6
Huxley Gdns WLSDN NW10 86 B2
Huxley Pde UED * N18 41 K4
Huxley Pl PLMGR N13 41 H3
Huxley Rd LEY E10 76 A1
UED N18 41 K3
WELL DA16 136 A2
Huxley Sayze UED * N18 41 K4
Huxley St NKENS W10 88 C2
Hyacinth Cl HPTN TW12 142 A5
Hyacinth Rd PUT/ROE SW15 126 D7
The Hyde CDALE/KGS NW9 51 H4
Hyde Cl BAR EN5 26 D2
PLSTW E13 94 E1
Hyde Crs CDALE/KGS NW9 51 G4
Hyde Estate Rd
CDALE/KGS NW9 51 H4
Hyde Farm Ms BAL SW12 129 J7
Hydefield Cl ED N9 29 K7
Hydefield Ct ED N9 42 A1
Hyde La BTSEA SW11 108 D7
Hyde Park Av WCHMH N21 41 J1
Hyde Park Cnr MYFR/PICC W1J 16 B1
Hyde Park Crs BAY/PAD W2 9 J5
Hyde Park Gdns BAY/PAD W2 9 H6
WCHMH N21 29 J7
Hyde Park Gardens Ms
BAY/PAD W2 9 H6
Hyde Park Ga KENS W8 14 E2
Hyde Park Gate Ms
SKENS * SW7 14 F2
Hyde Park Pl BAY/PAD W2 9 K6
Hyde Park Sq BAY/PAD W2 9 J5
Hyde Park St BAY/PAD W2 9 J6
Hyderabad Wy SRTFD E15 76 C6
Hyde Rd BXLYHN DA7 137 G1
IS N1 7 H4
RCHPK/HAM TW10 125 G4
WAT WD17 20 E2
Hydeside Gdns ED N9 42 B1
Hyde's Pl IS N1 6 C1
Hyde St DEPT SE8 112 D5
Hyde Ter SUN TW16 140 C5
Hydethorpe Av ED N9 42 B1
Hydethorpe Rd BAL SW12 129 H7
Hyde V GNWCH SE10 113 F6
Hyde Wk MRDN SM4 161 K6
Hyde Wy ED N9 42 B1
HYS/HAR UB3 101 J3
Hyland Cl EMPK RM11 63 K6
Hylands Rd WALTH E17 58 B1
Hyland Wy EMPK RM11 63 K6
Hylton St WOOL/PLUM SE18 116 A3
Hyndewood FSTH * SE23 151 F2
Hyndman St PECK SE15 111 J5
Hynton Rd BCTR RM8 79 J1
Hyperion Pl HOR/WEW KT19 173 F7
Hyson Rd BERM/RHTH SE16 111 J4
Hythe Av BXLYHN DA7 117 G6
Hythe Cl UED N18 42 C3
Hythe Rd THHTH CR7 164 E1
WLSDN NW10 87 H2
Hythe St DART DA1 139 H5
Hyver Hl MLHL NW7 25 F5

I

Ibbotson Av CAN/RD E16 94 D5
Ibbott St WCHPL E1 92 E3
Iberian Av WLGTN SM6 176 D3
Ibis La CHSWK W4 105 K7
Ibis Wy YEAD UB4 83 H5
Ibscott Cl DAGE RM10 80 E5
Ibsley Gdns PUT/ROE SW15 126 D7
Ibsley Wy EBAR EN4 27 J4
Iceland Rd BOW E3 75 J7
Ickburgh Est CLPT * E5 74 D1
Ickburgh Rd CLPT E5 74 D2
Ickenham Cl RSLP HA4 64 B1
Ickenham Rd RSLP HA4 46 B7
Ickleton Rd ELTH/MOT SE9 153 J3
Icknield Dr GNTH/NBYPK IG2 60 B4
Ickworth Park Rd WALTH E17 57 G3
Ida Rd SEVS/STOTM N15 55 K4
Ida St POP/IOD E14 94 A5
Iden Cl HAYES BR2 167 H2
Idlecombe Rd TOOT SW17 148 A5
Idmiston Rd SRTFD E15 76 D4
WNWD SE27 149 J2
WPK KT4 160 C6
Idmiston Sq WPK KT4 160 C6
Idol La MON EC3R 13 J7
Idonia St DEPT SE8 112 C6
Iffley Rd HMSMTH W6 106 E2
Ifield Rd WBPTN SW10 14 D9
Ightham Rd ERITH DA8 117 H6
Ilbert St NKENS W10 88 C2
Ilchester Gdns BAY/PAD W2 8 C6
Ilchester Pl WKENS W14 107 J2
Ilchester Rd BCTR RM8 79 H4
Ildersly Gv DUL SE21 149 K1
Ilderton Rd BERM/RHTH SE16 111 K5
Ilex Cl SUN TW16 156 B1
Ilex Rd WLSDN NW10 69 H5
Ilex Wy STRHM/NOR SW16 149 G4
Ilford Hl IL IG1 78 A2
Ilford La IL IG1 78 B3
Ilfracombe Gdns CHDH RM6 61 H6
Ilfracombe Rd BMLY BR1 152 D2
Iliffe St WALW SE17 18 D7
Iliffe Yd WALW SE17 18 D7
Ilkley Cl NRWD * SE19 149 K5
Ilkley Rd CAN/RD E16 95 G4
OXHEY WD19 33 H4
Illingworth Cl MTCM CR4 162 C2
Illingworth Wy EN EN1 30 A4
Ilmington Rd
KTN/HRWW/W HA3 49 K5
Ilminster Gdns BTSEA SW11 128 D3
Imber Cl STHGT/OAK N14 28 C6
Imber Cross THDIT * KT7 158 A6
Imber Gv ESH/CLAY KT10 157 J6
Imber Park Rd ESH/CLAY KT10 157 J7
Imber St IS N1 7 G4
Imperial Av STNW/STAM * N16 74 A3
Imperial Cl RYLN/HDSTN HA2 48 A5
Imperial College Rd SKENS SW7 15 G4
Imperial Dr RYLN/HDSTN HA2 48 A7
Imperial Gdns MTCM CR4 163 G2
Imperial Pl BORE * WD6 24 D2
CHST BR7 154 A7
Imperial Rd EBED/NFELT TW14 121 H6
FUL/PGN SW6 108 A7
WDGN N22 40 E6
Imperial Sq FUL/PGN SW6 108 A7
Imperial St BOW E3 94 A2
Imperial Wy CHST BR7 154 C2
CROY/NA CR0 177 G5
KTN/HRWW/W HA3 50 A5
Imre Cl SHB W12 87 K7
Inca Dr ELTH/MOT SE9 135 G6
Inchmery Rd CAT SE6 151 K1
Inchwood CROY/NA CR0 179 K3
Independent Pl HACK E8 74 B4
Independents Rd
BKHTH/KID SE3 133 J2
Inderwick Rd CEND/HSY/T N8 55 F5
Indescon Ct POP/IOD E14 112 E1
India St TWRH EC3N 13 L5
India Wy SHB W12 87 K6
Indigo Ms POP/IOD * E14 94 A6
STNW/STAM N16 73 K2
Indus Rd CHARL SE7 114 B6
Ingal Rd PLSTW E13 94 E3
Ingate Pl VX/NE SW8 109 G7
Ingatestone Rd MNPK E12 59 G7
SNWD SE25 165 J4
WFD IG8 45 F6
Ingelow St VX/NE SW8 129 G1
Ingersoll Rd SHB W12 87 K7
Ingestre Pl SOHO/CST W1F 10 F5
Ingestre Rd FSTGT E7 76 E3
KTTN NW5 72 B3
Ingham Cl SAND/SEL CR2 179 F7
Ingham Rd KIL/WHAMP NW6 70 E3
SAND/SEL CR2 178 E7
Inglebert St CLKNW EC1R 6 A7
Ingleborough St BRXN/ST SW9 130 B1
Ingleby Dr HRW HA1 66 D2
Ingleby Rd DAGE RM10 80 D5
HOLWY N7 72 E2
IL IG1 60 B7
Ingleby Wy CHST BR7 154 A4
WLGTN SM6 176 D7
Ingle Cl PIN HA5 47 K2
Ingledew Rd
WOOL/PLUM SE18 115 J4
Inglefield Sq WAP * E1W 92 D7
Inglehurst Gdns REDBR IG4 59 K4
Inglemere Rd FSTH SE23 151 F2
TOOT SW17 147 K6
Ingleside Cl BECK BR3 151 J6
Ingleside Gv BKHTH/KID SE3 113 J5
Inglethorpe St FUL/PGN SW6 107 G7
Ingleton Av WELL DA16 136 B4
Ingleton Rd CAR SM5 175 J7
UED N18 42 C5
Ingleton St BRXN/ST SW9 130 B1
Ingleway NFNCH/WDSP N12 39 H5
Inglewood CROY/NA CR0 179 G7
Inglewood Cl POP/IOD E14 112 D3
Inglewood Copse BMLY BR1 168 D1
Inglewood Rd BXLYHN DA7 138 A3
KIL/WHAMP NW6 70 E4
Inglis Rd CROY/NA CR0 165 G7
EA W5 86 B6
Inglis St CMBW SE5 110 C7
Ingram Av EFNCH N2 53 G6
Ingram Cl LBTH SE11 17 M5
STAN HA7 35 J4
Ingram Rd DART DA1 139 H7
EFNCH N2 53 J3
THHTH CR7 149 J7
Ingram Wy GFD/PVL UB6 66 D7
Ingrave Rd ROM RM1 63 F3
Ingrave St BTSEA SW11 128 C2
Ingrebourne Rd RAIN RM13 99 K3
Ingress St CHSWK W4 106 B4
Inigo Jones Rd CHARL SE7 114 C6
Inkerman Rd KTTN NW5 72 B5
Inks Gn CHING E4 44 A4
Inkwell Cl NFNCH/WDSP N12 39 G2
Inman Rd WAND/EARL SW18 128 B6
WLSDN NW10 69 G7
Inmans Rw WFD IG8 44 E3
Inner Cir CAMTN NW1 4 A8
Inner Park Rd
WIM/MER SW19 146 B1
Inner Ring East HTHAIR TW6 120 E2
Innes Cl RYNPK SW20 161 H1
Innes Gdns PUT/ROE SW15 126 E5
Innes Yd CROY/NA CR0 177 J2
Inniskilling Rd PLSTW E13 95 G1
Innovation Cl ALP/SUD HA0 68 A7
Inskip Cl LEY E10 75 K1
Inskip Rd BCTR RM8 61 K7
Institute Pl HACK E8 74 D4
Instone Rd DART DA1 139 G6
Integer Gdns WAN * E11 58 B6
International Av HEST TW5 102 B4
Inver Cl BAY/PAD W2 8 D5
Inveresk Gdns WPK KT4 173 H2
Inverforth Cl HAMP NW3 71 G1
Inverforth Rd FBAR/BDGN N11 40 B4
Inverine Rd CHARL SE7 114 A4
Invermore Pl
WOOL/PLUM SE18 115 H3
Inverness Gdns KENS W8 8 C9
Inverness Ms BAY/PAD W2 8 D6
Inverness Pl BAY/PAD W2 8 D6
Inverness Rd HSLW TW3 122 E3
NWDGN UB2 102 D3
UED N18 42 D4
WPK KT4 161 G7
Inverness St CAMTN NW1 4 C3
Inverness Ter BAY/PAD W2 8 D5
WDGN * N22 41 H7
Inverton Rd PECK SE15 132 A3
Invicta Cl CHST BR7 154 A4
EBED/NFELT TW14 121 J7
Invicta Gv NTHLT UB5 83 K2
Invicta Pde SCUP * DA14 155 H3
Invicta Plaza STHWK SE1 12 C8
Invicta Rd BKHTH/KID SE3 113 K6
Inville Rd WALW SE17 19 H8
Inwood Av HSLW TW3 123 H2
Inwood Cl CROY/NA CR0 179 G1
Inwood Rd HSLW TW3 123 H3
Inworth St BTSEA SW11 128 D1
Inworth Wk IS * N1 6 E3
Iona Cl CAT SE6 132 D6
MRDN SM4 162 A6
Ion Sq BETH * E2 92 C1
Ipswich Rd TOOT SW17 148 A5
Ireland Cl EHAM E6 95 K4
Ireland Pl WDGN N22 40 E6
Irene Ms HNWL * W7 85 F7
Irene Rd FUL/PGN SW6 107 K7
Ireton Cl MUSWH N10 40 A6
Ireton St BOW E3 93 J3
Iris Av BXLY DA5 137 F5
Iris Cl CROY/NA CR0 166 A7
EHAM E6 95 J4
SURB * KT6 159 G6
Iris Crs BXLYHN DA7 117 G5
Iris Rd HOR/WEW KT19 172 D4
Iris Wy CHING E4 43 H5
Iron Bridge Cl NWDGN UB2 84 C7
WLSDN NW10 69 G4
Iron Bridge Rd South
WDR/YW UB7 100 D1
Iron Mill La DART DA1 138 C3
Iron Mill Pl DART DA1 138 C3
WAND/EARL * SW18 128 A5
Iron Mill Rd WAND/EARL SW18 128 A5
Ironmonger La CITYW EC2V 13 G5
Ironmonger Rw FSBYE EC1V 6 F8
Ironside Cl BERM/RHTH SE16 112 A1
Irvine Av KTN/HRWW/W HA3 49 G2
Irvine Cl TRDG/WHET N20 39 J1
Irving Av NTHLT UB5 65 H7
Irving Gv BRXN/ST SW9 130 A1
Irving Ms IS N1 73 J5
Irving Rd WKENS W14 107 G2
Irving St LSQ/SEVD WC2H 11 H7
Irwell Est BERM/RHTH * SE16 111 K1
Irwin Av WOOL/PLUM SE18 115 K6
Irwin Gdns WLSDN NW10 69 K7
Isabella Cl STHGT/OAK N14 28 C6
Isabella Ct
RCHPK/HAM * TW10 125 G5
Isabella Rd HOM * E9 74 E4
Isabella St STHWK SE1 12 C9
Isabel St BRXN/ST SW9 110 A7
Isambard Ms POP/IOD E14 113 F2
Isambard Pl BERM/RHTH SE16 92 E7
Isham Rd STRHM/NOR SW16 163 K1
Isis Cl RSLP HA4 46 A5
Isis St WAND/EARL SW18 147 G1
Island Farm Av
E/WMO/HCT KT8 156 E4
Island Farm Rd
E/WMO/HCT KT8 156 E4
Island Rd MTCM CR4 147 K6
Island Rw POP/IOD E14 93 H5
Isla Rd WOOL/PLUM SE18 115 H5
Islay Gdns HSLWW TW4 122 C4
Islay Wk IS * N1 73 J5
Islay Whf POP/IOD * E14 94 A4
Isledon Rd HOLWY N7 73 G2
Islehurst Cl CHST BR7 154 A7
Islington Gn IS N1 6 C4
Islington High St IS N1 6 C5
Islington Park Ms IS N1 6 C1
Islington Park St IS N1 6 B1
Islip Gdns EDGW HA8 37 F5
NTHLT UB5 65 J6
Islip Manor Rd NTHLT UB5 65 J6
Islip St KTTN NW5 72 C4
Ismailia Rd FSTGT E7 77 F6
Isom Cl PLSTW E13 95 F2
Ivanhoe Dr KTN/HRWW/W HA3 49 H1
Ivanhoe Rd CMBW SE5 131 G2
HSLWW TW4 122 C2
Ivatt Pl WKENS W14 107 J4
Ivatt Wy SEVS/STOTM N15 55 H2
Iveagh Av WLSDN NW10 86 C1
Iveagh Cl HOM E9 75 F7
WLSDN NW10 86 C1
Ivedon Rd WELL DA16 136 D1
Ive Farm Cl LEY E10 75 J1
Ive Farm La LEY E10 75 J1
Iveley Rd CLAP SW4 129 H1
Ivere Dr BAR EN5 27 F5
Iverhurst Cl BXLYHS DA6 136 E4
Iverna Ct KENS W8 14 B3
Iverna Gdns
EBED/NFELT TW14 121 G4
KENS W8 14 B3
Iverson Rd KIL/WHAMP NW6 70 D5
Ivers Wy CROY/NA CR0 179 K6
Ives Gdns ROM RM1 63 H3
Ives Rd CAN/RD E16 94 C4
Ives St CHEL SW3 15 K5
Ivimey St BETH * E2 92 C2
Ivinghoe Cl EN EN1 30 A1
Ivinghoe Rd BCTR RM8 79 H4
BUSH WD23 22 D6
Ivor Gv ELTH/MOT SE9 135 G7
Ivor Pl CAMTN NW1 9 L1
Ivor St CAMTN NW1 4 E2
Ivory Ct FELT TW13 140 E1
Ivorydown BMLY BR1 152 E3
Ivybridge Cl TWK TW1 124 B5
Ivychurch Cl PGE/AN SE20 150 D6
Ivy Church La STHWK * SE1 19 L7
Ivy Cl DART DA1 139 K5
PIN HA5 47 G6
RYLN/HDSTN HA2 65 K3
SUN TW16 156 B1
Ivy Ct STHWK * SE1 111 H4
Ivy Crs CHSWK W4 105 K3
Ivydale Rd BROCKY SE4 132 A2
CAR SM5 175 K1
Ivyday Gv STRHM/NOR SW16 149 F2
Ivydene E/WMO/HCT KT8 156 E4
Ivydene Cl SUT SM1 175 G3
Ivy Gdns CEND/HSY/T N8 54 E5
MTCM CR4 163 J2
Ivyhouse Rd DAGW RM9 79 K5
Ivy La HSLWW TW4 122 E3
Ivymount Rd WNWD SE27 149 G2
Ivy Rd BROCKY SE4 132 C3
CAN/RD E16 94 E5
CRICK NW2 70 A3
HSLW TW3 123 G3
STHGT/OAK N14 28 D6
SURB * KT6 172 C1
TOOT SW17 147 J4
WALTH E17 57 J5
Ivy St IS N1 7 J5
Ivy Wk DAGW RM9 80 A5
NTHWD * HA6 32 C7
Ixworth Pl CHEL SW3 15 J6
Izane Rd BXLYHS DA6 137 G3

J

Jacaranda Cl NWMAL KT3 160 B2
Jacaranda Gv HACK E8 7 M2
Jackass La HAYES BR2 181 F5
Jack Clow Rd SRTFD E15 94 C1
Jack Cornwell St MNPK E12 78 A3
Jackman Ms WLSDN NW10 69 G2
Jackman St HACK E8 74 D7
Jackson Cl HOM E9 75 F6
Jackson Rd BARK IG11 78 D7
EBAR EN4 27 J5
HAYES BR2 181 J1
HOLWY N7 73 F3
Jackson's La HGT N6 54 A6
Jackson's Pl CROY/NA CR0 164 E7
Jackson St WOOL/PLUM SE18 115 F5
Jackson's Wy CROY/NA CR0 179 J2
Jack Walker Ct HBRY N5 73 H3
Jacobs Cl DAGE RM10 80 D3
Jacob St STHWK SE1 19 M1
Jacob's Well Ms MHST W1U 10 B4
Jacqueline Cl NTHLT UB5 65 J7
Jacqueline Creft Ter HGT * N6 54 A5
Jacqueline Vls WALTH * E17 58 A4
Jade Cl BCTR RM8 61 J7
CAN/RD E16 95 H5
CRICK NW2 52 B6
Jade Ter KIL/WHAMP * NW6 2 F1
Jaffe Rd IL IG1 60 C7
Jaffray Rd HAYES BR2 168 C3
Jaggard Wy BAL SW12 128 E6
Jago Cl WOOL/PLUM SE18 115 H5
Jago Wk CMBW SE5 110 E6
Jamaica Rd BERM/RHTH SE16 111 J2
STHWK SE1 19 L2
THHTH CR7 164 C5
Jamaica St WCHPL E1 92 E4
James Av BCTR RM8 62 B7
CRICK NW2 70 A4
James Cl BUSH WD23 21 J4
GLDGN * NW11 52 C5
GPK RM2 63 J4
PLSTW E13 94 E1
James Collins Cl MV/WKIL W9 88 D3
James Gdns WDGN N22 41 J6
James Joyes Wk HNHL * SE24 130 C3
James La LEY E10 58 A6
Jameson St KENS W8 8 B8
James Pl TOTM N17 42 B6
James Rd DART DA1 138 D6
James St BARK IG11 78 C6
COVGDN WC2E 11 K6
EN EN1 30 B4
HSLW TW3 123 J2
MHST W1U 10 B5
Jamestown Rd CAMTN NW1 4 C3
Jamestown Wy POP/IOD E14 94 B6
James Watt Wy ERITH DA8 118 C5
James Yd CHING * E4 44 B5
Jamuna Cl POP/IOD * E14 93 G4
Jane St WCHPL E1 92 D5
Janet St POP/IOD E14 112 D2
Janeway Pl BERM/RHTH SE16 111 J1
Janeway St BERM/RHTH SE16 111 H1
Janson Cl SRTFD E15 76 C4
WLSDN NW10 69 F2
Janson Rd SRTFD E15 76 C4
Jansons Rd SEVS/STOTM N15 56 A2
Japan Crs FSBYPK N4 55 F7
Japan Rd CHDH RM6 61 K5
Jardine Rd WAP E1W 93 F6
Jarrett Cl BRXS/STRHM SW2 130 C7
Jarrow Cl MRDN SM4 162 A4
Jarrow Rd BERM/RHTH SE16 111 K3
CHDH RM6 61 J5
TOTM N17 56 D3
Jarrow Wy HOM E9 75 G3
Jarvis Cl BAR EN5 26 B4
Jarvis Rd EDUL SE22 131 F3
SAND/SEL CR2 177 K5
Jasmin Cl NTHWD HA6 32 D7
Jasmine Cl IL IG1 78 B4
STHL UB1 83 J6
Jasmine Ct LEE/GVPK SE12 133 K5
Jasmine Gdns CROY/NA CR0 179 K2
RYLN/HDSTN HA2 66 A1
Jasmine Gv PGE/AN SE20 150 D7
Jasmine Rd HOR/WEW KT19 172 D5
ROMW/RG RM7 81 G1
Jasmine Ter WDR/YW UB7 100 D1
Jasmin Rd HOR/WEW KT19 172 D5
Jason Wk ELTH/MOT SE9 154 A3
Jasper Rd CAN/RD E16 95 H5
NRWD SE19 150 B5
Javelin Wy NTHLT UB5 83 H2
Jay Gdns CHST BR7 153 K3
Jay Ms SKENS SW7 14 F2
Jean Batten Cl CROY/NA CR0 177 F6
Jebb Av BRXS/STRHM SW2 129 K5
Jebb St BOW E3 93 J1
Jedburgh Rd PLSTW E13 95 G2
Jedburgh St BTSEA SW11 129 F3
Jeddo Ms SHB * W12 106 C1
Jeddo Rd SHB W12 106 C1
Jefferson Cl GNTH/NBYPK IG2 60 B4
WEA W13 104 C2
Jeffrey's Pl CAMTN NW1 4 E1
Jeffrey's Rd CLAP SW4 129 K1
PEND EN3 31 H3
Jeffrey's St CAMTN NW1 4 D1
Jeffs Cl HPTN * TW12 142 B5
Jeffs Rd SUT SM1 174 D3
Jeger Av BETH E2 7 L4
Jeken Rd ELTH/MOT SE9 134 B3
Jelf Rd BRXS/STRHM SW2 130 B4
Jellicoe Gdns STAN HA7 35 G5
Jellicoe Rd TOTM N17 41 K6
WATW WD18 20 E5
Jemmett Cl KUTN/CMB KT2 144 D7
Jem Paterson Ct HRW * HA1 66 E3
Jengar Cl SUT SM1 175 F3
Jenkins La BARK IG11 96 B1

Jenkins Rd PLSTW E13 95 F3
Jenner Av ACT W3 87 F4
Jenner Rd STNW/STAM N16 74 B1
Jennett Rd CROY/NA CR0 177 G2
Jennifer Rd BMLY BR1 152 D2
Jennings Cl SURB KT6 158 D6
Jennings Rd EDUL SE22 131 G5
Jennings Wy BAR EN5 26 A2
Jenningtree Rd ERITH DA8 118 E6
Jenningtree Wy BELV DA17 117 K1
Jenny Hammond Cl WAN E11 76 D2
Jenson Wy NRWD SE19 150 B6
Jenton Av BXLYHN DA7 117 F7
Jephson Rd FSTGT E7 77 G6
Jephson St CMBW SE5 110 E7
Jephtha Rd WAND/EARL SW18 127 K5
Jeppo's La MTCM CR4 162 E3
Jerdan Pl FUL/PGN SW6 107 K6
Jeremiah St POP/IOD E14 93 K5
Jeremy's Gn UED N18 42 D3
Jermyn St STJS SW1Y 10 E8
Jerningham Av CLAY IG5 60 B1
Jerningham Rd NWCR SE14 132 B1
Jerome Crs STJWD NW8 3 J9
Jerome St WCHPL E1 13 L2
Jerrard St LEW SE13 132 E2
Jerrold St IS * N1 7 K6
Jersey Av KTN/HRWW/W HA3 49 H1
Jersey Dr STMC/STPC BR5 169 J5
Jersey Rd CAN/RD E16 95 G4
HEST TW5 103 G7
HNWL W7 104 B1
IL IG1 78 B3
IS N1 73 J5
LEY E10 58 B7
RAIN RM13 81 J6
TOOT SW17 148 B6
Jersey St BETH E2 92 D2
Jersey Vls HNWL * W7 103 K1
Jerusalem Pas CLKNW EC1R 12 C1
Jerviston Gdns
STRHM/NOR SW16 149 G5
Jesmond Av WBLY HA9 68 B5
Jesmond Cl MTCM CR4 163 G2
Jesmond Dene HAMP * NW3 71 G5
Jesmond Rd CROY/NA CR0 165 G6
Jesmond Wy STAN HA7 36 A4
Jessam Av CLPT E5 56 D7
Jessamine Rd HNWL W7 84 E7
Jesse Rd LEY E10 58 A7
Jessett Cl ERITH DA8 118 A3
Jessica Rd WAND/EARL SW18 128 B5
Jessop Av NWDGN UB2 102 E3
Jessops Wy MTCM CR4 163 H5
Jessup Cl WOOL/PLUM SE18 115 H3
Jetstar Wy NTHLT UB5 83 J2
Jevington Wy LEE/GVPK SE12 134 A7
Jewel Rd WALTH E17 57 J2
Jewry St TWRH EC3N 13 L5
Jews Rw WAND/EARL SW18 128 A3
Jews Wk SYD SE26 150 D3
Jeymer Av CRICK NW2 69 K4
Jeymer Dr GFD/PVL UB6 66 C7
Jeypore Rd WAND/EARL SW18 128 B6
Jillian Cl HPTN TW12 142 A6
Jim Bradley Cl
WOOL/PLUM SE18 115 F3
Joan Crs ELTH/MOT SE9 134 C6
Joan Gdns BCTR RM8 80 A1
Joan Rd BCTR RM8 80 A1
Joan St STHWK SE1 12 C9
Jocelyn Rd RCH/KEW TW9 125 F2
Jocelyn St PECK SE15 111 H7
Jockey's Flds FSBYW WC1X 11 M2
Jodane Rd DEPT SE8 112 C3
Jodrell Cl ISLW TW7 104 B7
Jodrell Rd HOM E9 75 H7
Joel St NTHWD HA6 46 E1
Johanna St STHWK * SE1 18 A2
John Adam St CHCR WC2N 11 K8
John Aird Ct BAY/PAD W2 8 F2
John Archer Wy
WAND/EARL SW18 128 C5
John Ashby Cl
BRXS/STRHM SW2 129 K5
John Austin Cl KUTN/CMB KT2 144 B7
John Bradshaw Rd
STHGT/OAK N14 28 D7
John Burns Dr BARK IG11 78 E7
John Campbell Rd
STNW/STAM N16 74 A4
John Carpenter St EMB EC4Y 12 C6
John Felton Rd
BERM/RHTH * SE16 111 H1
John Fisher St WCHPL E1 92 C6
John Goodchild Wy KUT KT1 159 J2
John Harrison Wy
GNWCH SE10 113 J2
John Islip St WEST SW1P 17 H7
John Lamb Ct
KTN/HRWW/W HA3 34 E7
John Maurice Cl WALW SE17 19 G5
John McKenna Wk
BERM/RHTH * SE16 111 H2
John Parker Sq BTSEA * SW11 128 C2
John Penn St LEW SE13 112 E7
John Perrin Pl
KTN/HRWW/W HA3 50 A6
John Prince's St
CAVSQ/HST W1G 10 D4
John Rennie Wk WAP E1W 92 D6
John Roll Wy
BERM/RHTH SE16 111 H2
John Ruskin St CMBW SE5 110 C6
John's Av HDN NW4 52 A3
John's Cl ASHF TW15 140 A3
John Silkin La DEPT SE8 112 A4
Johns La MRDN SM4 162 B4
John's Ms BMSBY WC1N 11 M1
John Smith Av FUL/PGN SW6 107 J6
Johnson Cl HACK E8 74 C7
Johnson Rd CROY/NA CR0 164 E6
HAYES BR2 168 C4
HEST TW5 102 B6
WLSDN NW10 69 F7
Johnson's Cl CAR SM5 175 K2
Johnsons Dr HPTN TW12 142 C7
Johnson's Pl PIM SW1V 16 F8
Johnson St NWDGN UB2 102 B2
WCHPL E1 92 E5
Johnsons Wy WLSDN NW10 86 D3
John Spencer Sq IS * N1 73 H5
Johns Pl WCHPL E1 92 D5
John's Ter CROY/NA CR0 165 F7
Johnston Cl BRXN/ST SW9 110 A7
Johnstone Rd EHAM E6 95 K2
Johnston Rd WFD IG8 44 E4
John St BMSBY WC1N 11 M1
EN EN1 30 B4
HSLW TW3 122 D1
SNWD SE25 165 H3
SRTFD E15 76 D7
John Trundle Highwalk
BARB * EC2Y 12 E2
John Williams Cl NWCR SE14 112 A5
John Wilson St
WOOL/PLUM SE18 115 F3
John Wooley Cl LEW * SE13 133 H3
Joiners Arms Yd CMBW * SE5 110 E7
Joiner St STHWK SE1 13 G9
Joint Rd EFNCH N2 39 J7
Jollys La YEAD UB4 83 H4
Jonathan St LBTH SE11 17 L7
Jones Rd PLSTW E13 95 F3
Jonson Cl MTCM CR4 163 G3
YEAD UB4 82 E4
Jordan Cl RYLN/HDSTN HA2 65 K2
Jordan Rd GFD/PVL UB6 67 H7
Jordans Cl DAGE RM10 80 D3
Jordans Ms WHTN TW2 142 E1
Joseph Av ACT W3 87 F5
Josephine Av
BRXS/STRHM SW2 130 A4
Joseph Locke Wy
ESH/CLAY KT10 170 A1
Joseph Powell Cl BAL SW12 129 H5
Joseph Ray Rd WAN E11 76 C1
Joseph St BOW E3 93 H4
Joseph Trotter Cl CLKNW EC1R 6 B8
Joshua Cl MUSWH N10 40 B6
SAND/SEL CR2 177 H6
Joshua St POP/IOD E14 94 A5
Joslings Cl SHB W12 87 J6
Joubert St BTSEA SW11 128 E1
Jowett St PECK SE15 111 G6
Joyce Av UED N18 42 B4
Joyce Green La DART DA1 119 G7
Joydon Dr CHDH RM6 61 H5
Joyners Cl DAGW RM9 80 B3
The Jubilee GNWCH * SE10 112 E6
Jubilee Av CHING E4 44 A5
ROMW/RG RM7 62 E4
WHTN TW2 123 H7
Jubilee Cl CDALE/KGS NW9 51 F5
KUT KT1 143 J7
PIN HA5 47 G1
ROMW/RG RM7 62 D4
Jubilee Crs ED N9 30 C7
Jubilee Dr RSLP HA4 65 H3
Jubilee Gdns STHL UB1 84 A4
STHWK * SE1 11 M9
Jubilee Market COVGDN * WC2E 11 K6
Jubilee Pl CHEL SW3 15 K7
Jubilee Rd CHEAM SM3 174 B6
GFD/PVL UB6 67 H7
Jubilee St WCHPL E1 92 E5
Jubilee Ter FUL/PGN * SW6 127 H1
Jubilee Vls ESH/CLAY * KT10 157 K7
Jubilee Wy CHSGTN KT9 172 D2
EBED/NFELT TW14 121 K7
SCUP DA14 155 G1
WIM/MER SW19 147 F7
Judd St STPAN WC1H 5 J8
Jude St CAN/RD E16 94 D5
Judge Heath La HYS/HAR UB3 82 A5
Judges' Wk HAMP NW3 71 G2
Judge Wk ESH/CLAY KT10 170 E5
Juer St BTSEA SW11 108 D6
Jules Thorn Av EN EN1 30 C2
Julia Gdns BARK IG11 97 K1
Juliana Cl EFNCH N2 53 G2
Julian Av ACT W3 86 D6
Julian Cl BAR EN5 27 F2
Julian Hl HRW HA1 66 E1
Julian Pl POP/IOD E14 112 E4
Julian Tayler Pth FSTH * SE23 150 D1
Julien Rd EA W5 104 D2
Juliette Rd PLSTW E13 94 E1
Juliette Wy PUR RM19 119 J1
Julius Nyerere Cl IS N1 5 M4
Junction Ap BTSEA SW11 128 D2
LEW SE13 133 F2
Junction Ms BAY/PAD W2 9 J4
Junction Pl BAY/PAD * W2 9 H4
Junction Rd ARCH N19 72 C2
ASHF TW15 140 A4
DART DA1 139 G5
EA W5 104 D3
ED N9 30 C7
HRW HA1 48 E5
PLSTW E13 77 F7
ROM RM1 63 H3
SAND/SEL CR2 177 K5
TOTM N17 56 C2
Junction Rd East CHDH RM6 62 A6
Junction Rd West CHDH RM6 61 K6
Juniper Cl BAR EN5 26 B4
CHSGTN KT9 172 B4
Juniper Ct CHDH RM6 61 H5
KTN/HRWW/W * HA3 35 F7
NTHWD * HA6 32 E7
Juniper Crs CAMTN NW1 4 B2
Juniper Gdns MTCM CR4 148 C7
SUN TW16 140 D5
Juniper La EHAM E6 95 J4
Juniper Rd IL IG1 78 A3
Juniper St WCHPL * E1 92 E6
Juniper Wy HYS/HAR UB3 82 B6
Juno Wy NWCR SE14 112 A5
Jupiter Wy HOLWY N7 73 F5
Jupp Rd SRTFD E15 76 B6
Jupp Rd West SRTFD E15 76 B7
Justice Wk CHEL SW3 108 D5
Justin Cl BTFD TW8 104 E6
Justin Rd CHING E4 43 H5
Jute La PEND EN3 31 G1
Jutland Rd CAT SE6 133 F6
PLSTW E13 94 E3
Jutsums Av ROMW/RG RM7 62 D5
Jutsums La ROMW/RG RM7 62 D5
Juxon Cl RYLN/HDSTN HA2 34 B7
Juxon St LBTH SE11 17 M5

K

Kaduna Cl PIN HA5 47 F4
Kale Rd ERITHM DA18 116 E1
Kambala Rd BTSEA SW11 128 C1
Kangley Bridge Rd SYD SE26 151 H4
Kaplan Dr WCHMH N21 29 F4
Kara Wy CRICK NW2 70 B3
Karen Cl RAIN RM13 99 G1
Karen Ct BMLY BR1 152 D7
ELTH/MOT SE9 134 B4
Karenza Ct WBLY * HA9 49 J6
Kashgar Rd WOOL/PLUM SE18 116 A4
Kashmir Rd CHARL SE7 114 C6
Kassala Rd BTSEA SW11 108 E7
Katharine St CROY/NA CR0 177 J2
Katherine Cl BERM/RHTH SE16 93 F7
Katherine Gdns ELTH/MOT SE9 134 C3
Katherine Rd EHAM E6 77 H6
Katherine Sq NTGHL * W11 88 C7
Kathleen Av ACT W3 86 E4
ALP/SUD HA0 68 A6
Kathleen Rd BTSEA SW11 128 E2
Kayemoor Rd BELMT SM2 175 J6
Kay Rd BRXN/ST SW9 129 K1
Kays Ter SWFD * E18 58 D1
Kay St BETH E2 92 C1
SRTFD E15 76 B6
WELL DA16 116 C7
Kean St HOL/ALD WC2B 11 L5
Keatley Gn CHING E4 43 H5
Keats Av CAN/RD E16 95 F7
Keats Cl PEND EN3 31 F4
STHWK SE1 19 L6
WAN E11 59 F4
WIM/MER SW19 147 H5
YEAD UB4 82 E4
Keats Est STNW/STAM * N16 74 B1
Keats Gv HAMP NW3 71 J3
Keats Pde ED * N9 42 C1
Keats Rd BELV DA17 117 K2
WELL DA16 115 K7
Keats Wy CROY/NA CR0 165 K5
GFD/PVL UB6 84 B4
WDR/YW UB7 100 C3
Keble Cl NTHLT UB5 66 C4
WPK KT4 160 C7
Keble Pl BARN SW13 106 E5
Keble St TOOT SW17 147 G3
Kechill Gdns HAYES BR2 167 K6
Kedleston Wk BETH E2 92 D2
Keeble Cl WOOL/PLUM * SE18 115 G5
Keedonwood Rd BMLY BR1 152 C3
Keel Cl BARK IG11 97 J1
BERM/RHTH SE16 93 F7
Keele Cl WATN WD24 21 G1
Keeley Rd CROY/NA CR0 177 J1
Keeley St HOL/ALD WC2B 11 L5
Keeling Rd ELTH/MOT SE9 134 C4
Keely Cl EBAR EN4 27 J4
Keemor Cl WOOL/PLUM * SE18 115 F6
Keens Cl STRHM/NOR SW16 148 D4
Keen's Rd CROY/NA CR0 177 J3
Keen's Yd IS N1 73 H5
The Keep BKHTH/KID SE3 133 K1
KUTN/CMB KT2 144 B5
Keepers Ms TEDD TW11 143 J5
Keesey St WALW SE17 19 G9
Keeton's Rd BERM/RHTH SE16 111 J2
Keevil Dr WIM/MER SW19 127 G6
Keighley Cl HOLWY N7 72 E3
Keightley Dr ELTH/MOT SE9 135 H7
Keildon Rd BTSEA SW11 128 E3
Keir Hardie Est CLPT * E5 56 D7
Keir Hardie Wy BARK IG11 79 G6
YEAD * UB4 82 E2
Keith Connor Cl VX/NE SW8 129 G2
Keith Gv SHB W12 106 D1
Keith Rd BARK IG11 96 D1
HYS/HAR UB3 101 H2
WALTH E17 43 H7
Kelbrook Rd BKHTH/KID SE3 134 D1
Kelburn Wy RAIN RM13 99 J2
Kelceda Cl CRICK NW2 69 J1
Kelf Gv HYS/HAR UB3 82 D5
Kelfield Gdns NKENS W10 88 B5
Kelfield Ms NKENS W10 88 B4
Kelland Cl CEND/HSY/T * N8 54 D4
Kelland Rd PLSTW E13 94 E3
Kellaway Rd BKHTH/KID SE3 134 B1
Keller Cresent MNPK E12 77 H3
Kellerton Rd LEW SE13 133 H4
Kellett Rd BRXS/STRHM SW2 130 B3
Kelling Gdns CROY/NA CR0 164 C6
Kellino St TOOT SW17 147 K3
Kellner Rd THMD SE28 116 A2
Kell St STHWK SE1 18 D3
Kelly Av PECK SE15 111 G7
Kelly Cl BORE WD6 25 F1
WLSDN NW10 69 F2
Kelly Ms MV/WKIL * W9 88 D4
Kelly Rd MLHL NW7 38 C5
Kelly St CAMTN NW1 72 B5
Kelly Wy CHDH RM6 62 A4
Kelman Cl CLAP SW4 129 J1
Kelmore Gv EDUL SE22 131 H3
Kelmscott Cl WALTH E17 43 H7
WATW WD18 20 E5
Kelmscott Crs WATW WD18 20 E4
Kelmscott Gdns SHB W12 106 D2
Kelmscott Rd BTSEA SW11 128 E4
Kelross Rd HBRY N5 73 H3
Kelsall Cl BKHTH/KID SE3 134 A1
Kelsey La BECK BR3 166 D2
Kelsey Park Av BECK BR3 166 E2
Kelsey Park Rd BECK BR3 166 D1
Kelsey Sq BECK BR3 166 D1
Kelsey St BETH E2 92 C3
Kelsey Wy BECK BR3 166 D2
Kelso Pl KENS W8 14 C3
Kelso Rd CAR SM5 162 B6
Kelston Rd BARK/HLT IG6 60 B1
Kelton Vls KUT * KT1 159 G1
Kelvedon Cl KUTN/CMB KT2 144 C5
Kelvedon Rd FUL/PGN SW6 107 J6
Kelvedon Wy WFD IG8 45 K5
Kelvin Av PLMGR N13 41 F5
Kelvinbrook E/WMO/HCT KT8 157 G2
Kelvin Cl HOR/WEW KT19 172 C5
Kelvin Crs KTN/HRWW/W HA3 34 E6
Kelvin Dr TWK TW1 124 C5
Kelvin Gdns CROY/NA CR0 163 K6
STHL UB1 84 A5
Kelvin Gv SURB KT6 171 K2
SYD SE26 150 D2
Kelvington Cl CROY/NA CR0 166 B6
Kelvington Rd PECK SE15 132 A4
Kelvin Pde ORP BR6 169 K7
Kelvin Rd HBRY N5 73 H3
WELL DA16 136 B2
Kember St IS * N1 5 L2
Kemble Dr HAYES BR2 181 J2
Kemble Rd CROY/NA CR0 177 H2
FSTH SE23 132 A7
TOTM N17 42 C7
Kemble St HOL/ALD WC2B 11 L5
Kemerton Rd BECK BR3 166 E1
CMBW SE5 130 D2
CROY/NA CR0 165 G6
Kemey's St HOM E9 75 G4
Kemnal Rd CHST BR7 154 C5
Kempe Rd KIL/WHAMP NW6 88 B1
Kemp Gdns CROY/NA CR0 164 D5
Kemplay Rd HAMP NW3 71 H3
Kemp Pl BUSH WD23 22 A5
Kemps Dr NTHWD HA6 32 D6
POP/IOD E14 93 J6
Kempsford Gdns ECT SW5 14 B8
Kempsford Rd LBTH SE11 18 B6
Kempshott Rd
STRHM/NOR SW16 148 E6
Kempson Rd FUL/PGN SW6 107 K7
Kempthorne Rd DEPT SE8 112 B3
Kempton Av NTHLT UB5 66 A5
SUN TW16 141 F7
Kempton Cl ERITH DA8 117 K5
HGDN/ICK UB10 64 A3
Kempton Ct SUN TW16 141 F7
Kempton Pk SUN * TW16 141 G7
Kempton Rd EHAM E6 77 K7
HPTN TW12 156 E1
Kempton Wk CROY/NA CR0 166 B5
Kempt St WOOL/PLUM SE18 115 F5
Kemsing Cl BXLY DA5 137 F6
THHTH * CR7 164 D3
Kemsing Rd GNWCH SE10 113 K4
Kenbury St CMBW SE5 130 D1
Kenchester Cl VX/NE SW8 109 K6
Kendal Av ACT W3 86 C4
BARK IG11 78 E7
UED N18 41 K3
Kendal Cl CMBW SE5 110 C6
EBED/NFELT TW14 121 J7
WFD IG8 44 D1
YEAD UB4 82 C1
Kendal Ct ACT W3 86 C4
Kendal Cft HCH RM12 81 J4
Kendale Rd BMLY BR1 152 C4
Kendal Gdns SUT SM1 175 G1
UED N18 41 K3
Kendall Av BECK BR3 166 B1
SAND/SEL CR2 177 K7
Kendall Pl MHST W1U 10 A3
Kendall Rd BECK BR3 166 B1
ISLW TW7 124 B1
WOOL/PLUM SE18 114 D7
Kendalmere Cl MUSWH N10 40 B7
Kendal Pde UED * N18 41 K3
Kendal Pl PUT/ROE SW15 127 J4
Kendal Rd WLSDN NW10 69 J3
Kendal Steps BAY/PAD * W2 9 K5
Kendal St BAY/PAD W2 9 K5
Kender St NWCR SE14 111 K6
Kendoa Rd CLAP SW4 129 J3
Kendon Cl WAN E11 59 F4
Kendra Hall Rd SAND/SEL CR2 177 H6
Kendrey Gdns WHTN TW2 123 K5
Kendrick Ms SKENS SW7 15 G5
Kendrick Pl SKENS * SW7 15 G6
Kenelm Cl HRW HA1 67 G2
Kenerne Dr BAR EN5 26 C4
Kenilford Rd BAL SW12 129 G6
Kenilworth Av
RYLN/HDSTN HA2 65 K3
WALTH E17 57 J1
WIM/MER SW19 146 E4
Kenilworth Dr BORE WD6 24 E2
Kenilworth Gdns
GDMY/SEVK IG3 79 F1
OXHEY WD19 33 G4
STHL * UB1 83 K2
WOOL/PLUM SE18 135 G1
YEAD UB4 82 D4
Kenilworth Rd BOW E3 93 G1
EA W5 86 A7
EDGW HA8 36 E1
EW KT17 173 J5
KIL/WHAMP NW6 70 D7
PGE/AN SE20 151 F7
STMC/STPC BR5 169 H5
Kenilworth Ter BELMT * SM2 174 E6
Kenley Av CDALE/KGS NW9 37 G7
Kenley Cl BXLY DA5 137 H6
CHST BR7 169 K2
EBAR EN4 27 J3
Kenley Gdns THHTH CR7 164 C3
Kenley Rd KUT KT1 159 J1
TWK TW1 124 B5
WIM/MER SW19 161 K2
Kenley Wk CHEAM SM3 174 B3
NTGHL * W11 88 C7
Kenlor Rd TOOT SW17 147 H4
Kenmare Dr MTCM CR4 147 K6
Kenmare Gdns PLMGR N13 41 J3
Kenmare Rd THHTH CR7 164 B5
Kenmere Gdns ALP/SUD HA0 68 C7
Kenmere Rd WELL DA16 136 D1
Kenmont Gdns WLSDN NW10 87 K2
Kenmore Av KTN/HRWW/W HA3 49 G4
Kenmore Crs YEAD UB4 82 D2
Kenmore Gdns EDGW HA8 50 D1
Kenmore Rd
KTN/HRWW/W HA3 49 K2
Kenmure Rd HACK * E8 74 D4
Kenmure Yd HACK * E8 74 D4
Kennard Rd FBAR/BDGN N11 39 K4
SRTFD E15 76 B6
Kennard St BTSEA SW11 109 F7
CAN/RD E16 95 K7
Kennedy Av PEND EN3 30 E5
Kennedy Cl MTCM CR4 163 F1
PIN HA5 33 K5
PLSTW E13 94 E1
STMC/STPC BR5 169 J7
Kennedy Rd BARK IG11 78 E7
HNWL W7 84 E4
Kennedy Wk WALW SE17 19 H6
Kennet Cl BTSEA SW11 128 C3
Kennet Dr YEAD UB4 83 J4
Kenneth Av IL IG1 78 B3
Kenneth Crs CRICK NW2 69 K4
Kenneth Gdns STAN HA7 35 G5
Kenneth Moor Rd IL * IG1 78 B2
Kenneth Rd CHDH RM6 62 A6
Kennet Rd DART DA1 138 D2
ISLW TW7 124 A2
MV/WKIL W9 88 D3
Kennet St WAP E1W 92 C7
Kennett Wharf La BLKFR EC4V 12 F6
Kenninghall Rd CLPT E5 74 D2
UED N18 42 D4
Kenning St BERM/RHTH SE16 111 K1
Kennings Wy LBTH SE11 18 B7
Kennington Gdns KUT KT1 158 E2
Kennington Gv LBTH SE11 17 M9
Kennington La LBTH SE11 17 M8
Kennington Ov LBTH SE11 17 M9
Kennington Park Gdns
LBTH SE11 18 C9
Kennington Park Pl WALW SE17 18 B9
Kennington Park Rd LBTH SE11 18 C7
Kennington Rd LBTH SE11 18 A4
Kenny Dr CAR SM5 176 A7
Kenny Rd MLHL NW7 38 C5
Kenrick Pl MHST W1U 10 A2
Kensal Rd NKENS W10 88 C3
Kensal Whf NKENS * W10 88 C3
Kensington Av MNPK E12 77 K5
THHTH CR7 149 G7
WATW WD18 20 D3
Kensington Church Ct KENS W8 14 C2
Kensington Church St KENS W8 8 B8
Kensington Church Wk
KENS * W8 14 C1
Kensington Cl
FBAR/BDGN * N11 40 A4
Kensington Ct KENS W8 14 D2
Kensington Court Gdns
KENS * W8 14 D3
Kensington Court Ms
KENS * W8 14 D3
Kensington Court Pl KENS W8 14 D3
Kensington Dr WFD IG8 59 H1
Kensington Gdns IL IG1 59 K7
Kensington Gardens Sq
BAY/PAD W2 8 C5
Kensington Ga SKENS SW7 14 E3
Kensington Gore SKENS SW7 14 F2
Kensington Hall Gdns
WKENS * W14 107 J4
Kensington High St KENS W8 14 B3
WKENS W14 107 H3
Kensington Palace KENS * W8 8 D9
Kensington Palace Gdns
KENS W8 8 C8
Kensington Park Gdns
NTGHL W11 88 D6
Kensington Park Ms
NTGHL W11 88 D5
Kensington Park Rd
NTGHL W11 88 D6
Kensington Pl KENS W8 8 A9
Kensington Rd KENS W8 14 D2
NTHLT UB5 84 A1
ROMW/RG RM7 62 E5
SKENS SW7 15 J2
Kensington Sq KENS W8 14 C2
Kensington Ter SAND/SEL CR2 177 K6
Kensington Wy BORE WD6 25 F2
Kent Av DAGW RM9 98 C3
WEA W13 85 H4
WELL DA16 136 A4
Kent Cl STRHM/NOR SW16 163 K3
Kent Ct CDALE/KGS * NW9 51 G1
Kent Dr EBAR EN4 28 A3
TEDD TW11 142 E4
Kentford Wy NTHLT UB5 65 J7
Kent Gdns RSLP HA4 46 E5
WEA W13 85 H4
Kent Gate Wy CROY/NA CR0 179 H5
Kent House La BECK BR3 151 G5
Kent House Rd BECK BR3 151 F6
Kentish Rd BELV DA17 117 H3
Kentish Town Rd CAMTN NW1 4 D2
Kentish Wy BMLY BR1 168 A1
Kentlea Rd THMD SE28 96 E7
Kentmere Rd
WOOL/PLUM SE18 115 K3
Kenton Av HRW HA1 49 F6
STHL UB1 84 A6
SUN TW16 156 C1
Kenton Gdns
KTN/HRWW/W HA3 49 J4
Kenton La KTN/HRWW/W HA3 35 G7
Kenton Park Av
KTN/HRWW/W HA3 49 K3
Kenton Park Cl
KTN/HRWW/W HA3 49 J3
Kenton Park Crs
KTN/HRWW/W HA3 49 K3
Kenton Park Pde
KTN/HRWW/W * HA3 49 J4
Kenton Park Rd
KTN/HRWW/W HA3 49 J3
Kenton Rd HOM E9 75 F5
HRW HA1 49 F6
KTN/HRWW/W HA3 50 A4
Kenton St STPAN WC1H 5 J9
Kenton Wy YEAD UB4 82 C2
Kent Rd CHSWK W4 105 K2
DAGE RM10 80 D4
DART DA1 139 H5
E/WMO/HCT KT8 157 H3
KUT KT1 158 E2
RCH/KEW TW9 105 H6
WCHMH N21 29 K7
WWKM BR4 166 E7
Kent St BETH E2 7 M5
PLSTW E13 95 F2
Kent Ter CAMTN NW1 3 K8
Kent View Gdns
GDMY/SEVK IG3 78 E1
Kent Wy SURB KT6 172 A2
Kentwell Cl BROCKY * SE4 132 B3
Kentwode Gn BARN SW13 106 D6
Kent Yd SKENS SW7 15 K2
Kenver Av NFNCH/WDSP N12 39 H5
Kenward Rd ELTH/MOT SE9 134 B4
Kenway ROMW/RG RM7 62 E1
Ken Wy WBLY HA9 68 E1
Kenway Rd ECT SW5 14 C6
Kenwood Cl GLDGN NW11 53 H7
WDR/YW UB7 100 D5
Kenwood Dr BECK BR3 167 F2
Kenwood Gdns CLAY IG5 60 A3
SWFD E18 59 F2
Kenwood Rd ED N9 42 C1
HGT N6 53 K5
Kenworthy Rd HOM E9 75 G4
Kenwyn Dr CRICK NW2 69 G2
Kenwyn Rd CLAP SW4 129 J3
DART DA1 139 G4
RYNPK SW20 146 A7
Kenya Rd CHARL SE7 114 C6
Kenyngton Dr SUN TW16 140 E4
Kenyngton Pl
KTN/HRWW/W HA3 49 J4
Kenyon St FUL/PGN SW6 107 G7
Keogh Rd SRTFD E15 76 C5
Kepler Rd CLAP SW4 129 K3
Keppel Rd DAGW RM9 80 A3
EHAM E6 77 K6
Keppel St GWRST WC1E 11 H2
Kerbela St BETH E2 92 C3
Kerbey St POP/IOD E14 93 K5
Kerfield Crs CMBW SE5 110 E7
Kerfield Pl CMBW SE5 110 E7
Kerri Cl BAR EN5 26 A3
Kerrison Pl EA W5 85 K7
Kerrison Rd BTSEA SW11 128 D2
EA W5 85 K7
SRTFD E15 76 B7
Kerry Av PUR RM19 119 J1
STAN HA7 35 J3
Kerry Cl CAN/RD E16 95 F5

PLMGR N13 41 F1
Kerry Ct STAN HA7 35 K3
Kerry Pth NWCR SE14 112 C5
Kerry Rd NWCR SE14 112 C5
Kersfield Rd PUT/ROE SW15 127 G5
Kershaw Rd DAGE RM10 80 C2
Kersley Ms BTSEA SW11 108 E7
Kersley Rd STNW/STAM N16 74 A2
Kersley St BTSEA SW11 128 E1
Kerstin Cl HYS/HAR UB3 82 D6
Kerswell Cl SEVS/STOTM N15 56 A4
Kerwick Cl HOLWY N7 5 K1
Keslake Rd KIL/WHAMP NW6 88 B1
Kessock Cl TOTM N17 56 D4
Keston Av HAYES BR2 181 G4
Keston Cl UED N18 41 K2
WELL DA16 116 D6
Keston Gdns HAYES BR2 181 G3
Keston Ms WAT WD17 21 F1
Keston Park Cl HAYES BR2 181 K3
Keston Rd PECK SE15 131 H2
THHTH CR7 164 A5
TOTM N17 55 K2
Kestrel Av EHAM E6 95 J4
HNHL SE24 130 C4
Kestrel Cl CDALE/KGS NW9 51 G1
HCH RM12 81 K6
KUTN/CMB KT2 143 K3
WLSDN NW10 69 F4
Kestrel Pl NWCR * SE14 112 B5
Kestrel Wy CROY/NA CR0 180 B7
HYS/HAR UB3 101 G1
Keswick Av KUTN/CMB KT2 145 G4
WIM/MER SW19 161 K1
Keswick Cl SUT SM1 175 G3
Keswick Gdns REDBR IG4 59 J4
RSLP HA4 46 B5
WBLY HA9 68 A4
Keswick Ms EA W5 86 A7
Keswick Rd BXLYHN DA7 137 H1
PUT/ROE SW15 127 H4
WHTN TW2 123 H5
WWKM BR4 180 C1
Kettering St
STRHM/NOR SW16 148 B5
Kettlebaston Rd LEY E10 57 H7
Kettlewell Cl FBAR/BDGN N11 40 A5
Kevelioc Rd TOTM N17 41 J7
Kevin Cl HSLWW TW4 122 C1
Kew Br RCH/KEW TW9 105 H5
Kew Bridge Arches
CHSWK * W4 105 H5
Kew Bridge Rd BTFD TW8 105 G5
Kew Crs CHEAM SM3 174 D2
Kewferry Rd NTHWD HA6 32 A5
Kew Foot Rd RCH/KEW TW9 125 F3
Kew Gardens Rd
RCH/KEW TW9 105 G6
Kew Gn RCH/KEW TW9 105 G5
Kew Meadow Pth
RCH/KEW TW9 105 J7
Kew Rd RCH/KEW TW9 105 G5
RCH/KEW TW9 125 F3
Key Cl WCHPL E1 92 D3
Keyes Rd CRICK NW2 70 B4
DART DA1 139 K3
Keymer Rd BRXS/STRHM SW2 149 F1
Keynes Cl EFNCH N2 53 K2
Keynsham Av WFD IG8 44 C3
Keynsham Gdns
ELTH/MOT SE9 134 D4
Keynsham Rd ELTH/MOT SE9 134 C4
MRDN SM4 162 A7
Keyse Rd STHWK SE1 19 L4
Keysham Av HEST TW5 101 K7
Keystone Crs IS N1 5 K6
Keywood Dr SUN TW16 140 E5
Keyworth Cl CLPT E5 75 G3
Keyworth St STHWK SE1 18 D3
Kezia St DEPT SE8 112 B4
Khama Rd TOOT SW17 147 J3
Khartoum Rd IL IG1 78 B4
PLSTW E13 95 F2
TOOT SW17 147 H3
Khyber Rd BTSEA SW11 128 D1
Kibworth St VX/NE SW8 110 A6
Kidbrooke Gdns
BKHTH/KID SE3 133 K1
Kidbrooke Gv BKHTH/KID SE3 113 K7
Kidbrooke La ELTH/MOT SE9 134 D3
Kidbrooke Park Cl
BKHTH/KID SE3 114 A7
Kidbrooke Park Rd
BKHTH/KID SE3 114 A7
Kidbrooke Wy BKHTH/KID SE3 134 A1
Kidderminster Pl
CROY/NA CR0 164 C7
Kidderminster Rd
CROY/NA CR0 164 C7
Kidderpore Av HAMP NW3 70 E3
Kidderpore Gdns HAMP NW3 70 E3
Kidd Pl CHARL SE7 114 D4
Kidlington Wy CDALE/KGS NW9 51 G1
Kilberry Cl ISLW TW7 103 J7
Kilburn Br KIL/WHAMP NW6 2 B4
Kilburn La NKENS W10 88 B2
Kilburn Park Rd
KIL/WHAMP NW6 2 A8
Kilburn Pl KIL/WHAMP NW6 2 B4
Kilburn Priory KIL/WHAMP NW6 2 C4
Kilburn Sq KIL/WHAMP NW6 2 A4
Kilburn V KIL/WHAMP NW6 2 B4
Kildare Cl RSLP HA4 47 G7
Kildare Gdns BAY/PAD W2 8 B4
Kildare Rd CAN/RD E16 94 E4
Kildare Ter BAY/PAD W2 8 B4
Kildoran Rd BRXS/STRHM SW2 129 K4
Kildowan Rd GDMY/SEVK IG3 61 G7
Kilgour Rd FSTH SE23 132 B5
Kilkie St FUL/PGN SW6 128 B1
Killarney Rd WAND/EARL SW18 128 B5
Killburns Mill Cl WLGTN SM6 176 B1
Killearn Rd CAT SE6 133 G7
Killester Gdns EW KT17 173 K3
Killick St IS N1 5 L5
Killieser Av BRXS/STRHM SW2 148 E1
Killip Cl CAN/RD E16 94 D5
Killowen Av NTHLT UB5 66 C4
Killowen Rd HOM * E9 75 F5
Killyon Rd VX/NE SW8 129 H1
Kilmaine Rd FUL/PGN SW6 107 H6
Kilmarnock Gdns BCTR RM8 79 J2
Kilmarnock Rd OXHEY WD19 33 H3
Kilmarsh Rd HMSMTH W6 107 F3
Kilmartin Av
STRHM/NOR SW16 164 B2
Kilmartin Rd GDMY/SEVK IG3 79 G1
Kilmartin Wy HCH RM12 81 K4
Kilmington Rd BARN SW13 106 D5
Kilmorey Gdns TWK TW1 124 C4
Kilmorey Rd TWK TW1 124 C3
Kilmorie Rd FSTH SE23 132 B7
Kiln Cl HYS/HAR UB3 101 G5
Kilner St POP/IOD E14 93 J4
Kiln Ms TOOT SW17 147 H4
Kiln Pl KTTN NW5 72 A3
Kilnside ESH/CLAY KT10 171 G6
Kiln Wy NTHWD HA6 32 C5
Kilpatrick Wy YEAD UB4 83 J4
Kilravock St NKENS W10 88 C2
Kilross Rd EBED/NFELT TW14 121 G7
Kilsha Rd WOT/HER KT12 156 A5
Kimbell Gdns FUL/PGN SW6 107 H7
Kimbell Pl ELTH/MOT SE9 134 B3
Kimberley Av EHAM E6 95 J1
GNTH/NBYPK IG2 60 D6
PECK SE15 131 J1
ROMW/RG RM7 62 D5
Kimberley Dr SCUP DA14 155 K1
Kimberley Gdns EN EN1 30 B2
FSBYPK N4 55 H4
Kimberley Rd BECK BR3 166 A1
BRXN/ST SW9 129 K1
CAN/RD E16 94 D3
CROY/NA CR0 164 C5
KIL/WHAMP NW6 70 C7
TOTM N17 56 C1
UED N18 42 D5
WALTH E17 43 G7
WAN E11 76 B1
Kimber Rd WAND/EARL SW18 127 K6
Kimble Cl WATW * WD18 20 C5
Kimble Crs BUSH WD23 22 C6
Kimble Rd WIM/MER SW19 147 H5
Kimbolton Cl LEE/GVPK SE12 133 J5
Kimbolton Gn BORE WD6 24 E3
Kimmeridge Gdns
ELTH/MOT SE9 153 J3
Kimmeridge Rd ELTH/MOT SE9 153 J3
Kimpton Rd CHEAM SM3 174 D2
CMBW SE5 110 E7
Kinburn St BERM/RHTH * SE16 112 A1
Kincaid Rd PECK SE15 111 J6
Kincardine Gdns MV/WKIL * W9 8 A1
Kinch Gv WBLY HA9 50 B6
Kinder Cl THMD SE28 97 J6
Kinder St WCHPL E1 92 D5
Kinfauns Rd BRXS/STRHM SW2 149 G1
GDMY/SEVK IG3 61 H7
Kingaby Gdns RAIN RM13 81 J6
King Alfred Av CAT SE6 151 J3
King And Queen St WALW SE17 18 F7
King Arthur Cl PECK SE15 111 K6
King Charles Crs BRYLDS KT5 159 G6
King Charles I Island
CHCR WC2N 11 J8
King Charles' Rd BRYLDS KT5 159 G5
King Charles St WHALL SW1A 17 H1
King Charles Ter WAP * E1W 92 D6
King Charles Wk
WIM/MER * SW19 127 H7
Kingcup Cl CROY/NA CR0 166 A7
King David La WCHPL E1 92 E6
Kingdon Rd KIL/WHAMP NW6 70 E5
King Edward Av DART DA1 139 G5
King Edward Dr SURB KT6 172 A2
King Edward Rd BAR EN5 26 E3
LEY E10 58 A7
OXHEY WD19 21 J5
ROM RM1 63 H5
WALTH E17 57 G2
King Edward's Gdns ACT W3 86 C7
King Edward's Gv TEDD TW11 143 H5
King Edward's Rd BARK IG11 78 D7
ED N9 30 D6
HACK E8 74 D7
PEND EN3 31 F3
RSLP HA4 46 B7
King Edward St STBT EC1A 12 E4
King Edward the Third Ms
BERM/RHTH SE16 111 J1
King Edward Wk STHWK SE1 18 B4
Kingfield Rd EA W5 85 K3
Kingfield St POP/IOD E14 113 F3
Kingfisher Cl
KTN/HRWW/W HA3 35 F6
THMD SE28 97 J6
Kingfisher Dr
RCHPK/HAM TW10 143 J3
Kingfisher Pl WDGN * N22 55 F1
Kingfisher St EHAM E6 95 J4
Kingfisher Wy CROY/NA CR0 166 A4
WLSDN * NW10 69 F5
King Gdns CROY/NA CR0 177 H4
King Garth Ms FSTH SE23 150 E1
King George Av BUSH WD23 22 B5
CAN/RD E16 95 H5
GNTH/NBYPK IG2 60 D5
WOT/HER KT12 156 C7
King George Cl ROMW/RG RM7 62 E2
SUN * TW16 140 C4
King Georges Av WATW WD18 20 C4
King George Sq
RCHPK/HAM TW10 125 G5
King George St GNWCH SE10 113 F6
King George VI Av MTCM CR4 162 E3
Kingham Cl NTGHL W11 107 H1
WAND/EARL SW18 128 B6
King Harolds Wy BXLYHN DA7 116 E6
King Henry's Dr CROY/NA CR0 180 A7
King Henry's Rd HAMP NW3 3 J2
KUT KT1 159 J2
King Henry St STNW/STAM N16 74 A4
King Henry's Wk IS N1 74 A5
King Henry Ter WAP * E1W 92 D6
Kinghorn St STBT * EC1A 12 E3
King James St STHWK SE1 18 D2
King John Ct SDTCH EC2A 7 K9
King John St WCHPL E1 93 F4
King John's Wk
ELTH/MOT SE9 134 D6
Kinglake Est WALW * SE17 19 J7
Kinglake St WALW SE17 19 J8
Kingly Ct REGST * W1B 10 F6
Kingly St REGST W1B 10 E5
King & Queen Cl
ELTH/MOT * SE9 153 J3
King & Queen St WALW * SE17 18 F7
King & Queen Whf
BERM/RHTH * SE16 93 F7
Kingsand Rd LEE/GVPK SE12 152 E1
Kings Arbour NWDGN UB2 102 D4
King's Arms Yd LOTH EC2R 13 G4
Kingsash Dr YEAD UB4 83 J3
Kings Av BAL SW12 129 J7
BMLY BR1 152 E5
CAR SM5 175 J6
CHDH RM6 62 B5
CLAP SW4 129 K5
EA W5 85 K5
GFD/PVL UB6 84 B5
HEST TW5 103 G7
MUSWH N10 54 A2
NWMAL KT3 160 C3
SUN TW16 140 D4
WATW WD18 20 E3
WCHMH N21 29 H7
WFD IG8 45 G4
King's Bench St STHWK SE1 18 D1
King's Bench Wk EMB * EC4Y 12 B6
Kingsbridge Av ACT W3 105 G1
Kingsbridge Ct POP/IOD E14 112 D3
Kingsbridge Rd BARK IG11 96 D1
MRDN SM4 161 G6
NKENS W10 88 A5
NWDGN UB2 102 E3
WOT/HER KT12 156 A6
Kingsbury Gn CDALE/KGS * NW9 50 E4
Kingsbury Rd CDALE/KGS NW9 50 C4
IS N1 74 A5
Kingsbury Ter IS N1 74 A5
Kings Cha E/WMO/HCT KT8 157 H2
Kingsclere Cl PUT/ROE SW15 126 D6
Kingsclere Pl ENC/FH EN2 29 J1
Kingscliffe Gdns
WIM/MER SW19 127 J7
Kings Cl DART DA1 138 B3
HDN NW4 52 B3
LEY E10 57 K6
NTHWD HA6 32 D5
THDIT KT7 158 B5
WATW WD18 21 G3
WOT/HER * KT12 156 A7
King's College Rd HAMP NW3 3 J1
RSLP HA4 46 D5
Kingscote Rd CHSWK W4 106 A2
CROY/NA CR0 165 J6
NWMAL KT3 160 A2
Kingscote St EMB EC4Y 12 C6
Kings Ct PLSTW E13 77 F7
STHWK * SE1 18 D1
Kingscourt Rd
STRHM/NOR SW16 148 D2
King's Crs HBRY N5 73 J2
Kingscroft Rd CRICK NW2 70 D5
King's Cross Br FSBYW * WC1X 5 K7
King's Cross Rd FSBYW WC1X 5 M7
Kingsdale Gdns NTGHL W11 88 B7
Kingsdale Rd PGE/AN SE20 151 F7
WOOL/PLUM SE18 116 A5
Kingsdown Av ACT W3 87 G6
SAND/SEL CR2 177 J7
WEA W13 104 C1
Kingsdown Cl
BERM/RHTH * SE16 111 J4
NTGHL W11 88 B5
Kingsdowne Ct EA * W5 86 A6
Kingsdowne Rd SURB KT6 159 F6
Kingsdown Rd ARCH N19 72 E2
CHEAM SM3 174 C4
WAN E11 76 C2
Kingsdown Wy HAYES BR2 167 K5
Kings Dr BRYLDS KT5 159 H6
EDGW HA8 36 B3
THDIT KT7 158 C5
WBLY HA9 68 D1
Kingsend RSLP HA4 46 C7
Kingsend Ct RSLP * HA4 46 C7
Kings Farm WALTH * E17 43 K7
Kings Farm Av
RCHPK/HAM TW10 125 H3
Kingsfield Av
RYLN/HDSTN HA2 48 B4
Kingsfield Ct OXHEY WD19 21 H5
Kingsfield Rd HRW * HA1 48 D6
OXHEY WD19 21 H6
Kingsfield Ter DART * DA1 139 G5
Kingsford Av WLGTN SM6 176 E6
Kingsford St KTTN NW5 71 K4
Kingsford Wy EHAM E6 95 K4
Kings Gdns IL IG1 60 D7
KIL/WHAMP NW6 2 B2
Kingsgate WBLY HA9 68 E2
Kingsgate Av FNCH N3 52 E2
Kingsgate Cl BXLYHN DA7 117 F7
Kingsgate Est IS * N1 74 A5
Kingsgate Pl KIL/WHAMP NW6 2 A2
Kingsgate Rd KIL/WHAMP NW6 2 A1
KUT KT1 144 A7
Kingsground ELTH/MOT SE9 134 D6
King's Gv PECK SE15 111 J7
ROM RM1 63 J4
Kings Hall Ms LEW * SE13 133 F2
Kings Hall Rd BECK BR3 151 F6
Kings Head Hl CHING E4 31 K6
King's Hwy WOOL/PLUM SE18 115 K5
Kingshill Av KTN/HRWW/W HA3 49 H3
WPK KT4 160 D6
YEAD UB4 82 C2
Kingshill Ct BAR * EN5 26 C3
Kingshill Dr KTN/HRWW/W HA3 49 H2
Kingshold Rd HOM E9 74 E6
Kingsholm Gdns
ELTH/MOT SE9 134 C3
Kingshurst Rd LEE/GVPK SE12 133 K6
Kings Keep HAYES * BR2 167 H2
SURB * KT6 159 F3
Kingsland Gn STNW/STAM N16 74 A5
Kingsland High St HACK E8 74 B5
Kingsland Pas HACK E8 74 A5
Kingsland Rd BETH E2 7 K6
HACK E8 7 L2
PLSTW E13 95 G2
King's La SUT SM1 175 H4
Kingslawn Cl PUT/ROE SW15 126 E4
Kingsleigh Pl MTCM CR4 162 E2
Kingsleigh Wk HAYES BR2 167 J3
Kingsley Av BORE WD6 24 B1
DART DA1 139 K4
HSLW TW3 123 H1
STHL UB1 84 A6
SUT SM1 175 H3
WEA W13 85 G5
Kingsley Cl DAGE RM10 80 D3
GLDGN NW11 53 G6
Kingsley Ct EDGW * HA8 36 D1
GPK RM2 63 K4
Kingsley Dr WPK KT4 173 H1
Kingsley Gdns CHING E4 43 J4
Kingsley Ms CHST BR7 154 B5
KENS * W8 14 D4
WAP * E1W 92 D6
Kingsley Pl HGT N6 54 A6
Kingsley Rd CROY/NA CR0 164 B7
FSTGT E7 76 E6
HSLW TW3 123 H1
KIL/WHAMP NW6 70 D7
PIN HA5 47 K3
PLMGR N13 41 G3
RYLN/HDSTN HA2 66 C3
WALTH E17 58 A1
WIM/MER SW19 147 F4
Kingsley St BTSEA SW11 128 E2
Kingsley Wy EFNCH N2 53 G5
Kingsley Wood Dr
ELTH/MOT SE9 153 K2
Kingslyn Crs NRWD SE19 150 A7
Kings Ml HMSMTH * W6 107 F3
Kingsman St
WOOL/PLUM SE18 114 E3
Kingsmead BAR EN5 26 E3
RCHPK/HAM TW10 125 G5
Kingsmead Av CDALE/KGS NW9 51 F6
ED N9 30 D7
MTCM CR4 163 H2
ROM RM1 63 G5
SUN TW16 156 B2
SURB KT6 172 C1
WPK KT4 173 K2
Kingsmead Cl BFN/LL DA15 155 G1
HOR/WEW KT19 173 F6
TEDD TW11 143 H5
Kingsmead Dr NTHLT UB5 65 K6
Kingsmead Pde NTHLT * UB5 65 K6
Kings Mead Pk ESH/CLAY KT10 170 E6
Kingsmead Rd
BRXS/STRHM SW2 149 G1
Kingsmead Wy HOM E9 75 G3
Kingsmere Cl PUT/ROE SW15 127 G2
Kingsmere Pk CDALE/KGS NW9 50 E7
Kingsmere Pl
STNW/STAM * N16 55 K7
Kingsmere Rd WIM/MER SW19 146 B1
King's Ms BMSBY WC1N 11 M1
Kingsmill Gdns DAGW RM9 80 B4
Kingsmill Rd DAGW RM9 80 B4
Kingsmill Ter STJWD NW8 3 H5
Kingsnympton Pk
KUTN/CMB KT2 144 D6
Kings Oak ROMW/RG RM7 62 C2
King's Orch ELTH/MOT SE9 134 D5
King's Paddock HPTN TW12 142 C7
Kings Pde CAR * SM5 175 J2
SHB * W12 106 D2
TOTM * N17 56 B2
WLSDN * NW10 70 A7
Kingspark Ct SWFD E18 58 E2
Kings Pas WAN * E11 58 C6
Kings Pl BKHH IG9 45 H1
CHSWK W4 105 K4
STHWK SE1 18 E2
King Sq FSBYE EC1V 6 E8
King's Quay WBPTN * SW10 108 B7
Kings Reach EMB * EC4Y 12 B6
Kingsridge Gdns DART DA1 139 G5
Kings Rd BAR EN5 26 A2
BARK IG11 78 C6
BGVA SW1W 16 B5
CHEL * SW3 108 C5
EA W5 85 K4
EHAM E6 77 G7
FELT TW13 122 B7
FUL/PGN SW6 108 A7
KUTN/CMB KT2 144 B6
MORT/ESHN SW14 126 A2
MTCM CR4 163 F2
RCHPK/HAM TW10 125 G4
ROM RM1 63 J4
RYLN/HDSTN HA2 65 K1
SNWD SE25 165 H2
SURB KT6 158 D7
TEDD TW11 142 D4
TOTM N17 42 B7
TWK TW1 124 C5
UED * N18 42 C4
WAN E11 58 C6
WDGN N22 41 F7
WDR/YW UB7 100 C1
WIM/MER SW19 146 E5
WLSDN NW10 69 G7
WLSDN NW10 69 K6
King's Scholars' Pas
WEST SW1P 16 E4
King Stairs Cl
BERM/RHTH SE16 111 J1
King's Ter CAMTN NW1 4 E4
Kingsthorpe Rd SYD SE26 151 F3
Kingston Av CHEAM SM3 174 C2
EBED/NFELT TW14 121 H5
Kingston By-Pass BRYLDS KT5 159 K7
CHSGTN KT9 172 B2
ESH/CLAY KT10 170 E2
Kingston Cl CHDH RM6 62 A2
NTHLT UB5 65 K6
TEDD TW11 143 H5
Kingston Crs BECK BR3 151 H7
Kingston Gdns CROY/NA CR0 176 E2
Kingston Hall Rd KUT KT1 158 E2
Kingston Hl KUTN/CMB KT2 144 C7
Kingston Hill Av CHDH RM6 62 A2
Kingston Hill Pl KUTN/CMB KT2 144 E3
Kingston House Est
SURB * KT6 158 C5
Kingston La TEDD TW11 143 G4
WDR/YW UB7 100 C1
Kingston Ldg NWMAL KT3 160 B3
Kingston Rd BRYLDS KT5 172 D1
EBAR EN4 27 H4
ED N9 42 C1
EW KT17 173 H6
HOR/WEW KT19 173 F3
IL IG1 78 C3
NWDGN UB2 102 E1
NWMAL KT3 160 A3
PUT/ROE SW15 126 E7
ROM RM1 63 H3
RYNPK SW20 161 H1
TEDD TW11 143 H5
Kingston Sq NRWD SE19 149 K4
Kingston V PUT/ROE SW15 145 F3
Kingstown St CAMTN NW1 4 A3
King St CITYW EC2V 12 F5
COVGDN WC2E 11 J6
EFNCH N2 53 H2
HMSMTH W6 106 C3
NWDGN UB2 102 D2
PLSTW E13 94 E3
RCH/KEW TW9 124 E4
STJS SW1Y 10 F9
TOTM N17 42 B7
TWK TW1 124 B7
WATW WD18 21 G3
King St Cloisters
HMSMTH * W6 106 E3
King Street Pde TWK * TW1 124 B7
Kingswater Pl BTSEA * SW11 108 D6
Kings Wy CROY/NA CR0 177 F4
HRW HA1 48 E3
Kingsway HOL/ALD WC2B 11 L4
HYS/HAR UB3 82 A4
MORT/ESHN SW14 125 J2
NWMAL KT3 161 F3
PEND EN3 30 D4
STMC/STPC BR5 169 J4
STWL/WRAY TW19 120 A7
WBLY HA9 68 A3
WWKM BR4 180 D2
Kingsway Av SAND/SEL CR2 178 E7
Kingsway Crs RYLN/HDSTN HA2 48 C3
Kingsway Pde
STNW/STAM * N16 73 K2
Kingsway Pl CLKNW EC1R 6 B9
Kingsway Rd CHEAM SM3 174 C6
Kingswear Rd KTTN NW5 72 B2
RSLP HA4 64 E1
Kingswood Av BELV DA17 117 G3
HAYES BR2 167 H2
HEST TW5 122 E1
HPTN TW12 142 B5
KIL/WHAMP NW6 70 C7
THHTH CR7 164 B4
Kingswood Cl DART DA1 139 F5
EN EN1 30 B3
NWMAL KT3 160 C5
ORP BR6 169 J6
SURB KT6 159 F6
TRDG/WHET N20 27 G5
VX/NE SW8 109 K6
Kingswood Dr BELMT SM2 175 F7
CAR SM5 162 E7
NRWD SE19 150 A3
Kingswood Pk FNCH N3 52 D1
Kingswood Pl LEW SE13 133 H3
Kingswood Rd
BRXS/STRHM SW2 129 K5
CHSWK W4 105 K2
GDMY/SEVK IG3 61 G7
HAYES BR2 167 H2
PGE/AN SE20 150 E5
WAN E11 58 C6
WIM/MER SW19 146 D7
Kingswood Ter CHSWK W4 105 K2
Kingswood Wy WLGTN SM6 176 E4
Kingsworth Cl BECK BR3 166 B4
Kingsworthy Cl KUT KT1 159 G1
Kings Yd PUT/ROE * SW15 127 G2
SRTFD * E15 75 J5
Kingthorpe Rd WLSDN NW10 69 F6
Kingthorpe Ter WLSDN * NW10 69 F6
King William La GNWCH SE10 113 H4
King William St CANST EC4R 13 H7
King William Wk GNWCH SE10 113 F5
Kingwood Rd FUL/PGN SW6 107 H6
Kinlet Rd WOOL/PLUM SE18 115 H6
Kinloch Dr CDALE/KGS NW9 51 G6
Kinloch St HOLWY N7 73 F2
Kinloss Gdns FNCH N3 52 D2
Kinloss Rd CAR SM5 162 B6
Kinnaird Av BMLY BR1 152 D5
CHSWK W4 105 K6
Kinnaird Cl BMLY BR1 152 D5
Kinnaird Wy WFD IG8 45 K5
Kinnear Rd SHB W12 106 C1
Kinnerton Pl North
KTBR * SW1X 15 M2
Kinnerton Pl South
KTBR * SW1X 15 M2
Kinnerton St KTBR SW1X 16 A2
Kinnerton Yd KTBR * SW1X 16 A2
Kinnoul Rd HMSMTH W6 107 H5
Kinross Av WPK KT4 173 J1
Kinross Cl KTN/HRWW/W HA3 50 B4
SUN TW16 140 D4
Kinross Dr SUN TW16 140 D4
Kinross Ter WALTH E17 57 H1
Kinsale Rd PECK SE15 131 H2
Kintyre Cl STRHM/NOR SW16 164 A1
Kinveachy Gdns CHARL SE7 114 D4
Kinver Rd SYD SE26 150 E3
Kipling Dr WIM/MER SW19 147 H5
Kipling Est STHWK SE1 19 H2
Kipling Rd BXLYHN DA7 117 F7
Kipling St STHWK SE1 19 H2
Kipling Ter ED * N9 41 K2
Kippington Dr ELTH/MOT SE9 134 C7
Kirby Cl HOR/WEW KT19 173 H4
NTHWD HA6 32 D5
Kirby Est BERM/RHTH * SE16 111 J2
Kirby Gv STHWK SE1 19 J1
Kirby St HCIRC EC1N 12 B2
Kirchen Rd WEA W13 85 H6
Kirkcaldy Gn OXHEY WD19 33 G2
Kirkdale SYD SE26 150 D1
Kirkdale Cnr SYD * SE26 150 E3
Kirkdale Rd WAN E11 58 C7
Kirkfield Cl WEA W13 85 H7
Kirkham Rd EHAM E6 95 J5
Kirkham St WOOL/PLUM SE18 115 K5
Kirkland Av CLAY IG5 60 A1
Kirkland Cl BFN/LL DA15 135 K5
Kirkland Wk HACK E8 74 B5
Kirk La WOOL/PLUM SE18 115 H5
Kirkleas Rd SURB KT6 159 F7
Kirklees Rd BCTR RM8 79 J4
THHTH CR7 164 B4
Kirkley Rd WIM/MER SW19 146 E7
Kirkly Cl SAND/SEL CR2 178 A7
Kirkmichael Rd POP/IOD E14 94 A5
Kirk Rd WALTH E17 57 H5
Kirkside Rd BKHTH/KID SE3 113 K5
Kirk's Pl POP/IOD E14 93 H4
Kirkstall Av TOTM N17 55 K3
Kirkstall Gdns
BRXS/STRHM SW2 129 J7
Kirkstall Rd BRXS/STRHM SW2 129 K7
Kirksted Rd MRDN SM4 162 A7
Kirkstone Wy BMLY BR1 152 C6
Kirkton Rd SEVS/STOTM N15 56 A3
Kirkwall Pl BETH * E2 92 E2
Kirkwood Rd PECK SE15 111 J7
Kirn Rd WEA W13 85 H6
Kirrane Cl NWMAL KT3 160 C4
Kirtley Rd SYD SE26 151 G3
Kirtling St VX/NE SW8 109 H6
Kirton Cl CHSWK W4 106 A3
Kirton Gdns BETH E2 7 M8
Kirton Ldg WAND/EARL * SW18 128 A5
Kirton Rd PLSTW E13 95 G1
Kirton Wk EDGW HA8 36 E6
Kirwyn Wy CMBW SE5 110 D6
Kitcat Ter BOW E3 93 J2
Kitchener Rd EFNCH N2 53 J2
FSTGT E7 77 F5
THHTH CR7 164 E2
TOTM N17 56 A2
WALTH E17 43 K7
Kite Pl BETH * E2 92 C2
Kite Yd BTSEA * SW11 108 E7
Kitley Gdns NRWD SE19 150 B7
Kitson Rd BARN SW13 106 D7

CMBW SE5 110 D6
Kittiwake Rd NTHLT UB5 83 H2
Kittiwake Wy YEAD UB4 83 H4
Kitto Rd NWCR SE14 132 A1
Kiver Rd ARCH N19 72 E1
Klea Av CLAP SW4 129 H5
Knapdale Cl FSTH SE23 150 D1
Knapmill Rd CAT SE6 151 J1
Knapmill Wy CAT SE6 151 J1
Knapp Cl WLSDN NW10 69 G5
Knapp Rd BOW E3 93 J3
Knapton Ms TOOT SW17 148 A5
Knaresborough Dr
WAND/EARL SW18 128 A7
Knaresborough Pl ECT SW5 14 C5
Knatchbull Rd CMBW SE5 130 C1
WLSDN NW10 69 F7
Knebworth Av WALTH E17 43 J7
Knebworth Pth BORE WD6 25 F3
Knebworth Rd
STNW/STAM * N16 74 A3
Knee Hl ABYW SE2 116 D4
Knee Hill Crs ABYW SE2 116 D3
Kneller Gdns ISLW TW7 123 J5
Kneller Rd BROCKY SE4 132 B3
NWMAL KT3 160 B6
WHTN TW2 123 H5
Knight Cl BCTR RM8 79 J1
Knighten St WAP E1W 92 D7
Knighthead Point
POP/IOD * E14 112 D1
Knightland Rd CLPT E5 74 D1
Knighton Cl ROMW/RG RM7 63 F5
SAND/SEL CR2 177 H7
WFD IG8 45 F3
Knighton Dr WFD IG8 45 F3
Knighton La BKHH IG9 45 F1
Knighton Park Rd SYD SE26 151 F4
Knighton Rd FSTGT E7 76 E2
ROMW/RG RM7 62 E5
Knightrider Ct BLKFR * EC4V 12 D6
Knightrider St BLKFR EC4V 12 E6
Knight's Av EA W5 105 F1
Knightsbridge SKENS SW7 15 K2
Knightsbridge Gdns
ROMW/RG RM7 63 F4
Knightsbridge Gn KTBR * SW1X 15 L2
Knights Chambers ED * N9 42 C2
Knight's Hl WNWD SE27 149 H4
Knight's Hill Sq WNWD SE27 149 H3
Knight's La ED N9 42 C2
Knights Manor Wy DART DA1 139 J5
Knight's Pk KUT KT1 159 F2
Knights Rd CAN/RD E16 94 E7
STAN HA7 35 J3
Knights Wk LBTH SE11 18 C6
Knightswood Cl EDGW HA8 36 E1
Knightswood Rd RAIN RM13 99 H1
Knightwood Crs NWMAL KT3 160 B5
Knivet Rd FUL/PGN SW6 107 K5
Knobs Hill Rd SRTFD E15 75 K7
Knockholt Rd ELTH/MOT SE9 134 C4
The Knole ELTH/MOT SE9 154 A3
Knole Cl CROY/NA * CR0 165 K5
Knole Rd DART DA1 138 D6
The Knoll BECK BR3 151 K7
HAYES BR2 180 E1
PIN * HA5 47 H1
WEA W13 85 J4
Knoll Crs NTHWD HA6 46 C1
Knoll Dr STHGT/OAK N14 28 A6
Knollmead BRYLDS KT5 159 K7
Knoll Rd BXLY DA5 137 H6
SCUP DA14 155 H4
WAND/EARL SW18 128 B4
Knolls Cl WPK KT4 173 K2
Knolly's Cl STRHM/NOR SW16 149 G2
Knolly's Rd STRHM/NOR SW16 149 G2
Knottisford St BETH E2 93 F2
Knotts Green Rd LEY E10 57 K5
Knowle Av BXLYHN DA7 117 F6
Knowle Cl BRXN/ST SW9 130 B2
Knowle Rd HAYES BR2 181 J1
WHTN TW2 123 K7
Knowles Ct HRW HA1 49 F5
Knowles Hill Crs LEW SE13 133 G4
Knowlton Gn HAYES BR2 167 J4
Knowl Wy BORE WD6 24 B4
Knowsley Av STHL UB1 84 B7
Knowsley Rd BTSEA SW11 128 E1
Knox Rd FSTGT E7 76 E5
Knox St MBLAR W1H 9 L2
Knoyle St NWCR SE14 112 B5
Kohat Rd WIM/MER SW19 147 F4
Koh-i-noor Av BUSH WD23 22 A5
Kossuth St GNWCH SE10 113 H4
Kramer Ms ECT SW5 14 B8
Kreedman Wk HACK * E8 74 C4
Kuala Gdns STRHM/NOR SW16 149 F7
Kydbrook Cl STMC/STPC BR5 169 H6
Kylemore Cl EHAM E6 95 H1
Kylemore Rd KIL/WHAMP NW6 2 A1
Kymberley Rd HRW * HA1 48 E5
Kyme Rd ROM RM1 63 H5
Kynance Gdns STAN HA7 35 J7
Kynance Ms KENS W8 14 D4
Kynance Pl KENS W8 14 E4
Kynaston Av THHTH CR7 164 D4
Kynaston Cl KTN/HRWW/W HA3 34 D6
Kynaston Crs THHTH CR7 164 D4
Kynaston Rd BMLY BR1 152 E4
STNW/STAM N16 74 A2
THHTH CR7 164 D4
Kynaston Wd
KTN/HRWW/W HA3 34 D6
Kynersley Cl CAR SM5 175 K2
Kynoch Rd UED N18 43 F3
Kyrle Rd BTSEA SW11 129 F5
Kyverdale Rd STNW/STAM N16 56 B6

L

Laburnum Av DART DA1 139 F7
ED N9 42 A1
HCH RM12 81 J1
SUT SM1 175 J2
TOTM N17 41 K6
Laburnum Cl CHING E4 43 H5
Laburnum Ct STAN HA7 35 J3
Laburnum Crs SUN TW16 141 F7
Laburnum Gdns CROY/NA CR0 166 A6
Laburnum Gv CDALE/KGS NW9 50 E6
HSLW TW3 122 E3
NWMAL KT3 160 A1
STHL UB1 83 K3
WCHMH N21 41 J1
Laburnum Pl ELTH/MOT * SE9 135 F4
Laburnum Rd HYS/HAR UB3 101 J3
MTCM CR4 163 F1
WIM/MER SW19 147 G6
Laburnum St BETH E2 7 L4
Laburnum Wy HAYES BR2 169 G6
STWL/WRAY TW19 120 C7
Lacebark Cl BFN/LL DA15 136 A6
Lacey Cl ED N9 42 C1
Lacey Dr BCTR RM8 79 J2
EDGW HA8 36 A3
HPTN TW12 141 K7
Lackington St SDTCH EC2A 13 H2
Lacock Cl WIM/MER SW19 147 G5
Lacon Rd EDUL SE22 131 H3
Lacrosse Wy
STRHM/NOR SW16 148 D7
Lacy Rd PUT/ROE SW15 127 G3
Ladas Rd WNWD SE27 149 J4
Ladbroke Crs NTGHL W11 88 C5
Ladbroke Gdns NTGHL W11 88 D6
Ladbroke Gv NKENS W10 88 B3
Ladbroke Ms NTGHL W11 88 C7
Ladbroke Rd EN EN1 30 B5
NTGHL W11 88 D7
Ladbroke Sq NTGHL W11 88 D6
Ladbroke Ter NTGHL W11 88 D6
Ladbroke Wk NTGHL W11 88 D7
Ladbrook Cl PIN HA5 47 K4
Ladbrooke Crs SCUP DA14 155 K2
Ladbrook Rd SNWD SE25 164 E2
Ladderstile Ride
RCHPK/HAM TW10 144 D4
Ladderswood Wy
FBAR/BDGN N11 40 C4
Lady Alesford Av STAN HA7 35 H4
Lady Booth Rd KUT KT1 159 F1
Ladycroft Rd LEW SE13 132 E2
Ladycroft Wk STAN HA7 35 K7
Lady Forsdyke Wy
HOR/WEW KT19 172 C7
Ladygate La RSLP HA4 46 A5
Ladygrove CROY/NA CR0 179 G7
Lady Harewood Wy
HOR/WEW KT19 172 C7
Lady Hay WPK KT4 173 H1
Lady Margaret Rd ARCH N19 72 C3
STHL UB1 83 K3
Ladymount WLGTN SM6 176 D3
Lady's Cl WATW WD18 21 G3
Ladyship Ter EDUL * SE22 131 J6
Ladysmith Av EHAM E6 95 J1
GNTH/NBYPK IG2 60 D6
Ladysmith Rd CAN/RD E16 94 D2
ELTH/MOT SE9 135 F5
EN EN1 30 B1
KTN/HRWW/W HA3 48 E1
TOTM N17 56 C1
UED N18 42 D4
Lady Somerset Rd KTTN NW5 72 B3
Ladywell Rd LEW SE13 132 E4
Ladywell St SRTFD E15 76 D7
Ladywell Water Tower
BROCKY * SE4 132 C2
Ladywood Av STMC/STPC BR5 169 K4
Ladywood Rd SURB KT6 172 C1
Lafone Av FELT TW13 122 B7
Lafone St STHWK SE1 19 L1
Lagado Ms BERM/RHTH SE16 93 F7
Lagonda Wy DART DA1 139 F3
Laidlaw Dr WCHMH N21 29 F4
Laing Dean NTHLT UB5 65 G7
Laings Av MTCM CR4 162 E1
Lainlock Pl HSLW TW3 103 G7
Lainson St WAND/EARL SW18 127 K6
Lairdale Cl DUL SE21 130 D7
Lairs Cl HOLWY * N7 72 E5
Laitwood Rd BAL SW12 129 G7
The Lake BUSH WD23 22 D7
Lake Av BMLY BR1 152 E5
Lake Cl BCTR RM8 79 K2
Lakedale Rd WOOL/PLUM SE18 115 K4
Lake Dr BUSH WD23 34 C1
Lakefield Rd WDGN N22 55 H1
Lake Gdns DAGE RM10 80 C4
RCHPK/HAM TW10 143 H2
WLGTN SM6 176 B2
Lakehall Gdns THHTH CR7 164 C4
Lakehall Rd THHTH CR7 164 C4
Lake House Rd WAN E11 76 E2
Lakehurst Rd HOR/WEW KT19 173 G4
Lakeland Cl KTN/HRWW/W HA3 34 D5
Lakenheath STHGT/OAK N14 28 D4
Lake Ri ROM RM1 63 H2
Lake Rd CHDH RM6 61 K3
CROY/NA CR0 179 H1
DAGW RM9 98 D2
WIM/MER SW19 146 D4
Lakeside BECK BR3 166 E2
ENC/FH EN2 28 D3
HOR/WEW KT19 173 G5
WEA W13 85 J5
WLGTN SM6 176 B3
Lakeside Av REDBR IG4 59 H3
THMD SE28 97 G7
Lakeside Cl BFN/LL DA15 136 D4
RSLP HA4 46 B3
SNWD SE25 165 H1
Lakeside Crs EBAR EN4 27 K5
Lakeside Dr ESH/CLAY KT10 170 C5
HAYES BR2 181 J2
Lakeside Rd PLMGR N13 41 F3
WKENS W14 107 G2
Lakeside Wy WBLY HA9 68 C3
Lakes Rd HAYES BR2 181 G4
Lakeswood Rd
STMC/STPC BR5 169 G5
Lake Vw EDGW HA8 36 B4
Lake View Est BOW * E3 93 F1
Lakeview Rd WELL DA16 136 C3
WNWD SE27 149 G4
Lake View Ter UED * N18 42 B3
Lakis Cl HAMP NW3 71 G3
Laleham Av MLHL NW7 37 F2
Laleham Ct SUT * SM1 175 G4
Laleham Rd CAT SE6 133 F6
Lalor St FUL/PGN SW6 127 H1
Lambarde Av ELTH/MOT SE9 154 A3
Lamberhurst Rd BCTR RM8 62 A7
WNWD SE27 149 G3
Lambert Av RCH/KEW TW9 125 H2
Lambert Ct BUSH WD23 21 H3
Lambert Jones Ms BARB * EC2Y 12 E2
Lambert Rd BRXS/STRHM SW2 129 K4
CAN/RD E16 95 F5
NFNCH/WDSP N12 39 H4
Lambert's Pl CROY/NA CR0 164 E7
Lambert's Rd SURB KT6 159 F4
Lambert St IS N1 6 A2
Lambert Wy NFNCH/WDSP N12 39 G4
Lambeth Br WEST SW1P 17 K5
Lambeth High St STHWK SE1 17 L6
Lambeth Hl BLKFR * EC4V 12 E6
Lambeth Palace Rd STHWK SE1 17 L4
Lambeth Rd CROY/NA CR0 164 B7
STHWK SE1 18 A4
Lambeth Wk LBTH SE11 17 M6
Lamb La HACK E8 74 D6
Lamble St KTTN NW5 72 A4
Lambley Rd DAGW RM9 79 H5
Lambolle Pl HAMP NW3 71 J5
Lambolle Rd HAMP NW3 71 J5
Lambourn Cl HNWL W7 104 A1
KTTN * NW5 72 C3
Lambourne Av
WIM/MER SW19 146 D3
Lambourne Gdns BARK IG11 79 F6
CHING E4 43 J1
EN EN1 30 B1
Lambourne Gv KUT KT1 159 J1
Lambourne Pl BKHTH/KID SE3 114 A7
Lambourne Rd BARK IG11 78 E6
GDMY/SEVK IG3 78 E1
WAN E11 58 A6
Lambourn Rd CLAP SW4 129 G2
Lambrook Ter FUL/PGN SW6 107 H7
Lambs Cl ED * N9 42 C1
Lamb's Conduit Pas
FSBYW WC1X 11 L2
Lamb's Conduit St
BMSBY WC1N 11 L1
Lambscroft Av ELTH/MOT SE9 153 G2
Lambs Meadow WFD IG8 59 H1
Lambs Ms IS N1 6 C4
Lamb's Pas STLK EC1Y 13 G1
Lambs Ter ED * N9 41 K1
Lamb St WCHPL E1 13 L2
Lambs Wk ENC/FH EN2 29 J1
Lambton Pl NTGHL * W11 88 D6
Lambton Rd ARCH N19 54 E7
RYNPK SW20 146 A7
Lamb Wk STHWK SE1 19 J2
Lamerock Rd BMLY BR1 152 D3
Lamerton Rd BARK/HLT IG6 60 B1
Lamerton St DEPT SE8 112 D5
Lamford Cl TOTM N17 41 K6
Lamington St HMSMTH W6 106 E3
Lamlash St LBTH SE11 18 C5
Lammas Av MTCM CR4 163 F1
Lammas La ESH/CLAY KT10 170 A3
Lammas Park Gdns EA W5 85 J7
Lammas Rd HOM E9 75 F6
LEY E10 75 G1
RCHPK/HAM TW10 143 J3
WATW WD18 21 G4
Lammermoor Rd BAL * SW12 129 G6
Lamont Rd WBPTN SW10 108 C5
Lamont Road Pas
WBPTN * SW10 108 C5
Lamorbey Cl BFN/LL DA15 155 F1
Lamorbey Pk BFN/LL * DA15 136 C7
Lamorna Cl WALTH E17 58 A1
Lamorna Gv STAN HA7 35 K7
Lampard Gv STNW/STAM N16 56 B7
Lampern Sq BETH * E2 92 C2
Lampeter Sq HMSMTH W6 107 H5
Lamplighter Cl WCHPL E1 92 E3
Lamplighters Cl DART DA1 139 J5
Lampmead Rd LEW SE13 133 H4
Lamport Cl WOOL/PLUM SE18 114 E3
Lampton Av HEST TW5 103 F7
Lampton House Cl
WIM/MER SW19 146 B3
Lampton Park Rd HSLW TW3 123 G1
Lampton Rd HSLW TW3 123 G1
Lamson Rd RAIN RM13 99 H4
Lanacre Av CDALE/KGS NW9 37 G7
Lanark Cl EA W5 85 J4
Lanark Pl MV/WKIL W9 2 F9
Lanark Rd MV/WKIL W9 2 D6
Lanbury Rd PECK SE15 132 A3
Lancashire Ct MYFR/PKLN W1K 10 C6
Lancaster Av BARK IG11 78 E6
MTCM CR4 163 K4
WAN E11 59 F3
WIM/MER SW19 146 B4
WNWD SE27 149 H1
Lancaster Cl CDALE/KGS NW9 37 H6
HAYES BR2 167 J3
IS N1 7 K2
STWL/WRAY TW19 120 B5
TOTM * N17 42 C6
Lancaster Ct BAY/PAD W2 8 F6
Lancaster Dr HAMP NW3 71 J5
HCH RM12 81 K4
POP/IOD E14 94 A7
Lancaster Gdn
KUTN/CMB KT2 143 K4
Lancaster Gdns
WIM/MER SW19 146 C4
Lancaster Ga BAY/PAD W2 8 F7
Lancaster Gv HAMP NW3 71 H5
Lancaster Ms BAY/PAD W2 8 F6
RCHPK/HAM TW10 125 F5
WAND/EARL * SW18 128 A4
Lancaster Pk
RCHPK/HAM TW10 125 F4
Lancaster Pl TPL/STR WC2R 11 L6
TWK TW1 124 B6
WIM/MER SW19 146 B4
Lancaster Rd EBAR EN4 27 H4
FBAR/BDGN N11 40 D5
FSBYPK N4 55 G6
FSTGT E7 76 E6
NTGHL W11 88 C5
NTHLT UB5 66 C5
RYLN/HDSTN HA2 48 A4
SNWD SE25 165 G1
STHL UB1 83 J6
UED N18 42 B4
WALTH E17 57 F1
WAN E11 76 C1
WIM/MER SW19 146 B4
WLSDN NW10 69 H4
Lancaster Stables HAMP * NW3 71 J5
Lancaster St STHWK SE1 18 C2
Lancaster Ter BAY/PAD W2 9 G6
Lancaster Wk HYS/HAR UB3 82 A5
Lancaster West NTGHL * W11 88 C5
Lancastrian Rd WLGTN SM6 176 E6
Lancefield St MV/WKIL W9 88 D2
Lancell St STNW/STAM N16 74 A1
Lancelot Av ALP/SUD HA0 67 K3
Lancelot Crs ALP/SUD HA0 67 K3
Lancelot Gdns EBAR EN4 28 A6
Lancelot Pde ALP/SUD * HA0 68 A4
Lancelot Pl SKENS SW7 15 L2
Lancelot Rd ALP/SUD HA0 67 K3
WELL DA16 136 B3
Lance Rd HRW HA1 48 C6
Lancer Sq KENS W8 14 C1
Lancey Cl CHARL SE7 114 C3
Lanchester Rd HGT N6 53 K4
Lancing Gdns ED N9 30 B7
Lancing Rd CROY/NA CR0 164 A5
FELT TW13 140 D1
GNTH/NBYPK IG2 60 D5
WEA W13 85 H6
Lancing St CAMTN NW1 5 G8
Landale Gdns DART DA1 139 F7
Landau Wy ERITH DA8 119 G4
Landcroft Rd EDUL SE22 131 G5
Landells Rd EDUL SE22 131 G5
Landford Rd PUT/ROE SW15 127 F2
Landgrove Rd WIM/MER SW19 146 E4
Landleys Flds HOLWY * N7 72 D4
Landmann Wy NWCR SE14 112 A5
Landon Pl KTBR SW1X 15 L3
Landons Cl POP/IOD E14 94 A7
Landor Rd BRXN/ST SW9 129 K2
Landor Wk SHB W12 106 D1
Landra Gdns WCHMH N21 29 H5
Landridge Rd FUL/PGN SW6 127 H1
Landrock Rd CEND/HSY/T N8 54 E5
Landscape Rd WFD IG8 45 F6
Landseer Av MNPK E12 78 A4
Landseer Cl EDGW HA8 50 C1
EMPK RM11 63 K7
WIM/MER SW19 147 G7
Landseer Rd ARCH N19 72 E2
EN EN1 30 C4
NWMAL KT3 160 A6
SUT SM1 174 E5
Lands' End BORE WD6 23 K5
Landstead Rd
WOOL/PLUM SE18 115 J6
The Lane BKHTH/KID SE3 133 K2
STJWD NW8 2 E6
Lane Ap MLHL * NW7 38 C4
Lane Cl CRICK NW2 69 K2
Lane End BXLYHN DA7 137 J2
Lane Gdns BUSH WD23 22 E7
Lanercost Gdns STHGT/OAK N14 28 E5
Lanercost Rd
BRXS/STRHM SW2 149 G1
Laneside CHST BR7 154 B4
EDGW HA8 36 E4
Laneside Av BCTR RM8 62 B6
Laneway PUT/ROE SW15 126 E4
Lanfranc Rd BOW E3 93 G1
Lanfrey Pl WKENS W14 107 J4
Langbourne Av HGT N6 72 A1
Langbourne Wy
ESH/CLAY KT10 171 F5
Langbrook Rd BKHTH/KID SE3 134 C2
Langcroft Cl CAR SM5 175 K2
Langdale Av MTCM CR4 162 E2
Langdale Cl BCTR RM8 61 J7
MORT/ESHN SW14 125 J3
WALW SE17 18 E9
Langdale Crs BXLYHN DA7 117 H7
Langdale Dr YEAD UB4 82 C1
Langdale Gdns HCH RM12 81 J4
Langdale Pde MTCM * CR4 162 E1
Langdale Rd GNWCH SE10 113 F6
THHTH CR7 164 B3
Langdale St WCHPL * E1 92 D5
Langdale Ter BORE * WD6 25 F2
Langdon Ct WLSDN NW10 69 G7
Langdon Crs EHAM E6 96 A1
Langdon Dr CDALE/KGS NW9 50 E7
Langdon Park Rd HGT N6 54 B6
Langdon Pl MORT/ESHN SW14 125 K2
Langdon Rd EHAM E6 78 A7
HAYES BR2 168 A2
MRDN SM4 162 B4
Langdon Shaw SCUP DA14 155 F4
Langdon Wk MRDN SM4 162 B4
Langdon Wy STHWK SE1 111 H3
Langford Cl HACK E8 74 C4
SEVS/STOTM N15 56 A5
Langford Crs EBAR EN4 27 K3
Langford Gn CMBW SE5 131 F2
Langford Pl SCUP DA14 155 G2
STJWD NW8 2 F6
Langford Rd EBAR EN4 27 K3
FUL/PGN SW6 128 A1
WFD IG8 45 G5
Langfords BKHH IG9 45 H1
Langham Ct RSLP * HA4 65 F4
Langham Dr GDMY/SEVK IG3 61 H5
Langham Gdns ALP/SUD HA0 67 J1
EDGW HA8 36 E6
RCHPK/HAM TW10 143 J3
WCHMH N21 29 G4
WEA W13 85 H6
Langham House Cl
RCHPK/HAM TW10 143 K3
Langham Pde
SEVS/STOTM * N15 55 H2
Langham Park Pl HAYES BR2 167 J3
Langham Pl CAVSQ/HST W1G 10 D3
CHSWK W4 106 B5
SEVS/STOTM N15 55 H2
Langham Rd EDGW HA8 36 E5
RYNPK SW20 146 A7
SEVS/STOTM N15 55 H2
TEDD TW11 143 H4
Langham St REGST W1B 10 D3
Langhedge Cl UED N18 42 B5
Langhedge La UED N18 42 B4
Langholm Cl BAL SW12 129 J6
Langholme BUSH WD23 22 C7
Langhorn Dr WHTN TW2 123 K6
Langhorne Rd DAGE RM10 80 C6
Langland Ct NTHWD HA6 32 A6
Langland Crs STAN HA7 49 K2
Langland Dr PIN HA5 33 J6
Langland Gdns CROY/NA CR0 179 H1
HAMP NW3 71 F4
Langler Rd WLSDN NW10 88 A1
Langley Av RSLP HA4 65 F1
SURB KT6 158 E7
WPK KT4 174 B1
Langley Ct BECK * BR3 166 E3
COVGDN WC2E 11 J6
Langley Crs DAGW RM9 79 J6
EDGW HA8 36 E2
HYS/HAR UB3 101 J6
WAN E11 59 F6
Langley Dr ACT W3 105 J1
WAN E11 59 F6
Langley Gdns DAGW RM9 79 K6
STMC/STPC BR5 169 G5
Langley Gv NWMAL KT3 160 A1
Langley La VX/NE SW8 17 K9
Langley Pk EDGW HA8 37 G5
Langley Park Rd BELMT SM2 175 G5
Langley Rd BECK BR3 166 A3
ISLW TW7 124 A1
SAND/SEL CR2 179 F7
SURB KT6 159 F6
WELL DA16 116 D5
WIM/MER SW19 146 D7
Langley St LSQ/SEVD WC2H 11 J5
Langley Wy WWKM BR4 167 G7
Langley Wd BECK * BR3 167 H4
Langmead Dr BUSH WD23 22 D7
Langmead St WNWD SE27 149 H3
Langport Ct WOT/HER KT12 156 B7
Langridge Ms HPTN TW12 141 K5
Langroyd Rd TOOT SW17 147 K1
Langside Av PUT/ROE SW15 126 D3
Langside Crs STHGT/OAK N14 40 D2
Langston Hughes Cl
HNHL * SE24 130 C3
Lang St WCHPL E1 92 E3
Langthorn Ct LOTH * EC2R 13 H4
Langthorne Rd WAN E11 76 B2
Langthorne St FUL/PGN SW6 107 G7
Langton Av EHAM E6 96 A2
TRDG/WHET N20 27 G6
Langton Cl FSBYW WC1X 5 M8
Langton Gv NTHWD HA6 32 A4
Langton Ri FSTH SE23 131 J6
Langton Rd BRXN/ST SW9 110 C6
CRICK NW2 70 B2
E/WMO/HCT KT8 157 H4
KTN/HRWW/W HA3 34 C6
Langton St WBPTN SW10 108 B5
Langton Vls TOTM * N17 42 C7
Langton Wy BKHTH/KID SE3 113 K7
CROY/NA CR0 178 A3
Langtry Pl FUL/PGN SW6 14 B9
NTHLT UB5 83 H1
Langtry Rd KIL/WHAMP NW6 2 C4
Langtry Wk KIL/WHAMP NW6 2 F2
Langwood Cha TEDD TW11 143 J5
Langworth Dr YEAD UB4 83 F5
Lanhill Rd MV/WKIL W9 2 A9
Lanier Rd LEW SE13 133 F5
Lanigan Dr HSLW TW3 123 G4
Lankaster Gdns EFNCH N2 39 H7
Lankers Dr RYLN/HDSTN HA2 47 K5
Lankton Cl BECK BR3 152 A7
Lannock Rd HYS/HAR UB3 82 D7
Lannoy Rd ELTH/MOT SE9 135 H7
Lanrick Rd POP/IOD E14 94 B5
Lanridge Rd ABYW SE2 116 E2
Lansbury Av BARK IG11 79 G6
CHDH RM6 62 A4
EBED/NFELT TW14 122 A5
UED N18 41 K4
Lansbury Cl WLSDN NW10 68 E4
Lansbury Crs DART DA1 139 K4
Lansbury Dr YEAD UB4 82 D2
Lansbury Gdns POP/IOD * E14 94 B5
Lansbury Wy UED N18 42 A4
Lanscombe Wk VX/NE * SW8 109 K6
Lansdell Rd MTCM CR4 163 F1
Lansdown Cl WOT/HER KT12 156 B7
Lansdowne Av BXLYHN DA7 116 D6
ORP BR6 169 G7
Lansdowne Cl BRYLDS KT5 172 D1
RYNPK SW20 146 B6
TWK TW1 124 A7
Lansdowne Copse WPK * KT4 173 J1
Lansdowne Ct WPK KT4 173 J1
Lansdowne Crs NTGHL W11 88 C6
Lansdowne Dr HACK E8 74 D7
Lansdowne Gdns VX/NE SW8 109 K7
Lansdowne Gn VX/NE SW8 109 K6
Lansdowne Gv WLSDN NW10 69 G3
Lansdowne Hl WNWD SE27 149 H2
Lansdowne La CHARL SE7 114 C4
Lansdowne Ms CHARL SE7 114 C4
NTGHL W11 88 D7
Lansdowne Pl NRWD SE19 150 B6
STHWK SE1 19 H3
Lansdowne Ri NTGHL W11 88 C6
Lansdowne Rd BMLY BR1 152 E6
CHING E4 43 J1
CROY/NA CR0 177 J1
FNCH N3 38 D6
GDMY/SEVK IG3 61 F7
HACK E8 74 C6
HOR/WEW KT19 172 E6
HSLW TW3 123 G2
MUSWH N10 54 C1
NTGHL W11 88 C6
RYNPK SW20 146 A6
STAN HA7 35 J5
SWFD E18 58 E2
TOTM N17 42 C7
WALTH E17 57 J5
WAN E11 76 D1
Lansdowne Ter BMSBY WC1N 11 K1
Lansdowne Wk NTGHL W11 88 C7
Lansdowne Wy VX/NE SW8 109 K7
Lansdowne Wood Cl
WNWD SE27 149 H2
Lansdown Rd FSTGT E7 77 G6
SCUP DA14 155 H2
Lansfield Av UED N18 42 C3
Lantern Cl ALP/SUD HA0 67 K4
PUT/ROE SW15 126 D3
Lanterns Ct POP/IOD E14 112 D2
Lantern Wy WDR/YW UB7 100 B1
Lant St STHWK SE1 18 E1
Lanvanor Rd PECK SE15 131 K1
Lapford Cl MV/WKIL * W9 88 D3
Lapse Wood Wk FSTH SE23 131 J7
Lapstone Gdns
KTN/HRWW/W HA3 49 J5
Lapwing Cl ERITH * DA8 118 E6
Lapwing Wy YEAD UB4 83 H5
Lapworth Ct BAY/PAD W2 8 D2
Lara Cl CHSGTN KT9 172 A6
LEW SE13 133 F5
Larbert Rd STRHM/NOR SW16 148 C7
Larch Av ACT W3 87 G7
Larch Cl BAL SW12 148 B1
DEPT SE8 112 C5
FBAR/BDGN N11 40 A5
Larch Crs HOR/WEW KT19 172 D5
YEAD UB4 83 G4
Larch Dr CHSWK * W4 105 H4
The Larches BUSH WD23 21 J4
PLMGR N13 41 J2
Larches Av MORT/ESHN SW14 126 A3
Larch Gv BFN/LL DA15 136 A7
Larch Rd CRICK NW2 70 A3
DART DA1 139 G7
LEY E10 75 J1
Larch Tree Wy CROY/NA CR0 179 J2
Larch Wy HAYES BR2 169 F6
Larchwood Rd ELTH/MOT SE9 154 B1
Larcombe Cl CROY/NA CR0 178 B3
Larcom St WALW SE17 18 F6
Larden Rd ACT W3 106 B1
Largewood Av SURB KT6 172 C1
Larissa St WALW * SE17 19 H6

Larkbere Rd SYD SE26 151 G3
Larken Cl BUSH WD23 22 C7
Larken Dr BUSH WD23 22 C7
Larkfield Av KTN/HRWW/W HA3 49 H2
Larkfield Rd RCH/KEW TW9 125 F3
SCUP DA14 155 F2
Larkhall La CLAP SW4 129 K1
Larkhall Ri CLAP SW4 129 H2
Larkham Cl FELT TW13 140 C2
Larkhill Ter WOOL/PLUM * SE18 115 F6
Lark Rw BETH E2 74 E7
Larkshall Crs CHING E4 44 A3
Larkshall Rd CHING E4 44 A4
Larkspur Cl CDALE/KGS NW9 50 D4
TOTM N17 41 K6
Larkspur Gv EDGW HA8 36 E3
Larkspur Wy HOR/WEW KT19 172 E4
Larkswood Cl ERITH DA8 118 D7
Larkswood Ri PIN HA5 47 G3
Larkswood Rd CHING E4 43 J3
Lark Wy CAR SM5 162 D6
Larkway Cl CDALE/KGS NW9 51 F3
Larnach Rd HMSMTH W6 107 G5
Larne Rd RSLP HA4 46 D6
Larner Rd ERITH DA8 118 B6
Larpent Av PUT/ROE SW15 127 F4
Larwood Cl GFD/PVL UB6 66 D4
Lascelles Av HRW HA1 48 D6
Lascelles Cl WAN E11 76 B1
Lascott's Rd WDGN N22 41 F5
Lassa Rd ELTH/MOT SE9 134 D4
Lassell St GNWCH SE10 113 G4
Latchett Rd SWFD E18 45 F7
Latchingdon Gdns WFD IG8 45 J5
Latchmere Cl
RCHPK/HAM TW10 144 A4
Latchmere La KUTN/CMB KT2 144 B5
Latchmere Rd BTSEA SW11 128 E1
KUTN/CMB KT2 144 A5
Latchmere St BTSEA SW11 128 E1
Lateward Rd BTFD TW8 104 E5
Latham Cl EHAM E6 95 J5
Latham Rd BXLYHS DA6 137 H4
TWK TW1 124 A6
Latham's Wy CROY/NA CR0 164 A7
Lathkill Cl EN EN1 30 C6
Lathom Rd EHAM E6 77 K6
Latimer Av EHAM E6 77 K7
Latimer Cl PIN HA5 33 G7
WATW WD18 20 C6
WPK KT4 173 K3
Latimer Gdns PIN HA5 33 G7
Latimer Pl NKENS W10 88 A5
Latimer Rd BAR EN5 27 F2
CROY/NA * CR0 177 H2
FSTGT E7 77 F3
NKENS W10 88 A4
SEVS/STOTM N15 56 A5
TEDD TW11 143 F4
WIM/MER SW19 147 F5
Latona Rd PECK SE15 111 H5
Lattimer Pl CHSWK W4 106 B6
Latton Cl ESH/CLAY KT10 170 B3
WOT/HER KT12 156 E6
Latymer Gdns FNCH * N3 52 C1
Latymer Rd ED N9 30 B7
Latymer Wy ED N9 41 K1
Lauder Cl NTHLT UB5 83 H1
Lauderdale Dr
RCHPK/HAM TW10 143 K2
Lauderdale Pde MV/WKIL * W9 2 C8
Lauderdale Pl BARB * EC2Y 12 F3
Lauderdale Rd MV/WKIL W9 2 D8
Laud St CROY/NA CR0 177 J2
LBTH SE11 17 L7
Laughton Rd NTHLT UB5 83 H1
Launcelot Rd BMLY BR1 152 E3
Launcelot St STHWK SE1 18 A2
Launceston Gdns GFD/PVL UB6 67 J7
Launceston Pl KENS W8 14 E3
Launceston Rd GFD/PVL UB6 67 J7
Launch St POP/IOD E14 113 F2
Launders Ga ACT * W3 105 J1
Laundress La CLPT * E5 74 C2
Laundry Rd HMSMTH W6 107 H5
Laura Cl EN EN1 30 A4
WAN E11 59 G4
Lauradale Rd EFNCH N2 53 K3
Laura Pl CLPT E5 74 E3
Laura Ter FSBYPK * N4 73 H1
Laurel Av TWK TW1 124 A7
Laurel Bank
NFNCH/WDSP * N12 39 G3
Laurel Bank Gdns
FUL/PGN SW6 127 J1
Laurel Cl DART DA1 139 F7
SCUP DA14 155 G2
TOOT SW17 147 J4
Laurel Crs CROY/NA CR0 179 J2
ROMW/RG RM7 63 G7
Laurel Dr WCHMH N21 29 G6
Laurel Gdns CHING E4 31 K6
HNWL W7 84 E7
HSLWW TW4 122 D3
MLHL NW7 37 F2
Laurel Gv PGE/AN SE20 150 D6
SYD SE26 151 F4
Laurel La WDR/YW UB7 100 B3
Laurel Pk KTN/HRWW/W HA3 35 F6
Laurel Rd BARN SW13 126 D1
HPTN TW12 142 D4
RYNPK SW20 145 K7
The Laurels BUSH * WD23 34 E1
CMBW * SE5 110 C6
Laurel St HACK E8 74 B5
Laurel Vw NFNCH/WDSP N12 39 F2
Laurel Vls HNWL * W7 103 K1
Laurel Wy NFNCH/WDSP N12 38 E2
SWFD E18 58 D3
Laurence Ms SHB W12 106 D1
Laurence Pountney Hl
CANST * EC4R 13 G6
Laurence Pountney La
CANST EC4R 13 G6
Laurie Gv NWCR SE14 112 B7
Laurie Rd HNWL W7 84 E4
Laurier Rd CROY/NA CR0 165 G6
KTTN NW5 72 B2
Laurimel Cl STAN HA7 35 H5
Laurino Pl BUSH WD23 34 C1
Lauriston Rd HOM E9 75 F7
WIM/MER SW19 146 B5
Lausanne Rd CEND/HSY/T N8 55 G3
PECK SE15 111 K7
Lavender Av CDALE/KGS NW9 50 E7
MTCM CR4 147 J7
WPK KT4 174 A2
Lavender Cl CAR SM5 176 A3
CHEL SW3 108 C5
HAYES BR2 168 D5
Lavender Ct E/WMO/HCT KT8 157 G2
Lavender Gdns BTSEA SW11 128 E3
KTN/HRWW/W HA3 34 E5
Lavender Gv HACK E8 74 C6
MTCM CR4 147 J7
Lavender Hl BTSEA SW11 128 E2
Lavender Pl IL IG1 78 B4
Lavender Ri WDR/YW UB7 100 D1
Lavender Rd BERM/RHTH SE16 93 G7
BTSEA SW11 128 C2
CAR SM5 176 A4
CROY/NA CR0 164 A5
HOR/WEW KT19 172 D4
SUT SM1 175 H3
Lavender St SRTFD E15 76 C5
Lavender Sweep BTSEA SW11 128 E3
Lavender Ter BTSEA * SW11 128 D2
Lavender V WLGTN SM6 176 D5
Lavender Wy CROY/NA CR0 166 A5
Lavengro Rd WNWD SE27 149 J1
Lavenham Rd
WAND/EARL SW18 146 D1
Lavernock Rd BXLYHN DA7 137 H1
Lavers Rd STNW/STAM N16 74 A2
Laverstoke Gdns
PUT/ROE SW15 126 C6
Laverton Ms ECT * SW5 14 D6
Laverton Pl ECT SW5 14 D6
Lavidge Rd ELTH/MOT SE9 153 J1
Lavina Gv IS N1 5 L5
Lavington Cl HOM E9 75 H5
Lavington Rd CROY/NA CR0 177 F2
WEA W13 85 H7
Lavington St STHWK SE1 12 D9
Lavinia Rd DART DA1 139 J5
Lawdon Gdns CROY/NA CR0 177 H3
Lawford Cl WLGTN SM6 176 E7
Lawford Gdns DART DA1 139 F4
Lawford Rd CHSWK W4 105 K6
IS N1 7 J2
KTTN NW5 72 C5
Lawless St POP/IOD * E14 93 K6
Lawley Rd STHGT/OAK N14 28 B6
Lawley St CLPT E5 74 E3
The Lawn NWDGN UB2 103 F4
Lawn Cl BMLY BR1 153 F6
EN EN1 30 B6
NWMAL KT3 160 B1
RSLP HA4 64 D2
Lawn Crs RCH/KEW TW9 125 H1
Lawn Farm Gv CHDH RM6 62 A3
Lawn Gdns HNWL W7 84 E7
Lawn House Cl POP/IOD E14 113 F1
Lawn La VX/NE SW8 17 K9
Lawn Rd BECK BR3 151 H6
HAMP NW3 71 K4
The Lawns BELMT SM2 174 C6
BKHTH/KID * SE3 133 J2
CHING E4 43 J4
NRWD SE19 149 K7
PIN HA5 34 B6
SCUP DA14 155 H3
Lawns Ct WBLY * HA9 68 C1
Lawnswood BAR * EN5 26 C4
Lawn Ter BKHTH/KID SE3 133 J2
Lawn V PIN HA5 47 H1
Lawrence Av MLHL NW7 37 G3
MNPK E12 78 A3
NWMAL KT3 160 A5
PLMGR N13 41 H3
WALTH E17 43 F7
Lawrence Buildings
STNW/STAM N16 74 B2
Lawrence Cl SEVS/STOTM N15 56 A3
SHB * W12 87 K6
Lawrence Ct MLHL NW7 37 G4
OXHEY * WD19 33 H2
Lawrence Crs DAGE RM10 80 D2
EDGW HA8 50 A1
Lawrence Dr HGDN/ICK UB10 64 A3
Lawrence Gdns MLHL NW7 37 H2
Lawrence Hl CHING E4 43 J1
Lawrence Hill Gdns DART DA1 139 F5
Lawrence Hill Rd DART DA1 139 F5
Lawrence La CITYW EC2V 12 F5
Lawrence Pde ISLW * TW7 124 C2
Lawrence Pl IS N1 5 K3
Lawrence Rd EA W5 104 D3
EHAM E6 77 J7
ERITH DA8 117 J6
GPK RM2 63 K4
HPTN TW12 141 K6
HSLWW TW4 122 B3
PIN HA5 47 H4
PLSTW E13 77 F7
RCHPK/HAM TW10 143 J3
SEVS/STOTM N15 56 A2
SNWD SE25 165 G3
UED N18 42 D3
WWKM BR4 180 E3
YEAD UB4 82 A1
Lawrence St CAN/RD E16 94 D4
CHEL SW3 108 D5
MLHL NW7 37 H3
Lawrence Wy WLSDN NW10 68 E2
Lawrence Yd SEVS/STOTM N15 56 A3
Lawrie Park Av SYD SE26 150 D4
Lawrie Park Crs SYD SE26 150 D4
Lawrie Park Gdns SYD SE26 150 D4
Lawrie Park Rd SYD SE26 150 E5
Lawson Cl CAN/RD E16 95 G5
WIM/MER SW19 146 B2
Lawson Gdns DART DA1 139 G4
PIN HA5 47 F2
Lawson Rd DART DA1 139 G3
STHL UB1 83 K3
Law St STHWK SE1 19 H3
Lawton Rd BOW E3 93 G2
EBAR EN4 27 H2
LEY E10 58 A7
Laxcon Cl WLSDN NW10 69 F4
Laxley Cl CMBW SE5 110 C6
Laxton Pl CAMTN NW1 4 D9
Layard Rd BERM/RHTH SE16 111 J3
THHTH CR7 164 E1
Layard Sq BERM/RHTH SE16 111 J3
Laycock St IS N1 73 G5
Layer Gdns ACT W3 86 C6
Layfield Cl HDN NW4 51 K6
Layfield Crs HDN NW4 51 K6
Layfield Rd HDN NW4 51 K6
Layhams Rd HAYES BR2 180 E6
WWKM BR4 180 C3
Laymarsh Cl BELV DA17 117 G2
Laymead Cl NTHLT UB5 65 J5
Laystall St FSBYW WC1X 12 A1
Layton Crs CROY/NA CR0 177 G4
Layton Pl RCH/KEW TW9 105 H7
Layton Rd BTFD TW8 104 E4
HSLW TW3 123 G3
Layzell Wk ELTH/MOT SE9 134 C7
Lazenby Ct COVGDN * WC2E 11 J6
Leabank Cl HRW HA1 66 E2
Leabank Sq HOM E9 75 J5
Leabank Vw SEVS/STOTM N15 56 C5
Leabourne Rd STNW/STAM N16 56 C5
Lea Bridge Rd CLPT E5 74 E1
Lea Cl BUSH WD23 22 B4
WHTN TW2 122 E6
Lea Cottages MTCM * CR4 163 F1
Lea Crs RSLP HA4 64 D3
Leacroft Av BAL SW12 128 E6
Leacroft Cl WCHMH N21 41 H1
Leadale Av CHING E4 43 J1
Leadale Rd STNW/STAM N16 56 C5
Leadbeaters Cl FBAR/BDGN N11 39 K4
Leadenhall Pl FENCHST EC3M 13 J5
Leadenhall St BANK EC3V 13 J5
Leader Av MNPK E12 78 A4
The Leadings WBLY HA9 68 E2
Leaf Cl NTHWD HA6 32 B6
THDIT KT7 157 K4
Leaf Gv STRHM/NOR SW16 149 G4
Leafield Cl STRHM/NOR SW16 149 H5
Leafield Rd RYNPK SW20 161 J2
SUT SM1 174 E1
Leafy Gv HAYES BR2 181 G4
Leafy Oak Rd LEE/GVPK SE12 153 G3
Leafy Wy CROY/NA CR0 178 B1
Lea Gdns WBLY HA9 68 B4
Leagrave St CLPT E5 74 E2
Lea Hall Gdns LEY * E10 57 J7
Lea Hall Rd LEY E10 57 J7
Leahurst Rd LEW SE13 133 G4
Leake St STHWK SE1 17 M1
Lealand Rd SEVS/STOTM N15 56 B5
Leamington Av BMLY BR1 153 G4
MRDN SM4 161 J3
WALTH E17 57 J4
Leamington Cl BMLY BR1 153 G3
HSLW TW3 123 H4
Leamington Crs
RYLN/HDSTN HA2 65 J2
Leamington Gdns
GDMY/SEVK IG3 79 F1
Leamington Pk ACT W3 87 F4
Leamington Pl YEAD UB4 82 D3
Leamington Rd NWDGN UB2 102 C3
Leamington Road Vls
NTGHL W11 88 D4
Leamore St HMSMTH W6 106 E3
Leamouth Rd EHAM E6 95 J5
POP/IOD E14 94 B5
Leander Rd BRXS/STRHM SW2 130 A5
NTHLT UB5 84 A1
THHTH CR7 164 A3
Learner Dr RYLN/HDSTN HA2 66 A1
Lea Rd BECK BR3 166 D1
NWDGN UB2 102 D3
Learoyd Gdns EHAM E6 96 A6
The Leas BUSH WD23 21 K1
Leas Cl CHSGTN KT9 172 B6
Leas Dl ELTH/MOT SE9 154 A2
Leas Gn CHST BR7 155 F5
Leaside Av MUSWH N10 54 A2
Leaside Rd CLPT E5 56 E7
Leasowes Rd LEY E10 57 J7
Leathart Cl HCH RM12 81 K6
Leatherbottle Gn
ERITHM DA18 117 G2
Leather Cl MTCM CR4 163 F1
Leatherdale St WCHPL * E1 93 F2
Leather Gdns SRTFD E15 76 C7
Leatherhead Cl
STNW/STAM N16 56 A7
Leather La CLKNW EC1R 12 A1
Leathermarket Ct STHWK SE1 19 J2
Leathermarket St STHWK SE1 19 J2
Leathersellers Cl BAR * EN5 26 C2
Leathsale Rd RYLN/HDSTN HA2 66 B2
Leathwaite Rd BTSEA SW11 128 E3
Leathwell Rd DEPT SE8 132 E1
Lea V DART DA1 138 A3
Lea Valley Rd CHING E4 31 H5
Lea Valley Wk CLPT E5 56 D6
TOTM N17 56 D1
Leaveland Cl BECK BR3 166 D3
Leaver Gdns GFD/PVL UB6 84 D1
Leavesden Rd STAN HA7 35 G5
Leaway CLPT * E5 56 E7
Lebanon Av FELT TW13 141 H4
Lebanon Gdns
WAND/EARL SW18 127 K5
Lebanon Pk TWK TW1 124 C6
Lebanon Rd CROY/NA CR0 165 F7
WAND/EARL SW18 127 K4
Lebrun Sq BKHTH/KID SE3 134 A3
Lechmere Ap WFD IG8 59 H1
Lechmere Rd CRICK NW2 69 K5
Leckford Rd WAND/EARL SW18 147 G1
Leckwith Av ABYW SE2 117 F5
Lecky St SKENS SW7 15 G7
Leconfield Av BARN SW13 126 C2
Leconfield Rd HBRY N5 73 K3
Leda Rd WOOL/PLUM SE18 114 E2
Ledbury Ms North NTGHL W11 8 A6
Ledbury Ms West NTGHL * W11 8 A6
Ledbury Rd CROY/NA CR0 177 J3
NTGHL W11 88 D5
Ledbury St PECK SE15 111 H6
Ledrington Rd NRWD SE19 150 B5
Ledway Dr WBLY HA9 50 B6
The Lee NTHWD HA6 32 D6
Lee Av CHDH RM6 62 A5
Leechcroft Av BFN/LL DA15 136 A4
Leechcroft Rd WLGTN SM6 176 A2
Lee Church St LEW SE13 133 H3
Lee Cl WALTH E17 43 F7
Lee Conservancy Rd HOM E9 75 H4
Leecroft Rd BAR EN5 26 C4
Leeds Rd IL IG1 60 D7
Leeds St UED N18 42 C4
Lee High Rd LEW SE13 133 G3
Leeke St FSBYW WC1X 5 L7
Leeland Rd WEA W13 85 G7
Leeland Ter WEA W13 85 G7
Leeland Wy WLSDN NW10 69 G3
Leemount Cl HDN * NW4 52 B3
Lee Pk BKHTH/KID SE3 133 J3
Lee Park Wy UED N18 43 F4
Lee Rd BKHTH/KID SE3 133 J2
EN EN1 30 C5
GFD/PVL UB6 67 J7
MLHL NW7 38 B6
WIM/MER SW19 147 F7
The Lees CROY/NA CR0 179 H1
Lees Av NTHWD HA6 32 D7
Leeside BAR EN5 26 C4
Leeside Crs GLDGN NW11 52 C5
Leeside Rd TOTM N17 42 E5
Leeson Rd BRXN/ST * SW9 130 B4
Leesons Hl CHST BR7 169 K2
Lees Pl MYFR/PKLN W1K 10 A6
Lee St HACK E8 7 L3
Lee Ter BKHTH/KID SE3 133 H2
Leeward Gdns WIM/MER SW19 146 C5
Leeway DEPT SE8 112 C4
The Leeways CHEAM * SM3 174 C5
Leewood Cl LEE/GVPK * SE12 133 J5
Lefevre Wk BOW E3 75 H7
Leffern Rd SHB W12 106 D1
Lefroy Rd SHB W12 106 C1
Left Side STHGT/OAK * N14 28 D7
Legard Rd HBRY N5 73 H2
Legatt Rd ELTH/MOT SE9 134 C4
Leggatt Rd SRTFD E15 94 A1
Legge St LEW SE13 133 F4
Leghorn Rd WLSDN NW10 87 J1
WOOL/PLUM SE18 115 J4
Legion Cl IS N1 73 G5
Legion Ter BOW E3 75 J7
Legion Wy NFNCH/WDSP N12 39 J6
Legon Av ROMW/RG RM7 62 E7
Legrace Av HSLWW TW4 122 C1
Leicester Av MTCM CR4 163 K3
Leicester Cl WPK KT4 174 A3
Leicester Gdns GDMY/SEVK IG3 60 E6
Leicester Pl LSQ/SEVD * WC2H 11 H6
Leicester Rd BAR EN5 27 F4
CROY/NA CR0 165 F6
EFNCH N2 53 J2
WAN E11 59 F4
WLSDN NW10 69 F6
Leicester Sq LSQ/SEVD WC2H 11 H7
Leicester St SOHO/SHAV W1D 11 H6
Leigham Av STRHM/NOR SW16 148 E2
Leigham Court Rd
STRHM/NOR SW16 149 F2
Leigham Dr ISLW TW7 103 K6
Leigham Hall Pde
STRHM/NOR * SW16 148 E2
Leigham V STRHM/NOR SW16 149 G2
Leigh Av REDBR IG4 59 H3
Leigh Cl NWMAL KT3 160 A3
Leigh Ct BORE * WD6 25 F1
RYLN/HDSTN * HA2 48 E7
Leigh Crs CROY/NA CR0 179 K6
Leigh Gdns WLSDN NW10 88 A1
Leigh Hunt Dr STHGT/OAK N14 28 D7
Leigh Orchard Cl
STRHM/NOR SW16 149 F2
Leigh Pl WELL DA16 136 B1
Leigh Rd EHAM E6 78 A6
HBRY N5 73 H3
HSLW TW3 123 J3
LEY E10 58 A6
Leigh Rodd OXHEY WD19 33 J2
Leigh St STPAN WC1H 5 J9
Leighton Av MNPK E12 78 A4
PIN HA5 47 J2
Leighton Cl EDGW HA8 50 C1
Leighton Crs KTTN NW5 72 C4
Leighton Gdns WLSDN NW10 88 A1
Leighton Gv KTTN NW5 72 C4
Leighton Pl KTTN NW5 72 C4
Leighton Rd EN EN1 30 B4
KTN/HRWW/W HA3 48 D1
KTTN NW5 72 D4
WEA W13 104 B1
Leighton St CROY/NA CR0 164 C7
Leila Parnell Pl CHARL SE7 114 B5
Leinster Av MORT/ESHN SW14 125 K2
Leinster Gdns BAY/PAD W2 8 E5
Leinster Ms BAY/PAD W2 8 E7
Leinster Pl BAY/PAD W2 8 E5
Leinster Rd MUSWH N10 54 B3
Leinster Sq BAY/PAD W2 8 B6
Leinster Ter BAY/PAD W2 8 E6
Leisure Wy NFNCH/WDSP N12 39 H6
Leith Cl CDALE/KGS NW9 51 F7
Leithcote Gdns
STRHM/NOR SW16 149 F3
Leithcote Pth
STRHM/NOR SW16 149 F2
Leith Hl STMC/STPC BR5 155 G7
Leith Rd WDGN N22 41 H7
Leith Towers BELMT * SM2 175 F6
Leith Yd KIL/WHAMP * NW6 2 B3
Lela Av HSLWW TW4 122 B1
Lelitia Cl HACK E8 74 C7
Leman St WCHPL E1 13 M5
Lemark Cl STAN HA7 35 J5
Le May Av LEE/GVPK SE12 153 F2
Lemmon Rd GNWCH SE10 113 H5
Lemna Rd WAN E11 58 C6
Lemonwell Dr ELTH/MOT SE9 135 G4
Lemsford Cl SEVS/STOTM N15 56 C5
Lemsford Ct BORE WD6 24 E3
Lena Crs ED N9 42 E1
Lena Gdns HMSMTH W6 107 F2
Lena Kennedy Cl CHING E4 44 A5
Lendal Ter CLAP * SW4 129 K2
Lenelby Rd SURB KT6 159 H7
Len Freeman Pl FUL/PGN SW6 107 J5
Lenham Rd BXLYHN DA7 117 G5
LEW SE13 133 J3
SUT SM1 175 F3
THHTH CR7 164 E1
Lennard Av WWKM BR4 180 C1
Lennard Cl WWKM BR4 180 C1
Lennard Rd CROY/NA CR0 164 D7
HAYES BR2 168 E7
SYD SE26 150 E5
Lennard Ter SYD * SE26 151 F5
Lennon Rd CRICK NW2 70 A4
Lennox Cl ROM RM1 63 H5
Lennox Gdns CROY/NA CR0 177 H3
IL IG1 59 K7
KTBR SW1X 15 L4
WLSDN NW10 69 H3
Lennox Gardens Ms CHEL SW3 15 L5
Lennox Rd FSBYPK N4 73 F1
WALTH E17 57 H5
Lenor Cl BXLYHS DA6 137 F3
Lensbury Wy ABYW SE2 116 E2
Lens Rd FSTGT E7 77 G6
Lenthall Rd HACK E8 7 M1
Lenthorp Rd GNWCH SE10 113 J4
Lentmead Rd BMLY BR1 152 D2
Lenton Ri RCH/KEW TW9 125 F2
Lenton St WOOL/PLUM SE18 115 J3
Lenton Ter FSBYPK * N4 73 G1
Leof Crs CAT SE6 151 K4
Leominster Rd MRDN SM4 162 B5
Leominster Wk MRDN SM4 162 B5
Leonard Av MRDN SM4 162 B4
ROMW/RG RM7 63 F7
Leonard Ct KENS * W8 14 A3
Leonard Pl HAYES * BR2 181 J2
STNW/STAM * N16 74 A3
Leonard Rd CHING E4 43 J5
ED * N9 42 B2
FSTGT E7 76 E3
MTCM CR4 148 C7
NWDGN UB2 102 C2
Leonard St CAN/RD E16 95 J7
SDTCH EC2A 7 H9
Leontine Cl PECK SE15 111 H6
Leopold Av WIM/MER SW19 146 D4
Leopold Ms HOM E9 74 E7
Leopold Rd EA W5 86 B7
EFNCH N2 53 H2
WALTH E17 57 J4
WIM/MER SW19 146 D3
WLSDN NW10 69 G6
Leopold St BOW E3 93 H4
Leo St PECK SE15 111 J6
Leppoc Rd CLAP SW4 129 J4
Leroy St STHWK SE1 19 J5
Lerry Cl WKENS W14 107 J5
Lescombe Cl FSTH SE23 151 G2
Lescombe Rd FSTH SE23 151 G2
Lesley Cl BXLY DA5 137 J6
Leslie Gdns BELMT SM2 174 E6
Leslie Gv CROY/NA CR0 164 E7
Leslie Grove Pl CROY/NA * CR0 165 F7
Leslie Park Rd CROY/NA CR0 165 F7
Leslie Rd CAN/RD E16 95 F5
EFNCH N2 53 H2
WAN E11 76 B3
Lesney Pk ERITH DA8 118 A5
Lesney Park Rd ERITH DA8 118 A5
Lessar Av CLAP SW4 129 H4
Lessingham Av TOOT SW17 147 K3
Lessing St FSTH SE23 132 B6
Lessington Av ROMW/RG RM7 62 E5
Lessness Av BXLYHN DA7 116 E6
Lessness Pk BELV DA17 117 G4
Lessness Rd MRDN SM4 162 B5
Lester Av SRTFD E15 94 C3
Leston Cl RAIN RM13 99 K2
Leswin Pl STNW/STAM N16 74 B2
Leswin Rd STNW/STAM N16 74 B2
Letchford Gdns WLSDN NW10 87 J2
Letchford Ms WLSDN * NW10 87 J2
Letchford Ter
KTN/HRWW/W * HA3 34 B7
Letchworth Av
EBED/NFELT TW14 121 J6
Letchworth Cl HAYES BR2 167 K4
OXHEY WD19 33 H4
Letchworth Dr HAYES BR2 167 K4
Letchworth St TOOT SW17 147 K3
Letterstone Rd FUL/PGN SW6 107 J6
Lettice St FUL/PGN SW6 127 J1
Lett Rd SRTFD E15 76 B6
Leucha Rd WALTH E17 57 G4
Levana Cl WIM/MER SW19 127 H7
Levehurst Wy CLAP SW4 129 K1
Leven Cl OXHEY * WD19 33 H4
Levendale Rd FSTH SE23 151 G1
Leven Rd POP/IOD E14 94 A4
Leven Wy HYS/HAR UB3 82 C5
Leverett St CHEL SW3 15 K5
Leverholme Gdns
ELTH/MOT SE9 154 A3
Leverson St STRHM/NOR SW16 148 C5
Lever St FSBYE EC1V 6 E8
Leverton Pl KTTN NW5 72 C4
Leverton St KTTN NW5 72 C4
Levett Gdns GDMY/SEVK IG3 79 F3
Levett Rd BARK IG11 78 E5
Levine Gdns BARK IG11 97 K1
Lewes Cl NTHLT UB5 66 A5
Lewesdon Cl WIM/MER SW19 127 G7
Lewes Rd BMLY BR1 168 C1
NFNCH/WDSP N12 39 J4
Leweston Pl STNW/STAM N16 56 B6
Lewgars Av CDALE/KGS NW9 50 E5
Lewing Cl ORP BR6 169 K7
Lewin Rd BXLYHS DA6 137 F3
MORT/ESHN SW14 126 A2
STRHM/NOR SW16 148 D5
Lewis Av WALTH E17 43 J7
Lewis Cl STHGT/OAK N14 28 C6
Lewis Crs WLSDN NW10 69 F4
Lewis Gdns EFNCH N2 53 H1
Lewis Gv LEW SE13 133 F3
Lewisham High St LEW SE13 132 E5
Lewisham Hl LEW SE13 133 F1
Lewisham Pk LEW SE13 132 E5
Lewisham Rd LEW SE13 133 F1
Lewisham Wy BROCKY SE4 132 C1
NWCR SE14 112 C7
Lewis Pl HACK E8 74 C4
Lewis Rd MTCM CR4 162 D1
RCHPK/HAM * TW10 124 E4
SCUP DA14 155 J2
STHL UB1 102 D1
SUT SM1 175 F3
WELL DA16 136 D2
Lewis St CAMTN NW1 4 D1
Lewis Wy DAGE RM10 80 D5
Lexden Dr CHDH RM6 61 H5
Lexden Rd ACT W3 86 D6
MTCM CR4 163 J3
Lexham Gdns KENS W8 14 B5
Lexham Ms KENS W8 14 B5
Lexington Cl BORE WD6 24 B2
Lexington St SOHO/CST W1F 10 F5
Lexington Wy BAR EN5 26 B3
Lexton Gdns
BRXS/STRHM SW2 129 J7
Leyborne Av WEA W13 104 D1
Leyborne Pk RCH/KEW TW9 105 H7
Leybourne Cl HAYES BR2 167 K4
Leybourne Rd CAMTN NW1 4 D2
CDALE/KGS NW9 50 C4
HGDN/ICK UB10 64 A7
WAN E11 58 D7
Leybourne St CAMTN NW1 4 C2
Leyburn Cl WALTH E17 58 A3
Leyburn Gdns CROY/NA CR0 178 A1
Leyburn Gv UED N18 42 C5
Leyburn House
WOOL/PLUM SE18 114 D6
Leyburn Rd UED N18 42 C5
Leycroft Gdns ERITH DA8 118 E7
Leyden St WCHPL E1 13 L3
Leyes Rd CAN/RD E16 95 H6
Leyfield WPK KT4 173 G1
Leyland Av PEND EN3 31 G1
Leyland Rd LEE/GVPK SE12 133 J4
Leylang Rd NWCR SE14 112 A6
The Leys KTN/HRWW/W HA3 50 B5
Leys Av DAGE RM10 80 E7
Leys Cl DAGE RM10 80 E6
HRW HA1 48 D3
Leysdown Av BXLYHN DA7 137 K3
Leysdown Rd ELTH/MOT SE9 153 J1

Leysfield Rd *SHB* W12 ....106 D1
Leys Gdns *EBAR* EN4 ....28 A4
Leyspring Rd *WAN* E11 ....58 D7
Leys The *EFNCH* N2 ....53 G3
Ley St *IL* IG1 ....78 C1
Leyswood Dr *GNTH/NBYPK* IG2 ....60 E4
Leythe Rd *ACT* W3 ....105 K1
Leyton Gra *LEY* E10 ....75 J1
Leyton Green Rd *LEY* E10 ....58 A5
Leyton Park Rd *LEY* E10 ....76 A1
Leyton Rd *SRTFD* E15 ....76 B4
WIM/MER SW19 ....147 G6
Leytonstone Rd *SRTFD* E15 ....76 C5
Leywick St *SRTFD* E15 ....94 C1
Liardet St *NWCR* SE14 ....112 B5
Liberia Rd *HBRY* N5 ....73 H5
Liberty Av *WIM/MER* SW19 ....147 H7
Liberty Ms *WDGN* * N22 ....41 H7
Liberty St *BRXN/ST* SW9 ....110 A7
Libra Rd *BOW* E3 ....75 H7
PLSTW E13 ....94 E1
Library Pde *WLSDN* * NW10 ....69 G7
Library St *STHWK* SE1 ....18 D2
Lichfield Cl *EBAR* EN4 ....27 K2
Lichfield Gdns *RCH/KEW* * TW9 ....125 F4
Lichfield Gv *FNCH* N3 ....38 E7
Lichfield Rd *BCTR* RM8 ....79 H3
BOW E3 ....93 G2
CRICK NW2 ....70 C3
ED N9 ....42 C1
EHAM E6 ....95 H2
HSLWW TW4 ....122 B2
NTHWD HA6 ....46 E2
RCH/KEW TW9 ....105 G7
WFD IG8 ....44 C3
Lichfield Ter
RCHPK/HAM * TW10 ....125 F4
Lidbury Rd *MLHL* NW7 ....38 C5
Lidcote Gdns *BRXN/ST* * SW9 ....130 B1
Liddell Cl *KTN/HRWW/W* HA3 ....49 K2
Liddell Gdns *WLSDN* NW10 ....88 A1
Liddell Rd *KIL/WHAMP* NW6 ....70 E5
Lidding Rd *KTN/HRWW/W* HA3 ....49 K4
Liddington Rd *SRTFD* E15 ....76 D7
Liddon Rd *BMLY* BR1 ....168 B2
PLSTW E13 ....95 F2
Liden Cl *WALTH* E17 ....57 H6
Lidfield Rd *STNW/STAM* N16 ....73 K3
Lidgate Rd *PECK* * SE15 ....111 G6
Lidiard Rd *WAND/EARL* SW18 ....147 G1
Lido Sq *TOTM* N17 ....55 K1
Lidyard Rd *ARCH* N19 ....54 C7
Liffler Rd *WOOL/PLUM* SE18 ....115 K4
Lifford St *PUT/ROE* SW15 ....127 G3
Lightcliffe Rd *PLMGR* N13 ....41 G3
Lighterman Ms *WCHPL* E1 ....93 F5
Lighterman's Rd *POP/IOD* E14 ....112 D1
Lightfoot Rd *CEND/HSY/T* N8 ....54 E4
Ligonier St *BETH* E2 ....7 L9
Lilac Cl *CHING* E4 ....43 H5
Lilac Gdns *CROY/NA* CR0 ....179 J2
EA W5 ....104 E2
HYS/HAR UB3 ....82 C5
ROMW/RG RM7 ....63 G7
Lilac Pl *LBTH* SE11 ....17 L6
Lilac St *SHB* W12 ....87 J6
Lilburne Gdns *ELTH/MOT* SE9 ....134 D4
Lilburne Rd *ELTH/MOT* SE9 ....134 D4
Lile Crs *HNWL* W7 ....84 E4
Lilestone St *STJWD* NW8 ....3 J9
Lilford Rd *BRXN/ST* SW9 ....130 C1
Lilian Barker Cl *LEE/GVPK* SE12 ....133 K4
Lilian Board Wy *GFD/PVL* UB6 ....66 D4
Lilian Gdns *WFD* IG8 ....45 F7
Lilian Rd *MTCM* CR4 ....148 C7
Lillechurch Rd *BCTR* RM8 ....79 H5
Lilleshall Rd *MRDN* SM4 ....162 C5
Lilley Cl *WAP* E1W 92 C7
Lilley La *MLHL* * NW7 ....37 G4
Lillian Av *ACT* W3 ....105 H1
Lillian Rd *BARN* SW13 ....106 D5
Lillie Rd *FUL/PGN* SW6 ....107 G5
Lillieshall Rd *CLAP* SW4 ....129 G2
Lillie Yd *FUL/PGN* SW6 ....14 A9
Lillington Gardens Est
PIM SW1V 16 F6
Lilliput Av *NTHLT* UB5 ....65 J7
Lilliput Rd *ROMW/RG* RM7 ....63 F6
Lily Cl *WKENS* * W14 ....107 H3
Lily Dr *WDR/YW* UB7 ....100 A3
Lily Gdns *ALP/SUD* HA0 ....85 J1
Lily Pl *HCIRC* EC1N 12 B2
Lily Rd *LEY* E10 ....57 J5
Lilyville Rd *FUL/PGN* SW6 ....107 J7
Limbourne Av *BCTR* RM8 ....62 B6
Limburg Rd *BTSEA* SW11 ....128 D3
Limeburner La *STP* EC4M 12 C4
Lime Cl *BKHH* IG9 ....45 H1
BMLY BR1 ....168 D3
KTN/HRWW/W HA3 ....49 G1
OXHEY WD19 ....21 H6
ROMW/RG RM7 ....62 E4
RSLP HA4 ....46 D2
WAP E1W 92 C7
Lime Crs *SUN* TW16 ....156 B1
Limecroft Cl *HOR/WEW* KT19 ....173 F6
Limedene Cl *PIN* HA5 ....33 H7
Lime Gv *BFN/LL* DA15 ....136 A5
HYS/HAR UB3 ....82 B6
NWMAL KT3 ....160 A2
RSLP HA4 ....47 F5
SHB W12 ....107 F1
TRDG/WHET N20 ....26 C7
TWK TW1 ....124 A5
Limeharbour *POP/IOD* E14 ....112 E2
Limehouse *POP/IOD* * E14 ....93 J6
Limehouse Cswy *POP/IOD* E14 ....93 H6
Limehouse Link *POP/IOD* E14 ....93 G6
Lime Kiln Dr *CHARL* SE7 ....114 A5
Limerick Cl *BAL* SW12 ....129 H6
Limerston St *WBPTN* SW10 ....14 F9
The Limes *CMBW* * SE5 ....131 F2
The Limes Av *FBAR/BDGN* N11 ....40 B4
Limes Av *BARN* SW13 ....126 C1
CAR SM5 ....162 E7
CROY/NA CR0 ....177 F2
GLDGN NW11 ....52 C6
MLHL NW7 ....37 G5
NFNCH/WDSP N12 ....39 G3
PGE/AN SE20 ....150 D6
WAN E11 ....59 F3
Limes Cl *CAR* SM5 ....175 K1
FBAR/BDGN * N11 ....40 C4
Limesdale Gdns *EDGW* HA8 ....50 E1
Limes Field Rd *BARN* SW13 ....126 B2
Limesford Rd *PECK* SE15 ....132 A3
Limes Gdns *WAND/EARL* SW18 ....127 K5
Limes Gv *LEW* SE13 ....133 F3
Limes Rd *BECK* BR3 ....166 E1
CROY/NA CR0 ....164 E5
PUR RM19 ....119 K4
WAND/EARL * SW18 ....127 K5
Lime St *FENCHST* EC3M 13 J6
WALTH E17 ....57 G3
Lime Street Pas *BANK* * EC3V 13 J5
Limes Wk *EA* W5 ....104 E1
PECK * SE15 ....131 K3
Lime Tree Av *THDIT* KT7 ....157 K7
Limetree Cl *BRXS/STRHM* SW2 ....130 A7
Lime Tree Ct *PIN* * HA5 ....34 A6
Lime Tree Gv *CROY/NA* CR0 ....179 H2
Limetree Pl *MTCM* CR4 ....148 B7
Lime Tree Rd *HEST* TW5 ....103 G7
Lime Tree Ter *CAT* * SE6 ....132 C7
Lime Tree Wk *BUSH* WD23 ....22 E7
WWKM BR4 ....180 D3
Lime Wk *SRTFD* * E15 ....76 C7
Limewood Cl *BECK* BR3 ....167 F4
WALTH E17 ....57 H3
WEA W13 ....85 H5
Limewood Rd *ERITH* DA8 ....117 K6
Limpsfield Av *THHTH* CR7 ....164 A4
WIM/MER SW19 ....146 B1
Linacre Rd *CRICK* NW2 ....69 K5
Linchmere Rd *LEE/GVPK* SE12 ....133 K6
Lincoln Av *ROMW/RG* RM7 ....63 G7
STHGT/OAK N14 ....40 C2
WHTN TW2 ....142 C1
WIM/MER SW19 ....146 B2
Lincoln Cl *ERITH* DA8 ....138 C1
GFD/PVL UB6 ....66 C7
RYLN/HDSTN HA2 ....47 K4
Lincoln Ct *BORE* WD6 ....25 F4
Lincoln Crs *EN* EN1 ....30 A3
Lincoln Dr *OXHEY* WD19 ....33 G2
Lincoln Est *BOW* E3 ....93 J3
Lincoln Gdns *IL* IG1 ....59 J6
Lincoln Ms *KIL/WHAMP* NW6 ....70 D7
Lincoln Pde *EFNCH* * N2 ....53 J2
Lincoln Rd *ALP/SUD* HA0 ....67 K5
EFNCH N2 ....53 J2
EN EN1 ....30 A3
ERITH DA8 ....138 C1
FELT TW13 ....141 K2
MTCM CR4 ....163 K4
NTHWD HA6 ....46 D2
NWMAL KT3 ....159 K2
PLSTW E13 ....95 F3
RYLN/HDSTN HA2 ....47 K4
SCUP DA14 ....155 H4
SNWD SE25 ....165 J2
SWFD E18 ....44 D7
WPK KT4 ....160 E7
The Lincolns *MLHL* NW7 ....37 H2
Lincoln's Inn Flds *LINN* WC2A 11 L4
Lincoln St *CHEL* SW3 ....15 L6
WAN E11 ....76 C1
Lincoln Ter *BELMT* * SM2 ....174 E6
Lincoln Wy *EN* EN1 ....30 D4
SUN TW16 ....140 C7
Lincombe Rd *BMLY* BR1 ....152 D2
Lindal Crs *STHGT/OAK* N14 ....28 E4
The Lindales *TOTM* N17 ....42 C5
Lindal Rd *BROCKY* SE4 ....132 C4
Lindbergh Rd *WLGTN* SM6 ....176 E7
Linden Av *DART* DA1 ....139 F7
HSLW TW3 ....123 G4
RSLP HA4 ....46 E7
THHTH CR7 ....164 C3
WBLY HA9 ....68 B4
WLSDN NW10 ....88 B1
Linden Cl *RSLP* HA4 ....46 E7
STAN HA7 ....35 H4
STHGT/OAK N14 ....28 C5
THDIT KT7 ....158 B6
Linden Cottages
WIM/MER * SW19 ....146 C5
Linden Crs *GFD/PVL* UB6 ....67 F5
KUT KT1 ....159 G1
WFD IG8 ....45 F5
Lindenfield *CHST* BR7 ....169 G1
Linden Gdns *BAY/PAD* W2 ....8 B7
CHSWK W4 ....106 A4
Linden Gv *NWMAL* KT3 ....160 B2
PECK SE15 ....131 J2
SYD SE26 ....150 E5
Linden Lea *EFNCH* N2 ....53 G4
PIN * HA5 ....33 K6
Linden Leas *WWKM* BR4 ....180 B1
Linden Ms *BAY/PAD* W2 ....8 B7
IS N1 ....73 K4
Linden Pl *MTCM* CR4 ....162 D3
Linden Rd *FBAR/BDGN* N11 ....39 K1
HPTN TW12 ....142 A7
MUSWH N10 ....54 B3
SEVS/STOTM N15 ....55 J4
The Lindens *CHSWK* W4 ....105 K7
NFNCH/WDSP * N12 ....39 H4
WALTH * E17 ....57 K3
Linden St *ROMW/RG* RM7 ....63 F3
Linden Wy *STHGT/OAK* N14 ....28 C5
Lindfield Gdns *HAMP* NW3 ....71 G4
Lindfield Rd *CROY/NA* CR0 ....165 G5
EA W5 ....85 J3
Lindfield St *POP/IOD* E14 ....93 J5
Lindhill Cl *PEND* EN3 ....31 F1
Lindisfarne Md *HOM* E9 ....75 G3
Lindisfarne Rd *BCTR* RM8 ....79 J2
RYNPK SW20 ....145 J6
Lindley Est *PECK* * SE15 ....111 H6
Lindley Pl *RCH/KEW* TW9 ....105 H7
Lindley Rd *LEY* E10 ....76 A1
Lindley St *WCHPL* E1 ....92 E4
Lindore Rd *BTSEA* SW11 ....128 E3
Lindores Rd *CAR* SM5 ....162 B6
Lindo St *PECK* SE15 ....131 K1
Lind Rd *SUT* SM1 ....175 G4
Lindrop St *FUL/PGN* SW6 ....128 B1
Lindsay Cl *CHSGTN* KT9 ....172 A6
STWL/WRAY TW19 ....120 A5
Lindsay Dr *KTN/HRWW/W* HA3 ....50 A5
Lindsay Rd *HPTN* TW12 ....142 C4
WPK KT4 ....173 K1
Lindsay Sq *PIM* SW1V 17 H7
Lindsell St *GNWCH* SE10 ....113 F7
Lindsey Cl *BMLY* BR1 ....168 C2
MTCM CR4 ....163 K3
Lindsey Gdns
EBED/NFELT * TW14 ....121 G6
Lindsey Ms *IS* N1 ....6 F1
Lindsey Rd *BCTR* RM8 ....79 J2
Lindsey St *STBT* EC1A 12 D2
Lind St *DEPT* SE8 ....132 E1
Lindum Rd *TEDD* TW11 ....143 J6
Lindway *WNWD* SE27 ....149 H4
Linfield Cl *HDN* NW4 ....52 A2
Linford Rd *WALTH* E17 ....58 A2
Linford St *VX/NE* SW8 ....109 H7
Lingards Rd *LEW* SE13 ....133 F3
Lingey Cl *BFN/LL* DA15 ....155 F1
Lingfield Av *BRYLDS* KT5 ....159 F3
Lingfield Cl *EN* EN1 ....30 A5
NTHWD HA6 ....32 C6
Lingfield Ct *NTHLT* * UB5 ....84 A1
Lingfield Crs *ELTH/MOT* SE9 ....135 J3
Lingfield Gdns *ED* N9 ....30 D6
Lingfield Rd *WIM/MER* SW19 ....146 B5
WPK KT4 ....174 A2
Lingham St *BRXN/ST* SW9 ....129 K1
Lingholm Wy *BAR* EN5 ....26 B4
Ling Rd *CAN/RD* E16 ....94 E4
ERITH DA8 ....117 K5
Lingwell Rd *TOOT* SW17 ....147 J2
Lingwood Gdns *ISLW* TW7 ....103 K6
Lingwood Rd *STNW/STAM* N16 ....56 C6
Linhope St *CAMTN* NW1 ....3 L9
The Link *ACT* W3 ....86 D5
ALP/SUD HA0 ....49 J7
NTHLT * UB5 ....65 K4
PIN HA5 ....47 G5
TEDD TW11 ....143 F5
Linkfield *E/WMO/HCT* KT8 ....157 F2
Link Fld *HAYES* BR2 ....167 K5
Linkfield Rd *ISLW* TW7 ....124 A1
Link La *WLGTN* SM6 ....176 D5
Linklea Cl *CDALE/KGS* NW9 ....37 G6
Link Rd *DAGW* RM9 ....98 D1
EBED/NFELT TW14 ....121 J6
FBAR/BDGN N11 ....40 A3
WATN WD24 ....21 H1
WLGTN SM6 ....163 F7
The Links *WALTH* E17 ....57 G3
Links Av *GPK* RM2 ....63 K1
MRDN SM4 ....161 K3
Links Dr *BORE* WD6 ....24 B3
TRDG/WHET N20 ....26 E7
Links Gdns *STRHM/NOR* SW16 ....149 G6
Linkside *NFNCH/WDSP* N12 ....38 D5
NWMAL KT3 ....160 B1
Linkside Cl *ENC/FH* EN2 ....29 F2
Linkside Gdns *ENC/FH* EN2 ....29 F2
Links Rd *ACT* W3 ....86 C5
CRICK NW2 ....69 H1
TOOT SW17 ....148 A5
WFD IG8 ....44 E4
WWKM BR4 ....167 F7
Links Side *ENC/FH* EN2 ....29 F2
Link St *HOM* E9 ....74 E5
Links Vw *DART* DA1 ....139 F7
FNCH N3 ....38 D6
Links View Cl *STAN* HA7 ....35 G5
Linksview Ct *HPTN* * TW12 ....142 D3
Links View Rd *CROY/NA* CR0 ....179 J2
HPTN TW12 ....142 C4
Links Wy *BECK* BR3 ....166 D5
NTHWD HA6 ....32 A7
RKW/CH/CXG WD3 ....20 A2
Linksway *HDN* NW4 ....52 B1
NTHWD HA6 ....32 B7
Links Yd *WCHPL* E1 ....13 M2
Link Wy *HAYES* BR2 ....168 D6
RCHPK/HAM TW10 ....143 H1
Linkway *BCTR* RM8 ....79 J3
FSBYPK N4 ....55 J6
PIN HA5 ....33 H7
RYNPK SW20 ....160 E2
The Linkway *BAR* EN5 ....26 E5
BELMT SM2 ....175 G7
Linkwood Wk *CAMTN* NW1 ....5 H1
Linley Crs *ROMW/RG* RM7 ....62 D2
Linley Rd *TOTM* N17 ....56 A1
Linnell Cl *GLDGN* NW11 ....53 F5
Linnell Dr *GLDGN* NW11 ....53 F5
Linnell Rd *CMBW* SE5 ....131 F1
UED N18 ....42 C4
Linnet Cl *BUSH* WD23 ....22 C7
ED N9 ....31 F7
THMD SE28 ....97 J6
Linnet Ms *BAL* SW12 ....129 F6
Linnett Cl *CHING* E4 ....44 A3
Linom Rd *CLAP* SW4 ....129 K3
Linscott Rd *CLPT* E5 ....74 E3
Linsdell Rd *BARK* IG11 ....78 C7
Linsey St *BERM/RHTH* SE16 ....111 H3
Linslade Cl *HSLWW* TW4 ....122 D4
PIN HA5 ....47 F2
Linstead St *KIL/WHAMP* NW6 ....2 A1
Linstead Wy *WAND/EARL* SW18 ....127 H6
Linster Gv *BORE* WD6 ....24 E4
Lintaine Cl *FUL/PGN* * SW6 ....107 H5
Linthorpe Av *ALP/SUD* HA0 ....67 J5
Linthorpe Rd *EBAR* EN4 ....27 J2
STNW/STAM N16 ....56 A6
Linton Av *BORE* WD6 ....24 B1
Linton Cl *CAR* SM5 ....162 E6
CHARL SE7 ....114 B4
WELL DA16 ....116 B7
Linton Ct *ROM* RM1 ....63 G1
Linton Gdns *EHAM* E6 ....95 J5
Linton Gv *WNWD* SE27 ....149 H4
Linton Rd *BARK* IG11 ....78 C6
Linton St *IS* N1 ....6 F4
Lintott Ct *STWL/WRAY* TW19 ....120 A5
Linver Rd *FUL/PGN* SW6 ....127 J1
Linwood Cl *CMBW* SE5 ....131 G1
Linzee Rd *CEND/HSY/T* N8 ....54 E3
Lion Av *TWK* TW1 ....124 A7
Lion Cl *BROCKY* SE4 ....132 D5
Lionel Gdns *ELTH/MOT* SE9 ....134 C4
Lionel Ms *NKENS* * W10 ....88 C4
Lionel Rd *ELTH/MOT* SE9 ....134 C4
Lionel Rd North *BTFD* TW8 ....105 F2
Lionel Rd South *BTFD* TW8 ....105 G4
Lion Gate Gdns *RCH/KEW* TW9 ....125 G2
Lion Mills *BETH* * E2 ....92 C1
Lion Park Av *CHSGTN* KT9 ....172 C3
Lion Rd *BXLYHS* DA6 ....137 F3
CROY/NA CR0 ....164 D4
ED N9 ....42 C1
EHAM E6 ....95 K4
WHTN TW2 ....124 A7
Lions Cl *ELTH/MOT* SE9 ....153 G2
Lion Wy *BTFD* TW8 ....104 E6
Lion Wharf Rd *ISLW* TW7 ....124 C2
Liphook Cl *HCH* RM12 ....81 H3
Liphook Crs *FSTH* SE23 ....131 K6
Liphook Rd *OXHEY* WD19 ....33 H3
Lisbon Av *WHTN* TW2 ....142 C1
Lisbon Cl *WALTH* E17 ....57 H1
Lisburne Rd *HAMP* NW3 ....71 K3
Lisford St *PECK* SE15 ....111 G7
Lisgar Ter *WKENS* W14 ....107 J3
Liskeard Gdns *BKHTH/KID* SE3 ....113 K7
Lisle Cl *TOOT* SW17 ....148 B3
Lisle St *SOHO/SHAV* W1D 11 H6
Lismore *WIM/MER* * SW19 ....146 D4
Lismore Circ *HAMP* NW3 ....71 K4
Lismore Cl *ISLW* TW7 ....124 B1
Lismore Rd *SAND/SEL* CR2 ....178 A5
TOTM N17 ....55 K2
Lismore Wk *IS* N1 ....73 J5
Lissant Cl *SURB* KT6 ....158 D6
Lissenden Gdns *KTTN* NW5 ....72 A3
Lisson Gv *STJWD* NW8 ....9 J1
Lisson St *STJWD* NW8 ....9 J2
Lister Cl *ACT* W3 ....87 F4
WIM/MER SW19 ....147 J7
Lister Gdns *UED* N18 ....41 J4
Lister Ms *HOLWY* N7 ....73 F3
Lister Rd *WAN* E11 ....58 C7
Liston Rd *CLAP* SW4 ....129 H2
TOTM N17 ....42 C7
Liston Wy *WFD* IG8 ....45 G6
Listowel Cl *BRXN/ST* SW9 ....110 B6
Listowel Rd *DAGE* RM10 ....80 C2
Listria Pk *STNW/STAM* N16 ....74 A1
Litchfield Av *MRDN* SM4 ....161 J6
SRTFD * E15 ....76 C5
Litchfield Gdns *WLSDN* NW10 ....69 J5
Litchfield Rd *SUT* SM1 ....175 G3
Litchfield Wy *GLDGN* NW11 ....53 G4
Lithgow's Rd *HTHAIR* TW6 ....121 H3
Lithos Rd *HAMP* NW3 ....71 F5
Little Acre *BECK* BR3 ....166 D2
Little Albany St *CAMTN* NW1 ....4 D9
Little Argyll St *CONDST* * W1S 10 E5
Little Benty *WDR/YW* UB7 ....100 A4
Little Birches *BFN/LL* DA15 ....154 E1
The Little Boltons *WBPTN* SW10 ....14 D7
Little Bornes *DUL* SE21 ....150 A3
Little Britain *STBT* EC1A 12 E3
Littlebrook Cl *CROY/NA* CR0 ....166 A5
Littlebrook Manor Wy
DART DA1 ....139 K4
Littlebury Rd *CLAP* * SW4 ....129 J2
Little Bury St *ED* N9 ....30 A6
Little Bushey La *BUSH* WD23 ....22 A2
Little Cedars *NFNCH/WDSP* N12 ....39 G3
Little Chester St *KTBR* SW1X 16 C3
Little Cloisters *WEST* SW1P 17 J3
Littlecombe Cl
PUT/ROE * SW15 ....127 G5
Littlecote Cl *WIM/MER* SW19 ....127 G6
Littlecote Pl *PIN* HA5 ....33 J7
Little Ct *WWKM* BR4 ....180 C1
Littlecroft *ELTH/MOT* SE9 ....135 F2
Littledale *ABYW* SE2 ....116 B5
Little Deans Yd *WEST* SW1P 17 J3
Little Dimocks *BAL* SW12 ....148 B1
Little Dorrit Ct *STHWK* SE1 ....18 F1
Little Ealing La *EA* W5 ....104 D3
Little Edward St *CAMTN* * NW1 ....4 D7
Little Elms *HYS/HAR* UB3 ....101 G6
Little Essex St *TPL/STR* * WC2R 12 A6
Little Ferry Rd *TWK* * TW1 ....124 C7
Littlefield Cl *ARCH* N19 ....72 C3
KUT KT1 ....159 F1
Littlefield Rd *EDGW* HA8 ....36 E6
Little Friday Rd *CHING* E4 ....44 C1
Little Gearies *BARK/HLT* IG6 ....60 B3
Little George St *WEST* SW1P 17 J2
Little Green St *KTTN* * NW5 ....72 B3
Little Gv *BUSH* WD23 ....22 B3
Littlegrove *EBAR* EN4 ....27 J5
Little Heath *CHARL* SE7 ....114 D5
CHDH RM6 ....61 H3
Little Heath Rd *BXLYHN* DA7 ....117 G7
Littleheath Rd *SAND/SEL* CR2 ....178 D7
Little Ilford La *MNPK* E12 ....77 K3
Littlejohn Rd *HNWL* W7 ....85 F5
Little Marlborough St
REGST * W1B 10 E5
Little Martins *BUSH* WD23 ....22 B4
Littlemead *ESH/CLAY* KT10 ....170 D3
Littlemede *ELTH/MOT* SE9 ....153 K2
Littlemoor Rd *IL* IG1 ....78 D2
Littlemore Rd *ABYW* SE2 ....116 B1
Little Moss La *PIN* HA5 ....47 J1
Little Newport St
LSQ/SEVD WC2H 11 H6
Little New St *FLST/FETLN* EC4A 12 B4
Little Orchard Cl *PIN* * HA5 ....47 J1
Little Oxhey La *OXHEY* WD19 ....33 J4
Little Park Dr *FELT* TW13 ....141 H1
Little Park Gdns *ENC/FH* EN2 ....29 K2
Little Portland St *REGST* W1B 10 D4
Little Potters *BUSH* WD23 ....22 D6
Little Queens Rd *TEDD* TW11 ....143 F5
Little Queen St *DART* DA1 ....139 J6
Little Redlands *BMLY* BR1 ....168 D1
Little Rd *HYS/HAR* UB3 ....101 J1
Little Rownings *FSTH* SE23 ....150 D1
Littlers Cl *WIM/MER* SW19 ....147 H7
Little Russell St
NOXST/BSQ WC1A 11 J3
Little St James's St
WHALL SW1A 10 E9
Little St Leonards
MORT/ESHN SW14 ....125 K2
Little Smith St *WEST* SW1P 17 H3
Littlestone Cl *BECK* BR3 ....151 J5
Little Strd *CDALE/KGS* NW9 ....51 H1
Little Stream Cl *NTHWD* HA6 ....32 C4
Little Thrift *STMC/STPC* BR5 ....169 H3
Little Titchfield St *GTPST* W1W 10 E3
Littleton Crs *HRW* HA1 ....67 F1
Littleton Rd *ASHF* TW15 ....140 A6
HRW HA1 ....67 F1
Littleton St *WAND/EARL* SW18 ....147 G1
Little Trinity La *BLKFR* EC4V 12 F6
Little Turnstile *HHOL* WC1V 11 L3
Littlewood *LEW* SE13 ....133 F4
Little Wood Cl *STMC/STPC* BR5 ....155 G7
Littlewood Cl *WEA* W13 ....104 C2
Littleworth Av *ESH/CLAY* KT10 ....170 D4
Littleworth Common Rd
ESH/CLAY KT10 ....170 D2
Littleworth La *ESH/CLAY* KT10 ....170 D3
Littleworth Pl *ESH/CLAY* KT10 ....170 D3
Littleworth Rd *ESH/CLAY* KT10 ....170 D4
Livermere Rd *HACK* E8 ....7 M3
Liverpool Gv *WALW* SE17 ....19 G8
Liverpool Rd *CAN/RD* E16 ....94 C4
EA W5 ....104 E1
IS N1 ....6 B1
KUTN/CMB KT2 ....144 C6
LEY E10 ....58 A5
THHTH CR7 ....164 D2
WATW WD18 ....21 F4
Liverpool St *LVPST* EC2M 13 J3
Livesey Cl *KUT* KT1 ....159 G2
Livesey Pl *PECK* SE15 ....111 H5
Livingstone Rd *BTSEA* SW11 ....128 C2
HSLW TW3 ....123 H3
PLMGR N13 ....40 E5
SRTFD E15 ....76 A7
STHL UB1 ....83 H6
THHTH CR7 ....164 E1
WALTH E17 ....57 K5
Lizard St *FSBYE* EC1V 6 F8
Lizban St *BKHTH/KID* SE3 ....114 A6
Llanelly Rd *CRICK* NW2 ....70 D1
Llanover Rd *WBLY* HA9 ....67 K2
WOOL/PLUM SE18 ....115 F6
Llanthony Rd *MRDN* SM4 ....162 C5
Llanvanor Rd *CRICK* NW2 ....70 D1
Llewellyn St *BERM/RHTH* SE16 ....111 H1
Lloyd Av *STRHM/NOR* SW16 ....148 E7
Lloyd Baker St *FSBYW* WC1X 6 A8
Lloyd Ct *PIN* HA5 ....47 H4
Lloyd Park Av *CROY/NA* CR0 ....178 B3
Lloyd Rd *DAGW* RM9 ....80 B5
EHAM E6 ....77 K7
WALTH E17 ....57 F3
WPK KT4 ....174 A2
Lloyd's Av *TWRH* EC3N 13 K5
Lloyd's Pl *BKHTH/KID* * SE3 ....133 H1
Lloyd Sq *FSBYW* WC1X 6 A8
Lloyd's Rw *CLKNW* EC1R 6 B8
Lloyd St *FSBYW* WC1X 6 A7
Lloyds Wy *BECK* BR3 ....166 B4
Lloyd Thomas Ct *WDGN* * N22 ....41 F6
Lloyd Vls *BROCKY* SE4 ....132 D1
Loampit Hl *LEW* SE13 ....132 D1
Loampit V *LEW* SE13 ....132 E2
Loanda Cl *HACK* E8 ....7 L3
Loates La *WAT* WD17 ....21 G2
Loats Rd *BRXS/STRHM* SW2 ....129 K5
Local Board Rd *WAT* WD17 ....21 H4
Locarno Rd *ACT* W3 ....86 E7
GFD/PVL UB6 ....84 C3
Lochaber Rd *LEW* SE13 ....133 H3
Lochaline St *HMSMTH* W6 ....107 F5
Lochan Cl *YEAD* UB4 ....83 J3
Lochinvar St *BAL* SW12 ....129 G6
Lochmere Cl *ERITH* DA8 ....117 J5
Lochnagar St *POP/IOD* E14 ....94 A4
Lock Cha *LEW* SE13 ....133 H2
Lock Cl *NWDGN* * UB2 ....103 H1
Locke Cl *RAIN* RM13 ....81 H5
Locksley Sq *SURB* * KT6 ....158 E5
Locket Rd *KTN/HRWW/W* HA3 ....49 F1
Lockfield Av *PEND* EN3 ....31 G1
Lockgate Cl *HOM* E9 ....75 H4
Lockhart Cl *HOLWY* N7 ....73 F5
Lockhart St *BOW* E3 ....93 H3
Lockhurst St *CLPT* E5 ....75 F3
Lockington Rd *VX/NE* SW8 ....109 G7
Lockmead Rd *LEW* SE13 ....133 F2
SEVS/STOTM N15 ....56 C5
Lock Rd *RCHPK/HAM* TW10 ....143 J3
Lock's La *MTCM* CR4 ....148 A7
Locksley Est *POP/IOD* E14 ....93 H5
Locksley St *POP/IOD* E14 ....93 H4
Locksmeade Rd
RCHPK/HAM TW10 ....143 H3
Lockwood Cl *SYD* SE26 ....151 F3
Lockwood Sq
BERM/RHTH SE16 ....111 J2
Lockwood Wy *CHSGTN* KT9 ....172 C4
WALTH E17 ....57 F1
Lockyer St *STHWK* SE1 ....19 H2
Locomotive Dr
EBED/NFELT TW14 ....121 K7
Locton Gn *BOW* * E3 ....75 H7
Loddiges Rd *HOM* E9 ....74 E6
Loder St *PECK* SE15 ....111 K6
The Lodge *SHB* * W12 ....107 G1
Lodge Av *BORE* WD6 ....24 B4
CROY/NA CR0 ....177 F2
DAGW RM9 ....79 H7
DART DA1 ....139 F5
GPK RM2 ....63 J4
KTN/HRWW/W HA3 ....50 A3
Lodge Cl *EDGW* * HA8 ....36 B5
ISLW TW7 ....104 C7
UED N18 ....41 J4
WLGTN SM6 ....163 F7
Lodge Ct *ALP/SUD* * HA0 ....68 A4
Lodge Dr *PLMGR* N13 ....41 G3
Lodge End *RKW/CH/CXG* WD3 ....20 B3
Lodge Gdns *BECK* BR3 ....166 C4
Lodge Hl *REDBR* IG4 ....59 J3
WELL DA16 ....116 C6
Lodgehill Park Cl
RYLN/HDSTN HA2 ....66 B1
Lodge La *BXLY* DA5 ....136 E5
CROY/NA CR0 ....179 K6
NFNCH/WDSP N12 ....39 G4
Lodge Mansions Pde
PLMGR * N13 ....41 G3
Lodge Ms *HBRY* * N5 ....73 J3
Lodge Pl *SUT* SM1 ....175 F4
Lodge Rd *BMLY* BR1 ....153 G6
CROY/NA CR0 ....164 C5
HDN NW4 ....52 A3
RKW/CH/CXG WD3 ....20 B3
STJWD NW8 ....3 H8
SUT SM1 ....175 F4
WLGTN SM6 ....176 B4
Lodge Vls *WFD* IG8 ....44 D6
Lodore Gdns *CDALE/KGS* NW9 ....51 G4
Lodore St *POP/IOD* E14 ....94 A5
Lofthouse Pl *CHSGTN* KT9 ....171 J5
Loftie St *BERM/RHTH* SE16 ....111 H1
Lofting Rd *IS* N1 ....6 A2
Loftus Rd *SHB* W12 ....87 K7
Loftus Vls *SHB* * W12 ....87 K7
Logan Cl *HSLWW* TW4 ....122 E2
Logan Ms *KENS* W8 ....14 A5
ROM RM1 ....63 G4
Logan Pl *KENS* W8 ....14 A5
Logan Rd *ED* N9 ....42 D1
WBLY HA9 ....68 A1
The Logans *BAR* * EN5 ....26 B2
Logs Hl *CHST* BR7 ....153 J7
Logs Hill Cl *CHST* BR7 ....153 J7
Lolesworth Cl *WCHPL* * E1 ....13 M3
Lollard St *LBTH* SE11 ....17 M5
Loman St *STHWK* SE1 ....18 D1
Lomas Cl *CROY/NA* CR0 ....180 A6
Lomas St *WCHPL* E1 ....92 C4
Lombard Av *GDMY/SEVK* IG3 ....60 E7
Lombard Rd *BTSEA* SW11 ....128 C1
FBAR/BDGN N11 ....40 B4
WIM/MER SW19 ....162 A1
Lombard St *BANK* EC3V 13 H5
Lombard Vls *FBAR/BDGN* * N11 ....40 B4
Lombard Wall *CHARL* SE7 ....114 A2
Lombardy Pl *BAY/PAD* W2 ....8 C7
Lomond Cl *ALP/SUD* HA0 ....68 B6
SEVS/STOTM N15 ....56 A3
Lomond Gdns *SAND/SEL* CR2 ....179 G6
Lomond Gv *CMBW* SE5 ....110 E6
Loncroft Rd *CMBW* SE5 ....19 K9
Londesborough Rd
STNW/STAM N16 ....74 A3
London Br *CANST* EC4R 13 H7
London Bridge Wk
STHWK * SE1 ....13 H8

Londonderry Pde ERITH * DA8 118 A6
London Flds HACK * E8 74 D6
London Fields East Side
HACK E8 74 D6
London Fields West Side
HACK E8 74 C6
London La BMLY BR1 152 E6
HACK E8 74 D6
London Loop BORE WD6 24 D5
CROY/NA CR0 179 F2
MLHL NW7 24 E6
SAND/SEL CR2 179 F7
WWKM BR4 180 B2
London Ms BAY/PAD W2 9 H5
London Rd BARK IG11 78 B6
BMLY BR1 152 D6
BUSH WD23 21 J5
CHDH RM6 62 C5
CHEAM SM3 174 C1
CROY/NA CR0 164 C7
DART DA1 138 A4
EN EN1 29 K3
EW KT17 173 H7
FSTH SE23 131 K7
HRW HA1 66 E1
ISLW TW7 123 K1
KUT KT1 159 F1
MRDN SM4 161 K4
MTCM CR4 147 K7
MTCM CR4 162 D3
MTCM CR4 163 F6
PLSTW E13 94 E1
ROMW/RG RM7 62 E5
SOCK/AV RM15 119 J1
SOCK/AV RM15 119 K1
STAN HA7 35 J4
STAN HA7 35 K3
STHWK SE1 18 C3
STRHM/NOR SW16 149 F7
THHTH CR7 164 B5
TWK TW1 124 B7
WBLY HA9 68 A4
WLGTN SM6 176 B1
London Stile CHSWK W4 105 H4
London St BAY/PAD W2 9 G5
FENCHST * EC3M 13 K6
London Ter BETH * E2 92 C1
London Wall BARB EC2Y 12 F3
London Wall Buildings
LVPST EC2M 13 H3
Lonesome Wy MTCM CR4 148 B7
Long Acre COVGDN WC2E 11 J5
Long Acre Ct WEA * W13 85 G4
Longacre Pl CAR * SM5 176 A5
Longacre Rd WALTH E17 44 B7
Longbeach Rd BTSEA SW11 128 E2
Longboat Rw STHL UB1 83 K5
Longbridge Rd BARK IG11 78 D5
BCTR RM8 79 G3
Longbridge Wy LEW SE13 133 F4
Longcliffe Pth OXHEY WD19 32 E2
Long Ct PUR RM19 119 K3
Longcroft ELTH/MOT SE9 154 A2
Long Cft OXHEY WD19 21 F6
Longcrofte Rd EDGW HA8 35 K6
Longdon Wd HAYES BR2 181 J3
Longdown Rd CAT SE6 151 J3
Long Dr ACT W3 87 G5
GFD/PVL UB6 66 B7
RSLP HA4 65 G3
WDR/YW * UB7 100 B1
Long Elmes KTN/HRWW/W HA3 34 C7
Longfellow Rd BOW * E3 93 G2
WALTH E17 57 H5
WPK KT4 160 D7
Longfellow Wy STHWK * SE1 19 M6
Longfield BMLY BR1 152 D7
Long Fld CDALE/KGS NW9 37 G6
Longfield Av EA W5 85 J6
EMPK RM11 63 H6
MLHL NW7 37 J6
WALTH E17 57 G3
WBLY HA9 50 A7
WLGTN SM6 163 F7
Longfield Crs SYD SE26 150 E2
Longfield Dr
MORT/ESHN SW14 125 J4
WIM/MER SW19 147 J7
Longfield Est STHWK SE1 19 M5
Longfield Rd EA W5 85 J5
Longfield St WAND/EARL SW18 127 K6
Longford Av
EBED/NFELT TW14 121 H5
STHL UB1 84 A6
STWL/WRAY TW19 120 B7
Longford Cl FELT TW13 141 J2
HPTN TW12 142 A3
YEAD UB4 83 H6
Longford Ct HOR/WEW KT19 172 E3
HPTN TW12 142 B5
Longford Gdns SUT SM1 175 G2
YEAD UB4 83 H6
Longford Rd WHTN TW2 123 F7
Longford St CAMTN NW1 4 D9
Longford Wy
STWL/WRAY TW19 120 B7
Longhayes Av CHDH RM6 61 K2
Longheath Gdns CROY/NA CR0 165 K4
Longhedge St BTSEA SW11 129 F1
Longhill Rd CAT SE6 152 B1
Longhook Gdns NTHLT UB5 82 E1
Longhope Cl PECK SE15 111 F5
Longhurst Rd CROY/NA CR0 165 J5
LEW SE13 133 H4
Longland Dr TRDG/WHET N20 39 F2
Longlands Park Crs
BFN/LL DA15 154 E2
Longlands Rd BFN/LL DA15 154 E2
Long La BXLYHN DA7 117 F6
CROY/NA CR0 165 K5
FNCH N3 39 F7
STBT EC1A 12 D2
STHWK SE1 19 H2
STWL/WRAY TW19 120 C7
Longleat Rd EN EN1 30 A4
Longleat Wy
EBED/NFELT TW14 121 F6
Longleigh La ABYW SE2 116 D5
Longley Av ALP/SUD HA0 68 B7
Longley Rd CROY/NA CR0 164 C6
HRW HA1 48 D4
TOOT SW17 147 J5
Long Leys CHING E4 43 K5
Longley St STHWK SE1 111 H3
Longley Wy CRICK NW2 70 A2
Long Mark Rd CAN/RD E16 95 H5
Long Md CDALE/KGS NW9 37 H7
Longmead CHST BR7 169 F1
Longmead Dr SCUP DA14 155 K1
Long Meadow HOLWY * N7 72 D5
Long Meadow Cl BECK BR3 167 F6
Longmeadow Rd BFN/LL DA15 135 K7
Longmead Rd HYS/HAR UB3 82 E6
THDIT KT7 157 K6
TOOT SW17 147 K4
Longmoore St PIM SW1V 16 E6
Longmore Av BAR EN5 27 G5
Longnor Rd WCHPL E1 93 F2
Long Pond Rd BKHTH/KID SE3 113 H7
Long Reach Rd BARK IG11 97 F3
Longreach Rd ERITH DA8 118 E6
Longridge La STHL UB1 84 B6
Longridge Rd ECT SW5 14 A6
Long Rd CLAP SW4 129 H3
Longshaw Rd CHING E4 44 B2
Longshore DEPT SE8 112 C3
Longstaff Crs
WAND/EARL SW18 127 K5
Longstaff Rd
WAND/EARL SW18 127 K5
Longstone Av WLSDN NW10 69 H6
Longstone Rd
STRHM/NOR SW16 148 B4
Long St BETH E2 7 L7
Longthornton Rd
STRHM/NOR SW16 163 H1
Longton Av SYD SE26 150 C3
Longton Gv SYD SE26 150 D3
Longville Rd LBTH SE11 18 C5
Long Wk NWMAL KT3 159 K2
STHWK SE1 19 K3
Longwalk Rd STKPK * UB11 100 E1
Longwood Ct WPK KT4 173 J1
Longwood Dr PUT/ROE SW15 126 D5
Longwood Gdns CLAY IG5 59 K3
Longworth Cl THMD SE28 97 K5
Long Yd BMSBY WC1N 11 L1
The Loning CDALE/KGS NW9 51 H3
Lonsdale Av EHAM E6 95 H3
ROMW/RG RM7 62 E5
WBLY HA9 68 A4
Lonsdale Cl EHAM E6 95 J3
ELTH/MOT SE9 153 H2
UX/CGN UB8 82 A5
Lonsdale Crs GNTH/NBYPK IG2 60 B5
Lonsdale Dr ENC/FH EN2 28 D3
Lonsdale Dr North ENC/FH EN2 28 E4
Lonsdale Gdns
STRHM/NOR SW16 164 A3
Lonsdale Ms RCH/KEW * TW9 105 H7
Lonsdale Pl IS N1 6 B2
Lonsdale Rd BARN SW13 106 C6
BXLYHN DA7 137 G1
CHSWK W4 106 C3
KIL/WHAMP NW6 88 D1
NTGHL W11 88 D5
NWDGN UB2 102 C2
SNWD SE25 165 J3
WAN E11 58 D6
Lonsdale Sq IS N1 6 B2
Loobert Rd SEVS/STOTM N15 56 A2
Looe Gdns BARK/HLT IG6 60 B2
Loop Rd CHST BR7 154 B4
Lopen Rd UED N18 42 A3
Loraine Cl PEND EN3 30 E4
Loraine Cottages HOLWY * N7 73 F3
Loraine Rd CHSWK W4 105 J5
HOLWY N7 73 F3
Lord Av CLAY IG5 59 K3
Lord Chancellor Wk
KUTN/CMB KT2 144 E7
Lord Gdns CLAY IG5 59 J3
Lord Hills Rd BAY/PAD W2 8 D2
Lord Holland La BRXN/ST * SW9 130 B1
Lord Knyvett Cl
STWL/WRAY TW19 120 A5
Lord Knyvetts Ct
STWL/WRAY * TW19 120 B5
Lord Napier Pl HMSMTH W6 106 D4
Lord North St WEST SW1P 17 J4
Lord Roberts Ms
FUL/PGN * SW6 108 A6
Lords Cl DUL SE21 149 J1
FELT TW13 141 J1
Lordship Gv STNW/STAM N16 73 K1
Lordship La EDUL SE22 131 G5
WDGN N22 41 H7
Lordship Pk STNW/STAM N16 73 K1
Lordship Park Ms
STNW/STAM N16 73 J1
Lordship Pl CHEL SW3 108 D5
Lordship Rd NTHLT UB5 65 J6
STNW/STAM N16 55 K7
Lordship Ter STNW/STAM N16 73 K1
Lordsmead Rd TOTM N17 42 A7
Lord St CAN/RD E16 95 J7
WAT WD17 21 G2
Lords Vw STJWD NW8 3 J8
Lord Warwick St
WOOL/PLUM SE18 114 E2
Lorenzo St FSBYW WC1X 5 L7
Loretto Gdns
KTN/HRWW/W HA3 50 A3
Lorian Cl NFNCH/WDSP N12 39 F3
Loring Rd ISLW TW7 124 A1
TRDG/WHET N20 39 J1
Loris Rd HMSMTH W6 107 F2
Lorn Ct BRXN/ST SW9 130 B1
Lorne Av CROY/NA CR0 166 A6
Lorne Cl STJWD NW8 3 K8
Lorne Gdns CROY/NA CR0 166 B6
NTGHL W11 107 G1
WAN E11 59 G3
Lorne Rd FSBYPK N4 55 F7
FSTGT E7 77 F3
KTN/HRWW/W HA3 49 F1
RCHPK/HAM TW10 125 G4
WALTH E17 57 J4
Lorne Ter FNCH * N3 52 D1
Lorn Rd BRXN/ST SW9 130 A1
Lorraine Pk KTN/HRWW/W HA3 34 E6
Lorrimore Rd WALW SE17 110 C5
Lorrimore Sq WALW SE17 18 D9
Loseberry Rd ESH/CLAY KT10 170 D4
Lothair Rd EA W5 104 E1
Lothair Rd North FSBYPK N4 55 H5
Lothair Rd South FSBYPK N4 55 G6
Lothbury LOTH EC2R 13 G4
Lothian Av YEAD UB4 83 F4
Lothian Cl ALP/SUD HA0 67 G3
Lothian Rd BRXN/ST SW9 110 C7
Lothrop St NKENS W10 88 C2
Lots Rd WBPTN SW10 108 B6
Loubet St TOOT SW17 147 K5
Loudoun Av GNTH/NBYPK IG2 60 B4
Loudoun Rd STJWD NW8 2 F4
Loughborough Pk
BRXN/ST SW9 130 C3
Loughborough Rd
BRXN/ST SW9 130 C1
Loughborough St LBTH SE11 17 M7
Lough Rd HOLWY N7 73 F5
Louisa Cl HOM E9 74 E6
Louisa St WCHPL E1 93 F4
Louis Cl CHST BR7 153 K3
Louise Bennett Cl HNHL * SE24 130 C3
Louise Gdns RAIN RM13 99 G2
Louise Rd SRTFD E15 76 C5
Louisville Rd TOOT SW17 148 A2
Louvaine Rd BTSEA SW11 128 C3
Lovage Ap EHAM E6 95 J4
Lovat Cl CRICK NW2 69 H2
Lovat La FENCHST EC3M 13 J6
Lovatt Cl EDGW HA8 36 D5
Loveday Rd WEA W13 85 H7
Lovegrove St STHWK SE1 111 H4
Lovegrove Wk POP/IOD E14 94 A7
Lovekyn Cl KUTN/CMB KT2 159 F1
Lovelace Av HAYES BR2 169 F5
Lovelace Gdns BARK IG11 79 G3
SURB KT6 158 E6
Lovelace Gn ELTH/MOT SE9 134 E2
Lovelace Rd DUL SE21 149 J1
EBAR EN4 27 J6
SURB KT6 158 D6
Lovelace Vls THDIT * KT7 158 C6
Love La BXLY DA5 137 H5
CHEAM SM3 174 C5
CITYW EC2V 12 F4
MRDN SM4 161 K6
MTCM CR4 162 D2
PIN HA5 47 J2
SNWD SE25 165 J2
SURB KT6 171 K1
TOTM N17 42 B6
WFD IG8 45 K5
WOOL/PLUM SE18 115 F3
Lovel Av WELL DA16 136 B1
Lovelinch Cl PECK SE15 111 K5
Lovell Pl BERM/RHTH SE16 112 B2
Lovell Rd RCHPK/HAM TW10 143 J2
STHL UB1 84 B5
Lovell Wk RAIN RM13 81 J5
Loveridge Ms KIL/WHAMP NW6 70 D5
Loveridge Rd KIL/WHAMP NW6 70 D5
Lovett Dr CAR SM5 162 B6
Lovett Wy WLSDN NW10 68 E4
Love Wk CMBW SE5 130 E1
Lowbrook Rd IL IG1 78 B3
Lowden Rd ED N9 30 D7
HNHL SE24 130 C3
STHL UB1 83 J6
Lowe Av CAN/RD E16 94 E4
Lowell St POP/IOD E14 93 G5
Lowen Rd RAIN RM13 99 F1
Lower Addiscombe Rd
CROY/NA CR0 164 E7
Lower Addison Gdns
WKENS W14 107 H1
Lower Belgrave St BGVA SW1W 16 C4
Lower Boston Rd HNWL W7 84 E7
Lower Broad St DAGE RM10 80 C7
Lower Camden CHST BR7 153 K7
Lower Church St
CROY/NA * CR0 177 H1
Lower Clapton Rd CLPT E5 74 D3
Lower Clarendon Wk
NTGHL W11 88 C5
Lower Common South
PUT/ROE SW15 126 E2
Lower Coombe St
CROY/NA CR0 177 J3
Lower Derby Rd WAT WD17 21 G3
Lower Downs Rd RYNPK SW20 146 B7
Lower Gravel Rd HAYES BR2 168 D7
Lower Green Gdns WPK KT4 160 D7
Lower Green Rd
ESH/CLAY KT10 170 B1
Lower Gn West MTCM CR4 162 D2
Lower Grosvenor Pl KTBR SW1X 16 C3
Lower Grove Rd
RCHPK/HAM TW10 125 G5
Lower Hall La CHING E4 43 G4
Lower Hampton Rd SUN TW16 156 C1
Lower Ham Rd KUTN/CMB KT2 143 K5
Lower High St WAT WD17 21 G3
Lower James St
SOHO/CST * W1F 10 F6
Lower John St SOHO/CST W1F 10 F6
Lower Kenwood Av
STHGT/OAK N14 28 E4
Lower Lea Crossing
POP/IOD E14 94 C6
Lower Maidstone Rd
FBAR/BDGN N11 40 C5
Lower Mardyke Av RAIN RM13 98 E1
Lower Marsh STHWK SE1 18 A2
Lower Marsh La KUT KT1 159 H3
Lower Merton Ri HAMP NW3 3 J2
Lower Morden La MRDN SM4 161 G5
Lower Mortlake Rd
RCH/KEW TW9 125 F3
Lower Paddock Rd
OXHEY WD19 21 J5
Lower Park Rd BELV DA17 117 H2
FBAR/BDGN N11 40 C4
Lower Queen's Rd BKHH IG9 45 J1
Lower Richmond Rd
PUT/ROE SW15 127 F2
RCH/KEW TW9 125 H2
Lower Rd BELV DA17 117 K2
BERM/RHTH SE16 111 K2
RYLN/HDSTN HA2 66 D1
SUT SM1 175 H4
Lower Sand Hills SURB KT6 158 D6
Lower Sloane St BGVA SW1W 15 M6
Lower Station Rd DART DA1 138 B5
Lower Strd CDALE/KGS NW9 51 H1
Lower Sunbury Rd HPTN TW12 156 E1
Lower Tail OXHEY WD19 33 J2
Lower Teddington Rd KUT KT1 143 K7
Lower Ter HAMP NW3 71 G2
Lower Thames St MON EC3R 13 K7
Lower Tub BUSH WD23 22 D6
Lower Wood Rd
ESH/CLAY KT10 171 H5
Loweswater Cl WBLY HA9 67 K1
Lowfield Rd ACT W3 86 E5
KIL/WHAMP NW6 2 A1
Lowfield St DART DA1 139 H6
Low Hall Cl CHING E4 31 J6
Low Hall La WALTH E17 57 G5
Lowick Rd HRW HA1 48 E3
Lowland Gdns ROMW/RG RM7 62 D5
Lowlands Rd HRW HA1 48 E6
PIN HA5 47 G6
STWL/WRAY TW19 120 A4
Lowman Rd HOLWY N7 73 F3
Lowndes Cl KTBR SW1X 16 B4
Lowndes Ct REGST W1B 10 E5
Lowndes Pl KTBR * SW1X 16 A4
Lowndes Sq KTBR SW1X 15 M2
Lowndes St KTBR SW1X 15 M3
Lowood St WCHPL E1 92 D6
Lowry Crs MTCM CR4 162 D1
Lowry Rd BCTR RM8 79 H4
Lowson Gv OXHEY WD19 21 J6
Lowswood Cl NTHWD HA6 32 A7
Lowther Cl BORE WD6 24 B4
Lowther Dr ENC/FH EN2 28 E3
Lowther Hl FSTH SE23 132 B6
Lowther Man BARN * SW13 106 D7
Lowther Rd BARN SW13 106 C7
HOLWY * N7 73 G4
KUTN/CMB KT2 144 B7
STAN HA7 50 B2
WALTH E17 57 G1
Lowth Rd CMBW SE5 130 D1
Loxford Av EHAM E6 95 H1
Loxford La IL IG1 78 C4
Loxford Rd BARK IG11 78 B5
Loxham Rd CHING E4 43 K6
Loxham St STPAN * WC1H 5 K8
Loxley Cl SYD SE26 151 F4
Loxley Rd HPTN TW12 141 K3
WAND/EARL SW18 128 C7
Loxton Rd FSTH SE23 132 A7
Loxwood Cl EBED/NFELT TW14 121 G7
Loxwood Rd TOTM N17 56 A2
Lubbock Rd CHST BR7 153 K6
Lubbock St NWCR SE14 111 K6
Lucan Pl CHEL SW3 15 J6
Lucan Rd BAR EN5 26 C2
Lucas Av PLSTW E13 77 F7
RYLN/HDSTN HA2 66 A1
Lucas Gdns EFNCH N2 53 G1
Lucas Rd PGE/AN SE20 150 E5
Lucas Sq GLDGN NW11 52 E5
Lucas St DEPT SE8 132 D1
Lucerne Cl PLMGR N13 40 E2
Lucerne Gv WALTH E17 58 B3
Lucerne Ms KENS * W8 8 B8
Lucerne Rd HBRY N5 73 H3
THHTH CR7 164 C4
Lucey Rd BERM/RHTH SE16 111 H2
Lucey Wy BERM/RHTH SE16 111 H2
Lucien Rd TOOT SW17 148 A3
WAND/EARL SW18 147 F1
Lucknow St WOOL/PLUM SE18 115 K6
Lucorn Cl LEE/GVPK SE12 133 J5
Luddesdon Rd ERITH DA8 117 H6
Ludford Cl CDALE/KGS NW9 51 G1
CROY/NA CR0 177 H3
Ludgate Broadway
BLKFR * EC4V 12 D5
Ludgate Circ STP * EC4M 12 C5
Ludgate Hl STP EC4M 12 C5
Ludgate Sq BLKFR * EC4V 12 D5
Ludham Cl THMD SE28 97 J5
Ludlow Cl HAYES BR2 167 K2
RYLN/HDSTN HA2 65 K3
Ludlow Md OXHEY WD19 33 F2
Ludlow Rd EA W5 85 J3
FELT TW13 140 E2
Ludlow St FSBYE * EC1V 6 E9
Ludlow Wy EFNCH N2 53 G3
RKW/CH/CXG WD3 20 A3
Ludovick Wk PUT/ROE SW15 126 B3
Luffield Rd ABYW SE2 116 C2
Luffman Rd LEE/GVPK SE12 153 F2
Lugard Rd PECK SE15 131 J1
Lugg Ap MNPK E12 78 A2
Luke St SDTCH EC2A 7 J9
Lukin Crs CHING E4 44 B2
Lukin St WCHPL E1 92 E6
Lullingstone Cl
STMC/STPC BR5 155 H6
Lullingstone Crs
STMC/STPC BR5 155 G6
Lullingstone La LEW SE13 133 G5
Lullingstone Rd BELV DA17 117 G5
Lullington Garth BMLY * BR1 152 C6
BORE * WD6 24 E4
MLHL NW7 38 D4
Lullington Rd DAGW RM9 80 A6
PGE/AN SE20 150 C6
Lulworth Av HEST TW5 103 G7
WBLY HA9 49 J6
Lulworth Cl RYLN/HDSTN HA2 65 K2
Lulworth Crs MTCM CR4 162 D1
Lulworth Dr PIN HA5 47 H6
Lulworth Gdns
RYLN/HDSTN HA2 65 J1
Lulworth Rd ELTH/MOT SE9 153 J1
PECK * SE15 131 J1
WELL DA16 136 A1
Lulworth Waye YEAD UB4 83 F5
Lumen Rd WBLY * HA9 67 K1
Lumley Cl BELV DA17 117 H5
Lumley Gdns CHEAM SM3 174 C4
Lumley Rd CHEAM SM3 174 C5
Lumley St MYFR/PKLN W1K 10 B5
Luna Rd THHTH CR7 164 D2
Lundin Wk OXHEY * WD19 33 H3
Lundy Dr HYS/HAR UB3 101 H3
Lundy Wk IS * N1 73 J5
Lunham Rd NRWD SE19 150 A5
Lupin Cl BRXS/STRHM SW2 149 H1
CROY/NA CR0 166 A7
ROMW/RG RM7 81 F1
WDR/YW UB7 100 A4
Lupton Cl LEE/GVPK SE12 153 F3
Lupton St KTTN NW5 72 C3
Lupus St PIM SW1V 16 D8
PIM SW1V 17 G7
Lurgan Av HMSMTH W6 107 G5
Lurline Gdns BTSEA SW11 109 F7
Luscombe Wy VX/NE SW8 109 K6
Lushington Rd CAT SE6 151 K4
WLSDN NW10 87 K1
Lushington Ter HACK E8 74 C4
Luther Cl EDGW HA8 36 E1
Luther King Cl WALTH E17 57 G5
Luton Pl GNWCH SE10 113 F6
Luton Rd PLSTW E13 94 E3
SCUP DA14 155 J2
WALTH E17 57 G2
Luton St STJWD NW8 9 H1
Luttrell Av PUT/ROE SW15 126 E4
Lutwyche Rd FSTH SE23 151 H1
Luxborough La CHIG IG7 45 K3
Luxborough St MHST W1U 10 A1
Luxemburg Gdns HMSMTH W6 107 G3
Luxfield Rd ELTH/MOT SE9 134 D7
Luxford St BERM/RHTH SE16 112 A3
Luxmore St BROCKY SE4 112 C7
Luxor St CMBW SE5 130 C1
Lyall Av DUL SE21 150 A3
Lyall Ms KTBR SW1X 16 A4
Lyall Ms West KTBR * SW1X 16 A4
Lyall St KTBR SW1X 16 A4
Lyal Rd BOW E3 93 G1
Lycett Pl SHB W12 106 D1
Lych Gate Wk HYS/HAR UB3 82 D6
Lyconby Gdns CROY/NA CR0 166 B6
Lydd Cl BFN/LL DA15 154 E2
Lydden Gv WAND/EARL SW18 128 A6
Lydden Rd WAND/EARL SW18 128 A6
Lydd Rd BXLYHN DA7 117 G6
Lydeard Rd EHAM E6 77 K6
Lydford Cl STNW/STAM N16 74 A4
Lydford Rd CRICK NW2 70 B5
MV/WKIL W9 88 D3
SEVS/STOTM N15 55 K4
Lydhurst Av BRXS/STRHM SW2 149 F1
Lydia Rd ERITH DA8 118 C5
Lydney Cl PECK SE15 111 F6
WIM/MER SW19 146 C1
Lydon Rd CLAP SW4 129 H2
Lydstep Rd CHST BR7 154 A3
Lyford Rd WAND/EARL SW18 128 C6
Lyford St WOOL/PLUM SE18 114 D3
Lygon Pl BGVA * SW1W 16 C4
Lyham Cl BRXS/STRHM SW2 129 K5
Lyham Rd BRXS/STRHM SW2 129 K4
Lyle Cl MTCM CR4 163 F6
Lyme Farm Rd LEE/GVPK SE12 133 K3
Lyme Gv HOM E9 74 E6
Lymer Av NRWD SE19 150 B4
Lyme Rd WELL DA16 116 C7
Lymescote Gdns SUT SM1 174 E1
Lyme St CAMTN NW1 4 E2
Lyme Ter CAMTN NW1 4 E2
Lyminge Cl SCUP DA14 155 F3
Lyminge Gdns
WAND/EARL SW18 128 D7
Lymington Av WDGN N22 55 G1
Lymington Cl
STRHM/NOR SW16 163 J1
Lymington Dr RSLP HA4 64 B1
Lymington Gdns
HOR/WEW KT19 173 H4
Lymington Rd BCTR RM8 61 K7
KIL/WHAMP * NW6 71 F5
Lyminster Cl YEAD UB4 83 J4
Lympstone Gdns PECK SE15 111 H6
Lynbridge Gdns PLMGR N13 41 H3
Lynbrook Cl PECK SE15 111 F6
RAIN RM13 99 F1
Lynchen Cl HEST TW5 101 K7
Lyncourt BKHTH/KID * SE3 133 G1
Lyncroft Av PIN HA5 47 H4
Lyncroft Gdns EW KT17 173 H7
HSLW TW3 123 H4
KIL/WHAMP NW6 70 E4
WEA W13 104 D1
Lyndale CRICK NW2 70 D3
ESH/CLAY * KT10 157 K6
Lyndale Av CRICK NW2 70 D2
Lyndale Cl BKHTH/KID SE3 113 J5
Lyndale Hampton Court Wy
ESH/CLAY KT10 157 K6
Lyndhurst Av BRYLDS KT5 159 J7
MLHL NW7 37 G5
NFNCH/WDSP N12 39 K5
PIN HA5 33 F7
STHL UB1 84 B7
STRHM/NOR SW16 163 J1
WHTN TW2 122 E7
Lyndhurst Cl BXLYHN DA7 137 J2
CROY/NA CR0 178 B2
WLSDN NW10 69 F2
Lyndhurst Ct BELMT * SM2 174 E6
Lyndhurst Dr LEY E10 58 A6
NWMAL KT3 160 B5
Lyndhurst Gdns BARK IG11 78 E5
EN EN1 30 A3
FNCH N3 38 C7
GNTH/NBYPK IG2 60 D5
HAMP NW3 71 H4
PIN HA5 33 F7
Lyndhurst Gv CMBW SE5 131 F1
Lyndhurst Leys HAYES * BR2 167 G1
Lyndhurst Prior SNWD * SE25 165 F2
Lyndhurst Rd BXLYHN DA7 137 J2
CHING E4 44 A6
GFD/PVL UB6 84 B3
HAMP NW3 71 H4
THHTH CR7 164 B3
UED N18 42 C3
WDGN N22 41 G5
Lyndhurst Sq PECK SE15 111 G7
Lyndhurst Ter HAMP NW3 71 H4
Lyndhurst Wy BELMT SM2 174 E7
PECK SE15 111 G7
Lyndon Av BFN/LL DA15 136 A4
PIN HA5 33 J5
WLGTN SM6 176 A2
Lyndon Rd BELV DA17 117 H3
Lyndon Yd TOOT SW17 147 F3
Lyne Crs WALTH E17 43 H7
Lynegrove Av ASHF TW15 140 A4
Lyneham Wk CLPT * E5 75 G4
Lynette Av CLAP SW4 129 G5
Lynford Cl EDGW HA8 36 E7
Lynford Gdns EDGW HA8 36 D3
GDMY/SEVK IG3 79 F1
Lynford Ter ED * N9 30 B7
Lynhurst Crs HGDN/ICK UB10 64 A6
Lynhurst Rd HGDN/ICK UB10 64 A6
Lynmere Rd WELL DA16 136 C1
Lyn Ms STNW/STAM * N16 74 B3
Lynmouth Av EN EN1 30 B5
MRDN SM4 161 G6
Lynmouth Dr RSLP HA4 65 F1
Lynmouth Gdns GFD/PVL UB6 67 H7
HEST TW5 102 C7
Lynmouth Rd EFNCH N2 53 K2
GFD/PVL UB6 67 H7
STNW/STAM N16 56 B7
WALTH E17 57 G5
Lynn Cl ASHF TW15 140 B4
KTN/HRWW/W HA3 48 D1
Lynnett Rd BCTR RM8 79 K1
Lynne Wk ESH/CLAY KT10 170 C4
Lynne Wy NTHLT UB5 83 H1
WLSDN NW10 69 G5
Lynn Ms WAN E11 76 C1
Lynn Rd BAL SW12 129 G6
GNTH/NBYPK IG2 60 D6
WAN E11 76 C1
Lynscott Wy SAND/SEL CR2 177 H7
Lynstead Cl BMLY BR1 168 B1
Lynsted Cl BXLYHS DA6 137 J4
Lynsted Ct BECK BR3 166 B1
Lynsted Gdns ELTH/MOT SE9 134 C3
Lynton Av ACT W3 86 E5
CDALE/KGS NW9 51 H3
NFNCH/WDSP N12 39 H3
WEA W13 85 G5

Lynton Cl CHSGTN KT9 172 A3
ISLW TW7 124 A3
WLSDN NW10 69 G4
Lynton Crs GNTH/NBYPK IG2 60 B5
Lynton Est STHWK SE1 19 M6
Lynton Gdns EN EN1 30 A6
FBAR/BDGN N11 40 D5
Lynton Md TRDG/WHET N20 38 E2
Lynton Rd ACT W3 86 C6
CEND/HSY/T N8 54 D4
CHING E4 43 K4
CROY/NA CR0 164 B5
KIL/WHAMP NW6 70 D7
NWMAL KT3 160 A4
RYLN/HDSTN HA2 65 J1
STHWK SE1 19 M6
Lynton Ter ACT * W3 86 E5
Lynwood Cl RYLN/HDSTN HA2 65 J2
SWFD E18 45 G7
Lynwood Dr NTHWD HA6 32 C7
WPK KT4 173 J1
Lynwood Gdns CROY/NA CR0 177 F3
STHL UB1 83 K5
Lynwood Gv ORP BR6 169 K6
WCHMH N21 29 G7
Lynwood Rd EA W5 85 K2
ESH/CLAY KT10 171 F1
TOOT SW17 147 K2
Lynwood Ter WIM/MER * SW19 146 D7
Lyon Meade STAN HA7 35 J7
Lyon Park Av ALP/SUD HA0 68 A5
Lyon Rd HRW HA1 49 F5
ROM RM1 63 H6
WIM/MER SW19 147 G7
Lyonsdown Av BAR EN5 27 G5
Lyonsdown Rd BAR EN5 27 G5
Lyons Pl STJWD NW8 9 G1
Lyon St IS N1 5 L2
Lyons Wk WKENS W14 107 H3
Lyon Wy GFD/PVL UB6 66 E7
Lyric Dr GFD/PVL UB6 84 B3
Lyric Ms SYD SE26 150 E3
Lyric Rd BARN SW13 106 C7
Lysander CDALE/KGS * NW9 37 H7
Lysander Gdns SURB KT6 159 G5
Lysander Gv ARCH N19 54 D7
Lysander Ms ARCH * N19 54 E7
Lysander Rd CROY/NA CR0 177 F5
RSLP HA4 64 B1
Lysias Rd BAL SW12 129 F5
Lysia St FUL/PGN SW6 107 G6
Lysons Wk PUT/ROE * SW15 126 D4
Lytchet Rd BMLY BR1 152 E6
Lytchgate Cl SAND/SEL CR2 178 A6
Lytcott Dr E/WMO/HCT KT8 156 E2
Lytcott Gv EDUL SE22 131 G4
Lytham Av OXHEY WD19 33 H4
Lytham Cl THMD SE28 98 A5
Lytham Gv EA W5 86 A2
Lytham St WALW SE17 19 G8
Lyttelton Rd EFNCH N2 53 G4
LEY E10 75 K2
Lyttleton Cl HAMP NW3 3 J2
Lyttleton Rd CEND/HSY/T * N8 55 G2
Lytton Av PLMGR N13 41 G1
Lytton Cl EFNCH N2 53 H4
NTHLT UB5 65 K6
Lytton Gdns WLGTN SM6 176 D3
Lytton Gv PUT/ROE SW15 127 G4
Lytton Rd BAR EN5 27 G3
GPK RM2 63 K4
PIN HA5 33 J6
WAN E11 58 C6
Lyveden Rd BKHTH/KID SE3 114 A6
WIM/MER SW19 147 J5

M

Maberley Crs NRWD SE19 150 C6
Maberley Rd BECK BR3 166 A2
NRWD SE19 150 B7
Mabledon Pl CAMTN NW1 5 H8
Mablethorpe Rd FUL/PGN SW6 107 H6
Mabley St HOM E9 75 G4
Macaret Cl TRDG/WHET N20 27 F6
Macarthur Cl FSTGT E7 76 E5
Macarthur Ter CHARL * SE7 114 C5
Macaulay Av ESH/CLAY KT10 170 E1
Macaulay Rd CLAP SW4 129 G2
EHAM E6 95 H1
Macbean St WOOL/PLUM SE18 115 F2
Macbeth St HMSMTH W6 106 E4
Macclesfield Br STJWD NW8 3 K5
Macclesfield Rd FSBYE EC1V 6 E7
SNWD SE25 165 J4
Macclesfield St
SOHO/SHAV * W1D 11 H6
Macdonald Av DAGE RM10 80 D2
Macdonald Rd ARCH N19 72 C1
FBAR/BDGN N11 39 K4
FSTGT E7 76 E3
WALTH E17 58 A1
Macduff Rd BTSEA SW11 109 F7
Mace Cl WAP E1W 92 D7
Mace Gtwy CAN/RD E16 94 E6
Mace St BETH E2 93 F1
Macfarlane La ISLW TW7 104 A5
Macfarlane Rd SHB W12 88 A7
MacFarren Pl CAMTN NW1 10 B1
Macgregor Rd CAN/RD E16 95 G4
Machell Rd PECK SE15 131 K2
Mackay Rd CLAP SW4 129 G2
Mackennal St STJWD NW8 3 K6
Mackenzie Cl SHB * W12 87 K6
Mackenzie Rd BECK BR3 166 A1
HOLWY N7 73 F5
Mackeson Rd HAMP * NW3 71 K3
Mackie Rd BRXS/STRHM SW2 130 B6
Mackintosh La HOM E9 75 F4
Macklin St HOL/ALD * WC2B 11 K4
Macks Rd BERM/RHTH SE16 111 H3
Mackworth St CAMTN NW1 4 E7
Maclean Rd FSTH SE23 132 B5
Macleod House
WOOL/PLUM SE18 114 D6
Macleod Rd STHGT/OAK N14 28 E4
Macleod St WALW SE17 18 F8
Maclise Rd WKENS W14 107 H2
Macoma Rd WOOL/PLUM SE18 115 J5
Macoma Ter WOOL/PLUM SE18 115 J5
Maconochies Rd
POP/IOD * E14 112 E4
Macquarie Wy POP/IOD E14 112 E3
Macroom Rd MV/WKIL W9 88 D2
Maddams St BOW E3 93 K3
Maddison Cl TEDD TW11 143 F5
Maddocks Cl SCUP DA14 155 K5
Maddock Wy WALW SE17 110 C5
Maddox St MYFR/PKLN W1K 10 D6
Madeira Av BMLY BR1 152 C7
Madeira Gv WFD IG8 45 G5
Madeira Rd MTCM CR4 162 E3
PLMGR N13 41 H3
STRHM/NOR SW16 148 E4
WAN E11 58 B7
Madeley Rd EA W5 85 K6
Madeline Gv IL IG1 78 D4
Madeline Rd PGE/AN SE20 150 C6
Madge Gill Wy EHAM E6 77 J7
Madge Hl HNWL * W7 84 E6
Madinah Rd HACK E8 74 C5
Madison Crs WELL DA16 116 D6
Madison Gdns BXLYHN DA7 116 D6
Madras Pl HOLWY N7 73 G5
Madras Rd IL IG1 78 B3
Madrid Rd BARN SW13 106 D7
Madron St STHWK SE1 19 K7
Mafeking Av BTFD TW8 105 F5
EHAM E6 95 H1
GNTH/NBYPK IG2 60 D6
Mafeking Rd CAN/RD E16 94 D3
EN EN1 30 B2
TOTM N17 56 C1
Magazine Ga BAY/PAD * W2 9 K8
Magdala Av ARCH N19 72 C1
Magdala Rd ISLW TW7 124 B2
SAND/SEL CR2 177 K6
Magdalene Gdns EHAM E6 96 A3
Magdalen Rd
WAND/EARL SW18 128 B7
Magdalen St STHWK SE1 13 J9
Magee St LBTH SE11 18 A9
Magnaville Rd BUSH WD23 22 E6
Magnet Rd WBLY * HA9 67 K1
Magnin Cl HACK E8 74 C7
Magnolia Cl KUTN/CMB KT2 144 D5
LEY E10 75 J1
Magnolia Ct KTN/HRWW/W HA3 50 B6
Magnolia Gdns EDGW HA8 36 E3
Magnolia Pl CLAP * SW4 129 K4
EA * W5 85 K4
Magnolia Rd CHSWK W4 105 J5
Magnolia St WDR/YW UB7 100 A3
Magnolia Wy HOR/WEW KT19 172 E4
Magnolia Whf CHSWK * W4 105 J5
Magpie Cl CDALE/KGS NW9 51 G1
FSTGT E7 76 D4
Magpie Hall Cl HAYES BR2 168 D5
Magpie Hall La HAYES BR2 168 D6
Magpie Hall Rd BUSH WD23 34 E1
Magpie Pl NWCR * SE14 112 B5
Magri Wk WCHPL E1 92 E4
Maguire Dr RCHPK/HAM TW10 143 J3
Maguire St STHWK SE1 19 M1
Mahlon Av RSLP HA4 65 F4
Mahogany Cl BERM/RHTH SE16 93 G7
Maida Av BAY/PAD W2 8 F2
CHING E4 31 K6
Maida Rd BELV DA17 117 H2
Maida V MV/WKIL W9 2 D6
Maida Vale Rd DART DA1 138 D5
Maida Wy CHING E4 31 K6
Maiden Erlegh Av BXLY DA5 137 F7
Maiden La CAMTN NW1 5 H1
COVGDN WC2E 11 K7
DART DA1 138 D3
STHWK SE1 12 F9
Maiden Rd SRTFD E15 76 C6
Maidenstone Hl GNWCH SE10 113 F7
Maidstone Av CRW RM5 62 E1
Maidstone Buildings Ms
STHWK SE1 12 F9
Maidstone Rd FBAR/BDGN N11 40 D5
SCUP DA14 155 K5
Main Av EN EN1 30 B4
NTHWD HA6 32 A2
Main Barracks
WOOL/PLUM * SE18 114 E4
Main Dr GFD/PVL * UB6 85 G2
WBLY * HA9 67 K2
Mainridge Rd CHST BR7 154 A3
Main Rd BFN/LL DA15 154 E2
GPK RM2 63 H3
STMC/STPC BR5 155 J7
Main St FELT TW13 141 H4
Maise Webster Cl
STWL/WRAY * TW19 120 A6
Maismore St PECK SE15 111 H5
The Maisonettes SUT * SM1 174 D4
Maitland Cl GNWCH SE10 112 E6
HSLWW TW4 122 E2
Maitland Park Rd HAMP NW3 71 K5
Maitland Park Vls HAMP NW3 71 K5
Maitland Rd SRTFD * E15 76 D5
SYD SE26 151 F5
Majendie Rd WOOL/PLUM SE18 115 J4
Major Rd BERM/RHTH * SE16 111 H2
SRTFD E15 76 B4
Makepeace Av HGT N6 72 A1
Makepeace Rd NTHLT UB5 83 J1
WAN E11 58 E3
Makins St CHEL SW3 15 K6
Malabar St POP/IOD E14 112 D1
Malam Gdns POP/IOD E14 93 K6
Malan Sq RAIN RM13 81 K5
Malbrook Rd PUT/ROE SW15 126 E3
Malcolm Cl PGE/AN * SE20 150 E6
Malcolm Ct STAN HA7 35 J4
Malcolm Crs HDN NW4 51 J4
Malcolm Dr SURB KT6 158 E7
Malcolm Gavin Cl TOOT SW17 147 J1
Malcolm Pl BETH E2 92 E3
Malcolm Rd PGE/AN SE20 150 E6
SNWD SE25 165 H5
WCHPL E1 92 E3
WIM/MER SW19 146 C5
Malcolm Wy WAN E11 58 E4
Malden Av GFD/PVL UB6 66 E5
SNWD SE25 165 J3
Malden Flds BUSH WD23 21 H4
Malden Green Av WPK KT4 160 C7
Malden Hl NWMAL KT3 160 C3
Malden Hill Gdns NWMAL KT3 160 C2
Malden Pk NWMAL KT3 160 C5
Malden Pl KTTN NW5 72 A4
Malden Rd BORE WD6 24 C2
CHEAM SM3 174 B3
KTTN NW5 71 K4
NWMAL KT3 160 C6
WAT * WD17 21 F1
Malden Wy NWMAL KT3 160 A5
Malden Wy (Kingston By-Pass)
NWMAL KT3 160 B5
Maldon Cl CMBW * SE5 131 F2
IS N1 6 E3
Maldon Rd ACT W3 86 E6
ED N9 42 B2
ROMW/RG RM7 62 E6
WLGTN SM6 176 B4
Maldon Wk WFD IG8 45 G5
Malet St GWRST WC1E 11 G1
Maley Av WNWD SE27 149 H1
Malford Gv SWFD E18 58 E2
Malfort Rd CMBW SE5 131 F2
Malham Cl FBAR/BDGN N11 40 A5
Malham Rd FSTH SE23 132 A7
Malham Ter UED * N18 42 D5
Malins Cl BAR * EN5 25 K4
The Mall BTFD * TW8 104 E5
BXLYHS * DA6 137 H3
EA W5 86 A6
EMPK RM11 63 K7
KTN/HRWW/W HA3 50 B5
MORT/ESHN SW14 125 K4
SRTFD * E15 76 B6
STHGT/OAK N14 40 E2
SURB KT6 158 E4
WHALL SW1A 17 G1
Mallams Ms BRXN/ST SW9 130 B2
Mallard Cl BAR * EN5 27 H5
DART DA1 139 J4
KIL/WHAMP NW6 2 B4
WHTN TW2 123 F6
Mallard Ct WALTH * E17 58 B2
Mallard Pl TWK TW1 143 G2
WDGN * N22 55 F1
Mallards Ct OXHEY * WD19 33 K2
Mallards Rd BARK IG11 97 G2
WFD IG8 45 F6
Mallard Wk CROY/NA CR0 166 A4
Mallard Wy CDALE/KGS NW9 50 E6
NTHWD HA6 32 A6
WLGTN SM6 176 C7
Mall Chambers KENS * W8 8 B8
Mallet Dr NTHLT UB5 65 K4
Mallet Rd LEW SE13 133 G5
Malling Cl CROY/NA * CR0 165 K5
Malling Gdns MRDN SM4 162 B5
Malling Wy HAYES BR2 167 J6
Mallinson Rd BTSEA SW11 128 D4
CROY/NA CR0 176 D2
Mallord St CHEL SW3 15 H9
Mallory Cl BROCKY SE4 132 B3
Mallory Gdns EBAR EN4 28 A6
Mallory St STJWD NW8 9 K1
Mallow Cl CROY/NA CR0 166 A7
Mallow Md MLHL NW7 38 C6
Mallow St FSBYE EC1V 7 G9
Mall Rd HMSMTH W6 106 E4
Mall Vls HMSMTH * W6 106 E4
Malmains Cl BECK BR3 167 G4
Malmains Wy BECK BR3 167 F3
Malmesbury Cl PIN HA5 46 E3
Malmesbury Rd BOW E3 93 H2
CAN/RD E16 94 C4
MRDN SM4 162 B6
SWFD E18 44 D7
Malmesbury Ter CAN/RD E16 94 D4
Malmesbury West Est BOW E3 93 H2
Malpas Dr PIN HA5 47 H4
Malpas Rd BROCKY SE4 132 C1
DAGW RM9 79 K5
HACK E8 74 D5
Malta Rd LEY E10 57 J7
Malta St FSBYE EC1V 6 C9
Maltby Rd CHSGTN KT9 172 C5
Maltby St STHWK SE1 19 L3
Malthouse Dr FELT TW13 141 H4
Maltings Pl FUL/PGN SW6 108 A7
STHWK SE1 19 K1
The Maltings ROM RM1 63 H6
SNWD * SE25 165 F2
Malting Wy ISLW TW7 124 A2
Malton Ms NKENS * W10 88 C5
WOOL/PLUM SE18 115 K5
Malton Rd NKENS W10 88 C5
Malton St WOOL/PLUM SE18 115 K5
Maltravers St TPL/STR WC2R 11 M6
Malt St STHWK SE1 111 H5
Malva Cl WAND/EARL SW18 128 A4
Malvern Av BXLYHN DA7 117 F6
CHING E4 44 B6
RYLN/HDSTN HA2 65 J2
Malvern Cl MTCM CR4 163 H2
NKENS W10 88 D4
SURB KT6 159 F7
Malvern Dr FELT TW13 141 H4
GDMY/SEVK IG3 79 F3
WFD IG8 45 G4
Malvern Gdns CRICK NW2 70 C1
KTN/HRWW/W HA3 50 A3
Malvern Ms KIL/WHAMP NW6 2 A8
Malvern Pl MV/WKIL * W9 88 D2
Malvern Rd CEND/HSY/T N8 55 F2
EHAM E6 77 J7
EMPK RM11 63 J5
HACK E8 74 C6
HPTN TW12 142 A7
HYS/HAR UB3 101 H6
KIL/WHAMP NW6 2 A7
MV/WKIL * W9 88 D2
SURB KT6 172 A1
THHTH CR7 164 B3
TOTM N17 56 C2
WAN E11 76 C1
Malvern Ter ED N9 30 B7
IS N1 6 A3
Malvern Wy WEA W13 85 H4
Malwood Rd BAL SW12 129 G5
Malyons Rd LEW SE13 132 E4
Malyons Ter LEW SE13 132 E4
Managers St POP/IOD * E14 94 A7
Manaton Cl PECK SE15 131 J2
Manaton Crs STHL UB1 84 A5
Manbey Gv SRTFD E15 76 C5
Manbey Park Rd SRTFD E15 76 C5
Manbey Rd SRTFD * E15 76 C5
Manbey St SRTFD E15 76 C5
Manbre Rd HMSMTH W6 107 F5
Manbrough Av EHAM E6 95 K2
Manchester Dr NKENS * W10 88 C3
Manchester Gv POP/IOD E14 113 F4
Manchester Ms MHST W1U 10 A3
Manchester Rd POP/IOD E14 113 F4
SEVS/STOTM N15 55 K5
THHTH CR7 164 D2
Manchester Sq MBLAR W1H 10 B4
Manchester St MHST W1U 10 A3
Manchuria Rd BTSEA SW11 129 F5
Manciple St STHWK SE1 19 H2
Mandalay Rd CLAP SW4 129 H4
Mandarin Wy YEAD UB4 83 H5
Mandela Cl WLSDN NW10 68 E6
Mandela Pl WATN WD24 21 H1
Mandela Rd CAN/RD E16 94 E5
Mandela St BRXN/ST SW9 110 B6
CAMTN NW1 4 F3
Mandela Wy STHWK SE1 19 K5
Mandeville Cl WIM/MER SW19 146 C6
Mandeville Dr SURB KT6 158 E7
Mandeville Pl MHST W1U 10 B4
Mandeville Rd ISLW TW7 124 B1
NTHLT UB5 66 A5
STHGT/OAK N14 40 B1
Mandeville St CLPT E5 75 G2
Mandrake Rd TOOT SW17 147 K2
Mandrake Wy SRTFD * E15 76 C6
Mandrell Rd BRXS/STRHM SW2 129 K4
Manette St SOHO/SHAV W1D 11 H5
Manfred Rd PUT/ROE SW15 127 J4
Manger Rd HOLWY N7 72 E5
Manilla St POP/IOD E14 112 D1
Manister Rd ABYW SE2 116 B2
Manley Ct STNW/STAM N16 74 B2
Manley St CAMTN NW1 4 A3
Mann Cl CROY/NA CR0 177 J2
Manningford Cl FSBYE * EC1V 6 C7
Manning Gdns
KTN/HRWW/W HA3 49 K6
Manning Pl RCHPK/HAM TW10 125 G5
Manning Rd DAGE RM10 80 C6
WALTH E17 57 G3
Manningtree Cl
WIM/MER SW19 127 H7
Manningtree Rd RSLP HA4 65 F3
Manningtree St WCHPL E1 92 C5
Mannin Rd CHDH RM6 61 H6
Mannock Rd DART DA1 139 J2
WDGN N22 55 H2
Mann's Cl ISLW TW7 124 A4
Manns Rd EDGW HA8 36 C5
Manoel Rd WHTN TW2 142 C1
The Manor Dr WPK KT4 160 B7
Manor Av BROCKY SE4 132 C1
HSLWW TW4 122 C2
NTHLT UB5 65 K6
Manorbrook BKHTH/KID SE3 133 K3
Manor Cl BAR EN5 26 C3
CDALE/KGS NW9 50 D3
DAGE RM10 81 F5
DART DA1 138 A3
MLHL * NW7 37 F4
ROM RM1 63 J4
RSLP HA4 46 D7
THMD SE28 97 J5
WPK KT4 160 B7
Manor Cottages NTHWD HA6 32 D7
Manor Cottages Ap EFNCH N2 53 G1
Manor Ct ACT * W3 105 H3
E/WMO/HCT * KT8 157 F3
HRW * HA1 49 F5
KUTN/CMB * KT2 144 C7
WBLY * HA9 68 B3
Manor Court Rd HNWL W7 84 E6
Manor Crs BRYLDS KT5 159 H5
Manor Cft EDGW * HA8 36 C5
Manordene Cl THDIT KT7 158 B7
Manordene Rd THMD SE28 97 J5
Manor Dr BRYLDS KT5 159 H5
ESH/CLAY KT10 171 F2
FELT TW13 141 H4
HOR/WEW KT19 173 G5
MLHL NW7 37 F4
STHGT/OAK N14 28 B6
TRDG/WHET N20 39 J2
WBLY HA9 68 B3
Manor Dr North NWMAL KT3 160 A6
Manor Est BERM/RHTH SE16 111 J3
Manor Farm Dr CHING E4 44 C2
Manor Farm Rd ALP/SUD HA0 85 K1
STRHM/NOR SW16 164 B1
Manor Gdns ACT W3 105 H3
HOLWY N7 72 E2
HPTN TW12 142 B6
RCH/KEW TW9 125 G3
RSLP HA4 65 G4
RYNPK SW20 161 J1
SAND/SEL CR2 178 B5
SUN TW16 140 E7
VX/NE * SW8 129 H1
Manor Ga NTHLT UB5 65 J6
Manorgate Rd KUTN/CMB KT2 144 C7
Manor Gv BECK BR3 166 E1
PECK SE15 111 K5
RCH/KEW TW9 125 H3
Manor Hall Av HDN NW4 52 A1
Manor Hall Dr HDN NW4 52 B1
Manor Hall Gdns LEY E10 57 J7
Manor House Dr
KIL/WHAMP NW6 70 B6
Manor House Wy ISLW TW7 124 C2
Manor La FELT TW13 140 E1
HYS/HAR UB3 101 G5
LEW SE13 133 H4
SUN TW16 156 A1
SUT SM1 175 G4
Manor Lane Ter LEW SE13 133 H3
Manor Ms KIL/WHAMP NW6 2 B5
Manor Mt FSTH SE23 131 K7
Manor Pde HRW * HA1 49 F5
STNW/STAM * N16 74 B1
Manor Pk CHST BR7 169 J1
LEW SE13 133 G4
RCH/KEW TW9 125 G3
Manor Park Cl WWKM BR4 166 E7
Manor Park Crs EDGW HA8 36 C5
Manor Park Dr
RYLN/HDSTN HA2 48 B2
Manor Park Gdns EDGW HA8 36 C4
Manor Park Rd CHST BR7 154 C7
EFNCH N2 53 G2
MNPK E12 77 H3
SUT SM1 175 G4
WLSDN NW10 69 G7
WWKM BR4 166 E7
Manor Pl BORE * WD6 24 E2
CHST BR7 169 J1
EBED/NFELT TW14 121 K7
MTCM CR4 163 H2
SUT SM1 175 F4
WALW SE17 18 D8
Manor Rd BAR EN5 26 C3
BECK BR3 166 D1
BELMT SM2 174 D6
BFN/LL DA15 155 F2
BXLY DA5 137 J7
CAN/RD E16 94 C4
CHDH RM6 61 K5
DAGE RM10 80 E5
DART DA1 138 B3
E/WMO/HCT KT8 157 J3
ENC/FH EN2 29 K1
ERITH DA8 118 C5
HRW HA1 49 G5
HYS/HAR UB3 82 E5
LEY E10 57 J6
MTCM CR4 163 H2
RCH/KEW TW9 125 G2
ROM RM1 63 J4
RSLP HA4 46 B7
RYNPK SW20 161 J1
SNWD SE25 165 H2
STNW/STAM N16 56 A7
TEDD TW11 143 G4
TOTM N17 42 C7
WALTH E17 57 G1
WDGN N22 40 E5
WEA W13 85 G6
WHTN TW2 142 C1
WLGTN SM6 176 B3
WWKM BR4 179 K1
Manor Rd North
ESH/CLAY KT10 171 F2
WLGTN SM6 176 B3
Manor Rd South
ESH/CLAY KT10 170 E3
Manorside BAR EN5 26 C3
Manor Sq BCTR RM8 79 J1
Manor V BTFD TW8 104 D4
Manor Vw FNCH N3 53 F1
The Manor Wy WLGTN SM6 176 B3
Manor Wy BECK BR3 166 D2
BKHTH/KID SE3 133 K3
BORE WD6 24 E3
BXLY DA5 137 H7
BXLYHN DA7 138 A2
CDALE/KGS NW9 51 G3
CHING E4 44 B3
HAYES BR2 168 D5
MTCM CR4 163 H2
NWDGN UB2 102 C3
RAIN RM13 99 G3
RSLP HA4 46 C6
RYLN/HDSTN HA2 48 B3
SAND/SEL CR2 178 A5
STMC/STPC BR5 169 H3
WPK KT4 160 B7
Manorway EN EN1 30 A6
WFD IG8 45 G4
Manresa Rd CHEL SW3 15 H8
Mansard Beeches TOOT SW17 148 A4
Mansard Cl HCH RM12 81 J1
PIN HA5 47 H2
Manse Cl HYS/HAR UB3 101 G5
Mansel Gv WALTH E17 43 J7
Mansell Rd ACT W3 87 F7
GFD/PVL UB6 84 B4
Mansell St WCHPL E1 13 M5
Mansel Rd WIM/MER SW19 146 C5
Mansergh Cl WOOL/PLUM SE18 114 D6
Manse Rd STNW/STAM N16 74 B2
Manser Rd RAIN RM13 99 G2
Mansfield Av EBAR EN4 27 K5
RSLP HA4 47 F7
SEVS/STOTM N15 55 K3
Mansfield Cl ED N9 30 C5
Mansfield Dr YEAD UB4 82 C3
Mansfield Hl CHING E4 31 K7
Mansfield Ms CAVSQ/HST W1G 10 C3
Mansfield Rd ACT W3 86 D3
CHSGTN KT9 171 J4
HAMP NW3 71 K4
IL IG1 78 A1
SAND/SEL CR2 177 K5
WALTH E17 57 H3
WAN E11 59 F5
Mansfield St CAVSQ/HST W1G 10 C3
Mansford St BETH E2 92 C1
Manship Rd MTCM CR4 148 A7
Mansion House Pl
MANHO * EC4N 13 G5
Manson Ms SKENS SW7 14 F6
Manson Pl SKENS SW7 15 G6
Manstead Gdns CHDH RM6 61 J6
RAIN RM13 99 K5
Manston Av NWDGN UB2 103 F3
Manston Cl PGE/AN SE20 150 E7
Manstone Rd CRICK NW2 70 C4
Manston Gv KUTN/CMB KT2 143 K4
Manston Wy HCH RM12 81 K5
Manthorpe Rd
WOOL/PLUM SE18 115 H4
Mantilla Rd TOOT SW17 148 A3
Mantle Rd BROCKY SE4 132 B2
Mantlet Cl STRHM/NOR SW16 148 C6
Mantle Wy SRTFD E15 76 C6
Manton Av HNWL W7 104 A1
Manton Cl HYS/HAR UB3 82 C6
Manton Rd ABYW SE2 116 B3
Mantua St BTSEA SW11 128 C2
Mantus Cl WCHPL E1 92 E3
Mantus Rd WCHPL E1 92 E3
Manus Wy TRDG/WHET N20 39 G1
Manville Gdns TOOT SW17 148 B2
Manville Rd TOOT SW17 148 A1
Manwood Rd BROCKY SE4 132 C5
Manwood St CAN/RD E16 95 K7
Many Gates BAL SW12 148 B1
Mapesbury Rd CRICK NW2 70 C5
Mapeshill Pl CRICK NW2 70 A5
Mape St BETH E2 92 D3
Maple Av ACT W3 87 G7
CHING E4 43 H5
RYLN/HDSTN HA2 66 B1
Maple Cl BKHH IG9 45 H2
BUSH WD23 21 J1
CLAP SW4 129 J5
FNCH N3 38 E5
HCH RM12 81 K2
HPTN TW12 141 K5
MTCM CR4 148 B7
RSLP HA4 47 F5
STMC/STPC BR5 169 J4
STNW/STAM N16 56 C5
YEAD UB4 83 H2
Maple Ct NWMAL KT3 160 A2
Maple Crs BFN/LL DA15 136 B5
Maplecroft Cl EHAM E6 95 H5
Mapledale Av CROY/NA CR0 178 D2
Mapledene Est HACK * E8 74 C6
Mapledene Rd HACK E8 7 M1
Maple Gdns EDGW HA8 37 G6
Maple Gv BTFD TW8 104 C6
CDALE/KGS NW9 50 E6
EA W5 104 E2
STHL UB1 83 K4
Maplehurst Cl KUT KT1 159 F3
Maple Leaf Dr BFN/LL DA15 136 A7
Mapleleafe Gdns
BARK/HLT IG6 60 B2
Maple Leaf Sq
BERM/RHTH * SE16 112 A1
Maple Ms KIL/WHAMP * NW6 2 C5
STRHM/NOR SW16 149 F4
Maple Pl FITZ W1T 10 F2
Maple Rd DART DA1 139 F7
PGE/AN SE20 150 D7
SURB KT6 158 E4

WAN E11 58 C5
YEAD UB4 83 G2
The Maples E/WMO/HCT * KT8 143 J6
ESH/CLAY * KT10 171 G6
Maples Pl WCHPL * E1 92 D4
Maplestead Rd
BRXS/STRHM SW2 130 A6
DAGW RM9 79 H7
Maple St FITZ W1T 10 E2
ROMW/RG RM7 62 E3
Maplethorpe Rd THHTH CR7 164 B3
Mapleton Cl HAYES BR2 167 K4
Mapleton Crs
WAND/EARL SW18 128 A5
Mapleton Rd CHING E4 44 A2
EN EN1 30 D1
WAND/EARL SW18 127 K5
Maple Wk NKENS * W10 88 B3
Maple Wy FELT TW13 140 E2
Maplin Cl WCHMH N21 29 F5
Maplin Rd CAN/RD E16 94 E5
Maplin St BOW E3 93 H2
Mapperley Dr WFD IG8 44 C6
Maran Wy ERITHM DA18 116 E2
Marathon Wy THMD SE28 116 A1
Marban Rd MV/WKIL W9 88 D2
Marble Cl ACT W3 86 D7
Marble Dr CRICK NW2 52 B7
Marble Hill Cl TWK TW1 124 C6
Marble Hill Gdns TWK TW1 124 C6
Marble Quay WAP E1W 13 M8
Marbrook Ct LEE/GVPK SE12 153 G2
Marcella Rd BRXN/ST SW9 130 B1
Marcet Rd DART DA1 139 F4
Marchant Rd WAN E11 76 B1
Marchant St NWCR SE14 112 B5
Marchbank Rd WKENS W14 107 J5
Marchmont Rd
RCHPK/HAM TW10 125 G4
WLGTN SM6 176 C7
Marchmont St BMSBY WC1N 5 J9
March Rd TWK TW1 124 A6
Marchside Cl HEST TW5 102 C7
Marchwood Cl CMBW SE5 111 F6
Marchwood Crs EA W5 85 J5
Marcia Rd STHWK SE1 19 K6
Marcilly Rd WAND/EARL SW18 128 C4
Marconi Pl FBAR/BDGN N11 40 B3
Marconi Rd LEY E10 57 J7
Marconi Wy STHL UB1 84 B5
Marcon Pl HACK E8 74 D5
Marco Rd HMSMTH W6 106 E2
Marcus Garvey Ms EDUL SE22 131 J5
Marcus Garvey Wy
BRXN/ST SW9 130 B3
Marcus Rd DART DA1 138 D6
Marcus St SRTFD E15 76 C7
WAND/EARL SW18 128 A5
Marcus Ter WAND/EARL SW18 128 A5
Mardale Dr CDALE/KGS NW9 51 F4
Mardell Rd CROY/NA CR0 166 A4
Marden Av HAYES BR2 167 K5
Marden Crs BXLY DA5 137 K4
CROY/NA CR0 164 A5
Marden Rd CROY/NA CR0 164 A5
ROM RM1 63 G5
TOTM N17 56 A1
Marden Sq BERM/RHTH SE16 111 J2
Marder Rd WEA W13 104 B1
Marechal Niel Av BFN/LL DA15 154 D2
Marechal Niel Pde
BFN/LL * DA15 154 D2
Maresfield CROY/NA CR0 178 A2
Maresfield Gdns HAMP NW3 71 G4
Mare St HACK E8 74 D4
Marfleet Cl CAR SM5 175 J1
Margaret Av CHING E4 31 K5
Margaret Bondfield Av
BARK IG11 79 G6
Margaret Cl GPK RM2 63 K4
Margaret Gardner Dr
ELTH/MOT SE9 153 K1
Margaret Ingram Cl
FUL/PGN * SW6 107 J5
Margaret Lockwood Cl
KUT * KT1 159 G3
Margaret Rd BXLY DA5 136 E5
EBAR EN4 27 H4
GPK RM2 63 K4
STNW/STAM * N16 56 B7
Margaret St GTPST W1W 10 E4
Margaretta Ter CHEL SW3 15 J9
Margaretting Rd MNPK E12 77 G1
Margaret Wy REDBR IG4 59 J5
Margate Rd BRXS/STRHM SW2 129 K4
Margeholes OXHEY WD19 33 J1
Margery Rd BCTR RM8 79 K2
Margery St FSBYW WC1X 6 A8
Margin Dr WIM/MER SW19 146 B4
Margravine Gdns HMSMTH W6 107 G4
Margravine Rd HMSMTH W6 107 G5
Marguerite Vls RYNPK * SW20 145 K6
Marham Gdns MRDN SM4 162 B5
WAND/EARL SW18 128 D7
Maria Cl BERM/RHTH SE16 111 H3
Marian Cl YEAD UB4 83 H3
Marian Pl BETH E2 92 D1
Marian Rd STRHM/NOR SW16 148 C7
Marian Sq BETH E2 92 C1
Marian St BETH * E2 92 D1
Marian Wy WLSDN NW10 69 H6
Maria Ter WCHPL E1 93 F3
Maria Theresa Cl NWMAL KT3 160 A4
Maricas Av KTN/HRWW/W HA3 34 D7
Marie Curie CMBW * SE5 111 F7
Marie Lloyd Wk HACK * E8 74 C5
Mariette Wy WLGTN SM6 176 E7
Marigold Aly STHWK SE1 12 C7
Marigold Cl STHL UB1 83 J6
Marigold St BERM/RHTH SE16 111 J1
Marigold Wy CROY/NA CR0 166 A7
Marina Ap YEAD UB4 83 J4
Marina Av NWMAL KT3 160 E5
Marina Dr DART DA1 139 K7
WELL DA16 135 K1
Marina Gdns ROMW/RG RM7 62 D4
Marina Wy TEDD TW11 143 K6
Marine Ct PUR RM19 119 J3
Marine Dr BARK IG11 97 G3
WOOL/PLUM SE18 114 E3
Marinefield Rd FUL/PGN SW6 128 A1
Mariner Gdns
RCHPK/HAM TW10 143 H2
Mariner Rd MNPK E12 78 A3
Mariners Ms POP/IOD E14 113 G3
Marine St BERM/RHTH SE16 111 H2
Marion Gv WFD IG8 44 C4
Marion Rd CROY/NA CR0 164 D4
MLHL NW7 37 J4
Marischal Rd LEW SE13 133 G2
Maritime Quay POP/IOD E14 112 D4
Maritime St BOW E3 93 H3
Marius Rd TOOT SW17 148 A1
Marjorie Gv BTSEA SW11 128 E3
Markara Ms WALW SE17 18 E7
Mark Av CHING E4 31 K5
Mark Cl BXLYHN DA7 117 F7
HAYES BR2 181 J3
STHL UB1 84 A7
Markeston Gn OXHEY WD19 33 H3
The Market COVGDN * WC2E 11 K6
HNWL * W7 104 A1
PECK * SE15 131 H1
RCH/KEW * TW9 124 E4
SUT * SM1 162 B7
Market Chambers
ENC/FH * EN2 29 K2
Market Est HOLWY N7 72 E5
Market La EDGW HA8 36 E7
Market Link ROM RM1 63 G3
Market Ms MYFR/PICC W1J 10 C9
Market Pde BMLY * BR1 152 E7
ED * N9 42 C1
EW * KT17 173 H7
FELT * TW13 141 J1
LEY * E10 57 K5
SCUP * DA14 155 G3
SNWD * SE25 165 H3
STNW/STAM * N16 56 C7
WALTH * E17 57 J4
Market Pl ACT W3 86 E7
BERM/RHTH * SE16 111 H3
BTFD TW8 104 D6
BXLYHN DA7 137 H3
DART DA1 139 H6
EFNCH N2 53 H2
KUT * KT1 158 E1
ROM RM1 63 G4
SOHO/SHAV W1D 10 E4
WAT WD17 21 G3
Market Rd HOLWY N7 72 E5
RCH/KEW TW9 125 H2
Market Sq BMLY BR1 167 K1
ED N9 42 D1
Market St DART DA1 139 H6
EHAM E6 95 K1
WATW WD18 21 F3
WOOL/PLUM SE18 115 F3
Market Ter BTFD * TW8 105 F5
Markfield Gdns CHING E4 31 K6
Markfield Rd SEVS/STOTM N15 56 C3
Markham Pl CHEL * SW3 15 L7
Markham Sq CHEL SW3 15 L7
Markham St CHEL SW3 15 K7
Markhole Cl HPTN TW12 141 K6
Markhouse Av WALTH E17 57 G5
Markhouse Rd WALTH E17 57 H5
Mark La MON EC3R 13 K6
Markmanor Av WALTH E17 57 G6
Mark Rd WDGN N22 55 H1
Marksbury Av RCH/KEW TW9 125 H2
Marks Rd ROMW/RG RM7 62 E4
Mark St SDTCH EC2A 7 J9
SRTFD E15 76 C6
Mark Ter RYNPK * SW20 146 A6
The Markway SUN TW16 156 B1
Markwell Cl SYD SE26 150 D3
Markyate Rd BCTR RM8 79 H4
Marlands Rd CLAY IG5 59 J2
Marlborough Av EDGW HA8 36 D2
HACK * E8 74 C7
RSLP HA4 46 A5
STHGT/OAK N14 40 C2
Marlborough Cl
TRDG/WHET N20 39 K2
WALW SE17 18 D6
WIM/MER SW19 147 J5
Marlborough Ct REGST W1B 10 E5
Marlborough Crs CHSWK W4 106 A2
Marlborough Dr CLAY IG5 59 J2
Marlborough Gdns
TRDG/WHET N20 39 K2
Marlborough Ga BAY/PAD W2 9 G7
Marlborough Gv STHWK SE1 111 H4
Marlborough Hl HRW HA1 48 E3
STJWD NW8 2 F4
Marlborough La CHARL SE7 114 B5
Marlborough Ms
BRXN/ST SW9 130 A3
Marlborough Pde FSBYPK * N4 55 J7
Marlborough Park Av
BFN/LL DA15 136 B7
Marlborough Pl STJWD NW8 2 E6
Marlborough Rd ARCH N19 72 E1
BCTR RM8 79 J3
BXLYHN DA7 136 E2
CHING E4 43 K5
CHSWK W4 105 K4
DART DA1 139 F5
EA W5 104 E1
ED N9 30 B7
FELT TW13 141 H1
FSTGT E7 77 G6
HAYES BR2 168 B3
HPTN TW12 142 A5
HYS/HAR UB3 101 G6
NWDGN UB2 102 B2
RCHPK/HAM TW10 125 F5
ROMW/RG RM7 62 C3
SAND/SEL CR2 177 J6
SRTFD * E15 76 C3
SUT SM1 174 E2
SWFD E18 58 E3
WATW WD18 21 F3
WDGN N22 41 F6
WHALL SW1A 10 F9
WIM/MER SW19 147 J5
WOOL/PLUM SE18 115 G2
Marlborough St CHEL SW3 15 J6
Marlborough Yd ARCH N19 72 D1
Marler Rd FSTH SE23 132 C7
Marley Av BXLYHN DA7 116 E5
Marley Cl GFD/PVL UB6 84 A2
SEVS/STOTM N15 55 H3
Marlin Cl SUN TW16 140 C5
Marlingdene Cl HPTN TW12 142 A5
Marlings Cl CHST BR7 169 K3
Marlings Park Av CHST BR7 169 K3
The Marlins NTHWD HA6 32 D5
Marlins Cl SUT * SM1 175 G4
Marlins Meadow WATW WD18 20 B5
Marloes Cl ALP/SUD HA0 67 K3
Marloes Rd KENS W8 14 C3
Marlow Av PUR RM19 119 K3
Marlow Cl PGE/AN SE20 165 J2
Marlow Ct CDALE/KGS NW9 51 H2
Marlow Crs TWK TW1 124 A5
Marlow Dr CHEAM SM3 174 B2
Marlowe Cl CHST BR7 154 D5
Marlowe Rd WALTH E17 58 A3
The Marlowes DART DA1 138 A3
STJWD NW8 3 G4
Marlowe Wy CROY/NA CR0 176 E1
Marlow Gdns HYS/HAR UB3 101 G2
Marlow Rd EHAM E6 95 K2
NWDGN UB2 102 E2
PGE/AN SE20 165 J2
Marlow Wy BERM/RHTH SE16 112 A1
Marl Rd WAND/EARL SW18 128 A3
Marlton St GNWCH SE10 113 J4
Marlwood Cl BFN/LL DA15 154 E1
Marmadon Rd
WOOL/PLUM SE18 116 A3
Marmion Ap CHING E4 43 J3
Marmion Av CHING E4 43 H3
Marmion Cl CHING E4 43 H3
Marmion Ms BTSEA * SW11 129 F2
Marmion Rd BTSEA SW11 129 F3
Marmont Rd PECK SE15 111 H7
Marmora Rd EDUL SE22 131 K5
Marmot Rd HSLWW TW4 122 C2
Marne Av FBAR/BDGN N11 40 B3
WELL DA16 136 B2
Marnell Wy HSLWW TW4 122 C2
Marne St NKENS W10 88 C2
Marney Rd BTSEA SW11 129 F3
Marnfield Crs
BRXS/STRHM SW2 130 A7
Marnham Av CRICK NW2 70 C3
Marnham Crs GFD/PVL UB6 84 B2
Marnock Rd BROCKY SE4 132 C4
Maroon St POP/IOD E14 93 G4
Maroons Wy CAT SE6 151 J4
Marquess Rd IS N1 73 K5
Marquess Rd North IS N1 73 J5
Marquess Rd South IS * N1 73 J5
Marquis Cl ALP/SUD HA0 68 B6
Marquis Rd CAMTN NW1 72 D5
FSBYPK N4 55 F7
WDGN N22 41 F5
Marrabon Cl BFN/LL DA15 136 B7
Marrick Cl PUT/ROE SW15 126 D3
Marriner Ct HYS/HAR * UB3 82 C6
Marriot Rd MUSWH N10 39 K7
Marriott Cl EBED/NFELT TW14 121 G5
Marriott Rd BAR EN5 26 B2
DART DA1 139 K6
FSBYPK N4 55 F7
SRTFD E15 76 C7
Marriotts Cl CDALE/KGS NW9 51 H5
Marriotts Yd BAR * EN5 26 B2
Marryat Pl WIM/MER SW19 146 C3
Marryat Rd WIM/MER SW19 146 B4
Marryat Sq FUL/PGN * SW6 107 H7
Marsala Rd LEW SE13 132 E3
Marsden Rd ED N9 42 D1
PECK SE15 131 G2
Marsden St KTTN NW5 72 A5
Marshall Cl FBAR/BDGN N11 40 B3
HRW HA1 48 D6
HSLWW TW4 122 E4
WAND/EARL SW18 128 B5
Marshall Dr YEAD UB4 82 D4
Marshall Est MLHL * NW7 37 J3
Marshall Rd LEY E10 75 K3
TOTM N17 41 K7
Marshalls Dr ROM RM1 63 G2
Marshalls Gv
WOOL/PLUM SE18 114 D3
Marshalls Rd ROMW/RG RM7 63 F3
SUT SM1 175 F3
Marshall St SOHO/CST W1F 10 F5
Marshalsea Rd STHWK SE1 18 F1
Marsham Cl CHST * BR7 154 B4
Marsham St WEST SW1P 17 H5
Marsh Av MTCM CR4 162 E1
Marshbrook Cl BKHTH/KID SE3 134 C2
Marsh Cl MLHL NW7 37 H2
Marsh Dr CDALE/KGS NW9 51 H5
Marsh Farm Rd WHTN TW2 124 A7
Marshfield St POP/IOD E14 113 F2
Marshgate La SRTFD E15 75 K7
Marsh Green Rd DAGE RM10 80 C7
Marsh Hl HOM E9 75 G4
Marsh La LEY E10 75 H1
MLHL NW7 37 G2
STAN HA7 35 J5
TOTM N17 42 D6
Marsh Rd ALP/SUD HA0 85 K2
PIN HA5 47 K3
Marshside Cl ED N9 30 E7
Marsh St DART DA1 139 K2
POP/IOD * E14 112 E3
Marsh Wall POP/IOD E14 112 D1
Marsh Wy DAGW RM9 99 F3
Marsland Cl WALW SE17 18 D8
Marston Av CHSGTN KT9 172 A5
DAGE RM10 80 C2
Marston Cl DAGE RM10 80 C2
KIL/WHAMP NW6 2 F1
Marston Ct WOT/HER * KT12 156 B7
Marston Rd CLAY IG5 59 J1
TEDD TW11 143 H4
Marston Wy NRWD SE19 149 H6
Marsworth Av PIN HA5 33 H7
Marsworth Cl WATW * WD18 20 C5
YEAD UB4 83 J4
Martaban Rd STNW/STAM N16 74 A1
Martello St HACK E8 74 D6
Martell Rd DUL SE21 149 K2
Martel Pl HACK E8 74 B5
Marten Rd WALTH E17 57 J1
Martens Av BXLYHN DA7 137 K3
Martens Cl BXLYHN DA7 137 K3
Martham Cl THMD SE28 97 K6
Martha Rd SRTFD E15 76 C5
Martha's Buildings FSBYE EC1V 7 G9
Martha St WCHPL E1 92 E5
Marthorne Crs
KTN/HRWW/W HA3 48 D1
Martin Bowes Rd
ELTH/MOT SE9 134 E2
Martin Cl ED N9 31 F7
Martin Crs CROY/NA CR0 164 A7
Martindale MORT/ESHN SW14 125 K4
Martindale Av CAN/RD E16 94 E6
Martindale Rd BAL SW12 129 G6
HSLWW TW4 122 D3
Martin Dene BXLYHS DA6 137 G4
Martin Dr NTHLT UB5 65 K4
RAIN RM13 99 K3
Martineau Cl ESH/CLAY KT10 170 D3
Martineau Rd HBRY N5 73 H3
Martineau St WCHPL E1 92 E6
Martingales Cl
RCHPK/HAM TW10 143 K2
Martin Gdns BCTR RM8 79 J3
Martin Gv WIM/MER SW19 161 K2
Martin La CANST EC4R 13 H6
Martin Ri BXLYHS DA6 137 G4
Martin Rd BCTR RM8 79 J3
The Martins SYD SE26 150 D4
WBLY * HA9 68 B2
Martins Cl WWKM BR4 180 B1
Martins Mt BAR EN5 26 E3
Martin's Rd HAYES BR2 167 H1
Martin St THMD SE28 96 E7
Martins Wk MUSWH * N10 40 A7
Martin Wy RYNPK SW20 161 H2
Martlet Gv NTHLT UB5 83 H2
Martlett Ct HOL/ALD WC2B 11 K5
Martley Dr IL IG1 60 B4
Martock Cl KTN/HRWW/W HA3 49 G3
Marton Cl CAT SE6 151 J2
Marton Rd STNW/STAM * N16 74 A1
Martys Yd HAMP * NW3 71 H3
Marvell Av YEAD UB4 82 E4
Marvels Cl LEE/GVPK SE12 153 F1
Marvels La LEE/GVPK SE12 153 F1
Marville Rd FUL/PGN SW6 107 J6
Marvin St HACK * E8 74 D5
Marwell Cl ROM RM1 63 J5
WWKM BR4 180 D1
Marwood Cl WELL DA16 136 C2
Mary Adelaide Cl
PUT/ROE SW15 145 G2
Mary Ann Buildings DEPT SE8 112 D5
Maryatt Av RYLN/HDSTN HA2 66 B1
Marybank WOOL/PLUM SE18 114 E3
Mary Cl KTN/HRWW/W HA3 50 B3
Mary Datchelor Cl CMBW SE5 110 E7
Mary Gn STJWD * NW8 2 D3
Maryland Pk SRTFD E15 76 C4
Maryland Rd MV/WKIL W9 8 B1
SRTFD E15 76 B4
THHTH CR7 149 H7
WDGN N22 41 G5
Maryland Sq SRTFD E15 76 C4
Marylands Rd MV/WKIL W9 8 B1
Maryland St SRTFD E15 76 B4
Maryland Wk IS * N1 6 E3
Mary Lawrencson Pl
BKHTH/KID SE3 113 J6
Marylebone High St MHST W1U 10 B3
Marylebone La MHST W1U 10 B4
Marylebone Ms
CAVSQ/HST W1G 10 B3
Marylebone Pas GTPST W1W 10 F4
Marylebone Rd CAMTN NW1 9 K2
Marylebone St MHST W1U 10 B3
Marylee Wy LBTH SE11 17 M6
Maryon Gv WOOL/PLUM SE18 114 D3
Maryon Ms HAMP NW3 71 J3
Maryon Rd CHARL SE7 114 D3
Mary Peters Dr GFD/PVL UB6 66 D4
Mary Pl NTGHL W11 88 C6
Mary Rose Cl HPTN TW12 142 A7
Maryrose Wy TRDG/WHET N20 27 H7
Mary Seacole Cl HACK * E8 7 L3
Mary Secole Cl HACK E8 7 L3
Mary's Ter TWK TW1 124 B6
Mary St CAN/RD E16 94 D4
IS N1 6 F4
Mary Ter CAMTN NW1 4 D4
Masbro' Rd WKENS W14 107 G2
Mascalls Rd CHARL SE7 114 B5
Mascotts Cl CRICK NW2 69 K2
Masefield Av BORE WD6 24 D4
STAN HA7 35 F4
STHL UB1 84 A6
Masefield Cl ERITH DA8 118 C7
Masefield Crs STHGT/OAK N14 28 C4
Masefield Gdns EHAM E6 96 A3
Masefield La YEAD UB4 83 F3
Masefield Rd FELT TW13 141 K3
Masefield Wy
STWL/WRAY TW19 120 C7
Mashie Rd ACT W3 87 G5
Mashiters Wk ROM RM1 63 G2
Maskall Cl BRXS/STRHM * SW2 130 B7
Maskell Rd TOOT SW17 147 G2
Maskelyne Cl BTSEA SW11 108 D7
Mason Cl BERM/RHTH SE16 111 H4
BORE WD6 25 F1
BXLYHN DA7 137 J2
HPTN TW12 141 K7
RYNPK SW20 146 B7
Mason Ct WBLY * HA9 68 C1
Mason Rd WFD IG8 44 C3
Mason's Arms Ms
CONDST * W1S 10 D5
Mason's Av CITYW EC2V 13 G4
CROY/NA CR0 177 J2
KTN/HRWW/W HA3 48 E2
Masons Ct EW * KT17 173 J7
Masons Hl HAYES BR2 167 K2
WOOL/PLUM SE18 115 G3
Mason's Pl FSBYE EC1V 6 D7
MTCM CR4 147 K7
Mason St WALW SE17 19 H5
Masons Yd FSBYE EC1V 6 E9
STJS SW1Y 10 F8
Massey Cl FBAR/BDGN N11 40 B4
Massie Rd HACK E8 74 C5
Massingberd Wy TOOT SW17 148 B3
Massinger St WALW SE17 19 J6
Massingham St WCHPL E1 93 F3
Masson Av RSLP HA4 65 G5
Master Gunners Pl
WOOL/PLUM SE18 114 D7
Masterman Rd EHAM E6 95 J2
Masters Cl STRHM/NOR SW16 148 C5
Masters Dr BERM/RHTH SE16 111 J4
Master's St WCHPL E1 93 F4
Mast House Ter POP/IOD * E14 112 D3
Masthouse Ter POP/IOD E14 112 D3
Mastmaker Rd POP/IOD E14 112 D1
Maswell Park Crs HSLW TW3 123 H4
Maswell Park Rd HSLW TW3 123 G4
Matcham Rd WAN E11 76 C2
Matchless Dr
WOOL/PLUM SE18 115 F6
Matfield Cl HAYES BR2 167 K4
Matfield Rd BELV DA17 117 H5
Matham Gv EDUL SE22 131 G3
Matham Rd E/WMO/HCT KT8 157 J4
Matheson Rd WKENS W14 107 J3
Mathews Av EHAM E6 96 A1
Mathews Park Av SRTFD E15 76 D5
Mathews Yd LSQ/SEVD * WC2H 11 J5
Mathieson Ct STHWK SE1 18 D2
Matilda Cl NRWD SE19 149 K6
Matilda St IS N1 5 M4
Matlock Cl BAR EN5 26 B4
Matlock Crs CHEAM SM3 174 C3
OXHEY WD19 33 G2
Matlock Gdns CHEAM SM3 174 C3
Matlock Pl CHEAM SM3 174 C3
Matlock Rd LEY E10 58 A5
Matlock St WCHPL E1 93 G5
Matlock Wy NWMAL KT3 145 F7
Matthew Cl NKENS * W10 88 B3
Matthew Ct MTCM CR4 163 J4
Matthews Rd GFD/PVL UB6 66 D4
Matthews St BTSEA * SW11 128 E1
Matthias Rd STNW/STAM N16 73 K4
Mattingly Wy PECK SE15 111 G6
Mattison Rd FSBYPK N4 55 G5
Mattock La WEA W13 85 J7
Maud Cashmore Wy
WOOL/PLUM SE18 114 E2
Maude Rd CMBW SE5 131 F1
WALTH E17 57 G4
Maudesville Cottages
HNWL W7 84 E7
Maude Ter WALTH E17 57 G3
Maud Gdns BARK IG11 97 F1
PLSTW E13 94 D1
Maudlins Gn WAP * E1W 92 C7
Maud Rd LEY E10 76 A2
PLSTW E13 76 D7
Maudslay Rd ELTH/MOT SE9 134 E2
Maud St CAN/RD E16 94 D4
Maud Wilkes Cl KTTN NW5 72 C4
Mauleverer Rd
BRXS/STRHM SW2 129 K4
Maundeby Wk WLSDN * NW10 69 G4
Maunder Rd HNWL W7 84 E7
Maunsel St WEST SW1P 17 G5
Maurice Av WDGN N22 55 H1
Maurice Brown Cl MLHL * NW7 38 B4
Maurice St SHB W12 87 K5
Maurice Wk GLDGN NW11 53 G3
Maurier Cl NTHLT UB5 65 G7
Mauritius Rd GNWCH SE10 113 H3
Maury Rd STNW/STAM N16 74 C1
Mavelstone Rd BMLY BR1 153 H7
Maverton Rd BOW * E3 75 J7
Mavis Av HOR/WEW KT19 173 G4
Mavis Cl HOR/WEW KT19 173 G4
Mawbey Pl STHWK SE1 19 M8
Mawbey Rd STHWK SE1 19 M8
Mawbey St VX/NE SW8 109 K6
Mawney Cl ROMW/RG RM7 62 D1
Mawney Rd ROMW/RG RM7 62 D2
Mawson Cl RYNPK SW20 161 H1
Mawson La CHSWK W4 106 C5
Maxey Gdns DAGW RM9 80 A3
Maxey Rd DAGW RM9 80 A3
WOOL/PLUM SE18 115 H3
Maxfield Cl TRDG/WHET N20 27 G6
Maximfeldt Rd ERITH DA8 118 B4
Maxim Rd DART DA1 138 B4
ERITH DA8 118 B4
WCHMH N21 29 G5
Maxted Pk HRW HA1 48 E6
Maxted Rd PECK SE15 131 G2
Maxwell Cl CROY/NA CR0 163 K7
HYS/HAR UB3 82 E6
Maxwell Ri OXHEY WD19 21 J6
Maxwell Rd ASHF TW15 140 A5
BORE WD6 24 D2
FUL/PGN SW6 108 A6
NTHWD HA6 32 B6
WDR/YW UB7 100 B3
WELL DA16 136 B3
Maxwelton Av MLHL NW7 37 F4
Maxwelton Cl MLHL NW7 37 F4
Maya Cl PECK SE15 131 J1
Mayall Rd BRXN/ST SW9 130 C4
Maya Pl FBAR/BDGN N11 40 D6
Maya Rd EFNCH N2 53 G3
Maybank Av ALP/SUD HA0 67 G4
HCH RM12 81 K4
SWFD E18 59 F1
Maybank Gdns PIN HA5 46 E4
Maybank Rd SWFD E18 45 G7
May Bate Av KUTN/CMB KT2 143 K7
Maybery Pl BRYLDS KT5 159 G6
Maybourne Cl SYD * SE26 150 D5
Maybury Cl STMC/STPC BR5 169 G4
Maybury Gdns WLSDN NW10 69 J6
Maybury Rd BARK IG11 97 G1
PLSTW E13 95 G3
Maybury St TOOT SW17 147 J4
Maychurch Cl STAN HA7 35 K7
May Cl CHSGTN KT9 172 B5
Maycock Gv NTHWD HA6 32 D5
Maycroft PIN HA5 47 F1
Maycross Av MRDN SM4 161 J3
Mayday Gdns BKHTH/KID SE3 134 D1
Mayday Rd THHTH CR7 164 C5
Maydwell Ldg BORE WD6 24 B1
Mayefield Rd THHTH CR7 164 A3
Mayerne Rd ELTH/MOT SE9 134 C4
Mayesbrook Rd BARK IG11 79 F7
GDMY/SEVK IG3 79 G2
Mayesford Rd CHDH RM6 61 J6
Mayes Rd WDGN N22 55 F1
Mayeswood Rd
LEE/GVPK SE12 153 G3
Mayfair Av BXLYHN DA7 116 E7
CHDH RM6 61 K5
IL IG1 77 K1
WHTN TW2 123 H6
WPK KT4 160 D7
Mayfair Cl BECK BR3 151 K7
SURB KT6 159 F7
Mayfair Gdns TOTM N17 41 J5
WFD IG8 44 E6
Mayfair Ms HAMP * NW3 3 M2
Mayfair Pl MYFR/PICC W1J 10 D8
Mayfair Rd DART DA1 139 G4
Mayfair Ter STHGT/OAK N14 28 D6
Mayfare RKW/CH/CXG WD3 20 B4
Mayfield BXLYHN DA7 137 G2
Mayfield Av CHSWK W4 106 B3
KTN/HRWW/W HA3 49 H4
NFNCH/WDSP N12 39 G3
STHGT/OAK N14 40 C1
WEA W13 104 C2
WFD IG8 44 E5
Mayfield Cl CLAP SW4 129 J4
HACK E8 74 B5
PGE/AN * SE20 150 D7
THDIT KT7 158 C7
Mayfield Crs ED N9 30 D5
THHTH CR7 164 A3
Mayfield Dr PIN HA5 47 K3
Mayfield Gdns HDN NW4 52 B5
HNWL W7 84 D5
Mayfield Rd ACT W3 86 D6
BCTR RM8 61 J7
BELMT SM2 175 H5
BELV DA17 117 K3
BMLY BR1 168 D4
CEND/HSY/T N8 55 F5
CHING E4 44 B1
HACK E8 7 L2

PEND EN3 .... 31 F1
PLSTW E13 .... 94 D3
SAND/SEL CR2 .... 177 K7
SHB W12 .... 106 B1
WALTH E17 .... 57 G1
WIM/MER SW19 .... 146 D7
Mayfields WBLY HA9 .... 68 C1
Mayfields Cl WBLY HA9 .... 68 C1
Mayfield Vls SCUP * DA14 .... 155 J5
Mayflower Cl
BERM/RHTH SE16 .... 112 A3
RSLP HA4 .... 46 A5
Mayflower Rd
BRXN/ST SW9 .... 129 K2
Mayflower St
BERM/RHTH SE16 .... 111 K1
Mayfly Cl PIN HA5 .... 47 G6
Mayford Cl BAL SW12 .... 128 E6
BECK BR3 .... 166 A2
Mayford Rd BAL SW12 .... 128 E6
May Gdns BORE WD6 .... 23 K5
GFD/PVL UB6 .... 85 J1
Maygood St IS N1 .... 5 M5
Maygreen Crs EMPK RM11 .... 63 J6
Maygrove Rd KIL/WHAMP NW6 .... 70 D5
Mayhew Cl CHING E4 .... 43 J2
Mayhill Rd BAR EN5 .... 26 C4
CHARL SE7 .... 114 A5
Maylands Av HCH RM12 .... 81 K3
Maylands Dr SCUP DA14 .... 155 K2
Maylands Rd OXHEY WD19 .... 33 G3
Maynard Cl ERITH DA8 .... 118 C6
FUL/PGN SW6 .... 108 A6
SEVS/STOTM N15 .... 56 A4
Maynard Rd WALTH E17 .... 58 A4
Maynards Quay WAP * E1W 92 E6
Maynooth Gdns MTCM CR4 .... 162 E6
Mayola Rd CLPT E5 .... 74 E3
Mayo Rd CROY/NA CR0 .... 164 E4
WLSDN NW10 .... 69 G5
Mayow Rd SYD SE26 .... 151 F3
Mayplace Av DART DA1 .... 138 D3
Mayplace Cl BXLYHN DA7 .... 137 J2
Mayplace La WOOL/PLUM SE18 .... 115 G5
Mayplace Rd BXLYHN DA7 .... 137 K2
Mayplace Rd East BXLYHN DA7 .... 137 K2
Mayplace Rd West
BXLYHN DA7 .... 137 H3
Maypole Crs ERITH DA8 .... 119 G5
May Rd CHING E4 .... 43 J5
PLSTW E13 .... 94 E1
WHTN TW2 .... 123 K7
Mayroyd Av SURB KT6 .... 172 C1
May's Buildings Ms
GNWCH SE10 .... 113 G6
Mays Ct CHCR WC2N 11 J7
May's Hill Rd HAYES BR2 .... 167 H1
Mays La BAR EN5 .... 25 K6
Maysoule Rd BTSEA SW11 .... 128 C3
Mays Rd HPTN TW12 .... 142 D4
May St WKENS W14 .... 107 J4
Mayswood Gdns DAGE RM10 .... 80 E5
Maythorne Cl WATW WD18 .... 20 C3
Maythorne Cottages
LEW SE13 .... 133 G5
Mayton St HOLWY N7 .... 73 F2
Maytree Cl EDGW HA8 .... 36 E2
RAIN RM13 .... 99 G1
Maytree Ct MTCM CR4 .... 163 F2
Maytree La STAN HA7 .... 35 F5
Maytree Wk
BRXS/STRHM * SW2 .... 149 G1
Mayville Est STNW/STAM * N16 .... 74 A4
Mayville Rd IL IG1 .... 78 B4
WAN E11 .... 76 C1
Maywood Cl BECK * BR3 .... 151 K6
Maze Hl GNWCH SE10 .... 113 H5
Mazenod Av KIL/WHAMP NW6 .... 2 B2
Maze Rd RCH/KEW TW9 .... 105 H6
McAdam Dr ENC/FH EN2 .... 29 H1
McAuley Cl ELTH/MOT SE9 .... 135 F4
STHWK SE1 .... 18 A3
McCall Cl CLAP SW4 .... 129 K1
McCall Crs CHARL SE7 .... 114 D4
McCarthy Rd FELT TW13 .... 141 H4
McCoid Wy STHWK SE1 .... 18 E2
McCrone Ms HAMP NW3 .... 71 H5
McCudden Rd DART DA1 .... 139 J2
McCullum Rd BOW E3 .... 75 H7
McDermott Cl BTSEA SW11 .... 128 D1
McDermott Rd PECK SE15 .... 131 H2
McDonough Cl CHSGTN KT9 .... 172 A3
McDougall Ct RCH/KEW TW9 .... 125 H1
McDowall Cl CAN/RD E16 .... 94 E4
McEntee Av WALTH E17 .... 43 G7
McEwan Wy SRTFD * E15 .... 76 B7
McGrath Rd FSTGT E7 .... 76 E5
McGregor Rd NTGHL W11 .... 88 D5
McIntosh Cl ROM RM1 .... 63 G2
WLGTN SM6 .... 176 E6
McIntosh Rd ROM RM1 .... 63 G2
McKay Rd RYNPK SW20 .... 145 K6
McKellar Cl BUSH WD23 .... 34 C1
McKerrell Rd PECK SE15 .... 111 H7
McKillop Wy SCUP DA14 .... 155 J6
McLeod Rd ABYW SE2 .... 116 D3
McLeod's Ms SKENS SW7 .... 14 D4
McMillan St DEPT * SE8 .... 112 D5
McNair Rd NWDGN UB2 .... 103 F2
McNeil Rd CMBW SE5 .... 131 F1
McNicol Dr WLSDN NW10 .... 86 E1
McRae La MTCM CR4 .... 162 E6
The Mead BECK BR3 .... 167 F1
EFNCH N2 .... 53 G1
OXHEY WD19 .... 33 J2
WEA W13 .... 85 H4
WLGTN SM6 .... 176 D5
WWKM BR4 .... 167 G7
Mead Cl CAMTN * NW1 .... 4 B1
GPK RM2 .... 63 J1
KTN/HRWW/W HA3 .... 34 E7
Mead Ct CDALE/KGS NW9 .... 50 E4
Mead Crs CHING E4 .... 44 A3
DART DA1 .... 139 G7
SUT SM1 .... 175 J3
Meadcroft Rd LBTH SE11 .... 110 B5
Meade Cl CHSWK W4 .... 105 H5
Meadfield EDGW HA8 .... 36 D1
Mead Fld RYLN/HDSTN * HA2 .... 65 K2
Meadfoot Rd
STRHM/NOR SW16 .... 148 C7
Meadgate Av WFD IG8 .... 45 J4
Mead Gv CHDH RM6 .... 61 K2
Mead House La YEAD UB4 .... 82 B3
Meadhurst Pk SUN TW16 .... 140 C5
Meadlands Dr
RCHPK/HAM TW10 .... 143 K1
The Meadow CHST BR7 .... 154 C5
Meadow Av CROY/NA CR0 .... 166 A5
Meadowbank BKHTH/KID SE3 .... 133 J2
BRYLDS KT5 .... 159 G5
HAMP NW3 .... 3 L2
OXHEY WD19 .... 21 G6
WCHMH N21 .... 29 F5
Meadowbank Cl FUL/PGN SW6 .... 107 F6
Meadowbank Gdns HEST TW5 .... 101 K7
HSLWW TW4 .... 121 K1
Meadowbank Rd
CDALE/KGS NW9 .... 51 F6
Meadowbanks BAR EN5 .... 25 J4
Meadow Cl BAR EN5 .... 26 D5
BXLYHS DA6 .... 137 G4
CAT SE6 .... 151 J4
CHING E4 .... 31 K7
CHST BR7 .... 154 B4
ESH/CLAY KT10 .... 171 F2
HOM E9 .... 75 H4
HSLWW TW4 .... 123 F5
NTHLT UB5 .... 84 A1
RCHPK/HAM TW10 .... 125 F7
RSLP HA4 .... 46 D5
RYNPK SW20 .... 161 G3
Meadowcourt Rd
BKHTH/KID SE3 .... 133 J3
Meadow Cft BMLY BR1 .... 168 E2
Meadowcroft BUSH * WD23 .... 22 B5
Meadowcroft Cl PLMGR * N13 .... 41 H1
Meadowcroft Rd PLMGR N13 .... 41 G1
Meadow Dr HDN NW4 .... 52 A1
MUSWH N10 .... 54 A2
Meadowford Cl THMD SE28 .... 97 G6
Meadow Gdns EDGW HA8 .... 36 D5
Meadow Garth WLSDN NW10 .... 68 E5
Meadow Hl NWMAL KT3 .... 160 B5
Meadowlands BAR EN5 .... 25 H4
Meadow La LEE/GVPK SE12 .... 153 F2
Meadowlea Cl WDR/YW UB7 .... 100 A5
Meadow Ms VX/NE SW8 .... 110 A5
Meadow Pl CHSWK * W4 .... 106 B6
VX/NE SW8 .... 109 K6
Meadow Rd ASHF TW15 .... 140 B4
BARK IG11 .... 79 F6
BORE WD6 .... 24 D1
BUSH WD23 .... 22 B4
DAGW RM9 .... 80 B5
ESH/CLAY KT10 .... 170 E4
FELT TW13 .... 141 J1
HAYES BR2 .... 152 C7
PIN HA5 .... 47 H3
ROMW/RG RM7 .... 62 E7
STHL UB1 .... 83 K6
SUT SM1 .... 175 J3
VX/NE SW8 .... 110 A5
WIM/MER SW19 .... 147 G6
Meadow Rw STHWK SE1 .... 18 E4
Meadows Cl LEY E10 .... 75 J1
Meadows End SUN TW16 .... 140 E7
Meadowside DART DA1 .... 139 H7
ELTH/MOT SE9 .... 134 B3
TWK TW1 .... 124 E6
Meadowside Rd BELMT SM2 .... 174 C7
Meadow Stile CROY/NA CR0 .... 177 J2
Meadowsweet Cl CAN/RD E16 .... 95 H4
NWMAL KT3 .... 161 F4
Meadow Vw BFN/LL DA15 .... 136 C5
HRW HA1 .... 48 E7
Meadowview Rd BXLY DA5 .... 137 F5
CAT SE6 .... 151 H5
HOR/WEW KT19 .... 173 G7
Meadow View Rd THHTH CR7 .... 164 C4
YEAD UB4 .... 82 B3
Meadow Wk DAGW RM9 .... 80 B5
HOR/WEW KT19 .... 173 G5
SWFD E18 .... 58 E3
WLGTN SM6 .... 176 B2
The Meadow Wy
KTN/HRWW/W HA3 .... 34 E7
Meadow Wy CDALE/KGS NW9 .... 51 F4
CHSGTN KT9 .... 172 A4
RSLP HA4 .... 47 F5
WBLY HA9 .... 67 K3
Meadow Waye HEST TW5 .... 102 D6
Mead Pth WIM/MER SW19 .... 147 H5
Mead Pl CROY/NA CR0 .... 164 C7
HOM E9 .... 74 E5
Mead Plat WLSDN NW10 .... 68 E5
Mead Rd CHST BR7 .... 154 C5
DART DA1 .... 139 G7
EDGW HA8 .... 36 C5
RCHPK/HAM TW10 .... 143 J2
Mead Rw STHWK SE1 .... 18 A3
The Meads CHEAM SM3 .... 174 B2
EDGW HA8 .... 37 F5
MTCM * CR4 .... 162 D4
Meadside Cl BECK BR3 .... 151 G7
Meads La GDMY/SEVK IG3 .... 61 F6
Meads Rd WDGN N22 .... 55 H1
Meadvale Rd CROY/NA CR0 .... 165 G6
EA W5 .... 85 H3
The Meadway BKHTH/KID SE3 .... 133 G1
Mead Wy BUSH WD23 .... 21 J1
CROY/NA CR0 .... 179 G1
HAYES BR2 .... 167 K5
RSLP HA4 .... 46 B5
Meadway BAR EN5 .... 26 E3
BECK BR3 .... 152 A7
BRYLDS KT5 .... 159 K7
ESH/CLAY KT10 .... 170 B7
GDMY/SEVK IG3 .... 78 E3
GLDGN NW11 .... 53 F5
GPK RM2 .... 63 J1
RYNPK SW20 .... 161 F3
STHGT/OAK N14 .... 40 D1
WFD IG8 .... 45 G4
WHTN TW2 .... 123 J7
Meadway Cl BAR EN5 .... 26 E2
GLDGN NW11 .... 53 F5
PIN HA5 .... 34 B5
Meadway Ct EA * W5 .... 86 B4
Meadway Gdns RSLP HA4 .... 46 B5
Meaford Wy PGE/AN SE20 .... 150 D6
Meanley Rd MNPK E12 .... 77 J4
Meard St SOHO/CST W1F 11 G5
Meath Rd IL IG1 .... 78 C2
SRTFD E15 .... 94 D1
Meath St BTSEA SW11 .... 109 G7
Mecklenburgh Pl BMSBY WC1N 5 L9
Mecklenburgh Sq BMSBY WC1N 5 L9
Mecklenburgh St BMSBY WC1N 5 L9
Medburn St CAMTN NW1 .... 5 G5
Medcroft Gdns
MORT/ESHN SW14 .... 125 K3
Medebourne Cl
BKHTH/KID SE3 .... 133 K2
Medesenge Wy PLMGR N13 .... 41 H5
Medfield St PUT/ROE SW15 .... 126 D6
Medhurst Cl BOW E3 .... 93 G1
Median Rd CLPT E5 .... 74 E4
Medina Av ESH/CLAY KT10 .... 170 E2
Medina Rd HOLWY N7 .... 73 G2
Medland Cl WLGTN SM6 .... 163 F7
Medlar Cl NTHLT UB5 .... 83 H1
Medlar St CMBW SE5 .... 110 D7
Medley Rd KIL/WHAMP NW6 .... 70 E5
Medora Rd BRXS/STRHM SW2 .... 130 A5
ROMW/RG RM7 .... 63 F3
Medusa Rd LEW SE13 .... 132 E5
Medway Cl CROY/NA CR0 .... 165 K5
IL IG1 .... 78 C4
Medway Dr GFD/PVL UB6 .... 85 F1
Medway Gdns ALP/SUD HA0 .... 67 G3
Medway Pde GFD/PVL * UB6 .... 85 F1
Medway Rd BOW E3 .... 93 G1
DART DA1 .... 138 D2
Medway St WEST SW1P 17 G4
Medwin St BRXN/ST SW9 .... 130 A3
Meerbrook Rd BKHTH/KID SE3 .... 134 B2
Meeson Rd SRTFD E15 .... 76 D6
Meeson St CLPT E5 .... 75 G3
Meesons Whf SRTFD * E15 .... 94 A1
Meeting Aly WAT * WD17 .... 21 G3
Meeting Field Pth HOM * E9 .... 74 E5
Meeting House Aly WAP * E1W 92 D7
Meeting House La PECK SE15 .... 111 J7
Mehetabel Rd HOM E9 .... 74 E5
Meister Cl IL IG1 .... 60 D7
Melanda Cl CHST BR7 .... 153 K4
Melanie Cl BXLYHN DA7 .... 117 F7
Melaris Ms KIL/WHAMP NW6 .... 70 E4
Melbourne Av PLMGR N13 .... 41 F5
RYLN/HDSTN HA2 .... 48 B2
WEA W13 .... 85 G7
Melbourne Cl ORP BR6 .... 169 K6
WLGTN SM6 .... 176 C4
Melbourne Gdns CHDH RM6 .... 62 A4
Melbourne Gv EDUL SE22 .... 131 G3
Melbourne Ms BRXN/ST SW9 .... 110 B7
CAT SE6 .... 133 F6
Melbourne Pl HOL/ALD WC2B 11 M5
Melbourne Rd BUSH WD23 .... 22 B4
EHAM E6 .... 95 K1
IL IG1 .... 60 B7
LEY E10 .... 57 K6
TEDD TW11 .... 143 J5
WALTH E17 .... 57 G3
WIM/MER SW19 .... 146 E7
WLGTN SM6 .... 176 B4
Melbourne Sq BRXN/ST SW9 .... 110 B7
Melbourne Ter EDUL * SE22 .... 131 F3
FUL/PGN * SW6 .... 108 A6
Melbourne Wy EN EN1 .... 30 B5
Melbury Av NWDGN UB2 .... 103 G2
Melbury Cl CHST BR7 .... 153 K5
ESH/CLAY KT10 .... 171 H5
Melbury Ct WKENS W14 .... 107 J2
Melbury Dr CMBW SE5 .... 111 F6
Melbury Gdns RYNPK SW20 .... 145 K7
Melbury Rd KTN/HRWW/W HA3 .... 50 B4
WKENS W14 .... 107 J2
Melbury Ter CAMTN NW1 .... 9 K1
Melcombe Gdns
KTN/HRWW/W HA3 .... 50 B5
Melcombe Pl CAMTN NW1 .... 9 L2
Melcombe St CAMTN NW1 .... 9 M1
Meldon Cl FUL/PGN * SW6 .... 108 A7
Meldone Cl BRYLDS KT5 .... 159 J5
Meldrum Rd GDMY/SEVK IG3 .... 79 G1
Melfield Gdns CAT SE6 .... 151 K3
Melfont Av THHTH CR7 .... 164 C2
Melford Av BARK IG11 .... 78 E5
Melford Cl CHSGTN KT9 .... 172 B4
Melford Rd EDUL SE22 .... 131 H7
EHAM E6 .... 95 K3
IL IG1 .... 78 D1
WALTH E17 .... 57 G3
WAN E11 .... 76 C1
Melfort Rd THHTH CR7 .... 164 C2
Melgund Rd HBRY N5 .... 73 G4
Melina Cl HYS/HAR UB3 .... 82 B4
Melina Pl STJWD NW8 .... 3 G8
Melina Rd SHB W12 .... 106 E1
Melior Pl STHWK * SE1 .... 19 J1
Melior St STHWK SE1 .... 19 H1
Meliot Rd CAT SE6 .... 152 B1
Meller Cl CROY/NA CR0 .... 176 E2
Melling St WOOL/PLUM SE18 .... 115 K5
Mellish Gdns WFD IG8 .... 44 E4
Mellish St POP/IOD E14 .... 112 D2
Mellison Rd TOOT SW17 .... 147 J4
Melliss Av RCH/KEW TW9 .... 105 J7
Mellitus St SHB W12 .... 87 H5
Mellor Cl WOT/HER KT12 .... 156 E6
Mellow La East YEAD UB4 .... 82 A3
Mellows Rd CLAY IG5 .... 59 K2
WLGTN SM6 .... 176 D4
Mells Crs ELTH/MOT SE9 .... 153 K3
Mell St GNWCH SE10 .... 113 H4
Melody Rd WAND/EARL SW18 .... 128 B4
Melon Pl KENS * W8 .... 14 B1
Melon Rd PECK SE15 .... 111 H7
WAN E11 .... 76 C2
Melrose Av BORE WD6 .... 24 D4
CRICK NW2 .... 70 A4
DART DA1 .... 138 B6
GFD/PVL UB6 .... 84 B1
MTCM CR4 .... 148 B6
STRHM/NOR SW16 .... 164 A2
WDGN N22 .... 41 H7
WHTN TW2 .... 123 G6
WIM/MER SW19 .... 146 D1
Melrose Cl GFD/PVL UB6 .... 84 B1
LEE/GVPK SE12 .... 133 K7
YEAD UB4 .... 82 E4
Melrose Dr STHL UB1 .... 84 A7
Melrose Gdns EDGW HA8 .... 50 D2
HMSMTH W6 .... 107 F2
NWMAL KT3 .... 160 A2
Melrose Rd BARN SW13 .... 126 C1
RYLN/HDSTN HA2 .... 47 K3
WAND/EARL SW18 .... 127 J5
WIM/MER SW19 .... 161 K1
Melrose Ter HMSMTH W6 .... 107 F1
Melrose Vls BECK * BR3 .... 166 D1
Melsa Rd MRDN SM4 .... 162 B5
Melthorne Dr RSLP HA4 .... 65 G2
Melthorpe Gdns
WOOL/PLUM SE18 .... 114 C7
Melton Cl RSLP HA4 .... 47 G7
Melton Flds HOR/WEW KT19 .... 173 F7
Melton Gdns ROM RM1 .... 63 H6
Melton Pl HOR/WEW KT19 .... 173 F7
Melton St CAMTN NW1 .... 4 F8
Melville Av GFD/PVL UB6 .... 67 F4
RYNPK SW20 .... 145 J6
SAND/SEL CR2 .... 178 B4
Melville Cl HGDN/ICK UB10 .... 64 B2
Melville Ct DEPT SE8 .... 112 A3
Melville Gdns PLMGR N13 .... 41 G4
Melville Pl IS N1 .... 6 E2
Melville Rd BARN SW13 .... 106 D7
RAIN RM13 .... 99 J3
SCUP DA14 .... 155 J1
WALTH E17 .... 57 H3
WLSDN NW10 .... 69 F6
Melville Villas Rd ACT * W3 .... 87 F7
Melvin Rd PGE/AN SE20 .... 150 E7
Memel St STLK EC1Y 12 E1
Memorial Av SRTFD E15 .... 94 C2
Memorial Cl HEST TW5 .... 102 E5
Memorial Wy WAT WD17 .... 20 E2
Mendip Cl HYS/HAR UB3 .... 101 G6
SYD SE26 .... 150 E3
WPK KT4 .... 174 A1
Mendip Dr GLDGN NW11 .... 70 C1
Mendip Houses BETH * E2 .... 92 E2
Mendip Rd BTSEA SW11 .... 128 B2
BUSH WD23 .... 22 C5
BXLYHN DA7 .... 118 B7
EMPK RM11 .... 63 J6
GNTH/NBYPK IG2 .... 60 E4
Mendora Rd FUL/PGN SW6 .... 107 H6
Menelik Rd CRICK NW2 .... 70 C3
Menlo Gdns NRWD SE19 .... 149 K6
Menon Dr ED N9 .... 42 D2
Menotti St BETH * E2 .... 92 C3
Mentmore Cl
KTN/HRWW/W HA3 .... 49 J5
Mentmore Ter HACK E8 .... 74 D6
Meon Rd ACT W3 .... 105 K1
Meopham Rd MTCM CR4 .... 148 C7
Mepham Crs
KTN/HRWW/W HA3 .... 34 C6
Mepham Gdns
KTN/HRWW/W HA3 .... 34 C6
Mepham St STHWK SE1 .... 11 M9
Mera Dr BXLYHN DA7 .... 137 H3
Merantun Wy WIM/MER SW19 .... 147 F7
Merbury Cl LEW SE13 .... 133 F4
Merbury Rd THMD SE28 .... 96 D7
Merbury St WOOL/PLUM SE18 .... 115 G2
Mercator Pl POP/IOD E14 .... 112 D4
Mercator Rd LEW SE13 .... 133 G3
Mercer Cl THDIT KT7 .... 158 A6
Merceron Houses BETH * E2 .... 92 E2
Merceron St WCHPL E1 .... 92 D3
Mercer Pl PIN HA5 .... 47 G1
Mercers Cl GNWCH SE10 .... 113 J3
Mercers Cottages WCHPL * E1 .... 93 G5
Mercers Pl HMSMTH W6 .... 107 F3
Mercers Rd ARCH N19 .... 72 D2
Mercer St LSQ/SEVD WC2H 11 J5
Merchant St BOW * E3 .... 93 H2
Merchiston Rd CAT SE6 .... 152 B1
Merchland Rd ELTH/MOT SE9 .... 135 H7
Mercia Gv LEW SE13 .... 133 F2
Mercier Rd PUT/ROE SW15 .... 127 H4
Mercury Gdns ROM RM1 .... 63 H4
Mercury House
HYS/HAR * UB3 .... 101 J1
Mercury Rd BTFD TW8 .... 104 D4
Mercury Wy NWCR SE14 .... 112 A5
Mercy Ter LEW SE13 .... 132 E4
Merebank La WLGTN SM6 .... 177 F4
Mere Cl WIM/MER SW19 .... 127 G6
Meredith Av CRICK NW2 .... 70 A4
Meredith Cl PIN HA5 .... 33 H6
Meredith Ms BROCKY * SE4 .... 132 C3
Meredith St CLKNW EC1R 6 C8
PLSTW E13 .... 94 E2
Meredyth Rd BARN SW13 .... 126 D1
Mere End CROY/NA CR0 .... 166 A6
Mereside Pk ASHF * TW15 .... 140 A3
Meretone Cl BROCKY SE4 .... 132 B3
Merevale Crs MRDN SM4 .... 162 B5
Mereway Rd WHTN TW2 .... 123 J7
Merewood Cl BMLY BR1 .... 169 F1
Merewood Rd BXLYHN DA7 .... 137 K1
Mereworth Cl HAYES BR2 .... 167 J4
Mereworth Dr
WOOL/PLUM SE18 .... 115 G6
Meriden Cl BMLY BR1 .... 153 H6
Meridian Rd CHARL SE7 .... 114 C6
Meridian Sq SRTFD E15 .... 76 B6
Meridian Wy UED N18 .... 42 E5
Merifield Rd ELTH/MOT SE9 .... 134 B3
Merino Cl WAN E11 .... 59 G3
Merivale Rd HRW HA1 .... 48 C6
PUT/ROE SW15 .... 127 H3
Merlewood Dr CHST BR7 .... 153 K7
Merley Ct CDALE/KGS NW9 .... 50 E7
Merlin Cl CROY/NA CR0 .... 177 F5
CROY/NA CR0 .... 178 A3
MTCM CR4 .... 162 D2
NTHLT UB5 .... 83 G2
Merlin Crs EDGW HA8 .... 36 B7
Merlin Gv BECK BR3 .... 166 C3
Merlin Rd MNPK E12 .... 77 H1
WELL DA16 .... 136 B3
Merlin Rd North WELL DA16 .... 136 B3
Merlins Av RYLN/HDSTN HA2 .... 65 K2
Merlin St FSBYW WC1X 6 A8
Mermagen Dr RAIN RM13 .... 81 K6
Mermaid Ct STHWK SE1 .... 19 G1
Merredene St
BRXS/STRHM SW2 .... 130 A5
Merriam Cl CHING E4 .... 44 A4
Merrick Rd NWDGN UB2 .... 102 E3
Merrick Sq STHWK SE1 .... 19 G3
Merridene WCHMH N21 .... 29 H5
Merrielands Crs DAGW RM9 .... 98 B1
Merrilands Rd WPK KT4 .... 161 F7
Merrilees Rd BFN/LL DA15 .... 135 K6
Merrilyn Cl ESH/CLAY KT10 .... 171 G5
Merriman Rd BKHTH/KID SE3 .... 114 B7
Merrington Rd FUL/PGN SW6 .... 14 B9
Merrion Av STAN HA7 .... 35 K4
Merritt Gdns CHSGTN KT9 .... 171 J5
Merritt Rd BROCKY SE4 .... 132 C4
Merrivale STHGT/OAK N14 .... 28 D4
Merrivale Av REDBR IG4 .... 59 H4
Merrow Rd BELMT SM2 .... 174 B7
Merrow St WALW SE17 .... 19 G8
Merrow Wk WALW SE17 .... 19 H7
Merrow Wy CROY/NA CR0 .... 180 A5
Merrydown Wy CHST BR7 .... 153 J7
Merryfield BKHTH/KID SE3 .... 133 J1
Merryfield Cl BORE WD6 .... 24 B1
Merryfield Gdns STAN HA7 .... 35 J4
Merryhill Cl CHING E4 .... 31 K6
Merry Hill Mt BUSH WD23 .... 22 B7
Merry Hill Rd BUSH WD23 .... 22 A6
Merryhills Dr ENC/FH EN2 .... 28 E3
Merryweather Cl DART DA1 .... 139 J5
Merryweather Ct
NWMAL * KT3 .... 160 B4
Mersey Rd WALTH E17 .... 57 H2
Mersham Dr CDALE/KGS NW9 .... 50 C4
Mersham Pl PGE/AN SE20 .... 150 D7
THHTH CR7 .... 164 E1
Mersham Rd THHTH CR7 .... 164 E2
Merten Rd CHDH RM6 .... 62 A6
Merthyr Ter BARN SW13 .... 106 E5
Merton Av CHSWK W4 .... 106 C3
NTHLT UB5 .... 66 C4
Merton Gdns STMC/STPC BR5 .... 169 G4
Merton Hall Gdns RYNPK SW20 .... 146 C7
Merton Hall Rd
WIM/MER SW19 .... 146 C7
Merton High St
WIM/MER SW19 .... 147 G6
Merton La HGT N6 .... 71 K1
Merton Pl WIM/MER * SW19 .... 147 G7
Merton Ri HAMP NW3 .... 3 J1
Merton Rd BARK IG11 .... 79 F6
GDMY/SEVK IG3 .... 61 F6
RYLN/HDSTN HA2 .... 48 C7
SNWD SE25 .... 165 G4
WALTH E17 .... 58 A4
WAND/EARL SW18 .... 127 K7
WATW WD18 .... 21 F3
WIM/MER SW19 .... 147 F6
Merton Wy E/WMO/HCT KT8 .... 157 H3
Mertoun Ter MBLAR * W1H 9 L4
Merttins Rd PECK SE15 .... 132 A3
Meru Cl KTTN NW5 .... 72 A4
Mervan Rd BRXS/STRHM SW2 .... 130 B3
Mervyn Av ELTH/MOT SE9 .... 154 C2
Mervyn Rd WEA W13 .... 104 B2
Messaline Av ACT W3 .... 86 E5
Messent Rd ELTH/MOT SE9 .... 134 B4
Messeter Pl ELTH/MOT SE9 .... 135 F5
Messina Av KIL/WHAMP NW6 .... 2 A2
Meteor St BTSEA SW11 .... 129 F3
Meteor Wy WLGTN SM6 .... 176 E6
Metheringham Wy
CDALE/KGS NW9 .... 51 G1
Methley St LBTH SE11 .... 18 B8
Methuen Cl EDGW HA8 .... 36 C6
Methuen Pk MUSWH N10 .... 54 B1
Methuen Rd BELV DA17 .... 117 J3
BXLYHS DA6 .... 137 G3
EDGW HA8 .... 36 C6
Methwold Rd NKENS W10 .... 88 B4
Metropolitan Cl POP/IOD E14 .... 93 J4
Metropolitan Station Ap
WATW WD18 .... 20 D2
Metropolitan Whf WAP * E1W 92 E7
The Mews BECK * BR3 .... 151 J7
CEND/HSY/T N8 .... 55 G3
NFNCH/WDSP * N12 .... 39 F4
REDBR IG4 .... 59 H4
ROM RM1 .... 63 G3
STRHM/NOR * SW16 .... 149 F7
TWK * TW1 .... 124 C5
WATW * WD18 .... 21 G3
Mews North BGVA SW1W 16 C4
Mews Pl WFD IG8 .... 44 E3
Mews South PIM SW1V 16 F7
Mews St WAP E1W 13 M8
Mexfield Rd PUT/ROE SW15 .... 127 J4
Meyer Rd ERITH DA8 .... 117 K5
Meymott St STHWK SE1 .... 12 C9
Meynell Crs HOM E9 .... 75 F6
Meynell Gdns HOM E9 .... 75 F6
Meynell Rd HOM E9 .... 75 F6
Meyrick Rd BTSEA SW11 .... 128 C2
WLSDN NW10 .... 69 J5
Mezen Cl NTHWD HA6 .... 32 B4
Miah Ter WAP * E1W 92 C7
Micawber St IS N1 .... 6 E7
Michael Gaynor Cl HNWL W7 .... 85 F7
Michaelmas Cl RYNPK SW20 .... 161 F2
Michael Rd FUL/PGN SW6 .... 108 A7
SNWD SE25 .... 165 F2
WAN E11 .... 58 C7
Michaels Cl LEW SE13 .... 133 H2
Micheldever Rd LEW SE13 .... 133 H5
Michelham Gdns TWK TW1 .... 143 F2
Michigan Av MNPK E12 .... 77 J3
Michleham Down
NFNCH/WDSP N12 .... 38 D3
Mickleham Gdns CHEAM SM3 .... 174 C5
Mickleham Rd STMC/STPC BR5 .... 155 F7
Mickleham Wy CROY/NA CR0 .... 180 B6
Micklethwaite Rd
FUL/PGN SW6 .... 107 K5
Midcroft RSLP HA4 .... 46 C7
Middle Dartrey Wk
WBPTN * SW10 .... 108 B6
Middle Dene MLHL NW7 .... 37 F2
Middlefield STJWD NW8 .... 3 G3
Middlefields CROY/NA CR0 .... 179 G7
WEA W13 .... 85 H4
Middle Furlong BUSH WD23 .... 22 B3
Middle Green Cl BRYLDS KT5 .... 159 G5
Middleham Gdns UED N18 .... 42 C5
Middleham Rd UED N18 .... 42 C5
Middle La CEND/HSY/T N8 .... 54 E4
TEDD TW11 .... 143 F5
Middle Lane Ms CEND/HSY/T N8 .... 54 E4
Middle Park Av ELTH/MOT SE9 .... 134 C6
Middle Rd EBAR EN4 .... 27 J5
PLSTW E13 .... 94 E1
RYLN/HDSTN HA2 .... 66 D1
STRHM/NOR SW16 .... 163 H1
Middle Rw NKENS W10 .... 88 C3
Middlesborough Rd UED N18 .... 42 C5
Middlesex Pl HOM E9 .... 74 E5
Middlesex Rd MTCM CR4 .... 163 K4
Middlesex St WCHPL E1 .... 13 K3
Middle St CROY/NA CR0 .... 177 J1
STBT EC1A 12 E2
Middle Temple La
TPL/STR WC2R 12 A5
Middleton Av CHING E4 .... 43 H3
GFD/PVL UB6 .... 84 D1
SCUP DA14 .... 155 J5
Middleton Buildings
GTPST W1W 10 E3
Middleton Cl CHING E4 .... 43 H2
Middleton Dr
BERM/RHTH SE16 .... 112 A1
PIN HA5 .... 46 E2
Middleton Gdns
GNTH/NBYPK IG2 .... 60 B5
Middleton Gv HOLWY N7 .... 72 E4
Middleton Pl GTPST W1W 10 E3
Middleton Rd GLDGN NW11 .... 52 E6
HACK E8 .... 7 L2
HYS/HAR UB3 .... 82 B4
MRDN SM4 .... 162 B5
NWMAL KT3 .... 159 K2
Middleton St BETH E2 .... 92 D2
Middleton Wy LEW SE13 .... 133 G3
The Middle Wy
KTN/HRWW/W HA3 .... 49 F1
Middleway GLDGN NW11 .... 53 F4
Middle Wy STRHM/NOR SW16 .... 163 J1
Middle Yd STHWK SE1 .... 13 H8
Midfield Av BXLYHN DA7 .... 137 K2

Midfield Wy STMC/STPC BR5 155 H7
Midford Pl FITZ * W1T 10 F1
Midholm GLDGN NW11 53 F3
WBLY HA9 50 C7
Midholm Cl GLDGN * NW11 53 F3
Midholm Rd CROY/NA CR0 179 G2
Midhope St STPAN WC1H 5 K8
Midhurst Av CROY/NA CR0 164 B6
MUSWH N10 54 A2
Midhurst Cl HCH RM12 81 J3
Midhurst Gdns HGDN/ICK UB10 64 A6
Midhurst Hl BXLYHS DA6 137 H4
Midhurst Pde MUSWH * N10 54 A2
Midhurst Rd HNWL W7 104 B1
Midland Arches CRICK * NW2 69 K1
Midland Crs HAMP NW3 71 G5
Midland Rd CAMTN NW1 5 H6
LEY E10 58 A6
Midland Ter WLSDN NW10 87 G3
Midlothian Rd BOW E3 93 H3
Midmoor Rd BAL SW12 129 H7
WIM/MER SW19 146 B7
Midship Cl BERM/RHTH * SE16 93 F7
Midship Point POP/IOD * E14 112 D1
Midstrath Rd WLSDN NW10 69 G3
Midsummer Av HSLWW TW4 122 E3
Midway CHEAM SM3 161 J6
Midwinter Cl WELL DA16 136 B2
Mighell Av REDBR IG4 59 H4
Milan Rd STHL UB1 102 E1
Milborne Gv WBPTN SW10 14 F8
Milborne St HOM E9 74 E5
Milborough Crs
LEE/GVPK SE12 133 H5
Milbourne La ESH/CLAY KT10 170 C5
Milbrook ESH/CLAY KT10 170 C5
Milcote St STHWK SE1 18 C2
Mildenhall Rd CLPT E5 74 E3
Mildmay Av IS N1 73 K5
Mildmay Gv North IS N1 73 K4
Mildmay Gv South IS N1 73 K4
Mildmay Pk IS N1 73 K4
Mildmay Pl STNW/STAM * N16 74 A4
Mildmay Rd IL IG1 78 B2
IS N1 73 K4
ROMW/RG RM7 62 E4
Mildmay St IS N1 73 K5
Mildred Av BORE WD6 24 C3
HYS/HAR UB3 101 G3
NTHLT UB5 66 B4
WATW WD18 20 E3
Mildred Cl DART DA1 139 K5
Mildred Rd ERITH DA8 118 B4
The Mile End WALTH E17 43 F7
Mile End Pl WCHPL E1 93 F3
Mile End Rd WCHPL E1 92 E4
Mile Rd WLGTN SM6 163 F7
Miles Dr THMD SE28 96 E7
Milespit Hl MLHL NW7 37 K4
Miles Pl BRYLDS * KT5 159 G3
Miles Rd CEND/HSY/T N8 54 E2
MTCM CR4 162 D2
Miles St VX/NE SW8 109 K5
Milestone Cl BELMT SM2 175 H5
ED N9 42 C1
Milestone Rd NRWD SE19 150 B5
Miles Wy TRDG/WHET N20 39 J1
Milfoil St SHB W12 87 J6
Milford Cl ABYW SE2 117 F5
Milford Gdns ALP/SUD HA0 67 K4
EDGW HA8 36 C6
Milford Gv SUT SM1 175 G3
Milford La TPL/STR WC2R 12 A6
Milford Ms STRHM/NOR SW16 149 F2
Milford Rd STHL UB1 84 A6
WEA W13 85 H7
Milk St BMLY BR1 153 F5
CAN/RD E16 96 B7
CITYW EC2V 12 F4
Milkwell Gdns WFD IG8 45 F6
Milkwell Yd CMBW SE5 110 D7
Milkwood Rd HNHL SE24 130 C4
Milk Yd WAP E1W 92 E6
Millais Av MNPK E12 78 A4
Millais Gdns EDGW HA8 50 C1
Millais Rd EN EN1 30 B4
NWMAL KT3 160 B6
WAN E11 76 A3
Millais Wy HOR/WEW KT19 172 E3
Millard Cl STNW/STAM N16 74 A4
Millbank WEST SW1P 17 J5
Millbank Est WEST SW1P 17 H6
Millbank Wy LEE/GVPK SE12 133 K4
Millbourne Rd FELT TW13 141 J3
Mill Br BAR * EN5 26 D4
Millbrook Av WELL DA16 135 J3
Millbrook Gdns CHDH RM6 62 A5
GPK RM2 63 G1
Millbrook Rd BRXN/ST SW9 130 C2
ED N9 30 D7
Mill Cl CAR * SM5 176 A1
WDR/YW UB7 100 A2
Millennium Br STHWK SE1 12 E7
Millennium Cl CAN/RD E16 94 E5
Millennium Dr POP/IOD E14 113 G2
Millennium Pl BETH * E2 92 D1
Millennium Sq STHWK SE1 19 L1
Millennium Wy GNWCH SE10 113 H1
Millennium Whf POP/IOD E14 113 G3
Miller Cl MTCM CR4 162 E6
Miller Rd CROY/NA CR0 164 A7
WIM/MER SW19 147 H5
Miller's Av HACK E8 74 B4
Millers Cl MLHL NW7 37 J3
Miller's Ct CHSWK W4 106 C4
Millers Green Cl ENC/FH EN2 29 H2
Miller's Ter HACK E8 74 B4
Miller St CAMTN NW1 4 E5
Miller's Wy HMSMTH W6 107 F1
Millers Yd FNCH N3 39 F7
Miller Wk STHWK SE1 12 B9
Millet Rd GFD/PVL UB6 84 B2
Mill Farm Av SUN TW16 140 C6
Mill Farm Cl PIN HA5 47 G3
Mill Farm Crs HSLWW TW4 122 D7
Millfield SUN TW16 140 B7
Millfield Av WALTH E17 43 H7
Millfield La HGT N6 71 K1
Millfield Rd EDGW HA8 50 E1
HSLWW TW4 122 D7
Millfields Rd CLPT E5 74 E3
Mill Gdns SYD SE26 150 D3
Mill Gn MTCM * CR4 163 F6
Mill Green Rd MTCM CR4 163 F6
Millgrove St BTSEA SW11 109 F7
Millharbour POP/IOD E14 112 E2
Millhaven Cl CHDH RM6 61 H5
Mill Hl BARN SW13 126 D2
Mill Hill Gv ACT * W3 86 D7
Mill Hill Rd ACT W3 105 J1
BARN SW13 126 E2
Mill Hill Ter ACT W3 86 D7
Millhouse Pl WNWD SE27 149 H3
Millicent Rd LEY * E10 57 H7
Milligan St POP/IOD E14 93 H6
Milling Rd EDGW HA8 37 F6
Millington Rd HYS/HAR UB3 101 H2
Mill La CAR SM5 176 A3
CHDH RM6 62 A5
CHING E4 31 K2
CRICK NW2 70 C4
CROY/NA CR0 177 G2
EW KT17 173 H7
WFD IG8 44 D4
WOOL/PLUM SE18 115 F4
Millman Ms BMSBY * WC1N 11 L1
Millman Pl BMSBY * WC1N 11 L1
Millman St BMSBY WC1N 11 L1
Millmark Gv NWCR SE14 132 B1
Millmarsh La PEND EN3 31 G1
Mill Mead Rd TOTM N17 56 D2
Mill Pl CHST BR7 154 A7
DART DA1 138 D3
KUT KT1 159 G2
POP/IOD E14 93 G5
Mill Plat ISLW TW7 124 B2
Mill Plat Av ISLW TW7 124 B1
Millpond Est
BERM/RHTH * SE16 111 J1
Mill Pond Rd DART DA1 139 H5
Mill Rdg EDGW HA8 36 B4
Mill Rd CAN/RD E16 95 F7
ERITH DA8 117 K6
ESH/CLAY KT10 170 A1
IL IG1 78 A2
WDR/YW UB7 100 A2
WHTN TW2 142 C1
WIM/MER SW19 147 G6
Mill Rw BXLY * DA5 137 J6
IS N1 7 K4
Mills Gv HDN NW4 52 B2
POP/IOD E14 94 A4
Millshot Cl FUL/PGN SW6 107 F7
Millside CAR SM5 175 K1
Millside Pl ISLW TW7 124 C1
Millson Cl TRDG/WHET N20 39 H1
Mills Rw CHSWK W4 106 A3
Millstream Cl PLMGR N13 41 G4
Millstream Rd STHWK SE1 19 L2
Mill St CONDST W1S 10 D6
KUT KT1 159 F2
STHWK SE1 19 M2
Mill V HAYES BR2 167 K2
Mill View Cl EW KT17 173 H6
Mill View Gdns CROY/NA CR0 179 F2
Millwall Dock Rd POP/IOD E14 112 D2
Mill Wy BUSH WD23 21 J1
EBED/NFELT TW14 122 A4
MLHL NW7 37 G4
Millway Gdns NTHLT UB5 65 K5
Millwood Rd HSLW TW3 123 H4
Millwood St NKENS W10 88 C4
Milman Cl PIN HA5 47 H2
Milman Rd KIL/WHAMP NW6 88 B1
Milman's St WBPTN SW10 108 C5
Milne Fld PIN HA5 34 A6
Milne Gdns ELTH/MOT SE9 134 D4
Milner Ct BUSH WD23 22 B5
Milner Dr WHTN TW2 123 J6
Milner Pl IS N1 6 B3
Milner Rd BCTR RM8 79 J1
KUT KT1 158 E2
MRDN SM4 162 C4
SRTFD E15 94 C2
THHTH CR7 164 D2
WIM/MER SW19 147 F7
Milner Sq IS N1 6 C2
Milner St CHEL SW3 15 L5
Milnthorpe Rd CHSWK W4 106 A5
Milo Rd EDUL SE22 131 G5
Milroy Wk STHWK SE1 12 B8
Milson Rd WKENS W14 107 H2
Milton Av BAR EN5 26 D4
CDALE/KGS NW9 50 D3
CROY/NA CR0 164 E6
EHAM E6 77 H6
HCH RM12 81 H1
HGT N6 54 C6
SUT SM1 175 H2
WLSDN NW10 69 F7
Milton Cl EFNCH N2 53 G5
STHWK SE1 19 L6
SUT SM1 175 H2
YEAD UB4 82 E5
Milton Ct BARB EC2Y 13 G2
Milton Court Rd NWCR SE14 112 B5
Milton Crs GNTH/NBYPK IG2 60 C6
Milton Dr BORE WD6 24 D4
Milton Gdns STWL/WRAY TW19 120 C7
Milton Gv FBAR/BDGN N11 40 C4
STNW/STAM N16 73 K3
Milton Pk HGT N6 54 C6
Milton Rd ACT W3 87 F7
BELV DA17 117 H3
CDALE/KGS * NW9 51 J6
CROY/NA CR0 164 E6
HGT N6 54 C6
HNHL SE24 130 C4
HNWL W7 85 F6
HPTN TW12 142 A6
HRW HA1 48 E3
MLHL NW7 37 J4
MORT/ESHN SW14 126 A2
MTCM CR4 148 A7
ROM RM1 63 J5
SEVS/STOTM N15 55 H2
SUT SM1 174 E2
WALTH E17 57 J3
WELL DA16 116 A7
WIM/MER SW19 147 G5
WLGTN SM6 176 C5
Milton St BARB EC2Y 13 G2
Milton Wy WDR/YW UB7 100 C3
Milverton Dr HGDN/ICK UB10 64 A3
Milverton Gdns GDMY/SEVK IG3 79 F1
Milverton Rd KIL/WHAMP NW6 70 A6
Milverton St LBTH SE11 18 B8
Milverton Wy ELTH/MOT SE9 154 A3
Milward St WCHPL E1 92 D4
Mimosa Rd YEAD UB4 83 G4
Mimosa St FUL/PGN SW6 107 J7
Minard Rd CAT SE6 133 H7
Mina Rd WALW SE17 19 K8
WIM/MER SW19 146 E7
Minchenden Crs
STHGT/OAK N14 40 D2
Mincing La MON EC3R 13 J6
Minden Rd CHEAM SM3 174 C1
PGE/AN SE20 150 D7
Minehead Rd RYLN/HDSTN HA2 66 A2
STRHM/NOR SW16 149 F4
Mineral St WOOL/PLUM SE18 115 K3
Minera Ms BGVA SW1W 16 B5
Minerva Cl BRXN/ST SW9 110 B6
SCUP DA14 154 E3
Minerva Rd CHING E4 43 K6
KUT KT1 159 G1
WLSDN NW10 86 E3
Minerva St BETH E2 92 D1
Minet Av WLSDN NW10 87 G1
Minet Dr HYS/HAR UB3 82 E7
Minet Gdns HYS/HAR UB3 83 F7
WLSDN NW10 87 G1
Minet Rd CMBW SE5 130 C1
Minford Gdns WKENS W14 107 G1
Ming St POP/IOD E14 93 J6
Minimax Cl EBED/NFELT TW14 121 K5
Ministry Wy ELTH/MOT SE9 153 K1
Mink Ct HSLWW TW4 122 B1
Minniedale BRYLDS KT5 159 G4
Minnow Wk WALW SE17 19 K6
Minories TWRH EC3N 13 L5
Minshull Pl BECK * BR3 151 J6
Minshull St VX/NE * SW8 109 J7
Minson Rd HOM E9 75 F7
Minstead Gdns PUT/ROE SW15 126 C6
Minstead Wy NWMAL KT3 160 B5
Minster Av SUT SM1 174 E1
Minster Ct FENCHST * EC3M 13 J6
Minster Dr CROY/NA CR0 178 A3
Minster Gdns E/WMO/HCT KT8 156 E3
Minster Rd BMLY BR1 153 F6
CRICK NW2 70 C4
Minstrel Gdns BRYLDS KT5 159 G3
Mintern Cl PLMGR N13 41 H2
Minterne Av NWDGN UB2 103 F3
Minterne Rd KTN/HRWW/W HA3 50 B4
Minterne Waye YEAD UB4 83 G5
Mintern St IS N1 7 H5
Minton Ms KIL/WHAMP NW6 71 F5
Mint Rd WLGTN SM6 176 B4
Mint St STHWK SE1 18 E1
Mint Wk CROY/NA CR0 177 J2
Mirabel Rd FUL/PGN SW6 107 J6
Miranda Cl WCHPL E1 92 E4
Miranda Rd ARCH N19 54 C7
Mirfield St CHARL SE7 114 C2
Miriam Rd WOOL/PLUM SE18 115 K4
Mirren Cl RYLN/HDSTN HA2 65 K3
Miskin Rd DART DA1 139 F6
Missenden Cl
EBED/NFELT TW14 121 J7
Missenden Gdns MRDN SM4 162 B5
Mission Gv WALTH E17 57 H4
Mission Pl PECK SE15 111 H7
Mistletoe Cl CROY/NA CR0 166 A7
Misty's Fld WOT/HER KT12 156 B7
Mitali Pas WCHPL E1 92 C5
Mitcham La STRHM/NOR SW16 148 C4
Mitcham Pk MTCM CR4 162 E3
Mitcham Rd CROY/NA CR0 163 J5
EHAM E6 95 J2
GDMY/SEVK IG3 61 F6
TOOT SW17 147 K5
Mitchellbrook Wy WLSDN NW10 69 F5
Mitchell Cl ABYW SE2 116 D4
BELV DA17 117 K2
Mitchell Rd PLMGR N13 41 H4
Mitchell St FSBYE EC1V 6 E9
Mitchell Wy BMLY BR1 152 E7
WLSDN NW10 68 E5
Mitchison Rd IS N1 73 K5
Mitchley Rd TOTM N17 56 C2
Mitford Rd FSBYPK N4 72 E1
The Mitre POP/IOD E14 93 H6
Mitre Cl BELMT SM2 175 G6
HAYES BR2 167 J1
Mitre Rd SRTFD E15 94 C1
STHWK SE1 18 B1
Mitre Sq HDTCH EC3A 13 K5
Mitre St HDTCH EC3A 13 K5
Mitre Wy WLSDN NW10 87 K3
The Moat NWMAL KT3 145 G7
Moat Cl BUSH WD23 22 B4
Moat Ct ELTH/MOT * SE9 134 E5
Moat Crs EFNCH N2 53 F2
Moat Cft WELL DA16 136 D2
Moat Dr HRW HA1 48 C3
RSLP HA4 46 C6
Moat Farm Rd NTHLT UB5 65 K5
Moatfield Rd BUSH WD23 22 B4
Moat La ERITH DA8 118 D7
Moat Pl ACT W3 86 D5
BRXN/ST SW9 130 A2
Moat Side FELT TW13 141 G3
PEND EN3 30 E3
Moberly Rd CLAP SW4 129 J6
Modbury Gdns HAMP NW3 72 A5
Model Cottages WEA * W13 104 C1
Model Farm Cl ELTH/MOT SE9 153 J2
Moelyn Ms HRW HA1 49 G4
Moffat Rd PLMGR N13 40 E5
THHTH CR7 164 D1
TOOT SW17 147 J3
Mogden La ISLW TW7 124 A4
Mohammad Khan Rd
WAN * E11 58 D7
Moiety Rd POP/IOD E14 112 D1
Moira Cl TOTM N17 56 A1
Moira Rd ELTH/MOT SE9 134 E3
Moir Cl SAND/SEL CR2 178 C7
Mole Abbey Gdns
E/WMO/HCT KT8 157 F2
Mole Ct HOR/WEW KT19 172 E3
Molember Rd E/WMO/HCT KT8 157 K4
Molescroft ELTH/MOT SE9 154 C2
Molesey Av E/WMO/HCT KT8 156 E4
Molesey Dr CHEAM SM3 174 C1
Molesey Park Av
E/WMO/HCT KT8 157 G4
Molesey Park Cl
E/WMO/HCT KT8 157 H4
Molesey Park Rd
E/WMO/HCT KT8 157 G4
Molesey Rd E/WMO/HCT KT8 156 D4
Molesford Rd FUL/PGN * SW6 107 K7
Molesham Cl E/WMO/HCT KT8 157 G2
Molesham Wy
E/WMO/HCT KT8 157 G3
Molesworth St LEW SE13 133 F2
Mollison Av PEND EN3 31 G2
Mollison Dr WLGTN SM6 176 E6
Mollison Wy EDGW HA8 50 C1
Molly Huggins Cl BAL SW12 129 H6
Molyneux Dr TOOT SW17 148 B3
Molyneux St MBLAR W1H 9 K3
Monarch Cl EBED/NFELT TW14 121 H6
RAIN RM13 99 J1
WWKM BR4 180 D3
Monarch Dr CAN/RD E16 95 H4
Monarch Ms WNWD SE27 149 G4
Monarch Pde MTCM * CR4 162 E1
Monarch Pl BKHH IG9 45 G1
Monarch Rd BELV DA17 117 H2
Monarch's Wy RSLP * HA4 46 B7
Mona Rd PECK SE15 131 K1
Monastery Gdns ENC/FH EN2 29 K1
Mona St CAN/RD E16 94 D4
Monaveen Gdns
E/WMO/HCT KT8 157 G2
Monck's Rw PUT/ROE * SW15 127 J5
Monck St WEST SW1P 17 H4
Monclar Rd CMBW SE5 130 E3
Moncorvo Cl SKENS SW7 15 J2
Moncrieff St PECK SE15 131 H1
Mondial Wy WDR/YW UB7 101 F6
Monega Rd FSTGT E7 77 G5
Money La WDR/YW UB7 100 A2
Monica Cl WATN WD24 21 H1
Monier Rd BOW E3 75 J6
Monivea Rd BECK BR3 151 H6
Monk Dr CAN/RD E16 94 E6
Monkfrith Av STHGT/OAK N14 28 B5
Monkfrith Wy STHGT/OAK N14 28 B6
Monkham's Av WFD IG8 45 F4
Monkham's Dr WFD IG8 45 F4
Monkham's La WFD IG8 45 F3
Monkleigh Rd MRDN SM4 161 H2
Monks Av BAR EN5 27 G5
E/WMO/HCT KT8 156 E4
Monks Cl ABYW SE2 116 E3
ENC/FH EN2 29 J1
RSLP HA4 65 H3
RYLN/HDSTN * HA2 66 A1
Monks Crs WOT/HER KT12 156 A7
Monksdene Gdns SUT SM1 175 F2
Monks Dr ACT W3 86 C4
Monksmead BORE WD6 24 E3
Monks Orchard Rd BECK BR3 166 D7
Monks Pk WBLY HA9 68 E5
Monks Park Gdns WBLY HA9 68 D5
Monks Rd ENC/FH EN2 29 H1
Monk St WOOL/PLUM SE18 115 F3
Monks Wy BECK BR3 166 D5
GLDGN NW11 52 D3
STMC/STPC BR5 169 H7
Monkswood Gdns BORE WD6 25 F4
CLAY IG5 60 A2
Monkton Rd WELL DA16 136 A1
Monkton St LBTH SE11 18 B5
Monkville Av GLDGN NW11 52 D3
Monkville Pde GLDGN * NW11 52 D3
Monkwell Sq BARB EC2Y 12 F3
Monkwood Cl ROM RM1 63 J4
Monmouth Av KUT KT1 143 J6
SWFD E18 59 F3
Monmouth Cl CHSWK W4 106 A2
MTCM CR4 163 K3
WELL DA16 136 B3
Monmouth Gv BTFD TW8 105 F3
Monmouth Pl BAY/PAD W2 8 B5
Monmouth Rd BAY/PAD W2 8 B5
DAGW RM9 80 B4
ED N9 42 D1
EHAM E6 95 K2
HYS/HAR UB3 101 H3
WAT WD17 21 F2
Monmouth St LSQ/SEVD WC2H 11 J5
Monnery Rd ARCH N19 72 C2
Monnow Rd STHWK SE1 111 H4
Monoux Gv WALTH E17 43 J7
Monroe Dr MORT/ESHN SW14 125 J4
Monro Gdns KTN/HRWW/W HA3 34 E6
Monro Pl HOR/WEW KT19 172 C7
Monsell Rd FSBYPK N4 73 H2
Monson Rd NWCR SE14 112 A6
WLSDN NW10 87 J1
Mons Wy HAYES BR2 168 D5
Montacute Rd BUSH WD23 22 E6
CAT SE6 132 C6
CROY/NA CR0 180 A7
MRDN SM4 162 C5
Montagu Crs UED N18 42 D3
Montague Av BROCKY SE4 132 C3
HNWL W7 85 F7
Montague Cl STHWK SE1 13 G8
Montague Gdns EA W5 86 C6
Montague Hall Pl BUSH WD23 22 A5
Montague Pl GWRST WC1E 11 H2
Montague Rd CEND/HSY/T N8 55 F4
CROY/NA CR0 164 C7
HACK E8 74 C4
HNWL W7 104 A1
HSLW TW3 123 G2
NWDGN UB2 102 D3
RCHPK/HAM TW10 125 F5
TOTM * N17 56 C3
WAN E11 76 D1
WEA W13 85 H5
WIM/MER SW19 147 F6
Montague Sq NWCR SE14 111 K6
Montague St RSQ WC1B 11 J2
STBT EC1A 12 E3
Montague Ter HAYES * BR2 167 K3
Montagu Gdns UED N18 42 D3
WLGTN SM6 176 C3
Montagu Man MHST W1U 9 M3
Montagu Ms North MBLAR W1H 9 M3
Montagu Ms South MBLAR W1H 9 M4
Montagu Ms West MBLAR W1H 9 M4
Montagu Pl MBLAR W1H 9 L3
Montagu Rd HDN NW4 51 J5
UED N18 42 D4
Montagu Rw MHST W1U 9 M3
Montagu Sq MBLAR W1H 9 M3
Montagu St MBLAR W1H 9 M4
Montalt Rd WFD IG8 44 D4
Montana Gdns CAT SE6 151 H4
SUT SM1 175 G4
Montana Rd RYNPK SW20 146 A7
TOOT SW17 148 A2
Montbelle Rd ELTH/MOT SE9 154 B2
Montcalm Cl HAYES BR2 167 K5
YEAD UB4 83 F2
Montcalm Rd CHARL SE7 114 C6
Montclare St BETH E2 7 L8
Monteagle Av BARK IG11 78 C5
Monteagle Wy PECK SE15 131 J2
Montefiore St VX/NE SW8 129 G1
Montem Rd FSTH SE23 132 C6
NWMAL KT3 160 B3
Montem St FSBYPK N4 55 F7
Montenotte Rd CEND/HSY/T N8 54 C4
Montesquieu Ter CAN/RD * E16 94 D5
Montford Pl LBTH SE11 18 A9
Montfort Pl WIM/MER SW19 127 G7
Montgomery Av
ESH/CLAY KT10 170 E1
Montgomery Cl BFN/LL DA15 135 K4
MTCM * CR4 163 K3
Montgomery Rd CHSWK W4 105 K3
EDGW HA8 36 B5
Montholme Rd BTSEA SW11 128 E5
Monthorpe Rd WCHPL E1 92 C4
Montolieu Gdns
PUT/ROE SW15 126 E4
Montpelier Av BXLY DA5 136 E6
EA W5 85 J4
Montpelier Gdns CHDH RM6 61 J6
EHAM E6 95 H2
Montpelier Gv KTTN NW5 72 C4
Montpelier Ms SKENS SW7 15 K3
Montpelier Pl SKENS SW7 15 K3
WCHPL E1 92 E5
Montpelier Ri GLDGN NW11 52 C6
WBLY HA9 49 K7
Montpelier Rd EA W5 85 K4
FNCH N3 39 G7
PECK SE15 111 J7
SUT SM1 175 G3
Montpelier Rw BKHTH/KID SE3 133 J1
TWK TW1 124 C6
Montpelier Sq SKENS SW7 15 K3
Montpelier St SKENS SW7 15 K2
Montpelier Ter SKENS SW7 15 K2
Montpelier V BKHTH/KID * SE3 133 J1
Montpelier Wk SKENS SW7 15 K2
Montpelier Wy GLDGN NW11 52 C6
Montrave Rd PGE/AN SE20 150 E5
Montreal Pl HOL/ALD WC2B 11 L6
Montreal Rd IL IG1 60 C6
Montrell Rd BRXS/STRHM SW2 129 K7
Montrose Av BFN/LL DA15 136 B6
EDGW HA8 51 F1
KIL/WHAMP NW6 88 C1
WELL DA16 135 J2
WHTN TW2 123 G6
Montrose Cl ASHF TW15 140 A5
WELL DA16 136 A2
WFD IG8 44 E3
Montrose Crs ALP/SUD HA0 68 A5
NFNCH/WDSP N12 39 F5
Montrose Gdns MTCM CR4 162 E2
SUT SM1 175 F1
Montrose Pl KTBR SW1X 16 B2
Montrose Rd
EBED/NFELT TW14 121 G5
KTN/HRWW/W HA3 48 E1
Montrose Vls HMSMTH * W6 106 D4
Montrose Wy FSTH SE23 132 A7
Montserrat Av WFD IG8 44 B6
Montserrat Cl NRWD SE19 149 K4
Montserrat Rd PUT/ROE SW15 127 H3
Monument St MON EC3R 13 H7
Monument Wy TOTM N17 56 B2
Monza St WAP E1W 92 E6
Moodkee St BERM/RHTH SE16 111 K2
Moody St WCHPL E1 93 F2
Moon Ct LEE/GVPK * SE12 133 K3
Moon La BAR EN5 26 D2
Moon St IS N1 6 C3
Moorcroft EDGW * HA8 36 D7
Moorcroft Gdns HAYES BR2 168 D4
Moorcroft Rd
STRHM/NOR SW16 148 E2
Moorcroft Wy PIN HA5 47 J4
Moordown WOOL/PLUM SE18 115 G7
Moore Cl MORT/ESHN SW14 125 K2
MTCM * CR4 163 G1
WLGTN SM6 176 E6
Moore Crs DAGW RM9 79 H7
Moorefield Rd TOTM N17 56 B2
Mooreland Rd BMLY BR1 152 D6
Moore Park Rd FUL/PGN SW6 108 A6
Moore Rd NRWD SE19 149 J5
Moore St CHEL SW3 15 L5
Moore Wy BELMT SM2 174 E7
Moorey Cl SRTFD E15 76 D7
Moorfield Av EA W5 85 K3
Moorfield Rd CHSGTN KT9 172 A4
Moorfields LVPST EC2M 13 G3
Moorfields Highwalk
BARB EC2Y 13 G3
Moorgate LOTH EC2R 13 G4
Moorgate Pl LOTH * EC2R 13 G4
Moorhead Wy BKHTH/KID SE3 134 A3
Moorhen Cl ERITH DA8 118 E6
Moorhouse Rd BAY/PAD W2 8 A4
KTN/HRWW/W HA3 49 K2
The Moorings CHSWK * W4 105 H5
Moorland Cl HSLWW TW4 123 F6
Moorland Rd BRXN/ST SW9 130 C3
Moorlands Av MLHL NW7 37 K5
Moor La BARB EC2Y 13 G3
CHSGTN KT9 172 A3
Moor La Crossing WATW WD18 20 A6
Moormead Dr HOR/WEW KT19 173 G4
Moor Mead Rd TWK TW1 124 B5
Moor Park Gdns
KUTN/CMB KT2 145 G6
NTHWD * HA6 32 A1
Moor Park Rd NTHWD HA6 32 B5
Moorside Rd BMLY BR1 152 C3
Moor St SOHO/SHAV W1D 11 H5
Moortown Rd OXHEY WD19 33 G3
Moor Vw WATW WD18 20 E6
Morant St POP/IOD E14 93 J6
Mora Rd CRICK NW2 70 A3
Mora St FSBYE EC1V 6 F8
Morat St BRXN/ST SW9 110 A7
Moravian Pl WBPTN SW10 108 C5
Moravian St BETH E2 92 E1
Moray Av HYS/HAR UB3 82 D7
Moray Cl EDGW * HA8 36 D1
Moray Ms HOLWY N7 73 F1
Moray Rd HOLWY N7 73 F1
Morcambe St WALW SE17 18 F6
Mordaunt Gdns DAGW RM9 80 A6
Mordaunt Rd WLSDN NW10 69 F7
Mordaunt St BRXN/ST SW9 130 A2
Morden Ct MRDN SM4 162 A3
Morden Court Pde
WIM/MER * SW19 162 A2
Morden Gdns GFD/PVL UB6 67 F4
MTCM CR4 162 C3
Morden Hall Rd MRDN SM4 162 A2
Morden Hl LEW SE13 133 F1
Morden La LEW SE13 133 F1
Morden Rd BKHTH/KID SE3 133 K1
CHDH RM6 62 A6
WIM/MER SW19 162 A1
Morden Road Ms
BKHTH/KID SE3 133 K1
Morden St LEW SE13 112 E7
Morden Wy CHEAM SM3 161 K6
Morden Wharf Rd
GNWCH SE10 113 H2
Mordon Rd GDMY/SEVK IG3 61 F6
Mordred Rd CAT SE6 152 C1
Morecambe Cl HCH RM12 81 K4

WCHPL * E1 93 F4
Morecambe Gdns STAN HA7 35 K3
Morecambe Ter UED * N18 41 K3
More Cl CAN/RD E16 94 D5
WKENS W14 107 G3
Morecoombe Cl
KUTN/CMB KT2 144 D6
Moree Wy UED N18 42 C3
Moreland Cottages BOW * E3 93 J1
Moreland St FSBYE EC1V 6 D7
Moreland Wy CHING E4 43 K2
More La ESH/CLAY KT10 170 B2
Morella Rd BAL SW12 128 E6
Moremead Rd CAT SE6 151 H3
Morena St CAT SE6 132 E6
Moresby Av BRYLDS KT5 159 J6
Moresby Rd CLPT E5 56 D7
Mores Gdn CHEL * SW3 108 C5
Moreton Av ISLW TW7 103 J7
Moreton Cl CLPT E5 74 E1
MLHL NW7 38 A5
SEVS/STOTM N15 55 K5
Moreton Ct DART DA1 138 B2
Moreton Gdns WFD IG8 45 J4
Moreton Pl PIM SW1V 16 F7
Moreton Rd SAND/SEL CR2 177 K4
SEVS/STOTM N15 55 K5
WPK KT4 173 J1
Moreton St PIM SW1V 16 F7
Moreton Ter PIM SW1V 16 F7
Moreton Terrace Ms South
PIM SW1V 16 F7
Morford Cl RSLP HA4 47 F6
Morford Wy RSLP HA4 47 F6
Morgan Av WALTH E17 58 B3
Morgan Cl DAGE RM10 80 C6
NTHWD HA6 32 D4
Morgan Rd BMLY BR1 152 E6
HOLWY N7 73 G4
NKENS W10 88 D4
Morgan's La HYS/HAR UB3 82 B4
STHWK SE1 13 J9
Morgan St BOW E3 93 G2
CAN/RD E16 94 D4
Morgan Wy WFD IG8 45 J5
Moriatry Cl HOLWY N7 72 E3
Morie St WAND/EARL SW18 128 A3
Morieux Rd LEY E10 57 H7
Moring Rd TOOT SW17 148 A3
Morkyns Wk DUL * SE21 150 A2
Morland Av CROY/NA CR0 165 F7
DART DA1 138 E4
Morland Cl GLDGN NW11 53 F7
HPTN TW12 141 K4
MTCM CR4 162 D2
Morland Est HACK * E8 74 C6
Morland Gdns STHL UB1 84 B7
WLSDN NW10 69 F6
Morland Ms IS N1 6 B2
Morland Rd CROY/NA CR0 165 G6
DAGE RM10 80 C6
IL IG1 78 B1
KTN/HRWW/W HA3 50 A4
PGE/AN SE20 151 F6
SUT SM1 175 G4
WALTH E17 57 F4
Morley Av CHING E4 44 B6
UED N18 42 C3
WDGN N22 55 G1
Morley Crs EDGW HA8 36 E1
RSLP HA4 65 G1
Morley Crs East STAN HA7 49 J2
Morley Crs West STAN HA7 49 J2
Morley Rd BARK IG11 78 D7
CHDH RM6 62 A4
CHEAM SM3 161 J7
CHST BR7 154 C7
LEW SE13 133 F3
LEY E10 58 A7
SRTFD E15 94 D1
TWK TW1 124 E5
Morley St STHWK SE1 18 B2
Morna Rd CMBW SE5 130 D1
Morning La HOM E9 74 E5
Morningside Rd WPK KT4 173 K1
Mornington Av BMLY BR1 168 B2
IL IG1 60 A6
WKENS W14 107 J3
Mornington Ct BXLY DA5 138 A7
Mornington Crs CAMTN NW1 4 E5
HEST TW5 102 A7
Mornington Gv BOW E3 93 J2
Mornington Ms CMBW SE5 110 D7
Mornington Pl CAMTN NW1 4 D5
Mornington Rd ASHF TW15 140 A4
DEPT SE8 112 C6
GFD/PVL UB6 84 B4
WAN E11 58 D7
WFD IG8 44 E3
Mornington St CAMTN NW1 4 D5
Mornington Ter CAMTN NW1 4 D4
Mornington Wk
RCHPK/HAM TW10 143 J3
Morocco St STHWK SE1 19 J2
Morpeth Gv HOM E9 75 F7
Morpeth Rd HOM E9 74 E7
Morpeth St BETH E2 93 F2
Morpeth Ter WEST SW1P 16 E4
Morpeth Wk TOTM * N17 42 D6
Morrab Gdns GDMY/SEVK IG3 79 F2
Morrel Cl BAR EN5 27 G2
Morris Av MNPK E12 77 K4
Morris Bishop Ter HGT * N6 54 A5
Morris Cl CROY/NA CR0 166 B5
Morris Ct CHING E4 43 K2
Morris Gdns DART DA1 139 K4
WAND/EARL SW18 127 K6
Morrish Rd BRXS/STRHM SW2 129 K6
Morrison Av TOTM N17 56 A2
Morrison Rd BARK IG11 98 A1
DAGW RM9 80 A7
YEAD UB4 83 F2
Morrison St BTSEA SW11 129 F2
Morris Pl FSBYPK N4 73 G1
Morris Rd BCTR RM8 80 B1
ISLW TW7 124 A2
POP/IOD E14 93 K4
WAN E11 76 C3
Morris St WCHPL E1 92 D5
Morriston Cl OXHEY WD19 33 G4
Morse Cl PLSTW E13 94 E2
Morshead Rd MV/WKIL W9 2 B8
Morson Rd PEND EN3 31 G5
Morteyne Rd TOTM N17 41 K7
Mortham St SRTFD E15 76 C7
Mortimer Cl BAL SW12 148 D1
BUSH WD23 22 B5
CRICK NW2 70 D2
Mortimer Crs STJWD NW8 2 C4
WPK KT4 173 F2
Mortimer Dr EN EN1 29 K4
Mortimer Pl KIL/WHAMP NW6 2 C4
Mortimer Rd EHAM E6 95 K2
ERITH DA8 118 A5
IS N1 7 K2
MTCM CR4 147 K7
WEA W13 85 J5
WLSDN NW10 88 A2
Mortimer Sq NTGHL W11 88 B6
Mortimer St REGST W1B 10 D4
Mortimer Ter KTTN * NW5 72 B3
Mortlake Cl CROY/NA CR0 177 F2
Mortlake Dr MTCM CR4 147 J7
Mortlake High St
MORT/ESHN SW14 126 A2
Mortlake Rd CAN/RD E16 95 F5
IL IG1 78 C3
MORT/ESHN SW14 125 J2
Morton Cl CROY/NA CR0 177 F6
Morton Crs FBAR/BDGN N11 40 D3
Morton Gdns WLGTN SM6 176 C4
Morton Ms ECT * SW5 14 C6
Morton Pl STHWK SE1 18 A4
Morton Rd IS N1 6 F2
MRDN SM4 162 C4
SRTFD E15 76 D6
Morton Wy STHGT/OAK N14 40 C2
Morvale Cl BELV DA17 117 G3
Morval Rd BRXS/STRHM SW2 130 B4
Morven Rd TOOT SW17 147 K2
Morville St BOW E3 93 J1
Morwell St FITZ W1T 11 G3
Moscow Pl BAY/PAD W2 8 C6
Moscow Rd BAY/PAD W2 8 C6
Moselle Av WDGN N22 55 G1
Moselle Cl CEND/HSY/T N8 55 F2
Moselle St TOTM N17 42 B6
Mossborough Cl
NFNCH/WDSP N12 39 F5
Mossbury Rd BTSEA SW11 128 D2
Moss Cl PIN HA5 47 K1
WCHPL E1 92 C4
Mossdown Cl BELV DA17 117 H3
Mossford Gn BARK/HLT IG6 60 B2
Mossford La BARK/HLT IG6 60 C1
Mossford St BOW E3 93 H3
Moss Gdns SAND/SEL CR2 179 F6
Moss Hall Crs NFNCH/WDSP N12 39 F5
Moss Hall Gv FNCH N3 39 F5
Moss La PIN HA5 47 J1
ROM RM1 63 H5
Mosslea Rd HAYES BR2 168 C4
PGE/AN SE20 150 E6
Mossop St CHEL SW3 15 K5
Moss Rd DAGE RM10 80 C6
Mossville Gdns MRDN SM4 161 J2
Moston Cl HYS/HAR UB3 101 J4
Mostyn Av WBLY HA9 68 B4
Mostyn Gdns WLSDN NW10 88 B2
Mostyn Gv BOW E3 93 H1
Mostyn Rd BRXN/ST SW9 110 B7
BUSH WD23 22 C4
EDGW HA8 37 G6
WIM/MER SW19 161 J1
Mosul Wy HAYES BR2 168 D5
Motcomb St KTBR SW1X 16 A3
Moth Cl WLGTN SM6 176 E6
The Mothers Sq CLPT * E5 74 D3
Motley St VX/NE SW8 129 H1
Motspur Pk NWMAL KT3 160 C5
Mottingham Gdns
ELTH/MOT SE9 134 C7
Mottingham La ELTH/MOT SE9 134 B7
Mottingham Rd ED N9 31 F5
ELTH/MOT SE9 153 K2
Mottisfont Rd ABYW SE2 116 B2
Moulins Rd HOM E9 74 E6
Moulton Av HEST TW5 122 D1
Moundfield Rd STNW/STAM N16 56 C5
The Mount BMLY * BR1 153 J7
BXLYHS * DA6 137 J4
CLPT * E5 74 D1
ESH/CLAY KT10 170 A5
HAMP NW3 71 G3
NTHLT * UB5 66 B4
NWMAL KT3 160 C2
TRDG/WHET N20 39 G1
WBLY HA9 68 D1
WPK KT4 173 K3
Mountacre Cl SYD SE26 150 B3
Mount Adon Pk EDUL SE22 131 H6
Mountague Pl POP/IOD E14 94 A6
Mount Angelus Rd
PUT/ROE SW15 126 C6
Mount Ararat Rd
RCHPK/HAM TW10 125 F4
Mount Ash Rd SYD SE26 150 D2
Mount Av CHING E4 43 J2
STHL UB1 84 A5
Mountbatten Cl NRWD SE19 150 A4
WOOL/PLUM SE18 115 K5
Mountbatten Ct BKHH IG9 45 H1
Mountbel Rd
KTN/HRWW/W * HA3 49 G1
Mount Cl BMLY BR1 153 J7
CAR SM5 176 A7
EA * W5 85 J4
EBAR EN4 28 A3
Mountcombe Cl SURB KT6 159 F6
Mount Cottages BXLYHS * DA6 137 F3
Mount Ct WWKM BR4 180 C1
Mount Culver Av SCUP DA14 155 K5
Mount Dr CDALE/KGS NW9 68 E1
RYLN/HDSTN HA2 47 K4
Mountearl Gdns
STRHM/NOR SW16 149 F2
Mount Echo Av CHING E4 31 K7
Mount Echo Dr CHING E4 31 K7
Mount Ephraim La
STRHM/NOR SW16 148 D2
Mount Ephraim Rd
STRHM/NOR SW16 148 D2
Mountfield Cl LEW SE13 133 G6
Mountfield Rd EA W5 85 K5
EHAM E6 95 K1
FNCH N3 52 E2
Mountford St WCHPL E1 92 C5
Mountfort Ter IS N1 6 A2
Mount Gdns SYD SE26 150 D2
Mount Gv EDGW HA8 36 E2
Mountgrove Rd HBRY N5 73 J2
Mounthurst Rd HAYES BR2 167 K6
Mountington Park Cl
KTN/HRWW/W HA3 49 K5
Mountjoy Cl THMD SE28 116 C1
Mount Mills FSBYE EC1V 6 D8
Mount Nod Rd
STRHM/NOR SW16 149 F2
Mount Pde EBAR * EN4 27 J3
Mount Pk CAR SM5 176 A7
Mount Park Av HRW HA1 66 D1
SAND/SEL CR2 177 H7
Mount Park Crs EA W5 85 K5
Mount Park Rd EA W5 85 K4
HRW HA1 66 D1
PIN HA5 46 E4
Mount Pl ACT W3 86 D7
Mount Pleasant ALP/SUD HA0 68 A7
EBAR EN4 27 K3
FSBYW WC1X 11 M1
HRW * HA1 66 E1
RSLP HA4 65 G2
WNWD SE27 149 J3
Mount Pleasant Crs
FSBYPK * N4 55 F6
Mount Pleasant Hl CLPT E5 74 D1
Mount Pleasant La CLPT E5 56 D7
Mount Pleasant Pl
WOOL/PLUM SE18 115 J3
Mount Pleasant Rd DART DA1 139 J5
EA W5 85 J3
LEW SE13 133 F5
NWMAL KT3 159 K2
TOTM N17 56 A2
WALTH E17 57 G1
WLSDN NW10 70 A6
Mount Pleasant Vls FSBYPK N4 55 F6
Mount Ri FSTH SE23 150 E1
Mount Rd BCTR RM8 62 B7
BXLYHS DA6 137 F4
CHSGTN KT9 172 B4
CRICK NW2 69 K2
DART DA1 138 C5
EBAR EN4 27 J4
FELT TW13 141 J2
HDN NW4 51 J5
HYS/HAR UB3 101 K1
IL IG1 78 B4
MTCM CR4 162 C1
NRWD * SE19 149 K5
NWMAL KT3 160 A2
WAND/EARL SW18 146 E1
Mount Rw MYFR/PKLN W1K 10 C7
Mountside KTN/HRWW/W HA3 35 F7
Mounts Pond Rd LEW SE13 133 G1
The Mount Sq HAMP * NW3 71 G2
Mount Stewart Av
KTN/HRWW/W HA3 49 K5
Mount St MYFR/PKLN W1K 10 A7
Mount Ter WCHPL E1 92 D4
Mountview MLHL NW7 37 F2
NTHWD HA6 32 E5
Mount Vw NWDGN * UB2 102 C3
Mount View Rd
CDALE/KGS NW9 51 F3
ESH/CLAY KT10 171 H6
FSBYPK N4 55 F6
Mount Vls WNWD SE27 149 H2
Mount Wy CAR SM5 176 A7
Mountwood E/WMO/HCT KT8 157 G2
Movers La BARK IG11 78 D7
Mowatt Cl ARCH N19 54 D7
Mowbray Gdns NTHLT * UB5 66 A7
Mowbray Rd BAR EN5 27 G3
EDGW HA8 36 C3
KIL/WHAMP NW6 70 C6
NRWD SE19 150 B7
RCHPK/HAM TW10 143 J2
Mowbrays Rd CRW RM5 62 E1
Mowlem St BETH E2 92 D1
Mowll St BRXN/ST SW9 110 B6
Moxon Cl PLSTW E13 94 D1
Moxon St BAR EN5 26 D2
MHST W1U 10 A3
Moye Cl BETH * E2 92 C1
Moyers Rd LEY E10 58 A7
Moylan Rd HMSMTH W6 107 H5
Moyne Pl WLSDN NW10 86 C2
Moynihan Dr STHGT/OAK N14 28 E4
Moys Cl CROY/NA CR0 163 K5
Moyser Rd STRHM/NOR SW16 148 B4
Mozart St NKENS W10 88 D2
Muchelney Rd MRDN SM4 162 B5
Muggeridge Cl SAND/SEL CR2 177 K4
Muggeridge Rd DAGE RM10 80 D3
Muir Cl WAND/EARL SW18 128 D5
Muirdown Av
MORT/ESHN SW14 125 K3
Muirfield ACT W3 87 G5
Muirfield Cl
BERM/RHTH * SE16 111 J4
OXHEY * WD19 33 G4
Muirfield Crs POP/IOD E14 112 E2
Muirfield Gn OXHEY WD19 33 G3
Muirfield Rd OXHEY WD19 33 G3
Muirkirk Rd CAT SE6 133 F7
Muir Rd CLPT E5 74 C3
Muir St CAN/RD E16 95 K7
Mulberry Av STWL/WRAY TW19 120 B7
Mulberry Cl CHEL * SW3 108 C5
CHING E4 43 J1
EBAR EN4 27 H3
GPK RM2 63 K3
HDN NW4 52 A2
NTHLT UB5 83 J1
STRHM/NOR SW16 148 C3
Mulberry Crs BTFD TW8 104 C6
WDR/YW UB7 100 D1
Mulberry Dr PUR RM19 119 J3
Mulberry La CROY/NA CR0 165 G7
Mulberry Ms NWCR SE14 112 C7
Mulberry Pde WDR/YW UB7 100 D2
Mulberry Pl HMSMTH W6 106 D4
Mulberry Rd HACK E8 7 L2
Mulberry St WCHPL E1 92 C5
Mulberry Wk CHEL SW3 15 H9
Mulberry Wy BARK/HLT IG6 60 C3
BELV DA17 117 K1
SWFD E18 59 F1
Mulgrave Rd BELMT SM2 174 D6
CROY/NA CR0 177 K2
EA W5 85 K2
HRW HA1 67 G1
WKENS W14 107 J5
WLSDN NW10 69 H3
WOOL/PLUM SE18 114 E3
Mulholland Cl MTCM CR4 163 G1
Mulkern Rd ARCH N19 54 D7
Mullards Cl MTCM CR4 162 E7
Mullet Gdns BETH E2 92 C2
Mullins Pth MORT/ESHN SW14 126 A2
Mullion Cl KTN/HRWW/W HA3 34 B7
Mullion Wk OXHEY WD19 33 H3
Mull Wk IS N1 73 J5
Mulready St STJWD NW8 9 J1
Multi Wy ACT W3 106 B1
Multon Rd WAND/EARL SW18 128 C6
Mumford Ct CITYW EC2V 12 F4
Mumford Rd HNHL SE24 130 C4
Muncaster Rd CLAP SW4 128 E3
Muncies Ms CAT SE6 152 A1
Mundania Rd EDUL SE22 131 J5
Munday Rd CAN/RD E16 94 E5
Munden St WKENS W14 107 H3
Mundesly Cl OXHEY WD19 33 G3
Mundford Rd CLPT E5 74 E1
Mundon Gdns IL IG1 60 D7
Mund St WKENS W14 107 J4
Mundy St IS N1 7 J7
Mungo-park Cl BUSH * WD23 34 C1
Mungo Park Rd RAIN RM13 81 J5
Munnings Gdns ISLW TW7 123 J4
Munro Dr FBAR/BDGN * N11 40 C5
Munro Ms NKENS W10 88 C4
Munro Rd BUSH WD23 22 B4
Munslow Gdns SUT SM1 175 G3
Munster Av HSLWW TW4 122 D3
Munster Gdns PLMGR N13 41 J3
Munster Ms FUL/PGN * SW6 107 J6
Munster Rd FUL/PGN SW6 107 H6
TEDD TW11 143 J5
Munster Sq CAMTN NW1 4 D8
Munton Rd WALW SE17 18 F5
Murchison Av BXLY DA5 136 E7
Murchison Rd LEY E10 76 A1
Murdock Cl CAN/RD E16 94 D5
Murdock St PECK SE15 111 J5
Murfett Cl WIM/MER SW19 146 C1
Muriel Av WATW WD18 21 G4
Muriel St IS N1 5 M5
Murillo Rd LEW SE13 133 G3
Murphy St STHWK SE1 18 A2
Murray Av BMLY BR1 168 A2
HSLW TW3 123 G4
Murray Crs PIN HA5 33 H7
Murray Gv IS N1 7 G6
Murray Ms CAMTN NW1 5 G1
Murray Rd EA W5 104 D3
NTHWD HA6 32 C7
RCHPK/HAM TW10 143 H1
WIM/MER SW19 146 B5
Murray Sq CAN/RD E16 94 E5
Murray St CAMTN NW1 4 F1
Murray Ter HAMP NW3 71 G3
Musard Rd WKENS W14 107 H5
Musbury St WCHPL E1 92 E5
Muscatel Pl CMBW SE5 111 F7
Muschamp Rd CAR SM5 175 J1
PECK SE15 131 G2
Muscovy St TWRH EC3N 13 K7
Museum St NOXST/BSQ WC1A 11 J4
Musgrave Crs FUL/PGN SW6 107 K6
Musgrave Rd ISLW TW7 104 A7
Musgrove Rd NWCR SE14 112 A7
Musjid Rd BTSEA SW11 128 C1
Musquash Wy HSLWW TW4 122 B1
Muston Rd CLPT E5 74 D1
Muswell Av MUSWH N10 54 B1
Muswell Hl MUSWH N10 54 B2
Muswell Hill Broadway
MUSWH N10 54 B2
Muswell Hill Pl MUSWH N10 54 B3
Muswell Hill Rd MUSWH N10 54 A3
Muswell Ms MUSWH N10 54 B2
Muswell Rd MUSWH N10 54 B1
Mutrix Rd KIL/WHAMP NW6 2 B3
Mutton Pl CAMTN NW1 72 A5
Muybridge Rd NWMAL KT3 159 K1
Myatt Rd BRXN/ST SW9 110 C7
Mycenae Rd BKHTH/KID SE3 113 K5
Myddelton Gdns WCHMH N21 29 J6
Myddelton Pk TRDG/WHET N20 39 H2
Myddelton Pas CLKNW EC1R 6 B7
Myddelton Rd CEND/HSY/T N8 54 E2
Myddelton Sq CLKNW EC1R 6 B7
Myddelton St CLKNW EC1R 6 B8
Myddleton Av FSBYPK N4 73 H1
Myddleton Rd WDGN N22 40 E6
Myers La NWCR SE14 112 A5
Mylis Cl SYD SE26 150 D3
Mylne Cl HMSMTH * W6 106 D4
Mylne St CLKNW EC1R 6 A6
Myra St ABYW SE2 116 B4
Myrdle St WCHPL E1 92 C4
Myrna Cl WIM/MER SW19 147 J6
Myron Pl LEW SE13 133 F2
Myrtle Aly WOOL/PLUM SE18 115 F2
Myrtle Av EBED/NFELT TW14 121 H3
RSLP HA4 46 E6
Myrtleberry Cl HACK * E8 74 B5
Myrtle Cl EBAR EN4 27 K7
ERITH DA8 118 B6
WDR/YW UB7 100 C3
Myrtledene Rd ABYW SE2 116 B4
Myrtle Gdns HNWL W7 84 E7
Myrtle Gv NWMAL KT3 159 K1
Myrtle Rd ACT W3 86 E7
CROY/NA CR0 179 J2
EHAM E6 77 J7
HPTN TW12 142 C5
HSLW TW3 123 H1
IL IG1 78 B1
PLMGR N13 41 J2
SUT SM1 175 G4
WALTH E17 57 G5
Myrtleside Cl NTHWD HA6 32 B6
Myrtle St IS N1 7 J6
Myrtle Wk IS N1 7 J6
Mysore Rd BTSEA SW11 128 E3
Myton Rd DUL SE21 149 K2

N

Nadine St CHARL SE7 114 B4
Nagle Cl WALTH E17 58 B1
Nag's Head La WELL DA16 136 C2
Nags Head Rd PEND EN3 30 E3
Nairne Gv EDUL SE22 130 E4
Nairn Gn OXHEY WD19 32 E2
Nairn Rd RSLP HA4 65 G5
Nairn St POP/IOD E14 94 A4
Nallhead Rd FELT TW13 141 G4
Namba Roy Cl
STRHM/NOR SW16 149 F3
Namton Dr STRHM/NOR SW16 164 A3
Nan Clark's La MLHL NW7 37 H1
Nancy Downs OXHEY WD19 21 G6
Nankin St POP/IOD E14 93 J5
Nansen Rd BTSEA SW11 129 F3
Nansen Village
NFNCH/WDSP * N12 39 F3
Nantes Cl WAND/EARL SW18 128 B3
Nant Rd CRICK NW2 70 D1
Nant St BETH E2 92 D2
Naoroji St FSBYW WC1X 6 A8
Napier Av FUL/PGN SW6 127 J2
POP/IOD E14 112 D4
Napier Cl DEPT SE8 112 C6
EMPK RM11 63 K7
WDR/YW UB7 100 C2
Napier Ct LEE/GVPK SE12 153 F1
Napier Dr BUSH WD23 21 J3
Napier Gv IS N1 6 F6
Napier Pl WKENS W14 107 J2
Napier Rd ALP/SUD HA0 67 K4
ASHF TW15 140 B6
BELV DA17 117 G3
EHAM E6 78 A7
HAYES BR2 168 A2
ISLW TW7 124 B3
PEND EN3 31 F4
SAND/SEL CR2 177 K6
SNWD SE25 165 J3
SRTFD E15 94 C1
TOTM N17 56 A2
WAN E11 76 C2
WDR/YW UB7 100 A7
WKENS W14 107 J2
WLSDN NW10 87 K2
Napier Ter IS N1 6 C2
Napier Wk ASHF TW15 140 B6
Napoleon Rd CLPT E5 74 D2
TWK * TW1 124 C6
Napton Cl YEAD UB4 83 J3
Narbonne Av CLAP SW4 129 H5
Narboro Ct ROM RM1 63 J5
Narborough Cl HGDN/ICK UB10 64 A1
Narborough St FUL/PGN SW6 128 A1
Narcissus Rd KIL/WHAMP NW6 70 E4
Narford Rd CLPT E5 74 C2
Narrow Boat Cl THMD SE28 115 J1
Narrow St ACT W3 86 D7
POP/IOD E14 93 G6
Narrow Wy HAYES BR2 168 D5
Nascot Pl WAT WD17 21 F1
Nascot Rd WAT WD17 21 F1
Nascot St SHB W12 88 A5
WAT WD17 21 F1
Naseby Cl ISLW TW7 103 K7
KIL/WHAMP NW6 2 F1
Naseby Rd CLAY IG5 45 K7
DAGE RM10 80 C2
NRWD SE19 149 K5
Nash Cl BORE WD6 24 B3
SUT SM1 175 H2
Nash Gn BMLY BR1 152 E6
Nash La HAYES BR2 180 E5
Nash Rd BROCKY SE4 132 B4
CHDH RM6 61 K3
ED N9 42 E1
Nash St CAMTN NW1 4 D7
Nash Wy KTN/HRWW/W HA3 49 H5
Nasmyth St HMSMTH W6 106 E2
Nassau Rd BARN SW13 106 C7
Nassau St GTPST W1W 10 E3
Nassington Rd HAMP NW3 71 J3
Natalie Cl EBED/NFELT TW14 121 G6
Natal Rd FBAR/BDGN N11 40 E4
IL IG1 78 B3
STRHM/NOR SW16 148 D5
THHTH CR7 164 E2
Nathaniel Cl WCHPL E1 13 M3
Nathans Rd ALP/SUD HA0 67 J1
Nathan Wy THMD SE28 116 A2
National Ter
BERM/RHTH * SE16 111 J1
Naval Rw POP/IOD E14 94 A6
Navarino Gv HACK E8 74 C5
Navarino Rd HACK E8 74 C5
Navarre Rd EHAM E6 95 J1
Navarre St BETH E2 7 L9
Navestock Cl CHING * E4 44 A2
Navestock Crs WFD IG8 45 G7
Navestock Ter WFD IG8 45 G6
Navigator Dr NWDGN UB2 103 H1
Navy St CLAP SW4 129 J2
Nayim Pl HACK E8 74 D5
Naylor Gv PEND EN3 31 F4
Naylor Rd PECK SE15 111 J6
TRDG/WHET N20 39 G1
Nazareth Cl PECK SE15 131 J1
Nazrul St BETH E2 7 L7
Neal Av STHL UB1 83 K3
Neal Cl NTHWD HA6 32 E7
Nealden St BRXN/ST SW9 130 A2
Neale Cl EFNCH N2 53 G2
Neal St LSQ/SEVD WC2H 11 J5
WATW WD18 21 G4
Neal Ter FSTH * SE23 132 A7
Neal Yd LSQ/SEVD WC2H 11 J5
Near Acre CDALE/KGS NW9 37 H7
Neasden Cl WLSDN NW10 69 G4
Neasden La WLSDN NW10 69 F2
Neasden La North
WLSDN NW10 69 G2
Neasham Rd BCTR RM8 79 H4
Neate St CMBW SE5 111 F5
Neath Gdns MRDN SM4 162 B5
Neathouse Pl PIM SW1V 16 E5
Neats Acre RSLP HA4 46 B6
Neatscourt Rd EHAM E6 95 H4
Neckinger STHWK SE1 19 M3
Neckinger Est
BERM/RHTH SE16 19 M3
Neckinger St STHWK SE1 19 M2
Nectarine Wy LEW SE13 132 E1
Needham Rd NTGHL W11 8 A5
Needleman St
BERM/RHTH SE16 112 A1
Neeld Crs HDN NW4 51 K4
WBLY HA9 68 C4
Neil Cl ASHF TW15 140 A4
Neils Yd LSQ/SEVD * WC2H 11 J5
Nelgarde Rd CAT SE6 132 D6
Nella Rd HMSMTH W6 107 G5
Nelldale Rd BERM/RHTH SE16 111 J3
Nello James Gdns WNWD SE27 149 K3
Nelson Cl CROY/NA CR0 164 C7
EBED/NFELT * TW14 121 J7
KIL/WHAMP NW6 2 A7
WOT/HER KT12 156 A7
Nelson Gdns BETH E2 92 C2
HSLW TW3 123 F5
Nelson Grove Rd
WIM/MER SW19 147 F7
Nelson Mandela Cl MUSWH N10 53 K1
Nelson Mandela Rd
BKHTH/KID SE3 134 B2
Nelson Pl IS N1 6 D6
SCUP DA14 155 G3
Nelson Rd BELV DA17 117 G4
CEND/HSY/T N8 55 F4
CHING E4 43 K5
DART DA1 139 F5
ED N9 42 D2
GNWCH SE10 113 F5
HAYES BR2 168 B3
HRW HA1 48 D7

HSLW TW3 123 F5
NWMAL KT3 160 A4
PEND EN3 31 F5
RAIN RM13 99 H1
SCUP DA14 155 G3
SEVS/STOTM N15 56 A3
STAN HA7 35 J5
WAN E11 58 E3
WDR/YW UB7 100 C7
WHTN TW2 123 G6
WIM/MER SW19 147 F6
Nelson Sq STHWK SE1 18 C1
Nelsons Rw CLAP SW4 129 J3
Nelson St CAN/RD E16 94 D6
EHAM E6 95 K1
WCHPL E1 92 D5
Nelsons Yd CAMTN NW1 4 E5
Nelson Ter FSBYE EC1V 6 D6
Nelson Wk HOR/WEW KT19 172 C7
Nemoure Rd ACT W3 86 E6
Nene Gdns FELT TW13 141 K1
Nene Rd HTHAIR TW6 100 E7
Nepaul Rd BTSEA SW11 128 D1
Nepean St PUT/ROE SW15 126 D5
Neptune Cl RAIN RM13 99 H1
Neptune Ct BORE * WD6 24 C2
Neptune Rd HRW HA1 48 D5
HTHAIR * TW6 101 F7
Neptune St BERM/RHTH SE16 111 K2
Nesbit Cl BKHTH/KID SE3 133 H2
Nesbit Rd ELTH/MOT SE9 134 C3
Nesbitts Aly BAR * EN5 26 D2
Nesbitt Sq NRWD * SE19 150 A6
Nesham St WAP E1W 92 C7
Ness Rd ERITH DA8 119 G5
Ness St BERM/RHTH SE16 111 H2
Nesta Rd WFD IG8 44 D5
Nestle's Av HYS/HAR UB3 101 J2
Nestor Av WCHMH N21 29 H5
Netheravon Rd CHSWK W4 106 C4
HNWL W7 85 F7
Netheravon Rd South CHSWK W4 106 C5
Netherbury Rd EA W5 104 E2
Netherby Gdns ENC/FH EN2 28 E3
Netherby Rd FSTH SE23 131 K6
Nether Cl FNCH N3 38 E6
Nether Ct MLHL * NW7 38 D5
Nethercourt Av FNCH N3 38 E5
Netherfield Gdns BARK IG11 78 D5
Netherfield Rd NFNCH/WDSP N12 39 F4
TOOT SW17 148 A2
Netherford Rd CLAP SW4 129 H1
Netherhall Gdns HAMP NW3 71 G4
Netherhall Wy HAMP NW3 71 G4
Netherlands Rd BAR EN5 27 H5
Netherleigh Cl ARCH * N19 54 B7
Netherpark Dr GPK RM2 63 H1
Nether St FNCH N3 38 E7
Netherton Gv WBPTN SW10 108 B5
Netherton Rd SEVS/STOTM N15 55 K5
TWK TW1 124 B4
Netherwood Pl WKENS * W14 107 G2
Netherwood Rd WKENS W14 107 G2
Netherwood St KIL/WHAMP NW6 70 D6
Netley Cl CHEAM SM3 174 B4
CROY/NA CR0 180 A6
Netley Dr WOT/HER KT12 156 E6
Netley Gdns MRDN SM4 162 B6
Netley Rd BTFD TW8 105 F5
GNTH/NBYPK IG2 60 D4
MRDN SM4 162 B6
WALTH E17 57 H4
Netley St CAMTN NW1 4 E8
Nettlecombe Cl BELMT SM2 175 F7
Nettleden Av WBLY HA9 68 C5
Nettlefold Pl WNWD SE27 149 H2
Nettlestead Cl BECK BR3 151 H6
Nettleton Rd HTHAIR TW6 100 E7
NWCR SE14 112 A6
Nettlewood Rd STRHM/NOR SW16 148 D6
Neuchatel Rd CAT SE6 151 H1
Nevada Cl NWMAL KT3 159 K3
Nevada St GNWCH SE10 113 F6
Nevern Pl ECT SW5 14 B6
Nevern Rd ECT SW5 14 A6
Nevern Sq ECT SW5 14 B7
Nevil Cl NTHWD HA6 32 B4
Neville Av NWMAL KT3 145 F7
Neville Cl ACT W3 105 K1
BFN/LL DA15 155 F3
HSLW TW3 123 F1
KIL/WHAMP NW6 88 D1
PECK SE15 111 H6
WAN E11 76 D2
Neville Dr EFNCH N2 53 G5
Neville Gdns BCTR RM8 79 K2
Neville Gill Cl WAND/EARL SW18 127 K5
Neville Pl WDGN N22 41 F7
Neville Rd BCTR RM8 79 K1
CROY/NA CR0 164 E6
EA W5 85 K3
FSTGT E7 76 E6
KIL/WHAMP * NW6 88 D1
KUT KT1 159 H1
RCHPK/HAM TW10 143 J2
Neville St SKENS SW7 15 G7
Neville Ter SKENS * SW7 15 G7
Neville Wk CAR SM5 162 D6
Nevill Rd STNW/STAM N16 74 A3
Nevil Wk CAR * SM5 162 D6
Nevin Dr CHING E4 31 K7
Nevinson Cl WAND/EARL SW18 128 C5
Nevis Rd TOOT SW17 148 A1
New Acres Rd THMD SE28 96 E7
Newall Rd HTHAIR TW6 101 F7
Newark Ct WOT/HER KT12 156 B7
Newark Crs WLSDN NW10 87 F2
Newark Gn BORE WD6 25 G2
Newark Knok EHAM E6 96 A5
Newark Rd SAND/SEL CR2 177 K5
Newark St WCHPL E1 92 D4
Newark Wy HDN NW4 51 J3
New Ash Cl EFNCH N2 53 H2
New Barn Cl CROY/NA CR0 177 F5
New Barns Av MTCM CR4 163 J3
New Barn St PLSTW E13 94 E3
Newbery Rd ERITH DA8 118 C7
Newbiggin Pth OXHEY WD19 33 G3
Newbold Cottages WCHPL * E1 92 E5
Newbolt Av CHEAM SM3 174 A4
Newbolt Rd STAN HA7 35 F5
New Bond St MYFR/PICC W1J 10 D6
Newborough Gn NWMAL KT3 160 A3
New Brent St HDN NW4 52 A4
New Bridge St STP EC4M 12 C5
New Broad St LVPST EC2M 13 H3
New Broadway EA W5 85 K6
Newburgh Rd ACT W3 86 E7
Newburgh St SOHO/CST W1F 10 E5
New Burlington Ms CONDST W1S 10 E6
New Burlington Pl CONDST W1S 10 E6
New Burlington St CONDST W1S 10 E6
Newburn St LBTH SE11 17 M7
Newbury Cl NTHLT UB5 65 K5
Newbury Gdns HOR/WEW KT19 173 H3
Newbury Ms KTTN NW5 72 A5
Newbury Rd CHING E4 44 A5
GNTH/NBYPK IG2 60 D5
HAYES BR2 167 K2
WDR/YW UB7 100 C7
Newbury St STBT EC1A 12 E3
Newbury Wy NTHLT UB5 65 J5
New Butt La DEPT * SE8 112 D6
Newby Cl EN EN1 30 A1
Newby Pl POP/IOD E14 94 A6
Newby St VX/NE SW8 129 G2
Newcastle Cl STP EC4M 12 C4
Newcastle Pl BAY/PAD W2 9 H3
Newcastle Rw CLKNW EC1R 12 B1
New Cavendish St MHST W1U 10 B3
New Change STP EC4M 12 E5
New Charles St FSBYE EC1V 6 D7
New Church Rd CMBW SE5 110 E6
New City Rd PLSTW E13 95 G2
New Cl FELT TW13 141 J4
WIM/MER SW19 162 B2
New College Ms IS * N1 6 B1
New College Pde HAMP * NW3 71 G5
Newcombe Pk ALP/SUD HA0 68 B7
MLHL NW7 37 G4
Newcombe St KENS * W8 8 B8
Newcome Gdns STRHM/NOR SW16 148 E3
Newcomen Rd BTSEA SW11 128 C2
WAN * E11 76 D2
Newcomen St STHWK SE1 19 G1
New Compton St LSQ/SEVD * WC2H 11 H5
New Ct NTHLT UB5 66 B4
TPL/STR * WC2R 12 A6
Newcourt St STJWD NW8 3 J6
New Covent Garden Market VX/NE SW8 17 H9
New Crane Pl WAP * E1W 92 E7
New Crescent Yd WLSDN * NW10 87 H1
Newdales Cl ED N9 42 C1
Newdene Av NTHLT UB5 83 H1
Newdigate STRHM/NOR * SW16 149 G3
Newell St POP/IOD E14 93 H6
New End HAMP NW3 71 G3
New End Sq HAMP NW3 71 H3
Newent Cl CAR SM5 162 E7
PECK SE15 111 F6
New Era Est IS N1 7 J4
New Farm Av HAYES BR2 167 K3
New Farm La NTHWD HA6 32 C7
New Ferry Ap WOOL/PLUM SE18 115 F2
New Fetter La FLST/FETLN EC4A 12 B4
Newfield Cl HPTN TW12 142 A7
Newfield Ri CRICK NW2 69 J2
Newgale Gdns EDGW HA8 36 B7
New Garden Dr WDR/YW UB7 100 B1
Newgate CROY/NA CR0 164 D7
Newgate Cl FELT TW13 141 J1
Newgate St CHING E4 44 C2
STBT EC1A 12 D4
New Globe Wk STHWK SE1 12 E8
New Goulston St WCHPL E1 13 L4
New Green Pl NRWD SE19 150 A5
Newham's Rw STHWK SE1 19 K2
Newham Wy CAN/RD E16 94 D4
Newhaven Cl HYS/HAR UB3 101 J3
Newhaven Crs ASHF TW15 140 B4
Newhaven Gdns ELTH/MOT SE9 134 C3
Newhaven La CAN/RD E16 94 E4
Newhaven Rd SNWD SE25 164 E4
New Heston Rd HEST TW5 102 E6
Newhouse Av CHDH RM6 61 K2
Newhouse Cl NWMAL KT3 160 B6
Newhouse Wk MRDN SM4 162 B6
Newick Cl BXLY DA5 137 J5
Newick Rd CLPT E5 74 D2
Newing Gn BMLY BR1 153 H6
Newington Barrow Wy HOLWY N7 73 F2
Newington Butts LBTH SE11 18 D6
Newington Cswy STHWK SE1 18 E3
Newington Gn STNW/STAM N16 73 K4
Newington Green Rd IS N1 73 K4
New Inn Broadway SDTCH * EC2A 7 K9
New Inn Sq SDTCH * EC2A 7 K9
New Inn St SDTCH * EC2A 7 K9
New Inn Yd SDTCH EC2A 7 K9
New Kelvin Av TEDD TW11 142 E5
New Kent Rd STHWK SE1 18 E5
New Kings Rd FUL/PGN SW6 127 J1
New King St DEPT SE8 112 D5
Newland Cl PIN HA5 33 J5
Newland Gdns HNWL W7 104 B1
Newland Rd CEND/HSY/T N8 54 E2
Newlands Av THDIT KT7 157 K7
Newlands Cl ALP/SUD HA0 67 J5
EDGW HA8 36 A2
NWDGN UB2 102 D4
Newlands Ct WBLY HA9 68 C1
Newlands Pk SYD SE26 150 E5
Newlands Pl BAR EN5 26 B4
Newlands Quay WAP E1W 92 E6
Newlands Rd STRHM/NOR SW16 163 K1
WFD IG8 44 D1
The Newlands WLGTN SM6 176 C6
Newland St CAN/RD E16 95 J7
Newlands Wy CHSGTN KT9 171 J4
Newlands Wd CROY/NA CR0 179 H7
Newlands Woods CROY/NA * CR0 179 H7
Newling Cl EHAM E6 95 K5
Newling Est BETH E2 7 M8
New London St MON * EC3R 13 K6
New Lydenburg St CHARL SE7 114 B2
Newlyn Gdns RYLN/HDSTN HA2 47 K6
Newlyn Rd BAR EN5 26 D3
TOTM N17 42 B7
WELL DA16 136 A1
Newman Rd BMLY BR1 152 E7
CROY/NA CR0 164 A6
HYS/HAR UB3 83 F6
PLSTW E13 95 F2
WALTH E17 57 F4
Newman's Rw LINN WC2A 11 M3
Newman St FITZ W1T 10 F3
Newman's Wy EBAR EN4 27 G1
Newmarket Av NTHLT UB5 66 A4
Newmarsh Rd THMD SE28 97 F7
New Mill Rd STMC/STPC BR5 155 J7
Newminster Ct ENC/FH * EN2 29 H1
Newminster Rd MRDN SM4 162 B5
New Mount St SRTFD E15 76 B6
Newnham Av RSLP HA4 47 G7
Newnham Cl NTHLT UB5 66 C5
THHTH CR7 164 D1
Newnham Gdns NTHLT UB5 66 C5
Newnham Gn WDGN * N22 41 G7
Newnham Rd WDGN N22 41 F7
Newnhams Cl BMLY BR1 168 E2
Newnham Ter STHWK SE1 18 A3
Newnham Wy KTN/HRWW/W HA3 50 A4
New North Pl SDTCH EC2A 7 J9
New North Rd IS N1 6 F3
New North St BMSBY WC1N 11 L2
Newnton Cl FSBYPK N4 55 K6
New Oak Rd EFNCH N2 53 G1
New Oxford St NOXST/BSQ WC1A 11 H4
New Park Av PLMGR N13 41 J2
New Park Cl NTHLT UB5 65 J5
New Park Est UED N18 42 E4
New Park Rd ASHF TW15 140 A4
BRXS/STRHM SW2 129 K7
New Place Sq BERM/RHTH * SE16 111 J2
New Plaistow Rd SRTFD E15 76 C7
New Pond Pde RSLP * HA4 64 E2
Newport Av POP/IOD E14 94 B6
Newport Ct SOHO/SHAV W1D 11 H6
Newport Md OXHEY * WD19 33 H3
Newport Pl SOHO/SHAV * W1D 11 H6
Newport Rd BARN SW13 106 D7
HTHAIR TW6 100 D7
LEY E10 76 B1
WALTH * E17 57 G3
YEAD UB4 82 B4
Newport St LBTH SE11 17 L6
Newquay Crs RYLN/HDSTN HA2 65 J1
Newquay Gdns OXHEY WD19 33 F1
Newquay Rd CAT SE6 151 K1
New Quebec St MBLAR W1H 9 M5
New River Crs PLMGR N13 41 H3
New River Wy STNW/STAM N16 55 K6
New Rd ABYW SE2 116 E3
BTFD * TW8 104 E5
CEND/HSY/T N8 54 D4
CHING E4 43 K3
DAGW RM9 80 C7
E/WMO/HCT KT8 157 F2
EBED/NFELT TW14 121 G5
EBED/NFELT TW14 122 A7
ED N9 42 C2
ESH/CLAY KT10 170 C3
FELT TW13 141 J4
GDMY/SEVK IG3 78 E1
HGDN/ICK UB10 82 A3
HRW HA1 67 F3
HSLW TW3 123 G3
HYS/HAR UB3 101 F6
KUTN/CMB KT2 144 C6
MLHL NW7 38 C6
MTCM CR4 163 F7
RAIN RM13 99 J2
RCHPK/HAM TW10 143 J3
WAT WD17 21 G3
WCHPL E1 92 D4
WDGN N22 41 J7
WELL DA16 136 C1
New Road Hl HAYES BR2 181 J7
New Rw CHCR WC2N 11 J6
Newry Rd TWK TW1 124 B3
Newsam Av SEVS/STOTM N15 55 K4
Newsholme Dr WCHMH N21 29 F4
New Spring Gardens Wk LBTH * SE11 17 K8
New Sq LINN WC2A 11 M4
Newstead Cl NFNCH/WDSP N12 39 J5
Newstead Ct NTHLT * UB5 83 J2
Newstead Rd LEE/GVPK SE12 133 J6
Newstead Wk MRDN SM4 162 B6
Newstead Wy WIM/MER SW19 146 B3
New St LVPST EC2M 13 K3
WATW * WD18 21 G3
New Street Hl BMLY BR1 153 F4
New Street Sq FLST/FETLN EC4A 12 B4
Newton Av ACT W3 105 K1
MUSWH N10 40 A7
Newton Cl RYLN/HDSTN HA2 66 A1
WALTH E17 57 G5
Newton Crs BORE WD6 24 E3
Newton Gv CHSWK W4 106 B2
Newton Rd ALP/SUD HA0 68 B6
BAY/PAD W2 8 B5
CRICK NW2 70 A3
ISLW TW7 124 A1
KTN/HRWW/W HA3 34 E7
SEVS/STOTM N15 56 B4
SRTFD * E15 76 B4
WDR/YW UB7 100 B7
WELL DA16 136 B2
WIM/MER SW19 146 C6
Newtons Cl RAIN RM13 81 G6
Newton St HOL/ALD WC2B 11 K4
Newton's Yd WAND/EARL SW18 127 K4
Newton Ter HAYES BR2 168 C5
Newton Wk EDGW HA8 36 E7
Newton Wy UED N18 41 J4
New Tower Buildings WAP * E1W 92 D7
Newtown St BTSEA SW11 109 G7
New Trinity Rd EFNCH N2 53 H2
New Union Cl POP/IOD E14 113 F2
New Union St BARB EC2Y 13 G3
New Vls TOTM * N17 42 C7
New Wanstead WAN E11 58 E5
New Way Rd CDALE/KGS NW9 51 G3
New Wharf Rd IS N1 5 K5
New Zealand Wy RAIN RM13 99 H2
Niagara Av EA W5 104 D3
Niagara Cl IS N1 6 F5
Nibthwaite Rd HRW HA1 48 E4
Nicholas Cl GFD/PVL UB6 84 B1
Nicholas Gdns EA W5 85 K7
Nicholas La MANHO EC4N 13 H6
Nicholas Rd BCTR RM8 80 B1
BORE WD6 24 B5
CROY/NA CR0 176 E3
WCHPL E1 92 E3
Nicholas Wy NTHWD HA6 32 A7
Nicholay Rd ARCH N19 54 D7
Nicholes Rd HSLW TW3 123 F3
Nichol La BMLY BR1 152 E6
Nichollsfield Wk HOLWY N7 72 E4
Nicholl St BETH E2 74 C7
Nichols Cl FSBYPK * N4 55 G7
Nichols Gn EA W5 86 A4
Nicholson Dr BUSH WD23 22 C7
Nicholson Ms KUT KT1 159 F3
Nicholson Rd CROY/NA CR0 165 G7
Nicholson St STHWK SE1 12 C9
Nickelby Cl THMD SE28 97 J5
Nicola Cl KTN/HRWW/W HA3 48 D1
SAND/SEL CR2 177 J5
Nicoll Pl HDN NW4 51 K5
Nicoll Rd WLSDN NW10 69 G7
Nicoll Wy BORE WD6 25 F4
Nicosia Rd WAND/EARL SW18 128 D6
Niederwald Rd SYD SE26 151 G3
Nield Rd HYS/HAR UB3 101 J1
Nigel Cl NTHLT UB5 65 J7
Nigel Fisher Wy CHSGTN KT9 171 J6
Nigel Ms IL IG1 78 B3
Nigel Playfair Av HMSMTH W6 106 E4
Nigel Rd FSTGT E7 77 G4
PECK SE15 131 H2
Nigeria Rd CHARL SE7 114 B6
Nightingale Av CHING E4 44 C4
Nightingale Cl CAR SM5 176 A1
CHING E4 44 C3
CHSWK W4 105 K5
PIN HA5 47 G4
Nightingale Dr HOR/WEW KT19 172 D5
Nightingale Gv LEW SE13 133 G4
Nightingale La BAL SW12 128 E6
BMLY BR1 168 B1
CEND/HSY/T N8 54 E3
RCHPK/HAM TW10 125 F6
WAN E11 59 F4
Nightingale Ms KUT * KT1 158 E2
LBTH SE11 18 B5
Nightingale Pl WBPTN SW10 14 F9
WOOL/PLUM SE18 115 F5
Nightingale Rd BUSH WD23 22 A4
CAR SM5 175 K2
CLPT E5 74 D2
E/WMO/HCT KT8 157 G4
ED N9 30 E6
HNWL W7 85 F7
HPTN TW12 142 A5
STMC/STPC BR5 169 H5
WDGN N22 40 E7
WLSDN NW10 87 H1
WOT/HER * KT12 156 B6
The Nightingales STWL/WRAY TW19 120 C7
Nightingale Sq BAL SW12 129 F6
Nightingale V WOOL/PLUM SE18 115 F5
Nightingale Wk BAL SW12 129 G5
Nightingale Wy EHAM E6 95 J4
Nigntingale Av HRW HA1 49 H6
Nile Cl STNW/STAM N16 74 B2
Nile Dr ED N9 42 E2
Nile Rd PLSTW E13 95 G1
Nile St IS N1 7 G7
Nile Ter PECK SE15 19 M8
Nimmo Dr BUSH WD23 22 D6
Nimrod Cl NTHLT UB5 83 H2
Nimrod Pas IS N1 74 A5
Nimrod Rd STRHM/NOR SW16 148 B5
Nina Mackay Cl SRTFD * E15 76 C7
Nine Acres Cl MNPK E12 77 J4
Nine Elms Cl EBED/NFELT TW14 121 J7
Nine Elms La VX/NE SW8 109 H6
Nineteenth Rd MTCM CR4 163 K3
Ninth Av HYS/HAR UB3 82 E6
Nithdale Rd WOOL/PLUM SE18 115 G6
Nithsdale Gv HGDN/ICK UB10 64 A2
Niton Cl BAR EN5 26 B5
Niton Rd RCH/KEW * TW9 125 H2
Niton St FUL/PGN SW6 107 G6
No 1 St WOOL/PLUM SE18 115 G2
No 2 St WOOL/PLUM SE18 115 G2
Nobel Dr HYS/HAR UB3 101 H6
Nobel Rd UED N18 42 E3
Noble Cnr HEST * TW5 103 F7
Noble St CITYW EC2V 12 E4
Noel Rd ACT W3 86 C5
EHAM E6 95 J3
IS N1 6 C5
Noel St SOHO/CST * W1F 10 F5
Nolan Wy CLPT E5 74 C3
Nolton Pl EDGW HA8 36 B7
Nonsuch Pl CHEAM * SM3 174 B6
Norbiton Av KUT KT1 159 H1
KUTN/CMB KT2 144 C7
Norbiton Common Rd NWMAL KT3 159 J2
Norbiton Rd POP/IOD E14 93 H5
Norbroke St ACT W3 87 H6
Norburn St NKENS W10 88 C4
Norbury Av HSLW TW3 123 J4
STRHM/NOR SW16 149 F7
Norbury Cl STRHM/NOR SW16 149 G7
Norbury Court Rd STRHM/NOR SW16 163 K1
Norbury Crs STRHM/NOR SW16 164 B1
Norbury Cross STRHM/NOR SW16 163 K2
Norbury Gdns CHDH RM6 61 K4
Norbury Gv MLHL NW7 37 G2
Norbury Hl STRHM/NOR SW16 149 G6
Norbury Ri STRHM/NOR SW16 163 K2
Norbury Rd CHING E4 43 J4
THHTH CR7 164 D1
Norbury Vls KUT * KT1 159 G1
Norcombe Gdns KTN/HRWW/W HA3 49 J5
Norcott Cl YEAD UB4 83 G3
Norcott Rd STNW/STAM N16 74 C1
Norcroft Gdns EDUL SE22 131 H6
Norcutt Rd WHTN TW2 123 K7
Nordenfeldt Rd ERITH DA8 118 A4
Norfolk Av PLMGR N13 41 H5
SEVS/STOTM N15 56 B5
Norfolk Cl DART DA1 139 K5
EBAR EN4 28 A3
EFNCH N2 53 J2
PLMGR N13 41 H5
TWK * TW1 124 C5
Norfolk Ct BAR * EN5 26 C3
Norfolk Crs BAY/PAD W2 9 J4
BFN/LL DA15 135 K6
Norfolk Gdns BORE WD6 25 F3
BXLYHN DA7 117 G7
Norfolk House Rd STRHM/NOR SW16 148 D2
Norfolk Ms NKENS W10 88 C4
Norfolk Pl BAY/PAD W2 9 H4
WELL DA16 136 B1
Norfolk Rd BAR EN5 26 E2
BARK IG11 78 E6
DAGE RM10 80 D4
EHAM E6 77 K7
ESH/CLAY KT10 170 E4
FELT TW13 122 B7
GDMY/SEVK IG3 60 E7
HRW HA1 48 B4
PEND EN3 30 D4
ROMW/RG RM7 62 E5
STJWD NW8 3 H4
THHTH CR7 164 D2
WALTH E17 43 G7
WIM/MER SW19 147 J6
WLSDN NW10 69 G6
Norfolk Rw STHWK SE1 17 L5
Norfolk Sq BAY/PAD W2 9 H5
Norfolk Square Ms BAY/PAD W2 9 H5
Norfolk St FSTGT E7 76 E4
Norgrove St BAL SW12 129 F7
Norhyrst Av SNWD SE25 165 G2
Norland Pl NTGHL W11 88 C7
Norland Rd NTGHL W11 88 B7
Norlands Crs CHST BR7 154 B7
Norlands Ga CHST * BR7 154 B7
Norland Sq NTGHL W11 88 C7
Norley V PUT/ROE SW15 126 D7
Norlington Rd WAN E11 58 A7
Norman Av FELT TW13 141 J1
STHL UB1 83 J6
TWK TW1 124 C6
WDGN N22 41 J7
Normanby Cl PUT/ROE SW15 127 J4
Normanby Rd WLSDN NW10 69 H4
Norman Cl ROMW/RG RM7 62 D1
Norman Crs HEST TW5 102 C6
PIN HA5 33 G7
Normand Gdns WKENS * W14 107 H5
Normand Ms WKENS W14 107 H5
Normand Rd WKENS W14 107 J5
Normandy Av BAR EN5 26 D4
Normandy Cl SYD SE26 151 G2
Normandy Dr HYS/HAR UB3 82 A5
Normandy Rd BRXN/ST SW9 110 B7
Normandy Ter CAN/RD E16 95 F5
Normandy Wy ERITH DA8 118 B7
Norman Gv BOW E3 93 G1
Normanhurst Av WELL DA16 116 E7
Normanhurst Dr TWK TW1 124 C4
Normanhurst Rd BRXS/STRHM SW2 149 F1
Norman Rd ASHF TW15 140 B5
BELV DA17 98 D7
DART DA1 139 H7
EHAM E6 95 K3
EMPK RM11 63 J6
GNWCH SE10 112 E6
IL IG1 78 B4
SEVS/STOTM N15 56 B4
SUT SM1 174 E4
THHTH CR7 164 C4
WAN E11 76 C1
WIM/MER SW19 147 G6
Normans Cl WDGN * N22 41 J7
WLSDN NW10 69 F5
Normansfield Av E/WMO/HCT KT8 143 J6
Normansfield Cl BUSH WD23 22 B6
Normanshire Dr CHING E4 43 J3
Normans Md WLSDN NW10 69 F5
Norman St FSBYE EC1V 6 E8
Norman Ter KIL/WHAMP * NW6 70 D4
Normanton Av WAND/EARL SW18 146 E1
Normanton Pk CHING E4 44 C2
Normanton Rd SAND/SEL CR2 178 A5
Normanton St FSTH SE23 151 F1
Norman Wy ACT W3 86 D4
STHGT/OAK N14 40 E1
Normington Cl STRHM/NOR SW16 149 G4
Norrice Lea EFNCH N2 53 H4
Norris St STJS SW1Y 11 G7
Norris Wy DART DA1 138 C2
Norroy Rd PUT/ROE SW15 127 G3
Norrys Cl EBAR EN4 27 K4
Norrys Rd EBAR EN4 27 K3
Norseman Cl GDMY/SEVK IG3 61 H7
Norseman Wy GFD/PVL UB6 66 B7
Norstead Pl PUT/ROE SW15 145 J1
North Access Rd WALTH E17 57 F5
North Acre CDALE/KGS NW9 37 G7
North Acton Rd WLSDN NW10 87 F1
Northall Rd BXLYHN DA7 137 K1
Northampton Gv IS N1 73 J4
Northampton Pk IS N1 73 J5
Northampton Rd CLKNW EC1R 6 B9
CROY/NA CR0 178 C1
PEND EN3 31 G3
Northampton Rw CLKNW * EC1R 6 B9
Northampton Sq FSBYE EC1V 6 C8
Northampton St IS N1 6 E1
Northanger Rd STRHM/NOR SW16 148 E5
North Ap RKW/CH/CXG WD3 32 A1
North Audley St MYFR/PKLN W1K 10 A5
North Av CAR SM5 176 A6
HYS/HAR UB3 82 E6
RCH/KEW TW9 105 H7
RYLN/HDSTN HA2 48 B5
STHL UB1 83 K6
UED N18 42 C3
WEA W13 85 H5
North Bank STJWD NW8 3 J8
Northbank Rd WALTH E17 58 A1
North Birkbeck Rd WAN E11 76 B2
Northborough Rd STRHM/NOR SW16 163 K1
Northbourne HAYES BR2 167 K6
Northbourne Rd CLAP SW4 129 J3
Northbrook Dr NTHWD HA6 32 C7
Northbrook Rd BAR EN5 26 C5
CROY/NA CR0 164 E4
IL IG1 78 A1
LEW SE13 133 G4
WDGN N22 40 E5
Northburgh St FSBYE EC1V 12 D1
North Carriage Dr BAY/PAD W2 9 K6
Northchurch Rd IS N1 7 H1
WBLY HA9 68 C5
Northchurch Ter IS N1 7 J2
North Circular PLMGR N13 41 G4
WALTH E17 43 K7
North Circular Rd CHING * E4 43 G5
CRICK NW2 69 G2
EFNCH N2 53 G1

GLDGN NW11 52 C3
SWFD E18 59 G2
WLSDN NW10 86 B1
Northcliffe Cl WPK KT4 173 G2
Northcliffe Dr TRDG/WHET N20 26 D7
North Cl BAR EN5 26 A4
BXLYHS DA6 136 E3
DAGE RM10 80 C7
EBED/NFELT TW14 121 G5
MRDN SM4 161 H3
North Colonnade POP/IOD E14 93 J7
North Common Rd EA W5 86 A6
Northcote Av BRYLDS KT5 159 H6
EA W5 86 A6
ISLW TW7 124 B4
STHL UB1 83 J6
Northcote Rd BTSEA SW11 128 D3
CROY/NA CR0 164 E5
NWMAL KT3 159 K2
SCUP DA14 154 E3
TWK TW1 124 B4
WALTH E17 57 G3
WLSDN NW10 69 G6
Northcott Av WDGN N22 40 E7
North Countess Rd WALTH E17 57 H1
North Crs CAN/RD E16 94 B3
FITZ W1T 11 G2
FNCH N3 52 D1
Northcroft Rd HOR/WEW KT19 173 G6
WEA W13 104 C1
North Cross Rd BARK/HLT IG6 60 C3
EDUL SE22 131 G4
North Dene HEST TW5 103 G7
MLHL NW7 37 F2
Northdene Gdns
SEVS/STOTM N15 56 B5
Northdown Cl RSLP HA4 64 D2
Northdown Gdns
GNTH/NBYPK IG2 60 E4
Northdown Rd EMPK RM11 63 K6
WELL DA16 136 C1
Northdown St IS N1 5 L6
North Dr BECK BR3 166 E3
HSLW TW3 123 H1
RSLP HA4 46 C6
STRHM/NOR SW16 148 C3
North End CROY/NA CR0 164 D7
HAMP NW3 71 G1
North End Av HAMP NW3 71 G1
North End Crs WKENS W14 107 J3
Northend Rd ERITH DA8 118 C7
North End Rd FUL/PGN SW6 107 K6
GLDGN NW11 52 E7
WBLY HA9 68 C2
WKENS W14 107 H3
North End Wy HAMP NW3 71 G1
Northern Av ED N9 42 B1
Northernhay Wk MRDN SM4 161 H3
Northern Perimeter Rd
HTHAIR TW6 101 F7
Northern Perimeter Rd (West)
HTHAIR TW6 100 B7
Northern Relief Rd BARK IG11 78 C6
North Eyot Gdns
HMSMTH * W6 106 C4
Northey St POP/IOD E14 93 G6
Northfield Av PIN HA5 47 H3
WEA W13 85 H7
Northfield Cl BMLY BR1 153 J7
HYS/HAR UB3 101 J2
Northfield Crs CHEAM SM3 174 C3
Northfield Pde HYS/HAR * UB3 101 J2
Northfield Pk HYS/HAR UB3 101 H2
North Field Rd HEST TW5 102 C5
Northfield Rd DAGW RM9 80 B3
EBAR EN4 27 J2
EHAM E6 77 K5
PEND * EN3 30 D4
STNW/STAM N16 56 A6
WEA W13 104 C1
Northfields WAND/EARL SW18 127 K3
Northfields Rd ACT W3 86 E4
North Gdns WIM/MER SW19 147 H6
Northgate NTHWD HA6 32 A6
Northgate Dr CDALE/KGS NW9 51 G5
North Gower St CAMTN NW1 4 E8
North Gv HGT N6 54 A6
SEVS/STOTM N15 55 K4
North Hl HGT N6 53 K5
North Hill Av HGT N6 53 K5
North Hyde Gdns HYS/HAR UB3 101 K2
North Hyde La NWDGN UB2 102 D4
North Hyde Rd HYS/HAR UB3 101 H2
North Hyde Whf NWDGN * UB2 102 B3
Northiam NFNCH/WDSP N12 38 E3
Northiam St HACK E8 74 D7
Northington St BMSBY WC1N 11 L2
Northlands St CMBW SE5 130 D1
North La TEDD TW11 143 F5
North Lodge Cl PUT/ROE * SW15 127 G4
North Ms BMSBY WC1N 11 M1
North Mt TRDG/WHET * N20 39 G1
Northolm EDGW HA8 37 F3
Northolme Gdns EDGW HA8 36 C7
Northolme Rd HBRY N5 73 J3
Northolt Av RSLP HA4 65 F4
Northolt Gdns GFD/PVL UB6 67 F4
Northolt Rd RYLN/HDSTN HA2 66 B3
WDR/YW UB7 100 A7
Northover BMLY BR1 152 D3
North Pde CHSGTN KT9 172 B4
EDGW * HA8 50 C1
STHL * UB1 84 A5
North Pk ELTH/MOT SE9 134 E5
North Pas WAND/EARL SW18 127 K4
North Peckham Est PECK SE15 111 G6
North Pl TEDD TW11 143 F5
WIM/MER SW19 147 K6
North Pole La HAYES BR2 180 E5
North Pole Rd SHB W12 88 A5
Northport St IS N1 7 H4
North Ri BAY/PAD * W2 9 K5
North Rd BELV DA17 117 J2
BMLY BR1 153 F7
BTFD TW8 105 F5
CHDH RM6 62 A4
DART DA1 138 C5
EA W5 104 E2
EBED/NFELT TW14 121 G5
ED N9 30 D7
EDGW HA8 36 D7
EFNCH N2 39 J7
GDMY/SEVK IG3 78 E1
HEST TW5 102 B5
HGT N6 54 A6
HOLWY N7 72 E5
HYS/HAR UB3 82 D5
RCH/KEW TW9 125 H1
STHL UB1 84 A6
SURB KT6 158 E5
WDR/YW UB7 100 C2
WIM/MER SW19 147 H5
WOOL/PLUM SE18 115 K3
WWKM BR4 166 E7
Northrop Rd HTHAIR TW6 101 H7
North Rw MYFR/PKLN W1K 10 A6
North Several
BKHTH/KID * SE3 133 G1
Northside Rd BMLY BR1 152 E7
North Side
Wandsworth Common
WAND/EARL SW18 128 B4
Northspur Rd SUT SM1 174 E2
North Sq ED N9 42 D1
GLDGN NW11 52 E5
Northstead Rd
BRXS/STRHM SW2 149 G1
North St BARK IG11 78 C6
BMLY BR1 152 E7
BXLYHN DA7 137 H3
CAR SM5 175 K3
DART DA1 139 G6
HDN NW4 52 A4
ISLW TW7 124 B2
PLSTW E13 95 F1
ROM RM1 63 F3
VX/NE SW8 129 G2
North Tenter St WCHPL E1 13 M5
North Ter CHEL SW3 15 J5
Northumberland Aly
TWRH * EC3N 13 K5
Northumberland Av
CHCR WC2N 11 J8
ISLW TW7 104 A7
MNPK E12 59 G7
WELL DA16 135 K3
Northumberland Cl ERITH DA8 117 K6
STWL/WRAY TW19 120 B5
Northumberland Crs
EBED/NFELT TW14 121 H5
Northumberland Gdns
BMLY BR1 169 F3
ED N9 42 B2
MTCM CR4 163 J4
Northumberland Gv TOTM N17 42 D6
Northumberland Pk
ERITH DA8 117 K6
TOTM N17 42 C6
Northumberland Pl BAY/PAD W2 8 A4
Northumberland Rd BAR EN5 27 G5
EHAM E6 95 J5
RYLN/HDSTN HA2 47 K4
WALTH E17 57 J6
Northumberland St
CHCR WC2N 11 J8
Northumberland Wy
ERITH DA8 117 K7
Northumbria St POP/IOD E14 93 J5
North Verbena Gdns
HMSMTH * W6 106 D4
North Vw EA W5 85 J3
PIN HA5 47 G6
WIM/MER SW19 145 K4
Northview Crs WLSDN NW10 69 H3
Northview Dr WFD IG8 59 H1
Northview Pde HOLWY * N7 72 E2
North View Rd CEND/HSY/T N8 54 D2
North Vls CAMTN NW1 72 D5
North Wy CDALE/KGS NW9 50 D2
ED N9 42 E1
FBAR/BDGN N11 40 C5
PIN HA5 47 G2
Northway GLDGN NW11 53 F4
RYNPK SW20 161 H2
WLGTN SM6 176 C3
Northway Crs MLHL NW7 37 G3
Northway Rd CMBW SE5 130 D2
CROY/NA CR0 165 G5
Northways Pde HAMP NW3 3 G1
North Weald La
KUTN/CMB KT2 143 J4
North Western Av Elto
GSTN WD25 22 B1
North Western Av (Tylers Way)
BUSH WD23 22 C3
North Western Av
(Watford By-Pass)
STAN HA7 23 G5
North Wharf Rd BAY/PAD W2 9 G3
Northwick Av HRW HA1 49 G5
Northwick Cir
KTN/HRWW/W HA3 49 J5
Northwick Cl STJWD NW8 3 G9
Northwick Park Rd HRW HA1 49 F5
Northwick Rd ALP/SUD HA0 67 K7
OXHEY WD19 33 G3
Northwick Ter STJWD NW8 3 G9
Northwold Dr PIN HA5 47 G2
Northwold Rd STNW/STAM N16 74 C1
Northwood Av HCH RM12 81 J3
Northwood Gdns CLAY IG5 60 A3
GFD/PVL UB6 67 F4
NFNCH/WDSP N12 39 H4
Northwood Pl ERITHM DA18 117 G2
Northwood Rd CAR SM5 176 A5
FSTH SE23 132 C7
HGT N6 54 B6
HTHAIR TW6 100 A7
THHTH CR7 164 D1
Northwood Wy NTHWD HA6 32 E7
North Woolwich Rd
CAN/RD E16 95 F7
North Worple Wy
MORT/ESHN SW14 126 A2
Norton Av BRYLDS KT5 159 J6
Norton Cl CHING E4 43 J4
Norton Folgate WCHPL E1 13 K1
Norton Gdns
STRHM/NOR SW16 163 K1
Norton Rd ALP/SUD HA0 67 K5
DAGE RM10 81 F5
LEY E10 57 H7
Norval Gn BRXN/ST * SW9 130 B1
Norval Rd ALP/SUD HA0 67 H1
Norway Ga BERM/RHTH SE16 112 B2
Norway Pl POP/IOD E14 93 H5
Norway St GNWCH SE10 112 E5
Norwich Pl BXLYHS DA6 137 H3
Norwich Rd FSTGT E7 76 E5
GFD/PVL UB6 66 B7
PIN HA5 46 D2
THHTH CR7 164 D2
Norwich St FLST/FETLN EC4A 12 A4
Norwich Wk EDGW HA8 36 E6
Norwood Av ALP/SUD HA0 68 B7
ROMW/RG RM7 63 F6
Norwood Cl NWDGN UB2 103 F3
WHTN TW2 142 D1
Norwood Crs HTHAIR TW6 101 F7
Norwood Dr RYLN/HDSTN HA2 47 K5
Norwood Gdns NWDGN UB2 102 E3
YEAD UB4 83 G3
Norwood Green Rd
NWDGN UB2 103 F3
Norwood High St WNWD SE27 149 H2
Norwood Park Rd WNWD SE27 149 J4
Norwood Rd HNHL SE24 130 C7
NWDGN UB2 102 D2
Notley St CMBW SE5 110 E6
Notson Rd SNWD SE25 165 J3
Notting Barn Rd NKENS W10 88 B3
Nottingdale Sq NTGHL * W11 88 C7
Nottingham Av CAN/RD E16 95 G4
Nottingham Ct
LSQ/SEVD * WC2H 11 J5
Nottingham Pl MHST W1U 10 A1
Nottingham Rd ISLW TW7 124 A1
LEY E10 58 A5
SAND/SEL CR2 177 J4
TOOT SW17 128 E7
Nottingham St MHST W1U 10 A2
Nottingham Ter CAMTN NW1 10 A1
Notting Hill Ga KENS W8 8 B8
Nova Ms MRDN SM4 161 H6
Nova Rd CROY/NA CR0 164 C7
Novar Rd ELTH/MOT SE9 135 H7
Novello St FUL/PGN SW6 107 K7
Nowell Rd BARN SW13 106 D5
Nower Hl PIN HA5 47 K3
Noyna Rd TOOT SW17 147 K2
Nubia Wy BMLY BR1 152 C3
Nuding Cl LEW SE13 132 D2
Nugent Rd ARCH N19 54 E7
SNWD SE25 165 G2
Nugents Ct PIN * HA5 33 J7
Nugent's Pk PIN HA5 33 K7
Nugent Ter STJWD NW8 2 F6
Nuneaton Rd DAGW RM9 79 K6
Nunhead Gv PECK SE15 131 J2
Nunhead La PECK SE15 131 J2
Nunnington Cl ELTH/MOT SE9 153 J2
Nunn's Rd ENC/FH EN2 29 J1
Nupton Dr BAR EN5 26 A5
Nurse Cl EDGW HA8 36 E7
The Nursery ERITH DA8 118 C6
Nursery Av BXLYHN DA7 137 G2
CROY/NA CR0 179 F1
FNCH N3 53 F1
Nursery Cl BROCKY SE4 132 C1
CHDH RM6 61 K5
CROY/NA CR0 179 F1
EBED/NFELT TW14 122 A6
WFD IG8 45 F4
Nursery Gdns CHST BR7 154 B5
HSLWW TW4 122 E4
Nursery La BETH E2 7 L4
FSTGT E7 76 E5
NKENS W10 88 A4
Nurserymans Rd
FBAR/BDGN N11 40 A1
Nursery Rd BRXN/ST SW9 130 A3
EFNCH N2 39 H7
HOM E9 74 E5
MTCM CR4 162 D3
PIN HA5 47 G2
STHGT/OAK N14 28 C6
SUN TW16 140 E7
SUT SM1 175 G3
THHTH CR7 164 E3
WIM/MER SW19 146 C6
WIM/MER SW19 162 A1
Nursery Rw BAR * EN5 26 C2
WALW SE17 19 G6
Nursery St TOTM N17 42 B6
Nursery Wk HDN NW4 51 K2
Nurstead Rd ERITH DA8 117 H6
Nutbourne St NKENS W10 88 C2
Nutbrook St PECK SE15 131 G2
Nutbrowne Rd DAGW RM9 80 B7
Nutcroft Rd PECK SE15 111 J6
Nutfield Cl CAR SM5 175 J2
UED N18 42 C5
Nutfield Gdns GDMY/SEVK IG3 79 F1
NTHLT UB5 83 G1
Nutfield Rd CRICK NW2 69 J1
EDUL SE22 131 G4
SRTFD E15 76 A3
THHTH CR7 164 C3
Nutford Pl BAY/PAD W2 9 K4
Nuthatch Gdns THMD SE28 115 J1
Nuthurst Av BRXS/STRHM SW2 149 F1
Nutley Ter HAMP NW3 71 H5
Nutmead Cl BXLY DA5 137 K7
Nutmeg Cl CAN/RD E16 94 C3
Nutmeg La POP/IOD E14 94 B5
Nuttall St IS N1 7 K5
Nutter La WAN E11 59 G4
Nutt Gv EDGW HA8 35 K1
Nutt St PECK SE15 111 G6
Nutwell St TOOT SW17 147 J4
Nuxley Rd BELV DA17 117 G5
Nyanza St WOOL/PLUM SE18 115 J5
Nylands Av RCH/KEW TW9 125 H1
Nymans Gdns RYNPK SW20 160 E2
Nynehead St NWCR SE14 112 B6
Nyon Gv FSTH SE23 151 H1
Nyssa Cl WFD IG8 45 K5

O

Oak Av CEND/HSY/T N8 54 E3
CROY/NA CR0 179 J1
HEST TW5 102 C6
HPTN TW12 141 J4
MUSWH N10 40 B6
TOTM N17 41 K6
WDR/YW UB7 100 D2
Oakbank Av WOT/HER KT12 156 E6
Oakbank Gv HNHL SE24 130 D3
Oakbrook Cl BMLY BR1 153 F3
Oakbury Rd FUL/PGN SW6 128 A1
Oak Cl DART DA1 138 B3
STHGT/OAK N14 28 B6
Oakcombe Cl NWMAL KT3 145 G7
Oak Cottage Cl CAT SE6 133 H7
Oak Cottages HNWL * W7 103 K1
Oak Crs CAN/RD E16 94 C4
Oakcroft Cl PIN HA5 47 F1
Oakcroft Rd CHSGTN KT9 172 B3
LEW SE13 133 G1
Oakcroft Vls CHSGTN KT9 172 B3
Oakdale STHGT/OAK N14 28 B7
Oakdale Av KTN/HRWW/W HA3 50 A4
NTHWD HA6 46 E1
Oakdale Cl OXHEY WD19 33 G3
Oakdale Gdns CHING E4 44 A4
Oakdale Rd FSBYPK N4 55 J5
FSTGT E7 77 F6
HOR/WEW KT19 173 F7
OXHEY WD19 33 G2
PECK SE15 131 K2
STRHM/NOR SW16 148 E4
SWFD E18 59 F1
WAN E11 76 B1
Oakdale Wy MTCM CR4 163 F6
Oakdene Av CHST BR7 154 A4
ERITH DA8 117 K5
THDIT KT7 158 B7
Oakdene Cl PIN HA5 33 K6
Oak Dene Cl ROM RM1 63 K5
Oakdene Dr BRYLDS KT5 159 K7
Oakdene Ms CHEAM SM3 161 J7
Oakdene Pk FNCH N3 38 D6
Oakden St LBTH SE11 18 B5
Oaken Dr ESH/CLAY KT10 171 F5
Oaken La ESH/CLAY KT10 170 E3
Oakenshaw Cl SURB KT6 159 F6
Oakeshott Av HGT N6 72 A1
Oakey La STHWK SE1 18 A3
Oak Farm BORE WD6 24 E4
Oakfield CHING E4 43 K4
Oakfield Av
KTN/HRWW/W HA3 49 H2
Oakfield Cl NWMAL KT3 160 C4
Oakfield Ct BORE * WD6 24 D3
Oakfield Gdns BECK BR3 166 D4
CAR SM5 162 D7
GFD/PVL UB6 84 D3
UED N18 42 A3
Oakfield La HAYES BR2 181 G3
Oakfield Rd CROY/NA CR0 164 D7
EHAM E6 77 J7
FNCH N3 39 F7
FSBYPK N4 55 G5
IL IG1 78 B2
PGE/AN SE20 150 D7
STHGT/OAK N14 40 E1
WALTH E17 57 G1
WIM/MER SW19 146 B2
Oakfields Rd GLDGN NW11 52 C5
Oakfield St WBPTN SW10 14 E9
Oakford Rd KTTN NW5 72 C3
Oak Gdns CROY/NA CR0 179 J1
EDGW HA8 50 E1
Oak Gv CRICK NW2 70 B3
RSLP HA4 47 F7
SUN TW16 141 F6
WWKM BR4 180 A1
Oak Grove Rd PGE/AN SE20 150 E7
Oakhall Dr SUN TW16 140 D4
Oak Hall Rd WAN E11 59 F5
Oakham Cl CAT * SE6 151 H1
Oakham Dr HAYES BR2 167 K3
Oakhampton Rd MLHL NW7 38 B7
Oakhill ESH/CLAY KT10 171 G5
Oak Hl SURB KT6 159 F6
WFD IG8 44 B6
Oakhill Av HAMP NW3 71 F3
PIN HA5 47 J1
Oak Hill Crs SURB KT6 159 F6
WFD IG8 44 C6
Oak Hill Gdns WALTH E17 44 C7
Oak Hill Gv SURB KT6 159 F5
Oak Hill Pk HAMP NW3 71 F3
Oak Hill Park Ms HAMP NW3 71 G3
Oakhill Pl WAND/EARL SW18 127 K4
Oak Hill Rd SURB * KT6 159 F5
Oakhill Rd BECK BR3 167 F1
PUT/ROE SW15 127 J4
STRHM/NOR SW16 148 E7
SUT SM1 175 F2
Oak Hill Wy HAMP NW3 71 G3
Oakhouse Rd BXLYHS DA6 137 H4
Oakhurst Av BXLYHN DA7 117 F6
EBAR EN4 27 J6
Oakhurst Cl CHST BR7 153 K7
TEDD TW11 142 E4
WALTH E17 58 C3
Oakhurst Gdns BXLYHN DA7 117 F6
WALTH E17 58 C3
Oakhurst Gv EDUL SE22 131 H3
Oakhurst Pl WATW * WD18 20 D3
Oakhurst Rd HOR/WEW KT19 172 E5
Oakington Av HYS/HAR UB3 101 G3
RYLN/HDSTN HA2 48 A6
WBLY HA9 68 B2
Oakington Dr SUN TW16 156 B1
Oakington Manor Dr WBLY HA9 68 C4
Oakington Rd MV/WKIL W9 2 B9
Oakington Wy CEND/HSY/T N8 54 E5
Oakland Pl BKHH IG9 44 E1
Oakland Rd SRTFD E15 76 C3
Oaklands PLMGR N13 41 F1
Oaklands Av BFN/LL DA15 136 A6
ED N9 30 D5
ESH/CLAY KT10 157 J7
ISLW TW7 104 A5
OXHEY WD19 21 F7
ROM RM1 63 G2
THHTH CR7 164 B3
WWKM BR4 179 K2
Oaklands Cl ALP/SUD HA0 67 K4
BXLYHS DA6 137 G4
CHSGTN KT9 171 J3
STMC/STPC BR5 169 K5
Oaklands Ga NTHWD HA6 32 C5
Oaklands Gv SHB W12 87 J7
Oaklands La BAR EN5 25 K3
Oaklands Ms CRICK NW2 70 B3
Oaklands Park Av IL IG1 78 C1
Oaklands Pl CLAP SW4 129 J3
Oaklands Rd BMLY BR1 152 C6
BXLYHS DA6 137 G3
CRICK NW2 70 B3
HNWL W7 104 A1
MORT/ESHN SW14 126 A2
TRDG/WHET N20 26 D6
Oaklands Wy WLGTN SM6 176 C6
Oakland Wy HOR/WEW KT19 173 F5
Oak La EFNCH N2 53 H1
FBAR/BDGN N11 40 D5
ISLW TW7 123 K3
POP/IOD E14 93 H6
TWK TW1 124 B6
WFD IG8 44 D3
Oakleafe Gdns CLAY IG5 60 B2
Oakleigh Av EDGW HA8 50 D1
SURB KT6 159 H7
TRDG/WHET N20 27 H7
Oakleigh Cl TRDG/WHET N20 39 K2
Oakleigh Ct EDGW * HA8 50 E1
Oakleigh Crs TRDG/WHET N20 39 J2
Oakleigh Dr RKW/CH/CXG WD3 20 A5
Oakleigh Gdns EDGW HA8 36 B4
TRDG/WHET N20 27 G7
Oakleigh Ms TRDG/WHET * N20 39 G1
Oakleigh Park Av CHST BR7 169 F1
Oakleigh Pk North
TRDG/WHET N20 27 H7
Oakleigh Pk South
TRDG/WHET N20 27 J7
Oakleigh Rd HGDN/ICK UB10 64 A6
PIN HA5 33 K5
Oakleigh Rd North
TRDG/WHET N20 39 H1
Oakleigh Rd South
FBAR/BDGN N11 40 A3
Oakleigh Wy MTCM CR4 148 B7
SURB KT6 159 H7
Oakley Av BARK IG11 79 F5
CROY/NA CR0 176 E3
EA W5 86 C6
Oakley Cl CHING E4 44 A2
HNWL W7 84 E6
ISLW TW7 103 J7
Oakley Crs FSBYE * EC1V 6 D6
Oakley Dr BFN/LL DA15 135 J7
HAYES BR2 181 J2
LEW SE13 133 G5
Oakley Gdns CEND/HSY/T N8 55 F4
CHEL SW3 15 K9
Oakley Pk BFN/LL DA15 136 D6
Oakley Pl STHWK SE1 19 L8
Oakley Rd HAYES BR2 181 J2
HRW HA1 48 E5
IS N1 7 G1
SNWD SE25 165 J4
Oakley Sq CAMTN NW1 4 F5
Oakley St CHEL SW3 15 J9
Oakley Yd BETH * E2 7 M9
Oak Lodge Cl STAN HA7 35 J4
Oak Lodge Dr WWKM BR4 166 E6
Oakmead Av HAYES BR2 167 K5
Oakmeade PIN HA5 34 A5
Oakmead Gdns EDGW HA8 37 F3
Oakmead Pl MTCM CR4 147 J7
Oakmead Rd BAL SW12 129 G7
CROY/NA CR0 163 J5
Oakmere Rd ABYW SE2 116 B5
Oak Park Gdns
WIM/MER SW19 127 G7
Oakridge Dr EFNCH N2 53 H2
Oakridge Rd BMLY BR1 152 C3
Oak Ri BKHH IG9 45 H2
Oak Rd EA W5 85 K6
ERITH DA8 117 K6
ERITH DA8 118 D7
NWMAL KT3 160 A1
Oak Rw MTCM CR4 163 H1
Oaks Av CRW RM5 62 E1
FELT TW13 141 J1
NRWD SE19 150 A4
WPK KT4 173 K3
Oaksford Av SYD SE26 150 D2
Oaks Gv CHING E4 44 C1
Oakshade Rd BMLY BR1 152 B3
Oakshaw Rd
WAND/EARL SW18 128 A6
Oaks La CROY/NA CR0 178 E2
GNTH/NBYPK IG2 60 E4
Oaks Rd CROY/NA CR0 178 D4
STWL/WRAY TW19 120 A4
The Oaks FELT * TW13 141 J1
HAYES * BR2 169 F5
MRDN * SM4 161 H3
NFNCH/WDSP N12 39 F3
OXHEY WD19 21 G7
RSLP HA4 46 B6
SURB KT6 171 J2
WFD IG8 44 C6
WOOL/PLUM SE18 115 H4
YEAD UB4 82 A1
Oak St ROMW/RG RM7 62 E4
Oaks Wy CAR SM5 175 K6
SURB KT6 171 K1
Oakthorpe Rd PLMGR N13 41 G4
Oaktree Av PLMGR N13 41 G2
Oak Tree Cl STAN HA7 35 J6
WEA * W13 85 J5
Oak Tree Ct BORE * WD6 23 K5
Oak Tree Dell CDALE/KGS NW9 50 E4
Oak Tree Dr TRDG/WHET N20 27 F7
Oak Tree Gdns BMLY BR1 153 F4
Oaktree Gv IL IG1 78 D4
Oak Tree Rd STJWD NW8 3 H8
Oakview Gdns EFNCH N2 53 H3
Oakview Gv CROY/NA CR0 166 B7
Oakview Rd CAT SE6 151 K4
Oak Village HAMP NW3 72 A3
Oak Vls GLDGN * NW11 52 D5
Oak Wy ACT W3 87 G7
CROY/NA CR0 166 A5
EBED/NFELT TW14 121 H7
STHGT/OAK N14 28 B6
Oakway HAYES BR2 167 G1
RYNPK SW20 161 F3
Oakway Cl BXLY DA5 137 F5
Oakways ELTH/MOT SE9 135 G5
Oakwood WLGTN SM6 176 B7
Oakwood Av BECK BR3 167 F1
BORE WD6 24 D3
HAYES BR2 168 A2
HOR/WEW KT19 172 C7
MTCM CR4 162 C1
STHGT/OAK N14 28 D6
STHL UB1 84 A6
Oakwood Cl CHST BR7 153 K5
STHGT/OAK N14 28 C5
WFD IG8 45 J5
Oakwood Ct WKENS W14 107 J2
Oakwood Crs GFD/PVL UB6 67 G5
WCHMH N21 28 E5
Oakwood Dr BXLYHN DA7 137 K3
EDGW HA8 36 E5
NRWD SE19 149 K5
Oakwood Gdns GDMY/SEVK IG3 79 F1
SUT SM1 174 E1
Oakwood La WKENS W14 107 J2
Oakwood Pde EBAR * EN4 28 C4
Oakwood Park Cottages
STHGT/OAK * N14 29 F5
Oakwood Park Rd
STHGT/OAK N14 28 E5
Oakwood Pl CROY/NA CR0 164 B5
Oakwood Rd CROY/NA CR0 164 B5
GLDGN NW11 52 E4
PIN HA5 47 F1
RYNPK SW20 145 J7
Oakworth Rd NKENS W10 88 A4
Oak Yd WAT * WD17 21 G3
Oarsman Pl E/WMO/HCT KT8 157 K3
Oates Cl HAYES BR2 167 G2
Oatland Ri WALTH E17 57 G1
Oat La CITYW EC2V 12 E4
Oban Cl PLSTW E13 95 G3
Oban Rd PLSTW E13 95 G2
SNWD SE25 164 E3

Oban St POP/IOD E14 94 B5
Oberstein Rd BTSEA SW11 128 C3
Oborne Cl HNHL SE24 130 C4
Observatory Gdns KENS W8 14 A1
Observatory Rd
MORT/ESHN SW14 125 K3
SKENS SW7 15 H3
Occupation La EA W5 104 E3
WOOL/PLUM SE18 115 G7
Occupation Rd WALW SE17 18 E7
WATW WD18 21 F4
WEA W13 104 C1
Ocean Est WCHPL E1 93 F3
Ocean St WCHPL E1 93 F4
Ockendon Ms IS * N1 73 K5
Ockendon Rd IS N1 73 K5
Ockham Dr STMC/STPC BR5 155 G6
Ockley Rd CROY/NA CR0 164 A6
STRHM/NOR SW16 148 E3
Octagon Ar LVPST * EC2M 13 J3
Octavia Cl MTCM CR4 162 D4
Octavia Ct WATN WD24 21 G1
Octavia Ms CRICK * NW2 69 K5
Octavia Rd ISLW TW7 124 A2
Octavia St BTSEA SW11 108 D7
Octavius St DEPT SE8 112 D6
October Pl HDN * NW4 52 B2
Odard Rd E/WMO/HCT KT8 157 F3
Odeon Pde ELTH/MOT * SE9 134 D3
GFD/PVL * UB6 67 H5
HOLWY * N7 72 E2
ISLW * TW7 123 K1
Odessa Rd FSTGT E7 76 D3
WLSDN NW10 87 J1
Odessa St BERM/RHTH SE16 112 C2
Odger St BTSEA SW11 128 E1
Odhams Wk LSQ/SEVD * WC2H 11 J5
Odsey Vls FSBYPK * N4 55 G5
Offa's Md HOM E9 75 G3
Offenham Rd ELTH/MOT SE9 153 K3
Offerton Rd CLAP SW4 129 H2
Offham Slope
NFNCH/WDSP N12 38 D4
Offley Rd BRXN/ST SW9 110 B6
Offord Cl TOTM N17 42 C6
Offord Rd IS N1 5 M1
Offord St HOLWY N7 5 L1
Ogilby St WOOL/PLUM SE18 114 E3
Oglander Rd PECK SE15 131 G3
Ogle St GTPST W1W 10 E2
Oglethorpe Rd DAGE RM10 80 B2
Ohio Rd PLSTW E13 94 D3
Oil Mill La HMSMTH W6 106 D4
Okeburn Rd TOOT SW17 148 A4
Okehampton Crs WELL DA16 116 C7
Okehampton Rd WLSDN NW10 70 A7
Olaf St NTGHL W11 88 B6
Old Bailey STP EC4M 12 D5
Old Barn Cl BELMT SM2 174 C6
Old Barn Wy BXLYHN DA7 138 A3
Old Barrack Yd KTBR SW1X 16 A1
Oldberry Rd EDGW HA8 37 F5
Old Bethnal Green Rd BETH E2 92 D2
Old Bond St CONDST W1S 10 E7
Oldborough Rd ALP/SUD HA0 67 J1
Old Brewery Ms HAMP NW3 71 H3
Old Bridge Cl NTHLT UB5 84 A1
Old Bridge St KUT KT1 158 E1
Old Broad St LVPST EC2M 13 J4
Old Bromley Rd BMLY BR1 152 B4
Old Brompton Rd ECT SW5 14 B8
Old Buildings LINN WC2A 12 A4
Old Burlington St CONDST W1S 10 E6
Oldbury Pl MHST W1U 10 B2
Oldbury Rd EN EN1 30 C1
Old Castle St WCHPL E1 13 L4
Old Cavendish St
CAVSQ/HST W1G 10 C4
Old Chestnut Av
ESH/CLAY KT10 170 A5
Old Church La CDALE/KGS NW9 68 E1
GFD/PVL UB6 85 G2
STAN HA7 35 H5
Old Church Pth ESH/CLAY KT10 170 B3
Oldchurch Ri ROMW/RG RM7 63 G5
Old Church Rd CHING E4 43 J2
Oldchurch Rd ROMW/RG RM7 63 F6
Old Church Rd WCHPL * E1 93 F5
Old Church St CHEL SW3 15 H9
Old Claygate La
ESH/CLAY KT10 171 G5
Old Compton St
SOHO/SHAV W1D 11 G6
Old Cote Dr HEST TW5 103 F5
Old Court Pl KENS W8 14 C1
The Old Ctyd BMLY BR1 153 F7
Old Dairy Ms BAL SW12 129 F7
KTTN * NW5 72 B5
Old Deer Pk RCH/KEW * TW9 125 G2
Old Deer Park Gdns
RCH/KEW TW9 125 F2
Old Devonshire Rd BAL SW12 129 G6
Old Dock Cl RCH/KEW TW9 105 H5
Old Dover Rd BKHTH/KID SE3 113 K6
Old Farm Av BFN/LL DA15 135 J7
STHGT/OAK N14 28 C6
Old Farm Cl HSLW TW3 122 E3
Old Farm Rd EFNCH N2 39 H7
HPTN TW12 141 K5
WDR/YW UB7 100 A1
Old Farm Rd East BFN/LL DA15 155 G1
Old Farm Rd West
BFN/LL DA15 155 F1
Oldfield Cl BMLY BR1 168 E3
GFD/PVL UB6 66 E4
STAN HA7 35 G4
Oldfield Farm Gdns
GFD/PVL UB6 66 D7
Oldfield Gv DEPT SE8 112 A3
Oldfield La North GFD/PVL UB6 66 D5
Oldfield La South GFD/PVL UB6 84 C2
Oldfield Ms HGT N6 54 C6
Oldfield Rd ACT W3 106 C1
BMLY BR1 168 E3
BXLYHN DA7 137 F1
HPTN TW12 142 A7
STNW/STAM N16 74 A2
WIM/MER SW19 146 C5
WLSDN NW10 69 H6
Oldfields Circ NTHLT UB5 66 C5
Oldfields Rd CHEAM SM3 174 C2
Old Fish Street Hl BLKFR * EC4V 12 E6
Old Fleet La STP EC4M 12 C4
Old Fold Vw BAR EN5 26 A2
Old Ford Lock SRTFD * E15 75 J6
Old Ford Rd BETH E2 92 E1
BOW E3 75 H7
Old Forge Cl STAN HA7 35 G3
Old Forge Wy SCUP DA14 155 H3
Old Gannon Cl NTHWD HA6 32 A3
Old Gloucester St BMSBY WC1N 11 K2
Old Hall Cl PIN HA5 33 J7
Old Hall Dr PIN HA5 33 J7
Oldham Ter ACT W3 86 E7
Old Hl CHST BR7 154 A7
Oldhill St STNW/STAM N16 56 C7
Old Homesdale Rd HAYES BR2 168 B3
Old Hospital Cl TOOT * SW17 128 E7
Old House Cl WIM/MER SW19 146 C4
Old House Gdns TWK * TW1 124 D5
Old Howlett's La RSLP * HA4 46 B5
Old Jamaica Rd STHWK SE1 111 H2
Old James St PECK SE15 131 J2
Old Jewry LOTH * EC2R 13 G5
Old Kenton La CDALE/KGS NW9 50 D4
Old Kingston Rd WPK KT4 172 E2
Old Lodge Wy STAN HA7 35 G4
Old London Rd KUTN/CMB KT2 159 H1
Old Malden La WPK KT4 173 G1
Old Manor Dr ISLW TW7 123 H5
Old Manor Wy BXLYHN DA7 138 A1
ELTH/MOT SE9 153 K4
Old Manor Yd ECT SW5 14 C6
Old Market Sq BETH E2 7 L7
Old Marylebone Rd CAMTN NW1 9 K3
Old Mill Ct SWFD E18 59 G2
Old Mill Rd KUT KT1 159 G2
WOOL/PLUM SE18 115 J5
Old Mitre Ct EMB * EC4Y 12 B5
Old Montague St WCHPL E1 92 C4
Old Nichol St BETH E2 7 L9
Old North St FSBYW * WC1X 11 L2
Old Oak Common La
WLSDN NW10 87 G3
Old Oak La WLSDN NW10 87 H2
Old Oak Rd ACT W3 87 H6
The Old Orch HAMP * NW3 71 K3
Old Orch SUN TW16 156 B1
Old Palace Rd CROY/NA CR0 177 J2
Old Palace Yd RCH/KEW TW9 124 D4
Old Paradise St LBTH SE11 17 L5
Old Park Av BAL SW12 129 F5
ENC/FH EN2 29 J3
Old Park Gv WCHMH N21 29 J3
Old Park La MYFR/PICC W1J 10 B9
Old Park Ms HEST TW5 102 E6
Old Park Ridings WCHMH N21 29 H5
Old Park Rd ABYW SE2 116 B4
ENC/FH EN2 29 H2
PLMGR N13 41 F2
Old Park Rd South ENC/FH EN2 29 H3
Old Park Vw ENC/FH EN2 29 G2
Old Perry St CHST BR7 154 E6
Old Pound Cl ISLW TW7 104 B7
Old Pye St WEST SW1P 17 G3
Old Quebec St MBLAR W1H 9 M5
Old Queen St STJSPK SW1H 17 H2
Old Rectory Gdns EDGW HA8 36 C5
Old Redding KTN/HRWW/W HA3 34 B4
Oldridge Rd BAL SW12 129 F6
Old Rd DART DA1 138 A3
LEW SE13 133 H3
Old Royal Free Sq IS N1 6 B4
Old Ruislip Rd NTHLT UB5 83 H1
Old's Ap WATW WD18 20 A7
Old School Cl BECK BR3 166 A1
Old School Crs FSTGT E7 76 E5
Old Schools La EW KT17 173 H7
Old School Sq THDIT KT7 158 A5
Old School Ter CHEAM * SM3 174 B6
Old Seacoal La STP * EC4M 12 C5
Old South Cl PIN HA5 33 H7
Old South Lambeth Rd
VX/NE * SW8 109 K6
Old Sq LINN WC2A 11 M4
Old Stable Ms HBRY * N5 73 J2
Old Station Gdns TEDD * TW11 143 G5
Old Station Rd HYS/HAR UB3 101 J2
Oldstead Rd BMLY BR1 152 B3
Old St FSBYE EC1V 6 E9
IS N1 7 J8
PLSTW E13 95 F1
Old Swan Yd CAR SM5 175 K3
Old Town CLAP SW4 129 H3
CROY/NA CR0 177 H2
Old Tramyard
WOOL/PLUM SE18 115 K3
Old Woolwich Rd GNWCH SE10 113 G5
Old York Rd WAND/EARL SW18 128 A4
O'leary Sq WCHPL E1 92 E4
Olga St BOW E3 93 G1
Olinda Rd STNW/STAM N16 56 B5
Oliphant St NKENS W10 88 C2
Oliver Av SNWD SE25 165 G2
Oliver Cl CHSWK W4 105 J5
Oliver Gdns EHAM E6 95 J4
Oliver Gv SNWD SE25 165 G3
Oliver Ms PECK SE15 131 H1
Olive Rd CRICK NW2 70 A3
DART DA1 139 G7
EA W5 104 E2
PLSTW E13 95 G2
WIM/MER * SW19 147 G6
Oliver Rd LEY E10 75 K2
NWMAL KT3 159 K1
RAIN RM13 81 H7
SUT SM1 175 H3
WALTH E17 58 A4
Oliver's Yd STLK EC1Y 7 H9
Olive St ROMW/RG RM7 63 F4
Ollerton Gn BOW E3 75 H7
Ollerton Rd FBAR/BDGN N11 40 D4
Olley Cl WLGTN SM6 176 E6
Ollgar Cl ACT W3 87 H7
Olliffe St POP/IOD E14 113 F2
Olmar St STHWK SE1 111 H5
Olney Rd WALW SE17 18 E9
Olron Crs BXLYHS DA6 136 E4
Olven Rd WOOL/PLUM SE18 115 H6
Olveston Wk MRDN SM4 162 C5
Olwen Ms PIN HA5 47 H1
Olyffe Av WELL DA16 136 B1
Olyffe Dr BECK BR3 152 A7
Olympia Wy WKENS W14 107 H2
Olympic Wy GFD/PVL UB6 66 B7
WBLY HA9 68 C3
Oman Av CRICK NW2 70 A4
O'meara St STHWK SE1 12 F9
Omega Pl IS N1 5 K6
Omega St NWCR SE14 112 C7
Ommaney Rd NWCR SE14 112 A7
Omnibus Wy WALTH E17 57 J1
Ondine Rd EDUL SE22 131 G3
Onega Ga BERM/RHTH SE16 112 B2
One Tree Cl FSTH SE23 131 K5
Ongar Cl CHDH RM6 61 J4
Ongar Rd FUL/PGN SW6 14 B9
Ongar Wy RAIN RM13 81 G7
Onra Rd WALTH E17 57 J6
Onslow Av RCHPK/HAM TW10 125 F4
Onslow Cl CHING E4 44 B1
Onslow Crs CHST BR7 154 B7
Onslow Dr SCUP DA14 155 K2
Onslow Gdns MUSWH N10 54 B4
SKENS SW7 15 G7
SWFD E18 59 F2
THDIT KT7 157 K7
WCHMH N21 29 G4
WLGTN SM6 176 C6
Onslow Ms East SKENS SW7 15 G6
Onslow Ms West SKENS SW7 15 G6
Onslow Pde STHGT/OAK * N14 28 B7
Onslow Rd CROY/NA CR0 164 B6
NWMAL KT3 160 D3
RCHPK/HAM TW10 125 F5
Onslow Sq SKENS SW7 15 H6
Onslow St FARR EC1M 12 B1
Onslow Wy THDIT KT7 157 K7
Ontario St STHWK SE1 18 D4
Ontario Wy POP/IOD E14 93 J6
On the Hl OXHEY WD19 33 J1
Opal Cl CAN/RD E16 95 H5
Opal St LBTH SE11 18 C7
Openshaw Rd ABYW SE2 116 C4
Openview WAND/EARL SW18 128 B7
Ophir Ter PECK SE15 111 H7
Opossum Wy HSLWW TW4 122 B2
Oppenheim Rd LEW SE13 133 F1
Oppidans Rd HAMP NW3 3 L2
Optima Pk DART * DA1 138 D2
Orange Gv WAN E11 76 C2
Orange Hill Rd EDGW HA8 36 E6
Orange Pl BERM/RHTH SE16 111 K2
The Orangery
RCHPK/HAM TW10 143 J1
Orangery La ELTH/MOT SE9 134 E4
Orange St LSQ/SEVD WC2H 11 H7
WAP E1W 92 C7
Oransay Rd IS N1 73 J5
Oratory La CHEL * SW3 15 H7
Orbain Rd FUL/PGN SW6 107 H6
Orbel St BTSEA SW11 108 D7
Orb St WALW SE17 19 G6
The Orchard BKHTH/KID SE3 133 G1
CHSWK W4 106 A3
EW KT17 173 H6
GLDGN NW11 52 E4
WCHMH N21 29 K5
Orchard BUSH WD23 22 D7
Orchard Av ASHF TW15 140 A5
BELV DA17 117 G5
CROY/NA CR0 179 G1
DART DA1 138 E6
EBED/NFELT TW14 121 G4
FNCH N3 52 E2
HEST TW5 102 D6
MTCM CR4 163 F7
NWMAL KT3 160 B1
STHGT/OAK N14 28 C5
STHL UB1 103 F1
THDIT KT7 158 B7
TRDG/WHET N20 39 H1
Orchard Cl ALP/SUD HA0 68 A7
ASHF TW15 140 A5
BORE WD6 24 B3
BXLYHN DA7 117 F7
CHING E4 43 J3
CRICK NW2 69 J2
EDGW HA8 36 A5
FSTH SE23 131 K5
HOR/WEW * KT19 172 D5
NKENS W10 88 C4
RSLP HA4 46 A6
RYNPK SW20 161 F3
WAT WD17 20 D1
WOT/HER KT12 156 A6
Orchard Cottages
HYS/HAR * UB3 101 H1
KUTN/CMB * KT2 144 C7
Orchard Ct WLGTN * SM6 176 B4
WPK * KT4 160 D7
Orchard Crs EDGW HA8 36 E4
Orchard Dr BKHTH/KID SE3 133 H1
EDGW HA8 36 B4
Orchard Gdns CHSGTN KT9 172 A3
Orchard Ga CDALE/KGS NW9 51 G3
ESH/CLAY KT10 157 J7
GFD/PVL UB6 67 H5
Orchard Gv CROY/NA CR0 166 B6
EDGW HA8 36 C7
KTN/HRWW/W HA3 50 B4
PGE/AN SE20 150 C6
Orchard Hl DART DA1 138 B4
LEW SE13 132 E1
Orchard La E/WMO/HCT KT8 157 J5
RYNPK SW20 145 K7
WFD IG8 45 G3
Orchardleigh Av PEND EN3 30 E1
Orchardmede EN EN1 29 K5
Orchard Ms IS N1 7 H2
Orchard Pl POP/IOD E14 94 C6
TOTM N17 42 B6
Orchard Ri CROY/NA CR0 166 B7
KUTN/CMB KT2 144 E7
RCHPK/HAM TW10 125 J3
RSLP HA4 46 D2
Orchard Ri East BFN/LL DA15 135 K4
Orchard Ri West BFN/LL DA15 135 K4
Orchard Rd BAR EN5 26 C3
BELV DA17 117 H3
BMLY BR1 153 G7
BTFD TW8 104 D5
CHSGTN KT9 172 A3
DAGE RM10 80 C7
HGT N6 54 B6
HPTN TW12 141 K6
HSLWW TW4 122 E4
HYS/HAR UB3 82 E6
KUT KT1 159 F1
PEND EN3 31 F4
RCH/KEW TW9 125 H2
ROMW/RG RM7 62 D1
SCUP DA14 154 E3
SUN TW16 141 F6
SUT SM1 174 E4
TWK TW1 124 B4
WELL DA16 136 C2
Orchardson St STJWD NW8 9 G1
Orchard Sq WKENS * W14 107 J4
Orchard St DART DA1 139 H5
MBLAR W1H 10 A5
THDIT KT7 158 C7
WALTH E17 57 G3
Orchard Ter EN * EN1 30 C5
WLSDN * NW10 69 H3
Orchard Vls SCUP * DA14 155 J5
Orchard Wy CROY/NA CR0 166 B6
EN EN1 30 A2
ESH/CLAY KT10 170 C5
SUT SM1 175 H3
Orchid Cl CHSGTN KT9 171 J6
STHL UB1 83 J5
Orchid Rd STHGT/OAK N14 28 C6
Orchid St SHB W12 87 J6
Orde Hall St BMSBY * WC1N 11 L2
Ordell Rd BOW E3 93 H1
Ordnance Cl FELT TW13 140 E1
Ordnance Crs GNWCH SE10 113 H1
Ordnance Hl STJWD NW8 3 H4
Ordnance Ms STJWD NW8 3 H5
Ordnance Rd CAN/RD E16 94 D4
WOOL/PLUM SE18 115 F5
Oregon Av MNPK E12 77 K3
Oregon Cl NWMAL KT3 159 K3
Oregon Sq ORP BR6 169 J7
Orestes Ms KIL/WHAMP * NW6 70 E4
Orford Gdns TWK TW1 143 F1
Orford Rd CAT SE6 151 K2
SWFD E18 59 F2
WALTH E17 57 K4
Oriel Cl MTCM CR4 163 J3
Oriel Ct HAMP NW3 71 G3
Oriel Dr BARN SW13 107 F5
Oriel Gdns CLAY IG5 59 K2
Oriel Rd HOM E9 75 F5
Oriel Wy NTHLT UB5 66 B6
Oriental Rd CAN/RD E16 95 H7
Orient St LBTH SE11 18 C5
Orient Wy CLPT E5 75 F2
LEY E10 75 J2
Oriole Wy THMD SE28 97 H6
Orion Rd MUSWH N10 40 A5
Orion Wy NTHWD HA6 32 D3
Orissa Rd WOOL/PLUM SE18 115 K4
Orkney St BTSEA SW11 129 F1
Orlando Rd CLAP SW4 129 H2
Orleans Rd NRWD SE19 149 K5
TWK TW1 124 C6
Orleston Ms HOLWY N7 73 G5
Orleston Rd HOLWY N7 73 G5
Orley Farm Rd HRW HA1 66 E2
Ormanton Rd SYD SE26 150 C3
Orme Ct BAY/PAD W2 8 C7
Orme Court Ms BAY/PAD * W2 8 D7
Orme La BAY/PAD W2 8 C7
Ormeley Rd BAL SW12 129 G6
Orme Rd KUT KT1 159 J1
SUT SM1 175 F5
Ormerod Gdns MTCM CR4 163 F1
Ormesby Cl THMD SE28 97 K6
Ormesby Wy
KTN/HRWW/W HA3 50 B5
Orme Sq BAY/PAD W2 8 C7
Orme Square Ga KENS W8 8 C7
Ormiston Gv SHB W12 87 K7
Ormiston Rd GNWCH SE10 113 K4
Ormond Av HPTN TW12 142 B7
Ormond Cl BMSBY WC1N 11 K2
Ormond Crs HPTN TW12 142 B6
Ormond Dr HPTN TW12 142 B6
Ormonde Av HOR/WEW KT19 173 F7
Ormonde Ct STJWD * NW8 3 L4
Ormonde Ga CHEL SW3 15 M8
Ormonde Pl BGVA SW1W 16 B6
Ormonde Rd
MORT/ESHN SW14 125 J2
NTHWD HA6 32 C4
Ormonde Ter STJWD NW8 3 L4
Ormond Rd ARCH N19 54 E7
RCHPK/HAM TW10 124 E4
Ormond Yd STJS SW1Y 10 F8
Ormsby BELMT * SM2 175 F6
Ormsby Gdns GFD/PVL UB6 84 C1
Ormsby Pl STNW/STAM N16 74 B2
Ormsby St BETH E2 7 L5
Ormside St PECK SE15 111 K5
Ormskirk Rd OXHEY WD19 33 H3
Ornan Rd HAMP NW3 71 J4
Oronsay Wk IS * N1 73 J5
Orphanage Rd WAT WD17 21 G1
Orpheus St CMBW SE5 110 E7
Orpington Gdns ED N9 42 A2
Orpington Rd CHST BR7 169 K2
WCHMH N21 29 G7
Orpwood Cl HPTN TW12 141 K5
Orsett Ms BAY/PAD W2 8 E4
Orsett St LBTH SE11 17 M7
Orsett Ter BAY/PAD W2 8 E4
WFD IG8 45 G7
Orsman Rd IS N1 7 J4
Orton St WAP E1W 92 C7
Orville Rd BTSEA SW11 128 C1
Orwell Cl HYS/HAR UB3 82 C6
Orwell Ct WATN * WD24 21 H1
Orwell Rd PLSTW E13 95 G1
Osbaldeston Rd
STNW/STAM N16 74 C1
Osberton Rd LEE/GVPK SE12 133 K4
Osbert St WEST SW1P 17 G6
Osborn Cl HACK E8 74 C7
Osborne Av STWL/WRAY TW19 120 B7
Osborne Cl BECK BR3 166 B3
EBAR EN4 27 K2
EMPK RM11 63 K5
FELT TW13 141 H4
Osborne Ct EA * W5 86 A4
Osborne Gdns THHTH CR7 164 D1
Osborne Gv WALTH E17 57 H3
Osborne Rd ACT W3 105 J1
BELV DA17 117 G4
CRICK NW2 69 K5
EMPK RM11 63 K5
FSBYPK N4 55 G7
FSTGT E7 77 F4
HOM E9 75 H5
HSLW TW3 122 E2
KUTN/CMB KT2 144 A6
LEY E10 75 K2
PEND EN3 31 G1
PLMGR N13 41 G2
STHL UB1 84 C5
THHTH CR7 164 D1
Osborne Sq DAGW RM9 80 B3
Osborne Ter TOOT * SW17 148 A4
Osborne Wy CHSGTN KT9 172 B4
Osborn Gdns MLHL NW7 38 B6
Osborn La FSTH SE23 132 B6
Osborn St WCHPL E1 13 M3
Osborn Ter BKHTH/KID SE3 133 J3
Osbourne Ct RYLN/HDSTN * HA2 48 B3
Oscar Faber Pl IS * N1 7 K2
Oscar St DEPT SE8 112 D7
Oseney Crs KTTN NW5 72 C5
O'shea Gv BOW E3 75 H7
Osidge La STHGT/OAK N14 28 A7
Osier Crs MUSWH N10 39 K7
Osiers Rd WAND/EARL SW18 127 K3
Osier St WCHPL E1 92 E3
Osier Wy LEY E10 75 K2
MTCM CR4 162 D4
Oslac Rd CAT SE6 151 K4
Osman Rd ED N9 42 C2
HMSMTH * W6 107 F2
Osmond Cl RYLN/HDSTN HA2 66 C1
Osmond Gdns WLGTN SM6 176 C4
Osmund St SHB W12 87 H5
Osnaburgh St CAMTN NW1 10 D1
Osnaburgh Ter CAMTN NW1 4 D9
Osney Wk MRDN SM4 162 C5
Osprey Cl EHAM E6 95 J4
SWFD E18 58 E3
WALTH E17 43 G6
WDR/YW UB7 100 A1
Osprey Est BERM/RHTH SE16 112 A3
Osprey Ms PEND EN3 30 D4
Ospringe Cl PGE/AN SE20 150 E6
Ospringe Rd KTTN NW5 72 C3
Osram Rd WBLY * HA9 67 K2
Ossian Rd FSBYPK N4 55 F6
Ossington Buildings
MHST * W1U 10 A2
Ossington Cl BAY/PAD * W2 8 B7
Ossington St BAY/PAD W2 8 B6
Ossory Rd STHWK SE1 111 H5
Ossulston St CAMTN NW1 5 H6
Ossulton Pl EFNCH * N2 53 G2
Ossulton Wy EFNCH N2 53 G3
Ostade Rd BRXS/STRHM SW2 130 A6
Osten Ms SKENS SW7 14 D4
Osterberg Rd DART DA1 139 J3
Osterley Av ISLW TW7 103 J6
Osterley Crs ISLW TW7 103 K7
Osterley Gdns THHTH CR7 164 D1
Osterley La NWDGN UB2 103 G4
Osterley Park Rd
NWDGN * UB2 102 E2
Osterley Park View Rd
HNWL W7 103 K1
Osterley Rd ISLW TW7 103 K6
STNW/STAM N16 74 A3
Ostliffe Rd PLMGR N13 41 H4
Oswald Rd STHL UB1 83 J7
Oswald's Md CLPT E5 75 G3
Oswald St CLPT E5 75 F2
Oswald Ter CRICK * NW2 70 A2
Osward CROY/NA * CR0 179 H7
Osward Pl ED N9 42 C1
Osward Rd BAL SW12 147 K1
Oswin St LBTH SE11 18 D5
Oswyth Rd CMBW SE5 131 F1
Otford Cl BMLY BR1 169 F2
BXLY DA5 137 J5
PGE/AN SE20 150 E7
Otford Crs BROCKY SE4 132 C5
Othello Cl LBTH SE11 18 C7
Otis St BOW E3 94 A2
Otley Dr GNTH/NBYPK IG2 60 B5
Otley Rd CAN/RD E16 95 G5
Otley Ter CLPT E5 74 E1
Otley Wy OXHEY WD19 33 G2
Ottawa Gdns DAGE RM10 81 F6
Ottaway St CLPT E5 74 C2
Otterbourne Rd CHING E4 44 B2
CROY/NA CR0 177 J1
Otterburn Gdns ISLW TW7 104 B6
Otterburn St TOOT SW17 147 K5
Otterden St CAT SE6 151 J3
Otter Rd GFD/PVL UB6 84 C3
Otto Cl SYD * SE26 150 D1
Ottoman Ter WAT WD17 21 G2
Otto St WALW SE17 110 C5
Otway Gdns BUSH WD23 22 E6
Oulton Cl THMD SE28 97 J5
Oulton Crs BARK IG11 79 F5
Oulton Rd SEVS/STOTM N15 55 K4
Oulton Wy OXHEY WD19 33 K3
Oundle Av BUSH WD23 22 C5
Ouseley Rd BAL SW12 128 E7
Outer Cir CAMTN NW1 3 M5
Outgate Rd WLSDN NW10 69 H6
Outram Pl IS N1 5 K3
Outram Rd CROY/NA CR0 178 B1
EHAM E6 77 J7
WDGN N22 40 D7
Outwich St HDTCH * EC3A 13 K4
The Oval BETH E2 92 D1
BFN/LL DA15 136 B6
Oval Ct EDGW * HA8 36 E6
Oval Pl VX/NE SW8 110 A6
Oval Rd CAMTN NW1 4 C3
CROY/NA CR0 177 K1
Oval Rd North DAGE RM10 80 E7
Oval Rd South DAGE RM10 98 E1
Oval Wy LBTH SE11 17 M9
Overbrae BECK BR3 151 J5
Overbrook Wk EDGW HA8 36 C6
Overbury Av BECK BR3 166 E2
Overbury Rd SEVS/STOTM N15 55 K5
Overbury St CLPT E5 75 F3
Overcliff Rd LEW SE13 132 D2
Overcourt Cl BFN/LL DA15 136 C5
Overdale Av NWMAL KT3 159 K1
Overdale Rd EA W5 104 D2
Overdown Rd CAT SE6 151 J3
Overhill Cottages MTCM * CR4 163 F1
Overhill Rd EDUL SE22 131 H6
PUR/KEN CR8 177 G7
Overhill Wy BECK BR3 167 G4
Overlea Rd CLPT E5 56 C6
Overmead ELTH/MOT SE9 135 J6
Overstand Cl BECK BR3 166 D4
Overstone Gdns CROY/NA CR0 166 C6
Overstone Rd HMSMTH W6 107 F3
Overton Cl ISLW TW7 104 A7
WLSDN NW10 68 E5
Overton Dr CHDH RM6 61 J6
WAN E11 59 F6
Overton Rd ABYW SE2 116 D2
BELMT SM2 174 E6
BRXN/ST SW9 130 B1
LEY E10 57 G7
STHGT/OAK N14 28 E4
Overton's Yd CROY/NA CR0 177 J2
Overy Liberty DART DA1 139 H6
Overy St DART DA1 139 J5
Ovesdon Av RYLN/HDSTN HA2 47 K7
Ovett Cl NRWD SE19 150 A5
Ovex Cl POP/IOD E14 113 F2
Ovington Gdns CHEL SW3 15 K4
Ovington Ms CHEL SW3 15 K4
Ovington Sq CHEL SW3 15 K4
Ovington St CHEL SW3 15 K4
Owen Cl CROY/NA CR0 164 E5
NTHLT * UB5 83 F2
THMD SE28 97 J7
Owen Gdns WFD IG8 45 J5
Owenite St ABYW SE2 116 C3
Owen Rd PLMGR N13 41 J4
Owen's Rw FSBYE EC1V 6 C7
Owen St FSBYE EC1V 6 B6

Owens Wy FSTH SE23 132 B6
Owen Wy WLSDN NW10 68 E5
Owgan Cl CMBW SE5 110 E6
Oxberry Av FUL/PGN SW6 127 H1
Oxendon St SOHO/SHAV * W1D 11 G7
Oxenford St PECK SE15 131 G2
Oxenpark Av WBLY HA9 50 A6
Oxestalls Rd DEPT SE8 112 B4
Oxford Av HEST TW5 103 F4
HYS/HAR UB3 101 J6
RYNPK SW20 161 H1
Oxford Cl ASHF TW15 140 A6
ED N9 42 D1
MTCM CR4 163 H2
NTHWD HA6 32 A3
Oxford Ct MANHO EC4N 13 G6
Oxford Crs NWMAL KT3 160 A5
Oxford Dr RSLP HA4 65 G1
Oxford Gdns CHSWK W4 105 H4
NKENS W10 88 B5
TRDG/WHET N20 27 H7
WCHMH N21 29 J6
Oxford Ga WKENS * W14 107 G3
Oxford Ms BXLY DA5 137 H7
Oxford Rd CAR SM5 175 J5
EA W5 85 K6
ED N9 42 D1
FSBYPK N4 55 G7
HPTN TW12 142 D4
HRW HA1 48 C5
IL IG1 78 C3
KIL/WHAMP NW6 2 B5
KTN/HRWW/W HA3 49 F2
NRWD SE19 149 K5
PEND EN3 30 D4
PUT/ROE SW15 127 H3
SCUP DA14 155 H4
SRTFD E15 76 B5
WFD IG8 45 H4
WLGTN * SM6 176 C4
Oxford Rd North CHSWK W4 105 J4
Oxford Rd South CHSWK W4 105 H4
Oxford Rw SUN * TW16 156 B2
Oxford Sq BAY/PAD W2 9 K5
Oxford St SOHO/CST W1F 11 G4
WATW WD18 21 F4
Oxford Wk STHL UB1 83 K7
Oxford Wy FELT TW13 141 H3
Oxgate Court Pde CRICK * NW2 69 K1
Oxgate Gdns CRICK NW2 69 K2
Oxgate La CRICK NW2 69 K1
Oxhawth Crs HAYES BR2 169 F4
Oxhey Av OXHEY WD19 21 H6
Oxhey Dr OXHEY WD19 33 F3
Oxhey La OXHEY WD19 21 H6
PIN HA5 34 A4
Oxhey Ridge Cl OXHEY WD19 32 E4
Oxhey Rd OXHEY WD19 21 G6
Oxleas EHAM E6 96 B5
Oxleas Cl WELL DA16 135 J1
Oxleay Rd RYLN/HDSTN HA2 48 A7
Oxleigh Cl NWMAL KT3 160 B4
Oxley Cl STHWK SE1 19 M7
Oxleys Rd CRICK NW2 69 K2
Oxlow La DAGE RM10 80 C3
Oxonian St EDUL SE22 131 G3
Oxted Cl MTCM CR4 162 C2
Oxtoby Wy STRHM/NOR SW16 148 D7
Oyster Catchers Cl CAN/RD E16 95 F5
Oyster Rw WCHPL E1 92 E5
Ozolins Wy CAN/RD E16 94 D5

P

Pace Pl WCHPL E1 92 D5
Pacific Cl EBED/NFELT TW14 121 J7
Pacific Rd CAN/RD E16 94 E5
Packington Sq IS N1 6 E4
Packington St IS N1 6 D4
Packmores Rd ELTH/MOT SE9 135 J4
Padbury Cl EBED/NFELT TW14 121 G7
Padbury Ct BETH E2 7 M8
Paddenswick Rd
HMSMTH W6 106 D2
Paddington Cl NTHLT UB5 83 H3
Paddington Gn BAY/PAD W2 9 G3
Paddington St MHST W1U 10 A2
Paddock Cl BKHTH/KID SE3 133 K2
NTHLT UB5 84 A1
OXHEY WD19 21 J5
SYD SE26 151 F3
WPK KT4 160 B7
Paddock Gdns NRWD SE19 150 A5
Paddock La BAR EN5 25 G3
Paddock Rd BXLYHS DA6 137 F3
CRICK NW2 69 J2
RSLP HA4 65 H2
The Paddocks EA * W5 104 E2
EBAR EN4 27 K2
MLHL * NW7 38 D5
WBLY HA9 68 D1
Paddocks Cl RYLN/HDSTN HA2 66 B3
Paddock Wy CHST BR7 154 D6
Padfield Rd CMBW SE5 130 D2
Padley Cl CHSGTN KT9 172 B4
Padnall Rd CHDH RM6 61 K2
Padstow Rd ENC/FH EN2 29 H1
Padstow Wk
EBED/NFELT TW14 140 D1
Padua Rd PGE/AN SE20 150 E7
Pagden St VX/NE SW8 109 G7
Pageant Crs BERM/RHTH SE16 93 H6
Pageant Wk CROY/NA CR0 178 A2
Page Cl DAGW RM9 80 A4
FELT TW13 141 J5
KTN/HRWW/W HA3 50 B5
Page Crs CROY/NA CR0 177 H4
ERITH DA8 118 C6
Page Green Rd
SEVS/STOTM * N15 56 C4
Page Heath La BMLY BR1 168 C2
Page Heath Vls BMLY BR1 168 C2
Pagehurst Rd CROY/NA CR0 165 H6
Page Meadow MLHL NW7 37 J6
Page Rd EBED/NFELT TW14 121 G5
Page's Hl MUSWH N10 54 A1
Page's La MUSWH N10 54 A1
Page St MLHL NW7 37 J7
WEST SW1P 17 H5
Page's Wk STHWK SE1 19 J5
Pages Yd CHSWK * W4 106 B5
Paget Av SUT SM1 175 H2
Paget Cl HPTN TW12 142 D3
Paget Gdns CHST BR7 154 B7
Paget La ISLW TW7 123 J2
Paget Pl KUTN/CMB * KT2 144 E5
THDIT KT7 158 A7
Paget Ri WOOL/PLUM SE18 115 F6
Paget Rd HGDN/ICK UB10 82 A3
IL IG1 78 B3
STNW/STAM N16 55 K7
Paget St FSBYE EC1V 6 C7
Paget Ter WOOL/PLUM SE18 115 G5
Pagnell St NWCR SE14 112 C6
Pagoda Av RCH/KEW TW9 125 G2
Pagoda Gdns BKHTH/KID SE3 133 G1
Paignton Rd RSLP HA4 64 E2
SEVS/STOTM N15 56 A5
Paines Cl PIN HA5 47 J2
Paine's La PIN HA5 47 J1
Pain's Cl MTCM CR4 163 G1
Painsthorpe Rd
STNW/STAM N16 74 A2
Painters Rd GNTH/NBYPK IG2 61 G2
Paisley Rd CAR SM5 162 C7
WDGN N22 41 H7
Pakeman St HOLWY N7 73 F2
Pakenham Cl BAL SW12 129 F7
Pakenham St FSBYW WC1X 5 M8
Palace Av KENS W8 8 D9
Palace Ct BAY/PAD W2 8 C6
KTN/HRWW/W HA3 50 A5
Palace Court Gdns MUSWH N10 54 C2
Palace Garden Ms KENS W8 8 B8
Palace Gardens Ter KENS W8 8 B8
Palace Ga KENS W8 14 E2
Palace Gates Rd WDGN N22 40 E7
Palace Gn CROY/NA CR0 179 H6
KENS W8 8 C9
Palace Gv BMLY BR1 153 F7
NRWD SE19 150 B6
Palace Ms FUL/PGN * SW6 107 J6
Palace Pde WALTH * E17 57 H3
Palace Pl WESTW SW1E 16 E3
Palace Rd BMLY BR1 153 F7
BRXS/STRHM SW2 130 A7
CEND/HSY/T N8 54 D4
E/WMO/HCT KT8 157 H2
FBAR/BDGN N11 40 E6
KUT KT1 158 E3
NRWD SE19 150 B6
RSLP HA4 65 J3
Palace Sq NRWD SE19 150 B6
Palace St WESTW SW1E 16 E3
Palace Vw BMLY BR1 168 A2
CROY/NA CR0 179 H3
LEE/GVPK SE12 152 E1
Palace View Rd CHING E4 43 K4
Palamos Rd LEY E10 57 J7
Palatine Av STNW/STAM N16 74 A3
Palatine Rd STNW/STAM N16 74 A3
Palemead Cl FUL/PGN SW6 107 G7
Palermo Rd WLSDN NW10 87 J1
Palestine Gv WIM/MER SW19 147 H7
Palewell Common Dr
MORT/ESHN SW14 126 A4
Palewell Pk MORT/ESHN SW14 126 A4
Palfrey Pl BRXN/ST SW9 110 A6
Palgrave Av STHL UB1 84 A6
Palgrave Gdns CAMTN NW1 3 K9
Palgrave Rd SHB W12 106 C2
Palissy St BETH E2 7 L8
Pallet Wy WOOL/PLUM SE18 114 D7
Palliser Dr RAIN RM13 99 J4
Palliser Rd WKENS W14 107 H4
Pall Ml STJS SW1Y 11 G9
Pall Ml East STJS SW1Y 11 G8
Pall Mall Pl STJS SW1Y 10 F9
Palmar Crs BXLYHN DA7 137 H2
Palmar Rd BXLYHN DA7 137 H1
Palm Av SCUP DA14 155 K5
Palm Cl LEY E10 75 K2
Palmeira Rd BXLYHN DA7 136 E2
Palmer Av BUSH WD23 22 B5
CHEAM SM3 174 A3
Palmer Cl HEST TW5 103 F7
WWKM BR4 180 B1
Palmer Crs KUT KT1 159 F2
Palmer Gdns BAR EN5 26 B4
Palmer Pl HOLWY N7 73 G4
Palmer Rd BCTR RM8 61 K7
PLSTW E13 95 F3
Palmers Gv E/WMO/HCT KT8 157 F3
Palmers Rd BETH E2 93 F1
FBAR/BDGN N11 40 C4
MORT/ESHN SW14 125 K2
STRHM/NOR SW16 164 A1
Palmerston Crs PLMGR N13 41 F4
WOOL/PLUM SE18 115 H5
Palmerston Gv
WIM/MER SW19 146 E6
Palmerston Rd ACT W3 105 K2
BKHH IG9 45 G1
CAR SM5 175 K3
CROY/NA CR0 164 F4
FSTGT E7 77 F4
HSLW TW3 103 H7
KIL/WHAMP NW6 70 D6
KTN/HRWW/W * HA3 48 E2
MORT/ESHN SW14 125 K3
SUT SM1 175 G4
WALTH E17 57 H3
WDGN N22 41 F6
WHTN TW2 123 K5
WIM/MER SW19 146 E6
Palmerston Wy VX/NE * SW8 109 G6
Palmer St STJSPK SW1H 17 G3
Palmers Whf KUT * KT1 158 E1
Palm Gv EA W5 105 F2
Palm Rd ROMW/RG RM7 62 E4
Pamela Ct FNCH * N3 39 F5
Pamela Gdns PIN HA5 47 F4
Pams Wy HOR/WEW KT19 173 F4
Pancras La MANHO EC4N 12 F5
Pancras Rd CAMTN NW1 5 H5
Pandora Rd KIL/WHAMP NW6 70 E5
Panfield Ms GNTH/NBYPK IG2 60 A5
Panfield Rd ABYW SE2 116 B2
Pangbourne Av NKENS * W10 88 A4
Pangbourne Dr STAN HA7 35 K4
Panhard Pl STHL UB1 84 B6
Pank Av BAR EN5 27 H4
Pankhurst Cl ISLW TW7 124 A2
Pankhurst Pl WATN WD24 21 G2
Pankhurst Rd WOT/HER KT12 156 B6
Pankridge OXHEY * WD19 33 H1
Panmuir Rd RYNPK SW20 145 K7
Panmure Cl HBRY N5 73 H3
Panmure Rd SYD SE26 150 D2
Pansy Gdns SHB W12 87 J6
Panther Dr WLSDN NW10 69 F4
The Pantiles BMLY BR1 168 D2
BUSH WD23 22 D7
BXLYHN DA7 117 G6
Pantiles Cl PLMGR N13 41 H4
Panton Cl CROY/NA CR0 164 C7
Panton St STJS * SW1Y 11 G7
Paper Buildings EMB * EC4Y 12 B6
Papermill Cl CAR SM5 176 A3
Papillons Wk BKHTH/KID SE3 133 K1
Papworth Gdns HOLWY N7 73 F4
Papworth Wy
BRXS/STRHM SW2 130 B6
The Parade ALP/SUD * HA0 67 H5
BROCKY * SE4 112 C7
BTSEA * SW11 128 C3
CAR * SM5 175 K4
CROY/NA * CR0 163 K5
CROY/NA * CR0 177 F4
DART * DA1 138 C4
EA * W5 85 K5
EDUL * SE22 131 F2
ESH/CLAY KT10 170 E5
FSBYPK * N4 73 G1
KUT * KT1 159 F1
OXHEY * WD19 33 H2
PGE/AN * SE20 150 E7
RCH/KEW * TW9 125 H2
SUN TW16 140 D6
SUT * SM1 174 D2
SYD * SE26 150 D3
WATW WD18 21 F2
Parade Ms BRXS/STRHM SW2 149 H1
Parade Ter CDALE/KGS * NW9 51 J5
Paradise Pas HOLWY N7 73 G4
Paradise Rd CLAP SW4 129 K1
RCHPK/HAM TW10 125 F4
Paradise Rw BETH * E2 92 D2
Paradise St BERM/RHTH SE16 111 J1
Paradise Wk CHEL SW3 15 L9
The Paragon BKHTH/KID SE3 133 K1
Paragon Cl CAN/RD E16 94 E5
Paragon Gv BRYLDS KT5 159 G5
Paragon Ms WALW SE17 19 H5
Paragon Pl BKHTH/KID SE3 133 J1
Paragon Rd HACK E8 74 D5
Parbury Ri CHSGTN KT9 172 A5
Parbury Rd FSTH SE23 132 B5
Parchmore Rd THHTH CR7 164 C1
Parchmore Wy THHTH CR7 164 C1
Pardoner St STHWK SE1 19 H3
Pardon St FSBYE EC1V 6 D9
Parfett St WCHPL E1 92 C4
Parfrey St HMSMTH W6 107 F5
Parham Dr GNTH/NBYPK IG2 60 B5
Paris Gdn STHWK SE1 12 C8
Parish Cl EMPK RM11 81 K1
Parish Gate Dr BFN/LL DA15 135 K5
Parish La PGE/AN SE20 151 F6
Parish Whf WOOL/PLUM SE18 114 D3
The Park CAR SM5 175 K4
EA W5 85 K7
GLDGN NW11 53 F7
HGT N6 54 A6
SCUP DA14 155 F4
Park Ap BERM/RHTH * SE16 111 K2
WELL DA16 136 C3
Park Av BMLY BR1 152 E5
BUSH WD23 21 H1
CAR SM5 176 A5
CRICK NW2 70 A5
EHAM E6 78 A7
EN EN1 29 K4
FNCH N3 39 F7
GLDGN NW11 53 F7
HSLW TW3 123 G5
IL IG1 78 A1
MORT/ESHN SW14 126 A3
MTCM CR4 148 B6
ORP BR6 181 K1
PLMGR N13 41 G2
RSLP HA4 46 C5
SRTFD E15 76 C5
STHL UB1 102 E1
UED N18 42 C3
WATW WD18 20 E2
WDGN N22 54 E1
WFD IG8 45 F4
WLSDN NW10 86 B2
WWKM BR4 180 A1
Park Av East EW KT17 173 J5
Park Av North CEND/HSY/T N8 54 D3
WLSDN NW10 69 K4
Park Avenue Rd TOTM N17 42 D6
Park Av South CEND/HSY/T N8 54 D3
Park Av West EW KT17 173 J5
Park Cha WBLY HA9 68 B3
Park Cl BUSH WD23 21 H2
CAR SM5 175 K5
CRICK NW2 69 J2
HOM E9 74 E7
HPTN TW12 142 C7
HSLW TW3 123 H4
KTN/HRWW/W HA3 34 E7
KUTN/CMB KT2 144 C7
SKENS * SW7 15 L2
TRDG/WHET * N20 39 H3
WKENS W14 107 J2
WLSDN NW10 86 B2
Park Cottages FNCH * N3 52 D1
Park Ct DUL * SE21 149 K2
NWMAL KT3 160 A3
SYD * SE26 150 D5
WBLY HA9 68 A4
Park Crs BORE WD6 24 B2
EMPK RM11 63 K5
ENC/FH EN2 29 K3
ERITH DA8 117 K5
FNCH N3 39 F6
KTN/HRWW/W HA3 34 E7
REGST W1B 10 C1
WHTN TW2 123 J7
Park Crescent Ms East
REGST W1B 10 D1
Park Crescent Ms West
CAVSQ/HST W1G 10 C1
Park Cft EDGW HA8 36 E7
Parkcroft Rd LEE/GVPK SE12 133 J6
Parkdale Crs WPK KT4 173 F2
Parkdale Rd WOOL/PLUM SE18 115 K4
Park Dr ACT W3 105 H3
CHARL SE7 114 D5
DAGE RM10 80 E2
GLDGN NW11 53 F7
KTN/HRWW/W HA3 34 D5
MORT/ESHN SW14 126 A4
ROM RM1 63 F3
RYLN/HDSTN HA2 48 A6
WCHMH N21 29 J5
Park End BMLY BR1 152 D7
HAMP NW3 71 J3
Park End Rd ROM RM1 63 G3
Parker Cl CAN/RD E16 95 J7
CAR SM5 175 K5
Parker Ms HOL/ALD * WC2B 11 K4
Parke Rd BARN SW13 106 D7
Parker Rd CROY/NA CR0 177 J3
Parker's Rw STHWK SE1 19 M2
Parker St CAN/RD E16 95 J7
HOL/ALD WC2B 11 K4
Park Farm Cl EFNCH N2 53 G2
Park Farm Rd BMLY BR1 153 H7
KUTN/CMB KT2 144 A6
Parkfield Av FELT TW13 140 E2
MORT/ESHN SW14 126 B3
NTHLT UB5 83 H1
RYLN/HDSTN HA2 48 C1
Parkfield Cl EDGW HA8 36 D5
NTHLT UB5 83 J1
Parkfield Crs FELT TW13 140 E2
RSLP HA4 65 J1
RYLN/HDSTN HA2 48 C1
Parkfield Dr NTHLT UB5 83 H1
Parkfield Gdns
RYLN/HDSTN HA2 48 B2
Parkfield Pde FELT * TW13 140 E2
Parkfield Rd FELT TW13 140 E2
NTHLT UB5 83 J1
NWCR SE14 112 C7
RYLN/HDSTN HA2 66 C2
WLSDN NW10 69 J6
Parkfields CROY/NA CR0 166 C7
PUT/ROE SW15 127 F3
Parkfields Av CDALE/KGS NW9 51 F7
RYNPK SW20 145 K7
Parkfields Cl CAR SM5 176 A3
Parkfields Rd KUTN/CMB KT2 144 B4
Parkfield St IS N1 6 B5
Parkfield Wy HAYES BR2 168 E5
Park Gdns CDALE/KGS NW9 50 D2
ERITH DA8 118 A3
KUTN/CMB KT2 144 B4
Parkgate BKHTH/KID SE3 133 J2
Park Ga EA W5 85 K4
EFNCH N2 53 H2
WCHMH N21 29 F6
Parkgate Cl KUTN/CMB KT2 144 D5
Park Gate Ct HPTN * TW12 142 C4
Parkgate Gdns
MORT/ESHN SW14 126 A4
Parkgate Rd BTSEA SW11 108 D6
CAR SM5 176 A4
Park Gates RYLN/HDSTN * HA2 66 A3
Park Gv BMLY BR1 153 F7
BXLYHN DA7 137 K3
EDGW HA8 36 B4
FBAR/BDGN N11 40 D6
SRTFD E15 76 E7
Park Grove Rd WAN E11 76 C1
Park Hall Rd DUL SE21 149 K2
EFNCH N2 53 J3
Parkham St BTSEA SW11 108 C7
Park Hl BMLY BR1 168 D3
CAR SM5 175 K5
CLAP SW4 129 J4
EA W5 85 K4
FSTH SE23 150 D1
RCHPK/HAM TW10 125 G5
Park Hill Cl CAR SM5 175 J4
Park Hill Ri CROY/NA CR0 178 A1
Park Hill Rd CROY/NA CR0 178 A1
HAYES BR2 167 H1
WLGTN SM6 176 B6
Parkhill Rd BFN/LL DA15 154 E2
BXLY DA5 137 G6
HAMP NW3 71 K4
Parkhill Wk HAMP NW3 71 K4
Parkholme Rd HACK E8 74 C5
Park House Gdns TWK TW1 124 D4
Parkhouse St CMBW SE5 110 E6
Parkhurst Gdns BXLY DA5 137 H6
Parkhurst Rd BXLY DA5 137 H6
FBAR/BDGN N11 40 A3
HOLWY N7 72 E3
MNPK E12 78 A3
SUT SM1 175 H3
TOTM N17 56 C1
WALTH * E17 57 G3
WDGN N22 41 F6
Parkland Av ROM RM1 63 G1
Parkland Rd WDGN N22 55 F1
WFD IG8 45 F6
Parklands BRYLDS KT5 159 G4
BUSH * WD23 22 C5
HGT N6 54 B6
Parklands Cl GNTH/NBYPK IG2 60 C6
MORT/ESHN SW14 125 K4
Parklands Dr FNCH N3 52 C2
Parklands Pde HEST * TW5 122 C1
Parklands Rd TOOT SW17 148 B4
Parklands Wy WPK KT4 173 G1
Park La CAR SM5 176 A4
CHDH RM6 61 K5
CHEAM SM3 174 C5
CROY/NA CR0 177 K1
ED N9 42 B2
EMPK RM11 63 J6
HCH RM12 81 K5
HYS/HAR UB3 101 K6
MBLAR W1H 9 M6
MYFR/PICC W1J 16 B1
RCH/KEW * TW9 124 E3
RYLN/HDSTN HA2 66 B2
SRTFD * E15 76 A7
STAN HA7 35 G2
TEDD TW11 143 F5
TOTM N17 42 C6
WBLY HA9 68 B3
YEAD UB4 82 C4
Park Lane Cl TOTM N17 42 C6
Parklea Cl CDALE/KGS NW9 37 G7
Parkleigh Rd WIM/MER SW19 162 A1
Parkleys KUTN/CMB KT2 143 K3
Parkleys Pde KUTN/CMB * KT2 143 K3
Park Md BFN/LL DA15 136 B4
RYLN/HDSTN HA2 66 B2
Parkmead PUT/ROE SW15 126 E5
Parkmead Gdns MLHL NW7 37 H5
Park Ms CHST BR7 154 B5
NKENS W10 88 C1
STWL/WRAY TW19 120 C6
Park Pde ACT * W3 105 H2
HYS/HAR * UB3 82 C5
WLSDN NW10 87 H1
Park Pl ACT W3 105 H3
BMLY * BR1 153 F7
EA W5 85 K7
HPTN TW12 142 C5
POP/IOD E14 93 J7
WBLY HA9 68 B3
WHALL SW1A 10 E9
Park Place Vls BAY/PAD W2 8 F2
Park Ridings CEND/HSY/T N8 55 G2
Park Ri KTN/HRWW/W HA3 34 E7
Park Rise Rd FSTH SE23 132 B7
Park Rd ALP/SUD HA0 68 A5
BAR EN5 26 D3
BECK BR3 151 H6
BMLY BR1 153 F7
BRYLDS KT5 159 G5
BUSH WD23 22 A5
CAMTN NW1 9 M1
CDALE/KGS NW9 51 F6
CEND/HSY/T N8 54 D4
CEND/HSY/T N8 55 H3
CHEAM SM3 174 C5
CHST BR7 154 B5
CHSWK W4 106 A5
DART DA1 139 K6
E/WMO/HCT KT8 143 J7
E/WMO/HCT KT8 157 H3
EBAR EN4 27 H3
ED N9 42 B3
EFNCH N2 53 H2
EHAM E6 77 G7
ESH/CLAY KT10 170 B3
FBAR/BDGN N11 40 D6
FELT TW13 141 H3
HNWL W7 85 F6
HPTN TW12 142 C4
HSLW TW3 123 H4
IL IG1 78 D2
ISLW TW7 104 C7
KUT KT1 143 J7
KUTN/CMB KT2 144 B4
LEY E10 57 J7
MNPK E12 77 F1
MNPK E12 77 H3
NWMAL KT3 160 A3
RCHPK/HAM TW10 125 G5
SNWD SE25 165 F3
SRTFD E15 76 E7
STHGT/OAK N14 28 D6
STJWD NW8 3 K8
SUN TW16 141 F6
TEDD TW11 143 F6
TWK TW1 124 D5
WALTH E17 57 H4
WAN E11 59 F7
WIM/MER SW19 147 H6
WLGTN SM6 176 B4
WLGTN SM6 176 B1
WLSDN * NW10 69 G7
YEAD UB4 82 C4
Park Rd East ACT W3 105 K1
Park Rd North ACT W3 105 J1
CHSWK W4 106 A5
Park Rw GNWCH SE10 113 G5
Park Royal Rd WLSDN NW10 86 E2
Parkshot RCH/KEW TW9 124 E3
Park Side BKHH IG9 45 F1
CRICK NW2 69 J2
HYS/HAR * UB3 82 C6
Parkside BECK * BR3 166 E1
BKHTH/KID * SE3 113 J6
CHEAM SM3 174 C5
FNCH N3 39 F7
HPTN TW12 142 D4
MLHL NW7 37 J5
OXHEY * WD19 21 G5
SCUP DA14 155 H1
WIM/MER SW19 146 B3
Parkside Av BMLY BR1 168 D3
BXLYHN DA7 138 A1
ROM RM1 63 F1
WIM/MER SW19 146 B4
Parkside Cl PGE/AN SE20 150 E6
Parkside Crs BRYLDS KT5 159 K5
HOLWY N7 73 G2
Parkside Cross BXLYHN DA7 138 B1
Parkside Dr EDGW HA8 36 C2
WAT WD17 20 C1
Parkside Est HOM * E9 75 F7
Parkside Gdns EBAR EN4 27 K7
WIM/MER SW19 146 B3
Parkside Pde ERITH * DA8 138 C1
Parkside Rd BELV DA17 117 J3
HSLW TW3 123 G4
NTHWD HA6 32 D4
Parkside St BTSEA SW11 109 F7
Parkside Ter UED * N18 41 K3
Parkside Wy RYLN/HDSTN HA2 48 B3
Park Sq East CAMTN NW1 4 C9
Park Square Ms CAMTN NW1 10 C1
Park Sq West CAMTN NW1 4 C9
Parkstead Rd PUT/ROE SW15 126 D4
Park Steps BAY/PAD * W2 9 K6
Parkstone Av UED N18 42 B4
Parkstone Rd PECK * SE15 131 H1
Park St CROY/NA CR0 177 J2
MYFR/PKLN W1K 10 A7
STHWK SE1 12 E8
TEDD TW11 142 E5
Park Ter CAR * SM5 175 J2
WPK KT4 160 D7
Parkthorne Cl
RYLN/HDSTN * HA2 48 B5
Parkthorne Dr
RYLN/HDSTN HA2 48 A5
Parkthorne Rd BAL SW12 129 J6
Park Vw ACT W3 86 E4
NWMAL KT3 160 C2
PIN HA5 33 K7
WBLY HA9 68 D4
WCHMH N21 29 F6
Park View Ct
NFNCH/WDSP * N12 39 J3
Park View Crs FBAR/BDGN N11 40 B3
Park View Dr MTCM CR4 162 C1
Park View Est HBRY * N5 73 J3
Parkview Gdns CLAY IG5 59 K3
Park View Gdns HDN NW4 52 A4
WDGN * N22 41 G7
Park View Rd CRICK NW2 69 H3
EA W5 86 A4
ELTH/MOT SE9 135 G7
FNCH N3 39 F7
PIN HA5 33 F5
STHL UB1 84 A7
TOTM N17 56 C2
WELL DA16 136 E2
Parkview Rd CROY/NA CR0 165 H7
Park Village East CAMTN NW1 4 C5
Park Village West CAMTN NW1 4 C5
Park Vls TOOT * SW17 147 J4
Parkville Rd FUL/PGN SW6 107 J6
Park Vis GNWCH SE10 113 G5
Park Wk WBPTN SW10 14 F9
The Parkway HEST TW5 101 K5
HEST TW5 102 A3
NTHLT UB5 83 H2
Park Wy E/WMO/HCT KT8 157 H2
EBED/NFELT TW14 122 A6
EDGW HA8 36 D7
ENC/FH EN2 29 G1
GLDGN NW11 52 C4
RSLP HA4 46 E7
TRDG/WHET N20 39 K3

Parkway CAMTN NW1 4 D3
CROY/NA CR0 180 A7
ERITHM DA18 117 F2
GDMY/SEVK IG3 79 F2
GPK RM2 63 H1
RAIN RM13 99 J3
RYNPK SW20 161 G3
STHGT/OAK N14 40 E1
WFD IG8 45 G4
Park West BAY/PAD W2 9 K4
Park West Pl BAY/PAD W2 9 K4
Parkwood BECK BR3 151 J6
Parkwood Av ESH/CLAY KT10 157 H7
Parkwood Ms HGT N6 54 B5
Parkwood Rd BXLY DA5 137 G6
ISLW TW7 104 A7
WIM/MER SW19 146 D4
Parliament Ct WCHPL * E1 13 K3
Parliament Hl HAMP NW3 71 J3
Parliament Hill Flds KTTN * NW5 72 A2
Parliament Sq WEST SW1P 17 J2
Parliament St WHALL SW1A 17 J1
Parma Crs BTSEA SW11 128 E3
Parmiter St BETH E2 92 D1
Parnell Cl EDGW HA8 36 D3
SHB W12 106 E2
Parnell Rd BOW E3 75 H7
Parnham St POP/IOD * E14 93 G5
Parolles Rd ARCH N19 54 C7
Paroma Rd BELV DA17 117 H2
Parr Av EW KT17 173 K7
Parr Cl ED N9 42 D3
Parr Rd EHAM E6 77 H7
STAN HA7 35 K7
Parrs Cl SAND/SEL CR2 177 K7
Parr's Pl HPTN TW12 142 A6
Parr St IS N1 7 G5
Parry Av EHAM E6 95 K5
Parry Cl EW KT17 173 J6
Parry Pl WOOL/PLUM SE18 115 G3
Parry Rd NKENS W10 88 C2
SNWD SE25 165 F2
Parry St VX/NE SW8 17 K9
Parsifal Rd KIL/WHAMP NW6 70 E4
Parsloes Av DAGW RM9 80 A4
Parsonage Cl HYS/HAR UB3 82 D5
Parsonage Gdns ENC/FH EN2 29 J1
Parsonage La ENC/FH EN2 29 K1
Parsonage Manorway
ERITH DA8 117 H5
Parsonage St POP/IOD E14 113 F3
Parsons Crs EDGW HA8 36 C2
Parsons Gn FUL/PGN SW6 107 K7
Parsons Green La
FUL/PGN SW6 107 K7
Parsons Gv EDGW HA8 36 C2
Parson's Md CROY/NA CR0 164 C7
E/WMO/HCT KT8 157 H2
Parsons Rd PLSTW E13 95 G1
Parson St HDN NW4 52 A2
Parthenia Rd FUL/PGN SW6 107 K7
Partingdale La MLHL NW7 38 B4
Partridge Cl BAR EN5 26 A5
BUSH * WD23 22 C7
CAN/RD E16 95 H4
STAN HA7 36 A3
Partridge Gn ELTH/MOT SE9 154 A2
Partridge Rd HPTN TW12 141 K5
SCUP DA14 154 E2
Partridge Sq EHAM E6 95 J4
Partridge Wy WDGN N22 40 E7
Pasadena Cl HYS/HAR UB3 101 K1
Pascal St VX/NE SW8 109 J6
Pascoe Rd LEW SE13 133 G4
Pasley Cl WALW SE17 18 D8
Pasquier Rd WALTH E17 57 G2
Passey Pl ELTH/MOT SE9 134 E5
Passfield Dr POP/IOD E14 93 K4
Passmore Gdns
FBAR/BDGN N11 40 D5
Passmore St BGVA SW1W 16 A6
Pasteur Cl CDALE/KGS NW9 51 G1
Pasteur Gdns UED N18 41 J4
Paston Cl WLGTN SM6 176 C2
Paston Crs LEE/GVPK SE12 134 A6
Pastor St LBTH SE11 18 D5
Pasture Cl ALP/SUD HA0 67 H2
BUSH WD23 22 C6
Pasture Rd ALP/SUD HA0 67 H1
CAT SE6 133 H7
DAGW RM9 80 B4
The Pastures OXHEY WD19 21 F6
TRDG/WHET N20 26 D7
Patcham Ter VX/NE SW8 109 G7
Patching Wy YEAD UB4 83 J4
Paternoster Rw STP EC4M 12 D5
Pater St KENS W8 14 A4
Pates Manor Dr
EBED/NFELT TW14 121 G6
The Path WIM/MER SW19 147 F7
Pathfield Rd
STRHM/NOR SW16 148 D5
The Pathway OXHEY WD19 21 H7
Patience Rd BTSEA SW11 128 D1
Patio Cl CLAP SW4 129 J5
Patmore St VX/NE SW8 109 H7
Patmos Rd BRXN/ST SW9 110 C6
Paton Cl BOW E3 93 J2
Patricia Ct WELL DA16 116 C6
Patricia Vls TOTM * N17 42 D7
Patrick Rd PLSTW E13 95 G2
Patriot Sq BETH E2 92 D1
Patrol Pl CAT SE6 132 E5
Patshull Pl KTTN NW5 72 C5
Patshull Rd KTTN NW5 72 C5
Pattenden Rd CAT SE6 132 C7
Patten Rd WAND/EARL SW18 128 D6
Patterdale Cl BMLY BR1 152 C5
Patterdale Rd PECK SE15 111 K6
Patterson Rd NRWD SE19 150 B5
Pattina Wk BERM/RHTH SE16 93 G7
Pattison Rd CRICK NW2 70 E2
Paul Cl SRTFD E15 76 C6
Paulet Rd CMBW SE5 130 C1
Paul Gdns CROY/NA CR0 178 B1
Paulhan Rd KTN/HRWW/W HA3 49 K3
Paulin Dr WCHMH N21 29 G6
Pauline Crs WHTN TW2 123 H7
Paul Julius Cl POP/IOD E14 94 B6
Paul Robeson Cl EHAM E6 96 A2
Paul St SDTCH EC2A 7 J9
SRTFD E15 76 C7
Paultons Sq CHEL SW3 15 H9
Paultons St CHEL SW3 108 C5
Pauntley St ARCH N19 54 C7
Paveley Dr BTSEA SW11 108 D6
Paveley St STJWD NW8 3 K9
The Pavement CLAP SW4 129 H3
EA * W5 105 F2
TEDD * TW11 143 H6
WAN * E11 58 A7
WIM/MER * SW19 146 D5
WNWD * SE27 149 J3
Pavet Cl DAGE RM10 80 D5
The Pavilion VX/NE * SW8 109 J6
Pavilion Ldg RYLN/HDSTN * HA2 48 D7
Pavilion Pde SHB * W12 88 A5
Pavilion Rd IL IG1 59 K6
KTBR SW1X 15 M2
Pavilion St KTBR SW1X 15 M4
Pavilion Wy EDGW HA8 36 E6
RSLP HA4 65 G1
Pavillion Ter SHB * W12 88 A5
Pawleyne Cl PGE/AN SE20 150 E6
Pawsey Cl PLSTW E13 76 E7
Pawson's Rd CROY/NA CR0 164 D5
Paxford Rd ALP/SUD HA0 67 H1
Paxton Cl RCH/KEW TW9 125 G1
WOT/HER * KT12 156 B6
Paxton Pl WNWD SE27 150 A3
Paxton Rd BMLY BR1 152 E6
CHSWK W4 106 B5
FSTH SE23 151 G2
TOTM N17 42 C6
Paxton Ter PIM SW1V 16 D9
Payne Cl BARK IG11 78 E6
Payne Rd BOW E3 93 K1
Paynesfield Av
MORT/ESHN SW14 126 A2
Paynesfield Rd BUSH WD23 23 F6
Payne St DEPT SE8 112 C5
Paynes Wk HMSMTH W6 107 H5
Payzes Gdns WFD * IG8 44 D5
Peabody Av PIM SW1V 16 D8
Peabody Cl CROY/NA CR0 165 K7
GNWCH * SE10 112 E7
PIM SW1V 16 D8
Peabody Cottages
HNHL * SE24 130 D6
Peabody Est BTSEA * SW11 128 D3
CHEL * SW3 108 D5
CLKNW * EC1R 12 B1
CMBW * SE5 110 E7
HMSMTH * W6 107 F4
HNHL SE24 130 C6
NKENS * W10 88 A4
STHWK * SE1 12 B8
STHWK * SE1 12 E8
STLK * EC1Y 12 F1
TOTM * N17 42 A7
Peabody Hl DUL SE21 130 C7
Peabody Sq IS * N1 6 E3
Peabody Ter CLKNW * EC1R 12 B1
Peace Cl GFD/PVL UB6 66 D7
SNWD SE25 165 F3
STHGT/OAK N14 28 B4
Peace Gv WBLY HA9 68 D2
Peace Prospect WAT WD17 20 E2
Peace St WOOL/PLUM SE18 115 F5
Peaches Cl BELMT SM2 174 C6
Peach Rd NKENS W10 88 B2
Peachum Rd BKHTH/KID SE3 113 J5
Peacock Av EBED/NFELT TW14 121 G7
Peacock St WALW SE17 18 D6
Peacock Yd WALW SE17 18 D6
The Peak SYD SE26 150 E2
Peaketon Av REDBR IG4 59 H4
Peak Hl SYD SE26 150 E3
Peak Hill Av SYD SE26 150 E3
Peak Hill Gdns SYD SE26 150 E3
Peal Gdns WEA W13 85 G2
Peall Rd CROY/NA CR0 164 A5
Pearce Cl MTCM CR4 163 F1
Pearcefield Av FSTH SE23 131 K7
Pear Cl CDALE/KGS NW9 51 F3
NWCR SE14 112 B6
Pearcroft Rd WAN E11 76 B1
Peardon St VX/NE SW8 129 G1
Peareswood Gdns STAN HA7 35 K7
Peareswood Rd ERITH DA8 118 C7
Pearfield Rd FSTH SE23 151 G2
Pear Gv WAN E11 76 B2
Pearl Cl CRICK NW2 52 B6
EHAM E6 96 A5
Pearl Rd WALTH E17 57 J2
Pearl St WAP E1W 92 D7
Pearman St STHWK SE1 18 B3
Pear Pl STHWK SE1 18 A1
Pearscroft Ct FUL/PGN SW6 108 A7
Pearscroft Rd FUL/PGN SW6 128 A1
Pearson's Av NWCR SE14 112 D7
Pearson St BETH E2 7 L5
Pears Rd HSLW TW3 123 H2
Pear Tree Cl BETH E2 7 L4
ERITH DA8 118 A7
MTCM CR4 162 D1
Pear Tree Ct CLKNW EC1R 12 B1
Peartree Gdns BCTR RM8 79 H4
ROMW/RG RM7 62 D1
Peartree La WAP * E1W 92 E6
Pear Tree Rd ASHF TW15 140 A4
Peartree Rd EN EN1 30 A2
Peartree St FSBYE EC1V 6 D9
Peartree Wy GNWCH SE10 113 K3
Pearwood Cottages STAN * HA7 35 J1
Peary Pl BETH E2 92 E2
Pease Cl HCH RM12 81 K6
Peasmead Ter CHING * E4 44 A3
Peatfield Cl BFN/LL DA15 154 E2
Pebworth Rd HRW HA1 67 G1
Peckarmans Wd SYD SE26 150 C2
Peckett Sq HBRY * N5 73 J3
Peckford Pl BRXN/ST SW9 130 B1
Peckham Gv PECK SE15 111 F6
Peckham High St PECK SE15 111 H7
Peckham Hill St PECK SE15 111 H6
Peckham Park Rd PECK SE15 111 H6
Peckham Rd CMBW SE5 111 F7
Peckham Rye EDUL SE22 131 H3
Pecks Yd WCHPL * E1 13 L2
Peckwater St KTTN NW5 72 C4
Pedlars Wk HOLWY * N7 72 E4
Pedley Rd BCTR RM8 61 J7
Pedley St BETH E2 92 C3
WCHPL E1 13 M1
Pedro St CLPT E5 75 F2
Peek Crs WIM/MER SW19 146 B4
Peel Cl CHING E4 43 K1
ED N9 42 C2
Peel Dr CDALE/KGS NW9 51 H2
CLAY IG5 59 J2
Peel Gv BETH E2 92 E1
Peel Pas KENS * W8 8 A9
Peel Pl CLAY IG5 59 J1
Peel Prec KIL/WHAMP NW6 88 D1
Peel Rd ALP/SUD HA0 67 J2
KTN/HRWW/W HA3 48 E2
SWFD E18 44 D7
Peel St KENS W8 8 A9
Peerglow Est PEND * EN3 30 E4
Peerless St FSBYE EC1V 7 G8
Pegamoid Rd UED N18 42 E2
Pegasus Cl STNW/STAM * N16 73 K3
Pegasus Ct BTFD TW8 105 G4
Pegasus Pl FUL/PGN * SW6 107 K7
LBTH SE11 18 A9
Pegasus Rd CROY/NA CR0 177 G5
Pegasus Wy FBAR/BDGN N11 40 B5
Pegg Rd HEST TW5 102 C6
Pegley Gdns LEE/GVPK SE12 152 E1
Pegwell St WOOL/PLUM SE18 115 K6
Pekin St POP/IOD E14 93 J5
Peldon Wk IS * N1 6 D3
Pelham Av BARK IG11 79 F7
Pelham Cl CMBW SE5 131 F2
Pelham Cottages BXLY * DA5 137 J7
Pelham Crs SKENS SW7 15 J6
Pelham Pl SKENS SW7 15 J5
Pelham Rd BXLYHN DA7 137 H2
IL IG1 78 D1
PGE/AN SE20 165 K1
SEVS/STOTM N15 56 B3
SWFD E18 59 F2
WDGN N22 55 G1
WIM/MER SW19 146 E6
Pelhams Cl ESH/CLAY KT10 170 A3
Pelham St SKENS SW7 15 H5
Pelhams Wk ESH/CLAY KT10 170 A3
Pelier St WALW SE17 18 F9
Pelinore Rd CAT SE6 152 C1
Pellant Rd FUL/PGN SW6 107 H6
Pellatt Gv WDGN N22 41 G7
Pellatt Rd EDUL SE22 131 G4
WBLY HA9 67 K1
Pellerin Rd STNW/STAM N16 74 A4
Pelling St POP/IOD E14 93 H5
Pellipar Cl PLMGR N13 41 G2
Pellipar Rd WOOL/PLUM SE18 114 E4
Pelly Rd PLSTW E13 76 E7
Pelter St BETH E2 7 L7
Pelton Rd GNWCH SE10 113 H4
Pembar Av WALTH * E17 57 G2
Pemberley Cha
HOR/WEW KT19 172 D4
Pemberley Cl HOR/WEW KT19 172 D4
Pember Rd WLSDN NW10 88 B2
Pemberton Av GPK RM2 63 K2
Pemberton Gdns ARCH N19 72 C2
CHDH RM6 62 A4
Pemberton Pl ESH/CLAY KT10 170 C2
HACK E8 74 D6
Pemberton Rd
E/WMO/HCT KT8 157 H3
FSBYPK N4 55 G4
Pemberton Rw
FLST/FETLN EC4A 12 B4
Pemberton Ter ARCH N19 72 C2
Pembridge Av HSLWW TW4 122 E7
Pembridge Crs NTGHL W11 88 D6
Pembridge Gdns BAY/PAD W2 8 A7
Pembridge Ms NTGHL W11 8 A6
Pembridge Pl BAY/PAD W2 8 B6
Pembridge Rd NTGHL W11 8 A7
Pembridge Sq BAY/PAD W2 8 A7
Pembridge Vls NTGHL W11 8 A6
Pembroke Av BRYLDS KT5 159 J4
KTN/HRWW/W HA3 49 G2
RSLP HA4 47 H7
Pembroke Cl ERITH DA8 117 K3
KTBR SW1X 16 B2
Pembroke Gdns DAGE RM10 80 D2
KENS W8 107 J2
Pembroke Gardens Cl
KENS W8 107 J2
Pembroke Ldg STAN * HA7 35 J5
Pembroke Ms KENS * W8 14 A4
MUSWH N10 40 A7
Pembroke Pde ERITH * DA8 117 K4
Pembroke Pl EDGW HA8 36 C6
ISLW TW7 123 K1
KENS * W8 14 A4
Pembroke Rd BMLY BR1 168 B1
CEND/HSY/T N8 54 E3
ECT SW5 14 A5
EHAM E6 95 K4
ERITH DA8 117 K4
GDMY/SEVK IG3 61 F7
GFD/PVL UB6 84 B3
MTCM CR4 163 F1
MUSWH N10 40 A7
NTHWD HA6 32 A2
PLMGR N13 41 J2
RSLP HA4 46 C7
SEVS/STOTM N15 56 B4
SNWD SE25 165 F3
WALTH E17 57 K4
WBLY HA9 67 K2
Pembroke Sq KENS W8 14 A4
Pembroke St IS N1 5 K2
Pembroke Ter STJWD * NW8 3 G4
Pembroke Vls KENS W8 14 A4
Pembroke Wk KENS W8 14 A5
Pembrook Ms BTSEA * SW11 128 C3
Pembry Cl BRXN/ST SW9 110 B7
Pembury Av WPK KT4 160 D7
Pembury Cl CLPT * E5 74 D4
HAYES BR2 167 J6
Pembury Ct HYS/HAR UB3 101 G5
Pembury Rd BXLYHN DA7 117 F6
CLPT E5 74 D4
SNWD SE25 165 H3
TOTM N17 42 B7
Pemdevon Rd CROY/NA CR0 164 B6
Pemell Cl WCHPL E1 92 E3
Pemerich Cl HYS/HAR * UB3 101 J4
Pempath Pl WBLY HA9 67 K1
Penally Pl IS N1 7 H3
Penang St WAP E1W 92 D7
Penard Rd NWDGN UB2 103 F2
Penarth St PECK SE15 111 K5
Penates ESH/CLAY KT10 170 D3
Penberth Rd CAT SE6 152 A1
Penbury Rd NWDGN UB2 102 E4
Pencombe Ms NTGHL W11 88 D6
Pencraig Wy PECK * SE15 111 J5
Pencroft Dr DART DA1 139 F6
Pendall Cl EBAR EN4 27 J3
Penda Rd ERITH DA8 117 J6
Pendarves Rd RYNPK SW20 146 A7
Penda's Md HOM E9 75 G3
Pendell Av HYS/HAR UB3 101 J6
Pendennis Rd
STRHM/NOR SW16 148 E3
TOTM N17 55 K2
Penderel Rd HSLW TW3 123 F4
Penderry Ri CAT SE6 152 B1
Penderyn Wy HOLWY N7 72 D3
Pendlebury House
WOOL/PLUM SE18 114 D7
Pendle Rd STRHM/NOR SW16 148 B5
Pendlestone Rd WALTH E17 57 K4
Pendragon Rd BMLY BR1 152 E2
Pendrell Rd BROCKY SE4 132 B2
Pendrell St WOOL/PLUM SE18 115 J5
Pendula Dr YEAD UB4 83 H3
Pendulum Ms HACK * E8 74 B4
Penerley Rd CAT SE6 132 E7
RAIN RM13 99 K4
Penfold Cl CROY/NA CR0 177 G2
Penfold Pl BAY/PAD W2 9 J2
Penfold Rd ED N9 31 F7
Penfold St STJWD NW8 9 H1
Penford Gdns ELTH/MOT SE9 134 C3
Penford St CMBW SE5 130 C1
Pengarth Rd BXLY DA5 136 E4
Penge La PGE/AN SE20 150 E6
Penge Rd PLSTW E13 77 G6
SNWD SE25 165 H2
Penhall Rd CHARL SE7 114 C3
Penhill Rd BXLY DA5 136 D6
Penifather La GFD/PVL UB6 84 D2
Peninsular Cl
EBED/NFELT TW14 121 G5
Peninsular Park Rd CHARL SE7 113 K4
Penistone Rd
STRHM/NOR SW16 148 E6
Penmon Rd ABYW SE2 116 B2
Pennack Rd PECK SE15 111 G5
Pennant Ms KENS W8 14 C5
Pennant Ter WALTH E17 57 H1
Pennard Rd SHB W12 107 F1
The Pennards SUN TW16 156 B2
Penn Cl GFD/PVL UB6 84 B1
KTN/HRWW/W HA3 49 J3
Penner Cl WIM/MER SW19 146 C1
Penners Gdns SURB KT6 159 F6
Pennethorne Cl HOM E9 74 E7
Pennethorne Rd PECK SE15 111 J6
Penney Cl DART DA1 139 G6
Penn Gdns CHST BR7 169 G1
Pennine Dr CRICK NW2 70 C1
Pennine La CRICK NW2 70 C1
Pennine Pde CRICK * NW2 70 C1
Pennine Wy BXLYHN DA7 118 B7
HYS/HAR UB3 101 G6
Pennington Dr STHGT/OAK N14 28 E4
Pennington St WAP E1W 92 D6
Pennington Wy
LEE/GVPK SE12 153 F1
Penniston Cl WDGN N22 55 J1
Penn La BXLY DA5 136 E5
Penn Rd HOLWY N7 72 E4
Penn St IS N1 7 H4
Penny Cl RAIN RM13 99 K3
Pennycroft SAND/SEL CR2 179 G7
Pennyfields POP/IOD E14 93 J6
Pennymoor Wk MV/WKIL W9 88 D3
Pennyroyal Av EHAM E6 96 A5
Penpoll Rd HACK E8 74 D5
Penpool La WELL DA16 136 C2
Penrhyn Av WALTH E17 43 J7
Penrhyn Crs
MORT/ESHN SW14 125 K3
WALTH E17 43 J7
Penrhyn Gdns KUT * KT1 159 F3
Penrhyn Gv WALTH E17 43 J7
Penrhyn Rd KUT KT1 159 F2
Penrith Cl BECK BR3 151 K7
PUT/ROE SW15 127 H4
Penrith Crs HCH RM12 81 J4
Penrith Pl STRHM/NOR SW16 149 H1
Penrith Rd NWMAL KT3 160 A3
SEVS/STOTM N15 55 K4
THHTH CR7 164 D1
Penrith St STRHM/NOR SW16 148 C5
Penrose Av OXHEY WD19 33 J1
Penrose Gv WALW SE17 18 E8
Penrose St WALW SE17 18 E8
Penryn St CAMTN NW1 5 G5
Penry St STHWK SE1 19 K6
Pensbury Pl VX/NE SW8 129 H1
Pensbury St VX/NE SW8 129 H1
Penscroft Gdns BORE WD6 25 F3
Pensford Av RCH/KEW TW9 125 H1
Penshurst Av BFN/LL DA15 136 B5
Penshurst Gdns EDGW HA8 36 D4
Penshurst Gn HAYES BR2 167 J4
Penshurst Rd BXLYHN DA7 117 G7
HOM E9 75 F6
THHTH CR7 164 C4
TOTM N17 42 B6
Penshurst Wy BELMT SM2 174 E6
Pensilver Cl EBAR * EN4 27 J3
Penstemon Cl FNCH N3 38 E5
Penta Ct BORE * WD6 24 C3
Pentelow Gdns
EBED/NFELT TW14 121 K5
Pentire Rd WALTH E17 44 B7
Pentland Av EDGW HA8 36 D1
Pentland Cl CRICK NW2 70 C1
ED N9 42 E1
Pentland Pl NTHLT UB5 65 J7
Pentland Rd BUSH WD23 22 C5
Pentlands Cl MTCM CR4 163 G2
Pentland St WAND/EARL SW18 128 B5
Pentland Wy HGDN/ICK UB10 64 A2
Pentlow St PUT/ROE SW15 127 F1
Pentney Rd BAL SW12 129 H7
WIM/MER SW19 146 C7
Penton Gv IS N1 6 A6
Penton Pl WALW SE17 18 D6
Penton Ri FSBYW WC1X 5 M7
Penton St IS N1 6 A5
Pentonville Rd IS N1 5 M6
Pentridge St PECK SE15 111 G6
Pentyre Av UED N18 41 K4
Penwerris Av ISLW TW7 103 H6
Penwith Rd WAND/EARL SW18 147 F1
Penwortham Rd
STRHM/NOR SW16 148 B5
Penylan Pl EDGW * HA8 36 C7
Penywern Rd ECT SW5 14 B7
Penzance Pl NTGHL W11 88 C7
Penzance St NTGHL W11 88 C7
Peony Gdns SHB W12 87 J6
Peploe Rd KIL/WHAMP NW6 88 B1
Pepper Cl EHAM E6 95 K4
Peppercorn Cl THHTH CR7 164 E1
Peppermead Sq LEW * SE13 132 D4
Peppermint Cl CROY/NA CR0 163 K6
Peppermint Pl WAN E11 76 C2
Pepper St POP/IOD E14 112 E2
STHWK SE1 18 E1
Peppie Cl STNW/STAM N16 74 A1
Pepys Crs BAR EN5 26 A4
Pepys Est DEPT SE8 112 C4
Pepys Park Est DEPT SE8 112 C3
Pepys Rd NWCR SE14 112 A7
RYNPK SW20 146 A7
Pepys St TWRH EC3N 13 K6
Perceval Av HAMP NW3 71 J4
Percheron Rd BORE WD6 25 F5
Perch St HACK E8 74 B3
Percival Ct TOTM N17 42 B6
Percival Gdns CHDH RM6 61 J5
Percival Rd EN EN1 30 B3
FELT TW13 140 D1
MORT/ESHN SW14 125 K4
Percival St FSBYE EC1V 6 C9
Percival Wy HOR/WEW KT19 172 E3
Percy Bryant Rd SUN TW16 140 C6
Percy Bush Rd WDR/YW UB7 100 C2
Percy Gdns PEND EN3 31 F4
WPK KT4 160 A7
YEAD UB4 82 C2
Percy Ms FITZ W1T 11 G3
Percy Rd BXLYHN DA7 137 F1
CAN/RD E16 94 C4
GDMY/SEVK IG3 61 G6
HPTN TW12 142 A6
ISLW TW7 124 B3
MTCM CR4 163 F6
NFNCH/WDSP N12 39 G4
PGE/AN SE20 151 F7
ROMW/RG RM7 62 E2
SHB W12 106 D1
SNWD SE25 165 G4
WAN E11 58 C6
WATW WD18 21 F3
WCHMH N21 29 J6
WHTN TW2 123 G7
Percy St FITZ W1T 11 G3
Percy Wy WHTN TW2 123 H7
Peregrine Cl WLSDN NW10 69 F4
Peregrine Ct WELL DA16 116 A7
Peregrine Gdns CROY/NA CR0 179 G1
Peregrine Wy WIM/MER SW19 146 A6
Perham Rd WKENS W14 107 H4
Peridot St EHAM E6 95 J4
Perifield DUL SE21 130 D7
Perimeade Rd GFD/PVL UB6 85 J1
Periton Rd ELTH/MOT SE9 134 C3
Perivale Gdns WEA W13 85 H3
Perivale La GFD/PVL UB6 85 G2
Perivale Village GFD/PVL * UB6 85 J2
Perkin Cl ALP/SUD HA0 67 H4
Perkin's Rents WEST SW1P 17 G3
Perkins Rd BARK/HLT IG6 60 D4
Perkins Sq STHWK SE1 12 F8
Perks Cl BKHTH/KID SE3 133 H1
Perpins Rd ELTH/MOT SE9 135 K5
Perran Rd BRXS/STRHM SW2 149 H1
Perrers Rd HMSMTH W6 106 E2
Perrin Rd ALP/SUD HA0 67 G3
Perrin's Ct HAMP * NW3 71 G3
Perrin's Wk HAMP NW3 71 G3
Perry Av ACT W3 87 F5
Perry Cl RAIN RM13 99 F1
Perry Ct SEVS/STOTM * N15 56 A5
Perryfield Wy CDALE/KGS NW9 51 H5
RCHPK/HAM TW10 143 H1
Perry Gdns ED N9 42 A2
Perry Garth NTHLT UB5 65 G7
Perry Gv DART DA1 139 K3
Perry Hl CAT SE6 151 H1
Perry How WPK KT4 160 C7
Perry Mnr CHST BR7 154 E5
Perrymans Farm Rd
GNTH/NBYPK IG2 60 D5
Perry Md BUSH WD23 22 C5
ENC/FH EN2 29 H1
Perrymead St FUL/PGN SW6 107 K7
Perryn Rd ACT W3 87 F6
BERM/RHTH SE16 111 J2
Perry Oak Dr HTHAIR TW6 120 A1
Perry Ri FSTH SE23 151 G2
Perry St CHST BR7 154 E5
DART DA1 138 B2
Perry V FSTH SE23 150 E1
Persant Rd CAT SE6 152 C2
Perseverance Pl
BRXN/ST * SW9 110 B6
Pershore Cl GNTH/NBYPK IG2 60 B4
Pershore Gv CAR SM5 162 C5
Pert Cl MUSWH N10 40 B6
Perth Av CDALE/KGS NW9 51 F6
YEAD UB4 83 G3
Perth Cl RYNPK SW20 160 D1
Perth Rd BARK IG11 96 D1
BECK BR3 167 F1
FSBYPK N4 55 G7
GNTH/NBYPK IG2 60 B5
LEY E10 57 G7
PLSTW E13 95 F1
WDGN N22 41 H7
Perth Ter GNTH/NBYPK IG2 60 C6
Perwell Av RYLN/HDSTN HA2 47 K7
Petauel Rd TEDD TW11 142 E4
Petavel Rd TEDD TW11 142 E5
Peter Av WLSDN NW10 69 K6
Peterboat Cl GNWCH SE10 113 H3
Peterborough Ms
FUL/PGN SW6 127 K1
Peterborough Rd CAR SM5 162 D5
FUL/PGN SW6 127 K1
HRW HA1 48 E7
LEY E10 58 A4
Peterborough Vls
FUL/PGN SW6 108 A7
Petergate BTSEA SW11 128 B3
Peters Cl BCTR RM8 61 K7
EDGW HA8 35 K5
WELL DA16 135 K1
Petersfield Cl UED N18 41 J4
Petersfield Ri PUT/ROE SW15 126 E7
Petersfield Rd ACT W3 105 K1
Petersham Cl
RCHPK/HAM TW10 143 K1
SUT SM1 174 D4
Petersham La SKENS SW7 14 E3
Petersham Ms SKENS SW7 14 E4
Petersham Pl SKENS SW7 14 E4
Petersham Rd
RCHPK/HAM TW10 125 F5
RCHPK/HAM TW10 143 K2
Petersham Ter CROY/NA * CR0 176 E2
Peter's Hl BLKFR EC4V 12 E6
Peterstone Rd ABYW SE2 116 C1
Peterstow Cl WIM/MER SW19 146 C1
Peter St SOHO/CST W1F 11 G6
Peterwood Wy CROY/NA CR0 177 F1
Petherton Rd HBRY N5 73 J4
Petiver Cl HOM * E9 74 E6
Petley Rd HMSMTH W6 107 F5
Peto Pl CAMTN NW1 4 D9
Petrie Cl CRICK * NW2 70 C5
Petros Gdns HAMP * NW3 71 F4
Petro St South CAN/RD E16 94 D6
Pett Cl EMPK RM11 81 K1

Petticoat Sq WCHPL E1 13 L4
Petticoat Tower WCHPL * E1 13 L4
Pettits Bvd ROM RM1 63 G1
Pettits Cl ROM RM1 63 G1
Pettits La ROM RM1 63 G2
Pettit's Pl DAGE RM10 80 C4
Pettit's Rd DAGE RM10 80 C4
Pettiward Cl PUT/ROE SW15 127 F3
Pettley Gdns ROMW/RG RM7 63 F4
Pettman Crs THMD SE28 115 J3
Pettsgrove Av ALP/SUD HA0 67 J4
Pett's Hl RYLN/HDSTN HA2 66 B3
Pett St WOOL/PLUM SE18 114 D3
Petts Wood Rd
STMC/STPC BR5 169 J4
Petty France STJSPK SW1H 16 F3
Petworth Cl NTHLT UB5 65 K6
Petworth Gdns HGDN/ICK UB10 64 A7
RYNPK SW20 160 E2
Petworth Rd BXLYHS DA6 137 H4
NFNCH/WDSP N12 39 J4
Petworth St BTSEA SW11 108 D7
Petworth Wy HCH RM12 81 H3
Petyt Pl CHEL * SW3 108 D5
Petyward CHEL SW3 15 K6
Pevensey Av EN EN1 29 K1
FBAR/BDGN N11 40 D4
Pevensey Cl ISLW TW7 103 H6
Pevensey Rd FELT TW13 122 D7
FSTGT E7 76 E3
TOOT SW17 147 H3
Peveret Cl FBAR/BDGN * N11 40 B4
Peveril Dr TEDD TW11 142 D4
Pewsey Cl CHING E4 43 J4
Peyton Pl GNWCH SE10 113 F6
Pharaoh Cl MTCM CR4 162 E6
Pheasant Cl CAN/RD E16 95 F5
Phelp St WALW SE17 19 G8
Phelps Wy HYS/HAR UB3 101 J3
Phene St CHEL SW3 15 K9
Philbeach Gdns ECT SW5 14 A7
Philchurch Pl WCHPL E1 92 C5
Philimore Cl WOOL/PLUM SE18 115 K4
Philip Av ROMW/RG RM7 63 F7
Philip Gdns CROY/NA CR0 179 H1
Philip La SEVS/STOTM N15 55 K3
Philippa Gdns ELTH/MOT SE9 134 C4
Philip Rd PECK SE15 131 H2
RAIN RM13 99 G2
Philips Cl MTCM CR4 163 F7
Philip St PLSTW E13 94 E3
Phillimore Gdns KENS W8 14 A2
WLSDN NW10 70 A7
Phillimore Gardens Cl
KENS * W8 14 A3
Phillimore Pl KENS W8 14 A2
Phillimore Wk KENS W8 14 A3
Phillipp St IS N1 7 K4
Phillips Cl DART DA1 138 E5
Philpot La FENCHST EC3M 13 J6
Philpot St WCHPL * E1 92 D5
Phineas Pett Road Rd
ELTH/MOT SE9 134 D2
Phipp's Bridge Rd
WIM/MER SW19 162 B1
Phipp's Ms BGVA SW1W 16 C4
Phipp St SDTCH EC2A 7 J9
Phoebeth Rd LEW SE13 132 D4
Phoenix Cl HACK * E8 7 L3
NTHWD HA6 32 D3
WWKM BR4 180 B1
Phoenix Ct BTFD TW8 105 F4
Phoenix Dr HAYES BR2 181 H3
Phoenix Pk BTFD * TW8 104 E4
Phoenix Pl DART DA1 139 G6
FSBYW WC1X 5 M9
Phoenix Rd CAMTN NW1 5 G7
PGE/AN SE20 150 E5
Phoenix St LSQ/SEVD WC2H 11 H5
Phoenix Wy HEST TW5 102 C5
Phoenix Wharf Rd STHWK SE1 19 M2
Phyllis Av NWMAL KT3 160 E4
Picardy Manorway BELV DA17 117 J2
Picardy Rd BELV DA17 117 H4
Picardy St BELV DA17 117 H2
Piccadilly MYFR/PICC W1J 10 C9
Piccadilly Ar MYFR/PICC W1J 10 E8
Piccadilly Circ MYFR/PICC W1J 10 F7
Pickard St FSBYE EC1V 6 D7
Pickering Av EHAM E6 96 A1
Pickering Gdns FBAR/BDGN N11 40 A5
SNWD SE25 165 G5
Pickering Pl STJS * SW1Y 10 F9
Pickering St IS N1 6 D3
Pickets Cl BUSH WD23 22 D7
Pickets St BAL SW12 129 F6
Pickett Cft STAN HA7 35 K7
Pickett's Lock La ED N9 43 F1
Pickford Cl BXLYHN DA7 137 F1
Pickford La BXLYHN DA7 137 F1
Pickford Rd BXLYHN DA7 137 F2
Pickfords Whf IS * N1 6 E6
Pickhurst Gn HAYES BR2 167 J6
Pickhurst La HAYES BR2 167 H5
WWKM BR4 167 H5
Pickhurst Md HAYES BR2 167 J6
Pickhurst Pk HAYES BR2 167 H5
Pickhurst Ri WWKM BR4 167 G7
Pickwick Cl HSLWW TW4 122 D4
Pickwick Ms UED N18 42 A4
Pickwick Pl HRW HA1 48 E6
Pickwick Rd DUL SE21 130 E6
Pickwick St STHWK SE1 18 E2
Pickwick Wy CHST BR7 154 C5
Pickworth Cl VX/NE * SW8 109 K6
Picton Pl MBLAR W1H 10 B5
Picton St CMBW SE5 110 E6
Piedmont Rd
WOOL/PLUM SE18 115 J4
Pier Head WAP * E1W 92 D7
Piermont Pl BMLY BR1 168 D1
Piermont Rd EDUL SE22 131 J4
Pierrepoint Ar IS * N1 6 C5
Pierrepoint Rd ACT W3 86 D6
Pierrepoint Rw IS N1 6 C5
Pier Rd CAN/RD E16 114 E1
EBED/NFELT TW14 122 A4
ERITH DA8 118 B6
Pier St POP/IOD E14 113 F3
Pier Ter WAND/EARL SW18 128 A3
Pier Wy WOOL/PLUM SE18 115 J2
Pigeon La HPTN TW12 142 A3
Pigott St POP/IOD E14 93 J5
Pike Cl BMLY BR1 153 F4
Pike Rd MLHL NW7 37 F3
Pike's End PIN HA5 47 F3
Pikestone Cl YEAD * UB4 83 J3
Pilgrimage St STHWK SE1 19 G2
Pilgrim Cl MRDN SM4 162 A6
Pilgrim Hl WNWD SE27 149 J3
Pilgrims Cl NTHLT UB5 66 C4
PLMGR N13 41 F3
Pilgrims Ct DART DA1 139 K4
Pilgrim's La HAMP NW3 71 H3
Pilgrims Ms POP/IOD E14 94 B6
Pilgrim's Ri EBAR EN4 27 J4
Pilgrim St BLKFR * EC4V 12 C5
Pilgrims Wy ARCH N19 54 D7
SAND/SEL CR2 178 B5
WBLY HA9 50 D7
Pilkington Rd PECK SE15 131 J1
Pilot Cl DEPT SE8 112 C5
Pilsden Cl WIM/MER * SW19 127 G7
Piltdown Rd OXHEY WD19 33 H3
Pilton Pl WALW SE17 18 F7
Pimlico Rd BGVA SW1W 16 B7
Pinchin & Johnsons Yd
WCHPL * E1 92 C6
Pinchin St WCHPL E1 92 C6
Pincott Pl BROCKY SE4 132 A2
Pincott Rd BXLYHS DA6 137 H4
WIM/MER SW19 147 G7
Pindar St SDTCH EC2A 13 J2
Pindock Ms MV/WKIL W9 8 D1
Pine Apple Ct WESTW * SW1E 16 E3
Pine Av SRTFD E15 76 B4
WWKM BR4 166 E7
Pine Cl LEY E10 75 J1
NTHWD HA6 32 C5
PGE/AN SE20 150 E7
STAN HA7 35 H3
STHGT/OAK N14 28 C6
Pine Coombe CROY/NA CR0 179 F3
Pinecroft KTN/HRWW/W HA3 50 B4
WELL DA16 116 B6
Pinecroft Crs BAR EN5 26 C3
Pinefield Cl POP/IOD * E14 93 J6
Pine Gdns BRYLDS KT5 159 H5
RSLP HA4 47 F7
Pine Gld ORP BR6 181 K3
Pine Gv BUSH WD23 21 J1
FSBYPK N4 72 E1
TRDG/WHET N20 26 D7
WIM/MER SW19 146 D4
Pinelands Cl BKHTH/KID * SE3 113 J6
Pinelees Ct
MORT/ESHN * SW14 125 K3
Pinemartin Cl CRICK NW2 70 A2
Pine Rdg CAR SM5 176 A7
Pine Rd CRICK NW2 70 A3
FBAR/BDGN N11 40 A1
The Pines BORE WD6 24 B1
NRWD * SE19 149 H5
WFD IG8 44 E2
Pines Rd BMLY BR1 168 D1
Pine St CLKNW EC1R 6 A9
Pine Tree Cl HEST TW5 102 A7
Pine Wk BRYLDS KT5 159 H5
Pine Wd SUN TW16 140 E7
Pinewood Av BFN/LL DA15 135 K7
PIN HA5 34 B5
RAIN RM13 99 K3
Pinewood Cl CROY/NA CR0 179 G2
ORP BR6 169 J7
PIN HA5 34 B5
Pinewood Gv WEA W13 85 J5
Pinewood Ldg BUSH * WD23 22 D7
Pinewood Ms
STWL/WRAY TW19 120 A5
Pinewood Rd ABYW SE2 116 E5
FELT TW13 141 F2
HAYES BR2 167 K3
Pinfold Rd BUSH WD23 21 K1
STRHM/NOR SW16 148 E3
Pinglestone Cl WDR/YW UB7 100 B6
Pinkcoat Cl FELT TW13 141 F2
Pinkham Wy North Circular Rd
MUSWH N10 39 K6
Pinkwell Av HYS/HAR UB3 101 G3
Pinkwell La HYS/HAR UB3 101 F3
Pinley Gdns DAGW RM9 79 H7
Pinnacle Hl BXLYHN DA7 137 J3
Pinnacle Hl North BXLYHN DA7 137 J2
Pinnell Rd ELTH/MOT SE9 134 C3
Pinner Ct PIN HA5 48 A3
Pinner Gn PIN HA5 47 G1
Pinner Gv PIN HA5 47 J3
Pinner Hl PIN HA5 33 F6
Pinner Hill Rd PIN HA5 33 G7
Pinner Park Av
RYLN/HDSTN HA2 48 C1
Pinner Park Gdns
RYLN/HDSTN HA2 48 C1
Pinner Rd HRW HA1 48 B4
NTHWD HA6 32 D7
OXHEY WD19 21 H5
PIN HA5 47 K3
Pinner Vw RYLN/HDSTN HA2 48 C3
Pinn Wy RSLP HA4 46 B6
Pintail Cl EHAM E6 95 J4
Pintail Rd WFD IG8 45 F6
Pintail Wy YEAD UB4 83 H4
Pinto Cl BORE * WD6 25 F5
Pinto Wy BKHTH/KID SE3 134 A3
Pioneer Cl SHB W12 87 K5
Pioneer St PECK SE15 111 H7
Pioneer Wy SHB W12 88 A5
WATW WD18 20 D5
Piper Cl HOLWY N7 73 F4
Piper Rd KUT KT1 159 H2
Pipers Gdns CROY/NA CR0 166 B6
Pipers Gn CDALE/KGS NW9 50 E4
Pipers Green La EDGW HA8 36 A2
Pipewell Rd CAR SM5 162 D5
Pippin Cl CRICK NW2 69 J2
CROY/NA CR0 166 C7
Pippins Cl WDR/YW UB7 100 A2
Piquet Rd PGE/AN SE20 165 K1
Pirbright Crs CROY/NA CR0 180 A5
Pirbright Rd WAND/EARL SW18 127 J7
Pirie St CAN/RD E16 95 F7
Pitcairn Cl ROMW/RG RM7 62 C3
Pitcairn Rd MTCM CR4 147 K6
Pitchford St SRTFD E15 76 B6
Pitfield Crs THMD SE28 97 G7
Pitfield St IS N1 7 J7
Pitfield Wy WLSDN NW10 68 E5
Pitfold Rd LEE/GVPK SE12 133 K6
Pitlake CROY/NA CR0 177 H1
Pitman St CMBW SE5 110 D6
Pitsea Pl WCHPL E1 93 F5
Pitsea St WCHPL E1 93 F5
Pitshanger La EA W5 85 H3
Pitt Crs WIM/MER SW19 147 F3
Pittman Gdns IL IG1 78 C4
Pitt Rd RYLN/HDSTN HA2 66 C1
THHTH CR7 164 D4
Pitt's Head Ms
MYFR/PKLN W1K 10 B9
Pittsmead Av HAYES BR2 167 K6
Pitt St KENS W8 14 B1
Pittville Gdns SNWD SE25 165 H2
Pixley St POP/IOD E14 93 H5
Pixton Wy CROY/NA CR0 179 G7
Place Farm Av ORP BR6 169 J7
Plaistow Gv BMLY BR1 153 F6
SRTFD E15 76 D7
Plaistow La BMLY BR1 152 E6
Plaistow Park Rd PLSTW E13 95 F1
Plaistow Rd PLSTW E13 94 E1
SRTFD E15 76 D7
Plane St SYD SE26 150 D2
Plane Tree Crs FELT TW13 141 F2
Plantagenet Cl
HOR/WEW KT19 173 F3
Plantagenet Gdns CHDH RM6 61 K6
Plantagenet Pl CHDH RM6 61 K6
Plantagenet Rd BAR EN5 27 G3
Plantain Gdns WAN * E11 76 B2
Plantain Pl STHWK SE1 19 G1
The Plantation BKHTH/KID SE3 133 K1
Plantation Rd ERITH DA8 118 D7
Plashet Gv EHAM E6 77 G7
Plashet Rd PLSTW E13 76 E7
Plassy Rd CAT SE6 132 E6
Platina St SDTCH EC2A 7 H9
Plato Rd CLAP SW4 129 K3
Platt's La HAMP NW3 70 E2
Platt St CAMTN NW1 5 G5
Plawsfield Rd BECK BR3 151 F7
Plaxtol Cl BMLY BR1 153 G7
Plaxtol Rd ERITH DA8 117 H6
Playfair St HMSMTH * W6 107 F4
Playfield Crs EDUL SE22 131 F4
Playfield Rd EDGW HA8 50 E1
Playford Rd FSBYPK N4 73 G1
Playgreen Wy CAT SE6 151 J3
Playground Cl BECK BR3 166 A1
Playhouse Yd BLKFR EC4V 12 C5
Plaza Pde ALP/SUD * HA0 68 A5
The Pleasance PUT/ROE SW15 126 E3
Pleasance Rd PUT/ROE SW15 126 E4
Pleasant Gv CROY/NA CR0 179 H2
Pleasant Pl IS N1 6 D2
Pleasant Vw ERITH DA8 118 B4
Pleasant Wy ALP/SUD HA0 85 J1
Plender St CAMTN NW1 4 E4
Pleshey Rd HOLWY N7 72 D3
Plesman Wy WLGTN * SM6 176 E7
Plevna Crs SEVS/STOTM N15 56 A5
Plevna Rd ED N9 42 C2
HPTN TW12 142 B7
Plevna St POP/IOD E14 113 F2
Pleydell Av HMSMTH W6 106 C2
NRWD SE19 150 B6
Pleydell Est FSBYE * EC1V 6 F8
Pleydell Gdns NRWD * SE19 150 B5
Pleydell St EMB EC4Y 12 B5
Plimsoll Cl POP/IOD E14 93 K5
Plimsoll Rd FSBYPK N4 73 H2
Plough Farm Cl RSLP HA4 46 B5
Plough La CROY/NA CR0 176 E3
EDUL SE22 131 G5
TEDD * TW11 143 G4
WIM/MER SW19 147 F4
WLGTN SM6 176 E7
Plough Lane Cl WLGTN SM6 176 E4
Ploughmans Cl CAMTN NW1 5 G3
Ploughmans End ISLW TW7 123 J4
Plough Pl FLST/FETLN EC4A 12 B4
Plough Rd BTSEA SW11 128 C2
HOR/WEW KT19 173 F6
Plough St WCHPL * E1 92 C5
Plough Ter BTSEA SW11 128 C3
Plough Wy BERM/RHTH SE16 112 A3
Plough Yd SDTCH EC2A 13 K1
Plover Wy BERM/RHTH SE16 112 B2
YEAD UB4 83 H5
Plowden Buildings EMB * EC4Y 12 A6
Plowman Cl UED N18 41 K4
Plowman Wy BCTR RM8 61 J7
Plumbers Rw WCHPL E1 92 C4
Plumbridge St GNWCH * SE10 113 F7
Plum Cl FELT TW13 121 K7
Plum Garth BTFD TW8 104 E3
Plum La WOOL/PLUM SE18 115 G6
Plummer La MTCM CR4 147 K7
Plummer Rd CLAP SW4 129 H5
Plumpton Cl NTHLT UB5 66 A5
Plumpton Wy CAR SM5 175 J2
Plumstead Common Rd
WOOL/PLUM SE18 115 H5
Plumstead High St
WOOL/PLUM SE18 115 J3
Plumstead Rd
WOOL/PLUM SE18 115 H3
Plumtree Cl DAGE RM10 80 D5
Plumtree Ct FLST/FETLN EC4A 12 B4
Plymouth Rd BMLY BR1 153 F7
CAN/RD E16 94 E4
Plymouth Whf POP/IOD E14 113 G3
Plympton Av KIL/WHAMP NW6 70 D6
Plympton Cl BELV DA17 117 F2
Plympton Pl STJWD * NW8 9 J1
Plympton Rd KIL/WHAMP NW6 70 D6
Plympton St STJWD NW8 9 J1
Plymstock Rd WELL DA16 116 D6
Pocklington Cl CDALE/KGS NW9 51 G1
Pocock Av WDR/YW UB7 100 C2
Pocock St STHWK SE1 18 C1
Podmore Rd
WAND/EARL SW18 128 B3
Poet's Rd HBRY N5 73 K4
Poets Wy HRW HA1 48 E3
Pointalls Cl FNCH N3 53 G1
Point Cl GNWCH SE10 113 F7
Pointer Cl THMD SE28 97 K5
Pointers Cl POP/IOD E14 112 E4
Point Hl GNWCH SE10 113 F7
Point Pl WBLY HA9 68 D6
Point Pleasant
WAND/EARL SW18 127 K3
Poland St SOHO/CST W1F 10 F4
Polebrook Rd BKHTH/KID SE3 134 B2
Polecroft La CAT SE6 151 H1
Polesden Gdns RYNPK SW20 160 E2
Polesworth Rd DAGW RM9 98 B1
Pollard Cl CAN/RD E16 94 E6
HOLWY N7 73 F4
Pollard Rd MRDN SM4 162 C4
TRDG/WHET N20 39 J1
Pollard Rw BETH E2 92 C2
Pollards Crs STRHM/NOR SW16 163 K2
Pollards Hl East
STRHM/NOR SW16 164 A2
Pollards Hl North
STRHM/NOR SW16 164 A2
Pollards Hl South
STRHM/NOR SW16 163 K2
Pollards Hl West
STRHM/NOR SW16 163 K2
Pollard St BETH * E2 92 C2
Pollards Wood Rd
STRHM/NOR SW16 163 K1
Pollen St CONDST W1S 10 D5
Pollitt Dr STJWD NW8 3 G9
Polperro Ms LBTH SE11 18 B5
Polsted Rd CAT SE6 132 C6
Polthorne Gv
WOOL/PLUM SE18 115 H3
Polworth Rd
STRHM/NOR SW16 148 E4
The Polygon CLAP * SW4 129 H3
Polygon Rd CAMTN NW1 5 G6
Polytechnic St
WOOL/PLUM SE18 115 F3
Pomell Wy WCHPL E1 13 M4
Pomeroy St NWCR SE14 111 K6
Pomfret Rd CMBW SE5 130 C2
Pomoja La ARCH N19 72 E1
Pond Cl BKHTH/KID SE3 133 K1
NFNCH/WDSP N12 39 J5
Pond Cottage La BECK BR3 166 D7
Ponder St HOLWY * N7 5 L1
Pond Farm Est CLPT * E5 74 E2
Pondfield Rd DAGE RM10 80 D4
HAYES BR2 167 H7
Pond Gn RSLP HA4 64 C1
Pond Hill Gdns CHEAM * SM3 174 C5
Pond Md EDUL SE22 130 E5
Pond Pl CHEL SW3 15 J6
Pond Rd BKHTH/KID SE3 133 J2
SRTFD E15 94 C1
Pondside Cl HYS/HAR UB3 101 G6
Pond St HAMP NW3 71 J4
Pond Wy TEDD TW11 143 J5
Pondwood Ri ORP BR6 169 K6
Ponler St WCHPL E1 92 D5
Ponsard Rd WLSDN NW10 87 K2
Ponsford St HOM E9 74 E5
Ponsonby Pl WEST SW1P 17 H7
Ponsonby Rd PUT/ROE SW15 126 E6
Ponsonby Ter WEST SW1P 17 H7
Pontefract Rd BMLY BR1 152 E4
Ponton Rd VX/NE SW8 109 J6
Pont St KTBR SW1X 15 L4
Pont Street Ms CHEL SW3 15 L4
Pool Cl BECK BR3 151 J4
E/WMO/HCT KT8 156 E4
Pool Ct CAT SE6 151 J1
Poole Cl RSLP HA4 64 C1
Poole Court Rd HEST TW5 122 D1
Poole Rd HOM E9 75 F5
HOR/WEW KT19 173 F5
Pooles Buildings FSBYW WC1X 12 A1
Pooles La WBPTN * SW10 108 B6
Pooles Pk FSBYPK N4 73 G1
Poole St IS N1 7 G4
Poole Wy YEAD * UB4 82 C2
Poolmans St BERM/RHTH SE16 112 A1
Pool Rd E/WMO/HCT KT8 156 E4
HRW HA1 48 D6
Poolsford Rd CDALE/KGS NW9 51 G3
Poonah St WCHPL E1 92 E5
Pope Cl EBED/NFELT TW14 121 J7
WIM/MER * SW19 147 H5
Pope Rd HAYES BR2 168 C4
Pope's Av WHTN TW2 142 E1
Popes Dr FNCH N3 38 E7
Popes Gv CROY/NA CR0 179 H2
WHTN TW2 142 E1
Pope's La EA W5 104 E2
Pope's Rd BRXN/ST * SW9 130 B3
Pope St STHWK SE1 19 K2
Popham Cl FELT TW13 141 J2
Popham Gdns RCH/KEW * TW9 125 J2
Popham Rd IS N1 6 E3
Popham St IS N1 6 E3
Popinjays Rw CHEAM * SM3 174 B4
Poplar Av MTCM CR4 147 K7
NWDGN UB2 103 G2
Poplar Bath St POP/IOD E14 93 K6
Poplar Cl HOM E9 75 H4
PIN HA5 33 H7
Poplar Court Pde TWK * TW1 124 D5
Poplar Crs HMSMTH W6 107 F1
HOR/WEW KT19 172 E5
Poplar Farm Cl
HOR/WEW KT19 172 E5
Poplar Gdns NWMAL KT3 160 A1
Poplar Gv FBAR/BDGN N11 40 A5
NWMAL KT3 160 A2
WBLY HA9 68 E2
Poplar High St POP/IOD E14 93 K6
Poplar Ms SHB W12 88 A7
Poplar Mt BELV DA17 117 J3
Poplar Pl BAY/PAD W2 8 C6
HYS/HAR UB3 82 E6
THMD SE28 97 J6
Poplar Rd ASHF TW15 140 A4
CHEAM SM3 161 J7
HNHL SE24 130 D3
WIM/MER SW19 161 K1
Poplar Rd South WIM/MER SW19 161 K2
Poplars Cl RSLP HA4 46 C7
Poplars Rd WALTH E17 57 K5
Poplar St ROMW/RG RM7 62 E3
Poplar Vw WBLY * HA9 67 K1
Poplar Wk CROY/NA CR0 177 J1
HNHL SE24 130 D3
Poplar Wy BARK/HLT IG6 60 C3
FELT TW13 140 E2
Poppins Ct FLST/FETLN EC4A 12 C5
Poppleton Rd WAN E11 58 C5
Poppy Cl MTCM CR4 163 F7
Poppy La CROY/NA CR0 165 K6
Porchester Garden Ms
BAY/PAD * W2 8 D5
Porchester Gdns BAY/PAD W2 8 D6
Porchester Ga BAY/PAD * W2 8 E7
Porchester Md BECK BR3 151 K5
Porchester Pl BAY/PAD W2 9 K5
Porchester Rd BAY/PAD W2 8 D4
KUT KT1 159 J1
Porchester Sq BAY/PAD W2 8 D4
Porchester Square Ms BAY/PAD W2 8 D4
Porchester Ter BAY/PAD W2 8 E5
Porchester Ter North BAY/PAD W2 8 D4
Porch Wy TRDG/WHET N20 39 K2
Porcupine Cl ELTH/MOT SE9 153 J1
Porden Rd BRXS/STRHM SW2 130 A3
Porlock Av RYLN/HDSTN HA2 48 C7
Porlock Rd EN EN1 30 B6
Porlock St STHWK SE1 19 H1
Porrington Cl CHST BR7 153 K7
Portal Cl RSLP HA4 64 E3
WNWD SE27 149 G2
Portbury Cl PECK SE15 111 H7
Portchester Cl CMBW SE5 130 D3
Portchester Ga BAY/PAD W2 8 E7
Portcullis Lodge Rd
ENC/FH EN2 29 K2
Portelet Rd WCHPL E1 93 F2
Porten Houses WKENS * W14 107 H2
Porten Rd WKENS W14 107 H2
Porter Rd EHAM E6 95 K5
Porters Av DAGW RM9 79 H5
Porter St MHST W1U 9 M2
STHWK SE1 12 F8
Porters Wk WAP * E1W 92 D6
Porters Wy WDR/YW UB7 100 C2
Porteus Rd BAY/PAD W2 8 F3
Portgate Cl MV/WKIL W9 88 D3
Porthcawe Rd SYD SE26 151 G3
Porthkerry Av WELL DA16 136 B3
Portia Wy BOW E3 93 H3
The Porticos WBPTN * SW10 108 C5
Portinscale Rd PUT/ROE SW15 127 H4
Portland Av BFN/LL DA15 136 B5
NWMAL KT3 160 C6
STNW/STAM N16 56 B7
Portland Cl CHDH RM6 62 A4
Portland Cottages
CROY/NA * CR0 163 J6
Portland Crs ELTH/MOT SE9 153 J1
FELT TW13 140 B3
GFD/PVL UB6 84 B4
STAN HA7 49 K1
Portland Crs West STAN HA7 49 K2
Portland Gdns CHDH RM6 61 K4
FSBYPK N4 55 H5
Portland Gv VX/NE SW8 110 A7
Portland Ms SOHO/CST W1F 10 F5
Portland Pl CAVSQ/HST * W1G 10 D3
SNWD SE25 165 H3
Portland Ri FSBYPK N4 55 H7
Portland Rd BMLY BR1 153 G3
KUT KT1 159 F2
MTCM CR4 162 D1
NTGHL W11 88 C6
NWDGN UB2 102 E2
SEVS/STOTM N15 56 A3
SNWD SE25 165 J3
YEAD UB4 82 C2
Portland Sq WAP E1W 92 D7
Portland St WALW SE17 19 G8
Portland Ter RCH/KEW * TW9 124 E3
Portman Av MORT/ESHN SW14 126 A2
Portman Cl BXLY DA5 138 B7
BXLYHN DA7 136 E2
MBLAR W1H 10 A4
Portman Dr WFD IG8 59 H1
Portman Gdns CDALE/KGS NW9 51 F2
Portman Ga STJWD NW8 9 K1
Portman Ms South MBLAR W1H 10 A5
Portman Pl BETH E2 92 E2
Portman Rd KUT KT1 159 G1
Portman Sq MBLAR W1H 9 M4
Portman St MBLAR W1H 10 A5
Portman Towers MBLAR W1H 9 M4
Portmeers Cl WALTH * E17 57 H5
Portnall Rd MV/WKIL W9 88 D2
Portnoi Cl ROM RM1 63 F1
Portobello Ct NTGHL * W11 88 D6
Portobello Ms NTGHL * W11 8 A7
Portobello Rd NKENS W10 88 C4
Portpool La FSBYW WC1X 12 A2
Portree St POP/IOD E14 94 B5
Portsdown Av GLDGN NW11 52 D5
Portsdown Ms GLDGN NW11 52 D5
Portsea Ms BAY/PAD W2 9 K5
Portsea Pl BAY/PAD W2 9 K5
Portslade Rd VX/NE SW8 129 H1
Portsmouth Av THDIT KT7 158 B6
Portsmouth Rd
ESH/CLAY KT10 170 A5
KUT KT1 158 E2
PUT/ROE SW15 126 E7
Portsmouth St LINN WC2A 11 L4
Portsoken St TWRH EC3N 13 L6
Portugal Gdns WHTN * TW2 142 C1
Portugal St LINN WC2A 11 M5
Portway SRTFD E15 76 E7
Portway Crs EW KT17 173 J7
Portway Gdns
WOOL/PLUM SE18 114 C7
The Postern BARB * EC2Y 12 F3
Postern Gn ENC/FH EN2 29 G1
Post La WHTN TW2 123 J7
Postmill Cl CROY/NA CR0 178 E2
Post Office Ap FSTGT E7 77 F4
Post Rd NWDGN UB2 103 G2
Postway Ms IL IG1 78 B2
Potier St STHWK SE1 19 H4
Pott Cl MTCM * CR4 163 G1
The Potteries BAR * EN5 26 E4
Potterne Cl WIM/MER SW19 127 G6
Potters Cl CROY/NA CR0 166 B7
Potters Fld EN * EN1 30 A3
Potters Flds STHWK SE1 13 K9
Potters Gv NWMAL KT3 159 K3
Potters Heights Cl PIN HA5 33 F6
Potter's La BAR EN5 26 E3
STRHM/NOR * SW16 148 D5
Potter's Rd BAR EN5 27 F3
FUL/PGN SW6 128 B1
Potter St NTHWD HA6 32 E7
Potter Street Hl NTHWD HA6 33 F5
Pottery La NTGHL W11 88 C6
Pottery Rd BTFD TW8 105 F5
Pottery St BERM/RHTH * SE16 111 J1
Pott St BETH E2 92 D2
Poulett Gdns TWK TW1 143 F1
Poulett Rd EHAM E6 95 K1
Poulter Pk MTCM * CR4 162 D5
Poulters Wd HAYES BR2 181 H4
Poulton Av SUT SM1 175 H2
Poulton Cl HACK E8 74 D5
Poultry LOTH EC2R 13 G5
Pound Cl SURB KT6 158 D7
Pound Farm La ESH/CLAY KT10 157 J7
Pound La WLSDN NW10 69 J5
Pound Park Rd CHARL SE7 114 C3
Pound Pl ELTH/MOT SE9 135 F5
Pound St CAR SM5 175 K4
Pountney Rd BTSEA SW11 129 F2
Powder Mill La WHTN TW2 122 E7
Powell Cl EDGW HA8 36 B5
Powell Gdns DAGE RM10 80 C3
Powell Rd CLPT E5 74 D2
Power Rd CHSWK W4 105 H3
Powers Ct TWK TW1 124 E6
Powerscroft Rd CLPT E5 74 E3
SCUP DA14 155 J5
Powis Ct BUSH * WD23 22 D7
Powis Gdns GLDGN NW11 52 D6
NTGHL W11 88 D5
Powis Ms NTGHL W11 88 D5
Powis Pl BMSBY WC1N 11 K1

Powis Rd BOW E3 93 K2
Powis Sq NTGHL W11 88 D5
Powis St WOOL/PLUM SE18 115 F2
Powis Ter NTGHL W11 88 D5
Powlett Pl CAMTN NW1 4 B1
Pownall Gdns HSLW TW3 123 G3
Pownall Rd HACK E8 74 C7
HSLW TW3 123 G3
Pownsett Ter IL IG1 78 C4
Powster Rd BMLY BR1 152 E4
Powys Cl BXLYHN DA7 116 E5
Powys Ct BORE WD6 25 F2
Powys La PLMGR N13 40 E3
Poynders Rd CLAP SW4 129 H6
Poynings Rd ARCH N19 72 C2
Poynings Wy NFNCH/WDSP N12 38 E4
Poyntell Crs CHST BR7 154 D7
Poynter Rd EN EN1 30 B4
Poynton Rd TOTM N17 56 C1
Poyntz Rd BTSEA SW11 128 E1
Poyser St BETH E2 92 D2
Praed Ms BAY/PAD W2 9 H4
Praed St BAY/PAD W2 9 H4
Pragel St PLSTW E13 95 F1
Pragnell Rd LEE/GVPK SE12 153 F1
Prague Pl BRXS/STRHM SW2 129 K4
Prah Rd FSBYPK N4 73 G1
Prairie St VX/NE SW8 129 F1
Pratt Ms CAMTN NW1 4 E4
Pratt St CAMTN NW1 4 E4
Pratt Wk LBTH SE11 17 M5
Prayle Gv CRICK NW2 52 B7
Prebend Gdns CHSWK W4 106 C3
Prebend St IS N1 6 E4
The Precinct IS * N1 6 E5
Precinct Rd HYS/HAR UB3 82 E6
Premiere Pl POP/IOD E14 93 J6
Premier Park Rd WLSDN NW10 86 D1
Prentis Rd STRHM/NOR SW16 148 D3
Prentiss Ct CHARL SE7 114 C3
Presburg Rd NWMAL KT3 160 B4
Prescelly Pl EDGW HA8 36 B7
Prescot St WCHPL E1 13 M6
Prescott Av STMC/STPC BR5 169 G5
Prescott Cl EMPK RM11 63 K7
Prescott Pl CLAP SW4 129 J2
Presentation Ms
BRXS/STRHM SW2 149 F1
Presidents Dr WAP E1W 92 D7
President St FSBYE * EC1V 6 E7
Press Rd WLSDN NW10 69 F2
Prestage Wy POP/IOD E14 94 A6
Prestbury Rd FSTGT E7 77 G6
Prestbury Sq ELTH/MOT SE9 153 K3
Prested Rd BTSEA SW11 128 D3
Preston Av CHING E4 44 B5
Preston Cl STHWK * SE1 19 J5
WHTN TW2 142 E2
Preston Ct WOT/HER KT12 156 B7
Preston Dr BXLYHN DA7 116 E7
HOR/WEW KT19 173 G5
WAN E11 59 G4
Preston Gdns IL IG1 59 J5
WLSDN * NW10 69 G5
Preston Hl KTN/HRWW/W HA3 50 A6
Preston Pl RCHPK/HAM TW10 125 F4
WLSDN NW10 69 J5
Preston Rd NRWD SE19 149 H5
RYNPK SW20 145 J6
WAN E11 58 C5
WBLY HA9 68 A1
Prestons Rd HAYES BR2 180 E2
POP/IOD E14 94 A6
Preston Vls KUT * KT1 159 G1
Preston Waye
KTN/HRWW/W HA3 50 A7
Prestwich Ter CLAP * SW4 129 J4
Prestwick Cl NWDGN UB2 102 D4
Prestwick Rd OXHEY WD19 33 H2
Prestwood OXHEY * WD19 33 J1
Prestwood Av
KTN/HRWW/W HA3 49 H3
Prestwood Cl
KTN/HRWW/W HA3 49 H3
WOOL/PLUM SE18 116 B6
Prestwood Gdns CROY/NA CR0 164 D6
Prestwood St IS * N1 6 F6
Pretoria Av WALTH E17 57 G3
Pretoria Pde LEW * SE13 132 D1
Pretoria Rd CAN/RD E16 94 D2
IL IG1 78 B3
ROMW/RG RM7 62 E3
STRHM/NOR SW16 148 B5
TOTM N17 42 B5
WAN E11 58 B7
WATW WD18 20 E3
Pretoria Rd North UED N18 42 B5
Prevost Rd FBAR/BDGN N11 40 A1
Price Cl MLHL NW7 38 C5
TOOT SW17 147 K2
Price Rd CROY/NA CR0 177 H4
Price's St STHWK SE1 12 D9
Pricklers Hl BAR EN5 27 F4
Prickley Wd HAYES BR2 167 J7
Prideaux Pl ACT W3 87 F6
FSBYW WC1X 5 M7
Prideaux Rd BRXN/ST SW9 129 K2
Pridham Rd THHTH CR7 164 E3
Priestfield Rd FSTH SE23 151 G2
Priestlands Park Rd
BFN/LL DA15 155 F2
Priestley Cl STNW/STAM * N16 56 B6
Priestley Gdns CHDH RM6 61 H5
Priestley Rd MTCM CR4 163 F1
Priestley Wy CRICK NW2 51 J7
WALTH E17 57 F2
Priest Park Av
RYLN/HDSTN HA2 66 A1
Priests Av ROM RM1 63 F1
Priests Br MORT/ESHN SW14 126 B2
Prima Rd BRXN/ST SW9 110 B6
Primrose Av GDMY/SEVK IG3 61 G6
Primrose Cl CAT SE6 152 A4
RYLN/HDSTN HA2 65 K2
WLGTN SM6 163 G7
Primrose Dr WDR/YW UB7 100 A3
Primrose Gdns BUSH WD23 22 B6
HAMP NW3 71 J5
RSLP HA4 65 G4
Primrose Hl EMB EC4Y 12 B5
Primrose Hill Rd HAMP NW3 3 L2
Primrose Hill Studios
CAMTN NW1 4 A3
Primrose La CROY/NA CR0 165 K7
Primrose Ms CAMTN * NW1 3 M2
Primrose Rd LEY E10 57 K7
SWFD E18 59 F1
Primrose Sq HOM E9 74 E6
Primrose St SDTCH EC2A 13 J2
Primrose Wk EW KT17 173 H6
NWCR SE14 112 B6
Primrose Wy ALP/SUD HA0 85 K1
Primula St SHB W12 87 J6
Prince Albert STJWD NW8 3 K5
Prince Albert Rd STJWD NW8 3 K6
Prince Arthur Rd HAMP NW3 71 G4
Prince Charles Dr HDN NW4 52 A6
Prince Charles Rd
BKHTH/KID SE3 113 J7
Prince Charles Wy WLGTN SM6 176 B2
Prince Consort Dr CHST BR7 154 D7
Prince Consort Rd SKENS SW7 15 G3
Princedale Rd NTGHL W11 88 C7
Prince Edward Rd HOM E9 75 H5
Prince George Av
STHGT/OAK N14 28 C4
Prince George Rd
STNW/STAM N16 74 A3
Prince George's Av
RYNPK SW20 161 F1
Prince Georges Rd
WIM/MER SW19 147 H7
Prince Henry Rd CHARL SE7 114 C6
Prince Imperial Rd CHST BR7 154 B6
WOOL/PLUM SE18 114 E7
Prince John Rd ELTH/MOT SE9 134 D4
Princelet St WCHPL E1 13 M2
Prince of Orange La
GNWCH * SE10 113 F6
Prince of Wales Cl HDN NW4 51 K3
Prince of Wales Dr
BTSEA SW11 108 E7
Prince of Wales Ga SKENS SW7 15 J1
Prince of Wales Pas
CAMTN * NW1 4 E8
Prince of Wales Rd
BKHTH/KID SE3 113 J7
CAN/RD E16 95 G5
KTTN NW5 72 A5
SUT SM1 175 H1
Prince of Wales Ter CHSWK W4 106 B4
KENS W8 14 D2
Prince Regent La PLSTW E13 95 G3
Prince Regent Ms CAMTN NW1 4 E8
Prince Regent Rd HSLW TW3 123 H2
Prince Rd SNWD SE25 165 F4
Prince Rupert Rd
ELTH/MOT SE9 134 E3
Princes Ar MYFR/PICC W1J 10 F8
Princes Av ACT W3 105 H2
CAR SM5 175 K6
CDALE/KGS NW9 50 C3
FNCH N3 39 F7
MUSWH N10 54 B2
PLMGR N13 41 G4
STMC/STPC BR5 169 K4
SURB KT6 172 C1
WATW WD18 20 E4
WDGN N22 40 D7
WFD IG8 45 F3
Princes Cl CDALE/KGS NW9 50 C3
EDGW HA8 36 C4
HPTN TW12 142 D3
SCUP DA14 155 K2
Princes Ct WBLY HA9 68 A4
Princes Dr HRW HA1 48 E2
Princes Gdns ACT W3 86 C5
EA W5 85 J3
SKENS SW7 15 H3
Princes Ga SKENS SW7 15 H3
Princes Gate Ct SKENS SW7 15 G2
Princes Gate Ms SKENS SW7 15 H3
Princes La MUSWH N10 54 A2
Prince's Ms BAY/PAD W2 8 B6
HMSMTH * W6 106 E4
Princes Pde GLDGN * NW11 52 C5
Princes Pk RAIN RM13 81 J6
Princes Park Av GLDGN NW11 52 C5
HYS/HAR UB3 82 B6
Princes Park Cir HYS/HAR UB3 82 B6
Princes Park Cl HYS/HAR UB3 82 B6
Princes Park La HYS/HAR UB3 82 B6
Princes Park Pde HYS/HAR UB3 82 B6
Princes Pl NTGHL W11 88 C7
Prince's Pln HAYES BR2 168 D6
Princes Ri LEW SE13 133 F1
Princes Riverside Rd
BERM/RHTH SE16 93 F7
Princes Rd BARK/HLT IG6 60 D3
BKHH IG9 45 G1
DART DA1 138 E6
DART DA1 139 J7
FELT TW13 140 D2
HPTN TW12 142 D3
KUTN/CMB KT2 144 C7
MORT/ESHN SW14 126 A2
PGE/AN SE20 151 F5
RCH/KEW TW9 105 G7
RCHPK/HAM TW10 125 G4
ROM RM1 63 J4
UED N18 42 E3
WEA W13 85 H7
WIM/MER SW19 146 E5
Princess Alice Wy THMD SE28 115 J1
Princess Av WBLY HA9 68 A1
Princess Crs FSBYPK N4 73 H1
Princesses Pde DART * DA1 138 C4
Princess La RSLP HA4 46 C7
Princess Louise Cl BAY/PAD W2 9 H2
Princess May Rd
STNW/STAM N16 74 A3
Princess Ms HAMP NW3 71 H5
Prince's Sq BAY/PAD W2 8 C6
Princess Rd CAMTN NW1 4 A3
CROY/NA CR0 164 D5
KIL/WHAMP NW6 2 A6
Princess St BXLYHN DA7 137 G2
STHWK SE1 18 D4
Princes St CONDST W1S 10 D5
LOTH EC2R 13 G5
RCH/KEW TW9 125 F3
SUT SM1 175 H3
TOTM N17 42 A5
Prince's Ter PLSTW E13 77 F7
Prince St DEPT SE8 112 C5
WAT WD17 21 G2
Princes Vw DART DA1 139 K7
Princes Wy BKHH IG9 45 G1
CROY/NA CR0 177 F4
RSLP HA4 65 J3
WIM/MER SW19 127 G6
WWKM BR4 180 D3
Prince's Yd NTGHL W11 88 C7
Princethorpe Rd SYD SE26 151 F3
Princeton St GINN WC1R 11 L3
Pringle Gdns
STRHM/NOR SW16 148 C3
Printers Inn Ct
FLST/FETLN EC4A 12 A4
Printinghouse La
HYS/HAR UB3 101 H1
Printing House Yd BETH * E2 7 K8
Priolo Rd CHARL SE7 114 B4
Prior Av BELMT SM2 175 J6
Prior Bolton St IS N1 73 H5
Prioress Rd WNWD SE27 149 H2
Prioress St STHWK SE1 19 H4
The Priory BKHTH/KID SE3 133 J2
CROY/NA * CR0 177 G2
Prior Rd IL IG1 78 A2
Priors Cft WALTH E17 57 G1
Priors Fld NTHLT UB5 65 J5
Priors Gdns RSLP HA4 65 G4
Prior St GNWCH SE10 113 F6
Priory Av ALP/SUD HA0 67 F3
CEND/HSY/T N8 54 D3
CHEAM SM3 174 B3
CHING E4 43 H2
CHSWK W4 106 B2
STMC/STPC BR5 169 J5
WALTH E17 57 J4
Priory Cl ALP/SUD HA0 67 F3
BECK BR3 166 B2
BMLY BR1 153 K7
CHING E4 43 H2
DART DA1 139 F4
HPTN TW12 141 K7
HYS/HAR UB3 83 F6
RSLP HA4 46 D7
STAN HA7 35 F2
STHGT/OAK N14 28 B4
SUN TW16 140 E6
SWFD E18 44 E7
TRDG/WHET N20 26 D6
WIM/MER * SW19 147 F7
Priory Cottages EA * W5 86 B4
Priory Ct BLKFR * EC4V 12 D5
VX/NE SW8 109 J7
WALTH E17 57 H2
Priory Crs ALP/SUD HA0 67 G2
CHEAM SM3 174 B3
NRWD SE19 149 J6
Priory Dr ABYW SE2 116 E4
STAN HA7 35 F2
Priory Field Dr EDGW HA8 36 D3
Priory Gdns ALP/SUD HA0 67 G3
ASHF TW15 140 B4
BARN SW13 126 C2
CHSWK * W4 106 B3
DART DA1 139 G4
HGT N6 54 B5
HPTN TW12 141 K6
SNWD SE25 165 G3
Priory Green Est IS N1 5 L5
Priory Gv CLAP SW4 109 K7
Priory Hl ALP/SUD HA0 67 G3
DART DA1 139 G5
Priory La E/WMO/HCT KT8 157 F3
PUT/ROE SW15 126 C4
Priory Leas ELTH/MOT * SE9 134 D7
Priory Market Pl DART * DA1 139 H6
Priory Ms EMPK RM11 63 K7
Priory Pk BKHTH/KID SE3 133 J2
Priory Park Rd ALP/SUD HA0 67 G3
KIL/WHAMP NW6 70 D7
Priory Pl DART DA1 139 G5
Priory Rd BARK IG11 78 D6
CEND/HSY/T N8 54 D3
CHEAM SM3 174 B3
CHSGTN KT9 172 A2
CHSWK W4 106 A2
CROY/NA CR0 164 B6
DART DA1 139 G3
EHAM E6 77 H7
HPTN TW12 141 K6
HSLW TW3 123 H4
KIL/WHAMP NW6 2 C3
MUSWH N10 54 C3
RCH/KEW TW9 105 H5
WIM/MER SW19 147 H6
Priory St BOW E3 93 K2
Priory Ter KIL/WHAMP NW6 2 C3
Priory Vw BUSH WD23 22 E6
Priory Vls FBAR/BDGN * N11 39 K5
Priory Wk WBPTN SW10 14 F8
Priory Wy NWDGN UB2 102 C2
RYLN/HDSTN HA2 48 B3
WDR/YW UB7 100 B5
Pritchard's Rd BETH E2 92 C1
Priter Rd BERM/RHTH * SE16 111 H2
Private Rd EN EN1 29 K4
Probert Rd BRXS/STRHM SW2 130 B4
Probyn Rd BRXS/STRHM SW2 149 H1
Procter St GINN WC1R 11 L3
Proctor Cl MTCM CR4 148 A7
Proctors Cl EBED/NFELT TW14 121 K7
Progress Wy CROY/NA CR0 177 F1
EN EN1 30 C4
WDGN N22 41 G7
The Promenade CHSWK W4 106 B7
EDGW * HA8 36 C4
Promenade Approach Rd
CHSWK W4 106 B6
Prospect Cl BELV DA17 117 H3
HEST TW5 102 E7
RSLP HA4 47 H6
SYD SE26 150 D3
Prospect Cottages
WAND/EARL SW18 127 K3
Prospect Crs WHTN TW2 123 H5
Prospect Hl WALTH E17 57 K3
Prospect Pl CHSWK W4 106 A4
CRICK NW2 70 D2
DART DA1 139 H5
EFNCH N2 53 H3
HAYES BR2 168 A2
ROMW/RG RM7 62 E1
RYNPK SW20 145 K6
WAP E1W 92 E7
Prospect Rd BAR EN5 26 E3
CRICK NW2 70 D2
SURB KT6 158 D5
WFD IG8 45 G4
Prospect St BERM/RHTH SE16 111 J1
Prospect V WOOL/PLUM SE18 114 D3
Prospero Rd ARCH N19 54 D7
Prothero Gdns HDN NW4 51 K4
Prothero Rd FUL/PGN SW6 107 H6
Prout Gv WLSDN NW10 69 G3
Prout Rd CLPT E5 74 D2
Providence Cl HOM * E9 75 F7
Providence Ct MYFR/PKLN W1K 10 B6
Providence La HYS/HAR UB3 101 G6
Providence Pl IS N1 6 C4
Providence Row Cl BETH E2 92 D2
Providence Sq STHWK SE1 19 J1
Providence Yd BETH * E2 92 C2
Provincial Ter PGE/AN * SE20 151 F6
Provost Est IS N1 7 G7
Provost Rd HAMP NW3 3 M1
Provost St IS N1 7 G6
Prowse Av BUSH WD23 34 C1
Prowse Pl CAMTN NW1 4 E1
Pruden Cl STHGT/OAK * N14 40 C1
Prusom St WAP E1W 92 D7
Pudding La MON EC3R 13 H6
Pudding Mill La SRTFD E15 75 K7
Puddle Dock BLKFR EC4V 12 D6
Puffin Cl BARK IG11 97 H2
CROY/NA CR0 166 A4
Pulborough Rd
WAND/EARL SW18 127 J6
Pulborough Wy HSLWW TW4 122 B3
Pulford Rd SEVS/STOTM N15 55 K5
Pulham Av EFNCH N2 53 G3
Puller Rd BAR EN5 26 C1
Pulleyns Av EHAM E6 95 J2
Pullman Gdns PUT/ROE SW15 127 F5
Pullman Ms LEE/GVPK SE12 153 F2
Pullman Pl ELTH/MOT SE9 134 D4
Pulross Rd BRXN/ST SW9 130 A2
Pulteney Cl BOW E3 75 H7
Pulteney Rd SWFD E18 59 F2
Pulton Pl FUL/PGN SW6 107 K6
Puma Ct WCHPL E1 13 L2
Pump Aly BTFD TW8 104 E6
Pump Cl NTHLT UB5 84 A1
Pump Ct EMB * EC4Y 12 A5
Pump House Cl HAYES BR2 167 J1
Pumping Station Rd
CHSWK W4 106 B6
Pump La HYS/HAR UB3 101 K1
NWCR SE14 111 K6
Punderson's Gdns BETH E2 92 D2
Purbeck Av NWMAL KT3 160 C5
Purbeck Dr CRICK NW2 70 B1
Purbeck Rd EMPK RM11 63 J6
Purbrook St STHWK SE1 19 K3
Purcell Crs FUL/PGN * SW6 107 G5
Purcell Ms WLSDN * NW10 69 G6
Purcell Rd GFD/PVL UB6 84 B4
Purcells Av EDGW HA8 36 C4
Purcell St IS N1 7 J5
Purchese St CAMTN NW1 5 G5
Purdy St BOW E3 93 K3
Purelake Ms LEW * SE13 133 G2
Purland Cl BCTR RM8 62 B7
Purland Rd THMD SE28 116 A1
Purleigh Av WFD IG8 45 J5
Purley Av CRICK NW2 70 C1
Purley Cl CLAY IG5 60 A1
Purley Pl IS N1 6 C1
Purley Rd ED N9 41 K2
SAND/SEL CR2 177 K6
Purley Wy CROY/NA CR0 164 A7
Purlings Rd BUSH WD23 22 B4
Purneys Rd ELTH/MOT SE9 134 C3
Purrett Rd WOOL/PLUM SE18 116 A4
Pursers Cross Rd
FUL/PGN * SW6 107 J7
Pursewardens Cl WEA W13 85 J7
Pursley Rd MLHL NW7 37 K6
Purves Rd WLSDN NW10 87 K2
Putney Br PUT/ROE SW15 127 H2
Putney Bridge Ap
PUT/ROE SW15 127 H2
Putney Bridge Rd
PUT/ROE SW15 127 H3
Putney Common
PUT/ROE SW15 127 F2
Putney Ex PUT/ROE * SW15 127 G3
Putney Heath PUT/ROE SW15 126 E5
Putney Heath La
PUT/ROE SW15 127 G5
Putney High St PUT/ROE SW15 127 H3
Putney Hl PUT/ROE SW15 127 G6
Putney Park Av
PUT/ROE SW15 126 D3
Putney Park La
PUT/ROE SW15 126 E3
Puttenham Cl OXHEY WD19 33 G2
Pycombe Cnr
NFNCH/WDSP N12 38 D3
Pycroft Wy ED N9 42 C3
Pylbrook Rd SUT SM1 174 E2
Pym Cl EBAR EN4 27 H4
Pymers Md DUL SE21 130 D7
Pymmes Brook Trail EBAR EN4 27 K6
EBAR EN4 27 J4
PLMGR N13 40 E3
Pymmes Cl PLMGR N13 41 F4
TOTM N17 42 D7
Pymmes Gdns North ED N9 42 B2
Pymmes Gdns South ED N9 42 B2
Pymmes Green Rd
FBAR/BDGN N11 40 B3
Pymmes Rd PLMGR N13 40 E5
Pymms Brook Dr EBAR EN4 27 J3
Pyne Rd SURB KT6 159 H7
Pynham Cl ABYW SE2 116 B2
Pynnacles Cl STAN HA7 35 H4
Pyrland Rd HBRY N5 73 K4
RCHPK/HAM TW10 125 G5
Pyrmont Gv WNWD SE27 149 H2
Pyrmont Rd CHSWK W4 105 H5
Pytchley Crs NRWD SE19 149 J5
Pytchley Rd EDUL SE22 131 F2

Q

The Quadrangle BAY/PAD W2 9 J4
HNHL * SE24 130 D4
WBPTN * SW10 108 B7
The Quadrant BELMT SM2 175 G5
BXLYHN DA7 116 E6
EDGW * HA8 36 C5
NKENS * W10 88 B2
RCH/KEW TW9 124 E4
RYLN/HDSTN * HA2 48 D2
RYNPK SW20 146 C7
Quadrant Ar REGST W1B 10 F7
Quadrant Cl HDN * NW4 51 K4
Quadrant Gv HAMP NW3 71 K4
Quadrant Rd RCH/KEW TW9 124 E3
THHTH CR7 164 C3
Quad Rd WBLY * HA9 67 K2
Quaggy Wk BKHTH/KID SE3 133 K3
Quainton St WLSDN NW10 69 F2
Quaker La NWDGN UB2 103 F2
Quakers Course
CDALE/KGS NW9 37 H7
Quakers Pl FSTGT E7 77 H4
Quaker St WCHPL E1 13 L1
Quakers Wk WCHMH N21 29 K5
Quality Ct LINN WC2A 12 A4
Quantock Cl HYS/HAR UB3 101 G6
Quantock Gdns CRICK * NW2 70 B1
Quantock Rd BXLYHN DA7 138 B1
Quarrendon St FUL/PGN SW6 107 K7
Quarr Rd CAR SM5 162 C5
Quarry Ms PUR RM19 119 K3
Quarry Park Rd SUT SM1 174 D5
Quarry Ri SUT SM1 174 D5
Quarry Rd WAND/EARL SW18 128 B5
Quartermile La LEY E10 75 K3
Quatre Ports CHING * E4 44 B4
Quay House POP/IOD * E14 112 D1
Quebec Ms MBLAR W1H 9 M5
Quebec Rd GNTH/NBYPK IG2 60 C6
YEAD UB4 83 G6
Quebec Wy BERM/RHTH SE16 112 A1
Queen Adelaide Rd
PGE/AN SE20 150 E5
Queen Anne Av HAYES BR2 167 K2
Queen Anne Dr ESH/CLAY KT10 170 E6
Queen Anne Ga BXLYHN DA7 136 E2
Queen Anne Ms
CAVSQ/HST W1G 10 D3
Queen Anne Rd HOM E9 75 F5
Queen Annes Cl WHTN TW2 142 D2
Queen Anne's Gdns
CHSWK W4 106 B2
EA W5 105 F1
EN EN1 30 A5
MTCM * CR4 162 E2
Queen Anne's Ga STJSPK SW1H 17 G2
Queen Anne's Gv CHSWK W4 106 B2
EA W5 105 F1
EN EN1 29 K6
Queen Anne's Pl EN EN1 30 A5
Queen Anne St CAVSQ/HST W1G 10 C3
Queen Anne Ter WAP * E1W 92 D6
Queenborough Gdns
CHST BR7 154 D5
GNTH/NBYPK IG2 60 A3
Queen Caroline Est
HMSMTH W6 107 F4
Queen Caroline St
HMSMTH W6 107 F4
Queen Elizabeth Buildings
EMB * EC4Y 12 A6
Queen Elizabeth College
GNWCH * SE10 113 F6
Queen Elizabeth Gdns
MRDN SM4 161 K3
Queen Elizabeth Rd
KUTN/CMB * KT2 144 B7
WALTH E17 57 G2
Queen Elizabeth's Cl
STNW/STAM N16 73 K1
Queen Elizabeth's Dr
STHGT/OAK N14 28 E7
Queen Elizabeth St STHWK SE1 19 K1
Queen Elizabeth's Wk
STNW/STAM N16 55 K7
WLGTN SM6 176 D3
Queen Elizabeth Wk
BARN SW13 106 D7
Queenhithe BLKFR EC4V 12 F7
Queen Margaret's Gv IS N1 74 A4
Queen Mary Av MRDN SM4 161 G4
Queen Mary Cl CHSGTN KT9 172 C2
ROM RM1 63 H5
Queen Mary Rd NRWD SE19 149 H5
Queen Mary's Av CAR SM5 175 K6
WATW WD18 20 C3
Queen Mother Ga BAY/PAD W2 10 B9
Queens Acre CHEAM SM3 174 B6
Queens Av FELT TW13 141 G3
FNCH N3 39 G6
GFD/PVL UB6 84 B5
KTN/HRWW/W HA3 49 H2
MUSWH N10 54 A2
TRDG/WHET N20 39 H1
WATW WD18 20 D3
WCHMH N21 29 H7
WFD IG8 45 F4
Queensberry Ms West
SKENS * SW7 15 G5
Queensberry Pl FSTGT E7 77 H4
SKENS SW7 15 G5
Queensberry Wy SKENS * SW7 15 G5
Queensborough Ms
BAY/PAD * W2 8 E6
Queensborough Pas
BAY/PAD W2 8 E6
Queensborough Studios
BAY/PAD W2 8 E6
Queensborough Ter
BAY/PAD W2 8 D6
Queensbridge Pk ISLW TW7 123 J5
Queensbridge Rd HACK E8 7 M2
Queensbury Rd
CDALE/KGS NW9 51 F6
WLSDN NW10 86 B1
Queensbury Station Pde
EDGW HA8 50 B2
Queensbury St IS N1 6 F2
Queens Circ VX/NE SW8 109 G6
Queen's Cl EDGW HA8 36 C4
ESH/CLAY * KT10 170 B3
WLGTN SM6 176 B4
Queen's Club Gdns
WKENS W14 107 H5
Queens Club Ter WKENS * W14 107 J5
Queenscourt WBLY HA9 68 A3
Queen's Crs KTTN NW5 72 A5
RCHPK/HAM TW10 125 G4
Queenscroft Rd ELTH/MOT SE9 134 C4
Queensdale Crs NTGHL W11 88 B7
Queensdale Pl NTGHL W11 88 C7
Queensdale Rd NTGHL W11 88 B7
Queensdale Wk NTGHL W11 88 C7
Queens Down Rd CLPT E5 74 D3
Queens Dr BRYLDS KT5 159 H6
EA W5 86 B5
FSBYPK N4 73 H1
LEY E10 57 J6
THDIT KT7 158 B5
Queen's Elm Sq CHEL SW3 15 G8
Queen's Gdns BAY/PAD W2 8 E6
EA W5 85 J4
HDN NW4 52 A4
HEST TW5 102 D7
RAIN RM13 99 F1
Queens Garth FSTH * SE23 150 E1
Queens Ga SKENS SW7 14 F2
Queens Gate Gdns CHST BR7 154 D7
Queensgate Gdns
PUT/ROE SW15 126 E3
Queen's Gate Gdns SKENS SW7 14 E4
Queen's Gate Ms SKENS SW7 14 E3
Queensgate Pl KIL/WHAMP NW6 2 A2
Queen's Gate Pl SKENS SW7 14 F4
Queen's Gate Place Ms
SKENS SW7 14 F4
Queen's Gate Ter SKENS SW7 14 E3

Queen's Gv STJWD NW8 3 G4
Queen's Head St IS N1 6 D4
Queens Keep TWK * TW1 124 D5
Queensland Av UED N18 41 J5
WIM/MER SW19 147 F7
Queensland Pl HOLWY N7 73 G3
Queensland Rd HOLWY N7 73 G3
Queens La MUSWH N10 54 B2
Queensmead STJWD NW8 3 H3
Queen's Mead Rd HAYES BR2 167 J1
Queensmere Cl
WIM/MER SW19 146 B1
Queensmere Rd
WIM/MER SW19 146 B1
Queen's Ms BAY/PAD W2 8 D6
Queensmill Rd FUL/PGN SW6 107 G6
Queens Pde CEND/HSY/T * N8 55 H3
CRICK * NW2 70 A5
EA * W5 86 B5
FBAR/BDGN * N11 39 K4
FBAR/BDGN * N11 40 E6
HDN * NW4 51 K4
Queens Parade Cl
FBAR/BDGN N11 39 K4
Queens Park Gdns FELT * TW13 140 D2
Queen's Pl MRDN SM4 161 K3
WAT WD17 21 G2
Queens Prom KUT KT1 158 E3
Queen Sq BMSBY WC1N 11 K1
Queen's Ride BARN SW13 126 E2
Queen's Ri RCHPK/HAM TW10 125 G5
Queens Rd BAR EN5 26 B2
BARK IG11 78 C6
BECK BR3 166 B1
BKHH IG9 45 F1
BMLY BR1 167 K1
CHST BR7 154 B5
CROY/NA CR0 164 C5
EA W5 86 A5
ED N9 42 D1
EN EN1 30 A3
ERITH DA8 118 B5
FBAR/BDGN N11 40 E6
FELT TW13 122 A7
FNCH N3 39 G7
HDN NW4 52 A4
HPTN TW12 142 B3
HSLW TW3 123 G2
HYS/HAR UB3 82 C5
KUTN/CMB KT2 144 C6
MORT/ESHN SW14 126 A2
MRDN SM4 161 K3
MTCM CR4 162 C2
NWDGN UB2 102 C1
NWMAL KT3 160 C3
PECK SE15 111 K7
PLSTW E13 77 F7
RCHPK/HAM TW10 125 G5
TEDD TW11 143 F5
THDIT KT7 158 A4
TWK TW1 124 A7
WALTH E17 57 H5
WAN E11 58 C6
WAT WD17 21 G1
WDR/YW UB7 100 C1
WELL DA16 136 C1
WIM/MER SW19 146 E5
WLGTN SM6 176 B4
Queen's Rd West PLSTW E13 94 E1
Queen's Rw WALW SE17 19 G9
Queen's Ter ISLW TW7 124 B3
PLSTW E13 77 F7
STJWD NW8 3 G4
THDIT * KT7 158 B5
WCHPL * E1 92 E3
Queens Terrace Cottages
HNWL * W7 103 K1
Queensthorpe Ms SYD * SE26 151 F3
Queensthorpe Rd SYD SE26 151 F3
Queens Town Gdns RAIN RM13 99 H2
Queenstown Rd VX/NE SW8 129 G1
Queen St BXLYHN DA7 137 G2
CROY/NA CR0 177 J3
ERITH * DA8 118 B5
MANHO EC4N 12 F5
MYFR/PICC W1J 10 C8
ROMW/RG RM7 63 F5
TOTM N17 42 A5
Queen Street Pl CANST EC4R 12 F7
Queensville Rd CLAP SW4 129 J6
Queens Wk CDALE/KGS NW9 68 E1
EA W5 85 J3
HRW HA1 48 E3
RSLP HA4 65 G2
Queens Walk Ter RSLP * HA4 65 G2
Queens Wy FELT TW13 141 G3
HDN NW4 52 A4
Queensway BAY/PAD W2 8 D5
CROY/NA CR0 177 F4
PEND EN3 30 E3
STMC/STPC BR5 169 H4
SUN TW16 156 A1
WWKM BR4 180 E3
Queens Well Av TRDG/WHET N20 39 J3
Queenswood Av HEST TW5 122 E1
HPTN TW12 142 B5
THHTH CR7 164 B4
WALTH E17 44 A7
WLGTN SM6 176 D3
Queenswood Gdns WAN E11 58 E7
Queenswood Pk FNCH N3 52 C1
Queenswood Rd BFN/LL DA15 136 A4
FSTH SE23 151 G2
Queen's Wood Rd HGT N6 54 B5
Queen's Yd FITZ W1T 10 F1
Queen Victoria Av ALP/SUD HA0 67 K6
Queen Victoria St BLKFR EC4V 12 D6
Queen Victoria Ter WAP * E1W 92 D6
Quemerford Rd HOLWY N7 73 F4
Quentin Pl LEW SE13 133 H2
Quentin Rd BKHTH/KID SE3 133 H2
Quernmore Cl BMLY BR1 152 E5
Quernmore Rd BMLY BR1 152 E5
FSBYPK N4 55 G5
Querrin St FUL/PGN SW6 128 B1
Quex Ms KIL/WHAMP NW6 2 B3
Quex Rd KIL/WHAMP NW6 2 B3
Quick Rd CHSWK W4 106 B4
Quicks Rd WIM/MER SW19 147 F6
Quick St IS N1 6 D6
Quickswood HAMP NW3 3 K1
Quiet Nook HAYES BR2 181 H2
Quill St EA W5 86 A2
FSBYPK N4 73 G2
Quilp St STHWK SE1 18 E1
Quilter St BETH E2 92 C2
WOOL/PLUM SE18 116 A4
Quinta Dr BAR EN5 25 K4
Quintin Av RYNPK SW20 146 C7
Quinton Cl BECK BR3 167 F2
HEST TW5 102 A6
WLGTN SM6 176 B3
Quinton Rd THDIT KT7 158 B7
Quixley St POP/IOD E14 94 B6
Quorn Rd EDUL SE22 131 F3

R

Rabbit Rw KENS * W8 8 B8
Rabbits Rd MNPK E12 77 J3
Rabournmead Dr RSLP HA4 65 J4
Raby Rd NWMAL KT3 160 A3
Raby St POP/IOD * E14 93 G5
Raccoon Wy HSLWW TW4 122 B1
Rachel Cl BARK/HLT IG6 60 D2
Rackham Cl WELL DA16 136 C1
Rackham Ms
STRHM/NOR SW16 148 C5
Racton Rd FUL/PGN SW6 107 K5
Radbourne Av EA W5 104 D3
Radbourne Cl CLPT E5 75 F3
Radbourne Ct
KTN/HRWW/W * HA3 49 H5
Radbourne Crs WALTH E17 58 B2
Radbourne Rd BAL SW12 129 H6
Radcliffe Av WLSDN NW10 87 J1
Radcliffe Gdns CAR SM5 175 J6
Radcliffe Rd CROY/NA CR0 178 B1
KTN/HRWW/W HA3 49 G1
STHWK SE1 19 K3
WCHMH N21 29 H7
Radcliffe Wy NTHLT UB5 83 H2
Radcot St LBTH SE11 18 B8
Raddington Rd NKENS W10 88 C4
Radfield Wy ELTH/MOT SE9 135 J6
Radford Est WLSDN * NW10 87 G2
Radford Rd LEW SE13 133 F5
Radford Wy BARK IG11 97 F2
Radipole Rd FUL/PGN SW6 107 J7
Radius Pk EBED/NFELT * TW14 121 J3
Radland Rd CAN/RD E16 94 E5
Radlet Av SYD SE26 150 D2
Radlett Cl FSTGT E7 76 D5
Radlett Pl STJWD NW8 3 J4
Radlett Rd WATN WD24 21 G2
Radley Av GDMY/SEVK IG3 79 F3
Radley Cl EBED/NFELT TW14 121 J7
Radley Ct BERM/RHTH SE16 112 A1
Radley Gdns KTN/HRWW/W HA3 50 A3
Radley Ms KENS W8 14 B4
Radley Rd TOTM N17 56 A1
Radley's La SWFD E18 58 E1
Radleys Md DAGE RM10 80 D5
Radley Sq CLPT * E5 74 E1
Radley Ter CAN/RD * E16 94 D4
Radlix Rd LEY E10 57 J7
Radnor Av HRW HA1 48 E4
WELL DA16 136 C4
Radnor Cl CHST BR7 154 E5
MTCM CR4 163 K4
Radnor Crs REDBR IG4 59 K4
WOOL/PLUM SE18 116 B6
Radnor Gdns TWK TW1 143 F1
Radnor Hall BORE * WD6 24 A4
Radnor Ms BAY/PAD W2 9 H5
Radnor Pl BAY/PAD W2 9 J5
Radnor Rd HRW HA1 48 D4
KIL/WHAMP NW6 70 C7
PECK SE15 111 H6
TWK TW1 124 A7
Radnor St FSBYE EC1V 6 F8
Radnor Ter WKENS W14 107 J3
Radnor Wk CHEL SW3 15 K8
CROY/NA CR0 166 B6
Radnor Wy WLSDN NW10 86 D3
Radstock Av
KTN/HRWW/W HA3 49 G2
Radstock Cl FBAR/BDGN N11 40 A4
Radstock St BTSEA * SW11 108 D6
Raebarn Gdns BAR EN5 25 K4
Raeburn Av BRYLDS KT5 159 J5
DART DA1 138 E4
Raeburn Cl EFNCH N2 53 G5
KUT KT1 143 K6
Raeburn Rd BFN/LL DA15 135 K5
EDGW HA8 50 C1
YEAD UB4 82 B1
Raeburn St BRXS/STRHM SW2 129 K3
Rafford Wy BMLY BR1 168 A1
Raggleswood CHST BR7 154 A7
Raglan Cl HSLWW TW4 122 D4
Raglan Ct CROY/NA CR0 177 H4
Raglan Gdns OXHEY WD19 21 F7
Raglan Rd BELV DA17 117 G3
EN EN1 30 A6
HAYES BR2 168 B3
WALTH E17 58 A4
WOOL/PLUM SE18 115 H4
Raglan St KTTN NW5 72 B5
Raglan Ter RYLN/HDSTN * HA2 66 B3
Raglan Vls WALTH * E17 58 A4
Raglan Wy NTHLT UB5 66 C5
Ragley Cl ACT W3 105 K1
Railey Ms KTTN NW5 72 C4
Railshead Rd ISLW TW7 124 C3
Railton Rd HNHL SE24 130 B4
Railway Ap HRW HA1 49 F3
STHWK SE1 13 H8
TWK TW1 124 B6
WLGTN * SM6 176 B5
Railway Ar BRXN/ST * SW9 130 B3
Railway Av BERM/RHTH SE16 111 K1
Railway Cottages SHB * W12 107 F1
SRTFD * E15 94 C1
WIM/MER * SW19 147 F3
Railway Gv NWCR SE14 112 C6
Railway Pl BELV DA17 117 H2
Railway Ri EDUL SE22 131 F3
Railway Rd TEDD TW11 142 E3
Railway Side BARN SW13 126 B2
Railway Station Whf LEY * E10 57 G7
Railway St BCTR RM8 61 J7
IS N1 5 K6
Railway Ter FELT TW13 121 K7
LEW SE13 132 E4
WALTH E17 44 A7
Rainborough Cl WBLY HA9 68 E5
Rainbow Av POP/IOD E14 112 E4
Rainbow Ct OXHEY WD19 21 G5
Rainbow St CMBW SE5 111 F6
Raine St WAP E1W 92 D7
Rainham Cl BTSEA SW11 128 D5
ELTH/MOT SE9 135 K5
Rainham Rd RAIN RM13 81 H6
WLSDN NW10 88 A2
Rainham Rd North DAGE RM10 80 D1
Rainham Rd South DAGE RM10 80 E3
Rainhill Wy BOW E3 93 J2
Rainsborough Av DEPT SE8 112 B3
Rainsford Rd WLSDN NW10 86 D2
Rainsford St BAY/PAD W2 9 J4
Rainsford Wy HCH RM12 63 J7
Rainton Rd CHARL SE7 113 K4
Rainville Rd HMSMTH W6 107 F5
Raisins Hl PIN HA5 47 G2
Raith Av STHGT/OAK N14 40 D2
Raleana Rd POP/IOD E14 94 A7
Raleigh Av WLGTN SM6 176 D3
YEAD UB4 83 F4
Raleigh Cl ERITH DA8 118 C5
HDN NW4 52 A4
PIN HA5 47 H6
RSLP HA4 64 D1
Raleigh Dr BRYLDS KT5 159 K7
ESH/CLAY KT10 170 D4
TRDG/WHET N20 39 J2
Raleigh Gdns MTCM CR4 162 E2
Raleigh Ms IS N1 6 D4
Raleigh Rd CEND/HSY/T N8 55 G3
ENC/FH EN2 29 K3
FELT TW13 140 D1
MUSWH N10 39 J7
NWDGN UB2 102 D4
PGE/AN SE20 151 F6
RCH/KEW TW9 125 G2
Raleigh St IS N1 6 D4
Raleigh Wy FELT TW13 141 G4
STHGT/OAK N14 28 D7
Ralph Perring Ct BECK BR3 166 D3
Ralston St CHEL SW3 15 L8
Ralston Wy OXHEY WD19 33 H1
Rama Cl STRHM/NOR SW16 148 E6
Ramac Wy CHARL SE7 114 A3
Rambler Cl STRHM/NOR SW16 148 C3
Rame Cl TOOT SW17 148 A4
Ramilles Cl BRXS/STRHM SW2 129 K5
Ramillies Pl SOHO/CST W1F 10 E5
Ramillies Rd BFN/LL DA15 136 C5
CHSWK W4 106 A2
MLHL NW7 37 G1
Ramillies St SOHO/CST W1F 10 E5
Ramones Ter MTCM * CR4 163 H3
Rampart St WCHPL E1 92 D5
Ram Pas KUT KT1 158 E1
Rampayne St PIM SW1V 17 G7
Rampton Cl CHING E4 43 J2
Ramsay Rd ACT W3 105 K2
FSTGT E7 76 D3
Ramscroft Cl ED N9 30 A6
Ramsdale Rd TOOT SW17 148 A4
Ramsden Ga BAL * SW12 129 G6
Ramsden Rd BAL SW12 129 F6
ERITH DA8 118 A6
FBAR/BDGN N11 39 K4
Ramsey Cl CDALE/KGS NW9 51 H5
GFD/PVL UB6 66 D4
Ramsey Rd THHTH CR7 164 A5
Ramsey St BETH E2 92 C3
Ramsey Wk IS * N1 73 K5
Ramsey Wy STHGT/OAK N14 28 C6
Ramsgate St HACK * E8 74 B5
Ramsgill Ap GNTH/NBYPK IG2 61 F3
Ramsgill Dr GNTH/NBYPK IG2 61 F4
Rams Gv CHDH RM6 62 A3
Ram St WAND/EARL SW18 128 A4
Ramulis Dr YEAD UB4 83 J3
Rancliffe Gdns ELTH/MOT SE9 134 D3
Rancliffe Rd EHAM E6 95 J1
Randall Av CRICK NW2 69 G1
Randall Cl BTSEA SW11 108 D7
ERITH DA8 117 K5
Randall Pl GNWCH SE10 113 F6
Randall Rd LBTH SE11 17 L7
Randall Rw LBTH SE11 17 L6
Randell's Rd IS N1 5 K3
Randisbourne Gdns CAT * SE6 151 K2
Randle Rd RCHPK/HAM TW10 143 J3
Randlesdown Rd CAT SE6 151 J3
Randolph Ap CAN/RD E16 95 G5
Randolph Av MV/WKIL W9 2 C6
Randolph Cl BXLYHN DA7 137 K2
KUTN/CMB * KT2 144 E4
Randolph Crs MV/WKIL W9 8 E1
Randolph Gdns KIL/WHAMP NW6 2 C6
Randolph Ms MV/WKIL W9 8 F1
Randolph Rd HAYES BR2 168 E7
MV/WKIL W9 8 E1
STHL * UB1 102 E1
WALTH * E17 57 K4
Randolph St CAMTN NW1 4 E2
Randon Cl PIN HA5 48 B1
Ranelagh Av BARN SW13 126 D1
FUL/PGN SW6 127 J2
Ranelagh Cl EDGW HA8 36 C3
Ranelagh Dr EDGW HA8 36 C3
TWK TW1 124 C3
Ranelagh Gdns CHSWK W4 105 K6
FUL/PGN SW6 127 H2
IL IG1 60 A7
WAN E11 59 G4
Ranelagh Gv BGVA SW1W 16 B7
Ranelagh Pl NWMAL KT3 160 B4
Ranelagh Rd ALP/SUD HA0 67 K4
EA W5 104 E1
EHAM E6 78 A7
PIM SW1V 16 F8
SRTFD E15 76 C7
STHL UB1 83 H7
TOTM N17 56 A2
WAN E11 76 C3
WDGN N22 41 F7
WLSDN NW10 87 H1
Ranfurly Rd SUT SM1 174 E1
Rangefield Rd BMLY BR1 152 E5
Rangemoor Rd
SEVS/STOTM N15 56 B4
Rangeworth Pl BFN/LL DA15 155 F2
Rangoon St TWRH * EC3N 13 L5
Rankin Cl CDALE/KGS NW9 51 G2
Ranleigh Gdns BXLYHN DA7 117 G6
Ranmere St BAL SW12 129 G7
Ranmoor Gdns HRW HA1 48 D3
Ranmore Av CROY/NA CR0 178 B2
Ranmore Rd BELMT SM2 174 B7
Rannoch Cl EDGW HA8 36 D1
Rannoch Rd HMSMTH W6 107 F5
Rannock Av CDALE/KGS NW9 51 F6
Ransom Cl OXHEY WD19 21 G6
Ransom Rd CHARL * SE7 114 B4
Ranston St STJWD NW8 9 J2
Ranulf Rd CRICK NW2 70 D3
Ranwell Cl BOW * E3 75 H7
Ranworth Cl ERITH DA8 138 B1
Ranworth Rd ED N9 42 E1
Ranyard Cl CHSGTN KT9 172 B2
Raphael Av ROM RM1 63 H2
Raphael Dr THDIT KT7 158 A7
WATN WD24 21 H1
Raphael St SKENS SW7 15 L2
Rapier Cl PUR RM19 119 J3
Rasper Rd TRDG/WHET N20 39 G1
Rastell Av BRXS/STRHM SW2 148 D1
Ratcliffe Cl LEE/GVPK SE12 133 K6
Ratcliffe Cross St WCHPL * E1 93 F5
Ratcliffe La POP/IOD E14 93 G5
Ratcliff Rd FSTGT E7 77 G4
Rathbone Market CAN/RD * E16 94 D4
Rathbone Pl FITZ W1T 11 G3
Rathbone Sq CROY/NA * CR0 177 J3
Rathbone St CAN/RD E16 94 D4
FITZ W1T 10 F3
Rathcoole Av CEND/HSY/T N8 55 F4
Rathcoole Gdns
CEND/HSY/T N8 55 F4
Rathfern Rd CAT SE6 132 C7
Rathgar Av WEA W13 85 H7
Rathgar Cl FNCH N3 52 D1
Rathgar Rd BRXN/ST SW9 130 C2
Rathmell Dr CLAP SW4 129 J5
Rathmore Rd CHARL SE7 114 A4
Rattray Rd BRXS/STRHM SW2 130 B3
Raul Rd PECK SE15 131 H1
Raveley St KTTN NW5 72 C3
Raven Cl CDALE/KGS NW9 51 H1
Ravencroft Crs ELTH/MOT SE9 153 K2
Ravenet St BTSEA SW11 109 G7
Ravenfield Rd TOOT SW17 147 K2
Ravenhill Rd PLSTW E13 77 G7
Ravenna Rd PUT/ROE SW15 127 G4
Ravenor Park Rd GFD/PVL UB6 84 B2
Raven Rd SWFD E18 59 G1
Raven Rw WCHPL E1 92 D4
Ravens Ait SURB * KT6 158 E4
Ravensbourne Av HAYES BR2 152 B7
STWL/WRAY TW19 120 B7
Ravensbourne Gdns WEA W13 85 H4
Ravensbourne Pk BROCKY SE4 132 D6
Ravensbourne Park Crs
CAT SE6 132 C6
Ravensbourne Pl DEPT SE8 132 E1
Ravensbourne Rd BMLY BR1 167 K2
CAT SE6 132 C6
DART DA1 138 D2
TWK TW1 124 D5
Ravensbury Av MRDN SM4 162 B4
Ravensbury Gv MTCM CR4 162 C3
Ravensbury La MTCM CR4 162 C3
Ravensbury Rd
WAND/EARL SW18 147 F1
Ravensbury Ter
WAND/EARL SW18 147 F1
Ravenscar Rd BMLY BR1 152 C3
SURB KT6 172 B1
Ravens Cl CDALE/KGS NW9 51 G1
EN EN1 30 A1
HAYES BR2 167 J1
Ravenscourt SUN TW16 140 D7
Ravenscourt Av HMSMTH W6 106 D3
Ravenscourt Cl RSLP HA4 46 A6
Ravenscourt Gdns
HMSMTH W6 106 C3
Ravenscourt Pk HMSMTH W6 106 D3
Ravenscourt Pl HMSMTH W6 106 E3
Ravenscourt Rd HMSMTH W6 106 E3
Ravenscourt Sq HMSMTH W6 106 D2
Ravenscraig Rd
FBAR/BDGN N11 40 B3
Ravenscroft Av GLDGN NW11 52 D6
WBLY HA9 50 A7
Ravenscroft Cl CAN/RD E16 94 E4
Ravenscroft Cottages
BAR * EN5 26 E3
Ravenscroft Pk BAR EN5 26 B3
Ravenscroft Rd BECK BR3 165 K1
CAN/RD E16 94 E4
CHSWK W4 105 K3
Ravenscroft St BETH E2 7 M6
Ravensdale Av
NFNCH/WDSP N12 39 G3
Ravensdale Gdns NRWD SE19 149 K6
Ravensdale Rd HSLWW TW4 122 D2
STNW/STAM N16 56 B6
Ravensdon St LBTH SE11 18 B8
Ravensfield DAGW RM9 79 K3
Ravensfield Gdns
HOR/WEW KT19 173 G4
Ravenshaw St
KIL/WHAMP NW6 70 D4
Ravenshill CHST BR7 154 B7
Ravenshurst Av HDN NW4 52 A3
Ravenside Cl UED N18 43 F4
Ravenslea Rd BAL SW12 128 E6
Ravensmead Rd HAYES BR2 152 B6
Ravensmede Wy CHSWK W4 106 C3
Ravens Ms BKHTH/KID * SE3 133 K4
Ravenstone Rd
CDALE/KGS * NW9 51 H5
CEND/HSY/T N8 55 F2
Ravenstone St BAL SW12 129 F7
Ravens Wy LEE/GVPK SE12 133 K4
Ravenswood BXLY DA5 137 F7
Ravenswood Av SURB KT6 172 B1
WWKM BR4 167 F7
Ravenswood Ct
KUTN/CMB * KT2 144 E5
Ravenswood Crs
RYLN/HDSTN HA2 65 K1
WWKM BR4 167 F7
Ravenswood Gdns ISLW TW7 103 K7
Ravenswood Pk NTHWD HA6 32 E5
Ravenswood Rd BAL SW12 129 G6
CROY/NA CR0 177 H2
WALTH E17 58 A3
Ravensworth Rd
ELTH/MOT SE9 153 K3
WLSDN * NW10 87 K2
Ravent Rd LBTH SE11 17 M6
Ravey St SDTCH EC2A 7 J9
Ravine Gv WOOL/PLUM SE18 115 K5
Rav Pinter Cl STNW/STAM N16 56 A6
Rawlings St CHEL SW3 15 L5
Rawlins Cl FNCH N3 52 C2
SAND/SEL CR2 179 H6
Rawnsley Av MTCM CR4 162 C4
Rawreth Wk IS N1 6 F3
Rawson St BTSEA SW11 109 G7
Rawsthorne Cl CAN/RD E16 95 K7
Rawstorne Pl FSBYE * EC1V 6 C7
Rawstorne St FSBYE EC1V 6 C7
Ray Bell Ct BROCKY * SE4 132 C1
Raydean Rd BAR EN5 26 E4
Raydons Gdns DAGW RM9 80 A3
Raydons Rd DAGW RM9 80 A4
Raydon St ARCH N19 72 B1
Rayfield Cl HAYES BR2 168 D5
Rayford Av LEE/GVPK SE12 133 J6
Rayford Cl DART DA1 139 F4
Ray Gdns BARK IG11 97 G1
STAN HA7 35 H4
Ray Lamb Wy ERITH DA8 118 E5
Rayleas Cl WOOL/PLUM SE18 115 G7
Rayleigh Av TEDD TW11 142 E5
Rayleigh Cl PLMGR N13 41 K2
Rayleigh Ct KUT KT1 159 H1
Rayleigh Ri SAND/SEL CR2 178 A5
Rayleigh Rd CAN/RD E16 95 F7
PLMGR N13 41 J2
WFD IG8 45 G6
WIM/MER SW19 146 D7
Ray Lodge Rd WFD IG8 45 G5
Raymead Av THHTH CR7 164 B4
Raymere Gdns
WOOL/PLUM SE18 115 J6
Raymond Av HNWL W7 104 B2
SWFD E18 58 D2
Raymond Buildings
GINN * WC1R 11 M2
Raymond Cl SYD SE26 150 E4
Raymond Rd BECK BR3 166 B3
GNTH/NBYPK IG2 60 D6
PLSTW E13 77 G6
WIM/MER SW19 146 C5
Raymond Wy ESH/CLAY * KT10 171 G5
Raymouth Rd
BERM/RHTH SE16 111 J3
Rayne Ct SWFD E18 58 D3
Rayners Cl ALP/SUD HA0 67 K4
Rayners Gdns NTHLT UB5 83 F2
Rayners La PIN HA5 47 K5
Rayner's Rd PUT/ROE SW15 127 H4
Raynes Av WAN E11 59 G6
Raynham Av UED N18 42 C5
Raynham Rd HMSMTH W6 106 E3
UED N18 42 C4
Raynham Ter UED N18 42 C4
Raynor Cl STHL UB1 83 K7
Raynor Pl IS N1 6 F3
Raynton Cl RYLN/HDSTN HA2 47 J7
YEAD UB4 82 D3
Raynton Dr YEAD UB4 82 C1
Ray Rd E/WMO/HCT KT8 157 G4
Rays Av UED N18 42 E3
Rays Rd UED N18 42 E3
WWKM BR4 167 F6
Ray St CLKNW EC1R 12 B1
Ray Street Br CLKNW * EC1R 12 B1
Raywood Cl WDR/YW UB7 101 F6
Reachview Cl CAMTN NW1 4 F2
Reading La HACK E8 74 D5
Reading Rd NTHLT UB5 66 B4
SUT SM1 175 G4
Reading Wy MLHL NW7 38 C4
Reads Cl IL IG1 78 B2
Reapers Cl CAMTN NW1 5 G3
Reapers Wy ISLW TW7 123 J4
Reardon Pth WAP E1W 92 D7
Reardon St WAP E1W 92 D7
Reaston St NWCR SE14 111 K6
Reckitt Rd CHSWK W4 106 B4
Record St PECK SE15 111 K5
Recovery St TOOT SW17 147 J4
Recreation Av ROMW/RG RM7 62 E4
Recreation Rd HAYES BR2 167 J1
NWDGN UB2 102 D3
SYD SE26 151 F3
Recreation Wy MTCM CR4 163 K2
Rector St IS N1 6 E4
Rectory Cl CHING E4 43 J2
DART DA1 138 B3
FNCH N3 38 D7
RYNPK SW20 161 F1
SCUP DA14 155 H3
STAN HA7 35 H5
SURB KT6 158 D7
Rectory Field Crs CHARL SE7 114 B6
Rectory Gdns BECK * BR3 151 J7
CEND/HSY/T N8 54 E3
CHST * BR7 154 C7
NTHLT UB5 65 K7
Rectory Gn BECK BR3 151 H7
Rectory Gv CLAP SW4 129 H2
CROY/NA CR0 177 H1
FELT TW13 141 K3
Rectory La EDGW HA8 36 C5
SCUP DA14 155 H3
STAN HA7 35 H4
SURB KT6 158 D7
TOOT SW17 148 A4
WLGTN SM6 176 C3
Rectory Orch WIM/MER SW19 146 C3
Rectory Park Av NTHLT UB5 83 K2
Rectory Pl CHST * BR7 154 C7
WOOL/PLUM SE18 115 F3
Rectory Rd BARN SW13 126 D1
BECK BR3 151 J7
DAGE RM10 80 C5
HAYES BR2 181 H6
HEST TW5 122 A1
HYS/HAR UB3 82 E5
MNPK E12 77 K4
NWDGN UB2 102 E2
STNW/STAM N16 74 B2
SUT SM1 174 E2
WALTH E17 57 K3
Rectory Sq WCHPL E1 93 F4
Reculver Ms UED N18 42 C3
Reculver Rd BERM/RHTH SE16 111 K4
Red Anchor Cl CHEL * SW3 108 C5
Redan Pl BAY/PAD W2 8 C5
Redan St WKENS W14 107 G2
Redan Ter CMBW SE5 130 C1
Red Barracks Rd
WOOL/PLUM SE18 114 E3
Redberry Gv SYD SE26 150 E2
Redbourne Av FNCH N3 38 E7
Redbourne Dr THMD SE28 97 K5
Redbridge Gdns CMBW SE5 111 F6
Redbridge La East REDBR IG4 59 H5
Redbridge La West WAN E11 59 F5
Redburn St CHEL SW3 15 L9
Redbury Cl RAIN RM13 99 K3
Redcar Cl NTHLT UB5 66 B5
Redcar St CMBW * SE5 110 D6
Redcastle Cl WCHPL E1 92 E6
Red Cedars Rd ORP BR6 169 K6
Redchurch St BETH E2 7 L9
Redcliffe Cl ECT SW5 14 C8
Redcliffe Gdns IL IG1 60 A7
WBPTN SW10 14 D8
Redcliffe Ms WBPTN SW10 14 D8
Redcliffe Pl WBPTN SW10 108 B5
Redcliffe Rd WBPTN SW10 14 E8
Redcliffe Sq WBPTN SW10 14 D8
Redcliffe St WBPTN SW10 14 D9
Redclose Av MRDN SM4 161 K4
Redclyffe Rd EHAM E6 77 G7
Redcroft Rd STHL UB1 84 C6

Redcross Wy STHWK SE1 18 F1
The Reddings BORE WD6 24 B2
MLHL NW7 37 H2
Reddings Av BUSH WD23 22 B4
Reddings Cl MLHL NW7 37 H3
Reddington Cl SAND/SEL CR2 177 K7
Reddins Rd PECK SE15 111 H6
Reddons Rd BECK BR3 151 G6
Reddy Rd ERITH DA8 118 C5
Rede Pl BAY/PAD W2 8 B5
Redesdale Gdns ISLW TW7 104 B6
Redesdale St CHEL SW3 15 L9
Redfern Av HSLWW TW4 123 F6
Redfern Rd CAT SE6 133 F6
WLSDN NW10 69 G6
Redfield La ECT SW5 14 C5
Redford Av THHTH CR7 164 A3
WLGTN SM6 176 E5
Redford Cl FELT TW13 140 D1
Redford Wk IS * N1 6 D3
Redgate Dr HAYES BR2 181 F1
Redgate Ter PUT/ROE SW15 127 G5
Redgrave Cl SNWD SE25 165 G5
Redgrave Rd PUT/ROE SW15 127 G3
Redgrave Ter BETH * E2 92 C2
Redhall Ter EA * W5 86 C6
Red Hl CHST BR7 154 A4
Redhill Dr EDGW HA8 50 E1
Redhill St CAMTN NW1 4 D7
Red House La BXLYHS DA6 136 E3
Red House Rd CROY/NA CR0 163 J5
Red House Sq IS * N1 6 F1
Redington Gdns HAMP NW3 71 F3
Redington Rd HAMP NW3 71 F2
Redland Gdns
E/WMO/HCT * KT8 156 E3
Redlands Wy
BRXS/STRHM SW2 129 K6
Red La ESH/CLAY KT10 171 G5
Redleaf Cl BELV DA17 117 H5
Redlees Cl ISLW TW7 124 B3
Red Lion Cl WALW SE17 19 G9
Red Lion Ct FLST/FETLN EC4A 12 B5
HSLW * TW3 123 G2
Red Lion Hl EFNCH N2 53 H1
Red Lion La WOOL/PLUM SE18 115 F7
Red Lion Pde PIN * HA5 47 J2
Red Lion Pl
WOOL/PLUM * SE18 115 F7
Red Lion Rd SURB KT6 172 B1
Red Lion Rw WALW SE17 110 D5
Red Lion Sq BMSBY WC1N 11 L3
WAND/EARL * SW18 127 K4
Red Lion St GINN WC1R 11 L3
RCHPK/HAM TW10 124 E4
Red Lion Yd MYFR/PKLN * W1K 10 B8
Red Lodge Rd WWKM BR4 167 F7
Redman Cl NTHLT UB5 83 G1
Redman's Rd WCHPL E1 92 E4
Redmead La WAP E1W 92 C7
Redmead Rd HYS/HAR UB3 101 H3
Redmore Rd HMSMTH * W6 106 E3
Red Pl MYFR/PKLN W1K 10 A6
Red Post Hl HNHL SE24 130 E4
Redriffe Rd PLSTW E13 94 D1
Redriff Rd BERM/RHTH SE16 112 B2
ROMW/RG RM7 62 D1
Red Rd BORE WD6 24 B2
Redroofs Cl BECK BR3 151 K7
Redruth Cl WDGN N22 41 F6
Redruth Rd HOM E9 74 E7
Redstart Cl EHAM E6 95 J4
NWCR * SE14 112 B6
Redston Rd CEND/HSY/T N8 54 D3
Redvers Rd WDGN N22 55 G1
Redvers St IS N1 7 K7
Redwald Rd CLPT E5 75 F3
Redway Dr WHTN TW2 123 H6
Redwing Rd WLGTN SM6 176 E5
Redwood Cl BERM/RHTH SE16 93 G7
BFN/LL DA15 136 B7
OXHEY WD19 33 G3
STHGT/OAK N14 28 D6
Redwood Gdns CHING * E4 31 K6
Redwood Ms ASHF * TW15 140 B6
Redwood Wy BAR EN5 26 B4
Reece Ms SKENS SW7 15 G5
Reed Cl CAN/RD E16 94 E4
LEE/GVPK SE12 133 K4
Reede Rd DAGE RM10 80 C5
Reede Wy DAGE RM10 80 D5
Reedham Cl TOTM N17 56 D3
Reedham St PECK * SE15 131 H1
Reedholm Vls STNW/STAM N16 73 K3
Reed Pond Wk GPK RM2 63 H1
Reed Rd TOTM N17 56 B2
Reeds Crs WATN WD24 21 G1
Reed's Pl CAMTN NW1 4 E1
Reedworth St LBTH SE11 18 B6
Reenglass Rd STAN * HA7 35 K3
Rees Dr STAN HA7 36 A3
Rees Gdns CROY/NA CR0 165 G5
Reesland Cl MNPK E12 78 A5
Rees St IS N1 7 G4
Reets Farm Cl CDALE/KGS NW9 51 G5
Reeves Av CDALE/KGS NW9 51 F6
Reeves Cnr CROY/NA CR0 177 H1
Reeves Ms MYFR/PKLN W1K 10 A7
Reeves Rd BOW E3 93 K3
WOOL/PLUM SE18 115 G5
Reform Rw TOTM N17 56 B1
Reform St BTSEA SW11 128 E1
Regal Cl EA W5 85 K4
WCHPL E1 92 C4
Regal Ct MTCM CR4 162 E2
UED N18 42 B4
Regal Crs WLGTN SM6 176 B2
Regal Dr FBAR/BDGN N11 40 B4
Regal La CAMTN NW1 4 B4
Regal Wy KTN/HRWW/W HA3 50 A5
Regan Wy IS N1 7 J6
Regarth Av ROM RM1 63 G5
Regency Cl EA W5 86 A5
HPTN TW12 141 K4
Regency Ct EN EN1 29 K4
Regency Dr RSLP HA4 46 C7
Regency Gdns WOT/HER KT12 156 C7
Regency Lawn KTTN * NW5 72 B2
Regency Ms BECK BR3 152 A7
WLSDN NW10 69 J5
Regency Pde HAMP * NW3 3 G2
Regency Pl WEST * SW1P 17 G5
Regency St WEST SW1P 17 H6
Regency Ter HGT * N6 53 K5
SKENS * SW7 15 G7
Regency Wk CROY/NA CR0 166 B5
Regency Wy BXLYHN DA7 136 E2
Regent Cl HEST TW5 102 A7
KTN/HRWW/W HA3 50 A5
NFNCH/WDSP N12 39 G4
Regent Gdns GDMY/SEVK IG3 61 G5
Regent Pde BELMT * SM2 175 G5
STNW/STAM * N16 56 B6
Regent Pl WIM/MER SW19 147 G4
Regent Rd BRYLDS KT5 159 G4
HNHL SE24 130 C5
Regents Av PLMGR N13 41 G4
Regents Bridge Gdns
VX/NE SW8 109 K5
Regents Cl SAND/SEL CR2 178 A5
YEAD UB4 82 C4
Regents Dr HAYES BR2 181 H4
Regents Ms STJWD NW8 2 F5
Regent's Park Rd CAMTN NW1 3 M3
FNCH N3 52 D2
Regent's Park Ter CAMTN NW1 4 C3
Regents Plaza
KIL/WHAMP * NW6 2 C5
Regent Sq BELV DA17 117 J3
BOW E3 93 K2
STPAN WC1H 5 K8
Regent's Rw HACK E8 74 C7
Regent St CHSWK W4 105 H4
CONDST W1S 10 E5
WLSDN NW10 88 B2
Regents Whf IS * N1 5 L5
Reginald Rd DEPT SE8 112 D6
FSTGT E7 76 E6
NTHWD HA6 32 D7
Reginald Sq DEPT SE8 112 D6
Regina Rd FSBYPK N4 55 F7
NWDGN UB2 102 D3
SNWD SE25 165 H2
WEA W13 85 G7
Regina Ter WEA W13 85 G7
Regis Rd KTTN NW5 72 B4
Regnart Buildings CAMTN NW1 4 F8
Reid Cl PIN HA5 46 E2
Reidhaven Rd
WOOL/PLUM SE18 115 K3
Reigate Av SUT SM1 162 A7
Reigate Rd BMLY BR1 152 E1
GDMY/SEVK IG3 79 F1
Reigate Wy WLGTN SM6 176 E4
Reighton Rd CLPT E5 74 C2
Relay Rd SHB W12 88 A6
Relf Rd PECK SE15 131 H2
Reliance Ar BRXN/ST * SW9 130 B3
Relton Ms SKENS SW7 15 K3
Rembrandt Cl BGVA SW1W 16 A7
POP/IOD E14 113 G2
Rembrandt Ct HOR/WEW KT19 173 H5
Rembrandt Rd EDGW * HA8 50 C1
LEW SE13 133 H3
Remington Rd EHAM E6 95 J5
SEVS/STOTM N15 55 K5
Remington St IS N1 6 D6
Remnant St HOL/ALD WC2B 11 L4
Remus Rd BOW E3 75 J6
Rendle Cl CROY/NA CR0 165 G4
Rendlesham Rd CLPT E5 74 C3
Renforth St BERM/RHTH SE16 111 K1
Renfrew Cl EHAM E6 96 A6
Renfrew Rd HEST TW5 122 C1
KUTN/CMB KT2 144 E6
LBTH SE11 18 C5
Renmuir St TOOT SW17 147 K5
Rennell St LEW SE13 133 F2
Renness Rd WALTH E17 57 G2
Rennets Cl ELTH/MOT SE9 135 J4
Rennets Wood Rd
ELTH/MOT SE9 135 J4
Rennie Est BERM/RHTH SE16 111 J3
Rennie St STHWK SE1 12 C8
Renown Cl CROY/NA CR0 164 C7
Rensburg Rd WALTH E17 57 F4
Rensburg Vls WALTH * E17 57 F4
Renshaw Cl BELV DA17 117 G5
Renters Av HDN NW4 52 A5
Renton Cl BRXS/STRHM * SW2 130 A5
Renwick Rd BARK IG11 97 H3
Repens Wy YEAD UB4 83 H3
Rephidim St STHWK SE1 19 H4
Replingham Rd
WAND/EARL SW18 127 J7
Reporton Rd FUL/PGN SW6 107 H7
Repository Rd
WOOL/PLUM SE18 114 E5
Repton Av ALP/SUD HA0 67 J3
GPK RM2 63 J2
HYS/HAR UB3 101 G3
Repton Cl SUT SM1 175 J4
Repton Ct BECK BR3 151 K7
Repton Dr GPK RM2 63 J3
Repton Gdns GPK RM2 63 J2
Repton Gv CLAY IG5 45 K7
Repton Rd KTN/HRWW/W HA3 50 B3
Repton St POP/IOD E14 93 G5
Reservoir Cl THHTH CR7 164 E2
Reservoir Rd BROCKY SE4 132 B1
RSLP HA4 46 A4
STHGT/OAK N14 28 C4
Resolution Wy DEPT SE8 112 D6
Restell Cl BKHTH/KID SE3 113 H5
Restmor Wy WLGTN SM6 176 A1
Reston Pl SKENS SW7 14 E2
Restons Crs ELTH/MOT SE9 135 J5
Retford St BETH * E2 7 K6
Retingham Wy CHING E4 43 K1
The Retreat BARN SW13 126 B2
BRYLDS KT5 159 G5
CDALE/KGS NW9 51 F4
RYLN/HDSTN HA2 48 A6
THHTH CR7 164 E3
WPK KT4 173 K2
Retreat Cl KTN/HRWW/W HA3 49 J4
Retreat Pl HOM E9 74 E5
Retreat Rd RCH/KEW TW9 124 E4
Reunion Rw WAP * E1W 92 D6
Reveley Sq BERM/RHTH SE16 112 B1
Revell Ri WOOL/PLUM SE18 116 A5
Revell Rd KUT KT1 159 J1
SUT SM1 174 D5
Revelon Rd BROCKY SE4 132 B3
Revelstoke Rd
WAND/EARL SW18 146 E1
Reventlow Rd ELTH/MOT SE9 135 H7
Reverdy Rd STHWK SE1 111 H3
Reverend Cl RYLN/HDSTN HA2 66 B2
Revesby Rd CAR SM5 162 D5
Review Rd CRICK NW2 69 H1
DAGE RM10 98 D1
Rewell St FUL/PGN * SW6 108 B6
Rewley Rd CAR SM5 162 C5
Rex Pl MYFR/PKLN W1K 10 B8
Reydon Av WAN E11 59 G5
Reynard Cl BMLY BR1 168 E2
Reynard Dr NRWD SE19 150 B6
Reynard Pl NWCR * SE14 112 B5
Reynardson Rd TOTM N17 41 J6
Reynolds Av CHDH RM6 61 J6
CHSGTN KT9 172 A6
MNPK E12 78 A4
Reynolds Cl CAR SM5 162 E7
GLDGN NW11 53 F6
WIM/MER SW19 147 H7
Reynolds Dr EDGW HA8 50 B2
Reynolds Pl BKHTH/KID SE3 114 A6
RCHPK/HAM TW10 125 G5
Reynolds Rd CHSWK W4 105 K2
NWMAL KT3 160 A6
PECK SE15 131 K4
YEAD UB4 83 G3
Reynolds Wy CROY/NA CR0 178 A3
Rheidol Ms IS N1 6 E5
Rheidol Ter IS N1 6 D5
Rheingold Wy WLGTN SM6 176 E7
Rheola Cl TOTM N17 42 B7
Rhoda St BETH E2 7 M9
Rhodes Av WDGN N22 40 C7
Rhodesia Rd BRXN/ST SW9 129 K1
WAN E11 76 B1
Rhodes St HOLWY N7 73 F4
Rhodes Wy WATN WD24 21 H1
Rhodeswell Rd BOW E3 93 G4
Rhodrons Av CHSGTN KT9 172 A4
Rhondda Gv BOW E3 93 G2
Rhyl Rd GFD/PVL UB6 85 F1
Rhyl St KTTN NW5 72 A5
Rhys Av FBAR/BDGN N11 40 D6
Rialto Rd MTCM CR4 163 F1
Ribble Cl WFD IG8 45 G5
Ribblesdale Av FBAR/BDGN N11 39 K5
NTHLT UB5 66 B5
Ribblesdale Rd CEND/HSY/T N8 55 F3
STRHM/NOR SW16 148 B4
Ribbon Dance Ms CMBW SE5 110 E7
Ribchester Av GFD/PVL UB6 85 F2
Ribston Cl HAYES BR2 168 E7
Ricardo St POP/IOD E14 93 K5
Ricards Rd WIM/MER SW19 146 D4
Rice Pde STMC/STPC * BR5 169 J4
Richard Cl WOOL/PLUM SE18 114 D3
Richard House Dr CAN/RD E16 95 H5
Richards Av ROMW/RG RM7 62 E4
Richards Cl BUSH WD23 22 D6
HRW HA1 49 G4
HYS/HAR UB3 101 G5
Richards Cottages CAR * SM5 175 K4
Richards Fld HOR/WEW KT19 173 F7
Richardson Cl HACK * E8 7 L3
Richardson Rd SRTFD * E15 94 C1
Richardson's Ms FITZ W1T 10 E1
Richard's Pl CHEL SW3 15 K5
WALTH E17 57 J2
Richard St WCHPL E1 92 D5
Richbell Pl BMSBY WC1N 11 L2
Richborne Ter VX/NE SW8 110 A6
Richborough Rd CRICK NW2 70 B3
Richens Cl HSLW TW3 123 J1
Riches Rd IL IG1 78 C1
Richfield Rd BUSH WD23 22 C6
Richford Ga HMSMTH * W6 107 F2
Richford Rd SRTFD E15 76 D7
Richford St SHB W12 107 F1
Richlands Av EW KT17 173 J3
Richmer Rd ERITH DA8 118 D6
Richmond Av CHING E4 44 B4
EBED/NFELT TW14 121 H5
IS N1 5 M3
RYNPK SW20 146 C7
WLSDN NW10 69 K5
Richmond Buildings
SOHO/CST W1F 11 G5
Richmond Cl WALTH E17 57 H5
Richmond Crs CHING E4 44 B4
ED N9 30 C7
IS N1 5 M3
Richmond Dr WAT WD17 20 C1
Richmond Gdns HDN NW4 51 J4
KTN/HRWW/W HA3 35 F6
Richmond Gn CROY/NA CR0 176 E2
Richmond Gv IS N1 6 D2
Richmond Hl
RCHPK/HAM TW10 125 F5
Richmond Ms SOHO/CST W1F 11 G5
Richmond Pde TWK * TW1 124 D5
Richmond Park Rd
KUTN/CMB KT2 144 A6
MORT/ESHN SW14 125 K4
Richmond Pl
WOOL/PLUM SE18 115 H3
Richmond Rd BAR EN5 27 G4
CROY/NA CR0 176 E2
EA W5 105 F1
EFNCH * N2 53 G1
FBAR/BDGN N11 40 E5
FSTGT E7 77 F4
HACK E8 7 L1
HACK E8 74 C6
IL IG1 78 C2
ISLW TW7 124 B3
KUTN/CMB KT2 143 K4
ROM RM1 63 H5
RYNPK SW20 145 K7
SEVS/STOTM N15 56 A5
THHTH CR7 164 C3
TWK TW1 124 C6
WAN E11 76 B1
Richmond St PLSTW E13 94 E1
Richmond Ter WHALL SW1A 17 J1
Richmond Vls WALTH * E17 43 K7
Richmond Wy
RKW/CH/CXG WD3 20 A3
SHB W12 107 G1
WAN E11 76 E1
Richmount Gdns
BKHTH/KID SE3 133 K2
Rich St POP/IOD E14 93 H6
Rickard Cl BRXS/STRHM SW2 130 B7
HDN NW4 51 J3
WDR/YW UB7 100 A2
Rickards Cl SURB KT6 172 A1
Rickett St FUL/PGN SW6 14 B9
Rickman St WCHPL E1 92 E3
Rickmansworth Rd NTHWD HA6 32 B6
WATW WD18 20 C3
Rick Roberts Wy SRTFD E15 76 B7
Rickthorne Rd ARCH N19 72 E1
Ridding La GFD/PVL UB6 67 F4
Riddons Rd LEE/GVPK SE12 153 G2
The Ride BTFD TW8 104 C4
PEND EN3 30 E2
Rideout St WOOL/PLUM SE18 114 E3
Rider Cl BFN/LL DA15 135 K5
Ridgdale St BOW E3 93 J1
The Ridge BAR * EN5 26 D4
BRYLDS KT5 159 H4
BXLY DA5 137 G6
WHTN TW2 123 J6
Ridge Av DART DA1 138 C5
WCHMH N21 29 J6
Ridgebrook Rd BKHTH/KID SE3 134 B3
Ridge Cl CDALE/KGS NW9 51 F3
HDN NW4 52 B1
THMD SE28 115 J1
Ridgecroft Cl BXLY DA5 137 K7
Ridge Hl GLDGN NW11 52 C7
Ridgemead Cl STHGT/OAK N14 40 E1
Ridgemont Gdns EDGW HA8 36 E3
Ridgemount Av CROY/NA CR0 179 F1
Ridgemount Gdns ENC/FH EN2 29 H2
Ridge Rd CEND/HSY/T N8 55 F5
CHEAM SM3 161 J7
CRICK NW2 70 D2
MTCM CR4 148 B6
WCHMH N21 29 K7
Ridge Ter WCHMH * N21 29 J6
Ridgeview Cl BAR EN5 26 B5
Ridgeview Rd
NFNCH/WDSP N12 39 F2
Ridge Wy DART DA1 138 C5
FELT TW13 141 J2
Ridgeway HAYES BR2 180 E1
WFD IG8 45 G3
Ridgeway Av EBAR EN4 27 K5
Ridgeway Dr BMLY BR1 153 F3
Ridgeway East BFN/LL DA15 136 A4
Ridgeway Gdns REDBR IG4 59 J4
Ridgeway Rd ISLW TW7 103 K6
Ridgeway Rd North ISLW TW7 103 K6
The Ridgeway ACT W3 105 H2
CDALE/KGS NW9 51 F3
CROY/NA CR0 177 F2
FBAR/BDGN N11 39 K3
FNCH N3 39 F6
GLDGN NW11 52 D7
GPK RM2 63 J3
KTN/HRWW/W HA3 49 J5
MLHL NW7 37 K3
RSLP HA4 46 E6
RYLN/HDSTN HA2 47 K4
STAN HA7 35 J5
STHGT/OAK N14 40 E1
Ridgeway West BFN/LL DA15 135 K4
Ridgewell Cl DAGE RM10 80 D7
IS N1 6 F3
SYD SE26 151 H3
Ridgmount Gdns GWRST WC1E 11 G2
Ridgmount Rd
WAND/EARL SW18 128 A4
Ridgmount St GWRST WC1E 11 G2
Ridgway RCHPK/HAM * TW10 125 F5
WIM/MER SW19 146 A6
Ridgway Gdns WIM/MER SW19 146 B6
Ridgway Pl WIM/MER SW19 146 C5
Ridgway Rd BRXN/ST SW9 130 C2
The Ridgway BELMT SM2 175 H6
Ridgwell Rd CAN/RD E16 95 G4
Riding House St REGST * W1B 10 D3
Ridings Av WCHMH N21 29 H3
The Ridings BRYLDS KT5 159 H4
EA W5 86 B3
EBAR * EN4 27 J6
EW KT17 173 H7
SUN TW16 140 E7
The Riding GLDGN NW11 52 D6
Ridley Av WEA W13 104 C2
Ridley Rd FSTGT E7 77 G3
HACK E8 74 B4
HAYES BR2 167 J2
WELL DA16 116 C7
WIM/MER SW19 147 F6
WLSDN NW10 87 J1
Ridsdale Rd PGE/AN SE20 150 D7
Riefield Rd ELTH/MOT SE9 135 H3
Riesco Dr CROY/NA CR0 178 E5
Riffel Rd CRICK NW2 70 A4
Rifle Pl NTGHL W11 88 B7
Rifle Range La HRW HA1 49 F7
Rifle St POP/IOD E14 93 K4
Rigault Rd FUL/PGN SW6 127 H1
Rigby Cl CROY/NA CR0 177 G2
Rigby La HYS/HAR UB3 101 G1
Rigby Ms IL IG1 78 A1
Rigden St POP/IOD E14 93 K5
Rigeley Rd WLSDN NW10 87 J2
Rigg Ap LEY E10 57 F7
Rigge Pl CLAP SW4 129 J3
Riggindale Rd
STRHM/NOR SW16 148 D4
Right Side STHGT/OAK * N14 28 D7
Riley Rd STHWK SE1 19 L3
Riley St WBPTN SW10 108 C6
Rinaldo Rd BAL SW12 129 G6
Ring Cl BMLY BR1 153 F6
Ringcroft St HOLWY N7 73 G4
Ringer's Rd BMLY BR1 167 K2
Ringford Rd WAND/EARL SW18 127 J4
Ringlet Cl CAN/RD E16 95 F4
Ringmer Av FUL/PGN SW6 107 H7
Ringmer Pl WCHMH N21 29 K4
Ringmer Wy BMLY BR1 168 E4
Ringmore Ri FSTH SE23 131 J6
Ringslade Rd WDGN N22 55 F1
Ringstead Rd CAT SE6 132 E6
SUT SM1 175 H3
Ring Wy FBAR/BDGN N11 40 C5
Ringway NWDGN UB2 102 D4
Ringwold Cl BECK BR3 151 G6
Ringwood Av CROY/NA CR0 163 K6
EFNCH N2 53 K2
Ringwood Cl PIN * HA5 47 G2
Ringwood Gdns
PUT/ROE SW15 145 J1
Ringwood Rd WALTH E17 57 H5
Ringwood Wy HPTN TW12 142 A3
WCHMH N21 29 H7
Ripley Cl BMLY BR1 168 E4
CROY/NA CR0 180 A5
Ripley Gdns MORT/ESHN SW14 126 A2
Ripley Ms WAN * E11 58 C5
Ripley Rd BELV DA17 117 H3
CAN/RD E16 95 G5
GDMY/SEVK IG3 79 F1
HPTN TW12 142 A6
Ripleys Market DART * DA1 139 H6
Ripley Vls WEA * W13 85 J5
Ripon Cl NTHLT UB5 66 A4
Ripon Gdns CHSGTN KT9 171 K4
IL IG1 59 J5
Ripon Rd ED N9 30 D6
TOTM N17 55 K2
WOOL/PLUM SE18 115 G5
Ripon Wy BORE WD6 24 E4
Rippersley Rd WELL DA16 116 B7
Ripple Rd BARK IG11 78 C6
BARK IG11 78 E7
BARK IG11 79 H7
BARK IG11 80 A7
Ripplevale Gv IS N1 5 M2
Rippolson Rd
WOOL/PLUM SE18 116 A4
Ripston Rd ASHF TW15 140 B4
Risborough Cl MUSWH * N10 54 B2
Risborough Dr WPK KT4 160 D6
Risborough St STHWK SE1 18 D1
Risdon St BERM/RHTH SE16 111 K1
The Rise BORE WD6 24 B4
BXLY DA5 136 D6
DART DA1 138 C3
EDGW HA8 36 D4
GFD/PVL UB6 67 G4
MLHL NW7 37 H5
PLMGR N13 41 G3
SAND/SEL CR2 178 E7
WAN E11 58 E4
WLSDN NW10 69 F2
Risebridge Rd GPK RM2 63 H1
Risedale Rd BXLYHN DA7 137 J2
Riseldine Rd FSTH SE23 132 B5
Rise Park Pde ROM RM1 63 G1
Rising Hill Cl NTHWD * HA6 32 A5
Risinghill St IS N1 6 A5
Risingholme Cl BUSH WD23 22 B6
KTN/HRWW/W HA3 34 E7
Risingholme Rd
KTN/HRWW/W HA3 48 E1
The Risings WALTH E17 58 B3
Risley Av TOTM N17 41 J7
Rita Rd VX/NE SW8 109 K6
Ritches Rd SEVS/STOTM N15 55 J4
Ritchie Rd CROY/NA CR0 165 J5
Ritchie St IS N1 6 B5
Ritchings Av WALTH E17 57 G3
Ritherdon Rd TOOT SW17 148 A1
Ritson Rd HACK E8 74 B5
Ritter St WOOL/PLUM SE18 115 F5
Rivaz Pl HOM E9 74 E5
Rivenhall Gdns SWFD E18 58 D3
River Av PLMGR N13 41 H2
THDIT KT7 158 B6
Riverbank E/WMO/HCT KT8 157 K2
River Bank THDIT KT7 158 A4
WCHMH N21 29 J6
Riverbank Rd BMLY BR1 152 E2
Riverbank Wy BTFD TW8 104 D5
River Barge Cl POP/IOD E14 113 F1
River Cl NWDGN UB2 103 H1
RAIN RM13 99 K4
RSLP HA4 46 D5
WAN E11 59 G5
Rivercourt Rd HMSMTH W6 106 E3
Riverdale Dr WAND/EARL SW18 128 A7
Riverdale Gdns TWK TW1 124 D4
Riverdale Rd BXLY DA5 137 G6
ERITH DA8 117 J4
FELT TW13 141 J3
TWK TW1 124 D5
WOOL/PLUM SE18 116 A4
Riverdene EDGW HA8 36 E3
Riverdene Rd IL IG1 78 A2
River Front EN EN1 29 K2
River Gdns CAR SM5 176 A1
EBED/NFELT TW14 122 A4
River Grove Pk BECK BR3 151 H7
Riverhead Cl WALTH E17 57 F1
Riverholme Dr HOR/WEW KT19 173 F7
River La RCHPK/HAM TW10 124 E7
Rivermead E/WMO/HCT KT8 157 H2
SURB * KT6 158 E4
Rivermead Cl TEDD TW11 143 H4
Rivermead Rd UED * N18 43 F4
River Meads Av WHTN TW2 142 B2
Rivernook Cl WOT/HER KT12 156 B4
Riverpark Gdns HAYES BR2 152 B6
River Park Rd WDGN N22 55 F1
River Pl IS N1 6 E2
River Reach TEDD TW11 143 J5
River Rd BARK IG11 96 E1
Riversdale Rd HBRY N5 73 H2
THDIT KT7 158 B4
Riversfield Rd EN EN1 30 A2
The Riverside
E/WMO/HCT * KT8 157 J2
Riverside CHARL SE7 114 A2
HDN NW4 51 K6
RCH/KEW * TW9 105 H5
SUN * TW16 156 C1
TWK TW1 124 C7
Riverside Av E/WMO/HCT KT8 157 J4
Riverside Cl CLPT E5 56 E7
HNWL W7 84 E3
KUT KT1 158 E3
WLGTN SM6 176 B2
Riverside Ct CHING * E4 31 K5
Riverside Dr CHSWK W4 106 B6
ESH/CLAY KT10 170 A3
GLDGN * NW11 52 C5
MTCM CR4 162 D4
RCHPK/HAM TW10 143 H2
Riverside Gdns ALP/SUD HA0 86 A1
ENC/FH EN2 29 J1
HMSMTH W6 106 E4
Riverside Ms CROY/NA * CR0 176 E2
Riverside Pl FBAR/BDGN * N11 40 C2
STWL/WRAY TW19 120 A5
Riverside Rd IL IG1 78 B2
OXHEY WD19 21 F5
SEVS/STOTM N15 56 C5
SRTFD E15 94 A1
STWL/WRAY TW19 120 A4
TOOT SW17 147 F3
Riverside Vls SURB * KT6 158 D5
Riverside Wk ISLW TW7 123 K2
KUT KT1 158 E1
Riverside Wy DART DA1 139 H4
River St CLKNW EC1R 6 A7
River Ter HMSMTH W6 107 F4
Riverton Cl MV/WKIL * W9 88 D2
Riverview Gdns BARN SW13 106 E5
River View Gdns TWK TW1 143 F1
Riverview Pk CAT SE6 151 J1
Riverview Rd CHSWK W4 105 J6
HOR/WEW KT19 172 E3
River Wk SUN TW16 156 C1
River Wy FELT TW13 142 B1
GNWCH SE10 113 J2
HOR/WEW KT19 173 F4
Riverway PLMGR N13 41 G4
River Whf BELV * DA17 118 A1
Riverwood La CHST BR7 169 J1
Rivington Av WFD IG8 59 H1
Rivington Crs CDALE/KGS NW9 37 G6
Rivington Pl SDTCH EC2A 7 K8
Rivington St SDTCH EC2A 7 K8
Rivington Wk HACK * E8 74 C7
Rivulet Rd TOTM N17 41 J6
Rixon St HOLWY N7 73 G2
Rixsen Rd MNPK E12 77 J4

Roach Rd BOW E3 75 J6
Roads Pl FSBYPK N4 72 E1
Roan St GNWCH SE10 113 F5
Robarts Cl PIN HA5 47 F4
Robb Rd STAN HA7 35 G5
Robert Adam St MBLAR W1H 10 A4
Roberta St BETH E2 92 C2
Robert Cl MV/WKIL W9 8 F1
Robert Keen Cl PECK SE15 111 H7
Robert Lowe Cl NWCR SE14 112 A6
Roberton Dr BMLY BR1 168 B1
Robertsbridge Rd CAR SM5 162 B6
Roberts Cl CHEAM SM3 174 B6
ELTH/MOT SE9 135 J7
THHTH CR7 164 E2
Roberts Ct CHSGTN * KT9 171 K4
WLSDN NW10 69 G5
Roberts House
WOOL/PLUM SE18 114 D7
Roberts Ms KTBR * SW1X 16 A4
Robertson Rd SRTFD E15 76 A7
Robertson St VX/NE SW8 129 G2
Robert's Pl CLKNW * EC1R 6 B9
Roberts Rd BELV DA17 117 H4
MLHL NW7 38 C4
WALTH E17 43 K7
WATW WD18 21 G4
Robert St CAMTN NW1 4 D8
CHCR WC2N 11 K7
CROY/NA CR0 177 J2
WOOL/PLUM SE18 115 J4
Robeson St BOW E3 93 H4
Robina Cl BXLYHS DA6 136 E3
NTHWD HA6 46 D1
Robin Cl HPTN TW12 141 J4
MLHL NW7 37 G2
Robin Gv BTFD TW8 104 D5
HGT N6 72 A1
KTN/HRWW/W HA3 50 B5
Robin Hill Dr CHST BR7 153 J5
Robinhood Cl MTCM CR4 163 H3
Robin Hood Dr
KTN/HRWW/W HA3 35 F6
Robin Hood Gdns
POP/IOD * E14 94 A6
Robin Hood La BXLYHS DA6 137 F4
Robinhood La MTCM CR4 163 H2
Robin Hood La POP/IOD E14 94 A6
PUT/ROE SW15 145 G2
SUT SM1 174 E4
Robin Hood Rd PUT/ROE SW15 145 G3
Robin Hood Wy GFD/PVL UB6 67 F5
PUT/ROE SW15 145 G3
Robin Hood Wy
(Kingston By-Pass)
PUT/ROE SW15 145 G3
Robinia Cl PGE/AN SE20 150 C7
Robinia Crs LEY E10 75 K1
Robins Gv WWKM BR4 180 E2
Robinson Cl HCH RM12 81 K6
Robinson Crs BUSH WD23 22 C7
Robinson Rd BETH E2 92 E1
DAGE RM10 80 C3
WIM/MER SW19 147 J5
Robinson's Cl WEA W13 85 G4
Robinson St CHEL SW3 15 L9
Robinwood Pl
RCHPK/HAM TW10 145 F3
Robsart St BRXN/ST SW9 130 A1
Robson Av WLSDN NW10 69 J7
Robson Cl EHAM E6 95 J5
ENC/FH EN2 29 H1
Robson Rd WNWD SE27 149 H2
Roch Av EDGW HA8 50 B1
Rochdale Rd ABYW SE2 116 C4
Rochdale Wy DEPT SE8 112 D6
Rochelle Cl BTSEA SW11 128 C3
Rochelle St BETH E2 7 L8
Rochemont Wk HACK * E8 7 M4
Roche Rd STRHM/NOR SW16 148 E7
Rochester Av BMLY BR1 168 A1
FELT TW13 140 D1
PLSTW E13 77 G7
Rochester Cl BFN/LL DA15 136 C5
STRHM/NOR * SW16 148 E6
Rochester Dr BXLY DA5 137 H5
PIN HA5 47 H4
Rochester Gdns CROY/NA CR0 178 A2
IL IG1 59 K6
Rochester Ms CAMTN NW1 4 F1
EA * W5 104 D3
Rochester Pde FELT * TW13 140 E2
Rochester Pl CAMTN NW1 72 C5
Rochester Rd CAMTN NW1 72 C5
CAR SM5 175 K3
DART DA1 139 K6
NTHWD HA6 46 D2
Rochester Rw WEST SW1P 16 F5
Rochester Sq CAMTN NW1 4 F1
Rochester St WEST SW1P 17 G4
Rochester Ter CAMTN NW1 72 C5
Rochester Wk STHWK * SE1 13 G8
Rochester Wy BKHTH/KID SE3 114 A7
DART DA1 138 B6
Rochester Way Relief Rd
ELTH/MOT SE9 134 D4
Roche Wk MRDN SM4 162 C5
Rochford Av CHDH RM6 61 J4
Rochford Cl EHAM E6 95 H1
HCH RM12 81 K5
Rochford Wk HACK * E8 74 C6
Rochford Wy CROY/NA CR0 163 K5
Rock Av MORT/ESHN SW14 126 A2
Rockbourne Rd FSTH SE23 132 A7
Rock Cl MTCM CR4 162 C1
Rockell's Pl EDUL SE22 131 J5
Rockford Av GFD/PVL UB6 85 H1
Rock Grove Wy
BERM/RHTH SE16 111 H3
Rockhall Rd CRICK NW2 70 B3
Rockhampton Rd
SAND/SEL CR2 178 A5
STRHM/NOR SW16 149 G3
Rock Hl SYD SE26 150 B3
Rockingham Av EMPK RM11 63 K5
Rockingham Cl PUT/ROE SW15 126 C3
Rockingham Ga BUSH WD23 22 C5
Rockingham St STHWK SE1 18 E4
Rockland Rd PUT/ROE SW15 127 H3
Rocklands Dr
KTN/HRWW/W HA3 49 H1
Rockley Rd SHB W12 107 G1
Rockmount Rd NRWD SE19 149 K5
WOOL/PLUM SE18 116 A4
Rocks La BARN SW13 126 D2
Rock St FSBYPK N4 73 G1
Rockware Av GFD/PVL UB6 66 E7
Rockways BAR EN5 25 H5
Rockwell Gdns NRWD SE19 150 A3
Rockwell Rd DAGE RM10 80 D4
Rocliffe St IS N1 6 D6
Rocombe Crs FSTH * SE23 131 K6
Rocque La BKHTH/KID SE3 133 J2
Rodborough Rd GLDGN NW11 52 E7
Roden Gdns CROY/NA CR0 165 F5
Rodenhurst Rd CLAP SW4 129 H6
Roden St HOLWY N7 73 F2
IL IG1 78 A2
Rodeo Cl ERITH DA8 118 E7
Roderick Rd HAMP NW3 71 K3
Rodgers Cl BORE WD6 23 K5
Roding La North WFD IG8 59 J1
Roding La South REDBR IG4 59 H4
Roding Ms WAP E1W 92 C7
Roding Rd CLPT E5 75 F3
EHAM E6 96 B4
Rodings Rw BAR * EN5 26 C3
Rodmarton St MHST W1U 9 M3
Rodmell Cl YEAD UB4 83 J3
Rodmell Slope
NFNCH/WDSP N12 38 D4
Rodmere St GNWCH SE10 113 H4
Rodmill La BRXS/STRHM SW2 129 K6
Rodney Cl CROY/NA CR0 164 C7
NWMAL KT3 160 B4
PIN HA5 47 J6
WOT/HER * KT12 156 B7
Rodney Gdns PIN HA5 47 G4
WWKM BR4 180 E3
Rodney Pl STHWK SE1 18 F5
WALTH E17 57 G1
WIM/MER SW19 147 G7
Rodney Rd HSLW TW3 123 F5
MTCM CR4 162 D1
NWMAL KT3 160 B4
WALW SE17 18 F6
WAN E11 59 F3
Rodney St IS N1 5 M5
Rodway Rd BMLY BR1 153 F7
PUT/ROE SW15 126 D6
Rodwell Cl RSLP * HA4 47 G7
Rodwell Rd EDUL SE22 131 G5
Roebuck Cl FELT TW13 141 F3
Roebuck Rd CHSGTN KT9 172 C4
Roedean Crs PUT/ROE SW15 126 B5
Roe End CDALE/KGS NW9 50 E3
Roe Gn CDALE/KGS NW9 50 E4
Roehampton Cl
PUT/ROE SW15 126 D3
Roehampton Dr CHST BR7 154 C5
Roehampton Ga
PUT/ROE SW15 126 B5
Roehampton High St
PUT/ROE SW15 126 D6
Roehampton La
PUT/ROE SW15 126 D4
Roehampton V PUT/ROE SW15 145 H2
Roe La CDALE/KGS NW9 50 E3
Roe Wy WLGTN SM6 176 E6
Rofant Rd NTHWD HA6 32 C5
Roffey St POP/IOD E14 113 F1
Rogers Gdns DAGE RM10 80 C4
Rogers Rd CAN/RD E16 94 D5
DAGE RM10 80 C4
TOOT SW17 147 H3
Rogers Ruff NTHWD HA6 32 A7
Roger St BMSBY WC1N 11 M1
Rojack Rd FSTH SE23 132 A7
Rokeby Gdns WFD IG8 44 E7
Rokeby Pl RYNPK SW20 145 K6
Rokeby Rd BROCKY * SE4 132 C1
Rokeby St SRTFD E15 76 C7
Rokesby Cl WELL DA16 135 J1
Rokesby Pl ALP/SUD HA0 67 K4
Rokesly Av CEND/HSY/T N8 54 E4
Roland Gdns SKENS SW7 14 F7
Roland Ms WCHPL * E1 93 F4
Roland Rd WALTH E17 58 B3
Roland Wy WALW SE17 19 H8
WBPTN SW10 14 F7
WPK KT4 173 H1
Roles Gv CHDH RM6 61 K3
Rolfe Cl EBAR EN4 27 J3
Rolinsden Wy HAYES BR2 181 H3
Rollesby Rd CHSGTN KT9 172 C5
Rollesby Wy THMD SE28 97 J6
Rolleston Av STMC/STPC BR5 169 G6
Rolleston Cl STMC/STPC BR5 169 G6
Rolleston Rd SAND/SEL CR2 177 K6
Roll Gdns GNTH/NBYPK IG2 60 A4
Rollins St NWCR SE14 111 K5
Rolls Park Av CHING E4 43 J5
Rolls Park Rd CHING E4 43 K4
Rolls Rd STHWK SE1 19 M7
Rolt St DEPT SE8 112 B5
Rolvenden Gdns BMLY BR1 153 H7
Rolvenden Pl TOTM N17 42 C7
Roman Cl ACT W3 105 J1
EBED/NFELT TW14 122 B4
RAIN RM13 99 F1
Romanfield Rd
BRXS/STRHM SW2 130 A6
Romanhurst Av HAYES BR2 167 H3
Romanhurst Gdns BECK BR3 167 H3
Roman Ri NRWD SE19 149 K5
Roman Rd BETH E2 93 F1
BOW E3 75 H7
CHSWK W4 106 B3
EHAM E6 95 J3
IL IG1 78 B5
MUSWH N10 40 B6
Roman Sq THMD SE28 97 G7
Roman Wy CROY/NA CR0 177 H1
DART DA1 138 B4
EN EN1 30 B4
HOLWY N7 73 F5
Romany Gdns CHEAM SM3 161 K6
Romany Ri STMC/STPC BR5 169 H7
Roma Rd WALTH E17 57 G2
Romberg Rd TOOT SW17 148 A2
Romborough Gdns LEW SE13 133 F4
Romborough Wy LEW SE13 133 F4
Rom Crs ROMW/RG RM7 63 G6
Romeland BORE WD6 23 K5
Romero Sq BKHTH/KID SE3 134 B3
Romeyn Rd STRHM/NOR SW16 149 F2
Romford Rd MNPK E12 78 A2
SRTFD E15 76 C6
Romford St WCHPL E1 92 C4
Romilly Dr OXHEY WD19 33 J3
Romilly Rd FSBYPK N4 73 H1
Romilly St SOHO/SHAV W1D 11 H6
Rommany Rd WNWD SE27 149 K3
Romney Cl ASHF TW15 140 A4
CHSGTN KT9 172 A3
GLDGN NW11 53 F7
RYLN/HDSTN HA2 48 A6
TOTM N17 42 D7
Romney Dr BMLY BR1 153 H6
RYLN/HDSTN HA2 48 A6
Romney Gdns BXLYHN DA7 117 G7
Romney Rd GNWCH SE10 113 F5
NWMAL KT3 160 A5
WOOL/PLUM SE18 115 G2
YEAD UB4 82 B1
Romney Rw CRICK * NW2 70 B1
Romola Rd BRXS/STRHM SW2 130 C7
Romsey Rd DAGW RM9 79 K7
WEA * W13 85 G6
Rom Valley Wy ROMW/RG RM7 63 G5
Ronald Av SRTFD E15 94 C2
Ronald Cl BECK BR3 166 C4
Ronalds Rd BMLY BR1 152 E7
HBRY N5 73 H4
Ronaldstone Rd BFN/LL DA15 135 K5
Ronald St WCHPL E1 92 E5
Rona Rd HAMP NW3 72 A3
Ronart St KTN/HRWW/W HA3 49 F2
Rona Wk IS N1 73 K5
Rondu Rd CRICK NW2 70 C4
Ronelean Rd SURB KT6 172 B1
Roneo Cnr ROMW/RG RM7 63 H7
Roneo Link HCH RM12 63 H7
Ron Green Ct ERITH DA8 118 A4
Ron Leighton Wy EHAM E6 77 J7
Ronver Rd LEE/GVPK SE12 133 K7
Rood La FENCHST EC3M 13 J6
Rookby Ct WCHMH N21 41 H1
Rook Cl WBLY HA9 68 D2
Rookeries Cl FELT TW13 141 F2
The Rookery
STRHM/NOR * SW16 149 F5
Rookery Dr CHST BR7 154 A7
Rookery La HAYES BR2 168 C5
Rookery Rd CLAP SW4 129 H3
Rookery Wy CDALE/KGS NW9 51 H4
Rookfield Av MUSWH N10 54 C3
Rookfield Cl MUSWH N10 54 C3
Rooks Ter WDR/YW * UB7 100 B1
Rookstone Rd TOOT SW17 147 K4
Rookwood Av NWMAL KT3 160 D3
WLGTN SM6 176 D3
Rookwood Gdns CHING * E4 44 D1
Rookwood Rd STNW/STAM N16 56 B5
Roosevelt Wy DAGE RM10 81 F5
Rootes Dr NKENS W10 88 B3
Ropemaker Rd
BERM/RHTH SE16 112 B1
Ropemaker's Flds
POP/IOD * E14 93 H6
Ropemaker St BARB EC2Y 13 G2
Roper La STHWK SE1 19 K2
Ropers Av CHING E4 44 A4
Ropers Orch CHEL * SW3 108 D5
Roper St ELTH/MOT SE9 134 E4
Roper Wy MTCM CR4 163 F1
Ropery St BOW E3 93 H3
Rope St BERM/RHTH SE16 112 B2
Ropewalk Gdns WCHPL E1 92 C5
Ropewalk Ms HACK * E8 7 L2
Rope Yard Rails
WOOL/PLUM SE18 115 G2
Ropley St BETH E2 92 C1
Rosa Alba Ms HBRY N5 73 J3
Rosaline Rd FUL/PGN SW6 107 H6
Rosaline Ter FUL/PGN * SW6 107 H6
Rosamond St SYD SE26 150 D2
Rosamond Vls
MORT/ESHN * SW14 126 A3
Rosamund Cl SAND/SEL CR2 177 K3
Rosary Cl HSLW TW3 122 D1
Rosary Gdns BUSH WD23 22 E6
SKENS SW7 14 F6
Rosary Ga BTSEA SW11 109 G6
Rosaville Rd FUL/PGN SW6 107 J6
Roscoe St STLK EC1Y 12 F1
Roscoff Cl EDGW HA8 36 D7
Roseacre Cl WEA W13 85 H4
Roseacre Rd WELL DA16 136 C2
Rose Aly STHWK SE1 12 F8
Rose & Crown Yd STJS * SW1Y 10 F9
Roseary Cl WDR/YW UB7 100 A3
Rose Av MRDN SM4 162 B4
MTCM CR4 147 K7
SWFD E18 59 F1
Rosebank PGE/AN SE20 150 D6
Rosebank Av HRW HA1 67 F3
Rose Bank Cl NFNCH/WDSP N12 39 J4
Rosebank Cl TEDD TW11 143 G5
Rosebank Est BOW E3 93 H1
Rosebank Gdns ACT * W3 87 F5
BOW * E3 93 G1
Rosebank Gv WALTH E17 57 H2
Rosebank Rd HNWL W7 103 K1
WALTH E17 57 J5
Rosebank Wk CAMTN NW1 5 H2
Rosebank Wy ACT W3 87 F5
Rose Bates Dr CDALE/KGS NW9 50 C3
Roseberry Gdns DART DA1 139 F6
FSBYPK N4 55 H5
Roseberry Pl HACK E8 74 B5
Roseberry St
BERM/RHTH SE16 111 J3
Rosebery Av BFN/LL DA15 135 K6
CLKNW EC1R 12 A1
MNPK E12 77 J5
NWMAL KT3 160 C1
RYLN/HDSTN HA2 65 J3
THHTH CR7 164 D1
TOTM N17 56 C1
Rosebery Cl MRDN SM4 161 G5
Rosebery Ct CLKNW EC1R 6 A9
Rosebery Gdns
CEND/HSY/T * N8 54 E4
SUT SM1 175 F3
WEA W13 85 G5
Rosebery Ms MUSWH N10 54 C1
Rosebery Pde EW * KT17 173 H6
Rosebery Rd BUSH WD23 22 B7
CLAP SW4 129 K5
ED N9 42 C2
HSLW TW3 123 H4
KUT KT1 159 J1
MUSWH N10 54 C1
SUT SM1 174 D5
Rosebine Av WHTN TW2 123 J6
Rosebriars ESH/CLAY KT10 170 C4
Rosebury Rd FUL/PGN SW6 128 A1
Rosebury V RSLP HA4 64 E1
Rose Ct WCHPL E1 13 L3
Rosecourt Rd CROY/NA CR0 164 A5
Rosecroft Av HAMP NW3 70 E2
Rosecroft Ct NTHWD * HA6 32 A5
Rose Croft Gdns CRICK NW2 69 J2
Rosecroft Gdns WHTN TW2 123 J7
Rosecroft Rd STHL UB1 84 A3
Rosecroft Wk ALP/SUD HA0 67 K4
PIN HA5 47 H4
Rosedale Av HYS/HAR UB3 82 B4
Rosedale Cl ABYW SE2 116 C2
HNWL W7 104 A1
STAN HA7 35 H5
Rosedale Gdns DAGW RM9 79 H6
Rosedale Rd DAGW RM9 79 H6
EW KT17 173 J4
FSTGT E7 77 G4
RCH/KEW TW9 125 F3
ROM RM1 62 E2
Rosedene Av CROY/NA CR0 163 K6
GFD/PVL UB6 84 A2
MRDN SM4 161 K4
STRHM/NOR SW16 149 F2
Rosedene Cl DART DA1 139 F6
Rosedene Gdns
GNTH/NBYPK IG2 60 A3
Rosedene Ter LEY E10 75 K1
Rosedew Rd HMSMTH W6 107 G5
Rose End WPK KT4 161 G7
Rosefield POP/IOD E14 93 J6
Rosefield Cl CAR SM5 175 J4
Rosefield Gdns POP/IOD E14 93 J6
Rose Garden Cl EDGW HA8 36 A5
Rose Gdns EA W5 104 E2
FELT TW13 140 E1
STHL UB1 84 A3
STWL/WRAY TW19 120 A6
WATW WD18 20 E4
Rose Gln CDALE/KGS NW9 51 F3
ROMW/RG RM7 63 G7
Rosehart Ms NTGHL * W11 8 A5
Rosehatch Av CHDH RM6 61 K2
Roseheath Rd HSLWW TW4 122 E4
Rosehill ESH/CLAY KT10 171 G5
HPTN TW12 142 A7
Rose Hl SUT SM1 175 F1
Rosehill Av SUT SM1 162 B7
Rosehill Court Pde
MRDN * SM4 162 B6
Rosehill Gdns GFD/PVL UB6 67 F4
SUT SM1 175 F1
Rose Hill Pk West SUT SM1 162 B7
Rosehill Rd WAND/EARL SW18 128 B5
Roseland Cl TOTM N17 41 K6
Rose La CHDH RM6 62 A3
Rose Lawn BUSH WD23 22 C7
Roseleigh Av HBRY N5 73 H3
Roseleigh Cl TWK TW1 124 E5
Rosemary Av E/WMO/HCT KT8 157 F2
ED N9 30 D7
FNCH N3 53 F1
HSLWW TW4 122 C1
ROM RM1 63 H2
Rosemary Cl CROY/NA CR0 163 K6
Rosemary Dr POP/IOD E14 94 B5
REDBR IG4 59 H4
Rosemary Gdns BCTR RM8 62 B7
CHSGTN KT9 172 A3
Rosemary La
MORT/ESHN SW14 125 K2
Rosemary Rd PECK SE15 111 G6
TOOT SW17 147 F2
WELL DA16 116 A7
Rosemary St IS N1 7 G3
Rosemead CDALE/KGS NW9 51 H6
Rosemead Av FELT TW13 140 D1
MTCM CR4 163 H2
WBLY HA9 68 A4
Rosemont Av
NFNCH/WDSP N12 39 G5
Rosemont Rd ACT W3 86 D6
HAMP NW3 71 G5
NWMAL KT3 159 K2
RCHPK/HAM TW10 125 F5
Rosemoor St CHEL SW3 15 L6
Rosemount Cl WFD IG8 45 K5
Rosemount Dr BMLY BR1 168 E3
Rosemount Rd ALP/SUD HA0 68 A7
WEA W13 85 G5
Rosenau Crs BTSEA SW11 108 E7
Rosenau Rd BTSEA SW11 108 D7
Rosendale Rd DUL SE21 130 D7
Roseneath Av WCHMH N21 29 H7
Roseneath Rd BTSEA SW11 129 F5
Roseneath Wk EN EN1 30 A3
Rosens Wk EDGW HA8 36 D2
Rosenthal Rd CAT SE6 132 E5
Rosenthorpe Rd PECK SE15 132 A4
Rose Park Cl YEAD UB4 83 G3
Roserton St POP/IOD E14 113 F1
The Rosery CROY/NA CR0 166 A5
The Roses WFD * IG8 44 D6
Rose St COVGDN WC2E 11 J6
Rosethorn Cl BAL SW12 129 H6
Rosetta Cl VX/NE SW8 109 K6
Roseveare Rd LEE/GVPK SE12 153 G3
Roseville Av HSLW TW3 123 F4
Roseville Rd HYS/HAR UB3 101 K4
Rosevine Rd RYNPK SW20 146 A7
Rose Wk BRYLDS KT5 159 J4
WWKM BR4 180 B1
Roseway DUL SE21 130 E5
EDGW HA8 36 E3
Rose Wy LEE/GVPK SE12 133 K4
Rosewell Cl PGE/AN SE20 150 D6
Rosewood Av GFD/PVL UB6 67 G4
HCH RM12 81 J4
Rosewood Cl SCUP DA14 155 J2
Rosewood Ct KUTN/CMB KT2 144 C6
Rosewood Gv SUT SM1 175 G1
Rosewood Ter PGE/AN * SE20 150 E6
Rosher Cl SRTFD E15 76 B6
Rosina St HOM E9 75 F4
Roskell Rd PUT/ROE SW15 127 G2
Roslin Rd ACT W3 105 J2
Roslin Wy BMLY BR1 152 E4
Roslyn Cl MTCM CR4 162 C1
Roslyn Gdns GPK RM2 63 H1
Roslyn Ms SEVS/STOTM * N15 56 A4
Roslyn Rd SEVS/STOTM N15 55 K4
Rosmead Rd NTGHL W11 88 C6
Rosoman Pl CLKNW EC1R 6 B9
Rosoman St CLKNW EC1R 6 B8
Rossall Cl EMPK RM11 63 J5
Rossall Crs WLSDN NW10 86 B2
Ross Av BCTR RM8 80 B1
MLHL NW7 38 C4
Ross Cl HYS/HAR UB3 101 G3
KTN/HRWW/W HA3 34 C6
Rossdale SUT SM1 175 J4
Rossdale Dr CDALE/KGS NW9 50 E7
ED N9 30 E5
Rossdale Rd PUT/ROE SW15 127 F3
Rosse Ms BKHTH/KID SE3 114 A7
Rossendale St CLPT E5 74 D1
Rossendale Wy CAMTN NW1 4 F2
Rossetti Rd BERM/RHTH SE16 111 J4
Ross House WOOL/PLUM SE18 114 D7
Rossignol Gdns CAR SM5 176 A1
Rossindel Rd HSLW TW3 123 F4
Rossington St CLPT * E5 74 D1
Rossiter Flds BAR EN5 26 C5
Rossiter Rd BAL SW12 129 G7
Rossland Cl BXLYHS DA6 137 H4
Rosslyn Av BARN SW13 126 B2
BCTR RM8 62 B6
CHING E4 44 D1
EBAR EN4 27 J5
EBED/NFELT TW14 121 K5
Rosslyn Cl HYS/HAR UB3 82 B4
SUN TW16 140 C5
WWKM BR4 180 D2
Rosslyn Crs HRW HA1 49 F3
WBLY HA9 68 A2
Rosslyn Hl HAMP NW3 71 H4
Rosslyn Park Ms HAMP NW3 71 H4
Rosslyn Rd BARK IG11 78 D6
TWK TW1 124 D5
WALTH * E17 58 A3
WATW WD18 21 F2
Rossmore Cl STJWD * NW8 9 K1
Rossmore Rd STJWD NW8 3 K9
Ross Pde WLGTN SM6 176 B5
Ross Rd DART DA1 138 D5
SNWD SE25 165 F2
WHTN TW2 123 H7
WLGTN SM6 176 C5
Ross Wy ELTH/MOT SE9 134 D2
NTHWD HA6 32 D3
Rossway Dr BUSH WD23 22 C4
Rosswood Gdns WLGTN SM6 176 B5
Rostella Rd TOOT SW17 147 H3
Rostrever Gdns HYS/HAR UB3 82 C7
Rostrevor Av SEVS/STOTM N15 56 B5
Rostrevor Gdns NWDGN UB2 102 D4
Rostrevor Rd FUL/PGN SW6 107 J7
WIM/MER SW19 146 E4
Rotary St STHWK SE1 18 C3
Rothbury Av RAIN RM13 99 K4
Rothbury Gdns ISLW TW7 104 B6
Rothbury Rd HOM E9 75 H6
Rotherfield Rd CAR SM5 176 A3
Rotherfield St IS N1 6 F2
Rotherham Wk STHWK * SE1 12 D9
Rotherhill Av
STRHM/NOR SW16 148 D5
Rotherhithe New Rd
BERM/RHTH SE16 111 J4
Rotherhithe Old Rd
BERM/RHTH SE16 112 A3
Rotherhithe St
BERM/RHTH SE16 111 K1
Rotherhithe Tnl
BERM/RHTH SE16 111 K1
Rothermere Rd CROY/NA CR0 177 F4
Rotherwick Hl EA W5 86 B3
Rotherwick Rd GLDGN NW11 52 E6
Rotherwood Cl
WIM/MER SW19 146 C7
Rotherwood Rd
PUT/ROE SW15 127 G2
Rothery St IS * N1 6 D3
Rothery Ter BRXN/ST * SW9 110 C6
Rothesay Av GFD/PVL UB6 66 D5
RCHPK/HAM TW10 125 J3
RYNPK SW20 161 H1
Rothesay Rd SNWD SE25 164 E3
Rothsay Rd FSTGT E7 77 G6
Rothsay St STHWK SE1 19 J3
Rothschild Rd CHSWK W4 105 K3
Rothschild St WNWD SE27 149 H3
Rothwell Gdns DAGW RM9 79 J6
Rothwell Rd DAGW RM9 79 J7
Rothwell St CAMTN NW1 3 M3
Rotterdam Dr POP/IOD E14 113 F2
Rouel Rd BERM/RHTH SE16 111 H3
Rougemont Av MRDN SM4 161 K5
The Roughs NTHWD HA6 32 C2
Roundaway Rd CLAY IG5 59 K1
Roundel Cl BROCKY SE4 132 C3
Round Gv CROY/NA CR0 166 A6
Roundhay Cl FSTH SE23 151 F1
Round Hl SYD SE26 150 D1
Roundhill Dr ENC/FH EN2 29 F3
Roundtable Rd BMLY BR1 152 E2
Roundtree Rd ALP/SUD HA0 67 H4
The Roundway ESH/CLAY KT10 171 F5
TOTM N17 41 K7
WATW WD18 20 D6
Roundways RSLP HA4 64 D2
Roundwood CHST BR7 169 G1
Roundwood Av STKPK UB11 82 A7
Roundwood Cl RSLP * HA4 46 B6
Roundwood Pk WLSDN * NW10 69 J7
Roundwood Rd WLSDN NW10 69 G5
Rounton Rd BOW E3 93 J3
Roupell Rd BRXS/STRHM SW2 130 A7
Roupell St STHWK SE1 12 B9
Rousden St CAMTN NW1 4 E2
Rouse Gdns DUL SE21 150 A3
Routemaster Cl PLSTW E13 95 F2
Routh Rd WAND/EARL SW18 128 D6
Routh St EHAM E6 95 K4
Rowallan Rd FUL/PGN SW6 107 H6
Rowan Av CHING E4 43 H5
Rowan Cl ALP/SUD HA0 67 G2
EA W5 105 F1
IL IG1 78 D4
KTN/HRWW/W HA3 35 F5
NWMAL KT3 160 B1
STRHM/NOR SW16 148 C7
Rowan Crs DART DA1 139 F7
STRHM/NOR SW16 148 C7
Rowan Dr CDALE/KGS NW9 51 J2
Rowan Gdns CROY/NA CR0 178 B2
Rowan Pl HYS/HAR UB3 82 D6
Rowan Rd BTFD TW8 104 C6
BXLYHN DA7 137 F2
HMSMTH W6 107 G3
STRHM/NOR SW16 163 H1
WDR/YW UB7 100 A3
The Rowans PLMGR N13 41 J2
SUN TW16 140 D4
Rowan Ter PGE/AN * SE20 150 C7
WIM/MER * SW19 146 C6
Rowantree Cl WCHMH N21 29 K7
Rowantree Ms ENC/FH EN2 29 H1
Rowantree Rd ENC/FH EN2 29 H1
WCHMH N21 29 K7
Rowan Wk EFNCH N2 53 G5
HAYES BR2 181 K2
NKENS * W10 88 C3
Rowan Wy CHDH RM6 61 J2
Rowanwood Av BFN/LL DA15 136 B7
Rowben Cl TRDG/WHET N20 27 F7
Rowberry Cl FUL/PGN SW6 107 G6

Rowcross St STHWK SE1 19 L7
Rowdell Rd NTHLT UB5 66 A7
Rowden Pde CHING * E4 43 J5
Rowden Rd BECK BR3 151 G7
CHING E4 43 K5
HOR/WEW KT19 172 E3
Rowditch La BTSEA SW11 129 F1
Rowdon Av WLSDN NW10 69 K6
Rowdown Crs CROY/NA CR0 180 B7
Rowdowns Rd DAGW RM9 80 B7
Rowe Gdns BARK IG11 97 F1
Rowe La HOM E9 74 E4
Rowena Crs BTSEA SW11 128 D1
Rowe Wk RYLN/HDSTN HA2 66 A2
Rowfant Rd TOOT SW17 148 A1
Rowhill Rd CLPT E5 74 D3
Rowington Cl BAY/PAD W2 8 C2
Rowland Av KTN/HRWW/W HA3 49 J2
Rowland Gv SYD SE26 150 D2
Rowland Hill Av TOTM N17 41 J6
Rowland Hill St HAMP NW3 71 J4
Rowland Pl NTHWD * HA6 32 C6
Rowlands Av PIN HA5 34 A5
Rowlands Cl HGT * N6 54 A5
MLHL NW7 37 J6
Rowlands Rd BCTR RM8 80 B1
Rowland Wy ASHF TW15 140 A6
WIM/MER SW19 147 F7
Rowley Av BFN/LL DA15 136 C6
Rowley Cl ALP/SUD HA0 68 B6
OXHEY WD19 21 J5
Rowley Cottages
WKENS * W14 107 J3
Rowley Gdns FSBYPK N4 55 J6
Rowley Green Rd BAR EN5 25 J4
Rowley La BORE WD6 25 F2
Rowley Rd SEVS/STOTM N15 55 J4
Rowley Wy STJWD NW8 2 F3
Rowlheys Pl WDR/YW UB7 100 B2
Rowlls Rd KUT KT1 159 G2
Rowney Gdns DAGW RM9 79 J5
Rowney Rd DAGW RM9 79 H5
Rowntree Cl KIL/WHAMP * NW6 70 E5
PLSTW E13 95 F3
Rowntree Rd WHTN TW2 123 K7
Rowse Cl SRTFD E15 76 A7
Rowsley Av HDN NW4 52 A2
Rowstock Gdns HOLWY N7 72 D4
Rowton Rd WOOL/PLUM SE18 115 H6
Roxborough Av HRW HA1 48 D6
ISLW TW7 104 A6
Roxborough Pk HRW HA1 48 E6
Roxborough Rd HRW HA1 48 D4
Roxbourne Cl NTHLT UB5 65 H5
Roxburgh Rd WNWD SE27 149 H4
Roxburn Wy RSLP HA4 64 D2
Roxby Pl FUL/PGN SW6 14 B9
Roxeth Green Av
RYLN/HDSTN HA2 66 B2
Roxeth Gv RYLN/HDSTN HA2 66 B3
Roxeth Hl RYLN/HDSTN HA2 66 D1
Roxley Rd LEW SE13 132 E5
Roxton Gdns CROY/NA CR0 179 H5
Roxwell Rd BARK IG11 97 G1
SHB W12 106 D1
Roxwell Wy WFD IG8 45 G6
Roxy Av CHDH RM6 61 J6
Royal Albert Rd EHAM E6 96 A6
Royal Albert Wy CAN/RD E16 95 H6
Royal Ar CONDST W1S 10 E7
Royal Arsenal West
WOOL/PLUM * SE18 115 F4
Royal Av CHEL SW3 15 L7
WPK KT4 173 G1
Royal Circ WNWD SE27 149 G2
Royal Cl DEPT SE8 112 C5
GDMY/SEVK IG3 61 G6
STNW/STAM * N16 56 A7
WPK KT4 173 G1
Royal College St CAMTN NW1 4 F2
Royal Ct BANK EC3V 13 H5
ELTH/MOT * SE9 134 E7
EN * EN1 30 A5
Royal Crs NTGHL W11 107 G1
RSLP HA4 65 J3
Royal Crescent Ms NTGHL W11 107 G1
Royal Docks Rd EHAM E6 96 B4
Royal Herbert Pavilions
WOOL/PLUM * SE18 114 E7
Royal Hl GNWCH SE10 113 F6
Royal Hospital Rd CHEL SW3 15 L9
Royal Ms BAL SW12 129 G6
Royal Mint Pl WCHPL E1 13 M6
Royal Mint St TWRH EC3N 13 M6
Royal Naval Pl NWCR SE14 112 C6
Royal Oak Pl EDUL SE22 131 J5
Royal Oak Rd BXLYHS DA6 137 G4
HACK E8 74 D5
Royal Opera Ar STJS * SW1Y 11 G8
Royal Orchard Cl
WAND/EARL SW18 127 H6
Royal Pde BKHTH/KID SE3 133 J1
CHST BR7 154 C6
FUL/PGN * SW6 107 H6
Royal Pl GNWCH SE10 113 F6
Royal Rd CAN/RD E16 95 H5
SCUP DA14 155 K2
TEDD TW11 142 D4
WALW SE17 18 C9
Royal Route WBLY HA9 68 B3
Royal St STHWK SE1 17 M3
Royal Victor Pl BOW E3 93 F1
Roycraft Av BARK IG11 97 F1
Roycroft Cl
BRXS/STRHM * SW2 130 B7
SWFD E18 45 F7
Roydene Rd WOOL/PLUM SE18 115 K5
Roy Gdns GNTH/NBYPK IG2 60 E3
Roy Gv HPTN TW12 142 B5
Royle Cl GPK RM2 63 K4
Royle Crs WEA W13 85 G3
Roy Rd NTHWD HA6 32 D6
Royston Av CHING E4 43 J4
SUT SM1 175 H2
WLGTN SM6 176 D3
Royston Cl HEST TW5 102 A7
Royston Gdns IL IG1 59 H5
Royston Gv PIN HA5 33 K5
Royston Park Rd PIN HA5 33 K5
Royston Rd DART DA1 138 C5
PGE/AN SE20 151 F7
RCHPK/HAM TW10 125 F4
The Roystons BRYLDS KT5 159 J4
Royston St BETH E2 92 E1
Rozel Rd CLAP SW4 129 H1
Rubastic Rd NWDGN UB2 102 B2
Rubens Rd NTHLT UB5 83 G1
Rubens St CAT SE6 151 H1
Ruby Ms WALTH * E17 57 J2
Ruby Rd WALTH E17 57 J2
Ruby St PECK SE15 111 J5
Ruby Triangle PECK * SE15 111 J5
Ruckholt Cl LEY E10 75 K2
Ruckholt Rd LEY E10 75 K3
Rucklidge Av WLSDN NW10 87 H1
Rudall Crs HAMP NW3 71 H3
Ruddington Cl CLPT E5 75 G3
Ruddock Cl EDGW HA8 36 E6
Ruddstreet Cl
WOOL/PLUM SE18 115 G3
Rudgwick Ter STJWD * NW8 3 K4
Rudland Rd BXLYHN DA7 137 J2
Rudloe Rd BAL SW12 129 H6
Rudolf Pl VX/NE SW8 109 K5
Rudolph Rd BUSH WD23 22 A5
KIL/WHAMP NW6 2 B6
PLSTW E13 94 E1
Rudyard Gv EDGW HA8 36 E5
The Ruffetts SAND/SEL CR2 178 D6
Ruffetts Cl SAND/SEL CR2 178 D6
Ruffle Cl WDR/YW UB7 100 B1
Rufford Cl HRW HA1 49 G5
Rufford St IS N1 5 K3
Rufus Cl RSLP HA4 65 H2
Rufus St IS N1 7 J8
Rugby Av ALP/SUD HA0 67 J3
ED N9 30 B7
GFD/PVL UB6 66 D5
Rugby Cl HRW HA1 48 E3
Rugby Gdns DAGW RM9 79 J5
Rugby La BELMT SM2 174 B7
Rugby Rd CDALE/KGS NW9 50 C3
CHSWK W4 106 B1
DAGW RM9 79 H6
WHTN TW2 123 K5
Rugby St BMSBY WC1N 11 L1
Rugg St POP/IOD E14 93 J6
Ruislip Cl GFD/PVL UB6 84 B3
Ruislip Ct RSLP * HA4 64 D1
Ruislip Rd NTHLT UB5 65 G7
Ruislip Rd East GFD/PVL UB6 84 C3
Ruislip St TOOT SW17 147 K3
Rumbold Rd FUL/PGN SW6 108 A6
Rum Cl WAP E1W 92 D6
Rumsey Cl HPTN TW12 141 K5
Rumsey Rd BRXN/ST SW9 130 A2
Runbury Cir CDALE/KGS NW9 69 F1
Runcorn Cl TOTM N17 56 D3
Runcorn Pl NTGHL W11 88 C6
Rundell Crs HDN NW4 51 K4
Runes Cl MTCM CR4 162 C3
Runnelfield HRW HA1 66 E2
Runnymede WIM/MER SW19 147 H7
Runnymede Cl WHTN TW2 123 G5
Runnymede Crs
STRHM/NOR SW16 148 D7
Runnymede Gdns GFD/PVL UB6 84 D1
WHTN TW2 123 G5
Runnymede Rd HSLW TW3 123 G5
The Runway RSLP HA4 65 F4
Rupack St BERM/RHTH * SE16 111 K1
Rupert Av WBLY HA9 68 A4
Rupert Ct E/WMO/HCT * KT8 157 F3
SOHO/SHAV W1D 11 G6
Rupert Gdns BRXN/ST SW9 130 C1
Rupert Rd ARCH N19 72 D2
CHSWK W4 106 B2
KIL/WHAMP NW6 88 D1
Rupert St SOHO/SHAV * W1D 11 G6
Rural Cl EMPK RM11 63 K7
Rural Wy STRHM/NOR SW16 148 B6
Rusbridge Cl HACK E8 74 C4
Ruscoe Rd CAN/RD E16 94 D5
Ruscombe Wy
EBED/NFELT TW14 121 J6
Rusham Rd BAL SW12 128 E5
Rushbrook Crs WALTH E17 43 H7
Rushbrook Rd ELTH/MOT SE9 154 C1
Rush Common Ms
BRXS/STRHM SW2 129 K6
Rushcroft Rd
BRXS/STRHM SW2 130 B3
CHING E4 43 K6
Rushden Cl NRWD SE19 149 K6
Rushdene ABYW SE2 116 D2
Rushdene Av EBAR EN4 27 J6
Rushdene Cl NTHLT UB5 83 G1
Rushdene Crs NTHLT UB5 83 F1
Rushdene Rd PIN HA5 47 G5
Rushden Gdns CLAY IG5 60 A2
MLHL NW7 38 A5
Rushdon Cl ROM RM1 63 J4
Rushett Cl THDIT KT7 158 C7
Rushett Rd THDIT KT7 158 C6
Rushey Cl NWMAL KT3 160 A3
Rushey Gn CAT SE6 132 E6
Rushey Hl ENC/FH EN2 29 F3
Rushey Md BROCKY SE4 132 D4
Rushford Rd BROCKY SE4 132 C5
Rush Green Gdns
ROMW/RG RM7 62 E7
Rush Green Rd ROMW/RG RM7 62 E7
Rushgrove Av CDALE/KGS NW9 51 H3
Rushgrove Pde
CDALE/KGS * NW9 51 H4
Rushgrove St
WOOL/PLUM SE18 114 E3
Rush Hill Ms BTSEA SW11 129 F2
Rush Hill Rd BTSEA SW11 129 F2
Rushley Cl HAYES BR2 181 H3
Rushmead BETH E2 92 D2
RCHPK/HAM TW10 143 H2
Rushmead Cl CROY/NA CR0 178 B3
Rushmere Ct WPK KT4 173 J1
Rushmere Pl WIM/MER SW19 146 B4
Rushmon Pl CHEAM * SM3 174 C5
Rushmon Vls NWMAL * KT3 160 C3
Rushmoor Cl PIN HA5 47 F3
Rushmore Cl BMLY BR1 168 D2
Rushmore Ct WATW * WD18 20 B5
Rushmore Rd CLPT E5 74 E3
Rusholme Av DAGE RM10 80 C2
Rusholme Gv NRWD SE19 150 A4
Rusholme Rd PUT/ROE SW15 127 G5
Rushout Av KTN/HRWW/W HA3 49 H5
Rushton St IS N1 7 H5
Rushworth St STHWK SE1 18 D1
Rushy Meadow La CAR SM5 175 J1
Ruskin Av EBED/NFELT TW14 121 J6
MNPK E12 77 K5
RCH/KEW TW9 105 H6
WELL DA16 136 B2
Ruskin Cl GLDGN NW11 53 F5
Ruskin Dr WELL DA16 136 B2
WPK KT4 173 K1
Ruskin Gdns EA W5 85 K3
KTN/HRWW/W HA3 50 B4
Ruskin Gv DART DA1 139 K4
WELL DA16 136 B1
Ruskin Rd BELV DA17 117 H3
CAR SM5 176 A4
CROY/NA CR0 177 H1
ISLW TW7 124 A2
STHL UB1 83 J6
TOTM N17 42 B7
Ruskin Wk ED N9 42 C1
HAYES BR2 168 D5
HNHL SE24 130 D4
Ruskin Wy WIM/MER SW19 162 C1
Rusland Park Rd HRW HA1 48 E3
Rusper Cl CRICK NW2 70 A2
STAN HA7 35 J3
Rusper Rd DAGW RM9 79 J5
WDGN N22 55 H1
Russel Cl BECK BR3 166 E2
Russell Av WDGN N22 55 H1
Russell Cl BXLYHN DA7 137 H3
CHARL SE7 114 B6
DART DA1 138 D2
NTHWD HA6 32 A4
RSLP HA4 65 G1
WLSDN NW10 68 E6
Russell Ct BAR * EN5 27 G3
WHALL SW1A 10 F9
Russell Dr STWL/WRAY TW19 120 A5
Russell Gdns GLDGN NW11 52 C5
RCHPK/HAM TW10 143 J1
TRDG/WHET N20 39 J1
WDR/YW UB7 100 D4
WKENS * W14 107 H2
Russell Gardens Ms
WKENS W14 107 H1
Russell Gv BRXN/ST SW9 110 B7
MLHL NW7 37 G4
Russell Kerr Cl CHSWK * W4 105 K6
Russell La TRDG/WHET N20 39 K1
Russell Pde GLDGN * NW11 52 C5
Russell Pl HAMP NW3 71 J4
Russell Rd CAN/RD E16 94 E5
CDALE/KGS NW9 51 H5
CEND/HSY/T N8 54 D5
CHING E4 43 H3
LEY E10 57 K5
MTCM CR4 162 D2
NTHLT UB5 66 C4
NTHWD HA6 32 A2
SEVS/STOTM N15 56 A4
TRDG/WHET N20 39 J1
WALTH E17 57 H2
WDGN N22 41 F5
WHTN TW2 124 A5
WIM/MER SW19 146 E6
WKENS W14 107 H2
Russell Sq GWRST WC1E 11 H2
Russell St HOL/ALD WC2B 11 L5
Russell Wy OXHEY WD19 21 F6
SUT SM1 175 F4
Russet Cl HGDN/ICK UB10 82 A3
Russet Crs HOLWY * N7 73 F4
Russet Dr CROY/NA CR0 166 B7
Russets Cl CHING E4 44 B3
Russia Dock Rd
BERM/RHTH * SE16 93 G7
Russia La BETH E2 92 E1
Russia Rw CITYW EC2V 12 F5
Rusthall Av CHSWK W4 106 A2
Rusthall Cl CROY/NA CR0 165 K5
Rustic Av STRHM/NOR SW16 148 B6
Rustic Pl ALP/SUD HA0 67 K3
Rustington Wk MRDN SM4 161 J6
Ruston Av BRYLDS KT5 159 J6
Ruston Ms NTGHL * W11 88 C5
Ruston Rd WOOL/PLUM SE18 114 D2
Ruston St BOW E3 75 H7
Rust Sq CMBW SE5 110 E6
Rutford Rd STRHM/NOR SW16 148 E4
Ruth Cl KTN/HRWW/W HA3 50 B3
Rutherford Cl BELMT SM2 175 H5
BORE WD6 24 E1
Rutherford St WEST SW1P 17 G5
Rutherford Wy BUSH WD23 22 D7
WBLY HA9 68 C2
Rutherglen Rd ABYW SE2 116 B5
Rutherwyke Cl EW KT17 173 J5
Ruthin Cl CDALE/KGS NW9 51 G5
Ruthin Rd BKHTH/KID SE3 113 K5
Ruthven St HOM E9 75 F7
Rutland Av BFN/LL DA15 136 B6
Rutland Cl BXLY DA5 136 E7
DART DA1 139 G6
MORT/ESHN SW14 125 J2
Rutland Ct CHST BR7 154 A7
SKENS SW7 15 K2
Rutland Dr MRDN SM4 161 K6
RCHPK/HAM TW10 124 E7
Rutland Gdns BCTR RM8 79 J4
CROY/NA CR0 178 A3
FSBYPK N4 55 H5
SKENS SW7 15 K2
WEA * W13 85 G4
Rutland Ga BELV DA17 117 J4
HAYES BR2 167 J3
SKENS SW7 15 J3
Rutland Gate Ms SKENS * SW7 15 J2
Rutland Gv HMSMTH W6 106 E4
Rutland Ms STJWD NW8 2 D4
Rutland Ms South SKENS * SW7 15 J3
Rutland Pk CAT SE6 151 H1
CRICK NW2 70 A5
Rutland Pl BUSH * WD23 22 D7
FARR * EC1M 12 D2
Rutland Rd FSTGT E7 77 H6
HOM E9 75 F7
HRW HA1 48 C5
HYS/HAR UB3 101 G3
IL IG1 78 B3
STHL UB1 84 A3
WALTH E17 57 J5
WAN E11 59 F4
WHTN TW2 142 D1
WIM/MER SW19 147 J6
Rutland St SKENS SW7 15 K3
Rutland Wk CAT SE6 151 H1
Rutley Cl WALW SE17 18 C9
Rutlish Rd WIM/MER SW19 146 E7
Rutter Gdns MTCM CR4 162 C3
Rutters Cl WDR/YW UB7 100 D1
The Rutts BUSH WD23 22 D7
Rutt's Ter NWCR SE14 112 A7
Ruvigny Gdns PUT/ROE SW15 127 G2
Ruxley Cl HOR/WEW KT19 172 D4
SCUP DA14 155 K5
Ruxley Crs ESH/CLAY KT10 171 H6
Ruxley La HOR/WEW KT19 172 D5
Ruxley Ms HOR/WEW KT19 172 D4
Ruxley Rdg ESH/CLAY KT10 171 G6
Ruxley Towers
ESH/CLAY * KT10 171 G6
Ryan Cl BKHTH/KID SE3 134 A3
RSLP HA4 47 F7
Ryan Ct OXHEY * WD19 21 J6
Ryan Dr BTFD TW8 104 B5
Rycroft Wy TOTM * N17 56 B2
Ryculff Sq BKHTH/KID SE3 133 J1
Rydal Cl HDN NW4 38 C7
Rydal Crs GFD/PVL UB6 85 H2
Rydal Dr BXLYHN DA7 117 H7
WWKM BR4 180 C1
Rydal Gdns CDALE/KGS NW9 51 G4
HSLW TW3 123 G5
PUT/ROE SW15 145 G4
WBLY HA9 49 J7
Rydal Mt HAYES * BR2 167 J3
Rydal Rd STRHM/NOR SW16 148 D4
Rydal Wy PEND EN3 30 E5
RSLP HA4 65 G3
Ryde Pl TWK TW1 124 D5
Ryder Cl BUSH WD23 22 B5
Ryder Dr BERM/RHTH SE16 111 J4
Ryder Gdns RAIN RM13 81 H5
Ryder St STJS SW1Y 10 F8
Ryde Vale Rd BAL SW12 148 B1
Rydon St IS N1 6 F4
Rydston Cl HOLWY N7 5 K1
The Rye STHGT/OAK N14 28 C6
Rye Cl BXLY DA5 137 J5
Ryecotes Md DUL SE21 131 F7
Ryecroft Av CLAY IG5 60 B1
WHTN TW2 123 G7
Ryecroft Crs BAR EN5 25 K4
Ryecroft Rd LEW SE13 133 F4
STMC/STPC BR5 169 J5
STRHM/NOR SW16 149 G5
Ryecroft St FUL/PGN SW6 108 A7
Ryedale EDUL SE22 131 J5
Ryefield Av HGDN/ICK UB10 64 A7
Ryefield Crs PIN * HA5 46 E1
Ryefield Pde NTHWD * HA6 46 E1
Ryefield Rd NRWD SE19 149 J5
Rye Hill Pk PECK SE15 131 K3
Ryelands Crs LEE/GVPK SE12 134 B5
Rye La PECK SE15 111 H7
Rye Rd PECK SE15 132 A3
Rye Wk PUT/ROE SW15 127 G4
Rye Wy EDGW HA8 36 B5
Ryfold Rd WIM/MER SW19 146 E2
Ryhope Rd FBAR/BDGN N11 40 B3
Ryland Cl FELT TW13 140 D3
Rylandes Rd CRICK NW2 69 J2
SAND/SEL CR2 178 D7
Ryland Rd KTTN * NW5 72 B5
Rylett Crs SHB W12 106 C2
Rylett Rd SHB W12 106 C1
Rylston Rd FUL/PGN SW6 107 J5
PLMGR N13 41 K2
Rymer Rd CROY/NA CR0 165 F6
Rymer St HNHL SE24 130 C5
Rymill St CAN/RD E16 96 A7
Rysbrack St CHEL SW3 15 L3
Rythe Cl CHSGTN KT9 171 J6
Rythe Ct THDIT KT7 158 B6
Rythe Rd ESH/CLAY KT10 170 D4
Ryves Cottages MTCM * CR4 163 F1

S

Sabbarton St CAN/RD E16 94 D5
Sabine Rd BTSEA SW11 128 E2
Sable Cl HSLWW TW4 122 B2
Sable St IS N1 6 D1
Sach Rd CLPT E5 74 D1
Sackville Av HAYES BR2 167 K7
Sackville Cl RYLN/HDSTN HA2 66 D2
Sackville Est
STRHM/NOR SW16 148 E2
Sackville Gdns IL IG1 59 K7
Sackville Rd BELMT SM2 174 E6
Sackville St MYFR/PICC W1J 10 F7
Saddlebrook Pk SUN TW16 140 C6
Saddlers Cl BORE * WD6 25 F4
PIN HA5 34 A4
Saddlers Ms KUT * KT1 143 J7
Saddlescombe Wy
NFNCH/WDSP N12 38 E4
Sadler Cl MTCM CR4 162 E1
Sadlers Ride E/WMO/HCT KT8 157 H1
Saffron Av POP/IOD E14 94 B6
Saffron Cl CROY/NA CR0 163 K5
Saffron Hl HCIRC EC1N 12 B3
Saffron Rd CRW RM5 63 F1
Saffron St FARR EC1M 12 B2
Saffron Wy SURB KT6 158 E7
Sage Cl EHAM E6 95 K4
Sage St WCHPL E1 92 E6
Sage Wy FSBYW WC1X 5 L8
Sage Yd SURB * KT6 159 G7
Saigasso Cl CAN/RD E16 95 H5
Sail St LBTH SE11 17 M5
Sainfoin Rd TOOT SW17 148 A1
Sainsbury Rd NRWD SE19 150 A4
St Agatha's Dr KUTN/CMB KT2 144 B5
St Agatha's Gv CAR SM5 162 E7
St Agnes Cl HOM * E9 74 E7
St Agnes Pl CMBW SE5 110 C5
St Agnes Well STLK EC1Y 7 H9
St Aidan's Rd EDUL SE22 131 J5
WEA W13 104 C1
St Albans Av CHSWK W4 106 A2
EHAM E6 95 K2
FELT TW13 141 H4
St Albans Crs WDGN N22 41 G7
St Albans Farm HSLWW * TW4 122 B4
St Alban's Gdns TEDD TW11 143 G4
St Alban's Gv CAR SM5 162 D6
KENS W8 14 D3
St Albans La GLDGN NW11 52 E7
St Alban's Ms BAY/PAD W2 9 H2
St Alban's Pl IS N1 6 C4
St Alban's Rd DART DA1 139 J5
GDMY/SEVK IG3 61 F7
KTTN NW5 72 A2
KUTN/CMB KT2 144 A5
SUT SM1 174 D3
WAT WD17 21 F1
WFD IG8 44 E6
WLSDN NW10 69 G7
St Alban's St STJS SW1Y 11 G7
St Albans Ter HMSMTH * W6 107 H5
St Alfege Rd CHARL SE7 114 C5
St Alphage Gdn BARB EC2Y 12 F3
St Alphage Gdns BARB * EC2Y 12 F3
St Alphage Highwalk
BARB EC2Y 12 F3
St Alphage Wk EDGW * HA8 50 E1
St Alphege Rd ED N9 30 E6
St Alphonsus Rd CLAP SW4 129 H3
St Amunds Cl CAT SE6 151 J3
St Andrews Av ALP/SUD HA0 67 G3
HCH RM12 81 H4
St Andrews Cl
BERM/RHTH * SE16 111 J4
CRICK * NW2 69 K2
NFNCH/WDSP * N12 39 G3
RSLP HA4 65 H1
STAN * HA7 49 J1
THDIT KT7 158 C7
THMD SE28 97 K5
St Andrew's Ct
WAND/EARL SW18 147 G1
St Andrews Dr STAN HA7 35 J7
St Andrew's Gv
STNW/STAM N16 55 K7
St Andrew's Hl BLKFR EC4V 12 D6
St Andrews Ms BAL SW12 129 J7
STNW/STAM * N16 56 A6
St Andrew's Pl CAMTN NW1 4 C9
St Andrew's Rd ACT W3 87 G5
CAR SM5 175 J2
CDALE/KGS NW9 51 F7
CROY/NA CR0 177 J3
ED N9 30 E6
EN EN1 29 K2
GLDGN NW11 52 D4
HNWL W7 103 K1
IL IG1 59 K6
PLSTW E13 95 F2
ROMW/RG RM7 63 F5
SCUP DA14 155 K2
SURB KT6 158 E5
WALTH E17 57 F1
WAN E11 58 C5
WKENS W14 107 H5
WLSDN NW10 69 K5
St Andrew's Sq NTGHL * W11 88 C5
SURB KT6 158 E5
St Andrews Ter OXHEY * WD19 33 G4
St Andrew St HCIRC EC1N 12 B3
St Andrews Wy BOW E3 93 K3
St Anna Rd BAR * EN5 26 B4
St Anne's Av STWL/WRAY TW19 120 A6
St Annes Cl HGT N6 72 A2
OXHEY WD19 33 G3
St Annes Ct SOHO/CST W1F 11 G5
St Annes Gdns WLSDN NW10 86 B2
St Anne's Pas POP/IOD * E14 93 H5
St Anne's Rd ALP/SUD HA0 67 K4
LEY E10 76 B1
St Anne's Rw POP/IOD E14 93 H5
St Anne St POP/IOD E14 93 H5
St Ann's BARK IG11 78 C7
St Anns Ct HDN * NW4 51 K2
St Ann's Crs WAND/EARL SW18 128 A5
St Ann's Gdns HAMP NW3 72 A5
St Ann's Hl WAND/EARL SW18 128 A4
St Ann's Park Rd
WAND/EARL SW18 128 B5
St Ann's Rd BARK IG11 78 C7
BARN * SW13 126 C1
ED N9 42 B1
HRW HA1 48 E5
NTGHL W11 88 B6
SEVS/STOTM N15 55 K4
St Ann's St WEST SW1P 17 H4
St Ann's Ter STJWD NW8 3 H5
St Ann's Vls NTGHL W11 88 B7
St Ann's Wy CROY/NA CR0 177 H5
St Anselm's Pl MYFR/PKLN W1K 10 C6
St Anselms Rd HYS/HAR UB3 101 J1
St Anthony's Av WFD IG8 45 G5
St Anthonys Cl TOOT SW17 147 J1
WAP * E1W 92 C7
St Anthony's Ct HAYES BR2 169 G7
St Anthony's Wy
EBED/NFELT TW14 121 J3
St Antony's Rd FSTGT E7 77 F6
St Arvans Cl CROY/NA CR0 178 A2
St Asaph Rd BROCKY SE4 132 A2
St Aubyn's Av HSLW TW3 123 F4
WIM/MER SW19 146 D4
St Aubyn's Rd NRWD SE19 150 B5
St Audrey Av BXLYHN DA7 137 H1
St Augustine's Av BMLY BR1 168 D4
EA W5 86 A1
SAND/SEL CR2 177 J6
WBLY HA9 68 A2
St Augustine's Rd BELV DA17 117 G3
CAMTN NW1 5 G1
St Austell Cl EDGW HA8 50 B1
St Austell Rd BKHTH/KID SE3 133 F1
St Awdry's Rd BARK IG11 78 D6
St Barnabas Cl BECK BR3 167 F1
St Barnabas' Gdns
E/WMO/HCT KT8 157 F4
St Barnabas Rd MTCM CR4 148 A6
SUT SM1 175 H4
SWFD E18 45 F7
WALTH E17 57 J5
St Barnabas St BGVA * SW1W 16 B7
St Barnabas Ter HOM E9 75 F4
St Barnabas Vls VX/NE SW8 109 K7
St Barnabus St BGVA SW1W 16 B7
St Bartholomew's Cl SYD SE26 150 E3
St Bartholomew's Rd EHAM E6 77 J7
St Benets Cl TOOT * SW17 147 J1
St Benet's Gv MRDN SM4 162 B6
St Bernards CROY/NA CR0 178 A2
St Bernards Cl WNWD SE27 149 K3
St Bernard's Rd EHAM E6 77 H7
St Blaise Av BMLY BR1 168 A1
St Botolph St HDTCH EC3A 13 L4
St Bride's Av EDGW HA8 36 B7
St Brides Cl ERITHM DA18 116 E1
St Bride St FLST/FETLN EC4A 12 C4
St Catherines Cl CHSGTN KT9 171 K5
TOOT * SW17 147 J1
St Catherines Ct FELT TW13 121 K7
St Catherine's Dr NWCR SE14 132 A1
St Catherines Ms CHEL SW3 15 L5
St Catherines Rd RSLP HA4 46 A4
CHING E4 43 J1
St Chads Cl SURB KT6 158 D6
St Chad's Gdns CHDH RM6 62 A6
St Chad's Pl FSBYW WC1X 5 K7
St Chad's Rd CHDH RM6 62 A5
St Chad's St STPAN WC1H 5 K7
St Charles Pl NKENS W10 88 C4
St Charles Sq NKENS W10 88 C4
St Christopher's Cl ISLW TW7 103 K7
St Christophers Dr
HYS/HAR UB3 83 F6
St Christopher's Ms
WLGTN SM6 176 C4
St Christopher's Pl MHST W1U 10 B5
St Clair Cl CLAY IG5 59 K1
St Clair Dr WPK KT4 173 K2
St Clair Rd PLSTW E13 95 F1
St Clair's Rd CROY/NA CR0 178 A1
St Clare St TWRH EC3N 13 L5

St Clements Ct PUR RM19 119 K3
St Clement's La LINN WC2A 11M5
St Clements Yd EDUL * SE22 131 G4
St Cloud Rd WNWD SE27 149 J3
St Crispins Cl HAMP NW3 71 J3
STHL UB1 83 K5
St Cross St HCIRC EC1N 12 B2
St Cuthberts Gdns PIN * HA5 33 K6
St Cuthbert's Rd CRICK NW2 70 D5
PLMGR N13 41 G5
St Cyprian's St TOOT SW17 147 K3
St Davids Cl
BERM/RHTH * SE16 111 J4
WBLY HA9 68 E2
WWKM BR4 166 E6
St David's Dr EDGW HA8 36 B7
St Davids Ms BOW * E3 93 G2
St David's Pl HDN NW4 51 K6
St Davids Sq POP/IOD E14 112 E4
St Denis Rd WNWD SE27 149 K3
St Dionis Rd FUL/PGN SW6 127 J1
St Donatt's Rd NWCR SE14 112 C7
St Dunstan's Av ACT W3 87 F6
St Dunstans Cl HYS/HAR UB3 101 J3
St Dunstans Gdns ACT W3 87 F6
St Dunstan's Hl MON * EC3R 13 J7
SUT SM1 174 C3
St Dunstan's La BECK BR3 167 F5
MON * EC3R 13 J7
St Dunstan's Rd FELT TW13 140 D2
FSTGT E7 77 F5
HMSMTH W6 107 G4
HNWL W7 103 K1
HSLWW TW4 122 A1
SNWD SE25 165 G3
St Edmunds Av RSLP HA4 46 B5
St Edmunds Cl ABYW SE2 116 E1
STJWD NW8 3 L4
TOOT SW17 147 J1
St Edmunds Dr STAN HA7 35 G7
St Edmund's La WHTN TW2 123 G6
St Edmunds Rd DART DA1 139 J3
ED N9 30 C6
IL IG1 59 K5
St Edmunds Sq BARN SW13 107 F5
St Edmund's Ter STJWD NW8 3 K5
St Edward's Cl GLDGN NW11 52 E5
St Edwards Wy ROMW/RG RM7 63 F4
St Elmo Rd ACT W3 106 C1
St Elmos Rd BERM/RHTH SE16 112 B1
St Erkenwald Ms BARK IG11 78 D7
St Erkenwald Rd BARK IG11 78 D7
St Ervans Rd NKENS W10 88 C4
St Faith's Rd HNHL SE24 130 C7
St Fidelis' Rd ERITH DA8 118 A3
St Fillans Rd CAT SE6 133 F7
St Francis Cl ORP BR6 169 K5
OXHEY WD19 21 F7
St Francis Rd EDUL SE22 131 F3
St Francis Wy IL IG1 78 D3
St Gabriel's Cl WAN E11 59 F7
St Gabriel's Rd CRICK NW2 70 B4
St George's Av CDALE/KGS NW9 50 E3
EA W5 104 E1
FSTGT E7 77 F6
HOLWY N7 72 D3
STHL UB1 83 K6
St George's Circ STHWK SE1 18 C2
St Georges Cl ALP/SUD HA0 67 G2
GLDGN NW11 52 D5
THMD SE28 97 K5
St George's Dr OXHEY WD19 33 J2
PIM SW1V 16 E7
St Georges Flds BAY/PAD W2 9 K6
St George's Gdns SURB KT6 172 D1
St George's Gv TOOT SW17 147 H2
St George's La MON * EC3R 13 H6
St Georges Ms CHSWK * W4 105 K5
DEPT SE8 112 C3
HAMP NW3 3M2
St Georges Pde CAT * SE6 151 H1
St George's Rd BECK BR3 151 K7
BMLY BR1 168 E1
CHSWK W4 106 A1
DAGW RM9 80 A4
ED N9 42 C2
FELT TW13 141 H3
FSTGT E7 77 F6
GLDGN NW11 52 D5
HNWL W7 85 F7
IL IG1 59 K6
KUTN/CMB KT2 144 C6
LEY E10 76 A2
MTCM CR4 163 G2
PLMGR N13 41 F2
RCH/KEW TW9 125 G2
SCUP DA14 155 K5
STHWK SE1 18 C4
STMC/STPC BR5 169 J5
TWK TW1 124 C4
WIM/MER SW19 146 D5
WLGTN SM6 176 B4
St Georges Rd West BMLY BR1 168 D1
St George's Sq FSTGT E7 77 F6
St Georges's Ct STP * EC4M 12 C4
NWMAL * KT3 160 B2
PIM SW1V 17 G8
St George's Square Ms
PIM SW1V 17 G8
St George's Ter HAMP NW3 3M2
PECK * SE15 111 H6
St George St CONDST W1S 10 D6
St George's Wk CROY/NA CR0 177 J1
St George's Wy PECK SE15 111 F5
St Gerards Cl CLAP SW4 129 H4
St German's Pl BKHTH/KID SE3 113 K7
St German's Rd FSTH SE23 132 B7
St Giles Av DAGE RM10 80 D6
HGDN/ICK UB10 64 A3
St Giles Churchyard
BARB * EC2Y 12 F3
St Giles Cl DAGE RM10 80 D6
St Giles High St LSQ/SEVD WC2H 11 H4
St Giles Rd CMBW SE5 111 F7
St Gothard Rd WNWD SE27 149 K3
St Gregory Cl RSLP HA4 65 G3
St Helena Rd
BERM/RHTH SE16 112 A3
St Helena St FSBYW * WC1X 6 A8
St Helena Ter RCH/KEW * TW9 124 E4
St Helens THDIT * KT7 157 K6
St Helen's Crs
STRHM/NOR SW16 149 F7
St Helen's Gdns NKENS W10 88 B5
St Helen's Pl OBST EC2N 13 J4
St Helens Rd ERITH DA18 116 E1
IL IG1 59 K5
STRHM/NOR SW16 164 A1
WEA W13 85 H7
St Helier Av MRDN SM4 162 B6
St Heliers Av HSLWW TW4 123 F4
St Helier's Rd LEY E10 57 K5
St Hildas Cl KIL/WHAMP * NW6 70 B7
TOOT SW17 147 J1
St Hilda's Rd BARN SW13 106 E5
St Hughes Cl TOOT * SW17 147 J1
St Hugh's Rd PGE/AN * SE20 150 D7
St Ivians Dr GPK RM2 63 J2
St James Av SUT SM1 174 E4
TRDG/WHET N20 39 J2
WEA W13 85 G7
St James' Cl NWMAL KT3 160 C4
RSLP HA4 65 G1
STJWD NW8 3 L5
TRDG/WHET N20 39 J2
St James' Ct WESTW * SW1E 16 F3
St James' Gdns ALP/SUD HA0 67 K6
St James Ms POP/IOD * E14 113 F2
St James Pl DART DA1 139 G5
St James Rd CAR SM5 175 J2
EBAR EN4 27 H2
ED N9 42 D1
FSTGT E7 76 D4
MTCM CR4 148 A6
SURB KT6 158 E5
SUT SM1 174 E5
WATW WD18 21 F4
St James's NWCR SE14 112 B7
St James's Av BECK BR3 166 B2
BETH E2 92 E1
HPTN TW12 142 C4
St James's Chambers
STJS * SW1Y 10 F8
St James's Cl TOOT * SW17 147 K1
TOOT * SW17 148 A4
WOOL/PLUM SE18 115 H4
St James's Cottages
RCHPK/HAM * TW10 124 E4
St James's Ct KUT * KT1 159 F2
WESTW SW1E 16 F3
St James's Crs BRXN/ST SW9 130 B2
St James's Dr BAL SW12 128 E7
St James's Gdns CAMTN * NW1 4 E8
NTGHL W11 88 C7
St James's Gv BTSEA * SW11 128 E1
St James's La MUSWH N10 54 B3
St James's Market STJS * SW1Y 11 G7
St James's Ms WALTH E17 57 G4
St James's Pk CROY/NA CR0 164 D6
St James's Pl WHALL SW1A 10 E9
St James Sq SURB KT6 158 D6
St James's Rd CROY/NA CR0 164 D6
HPTN TW12 142 B4
KUT KT1 158 E1
STHWK SE1 111 H4
St James's Rw CHSGTN * KT9 171 K5
St James's Sq STJS SW1Y 11 G8
St James's St WALTH E17 57 G4
WHALL SW1A 10 E8
St James's Ter STJWD NW8 3 L4
St James's Terrace Ms
STJWD NW8 3 L4
St James St HMSMTH W6 107 F4
St James Ter BAL * SW12 129 F7
St James Wk CLKNW EC1R 6 C9
St Jerome's Gv HYS/HAR UB3 82 A5
St Joan's Rd ED N9 42 B1
St John Cl FUL/PGN * SW6 107 K6
St John's Av FBAR/BDGN N11 39 K4
PUT/ROE SW15 127 G4
WLSDN NW10 69 H7
St John's Church Rd HOM * E9 74 E4
St John's Cl FUL/PGN * SW6 107 K6
RAIN RM13 81 J6
STHGT/OAK * N14 28 C5
TRDG/WHET * N20 39 G1
WBLY HA9 68 A4
St Johns Cottages
PGE/AN * SE20 150 E6
St John's Ct ISLW TW7 124 A1
St John's Crs BRXN/ST SW9 130 B2
St John's Dr WAND/EARL SW18 128 A7
WOT/HER KT12 156 B7
St John's Gdns NTGHL W11 88 D6
St John's Gv ARCH N19 72 C1
BARN * SW13 126 C1
RCH/KEW * TW9 125 F3
St John's Hl BTSEA SW11 128 D3
St John's Hill Gv BTSEA SW11 128 C3
St John's La FARR EC1M 12 C1
St Johns Pde SCUP * DA14 155 H3
WEA * W13 85 H7
St John's Pk BKHTH/KID SE3 113 K6
St John's Pl FARR EC1M 12 C1
St John's Rd BARK IG11 78 E7
BTSEA SW11 128 D3
CAN/RD E16 94 E5
CAR SM5 175 J2
CHING E4 43 K2
CROY/NA CR0 177 H2
E/WMO/HCT KT8 157 J3
EHAM E6 77 J7
ERITH DA8 118 A4
FELT TW13 141 K3
GLDGN NW11 52 D5
GNTH/NBYPK IG2 60 E6
HRW HA1 49 F5
ISLW TW7 124 A1
KUT KT1 158 D1
NWDGN UB2 102 D2
NWMAL KT3 159 K2
PGE/AN SE20 150 E6
RCH/KEW TW9 125 F3
SCUP DA14 155 H3
SEVS/STOTM N15 56 A5
STMC/STPC BR5 169 J5
SUT SM1 174 E1
WALTH E17 57 K1
WAT WD17 21 F1
WBLY HA9 67 K3
WELL DA16 136 C2
WIM/MER SW19 146 C6
St John's Sq FARR EC1M 12 C1
St John's Ter FSTGT E7 77 F5
NKENS W10 88 B3
WOOL/PLUM SE18 115 H5
St John St FSBYE EC1V 6 B6
St John's V DEPT SE8 132 D1
St John's Vls ARCH N19 72 D1
KENS W8 14 D4
St John's Wy ARCH N19 72 C1
St John's Wood High St
STJWD NW8 3 H6
St John's Wood Pk STJWD NW8 3 G4
St John's Wood Rd STJWD NW8 3 G9
St John's Wood Ter STJWD NW8 3 J5
St Josephs Cl NKENS W10 88 C4
St Joseph's Dr STHL UB1 83 J7
St Josephs Gv HDN NW4 51 K3
St Joseph's Rd ED N9 30 D6
St Joseph's St VX/NE * SW8 109 G7
St Joseph's V BKHTH/KID SE3 133 G1
St Jude's Rd BETH E2 92 D1
St Jude St STNW/STAM N16 74 A4
St Julian's Cl STRHM/NOR * SW16 149 G3
St Julian's Farm Rd
WNWD SE27 149 G3
St Julian's Rd KIL/WHAMP NW6 70 D6
St Katharine's Prec
CAMTN * NW1 4 C5
St Katharine's Wy TWRH EC3N 13M8
St Katherines Rd ERITHM DA18 116 E1
St Katherines Wk NTGHL * W11 88 B6
St Keverne Rd ELTH/MOT SE9 153 J3
St Kilda Rd WEA W13 104 B1
St Kilda's Rd HRW HA1 48 E5
STNW/STAM N16 55 K7
St Kitts Ter NRWD SE19 150 A4
St Laurence's Cl
KIL/WHAMP NW6 70 B7
St Lawrence Cl EDGW HA8 36 B6
St Lawrence Cottages
POP/IOD * E14 94 A7
St Lawrence Dr PIN HA5 47 F4
St Lawrence St POP/IOD E14 94 A7
St Lawrence Ter NKENS W10 88 C4
St Lawrence Wy
BRXN/ST * SW9 130 B1
St Leonard's Av CHING E4 44 B5
KTN/HRWW/W HA3 49 J4
St Leonards Cl BUSH WD23 21 J3
WELL DA16 136 B2
St Leonard's Gdns HEST TW5 102 D6
IL IG1 78 C4
St Leonard's Rd CROY/NA CR0 177 H2
ESH/CLAY KT10 171 F5
MORT/ESHN SW14 125 K2
POP/IOD E14 94 A5
SURB KT6 158 E4
THDIT KT7 158 B5
WEA W13 85 J6
WLSDN NW10 87 F3
St Leonards Sq KTTN NW5 72 A5
St Leonard's St BOW E3 93 K2
St Leonard's Ter CHEL SW3 15 L8
St Leonard's Wk
STRHM/NOR SW16 149 F6
St Leonards Wy EMPK RM11 63 K7
St Loo Av CHEL SW3 15 K9
St Louis Rd WNWD SE27 149 J3
St Loy's Rd TOTM N17 56 A1
St Lucia Dr SRTFD E15 76 D7
St Luke's Av CLAP SW4 129 J3
IL IG1 78 B4
St Luke's Cl SNWD SE25 165 J5
St Luke's Ms NTGHL W11 88 D5
St Luke's Rd NTGHL W11 88 D4
St Lukes's Cl FSBYE EC1V 6 F9
St Luke's Sq CAN/RD E16 94 D5
St Luke's St CHEL SW3 15 J7
St Lukes Yd MV/WKIL * W9 88 D1
St Malo Av ED N9 42 E2
St Margarets BARK IG11 78 D7
RCHPK/HAM * TW10 144 E4
St Margarets Av BFN/LL DA15 154 D2
CHEAM SM3 174 C2
RYLN/HDSTN HA2 66 C2
SEVS/STOTM N15 55 H3
TRDG/WHET N20 27 G7
St Margarets Ct
PUT/ROE * SW15 126 E3
St Margaret's Crs
PUT/ROE * SW15 126 E4
St Margaret's Dr TWK TW1 124 C4
St Margaret's Gv TWK TW1 124 B5
WAN E11 76 D2
WOOL/PLUM SE18 115 H5
St Margarets La KENS W8 14 C4
St Margarets Ms
RCHPK/HAM * TW10 144 E4
St Margaret's Rd BROCKY SE4 132 C3
EDGW HA8 36 D4
HNWL W7 103 K1
MNPK E12 77 G1
RSLP HA4 46 B5
TOTM N17 56 A2
TWK TW1 124 C3
WLSDN NW10 88 A2
St Margaret's Ter
WOOL/PLUM SE18 115 H4
St Margaret St WEST SW1P 17 J2
St Mark's Cl BAR EN5 27 F2
FUL/PGN SW6 107 K7
St Mark's Crs CAMTN NW1 4 B3
St Marks Ga HOM E9 75 G6
St Mark's Gv WBPTN * SW10 108 A6
St Mark's Hl SURB KT6 159 F5
St Mark's Pl NTGHL W11 88 C5
WIM/MER * SW19 146 D5
St Mark's Ri HACK E8 74 B4
St Mark's Rd EA W5 86 A7
EN EN1 30 B5
HAYES BR2 168 A2
HNWL W7 103 K1
MTCM CR4 162 E1
NKENS W10 88 B5
SNWD SE25 165 H3
TEDD TW11 143 H6
St Mark's Sq CAMTN NW1 4 A3
St Mark St WCHPL E1 13M5
St Marks Vls FSBYPK * N4 73 F1
St Martin's Ap RSLP HA4 46 C6
St Martin's Av EHAM E6 95 H1
St Martin's Cl CAMTN NW1 4 E3
ERITH DA18 116 E1
OXHEY WD19 33 G3
St Martins Ct LSQ/SEVD WC2H 11 J6
St Martin's La BECK BR3 166 E4
CHCR WC2N 11 J6
St Martin's Le Grand
STBT EC1A 12 E4
St Martin's Pl CHCR WC2N 11 J7
St Martin's Rd BRXN/ST SW9 130 A1
DART DA1 139 J5
ED N9 42 D1
St Martin's St LSQ/SEVD * WC2H 11 H7
St Martins Wy TOOT SW17 147 G2
St Mary Abbot's Pl KENS W8 107 J2
St Mary Abbots Ter
WKENS * W14 107 J2
St Mary At Hl MON EC3R 13 J7
St Mary Av WLGTN SM6 176 A2
St Mary Axe HDTCH EC3A 13 J5
St Marychurch St
BERM/RHTH SE16 111 K1
St Mary Graces Ct TWRH * EC3N 13M7
St Mary Rd WALTH E17 57 J3
St Marys BARK IG11 96 D1
St Mary's Ap MNPK E12 77 K4
St Mary's Av FNCH N3 52 C1
HAYES BR2 167 H2
NTHWD HA6 32 C4
NWDGN UB2 103 G3
STWL/WRAY TW19 120 A6
TEDD * TW11 143 F5
WAN E11 59 F5
St Mary's Cl CHSGTN KT9 172 B6
EW KT17 173 H6
TOTM * N17 56 B1
WATW * WD18 21 G3
St Marys Ct SHB * W12 106 C2
St Mary's Crs HDN NW4 51 K2
HYS/HAR UB3 82 D6
ISLW TW7 103 J6
STWL/WRAY TW19 120 A6
St Mary's Dr EBED/NFELT TW14 121 F6
St Marys Est
BERM/RHTH * SE16 111 K1
St Mary's Gdns LBTH SE11 18 B5
St Mary's Ga KENS W8 14 C4
St Mary's Gn EFNCH N2 53 G2
St Mary's Gv BARN SW13 126 E2
CHSWK W4 105 J5
IS N1 73 H5
RCH/KEW TW9 125 G3
St Mary's Man BAY/PAD W2 8 F2
St Mary's Ms KIL/WHAMP NW6 2 C2
St Mary's Pth IS N1 6 D3
St Mary's Pl EA W5 104 E1
KENS W8 14 C4
St Mary's Rd BXLY DA5 137 K7
CEND/HSY/T * N8 54 E3
E/WMO/HCT KT8 157 J4
EA W5 104 E1
EBAR EN4 27 K6
ED N9 30 E7
GLDGN NW11 52 C6
HYS/HAR UB3 82 D6
IL IG1 78 C1
LEY E10 76 A2
PECK SE15 111 K7
PLSTW E13 95 F1
SNWD SE25 165 F2
SURB KT6 158 D6
WATW WD18 21 F3
WIM/MER SW19 146 C4
WLSDN NW10 69 G7
WPK KT4 173 G1
St Mary's Sq BAY/PAD W2 9 G2
EA * W5 104 E1
St Mary's Ter BAY/PAD W2 9 G2
BORE * WD6 23 K5
St Mary St WOOL/PLUM SE18 114 E3
St Marys Vw
KTN/HRWW/W HA3 49 J4
WATW * WD18 21 G3
St Mary's Wk HYS/HAR UB3 82 D6
LBTH SE11 18 B5
St Matthews Av SURB KT6 159 F7
St Matthews Cl OXHEY WD19 21 H5
RAIN RM13 81 J6
St Matthews Dr BMLY BR1 168 E2
St Matthew's Rd
BRXS/STRHM SW2 130 A4
EA W5 86 A7
St Matthew's Rw BETH E2 92 C2
St Matthew St WEST SW1P 17 G3
St Matthias Cl CDALE/KGS NW9 51 H4
St Maur Rd FUL/PGN SW6 107 J7
St Meddens CHST * BR7 154 D6
St Mellion Cl THMD SE28 97 K5
St Merryn Cl WOOL/PLUM SE18 115 J6
St Michael's Aly BANK EC3V 13 H5
St Michaels Av ED N9 30 E6
WBLY HA9 68 C5
St Michaels Cl BMLY BR1 168 D2
CAN/RD E16 95 H4
ERITHM * DA18 116 E1
FNCH N3 52 D1
NFNCH/WDSP N12 39 J4
WPK KT4 173 H1
St Michaels Ct GLDGN * NW11 52 D6
St Michael's Crs PIN HA5 47 J5
St Michael's Gdns NKENS W10 88 B4
St Michaels Ri WELL * DA16 116 C7
St Michael's Rd BRXN/ST SW9 130 A1
CRICK NW2 70 A3
CROY/NA * CR0 164 D7
WELL DA16 136 C2
WLGTN SM6 176 C5
St Michael's St BAY/PAD W2 9 H4
St Michaels Ter HGT * N6 54 A7
WDGN N22 54 E1
St Mildred's Ct LOTH * EC2R 13 G5
St Mildreds Rd CAT SE6 133 H6
St Nicholas Av HCH RM12 81 J2
St Nicholas Cl BORE WD6 23 K5
St Nicholas Glebe TOOT SW17 148 A5
St Nicholas Rd SUT SM1 175 F4
THDIT KT7 158 A5
WOOL/PLUM SE18 116 A4
St Nicholas St DEPT SE8 112 C7
St Nicholas Wy SUT SM1 175 F3
St Nicolas La CHST BR7 153 J7
St Ninian's Ct TRDG/WHET N20 39 K2
St Norbert Rd BROCKY SE4 132 B3
St Olaf's Rd FUL/PGN SW6 107 H6
St Olave's Rd EHAM E6 78 A7
St Olave's Wk
STRHM/NOR SW16 163 H1
St Onge Pde EN * EN1 29 K2
St Oswald's Pl LBTH SE11 17 L7
St Oswald's Rd
STRHM/NOR SW16 149 H7
St Oswulf St WEST * SW1P 17 H6
St Pancras Gdns CAMTN * NW1 5 H4
St Pancras Wy CAMTN NW1 4 F1
St Paul's Av BERM/RHTH * SE16 93 F7
CRICK NW2 69 K5
KTN/HRWW/W HA3 50 B4
St Paul's Church Yd
BLKFR * EC4V 12 D5
St Paul's Cl ASHF TW15 140 A4
CAR SM5 162 D6
CHARL SE7 114 C4
CHSGTN KT9 171 K3
EA W5 105 G1
HSLW TW3 122 E1
HYS/HAR UB3 101 G4
St Paul's Cray Rd CHST BR7 154 D7
St Pauls Crs CAMTN NW1 5 H1
St Paul's Dr SRTFD E15 76 B4
St Pauls Ms CAMTN NW1 5 H1
St Paul's Pl IS N1 73 K5
St Pauls Ri PLMGR N13 41 H5
St Pauls Rd BARK IG11 78 C7
BTFD TW8 104 E5
ERITH DA8 117 K6
IS N1 73 H5
RCH/KEW TW9 125 G2
THHTH CR7 164 D2
TOTM N17 42 C6
St Pauls Ter WALW SE17 18 D9
St Paul St IS N1 6 E4
St Paul's Wy FNCH N3 39 F6
POP/IOD E14 93 H4
WATN WD24 21 G1
St Paul's Wood Hl
STMC/STPC BR5 169 K1
St Peter's Av BETH E2 92 C1
UED N18 42 C3
St Petersburgh Ms BAY/PAD W2 8 C6
St Petersburgh Pl BAY/PAD W2 8 C6
St Peter's Cl BAR EN5 25 K4
BETH E2 92 C1
BUSH WD23 22 D7
CHST BR7 154 D6
GNTH/NBYPK IG2 60 E3
RSLP HA4 65 H1
TOOT SW17 147 J1
St Peters Ct E/WMO/HCT KT8 157 F3
HDN * NW4 52 A4
LEE/GVPK * SE12 133 J4
St Peter's Gdns WNWD SE27 149 G2
St Peter's Gv HMSMTH W6 106 D3
St Peter's Pth WALTH E17 58 C3
St Peters Pl MV/WKIL W9 8 C1
St Peter's Rd CROY/NA CR0 177 K3
E/WMO/HCT KT8 157 F3
ED N9 30 D7
HMSMTH * W6 106 D4
KUT KT1 159 H1
STHL UB1 84 A4
TWK TW1 124 C4
St Peter's Sq BETH * E2 92 C1
HMSMTH W6 106 C4
St Peter's St IS N1 6 D4
SAND/SEL CR2 177 K4
St Peter's Ter FUL/PGN SW6 107 H6
St Peter's Vls HMSMTH W6 106 D3
St Peter's Wy EA W5 85 K4
HYS/HAR UB3 101 G4
IS N1 7 K2
St Philip's Av WPK KT4 173 K1
St Philip Sq VX/NE * SW8 129 G1
St Philip's Rd HACK E8 74 C5
SURB KT6 158 E5
St Philip St VX/NE SW8 129 G1
St Philip's Wy IS N1 6 F4
St Quentin Rd WELL DA16 136 A2
St Quintin Av NKENS W10 88 A4
St Quintin Rd PLSTW E13 95 F2
St Raphael's Wy WLSDN NW10 68 E4
St Regis Cl MUSWH N10 54 B1
St Ronans Crs WFD IG8 44 E6
St Rule St VX/NE SW8 129 H1
St Saviour's Rd
BRXS/STRHM SW2 130 A4
CROY/NA CR0 164 D5
Saints Cl WNWD SE27 149 H3
Saints Dr FSTGT E7 77 H4
St Silas Pl KTTN NW5 72 A5
St Simon's Av PUT/ROE SW15 127 F4
St Stephen's Av SHB W12 87 K7
WALTH E17 58 A4
WEA W13 85 H5
St Stephens Cl KTTN * NW5 71 K4
STHL UB1 84 A4
STJWD NW8 3 J4
WALTH E17 57 K4
St Stephen's Crs BAY/PAD * W2 8 B4
THHTH CR7 164 B2
St Stephen's Gdns BAY/PAD W2 8 B4
TWK TW1 124 D5
St Stephen's Gv LEW SE13 133 F2
St Stephen's Ms BAY/PAD W2 8 B3
St Stephens Pde WHALL SW1A 17 J1
St Stephens Rd BAR EN5 26 B4
BOW E3 75 G7
BOW E3 93 H1
EHAM E6 77 G6
HSLW TW3 123 F5
WALTH E17 57 K4
WEA W13 85 H5
St Stephen's Ter VX/NE SW8 110 A6
St Stephen's Wk SKENS SW7 14 E5
St Swithin's La MANHO EC4N 13 G6
St Swithun's Rd LEW * SE13 133 G4
St Theresa's Rd
EBED/NFELT TW14 121 J3
St Thomas Cl SURB KT6 159 G7
St Thomas Ct BXLY DA5 137 H6
St Thomas' Dr PIN HA5 33 J7
STMC/STPC BR5 169 H7
St Thomas Gdns IL IG1 78 C5
St Thomas Rd BELV DA17 117 K1
CAN/RD E16 94 E5
CHSWK W4 105 K6
STHGT/OAK N14 28 D6
St Thomas's Gdns HAMP NW3 72 A5
St Thomas's Pl HOM * E9 74 E6
St Thomas's Rd FSBYPK N4 73 G1
WLSDN NW10 69 G7
St Thomas's Sq HACK E8 74 D6
St Thomas St STHWK SE1 13 H9
St Thomas's Wy FUL/PGN SW6 107 J6
St Ursula Gv PIN HA5 47 H4
St Ursula Rd STHL UB1 84 A5
St Vincent Cl WNWD SE27 149 H4
St Vincent Rd WHTN TW2 123 H5
St Vincents Cottages
WATW * WD18 21 F3
St Vincents Rd DART DA1 139 K5
St Vincent St MHST W1U 10 B3
St Wilfrid's Cl EBAR * EN4 27 J4
St Wilfrid's Rd EBAR EN4 27 H4
St Winefride's Av MNPK E12 77 K4
St Winifred's Rd TEDD TW11 143 H5
Saladin Dr PUR RM19 119 K3
Salamanca Pl LBTH SE11 17 L6
Salamanca St LBTH SE11 17 L6
Salamander Cl KUTN/CMB KT2 143 J4
Salamander Quay KUT * KT1 143 K7
Salamons Wy RAIN RM13 99 G5
Salcombe Dr CHDH RM6 62 B5
MRDN SM4 161 G7
Salcombe Gdns MLHL NW7 38 A5
Salcombe Rd STNW/STAM N16 74 B4
WALTH E17 57 H6
Salcombe Wy RSLP HA4 64 E1
Salcott Rd BTSEA SW11 128 E4
CROY/NA CR0 176 E2
Salehurst Cl KTN/HRWW/W HA3 50 A4
Salehurst Rd BROCKY SE4 132 C5
Salem Pl CROY/NA CR0 177 J2
Salem Rd BAY/PAD W2 8 D6
Sale Pl BAY/PAD W2 9 J3
Sale St BETH E2 92 C3
Salford Rd BRXS/STRHM SW2 129 J7
Salhouse Cl THMD SE28 97 J5

Salisbury Av DARK IG11 78 D6
FNCH N3 52 D1
SUT SM1 174 D5
Salisbury Cl WALW SE17 19 G5
WPK KT4 173 H2
Salisbury Ct EMB EC4Y 12 B5
Salisbury Gdns
WIM/MER * SW19 146 C6
Salisbury Pavement
FUL/PGN * SW6 107 K6
Salisbury Pl BRXN/ST SW9 110 C6
MBLAR W1H 9 L2
Salisbury Prom
CEND/HSY/T * N8 55 H4
Salisbury Rd BAR EN5 26 C2
BXLY DA5 137 H7
CAR SM5 175 K5
CHING E4 43 J2
CROY/NA CR0 165 H5
DAGE RM10 80 D5
ED N9 42 C2
FELT TW13 122 B7
FSBYPK N4 55 H4
FSTGT E7 76 E5
GDMY/SEVK IG3 78 E1
GPK RM2 63 K4
HAYES BR2 168 D4
HOR/WEW KT19 173 F3
HRW HA1 48 D4
HSLWW TW4 122 B2
LEY E10 76 A1
MNPK E12 77 H4
NWDGN * UB2 102 D3
NWMAL KT3 160 A2
PIN HA5 46 E3
RCH/KEW TW9 125 F3
WALTH E17 58 A4
WDGN N22 55 H1
WEA W13 104 C1
WIM/MER SW19 146 C6
Salisbury Sq EMB * EC4Y 12 B5
Salisbury St ACT W3 105 K1
STJWD NW8 9 H1
Salisbury Ter PECK SE15 131 K2
Salix Cl SUN TW16 141 F6
Sally Murray Cl MNPK E12 78 A3
Salmen Rd PLSTW E13 94 D1
Salmon La POP/IOD E14 93 G5
Salmon Ms KIL/WHAMP * NW6 70 E4
Salmon Rd BELV DA17 117 H4
DART DA1 139 J2
Salmons Rd CHSGTN KT9 172 A5
ED N9 30 C7
Salmon St CDALE/KGS NW9 68 E1
POP/IOD * E14 93 H5
Salomons Rd PLSTW E13 95 G4
Salop Rd WALTH E17 57 F5
Saltash Cl SUT SM1 174 D3
Saltash Rd WELL DA16 116 D7
Saltcoats Rd CHSWK W4 106 B1
Saltcote Cl DART DA1 138 B5
Saltcroft Cl WBLY HA9 50 D7
Salter Cl RYLN/HDSTN HA2 65 K2
Salterford Rd TOOT SW17 148 A5
Salter Rd BERM/RHTH SE16 93 F7
Salters' Hall Ct MANHO * EC4N 13 G6
Salter's Hl NRWD SE19 149 K4
Salters Rd NKENS W10 88 B3
WALTH E17 58 B3
Salters Rw IS * N1 73 K5
Salter St POP/IOD E14 93 J6
WLSDN NW10 87 J2
Salterton Rd HOLWY N7 72 E2
Saltford Cl ERITH DA8 118 B4
Saltley Cl EHAM E6 95 J5
Saltoun Rd BRXS/STRHM SW2 130 B3
Saltram Crs MV/WKIL W9 2 A8
Saltwell St POP/IOD E14 93 J6
Saltwood Gv WALW SE17 19 G8
Salusbury Rd KIL/WHAMP NW6 70 C7
Salvador TOOT SW17 147 J4
Salvia Gdns GFD/PVL UB6 85 G1
Salvin Rd PUT/ROE SW15 127 G2
Salway Cl WFD IG8 44 E6
Salway Pl SRTFD E15 76 B5
Salway Rd SRTFD E15 76 B5
Samantha Cl WALTH E17 57 H6
Sam Bartram Cl CHARL SE7 114 B4
Samels Ct HMSMTH W6 106 D4
Samford St STJWD NW8 9 J1
Samos Rd PGE/AN SE20 165 J1
Sampson Av BAR EN5 26 B4
Sampson Cl BELV DA17 116 E2
Sampson St WAP * E1W 92 C7
Samson St PLSTW E13 95 G1
Samuel Cl HACK E8 7 M3
NWCR SE14 112 A5
WOOL/PLUM SE18 114 D3
Samuel Gray Gdns
KUTN/CMB KT2 143 K7
Samuel St PECK SE15 111 G6
WOOL/PLUM SE18 114 E3
Sancroft Cl CRICK NW2 69 K2
Sancroft Rd KTN/HRWW/W HA3 49 F1
Sancroft St LBTH SE11 17 M7
The Sanctuary BXLY DA5 136 E5
WEST SW1P 17 H3
Sanctuary Cl DART DA1 139 F5
Sanctuary Rd
STWL/WRAY TW19 120 D5
Sanctuary St STHWK SE1 18 F2
Sandall Cl EA W5 86 A3
Sandall Rd EA W5 86 A3
KTTN NW5 72 C5
Sandal Rd NWMAL KT3 160 B3
UED N18 42 C4
Sandal St SRTFD E15 76 C7
Sandalwood Cl WCHPL E1 93 G3
Sandalwood Dr RSLP HA4 46 A6
Sandalwood Rd FELT TW13 141 F2
Sandbach Pl WOOL/PLUM SE18 115 H4
Sandbourne Av
WIM/MER SW19 162 A2
Sandbourne Rd BROCKY SE4 132 B1
Sandbrook Cl MLHL NW7 37 F5
Sandbrook Rd STNW/STAM N16 74 A2
Sandby Gn ELTH/MOT SE9 134 D2
Sandcliff Rd ERITH DA8 118 A3
Sandcroft Cl PLMGR N13 41 H5
Sandell's Av ASHF TW15 140 A3
Sandell St STHWK SE1 18 A1
Sanders Cl HPTN TW12 142 C4
Sanders La MLHL NW7 38 B6
Sanderson Cl KTTN * NW5 72 B3
Sanders Pde
STRHM/NOR * SW16 148 E5
Sanderstead Av CRICK NW2 70 C1
Sanderstead Cl CLAP SW4 129 H6
Sanderstead Rd LEY E10 57 G7
SAND/SEL CR2 177 K6
Sandfield Gdns THHTH CR7 164 C2
Sandfield Pl THHTH CR7 164 D2
Sandfield Rd THHTH CR7 164 C2
Sandford Av WDGN N22 41 H7
Sandford Rd BXLYHS DA6 137 F3
EHAM E6 95 K2
HAYES BR2 167 K3
Sandford Rw WALW SE17 19 G7
Sandford St FUL/PGN SW6 108 A6
Sandgate Cl ROMW/RG RM7 62 E6
Sandgate La WAND/EARL SW18 128 D7
Sandgate Rd WELL DA16 116 D6
Sandgate St PECK SE15 111 J5
Sandhills WLGTN SM6 176 D3
Sandhurst Av BRYLDS KT5 159 J6
RYLN/HDSTN HA2 48 B5
Sandhurst Cl CDALE/KGS NW9 50 C2
SAND/SEL CR2 178 A7
Sandhurst Dr GDMY/SEVK IG3 79 F3
Sandhurst Market CAT * SE6 133 F7
Sandhurst Pde CAT * SE6 133 F7
Sandhurst Rd BFN/LL DA15 155 F2
BXLY DA5 136 E4
CAT SE6 133 G7
CDALE/KGS NW9 50 C2
ED N9 30 E5
Sandhurst Wy SAND/SEL CR2 178 A6
Sandifer Dr CRICK NW2 70 B2
Sandiford Rd CHEAM SM3 174 D1
Sandiland Crs HAYES BR2 180 D1
Sandilands CROY/NA CR0 178 C2
Sandilands Rd FUL/PGN SW6 108 A7
Sandison St PECK SE15 131 G2
Sandland St GINN WC1R 11 M3
Sandling Ri ELTH/MOT SE9 154 A2
Sandlings Cl PECK SE15 131 J1
Sandmere Rd CLAP SW4 129 K3
Sandon Cl ESH/CLAY KT10 157 J6
Sandow Crs HYS/HAR UB3 101 J2
Sandown Av DAGE RM10 80 E5
ESH/CLAY KT10 170 C4
Sandown Cl HEST TW5 101 K7
Sandown Ct BELMT * SM2 175 F6
DAGE RM10 80 E6
SYD * SE26 150 D2
Sandown Dr CAR SM5 176 A7
Sandown Ga ESH/CLAY KT10 170 D1
Sandown Rd ESH/CLAY KT10 170 C3
SNWD SE25 165 J4
Sandown Wy NTHLT UB5 65 J5
Sandpiper Cl BERM/RHTH SE16 112 C1
WALTH E17 43 F6
Sandpiper Dr ERITH DA8 118 E6
Sandpiper Rd SUT SM1 174 D4
Sandpiper Ter CLAY * IG5 60 B2
Sandpit Pl CHARL SE7 114 D4
Sandpit Rd BMLY BR1 152 C4
DART DA1 139 F3
Sandpits Rd CROY/NA CR0 179 F3
RCHPK/HAM TW10 143 K1
Sandra Cl HSLW TW3 123 G4
WDGN N22 41 J7
Sandridge Cl HRW HA1 48 E3
Sandridge St ARCH N19 72 C1
Sandringham Av RYNPK SW20 146 C7
Sandringham Cl EN EN1 30 A1
WIM/MER * SW19 127 G7
Sandringham Crs
RYLN/HDSTN HA2 66 A2
Sandringham Dr WELL DA16 135 K1
Sandringham Gdns
BARK/HLT IG6 60 C2
CEND/HSY/T N8 54 E5
HEST TW5 101 K7
NFNCH/WDSP N12 39 H5
Sandringham Pl
E/WMO/HCT KT8 157 F3
Sandringham Rd BARK IG11 79 F5
BMLY BR1 152 E4
CRICK NW2 69 K4
CROY/NA CR0 164 D4
FSTGT E7 77 G4
GLDGN NW11 52 C6
HACK E8 74 C4
HTHAIR TW6 120 B4
LEY E10 58 B6
NTHLT UB5 66 A6
WDGN N22 55 J2
WPK KT4 173 J2
Sandrock Pl CROY/NA CR0 179 F3
Sandrock Rd LEW SE13 132 D2
Sands End La FUL/PGN SW6 108 A7
Sandstone Rd LEE/GVPK SE12 153 F1
Sands Wy WFD IG8 45 K5
Sandtoft Rd CHARL SE7 114 A5
Sandwell Crs KIL/WHAMP NW6 70 E5
Sandwich St STPAN WC1H 5 J8
Sandwick Cl MLHL NW7 37 J6
Sandycombe Rd
EBED/NFELT TW14 121 K7
RCH/KEW TW9 125 H1
Sandycoombe Rd TWK TW1 124 D5
Sandycroft ABYW SE2 116 B5
Sandy Dr EBED/NFELT TW14 121 H7
Sandy Hill Av
WOOL/PLUM SE18 115 G4
Sandy Hill La
WOOL/PLUM SE18 115 G3
Sandyhill Rd IL IG1 78 B3
Sandy Hill Rd WLGTN SM6 176 C7
WOOL/PLUM SE18 115 G4
Sandy La BELMT SM2 174 C7
BUSH WD23 22 C2
KTN/HRWW/W HA3 50 B5
MTCM CR4 148 A7
NTHWD HA6 32 D1
RCHPK/HAM TW10 143 J1
STMC/STPC BR5 155 K6
TEDD TW11 143 G6
Sandy La North WLGTN SM6 176 D4
Sandy La South WLGTN SM6 176 C7
Sandy Ldg PIN * HA5 34 A5
Sandy Lodge Ct NTHWD * HA6 32 C4
Sandy Lodge La NTHWD HA6 32 B1
Sandy Lodge Wy NTHWD HA6 32 C4
Sandymount Av STAN HA7 35 J4
Sandy Rdg CHST BR7 154 A5
Sandy Rd HAMP NW3 71 F1
Sandy's Rw WCHPL E1 13 K3
Sandy Wy CROY/NA CR0 179 H2
Sanford La STNW/STAM N16 74 B1
Sanford St NWCR SE14 112 B5
Sanford Ter STNW/STAM N16 74 B2
Sanger Av CHSGTN KT9 172 B4
Sangley Rd CAT SE6 132 E7
SNWD SE25 165 F3
Sangora Rd BTSEA SW11 128 C3
Sansom Rd WAN * E11 76 D1
Sansom St CMBW SE5 110 E6
Sans Wk CLKNW EC1R 6 C9
Santley St BRXS/STRHM SW2 129 K3
Santos Rd PUT/ROE SW15 127 K4
Saperton Wk LBTH SE11 17 M5
Sapphire Cl BCTR RM8 61 J7
Sapphire Rd DEPT SE8 112 B3
Saracen Cl CROY/NA CR0 164 E5
Saracen St POP/IOD E14 93 J5
Sarah St BETH E2 7 K7
Saratoga Rd CLPT E5 74 E3
Sardinia St HOL/ALD WC2B 11 L5
Sarita Cl KTN/HRWW/W HA3 48 D1
Sark Cl HEST TW5 103 F6
Sarnesfield Rd ENC/FH * EN2 29 K3
Sarre Rd KIL/WHAMP NW6 70 D4
Sarsen Av HSLW TW3 122 E1
Sarsfeld Rd BAL SW12 128 E7
Sarsfield Rd GFD/PVL UB6 85 H1
Sartor Rd PECK SE15 132 A3
Sarum Ter BOW * E3 93 H3
Satanita Cl CAN/RD E16 95 H5
Satchell Md CDALE/KGS NW9 37 H7
Satchwell Rd BETH E2 92 C2
Sattar Ms STNW/STAM * N16 73 K2
Sauls Gn WAN E11 76 C2
Saunders Cl POP/IOD * E14 93 H6
Saunders Ness Rd
POP/IOD E14 113 G3
Saunders Rd
WOOL/PLUM SE18 116 A4
Saunders St LBTH SE11 18 A5
Saunders Wy THMD SE28 97 H6
Saunderton Rd ALP/SUD HA0 67 H4
Saunton Av HYS/HAR UB3 101 J6
Saunton Rd HCH RM12 81 J1
Savage Gdns EHAM E6 95 K5
TWRH EC3N 13 K6
Savernake Ct STAN * HA7 35 H5
Savernake Rd ED N9 30 C5
HAMP NW3 71 K3
Savery Dr SURB KT6 158 D6
Savile Cl NWMAL KT3 160 B4
THDIT KT7 158 A7
Savile Gdns CROY/NA CR0 178 B1
Savile Rw CONDST W1S 10 E6
Saville Crs ASHF TW15 140 B5
Saville Rd CAN/RD E16 95 J7
CHDH RM6 62 B5
CHSWK W4 106 A2
TWK TW1 124 A7
Saville Rw HAYES BR2 167 J7
Savill Gdns RYNPK SW20 160 D2
Savill Rw WFD IG8 44 D5
Savona Cl WIM/MER SW19 146 B6
Savona St VX/NE SW8 109 H6
Savoy Av HYS/HAR UB3 101 H4
Savoy Cl EDGW HA8 36 C4
SRTFD E15 76 C7
Savoy Ct TPL/STR * WC2R 11 K7
Savoy Hl TPL/STR WC2R 11 L7
Savoy Pde EN * EN1 30 A2
Savoy Pl CHCR WC2N 11 K7
Savoy Rd DART DA1 139 F4
Savoy Rw TPL/STR WC2R 11 L6
Savoy Steps TPL/STR * WC2R 11 L7
Savoy St TPL/STR WC2R 11 L6
Savoy Wy TPL/STR WC2R 11 L7
Sawbill Cl YEAD UB4 83 H4
Sawkins Cl WIM/MER SW19 146 B1
Sawley Rd SHB W12 87 J7
Sawtry Cl CAR SM5 162 C6
Sawyer Cl ED N9 42 C1
Sawyer's Hl RCHPK/HAM TW10 125 G6
Sawyers Lawn WEA W13 85 F5
Sawyer St STHWK SE1 18 E1
Saxby Rd BRXS/STRHM SW2 129 K6
Saxham Rd BARK IG11 78 E7
Saxlingham Rd CHING E4 44 B2
Saxon Av FELT TW13 141 K1
Saxonbury Av SUN TW16 156 A2
Saxonbury Cl MTCM CR4 162 C2
Saxonbury Gdns SURB KT6 158 D7
Saxon Cl SURB KT6 158 E5
WALTH E17 57 J6
Saxon Dr ACT W3 86 D5
Saxonfield Cl
BRXS/STRHM SW2 130 A6
Saxon Rd ASHF TW15 140 B5
BMLY BR1 152 D6
BOW E3 93 H1
CROY/NA CR0 164 E4
EHAM E6 95 K3
IL IG1 78 B5
STHL UB1 83 J6
WBLY HA9 68 E2
WDGN N22 41 H7
Saxon Wy STHGT/OAK N14 28 D5
Saxony Pde HYS/HAR UB3 82 A4
Saxton Cl LEW SE13 133 G2
Sayesbury La UED N18 42 C4
Sayes Court St DEPT SE8 112 C4
Scala St FITZ W1T 10 F2
Scales Rd TOTM N17 56 B2
Scammell Wy WATW WD18 20 D5
Scampston Ms NKENS W10 88 B5
Scampton Rd HTHAIR TW6 120 C5
Scandrett St WAP * E1W 92 D7
Scarba Wk IS N1 73 K5
Scarborough Rd ED N9 30 E6
FSBYPK N4 55 G6
HTHAIR TW6 121 F5
WAN E11 58 B7
Scarborough St WCHPL E1 13 M5
Scarbrook Rd CROY/NA CR0 177 J2
Scarle Rd ALP/SUD HA0 67 K5
Scarlet Rd CAT SE6 152 C2
Scarsbrook Rd BKHTH/KID SE3 134 C2
Scarsdale Pl KENS * W8 14 C3
Scarsdale Rd RYLN/HDSTN HA2 66 C2
Scarsdale Vls KENS W8 14 B4
Scarth Rd BARN SW13 126 C2
Scawen Cl CAR SM5 176 A3
Scawen Rd DEPT SE8 112 B4
Scawfell St BETH E2 7 M6
Scaynes Link NFNCH/WDSP N12 38 E3
Sceptre Rd BETH E2 92 E2
Scholars Rd BAL SW12 129 H7
Scholefield Rd ARCH N19 54 D7
Schonfeld Sq STNW/STAM N16 73 K1
School Cl DART DA1 138 C3
School House La TEDD TW11 143 H6
Schoolhouse La WAP * E1W 93 F6
School La BUSH WD23 22 B6
KUT KT1 143 J7
PIN * HA5 47 J3
SURB KT6 159 H7
WELL DA16 136 C2
School Pas KUT KT1 159 G1
STHL UB1 83 K7
School Rd CHST BR7 154 C7
DAGE RM10 80 C7
E/WMO/HCT KT8 157 J3
HPTN TW12 142 C5
HSLW TW3 123 H2
KUT * KT1 143 J7
MNPK E12 77 K3
WDR/YW UB7 100 A5
WLSDN NW10 87 F3
School Road Av HPTN TW12 142 C5
School Wy BCTR RM8 79 H2
Schoolway NFNCH/WDSP N12 39 H5
Schooner Cl BARK IG11 97 H2
POP/IOD E14 113 G2
Schubert Rd BORE WD6 23 K5
PUT/ROE SW15 127 J4
Sclater St WCHPL E1 7 L9
Scoles Crs BRXS/STRHM SW2 130 B7
Scope Wy KUT KT1 159 F3
Scoresby St STHWK SE1 12 C9
Scorton Av GFD/PVL UB6 85 G1
Scotch Common WEA W13 85 G4
Scot Gv PIN HA5 33 H6
Scotia Rd BRXS/STRHM SW2 130 B6
Scotland Gn TOTM N17 56 B1
Scotland Green Rd PEND EN3 31 F4
Scotland Green Rd North
PEND EN3 31 F3
Scots Cl STWL/WRAY TW19 120 A7
Scotsdale Cl BELMT SM2 174 C6
CHST BR7 169 K3
Scotsdale Rd LEE/GVPK SE12 134 A4
Scotswood St CLKNW * EC1R 6 B9
Scotswood Wk TOTM * N17 42 D6
Scott Cl HOR/WEW KT19 172 E4
STRHM/NOR SW16 149 F7
WDR/YW UB7 100 C3
Scott Crs ERITH DA8 118 C7
RYLN/HDSTN HA2 48 B7
Scott Ellis Gdns STJWD NW8 3 G8
Scottes La BCTR RM8 61 K7
Scott Farm Cl THDIT KT7 158 C7
Scott Gdns HEST TW5 102 C6
Scott Lidgett Crs
BERM/RHTH SE16 111 H1
Scotts Av HAYES BR2 167 G1
SUN TW16 140 C6
Scotts Dr HPTN TW12 142 B6
Scotts Farm Rd
HOR/WEW KT19 172 E5
Scott's La HAYES BR2 167 G2
Scotts Pas WOOL/PLUM * SE18 115 G3
Scotts Rd BMLY BR1 152 E6
LEY E10 58 A7
NWDGN UB2 102 B2
SHB W12 106 E1
Scott St WCHPL E1 92 D3
Scotts Wy SUN TW16 140 C6
Scottswood Cl BUSH WD23 21 J1
Scottswood Rd BUSH WD23 21 J1
Scott Trimmer Wy HEST TW5 122 D1
Scottwell Dr CDALE/KGS NW9 51 H4
Scoulding Rd CAN/RD E16 94 D5
Scouler St POP/IOD E14 94 B6
Scout La CLAP SW4 129 H2
Scout Wy MLHL NW7 37 F3
Scovell Crs STHWK * SE1 18 E2
Scovell Rd STHWK SE1 18 E2
Scrattons Ter BARK IG11 97 K1
Scriven St HACK E8 7 M3
Scrooby St CAT SE6 132 E5
Scrubs La WLSDN NW10 87 J2
Scrutton St SDTCH EC2A 13 J1
Scutari Rd EDUL SE22 131 J4
Scylla Crs HTHAIR TW6 120 E6
Scylla Rd HTHAIR TW6 120 E5
PECK SE15 131 J2
Seabright St BETH E2 92 D2
Seabrook Dr WWKM BR4 180 C1
Seabrook Gdns ROMW/RG RM7 62 C6
Seabrook Rd BCTR RM8 79 K2
Seaburn Cl RAIN RM13 99 G2
Seacole Cl ACT W3 87 F5
Seacourt Rd ABYW SE2 116 E1
Seacroft Gdns OXHEY WD19 33 H2
Seafield Rd FBAR/BDGN N11 40 D3
Seaford Cl RSLP HA4 64 B1
Seaford Rd EN EN1 30 A3
HTHAIR TW6 120 A4
SEVS/STOTM N15 55 K4
WALTH E17 57 K2
WEA W13 85 H7
Seaford St STPAN WC1H 5 K8
Seaforth Av NWMAL KT3 160 E4
Seaforth Crs HBRY N5 73 J4
Seaforth Gdns HOR/WEW KT19 173 H3
WCHMH N21 29 F6
WFD IG8 45 G4
Seager Buildings DEPT * SE8 112 D7
Seager Pl BOW E3 93 H4
Seagrave Cl WCHPL * E1 93 F4
Seagrave Rd FUL/PGN SW6 14 B9
Seagry Rd WAN E11 58 E5
Sealand Rd HTHAIR TW6 120 D5
Seal St HACK E8 74 B3
Searles Cl BTSEA SW11 108 D6
Searles Dr EHAM E6 96 B4
Searles Rd STHWK SE1 19 H5
Sears St CMBW SE5 110 E6
Seasprite Cl NTHLT UB5 83 H2
Seaton Av GDMY/SEVK IG3 78 E4
Seaton Cl LBTH SE11 18 B7
PLSTW E13 94 E3
PUT/ROE SW15 126 E6
WHTN TW2 123 J5
Seaton Gdns RSLP HA4 64 E2
Seaton Rd ALP/SUD * HA0 86 A1
DART DA1 138 D6
HYS/HAR UB3 101 G3
MTCM CR4 162 D1
WELL DA16 116 D6
WHTN TW2 123 H5
Seaton St UED N18 42 C4
Sebastian St FSBYE EC1V 6 D8
Sebastopol Rd ED N9 42 C3
Sebbon St IS N1 6 D2
Sebergham Gv MLHL NW7 37 J6
Sebert Rd FSTGT E7 77 F4
Sebright Rd BAR EN5 26 B1
Secker Crs KTN/HRWW/W HA3 34 C7
Secker St STHWK SE1 12 A9
Second Av ACT W3 87 H7
CHDH RM6 61 J4
DAGE RM10 98 D1
EN EN1 30 B4
HDN NW4 52 B3
HYS/HAR UB3 82 D7
MNPK E12 77 J3
MORT/ESHN SW14 126 B2
NKENS W10 88 C3
PLSTW E13 94 E2
UED N18 42 E3
WALTH E17 57 J4
WBLY HA9 67 K1
WOT/HER KT12 156 A5
Second Cl E/WMO/HCT KT8 157 G3
Second Cross Rd WHTN TW2 142 D1
Second Wy WBLY HA9 68 D3
Sedan Wy WALW SE17 19 J7
Sedcombe Cl SCUP DA14 155 H3
Sedcote Rd PEND EN3 30 E4
Sedding St KTBR SW1X 16 A5
Seddon Rd MRDN SM4 162 C4
Seddon St FSBYW WC1X 5 L8
Sedgebrook Rd
BKHTH/KID SE3 134 C1
Sedgecombe Av
KTN/HRWW/W HA3 49 J4
Sedgeford Rd SHB W12 87 H7
Sedgehill Rd CAT SE6 151 J4
Sedgemere Av EFNCH N2 53 G2
Sedgemere Rd ABYW SE2 116 D2
Sedgemoor Dr DAGE RM10 80 C3
Sedge Rd TOTM N17 42 E6
Sedgeway CAT SE6 133 J7
Sedgewood Cl HAYES BR2 167 J6
Sedgmoor Pl CMBW SE5 111 F6
Sedgwick Rd LEY E10 76 A1
Sedgwick St HOM E9 75 F4
Sedleigh Rd WAND/EARL SW18 127 J5
Sedlescombe Rd FUL/PGN SW6 107 J5
Sedley Pl MYFR/PKLN W1K 10 C5
Sedum Cl CDALE/KGS NW9 50 D4
Seeley Dr DUL SE21 150 A3
Seelig Av CDALE/KGS NW9 51 J6
Seely Rd TOOT SW17 148 A5
Seething La TWRH EC3N 13 K6
Seething Wells La SURB KT6 158 D5
Sefton Av KTN/HRWW/W HA3 34 D7
MLHL NW7 37 F4
Sefton Ct ENC/FH * EN2 29 H1
Sefton Rd CROY/NA CR0 165 H7
Sefton St PUT/ROE SW15 127 F1
Sekforde St CLKNW EC1R 12 C1
Sekhon Ter FELT TW13 142 A2
Selan Gdns YEAD UB4 83 F4
Selbie Av WLSDN NW10 69 H4
Selborne Av BXLY DA5 137 F7
MNPK E12 78 A3
Selborne Gdns GFD/PVL UB6 85 G1
HDN NW4 51 J3
Selborne Rd CMBW SE5 130 E1
CROY/NA CR0 178 A2
IL IG1 78 A1
NWMAL KT3 160 B1
SCUP DA14 155 H3
STHGT/OAK N14 40 E2
WALTH E17 57 H4
WDGN N22 41 F7
Selbourne Av SURB KT6 172 B1
Selby Cha RSLP HA4 65 F1
Selby Cl CHSGTN KT9 172 A6
CHST BR7 154 A5
Selby Gdns STHL UB1 84 A3
Selby Gn CAR SM5 162 D6
Selby Rd ASHF TW15 140 A5
CAR SM5 162 D6
EA W5 85 H3
PGE/AN SE20 165 H1
PLSTW E13 95 F4
TOTM N17 42 A5
WAN E11 76 C2
Selby St WCHPL E1 92 C3
Selden Rd PECK SE15 131 K1
Selhurst Cl WIM/MER SW19 127 G7
Selhurst New Rd SNWD SE25 165 F5
Selhurst Pl CROY/NA CR0 165 F5
Selhurst Rd ED N9 41 K2
SNWD SE25 165 F4
Selinas La BCTR RM8 62 A6
Selkirk Dr ERITH DA8 118 B7
Selkirk Rd TOOT SW17 147 J3
WHTN TW2 142 C1
Sellers Hall Cl FNCH N3 38 E6
Sellincourt Rd TOOT SW17 147 J6
Sellindge Cl BECK BR3 151 H6
Sellons Av WLSDN NW10 69 H7
Sellwood Dr BAR EN5 26 B4
Selsdon Av SAND/SEL CR2 177 K5
Selsdon Cl SURB KT6 159 F4
Selsdon Rd CRICK NW2 69 H1
PLSTW E13 77 G7
SAND/SEL CR2 177 K4
WAN E11 58 E6
WNWD SE27 149 H2
Selsdon Wy POP/IOD E14 112 E2
Selsea Pl STNW/STAM N16 74 A4
Selsey Crs WELL DA16 116 E7
Selsey St POP/IOD E14 93 J4
Selvage La MLHL NW7 37 F4
Selway Cl PIN HA5 47 F3
Selwood Pl SKENS SW7 15 G7
Selwood Rd CHEAM SM3 161 J7
CHSGTN KT9 171 K3
CROY/NA CR0 178 D1
Selwood Ter SKENS SW7 15 G7
Selworthy Cl WAN E11 58 E5
Selworthy Rd CAT SE6 151 H2
Selwyn Av CHING E4 44 A5
GDMY/SEVK IG3 61 F5
RCH/KEW TW9 125 G2
Selwyn Cl HSLWW TW4 122 D3
Selwyn Ct EDGW HA8 36 D6
Selwyn Crs WELL DA16 136 C3
Selwyn Rd BOW E3 93 H1
NWMAL KT3 160 A4
PLSTW E13 77 F7
WLSDN NW10 69 G6
Semley Pl BGVA SW1W 16 B6
Semley Rd STRHM/NOR SW16 163 K1
Senate St PECK SE15 131 K1
Seneca Rd THHTH CR7 164 D3
Senga Rd WLGTN SM6 163 F7
Senhouse Rd CHEAM SM3 174 B2
Senior St BAY/PAD W2 8 C2
Senlac Rd LEE/GVPK SE12 134 A7
Sennen Rd EN EN1 30 B6
Senrab St WCHPL E1 93 F5
Sentinel Cl NTHLT UB5 83 J3
September Wy STAN HA7 35 H5
Sequoia Cl BUSH WD23 22 D7
Sequoia Pk PIN HA5 34 B5
Serbin Cl LEY E10 58 A6
Serenaders Rd BRXN/ST SW9 130 B1
Serjeant's Inn EMB * EC4Y 12 B5
Serle St LINN WC2A 11 M4
Sermon La BLKFR EC4V 12 E5
Serpentine Rd BAY/PAD W2 9 K9
Service Route No 1 SRTFD E15 76 B6
Service Route No 2 SRTFD E15 76 B6
Service Route No 3 SRTFD E15 76 B5
Serviden Dr BMLY BR1 153 H7

Setchell Est STHWK SE1 19 L5
Setchell Rd STHWK SE1 19 L5
Setchell Wy STHWK SE1 19 L5
Seton Gdns DAGW RM9 79 J6
Settles St WCHPL E1 92 C5
Settrington Rd FUL/PGN SW6 128 A1
Seven Acres CAR SM5 175 J1
NTHWD HA6 32 E5
Sevenex Pde WBLY * HA9 68 A4
Seven Kings Rd GDMY/SEVK IG3 60 E7
Sevenoaks Rd BROCKY SE4 132 C5
Seven Sisters Rd HOLWY N7 73 F2
Seventh Av HYS/HAR UB3 82 E7
MNPK E12 77 K3
Severnake Cl POP/IOD E14 112 D3
Severn Av GPK RM2 63 K2
NKENS W10 88 C2
Severn Dr ESH/CLAY KT10 171 G1
Severn Wy WLSDN NW10 69 H4
Severus Rd BTSEA SW11 128 D3
Seville Ms IS N1 7 J2
Seville St KTBR SW1X 15 M2
Sevington Rd HDN NW4 51 K5
Sevington St MV/WKIL W9 8 C1
Seward Rd BECK BR3 166 A1
HNWL W7 104 B1
Sewardstone Rd BETH E2 92 E1
CHING E4 31 K3
Seward St FSBYE EC1V 6 D9
Sewdley St CLPT E5 75 F2
Sewell Rd ABYW SE2 116 B2
Sewell St PLSTW E13 94 E2
Sextant Av POP/IOD E14 113 G3
Sexton Cl RAIN RM13 81 H7
Seymer Rd ROM RM1 63 F2
Seymour Av EW KT17 173 K7
MRDN SM4 161 G6
TOTM N17 56 C1
Seymour Cl E/WMO/HCT KT8 157 H4
PIN HA5 33 K7
Seymour Dr HAYES BR2 168 E7
Seymour Gdns BROCKY SE4 132 A2
BRYLDS KT5 159 G4
FELT TW13 141 F3
IL IG1 59 K7
RSLP HA4 47 H7
TWK TW1 124 C6
Seymour Ms MBLAR W1H 10 A4
Seymour Pl MBLAR W1H 9 L3
SNWD SE25 165 J3
Seymour Rd CAR SM5 176 A4
CEND/HSY/T N8 55 H4
CHING E4 31 K7
CHSWK W4 105 K3
E/WMO/HCT KT8 157 H4
ED N9 42 D1
EHAM E6 77 H7
FNCH N3 39 F6
HPTN TW12 142 C4
KUT KT1 143 K7
LEY E10 57 H7
MTCM CR4 163 F6
WAND/EARL SW18 127 J6
WIM/MER SW19 146 B2
Seymour St BAY/PAD W2 9 L5
WOOL/PLUM SE18 115 H3
Seymour Ter PGE/AN SE20 150 D7
Seymour Vls PGE/AN SE20 150 D7
Seymour Wk WBPTN SW10 14 E9
Seymour Wy SUN TW16 140 C5
Seyssel St POP/IOD E14 113 F3
Shaa Rd ACT W3 87 F6
Shacklegate La TEDD TW11 142 E3
Shackleton Cl FSTH SE23 150 D1
Shackleton Rd STHL UB1 83 K6
Shacklewell La HACK E8 74 B4
Shacklewell Rd
STNW/STAM N16 74 B3
Shacklewell Rw HACK E8 74 B3
Shacklewell St BETH E2 7 M9
Shadbolt Av CHING E4 43 G4
Shadbolt Cl WPK KT4 173 H1
Shad Thames STHWK SE1 13 M9
Shadwell Dr NTHLT UB5 83 K2
Shadwell Gdns WCHPL * E1 92 E6
Shadwell Pierhead WAP E1W 92 E6
Shady Bush Cl BUSH WD23 22 C6
Shady La WAT WD17 21 F1
Shaef Wy TEDD TW11 143 G6
Shafter Rd DAGE RM10 80 E5
Shaftesbury Av BAR EN5 27 G3
EBED/NFELT TW14 121 K5
KTN/HRWW/W HA3 49 K5
MYFR/PICC W1J 11 G6
NWDGN UB2 103 F3
PEND EN3 31 F1
RYLN/HDSTN HA2 48 C7
Shaftesbury Cir
RYLN/HDSTN * HA2 48 C7
Shaftesbury Ct
RKW/CH/CXG * WD3 20 A4
Shaftesbury Gdns WLSDN NW10 87 G3
Shaftesbury Ms KENS * W8 14 B4
Shaftesbury Pde
RYLN/HDSTN * HA2 48 C7
Shaftesbury Pl BARB * EC2Y 12 E3
Shaftesbury Rd ARCH N19 54 E7
BECK BR3 166 C1
CAR SM5 162 C6
FSTGT E7 77 G6
LEY * E10 57 J7
RCH/KEW TW9 125 F2
ROM RM1 63 H5
UED N18 42 A5
WALTH E17 57 K4
WAT WD17 21 G2
The Shaftesburys BARK IG11 96 C1
Shaftesbury St IS N1 6 F6
Shaftesbury Ter
HMSMTH * W6 106 C3
Shaftesbury Wy WHTN TW2 142 D2
Shaftesbury Waye YEAD UB4 83 F4
Shafto Ms KTBR SW1X 15 L4
Shafton Ms HOM * E9 75 F7
Shafton Rd HOM E9 75 F7
Shakespeare Av
EBED/NFELT TW14 121 K5
FBAR/BDGN N11 40 C4
WLSDN NW10 68 E7
YEAD UB4 82 E5
Shakespeare Crs MNPK E12 77 K6
WLSDN NW10 69 F7
Shakespeare Dr
KTN/HRWW/W HA3 50 B5
Shakespeare Gdns EFNCH N2 53 K3
Shakespeare Rd ACT W3 86 E7
BXLYHN DA7 117 F7
DART DA1 139 K3
FNCH * N3 38 E7
HNHL SE24 130 C4
HNWL W7 85 F6
MLHL NW7 37 J3
ROM RM1 63 H5
WALTH E17 57 F1
Shakespeare Ter
RCH/KEW * TW9 125 H2
Shakespeare Wy FELT TW13 141 G3
Shakspeare Ms
STNW/STAM N16 74 A3
Shakspeare Wk
STNW/STAM N16 74 A3
Shalbourne Sq HOM E9 75 H5
Shalcomb St WBPTN SW10 108 B5
Shaldon Dr MRDN SM4 161 H4
RSLP HA4 65 G2
Shaldon Rd EDGW HA8 50 B1
Shalfleet Dr NKENS W10 88 B6
Shalford Ct IS * N1 6 C5
Shalimar Gdns ACT W3 86 E6
Shalimar Rd ACT W3 86 E6
Shallons Rd ELTH/MOT SE9 154 B3
Shalstone Rd
MORT/ESHN SW14 125 J2
Shalston Vls SURB KT6 159 G5
Shamrock Rd CROY/NA CR0 164 A5
Shamrock St CLAP SW4 129 J2
Shamrock Wy STHGT/OAK N14 28 B7
Shandon Rd CLAP SW4 129 H5
Shand St STHWK SE1 19 K1
Shandy St WCHPL E1 93 F4
Shanklin Gdns OXHEY WD19 33 G3
Shanklin Rd CEND/HSY/T N8 54 D4
SEVS/STOTM N15 56 C3
Shannon Cl CRICK NW2 70 B2
HEST TW5 102 C4
Shannon Gv BRXN/ST SW9 130 A3
Shannon Pl STJWD NW8 3 K5
Shannon Wy BECK BR3 151 K5
Shap Crs CAR SM5 162 E7
Shapland Wy PLMGR N13 41 F4
Shapwick Cl FBAR/BDGN N11 39 K4
Shardcroft Av HNHL SE24 130 C4
Shardeloes Rd BROCKY * SE4 132 C4
BROCKY SE4 132 C1
Shard's Sq PECK SE15 111 H5
Sharland Cl THHTH CR7 164 B5
Sharman Ct SCUP DA14 155 G3
Sharnbrooke Cl WELL DA16 136 D2
Sharon Cl SURB KT6 158 D7
Sharon Gdns HOM E9 74 E7
Sharon Rd CHSWK W4 106 A4
PEND EN3 31 G1
Sharples Hall St CAMTN NW1 3 M2
Sharps La RSLP HA4 46 B7
Sharp Wy DART DA1 139 J2
Sharratt St PECK SE15 111 K5
Sharsted St WALW SE17 18 C8
Sharvel La NTHLT UB5 64 E7
Shavers Pl MYFR/PICC W1J 11 G7
Shaw Av BARK IG11 98 A1
Shawbrooke Rd
ELTH/MOT SE9 134 C3
Shawbury Rd EDUL SE22 131 G4
The Shaw CHST * BR7 154 C6
Shaw Cl BUSH WD23 34 E1
EMPK RM11 63 K7
THMD SE28 97 H7
Shaw Dr WOT/HER KT12 156 B6
Shawfield Pk BMLY BR1 168 C1
Shawfield St CHEL SW3 15 K8
Shawford Rd HOR/WEW KT19 173 F5
Shaw Gdns BARK IG11 98 A1
Shaw Rd BMLY BR1 152 D2
EDUL SE22 131 F3
Shaw's Cottages FSTH SE23 151 G2
Shaw Sq WALTH E17 43 G7
Shaw Wy WLGTN SM6 176 E6
Shaxton Crs CROY/NA CR0 180 A7
Sheaf Cottages THDIT * KT7 157 K7
Shearing Dr MRDN SM4 162 B6
Shearling Wy HOLWY N7 72 E5
Shearman Rd BKHTH/KID SE3 133 J3
Shearwater Rd SUT SM1 174 D4
Shearwater Wy YEAD UB4 83 H5
Shearwood Cresent DART DA1 138 C2
Sheaths Cottages THDIT * KT7 158 C6
Sheaveshill Av CDALE/KGS NW9 51 G2
Sheaveshill Pde
CDALE/KGS * NW9 51 G3
Sheen Common Dr
RCHPK/HAM TW10 125 H3
Sheen Court Rd
RCHPK/HAM TW10 125 H3
Sheendale Rd RCH/KEW TW9 125 G3
Sheenewood SYD SE26 150 D4
Sheen Gate Gdns
MORT/ESHN SW14 125 K3
Sheen Gv IS N1 6 A3
Sheen La MORT/ESHN SW14 125 K3
Sheen Pk RCH/KEW TW9 125 G3
Sheen Rd RCHPK/HAM TW10 125 F3
Sheen Wy WLGTN SM6 177 F5
Sheen Wd MORT/ESHN SW14 125 K4
Sheepcote Cl HEST TW5 101 K6
Sheepcote La BTSEA SW11 128 E1
Sheepcote Rd HRW HA1 49 F5
Sheepcotes Rd CHDH RM6 61 K3
Sheephouse Wy NWMAL KT3 160 A7
Sheep La HACK E8 74 D7
Sheep Walk Ms
WIM/MER SW19 146 B5
Sheerwater Rd CAN/RD E16 95 H4
Sheffield Rd HTHAIR TW6 121 F5
Sheffield St LINN * WC2A 11 L5
Sheffield Ter KENS W8 14 A1
Sheffield Wy HTHAIR TW6 121 G4
Shefton Ri NTHWD HA6 32 E6
Shelbourne Cl PIN HA5 47 K2
Shelbourne Rd TOTM N17 42 D7
Shelburne Dr HSLWW TW4 123 F5
Shelburne Rd HOLWY N7 73 F3
Shelbury Cl SCUP DA14 155 G2
Shelbury Rd EDUL SE22 131 J4
Sheldon Av CLAY IG5 60 B1
HGT N6 53 K6
Sheldon Cl LEE/GVPK SE12 134 A4
PGE/AN SE20 150 D7
Sheldon Rd BXLYHN DA7 117 G7
CRICK NW2 70 B3
DAGW RM9 80 A6
UED N18 42 A3
Sheldon St CROY/NA CR0 177 J2
Sheldrake Cl CAN/RD E16 95 K7
Sheldrake Pl KENS W8 107 J1
Sheldrick Cl MTCM CR4 162 C1
Shelduck Cl FSTGT E7 76 D4
Sheldwich Ter HAYES * BR2 168 D5
Shelford Pl STNW/STAM N16 73 K2
Shelford Ri NRWD SE19 150 A6
Shelford Rd BAR EN5 26 A5
Shelgate Rd BTSEA SW11 128 E4
Shell Cl HAYES BR2 168 D5
Shellduck Cl CDALE/KGS NW9 51 G1
Shelley Av GFD/PVL UB6 84 D2
HCH RM12 81 H1
MNPK E12 77 J5
Shelley Cl EDGW HA8 36 C3
GFD/PVL UB6 84 D2
NTHWD HA6 32 D4
YEAD UB4 82 E4
Shelley Crs HEST TW5 102 C7
STHL UB1 83 K5
Shelley Dr WELL DA16 115 K7
Shelley Gdns ALP/SUD HA0 67 J1
Shelley Rd WLSDN NW10 69 F7
Shelley Wy WIM/MER SW19 147 H5
Shellgrove Rd
STNW/STAM * N16 74 A4
Shellness Rd CLPT E5 74 D4
Shell Rd LEW SE13 132 E2
Shellwood Rd BTSEA SW11 128 E1
Shelmerdine Cl BOW E3 93 J4
Shelson Av FELT TW13 140 D3
Shelson Pde FELT * TW13 140 D2
Shelton Rd WIM/MER SW19 146 E7
Shelton St LSQ/SEVD * WC2H 11 J5
Shenfield Rd WFD IG8 45 F6
Shenfield St IS N1 7 K6
Shenley Av RSLP HA4 64 D1
Shenley Rd BORE WD6 24 C2
CMBW SE5 111 F7
DART DA1 139 K5
HEST TW5 102 D7
Shepherd Cl FELT TW13 141 J3
Shepherdess Pl FSBYE EC1V 6 F7
Shepherdess Wk IS N1 6 F6
Shepherd Market
MYFR/PICC * W1J 10 C9
Shepherd's Bush Gn SHB W12 107 F1
Shepherd's Bush Market
SHB W12 107 F1
Shepherd's Bush Pl SHB * W12 107 G1
Shepherd's Bush Rd
WKENS W14 107 F2
Shepherds Cl CHDH RM6 61 K4
HGT N6 54 B5
Shepherds Gn CHST BR7 154 D6
Shepherd's Hl HGT N6 54 B5
Shepherds La DART DA1 138 D7
HOM * E9 75 F4
Shepherd's Leas
ELTH/MOT * SE9 135 J3
Shepherds Pl MYFR/PKLN W1K 10 A6
Shepherds Rd WATW WD18 20 D2
Shepherd St MYFR/PICC W1J 10 C9
Shepherds Wk BUSH WD23 34 D1
CRICK NW2 69 J1
HAMP NW3 71 H4
Shepherds Wy SAND/SEL CR2 179 F6
Shepiston La WDR/YW UB7 100 E3
Shepley Cl CAR SM5 176 A2
Sheppard Cl SURB KT6 159 F3
Sheppard Dr BERM/RHTH SE16 111 J4
Sheppard St CAN/RD E16 94 D3
Shepperton Rd IS N1 6 F3
STMC/STPC BR5 169 H5
Sheppey Cl ERITH DA8 118 E6
Sheppey Gdns DAGW RM9 79 J6
Sheppey Rd DAGW RM9 79 H6
Sheppey Wk IS N1 6 F1
Shepton Houses BETH * E2 92 E2
Sherard Rd ELTH/MOT SE9 134 D4
Sheraton Cl BORE WD6 24 B4
Sheraton Ms WATW * WD18 20 C3
Sherborne Av NWDGN UB2 103 F3
PEND EN3 30 E1
Sherborne Cl YEAD UB4 83 G5
Sherborne Crs CAR SM5 162 D6
Sherborne Gdns
CDALE/KGS NW9 50 C2
WEA W13 85 H5
Sherborne La MANHO EC4N 13 G6
Sherborne Pl NTHWD HA6 32 B5
Sherborne Rd CHEAM SM3 174 E1
CHSGTN KT9 172 A4
EBED/NFELT TW14 121 G7
STMC/STPC BR5 169 K4
Sherborne St IS N1 7 G3
Sherborne Vls WEA * W13 85 H4
Sherboro Rd SEVS/STOTM N15 56 B5
Sherbrooke Cl BXLYHN DA7 137 H3
Sherbrooke Rd FUL/PGN SW6 107 H6
Sherbrooke Ter
FUL/PGN * SW6 107 H6
Sherbrook Gdns WCHMH N21 29 H6
Shere Cl CHSGTN KT9 171 K4
Sheredan Rd CHING E4 44 B4
Shere Rd GNTH/NBYPK IG2 60 A4
Sherfield Cl NWMAL KT3 159 J3
Sherfield Gdns
PUT/ROE SW15 126 C5
Sheridan Ct DART DA1 139 K3
HSLWW TW4 122 D4
Sheridan Crs CHST BR7 169 G1
Sheridan Gdns
KTN/HRWW/W HA3 49 K5
Sheridan Pl HPTN TW12 142 B7
Sheridan Rd BELV DA17 117 H3
BXLYHN DA7 137 F2
FSTGT E7 76 D2
MNPK E12 77 J4
OXHEY WD19 21 H6
RCHPK/HAM TW10 143 J2
WIM/MER SW19 146 D7
Sheridan St WCHPL E1 92 D5
Sheridan Ter NTHLT * UB5 66 B4
Sheridan Wk CAR SM5 175 K4
GLDGN NW11 52 E5
Sheridan Wy BECK BR3 151 H7
Sheringham Av MNPK E12 77 K3
ROMW/RG RM7 62 E5
STHGT/OAK N14 28 D4
WHTN TW2 122 E7
Sheringham Dr BARK IG11 79 F4
Sheringham Rd HOLWY N7 73 G5
PGE/AN SE20 165 J1
Sherington Av PIN HA5 34 A6
Sherington Rd CHARL SE7 114 A5
Sherland Rd TWK TW1 124 A7
Sherlock Ms MHST W1U 10 A2
Sherman Rd BMLY BR1 152 E7
Shernhall St WALTH E17 58 A2
Sherrard Rd FSTGT E7 77 G5
Sherrards Wy BAR EN5 26 E4
Sherrick Green Rd
WLSDN NW10 69 K4
Sherriff Rd KIL/WHAMP NW6 70 E5
Sherringham Av FELT TW13 140 E2
TOTM N17 56 C1
Sherrock Gdns HDN NW4 51 J3
Sherry Ms BARK IG11 78 D6
Sherwin Rd NWCR SE14 112 A7
Sherwood SURB KT6 171 K1
Sherwood Av GFD/PVL UB6 66 E5
RSLP HA4 46 C5
STRHM/NOR SW16 148 D6
SWFD E18 59 F2
YEAD UB4 83 F3
Sherwood Cl BXLY DA5 136 D5
WALTH E17 57 H1
WEA W13 85 H7
Sherwood Ct MBLAR * W1H 9 L3
Sherwood Gdns BARK IG11 78 D6
POP/IOD E14 112 D3
STHWK SE1 111 H4
Sherwood House
RYLN/HDSTN * HA2 66 C2
Sherwood Park Av
BFN/LL DA15 136 B6
Sherwood Park Rd MTCM CR4 163 H3
SUT SM1 174 E4
Sherwood Rd BARK/HLT IG6 60 D3
CROY/NA CR0 165 J6
HDN NW4 52 A2
HPTN TW12 142 C4
RYLN/HDSTN HA2 66 C1
WELL DA16 135 K2
WIM/MER SW19 146 D6
Sherwoods Rd OXHEY WD19 21 J6
Sherwood St SOHO/SHAV W1D 10 F6
TRDG/WHET N20 39 H2
Sherwood Ter TRDG/WHET N20 39 H2
Sherwood Wy WWKM BR4 180 A1
Shetland Cl BORE WD6 25 F5
Shetland Rd BOW E3 93 H1
Shield Dr BTFD TW8 104 C5
Shieldhall St ABYW SE2 116 D3
Shield Rd ASHF TW15 140 A3
Shifford Pth FSTH * SE23 151 F2
Shillibeer Pl MBLAR W1H 9 K3
Shillingford St IS * N1 6 D3
Shilling Pl HNWL * W7 85 G7
Shinfield St SHB W12 88 A5
Shinglewell Rd ERITH DA8 117 H6
Shinners Cl SNWD SE25 165 H4
Ship & Mermaid Rw
STHWK * SE1 19 H1
Shipka Rd BAL SW12 129 G7
Ship La MORT/ESHN SW14 125 K2
Shipman Rd CAN/RD E16 95 F5
FSTH SE23 151 F1
Ship St DEPT SE8 112 D7
Ship Tavern Pas BANK EC3V 13 J6
Shipton Cl BCTR RM8 79 K2
Shipton St BETH E2 7 M7
Shipwright Rd
BERM/RHTH SE16 112 B1
Shipwright Yd STHWK * SE1 13 J9
Shirburn Cl FSTH SE23 131 K6
Shirbutt St POP/IOD E14 93 J6
Shirebrook Rd BKHTH/KID SE3 134 C1
Shire Ct EW KT17 173 H6
Shirehall Cl HDN NW4 52 B5
Shirehall Gdns HDN NW4 52 B5
Shirehall La HDN NW4 52 B5
Shirehall Pk HDN NW4 52 B5
Shire Horse Wy ISLW TW7 124 A2
Shire La ORP BR6 181 K6
Shiremeade BORE WD6 24 B4
The Shires RCHPK/HAM TW10 144 A3
Shirland Ms MV/WKIL W9 88 D2
Shirland Rd MV/WKIL W9 2 B9
Shirley Av BXLY DA5 136 E6
CROY/NA CR0 165 K7
SUT SM1 175 J3
Shirley Church Rd
CROY/NA CR0 179 F2
Shirley Cl DART DA1 139 F3
HSLW TW3 123 H4
WALTH * E17 57 K4
Shirley Crs BECK BR3 166 B3
Shirley Dr HSLW TW3 123 H4
Shirley Gdns BARK IG11 78 E5
HNWL W7 85 F7
Shirley Gv BTSEA SW11 129 F2
ED N9 30 E6
Shirley Hills Rd CROY/NA CR0 179 F4
Shirley Oaks Rd CROY/NA CR0 166 A7
Shirley Park Rd CROY/NA CR0 165 J7
Shirley Rd BFN/LL DA15 154 E2
CHSWK W4 106 A1
CROY/NA CR0 165 J7
ENC/FH EN2 29 J2
SRTFD E15 76 C6
WLGTN SM6 176 C7
Shirley Rw SNWD * SE25 165 H1
Shirley St CAN/RD E16 94 D5
Shirley Wy CROY/NA CR0 179 H2
Shirlock Rd HAMP NW3 71 K3
Shobden Rd TOTM N17 41 K7
Shobroke Cl CRICK NW2 70 A2
Shoebury Rd EHAM E6 77 K6
Shoe La FLST/FETLN EC4A 12 B4
Shooters Av KTN/HRWW/W HA3 49 J3
Shooters Hl WOOL/PLUM SE18 114 E7
Shooters Hill Rd
BKHTH/KID SE3 113 H7
Shoot-Up Hl CRICK NW2 70 C5
Shore Cl EBED/NFELT TW14 121 K6
HPTN TW12 141 J4
Shoreditch High St BETH E2 7 K8
WCHPL E1 13 K2
Shore Gv FELT TW13 142 A1
Shoreham Cl CROY/NA CR0 165 K5
WAND/EARL SW18 128 A4
Shoreham Rd STMC/STPC BR5 155 H7
Shoreham Rd (East)
HTHAIR TW6 120 B4
Shoreham Rd (West)
HTHAIR TW6 120 B4
Shoreham Wy HAYES BR2 167 K5
Shore Pl HOM E9 74 E6
Shore Rd HOM E9 74 E6
Shorncliffe Rd CMBW SE5 19 L8
Shorndean St CAT SE6 133 F7
Shorne Cl BFN/LL DA15 136 C5
Shornefield Cl BMLY BR1 169 F2
Shorrolds Rd FUL/PGN SW6 107 K6
Shortcroft Rd EW KT17 173 H6
Shorter St WCHPL E1 13 L6
Shortgate NFNCH/WDSP N12 38 D3
Shortlands HMSMTH W6 107 G3
HYS/HAR UB3 101 G5
Shortlands Cl BELV DA17 117 G2
UED N18 41 K2
Shortlands Gdns HAYES BR2 167 H1
Shortlands Gv HAYES BR2 167 G2
Shortlands Rd HAYES BR2 167 G2
KUTN/CMB KT2 144 B6
LEY E10 57 K6
Short La STWL/WRAY TW19 120 C6
Short Rd CHSWK W4 106 B5
STWL/WRAY TW19 120 B5
WAN E11 76 C1
Shorts Cft CDALE/KGS NW9 50 D3
Shorts Gdns LSQ/SEVD * WC2H 11 J5
Shorts Rd CAR SM5 175 J3
Short St STHWK SE1 18 B1
Shortway ELTH/MOT SE9 134 D2
Short Wy NFNCH/WDSP N12 39 J5
WHTN TW2 123 H6
Shotfield WLGTN SM6 176 B5
Shott Cl SUT SM1 175 G4
Shottendane Rd
FUL/PGN * SW6 107 K7
Shottery Cl ELTH/MOT SE9 153 J2
Shottfield Av
MORT/ESHN SW14 126 B3
Shoulder of Mutton Aly
POP/IOD E14 93 G6
Shouldham St MBLAR W1H 9 K3
Showers Wy HYS/HAR UB3 82 E7
Shrapnel Cl WOOL/PLUM SE18 114 D6
Shrapnel Rd ELTH/MOT SE9 134 E2
Shrewsbury Av
KTN/HRWW/W HA3 50 A3
MORT/ESHN SW14 125 K3
Shrewsbury Cl SURB KT6 172 A1
Shrewsbury Crs WLSDN NW10 69 F7
Shrewsbury La
WOOL/PLUM SE18 115 G7
Shrewsbury Ms BAY/PAD W2 8 A4
Shrewsbury Rd BAY/PAD W2 8 A3
BECK BR3 166 B2
CAR SM5 162 D6
FBAR/BDGN N11 40 D5
HTHAIR TW6 121 F5
MNPK E12 77 H5
Shrewsbury St NKENS W10 88 A3
Shrewton Rd TOOT * SW17 147 K6
Shroffold Rd BMLY BR1 152 C3
Shropshire Cl MTCM CR4 163 K3
Shropshire Rd WDGN N22 41 F6
Shroton St CAMTN NW1 9 J2
The Shrubberies SWFD E18 58 E1
The Shrubbery SURB * KT6 159 F7
Shrubbery Gdns WCHMH N21 29 H6
Shrubbery Rd STHL UB1 83 K7
STRHM/NOR SW16 148 E3
Shrubland Cl TRDG/WHET * N20 39 H1
Shrubland Gv WPK KT4 174 A2
Shrubland Rd HACK E8 74 C7
WALTH E17 57 J4
Shrublands Av CROY/NA CR0 179 J3
Shrublands Cl SYD SE26 150 E2
Shrubsall Cl ELTH/MOT SE9 134 D7
Shuna Wk IS * N1 73 K5
Shurland Av EBAR EN4 27 H5
Shurland Gdns PECK * SE15 111 G6
Shuters Sq WKENS * W14 107 J4
Shuttle Cl BFN/LL DA15 136 A6
Shuttlemead BXLY DA5 137 G6
Shuttle Rd DART DA1 138 D2
Shuttle St WCHPL E1 92 C3
Shuttleworth Rd BTSEA SW11 128 C1
Sibella Rd CLAP SW4 129 J1
Sibley Cl BXLYHS DA6 137 F4
Sibley Ct UX/CGN UB8 82 A4
Sibley Gv MNPK E12 77 J6
Sibthorpe Rd LEE/GVPK SE12 134 A6
Sibthorp Rd MTCM * CR4 162 E1
Sibton Rd CAR SM5 162 D6
Sicilian Av NOXST/BSQ * WC1A 11 K3
Sidbury St FUL/PGN SW6 107 H7
Sidcup By-Pass Rd SCUP DA14 154 E3
Sidcup Hl SCUP DA14 155 H4
Sidcup Hill Gdns SCUP * DA14 155 J4
Sidcup Pl SCUP DA14 155 G4
Sidcup Rd ELTH/MOT SE9 134 C7
LEE/GVPK SE12 134 A4
Siddeley Dr HSLWW TW4 122 D2
Siddons La CAMTN NW1 9 M1
Siddons Rd CROY/NA CR0 177 G2
FSTH SE23 151 G1
TOTM N17 42 C7
Side Rd WALTH E17 57 H4
Sidewood Rd ELTH/MOT SE9 135 J7
Sidford Pl STHWK SE1 17 M4
The Sidings WAN E11 58 A7
Sidmouth Av ISLW TW7 123 K1
Sidmouth Cl OXHEY WD19 33 F1
Sidmouth Dr RSLP HA4 64 E2
Sidmouth Pde CRICK * NW2 70 A6
Sidmouth Rd LEY E10 76 A2
PECK SE15 111 G7
WELL DA16 116 D6
WLSDN NW10 70 A6
Sidmouth St STPAN WC1H 5 K8
Sidney Av PLMGR N13 41 F5
Sidney Elson Wy EHAM E6 96 A1
Sidney Gdns BTFD TW8 104 E5
Sidney Gv FSBYE EC1V 6 C6
Sidney Rd BECK BR3 166 B1
BRXN/ST SW9 130 A1
FSTGT E7 76 E2
RYLN/HDSTN HA2 48 C2
SNWD SE25 165 H4
TWK TW1 124 B5
WDGN N22 41 F6
Sidney Sq WCHPL * E1 92 E4
Sidney St WCHPL E1 92 D4
Sidworth St HACK E8 74 D6
Siebert Rd BKHTH/KID SE3 113 K5
Siemens Rd WOOL/PLUM SE18 114 C2
Sienna Ter CRICK * NW2 69 J1
Sierra Dr DAGW RM9 98 E1
Sigdon Rd HACK E8 74 C4
The Sigers RSLP HA4 47 F5
Signmakers Yd CAMTN * NW1 4 D4
Sigrist Sq KUTN/CMB KT2 144 A7
Silbury Av MTCM CR4 147 J7
Silbury St IS * N1 7 G7
Silchester Rd NKENS W10 88 B5
Silecroft Rd BXLYHN DA7 117 H7
Silesia Buildings HACK E8 74 D6
Silex St STHWK SE1 18 D2
Silk Cl LEE/GVPK SE12 133 K4
Silkfield Rd CDALE/KGS NW9 51 G4
Silk Mill Rd OXHEY WD19 21 F6
Silk Mills Pth LEW SE13 133 F2
Silkstream Pde EDGW * HA8 36 E7
Silkstream Rd EDGW HA8 36 E7
Silk St BARB EC2Y 12 F2
Silsoe Rd WDGN N22 55 F2
Silver Birch Av CHING E4 43 H4
Silver Birch Cl CAT SE6 151 H2
FBAR/BDGN N11 40 A5
THMD SE28 97 G7
Silverbirch Wk HAMP * NW3 71 K5
Silvercliffe Gdns EBAR EN4 27 J3
Silver Cl KTN/HRWW/W HA3 34 D6

NWCR * SE14 112 B6
Silver Crs CHSWK W4 105 J3
Silverdale CAMTN NW1 4 E6
ENC/FH EN2 28 E3
SYD SE26 150 E3
Silverdale Cl HNWL W7 84 E7
NTHLT UB5 65 K4
SUT SM1 174 D3
Silverdale Dr ELTH/MOT SE9 153 J1
HCH RM12 81 K4
SUN TW16 156 A1
Silverdale Gdns HYS/HAR UB3 101 K1
Silverdale Rd BUSH WD23 21 J4
BXLYHN DA7 137 J1
CHING E4 44 B5
HYS/HAR UB3 101 K1
STMC/STPC BR5 169 H3
Silverdene NFNCH/WDSP * N12 39 F5
Silver Dene PUT/ROE * SW15 127 F4
Silverhall St ISLW TW7 124 B2
Silverholme Cl
KTN/HRWW/W HA3 50 A6
Silver La WWKM BR4 180 B1
Silverleigh Rd THHTH CR7 164 A3
Silvermere Dr UED * N18 43 F4
Silvermere Rd LEW SE13 132 D5
Silvermere Rw SNWD * SE25 165 H1
Silver Rd SHB W12 88 B6
Silver Spring Cl ERITH DA8 117 J5
Silverston Wy STAN HA7 35 J5
Silver St EN EN1 29 K2
UED N18 41 K3
Silverthorne Rd VX/NE SW8 129 G1
Silverthorn Gdns CHING E4 43 J1
Silverton Rd HMSMTH W6 107 G6
Silvertown Wy CAN/RD E16 94 D6
Silvertree La GFD/PVL UB6 84 D2
Silver Wk BERM/RHTH SE16 93 H7
Silver Wy ROMW/RG RM7 62 D2
Silverwood Cl BECK BR3 151 J6
CROY/NA CR0 179 H7
NTHWD HA6 32 A7
Silvester Rd EDUL SE22 131 G4
Silvester St STHWK SE1 19 G2
Silwood St BERM/RHTH SE16 112 A4
Simmil Rd ESH/CLAY KT10 170 E4
Simmons Cl TRDG/WHET N20 27 J7
Simmons Ga ESH/CLAY KT10 170 C4
Simmons La CHING E4 44 B1
Simmons Rd
WOOL/PLUM SE18 115 G4
Simmons' Wy TRDG/WHET N20 39 J1
Simms Cl CAR SM5 175 J1
Simms Gdns EFNCH N2 53 G1
Simms Rd STHWK SE1 111 H3
Simnel Rd LEE/GVPK SE12 134 A6
Simon Cl NTGHL W11 88 D6
Simonds Rd LEY E10 75 J1
Simone Cl BMLY BR1 153 H7
Simons Wk SRTFD E15 76 B4
Simpson Cl WCHMH N21 29 F4
Simpson Dr ACT W3 87 F5
Simpson Rd HSLWW TW4 122 E5
RAIN RM13 81 H5
RCHPK/HAM TW10 143 J3
Simpson's Rd HAYES BR2 167 K2
POP/IOD E14 93 K6
Simpson St BTSEA SW11 128 D1
Simpson Wy SURB KT6 158 D5
Sims Cl ROM RM1 63 H3
Sinclair Dr BELMT SM2 175 F7
Sinclair Gdns WKENS W14 107 G1
Sinclair Gv GLDGN NW11 52 B5
Sinclair Rd CHING E4 43 H4
WKENS W14 107 H2
Singapore Rd HNWL W7 85 G7
Singer St FSBYE EC1V 7 H8
Singleton Cl CROY/NA CR0 164 D6
HCH RM12 81 H3
WIM/MER SW19 147 K6
Singleton Rd DAGW RM9 80 B4
Singleton Scarp
NFNCH/WDSP N12 38 E4
Sinnott Rd WALTH E17 43 F7
Sion Rd TWK TW1 124 C7
Sipson Cl WDR/YW UB7 100 D5
Sipson La WDR/YW UB7 100 E5
Sipson Rd WDR/YW UB7 100 E3
Sipson Wy WDR/YW UB7 100 D6
Sir Abraham Dawes Cottages
PUT/ROE * SW15 127 H3
Sir Alexander Cl ACT W3 87 H7
Sir Cyril Black Wy
WIM/MER SW19 146 D6
Sirdar Rd MTCM CR4 148 A5
NTGHL W11 88 B6
WDGN N22 55 H2
Sir John Kirk Cl CMBW SE5 110 D6
Sir Thomas Moore Est
CHEL SW3 108 C5
Sirus Rd NTHWD HA6 32 E4
Sise La MANHO * EC4N 13 G5
Siskin Cl BORE WD6 24 C3
BUSH WD23 21 J3
Sisley Rd BARK IG11 78 E7
Sispara Gdns
WAND/EARL SW18 127 J5
Sissinghurst Cl BMLY BR1 152 C4
Sissinghurst Rd CROY/NA CR0 165 H6
Sister Mabel's Wy PECK * SE15 111 H6
Sisters Av BTSEA SW11 128 E3
Sistova Rd BAL SW12 129 G7
Sisulu Pl BRXN/ST SW9 130 B2
Sittingbourne Av EN EN1 29 K5
Sitwell Gv STAN HA7 35 F4
Siverst Cl NTHLT UB5 66 B5
Siviter Wy DAGE RM10 80 D6
Siward Rd HAYES BR2 168 A2
TOOT SW17 147 G2
TOTM N17 41 K7
Sixth Av HYS/HAR UB3 82 D7
MNPK E12 77 K3
NKENS W10 88 C3
Sixth Cross Rd WHTN TW2 142 C2
Skardu Rd CRICK NW2 70 C4
Skeena Hl WAND/EARL SW18 127 H6
Skeffington Rd EHAM E6 77 K7
Skelbrook St
WAND/EARL SW18 147 F1
Skelgill Rd PUT/ROE SW15 127 J3
Skelley Rd SRTFD E15 76 D6
Skelton Cl HACK * E8 74 B5
Skelton Rd FSTGT E7 76 E5
Skelton's La LEY E10 57 K6
Skelwith Rd HMSMTH W6 107 F5
Skerne Rd KUTN/CMB KT2 143 K7
Sketchley Gdns
BERM/RHTH SE16 112 A4
Sketty Rd EN EN1 30 B2
Skiers St SRTFD E15 76 C7
Skiffington Cl
BRXS/STRHM SW2 130 B7
Skinner Pl BGVA * SW1W 16 A6
Skinners La BLKFR EC4V 12 F6
HEST TW5 103 G7
Skinner St CLKNW EC1R 6 B8
Skipsey Av EHAM E6 95 K2
Skipton Cl FBAR/BDGN N11 40 A5
Skipton Dr HYS/HAR UB3 101 F2
Skipworth Rd HOM E9 74 E7
Skylines Village POP/IOD * E14 113 F1
Sky Peals Rd WFD IG8 44 B7
Skyport Dr WDR/YW UB7 100 A6
The Slade WOOL/PLUM SE18 115 K5
Sladebrook Rd BKHTH/KID SE3 134 C2
Sladedale Rd
WOOL/PLUM SE18 115 K4
Slade Gdns ERITH DA8 118 C7
Slade Green Rd ERITH DA8 118 C7
Sladen Pl CLPT E5 74 D3
Slades Cl ENC/FH EN2 29 G2
Slades Dr CHST BR7 154 C3
Slades Gdns ENC/FH EN2 29 G1
Slades Hl ENC/FH EN2 29 G2
Slades Ri ENC/FH EN2 29 G2
Slade Wk WALW SE17 110 C5
Slagrove Pl LEW SE13 132 D4
Slaidburn St WBPTN SW10 108 B5
Slaithwaite Rd LEW SE13 133 F3
Slaney Pl HOLWY N7 73 G4
Slaney Rd ROM RM1 63 G4
Slattery Rd FELT TW13 122 B7
Sleaford Gn OXHEY WD19 33 H2
Sleaford St VX/NE SW8 109 H6
Slievemore Cl CLAP SW4 129 J2
Slingsby Pl COVGDN WC2E 11 J6
Slippers Pl BERM/RHTH SE16 111 J2
Sloane Av CHEL SW3 15 K6
Sloane Ct East CHEL SW3 16 A7
Sloane Ct West CHEL SW3 16 A7
Sloane Gdns BGVA SW1W 16 A6
Sloane Sq BGVA SW1W 15 M6
Sloane St KTBR SW1X 15 M2
Sloane Ter KTBR SW1X 15 M5
Sloane Wk CROY/NA CR0 166 C5
Slocum Cl THMD SE28 97 J6
Slough La CDALE/KGS NW9 50 E5
Sly St WCHPL * E1 92 D5
Smaldon Cl WDR/YW UB7 100 D2
Smallberry Av ISLW TW7 124 A1
Smallbrook Ms BAY/PAD W2 9 G5
Smalley Cl STNW/STAM N16 74 B2
Smallwood Rd TOOT SW17 147 H3
Smarden Cl BELV DA17 117 H4
Smart's Pl HHOL WC1V 11 K4
UED N18 42 C4
Smart St BETH E2 93 F2
Smeaton Rd WAND/EARL SW18 127 K6
WFD IG8 45 K4
Smeaton St WAP E1W 92 D7
Smedley St VX/NE SW8 129 J1
Smeed Rd BOW E3 75 J6
Smiles Pl LEW SE13 133 F1
Smith Cl BERM/RHTH SE16 93 F7
Smithfield St STBT EC1A 12 C3
Smithies Rd ABYW SE2 116 C3
Smith's Ct SOHO/SHAV * W1D 11 G6
Smithson Rd TOTM N17 41 K7
Smith St BRYLDS KT5 159 G5
CHEL SW3 15 L7
WATW WD18 21 G3
Smith Ter CHEL SW3 15 L8
Smithwood Cl WIM/MER SW19 127 H7
Smithy St WCHPL E1 92 E4
Smugglers Wy
WAND/EARL SW18 128 A3
Smyrk's Rd WALW SE17 19 K8
Smyrna Rd KIL/WHAMP NW6 2 A2
Smythe St POP/IOD E14 93 K6
Snakes La EBAR EN4 28 B2
Snakes La East WFD IG8 45 G5
Snakes La West WFD IG8 44 E5
Snaresbrook Dr STAN HA7 35 K3
Snaresbrook Rd WAN E11 58 D3
Snarsgate St NKENS W10 88 A4
Sneath Av GLDGN NW11 52 D6
Snell's Pk UED N18 42 B5
Sneyd Rd CRICK NW2 70 A4
Snipe Cl ERITH DA8 118 E6
Snowbury Rd FUL/PGN SW6 128 A1
Snowden Dr CDALE/KGS NW9 51 G5
Snowden Crs HYS/HAR UB3 101 F2
Snowdon Rd West
HTHAIR TW6 121 F5
Snowdown Cl PGE/AN SE20 150 E7
Snowdrop Cl HPTN TW12 142 A5
Snow Hl STBT EC1A 12 C3
Snowsfields STHWK SE1 19 H1
Snowshill Rd MNPK E12 77 J4
Snowy Fielder Waye ISLW TW7 124 C1
Soames St PECK SE15 131 G2
Soames Wk NWMAL KT3 145 G7
Soho Sq SOHO/SHAV W1D 11 G5
Soho St SOHO/SHAV W1D 11 G4
Sojourner Truth Cl HACK * E8 74 D5
Solander Gdns WCHPL E1 92 D6
Solar Ct WATW * WD18 20 D4
Solebay St WCHPL E1 93 G3
Solent Ri PLSTW E13 94 E2
Solent Rd KIL/WHAMP NW6 70 E4
Solna Av PUT/ROE SW15 127 F4
Solna Rd WCHMH N21 29 K7
Solomon Av UED N18 42 C3
Solomon's Pas PECK SE15 131 J3
Solon New Rd CLAP SW4 129 K3
Solon Rd BRXS/STRHM SW2 129 K3
Solway Cl HACK E8 74 B5
HSLWW TW4 122 D2
Solway Rd EDUL SE22 131 H3
WDGN N22 41 H7
Somaford Gv EBAR EN4 27 H5
Somali Rd CRICK NW2 70 D3
Somerby Rd BARK IG11 78 D6
Somercoates Cl EBAR EN4 27 J2
Somerfield Rd FSBYPK N4 73 H1
Somerford Cl PIN HA5 46 E3
Somerford Gv STNW/STAM N16 74 B3
TOTM N17 42 C6
Somerford St WCHPL * E1 92 D3
Somerford Wy
BERM/RHTH SE16 112 B1
Somerhill Av BFN/LL DA15 136 C6
Somerhill Rd WELL DA16 136 C1
Somerleyton Rd BRXN/ST SW9 130 B3
Somersby Gdns REDBR IG4 59 K4
Somers Cl CAMTN * NW1 5 G5
Somers Crs BAY/PAD W2 9 J5
Somerset Av CHSGTN KT9 171 K3
RYNPK SW20 160 E1
WELL DA16 136 A4
Somerset Cl NWMAL KT3 160 B5
TOTM N17 55 K1
WFD IG8 44 E7
Somerset Gdns HGT N6 54 A6
LEW SE13 132 E1
STRHM/NOR SW16 164 A2
TEDD TW11 142 E4
TOTM * N17 42 A6
Somerset Rd BAR EN5 27 F4
BTFD TW8 104 D5
CHSWK W4 106 A2
DART DA1 138 E5
HDN NW4 52 A3
HRW HA1 48 C5
KUT KT1 159 G1
STHL UB1 84 A4
TEDD TW11 142 E4
TOTM N17 56 B2
UED N18 42 B4
WALTH E17 57 J4
WEA W13 85 H7
WIM/MER SW19 146 C2
Somerset Sq WKENS * W14 107 H2
Somerset St Little TWRH EC3N 13 L5
Somerset Waye HEST TW5 102 D5
Somersham Rd BXLYHN DA7 137 F1
Somers Pl BRXS/STRHM SW2 130 A6
Somers Rd BRXS/STRHM SW2 130 A5
WALTH E17 57 H3
Somers Wy BUSH WD23 22 C6
Somerton Av RCH/KEW TW9 125 J2
Somerton Rd CRICK NW2 70 B2
PECK SE15 131 J3
Somertrees Av LEE/GVPK SE12 153 F1
Somervell Rd
RYLN/HDSTN HA2 65 K4
Somerville Av BARN SW13 107 F5
Somerville Rd CHDH RM6 61 J4
DART DA1 139 J5
PGE/AN SE20 151 F6
Sonderburg Rd HOLWY N7 73 F1
Sondes St WALW SE17 19 G9
Sonia Cl OXHEY WD19 21 G6
Sonia Gdns CRICK NW2 69 H3
HEST TW5 103 F6
NFNCH/WDSP N12 39 G3
Sonning Gdns HPTN TW12 141 J5
Sonning Rd CROY/NA CR0 165 H5
Soper Cl CHING E4 43 H4
FSTH SE23 132 A7
Sophia Cl HOLWY N7 73 F5
Sophia Rd CAN/RD E16 95 F5
LEY E10 57 K7
Sophia Sq BERM/RHTH SE16 93 G6
Sopwith Av CHSGTN KT9 172 A4
Sopwith Cl RCHPK/HAM TW10 144 B4
Sopwith Rd HEST TW5 102 B6
Sopwith Wy KUTN/CMB KT2 144 A7
VX/NE SW8 109 G6
Sorrel Bank CROY/NA CR0 179 G7
Sorrel Cl THMD SE28 97 G7
Sorrel Gdns EHAM E6 95 J4
Sorrel La POP/IOD E14 94 B5
Sorrell Cl BRXN/ST * SW9 130 B1
NWCR SE14 112 B6
Sorrel Wk ROM RM1 63 H2
Sorrento Rd SUT SM1 175 F2
Sotheby Rd HBRY N5 73 J3
Sotheran Cl HACK E8 74 C7
Sotheron Rd WAT WD17 21 G1
Soudan Rd BTSEA SW11 108 E7
Souldern Rd WKENS * W14 107 G2
Souldern St WATW WD18 21 F4
South Access Rd WALTH E17 57 G6
South Acre CDALE/KGS NW9 51 H1
Southacre Wy PIN HA5 33 G7
South Africa Rd SHB W12 87 K6
Southall Ct STHL * UB1 83 K6
Southall La HEST TW5 102 A4
Southall Pl STHWK SE1 19 G2
Southampton Buildings
LINN * WC2A 12 A3
Southampton Gdns
MTCM CR4 163 K4
Southampton Pl
NOXST/BSQ WC1A 11 K3
Southampton Rd HAMP NW3 71 K4
HTHAIR TW6 120 C5
Southampton Rw RSQ WC1B 11 K3
Southampton St COVGDN WC2E 11 K6
Southampton Wy CMBW SE5 110 E6
Southam St NKENS W10 88 C3
South Ap NTHWD HA6 32 B2
South Audley St
MYFR/PKLN W1K 10 B7
South Av CAR SM5 176 A6
CHING E4 31 K6
RCH/KEW * TW9 125 H1
STHL UB1 83 K6
South Avenue Gdns STHL UB1 83 K6
South Bank STHWK SE1 12 B7
SURB KT6 159 F5
Southbank THDIT KT7 158 C6
South Bank Ter SURB * KT6 159 F5
South Birkbeck Rd WAN E11 76 B2
South Black Lion La
HMSMTH W6 106 D4
South Bolton Gdns
WBPTN SW10 14 D7
Southborough Cl SURB KT6 158 E7
Southborough La HAYES BR2 168 E4
Southborough Rd BMLY BR1 168 D2
HOM E9 74 E7
SURB KT6 159 F7
Southborough Rd (The Lane)
SURB * KT6 159 F7
Southbourne HAYES BR2 167 K6
Southbourne Av
CDALE/KGS NW9 50 E1
Southbourne Cl PIN HA5 47 J6
Southbourne Crs HDN NW4 52 C3
Southbourne Gdns IL IG1 78 C4
LEE/GVPK SE12 134 A4
RSLP HA4 47 F7
Southbridge Pl CROY/NA CR0 177 J3
Southbridge Rd CROY/NA CR0 177 J3
Southbridge Wy NWDGN UB2 102 D1
Southbrook Rd LEW SE13 133 H5
STRHM/NOR SW16 148 E7
Southbury Av EN EN1 30 C3
Southbury Rd EN EN1 30 C3
South Carriage Dr SKENS SW7 15 J2
Southchurch Ct PLMGR N13 41 F4
Southchurch Rd EHAM E6 95 K1
South Cl BAR EN5 26 D2
BXLYHS DA6 136 E3
DAGE RM10 80 C7
FELT TW13 142 A2
HGT N6 54 B5
PIN HA5 47 K6
WDR/YW UB7 100 C2
South Colonnade POP/IOD E14 93 J7
The South Colonnade
POP/IOD E14 93 K7
Southcombe St WKENS W14 107 H3
Southcote Av BRYLDS KT5 159 J6
FELT TW13 140 E1
Southcote Ri RSLP HA4 46 B6
Southcote Rd ARCH N19 72 C3
SNWD SE25 165 J4
WALTH E17 57 F4
South Countess Rd WALTH E17 57 H2
South Crs CAN/RD E16 94 B4
Southcroft Av WELL DA16 135 K2
WWKM BR4 180 A1
Southcroft Rd
STRHM/NOR SW16 148 B5
South Cross Rd BARK/HLT IG6 60 C4
South Croxted Rd DUL SE21 149 K2
Southdean Gdns
WIM/MER SW19 146 D1
South Dene MLHL NW7 37 F2
Southdown Av HNWL W7 104 B2
Southdown Crs
GNTH/NBYPK IG2 60 E4
RYLN/HDSTN HA2 48 C7
Southdown Dr RYNPK SW20 146 B6
Southdown Rd CAR SM5 176 A7
EMPK RM11 63 K6
RYNPK SW20 146 B7
Southdown Vls
SEVS/STOTM * N15 55 H4
South Dr RSLP HA4 46 C7
South Ealing Rd EA W5 104 E1
South Eastern Av ED N9 42 B2
South Eaton Pl BGVA SW1W 16 B5
South Eden Park Rd BECK BR3 166 E4
South Edwardes Sq KENS W8 107 J2
South End CROY/NA CR0 177 J4
KENS W8 14 D3
Southend Cl ELTH/MOT SE9 135 G5
Southend Crs ELTH/MOT SE9 135 F5
Southend La CAT SE6 151 H3
Southend Rd BECK BR3 151 J7
South End Rd HAMP NW3 71 J3
RAIN RM13 81 J7
Southend Rd REDBR IG4 59 J2
Southend Rd (North Circular)
WALTH E17 44 B7
South End Rw KENS W8 14 D3
Southern Av EBED/NFELT TW14 121 K7
SNWD SE25 165 G2
Southern Down FELT * TW13 122 B7
Southerngate Wy NWCR SE14 112 B6
Southern Gv BOW E3 93 H2
Southern Perimeter Rd
HTHAIR TW6 121 F4
Southern Rd EFNCH N2 53 K3
PLSTW E13 95 F1
Southern Rw NKENS W10 88 B3
Southern St IS N1 5 L5
Southern Wy CHDH RM6 62 C5
Southerton Rd HMSMTH * W6 107 F3
South Esk Rd FSTGT E7 77 G5
Southey Rd BRXN/ST SW9 110 B7
SEVS/STOTM N15 56 A4
WIM/MER SW19 146 E6
Southey St PGE/AN SE20 151 F6
Southfield BAR EN5 26 B5
Southfield Gdns TWK TW1 143 F3
Southfield Pk RYLN/HDSTN HA2 48 B3
Southfield Rd CHSWK W4 106 A1
PEND EN3 30 D5
Southfields E/WMO/HCT KT8 157 K5
HDN NW4 51 K2
Southfields Ms
WAND/EARL * SW18 127 K5
Southfields Rd
WAND/EARL SW18 127 K5
South Gdns WBLY * HA9 68 C1
WIM/MER SW19 147 H6
South Gate Av FELT TW13 140 B3
Southgate Gv IS N1 7 H2
Southgate Rd IS N1 7 H2
South Gipsy Rd WELL DA16 136 E2
South Gv HGT N6 54 A7
SEVS/STOTM N15 55 K4
WALTH E17 57 H4
South Hall Dr RAIN RM13 99 K4
South Hl CHST BR7 153 K5
NTHWD * HA6 32 C7
South Hill Av HRW HA1 66 D2
South Hill Gv HRW HA1 66 E3
South Hill Pk HAMP NW3 71 J3
South Hill Park Gdns
HAMP NW3 71 J3
South Hill Rd HAYES BR2 167 H2
Southholme Cl NRWD SE19 150 A7
Southill La PIN HA5 46 E3
Southill Rd CHST BR7 153 J6
Southill St POP/IOD E14 93 K5
South Island Pl BRXN/ST SW9 110 A6
South Kensington Station Ar
SKENS SW7 15 H5
South Lambeth Pl VX/NE SW8 17 K9
South Lambeth Rd VX/NE SW8 109 K5
Southland Rd
WOOL/PLUM SE18 116 A6
Southlands Dr WIM/MER SW19 146 B1
Southlands Gv BMLY BR1 168 D2
Southlands Rd HAYES BR2 168 C3
Southland Wy HSLW TW3 123 J4
South La KUT KT1 158 E2
NWMAL KT3 160 A3
South La West NWMAL KT3 160 A3
South Lodge Av MTCM CR4 163 K3
South Lodge Crs ENC/FH EN2 28 D3
South Lodge Dr
STHGT/OAK N14 28 D3
South Md CDALE/KGS NW9 37 H7
HOR/WEW KT19 173 H6
Southmead Rd
WIM/MER SW19 127 H7
South Molton La
MYFR/PKLN W1K 10 C5
South Molton Rd CAN/RD E16 94 E5
South Molton St
MYFR/PKLN W1K 10 C5
Southmont Rd ESH/CLAY KT10 170 E1
Southmoor Wy HOM E9 75 H5
South Mt TRDG/WHET * N20 39 G1
South Norwood Hl SNWD SE25 165 F1
South Oak Rd
STRHM/NOR SW16 149 F3
Southold Ri ELTH/MOT SE9 153 K2
Southolm St VX/NE SW8 109 G7
Southover BMLY BR1 152 E4
NFNCH/WDSP N12 38 E3
South Pde CHEL SW3 15 H7
CHSWK W4 106 A3
EDGW * HA8 50 C1
WLGTN * SM6 176 C5
South Park Crs CAT SE6 133 H7
IL IG1 78 D2
South Park Dr IL IG1 78 E2
South Park Gv NWMAL KT3 159 K3
South Park Hill Rd
SAND/SEL CR2 177 K4
South Park Ms FUL/PGN SW6 128 A2
South Park Rd IL IG1 78 D2
WIM/MER SW19 146 E5
South Park Ter IL IG1 78 D2
South Park Wy RSLP HA4 65 G5
South Pl BRYLDS KT5 159 G6
LVPST EC2M 13 H3
PEND EN3 30 E4
South Place Ms LVPST EC2M 13 H3
Southport Rd
WOOL/PLUM SE18 115 J3
Southridge Pl RYNPK SW20 146 B6
South Ri BAY/PAD * W2 9 K6
CAR SM5 175 J7
South Rd CHDH RM6 61 J4
EA W5 104 E3
ED N9 30 C7
EDGW HA8 36 D7
ERITH DA8 118 C5
FELT TW13 141 H4
FSTH SE23 151 F1
NWDGN UB2 102 E1
STHL UB1 83 K7
WDR/YW UB7 100 D2
WHTN TW2 142 D2
WIM/MER SW19 147 H5
South Rw BKHTH/KID SE3 133 K1
Southsea Av WATW WD18 20 E3
Southsea Rd KUT KT1 159 F3
South Sea St BERM/RHTH SE16 112 C2
South Side HMSMTH W6 106 C2
SEVS/STOTM * N15 56 B3
Southside Common
WIM/MER SW19 146 B5
Southspring ELTH/MOT SE9 135 J6
South Sq GINN WC1R 12 A3
GLDGN NW11 52 E5
South St BMLY BR1 167 K1
ISLW TW7 124 B2
MYFR/PKLN W1K 10 B8
PEND EN3 31 F4
RAIN RM13 98 E1
ROM RM1 63 G4
South Tenter St WCHPL E1 13 M6
South Ter SKENS SW7 15 J5
SURB KT6 159 F5
WDGN N22 54 E1
South V HRW HA1 66 E3
NRWD SE19 150 A5
Southvale Rd BKHTH/KID SE3 133 H1
South Vale Rd SURB KT6 172 A1
South Vw BMLY BR1 168 B1
Southview Av WLSDN NW10 69 H4
South View Cl BXLY DA5 137 G5
Southview Cl TOOT SW17 148 A4
South View Ct NRWD * SE19 149 J6
South View Crs
GNTH/NBYPK IG2 60 B5
Southview Dr SWFD E18 59 F2
Southview Gdns WLGTN SM6 176 C6
Southview Rd BMLY BR1 152 B3
South View Rd CEND/HSY/T N8 54 D2
PIN HA5 33 F5
Southviews SAND/SEL CR2 179 F7
South Vls CAMTN NW1 72 D5
Southville VX/NE SW8 109 J7
Southville Cl
EBED/NFELT TW14 121 H6
HOR/WEW KT19 173 F7
Southville Crs
EBED/NFELT TW14 121 H7
Southville Rd
EBED/NFELT TW14 121 H7
THDIT KT7 158 B6
South Wk WWKM BR4 180 C2
Southwark Br CANST EC4R 12 F7
Southwark Bridge Rd
STHWK SE1 12 F8
Southwark Park Est
BERM/RHTH * SE16 111 J3
Southwark Park Rd
BERM/RHTH SE16 19 M5
Southwark Pl BMLY BR1 168 E2
Southwark St STHWK SE1 12 D8
Southwater Cl BECK BR3 151 K6
South Wy CROY/NA CR0 179 G2
FBAR/BDGN N11 40 C5
RYLN/HDSTN HA2 48 A3
WBLY HA9 68 C4
Southway GLDGN NW11 53 F5
HAYES BR2 167 K6
RYNPK SW20 161 G3
TRDG/WHET N20 38 E1
WLGTN SM6 176 C3
Southwell Av NTHLT UB5 66 A5
Southwell Gdns SKENS SW7 14 E5
Southwell Grove Rd WAN E11 76 C1
Southwell Rd CMBW SE5 130 D2
CROY/NA CR0 164 B5
KTN/HRWW/W HA3 49 K5
South Western Rd TWK TW1 124 B5
Southwest Rd WAN E11 58 B7
South Wharf Rd BAY/PAD W2 9 G4
Southwick Ms BAY/PAD W2 9 H4
Southwick Pl BAY/PAD W2 9 J5
Southwick St BAY/PAD W2 9 J4
Southwick Yd BAY/PAD * W2 9 K5
Southwold Dr BARK IG11 79 G4
Southwold Rd BXLY DA5 137 J5
CLPT E5 74 D1
Southwood Av HGT N6 54 B6
KUTN/CMB KT2 144 E7
Southwood Cl BMLY BR1 168 E3
WPK KT4 161 G7
Southwood Dr BRYLDS KT5 159 K6
Southwood Gdns BARK/HLT IG6 60 B3
ESH/CLAY KT10 171 G2
Southwood La HGT N6 54 A6
Southwood Lawn Rd HGT N6 54 B6
Southwood Pk HGT * N6 54 B6
Southwood Rd ELTH/MOT SE9 154 B1
THMD SE28 97 H7
South Worple Wy
MORT/ESHN SW14 126 A2
Sovereign Cl EA W5 85 J4
RSLP HA4 46 C7
WAP E1W 92 D6
Sovereign Ct E/WMO/HCT KT8 156 E3
Sovereign Crs BERM/RHTH SE16 93 G6
Sovereign Gv ALP/SUD HA0 67 K2
Sovereign Ms BETH * E2 7 L5
Sovereign Pk WLSDN * NW10 86 D3

Sovereign Rd BARK IG11 97 J2
Sowerby Cl ELTH/MOT SE9 134 E4
Sowrey Av RAIN RM13 81 H5
Space Waye EBED/NFELT TW14 121 K4
Spa Cl NRWD SE19 150 A7
Spafield St CLKNW * EC1R 6 A9
Spa Green Est CLKNW * EC1R 6 B7
Spa Hl THHTH CR7 149 K7
Spalding Cl EDGW HA8 37 G6
Spalding Rd HDN NW4 52 A5
TOOT SW17 148 B4
Spanby Rd BOW E3 93 J3
Spaniards Cl GLDGN NW11 53 G7
Spaniards End GLDGN NW11 53 G7
Spaniards Rd HAMP NW3 71 G1
Spanish Pl MHST * W1U 10 B4
Spanish Rd WAND/EARL SW18 128 B4
Sparkbridge Rd HRW HA1 48 E3
Sparke Ter CAN/RD * E16 94 D5
Sparkford Gdns
FBAR/BDGN N11 40 A4
Sparks Cl ACT W3 87 F5
BCTR RM8 79 K1
HPTN TW12 141 J5
Spa Rd BERM/RHTH SE16 19 L4
Sparrow Cl HPTN TW12 141 J5
Sparrow Dr STMC/STPC BR5 169 H7
Sparrow Farm Dr
EBED/NFELT TW14 122 C6
Sparrow Farm Rd EW KT17 173 J3
Sparrow Gn DAGE RM10 80 D2
Sparrows Herne BUSH WD23 22 B6
Sparrows La ELTH/MOT SE9 135 H7
Sparrows Wy BUSH * WD23 22 C6
Sparrows Wick BUSH * WD23 22 C7
Sparsholt Rd ARCH N19 55 F7
BARK IG11 78 E7
Sparta St GNWCH SE10 113 F7
Speakers Ct CROY/NA * CR0 164 E7
Spearman St
WOOL/PLUM * SE18 115 F5
Spear Ms ECT SW5 14 B6
Spears Rd ARCH N19 54 E7
Speart La HEST TW5 102 D6
Spedan Cl HAMP NW3 71 F2
Speedwell St DEPT SE8 112 D6
Speer Rd THDIT KT7 158 A5
Speirs Cl NWMAL KT3 160 C5
Spekehill ELTH/MOT SE9 153 K2
Speke Rd THHTH CR7 164 E1
Speldhurst Cl HAYES BR2 167 J4
Speldhurst Rd CHSWK W4 106 A2
HOM E9 75 F6
Spellbrook Wk IS * N1 6 F3
Spelman St WCHPL E1 92 C4
Spelthorne Gv SUN TW16 140 D6
Spelthorne La ASHF TW15 140 A6
Spence Cl BERM/RHTH SE16 112 C1
Spencer Av PLMGR N13 41 F5
YEAD UB4 82 E4
Spencer Cl FNCH N3 52 D1
WFD IG8 45 G4
WLSDN NW10 86 B2
Spencer Dr EFNCH N2 53 G5
Spencer Gdns
MORT/ESHN SW14 125 K4
Spencer Hl WIM/MER SW19 146 C5
Spencer Hill Rd
WIM/MER SW19 146 C6
Spencer House SURB * KT6 159 F4
Spencer Ms HMSMTH W6 107 H5
Spencer Pk WAND/EARL SW18 128 C4
Spencer Pl CROY/NA CR0 164 E6
IS N1 6 C1
WEST SW1P 16 F4
Spencer Ri KTTN NW5 72 B3
Spencer Rd ACT W3 86 E7
ALP/SUD HA0 67 J1
BMLY BR1 152 D6
BTSEA SW11 128 C3
CEND/HSY/T N8 55 F4
CHSWK W4 105 K6
E/WMO/HCT KT8 157 H3
EHAM E6 77 H7
FBAR/BDGN N11 40 B3
GDMY/SEVK IG3 61 F7
ISLW TW7 103 J7
KTN/HRWW/W HA3 48 E1
MTCM CR4 162 E6
MTCM CR4 163 F2
RAIN RM13 99 F2
RYNPK SW20 145 K7
SAND/SEL CR2 178 A4
TOTM N17 42 C7
WALTH E17 58 A1
WHTN TW2 142 E2
Spencer St FSBYE EC1V 6 C8
NWDGN UB2 102 C2
Spencer Wk PUT/ROE SW15 127 G3
Spenser Gv STNW/STAM N16 74 A3
Spenser Ms DUL SE21 130 E7
Spenser Rd HNHL SE24 130 C4
Spenser St WESTW SW1E 16 F3
Spensley Wk STNW/STAM N16 73 K2
Speranza St WOOL/PLUM SE18 116 A4
Sperling Rd TOTM N17 56 B1
Spert St POP/IOD E14 93 G6
Speyside STHGT/OAK N14 28 C5
Spey St POP/IOD E14 94 A4
Spezia Rd WLSDN NW10 87 J1
Spicer Cl CMBW SE5 130 C1
WOT/HER KT12 156 B5
Spices Yd CROY/NA CR0 177 J3
Spielman Rd DART DA1 139 J3
Spigurnell Rd TOTM N17 41 K7
Spikes Bridge Rd STHL UB1 83 J5
Spilsby Cl CDALE/KGS NW9 51 G1
Spindle Cl WOOL/PLUM SE18 114 D2
Spindlewood Gdns
CROY/NA CR0 177 K3
Spindrift Av POP/IOD E14 112 E3
Spinel Cl WOOL/PLUM SE18 116 A4
Spinnaker Cl BARK IG11 97 H2
Spinnells Rd RYLN/HDSTN HA2 47 K7
The Spinney ALP/SUD HA0 67 G2
BARN * SW13 106 E5
CHEAM SM3 174 A3
NFNCH/WDSP * N12 39 G6
STAN HA7 36 A3
STRHM/NOR SW16 148 C2
SUN TW16 140 E7
WCHMH N21 29 G6
Spinney Cl BECK BR3 166 E3
NWMAL KT3 160 B4
RAIN RM13 99 G1
WPK KT4 173 H2
Spinney Dr EBED/NFELT TW14 121 F6
Spinney Gdns DAGW RM9 80 A4
NRWD SE19 150 B4
Spinney Oak BMLY BR1 168 D1
The Spinneys BMLY BR1 168 E1
Spirit Quay WAP E1W 92 C7
Spital Sq WCHPL E1 13 K2
Spital St DART DA1 139 G5
WCHPL E1 92 C4
Spital Yd WCHPL * E1 13 K2
Spitfire Est HEST * TW5 102 B4
Spitfire Wy HEST TW5 102 B4
Spode Wk KIL/WHAMP * NW6 71 F4
Spondon Rd SEVS/STOTM N15 56 C3
Spoonbill Wy YEAD UB4 83 H4
Spooner Wk WLGTN SM6 176 D4
Sportsbank St CAT SE6 133 F6
Spottons Gv TOTM N17 41 J7
Spout Hl CROY/NA CR0 179 J4
Spratt Hall Rd WAN E11 58 E5
Spray St WOOL/PLUM SE18 115 G3
Spreighton Rd
E/WMO/HCT KT8 157 G3
Sprimont Pl CHEL SW3 15 L7
Springall St PECK SE15 111 J6
Springbank WCHMH N21 29 F5
Springbank Rd LEW SE13 133 H5
Springbank Wk CAMTN NW1 5 G2
Springbourne Ct BECK BR3 152 A7
Spring Bridge Rd EA W5 85 K6
Spring Cl BAR EN5 26 B4
BCTR RM8 61 K7
BORE WD6 24 C1
Springclose La CHEAM SM3 174 C5
Spring Cnr FELT * TW13 140 E2
Spring Cottages SURB * KT6 158 E4
Springcroft Av EFNCH N2 53 K2
Spring Crofts BUSH WD23 22 A4
Springdale Rd STNW/STAM N16 73 K3
Spring Dr PIN HA5 46 E5
Springfield BUSH WD23 22 D7
CLPT E5 56 D7
Springfield Av HPTN TW12 142 B5
MUSWH N10 54 C2
RYNPK SW20 161 J2
Springfield Cl
NFNCH/WDSP N12 39 F4
STAN HA7 35 G2
Springfield Dr GNTH/NBYPK IG2 60 C4
Springfield Gdns BMLY BR1 168 E3
CDALE/KGS NW9 51 F4
CLPT E5 56 D7
RSLP HA4 47 F7
WFD IG8 45 G6
WWKM BR4 179 K1
Springfield Gv CHARL SE7 114 B5
SUN TW16 140 E7
Springfield La KIL/WHAMP NW6 2 B4
Springfield Mt CDALE/KGS NW9 51 G4
Springfield Pl NWMAL KT3 159 K3
Springfield Ri SYD SE26 150 D3
Springfield Rd BMLY BR1 168 E3
BXLYHN DA7 137 J2
EHAM E6 77 K6
FBAR/BDGN N11 40 C4
HNWL W7 84 E7
HRW HA1 48 E5
HYS/HAR UB3 83 G7
KUT KT1 159 F3
SEVS/STOTM N15 56 C3
SRTFD * E15 94 C2
STJWD NW8 2 E4
SYD SE26 150 D4
TEDD TW11 143 G4
THHTH CR7 149 J7
WALTH E17 57 H5
WELL DA16 136 C2
WHTN TW2 123 F7
WIM/MER SW19 146 D4
WLGTN SM6 176 B4
Springfield Wk
KIL/WHAMP NW6 2 C4
Spring Gdns E/WMO/HCT KT8 157 H4
HBRY N5 73 J4
HCH RM12 81 K3
ROMW/RG RM7 62 E4
WFD IG8 45 G6
WHALL SW1A 11 J8
WLGTN SM6 176 C4
Spring Gv CHSWK W4 105 H4
HPTN TW12 142 B7
MTCM CR4 148 A7
Spring Grove Crs HEST TW5 103 H7
Spring Grove Rd HSLW TW3 103 H7
RCHPK/HAM TW10 125 G4
Springhead Rd ERITH DA8 118 C5
Spring Hl CLPT E5 56 C6
SYD SE26 150 E3
Springhurst Cl CROY/NA CR0 179 H3
Spring Lake STAN HA7 35 H3
Spring La CLPT E5 56 D7
MUSWH N10 54 A2
SNWD SE25 165 J5
Spring Ms MHST * W1U 9 M2
Spring Park Av CROY/NA CR0 179 F1
Springpark Dr BECK BR3 167 F2
FSBYPK N4 55 J7
Spring Park Rd CROY/NA CR0 179 F1
Spring Pl FNCH N3 52 E1
KTTN NW5 72 A4
Springpond Rd DAGW RM9 80 A4
Springrice Rd LEW SE13 133 F5
Spring Rd FELT TW13 140 D2
Spring Shaw Rd
STMC/STPC BR5 155 G7
Spring St BAY/PAD W2 9 G5
EW KT17 173 H7
Spring Tide Cl PECK * SE15 111 H7
Spring V BXLYHN DA7 137 J3
Springvale Av BTFD TW8 104 E4
Spring V North DART DA1 139 G6
Spring V South DART * DA1 139 G6
Springvale Ter WKENS W14 107 G2
Spring Villa Rd EDGW HA8 36 C6
Spring Vls WEA * W13 85 H7
Spring Wk WCHPL E1 92 C4
Springwater Cl
WOOL/PLUM * SE18 115 F7
Springwell Av WLSDN NW10 69 H7
Springwell Rd HEST TW5 102 C7
STRHM/NOR SW16 149 G3
Springwood Crs EDGW HA8 36 E1
Springwood Wy ROM RM1 63 J4
Sprowston Ms FSTGT E7 76 E5
Sprowston Rd FSTGT E7 76 E4
Sprucedale Gdns
CROY/NA CR0 179 F3
PUR/KEN CR8 176 E7
Spruce Hills Rd WALTH E17 57 K1
Sprules Rd BROCKY SE4 132 B1
Spurfield E/WMO/HCT KT8 157 G2
Spurgeon Av NRWD SE19 149 K7
Spurgeon Rd NRWD SE19 149 K6
Spurgeon St STHWK SE1 19 G4
Spurling Rd DAGW RM9 80 B5
EDUL * SE22 131 G3
Spur Rd BARK IG11 96 C2
EBED/NFELT TW14 122 A4
EDGW HA8 36 A3
ISLW TW7 104 B6
SEVS/STOTM * N15 55 K3
STHWK SE1 18 A1
WHALL SW1A 16 E2
Spurstowe Rd HACK E8 74 D5
Spurstowe Ter HACK E8 74 C4
The Square CAR SM5 176 A4
HMSMTH W6 107 F4
RCHPK/HAM TW10 125 F4
STKPK UB11 82 B7
WFD IG8 44 E4
Squarey St TOOT SW17 147 G2
Squire Gdns STJWD NW8 3 G8
Squires Ct WIM/MER SW19 146 E3
Squires La FNCH N3 53 F1
Squire's Mt HAMP NW3 71 H2
Squires Wk ASHF TW15 140 B6
Squires Wood Dr CHST * BR7 153 K6
Squirrel Cl HSLWW TW4 122 B2
Squirrel Ms HNWL * W7 85 G6
The Squirrels BUSH WD23 22 D5
LEW SE13 133 G2
PIN HA5 47 K2
Squirrels Cl NFNCH/WDSP N12 39 G3
Squirrels Gn WPK KT4 173 H1
Squirrel's Heath Av GPK RM2 63 K2
Squirries St BETH E2 92 C2
Stable Cl NTHLT UB5 84 A1
Stable Ms WNWD SE27 149 J4
The Stables Market
CAMTN * NW1 4 C2
Stables Wy LBTH SE11 18 A7
Stable Wk EFNCH * N2 39 H7
Stable Wy NKENS W10 88 A5
Stable Yard Rd WHALL SW1A 10 F9
Stacey Av UED N18 42 E3
Stacey Cl LEY E10 58 B4
Stacey St HOLWY N7 73 G2
LSQ/SEVD WC2H 11 H5
Stackhouse St KTBR SW1X 15 L3
Stacy Pth CMBW * SE5 111 F6
Stadium Rd WOOL/PLUM SE18 114 E6
Stadium St WBPTN SW10 108 B6
Stadium Wy DART DA1 138 B5
WBLY HA9 68 B3
Staffa Rd LEY E10 57 G7
Stafford Cl CHEAM SM3 174 C5
KIL/WHAMP NW6 2 A8
STHGT/OAK N14 28 C4
WALTH E17 57 H5
Stafford Gdns CROY/NA CR0 177 F4
Stafford Pl RCHPK/HAM TW10 125 G6
WESTW SW1E 16 E3
Stafford Rd BOW E3 93 H1
CROY/NA CR0 177 G3
FSTGT E7 77 G6
KIL/WHAMP NW6 2 A7
KTN/HRWW/W HA3 34 C6
NWMAL KT3 159 K2
RSLP HA4 64 D3
SCUP DA14 154 E3
WLGTN SM6 176 C5
Staffordshire St PECK SE15 111 H7
Stafford Ter KENS W8 14 A3
Stag Cl EDGW HA8 50 D1
Stag La BKHH IG9 45 F1
EDGW HA8 50 D1
PUT/ROE SW15 145 H2
Stag Pl WESTW SW1E 16 E3
Stags Wy ISLW TW7 104 A5
Stainbank Rd MTCM CR4 163 G2
Stainby Cl WDR/YW UB7 100 B2
Stainby Rd TOTM N17 56 B2
Stainer St STHWK SE1 13 H9
Staines Av CHEAM SM3 174 B1
Staines Rd EBED/NFELT TW14 121 F7
HSLWW TW4 122 C4
IL IG1 78 D3
WHTN TW2 142 C2
Staines Rd East SUN TW16 140 E6
Staines Rd West ASHF TW15 140 A6
Stainford Cl ASHF TW15 140 B4
Stainforth Rd GNTH/NBYPK IG2 60 D6
WALTH E17 57 J3
Staining La CITYW EC2V 12 F4
Stainmore Cl CHST BR7 154 D7
Stainsbury St BETH E2 92 E1
Stainsby Pl POP/IOD * E14 93 J5
Stainsby Rd POP/IOD E14 93 J5
Stainton Rd LEW SE13 133 G6
Stalbridge St CAMTN NW1 9 K2
Stalham St BERM/RHTH SE16 111 J2
Stambourne Wy NRWD SE19 150 A6
WWKM BR4 180 A2
Stamford Brook Av
HMSMTH W6 106 C2
Stamford Brook Gdns
HMSMTH W6 106 C2
Stamford Brook Rd
HMSMTH W6 106 C2
Stamford Cl KTN/HRWW/W HA3 34 E6
SEVS/STOTM N15 56 C3
STHL UB1 84 A6
Stamford Cottages
WBPTN * SW10 108 A6
Stamford Dr HAYES BR2 167 J3
Stamford Gdns DAGW RM9 79 J6
Stamford Gv East
STNW/STAM N16 56 C7
Stamford Gv West
STNW/STAM N16 56 C7
Stamford Hl STNW/STAM N16 56 B7
Stamford Rd DAGW RM9 79 G7
EHAM E6 77 J7
IS N1 7 K1
SEVS/STOTM N15 56 C4
WAT WD17 21 F1
Stamford St STHWK SE1 12 A8
Stamp Pl BETH E2 7 L7
Stanborough HACK E8 74 B5
Stanborough Cl HPTN TW12 141 K5
Stanborough Rd HSLW TW3 123 J2
Stanbridge Pl WCHMH N21 41 H1
Stanbridge Rd PUT/ROE SW15 127 F2
Stanbrook Rd ABYW SE2 116 C1
Stanbury Ct HAMP NW3 71 K5
Stanbury Rd PECK SE15 111 J7
Stancroft CDALE/KGS NW9 51 G3
Standale Gv RSLP HA4 46 A4
Standard Pl SDTCH EC2A 7 K8
Standard Rd BELV DA17 117 H4
BXLYHS DA6 137 F3
HSLWW TW4 122 D2
WLSDN NW10 86 E3
Standen Rd WAND/EARL SW18 127 K6
Standfield Rd DAGE RM10 80 C4
Standish Rd HMSMTH W6 106 D3
Stane Cl WIM/MER SW19 147 F6
Stane Wy WOOL/PLUM SE18 114 C6
Stanfield Rd BOW E3 93 G1
Stanford Cl HPTN TW12 141 K5
ROMW/RG RM7 62 D5
WFD IG8 45 J4
Stanford Pl STHWK SE1 19 J6
Stanford Rd FBAR/BDGN N11 39 K4
KENS W8 14 D4
STRHM/NOR SW16 163 K1
Stanford St WEST SW1P 17 G6
Stanford Wy
STRHM/NOR SW16 163 J1
Stangate Crs BORE WD6 25 G4
Stangate Gdns STAN HA7 35 H3
Stanger Rd SNWD SE25 165 H3
Stanham Pl DART DA1 138 D3
Stanham Rd DART DA1 139 F4
Stanhope Av FNCH N3 52 D2
HAYES BR2 167 K7
KTN/HRWW/W HA3 34 D7
Stanhope Cl
BERM/RHTH * SE16 112 A1
Stanhope Gdns FSBYPK N4 55 H5
HGT N6 54 B5
IL IG1 59 K7
MLHL NW7 37 H4
SKENS SW7 14 F6
Stanhope Ga BAY/PAD W2 9 L6
MYFR/PKLN W1K 10 B9
Stanhope Gv BECK BR3 166 C4
Stanhope Ms East SKENS SW7 14 F5
Stanhope Ms South SKENS SW7 14 F6
Stanhope Ms West SKENS SW7 14 F5
Stanhope Pde CAMTN NW1 4 D7
Stanhope Park Rd
GFD/PVL UB6 84 C3
Stanhope Pl BAY/PAD W2 9 L5
Stanhope Rd BAR EN5 26 B5
BCTR RM8 80 B1
BFN/LL DA15 155 G3
BXLYHN DA7 137 F1
CAR SM5 176 A6
CROY/NA CR0 178 A2
GFD/PVL UB6 84 C4
HGT N6 54 C5
NFNCH/WDSP N12 39 G4
RAIN RM13 99 J1
WALTH E17 57 K4
Stanhope Rw MYFR/PICC * W1J 10 C9
Stanhope St CAMTN NW1 4 E7
Stanhope Ter BAY/PAD W2 9 H6
TWK * TW1 124 A6
Stanier Cl WKENS W14 107 J4
Stanlake Rd SHB W12 88 A7
Stanlake Vls SHB W12 88 A7
Stanley Av ALP/SUD HA0 68 A6
BARK IG11 97 F2
BCTR RM8 62 B7
BECK BR3 167 F2
GFD/PVL UB6 66 C7
GPK RM2 63 J3
NWMAL KT3 160 D4
Stanley Cl ALP/SUD HA0 68 A6
GPK RM2 63 J3
Stanley Crs NTGHL W11 88 D6
Stanleycroft Cl ISLW TW7 103 K7
Stanley Gdns ACT W3 106 B1
CRICK NW2 70 A4
MTCM * CR4 148 A5
NTGHL W11 88 D6
WLGTN SM6 176 C5
Stanley Gardens Rd
TEDD TW11 142 E4
Stanley Gv THHTH CR7 164 B5
VX/NE SW8 129 F1
Stanley Park Dr ALP/SUD HA0 68 B6
Stanley Park Rd CAR SM5 175 K6
WLGTN SM6 176 B5
Stanley Pas CAMTN NW1 5 J6
Stanley Rd ACT W3 105 J2
BELMT SM2 175 F5
CAR SM5 176 A6
CROY/NA CR0 164 B6
ED N9 30 B7
EFNCH N2 53 H3
EN EN1 30 A2
FBAR/BDGN N11 40 D5
HAYES BR2 168 B2
HSLW TW3 123 H3
IL IG1 78 D1
MNPK E12 77 J4
MORT/ESHN SW14 125 J3
MRDN SM4 161 K3
MTCM CR4 148 A6
MUSWH N10 40 B6
NTHWD HA6 32 E7
RYLN/HDSTN HA2 66 C1
SCUP DA14 155 G2
SEVS/STOTM N15 55 H3
SRTFD E15 76 B7
STHL UB1 83 J6
SWFD E18 44 D7
WALTH E17 57 K5
WAT WD17 21 G2
WBLY HA9 68 B5
WHTN TW2 142 D2
WIM/MER SW19 146 E6
Stanley Rd North RAIN RM13 81 G7
Stanley Rd South RAIN RM13 99 H1
Stanley Sq CAR SM5 175 K7
Stanley St DEPT SE8 112 C6
Stanley Ter ARCH * N19 72 E1
BXLYHS * DA6 137 H3
Stanmer St BTSEA SW11 108 D7
Stanmore Gdns RCH/KEW TW9 125 G2
SUT SM1 175 G2
Stanmore Hl STAN HA7 35 H3
Stanmore Rd BELV DA17 117 K3
RCH/KEW TW9 125 G2
SEVS/STOTM N15 55 H3
WAN E11 58 D7
Stanmore St IS N1 5 L3
Stanmore Ter BECK BR3 166 D1
Stannard Ms HACK * E8 74 C5
Stannard Rd HACK E8 74 C5
Stannary St LBTH SE11 18 B9
Stannet Wy WLGTN SM6 176 C3
Stansfeld Rd CAN/RD E16 95 H5
Stansfield Rd BRXN/ST SW9 130 A2
HSLWW TW4 122 A1
Stansgate Rd DAGE RM10 80 C1
Stanstead Cl HAYES BR2 167 J4
Stanstead Gv CAT SE6 132 C7
Stanstead Rd FSTH SE23 132 B7
WAN E11 59 F4
Stansted Cl HCH RM12 81 K5
Stansted Crs BXLY DA5 136 E7
Stansted Rd HTHAIR TW6 120 C5
Stanswood Gdns CMBW SE5 111 F6
Stanthorpe Cl
STRHM/NOR * SW16 148 E4
Stanthorpe Rd
STRHM/NOR SW16 148 E4
Stanton Av TEDD TW11 142 E5
Stanton Cl HOR/WEW KT19 172 D4
WPK KT4 161 G7
Stanton Rd BARN SW13 126 C1
CROY/NA CR0 164 D6
RYNPK SW20 161 G1
Stanton St PECK * SE15 111 H7
Stanton Wy SYD SE26 151 H3
Stanway Gdns ACT W3 86 C7
EDGW HA8 36 E5
Stanway St IS N1 7 K5
Stanwell Cl STWL/WRAY TW19 120 A5
Stanwell Gdns
STWL/WRAY TW19 120 A5
Stanwell Rd EBED/NFELT TW14 120 E6
Stanwick Rd WKENS W14 107 J3
Stanworth St STHWK SE1 19 L2
Stapenhill Rd ALP/SUD HA0 67 H2
Staplefield Cl
BRXS/STRHM * SW2 129 K7
PIN HA5 33 J6
Stapleford Av GNTH/NBYPK IG2 60 E4
Stapleford Cl CHING E4 44 A2
KUT KT1 159 H1
WIM/MER SW19 127 H6
Stapleford Rd ALP/SUD HA0 67 K6
Stapleford Wy BARK IG11 97 H2
Staplehurst Rd CAR SM5 175 J6
LEW SE13 133 G4
Staple Inn HHOL WC1V 12 A3
Staples Cl BERM/RHTH SE16 93 G7
Staple St STHWK SE1 19 H2
Stapleton Crs RAIN RM13 81 J5
Stapleton Gdns CROY/NA CR0 177 G4
Stapleton Hall Rd FSBYPK N4 55 F6
Stapleton Rd BXLYHN DA7 117 G6
TOOT SW17 148 A2
Stapleton Vls
STNW/STAM * N16 74 A3
Stapley Rd BELV DA17 117 H4
Staplyton Rd BAR EN5 26 C2
Star & Garter Hl
RCHPK/HAM TW10 125 F7
Starboard Wy POP/IOD E14 112 D2
Starch House La BARK/HLT IG6 60 D1
Starcross St CAMTN NW1 4 F8
Starfield Rd SHB W12 106 D1
Star Hl DART DA1 138 B4
Star La CAN/RD E16 94 C3
Starling Cl PIN HA5 47 G2
Starmans Cl DAGW RM9 80 A7
Star Rd HGDN/ICK UB10 82 A3
ISLW TW7 123 J1
WKENS W14 107 J5
Star St BAY/PAD W2 9 H4
Starveall Cl WDR/YW UB7 100 C2
Star Yd LINN WC2A 12 A4
Staten Gdns TWK TW1 124 A7
Statham Gv STNW/STAM N16 73 K2
UED N18 42 A4
Station Ap ALP/SUD HA0 67 H5
BAR EN5 27 G3
BECK BR3 151 G7
BELMT SM2 174 C6
BKHH * IG9 45 H3
BKHTH/KID SE3 134 A2
BXLYHN DA7 137 F1
BXLYHN DA7 137 K1
CAMTN * NW1 10 A1
CAT SE6 151 H4
CHING * E4 44 B5
CHST BR7 153 J5
CHST BR7 154 A7
CROY/NA * CR0 177 K1
DART DA1 139 H5
ESH/CLAY KT10 171 F2
FBAR/BDGN N11 40 B4
FSTGT * E7 77 F3
FUL/PGN * SW6 127 H2
GFD/PVL UB6 66 C6
GLDGN * NW11 52 B6
HAYES BR2 167 K7
HOR/WEW KT19 173 H4
HPTN TW12 142 A7
HYS/HAR UB3 101 J2
KUT KT1 159 H1
NTHWD HA6 32 C6
OXHEY WD19 33 H2
PIN HA5 47 J2
RCH/KEW TW9 105 H7
RSLP HA4 46 C7
RSLP HA4 65 F4
SAND/SEL CR2 177 K7
STRHM/NOR SW16 148 D4
SUN TW16 140 E7
SWFD * E18 59 F1
WALTH * E17 57 J4
WAN E11 58 E4
WAN * E11 76 C3
WATW * WD18 20 D3
WELL DA16 136 B1
WFD * IG8 45 G5
WLSDN NW10 87 H2
Station Approach Rd
CHSWK W4 105 K6
Station Ar GTPST * W1W 10 D1
Station Av HOR/WEW KT19 173 G7
NWMAL KT3 160 B2
Station Buildings HAYES * BR2 167 K7
Station Chambers EA * W5 86 C3
Station Cl HPTN TW12 142 B7
Station Cottages WDGN * N22 54 E1
Station Crs ALP/SUD HA0 67 H5
BKHTH/KID SE3 113 K4
SEVS/STOTM N15 55 K3
Stationers Hall Ct STP * EC4M 12 D5
Station Est BECK BR3 166 A3
Station Estate Rd
EBED/NFELT TW14 122 A7
Station Garage Ms
STRHM/NOR * SW16 148 D5
Station Gdns CHSWK W4 105 K6
Station Gv ALP/SUD HA0 68 A5
Station Hl HAYES BR2 180 E1
Station House Ms ED N9 42 C3
Station Pde ACT * W3 86 C5
BAL * SW12 129 F7
BARK IG11 78 C6
BECK * BR3 166 A3
BELMT * SM2 175 G5
BMLY * BR1 152 E7
BXLYHN * DA7 137 F1
CHSWK * W4 105 K3
CHSWK * W4 105 K6

CLPT * E5 74 D2
CRICK NW2 70 A5
EA * W5 86 B7
EBAR * EN4 28 A3
EBED/NFELT * TW14 122 A6
EDGW * HA8 36 A6
EHAM * E6 77 G7
EHAM * E6 77 J6
HCH RM12 81 K3
KTN/HRWW/W * HA3 49 H1
NTHLT * UB5 66 A6
NTHLT * UB5 66 B4
RCH/KEW TW9 105 H7
ROM * RM1 63 G5
RSLP * HA4 64 A1
RYLN/HDSTN * HA2 66 B3
STHGT/OAK N14 28 D7
Station Pas PECK SE15 111 K7
SWFD E18 59 F1
Station Pl FSBYPK N4 73 G1
Station Ri WNWD SE27 149 H1
Station Rd ARCH N19 72 C2
BAR EN5 27 F4
BARK/HLT IG6 60 D2
BARN SW13 126 C1
BCTR RM8 61 K7
BELV DA17 117 H2
BFN/LL DA15 155 G1
BMLY BR1 152 E7
BORE WD6 24 C3
BXLYHN DA7 137 F2
CAR SM5 175 K3
CHSGTN KT9 172 A4
CROY/NA CR0 164 D7
DART DA1 138 C5
EA W5 86 B5
EDGW HA8 36 C5
ESH/CLAY KT10 157 J7
ESH/CLAY KT10 170 D4
FBAR/BDGN N11 40 B4
FNCH N3 38 E7
GPK RM2 63 K3
HAYES BR2 167 H1
HDN NW4 51 J5
HNWL W7 84 E7
HOLWY N7 72 C2
HPTN TW12 142 B7
HRW HA1 49 G3
HSLW TW3 123 G3
HYS/HAR UB3 101 H3
HYS/HAR UB3 101 J1
IL IG1 78 B2
KUT KT1 143 K7
KUTN/CMB KT2 144 C7
LEW SE13 133 F2
MLHL NW7 37 G5
MNPK E12 77 H3
NRWD SE19 150 C5
NWMAL KT3 160 E4
PGE/AN SE20 150 E5
RYLN/HDSTN HA2 48 B4
SCUP DA14 155 G3
SNWD SE25 165 G3
SUN TW16 140 E6
TEDD TW11 143 G5
THDIT KT7 158 A6
TOTM N17 56 C2
TWK TW1 124 A7
WALTH E17 57 G5
WAT WD17 21 F1
WCHMH N21 29 H7
WDGN N22 54 E1
WDGN N22 55 F1
WDR/YW UB7 100 B1
WIM/MER SW19 147 G7
WLSDN NW10 87 H1
WWKM BR4 167 F7
Station Rd North BELV DA17 117 J2
Station Sq STMC/STPC BR5 169 H4
Station St SRTFD E15 76 B6
Station Ter CMBW SE5 110 D7
WLSDN NW10 88 B1
Station Vw GFD/PVL UB6 66 D7
Station Wy BKHH IG9 45 H3
CHEAM SM3 174 C5
Station Yd RSLP * HA4 64 B1
STHL * UB1 102 E1
TWK TW1 124 B6
Staunton Rd KUTN/CMB KT2 144 B6
Staunton St DEPT SE8 112 C5
Staveley Cl HOLWY * N7 72 E3
PECK SE15 111 K7
Staveley Gdns CHSWK W4 106 A7
Staveley Rd ASHF TW15 140 B5
CHSWK W4 105 K5
Staverton Rd CRICK NW2 70 A6
Stave Yard Rd
BERM/RHTH SE16 93 G7
Stavordale Rd CAR SM5 162 B6
HBRY N5 73 G3
Stayner's Rd WCHPL E1 93 F3
Stayton Rd SUT SM1 174 E2
Steadfast Rd KUT KT1 143 K7
Stead St WALW SE17 19 G6
Steam Farm La
EBED/NFELT TW14 121 J3
Stean St HACK E8 7 L3
Stebbing Wy BARK IG11 97 G1
Stebondale St POP/IOD E14 113 F4
Stedly SCUP * DA14 155 G3
Steed Cl EMPK RM11 81 K1
Steedman St WALW SE17 18 E6
Steeds Rd MUSWH N10 39 K7
Steel Ap BARK IG11 97 H1
Steele Rd CHSWK W4 105 K2
ISLW TW7 124 B3
TOTM N17 56 A2
WAN E11 76 C3
WLSDN NW10 86 E1
Steele's Ms North HAMP * NW3 71 K5
Steele's Ms South HAMP NW3 71 K5
Steele's Rd HAMP NW3 71 K5
Steeles Studios HAMP * NW3 71 K5
Steel's La WCHPL E1 92 E5
Steelyard Pas CANST EC4R 13 G7
Steep Hl CROY/NA CR0 178 A3
STRHM/NOR SW16 148 D2
Steeplands BUSH WD23 22 B6
Steeple Cl FUL/PGN SW6 127 H2
WIM/MER SW19 146 C3
Steeplestone Cl UED N18 41 J4
Steeple Wk IS N1 6 F3
Steerforth St
WAND/EARL SW18 147 F1
Steers Md MTCM CR4 147 K7
Steers Wy BERM/RHTH SE16 112 B1
Stella Rd TOOT SW17 147 K5
Stelling Rd ERITH DA8 118 A6
Stellman Cl CLPT E5 74 C2
Stembridge Rd PGE/AN SE20 165 J1
Stephan Cl HACK E8 74 C7
Stephen Av RAIN RM13 81 J5
Stephendale Rd FUL/PGN SW6 128 A2
Stephen Ms FITZ W1T 11 G3
Stephen Pl CLAP SW4 129 H2
Stephen Rd BXLYHN DA7 137 K2
Stephenson Rd HNWL W7 85 F5
WALTH * E17 57 G4
WHTN TW2 123 F6
Stephenson St CAN/RD E16 94 C4
WLSDN NW10 87 G2
Stephenson Wy CAMTN NW1 4 F9
Stephen's Rd SRTFD E15 76 C7
Stephen St FITZ W1T 11 G4
Stepney Cswy WCHPL E1 93 F5
Stepney Gn WCHPL E1 92 E4
Stepney High St WCHPL E1 93 F4
Stepney Wy WCHPL E1 92 E4
Sterling Av EDGW HA8 36 B3
Sterling Cl WLSDN NW10 69 J6
Sterling Gdns NWCR SE14 112 B5
Sterling Pl BTFD TW8 105 F3
Sterling St SKENS SW7 15 K2
Sterling Wy (North Circular)
UED N18 41 K4
Stern Cl BARK IG11 97 J1
Sterndale Rd DART DA1 139 J6
WKENS * W14 107 G2
Sterne St SHB W12 107 G1
Sternhall La PECK SE15 131 H2
Sternhold Av
BRXS/STRHM SW2 148 E1
Sterry Crs DAGE RM10 80 C4
Sterry Dr HOR/WEW KT19 173 G3
THDIT KT7 157 K5
Sterry Gdns DAGE RM10 80 C5
Sterry Rd BARK IG11 79 F7
DAGE RM10 80 C3
Sterry St STHWK SE1 19 G2
Steucers La FSTH SE23 132 B7
Steve Biko La CAT SE6 151 J3
Steve Biko Rd HOLWY N7 73 G2
Steve Biko Wy HSLW TW3 123 F2
Stevedale Rd WELL DA16 136 D1
Stevedore St WAP E1W 92 D7
Stevenage Rd EHAM E6 78 A5
FUL/PGN SW6 107 G7
Stevens Av HOM E9 74 E5
Stevens Cl BECK BR3 151 J5
HPTN TW12 141 K5
PIN HA5 47 G4
Stevens Gn BUSH WD23 22 C7
Stevens' La ESH/CLAY KT10 171 G6
Stevenson Cl BAR EN5 27 H5
ERITH DA8 118 E6
Stevenson Crs
BERM/RHTH SE16 111 H4
Stevens Rd BCTR RM8 79 H1
Stevens St STHWK SE1 19 K3
Steventon Rd SHB W12 87 H6
Steward St WCHPL E1 13 K2
Stewart Cl CDALE/KGS * NW9 50 E5
CHST BR7 154 B4
HPTN TW12 141 J5
Stewart Rd WAN E11 76 B3
Stewartsby Cl UED N18 41 J4
Stewart's Gv CHEL SW3 15 H7
Stewart's La VX/NE SW8 109 G6
Stewart's Rd VX/NE SW8 109 H7
Stewart St POP/IOD E14 113 F1
Stew La BLKFR EC4V 12 E6
Steyne Rd ACT W3 86 D7
Steyning Gv ELTH/MOT SE9 153 K3
Steynings Wy
NFNCH/WDSP N12 38 E4
Steyning Wy HSLWW TW4 122 B3
Stickland Rd BELV DA17 117 H3
Stickleton Cl GFD/PVL UB6 84 B2
Stilecroft Gdns ALP/SUD HA0 67 H2
Stile Hall Gdns CHSWK W4 105 H4
Stiles Cl ERITH DA8 117 J4
HAYES BR2 168 E5
Stillingfleet Rd BARN SW13 106 D6
Stillington St WEST SW1P 16 F5
Stillness Rd FSTH SE23 132 B5
Stipularis Dr YEAD UB4 83 H3
Stirling Av PIN HA5 47 H6
Stirling Cl RAIN RM13 99 K2
STRHM/NOR SW16 148 C7
Stirling Gv HSLW TW3 123 H1
Stirling Rd ACT W3 105 J2
BRXN/ST SW9 129 K1
HYS/HAR UB3 83 F6
KTN/HRWW/W HA3 49 F2
PLSTW E13 95 F1
TOTM N17 42 C7
WALTH E17 57 G2
WDGN N22 41 H7
WHTN TW2 123 F6
Stirling Wk BRYLDS KT5 159 J5
Stirling Wy BORE WD6 25 F5
Stiven Crs RYLN/HDSTN HA2 65 K2
St John's Est IS N1 7 H6
STHWK SE1 19 L1
St Luke's Est FSBYE EC1V 7 G8
Stockbury Rd CROY/NA CR0 165 K5
Stockdale Rd BCTR RM8 80 B1
Stockdove Wy GFD/PVL UB6 85 F2
Stocker Gdns DAGW RM9 79 J6
Stockfield Rd ESH/CLAY KT10 170 E3
STRHM/NOR SW16 149 F2
Stockholm Rd
BERM/RHTH SE16 111 K4
Stockholm Wy WAP * E1W 92 C7
Stockhurst Cl PUT/ROE SW15 127 F1
Stockingswater La PEND EN3 31 G2
Stockland Rd ROMW/RG RM7 63 F5
Stockley Cl WDR/YW UB7 100 E1
Stockley Farm Rd
WDR/YW UB7 100 E2
Stockley Rd WDR/YW UB7 100 E2
Stock Orchard Crs HOLWY * N7 73 F3
Stock Orchard St HOLWY N7 73 F4
Stockport Rd
STRHM/NOR SW16 148 D7
Stocksfield Rd WALTH * E17 58 A2
Stocks Pl POP/IOD E14 93 H6
Stock St PLSTW E13 94 E1
Stockton Cl BAR EN5 27 G3
Stockton Gdns MLHL NW7 37 F2
TOTM N17 41 J6
Stockton Rd TOTM N17 41 J6
UED N18 42 C5
Stockwell Av BRXN/ST SW9 130 A2
Stockwell Cl BMLY BR1 168 A1
Stockwell Gdns BRXN/ST SW9 110 A7
Stockwell Gn BRXN/ST SW9 130 A1
Stockwell La BRXN/ST SW9 130 A1
Stockwell Park Crs
BRXN/ST SW9 130 A1
Stockwell Park Rd
BRXN/ST SW9 110 A7
Stockwell Park Wk
BRXN/ST SW9 130 A2
Stockwell Rd BRXN/ST SW9 130 A1
Stockwell St GNWCH SE10 113 F5
Stockwell Ter BRXN/ST SW9 110 A7
Stodart Rd PGE/AN SE20 150 E7
Stoford Cl WIM/MER SW19 127 H7
Stokenchurch St
FUL/PGN SW6 108 A7
Stoke Newington Church St
STNW/STAM N16 74 A1
Stoke Newington Common
STNW/STAM N16 74 B2
Stoke Newington High St
STNW/STAM N16 74 B2
Stoke Newington Rd
STNW/STAM N16 74 B4
Stoke Pl WLSDN NW10 87 H2
Stoke Rd KUTN/CMB KT2 144 E6
Stokesby Rd CHSGTN KT9 172 B5
Stokesley St SHB W12 87 H5
Stokes Rd CROY/NA CR0 166 A5
EHAM E6 95 J3
Stoll Cl CRICK NW2 70 A2
Stonard Rd BCTR RM8 79 H4
PLMGR N13 41 G2
Stondon Pk FSTH SE23 132 B6
Stonebridge Pk WLSDN NW10 69 F6
Stonebridge Rd
SEVS/STOTM N15 56 A4
Stonebridge Wy WBLY HA9 68 D5
Stone Buildings LINN WC2A 11 M3
Stonechat Sq EHAM E6 95 J4
Stone Cl BCTR RM8 80 B1
CLAP SW4 129 H1
Stonecot Cl MRDN SM4 161 H7
Stonecot Hl MRDN SM4 161 H7
Stone Crs EBED/NFELT TW14 121 J6
Stonecroft Cl BAR EN5 25 K3
Stonecroft Rd ERITH DA8 117 K6
Stonecroft Wy CROY/NA CR0 163 K6
Stonecutter St
FLST/FETLN EC4A 12 C4
Stonefield Cl BXLYHN DA7 137 H2
RSLP HA4 65 J4
Stonefield St IS N1 6 B3
Stonefield Wy CHARL SE7 114 C6
RSLP HA4 65 H4
Stone Gv EDGW HA8 36 A3
Stonegrove Gdns EDGW HA8 36 B4
Stonehall Av IL IG1 59 J5
Stone Hall Gdns KENS * W8 14 C4
Stone Hall Pl KENS * W8 14 C4
Stone Hall Rd WCHMH N21 29 F6
Stoneham Rd FBAR/BDGN N11 40 C4
Stonehill Cl MORT/ESHN SW14 126 A4
Stonehill Rd CHSWK W4 105 H4
MORT/ESHN SW14 125 K4
Stonehills Ct DUL SE21 150 A2
Stonehorse Rd PEND EN3 30 E4
Stone House Ct HDTCH EC3A 13 K4
Stoneleigh Av WPK KT4 173 J2
Stoneleigh Broadway
EW KT17 173 J4
Stoneleigh Crs HOR/WEW KT19 173 J4
Stoneleigh Park Av
CROY/NA CR0 166 A5
Stoneleigh Park Rd
HOR/WEW KT19 173 H5
Stoneleigh Pl NTGHL W11 88 B6
Stoneleigh Rd CAR SM5 162 D6
CLAY IG5 59 J2
TOTM N17 56 B1
Stoneleigh St NTGHL W11 88 B6
Stonemasons Cl
SEVS/STOTM * N15 55 K3
Stonenest St FSBYPK N4 55 F7
Stone Park Av BECK BR3 166 D3
Stone Pl WPK KT4 173 J1
Stone Rd HAYES BR2 167 J4
Stones End St STHWK SE1 18 E2
Stone St CROY/NA CR0 177 G4
Stonewall EHAM E6 96 A4
Stonewood Rd ERITH DA8 118 D4
Stoney Aly WOOL/PLUM SE18 135 F1
Stoneyard La POP/IOD E14 93 K6
Stoneycroft Cl LEE/GVPK SE12 133 J6
Stoneycroft Rd WFD IG8 45 J5
Stoneydown WALTH E17 57 G3
Stoneydown Av WALTH E17 57 G3
Stoneyfields Gdns EDGW HA8 36 E3
Stoneyfields La EDGW HA8 36 E4
Stoney La HDTCH EC3A 13 K4
NRWD SE19 150 B5
Stoney St STHWK SE1 13 G8
Stonhouse St CLAP SW4 129 H2
Stonnell's Rd BTSEA SW11 128 E4
Stonor Rd WKENS W14 107 J3
Stonycroft Cl PEND EN3 31 G1
Stopes St PECK SE15 111 G6
Stopford Rd PLSTW E13 76 E7
WALW * SE17 18 D8
Store Rd CAN/RD E16 115 F1
Storers Quay POP/IOD E14 113 G3
Store St GWRST WC1E 11 G3
SRTFD E15 76 B4
Storey Rd HGT N6 53 K5
WALTH E17 57 H3
Storey's Ga WEST SW1P 17 H2
Stories Ms CMBW * SE5 131 F1
Stories Rd CMBW SE5 131 F2
Stork Rd FSTGT E7 76 D5
Storksmead Rd EDGW HA8 37 G6
Storks Rd BERM/RHTH * SE16 111 H2
Stormont Rd BTSEA SW11 129 F3
HGT N6 53 K6
Stormont Wy CHSGTN KT9 171 J4
Stormount Dr HYS/HAR UB3 101 F1
Storrington Rd CROY/NA CR0 165 G7
Story St IS N1 5 L2
Stothard St WCHPL E1 92 E3
Stott Cl WAND/EARL SW18 128 C5
Stoughton Av CHEAM SM3 174 B4
Stoughton Cl PUT/ROE SW15 126 D7
Stour Av NWDGN UB2 103 F2
Stourcliffe St BAY/PAD W2 9 L5
Stour Cl HAYES BR2 181 G3
Stourhead Cl WIM/MER SW19 127 G6
Stourhead Gdns RYNPK SW20 160 D2
Stour Rd BOW E3 75 J6
DAGE RM10 80 C1
DART DA1 138 D2
Stourton Av FELT TW13 141 K3
Stowage DEPT SE8 112 E5
Stow Crs WALTH E17 43 G7
Stowe Gdns ED N9 30 B7
Stowe Pl SEVS/STOTM N15 56 A2
Stowe Rd SHB W12 106 E1
Stox Md KTN/HRWW/W HA3 34 D7
Stracey Rd WLSDN NW10 69 F7
Strachan Pl RYNPK SW20 146 A5
Stradbroke Gv CLAY IG5 59 J2
Stradbroke Rd HBRY N5 73 J3
Stradbrook Cl RYLN/HDSTN HA2 65 K2
Stradella Rd HNHL SE24 130 D5
Strafford Av CLAY IG5 60 A1
Strafford Rd ACT W3 105 K1
BAR EN5 26 C2
HSLW TW3 122 E2
TWK TW1 124 B6
Strafford St POP/IOD E14 112 D1
Strahan Rd BOW E3 93 G2
The Straight NWDGN UB2 102 C1
Straightsmouth GNWCH SE10 113 F6
Strait Rd EHAM E6 95 J6
Straker's Rd EDUL SE22 131 J3
Strand TPL/STR WC2R 11 K7
Strandfield Cl
WOOL/PLUM SE18 115 K4
Strand-on-the-Green
CHSWK W4 105 H5
Strand Pl UED N18 42 A3
Strangways Ter WKENS W14 107 J2
Stranraer Wy IS N1 5 L2
Strasburg Rd BTSEA SW11 109 F7
Stratfield Park Cl WCHMH N21 29 H6
Stratfield Rd BORE WD6 24 B2
Stratford Cl BARK IG11 79 G6
DAGE RM10 80 E6
Stratford Ct NWMAL KT3 160 A3
Stratford Gv PUT/ROE SW15 127 G3
Stratford House Av BMLY BR1 168 D2
Stratford Pl MHST W1U 10 C5
Stratford Rd HTHAIR TW6 120 E5
KENS W8 14 B4
NWDGN UB2 102 D3
PLSTW E13 76 E7
THHTH CR7 164 B3
WAT WD17 20 E1
YEAD UB4 83 F3
Stratford Vls CAMTN NW1 4 F1
Stratford Wy WAT WD17 20 D1
Strathan Cl WAND/EARL SW18 127 H5
Strathaven Rd LEE/GVPK SE12 134 A5
Strathblaine Rd BTSEA SW11 128 C4
Strathbrook Rd
STRHM/NOR SW16 149 F6
Strathcona Rd WBLY HA9 67 K1
Strathdale STRHM/NOR SW16 149 F4
Strathdon Dr TOOT SW17 147 H2
Strathearn Av HYS/HAR UB3 101 J6
WHTN TW2 123 H7
Strathearn Cottages
TRDG/WHET * N20 38 E2
Strathearn Pl BAY/PAD W2 9 J6
Strathearn Rd SUT SM1 174 E4
WIM/MER SW19 146 E4
Stratheden Rd BKHTH/KID SE3 113 K7
Strathfield Gdns BARK IG11 78 D5
Strathleven Rd
BRXS/STRHM SW2 129 K4
Strathmore Gdns EDGW HA8 50 D1
FNCH N3 39 F7
HCH RM12 63 H7
Strathmore Rd CROY/NA CR0 164 D6
TEDD TW11 142 E3
WIM/MER SW19 146 E2
Strathnairn St STHWK SE1 111 H3
Strathray Gdns HAMP * NW3 71 J5
Strath Ter BTSEA SW11 128 D3
Strathville Rd
WAND/EARL SW18 146 E1
Strathyre Av
STRHM/NOR SW16 164 B2
Stratton Av WLGTN SM6 176 D7
Stratton Cl BXLYHN DA7 137 F2
EDGW HA8 36 B5
HEST TW5 102 E7
WIM/MER SW19 161 J1
WOT/HER * KT12 156 B7
Strattondale St POP/IOD E14 113 F2
Stratton Dr BARK IG11 78 E4
Stratton Gdns STHL UB1 83 K5
Stratton Rd BXLYHN DA7 137 F2
WIM/MER SW19 161 K1
Stratton St MYFR/PICC W1J 10 D8
Strauss Rd CHSWK * W4 106 A1
Strawberry Hill Rd TWK TW1 143 F2
Strawberry La CAR SM5 175 K2
Strawberry Ter MUSWH * N10 39 K7
Strawberry V EFNCH N2 39 H7
TWK TW1 143 F2
Streakes Field Rd CRICK NW2 69 J1
Streamdale ABYW SE2 116 C5
Streamline Ms EDUL SE22 131 J7
Streamside Cl ED N9 30 B7
HAYES BR2 167 K3
Stream Wy BELV DA17 117 H5
Streatfeild Av EHAM E6 77 K7
Streatfeild Rd
KTN/HRWW/W HA3 49 J2
Streatham Cl
STRHM/NOR * SW16 148 E1
Streatham Common
STRHM/NOR * SW16 148 D6
Streatham Common North
STRHM/NOR SW16 149 F4
Streatham Common South
STRHM/NOR SW16 148 E5
Streatham Ct
STRHM/NOR SW16 148 E2
Streatham Gn
STRHM/NOR * SW16 148 E3
Streatham High Rd
STRHM/NOR SW16 148 E3
Streatham Hl
BRXS/STRHM SW2 129 K7
Streatham Pl
BRXS/STRHM SW2 129 K6
Streatham Rd MTCM CR4 148 A7
Streatham St
NOXST/BSQ WC1A 11 J4
Streatham V
STRHM/NOR SW16 148 C7
Streathbourne Rd TOOT SW17 148 A1
Streatleigh Pde
STRHM/NOR * SW16 148 E1
Streatley Pl HAMP NW3 71 H3
Streatley Rd KIL/WHAMP NW6 70 D6
Streeters La WLGTN SM6 176 D2
Streetfield Ms BKHTH/KID SE3 133 K1
Streimer Rd SRTFD E15 94 A1
Strelley Wy ACT W3 87 G6
Stretton Rd CROY/NA CR0 165 F6
RCHPK/HAM TW10 143 J1
Strickland Av DART DA1 139 J3
Strickland Rw
WAND/EARL SW18 128 C6
Strickland St DEPT SE8 132 D1
Stride Rd PLSTW E13 94 D1
Strimon Cl ED N9 42 E1
Stripling Wy WATW WD18 20 E5
Strode Cl MUSWH N10 40 A6
Strode Rd FSTGT E7 76 E3
FUL/PGN SW6 107 G6
TOTM N17 56 A1
WLSDN NW10 69 J5
Strone Rd FSTGT E7 77 G5
Strone Wy YEAD UB4 83 J3
Strongbow Crs
ELTH/MOT SE9 134 E4
Strongbow Rd
ELTH/MOT SE9 134 E4
Strongbridge Cl
RYLN/HDSTN HA2 48 A7
Stronsa Rd SHB W12 106 C1
Strood Av ROMW/RG RM7 63 F7
Stroud Crs PUT/ROE SW15 145 H2
Stroudes Cl WPK KT4 160 C6
Stroud Fld NTHLT UB5 65 J5
Stroud Ga RYLN/HDSTN HA2 66 B3
Stroud Green Rd FSBYPK N4 55 F7
Stroud Green Wy
CROY/NA CR0 165 J6
Stroud Rd SNWD SE25 165 H5
WIM/MER SW19 146 E2
Strouds Cl CHDH RM6 61 H4
Stroughton Cl LBTH SE11 17 M6
Strout's Pl BETH E2 7 L7
Strutton Gnd WEST SW1P 17 G3
Strype St WCHPL E1 13 L3
St Saviour's Est STHWK SE1 19 L3
Stuart Av CDALE/KGS NW9 51 J6
EA W5 105 G1
HAYES BR2 167 K7
RYLN/HDSTN HA2 65 K2
WOT/HER KT12 156 B7
Stuart Ct BORE WD6 23 K5
Stuart Crs CROY/NA CR0 179 H2
HYS/HAR UB3 82 A5
WDGN N22 41 F7
Stuart Evans Cl WELL DA16 136 D2
Stuart Gv TEDD TW11 142 E4
Stuart Mantle Wy ERITH DA8 118 A6
Stuart Pl MTCM CR4 147 K7
Stuart Rd ACT W3 86 E7
BARK IG11 79 F7
EBAR EN4 27 J6
KIL/WHAMP NW6 2 A8
KTN/HRWW/W HA3 49 F2
PECK SE15 131 K3
RCHPK/HAM TW10 143 H1
THHTH CR7 164 D3
WELL DA16 116 C7
WIM/MER SW19 146 E2
Stubbs Cl CDALE/KGS NW9 50 E4
Stubbs Dr BERM/RHTH SE16 111 J4
Stubbs Wy WIM/MER SW19 147 H7
Stucley Pl CAMTN NW1 4 D2
Stucley Rd ISLW TW7 103 H6
Studdridge St FUL/PGN SW6 127 K1
Studd St IS N1 6 C3
Studholme Ct HAMP * NW3 70 E3
Studholme St PECK SE15 111 J6
The Studios BUSH WD23 22 A5
Studio Pl KTBR * SW1X 15 M2
Studio Wy BORE WD6 24 E1
Studland Cl BFN/LL DA15 155 F2
Studland Rd HNWL W7 84 D5
KUTN/CMB KT2 144 A5
SYD SE26 151 F4
Studland St HMSMTH W6 106 E3
Studley Av CHING E4 44 B6
Studley Cl CLPT E5 75 G4
Studley Ct SCUP DA14 155 H4
Studley Dr REDBR IG4 59 H5
Studley Grange Rd HNWL W7 103 K2
Studley Rd CLAP SW4 109 K7
DAGW RM9 79 K6
FSTGT E7 77 F5
Stukeley Rd FSTGT E7 77 F6
Stukeley St HOL/ALD WC2B 11 K4
Stumps Hill La BECK BR3 151 J5
Sturdy Rd PECK SE15 131 J1
Sturge Av WALTH E17 43 K7
Sturgeon Rd WALW SE17 18 E8
Sturges Fld CHST BR7 154 D6
Sturgess Av HDN NW4 51 K6
Sturge St STHWK SE1 18 E2
Sturmer Wy HOLWY N7 73 F4
Sturminster Cl YEAD UB4 83 G5
Sturrock Cl SEVS/STOTM N15 55 K3
Sturry St POP/IOD E14 93 K5
Sturt St IS N1 6 F6
Stutfield St WCHPL E1 92 C5
Styles Gdns BRXN/ST SW9 130 C2
Styles Wy BECK BR3 167 F3
Sudbourne Rd
BRXS/STRHM SW2 129 K4
Sudbrooke Rd BAL SW12 128 E5
Sudbrook Gdns
RCHPK/HAM TW10 144 A2
Sudbrook La
RCHPK/HAM TW10 125 F7
Sudbury EHAM E6 96 A5
Sudbury Av ALP/SUD HA0 67 J2
Sudbury Court Dr HRW HA1 67 G1
Sudbury Court Rd ALP/SUD HA0 67 G2
Sudbury Crs ALP/SUD HA0 67 H4
BMLY BR1 152 E4
Sudbury Cft ALP/SUD HA0 67 F3
Sudbury Gdns CROY/NA CR0 178 A3
Sudbury Heights Av
GFD/PVL UB6 67 F4
Sudbury Hl HRW HA1 66 E2
Sudbury Hill Cl ALP/SUD HA0 67 F3
Sudbury Rd BARK IG11 79 F4
Sudeley St IS N1 6 D6
Sudlow Rd WAND/EARL SW18 127 K3
Sudrey St STHWK SE1 18 E2
Suez Av GFD/PVL UB6 85 F1
Suez Rd PEND EN3 31 G3
Suffield Rd CHING E4 43 K2
PGE/AN SE20 165 K1
SEVS/STOTM * N15 56 B4
Suffolk Cl BORE WD6 25 F4
Suffolk La CANST EC4R 13 G6
Suffolk Park Rd WALTH E17 57 G3
Suffolk Rd BARK IG11 78 D6
BARN SW13 106 C6
DAGE RM10 80 D4
DART DA1 139 H5
GDMY/SEVK IG3 60 E5
PEND EN3 30 D4
PLSTW E13 94 D2
RYLN/HDSTN HA2 47 K5
SCUP DA14 155 J5
SEVS/STOTM N15 55 K5

SNWD SE25 165 G3
WLSDN NW10 69 G6
WPK KT4 173 H1
Suffolk St *FSTGT* E7 76 E4
STJS SW1Y 11 H8
Suffolk Vls *WAND/EARL* * SW18 127 K6
Sugar House La *SRTFD* E15 94 A1
Sugar Loaf Wk *BETH* * E2 92 E2
Sugden Rd *BTSEA* SW11 129 F2
THDIT KT7 158 B7
Sugden Wy *BARK* IG11 97 F1
Sulgrave Gdns *SHB* W12 107 F1
Sulgrave Rd *SHB* W12 107 F1
Sulina Rd *BRXS/STRHM* SW2 129 K6
Sulivan Ct *FUL/PGN* SW6 127 K1
Sulivan Rd *FUL/PGN* SW6 127 K2
Sullivan Av *CAN/RD* E16 95 H4
Sullivan Cl *BTSEA* SW11 128 D2
DART DA1 138 E5
E/WMO/HCT KT8 157 G2
YEAD UB4 83 G4
Sullivan Rd *LBTH* SE11 18 B5
Sullivan Wy *BORE* WD6 23 J5
Sultan Rd *WAN* E11 59 F3
Sultan St *BECK* BR3 166 A1
CMBW SE5 110 D6
Sumatra Rd *KIL/WHAMP* NW6 70 E5
Sumburgh Rd *BAL* SW12 129 F5
Summer Av *E/WMO/HCT* KT8 157 K4
Summercourt Rd *WCHPL* E1 92 E5
Summerene Cl
STRHM/NOR SW16 148 C6
Summerfield Av
KIL/WHAMP NW6 88 C1
NFNCH/WDSP N12 39 J5
Summerfield La *SURB* KT6 171 K1
Summerfield Rd *WEA* W13 85 H3
Summerfield St
LEE/GVPK SE12 133 J6
Summer Gdns
E/WMO/HCT KT8 157 K4
Summer Gv *BORE* WD6 23 K5
Summer Hl *BORE* WD6 24 C4
CHST BR7 169 F1
Summerhill Gv *EN* EN1 30 A5
Summerhill Rd *DART* DA1 139 G6
SEVS/STOTM N15 55 K3
Summerhill Wy *MTCM* CR4 148 A7
Summerhouse Av *HEST* TW5 102 D7
Summerhouse La
WDR/YW UB7 100 A5
Summerhouse Rd
STNW/STAM N16 74 A1
Summerland Gdns *MUSWH* N10 54 B2
Summerlands Av *ACT* W3 86 E6
Summerlee Av *EFNCH* N2 53 K3
Summerlee Gdns *EFNCH* N2 53 K3
Summerley St
WAND/EARL SW18 147 F1
Summer Pl *WATW* * WD18 20 D5
Summer Rd *E/WMO/HCT* KT8 157 K4
Summersby Rd *HGT* N6 54 B5
Summers Cl *BELMT* SM2 174 E6
WBLY HA9 50 D7
Summerskille Cl *ED* N9 42 D1
Summers La *NFNCH/WDSP* N12 39 H6
Summers Rw
NFNCH/WDSP N12 39 J5
Summers St *CLKNW* EC1R 12 A1
Summerstown *TOOT* SW17 147 G2
Summers Wd *BORE* * WD6 24 D3
Summerton Wy *THMD* SE28 97 K6
Summer Trees *SUN* TW16 141 F7
Summerville Gdns *SUT* SM1 174 D5
Summerwood Rd *ISLW* TW7 124 A5
Summit Av *CDALE/KGS* NW9 51 F4
Summit Centre *WDR/YW* * UB7 100 A6
Summit Cl *CDALE/KGS* NW9 51 F3
EDGW HA8 36 C6
STHGT/OAK N14 40 C1
Summit Dr *WFD* IG8 59 H1
Summit Est *STNW/STAM* * N16 56 C6
Summit Rd *NTHLT* UB5 66 A6
WALTH E17 57 K3
Summit Wy *NRWD* SE19 150 A6
STHGT/OAK N14 40 B1
Sumner Av *PECK* SE15 111 G7
Sumner Gdns *CROY/NA* CR0 164 B7
Sumner Pl *SKENS* SW7 15 H6
Sumner Place Ms *SKENS* SW7 15 H6
Sumner Rd *CROY/NA* CR0 164 C7
HRW HA1 48 C6
PECK SE15 111 G5
Sumner Rd South
CROY/NA CR0 164 B7
Sumner St *STHWK* SE1 12 E8
Sumpter Cl *HAMP* NW3 71 G5
Sunbeam Crs *NKENS* W10 88 A3
Sunbeam Rd *WLSDN* NW10 86 E3
Sunbury Av *MLHL* NW7 37 F4
MORT/ESHN SW14 126 A3
Sunbury Ct *BAR* * EN5 26 C3
SUN TW16 156 C1
Sunbury Court Rd *SUN* TW16 156 B1
Sunbury Gdns *MLHL* NW7 37 F4
Sunbury La *BTSEA* SW11 108 C7
Sunbury Rd *CHEAM* SM3 174 B2
FELT TW13 140 D2
Sunbury St *WOOL/PLUM* SE18 114 E2
Sunbury Wy *FELT* TW13 141 G4
Sun Ct *ERITH* DA8 138 C1
Suncroft Pl *SYD* SE26 150 E2
Sunderland Mt *FSTH* * SE23 151 F1
Sunderland Rd *EA* W5 104 E2
FSTH SE23 132 A7
Sunderland Ter *BAY/PAD* W2 8 C4
Sunderland Wy *MNPK* E12 77 H1
Sundew Av *SHB* W12 87 J6
Sundew Ct *ALP/SUD* * HA0 86 A1
Sundial Av *SNWD* SE25 165 G1
Sundorne Rd *CHARL* SE7 114 A4
Sundown Rd *ASHF* TW15 140 A4
Sundridge Av *BMLY* BR1 153 H7
WELL DA16 135 J1
Sundridge Cl *DART* DA1 139 K5
Sundridge Pde *BMLY* * BR1 153 F6
Sundridge Rd *CROY/NA* CR0 165 G7
Sunfields Pl *BKHTH/KID* SE3 114 A6
Sun in Sands Rbt
BKHTH/KID SE3 114 A6
Sunken Rd *CROY/NA* CR0 178 E4
Sunkist Wy *WLGTN* SM6 176 E7
Sunland Av *BXLYHS* DA6 137 F3
Sun La *BKHTH/KID* SE3 114 A6
Sunleigh Rd *ALP/SUD* HA0 68 A7
Sunley Gdns *GFD/PVL* UB6 85 G1
Sunlight Cl *WIM/MER* * SW19 147 G5
Sunlight Sq *BETH* E2 92 D2
Sunna Gdns *SUN* TW16 156 A1
Sunningdale *STHGT/OAK* N14 40 D4
Sunningdale Av *ACT* W3 87 G6
BARK IG11 78 D7
FELT TW13 141 J1
RAIN RM13 99 K3
RSLP HA4 47 G7
Sunningdale Cl
BERM/RHTH * SE16 111 J4
STAN HA7 35 G6
SURB KT6 172 A1
THMD SE28 98 A5
Sunningdale Gdns
CDALE/KGS NW9 50 E4
KENS W8 14 B4
Sunningdale Ldg *EDGW* * HA8 36 B4
Sunningdale Rd *HAYES* BR2 168 D3
RAIN RM13 81 J6
SUT SM1 174 D2
Sunningfield Rd *HDN* NW4 51 K2
Sunningfields Crs *HDN* NW4 51 K1
Sunninghill Ct *ACT* * W3 105 K1
Sunninghill Rd *LEW* SE13 132 E1
Sunny Bank *SNWD* SE25 165 H2
Sunny Crs *WLSDN* NW10 68 E6
Sunnycroft Rd *HSLW* TW3 123 G1
SNWD SE25 165 H2
STHL UB1 84 A4
Sunnydale Gdns *MLHL* NW7 37 F5
Sunnydale Rd *LEE/GVPK* SE12 134 A4
Sunnydene Av *CHING* E4 44 B4
RSLP HA4 46 E7
Sunnydene Gdns *ALP/SUD* HA0 67 J5
Sunnydene St *SYD* SE26 151 G3
Sunnyfield *MLHL* NW7 37 H3
Sunny Gardens Rd *HDN* NW4 52 A2
Sunny Hl *HDN* NW4 51 K2
Sunnyhill Cl *CLPT* E5 75 G3
Sunnyhill Rd
STRHM/NOR SW16 148 E3
Sunnyhurst Cl *SUT* SM1 174 E2
Sunnymead Av *MTCM* CR4 163 J2
Sunnymead Rd
CDALE/KGS NW9 51 F6
PUT/ROE SW15 126 E4
Sunnymede Av
HOR/WEW KT19 173 G7
Sunnymede Dr *BARK/HLT* IG6 60 B3
Sunny Nook Gdns
SAND/SEL CR2 177 K5
Sunny Pl *HDN* NW4 52 A3
Sunnyside *CAT* * SE6 132 C6
CRICK NW2 70 D2
WIM/MER SW19 146 C5
WOT/HER KT12 156 B4
Sunnyside Rd *ARCH* N19 54 D6
EA W5 85 K7
IL IG1 78 C2
LEY E10 57 J7
TEDD TW11 142 D3
Sunnyside Rd East *ED* N9 42 C2
Sunnyside Rd North *ED* * N9 42 B2
Sunnyside Rd South *ED* * N9 42 B2
Sunny Vw *CDALE/KGS* NW9 51 F4
Sunny Wy *NFNCH/WDSP* N12 39 J6
Sun Pas *BERM/RHTH* SE16 111 H2
Sunray Av *BRYLDS* KT5 172 D1
CMBW SE5 130 E3
HAYES BR2 168 D5
WDR/YW UB7 100 A1
Sunrise Cl *FELT* TW13 141 K2
Sun Rd *WKENS* W14 107 J4
Sunset Av *CHING* E4 31 K7
WFD IG8 44 E4
Sunset Cl *ERITH* DA8 118 E6
Sunset Gdns *NRWD* SE19 165 F1
Sunset Rd *CMBW* SE5 130 D3
THMD SE28 97 G7
WIM/MER SW19 145 K4
Sunset Vw *BAR* EN5 26 C1
Sunshine Wy *MTCM* CR4 162 E1
Sun St *SDTCH* EC2A 13 H2
Surbiton Ct *SURB* KT6 158 D5
Surbiton Crs *SURB* KT6 159 F5
Surbiton Hall Cl *KUT* KT1 159 F3
Surbiton Hill Pk *BRYLDS* KT5 159 G4
Surbiton Hill Rd *SURB* KT6 159 F3
Surbiton Rd *KUT* KT1 158 E3
Surlingham Cl *THMD* SE28 97 K6
Surma Cl *WCHPL* E1 92 C3
Surmans Cl *DAGW* RM9 79 J7
Surrendale Pl *MV/WKIL* W9 8 B1
Surrey Canal Rd
BERM/RHTH SE16 111 K5
Surrey Crs *CHSWK* W4 105 H4
Surrey Gdns *FSBYPK* N4 55 J5
Surrey Gv *SUT* SM1 175 H2
WALW SE17 19 J8
Surrey La *BTSEA* SW11 108 D7
Surrey Ms *WNWD* SE27 150 A3
Surrey Quays Rd
BERM/RHTH SE16 111 K2
Surrey Rd *BARK* IG11 78 E6
DAGE RM10 80 E4
HRW HA1 48 C5
PECK SE15 132 A4
WWKM BR4 166 E7
Surrey Rw *STHWK* SE1 18 C1
Surrey Sq *WALW* SE17 19 J7
Surrey St *CROY/NA* CR0 177 J2
PLSTW E13 95 F2
TPL/STR WC2R 11 M6
Surrey Ter *WALW* SE17 19 K6
Surrey Water Rd
BERM/RHTH SE16 93 F7
Surridge Gdns *NRWD* SE19 149 K5
Surr St *HOLWY* N7 72 E4
Susan Cl *ROMW/RG* RM7 62 E2
Susannah St *POP/IOD* E14 93 K5
Susan Rd *BKHTH/KID* SE3 134 A1
Susan Wd *CHST* BR7 154 A7
Sussex Av *ISLW* TW7 123 K2
Sussex Cl *ARCH* * N19 72 E1
NWMAL KT3 160 B3
REDBR IG4 59 K5
TWK TW1 124 C5
Sussex Crs *NTHLT* UB5 66 A5
Sussex Gdns *BAY/PAD* W2 9 H6
CHSGTN KT9 171 K5
EFNCH N2 53 K4
FSBYPK N4 55 J4
Sussex Ga *EFNCH* * N2 53 K4
Sussex Ms East *BAY/PAD* * W2 9 H6
Sussex Ms West *BAY/PAD* W2 9 H6
Sussex Pl *BAY/PAD* W2 9 H5
CAMTN NW1 3 L9
HMSMTH W6 107 F4
NWMAL KT3 160 B3
Sussex Rd *CAR* SM5 175 K6
DART DA1 139 K6
EHAM E6 96 A1
ERITH DA8 117 J6
HGDN/ICK UB10 64 A3
HRW HA1 48 C4
MTCM * CR4 163 K4
NWDGN UB2 102 C2
NWMAL KT3 160 B3
SAND/SEL CR2 177 K5
SCUP DA14 155 H4
WWKM BR4 166 E7
Sussex Sq *BAY/PAD* W2 9 H6
Sussex St *PIM* SW1V 16 D8
PLSTW E13 95 F2
Sussex Ter *PGE/AN* * SE20 150 E6
Sussex Wy *ARCH* N19 54 D7
EBAR EN4 28 B4
Sutcliffe Cl *BUSH* WD23 22 C3
GLDGN NW11 53 F4
Sutcliffe Rd *WELL* DA16 136 D1
WOOL/PLUM SE18 115 K5
Sutherland Av *HYS/HAR* UB3 101 K3
MV/WKIL W9 2 E8
WEA W13 85 H5
WELL DA16 135 J3
Sutherland Cl *BAR* EN5 26 C3
Sutherland Ct *CDALE/KGS* NW9 50 D3
Sutherland Dr *WIM/MER* SW19 147 H7
Sutherland Gdns
MORT/ESHN SW14 126 B2
WPK KT4 160 E7
Sutherland Gv *TEDD* TW11 142 E4
WAND/EARL SW18 127 J6
Sutherland House *WALTH* * E17 57 G2
Sutherland Pl *BAY/PAD* W2 8 A4
Sutherland Rd *BELV* DA17 117 H2
BOW E3 93 H1
CHSWK W4 106 A5
CROY/NA CR0 164 B6
ED N9 30 C7
PEND EN3 31 F5
STHL UB1 83 K5
TOTM N17 42 C6
WALTH E17 57 F1
WEA W13 85 G5
Sutherland Rw *PIM* SW1V 16 D7
Sutherland Sq *WALW* SE17 18 E8
Sutherland St *PIM* SW1V 16 C7
Sutherland Vls *WEA* * W13 85 G6
Sutherland Wk *WALW* SE17 18 F8
Sutlej Rd *CHARL* SE7 114 B6
Sutterton St *HOLWY* N7 73 F5
Sutton Cl *BECK* BR3 151 K7
CHSWK * W4 105 K5
PIN HA5 46 E4
Sutton Common Rd
CHEAM SM3 161 J6
Sutton Ct *BELMT* SM2 175 G6
CHSWK * W4 105 K5
EA * W5 86 A7
Sutton Court Rd *CHSWK* W4 105 K5
PLSTW E13 95 G2
SUT SM1 175 G5
Sutton Crs *BAR* EN5 26 B4
Sutton Dene *HSLW* TW3 103 G7
Sutton Dwelling Est *CHEL* SW3 15 J7
The Sutton Est *IS* N1 6 C1
Sutton Est *IS* * N1 6 C1
Sutton Gdns *CROY/NA* CR0 165 G4
Sutton Gv *SUT* SM1 175 H4
Sutton Hall *HEST* TW5 103 F6
Sutton La *CHSWK* W4 105 K4
HSLW TW3 122 E1
Sutton La South *CHSWK* W4 105 K5
Sutton Park Rd *SUT* SM1 175 F5
Sutton Pl *HOM* E9 74 E4
Sutton Rd *BARK* IG11 96 E1
HEST TW5 103 F7
MUSWH N10 40 A7
PLSTW E13 94 D3
WALTH E17 43 F7
WAT WD17 21 G2
Sutton Rw *SOHO/SHAV* W1D 11 G4
Sutton Sq *HEST* TW5 102 E7
HOM * E9 74 E4
Sutton St *WCHPL* E1 92 E5
Sutton Wy *HEST* TW5 102 E7
NKENS W10 88 A4
Swaby Rd *WAND/EARL* SW18 147 G1
Swaffield Rd
WAND/EARL SW18 128 B6
Swain Cl *STRHM/NOR* SW16 148 B5
Swain Rd *THHTH* CR7 164 D4
Swains Cl *WDR/YW* UB7 100 B1
Swain's La *HGT* N6 54 A7
KTTN NW5 72 A2
Swainson Rd *ACT* W3 106 C1
Swains Rd *MTCM* CR4 147 K6
Swain St *STJWD* NW8 3 J9
Swaisland Rd *DART* DA1 138 E4
Swaislands Dr *DART* DA1 138 C4
Swaledale Cl *FBAR/BDGN* N11 40 A5
Swale Rd *DART* DA1 138 D2
Swallands Rd *CAT* SE6 151 J2
Swallow Cl *BUSH* WD23 22 B7
BXLYHN DA7 118 B7
NWCR SE14 111 K7
Swallow Ct *RSLP* * HA4 47 G7
Swallowdale *SAND/SEL* CR2 179 F7
Swallow Dr *NTHLT* UB5 84 A1
WLSDN NW10 69 F5
Swallowfield Rd *CHARL* SE7 114 A4
Swallowfield Wy
HYS/HAR UB3 101 G1
Swallow Gdns
STRHM/NOR SW16 148 D4
Swallow Pl *REGST* W1B 10 D5
Swallow St *CONDST* W1S 10 F7
EHAM E6 95 J4
Swanage Rd *CHING* E4 44 A6
WAND/EARL SW18 128 B5
Swanage Waye *YEAD* UB4 83 G5
Swan Ap *EHAM* E6 95 J4
Swanbridge Rd *BXLYHN* DA7 117 H7
Swan Cl *CROY/NA* * CR0 165 F6
FELT TW13 141 J3
WALTH E17 43 G7
Swandon Wy
WAND/EARL SW18 128 A3
Swan Dr *CDALE/KGS* NW9 51 G1
Swanfield St *BETH* E2 7 L8
Swan Island *TWK* * TW1 143 G2
Swan La *CANST* EC4R 13 H7
DART DA1 138 C6
TRDG/WHET N20 39 G2
Swanley Rd *WELL* DA16 116 D7
Swan Md *STHWK* SE1 19 J4
Swan Ms *BRXN/ST* SW9 130 A1
Swan Pas *WCHPL* E1 13 M7
Swan Pl *BARN* SW13 126 C1
Swan Rd *BERM/RHTH* SE16 111 K1
FELT TW13 141 J3
GFD/PVL UB6 84 B5
WDR/YW UB7 100 A1
Swanscombe Rd *CHSWK* W4 106 B4
NTGHL W11 88 B7
Swansea Rd *HTHAIR* TW6 121 F5
PEND EN3 30 E3
Swanston Pth *OXHEY* WD19 33 G2
Swan St *ISLW* TW7 124 C2
STHWK SE1 18 F2
Swanton Gdns
WIM/MER SW19 127 G7
Swanton Rd *ERITH* DA8 117 H6
Swan Wk *CHEL* SW3 15 L9
Swan Wy *PEND* EN3 31 F1
Swanwick Cl *PUT/ROE* SW15 126 C6
Swan Yd *IS* N1 73 H5
Swaton Rd *BOW* E3 93 J3
Swaylands Rd *BELV* DA17 117 H5
Swaythling Cl *UED* N18 42 D3
Sweden Ga *BERM/RHTH* SE16 112 B3
Sweeney Crs *STHWK* SE1 19 M2
Sweet Briar Gn *ED* N9 42 B2
Sweet Briar Gv *ED* N9 42 B2
Sweet Briar Wk *UED* N18 42 B3
Sweetmans Av *PIN* HA5 47 H2
Sweets Wy *TRDG/WHET* N20 39 H1
Swete St *PLSTW* E13 94 E1
Sweyn Pl *BKHTH/KID* SE3 133 K1
Swift Cl *RYLN/HDSTN* HA2 66 B1
WALTH E17 43 G6
YEAD UB4 82 D5
Swift Rd *FELT* TW13 141 H3
NWDGN UB2 102 E2
Swiftsden Wy *BMLY* BR1 152 C5
Swift St *FUL/PGN* SW6 107 H7
Swinbrook Rd *NKENS* W10 88 C4
Swinburne Crs *CROY/NA* CR0 165 K5
Swinburne Rd *PUT/ROE* SW15 126 D3
Swinderby Rd *ALP/SUD* HA0 68 A5
Swindon Cl *GDMY/SEVK* IG3 78 E1
Swindon Rd *HTHAIR* TW6 121 F4
Swindon St *SHB* * W12 87 K7
Swinfield Cl *FELT* TW13 141 J3
Swinford Gdns *BRXN/ST* SW9 130 C2
Swingate La *WOOL/PLUM* SE18 115 K6
Swinnerton St *HOM* E9 75 G4
Swinton Cl *WBLY* HA9 50 D7
Swinton Pl *FSBYW* WC1X 5 L7
Swinton St *FSBYW* WC1X 5 L7
Swires Shaw *HAYES* BR2 181 H3
Swiss Av *WATW* WD18 20 C3
Swiss Cl *WATW* WD18 20 C2
Swithland Gdns
ELTH/MOT SE9 153 K3
Swyncombe Av *BTFD* TW8 104 C3
Swynford Gdns *HDN* NW4 51 J3
Sybil Phoenix Cl *DEPT* SE8 112 A4
Sybourn St *WALTH* E17 57 H6
Sycamore Ap
RKW/CH/CXG WD3 20 A4
Sycamore Av *BFN/LL* DA15 136 A5
BOW E3 75 H7
EA W5 104 E2
HYS/HAR UB3 82 C6
Sycamore Cl *ACT* W3 87 G7
BUSH WD23 21 J1
CAN/RD E16 94 C3
CAR SM5 175 K3
EBAR EN4 27 H5
ED N9 42 C3
EDGW HA8 36 E3
FELT TW13 140 E2
NTHLT UB5 65 J7
SAND/SEL CR2 178 A4
Sycamore Gdns *MTCM* CR4 162 C1
SHB W12 106 E1
Sycamore Gv *CAT* SE6 133 F5
CDALE/KGS NW9 50 E6
NWMAL KT3 160 B2
PGE/AN SE20 150 C7
Sycamore Hl *FBAR/BDGN* N11 40 A5
Sycamore Ms *CLAP* SW4 129 H2
ERITH * DA8 118 A4
Sycamore Rd *DART* DA1 139 G6
RKW/CH/CXG WD3 20 A4
WIM/MER SW19 146 A5
Sycamore St *FSBYE* EC1V 12 E1
Sycamore Wk *NKENS* W10 88 C3
Sycamore Wy *TEDD* TW11 143 J5
Sydcote *DUL* * SE21 149 J1
Sydenham Av *SYD* SE26 150 D4
WCHMH N21 29 F4
Sydenham Cl *ROM* RM1 63 H3
Sydenham Cottages
LEE/GVPK * SE12 153 G1
Sydenham Hl *SYD* SE26 150 C2
Sydenham Pk *SYD* SE26 150 E2
Sydenham Park Rd *FSTH* SE23 150 E2
Sydenham Ri *FSTH* SE23 150 D1
Sydenham Rd *CROY/NA* CR0 177 J1
SYD SE26 151 F4
Sydenham Station Ap
SYD SE26 150 E3
Sydmons Ct *FSTH* * SE23 131 K6
Sydner Rd *STNW/STAM* N16 74 B3
Sydney Cl *SKENS* SW7 15 H6
Sydney Gv *HDN* NW4 52 A4
Sydney Ms *SKENS* SW7 15 H6
Sydney Pl *SKENS* SW7 15 H6
Sydney Rd *ABYW* SE2 116 E2
BARK/HLT IG6 60 C1
BXLYHS DA6 136 E3
CEND/HSY/T N8 55 G3
EBED/NFELT TW14 121 K7
ENC/FH EN2 29 K3
MUSWH N10 40 B7
RCH/KEW TW9 125 F3
RYNPK SW20 161 G1
SCUP DA14 154 E3
SUT SM1 174 E3
TEDD TW11 143 F4
WAN E11 59 F5
WATW WD18 20 C4
WEA W13 85 G7
Sydney St *CHEL* SW3 15 J7
Sydney Ter *ESH/CLAY* * KT10 171 F5
Sylvan Av *CHDH* RM6 62 B5
MLHL NW7 37 G5
WDGN N22 41 G6
Sylvan Gdns *SURB* KT6 158 E6
Sylvan Gv *CRICK* NW2 70 B3
PECK SE15 111 J5
Sylvan Hl *NRWD* SE19 150 A7
Sylvan Rd *FSTGT* E7 76 E5
IL IG1 78 C1
NRWD SE19 150 B7
WALTH * E17 57 J4
WAN E11 58 E4
Sylvan Ter *PECK* * SE15 111 J6
Sylvan Wy *BCTR* RM8 79 H2
WWKM BR4 180 C3
Sylverdale Rd *CROY/NA* CR0 177 H2
Sylvester Av *CHST* BR7 153 K5
Sylvester Pth *HACK* * E8 74 D5
Sylvester Rd *ALP/SUD* HA0 67 J4
EFNCH N2 53 K2
HACK * E8 74 D5
WALTH * E17 57 H6
Sylvia Av *PIN* HA5 33 K5
Sylvia Gdns *WBLY* HA9 68 D6
Symes Ms *CAMTN* NW1 4 E5
Symington Ms *HOM* * E9 75 F4
Symister Ms *IS* * N1 7 J8
Symons St *BGVA* SW1W 15 M6
Symphony Ms *NKENS* * W10 88 C2
Syon Gate Wy *BTFD* TW8 104 C6
Syon La *ISLW* TW7 104 A5
Syon Pk *ISLW* * TW7 124 C2
Syon Park Gdns *ISLW* TW7 104 A6

T

Tabard Garden Est *STHWK* SE1 19 G1
Tabard St *STHWK* SE1 19 G3
Tabernacle Av *PLSTW* E13 94 E3
Tabernacle St *SDTCH* EC2A 13 H1
Tableer Av *CLAP* SW4 129 H4
Tabley Rd *HOLWY* N7 72 E3
Tabor Gdns *CHEAM* SM3 174 D5
Tabor Gv *WIM/MER* SW19 146 C6
Tabor Rd *HMSMTH* W6 106 E2
Tachbrook Rd
EBED/NFELT TW14 121 J6
NWDGN UB2 102 C3
Tachbrook St *PIM* SW1V 16 F6
Tack Ms *BROCKY* SE4 132 D2
Tadema Rd *WBPTN* SW10 108 B6
Tadmor St *SHB* W12 88 B7
Tadworth Av *NWMAL* KT3 160 C3
Tadworth Pde *HCH* RM12 81 K3
Tadworth Rd *CRICK* NW2 69 J1
Taeping St *POP/IOD* E14 112 E3
Taffy's How *MTCM* CR4 162 D2
Tait Rd *CROY/NA* CR0 165 F6
Takeley Cl *CRW* RM5 63 F1
Talacre Rd *KTTN* NW5 72 A5
Talbot Av *EFNCH* N2 53 H2
OXHEY WD19 21 J6
Talbot Cl *SEVS/STOTM* N15 56 B3
Talbot Ct *BANK* EC3V 13 H6
Talbot Crs *HDN* NW4 51 J4
Talbot Gdns *GDMY/SEVK* IG3 79 G1
Talbot Pl *BKHTH/KID* SE3 133 H1
Talbot Rd *ALP/SUD* HA0 67 K4
BAY/PAD W2 8 B4
CAR SM5 176 A4
DAGW RM9 80 B6
EDUL SE22 131 F3
EHAM E6 95 K1
FSTGT E7 76 E3
HGT N6 54 A5
ISLW TW7 124 B3
KTN/HRWW/W HA3 49 F1
NTGHL W11 88 D5
NWDGN UB2 102 D3
SEVS/STOTM N15 56 B3
THHTH CR7 164 E3
WDGN N22 54 C1
WEA * W13 85 G6
WHTN TW2 123 K7
Talbot Sq *BAY/PAD* W2 9 G5
Talbot Wk *NTGHL* W11 88 C5
WLSDN * NW10 69 G5
Talbot Yd *STHWK* SE1 13 G9
Talcott Pth
BRXS/STRHM * SW2 130 B7
Talfourd Pl *PECK* SE15 111 G7
Talfourd Rd *PECK* SE15 111 G7
Talgarth Rd *HMSMTH* W6 107 G4
Talisman Cl *GDMY/SEVK* IG3 61 H7
Talisman Sq *SYD* SE26 150 C3
Talisman Wy *WBLY* HA9 68 B2
Tallack Rd *LEY* E10 57 H7
Tall Elms Cl *HAYES* BR2 167 J4
Tallis Cl *CAN/RD* E16 95 F5
Tallis Gv *CHARL* SE7 114 A5
Tallis St *EMB* EC4Y 12 B6
Tallis Vw *WLSDN* NW10 69 F5
Tall Trees *STRHM/NOR* SW16 164 A2
Talma Gdns *WHTN* TW2 123 K6
Talmage Cl *FSTH* SE23 131 K6
Talman Gv *STAN* HA7 35 K5
Talma Rd *BRXS/STRHM* SW2 130 B3
Talwin St *BOW* E3 93 K2
Tamar Cl *BOW* * E3 75 H7
Tamarind Yd *WAP* E1W 92 C7
Tamarisk Sq *SHB* W12 87 H6
Tamar St *WOOL/PLUM* SE18 114 D3
Tamesis Gdns *WPK* KT4 173 G1
Tamian Wy *HSLWW* TW4 122 B3
Tamworth Av *WFD* IG8 44 C5
Tamworth La *MTCM* CR4 163 G2
Tamworth Pk *MTCM* CR4 163 G3
Tamworth Pl *CROY/NA* * CR0 177 J1
Tamworth Rd *CROY/NA* CR0 177 J1
Tamworth St *FUL/PGN* SW6 14 A9
Tancred Rd *FSBYPK* N4 55 H5
Tandridge Dr *ORP* BR6 169 J7
Tanfield Av *CRICK* NW2 69 H3
Tanfield Rd *CROY/NA* CR0 177 J3
Tangier Rd *RCHPK/HAM* TW10 125 H3
Tangleberry Cl *BMLY* BR1 168 E3
Tangle Tree Cl *EFNCH* N2 53 F1
Tanglewood Cl *CROY/NA* CR0 178 E2
STAN HA7 34 E1
Tanglewood Wy *FELT* TW13 141 F2
Tangley Gv *PUT/ROE* SW15 126 C6
Tangley Park Rd *HPTN* * TW12 141 K4
Tangmere Crs *HCH* RM12 81 K5
Tangmere Gdns *NTHLT* UB5 83 G1
Tangmere Gv *KUTN/CMB* KT2 143 K4
Tangmere Wy *CDALE/KGS* NW9 51 G1
Tanhouse Fld *KTTN* * NW5 72 D4
Tankerton Houses *STPAN* * WC1H 5 K8
Tankerton Rd *SURB* KT6 172 B1
Tankerton St *STPAN* WC1H 5 K8
Tankerton Ter *CROY/NA* * CR0 164 A6
Tankerville Rd
STRHM/NOR SW16 148 D6
Tank Hill Rd *PUR* RM19 119 K3
Tank La *PUR* RM19 119 K3
Tankridge Rd *CRICK* NW2 69 K1
The Tanneries *WCHPL* * E1 92 E3
Tanners Cl *WOT/HER* KT12 156 A5
Tanners End La *UED* N18 42 A3
Tanner's Hl *DEPT* SE8 112 D7
Tanners La *BARK/HLT* IG6 60 C2
Tanner St *BARK* IG11 78 C5
STHWK SE1 19 K2

Tannery Cl CROY/NA CR0 166 A4
DAGE RM10 80 D2
Tannington Ter FSBYPK * N4 73 G2
Tannsfeld Rd SYD SE26 151 F4
Tansley Cl HOLWY * N7 72 D4
Tanswell St STHWK * SE1 18 A2
Tansy Cl EHAM E6 96 A5
Tantallon Rd BAL SW12 129 F7
Tant Av CAN/RD E16 94 D5
Tantony Gv CHDH RM6 61 K2
Tanworth Cl NTHWD HA6 32 A5
Tanworth Gdns PIN HA5 47 F1
Tan Yard La BXLY * DA5 137 H6
Tanza Rd HAMP NW3 71 K3
Tapestry Cl BELMT SM2 175 F6
Taplow Ct MTCM CR4 162 D3
Taplow St IS N1 6 F6
Tappesfield Rd PECK SE15 131 K2
Tapping Cl KUTN/CMB * KT2 144 C6
Tapp St BETH * E2 92 D3
Tapster St BAR EN5 26 D2
Taransay Wk IS N1 73 K5
Tara Ter BROCKY * SE4 132 B2
Tarbert Rd EDUL SE22 131 F4
Tarbert Wk WCHPL E1 92 E6
Target Cl EBED/NFELT TW14 121 H5
Tariff Rd UED N18 42 C5
Tarleton Gdns FSTH SE23 131 J7
Tarling Cl SCUP DA14 155 H2
Tarling Rd CAN/RD E16 94 D5
EFNCH N2 53 G1
Tarling St WCHPL E1 92 D5
Tarnbank STHGT/OAK N14 28 E4
Tarn St STHWK SE1 18 E4
Tarnwood Pk ELTH/MOT SE9 134 E7
Tarragon Cl NWCR * SE14 112 B6
Tarragon Gv SYD SE26 151 F5
Tarrant Pl MBLAR W1H 9 L3
Tarriff Crs DEPT SE8 112 C3
Tarrington Cl
STRHM/NOR * SW16 148 D3
Tarver Rd WALW SE17 18 D8
Tarves Wy GNWCH SE10 112 E6
Tash Pl FBAR/BDGN * N11 40 B4
Tasker Cl HYS/HAR UB3 101 F6
Tasker Rd HAMP NW3 71 K4
Tasmania Ter UED N18 41 J5
Tasman Rd BRXN/ST SW9 129 K2
Tasso Rd HMSMTH W6 107 H5
Tate Gdns BUSH WD23 22 E6
Tate Rd CAN/RD E16 95 K7
SUT SM1 174 E4
Tatnell Rd FSTH SE23 132 B5
Tattersall Cl ELTH/MOT SE9 134 D4
Tatton Crs STNW/STAM N16 56 B6
Tatum Rd WLSDN NW10 68 E6
Tatum St WALW SE17 19 H6
Tauber Cl BORE WD6 24 B3
Tauheed Cl FSBYPK N4 73 J1
Taunton Av HSLW TW3 123 H1
RYNPK SW20 160 E1
Taunton Cl BXLYHN DA7 138 A2
CHEAM SM3 161 K7
Taunton Dr EFNCH N2 53 G1
ENC/FH EN2 29 G2
Taunton Ms CAMTN NW1 9 L1
Taunton Pl CAMTN NW1 3 L9
Taunton Rd GFD/PVL UB6 66 B6
LEW SE13 133 H4
Taunton Wy STAN HA7 50 A1
Tavern Cl CAR SM5 162 D6
Taverners Cl NTGHL * W11 88 C7
Taverner Sq HBRY * N5 73 J3
Tavistock Av GFD/PVL UB6 85 G1
WALTH E17 57 F2
Tavistock Cl STNW/STAM * N16 74 A4
Tavistock Ct COVGDN * WC2E 11 K6
Tavistock Crs MTCM CR4 163 K3
NTGHL W11 88 D5
Tavistock Gdns GDMY/SEVK IG3 78 E3
Tavistock Gv CROY/NA CR0 164 E6
Tavistock Ms NTGHL * W11 88 D5
Tavistock Pl STHGT/OAK * N14 28 B5
STPAN WC1H 5 K9
Tavistock Rd CAR SM5 162 C7
CROY/NA CR0 164 E7
EDGW HA8 36 B7
FSBYPK N4 55 K5
HAYES BR2 167 K3
HGDN/ICK UB10 64 B4
NTGHL W11 88 D4
SWFD E18 58 E2
WAN E11 76 D3
WELL DA16 116 D7
WLSDN NW10 87 H1
Tavistock Sq STPAN WC1H 5 H9
Tavistock St COVGDN WC2E 11 K6
Tavistock Ter ARCH N19 72 D2
Taviton St STPAN WC1H 5 G9
Tavy Cl LBTH SE11 18 B7
Tawney Rd THMD SE28 97 H6
Tawny Cl FELT TW13 140 E2
WEA W13 85 H7
Tawny Wy BERM/RHTH SE16 112 A3
Tayben Av WHTN TW2 123 K5
Taybridge Rd BTSEA SW11 129 F2
Tayburn Cl POP/IOD E14 94 A5
Tayfield Cl HGDN/ICK UB10 64 A2
Taylor Av RCH/KEW TW9 125 J1
Taylor Cl DEPT SE8 112 C5
HPTN TW12 142 C4
HSLW TW3 103 H7
TOTM N17 42 C6
Taylor Rd WIM/MER SW19 147 J6
WLGTN SM6 176 B4
Taylor's Buildings
WOOL/PLUM SE18 115 G3
Taylors Cl SCUP DA14 155 F3
Taylors Ct FELT TW13 140 E1
Taylor's Gn ACT * W3 87 G5
Taylor's La SYD SE26 150 D3
WLSDN NW10 69 G6
Taylors Md MLHL * NW7 37 J4
Taymount Ri FSTH SE23 150 E1
Tayport Cl IS N1 5 L2
Tayside Dr EDGW HA8 36 D2
Taywood Rd STHL UB1 83 K2
Teak Cl BERM/RHTH SE16 93 G7
Teal Cl CAN/RD E16 95 H4
Teal Dr NTHWD HA6 32 A6
Teale St BETH E2 92 C1
Tealing Dr HOR/WEW KT19 173 F3
Teasel Cl CROY/NA CR0 166 A7
Teasel Wy SRTFD E15 94 C2
Tebworth Rd TOTM N17 42 B6
Technology Pk
CDALE/KGS * NW9 51 F2
Teck Cl ISLW TW7 124 B1
Tedder Cl CHSGTN KT9 171 J4
Tedder Rd SAND/SEL CR2 179 F6
Teddington Pk TEDD TW11 143 F4
Teddington Park Rd
TEDD TW11 143 F3
Tedworth Gdns CHEL SW3 15 L8
Tedworth Sq CHEL SW3 15 L8
The Tee ACT W3 87 G5
Tees Av GFD/PVL UB6 84 E1
Teesdale Av ISLW TW7 104 B7
Teesdale Cl BETH E2 92 C1
Teesdale Gdns ISLW TW7 104 B7
SNWD SE25 165 F1
Teesdale Rd WAN E11 58 D5
Teesdale St BETH E2 92 D1
Teesdale Yd BETH * E2 92 D1
Teevan Cl CROY/NA CR0 165 H6
Teevan Rd CROY/NA CR0 165 H6
Teignmouth Cl CLAP SW4 129 J3
EDGW HA8 50 B1
Teignmouth Rd CRICK NW2 70 B4
WELL DA16 136 D1
Telcote Wy RSLP * HA4 47 G6
Telegraph Hl HAMP NW3 71 F2
Telegraph La ESH/CLAY KT10 171 F3
Telegraph Pas
BRXS/STRHM SW2 129 K6
Telegraph Pl POP/IOD E14 112 E3
Telegraph Rd PUT/ROE SW15 126 E6
Telegraph St LOTH EC2R 13 G4
Telephone Pl WKENS * W14 107 J5
Telferscot Rd BAL SW12 129 J7
Telford Av BAL SW12 129 J7
Telford Cl NRWD SE19 150 B5
WALTH E17 57 G6
Telford Dr WOT/HER KT12 156 B6
Telford Rd CDALE/KGS NW9 51 H5
CHST BR7 154 D1
NKENS W10 88 C4
STHL UB1 84 B6
WHTN TW2 123 F6
Telford Rd North Circular Rd
FBAR/BDGN N11 40 C5
Telfords Yd WAP * E1W 92 C6
Telford Ter PIM SW1V 16 E9
Telford Wy ACT W3 87 G4
YEAD UB4 83 J4
Telham Rd EHAM E6 96 A1
Tell Gv EDUL SE22 131 G3
Tellisford ESH/CLAY KT10 170 B3
Tellson Av WOOL/PLUM SE18 114 C7
Temeraire St BERM/RHTH SE16 111 K1
Tempelhof Av HDN NW4 52 A6
Temperley Rd BAL SW12 129 F6
Tempest Wy RAIN RM13 81 J5
Templar Dr THMD SE28 97 K5
Templar Pl HPTN TW12 142 A6
Templars Av GLDGN NW11 52 D5
Templars Ct DART * DA1 139 K4
Templars Crs FNCH N3 52 E1
Templars Dr
KTN/HRWW/W * HA3 34 D5
Templar St CMBW SE5 130 C1
Temple Av BCTR RM8 62 C7
CROY/NA CR0 179 H2
EMB EC4Y 12 B6
TRDG/WHET N20 27 H6
Temple Cl FNCH N3 52 D1
WAN E11 58 C6
WAT WD17 20 D1
WOOL/PLUM SE18 115 H2
Templecombe Rd HOM E9 74 E7
Templecombe Wy MRDN SM4 161 H4
Templecroft ASHF TW15 140 B5
Temple Dwellings BETH * E2 92 D1
Temple Fortune Hl
GLDGN NW11 52 E4
Temple Fortune La
GLDGN NW11 52 D5
Temple Gdns BCTR RM8 79 K2
EMB * EC4Y 12 A6
GLDGN NW11 52 D5
WCHMH * N21 41 H1
Temple Gv ENC/FH EN2 29 H2
GLDGN NW11 52 E5
Temple Hl DART DA1 139 J4
Temple Hill Sq DART DA1 139 J4
Temple La EMB EC4Y 12 B5
Templeman Rd HNWL W7 85 F4
Templemead Cl ACT W3 87 G5
Temple Mead Cl STAN HA7 35 H5
Temple Mills La LEY E10 75 K3
Temple Pde BAR * EN5 27 H6
Temple Pl TPL/STR WC2R 11 M6
Temple Rd CEND/HSY/T N8 55 F3
CHSWK W4 105 K2
CRICK NW2 70 A3
CROY/NA CR0 177 K3
EA W5 104 E2
EHAM E6 77 J7
HSLW TW3 123 G3
RCH/KEW TW9 125 G1
Temple Sheen Rd
MORT/ESHN SW14 125 K3
Temple St BETH E2 92 D1
Temple Ter WDGN * N22 55 G1
Templeton Av CHING E4 43 J3
Templeton Cl STNW/STAM * N16 74 A4
THHTH CR7 149 K7
Templeton Pl ECT SW5 14 B6
Templeton Rd FSBYPK N4 55 K5
Temple Wy SUT SM1 175 H2
Templewood WEA W13 85 H4
Templewood Av HAMP NW3 71 F2
Templewood Gdns HAMP NW3 71 F2
Temple Yd BETH E2 92 C2
Tempsford Av BORE WD6 25 F3
Tempsford Cl ENC/FH EN2 29 J2
Temsford Cl RYLN/HDSTN HA2 48 C1
Tenbury Cl FSTGT E7 77 H4
Tenbury Ct BRXS/STRHM SW2 129 J7
Tenby Av KTN/HRWW/W HA3 49 H1
Tenby Cl CHDH RM6 62 A5
Tenby Gdns NTHLT UB5 66 A5
Tenby Rd CHDH RM6 62 A5
EDGW HA8 36 B7
PEND EN3 31 F2
WALTH E17 57 G4
WELL DA16 116 E7
Tench St WAP * E1W 92 D7
Tenda Rd BERM/RHTH SE16 111 J3
Tendring Wy CHDH RM6 61 J4
Tenham Av BRXS/STRHM SW2 148 D1
Tenniel Cl BAY/PAD W2 8 E5
Tennison Av BORE WD6 24 D4
Tennison Rd SNWD SE25 165 G3
Tennis St STHWK SE1 19 G1
Tennyson Av CDALE/KGS NW9 50 E2
MNPK E12 77 J6
NWMAL KT3 160 E4
TWK TW1 124 A7
WAN E11 58 E6
Tennyson Cl EBED/NFELT TW14 121 K5
PEND EN3 31 F4
WELL DA16 115 K7
Tennyson Rd DART DA1 139 K4
HNWL W7 85 F6
HSLW TW3 123 H1
KIL/WHAMP NW6 70 D7
LEY E10 57 K7
MLHL NW7 37 H4
PGE/AN SE20 151 F6
SRTFD E15 76 C6
WALTH E17 57 H5
WIM/MER SW19 147 G5
Tennyson St VX/NE SW8 129 G1
Tennyson Wy HCH RM12 63 H7
Tensing Rd NWDGN UB2 103 F2
Tentelow La NWDGN UB2 103 G2
Tenterden Cl ELTH/MOT SE9 153 K3
HDN NW4 52 B2
Tenterden Dr HDN NW4 52 B2
Tenterden Gdns CROY/NA CR0 165 H6
HDN NW4 52 B2
Tenterden Gv HDN NW4 52 A3
Tenterden Rd BCTR RM8 80 B1
CROY/NA CR0 165 H6
TOTM N17 42 B6
Tenterden St CONDST W1S 10 D5
Tenter Gnd WCHPL * E1 13 L3
Tent Peg La STMC/STPC BR5 169 H4
Tent St WCHPL E1 92 D3
Terling Cl WAN E11 76 D2
Terling Rd BCTR RM8 80 C1
Terling Wk IS * N1 6 E3
Terminus Pl PIM SW1V 16 D4
The Terrace BARN SW13 126 B1
BETH * E2 92 E2
CHING * E4 44 C2
DEPT * SE8 112 C3
EFNCH * N2 54 A3
FNCH * N3 52 D1
FSTH * SE23 132 B6
KIL/WHAMP NW6 2 A3
Terrace Gdns BARN SW13 126 C1
WAT WD17 21 F1
Terrace La RCHPK/HAM TW10 125 F5
Terrace Rd HOM E9 75 F6
PLSTW E13 76 E7
WOT/HER KT12 156 A6
Terrace Vls HMSMTH * W6 106 D4
Terrace Wk DAGW RM9 80 A4
Terrac St RCH/KEW TW9 125 G3
Terrapin Rd TOOT SW17 148 B2
Terretts Pl IS N1 6 C2
Terrick Rd WDGN N22 40 E7
Terrick St SHB W12 87 K5
Terrilands PIN HA5 47 K2
Terront Rd SEVS/STOTM N15 55 J4
Tessa Sanderson Wy
GFD/PVL UB6 66 D4
Testerton Wk NTGHL * W11 88 B6
Tetcott Rd WBPTN SW10 108 B6
Tetherdown MUSWH N10 54 A2
Tetty Wy HAYES BR2 167 K1
Teversham La VX/NE SW8 109 K7
Teviot Cl WELL DA16 116 C7
Teviot St POP/IOD E14 94 A4
Tewkesbury Av FSTH SE23 131 J7
PIN HA5 47 J4
Tewkesbury Gdns
CDALE/KGS NW9 50 D2
Tewkesbury Rd CAR SM5 162 C7
SEVS/STOTM N15 55 K6
WEA W13 85 G7
Tewkesbury Ter
FBAR/BDGN N11 40 C5
Tewson Rd WOOL/PLUM SE18 115 K4
Teynham Av EN EN1 29 K5
Teynham Gn HAYES BR2 167 K4
Teynton Ter TOTM N17 41 J7
Thackeray Av TOTM N17 56 C1
Thackeray Cl ISLW TW7 124 B1
RYLN/HDSTN HA2 48 A7
WIM/MER SW19 146 B6
Thackeray Dr CHDH RM6 61 G6
Thackeray Ms HACK * E8 74 C5
Thackeray Rd EHAM E6 95 H1
VX/NE SW8 129 G1
Thackeray St KENS W8 14 D3
Thakeham Cl SYD SE26 150 D4
Thalia Cl GNWCH SE10 113 G5
Thame Rd BERM/RHTH SE16 112 A1
Thames Av DAGW RM9 98 D3
GFD/PVL UB6 85 F1
WBPTN SW10 108 B7
Thames Bank
MORT/ESHN SW14 125 K1
Thamesbank Pl THMD SE28 97 J5
Thames Cir POP/IOD E14 112 D3
Thames Cl HPTN TW12 157 G1
RAIN RM13 99 K5
Thames Down Link
CHSGTN KT9 172 E3
Thames Dr RSLP HA4 46 A5
Thames Eyot TWK * TW1 143 G1
Thames Ga DART DA1 139 K4
Thamesgate Cl
RCHPK/HAM TW10 143 H3
Thameside TEDD TW11 143 K6
Thames Meadow
E/WMO/HCT KT8 157 F2
Thamesmere Dr THMD SE28 97 G6
Thames Pth BERM/RHTH SE16 112 C2
BOW E3 94 A1
CHSWK W4 106 C7
CLPT E5 75 F2
GNWCH SE10 113 F5
RCH/KEW TW9 124 D1
TWRH EC3N 13 K8
WEST SW1P 17 K4
WOT/HER KT12 156 B2
Thames Pl PUT/ROE SW15 127 G2
Thamespoint TEDD * TW11 143 K6
Thames Quay WBPTN * SW10 108 B7
Thames Reach KUT * KT1 143 K7
Thames Rd BARK IG11 97 G2
CAN/RD E16 95 H7
CHSWK W4 105 J5
DART DA1 138 D2
Thames Side KUTN/CMB KT2 143 K7
THDIT KT7 158 C5
Thames St GNWCH SE10 112 E5
HPTN TW12 157 G1
KUT KT1 158 E1
SUN TW16 156 A2
Thamesvale Cl HSLW TW3 123 F1
Thames Village CHSWK W4 105 K7
Thamley PUR RM19 119 K3
Thanescroft Gdns
CROY/NA CR0 178 A2
Thanet Dr HAYES BR2 181 H2
Thanet Pl CROY/NA CR0 177 J3
Thanet Rd BXLY DA5 137 H6
ERITH DA8 118 B6
Thanet St STPAN WC1H 5 J8
Thane Vls HOLWY N7 73 F2
Thant Cl LEY E10 75 K3
Tharp Rd WLGTN SM6 176 D4
Thatcham Gdns
TRDG/WHET N20 27 G6
Thatchers Wy ISLW TW7 123 J4
Thatches Gv CHDH RM6 62 A3
Thaxted Pl RYNPK SW20 146 B6
Thaxted Rd ELTH/MOT SE9 154 C1
Thaxton Rd WKENS W14 107 J5
Thayers Farm Rd BECK BR3 151 G7
Thayer St MHST W1U 10 B3
Theatre St BTSEA SW11 128 E2
Theberton St IS N1 6 B3
Theed St STHWK SE1 12 A9
Thelma Gv TEDD TW11 143 G5
Theobald Crs
KTN/HRWW/W HA3 34 B7
Theobald Rd CROY/NA CR0 177 H1
WALTH E17 57 H6
Theobald's Rd FSBYW WC1X 11 L2
Theobald St STHWK SE1 19 G4
Theodora Wy PIN HA5 46 D2
Theodore Rd LEW SE13 133 G5
Therapia La CROY/NA CR0 163 K6
Therapia Rd EDUL SE22 131 K5
Theresa Rd HMSMTH W6 106 D3
Theresa's Wk SAND/SEL CR2 177 K7
Thermopylae Ga POP/IOD E14 112 E3
Theseus Wk IS N1 6 D6
Thesiger Rd PGE/AN SE20 151 F6
Thessaly Rd VX/NE SW8 109 J7
Thetford Cl PLMGR N13 41 H5
Thetford Rd DAGW RM9 79 K6
NWMAL KT3 160 A5
Theydon Gdns RAIN RM13 81 G6
Theydon Gv WFD IG8 45 G5
Theydon Rd CLPT E5 74 E1
Theydon St WALTH E17 57 H6
Thicket Crs SUT SM1 175 G3
Thicket Gv DAGW RM9 79 J5
PGE/AN SE20 150 C6
Thicket Rd PGE/AN SE20 150 D6
SUT SM1 175 G3
Thicket Ter PGE/AN * SE20 150 C6
Third Av ACT W3 87 H7
CHDH RM6 61 J5
DAGE RM10 80 D7
EN EN1 30 B4
HYS/HAR UB3 82 D7
MNPK E12 77 J3
NKENS W10 88 C2
PLSTW E13 94 E2
WALTH E17 57 J4
WBLY HA9 67 K1
Third Cl E/WMO/HCT KT8 157 G3
Third Cross Rd WHTN TW2 142 D1
Third Wy WBLY HA9 68 D3
Thirleby Rd EDGW HA8 37 F7
WEST SW1P 16 F4
Thirlmere Av GFD/PVL UB6 85 J2
Thirlmere Gdns WBLY HA9 49 J7
Thirlmere Ri BMLY BR1 152 D5
Thirlmere Rd BXLYHN DA7 137 K1
MUSWH N10 40 B7
STRHM/NOR SW16 148 D3
Thirsk Cl NTHLT UB5 66 A5
Thirsk Rd BTSEA SW11 129 F2
MTCM CR4 148 A6
SNWD SE25 164 E3
Thirza Rd DART DA1 139 J5
Thisilefield Cl BXLY DA5 136 E7
Thistlebrook ABYW SE2 116 D2
Thistlecroft Gdns STAN HA7 35 K7
Thistledene THDIT KT7 157 K5
Thistledene Av
RYLN/HDSTN HA2 65 J2
Thistle Gv WBPTN SW10 14 F8
Thistlemead CHST BR7 169 G1
Thistlewaite Rd CLPT E5 74 D2
Thistlewood Cl HOLWY N7 73 F1
Thistleworth Cl ISLW TW7 103 J6
Thistley Cl NFNCH/WDSP N12 39 J5
Thomas a'Beckett Cl
ALP/SUD HA0 67 F3
Thomas Baines Rd
BTSEA SW11 128 C2
Thomas Cribb Ms EHAM E6 95 K5
Thomas Dean Rd SYD * SE26 151 H3
Thomas Dinwiddy Rd
LEE/GVPK SE12 153 F1
Thomas Doyle St STHWK SE1 18 C3
Thomas' La CAT SE6 132 E6
Thomas Moore Wy EFNCH N2 53 G2
Thomas More St WAP * E1W 92 C6
Thomas North Ter
CAN/RD * E16 94 D4
Thomas Pl KENS W8 14 C4
Thomas Rd POP/IOD E14 93 H5
Thomas St WOOL/PLUM SE18 115 F3
Thomas Wall Cl SUT SM1 175 F4
Thompson Av RCH/KEW TW9 125 J2
Thompson Cl CHEAM SM3 161 K7
IL IG1 78 C1
Thompson Rd DAGW RM9 80 B2
EDUL SE22 131 G5
HSLW TW3 123 G3
Thompson's Av CMBW * SE5 110 D6
Thomson Crs CROY/NA CR0 164 B7
Thomson Rd
KTN/HRWW/W HA3 48 E2
Thorburn Sq STHWK SE1 111 H3
Thorburn Wy
WIM/MER * SW19 147 H7
Thoresby St IS N1 6 F7
Thorkhill Gdns THDIT KT7 158 B7
Thorkhill Rd THDIT KT7 158 C7
Thornaby Gdns UED N18 42 C5
Thorn Av BUSH WD23 22 C7
Thornbury Av ISLW TW7 103 J6
Thornbury Cl STNW/STAM N16 74 A4
Thornbury Gdns BORE WD6 24 E3
Thornbury Rd CLAP SW4 129 K5
ISLW TW7 103 J6
Thornby Rd CLPT E5 74 E2
Thorncliffe Rd CLAP SW4 129 J5
NWDGN UB2 102 E4
Thorn Cl HAYES BR2 169 F5
NTHLT UB5 83 K2
Thorncombe Rd EDUL SE22 131 F4
Thorn Ct BELMT * SM2 175 F6
Thorncroft EMPK RM11 63 K5
Thorncroft Rd SUT SM1 175 F3
Thorncroft St VX/NE SW8 109 K6
Thorndean St
WAND/EARL SW18 147 G1
Thorndene Av TRDG/WHET N20 28 A7
Thorndike Av NTHLT UB5 65 H7
Thorndike Cl WBPTN SW10 108 B6
Thorndike St PIM * SW1V 17 G6
Thorndon Gdns
HOR/WEW KT19 173 G3
Thorndyke Ct PIN * HA5 33 K6
Thorne Cl ASHF TW15 140 A6
CAN/RD E16 94 E5
ERITH DA8 117 J5
WAN * E11 76 C3
Thorneloe Gdns CROY/NA CR0 177 H4
Thorne Rd VX/NE SW8 109 K6
Thorne's Cl BECK BR3 167 F2
Thorne St BARN SW13 126 B2
Thornet Wood Rd BMLY BR1 169 F2
Thorney Crs BTSEA * SW11 108 C6
Thorneycroft Cl
WOT/HER KT12 156 B5
Thorney Hedge Rd CHSWK W4 105 J3
Thorney St WEST SW1P 17 J5
Thornfield Av MLHL NW7 38 C7
Thornfield Pde MLHL * NW7 38 C6
Thornfield Rd SHB W12 106 E1
Thornford Rd LEW SE13 133 F4
Thorngate Rd MV/WKIL W9 2 B9
Thorngrove Rd PLSTW E13 77 F7
Thornham Gv SRTFD E15 76 B4
Thornham St GNWCH SE10 112 E5
Thornhaugh St STPAN WC1H 11 H1
Thornhill Av SURB KT6 172 A1
WOOL/PLUM SE18 115 K6
Thornhill Bridge Whf IS N1 5 L4
Thornhill Crs IS N1 5 M2
Thornhill Gdns BARK IG11 78 E6
LEY E10 75 K1
Thornhill Gv IS N1 6 A2
Thornhill Rd CROY/NA CR0 164 D6
IS N1 6 A1
LEY E10 75 K1
NTHWD HA6 32 A3
SURB KT6 172 A1
Thornhill Sq IS N1 5 M2
Thornlaw Rd WNWD SE27 149 G3
Thornley Cl TOTM N17 42 C6
Thornley Dr RYLN/HDSTN HA2 66 B1
Thornsbeach Rd CAT SE6 133 F7
Thornsett Pl PGE/AN SE20 165 J1
Thornsett Rd PGE/AN SE20 165 J1
WAND/EARL SW18 147 F1
Thornsett Ter PGE/AN * SE20 165 J1
Thornton Av BAL SW12 129 J7
CHSWK W4 106 B3
CROY/NA CR0 164 A5
WDR/YW UB7 100 C2
Thornton Cl WDR/YW UB7 100 C2
Thornton Dene BECK BR3 166 D1
Thornton Gdns BAL SW12 129 J7
Thornton Gv PIN HA5 34 A5
Thornton Hl WIM/MER SW19 146 C6
Thornton Pl MBLAR W1H 9 L2
Thornton Rd BAL SW12 129 J6
BAR EN5 26 C2
BELV * DA17 117 J3
BMLY BR1 152 E4
CAR SM5 162 C7
IL IG1 78 B3
MORT/ESHN SW14 126 A2
THHTH CR7 164 B4
UED N18 42 E2
WAN E11 76 B1
WIM/MER SW19 146 B5
Thornton Rw THHTH CR7 164 B4
Thorntons Farm Av
ROMW/RG RM7 80 E1
Thornton St BRXN/ST SW9 130 B1
Thornton Wy GLDGN NW11 53 F4
Thorntree Rd CHARL SE7 114 C4
Thornville Gv MTCM CR4 162 B1
Thornville St DEPT SE8 112 D7
Thornwood Cl SWFD E18 59 F1
Thornwood Rd LEW SE13 133 H4
Thorogood Gdns SRTFD E15 76 C4
Thorogood Wy RAIN RM13 81 G7
Thorold Rd IL IG1 78 B1
WDGN N22 40 E6
Thorparch Rd VX/NE SW8 109 J7
Thorpebank Rd SHB W12 87 J7
Thorpe Cl NKENS W10 88 C5
SYD * SE26 151 F3
Thorpe Crs OXHEY WD19 21 F6
WALTH E17 57 H1
Thorpedale Gdns
GNTH/NBYPK IG2 60 A3
Thorpedale Rd FSBYPK N4 54 E7
Thorpe Hall Rd WALTH E17 44 A7
Thorpe Rd BARK IG11 78 D6
EHAM E6 77 K7
FSTGT E7 76 E2
KUTN/CMB KT2 144 A6
SEVS/STOTM N15 56 A5
WALTH E17 58 A1
Thorpewood Av SYD SE26 150 D1
Thorpland Av HGDN/ICK UB10 64 A2
Thorsden Wy NRWD * SE19 150 A4
Thorverton Rd CRICK NW2 70 C2
Thoydon Rd BOW E3 93 G1
Thrale Rd STRHM/NOR SW16 148 C4
Thrale St STHWK SE1 12 F9
Thrasher Cl HACK * E8 7 L3
Thrawl St WCHPL E1 13 M3
Threadneedle St LOTH EC2R 13 H5
Three Colts La BETH E2 92 D3
Three Colt St POP/IOD * E14 93 H6
Three Corners BXLYHN DA7 137 J1
Three Kings Yd
MYFR/PKLN W1K 10 C6
Three Meadows Ms
KTN/HRWW/W HA3 35 F7
Three Mill La SRTFD E15 94 A2
Three Oak La STHWK SE1 19 L1
Three Valleys Wy BUSH WD23 21 H4
Threshers Pl NTGHL W11 88 C6
Thriffwood FSTH SE23 150 E2
Thrift Farm La BORE WD6 24 E1
Thrigby Rd CHSGTN KT9 172 B5
Throckmorten Rd CAN/RD E16 95 F5
Throgmorton Av OBST EC2N 13 H4
Throgmorton St LOTH EC2R 13 H4
Throwley Cl ABYW SE2 116 D2
Throwley Rd SUT SM1 175 F4
Throwley Wy SUT SM1 175 F3
Thrupp Cl MTCM CR4 163 G1
Thrush Gn RYLN/HDSTN HA2 48 A3
Thrush St WALW SE17 18 E7
Thunderer Rd DAGW RM9 98 A3
Thurbarn Rd CAT SE6 151 K4
Thurland Rd BERM/RHTH SE16 111 H2
Thurlby Cl WFD IG8 45 K5
Thurlby Rd ALP/SUD HA0 67 K5

WNWD SE27 149 G3
Thurleigh Av BAL SW12 129 F5
Thurleigh Rd BAL SW12 128 E5
Thurleston Av MRDN SM4 161 H4
Thurlestone Av GDMY/SEVK IG3 79 F3
NFNCH/WDSP N12 39 K5
Thurlestone Rd WNWD SE27 149 G2
Thurloe Cl SKENS SW7 15 J5
Thurloe Gdns ROM RM1 63 G5
Thurloe Pl SKENS SW7 15 H5
Thurloe Place Ms SKENS * SW7 15 H5
Thurloe Sq SKENS SW7 15 H5
Thurloe St SKENS SW7 15 H5
Thurlow Cl CHING E4 43 K5
Thurlow Gdns ALP/SUD * HA0 67 K4
Thurlow Hl DUL SE21 130 D7
Thurlow Park Rd DUL SE21 149 H1
Thurlow Rd HAMP NW3 71 H4
HNWL W7 104 B1
Thurlow St WALW SE17 19 J8
Thurlow Ter KTTN NW5 71 K4
Thurlow Wk WALW SE17 19 J8
Thurlston Rd RSLP HA4 64 E2
Thursley Crs CROY/NA CR0 180 B6
Thursley Gdns WIM/MER SW19 146 B1
Thursley Rd ELTH/MOT SE9 153 K2
Thurso St TOOT SW17 147 H3
Thurstan Rd RYNPK SW20 145 K6
Thurston Rd DEPT SE8 132 E1
STHL UB1 83 K5
Thurtle Rd BETH E2 7 M5
Thwaite Cl ERITH DA8 117 K5
Thyra Gv NFNCH/WDSP N12 39 F5
Tibbatt's Rd BOW E3 93 K3
Tibbenham Pl CAT SE6 151 J1
Tibberton Sq IS N1 6 E2
Tibbets Cl WIM/MER SW19 127 G7
Tibbet's Ride PUT/ROE SW15 127 G6
Tiber Gdns IS N1 5 K4
Ticehurst Cl STMC/STPC BR5 155 G6
Ticehurst Rd FSTH SE23 151 G1
Tickford Cl ABYW SE2 116 D1
Tidal Basin Rd CAN/RD E16 94 D6
Tidenham Gdns CROY/NA CR0 178 A2
Tideswell Rd CROY/NA CR0 179 J2
PUT/ROE SW15 127 F3
Tideway Cl RCHPK/HAM TW10 143 H3
Tideway Wk VX/NE * SW8 109 H5
Tidey St BOW E3 93 J4
Tidford Rd WELL DA16 136 A1
Tidworth Rd BOW E3 93 J3
Tiepigs La WWKM BR4 180 C1
Tierney Rd BRXS/STRHM SW2 129 K7
Tierney Ter
BRXS/STRHM * SW2 129 K7
Tiger La HAYES BR2 168 A3
Tiger Wy CLPT E5 74 D3
Tigres Cl ED N9 42 E1
Tilbrook Rd BKHTH/KID SE3 134 B2
Tilbury Cl PECK SE15 111 G6
Tilbury Rd EHAM E6 95 K1
LEY E10 58 A6
Tildesley Rd PUT/ROE SW15 127 F5
Tilehouse Cl BORE WD6 24 B2
Tilehurst Rd CHEAM SM3 174 C4
WAND/EARL SW18 128 C7
Tile Kiln La HGT N6 54 B7
PLMGR N13 41 J4
Tileyard Rd HOLWY N7 5 J1
Tilford Av CROY/NA CR0 180 A6
Tilford Gdns WIM/MER SW19 127 G7
Tilia Rd CLPT E5 74 D3
Tiller Rd POP/IOD E14 112 D2
Tillett Cl WLSDN NW10 68 E5
Tillet Wy BETH E2 92 C2
Tillingbourne Gdns FNCH N3 52 D2
Tillingbourne Wy GLDGN NW11 52 D3
Tillingham Wy
NFNCH/WDSP N12 38 E3
Tilling Rd CRICK NW2 51 K7
Tilling Wy WBLY * HA9 67 K2
Tillman St WCHPL E1 92 D5
Tilloch St IS * N1 5 L2
Tillotson Rd ED N9 42 B1
IL IG1 60 A6
KTN/HRWW/W HA3 34 B6
Tilney Gdns IS N1 73 K5
Tilney Rd DAGW RM9 80 B5
NWDGN UB2 102 B3
Tilney St MYFR/PKLN W1K 10 B8
Tilson Cl CMBW SE5 111 F6
Tilson Gdns BRXS/STRHM SW2 129 K6
Tilson Rd TOTM N17 42 C7
Tilston Cl WAN E11 76 D2
Tilton St FUL/PGN SW6 107 H5
The Tiltwood ACT W3 86 E6
Tilt Yard Ap ELTH/MOT SE9 134 E5
Timber Cl CHST BR7 169 F1
Timbercroft HOR/WEW KT19 173 G3
Timbercroft La
WOOL/PLUM SE18 115 K5
Timberland Cl PECK * SE15 111 H6
Timberland Rd WCHPL * E1 92 D5
Timber Mill Wy CLAP SW4 129 J2
Timber Pond Rd
BERM/RHTH SE16 112 A1
The Timbers CHEAM * SM3 174 C5
Timberslip Dr WLGTN SM6 176 D7
Timber St FSBYE * EC1V 6 E9
Timberwharf Rd
SEVS/STOTM N15 56 C5
Time Sq HACK * E8 74 B4
Times Sq SUT * SM1 175 F4
Timothy Cl BXLYHS DA6 137 F4
Timothy Rd POP/IOD E14 93 H4
Tindal St BRXN/ST SW9 110 C7
Tinniswood Cl HOLWY * N7 73 G4
Tinsley Rd WCHPL E1 92 E4
Tintagel Crs EDUL SE22 131 G3
Tintagel Dr STAN HA7 35 K4
Tintern Av CDALE/KGS NW9 50 D2
Tintern Cl PUT/ROE SW15 127 H4
WIM/MER SW19 147 G6
Tintern Gdns WCHMH N21 28 E6
Tintern Rd CAR SM5 162 C7
WDGN N22 41 J7
Tintern St CLAP SW4 129 K3
Tintern Wy RYLN/HDSTN HA2 48 B7
Tinto Rd CAN/RD E16 94 E4
Tinwell Ms BORE WD6 25 F4
Tinworth St LBTH SE11 17 K7
Tipthorpe Rd BTSEA SW11 129 F2
Tipton Dr CROY/NA CR0 178 A3
Tiptree Cl CHING E4 44 A2
Tiptree Crs CLAY IG5 60 A2
Tiptree Dr ENC/FH EN2 29 K3
Tiptree Rd RSLP HA4 65 F3
Tirlemont Rd SAND/SEL CR2 177 J6
Tirrell Rd CROY/NA CR0 164 D5
Tisbury Rd STRHM/NOR SW16 163 K1
Tisdall Pl WALW SE17 19 H6
Titan Ct BTFD TW8 105 G4
Titchborne Rw BAY/PAD W2 9 K5
Titchfield Rd CAR SM5 162 C7
STJWD NW8 3 K4
Titchfield Wk CAR SM5 162 C6
Titchwell Rd WAND/EARL SW18 128 C6
Tite St CHEL SW3 15 L9
Tithe Barn Cl KUTN/CMB KT2 144 B7
Tithe Barn Wy NTHLT UB5 83 F1
Tithe Cl MLHL NW7 37 J7
WOT/HER KT12 156 A5
YEAD UB4 82 D4
Tithe Ct HDN * NW4 37 J7
Tithe Farm Av RYLN/HDSTN HA2 66 A2
Tithe Farm Cl RYLN/HDSTN HA2 66 A2
Tithe Wk MLHL NW7 37 J7
Titian Av BUSH WD23 22 E6
Titley Cl CHING E4 43 J4
Titmus Cl UX/CGN UB8 82 A5
Titmuss Av THMD SE28 97 H6
Titmuss St SHB * W12 106 E1
Tiverton Av CLAY IG5 60 A2
Tiverton Dr ELTH/MOT SE9 135 H7
Tiverton Rd ALP/SUD HA0 86 A1
EDGW HA8 50 B1
HSLW TW3 123 G1
RSLP HA4 64 E2
SEVS/STOTM N15 55 K5
UED N18 42 A4
WLSDN NW10 70 B7
Tiverton St STHWK SE1 18 E3
Tiverton Wy CHSGTN KT9 171 J4
Tivoli Gdns WOOL/PLUM SE18 114 D3
Tivoli Rd CEND/HSY/T N8 54 D4
HSLWW TW4 122 D3
WNWD SE27 149 J4
Toad La HSLWW TW4 122 E3
Tobago St POP/IOD * E14 112 D1
Tobin Cl HAMP NW3 3 K1
Toby Wy SURB KT6 172 D1
Tokenhouse Yd LOTH EC2R 13 G4
Tokyngton Av WBLY HA9 68 C5
Toland Sq PUT/ROE SW15 126 D4
Tolcarne Dr PIN HA5 46 E1
Toley Av KTN/HRWW/W HA3 50 A6
Tollbridge Cl NKENS W10 88 C3
Tollesbury Gdns BARK/HLT IG6 60 D2
Tollet St WCHPL E1 93 F3
Tollgate Dr DUL SE21 150 A1
YEAD UB4 83 H6
Tollgate Gdns KIL/WHAMP NW6 2 C5
Tollgate Rd EHAM E6 95 J4
Tollhouse La WLGTN SM6 176 C7
Tollhouse Wy ARCH N19 72 C1
Tollington Pk FSBYPK N4 73 F1
Tollington Pl FSBYPK N4 73 F1
Tollington Rd HOLWY N7 73 F3
Tollington Wy HOLWY N7 72 E2
Tolmer's Sq CAMTN NW1 4 F9
Tolpits Cl WATW WD18 20 D4
Tolpits La WATW WD18 20 B6
Tolpuddle Av PLSTW E13 77 G7
Tolpuddle St IS N1 6 A5
Tolsford Rd CLPT E5 74 D4
Tolson Rd ISLW TW7 124 B2
Tolverne Rd RYNPK SW20 146 A7
Tolworth Cl SURB KT6 159 J7
Tolworth Gdns CHDH RM6 61 K4
Tolworth Park Rd SURB KT6 172 B1
Tolworth Ri North BRYLDS KT5 159 K6
Tolworth Ri South BRYLDS KT5 159 K7
Tolworth Rd SURB KT6 172 A1
Tom Cribb Rd
WOOL/PLUM SE18 115 H2
Tom Jenkinson Rd CAN/RD E16 94 E7
Tomlin's Gv BOW E3 93 J2
Tomlinson Cl BETH E2 7 M8
CHSWK W4 105 J4
Tomlins Orch BARK IG11 78 C7
Tomlin's Ter POP/IOD E14 93 G5
Tom Mann Cl BARK IG11 78 E7
Tom Nolan Cl SRTFD E15 94 C1
Tompion St FSBYE EC1V 6 C8
Tom Smith Cl GNWCH SE10 113 H5
Tonbridge Crs
KTN/HRWW/W HA3 50 A3
Tonbridge Rd E/WMO/HCT KT8 156 D3
Tonbridge St STPAN WC1H 5 J8
Tonfield Rd CHEAM SM3 161 J7
Tonsley Hl WAND/EARL SW18 128 A4
Tonsley Pl WAND/EARL SW18 128 A4
Tonsley Rd WAND/EARL SW18 128 A4
Tonsley St WAND/EARL SW18 128 A4
Tonstall Rd MTCM CR4 163 F1
Tooke Cl PIN HA5 33 J7
Tookey Cl WBLY HA9 50 B6
Took's Ct FLST/FETLN EC4A 12 A4
Tooley St STHWK SE1 13 H8
Toorack Rd KTN/HRWW/W HA3 48 D1
Tooting Bec Gdns
STRHM/NOR SW16 148 D3
Tooting Bec Rd TOOT SW17 148 A2
Tooting Gv TOOT SW17 147 J4
Tooting High St TOOT SW17 147 J3
Tooting Market TOOT * SW17 147 K3
Tootswood Rd HAYES BR2 167 H4
Topham Sq TOTM N17 41 J7
Topham St CLKNW * EC1R 6 A9
Topiary Sq RCH/KEW TW9 125 G2
Topley St ELTH/MOT SE9 134 B3
Topmast Point POP/IOD * E14 112 D1
Top Pk BECK BR3 167 H4
Topsfield Pde CEND/HSY/T * N8 54 E4
Topsfield Rd CEND/HSY/T N8 54 E4
Topsham Rd TOOT SW17 147 K2
Torbay Rd KIL/WHAMP NW6 70 D6
RYLN/HDSTN HA2 65 J1
Torbay St CAMTN NW1 4 D1
Torbridge Cl EDGW HA8 36 A6
Torcross Dr FSTH SE23 150 E1
Torcross Rd RSLP HA4 65 F2
Tor Gdns KENS W8 14 A1
Tormead Cl SUT SM1 174 E5
Tormount Rd
WOOL/PLUM SE18 115 K5
Toronto Av MNPK E12 77 K3
Toronto Rd IL IG1 60 B7
Torquay Gdns REDBR IG4 59 H3
Torquay St BAY/PAD W2 8 C3
Torrens Rd BRXS/STRHM SW2 130 A4
Torrens Sq SRTFD E15 76 D5
Torrens St FSBYE EC1V 6 C6
Torriano Av KTTN NW5 72 D4
Torriano Ms HOLWY N7 72 C4
Torridge Gdns PECK SE15 131 K3
Torridge Rd THHTH CR7 164 C4
Torridon Rd CAT SE6 133 G7
Torrington Av
NFNCH/WDSP N12 39 H4
Torrington Cl ESH/CLAY KT10 170 E5
Torrington Dr RYLN/HDSTN HA2 66 B3
Torrington Gdns
FBAR/BDGN N11 40 C5
GFD/PVL UB6 67 J7
Torrington Gv
NFNCH/WDSP N12 39 J4
Torrington Pk
NFNCH/WDSP N12 39 H3
Torrington Pl FITZ W1T 10 F2
WAP E1W 92 C7
Torrington Rd BCTR RM8 62 B7
ESH/CLAY KT10 170 E5
GFD/PVL UB6 67 J7
RSLP HA4 64 E2
Torrington Sq CROY/NA * CR0 164 E6
GWRST WC1E 11 H1
Torrington Wy MRDN SM4 161 K6
Tor Rd WELL DA16 116 D7
Torr Rd PGE/AN SE20 151 F6
Torver Rd HRW HA1 48 E3
Torwood Rd PUT/ROE SW15 126 D4
Tothill St STJSPK SW1H 17 G2
Totnes Rd WELL DA16 116 C6
Totnes Vls FBAR/BDGN * N11 40 C4
Totnes Wk EFNCH N2 53 H3
Tottan Ter WCHPL * E1 93 F5
Tottenhall Rd PLMGR N13 41 G5
Tottenham Court Rd FITZ W1T 10 F1
Tottenham Gn East
SEVS/STOTM N15 56 B3
Tottenham La CEND/HSY/T N8 54 E5
Tottenham Ms FITZ * W1T 10 F2
Tottenham Rd IS N1 74 A5
Tottenham South Side
SEVS/STOTM N15 56 B3
Tottenham St GTPST W1W 10 F3
Totterdown St TOOT SW17 147 K3
Totteridge Common
TRDG/WHET N20 37 J1
Totteridge La TRDG/WHET N20 38 E1
Totteridge Village
TRDG/WHET N20 26 D7
Totternhoe Cl
KTN/HRWW/W HA3 49 J4
Totton Rd THHTH CR7 164 B2
Toulmin St STHWK SE1 18 E2
Toulon St CMBW SE5 110 D6
Tournay Rd FUL/PGN SW6 107 J6
Toussaint Wk
BERM/RHTH SE16 111 H2
Tovil Cl PGE/AN SE20 165 H1
Towcester Rd BOW E3 93 K3
Tower Br TWRH EC3N 13 L8
Tower Bridge Ap TWRH EC3N 13 L8
Tower Bridge Rd STHWK SE1 19 J5
Tower Buildings WAP * E1W 92 D7
Tower Cl HAMP NW3 71 H4
PGE/AN SE20 150 D6
Tower Ct LSQ/SEVD * WC2H 11 J5
Tower Gdns ESH/CLAY KT10 171 H6
Tower Gardens Rd TOTM N17 41 J7
Tower Hamlets Rd FSTGT E7 76 D4
WALTH E17 57 J2
Tower Hl TWRH EC3N 13 K7
Tower Hill Ter MON EC3R 13 K7
Tower La WBLY * HA9 67 K2
Tower Ms CLPT * E5 75 G4
Tower Mill Rd PECK * SE15 111 F6
Tower Park Rd DART DA1 138 C4
Tower Pl MON EC3R 13 K7
Tower Ri RCH/KEW TW9 125 F2
Tower Rd BELV DA17 117 K3
BXLYHN DA7 137 J3
DART DA1 139 F6
WHTN TW2 142 E2
WLSDN NW10 69 J6
Tower Royal MANHO * EC4N 12 F6
Towers Av HGDN/ICK UB10 82 A2
Towers Ct HGDN/ICK * UB10 82 A2
Towers Pl RCHPK/HAM TW10 125 F4
Towers Rd PIN HA5 33 J7
STHL UB1 84 A3
Tower St LSQ/SEVD * WC2H 11 H5
Tower Ter WDGN N22 55 F1
Tower Vw CROY/NA CR0 166 B7
Towfield Rd FELT TW13 141 K1
Towncourt Crs
STMC/STPC BR5 169 H4
Towncourt La STMC/STPC BR5 169 J5
Towncourt Pth FSBYPK N4 55 J7
Town End Pde KUT * KT1 158 E2
Towney Md NTHLT UB5 83 K1
Town Farm Wy
STWL/WRAY * TW19 120 A6
Townfield Rd HYS/HAR UB3 82 E7
Townfield Sq HYS/HAR UB3 82 D7
Town Field Wy ISLW TW7 124 B1
Town Hall Approach Rd
SEVS/STOTM N15 56 B3
Townhall Av CHSWK W4 106 A4
Town Hall Pde
BRXS/STRHM * SW2 130 A3
Town Hall Rd BTSEA SW11 128 E2
Townholm Crs HNWL W7 104 A2
Town La STWL/WRAY TW19 120 A6
Townley Ct SRTFD E15 76 D5
Townley Rd BXLYHS DA6 137 G4
EDUL SE22 131 F4
Townley St WALW SE17 19 G7
Town Meadow BTFD TW8 104 E6
Townmead Rd FUL/PGN SW6 128 A2
RCH/KEW TW9 125 J1
Town Quay BARK IG11 78 B7
Town Rd ED N9 42 D1
Townsend Av STHGT/OAK N14 40 D3
Townsend La CDALE/KGS NW9 51 F6
Townsend Rd SEVS/STOTM N15 56 B4
STHL UB1 83 J7
WOOL/PLUM SE18 115 G2
Townsend St WALW SE17 19 H6
Townsend Wy NTHWD HA6 32 D6
Townsend Yd HGT N6 54 B7
Townshend Cl SCUP DA14 155 H5
Townshend Est STJWD NW8 3 J5
Townshend Rd CHST BR7 154 B4
RCH/KEW TW9 125 G3
STJWD NW8 3 J4
Townshend Ter RCH/KEW TW9 125 G3
Townson Av NTHLT UB5 83 F1
Townson Wy NTHLT UB5 82 E1
Town Wharf ISLW * TW7 124 C2
Towpath Rd UED * N18 43 F4
Towpath Wy CROY/NA CR0 165 G5
Towton Rd WNWD SE27 149 J1
Toynbec Cl CHST BR7 154 B3
Toynbee Rd RYNPK SW20 146 C7
Toynbee St WCHPL E1 13 L3
Toyne Wy HGT N6 53 K5
Tracey Av CRICK * NW2 70 A4
Trade Cl PLMGR N13 41 G3
Trader Rd EHAM E6 96 B5
Tradescant Rd VX/NE SW8 109 K6
Trading Estate Rd
WLSDN * NW10 86 E3
Trafalgar Av STHWK SE1 19 M8
TOTM N17 42 A5
WPK KT4 161 G7
Trafalgar Gdns WCHPL E1 93 F4
Trafalgar Gv GNWCH SE10 113 G5
Trafalgar Pl UED N18 42 C4
WAN E11 58 E3
Trafalgar Rd GNWCH SE10 113 H4
RAIN RM13 99 H1
WHTN TW2 142 D1
WIM/MER SW19 147 F6
Trafalgar Sq CHCR * WC2N 11 H8
Trafalgar St WALW SE17 19 G7
Trafalgar Wy CROY/NA CR0 177 F1
POP/IOD E14 94 A7
Trafford Cl SRTFD E15 75 K4
Trafford Rd THHTH CR7 164 A4
Tramway Av ED N9 30 D6
SRTFD E15 76 B6
Tramway Pth MTCM CR4 162 D3
Tranley Ms HAMP * NW3 71 J3
Tranmere Rd ED N9 30 B6
WAND/EARL SW18 147 G1
WHTN TW2 123 G6
Tranquil Ri ERITH DA8 118 B4
Tranquil V BKHTH/KID SE3 133 H1
Transept St CAMTN NW1 9 K3
Transmere Rd STMC/STPC BR5 169 H5
Transom Sq POP/IOD E14 112 E4
Transport Av BTFD TW8 104 B4
Tranton Rd BERM/RHTH SE16 111 J2
Traps La NWMAL KT3 160 B1
Travellers Site WALTH * E17 43 H6
Travellers Wy HEST TW5 122 B1
Travers Cl WALTH E17 43 F7
Travers Rd HOLWY N7 73 G2
Treacy Cl BUSH WD23 34 C1
Treadgold St NTGHL W11 88 B6
Treadway St BETH E2 92 D1
Treaty St IS N1 5 L4
Trebeck St MYFR/PICC W1J 10 C8
Trebovir Rd ECT SW5 14 B7
Treby St BOW E3 93 H3
Trecastle Wy HOLWY * N7 72 D3
Tredegar Rd BOW E3 93 H1
FBAR/BDGN N11 40 D6
Tredegar Sq BOW E3 93 H2
Trederwen Rd HACK E8 74 C7
Tredown Rd SYD SE26 150 E4
Tredwell Cl HAYES BR2 168 C3
Tredwell Rd WNWD SE27 149 H3
Tree Cl RCHPK/HAM TW10 124 E7
Treen Av BARN SW13 126 B2
Tree Rd CAN/RD E16 95 G5
Treeside Cl WDR/YW UB7 100 A3
Treetops Cl ABYW SE2 117 F4
NTHWD HA6 32 B4
Tree View Cl NRWD SE19 150 A7
Treewall Gdns BMLY BR1 153 F3
Trefgarne Rd DAGE RM10 80 C1
Trefoil Rd WAND/EARL SW18 128 B4
Tregaron Av CEND/HSY/T N8 54 E6
Tregaron Gdns NWMAL KT3 160 B3
Tregarvon Rd BTSEA SW11 129 F3
Tregenna Av RYLN/HDSTN HA2 66 A3
Tregenna Cl STHGT/OAK N14 28 C4
Trego Rd HOM E9 75 J6
Tregothnan Rd BRXN/ST SW9 129 K2
Tregunter Rd WBPTN SW10 14 E9
Treherne Ct BRXN/ST * SW9 110 C7
Trehern Rd MORT/ESHN SW14 126 A2
Trehurst St CLPT E5 75 G4
Trelawney Est HOM * E9 74 E5
Trelawn Rd BRXS/STRHM SW2 130 B4
WAN E11 76 C1
Trelawny Cl WALTH E17 57 K3
Treloar Gdns NRWD SE19 149 K5
Trelwney Est HOM * E9 74 E5
Tremadoc Rd CLAP SW4 129 J3
Tremaine Rd PGE/AN SE20 165 J1
Tremlett Gv ARCH N19 72 C2
Tremlett Ms ARCH * N19 72 C2
Trenance Gdns GDMY/SEVK IG3 79 G2
Trenchard Av RSLP HA4 65 F4
Trenchard Cl CDALE/KGS NW9 37 G7
STAN HA7 35 H5
Trenchard St GNWCH SE10 113 G4
Trenchold St VX/NE * SW8 109 K5
Trenholme Rd PGE/AN SE20 150 D6
Trenholme Ter PGE/AN SE20 150 D6
Trenmar Gdns WLSDN NW10 87 K2
Trent Av EA W5 104 D2
Trent Ct WAN E11 58 E4
Trent Gdns STHGT/OAK N14 28 B5
Trentham St WAND/EARL SW18 127 K7
Trent Pk EBAR * EN4 28 C1
Trent Rd BRXS/STRHM SW2 130 A4
Trent Wy WPK KT4 174 A2
YEAD UB4 82 C2
Trentwood Side ENC/FH EN2 29 F2
Treport St WAND/EARL SW18 128 A6
Tresco Cl BMLY BR1 152 C5
Trescoe Gdns PIN HA5 47 J6
Tresco Gdns GDMY/SEVK IG3 79 F1
Tresco Rd PECK SE15 131 J3
Tresham Crs STJWD NW8 3 J9
Tresham Rd BARK IG11 79 F6
Tresilian Av WCHMH N21 29 F4
Tressell Cl IS N1 6 D2
Tressillian Crs BROCKY SE4 132 D2
Tressillian Rd BROCKY SE4 132 D2
Trestis Cl YEAD UB4 83 H3
Treswell Rd DAGW RM9 80 A7
Tretawn Gdns MLHL NW7 37 G3
Tretawn Pk MLHL NW7 37 G3
Trevanion Rd WKENS * W14 107 H4
Treve Av HRW HA1 48 C6
Trevelyan Av MNPK E12 77 K3
Trevelyan Cl DART DA1 139 J3
Trevelyan Crs
KTN/HRWW/W HA3 49 K6
Trevelyan Gdns WLSDN * NW10 70 A7
Trevelyan Rd SRTFD E15 76 C3
TOOT SW17 147 K5
Treveris St STHWK SE1 12 D9
Treverton St NKENS W10 88 B3
Treves Cl WCHMH N21 29 F4
Treville St PUT/ROE SW15 126 E6
Treviso Rd FSTH SE23 151 F1
Trevithick Cl
EBED/NFELT TW14 121 J7
Trevithick Dr DART DA1 139 J3
Trevithick St DEPT SE8 112 D5
Trevone Gdns PIN HA5 47 J5
Trevor Cl EBAR EN4 27 H5
HAYES BR2 167 J6
ISLW TW7 124 A4
KTN/HRWW/W HA3 35 F6
NTHLT UB5 83 G1
Trevor Crs RSLP HA4 64 D3
Trevor Gdns EDGW HA8 37 F7
Trevor Pl SKENS SW7 15 K2
Trevor Rd EDGW HA8 37 F7
HYS/HAR UB3 101 H1
WFD IG8 44 E6
WIM/MER SW19 146 C6
Trevor Sq SKENS SW7 15 K2
Trevor St SKENS SW7 15 K2
Trevose Rd WALTH E17 44 B7
Trevose Wy OXHEY WD19 33 G2
Trewenna Dr CHSGTN KT9 171 K4
Trewince Rd RYNPK SW20 146 A7
Trewint St WAND/EARL SW18 147 G1
Trewsbury Rd SYD SE26 151 F4
Triandra Wy YEAD UB4 83 H4
The Triangle BFN/LL * DA15 136 B6
NWMAL KT3 159 K1
Triangle Pas BAR * EN5 27 G3
Triangle Pl CLAP SW4 129 J3
Triangle Rd HACK E8 74 D7
Trident St BERM/RHTH SE16 112 A3
Trident Wy NWDGN UB2 102 A2
Trig La BLKFR EC4V 12 E6
Trigon Rd VX/NE SW8 110 A6
Trilby Rd FSTH SE23 151 F1
Trim St NWCR SE14 112 C5
Trinder Rd ARCH N19 54 E7
BAR EN5 26 A4
Tring Av EA W5 86 B7
STHL UB1 83 K5
WBLY HA9 68 C5
Tring Cl BARK/HLT IG6 60 C4
Trinidad Gdns DAGE RM10 81 F6
Trinidad St POP/IOD E14 93 H6
Trinity Av EFNCH N2 53 H2
EN EN1 30 B5
Trinity Buoy Whf
POP/IOD * E14 94 B4
Trinity Church Rd BARN SW13 106 E5
Trinity Church Sq STHWK SE1 18 F3
Trinity Cl CLAP * SW4 129 H3
HACK * E8 74 B5
HAYES BR2 168 D7
HSLWW TW4 122 D2
LEW SE13 133 G3
NTHWD HA6 32 C5
SAND/SEL CR2 178 A7
WAN E11 76 C1
Trinity Ct ELTH/MOT SE9 135 G5
Trinity Crs TOOT SW17 147 K1
Trinity Gdns BRXN/ST SW9 130 A3
CAN/RD E16 94 D4
DART DA1 139 G5
Trinity Gn WCHPL * E1 92 E4
Trinity Gv GNWCH SE10 113 F7
Trinity Hall Cl WATN WD24 21 G2
Trinity Ms PGE/AN * SE20 150 E7
Trinity Pde HSLW * TW3 123 G2
Trinity Pk CHING * E4 43 H5
Trinity Pl BXLYHS DA6 137 G3
Trinity Ri BRXS/STRHM SW2 130 C6
Trinity Rd BARK/HLT IG6 60 C2
EFNCH N2 53 H2
RCH/KEW * TW9 125 G2
STHL UB1 83 J7
TOOT SW17 147 K1
WAND/EARL SW18 128 C5
WDGN N22 40 E6
WIM/MER SW19 146 E5
Trinity Sq TWRH EC3N 13 K7
Trinity St CAN/RD E16 94 D4
ENC/FH EN2 29 J1
STHWK SE1 18 F2
Trinity Wy ACT W3 87 G6
CHING E4 43 H5
Trio Pl STHWK SE1 18 F2
Tristan Ldg BUSH * WD23 21 J3
Tristan Sq BKHTH/KID SE3 133 H2
Tristram Cl WALTH E17 58 B2
Tristram Rd BMLY BR1 152 D3
Triton Sq CAMTN NW1 4 E9
Tritton Av CROY/NA CR0 176 E3
Tritton Rd WNWD SE27 149 K2
Triumph Cl HYS/HAR UB3 101 F7
Triumph Rd EHAM E6 95 K5
Trojan Wy CROY/NA CR0 177 F2
Troon Cl BERM/RHTH * SE16 111 J4
Troon St WCHPL E1 93 G5
Trosley Rd BELV DA17 117 H5
Trossachs Rd EDUL SE22 131 F4
Trothy Rd STHWK SE1 111 H3
Trott Rd MUSWH N10 40 A6
Trott St BTSEA SW11 108 C7
Troughton Rd CHARL SE7 114 A4
Troutbeck Rd NWCR SE14 112 B7
Trouville Rd CLAP SW4 129 H5
Trowbridge Rd HOM E9 75 H5
Trowlock Av TEDD TW11 143 J5
Trowlock Island TEDD TW11 143 K5
Trowlock Wy TEDD TW11 143 K5
Troy Ct KENS W8 14 A3
Troy Rd NRWD SE19 149 K5
Troy Town PECK SE15 131 H2
Trubshaw Rd NWDGN UB2 103 F2
Trueman Cl EDGW * HA8 36 D6
Trulock Rd TOTM N17 42 C6
Truman's Rd STNW/STAM N16 74 A4
Trumpers Wy HNWL W7 104 A2
Trumpington Rd FSTGT E7 76 D3
Trump St CITYW EC2V 12 F5
Trundlers Wy BUSH WD23 22 E7
Trundle St STHWK SE1 18 E1
Trundley's Rd DEPT SE8 112 A4
Trundley's Ter DEPT SE8 112 A3
Truro Gdns IL IG1 59 J6
Truro Rd WALTH E17 57 H3
WDGN N22 40 E6
Truro St KTTN NW5 72 A5
Truro Wy YEAD UB4 82 C2
Trusedale Rd EHAM E6 95 K5
Truslove Rd WNWD SE27 149 G4
Trussley Rd HMSMTH W6 107 F2
Trustons Gdns EMPK RM11 63 J6
Tryfan Cl REDBR IG4 59 H4
Tryon Crs HOM E9 74 E7
Tryon St CHEL SW3 15 L7
Trystings Cl ESH/CLAY KT10 171 G5
Tuam Rd WOOL/PLUM SE18 115 J5
Tubbs Rd WLSDN NW10 87 H1
Tucker St WATW WD18 21 G4
Tuck Rd RAIN RM13 81 J5
Tudor Av GPK RM2 63 J2
HPTN TW12 142 A5
WPK KT4 173 K2
Tudor Cl BRXS/STRHM * SW2 130 A5

CDALE/KGS NW9 68 E1
CHEAM SM3 174 B4
CHSGTN KT9 172 A4
CHST BR7 153 K7
DART DA1 138 E5
HAMP NW3 71 J4
HGT N6 54 C6
HPTN TW12 142 C4
MLHL NW7 37 J5
PIN HA5 46 E4
WFD IG8 45 F4
WLGTN SM6 176 C6
Tudor Ct BORE WD6 24 A1
ELTH/MOT * SE9 134 D3
WALTH E17 57 H6
Tudor Ct North WBLY HA9 68 C4
Tudor Ct South WBLY HA9 68 C4
Tudor Dr GPK RM2 63 J3
KUTN/CMB KT2 144 A4
MRDN SM4 161 G5
WOT/HER KT12 156 C7
Tudor Est WLSDN * NW10 86 D1
Tudor Gdns ACT W3 86 C5
BARN SW13 126 B2
CDALE/KGS NW9 68 E1
GPK RM2 63 J3
TWK TW1 124 A7
WWKM BR4 180 A2
Tudor Gv HOM E9 74 E6
Tudor Pde ELTH/MOT * SE9 134 D3
Tudor Pl NRWD * SE19 150 B6
WIM/MER SW19 147 J6
Tudor Rd ASHF TW15 140 B5
BAR EN5 26 E2
BARK IG11 79 F6
BECK BR3 167 F2
CHING E4 43 K5
ED N9 30 D6
EHAM E6 77 G7
HACK E8 74 D7
HPTN TW12 142 A6
HSLW TW3 123 J3
HYS/HAR UB3 82 B5
KTN/HRWW/W HA3 48 D1
KUTN/CMB KT2 144 C6
NRWD SE19 150 B6
PIN HA5 47 G1
SNWD SE25 165 J4
STHL UB1 83 J6
Tudor Sq HYS/HAR UB3 82 B6
Tudor St EMB EC4Y 12 B6
Tudor Wy ACT W3 105 H1
STHGT/OAK N14 28 D7
STMC/STPC BR5 169 J5
Tudor Well Cl STAN HA7 35 H4
Tudway Rd BKHTH/KID SE3 134 B3
Tufnail Rd DART DA1 139 J5
Tufnell Park Rd HOLWY N7 72 D3
Tufton Gdns E/WMO/HCT KT8 157 G1
Tufton Rd CHING E4 43 J3
Tufton St WEST SW1P 17 J4
Tugboat St THMD SE28 115 K1
Tugela Rd CROY/NA CR0 164 E5
Tugela St CAT SE6 151 H1
Tulip Cl CROY/NA CR0 166 A7
EHAM E6 95 K4
HPTN TW12 141 K5
NWDGN UB2 103 H1
Tulip Gdns CHING * E4 44 B2
IL IG1 78 B5
Tulip Wy WDR/YW UB7 100 A3
Tull St MTCM CR4 162 E6
Tulse Cl BECK BR3 167 F2
Tulse Hl BRXS/STRHM SW2 130 B6
Tulsemere Rd WNWD SE27 149 J1
Tummons Gdns SNWD SE25 165 F1
Tuncombe Rd UED N18 42 A3
Tunis Rd SHB W12 88 A7
Tunley Rd BAL SW12 148 A1
WLSDN NW10 69 G7
Tunmarsh La PLSTW E13 95 G2
Tunnan Leys EHAM E6 96 A5
Tunnel Av GNWCH SE10 113 G1
Tunnel Gdns FBAR/BDGN N11 40 C6
Tunnel Link Rd HTHAIR TW6 120 D4
Tunnel Rd BERM/RHTH SE16 111 K1
Tunnel Rd East WDR/YW UB7 100 E6
Tunnel Rd West WDR/YW UB7 100 D7
Tunstall Rd BRXN/ST SW9 130 A3
CROY/NA CR0 165 F7
Tunstock Wy BELV DA17 117 F2
Tunworth Cl CDALE/KGS NW9 50 E5
Tunworth Crs PUT/ROE SW15 126 C5
Tupelo Rd LEY E10 75 K1
Turene Cl BTSEA SW11 128 B3
Turin Rd ED N9 30 E6
Turin St BETH E2 92 C2
Turkey Oak Cl NRWD SE19 150 A7
Turks Rw CHEL SW3 15 M7
Turle Rd FSBYPK * N4 73 F1
STRHM/NOR SW16 163 K1
Turlewray Cl FSBYPK N4 55 F7
Turley Cl SRTFD E15 76 C7
Turnagain La STP * EC4M 12 C4
Turnage Rd BCTR RM8 62 A7
Turnant Rd TOTM N17 41 J7
Turnberry Cl
BERM/RHTH * SE16 111 J4
Turnberry Ct OXHEY * WD19 33 G2
Turnberry Wy ORP BR6 169 J7
Turnbury Cl THMD SE28 97 K5
Turner Av MTCM CR4 147 K7
SEVS/STOTM N15 56 A3
WHTN TW2 142 C2
Turner Cl ALP/SUD HA0 67 K4
CMBW SE5 110 C7
GLDGN NW11 53 F5
Turner Ct CMBW * SE5 130 E3
DART DA1 139 F4
Turner Dr GLDGN NW11 53 F5
Turner Rd BUSH WD23 22 C3
EDGW HA8 50 A1
NWMAL KT3 160 A6
WALTH E17 58 A3
Turners Meadow Wy
BECK BR3 151 H7
Turner's Rd POP/IOD E14 93 H4
Turner St CAN/RD E16 94 D5
WCHPL E1 92 D4
Turners Wy CROY/NA CR0 177 G1
Turner's Wd GLDGN NW11 53 G7
Turneville Rd WKENS W14 107 J5
Turney Rd DUL SE21 130 D6
Turnham Green Ter CHSWK W4 106 B3
Turnham Rd BROCKY SE4 132 B4
Turnmill St FARR EC1M 12 B1
Turnpike Cl DEPT SE8 112 C6
Turnpike La CEND/HSY/T N8 55 G3
SUT SM1 175 G4
Turnpike Link CROY/NA CR0 178 A1
Turnpike Ms CEND/HSY/T * N8 55 G2
Turnpike Pde CEND/HSY/T * N8 55 H2
Turnpike Wy ISLW TW7 104 B7
Turnstone Cl CDALE/KGS * NW9 51 G1
PLSTW E13 94 E2
Turnstone Ter WEA * W13 85 F3
Turpentine La PIM SW1V 16 D7
Turpington Cl HAYES BR2 168 D5
Turpington La HAYES BR2 168 D4
Turpin La ERITH DA8 118 D5
Turpin Rd EBED/NFELT TW14 121 J5
Turpin's La WFD IG8 45 K4
Turpins Yd CRICK * NW2 69 K1
Turpin Wy WLGTN SM6 176 B6
Turquand St WALW SE17 18 F6
Turret Gv CLAP SW4 129 H2
Turton Rd ALP/SUD HA0 68 A4
Turville St BETH * E2 7 L9
Tuscan Rd WOOL/PLUM SE18 115 J4
Tuskar St GNWCH SE10 113 H4
Tweeddale Gv HGDN/ICK UB10 64 A2
Tweeddale Rd CAR SM5 162 C7
Tweedmouth Rd PLSTW E13 95 F1
Tweedy Rd BMLY BR1 152 E7
Twelvetrees Crs BOW E3 94 A3
Twentyman Cl WFD IG8 44 E4
Twickenham Br TWK TW1 124 E4
Twickenham Cl CROY/NA CR0 177 F2
Twickenham Gdns
GFD/PVL UB6 67 G4
KTN/HRWW/W HA3 34 E6
Twickenham Rd FELT TW13 141 J3
ISLW TW7 124 A4
TEDD TW11 143 G3
WAN E11 76 B1
Twig Folly Cl BOW E3 93 F1
Twig Folly Whf BETH * E2 93 F1
Twigg Cl ERITH DA8 118 B6
Twilley St WAND/EARL SW18 128 A6
Twine Cl BARK IG11 97 H2
Twine Ct WCHPL E1 92 E6
Twineham Gn
NFNCH/WDSP N12 38 E3
Twine Ter BOW * E3 93 H3
Twining Av WHTN TW2 142 C2
Twinn Rd MLHL NW7 38 C5
Twisden Rd KTTN NW5 72 B3
Twisleton Ct DART DA1 139 G5
Twybridge Wy WLSDN NW10 68 E6
Twyford Abbey Rd
WLSDN NW10 86 B2
Twyford Av ACT W3 86 C6
EFNCH N2 53 K2
Twyford Crs ACT W3 86 C7
Twyford Rd CAR SM5 162 C7
IL IG1 78 C4
RYLN/HDSTN HA2 48 B6
Twyford St IS N1 5 L3
Tyas Rd CAN/RD E16 94 D3
Tybenham Rd WIM/MER SW19 161 K2
Tyberry Rd PEND EN3 30 D2
Tyburn La HRW HA1 48 E6
Tyburn Wy MBLAR W1H 9 M6
Tyers Ga STHWK SE1 19 J2
Tyers St LBTH SE11 17 L7
Tyers Ter LBTH SE11 17 L8
Tyeshurst Cl ABYW SE2 117 F4
Tylecroft Rd
STRHM/NOR SW16 163 K1
Tylehurst Gdns IL IG1 78 C4
Tyler Cl BETH E2 7 L5
Tylers Ga KTN/HRWW/W HA3 50 A5
Tyler St GNWCH SE10 113 H4
Tylney Av NRWD SE19 150 B4
Tylney Rd BMLY BR1 168 C1
FSTGT E7 77 G3
Tynan Cl EBED/NFELT TW14 121 K7
Tyndale La IS N1 6 C1
Tyndale Ter IS N1 6 C1
Tyndall Rd LEY E10 76 A1
WELL DA16 136 A2
Tyneham Cl BTSEA * SW11 129 F2
Tyneham Rd BTSEA SW11 129 F1
Tynemouth Cl EHAM E6 96 B5
Tynemouth Rd MTCM CR4 148 A6
SEVS/STOTM N15 56 B3
WOOL/PLUM SE18 115 K4
Tynemouth St FUL/PGN SW6 128 B1
Tynemouth Ter
SEVS/STOTM * N15 56 B3
Tyne St WCHPL E1 13 M4
Tynsdale Rd WLSDN NW10 69 G5
Type St BETH E2 93 F1
Tyrawley Rd FUL/PGN SW6 108 A7
Tyre La CDALE/KGS * NW9 51 G4
Tyrell Cl HRW HA1 66 E3
Tyrone Rd EHAM E6 95 K1
Tyron Wy SCUP DA14 154 E3
Tyrrell Av WELL DA16 136 B4
Tyrrell Rd EDUL SE22 131 H3
Tyrrel Wy CDALE/KGS NW9 51 H6
Tyrwhitt Rd LEW SE13 132 D2
Tysoe St CLKNW EC1R 6 A8
Tyson Gdns FSTH * SE23 131 K6
Tyson Rd FSTH SE23 131 K6
Tyssen Rd STNW/STAM * N16 74 B2
Tyssen St HACK E8 74 B5
Tytherton Rd ARCH N19 72 D2

U

Uamvar St POP/IOD E14 93 K4
Uckfield Gv MTCM CR4 148 A7
Udall St WEST SW1P 16 F6
Udney Park Rd TEDD TW11 143 G4
Uffington Rd WLSDN NW10 69 J7
WNWD SE27 149 G3
Ufford Cl KTN/HRWW/W HA3 34 B6
Ufford Rd KTN/HRWW/W HA3 34 B6
Ufford St STHWK SE1 18 B1
Ufton Rd IS N1 7 J2
Uhura Sq STNW/STAM * N16 74 A2
Ullathorne Rd
STRHM/NOR SW16 148 C3
Ulleswater Rd PLMGR N13 40 E5
Ulleswater Vls PLMGR * N13 40 E3
Ullin St POP/IOD E14 94 A4
Ullswater Cl BMLY BR1 152 C5
KUTN/CMB * KT2 145 F3
YEAD UB4 82 C1
Ullswater Ct RYLN/HDSTN * HA2 48 A6
Ullswater Crs PUT/ROE SW15 145 F3
Ullswater Rd BARN SW13 106 D6
WNWD SE27 149 H2
Ullswater Wy HCH RM12 81 J4
Ulster Gdns PLMGR N13 41 J3
Ulster Pl CAMTN NW1 10 C1
Ulundi Rd BKHTH/KID SE3 113 H5
Ulva Rd PUT/ROE SW15 127 G3
Ulverscroft Rd EDUL SE22 131 H4
Ulverston Rd WALTH E17 58 B1
Ulysses Rd KIL/WHAMP NW6 70 D4
Umberston St WCHPL * E1 92 C5
Umbria St PUT/ROE SW15 126 D5
Umfreville Rd FSBYPK N4 55 H5
Undercliff Rd LEW SE13 132 D2
Underhill BAR EN5 26 E4
Underhill Ct BAR * EN5 26 E4
Underhill Rd EDUL SE22 131 H4
Underhill St CAMTN NW1 4 D4
Underne Av STHGT/OAK N14 40 B1
Undershaft HDTCH EC3A 13 J5
Undershaw Rd BMLY BR1 152 C2
The Underwood
ELTH/MOT SE9 153 K1
Underwood Rd CHING E4 43 K4
WCHPL E1 92 C3
WFD IG8 45 H6
Underwood Rw IS N1 6 F7
Underwood St IS N1 6 F7
Undine Rd POP/IOD E14 112 E3
Undine St TOOT SW17 147 K4
Uneeda Dr GFD/PVL UB6 66 D7
Union Cl WAN E11 76 B3
Union Ct CLAP SW4 129 K1
Union Dr WCHPL * E1 93 G3
Union Gv VX/NE SW8 129 J1
Union Rd ALP/SUD HA0 68 A5
CROY/NA CR0 164 D6
FBAR/BDGN N11 40 D5
HAYES BR2 168 C4
NTHLT UB5 84 A1
VX/NE SW8 129 J1
Union Sq IS N1 6 E4
Union St BAR EN5 26 C3
KUT KT1 158 E1
SRTFD E15 76 B7
STHWK SE1 12 D9
Union Wk BETH E2 7 L7
Unity Cl CROY/NA CR0 179 K7
WLSDN NW10 69 J5
WNWD SE27 149 J4
Unity Ms CAMTN NW1 5 G5
Unity Wy WOOL/PLUM SE18 114 C2
University Cl BUSH WD23 21 K3
CDALE/KGS NW9 37 H6
University Gdns BXLY DA5 137 G6
University Rd WIM/MER SW19 147 H5
University St FITZ W1T 10 F1
University Wy DART DA1 139 K3
EHAM E6 96 A6
Unwin Av EBED/NFELT TW14 121 G4
Unwin Cl PECK SE15 111 H5
Unwin Rd ISLW TW7 123 K2
SKENS SW7 15 H3
Upbrook Ms BAY/PAD W2 8 F5
Upcerne Rd WBPTN SW10 108 B6
Upcroft Av EDGW HA8 36 E4
Updale Rd SCUP DA14 155 F3
Upfield CROY/NA CR0 178 D1
Upfield Rd HNWL W7 85 F3
Uphall Rd IL IG1 78 B4
Upham Park Rd CHSWK W4 106 B3
Uphill Dr CDALE/KGS NW9 50 E4
MLHL NW7 37 G4
Uphill Gv MLHL NW7 37 G3
Uphill Rd MLHL NW7 37 G3
Upland Rd BELMT SM2 175 H6
BXLYHN DA7 137 G2
EDUL SE22 131 H4
PLSTW E13 94 E3
SAND/SEL CR2 177 K4
The Uplands RSLP HA4 46 E7
Uplands BECK BR3 166 D1
Uplands Av WALTH E17 57 F2
Uplands Cl MORT/ESHN SW14 125 J4
Uplands Park Rd ENC/FH EN2 29 G1
Uplands Rd CEND/HSY/T N8 55 F4
CHDH RM6 61 K2
EBAR EN4 28 A7
WFD IG8 45 J6
Uplands Wy WCHMH N21 29 G4
Upminster Rd South RAIN RM13 99 J3
Upney La BARK IG11 79 F6
Upnor Wy WALW SE17 19 K7
Uppark Dr GNTH/NBYPK IG2 60 C5
Upper Abbey Rd BELV DA17 117 G3
Upper Addison Gdns
WKENS W14 107 H1
Upper Bardsey Wk IS * N1 73 J5
Upper Belgrave St KTBR SW1X 16 B3
Upper Berenger Wk
WBPTN * SW10 108 C6
Upper Berkeley St BAY/PAD W2 9 L5
Upper Beulah Hl NRWD SE19 150 A7
Upper Blantyre Wk
WBPTN * SW10 108 C6
Upper Brighton Rd SURB KT6 158 E5
Upper Brockley Rd
BROCKY SE4 132 C2
Upper Brook St
MYFR/PKLN W1K 10 A6
Upper Butts BTFD TW8 104 D5
Upper Caldy Wk IS * N1 73 J5
Upper Camelford Wk
NTGHL * W11 88 C5
Upper Cheyne Rw CHEL SW3 108 D5
Upper Clapton Rd CLPT E5 74 D1
Upper Clarendon Wk
NTGHL * W11 88 C5
Upper Dartrey Wk
WBPTN * SW10 108 B6
Upper Dengie Wk IS * N1 6 E3
Upper Elmers End Rd
BECK BR3 166 B3
Upper Farm Rd
E/WMO/HCT KT8 156 E3
Upper Gn East MTCM CR4 162 E2
Upper Gn West MTCM CR4 162 E1
Upper Grosvenor St
MYFR/PKLN W1K 10 A7
Upper Grotto Rd TWK TW1 143 F1
Upper Gnd STHWK SE1 12 A8
Upper Gv SNWD SE25 165 F3
Upper Grove Rd BELV DA17 117 G5
Upper Gulland Wk IS * N1 6 F1
Upper Ham Rd
RCHPK/HAM TW10 143 K3
Upper Handa Wk IS * N1 73 K5
Upper Harley St CAMTN NW1 10 B1
Upper Hawkwell Wk IS * N1 6 F3
Upper Hitch OXHEY WD19 21 J7
Upper Holly Hill Rd
BELV DA17 117 J4
Upper John St REGST W1B 10 F6
Upper Lismore Wk IS * N1 73 J5
Upper Ldg KENS * W8 8 D9
Upper Ml HMSMTH W6 106 D4
Upper Marsh STHWK SE1 17 M3
Upper Montagu St MBLAR W1H 9 L2
Upper Mulgrave Rd
BELMT SM2 174 C6
Upper North St POP/IOD E14 93 J4
Upper Paddock Rd
OXHEY WD19 21 J5
Upper Park Rd BELV DA17 117 J3
BMLY BR1 153 F7
FBAR/BDGN N11 40 B4
HAMP NW3 71 K5
KUTN/CMB KT2 144 C5
Upper Phillimore Gdns
KENS W8 14 A2
Upper Rainham Rd HCH RM12 63 H7
Upper Ramsey Wk IS N1 73 K5
Upper Rawreth Wk IS * N1 6 F3
Upper Richmond Rd
PUT/ROE SW15 126 E3
Upper Richmond Rd West
RCHPK/HAM TW10 125 H3
Upper Rd PLSTW E13 94 E2
WLGTN SM6 176 D4
Upper St Martin's La
LSQ/SEVD WC2H 11 J5
Upper Selsdon Rd
SAND/SEL CR2 178 B7
Upper Sheppey Wk IS N1 73 J5
Upper Sheridan Rd BELV DA17 117 H3
Upper Shirley Rd
CROY/NA CR0 178 E2
Upper Sq ISLW TW7 124 B2
Upper St IS N1 6 B6
IS N1 6 C1
Upper Sunbury Rd HPTN TW12 141 K7
Upper Sutton La HEST TW5 103 F7
Upper Tachbrook St PIM SW1V 16 F5
Upper Tail OXHEY WD19 33 J2
Upper Talbot Wk NTGHL * W11 88 C5
Upper Teddington Rd KUT KT1 143 J7
Upper Ter HAMP NW3 71 G2
Upper Thames St BLKFR EC4V 12 E6
Upper Tollington Pk FSBYPK N4 55 G7
Upperton Rd SCUP DA14 155 F4
Upperton Rd East PLSTW E13 95 G2
Upperton Rd West PLSTW E13 95 G2
Upper Tooting Pk TOOT SW17 147 K1
Upper Tooting Rd TOOT SW17 147 K3
Upper Town Rd GFD/PVL UB6 84 B3
Upper Tulse Hl
BRXS/STRHM SW2 130 A6
Upper Vernon Rd SUT SM1 175 H4
Upper Walthamstow Rd
WALTH E17 58 B3
Upper Whistler Wk
WBPTN * SW10 108 B6
Upper Wickham La
WELL DA16 136 C1
Upper Wimpole St
CAVSQ/HST W1G 10 B2
Upper Woburn Pl CAMTN NW1 5 H8
Uppingham Av STAN HA7 49 J2
Upsdell Av PLMGR N13 41 G5
Upstall St CMBW SE5 110 C7
Upton Av FSTGT E7 76 E6
Upton Cl BXLY DA5 137 G5
Upton Dene BELMT SM2 175 F6
Upton Gdns KTN/HRWW/W HA3 49 J5
Upton La FSTGT E7 77 F5
Upton Lodge Cl BUSH WD23 22 C6
Upton Park Rd FSTGT E7 77 F6
Upton Rd BXLYHS DA6 137 F3
HSLW TW3 123 F2
THHTH CR7 164 E1
UED N18 42 C4
WATW WD18 21 F3
WOOL/PLUM SE18 115 H5
Upton Rd South BXLY DA5 137 G5
Upway NFNCH/WDSP N12 39 J6
Upwood Rd LEE/GVPK SE12 133 K5
STRHM/NOR SW16 148 E7
Urlwin St CMBW SE5 110 D5
Urlwin Wk BRXN/ST SW9 110 B7
Urmston Dr WIM/MER SW19 127 H7
Ursula Ms FSBYPK N4 55 H7
Ursula St BTSEA SW11 108 D7
Urswick Rd CLPT E5 74 E4
DAGW RM9 80 A6
Usborne Ms VX/NE SW8 110 A6
Usher Rd BOW E3 75 H7
Usk Rd BTSEA SW11 128 B3
Usk St BETH E2 93 F2
Uvedale Rd DAGE RM10 80 C2
ENC/FH EN2 29 K4
Uverdale Rd WBPTN SW10 108 B6
Uxbridge Rd EA W5 86 A6
FELT TW13 141 H1
HGDN/ICK UB10 82 A3
HPTN TW12 142 A3
SHB W12 87 J7
STHL UB1 84 A7
SURB KT6 158 E3
WEA W13 85 H7
YEAD UB4 82 E5
Uxbridge Rd (Harrow Weald)
KTN/HRWW/W HA3 34 B6
Uxbridge Rd (Hatch End)
PIN HA5 33 J7
Uxbridge Rd High St STHL UB1 83 K7
Uxbridge Rd (Pinner) PIN HA5 47 H1
Uxbridge Rd (Stanmore)
STAN HA7 35 F5
Uxbridge Rd The Broadway
YEAD UB4 83 H6
Uxbridge St KENS W8 8 A8
Uxendon Crs WBLY HA9 50 A7
Uxendon Hl WBLY HA9 50 B7

V

Valan Leas HAYES BR2 167 H2
The Vale ACT W3 87 F7
CHEL SW3 15 G9
CRICK NW2 70 B2
CROY/NA CR0 179 F1
EBED/NFELT TW14 122 A5
GLDGN NW11 52 D7
HEST TW5 102 D5
MUSWH N10 40 A7
RSLP HA4 65 G3
STHGT/OAK N14 28 E6
SUN * TW16 140 E5
WFD IG8 44 E6
Vale Av BORE WD6 24 D4
Vale Cl EFNCH N2 53 K2
MV/WKIL W9 2 E8
TWK * TW1 143 G2
Vale Cottages
PUT/ROE * SW15 145 G2
Vale Ct ACT * W3 87 H7
Vale Crs PUT/ROE SW15 145 G3
Vale Cft ESH/CLAY KT10 171 F6
PIN HA5 47 J4
Vale Dr BAR EN5 26 D3
Vale End EDUL SE22 131 G3
Vale Gv ACT W3 87 F7
FSBYPK N4 55 J6
Vale La ACT W3 86 C4
Valence Av BCTR RM8 61 K7
Valence Circ BCTR RM8 79 K2
Valence Rd ERITH DA8 118 A6
Valence Wood Rd BCTR RM8 79 K2
Valencia Rd STAN HA7 35 J3
Valency Cl NTHWD HA6 32 D3
Valentia Pl BRXN/ST SW9 130 B3
Valentine Pl STHWK SE1 18 C1
Valentine Rd HOM * E9 75 F5
RYLN/HDSTN HA2 66 B2
Valentines Rd IL IG1 60 B7
Valentines Wy DAGE RM10 81 G1
Vale of Health HAMP NW3 71 G2
Valerian Wy SRTFD E15 94 C2
Vale Ri GLDGN NW11 52 D7
Vale Rd BMLY BR1 169 F1
BUSH WD23 21 J4
DART DA1 138 E7
ESH/CLAY KT10 170 E7
FSBYPK N4 55 J6
FSTGT E7 77 F5
MTCM CR4 163 J2
SUT SM1 175 F3
WPK KT4 173 H2
Vale Rd North SURB KT6 172 A1
Vale Royal HOLWY N7 5 J2
Valeswood Rd BMLY BR1 152 D4
Vale Ter FSBYPK N4 55 J5
Valetta Gv PLSTW E13 94 E1
Valetta Rd ACT W3 106 B1
Valette St HACK * E8 74 D5
Valiant Cl NTHLT UB5 83 H2
ROMW/RG RM7 62 C1
Valiant Wy EHAM E6 95 K4
Vallance Rd WCHPL E1 92 C3
WDGN N22 54 C1
Vallentin Rd WALTH E17 58 A3
Valley Av NFNCH/WDSP N12 39 H3
Valley Cl DART DA1 138 C5
PIN HA5 47 F1
Valley Dr CDALE/KGS NW9 50 D4
Valleyfield Rd
STRHM/NOR SW16 149 F4
Valley Fields Crs ENC/FH EN2 29 G1
Valley Gdns ALP/SUD HA0 68 B6
WIM/MER SW19 147 H6
Valley Gv CHARL SE7 114 B4
Valley Pk WATW * WD18 20 A6
Valley Rd DART DA1 138 C5
ERITH DA8 117 K3
HAYES BR2 167 H1
STMC/STPC BR5 155 H7
STRHM/NOR SW16 149 F3
Valley Side CHING E4 31 J7
Valley Vw BAR EN5 26 C5
Valley Wk CROY/NA CR0 178 E1
RKW/CH/CXG WD3 20 A4
Valliere Rd WLSDN NW10 87 J2
Valliers Wood Rd BFN/LL DA15 135 K7
Vallis Wy CHSGTN KT9 171 K3
WEA W13 85 G4
Valmar Rd CMBW SE5 110 D7
Valnay St TOOT SW17 147 K4
Valognes Av WALTH E17 43 G7
Valonia Gdns
WAND/EARL SW18 127 J5
Vambery Rd WOOL/PLUM SE18 115 H5
Vanbrough Crs NTHLT UB5 83 G1
Vanbrugh Dr WOT/HER KT12 156 B6
Vanbrugh Flds BKHTH/KID SE3 113 J5
Vanbrugh Hl GNWCH SE10 113 H4
Vanbrugh Pk BKHTH/KID SE3 113 K6
Vanbrugh Park Rd
BKHTH/KID SE3 113 J6
Vanbrugh Park Rd West
BKHTH/KID SE3 113 J6
Vanbrugh Rd CHSWK W4 106 A2
Vanbrugh Ter BKHTH/KID SE3 113 J7
Vanburgh Cl CAN/RD E16 95 H4
ORP BR6 169 K7
Vancouver Man EDGW * HA8 36 D7
Vancouver Rd EDGW HA8 36 D7
FSTH SE23 151 G1
RCHPK/HAM TW10 143 J3
YEAD UB4 83 F3
Vanderbilt Rd
WAND/EARL SW18 128 A7
Vanderbilt Vls SHB * W12 107 G1
Vandome Cl CAN/RD E16 95 F5
Vandon St STJSPK SW1H 16 F3
Van Dyck Av NWMAL KT3 160 A6
Vandyke Cl PUT/ROE SW15 127 G5
Vandyke Cross ELTH/MOT SE9 134 D4
Vandy St SDTCH EC2A 13 J1
Vane Cl HAMP NW3 71 H4
KTN/HRWW/W HA3 50 B5
Vanessa Cl BELV DA17 117 H4
Vanguard CDALE/KGS * NW9 37 G6
Vanguard Cl CAN/RD E16 94 E4
CROY/NA CR0 164 C7
ROMW/RG RM7 62 D1
Vanguard St DEPT SE8 112 D7
Vanguard Wy CROY/NA CR0 178 B3
HTHAIR TW6 121 H1
WLGTN SM6 176 E6
Vanneck Sq PUT/ROE * SW15 126 D4
Vanoc Gdns BMLY BR1 152 E3
Vansittart Rd FSTGT E7 76 E3
Vansittart St NWCR SE14 112 B6
Vanston Pl FUL/PGN SW6 107 K6
Vantage Pl KENS W8 14 B4
Vant Rd TOOT SW17 147 K4
Varcoe Rd BERM/RHTH SE16 111 J4
Vardens Rd BTSEA SW11 128 C3
Varden St WCHPL E1 92 D5
Vardley Rd CAN/RD E16 95 F5
Varley Wy MTCM CR4 162 C1
Varna Rd FUL/PGN SW6 107 H6
HPTN * TW12 142 B7
Varndell St CAMTN NW1 4 E7
Varsity Dr WHTN TW2 123 K4
Varsity Rw MORT/ESHN SW14 125 K1
Vartry Rd SEVS/STOTM N15 56 A5
Vassall Rd BRXN/ST SW9 110 B6
Vauban Est BERM/RHTH SE16 19 M4
Vauban St BERM/RHTH SE16 19 M4
Vaughan Av HDN NW4 51 J4
HMSMTH W6 106 C3
Vaughan Est BETH * E2 7 L7

Vaughan Gdns IL IG1 59 K6
Vaughan Rd CMBW SE5 130 D1
HRW HA1 48 C6
SRTFD E15 76 D5
THDIT KT7 158 C6
WELL DA16 136 A1
Vaughan St BERM/RHTH SE16 112 C1
Vaughan Wy WAP E1W 92 C6
Vaughan Williams Cl DEPT SE8 112 D6
Vauxhall Br LBTH SE11 17 J8
Vauxhall Bridge Rd PIM SW1V 16 E4
Vauxhall Gdns SAND/SEL CR2 177 J5
Vauxhall Gv VX/NE SW8 17 K9
Vauxhall Pl DART DA1 139 H6
Vauxhall St LBTH SE11 17 M8
Vauxhall Wk LBTH SE11 17 L7
Vawdrey Cl WCHPL E1 92 E3
Veals Md MTCM CR4 147 J7
Vectis Gdns TOOT SW17 148 B5
Vectis Rd TOOT SW17 148 B5
Veda Rd LEW SE13 132 D3
Vega Crs NTHWD HA6 32 D4
Vega Rd BUSH WD23 22 C6
Veldene Wy RYLN/HDSTN HA2 65 K2
Vellum Dr CAR SM5 176 A2
Venables Cl DAGE RM10 80 D3
Venables St STJWD NW8 9 H1
Vencourt Pl HMSMTH W6 106 D4
Venetian Rd CMBW SE5 130 D1
Venetia Rd EA W5 104 E1
FSBYPK N4 55 H5
Venette Cl RAIN RM13 99 K4
Venner Rd SYD SE26 150 E5
Venners Cl BXLYHN DA7 138 B1
Venn St CLAP SW4 129 H3
Ventnor Av STAN HA7 35 H7
Ventnor Dr NFNCH/WDSP N12 39 F2
Ventnor Gdns BARK IG11 78 E5
Ventnor Rd BELMT SM2 175 F6
NWCR SE14 112 A6
Ventnor Ter SEVS/STOTM * N15 56 C3
Venture Cl BXLY DA5 137 F6
Venue St POP/IOD E14 93 K4
Venus Rd WOOL/PLUM SE18 114 E2
Vera Av WCHMH N21 29 G4
Vera Ct OXHEY WD19 21 H6
Vera Lynn Cl FSTGT E7 76 E3
Vera Rd FUL/PGN SW6 107 H7
Verbena Cl CAN/RD E16 94 D3
WDR/YW UB7 100 A4
Verbena Gdns HMSMTH W6 106 D4
Ver-Colne Valley Wk
BUSH WD23 21 H2
Verdant La CAT SE6 133 H7
Verdayne Av CROY/NA CR0 166 A7
Verdun Rd BARN SW13 106 D6
WOOL/PLUM SE18 116 B5
Vereker Rd WKENS * W14 107 H4
Vere St MHST W1U 10 C5
Vermont Cl ENC/FH EN2 29 H3
Vermont Rd NRWD SE19 149 K5
SUT SM1 175 F2
WAND/EARL SW18 128 A5
Verney Gdns DAGW RM9 80 A3
Verney Rd BERM/RHTH SE16 111 J4
DAGW RM9 80 A4
Verney St WLSDN NW10 69 F2
Verney Wy BERM/RHTH SE16 111 J4
Vernham Rd
WOOL/PLUM SE18 115 H5
Vernon Av MNPK E12 77 K3
RYNPK SW20 161 G1
WFD IG8 45 F5
Vernon Cl HOR/WEW KT19 172 E5
Vernon Crs EBAR EN4 28 A4
Vernon Dr STAN HA7 35 G7
Vernon Pl BMSBY WC1N 11 K3
Vernon Ri FSBYW WC1X 5 M7
GFD/PVL UB6 66 D4
Vernon Rd BOW E3 93 H1
BUSH WD23 21 J4
CEND/HSY/T * N8 55 G2
FELT TW13 140 D1
GDMY/SEVK IG3 61 F7
MORT/ESHN SW14 126 A2
SRTFD E15 76 C6
SUT SM1 175 G4
WALTH E17 57 H3
WAN E11 58 C7
Vernon Sq FSBYW * WC1X 5 M7
Vernon St WKENS W14 107 H3
Vernon Yd NTGHL W11 88 D6
Veroan Rd BXLYHN DA7 137 F1
Verona Dr SURB KT6 172 A1
Veronica Gdns MTCM CR4 148 C7
Veronica Rd TOOT SW17 148 B2
Veronique Gdns
GNTH/NBYPK IG2 60 C4
Verran Rd BAL * SW12 129 G6
Versailles Rd PGE/AN SE20 150 C6
Verulam Av WALTH E17 57 H6
Verulam Ct CDALE/KGS * NW9 51 J6
Verulam Rd GFD/PVL UB6 84 A3
Verulam St FSBYW WC1X 12 A2
Verwood Dr EBAR EN4 27 K2
Verwood Rd RYLN/HDSTN HA2 48 C1
Vespan Rd SHB W12 106 D1
Vesta Rd BROCKY SE4 132 B1
Vestris Rd FSTH SE23 151 F1
Vestry Rd CMBW SE5 111 F7
WALTH E17 57 K4
Vestry St IS N1 7 G7
Vevey St FSTH SE23 151 H1
The Viaduct MUSWH * N10 54 B3
SWFD E18 58 E1
Viaduct Pl BETH E2 92 D2
Viaduct Rd EFNCH N2 53 H1
Viaduct St BETH E2 92 D2
Vian St LEW SE13 132 E2
Vibart Gdns BRXS/STRHM SW2 130 A6
Vibart Wk IS N1 5 K3
Vibia Cl STWL/WRAY TW19 120 A6
Vicarage Cl ERITH DA8 117 K5
NTHLT UB5 65 K7
RSLP HA4 46 B6
WPK KT4 160 B7
Vicarage Ct BECK * BR3 166 B2
Vicarage Crs BTSEA SW11 108 C7
Vicarage Dr BARK IG11 78 C6
BECK BR3 151 J7
MORT/ESHN SW14 126 A4
Vicarage Farm Rd HEST TW5 102 D7
HSLWW TW4 122 D1
Vicarage Flds WOT/HER KT12 156 B5
Vicarage Gdns KENS * W8 14 B1
MTCM CR4 162 D2
Vicarage Ga KENS W8 8 C9
Vicarage Gv CMBW SE5 110 E7
Vicarage La EHAM E6 95 K2
IL IG1 60 D7
SRTFD E15 76 C5
Vicarage Ms CHSWK * W4 106 B5
Vicarage Pde
SEVS/STOTM * N15 55 J3
Vicarage Pk WOOL/PLUM SE18 115 H4
Vicarage Rd BXLY DA5 137 J7
CROY/NA CR0 177 G2
DAGE RM10 80 D6
E/WMO/HCT KT8 143 J7
EMPK RM11 63 J7
HDN NW4 51 J5
LEY E10 57 K6
MORT/ESHN SW14 125 K4
SRTFD E15 76 D6
SUN TW16 140 D4
SUT SM1 174 E3
TEDD TW11 143 G4
TOTM N17 42 C6
WATW WD18 20 E6
WATW WD18 21 F3
WFD IG8 45 J6
WHTN TW2 123 H5
WHTN TW2 142 E1
WOOL/PLUM SE18 115 H4
Vicarage Wk BTSEA * SW11 108 C7
Vicarage Wy RYLN/HDSTN HA2 48 A6
WLSDN NW10 69 F2
Vicars Bridge Cl ALP/SUD HA0 86 A1
Vicar's Cl EN EN1 30 A1
HACK E8 74 E7
SRTFD E15 76 E7
Vicars Hl LEW SE13 132 E3
Vicar's Moor La WCHMH N21 29 G6
Vicars Oak Rd NRWD SE19 150 A5
Vicar's Rd KTTN NW5 72 A4
Viceroy Cl EFNCH * N2 53 J3
Viceroy Pde EFNCH * N2 53 J3
Viceroy Rd VX/NE SW8 109 K7
Vickers Cl CROY/NA CR0 177 F6
Vickers Rd ERITH DA8 118 A4
Victor Gv ALP/SUD HA0 68 A6
Victoria Ar PIM SW1V 16 D4
Victoria Av E/WMO/HCT KT8 157 G2
EHAM E6 77 H7
FNCH N3 38 D7
HSLW TW3 123 F4
SURB KT6 158 E5
WBLY HA9 68 D5
WLGTN SM6 176 A2
Victoria Cl E/WMO/HCT KT8 157 F2
EBAR EN4 27 H3
HRW * HA1 49 F5
HYS/HAR UB3 82 B5
Victoria Cottages
RCH/KEW TW9 105 G7
WCHPL * E1 92 C4
Victoria Ct WBLY HA9 68 C5
Victoria Crs NRWD SE19 150 A5
SEVS/STOTM N15 56 A4
WIM/MER * SW19 146 D6
Victoria Dock Rd CAN/RD E16 94 D5
CAN/RD E16 95 G6
Victoria Dr WIM/MER SW19 127 G7
Victoria Emb TPL/STR WC2R 11 L7
WHALL SW1A 17 K2
Victoria Embankment Gdns
CHCR * WC2N 11 K7
Victoria Gdns HEST TW5 102 D7
Victoria Ga BAY/PAD W2 9 H6
Victoria Gv KENS W8 14 E3
NFNCH/WDSP N12 39 H4
Victoria Grove Ms NTGHL * W11 8 C7
Victoria La HYS/HAR UB3 101 G4
Victoria Ms KIL/WHAMP NW6 2 A4
WAND/EARL SW18 128 B7
Victorian Gv STNW/STAM N16 74 A2
Victorian Rd STNW/STAM N16 74 A2
Victoria Pde RCH/KEW * TW9 105 H7
Victoria Park Rd HOM E9 75 F7
Victoria Park Sq BETH E2 92 E2
Victoria Park Studios HOM * E9 74 E5
Victoria Pl RCHPK/HAM TW10 124 E4
Victoria Ri CLAP SW4 129 G2
Victoria Rd ACT W3 87 F4
BARK IG11 78 B5
BFN/LL DA15 155 F2
BKHH IG9 45 H1
BUSH WD23 22 B7
BXLYHS DA6 137 H4
CHST BR7 154 A4
DAGE RM10 80 E4
DART DA1 139 G4
EBAR EN4 27 H3
ED N9 42 B2
ERITH DA8 118 B5
FELT TW13 122 A7
FSBYPK N4 55 F6
HAYES BR2 168 C4
HDN NW4 52 A3
KENS W8 14 E4
KIL/WHAMP NW6 2 A3
KUT KT1 159 G1
MLHL NW7 37 H4
MORT/ESHN SW14 126 A2
MTCM CR4 147 J6
NWDGN UB2 102 E2
PLSTW E13 94 E1
ROM RM1 63 H4
RSLP HA4 64 E1
SEVS/STOTM * N15 56 C3
SURB KT6 158 E5
SUT SM1 175 H4
SWFD E18 59 F2
TEDD TW11 143 G5
TWK TW1 124 C6
WALTH E17 58 A1
WAN E11 76 B3
WDGN N22 40 D7
WEA W13 85 H4
WLSDN NW10 87 G3
Victoria Sq BGVA SW1W 16 D3
Victoria St BELV DA17 117 G4
SRTFD E15 76 C6
WEST SW1P 16 E4
Victoria Ter EA * W5 85 K7
FSBYPK N4 55 G7
HRW HA1 48 E7
Victoria Vls RCH/KEW TW9 125 G2
Victoria Wy CHARL SE7 114 A4
Victoria Yd WCHPL * E1 92 C5
Victor Rd PGE/AN SE20 151 F6
RYLN/HDSTN HA2 48 C2
TEDD TW11 142 E4
WLSDN NW10 87 K2
Victors Dr HPTN * TW12 141 J5
Victors Wy BAR EN5 26 D2
Victor Vls UED * N18 41 K2
Victory Av MRDN SM4 162 B4
Victory Pk WBLY * HA9 67 K2
Victory Pl NRWD * SE19 150 A5
WALW SE17 18 F5
Victory Rd RAIN RM13 99 J1
WAN E11 59 F3
WIM/MER SW19 147 G6
Victory Wy BERM/RHTH SE16 112 B1
HEST TW5 102 B4
ROMW/RG RM7 62 D1
Vienna Cl CLAY IG5 59 H1
The View ABYW SE2 117 F4
View Cl HGT N6 53 K6
HRW HA1 48 D3
View Crs CEND/HSY/T N8 54 D4
Viewfield Cl KTN/HRWW/W HA3 50 A6
Viewfield Rd BFN/LL DA15 136 D7
WAND/EARL SW18 127 J5
Viewland Rd
WOOL/PLUM SE18 116 A4
View Rd HGT N6 53 K6
Viga Rd WCHMH N21 29 G5
Vigilant Cl SYD SE26 150 C3
Vignoles Rd ROMW/RG RM7 62 C6
Vigo St MYFR/PICC W1J 10 E7
Viking Gdns EHAM E6 95 J4
Viking Pl LEY E10 57 H7
Viking Rd STHL UB1 83 J6
Viking Wy BELV DA17 117 K2
Villacourt Rd WOOL/PLUM SE18 116 B6
The Village CHARL SE7 114 B5
HAMP * NW3 71 G1
Village Cl CHING E4 44 A4
HAMP * NW3 71 H4
Village Green Rd DART DA1 138 D3
Village Ms CDALE/KGS * NW9 69 F1
Village Mt HAMP * NW3 71 G3
Village Park Cl EN EN1 30 A5
Village Rd EN EN1 29 K5
FNCH N3 52 C1
Village Rw BELMT SM2 174 E6
Village Wy BECK BR3 166 D2
HNHL SE24 130 E5
PIN HA5 47 J6
WLSDN NW10 69 F3
Village Wy East
RYLN/HDSTN HA2 47 K6
Villa Rd BRXN/ST SW9 130 B2
Villas Rd WOOL/PLUM SE18 115 H3
Villa St WALW SE17 19 H8
Villiers Av BRYLDS KT5 159 G4
WHTN TW2 122 E7
Villiers Cl BRYLDS KT5 159 G3
Villiers Gv BELMT SM2 174 B7
Villiers Rd BECK BR3 166 A1
CRICK NW2 69 J5
ISLW TW7 123 K1
KUT KT1 159 G2
OXHEY WD19 21 J5
STHL UB1 83 K7
Villiers St CHCR WC2N 11 K8
Vincam Cl WHTN TW2 123 F6
Vincennes Est WNWD * SE27 149 K3
Vincent Av BRYLDS KT5 159 J7
Vincent Cl BAR EN5 26 E2
BFN/LL DA15 135 K7
ESH/CLAY KT10 170 B2
HAYES BR2 168 A3
WDR/YW UB7 100 D5
Vincent Gdns CRICK NW2 69 H2
Vincent Pde FSBYPK * N4 54 E7
Vincent Rd ACT W3 105 K2
ALP/SUD HA0 68 B6
CHING E4 44 B5
CROY/NA CR0 165 F6
DAGW RM9 80 A6
HSLWW TW4 122 C2
ISLW TW7 103 J7
KUT KT1 159 H2
SEVS/STOTM N15 55 J3
WDGN N22 55 G1
WOOL/PLUM * SE18 115 G3
Vincent Rw HPTN TW12 142 C5
Vincents Cl BERM/RHTH SE16 112 B1
Vincent Sq WDGN * N22 55 G1
WEST SW1P 16 F5
Vincent St CAN/RD E16 94 E4
WEST SW1P 17 G5
Vincent Ter IS N1 6 C5
Vincent Vls SEVS/STOTM * N15 55 J3
Vince St FSBYE EC1V 7 H8
Vine Cl BRYLDS KT5 159 G5
SUT SM1 175 G2
WDR/YW UB7 100 D3
Vine Cottages HNWL * W7 84 E7
WCHPL * E1 92 E5
Vine Ct KTN/HRWW/W HA3 50 A5
WCHPL E1 92 C4
Vine Gdns IL IG1 78 C4
Vinegar St WAP E1W 92 D7
Vinegar Yd STHWK SE1 19 J1
Vine Hl CLKNW EC1R 12 A1
Vine La STHWK SE1 13 K9
Vine Pl HSLW TW3 123 G3
The Vineries CAT * SE6 132 D7
EN EN1 30 A2
STHGT/OAK N14 28 C5
Vineries Bank MLHL NW7 37 K4
Vineries Cl WDR/YW UB7 100 D5
Vine Rd BARN SW13 126 C2
E/WMO/HCT KT8 157 H3
SRTFD E15 76 D6
Vine Rw RCHPK/HAM * TW10 125 F4
Viners Cl WOT/HER KT12 156 B5
Vines Av FNCH N3 39 F7
Vine Sq WKENS * W14 107 J4
Vine St CONDST W1S 10 F7
ROMW/RG RM7 62 E4
TWRH EC3N 13 L5
Vine Street Br FARR EC1M 12 B1
Vine Street Crs TWRH * EC3N 13 L6
The Vineyard
RCHPK/HAM TW10 124 E4
Vine Yd STHWK SE1 18 F1
Vineyard Av MLHL NW7 38 C6
Vineyard Cl CAT SE6 132 D7
KUT KT1 159 G2
Vineyard Gv FNCH N3 39 F7
Vineyard Hill Rd
WIM/MER SW19 146 E3
Vineyard Ms CLKNW * EC1R 6 A9
Vineyard Pth
MORT/ESHN SW14 126 A2
Vineyard Rd FELT TW13 140 E2
Vineyard Rw E/WMO/HCT KT8 143 J7
Vineyard Wk CLKNW EC1R 6 A9
Viney Bank CROY/NA CR0 179 H7
Viney Rd LEW SE13 132 E2
Vining St BRXN/ST SW9 130 B3
Vintry Ms WALTH E17 57 J3
Viola Av ABYW SE2 116 C3
EBED/NFELT TW14 122 B5
STWL/WRAY TW19 120 B7
Viola Sq SHB W12 87 H6
Violet Cl CAN/RD E16 94 C3
DEPT SE8 112 C5
WLGTN SM6 163 F7
Violet Gdns CROY/NA CR0 177 H4
Violet Hl STJWD NW8 2 E6
Violet La CROY/NA CR0 177 H4
Violet Rd BOW E3 93 K3
SWFD E18 59 F1
WALTH E17 57 J5
Violet St BETH E2 92 D3
Virgil St STHWK SE1 17 M3
Virginia Cl NWMAL KT3 159 K3
Virginia Gdns BARK/HLT IG6 60 D1
Virginia Rd BETH E2 7 L8
THHTH CR7 149 H7
Virginia St WAP * E1W 92 C6
Viscount Cl FBAR/BDGN N11 40 A4
Viscount Dr EHAM E6 95 K4
Viscount Gv NTHLT UB5 83 H2
Viscount Rd STWL/WRAY TW19 120 A6
Viscount St STLK EC1Y 12 E1
Viscount Wy HTHAIR TW6 121 H3
The Vista ELTH/MOT SE9 134 C6
Vista Av PEND EN3 31 F1
Vista Dr REDBR IG4 59 H4
Vista Wy KTN/HRWW/W HA3 50 A5
Viveash Cl HYS/HAR UB3 101 J2
Vivian Av HDN NW4 51 K4
WBLY HA9 68 C5
Vivian Cl OXHEY WD19 32 E1
Vivian Gdns OXHEY WD19 20 E7
WBLY HA9 68 C4
Vivian Rd BOW E3 93 G1
Vivian Sq PECK SE15 131 J2
Vivian Wy EFNCH N2 53 H4
Vivien Cl CHSGTN KT9 172 A6
Vivienne Cl TWK TW1 124 E5
Vixen Ms HACK * E8 7 L3
Voce Rd WOOL/PLUM SE18 115 J6
Voewood Cl NWMAL KT3 160 C5
Voltaire Rd CLAP SW4 129 J2
Volt Av WLSDN NW10 87 F2
Volta Wy CROY/NA CR0 164 A7
Voluntary Pl WAN E11 58 E5
Vorley Rd ARCH N19 72 C1
Voss Ct STRHM/NOR SW16 148 E5
Voss St BETH E2 92 C2
Voyagers Cl THMD SE28 97 J5
Vulcan Cl EHAM E6 96 A5
Vulcan Ga ENC/FH EN2 29 G1
Vulcan Rd BROCKY SE4 132 C1
Vulcan Ter BROCKY SE4 132 C1
Vulcan Wy HOLWY N7 73 F5
The Vyne BXLYHN DA7 137 J2
Vyner Rd ACT W3 87 F6
Vyner St BETH E2 92 D1
Vyse Cl BAR EN5 26 A3

W

Wadding St WALW SE17 19 G6
Waddington Cl EN EN1 30 A3
Waddington Rd SRTFD E15 76 B4
Waddington St SRTFD E15 76 B5
Waddington Wy NRWD SE19 149 J7
Waddon Cl CROY/NA CR0 177 G2
Waddon Court Rd
CROY/NA CR0 177 G3
Waddon Marsh Wy
CROY/NA CR0 177 F1
Waddon New Rd
CROY/NA CR0 177 H2
Waddon Park Av
CROY/NA CR0 177 G3
Waddon Rd CROY/NA CR0 177 H2
Waddon Wy CROY/NA CR0 177 G5
Wade House STHWK * SE1 111 H1
Wade Rd CAN/RD E16 95 G5
Wade's Gv WCHMH N21 29 G6
Wade's Hl WCHMH N21 29 G5
Wade's La TEDD TW11 143 G4
Wadeson St BETH E2 92 D1
Wade's Pl POP/IOD E14 93 K6
Wadeville Av CHDH RM6 62 A5
Wadeville Cl BELV DA17 117 H4
Wadham Av CHING E4 43 K6
Wadham Gdns GFD/PVL UB6 66 D5
HAMP NW3 3 J2
Wadham Rd CHING E4 43 K6
PUT/ROE SW15 127 H3
Wadhurst Cl PGE/AN SE20 165 J1
Wadhurst Rd CHSWK W4 106 A2
Wadley Rd WAN E11 58 C6
Wadsworth Cl GFD/PVL UB6 85 J1
PEND EN3 31 F4
Wadsworth Rd GFD/PVL UB6 85 H1
Wager St BOW E3 93 H3
Waghorn Rd
KTN/HRWW/W HA3 49 K2
PLSTW E13 77 G7
Waghorn St PECK SE15 131 H2
Wagner St PECK SE15 111 K6
Wagstaff Gdns DAGW RM9 79 J6
Wagtail Cl CDALE/KGS NW9 51 G1
Wagtail Wk BECK BR3 167 F4
Waid Cl DART DA1 139 J5
Waights Ct KUTN/CMB KT2 144 A7
Wainfleet Av CRW RM5 62 E1
Wainford Cl WIM/MER SW19 127 G7
Wainwright Gv ISLW TW7 123 J3
Waite Davies Rd
LEE/GVPK SE12 133 J6
Waite St PECK SE15 19 L9
Wakefield Gdns IL IG1 59 J5
NRWD SE19 150 A6
Wakefield Ms STPAN WC1H 5 K8
Wakefield Rd FBAR/BDGN N11 40 D4
RCHPK/HAM TW10 124 E4
SEVS/STOTM N15 56 B4
Wakefield St BMSBY WC1N 5 K9
EHAM E6 77 J7
UED N18 42 C4
Wakehams Hl PIN HA5 47 K2
Wakeham St IS N1 73 K5
Wakehurst Rd BTSEA SW11 128 E4
Wakeling Rd HNWL W7 85 F4
Wakeling St WCHPL * E1 93 G5
Wakelin Rd SRTFD E15 94 C1
Wakeman Rd WLSDN NW10 88 A2
Wakemans Hill Av
CDALE/KGS NW9 51 F4
Wakering Rd BARK IG11 78 C6
Wakerly Cl EHAM E6 95 K5
Wakley St FSBYE EC1V 6 C7
Walberswick St VX/NE SW8 109 K6
Walbrook MANHO EC4N 13 G6
Walburgh St WCHPL E1 92 D5
Walcorde Av WALW SE17 18 F6
Walcot Rd PEND EN3 31 H1
Walcot Sq LBTH SE11 18 B5
Walcott St WEST * SW1P 16 F5
Waldeck Gv WNWD SE27 149 H2
Waldeck Rd CHSWK W4 105 H5
DART DA1 139 J6
MORT/ESHN SW14 125 K2
SEVS/STOTM N15 55 H2
WEA W13 85 H5
Waldegrave Gdns TWK TW1 143 F1
Waldegrave Pk TWK TW1 143 F3
Waldegrave Rd BCTR RM8 79 J1
BMLY BR1 168 D4
CEND/HSY/T * N8 55 G2
EA W5 86 B6
NRWD SE19 150 B6
TWK TW1 143 F3
Waldegrove CROY/NA CR0 178 B2
Waldemar Av FUL/PGN SW6 107 H7
WEA W13 85 J7
Waldemar Rd WIM/MER SW19 146 E4
Walden Av CHST BR7 153 K3
PLMGR N13 41 J3
RAIN RM13 99 F1
Walden Cl BELV DA17 117 G4
Walden Gdns THHTH CR7 164 A3
Walden Pde CHST * BR7 153 K5
Walden Rd CHST BR7 153 K5
TOTM N17 41 K7
Waldenshaw Rd FSTH SE23 131 K7
Walden St WCHPL * E1 92 D5
Walden Wy MLHL NW7 38 B5
Waldo Cl CLAP SW4 129 H4
Waldo Pl WIM/MER SW19 147 J6
Waldorf Cl SAND/SEL CR2 177 H7
Waldo Rd BMLY BR1 168 B2
WLSDN NW10 87 K2
Waldram Crs FSTH SE23 131 K7
Waldram Park Rd FSTH SE23 132 A7
Waldrist Wy ERITHM DA18 117 G1
Waldron Gdns HAYES BR2 167 G2
Waldronhyrst CROY/NA CR0 177 H3
Waldron Ms CHEL SW3 15 H9
Waldron Rd HRW HA1 48 E7
WAND/EARL SW18 147 G2
The Waldrons CROY/NA CR0 177 J3
Waldron's Yd RYLN/HDSTN HA2 66 D1
Waldstock Rd THMD SE28 97 G6
Waleran Cl STAN HA7 35 F5
Walerand Rd LEW SE13 133 F1
Wales Av CAR SM5 175 K4
Wales Cl PECK SE15 111 J6
Wales Farm Rd ACT W3 87 F4
Waleton Acres WLGTN * SM6 176 C5
Waley St WCHPL * E1 93 F4
Walfield Av TRDG/WHET N20 27 F6
Walford Rd STNW/STAM N16 74 A3
Walfrey Gdns DAGW RM9 80 A6
Walham Green Ct
FUL/PGN * SW6 108 A6
Walham Gv FUL/PGN SW6 107 K6
Walham Ri WIM/MER SW19 146 C5
Walham Yd FUL/PGN SW6 107 K6
The Walk PLMGR * N13 41 G2
Walkden Rd CHST BR7 154 A3
Walker Cl DART DA1 138 C2
EBED/NFELT TW14 121 J6
FBAR/BDGN N11 40 C3
HNWL W7 84 E7
HPTN TW12 141 K5
WOOL/PLUM SE18 115 H3
Walker's Ct SOHO/CST W1F 11 G6
Walkerscroft Md DUL SE21 130 D7
Walker's Pl PUT/ROE * SW15 127 H3
Walkley Rd DART DA1 138 E4
The Walks EFNCH N2 53 H2
Wallace Cl THMD SE28 97 K6
Wallace Crs CAR SM5 175 K4
Wallace Rd IS N1 73 J5
Wallbutton Rd BROCKY SE4 132 B1
Wallcote Av CRICK NW2 52 B7
Wall End Rd EHAM E6 78 A6
Wallenger Av GPK RM2 63 K2
Waller Dr NTHWD HA6 46 E1
Waller Rd NWCR SE14 112 A7
Wallers Cl DAGW RM9 80 A7
WFD IG8 45 K5
Wallflower St SHB W12 87 H6
Wallgrave Rd ECT SW5 14 B5
Wallhouse Rd ERITH DA8 119 F6
Wallingford Av NKENS W10 88 B4
Wallington Cl RSLP HA4 46 A5
Wallington Rd GDMY/SEVK IG3 61 F6
Wallis Cl BTSEA SW11 128 C2
EMPK RM11 63 K7
Wallis Rd HOM E9 75 H5
STHL UB1 84 B5
Wallorton Gdns
MORT/ESHN SW14 126 A3
Wallside BARB * EC2Y 12 F3
Wall St IS N1 73 K5
Wallwood Rd WAN E11 58 B6
Wallwood St POP/IOD E14 93 H4
Walmer Cl CHING E4 43 K1
ROMW/RG RM7 62 D1
Walmer Gdns HNWL W7 104 B1
Walmer Rd NTGHL W11 88 C6
Walmer Ter WOOL/PLUM SE18 115 H3
Walmgate Rd GFD/PVL UB6 67 H7
Walmington Fold
NFNCH/WDSP N12 38 E5
Walm La CRICK NW2 70 B5
Walney Wk IS * N1 73 J5
Walnut Av WDR/YW UB7 100 D2
Walnut Cl BARK/HLT IG6 60 C3
CAR SM5 175 K4
DEPT SE8 112 C5
HYS/HAR UB3 82 C6
Walnut Ct EA * W5 105 F1
Walnut Gdns SRTFD E15 76 C4
Walnut Gn BUSH WD23 21 K1
Walnut Gv EN EN1 29 K4
Walnut Ms BELMT SM2 175 G6
Walnut Rd LEY E10 75 J1
Walnut Tree Av MTCM * CR4 162 D2
Walnut Tree Cl BARN SW13 106 C7
CHST BR7 154 C7
Walnut Tree Rd BCTR RM8 79 K1
BTFD TW8 105 F5
ERITH DA8 118 B4
GNWCH * SE10 113 H4
HEST * TW5 102 E5
Walnut Tree Wk LBTH SE11 18 A5
Walnut Wy BKHH IG9 45 H2
RSLP HA4 65 G5
Walpole Av RCH/KEW TW9 125 G1
Walpole Cl PIN HA5 34 A6
WEA W13 104 D1
Walpole Crs TEDD TW11 143 F4

Walpole Gdns CHSWK W4 105 K4
WHTN TW2 142 E1
Walpole Ms STJWD NW8 3 G4
Walpole Pl TEDD TW11 143 F4
Walpole Rd CROY/NA CR0 177 K1
EHAM E6 77 G6
HAYES BR2 168 C4
SURB KT6 159 F6
SWFD E18 44 D7
TEDD TW11 143 F4
TOTM N17 55 J1
WALTH E17 57 G3
WHTN TW2 142 E1
WIM/MER SW19 147 H5
Walpole St CHEL SW3 15 L7
Walrond Av WBLY HA9 68 A4
Walsham Cl STNW/STAM N16 56 C7
THMD SE28 97 K6
Walsham Rd
EBED/NFELT TW14 122 A6
NWCR SE14 132 A1
Walsingham Gdns
HOR/WEW KT19 173 G3
Walsingham Pk CHST BR7 169 J1
Walsingham Rd CLAP SW4 129 F5
CLPT E5 74 C2
ENC/FH EN2 29 K3
MTCM CR4 162 E4
STMC/STPC BR5 155 H7
WEA * W13 85 G7
Walsingham Wk BELV DA17 117 H5
Walters Rd PEND EN3 30 E4
SNWD SE25 165 F3
Walter St BETH E2 93 F2
KUTN/CMB * KT2 144 A7
Walters Wy FSTH SE23 132 A5
Walters Yd BMLY BR1 167 K1
Walter Ter WCHPL E1 93 F5
Walterton Rd MV/WKIL W9 88 D3
Walter Wk EDGW HA8 36 E5
Waltham Av CDALE/KGS NW9 50 C5
HYS/HAR UB3 101 F2
Waltham Cl DART DA1 138 D5
Waltham Dr EDGW HA8 50 C1
Waltham Pk WALTH E17 43 J6
Waltham Rd CAR SM5 162 C7
NWDGN UB2 102 D2
WFD IG8 45 J5
Walthamstow Av CHING E4 43 J6
Walthamstow Av (North Circular)
CHING E4 43 G4
Waltham Wy CHING E4 43 H2
Waltheof Av TOTM N17 41 K7
Waltheof Gdns TOTM N17 41 K7
Walton Av CHEAM SM3 174 D2
NWMAL KT3 160 C3
RYLN/HDSTN HA2 65 K4
Walton Cl CRICK NW2 69 K1
HRW HA1 48 D3
VX/NE SW8 109 K6
Walton Dr HRW HA1 48 D3
WLSDN NW10 69 F5
Walton Gdns ACT W3 86 D4
FELT TW13 140 D3
WBLY HA9 68 A1
Walton Gn CROY/NA CR0 179 K7
Walton Pl CHEL SW3 15 L3
Walton Rd BUSH WD23 21 H3
HRW HA1 48 D3
MNPK E12 78 A3
PLSTW E13 95 G1
SCUP DA14 155 H2
SEVS/STOTM * N15 56 B3
WOT/HER KT12 156 C4
Walton St CHEL SW3 15 K5
Walton Vls IS * N1 7 K2
Walton Wy ACT W3 86 D4
MTCM CR4 163 H3
Walt Whitman Cl HNHL * SE24 130 C3
Walverns Cl OXHEY WD19 21 G5
Walworth Pl WALW SE17 18 F8
Walworth Rd WALW SE17 18 E5
Walwyn Av BMLY BR1 168 C2
Wanborough Dr
PUT/ROE SW15 126 E7
Wanderer Dr BARK IG11 97 H2
Wandle Bank CROY/NA CR0 176 E2
WIM/MER SW19 147 H5
Wandle Ct HOR/WEW KT19 172 E3
Wandle Court Gdns
CROY/NA CR0 176 E2
Wandle Rd CROY/NA CR0 176 E2
CROY/NA CR0 177 J2
MRDN SM4 162 B2
TOOT SW17 147 J1
WLGTN SM6 176 B1
Wandle Side CROY/NA CR0 177 F2
WLGTN SM6 176 B2
Wandle Wy MTCM CR4 162 E4
WAND/EARL SW18 128 A7
Wandon Rd FUL/PGN SW6 108 A6
Wandsworth Br
WAND/EARL SW18 128 B2
Wandsworth Bridge Rd
FUL/PGN SW6 108 A7
Wandsworth Common
West Side
WAND/EARL SW18 128 B4
Wandsworth High St
WAND/EARL SW18 127 K4
Wandsworth Rd CLAP SW4 129 G2
VX/NE SW8 17 J9
Wangey Rd CHDH RM6 61 K6
Wanless Rd HNHL SE24 130 D2
Wanley Rd CMBW SE5 130 E3
Wanlip Rd PLSTW E13 95 F3
Wansbeck Rd HOM E9 75 H6
Wansdown Pl FUL/PGN SW6 108 A6
Wansey St WALW SE17 18 F6
Wansford Pk BORE WD6 25 F3
Wansford Rd WFD IG8 45 G7
Wanstead Cl BMLY BR1 168 B1
Wanstead La IL IG1 59 J5
Wanstead Park Av MNPK E12 77 H1
Wanstead Park Rd IL IG1 59 J7
Wanstead Pl WAN E11 58 E5
Wanstead Rd BMLY BR1 168 B1
Wansunt Rd BXLY DA5 137 K7
Wantage Rd LEE/GVPK SE12 133 J4
Wantz La RAIN RM13 99 K3
Wantz Rd DAGE RM10 80 D3
Wapping Dock St WAP * E1W 92 D7
Wapping High St WAP E1W 92 C7
Wapping La WAP E1W 92 D6
Wapping Wall WAP E1W 92 E7
Warbank La KUTN/CMB KT2 145 H6
Warbeck Rd SHB W12 87 K7
Warberry Rd WDGN N22 55 F1
Warboys Ap KUTN/CMB KT2 144 D5
Warboys Crs CHING E4 44 A4
Warboys Rd KUTN/CMB KT2 144 D5
Warburton Cl IS N1 74 A5
KTN/HRWW/W HA3 34 D5
Warburton Rd HACK E8 74 D7
WHTN TW2 123 G7
Warburton St HACK E8 74 D7
Warburton Ter WALTH E17 57 K1
Wardalls Gv NWCR * SE14 111 K6
Ward Cl ERITH DA8 118 A5
SAND/SEL CR2 178 A4
Wardell Cl CDALE/KGS NW9 37 G6
Warden Av RYLN/HDSTN HA2 47 J7
Warden Rd KTTN NW5 72 A5
Wardens Gv STHWK SE1 12 E9
Wardle St HOM E9 75 F4
Wardley St WAND/EARL SW18 128 A6
Wardo Av FUL/PGN SW6 107 H7
Wardour Ms SOHO/CST W1F 10 F5
Wardour St SOHO/CST W1F 10 F4
Ward Rd ARCH N19 72 C3
SRTFD * E15 76 B7
The Wardrobe RCH/KEW * TW9 124 E4
Wardrobe Pl BLKFR * EC4V 12 D5
Wards Rd GNTH/NBYPK IG2 60 D6
Wareham Cl HSLW TW3 123 G3
Waremead Rd GNTH/NBYPK IG2 60 B4
Warepoint Dr THMD SE28 115 J1
Warfield Rd EBED/NFELT TW14 121 H6
HPTN TW12 142 B7
WLSDN NW10 88 B2
Warfield Yd WLSDN * NW10 88 B2
Wargrave Av SEVS/STOTM N15 56 C5
Wargrave Rd RYLN/HDSTN HA2 66 C2
Warham Rd FSBYPK N4 55 G4
KTN/HRWW/W HA3 49 F2
SAND/SEL CR2 177 J4
Warham St CMBW SE5 110 C6
Waring Rd SCUP DA14 155 J5
Waring St WNWD SE27 149 J3
Warkworth Gdns ISLW TW7 104 B6
Warkworth Rd TOTM N17 41 K6
Warland Rd WOOL/PLUM SE18 115 J6
Warley Av ROMW/RG RM7 62 B6
YEAD UB4 82 E5
Warley Rd ED N9 42 E1
WFD IG8 45 F6
YEAD UB4 82 E4
Warley St BETH E2 93 F2
Warlingham Rd THHTH CR7 164 C3
Warlock Rd MV/WKIL W9 88 D3
Warlters Cl HOLWY * N7 72 E3
Warlters Rd HOLWY N7 72 E3
Warltersville Rd ARCH N19 54 E6
Warming Cl CLPT * E5 75 F2
Warmington Rd HNHL SE24 130 D5
Warmington St PLSTW E13 94 E3
Warminster Rd SNWD SE25 165 H1
Warminster Sq SNWD SE25 165 H1
Warminster Wy MTCM CR4 148 B7
Warndon St BERM/RHTH SE16 111 K3
Warneford Pl OXHEY WD19 21 J5
Warneford Rd
KTN/HRWW/W HA3 49 K2
Warneford St HOM E9 74 D7
Warne Pl BFN/LL DA15 136 C5
Warner Av CHEAM SM3 174 C1
Warner Cl CDALE/KGS NW9 51 H6
HPTN TW12 141 K4
HYS/HAR UB3 101 G6
SRTFD E15 76 C6
Warner Pl BETH E2 92 C1
Warner Rd BMLY BR1 152 D6
CEND/HSY/T N8 54 D3
CMBW SE5 110 D7
WALTH E17 57 G3
Warner St CLKNW EC1R 12 A1
Warner Ter POP/IOD * E14 93 J4
Warner Yd CLKNW EC1R 12 A1
Warnham Court Rd CAR SM5 175 K6
Warnham Rd
NFNCH/WDSP N12 39 H4
Warple Ms ACT * W3 106 B1
Warple Wy ACT W3 106 B1
Warren Av BMLY BR1 152 C6
RCHPK/HAM TW10 125 J3
SAND/SEL CR2 179 F6
WAN * E11 76 B2
Warren Cl BXLYHS DA6 137 H4
ED N9 31 F6
ESH/CLAY KT10 170 B3
WBLY HA9 67 K1
YEAD UB4 83 G4
Warren Crs ED N9 30 B6
Warren Cutting
KUTN/CMB KT2 145 F6
Warrender Rd ARCH N19 72 C2
Warrender Wy RSLP HA4 46 E6
The Warren CAR SM5 175 H7
HEST TW5 102 E6
HOR/WEW KT19 173 F3
MNPK E12 77 J3
YEAD UB4 82 E5
The Warren Dr WAN E11 59 G6
Warren Dr GFD/PVL UB6 84 B3
HCH RM12 81 J2
RSLP HA4 47 H6
Warren Dr North BRYLDS KT5 159 J7
Warren Dr South BRYLDS KT5 159 K7
Warren Flds STAN * HA7 35 J3
Warren Gv BORE WD6 25 F3
Warren La STAN HA7 35 G1
WOOL/PLUM SE18 115 G2
Warren Ms GTPST W1W 10 E1
Warren Pk KUTN/CMB KT2 144 E5
Warren Park Rd SUT SM1 175 H5
Warren Ri NWMAL KT3 145 F7
Warren Rd ASHF TW15 140 C6
BARK/HLT IG6 60 D4
BUSH WD23 22 C7
BXLYHS DA6 137 H4
CHING E4 44 A1
CRICK NW2 69 H1
CROY/NA CR0 165 F7
HAYES BR2 180 E1
KUTN/CMB KT2 144 E5
LEY E10 76 A2
SCUP DA14 155 J2
WAN E11 59 G5
WHTN TW2 123 J5
WIM/MER SW19 147 J5
Warrens Shawe La EDGW HA8 36 D1
Warren St FITZ W1T 10 D1
Warren Wy MLHL NW7 38 C5
Warren Wood Cl HAYES BR2 180 E1
Warriner Dr ED N9 42 C2
Warriner Gdns BTSEA SW11 108 E7
Warrington Crs MV/WKIL W9 8 E1
Warrington Gdns MV/WKIL W9 8 E1
Warrington Pl POP/IOD * E14 94 A7
Warrington Rd BCTR RM8 79 K1
CROY/NA CR0 177 H2
HRW HA1 48 E4
RCHPK/HAM TW10 124 E4
Warrington Sq BCTR RM8 79 K1
Warrior Sq MNPK E12 78 A3
Warsaw Cl RSLP HA4 65 F5
Warspite Rd WOOL/PLUM SE18 114 D2
Warton Rd SRTFD E15 76 A7
Warwall EHAM E6 96 B5
Warwick Av EDGW HA8 36 D2
MV/WKIL W9 8 E1
RYLN/HDSTN HA2 65 K3
Warwick Cl BUSH WD23 22 E6
BXLY DA5 137 G6
EBAR EN4 27 H4
HPTN TW12 142 C6
Warwick Ct HHOL WC1V 11 M3
Warwick Crs BAY/PAD W2 8 E2
YEAD UB4 82 D3
Warwick Dene EA W5 86 A7
Warwick Dr BARN SW13 126 E2
Warwick Gdns FSBYPK N4 55 J4
IL IG1 60 B7
THDIT KT7 158 A4
THHTH * CR7 164 B3
WKENS W14 107 J2
Warwick Gv BRYLDS KT5 159 G6
CLPT E5 56 D7
Warwick House St STJS SW1Y 11 G8
Warwick La STP EC4M 12 D4
Warwick Pde
KTN/HRWW/W * HA3 49 H1
Warwick Pl BORE * WD6 25 F2
EA W5 104 E1
MV/WKIL W9 8 E2
THDIT * KT7 158 B5
Warwick Pl North PIM * SW1V 16 E6
Warwick Rd BAR EN5 27 F3
BORE WD6 25 F2
CHING E4 43 J4
EA W5 86 A7
ECT SW5 14 A6
FBAR/BDGN N11 40 D5
FSTGT E7 76 D5
HSLWW TW4 122 A2
KUT KT1 143 J7
MNPK E12 77 J4
NWDGN UB2 102 E2
NWMAL KT3 159 K2
PGE/AN SE20 165 J2
SCUP DA14 155 H4
SUT SM1 175 G4
THDIT KT7 158 A4
THHTH CR7 164 B2
UED N18 42 A3
WALTH E17 43 H7
WAN E11 59 F4
WELL DA16 136 D2
WHTN TW2 123 K7
WKENS W14 107 J3
Warwick Rw WESTW SW1E 16 E3
Warwickshire Pth DEPT SE8 112 C6
Warwick Sq PIM SW1V 16 E7
STP * EC4M 12 D4
Warwick Square Ms PIM SW1V 16 E6
Warwick St REGST W1B 10 F6
Warwick Ter WALTH * E17 58 B4
WOOL/PLUM SE18 115 J5
Warwick Wy PIM SW1V 16 D6
RKW/CH/CXG WD3 20 A3
Warwick Yd STLK * EC1Y 12 F1
Washington Av MNPK E12 77 J3
Washington Cl BOW E3 93 K2
Washington Rd BARN SW13 106 D6
EHAM E6 77 G6
KUT KT1 159 H1
SWFD E18 58 D1
WPK KT4 173 K1
Wastdale Rd FSTH SE23 132 A7
The Watch NFNCH/WDSP * N12 39 G3
Watchfield Ct CHSWK * W4 105 K4
Watcombe Rd SNWD SE25 165 J4
Waterbank Rd CAT SE6 151 K2
Waterbeach Rd DAGW RM9 79 J5
Water Brook La HDN * NW4 52 A4
Watercress Pl IS N1 7 K2
Waterdale Rd ABYW SE2 116 B5
Waterden Rd SRTFD E15 75 J4
Waterer Ri WLGTN SM6 176 D5
Waterfall Cottages
WIM/MER SW19 147 H5
Waterfall Rd FBAR/BDGN N11 40 B3
WIM/MER SW19 147 H5
Waterfall Ter TOOT SW17 147 J5
Waterfield Cl BELV DA17 117 H2
THMD SE28 97 H7
Waterfield Cottages
MORT/ESHN * SW14 125 J3
Waterfield Gdns SNWD SE25 165 F3
Waterfields Wy WAT WD17 21 H3
Waterford Rd FUL/PGN SW6 108 A7
The Waterfront BORE * WD6 23 H5
The Water Gdns BAY/PAD W2 9 J4
Water Gdns STAN HA7 35 H5
The Watergate OXHEY WD19 33 H1
Watergate St DEPT SE8 112 D5
Waterhall Av CHING E4 44 C3
Waterhall Cl WALTH E17 43 F7
Waterhead Cl ERITH DA8 118 B6
Waterhouse Cl HAMP NW3 71 H4
Water La CAMTN NW1 4 D2
ED N9 30 D7
GDMY/SEVK IG3 79 F2
KUT KT1 143 K7
NWCR SE14 111 K6
PUR RM19 119 K3
RCH/KEW TW9 124 E4
SRTFD E15 76 C5
TWK TW1 124 B7
WAT WD17 21 G3
Water Lily Cl NWDGN UB2 103 H1
Waterloo Br STHWK SE1 11 M7
Waterloo Cl EBED/NFELT TW14 121 J7
Waterloo Gdns BETH E2 92 E1
ROMW/RG RM7 63 F5
Waterloo Pl CAR * SM5 175 K2
RCH/KEW TW9 105 H5
STJS SW1Y 11 G8
Waterloo Rd BARK/HLT IG6 60 C1
CRICK NW2 69 J1
EHAM E6 77 G6
FSTGT E7 76 D4
LEY E10 57 J6
ROMW/RG RM7 63 F4
STHWK SE1 11 M8
SUT SM1 175 H4
Waterloo Ter IS N1 6 C2
Waterlow Rd ARCH N19 54 C7
Waterman Cl OXHEY WD19 21 F5
Watermans Cl
KUTN/CMB * KT2 144 A6
Watermans Ms EA * W5 86 A6
Waterman St PUT/ROE SW15 127 G2
Waterman Wy WAP E1W 92 D7
Watermead EBED/NFELT TW14 121 H7
Watermead La MTCM CR4 162 E5
Watermeadow Cl ERITH DA8 118 E6
Watermeadow La
FUL/PGN SW6 128 B1
Watermead Rd CAT SE6 152 A3
Watermead Wy TOTM N17 56 D1
Watermens Sq PGE/AN * SE20 150 E6
Water Ms PECK SE15 131 K3
Watermill Cl
RCHPK/HAM TW10 143 J2
Watermill La UED N18 42 A4
Water Mill Wy FELT TW13 141 K1
Watermill Wy WIM/MER SW19 147 G7
Watermint Quay
STNW/STAM N16 56 C6
Water Rd ALP/SUD HA0 68 B7
Water's Edge FUL/PGN * SW6 107 G7
Watersedge HOR/WEW KT19 172 E3
Watersfield Wy EDGW HA8 35 K6
Waterside DART DA1 138 B4
WALTH E17 56 E5
Waterside Cl BARK IG11 79 G3
BERM/RHTH SE16 111 H1
HOM E9 75 H7
NTHLT UB5 83 K2
SURB KT6 172 A1
Waterside Ct LEW * SE13 133 G3
Waterside Dr WOT/HER KT12 156 A4
Waterside Pl CAMTN NW1 4 B3
Waterside Rd NWDGN UB2 103 F2
Waterside Wy TOOT SW17 147 G3
Watersmeet Wy THMD SE28 97 K5
Waterson St BETH E2 7 K7
Watersplash Cl KUT KT1 159 F2
Watersplash La HYS/HAR UB3 101 K3
Waters Rd CAT SE6 152 C2
KUT KT1 159 J1
Waters Sq KUT KT1 159 J2
Water St TPL/STR WC2R 12 A6
Water Tower Hl CROY/NA CR0 177 K3
Water Tower Pl IS N1 6 B4
Waterworks La CLPT E5 75 F1
Waterworks Rd
BRXS/STRHM SW2 129 K5
Watery La HYS/HAR UB3 101 G4
NTHLT UB5 83 G1
RYNPK SW20 161 J1
SCUP DA14 155 H5
Wates Wy MTCM CR4 162 E5
Wateville Rd TOTM N17 41 J7
Watford Cl BTSEA SW11 108 D7
Watford Field Rd WATW WD18 21 G4
Watford Heath OXHEY WD19 21 H6
Watford Rd BORE WD6 23 J5
CAN/RD E16 94 E4
HRW HA1 67 G1
NTHWD HA6 32 D6
RKW/CH/CXG WD3 20 B4
Watford Wy HDN NW4 51 J1
Watford Wy (Barnet By-Pass)
MLHL NW7 37 G3
Watkin Rd WBLY HA9 68 D2
Watkinson Rd HOLWY N7 73 F5
Watling Av EDGW HA8 36 E7
Watling Ct STP EC4M 12 F5
Watlings Cl CROY/NA CR0 166 B5
Watling St BXLYHS DA6 137 J3
STP EC4M 12 E5
Watlington Gv SYD SE26 151 G4
Watney Market WCHPL E1 92 D5
Watney Rd MORT/ESHN SW14 125 K2
Watneys Rd MTCM CR4 163 J4
Watney St WCHPL E1 92 D5
Watson Av CHEAM SM3 174 C1
EHAM E6 78 A6
Watson Cl STNW/STAM N16 73 K4
WIM/MER SW19 147 J5
Watson's Ms MBLAR W1H 9 K3
Watsons Rd WDGN N22 41 F7
Watson's St DEPT SE8 112 D6
Wattisfield Rd CLPT E5 74 E2
Watts Cl SEVS/STOTM N15 56 A4
Watts Gv BOW E3 93 J4
Watt's La CHST BR7 154 B7
TEDD TW11 143 G4
Watts Rd THDIT KT7 158 B6
Watts St WAP E1W 92 D7
Wat Tyler Rd BKHTH/KID SE3 133 F1
Wauthier Cl PLMGR N13 41 H4
Wavell Dr BFN/LL DA15 135 K5
Wavel Ms KIL/WHAMP NW6 2 C2
Wavel Pl SYD SE26 150 B3
Wavendon Av CHSWK W4 106 A4
Waveney Av PECK SE15 131 J3
Waveney Cl WAP E1W 92 C7
Waverley Av BRYLDS KT5 159 J5
CHING E4 43 H3
SUT SM1 175 F1
WALTH E17 58 B2
WBLY HA9 68 B4
WHTN TW2 122 E7
Waverley Cl E/WMO/HCT KT8 157 F4
HAYES BR2 168 C4
HYS/HAR UB3 101 G3
Waverley Crs
WOOL/PLUM SE18 115 J5
Waverley Gdns BARK IG11 96 E1
BARK/HLT IG6 60 C1
EHAM E6 95 J4
NTHWD HA6 32 E7
Waverley Gv HDN NW4 52 B2
Waverley Pl FSBYPK * N4 55 H7
STJWD NW8 3 G5
Waverley Rd CEND/HSY/T N8 54 D5
ENC/FH EN2 29 H3
EW KT17 173 K4
RAIN RM13 99 K2
RYLN/HDSTN HA2 47 J6
SNWD SE25 165 J3
STHL UB1 84 A6
SWFD E18 45 G7
TOTM N17 42 D6
WALTH E17 58 A2
WOOL/PLUM SE18 115 H4
Waverley Wy CAR SM5 175 J5
Waverton Rd
WAND/EARL SW18 128 B6
Waverton St MYFR/PICC W1J 10 B8
Wavertree Rd
BRXS/STRHM SW2 130 A7
SWFD E18 58 E1
Waxlow Crs STHL UB1 84 A5
Waxlow Rd WLSDN NW10 86 E1
Waxwell La PIN HA5 47 H2
Wayborne Gv RSLP HA4 46 A5
Waye Av HEST TW5 101 K7
Wayfarer Rd NTHLT UB5 83 J2
Wayford St BTSEA SW11 128 D1
Wayland Av HACK E8 74 C4
Waylands HYS/HAR UB3 82 B4
Waylett Pl ALP/SUD * HA0 67 K3
WNWD SE27 149 H2
Wayneflete Tower Av
ESH/CLAY KT10 170 A2
Waynflete Av CROY/NA CR0 177 H2
Waynflete Sq NKENS W10 88 B6
Waynflete St
WAND/EARL SW18 147 G1
Wayside CRICK NW2 52 C7
CROY/NA * CR0 179 K5
MORT/ESHN SW14 125 K3
Wayside Av BUSH WD23 22 D5
Wayside Cl ROM RM1 63 H2
STHGT/OAK N14 28 C5
Wayside Ct TWK TW1 124 D5
Wayside Gdns DAGE RM10 80 C4
Wayside Gv CHST BR7 153 K3
Wayside Ms GNTH/NBYPK IG2 60 A5
The Weald CHST BR7 153 K5
Weald Cl BERM/RHTH SE16 111 J4
HAYES BR2 181 J1
Weald La KTN/HRWW/W HA3 48 D1
Weald Ri KTN/HRWW/W HA3 35 F6
Weald Sq CLPT * E5 74 D1
Wealdstone Rd CHEAM SM3 174 D1
Weald Wy ROMW/RG RM7 62 D5
YEAD UB4 82 C2
Wealdwood Gdns PIN HA5 34 B5
Weale Rd CHING E4 44 B2
Weardale Rd LEW SE13 133 G4
Wear Pl BETH E2 92 D2
Wearside Rd LEW SE13 132 E3
Weaver Cl EHAM E6 96 B6
Weavers Cl ISLW TW7 123 K3
Weaver's La STHWK SE1 13 K9
Weavers Ter FUL/PGN * SW6 107 K5
Weaver St WCHPL E1 92 C3
Weavers Wy CAMTN NW1 5 G3
Weaver Wk WNWD SE27 149 H3
Webb Cl NKENS W10 88 A3
Webber Cl BORE WD6 23 K5
ERITH DA8 118 E6
Webber Rw STHWK SE1 18 B2
Webber St STHWK SE1 18 B1
Webb Est CLPT * E5 56 C6
Webb Pl WLSDN NW10 87 H2
Webb Rd BKHTH/KID SE3 113 J5
Webbscroft Rd DAGE RM10 80 D3
Webb's Rd BTSEA SW11 128 E4
YEAD UB4 82 E2
Webb St STHWK SE1 19 J4
Webster Gdns EA W5 85 K7
Webster Rd BERM/RHTH SE16 111 H2
WAN E11 76 A2
Wedderburn Rd BARK IG11 78 D7
HAMP NW3 71 H4
Wedgewood Cl NTHWD * HA6 32 A6
Wedgwood Wk
KIL/WHAMP * NW6 71 F4
Wedgwood Wy NRWD SE19 149 J6
Wedlake St NKENS W10 88 C3
Wedmore Gdns ARCH N19 72 E1
Wedmore Rd GFD/PVL UB6 84 D2
Wedmore St ARCH N19 72 D2
Weech Rd KIL/WHAMP NW6 70 E3
Weedington Rd KTTN NW5 72 A4
Weekley Sq BTSEA * SW11 128 C2
Weigall Rd LEE/GVPK SE12 133 K3
Weighhouse St
MYFR/PKLN W1K 10 B6
Weighton Rd
KTN/HRWW/W HA3 34 D7
PGE/AN SE20 165 J1
Weihurst Gdns SUT SM1 175 H4
Weimar St PUT/ROE SW15 127 H2
Weirdale Av TRDG/WHET N20 39 K1
Weir Hall Av UED N18 41 K5
Weir Hall Gdns UED N18 41 K4
Weir Hall Rd UED N18 41 K5
Weir Rd BAL SW12 129 H7
BXLY DA5 137 J6
WIM/MER SW19 147 F2
Weirs Pas CAMTN NW1 5 H7
Weiss Rd PUT/ROE SW15 127 G2
Welbeck Av BFN/LL DA15 136 B7
BMLY BR1 152 E3
YEAD UB4 83 F3
Welbeck Cl BORE WD6 24 C2
EW KT17 173 J6
NWMAL KT3 160 C4
Welbeck Rd CAR SM5 162 D7
EBAR EN4 27 H5
EHAM E6 95 H2
RYLN/HDSTN HA2 48 B7
SUT SM1 175 H1
Welbeck St MHST W1U 10 C4
Welbeck Vls WCHMH * N21 29 J7
Welbeck Wy MHST W1U 10 C4
Welby St CMBW SE5 110 C7
Welch Pl PIN * HA5 33 G7
Weldon Cl RSLP HA4 65 F5
Weldon Dr E/WMO/HCT KT8 156 E3
Weld Pl FBAR/BDGN N11 40 B4
Welfare Rd SRTFD E15 76 C6
Welford Cl CLPT E5 75 F2
Welford Pl WIM/MER SW19 146 C3
Welham Rd TOOT SW17 148 A4
Welhouse Rd CAR SM5 162 D7
Wellacre Rd KTN/HRWW/W HA3 49 H5
Wellan Cl BFN/LL DA15 136 C4
Welland Gdns GFD/PVL UB6 85 F1
Welland Ms WAP E1W 92 C7
Wellands Cl BMLY BR1 168 E1
Welland St GNWCH SE10 113 F5
Well Ap BAR EN5 26 A4
Well Cl RSLP HA4 65 J2
STRHM/NOR SW16 149 F3
Wellclose Sq WCHPL * E1 92 C6
Wellclose St WAP E1W 92 C6
Wellcome Av DART DA1 139 H3
Well Cottage Cl WAN E11 59 G6
Well Ct MANHO EC4N 12 F5
Welldon Crs HRW HA1 48 E5
Wellers Ct CAMTN NW1 5 J6
Weller St STHWK SE1 18 E1
Wellesley Av HMSMTH W6 106 E2
NTHWD HA6 32 D4
Wellesley Cl CHARL * SE7 114 B4
Wellesley Ct MV/WKIL W9 2 E7
Wellesley Court Rd
CROY/NA * CR0 177 K1
Wellesley Crs WHTN TW2 142 E1
Wellesley Gv CROY/NA CR0 177 K1
Wellesley Pde WHTN * TW2 142 E2

Wellesley Park Ms ENC/FH EN2......29 H1
Wellesley Pl CAMTN * NW1................5 G8
KTTN NW5..................................72 A4
Wellesley Rd BELMT SM2 ....175 G5
CHSWK W4..................................105 H4
CROY/NA CR0..............................164 D7
HRW HA1.....................................48 E4
IL IG1...78 B1
KTTN NW5..................................72 A4
WALTH E17..................................57 J5
WAN E11.....................................58 E4
WHTN TW2..................................142 D2
Wellesley St WCHPL E1....................93 F4
Wellesley Ter IS N1..........................6 F7
Wellfield Av MUSWH N10 ....54 B2
Wellfield Gdns CAR SM5 ....175 J7
Wellfield Rd STRHM/NOR SW16.....148 E3
Wellfit St HNHL SE24.......................130 C2
Wellgarth GFD/PVL UB6 ....67 H5
Wellgarth Rd GLDGN NW11 ....53 F7
Well Gv TRDG/WHET N20 ....27 G7
Well Hall Pde ELTH/MOT SE9 ....134 E3
Well Hall Rd ELTH/MOT SE9 ....134 E3
Wellhouse La BAR EN5 ....26 A3
Wellhouse Rd BECK BR3..................166 C3
Welling High St WELL DA16 ....136 C2
Wellington Av BFN/LL DA15...........136 B5
CHING E4....................................43 J1
ED N9..42 D2
HSLW TW3..................................123 F4
PIN HA5.......................................33 K7
SEVS/STOTM N15 ....56 C5
WOOL/PLUM SE18 ....115 H2
WPK KT4.....................................174 A2
Wellington Cl DAGE RM10 ....80 E6
NTGHL W11...................................8 A5
NWCR SE14 ....112 A7
OXHEY WD19 ....33 J2
Wellington Crs NWMAL KT3 ....159 K2
Wellington Dr DAGE RM10 ....80 E6
Wellington Gdns CHARL SE7 ....114 B4
HPTN TW12 ....142 D3
Wellington Gv GNWCH SE10...........113 G6
Wellington Ms HOLWY N7 ....73 F5
Wellington Pde BFN/LL * DA15 .....136 B4
Wellington Park Est
CRICK * NW2 ....69 J1
Wellington Pl EFNCH * N2 ....53 J4
STJWD NW8.....................................3 H7
Wellington Rd BELV DA17...............117 G4
BXLY DA5 ....136 E5
CROY/NA CR0..............................164 C6
DART DA1....................................139 F5
EA W5...104 D3
EBED/NFELT TW14 ....121 H4
EHAM E6 ....77 K7
EN EN1..30 A4
FSTGT E7 ....76 E4
HAYES BR2..................................168 B3
HPTN TW12.................................142 D3
KTN/HRWW/W HA3 ....48 E2
LEY E10 ....57 G7
PIN HA5.......................................33 K7
STJWD NW8...................................3 H6
WALTH E17...................................57 H3
WAN E11.....................................58 E4
WAT WD17...................................21 F1
WIM/MER SW19 ....146 E1
WLSDN * NW10 ....88 B2
Wellington Rd North
HSLWW TW4................................122 E2
Wellington Rd South
HSLWW TW4................................122 E3
Wellington Rw BETH E2 ....7M7
Wellington Sq CHEL SW3 ....15 L7
Wellington St COVGDN WC2E.........11 K6
WOOL/PLUM SE18 ....115 F3
Wellington Ter BAY/PAD W2 ....8 B7
CEND/HSY/T * N8 ....55 G2
HRW HA1 ....48 D7
WAP * E1W..................................92 D7
Wellington Wy BOW E3 ....93 J2
Welling Wy ELTH/MOT SE9.............135 J2
Well La MORT/ESHN SW14 ....125 K4
Wellmeadow Rd HNWL W7 ....104 B3
LEW SE13 ....133 H5
Well Rd BAR EN5 ....26 A4
HAMP NW3 ....71 H2
The Wells STHGT/OAK N14 ....28 D7
Wells Cl NTHLT UB5 ....83 G2
SAND/SEL CR2.............................178 A4
Wells Dr CDALE/KGS NW9...............51 F7
Wells Gdns IL IG1............................59 J6
RAIN RM13 ....81 H5
Wells House Rd WLSDN NW10........87 G4
Wellside Cl BAR EN5 ....26 A3
Wellside Gdns
MORT/ESHN SW14 ....125 K3
Wells Ms FITZ * W1T.......................10 F3
Wellsmoor Gdns BMLY BR1 ....169 F2
Wells Park Rd SYD SE26 ....150 C2
Wells Pl CMBW SE5 ....111 F6
WAND/EARL SW18.........................128 B6
Wells Ri STJWD NW8 ....3 L4
Wells Rd BMLY BR1 ....168 E1
SHB W12 ....107 F1
Wells Sq FSBYW WC1X.......................5 L8
Wells St GTPST W1W 10 E3
Wellstead Av ED N9 ....30 E6
Wellstead Rd EHAM E6....................96 A1
Wells Ter FSBYPK N4.......................73 G1
Wellstones WAT * WD17 ....21 F3
Well St HOM E9 ....74 E6
SRTFD E15 ....76 C5
Wells Wy SKENS SW7......................15 G3
Well Wk HAMP NW3 ....71 H2
Wellwood Rd GDMY/SEVK IG3 ....61 G7
Welsford St STHWK SE1 ....111 H4
Welsh Cl PLSTW E13 ....94 E2
Welshpool St HACK * E8 ....74 C7
Welshside CDALE/KGS * NW9..........51 G4
Welstead Wy CHSWK W4 ....106 C2
Weltje Rd HMSMTH W6...................106 D4
Welton Rd WOOL/PLUM SE18 ....115 K6
Welwyn Av EBED/NFELT TW14 ....121 J5
Welwyn St BETH E2..........................92 E2
Welwyn Wy YEAD UB4 ....82 C3
Wembley Hill Rd WBLY HA9 ....68 B4
Wembley Park Dr WBLY HA9............68 B3
Wembley Rd HPTN TW12 ....142 A7
Wembley Wy WBLY HA9..................68 D5
Wemborough Rd STAN HA7.............35 H7
Wembury Rd HGT N6 ....54 B6
Wemyss Rd BKHTH/KID SE3 ....133 J1
Wendela Ct HRW HA1 ....66 E2
Wendell Rd SHB W12 ....106 C1
Wendling Rd CAR SM5 ....162 C7
Wendon St BOW E3.........................75 H7
Wendover Cl YEAD UB4 ....83 H3
Wendover Dr NWMAL KT3 ....160 C5
Wendover Rd ELTH/MOT SE9 ......134 C2
HAYES BR2 ....168 A3
WLSDN NW10 ....87 H1
Wendover Wy BUSH WD23 ....22 C5
WELL DA16..................................136 B4
Wendy Cl EN EN1............................30 B5
Wendy Wy ALP/SUD HA0 ....68 A7
Wenlock Gdns HDN * NW4..............51 J3
Wenlock Rd EDGW HA8 ....36 D5
IS N1...6 E6
Wenlock St IS N1 ....6 F6
Wennington Rd BOW E3 ....93 F1
RAIN RM13 ....99 K4
Wensley Av WFD IG8 ....44 E6
Wensley Cl ELTH/MOT SE9 ....134 E5
FBAR/BDGN N11 ....40 A5
Wensleydale Av CLAY IG5 ....59 J1
Wensleydale Gdns HPTN TW12 ....142 B6
Wensleydale Rd HPTN TW12 ....142 A7
Wensley Rd UED N18......................42 D5
Wentland Cl CAT SE6 ....152 B1
Wentland Rd CAT SE6 ....152 B1
Wentworth Av BORE WD6 ....24 B4
FNCH N3......................................38 E6
Wentworth Cl FNCH N3 ....39 F6
HAYES * BR2 ....180 E1
MRDN SM4..................................161 K6
SURB KT6 ....171 K1
THMD SE28 ....97 K5
Wentworth Crs HYS/HAR UB3......101 G2
PECK SE15 ....111 H6
Wentworth Dr DART DA1..............138 D6
PIN HA5......................................46 E4
Wentworth Gdns PLMGR N13..........41 H2
Wentworth Hl WBLY HA9 ....50 B7
Wentworth Ms BOW E3 ....93 G3
Wentworth Pk FNCH N3 ....39 F6
Wentworth Pl STAN * HA7 ....35 H5
Wentworth Rd BAR EN5..................26 B1
CROY/NA CR0 ....164 B6
GLDGN NW11................................52 D5
MNPK E12 ....77 H3
NWDGN UB2 ....102 B3
Wentworth St WCHPL E1 ....13 L4
Wentworth Wy PIN HA5..................47 H3
RAIN RM13 ....99 K2
Wenvoe Av BXLYHN DA7...............137 J1
Wepham Cl YEAD UB4 ....83 H4
Wernbrook St
WOOL/PLUM SE18 ....115 H5
Werndee Rd SNWD SE25 ....165 H3
Werneth Hall Rd CLAY IG5 ....59 K2
Werrington St CAMTN NW1 ....4 F6
Werter Rd PUT/ROE SW15 ....127 H3
Wesleyan Pl KTTN NW5..................72 B3
Wesley Av CAN/RD E16 ....94 E7
HSLW TW3 ....122 D1
WLSDN NW10 ....87 F2
Wesley Cl HOLWY N7 ....73 F1
RYLN/HDSTN HA2 ....66 C1
WALW SE17 ....18 D6
Wesley Rd EFNCH N2 ....53 J1
HYS/HAR UB3 ....82 E6
LEY E10 ....58 A6
WLSDN NW10................................68 E7
Wesley Sq NTGHL W11 ....88 B5
Wesley St CAVSQ/HST W1G 10 B3
Wessex Av WIM/MER SW19 ....161 K1
Wessex Cl ESH/CLAY KT10............171 F1
GDMY/SEVK IG3.............................60 E5
KUTN/CMB KT2 ....144 D7
Wessex Ct BECK * BR3...................151 G7
Wessex Dr ERITH DA8 ....138 B1
PIN HA5..33 J6
Wessex Gdns CRICK NW2 ....52 C7
Wessex La GFD/PVL UB6................84 D1
Wessex St BETH E2.........................92 E2
Wessex Ter MTCM * CR4..............162 D4
Wessex Wy GLDGN NW11...............52 C6
Wesson Md CMBW * SE5...............110 D6
Westacott YEAD UB4......................82 C4
West Ap STMC/STPC BR5 ....169 H4
West Arbour St WCHPL E1 ....93 F5
West Av FNCH N3............................38 E5
HDN NW4 ....52 B4
HYS/HAR UB3 ....82 D6
PIN HA5 ....47 K6
STHL UB1 ....83 K6
WALTH E17 ....57 K4
WLGTN SM6 ....176 E4
West Avenue Rd WALTH E17 ....57 J3
West Bank BARK IG11 ....78 B7
ENC/FH EN2.................................29 J2
STNW/STAM N16............................56 A6
Westbank Rd HPTN TW12 ....142 C5
West Barnes La RYNPK SW20.......160 E2
Westbeech Rd WDGN N22 ....55 G2
Westbere Dr STAN HA7 ....35 K4
Westbere Rd CRICK NW2 ....70 C3
Westbourne Av ACT W3..................87 F5
CHEAM SM3 ....174 C1
Westbourne Cl YEAD UB4..............83 G3
Westbourne Crs BAY/PAD W2 ....9 G6
Westbourne Crescent Ms
BAY/PAD W2 ....9 G6
Westbourne Dr FSTH SE23............132 A7
Westbourne Gdns BAY/PAD W2 ......8 C4
Westbourne Ga BAY/PAD W2 ....9 H7
Westbourne Gv BAY/PAD W2 ....8 B5
Westbourne Grove Ms
NTGHL * W11 ....8 A5
Westbourne Grove Ter
BAY/PAD W2 ....8 C4
Westbourne Park Rd
BAY/PAD W2 ....8 B4
NTGHL W11 ....88 D5
Westbourne Park Vls
BAY/PAD W2 ....8 B3
Westbourne Pl ED N9......................42 D2
Westbourne Rd BXLYHN DA7.........116 E6
CROY/NA CR0 ....165 G5
FELT TW13 ....140 D2
HOLWY N7 ....73 G5
SYD SE26 ....151 F5
Westbourne St BAY/PAD W2 ....9 G6
Westbourne Ter BAY/PAD W2 ....8 E3
Westbourne Terrace Ms
BAY/PAD W2 ....8 E4
Westbourne Terrace Rd
BAY/PAD W2 ....8 E3
Westbridge Cl SHB W12 ....87 J7
Westbridge Rd BTSEA SW11 ....108 C7
Westbrook Av HPTN TW12 ....141 K6
Westbrook Cl EBAR EN4 ....27 H2
Westbrook Crs EBAR EN4...............27 H2
Westbrooke Crs WELL DA16 ....136 D2
Westbrooke Rd BFN/LL DA15 ....154 D1
WELL DA16..................................136 D2
Westbrook Rd BKHTH/KID SE3 ......113 K7
HEST TW5...................................102 E6
THHTH CR7 ....149 K7
Westbury Ar WDGN * N22 ....55 H2
Westbury Av ALP/SUD HA0 ....68 A6
ESH/CLAY KT10 ....171 F5
STHL UB1 ....84 A3
WDGN N22 ....55 H2
Westbury Cl RSLP HA4 ....46 E6
Westbury Gv FNCH N3 ....38 E5
Westbury La BKHH IG9 ....45 G1
Westbury Lodge Cl PIN HA5 ....47 H2
Westbury Pl BTFD TW8................104 E5
Westbury Rd ALP/SUD HA0 ....68 A6
BARK IG11 ....78 D7
BECK BR3 ....166 B2
BMLY BR1 ....153 H7
CROY/NA CR0..............................164 E5
EA W5...86 A5
FBAR/BDGN N11 ....40 E5
FELT TW13 ....122 C7
FSTGT E7 ....77 F4
IL IG1 ....59 K7
NFNCH/WDSP N12 ....38 E5
NTHWD HA6...................................32 C3
NWMAL KT3 ....160 A3
PGE/AN SE20 ....151 F7
WALTH E17 ....57 J3
WATW WD18 ....21 F4
Westbury Ter FSTGT E7..................77 F5
West Carriage Dr BAY/PAD W2 ....9 H7
West Central St
NOXST/BSQ WC1A..........................11 J4
West Chantry RYLN/HDSTN HA2 ....34 B7
Westchester Dr HDN NW4 ....52 B2
Westcliffe Vls KUT * KT1 ....159 G1
West Cl BAR EN5 ....25 K4
EBAR EN4......................................28 A3
ED N9 ....42 B2
GFD/PVL UB6.................................84 C1
RAIN RM13 ....99 K3
WBLY HA9 ....50 B7
Westcombe Av CROY/NA CR0 ....163 K5
Westcombe Dr BAR EN5..................26 E4
Westcombe Hl BKHTH/KID SE3 .....113 K5
Westcombe Park Rd
BKHTH/KID SE3 ....113 K6
West Common Rd HAYES BR2 ....180 E1
Westcoombe Av RYNPK SW20........145 H7
Westcote Ri RSLP HA4 ....46 A6
Westcote Rd
STRHM/NOR SW16 ....148 C4
Westcott Cl BMLY BR1 ....168 D4
CROY/NA CR0 ....179 K7
SEVS/STOTM N15 ....56 B5
Westcott Crs HNWL W7 ....84 E4
Westcott House POP/IOD * E14 .....93 J6
Westcott Rd WALW SE17 ....18 D9
West Ct ALP/SUD HA0 ....67 J1
Westcroft Cl CRICK NW2..................70 C3
Westcroft Gdns MRDN SM4............161 J2
Westcroft Ms HMSMTH * W6..........106 D3
Westcroft Rd CAR SM5 ....176 A3
Westcroft Sq HMSMTH W6 ....106 D3
Westcroft Wy CRICK NW2 ....70 C3
West Cross Route NTGHL W11.........88 B6
West Cross Wy BTFD TW8 ....104 C5
Westdale Rd
WOOL/PLUM SE18 ....115 G5
Westdean Av LEE/GVPK SE12 ....134 A7
Westdean Cl WAND/EARL SW18.....128 A5
Westdown Rd CAT SE6 ....132 D6
SRTFD E15 ....76 A3
West Drayton Park Av
WDR/YW UB7 ....100 B2
West Drayton Rd UX/CGN UB8 ....82 A4
West Dr BELMT SM2 ....174 B7
KTN/HRWW/W HA3 ....34 D5
TOOT SW17 ....148 B3
West Drive Gdns
KTN/HRWW/W HA3 ....34 D5
West Eaton Pl KTBR SW1X 16 A5
West Eaton Place Ms
KTBR SW1X...................................16 A5
West Ella Rd WLSDN NW10..............69 G6
West End Av PIN HA5 ....47 H3
WALTH E17 ....58 A4
West End Cl WLSDN NW10 ....68 E6
West End Ct PIN * HA5 ....47 H3
West End Gdns NTHLT UB5.............83 G1
West End La BAR EN5 ....26 B3
HYS/HAR UB3 ....101 F6
KIL/WHAMP NW6 ....2 B1
PIN HA5 ....47 H2
West End Rd RSLP HA4...................64 D2
STHL UB1 ....83 J7
Westerdale Rd GNWCH SE10 ....113 K4
Westerfield Rd
SEVS/STOTM * N15 ....56 B4
Westergate Rd ABYW SE2 ....117 F5
Westerham Av UED N18...................41 K5
Westerham Dr BFN/LL DA15 ....136 D5
Westerham Rd HAYES BR2 ....181 H5
LEY E10 ....57 K5
Westerley Crs SYD * SE26 ....151 H4
Western Av ACT W3.........................86 E3
DAGE RM10 ....80 E5
GFD/PVL UB6.................................85 F2
GLDGN NW11 ....52 B5
NTHLT UB5 ....65 F6
NTHLT UB5 ....65 J6
Western Ct FNCH * N3 ....38 E5
Western Gdns EA W5 ....86 C6
Western Gtwy CAN/RD E16 ....95 F6
Western La BAL SW12 ....129 F6
Western Man BAR * EN5..................27 F4
Western Ms MV/WKIL W9.................88 D3
Western Pde BAR EN5 ....26 E4
Western Rd BRXN/ST SW9 ....130 B2
EA W5 ....85 K6
EFNCH N2 ....53 K2
MTCM CR4 ....147 J7
NWDGN UB2 ....102 B3
PLSTW E13 ....77 F7
ROM RM1 ....63 H4
SUT SM1 ....174 E4
WALTH E17 ....58 A4
WDGN N22 ....55 F2
WLSDN NW10.................................86 E3
Western Ter HMSMTH * W6 ....106 D4
Western Vw HYS/HAR UB3.............101 J1
Westernville Gdns
GNTH/NBYPK IG2 ....60 C6
Western Wy BAR EN5 ....26 E5
THMD SE28 ....115 K1
Westferry Circ POP/IOD E14 ....93 J7
Westferry Rd POP/IOD E14 ....93 H6
Westfield Cl CDALE/KGS NW9 ....50 E2
FUL/PGN * SW6 ....108 B6
PEND EN3 ....31 G2
SUT SM1 ....174 D3
Westfield Dr
KTN/HRWW/W HA3 ....49 K4
Westfield Gdns
KTN/HRWW/W HA3 ....49 K3
Westfield La
KTN/HRWW/W HA3 ....49 K3
Westfield Pk PIN HA5 ....33 K6
Westfield Park Dr WFD IG8 ....45 J5
Westfield Rd BECK BR3 ....166 C1
BXLYHN DA7 ....137 K2
CROY/NA CR0 ....177 H1
DAGW RM9.....................................80 A3
MLHL NW7 ....37 F2
MTCM CR4 ....162 D1
SURB KT6 ....158 E4
SUT SM1 ....174 D3
WEA W13 ....85 G7
WOT/HER KT12 ....156 D6
Westfields BARN SW13 ....126 C2
Westfields Av BARN SW13 ....126 B2
Westfields Rd ACT W3.....................86 D4
Westfield St WOOL/PLUM SE18.....114 C2
Westfield Wy RSLP HA4 ....64 C2
WCHPL E1 ....93 G2
West Gdns WAP E1W 92 D6
WIM/MER SW19 ....147 J5
West Ga EA W5 ....86 A2
Westgate Est
EBED/NFELT * TW14 ....120 E7
Westgate Rd BECK BR3 ....152 A7
DART DA1 ....139 G5
SNWD SE25 ....165 J3
Westgate St HACK E8 ....74 D7
Westgate Ter WBPTN SW10 ....14 D8
Westglade Ct KTN/HRWW/W HA3...49 K4
West Green Pl GFD/PVL UB6 ....66 D7
West Green Rd SEVS/STOTM N15 ...55 K3
West Gv GNWCH SE10 ....113 F7
WFD IG8 ....45 G5
Westgrove La GNWCH SE10 ....113 F7
West Halkin St KTBR SW1X 16 A3
West Hallowes ELTH/MOT SE9 ......134 C7
West Hall Rd RCH/KEW TW9..........105 J7
West Ham La SRTFD E15..................76 C6
West Hampstead Ms
KIL/WHAMP NW6 ....71 F5
West Harding St
FLST/FETLN * EC4A 12 B4
West Hatch Mnr RSLP HA4..............46 D7
Westhay Gdns
MORT/ESHN SW14 ....125 J4
West Heath Av GLDGN NW11...........52 E7
West Heath Cl DART * DA1 ....138 C5
HAMP NW3 ....70 E2
West Heath Dr GLDGN NW11...........52 E7
West Heath Gdns HAMP NW3 ....70 E1
West Heath Rd BXLYHN DA7 ....116 E5
DART DA1 ....138 C5
HAMP NW3 ....70 E1
West Hl DART DA1 ....139 G5
HGT N6 ....54 A7
PUT/ROE SW15 ....127 G6
RYLN/HDSTN HA2 ....66 E1
SAND/SEL CR2 ....178 A7
WAND/EARL SW18.........................127 K4
WBLY HA9 ....50 B7
West Hill Dr DART DA1 ....139 F5
Westhill Pk HGT N6 ....71 K1
West Hill Ri DART DA1 ....139 G5
West Hill Rd PUT/ROE SW15..........127 J5
West Hill Wy TRDG/WHET N20.........27 F7
Westholm GLDGN NW11 ....53 F3
West Holme ERITH DA8 ....117 K7
Westholme ORP BR6.....................169 K6
Westholme Gdns RSLP HA4 ....46 E7
Westhorne Av ELTH/MOT SE9 ....134 B5
Westhorpe Gdns HDN NW4 ....52 A2
Westhorpe Rd PUT/ROE SW15 ......127 F2
West House Cl WIM/MER SW19.....127 H7
Westhurst Dr CHST BR7 ....154 B4
West India Av POP/IOD E14.............93 J7
West India Dock Rd
POP/IOD E14 ....93 H5
Westlake Cl PLMGR N13..................41 G2
YEAD UB4 ....83 J3
Westland Cl
STWL/WRAY * TW19 ....120 B5
Westland Dr HAYES BR2 ....180 D1
Westland Pl FSBYE EC1V 7 G8
Westland Rd WAT * WD17................21 F1
Westlands Cl HYS/HAR UB3 ....101 K3
Westlands Ter BAL SW12 ....129 H5
West La BERM/RHTH SE16 ....111 J1
Westlea Rd HNWL W7 ....104 B2
Westleigh Av PUT/ROE SW15.........127 F4
Westleigh Dr BMLY BR1 ....168 D1
Westleigh Gdns EDGW HA8 ....36 C7
West Links ALP/SUD HA0 ....85 K2
Westlinton Cl MLHL NW7 ....38 C5
West Lodge Av ACT W3....................86 C7
West Lodge Ct ACT * W3.................86 C7
Westmacott Dr
EBED/NFELT TW14 ....121 J7
West Malling Wy HCH RM12 ....81 K4
West Md HOR/WEW KT19 ....173 G5
RSLP HA4 ....65 G3
Westmead PUT/ROE SW15 ....126 E6
Westmead Rd SUT SM1 ....175 H3
Westmere Dr MLHL NW7 ....37 F2
West Ms PIM SW1V 16 D6
TOTM * N17 ....42 D6
Westminster Av THHTH CR7 ....164 C1
Westminster Br WEST SW1P 17 K2
Westminster Bridge Rd
STHWK SE1....................................17 L2
Westminster Cl
EBED/NFELT TW14 ....121 K7
TEDD TW11 ....143 G4
Westminster Dr PLMGR N13 ....40 E4
Westminster Gdns BARK IG11 ....96 E1
BARK/HLT IG6 ....60 D1
Westminster Rd ED N9....................30 D7
HNWL W7 ....84 E7
SUT SM1 ....175 H1
Westmoat Cl BECK BR3.................152 A6
Westmont Rd ESH/CLAY KT10 ....170 E1
Westmoor Gdns PEND EN3 ....31 F1
Westmoor Rd PEND EN3 ....31 F1
Westmoor St CHARL SE7 ....114 C3
Westmoreland Av WELL DA16........135 K2
Westmoreland Dr BELMT SM2 ....175 F7
Westmoreland Pl EA * W5 ....85 K4
HAYES * BR2 ....167 K2
PIM SW1V 16 D8
Westmoreland Rd BARN SW13 ......106 C7
CDALE/KGS NW9 ....50 B3
HAYES BR2 ....167 H4
WALW SE17 ....18 F9
Westmoreland St
CAVSQ/HST W1G 10 B3
Westmoreland Ter
PGE/AN * SE20............................150 D6
PIM SW1V 16 D7
Westmorland Cl MNPK E12 ....77 H1
TWK TW1 ....124 C5
Westmorland Rd HRW HA1 ....48 B4
WALTH E17 ....57 J5
Westmorland Wy MTCM CR4 ....163 J3
Westmount Ct EA * W5...................86 B4
Westmount Rd ELTH/MOT SE9 ......134 E2
West Oak BECK BR3......................152 B7
Westoe Rd ED N9 ....42 D1
Weston Av E/WMO/HCT KT8 ....156 D3
ESH/CLAY KT10 ....157 K6
Weston Dr KTN/HRWW/W HA3 ......35 H7
Weston Gdns ISLW TW7 ....103 J7
Weston Gn DAGW RM9 ....80 A3
THDIT KT7 ....157 K7
Weston Green Rd
ESH/CLAY KT10 ....157 J7
Weston Gv BMLY BR1 ....152 D6
Weston Pk CEND/HSY/T N8 ....54 E5
KUT KT1 ....159 F1
THDIT KT7 ....157 K7
Weston Park Cl THDIT * KT7.........157 K7
Weston Ri FSBYW WC1X...................5M7
Weston Rd BMLY BR1 ....152 D7
CHSWK W4 ....105 K2
DAGW RM9.....................................80 A3
EN EN1 ....29 K1
THDIT KT7 ....157 K7
Weston St STHWK SE1 ....13 H9
Weston Wk HACK E8 ....74 D6
Westover Cl BELMT SM2 ....175 F7
Westover Hl HAMP NW3..................70 E1
Westover Rd
WAND/EARL SW18.........................128 B5
Westow Hl NRWD SE19 ....150 A5
Westow St NRWD SE19.................150 A5
West Pk ELTH/MOT SE9 ....153 J1
West Park Av RCH/KEW TW9 ....105 H7
West Park Cl CHDH RM6 ....61 K4
HEST TW5 ....102 E5
West Park Rd NWDGN UB2..............84 C7
RCH/KEW TW9.............................105 H7
West Parkside GNWCH SE10 ....113 H1
West Pl NWDGN * UB2..................103 G3
WIM/MER SW19 ....146 A4
Westpole Av EBAR EN4...................28 B3
Westport Rd PLSTW E13..................95 F3
Westport St WCHPL E1 ....93 F5
West Poultry Av FARR EC1M 12 C3
West Quarters SHB W12 ....87 J5
West Quay Dr YEAD UB4.................83 J4
West Rp HTHAIR TW6 ....100 D7
West Ri BAY/PAD * W2 ....9 K6
West Rd CHDH RM6 ....62 A5
CHEL SW3 ....15M9
CLAP SW4 ....129 J4
EA W5 ....86 A4
EBAR EN4......................................28 A7
EBED/NFELT TW14 ....121 G6
EFNCH N2 ....53 H1
KUTN/CMB KT2 ....144 E7
ROMW/RG RM7 ....63 F6
SRTFD E15 ....76 D7
TOTM N17 ....42 D5
WDR/YW UB7 ....100 C2
West Rw NKENS W10 ....88 C3
Westrow Dr BARK IG11 ....79 F5
Westrow Gdns GDMY/SEVK IG3......79 F1
West Sheen V RCH/KEW TW9.........125 G3
Westside HDN NW4 ....51 K1
West Side Common
WIM/MER SW19 ....146 A5
West Smithfield STBT EC1A 12 D3
West Sq LBTH SE11 ....18 C4
West St BETH E2 ....92 D1
BMLY BR1 ....152 E7
BXLYHN DA7 ....137 G3
CAR SM5 ....175 K3
CROY/NA CR0 ....177 J3
ERITH DA8 ....118 A3
HRW HA1 ....48 D7
SUT SM1 ....175 F4
WALTH E17 ....57 K4
WAN E11 ....76 C2
WAT WD17 ....21 F1
West Street La CAR SM5 ....175 K3
West Street Pl CROY/NA * CR0 .....177 J3
West Temple Sheen
MORT/ESHN SW14 ....125 J4
West Tenter St WCHPL E1 ....13M5
West Ter BFN/LL * DA15 ....135 K7
West Towers PIN HA5 ....47 H5
West Vw EBED/NFELT TW14...........121 F7
Westview HNWL W7 ....84 E5
Westview Cl NKENS W10 ....88 A5
WLSDN NW10 ....69 H4
Westview Ct BORE WD6..................23 K5
Westview Crs EN EN1.....................30 A6
Westview Dr WFD IG8 ....59 H1
West View Gdns BORE WD6...........23 K5
West View Rd DART DA1 ....139 J5
Westville Rd SHB W12...................106 D1
THDIT KT7 ....158 B6
West Wk EBAR EN4 ....28 A7
HYS/HAR UB3 ....82 E7
Westward Rd CHING E4 ....43 H4
Westward Wy
KTN/HRWW/W HA3 ....50 A5
West Warwick Pl PIM * SW1V 16 E6
West Wy CROY/NA CR0.................179 G1
EDGW HA8 ....36 D5
HEST TW5 ....102 E7
PIN HA5 ....47 H3
RSLP HA4 ....46 D7
STMC/STPC BR5 ....169 J4
UED N18 ....41 K3
WLSDN NW10 ....69 F3
WWKM BR4 ....167 G5
Westway NTGHL W11 ....88 D4
RYNPK SW20 ....160 E3
SHB W12 ....87 J6
Westway Cl RYNPK SW20 ....160 E2
West Way Gdns CROY/NA CR0.......179 F1
Westways HOR/WEW KT19 ....173 H3
Westwell Rd
STRHM/NOR SW16 ....148 E5
Westwell Road Ap
STRHM/NOR SW16 ....148 E5
Westwick Gdns HEST TW5 ....122 A1
WKENS W14 ....107 G1
Westwood Av NRWD SE19 ....149 J7
RYLN/HDSTN HA2 ....66 B3
Westwood Cl BMLY BR1 ....168 C2
ESH/CLAY KT10 ....170 C2
Westwood Gdns BARN SW13..........126 C2
Westwood Hl SYD SE26 ....150 C4
Westwood La WELL DA16..............136 B3

Westwood Pk FSTH SE23 131 J6
Westwood Pl SYD * SE26 150 C4
Westwood Rd BARN SW13 126 C2
CAN/RD E16 95 F7
GDMY/SEVK IG3 61 F7
West Woodside BXLY DA5 137 F7
Wetheral Dr STAN HA7 35 H7
Wetherby Cl NTHLT UB5 66 B5
Wetherby Gdns ECT SW5 14 E6
Wetherby Ms ECT SW5 14 D7
Wetherby Pl ECT SW5 14 E6
Wetherby Wy CHSGTN KT9 172 A6
Wetherden St WALTH E17 57 H6
Wetherell Rd HOM E9 75 F7
Wetherill Rd MUSWH N10 40 A7
Wexford Rd BAL SW12 128 E6
Weybourne St
WAND/EARL SW18 147 G1
Weybridge Ct STHWK * SE1 111 J4
Weybridge Rd THHTH CR7 164 B3
Wey Ct HOR/WEW KT19 172 E3
Weydown Cl WIM/MER SW19 127 H7
Weyhill Rd WCHPL * E1 92 C5
Weylond Rd BCTR RM8 80 B2
Weyman Rd BKHTH/KID SE3 114 B7
Weymouth Av EA W5 104 D2
MLHL NW7 37 G4
Weymouth Cl EHAM E6 96 B5
Weymouth Ct BELMT * SM2 175 F6
Weymouth Ms CAVSQ/HST W1G 10 C2
Weymouth Rd YEAD UB4 82 C2
Weymouth St CAVSQ/HST W1G 10 B2
Weymouth Ter BETH E2 7 M5
Weymouth Vls FSBYPK * N4 73 F1
Weymouth Wk STAN HA7 35 G5
Whadcoat St FSBYPK N4 73 G1
Whalebone Av CHDH RM6 62 B5
Whalebone Gv CHDH RM6 62 B5
Whalebone La North
CHDH RM6 62 A3
Whalebone La South BCTR RM8 62 B7
Whales Yd SRTFD * E15 76 C6
Wharf Bridge Rd ISLW TW7 124 C2
Wharfdale Cl FBAR/BDGN N11 40 A5
Wharfdale Rd IS N1 5 K5
Wharfedale Gdns
STRHM/NOR SW16 164 A3
Wharfedale St WBPTN SW10 14 C8
Wharf La TWK TW1 124 B7
Wharf Pl BETH E2 74 C7
Wharf Rd IS N1 6 E6
PEND EN3 31 G5
SRTFD E15 76 B7
Wharfside Rd CAN/RD E16 94 C5
Wharf St CAN/RD E16 94 C4
Wharncliffe Dr STHL UB1 84 D7
Wharncliffe Gdns SNWD SE25 165 F1
Wharncliffe Rd SNWD SE25 164 E1
Wharton Cl WLSDN NW10 69 G5
Wharton Cottages
FSBYW * WC1X 5 M8
Wharton Rd BMLY BR1 153 F7
Wharton St FSBYW WC1X 5 M8
Whateley Rd EDUL SE22 131 G4
PGE/AN SE20 151 F6
Whatley Av RYNPK SW20 161 G2
Whatman Rd FSTH SE23 132 A6
Wheatestone Rd NKENS * W10 88 C4
Wheatfield Wy KUT KT1 159 F2
Wheathill Rd PGE/AN SE20 165 J1
Wheatlands HEST TW5 103 F5
Wheatlands Rd TOOT SW17 148 A2
Wheatley Cl HDN NW4 51 J1
Wheatley Crs HYS/HAR UB3 82 E6
Wheatley Gdns ED N9 42 A1
Wheatley Rd ISLW TW7 124 A2
Wheatley St CAVSQ/HST W1G 10 B3
Wheatley Terrace Rd
ERITH DA8 118 C5
Wheat Sheaf Cl POP/IOD E14 112 D3
Wheatsheaf Cl RSLP HA4 65 J4
Wheatsheaf La FUL/PGN SW6 107 F6
VX/NE SW8 109 K6
Wheatsheaf Rd ROM RM1 63 H5
Wheatsheaf Ter
FUL/PGN * SW6 107 J6
Wheatstone Cl
WIM/MER SW19 147 H7
Wheatstone Rd NKENS W10 88 C4
Wheeler Gdns IS N1 5 K3
Wheeler La WCHPL E1 13 L2
Wheelers Cross BARK IG11 96 D1
Wheelers Dr RSLP HA4 46 A5
Wheel Farm Dr DAGE RM10 80 E2
Wheelock Cl ERITH DA8 117 J6
Wheelright Cl BUSH WD23 22 B5
Wheelwright St HOLWY N7 5 L1
Whelan Wy WLGTN SM6 176 D2
Wheler St WCHPL E1 13 L1
Whellock Rd CHSWK W4 106 B2
Whetstone Cl TRDG/WHET N20 39 H1
Whetstone Pk LINN WC2A 11 L4
Whetstone Rd BKHTH/KID SE3 134 B1
Whewell Rd ARCH N19 72 E1
Whichcote St STHWK * SE1 12 A9
Whidborne Cl DEPT SE8 132 D1
Whidborne St STPAN WC1H 5 K8
Whimbrel Wy YEAD UB4 83 H5
Whinchat Rd THMD SE28 115 J2
Whinfell Cl STRHM/NOR SW16 148 D4
Whinyates Rd ELTH/MOT SE9 134 D2
Whippendell Cl
STMC/STPC BR5 155 H7
Whippendell Rd WATW WD18 20 C4
Whippendell Wy
STMC/STPC BR5 155 H7
Whipps Cross Rd WAN E11 58 C4
Whiskin St CLKNW EC1R 6 C8
Whistler Gdns EDGW HA8 50 B1
Whistlers Av BTSEA * SW11 108 C6
Whistler St HBRY N5 73 H3
Whistler Wk WBPTN * SW10 108 B6
Whiston Rd BETH E2 7 L5
Whitbread Cl TOTM N17 42 C7
Whitbread Rd BROCKY SE4 132 B3
Whitburn Rd LEW SE13 132 E4
Whitby Av WLSDN NW10 86 D2
Whitby Gdns CDALE/KGS NW9 50 C2
SUT SM1 175 H1
Whitby Pde RSLP * HA4 65 G1
Whitby Rd RSLP HA4 65 F2
RYLN/HDSTN HA2 66 C2
SUT SM1 175 H1
WOOL/PLUM SE18 114 E3
Whitby St WCHPL E1 7 L9
Whitcher Cl NWCR SE14 112 B5
Whitcher Pl KTTN NW5 72 C5
Whitchurch Av EDGW HA8 36 B6
Whitchurch Cl EDGW HA8 36 B5
Whitchurch Gdns EDGW HA8 36 B6
Whitchurch La EDGW HA8 36 A6
Whitchurch Pde EDGW * HA8 36 C6
Whitchurch Rd NTGHL W11 88 B6
Whitcomb St SOHO/SHAV W1D 11 H7
Whitcombe Ms RCH/KEW TW9 105 J7
Whitear Wk SRTFD E15 76 B5
Whitebarn La DAGE RM10 98 C1
Whitebeam Av HAYES BR2 169 F6
Whitebeam Cl BRXN/ST * SW9 110 A6
White Bear Pl HAMP * NW3 71 H3
White Bear Yd CLKNW * EC1R 12 A1
White Bridge Av MTCM CR4 162 C3
White Bridge Cl
EBED/NFELT TW14 121 J5
White Butts Rd RSLP HA4 65 H2
Whitechapel High St WCHPL E1 13 M4
Whitechapel Rd WCHPL E1 92 C5
White Church La WCHPL E1 92 C5
White City Cl SHB W12 88 A6
White City Rd SHB W12 87 K6
White Conduit St IS N1 6 B5
Whitecote Rd STHL UB1 84 B5
White Craig Cl PIN HA5 34 A4
Whitecroft Cl BECK BR3 167 G3
Whitecroft Wy BECK BR3 167 F3
Whitecross St STLK EC1Y 6 F9
Whitefield Av CRICK NW2 52 A6
Whitefield Cl
WAND/EARL SW18 127 H5
Whitefoot La CAT SE6 152 B3
Whitefoot Ter BMLY BR1 152 D2
Whitefriars Dr
KTN/HRWW/W HA3 48 E1
Whitefriars St EMB EC4Y 12 B5
White Gate Gdns
KTN/HRWW/W HA3 34 E6
Whitehall WHALL SW1A 11 J9
Whitehall Ct WHALL SW1A 11 J9
Whitehall Crs CHSGTN KT9 171 K4
Whitehall Gdns ACT W3 86 C7
CHSWK W4 105 J5
WHALL SW1A 11 J9
Whitehall La BKHH IG9 44 E1
ERITH DA8 138 C1
Whitehall Pk ARCH N19 54 C7
Whitehall Park Rd CHSWK W4 105 J5
Whitehall Pl CAR SM5 176 B3
WHALL SW1A 11 J9
Whitehall Rd CHING E4 44 C1
HAYES BR2 168 C4
HNWL W7 104 B1
HRW HA1 48 E6
THHTH CR7 164 B4
Whitehall St TOTM N17 42 B6
White Hart La BARN SW13 126 B1
WDGN N22 41 G7
White Hart Rd
WOOL/PLUM SE18 115 K3
White Hart St LBTH SE11 18 B7
White Hart Ter TOTM * N17 42 B6
White Hart Yd STHWK SE1 13 G9
Whitehaven Cl HAYES BR2 167 K3
Whitehaven St STJWD NW8 9 J1
Whitehead Cl UED N18 41 K4
WAND/EARL SW18 128 B6
Whitehead's Gv CHEL SW3 15 K7
White Heart Av UX/CGN UB8 82 A4
Whiteheath Av RSLP HA4 46 A6
White Heron Ms TEDD * TW11 143 F5
Whitehill Rd DART DA1 138 D4
White Horse Hl CHST BR7 154 A3
Whitehorse La SNWD SE25 165 F3
White Horse La WCHPL E1 93 F3
White Horse Rd EHAM E6 95 K2
Whitehorse Rd CROY/NA CR0 164 D6
WCHPL E1 93 G4
White Horse St MYFR/PICC W1J 10 D9
Whitehouse Av BORE WD6 24 D3
White House Dr STAN HA7 35 J3
Whitehouse Wy
STHGT/OAK N14 40 B1
Whitehurst Dr UED * N18 43 F4
White Kennett St WCHPL E1 13 K4
White Ledges WEA W13 85 J5
Whitelegg Rd PLSTW E13 94 D1
Whiteley Rd NRWD SE19 149 K4
Whiteleys Wy FELT TW13 142 A2
White Lion Ct BANK EC3V 13 J5
PECK * SE15 111 K5
White Lion Hl BLKFR EC4V 12 D6
White Lion St IS N1 6 A6
The White Ldg BAR * EN5 26 C2
White Ldg NRWD SE19 149 H6
White Lodge Cl BELMT SM2 175 G6
EFNCH N2 53 H5
White Lyon Ct BARB EC2Y 12 E2
White Oak Dr BECK BR3 167 F1
White Oak Gdns BFN/LL DA15 136 A6
Whiteoaks La GFD/PVL UB6 84 D1
White Orchards STAN HA7 35 G4
TRDG/WHET N20 26 D6
White Post La HOM E9 75 H6
White Post St PECK SE15 111 K6
White Rd SRTFD E15 76 C6
Whites Av GNTH/NBYPK IG2 60 E5
White's Grounds STHWK SE1 19 K1
Whites Grounds Est STHWK SE1 19 K1
Whites Meadow BMLY * BR1 169 F3
White's Rw WCHPL E1 13 L3
White's Sq CLAP SW4 129 J3
Whitestile Rd BTFD TW8 104 D4
Whitestone La HAMP NW3 71 G2
Whitestone Wk HAMP NW3 71 G2
White St NWDGN UB2 102 C1
Whitethorn Gdns
CROY/NA CR0 178 D1
ENC/FH EN2 29 K4
Whitethorn St BOW E3 93 J3
Whitewebbs Wy
STMC/STPC BR5 155 F7
Whitfield Pl FITZ W1T 10 E1
Whitfield Rd BXLYHN DA7 117 G6
EHAM E6 77 G6
GNWCH SE10 113 G7
Whitfield St FITZ W1T 10 F2
Whitford Gdns MTCM CR4 162 E2
Whitgift Av SAND/SEL CR2 177 J4
Whitgift St CROY/NA CR0 177 J2
LBTH SE11 17 L5
Whitings Rd BAR EN5 25 A4
Whitings Wy EHAM E6 96 A4
Whitland Rd CAR SM5 162 C7
Whitley Cl STWL/WRAY TW19 120 B5
Whitley Rd TOTM N17 56 A1
Whitlock Dr WAND/EARL SW18 127 H6
Whitman Rd BOW E3 93 G3
Whitmead Cl SAND/SEL CR2 177 K5
Whitmore Cl FBAR/BDGN N11 40 B4
Whitmore Est IS N1 7 K4
Whitmore Gdns WLSDN NW10 88 A1
Whitmore Rd BECK BR3 166 C2
HRW HA1 48 D6
IS N1 7 J4
Whitnell Wy PUT/ROE * SW15 127 F4
Whitney Av REDBR IG4 59 H3
Whitney Rd LEY E10 57 J6
Whitstable Cl BECK BR3 151 H7
Whitstable Pl CROY/NA CR0 177 J3
Whittaker Av RCH/KEW * TW9 124 E4
Whittaker Rd CHEAM SM3 174 D2
EHAM E6 77 G6
Whittaker St BGVA SW1W 16 A6
Whitta Rd MNPK E12 77 H3
Whittell Gdns SYD SE26 150 E2
Whittingstall Rd FUL/PGN SW6 107 J7
Whittington Av BANK EC3V 13 J5
YEAD UB4 82 D4
Whittington Ms
NFNCH/WDSP N12 39 G3
Whittington Rd WDGN N22 40 E6
Whittington Wy PIN HA5 47 J4
Whittlebury Cl CAR SM5 175 K6
Whittle Cl GFD/PVL UB6 84 B5
WALTH E17 57 G5
Whittle Rd HEST TW5 102 B6
NWDGN UB2 103 G1
Whittlesea Rd
KTN/HRWW/W HA3 34 C6
Whittlesey St STHWK SE1 12 B9
Whitton Av East GFD/PVL UB6 67 F4
Whitton Av West NTHLT UB5 66 B4
Whitton Cl GFD/PVL UB6 67 H5
Whitton Dene HSLW TW3 123 G4
Whitton Dr GFD/PVL UB6 67 G5
Whitton Manor Rd ISLW TW7 123 H5
Whitton Rd HSLW TW3 123 G4
WHTN TW2 123 K5
Whitton Waye HSLW TW3 123 F5
Whitwell Rd PLSTW E13 94 E2
Whitworth Rd SNWD SE25 165 F2
WOOL/PLUM SE18 115 F6
Whitworth St GNWCH SE10 113 H4
Whorlton Rd PECK SE15 131 H2
Whybridge Cl RAIN RM13 81 G7
Whymark Av WDGN N22 55 G2
Whytecroft HEST TW5 102 C6
Whyteville Rd FSTGT E7 77 F5
Wickersley Rd BTSEA SW11 129 F2
Wickers Oake NRWD * SE19 150 B3
Wicker St WCHPL * E1 92 C5
The Wicket CROY/NA CR0 179 J4
Wicket Rd GFD/PVL UB6 85 G2
Wickford St WCHPL E1 92 E3
Wickford Wy WALTH E17 57 F3
Wickham Av CHEAM SM3 174 A4
CROY/NA CR0 179 G1
Wickham Cha WWKM BR4 167 G6
Wickham Cl NWMAL KT3 160 C4
PEND EN3 30 D2
WCHPL E1 92 E4
Wickham Ct WWKM * BR4 180 B3
Wickham Court Rd
WWKM BR4 180 A1
Wickham Crs WWKM BR4 180 A1
Wickham Gdns BROCKY SE4 132 C2
Wickham La ABYW SE2 116 B5
Wickham Rd BECK BR3 166 E2
BROCKY SE4 132 C2
CHING E4 44 A6
CROY/NA CR0 166 C7
CROY/NA CR0 178 E1
KTN/HRWW/W HA3 48 D1
Wickham St LBTH SE11 17 L7
WELL DA16 135 K1
Wickham Wy BECK BR3 167 F3
Wick La BOW E3 75 J7
Wickliffe Av FNCH N3 52 C1
Wickliffe Gdns WBLY HA9 68 C1
Wicklow St FSBYW WC1X 5 L7
Wick Rd HOM E9 75 G5
TEDD TW11 143 H6
Wicks Cl ELTH/MOT SE9 153 H3
Wickwood St CMBW SE5 130 C1
Widdenham Rd HOLWY N7 73 F3
Widdicombe Av
RYLN/HDSTN HA2 65 J1
Widdin St SRTFD E15 76 C6
Widecombe Gdns REDBR IG4 59 J3
Widecombe Rd ELTH/MOT SE9 153 J2
Widecombe Wy EFNCH N2 53 H4
Widegate St WCHPL E1 13 K3
Widenham Cl PIN HA5 47 G4
Wide Wy STRHM/NOR SW16 163 J2
Widgeon Cl CAN/RD E16 95 F5
Widgeon Rd ERITH DA8 118 E6
Widley Rd MV/WKIL W9 2 B8
Widmore Lodge Rd BMLY BR1 168 C1
Widmore Rd BMLY BR1 168 B1
Wieland Rd NTHWD HA6 32 E6
Wigeon Wy YEAD UB4 83 H5
Wiggenhall Rd WATW WD18 21 F4
Wiggins Md CDALE/KGS NW9 37 H6
Wigginton Av WBLY HA9 68 C5
Wightman Rd CEND/HSY/T N8 55 G3
Wigley Rd FELT TW13 122 C7
Wigmore Pl CAVSQ/HST * W1G 10 C4
Wigmore Rd CAR SM5 175 H1
Wigmore St MBLAR W1H 10 B4
Wigram Rd WAN E11 59 G5
Wigram Sq WALTH E17 58 A2
Wigston Cl UED N18 42 A4
Wigston Rd PLSTW E13 95 F3
Wigton Gdns STAN HA7 36 A7
Wigton Pl LBTH * SE11 18 B8
Wigton Rd WALTH E17 43 H7
Wilberforce Rd CDALE/KGS NW9 51 H4
FSBYPK N4 73 H1
Wilberforce Wy
WIM/MER SW19 146 B5
Wilbraham Pl KTBR SW1X 16 A5
Wilbury Wy UED N18 41 K4
Wilby Ms NTGHL W11 88 D6
Wilcot Av OXHEY WD19 21 J6
Wilcot Cl OXHEY WD19 21 J6
Wilcox Cl VX/NE SW8 109 K6
Wilcox Rd SUT * SM1 175 F3
TEDD TW11 142 D3
VX/NE SW8 109 K6
Wildacres NTHWD HA6 32 D3
Wild Ct HOL/ALD WC2B 11 L4
Wildcroft Gdns STAN HA7 35 K5
Wildcroft Rd PUT/ROE SW15 127 F6
Wilde Cl HACK E8 74 C7
Wilde Pl PLMGR N13 41 H5
Wilder Cl RSLP HA4 47 F7
The Wilderness
E/WMO/HCT KT8 157 H4
HPTN * TW12 142 B3
Wilderness Rd CHST BR7 154 B6
Wilde Rd ERITH DA8 117 J6
Wilderton Rd STNW/STAM N16 56 A6
Wildfell Rd CAT SE6 132 E6
Wild Goose Dr PECK SE15 111 K7
Wild Hatch GLDGN NW11 52 E5
Wild Oaks Cl NTHWD HA6 32 D5
Wild's Rents STHWK SE1 19 J3
Wild St HOL/ALD WC2B 11 K5
Wildwood NTHWD HA6 32 B5
Wildwood Cl LEE/GVPK SE12 133 J6
Wildwood Gv HAMP NW3 53 G7
Wildwood Ri GLDGN NW11 53 G7
Wildwood Rd GLDGN NW11 53 G6
Wilford Cl ENC/FH * EN2 29 K2
NTHWD HA6 32 B6
Wilford Rd CROY/NA CR0 164 D5
Wilfred Av RAIN RM13 99 J4
Wilfred St WESTW SW1E 16 E3
Wilfrid Gdns ACT W3 86 E4
Wilkes Rd BTFD TW8 105 F5
Wilkes St WCHPL E1 13 M2
Wilkins Cl HYS/HAR UB3 101 J4
MTCM CR4 147 J7
Wilkinson Rd CAN/RD E16 95 G5
Wilkinson St VX/NE SW8 110 A6
Wilkinson Wy CHSWK W4 106 A1
Wilkin St KTTN NW5 72 A5
Wilkin Street Ms KTTN * NW5 72 B5
Wilks Gdns CROY/NA CR0 166 B7
Wilks Pl IS N1 7 K6
Willan Rd TOTM N17 55 K1
Willan Wall CAN/RD E16 94 D6
Willard St VX/NE SW8 129 G2
Willcocks Cl CHSGTN KT9 172 A2
Willcott Rd ACT W3 86 D7
Will Crooks Gdns
ELTH/MOT SE9 134 C3
Willenhall Av BAR EN5 27 G5
Willenhall Dr HYS/HAR UB3 82 C6
Willenhall Rd
WOOL/PLUM SE18 115 G4
Willerfield Rd WLSDN NW10 86 E2
Willersley Av BFN/LL DA15 136 A7
Willersley Cl BFN/LL DA15 136 A7
Willesden La KIL/WHAMP NW6 70 B6
Willes Rd KTTN NW5 72 B5
Willett Cl NTHLT UB5 83 G2
STMC/STPC BR5 169 K5
Willett Rd THHTH CR7 164 B4
Willett Wy STMC/STPC BR5 169 J4
William Barefoot Dr
ELTH/MOT SE9 154 A1
William Booth Rd
PGE/AN SE20 150 C7
William Carey Wy HRW HA1 48 E5
William Cl EFNCH N2 53 H1
LEW SE13 133 F2
NWDGN UB2 103 H1
William Ellis Wy
BERM/RHTH * SE16 111 H2
William Gdns PUT/ROE SW15 126 E4
William Guy Gdns BOW E3 93 K2
William IV St CHCR WC2N 11 J7
William Margrie Cl PECK * SE15 131 H1
William Ms KTBR SW1X 15 M2
William Morley Cl EHAM E6 77 H7
William Morris Cl WALTH E17 57 H2
William Morris Wy
FUL/PGN SW6 128 B2
William Rd CAMTN NW1 4 E8
SUT SM1 175 G4
WIM/MER SW19 146 C6
Williams Av WALTH E17 43 H7
William's Buildings BETH * E2 92 E3
Williams Cl CEND/HSY/T * N8 54 D5
FUL/PGN SW6 107 H6
Williams Dr HSLW TW3 123 F3
Williams Gv SURB KT6 158 D5
WDGN N22 41 G7
Williams La MORT/ESHN SW14 125 K2
MRDN SM4 162 B5
Williamson Cl GNWCH SE10 113 J4
Williamson Rd FSBYPK N4 55 H5
Williamson St HOLWY * N7 72 E3
Williamson Wy MLHL NW7 38 C5
William Sq BERM/RHTH SE16 93 G7
Williams Rd NWDGN UB2 102 D3
WEA * W13 85 G7
Williams Ter CROY/NA CR0 177 G5
William St BARK IG11 78 C6
BUSH WD23 21 H2
CAR SM5 175 J2
KTBR SW1X 15 M2
LEY E10 57 K5
TOTM N17 42 B6
Willifield Wy GLDGN NW11 52 E4
Willingdon Rd WDGN N22 55 H1
Willingham Cl KTTN NW5 72 C4
Willingham Ter KTTN * NW5 72 C4
Willingham Wy KUT KT1 159 H1
Willington Rd BRXN/ST SW9 129 K2
Willis Av BELMT SM2 175 J5
Willis Rd CROY/NA CR0 164 D6
ERITH DA8 117 K3
SRTFD E15 94 D1
Willis St POP/IOD E14 93 K5
Willmore End WIM/MER SW19 147 F7
Willoughby Av CROY/NA CR0 177 F3
Willoughby Dr RAIN RM13 81 G6
Willoughby Gv TOTM N17 42 D6
Willoughby La TOTM N17 42 D6
Willoughby Ms TOTM N17 42 D6
Willoughby Park Rd TOTM N17 42 D6
Willoughby Rd CEND/HSY/T N8 55 G2
HAMP NW3 71 H3
KUTN/CMB KT2 144 B7
TWK TW1 124 D4
Willoughby Wy CHARL SE7 114 A3
Willow Av BARN SW13 126 C1
BFN/LL DA15 136 B5
Willow Bridge Rd IS * N1 73 J5
Willowbrook HPTN * TW12 142 B4
Willowbrook Est PECK * SE15 111 G6
Willowbrook Rd NWDGN UB2 102 E2
PECK SE15 111 G5
STWL/WRAY TW19 120 B7
Willow Cl BKHH IG9 45 H2
BTFD TW8 104 D5
BXLY DA5 137 G5
HAYES BR2 168 E4
HCH RM12 81 K2
Willow Ct STAN * HA7 35 K6
Willowcourt Av
KTN/HRWW/W HA3 49 H4
Willow Dean PIN * HA5 47 H1
Willow Dene BUSH WD23 22 E6
Willowdene HGT * N6 53 K6
Willow Dene PIN HA5 47 H1
Willowdene Cl WHTN TW2 123 H6
Willow Dr BAR EN5 26 C3
Willow End NTHWD HA6 32 E5
TRDG/WHET N20 38 E1
Willowfields Cl
WOOL/PLUM SE18 115 K4
Willow Gdns HEST * TW5 103 F7
RSLP HA4 64 D1
Willow Gv CHST BR7 154 A5
RSLP HA4 64 D1
Willowhayne Dr
WOT/HER KT12 156 A6
Willowhayne Gdns WPK KT4 174 A3
Willow La MTCM CR4 162 E4
WATW WD18 20 E4
WOOL/PLUM SE18 114 E3
Willowmead Cl EA W5 85 K4
Willowmere ESH/CLAY KT10 170 C3
Willow Mt CROY/NA CR0 178 A3
Willow Pl WEST SW1P 16 F5
Willow Rd CHDH RM6 62 A5
DART DA1 139 F7
EA W5 105 F1
EN EN1 30 A1
ERITH DA8 118 D7
HAMP NW3 71 H3
NWMAL KT3 159 K3
WLGTN SM6 176 B6
The Willows BECK * BR3 151 J7
EBAR * EN4 27 J5
ESH/CLAY KT10 170 E5
OXHEY WD19 21 F6
Willows Av MRDN SM4 162 A4
Willows Cl PIN HA5 47 G1
Willows Ter WLSDN * NW10 87 H1
Willow St ROMW/RG RM7 62 E3
SDTCH EC2A 7 J9
Willow Ter PGE/AN * SE20 150 D7
Willowtree Cl HGDN/ICK UB10 64 A2
Willow Tree Cl HOM E9 75 G7
WAND/EARL SW18 128 A7
YEAD UB4 83 G3
Willow Tree La YEAD UB4 83 G3
Willow Tree Wk BMLY BR1 153 F7
Willowtree Wy
STRHM/NOR SW16 149 G7
Willow V CHST BR7 154 A5
SHB W12 87 J7
Willow Vw WIM/MER SW19 147 H7
Willow Wk CHEAM SM3 174 D2
DART * DA1 139 H4
SEVS/STOTM N15 55 H3
STHWK SE1 19 K5
WALTH E17 57 H4
WCHMH N21 29 F5
Willow Wy ALP/SUD * HA0 67 G2
FNCH N3 39 F6
HOR/WEW KT19 173 F5
NTGHL W11 88 B6
SYD SE26 150 D2
WHTN TW2 142 B1
Willow Wood Crs SNWD SE25 165 F5
Willow Wren Whf
NWDGN * UB2 102 A3
Willrose Crs ABYW SE2 116 C4
Wills Crs HSLW TW3 123 G5
Wills Gv MLHL NW7 37 J4
Willshaw St NWCR SE14 112 D7
Wilman Gv HACK E8 74 C6
Wilmar Cl YEAD UB4 82 B3
Wilmar Gdns WWKM BR4 166 E7
Wilmer Cl RCHPK/HAM TW10 144 B4
Wilmer Crs RCHPK/HAM TW10 144 B4
Wilmer Gdns IS N1 7 K4
Wilmer Lea Cl SRTFD E15 76 A6
Wilmer Pl STNW/STAM N16 74 B1
Wilmer Wy STHGT/OAK N14 40 D4
Wilmington Av CHSWK W4 106 A6
Wilmington Gdns BARK IG11 78 D6
Wilmington Sq FSBYW WC1X 6 A8
Wilmington St FSBYW WC1X 6 A8
Wilmot Cl PECK * SE15 111 H6
Wilmot Pl CAMTN NW1 4 E1
HNWL W7 84 E7
Wilmot Rd CAR * SM5 175 K4
DART DA1 138 E4
LEY E10 75 K1
TOTM N17 55 K2
Wilmot St BETH E2 92 D3
Wilmount St
WOOL/PLUM SE18 115 G3
Wilna Rd WAND/EARL SW18 128 B6
Wilsham St NTGHL W11 88 B7
Wilsmere Dr KTN/HRWW/W HA3 34 E6
NTHLT UB5 65 J5
Wilson Av MTCM CR4 147 J6
Wilson Cl SAND/SEL CR2 177 K4
WBLY HA9 50 B6
Wilson Dr WBLY HA9 50 B6
Wilson Gdns HRW HA1 48 C6
Wilson Gv BERM/RHTH SE16 111 J1
Wilson Rd CHSGTN KT9 172 B5
CMBW SE5 110 E7
IL IG1 59 K6
PLSTW E13 95 H2
Wilson's Av TOTM N17 56 B1
Wilson's Pl POP/IOD E14 93 H5
Wilson's Rd HMSMTH W6 107 G4
Wilson St SDTCH EC2A 13 H2
WALTH E17 58 A4
WCHMH N21 29 G6
Wilson Wk HMSMTH * W6 106 C3
Wilstone Cl NTHLT UB5 83 J3
Wilthorne Gdns DAGE RM10 80 D6
Wilton Av CHSWK W4 106 B4
Wilton Cl WDR/YW UB7 100 A5
Wilton Crs KTBR SW1X 16 A2
WIM/MER SW19 146 D7
Wilton Est HACK * E8 74 C5
Wilton Gdns E/WMO/HCT KT8 157 F2
WOT/HER KT12 156 C7
Wilton Gv NWMAL KT3 160 C5
WIM/MER SW19 146 D6
Wilton Ms HACK * E8 74 D5
KTBR SW1X 16 B3
Wilton Pl KTBR SW1X 16 A2
Wilton Rd ABYW SE2 116 D2
EBAR EN4 27 K3
HSLWW TW4 122 C2
MUSWH N10 54 A1
PIM SW1V 16 E5
WIM/MER SW19 147 J6
Wilton Rw KTBR SW1X 16 A2
Wilton Sq IS N1 7 G3
Wilton St KTBR SW1X 16 C3
Wilton Ter KTBR SW1X 16 A3
Wilton Vls IS N1 7 G4
Wilton Wk FELT * TW13 141 F1
Wilton Wy HACK E8 74 C5
Wiltshire Cl CHEL SW3 15 K6
MLHL * NW7 37 H4
Wiltshire Gdns FSBYPK N4 55 J5
WHTN TW2 123 H7

Wiltshire La RSLP HA4 46 D2
Wiltshire Rd BRXN/ST SW9 130 B2
THHTH CR7 164 B2
Wiltshire Rw IS N1 7 G4
Wilverley Crs NWMAL KT3 160 B5
Wimbart Rd
BRXS/STRHM * SW2 130 A6
Wimbledon Br
WIM/MER SW19 146 D5
Wimbledon Hill Rd
WIM/MER SW19 146 C5
Wimbledon Park Rd
WIM/MER SW19 146 C2
Wimbledon Park Side
WIM/MER SW19 146 B1
Wimbledon Rd TOOT SW17 147 G3
Wimbolt St BETH E2 92 C2
Wimborne Av NWDGN UB2 103 F3
YEAD UB4 83 F5
Wimborne Cl BKHH IG9 45 G1
LEE/GVPK SE12 133 J4
WPK KT4 161 F7
Wimborne Dr CDALE/KGS NW9 50 C2
PIN HA5 47 H6
Wimborne Gdns WEA W13 85 H5
Wimborne Rd ED N9 42 C1
TOTM N17 56 A1
Wimborne Wy BECK BR3 166 A2
Wimbourne St IS N1 7 G5
Wimpole Cl HAYES BR2 168 B3
KUT KT1 159 G1
Wimpole Ms CAVSQ/HST W1G 10 C2
Wimpole St CAVSQ/HST W1G 10 C4
Wimshurst Cl CROY/NA CR0 163 K7
Winans Wk BRXN/ST SW9 130 B1
Wincanton Crs NTHLT UB5 66 B4
Wincanton Gdns BARK/HLT IG6 60 B2
Wincanton Rd
WAND/EARL SW18 127 J6
Winchcombe Rd CAR SM5 162 C6
Winchcomb Gdns
ELTH/MOT SE9 134 D2
Winchelsea Av BXLYHN DA7 117 G6
Winchelsea Cl PUT/ROE SW15 127 G4
Winchelsea Rd FSTGT E7 76 E3
TOTM N17 56 A2
WLSDN NW10 69 F7
Winchelsey Ri SAND/SEL CR2 178 B5
Winchendon Rd FUL/PGN SW6 107 J6
TEDD TW11 142 D3
Winchester Av CDALE/KGS NW9 50 B2
HEST TW5 102 E5
KIL/WHAMP NW6 70 C7
Winchester Cl EN * EN1 30 A4
ESH/CLAY KT10 170 A3
HAYES BR2 167 J2
KUTN/CMB KT2 144 D6
LBTH * SE11 18 D6
Winchester Dr PIN HA5 47 H4
Winchester Pk HAYES BR2 167 J2
Winchester Pl HACK E8 74 B4
HGT N6 54 B7
Winchester Rd BXLYHN DA7 136 E1
CHING E4 44 A6
ED N9 30 B7
FELT TW13 141 K2
HAMP NW3 3 H1
HAYES BR2 167 J2
HGT N6 54 B7
HYS/HAR UB3 101 H6
IL IG1 78 D2
KTN/HRWW/W HA3 50 A3
TWK TW1 124 C5
Winchester Sq STHWK SE1 13 G8
Winchester St ACT W3 86 E7
PIM SW1V 16 D7
Winchester Wk STHWK SE1 13 G8
Winchfield Cl
KTN/HRWW/W HA3 49 J5
Winchfield Rd SYD SE26 151 G4
Winchilsea Crs
E/WMO/HCT KT8 157 H1
Winchmore Hill Rd
STHGT/OAK N14 28 E6
Winchmore Vls WCHMH * N21 29 F6
Winckley Cl KTN/HRWW/W HA3 50 B4
Wincott St LBTH SE11 18 B5
Wincrofts Dr ELTH/MOT SE9 135 J3
Windall Cl NRWD SE19 150 C7
Windborough Rd CAR SM5 176 A6
Windermere Av FNCH N3 52 E2
HCH RM12 81 J4
KIL/WHAMP NW6 70 C7
RSLP HA4 47 G6
WBLY HA9 49 J7
WIM/MER SW19 162 A2
Windermere Cl DART DA1 138 E7
EBED/NFELT TW14 121 H7
Windermere Gdns REDBR IG4 59 J4
Windermere Gv WBLY HA9 49 J7
Windermere Hall EDGW * HA8 36 B4
Windermere Rd ARCH * N19 72 C1
BXLYHN DA7 137 K1
CROY/NA CR0 165 G7
EA W5 104 D2
MUSWH N10 40 B7
PUT/ROE SW15 145 G3
STHL UB1 83 K4
STRHM/NOR SW16 148 C7
WWKM BR4 180 C1
Winders Rd BTSEA * SW11 128 D1
Windfield Cl SYD SE26 151 F3
Windham Rd RCH/KEW TW9 125 G2
Winding Wy BCTR RM8 79 J2
Windlass Pl DEPT SE8 112 B3
Windlesham Gv
WIM/MER SW19 127 G7
Windley Cl FSTH SE23 150 E1
Windmill Cl BERM/RHTH * SE16 111 H3
LEW * SE13 133 F1
SUN TW16 140 C6
SURB KT6 158 D7
Windmill Dr CLAP SW4 129 G4
HAYES BR2 181 G3
Windmill Gdns ENC/FH EN2 29 G1
Windmill Gv CROY/NA CR0 164 D6
Windmill Hl ENC/FH EN2 29 H2
HAMP * NW3 71 G2
RSLP HA4 46 D7
Windmill La BAR EN5 25 H5
BUSH WD23 22 E7
GFD/PVL UB6 84 C4
NWDGN UB2 84 C7
SRTFD E15 76 B5
THDIT KT7 158 C6
Windmill Pas CHSWK * W4 106 B3
Windmill Ri KUTN/CMB KT2 144 D6
Windmill Rd CHSWK W4 106 B3
CROY/NA CR0 164 D6
EA W5 104 D3
HPTN TW12 142 B4
MTCM CR4 163 H4
SUN TW16 140 C7
UED N18 41 K3
WAND/EARL SW18 128 C5
WIM/MER SW19 145 K4
Windmill Rd West SUN TW16 140 C7
Windmill Rw LBTH SE11 18 A8
Windmill St BUSH WD23 22 E7
FITZ W1T 11 G3
Windmill Wk STHWK * SE1 12 B9
Windmill Wy RSLP HA4 46 D7
Windrose Cl BERM/RHTH SE16 112 A1
Windrush NWMAL KT3 159 J3
Windrush Cl BTSEA * SW11 128 C3
CHSWK * W4 105 K6
Windrush La FSTH SE23 151 F2
Windrush Rd WLSDN NW10 69 F7
Windsor Av CHEAM SM3 174 C2
E/WMO/HCT KT8 157 F2
EDGW HA8 36 D3
NWMAL KT3 159 K4
WALTH E17 57 G1
WIM/MER SW19 147 G7
Windsor Cl CHST BR7 154 B4
FNCH N3 52 C1
NTHWD HA6 46 E1
RYLN/HDSTN HA2 66 A2
WNWD SE27 149 J3
Windsor Ct PIN * HA5 47 H2
STHGT/OAK N14 28 C6
Windsor Crs RYLN/HDSTN HA2 66 A2
WBLY HA9 68 C2
Windsor Dr DART DA1 138 D5
EBAR EN4 27 K5
Windsor Gdns CROY/NA CR0 176 E2
HYS/HAR UB3 101 G2
MV/WKIL * W9 8 A1
Windsor Gv WNWD SE27 149 J3
Windsor Ms CAT SE6 133 F7
Windsor Park Rd
HYS/HAR UB3 101 J6
Windsor Rd BAR EN5 26 B5
BCTR RM8 80 A2
BXLYHS DA6 137 F3
CHING E4 43 K3
CRICK NW2 69 K5
EA W5 86 A6
FNCH N3 52 C1
FSTGT E7 77 F4
HOLWY N7 72 E2
HSLWW TW4 122 A1
IL IG1 78 C3
KTN/HRWW/W HA3 34 C7
KUTN/CMB KT2 144 A6
LEY E10 75 K1
NWDGN UB2 102 E2
PLMGR N13 41 G2
RCH/KEW TW9 125 G1
SUN TW16 140 E6
TEDD TW11 142 D4
THHTH CR7 164 C1
TOTM N17 56 C1
WAN E11 58 E7
WPK KT4 173 J1
The Windsors BKHH IG9 45 J1
Windsor St IS N1 6 D4
Windsor Ter IS N1 6 F7
Windsor Wk CMBW SE5 130 E1
Windsor Wy WKENS W14 107 G3
Windspoint Dr PECK * SE15 111 H5
Windus Rd STNW/STAM N16 56 B7
Windy Rdg BMLY BR1 153 J7
Windy Ridge Cl
WIM/MER SW19 146 B4
Wine Cl WAP E1W 92 E6
Winery La KUT KT1 159 G2
Winey Cl CHSGTN KT9 171 J6
Winforton St GNWCH SE10 113 F7
Winfrith Rd WAND/EARL SW18 128 B6
Wingate Crs CROY/NA CR0 163 K5
Wingate Rd HMSMTH W6 106 E2
IL IG1 78 B4
SCUP DA14 155 J4
Wingfield Ct WATW * WD18 20 B5
Wingfield Ms PECK * SE15 131 H2
Wingfield Rd KUTN/CMB KT2 144 B5
SRTFD E15 76 C4
WALTH E17 57 K4
Wingfield St PECK SE15 131 H2
Wingfield Wy RSLP HA4 65 F5
Wingford Rd
BRXS/STRHM SW2 129 K5
Wingmore Rd HNHL SE24 130 D2
Wingrave Rd HMSMTH W6 107 F5
Wingrove Rd CAT SE6 152 C1
Wings Cl SUT SM1 174 E3
Winifred Cl MLHL NW7 25 H5
Winifred Pl NFNCH/WDSP N12 39 G4
Winifred Rd BCTR RM8 80 A1
DART DA1 138 E4
ERITH DA8 118 B4
HPTN TW12 142 A3
WIM/MER SW19 146 E7
Winifred St CAN/RD E16 95 K7
Winifred Ter EN EN1 30 B6
Winkfield Rd WDGN N22 41 G7
Winkley St BETH E2 92 D1
Winkworth Cottages
WCHPL * E1 92 E3
Winlaton Rd BMLY BR1 152 B3
Winmill Rd BCTR RM8 80 B2
Winn Bridge Cl WFD IG8 45 H7
Winn Common Rd
WOOL/PLUM SE18 115 K5
Winnett St SOHO/SHAV W1D 11 G6
Winnington Cl EFNCH N2 53 H5
Winnington Rd EFNCH N2 53 H6
Winn Rd LEE/GVPK SE12 133 K7
Winns Av WALTH E17 57 H2
Winns Ms SEVS/STOTM N15 56 A3
Winns Ter WALTH E17 57 J1
Winsbeach WALTH E17 58 B2
Winscombe Crs EA W5 85 K3
Winscombe St KTTN NW5 72 B2
Winscombe Wy STAN HA7 35 G4
Winsford Rd CAT SE6 151 H2
Winsford Ter UED * N18 41 K4
Winsham Gv BTSEA SW11 129 F4
Winslade Rd BRXS/STRHM SW2 129 K4
Winsland Ms BAY/PAD W2 9 G4
Winsland St BAY/PAD W2 9 G4
Winsley St GTPST W1W 10 E4
Winslow Cl PIN HA5 47 F5
WLSDN NW10 69 G2
Winslow Gv CHING E4 44 C1
Winslow Rd HMSMTH W6 107 F5
Winslow Wy FELT TW13 141 H2
Winsor Ter EHAM E6 96 B4
Winstanley Rd BTSEA SW11 128 C2
Winstead Gdns DAGE RM10 80 E4
Winston Av CDALE/KGS NW9 51 G6
Winston Cl KTN/HRWW/W HA3 35 F5
ROMW/RG RM7 62 D3
Winston Ct PIN HA5 34 B6
Winston House SURB * KT6 159 F4
Winston Rd STNW/STAM N16 73 K3
Winston Wy IL IG1 78 B2
Winter Av EHAM E6 77 J7
Winterbourne Rd BCTR RM8 79 J1
CAT SE6 132 C7
THHTH CR7 164 B3
Winter Box Wk
RCHPK/HAM TW10 125 G4
Winterbrook Rd HNHL SE24 130 D5
Winterburn Cl FBAR/BDGN N11 40 A5
Winterfold Cl WIM/MER SW19 146 C1
Winters Rd THDIT KT7 158 C6
Winterstoke Rd CAT SE6 132 C7
Winterton Pl WBPTN SW10 14 F9
Winterwell Rd
BRXS/STRHM SW2 129 K4
Winthorpe Rd PUT/ROE SW15 127 H3
Winthorpe St WCHPL E1 92 D4
Winthrop St WCHPL * E1 92 D4
Winton Ap RKW/CH/CXG WD3 20 A4
Winton Av FBAR/BDGN N11 40 C6
Winton Cl ED N9 31 F6
Winton Dr RKW/CH/CXG WD3 20 A4
Winton Gdns EDGW HA8 36 B6
The Wintons BUSH * WD23 22 D7
Winton Wy STRHM/NOR SW16 149 G4
Wirral Wood Cl CHST BR7 154 A5
Wisbeach Rd CROY/NA CR0 164 E4
Wisborough Rd SAND/SEL CR2 178 B7
Wisdons Cl DAGE RM10 62 D7
Wise La MLHL NW7 37 J5
WDR/YW UB7 100 A3
Wiseman Rd LEY * E10 75 J1
Wise Rd SRTFD E15 76 A7
Wiseton Rd TOOT SW17 128 D7
Wishart Rd BKHTH/KID SE3 114 C7
Wisley Rd BTSEA SW11 128 E4
STMC/STPC BR5 155 G6
Wisteria Cl IL IG1 78 B4
Wisteria Rd LEW SE13 133 G3
Witan St BETH E2 92 D2
Witham Rd DAGE RM10 80 C4
GPK RM2 63 K4
ISLW TW7 103 J7
PGE/AN SE20 165 K2
WEA W13 85 G7
Witherby Cl SAND/SEL CR2 178 A4
Witherington Rd HBRY * N5 73 G4
Withers Md CDALE/KGS NW9 37 H7
Witherston Wy ELTH/MOT SE9 154 A1
Withy La RSLP HA4 46 A4
Withy Md CHING E4 44 B2
Witley Crs CROY/NA CR0 180 A5
Witley Gdns NWDGN UB2 102 E3
Witley Rd ARCH N19 72 C1
Witney Cl PIN HA5 33 K5
Witney Pth FSTH * SE23 151 F2
Wittenham Wy CHING E4 44 B2
Wittering Cl KUTN/CMB KT2 143 K4
Wittersham Rd BMLY BR1 152 D4
Wivenhoe Cl PECK SE15 131 H2
Wivenhoe Ct HSLW TW3 122 E3
Wivenhoe Rd BARK IG11 97 G1
Wiverton Rd SYD SE26 150 E5
Wix Rd DAGW RM9 79 K7
Wix's La CLAP SW4 129 G3
Woburn WEA * W13 85 H4
Woburn Av HCH RM12 81 J3
Woburn Cl BUSH WD23 22 C5
WIM/MER SW19 147 G5
Woburn Pl STPAN WC1H 5 J9
Woburn Rd CAR SM5 162 D7
CROY/NA CR0 164 D7
Woburn Sq STPAN WC1H 11 H1
Woburn Wk STPAN WC1H 5 H8
Wodehouse Av PECK SE15 111 G7
Wodehouse Rd DART DA1 139 K3
Woffington Cl
E/WMO/HCT KT8 143 J7
Woking Cl PUT/ROE SW15 126 C3
Woldham Pl HAYES BR2 168 B3
Woldham Rd HAYES BR2 168 B3
Wolfe Cl HAYES BR2 167 K5
YEAD UB4 83 F2
Wolfe Crs CHARL SE7 114 C4
Wolferton Rd MNPK E12 77 K3
Wolfington Rd WNWD SE27 149 H3
Wolfram Cl LEW SE13 133 H4
Wolftencroft Cl BTSEA SW11 128 D2
Wollaston Cl WALW SE17 18 D6
Wolmer Cl EDGW HA8 36 C3
Wolmer Gdns EDGW HA8 36 C2
Wolseley Av WAND/EARL SW18 146 E1
Wolseley Gdns CHSWK W4 105 J5
Wolseley Rd CEND/HSY/T N8 54 D5
CHSWK W4 105 K3
FSTGT E7 77 F6
KTN/HRWW/W HA3 48 E2
MTCM CR4 163 F6
ROMW/RG RM7 63 F6
WDGN N22 41 F7
Wolseley St STHWK SE1 19 M2
Wolsey Av EHAM E6 96 A2
WALTH E17 57 H2
Wolsey Cl HSLW TW3 123 H3
KUTN/CMB KT2 144 D7
NWDGN UB2 103 H2
RYNPK SW20 145 K6
WPK KT4 173 J3
Wolsey Ct ELTH/MOT * SE9 134 E5
Wolsey Crs CROY/NA CR0 180 A7
MRDN SM4 161 J6
Wolsey Dr KUTN/CMB KT2 144 A4
WOT/HER KT12 156 C7
Wolsey Gv EDGW HA8 37 F6
ESH/CLAY KT10 170 B3
Wolsey Ms KTTN NW5 72 C5
Wolsey Rd E/WMO/HCT KT8 157 J3
EN EN1 30 D1
ESH/CLAY KT10 170 B3
HPTN TW12 142 B5
IS N1 73 K4
RKW/CH/CXG WD3 32 A1
SUN TW16 140 D6
Wolsey St WCHPL E1 92 E4
Wolsey Wy CHSGTN KT9 172 C4
Wolstonbury NFNCH/WDSP N12 38 E4
Wolvercote Rd ABYW SE2 116 E1
Wolverley St BETH * E2 92 D2
Wolverton Av KUTN/CMB KT2 144 C7
Wolverton Gdns EA W5 86 B6
HMSMTH W6 107 G3
Wolverton Rd STAN HA7 35 H5
Wolverton Wy STHGT/OAK N14 28 C4
Wolves La WDGN N22 41 G6
Womersley Rd CEND/HSY/T N8 55 F5
Wonersh Wy BELMT SM2 174 B7
Wonford Cl NWMAL KT3 145 G7
Wontner Cl IS N1 6 E2
Wontner Rd BAL SW12 147 K1
Woodall Cl CHSGTN KT9 171 J6
Woodall Rd PEND EN3 31 F5
Woodbank Rd BMLY BR1 152 D2
Woodbastwick Rd SYD SE26 151 F5
Woodberry Av
RYLN/HDSTN HA2 48 C3
WCHMH N21 41 G1
Woodberry Cl SUN TW16 140 E5
Woodberry Crs MUSWH N10 54 B2
Woodberry Down FSBYPK N4 55 J7
Woodberry Gdns
NFNCH/WDSP N12 39 G5
Woodberry Gv FSBYPK N4 55 J6
NFNCH/WDSP N12 39 G5
Woodberry Wy
NFNCH/WDSP N12 39 G5
Woodbine Cl WHTN TW2 142 D1
Woodbine Gv PGE/AN SE20 150 D6
Woodbine La WPK KT4 173 K2
Woodbine Pl WAN E11 58 E5
Woodbine Rd BFN/LL DA15 135 K7
Woodbines Av KUT KT1 158 E2
Woodbine Ter HOM E9 74 E5
Woodborough Rd
PUT/ROE SW15 126 E3
Woodbourne Av
STRHM/NOR SW16 148 D2
Woodbourne Dr
ESH/CLAY KT10 171 F5
Woodbourne Gdns
WLGTN SM6 176 B6
Woodbridge Cl HOLWY N7 73 F1
Woodbridge Rd BARK IG11 79 F4
Woodbridge St CLKNW EC1R 6 C9
Woodbrook Rd ABYW SE2 116 B5
Woodburn Cl HDN NW4 52 B4
Woodbury Cl CROY/NA CR0 178 B1
WAN E11 59 F3
Woodbury Park Rd WEA W13 85 H3
Woodbury Rd WALTH E17 57 K3
Woodbury St TOOT SW17 147 J4
Woodchester Sq BAY/PAD W2 8 C2
Woodchurch Cl BFN/LL DA15 154 D2
Woodchurch Dr BMLY BR1 153 H6
Woodchurch Rd
KIL/WHAMP NW6 2 B2
Wood Cl BETH E2 92 C3
CDALE/KGS NW9 51 F6
HRW HA1 48 D6
Woodclyffe Dr CHST BR7 169 F1
Woodcock Ct
KTN/HRWW/W HA3 50 A6
Woodcock Dell Av
KTN/HRWW/W HA3 49 J6
Woodcock Hl
KTN/HRWW/W HA3 49 J4
Woodcocks CAN/RD E16 95 G4
Woodcombe Crs FSTH SE23 131 K7
Woodcot Cl ED N9 30 E5
Woodcote Av HCH RM12 81 J3
MLHL NW7 38 A5
THHTH CR7 164 C3
WLGTN SM6 176 B7
Woodcote Cl KUTN/CMB KT2 144 B4
Woodcote Dr ORP BR6 169 J6
Woodcote Gn WLGTN SM6 176 C7
Woodcote Ms WLGTN SM6 176 B5
Woodcote Pl WNWD * SE27 149 H4
Woodcote Rd WAN E11 58 E6
WLGTN SM6 176 B5
Wood Crest BELMT * SM2 175 G6
Woodcroft ELTH/MOT SE9 153 K2
GFD/PVL UB6 67 G5
WCHMH N21 29 F7
Woodcroft Av MLHL NW7 37 G6
STAN HA7 35 G7
Woodcroft Ms DEPT SE8 112 B3
Woodcroft Rd THHTH CR7 164 C4
Wood Dene PECK * SE15 111 J7
Wood Dr CHST BR7 153 J5
Wooden Bridge Ter
WNWD * SE27 149 H2
The Wood End WLGTN SM6 176 B7
Woodend ESH/CLAY KT10 170 C1
Wood End HYS/HAR UB3 82 C5
Woodend NRWD SE19 149 J5
SUT SM1 175 G1
Wood End Av RYLN/HDSTN HA2 66 B3
Wood End Cl NTHLT UB5 66 D4
Woodend Gdns ENC/FH EN2 28 E3
Wood End Gdns NTHLT UB5 66 C4
Wood End Gn YEAD UB4 82 D4
Wood End Green Rd
HYS/HAR UB3 82 B4
Wood End La NTHLT UB5 66 B5
Wood End Rd HRW HA1 66 D3
Woodend Rd WALTH E17 58 A1
Wood End Wy NTHLT UB5 66 C4
Wooder Gdns FSTGT E7 76 D3
Wooderson Cl SNWD SE25 165 F3
Woodfall Av BAR EN5 26 D4
Woodfall Dr DART DA1 138 C3
Woodfall Rd FSBYPK N4 55 G7
Woodfall St CHEL SW3 15 L8
Woodfarrs CMBW SE5 130 E3
Wood Fld HAMP * NW3 71 K4
Woodfield Av ALP/SUD HA0 67 J2
CAR SM5 176 A5
CDALE/KGS NW9 51 G3
EA W5 85 J3
NTHWD HA6 32 C3
STRHM/NOR SW16 148 D2
Woodfield Cl EN EN1 30 A3
NRWD SE19 149 J6
Woodfield Crs EA W5 85 K3
Woodfield Dr EBAR EN4 28 A7
GPK RM2 63 J3
Woodfield Gdns NWMAL KT3 160 C4
Woodfield Gv
STRHM/NOR SW16 148 D2
Woodfield Pl MV/WKIL W9 88 D4
Woodfield Ri BUSH WD23 22 D6
Woodfield Rd EA W5 85 J3
ESH/CLAY KT10 171 F1
HSLWW TW4 122 A1
MV/WKIL W9 88 D4
Woodfields WATW * WD18 21 G3
Woodfield Wy FBAR/BDGN N11 40 D6
Woodford Av GNTH/NBYPK IG2 59 K4
Woodford Bridge Rd REDBR IG4 59 H2
Woodford Crs PIN HA5 47 F1
Woodford New Rd WALTH E17 58 C3
WFD IG8 44 D6
Woodford Pl WBLY HA9 50 A7
Woodford Rd FSTGT E7 77 F3
SWFD E18 58 E3
WAT WD17 21 F1
Woodgate Av CHSGTN KT9 171 K4
Woodgate Crs NTHWD HA6 32 E5
Woodgate Dr
STRHM/NOR SW16 148 D6
Woodger Rd SHB W12 107 F1
Woodget Cl EHAM E6 95 J5
Woodgrange Av EA W5 86 B7
EN EN1 30 C5
KTN/HRWW/W HA3 49 J4
NFNCH/WDSP N12 39 H5
Woodgrange Cl
KTN/HRWW/W HA3 49 K4
Woodgrange Gdns EN EN1 30 C5
Woodgrange Ter EN * EN1 30 C5
Woodgrave Rd FSTGT E7 76 E4
Woodhall Av DUL SE21 150 B2
PIN HA5 33 J7
Woodhall Dr DUL SE21 150 B2
PIN HA5 33 H7
Woodhall Ga PIN HA5 33 H6
Woodhall La OXHEY WD19 33 H2
Woodham Ct SWFD E18 58 D3
Woodham Rd CAT SE6 152 A2
Woodhatch Cl EHAM E6 95 J4
Woodhaven Gdns BARK/HLT IG6 60 C3
Woodhayes Rd RYNPK SW20 146 A6
Woodheyes Rd WLSDN NW10 69 G4
Woodhill WOOL/PLUM SE18 114 D3
Woodhill Crs
KTN/HRWW/W HA3 49 K5
Woodhouse Av GFD/PVL UB6 85 F1
Woodhouse Cl GFD/PVL UB6 85 F1
HYS/HAR UB3 101 H2
Woodhouse Eaves NTHWD HA6 32 E4
Woodhouse Gv MNPK E12 77 J5
Woodhouse Rd
NFNCH/WDSP N12 39 G5
WAN E11 76 D2
Woodhurst Av STMC/STPC BR5 169 H5
Woodhurst Rd ABYW SE2 116 B4
ACT W3 86 E7
Woodington Cl ELTH/MOT SE9 135 F5
Woodison St BOW E3 93 G3
Woodknoll Dr CHST BR7 153 K7
Woodland Ap GFD/PVL UB6 67 G5
Woodland Cl CDALE/KGS NW9 50 E5
HOR/WEW * KT19 173 G5
NRWD SE19 150 A5
WFD IG8 45 F2
Woodland Ct GLDGN * NW11 52 C4
Woodland Crs GNWCH SE10 113 H5
Woodland Gdns ISLW TW7 123 K2
MUSWH N10 54 B4
Woodland Hl NRWD SE19 150 A5
Woodland Ri GFD/PVL UB6 67 G5
MUSWH N10 54 B3
Woodland Rd FBAR/BDGN N11 40 B4
NRWD SE19 150 A4
THHTH CR7 164 B3
The Woodlands CMBW * SE5 110 C6
ESH/CLAY KT10 170 C1
HRW * HA1 66 E1
ISLW TW7 124 A1
LEW SE13 133 G6
NRWD SE19 149 J6
STAN * HA7 35 H4
STHGT/OAK N14 28 B7
WLGTN SM6 176 B7
Woodlands GLDGN NW11 52 C4
RYLN/HDSTN HA2 48 A3
RYNPK SW20 161 F3
Woodlands Av ACT W3 86 D7
BFN/LL DA15 135 K7
CHDH RM6 62 A5
FNCH N3 39 G6
NWMAL KT3 145 F7
RSLP HA4 47 G7
WAN E11 59 F7
WPK KT4 173 H1
Woodlands Cl BMLY BR1 168 E1
BORE WD6 24 D3
ESH/CLAY KT10 171 F6
GLDGN NW11 52 C4
Woodlands Dr STAN HA7 35 F5
SUN TW16 156 B1
Woodlands Gdns WALTH * E17 58 C3
Woodlands Gv GNWCH SE10 113 H4
ISLW TW7 123 K1
Woodlands Pde ASHF TW15 140 A5
Woodlands Park Rd
BKHTH/KID SE3 113 H5
SEVS/STOTM N15 55 J4
Woodlands Rd BARN SW13 126 C2
BMLY BR1 168 E1
BUSH WD23 21 J3
BXLYHN DA7 137 F2
ED N9 30 E7
HRW HA1 49 F4
IL IG1 78 C2
ISLW TW7 123 K2
ROM RM1 63 H2
STHL UB1 83 H7
SURB KT6 158 E6
WALTH E17 58 A2
WAN * E11 76 C1
Woodlands St LEW SE13 133 G6
Woodland St HACK * E8 74 B5
Woodlands Wy PUT/ROE SW15 127 J4
Woodland Ter CHARL SE7 114 D3
Woodland Wk HAMP NW3 71 J4
HOR/WEW KT19 172 C5
Woodland Wy ABYW SE2 116 E3
BRYLDS KT5 172 D1
CROY/NA CR0 166 B7
MLHL NW7 37 G5
MRDN SM4 161 J3
MTCM CR4 148 A6
STMC/STPC BR5 169 H3
WCHMH N21 41 G1
WFD IG8 45 F2
WWKM BR4 180 A2
Wood La CDALE/KGS NW9 51 F6
DAGE RM10 80 C1
HCH RM12 81 J4
HGT N6 54 B5
ISLW TW7 103 K5
RSLP HA4 64 C1
SHB W12 88 A5
STAN HA7 35 H2
WFD IG8 44 D4
Woodlawn Cl PUT/ROE SW15 127 J4
Woodlawn Crs WHTN TW2 142 B1
Woodlawn Dr FELT TW13 141 H1
Woodlawn Rd FUL/PGN SW6 107 G6
Woodlea Dr HAYES BR2 167 H4
Woodlea Gv NTHWD HA6 32 A5

Woodlea Rd STNW/STAM N16 ....74 A2
Woodleigh Av
NFNCH/WDSP N12 ....39 J5
Woodleigh Gdns
STRHM/NOR SW16 ....148 E2
Woodley Cl TOOT SW17 ....147 K6
Woodley La SUT SM1 ....175 J2
Wood Lodge Gdns BMLY BR1 ....153 J6
Wood Lodge La WWKM BR4 ....180 A2
Woodmans Gv WLSDN NW10 ....69 H4
Woodmansterne Rd
STRHM/NOR SW16 ....148 C6
Woodman St CAN/RD E16 ....96 A7
Woodmans Yd WAT WD17 ....21 G3
Wood Md TOTM * N17 ....42 C5
Woodmere ELTH/MOT SE9 ....134 E6
Woodmere Av CROY/NA CR0 ....166 A6
Woodmere Cl BTSEA SW11 ....129 F2
CROY/NA CR0 ....166 A6
Woodmere Gdns
CROY/NA CR0 ....166 A6
Woodmere Wy BECK BR3 ....167 G4
Woodnook Rd
STRHM/NOR SW16 ....148 B4
Woodpecker Cl BUSH WD23 ....22 C7
ED N9 ....30 D5
KTN/HRWW/W HA3 ....35 F7
Woodpecker Ms LEW SE13 ....133 G3
Woodpecker Mt
CROY/NA CR0 ....179 G7
Woodpecker Rd THMD SE28 ....97 J6
Woodquest Av HNHL SE24 ....130 C4
Wood Ride STMC/STPC BR5 ....169 J3
Woodridge Wy NTHWD HA6 ....32 C5
Woodridings Av PIN HA5 ....33 K7
Woodridings Cl PIN HA5 ....33 K6
Woodriffe Rd WAN E11 ....58 B6
Wood Ri PIN HA5 ....46 E4
Woodrow WOOL/PLUM SE18 ....114 D3
Woodrow Av YEAD UB4 ....82 D4
Woodrow Cl GFD/PVL UB6 ....67 H6
Woodrow Ct TOTM N17 ....42 D6
Woodrush Cl NWCR SE14 ....112 B6
Woodrush Wy CHDH RM6 ....61 K3
The Woods NTHWD HA6 ....32 E4
Woodseer St WCHPL E1 ....13 M2
Woodsford Sq WKENS W14 ....107 H1
Woodshire Rd DAGE RM10 ....80 E2
Woodshots Meadow
WATW WD18 ....20 B4
Woodside BKHH IG9 ....45 G1
BORE WD6 ....24 B3
GLDGN NW11 ....52 E4
WIM/MER SW19 ....146 D4
Woodside Av ALP/SUD HA0 ....68 A7
CHST BR7 ....154 C4
ESH/CLAY KT10 ....157 K6
HGT N6 ....53 K4
NFNCH/WDSP N12 ....39 G3
SNWD SE25 ....165 J5
Woodside Cl ALP/SUD HA0 ....68 A7
BRYLDS KT5 ....159 K6
BXLYHN DA7 ....138 A3
RSLP HA4 ....46 B5
STAN HA7 ....35 G4
Woodside Ct EA * W5 ....86 A7
Woodside Court Rd
CROY/NA CR0 ....165 H6
Woodside Crs BFN/LL DA15 ....154 E2
Woodside End ALP/SUD HA0 ....68 A7
Woodside Gdns CHING E4 ....43 K4
TOTM N17 ....56 B1
Woodside Grange Rd
NFNCH/WDSP N12 ....39 F3
Woodside Gn CROY/NA CR0 ....165 H6
Woodside Gv NFNCH/WDSP N12 ....39 G2
Woodside La BXLY DA5 ....136 E5
NFNCH/WDSP N12 ....39 F2
Woodside Pde BFN/LL * DA15 ....154 E2
Woodside Pk SNWD SE25 ....165 H5
Woodside Park Av WALTH E17 ....58 B3
Woodside Park Rd
NFNCH/WDSP N12 ....39 F3
Woodside Pl ALP/SUD HA0 ....68 A7
Woodside Rd BFN/LL DA15 ....154 E2
BMLY BR1 ....168 D4
BXLYHN DA7 ....138 A3
KUTN/CMB KT2 ....144 A6
NTHWD HA6 ....32 D6
NWMAL KT3 ....160 A1
PLSTW E13 ....95 G3
SNWD SE25 ....165 J5
SUT SM1 ....175 G2
WDGN N22 ....41 G6
WFD IG8 ....44 E3
Woodside Wy CROY/NA CR0 ....165 K5
MTCM CR4 ....148 B7
Wood's Ms MYFR/PKLN W1K 9 M6
Woodsome Rd KTTN NW5 ....72 A2
Wood's Pl STHWK SE1 ....19 K4
Woodspring Rd
WIM/MER SW19 ....146 C1
Wood's Rd PECK SE15 ....111 J7
Woodstead Gv EDGW HA8 ....36 A5
Woodstock Av CHEAM SM3 ....161 J6
GLDGN NW11 ....52 C6
HNWL W7 ....104 B2
ISLW TW7 ....124 B4
STHL UB1 ....83 K2
Woodstock Cl BXLY DA5 ....137 G7
STAN HA7 ....50 A1
Woodstock Crs ED N9 ....30 D5
Woodstock Gdns BECK BR3 ....151 K7
GDMY/SEVK IG3 ....79 G1
YEAD UB4 ....82 D4
Woodstock Gra EA * W5 ....86 A7
Woodstock Gv SHB W12 ....107 G1
Woodstock La North SURB KT6 ....171 J1
Woodstock La South
ESH/CLAY KT10 ....171 H4
Woodstock Ms
CAVSQ/HST W1G 10 B3
Woodstock Ri CHEAM SM3 ....161 J7
Woodstock Rd ALP/SUD HA0 ....68 B6
BUSH WD23 ....22 E6
CAR SM5 ....176 A4
CHSWK W4 ....106 B3
CROY/NA CR0 ....177 K2
FSBYPK N4 ....55 G7
FSTGT E7 ....77 G6
GLDGN NW11 ....52 D6
WALTH E17 ....58 B1
Woodstock St CAN/RD E16 ....94 D5
MYFR/PKLN W1K 10 C5
Woodstock Ter POP/IOD E14 ....93 K6
Woodstock Wy MTCM CR4 ....163 H1
Woodstone Av EW KT17 ....173 J4
Wood St BAR EN5 ....26 A3
CAN/RD E16 ....95 F6
CHSWK W4 ....106 B4
CITYW EC2V 12 F4
KUT KT1 ....143 K7
MTCM CR4 ....163 F6
WALTH E17 ....58 A2
Woodsyre SYD SE26 ....150 B3
Wood Ter CRICK * NW2 ....69 H1
Woodthorpe Rd
PUT/ROE SW15 ....126 E3
Woodtree Cl HDN NW4 ....52 A1
Wood V FSTH SE23 ....131 J7
MUSWH N10 ....54 C4
Woodvale Av SNWD SE25 ....165 G2
Woodvale Wy CRICK NW2 ....70 B2
Woodview Av CHING E4 ....44 A3
Woodview Cl KUTN/CMB KT2 ....145 F3
Woodville Cl LEE/GVPK SE12 ....133 K4
TEDD TW11 ....143 G3
Woodville Court Ms
WAT * WD17 ....20 E1
Woodville Gdns BARK/HLT IG6 ....60 B2
EA W5 ....86 A5
RSLP HA4 ....46 A6
SURB * KT6 ....158 E6
Woodville Gv WELL * DA16 ....136 B2
Woodville Rd BAR EN5 ....27 F2
EA W5 ....86 A5
GLDGN NW11 ....52 C6
KIL/WHAMP * NW6 ....88 D1
MRDN SM4 ....161 K3
RCHPK/HAM TW10 ....143 H2
STNW/STAM N16 ....74 A4
SWFD E18 ....59 F1
THHTH CR7 ....164 E2
WALTH E17 ....57 G3
WAN E11 ....58 D7
Woodville St
WOOL/PLUM SE18 ....114 D3
Woodward Av HDN NW4 ....51 J4
Woodward Cl ESH/CLAY KT10 ....171 F5
Woodwarde Rd EDUL SE22 ....131 F5
Woodward Gdns DAGW RM9 ....79 J6
STAN HA7 ....35 F6
Woodward Rd DAGW RM9 ....79 H6
Woodway Crs HRW HA1 ....49 G5
Woodwaye OXHEY WD19 ....21 G6
Woodwell St
WAND/EARL SW18 ....128 B4
Wood Whf GNWCH SE10 ....112 E5
Woodyard Cl KTTN NW5 ....72 A4
Woodyard La DUL SE21 ....131 F6
Woodyates Rd LEE/GVPK SE12 ....133 K5
Woolacombe Rd
BKHTH/KID SE3 ....134 B1
Woolacombe Wy
HYS/HAR UB3 ....101 H3
Woolands Rd WAN E11 ....76 C1
Woolbrook Rd DART DA1 ....138 B5
Wooler St WALW SE17 ....19 G8
Woolf Cl THMD SE28 ....97 H7
Woolf Ms STPAN WC1H 5 J9
Woollaston Rd FSBYPK N4 ....55 H5
Woollett Cl DART DA1 ....138 D3
Woolmead Av CDALE/KGS NW9 ....51 J6
Woolmerdine Ct BUSH WD23 ....21 H2
Woolmer Gdns UED N18 ....42 C5
Woolmer Rd UED N18 ....42 C4
Woolmore St POP/IOD E14 ....94 A6
Woolneigh St FUL/PGN SW6 ....128 A2
Woolridge Wy HOM * E9 ....74 E6
Wool Rd RYNPK SW20 ....145 K5
Woolstaplers Wy
BERM/RHTH SE16 ....111 H2
Woolston Cl WALTH E17 ....57 F1
Woolstone Rd FSTH SE23 ....151 G1
Woolwich Church St
CHARL SE7 ....114 C3
Woolwich Common
WOOL/PLUM SE18 ....115 F5
Woolwich High St
WOOL/PLUM SE18 ....115 F2
Woolwich Manor Wy
CAN/RD E16 ....96 B7
Woolwich Manorway
CAN/RD E16 ....115 G1
Woolwich Manor Wy EHAM E6 ....95 K3
Woolwich New Rd
WOOL/PLUM SE18 ....115 F5
Woolwich Rd ABYW SE2 ....116 E5
BXLYHN DA7 ....137 H2
GNWCH SE10 ....113 K4
Wooster Gdns POP/IOD E14 ....94 B5
Wootton Gv FNCH N3 ....38 E7
Wootton St STHWK SE1 ....18 B1
Worbeck Rd PGE/AN SE20 ....165 J1
Worcester Av TOTM N17 ....42 C6
Worcester Cl CRICK NW2 ....69 J2
CROY/NA CR0 ....179 H1
MTCM CR4 ....163 F1
Worcester Crs MLHL NW7 ....37 G2
WFD IG8 ....45 F4
Worcester Dr CHSWK W4 ....106 B2
Worcester Gdns GFD/PVL UB6 ....66 C5
IL IG1 ....59 J6
WPK KT4 ....173 G2
Worcester Ms
KIL/WHAMP NW6 ....71 F5
Worcester Park Rd WPK KT4 ....172 E2
Worcester Rd BELMT SM2 ....174 E6
MNPK E12 ....77 K2
WALTH E17 ....57 F1
WIM/MER SW19 ....146 D4
Wordsworth Av GFD/PVL UB6 ....84 D1
MNPK E12 ....77 J6
SWFD E18 ....58 D2
Wordsworth Dr CHEAM SM3 ....174 A3
Wordsworth Pde
CEND/HSY/T * N8 ....55 H3
Wordsworth Pl HAMP NW3 ....71 K4
Wordsworth Rd FELT TW13 ....141 K3
PGE/AN SE20 ....151 F6
STHWK SE1 ....19 L6
STNW/STAM N16 ....74 A3
WELL DA16 ....115 K7
WLGTN SM6 ....176 C5
Wordsworth Wk GLDGN NW11 ....52 D3
Wordsworth Wy DART DA1 ....139 K3
WDR/YW UB7 ....100 B3
Worfield St BTSEA SW11 ....108 D6
Worgan St BERM/RHTH SE16 ....112 A2
LBTH SE11 ....17 L7
Worland Rd SRTFD E15 ....76 C6
Worlds End Est WBPTN * SW10 ....108 C6
World's End La WCHMH N21 ....29 F4
Worlds End Pas WBPTN * SW10 ....108 C6
Worlidge St HMSMTH W6 ....107 F4
Worlingham Rd EDUL SE22 ....131 G3
Wormholt Rd SHB W12 ....87 J7
Wormholt Ter SHB * W12 ....87 J7
Wormwood St LVPST EC2M 13 J4
Wornington Rd NKENS W10 ....88 C4
Woronzow Rd STJWD NW8 ....3 H4
Worple Av ISLW TW7 ....124 B4
WIM/MER SW19 ....146 B6
Worple Cl RYLN/HDSTN HA2 ....47 K7
Worple Rd ISLW TW7 ....124 B3
RYNPK SW20 ....161 F1
Worple Road Ms
WIM/MER SW19 ....146 D5
Worple St MORT/ESHN SW14 ....126 A2
Worple Wy RCHPK/HAM TW10 ....125 F4
RYLN/HDSTN HA2 ....47 K7
Worship St SDTCH EC2A 13 H1
Worslade Rd TOOT SW17 ....147 H3
Worsley Bridge Rd CAT SE6 ....151 H4
Worsley Gv CLPT E5 ....74 C3
Worsley Rd WAN E11 ....76 C3
Worsopp Dr CLAP SW4 ....129 H4
Worthfield Cl HOR/WEW KT19 ....173 F6
Worth Gv WALW SE17 ....19 G8
Worthing Cl SRTFD E15 ....76 C7
Worthing Rd HEST TW5 ....102 E5
Worthington Cl MTCM CR4 ....163 G3
Worthington Rd SURB KT6 ....159 G7
Wortley Rd CROY/NA CR0 ....164 B6
EHAM E6 ....77 H6
Worton Gdns ISLW TW7 ....123 J1
Worton Rd ISLW TW7 ....124 A2
Worton Wy ISLW TW7 ....123 J1
Wotton Rd CRICK NW2 ....70 A3
Wouldham Rd CAN/RD E16 ....94 D5
Wragby Rd WAN * E11 ....76 C2
Wrampling Pl ED N9 ....42 C1
Wray Av CLAY IG5 ....60 A2
Wray Crs FSBYPK N4 ....72 E1
Wrayfield Rd CHEAM SM3 ....174 B2
Wray Rd BELMT SM2 ....174 D7
Wraysbury Cl HSLWW TW4 ....122 D4
Wrays Wy YEAD UB4 ....82 C4
Wrekin Rd WOOL/PLUM SE18 ....115 H6
Wren Av CRICK NW2 ....70 A3
NWDGN UB2 ....102 E3
Wren Cl CAN/RD E16 ....94 D5
ED N9 ....31 F7
Wren Crs BUSH WD23 ....22 C7
Wren Dr WDR/YW UB7 ....100 A2
Wren Gdns DAGW RM9 ....79 K4
HCH RM12 ....63 H7
Wren Ms LEW * SE13 ....133 H3
Wren Rd CMBW SE5 ....110 E7
DAGW RM9 ....79 K4
SCUP DA14 ....155 J2
Wren's Av ASHF TW15 ....140 A4
Wren St FSBYW WC1X 5 M9
Wrentham Av WLSDN NW10 ....88 B1
Wrenthorpe Rd BMLY BR1 ....152 C3
Wrenwood Wy PIN HA5 ....47 F3
Wrexham Rd BOW E3 ....93 J1
Wricklemarsh Rd
BKHTH/KID SE3 ....134 A1
Wrigglesworth St NWCR SE14 ....112 A6
Wright Cl LEW SE13 ....133 G3
Wright Rd HEST TW5 ....102 B6
Wrights Cl DAGE RM10 ....80 D3
Wright's La KENS W8 ....14 C3
Wrights Pl WLSDN * NW10 ....68 E5
Wright's Rd BOW E3 ....93 H1
SNWD SE25 ....165 F2
Wright's Rw CAR SM5 ....176 B3
Wrigley Cl CHING * E4 ....44 B4
Wrotham Rd BAR EN5 ....26 C1
CAMTN NW1 ....4 F2
WEA W13 ....85 J7
WELL DA16 ....116 D7
Wrottesley Rd WLSDN NW10 ....87 K1
WOOL/PLUM SE18 ....115 H5
Wroughton Rd BTSEA SW11 ....128 E5
Wroughton Ter HDN * NW4 ....51 K3
Wroxall Rd DAGW RM9 ....79 J5
Wroxham Gdns
FBAR/BDGN N11 ....40 C6
Wroxham Rd THMD SE28 ....97 K6
Wroxton Rd PECK SE15 ....131 J1
Wrythe Gn CAR SM5 ....175 K2
Wrythe Green Rd CAR SM5 ....175 K2
Wrythe La CAR SM5 ....162 C7
Wulfstan St SHB W12 ....87 H5
Wyatt Cl BUSH WD23 ....22 E6
FELT TW13 ....122 C7
YEAD UB4 ....82 E4
Wyatt Dr BARN SW13 ....106 E5
Wyatt Park Rd
BRXS/STRHM SW2 ....149 F1
Wyatt Rd DART DA1 ....138 C2
FSTGT E7 ....76 E5
HBRY N5 ....73 J2
Wyatt's La WALTH E17 ....58 A2
Wybert St CAMTN NW1 ....4 D9
Wyborne Wy WLSDN NW10 ....68 E6
Wyburn Av BAR EN5 ....26 D2
Wychcombe Studios
HAMP * NW3 ....71 K5
Wyche Gv SAND/SEL CR2 ....177 J6
Wycherley Cl BKHTH/KID SE3 ....113 J6
Wycherley Crs BAR EN5 ....27 F5
Wychwood Av EDGW HA8 ....35 K5
THHTH CR7 ....164 C2
Wychwood Cl EDGW HA8 ....35 K5
SUN TW16 ....140 E5
Wychwood End HGT N6 ....54 C6
Wychwood Gdns CLAY IG5 ....59 K3
Wychwood Wy NTHWD HA6 ....32 D6
Wycliffe Cl WELL DA16 ....116 A7
Wycliffe Rd BTSEA SW11 ....129 F1
WIM/MER SW19 ....147 F5
Wyclif St FSBYE EC1V 6 C8
Wycombe Gdns CRICK NW2 ....70 D1
Wycombe Pl
WAND/EARL SW18 ....128 B5
Wycombe Rd ALP/SUD HA0 ....68 C7
GNTH/NBYPK IG2 ....59 K4
TOTM N17 ....42 C7
Wydell Cl MRDN SM4 ....161 F5
Wydenhurst Rd CROY/NA CR0 ....165 H6
Wydeville Manor Rd
LEE/GVPK SE12 ....153 F3
Wye Cl RSLP HA4 ....46 A5
Wyemead Crs CHING E4 ....44 C1
Wye St BTSEA SW11 ....128 C2
Wyevale Cl PIN HA5 ....46 E2
Wyfold Rd FUL/PGN SW6 ....107 H7
Wyke Cl ISLW TW7 ....104 A5
Wyke Gdns HNWL W7 ....104 A2
Wykeham Av DAGW RM9 ....79 J5
Wykeham Cl WDR/YW UB7 ....100 D5
Wykeham Gn DAGW RM9 ....79 J5
Wykeham Hl WBLY HA9 ....50 B7
Wykeham Ri TRDG/WHET N20 ....26 C7
Wykeham Rd HDN NW4 ....52 A4
KTN/HRWW/W HA3 ....49 H3
Wyke Rd BOW E3 ....75 J6
RYNPK SW20 ....161 F1
Wylchin Cl PIN HA5 ....46 D3
Wyldes Cl GLDGN NW11 ....53 G7
Wyldfield Gdns ED N9 ....42 B1
Wyld Wy WBLY HA9 ....68 D5
Wyleu St FSTH SE23 ....132 B6
Wylie Rd NWDGN UB2 ....103 F2
Wyllen Cl WCHPL E1 ....92 E3
Wylo Dr BAR EN5 ....25 J5
Wymark Cl RAIN RM13 ....99 H1
Wymering Rd MV/WKIL W9 ....2 B8
Wymond St PUT/ROE SW15 ....127 F2
Wynan Rd POP/IOD E14 ....112 E4
Wynaud Ct WDGN N22 ....41 F5
Wyncham Av BFN/LL DA15 ....135 K7
Wynchgate
KTN/HRWW/W HA3 ....34 E6
STHGT/OAK N14 ....28 E6
Wyncote Wy SAND/SEL CR2 ....179 F7
Wyncroft Cl BMLY BR1 ....168 E2
Wyndale Av CDALE/KGS NW9 ....50 C5
Wyndcliff Rd CHARL SE7 ....114 A5
Wyndcroft Cl ENC/FH EN2 ....29 H2
Wyndham Cl BELMT SM2 ....174 E6
ORP BR6 ....169 H7
Wyndham Crs HSLWW TW4 ....122 E5
KTTN NW5 ....72 C2
Wyndham Est CMBW SE5 ....110 D6
Wyndham Ms MBLAR W1H 9 L3
Wyndham Pl MBLAR W1H 9 L3
Wyndham Rd CMBW SE5 ....110 D6
EBAR EN4 ....27 K7
EHAM E6 ....77 H6
KUTN/CMB KT2 ....144 B6
WEA W13 ....104 C2
Wyndham St MBLAR W1H 9 L2
Wyneham Rd HNHL SE24 ....130 E4
Wynell Rd FSTH SE23 ....151 F2
Wynford Pl BELV DA17 ....117 H5
Wynford Rd IS N1 ....5 L5
Wynford Wy ELTH/MOT SE9 ....153 K2
Wynlie Gdns PIN HA5 ....47 F1
Wynndale Rd SWFD E18 ....45 F7
Wynne Rd BRXN/ST SW9 ....130 B1
Wynn's Av BFN/LL DA15 ....136 B4
Wynnstay Gdns KENS W8 ....14 B3
Wynter St BTSEA SW11 ....128 B3
Wynton Gdns SNWD SE25 ....165 F4
Wynton Pl ACT W3 ....86 D5
Wynyard Ter LBTH SE11 ....17 M8
Wynyatt St FSBYE EC1V 6 C7
Wyre Gv EDGW HA8 ....36 E2
HYS/HAR UB3 ....101 K3
Wyresdale Crs GFD/PVL UB6 ....85 F2
Wyteleaf Cl RSLP HA4 ....46 A5
Wythburn Pl MBLAR W1H 9 L5
Wythenshawe Rd DAGE RM10 ....80 C2
Wythes Cl BMLY BR1 ....168 E1
Wythes Rd CAN/RD E16 ....95 J7
Wythfield Rd ELTH/MOT SE9 ....134 E5
Wyvenhoe Rd RYLN/HDSTN HA2 ....66 C2
Wyvern Cl DART DA1 ....139 F6
Wyvern Est NWMAL * KT3 ....160 D2
Wyvil Rd VX/NE SW8 ....109 K6
Wyvis St POP/IOD E14 ....93 K4

Y

Yabsley St POP/IOD E14 ....94 A7
Yalding Rd BERM/RHTH SE16 ....111 H2
Yale Cl HSLWW TW4 ....122 E4
Yale Wy HCH RM12 ....81 J3
Yarborough Rd WIM/MER SW19 ....147 H7
Yardley Cl CHING E4 ....31 K4
Yardley La CHING E4 ....31 K4
Yardley St FSBYW WC1X 6 A9
Yarmouth Crs TOTM N17 ....56 D4
Yarmouth Pl MYFR/PICC W1J 10 C9
Yarnton Wy ABYW SE2 ....116 D1
Yarrow Crs EHAM E6 ....95 J4
Yateley St WOOL/PLUM SE18 ....114 C2
Yeading Av RSLP HA4 ....65 J1
Yeading Fk YEAD UB4 ....83 G4
Yeading Gdns YEAD UB4 ....83 F4
Yeading La YEAD UB4 ....83 F5
Yeames Cl WEA W13 ....85 G5
Yeate St IS N1 ....7 G2
Yeatman Rd HGT N6 ....53 K5
Yeats Cl LEW * SE13 ....133 G1
WLSDN NW10 ....69 G5
Ye Cnr BUSH WD23 ....21 H5
Yeend Cl E/WMO/HCT KT8 ....157 F3
Yeldham Rd HMSMTH W6 ....107 G4
Yeldham Vls HMSMTH * W6 ....107 G4
Yelverton Rd BTSEA SW11 ....128 C1
Yenston Cl MRDN SM4 ....161 K5
Yeoman Cl EHAM E6 ....96 B6
Yeoman Rd NTHLT UB5 ....65 J6
Yeomans Acre RSLP HA4 ....46 E5
Yeoman's Rw CHEL SW3 ....15 K4
Yeoman St BERM/RHTH SE16 ....112 B3
Yeomans Wy PEND * EN3 ....30 D1
Yeo St BOW E3 ....93 K4
Yeovilton Pl KUTN/CMB KT2 ....143 K4
Yerbury Rd ARCH N19 ....72 D2
Yester Dr CHST BR7 ....153 J6
Yester Pk CHST BR7 ....153 K6
Yester Rd CHST BR7 ....153 K6
Yew Cl BKHH IG9 ....45 H1
Yewdale Cl BMLY BR1 ....152 C5
Yewfield Rd WLSDN NW10 ....69 H6
Yew Gv CRICK NW2 ....70 B3
Yewtree Cl RYLN/HDSTN HA2 ....48 B3
Yew Tree Cl WCHMH N21 ....29 G6
WELL DA16 ....116 B7
WPK KT4 ....160 B7
Yew Tree Ct BORE WD6 ....23 K5
Yew Tree Gdns CHDH RM6 ....62 A4
ROMW/RG RM7 ....63 F4
Yewtree Rd BECK BR3 ....166 C2
Yew Tree Rd SHB W12 ....87 H6
Yew Tree Wk HSLWW TW4 ....122 E4
Yew Wk HRW HA1 ....48 E7
Yoakley Rd STNW/STAM N16 ....74 A1
Yoke Cl HOLWY N7 ....72 E5
Yolande Gdns ELTH/MOT SE9 ....134 D4
Yonge Pk HOLWY N7 ....73 G2
York Av BFN/LL DA15 ....154 E1
HNWL W7 ....84 E7
HYS/HAR UB3 ....82 A5
KTN/HRWW/W HA3 ....35 H7
MORT/ESHN SW14 ....125 K4
York Br CAMTN NW1 ....4 A9
York Buildings CHCR WC2N 11 K7
York Cl CMBW * SE5 ....130 D1
EHAM E6 ....95 K5
HNWL W7 ....84 E7
MRDN SM4 ....162 A3
York Crs BORE WD6 ....25 F1
Yorke Ga WAT WD17 ....20 E1
York Ga CAMTN NW1 ....10 B1
STHGT/OAK N14 ....28 E6
York Gv PECK SE15 ....111 K7
York Hl STRHM/NOR SW16 ....149 H2
York House Pl KENS W8 ....14 C1
Yorkland Av WELL DA16 ....136 A3
York Ms IL IG1 ....78 A1
KTTN NW5 ....72 B4
York Pde BTFD * TW8 ....104 E4
CDALE/KGS * NW9 ....51 J5
York Pl BTSEA SW11 ....128 B2
IL IG1 ....78 A1
York Ri KTTN NW5 ....72 B2
ORP BR6 ....169 K7
York Rd ACT W3 ....86 E5
BAR EN5 ....27 G4
BELMT SM2 ....174 E5
BTFD TW8 ....104 E4
BTSEA SW11 ....128 B3
CHING E4 ....43 J4
CROY/NA CR0 ....164 B6
DART DA1 ....139 J6
EA W5 ....104 D2
FBAR/BDGN N11 ....40 D5
FSTGT E7 ....76 E5
HSLW TW3 ....123 G2
IL IG1 ....78 A2
KUTN/CMB KT2 ....144 B6
LEY E10 ....76 A2
NTHWD HA6 ....46 E1
RAIN RM13 ....81 F6
RCHPK/HAM TW10 ....125 G4
STHWK SE1 ....17 M1
TEDD TW11 ....142 E3
UED N18 ....42 D4
WALTH E17 ....57 F4
WATW WD18 ....21 G4
WCHMH N21 ....29 K6
WIM/MER SW19 ....147 F5
Yorkshire Cl STNW/STAM N16 ....74 A2
Yorkshire Gdns UED N18 ....42 D4
Yorkshire Grey Yd HHOL * WC1V 11 L3
Yorkshire Rd MTCM CR4 ....163 K4
POP/IOD E14 ....93 G5
York Sq POP/IOD * E14 ....93 G5
York St BARK IG11 ....78 B7
MHST W1U 9 M2
MTCM CR4 ....163 F6
TWK TW1 ....124 B7
York St Chambers MHST * W1U 9 M2
York Ter ERITH DA8 ....117 K7
York Ter East CAMTN NW1 ....10 B1
York Ter West CAMTN NW1 ....10 A1
Yorkton St BETH E2 ....92 C1
York Wy CHSGTN KT9 ....171 K6
FELT TW13 ....141 K2
IS N1 ....5 K5
TRDG/WHET N20 ....39 K2
York Way Ct IS N1 ....5 K4
York Way Est HOLWY N7 ....72 E5
Young Rd CAN/RD E16 ....95 G5
Youngs Rd GNTH/NBYPK IG2 ....60 D4
Young St KENS W8 ....14 C2
Yoxley Ap GNTH/NBYPK IG2 ....60 C5
Yoxley Dr GNTH/NBYPK IG2 ....60 C5
Yukon Rd BAL SW12 ....129 G6
Yuletide Cl WLSDN NW10 ....69 G5
Yunus Khan Cl WALTH E17 ....57 J4

Z

Zampa Rd BERM/RHTH SE16 ....111 K4
Zander Ct BETH E2 ....92 C2
Zangwill Rd BKHTH/KID SE3 ....114 C7
Zealand Av WDR/YW UB7 ....100 A6
Zealand Rd BOW E3 ....93 G1
Zennor Rd BAL SW12 ....129 H7
Zenoria St EDUL SE22 ....131 G3
Zermatt Rd THHTH CR7 ....164 D3
Zetland St POP/IOD E14 ....94 A4
Zion Pl THHTH CR7 ....164 E3
Zion Rd THHTH CR7 ....164 E3
Zoar St STHWK SE1 ....12 E8
Zoffany St ARCH N19 ....72 D1

AAIS
DART DA1 .... 139 H6
Aarotya Medical Centre
TOTM N17 .... 55 J3
Abbey Business Centre
VX/NE SW8 .... 109 H7
The Abbey Clinic
BELV DA17 .... 117 G4
Abbey Industrial Estate
ALP/SUD HA0 .... 68 B7
MTCM CR4 .... 162 E4
Abbey Medical Centre
STJWD NW8 .... 2 D4
Abbey Mills
WIM/MER SW19 .... 147 G7
Abbey Park Industrial Estate
BARK IG11 .... 96 B1
Abbey Primary School
ABYW SE2 .... 116 D2
Abbey (rems of)
ABYW SE2 .... 116 C5
Abbey Road Health Centre
SRTFD E15 .... 76 C7
Abbey School for the English Language
STJWD NW8 .... 2 F6
Abbey Sports Centre
BARK IG11 .... 78 C7
Abbey Trading Estate
SYD SE26 .... 151 G4
Abbey Tutorial College
BAY/PAD W2 .... 8 B5
Abbey Wharf Industrial Estate
BARK IG11 .... 96 D2
Abbey Wood School
ABYW SE2 .... 116 B2
Abbotsbury First School
MRDN SM4 .... 162 A4
ABC Cinema
CAT SE6 .... 132 E7
ESH/CLAY KT10 .... 170 B3
HAMP NW3 .... 71 J4
KUTN/CMB KT2 .... 159 F1
PUT/ROE SW15 .... 127 H2
STRHM/NOR SW16 .... 148 E1
Abercorn Place School
STJWD NW8 .... 2 F6
Abercorn Trading Estate
ALP/SUD HA0 .... 67 K7
Aberdeen Wharf
WAP E1W 92 D7
Aberglen Industrial Estate
HYS/HAR UB3 .... 101 G1
Abney Park Cemetery
STNW/STAM N16 .... 74 A1
Acacia Business Centre
WAN E11 .... 76 C2
Acland Burghley School
KTTN NW5 .... 72 B3
Acorn Industrial Park
DART DA1 .... 138 C5
Acre Road Health Clinic
KUTN/CMB KT2 .... 144 B6
Acton Business Centre
WLSDN NW10 .... 87 F3
Acton Central Industrial Estate
ACT W3 .... 86 D6
Acton Health Centre
ACT W3 .... 86 E7
Acton High School
ACT W3 .... 105 H1
Acton Hospital
ACT W3 .... 105 H1
Acton Lane Medical Centre
CHSWK W4 .... 106 A1
Acton Park Industrial Estate
ACT W3 .... 87 H7
CHSWK W4 .... 106 A1
Acton Superbowl
ACT W3 .... 86 C3
Acton Swimming Baths
ACT W3 .... 86 E7
Acumen (Anglo School)
NRWD SE19 .... 150 A6
Adams Bridge Business Centre
WBLY HA9 .... 68 D4
Adamsrill Primary School
FSTH SE23 .... 151 G2
Addey & Stanhope School
NWCR SE14 .... 112 C7
The Addington Golf Club
CROY/NA CR0 .... 179 H7
Addington Palace Golf Club
CROY/NA CR0 .... 179 G5
Addiscombe Cricket Club
CROY/NA CR0 .... 178 B2
Addison Primary School
WKENS W14 .... 107 G2
Adelphi Theatre
COVGDN WC2E 11 K7
Adler Industrial Estate
HYS/HAR UB3 .... 101 G1
Admiral Hyson Industrial Estate
BERM/RHTH SE16 .... 111 J3
Admiralty Arch
STJS SW1Y 11 H8
ADT Technology College
PUT/ROE SW15 .... 127 J4
The Adult College of Barking & Dagenham
BARK IG11 .... 78 E5
Adult Education Centre
DART DA1 .... 139 J6
POP/IOD E14 .... 113 F2
Africa Centre
COVGDN WC2E 11 K6
Agora Shopping Centre
PECK SE15 .... 131 H1
Ainslie Wood Primary School
CHING E4 .... 43 K4
Airbase Unity Elementary School
HGDN/ICK UB10 .... 64 A1
Airbus Coach Station
HTHAIR TW6 .... 120 C2
Air Call Business Centre
CDALE/KGS NW9 .... 51 F2
Airedale Physiotherapy Clinic
CHSWK W4 .... 106 C4
Airlinks Golf Club
NWDGN UB2 .... 102 B3
Air Links Industrial Estate
HEST TW5 .... 102 B4
Airport Gate Business Centre
WDR/YW UB7 .... 100 C6
Aksaray Sports Club
STNW/STAM N16 .... 73 K3
Albany Centre & Theatre
DEPT SE8 .... 112 C6
Albany Clinic
BFN/LL DA15 .... 155 G3
WIM/MER SW19 .... 147 F6
The Albany College
HDN NW4 .... 51 K4
Albany Park Canoe & Sailing Centre
KUTN/CMB KT2 .... 143 K5
The Albany School
HCH RM12 .... 81 K1
Albemarle Independant College
BAY/PAD W2 .... 8 D6
Albemarle Primary School
WIM/MER SW19 .... 146 C1
Albert Memorial
SKENS SW7 .... 15 G1
Albery Theatre
CHCR WC2N 11 J6
Albion Health Centre
WCHPL E1 .... 92 D4
Albion J & I School
BERM/RHTH SE16 .... 111 K1
Albion Street Health Centre
BERM/RHTH SE16 .... 111 K1
Albright Industrial Estate
RAIN RM13 .... 99 H4
The Alchemy Gallery
CLKNW EC1R 6 A9
Aldenham Country Park
BORE WD6 .... 23 H4
Aldenham School
BORE WD6 .... 23 F1
Alderbrook Primary School
BAL SW12 .... 129 G6
Aldersbrook County Secondary School
MNPK E12 .... 59 G7
Aldersbrook Primary School
WAN E11 .... 59 G7
Alderwood Primary School
ELTH/MOT SE9 .... 135 J5
Aldwych Theatre
HOL/ALD WC2B 11 L5
Alexander McLeod Primary School
ABYW SE2 .... 116 C4
Alexandra Avenue Clinic
RYLN/HDSTN HA2 .... 65 K1
Alexandra Business Centre
PEND EN3 .... 31 F3
Alexandra Infant School
KUTN/CMB KT2 .... 144 C6
PGE/AN SE20 .... 151 F6
Alexandra Junior School
HSLW TW3 .... 123 G1
SYD SE26 .... 151 F5
Alexandra Palace
WDGN N22 .... 54 D2
Alexandra Palace Ice Rink
WDGN N22 .... 54 D1
Alexandra Primary School
WDGN N22 .... 55 F1
Alexandra School
RYLN/HDSTN HA2 .... 65 K1
Alfred Mizen First School
MTCM CR4 .... 163 J2
Alfred Salter Primary School
BERM/RHTH SE16 .... 112 A1
Alfreds Way Industrial Estate
BARK IG11 .... 79 G7
Allegery Clinic
CAVSQ/HST W1G 10 C3
Allenby Infant School
STHL UB1 .... 84 A5
Allen Edwards Primary School
CLAP SW4 .... 109 K7
The All England Lawn Tennis & Croquet Club
WIM/MER SW19 .... 146 B2
Alleyns School
EDUL SE22 .... 131 F4
Allfarthing JMI School
WAND/EARL SW18 .... 128 B5
All Saints Benhilton School
SUT SM1 .... 175 F2
All Saints Catholic School
BCTR RM8 .... 62 C7
All Saints CE First School
WIM/MER SW19 .... 147 G6
All Saints CE Junior School
NRWD SE19 .... 150 A7
All Saints CE Primary School
BKHTH/KID SE3 .... 133 H1
CRICK NW2 .... 70 D2
FUL/PGN SW6 .... 127 H1
PUT/ROE SW15 .... 127 F2
TRDG/WHET N20 .... 39 H1
All Souls CE Primary School
GTPST W1W 10 E3
Allum Medical Centre
WAN E11 .... 58 B6
Alma Primary School
BERM/RHTH SE16 .... 111 H3
PEND EN3 .... 31 G4
Almeida Theatre
IS N1 .... 6 C2
Al Muntada Islamic School
FUL/PGN SW6 .... 107 J7
Alperton Cemetery
ALP/SUD HA0 .... 67 K7
Alperton Community School
ALP/SUD HA0 .... 68 A6
Alperton High School
ALP/SUD HA0 .... 67 K7
Alperton Sports Ground
ALP/SUD HA0 .... 85 K1
Alpha Business Centre
WALTH E17 .... 57 H4
Alpha Preparatory School
HRW HA1 .... 48 E4
Alpine Business Centre
EHAM E6 .... 96 A4
Alscot Road Industrial Estate
STHWK SE1 .... 19 M5
Altmore Infant School
EHAM E6 .... 77 K6
The Alton School
PUT/ROE SW15 .... 126 C6
Ambler Primary School
FSBYPK N4 .... 73 H2
Ambleside Junior School
WOT/HER KT12 .... 156 B7
AMC Business Centre
WLSDN NW10 .... 86 D2
American Intercontinental University
MHST W1U 10 B3
AMF Bowling
LEW SE13 .... 133 F2
Amherst Primary School
HACK E8 .... 74 C4
Ampthill Square Medical Centre
CAMTN NW1 .... 4 E6
Amy Johnson Primary School
WLGTN SM6 .... 176 E6
Anchorage Point Industrial Estate
CHARL SE7 .... 114 B2
Anchor Bay Industrial Estate
ERITH DA8 .... 118 C6
Anchor Retail Park
WCHPL E1 .... 92 E3
Andover Medical Centre
HOLWY N7 .... 73 F2
The Andrew Ewing Primary School
HEST TW5 .... 102 E6
Andrew Sketchley Theatre
WCHPL E1 .... 92 C4
Anerley Primary School
PGE/AN SE20 .... 150 C7
Anerley School
PGE/AN SE20 .... 150 C7
Angel Centre
DART DA1 .... 139 H5
Angerstein Business Park
GNWCH SE10 .... 113 K3
Anglian Industrial Estate
BARK IG11 .... 97 F3
Animal Cemetery
REDBR IG4 .... 59 H2
Annandale Primary School
GNWCH SE10 .... 113 J1
GNWCH SE10 .... 113 J4
Annemount School
EFNCH N2 .... 53 G5
Annunciation RC Infant School
EDGW HA8 .... 37 F7
The Annunciation RC Junior School
MLHL NW7 .... 37 F5
Anson Primary School
CRICK NW2 .... 70 B4
Ante Natal Clinic
MUSWH N10 .... 54 A2
Apex Industrial Estate
WLSDN NW10 .... 87 H3
Apex Retail Park
FELT TW13 .... 141 K2
Apollo Theatre
SOHO/SHAV W1D 11 G6
Apollo Victoria Theatre
PIM SW1V 16 E4
Apostolic Nuncio
WIM/MER SW19 .... 146 A2
Applegarth Primary School
CROY/NA CR0 .... 179 K5
Apsley House, The Wellington Museum
BAY/PAD W2 .... 16 A1
Aquarius Business Park
CRICK NW2 .... 51 J7
Aquarius Golf Club
PECK SE15 .... 131 K4
Arcadia Shopping Centre
EA W5 .... 85 K6
The Archbishop Lanfranc School
CROY/NA CR0 .... 163 K5
Archbishop Michael Ramsey Technology College
CMBW SE5 .... 110 C6
Archbishop Sumners CE Primary School
LBTH SE11 .... 18 B6
Archbishop Tenisons CE School
CROY/NA CR0 .... 178 B2
Archbishop Tenison's School
VX/NE SW8 .... 110 A5
Archdale Business Centre
RYLN/HDSTN HA2 .... 66 C1
Archdeacon Cambridge's CE Primary School
WHTN TW2 .... 142 E1
Arches Business Centre
NWDGN UB2 .... 102 E1
Arches Leisure Centre
GNWCH SE10 .... 113 G5
Archgate Business Centre
NFNCH/WDSP N12 .... 39 G3
Archway Business Centre
ARCH N19 .... 72 D2
Archway Leisure Centre
ARCH N19 .... 72 C1
Arena Estate
FSBYPK N4 .... 55 H5
Argyle Primary School
STPAN WC1H 5 J7
Arkley Golf Club
BAR EN5 .... 25 H4
Arklow Trading Estate
NWCR SE14 .... 112 B5
Armourers & Braziers' Hall
LOTH EC2R 13 G3
Arndale Health Centre
WAND/EARL SW18 .... 127 K5
Arnhem Wharf Primary School
POP/IOD E14 .... 112 C2
Arnold House School
STJWD NW8 .... 3 G5
Arnos Pool
FBAR/BDGN N11 .... 40 D4
Arnot Abbey
FARR EC1M 12 C2
Arsenal FC (Highbury)
HBRY N5 .... 73 G2
Art College
LBTH SE11 .... 18 C8
Arts Centre
BMLY BR1 .... 153 H7
HAMP NW3 .... 71 F4
Art School
BECK BR3 .... 166 B4
Arts Theatre
LSQ/SEVD WC2H 11 J6
PUT/ROE SW15 .... 127 G3
Ashbourne Independent Sixth Form College
KENS W8 .... 14 D1
Ashburnham Primary School
WBPTN SW10 .... 108 C6
Ashburton High School
CROY/NA CR0 .... 165 J6
Ashburton Primary School
CROY/NA CR0 .... 165 J5
Ashby Mill School
CLAP SW4 .... 129 K4
Ashfield Junior School
BUSH WD23 .... 22 B6
Ashford Industrial Estate
ASHF TW15 .... 140 A3
Ashford Sports Club
STWL/WRAY TW19 .... 120 C7
Ashgrove College
WALTH E17 .... 57 J2
Ashgrove Estate
BMLY BR1 .... 152 B5
Ashgrove School
BMLY BR1 .... 168 A1
Ashleigh Commercial Estate
CHARL SE7 .... 114 B3
Ashmead Primary School
DEPT SE8 .... 132 D1
Ashmole Centre
STHGT/OAK N14 .... 28 C7
Ashmole Primary School
VX/NE SW8 .... 110 A5
Ashmole School
STHGT/OAK N14 .... 28 C7
Ashmount Primary School
ARCH N19 .... 54 C6
Ashton House School
ISLW TW7 .... 103 J7
Ashton Playing Fields Track
WFD IG8 .... 45 J5
Aspen House School
LBTH SE11 .... 110 C5
Aspen House Secondary & Primary School
BRXS/STRHM SW2 .... 129 K7
Asquith Court School
KTN/HRWW/W HA3 .... 49 H5
Asquith School
PEND EN3 .... 30 E3
Assembly Rooms
KUT KT1 .... 159 F3
Associated Newspapers
BERM/RHTH SE16 .... 112 A2
Aston Clinic
NWMAL KT3 .... 160 B3
Aston House School
EA W5 .... 85 K5
Asylum Medical Centre
CEND/HSY/T N8 .... 55 G2
Athelney Primary School
CAT SE6 .... 151 J2
Athelstan House School
HPTN TW12 .... 142 A7
Athena Medical Centre
CLPT E5 .... 74 E3
Atherton Leisure Centre
FSTGT E7 .... 76 D5
Athlone House Hospital
HGT N6 .... 53 K7
Athlon Industrial Estate
ALP/SUD HA0 .... 85 K1
Atkinson Morley Hospital
RYNPK SW20 .... 145 K6
Atlas Business Centre
CRICK NW2 .... 69 K1
Atlas Transport Estate
BTSEA SW11 .... 128 B1
Auriol Junior School
HOR/WEW KT19 .... 173 H3
Australia House
HOL/ALD WC2B 11 M5
Aveling Park School
WALTH E17 .... 57 J1
Avenue House School
WEA W13 .... 85 H5
Avenue Industrial Estate
CHING E4 .... 43 H5
Avenue Primary School
KIL/WHAMP NW6 .... 70 C6
MNPK E12 .... 77 J3
Avigdor Primary School
STNW/STAM N16 .... 73 K1
Avondale Park Primary School
NTGHL W11 .... 88 B6
Avon House School
WFD IG8 .... 44 E3
Avon Trading Estate
WKENS W14 .... 107 J3
Axis Business Centre
SRTFD E15 .... 75 K7
The Aylesham Centre
PECK SE15 .... 111 H7
Ayloff Primary School
HCH RM12 .... 81 K3
Aylward First & Middle Schools
STAN HA7 .... 35 K4
Aylward School
UED N18 .... 41 K3
Aylwin Girls School
BERM/RHTH SE16 .... 19 M5
BAA Heathrow Visitor Centre
HTHAIR TW6 .... 100 E7
Babington House School
CHST BR7 .... 153 K5
Back Care Clinic
WPK KT4 .... 160 D7
Bacons City Technology College
BERM/RHTH SE16 .... 112 A1
Bacon's College
BERM/RHTH SE16 .... 93 G7
Baden Powell House
SKENS SW7 .... 14 F5
Baden Powell Primary School
CLPT E5 .... 74 D2
Bakers Hall
MON EC3R 13 K7
Balaam Leisure Centre
PLSTW E13 .... 94 E3
Bales College
NKENS W10 .... 88 B2
Balfour Business Centre
NWDGN UB2 .... 102 C2
Balgowan Primary School
BECK BR3 .... 166 B1
Balham Health Centre
BAL SW12 .... 148 B1
Balham Leisure Centre
TOOT SW17 .... 148 A1
Balham Preparatory School
TOOT SW17 .... 147 K3
Balmoral Trading
BARK IG11 .... 97 F4
Baltic Exchange
HDTCH EC3A 13 K4
Bancrofts School
WFD IG8 .... 44 E2
Bandon Hill Cemetery
WLGTN SM6 .... 176 D4
Bandon Hill Primary School
WLGTN SM6 .... 176 D5
Bangabandhu Primary School
BETH E2 .... 92 E2
Bank of England Extension
STP EC4M 12 E5
Bank of England (& Museum)
LOTH EC2R 13 G5
Bankside Gallery
STHWK SE1 .... 12 D7
Bankside Jetty
STHWK SE1 .... 12 E7
Bankside Park Industrial Estate
BARK IG11 .... 97 G2
Bannister Stadium
KTN/HRWW/W HA3 .... 34 C5
Bannockburn Primary School
WOOL/PLUM SE18 .... 116 A3
Banqueting House
WHALL SW1A 11 J9
Barber Surgeons' Hall
BARB EC2Y 12 F3
Barbican Cinema
BARB EC2Y 12 E2
Barbican Station
STBT EC1A 12 D2
The Barbican
BARB EC2Y 12 E2
Barbican Theatre
BARB EC2Y 12 F2
Barclay J & I School
LEY E10 .... 58 B5
Barham Primary School
ALP/SUD HA0 .... 67 J5
Baring Primary School
LEE/GVPK SE12 .... 133 K6
Baring Road Medical Centre
LEE/GVPK SE12 .... 152 E1
Barkantine Clinic
POP/IOD E14 .... 112 D1
Barking Abbey Comprehensive School
BARK IG11 .... 78 D4
BARK IG11 .... 79 F5
Barking Abbey Industrial Estate
BARK IG11 .... 78 B7
Barking Abbey Leisure Centre
BARK IG11 .... 79 G5
Barking College
ROMW/RG RM7 .... 81 F1
Barking FC
BCTR RM8 .... 79 H4
Barking Hospital
BARK IG11 .... 79 F6
Barking Industrial Park
BARK IG11 .... 79 F7
Barking RUFC
DAGW RM9 .... 79 K7
Barkingside Cemetery
BARK/HLT IG6 .... 60 B2
Barkingside FC
BARK/HLT IG6 .... 60 D3
Barlby Primary School
NKENS W10 .... 88 B3
Barley Lane Primary School
GDMY/SEVK IG3 .... 61 G6
Barnabas Medical Centre
NTHLT UB5 .... 66 C5
Barn Croft Primary School
WALTH E17 .... 57 G5
Barnehurst Primary School
BXLYHN DA7 .... 117 K7
Barnehurst Public Pay & Play Golf Club
BXLYHN DA7 .... 138 A2
Barn Elms Athletics Track
BARN SW13 .... 126 E1
Barn Elms Water Sports Centre
BARN SW13 .... 127 F1
Barnes Cray Primary School
DART DA1 .... 138 D3
Barnes Hospital
MORT/ESHN SW14 .... 126 B2
Barnes Sports Club
BARN SW13 .... 106 C7
Barnet College
BAR EN5 .... 26 D3
NFNCH/WDSP N12 .... 39 G4
Barnet Copthall Pool & Stadium
HDN NW4 .... 37 K6
Barnet Copthall Stadium
HDN NW4 .... 38 A7
Barnet County Court
BAR EN5 .... 27 G3
FNCH N3 .... 38 E7
Barnet FC (Underhill)
BAR EN5 .... 26 E4
Barnet General Hospital
BAR EN5 .... 26 B3
Barnet Health Centre
BAR EN5 .... 26 E4
Barnet Hill JMI School
BAR EN5 .... 26 D4
Barnet Hospital Chest Clinic
BAR EN5 .... 26 B3
Barnet Magistrates Court
BAR EN5 .... 26 D3
Barnet Museum
BAR EN5 .... 26 C3
Barnet Trading Estate
BAR EN5 .... 26 D2
Barnfield Primary School
EDGW HA8 .... 36 E7
Barnhill Community High School
YEAD UB4 .... 83 F2
Barnsbury School for Girls
IS N1 .... 6 A1
IS N1 .... 73 G5
Barons Court Theatre
WKENS W14 .... 107 H4
Barratt Industrial Park
BOW E3 .... 94 A3
Barrett Industrial Park
STHL UB1 .... 84 A7
Barrett Way Industrial Estate
HRW HA1 .... 48 D2
Barrington Primary School
BXLYHN DA7 .... 136 E1
Barrow Hedges Primary School
CAR SM5 .... 175 J6
Barrow Hill Junior School
STJWD NW8 .... 3 J6
Barton House Health Centre
STNW/STAM N16 .... 73 K2
Barwell Business Park
CHSGTN KT9 .... 171 K6
Bassett House School
NKENS W10 .... 88 B5
Baston School
HAYES BR2 .... 181 F1
Bath Factory Estate
HNHL SE24 .... 130 D5
Battersea Business Centre
BTSEA SW11 .... 129 F2
Battersea Dogs' Home
VX/NE SW8 .... 109 G6
Battersea Power Station (disused)
VX/NE SW8 .... 109 G5
Battersea Sports Centre
BTSEA SW11 .... 128 C2

Battersea Technology College BTSEA SW11 108 E7
Battersea Tutorial College TOOT SW17 148 A1
BBC Studios MV/WKIL W9 2 C9
BBC Television Centre SHB W12 88 A6
Beacon House School EA W5 86 B7
Beaconsfield Primary School HYS/HAR UB3 83 G7
Beal High School REDBR IG4 59 J2
Beam Primary School DAGE RM10 98 E1
Beatrix Potter Primary School WAND/EARL SW18 128 B7
Beauclerc Infant School SUN TW16 156 B2
Beaumont Primary School LEY E10 57 K6
The Beavers Community Primary School HSLWW TW4 122 B2
Beaverwood School for Girls CHST BR7 154 E5
Beckenham Business Centre BECK BR3 151 G5
Beckenham Crematorium SNWD SE25 165 K2
Beckenham Cricket Club BECK BR3 151 K6
Beckenham Hospital BECK BR3 166 C1
Beckenham Leisure Centre BECK BR3 151 G7
Beckenham Place Park Golf Course BECK BR3 151 K5
Beckenham RFC BECK BR3 166 B3
Beckenham Town FC BECK BR3 166 D4
Becket Sports Centre DART DA1 139 F5
Beckford Primary School KIL/WHAMP NW6 70 D4
Beckmead School BECK BR3 166 D7
The Beck Theatre HYS/HAR UB3 82 D5
Beckton Ski Centre EHAM E6 96 A3
Beckton Special School CAN/RD E16 95 H4
Beckton Triangle Retail Park EHAM E6 96 B2
Becontree Day Hospital BCTR RM8 80 A1
Becontree Primary School BCTR RM8 79 H2
Bective House Clinic PUT/ROE SW15 127 J3
Beddington Infants School WLGTN SM6 176 C2
Beddington Medical Centre CROY/NA CR0 176 E3
Beddington Park Primary School CROY/NA CR0 176 D2
Beddington Trading Estate CROY/NA CR0 163 K7
Bedelsford School KUT KT1 159 F2
Bedfont Health Clinic EBED/NFELT TW14 121 H6
Bedfont Industrial Park FELT TW13 140 B2
Bedfont J & I School EBED/NFELT TW14 121 H5
Bedfont Lakes Country Park EBED/NFELT TW14 140 A1
Bedington Infant School WLGTN SM6 176 C3
Bedonwell Clinic ABYW SE2 117 F5
Bedonwell Medical Centre BELV DA17 117 G4
Bedonwell Primary School BELV DA17 117 F5
Beecholme First School MTCM CR4 148 B7
Beechwood School STRHM/NOR SW16 148 E1
Beehive Preparatory School REDBR IG4 59 K3
The Beehive School ARCH N19 54 D6
Beis Rochel D'Satmar Girls School STNW/STAM N16 56 A6
Beis Yaakov Primary School CDALE/KGS NW9 51 F2
Bellamy's Wharf BERM/RHTH SE16 93 F7
Bellenden Primary School PECK SE15 131 H2
Bellenden Road Business Centre PECK SE15 131 G1
Bellenden Road Retail Park PECK SE15 111 G7
Belleville Primary School BTSEA SW11 128 E4
Belle Vue Cinema EDGW HA8 36 C5
WLSDN NW10 69 K6
Bell Industrial Estate CHSWK W4 105 K3
Bellingham Trading Estate CAT SE6 151 K2
Bell Lane JMI School HDN NW4 52 B3
Belmont First & Middle School KTN/HRWW/W HA3 49 F1
Belmont J & I School WDGN N22 55 J2
Belmont (Mill Hill Junior School) MLHL NW7 37 J2
Belmont Park School LEY E10 58 A5
Belmont Primary School BXLYHN DA7 117 H6
CHSWK W4 106 A3
Belmore Primary School YEAD UB4 83 F2
Belvedere Day Hospital WLSDN NW10 69 J7
Belvedere Industrial Estate BELV DA17 99 F7
Belvedere Link Business Park BELV DA17 117 K2
Belvedere Primary School BELV DA17 117 J3
Belvue Business Centre NTHLT UB5 66 B6
Belvue School NTHLT UB5 66 A7
Benedict House Preparatory School BFN/LL DA15 155 F3
Benhurst JMI School HCH RM12 81 K2
Ben Jonson Primary School WCHPL E1 93 G3
Bensham Manor School THHTH CR7 164 D4
Benson Primary School CROY/NA CR0 179 G2
Bentalls Shopping Centre KUT KT1 158 E1
Benthal Primary School STNW/STAM N16 74 C2
Bentley Wood Girls School STAN HA7 35 F4
Bentworth Primary School SHB W12 87 K5
Beormund School STHWK SE1 19 G2
Berger Primary School HOM E9 75 F5
Berkeley Primary School HEST TW5 102 C5
Berlitz Schools of Languages LINN WC2A 11 M3
Bermondsey Town Hall STHWK SE1 19 M4
Bermondsey Trading Estate BERM/RHTH SE16 111 K3
Berrymede Infant School ACT W3 105 J1
Berrymede Junior School ACT W3 105 J1
Bertram House School TOOT SW17 148 A1
Bessemer Grange J & I School EDUL SE22 131 F3
Bessemer Park Industrial Estate BRXN/ST SW9 130 C3
Bethlem Royal Hospital BECK BR3 166 D6
Bethnal Green Museum of Childhood BETH E2 92 D2
Bethnal Green Technology College BETH E2 7 M8
Beulah J & I School THHTH CR7 164 D1
Beverley School NWMAL KT3 160 D4
Beverley Trading Estate MRDN SM4 161 G6
Bevington Primary School NKENS W10 88 C4
Bexley College ABYW SE2 116 E5
ERITH DA8 117 K3
Bexley Cricket Club BXLY DA5 137 H7
Bexley Erith Technical High School BXLY DA5 137 H5
Bexley Grammar School WELL DA16 136 C3
Bexleyheath Centre BXLYHS DA6 137 F3
Bexleyheath Golf Club BXLYHS DA6 137 F4
Bexleyheath School BXLYHN DA7 137 H2
Bexley RFC BXLY DA5 137 H6
BFI London IMAX Cinema STHWK SE1 11 M9
Bickley Park Cricket Club BMLY BR1 168 D1
Bickley Park Prep School BMLY BR1 168 C2
Bickley Park School BMLY BR1 168 D2
Big Ben WEST SW1P 17 K2
Bigland Green Primary School WCHPL E1 92 D5
Billingsgate Fish Market POP/IOD E14 93 K7
Birch Court Colindale Hospital CDALE/KGS NW9 51 G1
Birkbeck College STPAN WC1H 5 G9
STPAN WC1H 11 H1
Birkbeck Primary School SCUP DA14 155 H2
Bishop Challenor RC School WCHPL E1 92 E6
Bishop Challoner RC Secondary School WCHPL E1 92 E5
Bishop Challoner School HAYES BR2 167 G1
Bishop Douglas RC School EFNCH N2 53 G1
Bishop Gilpin Primary School WIM/MER SW19 146 D4
Bishop John Robinson CE Primary THMD SE28 97 J6
Bishop Perrin CE Primary School WHTN TW2 123 G6
Bishop Ramsey CE School RSLP HA4 46 E6
RSLP HA4 46 D6
Bishopsgate Institute WCHPL E1 13 K3
Bishop Stopford School EN EN1 30 D1
Bishop Thomas Grant School STRHM/NOR SW16 149 F4
Bishop Winnington-Ingram CE Primary School RSLP HA4 46 B6
Bittacy Business Centre MLHL NW7 38 C5
Blackburn Trading Estate STWL/WRAY TW19 120 C5
Blackfen School for Girls BFN/LL DA15 136 C5
Blackfriars Millennium Pier EMB EC4Y 12 B6
Blackfriars Pier BLKFR EC4V 12 D6
Blackfriars Station BLKFR EC4V 12 C6
Blackheath Bluecoat CE School BKHTH/KID SE3 114 A6
Blackheath Business Estate GNWCH SE10 113 F7
The Blackheath Clinic BKHTH/KID SE3 133 K3
Blackheath High School BKHTH/KID SE3 133 J1
Blackheath High Senior School BKHTH/KID SE3 113 K6
Blackheath Hospital BKHTH/KID SE3 133 J2
Blackwall Trading Estate POP/IOD E14 94 B4
Blaire Peach School STHL UB1 83 H7
Blake College GTPST W1W 10 E2
Blanche Neville School WDGN N22 41 G7
Blenheim Business Centre MTCM CR4 147 K7
Blenheim Shopping Centre PGE/AN SE20 150 E6
Blessed Dominic RC Primary School CDALE/KGS NW9 51 G1
Blessed John Roche Catholic School POP/IOD E14 93 J5
Blessed Sacrament RC Primary School IS N1 5 K4
Blood Transfusion Centre EDGW HA8 36 D6
Bloomfield Clinic (Guys Hospital) STHWK SE1 19 H1
Bloomsbury College FUL/PGN SW6 107 K6
Bloomsbury Theatre STPAN WC1H 5 G9
Blossom House School RYNPK SW20 146 A6
Blossoms Inn Medical Centre BLKFR EC4V 12 F6
Blue Gate Fields Primary School WCHPL E1 92 E6
BMI Medical Centre CAVSQ/HST W1G 10 B3
Bnois Jerusalem School STNW/STAM N16 55 K6
The Bob Hope Theatre ELTH/MOT SE9 134 E5
Bodywise Natural Health Centre BETH E2 92 E2
Boleyn Cinema EHAM E6 95 H1
Bolingbroke Hospital BTSEA SW11 128 D4
Bolingbroke Primary School BTSEA SW11 108 C7
Bond First School MTCM CR4 162 E1
Bond Road School MTCM CR4 162 E1
Bonner Primary School BETH E2 93 F1
Bonneville Primary School CLAP SW4 129 H5
Bonus Pastor School BMLY BR1 152 C3
Boomes Industrial Estate RAIN RM13 99 H3
Booster Cushion Theatre WDGN N22 55 F1
Borehamwood FC BORE WD6 24 D1
Borehamwood Industrial Park BORE WD6 25 F1
Borough Market STHWK SE1 13 G8
Boston Business Park HNWL W7 103 K2
Botwell RC Primary School HYS/HAR UB3 101 J1
Boulevard 25 Retail Park BORE WD6 24 C2
Boundary Business Park MTCM CR4 162 C1
Bounds Green Health Centre FBAR/BDGN N11 40 D6
Bounds Green Industrial Estate FBAR/BDGN N11 40 C5
Bounds Green Primary School FBAR/BDGN N11 40 E6
Bourne CP School RSLP HA4 65 G4
Bourne Hall Health Centre EW KT17 173 H7
Bournehall J & I School BUSH WD23 22 A4
Bourne Hall Museum EW KT17 173 H7
Bourne Road Industrial Park DART DA1 138 A4
Bourneside Sports Club STHGT/OAK N14 28 E7
Bousfield Primary School WBPTN SW10 14 E7
Boutcher CE Primary School STHWK SE1 19 L4
Bowater House SKENS SW7 15 L2
Bow County Court SRTFD E15 76 D5
Bow County Secondary School BOW E3 93 J2
Bowden House Clinic HRW HA1 66 E1
Bowes Primary School FBAR/BDGN N11 40 D4
Bowes Road Clinic FBAR/BDGN N11 40 C4
Bow Industrial Park SRTFD E15 75 J6
Bowman Trading Estate CDALE/KGS NW9 50 C2
Bow Street Magistrates Court HOL/ALD WC2B 11 K5
Bow Triangle Business Centre BOW E3 93 J3
Boxgrove Primary School ABYW SE2 116 D2
Boys' Club EDGW HA8 36 C6
Brackenbury Health Centre HMSMTH W6 106 E2
Brackenbury Primary School HMSMTH W6 106 E2
Brady Recreation Centre WCHPL E1 92 C4
Braincroft Primary School CRICK NW2 69 H2
Braintree Road Industrial Estate RSLP HA4 65 F3
Bramah's Tea & Coffee Museum STHWK SE1 12 F9
Brampton Manor School PLSTW E13 95 H3
Brampton Primary School BXLYHN DA7 136 E1
EHAM E6 95 J2
Brandlehow Primary School PUT/ROE SW15 127 J3
Branollys Health Centre PLSTW E13 94 E3
Breakspear Crematorium RSLP HA4 46 A4
Breaside Pre Preparatory School BMLY BR1 152 E6
Brecknock Primary School HOLWY N7 72 D5
Bredinghurst School PECK SE15 131 K3
Brent Adult College WLSDN NW10 69 F7
Brent Arts Council CRICK NW2 69 J2
Brent Child & Family Clinic WLSDN NW10 69 H4
Brent Cross Shopping Centre HDN NW4 52 A6
Brentfield Medical Centre WLSDN NW10 69 F5
Brentfield Primary School WLSDN NW10 69 F5
Brentford Business Centre BTFD TW8 104 D6
The Brentford Clinic BTFD TW8 105 F5
Brentford County Court BTFD TW8 104 E6
Brentford FC (Griffin Park) BTFD TW8 104 E5
Brentford Fountain Leisure Centre CHSWK W4 105 G4
Brentford Health Centre BTFD TW8 104 D5
Brentford Medical Centre BTFD TW8 104 E6
Brentford School for Girls BTFD TW8 104 E5
Brent Knoll School FSTH SE23 151 F2
Brent Magistrates Court House WLSDN NW10 69 G5
Brent Park Industrial Estate NWDGN UB2 102 A2
Brentside First School HNWL W7 84 E4
Brentside High School HNWL W7 84 E3
Brentside Primary School HNWL W7 84 E3
Brent Trading Estate WLSDN NW10 69 G4
Brent Valley Golf Club HNWL W7 84 E6
Brentwaters Business Park BTFD TW8 104 D6
Brewers' Hall CITYW EC2V 12 F3
Brewery Industrial Estate IS N1 6 E6
Brewery Mews Business Centre ISLW TW7 124 A2
Brick Lane Music Hall SDTCH EC2A 7 K8
Brick Lane Music House WCHPL E1 13 M1
Bricklayer Arms Industrial Estate STHWK SE1 19 L6
The Bridewell Theatre EMB EC4Y 12 C5
The Bridge Business Centre NWDGN UB2 103 F1
Bridge Lane Theatre BTSEA SW11 108 D7
The Bridge Leisure Centre SYD SE26 151 H4
Bridge Park Business & Leisure Centre WLSDN NW10 68 D6
Bright Sparks Montessori School WKENS W14 107 G1
Bright Sparks School STRHM/NOR SW16 148 E3
Brigstock Medical Centre THHTH CR7 164 C4
Brimsdown Industrial Estate PEND EN3 30 E1
Brimsdown Primary School PEND EN3 31 F2
Brindishe Primary School LEE/GVPK SE12 133 J4
Britannia Business Centre CRICK NW2 70 B3
Britannia Leisure Centre IS N1 7 H4
Britannia Sports Ground WALTH E17 43 J6
Britannia Village Primary School CAN/RD E16 95 F7
British Airways London Eye WHALL SW1A 17 K1
British Cartoon Centre BMSBY WC1N 11 K1
British Dental Association CAVSQ/HST W1G 10 C3
British Library CAMTN NW1 5 H7
British Library Newspaper Library CDALE/KGS NW9 51 G2
British Medical Association STPAN WC1H 5 H9
British Museum RSQ WC1B 11 J3
The British Museum Shop HTHAIR TW6 120 E4
British Telecom Tower GTPST W1W 10 E2
The Brit School SNWD SE25 164 E5
Brittons School RAIN RM13 81 H6
Brixton Academy BRXN/ST SW9 130 B2
Brixton College for Further Education BRXS/STRHM SW2 130 A4
Brixton Recreation Centre BRXN/ST SW9 130 B2
Broadfields Infant School EDGW HA8 36 C1
Broadfields Junior School EDGW HA8 36 D1
Broadgate LVPST EC2M 13 H2
Broadgate Ice Arena LVPST EC2M 13 J3
Broadhurst School KIL/WHAMP NW6 2 E1
Broadmead Primary School CROY/NA CR0 164 E5
Broadwalk Shopping Centre EDGW HA8 36 C5
Broadwater Farm Primary School TOTM N17 55 K1
Broadwater Primary School TOOT SW17 147 H3
Broadway Clinic EDGW HA8 36 D7
Broadway Retail Park CRICK NW2 70 B3
Broadway Shopping Centre BXLYHS DA6 137 H3
HMSMTH W6 107 F4
Broadway Square Shopping Centre BXLYHN DA7 137 H3
Broadway Squash & Fitness Centre HMSMTH W6 107 G3
Brocklebank Health Centre WAND/EARL SW18 128 A6
Brocklebank Industrial Estate GNWCH SE10 113 K3
Brockley Cross Business Centre BROCKY SE4 132 B2
Brockley Primary School BROCKY SE4 132 C4
Brockwell Lido HNHL SE24 130 C5
Brockwell Primary School BRXS/STRHM SW2 130 B5
Bromet Primary School OXHEY WD19 21 H6
Bromley Cemetery BMLY BR1 152 D6
Bromley College of Further & Higher Education BMLY BR1 152 E7
HAYES BR2 168 C5
Bromley County Court BMLY BR1 152 E7
Bromley FC HAYES BR2 168 A4
Bromley Golf Club HAYES BR2 168 D6
Bromley High School BMLY BR1 169 F3
Bromley Hospital HAYES BR2 168 A3
Bromley Industrial Centre BMLY BR1 168 C2
Bromley Mall Indoor Market BMLY BR1 167 K1
Bromley Road Infant School BECK BR3 151 K7
Bromley Road Retail Park CAT SE6 151 K1
Brompton Medical Centre WBPTN SW10 14 D7
Brompton Oratory SKENS SW7 15 J4
Bromyard Leisure Centre ACT W3 87 G7
Brondesbury College for Boys KIL/WHAMP NW6 70 B6
Brooke Trading Estate ROM RM1 63 H6
Brookfield Primary School CHEAM SM3 161 H7
HGT N6 72 B1
Brook House FC YEAD UB4 82 D2
Brook Industrial Estate YEAD UB4 83 H7
Brookland Primary School GLDGN NW11 53 F3
Brooklands Primary School BKHTH/KID SE3 133 K2
Brook Lane Business Centre BTFD TW8 104 E4
Brookmarsh Trading Estate DEPT SE8 112 E6
Brookmead Industrial Estate MTCM CR4 163 H5
Brookside J & I School YEAD UB4 83 G2
Broomfield House School RCH/KEW TW9 105 G7
Broomfield School STHGT/OAK N14 40 D4
Broomsleigh Business Park CAT SE6 151 H4
Broomwood Hall School BAL SW12 129 F6
Brothwick Wharf DEPT SE8 112 D4
Brownlow Medical Centre FBAR/BDGN N11 40 E4
Bruce Castle Museum TOTM N17 42 A7
Bruce Grove Primary School TOTM N17 56 B1
Brunel Engine House BERM/RHTH SE16 111 K1
Brunel University ISLW TW7 103 K6
TWK TW1 124 C3
Brunel University (Osterley Campus) Track ISLW TW7 103 K6
Brunswick Health Centre FBAR/BDGN N11 40 A1

Brunswick Housing & Shopping Centre *BMSBY* WC1N 5 K9
Brunswick Industrial Park *FBAR/BDGN* N11 40 B3
Brunswick Medical Centre *BMSBY* WC1N 5 J9
Brunswick Park JMI School *FBAR/BDGN* N11 28 A7
Brunswick Park Primary School *CMBW* SE5 110 E6
BT Centre *STBT* EC1A 12 E4
Buckhurst Hill Primary School *BKHH* IG9 45 J1
Buckingham College Preparatory School *PIN* HA5 47 K5
Buckingham College School *HRW* HA1 48 E4
Buckingham Palace *WHALL* SW1A 16 D2
Buckingham Primary School *HPTN* TW12 141 K4
Buckingham Road Cemetery *IL* IG1 78 D1
Buckland Infant School *CHSGTN* KT9 172 B4
Building Centre *GWRST* WC1E 11 G3
Bullers Wood School *CHST* BR7 153 K7
Bullsbridge Industrial Estate *NWDGN* UB2 102 A3
The Bull Theatre *BAR* EN5 26 D3
Bupa Roding Hospital *REDBR* IG4 59 H2
Burbage School *IS* N1 7 J5
Burdett Coutts CE Primary School *WEST* SW1P 17 G5
Burgess Industrial Park *CMBW* SE5 110 E6
Burlington Danes School *SHB* W12 87 K5
Burlington Primary School *NWMAL* KT3 160 C3
Burnham Trading Estate *DART* DA1 139 G3
Burnhill Business Centre *BECK* BR3 166 D1
Burnley Road Clinic *WLSDN* NW10 69 J4
Burnt Ash Infant School *BMLY* BR1 152 E4
Burnt Ash School *BMLY* BR1 152 D4
Burnt Oak Junior School *BFN/LL* DA15 136 B7
Burntwood School *TOOT* SW17 147 H1
Burrels Wharf *POP/IOD* E14 112 E4
Bursted Woodprimary School *BXLYHN* DA7 137 J1
Burwell Industrial Estate *LEY* E10 57 G7
Bushey Golf & Country Club *BUSH* WD23 22 A5
Bushey Hall Golf Club *BUSH* WD23 21 K3
Bushey Hall School *BUSH* WD23 21 K5
Bushey Hall Swimming Pool *BUSH* WD23 21 K4
Bushey Health Centre *BUSH* WD23 21 K5
Bushey Heath Primary School *BUSH* WD23 22 D7
Bushey Manor Junior School *BUSH* WD23 21 K4
Bushey Meads School *BUSH* WD23 22 C4
Bushey Middle School *RYNPK* SW20 160 E2
Bushey Museum & Art Gallery *BUSH* WD23 22 A5
Bush Hill Park Golf Club *WCHMH* N21 29 J4
Bush Hill Park Medical Centre *EN* EN1 30 B5
Bush Hill Park Primary School *EN* EN1 30 C4
Bush House (BBC) *HOL/ALD* WC2B 11 L5
Bush Industrial Estate *ARCH* N19 72 C2
WLSDN NW10 87 F2
The Business Design Centre *IS* N1 6 B4
Bute House Preparatory School for Girls *HMSMTH* W6 107 F3
Butlers Wharf *STHWK* SE1 13 M9
Butler's Wharf Business Centre *STHWK* SE1 19 M1
Butler's Wharf Pier *STHWK* SE1 13 M9
Butterfly House *BTFD* TW8 104 C7
Butterfly Sports Club *ELTH/MOT* SE9 135 G5
Buxlow Preparatory School *WBLY* HA9 68 A2
Buzzard Creek Industrial Estate *BARK* IG11 97 F2
Byam Shaw School of Art *ARCH* N19 72 C1
Byfleet Industrial Estate *WATW* WD18 20 A7
Bygrove JMI School *POP/IOD* E14 93 K5
Byron Court Primary School *ALP/SUD* HA0 67 J1
Cabinet War Rooms *WHALL* SW1A 17 H1
Calder House School *BTSEA* SW11 108 E7
Caledonian Market *STHWK* SE1 19 K3
Cally Pool *IS* N1 5 L3
Calverton Primary School *CAN/RD* E16 95 H5
Cambell Primary School *DAGW* RM9 79 K6
Camberwell Business Centre *CMBW* SE5 110 E6
Camberwell College of Arts *CMBW* SE5 111 F7
Camberwell Leisure Centre *CMBW* SE5 110 E7
Camberwell New Cemetery *FSTH* SE23 132 A5
Camberwell Trading Estate *CMBW* SE5 130 C1
Cambridge Park Bowling & Sports Club *TWK* TW1 124 D5
Cambridge School *HMSMTH* W6 106 E3
Cambridge Theatre *LSQ/SEVD* WC2H 11 J5
Camden Community Trust Day Hospital *KTTN* NW5 72 C5
Camden House Clinic *BKHTH/KID* SE3 133 H1
Camden Junior School *CAR* SM5 175 K3
Camden Market *CAMTN* NW1 4 B2
Camden Mews Day Hospital *KTTN* NW5 4 F1
Camden Peoples Theatre *CAMTN* NW1 4 E8
Camden School for Girls *KTTN* NW5 72 C5
Camden Theatre *CAMTN* NW1 4 E5
Camden Town Hall & St Pancras Library *CAMTN* NW1 5 J7
Camelot Primary School *PECK* SE15 111 J6
Cameron House School *CHEL* SW3 15 H9
Camperdown House *WCHPL* E1 13 M5
Campion House College *ISLW* TW7 103 J6
Campsbourne Infant School *CEND/HSY/T* N8 54 E2
Campsbourne Junior School *CEND/HSY/T* N8 54 E2
Canada House *STJS* SW1Y 11 H8
Canada House Business Centre *RSLP* HA4 47 G7
Canada Square *POP/IOD* E14 93 J7
Canada Water Retail Park *BERM/RHTH* SE16 112 A2
Canada Wharf Museum *BERM/RHTH* SE16 93 H7
Canal Cafe Theatre *BAY/PAD* W2 8 D2
Canary Riverside *POP/IOD* E14 93 H7
Canary Wharf Pier *POP/IOD* E14 93 H7
Canary Wharf Tower *POP/IOD* E14 93 K7
Canberra Primary School *SHB* W12 87 K6
Canbury Business Centre *KUTN/CMB* KT2 144 A7
Canbury 2000 Business Park *KUTN/CMB* KT2 144 A7
Canbury Medical Centre *KUTN/CMB* KT2 144 B7
Canbury School *RCHPK/HAM* TW10 144 D5
Cann Hall Primary School *WAN* E11 76 D2
The Canning School *KENS* W8 14 A3
Cannon Hill Clinic *STHGT/OAK* N14 40 E2
Cannon Lane Primary School *PIN* HA5 47 H5
Cannon Sports Club *CANST* EC4R 12 F6
Cannon Street Station *CANST* EC4R 13 G6
Cannon Trading Estate *WBLY* HA9 68 D3
Cannon Wharf Business Centre *DEPT* SE8 112 B3
Cannon Workshops *POP/IOD* E14 93 J6
Canon Barnett Primary School *WCHPL* E1 13 M4
Canonbury Business Centre *IS* N1 6 F3
Canonbury Primary School *IS* N1 73 H5
Canon Palmer RC High School *IL* IG1 60 E7
Canons High School *EDGW* HA8 50 B1
The Canons Leisure Centrel *MTCM* CR4 162 E3
Canterbury Industrial Estate *NWCR* SE14 112 A5
Cantium Retail Park *STHWK* SE1 111 H5
Capital Business Centre *ALP/SUD* HA0 85 K1
MTCM CR4 162 E4
Capital Industrial Estate *BELV* DA17 98 E7
BELV DA17 117 J3
Capital Radio *LSQ/SEVD* WC2H 11 H7
Capital Wharf *WAP* E1W 92 C7
Capitol Industrial Park *CDALE/KGS* NW9 50 E2
Caplan Estate *MTCM* CR4 148 C7
Cardiff Road Industrial Estate *WATW* WD18 21 F5
Cardinal Hinsley High School *WLSDN* NW10 69 J7
Cardinal Pole RC School *HOM* E9 75 G5
Cardinal Pole RC Secondary Lower School *HOM* E9 75 F6
Cardinal Road Infant School *FELT* TW13 122 A7
Cardinal Vaughan Memorial School *WKENS* W14 107 H1
The Cardinal Wiseman ARC School Technology & Art College *GFD/PVL* UB6 84 C4
Cardwell Primary School *WOOL/PLUM* SE18 114 E3
Carew Manor School *WLGTN* SM6 176 D2
Carlisle Infant School *HPTN* TW12 142 B5
Carlton Gate Development *MV/WKIL* W9 8 B2
Carlton House *STJS* SW1Y 11 G9
Carlton Primary School *KTTN* NW5 72 A4
Carlton Vale Infant School *KIL/WHAMP* NW6 88 D2
Carlyle's House (NT) *CHEL* SW3 108 D5
Carnwath Road Industrial Estate *FUL/PGN* SW6 128 A2
Carolyn School Shop *PIN* HA5 47 J3
Carpenders Park Cemetery *OXHEY* WD19 33 K3
Carpenters Business Park *HOM* E9 75 J5
Carpenters' Hall *LVPST* EC2M 13 H3
Carpenters Primary School *SRTFD* E15 76 A7
Carshalton AFC *SUT* SM1 175 J2
Carshalton College of Further Education *CAR* SM5 175 K2
Carshalton High School for Boys *CAR* SM5 175 H1
Carshalton High School for Girls *CAR* SM5 175 J2
Carshalton War Memorial Hospital *CAR* SM5 175 K4
Caryl Thomas Clinic *HRW* HA1 48 E3
The Cassel Hospital *RCHPK/HAM* TW10 143 K3
Cassidy Medical Centre *FUL/PGN* SW6 107 K6
Castilion Primary School *THMD* SE28 97 J5
Castlebar Special School *WEA* W13 85 G4
Castlecombe Primary School *ELTH/MOT* SE9 153 J4
Castle Industrial Estate *WALW* SE17 18 E5
Caterham High School *CLAY* IG5 59 K1
Catford Cricket & Sports Club *CAT* SE6 132 E7
Catford Cyphers Cricket Club *CAT* SE6 151 H1
Catford Girls School *CAT* SE6 152 B2
Catford Trading Estate *CAT* SE6 151 K1
Catford Wanderers Sports Club *CAT* SE6 152 A3
Cathall Leisure Centre *WAN* E11 76 B2
Cathedral School of St Saviour & St Mary Overie *STHWK* SE1 18 F1
Cator Park School for Girls *BECK* BR3 151 G6
Cavendish College *FITZ* W1T 11 G3
Cavendish Primary School *CHSWK* W4 106 B6
The Cavendish School *CAMTN* NW1 4 C3
Cavendish Special School *HNWL* W7 85 F5
Caxton Hall *STJSPK* SW1H 17 G3
Caxton Trading Estate *HYS/HAR* UB3 101 H1
Cayley Primary School *POP/IOD* E14 93 G4
Cecil Park Clinic *PIN* HA5 47 J3
Cecil Sharpe House *CAMTN* NW1 4 B3
The Cedar School *FSTGT* E7 77 G5
Cedars First School *KTN/HRWW/W* HA3 34 C7
Cedars Middle School *KTN/HRWW/W* HA3 34 C7
The Cedars Primary School *HEST* TW5 101 K6
Cedar Way Industrial Estate *CAMTN* NW1 5 G2
Cenotaph *WHALL* SW1A 17 J1
Centaurs Business Centre *ISLW* TW7 104 B5
Centaurs RFC *ISLW* TW7 104 A5
Central Business Centre *WLSDN* NW10 69 G4
Central Criminal Court *STP* EC4M 12 C4
Central Foundation Boys School *SDTCH* EC2A 7 H9
Central Foundation Girls School *BOW* E3 93 G2
Central Hall *STJSPK* SW1H 17 H2
Central Hendon Clinic *HDN* NW4 51 K3
Central London County Court *CAVSQ/HST* W1G 10 C1
Central London Golf Club *TOOT* SW17 147 H1
Central London Markets *FARR* EC1M 12 C3
Central Medical Centre *MRDN* SM4 162 B3
Central Middlesex Hospital *WLSDN* NW10 86 E2
Central Park Arena *DART* DA1 139 H7
Central Park Primary School *EHAM* E6 95 H1
Central Primary School *WAT* WD17 21 G3
Central St Martins College of Art & Design *RSQ* WC1B 11 K3
Central School of Ballet *CLKNW* EC1R 12 B1
Central School of Fashion *GTPST* W1W 10 E3
Central School of Speech & Drama *HAMP* NW3 3 G1
Central School Speech & Drama *CAMTN* NW1 5 G4
Central Square Shopping Centre *ALP/SUD* HA0 68 A5
Centre Court Shopping Centre *WIM/MER* SW19 146 D5
Centre Point *LSQ/SEVD* WC2H 11 H4
Chadwell Heath Hospital *CHDH* RM6 61 H4
Chadwell Heath Industrial Park *BCTR* RM8 62 A7
Chadwell Heath Luncheon & Leisure Centre *CHDH* RM6 61 K5
Chadwell Heath School *CHDH* RM6 61 H5
Chadwell Primary School *CHDH* RM6 61 J6
Chaffinch Business Park *BECK* BR3 166 A2
Chailey Industrial Estate *HYS/HAR* UB3 101 K1
Chalcot School *CAMTN* NW1 4 C1
Chalgrove Primary School *FNCH* N3 52 C2
Chalkhill Primary School *WBLY* HA9 68 D2
Chambers Business Park *WDR/YW* UB7 100 D5
Chambers Wharf *BERM/RHTH* SE16 111 H1
Chandlers Field Primary School *E/WMO/HCT* KT8 157 F4
Chandos Business Centre *WLGTN* SM6 176 C5
Channelsea Business Centre *SRTFD* E15 94 B1
Channing School *HGT* N6 54 B7
Chapel End Infant School *WALTH* E17 43 K7
Chapel End Junior School *WALTH* E17 43 K7
Chapman Park Industrial Estate *WLSDN* NW10 69 H5
Charing Cross Hospital *HMSMTH* W6 107 G5
Charing Cross Station *CHCR* WC2N 11 K8
Charing Cross & Westminster Medical School *HMSMTH* W6 107 G4
The Charles Dickens Museum *BMSBY* WC1N 11 L1
Charles Dickens Primary School *STHWK* SE1 18 E2
Charles Edward Brook Lower School *CMBW* SE5 110 C7
Charles Edward Brook Upper School *CMBW* SE5 110 C7
Charles Lamb Primary School *IS* N1 6 E3
Charlotte Sharman Primary School *LBTH* SE11 18 C4
Charlton Athletic FC (The Valley) *CHARL* SE7 114 B4
Charlton Health & Fitness Centre *CHARL* SE7 114 B4
Charlton House *CHARL* SE7 114 C5
Charlton Manor Primary School *CHARL* SE7 114 C6
Charlton RFC *ELTH/MOT* SE9 135 G6
Charlton School *CHARL* SE7 114 D5
Charrington Bowl *SURB* KT6 172 D1
Charrville Primary School *YEAD* UB4 82 C1
Charter Clinic *CHEL* SW3 15 L8
Charterhouse *FARR* EC1M 12 D2
Charteris Road Sports Centre *HAMP* NW3 71 J4
KIL/WHAMP NW6 70 D7
Charter Nightingale Hospital & Counselling Centre *CAMTN* NW1 9 K2
The Charter School *EDUL* SE22 130 E4
Chartfield School *PUT/ROE* SW15 126 E4
Chartwell Business Centre *BMLY* BR1 168 C2
Chase Bridge Primary School *WHTN* TW2 123 K5
Chase Lane Primary School *CHING* E4 43 H3
Chase Road Trading Estate *WLSDN* NW10 87 F3
Chase Side J & I School *ENC/FH* EN2 29 J1
Chaseville Clinic *WCHMH* N21 29 F5
Chater Infant School *WATW* WD18 20 E3
Chater Junior School *WATW* WD18 20 E3
Chatsworth Infant School *BFN/LL* DA15 136 B7
Chatsworth J & I School *HSLW* TW3 123 H3
Chaucer Clinic *NWDGN* UB2 103 J1
Cheam Common Infant School *WPK* KT4 173 K1
Cheam Common Junior School *WPK* KT4 173 K2
Cheam Fields Primary School *CHEAM* SM3 174 C4
Cheam High School *CHEAM* SM3 174 C3
Cheam Leisure Centre *CHEAM* SM3 174 B3
Cheam Park Farm Junior School *CHEAM* SM3 174 C2
Cheam Sports Club *BELMT* SM2 174 B6
Chelsea Barracks *BGVA* SW1W 16 B8
Chelsea Bridge Business Centre *VX/NE* SW8 109 G6
Chelsea Centre & Theatre *WBPTN* SW10 108 C6
Chelsea Cinema *CHEL* SW3 15 K8
The Chelsea Club Leisure Centre *FUL/PGN* SW6 108 A5
Chelsea College of Art & Design *CHEL* SW3 15 H8
FUL/PGN SW6 128 B1
Chelsea FC (Stamford Bridge) *FUL/PGN* SW6 108 A6
Chelsea Fields Industrial Estate *WIM/MER* SW19 147 H7
Chelsea Leisure Centre *CHEL* SW3 15 K8
Chelsea Old Town Hall *CHEL* SW3 15 K8
Chelsea Physic Garden *CHEL* SW3 15 L9
Chelsea & Westminster Hospital *WBPTN* SW10 108 B5
Chelsea Wharf *WBPTN* SW10 108 C6
Chennestone Community School *SUN* TW16 156 A1
Cherington House Health Centre *HNWL* W7 85 F7
Cherry Garden School *BERM/RHTH* SE16 111 H3
Cherry Lane Primary School *WDR/YW* UB7 100 C3
Cherry Orchard Primary School *CHARL* SE7 114 B6
Chessington Community College & Sports Centre *CHSGTN* KT9 171 K6
Chessington Cricket Club *CHSGTN* KT9 171 J6
Chessington Golf Club *CHSGTN* KT9 171 K6
Chesterton Primary School *BTSEA* SW11 109 F7
Chestnut Grove School *BAL* SW12 129 F7
Cheyne Centre *CHEL* SW3 108 D5
Childeric Primary School *NWCR* SE14 112 B6
Childs Hill Clinic *CRICK* NW2 70 D1
Childs Hill Primary School *CRICK* NW2 70 C2
Childs Welfare Clinic *DAGW* RM9 79 J4
Chiltonian Industrial Estate *LEE/GVPK* SE12 133 J5
Chimnocks Wharf *POP/IOD* E14 93 G6
Chingford Hall Primary School *CHING* E4 43 H5
Chingford Health Centre *CHING* E4 43 H3
Chingford Industrial Centre *CHING* E4 43 G4
Chingford RFC *CHING* E4 31 J7
Chingford School *CHING* E4 31 K7
Chisenhale Primary School *BOW* E3 93 G1
Chislehurst Caves *CHST* BR7 154 A7
Chislehurst Cemetery *CHST* BR7 154 E4
Chislehurst Golf Club *CHST* BR7 154 B6
Chislehurst Natural Health Centre *CHST* BR7 154 B5
Chislehurst & Sidcup Grammar School *BFN/LL* DA15 155 H1
Chiswick & Bedford Park Preparatory School *CHSWK* W4 106 B3
Chiswick Business Park *CHSWK* W4 105 J3
Chiswick Community School *CHSWK* W4 106 A6
Chiswick House *CHSWK* W4 106 A5
Chrisp Street Health Centre *POP/IOD* E14 93 K5
Christ Church Bentinck CE Primary School *CAMTN* NW1 9 J2
Christ Church Brondesbury CE J & I School *KIL/WHAMP* NW6 70 D7
Christ Church CE Infant School *NWMAL* KT3 160 B2
Christ Church CE Junior School *NWMAL* KT3 160 A2
Christ Church CE Primary School *BAR* EN5 26 B1
BRXN/ST SW9 110 B7
BRXS/STRHM SW2 130 A7
BRYLDS KT5 159 H5
CHEL SW3 15 K9
FSTH SE23 151 F1
Christchurch CE Primary School *HAMP* NW3 71 H2
WCHPL E1 13 M3
Christ Church CE Primary School *WOOL/PLUM* SE18 115 F7
Christchurch CE School *NFNCH/WDSP* N12 39 H4
Christ Church CE Middle School *EA* W5 85 K6
Christchurch Industrial Centre *STHWK* SE1 12 C8
Christ Church Primary School *BTSEA* SW11 128 D2
Christchurch Primary School *IL* IG1 60 C7
Christ Church School *CAMTN* NW1 4 D6
Christian Meeting Hall *BECK* BR3 151 J7

Christine King 6th Form College
LEW SE13 ... 133 G2
Christopher Hutton Primary School
FSBYW WC1X ... 12 A1
Christs College
BKHTH/KID SE3 ... 113 K7
EFNCH N2 ... 53 F2
Christs College School
EFNCH N2 ... 53 F2
Christs School
RCHPK/HAM TW10 ... 125 G4
Christ the King RC First School
STWL/WRAY TW19 ... 120 A5
Christ the King RC Primary School
FSBYPK N4 ... 73 F1
Chrysalis Theatre
BAL SW12 ... 129 F7
Chrysanthemum Clinic
CHSWK W4 ... 105 K6
Chrysolyta Primary School
STHWK SE1 ... 19 H3
Church Down Adult School
LEE/GVPK SE12 ... 152 E1
Church End Medical Centre
WLSDN NW10 ... 69 G5
Church Farm House Museum
HDN NW4 ... 51 K2
Church Farm Swimming Pool
EBAR EN4 ... 27 K7
Churchfield Primary School
ED N9 ... 30 B7
Churchfield School
WOOL/PLUM SE18 ... 116 A3
Churchfields J & I School
SWFD E18 ... 44 E7
Churchfields Primary School
BECK BR3 ... 166 A2
Church Hill Primary School
EBAR EN4 ... 27 K6
Church House
WEST SW1P ... 17 H3
Churchill Clinic
STHWK SE1 ... 18 B3
Churchill College
RYNPK SW20 ... 161 F1
TOOT SW17 ... 147 K1
Churchill Gardens Primary School
PIM SW1V ... 16 E8
Churchill Theatre
HAYES BR2 ... 167 K1
Church Mead Infant School
LEY E10 ... 57 J7
Church Mead Junior School
LEY E10 ... 57 J7
The Church School
BTFD TW8 ... 105 F5
Church Stairs
WAP E1W ... 111 J1
Church Trading Estate
ERITH DA8 ... 118 D6
Cineworld Cinema
BXLYHS DA6 ... 137 J3
FELT TW13 ... 141 F1
WDGN N22 ... 55 G1
City Banking College
STHWK SE1 ... 19 H1
City Business Centre
BERM/RHTH SE16 ... 111 K1
City Business College
FSBYE EC1V ... 6 D8
City Central Estate
FSBYE EC1V ... 6 E8
City College of Higher Education
IS N1 ... 7 H7
City & Guilds of London Art School
LBTH SE11 ... 18 B8
City Health Centre
FSBYE EC1V ... 7 G9
City & Islington College
FSBYE EC1V ... 6 F8
FSBYPK N4 ... 73 H1
HOLWY N7 ... 72 E3
IS N1 ... 7 G3
STLK EC1Y ... 13 G1
City & Islington College Sixth Form Centre
HOLWY N7 ... 73 F3
City of London Cemetery
MNPK E12 ... 77 J1
City of London Club
OBST EC2N ... 13 J4
City of London College
WCHPL E1 ... 92 C5
City of London Crematorium
MNPK E12 ... 77 H2
City of London Magistrates Court
MANHO EC4N ... 13 G5
City of London Polytechnic Sports Ground
ELTH/MOT SE9 ... 153 G1
City of London School
BLKFR EC4V ... 12 D6
City of London School for Girls
BARB EC2Y ... 12 E2
City of Westminster Cemetery
HNWL W7 ... 85 F7
City of Westminster College
BAY/PAD W2 ... 9 G2
MV/WKIL W9 ... 2 A8
City of Westminster Vehicle Pound
BAY/PAD W2 ... 9 M7
City Thameslink Station
FLST/FETLN EC4A ... 12 C5
City University
FSBYE EC1V ... 6 C6
FSBYE EC1V ... 6 D8
City University Business School
BARB EC2Y ... 12 F2
Civic Centre & Bromley Palace
BMLY BR1 ... 168 A1
Civic Medical Centre
HRW HA1 ... 48 E4
Civil Service Recreation Centre
WEST SW1P ... 17 H4
Civil Service Sports Ground
ELTH/MOT SE9 ... 134 B5
Clapham Common Clinic
CLAP SW4 ... 129 J3
Clapham Manor Primary School
CLAP SW4 ... 129 H2
Clapham Manor Street Public Baths
CLAP SW4 ... 129 J2
Clapham North Business Centre
CLAP SW4 ... 129 J2
Clapham Park School
CLAP SW4 ... 129 J4
Clapham Picture House
CLAP SW4 ... 129 H3
Clapton Girls' Technology College
CLPT E5 ... 74 E3
Clapton Jewish Boys School
STNW/STAM N16 ... 56 B6
Clara Grant Primary School
BOW E3 ... 93 J3
Clare House Primary School
BECK BR3 ... 167 F1
Claremont Clinic
FSTGT E7 ... 77 F4
Claremont Fan Court School
ESH/CLAY KT10 ... 170 B5
Claremont High School
KTN/HRWW/W HA3 ... 50 A4
Claremont Way Industrial Estate
CRICK NW2 ... 52 A7
Clarence House
WHALL SW1A ... 16 F1
Clarendon Special School
HPTN TW12 ... 142 B5
Claridges Hotel
MYFR/PKLN W1K ... 10 C6
Claverings Industrial Estate
ED N9 ... 42 E1
Claygate Primary School
ESH/CLAY KT10 ... 170 E6
Clayhall Clinic
CLAY IG5 ... 59 J2
Clayponds Hospital
BTFD TW8 ... 105 F3
Cleeve Park School
SCUP DA14 ... 155 J2
Clementine Churchill Hospital
HRW HA1 ... 67 F2
Cleopatra's Needle
CHCR WC2N ... 11 L8
Clerkenwell County Court
IS N1 ... 6 C5
Clerkenwell Heritage Centre
FARR EC1M ... 12 C1
Clerkenwell Parochial CE Primary School
CLKNW EC1R ... 6 A8
Cleveland Primary School
IL IG1 ... 78 B3
Cleves Primary School
EHAM E6 ... 77 H7
C & L Golf & Country Club
NTHLT UB5 ... 65 F6
Clifton Lodge School
EA W5 ... 85 K6
Clifton Primary School
NWDGN UB2 ... 102 D3
Clink Exhibition
STHWK SE1 ... 13 G8
Clissold Leisure Centre
STNW/STAM N16 ... 73 K2
Clissold Park Natural Health Centre
STNW/STAM N16 ... 74 A1
Clitterhouse Primary School
CRICK NW2 ... 70 B1
C & L Leisure Centre
NTHLT UB5 ... 65 F6
Clockhouse Industrial Estate
EBED/NFELT TW14 ... 120 E7
Clock Museum
CITYW EC2V ... 12 F4
Cloisters Business Centre
VX/NE SW8 ... 109 G6
Clore Gallery
WEST SW1P ... 17 J6
The Clore Tikva School
BARK/HLT IG6 ... 60 C1
Clothworkers' Hall
FENCHST EC3M ... 13 K6
Clouster's Green
WAP E1W ... 92 C7
Cobbold Estate
WLSDN NW10 ... 69 H5
Cobourg Primary School
CMBW SE5 ... 19 L8
Cochrane Theatre
GINN WC1R ... 11 L3
Cockfosters Sports Ground
EBAR EN4 ... 27 K2
The Cockpit Theatre
STJWD NW8 ... 9 J1
Coldharbour Industrial Estate
CMBW SE5 ... 130 D1
Coldharbour Leisure Centre
ELTH/MOT SE9 ... 153 K1
Coldharbour Sports Ground
ELTH/MOT SE9 ... 154 A1
Colebrooke Primary School
IS N1 ... 6 C5
Colegrave Primary School
SRTFD E15 ... 76 B4
Coleraine Park Primary School
TOTM N17 ... 42 D7
Coleridge Primary School
HGT N6 ... 54 D6
Colfes Preparatory School
LEE/GVPK SE12 ... 134 A5
Colindale Business Park
CDALE/KGS NW9 ... 50 E2
Colindale Hospital
CDALE/KGS NW9 ... 51 G2
Colindale Primary School
CDALE/KGS NW9 ... 51 H3
Coliseum Theatre
CHCR WC2N ... 11 J7
College Fields Business Centre
WIM/MER SW19 ... 147 J7
College Library & Civic Centre
SUT SM1 ... 175 F4
College of Arms
BLKFR EC4V ... 12 E5
College of Central London
SDTCH EC2A ... 7 J9
College of Fuel Technology
HGT N6 ... 54 A5
College of Law
GWRST WC1E ... 11 G2
The College of Law
FLST/FETLN EC4A ... 12 A4
GWRST WC1E ... 11 G2
College of North East London
CEND/HSY/T N8 ... 55 G3
FBAR/BDGN N11 ... 40 C7
SEVS/STOTM N15 ... 56 B3
College of North West London
KIL/WHAMP NW6 ... 2 A3
WBLY HA9 ... 68 C2
WLSDN NW10 ... 69 H4
College of Organists
FLST/FETLN EC4A ... 12 B4
College Park School
BAY/PAD W2 ... 8 B5
Collingwood Business Centre
ARCH N19 ... 72 E2
Collingwood Preparatory School
WLGTN SM6 ... 176 B4
Collins Method School
CRICK NW2 ... 70 A5
Collis Primary School
TEDD TW11 ... 143 H5
Colnbrook School
OXHEY WD19 ... 33 G1
Colne Bridge Retail Park
WAT WD17 ... 21 H4
Colne Valley Retail Park
WAT WD17 ... 21 H4
Coloma Convent Girls School
CROY/NA CR0 ... 179 F2
The Colonnades Shopping Centre
BGVA SW1W ... 16 C5
Colours Sports Club
SUT SM1 ... 175 G4
Columbia Primary School
BETH E2 ... 7 M7
Colvestone Primary School
HACK E8 ... 74 B4
Colville Primary School
NTGHL W11 ... 88 D5
Colyers Lane Medical Centre
ERITH DA8 ... 118 A7
Colyers Primary School
ERITH DA8 ... 118 A7
Comber Grove Primary School
CMBW SE5 ... 110 D6
Comedy Theatre
STJS SW1Y ... 11 G7
Comelle House Trading Estate
DEPT SE8 ... 112 B4
Commonwealth Institute
KENS W8 ... 107 J2
Community Arts Centre
GNWCH SE10 ... 112 E6
Community Centre (Island History Trust)
POP/IOD E14 ... 113 F3
Community College & School
GNWCH SE10 ... 113 F6
Community Health Centre
HOM E9 ... 74 E7
Compass Theatre
HGDN/ICK UB10 ... 64 A2
Complementary Health Centre
LEW SE13 ... 133 H5
Compton Leisure Centre
NTHLT UB5 ... 65 J7
The Compton School
NFNCH/WDSP N12 ... 39 J5
Compton Sports Centre
NFNCH/WDSP N12 ... 39 J5
Concord Business Centre
ACT W3 ... 86 D4
Coney Hill School
HAYES BR2 ... 180 D1
Connaught Business Centre
CDALE/KGS NW9 ... 51 H4
CROY/NA CR0 ... 177 F5
MTCM CR4 ... 162 E4
Connaught Girls School
WAN E11 ... 58 C7
Connaught House School
BAY/PAD W2 ... 9 L5
Consort Clinic
PECK SE15 ... 131 J2
Consulate General of Monaco
SKENS SW7 ... 15 G5
Consulate General of the Republic of Guinea Bissau
KENS W8 ... 14 E3
Consulate of Burkina Faso
BTSEA SW11 ... 128 B2
Consulate of Chile
CAVSQ/HST W1G ... 10 C1
Consulate of Colombia
GTPST W1W ... 10 E4
Consulate of Eritrea
IS N1 ... 6 B5
Consulate of Guinea
MYFR/PKLN W1K ... 10 A7
Consulate of Panama
MYFR/PICC W1J ... 10 C9
Control Tower
HTHAIR TW6 ... 120 E2
Convent of Jesus & Mary Infant School
CRICK NW2 ... 70 A5
Convent of Jesus & Mary Language College
WLSDN NW10 ... 69 H7
Conway Hall
FSBYW WC1X ... 11 L2
Conway Medical Centre
WOOL/PLUM SE18 ... 115 J4
Conway Primary School
WOOL/PLUM SE18 ... 115 K3
Coombe Girls School
NWMAL KT3 ... 160 A1
Coombe Hill Golf Club
KUTN/CMB KT2 ... 145 F6
Coombe Hill J & I School
NWMAL KT3 ... 145 F7
Coombe Wood Golf Club
KUTN/CMB KT2 ... 144 D6
Coopers' Hall
LVPST EC2M ... 13 K3
Coopers Lane Primary School
LEE/GVPK SE12 ... 152 E1
Coopers School
CHST BR7 ... 154 C7
Copenhagen Primary School
IS N1 ... 5 K4
Copland Community School & Technology Centre
WBLY HA9 ... 68 B4
Coppermill Primary School
WALTH E17 ... 57 F4
Coppetts Wood Hospital
MUSWH N10 ... 39 K7
Coppetts Wood Primary School
MUSWH N10 ... 40 A7
Copthall School
MLHL NW7 ... 37 K5
Cordwainers College
HOM E9 ... 74 E6
Corinthian Casuals FC
CHSGTN KT9 ... 172 C2
Cornhill Sports Club
BECK BR3 ... 151 J4
Coronet Cinema
NTGHL W11 ... 8 A8
SEVS/STOTM N15 ... 55 H2
Corpus Christi RC Primary School
BRXS/STRHM SW2 ... 130 A4
Cosmopolitan College
IS N1 ... 5 L6
Coston Secondary Modern Girls School
GFD/PVL UB6 ... 84 C2
Coteford Infant School
RSLP HA4 ... 46 E5
Courtauld Institute
HOL/ALD WC2B ... 11 L6
Court Farm Industrial Estate
STWL/WRAY TW19 ... 120 C5
Courtfield Medical Centre
ECT SW5 ... 14 D6
Courtland JMI School
MLHL NW7 ... 37 G1
Covent Garden Medical Centre
LSQ/SEVD WC2H ... 11 J5
CPFC Soccer & Sports Centre
BRXN/ST SW9 ... 130 A2
Crafts Council
IS N1 ... 6 B6
Crampton Primary School
WALW SE17 ... 18 D6
Cranbrook College
IL IG1 ... 78 A1
Crane Infant School
FELT TW13 ... 141 K1
Crane Junior School
FELT TW13 ... 141 J1
Cranford Community College
HEST TW5 ... 102 A5
Cranford Infant School
HSLWW TW4 ... 121 K1
Cranford Junior School
HSLWW TW4 ... 122 A1
Cranford Park Junior School
HYS/HAR UB3 ... 101 J3
Cranford Park Primary School
HYS/HAR UB3 ... 101 J1
Cranleigh Gardens Industrial Estate
STHL UB1 ... 83 K4
Cranmer School
MTCM CR4 ... 162 E4
The Craven Clinic
HMSMTH W6 ... 106 E3
Craven Park Health Centre
WLSDN NW10 ... 69 F7
Craven Park Medical Centre
WLSDN NW10 ... 69 F7
Craven Park Primary School
SEVS/STOTM N15 ... 56 C5
Crawford Primary School
CMBW SE5 ... 110 D7
Crawford Upper School
MBLAR W1H ... 9 L3
Crayfields Business Park
STMC/STPC BR5 ... 155 J7
Crayford Commercial Centre
DART DA1 ... 138 B4
Crayford Industrial Estate
DART DA1 ... 138 C4
Crayford Leisure Centre & Greyhound Stadium
DART DA1 ... 138 B5
Crayford Medical Centre
DART DA1 ... 138 C4
Crayside Industrial Estate
DART DA1 ... 138 D2
Creekmouth Industrial Estate
BARK IG11 ... 97 F3
Creek Road Health Centre
DEPT SE8 ... 112 D5
Creek Road Industrial Estate
DEPT SE8 ... 112 E5
Cremer Business Centre
BETH E2 ... 7 L6
Crewe House
MYFR/PICC W1J ... 10 C8
Cricket Pavilion
WEST SW1P ... 17 G5
Cricklefield Stadium
IL IG1 ... 78 E1
Cricklewood Trading Estate
CRICK NW2 ... 70 C2
Crispin Industrial Centre
UED N18 ... 42 E4
Criterion Theatre
MYFR/PICC W1J ... 10 F7
Crofton Leisure Centre
BROCKY SE4 ... 132 D5
Crofton School
BROCKY SE4 ... 132 D5
Croham Hurst Golf Club
SAND/SEL CR2 ... 178 B5
Croham Hurst School
SAND/SEL CR2 ... 178 B4
Cromer Road JMI School
BAR EN5 ... 27 F2
Cromwell Business Centre
BARK IG11 ... 96 E2
Cromwell Hospital
KENS W8 ... 14 C5
Cromwell Industrial Estate
LEY E10 ... 57 G7
Crook Log Primary School
BXLYHS DA6 ... 136 E3
Crook Log Sports Centre
WELL DA16 ... 136 E2
Crouch End Art School
CEND/HSY/T N8 ... 54 E4
Crouch End Health Centre
CEND/HSY/T N8 ... 54 E4
Crouch Hill Recreation Centre
ARCH N19 ... 54 E6
Crowland Primary School
SEVS/STOTM N15 ... 56 B4
Crowlands Primary School
ROMW/RG RM7 ... 62 E5
Crown Close Business Centre
BOW E3 ... 75 J7
Crown Court at the Borough
STHWK SE1 ... 18 D1
Crowndale Health Centre
CAMTN NW1 ... 4 F5
Crownfield Primary School
ROMW/RG RM7 ... 62 C1
Crown Lane Clinic
STHGT/OAK N14 ... 28 C7
Crown Lane Primary School
WNWD SE27 ... 149 H4
Crown Trading Centre
HYS/HAR UB3 ... 101 H1
Crown Woods School
ELTH/MOT SE9 ... 135 H4
Croydon Airport Industrial Estate
CROY/NA CR0 ... 177 G6
Croydon Cemetery
THHTH CR7 ... 164 A4
Croydon Clocktower Cinema
CROY/NA CR0 ... 177 J2
Croydon College
CROY/NA CR0 ... 177 K1
Croydon Fairfield Halls Cinema
CROY/NA CR0 ... 177 K2
Croydon FC
SNWD SE25 ... 165 K4
Croydon Indoor Bowling Club
SAND/SEL CR2 ... 177 J4
Croydon Road Industrial Estate
SNWD SE25 ... 165 K3
Croydon Sports Arena
SNWD SE25 ... 165 K4
Crusader Industrial Estate
FSBYPK N4 ... 55 J5
Crusoe House School
IS N1 ... 7 G7
Crystal Palace
NRWD SE19 ... 150 C5
Crystal Palace Athletics Stadium
NRWD SE19 ... 150 C5
Crystal Palace FC 1986 (Selhurst Park)
SNWD SE25 ... 165 F3
Crystal Palace Museum
NRWD SE19 ... 150 B5
Cuaco Sports Ground
BECK BR3 ... 151 J5
Cubitt Town Primary School
POP/IOD E14 ... 113 F2
Cuddington Cemetery
WPK KT4 ... 173 K1
Cuddington CP School
HOR/WEW KT19 ... 173 H2
Culloden Primary School
POP/IOD E14 ... 94 B5
Culvers House Primary School
MTCM CR4 ... 163 F7
Cumberland Business Park
WLSDN NW10 ... 86 D2
Cumberland Comprehensive School
CAN/RD E16 ... 94 D4
Cumberland Park Industrial Estate
WLSDN NW10 ... 87 J2
The Cuming Museum
WALW SE17 ... 18 E6
Cumnor House School
SAND/SEL CR2 ... 177 H7
Curwen Primary School
PLSTW E13 ... 94 E1
Curzon Mayfair Cinema
MYFR/PICC W1J ... 10 C9
Curzon Soho Cinema
SOHO/SHAV W1D ... 11 H6
Custom House
MON EC3R ... 13 J7
Cutlers' Hall
STP EC4M ... 12 D4
Cutty Sark
GNWCH SE10 ... 113 F5
Cygnet Clinic Beckton
EHAM E6 ... 96 B4
Cygnus Business Centre
WLSDN NW10 ... 69 H4
Cypress Infant School
SNWD SE25 ... 165 F1
Cypress Junior School
SNWD SE25 ... 165 F1
Cyprus College of Art
WNWD SE27 ... 149 H3
Cyril Jackson Primary School
POP/IOD E14 ... 93 H6
Dagenham Chest Clinic
BCTR RM8 ... 80 B2
Dagenham Civic Centre
DAGE RM10 ... 80 D1
Dagenham Priory Comprehensive School
DAGE RM10 ... 80 D6
Dagenham & Redbridge FC
DAGE RM10 ... 80 D4
Dagenham Superbowl
DAGE RM10 ... 98 D1
Dagenham Swimming Pool
BCTR RM8 ... 80 B1
Daily Mirror Office
FLST/FETLN EC4A ... 12 B3
Daily Telegraph
POP/IOD E14 ... 112 D2
Dairy Meadow Primary School
NWDGN UB2 ... 102 E2
D'Albiac House
HTHAIR TW6 ... 120 D1
Dali Universal Exhibition
STHWK SE1 ... 17 L1
Dallington School
FSBYE EC1V ... 6 D9
Dalmain Primary School
FSTH SE23 ... 132 B7
Damilola Taylor Centre
PECK SE15 ... 111 G6
Danegrove Primary School
EBAR EN4 ... 27 J5
Danetree School
HOR/WEW KT19 ... 172 E6
Danson Primary School
WELL DA16 ... 136 C3
Danson Watersports Centre
BXLYHS DA6 ... 136 D4
Darell Primary School
RCH/KEW TW9 ... 125 H2
Darent Industrial Park
ERITH DA8 ... 119 G4
Dartford County Court
DART DA1 ... 139 H5
Dartford Grammar School for Boys
DART DA1 ... 139 F5
Dartford Grammar School for Girls
DART DA1 ... 139 F6
Dartford Magistrates Court
DART DA1 ... 139 G5
Dartford Museum & Library
DART DA1 ... 139 H6
Dartford Natural Health Centre
DART DA1 ... 139 H6
Dartford West Health Centre
DART DA1 ... 139 F5

Dartford West Technology College *DART* DA1 139 F6
Darwin Centre *SKENS* SW7 15 G4
Datapoint Business Centre *CAN/RD* E16 94 B3
Daubeney Primary School *CLPT* E5 75 G3
David Game College *KENS* W8 8 A8
David Game Tutorial College *SKENS* SW7 15 G6
David Livingstone Primary School *THHTH* CR7 149 J7
David Lloyd Leisure Centre *SKENS* SW7 14 D5
David Lloyd Sports Centre *EN* EN1 30 C1
David Lloyd Tennis Centre *SCUP* DA14 155 J4
Davidson J & I School *CROY/NA* CR0 165 G6
Davies Lane Infant School *WAN* E11 76 D1
Davies's College *STHWK* SE1 18 F1
Dawlish Primary School *LEY* E10 76 A1
Days Lane Primary School *BFN/LL* DA15 136 A5
Deanesfield Primary School *RSLP* HA4 65 H3
Deansbrook Primary School *MLHL* NW7 36 E5
Deansfield Primary School *ELTH/MOT* SE9 135 F2
De Beauvoir Primary School *IS* N1 74 A5
De Bohun Primary School *STHGT/OAK* N14 28 A4
Delta Wharf *GNWCH* SE10 113 G1
De Lucy Primary School *ABYW* SE2 116 C1
Denmead School *HPTN* TW12 142 A6
Denver Industrial Estate *RAIN* RM13 99 H4
Department for Environment, Food & Rural Affairs *WHALL* SW1A 11 J8
Department of Health *WHALL* SW1A 17 J1
Department of Trade & Industry *STJSPK* SW1H 17 H3
Deptford Business Centre *DEPT* SE8 112 A4
Deptford Green School *NWCR* SE14 112 C6
Deptford Park Business Centre *DEPT* SE8 112 B4
Deptford Park Primary School *DEPT* SE8 112 B4
Deptford Trading Estate *DEPT* SE8 112 B4
Dersingham Infant School *MNPK* E12 77 K4
Derwentwater Primary School *ACT* W3 86 E7
Descovery Business Park *BERM/RHTH* SE16 111 H2
Design Museum *STHWK* SE1 13 M9
Deutsche Schule *RCHPK/HAM* TW10 124 E7
Devonshire Hill Primary School *TOTM* N17 41 K5
Devonshire Hospital *MHST* W1U 10 B2
Devonshire House Preparatory School *HAMP* NW3 71 H4
Devonshire House School *HAMP* NW3 71 G4
Devonshire Primary School *BELMT* SM2 175 G6
Diamond College *SOHO/SHAV* W1D 11 H4
Diana Fountain *E/WMO/HCT* KT8 158 A1
Diane Matthews Clinic *ROMW/RG* RM7 63 F3
Dilloway Industrial Estate *NWDGN* UB2 102 D1
Docklands Medical Centre *POP/IOD* E14 112 D3
Docklands Sailing Centre *POP/IOD* E14 112 D2
Docklands Sailing & Watersports Centre *POP/IOD* E14 112 C2
Dockmaster's House *POP/IOD* E14 93 J6
Dockwell's Industrial Estate *EBED/NFELT* TW14 122 A4
Dockyard Industrial Estate *WOOL/PLUM* SE18 114 D2
Dog Kennel Hill Primary School *CMBW* SE5 131 F2
Dokal Industrial Estate *NWDGN* UB2 102 D1
Dollis Hill Synagogue & Torah Temimah Primary School *CRICK* NW2 69 K3
Dollis Infant School *MLHL* NW7 38 A6
Dollis Junior School *MLHL* NW7 38 A6
The Dolphin Leisure Centre *ROM* RM1 63 H3
Dolphin School *BTSEA* SW11 128 E4
Dome *GNWCH* SE10 94 C7
Dominion Business Park *ED* N9 43 F1
Dominion Theatre *NOXST/BSQ* WC1A 11 H4
Donmar Warehouse Theatre *LSQ/SEVD* WC2H 11 J5
Donnington Primary School *WLSDN* NW10 69 K6
Dorchester Primary School *WPK* KT4 161 F7
Dorma Trading Park *LEY* E10 57 F7
Dormers Wells Leisure Centre *STHL* UB1 84 B5
Dormers Wells Medical Centre *STHL* UB1 84 A5
Dormers Wells Primary School *STHL* UB1 84 B6
Dormers Wells School *STHL* UB1 84 A5
Dorothy Barley Primary School *BCTR* RM8 79 H4
Dorset Road Infant School *ELTH/MOT* SE9 153 J1
Douglas Bader Foundation *PUT/ROE* SW15 126 D5
Dovers Corner Industrial Estate *RAIN* RM13 99 H2
Downderry Primary School *BMLY* BR1 152 C3
Downe Manor Primary School *NTHLT* UB5 83 F2
Downham Health Centre *BMLY* BR1 152 C3
Downhills Primary School *TOTM* N17 55 K3
Down Lane Junior School *TOTM* N17 56 B1
Downsell Junior School *WAN* E11 76 B3
Downshall Primary School *GNTH/NBYPK* IG2 60 E6
Downsview Primary School *NRWD* SE19 149 J6
Downsview School *CLPT* E5 74 D3
Drapers Hall *LOTH* EC2R 13 H4
Drapers Sports Ground *SRTFD* E15 76 A3
Drayton Green Primary School *WEA* W13 85 G6
Drayton Manor High School *HNWL* W7 85 F6
Drayton Park Primary School *HBRY* N5 73 G4
DRCA Business Centre *BTSEA* SW11 109 F7
Drew Primary School *CAN/RD* E16 95 J7
Driving School & Road Safety Centre *KTN/HRWW/W* HA3 49 G2
Dr Johnson's House *FLST/FETLN* EC4A 12 B5
Dr Tripletts CE J & I School *HYS/HAR* UB3 82 D5
Drummond Shopping Centre *CROY/NA* CR0 177 J1
Drury Way Industrial Estate *WLSDN* NW10 69 F3
Duchess Theatre *COVGDN* WC2E 11 L6
Duff Miller College *SKENS* SW7 14 F5
Duke of York Column *STJS* SW1Y 11 G9
Duke of York's HQ *CHEL* SW3 15 M6
Duke of York Theatre *CHCR* WC2N 11 J7
Dulverton Primary School *BFN/LL* DA15 154 D1
Dulwich College *DUL* SE21 131 F7
Dulwich College Preparatory School *DUL* SE21 150 A2
Dulwich College Track *DUL* SE21 150 A1
Dulwich Hamlet FC *EDUL* SE22 131 F3
Dulwich Hamlet Junior School *DUL* SE21 130 E5
Dulwich Hospital *EDUL* SE22 131 F3
Dulwich Leisure Centre *EDUL* SE22 131 H3
Dulwich Medical Centre *EDUL* SE22 131 H4
Dulwich Picture Gallery *DUL* SE21 130 E6
Dulwich & Sydenham Hill Golf Club *DUL* SE21 150 C1
Dulwich Village CE Infant School *DUL* SE21 131 F5
Dunbar Wharf *POP/IOD* E14 93 H6
Duncombe Primary School *ARCH* N19 54 E7
Dundee Wharf *POP/IOD* E14 93 H6
Dundonald First School *WIM/MER* SW19 146 D6
Dunningford Primary School *HCH* RM12 81 H4
Dunraven School (Lower School) *STRHM/NOR* SW16 149 F2
Dunraven School (Upper School) *STRHM/NOR* SW16 149 F2
Duppas Junior School *CROY/NA* CR0 177 H4
Durand Primary School *BRXN/ST* SW9 110 A7
Durands Wharf *BERM/RHTH* SE16 112 C1
Durdans Park Primary School *STHL* UB1 83 K4
Durston House School *EA* W5 85 K5
Dysart School *KUTN/CMB* KT2 143 K3
Dysart Special School *SURB* KT6 159 F6
Eaglesfield School *WOOL/PLUM* SE18 115 F7
Eagle Trading Estate *MTCM* CR4 162 E5
Ealdham Primary School *ELTH/MOT* SE9 134 B3
Ealing Abbey *EA* W5 85 J5
Ealing Abbey Scriptorium *WEA* W13 85 J5
The Ealing Broadway Centre *EA* W5 85 K6
Ealing Central Sports Ground *GFD/PVL* UB6 85 G1
Ealing Civic Centre *EA* W5 85 J6
Ealing College Upper School *WEA* W13 85 H5
Ealing Cricket Club *EA* W5 86 A5
Ealing Film Studios *EA* W5 85 J7
Ealing Golf Club *GFD/PVL* UB6 85 H2
Ealing Hospital *NWDGN* UB2 103 J1
Ealing Northern Sports Centre *GFD/PVL* UB6 66 D3
Ealing Park Health Centre *EA* W5 104 E3
Ealing Road Trading Estate *BTFD* TW8 104 E4
Ealing Sports Centre *EA* W5 86 A6
Ealing Tertiary College *EA* W5 85 J7
Ealing Tutorial College *EA* W5 85 J6
Eardley Primary School *STRHM/NOR* SW16 148 C5
Earlham J & I School *WDGN* N22 41 G6
Earlham Primary School *FSTGT* E7 76 D4
Earl's Court Exhibition Centre *ECT* SW5 14 A8
Earlsfield Primary School *WAND/EARL* SW18 147 G1
Earlsmead First & Middle School *RYLN/HDSTN* HA2 65 K3
Earlsmead Primary School *SEVS/STOTM* N15 56 B3
Earth Gallery *SKENS* SW7 15 H4
East Acton Primary School *ACT* W3 87 G6
East Barking Luncheon & Leisure Centre *BCTR* RM8 79 J4
East Barnet Health Centre *EBAR* EN4 27 H4
East Barnet School *EBAR* EN4 27 H2
EBAR EN4 27 K5
East Beckton District Centre *EHAM* E6 95 K5
Eastbrook Comprehensive School *DAGE* RM10 80 E3
Eastbrook End Cemetery *DAGE* RM10 81 G2
Eastbrookend Country Park *DAGE* RM10 81 F3
Eastbury Comprehensive School *BARK* IG11 78 E6
Eastbury Farm JMI School *NTHWD* HA6 32 D3
Eastbury Infant School *BARK* IG11 79 F6
Eastcote Cricket Club *PIN* HA5 47 F4
Eastcote Health Centre *PIN* HA5 47 G6
Eastcote Industrial Estate *RSLP* HA4 47 G6
Eastcote Lane Cemetery *RYLN/HDSTN* HA2 66 B2
Eastcote Primary School *ELTH/MOT* SE9 135 J2
Eastcourt Independent School *GDMY/SEVK* IG3 61 G7
Eastern Business Park *HTHAIR* TW6 121 J1
Eastfields High School *MTCM* CR4 163 G1
East Finchley Cemetery *EFNCH* N2 53 F2
East Finchley Medical Centre *EFNCH* N2 53 J3
East Finchley School of English *EFNCH* N2 53 J2
East Greenwich Christ Church CE Primary School *GNWCH* SE10 113 H3
East Ham Industrial Estate *CAN/RD* E16 95 H3
East Ham Jewish Cemetery *EHAM* E6 95 J2
East Ham Leisure Centre *EHAM* E6 77 K7
East Ham Memorial Hospital *FSTGT* E7 77 H6
East Ham Nature Reserve *EHAM* E6 95 K3
East Lane Business Park *WBLY* HA9 67 K1
Eastlea Community School *CAN/RD* E16 94 C3
East London Business College *WAN* E11 58 C7
East London Cemetery *PLSTW* E13 94 D2
East London Crematorium *PLSTW* E13 94 D2
East London RFC *EHAM* E6 95 K4
East London RUFC *PLSTW* E13 94 D1
Eastman Dental Hospital *FSBYW* WC1X 5 L9
East Molesey Cricket Club *E/WMO/HCT* KT8 157 H2
East Sheen Cemetery *RCHPK/HAM* TW10 125 H4
East Sheen Primary School *MORT/ESHN* SW14 126 B3
East Thamesmead Business Park *ERITHM* DA18 117 G1
East Wickham Primary School *WELL* DA16 116 A7
Eaton House School *KTBR* SW1X 16 A5
Eaton Manor RFC *WAN* E11 59 G4
Eaton Square Preparatory School *BGVA* SW1W 16 C5
Eaton Square School *PIM* SW1V 16 E6
Ecclesbourne Primary School *IS* N1 7 G1
THHTH CR7 164 D4
Eckerd College *GWRST* WC1E 11 G2
Ecole De Mime Corporel Theatre De Lange Fou *FSBYPK* N4 72 E1
Eden College *STHWK* SE1 18 D3
Edenham High School *CROY/NA* CR0 166 B6
Eden Medical Centre *WKENS* W14 107 J3
Edenvale Child Health Clinic *TOOT* SW17 148 A6
Eden Walk Shopping Centre *KUT* KT1 159 F1
Edes Business Park *WLGTN* SM6 176 A1
Edgebury Primary School *CHST* BR7 154 C3
Edge Business Centre *CRICK* NW2 69 K1
Edgwarebury Cemetery *EDGW* HA8 36 C1
Edgware Clinic *EDGW* HA8 36 C5
Edgware College *HAMP* NW3 71 G5
Edgware Community Hospital *EDGW* HA8 36 D6
Edgware FC & Wealdstone FC *EDGW* HA8 36 C6
Edgware Infant School *EDGW* HA8 36 C5
Edgware Junior School *EDGW* HA8 36 C5
The Edgware School *EDGW* HA8 36 B3
Edinburgh Primary School *WALTH* E17 57 H4
Edith Neville Primary School *CAMTN* NW1 5 G6
Edmonton Cemetery *ED* N9 41 K1
Edmonton County Court *UED* N18 42 C4
Edmonton Green Shopping Centre *ED* N9 42 D1
Edmonton Leisure Centre *ED* N9 42 C2
Edmonton Upper School *EN* EN1 30 B6
Edmund Waller Primary School *NWCR* SE14 132 A1
Education Centre *WOOL/PLUM* SE18 115 G4
Edward Betham CE Primary School *GFD/PVL* UB6 84 D2
Edward Pauling School *FELT* TW13 140 C1
Edward Redhead Primary School *WALTH* E17 57 G2
Edward Wilson Primary School *BAY/PAD* W2 8 C2
Edwin Lambert Schooll *EMPK* RM11 63 J5
Effra Primary School *BRXS/STRHM* SW2 130 B4
Effra Road Retail Park *BRXS/STRHM* SW2 130 B4
Eglinton Infant School *WOOL/PLUM* SE18 115 F6
Eglinton Junior School *WOOL/PLUM* SE18 115 F5
Elbourne Trading Estate *BELV* DA17 117 J2
Eldenwall Industrial Estate *BCTR* RM8 62 A7
Eldon JMI School *ED* N9 30 E7
Eleanor Palmer Primary School *KTTN* NW5 72 C3
Eleanor Smith Special School & Primary Support Service *PLSTW* E13 94 E1
Electrical Trades Union College *ESH/CLAY* KT10 170 A3
Electric Cinema *NTGHL* W11 88 D5
Elephant & Castle Station *STHWK* SE1 18 E5
Elephant & Castle Leisure Centre *LBTH* SE11 18 D5
Elephant & Castle Shopping Centre *STHWK* SE1 18 D4
Elers Clinic *HYS/HAR* UB3 101 G3
Elfrida Primary School *CAT* SE6 151 K3
Eliot Bank Primary School *FSTH* SE23 150 D1
Elizabeth Garrett Anderson Hospital *CAMTN* NW1 5 H8
Elizabeth Garrett Anderson School *IS* N1 5 M5
Elizabeth Selby Infant School *BETH* E2 92 C2
Elizabeth Trading Estate *NWCR* SE14 112 A5
Ellen Wilkinson Primary School *EHAM* E6 95 H4
Ellen Wilkinson School for Girls *ACT* W3 86 B5
Ellerslie Square Industrial Estate *BRXS/STRHM* SW2 129 K3
Ellingham Primary School *CHSGTN* KT9 171 K6
Elliott Foundation School *PUT/ROE* SW15 127 F5
Elmbridge Leisure Centre *WOT/HER* KT12 156 A4
Elm Court School *WNWD* SE27 149 H1
Elmgrove First & Middle School *KTN/HRWW/W* HA3 49 G3
Elmhurst Preparatory School *BECK* BR3 166 A3
Elmhurst Primary School *FSTGT* E7 77 F6
Elmhurst School *CROY/NA* CR0 177 K3
Elm Lea Trading Estate *TOTM* N17 42 C6
Elmwood Primary School *CROY/NA* CR0 164 C6
Elm Wood Primary School *WNWD* SE27 149 K2
Elsdale Street Health Centre *HOM* E9 74 E6
Elsley Primary School *WBLY* HA9 68 B5
Elsley School *BTSEA* SW11 129 F2
Elstree Aerodrome *BORE* WD6 23 F2
Elstree Golf Club *BORE* WD6 23 K2
Elstree Studios *BORE* WD6 24 C2
Elstree Way Clinic *BORE* WD6 24 D1
Eltham Bus Station *ELTH/MOT* SE9 134 E4
Eltham Cemetery *ELTH/MOT* SE9 135 H3
Eltham CE Primary School *ELTH/MOT* SE9 134 E4
Eltham College *ELTH/MOT* SE9 153 H1
Eltham College Junior School *ELTH/MOT* SE9 134 C7
Eltham Crematorium *ELTH/MOT* SE9 135 J3
Eltham Green School *ELTH/MOT* SE9 134 C5
Eltham Health Clinic *ELTH/MOT* SE9 134 D4
Eltham Health & Fitness Centre *ELTH/MOT* SE9 135 F5
Eltham Hill Technology College *ELTH/MOT* SE9 134 D5
Eltham Palace (remains) *ELTH/MOT* SE9 134 D6
Eltham Pools *ELTH/MOT* SE9 134 D4
Eltham Warren Golf Club *ELTH/MOT* SE9 135 G4
Elthorne Park High School *HNWL* W7 104 A2
Elthorne Sports Centre *HNWL* W7 104 A2
Elystan Business Centre *HYS/HAR* UB3 83 G6
Emanuel School *WAND/EARL* SW18 128 C4
Embankment Pier *CHCR* WC2N 11 L8
Embass of Thailand *SKENS* SW7 14 F4
Embassy of Afghanistan *SKENS* SW7 15 G2
Embassy of Albania *BGVA* SW1W 16 D4
Embassy of Algeria *NTGHL* W11 88 C7
Embassy of Angola *MYFR/PKLN* W1K 10 A7
Embassy of Argentina *MYFR/PKLN* W1K 10 C6
Embassy of Armenia *KENS* W8 14 C3
Embassy of Austria *KTBR* SW1X 16 A3
Embassy of Bahrain *SKENS* SW7 14 E4
Embassy of Belarus *KENS* W8 14 D2
Embassy of Belgium *KTBR* SW1X 16 B4
Embassy of Bolivia *KTBR* SW1X 16 B4
Embassy of Bosnia-Herzegovina *CAVSQ/HST* W1G 10 D4
Embassy of Brazil *MYFR/PKLN* W1K 10 A6
Embassy of Bulgaria *SKENS* SW7 14 F3
Embassy of Cameroon *NTGHL* W11 88 C7
Embassy of China *CAVSQ/HST* W1G 10 C2
Embassy of Costa Rica *BAY/PAD* W2 8 F6
Embassy of Cote d'Ivoire *KTBR* SW1X 16 B3
Embassy of Croatia *GTPST* W1W 10 D1
Embassy of Cuba *LSQ/SEVD* WC2H 11 J4
Embassy of Democratic Republic of the Congo *KTBR* SW1X 15 M4
Embassy of Denmark *KTBR* SW1X 15 L3
Embassy of Dominican Republic *BAY/PAD* W2 8 D5
Embassy of Ecuador *KTBR* SW1X 15 L3
Embassy of Egypt *MYFR/PICC* W1J 10 C8
Embassy of Estonia *SKENS* SW7 14 F2
Embassy of Ethiopia *SKENS* SW7 15 H2
Embassy of Finland *KTBR* SW1X 16 A3
Embassy of France *KTBR* SW1X 15 M1
Embassy of Gabon *SKENS* SW7 14 F4
Embassy of Georgia *KENS* W8 14 C2
Embassy of Germany *KTBR* SW1X 16 A3
Embassy of Ghana *HGT* N6 54 B7
Embassy of Greece *KENS* W8 88 D7
Embassy of Guatemala *WBPTN* SW10 14 E9
Embassy of Honduras *MBLAR* W1H 9 M2
Embassy of Hungary *KTBR* SW1X 16 B4
Embassy of Iceland *KTBR* SW1X 16 A5
Embassy of Indonesia *MYFR/PKLN* W1K 10 B7
Embassy of Iran *SKENS* SW7 15 H2
Embassy of Iraq *SKENS* SW7 14 F3
Embassy of Ireland *KTBR* SW1X 16 C2
Embassy of Israel *KENS* W8 14 D1
Embassy of Italy *MYFR/PKLN* W1K 10 B6
Embassy of Japan *MYFR/PICC* W1J 10 D9
Embassy of Jordan *KENS* W8 14 A2

Embassy of Korea *WESTW* SW1E 16 F3
Embassy of Krygyzstan *MBLAR* W1H 9 L3
Embassy of Kuwait *KTBR* SW1X 15 M1
Embassy of Latvia *CAMTN* NW1 10 A1
Embassy of Lebanon *KENS* W8 8 C8
Embassy of Liberia *BAY/PAD* W2 8 B6
Embassy of Lithuania *MBLAR* W1H 9 L3
Embassy of Luxembourg *KTBR* SW1X 16 A2
Embassy of Mexico *MYFR/PICC* W1J 10 C9
Embassy of Mongolia *KENS* W8 14 D2
Embassy of Morocco *SKENS* SW7 14 E5
Embassy of Mozambique *FITZ* W1T 10 E1
Embassy of Myanmar *MYFR/PICC* W1J 10 C8
Embassy of Nepal *KENS* W8 8 C8
Embassy of Netherlands *SKENS* SW7 14 F2
Embassy of Norway *KTBR* SW1X 16 B3
Embassy of Paraguay *SKENS* SW7 14 D4
Embassy of Peru *KTBR* SW1X 15 M3
Embassy of Philippines *KENS* W8 8 C9
Embassy of Poland *CAVSQ/HST* W1G 10 C2
Embassy of Portugal *KTBR* SW1X 16 A2
Embassy of Qatar *MYFR/PKLN* W1K 10 B8
Embassy of Republic of Senegal *CRICK* NW2 70 A6
Embassy of Romania *KENS* W8 14 C1
Embassy of Russian Federation *KENS* W8 8 C9
Embassy of Saudi Arabia *MYFR/PICC* W1J 10 C8
Embassy of Slovak Republic *KENS* W8 8 C8
Embassy of Slovenia *CAVSQ/HST* W1G 10 C4
Embassy of South Vietnam *KENS* W8 14 D3
Embassy of Spain *KTBR* SW1X 16 B3
Embassy of Sudan *WHALL* SW1A 10 E9
Embassy of Sweden *MBLAR* W1H 9 L3
Embassy of Switzerland *MBLAR* W1H 9 L3
Embassy of Syria *KTBR* SW1X 16 A2
Embassy of Tunisia *SKENS* SW7 15 H2
Embassy of Turkey *KTBR* SW1X 16 B2
Embassy of Turkmenistan *GTPST* W1W 10 F3
Embassy of Ukraine *NTGHL* W11 88 C7
Embassy of United Arab Emirates *SKENS* SW7 15 H1
Embassy of Uruguay *SKENS* SW7 15 K3
Embassy of USA *MYFR/PKLN* W1K 10 A6
Embassy of Uzbekistan *NTGHL* W11 88 D7
Embassy of Venezuela *SKENS* SW7 15 H4
Embassy of Yemen *SKENS* SW7 15 G5
Ember Sports Club *ESH/CLAY* KT10 157 H7
Embroidery World Business Centre *WFD* IG8 59 H1
EMD Walthamstow Cinema *WALTH* E17 57 J3
Emery Theatre *POP/IOD* E14 93 K5
Emmanuel CE Primary School *KIL/WHAMP* NW6 70 E4
Emmanuel CE School *NTHWD* HA6 32 D6
Empire Cinema *LSQ/SEVD* WC2H 11 H6
Endsleigh Industrial Estate *NWDGN* UB2 102 D3
Enfield Business Centre *PEND* EN3 30 E1
Enfield College *PEND* EN3 30 E2
Enfield County Upper School *ENC/FH* EN2 29 K2
Enfield Cricket Club *EN* EN1 30 A3
Enfield FC *ED* N9 42 E1
Enfield Golf Club *ENC/FH* EN2 29 H3
Enfield Grammar School (Upper) *ENC/FH* EN2 29 K2
Enfield Lower Grammar School *ENC/FH* EN2 29 K1
English Martyrs RC Primary School *WALW* SE17 19 G6
WCHPL E1 13 M5
Ennersdale Primary School *LEW* SE13 133 G4
Ensham Secondary School *TOOT* SW17 147 K4
Enterprise Business Park *POP/IOD* E14 112 E1
Enterprise Industrial Estate *BERM/RHTH* SE16 111 K4
Epsom & Ewell High School *HOR/WEW* KT19 172 E5
Eric Liddell Sports Centre *ELTH/MOT* SE9 153 H1
Erith Cemetery *BELV* DA17 117 J5
Erith & District Hospital *ERITH* DA8 118 A5
Erith Health Centre *ERITH* DA8 118 B5
Erith Library & Museum *ERITH* DA8 118 B4
Erith School *ERITH* DA8 117 K6
Erith School Community Sports Centre *ERITH* DA8 117 K6
Erith Small Business Centre *ERITH* DA8 118 C5
Erith Sports Centre *ERITH* DA8 118 B5
Erith Stadium *ERITH* DA8 118 B5
Erith Theatre Guild *ERITH* DA8 118 C4
Ernest Bevin School *TOOT* SW17 147 J2
Eros *MYFR/PICC* W1J 11 G7
Esher Church School (Primary) *ESH/CLAY* KT10 170 C5
Esher College *THDIT* KT7 157 K6
Essendine Primary School *KIL/WHAMP* NW6 2 B8
Essex Primary School *MNPK* E12 77 J5
Ethelburga GM School *BTSEA* SW11 108 D7
Ethel Davis School *CHDH* RM6 61 H4
Euro Business Centre *SRTFD* E15 76 D7
Eurolink Business Centre *BRXS/STRHM* SW2 130 B3
Europa Trading Estate *ERITH* DA8 118 A4
European Business Centre *CDALE/KGS* NW9 51 F2
European School of Economics *KTBR* SW1X 16 B2
European Vocational College *HDTCH* EC3A 13 K5
Euro Way School *CEND/HSY/T* N8 55 G2
Euro Way School London *FSBYPK* N4 55 H6
Euston Centre *CAMTN* NW1 4 E9
Euston Station *CAMTN* NW1 5 G8
Euston Tower *CAMTN* NW1 4 E9
Eveline Lowe Primary School *STHWK* SE1 111 H4
Evendine College *SOHO/SHAV* W1D 11 G4
Eversley Medical Centre *THHTH* CR7 164 B5
Eversley Primary School *WCHMH* N21 28 E4
Everyman Cinema *HAMP* NW3 71 G3
Evolution House *RCH/KEW* TW9 125 F1
Ewell Athletics Track *HOR/WEW* KT19 173 F5
Ewell Castle School *EW* KT17 173 J7
Ewell Grove Infant School *EW* KT17 173 H7
EW Fact/Emile Woolf Colleges *HOLWY* N7 72 E5
ExCeL Exhibition Centre *CAN/RD* E16 95 G7
Exchange Square *SDTCH* EC2A 13 J2
The Exchange *IL* IG1 78 B1
Exhibition Halls *STLK* EC1Y 12 F2
WBLY HA9 68 C3
Eye Clinic *LSQ/SEVD* WC2H 11 H4
Fairbrook Medical Centre *BORE* WD6 24 D1
Faircharm Trading Estate *DEPT* SE8 112 E6
IS N1 6 E5
The Faircross Complementary Medical Centre *BARK* IG11 78 E5
Fairfield Industrial Estate *KUT* KT1 159 G2
Fairfield Pool & Leisure Centre *DART* DA1 139 H6
Fairholme J & I School *EBED/NFELT* TW14 121 G7
Fairlawn Primary School *FSTH* SE23 131 K6
Fairley House School *WEST* SW1P 17 G6
Fairview Industrial Centre *DAGW* RM9 99 F5
Fairview Industrial Estate *HYS/HAR* UB3 101 J1
Fairview Medical Centre *STRHM/NOR* SW16 148 E7
Fairway JMI School *MLHL* NW7 37 F1
Fairway Primary School *MLHL* NW7 37 F1
Fairways Business Park *LEY* E10 75 G1
Falconbrook JMI School *BTSEA* SW11 128 C1
Falcon Business Centre *BTSEA* SW11 128 D3
Falconer School *BUSH* WD23 21 K4
Falcon Park Industrial Estate *WLSDN* NW10 69 G4
Falkner House School *ECT* SW5 14 F7
Family Records Centre *CLKNW* EC1R 6 A8
Fanmakers' Hall *LVPST* EC2M 13 J4
Fan Museum *GNWCH* SE10 113 F6
Faraday Building *BLKFR* EC4V 12 D5
Farm Lane Trading Estate *FUL/PGN* SW6 107 K5
Farnell House Medical Centre *HSLW* TW3 103 G7
Farnham Green Primary School *GDMY/SEVK* IG3 61 G5
Farringdon Station *FARR* EC1M 12 B2
Farrington & Stratford House School *CHST* BR7 154 D6
Fashion & Textile Design Museum *STHWK* SE1 19 K2
Featherstone Industrial Estate *NWDGN* UB2 102 D1
Featherstone Primary School *NWDGN* UB2 102 D2
Featherstone Road Health Clinic *NWDGN* UB2 102 D2
Featherstone School *NWDGN* UB2 102 C3
Felnex Trading Estate *WLGTN* SM6 176 A1
Feltham Airparcs Leisure Centre *FELT* TW13 141 H1
Feltham Athletics Arena *EBED/NFELT* TW14 121 K6
Felthambrook Industrial Estate *FELT* TW13 141 F2
Feltham Community College *FELT* TW13 141 G1
Feltham Hill Infant School *FELT* TW13 140 C2
Feltham Hill Junior School *FELT* TW13 140 D2
Feltham & Hounslow Boro FC *EBED/NFELT* TW14 121 K6
Feltham Superbowl *FELT* TW13 141 F1
Fenchurch Street Station *FENCHST* EC3M 13 K6
Fenstanton J & I School *BRXS/STRHM* SW2 130 B7
Fenton House *HAMP* NW3 71 G2
Fern Hill Primary School *KUTN/CMB* KT2 144 A5
Ferrier Industrial Estate *WAND/EARL* SW18 128 A3
Ferry Island Retail Park *TOTM* N17 56 B2
Ferry Lane Industrial Estate *RAIN* RM13 99 J4
WALTH E17 56 E2
Ferry Lane Primary School *TOTM* N17 56 D3
Festival Pier *STHWK* SE1 11 M8
Field End Primary School *RSLP* HA4 65 H1
Fielding Primary School *WEA* W13 104 C2
Field Junior School *WATW* WD18 21 G4
Film House Cinema *RCH/KEW* TW9 124 E4
Financial Times *POP/IOD* E14 94 A5
STHWK SE1 12 F8
Finchley Lido *NFNCH/WDSP* N12 39 H6
Finchley Catholic High School *NFNCH/WDSP* N12 39 G2
Finchley Cricket Club *FNCH* N3 53 F1
Finchley Golf Club *MLHL* NW7 38 D5
The Finchley Industrial Centre *NFNCH/WDSP* N12 39 G3
Finchley Memorial Hospital *FNCH* N3 39 G6
Finchley Youth Theatre *EFNCH* N2 53 J2
Fine Arts College *HAMP* NW3 71 J5
Finsbury Circus Medical Centre *LVPST* EC2M 13 H3
Finsbury Health Centre *CLKNW* EC1R 6 A9
Finsbury Leisure Centre *FSBYE* EC1V 6 F8
Finsbury Park Track *FSBYPK* N4 55 H6
Finton House School *TOOT* SW17 147 K1
Fircroft Primary School *TOOT* SW17 147 K1
Fire & Ambulance Station *HTHAIR* TW6 100 D7
Fire Brigade HQ *STHWK* SE1 17 L5
Fire Brigade Museum *STHWK* SE1 18 E1
Firepower (Museum of Artillery) *WOOL/PLUM* SE18 115 G2
Firs Farm Primary School *PLMGR* N13 41 K2
Fisher Athletic FC *BERM/RHTH* SE16 93 F7
Fisher Industrial Estate *WATW* WD18 21 G4
Fishmonger's Hall *CANST* EC4R 13 G7
Fitness Unlimited Leisure Centre *BOW* E3 93 J1
Fitzjohns Primary School *HAMP* NW3 71 H4
Fitzrovia Medical Centre *GTPST* W1W 10 E1
Fitzroy Nuffield Hospital *MBLAR* W1H 9 L4
Five Bridges Special School *LBTH* SE11 17 M8
Five Elms Primary School *DAGW* RM9 80 B2
Five Ways Business Centre *FELT* TW13 141 F2
Flamsteed House Museum *GNWCH* SE10 113 G6
Flaxman Sports Centre *CMBW* SE5 130 D1
Fleecefield Primary School *ED* N9 42 C3
Fleet Primary School *HAMP* NW3 71 K4
Fleetway Business Park *GFD/PVL* UB6 85 H1
Fleming Lab Museum *BAY/PAD* W2 9 H4
Flora Gardens Primary School *HMSMTH* W6 106 E3
Florence Nightingale Museum *STHWK* SE1 17 L2
Florida State University *RSQ* WC1B 11 H3
Flutters Leisure Centre *FUL/PGN* SW6 107 K6
FOB School *STNW/STAM* N16 56 C6
Follys End Christian High School *SNWD* SE25 165 F5
The Foot Clinic *WIM/MER* SW19 146 C4
The Ford College *CONDST* W1S 10 D6
Ford Industrial Park *DAGW* RM9 98 D2
Fordview Industrial Estate *RAIN* RM13 99 F2
Foreign & Commonwealth Office *WHALL* SW1A 17 H1
Foreland Medical Centre *NTGHL* W11 88 C6
Forest Business Park *WALTH* E17 57 F6
Forestdale Primary School *CROY/NA* CR0 179 G7
Foresters Primary School *WLGTN* SM6 176 D5
Forest Gate Community School *FSTGT* E7 76 E4
Forest Hill Business Centre *FSTH* SE23 150 E1
Forest Hill Industrial Estate *FSTH* SE23 150 E1
Forest Hill School *FSTH* SE23 151 F2
Forest Hills Pools *FSTH* SE23 150 E1
Forest House Business Centre *WAN* E11 58 D6
Forest Road Medical Centre *WALTH* E17 57 H2
Forest School *WALTH* E17 58 C3
Forest Trading Estate *WALTH* E17 57 F2
Forge Close Clinic *HAYES* BR2 167 K7
Forge Lane Primary School *FELT* TW13 141 J4
The Former Health Centre *CHARL* SE7 114 C3
Forster Park Primary School *CAT* SE6 152 C2
Fortismere School *EFNCH* N2 53 K1
Fortismere Secondary School *MUSWH* N10 54 A2
Fortune Theatre *HOL/ALD* WC2B 11 K5
The Forum *EDGW* HA8 36 C5
Fossdene Primary School *CHARL* SE7 114 A4
Fosters Primary School *WELL* DA16 136 D1
Foster's Primary School *WELL* DA16 136 D1
Foulds School *BAR* EN5 26 B2
The Foundling Museum *BMSBY* WC1N 5 K9
Fountayne Business Centre *SEVS/STOTM* N15 56 C3
Fountayne Road Health Centre *CLPT* E5 74 C1
Foxfield Primary School *WOOL/PLUM* SE18 115 H4
Fox Primary School *KENS* W8 8 A9
Frances Bardsley School for Girls *ROM* RM1 63 J4
Frances King School of English *SKENS* SW7 14 E5
Franciscan Primary School *TOOT* SW17 148 A3
Francis Holland School *BGVA* SW1W 16 B6
CAMTN NW1 9 L1
Frank Barnes Primary School *HAMP* NW3 3 H2
Franklin Industrial Estate *PGE/AN* SE20 150 E7
Freehold Industrial Centre *HSLWW* TW4 122 B4
Free Trade Wharf *WAP* E1W 93 F6
Fresh Wharf Estate *BARK* IG11 78 B7
Freuchen Medical Centre *WLSDN* NW10 87 H1
Freud Museum *HAMP* NW3 71 H5
Friars Primary Foundation School *STHWK* SE1 18 C1
Friends House *CAMTN* NW1 5 G8
Friends of Bar Ilan University *GLDGN* NW11 52 E7
Friends of the Hebrew University *CAMTN* NW1 4 C4
Friern Barnet School *FBAR/BDGN* N11 39 K4
Friern Bridge Retail Park *FBAR/BDGN* N11 40 B5
Frithwood Primary School *NTHWD* HA6 32 D5
Froebel College *PUT/ROE* SW15 126 D5
Frogmore Industrial Estate *HBRY* N5 73 J3
HYS/HAR UB3 101 H1
WLSDN NW10 86 E2
Fryent Country Park *WBLY* HA9 50 C6
Fryent Medical Centre *CDALE/KGS* NW9 50 E6
Fryent Primary School *CDALE/KGS* NW9 50 E6
Fulham Clinic *FUL/PGN* SW6 107 J5
Fulham Cross School *FUL/PGN* SW6 107 G6
Fulham FC (Craven Cottage) *BARN* SW13 107 F7
Fulham Medical Centre *FUL/PGN* SW6 108 A6
Fulham Palace *FUL/PGN* SW6 127 H1
Fulham Preparatory School *FUL/PGN* SW6 127 H1
Fulham Primary School *FUL/PGN* SW6 107 K5
Fulham Warner Village Cinema *FUL/PGN* SW6 107 K6
Fuller Smith & Turner Sports Club *CHSWK* W4 106 B7
Fullwell Cross Health Centre *BARK/HLT* IG6 60 C1
Fullwell Cross Swimming Pool & Recreation Centre *BARK/HLT* IG6 60 C1
Fullwood Primary School *BARK/HLT* IG6 60 C3
Fulwell Golf Club *HPTN* TW12 142 D3
Furzedown Primary School *TOOT* SW17 148 B5
Furzehill School *BORE* WD6 24 C3
Furze Infant School *CHDH* RM6 62 A5
Future Business College *CONDST* W1S 10 D5
Gaflac Sports Ground Pavilion *SUN* TW16 140 E7
Gainsborough Clinic *PLMGR* N13 41 F3
Gainsborough Primary School *HOM* E9 75 H5
SRTFD E15 94 C2
Galleywall Primary School *BERM/RHTH* SE16 111 J3
Galliard Primary School *ED* N9 30 C5
Gallions Mount Primary School *WOOL/PLUM* SE18 116 A4
Gallions Primary School *EHAM* E6 96 B5
Gants Hill Medical Centre *GNTH/NBYPK* IG2 60 A5
Gardener Industrial Estate *BECK* BR3 151 G4
Garden House Boys School *KTBR* SW1X 15 L4
Garden House Girls School *BGVA* SW1W 15 M7
Garden Suburb Primary School *GLDGN* NW11 52 D4
Garfield Primary School *FBAR/BDGN* N11 40 B4
WIM/MER SW19 147 G5
Garratt Park Secondary Special School *WAND/EARL* SW18 147 F2
Garrick Industrial Centre *CDALE/KGS* NW9 51 H4
Garrick Theatre *LSQ/SEVD* WC2H 11 J7
Garth Primary School *MRDN* SM4 162 C4
The Garth Road Industrial Centre *MRDN* SM4 161 F6
Gascoigne Primary School *BARK* IG11 78 C7
Gate Cinema *NTGHL* W11 8 A8
Gatehouse School *BETH* E2 93 F1
The Gatehouse Theatre *HGT* N6 54 A6
The Gate Theatre *NTGHL* W11 8 A8
Gateway Industrial Estate *WLSDN* NW10 87 H2
Gateway Primary School *STJWD* NW8 3 H9
Gayhurst Primary School *HACK* E8 74 C6
Gazelda Industrial Estate *WAT* WD17 21 G4
Gearies Infant School *GNTH/NBYPK* IG2 60 A4
Gearies Junior School *GNTH/NBYPK* IG2 60 B4
Geffrye Museum *BETH* E2 7 K6
Gemini Business Estate *NWCR* SE14 112 A4
General Medical Clinics *WCHPL* E1 13 L2
Genesis Cinema *WCHPL* E1 92 E3
Geoffrey Chaucer School *STHWK* SE1 19 G4
The Geoffrey Lloyd Foulkes Clinic *IL* IG1 78 A1
Geoffrey Whitworth Theatre *DART* DA1 138 D3
George Elliot Primary School *STJWD* NW8 2 F3
George Green Mixed School *POP/IOD* E14 113 F4
George Lowe Court *BAY/PAD* W2 8 C2
George Mitchell School *LEY* E10 57 K7
George Mitchell School Annexe *LEY* E10 57 K7
George Spicer Primary School *EN* EN1 30 B2
George Tomlinson Primary School *WAN* E11 58 C7
Germal College *FSBYPK* N4 55 G7
Gibbs Green Special School *WKENS* W14 107 J4
Gibson Business Centre *TOTM* N17 42 B5
The Gibson Business Centre *TOTM* N17 42 B6
Gidea Park College *GPK* RM2 63 J2
Gidea Park Primary School *GPK* RM2 63 H3
The Gielgud Theatre *SOHO/SHAV* W1D 11 G6
Giffin Business Centre *DEPT* SE8 112 D6
Gifford Primary School *NTHLT* UB5 83 K1
Gilbert Collection *TPL/STR* WC2R 11 L6

Gilbert Scott Primary School
SAND/SEL CR2 179 G6
Gillespie Primary School
FSBYPK N4 73 H2
Girdlers' Hall
CITYW EC2V 12 F3
Glade Primary School
CLAY IG5 45 K7
Gladesmore Community School
SEVS/STOTM N15 56 C4
The Glades Shopping Centre
BMLY BR1 167 K1
Gladstone Court Business Centre
VX/NE SW8 109 H7
Gladstone Medical Centre
CRICK NW2 69 H3
Gladstone Park Primary School
WLSDN NW10 69 K4
Glaziers/Scientific Instrument Makers Hall
STHWK SE1 13 G8
Glebe First & Middle School
KTN/HRWW/W HA3 49 K3
Glebe Primary School
HGDN/ICK UB10 64 B3
Glebe School
WWKM BR4 167 G7
Gleen Lecky Health Centre
PUT/ROE SW15 127 G3
Glenbrook Primary School
CLAP SW4 129 J5
Glencairn Sports Club
FBAR/BDGN N11 40 C6
Glendower Preparatory School
SKENS SW7 14 F5
Glenham College
IL IG1 78 B1
Glenlyn Medical Centre
E/WMO/HCT KT8 157 H4
Glenthorne High School
CHEAM SM3 161 K7
Globe Primary School
BETH E2 92 E2
Globe Wharf
BERM/RHTH SE16 93 F6
Gloucester Primary School
PECK SE15 111 F6
Godolphin & Latymer School
HMSMTH W6 106 E3
Godwin Junior School
FSTGT E7 77 F3
Godwin Primary School
DAGW RM9 80 A6
Golborne Medical Centre
NKENS W10 88 D3
Goldbeaters Primary School
EDGW HA8 37 F7
Golden Hinde Educational Museum
STHWK SE1 13 G7
Golders Green Crematorium
GLDGN NW11 52 E6
Golders Green Health Centre
GLDGN NW11 53 F7
Golders Hill Health Centre
EFNCH N2 53 G5
Golders Hill School
GLDGN NW11 52 E6
Goldhawk Industrial Estate
SHB W12 106 E2
Goldsmiths College
BROCKY SE4 132 C2
DEPT SE8 112 D5
LEW SE13 133 H3
NWCR SE14 112 B7
Goldsmiths Hall
STBT EC1A 12 E4
Gonville Primary School
THHTH CR7 164 A4
Goodinge Health Centre
HOLWY N7 72 E5
Goodmayes Primary School
GDMY/SEVK IG3 61 H7
Goodmayes Retail Park
CHDH RM6 61 H6
Goodrich J & I School
EDUL SE22 131 H5
Good Shepherd RC Primary School
BMLY BR1 152 D3
CROY/NA CR0 179 K6
The Good Shepherd RC Primary School
SHB W12 106 C1
Goodwyn School
MLHL NW7 37 J4
Goose Green Primary School
EDUL SE22 131 G3
Goose Green Trading Estate
EDUL SE22 131 H3
Gordonbrock Primary School
BROCKY SE4 132 D4
Gordon Hospital
WEST SW1P 17 G6
Gordon House Health Centre
WEA W13 85 J7
Gordon Infant School
IL IG1 78 D2
Gordon Primary School
ELTH/MOT SE9 134 E3
Goresbrook Leisure Centre
DAGW RM9 79 K7
Goresbrook Sports Centre
DAGW RM9 80 A7
Gorringe Park Middle School
MTCM CR4 148 A7
Gosai Cinema
WEA W13 85 H7
Gosbury Hill Health Centre
CHSGTN KT9 172 A3
Gosford Primary School
REDBR IG4 59 K4
Gospel Oak Primary School
HAMP NW3 72 A3
Gower House School
CDALE/KGS NW9 68 E1
Grace Business Centre
MTCM CR4 162 E5
Grace Theatre at the Latchmere
BTSEA SW11 128 E1
Graduate School of Management
TOTM N17 42 B7
Grafton Primary School
BCTR RM8 80 A1
HOLWY N7 72 E2
Grahame Park Health Centre
CDALE/KGS NW9 37 G7
Grahame Park J & I School
CDALE/KGS NW9 37 G7
Granard Business Centre
EDGW HA8 37 G5
Granard Primary School
PUT/ROE SW15 126 E5
Granby Sports Club
ELTH/MOT SE9 153 J4
Grand Avenue Primary School
BRYLDS KT5 159 K6
Grande Vitesse Industrial Centre
STHWK SE1 12 D9
Grand Union Industrial Estate
WLSDN NW10 86 D1
Grange First & Middle School
RYLN/HDSTN HA2 48 B7
Grange Infant School
CAN/RD E16 94 D2
The Grange Museum
CRICK NW2 69 H3
Grange Park Clinic
YEAD UB4 82 D3
Grange Park Preparatory School
WCHMH N21 29 H5
Grange Park Primary School
ENC/FH EN2 29 G3
YEAD UB4 82 D3
Grange Primary School
EA W5 104 E1
STHWK SE1 19 J4
Grangewood Independent School
FSTGT E7 77 H6
Grangewood School
RSLP HA4 46 E4
Granton Primary School
STRHM/NOR SW16 148 C6
Granville Road Industrial Estate
CRICK NW2 70 D1
Grasmere Primary School
STNW/STAM N16 73 K3
Grasshoppers RFC
ISLW TW7 104 A5
Grassroots School
HPTN TW12 142 A7
Grasvenor Avenue Infant School
BAR EN5 26 E5
Gravel Hill Primary School
BXLYHS DA6 137 J4
Graveney School
TOOT SW17 148 B5
Graves Yard Industrial Estate
WELL DA16 136 B1
Grays Farm Primary School
STMC/STPC BR5 155 H7
Grazebrook Primary School
STNW/STAM N16 74 A1
Great Cambridge Industrial Estate
EN EN1 30 D4
Great Chapel Street Medical Centre
SOHO/SHAV W1D 11 G4
Greater London Authority Headquarters (City Hall)
STHWK SE1 13 K9
Greatham Road Industrial Estate
BUSH WD23 21 J3
Great Jubilee Wharf
WAP E1W 92 E7
Great Western Industrial Park
NWDGN UB2 103 G1
Great West Trading Estate
BTFD TW8 104 C5
Greenacres Primary School
ELTH/MOT SE9 154 A1
The Green CE Primary School
TOTM N17 56 B2
Green Dragon School
BTFD TW8 105 F4
Greenfield Medical Centre
CRICK NW2 70 C2
Greenfields Junior School
SHB W12 87 H6
Greenfields Primary School
OXHEY WD19 33 G4
Greenfields Special School
MUSWH N10 39 K7
Greenford Avenue Medical Centre
HNWL W7 84 E4
Greenford Green Clinic
GFD/PVL UB6 66 E4
Greenford High School
STHL UB1 84 A2
Greenford Industrial Estate
GFD/PVL UB6 66 B7
Greenford Park Cemetery
GFD/PVL UB6 84 B4
Greenford Road Medical Centre
GFD/PVL UB6 84 D1
Greenford Sports Centre
STHL UB1 84 A2
Greengate Medical Centre
PLSTW E13 95 F2
Greengrove College
STHGT/OAK N14 40 E1
Greenheath Business Centre
BETH E2 92 D2
Greenhill College
HRW HA1 49 F4
Greenhill Park Medical Centre
WLSDN NW10 69 G7
Greenland Pier
BERM/RHTH SE16 112 C2
Green Lane Business Park
ELTH/MOT SE9 154 A1
Green Lane Primary School
WPK KT4 160 E6
Greenleaf Primary School
WALTH E17 57 H2
Greenmead Primary School
PUT/ROE SW15 126 E4
The Green School for Girls
ISLW TW7 104 B6
Greenshaw High School
SUT SM1 175 G1
Greenshields Industrial Estate
CAN/RD E16 94 E7
Greenside Primary School
SHB W12 106 D1
Greenslade Primary School
WOOL/PLUM SE18 115 J5
Greenvale School
FSTH SE23 151 G2
Greenwich Centre Business Park
DEPT SE8 112 E6
Greenwich Cinema
GNWCH SE10 113 F6
Greenwich College
GNWCH SE10 113 F6
Greenwich Community College
WOOL/PLUM SE18 115 G3
WOOL/PLUM SE18 115 J5
Greenwich Hospital
GNWCH SE10 113 J4
Greenwich Industrial Estate
CHARL SE7 114 A3
GNWCH SE10 112 E6
Greenwich Natural Health Centre
GNWCH SE10 113 F6
Greenwich Pier
GNWCH SE10 113 F4
Greenwich Theatre & Art Gallery
GNWCH SE10 113 G6
Greenwich University Library
GNWCH SE10 113 F5
Greenwood First School
MTCM CR4 163 J2
Greenwood Primary School
NTHLT UB5 66 C4
Greenwood School
WOOL/PLUM SE18 115 K7
Greenwood Theatre
STHWK SE1 19 H1
Green Wrythe Primary School
CAR SM5 162 C5
Gresham College
FLST/FETLN EC4A 12 A3
Gresham Way Industrial Estate
WIM/MER SW19 147 F2
The Greycoat Hospital
WEST SW1P 17 G6
Grey Coat Hospital Upper School
WEST SW1P 17 G4
Grey Court School
RCHPK/HAM TW10 143 K2
Griffen Manor School
WOOL/PLUM SE18 115 K7
Grimsdyke First & Middle School
PIN HA5 33 K5
Grims Dyke Golf Club
PIN HA5 34 A3
Grinling Gibbons Primary School
DEPT SE8 112 C5
Grist Memorial Sports Club
E/WMO/HCT KT8 157 K4
Grocers' Hall
CITYW EC2V 13 G5
Grosvenor Hospitals
HDN NW4 51 K4
Grove Health Centre
KENS W8 8 B8
The Grove Health Centre
SHB W12 106 E1
Grove House School
WNWD SE27 149 H1
Grovelands Priory Hospital
STHGT/OAK N14 28 E7
Grovelands School
WOT/HER KT12 156 A5
Grove Medical Centre
DEPT SE8 112 B3
The Grove Medical Centre
ARCH N19 72 C1
Grove Park Industrial Estate
CDALE/KGS NW9 51 F3
Grove Park Primary School
CHSWK W4 105 K5
Grove Park School
CDALE/KGS NW9 50 E3
Grove Primary School
CHDH RM6 61 H4
Grove Road Primary School
HSLW TW3 123 F3
The Groves Medical Centre
NWMAL KT3 160 B2
Grove Village Medical Centre
EBED/NFELT TW14 121 H7
Guardian Angels RC Primary School
BOW E3 93 G3
Guardian Newspapers
POP/IOD E14 112 E1
Guards' Chapel & Museum
WHALL SW1A 17 G2
Guildhall Annex
KUT KT1 158 E2
Guildhall Art Gallery
LOTH EC2R 12 F4
Guildhall School
BARB EC2Y 12 F2
Guildhall School of Music & Drama
STLK EC1Y 12 F1
Guildhall University
WCHPL E1 92 C5
Gumley House Convent School
ISLW TW7 124 B2
Gunnersbury Catholic School
BTFD TW8 104 D4
Gunnersbury Park Museum
ACT W3 105 H2
Gurnell Leisure Centre
WEA W13 85 F2
Guru Nanak Medical Centre
STHL UB1 83 H7
Guys Hospital
STHWK SE1 13 H9
Guys Kings & St Thomas School of Medicine
CMBW SE5 130 D1
Gwyn Jones Primary School
WAN E11 58 B6
GX Superbowl
EHAM E6 96 A4
Gypsy Moth IV
GNWCH SE10 113 F5
Haberdashers' Aske's Boys' School
BORE WD6 23 H2
Haberdashers' Aske's Girls' School
BORE WD6 23 H3
Haberdashers Askes Hatcham College
NWCR SE14 112 B7
NWCR SE14 132 A1
Haberdashers' Hall
CITYW EC2V 12 F4
Haberdashers RUFC
BORE WD6 24 B1
Hackbridge Primary School
WLGTN SM6 163 F7
Hackney Business Centre
HACK E8 74 D5
Hackney Community College
CLPT E5 74 D2
IS N1 7 J6
Hackney Empire Variety Theatre
HACK E8 74 D5
Hackney Free & Parochial CE School
HOM E9 74 E5
Hackney Hospital
HOM E9 75 G4
The Hackney Museum
HOM E9 74 E7
Hackney Sports Centre
HOM E9 75 J3
Hadlow College
LEE/GVPK SE12 134 B7
The Haelan Clinic
CEND/HSY/T N8 54 D5
Haggerston School
BETH E2 7 M5
Haggerston Swimming Pool
BETH E2 7 M4
Hague Primary School
BETH E2 92 D3
Hailey Road Business Park
ERITHM DA18 117 H1
Haimo Primary School
ELTH/MOT SE9 134 C4
Hakim Qureshi Clinic
NWDGN UB2 102 D2
The Hale Clinic
REGST W1B 10 D1
Half Moon Theatre
WCHPL E1 93 F3
Haling Manor High School
CROY/NA CR0 177 H6
Halley Primary School
POP/IOD E14 93 G4
Hallfield Clinic
BAY/PAD W2 8 E5
Hallfield J & I School
BAY/PAD W2 8 D5
The Hall Junior School
HAMP NW3 71 H5
Hallmark Trading Estate
WBLY HA9 68 E3
Hall Place
BXLY DA5 137 K5
Halls Business Centre
HYS/HAR UB3 101 K2
Hall School Wimbledon
PUT/ROE SW15 145 J2
The Hall Senior School
HAMP NW3 71 H5
Hallsville Primary School
CAN/RD E16 94 E5
Halstow Primary School
GNWCH SE10 113 J4
Hambrough Primary School
STHL UB1 83 J7
Hamer Indoor Market
BOW E3 93 H1
Ham Health Clinic
RCHPK/HAM TW10 143 J2
Ham House (NT)
RCHPK/HAM TW10 124 D7
Hamilton Road Industrial Estate
WNWD SE27 149 K3
Hamlet International Industrial Estate
ERITH DA8 118 A4
Hammersmith Apollo
HMSMTH W6 107 F4
Hammersmith Cemetery
HMSMTH W6 107 G4
The Hammersmith Hospitals
SHB W12 87 J5
Hammersmith Industrial Estate
HMSMTH W6 107 F5
Hammersmith New Cemetery
RCH/KEW TW9 125 J1
Hammersmith Palais
HMSMTH W6 107 F3
Hammersmith Physio & Sportsinjury Clinic
HMSMTH W6 107 F3
Hammersmith & West London College
WKENS W14 107 G3
Hampden Gurney School
MBLAR W1H 9 K4
Ham & Petersham Cricket Club
RCHPK/HAM TW10 143 K3
The Hampshire School (Knightsbridge)
SKENS SW7 15 J2
The Hampshire School
BAY/PAD W2 8 D6
Hampstead Cricket Club
KIL/WHAMP NW6 71 F4
Hampstead Golf Club
EFNCH N2 53 G6
Hampstead Hill School
HAMP NW3 71 K3
Hampstead Medical Centre
HAMP NW3 71 G3
Hampstead Parochial CE School
HAMP NW3 71 G3
Hampstead School
CRICK NW2 70 C3
Hampstead School of English
KIL/WHAMP NW6 70 E3
Hampstead Theatre
HAMP NW3 3 G1
Hampton Cemetery
HPTN TW12 142 A6
Hampton Community College
HPTN TW12 142 A4
Hampton Court Palace
E/WMO/HCT KT8 158 A2
Hampton Farm Industrial Estate
FELT TW13 141 J2
Hampton FC
HPTN TW12 142 B7
Hampton Hill Junior School
HPTN TW12 142 C4
Hampton Infant School
HPTN TW12 141 K6
Hampton Junior School
HPTN TW12 142 A7
The Hampton Medical Centre
HPTN TW12 142 A6
Hampton Open Air Pool
HPTN TW12 142 C6
Hampton Road Industrial Park
CROY/NA CR0 164 D5
Hampton School
HPTN TW12 142 A4
Hampton Wick Infants School
KUT KT1 143 J6
Handel's House
MYFR/PKLN W1K 10 C6
Handsworth Health Clinic
CHING E4 44 B5
Handsworth Primary School
CHING E4 44 B5
Hanover Primary School
IS N1 6 D5
Hanover Trading Estate
HOLWY N7 72 E4
Hanover West Industrial Estate
WLSDN NW10 86 E2
Hanworth Trading Estate
FELT TW13 141 J2
Harbinger Primary School
POP/IOD E14 112 D3
Harborough School
ARCH N19 72 D1
Harenc School
SCUP DA14 155 J4
Hargrave Park Primary School
ARCH N19 72 C1
Haringey Arts Council
ED N9 42 C1
Haringey Community Health Clinic
SEVS/STOTM N15 56 B3
Haringey Health Care
SEVS/STOTM N15 56 B3
Haringey Magistrates Court
HGT N6 54 A5
Harkness Industrial Estate
BORE WD6 24 C3
Harland Primary School
WIM/MER SW19 162 B1
Harlequin Shopping Centre
WAT WD17 21 G3
Harlesden Primary School
WLSDN NW10 87 G1
Harley Medical Centre
CAVSQ/HST W1G 10 C4
The Harley Medical Centre
CANST EC4R 12 F6
Harley Street Clinic
CAVSQ/HST W1G 10 C3
Harlington Community School
HYS/HAR UB3 101 G3
Harlyn Primary School
PIN HA5 47 F2
The Harold Macmillan Medical Centre
HRW HA1 48 D6
Harp Business Centre
CRICK NW2 69 J1
Harpley School
WCHPL E1 92 E3
Harrington Hill Primary School
CLPT E5 56 D7
Harris City Technology College
NRWD SE19 150 B7
Harrodian School
BARN SW13 106 C6
Harrods Store
CHEL SW3 15 L3
Harrovian Business Village
HRW HA1 48 D6
Harrow Arts Centre
PIN HA5 34 A6
Harrow Borough FC
RYLN/HDSTN HA2 66 A3
Harrow College
HRW HA1 48 E6
Harrow Cricket Club
HRW HA1 66 E3
Harrow Crown Courts
HRW HA1 48 D2
Harrow Heritage Museum
RYLN/HDSTN HA2 48 C2
Harrow High School
HRW HA1 49 G5
Harrow Magistrates Court
HRW HA1 49 F3
Harrow RFC
STAN HA7 35 H2
Harrow Road Health Centre
BAY/PAD W2 8 B2
Harrow School
HRW HA1 48 E6
RYLN/HDSTN HA2 66 E1
Harrow Superbowl
RYLN/HDSTN HA2 48 B4
Harrow Town Cricket Club
RYLN/HDSTN HA2 48 A7
Harrow Weald Cemetery
KTN/HRWW/W HA3 34 E5
Harry Gosling Primary School
WCHPL E1 92 C5
Hartley Primary School
EHAM E6 77 J7
Hartsbourne Golf & Country Club
BUSH WD23 34 C1
Hartsbourne JMI School
BUSH WD23 34 D1
Hartspring Industrial Park
GSTN WD25 22 A1
Hartspring Sports Centre
BUSH WD23 22 A1
Harvington School
EA W5 85 J5
Haselrigge School
CLAP SW4 129 J3
Haseltine Primary School
CAT SE6 151 H3
Haslemere Business Centre
EN EN1 30 D3
Haslemere Industrial Estate
EBED/NFELT TW14 121 K4
WAND/EARL SW18 147 F1
Haslemere Primary School
MTCM CR4 162 C1
Hasmonean High School
HDN NW4 52 B1
MLHL NW7 37 J7
Hasmonean Primary School
HDN NW4 52 B4
Haste Hill Golf Club
NTHWD HA6 46 C1
Hastings Clinic
BRXS/STRHM SW2 130 A4
Hastingwood Trading Estate
UED N18 43 G5
Hatcham Mews Business Centre
NWCR SE14 112 A6
Hatch End High School
KTN/HRWW/W HA3 34 B6
Hatch End Swimming Pool
PIN HA5 34 A6

Hathaway Primary School *WEA* W13 85 F4
Hatton School *REDBR* IG4 59 H2
Havelock Primary School *NWDGN* UB2 102 E2
Haven Green Clinic *EA* W5 85 K5
Havering College of Further & Higher Education *EMPK* RM11 63 K6
Havering Magistrates Court *ROM* RM1 63 G3
Haverstock School *CAMTN* NW1 72 A5
Hawes Down Clinic *WWKM* BR4 180 B1
Hawes Down primary School *WWKM* BR4 167 G7
The Hawker Centre *KUTN/CMB* KT2 143 K4
Hawkins Clinic *PUT/ROE* SW15 127 G3
RYNPK SW20 145 H7
Hawksmoor Primary School *THMD* SE28 97 H6
Hawley Infant School *CAMTN* NW1 4 D2
Haydon School *PIN* HA5 46 D2
Hayes Bridge Middle School *NWDGN* UB2 102 D1
Hayes Bridge Retail Park *HYS/HAR* UB3 83 G6
Hayes Cricket Club *HYS/HAR* UB3 82 D5
Hayes FC *HYS/HAR* UB3 82 D6
Hayes Grove Priory Hospital *HAYES* BR2 180 E1
The Hayes Manor School *HYS/HAR* UB3 82 B5
Hayes Park J & I School *YEAD* UB4 82 D3
Hayes Pool *HYS/HAR* UB3 82 D7
Hayes Primary School *HAYES* BR2 168 A7
Hayes School *HAYES* BR2 181 F1
Hayes Social & Sports Club *HYS/HAR* UB3 82 D6
Hayes Stadium Sports Centre *HYS/HAR* UB3 82 B5
Hay Lane School *CDALE/KGS* NW9 50 E3
Haymerle School *PECK* SE15 111 H5
Hays Galleria *STHWK* SE1 13 J8
Hayward Gallery *STHWK* SE1 11 M9
Hazelbury Primary School *ED* N9 42 A2
Hazeldene Medical Centre *WBLY* HA9 68 D5
Hazelhurst School *RYNPK* SW20 146 B7
Hazelwood Infant School *PLMGR* N13 41 H3
Hazelwood Junior School *PLMGR* N13 41 G3
Healy Medical Centre *CLPT* E5 56 D7
The Heart Hospital *CAVSQ/HST* W1G 10 B3
Heathbrook Primary School *VX/NE* SW8 129 H1
Heath Business Centre *HSLW* TW3 123 H3
Heathcote School *CHING* E4 44 C1
Heathfield College *HAYES* BR2 181 G5
Heathfield Primary School *WHTN* TW2 123 F7
Heathfield School (Senior) *PIN* HA5 47 H5
Heath House Preparatory School *BKHTH/KID* SE3 133 J1
Heathland School *HSLWW* TW4 122 E5
Heathmere Primary School *PUT/ROE* SW15 126 D7
Heathpark Golf Club *WDR/YW* UB7 100 D2
Heathrow Airport *HTHAIR* TW6 120 E1
Heathrow Airport Central Bus & Coach Station *HTHAIR* TW6 120 D2
Heathrow International Trading Estate *HSLWW* TW4 122 A2
Heathrow Medical Centre *HYS/HAR* UB3 101 G4
Heathrow Primary School *WDR/YW* UB7 100 C5
Heathrow World Cargo Centre *HTHAIR* TW6 120 C4
Heathside Preparatory School *HAMP* NW3 71 G3
Heathway Industrial Estate *DAGE* RM10 80 D3
Heathway Medical Centre *DAGW* RM9 80 B3
Heavers Farm Primary School *SNWD* SE25 165 G4
Heber Primary School *EDUL* SE22 131 G5
Heckford Street Business Centre *WAP* E1W 93 F6
Hedges & Butler Estate *SRTFD* E15 94 A1
Hedgewood School *YEAD* UB4 82 C2
Helena Road Clinic *WLSDN* NW10 69 K3
Heliport Industrial Estate *BTSEA* SW11 128 C1
Hellenic College of London *KTBR* SW1X 15 L4
Helston Court Business Centre *WIM/MER* SW19 145 K4
Henderson Hospital *BELMT* SM2 174 E7
Hendon Cemetery *HDN* NW4 38 B7
Hendon College *CDALE/KGS* NW9 37 H7
Hendon Crematorium *HDN* NW4 38 B6
Hendon FC *CRICK* NW2 70 B1
Hendon Golf Club *HDN* NW4 38 A6
Hendon Preparatory School *HDN* NW4 52 B2
Hendon School *HDN* NW4 52 B4
Hendon Secretarial College *HDN* NW4 51 K4
Hendon Youth Sports Centre *CRICK* NW2 52 B6
Henry Cavendish Primary School *BAL* SW12 129 H7
Henry Compton School *FUL/PGN* SW6 107 G7
Henry Fawcett Primary School *LBTH* SE11 18 A9
Henry Green Primary School *BCTR* RM8 61 K7
Henry Maynard Infant School *WALTH* E17 58 A4
Henry Maynard Junior School *WALTH* E17 58 A4
Henwick Primary School *ELTH/MOT* SE9 134 C2
Herbert Morrison Primary School *VX/NE* SW8 109 K6
Hereward House School *HAMP* NW3 71 J5
Her Majestys' Theatre *STJS* SW1Y 11 H8
Hermitage Primary School *WAP* E1W 92 C7
Herne Hill School *HNHL* SE24 130 D4
Herne Hill Stadium (Cycle Centre) *DUL* SE21 130 E5
Heron Industrial Estate *SRTFD* E15 93 K1
Heronsgate Primary School *THMD* SE28 115 J2
Heron Trading Estate *ACT* W3 86 D4
Heston Community School *HEST* TW5 103 F6
Heston Community Sports Hall *HEST* TW5 103 F6
Heston Industrial Mall *HEST* TW5 102 E6
Heston Infant School *HEST* TW5 103 F6
Heston Junior School *HEST* TW5 103 F5
Heston Park Cricket Club *HEST* TW5 102 E5
Heston Swimming Baths *HEST* TW5 102 E5
Heythrop College *KENS* W8 14 C3
HGS Institute Centre *GLDGN* NW11 53 F4
Higgs Industrial Estate *BRXN/ST* SW9 130 C2
Highams Lodge Business Centre *WALTH* E17 57 F2
Highams Park School *CHING* E4 44 B5
Highbury Corner Magistrates Court *HOLWY* N7 73 G5
Highbury Fields School *HBRY* N5 73 H4
Highbury Grove School *HBRY* N5 73 J4
Highbury Park Clinic *HBRY* N5 73 H2
Highbury Pool *HBRY* N5 73 H5
Highbury Quadrant Primary School *HBRY* N5 73 J3
High Commission of Angola *MYFR/PKLN* W1K 10 B6
High Commission of Antigua & Barbuda *MHST* W1U 10 A4
High Commission of Bahamas *MYFR/PICC* W1J 10 B8
High Commission of Bangladesh *SKENS* SW7 14 F3
High Commission of Barbados *FITZ* W1T 11 G4
High Commission of Belize *CAVSQ/HST* W1G 10 C4
High Commission of Botswana *OXSTW* W1C 10 C5
High Commission of Brunei *KTBR* SW1X 16 A3
High Commission of Cyprus *CONDST* W1S 10 D5
MYFR/PKLN W1K 10 A6
High Commission of Dominica *ECT* SW5 14 D6
High Commission of Fiji *SKENS* SW7 14 E2
High Commission of Gambia *KENS* W8 14 D2
High Commission of Guyana *NTGHL* W11 8 C7
High Commission of Jamaica *SKENS* SW7 15 G2
High Commission of Kenya *CAVSQ/HST* W1G 10 C2
High Commission of Lesotho *KTBR* SW1X 16 A3
High Commission of Malawi *MYFR/PKLN* W1K 10 C6
High Commission of Malaysia *KTBR* SW1X 16 B2
MBLAR W1H 9 L4
High Commission of Maldives *MHST* W1U 10 A2
High Commission of Malta *MYFR/PICC* W1J 10 F7
High Commission of Mauritius *SKENS* SW7 14 F4
High Commission of Namibia *CAVSQ/HST* W1G 10 D3
High Commission of New Zealand *STJS* SW1Y 11 G8
High Commission of Nigeria *CHCR* WC2N 11 J8
EMB EC4Y 12 B5
High Commission of Pakistan *KTBR* SW1X 15 M3
High Commission of Papua New Guinea *STJS* SW1Y 11 G8
High Commission of St Vincent & The Grenadines *KENS* W8 14 D2
High Commission of Seychelles *MBLAR* W1H 9 M2
High Commission of Sierra Leone *OXSTW* W1C 10 E4
High Commission of Singapore *KTBR* SW1X 15 M2
KTBR SW1X 16 A4
STJS SW1Y 11 G8
WEST SW1P 16 F5
High Commission of South Africa *CHCR* WC2N 11 J8
High Commission of Sri Lanka *BAY/PAD* W2 9 H6
High Commission of Swaziland *WESTW* SW1E 16 E3
High Commission of Tonga *MBLAR* W1H 9 K3
High Commission of Trinidad & Tobago *KTBR* SW1X 16 A3
High Commission of Uganda *STJS* SW1Y 11 H8
High Commission of Zambia *SKENS* SW7 14 E2
High Commission of Zimbabwe *CHCR* WC2N 11 J7
High Comm of Brunei *BAY/PAD* W2 9 H4
High Cross Centre *SEVS/STOTM* N15 56 C3
Highfield Infant School *HAYES* BR2 167 H3
Highfield Junior School *HAYES* BR2 167 H3
Highfield Primary School *WCHMH* N21 29 H7
Highfield School *WAND/EARL* SW18 128 D6
Highgate Cemetery *HGT* N6 54 A7
Highgate Golf Club *HGT* N6 53 J5
Highgate Junior School *HGT* N6 53 K6
Highgate Pre-Preparatory School *HGT* N6 53 K6
Highgate Primary School *HGT* N6 53 K5
Highgate Private Hospital *HGT* N6 53 K5
Highgate School *HGT* N6 53 K6
Highgate Wood School *CEND/HSY/T* N8 54 C4
Highgrove Pool *RSLP* HA4 46 E6
Highlands J & I School *IL* IG1 59 K7
Highlands Primary School *IL* IG1 59 K7
Highshore School *PECK* SE15 111 G7
High View Primary School *BTSEA* SW11 128 C3
Highview Primary School *WLGTN* SM6 176 E4
The Highway Trading Centre *WAP* E1W 93 F6
Hillbrook Primary School *TOOT* SW17 147 K3
Hillcroft College *SURB* KT6 159 F5
Hillcross Primary School *MRDN* SM4 161 J3
Hill House School *CHEL* SW3 15 K9
Hill Mead Infant School *BRXN/ST* SW9 130 C3
Hillmead Primary School *BRXN/ST* SW9 130 C3
Hills Grove Primary School *WELL* DA16 116 D6
Hillside Primary School *NTHWD* HA6 32 E6
Hillside School *BORE* WD6 24 E3
Hilly Fields Medical Centre *BROCKY* SE4 132 D4
The Hiltongrove Business Centre *WALTH* E17 57 J3
Hinchley Wood School *ESH/CLAY* KT10 171 G1
Hinley Clinic *LBTH* SE11 18 C6
Hispaniola *WHALL* SW1A 11 K9
Hitherfield Primary School *STRHM/NOR* SW16 149 G1
Hither Green Cemetery *CAT* SE6 152 D1
Hither Green Primary School *LEW* SE13 133 G5
HM Prison *BRXS/STRHM* SW2 129 K5
HOLWY N7 72 E3
HOLWY N7 73 F5
SHB W12 87 J5
THMD SE28 115 K2
WAND/EARL SW18 128 C5
HMS Belfast *STHWK* SE1 13 K8
HMS President *EMB* EC4Y 12 B6
HM Young Offender Institution *FELT* TW13 140 B2
Hobbayne First & Middle School *HNWL* W7 85 F5
Hobbayne Primary School *HNWL* W7 84 E5
Hogarth Business Park *CHSWK* W4 106 B5
Hogarth Industrial Estate *WLSDN* NW10 87 J3
Hogarth Primary School *CHSWK* W4 106 B4
Hogarth's House *CHSWK* W4 106 A5
Holbeach Primary School *CAT* SE6 132 D6
Holborn College *WKENS* W14 107 H5
Holborn Medical Centre *BMSBY* WC1N 11 L1
Holborn Town Hall *HHOL* WC1V 11 K4
Holland House School *EDGW* HA8 36 C3
Holland Park School *KENS* W8 107 J1
Holland Park Theatre *KENS* W8 107 J1
Holland Street Clinic *KENS* W8 14 B2
Hollickwood JMI School *MUSWH* N10 40 B6
Holloway School *HOLWY* N7 72 D4
Hollydale Primary School *PECK* SE15 131 K1
The Hollyfield School *SURB* KT6 159 F4
Holly House Private Hospital *BKHH* IG9 45 F1
Hollymount Primary School *RYNPK* SW20 146 A7
Holly Park JMI School *FBAR/BDGN* N11 40 A3
Holmefield Preparatory School *SUT* SM1 174 E4
The Holme *CAMTN* NW1 3 M8
Holmleigh Primary School *STNW/STAM* N16 56 B7
Holmshill School *BORE* WD6 24 E1
Holy Cross Convent School *NWMAL* KT3 160 A3
Holy Cross Preparatory School *KUTN/CMB* KT2 144 E6
Holy Cross Primary School *FUL/PGN* SW6 107 K7
Holy Cross RC Primary School *CAT* SE6 133 F7
Holy Family College *WALTH* E17 58 A2
Holy Family RC Primary School *BKHTH/KID* SE3 134 A3
POP/IOD E14 93 J6
Holy Family Technology College *WALTH* E17 57 K3
Holy Ghost RC Primary School *BAL* SW12 128 E6
Holy Trinity CE First School *WIM/MER* SW19 146 E5
Holy Trinity CE Junior School *WLGTN* SM6 176 C3
Holy Trinity CE Primary School *BGVA* SW1W 16 A5
BRXS/STRHM SW2 130 A6
DART DA1 139 F4
EFNCH N2 53 H2
FSTH SE23 150 E1
KIL/WHAMP NW6 71 G5
NTHWD HA6 32 A5
RCHPK/HAM TW10 125 H3
Holy Trinity College *BMLY* BR1 153 G7
Holy Trinity Haverstock Hill CE Primary School *CAMTN* NW1 4 C1
Holy Trinity Lamorbey CE Primary School *BFN/LL* DA15 136 B7
Holy Trinity Primary School *HACK* E8 74 B5
Holy Trinity School *CHEL* SW3 15 M5
Holywell School *WATW* WD18 20 D5
Home Park Golf Club *E/WMO/HCT* KT8 158 D4
Homerton Hospital *CLPT* E5 75 F4
Homerton House School *HOM* E9 74 E4
Homoeopathic Health Centre *PLSTW* E13 94 E3
The Homoeopathic Health Centre *MLHL* NW7 37 H4
Honeypot Business Centre *STAN* HA7 36 A7
Honeypot Lane Centre *STAN* HA7 35 K7
Honeypot Medical Centre *STAN* HA7 50 A1
Honeywell Primary School *BTSEA* SW11 128 E5
Hong Kong & Shanghai Sports Club *BECK* BR3 151 G5
Honor Oak Crematorium *FSTH* SE23 132 A4
Honor Oak Gallery *FSTH* SE23 132 A5
Honor Oak Health Centre *BROCKY* SE4 132 B3
Honourable Artillery Company HQ *STLK* EC1Y 13 G1
Hook Lane Primary School *WELL* DA16 136 B2
Hook Rise South Industrial Park *CHSGTN* KT9 172 C2
Horizon Business Centre *ED* N9 43 F1
Horizon Industrial Estate *PECK* SE15 111 H5
Horizon School *STNW/STAM* N16 74 A3
The Horniman Museum & Gardens *FSTH* SE23 131 J7
Horniman Primary School *FSTH* SE23 131 J7
Horn Park Primary School *LEE/GVPK* SE12 134 A6
Hornsby House School *BAL* SW12 129 F7
Hornsey Central Hospital *CEND/HSY/T* N8 54 C4
Hornsey County School *FSBYPK* N4 55 H4
Hornsey Rise Health Centre *ARCH* N19 54 D6
Hornsey School for Girls *CEND/HSY/T* N8 55 F4
Horseferry Road Magistrates Court *WEST* SW1P 17 H4
Horse Guards Parade *WHALL* SW1A 11 H9
Horsenden Hill Golf Club *GFD/PVL* UB6 67 H5
Horsenden Primary School *GFD/PVL* UB6 66 E5
Horton Country Park *HOR/WEW* KT19 172 C7
Horton Park Golf & Country Club *HOR/WEW* KT19 172 E6
Hortus Cemetery *NWDGN* UB2 102 E1
Hospital of St John & St Elizabeth *STJWD* NW8 3 G6
Hotham Primary School *PUT/ROE* SW15 127 G3
Hotspur Industrial Estate *TOTM* N17 42 D5
Houndsfield Primary School *ED* N9 30 C6
Hounslow Business Park *HSLW* TW3 123 F3
Hounslow Cemetery *HSLWW* TW4 122 E6
Hounslow College Independent School *FELT* TW13 141 H3
Hounslow Cricket Club *HSLW* TW3 122 E1
Hounslow Heath Golf Club *HSLWW* TW4 122 C4
Hounslow Heath Infant School *HSLWW* TW4 122 D2
Hounslow Heath Junior School *HSLWW* TW4 122 D2
Hounslow Manor School *HSLW* TW3 123 G2
Hounslow Manor Sports Hall *HSLW* TW3 123 G2
Hounslow Town Primary School *HSLW* TW3 123 H2
House of Detention *CLKNW* EC1R 6 B9
House of St Barnabus *SOHO/SHAV* W1D 11 G5
Houses of Parliament *WEST* SW1P 17 K2
Houston Business Park *YEAD* UB4 83 G7
Howard Primary School *CROY/NA* CR0 177 J3
Howland Quay *BERM/RHTH* SE16 112 A2
Hoxton Hall Community Theatre *IS* N1 7 J5
HQS Wellington (Master Mariners) *TPL/STR* WC2R 12 A7
Hubbinet Industrial Estate *ROMW/RG* RM7 62 E2
Hughesfields Primary School *DEPT* SE8 112 D5
Hugh Myddelton Primary School *CLKNW* EC1R 6 B8
The Humana Wellington Hospital *STJWD* NW8 3 H7
Humber Trading Estate *CRICK* NW2 69 K1
Hungerford Primary School *HOLWY* N7 72 D5
Hunters Hall Primary School *DAGE* RM10 80 D4
Hunter Street Health Centre *STPAN* WC1H 5 J9
Huntsman Sports Club *BKHTH/KID* SE3 133 K3
Hurlingham Business Park *FUL/PGN* SW6 127 K2
Hurlingham & Chelsea School *FUL/PGN* SW6 127 K2
Hurlingham House *FUL/PGN* SW6 127 J2
Hurlingham Private School *PUT/ROE* SW15 127 J3
Huron College *SKENS* SW7 14 F5
Huron University *SKENS* SW7 15 H3
Hurricane Trading Centre *CDALE/KGS* NW9 37 H7
Hurstmere School *BFN/LL* DA15 136 C7
Hurst Park School *E/WMO/HCT* KT8 157 F2
Hurst Primary School *BXLY* DA5 136 E7
The Hyde Industrial Estate *CDALE/KGS* NW9 51 H4
The Hyde School *CDALE/KGS* NW9 51 H4
Hyland House School *WALTH* E17 58 B1
Hyleford Leavers Unit School *BARK/HLT* IG6 60 D1
Hyleford School *IL* IG1 78 E4
Hythe Road Industrial Estate *WLSDN* NW10 87 J3
Ian Mikardo High School *BOW* E3 93 K2
Ibstock Place School *PUT/ROE* SW15 126 B5
ICA Cinema *STJS* SW1Y 11 H9
Ichthus Primary School *CMBW* SE5 110 E6
Ickburgh School *CLPT* E5 74 D2
Ickenham Clinic *HGDN/ICK* UB10 64 A2
Ihlara Sport FC *HBRY* N5 73 J3
Ikra Primary School *STNW/STAM* N16 74 A3
Ilderton Primary School *BERM/RHTH* SE16 111 K5
Ilford County Court *IL* IG1 78 D1
Ilford County High School *BARK/HLT* IG6 60 C1
Ilford Golf Club *IL* IG1 59 K7

Ilford Jewish Primary School BARK/HLT IG6 60 D2
Ilford Medical Centre IL IG1 78 B2
Ilford Preparatory School GDMY/SEVK IG3 61 F7
Ilford Retail Park IL IG1 78 C1
Ilford Swimming Pool IL IG1 78 D1
Imber Court Trading Estate E/WMO/HCT KT8 157 J5
Immanuel CE Primary School STRHM/NOR SW16 148 E5
Immanuel College BUSH WD23 22 E6
Imperial College PUT/ROE SW15 127 G1; SKENS SW7 15 G3; SKENS SW7 15 G8
Imperial College Athletic Ground WDR/YW UB7 101 F5
Imperial College of Science FUL/PGN SW6 14 A9
Imperial College of Science & Technology SKENS SW7 15 H2
Imperial College of Science Technology & Medicine SKENS SW7 14 F3
Imperial College School of Medicine PIM SW1V 17 G6
Imperial War Museum STHWK SE1 18 B4
Imperial War Museum Annexe STHWK SE1 18 B4
Independent Jewish School HDN NW4 52 B4
India House HOL/ALD WC2B 11 L6
Indoor Market WAT WD17 21 G2
Industrial Estate WATW WD18 20 B4
Infant College IL IG1 78 A1
The Infirmary Royal Hospital CHEL SW3 16 A8
Innellan House School PIN HA5 47 H2
Inner London Sessions House (Crown Court) STHWK SE1 18 E3
Inner Temple EMB EC4Y 12 B6
Innholders Hall CANST EC4R 12 F6
Inns of Court & Chancery TPL/STR WC2R 12 A5
Inns of Court School of Law GINN WC1R 11 M2
Institut Francais SKENS SW7 15 G5
International Community School CAMTN NW1 10 A1
International Financial Centre OBST EC2N 13 J4
International Medical Centre ECT SW5 14 B6
International Rail Terminal STHWK SE1 17 M1
International School of London ACT W3 105 H3
International Trading Estate NWDGN UB2 102 A2
International University BUSH WD23 21 K3
Invicta Industrial Estate SRTFD E15 94 A2
Invicta Primary School BKHTH/KID SE3 113 K5
Invicta Sports Club DART DA1 139 G4
Inwood Business Centre HSLW TW3 123 G3
IQRA Independent School BRXN/ST SW9 130 B2
Ironmonger Row Baths FSBYE EC1V 6 E8
Ironmongers Hall STBT EC1A 12 E3
Islamia Girls School KIL/WHAMP NW6 70 C7
Islamic College for Advanced Studies WLSDN NW10 69 K6
The Islamic Grammar School WAND/EARL SW18 127 J6
Island Clinic POP/IOD E14 113 F1
Isleworth Blue CE Primary School ISLW TW7 124 B2
Isleworth Cemetery ISLW TW7 124 B1
Isleworth Recreation Centre ISLW TW7 124 A3
Isleworth & Syon School for Boys ISLW TW7 103 K6
Isleworth Town Primary School ISLW TW7 124 A1
Islington Arts & Media School FSBYPK N4 55 F7
Islington Business Centre IS N1 6 E3
Islington Crematorium EFNCH N2 39 J7
Islington Green Medical Centre IS N1 6 C3
Islington Green School IS N1 6 D4
Islington Tennis Centre HOLWY N7 72 E5
Islington Town Hall IS N1 6 C1
Ismaili Centre SKENS SW7 15 H5
Italia Conti Academy of Theatre Arts BRXN/ST SW9 129 K2
Italian Hospital WEST SW1P 16 E5
Ivybridge Primary School TWK TW1 124 A5
Ivybridge Retail Park ISLW TW7 124 A4
Ivydale Primary School BROCKY SE4 132 A3
Jack & Jill School HPTN TW12 142 A5; WHTN TW2 142 E1
Jack Taylor School STJWD NW8 2 E3
Jack Tizzard School FUL/PGN SW6 107 G7
Jacques Prevert School WKENS W14 107 G3
Jamahiriya School CHEL SW3 15 J9
James Allens Preparatory Girls School EDUL SE22 130 E4
James Dixon Primary School PGE/AN SE20 150 C6
Jamestown Mental Health Centre HAMP NW3 3 L1
James Wolfe Primary School GNWCH SE10 112 E6
Janet Adegoke Leisure Centre SHB W12 87 J6
The Japanese School ACT W3 86 C6
Japan Green Medical Centre ACT W3 86 D7
Jenner Health Centre FSTH SE23 132 B7
Jenny Hammond Primary School WAN E11 76 C3
Jermyn Street Theatre STJS SW1Y 10 F7
Jessop Primary School HNHL SE24 130 C3
Jewel Tower WEST SW1P 17 J3
Jewish Cemetery GLDGN NW11 52 E5
Jewish Community Theatre CMBW SE5 130 E2
Jewish Free School KTTN NW5 72 D5
The Jewish Museum CAMTN NW1 4 C4; FNCH N3 52 E1
Jews College London HDN NW4 52 B3
Johanna Primary School STHWK SE1 18 A2
John Ball Primary School BKHTH/KID SE3 133 H1
John Betts Primary School HMSMTH W6 106 D2
John Burns Primary School BTSEA SW11 129 F1
John Chilton School NTHLT UB5 65 J6
John Dixon Clinic BERM/RHTH SE16 111 J2
John Donne Primary School PECK SE15 111 J7
John F Kennedy Special School SRTFD E15 76 B7
John Keble CE Primary School WLSDN NW10 69 H7
John Kelly Boys & Girls Technology College CRICK NW2 69 H2
The John Loughborough School TOTM N17 56 B1
John Lyon School RYLN/HDSTN HA2 48 D7
John Milton Primary School VX/NE SW8 109 H6
John Nightingale School E/WMO/HCT KT8 156 E2
John Orwell Sports Centre WAP E1W 92 C7
John Paul II RC School WIM/MER SW19 127 G6
John Perryn Primary School ACT W3 87 G4
John Perry Primary School DAGE RM10 81 F5
John Roan Lower School BKHTH/KID SE3 113 J5
John Roan School BKHTH/KID SE3 113 H6
John Ruskin College SAND/SEL CR2 179 G6
John Ruskin Primary School WALW SE17 18 E9
John Scott Health Centre FSBYPK N4 55 J7
John Scurr JMI School WCHPL E1 92 E3
John Smith House WALW SE17 18 E6
Johnsons Industrial Estate HYS/HAR UB3 101 K2
John Stainer Primary School BROCKY SE4 132 B2
Joseph Clarke Special School CHING E4 44 B5
Joseph Hood Primary School RYNPK SW20 161 H1
Joseph Lancaster School STHWK SE1 18 F4
Joseph Tritton Primary School BTSEA SW11 128 B3
Jubilee Country Park HAYES BR2 169 G3
Jubilee JMI School STNW/STAM N16 56 C7
Jubilee Market COVGDN WC2E 11 K6
Jubilee Primary School THMD SE28 97 J6
Jubilee Sports Ground CHING E4 44 B3
Julians Primary School STRHM/NOR SW16 149 G3
Junior & Youth Centre POP/IOD E14 93 H4
Juno Way Industrial Estate NWCR SE14 112 A5
JVC Business Park CRICK NW2 51 J7
Kangley Business Centre SYD SE26 151 H4
Katella Trading Estate BARK IG11 96 E2
Katherine Road Medical Centre FSTGT E7 77 G5
Keats House Museum HAMP NW3 71 H3
Keble Preparatory School WCHMH N21 29 G6
Keen Students Supplementary School WCHPL E1 92 C4
Keir Hardie Primary School CAN/RD E16 94 E4
Keith Davis Cue Sports Club DAGW RM9 79 K6
Kelmscott Leisure Centre WALTH E17 57 H5
Kelmscott School WALTH E17 57 H5
Kelsey Park School BECK BR3 166 D2
Kelvin Grove Primary School SYD SE26 150 D2
Kelvin Industrial Estate GFD/PVL UB6 66 B7; GFD/PVL UB6 84 D2
Kemnal Technology College STMC/STPC BR5 155 H6
Kempton Park Racecourse SUN TW16 141 F6
Ken Barrington Centre LBTH SE11 110 A5
Kender Primary School NWCR SE14 111 K7
Kenilworth First School BORE WD6 25 F2
Kenmont Primary School WLSDN NW10 87 J2
Kenmore Park Middle School KTN/HRWW/W HA3 49 K2
Kenneth More Theatre IL IG1 78 C2
Kensal Rise Primary School WLSDN NW10 88 B1
Kensington & Chelsea Town Hall KENS W8 14 B2
Kensington Ave Primary School THHTH CR7 149 G7
Kensington Business Centre SKENS SW7 15 K3
Kensington & Chelsea College NKENS W10 88 C4; WBPTN SW10 108 B6
The Kensington Clinic KENS W8 14 C4
Kensington Leisure Centre NTGHL W11 88 B6
Kensington Market KENS W8 14 C2
Kensington Palace State Apartments & Royal Ceremonial Dress Collection KENS W8 8 D9
Kensington Park School REGST W1B 10 D2
Kensington Preparatory School FUL/PGN SW6 107 J7
Kensington Primary School MNPK E12 77 K5
Kensington School of Business HCIRC EC1N 12 B2
Kensington Wharf WBPTN SW10 108 C6
Kensit Memorial College FNCH N3 52 C1
Kentish Town Church CE Primary School KTTN NW5 72 C4
Kentish Town Health Centre KTTN NW5 72 C5
Kentish Town Industrial Estate KTTN NW5 72 B4
Kentish Town Sports Centre KTTN NW5 72 A5
Kenton Clinic KTN/HRWW/W HA3 50 A4
Kenton Cricket Club KTN/HRWW/W HA3 49 J3
Kent Park Industrial Estate PECK SE15 111 J5
Kenwood House HGT N6 53 J7
Kenyngton Manor Primary School SUN TW16 140 E5
Kerem House School EFNCH N2 53 G4
The Kerem School EFNCH N2 53 H4
Keston CE Primary School HAYES BR2 181 H4
Kew Bridge Steam Museum BTFD TW8 105 G4
Kew College RCH/KEW TW9 105 H6
Kew Gardens (Royal Botanic Gardens) RCH/KEW TW9 105 F7
Kew Palace RCH/KEW TW9 105 F6
Kew Retail Park RCH/KEW TW9 105 J7
Keyplan & Roxburghe Collegel FITZ W1T 10 F1
Keyworth Primary School WALW SE17 18 C8
Khalsa College London HRW HA1 49 F5
Kidbrooke Park Primary School BKHTH/KID SE3 134 B1
Kidbrooke School BKHTH/KID SE3 134 C1
Kilburn Park Junior School KIL/WHAMP NW6 2 A6; KIL/WHAMP NW6 88 D2
Killick Street Medical Centre IS N1 5 L5
Kilmorie Primary School FSTH SE23 151 G1
Kimberley Industrial Estate WALTH E17 43 H6
Kimpton Industrial Estate CHEAM SM3 174 D1
Kinetic Business Centre BORE WD6 24 B2
King Alfred School GLDGN NW11 53 F7
King Athelstan Primary School KUT KT1 159 G2
King Edwards Road Clinic RSLP HA4 46 B7
King Edward VII Hospital for Officers MHST W1U 10 B2
King Fahad Academy (Boys School & Girls Lower School) ACT W3 87 G6
King Fahad Academy (Girls Upper School) EA W5 104 D3
The Kingfisher Medical Centre DEPT SE8 112 C5
The Kingfisher Sports Centre KUT KT1 159 F1
Kingford Community School PLSTW E13 95 G3
King George Hospital GDMY/SEVK IG3 61 G4
Kingham Industrial Estate WLSDN NW10 87 F2
King Henry's Reach Development BARN SW13 107 F5
King & Queen Wharf WAP E1W 93 F6
Kings Acre Primary School CLAP SW4 129 K4
Kings Avenue Medical Centre GFD/PVL UB6 84 C5
Kingsbury Green Primary School CDALE/KGS NW9 50 D4
Kingsbury High School CDALE/KGS NW9 50 D3
Kingsbury Hospital CDALE/KGS NW9 50 C3
Kingsbury Tamil School CDALE/KGS NW9 50 D2
Kingsbury Trading Estate CDALE/KGS NW9 50 E5
Kings College Hospital CMBW SE5 130 D2
Kings College London CHEL SW3 15 J8; CMBW SE5 130 E1; HAMP NW3 70 E3; LSQ/SEVD WC2H 11 K5; STHWK SE1 12 D8; STHWK SE1 12 F9; TPL/STR WC2R 11 M6; WBPTN SW10 108 B6; WEST SW1P 16 F5
King's College School WIM/MER SW19 146 A5
Kings College School of Medicine & Dentistry DUL SE21 130 E5
Kings College Sports Ground RSLP HA4 46 C5
King's Cross Station CAMTN NW1 5 J6
King's Cross Thameslink Station FSBYW WC1X 5 L7
Kingsdale School DUL SE21 150 A2
Kings Estate HCH RM12 81 J3
Kingsgate Business Centre KUTN/CMB KT2 144 A7
Kingsgate Infant School KIL/WHAMP NW6 2 A1
Kingsgate Junior School KIL/WHAMP NW6 2 A2
Kings Hall Leisure Centre CLPT E5 74 E4
Kings Head Theatre IS N1 6 C3
Kings House School RCHPK/HAM TW10 125 G4
Kingsland Health Centre IS N1 7 K1
Kingsland School HACK E8 74 B4
Kingsland Shopping Centre HACK E8 74 B5
Kingsley Primary School CROY/NA CR0 164 A7
Kings Mall Shopping Centre HMSMTH W6 107 F3
Kingsmeadow Athletics Centre KUT KT1 159 H2
Kingsmead Primary School CLPT E5 75 G3
Kingsmead School EN EN1 30 C3
King Solomon High School BARK/HLT IG6 60 D1
Kings Private Clinic GDMY/SEVK IG3 61 F7; MHST W1U 10 A2
Kings School of English BECK BR3 166 C1
Kings Stairs BERM/RHTH SE16 111 J1
Kingston Business Centre CHSGTN KT9 172 A2
Kingston College of Further Education KUT KT1 158 E2
Kingston Crematorium KUT KT1 159 H2
Kingston Crown Court KUT KT1 158 E2
Kingston Grammar School KUT KT1 159 G1
Kingston Hospital NHS Trust KUTN/CMB KT2 144 C7
Kingstonian FC NWMAL KT3 159 J2
Kingston University KUT KT1 159 F2; KUTN/CMB KT2 145 F4; KUTN/CMB KT2 145 F6
King Street College HMSMTH W6 107 F3
Kingsway Business Park HPTN TW12 141 K7
Kingsway College CLKNW EC1R 6 B9; KTTN NW5 72 B5; STPAN WC1H 5 L8
Kingswood Primary School WNWD SE27 149 K3
Kisharon School GLDGN NW11 52 D5
KLC School of Design WBPTN SW10 108 B7
Knightsbridge Barracks SKENS SW7 15 K2
Knightsbridge Medical Centre KTBR SW1X 15 M3
Knollmead Primary School WPK KT4 172 E1
Knowledge Point School HOLWY N7 73 F5
Kobi Nazrul Primary School WCHPL E1 92 C5
KP Estate RAIN RM13 99 G6
KS Medical Centre STHL UB1 84 B6
Kubrick Business Estate FSTGT E7 77 F3
Laban Centre DEPT SE8 112 E6
Laburnum Health Centre DAGE RM10 80 C1
Laburnum Primary School HACK E8 7 L4
Lady Bankes Primary School RSLP HA4 64 E1
Lady Edens School KENS W8 14 E3
The Lady Eleanor Holles School HPTN TW12 142 B4
Lady Margaret Primary School STHL UB1 83 K4
Lady Margaret School FUL/PGN SW6 107 K7
Ladywell arena LEW SE13 132 E5
Ladywell Cemetery BROCKY SE4 132 C4
Ladywell Leisure Centre LEW SE13 133 F4
Laings Sports Ground BAR EN5 25 G3
Lake Business Centre TOTM N17 42 C5
Laker Industrial Estate BECK BR3 151 G4
Lambeth Cemetery TOOT SW17 147 G4
Lambeth College CLAP SW4 129 H4; STHWK SE1 13 K9
Lambeth County Court LBTH SE11 18 B7
Lambeth Crematorium TOOT SW17 147 G3
Lambeth Palace STHWK SE1 17 L4
Lambs Court POP/IOD E14 93 G6
Lamont Business Centre CROY/NA CR0 163 K6
Lamorbey Swimming Centre BFN/LL DA15 155 G1
Lampton School HEST TW5 103 F7
The Lanark Medical Centre MV/WKIL W9 2 D7
Lancaster House WHALL SW1A 16 E1
Lancasterian Primary School TOTM N17 42 A7
Lancaster Road Industrial Estate EBAR EN4 27 H4
Lancelot Medical Centre ALP/SUD HA0 67 K4
Lanford Obesity Clinic ED N9 30 D6
Langbourne Primary School DUL SE21 150 A2
Langdon Park Secondary School POP/IOD E14 93 K5
Langdon School EHAM E6 96 B1
Langford Primary School FUL/PGN SW6 128 A1
The Langham School SEVS/STOTM N15 55 J3
Langhedge Lane Industrial Estate UED N18 42 B5
Langley Park Girls School & Sports Centre BECK BR3 166 E4
Langley Park Golf Club BECK BR3 167 G5
Langley Park School for Boys BECK BR3 166 E5
Langthorne Health Centre WAN E11 76 B2
Langthorne Hospital WAN E11 76 B3
Lansbury Lawrence Primary School POP/IOD E14 93 K5
Lansdownecollege BAY/PAD W2 8 C7
Lansdowne School BRXN/ST SW9 130 A2
La Retraite RC Girls School BAL SW12 129 H6
Lark Hall Junior School CLAP SW4 129 J1
Lark Hall Primary School CLAP SW4 129 J1
Larkshall Business Centre CHING E4 44 B1
Larkswood Primary School CHING E4 43 K3
Larmenier Infant School HMSMTH W6 107 G3
La Sainte Union Convent School KTTN NW5 72 A2
La Salette RC Primary School RAIN RM13 99 J2
Lasnding Stage DEPT SE8 112 D4
Latchmere J & I School KUTN/CMB KT2 144 B5
Latchmere Leisure Centre BTSEA SW11 128 E1
Lathom Junior School EHAM E6 77 J6
Latimer Industrial Estate SHB W12 88 A5
Latymer All Saints CE Primary School ED N9 42 B1
The Latymer School ED N9 42 A1
Latymer Upper School HMSMTH W6 106 D3
Launcelot Primary School BMLY BR1 152 E3
Laurel Clinic EA W5 104 D3
Laurence Haines School WATW WD18 20 E5
Lauriston Primary School HOM E9 75 F7
Lawdale Junior School BETH E2 92 C2

Lawrence Trading Estate
GNWCH SE10 113 H3
Lawrence University
SKENS SW7 14 F6
Lawrence Wharf
BERM/RHTH SE16 93 H7
Laycock Primary School
IS N1 73 G5
Lazards Sports Club
SUN TW16 141 F7
Lea Bridge Industrial Estate
LEY E10 57 G7
Leadenhall Market
BANK EC3V 13 J5
Lea Park Trading Estate
LEY E10 57 H6
Leaside Business Centre
PEND EN3 31 H1
Leathermarket Gardens
STHWK SE1 19 J2
Leathersellers Sports Ground
ELTH/MOT SE9 134 B6
Leathers Hall
HDTCH EC3A 13 J4
Lea Valley Primary School
TOTM N17 42 C6
Lea Valley Trading Estate
UED N18 42 E3
UED N18 43 F5
L'écoles Des Petits
FUL/PGN SW6 128 A1
Lee Manor Primary School
LEW SE13 133 H5
Leeside Court
BERM/RHTH SE16 93 F7
Leeside Trading Estate
TOTM N17 42 E6
Lee Valley Campsite
CHING E4 31 K1
Lee Valley Ice Centre
LEY E10 75 F1
Lee Valley Leisure Centre Camping & Caravan
ED N9 31 F7
Lee Valley Leisure Golf Club
ED N9 31 G6
Lee Valley Watersports Centre
CHING E4 43 G5
The Leigh City Technology College (East Campus)
DART DA1 139 K7
The Leigh City Technology College (West Campus)
DART DA1 139 K7
Leigh Close Industrial Estate
NWMAL KT3 160 A3
Leighton House Museum & Art Gallery
WKENS W14 107 J2
Lena Gardens Primary School
HMSMTH W6 107 F2
Leopold Primary School
WLSDN NW10 69 H6
Leopold Street Clinic
BOW E3 93 H4
Lesnes Abbey
ABYW SE2 116 E3
Lesney Park Primary School
ERITH DA8 118 A5
Lessness Heath Primary School
BELV DA17 117 H4
Lewin Mead Community Mental Health Centre
STRHM/NOR SW16 148 D5
Lewis Clinic
CAR SM5 176 A3
Lewisham Bridge Primary School
LEW SE13 132 E2
Lewisham Business Centre
NWCR SE14 112 A5
Lewisham Centre
LEW SE13 133 F2
Lewisham College
DEPT SE8 112 D7
Lewisham Crematorium
CAT SE6 152 D1
The Leys Primary School
DAGE RM10 80 E6
Leyton Business Centre
LEY E10 75 H1
Leyton FC
LEY E10 57 H7
Leyton Industrial Village
LEY E10 57 F6
Leyton Leisure Centre
LEY E10 57 K6
Leyton Orient FC (Matchroom Stadium)
LEY E10 75 K2
Leytonstone School
WAN E11 58 C5
Leyton VI Form College
LEY E10 58 B5
Leyton Youth Sports Ground
LEY E10 57 K7
The Liberty City Clinic
SDTCH EC2A 7 J9
Liberty II Centre
ROM RM1 63 G3
Liberty Middle School
MTCM CR4 162 D1
Library & Community Centre
BTSEA SW11 128 C2
Lillian Baylis School
LBTH SE11 17 M6
Lillian Baylis Theatre
FSBYE EC1V 6 C7
Lillian Bishop School of English
SKENS SW7 15 G5
Lillie Road Fitness Centre
FUL/PGN SW6 107 G5
Limehouse Town Hall
POP/IOD E14 93 H5
Lime Trees Park Golf Club
NTHLT UB5 65 G7
Lincoln Road Clinic
EN EN1 30 C4
Lincoln's Inn
LINN WC2A 11 M4
Linden Bridge School
WPK KT4 173 G2
Linden Lodge School
WIM/MER SW19 127 H7
Lindon Bennett School
FELT TW13 141 H4
Linford Christie Stadium
SHB W12 87 J4
The Link Day Primary School
CROY/NA CR0 176 E3
The Link Secondary School
CROY/NA CR0 177 F3
Links Primary School
TOOT SW17 148 A5
Linley Sambourne House
KENS W8 14 A2
KENS W8 107 J1
Linnet House Clinic
STJWD NW8 3 J6
Linton Mead Primary School
THMD SE28 97 H6
Lionel Road Primary School
BTFD TW8 105 F3
Lion House School
PUT/ROE SW15 127 G3
Lismarrine Industrial Park
BORE WD6 23 H5
Lisson Grove Health Centre
STJWD NW8 3 J9
Lister Community School
PLSTW E13 95 F1
The Lister Hospital
BGVA SW1W 16 C8
Lister House Clinic
CAVSQ/HST W1G 10 C4
Little Danson Welfare Clinic
WELL DA16 136 B3
Little Eden & Eden High School
FELT TW13 141 H3
Little Furze School
OXHEY WD19 33 F2
Little Hands Theatre
HDN NW4 52 A3
Little Heath School
CHDH RM6 61 H3
Little Ilford School
MNPK E12 77 K4
Little Reddings Primary School
BUSH WD23 22 B4
Little St Helens School
NTHWD HA6 32 D5
Little Stanmore First & Middle School
EDGW HA8 36 A7
Little Wandsworth School
TOOT SW17 148 A1
Liverpool Street Station
LVPST EC2M 13 J2
Livesey Museum for Children
PECK SE15 111 J5
Livingstone Hospital
DART DA1 139 J6
Livingstone Primary School
EBAR EN4 27 H2
Lloyd's
BANK EC3V 13 J5
Lloyds Register Cricket Club
DUL SE21 130 E7
Locks View Court
POP/IOD E14 93 G6
Lockwood Industrial Park
TOTM N17 56 D2
Lombard Business Centre
BTSEA SW11 128 C1
Lombard Business Park
CROY/NA CR0 164 A6
WAND/EARL SW18 128 C5
WIM/MER SW19 162 B1
Lombard Trading Estate
CHARL SE7 114 A3
Lombardy Retail Park
HYS/HAR UB3 83 F6
London Academy of Music & Dramatic Art
HMSMTH W6 107 G4
London Aquarium
STHWK SE1 17 L2
London Area Terminal Control Centre
WDR/YW UB7 100 C1
London Arena
POP/IOD E14 112 E2
London Balloon
LBTH SE11 17 L8
London Bible College
NTHWD HA6 32 B5
London Bridge City Pier
STHWK SE1 13 J8
London Bridge Hospital
STHWK SE1 13 H8
London Bridge Sports Centre
CANST EC4R 13 G7
London Bridge Station
STHWK SE1 13 J9
London Broncos RLFC (Griffin Park)
BTFD TW8 104 E5
London Business School
CAMTN NW1 3 L9
The London Canal Museum
IS N1 5 K5
London Capital College
CAMTN NW1 4 D3
London Chest Hospital
BETH E2 92 E1
London City Airport
CAN/RD E16 95 J7
London City College
STHWK SE1 12 A9
London City Mission
STHWK SE1 19 K1
The London Clinic
MHST W1U 10 B1
London College of Business & Computing
BETH E2 92 D1
London College of Fashion
CAVSQ/HST W1G 10 D4
MHST W1U 10 B5
SDTCH EC2A 7 K9
London College of Further Education
LBTH SE11 18 C6
London College of Higher Education
CLAP SW4 129 G2
London College of International Business Studies
HHOL WC1V 11 K3
London College of Printing
LBTH SE11 18 D4
The London College
KENS W8 8 A8
London Commodity Exchange
WAP E1W 13 M7
London Dungeon
STHWK SE1 13 H8
London Electronics College
ECT SW5 14 C7
London Executive College
TOOT SW17 148 A2
London Eye Clinic
CAVSQ/HST W1G 10 C3
London Fields Primary School
HACK E8 74 D7
London Foot Hospital
FITZ W1T 10 E1
London Gender Clinic
HDN NW4 51 K5
London Group Business Park
CRICK NW2 51 H7
London Guildhall University
LVPST EC2M 13 H3
TWRH EC3N 13 L5
London Guildhall University Sports Ground
LEE/GVPK SE12 153 G1
London Heart Clinic
CAVSQ/HST W1G 10 C3
London Hospital Medical College
WCHPL E1 92 D4
The London Industrial Estate
EHAM E6 96 A4
London Industrial Park
EHAM E6 96 B4
The London Institute
WEST SW1P 17 J7
London International Film School
LSQ/SEVD WC2H 11 J5
London Irish RFC
SUN TW16 140 E7
The London Irish Youth Theatre
HGT N6 54 B7
London Islamic School/Madrasah
WCHPL E1 92 D5
London Ladies & Girls FC
CAT SE6 151 K4
London Lane Clinic
BMLY BR1 152 D6
London Lighthouse
NTGHL W11 88 C5
London Living Theatre
SYD SE26 151 F3
London Nautical School
STHWK SE1 12 B8
London Open College
FSBYE EC1V 6 D7
London Oratory School
FUL/PGN SW6 107 K6
London Pavilion
REGST W1B 11 G7
London Road Medical Centre
THHTH CR7 164 B5
London School of Economics
HHOL WC1V 11 J4
LINN WC2A 11 M5
STHWK SE1 12 E8
London School of Hygiene & Tropical Medicine
GWRST WC1E 11 H2
London Scottish Golf Club
WIM/MER SW19 145 K2
London Silver Vaults
LINN WC2A 12 A3
The London Television Centre (LWT)
STHWK SE1 12 A8
London Tourist Board & Convention Centre
BGVA SW1W 16 C3
London Toy & Model Museum
BAY/PAD W2 8 F6
London Transport Bus Depot
BXLYHN DA7 137 J2
London Transport Museum
COVGDN WC2E 11 K6
London Underwriting Centre
MON EC3R 13 K6
London Weather Centre
CLKNW EC1R 12 A2
London Welsh FC
RCH/KEW TW9 125 F2
London Welsh School
CRICK NW2 70 A5
London Wetland Centre
BARN SW13 106 E7
London Zoo
CAMTN NW1 4 A5
Lonesome First School
MTCM CR4 163 G1
Long Ditton County Infant School
SURB KT6 158 D7
Long Ditton Ferry
THDIT KT7 158 C5
Longfield Primary School
RYLN/HDSTN HA2 48 A5
Longford Community School
EBED/NFELT TW14 121 J6
Longford Industrial Estate
HPTN TW12 142 B5
Longlands Primary School
BFN/LL DA15 154 E2
Long Lane AFC
BKHTH/KID SE3 134 B1
Longmead Primary School
WDR/YW UB7 100 A2
Longshaw Primary School
CHING E4 44 B2
Lord Lister Health Centre
FSTGT E7 76 E3
Lordship Lane Clinic
TOTM N17 56 A1
Lordship Lane Primary School
WDGN N22 41 J7
Lord's Tour & Mcc Museum
STJWD NW8 3 G8
Lorimar Business Centre
RAIN RM13 99 G5
Loughborough Primary School
BRXN/ST SW9 130 C1
Lovelace Primary School
CHSGTN KT9 171 J4
Lovell's Wharf
GNWCH SE10 113 G4
Lower Clapton Health Centre
CLPT E5 74 E4
Lower Place Business Centre
WLSDN NW10 86 E1
Lower Sydenham Industrial Estate
CAT SE6 151 H4
Lowfield Medical Centre
DART DA1 139 H6
Low Hall Sports Ground
WALTH E17 57 F5
Lowther Primary School
BARN SW13 106 D5
Loxford School of Science & Technology
IL IG1 78 D4
LSE Sports Club
NWMAL KT3 160 A5
LT Lost Property Office
CAMTN NW1 9 M1
LTR Depot
SHB W12 88 B7
Lubavitch House School
STNW/STAM N16 56 B6
Lucas Vale Primary School
DEPT SE8 112 D7
Lucie Clayton Secretarial/Fashion Design College
SKENS SW7 14 E4
Lutomer House Business Centre
POP/IOD E14 93 K7
Lux Cinema
IS N1 7 J8
Lycee Francais
SKENS SW7 15 G5
The Lyceum Theatre
TPL/STR WC2R 11 L6
Lyndean Industrial Estate
ABYW SE2 116 D2
Lyndhurst House Preparatory School
HAMP NW3 71 H4
Lyndhurst Primary School
CMBW SE5 130 E1
Lyon Business Park
BARK IG11 96 E1
Lyon Park J & I School
ALP/SUD HA0 68 B6
Lyonsdown School
BAR EN5 27 G4
Lyric Theatre
HMSMTH W6 107 F3
SOHO/SHAV W1D 11 G6
Mabwin Supplementary School
ED N9 42 D1
Macaulay CE Primary School
CLAP SW4 129 G3
Madame Tussaud's
CAMTN NW1 10 A1
Madeira Grove Clinic
WFD IG8 45 F4
Madison Bowl
NTHWD HA6 32 C6
Madni Girls School
WCHPL E1 92 D5
Mahatma Gandhi Industrial Estate
BRXN/ST SW9 130 C2
Maida Vale Hospital
STJWD NW8 2 F9
Maida Vale Medical Centre
MV/WKIL W9 2 C8
Malcolm Primary School
PGE/AN SE20 150 E6
The Malden Centre
NWMAL KT3 160 C3
Malden Golf Club
NWMAL KT3 160 B1
Malden Manor Junior School
NWMAL KT3 160 B6
Malden Parochial Primary School
WPK KT4 160 B7
Malden Road Baths
CHEAM SM3 174 B3
Malham Road Industrial Estate
FSTH SE23 132 A7
Mall Galleries
STJS SW1Y 11 H8
The Mall School
WHTN TW2 142 D2
Malmesbury Middle School
MRDN SM4 162 B5
Malmesbury Primary School
BOW E3 93 H2
MRDN SM4 162 B6
Malorees J & I School
KIL/WHAMP NW6 70 B6
Malory School
BMLY BR1 152 E3
Malvern Way Infant School
RKW/CH/CXG WD3 20 A4
Mandeville Primary School
CLPT E5 75 G2
Mandeville Special School
NTHLT UB5 65 K5
Manford Industrial Estate
ERITH DA8 118 E5
Manor Brook Medical Centre
BKHTH/KID SE3 134 A1
Manor Drive Health Centre
WPK KT4 160 C7
Manorfield Primary School
POP/IOD E14 93 K4
Manor House Hospital
GLDGN NW11 53 F7
Manor House School
HNWL W7 84 E6
Manor Infant School
BARK IG11 79 F5
Manor Park Cemetery
FSTGT E7 77 H3
Manor Park Crematorium
FSTGT E7 77 G3
Manor Park Methodist School
MNPK E12 77 J3
Manor Park Primary School
SUT SM1 175 G4
Manor Place Industrial Estate
BORE WD6 24 E2
Manor Primary School
SRTFD E15 94 C1
The Manor Primary School
ROM RM1 63 H4
Manorside Primary School
FNCH N3 39 F7
Manor Special School
WLSDN NW10 88 B1
Manor Way Business Centre
DAGW RM9 99 F4
Mansion House
MANHO EC4N 13 G5
Mapledown School
CRICK NW2 52 B6
Maple Grove Business Centre
HSLWW TW4 122 B3
Maple Industrial Estate
FELT TW13 140 E1
Maple Infant School
SURB KT6 158 E4
Maples Business Centre
IS N1 6 B3
Marble Arch
BAY/PAD W2 9 M6
Marble Hill House
TWK TW1 124 D6
Maria Fidelis Convent Lower School
CAMTN NW1 4 F8
Maria Fidelis Convent Upper School
CAMTN NW1 5 G7
Marion Richardson Primary School
WCHPL E1 93 F5
Marion Vian Primary School
BECK BR3 166 A4
Maritime Industrial Estate
CHARL SE7 114 A3
Maritime Museum
GNWCH SE10 113 H3
The Marjory Kinnon School
EBED/NFELT TW14 121 H4
The Market
COVGDN WC2E 11 K6
Market Trading Estate
NWDGN UB2 102 A3
Marks Gate Junior School
CHDH RM6 62 A2
Marlborough Cricket Club
DUL SE21 131 H7
Marlborough Day Hospital
STJWD NW8 2 E5
Marlborough First & Middle School
HRW HA1 48 E3
Marlborough House
STJS SW1Y 10 F9
Marlborough Park School
BFN/LL DA15 136 B7
Marlborough Primary School
CHEL SW3 15 K6
ISLW TW7 104 B7
Marlborough Trading Estate
RCH/KEW TW9 105 J7
Marlowe Business Centre
NWCR SE14 112 B6
Marner Primary School
BOW E3 93 K3
Marshalls Park School
ROM RM1 63 G1
Marshall Street Leisure Centre
SOHO/CST W1F 10 F5
Marsh Gate Business Centre
SRTFD E15 94 A1
Marshgate Trading Estate
SRTFD E15 75 K6
Marsh Green School
DAGW RM9 98 C1
Martan College
HOL/ALD WC2B 11 K4
Martinbridge Industrial Estate
EN EN1 30 C4
Martindale Industrial Estate
EN EN1 30 A4
Martin Infant School
EFNCH N2 53 J1
Marvels Lane Primary School
LEE/GVPK SE12 153 G3
Mary Boone School
WKENS W14 107 H3
Maryland Industrial Estate
SRTFD E15 76 C4
Maryland Primary School
SRTFD E15 76 C4
Marylebone Health Centre
MHST W1U 10 B1
Marylebone Magistrates Court
CAMTN NW1 9 K2
Marylebone Station
CAMTN NW1 9 K1
Marymount International School
KUTN/CMB KT2 144 E6
Mary Wallace Theatre
TWK TW1 124 B7
Maswell Park Health Centre
HSLW TW3 123 H4
Matilda Marks School
MLHL NW7 37 F4
Matrix Business Centre
DART DA1 139 H4
The Maudsley Hospital
CMBW SE5 130 E1
Mawbrey Brough Health Centre
VX/NE SW8 109 K6
The Mawney School
ROMW/RG RM7 63 F4
Mayday University Hospital
THHTH CR7 164 C5
Mayesbrook Park Arena
BCTR RM8 79 G4
Mayespark Primary School
GDMY/SEVK IG3 79 G2
Mayfair Medical Centre
MYFR/PKLN W1K 10 B5
Mayfield Primary School
GFD/PVL UB6 84 D5
Mayfield School
PIN HA5 47 J2
Mayfield School & College
BCTR RM8 61 J7
Mayflower Primary School
POP/IOD E14 93 J5
Mayplace Primary School
BXLYHN DA7 138 A3
Maytime School
IL IG1 78 A2
Mayville Infant School
WAN E11 76 C2
Mayville Junior School
WAN E11 76 C1
Maze Hill School
GNWCH SE10 113 H5
McEntee School
WALTH E17 43 H7
McKay Trading Estate
NKENS W10 88 C3
McMillan Clinic
HYS/HAR UB3 82 A6
MDQ Majidiah (UK)
WCHPL E1 92 D6
The Mead Infant School
HOR/WEW KT19 173 H2
Meadlands Primary School
RCHPK/HAM TW10 143 J3
Meadowgate School
BROCKY SE4 132 A2
Meadowside Leisure Centre
BKHTH/KID SE3 134 B3
Meadow Wood School
BUSH WD23 22 C4

Mead Road Infant School *CHST* BR7 154 C5
Medical Express Clinic *CAVSQ/HST* W1G 10 C2
Mednurs Clinic *SEVS/STOTM* N15 55 K5
Megabowl *BRXS/STRHM* SW2 148 E1
Melcombe Primary School *HMSMTH* W6 107 G5
Mellish Industrial Estate *WOOL/PLUM* SE18 114 C2
Mellow Lane School *YEAD* UB4 82 A3
Melrose Special School *MTCM* CR4 162 D2
Memorial Hospital *WOOL/PLUM* SE18 135 F1
The Menorah Foundation School *EDGW* HA8 36 E6
Menorah Grammar School *GLDGN* NW11 52 C6
Menorah Primary School *GLDGN* NW11 52 C6
Mercers' Hall *CITYW* EC2V 12 F5
The Merchant Taylors Hall *BANK* EC3V 13 H5
Merchant Taylors School *NTHWD* HA6 20 C7
Meridian Clinic *BRXN/ST* SW9 130 A2
Meridian Locality Mental Health Centre *CHARL* SE7 114 B5
Meridian Primary School *GNWCH* SE10 113 G4
Meridian Sports Club *CHARL* SE7 114 D5
Meridian Trading Estate *CHARL* SE7 114 A3
Merlin Primary School *BMLY* BR1 152 E2
Merlin School *PUT/ROE* SW15 127 G4
Mermaid Theatre *BLKFR* EC4V 12 D6
Merrielands Retail Park *DAGW* RM9 80 B7
Merryhills Clinic *ENC/FH* EN2 29 F2
Merryhills Primary School *ENC/FH* EN2 29 F3
Merton Abbey First School *WIM/MER* SW19 147 F7
Merton Adult College *RYNPK* SW20 161 H2
Merton College *MRDN* SM4 161 J4
Merton Court Preparatory School *SCUP* DA14 155 J3
Merton Industrial Park *WIM/MER* SW19 147 G7
Merton Park Primary School *WIM/MER* SW19 161 J1
Merton Road Industrial Estate *WAND/EARL* SW18 127 K6
Metro Business Centre *SYD* SE26 151 H5
The Metro Golf Centre *HDN* NW4 38 A7
Metro Industrial Centre *ISLW* TW7 123 K1
Metropolitan Business Centre *HACK* E8 7 K2
Metropolitan Hospital *STHWK* SE1 18 B3
Metropolitan Police FC *E/WMO/HCT* KT8 157 J5
Metropolitan Police Hayes Sports Club *HAYES* BR2 180 D1
Metropolitan Police (Hendon) Track *CDALE/KGS* NW9 51 H2
Metropolitan Police Training School, Hendon *CDALE/KGS* NW9 51 H2
Metropolitan Tabernacle *LBTH* SE11 18 D5
Metro Trading Centre *WBLY* HA9 68 D3
Michael Faraday Primary School *WALW* SE17 19 H8
Michael Manley Industrial Estate *VX/NE* SW8 129 H1
Michael Sobell Sinai School *KTN/HRWW/W* HA3 50 C5
The Michael Tippett School *LBTH* SE11 18 B6
Midas Business Centre *DAGE* RM10 80 C3
Midas Industrial Estate *DAGE* RM10 80 C3
Middle Park Primary School *ELTH/MOT* SE9 134 C6
Middle Row Primary School *NKENS* W10 88 C3
Middlesex Business Centre *NWDGN* UB2 103 F1
Middlesex CCC (Lord's Cricket Ground) *STJWD* NW8 3 H7
Middlesex Guildhall *WEST* SW1P 17 H2
Middlesex Hospital *GTPST* W1W 10 F3
Middlesex Hospital Medical School *FITZ* W1T 10 F2
Middlesex Hospital Nurses Home *GTPST* W1W 10 E2
Middlesex Hospital School of Physiotherapy *FITZ* W1T 10 F2
Middlesex Hospital Sports Ground *CHST* BR7 155 F4
Middlesex University *EBAR* EN4 28 A5
GLDGN NW11 53 F7
TOTM N17 42 A5
WDGN N22 54 E1
Middlesex University Business School *HDN* NW4 51 K3
Middle Temple Hall *TPL/STR* WC2R 12 A6
Midfield Primary School *CHST* BR7 155 G6
Midway Mission Hospital *BETH* E2 7 L8
Milbourne Lodge School *ESH/CLAY* KT10 170 D5
Mile End & Bow Business Centre *WCHPL* E1 92 D4
Mile End Hospital *WCHPL* E1 93 F2
Mile End Stadium *BOW* E3 93 H4
Milehams Industrial Estate *PUR* RM19 119 K2
Miles Coverdale Primary School *SHB* W12 107 F1
Millbank Millennium Pier *WEST* SW1P 17 J6
Millbank Primary School *WEST* SW1P 17 H6
Millbank Tower *WEST* SW1P 17 J6
Millbourne Lodge Junior School *ESH/CLAY* KT10 170 C4
Millennium Arena *BTSEA* SW11 109 F6
Millennium Balloon *STHWK* SE1 13 K9
Millennium Harbour Development *POP/IOD* E14 112 C1
Millennium Quay *DEPT* SE8 112 E5
Millennium Wharf Development *POP/IOD* E14 113 G2
Mill Farm Business Park *HSLWW* TW4 122 D6
Millfields J & I School *CLPT* E5 74 E3
Millfield Theatre *UED* N18 41 K3
Mill Green Business Park *MTCM* CR4 162 E6
Mill Hill Cemetery *MLHL* NW7 38 A5
Mill Hill County High School *MLHL* NW7 37 G1
The Mill Hill Cricket Club *MLHL* NW7 38 A2
Mill Hill Golf Club *MLHL* NW7 37 G1
Mill Hill Industrial Estate *MLHL* NW7 37 H5
Mill Hill School *MLHL* NW7 37 K3
Mill Lane Medical Centre *KIL/WHAMP* NW6 70 E4
Mill Lane Trading Estate *CROY/NA* CR0 177 F2
Mill River Trading Estate *PEND* EN3 31 G3
Millside Industrial Estate *DART* DA1 139 G3
Mill Street Clinic *STHWK* SE1 19 M1
Mill Trading Estate *WLSDN* NW10 86 D1
Millwall FC (The New Den) *BERM/RHTH* SE16 111 K4
Milmead Industrial Centre *TOTM* N17 56 D1
Milton Natural Health Centre *HGT* N6 54 C6
Minet Clinic *HYS/HAR* UB3 82 E7
Minet J & I School *HYS/HAR* UB3 83 F7
Ministry of Defence *WHALL* SW1A 11 J9
Mini Town Hall *WOOL/PLUM* SE18 116 A4
Mint Business Park *CAN/RD* E16 94 E4
Mirravale Trading Estate *BCTR* RM8 62 A6
Mission Grove Primary School *WALTH* E17 57 H3
Mitcham Cricket Club *MTCM* CR4 162 D3
Mitcham Golf Club *MTCM* CR4 163 F4
Mitcham Industrial Estate *MTCM* CR4 148 A7
Mitcham Road Crematorium *THHTH* CR7 163 K4
Mitchell Brook Primary School *WLSDN* NW10 69 F5
Mitre Bridge Industrial Park *WLSDN* NW10 87 K3
Moatbridge School *ELTH/MOT* SE9 134 C5
Moberly Sports & Education Centre *NKENS* W10 88 B2
Molesey Hospital *E/WMO/HCT* KT8 157 F4
Molesey Lock *E/WMO/HCT* KT8 157 K2
Mollison Drive Health Centre *WLGTN* SM6 176 E6
Monega Primary School *MNPK* E12 77 H4
Monkfrith Primary School *EBAR* EN4 28 A6
Monks Hill Sports Centre *SAND/SEL* CR2 179 F6
Monksmead School *BORE* WD6 24 E2
Monks Orchard Primary School *CROY/NA* CR0 166 A4
Monson Primary School *NWCR* SE14 112 A6
Montbelle Primary School *ELTH/MOT* SE9 154 B2
Monteagle Primary School *DAGW* RM9 79 H7
Montem Primary School *HOLWY* N7 73 F2
Montpelier Primary School *EA* W5 85 K4
The Monument *CANST* EC4R 13 H6
Moore Place Golf Club *ESH/CLAY* KT10 170 A4
Moorfields Eye Hospital *FSBYE* EC1V 7 G8
Moorfields Primary School *STLK* EC1Y 7 G9
Moorgate Station *BARB* EC2Y 13 G3
Moor Lane Junior School *CHSGTN* KT9 172 B4
Moor Park Industrial Estate *WATW* WD18 20 A6
Mora Primary School *CRICK* NW2 70 A3
Morden Cemetery *MRDN* SM4 161 F5
Morden College Homes *BKHTH/KID* SE3 133 K1
Morden First School *MRDN* SM4 161 K4
Morden Hall Medical Centre *WIM/MER* SW19 162 A2
Morden Mount Primary School *LEW* SE13 132 E1
Morden Park Pool *MRDN* SM4 161 J5
Morden Road Clinic *WIM/MER* SW19 162 A2
More House School *ISLW* TW7 103 K7
KTBR SW1X 15 M4
Moreland Primary School *FSBYE* EC1V 6 D8
Moriah Jewish Day School *PIN* HA5 47 J7
Morningside Primary School *HOM* E9 74 E5
Mornington Sports & Fitness Centre *CAMTN* NW1 4 D3
Morpeth School *BETH* E2 92 E2
Mortimer Road Clinic *WLSDN* NW10 88 A2
Mortimer School *STRHM/NOR* SW16 148 D1
Mortlake Cemetery *MORT/ESHN* SW14 126 B2
Mortlake Crematorium *RCH/KEW* TW9 125 J1
Moselle School *TOTM* N17 56 A1
Mosiah Foundation Supplementary School *STNW/STAM* N16 56 A7
Mossford Green Primary School *BARK/HLT* IG6 60 C1
Moss Hall Primary School *FNCH* N3 39 F5
The Mother & Baby Clinic *HOM* E9 74 E5
Mottingham Community Health Clinic *ELTH/MOT* SE9 153 J3
Mottingham Primary School *ELTH/MOT* SE9 153 K2
Mount Carmel RC Primary School *EA* W5 104 D2
Mount Carmel School *ARCH* N19 54 D7
The Mount Infant School *NWMAL* KT3 159 J2
Mount Medical Centre *FELT* TW13 141 J1
Mount School *MLHL* NW7 37 K4
Mount Stewart Primary School *KTN/HRWW/W* HA3 49 K5
Mowlem Primary School *BETH* E2 92 E1
Mowlem Trading Estate *TOTM* N17 42 E6
MS Business Centre *PIN* HA5 47 H2
MSP Business Centre *WBLY* HA9 68 D3
Mudchute City Farm *POP/IOD* E14 113 F3
Mudlands Estate *RAIN* RM13 99 G2
Mulberry Business Centre *BERM/RHTH* SE16 112 A1
Mulberry House School *CRICK* NW2 70 C4
Mulberry School for Girls *WCHPL* E1 92 D5
Mulgrave Primary School *WOOL/PLUM* SE18 115 F3
WOOL/PLUM SE18 115 G2
Murky Puddle Theatre *NWMAL* KT3 160 C2
Muschamp Primary School *CAR* SM5 175 J1
Museum in Docklands *POP/IOD* E14 93 J6
Museum of Artillery in the Rotunda *CHARL* SE7 114 E4
Museum of Domestic Design & Architecture *EBAR* EN4 27 K4
Museum of Fulham Palace *FUL/PGN* SW6 127 G1
Museum of Garden History *STHWK* SE1 17 K4
Museum of London *STBT* EC1A 12 E3
Museum of London (Archaeological Research Centre) *IS* N1 6 F4
Museum of Richmond *RCH/KEW* TW9 124 E4
Museum of Rugby & Twickenham Stadium Tours *WHTN* TW2 123 K5
Museum of the Order of St John *FARR* EC1M 12 D1
Museums of the Royal College of Surgeons *LINN* WC2A 11 M4
The Musical Museum *BTFD* TW8 105 F5
Muswell Hill Bowling Club *MUSWH* N10 54 A2
Muswell Hill Golf Club *FBAR/BDGN* N11 40 B7
Muswell Hill Primary School *MUSWH* N10 54 B2
Myatt Garden Primary School *BROCKY* SE4 132 C1
Myatts Field Clinic *BRXN/ST* SW9 110 C7
Nagi Business Centre *ALP/SUD* HA0 85 K1
Nags Head Shopping Centre *HOLWY* N7 73 F3
Naima Jewish Preparatory School *KIL/WHAMP* NW6 2 C5
National Army Museum *CHEL* SW3 15 M9
National Film Theatre *STHWK* SE1 11 M8
National Gallery *LSQ/SEVD* WC2H 11 H7
National Hospital for Neurology & Neurosurgery *BMSBY* WC1N 11 J1
National Hospital for Sick Children (Great Ormond St) *BMSBY* WC1N 11 K1
National Maritime Museum *GNWCH* SE10 113 G5
National Physical Laboratory *TEDD* TW11 142 E5
National Portrait Gallery *LSQ/SEVD* WC2H 11 H7
National Temperance Hospital *CAMTN* NW1 4 F8
National Youth Theatre of GB *HOLWY* N7 72 E2
Natural History Museum *SKENS* SW7 15 G4
Natural Therapy Clinic *TOOT* SW17 148 B4
Natwest Sports Club *BECK* BR3 151 H5
Navigation College *MANHO* EC4N 12 F6
NEC Harlequins RFC (The Stoop Memorial Ground) *WHTN* TW2 123 K6
Negus 6th Form Centre *WOOL/PLUM* SE18 115 J5
Nelson Dock Museum *BERM/RHTH* SE16 93 H7
Nelson Hospital *WIM/MER* SW19 161 J1
Nelson Primary School *EHAM* E6 96 A1
WHTN TW2 123 G5
Nelson's Column *CHCR* WC2N 11 J8
Nelson Trading Estate *WIM/MER* SW19 147 F7
Neo Clinic *PIM* SW1V 16 E6
Netley Primary School *CAMTN* NW1 4 E8
The New Ambassadors Theatre *LSQ/SEVD* WC2H 11 J5
New Atlas Wharf Development *POP/IOD* E14 112 C2
The New Aylesbury Medical Centre *WALW* SE17 19 H7
New Brentford Cemetery *HSLW* TW3 122 E1
Newbury Park Health Centre *GNTH/NBYPK* IG2 60 D5
Newbury Park Primary School *GNTH/NBYPK* IG2 60 D5
The New Business Centre *WLSDN* NW10 87 H2
New Caledonian Wharf *BERM/RHTH* SE16 112 C2
New Chiswick Pool *CHSWK* W4 106 B6
New City Primary School *PLSTW* E13 95 G2
New Connaught Rooms *HOL/ALD* WC2B 11 K4
New Covent Garden Market *VX/NE* SW8 109 J5
New Crane Wharf *WAP* E1W 92 E7
New Cross Sports Arena *NWCR* SE14 112 B6
New End Primary School *HAMP* NW3 71 G3
New End Theatre *HAMP* NW3 71 G2
New England Industrial Estate *BARK* IG11 96 C1
Newfield Primary School *WLSDN* NW10 69 H6
The New Furness Primary School *WLSDN* NW10 87 J1
Newham College of Further Education *EHAM* E6 95 K1
SRTFD E15 76 C6
Newham Community College *CAN/RD* E16 94 C3
Newham General Hospital *PLSTW* E13 95 G3
Newham Leisure Centre *PLSTW* E13 95 G4
Newham Medical Centre *PLSTW* E13 95 G1
Newham Sixth Form College *PLSTW* E13 95 F3
New Health Centre *TOTM* N17 42 A7
Newington Court Business Centre *STHWK* SE1 18 E4
Newington Green Primary School *STNW/STAM* N16 74 A4
Newington Industrial Estate *WALW* SE17 18 D6
New Kings Primary School *FUL/PGN* SW6 127 J1
Newland House School *TWK* TW1 143 F3
New London Theatre *LSQ/SEVD* WC2H 11 K4
Newnham J & I School *RSLP* HA4 47 G7
Newport J & I School *LEY* E10 76 A1
New River Stadium *WDGN* N22 41 H6
New Rush Hall School *IL* IG1 78 C1
New School *FUL/PGN* SW6 107 J7
New Scotland Yard *STJSPK* SW1H 17 G3
News International *WAP* E1W 92 D6
New Southgate Cemetery *FBAR/BDGN* N11 40 B2
New Southgate Crematorium *FBAR/BDGN* N11 40 B2
New Southgate Industrial Estate *FBAR/BDGN* N11 40 C4
New Southgate Pain Clinic & Medical Centre *FBAR/BDGN* N11 40 C4
New Spitalfields Market *LEY* E10 75 J2
Newton Farm First & Middle School *RYLN/HDSTN* HA2 65 K1
Newton Industrial Estate *CHDH* RM6 61 K3
Newton Medical Centre *BAY/PAD* W2 8 B4
Newton Preparatory School *VX/NE* SW8 109 G6
Newtons Primary School *RAIN* RM13 99 F1
New Victoria Hospital *KUTN/CMB* KT2 145 G6
New Woodlands School *BMLY* BR1 152 C3
New York University in London *RSQ* WC1B 11 H3
Nightingale Clinic *PLSTW* E13 95 G1
Nightingale Primary School *CLPT* E5 74 C3
SWFD E18 59 G3
WDGN N22 40 E7
WOOL/PLUM SE18 115 G4
Nightingale School *STHWK* SE1 17 L2
TOOT SW17 147 J1
Nineacres School *WOOL/PLUM* SE18 115 J4
Noel Park Primary School *WDGN* N22 55 H1
Nonsuch High School for Girls *EW* KT17 174 B6
Nonsuch Primary School *EW* KT17 173 K4
Norbury Complementary Therapy Clinic *STRHM/NOR* SW16 149 F7
Norbury First & Middle School *HRW* HA1 48 E4
Norbury Health Centre *STRHM/NOR* SW16 164 A1
Norbury Manor Primary School *STRHM/NOR* SW16 148 E7
Norbury Manor Secondary Girls School *STRHM/NOR* SW16 149 F7
Norbury Trading Estate *STRHM/NOR* SW16 164 A1
Norfolk House School *MUSWH* N10 54 B1
Norland Place School *NTGHL* W11 88 C7
Norlington School *WAN* E11 58 B7
Normand Park Primary School *WKENS* W14 107 J5
Normandy Primary School *ERITH* DA8 118 A7
Norman Park Athletics Track *HAYES* BR2 168 A5
Norman Shaw Building (MP's Offices) *WHALL* SW1A 17 J1
North Acton Business Park *ACT* W3 87 F5
North Beckton Primary School *EHAM* E6 95 K4
North Bridge House *HAMP* NW3 71 G5
North Bridge House School *HAMP* NW3 71 H5
North Bridge House Senior School *CAMTN* NW1 4 C4
Northbrook CE School *LEW* SE13 133 H4
Northbury Primary School *BARK* IG11 78 B5
North Clinic *BMLY* BR1 152 E7
Northcote Lodge School *BTSEA* SW11 128 D5
North Croydon Medical Centre *THHTH* CR7 164 C5
North Ealing Primary School *WEA* W13 85 H3
North East Surrey Crematorium *NWMAL* KT3 161 F5
Northend Primary School *ERITH* DA8 118 C7
North End Trading Estate *ERITH* DA8 118 B6
North Feltham Trading Estate *EBED/NFELT* TW14 122 A3
Northfields Industrial Estate *ALP/SUD* HA0 68 C7
Northfields Prospect Business Centre *WAND/EARL* SW18 127 J3
Northgate Business Centre *EN* EN1 30 D2
Northgate Clinic *CDALE/KGS* NW9 51 G5
Northgate Industrial Park *ROMW/RG* RM7 62 B1
North Harringey Primary School *CEND/HSY/T* N8 55 G3
North Havering College of Adult Education *ROM* RM1 63 G3
North London Collegiate School *EDGW* HA8 36 A5
The North London Hospice *NFNCH/WDSP* N12 39 F2
North London School of Physiotherapy *ARCH* N19 54 C7
North London Tutorial College *HDN* NW4 52 A5
North Middlesex Golf Club *TRDG/WHET* N20 39 H2
North Middlesex Hospital *UED* N18 42 A4
Northolt Aerodrome *RSLP* HA4 64 E5
Northolt High School *NTHLT* UB5 65 K5

Northolt Park Infant School NTHLT UB5 66 B4
Northolt Primary School NTHLT UB5 65 H6
Northolt Road Clinic RYLN/HDSTN HA2 66 C2
Northolt Swimarama NTHLT UB5 66 A5
North Primary School STHL UB1 83 K6
Northside Primary NFNCH/WDSP N12 39 F4
The North Street Health Centre CLAP SW4 129 H2
Northumberland Heath Medical Centre ERITH DA8 118 A6
Northumberland Heath Primary School ERITH DA8 117 J6
Northumberland Park Industrial Estate TOTM N17 42 D5
Northumberland Park School TOTM N17 42 C6
Northview Primary School WLSDN NW10 69 G3
Northway School MLHL NW7 36 E2
North West Kent College of Technology DART DA1 139 F6
North West London Jewish J & I School CRICK NW2 70 C6
North West London Medical Centre STJWD NW8 2 E6
North Westminster Community School
BAY/PAD W2 9 G3
STJWD NW8 9 J2
North Westminster Community Secondary School MV/WKIL W9 2 B9
Northwick Park Hospital & Clinical Research Centre HRW HA1 49 H6
Northwold Primary School CLPT E5 74 C1
Northwood Cemetery NTHWD HA6 46 D1
Northwood College NTHWD HA6 32 B6
Northwood FC NTHWD HA6 46 D1
Northwood Golf Club NTHWD HA6 32 B6
Northwood & Pinner Community Hospital NTHWD HA6 32 E7
Northwood Preparatory School RKW/CH/CXG WD3 32 A1
Northwood Primary School ERITHM DA18 117 F2
Northwood School NTHWD HA6 33 F7
Northwood Sports Centre PIN HA5 33 F7
Norwegian/British Monument BAY/PAD W2 9 J8
The Norwegian School WIM/MER SW19 146 A6
Norwood Green Infant School NWDGN UB2 102 D4
Norwood Green Junior School NWDGN UB2 102 D4
Norwood Heights Shopping Centre NRWD SE19 150 A5
Norwood Park Primary School WNWD SE27 149 J3
Norwood School WNWD SE27 149 J4
Notre Dame RC Girls School STHWK SE1 18 C3
Notre Dame RC Primary School WOOL/PLUM SE18 115 G5
Notting Hill & Ealing High School WEA W13 85 H4
Nower Hill High School PIN HA5 48 A3
N1 Shopping Centre IS N1 6 B5
NTGB Sports Ground EHAM E6 78 A5
Nuffield Hospital ENC/FH EN2 29 G1
Nutrition Clinic MHST W1U 10 A2
Oakdale Infant School SWFD E18 59 F1
Oakdale Junior School SWFD E18 59 G1
Oakfield Preparatory School DUL SE21 149 K1
Oakfield Road Industrial Estate PGE/AN SE20 150 D6
Oak Hill College EBAR EN4 28 A5
Oak Hill Health Centre SURB KT6 159 F5
Oakhill Primary School WFD IG8 44 C5
Oakington Manor School WBLY HA9 68 D4
Oakland CP School EBAR EN4 27 K5
Oaklands College BORE WD6 24 E1
Oaklands Primary School HNWL W7 104 A1
Oaklands School ISLW TW7 123 J2
Oaklands Secondary School BETH E2 92 C2
Oak Lane Cemetery TWK TW1 124 B6
Oak Lane Medical Centre TWK TW1 124 C6
Oakleigh School TRDG/WHET N20 39 J2
Oak Lodge JMI School WWKM BR4 166 E6
Oak Lodge Medical Centre EDGW HA8 36 D6
Oak Lodge School
BAL SW12 128 E6
EFNCH N2 53 G2
Oakthorpe Primary School PLMGR N13 41 J4
Oak Tree Medical Centre GDMY/SEVK IG3 78 E1
Oakwood Business Park WLSDN NW10 87 F2
Oakwood Medical Centre STHGT/OAK N14 28 C4
Oasis Sports Centre LSQ/SEVD WC2H 11 J4
Obstetrics Hospital GWRST WC1E 10 F1
Occupational Health Centre CROY/NA CR0 177 K2
Odeon Cinema
ARCH N19 72 E2
BAR EN5 26 E4
BECK BR3 166 D1
CAMTN NW1 4 D3
ELTH/MOT SE9 134 D3
ESH/CLAY KT10 170 B3
FITZ W1T 11 G3
GNTH/NBYPK IG2 60 A5
HAYES BR2 167 K1
KENS W8 14 A3
KIL/WHAMP NW6 3 G2
KUTN/CMB KT2 159 F1
LSQ/SEVD WC2H 11 H7
MBLAR W1H 9 M5
MUSWH N10 54 A3
RCHPK/HAM TW10 124 E4
ROM RM1 63 H4
STJS SW1Y 11 G7
STRHM/NOR SW16 148 E2
SWFD E18 58 E1
WIM/MER SW19 146 E6
Odeon Covent Gardens Cinema LSQ/SEVD WC2H 11 H5
Odeon Wardour Street Cinema SOHO/SHAV W1D 11 G6
Odessa Infant School FSTGT E7 76 E4
Odyssey Business Park RSLP HA4 65 F4
Old Actonians Sports Club EA W5 105 G1
Old Admiralty WHALL SW1A 11 H9
Old Bancroftians FC BKHH IG9 45 H3
Old Barnes Cemetery BARN SW13 126 E1
Old Beckenhamian RFC WWKM BR4 180 B2
Old Bellgate Wharf Development POP/IOD E14 112 C2
Old Bexley Business Park BXLY DA5 137 J6
Old Bexley CE Primary School BXLY DA5 137 G7
Old Brockleians Sports Ground ELTH/MOT SE9 134 B5
Old Bromlians Cricket Club HAYES BR2 168 A4
Old Cemetery EDUL SE22 131 J5
Oldchurch Hospital ROMW/RG RM7 63 F5
Old Colfeian Sports Club LEE/GVPK SE12 133 K4
Old Curiosity Shop LINN WC2A 11 L4
Old Elthamians Sports Club CHST BR7 154 E5
Oldfield House Special School HPTN TW12 141 K7
Oldfields Primary School GFD/PVL UB6 84 D1
Oldfields Trading Estate SUT SM1 174 E2
Old Ford Primary School BOW E3 93 H1
Oldhill Medical Centre STNW/STAM N16 56 B7
Old Jamaica Business Estate BERM/RHTH SE16 19 M3
Old Lyonian Sports Ground RYLN/HDSTN HA2 48 C4
Old Millhillians Sports Ground PIN HA5 34 A7
Old Oak Primary School SHB W12 87 H5
Old Operating Theatre Museum STHWK SE1 13 G9
Old Owens Sports Ground TRDG/WHET N20 27 H7
Old Palace Primary School BOW E3 93 K2
Old Palace School CROY/NA CR0 177 H2
Old Royal Naval College GNWCH SE10 113 G4
Old Royal Observatory Greenwich GNWCH SE10 113 G6
Old Station Museum CAN/RD E16 115 F1
Old Street Station FSBYE EC1V 7 G8
Old Sun Wharf POP/IOD E14 93 G6
Old Tiffinians Sports Ground E/WMO/HCT KT8 157 K4
Old Treasury WHALL SW1A 17 J1
Old Vicarage School RCHPK/HAM TW10 125 F5
Old Vic Theatre STHWK SE1 18 B1
Old War Office WHALL SW1A 11 J9
Old Wilsonians Sports Club WWKM BR4 167 H7
Olga Primary School BOW E3 93 G1
Oliver Business Park WLSDN NW10 86 E1
Oliver Goldsmith Primary School
CDALE/KGS NW9 51 F4
CMBW SE5 111 G7
Olympia WKENS W14 107 H2
Olympia Industrial Estate WDGN N22 55 F1
Olympic Industrial Estate WBLY HA9 68 D3
Olympic Retail Park WBLY HA9 68 C3
Olympic Trading Estate WBLY HA9 68 D3
The One Stanley Medical Centre ALP/SUD HA0 68 A6
On Sai Clinic ECT SW5 14 C6
On the Road Tours CC WAND/EARL SW18 128 B5
Open Air Theatre CAMTN NW1 4 A8
The Open University
FSBYW WC1X 5 L7
HAMP NW3 70 E3
Ophaboom Theatre WLSDN NW10 87 K2
Optimax Laser Eye Clinic HAMP NW3 71 G5
Orange Tree Theatre RCH/KEW TW9 125 F3
Oratory RC Primary School CHEL SW3 15 J7
Orchard Business Centre SYD SE26 151 H4
The Orchard Health Centre BARK IG11 96 C1
Orchard House School CHSWK W4 106 A3
The Orchard Junior School HSLW TW3 123 F3
Orchard Primary School HOM E9 74 E6
The Orchard School E/WMO/HCT KT8 157 J4
Orchard Shopping Centre DART DA1 139 H5
The Orchard Theatre DART DA1 139 H5
Orchard Way Primary School CROY/NA CR0 166 B6
Oriel Primary School FELT TW13 141 J2
Orient Industrial Park LEY E10 75 J1
Orion Business Centre BERM/RHTH SE16 112 A4
Orleans House Gallery TWK TW1 124 C7
Orleans Infant School TWK TW1 124 C6
Orleans Park School TWK TW1 124 C6
Orley Farm School HRW HA1 66 D2
Osidge JMI School STHGT/OAK N14 28 C7
Osmani Primary School WCHPL E1 92 C4
Osteopathic Clinic HOR/WEW KT19 173 F4
Osterley RFC NWDGN UB2 103 G2
Our Lady Immaculate RC Primary School BRYLDS KT5 159 J7
Our Lady of Dolours RC Primary School BAY/PAD W2 8 C2
Our Lady of Grace RC Junior School CRICK NW2 69 K2
Our Lady of Lourdes RC Primary School
FBAR/BDGN N11 40 C4
FNCH N3 39 G6
LEW SE13 133 G2
WAN E11 58 D5
WLSDN NW10 68 E7
Our Lady of Muswell RC Primary School MUSWH N10 54 A1
Our Lady of St Johns BTFD TW8 104 D4
Our Lady of the Assumption RC Infant School BETH E2 92 E1
Our Lady of the Rosary RC Primary School BFN/LL DA15 135 K5
Our Lady of the Sacred Heart School HOLWY N7 73 F4
Our Lady of the Visitation RC Combined Primary School GFD/PVL UB6 84 C3
Our Lady of Victories RC Primary School
PUT/ROE SW15 127 G3
SKENS SW7 15 G6
Our Lady Queen of Heaven RC Primary School WIM/MER SW19 127 G6
Our Lady RC Primary School
CAMTN NW1 4 F3
POP/IOD E14 93 H5
Our Lady & St Joseph Primary School IS N1 74 A5
Our Lady & St Philip Neri RC Primary School FSTH SE23 151 F2
Our Ladys Catholic Primary School DART DA1 139 F5
Our Ladys Convent High School STNW/STAM N16 56 A6
Oval Business Centre LBTH SE11 17 M8
Oval House Theatre LBTH SE11 110 B5
Oval Primary School CROY/NA CR0 165 F7
Overton Grange School BELMT SM2 175 F6
Oxford Gardens Primary School NKENS W10 88 B5
Oxford House College SOHO/SHAV W1D 11 G4
Oxhey Infant School BUSH WD23 21 J5
Oxhey Park Golf Centre OXHEY WD19 21 H7
Oxhey Wood Primary School OXHEY WD19 33 G3
Oxo Tower Wharf STHWK SE1 12 B7
Paddington Bowling & Sports Club MV/WKIL W9 2 C9
Paddington Community Hospital MV/WKIL W9 8 A2
Paddington Green Primary School BAY/PAD W2 9 G1
Paddington Recreation Ground Athletics Track MV/WKIL W9 2 B7
Paddington Station BAY/PAD W2 9 G4
Paddock School PUT/ROE SW15 126 C3
Pain Relief Clinic HDN NW4 51 K5
Pakeman Primary School HOLWY N7 73 F2
Palace Gardens Shopping Centre ENC/FH EN2 29 K2
Palace Theatre WAT WD17 21 F2
Palladium Theatre REGST W1B 10 E5
Palmers Green High School WCHMH N21 41 G1
Palmerston Business Centre SUT SM1 175 G4
Palm House RCH/KEW TW9 105 G7
Panorama Pier STHWK SE1 12 D7
Paradise Swimming Pools MLHL NW7 37 G4
Parayhouse School WBPTN SW10 108 B6
Parchmore Medical Centre THHTH CR7 164 D2
Pardes House & Beis Yaakov Boys School FNCH N3 52 D1
Parent Infant Clinic HAMP NW3 71 G4
Parish CE Primary School BMLY BR1 152 E6
Parish Church CE Primary School CROY/NA CR0 177 H2
Park Avenue Clinic WAT WD17 20 E1
Park Business Centre KIL/WHAMP NW6 2 A8
Parkfield Industrial Estate BTSEA SW11 129 F1
Parkfield JMI School HDN NW4 51 K6
Parkgate House School BTSEA SW11 129 F3
Park Hall Trading Estate WNWD SE27 149 J2
Park High School STAN HA7 49 K1
Park Hill Junior School CROY/NA CR0 177 K2
Parkhill Primary School CLAY IG5 59 K2
Park Hill School KUTN/CMB KT2 144 C6
Park House Medical Centre KIL/WHAMP NW6 88 C1
Parkhouse Middle School WIM/MER SW19 146 D3
Park House RFC HAYES BR2 181 G1
Parkhurst Infant School TOTM N17 56 B1
Parklands Primary School ROM RM1 63 F2
Park Lane Primary School WBLY HA9 68 A3
Park Medical Centre BERM/RHTH SE16 112 A3
Park Mews Small Business Centre HNHL SE24 130 D5
Park Primary School SRTFD E15 76 D6
Park Road Clinic CEND/HSY/T N8 54 D4
Park Road Swimming Centre CEND/HSY/T N8 54 D4
Park Royal Business Centre WLSDN NW10 86 E3
Park School for Girls IL IG1 60 B7
Parkside Business Estate DEPT SE8 112 C5
Parkside Clinic NTGHL W11 88 C5
Parkside Health NTGHL W11 88 C5
Parkside Hospital WIM/MER SW19 146 B2
Park Walk Primary School WBPTN SW10 108 C5
Parkway Primary School ERITHM DA18 117 F2
Parkway Trading Estate HEST TW5 102 B5
Parkwood Primary School FSBYPK N4 73 H1
Parliament Hill Fields Athletics Track KTTN NW5 71 K3
Parliament Hill School KTTN NW5 72 A3
Parmiter Industrial Centre BETH E2 92 D1
Parnells Sports Ground KTN/HRWW/W HA3 50 B5
Parsloes Primary School DAGW RM9 80 B5
Parsons Green Health Clinic FUL/PGN SW6 107 K7
Passport Language Schools BMLY BR1 153 F7
Patent Office HHOL WC1V 12 A3
The Patrick Doody Clinic & Health Centre WIM/MER SW19 146 E6
Pattinson Clinic RCHPK/HAM TW10 124 E4
The Paul Robeson Theatre HSLW TW3 123 G2
Pavilion Barclays Sports Ground EA W5 86 A4
The Pavilion Leisure Centre BMLY BR1 167 K1
Pavilion Restaurant RCH/KEW TW9 125 F1
Paxton Primary School NRWD SE19 150 B5
PDSA Hospital REDBR IG4 59 H2
Peace Pagoda BTSEA SW11 108 E6
Peacock Estate TOTM N17 42 B5
Peacock Industrial Estate TOTM N17 42 B6
The Peacock Theatre HOL/ALD WC2B 11 L5
Peall Road Industrial Estate CROY/NA CR0 164 A5
Peckham Leisure Centre PECK SE15 111 H7
Peckham Park Primary School PECK SE15 111 H6
Peckham Pulse Healthy Living Centre PECK SE15 111 H7
Peckham Rye Primary School PECK SE15 131 J2
Pelham Primary School
BXLYHN DA7 137 G2
WIM/MER SW19 146 E6
Pembridge Hall BAY/PAD W2 8 B7
Pendragon Secondary School BMLY BR1 152 E2
Pentavia Retail Park MLHL NW7 37 H6
Penton Primary School IS N1 6 B5
Penwortham Primary School STRHM/NOR SW16 148 B5
Percival David Foundation of Chinese Art STPAN WC1H 5 H9
Perivale Industrial Park GFD/PVL UB6 67 G7
Perivale New Business Centre GFD/PVL UB6 85 J1
Perivale Park Athletics Track GFD/PVL UB6 84 E2
Perivale Park Golf Course GFD/PVL UB6 84 E2
Perivale Primary School GFD/PVL UB6 85 J1
Perrin Road Clinic ALP/SUD HA0 67 H3
Perrymount Primary School FSTH SE23 151 F1
Peterborough Primary School FUL/PGN SW6 127 K1
Peterborough & St Margarets High School STAN HA7 34 E2
Peter Hills School BERM/RHTH SE16 93 F7
Peter James Business Centre HYS/HAR UB3 101 K1
Peterley Business Centre BETH E2 92 D1
Peter Pan Statue BAY/PAD W2 9 G8
Petric Museum of Egyptia Archaeology GWRST WC1E 11 G1
Pewterers' Hall CITYW EC2V 12 F3
Phoenix Business Centre POP/IOD E14 93 J4
Phoenix Cinema EFNCH N2 53 J3
Phoenix College
MRDN SM4 162 A4
TOOT SW17 147 J1
Phoenix Court POP/IOD E14 112 D3
Phoenix High School SHB W12 87 J6
Phoenix Industrial Estate HRW HA1 49 F3
Phoenix Leisure Centre CAT SE6 132 E6
Phoenix School BOW E3 93 H2
Phoenix Theatre LSQ/SEVD WC2H 11 H5
Phoenix Trading Estate GFD/PVL UB6 67 J7
Photographer's Gallery LSQ/SEVD WC2H 11 H6
Physical Energy Statue BAY/PAD W2 9 G9
Piccadilly Theatre SOHO/SHAV W1D 11 G6
Pickford Lane Medical Centre BXLYHN DA7 117 F7
Pickhurst Infant School HAYES BR2 167 H5
Pickhurst Junior School HAYES BR2 167 J5
Picture House Cinema SRTFD E15 76 B5
Pilgrims Way J & I School PECK SE15 111 K5
Pilot Industrial Centre WLSDN NW10 87 G3
Pilton Estate CROY/NA CR0 177 H1
Pimlico School PIM SW1V 16 F8
Pinkwell Primary School WDR/YW UB7 101 F3
Pinner Hill Golf Club PIN HA5 33 F5
Pinner Park Primary School RYLN/HDSTN HA2 48 B2
Pinner View Medical Centre HRW HA1 48 C4
Pinner Wood Primary School PIN HA5 33 G7
Pinn Medical Centre PIN HA5 47 J3
Pioneers Industrial Park CROY/NA CR0 163 K7
Pitshanger Manor Museum EA W5 85 J7
Plaisterers Hall CITYW EC2V 12 E3
Plaistow Hospital PLSTW E13 95 F1
Planetarium CAMTN NW1 10 A1

Plantation House Medical Centre *LOTH* EC2R 13 H4
Plashet Jewish Cemetery *MNPK* E12 77 H5
Plashet Road Medical Centre *FSTGT* E7 77 F6
Plashet School *EHAM* E6 77 J6
Players Theatre *CHCR* WC2N 11 J8
The Playhouse *CHCR* WC2N 11 K8
Plaza Business Centre *PEND* EN3 31 H1
Pleasance Theatre *HOLWY* N7 72 E5
Plumcroft Primary School *WOOL/PLUM* SE18 115 H5
Plumstead Leisure Centre *WOOL/PLUM* SE18 116 A4
Plumstead Manor School *WOOL/PLUM* SE18 115 J4
The Pointer School *BKHTH/KID* SE3 113 K7
Police Cadet School *WAN* E11 58 E7
The Polish Institute & Sikorski Museum *SKENS* SW7 15 H2
Polka Theatre for Children *WIM/MER* SW19 147 F5
Pollock's Toy Museum *FITZ* W1T 10 F2
Ponders End Industrial Estate
PEND EN3 31 F1
PEND EN3 31 H3
Poole's Park Primary School *HOLWY* N7 73 F1
Pools in the Park *RCH/KEW* TW9 124 E3
Pope John Primary School *SHB* W12 87 K6
Pop In Business Centre *WBLY* HA9 68 D4
Poplar Business Park *POP/IOD* E14 94 A6
Poplar First School *WIM/MER* SW19 161 K2
Pop Up Theatre *IS* N1 6 B6
Porchester Leisure Centre *BAY/PAD* W2 8 C4
Portcullis House *WHALL* SW1A 17 K2
The Portland Hospital *REGST* W1B 10 D1
Portland House Medical Centre *GFD/PVL* UB6 84 B3
Portland Medical Centre *SNWD* SE25 165 J4
Portland Place School *REGST* W1B 10 D2
The Portman Clinic *HAMP* NW3 71 H5
Portobello Market *NKENS* W10 88 C4
Portobello Medical Centre *NTGHL* W11 88 C5
Portway Primary School *SRTFD* E15 76 E7
Pound Park Nursery School *CHARL* SE7 114 C4
The Pountney Clinic *HSLW* TW3 123 F2
Powergate Business Park *WLSDN* NW10 87 F2
Power Industrial Estate *ERITH* DA8 118 C7
Premier Cinema *PECK* SE15 131 H1
Prendergast School *BROCKY* SE4 132 D3
Preston Manor School *WBLY* HA9 68 B1
Preston Medical Centre *WBLY* HA9 68 A2
Preston Park Primary School *WBLY* HA9 49 K7
PR for Schools *SYD* SE26 150 E2
Priestmead First & Middle Schools *KTN/HRWW/W* HA3 49 H2
Primrose Hill School *CAMTN* NW1 4 B3
Primrose Montessori School *HBRY* N5 73 J2
Prince Charles Cinema *SOHO/SHAV* W1D 11 H6
Prince Edward Theatre *SOHO/SHAV* W1D 11 G5
Prince of Wales Theatre *STJS* SW1Y 11 G7
Princes College *NOXST/BSQ* WC1A 11 J4
Princes Court Business Centre *WAP* E1W 92 D6
Princess Avenue School *MUSWH* N10 54 B2
Princess Frederica CE J & I School *WLSDN* NW10 87 K1
Princess Grace Hospital *MHST* W1U 10 A1
Princess Louise Hospital *NKENS* W10 88 A4
Princess May Primary School *STNW/STAM* N16 74 A4
Princess of Wales Conservatory *RCH/KEW* TW9 105 G6
Prior Western Primary School *STLK* EC1Y 12 F1
Priory CE Middle School *WIM/MER* SW19 147 F4
Priory House School *CAT* SE6 132 E7
Priory Retail Park *WIM/MER* SW19 147 H6
Priory Shopping Centre *DART* DA1 139 G5
Priory Special School *SNWD* SE25 165 G3
Privy Council *STJS* SW1Y 11 G9
Privy Council Office *WHALL* SW1A 11 J9
Progress Business Park *CROY/NA* CR0 177 F1
Pronto Trading Estate *YEAD* UB4 82 C4
Prospect House School *PUT/ROE* SW15 127 G6
Prospect of Whitby *WAP* E1W 92 E7
Proud Gallery *CHCR* WC2N 11 J7
Provident Industrial Estate *HYS/HAR* UB3 101 K1
Psychiatric Home *BRXN/ST* SW9 129 K2
Public Record Office *LINN* WC2A 12 A4
Public Record Office Museum *RCH/KEW* TW9 105 J6
Pump House *BERM/RHTH* SE16 93 G7
Pump House Theatre *WAT* WD17 21 G4
Pumping Station *HAYES* BR2 167 H1
Pump Lane Industrial Estate *HYS/HAR* UB3 102 A1
The Purcell School
BUSH WD23 21 K1
HRW HA1 66 D2
Purdy Hicks Gallery *STHWK* SE1 12 C8
Purfleet Industrial Park *PUR* RM19 119 J1
Purfleet Primary School *PUR* RM19 119 K3
Purley Oaks Primary School *SAND/SEL* CR2 177 K6
Pursuit Centre *WAP* E1W 92 E6
Putney Animal Hospital *PUT/ROE* SW15 127 G3
Putney Exchange Shopping Centre *PUT/ROE* SW15 127 G3
Putney High School *PUT/ROE* SW15 127 G4
Putney Hospital *PUT/ROE* SW15 127 F2
Putney Leisure Centre *PUT/ROE* SW15 127 F3
Putney Lower Common Cemetery *PUT/ROE* SW15 126 E1
Putneymead Medical Centre *PUT/ROE* SW15 127 F3
Putney Park School *PUT/ROE* SW15 126 E3
Putney School of Art *PUT/ROE* SW15 127 H3
Putney Vale Cemetery *PUT/ROE* SW15 145 J1
Putney Vale Crematorium *PUT/ROE* SW15 145 J1
Pylon Trading Estate *CAN/RD* E16 94 B3
Quadrant Business Park *KIL/WHAMP* NW6 70 C7
Quebec Industrial Estate *BERM/RHTH* SE16 112 B1
Queen Charlottes & Chelsea Hospital *HMSMTH* W6 106 D2
Queen Charlotte's Cottage *RCH/KEW* TW9 105 G6
Queen Elizabeth Centre *BAR* EN5 26 D3
Queen Elizabeth College *KENS* W8 14 A1
Queen Elizabeth Conference Centre *WEST* SW1P 17 H2
Queen Elizabeth Hall *STHWK* SE1 11 L8
Queen Elizabeth Hospital *CHARL* SE7 114 E5
Queen Elizabeth II School *MV/WKIL* W9 88 D3
Queen Elizabeths Boys School *BAR* EN5 26 B2
Queen Elizabeths Girls School *BAR* EN5 26 D3
Queen Elizabeth Stadium *EN* EN1 30 B1
Queenhithe Stairs *BLKFR* EC4V 12 E7
Queen Mary's Hospital *HAMP* NW3 71 G2
Queen Marys Hospital *SCUP* DA14 155 G4
Queen Marys Hospital for Children *CAR* SM5 175 K7
Queen Mary's University Hospital *PUT/ROE* SW15 126 D5
Queen Mary & Westfield College
SWFD E18 44 E7
WCHPL E1 93 F3
Queen Mother Sports Centre *PIM* SW1V 16 E5
Queensbridge Infant School *HACK* E8 7 M2
Queensbridge Sports Centre *HACK* E8 7 M1
Queen's Building *HTHAIR* TW6 120 E2
Queens CE Primary School *RCH/KEW* TW9 105 G6
Queen's Club *WKENS* W14 107 H4
Queens College *CAVSQ/HST* W1G 10 C3
Queen's Gallery *WHALL* SW1A 16 D2
Queens Gate School *SKENS* SW7 15 G5
The Queens House *GNWCH* SE10 113 G5
Queens Ice Skating Club *BAY/PAD* W2 8 D7
Queens Manor Primary School *FUL/PGN* SW6 107 F6
Queensmead School *RSLP* HA4 65 H3
Queensmead Sports Centre
RSLP HA4 64 E1
RSLP HA4 65 H4
Queens Medical Centre *RCHPK/HAM* TW10 125 G4
Queensmill School *FUL/PGN* SW6 127 K1
Queens Park Community School Gm *KIL/WHAMP* NW6 70 A7
Queens Park Health Centre *NKENS* W10 88 C2
Queens Park Primary School *NKENS* W10 88 C2
Queens Park Rangers FC (Loftus Road Stadium) *SHB* W12 87 K6
Queen's Road Cemetery *CROY/NA* CR0 164 D5
Queens Road Practice *NWCR* SE14 112 A7
Queens School *BUSH* WD23 21 K2
Queens Theatre *SOHO/SHAV* W1D 11 G6
Queensway Business Centre *PEND* EN3 30 E3
Queenswell Infant School *TRDG/WHET* N20 39 H1
Queen Victoria Memorial *WHALL* SW1A 16 E2
The Questors Theatre *EA* W5 85 J6
Quintin Kynaston School *STJWD* NW8 2 F4
Radcliffe College *SOHO/CST* W1F 10 E5
Raglan Infant School *EN* EN1 30 A5
Raglan Junior School *EN* EN1 30 A6
Raglan Primary School *HAYES* BR2 168 B3
Railton Road Clinic *BRXN/ST* SW9 130 C4
Rainbow Industrial Estate *RYNPK* SW20 160 E1
Rainbow Quay *BERM/RHTH* SE16 112 B2
Raines Foundation School *BETH* E2 92 D2
Rainham Hall NT *RAIN* RM13 99 J3
Rainham Trading Estate *RAIN* RM13 99 G2
Rainham Village Primary School *RAIN* RM13 99 J3
Ramac Industrial Estate *CHARL* SE7 113 K4
Ram Brewery & Visitor Centre *WAND/EARL* SW18 128 A4
Randal Cremer Primary School *BETH* E2 7 L5
Ranelagh Gardens (site of Chelsea Flower Show) *CHEL* SW3 16 B8
Ranelagh Primary School *SRTFD* E15 94 C1
Rangefield Primary School *BMLY* BR1 152 C4
Rangers House (The Wernher Collection) *GNWCH* SE10 113 G7
Ransomes Dock Business Centre *BTSEA* SW11 108 D6
Raphael School *EMPK* RM11 63 J5
Rathfern Primary School *CAT* SE6 132 C7
Ravenor Primary School *GFD/PVL* UB6 84 A2
Ravensbourne College of Design & Communication *CHST* BR7 153 K4
The Ravensbourne School *HAYES* BR2 168 A3
Ravenscourt Park Preparatory School *HMSMTH* W6 106 D3
Ravenscroft Medical Centre *GLDGN* NW11 52 D6
Ravenscroft Primary School *PLSTW* E13 94 E3
Ravenscroft School *TRDG/WHET* N20 26 D6
Ravenside Retail Park *UED* N18 43 F4
Ravenstone Primary School *BAL* SW12 129 F7
Ravenswood Industrial Estate *WALTH* E17 58 A3
Ravens Wood School *HAYES* BR2 181 H2
Ray Lodge Primary School *WFD* IG8 45 H5
Raynes Park High School *NWMAL* KT3 160 E2
Raynes Park Sports Ground *RYNPK* SW20 160 D1
Raynes Park Vale FC *RYNPK* SW20 161 G4
Raynham Primary School *UED* N18 42 C4
RCA *SKENS* SW7 14 F4
RCA Sculpture School *BTSEA* SW11 108 D6
Reay Primary School *BRXN/ST* SW9 110 A6
Records Office *CLKNW* EC1R 6 B9
Rectory Business Centre *SCUP* DA14 155 H3
Redbridge College *CHDH* RM6 61 H4
Redbridge Museum *IL* IG1 78 B2
Redbridge Primary School *REDBR* IG4 59 J4
Redburn Industrial Estate *PEND* EN3 31 F5
Redcliffe School *WBPTN* SW10 14 D9
Reddiford School *PIN* HA5 47 J3
Redford Lodge Psychiatric Hospital *ED* N9 42 C1
Redhill Junior School *CHST* BR7 154 B4
Redlands Primary School *WCHPL* E1 92 E4
Red Lion Business Park *SURB* KT6 172 B1
Redriff Community Primary School *BERM/RHTH* SE16 93 G7
Red Rose Trading Estate *EBAR* EN4 27 H4
Regent Business Centre *HYS/HAR* UB3 102 A1
Regent Clinic *CAVSQ/HST* W1G 10 C3
Regent's College *CAMTN* NW1 4 A7
Regent's Park Barracks *CAMTN* NW1 4 C5
Regents Park Clinic *CAMTN* NW1 3 L9
Regents Park Medical Centre *CAMTN* NW1 4 D7
Regent's Park Track *CAMTN* NW1 3 L5
Regina Coeli RC Primary School *CROY/NA* CR0 177 H6
Renoir Cinema *BMSBY* WC1N 5 K9
Renwick Industrial Estate *BARK* IG11 97 H1
Reynard Mills Trading Estate *BTFD* TW8 104 D4
Reynolds Sports Centre *EA* W5 105 H1
Rhodes Avenue Primary School *FBAR/BDGN* N11 40 C7
Rhodes Farm Clinic *MLHL* NW7 38 A3
Rhyl Primary School *KTTN* NW5 72 A5
RIBA Library Drawings & Manuscript Collection *MBLAR* W1H 9 M4
Ricards Lodge High School *WIM/MER* SW19 146 D4
Richard Alibon Primary School *DAGE* RM10 80 C4
Richard Atkins Primary School *BRXS/STRHM* SW2 129 K6
Richard Cloudesley School *STLK* EC1Y 12 E1
Richard Cobden Primary School *CAMTN* NW1 4 F4
Rich Industrial Estate
PECK SE15 111 J5
STHWK SE1 19 K4
STHWK SE1 19 M7
Richmond Adult & Community College
RCH/KEW TW9 124 E3
TWK TW1 124 A7
The Richmond Clinic *RCHPK/HAM* TW10 125 G3
Richmond College
KENS W8 14 C3
RCHPK/HAM TW10 125 F6
Richmond FC *RCH/KEW* TW9 124 E3
The Richmond Golf Club *RCHPK/HAM* TW10 144 A1
The Richmond Green Medical Centre *RCH/KEW* TW9 124 E4
Richmond House School *HPTN* TW12 141 K4
Richmond Magistrates Court *RCH/KEW* TW9 124 E3
Richmond Park Golf Club *PUT/ROE* SW15 126 B6
Richmond Road Medical Centre *KUTN/CMB* KT2 144 A6
Richmond Theatre *RCH/KEW* TW9 124 E3
Richmond upon Thames College *WHTN* TW2 123 K6
Ridge House Clinic *WCHMH* N21 29 K6
Ridgeway Primary School *SAND/SEL* CR2 178 A7
Rio Cinema *HACK* E8 74 B4
Ripple J & I School *BARK* IG11 78 D7
Risley Avenue Primary School *TOTM* N17 42 A7
Ritzy Cinema *BRXN/ST* SW9 130 B3
River Brent Business Park *NWDGN* UB2 103 K2
River Gardens Business Centre *EBED/NFELT* TW14 122 A3
River Mole Business Park *ESH/CLAY* KT10 157 F7
River Place Health Centre *IS* N1 6 E2
River Road Business Park *BARK* IG11 96 E2
Riversdale Primary School *WAND/EARL* SW18 127 K7
Riverside Business Centre *WAND/EARL* SW18 128 A7
Riverside Business Park *WIM/MER* SW19 147 G7
Riverside Community Health Care *WKENS* W14 107 G2
Riverside Golf Club *THMD* SE28 98 A5
Riverside Industrial Estate
BARK IG11 97 G2
DART DA1 139 H4
ED N9 31 G5
Riverside Primary School *BERM/RHTH* SE16 111 H1
Riverside Studios Cinema *BARN* SW13 107 F4
Riverside Swimming Centre *ERITH* DA8 118 B4
Riverside Wandle Trading Estate *MTCM* CR4 162 E6
Riverston School *LEE/GVPK* SE12 133 K4
Riverview C E Primary School *HOR/WEW* KT19 172 E3
RJ Mitchell Primary School *HCH* RM12 81 K5
RNIB Sunshine House School *NTHWD* HA6 32 B5
RNLI Lifeboat Station *TWRH* EC3N 13 K8
Roan Industrial Estate *MTCM* CR4 147 J7
Robert Blair Primary School *HOLWY* N7 72 E5
Robert Browning Primary School *WALW* SE17 18 F7
Robert Clack School *BCTR* RM8 62 B7
Robin Hood Infant School *SUT* SM1 174 E4
Robin Hood Junior School *SUT* SM1 175 F4
Robin Hood Lane Health Centre *SUT* SM1 174 E4
Robin Hood Primary School *KUTN/CMB* KT2 145 F4
Robinsfield Infant School *STJWD* NW8 3 H5
The Roche School *WAND/EARL* SW18 127 K4
Rockcliffe Manor Primary School *WOOL/PLUM* SE18 115 K6
Rockmount School *NRWD* SE19 149 J5
Rockware Business Centre *GFD/PVL* UB6 66 D7
Roding Primary School
BCTR RM8 79 J3
WFD IG8 45 J6
Roe Green J & I School *CDALE/KGS* NW9 50 D3
Roehampton Church School *PUT/ROE* SW15 126 E6
Roehampton Golf Club *PUT/ROE* SW15 126 C3
Roehampton Institute
PUT/ROE SW15 126 C4
WAND/EARL SW18 127 H5
The Roehampton Priory Hospital *PUT/ROE* SW15 126 C3
Roehampton Recreation Centre *PUT/ROE* SW15 126 D6
Roger Ascham Primary School *WALTH* E17 43 H7
Roger Bannister Sports Ground *KTN/HRWW/W* HA3 34 C5
Rokeby School
KUTN/CMB KT2 144 E6
SRTFD E15 76 B6
Rokesly Primary School *CEND/HSY/T* N8 54 E4
Roman Bath *TPL/STR* WC2R 11 M6
Roman Industrial Estate *CROY/NA* CR0 165 F6
Roman Road Primary School *EHAM* E6 95 H3
Roman Wall Remains *BARB* EC2Y 12 E3
Romford Cemetery *ROMW/RG* RM7 62 E6
Romford Clinic *ROM* RM1 63 H3
Romford County Court *ROM* RM1 63 H3
Romford Golf Club *GPK* RM2 63 J2
Romford Ice Rink *ROMW/RG* RM7 63 G6
Ronald Rose Primary School *WIM/MER* SW19 127 G6
Rood Lane Medical Centre *FENCHST* EC3M 13 J6
Rooks Heath School *RYLN/HDSTN* HA2 66 A2
Roosevelt Memorial *MYFR/PKLN* W1K 10 B6
Ropery Business Park *CHARL* SE7 114 B3
Rosary Priory High School *BUSH* WD23 22 E5
Rosary RC Infant School *HEST* TW5 102 E5
The Rosary RC Primary School *HAMP* NW3 71 J4
Rosebery Industrial Park *TOTM* N17 56 D1
Rose Bruford College of Speech & Drama *BFN/LL* DA15 136 C7
Roselands Clinic *NWMAL* KT3 159 K3
Rosemary Primary School *IS* N1 6 E3
Rosemary Secondary School *CLKNW* EC1R 6 C9
Rose McAndrew Clinic *BRXN/ST* SW9 130 A1
Rosemead Preparatory School *DUL* SE21 149 J1
Rosendale Primary School *DUL* SE21 130 D6
Rose Theatre Exhibition *STHWK* SE1 12 E8
Rosetta Primary School *CAN/RD* E16 95 F4
Rosewood Medical Centre *HCH* RM12 81 K4
Rosh Pinah Primary School *EDGW* HA8 36 D1
Rosslyn Park RFC *PUT/ROE* SW15 126 C3
Rotherfield Primary School *IS* N1 6 F3
Rotherhithe Civic Centre *BERM/RHTH* SE16 111 K1
Rotherhithe Primary School *BERM/RHTH* SE16 111 K3
The Rotunda *KUT* KT1 159 F1
The Roundhouse Theatre *CAMTN* NW1 4 A1
Roundwood Park Medical Centre *WLSDN* NW10 69 J6
Rowan High School
CLAP SW4 129 J5
MTCM CR4 163 H1
Rowans School *RYNPK* SW20 145 J6
Rowley Industrial Park *ACT* W3 105 J2
Roxbourne Medical Centre *RYLN/HDSTN* HA2 66 B1
Roxbourne Middle School *RSLP* HA4 65 H1
Roxeth First & Middle School *RYLN/HDSTN* HA2 66 D1
Roxeth Manor First School *RYLN/HDSTN* HA2 66 A2
Roxeth Mead School *RYLN/HDSTN* HA2 66 D1
Roxwell Trading Park *WALTH* E17 57 G6

Royal Academy of Arts *MYFR/PICC* W1J 10 E7
Royal Academy of Dramatic Art *GWRST* WC1E 11 H1
Royal Academy of Music *CAMTN* NW1 10 B1
Royal Air Force Museum *CDALE/KGS* NW9 51 J1
Royal Albert Hall *SKENS* SW7 15 G2
Royal Arsenal *WOOL/PLUM* SE18 115 G2
Royal Ballet School *LSQ/SEVD* WC2H 11 K5
The Royal Ballet School *RCHPK/HAM* TW10 126 A7
Royal Blackheath Golf Club *ELTH/MOT* SE9 134 E6
Royal Botanic Gardens Kew School *RCH/KEW* TW9 105 G6
Royal Brompton & National Heart Hospitals *CHEL* SW3 15 H7
Royal College of Anaesthetists *RSQ* WC1B 11 J2
Royal College of Art *SKENS* SW7 14 F2
Royal College of Music *SHB* W12 106 D2
SKENS SW7 15 G3
Royal College of Nursing *CAMTN* NW1 4 F9
IS N1 6 C4
Royal College of Obstetricians & Gynaecologists *CAMTN* NW1 3 L9
Royal College of Ophthalmologists *CAMTN* NW1 10 A1
Royal College of Paediatrics & Child Health *GTPST* W1W 10 D2
The Royal College of Pathology *STJS* SW1Y 11 G9
Royal College of Physicians *CAMTN* NW1 4 C9
Royal College of Surgeons *LINN* WC2A 11 M4
Royal Courts of Justice *LINN* WC2A 11 M5
Royal Court Theatre *BGVA* SW1W 16 A6
Royal Court Young Peoples Theatre *NKENS* W10 88 C4
The Royal Dock Community School *CAN/RD* E16 95 G5
Royal Docks Medical Centre *EHAM* E6 96 A5
Royal Exchange *LOTH* EC2R 13 H5
Royal Festival Hall *STHWK* SE1 11 L9
Royal Foundation of Grey Coat Hospital *WESTW* SW1E 16 E3
Royal Free Hospital *HAMP* NW3 71 J4
Royal Free Hospital School of Medicine *HAMP* NW3 71 J4
Royal Geographical Soc *SKENS* SW7 15 G2
Royal Horticultural Society New Hall *WEST* SW1P 17 G4
Royal Horticultural Society Old Hall *WEST* SW1P 17 G5
Royal Hospital *RCH/KEW* TW9 125 F2
Royal Hospital Chelsea *CHEL* SW3 16 A9
Royal Hospital for Neuro-Disability *WAND/EARL* SW18 127 H5
Royal Hospital & Home *PUT/ROE* SW15 126 E6
Royal Hospital Museum *CHEL* SW3 16 A8
Royal Institute of British Architects *REGST* W1B 10 D2
Royal Institution's Faraday Museum *MYFR/PICC* W1J 10 D7
The Royal London Estate *TOTM* N17 42 D6
Royal London Homeopathic Hospital *BMSBY* WC1N 11 K2
The Royal London Hospital (Whitechapel) A & E *WCHPL* E1 92 D4
Royal Marsden Hospital *CHEL* SW3 15 H7
The Royal Mews *WHALL* SW1A 16 D3
Royal Mid-Surrey Golf Club *RCH/KEW* TW9 124 E2
Royal Mint Court *TWRH* EC3N 13 M7
Royal National Orthopaedic Hospital *GTPST* W1W 10 D1
STAN HA7 23 H7
Royal National Theatre *CMBW* SE5 110 B6
STHWK SE1 12 A8
Royal National Throat, Nose & Ear Hospital *FSBYW* WC1X 5 L7
Royal Observatory Greenwich *GNWCH* SE10 113 G5
Royal Opera House *COVGDN* WC2E 11 K5
Royal Russell School *CROY/NA* CR0 178 D5
The Royal School *HAMP* NW3 71 H3
Royal Society of Arts *TPL/STR* WC2R 11 K7
Royal Society of Medicine *CAVSQ/HST* W1G 10 C4
Royal Veterinary College *CAMTN* NW1 4 F4
Royal Victoria Docks Watersports Centre *CAN/RD* E16 94 E6
Royal Wimbledon Golf Club *WIM/MER* SW19 145 K4
Royston Primary School *BECK* BR3 151 F7
RSPCA Animal Hospital *HOLWY* N7 73 F1
Rudolph Steiner Hall *CAMTN* NW1 3 L9
Rufus Business Centre *WAND/EARL* SW18 147 F1
Ruislip Gardens Primary School *HGDN/ICK* UB10 64 C3
Ruislip Golf Club *RSLP* HA4 64 A1
Ruislip Manor FC *RSLP* HA4 64 D1
Ruislip RFC *RSLP* HA4 64 C1
Rumford Shopping Hall *ROM* RM1 63 G3
Rush Croft School *CHING* E4 43 K6
Rushey Green Primary School *CAT* SE6 132 E7
Rush Green Primary School *ROMW/RG* RM7 63 F7
Rushmore Junior School *CLPT* E5 74 E3
Ruskin House School *HNHL* SE24 130 D4
The Russell JMI School *RCHPK/HAM* TW10 143 K1
The Russell School *RCHPK/HAM* TW10 124 E7
Rutlish School *RYNPK* SW20 161 J1
Ruxley Corner Industrial Estate *SCUP* DA14 155 K5
Ruxley Manor School *ELTH/MOT* SE9 154 A3
Ruxley Park Golf Centre *STMC/STPC* BR5 155 K7
Ryde College *WATW* WD18 20 C5
Ryefield Primary School *HGDN/ICK* UB10 64 B7
Ryelands Primary School *SNWD* SE25 165 J4
Saatchi Gallery *STHWK* SE1 17 L1
Sacred Heart High School *HMSMTH* W6 107 F3
Sacred Heart High School for Girls *KTN/HRWW/W* HA3 48 E1
Sacred Heart JMI School *OXHEY* WD19 21 K5
Sacred Heart Junior School *HMSMTH* W6 107 G3
Sacred Heart RC Infant School *BTSEA* SW11 128 D1
Sacred Heart RC J & I School *RSLP* HA4 64 C1
Sacred Heart RC Junior & Middle School *BTSEA* SW11 128 D2
Sacred Heart RC Primary School *NWMAL* KT3 160 D3
PUT/ROE SW15 126 D4
TEDD TW11 143 H6
Sacred Heart RC School *CMBW* SE5 110 D7
Sacred Heart School *HOLWY* N7 73 F4
Saddlers Hall *CITYW* EC2V 12 E5
Sadler's Wells Theatre *CLKNW* EC1R 6 B7
SAE Technology College *HOLWY* N7 72 E4
Safari Cinema *CROY/NA* CR0 164 C6
Safari Cinema & Bingo *HRW* HA1 49 F4
Saffron Green Primary School *BORE* WD6 25 G3
Sai Medical Centre *POP/IOD* E14 94 A7
St Agathas RC Primary School *KUTN/CMB* KT2 144 B5
St Agnes RC Primary School *BOW* E3 93 J2
CRICK NW2 70 C2
St Aidans Primary School *FSBYPK* N4 55 G6
St Aidans RC Primary School *IL* IG1 60 D7
St Albans CE Primary School *FSBYW* WC1X 12 A2
St Albans Health Clinic *KTTN* NW5 72 A2
St Albans RC Aided Primary School *E/WMO/HCT* KT8 157 G4
St Albans RC Church & School Presbytery *HCH* RM12 81 J4
St Albans RC JMI School *HCH* RM12 81 K6
St Albans Road Infant School *DART* DA1 139 J5
St Alfege with St Peter CE Primary School *GNWCH* SE10 113 F5
St Aloysius College *ARCH* N19 54 C7
St Aloysius RC Infant School *CAMTN* NW1 5 G7
St Aloysius RC Junior School *CAMTN* NW1 4 F6
St Andrew & St Francis CE JMI School *CRICK* NW2 69 J5
St Andrews CE JMI School *TRDG/WHET* N20 38 D1
St Andrews CE Primary School *EN* EN1 29 K1
STHGT/OAK N14 28 D7
St Andrews Greek School *CAMTN* NW1 72 B5
St Andrews Hospital *BOW* E3 93 K3
St Andrews Primary School *BRXN/ST* SW9 130 A1
IS N1 5 M3
St Andrews School *RYLN/HDSTN* HA2 48 B4
WLSDN NW10 69 K6
St Angelas RC School *FSTGT* E7 77 F5
St Annes Catholic High School *PLMGR* N13 41 G3
St Annes CE Primary School *WAND/EARL* SW18 128 A4
St Annes Convent School *EN* EN1 29 K3
St Annes Primary School *STWL/WRAY* TW19 120 B6
St Annes RC Primary School *LBTH* SE11 17 L9
St Annes Special School *MRDN* SM4 162 A4
St Anne's Trading Estate *POP/IOD* E14 93 H5
St Anns CE Primary School *SEVS/STOTM* N15 55 K4
St Ann's General Hospital *SEVS/STOTM* N15 55 J4
St Anns School *HNWL* W7 84 E7
St Ann's Shopping Centre *HRW* HA1 48 E5
St Anselms RC First & Middle School *HRW* HA1 48 E6
St Anselms RC Primary School *DART* DA1 139 K4
NWDGN UB2 102 E2
St Anslems RC Primary School *TOOT* SW17 148 A2
St Anthonys Hospital *WPK* KT4 161 G7
St Anthony's Preparatory School *HAMP* NW3 71 H3
St Anthonys RC Junior School *WATW* WD18 20 C4
St Anthonys RC Primary School *EDUL* SE22 131 G5
FSTGT E7 76 E6
PGE/AN SE20 150 D7
St Anthony's School *HAMP* NW3 71 G4
St Antonys RC Primary School *WFD* IG8 44 E3
St Aubyns School *WFD* IG8 44 D6
St Augustines CE School *KIL/WHAMP* NW6 2 B6
St Augustines Primary School *BELV* DA17 117 G2
KIL/WHAMP NW6 2 B5
St Augustines Priory School *EA* W5 86 A4
St Augustines RC Infant School *GNTH/NBYPK* IG2 60 B4
St Augustines RC Primary School *CAT* SE6 151 K4
GNTH/NBYPK IG2 60 B4
WKENS W14 107 H5
St Barnabas CE Primary School *BGVA* SW1W 16 B7
St Barnabas & Philip CE Primary *KENS* W8 14 A4
St Barnabas & St Philips CE Primary School *KENS* W8 14 A4
St Bartholomews CE Primary School *SYD* SE26 150 E3
St Bartholomews Hospital *STBT* EC1A 12 D3
St Bartholomews Medical School *FARR* EC1M 12 D1
St Bartholomews & Royal London School of Medicine *FARR* EC1M 12 E2
St Bartholomew's the Great *STBT* EC1A 12 D3
St Barts Hospital Sports Ground *CHST* BR7 154 D5
St Bedes RC Infant School *BAL* SW12 129 J7
St Bedes RC Primary School *CHDH* RM6 61 J4
St Benedicts Junior School *EA* W5 85 J4
St Benedicts School *EA* W5 85 K4
St Bernadettes RC First & Middle School *KTN/HRWW/W* HA3 50 B3
St Bonaventure's School *FSTGT* E7 76 E6
St Boniface RC Primary School *TOOT* SW17 147 K4
St Catherines RC Girls School *BXLYHS* DA6 137 J4
St Catherines RC Middle School *NWMAL* KT3 161 F4
St Catherines RC Primary School *WDR/YW* UB7 100 A1
St Catherines School *TWK* TW1 143 F1
St Cecilias RC Primary School *WPK* KT4 174 B1
St Chads RC Primary School *SNWD* SE25 165 F4
St Charles Hospital *NKENS* W10 88 B4
St Charles RC Primary School *NKENS* W10 88 B4
St Christinas Preparatory School *STJWD* NW8 3 K5
St Christopher House *STHWK* SE1 12 E8
St Christophers School *BECK* BR3 167 F1
HAMP NW3 71 H4
WBLY HA9 68 B2
St Clare Business Park *HPTN* TW12 142 C5
St Clement Danes CE Primary School *HOL/ALD* WC2B 11 L5
St Clement & James CE Primary School *NTGHL* W11 88 C7
St Clements Hospital *BOW* E3 93 H2
St Clements RC Primary School *EW* KT17 173 H7
St Columbas RC Boys School *BXLYHS* DA6 137 J4
St Cuthbert With St Matthias CE Primary School *ECT* SW5 14 B7
St Davids College *WWKM* BR4 166 E6
St Davids Health Centre *STWL/WRAY* TW19 120 A6
St Dominics RC J & I School *HOM* E9 75 F5
St Dominics RC Primary School *HAMP* NW3 71 K4
St Dominics 6th Form College *HRW* HA1 66 E1
St Dunstans CE Primary School *CHEAM* SM3 174 C6
St Dunstans College *CAT* SE6 132 C7
St Ebba's Hospital *HOR/WEW* KT19 172 E7
St Edmunds RC Primary School *ED* N9 30 D7
POP/IOD E14 112 D3
WHTN TW2 123 G6
St Edwards CE Comprehensive School *CHDH* RM6 62 C5
St Edwards CE Primary School *ROM* RM1 63 F3
St Edwards RC JMI School *STJWD* NW8 9 J1
St Elizabeths RC Primary School *RCHPK/HAM* TW10 125 G5
St Elpheges RC Primary School *WLGTN* SM6 176 E5
St Eugene de Mazenod RC Primary School *KIL/WHAMP* NW6 2 B2
St Faiths CE School *WAND/EARL* SW18 128 A4
St Fidelis Catholic Primary School *ERITH* DA8 117 K5
St Francesca Cabrini Primary School *FSTH* SE23 131 K5
St Francis of Assisi Primary School *NTGHL* W11 88 B6
St Francis RC Primary School *PECK* SE15 111 H5
SRTFD E15 76 C4
St Francis Xavier College *BAL* SW12 129 G5
St Gabriels CE Primary School *PIM* SW1V 16 E8
St George's Cathedral *STHWK* SE1 18 B3
St George's Cathedral RC Primary *STHWK* SE1 18 C3
St Georges CE Primary School *BMLY* BR1 168 B1
PECK SE15 111 F6
VX/NE SW8 109 H6
St Georges College *HOLWY* N7 73 G2
St Georges Elizabethan Theatre *HOLWY* N7 72 D3
St Georges Hanover Square CE Primary School *MYFR/PKLN* W1K 10 B7
St Georges Hospital *TOOT* SW17 147 J4
St Georges Industrial Estate *KUTN/CMB* KT2 143 K4
WDGN N22 41 H6
St Georges Medical Centre *HDN* NW4 51 K2
St Georges Pool *WCHPL* E1 92 C6
St Georges RC First & Middle School *HRW* HA1 67 F2
St Georges RC Primary School *ENC/FH* EN2 29 K1
St Georges RC School *MV/WKIL* W9 2 D6
St Georges Shopping Centre & Cinema *HRW* HA1 48 D5
St George the Martyr CE Primary School *BMSBY* WC1N 11 L1
St George Wharf *VX/NE* SW8 17 J9
St Gildas RC Junior School *CEND/HSY/T* N8 54 E6
St Giles College London Central *RSQ* WC1B 11 J2
St Giles School *CROY/NA* CR0 177 H5
St Gregorys High School *KTN/HRWW/W* HA3 49 K4
St Gregorys RC Primary School *EA* W5 85 J3
St Helens Catholic Infant School *WALTH* E17 58 A4
St Helens RC Primary School *BRXN/ST* SW9 130 B2
PLSTW E13 94 D3
St Helens School for Girls *NTHWD* HA6 32 C5
St Helier Hospital *SUT* SM1 162 B7
St Hildas School *BUSH* WD23 22 B6
St Ignatius RC Primary School *SEVS/STOTM* N15 56 A5
SUN TW16 140 E7
St James & St Michaels CE Primary School *BAY/PAD* W2 8 F6
St James CE J & I School *BERM/RHTH* SE16 111 H2
St James CE Primary School *MUSWH* N10 54 A3
PEND EN3 30 E1
St James CE Junior School *FSTGT* E7 76 D4
St James Hatcham CE Primary School *NWCR* SE14 112 B7
St James Independent School *TWK* TW1 143 G1
St James Independent School for Girls *BAY/PAD* W2 8 A6
St James Medical Centre *CROY/NA* CR0 164 E6
St James RC Primary School *HAYES* BR2 169 G4
WHTN TW2 142 E2
St James's Health Centre *WALTH* E17 57 G4
St James's Palace *WHALL* SW1A 10 F9
St James the Great Catholic School *PECK* SE15 111 G7
St James the Great RC Primary School *THHTH* CR7 164 C1
St Joachims RC Primary School *CAN/RD* E16 95 G5
St Joan of Arc RC Primary School *HBRY* N5 73 H3
St John Fisher RC First & Middle School *RYLN/HDSTN* HA2 48 A3
St John Fisher RC Primary School *ERITHM* DA18 117 F2
GFD/PVL UB6 85 J2
NWMAL KT3 161 F4
St John of Jerusalem CE Primary School *HOM* E9 74 E6
St John Rigby Catholic College *WWKM* BR4 180 B3
St John & St James CE Primary School *HACK* E8 74 E4
St Johns & St James CE School *UED* N18 42 B4
St Johns Angell Town CE Primary School *BRXN/ST* SW9 130 B1
St Johns CE First School *STAN* HA7 35 G3
St Johns CE Middle School *STAN* HA7 35 G3
St Johns CE Primary School *BETH* E2 92 E1
FBAR/BDGN N11 39 K3
KUT KT1 159 F2
PGE/AN SE20 150 E6
TRDG/WHET N20 39 G1
WALW SE17 18 F6
St Johns C E School *CDALE/KGS* NW9 51 G4
St John's CE Walham Green *FUL/PGN* SW6 107 H7
St Johns CE Infant School *HDN* NW4 51 K4
St John's Concert Hall *WEST* SW1P 17 J4
St Johns Highbury Vale CE Primary School *HBRY* N5 73 H2
St John's Hospital *SOHO/SHAV* W1D 11 H6
St John's Hospital Day Centre *BTSEA* SW11 128 C3
St Johns Primary School *WEA* W13 85 G6
St Johns RC Primary School *BERM/RHTH* SE16 112 B1
St Johns School *ENC/FH* EN2 29 G1
NTHWD HA6 33 F5
St Johns Upper Holloway CE Primary School *ARCH* N19 72 D2
St Johns Way Medical Centre *ARCH* N19 54 D7
St Johns Wood School *STJWD* NW8 3 J7
St John the Baptist CE Junior School *KUT* KT1 143 K6
St John the Baptist CE Primary School *CAT* SE6 152 A3
IS N1 7 J6
St John the Baptist RC Junior School *BETH* E2 92 E1
St John the Divine CE Primary School *CMBW* SE5 110 C6
St John the Evangelist RC Primary School *IS* N1 6 C5
St John Vianney RC Primary School *SEVS/STOTM* N15 55 H3
St Josephs Academic RC School *BKHTH/KID* SE3 133 H2
St Josephs Catholic Infant School *LEY* E10 57 H7
St Josephs Catholic Primary School *BMLY* BR1 153 G6
St Josephs College *STRHM/NOR* SW16 149 H5
St Josephs Convent School *WAN* E11 58 E5
St Josephs Primary School *HDN* NW4 51 K3
PUT/ROE SW15 127 K4
St Joseph's RC College *MLHL* NW7 37 H3
St Josephs RC First & Middle School *KTN/HRWW/W* HA3 49 G1
St Josephs RC Infant School *NRWD* SE19 149 J5
WBLY HA9 68 B5
St Josephs RC Junior School *CMBW* SE5 110 D6
LEY E10 57 K7
NRWD SE19 149 J5
WBLY HA9 68 B4
St Josephs RC Primary School *ARCH* N19 54 B7
BARK IG11 78 C7
BERM/RHTH SE16 111 K2
CHEL SW3 15 L6
DAGW RM9 80 B3
DART DA1 138 A3
DEPT SE8 112 D6
GNWCH SE10 113 H4
HNWL W7 84 E7
HOL/ALD WC2B 11 K4
KUT KT1 159 F1
MV/WKIL W9 2 E8
STHWK SE1 18 F1
STHWK SE1 111 H1

WLSDN NW10 69 G6
St Josephs RC School
OXHEY WD19 33 F2
St Judes CE Primary School
STHWK SE1 18 C4
St Jude's CE Prim School
HNHL SE24 130 C5
St Judes & St Pauls CE Primary School
IS N1 74 A5
St Katharine Pier
TWRH EC3N 13 M8
St Lawrence Business Centre
FELT TW13 141 F1
St Lawrence Catholic School
FELT TW13 141 F1
St Lawrence Junior School
E/WMO/HCT KT8 157 J2
St Lawrence University
FSBYW WC1X 11 M1
St Leonards CE Primary School
STRHM/NOR SW16 148 D4
St Leonards Hospital
IS N1 7 K5
St Lukes CE Primary School
CAN/RD E16 94 D5
FSBYE EC1V 6 F8
KUTN/CMB KT2 144 B7
MV/WKIL W9 88 D1
POP/IOD E14 113 G3
WNWD SE27 149 J4
St Luke's Health Centre
CAN/RD E16 94 D5
St Lukes Hospital for the Clergy
FITZ W1T 10 E1
St Lukes School
THHTH CR7 164 B3
St Lukes Woodside Hospital
MUSWH N10 54 A3
St Margaret Clitherow RC Primary
THMD SE28 97 H7
St Margaret Lee CE Primary School
LEW SE13 133 H3
St Margarets Business Centre
TWK TW1 124 B6
St Margarets CE Primary School
WOOL/PLUM SE18 115 H5
St Margarets Clitherow RC Primary School
WLSDN NW10 69 F2
St Margarets Primary School
BARK IG11 78 B7
St Margarets School
BUSH WD23 22 A6
HAMP NW3 71 F3
St Marks CE Primary School
ARCH N19 72 E1
HAYES BR2 167 K2
LBTH SE11 17 M9
SNWD SE25 165 H3
St Marks Industrial Estate
CAN/RD E16 95 H7
St Marks Primary School
MTCM CR4 162 E1
NWDGN UB2 103 K1
St Marks RC School
HSLW TW3 122 E2
St Martin-in-the-Fields High School
BRXS/STRHM SW2 130 C7
St Martin of Pores RC Primary School
FBAR/BDGN N11 40 C5
St Martins Hospital
MYFR/PKLN W1K 10 A6
St Martins Medical Centre
RSLP HA4 46 C6
St Martins School
MLHL NW7 37 G4
NTHWD HA6 32 B4
St Martins School of Art
SOHO/SHAV W1D 11 H5
St Martins Theatre
LSQ/SEVD WC2H 11 H6
St Mary Abbots CE Primary School
KENS W8 14 C2
St Mary Abbots Church Hall
KENS W8 14 C1
St Mary & St Josephs Gm School
SCUP DA14 155 F4
St Mary CE Primary School
PUT/ROE SW15 127 G2
St Marylebone CE Secondary School
MHST W1U 10 B2
St Marylebone Crematorium
EFNCH N2 53 F2
St Mary Magdalene CE Primary School
MV/WKIL W9 8 C2
WOOL/PLUM SE18 114 E3
PECK SE15 131 J1
St Mary Magdalene Primary School
HOLWY N7 73 G5
St Mary Magdalen RC Junior School
CRICK NW2 69 K5
St Mary Magdalens RC Primary School
MORT/ESHN SW14 126 A2
St Mary of the Angels RC Primary School
BAY/PAD W2 8 A4
St Marys Abbey
MLHL NW7 37 J2
St Mary & St Pancras CE Primary School
CAMTN NW1 5 G6
St Marys Bryanston Square CE Primary School
MBLAR W1H 9 L3
St Marys CE High School
HDN NW4 52 A2
St Marys CE Infant School
CEND/HSY/T N8 55 F3
St Marys CE Junior School
CEND/HSY/T N8 54 E3
STWL/WRAY TW19 120 B5
THDIT KT7 158 C7
St Mary's Cemetery
BTSEA SW11 128 D4
St Marys CE Primary School
CHSGTN KT9 172 A5
EBAR EN4 27 J5
FNCH N3 38 D7
IS N1 6 D2
LEW SE13 132 E4
TWK TW1 124 B6
WALTH E17 57 K3
WLSDN NW10 69 G5
St Marys Church of England High School
HDN NW4 52 A2
St Marys Greek Cathedral
WDGN N22 41 F7
St Marys High School
CROY/NA CR0 164 D7
St Marys Hospital
BAY/PAD W2 9 H4
St Marys Hospital Medical School
BAY/PAD W2 9 H4
St Marys Infant School
CAR SM5 175 J3
St Mary's Kilburn Primary School
KIL/WHAMP NW6 2 B3
St Marys Magdalens RC Primary School
BROCKY SE4 132 B3
St Mary's Primary School
WKENS W14 107 G2
St Marys RC Infant School
CAR SM5 175 K3
CROY/NA CR0 164 E7
St Marys RC JMI School
HCH RM12 63 J7
St Marys RC Junior School
CROY/NA CR0 164 E7
WALTH E17 58 A2
St Marys RC Primary School
BECK BR3 152 A6
CHSWK W4 106 A4
CLAP SW4 129 H4
ELTH/MOT SE9 135 F4
ISLW TW7 124 B2
KIL/WHAMP NW6 2 A5
NKENS W10 88 C3
PEND EN3 31 F3
SEVS/STOTM N15 55 K4
VX/NE SW8 109 G7
WIM/MER SW19 146 E6
St Marys & St Peters CE Primary School
TEDD TW11 142 E4
St Marys School
CEND/HSY/T N8 55 F4
HAMP NW3 71 G4
St Marys Stoke Newington CE Primary School
STNW/STAM N16 74 A1
St Marys University College
TWK TW1 143 F2
St Matthews CE Primary School
PEND EN3 30 E4
RYNPK SW20 145 J7
SURB KT6 159 F6
WEST SW1P 17 H4
St Matthias CE Primary School
BETH E2 7 M9
STNW/STAM N16 74 A4
St Meryl JMI School
OXHEY WD19 33 J2
St Michael At Bowes CE Junior School
PLMGR N13 41 G5
St Michaels & St Martins RC Primary School
HSLWW TW4 122 E2
St Michaels Catholic Grammar School
NFNCH/WDSP N12 39 F4
St Michaels CE Primary School
CAMTN NW1 4 E3
HGT N6 54 A6
WAND/EARL SW18 127 J6
WDGN N22 41 F7
St Michaels CE Aided Primary School Hall
WELL DA16 116 D7
St Michaels RC Primary School
EHAM E6 95 K1
St Michaels RC Secondary School
BERM/RHTH SE16 111 H1
St Michaels Sydenham CE Primary
SYD SE26 151 G3
St Monicas RC Primary School
IS N1 7 J7
St Monica's RC Primary School
IS N1 7 J7
St Monicas RC Primary School
STHGT/OAK N14 40 E2
St Nicholas Centre
SUT SM1 175 F4
St Nicholas Preparatory School
CDALE/KGS NW9 68 E1
St Nicholas School
BORE WD6 24 A5
CHST BR7 154 C6
St Olaves Preparatory School
ELTH/MOT SE9 154 B1
St Osmunds RC Primary School
BARN SW13 106 C7
St Pancras & Islington Cemetery
EFNCH N2 39 J7
St Pancras Hospital
CAMTN NW1 5 G4
St Pancras Station
CAMTN NW1 5 J7
St Patricks Church School
STHWK SE1 12 A9
St Patricks Infants School
WAP E1W 92 D7
St Patricks International School
SOHO/CST W1F 10 F4
St Patricks Primary School
KTTN NW5 72 B5
St Patricks RC Primary School
WALTH E17 57 G3
WAP E1W 92 D7
WOOL/PLUM SE18 115 J3
St Paulinus CE Primary School
DART DA1 138 B3
St Pauls & All Hallows CE Infant School
TOTM N17 42 C6
St Paul's Cathedral
STP EC4M 12 D5
St Paul's Cathedral School
STP EC4M 12 E5
St Pauls Catholic College
SUN TW16 140 E7
St Pauls CE JMI School
MLHL NW7 37 K3
St Pauls CE Primary School
BTFD TW8 104 E5
CHSGTN KT9 172 A3
FBAR/BDGN N11 40 A4
HAMP NW3 3 K2
WALW SE17 18 D8
WCHMH N21 29 H6
St Pauls CE Junior School
KUTN/CMB KT2 144 C6
St Pauls CE Primary School
WCHPL E1 92 C6
St Pauls Girls School
HMSMTH W6 107 G3
St Pauls Preparatory School
BARN SW13 106 D4
St Paul's Primary School
HMSMTH W6 107 F4
St Pauls RC Primary School
THDIT KT7 157 K6
WDGN N22 55 F1
St Pauls RC School
WOOL/PLUM SE18 116 B5
St Pauls Road Medical Centre
IS N1 73 H5
St Pauls Way School
BOW E3 93 J3
St Pauls With St Lukes CE Primary School
BOW E3 93 H4
St Paul's with St Michael's CE Primary School
HACK E8 74 C7
St Paul with St. Luke CE Primary School
POP/IOD E14 93 H4
St Peter & St Paul RC Primary School
MTCM CR4 162 E3
St Peter Chanel RC Primary School
SCUP DA14 155 J4
St Peter & Pauls RC Primary School
IL IG1 78 D2
St Peter & St Pauls Primary School
FSBYE EC1V 6 D9
St Peters Catholic Primary School
ROM RM1 63 F2
St Peters CE Primary School
HMSMTH W6 106 D4
MV/WKIL W9 8 A1
WALW SE17 19 G8
St Peters Eaton Square CE Primary School
BGVA SW1W 16 C4
St Peter's Hospital
COVGDN WC2E 11 K6
St Peters Primary School
SAND/SEL CR2 177 K5
WAP E1W 92 F7
St Peters RC Primary School
DAGW RM9 80 B7
WOOL/PLUM SE18 115 G4
St Philips School
CHSGTN KT9 171 K5
SKENS SW7 14 F6
St Phillips Infant School
SYD SE26 150 D3
St Philomenas RC High School
CAR SM5 175 K4
St Quintins Health Centre
NKENS W10 88 A4
St Raphaels Hospice
WPK KT4 174 B1
St Raphael's RC Primary School
NTHLT UB5 83 F1
St Raphaels Way Medical Centre
WBLY HA9 68 E4
St Richards with St Andrews CE Primary School
RCHPK/HAM TW10 143 H2
St Robert Southwell RC Primary School
CDALE/KGS NW9 50 E5
St Saviour & St Olaves School
STHWK SE1 19 H4
St Saviours CE Infant School
EA W5 85 K7
St Saviours CE Primary School
HNHL SE24 130 D2
MV/WKIL W9 8 D1
POP/IOD E14 93 K4
WALTH E17 57 H6
St Saviours RC Primary School
LEW SE13 133 F3
St Scholastica's RC Primary School
STNW/STAM N16 74 C2
St Stephens CE Junior School
TWK TW1 124 B5
St Stephens CE Primary School
BAY/PAD W2 8 B3
DEPT SE8 132 D1
SHB W12 88 A7
St Stephens CE School
VX/NE SW8 109 K6
St Stephens Primary School
EHAM E6 77 G6
St Stephens RC Primary School
WELL DA16 136 B2
St Swithun Wells RC Primary School
RSLP HA4 65 H2
St Teresa RC Primary School
BCTR RM8 79 J3
St Teresa's RC Primary School
BORE WD6 24 D1
St Teresas RC School
KTN/HRWW/W HA3 34 C7
St Theresas RC Primary School
FNCH N3 52 E2
St Thomas a' Becket RC Primary School
ABYW SE2 116 B2
St Thomas CE Primary School
NKENS W10 88 C3
STNW/STAM N16 56 B7
St Thomas Childrens Day Hospital
LBTH SE11 17 M7
St Thomas' Hospital
STHWK SE1 17 L3
St Thomas' Hospital Operation Theatre
STHWK SE1 13 G9
St Thomas More RC Primary School
BXLYHN DA7 137 G1
ELTH/MOT SE9 134 D2
St Thomas More RC School
CHEL SW3 15 L6
ELTH/MOT SE9 135 F5
St Thomas More School
WDGN N22 41 F6
St Thomas of Canterbury RC Middle School
MTCM CR4 163 F2
St Thomas of Canterbury RC Primary School
FUL/PGN SW6 107 J6
St Thomas the Apostle College
PECK SE15 111 K7
St Ursulas Convent School
GNWCH SE10 113 G6
St Vincent de Paul RC Primary School
WEST SW1P 16 E4
St Vincents Catholic Primary School
ELTH/MOT SE9 153 J3
St Vincents Hospital
RSLP HA4 46 C2
St Vincents RC Primary School
ACT W3 86 D6
BCTR RM8 79 J1
MHST W1U 10 A3
MLHL NW7 38 A3
St Walter & St John Sports Ground
TOOT SW17 128 D7
St William of York Primary School
FSTH SE23 132 B7
St Winefrides Catholic Primary School
MNPK E12 77 K4
St Winifreds Junior School
LEE/GVPK SE12 133 J5
St Winifreds RC Infant School
LEW SE13 133 H4
Salcombe School
STHGT/OAK N14 28 D6
Salesian College
BTSEA SW11 108 D7
Salisbury Primary School
MNPK E12 77 H4
Salisbury School
ED N9 30 E7
Salisbury Upper School
ED N9 30 E6
Salters' Hall
BARB EC2Y 12 F3
Salusbury Primary School
KIL/WHAMP NW6 70 C7
Salvation Army Heritage Centre
BLKFR EC4V 12 E6
Salvatorian College
KTN/HRWW/W HA3 48 E1
Samaritan & Western Ophthalmic Hospital
MBLAR W1H 9 L2
Samuel Jones Industrial Estate
PECK SE15 111 F6
Samuel Rhodes School
IS N1 6 A3
Sanderstead Junior School
SAND/SEL CR2 177 K7
Sandgate Trading Estate
BERM/RHTH SE16 111 J4
Sandhurst Primary School
CAT SE6 133 H6
Sandown Golf Centre
ESH/CLAY KT10 170 B2
Sandown Industrial Park
ESH/CLAY KT10 170 A1
Sandown Park Racecourse
ESH/CLAY KT10 170 B2
Sandringham Primary School
FSTGT E7 77 G5
Sandy Lodge Golf Club
NTHWD HA6 32 B1
Sapcote Trading Centre
WLSDN NW10 69 H4
Sarah Bonnell School
SRTFD E15 76 C5
Sarum Hall School
HAMP NW3 3 K1
Satmer Trust School
STNW/STAM N16 74 C1
Savoy Pier
TPL/STR WC2R 11 L7
Savoy Theatre
TPL/STR WC2R 11 L7
Saxon Business Centre
WIM/MER SW19 162 B1
Sayer Clinic
CROY/NA CR0 177 F3
Sayer Clinics
MBLAR W1H 9 M5
Scarsdale Place Medical Centre
KENS W8 14 C3
Schiller International School
STHWK SE1 12 A9
Schomberg House
STJS SW1Y 10 F9
School of Art
RCH/KEW TW9 125 F3
School of English
GLDGN NW11 52 E7
School of Oriental & African Studies
STPAN WC1H 11 H1
The School of Pharmacy
BMSBY WC1N 5 K9
The School of St David & St Katharine
CEND/HSY/T N8 54 E3
Science Museum
SKENS SW7 15 H4
Science Museum IMAX Cinema
SKENS SW7 15 G4
The Science Museum Library
SKENS SW7 15 G3
Scotts Park Primary School
BMLY BR1 153 G7
Scott Wilkie Primary School
CAN/RD E16 95 G5
Screen on Baker Street Cinema
MHST W1U 9 M2
Screen on the Green Cinema
IS N1 6 C4
Screen on the Hill Cinema
HAMP NW3 71 J4
Sebright Primary School
BETH E2 92 C1
Secombe Centre
SUT SM1 174 E4
Sedgehill School
CAT SE6 151 K4
Sedgewick Centre
WCHPL E1 13 M4
Selborne Primary School
GFD/PVL UB6 85 F1
The Selhurst Medical Centre
SNWD SE25 164 E5
Sellincourt School
TOOT SW17 147 J5
Selsdon High School
SAND/SEL CR2 179 F6
Selsdon Primary School
SAND/SEL CR2 178 E7
Selsdon Road Industrial Estate
SAND/SEL CR2 177 K6
Selwyn Primary School
CHING E4 44 A5
PLSTW E13 76 E7
Sergeant Industrial Estate
WAND/EARL SW18 128 A5
Serpentine Gallery
BAY/PAD W2 9 H9
Servite RC Primary School
WBPTN SW10 14 E9
Seven Islands Leisure Centre
BERM/RHTH SE16 111 K2
Seven Kings Health Centre
GDMY/SEVK IG3 60 E7
Seven Kings High School
GNTH/NBYPK IG2 60 D6
Seven Mills Primary School
POP/IOD E14 112 D1
Seven Sisters Primary School
SEVS/STOTM N15 56 A4
Seymour Gardens Medical Centre
IL IG1 59 K7
Seymour Leasure Centre
MBLAR W1H 9 L3
Shaare Zedek Medical Centre
GLDGN NW11 52 D5
Shacklewell Primary School
STNW/STAM N16 74 B3
Shaftesbury High School
KTN/HRWW/W HA3 34 B7
Shaftesbury Hospital
LSQ/SEVD WC2H 11 H5
Shaftesbury Medical Centre
RYLN/HDSTN HA2 48 C7
Shaftesbury Park Primary School
BTSEA SW11 129 F2
Shaftesbury Primary School
FSTGT E7 77 G6
Shaftesbury Theatre
LSQ/SEVD WC2H 11 J4
Shahjalal Medical Centre
WCHPL E1 92 C5
Shakespeare Business Centre
BRXN/ST SW9 130 C2
Shakespeare's Globe Theatre
STHWK SE1 12 D7
The Shamrock Sports Club
ACT W3 86 E5
Shannon Corner Retail Park
NWMAL KT3 160 D3
Shapla J & I School
WCHPL E1 92 C6
Sharp Sports Centre
EDGW HA8 36 C5
Sheen Lane Health Centre
MORT/ESHN SW14 125 K2
Sheen Mount Primary School
RCHPK/HAM TW10 125 J4
Sheen School
MORT/ESHN SW14 126 B3
Sheen Sports Centre
MORT/ESHN SW14 126 B3
Shell Centre
STHWK SE1 11 M9
Shelley School
CLAP SW4 129 H2
Shenstone School
DART DA1 138 A4
Shepherd's Bush Cricket Club
ACT W3 87 G6
Shepherd's Bush Empire
SHB W12 107 F1
Shepherds Community School YWAM
BROCKY SE4 132 D2
Sheraton Business Centre
GFD/PVL UB6 85 J1
Sheringdale Primary School
WAND/EARL SW18 127 J7
Sheringham Junior School
MNPK E12 77 K3
Sherington Primary School
CHARL SE7 114 A5
Sherlock Holmes Museum
CAMTN NW1 9 M1
Sherwood First School
MTCM CR4 163 H3
Sherwood Park Primary School
BFN/LL DA15 136 C5
Sherwood Park School
WLGTN SM6 176 D2
Shirley Clinic
CROY/NA CR0 165 K7
Shirley High School
CROY/NA CR0 179 F2
Shirley Park Golf Club
CROY/NA CR0 178 D1
Shirley Wanderers RFC
WWKM BR4 180 A3
Shooters Hill Golf Club
WOOL/PLUM SE18 115 H7
The Shopping Hall
EHAM E6 77 J7
Shore Business Centre
HOM E9 74 E6
Shoreditch Comprehensive School
IS N1 7 K6
Shoreditch County Court
STLK EC1Y 7 H9
Shortlands Golf Club
HAYES BR2 152 C7
Shotfield Health Clinic
WLGTN SM6 176 B5
Showcase Cinema
WDGN N22 55 G1
Showcase Newham Cinema
BARK IG11 96 C2
Shrewsbury House School
SURB KT6 171 K1
Shrewsbury Road Health Centre
FSTGT E7 77 H6
Sidcup Cemetery
BXLY DA5 155 K1

Sidcup Golf Club *BFN/LL* DA15 155 G1
Sidcup Health Centre *SCUP* DA14 155 G2
Sidcup Hill Primary School *SCUP* DA14 155 H4
Sidcup Sports Club *SCUP* DA14 155 F3
Sidney Russell School *DAGW* RM9 80 A3
Silicon Business Centre *GFD/PVL* UB6 85 J1
Silverdale Industrial Estate *HYS/HAR* UB3 82 E7
Silver Industrial Estate *TOTM* N17 56 B1
Silver Street Medical Centre *UED* N18 42 A3
Silver Wing Industrial Estate *CROY/NA* CR0 177 F5
Simon Marks Jewish Primary School *STNW/STAM* N16 56 B7
Sinclair House School *FUL/PGN* SW6 107 H7
Singlegate First School *WIM/MER* SW19 147 H6
Sion College *EMB* EC4Y 12 B6
Sion Manning RC Girls School *NKENS* W10 88 B4
Sir Francis Drake Primary School *DEPT* SE8 112 B4
Sir George Monoux College *WALTH* E17 57 K1
Sir James Barrie School *VX/NE* SW8 109 H7
Sir John Cass Foundation/redcoat School *WCHPL* E1 93 F4
Sir John Cass Foundation School *TWRH* EC3N 13 L5
Sir John Lillie Primary School *HMSMTH* W6 107 H5
Sir John Soane's Museum *LINN* WC2A 11 M4
Sir Thomas Abney Primary School *STNW/STAM* N16 55 K6
Sir Thomas Lipton Memorial Hospital *STHGT/OAK* N14 28 B6
Sir William Burrough Primary School *POP/IOD* E14 93 G5
Six Bridges Trading Estate *STHWK* SE1 111 H4
Sixth Form Centre *FSTGT* E7 77 F5
Skillion Business Park *BARK* IG11 97 F2
Skinners Companys Lower Girls School *CLPT* E5 56 D7
Skinners Companys School For Girls *STNW/STAM* N16 56 B6
Ski Slope *STMC/STPC* BR5 155 K7
Slade Green FC *ERITH* DA8 118 E7
Slade Green Primary School *ERITH* DA8 118 D6
Slade School of Fine Art *STPAN* WC1H 5 H8
Sleaford Industrial Estate *VX/NE* SW8 109 H6
Sloane Hospital *BECK* BR3 152 B7
Smallberry Green Primary School *ISLW* TW7 124 B1
Smallwood Primary School *TOOT* SW17 147 H3
SMA Medical Centre *LEY* E10 57 K6
Smithy Street School *WCHPL* E1 92 E4
Snaresbrook College *SWFD* E18 58 E1
Snaresbrook Crown Court *WAN* E11 58 D4
Snaresbrook Primary School *SWFD* E18 58 E3
Snooker Club *WEA* W13 85 H7
Snowsfields Primary School *STHWK* SE1 19 J1
Sobell Leisure Centre *HOLWY* N7 73 F2
Sobell Medical Centre *HOLWY* N7 73 G3
Soho Parish CE Primary School *SOHO/CST* W1F 11 G6
Solent Road Health Centre *KIL/WHAMP* NW6 70 E5
Somerset House *COVGDN* WC2E 11 L6
Somers Town Community Sports Centre *CAMTN* NW1 4 F6
Sorsby Health Centre *CLPT* E5 75 F3
South Bank Business Centre *BTSEA* SW11 109 F7; *VX/NE* SW8 109 J5
Southbank International School *HAMP* NW3 71 G5; *NTGHL* W11 8 A7
Southbank University *STHWK* SE1 18 C2; *STHWK* SE1 18 E3; *VX/NE* SW8 109 J7
Southborough Primary School *HAYES* BR2 169 F4
Southborough School *SURB* KT6 172 A2
Southbury Primary School *PEND* EN3 30 D3
South Camden Community School *CAMTN* NW1 4 F5
South Chelsea College *BRXN/ST* SW9 130 A3
South Croydon Medical Centre *SAND/SEL* CR2 177 J6
South Croydon Sports Club *SAND/SEL* CR2 178 A4
South Eastern University *HOLWY* N7 73 F2
Southern Road Primary School *PLSTW* E13 95 F1
Southfield First & Middle School *CHSWK* W4 106 B1
Southfield Medical Centre *CHSWK* W4 106 A1
The Southfields Clinic *WAND/EARL* SW18 127 K5
Southfields Community School *WAND/EARL* SW18 127 K7
Southgate Cemetery *STHGT/OAK* N14 40 C1
Southgate College *STHGT/OAK* N14 40 C1
Southgate Compton Cricket Club *EBAR* EN4 27 K3
Southgate Leisure Centre *STHGT/OAK* N14 28 D6
Southgate Road Medical Centre *IS* N1 7 H1
Southgate School *EBAR* EN4 28 B4
South Grove Primary School *WALTH* E17 57 G5
South Hampstead Cricket Club *CRICK* NW2 70 A6
South Hampstead High School (Senior) *HAMP* NW3 71 H5
South Harringay Junior School *FSBYPK* N4 55 G4
South Herts Golf Club *TRDG/WHET* N20 26 E7
Southlake Primary School *ABYW* SE2 116 E1
Southlands College *PUT/ROE* SW15 126 C3
South Lewisham Health Centre *CAT* SE6 152 A3
South London Crematorium *MTCM* CR4 163 H1
South London Gallery *CMBW* SE5 111 F7
South London Montessori School *BTSEA* SW11 108 D7
The South London Natural Health Centre *CLAP* SW4 129 H3
South London Tamil School *CROY/NA* CR0 164 D6
South London Theatre *WNWD* SE27 149 J2
Southmead Primary School *WIM/MER* SW19 127 H7
South Norwood Country Park *SNWD* SE25 165 K3
South Norwood Hill Medical Centre *SNWD* SE25 165 F1
South Norwood Medical Centre *SNWD* SE25 165 F3
South Norwood Primary School *SNWD* SE25 165 H3
South Park Business Centre *IL* IG1 78 E1
South Park Clinic *IL* IG1 78 E3
South Park Primary School *GDMY/SEVK* IG3 78 E2
South Quay Plaza *POP/IOD* E14 112 E1
South Rise Primary School *WOOL/PLUM* SE18 115 J4
Southside Industrial Estate *VX/NE* SW8 109 H6
South Thames College *PUT/ROE* SW15 127 G4
South Thames College/Wandsworth Adult College *PUT/ROE* SW15 126 C5
Southville Junior School *EBED/NFELT* TW14 121 J7
Southwark Bridge Business Centre *STHWK* SE1 12 F9
Southwark Bridge Stairs *BLKFR* EC4V 12 E7
Southwark Cathedral *STHWK* SE1 13 G8
Southwark College *BERM/RHTH* SE16 111 J2; *CMBW* SE5 111 F6; *STHWK* SE1 18 C1; *STHWK* SE1 19 K3
Southwark Crown Court *STHWK* SE1 13 J8
Southwark Park Primary School *BERM/RHTH* SE16 111 J2
Southwark Park Sports Centre *BERM/RHTH* SE16 111 K3
Southwark Sports Ground *DUL* SE21 131 G7
South West Middlesex Crematorium *FELT* TW13 122 D7
Southwold Primary School *CLPT* E5 74 E1
South Woodford Health Centre *SWFD* E18 44 E7
Southwood Hospital *HGT* N6 54 A6
Southwood Primary School *DAGW* RM9 80 A3
Sovereign Business Centre *PEND* EN3 31 H2
The Space Arts Centre Cinema *POP/IOD* E14 112 C3
Sparrow Farm County Junior School *EW* KT17 173 K4
Sparrow Farm Junior School *EBED/NFELT* TW14 122 B6
Sparrow Farm Nursery School *EBED/NFELT* TW14 122 B6
Speakers Corner *BAY/PAD* W2 9 M6
Spectators Viewing Area *HTHAIR* TW6 120 E2
Speedway Industrial Estate *HYS/HAR* UB3 101 G1
Speke's Monument *BAY/PAD* W2 8 F8
Spelthorne Clinic *ASHF* TW15 140 B5
Spelthorne Primary School *ASHF* TW15 140 B5
Spelthorne Sports Club *ASHF* TW15 140 B6
Spencer House *WHALL* SW1A 10 E9
The Spires Shopping Centre *BAR* EN5 26 C2
Spiritualist University *WLSDN* NW10 69 J6
Spitalfields Health Centre *WCHPL* E1 13 M3
Spitalfields Market Hall *WCHPL* E1 13 L2
Splashworld Swimming Centre *WELL* DA16 136 E3
Springfield Christian School *PECK* SE15 111 G6
Springfield Hospital *TOOT* SW17 147 J2
Springfield Primary School *SUN* TW16 140 C7; *VX/NE* SW8 109 J6
Spring Grove Primary School *ISLW* TW7 123 J1
Springhallow School *HNWL* W7 85 F5
Spring Park Primary School *CROY/NA* CR0 179 J2
Springwell Infant School *HEST* TW5 102 D6
Springwell Junior School *HEST* TW5 102 D6
Spurgeons College *SNWD* SE25 165 F1
Squash & Badminton Club *WIM/MER* SW19 146 C6
Squirrels Heath Junior School *GPK* RM2 63 K4
Squirrels Trading Estate *HYS/HAR* UB3 101 J2
The Stables Gallery & Art Centre *CRICK* NW2 69 J3
Stadium Business Centre *WBLY* HA9 68 D2
Stadium Industrial Estate *WBLY* HA9 68 D4
Stadium Retail Park *WBLY* HA9 68 C2
Stafford Cross Business Park *CROY/NA* CR0 177 F4
Stag Lane Medical Centre *CDALE/KGS* NW9 50 E2
Stag Lane Primary School *EDGW* HA8 50 C1
Staines RFC *FELT* TW13 140 E4
Stamford Clinic *HMSMTH* W6 106 D3
Stamford Hill Primary School *SEVS/STOTM* N15 55 K5
Stanburn Middle School *STAN* HA7 35 J6
Standard Industrial Estate *CAN/RD* E16 114 C1; *CAN/RD* E16 114 E1
Stanford Middle School *STRHM/NOR* SW16 148 D7
Stanhope Primary School *GFD/PVL* UB6 84 C3
Stanley Infant School *TEDD* TW11 142 E3
Stanley Junior School *TEDD* TW11 142 E3
Stanley Park High School *CAR* SM5 176 A5
Stanley Park Junior School *CAR* SM5 175 K6
Stanley Technical Boys High School *SNWD* SE25 165 G2
Stanmore College *STAN* HA7 35 H5
Stanmore Golf Club *STAN* HA7 35 H6
Stanton Square Industrial Estate *CAT* SE6 151 H3
Staple Inn Buildings *HHOL* WC1V 12 A3
Staples Corner Business Park *CRICK* NW2 51 J7
Star Business Centre *DAGW* RM9 99 F4
Star Primary School *CAN/RD* E16 94 C3
Stationers Hall *STP* EC4M 12 D5
Stationery Office *HOL/ALD* WC2B 11 L4
Stephen Hawking Primary School *POP/IOD* E14 93 G5
Stepney Day Hospital *WCHPL* E1 92 E5
Stepney Greencoat CE Primary School *POP/IOD* E14 93 H5
Stepney Green School *WCHPL* E1 93 F4
Ster Century Cinema *ROM* RM1 63 G4
Sterling Industrial Estate *DAGE* RM10 80 D3
Sterling Way Clinic *UED* N18 42 B4
Stewart Fleming Primary School *PGE/AN* SE20 165 K2
Stewart Headlam Primary School *WCHPL* E1 92 D3
Stillness Primary School *BROCKY* SE4 132 B5
Stirling Industrial Centre *BORE* WD6 25 F4
Stirling Retail Park *BORE* WD6 25 F5
Stirling Way Industrial Estates *CROY/NA* CR0 163 K6
Stock Exchange *OBST* EC2N 13 H4
Stockley Park Business Centre *STKPK* UB11 82 A7
Stockley Park Golf Club *STKPK* UB11 82 A6
Stockwell Park School *BRXN/ST* SW9 110 A7
Stockwell Primary School *BRXN/ST* SW9 130 A2
Stoke Newington School *STNW/STAM* N16 73 K2
The Stonebridge Primary School *WLSDN* NW10 68 E7
Stonebridge Shopping Centre *WLSDN* NW10 69 F7
Stonehill Business Centre *UED* N18 43 F5
Stonehill Business Park *UED* N18 43 F4
Stone Lake Retail Park *CHARL* SE7 114 B3
Stoneydown Park Primary School *WALTH* E17 57 G3
Storey Primary School *CAN/RD* E16 96 A7
Stormont House School *CLPT* E5 74 D3
Stowford College *BELMT* SM2 175 G6
Strand on the Green J & I School *CHSWK* W4 105 H5
Strand Theatre *HOL/ALD* WC2B 11 L6
Stratford Magistrates Court *SRTFD* E15 76 B6
Stratford School *FSTGT* E7 76 E6
Stratford Shopping Centre *SRTFD* E15 76 B6
Strathmore School *RCHPK/HAM* TW10 124 E7
Strawberry Fields School *BAY/PAD* W2 8 B5
Strawberry Hill Golf Club *WHTN* TW2 142 E2
Streatham Cemetery *TOOT* SW17 147 J2
Streatham & Clapham High School *STRHM/NOR* SW16 148 C2
Streatham & Clapham High School Preparatory Site *BRXS/STRHM* SW2 130 A7
Streatham & Croydon RFC *THHTH* CR7 164 B4
Streatham Ice Rink *STRHM/NOR* SW16 148 E4
Streatham Modern School *STRHM/NOR* SW16 148 E5
Streatham Park Cemetery *MTCM* CR4 163 H1
Streatham Swimming Pool *STRHM/NOR* SW16 148 E4
Streatham Vale Sports Club *STRHM/NOR* SW16 148 C6
Streatham Wells Primary School *BRXS/STRHM* SW2 149 F1
Stroud Green Primary School *FSBYPK* N4 55 G7
The Study Preparatory School *WIM/MER* SW19 146 B4
The Study School *NWMAL* KT3 160 B4
Sudbourne Primary School *BRXS/STRHM* SW2 130 A4
Sudbury Court Sports Club *ALP/SUD* HA0 67 J2
Sudbury Golf Club *GFD/PVL* UB6 67 J5
Sudbury Primary School *ALP/SUD* HA0 67 H3
Suffolks Primary School *EN* EN1 30 D1
Sulivan Primary School *FUL/PGN* SW6 127 K1
Summerside JMI School *NFNCH/WDSP* N12 39 H5
Summerswood Primary School *BORE* WD6 24 D3
Summit Business Park *SUN* TW16 140 E6
Sunbury Business Centre *SUN* TW16 140 C7
Sunbury Court *SUN* TW16 156 C1
Sunbury Leisure Centre *SUN* TW16 140 D7
Sunbury Lock *WOT/HER* KT12 156 A2
Sunbury Manor School *SUN* TW16 140 D7
Sundridge Park Golf Club *BMLY* BR1 153 G5
Sun Life Trading Estate *EBED/NFELT* TW14 121 K2
Sunnyfields Primary School *HDN* NW4 51 K2
Sunnyhill Primary School *STRHM/NOR* SW16 149 F3
Super Bowl *BXLYHS* DA6 137 G3
Surbiton Business Centre *SURB* KT6 158 E5
Surbiton Cemetery *BRYLDS* KT5 159 H3
Surbiton Golf Club *ESH/CLAY* KT10 171 H3
Surbiton High School *KUT* KT1 159 F3
Surbiton Hospital *SURB* KT6 159 F5
Surbiton Natural Health Centre *SURB* KT6 159 F5
Surrey County Cricket Club (The Oval) *LBTH* SE11 17 M9
Surrey Docks Farm *BERM/RHTH* SE16 112 C1
Surrey Docks Health Centre *BERM/RHTH* SE16 112 B1
Surrey Docks Watersports Centre *BERM/RHTH* SE16 112 B2
Surrey Quays Leisure Park *BERM/RHTH* SE16 112 A2
Surrey Quays Shopping Centre *BERM/RHTH* SE16 112 A2
Surrey Square Primary School *WALW* SE17 19 J7
Sussex House Preparatory School *KTBR* SW1X 15 L5
Sutcliffe Park Athletics Track *ELTH/MOT* SE9 134 A4
Sutton Alternative Health Centre *SUT* SM1 175 F4
Sutton Arena *CAR* SM5 162 C6
Sutton Bowling Club *BELMT* SM2 174 E7
Sutton Cemetery *CHEAM* SM3 174 D1
Sutton Grammar School for Boys *SUT* SM1 175 G4
Sutton High Junior School *SUT* SM1 175 F5
Sutton High School for Girls Gdst *SUT* SM1 174 E5
Sutton House *HOM* E9 74 E4
Suttons Business Park *RAIN* RM13 99 F2
Sutton Superbowl *SUT* SM1 175 F4
Sutton United FC *SUT* SM1 174 E3
Sutton West Centre *SUT* SM1 174 E4
Swaffield Primary School *WAND/EARL* SW18 128 B5
Swakeleys School *HGDN/ICK* UB10 82 A1
Swaminarayan School *WLSDN* NW10 69 F5
Swan Business Centre *CHSWK* W4 106 A3
Swan Business Park *DART* DA1 139 G3
Swan Lane Pier *CANST* EC4R 13 G7
Swanlea School *WCHPL* E1 92 D3
Swansmere School *WOT/HER* KT12 156 B7
Swedish School *BARN* SW13 106 D5
Swiss Cottage School *HAMP* NW3 3 H2
Swiss Re-Insurance Tower *LVPST* EC2M 13 K5
Sybil Elgar School *EA* W5 86 A6; *NWDGN* UB2 102 E2
Sybourn Infant School *LEY* E10 57 G7
Sybourn Junior School *WALTH* E17 57 H6
Sydenham Girls School *SYD* SE26 150 D2
Sydenham High School *SYD* SE26 150 D4
Sydenham (Junior) High School *SYD* SE26 150 D3
Sydney Russell Comprehensive School *DAGW* RM9 79 K4
Syon House *BTFD* TW8 104 D7
Syon Park *BTFD* TW8 124 D1
Syon Park School *ISLW* TW7 104 C7
Syracuse University London Centre *NTGHL* W11 88 D6
Tabard Theatre *CHSWK* W4 106 B3
Taberner House *CROY/NA* CR0 177 J2
TA Centre *EDGW* HA8 36 D6; *HRW* HA1 49 F4; *NFNCH/WDSP* N12 39 H7
Tait Road Industrial Estate *CROY/NA* CR0 164 E6
Talmud Torah School *STNW/STAM* N16 55 K6
Tamian Industrial Estate *HSLWW* TW4 122 B3
Tamworth Manor High School *STRHM/NOR* SW16 163 J2
Tandem Centre *WIM/MER* SW19 147 H7
Tate Britain *WEST* SW1P 17 J6
Tate Modern *STHWK* SE1 12 D8
Tavistock Clinic *HAMP* NW3 71 H5
TAVR Centre *KUT* KT1 158 E3
Tavy Clinic *ABYW* SE2 116 D1
Teddington Business Park *TEDD* TW11 143 F4
Teddington Cemetery *TEDD* TW11 142 E3
Teddington Clinic *TEDD* TW11 142 E5
Teddington Lock *TEDD* TW11 143 H3
Teddington Memorial Hospital *TEDD* TW11 142 E5
Teddington Pool & Fitness Centre *TEDD* TW11 143 G4
Teddington School *TEDD* TW11 143 K5
The Teddington Theatre Club *E/WMO/HCT* KT8 157 J4
Telegraph Hill School *BROCKY* SE4 132 B1
Telferscot Primary School *BAL* SW12 129 H7
Temperate House *RCH/KEW* TW9 125 G1
Temple Hill Primary School *DART* DA1 139 K4
Temple of Bacchus *CMBW* SE5 130 D1
Temple of Mithras *MANHO* EC4N 13 G5
Tenby Road Clinic *EDGW* HA8 50 B1
Tennis & Squash Club *FNCH* N3 38 C7
Tennis Club *HAYES* BR2 168 A3; *STAN* HA7 35 H4
Tenterden Sports Ground *KTN/HRWW/W* HA3 50 A6
Terence McMillan Stadium *PLSTW* E13 95 G3
Tetherdown Primary School *MUSWH* N10 54 A3
Thames Barrier *CAN/RD* E16 114 C1

Thames Barriervisitor Centre
WOOL/PLUM SE18 114 C2
Thames Christian College
BTSEA SW11 128 C2
Thames Ditton Infant School
THDIT KT7 158 A5
Thames Ditton Junior School
THDIT KT7 158 A6
Thames House
WEST SW1P 17 J5
Thameside Industrial Estate
CAN/RD E16 95 H7
Thames Magistrates Court
BOW E3 93 J2
Thamesmead Community College
ERITHM DA18 117 F1
Thamesmead Leisure Centre
THMD SE28 97 G6
Thamesmead Shopping Centre
THMD SE28 97 G6
Thames Valley University
EA W5 85 K7
Thamesview Business Centre
RAIN RM13 99 G4
Thames View Clinic
BARK IG11 97 F1
Thames View J & I School
BARK IG11 97 G1
Thames Water Tower
NTGHL W11 107 G1
Theatre Centre
BECK BR3 166 E1
Théatre De Complicité
HOLWY N7 73 F4
Theatre for Mankind
FSBYPK N4 55 F7
Theatre Museum Library & Archive
COVGDN WC2E 11 K6
Theatre of the Dispossessed
WIM/MER SW19 127 G7
Theatre Royal
HOL/ALD WC2B 11 K5
SRTFD E15 76 B5
Theatre Royal Haymarket
STJS SW1Y 11 H7
Theodore McLeary Primary School
BRXS/STRHM SW2 130 A3
Therapia Trading Estate
CROY/NA CR0 163 J6
Thistlebrook Industrial Estate
ABYW SE2 116 D2
Thomas Arnold Primary School
DAGW RM9 80 B6
Thomas Becket RC Primary School
SNWD SE25 165 H5
Thomas Buxton Primary School
WCHPL E1 92 C3
Thomas Fairchild Primary School
IS N1 7 G5
Thomas Gamuel Primary School
WALTH E17 57 J5
Thomas Jones Primary School
NTGHL W11 88 C5
Thomas London Independent Day School
KENS W8 14 D3
Thomas Road Industrial Estate
POP/IOD E14 93 J4
Thomas's Preparatory School
BTSEA SW11 108 C7
Thomas Tallis School
BKHTH/KID SE3 134 A2
Thornhill Primary School
IS N1 6 A2
Thornton Heath Health Centre
THHTH CR7 164 D3
Thornton Heath Pools & Fitness Centre
SNWD SE25 165 H4
THHTH CR7 164 D3
Thornton Road Industrial Estate
CROY/NA CR0 163 K5
Thorntree Primary School
CHARL SE7 114 C4
Thorpe Hall Primary School
WALTH E17 44 A7
Three Bridges Business Centre
NWDGN UB2 103 H1
Three Bridges Primary School
NWDGN UB2 102 B3
NWDGN UB2 103 G2
Three Mills Heritage Centre
SRTFD E15 94 A2
Thurlow Park School
WNWD SE27 149 H1
Thurston Industrial Estate
LEW SE13 132 E2
Tidemill Primary School
DEPT SE8 112 D6
Tideway Industrial Estate
VX/NE SW8 109 H5
Tiffin Girls School
KUTN/CMB KT2 144 A5
Tiffin School
KUTN/CMB KT2 159 G1
Tiller Centre (Swimming Baths)
POP/IOD E14 112 D2
Tiller Leisure Centre
POP/IOD E14 112 D2
Timbercroft Primary School
WOOL/PLUM SE18 115 K6
Timbers Clinic
KTN/HRWW/W HA3 34 D5
Times Square Shopping Centre
SUT SM1 175 F4
Tiverton Primary School
SEVS/STOTM N15 55 K5
Tobacco Dock
WAP E1W 92 D6
Tokyngton Community Centre
WBLY HA9 68 D4
Toldos School
STNW/STAM N16 55 K7
Tollgate Primary School
CROY/NA CR0 165 K5
PLSTW E13 95 G3
Tolworth CP School
SURB KT6 159 G7
Tolworth Girls School & Centre for Continuing Education
SURB KT6 172 B2
Tolworth Recreation Centre
CHSGTN KT9 172 B2
Tolworth Tower
SURB KT6 159 J7
Tom Hood School
WAN E11 76 D2
Tooting Bec Athletics Track
TOOT SW17 148 B3
Tooting Leisure Centre
TOOT SW17 147 H3
Tooting & Mitcham United FC
MTCM CR4 148 A7
Torriano J & I School
KTTN NW5 72 C4
Torridon Primary School
CAT SE6 152 B1
Torrington Clinic
NFNCH/WDSP N12 39 G4
Torrington Park Health Centre
NFNCH/WDSP N12 39 G3
Total Health Clinic
SHB W12 106 E1
Tottenhall Infants School
PLMGR N13 41 G4
Tottenham Green Leisure Centre
SEVS/STOTM N15 56 A3
Tottenham Hale Retail Park
SEVS/STOTM N15 56 C3
Tottenham Hotspur FC (White Hart Lane)
TOTM N17 42 B6
Tottenham Park Cemetery
ED N9 42 D2
Tottenham Sports Centre
TOTM N17 42 B7
Totteridge Cricket Club
TRDG/WHET N20 38 E1
The Tower Bridge Experience
STHWK SE1 13 L9
Tower Bridge Primary School
STHWK SE1 19 L1
Tower Bridge Wharf
WAP E1W 92 C7
Tower Hamlets College
POP/IOD E14 93 K6
WCHPL E1 92 E4
Tower House School
MORT/ESHN SW14 125 K3
Tower Industrial Estate
SNWD SE25 165 H3
Tower Medical Centre
WCHPL E1 92 C5
Tower Millennium Pier
MON EC3R 13 K8
Tower of London
TWRH EC3N 13 L7
Tower Retail Park
DART DA1 138 C4
Towers Business Park
WBLY HA9 68 D3
Tower Stairs
MON EC3R 13 J7
Town Farm Primary School
STWL/WRAY TW19 120 A6
Townley Grammar School for Girls
BXLYHS DA6 137 G5
Townmead Business Centre
FUL/PGN SW6 128 B2
Townsend Industrial Estate
WLSDN NW10 68 E7
Townsend Primary School
STHWK SE1 19 J5
Toynbee Hall & Curtain Theatre
WCHPL E1 13 L4
Trabzon Spor FC
STNW/STAM N16 73 K3
Trade Union Congress
NOXST/BSQ WC1A 11 H4
Trafalgar Business Centre
BARK IG11 97 F3
Trafalgar Primary School
WHTN TW2 142 D1
Trafalgar Square
CHCR WC2N 11 H8
Trafalgar Trading Estate
PEND EN3 31 H3
Tramshed Theatre
WOOL/PLUM SE18 115 G3
Trans Atlantic College
BETH E2 7 L5
Transport House
WEST SW1P 17 J4
Treasury
WHALL SW1A 17 J2
The Treaty Centre
HSLW TW3 123 G2
The Treehouse School
BMSBY WC1N 5 L9
Trent CE Primary School
EBAR EN4 27 K3
Trent Country Park
EBAR EN4 28 A1
Trent Park Cemetery
EBAR EN4 28 A2
Trent Park Golf Club
EBAR EN4 28 C3
Trevor Roberts School
HAMP NW3 3 H1
Tricycle Cinema
KIL/WHAMP NW6 70 D6
Trident Business Centre
TOOT SW17 147 K4
Trinity Business Centre
BERM/RHTH SE16 112 C1
Trinity Catholic Lower High School
WFD IG8 44 E3
Trinity College Centre
PECK SE15 111 F6
Trinity College of Music
GNWCH SE10 113 F5
MHST W1U 10 B3
Trinity Hospital
GNWCH SE10 113 G4
Trinity House
TWRH EC3N 13 K6
Trinity RC High School (Upper)
WFD IG8 44 E3
Trinity St Marys Primary School
BAL SW12 129 F7
Trinity School
CROY/NA CR0 178 E1
DAGE RM10 80 C2
Trinity School Belvedere
BELV DA17 117 K3
Trinity Trading Estate
HYS/HAR UB3 101 K2
Triumph Trading Estate
TOTM N17 42 C5
Trocadero Centre
MYFR/PICC W1J 11 G7
Trojan Business Centre
WLSDN NW10 69 H5
Troy Industrial Estate
HRW HA1 49 F4
True Buddha School
IS N1 5 L4
Tudor Lodge Health Centre
WIM/MER SW19 127 G6
Tudor Primary School
FNCH N3 39 G7
STHL UB1 83 J6
Tufnell Park Primary School
HOLWY N7 72 D3
Tuke School
PECK SE15 111 J7
Tulloch Clinic
SHB W12 88 B7
Tunnel Avenue Trading Estate
GNWCH SE10 113 G1
Turney School
DUL SE21 130 D6
Turnham Primary School
BROCKY SE4 132 B3
Tweeddale Infant School
CAR SM5 162 C6
Tweeddale Junior School
CAR SM5 162 C6
Twickenham Cemetery
WHTN TW2 123 G7
Twickenham Golf Club
FELT TW13 142 A2
Twickenham Park Health Centre
TWK TW1 124 D5
Twickenham Stadium
WHTN TW2 123 K5
Twickenham Trading Centre
TWK TW1 124 A5
Two Bridges Business Park
SAND/SEL CR2 177 K5
Twyford CE High School
ACT W3 86 D7
Twyford Sports Centre
ACT W3 86 D7
Tyburn Infant School
STJWD NW8 3 H9
The Type Museum
BRXN/ST SW9 110 A7
Tyssen Primary School
STNW/STAM N16 56 C7
UCI Cinema
BAY/PAD W2 8 D5
BERM/RHTH SE16 112 A2
ED N9 31 F6
SUT SM1 175 F4
UCI Empire Cinema
LSQ/SEVD WC2H 11 H7
UCI Filmworks Cinema
GNWCH SE10 113 J3
UCL Hospitals
FITZ W1T 10 F1
UGC Cinema
CHEL SW3 15 H9
CRICK NW2 51 K7
EA W5 85 K6
EN EN1 30 C3
HMSMTH W6 106 E3
SOHO/SHAV W1D 11 G6
WBPTN SW10 14 F8
Underhill J & I School
BAR EN5 26 C4
Unicorn School
RCH/KEW TW9 105 G7
United Medical & Dental Schools
STHWK SE1 17 L3
United Services Sports Ground
CHSWK W4 106 B7
Unity College
KTTN NW5 72 B3
Unity Trading Estate
WFD IG8 59 H2
University Church of Christ the King
STPAN WC1H 11 G1
University College Hospital
GWRST WC1E 10 F1
HAMP NW3 71 H5
University College Junior School
HAMP NW3 71 G3
University College London
FITZ W1T 10 F2
GWRST WC1E 11 G1
STPAN WC1H 5 G9
University College London, Astor College
FITZ W1T 10 F2
University College London, Department of Clinical Haematology
GWRST WC1E 11 G1
University College London Medical School
FITZ W1T 10 E2
University College School
HAMP NW3 71 G4
University Hospital Lewisham
LEW SE13 132 E4
University of California
WHALL SW1A 10 E9
University of East London
BCTR RM8 79 G3
PLSTW E13 95 F2
University of East London Campus
EHAM E6 96 A6
University of Greenwich
GNWCH SE10 113 G4
WOOL/PLUM SE18 115 F2
University of Greenwich (Mansion Site)
ELTH/MOT SE9 135 H5
University of Greenwich (Southwood Site)
ELTH/MOT SE9 135 H5
University of Greenwich Sports Ground
ELTH/MOT SE9 134 D3
ELTH/MOT SE9 135 H6
University of London
BAY/PAD W2 9 G5
BMSBY WC1N 11 K1
FITZ W1T 11 G4
GWRST WC1E 11 H2
NWCR SE14 112 B7
STPAN WC1H 5 H9
University of London Athletics Ground
NWMAL KT3 160 D4
University of Middlesex
EBAR EN4 28 C1
PEND EN3 30 D4
University of North London
HOLWY N7 73 F3
University of Notre Dame
LSQ/SEVD WC2H 11 H7
University of Westminster
CAMTN NW1 4 E9
CHSWK W4 105 K7
GTPST W1W 10 D2
HGT N6 54 B7
MHST W1U 10 A2
University of Westminster (Harrow Campus)
HRW HA1 49 G6
Uphall Primary School
IL IG1 78 B4
Upland Primary School
BXLYHN DA7 137 G2
Uplands Business Park
WALTH E17 57 F1
Upper Montagu Street Clinic
MBLAR W1H 9 L2
Upper Tooting Independent High School
TOOT SW17 147 J1
Upton Cross Primary School
PLSTW E13 77 F7
Upton Day Hospital
BXLYHS DA6 137 F3
Upton Lane Medical Centre
FSTGT E7 77 F5
Upton Primary School
BXLY DA5 137 F4
Upton Road School
BXLYHS DA6 137 F4
Ursuline High School
IL IG1 78 B1
RYNPK SW20 146 B6
Uxbridge College
HYS/HAR UB3 82 E6
Uxbridge County Court
YEAD UB4 82 C4
Uxendon Manor JMI School
KTN/HRWW/W HA3 50 A4
Vale Farm Sports Centre
ALP/SUD HA0 67 H3
Vale Industrial Estate
WATW WD18 20 A7
The Vale Medical Centre
FSTH SE23 151 G1
Valence House Museum & Library
BCTR RM8 79 K1
Valence Junior School
BCTR RM8 79 K1
Valentine High School
IL IG1 60 A5
Valentines High Lower School
GNTH/NBYPK IG2 60 B4
Vale Park Industrial
ACT W3 106 B1
The Vale School
SKENS SW7 14 E4
Valley Primary School
HAYES BR2 167 J1
Valmar Trading Estate
CMBW SE5 110 D7
Vanbrugh Theatre
GWRST WC1E 11 G1
Vanguard Trading Estate
SRTFD E15 76 A7
Vaudeville Theatre
COVGDN WC2E 11 K6
Vaughan First & Middle School
RYLN/HDSTN HA2 48 C5
Vauxhall Primary School
LBTH SE11 17 L7
Vauxhall Station
LBTH SE11 17 K8
Vernon House Special School
WLSDN NW10 68 E4
Vestry Hall
MTCM CR4 162 E2
Vestry House Museum
WALTH E17 57 K3
Vicarage Fields Health Clinic
BARK IG11 78 C6
The Vicarage Field Shopping Centre
BARK IG11 78 C6
Vicarage Primary School
EHAM E6 95 K2
Vicarage Road Cemetery
WATW WD18 20 E3
Vicars Green Primary School
GFD/PVL UB6 85 J1
VI Components Industrial Park
ERITH DA8 118 B4
Victoria & Albert Museum
SKENS SW7 15 H4
Victoria Business Centre
WELL DA16 136 B1
Victoria Chiropractic Clinic
CHEL SW3 15 L2
Victoria Coach Station
BGVA SW1W 16 C6
Victoria Hall
FNCH N3 38 D7
Victoria Industrial Estate
ACT W3 87 F4
Victoria Industrial Park
DART DA1 139 G4
Victoria Junior School
FELT TW13 122 A7
Victoria Medical Centre
PIM SW1V 16 E6
Victoria Palace Theatre
WESTW SW1E 16 D4
Victoria Park Industrial Centre
HOM E9 75 H6
Victoria Place Shopping Centre
PIM SW1V 16 D5
Victoria Rail/Air Terminal
PIM SW1V 16 D5
Victoria Retail Park
RSLP HA4 65 H4
Victoria Station
PIM SW1V 16 D5
Victoria Wharf
POP/IOD E14 93 G6
Victoria Wharf Industrial Estate
DEPT SE8 112 C4
Victor Seymour Infant School
CAR SM5 175 K2
Victory Business Centre
ISLW TW7 124 A3
Victory Primary School
WALW SE17 18 F5
Viking Business Centre
ROMW/RG RM7 62 E6
Viking Primary School
NTHLT UB5 83 H2
Village Infant School
DAGE RM10 80 C6
The Village School
HAMP NW3 71 K5
Villiers High School
STHL UB1 84 A7
The Vine Clinic
KUTN/CMB KT2 144 A5
Vine Medical Centre
E/WMO/HCT KT8 157 H2
The Vines School
BTSEA SW11 129 F3
The Vineyard Primary School
RCHPK/HAM TW10 125 F5
Vinopolis, City of Wine
STHWK SE1 12 F8
Vinters' Hall
BLKFR EC4V 12 F6
VIP Trading Estate
CHARL SE7 114 B3
Virginia Primary School
BETH E2 7 L8
Virgo Fidelis Convent Schools
NRWD SE19 149 J5
Vitoria Primary School
IS N1 5M4
Voyager Business Estate
BERM/RHTH SE16 111 H2
Vulcan Business Centre
CROY/NA CR0 180 C7
Waddon Clinic
CROY/NA CR0 177 G4
Waddon Infant School
CROY/NA CR0 177 G4
Wadham Lodge Sports Centre
WALTH E17 43 K7
Wadsworth Business Centre
GFD/PVL UB6 85 J1
The Waldegrave Clinic
TEDD TW11 143 F4
Waldegrave Girls School
WHTN TW2 142 D2
Waldo Industrial Estate
BMLY BR1 168 B2
Waldorf School of SW London
STRHM/NOR SW16 148 C1
Waldorf Steiner School of SW London
STRHM/NOR SW16 148 D3
Walford Secondary School
NTHLT UB5 65 J7
Walker Primary School
STHGT/OAK N14 40 D1
Wallace Collection
MHST W1U 10 A4
Wallbrook Business Centre
HSLWW TW4 122 A2
Wallington County Grammar School
WLGTN SM6 176 B2
Wallington High School for Girls
WLGTN SM6 176 B7
Walmer Road Clinic
NTGHL W11 88 C6
Walm Lane Clinic
CRICK NW2 70 B4
Walnut Tree Walk Primary School
LBTH SE11 18 A5
Waltham Forest College
WALTH E17 57 F1
WALTH E17 57 K2
Waltham Forest Magistrates Court
WALTH E17 57 K2
Waltham Forest Theatre
WALTH E17 57 H2
Waltham Forest Track
WALTH E17 57 K1
Walthamstow Business Centre
WALTH E17 58 A1
Walthamstow Greyhound Stadium
CHING E4 43 K6
Walthamstow School for Girls
WALTH E17 57 K3
Walton Business Centre
WOT/HER KT12 156 A6
Walton Casuals FC
WOT/HER KT12 156 A4
Walton Swimming Pool
WOT/HER KT12 156 A7
Walworth Lower School
WALW SE17 19 H7
Walworth Town Hall
WALW SE17 18 E6
Walworth Upper School
WALW SE17 19 K8
Wandle Primary School
WAND/EARL SW18 128 A7
Wandle Recreation Centre
WAND/EARL SW18 128 A5
Wandle Trading Estate
MTCM CR4 162 E6
Wandsworth Adult College
TOOT SW17 147 J3
The Wandsworth Arndale Centre
WAND/EARL SW18 128 A5
Wandsworth Cemetery
WAND/EARL SW18 128 B7
Wandsworth Community Health Trust
TOOT SW17 148 A4
Wandsworth County Court
PUT/ROE SW15 127 H4
Wandsworth Trading Estate
WAND/EARL SW18 128 A6
Wanstead CE Primary School
WAN E11 58 E4
Wanstead Cricket Club
WAN E11 59 F6
Wanstead Golf Club
WAN E11 59 G6
Wanstead High School
WAN E11 59 G5
Wanstead Hospital
WAN E11 59 F3
Wanstead Leisure Centre
WAN E11 59 G5
Wapping Sports Centre
WAP E1W 92 D7
Wapping Wharf
WAP E1W 92 E7
Warehouse Theatre
CROY/NA CR0 177 K1
War Memorial
EDGW HA8 36 C5
War Memorial Sports Ground
SUT SM1 175 J3
Warner Village Cinema
ACT W3 86 C3
CROY/NA CR0 177 F1
DAGW RM9 80 A7
HAMP NW3 71 F5
HRW HA1 48 E5

NFNCH/WDSP N12 39 H7
SHB W12 107 G1
SOHO/SHAV W1D 11 H6
Warnford Industrial Estate *HYS/HAR* UB3 101 H1
Warren Comprehensive School *CHDH* RM6 62 B4
Warren Dell Primary School *OXHEY* WD19 33 G2
Warrender School *RSLP* HA4 46 D6
Warren Junior School *CHDH* RM6 62 B4
The Warren Medical Centre *YEAD* UB4 83 F5
Warren Sports Centre *CHDH* RM6 62 B4
Warwick Estate *BAY/PAD* W2 8 D3
Warwick Leadlay Gallery *GNWCH* SE10 113 F5
Warwick Park School *PECK* SE15 111 G7
Warwick School for Boys *WALTH* E17 58 A3
Waterfront Leisure Centre *WOOL/PLUM* SE18 115 F2
Watergate School *LEW* SE13 132 E3
Waterloo East Station *STHWK* SE1 12 B9
Waterloo Health Centre *STHWK* SE1 18 A2
Waterloo Station *STHWK* SE1 18 A1
Watermans Arts, Cinema & Theatre Centre *BTFD* TW8 105 F5
The Watermans Hall *MON* EC3R 13 J7
Watermeads High School *MRDN* SM4 162 C5
Watermill Business Centre *PEND* EN3 31 H1
Water Rats Theatre *STPAN* WC1H 5 K7
Waterside Business Centre *ISLW* TW7 124 C3
The Waterside Trading Centre *HNWL* W7 103 K2
Watersports Centre *FSBYPK* N4 55 J7
Watford Arches Retail Park *WATW* WD18 21 G4
Watford Business Centre *WATW* WD18 21 F2
Watford Central Swimming Bath *WAT* WD17 20 E2
Watford County Court *WAT* WD17 21 F1
Watford FC & Saracens RFC (Vicarage Road Stadium) *WATW* WD18 21 F4
Watford General Hospital *WATW* WD18 21 F4
Watford Grammar School for Boys *WATW* WD18 20 D3
Watford Grammar School for Girls *WATW* WD18 21 G4
Watford Museum *WAT* WD17 21 G4
Watling Clinic *EDGW* HA8 37 F6
Watling Medical Centre *EDGW* HA8 36 E7
Wavelengths Leisure Pool & Library *DEPT* SE8 112 D6
Waverley Industrial Estate *HRW* HA1 48 D2
Waverley Lower Secondary School *EDUL* SE22 131 J4
Waverley School
PECK SE15 131 K4
PEND EN3 30 E3
Waxchandlers' Hall *CITYW* EC2V 12 F4
Weald College *KTN/HRWW/W* HA3 34 E5
Weald First & Middle School *KTN/HRWW/W* HA3 35 F6
Welbeck Clinic *CRICK* NW2 70 E2
Welbourne Primary School *TOTM* N17 56 C3
Welfare Clinic
CMBW SE5 130 E2
GNWCH SE10 113 F6
HGT N6 54 A5
Wellcome Institute *CAMTN* NW1 5 G9
Welldon Park Middle School *RYLN/HDSTN* HA2 66 C3
The Welling Clinic *WELL* DA16 136 B1
Welling Medical Centre *WELL* DA16 136 A3
Welling School *WELL* DA16 116 C7
Wellington Arch *MYFR/PICC* W1J 16 B1
Wellington Barracks *STJSPK* SW1H 16 F2
Wellington Primary School
BOW E3 93 J2
HSLW TW3 122 E1
Welling United FC *WELL* DA16 136 D2
Wells Primary School *WFD* IG8 45 F3
Wembley Arena *WBLY* HA9 68 C3
Wembley Conference Centre *WBLY* HA9 68 B3
Wembley FC *ALP/SUD* HA0 67 H3
Wembley High School *ALP/SUD* HA0 67 J2
Wembley Hospital *ALP/SUD* HA0 67 K5
Wembley Manor Primary School *WBLY* HA9 68 A2
Wembley Park Business Centre *WBLY* HA9 68 D2
Wembley Stadium Industrial Estate
WBLY HA9 68 C3
WBLY HA9 68 E2
Wembley Stadium (under development) *WBLY* HA9 68 C3
Wendell Park Primary School *SHB* W12 106 C1
Wentworth Primary School *DART* DA1 138 C6
Wentworth Tutorial College *GLDGN* NW11 52 B5
Wesley's Chapel, House & Museum *STLK* EC1Y 7 G9
Wessex Gardens Primary School *CRICK* NW2 52 C7
West Acton Primary School *ACT* W3 86 D5
West Becton Health Centre *CAN/RD* E16 95 H5
Westbourne Green Sports Complex *BAY/PAD* W2 8 B3
Westbourne Primary School *SUT* SM1 174 E2
Westbridge College *BTSEA* SW11 108 D7
Westbrooke School *WELL* DA16 136 E2
Westbury Medical Centre *WDGN* N22 55 J1
Westcroft Leisure Centre *CAR* SM5 176 A3
West Drayton Primary School *WDR/YW* UB7 100 B1
West Ealing Business Centre *WEA* W13 85 G6
Western Avenue Business Park *ACT* W3 86 D3
Western Trading Estate *WLSDN* NW10 86 E3
West Ewell County Infant School *HOR/WEW* KT19 173 F4
Westfield School *WATW* WD18 20 D5
Westfields Primary School *BARN* SW13 126 C1
Westgate Business Centre *NKENS* W10 88 C3
Westgate Primary School *DART* DA1 139 G6
West Green Primary School *SEVS/STOTM* N15 55 J3
West Grove Primary School *STHGT/OAK* N14 28 D6
West Ham Church Primary School *SRTFD* E15 76 D7
West Ham Lane Clinic *SRTFD* E15 76 C7
West Hampstead Clinic *KIL/WHAMP* NW6 2 B1
West Ham United FC (Upton Park) *EHAM* E6 95 H1
West Hatch High School *CHIG* IG7 45 K4
West Hendon Clinic *CDALE/KGS* NW9 51 H5
West Herts Business Centre *BORE* WD6 24 D2
West Herts College *BUSH* WD23 21 H2
West Herts Golf Club *RKW/CH/CXG* WD3 20 B2
West Hill Primary School
DART DA1 139 F5
WAND/EARL SW18 127 K4
West India Pier *POP/IOD* E14 112 C1
West India Shopping Centre *POP/IOD* E14 93 J7
Westland Heliport *BTSEA* SW11 128 C2
West Lea School *ED* N9 42 A2
West Lodge Preparatory School *BFN/LL* DA15 155 F2
West Lodge Primary School *PIN* HA5 47 H3
West London County Court *WKENS* W14 107 H3
West London Magistrates Court *HMSMTH* W6 107 G4
West London Tamil School *WLSDN* NW10 87 H1
West Mead Clinic *RSLP* HA4 65 G2
West Middlesex Golf Club *STHL* UB1 84 C6
West Middlesex University Hospital *ISLW* TW7 124 B1
Westminster Abbey *WEST* SW1P 17 J3
Westminster Abbey Choir School *WEST* SW1P 17 H3
Westminster Business Square *LBTH* SE11 17 L8
Westminster Cathedral *WEST* SW1P 16 E4
Westminster Cathedral Choir School *WEST* SW1P 16 F5
Westminster Cathedral RC Primary School *PIM* SW1V 17 H7
Westminster City Hall *WESTW* SW1E 16 F3
Westminster City School *WESTW* SW1E 16 F3
Westminster College
BTSEA SW11 109 F7
SOHO/SHAV W1D 10 F6
Westminster Industrial Estate *WOOL/PLUM* SE18 114 C2
Westminster Natural Health Centre *PIM* SW1V 16 E6
Westminster Pier *WHALL* SW1A 17 K2
Westminster School *WEST* SW1P 17 J3
Westminster Technical College *WEST* SW1P 16 F5
Westminster Theatre *WESTW* SW1E 16 E3
Westminster Under School *WEST* SW1P 17 G6
Westmoor Community Clinic *PUT/ROE* SW15 126 D6
West Norwood Clinic *WNWD* SE27 149 J1
West Norwood Crematorium *WNWD* SE27 149 J2
West One Shopping Centre *MYFR/PKLN* W1K 10 B5
Weston Green School *THDIT* KT7 157 K7
Weston Park Clinic *CEND/HSY/T* N8 54 E4
Weston Park Primary School *CEND/HSY/T* N8 55 F4
Westpoint Trading Estate *ACT* W3 86 D4
West Ramp Coach Park *WDR/YW* UB7 100 D7
West Ruislip Elementary School *HGDN/ICK* UB10 64 A2
West 12 Shopping & Leisure Centre *WKENS* W14 107 G1
West Thames College *ISLW* TW7 103 K7
West Thornton Primary School *CROY/NA* CR0 164 A6
West Twyford Primary School *WLSDN* NW10 86 C1
Westway Business Centre *BAY/PAD* W2 8 C3
Westway Sports Centre *NKENS* W10 88 B5
West Wickham Swimming Baths *WWKM* BR4 167 F7
Westwood High School for Girls *NRWD* SE19 149 J6
Westwood Primary School *WELL* DA16 135 K3
Westwood School *BUSH* WD23 34 D1
Westwood Technology College *WELL* DA16 135 J3
Whaddon House Clinic *CMBW* SE5 131 F2
Whipps Cross Hospital *LEY* E10 58 B5
Whitechapel Art Gallery *WCHPL* E1 13 M4
Whitechapel Sports Centre *WCHPL* E1 92 C3
Whitefield School *CRICK* NW2 52 B6
Whitefield School & Leisure Centre *WALTH* E17 44 B7
Whitefriars First & Middle School *KTN/HRWW/W* HA3 48 E1
Whitefriars Trading Estate *KTN/HRWW/W* HA3 48 D1
Whitehall Primary School *CHING* E4 44 C1
Whitehall Theatre *WHALL* SW1A 11 H8
White Hart Lane School *WDGN* N22 41 H6
Whiteheath Junior School *RSLP* HA4 46 A5
Whitehorse Manor Primary School *THHTH* CR7 164 E3
Whiteleys Shopping Centre *BAY/PAD* W2 8 C5
Whiterose Trading Estate *EBAR* EN4 27 J6
Whitgift School *SAND/SEL* CR2 177 J4
Whitgift Shopping Centre *CROY/NA* CR0 177 J1
Whitings Hill Primary School *BAR* EN5 26 A4
Whitmore High School *RYLN/HDSTN* HA2 48 C7
Whitmore Primary School *IS* N1 7 H4
Whittingham Community Primary School *WALTH* E17 43 G7
Whittington Hospital *ARCH* N19 72 B1
Whittlesea School *KTN/HRWW/W* HA3 34 C6
Whitton Health Centre *WHTN* TW2 123 H7
Whitton Health Clinic *WHTN* TW2 123 G7
Whitton School *WHTN* TW2 142 B1
Whitton Sports & Fitness Centre *WHTN* TW2 142 B1
Whybridge Infant School *RAIN* RM13 81 J7
Whybridge Junior School *RAIN* RM13 81 H7
Wickham Theatre *WWKM* BR4 180 B2
Wide Way Health Clinic *MTCM* CR4 163 J2
Widmore Centre *BMLY* BR1 168 B1
Wigmore Hall *MHST* W1U 10 C4
Wilberforce Primary School *NKENS* W10 88 C2
Wilbury Primary School *UED* N18 41 K4
Willesden Community Hospital *WLSDN* NW10 69 J6
Willesden County Court *WLSDN* NW10 87 G1
Willesden High School *WLSDN* NW10 69 K7
Willesden Medical Centre *CRICK* NW2 69 K5
Willesden Sports Centre *WLSDN* NW10 69 K7
Willesden Sports Stadium *WLSDN* NW10 69 K7
William Bellamy J & I School *DAGE* RM10 80 C1
William Byrd School *HYS/HAR* UB3 101 F5
William C Harvey Special School *TOTM* N17 55 K1
William Davies Primary School *FSTGT* E7 77 H5
William Ellis School *KTTN* NW5 72 A2
William Ellis Sports Ground *EDGW* HA8 36 C7
William Ford CE Junior School *DAGE* RM10 80 C6
William Morris Academy *HMSMTH* W6 107 G4
William Morris Gallery *WALTH* E17 57 J2
William Morris Middle School *MTCM* CR4 163 J2
William Morris School *WALTH* E17 43 G7
William Patten Primary School *STNW/STAM* N16 74 B1
William Torbitt J & I School *GNTH/NBYPK* IG2 60 E4
William Tyndale Primary School *IS* N1 6 D1
Willington School *WIM/MER* SW19 146 D5
Willoughby Hall School *HAMP* NW3 71 H3
Willow Business Centre *MTCM* CR4 162 E4
Willow Business Park *SYD* SE26 150 E2
Willow Court Colindale Hospital *CDALE/KGS* NW9 51 F1
Willowfield Adult Education Centre *WALTH* E17 57 F2
Willowfield School
HNHL SE24 130 D3
WALTH E17 57 G2
The Willows Clinic *CHST* BR7 154 A5
The Willows *YEAD* UB4 83 H3
Willow Tree Primary School *NTHLT* UB5 65 J5
Wilsons School *WLGTN* SM6 176 E5
Wimbledon Chase Middle School *RYNPK* SW20 146 C7
Wimbledon College High School *WIM/MER* SW19 146 B6
Wimbledon Common Golf Club *WIM/MER* SW19 145 K4
Wimbledon Common Pre-Preparatory School *WIM/MER* SW19 146 A5
Wimbledon FC (Selhurst Park) *SNWD* SE25 165 F3
Wimbledon (Gap Road) Cemetery *WIM/MER* SW19 147 F3
Wimbledon High School *WIM/MER* SW19 146 C5
Wimbledon House School *WIM/MER* SW19 146 E7
Wimbledon Magistrates Court *WIM/MER* SW19 146 E5
Wimbledon Park Athletics Track *WIM/MER* SW19 146 D1
Wimbledon Park Golf Club *WIM/MER* SW19 146 D2
Wimbledon Park Primary School *WIM/MER* SW19 146 E1
Wimbledon Recreation Centre *WIM/MER* SW19 147 F5
Wimbledon RFC *RYNPK* SW20 145 H6
Wimbledon School of Art
WIM/MER SW19 146 C7
WIM/MER SW19 146 E6
Wimbledon School of English *WIM/MER* SW19 146 C5
Wimbledon Stadium *TOOT* SW17 147 F3
Wimbledon Stadium Business Centre *WIM/MER* SW19 147 F2
Wimbledon Theatre *WIM/MER* SW19 146 E6
Winchcombe Business Centre *PECK* SE15 111 F5
Winchmore Hill Clinic *WCHMH* N21 29 H7
Winchmore Hill Cricket Club *WCHMH* N21 29 J7
Winchmore School *WCHMH* N21 41 J1
Windmill Business Centre *NWDGN* UB2 84 C7
Windmill School *BRXS/STRHM* SW2 129 K4
Windmill Trading Estate
MTCM CR4 163 H4
SUN TW16 140 B7
Windrush Primary School *THMD* SE28 97 H7
Winfield House *CAMTN* NW1 3 K7
Wingate & Finchley FC *NFNCH/WDSP* N12 39 H6
Wingate Trading Estate *TOTM* N17 42 B6
Wingfield Primary School *BKHTH/KID* SE3 133 K2
Winns Primary School *WALTH* E17 57 H1
Winsor Primary School *EHAM* E6 96 A5
Winston Churchill's Britain at War Experience *STHWK* SE1 13 H9
Winterbourne Junior Girls School *THHTH* CR7 164 B3
Winton Primary School *IS* N1 5 L6
Witley Industrial Estate *NWDGN* UB2 102 E3
Witnitz School *STNW/STAM* N16 56 B7
Wix Primary School *CLAP* SW4 129 G2
Wolf Fields Primary School *NWDGN* UB2 102 E3
Wolfson-Hillel Primary School *STHGT/OAK* N14 28 D5
Wolfson Medical Centre *RYNPK* SW20 145 J6
Wolsey Business Park *WATW* WD18 20 B6
The Woodberry Clinic *MUSWH* N10 54 B2
Woodbridge High School & Language College *WFD* IG8 45 F6
Woodbrook School *BECK* BR3 151 H7
Woodbury Down Primary Sschool *FSBYPK* N4 55 J6
Woodcroft Primary School *EDGW* HA8 37 F6
Wood End J & I Schools *GFD/PVL* UB6 66 D4
Wood End Park Junior School *HYS/HAR* UB3 82 A6
Woodentops School *BAL* SW12 129 J7
Woodfield School *CDALE/KGS* NW9 51 G7
Woodford County High School *WFD* IG8 44 D5
Woodford Golf Club *WFD* IG8 44 D4
Woodford Green Preparatory School *WFD* IG8 44 E5
Woodford Green Primary School *WFD* IG8 44 D4
Woodford Trading Estate *WFD* IG8 59 G1
Woodgrange Infant School *FSTGT* E7 77 F3
Woodgrange Park Cemetery *FSTGT* E7 77 H4
Wood Green Crown Court *WDGN* N22 41 G7
Wood Green Health Centre *WDGN* N22 41 F7
Wood Green Old Boys FC *WDGN* N22 41 G6
Woodhall School *OXHEY* WD19 33 J3
Woodhill Primary School *CHARL* SE7 114 D3
Woodhouse Sixth Form College *NFNCH/WDSP* N12 39 H4
Woodlands Infant & Junior School *IL* IG1 78 D4
Woodlands Park Primary School *SEVS/STOTM* N15 55 J4
Wood Lane Medical Centre *RSLP* HA4 46 C7
Wood Lane School *FUL/PGN* SW6 108 B7
Wood Lane Sports Centre *BCTR* RM8 62 D7
Woodmansterne Primary School *STRHM/NOR* SW16 148 D7
Woodridge Primary School *NFNCH/WDSP* N12 38 D2
Woodside Health Centre *SNWD* SE25 165 J4
Woodside Junior School
CROY/NA CR0 165 H6
WALTH E17 58 A2
Woodside Park Golf Club *NFNCH/WDSP* N12 38 E3
Woodside Park School
FBAR/BDGN N11 39 K4
NFNCH/WDSP N12 39 F3
Woodside School *BELV* DA17 117 J3
Wood Street Medical Centre *WALTH* E17 58 A2
Wood Wharf *POP/IOD* E14 93 K7
Wood Wharf Business Park *POP/IOD* E14 113 F1
Woolmore Primary School *POP/IOD* E14 94 A6
Woolwich Cemetery *WOOL/PLUM* SE18 116 A6
Woolwich College
WOOL/PLUM SE18 114 C3
WOOL/PLUM SE18 115 H3
Woolwich County Court *WOOL/PLUM* SE18 115 F2
Woolwich Crown Court *THMD* SE28 115 K1
Woolwich Polytechnic School *THMD* SE28 97 G7
Working Mens College *CAMTN* NW1 4 F5
World Business Centre Heathrow *HTHAIR* TW6 101 F7
Worlds End Place *WBPTN* SW10 108 B6
World Trade Centre *TWRH* EC3N 13 M7
World University Service *STLK* EC1Y 13 G1
Wormholt Park Primary School *SHB* W12 87 J6
Worple Primary School *ISLW* TW7 124 B3
Worsley Bridge Junior School *BECK* BR3 151 J6
Worton Hall Industrial Estate *ISLW* TW7 123 K3
Wrencote *CROY/NA* CR0 177 J2
Wyborne Primary School *ELTH/MOT* SE9 135 G7
Wyke Green Golf Club *ISLW* TW7 104 A5
Wykeham Primary School
HCH RM12 63 J7
WLSDN NW10 69 F2
Wyndhams Theatre *LSQ/SEVD* WC2H 11 H6
Wyvil Primary School *VX/NE* SW8 109 K6
Yale University Press *HAMP* NW3 71 J3
Yardley Primary School *CHING* E4 31 K4
Yeading FC *HYS/HAR* UB3 83 G7
Yeading Medical Centre *NTHLT* UB5 83 G2
Yeading Primary School *YEAD* UB4 83 G4
Yerbury Primary School *ARCH* N19 72 D2
Yeshivo Horomo Talmudical College *STNW/STAM* N16 55 K7
Yesodey Hatorah Jewish School *STNW/STAM* N16 56 B6
Yetev Lev Day School for Boys *STNW/STAM* N16 56 C7
York Clinic *STHWK* SE1 13 G9
York Hall *BETH* E2 92 D1
York Road Junior School *DART* DA1 139 J6
York Water Gate *CHCR* WC2N 11 K8
Young England RFC *VX/NE* SW8 109 K5
Young Vic Theatre *STHWK* SE1 18 B1
Zennor Road Industrial Estate *BAL* SW12 129 H7
Zephyr Business Centre *SEVS/STOTM* N15 56 A3
Ziam Trading Estate *WALTH* E17 56 E7

The Post Office is a registered trademark of Post Office Ltd. in the UK and other countries.

Schools address data provided by Education Direct.

Petrol station information supplied by Johnsons

One-way street data provided by © Tele Atlas N.V. Tele Atlas

The boundary of the London congestion charging zone supplied by  Transport for London